CFA Institute®
CFA Program

AF888955

ASSET ALLOCATION

CFA® Program Curriculum
2026 • LEVEL III CORE • VOLUME 1

WILEY

ISBN 978-1-39436-057-4

May 2025

Please visit our website at
www.WileyGlobalFinance.com.

WILEY

SKY3EC54C31-5357-4E0E-A4D6-BC79DC5F3A7C_022825

CONTENTS

How to Use the CFA Program Curriculum

The CFA® Program exams measure your mastery of the core knowledge, skills, and abilities required to succeed as an investment professional. These core competencies are the basis for the Candidate Body of Knowledge (CBOK™). The CBOK consists of four components:

A broad outline that lists the major CFA Program topic areas (www .cfainstitute.org/programs/cfa/curriculum/cbok/cbok)

Topic area weights that indicate the relative exam weightings of the top-level topic areas (www.cfainstitute.org/en/programs/cfa/curriculum)

Learning outcome statements (LOS) that tell you the specific knowledge, skills, and abilities you should gain from each curriculum topic area. You will find these statements at the start of each learning module and lesson. We encourage you to review the information about the LOS on our website (www.cfainstitute.org/programs/cfa/curriculum/study-sessions), including the descriptions of LOS "command words" on the candidate resources page at www.cfainstitute.org/-/media/documents/support/programs/cfa-and -cipm-los-command-words.ashx.

The CFA Program curriculum that candidates receive access to upon exam registration.

Therefore, the key to your success on the CFA exams is studying and understanding the CBOK. You can learn more about the CBOK on our website: www.cfainstitute .org/programs/cfa/curriculum/cbok.

The curriculum, including the practice questions, is the basis for all exam questions. The curriculum is selected/developed specifically to provide candidates with the knowledge, skills, and abilities reflected in the CBOK.

CFA INSTITUTE LEARNING ECOSYSTEM (LES)

Your exam registration fee includes access to the CFA Institute Learning Ecosystem (LES). This digital learning platform provides access to all the curriculum content and practice questions. The LES is organized as a series of learning modules consisting of short online lessons and associated practice questions. This tool is your source for all study materials, including practice questions and mock exams. The LES is the primary method by which CFA Institute delivers your curriculum experience. Here, you will find additional practice questions to test your knowledge, including some interactive questions.

DESIGNING YOUR PERSONAL STUDY PROGRAM

An orderly, systematic approach to exam preparation is critical. You should dedicate a consistent block of time every week to reading and studying. Review the LOS both before and after you study curriculum content to ensure you can demonstrate

the knowledge, skills, and abilities described by the LOS and the assigned learning module. Use the LOS as a self-check to track your progress and highlight areas of weakness for later review.

Successful candidates report an average of more than 300 hours preparing for each exam. Your preparation time will vary based on your prior education and experience, and you will likely spend more time on some topics than on others.

ERRATA

The curriculum development process is rigorous and involves multiple rounds of reviews by content experts. Despite our efforts to produce a curriculum that is free of errors, we must make corrections in some instances. Curriculum errata are periodically updated and posted by exam level and test date on the Curriculum Errata webpage (www.cfainstitute.org/en/programs/submit-errata). If you believe you have found an error in the curriculum, you can submit your concerns through our curriculum errata reporting process found at the bottom of the Curriculum Errata webpage.

OTHER FEEDBACK

Please send any comments or suggestions to info@cfainstitute.org, and we will review your feedback thoughtfully.

Asset Allocation

LEARNING MODULE

1

Capital Market Expectations, Part 1: Framework and Macro Considerations

by Christopher D. Piros, PhD, CFA (USA).

LEARNING OUTCOMES

Mastery	The candidate should be able to:
☐	discuss the role of, and a framework for, capital market expectations in the portfolio management process
☐	discuss challenges in developing capital market forecasts
☐	explain how exogenous shocks may affect economic growth trends
☐	discuss the application of economic growth trend analysis to the formulation of capital market expectations
☐	compare major approaches to economic forecasting
☐	discuss how business cycles affect short- and long-term expectations
☐	explain the relationship of inflation to the business cycle and the implications of inflation for cash, bonds, equity, and real estate returns
☐	discuss the effects of monetary and fiscal policy on business cycles
☐	interpret the shape of the yield curve as an economic predictor and discuss the relationship between the yield curve and fiscal and monetary policy
☐	identify and interpret macroeconomic, interest rate, and exchange rate linkages between economies

Parts of this reading have been adapted from a former Capital Market Expectations reading authored by John P. Calverley, Alan M. Meder, CPA, CFA, Brian D. Singer, CFA, and Renato Staub, PhD

1 INTRODUCTION & FRAMEWORK FOR DEVELOPING CAPITAL MARKET EXPECTATIONS

☐ discuss the role of, and a framework for, capital market expectations in the portfolio management process

A noted investment authority has written that the "fundamental law of investing is the uncertainty of the future."[1] Investors have no choice but to forecast elements of the future because nearly all investment decisions look toward it. Specifically, investment decisions incorporate the decision maker's expectations concerning factors and events believed to affect investment values. The decision maker integrates these views into expectations about the risk and return prospects of individual assets and groups of assets.

This reading's focus is **capital market expectations (CME)** expectations concerning the risk and return prospects of asset classes, however broadly or narrowly the investor defines those asset classes. Capital market expectations are an essential input to formulating a strategic asset allocation. For example, if an investor's investment policy statement specifies and defines eight permissible asset classes, the investor will need to have formulated long-term expectations concerning each of those asset classes. The investor may also act on short-term expectations. Insights into capital markets gleaned during CME setting should also help in formulating the expectations concerning individual assets that are needed in security selection and valuation.

This is the first of two readings on capital market expectations. A central theme of both readings is that a disciplined approach to setting expectations will be rewarded. With that in mind, Sections 1 and 2 of this reading present a general framework for developing capital market expectations and alert the reader to the range of problems and pitfalls that await investors and analysts in this arena. Sections 3–11 focus on the use of macroeconomic analysis in setting expectations. The second of the two CME readings builds on this foundation to address setting expectations for specific asset classes: equities, fixed income, real estate, and currencies. Various analytical tools are reviewed as needed throughout both readings.

Framework and Challenges

In this section, we provide a guide to collecting, organizing, combining, and interpreting investment information. After outlining the process, we turn to a discussion of typical problems and challenges to formulating the most informed judgments possible.

Before laying out the framework, we must be clear about what it needs to accomplish. The ultimate objective is to develop a set of projections with which to make informed investment decisions, specifically asset allocation decisions. As obvious as this goal may seem, it has important implications.

Asset allocation is the primary determinant of long-run portfolio performance.[2] The projections underlying these decisions are among the most important determinants of whether investors achieve their long-term goals. It thus follows that it is vital to get the long-run *level* of returns (approximately) right. Until the late 1990s, it was standard practice for institutional investors to extrapolate historical return

1 Peter L. Bernstein in the foreword to Rapaport and Mauboussin (2001), p. xiii.
2 See Brinson, Hood, and Beebower (1986) and Ibbotson and Kaplan (2000).

data into forecasts. At the height of the technology bubble,[3] this practice led many to project double-digit portfolio returns into the indefinite future. Such inflated projections allowed institutions to underfund their obligations and/or set unrealistic goals, many of which have had to be scaled back. Since that time, most institutions have adopted explicitly forward-looking methods of the type(s) discussed in our two CME readings, and return projections have declined sharply. Indeed, as of the beginning of 2018, consensus rate of return projections seemed to imply that US private foundations, which must distribute at least 5% of assets annually, could struggle to prudently generate long-run returns sufficient to cover their required distributions, their expenses, and inflation. To reiterate, projecting a realistic overall level of returns has to be a top priority.

As appealing as it is to think we could project asset returns with precision, that idea is unrealistic. Even the most sophisticated methods are likely to be subject to frustratingly large forecast errors over relevant horizons. We should, of course, seek to limit our forecast errors. We should not, however, put undue emphasis on the precision of projections for individual asset classes. Far more important objectives are to ensure internal consistency across asset classes (**cross-sectional consistency**) and over various time horizons (**intertemporal consistency**). This emphasis stems once again from the primary use of the projections—asset allocation decisions. Inconsistency across asset classes is likely to result in portfolios with poor risk–return characteristics over any horizon, whereas intertemporal inconsistency is likely to distort the connection between portfolio decisions and investment horizon.

Our discussion adopts the perspective of an analyst or team responsible for developing projections to be used by the firm's investment professionals in advising and/or managing portfolios for its clients. As the setting of explicit capital market expectations has become both more common and more sophisticated, many asset managers have adopted this centralized approach, enabling them to leverage the requisite expertise and deliver more consistent advice to all their clients.

A Framework for Developing Capital Market Expectations

The following is a framework for a disciplined approach to setting CME.

1. *Specify the set of expectations needed, including the time horizon(s) to which they apply.* This step requires the analyst to formulate an explicit list of the asset classes and investment horizon(s) for which projections are needed.
2. *Research the historical record.* Most forecasts have some connection to the past. For many markets, the historical record contains useful information on the asset's investment characteristics, suggesting at least some possible ranges for future results. Beyond the raw historical facts, the analyst should seek to identify and understand the factors that affect asset class returns.
3. *Specify the method(s) and/or model(s) to be used and their information requirements.* The analyst or team responsible for developing CME should be explicit about the method(s) and/or model(s) that will be used and should be able to justify the selection.
4. *Determine the best sources for information needs.* The analyst or team must identify those sources that provide the most accurate and timely information tailored to their needs.

3 Explosive growth of the internet in the late 1990s was accompanied by soaring valuations for virtually any internet-related investment. The NASDAQ composite index, which was very heavily weighted in technology stocks, nearly quintupled from 1997 to early 2000, then gave up all of those gains by mid-2002. A variety of names have been given to this episode including the tech or technology bubble.

5. *Interpret the current investment environment using the selected data and methods, applying experience and judgment.* Care should be taken to apply a common set of assumptions, compatible methodologies, and consistent judgments in order to ensure mutually consistent projections across asset classes and over time horizons.
6. *Provide the set of expectations needed, documenting conclusions.* The projections should be accompanied by the reasoning and assumptions behind them.
7. *Monitor actual outcomes and compare them with expectations, providing feedback to improve the expectations-setting process.* The most effective practice is likely to synchronize this step with the expectations-setting process, monitoring and reviewing outcomes on the same cycle as the projections are updated, although several cycles may be required to validate conclusions.

The first step in the CME framework requires the analyst to define the universe of asset classes for which she will develop expectations. The universe should include all of the asset classes that will typically be accorded a distinct allocation in client portfolios. To put it another way, the universe needs to reflect the key dimensions of decision making in the firm's investment process. On the other hand, the universe should be as small as possible because even pared down to minimum needs, the expectations-setting process can be quite challenging.

Steps 2 and 3 in the process involve understanding the historical performance of the asset classes and researching their return drivers. The information that needs to be collected mirrors considerations that defined the universe of assets in step 1. The more granular the classification of assets, the more granular the breakdown of information will need to be to support the investment process. Except in the simplest of cases, the analyst will need to slice the data in multiple dimensions. Among these are the following:

- Geography: global, regional, domestic versus non-domestic, economic blocs (e.g., the European Union), individual countries;
- Major asset classes: equity, fixed-income, real assets;
- Sub-asset classes:
  - Equities: styles, sizes, sectors, industries;
  - Fixed income: maturities, credit quality, securitization, fixed versus floating, nominal or inflation-protected;
  - Real assets: real estate, commodities, timber.

How each analyst approaches this task depends on the hierarchy of decisions in their investment process. One firm may prioritize segmenting the global equity market by Global Industry Classification Standard (GIC) sector, with geographic distinctions accorded secondary consideration, while another firm prioritizes decisions with respect to geography considering sector breakdowns as secondary.[4]

In Step 3, the analyst needs to be sensitive to the fact that both the effectiveness of forecasting approaches and relationships among variables are related to the investor's time horizon. As an example, a discounted cash flow approach to setting equity market expectations is usually considered to be most appropriate to long-range forecasting. If forecasts are also to be made for shorter, finite horizons, intertemporal consistency dictates that the method used for those projections must be calibrated so that its projections converge to the long-range forecast as the horizon extends.

4 There is extensive literature on the relative importance of country versus industry factors in global equity markets. Marcelo, Quiros, and Martins (2013) summarized the evidence as "vast and contradictory."

Executing the fourth step—determining the best information sources—requires researching the quality of alternative data sources and striving to fully understand the data. Using flawed or misunderstood data is a recipe for faulty analysis. Furthermore, analysts should be alert to new, superior data sources. Large, commercially available databases and reputable financial publications are likely the best avenue for obtaining widely disseminated information covering the broad spectrum of asset classes and geographies. Trade publications, academic studies, government and central bank reports, corporate filings, and broker/dealer and third-party research often provide more specialized information. Appropriate data frequencies must be selected. Daily series are of more use for setting shorter-term expectations. Monthly, quarterly, or annual data series are useful for setting longer-term CME.

The first four steps lay the foundation for the heart of the process: the fifth and sixth steps. Monitoring and interpreting the economic and market environment and assessing the implications for relevant investments are activities the analyst should be doing every day. In essence, step five could be labelled "implement your investment/research process" and step six could be labelled "at designated times, synthesize, document, and defend your views." Perhaps what most distinguishes these steps from the day-to-day investment process is that the analyst must make simultaneous projections for all asset classes and all designated, concrete horizons.

Finally, in step 7 we use experience to improve the expectations-setting process. We measure our previously formed expectations against actual results to assess the level of accuracy the process is delivering. Generally, good forecasts are:

- unbiased, objective, and well researched;
- efficient, in the sense of minimizing the size of forecast errors; and
- internally consistent, both cross-sectionally and intertemporally.

Although it is important to monitor outcomes for ways in which our forecasting process can be improved, our ability to assess the accuracy of our forecasts may be severely limited. A standard rule of thumb in statistics is that we need at least 30 observations to meaningfully test a hypothesis. Quantitative evaluation of forecast errors in real time may be of limited value in refining a process that is already reasonably well constructed (i.e., not subject to obvious gross errors). Hence, the most valuable part of the feedback loop will often be qualitative and judgmental.

EXAMPLE 1

Capital Market Expectations Setting: Information Requirements

1. Consider two investment strategists charged with developing capital market expectations for their firms, John Pearson and Michael Wu. Pearson works for a bank trust department that runs US balanced separately managed accounts (SMAs) for high-net-worth individuals. These accounts' mandates restrict investments to US equities, US investment-grade fixed-income instruments, and prime US money market instruments. The investment objective is long-term capital growth and income. In contrast, Wu works for

a large Hong Kong SAR–based, internationally focused asset manager that uses the following types of assets within its investment process:

Equities	Fixed Income	Alternative Investments
Asian equities	Eurozone sovereign	Eastern European venture capital
Eurozone	US government	New Zealand timber
US large-cap		US commercial real estate
US small-cap		
Canadian large-cap		

Wu's firm runs SMAs with generally long-term time horizons and global tactical asset allocation (GTAA) programs. Compare and contrast the information and knowledge requirements of Pearson and Wu.

Guideline Answer:

Pearson's in-depth information requirements relate to US equity and fixed-income markets. By contrast, Wu's information requirements relate not only to US and non-US equity and fixed-income markets but also to three alternative investment types with non-public markets, located on three different continents. Wu has a more urgent need to be current on political, social, economic, and trading-oriented operational details worldwide than Pearson. Given their respective investment time horizons, Pearson's focus is on the long term whereas Wu needs to focus not only on the long term but also on near-term disequilibria among markets (for GTAA decisions). One challenge that Pearson has in US fixed-income markets that Wu does not face is the need to cover corporate and municipal as well as government debt securities. Nevertheless, Wu's overall information and knowledge requirements are clearly more demanding than Pearson's.

2 CHALLENGES IN FORECASTING

☐ discuss challenges in developing capital market forecasts

A range of problems can frustrate analysts' expectations-setting efforts. Expectations reflecting faulty analysis or assumptions may cause a portfolio manager to construct a portfolio that is inappropriate for the client. At the least, the portfolio manager may incur the costs of changing portfolio composition without any offsetting benefits. The following sections provide guidance on points that warrant special caution. The discussion focuses on problems in the use of data and on analyst mistakes and biases.

Limitations of Economic Data

The analyst needs to understand the definition, construction, timeliness, and accuracy of any data used, including any biases. The time lag with which economic data are collected, processed, and disseminated can impede their use because data that are not timely may be of little value in assessing current conditions. Some economic data may be reported with a lag as short as one week, whereas other important data may be reported with a lag of more than a quarter. The International Monetary Fund sometimes reports data for developing economies with a lag of two years or more. Older data increase the uncertainty concerning the current state of the economy with respect to that variable.

Furthermore, one or more official revisions to initial data values are common. Sometimes these revisions are substantial, which may give rise to significantly different inferences. Often only the most recent data point is revised. Other series are subject to periodic "benchmark revisions" that simultaneously revise all or a portion of the historical data series. In either case—routine updating of the most recent release or benchmark revision—the analyst must be aware that using revised data as if it were known at the time to which it applies often suggests strong historical relationships that are unreliable for forecasting.

Definitions and calculation methods change too. For example, the US Bureau of Labor Statistics (BLS) made significant changes to the Consumer Price Index for All Urban Consumers (CPI-U) in 1983 (treatment of owner-occupied housing) and again in 1991 (regression-based product quality adjustments). Analysts should also be aware that suppliers of economic and financial indexes periodically **re-base** these indexes, meaning that the specific period used as the base of the index is changed. Analysts should take care to avoid inadvertently mixing data relating to different base periods. Exhibit 1 illustrates the impact of re-basing a time series: Statistics Denmark announced that beginning January 2016, the Danish Consumer Price Index (CPI) was revised and the new base year is 2015. The CPI series based on the old base was no longer published, and the new series was computed back to 1980 retrospectively, such that the CPI took a value of 100.00 on 31 August 2015.

Exhibit 1: Danish CPI before and after Re-Basement (31 August 2015 = 100)

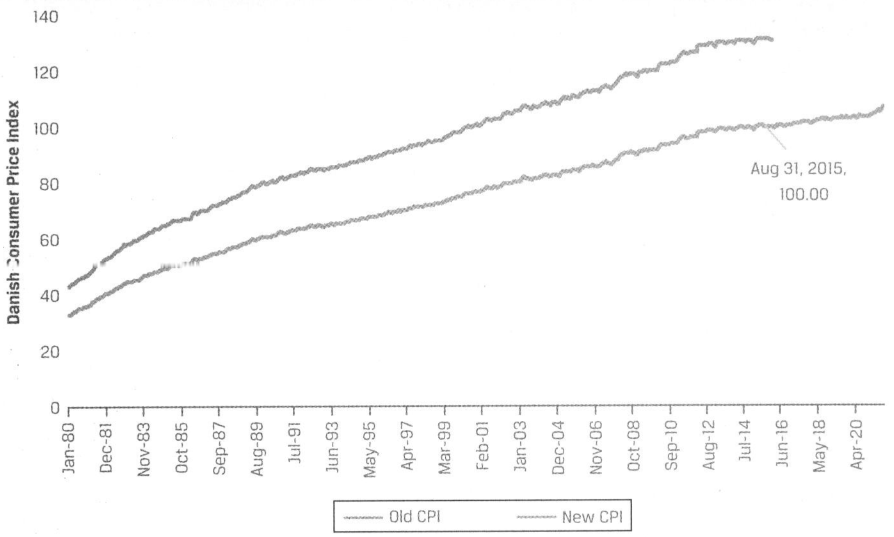

Sources: Statistics Denmark; Bloomberg

Data Measurement Errors and Biases

Analysts need to be aware of possible biases and/or errors in data series, including the following:

- Transcription errors. These are errors in gathering and recording data.

- Survivorship bias. This bias arises when a data series reflects only entities that survived to the end of the period. Without correction, statistics from such data can be misleading. Data on alternative assets such as hedge funds are notorious for survivorship bias.
- Appraisal (smoothed) data. For certain assets without liquid public markets, notably but not only real estate, appraisal data are used in lieu of transaction data. Appraised values tend to be less volatile than market-determined values. As a result, measured volatilities are biased downward and correlations with other assets tend to be understated.

The Limitations of Historical Estimates

Although history is often a helpful guide, the past should not be extrapolated uncritically. There are two primary issues with respect to using historical data. First, the data may not be representative of the future period for which an analyst needs to forecast. Second, even if the data are representative of the future, statistics calculated from that data may be poor estimates of the desired metrics. Both of these issues can be addressed to some extent by imposing structure (that is, a model) on how data is presumed to have been generated in the past and how it is expected to be generated in the future.

Changes in technological, political, legal, and regulatory environments; disruptions such as wars and other calamities; and changes in policy stances can all alter risk–return relationships. Such shifts are known as changes in **regime** (the governing set of relationships) and give rise to the statistical problem of **nonstationarity** (meaning, informally, that different parts of a data series reflect different underlying statistical properties). Statistical tools are available to help identify and model such changes or turning points.

A practical approach for an analyst to decide whether to use the whole of a long data series or only part of it involves answering two questions.

1. Is there any reason to believe that the entirety of the sample period is no longer relevant? In other words, has there been a fundamental regime change (such as political, economic, market, or asset class structure) during the sample period?
2. Do the data support the hypothesis that such a change has occurred?

If the answer to both questions is yes, the analyst should use only that part of the time series that appears relevant to the present. Alternatively, he may apply statistical techniques that account for regime changes in the past data as well as the possibility of subsequent regime changes. Example 2 illustrates examples of changes in regime.

EXAMPLE 2

Regimes and the Relevance of Historical Bond Returns

In the 1970s, oil price shocks combined with accommodative monetary policy by the US Federal Reserve fueled sharply rising inflation. In 1980, the Fed abruptly shifted to an aggressively tight stance. After the initial shock of sharply higher interest rates, US bond yields trended downward for roughly 35 years as the Fed kept downward pressure on inflation. Throughout the 1980s and 1990s, the Fed eased monetary policy in the aftermath of the technology bubble. Then, switching to an extraordinarily expansionary policy in the midst of the 2008–2009 global financial crisis, the Fed reduced its policy rate to 0% in December 2008. Subsequently, it aggressively bought Treasury bonds and mortgage-backed securities. The Fed finally raised its policy rate target in December 2015 and continued hiking it up until it reached 2.5% at the end of 2018. In October 2017, it stopped rolling over maturing bonds, allowing its balance sheet to shrink, albeit very slowly. After the outbreak of COVID-19, the Fed once again cut its policy rate target, to 0%–0.25% in March 2020. It can be argued that bond returns from the 1970s through 2021 reflect at least three distinct regimes: the inflationary 1970s, with accommodative Fed policy; the 1980–2008 period of disinflationary policy and secularly falling yields; and the unprecedented 2009–21 period of zero interest rates and explosive liquidity provision. The years after the 2008-09 global financial crisis were dominated by multiple waves of central bank asset buying, not only in the United States but also globally. The most recent wave of asset purchases (quantitative easing, or QE) came after the outbreak of COVID-19. Exhibit 2 illustrates how QE by the Fed, the European Central Bank, and the Bank of Japan drove long-term government yields lower—even to negative territory in some cases.

Exhibit 2: Effects of QE on Long-Term Government Yield

Source: Bloomberg.

As of mid-2021, nominal interest rates were still negative in some developed markets, and major central banks including the Fed were aiming to "normalize" policy over the next few years. There is ample reason to believe that future bond returns will reflect a regime like none before.

In general, the analyst should use the longest data history for which there is reasonable assurance of stationarity. This guideline follows from the fact that sample statistics from a longer history are more precise than those with fewer observations.

Although it is tempting to assume that using higher-frequency data (e.g., monthly rather than annual observations) will also provide more-precise estimates, this assumption is not necessarily true. Although higher-frequency data improve the precision of sample variances, covariances, and correlations, they do *not* improve the precision of the sample mean.

When many variables are considered, a large number of observations may be a statistical necessity. For example, to calculate a sample covariance matrix, the number of observations must exceed the number of variables (assets). Otherwise, some asset combinations (i.e., portfolios) will spuriously appear to have zero volatility. This problem arises frequently in investment analysis, and a remedy is available. Covariance matrices are routinely estimated even for huge numbers of assets by assuming that returns are driven by a smaller set of common factors plus uncorrelated asset-specific components.

As the frequency of observations increases, the likelihood increases that data may be asynchronous (i.e., not simultaneous or concurrent in time) across variables. This means that data points for different variables may not reflect exactly the same period even though they are labeled as if they do. For example, daily data from different countries are typically asynchronous because of time zone differences. Asynchronicity can be a significant problem for daily, and perhaps even weekly data, because it distorts measured correlations and induces lead–lag relationships that might not exist if the data were measured synchronously. Lower-frequency data (e.g., monthly or quarterly) are less susceptible to asynchrony, although it can still arise. For example, two series that are released and labeled as monthly could reflect data collected at different times of the month.

As a final note on historical data, some care should be taken with respect to whether data are normally distributed. Historical asset returns, in particular, routinely exhibit skewness and "fat tails," which cause them to fail formal tests of normality. The cost in terms of analytical complexity of accounting for non-normality, however, can be quite high. As a practical matter, the added complexity is often not worth the cost.[5]

Ex Post Risk Can Be a Biased Measure of Ex Ante Risk

In interpreting historical prices and returns over a given sample period, the analyst needs to evaluate whether asset prices reflected the possibility of a very negative event that did not materialize during the period. This phenomenon is often referred to as the "peso problem." Looking backward, we are likely to underestimate *ex ante* risk and overestimate *ex ante* anticipated returns. The key point is that high *ex post* returns that reflect fears of adverse events that did not materialize provide a poor estimate of *ex ante* expected returns.

THE ARGENTINE PESO DEVALUATIONS

Starting in 1992, the Argentine peso (ARS) was pegged to the US dollar at a 1:1 ratio, and the ARS/USD exchange rate remained fixed at 1.0 until the Argentine great depression of 1998–2002, which was characterized by bank runs, riots, and sovereign debt default. In January 2002, the government decided to abandon the fixed exchange rate policy and devalued the peso to a rate of 1.4 ARS/USD. The currency was allowed to fluctuate freely, and the peso further depreciated to 3.8 ARS/USD by June 2002. Over the following years, additional default waves took place, and Argentina suffered from elevated inflation, fluctuating around

5 See Chapter 5 of Stewart, Piros, and Heisler (forthcoming 2019) for discussion of the effect of alternative probability distributions on asset allocation decisions.

20%–40%, with fiscal imbalances over the 2010s. The 2018 Argentine monetary crisis led to a further severe devaluation of the peso, trading at a rate of 18.6 ARS/USD at the end of 2017 but closing the year at 37.7.

The opposite situation is also a problem, especially for risk measures that consider only the subset of worst-case outcomes (e.g., value at risk, or VaR). If our data series includes even one observation of a rare event, we may substantially overstate the likelihood of such events happening in the future. Within a finite sample, the observed frequency of this bad outcome will far exceed its true probability. As a simple example, there were 22 trading days in March 2020, the month of the COVID-19-related market panic. On 16 March, the price of Facebook (now named as Meta Platforms) stock closed down –14.3%. The second worst day in the same month was 12 March, with the stock price down –9.3%. Based on this sample, the (interpolated) daily 5% VaR on Facebook stock was 13.4%. That is, an investor in Facebook shares would expect to lose at least 13.4% once every 20 days. Note that the stock did not experience any such loss over the subsequent 19 months.

Biases in Analysts' Methods

Analysts naturally search for relationships that will help in developing better capital market expectations. Among the preventable biases that the analyst may introduce are the following:

- Data-mining bias arises from repeatedly searching a dataset until a statistically significant pattern emerges. It is almost inevitable that some relationship will appear. Such patterns cannot be expected to have predictive value. Lack of an explicit economic rationale for a variable's usefulness is a warning sign of a data-mining problem: no story, no future.[6] Of course, the analyst must be wary of inventing the story after discovering the relationship and bear in mind that correlation does not imply causation.
- Time-period bias relates to results that are period specific. Research findings often turn out to be sensitive to the selection of specific starting and/or ending dates.

SMALL-CAP OUTPERFORMANCE AND TIME-PERIOD BIAS

Evidence suggesting that small-cap stocks outperform large-cap stocks over time (the so-called small firm effect) is very sensitive to the choice of sample period. From 1926 through 1974, US small-cap stocks outperformed large caps by 0.43% per year, but if we skip the Great Depression and start in 1932, the differential becomes 3.49% per year. Similarly, small caps outperformed by 4.5% per year from 2000 through 2010 but underperformed by –2.8% per year from 2010 through 2020.[7]

How might analysts avoid using an irrelevant variable in a forecasting model? The analyst should scrutinize the variable selection process for data-mining bias and be able to provide an economic rationale for the variable's usefulness in a forecasting model. A further practical check is to examine the forecasting relationship out of sample (i.e., on data that was not used to estimate the relationship).

6 See McQueen and Thorley (1999).

7 Source: Ibbotson Associates database (Morningstar). Returns calculated by the author.

The Failure to Account for Conditioning Information

The discussion of regimes introduced the notion that assets' risk and return characteristics vary with the economic and market environment. That fact explains why economic analysis is important in expectation setting. The analyst should not ignore relevant information or analysis in formulating expectations. Unconditional forecasts, which dilute this information by averaging over environments, can lead to misperception of prospective risk and return. Example 3 illustrates how an analyst may use conditioning information.

EXAMPLE 3

Incorporating Conditioning Information

Noah Sota uses the CAPM to set capital market expectations. He estimates that one asset class has a beta of 0.8 in economic expansions and 1.2 in recessions. The expected return on the market is 12% in an expansion and 4% in a recession. The risk-free rate is assumed to be constant at 2%. Expansion and recession are equally likely. Sota aims to calculate the unconditional expected return for the asset class.

The conditional expected returns on the asset are 10% = 2% + 0.8 × (12% – 2%) in an expansion and 4.4% = 2% + 1.2 × (4% – 2%) in a recession. Weighting by the probabilities of expansion and recession, the unconditional expected return is 7.2% = [(0.5 × 10%) + (0.5 × 4.4%)].

EXAMPLE 4

Ignoring Conditioning Information

1. Following on from the scenario in Example 3, one of Noah Sota's colleagues suggests an alternative approach to calculate the unconditional expected return for the asset class. His method is to calculate the unconditional beta to be used in the CAPM formula, 1.0 = (0.5 × 0.8) + (0.5 × 1.2). He then works out the unconditional expected return on the market portfolio, 8% = (0.5 × 12%) + (0.5 × 4%). Finally, using the unconditional beta and the unconditional market return, he calculates the unconditional expected return on the asset class as 8.0% = 2.0% + 1.0 × (8% – 2%).

   Explain why the alternative approach is right or wrong.

   Guideline Answer:

   The approach suggested by Sota's colleague is wrong. It ignores the fact that the market excess return and the asset's beta vary with the business cycle. The expected return of 8% calculated this way would overestimate the (unconditional) expected return on this asset class. Such a return forecast would ignore the fact that the beta differs for expansion (0.8) and recession (1.2).

Misinterpretation of Correlations

When a variable *A* is found to be significantly correlated with another variable *B*, there are at least four possible explanations: (1) A predicts B, (2) B predicts A, (3) a third variable C predicts both A and B, or (4) the relationship is spurious. The observed correlation alone does not allow us to distinguish among these situations. Consequently, correlation relationships should not be used in a predictive model without investigating the underlying linkages.

Although apparently significant correlations can be spurious, it is also true that lack of a strong correlation can be misleading. A negligible measured correlation may reflect a strong but *nonlinear* relationship. Analysts should explore this possibility if they have a solid reason for believing a relationship exists.

Psychological Biases

The behavioral finance literature documents a long and growing list of psychological biases that can affect investment decisions. Only a few of the more prominent ones that could undermine the analyst's ability to make accurate and unbiased forecasts are outlined here. Furthermore, note that the literature contains various names and definitions of behavioral biases, which are not necessarily mutually exclusive.

- Anchoring bias is the tendency to give disproportionate weight to the first information received or first number envisioned, which is then adjusted. Such adjustment is often insufficient, and approximations are consequently biased. Analysts can try to avoid anchoring bias by consciously attempting to avoid premature conclusions.
- Status quo bias reflects the tendency for forecasts to perpetuate recent observations—that is, to avoid making changes and preserve the status quo, and/or to accept a default option. This bias may reflect greater pain from errors of commission (making a change) than from errors of omission (doing nothing). Status quo bias can be mitigated by disciplined effort to avoid "anchoring" on the status quo.
- Confirmation bias is the tendency to seek and overweight evidence or information that confirms one's existing or preferred beliefs and to discount evidence that contradicts those beliefs. This bias can be mitigated by examining all evidence with equal rigor and/or debating with a knowledgeable person capable of arguing against one's own views.
- Overconfidence bias is unwarranted confidence in one's own intuitive reasoning, judgment, knowledge, and/or ability. This bias may lead an analyst to overestimate the accuracy of her forecasts and/or fail to consider a sufficiently broad range of possible outcomes or scenarios. Analysts may not only fail to fully account for uncertainty about which they are aware (sometimes described as "known unknowns") but they also are very likely to ignore the possibility of uncertainties about which they are not even aware (sometimes described as "unknown unknowns").
- Prudence bias reflects the tendency to temper forecasts so that they do not appear extreme or the tendency to be overly cautious in forecasting. In decision-making contexts, one may be too cautious when making decisions that could damage one's career or reputation. This bias can be mitigated by conscious effort to identify plausible scenarios that would give rise to more extreme outcomes and to give greater weight to such scenarios in the forecast.

- Availability bias is the tendency to be overly influenced by events that have left a strong impression and/or for which it is easy to recall an example. Recent events may likewise be overemphasized. The effect of this bias can be mitigated by attempting to base conclusions on objective evidence and analytical procedures.

EXAMPLE 5

Biases in Forecasting and Decision Making

1. Cynthia Casey is a London-based investment adviser with a clientele of ultra-high-net-worth individuals in the UK, the US, and the EU. Within the equity portion of her portfolios, she rarely deviates significantly from the country weightings of the MSCI World Index, even though more often than not she tilts the allocation in the right direction. Hence, she can claim a good tactical track record despite having added little value in terms of return through tactical allocation. Because most investors have an implicit "home bias," her European clients tend to view their portfolios as significantly overweight the US (nearly 50% of the World index) and are happy because the US market outperformed the MSCI World ex-US Index by about 8% per year over the 10 years ending 31 December 2020. Conversely, her US clients are unhappy because Casey persistently projected US outperformance but maintained what they instinctively perceive as a significant underweight in the United States. Citing year-to-date performance as of 31 December 2020—US performance was up 21%, while World ex-US performance was up 8%, largely lagging behind the United States, with 8 of 15 European markets actually down in local currencies—Casey's US clients are pressuring her to aggressively increase allocations to US equities. Although experience has taught her to be wary of chasing a strong market, Casey vividly remembers losing clients in the late 1990s because she doubted that the explosive rally in technology stocks would be sustained. With that in mind, she has looked for and found a rationale for a bullish view on US stocks—very robust year-to-date earnings growth.

   What psychological biases are Casey and her clients exhibiting?

   Guideline Answer:

   Casey's clients are implicitly anchoring their expectations on the performance of their respective domestic markets. In pressing Casey to increase the allocation to US stocks based on recent outperformance, her US clients are clearly projecting continuation of the trend, a status quo bias. Casey herself is exhibiting several biases. Prudence bias is apparent in the fact that she has a good record of projecting the correct direction of relative performance among markets but has not translated that into reallocations large enough to add meaningful value. We cannot assess whether that bias affects the magnitude of her forecasts, the extent to which she responds to the opportunities, or both. Losing clients when she doubted the sustainability of the late 1990s technology rally made a very strong impression on Casey, so much so that she has apparently convinced herself to look for a reason to believe the recent relative performance trends will persist. This is indicative of availability bias. Searching for evidence to support a favored view (continued strength of the US market) is a clear sign of confirmation bias, whereas finding support for that view in the recent strength of earnings growth reflects status quo bias.

Model Uncertainty

The analyst usually encounters at least three kinds of uncertainty in conducting an analysis. **Model uncertainty** pertains to whether a selected model is structurally and/or conceptually correct. **Parameter uncertainty** arises because a quantitative model's parameters are invariably estimated with error. **Input uncertainty** concerns whether the inputs are correct. Any or all of these may give rise to erroneous forecasts and/or cause the unwary analyst to overestimate the accuracy and reliability of his forecasts.

The effects of parameter uncertainty can be mitigated through due attention to estimation errors. Input uncertainty arises primarily from the need to proxy for an unobservable variable such as "the market portfolio" in the CAPM. Whether or not this is a serious issue depends on the context. It is a problem if the analyst wants to test the validity of the underlying theory or identify "anomalies" relative to the model. It is less of an issue if the analyst is merely focused on useful empirical relationships rather than proof of concept/theory. Model uncertainty is potentially the most serious issue because the wrong model may lead an analyst to fundamentally flawed conclusions.

Our discussion of the limitations of historical data touched on a model that led many investors far astray in the late 1990s. Up to that point, the implicit model used by many, if not most, institutional investors for setting long-term equity expectations was, "The *ex ante* expected return is, was, and always will be a constant number μ, and the best estimate of that number is the mean over the longest sample available." As the market soared in the late 1990s, the historical estimate of μ rose steadily, leading investors to shift more heavily into equities, which fueled further price appreciation and more reallocation toward equities, and so on, until the technology bubble burst. Ironically, belief in the sanctity of historical estimates coincided with the diametrically opposed notion that the "new economy" made historical economic and market relationships obsolete. There seemed to be no limits to growth or to valuations, at least in some segments of the market. But, of course, there were. This description of the technology bubble illustrates the breakdown of a particular forecasting model. It is not a literal description of anyone's thought process. For various reasons, however—competitive pressures, status quo/availability/prudence biases—many investors acted *as if* they were following the model.

Another flawed model unraveled during the global financial crisis of 2007–2009. One component of that model was the notion that housing price declines are geographically isolated events: There was no risk of a nationwide housing slump. A second component involved "originate to sell" loan pipelines: businesses that made loans with the intention of immediately selling them to investors and therefore had very little incentive to vet loan quality. A third component was the notion that the macro risk of an ever-growing supply of increasingly poor-quality mortgages could be diversified away by progressive layers of securitization. End investors were implicitly sold the notion that the securities were low risk because numerous computer simulations showed that the "micro" risk of individual loans was well diversified. The macro risk of a housing crisis, however, was not reflected in prices and yields—until, of course, the model proved to be flawed. The scenario highlighted here provides another illustration of a particular model breaking down. In this case, it was a flawed model of risk and diversification, and its breakdown was one of many aspects of the financial crisis.

ECONOMIC AND MARKET ANALYSIS: EXOGENOUS SHOCKS TO GROWTH

3

☐ explain how exogenous shocks may affect economic growth trends

The previous section outlined various pitfalls in forecasting. Each of these is important. Yet they pale in comparison to a fundamental mistake: losing sight of the fact that investment outcomes are inherently linked to the economy. The technology bubble and the global financial crisis offer two extreme illustrations of the consequences of falling into this trap. Less dramatic, but still consequential, instances of this mistake regularly contribute to the differential investment performance that separates "winners" and "losers." The remainder of this reading is dedicated to effective incorporation of economic and market analysis into capital market expectations.

The Role of Economic Analysis

History has shown that there is a direct yet variable relationship among actual realized asset returns, expectations for future asset returns, and economic activity. Analysts need to be familiar with the historical relationships that empirical research has uncovered concerning the direction, strength, and lead–lag relationships between economic variables and capital market returns.

The analyst who understands which economic variables may be most relevant to the current economic environment has a competitive advantage, as does the analyst who can discern or forecast changes in acceleration and deceleration of a trend.

Economic output has both cyclical and trend growth components. Trend growth is of obvious relevance for setting long-term return expectations for asset classes such as equities. Cyclical variation affects variables such as corporate profits and interest rates, which are directly related to asset class returns and risk. In the following sections, we address trend growth, business cycles, the role of monetary and fiscal policies, and international interactions.

Analysis of Economic Growth

The economic growth trend is the long-term average growth path of GDP around which the economy experiences semi-regular business cycles. The analyst needs to understand and analyze both the trend and the cycles. Though each could exist without the other, they are related.

It might seem that trends are inherently easier to forecast than cycles. After all, trends are about long-term averages, whereas cycles are about shorter-term movements and turning points. The assumption that trends are easier to forecast would be true if trend growth rates were constant. But trend growth rates do change, which is what makes forecasting them relevant for investment analysis. Some changes are fairly easy to forecast because they are driven by slowly evolving and easily observable factors such as demographics. Trend changes that arise from significant "exogeneous shocks" to underlying economic and/or market relationships are not only impossible to foresee but also difficult to identify, assess, and quantify until the change is well-established and retrospectively revealed in the data. Virtually by definition, the effect of truly exogenous shocks on the level and/or growth rate of the economy will not have been built into asset prices in advance—although the risk of such events will likely have been reflected in prices to some degree.

Exogenous Shocks to Growth

Shocks arise from various sources. Some are purely domestic. Others are transmitted from other parts of the globe. Some are negative for potential growth, while others enhance it. Significant shocks typically arise from the following:

- Policy changes. Elements of pro-growth government policies include sound fiscal policy, minimal intrusion on the private sector, encouraging competition within the private sector, support for infrastructure and human capital development, and sound tax policies. Any significant, unexpected change in these policies that is likely to persist will change the expected trend rate of growth. The overhaul of US business taxes at the end of 2017, although not entirely unexpected, was intended to be a pro-growth change in policy. On the other hand, standard economic arguments indicate that erecting trade barriers will diminish trend growth.
- New products and technologies. Creation and assimilation of new products, markets, and technologies enhances potential growth. Consider the printing press, steam engine, telegraph and telephone, railroad, automobile, airplane, transistor, random-access memory (RAM), integrated circuits, internet, wireless communication (radio, TV, smartphone), rockets, and satellites, to name just a few.
- Geopolitics. Geopolitical conflict has the potential to reduce growth by diverting resources to less economically productive uses (e.g., accumulating and maintaining weapons, discouraging beneficial trade). The fall of the Berlin wall, which triggered German reunification and a "peace dividend" for governments as they cut defense spending, was a growth-enhancing geopolitical shock. Interestingly, geopolitical tensions (e.g., the space race) can also spur innovation that results in growth-enhancing technologies.
- Natural disasters. Natural disasters destroy productive capacity. In the short run, a disaster is likely to reduce growth, but it may actually enhance long-run growth if old capacity is replaced with more efficient facilities.
- Natural resources/critical inputs. Discovery of new natural resources or of new ways to recover them (e.g., fracking) can be expected to enhance potential growth, directly via production of those resources and indirectly by reducing the cost of production for other products. Conversely, sustained reduction in the supply of important resources diminishes growth (e.g., the OPEC oil shock in 1973).
- Financial crises. The financial system allows the economy to channel resources to their most efficient use. Financial crises arise when market participants lose confidence in others' ability (or willingness) to meet their obligations and cease to provide funding—first to specific counterparties and then more broadly as potential losses cascade through the system. As discussed in Example 6, a financial crisis may affect both the level of output and the trend growth rate.

EXAMPLE 6

Trend Growth after a Financial Crisis

An extensive study of growth and debt dynamics in the wake of the 2007–2009 global financial crisis identified three types of crises:

- Type 1: A persistent (permanent, one-time) decline in the level of output, but the subsequent trend rate of growth is unchanged.

- Type 2: No persistent decline in the level of output, but the subsequent trend rate of growth is reduced.
- Type 3: Both a persistent decline in the level of output and a reduction in the subsequent trend rate of growth.

The eurozone experienced a sharp, apparently permanent drop in output after the global financial crisis, and subsequent growth was markedly lower than before the crisis, suggesting a Type 3 crisis.

The eurozone's stagnant growth may be traced to structural problems in conjunction with policy missteps. Structural issues included rigid labor markets, a relatively rapid aging of the population, legal and regulatory barriers, cultural differences among countries, use of a common currency in dissimilar economies, and lack of a unified fiscal policy. In terms of policy response, the European Central Bank was slow to cut rates, was slow to expand its balance sheet, and failed to sustain that expansion. Insolvent banks were allowed to remain operational, thwarting deleveraging of the financial system. In part as the result of a lack of fiscal integration that would have facilitated cross-country transfers, several countries were forced to adopt drastic budget cuts that magnified the impact on their particular economies, the differential impact across countries, and the consequences of structural impediments.

Note: See Buttiglione, Lane, Reichlin, and Reinhart (2014).

It should be clear that any of the shocks listed would likely constitute a "regime change" as discussed earlier.

EXAMPLE 7

Impact of Exogenous Shocks on Trend Growth

1. Philippe Leblanc, an analyst focusing on economic forecasting, recently read about a discovery by scientists at a major university that may allow the efficiency of solar panels to double every two to three years, a result similar to Moore's Law with respect to computer chips. In further reading, he found new research at Tsinghua University that may rapidly increase the distance over which electricity can be transmitted.

   What implications should Leblanc draw with regard to growth trends if either, or both, of these developments come to fruition? What government policy changes might offset the impact?

   Guideline Answer:

   Either of these developments would be expected to increase trend growth. They would be especially powerful together. Rapid increases in solar panel efficiency would drive down the cost of energy over time, especially in areas with long days and intense sunlight. The closer to the equator, the larger the potential effect. The developments would also make it increasingly possible to bring large-scale power production to remote areas, thereby expanding the range and scale of economically viable businesses in those areas. Extending the range of electrical transmission would allow moving lower-cost energy (regardless of how it is generated) to where it is most efficiently used. A variety of government actions could undermine the pro-growth nature of these developments; for example, tariffs on solar panels, restrictions on electrical transmission lines, subsidies to support less efficient energy sources, failure to protect intellectual property rights, or prohibition on transfer of technology.

4 APPLYING GROWTH ANALYSIS TO CAPITAL MARKET EXPECTATIONS

☐ discuss the application of economic growth trend analysis to the formulation of capital market expectations

The expected trend rate of economic growth is a key consideration in a variety of contexts. First, it is an important input to discounted cash flow models of expected return. The trend growth rate imposes discipline on forecasts of fundamental metrics such as earnings because these must be kept consistent with aggregate long-run growth at the trend rate. Second, a country with a higher trend rate of growth may offer equity investors a particularly good return if that growth has not already been priced into the market. Third, a higher trend rate of growth in the economy allows actual growth to be faster before accelerating inflation becomes a significant concern. This fact is especially important in projecting the likely path of monetary policy and bond yields. Fourth, theory implies, and empirical evidence confirms, that the average level of real government bond yields is linked to the trend growth rate. Faster trend growth implies higher average real yields.

Most countries have had periods of faster and slower trend growth during their development. Emerging countries often experience rapid growth as they catch up with the leading industrial countries, but the more developed they become, the more likely it is that their growth will slow.

A Decomposition of GDP Growth and Its Use in Forecasting

The simplest way to analyze an economy's aggregate trend growth is to split it into the following components:

- growth from labor inputs, consisting of
  - growth in potential labor force size and
  - growth in actual labor force participation, plus
- growth from labor productivity, consisting of
  - growth from increasing capital inputs and
  - growth in total factor productivity.

Labor input encompasses both the number of workers and the average number of hours they work. Growth in the potential labor force size is driven by demographics such as the population's age distribution, net migration, and workplace norms such as the length of the work week. All of these factors tend to change slowly, making growth in the potential labor force relatively predictable. Trends in net migration and workplace norms, however, may change abruptly in response to sudden structural changes, such as changes in government policies.

Labor force participation primarily reflects labor versus leisure decisions by workers. All else the same, we should expect labor force participation to decline (or at least grow more slowly) as a country becomes more affluent. On the other hand, rising real wages tend to attract workers back into the labor force. Social norms and government policies also play a large role.

Growth in labor productivity comes from investment in additional capital per worker ("capital deepening") and from increases in **total factor productivity** (TFP), which is often taken to be synonymous with technological improvement.[8] Government policy (e.g., regulations) can also influence TFP. In historical analyses, TFP is often measured as a "residual"—that is, output growth that is not accounted for by the other factors.

The trend rate of growth in mature, developed markets is generally fairly stable. As a result, extrapolating past trends in the components outlined in the foregoing can be expected to provide a reasonable initial estimate of the future growth trend. This forecast should then be adjusted to reflect observable information indicating how future patterns are likely to differ from past patterns. This same approach can be applied to less developed markets. It must be recognized, however, that these economies are likely to be undergoing rapid structural changes that may require the analyst to make more significant adjustments relative to past trends.

Anchoring Asset Returns to Trend Growth

Both theory and empirical evidence indicate that the average level of real (nominal) default-free bond yields is linked to the trend rate of real (nominal) growth.[9] To put it another way, bond yields will be pulled toward this level over time. Thus, the trend rate of growth provides an important anchor for estimating bond returns over horizons long enough for this reversion to prevail over cyclical and short-term forces. Intertemporal consistency demands that this anchor be factored into forecasts even for shorter horizons.

The trend growth rate also provides an anchor for long-run equity appreciation.[10] We can express the aggregate market value of equity, V^e, as the product of three factors: the level of nominal GDP, the share of profits in the economy, S^k (earnings/GDP), and the P/E ratio (PE).

$$V_t^e = \text{GDP}_t \times S_t^k \times PE_t$$

It is clear that over long periods, capital's share of income cannot continually increase or decrease. The same is true for the P/E multiple applied to earnings. As a result, in the long run, the growth rate of the total value of equity in an economy is linked to the growth rate of GDP. Over finite horizons, the way in which the share of capital and the P/E multiple are expected to change will also affect the forecast of the total value of equity, as well as its corresponding growth rate over that period.

This argument applies to the capital appreciation component of equity returns. It does not supply a way to estimate the other component: the dividend yield. An estimate for the dividend yield (annual dividends/market value) can be obtained by noting that the dividend yield equals the dividend payout ratio (dividends/profit) divided by the profit multiple (market value/profit). The analyst may set any two of these three ratios and infer the third.

8 Total factor productivity captures a variety of effects, such as the impact of adding not just *more* physical capital (i.e., "capital deepening") but *better* capital, as well as the impact of increasingly skilled labor (i.e., increases in "human capital"). Earlier readings provide a more granular breakdown of the drivers/components of growth.

9 With regard to nominal yields and growth, it is assumed that inflation is sufficiently well behaved.

10 See Stewart, Piros, and Heisler (forthcoming 2019) for more thorough development of these arguments.

EXAMPLE 8

Long-Run Equity Returns and Economic Growth

In January 2021, Alena Bjornsdottir, CFA, was updating her firm's projections for US equity returns. The firm had always used the historical average return with little adjustment. Alena was aware that historical averages are subject to large sampling errors and was especially concerned about this fact because of the sequence of very high returns in the late 1990s, as well as over the past few years partly due to very low levels of interest rates. She decided to examine whether US equity returns since World War II had been consistent with economic growth. For the period 1946–2020, the continuously compounded (i.e., logarithmic) return was 10.7% per annum, which reflected the following components:

Real GDP Growth	Inflation	EPS/GDP (Chg)	P/E (Chg)	Dividend Yield
2.9%	3.5%	0.00%	0.9%	3.4%

1. What conclusion was Alena likely to have drawn from this analysis?

   Guideline Answer:

   Alena is likely have concluded that the post-war stock return exceeded what would have been consistent with growth of the economy. In particular, the rising P/E added 0.9% of "extra" return per year for 74 years, adding 67% (= 74 × 0.9%) to the cumulative, continuously compounded return and leaving the market 95% (exp[67%] = 1.95) above "fair value."

2. If she believed that in the long run that the US labor input would grow by 0.9% per annum and labor productivity by 1.5%, that inflation would be 2.1%, that the dividend yield would be 2.25%, and that there would be no further growth in P/E, what is likely to have been her baseline projection for continuously compounded long-term US equity returns?

   Guideline Answer:

   Her baseline projection is likely to have been 6.75% = 0.9% + 1.5% + 2.1% + 2.25%.

3. In light of her analysis, how might she have adjusted her baseline projection?

   Guideline Answer:

   She is likely to have adjusted her projection downward to some degree to reflect the likelihood that the effect of the P/E would decline toward zero over time. Assuming, for example, that this would occur over 30 years would imply reducing the baseline projection by 2.2% = (67%/30) per year.

Studies have shown that countries with higher economic growth rates do not reliably generate higher equity market returns.[11] A partial explanation is likely to be that the higher growth rate was already reflected in market prices. The sources of growth may be a second factor. Stock market returns ultimately reflect the rate of return on invested capital. If the capital stock is growing rapidly, the rate of return on invested capital may be driven down. Both of these explanations are consistent with the arguments outlined earlier. High growth need not translate one-for-one into higher

11 Joachim Klement, "What's Growth Got to Do with It? Equity Returns and Economic Growth," *Journal of Investing* Summer 2015 is one such study covering 44 countries.

return unless it can be expected to continue forever. Declining return on investment essentially means that either GDP growth slows or profits decline as a share of GDP, or both. And, of course, valuation multiples do matter.

APPROACHES TO ECONOMIC FORECASTING 5

☐ compare major approaches to economic forecasting

Whereas the trend growth rate is a long-term average and reflects only the supply side of the economy, most macroeconomic forecasting focuses on short- to intermediate-term fluctuations around the trend—that is, the business cycle. These fluctuations are usually ascribed primarily to shifts in aggregate demand, although shifts in the short-term aggregate supply curve also play a role.

Before discussing the business cycle, we outline the main approaches available for tracking and projecting these movements. There are at least three distinct approaches:

- Econometric models: the most formal and mathematical.
- Indicators: variables that lead, lag, or coincide with turns in the economy.
- Checklists: subjective integration of the answers to relevant questions.

These approaches are not mutually exclusive. Indeed, thorough analysis is likely to incorporate elements of all three.

Econometric Modeling

Econometrics is the application of statistical methods to model relationships among economic variables. **Structural models** specify functional relationships among variables based on economic theory. The functional form and parameters of these models are derived from the underlying theory. **Reduced-form models** have a looser connection to theory. As the name suggests, some such models are simply more-compact representations of underlying structural models. At the other end of the spectrum are models that are essentially data driven, with only a heuristic rationale for selection of variables and/or functional forms.

Econometric models vary from small models with a handful of equations to large, complex models with hundreds of equations. They are all used in essentially the same way, however. The estimated system of equations is used to forecast the future values of economic variables, with the forecaster supplying values for the exogenous variables. For example, such a model may require the forecaster to enter exchange rates, interest rates, commodity prices, and/or policy variables. The model then uses the estimated past relationships to forecast the future. It is important to consider that the forecaster's future values for the exogenous variables are themselves subject to estimation error. This fact will increase the variability of potential forecast errors of the endogenous variables beyond what results from errors in the estimated parameter values. The analyst should examine a realistic range of values for the exogenous variables to assess the forecast's sensitivity to these inputs.

Econometric models are widely regarded as very useful for simulating the effects of changes in key variables. The great merit of the econometric approach is that it constrains the forecaster to a certain degree of consistency and also challenges the modeler to reassess prior views based on what the model concludes. It does have important limitations, however. Econometric models require the user to find adequate measures for the real-world activities and relationships to be modeled. These measures may be unavailable. Variables may also be measured with error. Relationships among the variables may change over time because of changes in economic structure and/or because the model may have been based on faulty assumptions as to how the world works. As a result, the econometric model may be mis-specified. In practice, therefore, skillful econometric modelers monitor the model's recent forecasts for signs of systematic errors. Persistent forecast errors should ideally lead to a complete overhaul of the model. In practice, however, a more pragmatic approach is often adopted: Past forecast errors are incorporated into the model as an additional explanatory variable.

Economic Indicators

Economic indicators are economic statistics published by official agencies and/or private organizations. These indicators contain information on an economy's recent past activity or its current or future position in the business cycle. Lagging economic indicators and coincident indicators reflect recent past and current economic activity, respectively. A **leading economic indicator** (LEI) moves ahead of the business cycle by a fairly consistent time interval. Most analysts focus primarily on leading indicators because they purport to provide information about upcoming changes in economic activity, inflation, interest rates, and security prices.

Leading indicator–based analysis is the simplest forecasting approach to use because it requires following only a limited number of statistics. It also has the advantage of not requiring the analyst to make assumptions about the path of exogenous variables. Analysts use both individual LEIs and composite LEIs, reflecting a collection of economic data releases combined to give an overall reading. The OECD composite LEI for each country or region is based on five to nine variables such as share prices, manufacturing metrics, inflation, interest rates, and monetary data that exhibit cyclical fluctuations similar to GDP, with peaks and troughs occurring six to nine months earlier with reasonable consistency. Individual LEIs can also be combined into a so-called **diffusion index**, which measures how many indicators are pointing up and how many down. For example, if 7 out of 10 are pointing upward, then the odds are that the economy is accelerating.

One of the drawbacks of the (composite) leading indicator methodology is that the entire history may be revised each month. As a result, the most recently published historical indicator series will almost certainly appear to have fit past business cycles (i.e., GDP) better than it actually did in real time. This distortion is known as "look ahead" bias. Correspondingly, the LEI may be less reliable in predicting the current/next cycle than history suggests.

Business cycle indicators have been published for decades. A new methodology for tracking the business cycle, known generically as "nowcasting," emerged in the United States in the wake of the global financial crisis. The best-known of these forecasts, the Federal Reserve Bank of Atlanta's "GDPNow," was first published on 1 May 2014 for the second quarter of that year. The objective is to forecast GDP for the current quarter (which will not be released until after quarter-end) based on data as it is released throughout the quarter. To do this, the Atlanta Fed attempts to use the same methodology and data as will be used by the Bureau of Economic Analysis (BEA) to estimate GDP, replacing data that has not yet been released with forecasts based on the data already observed. As the quarter progresses, more of the actual data will have been observed, and GDPNow should, at least on average, converge to what will be released by the BEA.

BEA RELEASES OF ESTIMATES

The BEA releases a sequence of three GDP estimates for each quarter. The first, labeled the "advance" estimate, is released four weeks after the end of the quarter and tends to have the greatest market impact. The "preliminary" estimate is released a month later, and the "final" estimate comes at the end of the following quarter. The Atlanta Fed's GDPNow is actually a forecast of the BEA's advance estimate, not of the final GDP release. Exhibit 3 compares the history of Atlanta Fed's GDPNow model forecast with the actual GDP change.

Exhibit 3: GDPNow Model Forecast vs. Actual GDP Change

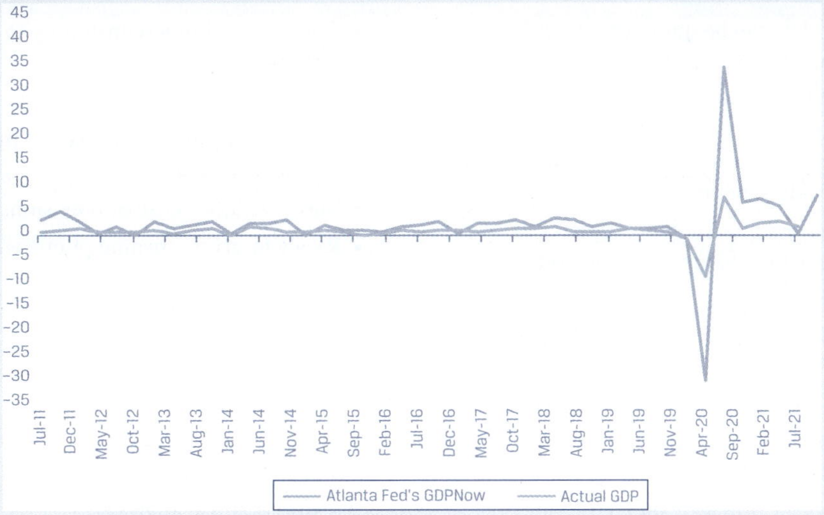

Sources: Federal Reserve Economic Data; St. Louis Fed.

It remains to be seen how useful nowcasting will be for investment analysts. It has a couple of clear advantages: It is updated in real time, and it is focused directly on a variable of primary interest (GDP and its components). Nowcasting is not designed to be predictive of anything beyond the end of the current quarter, however. In addition, it tends to be very volatile until a significant portion of the data for the quarter has been observed, at which point it may have lost some of its usefulness as a guide for investment decisions.

Checklist Approach

Formally or informally, many forecasters consider a whole range of economic data to assess the economy's future position. Checklist assessments are straightforward but time-consuming because they require continually monitoring the widest possible range of data. The data may then be extrapolated into forecasts via objective statistical methods, such as time-series analysis, or via more subjective or judgmental means. An analyst may then assess whether the measures are in an equilibrium state or nearer to an extreme reading.

The subjectivity of the checklist approach is perhaps its main weakness. The checklist's strength is its flexibility. It allows the forecaster to quickly take into account changes in economic structure by changing the variables or the weights assigned to variables within the analysis.

Economic Forecasting Approaches: Summary of Strengths and Weaknesses

Exhibit 4 summarizes the advantages and disadvantages of forecasting using econometric models, leading indicators, and checklists.

Exhibit 4: Economic Forecasting Approaches: Strengths and Weaknesses

Strengths	Weaknesses
Econometric Models Approach	
▪ Models can be quite robust, with many factors included to approximate reality. ▪ New data may be collected and consistently used within models to quickly generate output. ▪ Delivers quantitative estimates of impact of changes in exogenous variables. ▪ Imposes discipline/consistency on analysis.	▪ Complex and time-consuming to formulate. ▪ Data inputs not easy to forecast. ▪ Relationships not static. Model may be mis-specified. ▪ May give false sense of precision. ▪ Rarely forecasts turning points well.
Leading Indicator–Based Approach	
▪ Usually intuitive and simple in construction. ▪ Focuses primarily on identifying turning points. ▪ May be available from third parties. Easy to track.	▪ History subject to frequent revision. • "Current" data not reliable as input for historical analysis. • Overfitted in-sample. Likely overstates forecast accuracy. ▪ Can provide false signals. ▪ May provide little more than binary (no/yes) directional guidance.
Checklist Approach	
▪ Limited complexity. ▪ Flexible. • Structural changes easily incorporated. • Items easily added/dropped. • Can draw on any information, from any source, as desired. ▪ Breadth: Can include virtually any topics, perspectives, theories, and assumptions.	▪ Subjective. Arbitrary. Judgmental. ▪ Time-consuming. ▪ Manual process limits depth of analysis. No clear mechanism for combining disparate information. ▪ Imposes no consistency of analysis across items or at different points in time. May allow use of biased and/or inconsistent views, theories, assumptions.

EXAMPLE 9

Approaches to Forecasting

Sara Izek and Adam Berke are members of the asset allocation committee at Cycle Point Advisors, which emphasizes the business cycle within its tactical asset allocation process. Berke has developed a time series model of the business cycle that uses a published LEI series as a key input. He presents forecasts based on the model at each asset allocation meeting. Izek is eclectic in her approach, preferring to sample research from a wide variety of sources each month and then focus on whatever perspectives and results seem most interesting. She usually brings a stack of charts she has copied to the asset allocation meeting.

1. Which of the main forecasting approaches (or combination of approaches) best describe(s) each analyst's own practice?

   Guideline Answer:

   Berke uses the econometric modeling approach in conjunction with the LEI approach. Izek's practice is essentially a checklist approach.

2. What strength(s) are likely to have appealed to each analyst?

   Guideline Answer:

   Berke is probably attracted to the quantitative output provided by a model, the consistency and discipline it imposes on the process, and the ability to generate explicit forecasts. He may have included the LEI in the model because it is designed to capture cyclical turning points or simply because doing so improves the model's statistical fit of the model.

   Izek is probably drawn to the flexibility of the checklist approach with respect to what is included/excluded and how to evaluate the information.

3. What weaknesses might each analyst be overlooking?

   Guideline Answer:

   Berke may be overlooking potential mis-specification of his model, which is apt to make his forecasts systematically inaccurate (i.e., biased). He may also be failing to recognize the likely magnitude of the forecast errors that will be present even if the model is unbiased (i.e., overestimating the precision of the forecasts). By using the historical LEI series as an input to the model, he may be incorporating look-ahead bias into the model.

   Izek is likely overlooking the subjective, judgmental, and idiosyncratic nature of her approach. Her practice of basing her "checklist" on what seems most interesting in other analysts' current research makes her process especially vulnerable to inconsistency and cognitive biases.

6 BUSINESS CYCLE ANALYSIS, PHASES OF THE BUSINESS CYCLE AND MARKET EXPECTATIONS AND THE BUSINESS CYCLE

☐ discuss how business cycles affect short- and long-term expectations

The trend rate of economic growth provides a vital anchor for setting very long-run investment expectations, which in turn provide a starting point for developing projections over short- to intermediate-term horizons. Virtually by definition, deviations from trend wash out in the long run, making information about the current economic and market environment of limited value over very long horizons. Over short to intermediate horizons, however, such information can be very important. From a macroeconomic perspective, the most useful such information typically pertains to fluctuations associated with the **business cycle**.

It is useful to think of fluctuations in economic activity as a superposition of many cycles varying in frequency from very short (days) to very long (decades), each with stochastic amplitude. The business cycle is not a specific, well-defined cycle. It is the result of many intermediate frequency cycles that jointly generate most of the variation in aggregate economic activity (i.e., GDP) around the trend. This fact explains why historical business cycles have varied in both duration and intensity—each was a different realization of a range of underlying stochastic cycles. It also helps to explain why it is difficult to project turning points in real time.

BUSINESS CYCLE PEAKS AND TROUGHS

The best-known record of business cycle peaks and troughs is published for the United States by the National Bureau of Economic research (NBER). According to NBER, the United States has experienced 34 complete business cycles since 1854, averaging 59 months from peak to peak. The longest cycle was 146 months, the shortest only 17 months. Fifty percent of the cycles lasted between 38 and 69 months. On average, the cycle's contraction phase (peak to trough) lasted 17 months, whereas the expansion phase (trough to peak) lasted 42 months.

At a fundamental level, the business cycle arises in response to the interaction of uncertainty, expectational errors, and rigidities that prevent instantaneous adjustment to unexpected events. It reflects decisions that

a. are made based on imperfect information and/or analysis with the expectation of future benefits,

b. require significant current resources and/or time to implement, and

c. are difficult and/or costly to reverse.

Such decisions are, broadly defined, investment decisions. Much of the uncertainty that sustains the cycle is endogenous to the system. Competitors, suppliers, employers, creditors, customers, and policymakers do not behave as expected. Prices and quantities adjust more or less than expected. Other sources of uncertainty are more exogenous. Technological breakthroughs threaten to disrupt whole industries and/or create new ones. Fracking, gene sequencing, e-commerce, "big data," digital advertising, cybersecurity, 3-D printing, the internet of things, and driverless cars are among those now playing out. Weather patterns affect agriculture, construction, and transportation. Natural disasters devastate local economies. Political and geopolitical shifts favor some entities and disadvantage others. And, of course, shocks in one part of the global economy are often transmitted to other parts of the world through trade relations, financial markets, and the prices of goods and services.

Numerous variables can be used to monitor the business cycle. Among them are GDP growth, industrial production (IP), employment/unemployment, purchasing managers indexes, orders for durable goods, the output gap (the difference between GDP estimated as if the economy were on its trend growth path and the actual value of GDP), and the leading indicator indexes discussed earlier.

Phases of the Business Cycle

There are various ways to delineate phases of the business cycle. The most obvious is to divide it into two primary segments (the expansion and the contraction) with two key turning points at which growth changes sign (the peak and the trough). These two periods are fairly easy to identify, at least in retrospect. Subdividing the cycle more finely is more ambiguous, even in retrospect, because it requires identifying more nuanced changes such as acceleration or deceleration of growth without a change in direction. Nonetheless, it is useful to divide the cycle into several phases distinguished through both economic and financial market characteristics. For the purpose of setting expectations for capital markets, we use five phases of the business cycle here: initial recovery, early expansion, late expansion, slowdown, and contraction. The first four occur within the overall expansion.

1. Initial recovery. This period is usually a short phase of a few months beginning at the trough of the cycle in which the economy picks up, business confidence rises, stimulative policies are still in place, the negative output gap is large, and inflation is typically decelerating. Recovery is often supported by an upturn in spending on housing and consumer durables.

   Capital market effects: Short-term rates and government bond yields are low. Bond yields may continue to decline in anticipation of further disinflation but are likely to be bottoming. Stock markets may rise briskly as fears of a longer recession (or even a depression) dissipate. Cyclical assets—and riskier assets, such as small stocks, higher-yield corporate bonds, and emerging market equities and bonds—attract investors and typically perform well.

2. Early expansion. The economy is gaining some momentum, unemployment starts to fall but the output gap remains negative, consumers borrow and spend, and businesses step up production and investment. Profits typically rise rapidly. Demand for housing and consumer durables is strong.

   Capital market effects: Short rates are moving up as the central bank starts to withdraw stimulus put in place during the recession. Longer-maturity bond yields are likely to be stable or rising slightly. The yield curve is flattening. Stocks trend upward.

3. Late expansion. The output gap has closed, and the economy is increasingly in danger of overheating. A boom mentality prevails. Unemployment is low, profits are strong, both wages and inflation are rising, and capacity pressures boost investment spending. Debt coverage ratios may deteriorate as balance sheets expand and interest rates rise. The central bank may aim for a "soft landing" while fiscal balances improve.

   Capital market effects: Interest rates are typically rising as monetary policy becomes restrictive. Bond yields are usually rising, more slowly than short rates, so the yield curve continues to flatten. Private sector borrowing puts pressure on credit markets. Stock markets often rise but may be volatile as nervous investors endeavor to detect signs of looming deceleration. Cyclical assets may underperform while inflation hedges such as commodities outperform.

4. Slowdown. The economy is slowing and approaching the eventual peak, usually in response to rising interest rates, fewer viable investment projects, and accumulated debt. It is especially vulnerable to a shock at this juncture. Business confidence wavers. Inflation often continues to rise as firms raise prices in an attempt to stay ahead of rising costs imposed by other firms doing the same.

   Capital market effects: Short-term interest rates are high, perhaps still rising, but likely to peak. Government bond yields top out at the first clear sign of a slowing economy and may then decline sharply. The yield curve may invert, especially if the central bank continues to exert upward pressure on short rates. Credit spreads, especially for weaker credits generally widen. The stock market may fall, with interest-sensitive stocks such as utilities and "quality" stocks with stable earnings performing best.

5. Contraction. Recessions typically last 12 to 18 months. Investment spending, broadly defined, typically leads the contraction. Firms cut production sharply. Once the recession is confirmed, the central bank eases monetary policy. Profits drop sharply. Tightening credit magnifies downward pressure on the economy. Recessions are often punctuated by major bankruptcies, incidents of uncovered fraud, exposure of aggressive accounting practices, or a financial crisis. Unemployment can rise quickly, impairing household financial positions.

   Capital market effects: Short-term interest rates drop during this phase, as do bond yields. The yield curve steepens substantially. The stock market declines in the earlier stages of the contraction but usually starts to rise in the later stages, well before the recovery emerges. Credit spreads typically widen and remain elevated until signs of a trough emerge and it becomes apparent that firms will be able to roll over near-term debt maturities.

Exhibit 5 summarizes the fives phases of the business cycle, together with their impact on capital markets.

Exhibit 5: The Five Phases of the Business Cycle

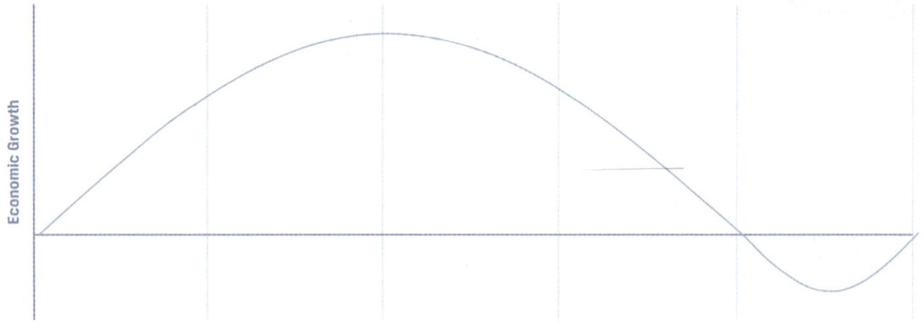

Initital Recovery	Early Expansion	Late Expansion	Slowdown	Contraction
Short-term and bond yield low Bond yields may still decline Stock markets may rise briskly Cyclical assets—small stocks, high yield, EM equities and bonds—attract investors	Short-term rates move up Yield curve flattens Stocks trend upward	Short-term interest rates rise Long-term rates rise slowly Pressure on credit market builds up Stocks rise, but more volatile Cyclical assets underperform	Short-term rates peak Bond yields top out Yield curve may invert Credit spreads widen Stocks may fall Utility and quality stocks outperform	Short-term rates drop Bond yields decline Yield curve steepens Credit spreads stay elevated Stocks reach bottom, may start to rise at the end of the contraction phase

Market Expectations and the Business Cycle

This description of a typical business cycle may suggest that forming capital market expectations for short and intermediate horizons should be relatively straightforward. If an investor can identify the current phase of the cycle and correctly predict when the next phase will begin, is it not easy to make money? Unfortunately, it is not that simple.

First, the phases of the business cycle vary in length and amplitude. Recessions can be steep, and downturns (such as in the 1930s and in 2007–2009) can be frightening. On the other hand, recessions also can be short lived, with only a small decline in output and only a modest rise in unemployment. Sometimes, the weakest phase of the cycle does not even involve a recession but merely a period of slower economic growth or a "growth recession." Similarly, expansions vary in length and intensity.

Second, it is not always easy to distinguish between cyclical forces and secular forces acting on the economy and the markets. The prolonged recovery following the 2007–2009 global financial crisis is a prime example. Interest rates and inflation went far lower and remained extraordinarily low far longer than virtually anyone would have predicted based on a purely cyclical view.

Third, although the connection between the real economy and capital market returns is strong, it is subject to substantial uncertainty. Capital market prices reflect a composite of investors' expectations and attitudes toward risk with respect to all future horizons. How, when, and by how much the markets respond to the business cycle are as uncertain as the cycle itself—perhaps more so.

What does all of this variation and uncertainty imply for setting capital market projections? First, as with virtually any investment information, business cycle analysis generates a noisy signal with respect to prospective opportunities. Second, the signal is likely to be most reliable (a higher "signal-to-noise" ratio), and hence most valuable, over horizons within the range of likely expansion and contraction phases—perhaps one to three years. Returns over substantially shorter horizons are likely to be driven primarily by market reactions to more transitory developments, undermining the cycle's predictive value. On the other hand, as the forecast horizon extends beyond this range, it becomes increasingly likely that one or more turning points will occur within the horizon, implying returns that increasingly reflect averaging over the cycle.

EXAMPLE 10

Cycles, Horizons, and Expectations

Lee Kim uses a statistical model that divides the business cycle into two "regimes": expansion and contraction. The expected (continuously compounded) return on equities is +2% per month during expansions and –2% per month during contractions. Consistent with NBER's historical record (see earlier sidebar), the probabilities of transitioning between regimes imply that expansions last 39 months on average, whereas contractions average 20 months. Correspondingly, over the long run, the economy expands roughly two-thirds of the time and contracts one-third of the time. Hence, the long-term expected equity return is 0.67% = [(2% × 2/3) + (–2% × 1/3)] per month, or 8% per year. Kim's model indicates that the economy recently transitioned into contraction. For the upcoming asset allocation committee meeting, he will prepare equity return forecasts for horizons of 3 months, 1 year, 5 years, and 10 years.

1. Explain how you would expect the choice of time horizon to affect Kim's projections.

   Guideline Answer:

   The longer the horizon, the more likely that one or more transitions will occur between contraction and expansion; more generally, the more likely it is that the horizon spans more than one business cycle phase or even more than one full cycle. As a result, the longer the horizon, the more Kim's forecast should reflect averaging over periods of expansion and contraction and the closer it will be to the "information-less" average of 8% per year.

   Over the next three months, it is highly likely that the economy will remain in contraction, so Kim's forecast for that period should be very close to –2% per month [cumulatively –6%]. Because contractions last 20 months on average in the model, Kim's forecast for a one-year horizon should reflect only a modestly higher probability of having transitioned to expansion at some point within the period. So, his forecast might be –18% (an average of –1.5% per month) instead of –24% (–2% per month). Over a five-year horizon, it is very likely that the economy will have spent time in both contraction and expansion. As a result, Kim's forecast will put significant weight on each phase. Because the economy starts in contraction (i.e., the starting point is not random), the weight on that phase will probably be somewhat higher than its long-term frequency of 1/3, say 0.40. This assumption implies a forecast of 4.8% per year [= 12 × [(0.6 × 2%) + (0.4 × −2%)]. Over a 10-year horizon, the frequency of expansion and contraction months is likely to be very close to the 2-to-1 long-run ratio. So, Kim's forecast should be very close to 8% per year.

7 INFLATION AND DEFLATION: TRENDS AND RELATIONS TO THE BUSINESS CYCLE

☐ explain the relationship of inflation to the business cycle and the implications of inflation for cash, bonds, equity, and real estate returns

Until the early 20th century, the money supply was largely dictated by the supply of specie—gold and/or silver used in coins and to back bank deposits. Periods of both inflation and deflation were common. Today, currencies are backed by the credibility of governments and central banks rather than specie, and people expect the prices of goods and services to trend upward. Persistent deflation is rare. Expectation of an upward trend in prices reflects recognition of an asymmetry in a central bank's so-called "reaction function." It is generally accepted that a central bank's policy tools are more effective in slowing economic activity than in accelerating sluggish activity. Hence, central banks may tend to be more aggressive in combating downward pressure on demand than in reining in strong demand. In addition, it is widely believed that outright deflation damages the economy because it undermines:

- debt-financed investments. Servicing and repayment of nominally fixed debt becomes more onerous as nominal income flows and the nominal value of real assets both decline; and
- the power of central banks. In a deflationary environment, interest rates fall to levels close to (or even below) zero. When interest rates are already very low, the central bank has less leeway to stimulate the economy by lowering interest rates.

In contrast, moderate inflation is generally considered to impose only modest costs on the economy. Both the differential effectiveness of policy and the differential costs of inflation versus deflation suggest that central banks will, implicitly or explicitly, target positive inflation, and investors set their expectations accordingly. The result is that asset prices in general and bond yields in particular generally build in compensation for a positive average inflation rate.

Inflation is procyclical, accelerating in the later stages of the business cycle when the output gap has closed and decelerating when, during a recession or the early years afterward, there is a large output gap, which puts downward pressure on wages and prices. If the central bank's target is credible, the average rate of inflation over the cycle should be near the target.

Because the cyclical pattern of inflation is well known, inflation expectations will also be procyclical. It is important, however, to differentiate inflation expectations by horizon. Very long-term inflation expectations should be virtually unaffected by cyclical fluctuations provided investors maintain confidence in the central bank's target. Short horizon expectations will tend to have about the same amplitude as actual inflation. Inflation, and therefore inflation expectations, over intermediate horizons will be a blend of the different phases of the current and subsequent cycles. Hence, the amplitude of expectations will decline with horizon—again, provided investors do not lose confidence in the central bank's target.

The pattern just described implies a "horizon structure" of inflation expectations that is countercyclical—upward sloping at the trough of the business cycle and inverted at the peak. Because inflation expectations are an important component of bond yields, this countercyclical pattern is one of the reasons that the yield curve's slope is countercyclical.[12]

To assess the effect of inflation on asset classes, we must consider both the cash flows and the discount rates. We consider "cash," nominal bonds, stocks, and real estate.

- *Cash:* In this context, cash is taken to mean short-term interest-bearing instruments, not currency or zero-interest deposits. As long as short-term interest rates adjust with expected inflation, cash is essentially a zero-duration, inflation-protected asset that earns a floating real rate. Inflation above or below expectation contributes to temporary fluctuations in the realized real return. Because central banks aim to stabilize actual and expected inflation, they tend to make the real rate on cash procyclical around a long-term level consistent with their target inflation rate. Hence, cash is relatively attractive (unattractive) in a rising (declining) rate environment. Deflation may make cash particularly attractive if a zero-lower-bound is binding on the nominal interest rate. Otherwise deflation is simply a component of the required short-term real rate.
- *Bonds:* Because the cash flows are fixed in nominal terms, the effect of inflation is transmitted solely through the discount rates (i.e., the yield curve). Rising (falling) inflation induces capital losses (gains) as the expected inflation component of yields rises (falls). If inflation remains within the expected cyclical range, shorter-term yields rise/fall more than longer yields but have less price impact as a result of shorter duration. If, however, inflation moves out of the expected range, longer-term yields may rise/fall more sharply as investors reassess the likelihood of a change in the long-run average level of inflation. Persistent deflation benefits the highest-quality bonds because it increases the purchasing power of the cash flows, but it is likely to impair the creditworthiness of lower-quality debt.
- *Stocks:* As long as inflation stays within the expected cyclical range, there should be little effect on stocks because both expected future cash flows (earnings and dividends) and associated discount rates rise/fall in line with the horizon structure of inflation expectations. Signs that inflation is moving out of the expected range, however, indicate a potential threat. Unexpectedly high and/or rapidly rising inflation could mean that the central bank needs to act to slow the economy, whereas very low and/or falling inflation (possibly deflation) threatens a recession and a decline in asset

12 As will be discussed later, compensation for taking duration risk (the "term premium") is procyclical. As a result, an inverted "horizon structure" of expected inflation does not necessarily imply an inverted yield curve.

prices. Within the stock market, higher inflation benefits firms that are able to pass along rising costs, whereas deflation is especially detrimental for asset-intensive, commodity-producing, and/or highly leveraged firms.

- *Real estate:* Short- to intermediate-term nominal cash flows are generally dictated by existing leases, with the speed of adjustment depending on the type of real estate asset held. As long as inflation remains within the expected range, renewal of leases will likely generate rental income rising with expected inflation, accompanied by stable asset values. Higher-than-expected inflation is likely to coincide with high demand for real estate, expectations that rental income will rise even faster than general inflation, and rising property values. The impact may be quite idiosyncratic, however, depending on the length of leases, the existing supply of similar properties, and the likelihood of new supply hitting the market when leases come up for renewal. On the other hand, unexpectedly low inflation (or deflation) will put downward pressure on expected rental income and property values, especially for less-than-prime properties, which may have to cut rents sharply to avoid rising vacancies.

EXAMPLE 11

Inflation

1. Kesia Jabari believes the quantitative easing undertaken by major central banks in the wake of the global financial crisis is finally about to induce a surge in inflation. She believes that without extraordinary policy actions from the central banks, the inflation rate will ultimately rise to the upper end of central banks' tolerance ranges at the peak of the current business cycle.

   Assuming Jabari is correct, discuss the likely implications for floating-rate instruments ("cash"), bonds, stocks, and real estate if:

   a. the market shares Jabari's view, or

   b. once inflation begins to rise, the market doubts that the central banks will be able to contain it.

   Guideline Answer:

   a. If the market agrees with Jabari, then the relationship of inflation and the asset classes to the business cycle should be fairly normal. Short-term rates and bond yields will rise with inflation expectations. The yield curve should flatten because long-term inflation expectations should remain well anchored. Floating-rate instruments (cash) will be relatively attractive, and intermediate maturities ("the belly of the curve") will be the most vulnerable. In general, the rise in inflation should not have much independent impact on stocks or real estate because both cash flows and discount rates will be expected to rise. Firms with pricing power and real estate with relatively short lease-renewal cycles are set to perform best.

   b. If the market doubts that central banks can contain inflation within previously perceived tolerances, then long-run inflation expectations will rise and the yield curve may steepen rather than flatten, at least initially. Floating-rate instruments will still be relatively attractive, but now it is the longest maturities that will be the most vulnerable.

Stocks are likely to suffer because the market expects central banks to be aggressive in fighting inflation. Real estate with long-term leases and little long-term, fixed-rate debt will suffer. Real estate with substantial long-term, fixed-rate debt should do relatively well, especially high-quality properties with little new supply nearby, which are likely to avoid significant vacancies even in a recession.

In the interest of completeness, we should note a caveat before leaving the topic of inflation. The preceding discussion implicitly assumes that the short-run aggregate supply curve is upward sloping and that the business cycle is primarily driven by fluctuations in aggregate demand. Together, these assumptions imply that inflation is pro-cyclical. Although globalization may have reduced the sensitivity of domestic prices to domestic output, it seems unlikely that domestic output/growth no longer matters. Thus, the aggregate supply curve may be *flatter* but is unlikely to be *flat*. With regard to what drives the cycle, if aggregate supply shocks predominate, then inflation will tend to be *counter*cyclical, reflecting alternating periods of "stagflation" and disinflationary boom. The 1970s oil crisis is a prime example. This pattern is more likely to be the exception rather than the rule, however.

ANALYSIS OF MONETARY AND FISCAL POLICIES 8

☐ discuss the effects of monetary and fiscal policy on business cycles

Actual and anticipated actions by monetary and fiscal authorities affect the decisions and actions of all other participants in the economy and the markets. As a result, it is somewhat difficult to isolate their role(s) from our broader discussion. Indeed, the foregoing sections have made numerous references to these policies. Nonetheless it is worthwhile to focus directly on these policies from the perspective of setting capital market expectations.

Monetary policy is often used as a mechanism for intervention in the business cycle. Indeed, this use is inherent in the mandates of most central banks to maintain price stability and/or growth consistent with the economy's potential. Each central bank interprets its mandate somewhat differently, sets its own operational objectives and guidelines, and selects its own mix of the tools (e.g., policy rates and liquidity provision) at its disposal. The common theme is that central banks virtually always aim to moderate the cyclical behavior of growth and inflation, in both directions. Thus, monetary policy aims to be countercyclical. The impact of monetary policy, however, is famously subject to "long and variable lags," as well as substantial uncertainty. As a result, a central bank's ability to fine-tune the economy is limited, and there is always risk that policy measures will exacerbate rather than moderate the business cycle. This risk is greatest at the top of the cycle, when the central bank may overestimate the economy's momentum and/or underestimate the effects of restrictive policies. In such situations, monetary policy may trigger a contraction that it cannot immediately counteract. In contrast, expansionary monetary policy rarely, if ever, suffices to turn a contraction into a strong recovery. This asymmetry is captured in a classic analogy: Expansionary policy is like "pushing" on a string, whereas restrictive policy is like "pulling" on a string.

Fiscal policy (government spending and taxation) can also be used to counteract cyclical fluctuations in the economy. Aside from extreme situations, however—such as the Great Depression of the 1930s and recovery from the 2007–2009 global financial crisis—fiscal policy typically addresses objectives other than regulating short-term growth, for at least two main reasons. First, in all but the most authoritarian regimes, the fiscal decision-making process is too lengthy to make timely adjustments to aggregate spending and taxation aimed at short-term objectives. Second, frequent changes of a meaningful magnitude would be disruptive to the ongoing process of providing and funding government services.

Notwithstanding these considerations, fiscal policy often does play a role in mitigating cyclical fluctuations. Progressive tax regimes imply that the effective tax rate on the private sector is pro-cyclical—rising as the economy expands and falling as the economy contracts. Similarly, means-based transfer payments vary inversely with the economy, helping to mitigate fluctuations in disposable income for the most vulnerable households. The effect of these so-called automatic stabilizers should not be overlooked in setting expectations for the economy and the markets.

From the perspective of an investment analyst focused on establishing expectations for broad asset classes, having a handle on monetary policy is mission-critical with respect to cyclical patterns. Under normal conditions, fiscal adjustments are important but likely to be secondary considerations. The reverse is likely with respect to assessing the long run. Of course, if a major change in fiscal stance is contemplated or has been implemented, the impact warrants significant attention with respect to all horizons. The major overhaul of the US tax code (the Tax Cuts and Jobs Act) at the end of 2017 is a good example of these points. Among the main provisions of this tax code change was a corporate tax rate reduction from 35% to 21% and a one-time reduced tax rate for US corporations' foreign earnings if these earnings held in off-shore cash accounts are repatriated to on-shore accounts. These were significant changes with an impact on how US-based global firms handled their foreign earnings. It almost certainly provided a short-term stimulus, especially with respect to capital expenditures. But it was not a short-term policy adjustment. It was the most significant change to the tax code in decades, a major structural change that may affect the path of both the economy and the markets for many years.

Monetary Policy

Central banks can, and do, carry out their mandates somewhat differently. In general, they seek to mitigate extremes in inflation and/or growth via countercyclical policy measures. As a generic illustration of how this might work, we briefly review the **Taylor rule**. In the current context, it can be viewed as a tool for assessing a central bank's stance and a guide to predicting how that stance is likely to evolve.

In essence, the Taylor rule links a central bank's target short-term nominal interest rate to the expected growth rate of the economy and inflation, relative to trend growth and the central bank's inflation target.

$$i^* = r_{\text{neutral}} + \pi_e + 0.5\left(\hat{Y}_e - \hat{Y}_{\text{trend}}\right) + 0.5(\pi_e - \pi_{\text{target}})$$

where

i^* = target nominal policy rate

r_{neutral} = real policy rate that would be targeted if growth is expected to be at trend and inflation on target

π_e, π_{target} = respectively, the expected and target inflation rates

$\hat{Y}_e$, $\hat{Y}_{\text{trend}}$ = respectively, the expected and trend real GDP growth rates

The rule can be re-expressed in terms of the real, inflation-adjusted target rate by moving the expected inflation rate to the left-hand side of the equation.

$$i^* - \pi_e = r_{\text{neutral}} + 0.5\left(\hat{Y}_e - \hat{Y}_{\text{trend}}\right) + 0.5(\pi_e - \pi_{\text{target}})$$

From this rearrangement, we see that the real, inflation-adjusted policy rate deviates from neutral by one-half the amount by which growth and inflation deviate from their respective targets. As an example, suppose the neutral real policy rate is 2.25%, the target inflation rate is 2%, and trend growth is estimated to be 2.5%. If growth is expected to be 3.5% and inflation is expected to be 3%, the Taylor rule would call for a 6.25% nominal policy rate:

2.25% + 3% + 0.5 (3.5% − 2.5%) + 0.5 (3.0% − 2.0%) = 6.25%.

With expected inflation at 3%, this calculation corresponds to a 3.25% real policy rate.

Even if a central bank were to set its policy rate according to the Taylor rule, there could still be substantial judgment left in the process. None of the inputs to the rule are objectively observable. To make the rule operational, policymakers and their staffs have to specify how the requisite expectations will be generated, and by whom. Whose estimate of trend growth is to be used? What is the appropriate neutral real policy rate? Over what horizon(s) do the expectations apply? Models could be developed to answer all these questions, but there would be judgments to be made in doing so. The upshot for the investment analyst is that monetary policy cannot be reduced to a simple equation. The Taylor rule, or some customized variant, provides a good framework for analyzing the thrust and likely evolution of monetary policy, but the analyst must pay careful attention to situational signals from the central bank. This is why, for example, the investment community literally scrutinizes every word in the Federal Reserve's post-meeting statements and speeches by officials, looking for any hint of a change in the Fed's own interpretation of the environment.

EXAMPLE 12

Policies and the Business Cycle

Albert Grant, CFA, is an institutional portfolio strategist at Camford Advisors. After a period of trend growth, inflation at the central bank's target, and neutral monetary policy, the economy has been hit by a substantial deflationary shock.

1. How are monetary and fiscal policies likely to respond to the shock?

Camford's economics department estimates that growth is now 1% below trend and inflation is 2% below the central bank's target. Camford's chief investment officer (CIO) has asked Grant to put together a projection of the likely path of policy rates for the next five years.

Guideline Answer:

A countercyclical response can be expected from both monetary and fiscal policy. Assuming the central bank uses a policy rate target as its primary tool, it will cut that rate. On the fiscal side, there may be no explicit expansionary policy action (tax cut or spending increase), but automatic stabilizers built into tax and transfer programs can be expected to cushion the shock's impact on private sector disposable incomes.

2. If Grant believes the central bank will respond in accordance with the Taylor Rule, what other information will he need in order to project the path of policy rates?

   Guideline Answer:

   Grant will need to know what values the central bank uses for the neutral real rate, trend growth rate, and inflation target. He will also need to know how the central bank forms its expectations of growth and inflation. Finally, he will need to know how growth and inflation are likely to evolve, including how they will be affected by the path of policy rates.

3. What pattern should Grant expect for growth, inflation, and market interest rates if the central bank does *not* respond to the shock?

   Guideline Answer:

   The deflationary shock is very likely to induce a contractionary phase of the business cycle, putting additional downward pressure on growth and inflation. Short-term market interest rates will be dragged downward by weak demand and deflation. Risky asset prices are likely to fall sharply. A deep and/or protracted recession may be required before conditions conducive to recovery are in place. Grant should therefore expect a deep "U-shaped" path for growth, inflation, and short-term rates.

4. Assuming the central bank does respond and that its reaction function is well approximated by the Taylor Rule, how will this alter Grant's expectations regarding the paths of growth, inflation, and short-term rates over the next five years?

   Guideline Answer:

   If the central bank responds as expected, it will push short-term rates down farther and faster than they would otherwise fall in an effort to mitigate the downward momentum of growth and inflation. If the central bank correctly calibrates its policy, growth and inflation should decline less, bottom out sooner, and recover more quickly toward trend growth and the target inflation level, respectively, than in the absence of a policy response. Whereas the central bank is virtually certain to drive short rates down farther and faster, it may be inclined to let the market dictate the pace at which rates eventually rise. That is, it may simply "accommodate" the need for higher rates rather than risk unduly restraining the recovery once it is established.

9 ZERO OR NEGATIVE INTEREST RATES AND IMPLICATIONS FOR CAPITAL MARKETS EXPECTATIONS

☐ discuss the effects of monetary and fiscal policy on business cycles

Prior to the 2007–2009 global financial crisis, it was generally accepted that central banks could not successfully implement negative interest rate policies. Belief in a "zero lower bound" on policy rates assumed that individuals would choose to hold currency (coins and notes) if faced with earning a negative interest rate on short-term instruments, including deposits. The move toward holding currency would drain deposits and reserves from the banking system, causing bank balance sheets to shrink. The resulting credit contraction would put upward pressure on interest rates, thwarting the central bank's attempt to maintain negative rates. The contraction of credit would likely also put additional downward pressure on economic growth, thereby reinforcing the need for stimulative policies.

This line of reasoning raised questions about the effectiveness of traditional monetary policy when the economy is so weak that economic growth fails to respond to (nominal) interest rates approaching zero. Following the global financial crisis, as well as after the COVID-19 pandemic began, central banks faced with this situation pursued less conventional measures.

One important measure was quantitative easing, in which central banks committed to large-scale, ongoing purchases of high-quality domestic fixed-income securities. These purchases were funded by creating an equally large quantity of bank reserves in the form of central bank deposits. As a result of QE, central bank balance sheets and bank reserves grew significantly and sovereign bond yields fell. QE was pursued by (among others) the US Federal Reserve, the European Central Bank, the Bank of Japan, and the Bank of England.

Conventional reasoning suggests that QE should have resulted in the desired growth in nominal spending. In theory, banks could use the increased reserves to extend loans, and low interest rates would stimulate businesses and households to borrow. The borrowing was expected to fund capital expenditure by businesses as well as current consumption and purchases of durables (e.g., houses and cars) by households, thereby stimulating the economy. With interest rates low, investors were expected to bid up the prices of stocks and real estate. Although asset prices did increase and businesses that could issue bonds borrowed heavily, proceeds were more often used to fund dividends and stock buybacks rather than capital expenditures. At the same time, household spending ability was significantly curtailed by the legacy of the global financial crisis.

Whether or not QE was effective remains subject to debate. To achieve desired levels of economic growth, central banks tried the previously unthinkable: targeting negative interest rates. The central banks of Denmark, Sweden, Japan, Switzerland, and the euro area were among those that adopted negative policy rates. Contrary to the notion of a "zero lower bound," negative policy rates proved to be sustainable. As of November 2021, 23% of the 1,744 bonds in the Bloomberg Global Aggregate Treasuries Index had negative nominal yield to maturity. These bonds represent 27% of the index's market value. The issuers of such bonds are governments in the eurozone, as well as Switzerland, Denmark, Sweden, and Japan.

The move into currency did not occur as expected because the scale and speed of transactions inherent in modern economies cannot be supported using physical cash as the primary method of exchange.[13] Trillions of dollars change hands daily to facilitate trade in goods, services, and financial instruments, and these transactions cannot be accomplished using physical cash. Bank deposits and bank reserves held at the central bank, rather than as vault cash, have an implicit yield or convenience value that cash does not. As long as this value exceeds the explicit cost of holding those deposits—in the form of a negative interest rate—there is no incentive to convert deposits into cash. In such circumstances, negative policy rates may be achievable and sustainable.

13 It should also be noted that banks were reluctant to directly impose negative rates on their retail and commercial deposit customers. In general, rates on these accounts remained non-negative. Thus, the aggregate incentive to move into cash was mitigated somewhat. Various fees (e.g., for overdraft protection) and conditions imposed on the accounts (e.g., compensating balance requirements), however, may still have resulted in a net cost for deposit customers.

In theory, using negative nominal rates to stimulate an economy should work similarly to using low but still positive rates. Businesses and consumers are encouraged to hold fewer deposits for transaction purposes; investors are encouraged to seek higher expected returns on other assets; consumers are encouraged to save less and/or borrow more against future income; businesses are encouraged to invest in profitable projects; and banks are encouraged to use their reserves in support of larger loan books. All of this is expected to stimulate economic growth.

For consumers, investors, businesses, and banks to behave as described, however, each must believe they will be adequately rewarded for taking the inherent risks. In a negative interest rate environment, these entities are likely to have greater levels of uncertainty as to whether they will be adequately compensated for risks taken, and therefore they may not act as desired by monetary policy makers. As a result, the effectiveness of expansionary monetary policy is more tenuous at low and negative interest rate levels than at higher interest rate levels.

Implications of Negative Interest Rates for Capital Market Expectations

Long-run capital market expectations typically take the level of the "risk-free rate" as a baseline to which various risk premiums are added to arrive at long-run expected returns for risky assets such as long-term bonds and equities. The implicit assumption is that the risk-free rate is at its long-term equilibrium level. When short-term rates are negative, the long-run equilibrium short-term rate can be used as the baseline rate in these models instead of the observed negative rate. This rate can be estimated using the neutral policy rate ($r_{neutral}$) in the Taylor rule (or more generally in the central bank's presumed reaction function), adjusted for a modest spread between policy rates and default-free rates available to investors.

In forming capital market expectations for shorter time horizons, analysts and investors must consider the expected path of interest rates. Paths should be considered that, on average, converge to the long-run equilibrium rate estimate. With negative policy rates in place, this approach means a negative starting point. In theory, many possible scenarios, each appropriately weighted by its likelihood, should be considered. In practice, it may suffice to consider only a few scenarios. Because shorter horizons provide less opportunity for the impact of events to average out, the shorter the forecast horizon, the more important it is to consider deviations from the most likely path.

Negative policy rates are expected to produce asset class returns similar to those occurring in the contraction and early recovery phases of a "more normal" business/policy cycle. Although such historical periods may provide a reasonable starting point in formulating appropriate scenarios, it is important to note that negative rate periods may indicate severe distress in the economy and thus involve greater uncertainty regarding the timing and strength of recovery.

Key considerations when forming capital market expectations in a negative interest rate environment include the following:

- Historical data are less likely to be reliable.
    - Useful data may exist on only a few historical business cycles, which may not include instances of negative rates. In addition, fundamental structural/institutional changes in markets and the economy may have occurred since this data was generated.
    - Quantitative models, especially statistical models, tend to break down in situations that differ from those on which they were estimated/calibrated.

- Forecasting must account for differences between the current environment and historical averages. Historical averages, which average out differences across phases of the cycle, will be even less reliable than usual.
- The effects of other monetary policy measures occurring simultaneously (e.g., quantitative easing) may distort market relationships such as the shape of the yield curve or the performance of specific sectors.

Incorporating uncertain dynamics, including negative interest rates, into capital market expectations over finite horizons is much more difficult than projecting long-term average levels. The challenge arises from the fact that asset prices depend not only on investor expectations regarding longer term "equilibrium" levels but also on the path taken to get there.

THE MONETARY AND FISCAL POLICY MIX AND THE SHAPE OF THE YIELD CURVE AND THE BUSINESS CYCLE 10

- ☐ discuss the effects of monetary and fiscal policy on business cycles
- ☐ interpret the shape of the yield curve as an economic predictor and discuss the relationship between the yield curve and fiscal and monetary policy

Fiscal policy is inherently political. Central banks ultimately derive their powers from governments, but most strive to be, or at least appear to be, independent of the political process in order to maintain credibility. As a result, to the extent that monetary and fiscal policy are coordinated, it is usually the case that the central bank takes the expected fiscal stance as given in formulating its own policy and disdains guidance from politicians regarding its policy.

The mix of monetary and fiscal policies has its most apparent impact on the level of interest rates and the shape of the yield curve. We first consider the effect of persistently loose or tight policies on the average level of rates. All else the same, loose fiscal policies (large deficits) increase the level of *real* interest rates because the domestic private sector must be induced to save more/investing less and/or additional capital must be attracted from abroad. Conversely, tight fiscal policies reduce real rates. Persistently loose monetary policy generally results in higher actual and expected inflation. Attempts by the central bank to hold down nominal rates will prove self-defeating, ultimately resulting in higher rather than lower nominal interest rates.[14] Conversely, persistently tight monetary policy ultimately reduces actual and expected inflation resulting in lower, rather than higher, nominal rates. Exhibit 6 summarizes the impact of persistent policy mixes on the level of real and nominal rates. In each case, the impact on real rates and on expected inflation is clear. Two cases involve a mix of loose and tight policy. In these cases, the combined impact could be higher or lower nominal rates. Nominal rates are labelled as "mid" level for these cases.

14 This was one of the crucial insights presented in Friedman (1968).

Exhibit 6: Effect of Persistent Policy Mix on the Average Level of Rates

		Fiscal Policy	
		Loose	**Tight**
Monetary Policy	**Loose**	High Real Rates + High Expected Inflation = High Nominal Rates	Low Real Rates + High Expected Inflation = Mid Nominal Rates
	Tight	High Real Rates + Low Expected Inflation = Mid Nominal Rates	Low Real Rates + Low Expected Inflation = Low Nominal Rates

The second impact of policy is on the slope of the yield curve. The slope of the term structure of (default-free) interest rates depends primarily on (1) the expected future path of short-term rates and (2) a risk premium required to compensate for the greater price volatility inherent in longer-maturity bonds. The maturity premium explains why the term structure is normally upward sloping. Changes in the curve's slope—flattening and steepening—are primarily driven by the evolution of short rate expectations, which are mainly driven by the business cycle and policies. This dynamic was described in an earlier discussion on business cycles. Exhibit 7 summarizes the main points regarding the evolution of rates, policy, and the yield curve.

Exhibit 7: Rates, Policy, and the Yield Curve over the Business Cycle

Cycle Phase	Monetary Policy & Automatic Stabilizers	Money Market Rates	Bond Yields and the Yield Curve
Initial recovery	Stimulative stance. Transitioning to tightening mode.	Low/bottoming. Increases expected over progressively shorter horizons.	Long rates bottoming. Shortest yields begin to rise first. Curve is steep.
Early expansion	Withdrawing stimulus	Moving up. Pace may be expected to accelerate.	Yields rising. Possibly stable at longest maturities. Curve is flattening. Front section of yield curve steepening, back half likely flattening.
Late expansion	Becoming restrictive	Above average and rising. Expectations tempered by eventual peak/decline.	Rising. Pace slows. Curve flattening from longest maturities inward.
Slowdown	Tight. Tax revenues may surge as accumulated capital gains are realized.	Approaching/reaching peak.	Peak. May then decline sharply. Curve flat to inverted.
Contraction	Progressively more stimulative. Aiming to counteract downward momentum.	Declining.	Declining. Curve steepening. Likely steepest on cusp of Initial Recovery phase.

Exhibit 8 illustrates the yield curve slope measured by the difference between the 10-year and three-month Treasury yield in the context of real GDP growth.

Exhibit 8

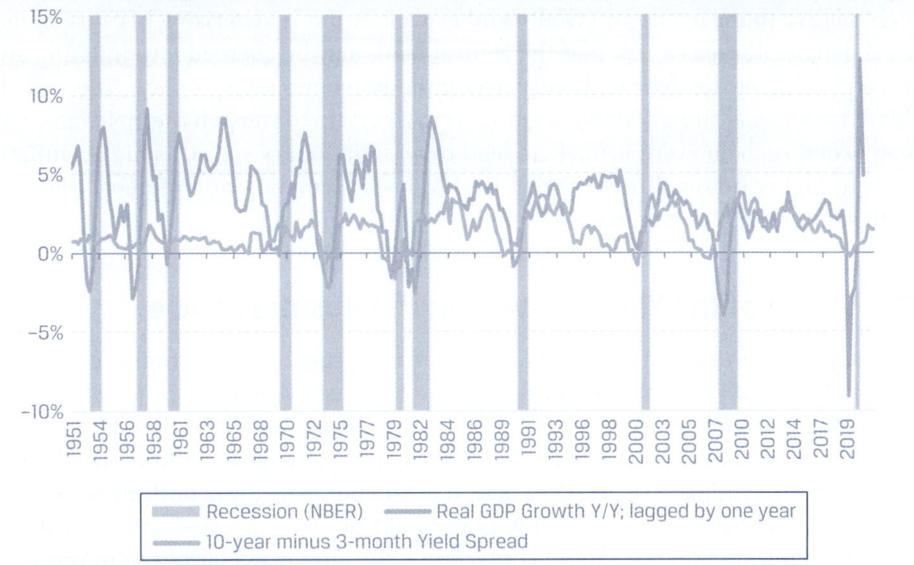

Sources: Bloomberg; NBER.

There is a third factor related to monetary and fiscal policy that may, or may not, be significant with respect to the shape of the yield curve and the effectiveness of policy: the relative supply of (government) bonds at various maturities. Does it matter what maturities the government issues in order to fund deficits? Does it matter what maturities the central bank chooses to buy/sell in its open market operations or its quantitative easing? There is no clear answer. The issue became important, however, in the wake of the global financial crisis for at least two reasons.

First, although it is now apparent that there is no clear lower bound on nominal interest rates, the effectiveness of conventional interest rate policies at very low rate levels remains in question. In particular, the central bank's ability to influence long-term rates may be even more tenuous than usual. Second, governments have run, and continue to run, large deficits while quantitative easing by major central banks has caused them to accumulate massive holdings of government debt (and other securities), which they may ultimately need or want to sell. If relative supply of debt along the yield curve really matters, then how governments fund their deficits in the future and how the central banks manage the maturity of their holdings could have significant implications for the yield curve and the broader financial markets.

It is difficult to draw firm conclusions with respect to maturity management. The existing evidence in conjunction with broader observation of markets, however, suggests the following: Sufficiently large purchases/sales at different maturities are likely to have a meaningful effect on the curve while they are occurring, but the effect is unlikely to be sustained for long once the buy/sell operation ends. To put it another way, a sufficiently large *flow* of supply may have a noticeable impact on relative yields, but discrete changes in the quantity of each maturity outstanding are much less likely to have a lasting impact. Government bonds are very liquid, and investors can and do move up and down the yield curve to exploit even very small yield differentials. Having said that, an important caveat pertaining to very long maturities is appropriate. Pension funds and other entities with very long-dated liabilities need correspondingly very long-maturity assets. Severely limiting the available supply of those assets would undoubtedly drive down their yield. Low yields at the very long end of the UK yield curve have been attributed to this effect at various times.

As a final comment on the interaction of monetary and fiscal policy, we acknowledge the potential for politicization of the central bank. If the level of government debt is high relative to the economy (GDP), and especially if it is also rising because of large fiscal deficits, there is a risk that the central bank may be coerced into inflating away the real value of the debt with very accommodative monetary policy. The risk that this dynamic *may* subsequently occur is almost certain to steepen the yield curve. If it *does* occur, such an event is likely to lead to an inflationary spiral, as higher inflation leads to higher nominal rates, which lead to faster accumulation of debt, which call forth even more accommodative monetary policy, and so on.

The Shape of the Yield Curve and the Business Cycle

The shape of the yield curve is frequently cited as a predictor of economic growth and as an indicator of where the economy is in the business cycle. Both casual observation and formal econometric analysis support its usefulness (an extensive bibliography is available at www.newyorkfed.org). The underlying rationale was summarized earlier in Exhibit 7. In simplest terms, the curve tends to be steep at the bottom of the cycle, flatten during the expansion until it is very flat or even inverted at the peak, and re-steepen during the subsequent contraction. Because expectations with respect to the path of short-term rates are the primary determinant of the curve's shape, the shape of the curve contains information about how market participants perceive the state and likely evolution of the economy as well as the impact they expect policymakers to have on that path. Thus, the empirical link between the shape of the yield curve and subsequent growth passes the test set out earlier for a good model—there is a solid rationale for believing it should be predictive. One must, of course, be aware that very few macroeconomic variables are truly exogenous and very few endogenous variables are completely unaffected by the past. "A" (shape of the yield curve) may predict "B" (growth next period), but it may also be the case that "B" predicts "A" in the period after that. The point is that the analyst should be aware of the fact that both the shape of the yield curve and economic growth (i.e., the business cycle) are endogenous within the economy. This is not to suggest throwing out a useful relationship but merely a reminder to interpret results with care.

EXAMPLE 13

The Business Cycle and the Yield Curve

Camford's quantitative analysis team helped Albert Grant incorporate the central bank's reaction function into a reduced-form model of growth and inflation. With this model, he will be able to project the path of short-term rates in the wake of the deflationary shock described in Example 12. Camford's CIO has now asked him to extend the analysis to project the path of bond yields as well.

1. What will Grant need in order to project the path of bond yields?

   Guideline Answer:

   Grant will need a model linking bond yields to the policy rate. In essence, he needs a model of the yield curve.

2. Even before he can undertake the formal analysis, a large client asks Grant to explain the likely implications for the yield curve. What can he say?

   Guideline Answer:

   Following the deflationary shock, the economy is very likely to enter into the contraction phase of the business cycle. The central bank will be cutting the policy rate, perhaps sharply. Long-term yields could drop even faster initially as the market anticipates that policy, but then the curve will steepen as the central bank cuts rates because long-maturity yields will incorporate the expectation of short-term rates rising again once the economy gains sufficient traction. The curve will likely reach its steepest point near the trough of the policy cycle and then gradually flatten as the economy gains strength and the central bank begins to tighten policy.

INTERNATIONAL INTERACTIONS

11

☐ identify and interpret macroeconomic, interest rate, and exchange rate linkages between economies

In general, the dependence of any particular country on international interactions is a function of its relative size and its degree of specialization. Large countries with diverse economies, such as the so-called G–7 (the United States, United Kingdom, Germany, France, Italy, Japan, and Canada), tend to be less influenced by developments elsewhere than smaller economies, such as Chile, whose output depends significantly on a few commodities like copper. Nonetheless, increasing globalization of trade, capital flows, and direct investment in recent decades has increased the importance of international interactions for nearly all countries.

Macroeconomic Linkages

Macroeconomic linkages between countries are expressed through their respective current and capital accounts. The current account reflects net exports of goods and services, net investment income flows, and unilateral transfers. The capital account, which for the purposes of this discussion also includes what is known as the financial account, reflects net investment flows for Foreign Direct Investment (FDI)—purchase and sale of productive assets across borders—and Portfolio Investment (PI) flows involving transactions in financial assets. By construction, if a country has a surplus on current account, it must have a matching deficit on capital account, or vice versa. Anything that affects one account must induce an equal and opposite change in the other account.

A nation's current and capital accounts are linked to the broader economy by the fact that net exports, virtually always the most significant component of the current account, contributes directly to aggregate demand for the nation's output. National income accounting also implies the following important relationship among net exports (X – M), saving (S), investment (I), and the government surplus (T – G):

$$(X - M) = (S - I) + (T - G).$$

Net exports always equal net private saving (the excess of domestic private saving over investment spending) plus the government surplus. Anything that changes net exports must also change net private saving, the government surplus, or both. Conversely, changes in either of these will be transmitted to the rest of the world through the current account. Of course, because the current account and capital accounts are mirror images, we can reverse all the signs in the foregoing equation and make corresponding statements about the capital account. A surplus on capital account is how a nation funds an excess of investment and government spending over domestic saving plus taxes.

There are four primary mechanisms by which the current and capital accounts are kept in balance: changes in income (GDP), relative prices, interest rates and asset prices, and exchange rates. Strictly speaking, all of these tools can play a role in both the real economy (the current account and FDI) and the financial markets, and they are determined simultaneously. However, markets do not all move at the same pace. In particular, investment markets adjust much more quickly than the real economy. In the short run, interest rates, exchange rates, and financial asset prices must adjust to keep the capital account in balance with the more slowly evolving current account. Meanwhile, the current account, in conjunction with real output and the relative prices of goods and services, tends to reflect secular trends and the pace of the business cycle.

EXAMPLE 14

International Macroeconomic Linkages

A large, diversified economy recently instituted a substantial tax cut, primarily aimed at reducing business taxes. Some provisions of the new law were designed to stem the tide of domestic firms moving production facilities abroad and encourage an increase in corporate investment in the domestic economy. There was no reduction in government spending. Prior to the tax cut, the country had both a current account deficit and a government deficit.

1. What impact is this tax cut likely to have on:

   a. the country's current account balance?

   b. the country's capital account balance?

   c. growth in other countries?

   d. the current and capital accounts of other countries?

Guideline Answer:

a. The deficit on current account will almost certainly increase. The government deficit will increase which, all else the same, will result in a one-for-one increase in the current account deficit. If the tax cut works as intended, domestic investment will increase, reducing net private saving and further increasing the current account deficit. Private saving will increase as a result of rising income (GDP), which will diminish the impact on the current account somewhat. Unless saving increases by the full amount of the tax cut plus the increase in investment spending, however, the net effect will be an increase in the current account deficit. In principle, this increase could be thwarted by movements in the financial markets that make it impossible to fund it, but this is unlikely.

b. Because the current account deficit will increase, the country's capital account surplus must increase by the same amount. In effect, the tax cut will be funded primarily by borrowing from abroad and/or selling assets to non-domestic investors. Part of the adjustment is likely to come from a reduction in FDI by domestic firms (i.e., purchases of productive assets abroad) provided the new tax provisions work as intended.

c. Growth in other countries is likely to increase as the tax cut stimulates demand for their exports and that increase in turn generates additional demand within their domestic economies.

d. In the aggregate, other countries must already be running current account surpluses and capital account deficits matching the balances of the country that has cut taxes. Their aggregate current account surplus and capital account deficit will increase by the same amount as the increase in current account deficit and capital account surplus of the tax-cutting country.

2. What adjustments is the tax cut likely to induce in the financial markets?

Guideline Answer:

The country must attract additional capital flows from abroad. This endeavor is likely to be facilitated, at least in part, by the expectation of rising after-tax profits resulting from the business taxes. Equity values should therefore rise. The adjustment may also require interest rates and bond yields to rise relative to the rest of the world. The impact on the exchange rate is less clear. Because the current account and the capital account represent exactly offsetting flows, there is no *a priori* change in demand for the currency. The net impact will be determined by what investors *expect* to happen. (See the following section for a discussion of exchange rate linkages.)

Interest Rate/Exchange Rate Linkages

One of the linkages of greatest concern to investors involves interest rates and exchange rates. The two are inextricably linked. This fact is perhaps most evident in the proposition that a country cannot simultaneously

- allow unrestricted capital flows;
- maintain a fixed exchange rate; and
- pursue an independent monetary policy.

The essence of this proposition is that if the central bank attempts to push interest rates down (up), capital will flow out (in), putting downward (upward) pressure on the exchange rate, forcing the bank to buy (sell) its own currency, and thereby reversing the expansionary (contractionary) policy. Carrying this argument to its logical conclusion suggests that, with perfect capital mobility and a fixed exchange rate, "the" interest rate must be the same in countries whose currencies are pegged to each other.

Can we extend this proposition to encompass the whole (default-free) yield curve? Yes, but in doing so, we have to be somewhat more precise. Under what conditions would two markets share a yield curve? First, there must be unrestricted capital mobility between the markets ensuring that risk-adjusted expected returns will be equalized. The second condition is more difficult: The exchange rate between the currencies must be credibly fixed *forever*.[15] That is, investors must believe there is no risk that the currencies will exchange at a different rate in the future. Otherwise, yield differentials will emerge, giving rise to differential risk and return expectations in the two markets and allowing each market to trade on its own fundamentals. Thus, it is the lack of credibly fixed exchange rates that allows (default-free) yield curves, and hence bond returns, to be less than perfectly correlated across markets.

15 These conditions are necessary and sufficient for permanent convergence. See Chapter 10 of Stewart, Piros, and Heisler (forthcoming 2019) for a full exposition.

If a currency is linked to another without full credibility, then bond yields in the weaker currency are nearly always higher. This has been true even in the eurozone where, technically, separate currencies no longer exist—Greece, Italy, and Spain have always traded at meaningful, but varying, spreads over Germany and France. As long as there is no imminent risk of a devaluation, spreads at the very shortest maturities should be comparatively narrow. As demonstrated by the Greek exit ("Grexit") crisis, however, the situation changes sharply when the market perceives an imminent threat of devaluation (or a withdrawal from the common currency). Spreads then widen throughout the curve, but especially at the shortest maturities, and the curve will almost certainly invert. Why? Because in the event of a devaluation, yields in the devaluing currency will decline sharply (as the currency-risk premium collapses), generating much larger capital gains on longer-term bonds and thereby mitigating more of the currency loss.

When the exchange rate is allowed to float, the link between interest rates and exchange rates is primarily expectational. To equalize risk-adjusted expected returns across markets, interest rates must generally be higher (lower) in a currency that is expected to depreciate (appreciate). Ironically, this dynamic can lead to seemingly perverse situations in which the exchange rate "overshoots" in one direction to generate the expectation of movement in the opposite direction. The expectational linkage among exchange rates, interest rates, and asset prices is covered in detail at a later stage.

Capital mobility alone is clearly insufficient to eliminate differences in *nominal* interest rates and bond yields across countries. To a greater or lesser extent, each market responds to its own fundamentals, including policies. But what about *real* yields? We need to look at this question from two perspectives: the financial markets and the real economy.

An investor cares about the real return that she expects to earn *in her owncurrency*. In terms of a non-domestic asset, what matters is the *nominal* return and the change in the exchange rate. Even if non-domestic interest rates remain unchanged, the real return earned by the investor will not equal the non-domestic real interest rate unless purchasing power parity (PPP) holds over the investor's horizon. The empirical evidence overwhelmingly indicates that PPP does not hold over relevant investment horizons. Hence, we cannot rely on the simplistic notion that real interest rate differentials represent exploitable opportunities and should be eliminated by portfolio investment flows.

The preceding point is somewhat subtle and should not be construed to mean that real interest rate differentials are irrelevant for cross-market investment decisions. On the contrary, they can, but do not always, point to the likelihood of favorable *nominal* yield and exchange rate movements. The investor needs to assess non-domestic real rates from that perspective.

Ultimately, real interest rates must be consistent with the real saving and investment decisions that drive economic growth and the productivity of capital. As discussed earlier, saving and investment decisions are linked across countries through their current accounts. "Excess" saving in one country funds "excess" investment in another. In essence, there is a global market in which capital flows to where it is expected to be most productive. Although real rates around the world need not be equal, they are linked through the requirement that global savings must always equal global investment. Hence, they will tend to move together. As an example, the widespread low level of real interest rates that persisted in the aftermath of the global financial crisis was widely attributed to a very high level of global saving—primarily in Asia—and an unusually low level of capital investment in many developed markets, notably the United States.

SUMMARY

This is the first of two readings on how investment professionals should address the setting of capital market expectations. The reading began with a general framework for developing capital market expectations followed by a review of various challenges and pitfalls that analysts may encounter in the forecasting process. The remainder of the reading focused on the use of macroeconomic analysis in setting expectations. The following are the main points covered in the reading:

- Capital market expectations are essential inputs for strategic as well as tactical asset allocation.
- The ultimate objective is a set of projections with which to make informed investment decisions, specifically asset allocation decisions.
- Undue emphasis should not be placed on the accuracy of projections for individual asset classes. Internal consistency across asset classes (cross-sectional consistency) and over various time horizons (intertemporal consistency) are far more important objectives.
- The process of capital market expectations setting involves the following steps:

  1. Specify the set of expectations that are needed, including the time horizon(s) to which they apply.
  2. Research the historical record.
  3. Specify the method(s) and/or model(s) that will be used and their information requirements.
  4. Determine the best sources for information needs.
  5. Interpret the current investment environment using the selected data and methods, applying experience and judgment.
  6. Provide the set of expectations and document the conclusions.
  7. Monitor outcomes, compare to forecasts, and provide feedback.

- Among the challenges in setting capital market expectations are:

  - *limitations of economic data* including lack of timeliness as well as changing definitions and calculations;
  - *data measurement errors and biases* including transcription errors, survivorship bias, and appraisal (smoothed) data;
  - *limitations of historical estimates* including lack of precision, nonstationarity, asynchronous observations, and distributional considerations such as fat tails and skewness;
  - ex post *risk as a biased risk measure* such as when historical returns reflect expectations of a low-probability catastrophe that did not occur or capture a low-probability event that did happen to occur;
  - *bias in methods* including data-mining and time-period biases;
  - *failure to account for conditioning information*;
  - *misinterpretation of correlations*;
  - *psychological biases* including anchoring, status quo, confirmation, overconfidence, prudence, and availability biases.
  - *model uncertainty*.

- Losing sight of the connection between investment outcomes and the economy is a fundamental, and potentially costly, mistake in setting capital market expectations.
- Some growth trend changes are driven by slowly evolving and easily observable factors that are easy to forecast. Trend changes arising from exogenous shocks are impossible to forecast and difficult to identify, assess, and quantify until the change is well established.
- Among the most important sources of shocks are policy changes, new products and technologies, geopolitics, natural disasters, natural resources/critical inputs, and financial crises.
- An economy's aggregate trend growth rate reflects growth in labor inputs and growth in labor productivity. Extrapolating past trends in these components can provide a reasonable initial estimate of the future growth trend, which can be adjusted based on observable information. Less developed economies may require more significant adjustments because they are likely to be undergoing more rapid structural changes.
- The average level of real (nominal) default-free bond yields is linked to the trend rate of real (nominal) growth. The trend rate of growth provides an important anchor for estimating bond returns over horizons long enough for this reversion to prevail over cyclical and short-term forces.
- The trend growth rate provides an anchor for long-run equity appreciation. In the very long run, the aggregate value of equity must grow at a rate very close to the rate of GDP growth.
- There are three main approaches to economic forecasting:
    - *Econometric models*: structural and reduced-form statistical models of key variables generate quantitative estimates, impose discipline on forecasts, may be robust enough to approximate reality, and can readily forecast the impact of exogenous variables or shocks. However, they tend to be complex, time-consuming to formulate, and potentially mis-specified, and they rarely forecast turning points well.
    - *Indicators*: variables that lead, lag, or coincide with turns in the economy. This approach is the simplest, requiring only a limited number of published statistics. It can generate false signals, however, and is vulnerable to revisions that may overfit past data at the expense of the reliability of out-of-sample forecasts.
    - *Checklist(s)*: subjective integration of information deemed relevant by the analyst. This approach is the most flexible but also the most subjective. It readily adapts to a changing environment, but ongoing collection and assessment of information make it time-consuming and also limit the depth and consistency of the analysis.
- The business cycle is the result of many intermediate frequency cycles that jointly generate most of the variation in aggregate economic activity. This explains why historical business cycles have varied in both duration and intensity and why it is difficult to project turning points in real time.
- The business cycle reflects decisions that (a) are made based on imperfect information and/or analysis with the expectation of future benefits, (b) require significant current resources and/or time to implement, and (c) are difficult and/or costly to reverse. Such decisions are, broadly defined, investment decisions.
- A typical business cycle has a number of phases. We split the cycle into five phases with the following capital market implications:

- Initial Recovery. Short-term interest rates and bond yields are low. Bond yields are likely to bottom. Stock markets may rise strongly. Cyclical/riskier assets such as small stocks, high-yield bonds, and emerging market securities perform well.
- Early Expansion. Short rates are moving up. Longer-maturity bond yields are stable or rising slightly. Stocks are trending up.
- Late Expansion. Interest rates rise, and the yield curve flattens. Stock markets often rise but may be volatile. Cyclical assets may underperform while inflation hedges outperform.
- Slowdown. Short-term interest rates are at or nearing a peak. Government bond yields peak and may then decline sharply. The yield curve may invert. Credit spreads widen, especially for weaker credits. Stocks may fall. Interest-sensitive stocks and "quality" stocks with stable earnings perform best.
- Contraction. Interest rates and bond yields drop. The yield curve steepens. The stock market drops initially but usually starts to rise well before the recovery emerges. Credit spreads widen and remain elevated until clear signs of a cycle trough emerge.

- At least three factors complicate translation of business cycle information into capital market expectations and profitable investment decisions. First, the phases of the cycle vary in length and amplitude. Second, it is not always easy to distinguish between cyclical forces and secular forces acting on the economy and the markets. Third, how, when, and by how much the markets respond to the business cycle is as uncertain as the cycle itself—perhaps more so.
- Business cycle information is likely to be most reliable/valuable in setting capital market expectations over horizons within the range of likely expansion and contraction phases. Transitory developments cloud shorter-term forecasts, whereas significantly longer horizons likely cover portions of multiple cycle phases. Information about the current cyclical state of the economy has no predictive value over very long horizons.
- Monetary policy is often used as a mechanism for intervention in the business cycle. This mechanism is inherent in the mandates of most central banks to maintain price stability and/or growth consistent with potential.
- Monetary policy aims to be countercyclical, but the ability to fine-tune the economy is limited and policy measures may exacerbate rather than moderate the business cycle. This risk is greatest at the top of the cycle when the central bank may overestimate the economy's momentum and/or underestimate the potency of restrictive policies.
- Fiscal policy—government spending and taxation—can be used to counteract cyclical fluctuations in the economy. Aside from extreme situations, however, fiscal policy typically addresses objectives other than regulating short-term growth. So-called automatic stabilizers do play an important role in mitigating cyclical fluctuations.
- The Taylor Rule is a useful tool for assessing a central bank's stance and for predicting how that stance is likely to evolve.
- The expectation that central banks could not implement negative policy rates proved to be unfounded in the aftermath of the 2007–2009 global financial crisis. Because major central banks combined negative policy rates

with other extraordinary measures (notably quantitative easing), however, the effectiveness of the negative rate policy is unclear. The effectiveness of quantitative easing is also unclear.

- Negative interest rates, and the environment that gives rise to them, make the task of setting capital market expectations even more complex. Among the issues that arise are the following:
  - It is difficult to justify negative rates as a "risk-free rate" to which risk premiums can be added to establish long-term "equilibrium" asset class returns.
  - Historical data and quantitative models are even less likely to be reliable.
  - Market relationships (e.g., the yield curve) are likely to be distorted by other concurrent policy measures.
- The mix of monetary and fiscal policies has its most apparent effect on the average level of interest rates and inflation. Persistently loose (tight) fiscal policy increases (reduces) the average level of real interest rates. Persistently loose (tight) monetary policy increases (reduces) the average levels of actual and expected inflation. The impact on nominal rates is ambiguous if one policy is persistently tight and the other persistently loose.
- Changes in the slope of the yield curve are driven primarily by the evolution of short rate expectations, which are driven mainly by the business cycle and policies. The slope of the curve may also be affected by debt management.
- The slope of the yield curve is useful as a predictor of economic growth and as an indicator of where the economy is in the business cycle.
- Macroeconomic linkages between countries are expressed through their respective current and capital accounts.
- There are four primary mechanisms by which the current and capital accounts are kept in balance: changes in income (GDP), relative prices, interest rates and asset prices, and exchange rates.
- In the short run, interest rates, exchange rates, and financial asset prices must adjust to keep the capital account in balance with the more slowly evolving current account. The current account, in conjunction with real output and the relative prices of goods and services, tends to reflect secular trends and the pace of the business cycle.
- Interest rates and currency exchange rates are inextricably linked. This relationship is evident in the fact that a country cannot simultaneously allow unfettered capital flows, maintain a fixed exchange rate, and pursue an independent monetary policy.
- Two countries will share a default-free yield curve if (and only if) there is perfect capital mobility and the exchange rate is credibly fixed *forever*. It is the lack of credibly fixed exchange rates that allows (default-free) yield curves, and hence bond returns, to be less than perfectly correlated across markets.
- With floating exchange rates, the link between interest rates and exchange rates is primarily expectational. To equalize risk-adjusted expected returns across markets, interest rates must be higher (lower) in a currency that is expected to depreciate (appreciate). This dynamic can lead to the exchange rate "overshooting" in one direction to generate the expectation of movement in the opposite direction.

- An investor cares about the real return that he or she expects to earn *in his or her owncurrency.* In terms of a foreign asset, what matters is the *nominal* return and the change in the exchange rate.
- Although real interest rates around the world need not be equal, they are linked through the requirement that global savings must always equal global investment. Hence, they will tend to move together.

REFERENCES

Brinson, Gary, Randolph Hood, and Gilbert Beebower. 1986. "Determinants of Portfolio Performance." *Financial Analysts Journal* 42, vol. (4): 39–44.

Buttiglione, Luigi, Philip R. Lane, Lucrezia Reichlin, and Vincent Reinhart. 2014. *Deleveraging? What Deleveraging?*, International Center for Monetary and Banking Studies.

Friedman, Milton. 1968. "The Role of Monetary Policy." *American Economic Review* 58, vol. (1): 1–17.

Ibbotson, Roger and Paul Kaplan. 2000. "Does Asset Allocation Policy Explain 40, 90, or 100 Percent of Performance?" *Financial Analysts Journal* 56, vol. (1): 26–33.

Klement, Joachim. 2015. "What's Growth Got to Do With It? Equity Returns and Economic Growth." *Journal of Investing* 24, vol. (2): 74–78.

Marcelo, Jose Luis Miralles, Luis Miralles Quiros Jose, and Jose Luis Martins. 2013. "The Role of Country and Industry Factors During Volatile Times." *Journal of International Financial Markets, Institutions and Money* 26:273–90. 10.1016/j.intfin.2013.06.005

Marcelo, José Luis Miralles, José Luis Miralles Quirós, and José Luís Martins. 2013. "The Role of Country and Industry Factors During Volatile Times." *Journal of International Financial Markets, Institutions and Money* 26, vol. :273–90.

McQueen, Grant and Steven Thorley. 1999. "Mining Fools Gold." *Financial Analysts Journal* 55, vol. (2): 61–72.

Rapaport, Alfred and Michael Mauboussin. 2001. *Expectations Investing: Reading Stock Prices for Better Returns*. Boston: Harvard Business School Press.

Stewart, Scott D., Christopher D. Piros, and Jeffrey C. Heisler. 2019, Forthcoming. *Portfolio Management: Theory and Practice*. Hoboken, NJ: John Wiley & Sons.

PRACTICE PROBLEMS

The following information relates to questions 1-2

Jennifer Wuyan is an investment strategist responsible for developing long-term capital market expectations for an investment firm that invests in domestic equities. She presents a report to the firm's investment committee describing the statistical model used to formulate capital market expectations, which is based on a dividend discount method. In the report, she notes that in developing the model, she researched the historical data seeking to identify the relevant variables and determined the best source of data for the model. She also notes her interpretation of the current economic and market environment.

1. Explain what additional step(s) Wuyan should have taken in the process of setting capital market expectations.

   Wuyan reports that after repeatedly searching the most recent 10 years of data, she eventually identified variables that had a statistically significant relationship with equity returns. Wuyan used these variables to forecast equity returns. She documented, in a separate section of the report, a high correlation between nominal GDP and equity returns. Based on this noted high correlation, Wuyan concludes that nominal GDP predicts equity returns. Based on her statistical results, Wuyan expects equities to underperform over the next 12 months and recommends that the firm underweight equities.

   Commenting on the report, John Tommanson, an investment adviser for the firm, suggests extending the starting point of the historical data back another 20 years to obtain more robust statistical results. Doing so would enable the analysis to include different economic and central bank policy environments. Tommanson is reluctant to underweight equities for his clients, citing the strong performance of equities over the last quarter, and believes the most recent quarterly data should be weighted more heavily in setting capital market expectations.

2. Discuss how *each* of the following forecasting challenges evident in Wuyan's report and in Tommanson's comments affects the setting of capital market expectations:

   i. Status quo bias
   ii. Data-mining bias
   iii. Risk of regime change
   iv. Misinterpretation of correlation

The following information relates to questions 3-5

Jan Cambo is chief market strategist at a US asset management firm. While preparing a report for the upcoming investment committee meeting, Cambo updates her long-term forecast for US equity returns. As an input into her forecasting model, she uses the following long-term annualized forecasts from the firm's chief economist:

- Labor input will grow 0.5%.
- Labor productivity will grow 1.3%.
- Inflation will be 2.2%.
- Dividend yield will be 2.8%.

Based on these forecasts, Cambo predicts a long-term 9.0% annual equity return in the US market. Her forecast assumes no change in the share of profits in the economy, and she expects some contribution to equity returns from a change in the price-to-earnings ratio (P/E).

3. Calculate the implied contribution to Cambo's US equity return forecast from the expected change in the P/E.

   At the investment committee meeting, the firm's chief economist predicts that the economy will enter the late expansion phase of the business cycle in the next 12 months.

4. **Discuss**, based on the chief economist's prediction, the implications for the following:

   i. Bond yields
   ii. Equity returns
   iii. Short-term interest rates

5. Cambo compares her business cycle forecasting approach to the approach used by the chief economist. Cambo bases her equity market forecast on a time-series model using a composite index of leading indicators as the key input, whereas the chief economist uses a detailed econometric model to generate his economic forecasts.

   Discuss strengths and weaknesses of the economic forecasting approaches used by Cambo and the chief economist.

	Cambo's Forecasting Approach	Chief Economist's Forecasting Approach
Strengths		
Weaknesses		

The following information relates to questions 6-13

Neshie Wakuluk is an investment strategist who develops capital market expectations for an investment firm that invests across asset classes and global markets. Wakuluk started her career when the global markets were experiencing significant volatility and poor returns; as a result, she is now careful to base her conclusions on objective evidence and analytical procedures to mitigate any potential biases.

Wakuluk's approach to economic forecasting utilizes a structural model in conjunction with a diffusion index to determine the current phase of a country's business cycle. This approach has produced successful predictions in the past, thus Wakuluk has high confidence in the predictions. Wakuluk also determines whether any adjustments need to be made to her initial estimates of the respective aggregate economic growth trends based on historical rates of growth for Countries X and Y (both developed markets) and Country Z (a developing market). Exhibit 1 summarizes Wakuluk's predictions:

Exhibit 1: Prediction for Current Phase of the Business Cycle

Country X	Country Y	Country Z
Initial Recovery	Contraction	Late Upswing

Wakuluk assumes short-term interest rates adjust with expected inflation and are procyclical. Wakuluk reviews the historical short-term interest rate trends for each country, which further confirms her predictions shown in Exhibit 1.

Wakuluk decides to focus on Country Y to determine the path of nominal interest rates, the potential economic response of Country Y's economy to this path, and the timing for when Country Y's economy may move into the next business cycle. Wakuluk makes the following observations:

Observation 1	Monetary policy has been persistently loose for Country Y, while fiscal policies have been persistently tight.
Observation 2	Country Y is expected to significantly increase transfer payments and introduce a more progressive tax regime.
Observation 3	The current yield curve for Country Y suggests that the business cycle is in the slowdown phase, with bond yields starting to reflect contractionary conditions.

6. Wakuluk *most likely* seeks to mitigate which of the following biases in developing capital market forecasts?

   A. Availability

   B. Time period

   C. Survivorship

7. Wakuluk's approach to economic forecasting:

   A. is flexible and limited in complexity.

   B. can give a false sense of precision and provide false signals.

   C. imposes no consistency of analysis across items or at different points in time.

8. Wakuluk is *most likely* to make significant adjustments to her estimate of the future growth trend for which of the following countries?

   A. Country Y only

   B. Country Z only

   C. Countries Y and Z

9. Based on Exhibit 1 and Wakuluk's assumptions about short-term rates and expected inflation, short-term rates in Country X are *most likely* to be:

   A. low and bottoming.

   B. approaching a peak.

   C. above average and rising.

10. Based on Exhibit 1, what capital market effect is Country Z *most likely* to experience in the short-term?

    A. Cyclical assets attract investors.

    B. Monetary policy becomes restrictive.

    C. The yield curve steepens substantially.

11. Based on Observation 1, fiscal and monetary policies in Country Y will *most likely* lead to:

    A. low nominal rates.

    B. high nominal rates.

    C. either high or low nominal rates.

12. Based on Observation 2, what impact will the policy changes have on the trend rate of growth for Country Y?

    A. Negative

    B. Neutral

    C. Positive

13. Based on Observation 3, Wakuluk *most likely* expects Country Y's yield curve in the near term to:

    A. invert.

    B. flatten.

    C. steepen.

The following information relates to questions 14-16

Robert Hadpret is the chief economist at Agree Partners, an asset management firm located in the developed country of Eastland. He has prepared an economic report on Eastland for the firm's asset allocation committee. Hadpret notes that the composite index of leading economic indicators has declined for three consecutive months and that the yield curve has inverted. Private sector borrowing is also projected to decline. Based on these recent events, Hadpret predicts an economic contraction and forecasts lower inflation and possibly deflation over the next 12 months.

Helen Smitherman, a portfolio manager at Agree, considers Hadpret's economic forecast when determining the tactical allocation for the firm's Balanced Fund (the fund). Smitherman notes that the fund has considerable exposure to real estate, shares of asset-intensive and commodity-producing firms, and high-quality debt. The fund's cash holdings are at cyclical lows.

14. **Discuss** the implications of Hadpret's inflation forecast on the expected returns of the fund's holdings of:

    i. cash.

    ii. bonds.

    iii. equities.

    iv. real estate.

15. In response to the projected cyclical decline in the Eastland economy and in private sector borrowing over the next year, Hadpret expects a change in the monetary and fiscal policy mix. He forecasts that the Eastland central bank will ease monetary policy. On the fiscal side, Hadpret expects the Eastland government to enact a substantial tax cut. As a result, Hadpret forecasts large government deficits that will be financed by the issuance of long-term government securities.

    Discuss the relationship between the shape of the yield curve and the monetary and fiscal policy mix projected by Hadpret.

16. Currently, Eastland's currency is fixed relative to the currency of the country of Northland, and Eastland maintains policies that allow unrestricted capital flows. Hadpret examines the relationship between interest rates and exchange rates. He considers three possible scenarios for the Eastland economy:

Scenario 1	Shift in policy restricting capital flows
Scenario 2	Shift in policy allowing the currency to float
Scenario 3	Shift in investor belief toward a lack of full credibility that the exchange rate will be fixed forever

Discuss how interest rate and exchange rate linkages between Eastland and Northland might change under *each* scenario.

Note: Consider *each* scenario independently.

SOLUTIONS

1. The process of setting capital market expectations (CMEs) involves the following seven steps:

   1. Specify the set of expectations needed, including the time horizon(s) to which they apply.
   2. Research the historical record.
   3. Specify the method(s) and/or model(s) to be used and their information requirements.
   4. Determine the best sources for information needs.
   5. Interpret the current investment environment using the selected data and methods, applying experience and judgment.
   6. Provide the set of expectations needed, documenting conclusions.
   7. Monitor actual outcomes and compare them with expectations, providing feedback to improve the expectation-setting process.

   The first step, which specifies the set of expectations needed, is carried out by the firm. Wuyan, in developing a statistical model based on a dividend discount method, researched the historical data seeking to identify the relevant variables and determined the best source of data for the model. In her report, she also noted her interpretation of the current economic and market environment. To complete the process, Wuyan should complete Steps 6 and 7. Wuyan should provide the set of expectations needed, documenting the conclusions, and include the reasoning and assumptions underlying the projections. Then, she should monitor the actual outcomes and compare them with the expectations, providing feedback to assess and improve the accuracy of the process. The comparison of the capital market expectations estimated by the model against actual results provides a quantitative evaluation of forecast error. The feedback from this step can be used to improve the expectation-setting process.

2. **Discuss** how *each* of the following forecasting challenges evident in Wuyan's report and in Tommanson's comments affects the setting of capital market expectations:

Status quo bias	Tommanson's statement that he is reluctant to underweight equities given the strong performance of equities over the last quarter is an example of status quo bias. His statement that the most recent quarterly data should be weighted more heavily in setting capital market expectations is also an example of this bias. Status quo bias reflects the tendency for forecasts to perpetuate recent observations and for managers to then avoid making changes. Status quo bias can be mitigated by a disciplined effort to avoid anchoring on the status quo.
Data-mining bias	In Wuyan's report, data-mining bias arises from repeatedly searching a data set until a statistically significant pattern emerges. Such a pattern will almost inevitably occur, but the statistical relationship cannot be expected to have predictive value. As a result, the modeling results are unreliable. Irrelevant variables are often included in the forecasting model. As a solution, the analyst should scrutinize the variables selected and provide an economic rationale for each variable selected in the forecasting model. A further test is to examine the forecasting relationship out of sample.

Risk of regime change	The suggestion by Tommanson to extend the data series back increases the risk of the data representing more than one regime. A change in regime is a shift in the technological, political, legal, economic, or regulatory environments. Regime change alters the risk–return relationship since the asset's risk and return characteristics vary with economic and market environments. Analysts can apply statistical techniques that account for the regime change or simply use only part of the whole data series.
Misinterpretation of correlation	Wuyan states that the high correlation between nominal GDP and equity returns implies nominal GDP predicts equity returns. This statement is incorrect since high correlation does not imply causation. In this case, nominal GDP could predict equity returns, equity returns could predict nominal GDP, a third variable could predict both, or the relationship could merely be spurious. Correlation does not allow the analyst to distinguish between these cases. As a result, correlation relationships should not be used in a predictive model without understanding the underlying linkages between the variables.

3. The growth rate in the aggregate market value of equity is expressed as a sum of the following four factors: (1) growth rate of nominal GDP, (2) the change in the share of profits in GDP, (3) the change in P/E, and (4) the dividend yield. The growth rate of nominal GDP is the sum of the growth of real GDP and inflation. The growth rate of real GDP is estimated as the sum of the growth rate in the labor input and the growth rate in labor productivity. Based on the chief economist's estimates, the macroeconomic forecast indicates that nominal GDP will increase by 4.0% (= 0.5% labor input + 1.3% productivity + 2.2% inflation).

   Assuming a 2.8% dividend yield and no change in the share of profits in the economy, Cambo's forecast of a 9.0% annual increase in equity returns implies a 2.2% long-term contribution (i.e., 9.0% equity return – 4.0% nominal GDP – 2.8% dividend yield) from an expansion in the P/E.

4.

Discuss, based on the chief economist's prediction, the implications for the following:

Bond yields	In the late expansion phase of the business cycle, bond yields are usually rising but more slowly than short-term interest rates are, so the yield curve flattens. Private sector borrowing puts upward pressure on rates while fiscal balances typically improve.
Equity returns	In the late expansion phase of the business cycle, stocks typically rise but are subject to high volatility as investors become nervous about the restrictive monetary policy and signs of a looming economic slowdown. Cyclical assets may underperform while inflation hedges, such as commodities, outperform.
Short-term interest rates	In the late expansion phase of the business cycle, short-term interest rates are typically rising as monetary policy becomes restrictive because the economy is increasingly in danger of overheating. The central bank may aim for a soft landing.

5.

Discuss strengths and weaknesses of the economic forecasting approaches used by Cambo and the chief economist.

	Cambo's Forecasting Approach	Chief Economist's Forecasting Approach

Strengths	• The leading indicator–based approach is simple since it requires following a limited number of economic/financial variables. • Can focus on individual or composite variables that are readily available and easy to track. • Focuses on identifying/forecasting turning points in the business cycle.	• Econometric models can be quite robust and can examine impact of many potential variables. • New data may be collected and consistently used within models to quickly generate output. • Models are useful for simulating effects of changes in exogenous variables. • Imposes discipline and consistency on the forecaster and challenges modeler to reassess prior view based on model results.
Weaknesses	• Data subject to frequent revisions resulting in "look-ahead" bias. • "Current" data not reliable as input for historical analysis. • Overfitted in sample. Likely overstates forecast accuracy. • Can provide false signals on the economic outlook. • May provide little more than binary directional guidance (no/yes).	• Models are complex and time consuming to formulate. • Requires future forecasts for the exogenous variables, which increases the estimation error for the model. • Model may be mis-specified, and relationships among variables may change over time. • Models may give false sense of precision. • Models perform badly at forecasting turning points.

6. A is correct. Wakuluk started her career when the global markets were experiencing significant volatility and poor returns. She is careful to base her conclusions on objective evidence and analytical procedures to mitigate potential biases, which suggests she is seeking to mitigate an availability bias. Availability bias is the tendency to be overly influenced by events that have left a strong impression and/or for which it is easy to recall an example.

7. B is correct. Wakuluk's approach to economic forecasting utilizes both a structural model (e.g., an econometric model approach) and a diffusion index (e.g., a leading indicator-based approach). However, the two approaches have weaknesses: An econometric model approach may give a false sense of precision, and a leading indicator-based approach can provide false signals. Two strengths of the checklist approach are its flexibility and limited complexity, although one weakness is that it imposes no consistency of analysis across items or at different points in time.

8. B is correct. Country Z is a developing market. Less-developed markets are likely to be undergoing more rapid structural changes, which may require the analyst to make more significant adjustments relative to past trends.

9. A is correct. Country X is predicted to be in the initial recovery phase of the business cycle, which suggests short-term (money market) rates are low or bottoming. Inflation is procyclical. It accelerates in the later stages of the business cycle when the output gap has closed, and it decelerates when a large output gap puts downward pressure on wages and prices, which often happens during a recession or the early years afterward. As long as short-term interest rates adjust with expected inflation, cash is essentially a zero-duration, inflation-protected asset that earns a floating real rate, which is typically procyclical. Wakuluk assumes short-term interest rates adjust with expected inflation and are procyclical. Thus, short-term rates are most likely to be low and bottoming if Country X is in the

initial recovery phase of the business cycle.

10. B is correct. Wakuluk's model predicts that Country Z's business cycle is currently in the late upswing phase. In the late upswing phase, interest rates are typically rising as monetary policy becomes more restrictive. Cyclical assets may underperform, whereas the yield curve is expected to continue to flatten.

11. C is correct. Monetary policy has been persistently loose for Country Y, while fiscal policies have been persistently tight. With this combination of persistently loose and tight policies, the impact could lead to higher or lower nominal rates (typically labeled as mid-nominal rates).

12. C is correct. Country Y is expected to significantly increase transfer payments and introduce a more progressive tax regime. Both of these changes are pro-growth government policies and should have a positive impact on the trend rate of growth for a business cycle that is in slowdown or contraction. Transfer payments help mitigate fluctuations in disposable income for the most vulnerable households, while progressive tax regimes imply that the effective tax rate on the private sector is pro-cyclical (i.e., rising as the economy expands and falling as the economy contracts).

13. C is correct. The current yield curve for Country Y suggests that the business cycle is in the slowdown phase (curve is flat to inverted), with bond yields starting to reflect contractionary conditions (i.e., bond yields are declining). The curve will most likely steepen near term, consistent with the transition to the contractionary phase of the business cycle, and be the steepest on the cusp of the initial recovery phase.

14. Discuss the implications of Hadpret's inflation forecast on the expected returns of the fund's holdings of:

Cash	The fund benefits from its cyclically low holdings of cash. With the economy contracting and inflation falling, short-term rates will likely be in a sharp decline. Cash, or short-term interest-bearing instruments, is unattractive in such an environment. However, deflation may make cash particularly attractive if a "zero lower bound" is binding on the nominal interest rate. Otherwise, deflation is simply a component of the required short-term real rate.
Bonds	The fund's holdings of high-quality bonds will benefit from falling inflation or deflation. Falling inflation results in capital gains as the expected inflation component of bond yields falls. Persistent deflation benefits the highest-quality bonds because it increases the purchasing power of their cash flows. It will, however, impair the creditworthiness of lower-quality debt.
Equities	The fund's holdings of asset-intensive and commodity-producing firms will be negatively affected by falling inflation or deflation. Within the equity market, higher inflation benefits firms with the ability to pass along rising costs. In contrast, falling inflation or deflation is especially detrimental for asset-intensive and commodity-producing firms unable to pass along the price increases.
Real Estate	The fund's real estate holdings will be negatively affected by falling inflation or deflation. Falling inflation or deflation will put downward pressure on expected rental income and property values. Especially negatively affected will be sub-prime properties that may have to cut rents sharply to avoid rising vacancies.

15. Hadpret expects that, in response to a forecasted contraction in the Eastland economy, the central bank will ease monetary policy and the government will enact an expansionary fiscal policy. This policy mix has an impact on the shape of the yield curve.

    The impact of changes in monetary policy on the yield curve are fairly clear, because changes in the yield curve's slope—its flattening or steepening—are largely determined by the expected movement in short rates. This movement, in turn, is determined by the expected path of monetary policy and the state of the economy. With the central bank easing and the economy contracting, policy rates will be declining and will be expected to decline further as the central bank aims to counteract downward momentum in the economy. Bond yields also decline but by a lesser amount, so the yield curve steepens. The yield curve will typically continue to steepen during the contraction phase as the central bank continues to ease, reaching its steepest point just before the initial recovery phase.

    Fiscal policy may affect the shape of the yield curve through the relative supply of bonds at various maturities that the government issues to fund deficits. Unlike the impact of monetary policy, the impact of changes in the supply of securities on the yield curve is unclear. The evidence seems to suggest that sufficiently large purchases/sales at different maturities will have only a temporary impact on yields. As a result, the large government budget deficits forecasted by Hadpret are unlikely to have much of a lasting impact on the yield curve, especially given that private sector borrowing will be falling during the contraction, somewhat offsetting the increase in the supply of government securities.

16. **Discuss** how interest rate and exchange rate linkages between Eastland and Northland might change under *each* scenario. (Note: Consider *each* scenario independently.)

Scenario 1	Eastland currently has a fixed exchange rate with unrestricted capital flows. It is unable to pursue an independent monetary policy, and interest rates will be equal to those in Northland. By restricting capital flows along with a fixed exchange rate, Eastland will be able to run an independent monetary policy with the central bank setting the policy rate. Thus, interest rates can be different in the two countries.
Scenario 2	Eastland currently has a fixed exchange rate pegged to Northland with unrestricted capital flows. Eastland is unable to pursue an independent monetary policy with interest rates in Eastland equal to the interest rates prevailing in Northland (the country to which the currency is pegged). If Eastland allows the exchange rate to float, it will now be able to run an independent monetary policy with interest rates determined in its domestic market. The link between interest rates and exchange rates will now be largely expectational and will depend on the expected future path of the exchange rate. To equalize risk-adjusted returns across countries, interest rates must generally be higher (lower) in the country whose currency is expected to depreciate (appreciate). This dynamic often leads to a situation where the currency overshoots in one direction or the other.
Scenario 3	Eastland and Northland (with currencies pegged to each other) will share the same yield curve if two conditions are met. First, unrestricted capital mobility must occur between them to ensure that risk-adjusted expected returns will be equalized. Second, the exchange rate between the currencies must be credibly fixed forever. Thus, as long as investors believe that there is no risk in the future of a possible currency appreciation or depreciation, Eastland and Northland will share the same yield curve. A shift in investors' belief in the credibility of the fixed exchange rate will likely cause risk and yield differentials to emerge. This situation will cause the (default-free) yield curve to differ between Eastland and Northland.

LEARNING MODULE

2

Capital Market Expectations, Part 2: Forecasting Asset Class Returns

by Christopher D. Piros, PhD, CFA.

Christopher D. Piros, PhD, CFA (USA).

LEARNING OUTCOMES

Mastery	*The candidate should be able to:*
☐	discuss approaches to setting expectations for fixed-income returns
☐	discuss risks faced by investors in emerging market fixed-income securities and the country risk analysis techniques used to evaluate emerging market economies
☐	discuss approaches to setting expectations for equity investment market returns
☐	discuss risks faced by investors in emerging market equity securities
☐	explain how economic and competitive factors can affect expectations for real estate investment markets and sector returns
☐	discuss major approaches to forecasting exchange rates
☐	discuss methods of forecasting volatility
☐	recommend and justify changes in the component weights of a global investment portfolio based on trends and expected changes in macroeconomic factors

Parts of this reading have been adapted from a former Capital Market Expectations reading authored by John P. Calverley, Alan M. Meder, CPA, CFA, Brian D. Singer, CFA, and Renato Staub, PhD.

1 INTRODUCTION

This is the second of two readings focusing on capital market expectations. A central theme of both readings is that a disciplined approach to setting expectations will be rewarded. After outlining a framework for developing expectations and reviewing potential pitfalls, the first reading focused on the use of macroeconomic analysis in setting expectations. This reading builds on that foundation and examines setting expectations for specific asset classes—fixed income, equities, real estate, and currencies. Estimation of variance–covariance matrices is covered as well.

The reading begins with an overview of the techniques frequently used to develop capital market expectations. The discussion of specific asset classes begins with fixed income in Sections 3 and 4, followed by equities, real estate, and currencies in Sections 5–7. Estimation of variance–covariance structures is addressed in Section 8. Section 9 illustrates the use of macroeconomic analysis to develop and justify adjustments to a global portfolio.

2 OVERVIEW OF TOOLS AND APPROACHES

This section provides a brief overview of the main concepts, approaches, and tools used in professional forecasting of capital market returns. Whereas subsequent sections focus on specific asset classes, the emphasis here is on the commonality of techniques.

The Nature of the Problem

Few investment practitioners are likely to question the notion that investment opportunities change in systematic, but imperfectly predictable, ways over time. Yet the ramifications of that fact are often not explicitly recognized. Forecasting returns is not simply a matter of estimating constant, but unknown, parameters—for example, expected returns, variances, and correlations. Time horizons matter. The previous reading highlighted two aspects of this issue: the need to ensure intertemporal consistency and the relative usefulness of specific information (e.g., the business cycle) over short, intermediate, and long horizons. The choice among forecasting techniques is effectively a choice of the information on which forecasts will be based (in statistical terms, the information on which the forecast is "conditioned") and how that information will be incorporated into the forecasts. The fact that opportunities change over time should, at least in principle, affect strategic investment decisions and how positions respond to changing forecasts.[1]

Although investment opportunities are not constant, virtually all forecasting techniques rely on notions of central tendency, toward which opportunities tend to revert over time. This fact means that although asset prices, risk premiums, volatilities, valuation ratios, and other metrics may exhibit momentum, persistence, and clustering in the short run, over sufficiently long horizons, they tend to converge to levels consistent with economic and financial fundamentals.

What are we trying to forecast? In principle, we are interested in the whole probability distribution of future returns. In practice, however, forecasting expected return is by far the most important consideration, both because it is the dominant driver

1 For example, in general, it is not optimal to choose a portfolio on the mean–variance-efficient frontier based on forecasts for the coming period. In addition, the distinction between "strategic" and "tactical" asset allocation is less clear cut since, in general, the optimal allocation evolves with the investor's remaining investment horizon. See Piros (2015) for a non-technical exposition of these issues.

of most investment decisions and because it is generally more difficult to forecast within practical tolerances than such risk metrics as volatility. Hence, the primary focus here is on expected return. In terms of risk metrics, we limit our attention to variances and covariances.

Approaches to Forecasting

At a very high level, there are essentially three approaches to forecasting: (1) formal tools, (2) surveys, and (3) judgment. Formal tools are established research methods amenable to precise definition and independent replication of results. Surveys involve asking a group of experts for their opinions. Judgment can be described as a qualitative synthesis of information derived from various sources and filtered through the lens of experience.

Surveys are probably most useful as a way to gauge consensus views, which can serve as inputs into formal tools and the analyst's own judgment. Judgment is always important. There is ample scope for applying judgment—in particular, economic and psychological insight—to improve forecasts and numbers, including those produced by elaborate quantitative models. In using survey results and applying their own judgment, analysts must be wary of the psychological traps discussed in the Capital Market Expectations Part 1 reading. Beyond these brief observations, however, there is not much new to be said about surveys and judgment.

The formal forecasting tools most commonly used in forecasting capital market returns fall into three broad categories: statistical methods, discounted cash flow models, and risk premium models. The distinctions among these methods will become clear as they are discussed and applied throughout the reading.

Statistical Methods

All the formal tools involve data and statistical analysis to some degree. Methods that are primarily, if not exclusively, statistical impose relatively little structure on the data. As a result, the forecasts inherit the statistical properties of the data with limited, if any, regard for economic or financial reasoning. Three types of statistical methods will be covered in this reading. The first approach is to use well-known sample statistics, such as sample means, variances, and correlations, to describe the distribution of future returns. This is undoubtedly the clearest example of simply taking the data at face value. Unfortunately, sampling error makes some of these statistics—in particular, the sample mean—very imprecise. The second approach, **shrinkage estimation**, involves taking a weighted average of two estimates of the same parameter—one based on historical sample data and the other based on some other source or information, such as the analyst's "prior" knowledge. This "two-estimates-are-better-than-one" approach has the desirable property of reducing forecast errors relative to simple sample statistics. The third method, **time-series estimation**, involves forecasting a variable on the basis of lagged values of the variable being forecast and often lagged values of other selected variables. These models have the benefit of explicitly incorporating dynamics into the forecasting process. However, since they are reduced-form models, they may summarize the historical data well without providing much insight into the underlying drivers of the forecasts.

Discounted Cash Flow

Discounted cash flow (DCF) models express the idea that an asset's value is the present value of its expected cash flows. They are a basic method for establishing the intrinsic value of an asset on the basis of fundamentals and its fair required rate of return. Conversely, they are used to estimate the required rate of return implied by the asset's current price.

Risk Premium Models

The risk premium approach expresses the expected return on a risky asset as the sum of the risk-free rate of interest and one or more risk premiums that compensate investors for the asset's exposure to sources of *priced risk* (risk for which investors demand compensation). There are three main methods for modeling risk premiums: (1) an equilibrium model, such as the CAPM, (2) a factor model, and (3) building blocks. Each of these methods was discussed in earlier readings. Equilibrium models and factor models both impose a structure on how returns are assumed to be generated. Hence, they can be used to generate estimates of (1) expected returns and (2) variances and covariances.

3 FORECASTING FIXED INCOME RETURNS

☐ discuss approaches to setting expectations for fixed-income returns

There are three main ways to approach forecasting fixed-income returns. The first is discounted cash flow. This method is really the only one that is precise enough to use in support of trades involving individual fixed-income securities. This type of "micro" analysis will not be discussed in detail here since it is covered extensively elsewhere in CFA Program curriculum readings that focus on fixed income. DCF concepts are also useful in forecasting the more aggregated performance needed to support asset allocation decisions. The second approach is the risk premium approach, which is often applied to fixed income, in part because fixed-income premiums are among the building blocks used to estimate expected returns on riskier asset classes, such as equities. The third approach is to include fixed-income asset classes in an equilibrium model. Doing so has the advantage of imposing consistency across asset classes and is especially useful as a first step in applying the Black–Litterman framework, which will be discussed in a later reading.

Applying DCF to Fixed Income

Fixed income is really all about discounted cash flow. This stems from the facts that almost all fixed-income securities have finite maturities and that the (promised) cash flows are known, governed by explicit rules, or can be modeled with a reasonably high degree of accuracy (e.g., mortgage-backed security prepayments). Using modern arbitrage-free models, we can value virtually any fixed-income instrument. The most straightforward and, undoubtedly, most precise way to forecast fixed-income returns is to explicitly value the securities on the basis of the assumed evolution of the critical inputs to the valuation model—for example, the spot yield curve, the term structure of volatilities, and prepayment speeds. A whole distribution of returns can be generated by doing this for a variety of scenarios. As noted previously, this is essentially the only option if we need the "micro" precision of accounting for rolling down the yield curve, changes in the shape of the yield curve, changes in rate volatilities, or changes in the sensitivity of contingent cash flows. But for many purposes—for example, asset allocation—we usually do not need such granularity.

Yield to maturity (YTM)—the single discount rate that equates the present value of a bond's cash flows to its market price—is by far the most commonly quoted metric of valuation and, implicitly, of expected return for bonds. For bond portfolios, the YTM is usually calculated as if it were simply an average of the individual bonds' YTM, which is not exactly accurate but is a reasonable approximation.[2] Forecasting bond returns would be very easy if we could simply equate yield to maturity with expected return. It is not that simple, but YTM does provide a reasonable and readily available first approximation.

Assuming cash flows are received in full and on time, there are two main reasons why realized return may not equal the initial yield to maturity. First, if the investment horizon is shorter than the amount of time until the bond's maturity, any change in interest rate (i.e., the bond's YTM) will generate a capital gain or loss at the horizon. Second, the cash flows may be reinvested at rates above or below the initial YTM. The longer the horizon, the more sensitive the realized return will be to reinvestment rates. These two issues work in opposite directions: Rising (falling) rates induce capital losses (gains) but increase (decrease) reinvestment income. If the investment horizon equals the (Macaulay) duration of the bond or portfolio, the capital gain/loss and reinvestment effects will roughly offset, leaving the realized return close to the original YTM. This relationship is exact if (a) the yield curve is flat and (b) the change in rates occurs immediately in a single step. In practice, the relationship is only an approximation. Nonetheless, it provides an important insight: *Over horizons shorter than the duration, the capital gain/loss impact will tend to dominate such that rising (declining) rates imply lower (higher) return, whereas over horizons longer than the duration, the reinvestment impact will tend to dominate such that rising (declining) rates imply higher (lower) return.*

Note that the timing of rate changes matters. It will not have much effect, if any, on the capital gain/loss component because that ultimately depends on the beginning and ending values of the bond or portfolio. But it does affect the reinvestment return. The longer the horizon, the more it matters. Hence, for long-term forecasts, we should break the forecast horizon into subperiods corresponding to when we expect the largest rate changes to occur.

EXAMPLE 1

Forecasting Return Based on Yield to Maturity

1. Jesper Bloch works for Discrete Asset Management (DAM) in Zurich. Many of the firm's more risk-averse clients invest in a currency-hedged global government bond strategy that uses cash flows to purchase new issues and seasoned bonds all along the yield curve to maintain a roughly constant maturity and duration profile. The yield to maturity of the portfolio is 1% (compounded annually), and the modified duration is 4.84. DAM's chief investment officer believes global government yields are likely to rise by 200 bps over the next two years as central banks remove extraordinarily accommodative policies and inflation surges. Bloch has been asked to project approximate returns for this strategy over horizons of two, five, and seven years. What conclusions is Bloch likely to draw?

Solution:

If yields were not expected to change, the return would be very close to the yield to maturity (1%) over each horizon. The Macaulay duration is 4.89 (= 4.84 × 1.01), so if the yield change occurred immediately, the capital gain/loss and reinvestment impacts on return would roughly balance over five

2 Bear in mind that yield to maturity does not account for optionality. However, various yield measures derived from option-adjusted valuation can be viewed as conveying similar information. To keep the present discussion as simple as possible, we ignore the distinction here. If optionality is critical to the forecast, it may be necessary to apply the more granular DCF framework discussed previously.

years. Ignoring convexity (which is not given), the capital loss at the end of two years will be approximately 9.68% (= 4.84 × 2%). Assuming yields rise linearly over the initial two-year period, the higher reinvestment rates will boost the cumulative return by approximately 1.0% over two years, so the annual return over two years will be approximately −3.3% [= 1 + (−9.68 + 1.0)/2]. Reinvesting for three more years at the 2.0% higher rate adds another 6.0% to the cumulative return, so the five-year annual return would be approximately 0.46% [= 1 + (-9.68 + 1.0 + 6.0)/5]. With an additional two years of reinvestment income, the seven-year annual return would be about 1.19% [= 1 + (−9.68 + 1.0 + 6.0 + 4.0)/7]. As expected, the capital loss dominated the return over two years, and higher reinvestment rates dominated over seven years. The gradual nature of the yield increase extended the horizon over which the capital gain/loss and reinvestment effects would balance beyond the initial five-year Macaulay duration.

We have extended the DCF approach beyond simply finding the discount rates implied by current market prices (e.g., YTMs), which might be considered the "pure" DCF approach. For other asset classes (e.g., equities), the connection between discount rates and valuations/returns is vague because there is so much uncertainty with respect to the cash flows. For these asset classes, discounted cash flow is essentially a conceptual framework rather than a precise valuation model. In contrast, in fixed income there is a tight connection between discount rates, valuations, and returns. We are, therefore, able to refine the "pure" DCF forecast by incorporating projections of how rates will evolve over the investment horizon. Doing so is particularly useful in formulating short-term forecasts.

The Building Block Approach to Fixed-Income Returns

The building block approach forms an estimate of expected return in terms of required compensation for specific types of risk. The required return for fixed-income asset classes has four components: the one-period default-free rate, the term premium, the credit premium, and the liquidity premium. As the names indicate, the premiums reflect compensation for interest rate risk, duration risk, credit risk, and illiquidity, respectively. Only one of the four components—the short-term default-free rate—is (potentially) observable. For example, the term premium and the credit premium are implicitly embedded in yield spreads, but they are not *equal* to observed yield spreads. Next, we will consider each of these components and summarize applicable empirical regularities.

The Short-term Default-free Rate

In principle, the short-term default-free rate is the rate on the highest-quality, most liquid instrument with a maturity that matches the forecast horizon. In practice, it is usually taken to be a government zero-coupon bill at a maturity that is issued frequently—say, every three months. This rate is virtually always tied closely to the central bank's policy rate and, therefore, mirrors the cyclical dynamics of monetary policy. Secular movements are closely tied to expected inflation levels.

Under normal circumstances, the observed rate is a reasonable base on which to build expected returns for risky assets. In extreme circumstances, however, it may be necessary to adopt a normalized rate. For example, when policy rates or short-term government rates are negative, using the observed rate without adjustment may unduly reduce the required/expected return estimate for risky instruments. An alternative to normalizing the short rate in this circumstance would be to raise the estimate of one or more of the risk premiums on the basis of the notion that the observed negative short rate reflects an elevated willingness to pay for safety or, conversely, elevated required compensation for risk.

Forecast horizons substantially longer than the maturity of the standard short-term instrument call for a different type of adjustment. There are essentially two approaches. The first is to use the yield on a longer zero-coupon bond with a maturity that matches the horizon. In theory, that is the right thing to do. It does, however, call into question the role of the term premium since the longer-term rate will already incorporate the term premium. The second approach is to replace today's observed short-term rate with an estimate of the return that would be generated by rolling the short-term instrument over the forecast horizon; that is, take account of the likely path of short-term rates. This approach does not change the interpretation of the term premium. In addition to helping establish the baseline return to which risk premiums will be added, explicitly projecting the path of short-term rates may help in estimating the term premium.

In many markets, there are futures contracts for short-term instruments. The rates implied by these contracts are frequently interpreted as the market's expected path of short-term rates. As such, they provide an excellent starting point for analysts in formulating their own projections. Some central banks—for example, the US Federal Reserve Board—publish projections of future policy rates that can also serve as a guide for analysts. Quantitative models, such as the Taylor rule, provide another tool.[3]

The Term Premium

The default-free spot rate curve reflects the expected path of short-term rates and the required term premiums for each maturity. It is tempting to think that given a projected path of short-term rates, we can easily deduce the term premiums from the spot curve. We can, of course, derive a set of forward rates in the usual way and subtract the projected short-term rate for each future period. Doing so would give an implied sequence of period-by-period premiums. This may be a useful exercise, but it will not give us what we really want—the expected returns for bonds of different maturities over our forecast horizon. The implication is that although the yield curve contains the information we want and may be useful in forecasting returns, we cannot derive the term premium directly from the curve itself.

A vast amount of academic research has been devoted over many decades to addressing three fundamental questions: Do term premiums exist? If so, are they constant? And if they exist, how are they related to maturity? The evidence indicates that term premiums are positive and increase with maturity, are roughly proportional to duration, and vary over time. The first of these properties implies that term premiums are important. The second allows the analyst to be pragmatic, focusing on a single term premium, which is then scaled by duration. The third property implies that basing estimates on current information is essential.

Ilmanen (2012) argued that there are four main drivers of the term premium for nominal bonds.

- *Level-dependent inflation uncertainty:* Inflation is arguably the main driver of long-run variation in both nominal yields and the term premium. Higher (lower) levels of inflation tend to coincide with greater (less) inflation uncertainty. Hence, nominal yields rise (fall) with inflation because of changes in both expected inflation and the inflation risk component of the term premium.
- *Ability to hedge recession risk:* In theory, assets earn a low (or negative) risk premium if they tend to perform well when the economy is weak. When growth and inflation are primarily driven by aggregate demand, nominal

3 See the Capital Market Expectations Part 1 reading for discussion of the Taylor rule.

bond returns tend to be negatively correlated with growth and a relatively low term premium is warranted. Conversely, when growth and inflation are primarily driven by aggregate supply, nominal bond returns tend to be positively correlated with growth, necessitating a higher term premium.

- *Supply and demand:* The relative outstanding supply of short-maturity and long-maturity default-free bonds influences the slope of the yield curve.[4] This phenomenon is largely attributable to the term premium since the maturity structure of outstanding debt should have little impact on the expected future path of short-term rates.[5]
- *Cyclical effects:* The slope of the yield curve varies substantially over the business cycle: It is steep around the trough of the cycle and flat or even inverted around the peak. Much of this movement reflects changes in the expected path of short-term rates. However, it also reflects countercyclical changes in the term premium.

Although the slope of the yield curve is useful information on which to base forecasts of the term premium, other indicators work as well or better. Exhibit 1 shows correlations with subsequent excess bond returns (7- to 10-year Treasury bond return minus 3-month Treasury bill return) over 1-quarter, 1-year, and 5-year horizons for eight indicators. The indicators are listed in descending order of the (absolute value of the) correlation with one-year returns. The first four are derived from the bond market. The *ex ante* real yield has the strongest relationship over each horizon. Next on the list are the two most complex indicators. The Cochrane and Piazzesi curve factor is a composite measure capturing both the slope and the curvature of the yield curve.[6] The Kim and Wright premium is derived from a three-factor term structure model.[7] The slope of the yield curve is next on the list. Note that it has the weakest relationship over the five-year horizon. The supply indicator—the share of debt with maturity greater than 10 years—has a particularly strong relationship over the longest horizon. Since this variable tends to change gradually over time, it is not surprising that it is more closely related to long-run average returns than it is to shorter-term returns. The three cyclical proxies—the corporate profit-to-GDP ratio, business confidence, and the unemployment rate—are at the bottom of the list since they had the weakest correlation with return over the next year.

Exhibit 1: Correlations with Future Excess Bond Returns, 1962–2009

	Return Horizon		
Current Indicator	**1 Quarter**	**1 Year**	**5 Years**
Ex ante real yield	0.28	0.48	0.69
Cochrane and Piazzesi curve factor	0.24	0.44	0.32
Kim and Wright model premium*	0.25	0.43	0.34
Yield curve slope (10 year – 3 month)	0.21	0.34	0.06

4 As discussed in the Capital Market Expectations Part 1 reading, temporary changes in the relative *flow* of bonds to the market may not have a lasting impact on the curve unless they result in a significant, permanent change in the amounts outstanding.

5 Supply/demand effects will be more pronounced if there are reasons for certain investors to prefer or require bonds of specific maturities. This is most likely to occur at the very long end of the curve because the supply of very long-term bonds is typically limited and some institutions must fund very long-term liabilities. As an example, the long end of the UK curve was severely squeezed in the 1990s.

6 See Cochrane and Piazzesi (2005).

7 See Kim and Wright (2005). The three factors in the theoretical model do not correspond directly with observable variables but may be thought of as proxies for the level, slope, and curvature of the term structure.

	Return Horizon		
Current Indicator	**1 Quarter**	**1 Year**	**5 Years**
Share of debt > 10 years	0.13	0.28	0.66
Corporate profit/GDP	−0.13	−0.25	−0.52
ISM business confidence	−0.10	−0.20	−0.30
Unemployment rate	0.11	0.18	0.24

* *Kim and Wright model results are for 1990–2009.*
Source: Ilmanen (2012, Exhibit 3.14).

The Credit Premium

The credit premium is the additional expected return demanded for bearing the risk of default losses—importantly, in addition to compensation for the *expected* level of losses. Both expected default losses and the credit premium are embedded in credit spreads. They cannot be recovered from those spreads unless we impose some structure (i.e., a model) on default-free rates, default probabilities, and recovery rates. The two main types of models—structural credit models and reduced-form credit models—are described in detail in other readings.[8] In the following discussion, we will focus on the empirical behavior of the credit premium.

An analysis of 150 years of defaults among US non-financial corporate bonds showed that the severity of default losses accounted for only about half of the 1.53% average yield spread.[9] Hence, holders of corporate bonds did, on average, earn a credit premium to bear the risk of default. However, the pattern of actual defaults suggests the premium was earned very unevenly over time. In particular, high and low default rates tended to persist, causing clusters of high and low annual default rates and resultant losses. The study found that the previous year's default rate, stock market return, stock market volatility, and GDP growth rate were predictive of the subsequent year's default rate. However, the aggregate credit spread was not predictive of subsequent defaults. Contemporaneous financial market variables—stock returns, stock volatility, and the riskless rate—were significant in explaining the credit spread, but neither GDP growth nor changes in the default rate helped explain the credit spread. This finding suggests that credit spreads were driven primarily by the credit risk premium and financial market conditions and only secondarily by fundamental changes in the expected level of default losses. Thus, credit spreads do contain information relevant to predicting the credit premium.

Ilmanen (2012) hypothesized that credit spreads and the credit premiums embedded in them are driven by different factors, depending on credit quality. Default rates on top-quality (AAA and AA) bonds are extremely low, so very little of the spread/premium is due to the likelihood of actual default in the absence of a change in credit quality. Instead, the main driver is "downgrade bias"—the fact that a deterioration in credit quality (resulting in a rating downgrade) is much more likely than an improvement in credit quality (leading to an upgrade) and that downgrades induce larger spread changes than upgrades do.[10] Bonds rated A and BBB have moderate default rates. They still do not have a high likelihood of actual default losses, but their prospects are more

8 See the CFA Program curriculum reading "Credit Analysis Models." More in-depth coverage can be found in Jarrow and van Deventer (2015).

9 See Giesecke, Longstaff, Schaefer, and Strebulaev (2011). Default rates were measured as a fraction of the par value of outstanding bonds. The authors did not document actual recovery rates, instead assuming 50% recovery. Hence, the true level of losses could have been somewhat higher or lower.

10 Liquidity relative to government bonds is also an important contributor to yield spreads on very high-quality private sector bonds. By definition, of course, this is really the liquidity premium, rather than part of the credit premium.

sensitive to cyclical forces and their spreads/premiums vary more (countercyclically) over the cycle. Default losses are of utmost concern for below-investment-grade bonds. Defaults tend to cluster in times when the economy is in recession. In addition, the default rate and the severity of losses in default tend to rise and fall together. These characteristics imply big losses at the worst times, necessitating substantial compensation for this risk. Not too surprisingly, high-yield spreads/premiums tend to rise ahead of realized default rates.

Exhibit 2 shows three variables that have tended to predict excess returns (over T-bills) for an index of US investment-grade corporate bonds over the next quarter and the next year. Not surprisingly, a high corporate option-adjusted spread is bullish for corporate bond performance because it indicates a large cushion against credit losses—that is, a higher credit premium. A steep Treasury curve is also bullish because, as mentioned earlier, it tends to correspond to the trough of the business cycle when default rates begin to decline. Combining these insights with those from Exhibit 1, the implication is that a steep yield curve predicts both a high term premium and a high credit premium. Higher implied volatility in the equity market was also bullish for corporates, most likely reflecting risk-averse pricing—that is, high risk premiums—across all markets.

Exhibit 2: Correlations with US Investment-Grade Corporate Excess Returns, 1990–2009

	Return Horizon	
Current Indicator	**1 Quarter**	**1 Year**
Corporate option-adjusted spread	0.25	0.46
VIX implied equity volatility	0.28	0.39
Yield curve slope (10 year − 2 year)	0.20	0.27

Source: Ilmanen (2012, Exhibit 4.15).

How are credit premiums related to maturity? Aside from situations of imminent default, there is greater risk of default losses the longer one must wait for payment. We might, therefore, expect that longer-maturity corporate bonds would offer higher credit risk premiums. The historical evidence suggests that this has not been the case. Credit premiums tend to be especially generous at the short end of the curve. This may be due to "event risk," in the sense that a default, no matter how unlikely, could still cause a huge proportional loss but there is no way that the bond will pay more than the issuer promised. It may also be due, in part, to illiquidity since many short-maturity bonds are old issues that rarely trade as they gradually approach maturity. As a result, many portfolio managers use a strategy known as a "credit barbell" in which they concentrate credit exposure at short maturities and take interest rate/duration risk via long-maturity government bonds.

The Liquidity Premium

Relatively few bond issues trade actively for more than a few weeks after issuance. Secondary market trading occurs primarily in the most recently issued sovereign bonds, current coupon mortgage-backed securities, and a few of the largest high-quality corporate bonds. The liquidity of other bonds largely depends on the willingness of dealers to hold them in inventory long enough to find a buyer. In general, liquidity tends to be better for bonds that are (a) priced near par/reflective of current market levels, (b) relatively new, (c) from a relatively large issue, (d) from a well-known/

frequent issuer, (e) standard/simple in structure, and (f) high quality. These factors tend to reduce the dealer's risk in holding the bond and increase the likelihood of finding a buyer quickly.

As a baseline estimate of the "pure" liquidity premium in a particular market, the analyst can look to the yield spread between fixed-rate, option-free bonds from the highest-quality issuer (virtually always the sovereign) and the next highest-quality large issuer of similar bonds (often a government agency or quasi-agency). Adjustments should then be made for the factors listed previously. In general, the impact of each factor is likely to increase disproportionately as one moves away from baseline attributes. For example, each step lower in credit quality is likely to have a bigger impact on liquidity than that of the preceding step.

EXAMPLE 2

Fixed-Income Building Blocks

Salimah Rahman works for SMECo, a Middle Eastern sovereign wealth fund. Each year, the fund's staff updates its projected returns for the following year on the basis of developments in the preceding year. The fund uses the building block approach in making its fixed-income projections. Rahman has been assigned the task of revising the key building block components for a major European bond market. The following table shows last year's values:

	Description	Value
Risk-free rate	3-month government bill	1.00%
Term premium	5-year duration	0.50%
Credit premium	Baa/BBB corporate	0.90%
Liquidity premium	Government-guaranteed agency	0.15%

Although inflation rose modestly, the central bank cut its policy rate by 50 bps in response to weakening growth. Aggregate corporate profits have remained solid, and after a modest correction, the stock market finished higher for the year. However, defaults on leveraged loans were unexpectedly high this year, and confidence surveys weakened again recently. Equity option volatility spiked mid year but ended the year somewhat lower. The interest rate futures curve has flattened but remains upward sloping. The 10-year government yield declined only a few basis points, while the yield on comparable government agency bonds remained unchanged and corporate spreads—both nominal and option adjusted—widened.

1. Indicate the developments that are likely to cause Rahman to increase/decrease each of the key building blocks relative to last year.

Guideline answer:

Based on the reduction in policy rates and the flattening of the interest rate futures curve, Rahman is virtually certain to reduce the short-term rate component. Steepening of the yield curve (10-year yield barely responded to the 50 bp rate cut) indicates an increase in both the term premium and the credit premium. Declining confidence also suggests a higher term premium. Widening of credit spreads is also indicative of a higher credit premium. However, the increase in loan defaults suggests that credit losses are likely to be higher next year as well, since defaults tend to cluster. All else the same, this reduces the expected return on corporate bonds/loans. Hence, the credit premium should increase less than would otherwise be implied by the steeper yield curve and wider credit spreads. Modest widening of the government agency spread indicates an increase in the liquidity premium. The resilience of the equity market and the decline in equity option volatility suggest that investors are not demanding a general increase in risk premiums.

4 RISKS IN EMERGING MARKET BONDS

☐ discuss risks faced by investors in emerging market fixed-income securities and the country risk analysis techniques used to evaluate emerging market economies

Emerging market debt was once nearly synonymous with crisis. The Latin American debt crisis of the 1980s involved bank loans but essentially triggered development of a market for emerging market bonds. In the early 1990s, the Mexican crisis occurred. In the late 1990s, there was the Asian crisis, followed by the Russian crisis, which contributed to the turmoil that sank the giant hedge fund Long-Term Capital Management. There have been other, more isolated, events, such as Argentina's forced restructuring of its debt, but the emerging market bond market has grown, deepened, and matured. What started with only a few government issuers borrowing in hard currencies (from their perspective foreign, but widely used, currencies) has grown into a market in which corporations as well as governments issue in their local currencies and in hard currencies. The discussion here applies not just to emerging markets but also to what are known as "frontier" markets (when they are treated separately or as a subset of emerging markets).

Investing in emerging market debt involves all the same risks as investing in developed country debt, such as interest rate movements, currency movements, and potential defaults. In addition, it poses risks that are, although not entirely absent, less significant in developed markets. These risks fall roughly into two categories: (1) economic and (2) political and legal. A slightly different breakdown would be "ability to pay" and "willingness to pay."

Before discussing these country risks, note that some countries that are labeled as emerging markets may in fact be healthy, prosperous economies with strong fundamentals. Likewise, the political and legal issues discussed in this section may or may not apply to any particular country. Furthermore, these risks will, in general, apply in varying degrees across countries. Emerging markets are widely recognized as a very heterogeneous group. It is up to the analyst to assess which considerations are relevant to a particular investment decision.

Economic Risks/Ability to Pay

Emerging market economies as a whole have characteristics that make them potentially more vulnerable to distress and hence less likely to be able to pay their debts on time or in full, such as the following:

- Greater concentration of wealth and income; less diverse tax base
- Greater dependence on specific industries, especially cyclical industries, such as commodities and agriculture; low potential for pricing power in world markets

- Restrictions on trade, capital flows, and currency conversion
- Poor fiscal controls and monetary discipline
- Less educated and less skilled work force; poor or limited physical infrastructure; lower level of industrialization and technological sophistication
- Reliance on foreign borrowing, often in hard currencies not their own
- Small/less sophisticated financial markets and institutions
- Susceptibility to capital flight; perceived vulnerability contributing to actual vulnerability

Although history is at best an imperfect guide to the future, the analyst should examine a country's track record on critical issues. Have there been crises in the past? If so, how were they handled/resolved? Has the sovereign defaulted? Is there restructured debt? How have authorities responded to fiscal challenges? Is there inflation or currency instability?

The analyst should, of course, examine the health of the macroeconomy in some detail. A few indicative guidelines can be helpful. If there is one ratio that is most closely watched, it is the ratio of the fiscal deficit to GDP. Most emerging countries have deficits and perpetually struggle to reduce them. A persistent ratio above 4% is likely a cause for concern. A debt-to-GDP ratio exceeding 70%–80%, perhaps of only mild concern for a developed market, is a sign of vulnerability for an emerging market. A persistent annual real growth rate less than 4% suggests that an emerging market is catching up with more advanced economies only slowly, if at all, and per capita income might even be falling—a potential source of political stress. Persistent current account deficits greater than 4% of GDP probably indicate lack of competitiveness. Foreign debt greater than 50% of GDP or greater than 200% of current account receipts is also a sign of danger. Finally, foreign exchange reserves less than 100% of short-term debt is risky, whereas a ratio greater than 200% is ample. It must be emphasized that the numbers given here are merely suggestive of levels that may indicate a need for further scrutiny.

When all else fails, a country may need to call on external support mechanisms. Hence, the analyst should consider whether the country has access to support from the International Monetary Fund (IMF), the World Bank, or other international agencies.

Political and Legal Risks/Willingness to Pay

Investors in emerging market debt may be unable to enforce their claims or recover their investments. Weak property rights laws and weak enforcement of contract laws are clearly of concern in this regard. Inability to enforce seniority structures within private sector claims is one important example. The principle of sovereign immunity makes it very difficult to force a sovereign borrower to pay its debts. Confiscation of property, nationalization of companies, and corruption are also relevant hazards. Coalition governments may also pose political instability problems. Meanwhile, the imposition of capital controls or restrictions on currency conversion may make it difficult, or even impossible, to repatriate capital.

As with economic risks, history may provide some guidance with respect to the severity of political and legal risks. The following are some pertinent questions: Is there a history of nationalization, expropriation, or other violations of property rights? How have international disputes been resolved and under which legal jurisdiction? Has the integrity of the judicial system and process been questioned? Are political institutions stable? Are they recognized as legitimate and subject to reasonable checks and balances? Has the transfer of power been peaceful, orderly, and lawful? Does the political process give rise to fragile coalitions that collapse whenever events strain the initial compromises with respect to policy?

EXAMPLE 3

Emerging Market Bonds

1. Belvia has big aspirations. Although still a poor country, it has been growing rapidly, averaging 6% real and 10% nominal growth for the last five years. At the beginning of this period of growth, a centrist coalition gained a narrow majority over the authoritarian, fiscally irresponsible, anti-investor, anti-business party that had been in power for decades. The government has removed the old barriers to trade, including the signing of a regional free-trade agreement, and removed capital controls. Much of its growth has been fueled by investment in its dominant industry—natural resources—financed by debt and foreign direct investment flows. These policies have been popular with the business community, as has the relaxation of regulations affecting key constituencies. Meanwhile, to ensure that prosperity flows rapidly to the people, the government has allowed redistributive social payments to grow even faster than GDP, resulting in a large and rising fiscal deficit (5% of GDP this year, projected to be 7% in two years). The current account deficit is 8% of GDP. Despite the large current account deficit, the local currency has appreciated significantly since it was allowed to float two years ago. The government has just announced that it will issue a large 10-year local currency bond under Belvian law—the first issue of its kind in many years.

   Despite a very strong relationship with the bank marketing the bond, Peter Valt has decided not to invest in it. When pressed for his reasoning, what risks is he likely to identify?

Solution:

There are several significant risks and warning signs. Coalition governments are often unstable, and the most likely alternative would appear to be a return to the previously dominant party that lacks fiscal discipline. That regime is likely to undo the recent pro-growth policies and might even disavow the debt, including this new bond. The bond will be governed by Belvian law, which, combined with the principle of sovereign immunity, will make it very difficult for foreigners to enforce their claims. In addition, the relaxation of regulations affecting key constituencies hints strongly at corruption and possibly at payoffs within the current regime. With respect to the economy, fiscal discipline remains poor, there is heavy reliance on a single industry, and the current account deficit is almost certainly unsustainable (e.g., over the 10-year life of this bond). In addition, the currency is very likely to be overvalued, which will both make it very difficult to broaden global competitiveness beyond natural resources and increase the investor's risk of substantial currency losses.

FORECASTING EQUITY RETURNS

5

- ☐ discuss approaches to setting expectations for equity investment market returns
- ☐ discuss risks faced by investors in emerging market equity securities

The task of forecasting equity market returns is often the central focus of setting capital market expectations. In this section, we discuss applying each of the major methodologies to equities.

Historical Statistics Approach to Equity Returns

Exhibit 3 shows the mean real return for each market portfolio centered within a 95% confidence interval. Results are also shown for a world portfolio, a world ex-US portfolio, and Europe. The portfolios are ordered from left to right on the basis of the mean return.

The means range from a low of 5.0% for Austria to a high of 9.4% in South Africa. Note that both of these values lie within the confidence interval for every country. From a statistical perspective, there is really no difference among these markets in terms of mean real return. This illustrates the fact that sample averages, even derived from seemingly long histories, are very imprecise estimates unless the volatility of the data is small relative to the mean. Clearly that is not the case for equity returns. Nonetheless, sample means are frequently cited without regard to the quality of information they convey.

Exhibit 3: Historical Mean Returns with Confidence Intervals by Country, 1900–2017

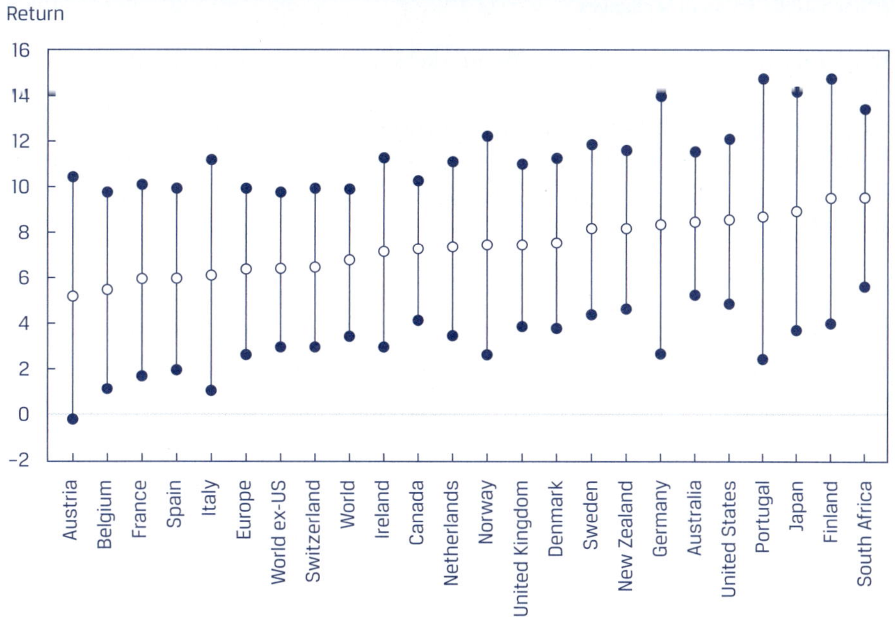

As indicated in Section 2, shrinkage estimators can often provide more reliable estimates by combining the sample mean with a second estimate of the mean return. However, the application of a common shrinkage estimator confirms that there is no basis for believing that the true expected returns for the countries in Exhibit 3 are different.

DCF Approach to Equity Returns

Analysts have frequently used the Gordon (constant) growth model form of the dividend discount model, solved for the required rate of return, to formulate the long-term expected return of equity markets. Although this model is quite simple, it has a big advantage over using historical stock returns to project future returns. The vast majority of the "noise" in historical stock returns comes from fluctuations in the price-to-earnings ratio (P/E) and the ratio of earnings to GDP. Since the amount of earnings appears in the numerator of one ratio and the denominator of the other, the impact of these ratios tends to cancel out over time, leaving the relationship between equity market appreciation and GDP growth much more stable. And GDP growth itself, especially the real growth component, is much less volatile and hence relatively predictable.[11] As an illustration, Exhibit 4 shows historical volatilities (defined as the standard deviation of percentage changes) for the S&P 500 Index return, P/E, the earnings-to-GDP ratio, real US GDP growth, and inflation for 1946–2016. The Gordon growth model allows us to take advantage of this relative stability by linking long-term equity appreciation to a more stable foundation—economic growth.

Exhibit 4: Historical Comparison of Standard Deviations in the United States, 1946–2020

S&P 500	P/E	Earnings/GDP	Real GDP Growth	Inflation
16.09	21.75	31.1	2.4	2.8

Note: Standard deviation of % changes

In the United States and other major markets, share repurchases have become an important way for companies to distribute cash to shareholders. Grinold and Kroner (2002) provided a restatement of the Gordon growth model that takes explicit account of repurchases. Their model also provides a means for analysts to incorporate expectations of valuation levels through the familiar price-to-earnings ratio. The **Grinold–Kroner model**[12] is

$$E\left(R_e\right) \approx \frac{D}{P} + (\%\Delta E - \%\Delta S) + \%\Delta \mathrm{P/E}, \tag{1}$$

where $E(R_e)$ is the expected equity return, D/P is the dividend yield, $\%\Delta E$ is the expected percentage change in total earnings, $\%\Delta S$ is the expected percentage change in shares outstanding, and $\%\Delta$P/E is the expected percentage change in the price-to-earnings ratio. The term in parentheses, $(\%\Delta E - \%\Delta S)$, is the growth rate of earnings per share. Net share repurchases ($\%\Delta S < 0$) imply that earnings per share grows faster than total earnings.

With a minor rearrangement of the equation, the expected return can be divided into three components:

- Expected cash flow ("income") return: $D/P - \%\Delta S$

11 See the previous reading for a discussion of projecting trend growth.
12 See Grinold and Kroner (2002) for a derivation. The model is shown here in a slightly modified form.

- Expected nominal earnings growth return: $\%\Delta E$
- Expected repricing return: $\%\Delta P/E$

The expected nominal earnings growth return and the expected repricing return constitute the expected capital gains.

In principle, the Grinold–Kroner model assumes an infinite horizon. In practice, the analyst typically needs to make projections for finite horizons, perhaps several horizons. In applying the model, the analyst needs to be aware of the implications of constant growth rate assumptions over different horizons. Failure to tailor growth rates to the horizon can easily lead to implausible results. As an example, suppose the P/E is currently 16.0 and the analyst believes that it will revert to a level of 20 and be stable thereafter. The P/E growth rates for various horizons that are consistent with this view are 4.56% for 5 years, 2.26% for 10 years, 0.75% for 30 years, and an arbitrarily small positive number for a truly long-term horizon. Treating, say, the 2.26% 10-year number as if it is appropriate for the "long run" would imply an ever-rising P/E rather than convergence to a plausible long-run valuation. The only very long-run assumptions that are consistent with economically plausible relationships are $\%\Delta E$ = Nominal GDP growth, $\%\Delta S = 0$, and $\%\Delta P/E = 0$. The longer the (finite) horizon, the less the analyst's projection should deviate from these values.

EXAMPLE 4

Forecasting the Equity Return Using the Grinold–Kroner Model

Cynthia Casey uses the Grinold–Kroner model in forecasting developed market equity returns. Casey makes the following forecasts:

- a 2.25% dividend yield on Canadian equities, based on the S&P/TSE Composite Index;
- a 1% rate of net share repurchases for Canadian equities;
- a long-term corporate earnings growth rate of 6% per year, based on a 1 percentage point (pp) premium for corporate earnings growth over her expected Canadian (nominal) GDP growth rate of 5%; and
- an expansion rate for P/E multiples of 0.25% per year.

1. Based on the information given, what expected rate of return on Canadian equities is implied by Casey's assumptions?

Solution:

The expected rate of return on Canadian equities based on Casey's assumptions would be 9.5%, calculated as

$$E(R_e) \approx 2.25\% + [6.0\% - (-1.0\%)] + 0.25\% = 9.5\%.$$

2. Are Casey's assumptions plausible for the long run and for a 10-year horizon?

Solution:

Casey's assumptions are not plausible for the very long run. The assumption that earnings will grow 1% faster than GDP implies one of two things: either an ever-rising ratio of economy-wide earnings to GDP or the earnings accruing to businesses not included in the index (e.g., private firms) continually shrinking relative to GDP. Neither is likely to persist indefinitely. Similarly, perpetual share repurchases would eventually eliminate all shares, whereas a perpetually rising P/E would lead to an arbitrarily high price per Canadian dollar of earnings per share. Based on Casey's economic growth forecast, a more reasonable long-run expected return would be 7.25% = 2.25% + 5.0%.

Casey's assumptions are plausible for a 10-year horizon. Over 10 years, the ratio of earnings to GDP would rise by roughly 10.5% = $(1.01)^{10} - 1$, shares outstanding would shrink by roughly 9.6% = $1 - (0.99)^{10}$, and the P/E would rise by about 2.5% = $(1.0025)^{10} - 1$.

Most of the inputs to the Grinold–Kroner model are fairly readily available. Economic growth forecasts can easily be found in investment research publications, reports from such agencies as the IMF, the World Bank, and the OECD, and likely from the analyst firm's own economists. Data on the rate of share repurchases are less straightforward but are likely to be tracked by sell-side firms and occasionally mentioned in research publications. The big question is how to gauge valuation of the market in order to project changes in the P/E.

The fundamental valuation metrics used in practice typically take the form of a ratio of price to some fundamental flow variable—such as earnings, cash flow, or sales—with seemingly endless variations in how the measures are defined and calculated. Whatever the metric, the implicit assumption is that it has a well-defined long-run mean value to which it will revert. In statistical terms, it is a stationary random variable. Extensive empirical evidence indicates that these valuation measures are poor predictors of short-term performance. Over multi-year horizons, however, there is a reasonably strong tendency for extreme values to be corrected. Thus, these metrics do provide guidance for projecting intermediate-term movements in valuation.

Gauging what is or is not an extreme value is complicated by the fact that all the fundamental flow variables as well as stock prices are heavily influenced by the business cycle. One method of dealing with this issue is to "cyclically adjust" the valuation measure. The most widely known metric is the cyclically adjusted P/E (CAPE). For this measure, the current price level is divided by the average level of earnings for the last 10 years (adjusted for inflation), rather than by the most current earnings. The idea is to average away cyclical variation in earnings and provide a more reliable base against which to assess the current market price.

Risk Premium Approaches to Equity Returns

The Grinold–Kroner model and similar models are sometimes said to reflect the "supply" of equity returns since they outline the sources of return. In contrast, risk premiums reflect "demand" for returns.

Defining and Forecasting the Equity Premium

The term "equity premium" is most frequently used to describe the amount by which the expected return on equities exceeds the riskless rate ("equity versus bills"). However, the same term is sometimes used to refer to the amount by which the expected return on equities exceeds the expected return on default-free bonds ("equity versus bonds"). From the discussion of fixed-income building blocks in Sections 3 and 4, we know that the difference between these two definitions is the term premium built into the expected return on default-free bonds. The equity-versus-bonds premium reflects an incremental/building block approach to developing expected equity returns, whereas the equity-versus-bills premium reflects a single composite premium for the risk of equity investment.

Exhibit 5 shows historical averages for both of these equity premium concepts by country for the period 1900–2020.[13] For each country, the bottom portion of the column is the realized term premium (i.e., bonds minus bills) and the top segment is the realized equity-versus-bonds premium. The whole column represents the equity-versus-bills premium. The equity-versus-bills premiums range from 3.0% to 6.3%, the equity-versus-bonds premiums range from 1.8% to 5.2%, and the term premiums range from –0.6% to 2.9%.

Exhibit 5: Worldwide Annualized Bonds vs. Bills and Equity vs. Bonds Premium (%), 1900–2020

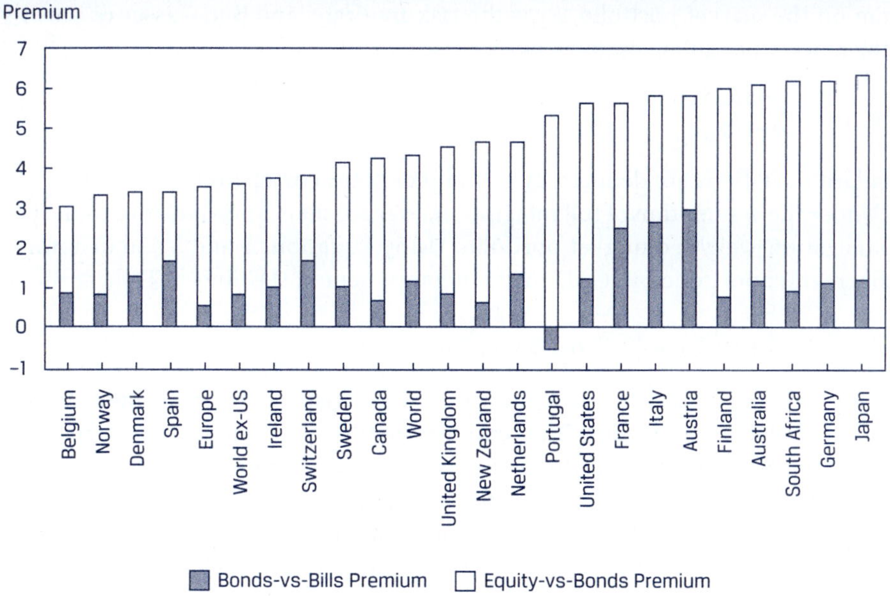

Notes: Germany excludes 1922–1923. Austria excludes 1921–1922. Returns are shown in percentages.

Source: Dimson et al. (2021, Chapter 2, Tables 8 and 9).

As with the mean equity returns in Exhibit 3, these historical premiums are subject to substantial estimation error. Statistically, there is no meaningful difference among them. Thus, the long-run cross section of returns/premiums provides virtually no reliable information with which to differentiate among countries.

Since equity returns are much more volatile than returns on either bills or bonds, forecasting either definition of the equity premium is just as difficult as projecting the absolute level of equity returns. That is, simply shifting to focus on risk premiums provides little, if any, specific insight with which to improve forecasts. The analyst must, therefore, use the other modes of analysis discussed here to forecast equity returns/premiums.

An Equilibrium Approach

There are various global/international extensions of the familiar capital asset pricing model (CAPM). We will discuss a version proposed by Singer and Terhaar (1997) that is intended to capture the impact of incomplete integration of global markets.

13 These premiums reflect geometric returns. Therefore, the equity-vs-bills premium is the sum of the term premium and the equity-vs-bonds premium. Premiums using arithmetic returns are systematically higher and are not additive.

The Singer–Terhaar model is actually a combination of two underlying CAPM models. The first assumes that all global markets and asset classes are fully integrated. The full integration assumption allows the use of a single global market portfolio to determine equity-versus-bills risk premiums for all assets. The second underlying CAPM assumes complete segmentation of markets such that each asset class in each country is priced without regard to any other country/asset class. For example, the markets for German equities and German bonds are completely segmented. Clearly, this is a very extreme assumption.

Recall the basic CAPM pricing relationship:

$$RP_i = \beta_{i,M} RP_M, \tag{2}$$

where $RP_i = [E(R_i) - R_F]$ is the risk premium on the ith asset, RP_M is the risk premium on the market portfolio, R_F is the risk-free rate, and $\beta_{i,M}$—asset i's sensitivity to the market portfolio—is given by

$$\beta_{i,M} = \frac{\text{Cov}\left(R_i, R_M\right)}{\text{Var}\left(R_M\right)} = \rho_{i,M}\left(\frac{\sigma_i}{\sigma_M}\right). \tag{3}$$

Standard deviations are denoted by σ, and ρ denotes correlation.

Under the assumption of full integration, every asset is priced relative to the global capitalization-weighted market portfolio. Using Equations 2 and 3 and denoting the global market portfolio by "*GM*," the first component of the Singer–Terhaar model is

$$RP_i^G = \beta_{i,GM} RP_{GM} = \rho_{i,GM}\sigma_i\left(\frac{RP_{GM}}{\sigma_{GM}}\right). \tag{4}$$

A superscript "*G*" has been added on the asset's risk premium to indicate that it reflects the global equilibrium. The term in parentheses on the far right is the Sharpe ratio for the global market portfolio, the risk premium per unit of global market risk.

Now consider the case of completely segmented markets. In this case, the risk premium for each asset will be determined in isolation without regard to other markets or opportunities for diversification. The risk premium will be whatever is required to induce investors with access to that market/asset to hold the existing supply. In terms of the CAPM framework, this implies treating each asset as its own "market portfolio." Formally, we can simply set β equal to 1 and ρ equal to 1 in the previous equations since each asset is perfectly correlated with itself. Using a superscript "*S*" to denote the segmented market equilibrium and replacing the global market portfolio with asset i itself in Equation 4, the segmented market equilibrium risk premium for asset i is

$$RP_i^S = 1 \times RP_i^S = 1 \times \sigma_i\left(\frac{RP_i^S}{\sigma_i}\right). \tag{5}$$

This is the second component of the Singer–Terhaar model. Note that the first equality in Equation 5 is an identity; it conveys no information. It reflects the fact that in a completely segmented market, the required risk premium could take any value. The second equality is more useful because it breaks the risk premium into two parts: the risk of the asset (σ_i) and the Sharpe ratio (i.e., compensation per unit of risk) in the segmented market.[14]

The final Singer–Terhaar risk premium estimate for asset i is a weighted average of the two component estimates

$$RP_i = \varphi RP_i^G + (1 - \varphi) RP_i^S. \tag{6}$$

14 A somewhat more complex model would allow for integration of asset classes within each country. Doing so would entail incorporating local market portfolios and allowing assets to be less than perfectly correlated with those portfolios. Equation (5) would then look exactly like equation (4) with the local segmented market portfolio replacing the global market portfolio ("GM").

To implement the model, the analyst must supply values for the Sharpe ratios in the globally integrated market and the asset's segmented market; the degree to which the asset is globally integrated, denoted by ϕ; the asset's volatility; and the asset's β with respect to the global market portfolio. A pragmatic approach to specifying the Sharpe ratios for each asset under complete integration is to assume that compensation for non-diversifiable risk (i.e., "market risk") is the same in every market. That is, assume all the Sharpe ratios equal the global Sharpe ratio.

In practice, the analyst must make a judgment about the degree of integration/segmentation—that is, the value of ϕ in the Singer–Terhaar model. With that in mind, some representative values that can serve as starting points for refinement can be helpful. Developed market equities and bonds are highly integrated, so a range of 0.75–0.90 would be reasonable for ϕ. Emerging markets are noticeably less integrated, especially during stressful periods, and there are likely to be greater differences among these markets, so a range of 0.50–0.75 would be reasonable for emerging market equities and bonds. Real estate market integration is increasing but remains far behind developed market financial assets, perhaps on par with emerging market stocks and bonds overall. In general, relative real estate market integration is likely to reflect the relative integration of the associated financial markets. Commodities for which there are actively traded, high-volume futures contracts should be on the higher end of the integration scale.

To illustrate the Singer–Terhaar model, suppose that an investor has developed the following projections for German shares and bonds.

	German Shares	German Bonds
Volatility (σ_i)	17.0%	7.0%
Correlation with global market ($\rho_{i,M}$)	0.70	0.50
Degree of integration (ϕ)	0.85	0.85
Segmented market Sharpe ratio $\left(RP_i^S/\sigma_i\right)$	0.35	0.25

The risk-free rate is 1.0%, and the investor's estimate of the global Sharpe ratio is 0.30. Note that the investor expects compensation for undiversifiable risk to be higher in the German stock market and lower in the German bond market under full segmentation. The following are the fully integrated risk premiums for each of the assets (from Equation 4):

Equities: 0.70 × 17.0% × 0.30 = 3.57%.

Bonds: 0.50 × 7.0% × 0.30 = 1.05%.

The following are the fully segmented risk premiums (from Equation 5):

Equities: 17.0% × 0.35 = 5.95%.

Bonds: 7.0% × 0.25 = 1.75%.

Based on 85% integration (ϕ = 0.85), the final risk estimates (from Equation 6) would be as follows:

Equities: (0.85 × 3.57%) + (1 − 0.85) × 5.95% = 3.93%.

Bonds: (0.85 × 1.05%) + (1 − 0.85) × 1.75% = 1.16%.

Adding in the risk-free rate, the expected returns for German shares and bonds would be 4.93% and 2.16%, respectively.

Virtually all equilibrium models implicitly assume perfectly liquid markets. Thus, the analyst should assess the actual liquidity of each asset class and add appropriate liquidity premiums. Although market segmentation and market liquidity are conceptually distinct, in practice they are likely to be related. Highly integrated markets are likely to be relatively liquid, and illiquidity is one reason that a market may remain segmented.

EXAMPLE 5

Using the Singer–Terhaar Model

1. Stacy Adkins believes the equity market in one of the emerging markets that she models has become more fully integrated with the global market. As a result, she expects it to be more highly correlated with the global market. However, she thinks its overall volatility will decline. Her old and new estimates are as follows:

	Previous Data	New Data
Volatility (σ_i)	22.0%	18.0%
Correlation with global market ($\rho_{i,M}$)	0.50	0.70
Degree of integration (ϕ)	0.55	0.75
Sharpe ratio (global and segmented markets)	0.30	0.30

If she uses the Singer–Terhaar model, what will the net impact of these changes be on her risk premium estimate for this market?

Solution:

The segmented market risk premium will decline from 6.6% (calculated as 22.0% × 0.30 = 6.6%) to 5.4% (= 18% × 0.30). The fully integrated risk premium will increase from 3.30% (= 0.50 × 22.0% × 0.30) to 3.78% (= 0.70 × 18.0% × 0.30). The weighted average premium will decline from 4.79% [= (0.55 × 3.30%) + (0.45 × 6.60%)] to 4.19% [= (0.75 × 3.78%) + (0.25 × 5.40%)], so the net effect is a decline of 60 bps.

Risks in Emerging Market Equities

Most of the issues underlying the risks of emerging market (and "frontier market" if they are classified as such) bonds also present risks for emerging market equities: more fragile economies, lower degree of informational efficiency, less stable political and policy frameworks, and weaker legal protections. However, the risks take somewhat different forms because of the different nature of equity and debt claims. Again, note that emerging markets are a very heterogeneous group. The political, legal, and economic issues that are often associated with emerging markets may not, in fact, apply to a particular market or country being analyzed.

There has been a debate about the relative importance of "country" versus "industry" risk factors in global equity markets for over 40 years. The empirical evidence has been summarized quite accurately as "vast and contradictory."[15] Both matter, but on the whole, country effects still tend to be more important than (global) industry

15 Marcelo, Quirós, and Martins (2013).

effects. This is particularly true for emerging markets. Emerging markets are generally less fully integrated into the global economy and the global markets. Hence, local economic and market factors exert greater influence on risk and return in these markets than in developed markets.

Political, legal, and regulatory weaknesses—in the form of weak standards and/or weak enforcement—affect emerging market equity investors in various ways. The standards of corporate governance may allow interested parties to manipulate the capital structure of companies and to misuse business assets. Accounting standards may allow management and other insiders to hide or misstate important information. Weak disclosure rules may also impede transparency and favor insiders. Inadequate property rights laws, lack of enforcement, and weak checks and balances on governmental actions may permit seizure of property, nationalization of companies, and prejudicial and unpredictable regulatory actions.

Whereas the emerging market debt investor needs to focus on ability and willingness to pay specific obligations, emerging market equity investors need to focus on variety of risks beyond the traditional credit and counterparty risks, especially in times of macroeconomic and political distress.

EXAMPLE 6

Emerging Market Equity Risks

Bill Dwight has been discussing investment opportunities in Belvia with his colleague, Peter Valt (see Example 3). He is aware that Valt declined to buy the recently issued government bond, but he believes the country's equities may be attractive. He notes the rapid growth, substantial investment spending, free trade agreement, deregulation, and strong capital inflows as factors favoring a strong equity market. In addition, solid global growth has been boosting demand for Belvia's natural resources. Roughly half of the public equity market is represented by companies in the natural resources sector. The other half is a reasonably diversified mix of other industries. Many of these firms remain closely held, having floated a minority stake on the local exchange in the last few years. Listed firms are required to have published two years of financial statements conforming to standards set by the Belvia Public Accounting Board, which is made up of the heads of the three largest domestic accounting firms. With the help of a local broker, Dwight has identified a diversified basket of stocks that he intends to buy.

Discuss the risks Dwight might be overlooking.

Guideline answer:

Dwight might be overlooking several risks. He is almost certainly underestimating the vulnerability of the local economy and the vulnerability of the equity market to local developments. The economy's rapid growth is being driven by a large and growing fiscal deficit, in particular, rapidly rising redistributive social payments, and investment spending financed by foreign capital. Appreciation of the currency has made industries other than natural resources less competitive, so the free trade agreement provides little support for the economy. When the government is forced to tighten fiscal policy or capital flows shrink, the domestic economy is likely to be hit hard. Political risk is also a concern. A return to the prior regime is likely to result in a less pro-growth, less business-friendly environment, which would most likely result in attempts by foreign investors to repatriate their capital. Dwight should also have serious concerns about corporate governance, given that most listed companies are closely held, with dominant shareholders posing expropriation risk. He should also be concerned about transparency (e.g., limited history available) and accounting standards (local standards set by the auditing firms themselves).

6 FORECASTING REAL ESTATE RETURNS

☐ explain how economic and competitive factors can affect expectations for real estate investment markets and sector returns

Real estate is inherently quite different from equities, bonds, and cash. It is a physical asset rather than a financial asset. It is heterogeneous, indivisible, and immobile. It is a factor of production, like capital equipment and labor, and as such, it directly produces a return in the form of services. Its services can be sold but can be used/consumed only in one location. Owning and operating real estate involves operating and maintenance costs. All these factors contribute to making real estate illiquid and costly to transfer. The characteristics just described apply to direct investment in real estate (raw land, which does not produce income, is an exception). We will address the investment characteristics of equity REITs versus direct real estate, but unless otherwise stated, the focus is on directly held, unlevered, income-producing real estate.

Historical Real Estate Returns

The heterogeneity, indivisibility, immobility, and illiquidity of real estate pose a severe problem for historical analysis. Individual properties trade infrequently and erratically in time, so there is little chance of getting a sequence of simultaneous, periodic (say, quarterly) transaction prices for a cross section of properties. Even in mor e developed real estate markets, there is a tendence for market transactions to occur predominantly in properties with lower to moderate historical price growth. As a result, real estate owners/investors must rely heavily on appraisals, rather than transactions, in valuing properties. Owing to infrequent transactions and the heterogeneity of properties, these appraisals tend to reflect slowly moving averages of past market conditions. As a result, returns calculated from appraisals represent weighted averages of (unobservable) "true" returns—returns that would have been observed if there had been transaction prices—in previous periods. This averaging does not, in general, bias the mean return. It does, however, significantly distort estimates of volatility and correlations. The published return series is too smooth; that is, the usual sample volatility substantially understates the true volatility of returns. Meanwhile, by disguising the timing of response to market information, the smoothing tends to understate the strength of contemporaneous correlation with other market variables and spuriously induce a lead/lag structure of correlations.

In order to undertake any meaningful analysis of real estate as an asset class, the analyst must first deal with this data issue. It has become standard to "unsmooth" appraisal-based returns using a time-series model. Such techniques, which also apply to private equity funds, private debt funds, and hedge funds, are briefly described in a later section.

Real Estate Cycles

Real estate is subject to cycles that both drive and are driven by the business cycle. Real estate is a major factor of production in the economy. Virtually every business requires it. Every household consumes "housing services." Demand for the services provided by real estate rises and falls with the pace of economic activity. The supply of real estate is vast but essentially fixed at any point in time.[16] As a result, there is a strong cyclical pattern to property values, rents, and occupancy rates. The extent to which this pattern is observable depends on the type of real estate. As emphasized previously, changes in property values are obscured by the appraisal process, although indications can be gleaned from transactions as they occur. The extent to which actual rents and occupancy rates fully reflect the balance of supply and demand depends primarily on the type of property and the quality of the property. High-quality properties with long leases will tend to have little turnover, so fluctuations in actual rents and occupancy rates are likely to be relatively small. In contrast, demand for low-quality properties is likely to be more sensitive to the economy, leading to more substantial swings in occupancy and possibly rents as well. Properties with short leases will see rents adjust more completely to current supply/demand imbalances. Room rates and occupancy at low-quality hotels will tend to be the most volatile.

Fluctuations in the balance of supply and demand set up a classic boom–bust cycle in real estate. First, the boom: Perceptions of rising demand, property values, lease rates, and occupancy induce development of new properties. This investment spending helps drive and/or sustain economic activity, which, in turn, reinforces the perceived profitability of building new capacity. Then, the bust: Inevitably, optimistic projections lead to overbuilding and declining property values, lease rates, and occupancy. Since property has a very long life and is immobile, leases are typically for multiple years and staggered across tenants. In addition, since moving is costly for tenants, it may take many months or years for the excess supply to be absorbed.

A study by Clayton, Fabozzi, Gilberto, Gordon, Hudson-Wilson, Hughes, Liang, MacKinnon, and Mansour (2011) suggested that the US commercial real estate crash following the global financial crisis was the first to have been driven by the capital markets rather than by a boom–bust cycle in real estate fundamentals.[17] The catalyst was not overbuilding, Clayton et al. argued, but rather excess leverage and investment in more speculative types of properties. Consistent with that hypothesis, both the collapse in property prices and the subsequent recovery were unusually rapid. The authors attributed the accelerated response to underlying conditions to appraisers responding more vigorously to signals from the REIT and commercial mortgage-backed security markets. It remains to be seen whether this phenomenon will persist in less extreme circumstances.

Capitalization Rates

The capitalization (cap) rate, defined as net operating income (NOI) in the current period divided by the property value, is the standard valuation metric for commercial real estate. It is analogous to EBITDA as a percentage of EV (reciprocal of EV/EBITDA valuation multiple) for a typical corporate issuer. It is not, strictly speaking, a cash

16 Yau, Schneeweis, Szado, Robinson, and Weiss (2018) found that real estate represents from one-third to as much as two-thirds of global wealth.

17 Data from the Investment Property Databank indicate that commercial property values dropped by 21.8% globally and US property values decreased by 33.2% in 2008–2009. Other countries suffered steep losses as well, notably Ireland (55.5%) and Spain (20.1%).

flow yield because a portion of operating income may be reinvested in the property.[18] As with any equity, an estimate of the long-run expected/required rate of return can be derived from this ratio by assuming a constant growth rate for NOI—that is, by applying the Gordon growth model.

$$E(R_{re}) = \text{Cap rate} + \text{NOI growth rate}. \quad (7)$$

The long-run, steady-state NOI growth rate for commercial real estate as a whole should be reasonably close to the growth rate of GDP. The observation that over a 30-year period UK nominal rental income grew about 6.5% per annum, roughly 2.5% in real terms,[19] is consistent with this relationship.

Over finite horizons, it is appropriate to adjust this equation to reflect the anticipated rate of change in the cap rate.

$$E(R_{re}) = \text{Cap rate} + \text{NOI growth rate} - \%\Delta\text{Cap rate}. \quad (8)$$

This equation is analogous to the Grinold–Kroner model for equities, except there is no term for share buybacks. The growth rate of NOI could, of course, be split into a real component and inflation.

Exhibit 6 shows private market cap rates as of 30 June 2021 for US commercial properties differentiated by type, location, and quality. The rates range from 34.7% for industrial properties to 6.8% for retail. The relatively high cap rate for retail reflects the investors' perception that of short-term risks related to in-person shopping during the COVID-19 pandemic and longer-term risks related to ecommerce continuing to take market share from in-store retail.

Exhibit 6: Private Market Cap Rates (%) as of 30 June 2021

Property Type	Average	Higher Risk	Lower Risk
Hotels	53.0	Limited Service 7.7	Full Service 7.1
Health Care	4.86	Skilled Nursing 9.5	Medical Office 5.7
Retail Malls	6.8	Low Productivity 8.8	High Productivity 5.0
Industrial	3.74		
Office	5.0	Secondary Cities 6.6	Gateway Cities 4.7
Apartments	4.55		

Source: CenterSquare Investment Management (2018).

In-store share losses to ecommerce is especially intense for lower-productivity (less profitable) locations. Cap rates for high- and low-productivity shopping malls began to diverge even before the global financial crisis. In 2006, the difference in cap rates was 1.2 percentage points; by 2018, it was 3.2 percentage points.[20]

Cap rates reflect long-term discount rates. As such, we should expect them to rise and fall with the general level of long-term interest rates, which tends to make them pro-cyclical. However, they are also sensitive to credit spreads and the availability of credit. Peyton (2009) found that the spread between cap rates and the 10-year Treasury yield is positively related to the option-adjusted spread on three- to five-year B-rated corporate bonds and negatively related to ratios of household and non-financial-sector

18 Ilmanen (2012) indicated that the difference between cap rates and cash flow yields may be on the order of 3 percentage points. Although significant reinvestment of NOI reduces the cash flow yield, it should increase the growth rate of NOI if the investment is productive.

19 Based on data from Investment Property Databank Limited.

20 CenterSquare Investment Management (2018). These are cap rates implied by REIT pricing, which is why the 2018 differential does not exactly match the private market figures given in Exhibit 6.

debt to GDP. The countercyclical nature of credit spreads mitigates the cyclicality of cap rates. The debt ratios are effectively proxies for the availability of debt financing for leveraged investment in real estate. Since real estate transactions typically involve substantial leverage, greater availability of debt financing is likely to translate into a lower required liquidity premium component of expected real estate returns. Not surprisingly, higher vacancy rates induce higher cap rates.

The Risk Premium Perspective on Real Estate Expected Return

As a very long-lived asset, real estate is quite sensitive to the level of long-term rates; that is, it has a high effective duration. Indeed, this is often the one and only characteristic mentioned in broad assessments of the likely performance of real estate as an asset class. Hence, real estate must earn a significant term premium. Income-earning properties are exposed to the credit risk of the tenants. In essence, a fixed-term lease with a stable stream of payments is like a corporate bond issued by the tenant secured with physical assets. The landlord must, therefore, demand a credit premium commensurate with what his or her average tenant would have to pay to issue such debt. Real estate must also earn a significant equity risk premium (relative to corporate debt) since the owner bears the full brunt of fluctuations in property values as well as uncertainty with respect to rent growth, lease rollover/termination, and vacancies. The most volatile component of return arises, of course, from changes in property values. As noted previously, these values are strongly pro-cyclical, which implies the need for a significant equity risk premium. Combining the bond-like components (term premium plus credit premium) with a stock-like component implies a risk premium somewhere between those of corporate bonds and equities.

Liquidity is an especially important risk for direct real estate ownership. There are two main ways to view illiquidity. For publicly traded equities and bonds, the question is not whether one can sell the security quickly but, rather, at what price. For real estate, however, it may be better to think of illiquidity as a total inability to sell the asset except at randomly spaced points in time. From this perspective, the degree of liquidity depends on the average frequency of these trading opportunities. By adopting this perspective, one can ask how large the liquidity premium must be to induce investors to hold an asset with a given level of liquidity. Ang, Papanikolaou, and Westerfield (2014) analyzed this question. Their results suggest liquidity premiums on the order of 0.60% for quarterly average liquidity, 0.90% for annual liquidity, and 2%, 4%, and 6% for liquidity on average every 2, 5, and 10 years, respectively.[21] All things considered, a liquidity premium of 2%–4% would seem reasonable for commercial real estate.

Real Estate in Equilibrium

Real estate can be incorporated into an equilibrium framework (such as the Singer–Terhaar model). Indeed, doing so might be deemed a necessity given the importance of real estate in global wealth. There are, however, a few important considerations. First, the impact of smoothing must have been removed from the risk/return data and metrics used for real estate. Otherwise, inclusion of real estate will distort the results for all asset classes. Second, it is important to recognize the implicit assumption of fully liquid assets in equilibrium models. Adjusting the equilibrium for illiquidity—that is, adding a liquidity premium—is especially important for real estate and other private

21 See Table 3 in Ang et al. (2014). The numbers cited here reflect an assumption of zero correlation between the investor's liquid and illiquid assets.

assets. Third, although real estate investors increasingly venture outside their home markets, real estate is still location specific and may, therefore, be more closely related to local, as opposed to global, economic/market factors than are financial claims.

Public vs. Private Real Estate

Many institutional investors and some ultra-wealthy individuals are able to assemble diversified portfolios of direct real estate holdings. Investors with smaller portfolios must typically choose between limited, undiversified direct real estate holdings or obtaining real estate exposure through financial instruments, such as REIT shares. Assessing whether these alternatives—direct real estate and REITs—have similar investment characteristics is difficult because of return smoothing, heterogeneity of properties, and variations in leverage.

A careful analysis of this issue requires (1) transaction-based returns for unlevered direct real estate holdings, (2) firm-by-firm deleveraging of REIT returns based on their individual balance sheets over time, and (3) carefully constructing direct real estate and REIT portfolios with matching property characteristics. Exhibit 7 shows the results of such an analysis.

Exhibit 7: Direct Real Estate vs. REITs: Four Property Types, 1994–2012

	Mean Return (%)			Standard Deviation (%)		
	Direct Real Estate	REITs		Direct Real Estate	REITs	
		Unlevered	Levered		Unlevered	Levered
Aggregate	8.80	9.29		11.09	9.71	
Apartment	9.49	9.08	11.77	11.42	9.50	20.69
Office	8.43	9.37	10.49	10.97	10.58	23.78
Industrial	9.00	9.02	9.57	11.14	11.65	23.46
Retail	8.96	9.90	12.04	11.54	10.03	23.73

Source: Ling and Naranjo (2015, Table 1).

Deleveraging the REITs substantially reduces both their mean returns and their volatilities. The volatilities are roughly cut in half. Clearly, the deleveraged REIT returns are much more similar to the direct real estate returns than are the levered REIT returns. In the aggregate, REITs outperformed direct real estate by 49 bps per year with lower volatility. Looking at specific property types, REITs had higher returns and lower volatility in two categories—office and retail. Industrial REITs had essentially the same return as directly owned industrial properties but with higher volatility. Apartment REITs lagged the direct market but with significantly lower volatility.

Exhibit 7 certainly shows some interesting differences. The pattern of unlevered REIT returns by property type is not the same as for direct real estate. Retail REITs had the highest return, and industrial REITs had the lowest. Among directly owned properties, apartments had the highest return and offices the lowest. A similar mismatch appears with respect to volatilities.

Overall, this study tends to support the general conclusion reached by most comparisons: Public and private commercial real estate are different. The extent of the difference is less clear. It does appear that once we account for differences in leverage, REIT investors are not sacrificing performance to obtain the liquidity afforded by publicly traded shares. Perhaps REIT investors are able to capture a significant portion of the liquidity risk premium garnered by direct investors (because the REIT is a direct investor) as well as benefit from professional management.

What about the diversification benefits of real estate as an asset class? REITs are traded securities, and that fact shows up in their much higher short-term correlation with equities. In contrast, direct real estate is often touted as a good diversifier based on the notion that it is not very highly correlated with equities. As noted previously, the smoothed nature of most published real estate returns is a major contributor to the appearance of low correlation with financial assets, including with REITs. Once that is corrected, however, the correlation is higher, even over reasonably short horizons, such as a quarter or a year. Importantly, REITs are more highly correlated with direct real estate and less highly correlated with equities over multi-year horizons.[22] Thus, although REITs tend to act like "stocks" in the short run, they act like "real estate" in the longer run. From a strategic asset allocation perspective, REITs and direct real estate are more comparable than conventional metrics suggest.

Long-Term Housing Returns

Savills World Research (2016) estimated that residential real estate accounts for 75% of the total value of developed properties globally. Most individuals' homes are their primary, perhaps only, real estate investment. A relatively new database provides a global perspective on the long-term performance of residential real estate (housing), equities, and bonds.[23] The database covers 145 years (1870–2015) and 16 countries.

Jordà, Knoll, Kuvshinov, Schularick, and Taylor (2017) found that residential real estate was the best performing asset class over the entire sample period, with a higher real return and much lower volatility than equities. However, performance characteristics differed before and after World War II:

- Residential real estate had a higher (lower) real return than equities before (after) World War II.
- Residential real estate had a higher real return than equities in every country except Switzerland, the United Kingdom, and the United States over 1950–1980 but a lower return than equities in every country for 1980–2015.
- Residential real estate and equities had similar patterns—that is, a strong correlation prior to the war but a low correlation after the war.
- Equity returns became increasingly correlated across countries after the war, but residential real estate returns are essentially uncorrelated across countries.

Exhibit 8 shows the real returns for equities and residential real estate in each country since 1950.

22 Stefek and Suryanarayanan (2012).

23 The database was developed for and is described in Jordà, Knoll, Kuvshinov, Schularick, and Taylor (2017).

Exhibit 8: Real Equity and Housing Returns by Country, 1950–2015

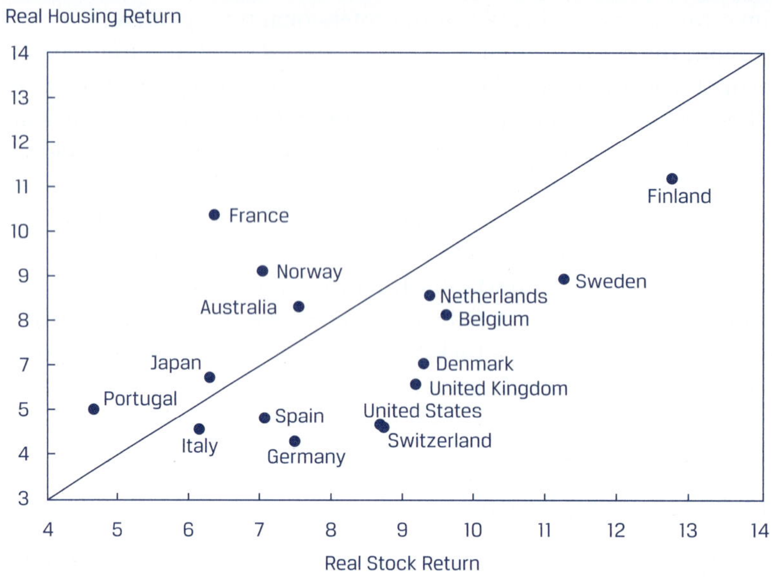

Note: Annual percentage returns are shown.

Source: Jordà et al. (2017).

EXAMPLE 7

Assessing Real Estate Investments

Tammi Sinclair, an analyst at a large retirement fund, recently attended investor presentations by three private real estate firms looking to fund new projects. Office Growth Partners specializes in building and owning low-cost, standardized office space for firms seeking to place sales representatives in the most rapidly growing small population areas across the region. Mega-Box Properties builds and owns large, custom-designed distribution facilities for multinational makers of brand-name products. The facilities are strategically located near major global transportation hubs. Exclusive Elegance Inc. develops and then manages some of the world's most luxurious, sought-after residential buildings in prime locations. It never breaks ground on a new property until at least 85% of the units have been sold and, to date, has never failed to sell out before construction is complete.

Identify important characteristics of each business that Sinclair will need to consider in establishing a required rate of return for each potential investment.

Guideline answer:

Office Growth Partners (OGP) is likely to be a very high-risk investment. It essentially chases hot markets, it builds generic office space, and its typical tenants (opportunistic sales forces) are apt to opt out as soon as the market cools. All these aspects suggest that its business is very exposed to a boom-and-bust cycle. It is likely to end up owning properties with persistently high vacancy rates and high turnover. Hence, Sinclair will likely require a rather high expected return on an investment in OGP.

Mega-Box's business should be fairly stable. The distribution centers are strategically located and designed to meet the needs of the tenant, which suggests long-term leases and low turnover will benefit both Mega-Box and the tenant firms. The average credit quality of the tenants—multinational makers of brand-name products—is likely to be solid and disciplined by the public bond and loan markets. All things considered, Sinclair should probably require a significantly lower expected return on an investment in Mega-Box than in OGP.

Exclusive Elegance appears to be even lower risk. First, it deals only in the very highest-quality, most sought-after properties in prime locations. These should be relatively immune to cyclical fluctuations. Second, it does not retain ownership of the properties, so it does not bear the equity/ownership risks. Third, it is fairly conservative in the riskiest portion of its business—developing new properties. However, Sinclair will need to investigate its record with respect to completing development projects within budget, maintaining properties, and delivering top-quality service to residents.

FORECASTING EXCHANGE RATES

7

☐ discuss major approaches to forecasting exchange rates

Forecasting exchange rates is generally acknowledged to be especially difficult—so difficult that many asset managers either passively accept the impact of currency movements on their portfolio returns or routinely hedge out the currency exposure even if doing so is costly.

To get a sense for why exchange rates are so difficult to forecast, it is useful to distinguish between "money" and the currency in which it is denominated. Like equities and bonds, money is an asset denominated in a currency. Currencies are the units of account in which the prices of everything else—goods, services, real assets, financial assets, liabilities, flows, and balances—are quoted. An exchange rate movement changes the values of everything denominated in one currency relative to everything denominated in every other currency. That is a very powerful force. It works in the other direction as well. Anything that affects quantities, prices, or values within one currency relative to those in another will exert some degree of pressure on exchange rates. Perhaps even more importantly, anything that changes *expectations* of prices, quantities, or values within any currency can change expectations about the future path of currencies, causing an immediate reaction in exchange rates as people adjust their exposures.

Of course, currencies are not abstract accounting ledgers. They are inherently tied to governments, financial systems, legal systems, and geographies. The laws, regulations, customs, and conventions within and between these systems also influence exchange rates, especially when exchange rates are used as instruments or targets of policy. The consequence of all these aspects is that there is very little firm ground on which to stand for analysts trying to forecast exchange rates. The best we can hope to do is to identify the forces that are likely to be exerting the most powerful influences and assess their relative strength. On a related note, it is not possible to identify mutually exclusive approaches to exchange rate forecasting that are each complete enough to stand alone. Hence, the perspectives discussed in this section should be viewed as complementary rather than as alternatives.

Focus on Goods and Services, Trade, and the Current Account

There are three primary ways in which trade in goods and services can influence the exchange rate. The first is directly through flows. The second is through quasi-arbitrage of prices. The third is through competitiveness and sustainability.

Trade Flows

Trade flows do not, in general, exert a significant impact on contemporaneous exchange rate movements, provided they can be financed. Although gross trade flows may be large, net flows (exports minus imports) are typically much smaller relative to the economy and relative to actual and potential financial flows. If trade-related flows through the foreign exchange market become large relative to financing/investment flows, it is likely that a crisis is emerging.

Purchasing Power Parity

Purchasing power parity (PPP) is based on the notion that the prices of goods and services should change at the same rate regardless of currency denomination.[24] Thus, *the expected percentage change in the exchange rate should be equal to the difference in expected inflation rates.* If we define the *real exchange rate* as the ratio of price levels converted to a common currency, then PPP says that *the expected change in the real exchange rate should be zero.*

The mechanism underlying PPP is a quasi-arbitrage. Free and competitive trade should force alignment of the prices of similar products after conversion to a common currency. This is a very powerful force. It works, but it is slow and incomplete. As a result, the evidence indicates that PPP is a poor predictor of exchange rates over short to intermediate horizons but is a better guide to currency movements over progressively longer multi-year horizons.[25]

There are numerous reasons for deviations from PPP. The starting point matters. Relative PPP implicitly assumes that prices and exchange rates are already well aligned. If not, it will take time before the PPP relationship re-emerges. Not all goods are traded, and virtually every country imposes some trade barriers. PPP completely ignores the impact of capital flows, which often exert much more acute pressure on exchange rates over significant periods of time. Finally, economic developments may necessitate changes in the country's terms of trade; that is, contrary to PPP, the real exchange rate may need to change over time.

The impact of relative purchasing power on exchange rates tends to be most evident when inflation differentials are large, persistent, and driven primarily by monetary conditions. Under these conditions, PPP may describe exchange rate movements reasonably well over all but the shortest horizons. Indeed, the well-known "monetary approach" to exchange rates essentially boils down to two assumptions: (1) PPP holds, and (2) inflation is determined by the money supply.

Competitiveness and Sustainability of the Current Account

It is axiomatic that in the absence of capital flows prices, quantities, and exchange rates would have to adjust so that trade is always balanced. Since the prices of goods and services, production levels, and spending decisions tend to adjust only gradually, the onus of adjustment would fall primarily on exchange rates. Allowing for capital flows mitigates this pressure on exchange rates. The fact remains, however, that imposition

---

24 This version of PPP is usually referred to as "relative PPP" to distinguish it from a stricter notion called "absolute PPP." Absolute PPP is an important concept but is not useful for practical forecasting. See previous CFA Program currency readings for a broader discussion of PPP concepts.

25 See, for example, Abuaf and Jorion (1990); Exhibit 2 in "Currency Exchange Rates: Understanding Equilibrium Value" provides a useful visual illustration of PPP over different horizons.

of restrictions on capital flows will increase the sensitivity of exchange rates to the trade balance or, more generally, the current account balance.[26] This is not usually a major consideration for large, developed economies with sophisticated financial markets but can be important in small or developing economies.

Aside from the issue of restrictions on capital mobility, the extent to which the current account balance influences the exchange rate depends primarily on whether it is likely to be persistent and, if so, whether it can be sustained. These issues, in turn, depend mainly on the size of the imbalance and its source. Small current account balances—say, less than 2% of GDP—are likely to be sustainable for many years and hence would exert little influence on exchange rates. Similarly, larger imbalances that are expected to be transitory may not generate a significant, lasting impact on currencies.

The current account balance equals the difference between national saving and investment.[27] A current account surplus indicates that household saving plus business profits and the government surplus/deficit exceeds domestic investment spending. A current account deficit reflects the opposite. A current account deficit that reflects strong, profitable investment spending is more likely to be sustainable than a deficit reflecting high household spending (low saving), low business profits, or substantial government deficits because it is likely to attract the required capital inflow for as long as attractive investment opportunities persist. A large current account surplus may not be very sustainable either because it poses a sustainability problem for deficit countries or because the surplus country becomes unwilling to maintain such a high level of aggregate saving.

Whether an imbalance is likely to persist in the absence of terms-of-trade adjustments largely depends on whether the imbalance is structural. Structural imbalances arise from (1) persistent fiscal imbalances; (2) preferences, demographics, and institutional characteristics affecting saving decisions; (3) abundance or lack of important resources; (4) availability/absence of profitable investment opportunities associated with growth, capital deepening, and innovation; and, of course, (5) the prevailing terms of trade. Temporary imbalances mainly arise from business cycles (at home and abroad) and associated policy actions.

If a change in the (nominal) exchange rate is to bring about a necessary change in the current account balance, it will have to induce changes in spending patterns, consumption/saving decisions, and production/investment decisions. These adjustments typically occur slowly and are often resisted by decision makers who hope they can be avoided. Rapid adjustment of the exchange rate may also be resisted because people only gradually adjust their expectations of its ultimate level. Hence, both the exchange rate and current account adjustments are likely to be gradual.

Focus on Capital Flows

Since the current account and the capital account must always balance and the drivers of the current account tend to adjust only gradually, virtually all of the short-term adjustment and much of the intermediate-term adjustment must occur in the capital account. Asset prices, interest rates, and exchange rates are all part of the equilibrating mechanism. Since a change in the exchange rate simultaneously affects the relative values of all assets denominated in different currencies, we should expect significant pressure to be exerted on the exchange rate whenever an adjustment of capital flows is required.

26 The Mundell–Fleming model of monetary and fiscal policy effects on the exchange rate with high/low capital mobility provides an important illustration of this point. See the CFA Program reading "Currency Exchange Rates: Understanding Equilibrium Value."

27 See Chapter 4 of Piros and Pinto (2013) for discussion of balance of payments accounting.

Implications of Capital Mobility

Capital seeks the highest risk-adjusted expected return. The investments available in each currency can be viewed as a portfolio. Designating one as domestic (*d*) and one as foreign (*f*), in a world of perfect capital mobility the exchange rate (expressed as domestic currency per foreign currency unit) will be driven to the point at which the expected percentage change in the exchange rate equals the "excess" risk-adjusted expected return on the domestic portfolio over the foreign portfolio. This idea can be expressed concretely using a building block approach to expected returns.

$$\begin{aligned}&E(\%\Delta S_{d/f})\\&= (r^d - r^f) + (\text{Term}^d - \text{Term}^f) + (\text{Credit}^d - \text{Credit}^f) + (\text{Equity}^d - \text{Equity}^f) +\\&(\text{Liquid}^d - \text{Liquid}^f).\end{aligned} \tag{9}$$

The expected change in the exchange rate ($\%\Delta S_{d/f}$) will reflect the differences in the nominal short-term interest rates (r), term premiums (Term), credit premiums (Credit), equity premiums (Equity), and liquidity premiums (Liquid) in the two markets. The components of this equation can be associated with the expected return on various segments of the portfolio: the money market (first term), government bonds (first and second), corporate bonds (first–third), publicly traded equities (first–fourth), and private assets (all terms), including direct investment in plant and equipment.

As an example, suppose the domestic market has a 1% higher short-term rate, a 0.25% lower term premium, a 0.50% higher credit premium, and the same equity and liquidity premiums as the foreign market. Equation 9 implies that the domestic currency must be expected to depreciate by 1.25% (= 1% – 0.25% + 0.5%)—that is, $E(\%\Delta S_{d/f}) = 1.25\%$—to equalize risk-adjusted expected returns.

It may seem counterintuitive that the domestic currency should be expected to depreciate if its portfolio offers a higher risk-adjusted expected return. The puzzle is resolved by the key phrase "driven to the point . . . " in this subsection's opening paragraph. In theory, the exchange rate will instantly move ("jump") to a level where the currency with higher (lower) risk-adjusted expected return will be so strong (weak) that it will be expected to depreciate (appreciate) going forward. This is known as the *overshooting* mechanism, introduced by Dornbusch (1976). In reality, the move will not be instantaneous, but it may occur very quickly if there is a consensus about the relative attractiveness of assets denominated in each currency. Of course, asset prices will also be adjusting.

The overshooting mechanism suggests that there are likely to be three phases in response to relative improvement in investment opportunities. First, the exchange rate will appreciate ($S_{d/f}$ will decline) as capital flows toward the more attractive market. The more vigorous the flow, the faster and greater the appreciation of the domestic currency and the more the flow will also drive up asset prices in that market. Second, in the intermediate term, there will be a period of consolidation as investors begin to question the extended level of the exchange rate and to form expectations of a reversal. Third, in the longer run, there will be a retracement of some or all of the exchange rate move depending on the extent to which underlying opportunities have been equalized by asset price adjustments. This is the phase that is reflected in Equation 9.

Importantly, these three phases imply that the relationship between currency appreciation/depreciation and apparent investment incentives will not always be in the same direction. This fact is especially important with respect to interest rate differentials since they are directly observable. At some times, higher–interest rate currencies appreciate; at other times, they depreciate.

Uncovered Interest Rate Parity and Hot Money Flows

Uncovered interest rate parity (UIP) asserts that the expected percentage change in the exchange rate should be equal to the nominal interest rate differential. That is, only the first term in Equation 9 matters. The implicit assumption is that the response to short-term interest rate differentials will be so strong that it overwhelms all other considerations.

Contrary to UIP, the empirical evidence consistently shows that *carry trades*—borrowing in low-rate currencies and lending in high-rate currencies—earn meaningful profits on average. For example, Burnside, Eichenbaum, Kleshchelski, and Rebelo (2011) found that from February 1976 to July 2009, a strategy of rolling carry trades involving portfolios of high- and low-rate currencies returned 4.31% per annum after transaction costs versus the US dollar and 2.88% per annum versus the British pound.

The profitability of carry trades is usually ascribed to a risk premium, which is clearly consistent with the idea that the risk premiums in Equation 9 matter. The empirical results may also be capturing primarily the overshooting phase of the response to interest rate differentials. In any case, carry trades tend to be profitable on average, and UIP does not hold up well as a predictor of exchange rates.

Vigorous flows of capital in response to interest rate differentials are often referred to as *hot moneyflows*. Hot money flows are problematic for central banks. First, they limit the central bank's ability to run an effective monetary policy. This is the key message of the Mundell–Fleming model with respect to monetary policy in economies characterized by the free flow of capital. Second, a flood of readily available short-term financing may encourage firms to fund longer-term needs with short-term money, setting the stage for a crisis when the financing dries up. Third, the nearly inevitable overshooting of the exchange rate is likely to disrupt non-financial businesses. These issues are generally most acute for emerging markets since their economies and financial markets tend to be more fragile. Central banks often try to combat hot money flows by intervening in the currency market to offset the exchange rate impact of the flows. They may also attempt to *sterilize* the impact on domestic liquidity by selling government securities to limit the growth of bank reserves or maintain a target level of interest rates. If the hot money is flowing *out* rather than *in*, the central bank would do the opposite: sell foreign currency (thereby draining domestic liquidity) to limit/avoid depreciation of the domestic currency and buy government securities (thereby providing liquidity) to sterilize the impact on bank reserves and interest rates. In either case, if intervention is not effective or sufficient, capital controls may be imposed.

Portfolio Balance, Portfolio Composition, and Sustainability Issues

The earlier discussion on the implications of capital mobility implicitly introduced a portfolio balance perspective. Each country/currency has a unique portfolio of assets that makes up part of the global "market portfolio." Exchange rates provide an across-the-board mechanism for adjusting the relative sizes of these portfolios to match investors' desire to hold them. We will look at this from three angles: tactical allocations, strategic/secular allocations, and the implications of wealth transfer.

The relative sizes of different currency portfolios within the global market portfolio do not, in general, change significantly over short to intermediate horizons. Hence, investors do not need to be induced to make changes in their long-term allocations. However, they are likely to want to make tactical allocation changes in response to evolving opportunities—notably, those related to the relative strength of various economies and related policy measures. Overall, capital is likely to flow into the currencies of countries in the strongest phases of the business cycle. The attraction should be especially strong if the economic expansion is led by robust investment in real, productive assets (e.g., plant and equipment) since that can be expected to generate a new stream of long-run profits.

In the long run, the relative size of each currency portfolio depends primarily on relative trend growth rates and current account balances. Rapid economic growth is almost certain to be accompanied by an expanding share of the global market portfolio being denominated in the associated currency. Thus, investors will have to be induced to increase their strategic allocations to assets in that country/currency. All else the same, this would tend to weaken that currency—partially offsetting the increase in the currency's share of the global portfolio—and upward pressure on risk premiums in that market. However, there are several mitigating factors.

- *With growth comes wealth accumulation:* The share of global wealth owned by domestic investors will be rising along with the supply of assets denominated in their currency. Since investors generally exhibit a strong *home country bias* for domestic assets, domestic investors are likely to willingly absorb a large portion of the newly created assets.
- *Productivity-driven growth:* If high growth reflects strong productivity gains, both foreign and domestic investors are likely to willingly fund it with both financial flows and foreign direct investment.
- *Small initial weight in global portfolios:* Countries with exceptionally high trend growth rates are typically relatively small, have previously restricted foreign access to their local-currency financial markets, and/or have previously funded external deficits in major currencies (not their own). Almost by definition, these are emerging and frontier markets. Any of these factors would suggest greater capacity to increase the share of local-currency-denominated assets in global portfolios without undermining the currency.

Large, persistent current account deficits funded in local currency will also put downward pressure on the exchange rate over time as investors are required to shift strategic allocations toward that currency. Again, there are mitigating considerations.

- *The source of the deficit matters:* As discussed previously, current account deficits arising from strong investment spending are relatively easy to finance as long as they are expected to be sufficiently profitable. Deficits due to a low saving rate or weak fiscal discipline are much more problematic.
- *Special status of reserve currencies:* A few currencies—notably, the US dollar—have a special status because the bulk of official reserves are held in these currencies, the associated sovereign debt issuer is viewed as a safe haven, major commodities (e.g., oil) are priced in these currencies, and international trade transactions are often settled in them. A small current account deficit in a reserve-currency country is welcome because it helps provide liquidity to the global financial system. Historically, however, reserve currency status has not proven to be permanent.

Current account surpluses/deficits reflect a transfer of wealth from the deficit country to the surplus country. In an ideal world of fully integrated markets, perfect capital mobility, homogeneous expectations, and identical preferences,[28] a transfer of wealth would have virtually no impact on asset prices or exchange rates because everyone would be happy with the same portfolio composition. This is not the case in practice. To pick just one example, as long as investors have a home country bias, the transfer of wealth will increase the demand for the current-account-surplus country's assets and currency and decrease demand for those of the deficit country.

28 Note that these are essentially the assumptions underlying the standard CAPM.

Does the composition of a particular currency's portfolio matter? A look back at Equation 9 suggests that it should matter to some degree. For the most part, however, we would expect asset price adjustments (changes in interest rates and risk premiums) to eliminate most of the pressure that might otherwise be exerted on the exchange rate. Nonetheless, some types of flows and holdings are often considered to be more or less supportive of the currency. Foreign direct investment flows are generally considered to be the most favorable because they indicate a long-term commitment and they contribute directly to the productivity/profitability of the economy. Similarly, investments in private real estate and private equity represent long-term capital committed to the market, although they may or may not represent the creation of new real assets. Public equity would likely be considered the next most supportive of the currency. Although it is less permanent than private investments, it is still a residual claim on the profitability of the economy that does not have to be repaid. Debt has to be serviced and must either be repaid or refinanced, potentially triggering a crisis. Hence, a high and rising ratio of debt to GDP gives rise to *debt sustainability* concerns with respect to the economy. This issue could apply to private sector debt. But it is usually associated with fiscal deficits because the government is typically the largest single borrower; typically borrows to fund consumption and transfers, rather than productive investment; and may be borrowing in excess of what can be serviced without a significant increase in taxes. Finally, as noted previously with respect to hot money flows, large or rapid accumulation of short-term borrowing is usually viewed as a clear warning sign for the currency.

EXAMPLE 8

Currency Forecasts

1. After many years of running moderately high current account deficits (2%–4% of GDP) but doing little infrastructure investment, Atlandia plans to increase the yearly government deficit by 3% of GDP and maintain that level of deficit for the next 10 years, devoting the increase to infrastructure spending. The deficits will be financed with local-currency government debt. Pete Stevens, CFA, is faced with the task of assessing the impact of this announcement on the Atlandian currency. After talking with members of the economics department at his firm, he has established the following baseline assumptions:

   - All else the same, current account deficits will persistently exceed 6% of GDP while the program is in place. Setting aside any lasting impact of the policy/spending, the current account deficit will then fall back to 3% of GDP provided the economy has remained competitive.
   - Pressure on wages will boost inflation to 1.5% above the global inflation rate. Because of limitations on factor substitutability, costs in the traded good sector will rise disproportionately.
   - Expectations of faster growth will raise the equity premium.
   - The central bank will likely tighten policy—that is, raise rates.

Questions:

1. What would purchasing power parity imply about the exchange rate?
2. What are the implications for competitiveness for the currency?
3. What is the likely short-term impact of capital flows on the exchange rate?

4. What does the overshooting mechanism imply about the path of the exchange rate over time? How does this fit with the answers to Questions 1–3?
5. What does a sustainability perspective imply?

Solutions:

1. Purchasing power parity would imply that the Atlandian currency will depreciate by 1.5% per year. The exchange rate, quoted in domestic (Atlandian) units per foreign unit as in Equation 9, will rise by a factor of $1.015^{10} = 1.1605$, corresponding to a 13.83% (= 1 – 1/1.1605) decline in the value of the domestic currency.[29]
2. Since costs in the traded sector will rise faster than inflation, the exchange rate would need to depreciate faster than PPP implies in order to maintain competitiveness. Thus, to remain competitive and re-establish a 3% current account deficit after 10 years, the *real* exchange rate needs to depreciate.
3. Both the increase in short-term rates and the increase in the equity premium are likely to induce strong short-term capital inflows even before the current account deficit actually increases. This should put significant pressure on the Atlandian currency to appreciate (i.e., the $S_{d/f}$ exchange rate will decline if the Atlandian currency is defined as the domestic currency). The initial impact may be offset to some extent by flows out of government bonds as investors push yields up in anticipation of increasing supply, but as bonds are repriced to offer a higher expected return (a higher term premium), it will reinforce the upward pressure on the exchange rate.
4. The overshooting mechanism would imply that the initial appreciation of the Atlandian currency discussed previously will extend to a level from which the currency is then expected to depreciate at a pace that equalizes risk-adjusted expected returns across markets and maintains equality between the current and capital accounts. The initial appreciation of the currency in this scenario is clearly inconsistent with PPP, but the subsequent longer-term depreciation phase (from a stronger level) is likely to bring the exchange rate into reasonable alignment with PPP and competitiveness considerations in the long run.
5. It is highly unlikely that a current account deficit in excess of 6% of GDP is sustainable for 10 years. It would entail an increase in net foreign liabilities equaling 60% (= 6% × 10) of GDP. Servicing that additional obligation would add, say, 2%–3% of GDP to the current account deficit forever. Adding that to the baseline projection of 3% would mean that the current account deficit would remain in the 5%–6% range even after the infrastructure spending ended, so net foreign liabilities would still be accumulating rapidly. Closing that gap will require a very large increase in net national saving: 5%–6% of annual GDP *in addition to* the 3% reduction in infrastructure spending when the program ends. Standard macroeconomic analysis implies that such an adjustment would require some combination of a very deep recession and a very large depreciation in the real value of the

29 Note that a slightly different number is obtained if the 1.5% rate is applied directly to the foreign currency value of the Atlandian currency (i.e., the exchange rate expressed as foreign units per domestic unit). That calculation would give a cumulative depreciation of 14.03% (= $1 - 0.985^{10}$). The difference arises because (1/1.015) is not exactly equal to 0.985.

Atlandian currency (i.e., the real $S_{d/f}$ exchange rate must increase sharply). As soon as investors recognize this, a crisis is almost certain to occur. Bond yields would increase sharply, and equity prices and the currency will fall substantially.

FORECASTING VOLATILITY

8

☐ discuss methods of forecasting volatility

In some applications, the analyst is concerned with forecasting the variance for only a single asset. More often, however, the analyst needs to forecast the variance–covariance matrix for several, perhaps many, assets in order to analyze the risk of portfolios. Estimating a single variance that is believed to be constant is straightforward: The familiar sample variance is unbiased and its precision can be enhanced by using higher-frequency data. The analyst's task becomes more complicated if the variance is not believed to be constant or the analyst needs to forecast a variance–covariance (VCV) matrix. These issues are addressed in this section. In addition, we elaborate on de-smoothing real estate and other returns.

Estimating a Constant VCV Matrix with Sample Statistics

The simplest and most heavily used method for estimating constant variances and covariances is to use the corresponding sample statistic—variance or covariance—computed from historical return data. These elements are then assembled into a VCV matrix. There are two main problems with this method, both related to sample size. First, given the short to intermediate sample periods typical in finance, the method cannot be used to estimate the VCV matrix for large numbers of assets. If the number of assets exceeds the number of historical observations, then some portfolios will erroneously appear to be riskless. Second, given typical sample sizes, this method is subject to substantial sampling error. A useful rule of thumb that addresses both of these issues is that the number of observations should be at least 10 times the number of assets in order for the sample VCV matrix to be deemed reliable. In addition, since each element is estimated without regard to any of the others, this method does not address the issue of imposing cross-sectional consistency.

VCV Matrices from Multi-Factor Models

Factor models have become the standard method of imposing structure on the VCV matrix of asset returns. From this perspective, their main advantage is that the number of assets can be very large relative to the number of observations. The key to making this work is that the covariances are fully determined by exposures to a small number of common factors whereas each variance includes an asset-specific component.

In a model with K common factors, the return on the ith asset is given by

$$r_i = \alpha_i + \sum_{k=1}^{K} \beta_{ik} F_k + \varepsilon_i, \tag{10}$$

where α_i is a constant intercept, β_{ik} is the asset's sensitivity to the kth factor, F_k is the kth common factor return, and ε_i is a stochastic term with a mean of zero that is unique to the ith asset. In general, the factors will be correlated. Given the model, the variance of the ith asset is

$$\sigma_i^2 = \sum_{m=1}^{K}\sum_{n=1}^{K}\beta_{im}\beta_{in}\rho_{mn} + v_i^2 \quad (11)$$

where ρ_{mn} is the covariance between the mth and nth factors and v_i^2 is the variance of the unique component of the ith asset's return. The covariance between the ith and jth assets is

$$\sigma_{ij} = \sum_{m=1}^{K}\sum_{n=1}^{K}\beta_{im}\beta_{jn}\rho_{mn} \quad (12)$$

As long as none of the factors are redundant and none of the asset returns are completely determined by the factors (so $v_i^2 \neq 0$), there will not be any portfolios that erroneously appear to be riskless. That is, we will not encounter the first problem mentioned in Section 8, with respect to using sample statistics.

Imposing structure with a factor model makes the VCV matrix much simpler. With N assets, there are $[N(N - 1)/2]$ distinct covariance elements in the VCV matrix. For example, if N =100, there are 4,950 distinct covariances to be estimated. The factor model reduces this problem to estimating $[N \times K]$ factor sensitivities plus $[K(K + 1)/2]$ elements of the factor VCV matrix, Ω. With N = 100 and K = 5, this would mean "only" 500 sensitivities and 15 elements of the factor VCV matrix—almost a 90% reduction in items to estimate. (Of course, we also need to estimate the asset-specific variance terms, v_i^2, in order to get the N variances, σ_i^2.) If the factors are chosen well, the factor-based VCV matrix will contain substantially less estimation error than the sample VCV matrix does.

A well-specified factor model can also improve cross-sectional consistency. To illustrate, suppose we somehow know that the true covariance of any asset i with any asset j is proportional to asset i's covariance with any third asset, k, so

$$\frac{\sigma_{ij}}{\sigma_{ik}} = \text{Constant} \quad (13)$$

for any assets i, j, and k. We would want our estimates to come as close as possible to satisfying this relationship. Sample covariances computed from any given sample of returns will not, in general, do so. However, using Equation 12 with only one factor (i.e., K = 1) shows that the covariances from a single-factor model will satisfy

$$\frac{\sigma_{ij}}{\sigma_{ik}} = \frac{\beta_j}{\beta_k} \quad (14)$$

for all assets i, j, and k. Thus, in this simple example, a single-factor model imposes exactly the right cross-sectional structure.

The benefits obtained by imposing a factor structure—handling large numbers of assets, a reduced number of parameters to be estimated, imposition of cross-sectional structure, and a potentially substantial reduction of estimation error—come at a cost. In contrast to the simple example just discussed, in general, the factor model will almost certainly be mis-specified. The structure it imposes will not be exactly right. As a result, the factor-based VCV matrix is *biased*; that is, the expected value is not equal to the true (unobservable) VCV matrix of the returns. To put it differently, the matrix is not correct even "on average." The matrix is also *inconsistent*; that is, it does not converge to the true matrix as the sample size gets arbitrarily large. In contrast, the sample VCV matrix is unbiased and consistent. Thus, when we use a factor-based matrix instead of the sample VCV matrix, we are choosing to estimate something that is "not quite right" with relative precision rather than the "right thing" with a lot of noise. The point is that although factor models are very useful, they are not a panacea.

Shrinkage Estimation of VCV Matrices

As with shrinkage estimation in general, the idea here is to combine the information in the sample data, the sample VCV matrix, with an alternative estimate, the target VCV matrix—which reflects assumed "prior" knowledge of the structure of the true VCV matrix—and thereby mitigate the impact of estimation error on the final matrix. Each element (variance or covariance) of the final shrinkage estimate of the VCV matrix is simply a weighted average of the corresponding elements of the sample VCV matrix and the target VCV matrix. The same weights are used for all elements of the matrix. The analyst must determine how much weight to put on the target matrix (the "prior" knowledge) and how much weight to put on the sample data (the sample VCV matrix).

Aside from a technical condition that rules out the appearance of riskless portfolios, virtually any choice of target VCV matrix will increase (or at least not decrease) the efficiency of the estimates versus the sample VCV matrix. "Efficiency" in this context means a smaller mean-squared error (MSE), which is equal to an estimator's variance plus the square of its bias. Although the shrinkage estimator is biased, its MSE will in general be smaller than the MSE of the (unbiased) sample VCV matrix. The more plausible (and presumably less biased) the selected target matrix, the greater the improvement will be. A factor-model-based VCV matrix would be a reasonable candidate for the target.

EXAMPLE 9

Estimating the VCV Matrix

1. Isa Berkitz is an analyst at Barnsby & Culp (B&C), a recently formed multi-family office. Berkitz has been asked to propose the method for estimating the variance–covariance matrix to be used in B&C's asset allocation process for all clients. After examining the existing client portfolios and talking with the clients and portfolio managers, Berkitz concludes that in order to support B&C's strategic and tactical allocation needs, the VCV matrix will need to include 25 asset classes. For many of these classes, she will be able to obtain less than 10 years of monthly return data. Berkitz has decided to incorporate both the sample statistics and factor-model approaches using shrinkage estimation.

   Explain the strengths and weaknesses of the two basic approaches and why Berkitz would choose to combine them using the shrinkage framework.

Solution:

The VCV matrix based on sample statistics is correct on average (it is unbiased) and convergences to the true VCV matrix as the sample size gets arbitrarily large (it is "consistent"). The sample VCV method cannot be used if the number of assets exceeds the number of observations, which is not an issue in this case. However, it is subject to large sampling errors unless the number of observations is large relative to the number of assets. A 10-to-1 rule of thumb would suggest that Berkitz needs more than 250 observations (20+ years of monthly data) in order for the sample VCV matrix to give her reliable estimates, but she has at most 120 observations. In addition, the sample VCV matrix does not impose any cross-sectional consistency on the estimates. A factor-model-based VCV matrix can be used even if the number of assets exceeds the number of observations. It can substantially reduce the number of unique parameters to be estimated, it imposes cross-sectional structure, and it can substantially reduce estimation errors. However, unless the structure imposed by the factor model is exactly correct, the VCV matrix will not be correct on average (it will be biased). Shrinkage estimation—a weighted average of the sample VCV and factor-based VCV matrices—will increase (or at least not decrease) the efficiency of the estimates. In effect, the shrinkage estimator captures the benefits of each underlying methodology and mitigates their respective limitations.

Estimating Volatility from Smoothed Returns

The available return data for such asset classes as private real estate, private equity, and hedge funds generally reflect smoothing of unobservable underlying "true" returns. The smoothing dampens the volatility of the observed data and distorts correlations with other assets. Thus, the raw data tend to understate the risk and overstate the diversification benefits of these asset classes. Failure to adjust for the impact of smoothing will almost certainly lead to distorted portfolio analysis and hence poor asset allocation decisions.

The basic idea is that the observed returns are a weighted average of current and past true, unobservable returns. One of the simplest and most widely used models implies that the current observed return, R_t, is a weighted average of the current true return, r_t, and the previous observed return:

$$R_t = (1 - \lambda) r_t + \lambda R_{t-1}, \quad (15)$$

where $0 < \lambda < 1$. From this equation, it can be shown that

$$\text{var}(r) = \left(\frac{1+\lambda}{1-\lambda}\right) \text{var}(R) > \text{var}(R). \quad (16)$$

As an example, if $\lambda = 0.8$, then the true variance, var(r), of the asset is 9 times the variance of the observed data. Equivalently, the standard deviation is 3 times larger.

This model cannot be estimated directly because the true return, r_t, is not observable. To get around this problem, the analyst assumes a relationship between the unobservable return and one or more observable variables. For private real estate, a natural choice might be a REIT index, whereas for private equity, an index of similar publicly traded equities could be used.

EXAMPLE 10

Estimating Volatility from Smoothed Data

While developing the VCV matrix for B&C, Isa Berkitz noted that the volatilities for several asset classes—notably, real estate and private equity categories—calculated directly from available return data appear to be very low. The data are from reputable sources, but Berkitz is skeptical because similar publicly traded classes—for example, REITs and small-cap equities—exhibit much higher volatilities. What is the likely cause of the issue?

Guideline answer:

The very low volatilities are very likely due to smoothing within the reported private asset returns. That is, the observed data reflect a weighted average of current and past true returns. For real estate, this smoothing arises primarily because the underlying property values used to calculate "current" returns are based primarily on backward-looking appraisals rather than concurrent transactions.

Time-Varying Volatility: ARCH Models

The discussion up to this point has focused on estimating variances and covariances under the assumption that their true values do not change over time. It is well known, however, that financial asset returns tend to exhibit **volatility clustering**, evidenced by periods of high and low volatility. A class of models known collectively as autoregressive conditional heteroskedasticity (ARCH) models has been developed to address these time-varying volatilities.[30]

One of the simplest and most heavily used forms of this broad class of models specifies that the variance in period t is given by

$$\begin{aligned}\sigma_t^2 &= \gamma + \alpha\sigma_{t-1}^2 + \beta\eta_t^2 \\ &= \gamma + (\alpha+\beta)\sigma_{t-1}^2 + \beta\left(\eta_t^2 - \sigma_{t-1}^2\right),\end{aligned} \tag{17}$$

where α, β, and γ are non-negative parameters such that (α + β) < 1. The term η_t is the unexpected component of return in period t; that is, it is a random variable with a mean of zero conditional on information at time (t – 1). Rearranging the equation as in the second line shows that $\left(\eta_t^2 - \sigma_{t-1}^2\right)$ can be interpreted as the "shock" to the variance in period t. Thus, the variance in period t depends on the variance in period (t – 1) plus a shock. The parameter β controls how much of the current "shock" feeds into the variance. In the extreme, if β = 0, then variance would be deterministic. The quantity (α + β) determines the extent to which the variance in future periods is influenced by the current level of volatility. The higher (α + β) is, the more the variance "remembers" what happened in the past and the more it "clusters" at high or low levels. The unconditional expected value of the variance is [γ/(1 – α – β)].

As an example, assume that γ = 0.000002, α = 0.9, and β = 0.08 and that we are estimating daily equity volatility. Given these parameters, the unconditional expected value of the variance is 0.0001, implying that the daily standard deviation is 1% (0.01). Suppose the estimated variance at time (t – 1) was 0.0004 (= 0.02^2) and the return in period t was 3% above expectations (η_t = 0.03). Then the variance in period t would be

$$\sigma_t^2 = 0.000002 + (0.9 \times 0.0004) + (0.08 \times 0.03^2) = 0.000434,$$

which is equivalent to a standard deviation of 2.0833%. Without the shock to the variance (i.e., with $\eta_t^2 = \sigma_{t-1}^2 = 0.0004$), the standard deviation would have been 1.9849%. Even without the shock, the volatility would have remained well above its long-run mean of 1.0%. Including the shock, the volatility actually increased. Note that the impact on volatility would have been the same if the return had been 3% *below* expectations rather than above expectations.

The ARCH methodology can be extended to multiple assets—that is, to estimation of a VCV matrix. The most straightforward extensions tend to be limited to only a few assets since the number of parameters rises very rapidly. However, Engle (2002) developed a class of models with the potential to handle large matrices with relatively few parameters.

EXAMPLE 11

ARCH

Sam Akai has noticed that daily returns for a variety of asset classes tend to exhibit periods of high and low volatility but the volatility does seem to revert toward a fairly stable average level over time. Many market participants capture this tendency by estimating volatilities using a 60-day moving window. Akai

30 Chapter 12 of Campbell, Lo, and MacKinlay (1997) provides an excellent, detailed explanation of these models. The present discussion draws on that book.

notes that this method implicitly assumes volatility is constant within each 60-day window but somehow not constant from one day to the next. He has heard that ARCH models can explicitly incorporate time variation and capture the observed clustering pattern.

Explain the models to him.

Guideline answer:

The key idea is to model variance as a linear time-series process in which the current volatility depends on its own recent history or recent shocks. The shocks to volatility arise from unexpectedly large or small returns. In one of the simplest ARCH models, the current variance depends only on the variance in the previous period and the unexpected component of the current return (squared). Provided the coefficients are positive and not "too large," the variance will exhibit the properties Akai has observed: periods of time at high/low levels relative to a well-defined average level.

9 ADJUSTING A GLOBAL PORTFOLIO

☐ recommend and justify changes in the component weights of a global investment portfolio based on trends and expected changes in macroeconomic factors

The coverage of capital market expectations has provided an intensive examination of topics with which analysts need to be familiar in order to establish capital market expectations for client portfolios. This section brings some of this material together to illustrate how analysts can develop and justify recommendations for adjusting a portfolio. The discussion that follows is selective in the range of assets and scenarios it considers. It focuses on connecting expectations to the portfolio and is about "direction of change" rather than the details of specific forecasts.

Macro-Based Recommendations

Suppose we start with a fairly generic portfolio of global equities and bonds (we assume no other asset classes are included or considered) and we are asked to recommend changes based primarily on macroeconomic considerations. Further assume that the portfolio reflects a reasonable strategic allocation for our clients. Hence, we do not need to make any wholesale changes and can focus on incremental improvements based on assessment of current opportunities. To be specific, we limit our potential recommendations to the following:

- Change the overall allocations to equities and bonds.
- Reallocate equities/bonds between countries.
- Adjust the average credit quality of our bond portfolios.
- Adjust duration and positioning on the yield curves.
- Adjust our exposures to currencies.

To approach the task systematically, we begin with a checklist of questions.

1. Have there been significant changes in the drivers of trend growth, globally or in particular countries?

2. Are any of the markets becoming more/less globally integrated?
3. Where does each country stand within its business cycle? Are they synchronized?
4. Are monetary and fiscal policies consistent with long-term stability and the phases of the business cycle?
5. Are current account balances trending and sustainable?
6. Are any currencies under pressure to adjust or trending? Have capital flows driven any currencies to extended levels? Have any of the economies become uncompetitive/super-competitive because of currency movements?

There are certainly many more questions we could ask. In practice, the analyst will need to look into the details. But these questions suffice for our illustration. We will examine each in turn. It must be noted, however, that they are inherently interrelated.

Trend Growth

All else the same, an increase in trend growth favors equities because it implies more rapid long-run earnings growth. Faster growth due to productivity is especially beneficial. In contrast, higher trend growth generally results in somewhat higher real interest rates, a negative for currently outstanding bonds. Identifiable changes in trend growth that have not already been fully factored into asset prices are most likely to have arisen from a shock (e.g., new technology). A global change would provide a basis for adjusting the overall equity/bond allocation. Country-specific or regional changes provide a basis for reallocation within equities toward the markets experiencing enhanced growth prospects that have not already been reflected in market prices.

Global Integration

All else the same, the Singer–Terhaar model implies that when a market becomes more globally integrated, its required return should decline. As prices adjust to a lower required return, the market should deliver an even higher return than was previously expected or required by the market. Therefore, expected increases in integration provide a rationale for adjusting allocations toward those markets and reductions in markets that are already highly integrated. Doing so will typically entail a shift from developed markets to emerging markets.

Phases of the Business Cycle

The best time to buy equities is generally when the economy is approaching the trough of the business cycle. Valuation multiples and expected earnings growth rates are low and set to rise. The Grinold–Kroner model could be used to formalize a recommendation to buy equities. At this stage of the cycle, the term premium is high (the yield curve is steep) and the credit premium is high (credit spreads are wide). However, (short-term) interest rates are likely to start rising soon and the yield curve can be expected to flatten again as the economy gains strength. All else the same, the overall allocation to bonds will need to be reduced to facilitate the increased allocation to equities. Within the bond portfolio, overall duration should be reduced, positions with intermediate maturities should be reduced in favor of shorter maturities (and perhaps a small amount of longer maturities) to establish a "barbell" posture with the desired duration, and exposure to credit should be increased (a "down in quality" trade). The opposite recommendations would apply when the analyst judges that the economy is at or near the peak of the cycle.

To the extent that business cycles are synchronized across markets, this same prescription would apply to the overall portfolio. It is likely, however, that some markets will be out of phase—leading or lagging other markets—by enough to warrant reallocations between markets. In this case, the recommendation would be to reallocate equities from (to) markets nearest the peak (trough) of their respective cycles and to do the opposite within the bond portfolio with corresponding adjustments to duration, yield curve positioning, and credit exposure within each market.

Monetary and Fiscal Policies

Investors devote substantial energy dissecting every nuance of monetary and fiscal policy. If policymakers are doing what we would expect them to be doing at any particular stage of the business cycle—for example, moderate countercyclical actions and attending to longer-term objectives, such as controlling inflation and maintaining fiscal discipline—their activities may already be reflected in asset prices. In addition, the analyst should have factored expected policy actions into the assessment of trend growth and business cycles.

Significant opportunities to add value by reallocating the portfolio are more likely to arise from structural policy changes (e.g., a shift from interest rate targeting to money growth targeting, quantitative easing, and restructuring of the tax code) or evidence that the response to policy measures is not within the range of outcomes that policymakers would have expected (e.g., if massive quantitative easing induced little inflation response). Structural policy changes are clearly intentional and the impact on the economy and the markets is likely to be consistent with standard macroeconomic analysis, so the investment recommendations will follow from the implications for growth trends and business cycles. Almost by definition, standard modes of analysis may be ineffective if policy measures have not induced the expected responses. In this case, the analyst's challenge is to determine what, why, and how underlying linkages have changed and identify the value-added opportunities.

Current Account Balances

Current account balances ultimately reflect national saving and investment decisions, including the fiscal budget. Current accounts must, of course, net out across countries. In the short run, this is brought about in large measure by the fact that household saving and corporate profits (business saving) are effectively residuals whereas consumption and capital expenditures are more explicitly planned. Hence, purely cyclical fluctuations in the current account are just part of the business cycle. Longer-term trends in the current account require adjustments to induce deliberate changes in saving/investment decisions. A rising current account deficit will tend to put upward pressure on real required returns (downward pressure on asset prices) in order to induce a higher saving rate in the deficit country (to mitigate the widening deficit) and to attract the increased flow of capital from abroad required to fund the deficit. An expanding current account surplus will, in general, require the opposite in order to reduce "excess" saving. This suggests that the analyst should consider reallocation of portfolio assets from countries with secularly rising current account deficits to those with secularly rising current account surpluses (or narrowing deficits).

Capital Accounts and Currencies

Setting aside very high inflation situations in which purchasing power parity may be important even in the short term, currencies are primarily influenced by capital flows. When investors perceive that the portfolio of assets denominated in a particular currency offers a higher risk-adjusted expected return than is available in other currencies, the initial surge of capital tends to drive the exchange rate higher, often to a level from which it is more likely to depreciate rather than continue to appreciate. At that point, the underlying assets may remain attractive in their native currency but not in conjunction with the currency exposure. An analyst recommending reallocation of a portfolio toward assets denominated in a particular currency must, therefore, assess whether the attractiveness of the assets has already caused an "overshoot" in the currency or whether a case can be made that there is meaningful appreciation yet to come. In the former case, the analyst needs to consider whether the assets remain attractive after taking account of the cost of currency hedging.

There is one final question that needs to be addressed for all asset classes and currencies. The previous discussion alluded to it, but it is important enough to be asked directly: *What is already reflected in asset prices?* There is no avoiding the fact that valuations matter.

Quantifying the Views

Although the analyst may not be required to quantify the views underlying his or her recommendations, we can very briefly sketch a process that may be used for doing so using some of the tools discussed in earlier sections.

Step 1 Use appropriate techniques to estimate the VCV matrix for all asset classes.

Step 2 Use the Singer–Terhaar model and the estimated VCV matrix to determine equilibrium expected returns for all asset classes.

Step 3 Use the Grinold–Kroner model to estimate returns for equity markets based on assessments of economic growth, earnings growth, valuation multiples, dividends, and net share repurchases.

Step 4 Use the building block approach to estimate expected returns for bond classes based primarily on cyclical and policy considerations.

Step 5 Establish directional views on currencies relative to the portfolio's base currency based on the perceived attractiveness of assets and the likelihood of having overshot sustainable levels. Set modest rates of expected appreciation/depreciation.

Step 6 Incorporate a currency component into expected returns for equities and bonds.

Step 7 Use the Black–Litterman framework (described in a later reading) to combine equilibrium expected returns from Step 2 with the expected returns determined in Steps 3–6.

SUMMARY

The following are the main points covered in the reading.

- The choice among forecasting techniques is effectively a choice of the information on which forecasts will be conditioned and how that information will be incorporated into the forecasts.
- The formal forecasting tools most commonly used in forecasting capital market returns fall into three broad categories: statistical methods, discounted cash flow models, and risk premium models.
- Sample statistics, especially the sample mean, are subject to substantial estimation error.
- Shrinkage estimation combines two estimates (or sets of estimates) into a more precise estimate.

- Time-series estimators, which explicitly incorporate dynamics, may summarize historical data well without providing insight into the underlying drivers of forecasts.
- Discounted cash flow models are used to estimate the required return implied by an asset's current price.
- The risk premium approach expresses expected return as the sum of the risk-free rate of interest and one or more risk premiums.
- There are three methods for modeling risk premiums: equilibrium models, such as the CAPM; factor models; and building blocks.
- The DCF method is the only one that is precise enough to use in support of trades involving individual fixed-income securities.
- There are three main methods for developing expected returns for fixed-income asset classes: DCF, building blocks, and inclusion in an equilibrium model.
- As a forecast of bond return, YTM, the most commonly quoted metric, can be improved by incorporating the impact of yield changes on reinvestment of cash flows and valuation at the investment horizon.
- The building blocks for fixed-income expected returns are the short-term default-free rate, the term premium, the credit premium, and the liquidity premium.
- Term premiums are roughly proportional to duration, whereas credit premiums tend to be larger at the short end of the curve.
- Both term premiums and credit premiums are positively related to the slope of the yield curve.
- Credit spreads reflect both the credit premium (i.e., additional expected return) and expected losses due to default.
- A baseline estimate of the liquidity premium can be based on the yield spread between the highest-quality issuer in a market (usually the sovereign) and the next highest-quality large issuer (often a government agency).
- Emerging market debt exposes investors to heightened risk with respect to both ability to pay and willingness to pay, which can be associated with the economy and political/legal weaknesses, respectively.
- The Grinold–Kroner model decomposes the expected return on equities into three components: (1) expected cash flow return, composed of the dividend yield minus the rate of change in shares outstanding, (2) expected return due to nominal earnings growth, and (3) expected repricing return, reflecting the rate of change in the P/E.
- Forecasting the equity premium directly is just as difficult as projecting the absolute level of equity returns, so the building block approach provides little, if any, specific insight with which to improve equity return forecasts.
- The Singer–Terhaar version of the international capital asset pricing model combines a global CAPM equilibrium that assumes full market integration with expected returns for each asset class based on complete segmentation.
- Emerging market equities expose investors to the same underlying risks as emerging market debt does: more fragile economies, less stable political and policy frameworks, and weaker legal protections.

- Emerging market investors need to pay particular attention to the ways in which the value of their ownership claims might be expropriated. Among the areas of concern are standards of corporate governance, accounting and disclosure standards, property rights laws, and checks and balances on governmental actions.
- Historical return data for real estate is subject to substantial smoothing, which biases standard volatility estimates downward and distorts correlations with other asset classes. Meaningful analysis of real estate as an asset class requires explicit handling of this data issue.
- Real estate is subject to boom–bust cycles that both drive and are driven by the business cycle.
- The cap rate, defined as net operating income in the current period divided by the property value, is the standard valuation metric for commercial real estate.
- A model similar to the Grinold–Kroner model can be applied to estimate the expected return on real estate:

$E(R_{re})$ = Cap rate + NOI growth rate − %ΔCap rate.

- There is a clear pattern of higher cap rates for riskier property types, lower-quality properties, and less attractive locations.
- Real estate expected returns contain all the standard building block risk premiums:
  - Term premium: As a very long-lived asset with relatively stable cash flows, income-producing real estate has a high duration.
  - Credit premium: A fixed-term lease is like a corporate bond issued by the leaseholder and secured by the property.
  - Equity premium: Owners bear the risk of property value fluctuations, as well as risk associated with rent growth, lease renewal, and vacancies.
  - Liquidity premium: Real estate trades infrequently and is costly to transact.
- Currency exchange rates are especially difficult to forecast because they are tied to governments, financial systems, legal systems, and geographies. Forecasting exchange rates requires identification and assessment of the forces that are likely to exert the most influence.
- Provided they can be financed, trade flows do not usually exert a significant impact on exchange rates. International capital flows are typically larger and more volatile than trade-financing flows.
- PPP is a poor predictor of exchange rate movements over short to intermediate horizons but is a better guide to currency movements over progressively longer multi-year horizons.
- The extent to which the current account balance influences the exchange rate depends primarily on whether it is likely to be persistent and, if so, whether it can be sustained.
- Capital seeks the highest risk-adjusted expected return. In a world of perfect capital mobility, in the long run, the exchange rate will be driven to the point at which the expected percentage change equals the "excess" risk-adjusted expected return on the portfolio of assets denominated in the domestic currency over that of the portfolio of assets denominated in the foreign currency. However, in the short run, there can be an exchange rate overshoot in the opposite direction as hot money chases higher returns.

- Carry trades are profitable on average, which is contrary to the predictions of uncovered interest rate parity.
- Each country/currency has a unique portfolio of assets that makes up part of the global "market portfolio." Exchange rates provide an across-the-board mechanism for adjusting the relative sizes of these portfolios to match investors' desire to hold them.
- The portfolio balance perspective implies that exchange rates adjust in response to changes in the relative sizes and compositions of the aggregate portfolios denominated in each currency.
- The sample variance–covariance matrix is an unbiased estimate of the true VCV structure; that is, it will be correct on average.
- There are two main problems with using the sample VCV matrix as an estimate/forecast of the true VCV matrix: It cannot be used for large numbers of asset classes, and it is subject to substantial sampling error.
- Linear factor models impose structure on the VCV matrix that allows them to handle very large numbers of asset classes. The drawback is that the VCV matrix is biased and inconsistent unless the assumed structure is true.
- Shrinkage estimation of the VCV matrix is a weighted average of the sample VCV matrix and a target VCV matrix that reflects assumed "prior" knowledge of the true VCV structure.
- Failure to adjust for the impact of smoothing in observed return data for real estate and other private assets will almost certainly lead to distorted portfolio analysis and hence poor asset allocation decisions.
- Financial asset returns exhibit volatility clustering, evidenced by periods of high and low volatilities. ARCH models were developed to address these time-varying volatilities.
- One of the simplest and most used ARCH models represents today's variance as a linear combination of yesterday's variance and a new "shock" to volatility. With appropriate parameter values, the model exhibits the volatility clustering characteristic of financial asset returns.

REFERENCES

Abuaf, Niso and Philippe Jorion. 1990. "Purchasing Power Parity in the Long Run." *Journal of Finance* (March): 157–74. 10.1111/j.1540-6261.1990.tb05085.x

Ang, Andrew, Dimitris Papanikolaou, and Mark M. Westerfield. 2014. "Portfolio Choice with Illiquid Assets." *Management Science* 6 (11). 10.1287/mnsc.2014.1986

Burnside, Craig, Martin Eichenbaum, Isaac Kleshchelski, and Sergio Rebelo. 2011. "Do Peso Problems Explain the Returns to the Carry Trade?" *Review of Financial Studies* 24 (3): 853–91. 10.1093/rfs/hhq138

Clayton, Jim, Frank J. Fabozzi, S. Michael Gilberto, Jacques N. Gordon, Susan Hudson-Wilson, William Hughes, Youguo Liang, Greg MacKinnon, and Asieh Mansour. 2011. "The Changing Face of Real Estate Investment Management." Special Real Estate Issue*Journal of Portfolio Management*:12–23.

Cochrane, John H. and Monika Piazzesi. 2005. "Bond Risk Premia." *American Economic Review* (March): 138–60. 10.1257/0002828053828581

Dimson, Elroy, Paul Marsh, and Mike Staunton. 2021. *Credit Suisse Global Investment Returns Yearbook 2021*. Zurich: Credit Suisse Research Institute.

Dornbusch, R. Dec 1976. "Expectations and Exchange Rate Dynamics." *Journal of Political Economy* 84 (6): 1161–76. 10.1086/260506

Engle, Robert. 2002. "Dynamic Conditional Correlation: A Simple Class of Multivariate Generalized Autoregressive Conditional Heteroskedasticity Models." *Journal of Business & Economic Statistics* (July): 339–50. 10.1198/073500102288618487

Giesecke, Kay, Francis A. Longstaff, Stephen Schaefer, and Ilya Strebulaev. 2011. "Corporate Bond Default Risk: A 150-Year Perspective." *Journal of Financial Economics* 102 (2): 233–50. 10.1016/j.jfineco.2011.01.011

Grinold, Richard and Ken Kroner. 2002. "*The Equity Risk Premium: Analyzing the Long-Run Prospects for the Stock Market.*" *InvestmentInsights* 5 (3).

Ilmanen, Antti. 2012. *Expected Returns on Major Asset Classes*. Charlottesville, VA: Research Foundation of CFA Institute.

Jarrow, Robert A. and Donald R. van Deventer. 2015. "Credit Analysis Models." In *Fixed Income Analysis*, 3rd ed. CFA Institute Investment Series/Wiley.

Jordà, Òscar, Katharina Knoll, Dmitry Kuvshinov, Moritz Schularick, and Alan M. Taylor. 2017. "*The Rate of Return on Everything, 1870–2015.*" NBER Working Paper No. 24112 (December). 10.3386/w24112

Kim, Don H. and Jonathan H. Wright. 2005. "*An Arbitrage-Free Three-Factor Term Structure Model and the Recent Behavior of Long-Term Yields and Distant-Horizon Forward Rates.*" Federal Reserve Board Working Paper 2005-33 (August). 10.2139/ssrn.813267

Ling, David C. and Andy Naranjo. 2015. "Returns and Information Transmission Dynamics in Public and Private Real Estate Markets." *Real Estate Economics* 43 (1): 163–208. 10.1111/1540-6229.12069

Peyton, Martha S. 2009. "Capital Markets Impact on Commercial Real Estate Cap Rates: A Practitioner's View." Special Real Estate Issue*Journal of Portfolio Management*38–49. 10.3905/JPM.2009.35.5.038

Piros, Christopher D. 2015. "*Strategic Asset Allocation: Plus ça change, plus c'est la meme chose.*" *Investments & Wealth Monitor* (March/April): 5–8.

Piros, Christopher D. and Jerald E. Pinto. 2013. *Economics for Investment Decision Makers Workbook: Micro, Macro, and International Economics*. Hoboken, NJ: John Wiley & Sons, Inc.

Savills World Research. 2016. *Around the World in Dollars and Cents*. London: Savills.

Singer, Brian D. and Kevin Terhaar. 1997. *Economic Foundations of Capital Market Returns*. Charlottesville, VA: Research Foundation of the Institute of Chartered Financial Analysts.

Stefek, Daniel and Raghu Suryanarayanan. 2012. "Private and Public Real Estate: What Is the Link?" *Journal of Alternative Investments* (Winter): 66–75.

Yau, Jot K., Thomas Schneeweis, Edward A. Szado, Thomas R. Robinson, and Lisa R. Weiss. 2018. "*Alternative Investments Portfolio Management.*" CFA Program Level III Curriculum Reading 26.

PRACTICE PROBLEMS

The following information relates to questions 1-2

An investor is considering adding three new securities to her internationally focused fixed income portfolio. She considers the following non-callable securities:

- 1-year government bond
- 10-year government bond
- 10-year BBB rated corporate bond

She plans to invest equally in all three securities being analyzed or will invest in none of them at this time. She will only make the added investment provided that the expected spread/premium of the equally weighted investment is at least 1.5 percent (150bp) over the 1-year government bond. She has gathered the following information:

Risk free interest rate (1-year, incorporating 0.6% inflation expectation)	1.0%
Term premium (10-year vs. 1-year government bond)	1%
10-year BBB credit premium (over 10-year government bond)	75bp
Estimated liquidity premium on 10-year corporate bonds	55bp

Using only the information given, address the following problems using the risk premium approach:

1. Calculate the expected return that an equal-weighted investment in the three securities could provide.

2. Calculate the expected total risk premium of the three securities and determine the investor's probable course of action.

The following information relates to questions 3-10

Richard Martin is chief investment officer for the Trunch Foundation (the foundation), which has a large, globally diversified investment portfolio. Martin meets with the foundation's fixed-income and real estate portfolio managers to review expected return forecasts and potential investments, as well as to consider short-term modifications to asset weights within the total fund strategic asset allocation.

Martin asks the real estate portfolio manager to discuss the performance characteristics of real estate. The real estate portfolio manager makes the following statements:

Statement 1 Adding traded REIT securities to an equity portfolio should substantially improve the portfolio's diversification over the next year.

Statement 2 Traded REIT securities are more highly correlated with direct real estate and less highly correlated with equities over multi-year horizons.

Martin looks over the long-run valuation metrics the manager is using for commercial real estate, shown in Exhibit 1.

Exhibit 1: Commercial Real Estate Valuation Metrics

Cap Rate	GDP Growth Rate
4.70%	4.60%

The real estate team uses an in-house model for private real estate to estimate the true volatility of returns over time. The model assumes that the current observed return equals the weighted average of the current true return and the previous observed return. Because the true return is not observable, the model assumes a relationship between true returns and observable REIT index returns; therefore, it uses REIT index returns as proxies for both the unobservable current true return and the previous observed return.

Martin asks the fixed-income portfolio manager to review the foundation's bond portfolios. The existing aggregate bond portfolio is broadly diversified in domestic and international developed markets. The first segment of the portfolio to be reviewed is the domestic sovereign portfolio. The bond manager notes that there is a market consensus that the domestic yield curve will likely experience a single 20 bp increase in the near term as a result of monetary tightening and then remain relatively flat and stable for the next three years. Martin then reviews duration and yield measures for the short-term domestic sovereign bond portfolio in Exhibit 2.

Exhibit 2: Short-Term Domestic Sovereign Bond Portfolio

Macaulay Duration	Modified Duration	Yield to Maturity
3.00	2.94	2.00%

The discussion turns to the international developed fixed-income market. The foundation invested in bonds issued by Country XYZ, a foreign developed country. XYZ's sovereign yield curve is currently upward sloping, and the yield spread between 2-year and 10-year XYZ bonds is 100 bps.

The fixed-income portfolio manager tells Martin that he is interested in a domestic market corporate bond issued by Zeus Manufacturing Corporation (ZMC). ZMC has just been downgraded two steps by a major credit rating agency. In addition to expected monetary actions that will raise short-term rates, the yield spread between three-year sovereign bonds and the next highest-quality government agency bond widened by 10 bps.

Although the foundation's fixed-income portfolios have focused primarily on developed markets, the portfolio manager presents data in Exhibit 3 on two emerging markets for Martin to consider. Both economies increased exports of their mineral resources over the last decade.

Exhibit 3: Emerging Market Data

Factor	Emerging Republic A	Emerging Republic B
Fiscal deficit/GDP	6.50%	8.20%
Debt/GDP	90.10%	104.20%
Current account deficit	5.20% of GDP	7.10% of GDP
Foreign exchange reserves	90.30% of short-term debt	70.10% of short-term debt

The fixed-income portfolio manager also presents information on a new investment opportunity in an international developed market. The team is considering the bonds of Xdelp, a large energy exploration and production company. Both the domestic and international markets are experiencing synchronized growth in GDP midway between the trough and the peak of the business cycle. The foreign country's government has displayed a disciplined approach to maintaining stable monetary and fiscal policies and has experienced a rising current account surplus and an appreciating currency. It is expected that with the improvements in free cash flow and earnings, the credit rating of the Xdelp bonds will be upgraded. Martin refers to the foundation's asset allocation policy in Exhibit 4 before making any changes to either the fixed-income or real estate portfolios.

Exhibit 4: Trunch Foundation Strategic Asset Allocation—Select Data

Asset Class	Minimum Weight	Maximum Weight	Actual Weight
Fixed income—Domestic	40.00%	80.00%	43.22%
Fixed income—International	5.00%	10.00%	6.17%
Fixed income—Emerging markets	0.00%	2.00%	0.00%
Alternatives—Real estate	2.00%	6.00%	3.34%

3. Which of the real estate portfolio manager's statements is correct?
   A. Only Statement 1
   B. Only Statement 2
   C. Both Statement 1 and Statement 2

4. Based only on Exhibit 1, the long-run expected return for commercial real estate:
   A. is approximately double the cap rate.
   B. incorporates a cap rate greater than the discount rate.
   C. needs to include the cap rate's anticipated rate of change.

5. Based on the private real estate model developed to estimate return volatility, the true variance is *most likely*:
   A. lower than the variance of the observed data.
   B. approximately equal to the variance of the observed data.

C. greater than the variance of the observed data.

6. Based on Exhibit 2 and the anticipated effects of the monetary policy change, the expected annual return over a three-year investment horizon will *most likely* be:

   A. lower than 2.00%.

   B. approximately equal to 2.00%.

   C. greater than 2.00%.

7. Based on the building block approach to fixed-income returns, the dominant source of the yield spread for Country XYZ is *most likely* the:

   A. term premium.

   B. credit premium.

   C. liquidity premium.

8. Using the building block approach, the required rate of return for the ZMC bond will *most likely*:

   A. increase based on the change in the credit premium.

   B. decrease based on the change in the default-free rate.

   C. decrease based on the change in the liquidity premium.

9. Based only on Exhibit 3, the foundation would *most likely* consider buying bonds issued by:

   A. only Emerging Republic A.

   B. only Emerging Republic B.

   C. neither Emerging Republic A nor Emerging Republic B.

10. Based only on Exhibits 3 and 4 and the information provided by the portfolio managers, the action *most likely* to enhance returns is to:

   A. decrease existing investments in real estate by 2.00%.

   B. initiate a commitment to emerging market debt of 1.00%.

   C. increase the investments in international market bonds by 1.00%.

---

11. Jo Akumba's portfolio is invested in a range of developed markets fixed income securities. She asks her adviser about the possibility of diversifying her investments to include emerging and frontier markets government and corporate fixed income securities. Her adviser makes the following comment regarding risk:

    "All emerging and frontier market fixed income securities pose economic, political and legal risk. Economic risks arise from the fact that emerging market countries have poor fiscal discipline, rely on foreign borrowing, have less diverse tax base and significant dependence on specific industries. They are susceptible to capital flight. Their ability to pay is limited. In addition, weak property rights, weak enforcement of contract laws and political instability pose hazard for emerging markets debt investors."

    Discuss the statement made.

The following information relates to questions 12-14

An Australian investor currently holds a A$240 million equity portfolio. He is considering rebalancing the portfolio based on an assessment of the risk and return prospects facing the Australian economy. Information relating to the Australian investment markets and the economy has been collected in the following table:

10-Year Historical	Current	Capital Market Expectations
Average government bond yield: 2.8%	10-year government bond yield: 2.3%	
Average annual equity return: 4.6%	Year-over-year equity return: −9.4%	
Average annual inflation rate: 2.3%	Year-over-year inflation rate: 2.1%	Expected annual inflation: 2.3%
Equity market P/E (beginning of period): 15×	Current equity market P/E: 14.5×	Expected equity market P/E: 14.0×
Average annual dividend income return: 2.6%		Expected annual income return: 2.4%
Average annual real earnings growth: 6.0%		Expected annual real earnings growth: 5.0%

Using the information in the table, address the following problems:

12. Calculate the historical Australian equity risk premium using the "equity-vs-bonds" premium method.

13. Calculate the expected annual equity return using the Grinold–Kroner model (assume no change in the number of shares outstanding).

14. Using your answers to the calculations above, calculate the expected annual equity risk premium.

The following information relates to questions 15-16

An analyst is reviewing various asset alternatives and is presented with the following information relating to the broad equity market of Switzerland and various industries within the Swiss market that are of particular investment interest.

Expected risk premium for overall global investable market (GIM) portfolio	3.5%
Expected standard deviation for the GIM portfolio	8.5%
Expected standard deviation for Swiss Healthcare Industry equity investments	12.0%
Expected standard deviation for Swiss Watch Industry equity investments	6.0%
Expected standard deviation for Swiss Consumer Products Industry equity investments	7.5%

Assume that the Swiss market is perfectly integrated with the world markets. Swiss Healthcare has a correlation of 0.7 with the GIM portfolio.

Swiss Watch has a correlation of 0.8 with the GIM portfolio.

Swiss Consumer Products has a correlation of 0.8 with the GIM portfolio.

15. Basing your answers only upon the data presented in the table above and using the international capital asset pricing model—in particular, the Singer–Terhaar approach—estimate the expected risk premium for the following:

    i. Swiss Health Care Industry

    ii. Swiss Watch Industry

    iii. Swiss Consumer Products Industry

16. Judge which industry is most attractive from a valuation perspective.

17. Identify risks faced by investors in emerging market equities over and above those that are faced by fixed income investors in such markets.

The following information relates to questions 18-25

Judith Bader is a senior analyst for a company that specializes in managing international developed and emerging markets equities. Next week, Bader must present proposed changes to client portfolios to the Investment Committee, and she is preparing a presentation to support the views underlying her recommendations.

Bader begins by analyzing portfolio risk. She decides to forecast a variance–covariance matrix (VCV) for 20 asset classes, using 10 years of monthly returns and incorporating both the sample statistics and the factor-model methods. To mitigate the impact of estimation error, Bader is considering combining the results of the two methods in an alternative target VCV matrix, using shrinkage estimation.

Bader asks her research assistant to comment on the two approaches and the benefits of applying shrinkage estimation. The assistant makes the following statements:

Statement 1	Shrinkage estimation of VCV matrices will decrease the efficiency of the estimates versus the sample VCV matrix.
Statement 2	Your proposed approach for estimating the VCV matrix will not be reliable because a sample VCV matrix is biased and inconsistent.
Statement 3	A factor-based VCV matrix approach may result in some portfolios that erroneously appear to be riskless if any asset returns can be completely determined by the common factors or some of the factors are redundant.

Bader then uses the Singer–Terhaar model and the final shrinkage-estimated VCV matrix to determine the equilibrium expected equity returns for all international asset classes by country. Three of the markets under consideration are located in Country A (developed market), Country B (emerging market), and Country C (emerging market). Bader projects that in relation to the global market, the equity market in Country A will remain highly integrated, the equity market in Country B will become more segmented, and the equity market in

Country C will become more fully integrated.

Next, Bader applies the Grinold–Kroner model to estimate the expected equity returns for the various markets under consideration. For Country A, Bader assumes a very long-term corporate earnings growth rate of 4% per year (equal to the expected nominal GDP growth rate), a 2% rate of net share repurchases for Country A's equities, and an expansion rate for P/E multiples of 0.5% per year.

In reviewing Countries B and C, Bader's research assistant comments that emerging markets are especially risky owing to issues related to politics, competition, and accounting standards. As an example, Bader and her assistant discuss the risk implications of the following information related to Country B:

- Experiencing declining per capita income
- Expected to continue its persistent current account deficit below 2% of GDP
- Transitioning to International Financial Reporting Standards, with full convergence scheduled to be completed within two years

Bader shifts her focus to currency expectations relative to clients' base currency and summarizes her assumptions in Exhibit 1.

Exhibit 1: Baseline Assumptions for Currency Forecasts

	Country A	Country B	Country C
Historical current account	Persistent current account deficit of 5% of GDP	Persistent current account deficit of 2% of GDP	Persistent current account surplus of 2% of GDP
Expectation for secular trend in current account	Rising current account deficit	Narrowing current account deficit	Rising current account surplus
Long-term inflation expectation relative to global inflation	Expected to rise	Expected to keep pace	Expected to fall
Capital flows	Steady inflows	Hot money flowing out	Hot money flowing in

During a conversation about Exhibit 1, Bader and her research assistant discuss the composition of each country's currency portfolio and the potential for triggering a crisis. Bader notes that some flows and holdings are more or less supportive of the currency, stating that investments in private equity make up the majority of Country A's currency portfolio, investments in public equity make up the majority of Country B's currency portfolio, and investments in public debt make up the majority of Country C's currency portfolio.

18. Which of the following statements made by Bader's research assistant is correct?

    A. Statement 1

    B. Statement 2

    C. Statement 3

19. Based on expectations for changes in integration with the global market, all else being equal, the Singer–Terhaar model implies that Bader should shift capital from Country A to:

    A. only Country B.

B. only Country C.

C. both Countries B and C.

20. Using the Grinold–Kroner model, which of the following assumptions for forecasting Country A's expected equity returns is plausible for the very long run?

A. Rate of net share repurchases

B. Corporate earnings growth rate

C. Expansion rate for P/E multiples

21. Based only on the emerging markets discussion, developments in which of the following areas *most likely* signal increasing risk for Country B's equity market?

A. Politics

B. Competitiveness

C. Accounting standards

22. Based on Bader's expectations for current account secular trends as shown in Exhibit 1, Bader should reallocate capital, all else being equal, from:

A. Country A to Country C.

B. Country B to Country A.

C. Country C to Country A.

23. Based on Bader's inflation expectations as shown in Exhibit 1, purchasing power parity implies that which of the following countries' currencies should depreciate, all else being equal?

A. Country A

B. Country B

C. Country C

24. Based on Exhibit 1, which country's central bank is *most likely* to buy domestic bonds near term to sterilize the impact of money flows on domestic liquidity?

A. Country A

B. Country B

C. Country C

25. Based on the composition of each country's currency portfolio, which country is most vulnerable to a potential crisis?

A. Country A

B. Country B

C. Country C

---

26. Describe the main issues that arise when conducting historical analysis of real

estate returns.

27. An analyst at a real estate investment management firm seeks to establish expectations for rate of return for properties in the industrial sector over the next year. She has obtained the following information:

Current industrial sector capitalization rate ("cap" rate)	5.7%
Expected cap rate at the end of the period	5.5%
NOI growth rate (real)	1%
Inflation expectation	1.5%

Estimate the expected return from the industrial sector properties based on the data provided.

28. A client has asked his adviser to explain the key considerations in forecasting exchange rates. The adviser's firm uses two broad complementary approaches when setting expectations for exchange rate movements, namely focus on trade in goods and services and, secondly, focus on capital flows. Identify the main considerations that the adviser should explain to the client under the two approaches.

29. Looking independently at each of the economic observations below, indicate the country where an analyst would expect to see a strengthening currency for each observation.

	Country X	**Country Y**
Expected inflation over next year	2.0%	3.0%
Short-term (1-month) government rate	Decrease	Increase
Expected (forward-looking) GDP growth over next year	2.0%	3.3%
New national laws have been passed that enable foreign direct investment in real estate/financial companies	Yes	No
Current account surplus (deficit)	8%	−1%

30. Fap is a small country whose currency is the Fip. Three years ago, the exchange rate was considered to be reflecting purchasing power parity (PPP). Since then, the country's inflation has exceeded inflation in the other countries by about 5% per annum. The Fip exchange rate, however, remained broadly unchanged.

What would you have expected the Fip exchange rate to show if PPP prevailed? Are Fips over or undervalued, according to PPP?

SOLUTIONS

1.

	Risk free interest rate (nominal) (%)	+	Premiums (%)	=	Expected annual fixed-income return (%)
1-year government bond	1	+	0	=	1
10-year government bond	1	+	1	=	2
10-year corporate bond	1	+	1 + 0.75 + 0.55	=	3.3

Estimate of the expected return of an equal-weighted investment in the three securities: (1% + 2% + 3.3%)/3 = 2.1%.

2. The average spread (over 1-year government bond) at issue is [0 + 1 + (1 + 0.75 + 0.55)] = 3.3%/3 = 1.1%.

   As the 1.1% is less than 1.5%, the investor will not make the investment.

3. B is correct. Statement 2 is correct because traded REIT securities are more highly correlated with direct real estate and less highly correlated with equities over multi-year horizons. Thus, although REITs tend to act like stocks in the short run, they act like real estate in the longer run.

   A and C are incorrect because Statement 1 is not correct. Traded REIT securities have relatively high correlations with equity securities over short time horizons, such as one year. The higher correlations suggest that traded REIT securities will not act as a good diversifier for an equity portfolio over a one-year period.

4. A is correct. An estimate of the long-run expected or required return for commercial real estate equals the sum of the capitalization rate (cap rate) plus the growth rate (constant) of net operating income (NOI). An approximation of the steady-state NOI growth rate for commercial real estate is equal to the growth rate in GDP. Thus, from Equation 7 and the information provided in Exhibit 1, $E(R_{re})$ = Cap rate + NOI growth rate = 4.70% + 4.60% = 9.30%, which is approximately double the cap rate.

   B is incorrect because the discount rate (expected or required return) equals the sum of the cap rate and the NOI growth rate. Based on the information in Exhibit 1, the 4.70% cap rate is less than (not greater than) the 9.30% discount rate.

   C is incorrect because the discount rate over finite horizons (not long-run horizons) needs to include the anticipated rate of change in the cap rate. For long-run expected return calculations, the anticipated rate of change in the cap rate is not included.

5. C is correct. The in-house model assumes that the current observed return equals the weighted average of the current true return and the previous observed return. The model uses REIT index returns as proxies for the returns in the model. The smoothed nature of most published (observed) real estate returns is a major contributor to the appearance of low correlation with financial assets. This smoothing dampens the volatility of the observed data and distorts correlations with other assets. Thus, the raw observable data tend to understate the risk and

overstate the diversification benefits of these asset classes. It is generally accepted that the true variance of real estate returns is greater than the variance of the observed data.

6. B is correct. If the investment horizon equals the (Macaulay) duration of the portfolio, the capital loss created by the increase in yields and the reinvestment effects (gains) will roughly offset, leaving the realized return approximately equal to the original yield to maturity. This relationship is exact if (a) the yield curve is flat and (b) the change in rates occurs immediately in a single step. In practice, the relationship is only an approximation. In the case of the domestic sovereign yield curve, the 20 bp increase in rates will likely be offset by the higher reinvestment rate, creating an annual return approximately equal to 2.00%.

7. A is correct. From the building block approach to fixed-income returns, the required return for fixed-income asset classes has four components: the one-period default-free rate, the term premium, the credit premium, and the liquidity premium. Since sovereign bonds are considered the highest-quality bonds, they likely do not have a significant credit premium nor are they likely to have a significant premium for illiquidity. The slope of the yield curve is useful information on which to base forecasts of the term premium. Therefore, the dominant source of the yield spread is most likely the term premium for XYZ's sovereign bond.

8. A is correct. The credit premium is the additional expected return demanded for bearing the risk of default losses. A credit downgrade two steps lower will increase the credit premium and the required rate of return. The change in the default-free rate associated with the monetary tightening will increase (not decrease) the required rate of return. The widening of the spread between the sovereign bond and the next highest-quality government agency security indicates an increase in the liquidity premium, which will increase (not decrease) the required rate of return.

   B is incorrect because the required rate of return would increase (not decrease) based on the change in the default-free rate associated with the monetary tightening.

   C is incorrect because the rate of return would increase (not decrease) based on a change in the liquidity premium. The liquidity premium can be estimated from the yield spread between the highest-quality issuer (typically a sovereign bond) and the next highest-quality large issuer of similar bonds (often a government agency). A widening yield spread indicates an increase in the liquidity premium and required rate of return.

9. C is correct. Emerging market debt requires an analysis of economic and political/legal risks. Based on the macroeconomic factors, the risk of a bond investment in either Republic A or Republic B appears to be high. Thresholds such as the risk guidelines listed in the table below can be used to assess the attractiveness of the two emerging market (EM) opportunities in Republic A and Republic B. Most notably, both republics raise concern based solely on their fiscal deficit-to-GDP ratios greater than 4.00% (Republic A's is 6.50% and Republic B's is 8.20%).

Emerging Market Analysis

Country Political/Economic Risk	Emerging Market Risk Guidelines	Emerging Republic A	Emerging Republic B
Fiscal deficit/GDP	4.00%	Negative	Negative
Debt/GDP	70.00%	Negative	Negative
Current account deficit	4.00% of GDP	Negative	Negative
Foreign exchange reserves	100.00% of short-term debt	Negative	Negative

Analysis of the economic and political risks associated with the two EM opportunities is suggestive of the need for further scrutiny; therefore, the foundation should not invest in Emerging Republic A or Emerging Republic B based only on the information provided.

10. C is correct. An investment in the bonds of the international energy exploration and production company (Xdelp) looks attractive. The international market benefits from positive macroeconomic fundamentals: point in the business cycle, monetary and fiscal discipline, rising current account surplus, and an appreciating currency. The anticipated credit rating improvement will add to the potential for this to become a profitable investment and enhance returns. An increase in the investments within the international fixed-income segment by 1.00% (existing weight is 6.17%) would take advantage of this opportunity and remain in compliance with the foundation's 5.00%–10.00% strategic asset allocation limits.

    A is incorrect because a decrease in the existing weight of real estate by 2.00% would put the portfolio weight below the minimum threshold of 2.00% (i.e., 3.34% ⊠ 2.00% = 1.34%) of the foundation's strategic asset allocation.

    B is incorrect because the information presented in Exhibit 3 would lead the chief investment officer to avoid the two opportunities in emerging market debt (Emerging Republic A and Emerging Republic B) and not initiate a commitment to emerging market debt of 1.00% (i.e., increase the existing weight above 0.00%).

11. The statement correctly identifies economic, political and legal risk. The adviser has correctly identified some of the characteristics typically associated with emerging and frontier markets that may affect their governments' and corporate borrowers' ability and willingness to pay bondholders. However, the assertion that all emerging and frontier market fixed income securities pose such risk is incorrect, as many countries classified as "emerging" are considered to be healthy and prosperous economies.

12. The historical equity risk premium is 1.8%, calculated as follows:

    Historical equity returns − Historical 10-year government bond yield
    = Historical equity risk premium

    4.6% − 2.8% = 1.8%

13. The Grinold–Kroner model states that the expected return on equity is the sum of the expected income return (2.4%), the expected nominal earnings growth return (7.3% = 2.3% from inflation + 5.0% from real earnings growth) and the expected repricing return (–3.45%). The expected change in market valuation of –3.45% is calculated as the percentage change in the P/E level from the current 14.5× to the expected level of 14.0×: (14 – 14.5)/14.5 = –3.45%. Thus, the expected return is 2.4% + 7.3% – 3.45% = 6.25%.

14. Using the results from Part B, the expected equity return is 6.25 percent.

    Expected equity return − Current 10-year government bond yield
    = Expected equity risk premium

    6.25% − 2.3% = 3.95%.

15. Using the formula $RP_i^G = \rho_{i,GM}\sigma_i\left(\frac{RP_{GM}}{\sigma_{GM}}\right)$ we can solve for each expected industry risk premium. The term in brackets is the Sharpe ratio for the GIM, computed as 3.5/8.5 = 0.412.

    i. $RP_{\text{Healthcare}}$ = (12)(0.7)(0.412) = 3.46%

    ii. RP_{Watch} = (6)(0.8)(0.412) = 1.98%

    iii. $RP_{\text{Consumer Products}}$ = (7.5)(0.8)(0.412) = 2.47%

16. Based on the above analysis, the Swiss Healthcare Industry would have the highest expected return. However, that expected return reflects compensation for systematic risk. Based on the data provided we cannot conclude which industry is most attractive from a valuation standpoint.

17. In addition to the economic, political and legal risks faced by fixed income investors, equity investors in emerging markets face corporate governance risks. Their ownership claims may be expropriated by corporate insiders, dominant shareholders or the government. Interested parties may misuse the companies' assets. Weak disclosure and accounting standards may result in limited transparency that favors insiders. Weak checks and balances on governmental actions may bring about regulatory uncertainty, seizure of property or nationalization.

18. C is correct. Statement 3 is correct. As long as none of the factors used in a factor-based VCV model are redundant and none of the asset returns are completely determined by the common factors, there will not be any portfolios that erroneously appear to be riskless. Therefore, a factor-based VCV matrix approach may result in some portfolios that erroneously appear to be riskless if any asset returns can be completely determined by the common factors or some of the factors are redundant.

    A is incorrect because shrinkage estimation of VCV matrices will increase the efficiency of the estimates versus the sample VCV matrix, because its mean squared error (MSE) will in general be smaller than the MSE of the (unbiased) sample VCV matrix. Efficiency in this context means a smaller MSE.

    B is incorrect because, although the proposed approach is not reliable, the reason is not that the sample VCV matrix is biased and inconsistent; on the contrary, it is unbiased and consistent. Rather, the estimate of the VCV matrix is not reliable because the number of observations is not at least 10 times the number of assets (i.e., with 10 years of monthly return data, there are only 120 observations, but the rule of thumb suggests there should be at least 200 observations for 20 asset classes).

19. B is correct. Bader expects the equity market in Country C (an emerging market) to become more fully integrated with the global market while Country A (a developed market) remains highly integrated. All else being equal, the Singer–Terhaar model implies that when a market becomes more globally integrated (segmented), its required return should decline (rise). As prices adjust to a lower (higher) required return, the market should deliver an even higher (lower) return than was previously expected or required by the market. Therefore, the allocation to markets that are moving toward integration should be increased. If a market

is moving toward integration, its increased allocation will come at the expense of markets that are already highly integrated. This will typically entail a shift from developed markets to emerging markets.

20. B is correct. Country A's long-term corporate earnings growth rate of 4% per year is equal to the expected nominal GDP growth rate of 4%, which is an economically plausible long-run assumption. The only very long-run assumptions that are consistent with economically plausible relationships are $\%\Delta E$ = Nominal GDP growth, $\%\Delta S = 0$, and $\%\Delta P/E = 0$, where $\%\Delta E$ is the expected nominal earnings growth rate, $\%\Delta S$ is the expected percentage change in shares outstanding, and $\%\Delta P/E$ is the expected percentage change in the price-to-earnings ratio.

    A is incorrect because a 2% rate of net share repurchases would eventually eliminate all shares, which is not an economically plausible very long-run assumption. The only very long-run assumptions that are consistent with economically plausible relationships are $\%\Delta E$ = Nominal GDP growth, $\%\Delta S = 0$, and $\%\Delta P/E = 0$, where $\%\Delta E$ is the expected nominal earnings growth rate, $\%\Delta S$ is the expected percentage change in shares outstanding, and $\%\Delta P/E$ is the expected percentage change in the price-to-earnings ratio.

    C is incorrect because Country A's perpetually rising P/E would lead to an arbitrarily high price per currency unit of earnings per share. The only very long-run assumptions that are consistent with economically plausible relationships are $\%\Delta E$ = Nominal GDP growth, $\%\Delta S = 0$, $\%\Delta P/E = 0$, where $\%\Delta E$ is the expected nominal earnings growth rate, $\%\Delta S$ is the expected percentage change in shares outstanding, and $\%\Delta P/E$ is the expected percentage change in the price-to-earnings ratio.

21. A is correct. Per capita income for Country B has been falling, which is a potential source of political stress.

    B is incorrect because the persistent current account deficit has been below 2% of GDP. Persistent current account deficits greater than 4% of GDP probably indicate a lack of competitiveness.

    C is incorrect because Country B has been transitioning to International Financial Reporting Standards, with full convergence expected within two years, which is a positive development for better accounting standards.

22. A is correct. Bader should reallocate capital from Country A, which is expected to have a secularly rising current account deficit, to Country C, which is expected to have a secularly rising current account surplus. A rising current account deficit will tend to put upward pressure on real required returns and downward pressure on asset prices, whereas a rising current account surplus (or narrowing deficit) will put downward pressure on real required returns and upward pressure on asset prices. Analysts should consider reallocation of portfolio assets from countries with secularly rising current account deficits to those with secularly rising current account surpluses (or narrowing deficits).

23. A is correct. Purchasing power parity implies that the value of Country A's currency will decline. Inflation for Country A is expected to rise relative to global inflation. Purchasing power parity implies that the expected percentage change in Country A's exchange rate should be equal to the difference in expected inflation rates. If Country A's inflation is rising relative to global inflation, then the currency will be expected to depreciate.

    B is incorrect because purchasing power parity implies that the value of Country B's currency will remain stable. Inflation for Country B is expected to keep pace with global inflation. Purchasing power parity implies that the expected percentage change in Country B's exchange rate should be equal to the difference in expected inflation rates. If Country B's inflation is keeping pace with global inflation, then the exchange rate will be expected to stay the same, corresponding to a stable value of Country B's currency.

C is incorrect because purchasing power parity implies that the value of Country C's currency will rise. Inflation for Country C is expected to fall relative to global inflation. Purchasing power parity implies that the expected percentage change in Country C's exchange rate should be equal to the difference in expected inflation rates. If Country C's inflation is falling relative to global inflation, then the currency will be expected to appreciate.

24. B is correct. Hot money is flowing out of Country B; thus, Country B's central bank is the most likely to sell foreign currency (thereby draining domestic liquidity) to limit/avoid depreciation of the domestic currency and buy government securities (thereby providing liquidity) to sterilize the impact on bank reserves and interest rates.

    A is incorrect because Country A is not experiencing hot money flows and, therefore, would not need to sterilize the impact of money flows on domestic liquidity.

    C is incorrect because hot money is flowing into Country C; thus, Country C's central bank is most likely to sell government securities to limit the growth of bank reserves and/or maintain a target level of interest rates.

25. C is correct. Public debt makes up the majority of Country C's currency portfolio, which is the least supportive flow (or holding) to a currency. Public debt is less supportive because it has to be serviced and must be either repaid or refinanced, potentially triggering a crisis. Some types of flows and holdings are considered to be more or less supportive of the currency. Investments in private equity represent long-term capital committed to the market and are most supportive of the currency. Public equity would likely be considered the next most supportive of the currency. Debt investments are the least supportive of the currency.

26. Properties trade infrequently so there is no data on simultaneous periodic transaction prices for a selection of properties. Analysis therefore relies on appraisals. Secondly, each property is different, it is said to be heterogenous. The returns calculated from appraisals represent weighted averages of unobservable returns. Published return series is too smooth and the sample volatility understates the true volatility of returns. It also distorts estimates of correlations.

27. The expected change in the cap rate from 5.7% to 5.5% represents a (5.5% – 5.7%)/5.7% = 3.5% decrease.

    Using the expression $E(R_{re})$ = CapRate + NOI growth rate – %ΔCapRate = 5.7% + (1% + 1.5%) – (–3.5%) = 11.7%.

    Note: As the cap rate is expected to decrease, property values are expected to increase, hence the cap rate change contributes to the expected return.

28. Under the first approach analysts focus on flows of export and imports to establish what the net trade flows are and how large they are relative to the economy and other, potentially larger financing and investment flows. The approach also considers differences between domestic and foreign inflation rates that relate to the concept of purchasing power parity. Under PPP, the expected percentage change in the exchange rate should equal the difference between inflation rates. The approach also considers the sustainability of current account imbalances, reflecting the difference between national saving and investment.

    Under the second approach the analysis focuses on capital flows and the degree of capital mobility. It assumes that capital seeks the highest risk-adjusted return. The expected changes in the exchange rate will reflect the differences in the respective countries' assets' characteristics such as relative short-term interest rates, term, credit, equity and liquidity premiums. The approach also considers hot money flows and the fact that exchange rates provide an across the board mechanism for adjusting the relative sizes of each country's portfolio of assets.

29.

	Country X	Country Y
Expected inflation over next year	2.0%	3.0%
Short-term (1-month) government rate	Decrease	Increase
Expected (forward-looking) GDP growth over next year	2.0%	3.3%
New national laws have been passed that enable foreign direct investment in real estate/financial companies	Yes	No
Current account surplus (deficit)	8%	−1%

Note: The shaded cells represent the comparatively stronger measure, where an analyst could expect to see a strengthening currency based on the factor being independently reviewed.

30. According to PPP, to offset the effect of the higher inflation in Fap, the Fip should have depreciated against the other currencies by approximately the difference between Fap inflation and that in the other countries.

According to PPP, Fip is overvalued.

LEARNING MODULE

3

Overview of Asset Allocation

by William W. Jennings, PhD, CFA, and Eugene L. Podkaminer, CFA.

William W. Jennings, PhD, CFA, is at the US Air Force Academy (USA). Eugene L. Podkaminer, CFA, is at Franklin Templeton Investments (USA).

LEARNING OUTCOMES

Mastery	The candidate should be able to:
☐	describe elements of effective investment governance and investment governance considerations in asset allocation
☐	formulate an economic balance sheet for a client and interpret its implications for asset allocation
☐	compare the investment objectives of asset-only, liability-relative, and goals-based asset allocation approaches
☐	contrast concepts of risk relevant to asset-only, liability-relative, and goals-based asset allocation approaches
☐	explain how asset classes are used to represent exposures to systematic risk and discuss criteria for asset class specification
☐	explain the use of risk factors in asset allocation and their relation to traditional asset class–based approaches
☐	recommend and justify an asset allocation based on an investor's objectives and constraints
☐	describe the use of the global market portfolio as a baseline portfolio in asset allocation
☐	discuss strategic implementation choices in asset allocation, including passive/active choices and vehicles for implementing passive and active mandates
☐	discuss strategic considerations in rebalancing asset allocations

1 INTRODUCTION

☐ describe elements of effective investment governance and investment governance considerations in asset allocation

Asset owners are concerned with accumulating and maintaining the wealth needed to meet their needs and aspirations. In that endeavor, investment portfolios—including individuals' portfolios and institutional funds—play important roles. Asset allocation is a strategic—and often a first or early—decision in portfolio construction. Because it holds that position, it is widely accepted as important and meriting careful attention. Among the questions addressed in this reading are the following:

- What is a sound governance context for making asset allocation decisions?
- How broad a picture should an adviser have of an asset owner's assets and liabilities in recommending an asset allocation?
- How can an asset owner's objectives and sensitivities to risk be represented in asset allocation?
- What are the broad approaches available in developing an asset allocation recommendation, and when might one approach be more or less appropriate than another?
- What are the top-level decisions that need to be made in implementing a chosen asset allocation?
- How may asset allocations be rebalanced as asset prices change?

The strategic asset allocation decision determines return levels[1] in which allocations are invested, irrespective of the degree of active management. Because of its strategic importance, the investment committee, at the highest level of the governance hierarchy, typically retains approval of the strategic asset allocation decision. Often a proposal is developed only after a formal asset allocation study that incorporates obligations, objectives, and constraints; simulates possible investment outcomes over an agreed-on investment horizon; and evaluates the risk and return characteristics of the possible allocation strategies.

In providing an overview of asset allocation, this reading's focus is the alignment of asset allocation with the asset owner's investment objectives, constraints, and overall financial condition. This is the first reading in several sequences of readings that address, respectively, asset allocation and portfolio management of equities, fixed income, and alternative investments. Asset allocation is also linked to other facets of portfolio management, including risk management and behavioral finance. As coverage of asset allocation progresses in the sequence of readings, various connections to these topics, covered in detail in other areas of the curriculum, will be made.[2]

In the asset allocation sequence, the role of this reading is the "big picture." It also offers definitions that will provide a coordinated treatment of many later topics in portfolio management. The second reading provides the basic "how" of developing an asset allocation, and the third reading explores various common, real-world complexities in developing an asset allocation.

1 See Ibbotson and Kaplan (2000, p. 30) and Xiong, Ibbotson, and Chen (2010). The conclusion for the aggregate follows from the premise that active management is a zero-sum game overall (Sharpe 1991).

2 Among these readings, see Blanchett, Cordell, Finke, and Idzorek (2016) concerning human capital and longevity and other risks and Pompian (2011a and 2011b) and Pompian, McLean, and Byrne (2011) concerning behavioral finance.

This reading is organized as follows: Section 1 explains the importance of asset allocation in investment management. Section 2 addresses the investment governance context in which asset allocation decisions are made. Section 3 considers asset allocation from the comprehensive perspective offered by the asset owner's economic balance sheet. Sections 4 and 5 distinguish three broad approaches to asset allocation and explain how they differ in investment objective and risk. In Sections 6–9, these three approaches are discussed at a high level in relation to three cases. Section 10 provides a top-level orientation to how a chosen asset allocation may be implemented, providing a set of definitions that underlie subsequent readings. Section 11 discusses rebalancing considerations.

Asset Allocation: Importance in Investment Management

Exhibit 1 places asset allocation in a stylized model of the investment management process viewed as an integrated set of activities aimed at attaining investor objectives.

Exhibit 1: The Portfolio Management Process

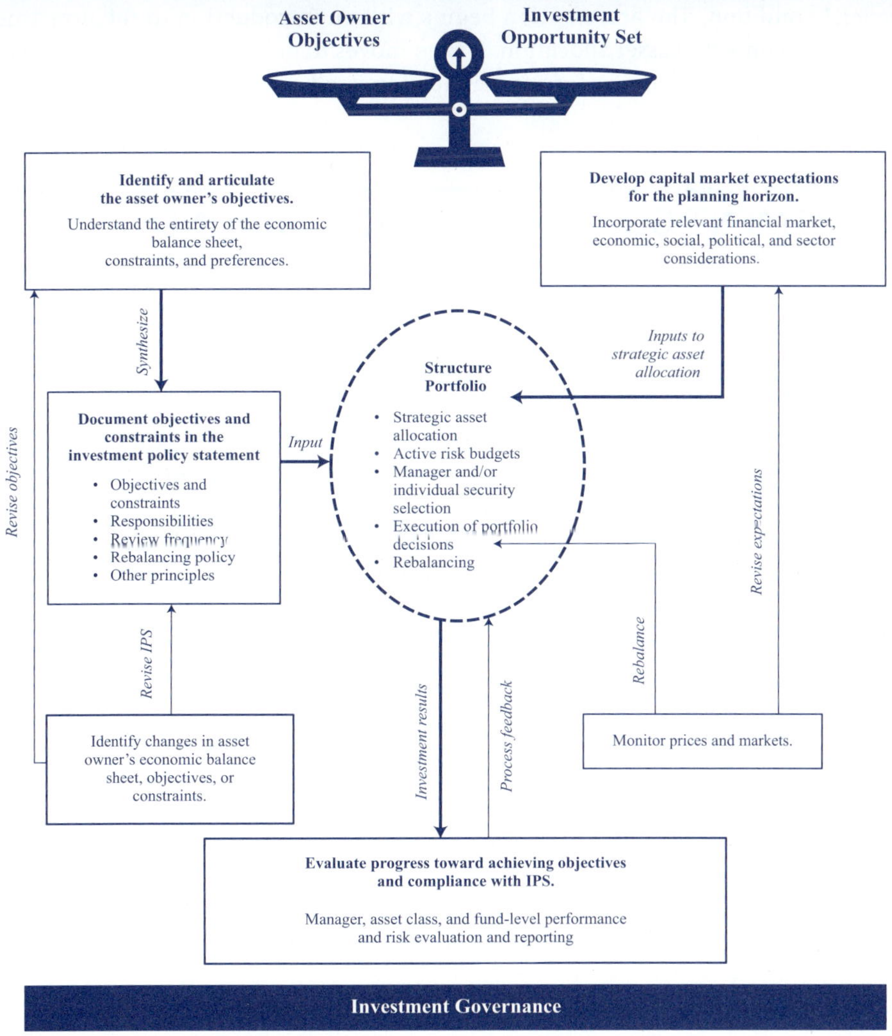

Exhibit 1 shows that an investment process that is in the asset owner's best interest rests on a foundation of good investment governance, which includes the assignment of decision-making responsibilities to qualified individuals and oversight of processes. The balance at the top of the chart suggests that the portfolio management process must reconcile (balance) investor objectives (on the left) with the possibilities offered by the investment opportunity set (on the right).

The investment process shows a sequence of activities that begins with understanding the asset owner's entire circumstance; objectives, including any constraints; and preferences. These factors, in conjunction with capital market inputs,[3] form the basis for asset allocation as a first step in portfolio construction and give a structure within which other decisions—such as the decision to invest passively or actively—take place. In the flow chart, thick lines show initial flows (or relations of logic) and thin lines show feedback flows.

Asset allocation is widely considered to be the most important decision in the investment process. The strategic asset allocation decision completely determines return levels[4] in which allocations are invested passively and also in the aggregate of all investors, irrespective of the degree of active management.

In providing an overview of asset allocation, this reading's focus is the alignment of asset allocation with the asset owner's investment objectives, constraints, and overall financial condition. The presentation begins with an introduction to the investment governance context of asset allocation. It then moves to present the economic balance sheet as the financial context for asset allocation itself.

2 INVESTMENT GOVERNANCE BACKGROUND

☐ describe elements of effective investment governance and investment governance considerations in asset allocation

Investment governance represents the organization of decision-making responsibilities and oversight activities. Effective investment governance ensures that assets are invested to achieve the asset owner's investment objectives within the asset owner's risk tolerance and constraints, and in compliance with all applicable laws and regulations. In addition, effective governance ensures that decisions are made by individuals or groups with the necessary skills and capacity.

Investment performance depends on asset allocation *and* its implementation. Sound investment governance practices seek to align asset allocation and implementation to achieve the asset owner's stated goals.

Investment governance structures are relevant to both institutional and individual investors. Because such structures are often formalized and articulated in detail for defined benefit pension plans, we will build our discussion using a pension plan governance framework. Elements of pension plan governance that are not directly related to the management of plan assets—plan design, funding policy, and communications to participants—are not discussed in this reading. Instead, we focus on those aspects of governance that directly affect the asset allocation decision.

3 The set of potential inputs to portfolio construction shown in Exhibit 1 is not exhaustive. For example, for investors delegating asset management, investment managers' performance records are relevant.
4 See Ibbotson and Kaplan (2000, p.30) and Xiong, Ibbotson, Idzorek, and Chen (2010). The conclusion for the aggregate follows from the premise that active management is a zero-sum game overall (Sharpe 1991).

Governance Structures

Governance and management are two separate but related functions. Both are directed toward achieving the same end. But governance focuses on clarifying the mission, creating a plan, and reviewing progress toward achieving long- and short-term objectives, whereas management efforts are geared to outcomes—the execution of the plan to achieve the agreed-on goals and objectives. A common governance structure in an institutional investor context will have three levels within the governance hierarchy:

- governing investment committee
- investment staff
- third-party resources

The investment committee may be a committee of the board of directors, or the board of directors may have delegated its oversight responsibilities to an internal investment committee made up of staff. Investment staff may be large, with full in-house asset management capabilities, or small—for example, two to five investment staff responsible for overseeing external investment managers and consultants. It may even be part time—a treasurer or chief financial officer with many other, competing responsibilities. The term "third-party resources" is used to describe a range of professional resources—investment managers, investment consultants, custodians, and actuaries, for example.

Although there are many governance models in use, most effective models share six common elements. Effective governance models perform the following tasks:

1. Articulate the long- and short-term objectives of the investment program.
2. Allocate decision rights and responsibilities among the functional units in the governance hierarchy effectively, taking account of their knowledge, capacity, time, and position in the governance hierarchy.
3. Specify processes for developing and approving the investment policy statement that will govern the day-to-day operations of the investment program.
4. Specify processes for developing and approving the program's strategic asset allocation.
5. Establish a reporting framework to monitor the program's progress toward the agreed-on goals and objectives.
6. Periodically undertake a governance audit.

In the sections that follow, we will discuss selected elements from this list.

Articulating Investment Objectives

Articulating long- and short-term objectives for an investor first requires an understanding of purpose—that is, what the investor is trying to achieve. Below are examples of simple investment objective statements that can be clearly tied to purposes:

- *Defined benefit pension fund.* The investment objective of the fund is to ensure that plan assets are sufficient to meet current and future pension liabilities.
- *Endowment fund.* The investment objective of the endowment is to earn a rate of return in excess of the return required to fund, after accounting for inflation, ongoing distributions consistent with the endowment's mission.
- *Individual investor.* The investment objective is to provide for retirement at the investor's desired retirement age, family needs, and bequests, subject to stated risk tolerance and investment constraints.

A return requirement is often considered the essence of an investment objective statement, but for that portion of the objective statement to be properly understood requires additional context, including the obligations the assets are expected to fund, the nature of cash flows into and out of the fund, and the asset owner's willingness and ability to withstand interim changes in portfolio value. The ultimate goal is to find the best risk/return trade-off consistent with the asset owner's resource constraints and risk tolerance.

As an example of how the overall context can affect decision making, the pension fund may be an active plan, with new participants added as they are hired, or it may be "frozen" (no additional benefits are being accrued by participants in the plan). The status of the plan, considered in conjunction with its funded ratio (the ratio of pension assets to pension liabilities), has a bearing on future contributions and benefit payments. The company offering the pension benefit may operate in a highly cyclical industry, where revenues ebb and flow over the course of the economic cycle. In this case, the plan sponsor may prefer a more conservative asset allocation to minimize the year-to-year fluctuations in its pension contribution.

The nature of inflows and outflows for an endowment fund can be quite different from those of a pension fund. An endowment fund may be used to support scholarships, capital improvements, or university operating expenses. The fund sponsor has some degree of control over the outflows from the fund but very little control over the timing and amounts of contributions to the fund because the contributions are typically coming from external donors.

These cash inflow and outflow characteristics must be considered when establishing the goals and objectives of the fund.

A third, inter-related aspect of defining the sponsor's goals and objectives is determining and communicating risk tolerance. There are multiple dimensions of risk to be considered: liquidity risk, volatility, risk of loss, and risk of abandoning a chosen course of action at the wrong time.

Effective investment governance requires consideration of the liquidity needs of the fund and the liquidity characteristics of the fund's investments. For example, too large an allocation to relatively illiquid assets, such as real estate or private equity, might impair the ability to make payouts in times of market stress.

A high risk/high expected return asset allocation is likely to lead to wider swings in interim valuations. Any minimum thresholds for funded status that, if breached, would trigger an adverse event, such as higher pension insurance premiums, must be considered in the asset allocation decision.

For individual investors, the risk of substantial losses may be unacceptable for a variety of financial and psychological reasons. When such losses occur after retirement, lost capital cannot be replaced with future earnings.

Asset owners have their own unique return requirements and risk sensitivities. Managing an investment program without a clear understanding of long- and short-term objectives is similar to navigating without a map: Arriving at the correct destination on time and intact is not compatible with leaving much to chance.

Allocation of Rights and Responsibilities

The rights and responsibilities necessary to execute the investment program are generally determined at the highest level of investment governance. The allocation of those rights and responsibilities among the governance units is likely to vary depending on the size of the investment program; the knowledge, skills, and abilities of the internal staff; and the amount of time staff can devote to the investment program if they have other, competing responsibilities. Above all, good governance requires that decisions be delegated to those best qualified to make an informed decision.

The resources available to an organization will affect the scope and complexity of the investment program and the allocation of rights and responsibilities. A small investment program may result in having a narrower opportunity set because of either asset size (too small to diversify across the range of asset classes and investment managers) or staffing constraints (insufficient asset size to justify a dedicated internal staff). Complex strategies may be beyond the reach of entities that have chosen not to develop investment expertise internally or whose oversight committee lacks individuals with sufficient investment understanding. Organizations willing to invest in attracting, developing, and retaining staff resources and in developing strong internal control processes, including risk management systems, are better able to adopt more complex investment programs. The largest investors, however, may find their size creates governance issues: Manager capacity constraints might lead to so many managers that it challenges the investor's oversight capacity.

Allocation of rights and responsibilities across the governance hierarchy is a key element in the success of an investment program. Effective governance requires that the individuals charged with any given decision have the required *knowledge* and expertise to thoroughly evaluate the alternative courses of action and the *capacity* to take on the ongoing responsibility of those decisions, and they must be able to execute those decisions in a timely fashion. (Individual investors engaging a private wealth manager are delegating these expertise, capacity, and execution responsibilities.)

Exhibit 2 presents a systematic way of allocating among governance units the primary duties and responsibilities of running an investment program.

Exhibit 2: Allocation of Rights and Responsibilities

Investment Activity	Investment Committee	Investment Staff	Third-Party Resource
Mission	Craft and approve	n/a	n/a
Investment policy statement	Approve	Draft	Consultants provide input
Asset allocation policy	Approve with input from staff and consultants	Draft with input from consultants	Consultants provide input
Investment manager and other service provider selection	Delegate to investment staff; approval authority retained for certain service providers	Research, evaluation, and selection of investment managers and service providers	Consultants provide input
Portfolio construction (individual asset selection)	Delegate to outside managers, or to staff if sufficient internal resources	Execution if assets are managed in-house	Execution by independent investment manager
Monitoring asset prices & portfolio rebalancing	Delegate to staff within confines of the investment policy statement	Assure that the sum of all sub-portfolios equals the desired overall portfolio positioning; approve and execute rebalancing	Consultants and custodian provide input
Risk management	Approve principles and conduct oversight	Create risk management infrastructure and design reporting	Investment manager manages portfolio within established risk guidelines; consultants may provide input and support
Investment manager monitoring	Oversight	Ongoing assessment of managers	Consultants and custodian provide input

Investment Activity	Investment Committee	Investment Staff	Third-Party Resource
Performance evaluation and reporting	Oversight	Evaluate manager's continued suitability for assigned role; analyze sources of portfolio return	Consultants and custodian provide input
Governance audit	Commission and assess	Responds and corrects	Investment Committee contracts with an independent third party for the audit

The available knowledge and expertise at each level of the hierarchy, the resource capacity of the decision makers, and the ability to act on a timely basis all influence the allocation of these rights and responsibilities.

Investment Policy Statement

The investment policy statement (IPS) is the foundation of an effective investment program. A well-crafted IPS can serve as a blueprint for ongoing fund management and assures stakeholders that program assets are managed with the appropriate care and diligence.

Often, the IPS itself will be a foundation document that is revised slowly over time, whereas information relating to more variable aspects of the program—the asset allocation policy and guidelines for individual investment managers—will be contained in a more easily modified appendix.

Asset Allocation and Rebalancing Policy

Because of its strategic importance, the investment committee, at the highest level of the governance hierarchy, typically retains approval of the strategic asset allocation decision. A proposal is often developed only after a formal asset allocation study that incorporates obligations, objectives, and constraints; simulates possible investment outcomes over an agreed-on investment horizon; and evaluates the risk and return characteristics of the possible allocation strategies.

Governance considerations inform not only the overall strategic asset allocation decision but also rebalancing decisions. The IPS should contain at least general orienting information relevant to rebalancing. In an institutional setting, rebalancing policy might be the responsibility of the investment committee, organizational staff, or the external consultant. Likewise, individual investors might specify that they have delegated rebalancing authority to their investment adviser. Specification of rebalancing responsibilities is good governance.

Reporting Framework

The reporting framework in a well-run investment program should be designed in a manner that enables the overseers to evaluate quickly and clearly how well the investment program is progressing toward the agreed-on goals and objectives. The reporting should be clear and concise, accurately answering the following three questions:

- Where are we now?
- Where are we relative to the goals and objectives?
- What value has been added or subtracted by management decisions?

Key elements of a reporting framework should address performance evaluation, compliance with investment guidelines, and progress toward achieving the stated goals and objectives.

- Benchmarking is necessary for performance measurement, attribution, and evaluation. Effective benchmarking allows the investment committee to evaluate staff and external managers. Two separate levels of benchmarks are appropriate: one that measures the success of the investment managers relative to the purpose for which they were hired and another to measure the gap between the policy portfolio and the portfolio as actually implemented.
- Management reporting, typically prepared by staff with input from consultants and custodians, provides responsible parties with the information necessary to understand which parts of the portfolio are performing ahead of or behind the plan and why, as well as whether assets are being managed in accordance with investment guidelines.
- Governance reporting, which addresses strengths and weaknesses in program execution, should be structured in such a way that regular committee meetings can efficiently address any concerns. Although a crisis might necessitate calling an extraordinary meeting, good governance structures minimize this need.

The Governance Audit

The purpose of the governance audit is to ensure that the established policies, procedures, and governance structures are effective. The audit should be performed by an independent third party. The governance auditor examines the fund's governing documents, assesses the capacity of the organization to execute effectively within the confines of those governing documents, and evaluates the existing portfolio for its "efficiency" given the governance constraints.

Effective investment governance ensures the durability or survivability of the investment program. An investment program must be able to survive unexpected market turmoil, and good investment governance makes certain that the consequences of such turmoil are considered before it is experienced. Good governance seeks to avoid **decision-reversal risk**—the risk of reversing a chosen course of action at exactly the wrong time, the point of maximum loss. Good investment governance also considers the effect of investment committee member and staff turnover on the durability of the investment program. Orientation sessions for new committee members and proper documentation of investment beliefs, policies, and decisions enhance the likelihood that the chosen course of action will be given sufficient time to succeed. New staff or investment committee members should be able to perceive easily the design and intent of the investment program and be able to continue to execute it. Similarly, good investment governance prevents key person risk—overreliance on any one staff member or long-term, illiquid investments dependent on a staff member.

Good governance works to assure accountability. O'Barr and Conley (1992, p.21), who studied investment management organizations using anthropological techniques, found that blame avoidance (not accepting personal responsibility when appropriate to do so) is a common feature of institutional investors. Good governance works to prevent such behavior.

EXAMPLE 1

Investment Governance: Hypothetical Case 1

In January 2016, the Caflandia Office Workers Union Pension (COWUP) made the following announcement:

"COWUP will fully exit all hedge funds and funds of funds. Assets currently amounting to 15% of its investment program are involved. Although hedge funds are a viable strategy for some, when judged against their complexity and cost, hedge fund investment is no longer warranted for COWUP."

One week later, a financial news service reported the following:

"The COWUP decision on hedge funds was precipitated by an allegation of wrongdoing by a senior executive with hedge fund selection responsibilities in COWUP's alternative investments strategy group."

1. Considering only the first statement, state what facts would be relevant in evaluating whether the decision to exit hedge funds was consistent with effective investment governance.

Solution:

The knowledge, capacity, and time available within COWUP to have an effective hedge fund investment program would need to be assessed against the stated concern for complexity and cost. The investment purpose served by hedge funds in COWUP's investment program before it exited them needs to be analyzed.

2. Considering both statements, identify deficiencies in COWUP's investment governance.

Solution:

The second statement raises these concerns about the decision described in the first statement:

- Hiring and oversight of COWUP executives may have been inadequate.
- The initial COWUP information release was incomplete and possibly misleading. Public communications appear not to have received adequate oversight.
- Divesting hedge funds may be a reaction to the personnel issue rather than being based on investment considerations.

EXAMPLE 2

Investment Governance: Hypothetical Case 2

1. The imaginary country of Caflandia has a sovereign wealth fund with assets of CAF$40 billion. A governance audit includes the following:

"The professional chief investment officer (CIO) reports to a nine-member appointed investment committee board of directors headed by an executive director. Investment staff members draft asset allocation policy in conjunction with consultants and make recommendation to the investment committee; the investment committee reviews and approves policy and any changes in policy, including the strategic asset allocation. The investment committee makes manager structure, conducts manager analysis, and makes manager selection decisions. The CIO has built a staff organization, which includes heads for each major asset class. In examining decisions over the last five years, we have noted several instances in which political or non-economic considerations appear to have influenced the investment program, including the selection of local private equity investments. Generally, the board spends much of its time debating individual manager strategies for inclusion in the portfolio and in evaluating investment managers' performance with comparatively little time devoted to asset allocation or risk management."

Based on this information and that in Exhibit 2, identify sound and questionable governance practices in the management of the Caflandia sovereign wealth fund.

Solution:

Sound practices: The allocation of responsibilities for asset allocation between investment staff and the investment committee is sound practice. Staff investment expertise should be reflected in the process of asset allocation policy and analysis. The investment committee assumes final responsibility for choices and decisions, which is appropriate given its position in receiving information from all parts of the organization and from all interested parties.

Questionable practices: The investment committee's level of involvement in individual manager selection and evaluation is probably too deep. Exhibit 2 indicates that these functions more effectively reside with staff. Individual manager selection is an implementation and execution decision designed to achieve strategic decisions made by the investment committee and is typically not a strategic decision itself. Manager evaluation has substantial data analysis and technical elements that can be efficiently provided by staff experts and consultants. The finding about political/non-economic influences indicates multiple problems. It confirms that the investment manager analysis and selection processes were misplaced. It also suggests that the investment committee has an inadequate set of governance principles or checks and balances as relates to the investment committee itself.

THE ECONOMIC BALANCE SHEET AND ASSET ALLOCATION 3

☐ formulate an economic balance sheet for a client and interpret its implications for asset allocation

An accounting balance sheet reflects a point-in-time snapshot of an organization's financial condition and shows the assets, liabilities, and owners' equity recognized by accountants. An **economic balance sheet** includes conventional assets and liabilities (called "financial assets" and "financial liabilities" in this reading) as well as additional assets and liabilities—known as **extended portfolio assets and liabilities**—that are relevant in making asset allocation decisions but do not appear on conventional balance sheets.

For individual investors, extended portfolio assets include human capital (the present value of future earnings), the present value of pension income, and the present value of expected inheritances. Likewise, the present value of future consumption is an extended portfolio liability.

For an institutional investor, extended portfolio assets might include underground mineral resources or the present value of future intellectual property royalties. Extended portfolio liabilities might include the present value of prospective payouts for foundations, whereas grants payable would appear as conventional liabilities.

Theory and, increasingly, practice suggest that asset allocation should consider the full range of assets and liabilities—both the financial portfolio and extended portfolio assets and liabilities—to arrive at an appropriate asset allocation choice. For example, an asset allocation process that considers the extended balance sheet, including the sensitivity of an individual investor's earnings to equity market risk (and that of the industry in which the individual is working), may result in a more appropriate allocation to equities than one that does not.

Life-cycle balanced funds (also known as target date funds) are examples of investments that seek to coordinate asset allocation with human capital. A 2040 life-cycle balanced fund that seeks to provide a retirement investment vehicle appropriate for many individuals retiring in 2040. Exhibit 3 illustrates a typical path for the composition of an individual's economic balance sheet from age 25 through age 65.

Exhibit 3: Human Capital (HC) and Financial Capital (FC) relative to Total Wealth

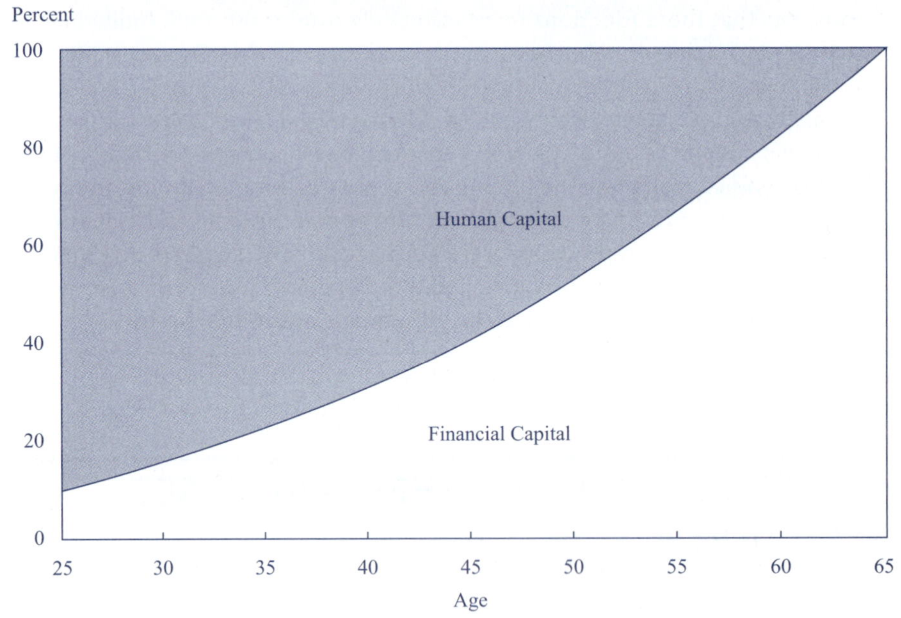

At age 25, with most of the individual's working life ahead of him, human capital dominates the economic balance sheet. As the individual progresses through life, the present value of human capital declines as human capital is transformed into earnings. Earnings saved and invested build financial capital balances. By a retirement age of 65, the conversion of human capital to earnings and financial capital is assumed to be complete.

Life-cycle balanced funds reflect these extended portfolio assets. Research indicates that, on average, human capital is roughly 30% equity-like and 70% bond-like, with significant variation among industries.[5] Making the simplifying assumption that investors have approximately constant risk tolerance through life, their asset allocation for total overall wealth (including human capital and financial capital) should be, in theory, constant over time. In this case, the asset allocation chosen for financial capital should reflect an increasing allocation to bonds as human capital declines to age 65, holding all else constant. Exhibit 4 shows the glide path for the equity/bond allocation chosen by one US mutual fund family. The increasing allocation to bonds is consistent with the view that human capital has preponderant bond-like characteristics.

Exhibit 4: Glide Path of Target Date Investment Funds in One Family

Assumed Age	Equity Allocation	Bond Allocation
25	85%	15%
35	82	18
45	77	23
55	63	37
65	49	51

Source: Based on data in Idzorek, Stempien, and Voris (2013).

Although estimating human capital is quite complex, including human capital and other extended portfolio assets and economic liabilities in asset allocation decisions is good practice.[6]

EXAMPLE 3

The Economic Balance Sheet of Auldberg University Endowment

- *Name*: Auldberg University Endowment (AUE)
- *Narrative*: AUE was established in 1852 in Caflandia and largely serves the tiny province of Auldberg. AUE supports about one-sixth of Auldberg University's CAF$60 million operating budget; real estate income and provincial subsidies provide the remainder and have been relatively stable. The endowment has historically had a portfolio limited to domestic equities, bonds, and real estate holdings; that policy is under current review. Auldberg University itself (not the endowment) has a CAF$350 million investment in domestic commercial real estate assets, including office buildings and industrial parks, much of it near the campus. AUE employs a well-qualified staff with substantial diverse experience in equities, fixed income, and real estate.

5 See Blanchett and Straehl (2015) and Blanchett and Straehl (2017).

6 Human capital is non-tradable, cannot be hedged, is subject to unspecified future taxes, and is a function of an individual's mortality. Human capital is technically defined as the net present value of an investor's future expected labor income weighted by the probability of surviving to each future age (see Ibbotson, Milevsky, Chen, and Zhu 2007). Thus, the present value of future earnings and pensions should be valued with mortality-weighted probabilities of receiving future cash flows, not the present value over life expectancy. There is meaningful extra value from the low-odds event of extreme longevity, which has an important portfolio implication in that individual investors can outlive their financial portfolios but not lifetime annuity payments.

- *Assets*: Endowment assets include CAF$100 million in domestic equities, CAF$60 million in domestic government debt, and CAF$40 million in Class B office real estate. The present value of expected future contributions (from real estate and provincial subsidies) is estimated to be CAF$400 million.
- *Liabilities*: These include CAF$10 million in short-term borrowings and CAF$35 million in mortgage debt related to real estate investments. Although it has no specific legal requirement, AUE has a policy to distribute to the university 5% of 36-month moving average net assets. In effect, the endowment supports $10 million of Auldberg University's annual operating budget. The present value of expected future support is CAF$450 million.

1. Prepare an economic balance sheet for AUE.

Solution:

The economic balance sheet for the endowment (given in the following table) does not include the real estate owned by Auldberg University. The economic net worth is found as a plug item (600 – 10 – 35 – 450 = 105).

AUE Economic Balance Sheet (in CAF$ millions) 31 December 20x6

Assets		Liabilities and Economic Net Worth	
Financial Assets		*Financial Liabilities*	
Domestic equities	100	Short-term borrowing	10
Domestic fixed income	60	Mortgage debt	35
Class B office real estate	40		
Extended Assets		*Extended Liabilities*	
Present value of expected future contributions to AUE	400	Present value of expected future support	450
		Economic Net Worth	
		Economic net worth (Economic assets – Economic liabilities)	105
Total	600		600

2. Describe elements in Auldberg University's investments that might affect AUE's asset allocation choices.

Solution:

AUE's Class B real estate investments' value and income are likely to be stressed during the same economic circumstances as the university's own real estate investments. In such periods, the university may look to the endowment for increased operating support and AUE may not be well positioned to meet that need. Thus, the AUE's real estate investment is actually less diversifying than it may appear and the allocation to it may need to be re-examined. Similar considerations apply to AUE's holdings in equities in relation to Auldberg University's.

APPROACHES TO ASSET ALLOCATION

4

- ☐ compare the investment objectives of asset-only, liability-relative, and goals-based asset allocation approaches
- ☐ contrast concepts of risk relevant to asset-only, liability-relative, and goals-based asset allocation approaches

We can identify three broad approaches to asset allocation: (1) **asset-only**, (2) **liability-relative**, and (3) **goals-based**. These are decision-making frameworks that take account of or emphasize different aspects of the investment problem.

Asset-only approaches to asset allocation focus solely on the asset side of the investor's balance sheet. Liabilities are not explicitly modeled. Mean–variance optimization (MVO) is the most familiar and deeply studied asset-only approach. MVO considers only the expected returns, risks, and correlations of the asset classes in the opportunity set. In contrast, liability-relative and goals-based approaches explicitly account for the liabilities side of the economic balance sheet, dedicating assets to meet, respectively, legal liabilities and quasi-liabilities (other needs that are not strictly liabilities but are treated as such) or goals.

Liability-relative approaches to asset allocation choose an asset allocation in relation to the objective of funding liabilities. The phrase "funding of liabilities" means to provide for the money to pay liabilities when they come due. An example is surplus optimization: mean–variance optimization applied to surplus (defined as the value of the investor's assets minus the present value of the investor's liabilities). In modeling, liabilities might be represented by a short position in a bond or series of bonds matched to the present value and duration of the liabilities. Another approach involves constructing a liability-hedging portfolio focused on funding liabilities and, for any remaining balance of assets, a risky-asset portfolio (so called because it is risky or riskier in relation to liabilities—often also called a "return-seeking portfolio" because it explicitly seeks return above and beyond the liability benchmark). **Liability-driven investing** (LDI) is an investment industry term that generally encompasses asset allocation that is focused on funding an investor's liabilities. Related fixed-income techniques are covered in the fixed-income sequence under liability-based mandates.

All approaches to asset allocation can be said to address goals. In investment practice and literature, however, the term "goals based" has come be widely associated with a particular type of approach to asset allocation and investing.

Goals-based approaches to asset allocation, as discussed here, are used primarily for individuals and families, involve specifying asset allocations for sub-portfolios, each of which is aligned to specified goals ranging from supporting lifestyle needs to aspirational. Each goal is associated with regular, irregular, or bulleted cash flows; a distinct time horizon; and a risk tolerance level expressed as a required probability of achieving the goal.[7] For example, a middle-aged individual might specify a goal of maintaining his current lifestyle and require a high level of confidence that this goal will be attained. That same individual might express a goal of leaving a bequest to his alma mater. This would be a very long-term goal and might have a low required probability. Each goal is assigned to its own sub-portfolio, and an asset allocation strategy specific to that sub-portfolio is derived. The sum of all sub-portfolio asset allocations results in an overall strategic asset allocation for the total portfolio. **Goals-based investing** (GBI) is an investment industry term that encompasses the asset allocation focused on addressing an investor's goals.

7 See Shefrin and Statman (2000) and Brunel (2015).

INSTITUTIONS AND GOALS-BASED ASSET ALLOCATION

Asset segmentation as practiced by some life insurers has some similarities to goals-based investing. Asset segmentation involves notionally or actually segmenting general account assets into sub-portfolios associated with specific lines of business or blocks of liabilities. On one hand, such an approach may be distinguished from goals-based asset allocation for individual investors in being motivated by competitive concerns (to facilitate offering competitive crediting rates on groups of contracts) rather than behavioral ones. On the other hand, Fraser and Jennings (2006) described a behaviorally motivated goals-based approach to asset allocation for foundations and endowments. Following their approach, components of an overall appropriate mean–variance optimal portfolio are allocated to time-based sub-portfolios such that uncomfortably novel or risky positions for the entity's governing body are made acceptable by being placed in longer-term sub-portfolios.

Although any asset allocation approach that considers the liabilities side of the economic balance sheet might be termed "liability relative," there are several important distinctions between liabilities for an institutional investor and goals for an individual investor. These distinctions have meaningful implications for asset allocation:[8]

- Liabilities of institutional investors are legal obligations or debts, whereas goals, such as meeting lifestyle or aspirational objectives, are not. Failing to meet them does not trigger similar consequences.
- Whereas institutional liabilities, such as life insurer obligations or pension benefit obligations, are uniform in nature (all of a single type), an individual's goals may be many and varied.
- Liabilities of institutional investors of a given type (e.g., the pension benefits owed to retirees) are often numerous and so, through averaging, may often be forecast with confidence. In contrast, individual goals are not subject to the law of large numbers and averaging. Contrast an estimate of expected death benefits payable for a group of life insurance policies against an individual's uncertainty about the resources needed in retirement: For a 65-year-old individual, the number of remaining years of life is very uncertain, but insurers can estimate the average for a group of 65-year-olds with some precision.

LIABILITY-RELATIVE AND GOALS-BASED APPROACHES TO INVESTING

Various perspectives exist concerning the relationship between liability-relative and goals-based approaches to investing. Professor Lionel Martellini summarizes one perspective in the following three statements:[9]

1. Goals-based investing is related to a new paradigm that advocates more granular and investor-centric investment solutions.
2. This new investment solutions paradigm translates into goals-based investing (GBI) approaches in individual money management, in which investors' problems can be summarized in terms of their goals,

8 See Rudd and Siegel (2013), which recognizes goals-based planning as a distinct approach. This discussion draws on Brunel (2015).

9 Communication of 3 June 2016, used with permission.

and it translates into liability-driven investing (LDI) approaches in institutional money management, where the investors' liability is treated as a proxy for their goal.

3. GBI and LDI are therefore related, but each of these approaches has its own specific characteristics. For example, GBI implies the capacity to help individual investors identify a hierarchical list of goals, with a distinction between different types of goals (affordable versus non affordable, essential versus aspirational, etc.) for which no exact counterpart exists in institutional money management.

Relevant Objectives

All three of the asset allocation approaches listed here seek to make optimal use of the amount of risk that the asset owner is comfortable bearing to achieve stated investment objectives, although they generally define risk differently. Exhibit 5 summarizes typical objectives.

Exhibit 5: Asset Allocation Approaches: Investment Objective

Asset Allocation Approach	Relation to Economic Balance Sheet	Typical Objective	Typical Uses and Asset Owner Types
Asset only	Does not explicitly model liabilities or goals	Maximize Sharpe ratio for acceptable level of volatility	Liabilities or goals not defined and/or simplicity is important ▪ Some foundations, endowments ▪ Sovereign wealth funds ▪ Individual investors
Liability relative	Models legal and quasi-liabilities	Fund liabilities and invest excess assets for growth	Penalty for not meeting liabilities high ▪ Banks ▪ Defined benefit pensions ▪ Insurers
Goals based	Models goals	Achieve goals with specified required probabilities of success	Individual investors

In a mean–variance asset-only approach, the objective is to maximize expected portfolio return per unit of portfolio volatility over some time horizon, consistent with the investor's tolerance for risk and consistent with any constraints stated in the IPS. A portfolio's Sharpe ratio is a characteristic metric for evaluating portfolios in an asset-only mean–variance approach.

The basic objective of a liability-relative asset allocation approach is to ensure payment of liabilities when they are due.

A goals-based approach is similar to a liability-relative approach in that it also seeks to ensure that there are sufficient assets to meet the desired payouts. In goals-based approaches, however, goals are generally associated with individual sub-portfolios, and an asset allocation is designed for each sub-portfolio that reflects the time horizon and required probability of success such that the sum of the sub-portfolios addresses the totality of goals satisfactorily.

Relevant Risk Concepts

Asset-only approaches focus on asset class risk and effective combinations of asset classes. The baseline asset-only approach, mean–variance optimization, uses volatility (standard deviation) of portfolio return as a primary measure of risk, which is a function of component asset class volatilities and the correlations of asset class returns. A mean–variance asset allocation can also incorporate other risk sensitivities, including risk relative to benchmarks and downside risk. Risk relative to benchmarks is usually measured by tracking risk (tracking error). Downside risk can be represented in various ways, including semi-variance, peak-to-trough maximum drawdown, and measures that focus on the extreme (tail) segment of the downside, such as value at risk.

Mean–variance results, although often the starting point for understanding portfolio risk, are regularly augmented by Monte Carlo simulation. By providing information about how an asset allocation performs when one or more variables are changed—for example, to values representing conditions of financial market stress—simulation helps complete the picture of risk, including downside and tail risk. Insights from simulation can then be incorporated as refinements to the asset allocation.

Liability-relative approaches focus on the risk of having insufficient assets to pay obligations when due, which is a kind of shortfall risk. Other risk concerns include the volatility of contributions needed to fund liabilities. Risk in a liability-relative context is generally underpinned by the differences between asset and liability characteristics (e.g., their relative size, their interest rate sensitivity, their sensitivity to inflation).

Goals-based approaches are concerned with the risk of failing to achieve goals.[10] The risk limits can be quantified as the maximum acceptable probability of not achieving a goal.[11] The plural in "liabilities" and "goals" underscores that these risks are generally related to multiple future points in time. Overall portfolio risk is thus the weighted sum of the risks associated with each goal.

Generally, a given statistical risk measure may be relevant in any of the three approaches. For example, standard deviation can be used to assess overall portfolio volatility in asset-only approaches, and it may be used to measure surplus volatility (the volatility of the difference between the values of assets and liabilities) or the volatility of the funded ratio (the ratio of the values of assets and liabilities) in liability-relative asset allocation.

5 MODELING ASSET CLASS RISK

- ☐ explain how asset classes are used to represent exposures to systematic risk and discuss criteria for asset class specification
- ☐ explain the use of risk factors in asset allocation and their relation to traditional asset class–based approaches

10 See Das, Markowitz, Scheid, and Statman (2010), who call goals "mental accounts."

11 See Brunel (2015).

Asset classes are one of the most widely used investment concepts but are often interpreted in distinct ways. Greer (1997) defines an asset class as "a set of assets that bear some fundamental economic similarities to each other, and that have characteristics that make them distinct from other assets that are not part of that class." He specifies three "super classes" of assets:

- *Capital assets.* An ongoing source of something of value (such as interest or dividends); capital assets can be valued by net present value.
- *Consumable/transformable assets.* Assets, such as commodities, that can be consumed or transformed, as part of the production process, into something else of economic value, but which do not yield an ongoing stream of value.
- *Store of value assets.* Neither income generating nor valuable as a consumable or an economic input; examples include currencies and art, whose economic value is realized through sale or exchange.

EXAMPLE 4

Asset Classes (1)

Classify the following investments based on Greer's (1997) framework, or explain how they *do not* fit in the framework:

1. Precious metals

   Precious metals are a store of value asset except in certain industrial applications (e.g., palladium and platinum in the manufacture of catalytic converters).

2. Petroleum

   Petroleum is a consumable/transformable asset; it can be consumed to generate power or provide fuel for transport.

3. Hedge funds

   Hedge funds do not fit into Greer's (1997) super class framework; a hedge fund strategy invests in underlying asset classes.

4. Timberland

   Timberland is a capital asset or consumable/transformable asset. It is a capital asset in the sense that timber can be harvested and replanted cyclically to generate a stream of cash flows; it is a consumable asset in that timber can be used to produce building materials/ packaging or paper.

5. Inflation-linked fixed-income securities

   Inflation-linked fixed-income securities is a capital asset because cash flows can be determined based on the characteristics of the security.

6. Volatility

   Volatility does not fit; it is a measurable investment characteristic. Because equity volatility is the underlying for various derivative contracts and an investable risk premium may be associated with it, it is mentioned by some as an asset.

Greer (1997) approaches the classification of asset classes in an abstract or generic sense. The next question is how to specify asset classes to support the purposes of strategic asset allocation.[12] For example, if a manager lumps together very different investments, such as distressed credit and Treasury securities, into an asset class called "fixed income," asset allocation becomes less effective in diversifying and controlling risk. Furthermore, the investor needs a logical framework for distinguishing an asset class from an investment strategy. The following are five criteria that will help in effectively *specifying asset classes for the purpose of asset allocation:*[13]

1. *Assets within an asset class should be relatively homogeneous.* Assets within an asset class should have similar attributes. In the example just given, defining equities to include both real estate and common stock would result in a non-homogeneous asset class.
2. *Asset classes should be mutually exclusive.* Overlapping asset classes will reduce the effectiveness of strategic asset allocation in controlling risk and could introduce problems in developing asset class return expectations. For example, if one asset class for a US investor is domestic common equities, then world equities ex-US is more appropriate as another asset class rather than global equities, which include US equities.
3. *Asset classes should be diversifying.* For risk control purposes, an included asset class should not have extremely high expected correlations with other asset classes or with a linear combination of other asset classes. Otherwise, the included asset class will be effectively redundant in a portfolio because it will duplicate risk exposures already present. In general, a pairwise correlation above 0.95 is undesirable (given a sufficient number of observations to have confidence in the correlation estimate).
4. *The asset classes as a group should make up a preponderance of world investable wealth.* From the perspective of portfolio theory, selecting an asset allocation from a group of asset classes satisfying this criterion should tend to increase expected return for a given level of risk. Furthermore, the inclusion of more markets expands the opportunities for applying active investment strategies, assuming the decision to invest actively has been made. However, such factors as regulatory restrictions on investments and government-imposed limitations on investment by foreigners may limit the asset classes an investor can invest in.
5. *Asset classes selected for investment should have the capacity to absorb a meaningful proportion of an investor's portfolio.* Liquidity and transaction costs are both significant considerations. If liquidity and expected transaction costs for an investment of a size meaningful for an investor are unfavorable, an asset class may not be practically suitable for investment.

Note that Criteria 1 through 3 strictly focus on assets themselves, while Criterion 5, and to some extent Criterion 4, involve potential investor-specific considerations.

ASSET CLASSES SHOULD BE DIVERSIFYING

Pairwise asset class correlations are often useful information and are readily obtained. However, in evaluating an investment's value as a diversifier at the portfolio level, it is important to consider an asset in relation to all other assets as a group rather than in a one-by-one (pairwise) fashion. It is possible to reach limited or incorrect conclusions by solely considering pairwise correlations. To

12 See Kritzman (1999).

13 As opposed to criteria for asset class definition in an absolute sense.

give an example, denote the returns to three assets by X, Y, and Z, respectively. Suppose that $Z = aX + bY$; a and b are constants, not both equal to zero. Asset Z is an exact weighted combination of X and Y and so has no value as a diversifier added to a portfolio consisting of assets X and Y. Yet, if the correlation between X and Y is −0.5, it can be shown that Z has a correlation of just 0.5 with X as well as with Y.

Examining return series' correlations during times of financial market stress can provide practically valuable insight into potential diversification benefits beyond typical correlations that average all market conditions.

In current professional practice, the listing of asset classes often includes the following:

- *Global public equity*—composed of developed, emerging, and sometimes frontier markets and large-, mid-, and small-cap asset classes; sometimes treated as several sub-asset classes (e.g., domestic and non-domestic).
- *Global private equity*—includes venture capital, growth capital, and leveraged buyouts (investment in special situations and distressed securities often occurs within private equity structures too).
- *Global fixed income*—composed of developed and emerging market debt and further divided into sovereign, investment-grade, and high-yield sub-asset classes, and sometimes inflation-linked bonds (unless included in real assets; see the following bullet). Cash and short-duration securities can be included here.
- *Real assets*—includes assets that provide sensitivity to inflation, such as private real estate equity, private infrastructure, and commodities. Sometimes, global inflation-linked bonds are included as a real asset rather than fixed income because of their sensitivity to inflation.

EMERGING MARKET EQUITIES AND FIXED INCOME

Investment practice distinguishes between developed and emerging market equities and fixed income within global equities. The distinction is based on practical differences in investment characteristics, which can be related to typical market differences including the following:

- diversification potential, which is related to the degree to which investment factors driving market returns in developed and emerging markets are not identical (a topic known as "market integration");
- perceived level of informational efficiency; and
- corporate governance, regulation, taxation, and currency convertibility.

As of mid-2016, emerging markets represent approximately 10% of world equity value based on MSCI indices.[14] In fixed income, investment opportunities have expanded as governments and corporations domiciled in emerging markets have increasingly issued debt in their own currency. Markets in local currency inflation-indexed emerging market sovereign debt have become more common.[15]

"Asset classes" are, by definition, groupings of assets. Investment vehicles, such as hedge funds, that apply strategies to asset classes and/or individual investments with the objective of earning a return to investment skill or providing attractive risk characteristics may be treated as a category called "strategies" or "diversifying strategies." When that is the case, this category is assigned a percentage allocation of assets, similar to a true asset class. Economically, asset classes contrast with "strategies" by offering, in general, an inherent, non-skill-based *ex ante* expected return premium.[16]

Effective portfolio optimization and construction may be hindered by excessive asset class granularity. Consider Exhibit 6.

Exhibit 6: Examples of Asset Classes and Sub-Asset Classes

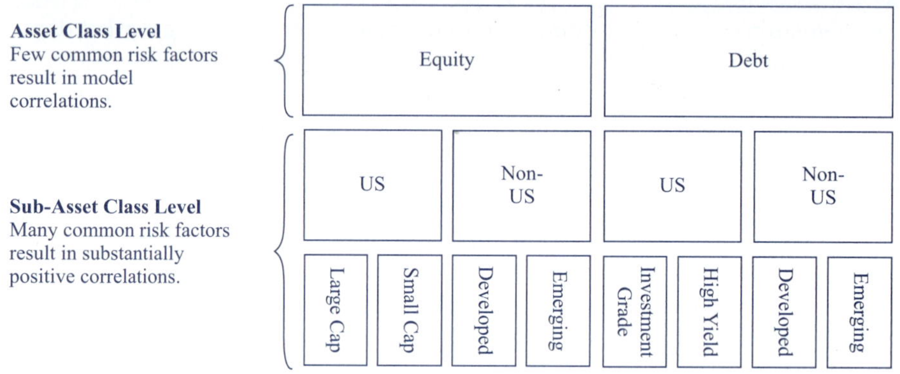

As more and more sub-asset classes are defined, they become less distinctive. In particular, the sources of risk for more broadly defined asset classes are generally better distinguished than those for narrowly defined subgroups. For example, the overlap in the sources of risk of US large-cap equity and US small-cap equity would be greater than the overlap between US and non-US equity. Using broadly defined asset classes with fewer risk source overlaps in optimization is consistent with achieving a diversified portfolio. Additionally, historical data for broadly defined asset classes may be more readily available or more reliable. The question of how much to allocate to equity versus fixed income versus other assets is far more important in strategic asset allocation than *precisely* how much to allocate to the various sub-classes of equity and fixed income. However, when the investor moves from the strategic asset allocation phase to policy implementation, sub-asset class choices become relevant.

14 MSCI uses three broad definitions to sort countries into developed, emerging, and frontier: 1) economic development, 2) size and liquidity requirements, and 3) market accessibility criteria (see the MSCI Market Classification Framework at www.msci.com/market-classification).

15 For a discussion of their potential benefits, see Burger, Warnock, and Warnock (2012), Perry (2011), and Swinkels (2012). Kozhemiakin (2011) discusses how emerging market bonds can facilitate broader representation than an equity-only portfolio because some countries (e.g., Argentina) have small equity markets but larger bond markets.

16 See Idzorek and Kowara (2013), p.20.

EXAMPLE 5

Asset Classes (2)

1. Discuss a specification of asset classes that distinguishes between "domestic intermediate-duration fixed income" and "domestic long-duration fixed income." Contrast potential relevance in asset-only and liability-relative contexts.

   Solution:

   These two groups share key risk factors, such as interest rate and credit risk. For achieving diversification in asset risk—for example, in an asset-only context—asset allocation using domestic fixed income, which includes intermediate and long duration, should be effective and simple. Subsequently, allocation within domestic fixed income could address other considerations, such as interest rate views. When investing in relation to liabilities, distinctions by duration could be of first-order importance and the specification could be relevant.

Any asset allocation, by whatever means arrived at, is expressed ultimately in terms of money allocations to assets. Traditionally—and still in common practice—asset allocation uses asset classes as the unit of analysis. Thus, mean–variance optimization based on four asset classes (e.g., global public equity, global private equity, global fixed income, and real assets) would be based on expected return, return volatility, and return correlation estimates for these asset classes. (The development of such capital market assumptions is the subject of another reading.) Factor-based approaches, discussed in more detail later, do not use asset classes as the basis for portfolio construction. Technically, the set of achievable investment outcomes cannot be enlarged simply by developing an asset allocation by a different means (for instance, using asset classes as the unit of analysis), all else being equal, such as constraints against short selling (non-negativity constraints).[17] Put another way, adopting a factor-based asset allocation approach does not, by default, lead to superior investment outcomes.

There are allocation methods that focus on assigning investments to the investor's desired exposures to specified risk factors. These methods are premised on the observation that asset classes often exhibit some overlaps in sources of risk, as illustrated in Exhibit 7.[18]

17 Stated more formally and demonstrated in Idzorek and Kowara (2013).

18 See Podkaminer (2013).

Exhibit 7: Common Factor Exposures across Asset Classes

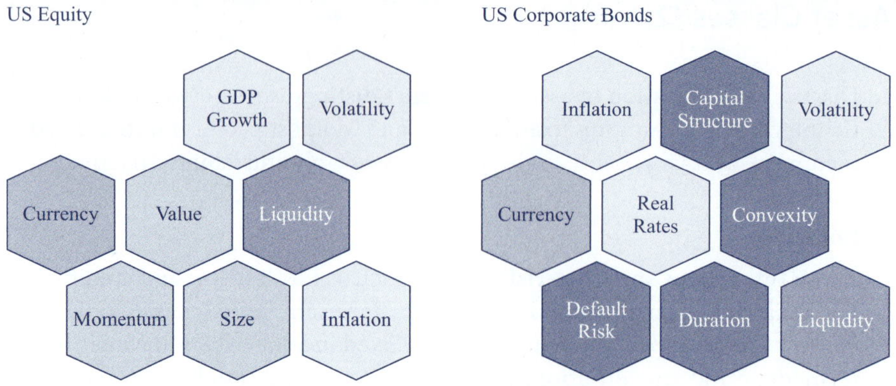

The overlaps seen in Exhibit 7 help explain the correlation of equity and credit assets. Modeling using asset classes as the unit of analysis tends to obscure the portfolio's sensitivity to overlapping risk factors, such as inflation risk in this example. As a result, controlling risk exposures may be problematic. Multifactor risk models, which have a history of use in individual asset selection, have been brought to bear on the issue of controlling systematic risk exposures in asset allocation.

In broad terms, when using factors as the units of analysis, we begin with specifying risk factors and the desired exposure to each factor. Asset classes can be described with respect to their sensitivities to each of the factors. Factors, however, are not directly investable. On that basis, asset class portfolios that isolate exposure to the risk factor are constructed; these factor portfolios involve both long and short positions. A choice of risk exposures in factor space can be mapped back to asset class space for implementation. Uses of multifactor risk models in asset allocation have been labeled "factor-based asset allocation" in contrast to "asset class-based asset allocation," which uses asset classes directly as the unit of analysis.

FACTOR REPRESENTATION

Although risk factors can be thought of as the basic building blocks of investments, most are not directly investable. In this context, risk factors are associated with expected return premiums. Long and short positions in assets (spread positions) may be needed to isolate the respective risks and associated expected return premiums. Other risk factors may be accessed through derivatives. The following are a few examples of how risk factor exposures can be achieved.

- *Inflation.* Going long nominal Treasuries and short inflation-linked bonds isolates the inflation component.
- *Real interest rates.* Inflation-linked bonds provide a proxy for real interest rates.
- *US volatility.* VIX (Chicago Board Options Exchange Volatility Index) futures provide a proxy for implied volatility.
- *Credit spread.* Going long high-quality credit and short Treasuries/government bonds isolates credit exposure.
- *Duration.* Going long 10+ year Treasuries and short 1–3 year Treasuries isolates the duration exposure being targeted.

FACTOR MODELS IN ASSET ALLOCATION

The interest in using factors for asset allocation stems from a number of considerations, including the following:

- The desire to shape the asset allocation based on goals and objectives that cannot be expressed by asset classes (such as matching liability characteristics in a liability-relative approach).
- An intense focus on portfolio risk in all of its various dimensions, helped along by availability of commercial factor-based risk measurement and management tools.
- The acknowledgment that many highly correlated so-called asset classes are better defined as parts of the same high-level asset class. For example, domestic and foreign equity may be better seen as subclasses of global public equity.
- The realization that equity risk can be the dominant risk exposure even in a seemingly well-diversified portfolio.

STRATEGIC ASSET ALLOCATION 6

☐ recommend and justify an asset allocation based on an investor's objectives and constraints

An asset allocation that arises in long-term investment planning is often called the "strategic asset allocation" or "policy portfolio": It is an asset allocation that is expected to be effective in achieving an asset owner's investment objectives, given his or her investment constraints and risk tolerance, as documented in the investment policy statement.

A theoretical underpinning for quantitative approaches to asset allocation is utility theory, which uses a utility function as a mathematical representation of preferences that incorporates the investor's risk aversion. According to utility theory, the optimal asset allocation is the one that is expected to provide the highest utility to the investor at the investor's investment time horizon. The optimization program, in broad terms, is

$$\underset{\text{by choice of asset class weights } w_i}{\text{Maximize}} \quad E[U(W_T)] = f\begin{pmatrix} W_0,\ w_i, \\ \text{asset class return distributions,} \\ \text{degree of risk aversion} \end{pmatrix}$$

$$\text{subject to} \sum_{i=1}^{n} w_i = 1 \text{ and any other constraints on } w_i$$

The first line is the objective function, and the second line consists of constraints on asset class weights; other constraints besides those on weights can also be incorporated (for example, specified levels of bond duration or portfolio yield may be targeted). With W_0 and W_T (the values of wealth today and at time horizon T, respectively) the investor's problem is to select the asset allocation that maximizes the expected utility of ending wealth, $E[U(W_T)]$, subject to the constraints that asset class weights sum to 1 and that weights observe any limits the investor places on them. Beginning wealth, asset class weights, and asset class returns imply a distribution of values for ending wealth, and the utility function assigns a value to each of them; by weighting these values by their probability of occurrence, an expected utility for the asset allocation is determined.

An expected utility framework underlies many, but not all, quantitative approaches to asset allocation. A widely used group in asset allocation consists of power utility functions,[19] which exhibit the analytically convenient characteristic that risk aversion does not depend on the level of wealth. Power utility can be approximated by mean–variance utility, which underlies mean–variance optimization.

OPTIMAL CHOICE IN THE SIMPLEST CASE

The simplest asset allocation decision problem involves one risky asset and one risk-free asset. Let λ, μ, r_f, and σ^2 represent, respectively, the investor's degree of risk aversion, the risk asset's expected return, the risk-free interest rate, and the variance of return. With mean–variance utility, the optimal allocation to the risky asset, w^*, can be shown to equal

$$w^* = \frac{1}{\lambda}\left(\frac{\mu - r_f}{\sigma^2}\right)$$

The allocation to the risky asset is inversely proportional to the investor's risk aversion and directly proportional to the risk asset's expected return per unit of risk (represented by return variance).[20]

Selection of a strategic asset allocation generally involves the following steps:[21]

1. Determine and quantify the investor's objectives. What is the pool of assets meant for (e.g., paying future benefit payments, contributing to a university's budget, securing ample assets for retirement)? What is the investor trying to achieve? What liabilities or needs or goals need to be recognized (explicitly or implicitly)? How should objectives be modeled?
2. Determine the investor's risk tolerance and how risk should be expressed and measured. What is the investor's overall tolerance for risk and specific risk sensitivities? How should these be quantified in the process of developing an appropriate asset allocation (risk measures, factor models)?
3. Determine the investment horizon(s). What are the appropriate planning horizons to use for asset allocation; that is, over what horizon(s) should the objectives and risk tolerance be evaluated?
4. Determine other constraints and the requirements they impose on asset allocation choices. What is the tax status of the investor? Should assets be managed with consideration given to ESG issues? Are there any legal and regulatory factors that need to be considered? Are any political sensitivities relevant? Are there any other constraints that the investor has imposed in the IPS and other communications?
5. Determine the approach to asset allocation that is most suitable for the investor.
6. Specify asset classes, and develop a set of capital market expectations for the specified asset classes.

19 Power utility has the form

$$U = \frac{w_T^{1-\lambda}}{1-\lambda},$$

where $\lambda > 0$ is the parameter of risk aversion (if $\lambda \to 0$, the investor is risk neutral).

20 See Ang (2014), Chapter 4, for further analysis.

21 Arjan Berkelaar, CFA, contributed to this formulation of steps.

7. Develop a range of potential asset allocation choices for consideration. These choices are often developed through optimization exercises. Specifics depend on the approach taken to asset allocation.
8. Test the robustness of the potential choices. This testing often involves conducting simulations to evaluate potential results in relation to investment objectives and risk tolerance over appropriate planning horizon(s) for the different asset allocations developed in Step 7. The sensitivity of the outcomes to changes in capital market expectations is also tested.
9. Iterate back to Step 7 until an appropriate and agreed-on asset allocation is constructed.

Subsequent readings on asset allocation in practice will address the "how." The following sections give an indication of thematic considerations. We use investors with specific characteristics to illustrate the several approaches distinguished: sovereign wealth fund for asset-only allocation; a frozen corporate DB plan for liability-relative allocation; and an ultra-high-net-worth family for goals-based allocation. In practice, any type of investor could approach asset allocation with varying degrees of focus on modeling and integrating liabilities-side balance sheet considerations. How these cases are analyzed in this reading should not be viewed as specifying normative limits of application for various asset allocation approaches. For example, a liability-relative perspective has wide potential relevance for institutional investors because it has the potential to incorporate all information on the economic balance sheet. Investment advisers to high-net-worth investors may choose to use any of the approaches.

STRATEGIC ASSET ALLOCATION: ASSET ONLY 7

- ☐ recommend and justify an asset allocation based on an investor's objectives and constraints
- ☐ describe the use of the global market portfolio as a baseline portfolio in asset allocation

Asset-only allocation is based on the principle of selecting portfolios that make efficient use of asset risk. The focus here is mean–variance optimization, the mainstay among such approaches. Given a set of asset classes and assumptions concerning their expected returns, volatilities, and correlations, this approach traces out an efficient frontier that consists of portfolios that are expected to offer the greatest return at each level of portfolio return volatility. The Sharpe ratio is a key descriptor of an asset allocation: If a portfolio is efficient, it has the highest Sharpe ratio among portfolios with the same volatility of return.

An example of an investor that might use an asset-only approach is the (hypothetical) Government Petroleum Fund of Caflandia (GPFC) introduced next.

INVESTOR CASE FACTS: GPFC, A SOVEREIGN WEALTH FUND

- *Name*: Government Petroleum Fund of Caflandia (GPFC)
- *Narrative*: The imaginary emerging country of Caflandia has established a sovereign wealth fund to capture revenue from its abundant petroleum reserves. The government's goal in setting up the fund is to promote a fair sharing of the benefits between current and future

generations (intergenerational equity) from the export of the country's petroleum resources. Caflandia's equity market represents 0.50% of global equity market capitalization. Economists estimate that distributions in the interest of intergenerational equity may need to begin in 20 years. Future distribution policy is undetermined.

- *Tax status*: Non-taxable.
- *Financial assets and financial liabilities*: Financial assets are CAF$40 billion at market value, making GPFC among the largest investors in Caflandia. GPFC has no borrowings.
- *Extended assets and liabilities*: Cash inflows from petroleum exports are assumed to grow at inflation + 1% for the next 15 years and may change depending on reserves and global commodity demand. The present value of expected future income from state-owned reserves is estimated to be CAF$60 billion. Future spending needs are positively correlated with consumer inflation and population growth. In Exhibit 8, the amount for the present value (PV) of future spending, which GPFC has not yet determined, is merely a placeholder to balance assets and liabilities; as a result, no equity is shown.

Exhibit 8: GPFC Economic Balance Sheet (in CAF$ billions) 31 December 20x6

Assets		Liabilities and Economic Net Worth	
Financial Assets		*Financial Liabilities*	
Investments (includes cash, equities, fixed income, and other investments)	40		
Extended Assets		*Extended Liabilities*	
PV of expected future income	60	PV of future spending	100
		Economic Net Worth	
		Economic net worth	0
Total	100		100

For GPFC, the amount and timing of funds needed for future distributions to Caflandia citizens are, as yet, unclear. GPFC can currently focus on asset risk and its efficient use to grow assets within the limits of the fund's risk tolerance. In addition to considering expected return in relation to volatility in selecting an asset allocation, GPFC might include such considerations as the following:

- diversification across global asset classes (possibly quantified as a constraint on the proportion allocated to any given asset classes);
- correlations with the petroleum sources of income to GPFC;
- the potential positive correlation of future spending with inflation and population growth in Caflandia;
- long investment horizon (as a long-term investor, GPFC may be well positioned to earn any return premium that may be associated with the relatively illiquid asset classes); and

- return outcomes in severe financial market downturns.

Suppose GPFC quantifies its risk tolerance in traditional mean–variance terms as willingness to bear portfolio volatility of up to 17% per year. This risk tolerance is partly based on GPFC's unwillingness to allow the fund to fall below 90% funded. GPFC's current strategic asset allocation, along with several alternatives that have been developed by its staff during an asset allocation review, are shown in Exhibit 9. The category "Diversifying strategies" consists of a diversified allocation to hedge funds.

Exhibit 9: GPFC Strategic Asset Allocation Decision[22]

	Asset Allocation			
		Proposed		
	Current	A	B	C
Investment				
Equities				
Domestic	50%	40%	45%	30%
Global ex-domestic		10%	20%	25%
Bonds				
Nominal	30%	30%	20%	10%
Inflation linked				10%
Real estate	20%	10%	15%	10%
Diversifying strategies		10%		15%
Portfolio statistics				
Expected arithmetic return	8.50%	8.25%	8.88%	8.20%
Volatility (standard deviation)	15.57%	14.24%	16.63%	14.06%
Sharpe ratio	0.353	0.369	0.353	0.370
One-year 5% VaR	−17.11%	−15.18%	−18.48%	−14.93%

Notes: The government bond rate is 3%. The acceptable level of volatility is ≤ 17% per year. The value at risk (VaR) is stated as a percent of the initial portfolio value over one year (e.g., −16% means a decline of 16%).

GPFC decides it is willing to tolerate a 5% chance of losing 22% or more of portfolio value in a given year. This risk is evaluated by examining the one-year 5% VaR of potential asset allocations.

Let us examine GPFC's decision. The current asset allocation and the alternatives developed by staff all satisfy the GPFC's tolerance for volatility and VaR limit. The staff's alternatives appear to represent incremental, rather than large-scale, changes from the current strategic asset allocation. We do not know whether capital market assumptions have changed since the current strategic asset allocation was approved.

22 The assumed expected returns and return volatilities are (given in that order in parentheses and expressed as decimals, rather than percentages): domestic equities (0.11, 0.25), non-domestic equities (0.09, 0.18), nominal bonds (0.05, 0.10), inflation-linked bonds (0.035, 0.06), real estate (0.075, 0.16), and diversifying strategies (0.07, 0.09). A correlation matrix with hypothetical values and a hypothetical relationship between the allocations and VaR also lies behind the exhibit. Because the purpose here is to illustrate concepts rather than mechanics, inputs are not discussed although they are very important in asset allocation.

Mix A, compared with the current asset allocation, diversifies the equity allocation to include non-domestic (global ex-domestic) equities and spreads the current allocation to real estate over real estate and diversifying strategies. Given GPFC's long investment horizon and absence of liquidity needs, an allocation to diversifying strategies at 10% should not present liquidity concerns. Because diversifying strategies are more liquid than private real estate, the overall liquidity profile of the fund improves. It is important to note that given the illiquid nature of real estate, it could take considerable time to reallocate from real estate to diversifying strategies. Mix A has a lower volatility (by 133 bps) than the current allocation and slightly lower tail risk (the 5% VaR for Mix A is −15%, whereas the 5% VaR for the current asset mix is −17%). Mix A's Sharpe ratio is slightly higher. On the basis of the facts given, Mix A appears to be an incremental improvement on the current asset allocation.

Compared with Mix A and the current asset allocation, Mix B increases the allocation to equities by 15 percentage points and pulls back from the allocation to bonds and, in relation to Mix A, diversifying strategies. Although Mix B has a higher expected return and its VaR is within GPFC's tolerance of 22%, Mix B's lower Sharpe ratio indicates that it makes inefficient use of its additional risk. Mix B does not appear to deserve additional consideration.

Compared with the current asset allocation and Mix A, Mix C's total allocation to equities, at 55%, is higher and the mix is more diversified considering the allocation of 25% non-domestic equities. Mix C's allocation to fixed income is 20% compared with 30% for Mix A and the current asset mix. The remaining fixed-income allocation has been diversified with an exposure to both nominal and inflation-linked bonds. The diversifying strategies allocation is funded by a combination of the reduced weights to fixed income and real estate. The following observations may be made:

- Mix C's increase in equity exposure (compared with the equity exposure of Mix A and the current mix) has merit because more equity-like choices in the asset allocation could be expected to give GPFC more exposure to such a factor as a GDP growth factor (see Exhibit 9); population growth is one driver of GDP.
- Within fixed income, Mix C's allocation to inflation-linked bonds could be expected to hedge the inflation risk inherent in future distributions.
- Mix C has the lowest volatility and the lowest VaR among the asset allocations, although the differences compared with Mix A are very small. Mix C's Sharpe ratio is comparable to (insignificantly higher than) Mix A's.

Based on the facts given, Mix A and Mix C appear to be improvements over the current mix. Mix C may have the edge over Mix A based on the discussion. As a further step in the evaluation process, GPFC may examine the robustness of the forecasted results by changing the capital market assumptions and simulating shocks to such variables as inflation. The discussion of Mix C shows that there are means for potential liability concerns (the probable sensitivity of spending to inflation and population growth) to enter decision making even from a mean–variance optimization perspective.

EXAMPLE 6

Asset-Only Asset Allocation

1. Describe how the Sharpe ratio, considered in isolation, would rank the asset allocation in Exhibit 9.

Solution:

The ranking by Sharpe ratios in isolation is C (3.70), A (3.69), and current and B (both 3.53). Using only the Sharpe ratio, Mix C appears superior to the other choices, but such an approach ignores several important considerations.

2. State a limitation of basing a decision only on the Sharpe ratio addressed in Question 1.

Solution:

The Sharpe ratio, while providing a means to rank choices on the basis of return per unit of volatility, does not capture other characteristics that are likely to be important to the asset owner, such as VaR and funded ratio. Furthermore, the Sharpe ratio by itself cannot confirm that the absolute level of portfolio risk is within the investor's specified range.

3. An assertion is heard in an investment committee discussion that because the Sharpe ratio of diversifying strategies (0.55) is higher than real estate's (0.50), any potential allocation to real estate would be better used in diversifying strategies. Describe why the argument is incomplete.

Solution:

It is true that the higher the Sharpe ratio of an investment, the greater its contribution to the Sharpe ratio of the overall portfolio, *holding all other things equal*. However, that condition is not usually true. Diversification potential in a portfolio (quantified by correlations) may differ. For example, including both diversifying strategies and real estate in an allocation may ultimately decrease portfolio-level risk through favorable correlation characteristics. Also, as in the solution to Question 2, other risk considerations besides volatility may be relevant.

Financial theory suggests that investors should consider the global market-value weighted portfolio as a baseline asset allocation. This portfolio, which sums all investable assets (global stocks, bonds, real estate, and so forth) held by investors, reflects the balancing of supply and demand across world markets. In financial theory, it is the portfolio that minimizes diversifiable risk, which in principle is uncompensated. Because of that characteristic, theory indicates that the global market portfolio should be the available portfolio that makes the most efficient use of the risk budget.[23] Other arguments for using it as a baseline include its position as a reference point for a highly diversified portfolio and the discipline it provides in relation to mitigating any investment biases, such as home-country bias (discussed below).

At a minimum, the global market portfolio serves as a starting point for discussion and ensures that the investor articulates a clear justification for moving away from global capitalization market weights. The global market portfolio is expressed in two phases. The first phase allocates assets in proportion to the global portfolio of stocks,

23 According to the two-fund separation theorem, all investors optimally hold a combination of a risk-free asset and an optimal portfolio of all risky assets. This optimal portfolio is the global market value portfolio.

bonds, and real assets. The second phase disaggregates each of these broad asset classes into regional, country, and security weights using capitalization weights. The second phase is typically used within a global equity portfolio where an asset owner will examine the global capitalization market weights and either accept them or alter them. Common tilts (biases) include overweighting the home-country market, value, size (small cap), and emerging markets. For many investors, allocations to foreign fixed income have been adopted more slowly than allocations to foreign equity. Most investors have at least some amount in non-home-country equity.

HOME-COUNTRY BIAS

A given for GPFC was that Caflandia's equity markets represent only 0.50% of the value of world equity markets. However, in all asset allocations in Exhibit 9, the share of domestic equity ranged from 50% for the current asset allocation to 30% for Mix C. The favouring of domestic over non-domestic investment relative to global market value weights is called **home-country bias** and is very common. Even relatively small economies feature pension plans, endowments, and other funds, which are disproportionately tilted toward the equity and fixed-income offerings in the domestic market. The same tendency is true for very large markets, such as the United States and the eurozone. By biasing toward the home market, asset owners may not be optimally aligning regional weights with the global market portfolio and are implicitly implementing a market view. Investment explanations for the bias, such as offsetting liabilities that are denominated in the home currency, may be relevant in some cases, however.

For reference, the MSCI All Country World Portfolio (ACWI), a proxy for the public equities portion of the global equity market portfolio, contains the following capitalization weights as of 31 December 2015:

- Developed Europe and the Middle East: 22.8%
- Developed Pacific: 11.7%
- North America: 55.9%
- Emerging markets: 9.6%

Investing in a global market portfolio faces several implementation hurdles. First, estimating the size of each asset class on a global basis is an imprecise exercise given the uneven availability of information on non-publicly traded assets. Second, the practicality of investing proportionately in residential real estate, much of which is held in individual homeowners' hands, has been questioned. Third, private commercial real estate and global private equity assets are not easily carved into pieces of a size that is accessible to most investors. Practically, proxies for the global market portfolio are often based only on traded assets, such as portfolios of exchange-traded funds (ETFs). Furthermore, some investors have implemented alternative weighting schemes, such as GDP weight or equal weight. However, it is a useful discipline to articulate a justification for any deviation from the capitalization-weighted global market portfolio.

8 STRATEGIC ASSET ALLOCATION: LIABILITY RELATIVE

☐ recommend and justify an asset allocation based on an investor's objectives and constraints

To illustrate the liability-relative approach, we take the defined benefit (DB) pension plan of (hypothetical) GPLE Corporation, with case facts given below.

A FROZEN DB PLAN, GPLE CORPORATION PENSION

- *Name*: GPLE Corporation Pension
- *Narrative*: GPLE is a machine tool manufacturer with a market value of $2 billion. GPLE is the sponsor of a $1.25 billion legacy DB plan, which is now frozen (i.e., no new plan participants and no new benefits accruing for existing plan participants). GPLE Pension has a funded ratio (the ratio of pension assets to liabilities) of 1.15. Thus, the plan is slightly overfunded. Responsibility for the plan's management rests with the firm's treasury department (which also has responsibility for GPLE Corporation treasury operations).
- *Tax status*: Non-taxable.
- *Financial assets and financial liabilities*: Assets amount to $1.25 billion at market values. Given a funded ratio of 1.15, that amount implies that liabilities are valued at about $1.087 billion. Projected distributions to pension beneficiaries have a present value of $1.087 billion at market value.

GPLE does not reflect any extended assets or liabilities; thus, economic net worth is identical to traditional accounting net worth.

Exhibit 10: GPLE Pension Economic Balance Sheet (in US$ billions) 31 December 20x6

Assets		Liabilities and Economic Net Worth	
Financial Assets		*Financial Liabilities*	
Pension assets	1.250	PV of pension liability	1.087
		Economic Net Worth	
		Economic net worth	0.163
Total	1.250		1.250

GPLE, the plan sponsor, receives two asset allocation recommendations. Recommendation A does not explicitly consider GPLE's pension's liabilities but is instead based on an asset-only perspective: the mean–variance efficient frontier given a set of capital market assumptions. A second recommendation, "Recommendation B," does explicitly consider liabilities, incorporating a liability-hedging portfolio based on an analysis of GPLE pension liabilities and a return-seeking portfolio.

In evaluating asset allocation choices, consider the pensioners' and the plan sponsor's interests. Pensioners want to receive the stream of promised benefits with as little risk, or chance of interruption, as possible. Risk increases as the funded ratio declines. When the funded ratio is 1.0, pension assets just cover pension liabilities with no safety buffer. When the funded ratio is less than 1.0, the plan sponsor generally needs to make up the deficit in pension assets by contributions to the plan. For example, with a 10-year investment time horizon and a choice between two asset allocations, the allocation with the lower expected present value of cumulative contributions to Year 10 would generally be preferred by the sponsor, all else being equal. In practice, all else is usually not equal. For example, the alternative with the lower *expected* present value of contributions may involve more risk to the level of contributions in adverse market conditions. For example, the 5% of *worst outcomes* for the present value of cumulative contributions may be more severe for the lower expected contribution alternative. Thus, possible asset allocations generally involve risk trade-offs.[24] Now consider the recommendations.

Recommendation A, based on asset-only analysis, involves a 65% allocation to global equities and a 35% allocation to global fixed income. Assume that this asset allocation is mean–variance efficient and has the highest Sharpe ratio among portfolios that meet the pension's assumed tolerance for asset return volatility. Capital market assumptions indicate that equities have a significantly higher expected return and volatility than fixed income.

Recommendation B, based on a liability-relative approach to asset allocation, involves an allocation of $1.125 billion to a fixed-income portfolio that is very closely matched in interest rate sensitivity to the present value of plan liabilities (and to any other liability factor risk exposures)—the liability hedging portfolio—and a $0.125 allocation to equities (the return-seeking portfolio). This is a proportional allocation of 10% to equities and 90% to fixed income. The equities allocation is believed to provide potential for increasing the size of the buffer between pension assets and liabilities with negligible risk to funded status. Recommendation B lies below the asset-only efficient frontier with a considerably lower expected return vis-à-vis Recommendation A.

What are the arguments for and against each of these recommendations? Recommendation A is expected, given capital market assumptions, to increase the size of the buffer between pension assets and liabilities. But the sponsor does not benefit from increases in the buffer if the current buffer is adequate.[25] However, with a 0.65 × $1.25 billion = $0.8125 allocation to equities and a current buffer of assets of $1.25 billion – $1.087 billion = $0.163 billion, a decline of that amount or more in equity values (a 20% decline) would put the plan into underfunded status (assuming no commensurate changes in the liability). Thus, Recommendation A creates contribution risk for the plan sponsor without a potential upside clearly benefiting either the sponsor or beneficiaries.

For Recommendation B, because the risk characteristics of the $1.125 billion fixed-income portfolio are closely matched with those of the $1.087 billion of pension liabilities with a buffer, the plan sponsor should not face any meaningful risk of needing to make further contributions to the pension. Pensioners expect the plan to be fully funded on an ongoing basis without any reliance on the sponsor's ability to make additional contributions. This is an excellent outcome for both. The pension liabilities are covered (defeased).

The example is highly stylized—the case facts were developed to make points cleanly—but does point to the potential value of managing risk in asset allocation explicitly in relation to liabilities. A typical use of fixed-income assets in liability-relative asset allocation should be noted: Liability-relative approaches to asset allocation tend to give fixed income a larger role than asset-only approaches in such cases as the one examined here because interest rates are a major financial market driver of both liability and bond values. Thus, bonds can be important in hedging liabilities, but equities can be relevant for liability hedging too. With richer case facts, as when liabilities accrue with inflation (not the case in the frozen DB example), equities may

24 Collie and Gannon (2009) explore the contribution risk trade-off considered here in more detail.

25 Real-world complexities, such as DB plan termination to capture a positive surplus or pension risk transfer (annuitization), are beyond the scope of this reading; generally, there are restrictions and penalties involved in such actions, and the point made here is valid.

have a long-term role in matching the characteristics of liabilities. In underfunded plans, the potential upside of equities would often have greater value for the plan sponsor than in the fully funded case examined.

LIABILITY GLIDE PATHS

If GPLE were underfunded, it might consider establishing a liability glide path. A **liability glide path** is a technique in which the plan sponsor specifies in advance the desired proportion of liability-hedging assets and return-seeking assets and the duration of the liability hedge as funded status changes and contributions are made. The technique is particularly relevant to underfunded pensions. The idea reflects the fact that the optimal asset allocation in general is sensitive to changes in the funded status of the plan. The objective is to increase the funded status by reducing surplus risk over time. Although a higher contribution rate may be necessary to align assets with liabilities, the volatility of contributions should decrease, providing more certainty for cash flow planning purposes and decreasing risk to plan participants. Eventually, GPLE would hope to achieve and maintain a sufficiently high funded ratio so that there would be minimal risk of requiring additional contributions or transferring pension risk to an annuity provider.

The importance of such characteristics as interest rate sensitivity (duration), inflation, and credit risk in constructing a liability-hedging asset portfolio suggests the relevance of risk-factor modeling in liability-relative approaches. A risk factor approach can be extended to the return-seeking portfolio in order to minimize unintentional overlap among common factors across both portfolios—for example, credit. Exploring these topics is outside the scope of the current reading.

The next section addresses an approach to asset allocation related to liability relative in its focus on funding needs.

STRATEGIC ASSET ALLOCATION: GOALS BASED 9

☐ recommend and justify an asset allocation based on an investor's objectives and constraints

We use the hypothetical Lee family to present some thematic elements of a goals-based approach.

INVESTOR CASE FACTS: THE LEE FAMILY

- *Name*: Ivy and Charles Lee
- *Narrative*: Ivy is a 54-year-old life sciences entrepreneur. Charles is 55 years old and employed as an orthopedic surgeon. They have two unmarried children aged 25 (Deborah) and 18 (David). Deborah has a daughter with physical limitations.
- *Financial assets and financial liabilities*: Portfolio of SGD 25 million with SGD 1 million in margin debt as well as residential real estate of SGD 3 million with $1 million in mortgage debt.
- *Other assets and liabilities*:

- Pre-retirement earnings are expected to total SGD 16 million in present value terms (human capital).
- David will soon begin studying at a four-year private university; the present value of the expected parental contribution is SGD 250,000.
- The Lees desire to give a gift to a local art museum in five years. In present value terms, the gift is valued at SGD 750,000.
- The Lees want to establish a trust for their granddaughter with a present value of SGD 3 million to be funded at the death of Charles.
- The present value of future consumption expenditures is estimated at SGD 20 million.

Exhibit 11: Lee Family Economic Balance Sheet (in SGD millions) 31 December 2016

Assets		Liabilities and Economic Net Worth	
Financial Assets		*Financial Liabilities*	
Investment portfolio	25	Margin debt	1
Real estate	3	Mortgage	1
Extended Assets		*Extended Liabilities*	
Human capital	16	David's education	0.25
		Museum gift	0.75
		Special needs trust	3
		PV of future consumption	20
		Economic Net Worth	
		Economic net worth (economic assets less economic liabilities)	18
Total	44		44

The financial liabilities shown are legal liabilities. The extended liabilities include funding needs that the Lees want to meet. The balance sheet includes an estimate of the present value of future consumption, which is sometimes called the "consumption liability." The amount shown reflects expected values over their life expectancy given their ages. If they live longer, consumption needs will exceed the SGD 20 million in the case facts and erode the SGD 18 million in equity. If their life span is shorter, SGD 18 million plus whatever they do not consume of the SGD 20 million in PV of future consumption becomes part of their estate. Note that for the Lees, the value of assets exceeds the value of liabilities, resulting in a positive economic net worth (a positive difference between economic assets and economic liabilities); this is analogous to a positive owners' equity on a company's financial balance sheet.

From Exhibit 11, we can identify four goals totaling SGD 24 million in present value terms: a lifestyle goal (assessed as a need for SGD 20 million in present value terms), an education goal (SGD 0.25 million), a charitable goal (SGD 0.75 million), and the special needs trust (SGD 3 million).

The present value of expected future earnings (human capital) at SGD 16 million is less than the lifestyle present value of SGD 20 million, which means that some part of the investment portfolio must fund the Lees' standard of living. It is important to note that although the Lee family has SGD 18 million of economic net worth, most of this comes from the SGD 16 million extended asset of human capital. Specific investment portfolio assets have not yet been dedicated to specific goals.

Goals-based asset allocation builds on several insights from behavioral finance. The approach's characteristic use of sub-portfolios is grounded in the behavioral finance insight that investors tend to ignore money's fungibility[26] and assign specific dollars to specific uses—a phenomenon known as mental accounting. Goals-based asset allocation, as described here, systemizes the fruitful use of mental accounts. This approach may help investors embrace more-optimal portfolios (as defined in an asset-only or asset–liability framework) by adding higher risk assets—that, without context, might frighten the investor—to longer-term, aspirational sub-portfolios while adopting a more conservative allocation for sub-portfolios that address lifestyle preservation.

In Exhibit 11, the Lees' lifestyle goal is split into three components: a component called "lifestyle—minimum" intended to provide protection for the Lees' lifestyle in a disaster scenario, a component called "lifestyle—baseline" to address needs outside of worst cases, and a component called "lifestyle—aspirational" that reflects a desire for a chance at a markedly higher lifestyle. These sum to the present value of future consumption shown in the preceding Exhibit 11. Exhibit 12 describes these qualitatively; a numerical characterization could be very relevant for some advisers, however. By eliciting information on the Lees' perception of the goals' importance, the investment adviser might calibrate the required probabilities of achieving the goals quantitatively. For example, the three lifestyle goals might have 99%, 90%, and 50% assigned probabilities of success, respectively.

Exhibit 12: Lee Family: Required Probability of Meeting Goals and Goal Time Horizons

Goal	Required Probability of Achieving	Time Horizon
Lifestyle—minimum	Extremely high	Short to distant
Lifestyle—baseline	Very high	Short to distant
Lifestyle—aspirational	Moderate	Distant
Education	Very high	Short
Trust	High	Long
Charitable	Moderate	Short

Because the Lees might delay or forego making a gift to the museum if it would affect the trust goal, the trust goal is more urgent for the Lees. Also note that although parts of the Lees' lifestyle goals run the full time horizon spectrum from short to distant, they also have significant current earnings and human capital (which transforms into earnings as time passes). This fact puts the investment portfolio's role in funding the lifestyle goal further into the future.

26 "Fungibility" is the property of an asset that a quantity of it may be replaced by another equal quantity in the satisfaction of an obligation. Thus, any 5,000 Japanese yen note can be used to pay a yen obligation of that amount, and the notes can be said to be fungible.

Goals-based approaches generally set the strategic asset allocation in a bottom-up fashion. The Lees' lifestyle goal might be addressed with three sub-portfolios, with the longest horizon sub-portfolio being less liquid and accepting more risk than the others. Although for the GPLE pension, no risk distinction was made among different parts of the pension liability vis-à-vis asset allocation, such distinctions are made in goals-based asset allocation.

What about the Lees' other goals? Separate sub-portfolios could be assigned to the special needs and charitable goals with asset allocations that reflect the associated time horizons and required probabilities of not attaining these goals. A later reading on asset allocation in practice addresses implementation processes in detail.

TYPES OF GOALS

As goals-based asset allocation has advanced, various classification systems for goals have been proposed. Two of those classification systems are as follows.

Brunel (2012):

- *Personal goals*—to meet current lifestyle requirements and unanticipated financial needs
- *Dynastic goals*—to meet descendants' needs
- *Philanthropic goals*

Chhabra (2005):

- *Personal risk bucket*—to provide protection from a dramatic decrease in lifestyle (i.e., safe-haven investments)
- *Market risk bucket*—to ensure the current lifestyle can be maintained (allocations for average risk-adjusted market returns)
- *Aspirational risk bucket*—to increase wealth substantially (greater than average risk is accepted)

EXAMPLE 7

Goals-Based Asset Allocation

The Lees are presented with the following optimized asset allocations:

Asset Allocation	Cash	Global Bonds	Global Equities	Diversifying Strategies
A	40%	50%	10%	0%
B	10%	30%	45%	15%

Assume that a portfolio of 70% global equities and 30% bonds reflects an appropriate balance of expected return and risk for the Lees with respect to a 10-year time horizon for most moderately important goals. Based on the information given:

Because of her industry connections in the life sciences, Ivy Lee is given the opportunity to be an early-stage venture capital investor in what she assesses is a very promising technology.

1. What goal(s) may be addressed by Allocation A?

   Solution:

   Allocation A stresses liquidity and stability. It may be appropriate to meet short-term lifestyle and education goals.

2. What goal(s) may be addressed by Allocation B?

   Solution:

   Allocation B has a greater growth emphasis, although it is somewhat conservative in relation to a 70/30 equity/bond baseline. It may be appropriate for funding the trust because of the goal's long time horizon and the Lees' desire for a high probability of achieving it.

3. What insights does goals-based asset allocation offer on this opportunity?

   Solution:

   Early-stage venture capital investments are both risky and illiquid; therefore, they belong in the longer-term and more risk-tolerant sub-portfolios. Ivy's decision about how much money she can commit should relate to how much excess capital remains after addressing goals that have a higher priority associated with them. Note that economic balance sheet thinking would stress that the life sciences opportunity is not particularly diversifying to her human capital.

DISCOUNT RATES AND LONGEVITY RISK

Although calculation of assets needed for sub-portfolios is outside the scope of this reading, certain themes can be indicated. Consider a retiree with a life expectancy of 20 years. The retiree has two goals:

- To maintain his current lifestyle upon retirement. This goal has a high required probability of achievement that is evaluated at 95%.
- To gift $1 million to a university in five years. This is viewed as a "desire" rather than a "need" and has a required probability evaluated at 75%.

Suppose that the investor's adviser specifies sub-portfolios as follows:

- for the first decade of lifestyle spending, a 3% expected return;
- for the second decade of lifestyle spending, a 4.6% expected return; and
- for the planned gift to the university, a 5.4% expected return.

Based on an estimate of annual consumption needs and the amount of the gift and given expected returns for the assigned sub-portfolios, the assets to be assigned to each sub-portfolio could be calculated by discounting amounts back to the present using their expected returns. However, this approach does not reflect the asset owner's required probability of achieving a goal. The higher the probability requirement for a future cash need, the greater the amount of assets needed in relation to it. Because of the inverse relation between present value and the discount rate, to reflect a 95% required probability, for example, the discount rates could be set at a lower level so that more assets are assigned to the sub-portfolio, increasing the probability of achieving the goal to the required level of 95% level.

Another consideration in determining the amount needed for future consumption is longevity risk. Life expectancies are median (50th percentile) outcomes. The retiree may outlive his life expectancy. To address longevity risk, the calculation of the present value of liabilities might use a longer life expectancy, such as a 35-year life expectancy instead of his actuarial 20-year expectation. Another approach is to transfer the risk to an insurer by purchasing an annuity that begins in 20 years and makes payments to the retiree for as long as he lives. Longevity risk and this kind of deferred annuity (sometimes called a "longevity annuity") are discussed in another curriculum reading on risk management.[27]

There are some drawbacks to the goals-based approach to asset allocation. One is that the sub-portfolios add complexity. Another is that goals may be ambiguous or may change over time. Goals-based approaches to asset allocation raise the question of how sub-portfolios coordinate to constitute an efficient whole. The subject will be taken up in a later reading, but the general finding is that the amount of sub-optimality is small.[28]

10 IMPLEMENTATION CHOICES

☐ discuss strategic implementation choices in asset allocation, including passive/active choices and vehicles for implementing passive and active mandates

Having established the strategic asset allocation policy, the asset owner must address additional strategic considerations before moving to implementation. One of these is the passive/active choice.

There are two dimensions of passive/active choices. One dimension relates to the management of the strategic asset allocation itself—for example, whether to deviate from it tactically or not. The second dimension relates to passive and active implementation choices in investing the allocation to a given asset class. Each of these are covered in the sections that follow.

In an advisory role, asset managers have an unequivocal responsibility to make implementation and asset selection choices that are initially, and on an ongoing basis, suitable for the client.[29]

Passive/Active Management of Asset Class Weights

Tactical asset allocation (TAA) involves deliberate short-term deviations from the strategic asset allocation. Whereas the strategic asset allocation incorporates an investor's long-term, equilibrium market expectations, tactical asset allocation involves short-term tilts away from the strategic asset mix that reflect short-term views—for example, to exploit perceived deviations from equilibrium.

Tactical asset allocation is active management at the asset class level because it involves intentional deviations from the strategic asset mix to exploit perceived opportunities in capital markets to improve the portfolio's risk–return trade-off. TAA mandates are often specified to keep deviations from the strategic asset allocation within

27 See Blanchett et al. (2016) for the management of longevity risk. Milevsky (2016) is a further reference.

28 This is addressed technically in Das et al. (2010). See also Brunel (2015).

29 See Standard III (C) in the Standards of Practice Handbook (CFA Institute 2014).

rebalancing ranges or within risk budgets. Tactical asset allocation decisions might be responsive to price momentum, perceived asset class valuation, or the particular stage of the business cycle. A strategy incorporating deviations from the strategic asset allocation that are motivated by longer-term valuation signals or economic views is sometimes distinguished as **dynamic asset allocation** (DAA).

Tactical asset allocation may be limited to tactical changes in domestic stock–bond or stock–bond–cash allocations or may be a more comprehensive multi-asset approach, as in a global tactical asset allocation (GTAA) model. Tactical asset allocation inherently involves market timing as it involves buying and selling in anticipation of short-term changes in market direction; however, TAA usually involves smaller allocation tilts than an invested-or-not-invested market timing strategy.

Tactical asset allocation is a source of risk when calibrated against the strategic asset mix. An informed approach to tactical asset allocation recognizes the trade-off of any potential outperformance against this tracking error. Key barriers to successful tactical asset allocation are monitoring and trading costs. For some investors, higher short-term capital gains taxes will prove a significant obstacle because taxes are an additional trading cost. A program of tactical asset allocation must be evaluated through a cost–benefit lens. The relevant cost comparisons include the expected costs of simply following a rebalancing policy (without deliberate tactical deviations).

Passive/Active Management of Allocations to Asset Classes

In addition to active and passive decisions about the asset class mix, there are active and passive decisions about how to implement the individual allocations within asset classes. An allocation can be managed passively or actively or incorporate both active and passive sub-allocations. For investors who delegate asset management to external firms, these decisions would come under the heading of manager structure,[30] which includes decisions about how capital and active risk are allocated to points on the passive/active spectrum and to individual external managers selected to manage the investor's assets.[31]

With a **passive management** approach, portfolio composition does not react to changes in the investor's capital market expectations or to information on or insights into individual investments. (The word *passive* means *not reacting.*) For example, a portfolio constructed to track the returns of an index of European equities might add or drop a holding in response to a change in the index composition but not in response to changes in the manager's expectations concerning the security's investment value; the market's expectations reflected in market values and index weights are taken as is. Indexing is a common passive approach to investing. (Another example would be buying and holding a fixed portfolio of bonds to maturity.)

In contrast, a portfolio manager for an active management strategy will respond to changing capital market expectations or to investment insights resulting in changes to portfolio composition. The objective of active management is to achieve, after expenses, positive excess risk-adjusted returns relative to a passive benchmark.

The range of implementation choices can be practically viewed as falling along a passive/active spectrum because some strategies use both passive and active elements. In financial theory, the pure model of a passive approach is indexing to a broad market-cap-weighted index of risky assets—in particular, the global market portfolio. This portfolio sums all investments in index components and is macro-consistent in the sense that all investors could hold it, and it is furthermore self-rebalancing to the extent it is based on market-value-weighted indices. A buy-and-hold investment as

30 Manager structure is defined by the number of managers, types of managers, as well as which managers are selected.

31 See, for example, Waring, Whitney, Pirone, and Castille (2000).

a proxy for the global market portfolio would represent a theoretical endpoint on the passive/active spectrum. However, consider an investor who indexes an equity allocation to a broad-based value equity style index. The investment could be said to reflect an active decision in tilting an allocation toward value but be passive in implementation because it involves indexing. An even more active approach would be investing the equity allocation with managers who have a value investing approach and attempt to enhance returns through security selection. Those managers would show positive tracking risk relative to the value index in general. Unconstrained active investment would be one that is "go anywhere" or not managed with consideration of any traditional asset class benchmark (i.e., "benchmark agnostic"). The degree of active management has traditionally been quantified by tracking risk and, from a different perspective, by active share.

Indexing is generally the lowest-cost approach to investing. Indexing involves some level of transaction costs because, as securities move in and out of the index, the portfolio holdings must adjust to remain in alignment with the index. Although indexing to a market-cap-weighted index is self-rebalancing, tracking an index based on other weighting schemes requires ongoing transactions to ensure the portfolio remains in alignment with index weights. An example is tracking an equally weighted index: As changes in market prices affect the relative weights of securities in the portfolio over time, the portfolio will need to be rebalanced to restore equal weights. Portfolios tracking fixed-income indices also incur ongoing transaction costs as holdings mature, default, or are called away by their issuers.

Exhibit 13 diagrams the passive/active choice as a continuum rather than binary (0 or 1) characteristic. Tracking risk and active share are widely known quantitative measures of the degree of active management that capture different aspects of it. Each measure is shown as tending to increase from left to right on the spectrum; however, they do not increase (or decrease) in lockstep with each other, in general.

Exhibit 13: Passive/Active Spectrum

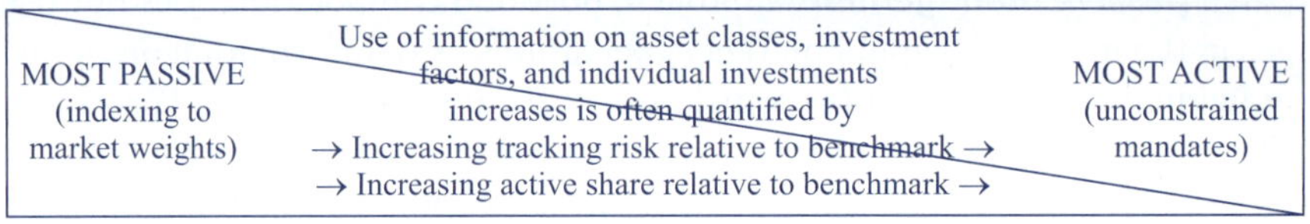

Asset class allocations may be managed with different approaches on the spectrum. For example, developed market equities might be implemented purely passively, whereas emerging market bonds might be invested with an unconstrained, index-agnostic approach.

Factors that influence asset owners' decisions on where to invest on the passive/active spectrum include the following:

- *Available investments.* For example, the availability of an investable and representative index as the basis for indexing.
- *Scalability of active strategies being considered.* The prospective value added by an active strategy may begin to decline at some level of invested assets. In addition, participation in it may not be available below some asset level, a consideration for small investors.
- *The feasibility of investing passively while incorporating client-specific constraints.* For example, an investor's particular ESG investing criteria may not align with existing index products.

- *Beliefs concerning market informational efficiency.* A strong belief in market efficiency for the asset class(es) under consideration would orient the investor away from active management.
- *The trade-off of expected incremental benefits relative to incremental costs and risks of active choices.* Costs of active management include investment management costs, trading costs, and turnover-induced taxes; such costs would have to be judged relative to the lower costs of index alternatives, which vary by asset class.
- *Tax status.* Holding other variables constant, taxable investors would tend to have higher hurdles to profitable active management than tax-exempt investors.[32] For taxable investors who want to hold both passive and active investments, active investments would be held, in general, in available tax-advantaged accounts.

The curriculum readings on equity, fixed-income, and alternative investments will explore many strategies and the nature of any active decisions involved. Investors do need to understand the nature of the active decisions involved in implementing their strategic asset allocations and their appropriateness given the factors described. Exhibit 14 shows qualitatively (rather than precisely) some choices that investors may consider for equity and fixed-income allocations. In the exhibit, non-cap-weighted indexing includes such approaches as equal weighting and quantitative rules-based indexing approaches (discussed further in the equity readings).[33]

Exhibit 14: Placement on the Passive/Active Spectrum: Examples of Possible Choices

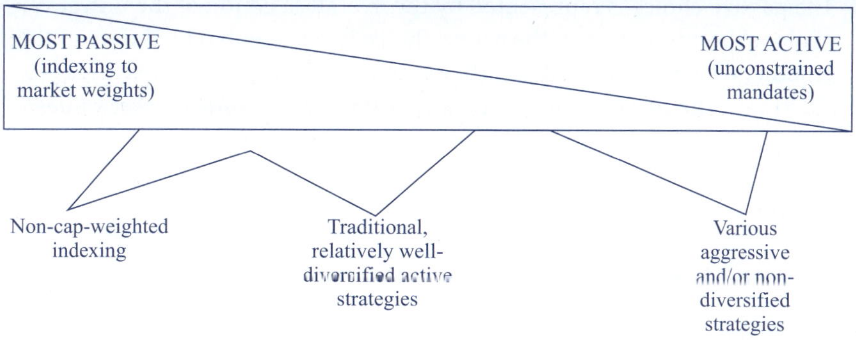

EXAMPLE 8

Implementation Choices (1)

1. Describe two kinds of passive/active choices faced by investors related to asset allocation.

   Solution:

   One choice relates to whether to allow active deviations from the strategic asset allocation. Tactical asset allocation and dynamic asset allocation are

32 See Jeffrey and Arnott (1993).

33 Podkaminer (2015) provides a survey.

examples of active management of asset allocations. A second set of choices relates to where to invest allocations to asset classes along the passive/active spectrum.

2. An equity index is described as "a rules-based, transparent index designed to provide investors with an efficient way to gain exposure to large-cap and small-cap stocks with low total return variability." Compared with the market-cap weighting of the parent index (with the same component securities), the weights in the low-volatility index are proportional to the inverse of return volatility, so that the highest-volatility security receives the lowest weight. Describe the active and passive aspects of a decision to invest an allocation to equities in ETFs tracking such indices.

   Solution:

   The active element is the decision, relative to the parent index, to overweight securities with low volatility and underweight securities with high volatility. This management of risk is distinct from reducing portfolio volatility by combining a market-cap-weighted index with a risk-free asset proxy because it implies a belief in some risk–return advantage to favoring low-volatility equities on an individual security basis. The passive element is a transparent rules-based implementation of the weighting scheme based on inverse volatilities.

3. Describe how investing in a GDP-weighted global bond index involves both active and passive choices.

   Solution:

   The passive choice is represented by the overall selection of the universe of global bonds; however, the active choice is represented by the weighting scheme, which is to use GDP rather than capital market weights. This is a tilt toward the real economy and away from fixed-income market values.

EXAMPLE 9

Implementation Choices (2)

Describe characteristic(s) of each of the following investors that are likely to influence the decision to invest passively or actively.

1. Caflandia sovereign wealth fund

   For a large investor like the Caflandia sovereign wealth fund (CAF$40 billion), the scalability of active strategies that it may wish to employ may be a consideration. If only a small percentage of portfolio assets can be invested effectively in an active strategy, for example, the potential value added for the overall portfolio may not justify the inherent costs and management time. Although the equities and fixed-income allocations could be invested using passive approaches, investments in the diversifying strategies category are commonly active.

2. GPLE corporate pension

   The executives responsible for the GPLE corporate pension also have other, non-investment responsibilities. This is a factor favoring a more passive approach; however, choosing an outsourced chief investment officer or delegated fiduciary consultant to manage active manager selection could facilitate greater use of active investment.

3. The Lee family

The fact that the Lees are taxable investors is a factor generally in favor of passive management for assets not held in tax-advantaged accounts. Active management involves turnover, which gives rise to taxes.

4. Auldberg University Endowment

According to the vignette in Example 3, the Auldberg University Endowment has substantial staff resources in equities, fixed income, and real estate. This fact suggests that passive/active decisions are relatively unconstrained by internal resources. By itself, it does not favor passive or active, but it is a factor that allows active choices to be given full consideration.

Risk Budgeting Perspectives in Asset Allocation and Implementation

Risk budgeting addresses the questions of which types of risks to take and how much of each to take. Risk budgeting provides another view of asset allocation—through a risk lens. Depending on the focus, the risk may be quantified in various ways. For example, a concern for volatility can be quantified as variance or standard deviation of returns, and a concern for tail risk can be quantified as VaR or drawdown. Risk budgets (budgets for risk taking) can be stated in absolute or in relative terms and in money or percent terms. For example, it is possible to state an overall risk budget for a portfolio in terms of volatility of returns, which would be an example of an absolute risk budget stated in percent terms (for example, 20% for portfolio return volatility). Risk budgeting is a tool that may be useful in a variety of contexts and asset allocation approaches.

Some investors may approach asset allocation with an exclusive focus on risk. A risk budgeting approach to asset allocation has been defined as an approach in which the investor specifies how risk (quantified by some measure, such as volatility) is to be distributed across assets in the portfolio, without consideration of the assets' expected returns.[34] An example is aiming for equal expected risk contributions to overall portfolio volatility from all included asset classes as an approach to diversification, which is a risk parity (or equal risk contribution) approach. A subsequent reading in asset allocation addresses this in greater detail.

More directly related to the choice of passive/active implementation are active risk budgets and active risk budgeting. **Active risk budgeting** addresses the question of how much benchmark-relative risk an investor is willing to take in seeking to outperform a benchmark. This approach is risk budgeting stated in benchmark-relative terms. In parallel to the two dimensions of the passive/active decision outlined previously are two levels of active risk budgeting, which can be distinguished as follows:

- At the level of the overall asset allocation, active risk can be defined relative to the strategic asset allocation benchmark. This benchmark may be the strategic asset allocation weights applied to specified (often, broad-based market-cap-weighted) indices.
- At the level of individual asset classes, active risk can be defined relative to the asset class benchmark.

34 See Roncalli (2013).

Active risk budgeting at the level of overall asset allocation would be relevant to tactical asset allocation. Active risk budgeting at the level of each asset class is relevant to how the allocation to those asset classes is invested. For example, it can take the form of expected-alpha versus tracking-error optimization in a manner similar to classic mean–variance optimization. If investment factor risks are the investor's focus, risk budgeting can be adapted to have a focus on allocating factor risk exposures instead. Later readings revisit risk budgeting in investing in further detail.

11 REBALANCING: STRATEGIC CONSIDERATIONS

☐ discuss strategic considerations in rebalancing asset allocations

Rebalancing is the discipline of adjusting portfolio weights to more closely align with the strategic asset allocation. Rebalancing is a key part of the monitoring and feedback step of the portfolio construction, monitoring, and revision process. An investor's rebalancing policy is generally documented in the IPS.

Even in the absence of changing investor circumstances, a revised economic outlook, or tactical asset allocation views, normal changes in asset prices cause the portfolio asset mix to deviate from target weights. Industry practice defines "rebalancing" as portfolio adjustments triggered by such price changes. Other portfolio adjustments, even systematic ones, are not rebalancing.

Ordinary price changes cause the assets with a high forecast return to grow faster than the portfolio as a whole. Because high-return assets are typically also higher risk, in the absence of rebalancing, overall portfolio risk rises. The mix of risks within the portfolio becomes more concentrated as well. Systematic rebalancing maintains the original strategic risk exposures. The discipline of rebalancing serves to control portfolio risks that have become different from what the investor originally intended.

Consider the example from the internet bubble (1995–2001) in Exhibit 15. The example assumes a 60/40 stock/bond portfolio, in which stocks are represented by the large-cap US growth stocks that characterized the internet bubble. In Panel B, the left-hand scale and upper two lines show month-by-month total portfolio *values* with and without monthly rebalancing ("wealth rebalanced" and "wealth unrebalanced," respectively). The right-hand scale and lower two lines show month-by-month portfolio *risk* as represented by the 5th percentile drawdown (in a VaR model) with and without monthly rebalancing ("risk rebalanced" and "risk unrebalanced," respectively).

Exhibit 15: Rebalancing

Panel A. Asset Mix

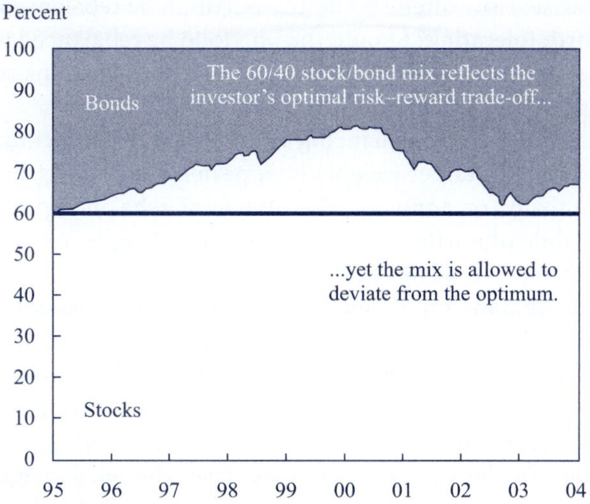

Panel B. Portfolio Value and Risk

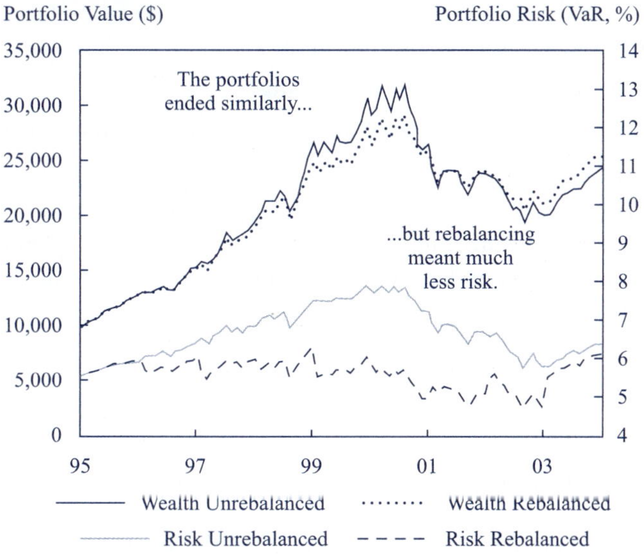

Note: The data are a 60/40 mix of the S&P 500 Growth Index and the Barclays Capital Aggregate Bond Index.

Because rebalancing is countercyclical, it is fundamentally a contrarian investment approach.[35] Behavioral finance tells us that such contrarianism will be uncomfortable; no one likes to sell the most recently best-performing part of the portfolio to buy the worst. Thus, rebalancing is a *discipline* of adjusting the portfolio to better align with the strategic asset allocation in both connotations of discipline—the sense of a typical practice and the sense of a strengthening regime.

35 A quantitative interpretation of rebalancing, given by Ang (2014), is that the return to rebalancing is selling out of the money puts and calls.

A Framework for Rebalancing

The actual mechanics of rebalancing are more complex than they first appear. A number of questions arise: How often should the portfolio be rebalanced? What levels of imbalance are worth tolerating? Should the portfolio be rebalanced to the edge of the policy range or to some other point? These non-trivial questions represent the key strategic decisions in rebalancing.

The simplest approach to rebalancing is **calendar rebalancing**, which involves rebalancing a portfolio to target weights on a periodic basis—for example, monthly, quarterly, semiannually, or annually. The choice of rebalancing frequency may be linked to the schedule of portfolio reviews. Although simple, rebalancing points are arbitrary and have other disadvantages.

Percent-range rebalancing permits tighter control of the asset mix compared with calendar rebalancing. Percent-range approach involves setting rebalancing thresholds or trigger points, stated as a percentage of the portfolio's value, around target values. For example, if the target allocation to an asset class is 50% of portfolio value, **trigger points** at 45% and 55% of portfolio value define a 10 percentage point **rebalancing range** (or corridor) for the value of that asset class. The rebalancing range creates a no-trade region. The portfolio is rebalanced when an asset class's weight first passes through one of its trigger points. Focusing on percent-range rebalancing, the following questions are relevant:

- How frequently is the portfolio valued?
- What size deviation triggers rebalancing?
- Is the deviation from the target allocation fully or partially corrected?

How frequently is the portfolio valued? The percent-range discipline requires monitoring portfolio values for breaches of a trigger point at an agreed-on frequency; the more frequent the monitoring, the greater the precision in implementation. Such monitoring may be scheduled daily, weekly, monthly, quarterly, or annually. A number of considerations—including governance resources and asset custodian resources—can affect valuation frequency. For many investors, monthly or quarterly evaluation efficiently balances the costs and benefits of rebalancing.

What size deviation triggers rebalancing? Trigger points take into account such factors as traditional practice, transaction costs, asset class volatility, volatility of the balance of the portfolio, correlation of the asset class with the balance of the portfolio, and risk tolerance.[36]

Before the rise of modern multi-asset portfolios, the stock/bond split broadly characterized the asset allocation and a traditional $\pm x\%$ rebalancing band was common. These fixed ranges would apply no matter the size or volatility of the allocation target. For example, both a 40% domestic equity allocation and a 15% real asset allocation might have ±5% rebalancing ranges. Alternatively, proportional bands reflect the size of the target weight. For example, a 60% target asset class might have a ±6% band, whereas a 5% allocation would have a ±0.5% band. Proportional bands might also be set to reflect the relative volatility of the asset classes. A final approach is the use of cost–benefit analysis to set ranges.

Is the deviation from the target allocation fully or partially corrected? Once the portfolio is evaluated and an unacceptably large deviation found, the investor must determine rebalancing trade size, as well as the timeline for implementing the rebalancing. In practice, three main approaches are used: rebalance back to target weights, rebalance to range edge, or rebalance halfway between the range-edge trigger point and the target weight.

36 See Masters (2003) for details on these factors apart from traditional factors.

Strategic Considerations in Rebalancing

The four-part rebalancing framework just described highlights important questions to address in setting rebalancing policy. Strategic considerations generally include the following, all else being equal:

- Higher transaction costs for an asset class imply wider rebalancing ranges.
- More risk-averse investors will have tighter rebalancing ranges.
- Less correlated assets also have tighter rebalancing ranges.
- Beliefs in momentum favor wider rebalancing ranges, whereas mean reversion encourages tighter ranges.
- Illiquid investments complicate rebalancing.
- Derivatives create the possibility of synthetic rebalancing.
- Taxes, which are a cost, discourage rebalancing and encourage asymmetric and wider rebalancing ranges.

Asset class volatility is also a consideration in the size of rebalancing ranges.

A cost–benefit approach to rebalancing sets ranges, taking transaction costs, risk aversion, asset class risks, and asset class correlations into consideration. For example, an asset that is more highly correlated with the rest of the portfolio than another would merit a wider rebalancing range, all else equal, because it would be closer to being a substitute for the balance of the portfolio; thus, larger deviations would have less impact on portfolio risk.

EXAMPLE 10

Different Rebalancing Ranges

1. The table shows a simple four-asset strategic mix along with rebalancing ranges created under different approaches. The width of the rebalancing range under the proportional range approach is 0.20 of the strategic target.

   State a reason that could explain why the international equity range is wider than the domestic equity range using the cost–benefit approach.

Asset Class	Strategic Target	Fixed Width Ranges	Proportional Ranges (±1,000 bps)	Cost–Benefit Ranges
Domestic equity	40%	35%–45%	36%–44%	35%–45%
International equity	25%	20%–30%	22½%–27½%	19%–31%
Emerging markets	15%	10%–20%	13½%–16½%	12%–18%
Fixed income	20%	15%–25%	18%–22%	19%–21%

Solution:

Higher transaction costs for international equity compared with domestic equity could explain the wider range for international equity compared with domestic equity under the cost–benefit approach. Another potential explanation relates to the possibility that international equity has a higher correlation with the balance of the portfolio (i.e., the portfolio excluding international equity) than does domestic equity (i.e., with the portfolio excluding domestic equity). If that is the case then, all else being equal, a wider band would be justified for international equity.

Investors' perspectives on capital markets can affect their approach to rebalancing. A belief in momentum and trend following, for example, encourages wider rebalancing ranges. In contrast, a belief in mean reversion encourages stricter adherence to rebalancing, including tighter ranges.

Illiquid assets complicate rebalancing. Relatively illiquid investments, such as hedge funds, private equity, or direct real estate, cannot be readily traded without substantial trading costs and/or delays. Accordingly, illiquid investments are commonly assigned wide rebalancing ranges. However, rebalancing of an illiquid asset may be affected indirectly when a highly correlated liquid asset can be traded or when exposure can be adjusted by means of positions in derivatives. For example, public equity could be reduced to offset an overweight in private equity. Rebalancing by means of highly correlated liquid assets and derivatives, however, involves some imprecision and basis risk.

This insight about liquidity is an instance where thinking ahead about rebalancing can affect the strategic asset allocation. It is one reason that allocations to illiquid assets are often smaller than if trading were possible.

Factor-based asset allocation, liability-relative investing, and goals-based investing, each a valid approach to asset allocation, can give rise to different rebalancing considerations. Factor exposures and liability hedges require monitoring (and rebalancing) the factors weights and surplus duration in addition to asset class weights. Goals-based investing in private wealth management may require both asset class rebalancing and moving funds between different goal sub-portfolios.

Tax considerations also complicate rebalancing. Rebalancing typically realizes capital gains and losses, which are taxable events in many jurisdictions. For private wealth managers, any rebalancing benefit must be compared with the tax cost. Taxes, as a cost, are much larger than other transaction costs, which often leads to wider rebalancing ranges in taxable portfolios than in tax-exempt portfolios. Because loss harvesting generates tax savings and realizing gains triggers taxes, rebalancing ranges in taxable accounts may also be asymmetric. (For example, a 25% target asset class might have an allowable range of 24%–28%, which is −1% to +3%.)

Modern cost–benefit approaches to rebalancing suggest considering derivatives as a rebalancing tool. Derivatives can often be used to rebalance synthetically at much lower transaction costs than the costs of using the underlying stocks and bonds. Using a derivatives overlay also avoids disrupting the underlying separate accounts in a multi-manager implementation of the strategic asset allocation. Tax considerations are also relevant; it may be more cost effective to reduce an exposure using a derivatives overlay than to sell the underlying asset and incur the capital gains tax liability. Lastly, trading a few derivatives may be quicker and easier than hundreds of underlying securities. Of course, using derivatives may require a higher level of risk oversight, but then risk control is the main rationale for rebalancing.

Estimates of the benefits of rebalancing vary. Many portfolios are statistically indistinguishable from each other, suggesting that much rebalancing is unnecessary. In contrast, Willenbrock (2011) demonstrates that even zero-return assets can, in theory, generate positive returns through rebalancing, which is a demonstrable (and surprising) benefit. Whatever the return estimate for the value added from rebalancing, the key takeaway is that rebalancing is chiefly about risk control, not return enhancement.

SUMMARY

This reading has introduced the subject of asset allocation. Among the points made are the following:

- Effective investment governance ensures that decisions are made by individuals or groups with the necessary skills and capacity and involves articulating the long- and short-term objectives of the investment program; effectively allocating decision rights and responsibilities among the functional units in the governance hierarchy; taking account of their knowledge, capacity, time, and position on the governance hierarchy; specifying processes for developing and approving the investment policy statement, which will govern the day-to-day operation of the investment program; specifying processes for developing and approving the program's strategic asset allocation; establishing a reporting framework to monitor the program's progress toward the agreed-on goals and objectives; and periodically undertaking a governance audit.
- The economic balance sheet includes non-financial assets and liabilities that can be relevant for choosing the best asset allocation for an investor's financial portfolio.
- The investment objectives of asset-only asset allocation approaches focus on the asset side of the economic balance sheet; approaches with a liability-relative orientation focus on funding liabilities; and goals-based approaches focus on achieving financial goals.
- The risk concepts relevant to asset-only asset allocation approaches focus on asset risk; those of liability-relative asset allocation focus on risk in relation to paying liabilities; and a goals-based approach focuses on the probabilities of not achieving financial goals.
- Asset classes are the traditional units of analysis in asset allocation and reflect systematic risks with varying degrees of overlap.
- Assets within an asset class should be relatively homogeneous; asset classes should be mutually exclusive; asset classes should be diversifying; asset classes as a group should make up a preponderance of the world's investable wealth; asset classes selected for investment should have the capacity to absorb a meaningful proportion of an investor's portfolio.
- Risk factors are associated with non-diversifiable (i.e., systematic) risk and are associated with an expected return premium. The price of an asset and/or asset class may reflect more than one risk factor, and complicated spread positions may be necessary to identify and isolate particular risk factors. Their use as units of analysis in asset allocation is driven by considerations of controlling systematic risk exposures.
- The global market portfolio represents a highly diversified asset allocation that can serve as a baseline asset allocation in an asset-only approach.
- There are two dimensions of passive/active choices. One dimension relates to the management of the strategic asset allocation itself—for example, whether to deviate from it tactically or not. The second dimension relates to passive and active implementation choices in investing the allocation to a given asset class. Tactical and dynamic asset allocation relate to the first dimension; active and passive choices for implementing allocations to asset classes relate to the second dimension.

- Risk budgeting addresses the question of which types of risks to take and how much of each to take. Active risk budgeting addresses the question of how much benchmark-relative risk an investor is willing to take. At the level of the overall asset allocation, active risk can be defined relative to the strategic asset allocation benchmark. At the level of individual asset classes, active risk can be defined relative to the benchmark proxy.
- Rebalancing is the discipline of adjusting portfolio weights to more closely align with the strategic asset allocation. Rebalancing approaches include calendar-based and range-based rebalancing. Calendar-based rebalancing rebalances the portfolio to target weights on a periodic basis. Range-based rebalancing sets rebalancing thresholds or trigger points around target weights. The ranges may be fixed width, percentage based, or volatility based. Range-based rebalancing permits tighter control of the asset mix compared with calendar rebalancing.
- Strategic considerations in rebalancing include transaction costs, risk aversion, correlations among asset classes, volatility, and beliefs concerning momentum, taxation, and asset class liquidity.

REFERENCES

Ang, Andrew. 2014. *Asset Management: A Systematic Approach to Factor Investing.* New York: Oxford University Press.

Blanchett, David M., David M. Cordell, Michael S. Finke, and Thomas Idzorek. 2016. "Risk Management for Individuals." CFA Institute.

Blanchett, David M. and Philip U. Straehl. 2015. "No Portfolio is an Island." *Financial Analysts Journal* 71, vol. , no. 3 (May/June): 15–33. 10.2469/faj.v71.n3.5

Blanchett, David M. and Philip U. Straehl. 2017. "Portfolio Implications of Job-Specific Human Capital Risk." *Journal of Asset Management* 18, vol. , no. 1:1–15.

Brunel, Jean L.P. 2012. "Goals-Based Wealth Management in Practice." *Conference Proceedings Quarterly*, vol. 29, no. 1 (March): 57–65.

Brunel, Jean L.P. 2015. *Goals-Based Wealth Management: An Integrated and Practical Approach to Changing the Structure of Wealth Advisory Practices.* Hoboken, NJ: John Wiley.

Burger, John D., Francis E. Warnock, and Veronica Cacdac Warnock. 2012. "Emerging Local Currency Bond Markets." *Financial Analysts Journal* 68, vol. , no. 4 (July/August): 73–93. 10.2469/faj.v68.n4.4

CFA Institute. *Standards of Practice Handbook*, 11th edition. 2014. CFA Institute.

Chhabra, Ashvin. 2005. "Beyond Markowitz: A Comprehensive Wealth Allocation Framework for Individual Investors." *Journal of Wealth Management* 7, vol. , no. 4 (Spring): 8–34. 10.3905/jwm.2005.470606

Collie, Bob and James A. Gannon. 2009. "Liability-Responsive Asset Allocation: A Dynamic Approach to Pension Plan Management." Russell Investments Insights (April).

Das, Sanjiv, Harry Markowitz, Jonathan Scheid, and Meir Statman. 2010. "Portfolio Optimization with Mental Accounts." *Journal of Financial and Quantitative Analysis* 45, vol. , no. 2 (April): 311–334. 10.1017/S0022109010000141

Fraser, Steve P. and William W. Jennings. 2006. "Behavioral Asset Allocation for Foundations and Endowments." *Journal of Wealth Management* 9, vol. , no. 3 (Winter): 38–50. 10.3905/jwm.2006.661431

Greer, Robert J. 1997. "What is an Asset Class, Anyway?" *Journal of Portfolio Management* 23, vol. , no. 2 (Winter): 86–91. 10.3905/jpm.23.2.86

Ibbotson, Roger G. and Paul D. Kaplan. 2000. "Does Asset Allocation Policy Explain 40, 90, or 100 Percent of Performance?" *Financial Analysts Journal* 56, vol. , no. 1 (January/February): 26–33. 10.2469/faj.v56.n1.2327

Ibbotson, Roger G., Moshe A. Milevsky, Peng Chen, and Kevin X. Zhu. 2007. *Lifetime Financial Advice: Human Capital, Asset Allocation, and Insurance.* Charlottesville, VA: CFA Institute Research Foundation.

Idzorek, Thomas M. and Maciej Kowara. 2013. "Factor-Based Asset Allocation versus Asset-Class-Based Asset Allocation." *Financial Analysts Journal* 69, vol. , no. 3 (May/June): 19–29. 10.2469/faj.v69.n3.7

Idzorek, Thomas, Jeremy Stempien, and Nathan Voris. 2013. "Bait and Switch: Glide Path Instability." *Journal of Investing* 22, vol. , no. 1 (Spring): 74–82. 10.3905/joi.2013.22.1.074

Jeffrey, Robert H. and Robert D. Arnott. 1993. "Is Your Alpha Big Enough to Cover Its Taxes?" *Journal of Portfolio Management* 19, vol. , no. 3 (Spring): 15–25. 10.3905/jpm.1993.710867

Kozhemiakin, Alexander. 2011. "Emerging Markets Local Currency Debt: Capitalizing on Improved Sovereign Fundamentals." BNY Mellon Asset Management.

Kritzman, Mark. 1999. "Toward Defining an Asset Class." *Journal of Alternative Investments* 2, vol. , no. 1 (Summer): 79–82. 10.3905/jai.1999.318919

Masters, Seth J. 2003. "Rebalancing." *Journal of Portfolio Management* 29, vol. , no. 3 (Spring): 52–57. 10.3905/jpm.2003.319883

Milevsky, Moshe A. 2016. "It's Time to Retire Ruin (Probabilities)." *Financial Analysts Journal* 72, vol. , no. 2 (March/April): 8–12. 10.2469/faj.v72.n2.4

Perry, William. 2011. "The Case For Emerging Market Corporates." *Journal of Indexes* 14, vol. , no. 5 (September/October): 10–17.

Podkaminer, Eugene. 2013. "Risk Factors as Building Blocks for Portfolio Diversification: The Chemistry of Asset Allocation." CFA Institute Investment Risk and Performance papers (January).

Podkaminer, Eugene. 2015. "The Education of Beta: Can Alternative Indexes Make Your Portfolio Smarter?" *Journal of Investing* 24, vol. , no. 2 (Summer): 7–34. 10.3905/joi.2015.24.2.007

Pompian, Michael M. 2011a. "The Behavioral Biases of Individuals." CFA Institute.

Pompian, Michael M. 2011b. "The Behavioral Finance Perspective." CFA Institute.

Pompian, Michael, Colin McLean, and Alistair Byrne. 2011. "Behavioral Finance and Investment Processes." CFA Institute.

Roncalli, Thierry. 2013. *Introduction to Risk Parity and Budgeting.* New York: CRC Press.

Rudd, Andrew and Laurence B. Siegel. 2013. "Using an Economic Balance Sheet for Financial Planning." *Journal of Wealth Management* 16, vol. , no. 2 (Fall): 15–23. 10.3905/jwm.2013.16.2.015

Shefrin, H. and M. Statman. 2000. "Behavioral Portfolio Theory." *Journal of Financial and Quantitative Analysis* 35, vol. , no. 2 (June): 127–151. 10.2307/2676187

Swinkels, Laurens. 2012. "Emerging Market Inflation-Linked Bonds." *Financial Analysts Journal* 68, vol. , no. 5 (September/October): 38–56. 10.2469/faj.v68.n5.2

Waring, M. Barton, Duane Whitney, John Pirone, and Charles Castille. 2000. "Optimizing Manager Structure and Budgeting Manager Risk." *Journal of Portfolio Management* 26, vol. , no. 3 (Spring): 90–104. 10.3905/jpm.2000.319719

Willenbrock, Scott. 2011. "Diversification Return, Portfolio Rebalancing, and the Commodity Return Puzzle." *Financial Analysts Journal* 67, vol. , no. 4 (July/August): 42–49. 10.2469/faj.v67.n4.1

PRACTICE PROBLEMS

The following information relates to questions 1-8

Meg and Cramer Law, a married couple aged 42 and 44, respectively, are meeting with their new investment adviser, Daniel Raye. The Laws have worked their entire careers at Whorton Solutions (WS), a multinational technology company. The Laws have two teenage children who will soon begin college.

Raye reviews the Laws' current financial position. The Laws have an investment portfolio consisting of \$800,000 in equities and \$450,000 in fixed-income instruments. Raye notes that 80% of the equity portfolio consists of shares of WS. The Laws also own real estate valued at \$400,000, with \$225,000 in mortgage debt. Raye estimates the Laws' pre-retirement earnings from WS have a total present value of \$1,025,000. He estimates the Laws' future expected consumption expenditures have a total present value of \$750,000.

The Laws express a very strong desire to fund their children's college education expenses, which have an estimated present value of \$275,000. The Laws also plan to fund an endowment at their alma mater in 20 years, which has an estimated present value of \$500,000. The Laws tell Raye they want a high probability of success funding the endowment. Raye uses this information to prepare an economic balance sheet for the Laws.

In reviewing a financial plan written by the Laws' previous adviser, Raye notices the following asset class specifications.

Equity:	US equities
Debt:	Global investment-grade corporate bonds and real estate
Derivatives:	Primarily large-capitalization foreign equities

The previous adviser's report notes the asset class returns on equity and derivatives are highly correlated. The report also notes the asset class returns on debt have a low correlation with equity and derivative returns.

Raye is concerned that the asset allocation approach followed by the Laws' previous financial adviser resulted in an overlap in risk factors among asset classes for the portfolio. Raye plans to address this by examining the portfolio's sensitivity to various risk factors, such as inflation, liquidity, and volatility, to determine the desired exposure to each factor.

Raye concludes that a portfolio of 75% global equities and 25% bonds reflects an appropriate balance of expected return and risk for the Laws with respect to a 20-year time horizon for most moderately important goals. Raye recommends the Laws follow a goals-based approach to asset allocation and offers three possible portfolios for the Laws to consider. Selected data on the three portfolios are presented in Exhibit 1.

Exhibit 1: Proposed Portfolio Allocations for the Law Family

	Cash	Fixed Income	Global Equities	Diversifying Strategies*
Portfolio 1	35%	55%	10%	0%
Portfolio 2	10%	15%	65%	10%
Portfolio 3	10%	30%	40%	20%

** Diversifying strategies consists of hedge funds*

Raye uses a cost–benefit approach to rebalancing and recommends that global equities have a wider rebalancing range than the other asset classes.

1. Using the economic balance sheet approach, the Laws' economic net worth is *closest* to:

   A. $925,000.

   B. $1,425,000.

   C. $1,675,000.

2. Using an economic balance sheet, which of the Laws' current financial assets is *most* concerning from an asset allocation perspective?

   A. Equities

   B. Real estate

   C. Fixed income

3. Raye believes the previous adviser's specification for debt is incorrect given that, for purposes of asset allocation, asset classes should be:

   A. diversifying.

   B. mutually exclusive.

   C. relatively homogeneous.

4. Raye believes the previous adviser's asset class specifications for equity and derivatives are inappropriate given that, for purposes of asset allocation, asset classes should be:

   A. diversifying.

   B. mutually exclusive.

   C. relatively homogeneous.

5. To address his concern regarding the previous adviser's asset allocation approach, Raye should assess the Laws' portfolio using:

   A. a homogeneous and mutually exclusive asset class–based risk analysis.

   B. a multifactor risk model to control systematic risk factors in asset allocation.

   C. an asset class–based asset allocation approach to construct a diversified portfolio.

6. Based on Exhibit 1, which portfolio *best* meets the Laws' education goal for their children?

   A. Portfolio 1

   B. Portfolio 2

   C. Portfolio 3

7. Based on Exhibit 1, which portfolio *best* meets the Laws' goal to fund an endowment for their alma mater?

   A. Portfolio 1

   B. Portfolio 2

   C. Portfolio 3

8. Raye's approach to rebalancing global equities is consistent with:

   A. the Laws' being risk averse.

   B. global equities' having higher transaction costs than other asset classes.

   C. global equities' having lower correlations with other asset classes.

SOLUTIONS

1. A is correct. The Laws' economic net worth is closest to $925,000. An economic balance sheet includes conventional financial assets and liabilities, as well as extended portfolio assets and liabilities that are relevant in making asset allocation decisions. The economic balance sheet for the Law family is shown in the following exhibit.

Assets		Liabilities and Economic Net Worth	
Financial Assets		*Financial Liabilities*	
Fixed income	450,000	Mortgage debt	225,000
Real estate	400,000		
Equity	800,000		
Extended Assets		*Extended Liabilities*	
Human capital	1,025,000	Children's education	275,000
		Endowment funding	500,000
		Present value of consumption	750,000
Total Economic Assets	2,675,000	*Total Economic Liabilities*	1,750,000
		Economic Net Worth	925,000

Economic net worth is equal to total economic assets minus total economic liabilities ($2,675,000 – $1,750,000 = $925,000).

2. A is correct. The Laws' equity portfolio is heavily concentrated in WS stock (80% of the equity portfolio), and both Laws work at WS. Should WS encounter difficult economic circumstances, the investment value of WS stock and the Laws' human capital are both likely to be adversely affected. Thus, their investment in WS should be reviewed and their equity portfolio diversified further.

3. C is correct. In order to effectively specify asset classes for the purpose of asset allocation, assets within an asset class should be relatively homogeneous and have similar attributes. The previous adviser's specification of the debt asset class includes global investment-grade corporate bonds and real estate. This definition results in a non-homogeneous asset class.

4. A is correct. For risk control purposes, an asset class should be diversifying and should not have extremely high expected correlations with other classes. Because the returns to the equity and the derivatives asset classes are noted as being highly correlated, inclusion of both asset classes will result in duplication of risk exposures. Including both asset classes is not diversifying to the asset allocation.

5. B is correct. Raye believes the Laws' previous financial adviser followed an asset allocation approach that resulted in an overlap in risk factors among asset classes. A multifactor risk model approach can be used to address potential risk factor overlaps. Risk factor approaches to asset allocation focus on assigning investments to the investor's desired exposures to specified risk factors. These methods are premised on the observation that asset classes often exhibit some overlaps in

sources of risk.

6. A is correct. Portfolio 1 best meets the Laws' education goal for their children. The estimated present value of the Laws' expected education expense is $275,000. Given that the children will be starting college soon, and the Laws have a very strong desire to achieve this goal, Portfolio 1, which stresses liquidity and stability, is most appropriate to meet the Laws' short-term education goal.

7. B is correct. Portfolio 2 best meets the Laws' goal to fund an endowment for their alma mater in 20 years. In present value terms, the gift is valued at $500,000, with the Laws desiring a high probability of achieving this goal. Although slightly more conservative than the 75/25 global equity/bond mix, Portfolio 2 has a greater growth emphasis compared with Portfolios 1 and 3. Therefore, Portfolio 2 is best for funding the endowment at their alma mater given the goal's long-term horizon and the Laws' desire for a high probability of achieving it.

8. B is correct. Using the cost–benefit approach, higher transaction costs for an asset class imply wider rebalancing ranges. Raye's recommendation for a wider rebalancing range for global equities is consistent with the presence of higher transaction costs for global equities.

LEARNING MODULE

4

Principles of Asset Allocation

by Jean L.P. Brunel, CFA, Thomas M. Idzorek, CFA, and John M. Mulvey, PhD.

Jean L.P. Brunel, CFA, is at Brunel Associates LLC (USA). Thomas M. Idzorek, CFA, is at Morningstar (USA). John M. Mulvey, PhD, is at the Bendheim Center for Finance at Princeton University (USA).

LEARNING OUTCOMES

Mastery	*The candidate should be able to:*
☐	describe and evaluate the use of mean–variance optimization in asset allocation
☐	recommend and justify an asset allocation using mean–variance optimization
☐	interpret and evaluate an asset allocation in relation to an investor's economic balance sheet
☐	recommend and justify an asset allocation based on the global market portfolio
☐	discuss the use of Monte Carlo simulation and scenario analysis to evaluate the robustness of an asset allocation
☐	discuss asset class liquidity considerations in asset allocation
☐	explain absolute and relative risk budgets and their use in determining and implementing an asset allocation
☐	describe how client needs and preferences regarding investment risks can be incorporated into asset allocation
☐	describe the use of investment factors in constructing and analyzing an asset allocation
☐	describe and evaluate characteristics of liabilities that are relevant to asset allocation
☐	discuss approaches to liability-relative asset allocation
☐	recommend and justify a liability-relative asset allocation

LEARNING OUTCOMES	
Mastery	***The candidate should be able to:***
☐	recommend and justify an asset allocation using a goals-based approach
☐	describe and evaluate heuristic and other approaches to asset allocation
☐	discuss factors affecting rebalancing policy

1 INTRODUCTION

Determining a strategic asset allocation is arguably the most important aspect of the investment process. This reading builds on the "Introduction to Asset Allocation" reading and focuses on several of the primary frameworks for developing an asset allocation, including asset-only mean–variance optimization, various liability-relative asset allocation techniques, and goals-based investing. Additionally, it touches on various other asset allocation techniques used by practitioners, as well as important related topics, such as rebalancing.

The process of creating a diversified, multi-asset class portfolio typically involves two separate steps. The first step is the asset allocation decision, which can refer to both the process and the result of determining long-term (strategic) exposures to the available asset classes (or risk factors) that make up the investor's opportunity set. Asset allocation is the first and primary step in translating the client's circumstances, objectives, and constraints into an appropriate portfolio (or, for some approaches, multiple portfolios) for achieving the client's goals within the client's tolerance for risk. The second step in creating a diversified, multi-asset-class portfolio involves implementation decisions that determine the specific investments (individual securities, pooled investment vehicles, and separate accounts) that will be used to implement the targeted allocations.

Although it is possible to carry out the asset allocation process and the implementation process simultaneously, in practice, these two steps are often separated for two reasons. First, the frameworks for simultaneously determining an asset allocation and its implementation are often complex. Second, in practice, many investors prefer to revisit their strategic asset allocation policy somewhat infrequently (e.g., annually or less frequently) in a dedicated asset allocation study, while most of these same investors prefer to revisit/monitor implementation vehicles (actual investments) far more frequently (e.g., monthly or quarterly).

Sections 2–9 cover the traditional mean–variance optimization (MVO) approach to asset allocation. We apply this approach in what is referred to as an "asset-only" setting, in which the goal is to create the most efficient mixes of asset classes in the absence of any liabilities. We highlight key criticisms of mean–variance optimization and methods used to address them. This section also covers risk budgeting in relation to asset allocation, factor-based asset allocation, and asset allocation with illiquid assets. The observation that almost all portfolios exist to help pay for what can be characterized as a "liability" leads to the next subject.

Sections 10–14 introduce liability-relative asset allocation—including a straightforward extension of mean–variance optimization known as surplus optimization. Surplus optimization is an economic balance sheet approach extended to the liability side of the balance sheet that finds the most efficient asset class mixes in the presence of liabilities. Liability-relative optimization is simultaneously concerned with the return of the assets, the change in value of the liabilities, and how assets and liabilities interact to determine the overall value or health of the total portfolio.

Sections 15–18 cover an increasingly popular approach to asset allocation called goals-based asset allocation. Conceptually, goals-based approaches are similar to liability-relative asset allocation in viewing risk in relation to specific needs or objectives associated with different time horizons and degrees of urgency.

Section 19 introduces some informal (heuristic) ways that asset allocations have been determined and other approaches to asset allocation that emphasize specific objectives.

Section 20 addresses the factors affecting choices that are made in developing specific policies relating to rebalancing to the strategic asset allocation. Factors discussed include transaction costs, correlations, volatility, and risk aversion[1]

ASSET-ONLY ASSET ALLOCATIONS AND MEAN–VARIANCE OPTIMIZATION

2

- ☐ describe and evaluate the use of mean–variance optimization in asset allocation
- ☐ recommend and justify an asset allocation using mean–variance optimization
- ☐ interpret and evaluate an asset allocation in relation to an investor's economic balance sheet
- ☐ recommend and justify an asset allocation based on the global market portfolio

In this section, we discuss several of the primary techniques and considerations involved in developing strategic asset allocations, leaving the issue of considering the liabilities to Sections 10–14 and the issue of tailoring the strategic asset allocation to meet specific goals to Sections 15–18.

We start by introducing mean–variance optimization, beginning with unconstrained optimization, prior to moving on to the more common mean–variance optimization problem in which the weights, in addition to summing to 1, are constrained to be positive (no shorting allowed). We present a detailed example, along with several variations, highlighting some of the important considerations in this approach. We also identify several criticisms of mean–variance optimization and the major ways these criticisms have been addressed in practice.

Mean–Variance Optimization: Overview

Mean–variance optimization (MVO), as introduced by Markowitz (1952, 1959), is perhaps the most common approach used in practice to develop and set asset allocation policy. Widely used on its own, MVO is also often the basis for more sophisticated approaches that overcome some of the limitations or weaknesses of MVO.

Markowitz recognized that whenever the returns of two assets are not perfectly correlated, the assets can be combined to form a portfolio whose risk (as measured by standard deviation or variance) is less than the weighted-average risk of the assets

1 In this reading, "volatility" is often used synonymously with "standard deviation."

themselves. An additional and equally important observation is that as one adds assets to the portfolio, one should focus not on the individual risk characteristics of the additional assets but rather on those assets' effect on the risk characteristics of the entire portfolio. Mean–variance optimization provides us with a framework for determining how much to allocate to each asset in order to maximize the *expected* return of the portfolio for an *expected* level of risk. In this sense, mean–variance optimization is a risk-budgeting tool that helps investors to spend their risk budget—the amount of risk they are willing to assume—wisely. We emphasize the word "expected" because the inputs to mean–variance optimization are necessarily forward-looking estimates, and the resulting portfolios reflect the quality of the inputs.

Mean–variance optimization requires three sets of inputs: returns, risks (standard deviations), and pair-wise correlations for the assets in the opportunity set. The objective function is often expressed as follows:

$$U_m = E\left(R_m\right) - 0.005\lambda\sigma_m^2 \quad (1)$$

where

U_m = the investor's utility for asset mix (allocation) m

R_m = the return for asset mix m

λ = the investor's risk aversion coefficient

σ_m^2 = the expected variance of return for asset mix m

The risk aversion coefficient (λ) characterizes the investor's risk–return trade-off; in this context, it is the rate at which an investor will forgo expected return for less variance. The value of 0.005 in Equation 1 is based on the assumption that $E(R_m)$ and σ_m are expressed as percentages rather than as decimals. (In using Equation 1, omit % signs.) If those quantities were expressed as decimals, the 0.005 would change to 0.5. For example, if $E(R_m) = 0.10$, $\lambda = 2$, and $\sigma = 0.20$ (variance is 0.04), then U_m is 0.06, or 6% [= 0.10 – 0.5(2)(0.04)]. In this case, U_m can be interpreted as a certainty-equivalent return—that is, the utility value of the risky return offered by the asset mix, stated in terms of the risk-free return that the investor would value equally. In Equation 1, 0.005 merely scales the second term appropriately.

In words, the objective function says that the value of an asset mix for an investor is equal to the expected return of the asset mix minus a penalty that is equal to one-half of the expected variance of the asset mix scaled by the investor's risk aversion coefficient. Optimization involves selecting the asset mix with the highest such value (certainty equivalent). Smaller risk aversion coefficients result in relatively small penalties for risk, leading to aggressive asset mixes. Conversely, larger risk aversion coefficients result in relatively large penalties for risk, leading to conservative asset mixes. A value of $\lambda = 0$ corresponds to a risk-neutral investor because it implies indifference to volatility. Most investors' risk aversion is consistent with λ between 1 and 10.[2] Empirically, $\lambda = 4$ can be taken to represent a moderately risk-averse investor, although the specific value is sensitive to the opportunity set in question and to market volatility.

In the absence of constraints, there is a closed-form solution that calculates, for a given set of inputs, the single set of weights (allocation) to the assets in the opportunity set that maximizes the investor's utility. Typically, this single set of weights is relatively extreme, with very large long and short positions in each asset class. Except in the special case in which the expected returns are derived using the reverse-optimization process of Sharpe (1974), the expected-utility-maximizing weights will not add up to 100%. We elaborate on reverse optimization in Section 19.

---

2 See Ang (2014, p. 44).

In most real-world applications, asset allocation weights must add up to 100%, reflecting a fully invested, non-leveraged portfolio. From an optimization perspective, when seeking the asset allocation weights that maximize the investor's utility, one must constrain the asset allocation weights to sum to 1 (100%). This constraint that weights sum to 100% is referred to as the "budget constraint" or "unity constraint." The inclusion of this constraint, or any other constraint, moves us from a problem that has a closed-form solution to a problem that must be solved numerically using optimization techniques.

In contrast to the single solution (single set of weights) that is often associated with unconstrained optimization (one could create an efficient frontier using unconstrained weights, but it is seldom done in practice), Markowitz's mean–variance optimization paradigm is most often identified with an efficient frontier that plots all potential efficient asset mixes subject to some common constraints. In addition to a typical budget constraint that the weights must sum to 1 (100% in percentage terms), the next most common constraint allows only positive weights or allocations (i.e., no negative or short positions).

Efficient asset mixes are combinations of the assets in the opportunity set that maximize expected return per unit of expected risk or, alternatively (and equivalently), minimize expected risk for a given level of expected return. To find all possible efficient mixes that collectively form the efficient frontier, *conceptually* the optimizer iterates through all the possible values of the risk aversion coefficient (λ) and for each value finds the combination of assets that maximizes expected utility. We have used the word *conceptually* because there are different techniques for carrying out the optimization that may vary slightly from our description, even though the solution (efficient frontier and efficient mixes) is the same. The efficient mix at the far left of the frontier with the lowest risk is referred to as the global minimum variance portfolio, while the portfolio at the far right of the frontier is the maximum expected return portfolio. In the absence of constraints beyond the budget and non-negativity constraints, the maximum expected return portfolio consists of a 100% allocation to the single asset with the highest expected return (which is not necessarily the asset with the highest level of risk).

RISK AVERSION

Unfortunately, it is extremely difficult to precisely estimate a given investor's risk aversion coefficient (λ). Best practices suggest that when estimating risk aversion (or, conversely, risk tolerance), one should examine both the investor's *preference* for risk (willingness to take risk) and the investor's *capacity* for taking risk. Risk preference is a subjective measure and typically focuses on how an investor feels about and potentially reacts to the ups and downs of portfolio value. The level of return an investor hopes to earn can influence the investor's willingness to take risk, but investors must be realistic when setting such objectives. Risk capacity is an objective measure of the investor's ability to tolerate portfolio losses and the potential decrease in future consumption associated with those losses.[3] The psychometric literature has developed validated questionnaires, such as that of Grable and Joo (2004), to approximately locate an investor's risk preference, although this result then needs to be blended with risk capacity to determine risk tolerance. For individuals, risk capacity is affected by factors such as net worth, income, the size of an emergency fund in relation to consumption needs, and the rate at which the individual saves out of gross income, according to the practice of financial planners noted in Grable (2008).

3 *Risk preference* and *risk capacity* are sometimes referred to as the willingness and the ability to take risk, respectively.

With this guidance in mind, we move forward with a relatively global opportunity set, in this case defined from the point of view of an investor from the United Kingdom with an approximate 10-year time horizon. The analysis is carried out in British pounds (GBP), and none of the currency exposure is hedged. Exhibit 1 identifies 12 asset classes within the universe of available investments and a set of plausible forward-looking capital market assumptions: expected returns, standard deviations, and correlations. The reading on capital market expectations covers how such inputs may be developed.[4] In the exhibit, three significant digits at most are shown, but the subsequent analysis is based on full precision.

TIME HORIZON

Mean–variance optimization is a "single-period" framework in which the single period could be a week, a month, a year, or some other time period. When working in a "strategic" setting, many practitioners typically find it most intuitive to work with annual capital market assumptions, even though the investment time horizon could be considerably longer (e.g., 10 years). If the strategic asset allocation will not be re-evaluated within a long time frame, capital market assumptions should reflect the average annual distributions of returns expected over the entire investment time horizon. In most cases, investors revisit the strategic asset allocation decision more frequently, such as annually or every three years, rerunning the analysis and making adjustments to the asset allocation; thus, the annual capital market assumption often reflects the expectations associated with the evaluation horizon (e.g., one year or three years).

Exhibit 1: Hypothetical UK-Based Investor's Opportunity Set with Expected Returns, Standard Deviations, and Correlations

Panel A: Expected Returns and Standard Deviations

Asset Class	Expected Return (%)	Standard Deviation (%)
UK large cap	6.6	14.8
UK mid cap	6.9	16.7
UK small cap	7.1	19.6
US equities	7.8	15.7
Europe ex UK equities	8.6	19.6
Asia Pacific ex Japan equities	8.5	20.9
Japan equities	6.4	15.2
Emerging market equities	9.0	23.0
Global REITs	9.0	22.5
Global ex UK bonds	4.0	10.4
UK bonds	2.9	6.1
Cash	2.5	0.7

4 The standard deviations and correlations in Exhibit 1 are based on historical numbers, while expected returns come from reverse optimization (described later).

Panel B: Correlations

	UK Large Cap	UK Mid Cap	UK Small Cap	US Equities	Europe ex UK Equities	Asia Pacific ex Japan Equities	Japan Equities	Emerging Market Equities	Global REITs	Global ex UK Bonds	UK Bonds	Cash
UK large cap	1.00	0.86	0.79	0.76	0.88	0.82	0.55	0.78	0.64	−0.12	−0.12	−0.06
UK mid cap	0.86	1.00	0.95	0.76	0.84	0.75	0.51	0.74	0.67	−0.16	−0.10	−0.17
UK small cap	0.79	0.95	1.00	0.67	0.79	0.70	0.49	0.71	0.61	−0.22	−0.15	−0.17
US equities	0.76	0.76	0.67	1.00	0.81	0.72	0.62	0.69	0.77	0.14	0.00	−0.12
Europe ex UK equities	0.88	0.84	0.79	0.81	1.00	0.82	0.60	0.80	0.72	0.04	−0.04	−0.03
Asia Pacific ex Japan equities	0.82	0.75	0.70	0.72	0.82	1.00	0.54	0.94	0.67	0.00	−0.02	0.02
Japan equities	0.55	0.51	0.49	0.62	0.60	0.54	1.00	0.56	0.52	0.18	0.07	−0.01
Emerging market equities	0.78	0.74	0.71	0.69	0.80	0.94	0.56	1.00	0.62	−0.02	−0.03	0.04
Global REITs	0.64	0.67	0.61	0.77	0.72	0.67	0.52	0.62	1.00	0.16	0.18	−0.15
Global ex UK bonds	−0.12	−0.16	−0.22	0.14	0.04	0.00	0.18	−0.02	0.16	1.00	0.62	0.24
UK bonds	−0.12	−0.10	−0.15	0.00	−0.04	−0.02	0.07	−0.03	0.18	0.62	1.00	0.07
Cash	−0.06	−0.17	−0.17	−0.12	−0.03	0.02	−0.01	0.04	−0.15	0.24	0.07	1.00

The classification of asset classes in the universe of available investments may vary according to local practices. For example, in the United States and some other larger markets, it is common to classify equities by market capitalization, whereas the practice of classifying equities by valuation ("growth" versus "value") is less common outside of the United States. Similarly, with regard to fixed income, some asset allocators may classify bonds based on various attributes—nominal versus inflation linked, corporate versus government issued, investment grade versus non-investment grade (high yield)—and/or by maturity/duration (short, intermediate, and long). By means of the non-negativity constraint and using a reverse-optimization procedure (to be explained later) based on asset class market values to generate expected return estimates, we control the typically high sensitivity of the composition of efficient portfolios to expected return estimates (discussed further in Sections 19 and 20). Without such precautions, we would often find that efficient portfolios are highly concentrated in a subset of the available asset classes.

Running this set of capital market assumptions through a mean–variance optimizer with the traditional non-negativity and unity constraints produces the efficient frontier depicted in Exhibit 2. We have augmented this efficient frontier with some non-traditional information that will assist with the understanding of some key concepts related to the efficient frontier. A risk-free return of 2.5% is used in calculating the reserve-optimized expected returns as well as the Sharpe ratios in Exhibit 2.

Exhibit 2: Efficient Frontier—Base Case

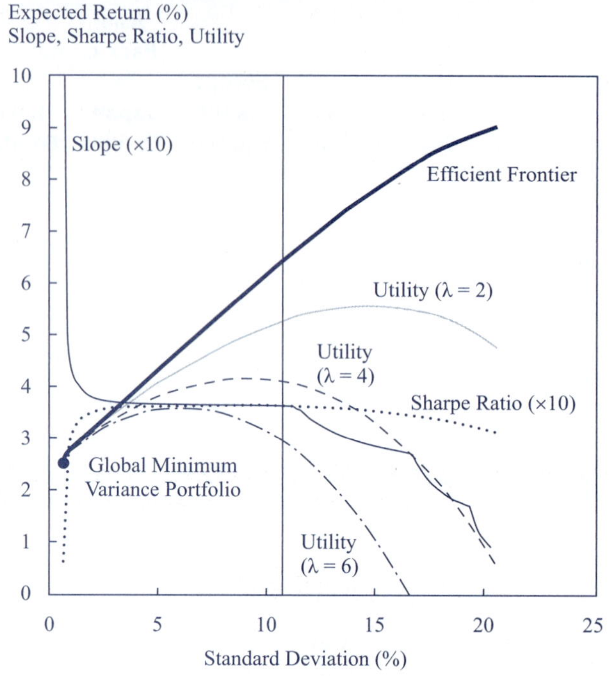

The slope of the efficient frontier is greatest at the far left of the efficient frontier, at the point representing the global minimum variance portfolio. Slope represents the rate at which expected return increases per increase in risk. As one moves to the right, in the direction of increasing risk, the slope decreases; it is lowest at the point representing the maximum return portfolio. Thus, as one moves from left to right along the efficient frontier, the investor takes on larger and larger amounts of risk for smaller and smaller increases in expected return. The "kinks" in the line representing the slope (times 10) of the efficient frontier correspond to portfolios (known as corner portfolios) in which an asset either enters or leaves the efficient mix.

For most investors, at the far left of the efficient frontier, the increases in expected return associated with small increases in expected risk represent a desirable trade-off. The risk aversion coefficient identifies the specific point on the efficient frontier at which the investor refuses to take on additional risk because he or she feels the associated increase in expected return is not high enough to compensate for the increase in risk. Of course, each investor makes this trade-off differently.

For this particular efficient frontier, the three expected utility curves plot the solution to Equation 1 for three different risk aversion coefficients: 2.0, 4.0, and 6.0, respectively.[5] For a given risk aversion coefficient, the appropriate efficient mix from the efficient frontier is simply the mix in which expected utility is highest (i.e., maximized). As illustrated in Exhibit 2, a lower risk aversion coefficient leads to a riskier (higher) point on the efficient frontier, while a higher risk aversion coefficient leads to a more conservative (lower) point on the efficient frontier.

The vertical line (at volatility of 10.88%) identifies the asset mix with the highest Sharpe ratio; it intersects the Sharpe ratio line at a value of 3.7 (an unscaled value of 0.37). This portfolio is also represented by the intersection of the slope line and the Sharpe ratio line.

5 Numbers have been rounded to increase readability.

Exhibit 3 is an efficient frontier asset allocation area graph. Each vertical cross section identifies the asset allocation at a point along the efficient frontier; thus, the vertical cross section at the far left, with nearly 100% cash, is the asset allocation of the minimum variance portfolio, and the vertical cross section at the far right, with 45% in emerging markets and 55% in global REITs, is the optimal asset allocation for a standard deviation of 20.5%, the highest level of portfolio volatility shown. In this example, cash is treated as a risky asset; although its return volatility is very low, because it is less than perfectly correlated with the other asset classes, mixing it with small amounts of other asset classes reduces risk further. The vertical line identifies the asset mix with the highest Sharpe ratio and corresponds to the similar line shown on the original efficient frontier graph (Exhibit 2). The asset allocation mixes are well diversified for most of the first half of the efficient frontier, and in fact, for a large portion of the efficient frontier, all 12 asset classes in our opportunity set receive a positive allocation.[6]

Exhibit 3: Efficient Frontier Asset Allocation Area Graph—Base Case

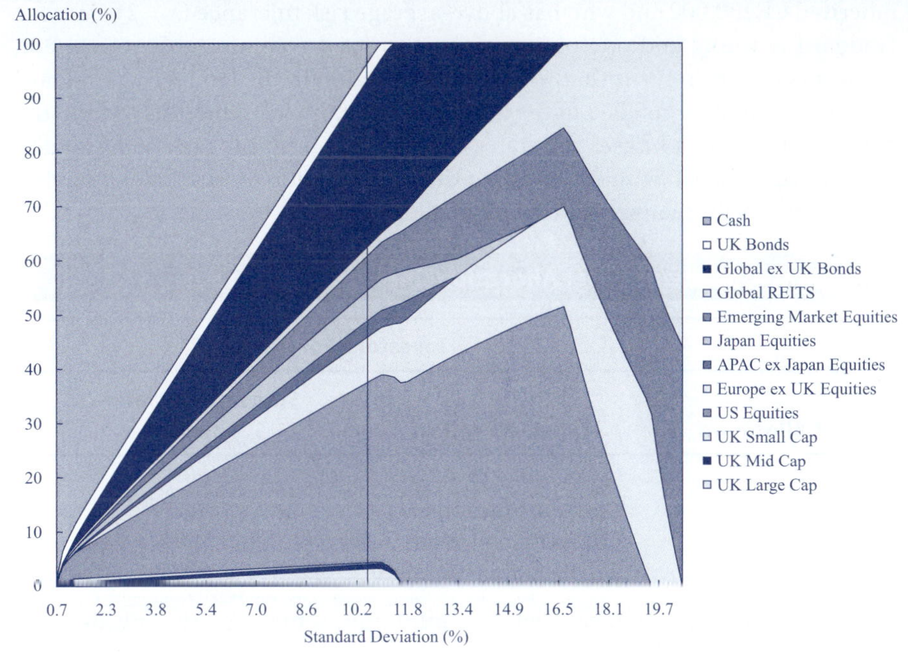

The investment characteristics of potential asset mixes based on mean–variance theory are often further investigated by means of Monte Carlo simulation, as discussed in Section 3. Several observations from theory and practice are relevant to narrowing the choices.

Equation 1 indicates that the basic approach to asset allocation involves estimating the investor's risk aversion parameter and then finding the efficient mix that maximizes expected utility. When the risk aversion coefficient has not been estimated, the investor may be able to identify the maximum tolerable level of portfolio return volatility. If

6 Studying Exhibit 3 closely, one notices distinct regime shifts where the rate at which allocations are made to asset classes changes so that a line segment with a different slope begins. These regime shifts occur at what are called *corner portfolios*. The efficient mixes between two adjacent corner portfolios are simply linear combinations of those portfolios. The efficient frontier asset allocation area graph helps to clarify this result. More formally, corner portfolios are points on the efficient frontier at which an asset class either enters or leaves the efficient mix or a constraint either becomes binding or is no longer binding.

that level is 10% per annum, for example, only the part of the efficient frontier associated with volatility less than or equal to 10% is relevant. This approach is justifiable because for a given efficient frontier, every value of the risk aversion coefficient can be associated with a value of volatility that identifies the best point on the efficient frontier for the investor; the investor may also have experience with thinking in terms of volatility. In addition, when the investor has a numerical return objective, he or she can further narrow the range of potential efficient mixes by identifying the efficient portfolios expected to meet that return objective. For example, if the return objective is 5%, one can select the asset allocation with a 5% expected return.

Example 1 illustrates the use of Equation 1 and shows the adaptability of MVO by introducing the choice problem in the context of an investor who also has a shortfall risk concern.

EXAMPLE 1

Mean–Variance-Efficient Portfolio Choice 1

An investment adviser is counseling Aimée Goddard, a client who recently inherited €1,200,000 and who has above-average risk tolerance ($\lambda = 2$). Because Goddard is young and one of her goals is to fund a comfortable retirement, she wants to earn returns that will outpace inflation in the long term. Goddard expects to liquidate €60,000 of the inherited portfolio in 12 months to fund the down payment on a house. She states that it is important for her to be able to take out the €60,000 without invading the initial capital of €1,200,000. Exhibit 4 shows three alternative strategic asset allocations.

Exhibit 4: Strategic Asset Allocation Choices for Goddard

	Investor's Forecasts	
Asset Allocation	**Expected Return**	**Standard Deviation of Return**
A	10.00%	20%
B	7.00	10
C	5.25	5

Note: In addressing 2, calculate the minimum return, R_L, that needs to be achieved to meet the investor's objective not to invade capital, using the expression ratio $[E(R_P) - R_L]/\sigma_P$, which reflects the probability of exceeding the minimum given a normal return distribution assumption in a safety-first approach.[7]

1. Based only on Goddard's risk-adjusted expected returns for the asset allocations, which asset allocation would she prefer?

   Solution:

   Using Equation 1,

7 See the Level I CFA Program reading "Common Probability Distributions" for coverage of Roy's safety-first criterion.

$$U_m = E(R_m) - 0.005\lambda\sigma_m^2$$
$$= E(R_m) - 0.005(2)\sigma_m^2$$
$$= E(R_m) - 0.01\sigma_m^2$$

So Goddard's utility for Asset Allocations A, B, and C are as follows:

$U_A = E(R_A) - 0.01\sigma_A^2$

$= 10.0 - 0.01(20)^2$

$= 10.0 - 4.0$

$= 6.0$ or 6.0%

$U_B = E(R_B) - 0.01\sigma_B^2$

$= 7.0 - 0.01(10)^2$

$= 7.0 - 1.0$

$= 6.0$ or 6.0%

$U_C = E(R_C) - 0.01\sigma_C^2$

$= 5.25 - 0.01(5)^2$

$= 5.25 - 0.25$

$= 5.0$ or 5.0%

Goddard would be indifferent between A and B based only on their common perceived certainty-equivalent return of 6%.

2. Recommend and justify a strategic asset allocation for Goddard.

Solution:

Because €60,000/€1,200,000 is 5.0%, for any return less than 5.0%, Goddard will need to invade principal when she liquidates €60,000. So 5% is a threshold return level.

To decide which of the three allocations is best for Goddard, we calculate the ratio $[E(R_P) - R_L]/\sigma_P$:

Allocation A: (10% – 5%)/20% = 0.25

Allocation B: (7% – 5%)/10% = 0.20

Allocation C: (5.25% – 5%)/5% = 0.05

Both Allocations A and B have the same expected utility, but Allocation A has a higher probability of meeting the threshold 5% return than Allocation B. Therefore, A would be the recommended strategic asset allocation.

There are several different approaches to determining an allocation to cash and cash equivalents, such as government bills. Exhibit 1 included cash among the assets for which we conducted an optimization to trace out an efficient frontier. The return to cash over a short time horizon is essentially certain in nominal terms. One approach to asset allocation separates out cash and cash equivalents as a (nominally) risk-free asset and calculates an efficient frontier of risky assets. Alternatively, a ray from the risk-free rate (a point on the return axis) tangent to the risky-asset efficient frontier (with cash excluded) then defines a linear efficient frontier. The efficient frontier then consists of combinations of the risk-free asset with the tangency portfolio (which has the highest Sharpe ratio among portfolios on the risky-asset efficient frontier).

A number of standard finance models (including Tobin two-fund separation) adopt this treatment of cash. According to two-fund separation, if investors can borrow or lend at the risk-free rate, they will choose the tangency portfolio for the risky-asset holdings and borrow at the risk-free rate to leverage the position in that portfolio to achieve a higher expected return, or they will split money between the tangency portfolio and the risk-free asset to reach a position with lower risk and lower expected return than that represented by the tangency portfolio. Since over horizons that are longer than the maturity of a money market instrument, the return earned would not be known, another approach that is well established in practice and reflected in Exhibit 1 is to include cash in the optimization. The amount of cash indicated by an optimization may be adjusted in light of short-term liquidity needs; for example, some financial advisers advocate that individuals hold an amount of cash equivalent to six months of expenses. All of these approaches are reasonable alternatives in practice.

Although we will treat cash as a risky asset in the following discussions, in Example 2, we stop to show the application of the alternative approach based on distinguishing a risk-free asset.

EXAMPLE 2

A Strategic Asset Allocation Based on Distinguishing a Nominal Risk-Free Asset

The Caflandia Foundation for the Fine Arts (CFFA) is a hypothetical charitable organization established to provide funding to Caflandia museums for their art acquisition programs.

CFFA's overall investment objective is to maintain its portfolio's real purchasing power after distributions. CFFA targets a 4% annual distribution of assets. CFFA has the following current specific investment policies.

Return objective

CFFA's assets shall be invested with the objective of earning an average nominal 6.5% annual return. This level reflects a spending rate of 4%, an expected inflation rate of 2%, and a 40 bp cost of earning investment returns. The calculation is (1.04)(1.02)(1.004) – 1 = 0.065, or 6.5%.

Risk considerations

CFFA's assets shall be invested to minimize the level of standard deviation of return subject to satisfying the expected return objective.

The investment office of CFFA distinguishes a nominally risk-free asset. As of the date of the optimization, the risk-free rate is determined to be 2.2%.

Exhibit 5 gives key outputs from a mean–variance optimization in which asset class weights are constrained to be non-negative.

Exhibit 5: Corner Portfolios Defining the Risky-Asset Efficient Frontier

Portfolio Number	Expected Nominal Returns	Standard Deviation	Sharpe Ratio
1	9.50%	18.00%	0.406
2	8.90	15.98	0.419

Portfolio Number	Expected Nominal Returns	Standard Deviation	Sharpe Ratio
3	8.61	15.20	0.422
4	7.24	11.65	0.433
5	5.61	7.89	0.432
6	5.49	7.65	0.430
7	3.61	5.39	0.262

The portfolios shown are corner portfolios (see footnote 6), which as a group define the risky-asset efficient frontier in the sense that any portfolio on the frontier is a combination of the two corner portfolios that bracket it in terms of expected return.

1. Based only on the facts given, determine the most appropriate strategic asset allocation for CFFA given its stated investment policies.

Solution:

An 85%/15% combination of Portfolio 4 and the risk-free asset is the most appropriate asset allocation. This combination has the required 6.5% expected return with the minimum level of risk. Stated another way, this combination defines the efficient portfolio at a 6.5% level of expected return based on the linear efficient frontier created by the introduction of a risk-free asset. Note that Portfolio 4 has the highest Sharpe ratio and is closest to the tangency portfolio. With an expected return of 7.24%, it can be combined with the risk-free asset, with a return of 2.2%, to achieve an expected return of 6.5%:

$$6.50 = 7.24w + 2.2(1 - w)$$

$$w = 0.853$$

Placing about 85% of assets in Portfolio 4 and 15% in the risk-free asset achieves an efficient portfolio with expected return of 6.5 with a volatility of 0.853(11.65) = 9.94%. (The risk-free asset has no return volatility by assumption and, also by assumption, zero correlation with any risky portfolio return.) This portfolio lies on a linear efficient frontier formed by a ray from the risk-free rate to the tangency portfolio and can be shown to have the same Sharpe ratio as the tangency portfolio, 0.433. The combination of Portfolio 4 with Portfolio 5 to achieve a 6.5% expected return would have a lower Sharpe ratio and would not lie on the efficient frontier.

Asset allocation decisions have traditionally been made considering only the investor's investment portfolio (and financial liabilities) and not the total picture that includes human capital and other non-traded assets (and liabilities), which are missing in a traditional balance sheet. Taking such extended assets and liabilities into account can lead to improved asset allocation decisions, however.

Depending on the nature of an individual's career, human capital can provide relatively stable cash flows similar to bond payments. At the other extreme, the cash flows from human capital can be much more volatile and uncertain, reflecting a lumpy, commission-based pay structure or perhaps a career in a seasonal business. For many individuals working in stable job markets, the cash flows associated with their human capital are somewhat like those of an inflation-linked bond, relatively consistent and tending to increase with inflation. If human capital is a relatively large component of the individual's total economic worth, accounting for this type of hidden asset in an asset allocation setting is extremely important and would presumably increase the individual's capacity to take on risk.

Let us look at a hypothetical example. Emma Beel is a 45-year-old tenured university professor in London. Capital market assumptions are as before (see Exhibit 1). Beel has GBP 1,500,000 in liquid financial assets, largely due to a best-selling book. Her employment as a tenured university professor is viewed as very secure and produces cash flows that resemble those of a very large, inflation-adjusted, long-duration bond portfolio. The net present value of her human capital is estimated at GBP 500,000. Beel inherited her grandmother's home on the edge of the city, valued at GBP 750,000. The results of a risk tolerance questionnaire that considers both risk preference and risk capacity suggest that Beel should have an asset allocation involving moderate risk. Furthermore, given our earlier assumption that the collective market risk aversion coefficient is 4.0, we assume that the risk aversion coefficient of a moderately risk-averse investor is approximately 4.0, from a total wealth perspective.

To account for Beel's human capital and residential real estate, these two asset classes were modeled and added to the optimization. Beel's human capital of GBP 500,000 was modeled as 70% UK long-duration inflation-linked bonds, 15% UK corporate bonds, and 15% UK equities.[8] Residential real estate was modeled based on a de-smoothed residential property index for London. (We will leave the complexities of modeling liabilities to Sections 10–14.) Beel's assets include those shown in Exhibit 6.

Exhibit 6: Emma Beel's Assets

Asset	Value (GBP)	Percentage
Liquid financial assets	1,500,000	54.55
UK residential real estate	750,000	27.27
Human capital	500,000	18.18
	2,750,000	100

Beel's UK residential real estate (representing the London house) and human capital were added to the optimization opportunity set. Additionally, working under the assumption that Beel's house and human capital are non-tradable assets, the optimizer was forced to allocate 27.27% or more to UK residential real estate and 18.18% to human capital and then determined the optimal asset allocation based on a risk aversion coefficient of 4. Beel's expected utility is maximized by an efficient asset allocation with volatility of approximately 8.2%. Exhibit 7 displays the resulting asset allocation area graph.

8 These weights were used to create the return composite representing Beel's human capital that was used in the asset allocation optimization.

Exhibit 7: Efficient Frontier Asset Allocation Area Graph—Balance Sheet Approach

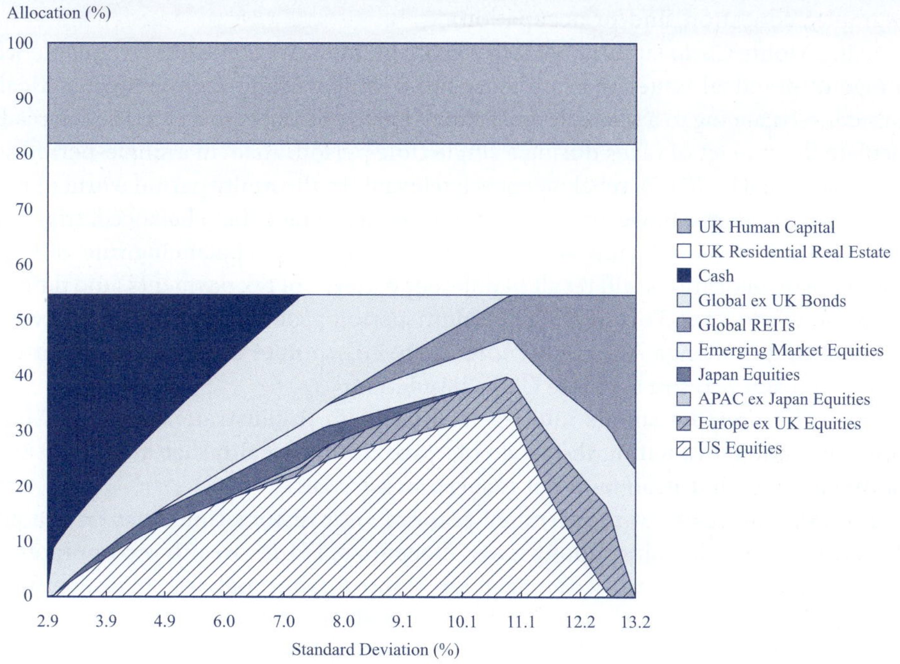

Looking past the constrained allocations to human capital and UK residential real estate, the remaining allocations associated with Beel's liquid financial assets do not include UK equities or UK fixed income. Each of these three asset classes is relatively highly correlated with either UK residential real estate or UK human capital.[9]

MONTE CARLO SIMULATION

3

- ☐ discuss the use of Monte Carlo simulation and scenario analysis to evaluate the robustness of an asset allocation
- ☐ recommend and justify an asset allocation using mean–variance optimization

Monte Carlo simulation complements MVO by addressing the limitations of MVO as a single-period framework. Additionally, in the case in which the investor's risk tolerance is either unknown or in need of further validation, Monte Carlo simulation can help paint a realistic picture of potential future outcomes, including the likelihood of meeting various goals, the distribution of the portfolio's expected value through time, and potential maximum drawdowns. Simulation also provides a tool for investigating the effects of trading/rebalancing costs and taxes and the interaction of evolving financial markets with asset allocation. It is important to note that not all Monte Carlo simulation tools are the same: They vary significantly in their ability

9 For additional information on applying a total balance sheet approach, see, for example, Blanchett and Straehl (2015) or Rudd and Siegel (2013).

to model non-normal multivariate returns, serial and cross-correlations, tax rates, distribution requirements, an evolving asset allocation schedule (target-date glide path), non-traditional investments (e.g., annuities), and human capital (based on age, geography, education, and/or occupation).

Using Monte Carlo simulation, an investment adviser can effectively grapple with a range of practical issues that are difficult or impossible to formulate analytically. Consider rebalancing to a strategic asset allocation for a taxable investor. We can readily calculate the impact of taxes during a single time period. Also, in a single-period setting, as assumed by MVO, rebalancing is irrelevant. In the multi-period world of most investment problems, however, the portfolio will predictably be rebalanced, triggering the realization of capital gains and losses. Given a specific rebalancing rule, different strategic asset allocations will result in different patterns of tax payments (and different transaction costs too). Formulating the multi-period problem mathematically would be a daunting challenge. We could more easily incorporate the interaction between rebalancing and taxes in a Monte Carlo simulation.

We will examine a simple multi-period problem to illustrate the use of Monte Carlo simulation, evaluating the range of outcomes for wealth that may result from a strategic asset allocation (and not incorporating taxes).

The value of wealth at the terminal point of an investor's time horizon is a possible criterion for choosing among asset allocations. Future wealth incorporates the interaction of risk and return. The need for Monte Carlo simulation in evaluating an asset allocation depends on whether there are cash flows into or out of the portfolio over time. For a given asset allocation with no cash flows, the sequence of returns is irrelevant; ending wealth will be path independent (unaffected by the sequence or path of returns through time). With cash flows, the sequence is also irrelevant if simulated returns are independent, identically distributed random variables. We could find expected terminal wealth and percentiles of terminal wealth analytically.[10] Investors save/deposit money in and spend money out of their portfolios; thus, in the more typical case, terminal wealth is path dependent (the sequence of returns matters) because of the interaction of cash flows and returns. When terminal wealth is path dependent, an analytical approach is not feasible but Monte Carlo simulation is. Example 3 applies Monte Carlo simulation to evaluate the strategic asset allocation of an investor who regularly withdraws from the portfolio.

EXAMPLE 3

Monte Carlo Simulation for a Retirement Portfolio with a Proposed Asset Allocation

Malala Ali, a resident of the hypothetical country of Caflandia, has sought the advice of an investment adviser concerning her retirement portfolio. At the end of 2017, she is 65 years old and holds a portfolio valued at CAF$1 million. Ali would like to withdraw CAF$40,000 a year to supplement the corporate pension she has begun to receive. Given her health and family history, Ali believes she should plan for a retirement lasting 25 years. She is also concerned about passing along a portion of her portfolio to the families of her three children; she hopes that at least the portfolio's current real value can go to them. Consulting with her adviser, Ali has expressed this desire quantitatively: She wants the median value of her bequest to her children to be no less than her portfolio's current value of CAF$1 million in real terms. The median is the 50th percentile outcome.

10 Making a plausible statistical assumption, such as a lognormal distribution, for ending wealth.

The asset allocation of her retirement portfolio is currently 50/50 Caflandia equities/Caflandia intermediate-term government bonds. Ali and her adviser have decided on the following set of capital market expectations (Exhibit 8):

Exhibit 8: Caflandia Capital Market Expectations

	Investor's Forecasts	
Asset Class	**Expected Return**	**Standard Deviation of Return**
Caflandia equities	9.4%	20.4%
Caflandia bonds	5.6%	4.1%
Inflation	2.6%	

The predicted correlation between returns of Caflandia equities and Caflandia intermediate-term government bonds is 0.15.

With the current asset allocation, the expected nominal return on Ali's retirement portfolio is 7.5% with a standard deviation of 11%. Exhibit 9 gives the results of the Monte Carlo simulation.[11] In Exhibit 9, the lowest curve represents, at various ages, levels of real wealth at or below which the 10% of worst real wealth outcomes lie (i.e., the 10th percentile for real wealth); curves above that represent, respectively, 25th, 50th, 75th, and 90th percentiles for real wealth.

Exhibit 9: Monte Carlo Simulation of Ending Real Wealth with Annual Cash Outflows

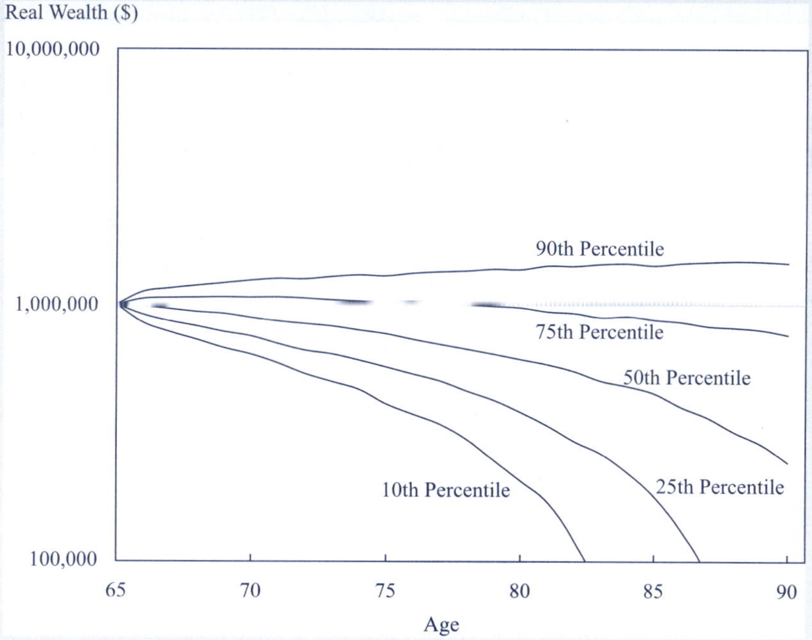

Based on the information given, address the following:

11 Note that the y-axis in this exhibit is specified using a logarithmic scale. The quantity CAF\$1 million is the same distance from CAF\$100,000 as CAF\$10 million is from CAF\$1 million because CAF\$1 million is 10 times CAF\$100,000, just as CAF\$10 million is 10 times CAF\$1 million. CAF\$100,000 is 10^5, and CAF \$1 million is 10^6. In Exhibit 9, a distance halfway between the CAF\$100,000 and CAF\$1 million hatch marks is $10^{5.5}$ = CAF\$316,228.

1. Justify the presentation of ending wealth in terms of real rather than nominal wealth in Exhibit 9.

   Solution:

   Ali wants the median real value of her bequest to her children to be "no less than her portfolio's current value of CAF$1 million." We need to state future amounts in terms of today's values (i.e., in real dollars) to assess the purchasing power of those amounts relative to CAF$1 million today. Exhibit 9 thus gives the results of the Monte Carlo simulation in real dollar terms. The median real wealth at age 90 is clearly well below the target ending wealth of real CAF$1 million.

2. Is the current asset allocation expected to satisfy Ali's investment objectives?

   Solution:

   From Exhibit 9, we see that the median terminal (at age 90) value of the retirement portfolio in real dollars is less than the stated bequest goal of CAF$1 million. Therefore, the most likely bequest is less than the amount Ali has said she wants. The current asset allocation is not expected to satisfy all her investment objectives. Although one potential lever would be to invest more aggressively, given Ali's age and risk tolerance, this approach seems imprudent. An adviser may need to counsel that the desired size of the bequest may be unrealistic given Ali's desired income to support her expenditures. Ali will likely need to make a relatively tough choice between her living standard (spending less) and her desire to leave a CAF$1 million bequest in real terms. A third alternative would be to delay retirement, which may or may not be feasible.

4 CRITICISMS OF MEAN–VARIANCE OPTIMIZATION

☐ describe and evaluate the use of mean–variance optimization in asset allocation

With this initial understanding of mean–variance optimization, we can now elaborate on some of the most common criticisms of it. The following criticisms and the ways they have been addressed motivate the balance of the coverage of MVO:

1. The outputs (asset allocations) are highly sensitive to small changes in the inputs.
2. The asset allocations tend to be highly concentrated in a subset of the available asset classes.
3. Many investors are concerned about more than the mean and variance of returns, the focus of MVO.
4. Although the asset allocations may appear diversified across assets, the sources of risk may not be diversified.
5. Most portfolios exist to pay for a liability or consumption series, and MVO allocations are not directly connected to what influences the value of the liability or the consumption series.
6. MVO is a single-period framework that does not take account of trading/rebalancing costs and taxes.

In the rest of Sections 2–9, we look at various approaches to addressing criticisms 1 and 2, giving some attention also to criticisms 3 and 4. Sections 10–18 present approaches to addressing criticism 5. “Asset Allocation with Real World Constraints” addresses some aspects of criticism 6.

It is important to understand that the first criticism above is not unique to MVO. Any optimization model that uses forward-looking quantities as inputs faces similar consequences of treating input values as capable of being determined with certainty. Sensitivity to errors in inputs is a problem that cannot be fully solved because it is inherent in the structure of optimization models that use as inputs forecasts of uncertain quantities.

To illustrate the importance of the quality of inputs, the sensitivity of asset weights in efficient portfolios to small changes in inputs, and the propensity of mean–variance optimization to allocate to a relatively small subset of the available asset classes, we made changes to the expected return of two asset classes in our base-case UK-centric opportunity set in Exhibit 1. We increased the expected return of Asia Pacific ex Japan equities from 8.5% to 9.0% and decreased the expected return of Europe ex UK equities from 8.6% to 8.1% (both changes are approximately 50 bps). We left all of the other inputs unchanged and reran the optimization. The efficient frontier as depicted in mean–variance space appears virtually unchanged (not shown); however, the efficient asset mixes of this new efficient frontier are dramatically different. Exhibit 10 displays the efficient frontier asset allocation area graph based on the slightly changed capital market assumptions. Notice the dramatic difference between Exhibit 10 and Exhibit 3. The small change in return assumptions has driven UK large cap, Europe ex-UK equities, and emerging market equities out of the efficient mixes, and the efficient mixes are now highly concentrated in a smaller subset of the available asset classes. Given that the expected returns of UK large cap and emerging market equities were unchanged, their disappearance from the efficient frontier is not intuitive.

Exhibit 10: Efficient Frontier Asset Allocation Area Graph—Changed Expected Returns

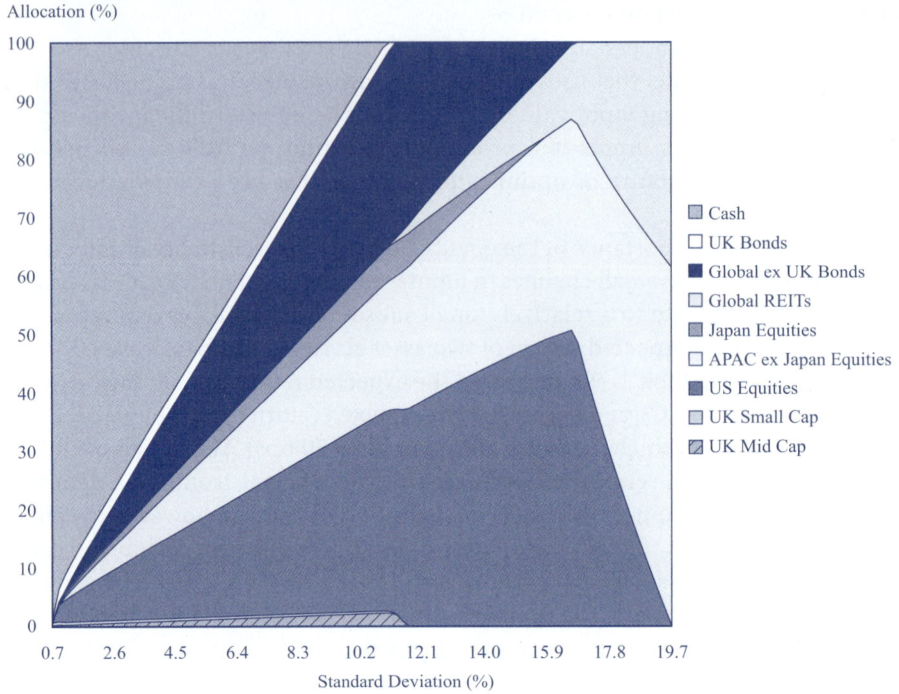

To aid with the comparison of Exhibit 10 with Exhibit 3, we identified three specific efficient asset allocation mixes and compared the version based on the ad hoc modification of expected returns to that of the base case. This comparison is shown in Exhibit 11.

Exhibit 11: Comparison of Select Efficient Asset Allocations—Ad Hoc Return Modification Allocations vs. Base-Case Allocations

	Modified 25/75	Base Case 25/75	Difference	Modified 50/50	Base Case 50/50	Difference	Modified 75/25	Base Case 75/25	Difference
UK large cap	0.0%	1.2%	−1.2%	0.0%	2.5%	−2.5%	0.0%	0.0%	0.0%
UK mid cap	0.8%	0.6%	0.3%	1.7%	0.8%	0.9%	0.0%	0.0%	0.0%
UK small cap	0.5%	0.5%	−0.1%	0.4%	0.4%	0.0%	0.0%	0.0%	0.0%
US equities	13.7%	13.8%	−0.1%	26.6%	26.8%	−0.2%	40.1%	40.5%	−0.4%
Europe ex UK equities	0.0%	2.7%	−2.7%	0.0%	6.5%	−6.5%	0.0%	13.2%	−13.2%
Asia Pacific ex Japan equities	7.5%	1.0%	6.5%	16.6%	2.3%	14.2%	26.8%	1.5%	25.3%
Japan equities	2.2%	2.3%	−0.1%	4.5%	4.5%	0.0%	4.4%	4.3%	0.1%
Emerging market equities	0.0%	2.0%	−2.0%	0.0%	4.9%	−4.9%	0.0%	10.0%	−10.0%
Global REITs	0.3%	0.9%	−0.6%	0.2%	1.4%	−1.3%	3.8%	5.6%	−1.8%

	Modified 25/75	Base Case 25/75	Difference	Modified 50/50	Base Case 50/50	Difference	Modified 75/25	Base Case 75/25	Difference
Global ex UK bonds	10.9%	10.6%	0.3%	24.7%	23.9%	0.7%	25.0%	25.0%	0.0%
UK bonds	2.5%	2.7%	−0.2%	2.4%	3.0%	−0.6%	0.0%	0.0%	0.0%
Cash	61.6%	61.7%	−0.1%	22.9%	23.1%	−0.1%	0.0%	0.0%	0.0%
Subtotal equities	25.0%	25.0%		50.0%	50.0%		75.0%	75.0%	
Subtotal fixed income	75.0%	75.0%		50.0%	50.0%		25.0%	25.0%	

ADDRESSING THE CRITICISMS OF MEAN–VARIANCE OPTIMIZATION

5

☐ describe and evaluate the use of mean–variance optimization in asset allocation

In this section, we explore several methods for overcoming some of the potential short-comings of mean–variance optimization. Techniques that address the first two criticisms mostly take three approaches: improving the quality of inputs, constraining the optimization, and treating the efficient frontier as a statistical construct. These approaches are treated in the following three subsections.

In MVO, the composition of efficient portfolios is typically more sensitive to expected return estimates than it is to estimates of volatilities and correlations. Furthermore, expected returns are generally more difficult to estimate accurately than are volatilities and correlations. Thus, in addressing the first criticism of MVO—that outputs are highly sensitive to small changes in inputs—the reading will focus on expected return inputs. However, volatility and correlation inputs are also sources of potential error.

Reverse Optimization

Reverse optimization is a powerful tool that helps explain the implied returns associated with any portfolio. It can be used to estimate expected returns for use in a forward-looking optimization. MVO solves for optimal asset weights based on expected returns, covariances, and a risk aversion coefficient. Based on predetermined inputs, an optimizer solves for the optimal asset allocation weights. As the name implies, *reverse* optimization works in the opposite direction. Reverse optimization takes as its inputs a set of asset allocation weights *that are assumed to be optimal* and, with the additional inputs of covariances and the risk aversion coefficient, solves for expected returns. These reverse-optimized returns are sometimes referred to as implied or imputed returns.

When using reverse optimization to estimate a set of expected returns for use in a forward-looking optimization, the most common set of starting weights is the observed market-capitalization value of the assets or asset classes that form the opportunity set. The market capitalization of a given asset or asset classes should reflect the collective information of market participants. In representing the world market portfolio, the use of non-overlapping asset classes representing the majority of the world's investable assets is most consistent with theory.

Some practitioners will find the link between reverse optimization and CAPM equilibrium elegant, while others will see it as a shortcoming. For those who truly object to the use of market-capitalization weights in estimating inputs, the mechanics of reverse optimization can work with any set of starting weights—such as those of an existing policy portfolio, the average asset allocation policy of a peer group, or a fundamental weighting scheme. For those with more minor objections, we will shortly introduce the Black–Litterman model, which allows the expression of alternative forecasts or views.

In order to apply reverse optimization, one must create a working version of the all-inclusive market portfolio based on the constituents of the opportunity set. The market size or capitalization for most of the traditional stock and bond asset classes can be easily inferred from the various indexes that are used as asset class proxies. Many broad market-capitalization-weighted indexes report that they comprise over 95% of the securities, by market capitalization, of the asset classes they are attempting to represent. Exhibit 12 lists approximate values and weights for the 12 asset classes in our opportunity set, uses the weights associated with the asset classes to form a working version of the global market portfolio, and then uses the beta of each asset relative to our working version of the global market portfolio to infer what expected returns would be if all assets were priced by the CAPM according to their market beta. We assume a risk-free rate of 2.5% and a global market risk premium of 4%. Note that expected returns are rounded to one decimal place from the more precise values shown later (in Exhibit 13); expected returns cannot in every case be exactly reproduced based on Exhibit 12 alone because of the approximations mentioned. Also, notice in the final row of Exhibit 12 that the weighted average return and beta of the assets are 6.5% and 1, respectively.

Exhibit 12: Reverse-Optimization Example (Market Capitalization in £ billions)

Asset Class	Mkt Cap	Weight	Return $E[R_i]$		Risk-Free Rate r_f		Beta $\beta_{i,mkt}$	Market Risk Premium
UK large cap	£1,354.06	3.2%	6.62%	=	2.5%	+	1.03	(4%)
UK mid cap	£369.61	0.9%	6.92%	=	2.5%	+	1.11	(4%)
UK small cap	£108.24	0.3%	7.07%	=	2.5%	+	1.14	(4%)
US equities	£14,411.66	34.4%	7.84%	=	2.5%	+	1.33	(4%)
Europe ex UK equities	£3,640.48	8.7%	8.63%	=	2.5%	+	1.53	(4%)
Asia Pacific ex Japan equities	£1,304.81	3.1%	8.51%	=	2.5%	+	1.50	(4%)
Japan equities	£2,747.63	6.6%	6.43%	=	2.5%	+	0.98	(4%)
Emerging market equities	£2,448.60	5.9%	8.94%	=	2.5%	+	1.61	(4%)
Global REITs	£732.65	1.8%	9.04%	=	2.5%	+	1.64	(4%)
Global ex UK bonds	£13,318.58	31.8%	4.05%	=	2.5%	+	0.39	(4%)
UK bonds	£1,320.71	3.2%	2.95%	=	2.5%	+	0.112	(4%)
Cash	£83.00	0.2%	2.50%	=	2.5%	+	0.00	(4%)
	£41,840.04	100.0%	6.50%				1	

Notes: For the Mkt Cap and Weight columns, the final row is the simple sum. For the Return and Beta columns, the final row is the weighted average.

Looking back at our original asset allocation area graph (Exhibit 3), the reason for the well-behaved and well-diversified asset allocation mixes is now clear. By using reverse optimization, we are consistently relating assets' expected returns to their systematic risk. If there isn't a consistent relationship between the expected return and systematic risk, the optimizer will see this inconsistency as an opportunity and seek to take advantage of the more attractive attributes. This effect was clearly visible in our second asset allocation area graph after we altered the expected returns of Asia Pacific ex Japan equities and Europe ex UK equities.

As alluded to earlier, some practitioners find that the reverse-optimization process leads to a nice starting point, but they often have alternative forecasts or views regarding the expected return of one or more of the asset classes that differ from the returns implied by reverse optimization based on market-capitalization weights. One example of having views that differ from the reverse-optimized returns has already been illustrated, when we altered the returns of Asia Pacific ex Japan equities and Europe ex UK equities by approximately 50 bps. Unfortunately, due to the sensitivity of mean–variance optimization to small changes in inputs, directly altering the expected returns caused relatively extreme and unintuitive changes in the resulting asset allocations. If one has strong views on expected returns that differ from the reverse-optimized returns, an alternative or additional approach is needed; the next section presents one alternative.

Black–Litterman Model

A complementary addition to reverse optimization is the Black–Litterman model, created by Fischer Black and Robert Litterman (see Black and Litterman 1990, 1991, 1992). Although the Black–Litterman model is often characterized as an asset allocation model, it is really a model for deriving a set of expected returns that can be used in an unconstrained or constrained optimization setting. The Black–Litterman model starts with excess returns (in excess of the risk-free rate) produced from reverse optimization and then provides a technique for altering reverse-optimized expected returns in such a way that they reflect an investor's own distinctive views yet still behave well in an optimizer.

The Black–Litterman model has helped make the mean–variance optimization framework more useful. It enables investors to combine their unique forecasts of expected returns with reverse-optimized returns in an elegant manner. When coupled with a mean–variance or related framework, the resulting Black–Litterman expected returns often lead to well-diversified asset allocations by improving the consistency between each asset class's expected return and its contribution to systematic risk. These asset allocations are grounded in economic reality—via the market capitalization of the assets typically used in the reverse-optimization process—but still reflect the information contained in the investor's unique forecasts (or views) of expected return.

The mathematical details of the Black–Litterman model are beyond the scope of this reading, but many practitioners have access to asset allocation software that includes the Black–Litterman model.[12] To assist with an intuitive understanding of the model and to show the model's ability to blend new information (views) with reverse-optimized returns, we present an example based on the earlier views regarding the expected returns of Asia Pacific ex Japan equities and Europe ex UK equities. The Black–Litterman model has two methods for accepting views: one in which an absolute return forecast is associated with a given asset class and one in which the return differential of an asset (or group of assets) is expressed relative to another asset

12 For those interested in the mathematical details of the Black–Litterman model, see Idzorek (2007); a pre-publication version is available here: http://corporate.morningstar.com/ib/documents/MethodologyDocuments/IBBAssociates/BlackLitterman.pdf).

(or group of assets). Using the relative view format of the Black–Litterman model, we expressed the view that we believe Asia Pacific ex Japan equities will outperform Europe ex UK equities by 100 bps. We placed this view into the Black–Litterman model, which blends reverse-optimized returns with such views to create a new, mixed estimate.

Exhibit 13 compares the Black–Litterman model returns to the original reverse-optimized returns (as in Exhibit 12 but showing returns to the second decimal place based on calculations with full precision). The model accounts for the correlations of the assets with each other, and as one might expect, all of the returns change slightly (the change in return on cash was extremely small).

Exhibit 13: Comparison of Black–Litterman and Reverse-Optimized Returns

Asset Class	Reverse-Optimized Returns	Black–Litterman Returns	Difference
UK large cap	6.62%	6.60%	−0.02%
UK mid cap	6.92	6.87	−0.05
UK small cap	7.08	7.03	−0.05
US equities	7.81	7.76	−0.05
Europe ex UK equities	8.62	8.44	−0.18
Asia Pacific ex Japan equities	8.53	8.90	0.37
Japan equities	6.39	6.37	−0.02
Emerging market equities	8.96	9.30	0.33
Global REITs	9.02	9.00	−0.01
Global ex UK bonds	4.03	4.00	−0.03
UK bonds	2.94	2.95	0.01
Cash	2.50	2.50	0.00

Next, we created another efficient frontier asset allocation area graph based on these new returns from the Black–Litterman model, as shown in Exhibit 14. The allocations look relatively similar to those depicted in Exhibit 3. However, if you compare the allocations to Asia Pacific ex Japan equities and Europe ex UK equities to their allocations in the original efficient frontier asset allocation graph, you will notice that allocations to Asia Pacific ex Japan equities have increased across the frontier and allocations to Europe ex UK equities have decreased across the frontier with very little impact on the other asset allocations.

Exhibit 14: Efficient Frontier Asset Allocation Area Graph, Black–Litterman Returns

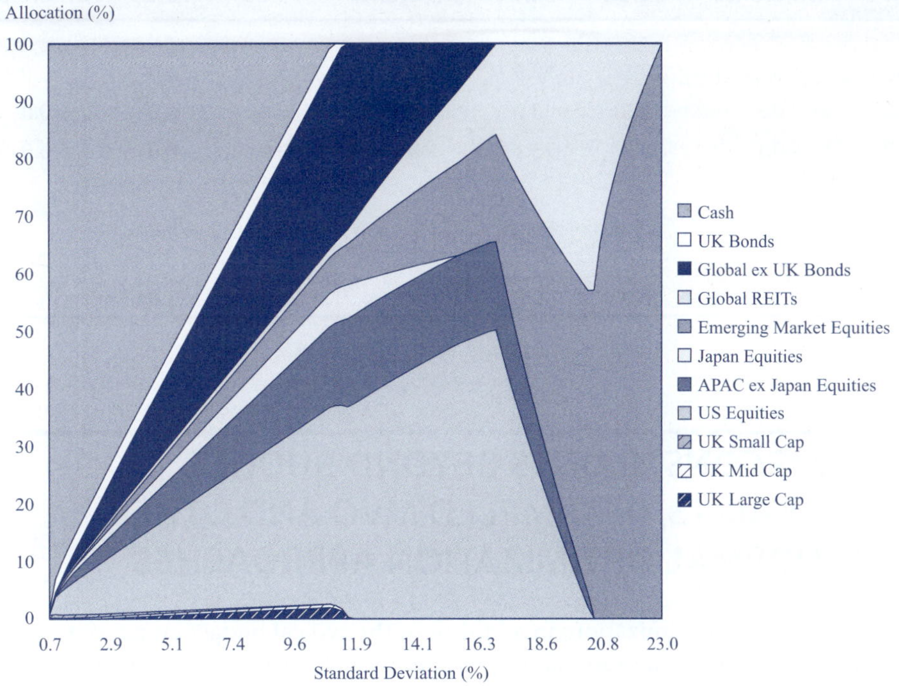

As before, to aid in the comparison of Exhibit 14 (Black–Litterman allocations) with Exhibit 3 (the base-case allocations), we identified three specific mixes in Exhibit 14 and compared those efficient asset allocation mixes based on the expected returns from the Black–Litterman model to those of the base case. The results are shown in Exhibit 15.

Exhibit 15: Comparison of Select Efficient Asset Allocations, Black–Litterman Allocations vs. Base-Case Allocations

	Modified 25/75	Base Case 25/75	Difference	Modified 50/50	Base Case 50/50	Difference	Modified 75/25	Base Case 75/25	Difference
UK large cap	0.4%	1.2%	−0.8%	1.4%	2.5%	−1.1%	0.0%	0.0%	0.0%
UK mid cap	0.4	0.6	−0.2	0.5	0.8	−0.3	0.0	0.0	0.0
UK small cap	0.4	0.5	−0.1	0.2	0.4	−0.2	0.0	0.0	0.0
US equities	13.8	13.8	0.0	26.8	26.8	0.0	40.0	40.5	−0.5
Europe ex UK equities	0.0	2.7	−2.7	0.0	6.5	−6.5	0.0	13.2	−13.2
Asia Pacific ex Japan equities	5.2	1.0	4.2	10.8	2.3	8.5	15.4	1.5	14.0
Japan equities	2.2	2.3	0.0	4.5	4.5	0.0	4.2	4.3	−0.1
Emerging market equities	1.8	2.0	−0.1	4.6	4.9	−0.2	9.8	10.0	−0.1
Global REITs	0.8	0.9	−0.1	1.3	1.4	−0.2	5.5	5.6	−0.1

	Modified 25/75	Base Case 25/75	Difference	Modified 50/50	Base Case 50/50	Difference	Modified 75/25	Base Case 75/25	Difference
Global ex UK bonds	10.3	10.6	−0.2	23.6	23.9	−0.3	25.0	25.0	0.0
UK bonds	3.1	2.7	0.3	3.5	3.0	0.5	0.0	0.0	0.0
Cash	61.6	61.7	−0.1	22.9	23.1	−0.1	0.0	0.0	0.0
Subtotal equities	25.0%	25.0%		50.0%	50.0%		75.0%	75.0%	
Subtotal fixed income	75.0%	75.0%		50.0%	50.0%		25.0%	25.0%	

6 ADDING CONSTRAINTS BEYOND BUDGET CONSTRAINTS, RESAMPLED MVO AND OTHER NON-NORMAL OPTIMIZATION APPROACHES

When running an optimization, in addition to the typical budget constraint and the non-negativity constraint, one can impose additional constraints. There are two primary reasons practitioners typically apply additional constraints: (1) to incorporate real-world constraints into the optimization problem and (2) to help overcome some of the potential shortcomings of mean–variance optimization elaborated above (input quality, input sensitivity, and highly concentrated allocations).

Most commercial optimizers accommodate a wide range of constraints. Typical constraints include the following:

1. Specify a set allocation to a specific asset—for example, 30% to real estate or 45% to human capital. This kind of constraint is typically used when one wants to include a non-tradable asset in the asset allocation decision and optimize around the non-tradable asset.
2. Specify an asset allocation range for an asset—for example, the emerging market allocation must be between 5% and 20%. This specification could be used to accommodate a constraint created by an investment policy, or it might reflect the user's desire to control the output of the optimization.
3. Specify an upper limit, due to liquidity considerations, on an alternative asset class, such as private equity or hedge funds.
4. Specify the relative allocation of two or more assets—for example, the allocation to emerging market equities must be less than the allocation to developed equities.
5. In a liability-relative (or surplus) optimization setting, one can constrain the optimizer to hold one or more assets representing the systematic characteristics of the liability short. (We elaborate on this scenario in Sections 10–14.)

In general, good constraints are those that model the actual circumstances/context in which one is attempting to set asset allocation policy. In contrast, constraints that are simply intended to control the output of a mean–variance optimization should be used cautiously. A perceived need to add constraints to control the MVO output would suggest a need to revisit one's inputs. If a very large number of constraints are imposed, one is no longer optimizing but rather specifying an asset allocation through a series of binding constraints.

Resampled Mean–Variance Optimization

Another technique used by asset allocators is called resampled mean–variance optimization (or sometimes "resampling" for short).[13] Resampled mean–variance optimization combines Markowitz's mean–variance optimization framework with Monte Carlo simulation and, all else equal, leads to more-diversified asset allocations. In contrast to reverse optimization, the Black–Litterman model, and constraints, resampled mean–variance optimization is an attempt to build a better optimizer that recognizes that forward-looking inputs are inherently subject to error.

Resampling uses Monte Carlo simulation to estimate a large number of potential capital market assumptions for mean–variance optimization and, eventually, for the resampled frontier. Conceptually, resampling is a large-scale sensitivity analysis in which hundreds or perhaps thousands of variations on baseline capital market assumptions lead to an equal number of mean–variance optimization frontiers based on the Monte Carlo–generated capital market assumptions. These intermediate frontiers are referred to as simulated frontiers. The resulting asset allocations, or portfolio weights, from these simulated frontiers are saved and averaged (using a variety of methods). To draw the resampled frontier, the averaged asset allocations are coupled with the starting capital market assumptions.

To illustrate how resampling can be used with other techniques, we conducted a resampled mean–variance optimization using the Black–Litterman returns from Exhibit 10, above. Exhibit 16 provides the asset allocation area graph from this optimization. Notice that the resulting asset allocations are smoother than in any of the previous asset allocation area graphs. Additionally, relative to Exhibit 15, based on the same inputs, the smallest allocations have increased in size while the largest allocations have decreased somewhat.

13 The current embodiments of resampling grew out of the work of Jobson and Korkie (1980, 1981); Jorion (1992); DiBartolomeo (1993); and Michaud (1998).

Exhibit 16: Efficient Frontier Asset Allocation Area Graph, Black–Litterman Returns with Resampling

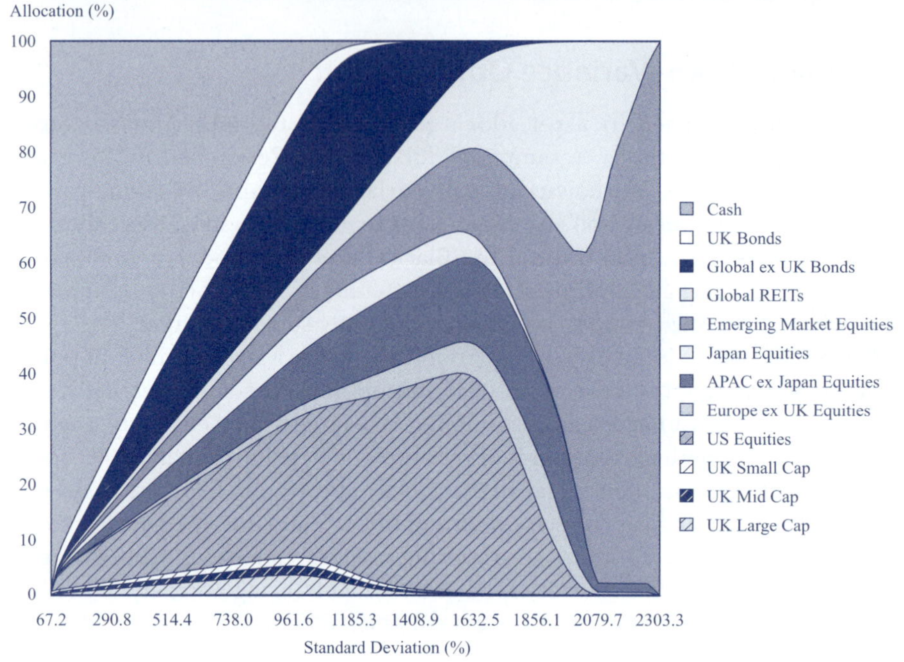

The asset allocations from resampling as depicted in Exhibit 16 are appealing. Criticisms include the following: (1) Some frontiers have concave "bumps" where expected return decreases as expected risk increases; (2) the "riskier" asset allocations are over-diversified; (3) the asset allocations inherit the estimation errors in the original inputs; and (4) the approach lacks a foundation in theory.[14]

Other Non-Normal Optimization Approaches

From our list of shortcomings/criticisms of mean–variance optimization, the third is that investor preferences may go beyond the first two moments (mean and variance) of a portfolio's return distribution. The third and fourth moments are, respectively, skewness and kurtosis. Skewness measures the degree to which return distributions are asymmetrical, and kurtosis measures the thickness of the distributions' tails (i.e., how frequently extreme events occur). A normal distribution is fully explained by the first two moments because the skewness and (excess) kurtosis of the normal distribution are both zero.

Returning to the discussion of Equation 1, the mean–variance optimization program involves maximizing expected utility, which is equal to expected return minus a penalty for risk, where risk is measured as variance (standard deviation). Unfortunately, variance or standard deviation is an incomplete measure of risk when returns are not normally distributed. By studying historical return distributions for the major asset classes and comparing those historical distributions to normal distributions, one will quickly see that, historically, asset class returns are not normally distributed. In fact, empirically extreme returns seem to occur approximately 10 times more often than the normal distribution would suggest. Coupling this finding with the asymmetrical risk preferences observed in investors—whereby the pain of a loss is approximately

14 For more details, see Scherer (2002).

twice as significant as the joy from an equivalent gain (according to Prospect theory)—has led to more complex utility functions and optimizers that expressly account for non-normal returns and asymmetric risk preference.[15] A number of variations of these more sophisticated optimization techniques have been put forth, making them challenging to cover. In general, most of them consider the non-normal return distribution characteristics and use a more sophisticated definition of risk, such as conditional value-at-risk. We view these as important advancements in the toolkit available to practitioners.

Exhibit 17 summarizes selected extensions of quantitative asset allocation approaches outside the sphere of traditional mean–variance optimization.

Exhibit 17: Selected Non-Mean–Variance Developments

Key Non-Normal Frameworks	Research/Recommended Reading
Mean–semivariance optimization	Markowitz (1959)
Mean–conditional value-at-risk optimization	Goldberg, Hayes, and Mahmoud (2013) Rockafellar and Uryasev (2000) Xiong and Idzorek (2011)
Mean–variance-skewness optimization	Briec, Kerstens, and Jokung (2007) Harvey, Liechty, Liechty, and Müller (2010)
Mean–variance-skewness-kurtosis optimization	Athayde and Flôres (2003) Beardsley, Field, and Xiao (2012)

Long-Term versus Short-Term Inputs

Strategic asset allocation is often described as "long term," while tactical asset allocation involves short-term movements away from the strategic asset allocation. In this context, "long term" is often defined as 10 or perhaps 20 or more years, yet in practice, very few asset allocators revisit their strategic asset allocation this infrequently. Many asset allocators update their strategic asset allocation annually, which makes it a bit more challenging to distinguish between strategic and tactical asset allocations. This frequent revisiting of the asset allocation policy brings up important questions about the time horizon associated with the inputs. In general, long-term (10-plus-year) capital market assumptions that ignore current market conditions, such as valuation levels, the business cycle, and interest rates, are often thought of as *unconditional* inputs. Unconditional inputs focus on the average capital market assumptions over the 10-plus-year time horizon. In contrast, shorter-term capital market assumptions that explicitly attempt to incorporate current market conditions (i.e., that are "conditioned" on them) are conditional inputs. For example, a practitioner who believes that the market is overvalued and that as a result we are entering a period of low returns, high volatility, and high correlations might prefer to use conditional inputs that reflect these beliefs.[16]

15 For more on prospect theory, see Kahneman and Tversky (1979) and Tversky and Kahneman (1992).

16 Relatedly, Chow, Jacquier, Kritzman, and Lowry (1999) showed a procedure for blending the optimal portfolios for periods of normal and high return volatility. The approach accounts for the tendency of asset returns to be more highly correlated during times of high volatility.

EXAMPLE 4

Problems in Mean–Variance Optimization

In a presentation to US-based investment clients on asset allocation, the results of two asset allocation exercises are shown, as presented in Exhibit 18.

Exhibit 18: Asset Allocation Choices

Panel A: Area Graph 1

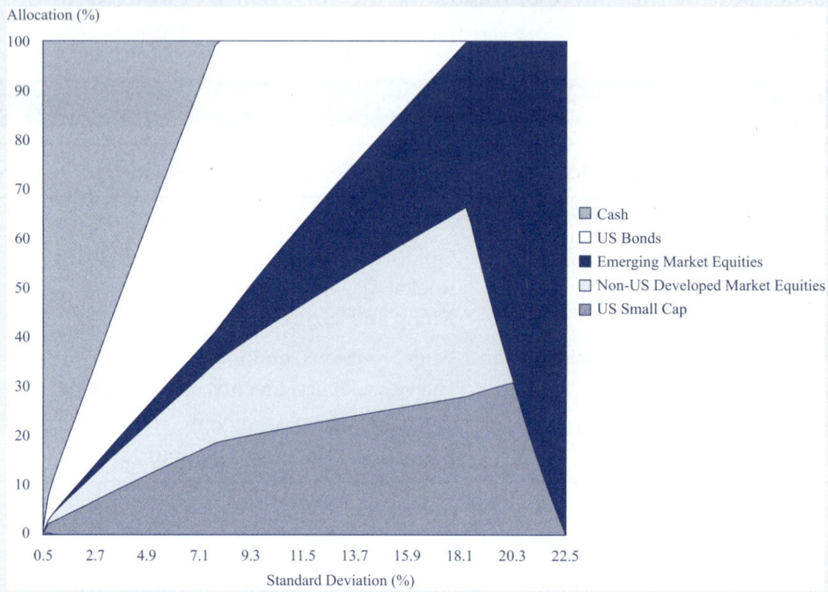

Panel B: Area Graph 2

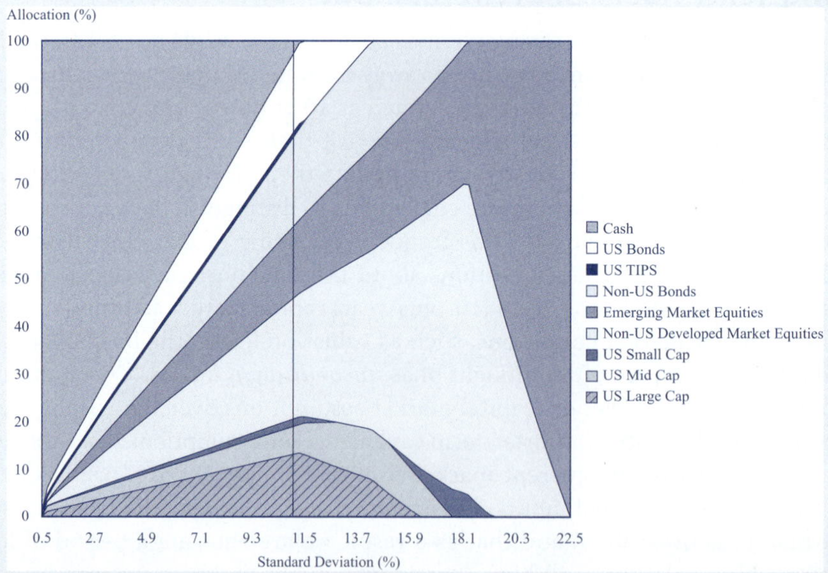

1. Based on Panel A, address the following:

   A. Based on mean–variance analysis, what is the asset allocation that would most likely be selected by a risk-neutral investor?

   B. Based only on the information that can be inferred from Panel A, discuss the investment characteristics of non-US developed market equity (NUSD) in efficient portfolios.

C. Critique the efficient asset mixes represented in Panel A.

Solution to 1A:

For a risk-neutral investor, the optimal asset allocation is 100% invested in emerging market equities. For a risk-neutral investor ($\lambda = 0$), expected utility is simply equal to expected return. The efficient asset allocation that maximizes expected return is the one with the highest level of volatility, as indicated on the x-axis. Panel A shows that that asset allocation consists entirely of emerging market equities.

Solution to 1B:

The weights of NUSD as the efficient frontier moves from its minimum to its maximum risk point suggest NUSD's investment characteristics. This asset class is neither the lowest-volatility asset (which can be inferred to be cash) nor the highest-volatility asset (which is emerging market equity). At the point of the peak of NUSD, when the weight in NUSD is about to begin its decline in higher-risk efficient portfolios, US bonds drop out of the efficient frontier. Further, NUSD leaves the efficient frontier portfolio at a point at which US small cap reaches its highest weight. These observations suggest that NUSD provided diversification benefits in portfolios including US bonds—a relatively low correlation with US bonds can be inferred—that are lost at this point on the efficient frontier. Beyond a volatility level of 20.3%, representing a corner portfolio, NUSD drops out of the efficient frontier.

Solution to 1C:

Of the nine asset classes in the investor's defined opportunity set, five at most are represented by portfolios on the efficient frontier. Thus, a criticism of the efficient frontier associated with Panel A is that the efficient portfolios are highly concentrated in a subset of the available asset classes, which likely reflects the input sensitivity of MVO.

2. Compare the asset allocations shown in Panel A with the corresponding asset allocations shown in Panel B. (Include a comparison of the panels at the level of risk indicated by the line in Panel B.)

Solution to 2:

The efficient asset mixes in Panels A and B cover a similar risk range: The risk levels of the two minimum-variance portfolios are similar, and the risk levels of the two maximum-return portfolios are similar. Over most of the range of volatility, however, the efficient frontier associated with Panel B is better diversified. For example, at the line in Panel B, representing a moderate level of volatility likely relevant to many investors, the efficient portfolio contains nine asset classes rather than four, as in Panel A. At that point, for example, the allocation to fixed income is spread over US bonds, non-US bonds, and US TIPS in Panel B, as opposed to just US bonds in Panel A.

3.

A. Identify three techniques that the asset allocations in Panel B might have incorporated to improve the characteristics relative to those of Panel A.

B. Discuss how the techniques described in your answer to 3A address the high input sensitivity of MVO.

Solution to 3A:

To achieve the better-diversified efficient frontier shown in Panel B, several methods might have been used, including reverse optimization, the Black–Litterman model, and constrained asset class weights.

Solution to 3B:

Reverse optimization and the Black–Litterman model address the issue of MVO's sensitivity to small differences in expected return estimates by anchoring expected returns to those implied by the asset class weights of a proxy for the global market portfolio. The Black–Litterman framework provides a disciplined way to tilt the expected return inputs in the direction of the investor's own views. These approaches address the problem by improving the balance between risk and return that is implicit in the inputs.

A very direct approach to the problem can be taken by placing constraints on weights in the optimization to force an asset class to appear in a constrained efficient frontier within some desired range of values. For example, non-US bonds did not appear in any efficient portfolio in Panel A. The investor could specify that the weight on non-US bonds be strictly positive. Another approach would be to place a maximum on the weight in US bonds to make the optimizer spread the fixed-income allocation over other fixed-income assets besides US bonds.

7 ALLOCATING TO LESS LIQUID ASSET CLASSES

☐ discuss asset class liquidity considerations in asset allocation

Large institutional investors have the ability to invest in less liquid asset classes, such as direct real estate, infrastructure, and private equity. These less liquid asset classes represent unique challenges to many of the common asset allocation techniques, such as mean–variance optimization.

For traditional, highly liquid asset classes, such as publicly listed equities and bonds, almost all of the major index providers have indexes that do an outstanding job of representing the performance characteristics of the asset class (and its various sub–asset classes). For example, over any reasonably long time period, the risk and return characteristics of a given asset class are nearly identical across the major global equity indexes and the correlations between the returns of the indexes are close to 1. Additionally, in most cases, there are passive, low-cost investment vehicles that allow investors to capture the performance of the asset class with very little tracking error.

CASH, THE RISK-FREE ASSET, AND LIQUIDITY NEEDS

The so called "risk-free asset" has a special and somewhat tricky spot in the world of finance. Asset allocators typically use indexes for either 30-day or 90-day government bills to represent the characteristics associated with holding cash, which they may or may not treat as the risk-free asset. The volatility associated with these total return indexes is extremely low, but it isn't zero. An alternative to using a cash index as a proxy for the risk-free asset is to use a government bond with a duration/maturity that matches the time horizon of the investor. Some asset allocators like to include cash or another asset that could be considered a risk-free asset in the optimization and to allow the optimizer to determine how to mix it with the other asset classes included in the optimization. Other asset allocators prefer to exclude the risk-free asset from the optimization and allow real-world needs, such as liquidity needs, to determine how much to allocate to cash-like assets.

Illiquid assets may offer an expected return premium as compensation for illiquidity as well as diversification benefits. Determining an appropriate allocation to these assets is associated with various challenges, however. Common illiquid asset classes cannot be readily diversified to eliminate idiosyncratic risk, so representing an overall asset class performance is problematic. Furthermore, for less liquid asset classes, such as direct real estate, infrastructure, and private equity, there are, in general, far fewer indexes that attempt to represent aggregate performance. If one were to compare the performance characteristics of multiple indexes representing one of these less liquid asset classes, there would be noticeable risk and return differences, suggesting that it is difficult to accurately measure the risk and return characteristics of these asset classes. Also, due to the illiquid nature of the constituents that make up these asset classes, it is widely believed that the indexes don't accurately reflect their true volatility. In contrast to the more traditional, highly liquid asset classes, there are no low-cost passive investment vehicles that would allow investors to closely track the aggregate performance of these less liquid asset classes.

Thus, the problem is twofold: (1) Due to the lack of accurate indexes, it is more challenging to make capital market assumptions for these less liquid asset classes, and (2) even if there were accurate indexes, there are no low-cost passive investment vehicles to track them.

Compounding the asset allocator's dilemma is the fact that the risk and return characteristics associated with actual investment vehicles, such as direct real estate funds, infrastructure funds, and private equity funds, are typically significantly different from the characteristics of the asset classes themselves. For example, the private equity "asset class" should represent the risk and return characteristics of owning all private equity, just as the MSCI All Country World Index represents the risk and return characteristics of owning all public equity. Purchasing the exchange-traded fund (ETF) that tracks the MSCI All Country World Index completely diversifies public company-specific risk. This scenario is in direct contrast to the typical private equity fund, in which the risk and return characteristics are often dominated by company-specific (idiosyncratic) risk.

In addressing asset allocation involving less liquid asset classes, practical options include the following:

1. Exclude less liquid asset classes (direct real estate, infrastructure, and private equity) from the asset allocation decision and then consider real estate funds, infrastructure funds, and private equity funds as potential implementation vehicles when fulfilling the target strategic asset allocation.
2. Include less liquid asset classes in the asset allocation decision and attempt to model the inputs to represent the *specific risk* characteristics associated with the likely *implementation vehicles.*
3. Include less liquid asset classes in the asset allocation decision and attempt to model the inputs to represent the *highly diversified* characteristics associated with the *true asset classes.*

Related to this last option, some practitioners use listed real estate indexes, listed infrastructure, and public equity indexes that are deemed to have characteristics similar to their private equity counterparts to help estimate the risk of the less liquid asset classes and their correlation with the other asset classes in the opportunity set. It should be noted that the use of listed alternative indexes often violates the recommendation that asset classes be mutually exclusive—the securities in these indexes are likely also included in indexes representing other asset classes—and thus typically results in higher correlations among different asset classes, which has the negative impact of increasing input sensitivity in most optimization settings.

For investors who do not have access to direct real estate funds, infrastructure funds, and private equity funds—for example, small investors—the most common approach is to use one of the indexes based on listed equities to represent the asset class and then to implement the target allocation with a fund that invests similarly. Thus global REITs might be used to represent (approximately) global real estate.

8 RISK BUDGETING

- ☐ explain absolute and relative risk budgets and their use in determining and implementing an asset allocation
- ☐ describe how client needs and preferences regarding investment risks can be incorporated into asset allocation

> [A] risk budget is simply a particular allocation of portfolio risk. An optimal risk budget is simply the allocation of risk such that the first order of conditions for portfolio optimization are satisfied. The risk budgeting process is the process of finding an optimal risk budget.
>
> Kurt Winkelmann (2003, p. 173)

As this quote from Kurt Winkelmann suggests, there are three aspects to risk budgeting:

- The risk budget identifies the total amount of risk and allocates the risk to a portfolio's constituent parts.
- An optimal risk budget allocates risk efficiently.
- The process of finding the optimal risk budget is risk budgeting.

Although its name suggests that risk budgeting is all about risk, risk budgeting is really using risk in relation to seeking return. The goal of risk budgeting is to maximize return per unit of risk—whether overall market risk in an asset allocation setting or active risk in an asset allocation implementation setting.

The ability to determine a position's marginal contribution to portfolio risk is a powerful tool that helps one to better understand the sources of risk. The marginal contribution to a type of risk is the partial derivative of the risk in question (total risk, active risk, or residual risk) with respect to the applicable type of portfolio holding (asset allocation holdings, active holdings, or residual holdings). Knowing a position's marginal contribution to risk allows one to (1) approximate the change in portfolio risk (total risk, active risk, or residual risk) due to a change in an individual holding, (2) determine which positions are optimal, and (3) create a risk budget. *Risk-budgeting tools assist in the optimal use of risk in the pursuit of return.*

Exhibit 19 contains risk-budgeting information for the Sharpe ratio–maximizing asset allocation from our original UK example. The betas are from Exhibit 12. The marginal contribution to total risk (MCTR) identifies the rate at which risk would change with a small (or marginal) change in the current weights. For asset class *i*, it is calculated as $MCTR_i$ = (Beta of asset class *i* with respect to portfolio)(Portfolio return volatility). The absolute contribution to total risk (ACTR) for an asset class measures how much it contributes to portfolio return volatility and can be calculated as the weight of the asset class in the portfolio times its marginal contribution to total risk: $ACTR_i = (Weight_i)(MCTR_i)$. Critically, beta takes account not only of the asset's own volatility but also of the asset's correlations with other portfolio assets.

The sum of the ACTR in Exhibit 19 is approximately 10.88%, which is equal to the expected standard deviation of this asset allocation mix. Dividing each ACTR by the total risk of 10.88% gives the percentage of total risk that each position contributes. Finally, an asset allocation is optimal from a risk-budgeting perspective when the ratio of excess return (over the risk-free rate) to MCTR is the same for all assets and matches the Sharpe ratio of the tangency portfolio. So in this case, which is based on reverse-optimized returns, we have an optimal risk budget.

Exhibit 19: Risk-Budgeting Statistics

Asset Class	Weight	MCTR	ACTR	Percent Contribution to Total Standard Deviation	Ratio of Excess Return to MCTR
UK large cap	3.2%	11.19%	0.36%	3.33%	0.368
UK mid cap	0.9	12.02	0.11	0.98	0.368
UK small cap	0.3	12.44	0.03	0.30	0.368
US equities	34.4	14.51	5.00	45.94	0.368
Europe ex UK equities	8.7	16.68	1.45	13.34	0.368
Asia Pacific ex Japan equities	3.1	16.35	0.51	4.69	0.368
Japan equities	6.6	10.69	0.70	6.46	0.368
Emerging market equities	5.9	17.51	1.02	9.42	0.368
Global REITs	1.8	17.79	0.31	2.86	0.368
Global ex UK bonds	31.8	4.21	1.34	12.33	0.368
UK bonds	3.2	1.22	0.04	0.35	0.368
Cash	0.2	0.00	0.00	0.00	0.368
	100.0		10.88	100.00	

For additional clarity, the following are the specific calculations used to derive the calculated values for UK large-cap equities (where we show some quantities with an extra decimal place in order to reproduce the values shown in the exhibit):

- Marginal contribution to risk (MCTR):

Asset beta relative to portfolio × Portfolio standard deviation

$1.0289 \times 10.876 = 11.19\%$

- ACTR:

Asset weight in portfolio × MCTR

$3.2\% \times 11.19\% = 0.36\%$

- Ratio of excess return to MCTR:

(Expected return − Risk-free rate)/MCTR

$(6.62\% - 2.5\%)/11.19\% = 0.368$

EXAMPLE 5

Risk Budgeting in Asset Allocation

1. Describe the objective of risk budgeting in asset allocation.

   Solution:

   The objective of risk budgeting in asset allocation is to use risk efficiently in the pursuit of return. A risk budget specifies the total amount of risk and how much of that risk should be budgeted for each allocation.

2. Consider two asset classes, A and B. Asset class A has two times the weight of B in the portfolio. Under what condition would B have a larger ACTR than A?

   Solution:

   Because $ACTR_i$ = ($Weight_i$)(Beta with respect to portfolio)$_i$(Portfolio return volatility), the beta of B would have to be more than twice as large as the beta of A for B to contribute more to portfolio risk than A.

3. When is an asset allocation optimal from a risk-budgeting perspective?

   Solution:

   An asset allocation is optimal when the ratio of excess return (over the risk-free rate) to MCTR is the same for all assets.

9 FACTOR-BASED ASSET ALLOCATION

☐ describe the use of investment factors in constructing and analyzing an asset allocation

Until now, we have primarily focused on the mechanics of asset allocation optimization as applied to an opportunity set consisting of traditional, non-overlapping asset classes. An alternative approach used by some practitioners is to move away from an opportunity set of *asset classes* to an opportunity set consisting of investment *factors*.

In factor-based asset allocation, the factors in question are typically similar to the fundamental (or structural) factors in widely used multi-factor investment models. Factors are typically based on observed market premiums and anomalies. In addition to the all-important market (equity) exposure, typical factors used in asset allocation include size, valuation, momentum, liquidity, duration (term), credit, and volatility. Most of these factors were identified as return drivers that help to explain returns that were not explained by the CAPM. These factors can be constructed in a number of different ways, but with the exception of the market factor, typically, the factor represents what is referred to as a zero (dollar) investment, or self-financing investment, in which the underperforming attribute is sold short to finance an offsetting long position in the better-performing attribute. For example, the size factor is the combined return from shorting large-cap stocks and going long small-cap stocks (Size factor return = Small-cap stock return − Large-cap stock return). Of course, if large-cap stocks outperform small-cap stocks, the realized size return would be negative. Constructing factors in this manner removes most market exposure from the factors (because of the short positions that offset long positions); as a result, the factors generally have low correlations with the market and with one another.

We next present an example of a factor-based asset allocation optimization. Exhibit 20 shows the list of factors, how they were specified, and their historical returns and standard deviations (in excess of the risk-free rate as proxied by the return on three-month Treasury bills). The exhibit also includes historical statistics for three-month Treasury bills.

Thus far, our optimization examples have taken place in "total return space," where the expected return of each asset has equaled the expected return of the risk-free asset plus the amount of expected return in excess of the risk-free rate. In order to stay in this familiar total return space when optimizing with risk factors, the factor return needs to include the return on the assumed collateral (in this example, cash, represented by three-month Treasury bills). This adjustment is also needed if one plans to include both risk factors and some traditional asset classes in the same optimization, so that the inputs for the risk factors and traditional asset classes are similarly specified. Alternatively, one could move in the opposite direction, subtracting the return of the three-month Treasury bills from asset class returns and then conducting the optimization in excess-return space. One way to think about a self-financing allocation to a risk factor is that in order to invest in the risk factor, one must put up an equivalent amount of collateral that is invested in cash.

Exhibit 20: Factors/Asset Classes, Factor Definitions, and Historical Statistics (US data, January 1979 to March 2016)

Factor/Asset Class	Factor Definition	Compound Annual Factor Return	Standard Deviation	Total Return	Standard Deviation
Treasury bonds	Long-term Treasury bonds			7.77%	5.66%
Market	Total market return – Cash	7.49%	16.56%	12.97	17.33
Size	Small cap – Large cap	0.41	10.15	5.56	10.65
Valuation	Value – Growth	0.68	9.20	5.84	9.76
Credit	Corporate – Treasury	0.70	3.51	5.87	3.84
Duration	Long Treasury bonds – Treasury bills	4.56	11.29	9.91	11.93
Mortgage	Mortgage-backed – Treasury bonds	0.30	3.38	5.45	3.83
Large growth	—	—	—	12.64	19.27
Large value	—	—	—	13.23	16.52
Small growth	—	—	—	12.30	25.59
Small value	—	—	—	14.54	19.84
Mortgage-backed sec.	—	—	—	8.09	6.98
Corporate bonds	—	—	—	8.52	7.52
Treasury bonds	—	—	—	7.77	5.66
Cash	—	—	—	5.13	1.23

Because of space considerations, we have not included the full correlation matrix, but it is worth noting that the average pair-wise correlation of the risk factor–based opportunity set (in excess of the risk-free rate collateral return) is 0.31, whereas that of the asset class–based opportunity set is 0.57. Given the low pair-wise correlations of the risk factors, there has been some debate among practitioners around whether it is better to optimize using asset classes or risk factors. The issue was clarified by Idzorek and Kowara (2013), who demonstrated that in a proper comparison, neither approach is inherently superior. To help illustrate risk factor optimization and to demonstrate that if the two opportunity sets are constructed with access to similar exposures, neither approach has an inherent advantage, we present two side-by-side optimizations. These optimizations are based on the data given in Exhibit 20.

Exhibit 21 contains the two efficient frontiers. As should be expected, given that the opportunity sets provide access to similar exposures, the two historical efficient frontiers are very similar. This result illustrates that when the same range of potential exposures is available in two opportunity sets, the risk and return possibilities are very similar.

Exhibit 21: Efficient Frontiers Based on Historical Capital Market Assumptions (January 1979 to March 2016)

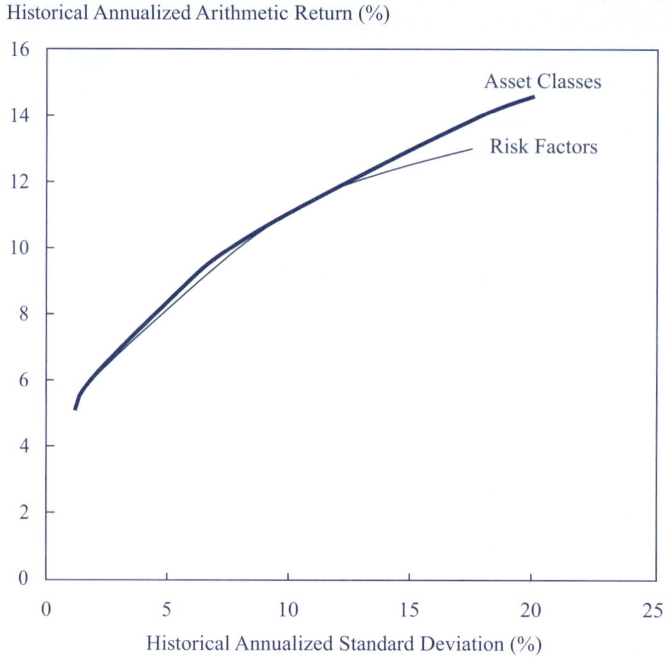

Moving to Exhibit 22, examining the two asset allocation area graphs associated with the two efficient frontiers reveals that the efficient mixes have some relatively clear similarities. For example, in Panel A (risk factors), the combined market, size, and valuation exposures mirror the pattern (allocations) in Panel B (asset classes) of combined large value and small value exposures.

Exhibit 22: Asset Allocation Area Graphs—Risk Factors and Asset Classes

Panel A: Risk Factor Asset Allocation Area Graph

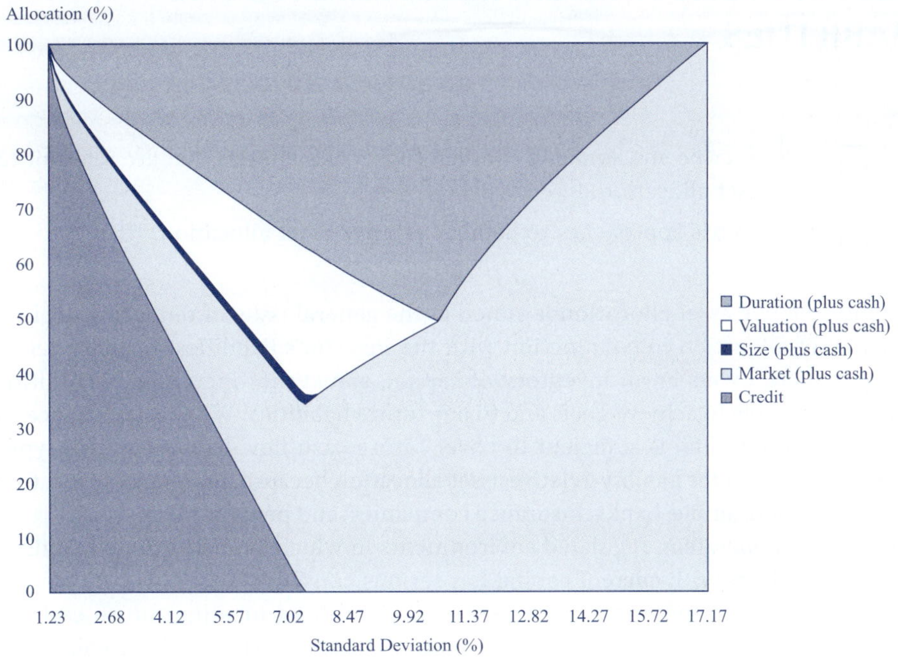

Panel B: Asset Class Asset Allocation Area Graph

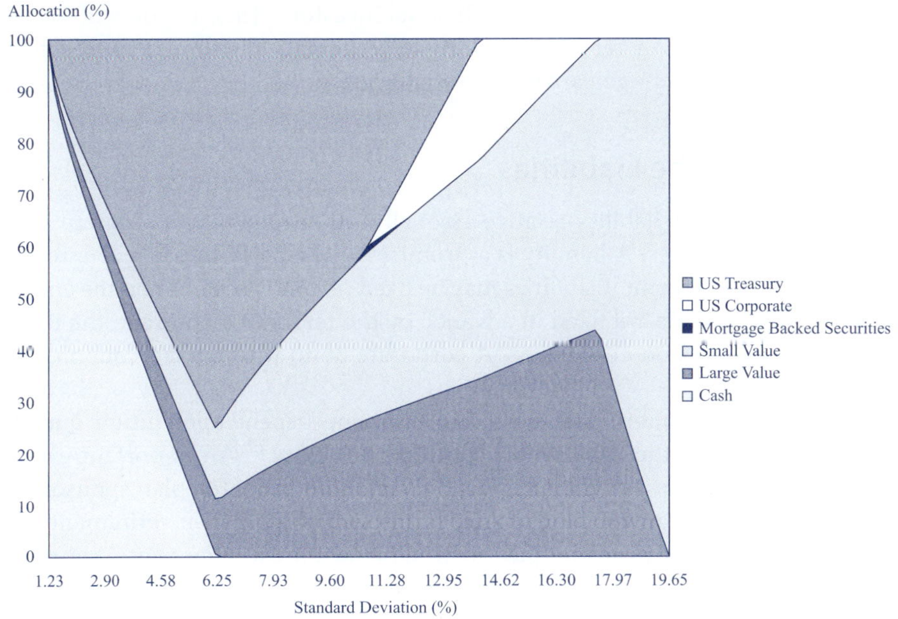

Practitioners should choose to carry out asset allocation in the particular space—risk factors or asset classes—in which they are most equipped to make capital market assumptions. Regardless of which space a practitioner prefers, expanding one's opportunity set to include new, weakly correlated risk factors or asset classes should improve the potential risk–return trade-offs.

10 DEVELOPING LIABILITY-RELATIVE ASSET ALLOCATIONS AND CHARACTERIZING THE LIABILITIES

- ☐ describe and evaluate characteristics of liabilities that are relevant to asset allocation
- ☐ discuss approaches to liability-relative asset allocation

Liability-relative asset allocation is aimed at the general issue of rendering decisions about asset allocation in conjunction with the investor's liabilities. Liability-relative investors view assets as an inventory of capital, sometimes increased by additions, which is available to achieve goals and to pay future liabilities. What is the chance that an institution's capital is sufficient to cover future cash flow liabilities? This type of question is critical for liability-relative asset allocation because many large institutional investors—for example, banks, insurance companies, and pension plans—possess legal liabilities and operate in regulated environments in which an institution's inability to meet its liabilities with current capital has serious consequences. This concern gives rise to unique risk measures, such as the probability of meeting future cash flow requirements, and the restatement of traditional risk metrics, such as volatility, in relation to liabilities.

Liability-relative methods were developed in an institutional investor context, but these ideas have also been applied to individual investors. This section will focus on institutional investors. A later section addresses a thematically similar approach with behavioral finance roots—goals-based asset allocation.

Characterizing the Liabilities

To be soundly applied, liability-relative asset allocation requires an accurate understanding of the liabilities. A liability is a promise by one party to pay a counterparty based on a prior agreement. Liabilities may be fixed or contingent. When the amounts and timing of payments are fixed in advance by the terms of a contract, the liability is said to be fixed or non-contingent. A corporate bond with a fixed coupon rate is an example.

In many cases relevant to asset allocation, payments depend upon future, uncertain events. In such cases, the liability is a contingent liability.[17] An important example involves the liabilities of a defined benefit (DB) pension plan. The plan sponsor has a legal commitment to pay the beneficiaries of the plan during their retirement years. However, the exact dates of the payments depend on the employees' retirement dates, longevity, and cash payout rules. Insurance companies' liabilities—created by the sale of insurance policies—are also contingent liabilities: The insurance company promises to pay its policyholders a specified amount contingent on the occurrence of a predefined event.

We distinguish legal liabilities from cash payments that are expected to be made in the future and are essential to the mission of an institution but are not legal liabilities. We call these quasi-liabilities. The endowment of a university can fit this category because, in many cases, the endowment contributes a major part of the university's operating budget. The endowment assures its stakeholders that it will continue to

17 Note that the term "contingent liability" has a specific definition in accounting. We are using the term more broadly here.

support its essential activities through spending from the endowment capital, and failure to provide such support will often lead to changes in how the endowment is managed. Accordingly, the asset allocation decisions are made in conjunction with the university's spending rules and policies. Asset allocation is just one portion of the investment problem. Although we do not explicitly discuss them here, as suggested in Sections 2–9, the spending needs of an individual represent another type of quasi-liability. Exhibit 23 summarizes the characteristics of liabilities that can affect asset allocation.

Exhibit 23: Characteristics of Liabilities That Can Affect Asset Allocation

1. Fixed versus contingent cash flows
2. Legal versus quasi-liabilities
3. Duration and convexity of liability cash flows
4. Value of liabilities as compared with the size of the sponsoring organization
5. Factors driving future liability cash flows (inflation, economic conditions, interest rates, risk premium)
6. Timing considerations, such as longevity risk
7. Regulations affecting liability cash flow calculations

The above liability characteristics are relevant to liability-relative asset allocation in various ways. For example, they affect the choice of appropriate discount rate(s) to establish the present value of the liabilities and thus the degree to which assets are adequate in relation to those liabilities. Liability characteristics determine the composition of the liability-matching portfolio and that portfolio's basis risk with respect to the liabilities. (Basis risk in this context quantifies the degree of mismatch between the hedging portfolio and the liabilities.)

We will discuss the following case study in detail. It involves a frozen pension plan for LOWTECH, a hypothetical US company. The company has decided to close its defined benefit pension plan and switch to a defined contribution plan. The DB plan has the fixed liabilities (accumulated benefit obligations) shown in Exhibit 24.

Exhibit 24: Projected Liability Cash Flows for Company LOWTECH (US$ billions)

		PV(Liabilities)	
Beginning of Year	Cash Outflow (Liability)	4% Discount Rate	2% Discount Rate
2015	—	$2.261	$3.039
2016	$0.100	2.352	3.10
2017	0.102	2.342	3.06
2018	0.104	2.329	3.02
2019	0.106	2.314	2.97
2020	0.108	2.297	2.92
2021	0.110	2.276	2.87
2022	0.113	2.252	2.82
2023	0.115	2.225	2.76
2024	0.117	2.195	2.69

		PV(Liabilities)	
Beginning of Year	Cash Outflow (Liability)	4% Discount Rate	2% Discount Rate
2025	0.120	2.161	2.63
2026	0.122	2.123	2.56
2027	0.124	2.081	2.49
2028	0.127	2.035	2.41
2029	0.129	1.984	2.33
2030	0.132	1.929	2.24
2031	0.135	1.869	2.15
2032	0.137	1.804	2.06
2033	0.140	1.733	1.96
2034	0.143	1.657	1.86
2035	0.146	1.575	1.75
2036	0.149	1.486	1.63
2037	0.152	1.391	1.52
2038	0.155	1.289	1.39
2039	0.158	1.180	1.26
2040	0.161	1.063	1.13
2041	0.164	0.938	0.98
2042	0.167	0.805	0.84
2043	0.171	0.663	0.68
2044	0.174	0.512	0.52
2045	0.178	0.352	0.36
2046	0.181	0.181	0.181

In the Cash Outflow (Liability) column, the assumption is made that payments for a given year are made at the beginning of the year (in the exhibit, outflows have a positive sign). As of the beginning of 2015, the present value of these liabilities, given a 4% discount rate for high-quality corporate bonds (required in the United States by the Pension Protection Act of 2006, which applies to private DB pension plans), is US$2.261 billion. The current market value of the assets is assumed to equal US$2.5 billion, for a surplus of US$0.239 billion. On the other hand, if the discount rate is equal to the long-term government bond rate at 2% (required before the 2006 US legislation), the surplus becomes a deficit at –$0.539 billion. In many cases, regulations set the appropriate discount rates; these rates have an impact on the determination of surplus or deficit and thus on future contribution rules.

Like other institutions with legal liabilities, the LOWTECH company must analyze its legal future cash flows under its DB pension system and evaluate them in conjunction with the current market value of its assets on an annual basis. The following steps of the valuation exercise for a DB pension plan occur on a fixed annual date:

1. Calculate the market value of assets.
2. Project liability cash flows (via actuarial principles and rules).
3. Determine an appropriate discount rate for liability cash flows.
4. Compute the present value of liabilities, the surplus value, and the funding ratio.

Surplus = Market value (assets) – Present value (liabilities).

The surplus for the LOWTECH company is US$2.500 billion – US$2.261 billion = US$0.239 billion, given the 4% discount rate assumption.

The funding ratio is another significant measure: Funding ratio = Market value (assets)/Present value (liabilities). We say that an investor is fully funded if the investor's funding ratio equals 1 (or the surplus is 0). A state of overfunding occurs when the funding ratio is greater than 1, and a state of underfunding takes place when the funding ratio is less than 1. Based on a discount rate of 4%, the funding ratio for LOWTECH = US$2.5 billion/US$2.261 billion = 1.1057, so that the company is about 10.6% overfunded.

The surplus value and the funding ratio are highly dependent upon the discount rate assumption. For example, if the discount rate is equal to 2.0% (close to the 10-year US Treasury bond rate in early 2016), the surplus drops to –US$0.539 billion and the funding ratio equals 0.8226. The company's status changes from overfunded to underfunded. The choice of discount rate is generally set by regulations and tradition. Rate assumptions are different across industries, countries, and domains. From the standpoint of economic theory, if the liability cash flows can be hedged perfectly by a set of market-priced assets, the discount rate can be determined by reference to the discount rate for the assets. For example, if the pension plan liabilities are fixed (without any uncertainty), the discount rate should be the risk-free rate with reference to the duration of the liability cash flows—for example, a five-year zero-coupon bond yield for a liability with a (modified) duration of 5. In other cases, it can be difficult to find a fully hedged portfolio because an ongoing DB pension plan's liabilities will depend upon future economic growth and inflation, which are clearly uncertain. Even a frozen pension plan can possess uncertainty due to the changing longevity of the retirees over the long-term future.

APPROACHES TO LIABILITY-RELATIVE ASSET ALLOCATION: SURPLUS OPTIMIZATION

11

- ☐ describe and evaluate characteristics of liabilities that are relevant to asset allocation
- ☐ discuss approaches to liability-relative asset allocation
- ☐ recommend and justify a liability-relative asset allocation

Various approaches to liability-relative asset allocation exist. These methods are influenced by tradition, regulations, and the ability of the stakeholders to understand and extend portfolio models that come from the asset-only domain.

There are several guiding principles. The first is to gain an understanding of the make-up of the investor's liabilities and especially the factors that affect the amount and timing of the cash outflows. Given this understanding, the present value of the liabilities is calculated, along with the surplus and funding ratio. These measures are used to track the results of ongoing investment and funding policies and for other tasks. Next come the decisions regarding the asset allocation taking account of the liabilities. There are a number of ways to proceed. We will discuss three major approaches:

- *Surplus optimization.* This approach involves applying mean–variance optimization (MVO) to an efficient frontier based on the volatility of the surplus ("surplus volatility," or "surplus risk") as the measure of risk. Surplus optimization is thus an extension of MVO based on asset volatility.[18] Depending on context, surplus risk may be stated in money or percentage terms ("surplus return volatility" is then another, more precise term for this measure).

- *Hedging/return-seeking portfolios approach.* This approach involves separating assets into two groups: a hedging portfolio and a return-seeking portfolio. The reading also refers to this as the two-portfolio approach. The concept of allocating assets to two distinct portfolios can be applied for various funding ratios, but the reading distinguishes as the basic approach the case in which there is a positive surplus available to allocate to the return-seeking portfolio.
- *Integrated asset–liability approach.* For some institutional investors, such as banks and insurance companies and long–short hedge funds, asset and liability decisions can be integrated and jointly optimized.

We cover these three approaches in turn.

Surplus Optimization

Surplus optimization involves adapting asset-only mean–variance optimization by substituting surplus return for asset return over any given time horizon. The quadratic optimization program involves choosing the asset allocation (mix) that maximizes expected surplus return net of a penalty for surplus return volatility at the chosen time horizon. The objective function is

$$U_m^{LR} = E\left(R_{s,m}\right) - 0.005\lambda\sigma^2\left(R_{s,m}\right) \quad (2)$$

where U_m^{LR} is the surplus objective function's expected value for a particular asset mix m; $E(R_{s,m})$ is the expected surplus return for asset mix m, with surplus return defined as (Change in asset value − Change in liability value)/(Initial asset value); and the parameter λ (lambda) indicates the investor's risk aversion. The more risk averse the investor, the greater the penalty for surplus return volatility. Note that the change in liability value (liability return) measures the time value of money for the liabilities plus any expected changes in the discount rate and future cash flows over the planning horizon.

This surplus efficient frontier approach is a straightforward extension of the asset-only portfolio model. Surplus optimization assumes that the relationship between the value of liabilities and the value of assets can be approximated through a correlation coefficient. Surplus optimization exploits natural hedges that may exist between assets and liabilities as a result of their systematic risk characteristics.

The following steps describe the surplus optimization approach:

1. Select asset categories and determine the planning horizon. One year is often chosen for the planning exercise, although funding status analysis is based on an analysis of all cash flows.
2. Estimate expected returns and volatilities for the asset categories and estimate liability returns (expanded matrix).
3. Determine any constraints on the investment mix.
4. Estimate the expanded correlation matrix (asset categories and liabilities) and the volatilities.[19]

18 Among the papers that discuss the surplus optimization model are Leibowitz and Henriksson (1988); Mulvey (1989, 1994); Sharpe and Tint (1990); Elton and Gruber (1992).

19 A covariance matrix is computed by combining the correlation matrix and the volatilities.

5. Compute the surplus efficient frontier and compare it with the asset-only efficient frontier.
6. Select a recommended portfolio mix.

Exhibit 25 lists LOWTECH's asset categories and current allocation for a one-year planning horizon. The current allocation for other asset categories, such as cash, is zero. LOWTECH has been following an asset-only approach but has decided to adopt a liability-relative approach. The company is exploring several liability-relative approaches. With respect to surplus optimization, the trustees want to maintain surplus return volatility at a level that tightly controls the risk that the plan will become underfunded, and they would like to keep volatility of surplus below US$0.25 billion (10%).

Exhibit 25: Asset Categories and Current Allocation for LOWTECH

	Private Equity	Real Estate	Hedge Funds	Real Assets	US Equities	Non-US Equities (Developed Markets)	Non-US Equities (Emerging Markets)	US Corporate Bonds
Allocation	20.0%	12.0%	18.0%	7.0%	15.0%	12.0%	8.0%	8.0%

The second step is to estimate future expected asset and liability returns, the expected present value of liabilities, and the volatility of both assets and PV(liabilities). The capital market projections can be made in several ways—based on historical data, economic analysis, or expert judgment, for example. The plan sponsor and its advisers are responsible for employing one or a blend of these approaches. Exhibit 26 shows the plan sponsor's capital market assumptions over a three- to five-year horizon. Note the inclusion of the present value of liabilities in Exhibit 26.

Exhibit 26: LOWTECH's Capital Market Assumptions: Expected Annual Compound Returns and Volatilities

	Private Equity	Real Estate	Hedge Funds	Real Assets	US Equities	Non-US Equities (Developed Markets)	Emerging Markets	US Corporate Bonds	Cash	PV (Liabilities)
Expected returns	8.50%	7.50%	7.00%	6.00%	7.50%	7.20%	7.80%	4.90%	1.00%	4.90%
Volatilities	14.20%	9.80%	7.70%	6.10%	18.00%	19.50%	26.30%	5.60%	1.00%	5.60%

Typically, in the third step, the investor imposes constraints on the composition of the asset mix, including policy and legal limits on the amount of capital invested in individual assets or asset categories (e.g., a constraint that an allocation to equities must not exceed 50%). In our example, we simply constrain portfolio weights to be non-negative and to sum to 1.

The fourth step is to estimate the correlation matrix and volatilities. We assume that the liabilities have the same expected returns and volatilities as US corporate bonds; thus, the expanded matrix has a column and a row for liabilities with values equal to the corporate bond values. For simplicity, the investor may employ historical performance. Exhibit 27 shows the correlation matrix of asset categories based on historical quarterly returns. Recall that we assume that liability returns (changes in liabilities) are driven by changes in the returns of US corporate bonds. An alternative approach is to deploy a set of underlying factors that drive the returns of the assets.

Factors include changes in nominal and real interest rates, changes in economic activity (such as employment levels), and risk premiums. This type of factor investment model can be applied in an asset-only or a liability-relative asset allocation context.

Exhibit 27: Correlation Matrix of Returns

	Private Equity	Real Estate	Hedge Funds	Real Assets	US Equities	Non-US Equities (Developed Markets)	Non-US Equities (Emerging Markets)	US Corporate Bonds	Cash	PV (Liabilities)
Private equity	1	0.41	0.57	0.32	0.67	0.59	0.49	−0.27	0	−0.27
Real estate	0.41	1	0.45	0.41	0.31	0.33	0.17	−0.08	0	−0.08
Hedge funds	0.57	0.45	1	0.11	0.68	0.61	0.54	−0.23	0	−0.23
Real assets	0.32	0.41	0.11	1	0.04	0.06	−0.06	0.34	0	0.34
US equities	0.67	0.31	0.68	0.04	1	0.88	0.73	−0.38	0	−0.38
Non-US equities (developed)	0.59	0.33	0.61	0.06	0.88	1	0.81	−0.39	0	−0.39
Non-US equities (emerging)	0.49	0.17	0.54	−0.06	0.73	0.81	1	−0.44	0	−0.44
US corporate bonds	−0.27	−0.08	−0.23	0.34	−0.38	−0.39	−0.44	1	0	1
Cash	0	0	0	0	0	0	0	0	1	0
PV(liabilities)	−0.27	−0.08	−0.23	0.34	−0.38	−0.39	−0.44	1	0	1

Exhibit 28 shows a surplus efficient frontier that results from the optimization program based on the inputs from Exhibit 26 and Exhibit 27. Surplus risk (i.e., volatility of surplus) in money terms (US$ billions) is on the *x*-axis, and expected surplus in money terms (US$ billions) is on the *y*-axis. By presenting the efficient frontier in money terms, we can associate the level of risk with the level of plan surplus, US$0.329 billion. Like the asset-only efficient frontier, the surplus efficient frontier has a concave shape.

Exhibit 28: Surplus Efficient Frontier

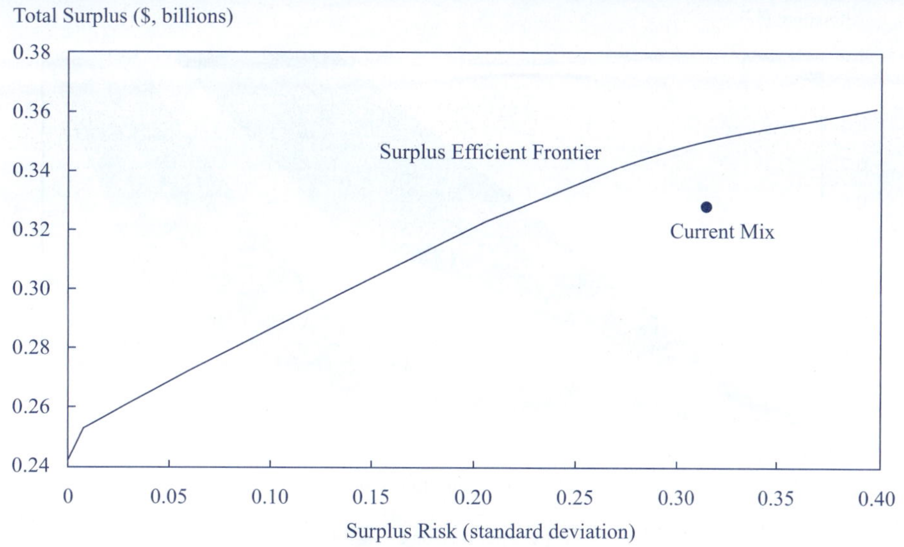

The first observation is that the current mix in Exhibit 28 lies below the surplus efficient frontier and is thus suboptimal.[20] We can attain the same expected total surplus as that of the current mix at a lower level of surplus volatility by choosing the portfolio on the efficient frontier at the current mix's level of expected total surplus. Another observation is that by uncovering the implications of asset mixes for surplus and surplus volatility, this approach allows the deliberate choice of an asset allocation in terms of the tolerable level of risk in relation to liabilities. It may be the case, for example, that neither the surplus volatility of the current mix nor that of the efficient mix with equal expected surplus is the appropriate level of surplus risk for the pension.

The surplus efficient frontier in Exhibit 28 shows efficient reward–risk combinations but does not indicate the asset class composition of the combinations. Exhibit 29 shows the asset class weights for surplus efficient portfolios.

20 The current mix can also be shown to lie below the asset-only mean–variance frontier.

Exhibit 29: Surplus Efficient Frontier Asset Allocation Area Graph

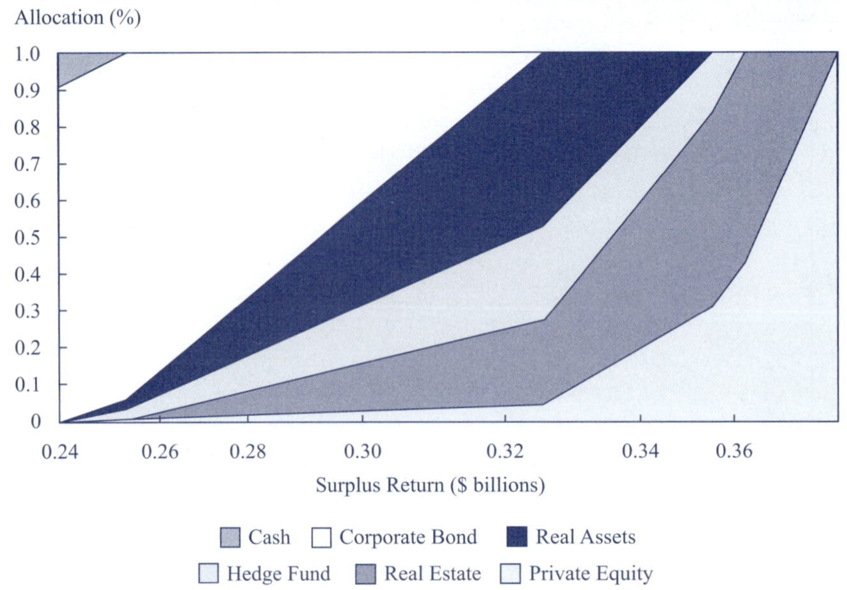

Exhibit 30, showing weights for portfolios on the usual *asset-only* efficient frontier based on the same capital market assumptions reflected in Exhibit 29, makes the point that efficient portfolios from the two perspectives are meaningfully different.[21]

Exhibit 30: Asset-Only Efficient Frontier Asset Allocation Area Graph

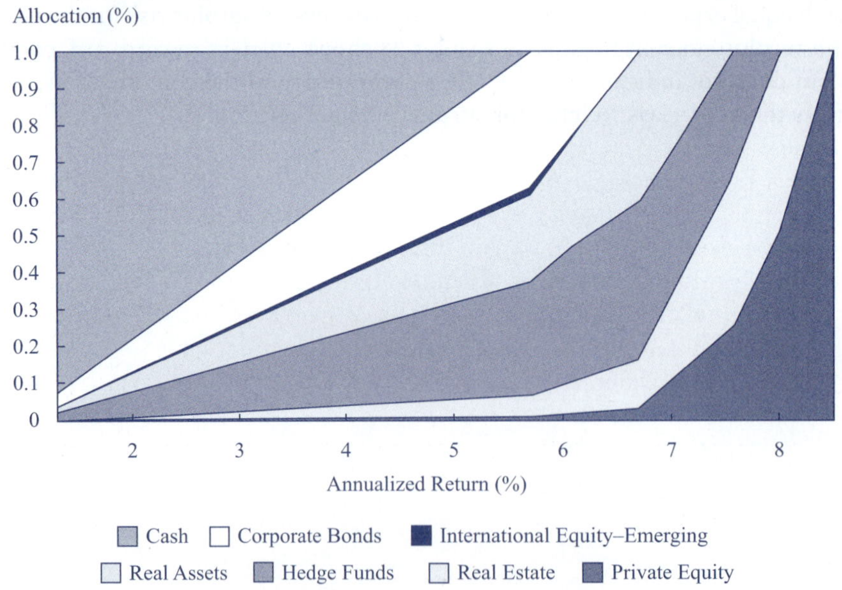

21 In Exhibit 30, the annualized percentage returns can be equated to monetary surplus returns by multiplying by the asset value, US$2.5 billion.

The asset mixes are very different on the conservative side of the two frontiers. The most conservative mix for the surplus efficient frontier (in Exhibit 29) consists mostly of the US corporate bond index (the hedging asset) because it results in the lowest volatility of surplus over the one-year horizon. Bonds are positively correlated with changes in the present value of the frozen liability cash flows (because the liabilities indicate negative cash flows). In contrast, the most conservative mix for the asset-only efficient frontier (in Exhibit 30) consists chiefly of cash. As long as there is a hedging asset and adequate asset value, the investor can achieve a very low volatility of surplus, and for conservative investors, the asset value at the horizon will be uncertain but the surplus will be constant (or as constant as possible).

The two asset mixes (asset-only and surplus) become similar as the degree of risk aversion decreases, and they are identical for the most aggressive portfolio (private equity). Bonds disappear from the frontier about halfway between the most conservative and the most aggressive mixes, as shown in Exhibit 29 and Exhibit 30.

To summarize, the current asset mix is moderately aggressive and below the surplus efficient frontier. Thus, a mean–variance improvement is possible: either higher expected surplus with the same surplus risk or lower surplus risk for the same expected surplus. The current portfolio is also poorly hedged with regard to surplus volatility; the hedging asset (long bonds in this case) has a low commitment.

The LOWTECH plan has been frozen, and the investment committee is interested in lowering the volatility of the surplus. Accordingly, it seems appropriate to choose an asset allocation toward the left-hand side of the surplus efficient frontier. For instance, a surplus efficient portfolio with about 60% bonds and the remainder in other assets (as can be approximately identified from Exhibit 29) will drop surplus volatility by about 50%.

In the end, the investment committee for the plan sponsor and its advisers and stakeholders are responsible for rendering the best decision, taking into account all of the above considerations. And as always, the recommendations of a portfolio-modeling exercise are only as good as the input data and assumptions.

MULTI-PERIOD PORTFOLIO MODELS

The traditional mean–variance model assumes that the investor follows a buy-and-hold strategy over the planning horizon. Thus, the portfolio is not rebalanced at intermediate dates. A portfolio investment model requires multiple time periods if rebalancing decisions are to be directly incorporated into the model. Mulvey, Pauling, and Madey (2003) discuss the pros and cons of building and implementing multi-period portfolio models. Applicable to both asset-only and liability-relative asset allocation, multi-period portfolio models are more comprehensive than single-period models but are more complex to implement. These models are generally implemented by means of the integrated asset–liability methods discussed in Section 11.

EXAMPLE 6

Surplus Optimization

1. Explain how surplus optimization solutions differ from mean–variance optimizations based on asset class risk alone.

   Solution:

   The surplus optimization model considers the impact of asset decisions on the (Market value of assets – Present value of liabilities) at the planning horizon.

2. What is a liability return?

   Solution:

   Liability returns measure the time value of money for the liabilities plus any expected changes in the discount rate over the planning horizon.

3. Compare the composition of a surplus optimal portfolio at two points on the surplus efficient frontier. In particular, take one point at the lower left of the surplus frontier (surplus return = US$0.26 billion) and the other point higher on the surplus efficient frontier (surplus return = US$0.32 billion). Refer to Exhibit 29. Explain the observed relationship in terms of the use of corporate bonds as the hedging asset for the liabilities.

   Solution:

   Whereas the portfolio at the US$0.26 billion surplus return point on the efficient frontier has a substantial position in corporate bonds, the efficient mix with US$0.32 billion surplus return does not include them. The observed relationship that the allocation to corporate bonds declines with increasing surplus return can be explained by the positive correlation of bond price with the present value of liabilities. The hedging asset (corporate bonds) is employed to a greater degree at the low end of the surplus efficient frontier.

12 APPROACHES TO LIABILITY-RELATIVE ASSET ALLOCATION

- ☐ describe and evaluate characteristics of liabilities that are relevant to asset allocation
- ☐ discuss approaches to liability-relative asset allocation
- ☐ recommend and justify a liability-relative asset allocation

Hedging/Return-Seeking Portfolio Approach

In this approach, the liability-relative asset allocation task is divided into two parts. We distinguish as "basic" the two-portfolio approach in the case in which there is a surplus available to allocate to a return-seeking portfolio and as "variants" the approach as applied when there is not a positive surplus. In the basic case, the first part of the asset allocation task consists of hedging the liabilities through a hedging portfolio. In the second part, the surplus (or some part of it) is allocated to a return-seeking portfolio, which can be managed independently of the hedging portfolio (for example, using mean–variance optimization or another method). An essential issue involves the composition of the hedging portfolio. In some cases, such as the LOWTECH frozen DB pension plan, the hedging portfolio is straightforward to identify. The designated cash flows can be hedged via cash flow matching, duration matching, or immunization (as explained in the fixed-income readings). This hedge will support the future cash flows with little or no risk.

In LOWTECH's application of the basic two-portfolio approach, the small surplus causes the pension plan to invest most of its capital in the hedging portfolio. The hedging portfolio can be approximated by the long-bond indexed investment as a first cut. Thus, given a 4% discount rate, US$2.261 billion is placed in long bonds. The remaining US$0.239 billion is invested in a portfolio of higher expected return assets, such as stocks, real estate, and hedge funds. This approach guarantees that the capital is adequate to pay future liabilities, as long as the hedging portfolio does not experience defaults.

Note that if the discount rate were 2% rather than 4%, the pension plan would be underfunded even if all assets were placed in a hedging portfolio. In such a case, the pension plan sponsor would either develop a strategy to increase the funding ratio so that the liabilities would be eventually paid or apply a variant of the two-portfolio approach. An underfunded plan will require higher contributions from the sponsor than a plan that is fully funded or overfunded.

The basic two-portfolio approach is most appropriate for conservative investors, such as insurance companies, and for overfunded pension plans that wish to reduce or eliminate the risk of not being able to pay future liabilities.

Several variants of the two-portfolio approach are possible. These include a partial hedge, whereby capital allocated to the hedging portfolio is reduced in order to generate higher expected returns, and dynamic versions whereby the investor increases the allotment to the hedging portfolio as the funding ratio increases. The specification of this allotment is often referred to as the liability glide path. These variants do not hedge the liabilities to the full extent possible given the assets and thus are less conservative than the basic approach discussed above. Still, there can be benefits to a partial hedge when the sponsor is able to increase contributions if the funding ratio does not increase in the future to 1 or above.

In the following discussion, we focus on determining the hedging portfolio.

Forming the Hedging Portfolio

The hedging portfolio must include assets whose returns are driven by the same factor(s) that drive the returns of the liabilities. Otherwise, even if the assets and liabilities start with equal values, the assets and liabilities will likely become inconsistent over time. One example involves promises (cash outflows) that are dependent upon future inflation. The hedging portfolio in this situation would often include index-linked (inflation-linked) Treasury bonds, again cash matched to the liabilities or immunized to the degree possible.

If there is an active market for the hedging portfolio (securities) in question, the present value of future cash flows is equal to a market value of the assets contained in the hedging portfolio. In this case, the date of valuation for the assets must be the same as the date of valuation for the liabilities. Absent market values, some form of appraised value is used.

The task of forming the hedging portfolio is complicated by the discount rate assumption and by the need to identify assets that are driven by the same factors that affect the liabilities. For example, if the discount rate is set by reference to a marketable instrument, such as the long government bond index, but the liability cash flows are driven by a factor such as inflation, the hedging task may require the use of instruments beyond nominal bonds (perhaps multiple instruments, such as interest rate swaps, inflation-linked bonds, and real assets). And in many applications, the hedge cannot be fully accomplished due to the nature of the driving factors (e.g., if they are non-marketable factors, such as economic growth).

If the uncertainties in the cash flows are related to non-market factors, such as future salary increases, the discount rate will depend upon regulations and tradition. Clearly, high discount rates lead to high funding ratios and in most cases require lower contributions from the sponsoring organization (at least in the short run). Conversely, lower discount rates give rise to lower funding ratios and thereby higher contributions. In the former case, investors with high discount rates will need to generate higher asset returns to achieve their promises if the pension plan sponsor wishes to avoid future contributions. A more conservative route is to designate a lower discount rate, as is the case in much of Europe and Asia. In all cases, it is the regulator's responsibility to set the guidelines, rules, and penalties involved in determining contribution policy.

Several issues complicate the valuation of liability cash flows. In many situations, investors must satisfy their promises without being able to go to a market and purchase a security with positive cash flows equal in magnitude to the liability cash flows.

At times, uncertain liabilities can be made more certain through the law of large numbers. For example, life insurance companies promise to pay beneficiaries when a policyholder dies. The life insurance company can minimize the risk of unexpected losses by insuring large numbers of individuals. Then, valuation of liabilities will use present value of expected cash flows based on a low (or even zero) risk premium in the discount rate. The field of application of the law of large numbers can be limited. For example, averages do not eliminate longevity risk.

Limitations

The basic two-portfolio approach cannot be directly applied under several circumstances. First, if the funding ratio is less than 1, the investor cannot create a fully hedging portfolio unless there is a sufficiently large positive cash flow (contribution). In this case, the sponsor might increase contributions enough to generate a positive surplus. As an alternative, there are conditional strategies that might help improve the investor's funding ratio, such as the glide path rules.[22]

A second barrier occurs when a true hedging portfolio is unavailable. An example involves losses due to weather-related causes, such as hurricanes or earthquakes. In these cases, the investor might be able to partially hedge the portfolio with instruments that share some of the same risks. The investor has "basis risk" when imperfect hedges are employed. (As an aside, the investor might be able to set up a contract with someone who, for a fee, will take on the liability risk that cannot be hedged. Insurance contracts have this defining characteristic.)

EXAMPLE 7

The Hedging/Return-Seeking Portfolios Approach

1. Compare how surplus optimization and the hedging/return-seeking portfolio approach take account of liabilities.

Solution:

The surplus optimization approach links assets and the present value of liabilities through a correlation coefficient. The two-portfolio model does

22 See Gannon and Collins (2009).

not require this input. Surplus optimization considers the asset allocation problem in one step; the hedging/return-seeking portfolio approach divides asset allocation into two steps.

2. How does funding status affect the use of the basic hedging/return-seeking portfolio approach?

Solution:

Implementation of the basic two-portfolio approach depends on having an overfunded plan. A variant of the two-portfolio approach might be applied, however. Surplus optimization does not require an overfunded status. Both approaches address the present value of liabilities, but in different ways.

Integrated Asset–Liability Approach

The previous two approaches are most appropriate when asset allocation decisions are made after, and relatively independently of, decisions regarding the portfolio of liabilities. However, there are numerous applications of the liability-relative perspective in which the institution must render significant decisions regarding the composition of its liabilities *in conjunction with the asset allocation.* Banks, long–short hedge funds (for which short positions constitute liabilities), insurance companies, and re-insurance companies routinely fall into this situation. Within this category, the liability-relative approaches have several names, including asset–liability management (ALM) for banks and some other investors and dynamic financial analysis (DFA) for insurance companies. These approaches are often implemented in the context of multi-period models. Using the following two cases, we review the major issues.

INTEGRATED ASSET–LIABILITY APPROACH FOR PROPERTY/CASUALTY INSURANCE COMPANIES

A property/casualty insurance company must make asset investment decisions in conjunction with business decisions about the portfolio of insured properties, its liabilities. To that end, asset and liability decisions are frequently integrated in an enterprise risk management system. In fact, the liability portfolio is essential to the company's long-term viability. For example, a particular property/casualty (PC) insurance company might engage (accept) liabilities for catastrophic risks such as earthquakes and hurricanes. In this case, the liabilities depend upon rare events and thus are most difficult to hedge against. Specialized firms calculate insured losses for a chosen set of properties for property/casualty insurance companies, and these firms provide liability cash flows on a probabilistic (scenario) basis. In this way information is gathered about the probability of losses over the planning horizon and the estimated losses for each loss event. An important issue involves the amount of capital needed to support the indicated liabilities. This issue is addressed by evaluating the tail risks, such as the 1% Value-at-Risk or Conditional-Value-at-Risk amount. To reduce this risk, there are major advantages to forming a diversified global portfolio of liabilities and rendering asset allocation decisions in conjunction with the liability portfolio decisions. The hedging portfolio in this case is not well defined. Therefore, it is difficult to hedge liabilities for a book of catastrophic risk policies. Liabilities might be addressed via customized products or by purchasing re-insurance. The assets and liabilities are integrated so that the worst-case events can be analyzed with regard to both sides of the balance sheet.

INTEGRATED ASSET–LIABILITY APPROACH FOR BANKS

Large global banks are often required to analyze their ability to withstand stress scenarios, in accordance with the Basel III framework. These institutions must be able to show that their current capital is adequate to withstand losses in their business units, such as asset trading, in conjunction with increases in liabilities. The chief risk officer evaluates these scenarios by means of integrated asset–liability approaches. The asset and liability decisions are linked in an enterprise manner. Both the portfolio of assets and the portfolio of liabilities have major impacts on the organization's risk. Thus, decisions to take on new products or expand an existing product—thereby generating liabilities—must take into account the associated decisions on the asset side. The integrated asset–liability management system provides a mechanism for discovering the optimal mix of assets and liabilities (products). These applications often employ multi-period models via a set of projected scenarios.

Decisions about asset allocation will affect the amount of business available to a financial intermediary, such as a bank or insurance company. Similarly, decisions about the portfolio of liabilities and concentration risks will feed back to the asset allocation decisions. Accordingly, we can set up a linked portfolio model. In a similar fashion, the performance of the assets of an institution possessing quasi-liabilities, such as a university endowment, will affect the spending rules for the institution. We can reduce worst-case outcomes by adjusting spending during crash periods, for example. Portfolio models linked to liabilities can provide significant information, helping the institution make the best compromise decisions for both the assets and the liabilities under its control. The twin goals are to maximize the growth of surplus over time subject to constraints on worst-case and other risk measures relative to the institution's surplus.

Comparing the Approaches

We have introduced three approaches for addressing asset allocation decisions in the context of liability issues; Exhibit 31 summarizes their characteristics. Each of these approaches has been applied in practice. The surplus optimization approach is a straightforward extension of the traditional (asset-only) mean–variance model. Surplus optimization demonstrates the importance of the hedging asset for risk-averse investors and provides choices for investors who are less risk averse in the asset mixes located on the middle and the right-hand side of the efficient frontier. The assumptions are similar to those of the traditional Markowitz model, where the inputs are expected returns and a covariance matrix. Thus, the assets and liabilities are linked through correlation conditions. The second approach, separating assets into two buckets, has the advantage of simplicity. The basic approach is most appropriate for conservative investors, such as life insurance companies, and for overfunded/fully funded institutional investors that can fully hedge their liabilities. Another advantage of this approach is a focus on the hedging portfolio and its composition. The hedging portfolio can be constructed using a factor model and then linked to the assets via the same factors. Unfortunately, underfunded investors do not have the luxury of fully hedging their liabilities and investing the surplus in the risky portion; they must apply variants of the two-portfolio approach. The third approach, integrating the liability portfolio with the asset portfolio, is the most comprehensive of the three. It requires a formal method for selecting liabilities and for linking the asset performance with changes in the liability values. This approach can be implemented in a factor-based model, linking the assets and liabilities to the underlying driving factors. It has the potential to improve the institution's overall surplus. It does not require the linear correlation assumption and is capable of modeling transaction costs, turnover constraints, and other real-world constraints. The capital required for this approach is often determined by reference to the output of integrated asset–liability systems in banks and property/casualty insurance and re-insurance companies.

Exhibit 31: Characteristics of the Three Liability-Relative Asset Allocation Approaches

Surplus Optimization	Hedging/Return-Seeking Portfolios	Integrated Asset–Liability Portfolios
Simplicity	Simplicity	Increased complexity
Linear correlation	Linear or non-linear correlation	Linear or non-linear correlation
All levels of risk	Conservative level of risk	All levels of risk
Any funded ratio	Positive funded ratio for basic approach	Any funded ratio
Single period	Single period	Multiple periods

EXAMPLE 8

Liability-Relative Asset Allocation: Major Approaches

1. Discuss how the probability of not being able to pay future liabilities when they come due is or is not addressed by each of the major approaches to liability-relative asset allocation.

   Solution:

   Such issues are best addressed by means of multi-period integrated asset–liability models. Surplus optimization and the two-portfolio approach, being single-period models, have difficulty estimating the probability of meeting future obligations.

2. What are the advantages of the three approaches for investors who are more interested in protecting the surplus than growing their assets? Assume that the investor has a positive surplus.

   Solution:

   The three liability-relative approaches are appropriate for conservative investors (investors who are more interested in protecting the surplus than growing their assets). All of the three approaches force investors to understand the nature of their liabilities. This type of information can help inform the decision-making process.

13 EXAMINING THE ROBUSTNESS OF ASSET ALLOCATION ALTERNATIVES

☐ discuss approaches to liability-relative asset allocation

As part of a liability-relative asset allocation study, the institutional investor can evaluate performance over selected events and "simulated" historical time periods. Each of the selected events can be interpreted as a "what if" sensitivity analysis. For example, we might wish to consider the effect of a 100 bp increase in interest rates across all maturities—that is, a parallel shift in the yield curve. This event would have a significant impact on the value of government bonds, clearly. Also, there would be a corresponding positive impact on the present discounted value of liabilities that are discounted at the government bond rate. The effect on other liability-relative asset allocation elements is less direct, and assumptions must be made. Suppose, for example, that the investor must discount at the high-quality corporate rate. In that case, we need to estimate the effect of changing government rates on corporate rates. These designated studies are part of the stress tests required by banking and other regulators.

Another type of event study is the construction of scenarios based on carefully selected historical time periods. For example, we might select late 2008 as a reference point. In such a scenario, we are interested in the changes in the economic factors and the associated changes in the values of the institution's assets and liabilities. What would be the impact on our current (or projected) portfolio—assets and PV(liabilities)—if the conditions seen in late 2008 occurred again?

A more comprehensive method for examining robustness involves setting up a multi-stage simulation analysis. Here, we use scenarios to model uncertainty and replace decisions with "rules." The process begins with a set of scenarios for the underlying driving economic factors. Each scenario designates a path for the asset returns and the liability values at each stage of the planning horizon. The result is a set of probabilistic outcomes for the institutional investor's asset portfolio and the cash flows for its liabilities. In such modeling, one must take care to be consistent between asset returns and corresponding liabilities within a scenario; for example, if interest rates are a common factor driving both asset performance and the PV (liabilities), the interest rate effects should be based on the same assumptions.

Through the scenario analysis, the probability of both good and bad outcomes can be estimated. For example, we can measure the probability that an institutional investor will make a capital contribution in the future. Exhibit 32 shows the decision structure for the simulation of an insurance company over several periods, including modeling of the company's business strategy and the required capital rules.

To evaluate robustness, we can apply the simulation system with different assumptions. For instance, if we change the expected return of US equities, what is the effect on the probability of meeting the liabilities over an extended horizon, such as 10 years? This type of sensitivity analysis is routinely done in conjunction with the modeling exercise.

Exhibit 32: Simulation Analysis

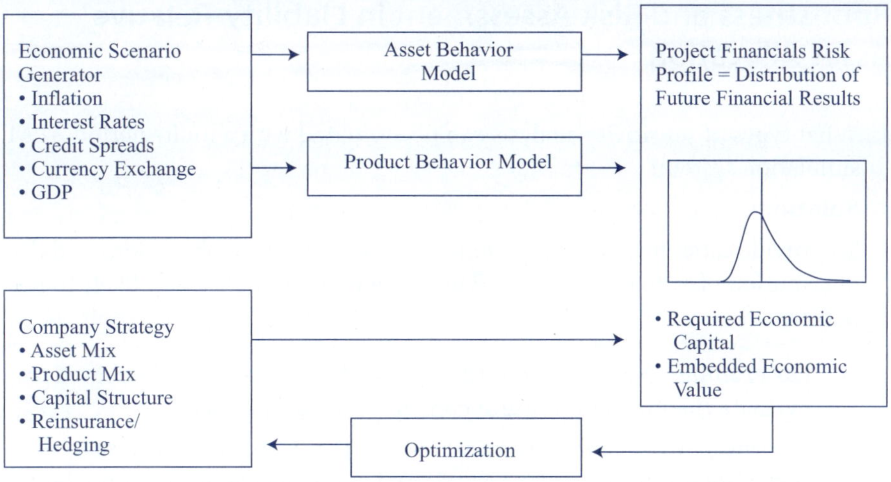

14 FACTOR MODELING IN LIABILITY-RELATIVE APPROACHES

- ☐ describe the use of investment factors in constructing and analyzing an asset allocation
- ☐ discuss approaches to liability-relative asset allocation

A factor-based approach for liability-relative asset allocation has gained interest and credibility for several reasons. First, in many applications, the liability cash flows are dependent on multiple uncertainties. The two primary macro factors are future economic conditions and inflation. Many pension payments to beneficiaries will be based on inflation and salary changes over the employees' work span. A fully hedged portfolio cannot be constructed when the liabilities are impacted by these uncertain factors. Recall that a hedged portfolio can be constructed for a frozen plan with fixed liabilities. For ongoing pension schemes, the best that can be done is to add asset categories to the portfolio that are positively correlated with the underlying driving risk factors, such as inflation-linked bonds. A factor-based approach can be implemented with any of the three liability-relative asset allocation methods discussed above.

EXAMPLE 9

Robustness and Risk Assessment in Liability-Relative Asset Allocation

1. What types of sensitivity analysis can be evaluated with a multi-period ALM simulation system?

Solution:

To provide estimates of the probability of meeting future obligations and the distribution of outcomes, several types of sensitivity analysis are likely to be performed.

- For example, the expected returns could be increased or decreased to evaluate the impact on future contributions to the plan.
- Likewise, by analyzing historical events, the investor can estimate the size of losses during crash periods and make decisions about the best asset allocation to protect against these worst-case events. Multiple risk measures over time (temporal risk measures) can be readily included in a simulation system.

15 DEVELOPING GOALS-BASED ASSET ALLOCATIONS

☐ recommend and justify an asset allocation using a goals-based approach

In this section, we review the concept of goals-based asset allocation, focusing first on the rationale behind this different approach and its investment implications. We then discuss the major elements of the process, illustrating them with specific, simplified examples when necessary. We conclude with a discussion of the applicability of the approach and its major shortcomings.

A goals-based asset allocation process disaggregates the investor's portfolio into a number of sub-portfolios, each of which is designed to fund an individual goal (or "mental account") with its own time horizon and required probability of success. The literature behind the development of this approach is very rich. Initially, goals-based wealth management was specifically proposed by a small group of practitioners,[23] each of whom offered his own solution for taking into account the tendency of individuals to classify money into non-fungible mental accounts. Shefrin and Statman (2000) developed the concept of the behavioral portfolio, which can be related to the Maslow (1943) hierarchy of needs. Das, Markowitz, Scheid, and Statman (2010, 2011) showed that traditional and behavioral finance could be viewed as equivalent if one were prepared to change the definition of risk from volatility of returns to the probability of not achieving a goal.[24] The essential point is that optimality requires

23 See Brunel (2003, 2005); Nevins (2004); Pompian and Longo (2004); Chhabra (2005).

24 We apologize to these authors for grossly oversimplifying their work, but our aim is to make their insights more readily available without going into excruciating detail.

both a suitably structured portfolio that can meet the given need *and* the correct capital allocation based on an appropriate discount rate, reflecting considerations of time horizon and the required probability of success.

Individuals have needs that are different from those of institutions. The most important difference is that individuals often have multiple goals, each with its own time horizon and its own "urgency," which can be expressed as a specific required probability of success. Exhibit 33 summarizes differences in institutional and individual investor definitions of goals. An individual's goals are not necessarily mutually compatible in two senses: The investor may not be able to address them all given the financial assets available, and there may be internal contradictions among the goals. An alternative process using one set of overall investment objectives—and thus effectively ignoring or "averaging" the different time horizons and required probabilities of success of individual goals—ostensibly loses the granular nature of client goals; as a result, the inherent complexities of the investment problem are less likely to be addressed fully. An approach that breaks the problem into sub-portfolios carries a higher chance of fully addressing an investor's goals, although it may require several iterations to ensure that the investor's portfolio is internally consistent and satisfactory.

Exhibit 33: Institutional and Individual Ways of Defining Goals

	Institutions	Individuals
Goals	Single	Multiple
Time horizon	Single	Multiple
Risk measure	Volatility (return or surplus)	Probability of missing goal
Return determination	Mathematical expectations[a]	Minimum expectations
Risk determination	Top-down/bottom-up	Bottom-up
Tax status	Single, often tax-exempt	Mostly taxable

[a] *"Mathematical expectations" here means the weighted expected return of portfolio components.*

The characteristics of individuals' goals have three major implications for an investment process that attempts to address the characteristics directly:

- The overall portfolio needs to be divided into sub-portfolios to permit each goal to be addressed individually.
- Both taxable and tax-exempt investments are important.
- Probability- and horizon-adjusted expectations (called "minimum expectations" in Exhibit 33) replace the typical use of mathematically expected average returns in determining the appropriate funding cost for the goal (or "discount rate" for future cash flows).

Compared with average return expectations—the median or average return anticipated for a combination of assets that is appropriate to address a goal—minimum expectations reflect a more complex concept. Minimum expectations are defined as the minimum return expected to be earned over the given time horizon with a given minimum required probability of success.

To illustrate, assume that a portfolio associated with a goal has an expected return of 7% with 10% expected volatility and the investor has indicated that the goal is to be met over the next five years with at least 90% confidence. Over the next five years, that portfolio is expected to produce returns of 35% with a volatility of 22.4%.[25] In short, this portfolio is expected to experience an average compound return of only 1.3% per year over five years with a probability of 90%; this result is quite a bit lower than the portfolio's average 7% expected return (see Exhibit 34). Thus, rather than discounting expected cash outflows by 7% to compute the dollar amount needed to defease the goal over that five-year horizon, one must use a considerably lower discount rate and by implication reserve a higher level of capital to meet that goal. Under moderate simplifying assumptions, that computation is valid whether or not return and volatility numbers are pretax or after-tax. Exhibit 34 shows, for the case of a normal distribution of returns, a return level that is expected to be exceeded 90% of the time (the 40% of the probability that lies between the vertical lines plus the 50% to the right of the median).

Exhibit 34: Probability-Weighted Return vs. Expected (= Median) Return

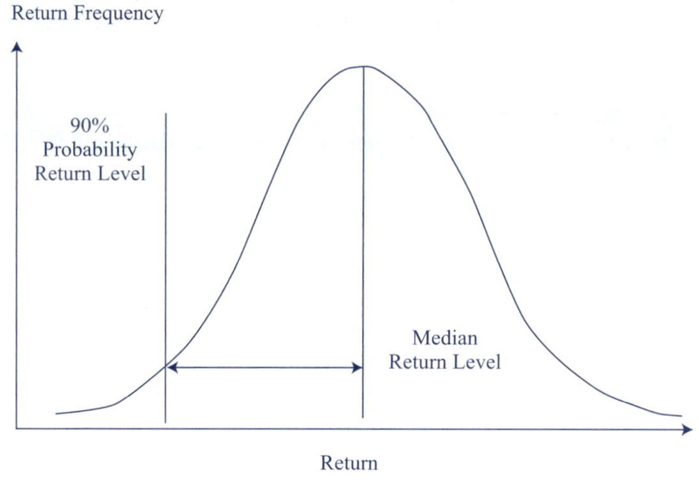

The Goals-Based Asset Allocation Process

Investment advisers taking a goals-based approach to investing client assets may implement this approach in a variety of ways. Exhibit 35 illustrates the major elements of the goals-based asset allocation process described in this reading. Ostensibly, there are two fundamental parts to this process. The first centers on the creation of portfolio modules, while the second involves identifying client goals and matching each of these goals to the appropriate sub-portfolio of a suitable asset size.

25 The return is the product of the annual return times the number of years, while the volatility is the product of the annual volatility times the square root of the number of years (under the assumption of independently and identically distributed returns).

Exhibit 35: A Stylized Representation of the Goals-Based Asset Allocation Process

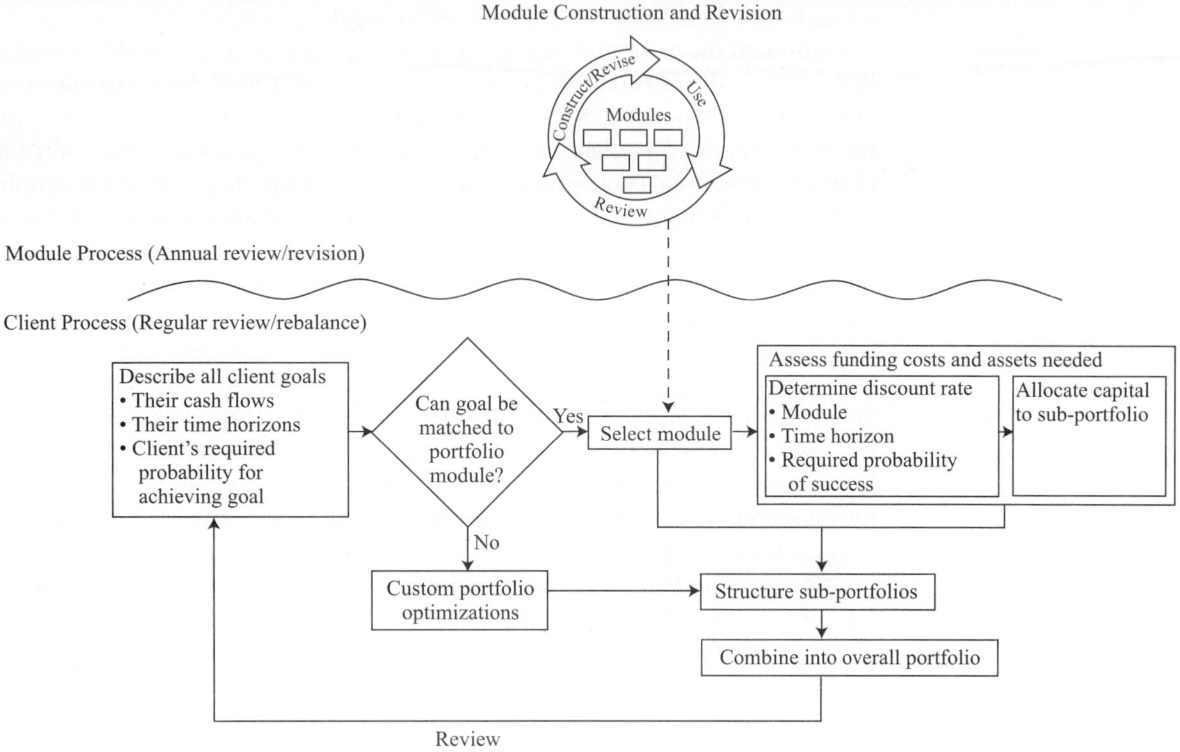

Determining the lowest-cost funding for any given goal requires the formulation of an optimized portfolio that will be used to defease that goal optimally in the sense that risks are not taken for which the investor is not fairly compensated. Note that this process is most often generic and internal to the adviser and his or her firm. The adviser will typically not create a specific sub-portfolio for each goal of each client but rather will select, from a pre-established set, one of a few modules—or model portfolios—that best meet each goal.[26] As discussed above, adjusting the expected return on that portfolio to account for the time horizon and the required probability of success allows one to formulate the relevant discount rate which, when applied to the expected cash flows, will help determine the capital required at the outset. That capital will then be invested in the optimized portfolio asset allocation, where the balance will decline until the end of the horizon, when it runs out.[27] Note that the process is somewhat iterative because individual investors may describe a certain horizon as set when in fact they view it as "the next *x* years," with the horizon rolling by one year every year. Note also that discounting needs based on probability- and

26 See the next paragraph for a discussion of when it makes sense to create specific optimal sub-portfolios.

27 An important reason for the use of a declining-balance portfolio relates to the need for individuals and families to plan for the transfer of assets at death. In order for the income from assets to be used by an individual, these assets must be in the individual's name, or at least in a structure of which he or she is a beneficiary. Such assets would then be a part of the estate of the individual. Using a declining-balance portfolio allows the individual to receive the income—and some of the principal liquidated every year—while still ensuring that the amount of assets kept in the individual's name remains as low as appropriate given the individual's goals. An exception to this scenario would be the case of families whose income needs are so modest in relation to total assets that there is no need to provide income in planning for generational transfers or families that have such large eventual philanthropic intentions that assets kept in some beneficiaries' names are meant to be transferred to charity at death.

horizon-adjusted minimum expectations naturally means that these expectations will be exceeded under "normal circumstances." Thus, it is not unusual for the funding for a goal to seem excessive with the benefit of hindsight.

Although the great majority of advisers will likely create individual client portfolios using model portfolios—precisely, pre-optimized modules—a greater degree of customization is possible. Such customization involves creating specific sub-portfolios for each goal of each client. Indeed, it is conceivable, and mathematically possible, to create an optimal sub-portfolio for each goal. In fact, in practice, one would often proceed in this way when dealing with complex situations and with clients who have highly differentiated needs and constraints.[28] The adviser may find it impossible to use pre-optimized modules if the investment constraints imposed by the client are incompatible with those used in the creation of the module set. These might include, for instance, geographical or credit emphases—or de-emphases—that conflict with the market portfolio concept. Other restrictions might concern base currency, the use of alternative strategies, or the acceptability of illiquid investments, for example. Thus, although it is feasible for advisers to create client-specific modules, this approach can become prohibitively expensive. In short, one would likely use standardized modules for most individuals, except for those whose situation is so complex as to require a fully customized approach.

Many multi-client advisers may prefer to create a set of "goal modules" whose purpose is, collectively, to cover a full range of capital market opportunities and, individually, to represent a series of return–risk trade-offs that are sufficiently differentiated to offer adequate but not excessive choices to meet all the goals they expect their clients to express. These modules should therefore collectively appear to create a form of efficient frontier, though the frontier they depict in fact does not exist because the modules may well be based on substantially different sets of optimization constraints.

The two most significant differences from one module to the next, besides the implied return–risk trade-offs, are liquidity requirements and the eligibility of certain asset classes or strategies. Additionally, while intra–asset class allocation to individual sub–asset classes or strategies may typically be guided by the market portfolio for that asset class, one can conceive of instances where the selection of a specific sub–asset class or strategy is justified, even though the asset class per se may seem inappropriate. For instance, one might agree to hold high-yield bonds in an equity-dominated portfolio because of the equity risk factor exposure inherent in lower-credit fixed income. Conversely, the fixed-income market portfolio might be limited to investment-grade bonds and possibly the base-currency-hedged variant of non-domestic investment-grade bonds. We will return to the construction of these modules in Section 17.

Describing Client Goals

At this point, it is important to note that individual investors do not always consider all goals as being equal and similarly well-formulated in their own minds. Thus, while certain investors will have a well-thought-out set of goals—which may at times not be simultaneously achievable given the financial assets available—others will focus only on a few "urgent" goals and keep other requirements in the background.

Thus, a first step is to distinguish between goals for which anticipated cash flows are available—whether regularly or irregularly timed across the horizon or represented by a bullet payment at some future point—and those we call "labeled goals," for which details are considerably less precise. The term "labeled" here simply means that the individual has certain "investment features" in mind—such as minimal risk, capital

28 Note that such an approach, being more complex, is also costlier. It would therefore be more likely to be economically feasible for those advisory clients who also have the ability to pay a higher fee.

preservation, purchasing power preservation, and long-term growth—but has not articulated the actual need that stands behind each label. The individual may already have mentally allocated some portion of his or her assets, in currency or percentage terms, to one or several of these labels. For cash flow–based goals,[29] the time horizon over which the goal is to be met is usually not difficult to ascertain: It is either the period over which cash outflows are expected to be made or the point in time at which a bullet payment is expected. More complex, however, is the issue of the urgency of the goal and thus of the required minimum probability of success.

By working to preserve a human (as opposed to a technical) tone in the advisory conversations, the adviser can serve the client without forcing him or her to come up with a quantified probability of success. The adviser may start with the simple observation that there are two fundamental types of goals: those that one seeks to achieve and those whose consequences one seeks to avoid. Dividing the goals the investor seeks to achieve into "needs, wants, wishes, and dreams" provides the adviser with an initial sense of the urgency of each goal. A need typically must be met and so should command a 90%–99% probability of success, while at the other end of the spectrum, it is an unfortunate fact that we all live with unfulfilled dreams, whose required probabilities of success probably fall below 60%. A parallel—and analogous—structure can be created to deal with goals one seeks to avoid:[30] "nightmares, fears, worries, and concerns," with similar implications in terms of required probabilities of success. In short, while some discussion of probability level may well take place, it can be informed and guided by the use of commonly accepted everyday words that will ensure that the outcome is internally consistent. The adviser avoids the use of jargon, which many clients dislike, and yet is able to provide professional advice.[31]

The simplest way to bring this concept to life is to work with a basic case study. Imagine a family, the Smiths, with financial assets of US$25 million. (For the sake of simplicity, we are assuming that they do not pay taxes and that all assets are owned in a single structure.) The parents are in their mid-fifties, and the household spends about US$500,000 a year. They expect that inflation will average about 2% per year for the foreseeable future. They express four important goals and are concerned that they may not be able to meet all of them:

1. They *need* a 95% chance of being able to maintain their current expenditures over the next five years.
2. They *want* an 85% chance of being able to maintain their current expenditures over the ensuing 25 years, which they see as a reasonable estimate of their joint life expectancy.
3. They *need* a 90% chance of being able to transfer US$10 million to their children in 10 years.
4. They *wish* to have a 75% chance to be able to create a family foundation, which they wish to fund with US$10 million in 20 years.

---

29 Note that all cash flows do not have to be negative (i.e., outflows). One can easily imagine circumstances where certain future inflows are anticipated and yet are not seen, individually, as sufficient to meet the specified goal.

30 Although negative goals may sound surprising, they do exist and play a double role. First, when a negative goal is explicitly stated, it can be "replaced" by a specific positive goal: Avoiding the nightmare of running out of capital, for example, can be turned into the need to meet a certain expense budget. Second, negative goals serve as a useful feedback loop to check the internal consistency of the investor's goal set.

31 Note that the adviser can also identify a series of "secondary" words to help determine whether a need, for instance, means that the required probability of success should be set at 99%, 95%, or 90%. An *indispensable* need could require a 99% probability of being met, while an *urgent* need might require only a 95% probability of success, and a *serious* need a 90% probability.

EXAMPLE 10

Understanding Client Goals

1. A client describes a desire to have a reserve of €2 million for business opportunities that may develop when he retires in five years. What are the important features of this goal?

   Solution:

   The time horizon is five years. Words such as "desire" in describing a goal, compared with expressions indicating "need," indicate that there is room for "error" in the event that capital markets are not supportive. The portfolio required to meet the goal described as a desire will likely be able to involve a riskier profile. One would want to verify this assumption by comparing the size of that goal compared with the total financial assets available to the client.

2. A 70-year-old client discusses the need to be able to maintain her lifestyle for the balance of her life and wishes to leave US$3 million to be split among her three grandchildren at her death. What are the important features of this situation?

   Solution:

   The key takeaway is that although the two goals have the same time horizon, the two portfolios designed to defease them will have potentially significantly different risk profiles. The time horizon is approximately 20 years. The first goal relates to maintaining the client's lifestyle and must be defeased with an appropriately structured portfolio. The second goal, relating to the wish to leave some money to grandchildren, will allow more room for risk taking.

16 CONSTRUCTING SUB-PORTFOLIOS AND THE OVERALL PORTFOLIO

☐ recommend and justify an asset allocation using a goals-based approach

Having defined the needs of the investor in as much detail as possible, the next step in the process is to identify the amount of money that needs to be allocated to each goal and the asset allocation that will apply to that sum. For most advisers, the process will start with a set of sub-portfolio modules (such as those we briefly discussed in Section 15 and will study in more depth in Section 17). When using a set of pre-optimized modules, the adviser will then need to identify the module best suited to each of the specific goals of the client. That process is always driven by the client's time horizon and required probability of success, and it involves identifying the module that offers the highest possible return given the investor's risk tolerance as characterized by a given required probability of success over a given time horizon.

To illustrate, consider the set of six modules shown in Exhibit 36;[32] these modules result from an optimization process that will be explained later.[33] In the exhibit, the entries for minimum expected return are shown rounded to one decimal place; subsequent calculations for required capital are based on full precision.

Exhibit 36: "Highest Probability- and Horizon-Adjusted Return" Sub-Portfolio Module under Different Horizon and Probability Scenarios

	A	B	C	D	E	F
Portfolio Characteristics						
Expected return	4.3%	5.5%	6.4%	7.2%	8.0%	8.7%
Expected volatility	2.7%	4.5%	6.0%	7.5%	10.0%	12.5%
Annualized Minimum Expectation Returns						
Time Horizon (years)				5		
Required Success						
99%	1.5%	0.9%	0.2%	−0.6%	−2.4%	−4.3%
95	2.3	2.2	2.0	1.7	0.7	−0.5
90	2.7	3.0	3.0	2.9	2.3	1.5
75	3.5	4.2	4.6	4.9	5.0	4.9
Time Horizon (years)				10		
Required Success						
99%	2.3%	2.2%	2.0%	1.7%	0.7%	−0.5%
90	3.2	3.7	4.0	4.1	4.0	3.6
75	3.7	4.6	5.1	5.6	5.9	6.0%
60	4.1	5.2	5.9	6.6	7.2	7.7
Time Horizon (years)				20		
Required Success						
95%	3.3%	3.9%	4.2%	4.4%	4.4%	4.1%
90	3.5	4.3	4.7	5.0	5.2	5.1
85	3.7	4.5	5.0	5.4	5.7	5.8
75	3.9	4.9	5.5	6.0	6.5	6.8
Time Horizon (years)				25		
Required Success						
95%	3.4%	4.1%	4.4%	4.7%	4.7%	4.6%
90	3.6	4.4	4.9	5.2	5.5	5.5
85	3.7	4.6	5.2	5.6	6.0	6.1
75	3.9	4.9	5.6	6.2	6.7	7.0

In Exhibit 36, the top section, on portfolio characteristics, presents the expected return and expected volatility of each module. Below that are four sections, one for each of four time horizons: 5, 10, 20, and 25 years. In a given section, the entries are

32 The different ranges of required probabilities of success for various time horizons reflect the fact that the differentiation across modules can occur more or less rapidly, reflecting the different ratios of return per unit of risk.

33 Exhibit 38 presents the details of the asset allocation of these modules and the constraints underpinning their optimization.

the returns that are expected for a given required probability of achieving success. For example, at a 10-year horizon and a 90% required probability of success, Modules A, B, C, D, E, and F are expected to return, respectively, 3.2%, 3.7%, 4.0%, 4.1%, 4.0%, and 3.6%. In this case, Module D would be selected to address a goal with this time horizon and required probability of success because its 4.1% expected return is higher than those of all the other modules. Thus, Module D offers the lowest "funding cost" for the given goal. The highest expected return translates to the lowest initially required capital when the expected cash flows associated with the goal are discounted using that expected return.

EXAMPLE 11

Selecting a Module

Address the following module selection problems using Exhibit 36:

1. A client describes a desire to have a reserve of €2 million for business opportunities that may develop when he retires in five years. Assume that the word "desire" points to a wish to which the adviser will ascribe a probability of 75%.

   Solution:

   The time horizon is five years. Exhibit 36 shows that Module E has the highest expected return (5.0%) over the five-year period and with the assumed 75% required probability of success.

2. A 70-year-old client with a 20-year life expectancy discusses the need to be able to maintain her lifestyle for the balance of her life and wishes to leave US$3 million to be split among her three grandchildren at her death.

   Solution:

   The time horizon is 20 years. The first goal is a need, while the second is a wish. We assume a required probability of success of 95% for a need and 75% for a wish. Exhibit 36 shows that Module D provides the highest horizon- and required-probability-adjusted return (4.4%) for the first goal. Module F is better suited to the second goal because, even though the second goal has the same time horizon, it involves only a 75% required probability of success; the appropriately adjusted return is 6.8%, markedly the highest, which means the initially required capital is lower.

Returning to the Smiths, let us use that same set of modules to look at their four specific goals. The results of our analysis are presented in Exhibit 37.

1. The first goal is a need, with a five-year time horizon and a 95% required probability of success. Looking at the 95% required probability line in the five-year time horizon section of Exhibit 36, we can see that the module with the highest expected return on a time horizon- and required probability-adjusted basis is Module A and that the appropriately adjusted expected return for that module is 2.3%. Discounting a US$500,000 annual cash flow, inflated by 2% a year from Year 2 onwards, required a US$2,430,000 initial investment. This amount represents 9.7% of the total financial wealth of the Smiths.
2. The second goal is a want, with a 25-year time horizon and an 85% required probability of success. The corresponding line of the table in Exhibit 36 points to Module F and a discount rate of 6.1%. Discounting their current

expenses with the same assumption over the 25 years starting in Year 6 with a 6.1% rate points to an initially required capital of US$6,275,000, representing 25.1% of the Smiths' wealth.

3. The third goal is another need, with a 10-year time horizon and a 90% required probability of success. Module D is the best module, and the US$6,691,000 required capital reflects the discounting of a US$10 million payment in 10 years at the 4.1% indicated in Exhibit 36.
4. Finally, the fourth goal is a wish with a 20-year time horizon and a 75% required probability of success. Module F is again the best module, and the discounting of a US$10 million payment 20 years from now at the 6.8% expected return from Exhibit 36 points to a required capital of US$2,683,000 today.

Note that different goals may, in fact, be optimally addressed using the same module; thus, an individual module may be used more than once in the allocation of the individual's overall financial assets. Here, Goals 2 and 4 can both be met with the riskiest of the six modules, although their time horizons differ, as do the required probabilities of success, with Goal 2 being characterized as a want and Goal 4 as a wish.

Exhibit 37: Module Selection and Dollar Allocations (US$ thousands)

	Total Financial Assets				25,000	
	Goals					Overall Asset Allocation
	1	2	3	4	Surplus	
Horizon (years)	5	25	10	20		
Required probability of success	95%	85%	90%	75%	$E(R_t)$	7.2%
Discount rate	2.3%	6.1%	4.1%	6.8%	$\sigma(R_t)$	8.0%
Module	**A**	**F**	**D**	**F**	**C**	
Required capital						
In currency	2,430	6,275	6,691	2,683	6,921	25,000
As a % of total	9.7%	25.1%	26.8%	10.7%	27.7%	100.0%

Note also that the Smiths' earlier worry, that they might not be able to meet all their goals, can be addressed easily. Our assumptions suggest that, in fact, they have excess capital representing 27.7% of their total financial wealth. They can either revisit their current goals and bring the timing of payments forward or raise their probability of success. The case suggests that they would rather think of additional goals but will want to give themselves some time to refine their intentions. Their adviser then suggests that a "middle of the road" module be used as a "labeled goal" for that interim period, and they call this module (Module C) "capital preservation."

The Overall Portfolio

Assuming the same six modules, with their detailed composition shown in Exhibit 38, one can then derive the overall asset allocation by aggregating the individual exposures to the various modules. In short, the overall allocation is simply the weighted average exposure to each of the asset classes or strategies within each module, with the weight being the percentage of financial assets allocated to each module. Exhibit

39 presents these computations and the overall asset allocation, which is given in bold in the right-most column. The overall portfolio's expected return and volatility are also shown. In Exhibit 38, liquidity[34] is measured as one minus the ratio of the average number of days that might be needed to liquidate a position to the number of trading days in a year. (Note that the column B values add up to 101 because of rounding.)

Exhibit 38: Asset Allocation of Each Module

	A	B	C	D	E	F
Portfolio Characteristics						
Expected return	4.3%	5.5%	6.4%	7.2%	8.0%	8.7%
Expected volatility	2.7%	4.5%	6.0%	7.5%	10.0%	12.5%
Expected liquidity	100.0%	96.6%	90.0%	86.1%	83.6%	80.0%
Portfolio Allocations						
Cash	80%	26%	3%	1%	1%	1%
Global investment-grade bonds	20	44	45	25	0	0
Global high-yield bonds	0	5	11	25	34	4
Lower-volatility alternatives	0	9	13	0	0	0
Global developed equities	0	9	13	19	34	64
Global emerging equities	0	2	2	3	6	11
Equity-based alternatives	0	0	0	8	0	0
Illiquid global equities	0	0	5	10	15	20
Trading strategy alternatives	0	1	3	6	7	0
Global real estate	0	5	5	3	3	0
Total	100%	100%	100%	100%	100%	100%

34 Note that we need to incorporate some estimate of liquidity for all asset classes and strategies to ensure that the client's and the goals' liquidity constraints can be met.

Exhibit 39: Goals-Based Asset Allocation (US$ thousands)

	Total Financial Assets				25,000	
	Goals					Overall Asset Allocation
	1	2	3	4	Surplus	
Horizon	5	25	10	20		
Required success	95%	85%	90%	75%	$E(R_t)$	7.2%
Discount rate	2.3%	6.1%	4.1%	6.8%	$\sigma(R_t)$	8.0%
Module	**A**	**F**	**D**	**F**	**C**	
Required capital						
In currency	2,430	6,275	6,691	2,683	6,921	25,000
As a % of total	9.7	25.1	26.8	10.7	27.7	100.0
Cash	80%	1%	1%	1%	3%	**9%**
Global investment-grade bonds	20	0	25	0	45	**24**
Global high-yield bonds	0	4	25	4	11	**12**
Lower-volatility alternatives	0	0	0	0	13	**4**
Global developed equities	0	64	19	64	13	**28**
Global emerging equities	0	11	3	11	2	**5**
Equity-based alternatives	0	0	8	0	0	**2**
Illiquid global equities	0	20	10	20	5	**10**
Trading strategy alternatives[a]	0	0	6	0	3	**3**
Global real estate	0	0	3	0	5	**2**
Total	100	100	100	100	100	**100**

[a] *"Trading strategy alternatives" refers to discretionary or systematic trading strategies such as global macro and managed futures.*

REVISITING THE MODULE PROCESS IN DETAIL 17

☐ recommend and justify an asset allocation using a goals-based approach

Having explained and illustrated the client process in Exhibit 35, we now explore how modules are developed. Creating an appropriate set of optimized modules starts with the formulation of capital market assumptions. Exhibit 40 presents a possible set of forward-looking pretax capital market expectations for expected return, volatility, and liquidity[35] in Panel A and a historical 15-year correlation matrix in Panel B.[36]

Exhibit 40: Example of Capital Market Expectations for a Possible Asset Class Universe

Panel A

	Expected		
	Return	Volatility	Liquidity
Cash	4.0%	3.0%	100%
Global investment-grade bonds	5.5	6.5	100
Global high-yield bonds	7.0	10.0	100
Lower-volatility alternatives	5.5	5.0	65
Global developed equities	8.0	16.0	100
Global emerging equities	9.5	22.0	100
Equity-based alternatives	6.0	8.0	65
Illiquid global equities	11.0	30.0	0
Trading strategy alternatives	6.5	10.0	80
Global real estate	7.0	15.0	100

Panel B

		Global			Global					
	Cash	IG Bonds	HY Bonds	Lower-Volatility Alts	Developed Equities	Emerging Equities	Equity-Based Alts	Trading Strategy Alts	Illiquid Equities	Global Real Estate
Cash	**1.00**	0.00	−0.12	0.08	−0.06	−0.04	0.02	0.04	−0.26	−0.01
Global investment-grade bonds	0.00	**1.00**	0.27	0.14	0.28	0.09	0.07	0.16	0.20	0.24
Global high-yield bonds	−0.12	0.27	**1.00**	0.46	0.70	0.17	0.31	−0.08	0.35	0.28
Lower-volatility alternatives	0.08	0.14	0.46	**1.00**	0.44	0.61	0.86	0.12	0.65	0.47
Global developed equities	−0.06	0.28	0.70	0.44	**1.00**	0.17	0.32	−0.03	0.47	0.38
Global emerging equities	−0.04	0.09	0.17	0.61	0.17	**1.00**	0.72	−0.03	0.67	0.49
Equity-based alternatives	0.02	0.07	0.31	0.86	0.32	0.72	**1.00**	0.11	0.72	0.45

35 For clients who might invest in traditional asset classes by means of vehicles such as mutual funds or ETFs, these asset classes can be treated as providing virtually instant liquidity. For clients with particularly large asset pools who might use separately managed accounts, the liquidity factor for high-yield or emerging market bonds, small-capitalization equities, and certain real assets might be adjusted downward.
36 For illiquid equities, data availability reduces the time period to seven years. The correlation matrix is based on the 15 years ending with March 2016.

	Cash	Global IG Bonds	Global HY Bonds	Lower-Volatility Alts	Global Developed Equities	Global Emerging Equities	Equity-Based Alts	Trading Strategy Alts	Illiquid Equities	Global Real Estate
Trading strategy alternatives	0.04	0.16	−0.08	0.12	−0.03	−0.03	0.11	**1.00**	−0.09	0.07
Illiquid global equities	−0.26	0.20	0.35	0.65	0.47	0.67	0.72	−0.09	**1.00**	0.88
Global real estate	−0.01	0.24	0.28	0.47	0.38	0.49	0.45	0.07	0.88	**1.00**

Ostensibly, in the real world, the process ought to be associated with a set of after-tax expectations, which usually cannot be limited to broad asset classes or sub–asset classes. Indeed, the tax impact of management processes within individual asset classes or strategies (for instance, index replication, index replication with systematic tax-loss harvesting, broadly diversified portfolios, or concentrated portfolios) requires that each management process within each asset class or strategy be given its own expected return and volatility. We will dispense with that step here for the sake of simplicity, both in absolute terms and with respect to jurisdictional differences.

Exhibit 41 presents a possible set of such modules based on the capital market expectations from Exhibit 40. The optimization uses a mean–variance process and is subject to a variety of constraints that are meant to reflect both market portfolio considerations and reasonable asset class or strategy suitability given the goals that we expect to correspond to various points on the frontier. Note that the frontier is not "efficient" in the traditional sense of the term because the constraints applied to the portfolios differ from one to the next. Three elements within the set of constraints deserve special mention. The first is the need to be concerned with the liquidity of the various strategies: It would make little sense, even if it were appropriate based on other considerations, to include any material exposure to illiquid equities in a declining-balance portfolio expected to "mature" within 10 years, for instance. Any exposure thus selected would be bound to increase through time because portfolio liquidation focuses on more-liquid assets. The second relates to strategies whose return distributions are known not to be "normal." This point applies particularly to a number of alternative strategies that suffer from skew and kurtosis,[37] which a mean–variance optimization process does not take into account (see Section 6). Finally, the constraints contain a measure of drawdown control to alleviate the problems potentially associated with portfolios that, although apparently optimal, appear too risky in overly challenging market circumstances. Drawdown controls are an important element in that they help deal with the often-observed asymmetric tolerance of investors for volatility: upward volatility is much preferred to downward volatility.

37 Kat (2003) described the challenge, and Davies, Kat, and Lu (2009) presented a solution that involves the use of mean–variance-skew-kurtosis optimization, which is typically too complex for most real-life circumstances.

Exhibit 41: Six Possible Sub-Portfolio Modules

	A	B	C	D	E	F
Portfolio Characteristics						
Expected return	4.3%	5.5%	6.4%	7.2%	8.0%	8.7%
Expected volatility	2.7	4.5	6.0	7.5	10.0	12.5
Expected liquidity	100.0	96.6	90.0	86.1	83.6	80.0
Portfolio Allocations						
Cash	80%	26%	3%	1%	1%	1%
Global investment-grade bonds	20	44	45	25	0	0
Global high-yield bonds	0	5	11	25	34	4
Lower-volatility alternatives	0	9	13	0	0	0
Global developed equities	0	9	13	19	34	64
Global emerging equities	0	2	2	3	6	11
Equity-based alternatives	0	0	0	8	0	0
Illiquid global equities	0	0	5	10	15	20
Trading strategy alternatives	0	1	3	6	7	0
Global real estate	0	5	5	3	3	0
Total	100%	100%	100%	100%	100%	100%
Constraints						
Maximum volatility	3.0%	4.5%	6.0%	7.5%	10.0%	12.5%
Minimum liquidity	100.0	95.0	90.0	85.0	80.0	70.0
Maximum alternatives	0.0	10.0	20.0	30.0	30.0	30.0
Minimum cash	80.0	20.0	0.3	0.5	0.7	1.0
Maximum HY as a percent of total fixed income	0.0	10.0	20.0	50.0	100.0	100.0
Maximum equity spectrum	0.0	10.0	20.0	40.0	75.0	100.0
Maximum EM as a percent of public equities	15.0	15.0	15.0	15.0	15.0	15.0
Maximum illiquid equities	0.0	0.0	5.0	10.0	15.0	20.0
Maximum trading as a percent of equity spectrum	0.0	10.0	15.0	15.0	20.0	25.0
Maximum real estate	0.0	5.0	10.0	15.0	20.0	25.0
Escrow cash as a percent of illiquid equities	5.0	5.0	5.0	5.0	5.0	5.0
Maximum probability of return < drawdown	1.0	1.5	2.0	2.0	2.5	2.5
Drawdown horizon	3	3	3	3	3	3
Drawdown amount	0.0	–5.0	–7.5	–10.0	–15.0	–20.0

The six sub-portfolios shown in Exhibit 41 satisfy two major design goals: First, they cover a wide spectrum of the investment universe, ranging from a nearly all-cash portfolio (Portfolio A) to an all-equity alternative (Portfolio F). Second, they are sufficiently differentiated to avoid creating distinctions without real differences. These portfolios are graphed in Exhibit 42.

Exhibit 42: Sub-Portfolio Modules Cover a Full Range

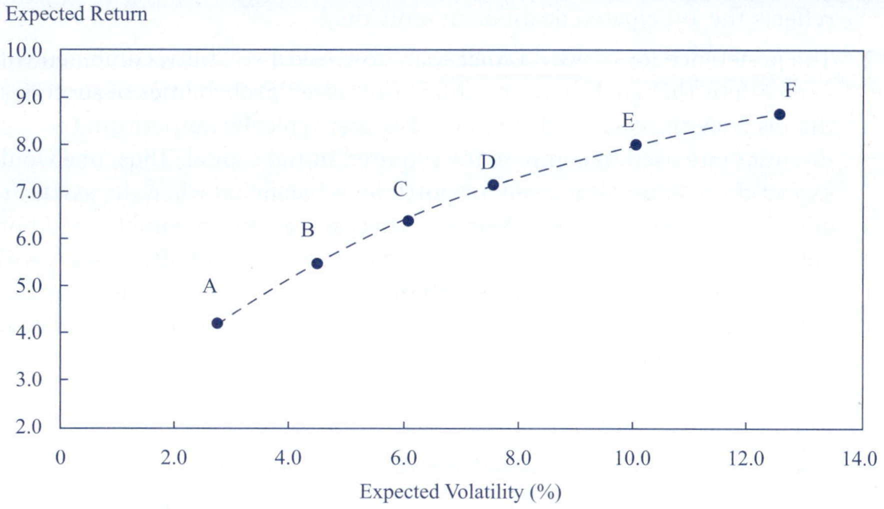

Returning to an earlier point about "labeled goals," one can easily imagine "aspirations" to describe each of these modules, ranging from "immediate- to short-term lifestyle" for Module A to "aggressive growth" for Module F. Module B might be labeled "long-term lifestyle," while C and D might represent forms of capital preservation and E a form of "balanced growth."

A final point deserves special emphasis: Modules need to be revisited on a periodic basis. While equilibrium assumptions will likely not change much from one year to the next, the need to identify one's position with respect to a "normal" market cycle can lead to modest changes in forward-looking assumptions. It would indeed be foolish to keep using long-term equilibrium assumptions when it becomes clear that one is closer to a market top than to a market bottom. The question of the suitability of revisions becomes moot when using a systematic approach such as the Black–Litterman model. One may also need to review the continued suitability of constraints, not to mention (when applicable) the fact that the make-up of the market portfolio may change in terms of geography or credit distribution.

ISSUES RELATED TO GOALS-BASED ASSET ALLOCATION 18

☐ recommend and justify an asset allocation using a goals-based approach

Once set, the goals-based allocation must be regularly reviewed. Two considerations dominate:

1. Goals with an initially fixed time horizon are not necessarily one year closer to maturity after a year. Superficially, one would expect that someone who says that his or her need is to meet lifestyle expenditures over the next five years, for instance, means exactly this. Accordingly, next year, the time horizon should shift down to four years. Yet experience suggests that certain

horizons are "placeholders": One year on, the time horizon remains five years. This is particularly—and understandably—relevant when the horizon reflects the anticipated death of an individual.

2. The preference for upward rather than downward volatility, combined with perceptions that goals may have higher required probabilities of success than is truly the case, leads to portfolios that typically outperform the discount rate used to compute the required initial capital. Thus, one would expect there to be some need for portfolio rebalancing when the assets allocated to certain goals appear excessive, at least in probability- and horizon-adjusted terms. This situation gives rise to important discussions with taxable clients because any form of portfolio rebalancing is inherently more complex and costly in a taxable environment than when taxes do not come into consideration.

Issues Related to Goals-Based Asset Allocation

Although goals-based asset allocation offers an elegant and mathematically sound way to deal with the circumstances of individuals, it is not a panacea. By definition, goals-based asset allocation applies best to individuals who have multiple goals, time horizons, and urgency levels. The classic example of the professional who is just starting to save for retirement and who has no other significant goal (as in the case of Aimée Goddard in Example 1) can be easily be handled with the traditional financial tools discussed in the earlier sections of this reading.[38] However, one should always be cautious to ensure that there is no "hidden" goal that should be brought out and that the apparently "single" retirement goal is not in fact an aggregation of several elements with different levels of urgency, if not also different time horizons. Single-goal circumstances may still be helped by the goals-based asset allocation process when there are sustainability or behavioral questions. In that case, one can look at the single goal as being made up of several similar goals over successive time periods with different required probabilities of success. For instance, one might apply a higher sense of urgency—and thus require a lower risk profile—to contributions made in the first few years, on the ground that adverse market circumstances might negatively affect the willingness of the client to stay with the program. In many ways, this approach can be seen as a conceptual analog to the dollar-cost-averaging investment framework.

Goals-based asset allocation is ideally suited to situations involving multiple goals, time horizons, and urgency levels, whether the assets are large or more modest. In fact, in cases where "human capital" is considered, a multi-goal approach can help investors understand the various trade-offs they face. Ostensibly, the larger the assets, the more complex the nature of the investment problem, the more diverse the list of investment structures, and the more one should expect a client-focused approach to offer useful benefits. However, the ratio of cash outflows to assets under consideration is a more germane issue than the overall size of the asset pool.

38 However, an adviser may find it appropriate to help the individual divide the funds he or she believes are needed for retirement into several categories. For instance, there may be some incompressible lifestyle expenditure that represents a minimum required spending level, but there may also be some luxury or at least compressible spending that does not have such a high level of urgency or that applies over a different time frame (say, the early or late years). Thus, one could still describe the problem as involving multiple goals, multiple time horizons, and multiple urgency levels. Then, one could compare the costs associated with the funding of these goals and have the individual weigh potential future satisfaction against the loss of current purchasing power.

Advisers using goals-based wealth management must contend with a considerably higher level of business management complexity. They will naturally expect to have a different policy for each client and potentially more than one policy per client. Thus, managing these portfolios day to day and satisfying the usual regulatory requirement that all clients be treated in an equivalent manner can appear to be a major quandary.

Typically, the solution would involve developing a systematic approach to decision making such that it remains practical for advisers to formulate truly individual policies that reflect their investment insights. Exhibit 43 offers a graphical overview of advisers' activities, divided into those that involve "firm-wide" processes, defined as areas where no real customization is warranted, and those that must remain "client focused." The result is analogous to a customized racing bicycle, whose parts are mass produced but then combined into a truly unique bike custom-designed for the individual racer.

Exhibit 43: Goals-Based Wealth Management Advisory Overview

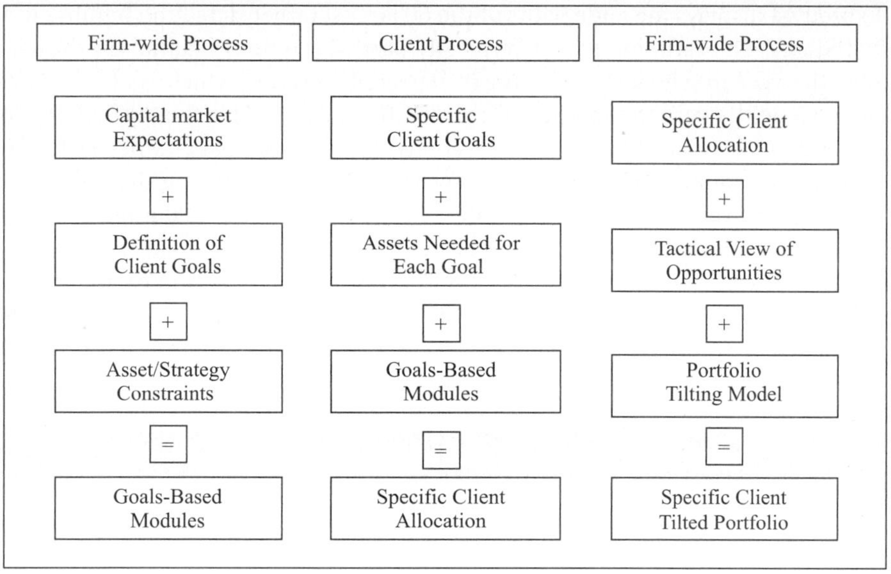

19 HEURISTICS AND OTHER APPROACHES TO ASSET ALLOCATION

☐ describe and evaluate heuristic and other approaches to asset allocation

In addition to the various asset allocation approaches already covered, a variety of heuristics (rules that provide a reasonable but not necessarily optimal solution) and other techniques deserve mention:

The "120 Minus Your Age" Rule

The phrase "120 minus your age" is a heuristic for inferring a hidden, age-driven risk tolerance coefficient that then leads directly to an age-based stock versus fixed income split: 120 − Age = Percentage allocated to stocks. Thus, a 25-year-old man would allocate 95% of his investment portfolio to stocks. Although we are aware of no theoretic basis for this heuristic—or its older and newer cousins, "100 minus your age" and "125 minus your age," respectively—it results in a linear decrease in equity exposure that seems to fit the general equity glide paths associated with target-date funds, including those that are based on a total balance sheet approach that includes human capital. A number of target-date funds (sometimes called life-cycle or age-based funds) and some target-date index providers report that their glide path (the age-based change in equity exposure) is based on the evolution of an individual's human capital. For example, one set of indexes[39] explicitly targets an investable proxy for the world market portfolio in which the glide path is the result of the evolving relationship of financial capital to human capital.[40]

Exhibit 44 displays the glide paths of the 60 largest target-date fund families in the United States. The retirement year (typically part of the fund's name) on the x-axis denotes the year in which the investor is expected to retire, which is almost always assumed to be the year the investor turns 65. Thus, as of 2016, the 2060 allocations correspond to a 21-year-old investor (79% equity, using the heuristic), whereas the 2005 allocation corresponds to a 76-year-old investor (24% equity, using the heuristic).[41] One dashed line represents the equity allocation based on the "100 minus your age" heuristic, while another dashed line represents the "120 minus your age" heuristic. The heuristic lines lack some of the nuances of the various glide path lines, but it would appear that an age-based heuristic leads to asset allocations that are broadly similar to those used by target-date funds.

Exhibit 44: Target-Date Funds and Age Heuristics (as of January 2016)

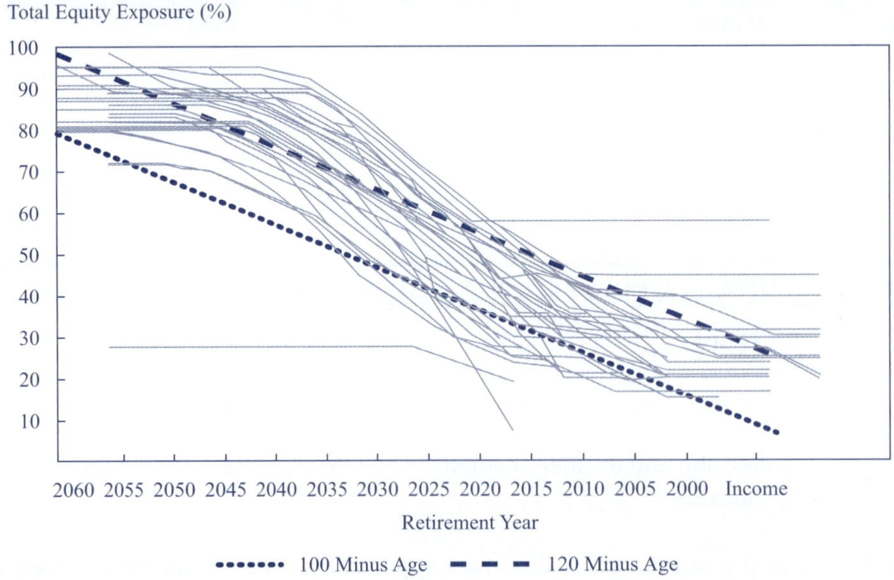

39 Morningstar's Lifetime Allocation (target-date) indexes.

40 See Idzorek (2008).

41 Many target-date funds continue to offer a "2005" vintage that would have been marketed/sold to people retiring in 2005.

The 60/40 Stock/Bond Heuristic

Some investors choose to skip the various optimization techniques and simply adopt an asset allocation consisting of 60% equities and 40% fixed income.

The equity allocation is viewed as supplying a long-term growth foundation, and the fixed-income allocation as supplying risk reduction benefits. If the stock and bond allocations are themselves diversified, an overall diversified portfolio should result.

There is some evidence that the global financial asset market portfolio is close to this prototypical 60/40 split. Exhibit 45 displays the estimated market value of eight major components of the market portfolio from 1990 to 2012. In approximately 7 of the 23 years, equities, private equity, and real estate account for slightly more than 60%, while for the rest of the time, the combined percentage is slightly less.

Exhibit 45: Global Market Portfolio, 1990 to 2012

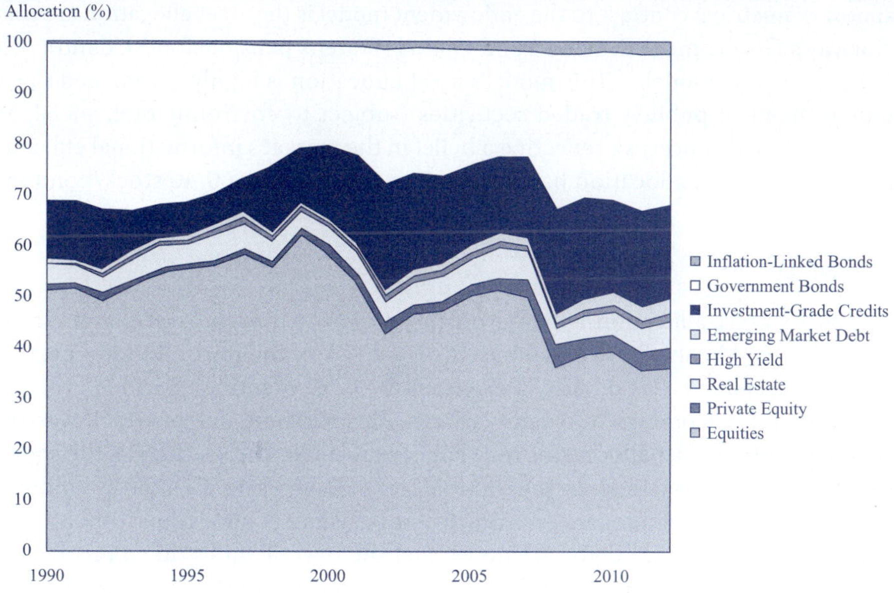

Source: Doeswijk, Lam, and Swinkels (2014).

The Endowment Model

An approach to asset allocation that emphasizes large allocations to non-traditional investments, including equity-oriented investments driven by investment manager skill (e.g., private equities), has come to be known as the endowment model or Yale model. The label "Yale model" reflects the fact that the Yale University Investments Office under David Swensen pioneered the approach in the 1990s; the label "endowment model" reflects the influence of this approach among US university endowments. Swensen (2009) stated that most investors should not pursue the Yale model but should instead embrace a simpler asset allocation implemented with low-cost funds. Besides high allocations to non-traditional assets and a commitment to active management, the approach characteristically seeks to earn illiquidity premiums, which endowments with long time horizons are well positioned to capture. Exhibit 46, showing the Yale endowment asset allocation, makes these points. In the exhibit, "absolute return" indicates investment in event-driven and value-driven strategies.

Exhibit 46: Yale University Endowment Asset Allocation as of June 2014

	Yale University	US Educational Institution Mean
Absolute return	17.4%	23.3%
Domestic equity	3.9	19.3
Fixed income	4.9	9.3
Foreign equity	11.5	22.0
Natural resources	8.2	8.5
Private equity	33.0	10.0
Real estate	17.6	4.2
Cash	3.5	3.5

Source: Yale University (2014, p. 13).

In almost diametrical contrast to the endowment model is the asset allocation approach of Norway's Government Pension Fund Global (Statens pensjonsfond Utland), often called the Norway model.[42] This model's asset allocation is highly committed to passive investment in publicly traded securities (subject to environmental, social, and governance [ESG] concerns), reflecting a belief in the market's informational efficiency. Since 2009, the asset allocation has followed an approximate 60/40 stock/bond mix.

Risk Parity

A risk parity asset allocation is based on the notion that each asset (asset class or risk factor) should contribute equally to the total risk of the portfolio for a portfolio to be well diversified. Recall that in Sections 2–9, we identified various criticisms and potential shortcomings of mean–variance optimization, one of which was that, while the resulting asset allocations may appear diversified across assets, the sources of risk may not be diversified. In the section on risk budgeting, Exhibit 19 contained a risk decomposition of a reverse-optimization-based asset allocation from a United Kingdom–based investor. There, we noted that the overall equity/fixed income split was approximately 54% equities and 46% fixed income, yet of the 10% standard deviation, approximately 74% of the risk came from equities while only 26% came from fixed income.

Risk parity is a relatively controversial approach. Although there are several variants, the most common risk parity approach has the following mathematical form:

$$w_i \times \text{Cov}\left(r_i, r_P\right) = \frac{1}{n}\sigma_P^2 \tag{3}$$

where

w_i = the weight of asset i

$\text{Cov}(r_i, r_P)$ = the covariance of asset i with the portfolio

n = the number of assets

σ_P^2 = the variance of the portfolio

In general, there is not a closed-form solution to the problem, and it must be solved using some form of optimization (mathematical programming). Prior to Markowitz's development of mean–variance optimization, which simultaneously considered both risk and return, most asset allocation approaches focused only on return *and ignored*

42 See Curtis (2012).

risk (or accounted for it in an ad hoc manner). The primary criticism of risk parity is that it makes the opposite mistake: It *ignores expected returns*. In general, most of the rules-based risk approaches—such as other forms of volatility weighting, minimum volatility, and target volatility—suffer from this shortcoming.

With risk parity, the contribution to risk is highly dependent on the formation of the opportunity set. For example, if the opportunity set consists of seven equity asset classes and three fixed-income asset classes, intuitively, 70% of risk will come from the equities and 30% of risk will come from fixed income. Conversely, if the opportunity set consists of three equity asset classes and seven fixed-income asset classes, intuitively, 70% of risk will come from fixed income and 30% of risk will come from equities. The point is that practitioners of risk parity must be very cognizant of the formation of their opportunity set.

Exhibit 47 gives a US-centric example consisting of five equity asset classes and three fixed-income asset classes. A constrained optimization routine (weights must sum to 100%) was used to determine the weight to each asset class, such that all asset classes contributed the same amount to total risk. In this case, each asset class contributed 0.8%, resulting in an asset allocation with a total standard deviation of 6.41%. In this example, 5/8 of total risk comes from equity asset classes and 3/8 comes from fixed-income asset classes. Earlier, we explained that reverse optimization can be used to infer the expected return of any set of presumed efficient weights. In Exhibit 47, based on a total market risk premium of 2.13% and a risk-free rate of 3%, we inferred the reverse-optimized total returns (final column). In this case, these seem to be relatively reasonable expected returns.

Exhibit 47: Risk Parity Portfolio Weights and Risk-Budgeting Statistics Based on Reverse-Optimized Returns

Asset Class	Weight	Marginal Contribution to Total Risk (MCTR)	ACTR	Percentage Contribution to Total Standard Deviation	Reverse-Optimized Total Returns
US large-cap equities	7.7%	10.43%	0.80%	12.50%	6.47%
US mid-cap equities	6.1	13.03	0.80	12.50	7.33
US small-cap equities	5.9	13.61	0.80	12.50	7.52
Non-US developed market equities	5.6	14.38	0.80	12.50	7.78
Emerging market equities	4.5	17.74	0.80	12.50	8.89
Non-US bonds	15.5	5.17	0.80	12.50	4.72
US TIPS	23.9	3.36	0.80	12.50	4.12
US bonds	30.8	2.60	0.80	12.50	3.86
Total	100.0%		6.41%	100.00%	5.13%

After deriving a risk parity–based asset allocation, the next step in the process is to borrow (use leverage) or to lend (save a portion of wealth, presumably in cash) so that the overall portfolio corresponds to the investor's risk appetite. Continuing with our example, the market risk premium is 2.13% (above the assumed risk-free rate of 3%) and the market variance is 0.41% (i.e., 6.41% squared); thus, the implied market trade-off of expected return (in excess of the risk-free rate) for risk is 2.13% divided by 0.41%, which equals approximately 5.2. Investors with a greater appetite for risk than the market as a whole would borrow money to lever up the risk parity portfolios, while investors with a lower appetite for risk would invest a portion of their wealth in cash.

Back tests of levered risk parity portfolios have produced promising results, although critics of these back tests argue that they suffer from look-back bias and are very dependent on the ability to use extremely large amounts of leverage at low borrow rates (which may not have been feasible); see, for example, Anderson, Bianchi, and Goldberg (2012). Proponents of risk parity have suggested that the idea of "leverage aversion" contributes to the success of the strategy. Black (1972) suggested that restrictions on leverage and a general aversion to leverage may cause return-seeking investors to pursue higher-returning assets, such as stocks. All else equal, this behavior would reduce the price of bonds, thus allowing the investor to buy bonds at a small discount, hold them to maturity, and realize the full value of the bond. Asness, Frazzini, and Pedersen (2012) have offered this idea as a potential explanation for why a levered (bond-centric) asset allocation might outperform an equity-centric asset allocation with equivalent or similar risk.

The 1/N Rule

One of the simplest asset allocation heuristics involves equally weighting allocations to assets. DeMiguel, Garlappi, and Uppal (2009) define an approach in which $1/N$ of wealth is allocated to each of N assets available for investment at each rebalancing date. Calendar rebalancing to equal weighting at quarterly intervals is one common rebalancing discipline used. By treating all assets as indistinguishable in terms of mean returns, volatility, and correlations, in principle, $1/N$ rule portfolios should be dominated by methods that optimize asset class weights to exploit differences in investment characteristics. In empirical studies comparing approaches, however, the $1/N$ rule has been found to perform considerably better, based on Sharpe ratios and certainty equivalents, than theory might suggest. One possible explanation is that the $1/N$ rule sidesteps problems caused by optimizing when there is estimation error in inputs.

20 PORTFOLIO REBALANCING IN PRACTICE

☐ discuss factors affecting rebalancing policy

The reading "Introduction to Asset Allocation" provided an introduction to rebalancing, including some detailed comments on strategic considerations. This section aims to present useful additional insight and information.

MEANINGS OF "REBALANCING"

Rebalancing has been defined as the discipline of adjusting portfolio weights to more closely align with the strategic asset allocation. In that sense, rebalancing includes policy regarding the correction of any drift away from strategic asset allocation weights resulting from market price movements and the passage of time for finite-lived assets, such as bonds. In liability-relative asset allocation, adjusting a liability-hedging portfolio to account for changes in net duration exposures from the passage of time, for example, would fall under the rubric of rebalancing.

Some use the term "rebalancing" more expansively, to include the combined effects on asset class weights not only of rebalancing in the above sense but also of active allocation activities. In that sense, rebalancing would include tactical allocations. Although rebalancing policy can be established to accommodate tactical adjustments, tactical asset allocation per se is not covered under "rebalancing" as the term is used here.

Changes in asset allocation weights in response to changes in client circumstances, goals, or other client factors are sometimes also referred to as "rebalancing" (especially if the adjustments are minor). These activities fall under the scope of client monitoring and asset allocation review, as described elsewhere in the CFA curriculum.

An appropriate rebalancing policy involves a weighing of benefits and costs. Benefits depend on the idea that if an investor's strategic asset allocation is optimal, then any divergence in the portfolio from that asset allocation represents an expected utility loss to the investor. Rebalancing benefits the investor by reducing the present value of expected losses from not tracking the optimum. In theory, the basic cost of not rebalancing is this present value of expected utility losses from straying from the optimum.[43]

Apart from the above considerations of trade-offs, disciplined rebalancing has tended to reduce risk while incrementally adding to returns. Several interpretations of this empirical finding have been offered, including the following:

- *Rebalancing earns a diversification return.* The compound growth rate of a portfolio is greater than the weighted average compound growth rates of the component portfolio holdings (given positive expected returns and positive asset weights). Given sufficiently low transaction costs, this effect leads to what has been called a *diversification return* to frequent rebalancing to a well-diversified portfolio.[44]
- *Rebalancing earns a return from being short volatility.* In the case of a portfolio consisting of a risky asset and a risk-free asset, the return to a rebalanced portfolio can be replicated by creating a buy-and-hold position in the portfolio, writing out-of-the-money puts and calls on the risky asset, and investing the premiums in risk-free bonds.[45] As the value of puts and calls is positively related to volatility, such a position is called being short volatility (or being short gamma, by reference to the option Greeks).

Practice appears not to have produced a consensus on the most appropriate rebalancing discipline. Introduction to Asset Allocation defined and discussed calendar rebalancing[46]—sometimes mentioned as common in portfolios managed for individual investors—and percent-range rebalancing. Calendar rebalancing involves lower overhead because of lower monitoring costs. Percent-range rebalancing is a more disciplined risk control policy, however, because it makes rebalancing contingent on market movements. Without weighing costs and benefits in the abstract, Exhibit 48 assumes percent-range rebalancing and summarizes the effects of each of several key factors on the corridor width of an asset class, holding all else equal, except for the factor of the asset class's own volatility.[47] For taxable investors, transactions trigger capital gains in jurisdictions that tax them; therefore, for such investors, higher tax rates on capital gains should also be associated with wider corridors.

43 See Leland (2000).

44 See Willenbrock (2011). This phenomenon was called *rebalancing return* by Mulvey and Kim (2009). Luenberger (2013) suggests that the phenomenon could be exploited by a strategy of buying high-volatility assets and rebalancing often, a process he called *volatility pumping*.

45 As shown in Ang (2014, pp. 135–139).

46 Rebalancing a portfolio to target weights on a periodic basis—for example, monthly, quarterly, semi-annually, or annually.

47 See Masters (2003).

Exhibit 48: Factors Affecting the Optimal Corridor Width of an Asset Class

Factor	Effect on Optimal Width of Corridor (All Else Equal)	Intuition
Factors Positively Related to Optimal Corridor Width		
Transaction costs	The higher the transaction costs, the wider the optimal corridor.	High transaction costs set a high hurdle for rebalancing benefits to overcome.
Risk tolerance	The higher the risk tolerance, the wider the optimal corridor.	Higher risk tolerance means less sensitivity to divergences from the target allocation.
Correlation with the rest of the portfolio	The higher the correlation, the wider the optimal corridor.	When asset classes move in sync, further divergence from target weights is less likely.
Factors Inversely Related to Optimal Corridor Width		
Volatility of the rest of the portfolio	The higher the volatility, the narrower the optimal corridor.	Higher volatility makes large divergences from the strategic asset allocation more likely.

Among positive factors, the cases of transaction costs and risk tolerance are obvious. Transaction costs can be reduced to the extent that portfolio cash flows can be used to rebalance. The case of correlation is less obvious. Because of correlations, the rebalancing triggers among different asset classes are linked.

Consider correlation in a two–asset class scenario. Suppose one asset class is above its target weight, so the other asset class is below its target weight. A further increase in the value of the overweight asset class implies, on average, a smaller divergence in the asset mix if the asset classes' returns are more highly positively correlated (because the denominator in computing the overweight asset class's weight is the sum of the values of the two asset classes). In a multi-asset-class scenario, all pair-wise asset class correlations would need to be considered, making the interpretation of correlations complex. To expand the application of the two-asset case's intuition, one simplification involves considering the balance of a portfolio to be a single hypothetical asset and computing an asset class's correlation with it.

As indicated in Exhibit 48, the higher the volatility of the rest of the portfolio, excluding the asset class being considered, the more likely a large divergence from the strategic asset allocation becomes. That consideration should point to a narrower optimal corridor, all else being equal.

In the case of an asset class's own volatility, "holding all else equal" is not practically meaningful. If rebalancing did not involve transaction costs, then higher volatility would lead to a narrower corridor, all else equal, for a risk-averse investor.[48] Higher volatility implies that if an asset class is not brought back into the optimal range after a given move away from it, the chance of an even further divergence from optimal is greater. In other words, higher volatility makes large divergence from the strategic asset allocation more likely. However, reducing a corridor's width means more frequent rebalancing and higher transaction costs. Thus, the effect of volatility on optimal corridor width involves a trade-off between controlling transaction costs and controlling risk. Conclusions also depend on the assumptions made about asset price return dynamics.

In practice, corridor width is often specified to be proportionally greater, the higher an asset class's volatility, with a focus on transaction cost control. In *volatility-based rebalancing*, corridor width is set proportionally to the asset class's own volatility. In one variation of *equal probability rebalancing* (McCalla 1997), the manager specifies a corridor for each asset class in terms of a common multiple of the standard deviation of the asset class's returns such that, under a normal probability assumption, each asset class is equally likely to trigger rebalancing.

48 As in Masters (2003).

EXAMPLE 12

Tolerance Bands for an Asset Allocation

An investment committee is reviewing the following strategic asset allocation:

Domestic equities 50% ± 5% (i.e., 45% to 55% of portfolio value)

International equities 15% ± 1.5%

Domestic bonds 35% ± 3.5%

The market for the domestic bonds is relatively illiquid. The committee views the above corridors as appropriate *if* each asset class's risk and transaction cost characteristics remain unchanged. The committee now wants to account for differences among the asset classes in setting the corridors.

Evaluate the implications of the following sets of facts for the stated tolerance bands, given an all-else-equal assumption in each case:

1. Tax rates for international equities increase by 10 percentage points.

Solution:

The tolerance band for international equities should increase if the entity is a taxable investor.

2. Transaction costs in international equities increase by 20% relative to domestic equities, but the correlation of international equities with domestic equities and bonds declines. What is the expected effect on the tolerance band for international equities?

Solution:

Increased transaction costs point to widening the tolerance band for international equities, but declining correlations point to narrowing it. The overall effect is indeterminate.

3. The volatility of domestic bonds increases. What is the expected effect on their tolerance band? Assume that domestic bonds are relatively illiquid.

Solution:

Given that the market for domestic bonds is relatively illiquid, the increase in volatility suggests widening the rebalancing band. Containing transaction costs is more important than the expected utility losses from allowing a larger divergence from the strategic asset allocation.

One decision involved in rebalancing policy is whether to adjust asset class holdings to their target proportions, to the limits of the corridors, or to within the corridors but not to target weights. Compared with rebalancing to target weights, rebalancing to the upper or lower limit of the allowed range results in less close alignment with target proportions but lower transaction costs—an especially important consideration in the case of relatively illiquid assets. The choice among alternatives may be influenced by judgmental tactical considerations.

Because one rebalancing decision affects later rebalancing decisions, the optimal rebalancing decisions at different points in time are linked. However, optimal rebalancing in a multi-period, multi-asset case is an unsolved problem.

The analysis of Dybvig (2005) suggests that fixed transaction costs favor rebalancing to the target weights and variable transaction costs favor rebalancing to the nearest corridor border (the interior of the corridor being therefore a "no trade zone"). A number of studies have contrasted rebalancing to target weights and rebalancing to the allowed range based on particular asset classes, time periods, and measures of the benefits of rebalancing. These studies have reached a variety of conclusions, suggesting that no simple, empirically based advice can be provided.

REBALANCING IN A GOALS-BASED APPROACH

The use of probability- and horizon-adjusted discount rates to size the various goal-defeasing sub-portfolios means that portfolios will usually produce returns that are higher than assumed. Thus, as time passes, the dollars allocated to the various sub-portfolios—other than labeled-goal portfolios—may be expected to exceed the actual requirements. For example, in average markets, returns should exceed the conservative requirements of a goal associated with a 90% required probability of success. Sub-portfolios with shorter time horizons for goals with high required probabilities of success will tend to contain relatively low-risk assets, whereas riskier assets may have high allocations in longer-horizon portfolios for goals with lower required probabilities of success. Thus, there is a greater chance that the exposure to lower-risk assets will creep up before one experiences the same for riskier assets. Thus, failing to rebalance the portfolio will gradually move it down the risk axis—and the defined efficient frontier—and thus lead the client to take less risk than he or she can bear.

SUMMARY

This reading has surveyed how appropriate asset allocations can be determined to meet the needs of a variety of investors. Among the major points made have been the following:

- The objective function of asset-only mean–variance optimization is to maximize the expected return of the asset mix minus a penalty that depends on risk aversion and the expected variance of the asset mix.
- Criticisms of MVO include the following:
  - The outputs (asset allocations) are highly sensitive to small changes in the inputs.
  - The asset allocations are highly concentrated in a subset of the available asset classes.
  - Investors are often concerned with characteristics of asset class returns such as skewness and kurtosis that are not accounted for in MVO.
  - While the asset allocations may appear diversified across assets, the sources of risk may not be diversified.
  - MVO allocations may have no direct connection to the factors affecting any liability or consumption streams.
  - MVO is a single-period framework that tends to ignore trading/rebalancing costs and taxes.
- Deriving expected returns by reverse optimization or by reverse optimization tilted toward an investor's views on asset returns (the Black–Litterman model) is one means of addressing the tendency of MVO to produce efficient portfolios that are not well diversified.

- Placing constraints on asset class weights to prevent extremely concentrated portfolios and resampling inputs are other ways of addressing the same concern.
- For some relatively illiquid asset classes, a satisfactory proxy may not be available; including such asset classes in the optimization may therefore be problematic.
- Risk budgeting is a means of making optimal use of risk in the pursuit of return. A risk budget is optimal when the ratio of excess return to marginal contribution to total risk is the same for all assets in the portfolio.
- Characteristics of liabilities that affect asset allocation in liability-relative asset allocation include the following:
  - Fixed versus contingent cash flows
  - Legal versus quasi-liabilities
  - Duration and convexity of liability cash flows
  - Value of liabilities as compared with the size of the sponsoring organization
  - Factors driving future liability cash flows (inflation, economic conditions, interest rates, risk premium)
  - Timing considerations, such longevity risk
  - Regulations affecting liability cash flow calculations
- Approaches to liability-relative asset allocation include surplus optimization, a hedging/return-seeking portfolios approach, and an integrated asset–liability approach.
  - Surplus optimization involves MVO applied to surplus returns.
  - A hedging/return-seeking portfolios approach assigns assets to one of two portfolios. The objective of the hedging portfolio is to hedge the investor's liability stream. Any remaining funds are invested in the return-seeking portfolio.
  - An integrated asset–liability approach integrates and jointly optimizes asset and liability decisions.
- A goals-based asset allocation process combines into an overall portfolio a number of sub-portfolios, each of which is designed to fund an individual goal with its own time horizon and required probability of success.
- In the implementation, there are two fundamental parts to the asset allocation process. The first centers on the creation of portfolio modules, while the second relates to the identification of client goals and the matching of these goals to the appropriate sub-portfolios to which suitable levels of capital are allocated.
- Other approaches to asset allocation include "120 minus your age," 60/40 stocks/bonds, the endowment model, risk parity, and the 1/*N* rule.
- Disciplined rebalancing has tended to reduce risk while incrementally adding to returns. Interpretations of this empirical finding include that rebalancing earns a diversification return, that rebalancing earns a return from being short volatility, and that rebalancing earns a return to supplying liquidity to the market.

- Factors positively related to optimal corridor width include transaction costs, risk tolerance, and an asset class's correlation with the rest of the portfolio. The higher the correlation, the wider the optimal corridor, because when asset classes move in sync, further divergence from target weights is less likely.
- The volatility of the rest of the portfolio (outside of the asset class under consideration) is inversely related to optimal corridor width.
- An asset class's own volatility involves a trade-off between transaction costs and risk control. The width of the optimal tolerance band increases with transaction costs for volatility-based rebalancing.

REFERENCES

Anderson, Robert M., Stephen W. Bianchi, and Lisa R. Goldberg. 2012. "Will My Risk Parity Strategy Outperform?" *Financial Analysts Journal* 68, vol. , no. 6 (November/December): 75–93. 10.2469/faj.v68.n6.7

Ang, Andrew. 2014. *Asset Management*. New York: Oxford University Press.

Asness, Clifford S., Andrea Frazzini, and Lasse H. Pedersen. 2012. "Leverage Aversion and Risk Parity." *Financial Analysts Journal* 68, vol. , no. 1 (January/February): 47–59. 10.2469/faj.v68.n1.1

Athayde, Gustavo M. de and Renato G. Flôres. 2003. "Incorporating Skewness and Kurtosis in Portfolio Optimization: A Multideminsional Efficient Set." In *Advances in Portfolio Construction and Implementation*, edited by Stephen Satchell and Alan Scowcroft. Oxford, UK: Butterworth–Heinemann.

Beardsley, Xiaoxin W., Brian Field, and Mingqing Xiao. 2012. "Mean–Variance-Skewness-Kurtosis Portfolio Optimization with Return and Liquidity." *Communications in Mathematical Finance* 1, vol. , no. 1: 13–49.

Black, Fischer. 1972. "Capital market equilibrium with restricted borrowing." *Journal of Business* 45, vol. , no. 3: 444–455. 10.1086/295472

Black, Fischer and Robert Litterman. 1990. "Asset Allocation: Combining Investors Views with Market Equilibrium." Fixed Income Research, Goldman, Sachs & Company, September.

Black, Fischer and Robert Litterman. 1991. "Global Asset Allocation with Equities, Bonds, and Currencies." Fixed Income Research, Goldman, Sachs & Company, October.

Black, Fischer and Robert Litterman. 1992. "Global Portfolio Optimization." *Financial Analysts Journal* 48, vol. , no. 5 (September/October): 28–43. 10.2469/faj.v48.n5.28

Blanchett, David M. and Philip U. Straehl. 2015. "No Portfolio is an Island." *Financial Analysts Journal* 71, vol. , no. 3 (May/June): 15–33. 10.2469/faj.v71.n3.5

Briec, W., K. Kerstens, and O. Jokung. 2007. "Mean–Variance-Skewness Portfolio Performance Gauging: A General Shortage Function and Dual Approach." *Management Science* 53, vol. , no. 1 (January): 135–149. 10.1287/mnsc.1060.0596

Brunel, Jean L.P. 2003. "Revisiting the Asset Allocation Challenge through a Behavioral Finance Lens." *Journal of Wealth Management* 6, vol. , no. 2 (Fall): 10–20. 10.3905/jwm.2003.320479

Brunel, Jean L.P. 2005. "A Behavioral Finance Approach to Strategic Asset Allocation—A Case Study." *Journal of Investment Consulting* 7, vol. , no. 3 (Winter): 61–69.

Chhabra, Ashvin. 2005. "Beyond Markowitz: A Comprehensive Wealth Allocation Framework for Individual Investors." *Journal of Wealth Management* 7, vol. , no. 4 (Spring): 8–34. 10.3905/jwm.2005.470606

Chow, George, Eric Jacquier, Mark Kritzman, and Kenneth Lowry. 1999. "Optimal Portfolios in Good Times and Bad." *Financial Analysts Journal* 55, vol. , no. 3 (May/June): 65–73. 10.2469/faj.v55.n3.2273

Curtis, Gregory. 2012. "Yale versus Norway." White Paper 55, Greycourt (September).

Das, Sanjiv, Harry Markowitz, Jonathan Scheid, and Meir Statman. 2010. "Portfolio Optimization with Mental Accounts." *Journal of Financial and Quantitative Analysis* 45, vol. , no. 2 (April): 311–334. 10.1017/S0022109010000141

Das, Sanjiv, Harry Markowitz, Jonathan Scheid, and Meir Statman. 2011. "Portfolios for Investors Who Want to Reach Their Goals While Staying on the Mean–Variance Efficient Frontier." *Journal of Wealth Management* 14, vol. , no. 2 (Fall): 25–31. 10.3905/jwm.2011.14.2.025

Davies, Ryan, Harry M. Kat, and Sa Lu. 2009. "Fund of Hedge Funds Portfolio Selection: A Multiple-Objective Approach." *Journal of Derivatives & Hedge Funds* 15, vol. , no. 2: 91–115. 10.1057/jdhf.2009.1

DeMiguel, V., L. Garlappi, and R. Uppal. 2009. "Optimal versus Naive Diversification: How Inefficient Is the 1/*N* Portfolio Strategy?" *Review of Financial Studies* 22, vol. , no. 5: 1915–1953. 10.1093/rfs/hhm075

DiBartolomeo, Dan. 1993. "Portfolio Optimization: The Robust Solution." Prudential Securities Quantitative Conference. Available online at http://www.northinfo.com/documents/45.pdf

Doeswijk, Ronald, Trevin Lam, and Laurens Swinkels. 2014. “The Global Multi-Asset Market Portfolio, 1959–2012.” *Financial Analysts Journal* 70, vol. , no. 2 (March/April): 26–41. 10.2469/faj.v70.n2.1

Dybvig, Philip H. 2005. “Mean-variance portfolio rebalancing with transaction costs.” Working paper, Washington University in Saint Louis.

Elton, Edwin J and Martin J. Gruber. 1992. “Optimal Investment Strategies with Investor Liabilities.” *Journal of Banking & Finance* 16, vol. , no. 5: 869–890. 10.1016/0378-4266(92)90030-4

Gannon, James A. and Bob Collins. 2009. “Liability-Responsive Asset Allocation.” Russell Research Viewpoint.

Goldberg, Lisa R., Michael Y. Hayes, and Ola Mahmoud. 2013. “Minimizing Shortfall.” *Quantitative Finance* 13, vol. , no. 10: 1533–1545.

Grable, John E. 2008. “RiskCAT: A Framework for Identifying Maximum Risk Thresholds in Personal Portfolios.” *Journal of Financial Planning* 21, vol. , no. 10: 52–62.

Grable, John E. and Soo-Hyun Joo. 2004. “Environmental and Biopsychosocial Factors Associated with Financial Risk Tolerance.” *Financial Counseling and Planning* 15, vol. , no. 1: 73–88.

Harvey, Campbell R., John C. Liechty, Merrill W. Liechty, and Peter Müller. 2010. “Portfolio Selection with Higher Moments.” *Quantitative Finance* 10, vol. , no. 5 (May): 469–485. 10.1080/14697681003756877

Idzorek, Thomas M. and Maciej Kowara. 2013. “Factor-Based Asset Allocation vs. Asset-Class-Based Asset Allocation.” *Financial Analysts Journal* 69, vol. , no. 3 (May/June): 19–29. 10.2469/faj.v69.n3.7

Idzorek, Thomas. 2008. “Lifetime Asset Allocations: Methodologies for Target Maturity Funds.” Ibbotson Associates Research Report.

Jobson, David J. and Bob Korkie. 1980. “Estimation for Markowitz Efficient Portfolios.” *Journal of the American Statistical Association* 75, vol. , no. 371 (September): 544–554. 10.1080/01621459.1980.10477507

Jobson, David J. and Bob Korkie. 1981. “Putting Markowitz Theory to Work.” *Journal of Portfolio Management* 7, vol. , no. 4 (Summer): 70–74. 10.3905/jpm.1981.408816

Jorion, Phillipe. 1992. “Portfolio Optimization in Practice.” *Financial Analysts Journal* 48, vol. , no. 1 (January/February): 68–74. 10.2469/faj.v48.n1.68

Kahneman, Daniel and Amos Tversky. 1979. “Prospect Theory: An Analysis of Decision under Risk.” *Econometrica* 47, vol. , no. 2: 263–292. 10.2307/1914185

Kat, Harry M. 2003. “10 Things That Investors Should Know about Hedge Funds.” *Journal of Wealth Management* 5, vol. , no. 4 (Spring): 72–81. 10.3905/jwm.2003.320466

Leibowitz, Martin L. and Roy D. Henriksson. 1988. “Portfolio Optimization Within a Surplus Framework.” *Financial Analysts Journal* 44, vol. , no. 2: 43–51. 10.2469/faj.v44.n2.43

Leland, Hayne. 2000. “Optimal Portfolio Implementation with Transaction Costs and Capital Gains Taxes.” Working paper, University of California, Berkeley.

Luenberger, David G. 2013. *Investment Science*, 2nd ed. New York: Oxford University Press.

Markowitz, Harry M. 1952. “Portfolio Selection.” *Journal of Finance* 7, vol. , no. 1 (March): 77–91.

Markowitz, Harry M. 1959. *Portfolio Selection: Efficient Diversification of Investments.* New York: John Wiley & Sons.

Maslow, A. H. 1943. “A Theory of Human Motivation.” *Psychological Review* 50, vol. , no. 4: 370–396. 10.1037/h0054346

Masters, Seth J. 2003. “Rebalancing.” *Journal of Portfolio Management* 29, vol. , no. 3: 52–57. 10.3905/jpm.2003.319883

McCalla, Douglas B. 1997. “Enhancing the Efficient Frontier with Portfolio Rebalancing.” *Journal of Pension Plan Investing* 1, vol. , no. 4: 16–32.

Michaud, Richard O. 1998. *Efficient Asset Management.* Boston: Harvard Business School Press.

Mulvey, J.M. and W. Kim. 2009. “Constantly Rebalanced Portfolio—Is Mean Reversion Necessary?” in Rama Cont, ed. *Encyclopedia of Quantitative Finance*, vol 2, Hoboken, NJ: John Wiley & Sons.

Mulvey, John M. 1989. “A Surplus Optimization Perspective.” *Investment Management Review* 3, vol. : 31–39.

Mulvey, John M. 1994. "An Asset-Liability System." *Interfaces* 24, vol. , no. 3: 22–33. 10.1287/inte.24.3.22

Mulvey, John M., Bill Pauling, and Ron E. Madey. 2003. "Advantages of Multi-Period Portfolio Models." *Journal of Portfolio Management* 29, vol. , no. 2 (Winter): 35–45. 10.3905/jpm.2003.319871

Nevins, Daniel. 2004. "Goal-Based Investing: Integrating Traditional and Behavioral Finance." *Journal of Wealth Management* 6, vol. , no. 4 (Spring): 8–23. 10.3905/jwm.2004.391053

Pompian, Michael M. and John B. Longo. 2004. "A New Paradigm for Practical Application of Behavioral Finance." *Journal of Wealth Management* 7, vol. , no. 2 (Fall): 9–15. 10.3905/jwm.2004.434561

Rockafellar, R. Tyrrell and Stanislav Uryasev. 2000. "Optimization of Conditional Value-at-Risk." *Journal of Risk* 2, vol. , no. 3 (Spring): 21–41. 10.21314/JOR.2000.038

Rudd, Andrew and Laurence B. Siegel. 2013. "Using an Economic Balance Sheet for Financial Planning." *Journal of Wealth Management* 16, vol. , no. 2 (Fall): 15–23. 10.3905/jwm.2013.16.2.015

Scherer, Bernd. 2002. "Portfolio Resampling: Review and Critique." *Financial Analysts Journal* 58, vol. , no. 6 (November/December): 98–109.

Sharpe, William. 1974. "Imputing Expected Security Returns from Portfolio Composition." *Journal of Financial and Quantitative Analysis* 9, vol. , no. 3 (June): 463–472. 10.2307/2329873

Sharpe, William and Lawrence G. Tint. 1990. "Liabilities: A New Approach." *Journal of Portfolio Management* 16, vol. , no. 2: 5–10. 10.3905/jpm.1990.409248

Shefrin, H. and M. Statman. 2000. "Behavioral Portfolio Theory." *Journal of Financial and Quantitative Analysis* 35, vol. , no. 2: 127–151. 10.2307/2676187

Swensen, D. 2009. *Pioneering Portfolio Management: An Unconventional Approach to Institutional Investment*, 2nd ed. New York: Free Press.

Tversky, Amos and Daniel Kahneman. 1992. "Advances in prospect theory: Cumulative representation of uncertainty." *Journal of Risk and Uncertainty* 5, vol. , no. 4: 297–323. 10.1007/BF00122574

Willenbrock, Scott. 2011. "Diversification Return, Portfolio Rebalancing, and the Commodity Return Puzzle." *Financial Analysts Journal* 67, vol. , no. 4 (July/August): 42–49. 10.2469/faj.v67.n4.1

Winkelmann, Kurt. 2003. "Developing an Optimal Active Risk Budget," in *Modern Investment Management: An Equilibrium Approach* Bob Litterman, ed. New York: John Wiley & Sons.

Xiong, James X. and Thomas M. Idzorek. 2011. "The Impact of Skewness and Fat Tails on the Asset Allocation Decision." *Financial Analysts Journal* 67, vol. , no. 2 (March/April): 23–35. 10.2469/faj.v67.n2.5

Yale University. 2014. "The Yale Endowment 2014" (http://investments.yale.edu/s/Yale_Endowment_14.pdf).

PRACTICE PROBLEMS

The following information relates to questions 1-8

Megan Beade and Hanna Müller are senior analysts for a large, multi-divisional money management firm. Beade supports the institutional portfolio managers, and Müller does the same for the private wealth portfolio managers.

Beade reviews the asset allocation in Exhibit 1, derived from a mean–variance optimization (MVO) model for an institutional client, noting that details of the MVO are lacking.

Exhibit 1: Asset Allocation and Market Weights (in percent)

Asset Classes	Asset Allocation	Investable Global Market Weights
Cash	0	—
US bonds	30	17
US TIPS	0	3
Non-US bonds	0	22
Emerging market equity	25	5
Non-US developed equity	20	29
US small- and mid-cap equity	25	4
US large-cap equity	0	20

The firm's policy is to rebalance a portfolio when the asset class weight falls outside of a corridor around the target allocation. The width of each corridor is customized for each client and proportional to the target allocation. Beade recommends wider corridor widths for high-risk asset classes, narrower corridor widths for less liquid asset classes, and narrower corridor widths for taxable clients with high capital gains tax rates.

One client sponsors a defined benefit pension plan where the present value of the liabilities is $241 million and the market value of plan assets is $205 million. Beade expects interest rates to rise and both the present value of plan liabilities and the market value of plan assets to decrease by $25 million, changing the pension plan's funding ratio.

Beade uses a surplus optimization approach to liability-relative asset allocation based on the objective function

$$U_m^{LR} = E\left(R_{s,m}\right) - 0.005\lambda\sigma^2\left(R_{s,m}\right)$$

where $E(R_{s,m})$ is the expected surplus return for portfolio m, λ is the risk aversion coefficient, and $\sigma^2(R_{s,m})$ is the variance of the surplus return. Beade establishes the expected surplus return and surplus variance for three different asset allocations, shown in Exhibit 2. Given $\lambda = 1.50$, she chooses the optimal asset mix.

Exhibit 2: Expected Surplus Return and Volatility for Three Portfolios

	Return	Standard Deviation
Portfolio 1	13.00%	24%
Portfolio 2	12.00%	18%
Portfolio 3	11.00%	19%

Client Haunani Kealoha has a large fixed obligation due in 10 years. Beade assesses that Kealoha has substantially more funds than are required to meet the fixed obligation. The client wants to earn a competitive risk-adjusted rate of return while maintaining a high level of certainty that there will be sufficient assets to meet the fixed obligation.

In the private wealth area, the firm has designed five subportfolios with differing asset allocations that are used to fund different client goals over a five-year horizon. Exhibit 3 shows the expected returns and volatilities of the subportfolios and the probabilities that the subportfolios will exceed an expected minimum return. Client Luis Rodríguez wants to satisfy two goals. Goal 1 requires a conservative portfolio providing the highest possible minimum return that will be met at least 95% of the time. Goal 2 requires a riskier portfolio that provides the highest minimum return that will be exceeded at least 85% of the time.

Exhibit 3: Characteristics of Subportfolios

Subportfolio	A	B	C	D	E
Expected return, in percent	4.60	5.80	7.00	8.20	9.40
Expected volatility, in percent	3.46	5.51	8.08	10.80	13.59
Required Success Rate	**Minimum Expected Return for Success Rate**				
99%	1.00	0.07	−1.40	−3.04	−4.74
95%	2.05	1.75	1.06	0.25	−0.60
90%	2.62	2.64	2.37	2.01	1.61
85%	3.00	3.25	3.26	3.19	3.10
75%	3.56	4.14	4.56	4.94	5.30

Müller uses a risk parity asset allocation approach with a client's four–asset class portfolio. The expected return of the domestic bond asset class is the lowest of the asset classes, and the returns of the domestic bond asset class have the lowest covariance with other asset class returns. Müller estimates the weight that should be placed on domestic bonds.

Müller and a client discuss other approaches to asset allocation that are not based on optimization models or goals-based models. Müller makes the following comments to the client:

Comment 1 An advantage of the "120 minus your age" heuristic over the 60/40 stock/bond heuristic is that it incorporates an age-based stock/bond allocation.

Comment 2 The Yale model emphasizes traditional investments and a commitment to active management.

Comment 3 A client's asset allocation using the $1/N$ rule depends on the investment characteristics of each asset class.

1. The asset allocation in Exhibit 1 *most likely* resulted from a mean–variance optimization using:

   A. historical data.

   B. reverse optimization.

   C. Black–Litterman inputs.

2. For clients concerned about rebalancing-related transactions costs, which of Beade's suggested changes in the corridor width of the rebalancing policy is correct? The change with respect to:

   A. high-risk asset classes.

   B. less liquid asset classes.

   C. taxable clients with high capital gains tax rates.

3. Based on Beade's interest rate expectations, the pension plan's funding ratio will:

   A. decrease.

   B. remain unchanged.

   C. increase.

4. Based on Exhibit 2, which portfolio provides the greatest objective function expected value?

   A. Portfolio 1

   B. Portfolio 2

   C. Portfolio 3

5. The asset allocation approach most appropriate for client Kealoha is *best* described as:

   A. a surplus optimization approach.

   B. an integrated asset–liability approach.

   C. a hedging/return-seeking portfolios approach.

6. Based on Exhibit 3, which subportfolios *best* meet the two goals expressed by client Rodríguez?

   A. Subportfolio A for Goal 1 and Subportfolio C for Goal 2

   B. Subportfolio B for Goal 1 and Subportfolio C for Goal 2

   C. Subportfolio E for Goal 1 and Subportfolio A for Goal 2

7. In the risk parity asset allocation approach that Müller uses, the weight that

Müller places on domestic bonds should be:

A. less than 25%.

B. equal to 25%.

C. greater than 25%.

8. Which of Müller's comments about the other approaches to asset allocation is correct?

A. Comment 1

B. Comment 2

C. Comment 3

The following information relates to questions 9-13

Investment adviser Carl Monteo determines client asset allocations using quantitative techniques such as mean–variance optimization (MVO) and risk budgets. Monteo is reviewing the allocations of three clients. Exhibit 1 shows the expected return and standard deviation of returns for three strategic asset allocations that apply to several of Monteo's clients.

Exhibit 1: Strategic Asset Allocation Alternatives

	Adviser's Forecasts	
Asset Allocation	**Expected Return (%)**	**Standard Deviation of Returns (%)**
A	10	12.0
B	8	8.0
C	6	2.0

Monteo interviews client Mary Perkins and develops a detailed assessment of her risk preference and capacity for risk, which is needed to apply MVO to asset allocation. Monteo estimates the risk aversion coefficient (λ) for Perkins to be 8 and uses the following utility function to determine a preferred asset allocation for Perkins:

$$U_m = E\left(R_m\right) - 0.005\lambda\sigma_m^2$$

Another client, Lars Velky, represents Velky Partners (VP), a large institutional investor with $500 million in investable assets. Velky is interested in adding less liquid asset classes, such as direct real estate, infrastructure, and private equity, to VP's portfolio. Velky and Monteo discuss the considerations involved in applying many of the common asset allocation techniques, such as MVO, to these asset classes. Before making any changes to the portfolio, Monteo asks Velky about his knowledge of risk budgeting. Velky makes the following statements:

Statement 1 An optimum risk budget minimizes total risk.

Statement 2 Risk budgeting decomposes total portfolio risk into its constituent parts.

Statement 3 An asset allocation is optimal from a risk-budgeting perspective when the ratio of excess return to marginal contribution to risk is different for all assets in the portfolio.

Monteo meets with a third client, Jayanta Chaterji, an individual investor. Monteo and Chaterji discuss mean–variance optimization. Chaterji expresses concern about using the output of MVOs for two reasons:

Criticism 1: The asset allocations are highly sensitive to changes in the model inputs.

Criticism 2: The asset allocations tend to be highly dispersed across all available asset classes.

Monteo and Chaterji also discuss other approaches to asset allocation. Chaterji tells Monteo that he understands the factor-based approach to asset allocation to have two key characteristics:

Characteristic 1 The factors commonly used in the factor-based approach generally have low correlations with the market and with each other.

Characteristic 2 The factors commonly used in the factor-based approach are typically different from the fundamental or structural factors used in multifactor models.

Monteo concludes the meeting with Chaterji after sharing his views on the factor-based approach.

9. Based on Exhibit 1 and the risk aversion coefficient, the preferred asset allocation for Perkins is:

   A. Asset Allocation A.

   B. Asset Allocation B.

   C. Asset Allocation C.

10. In their discussion of the asset classes that Velky is interested in adding to the VP portfolio, Monteo should tell Velky that:

    A. these asset classes can be readily diversified to eliminate idiosyncratic risk.

    B. indexes are available for these asset classes that do an outstanding job of representing the performance characteristics of the asset classes.

    C. the risk and return characteristics associated with actual investment vehicles for these asset classes are typically significantly different from the characteristics of the asset classes themselves.

11. Which of Velky's statements about risk budgeting is correct?

    A. Statement 1

    B. Statement 2

    C. Statement 3

12. Which of Chaterji's criticisms of MVO is/are valid?
   A. Only Criticism 1
   B. Only Criticism 2
   C. Both Criticism 1 and Criticism 2

13. Which of the characteristics put forth by Chaterji to describe the factor-based approach is/are correct?
   A. Only Characteristic 1
   B. Only Characteristic 2
   C. Both Characteristic 1 and Characteristic 2

---

14. John Tomb is an investment advisor at an asset management firm. He is developing an asset allocation for James Youngmall, a client of the firm. Tomb considers two possible allocations for Youngmall. Allocation A consists of four asset classes: cash, US bonds, US equities, and global equities. Allocation B includes these same four asset classes, as well as global bonds.

   Youngmall has a relatively low risk tolerance with a risk aversion coefficient (λ) of 7. Tomb runs mean–variance optimization (MVO) to maximize the following utility function to determine the preferred allocation for Youngmall:

   $$U_m = E\left(R_m\right) - 0.005\lambda\sigma_m^2$$

   The resulting MVO statistics for the two asset allocations are presented in Exhibit 1.

Exhibit 1: MVO Portfolio Statistics

	Allocation A	Allocation B
Expected return	6.7%	5.9%
Expected standard deviation	11.9%	10.7%

   Determine which allocation in Exhibit 1 Tomb should recommend to Youngmall. **Justify** your response.

Determine which allocation in Exhibit 1 Tomb should recommend to Youngmall. (circle one)

Allocation A	Allocation B
Justify your response.	

15. Walker Patel is a portfolio manager at an investment management firm. After successfully implementing mean–variance optimization (MVO), he wants to apply reverse optimization to his portfolio. For each asset class in the portfolio, Patel obtains market capitalization data, betas computed relative to a global market portfolio, and expected returns. This information, along with the MVO asset

allocation results, are presented in Exhibit 1.

Exhibit 1: Asset Class Data and MVO Asset Allocation Results

Asset Class	Market Cap (trillions)	Beta	Expected Returns	MVO Asset Allocation
Cash	$4.2	0.0	2.0%	10%
US bonds	$26.8	0.5	4.5%	20%
US equities	$22.2	1.4	8.6%	35%
Global equities	$27.5	1.7	10.5%	20%
Global bonds	$27.1	0.6	4.7%	15%
Total	$107.8			

The risk-free rate is 2.0%, and the global market risk premium is 5.5%.

Contrast, using the information provided above, the results of a reverse optimization approach with that of the MVO approach for each of the following:

i. The asset allocation mix

ii. The values of the expected returns for US equities and global bonds

Justify your response.

16. Viktoria Johansson is newly appointed as manager of ABC Corporation's pension fund. The current market value of the fund's assets is $10 billion, and the present value of the fund's liabilities is $8.5 billion. The fund has historically been managed using an asset-only approach, but Johansson recommends to ABC's board of directors that they adopt a liability-relative approach, specifically the hedging/return-seeking portfolios approach. Johansson assumes that the returns of the fund's liabilities are driven by changes in the returns of index-linked government bonds. Exhibit 1 presents three potential asset allocation choices for the fund.

Exhibit 1: Potential Asset Allocations Choices for ABC Corp's Pension Fund

Asset Class	Allocation 1	Allocation 2	Allocation 3
Cash	15%	5%	0%
Index-linked government bonds	70%	15%	85%
Corporate bonds	0%	30%	5%
Equities	15%	50%	10%
Portfolio Statistics			
Expected return	3.4%	6.2%	3.6%
Expected standard deviation	7.0%	12.0%	8.5%

Determine which asset allocation in Exhibit 1 would be *most appropriate* for Johansson given her recommendation. **Justify** your response.

Determine which asset allocation in Exhibit 1 would be *most appropriate* for Johansson given her recommendation.
(circle one)

Allocation 1	Allocation 2	Allocation 3

Justify your response.

The following information relates to questions 17-18

Mike and Kerry Armstrong are a married couple who recently retired with total assets of $8 million. The Armstrongs meet with their financial advisor, Brent Abbott, to discuss three of their financial goals during their retirement.

Goal 1: An 85% chance of purchasing a vacation home for $5 million in five years.

Goal 2: A 99% chance of being able to maintain their current annual expenditures of $100,000 for the next 10 years, assuming annual inflation of 3% from Year 2 onward.

Goal 3: A 75% chance of being able to donate $10 million to charitable foundations in 25 years.

Abbott suggests using a goals-based approach to construct a portfolio. He develops a set of sub-portfolio modules, presented in Exhibit 1. Abbott suggests investing any excess capital in Module A.

Exhibit 1: "Highest Probability- and Horizon-Adjusted Return" Sub-Portfolio Modules under Different Horizon and Probability Scenarios

	A	B	C	D
Portfolio Characteristics				
Expected return	6.5%	7.9%	8.5%	8.8%
Expected volatility	6.0%	7.7%	8.8%	9.7%
	Annualized Minimum Expectation Returns			
Time Horizon	**5 Years**			
Required Success				
99%	0.3%	−0.1%	−0.7%	−1.3%
85%	3.7%	4.3%	4.4%	4.3%
75%	4.7%	5.6%	5.8%	5.9%
Time Horizon	**10 Years**			
Required Success				
99%	2.1%	2.2%	2.0%	1.7%
85%	4.5%	5.4%	5.6%	5.6%
75%	5.2%	6.3%	6.6%	6.7%
Time Horizon	**25 Years**			
Required Success				
99%	3.7%	4.3%	4.4%	4.3%
85%	5.3%	6.3%	6.7%	6.8%
75%	5.7%	6.9%	7.3%	7.5%

17. **Select**, for each of Armstrong's three goals, which sub-portfolio module from Exhibit 1 Abbott should choose in constructing a portfolio. **Justify** each selection.

Select, for each of Armstrong's three goals, which sub-portfolio module from Exhibit 1 Abbott should choose in constructing a portfolio.
(circle one module for each goal)

Goal 1	Goal 2	Goal 3
Module A	Module A	Module A
Module B	Module B	Module B
Module C	Module C	Module C
Module D	Module D	Module D

Justify each selection.

18. **Construct** the overall goals-based asset allocation for the Armstrongs given their

three goals and Abbott's suggestion for investing any excess capital. **Show** your calculations.

Construct the overall goals-based asset allocation for the Armstrongs given their three goals and Abbott's suggestion for investing any excess capital.
(insert the percentage of the total assets to be invested in each module)

Module A	Module B	Module C	Module D

Show your calculations.

SOLUTIONS

1. A is correct. The allocations in Exhibit 1 are most likely from an MVO model using historical data inputs. MVO tends to result in asset allocations that are concentrated in a subset of the available asset classes. The allocations in Exhibit 1 have heavy concentrations in four of the asset classes and no investment in the other four asset classes, and the weights differ greatly from global market weights. Compared to the use of historical inputs, the Black–Litterman and reverse-optimization models most likely would be less concentrated in a few asset classes and less distant from the global weights.

2. A is correct. Theoretically, higher-risk assets would warrant a narrow corridor because high-risk assets are more likely to stray from the desired strategic asset allocation. However, narrow corridors will likely result in more frequent rebalancing and increased transaction costs, so in practice corridor width is often specified to be proportionally greater the higher the asset class's volatility. Thus, higher-risk assets should have a wider corridor to avoid frequent, costly rebalancing costs. Her other suggestions are not correct. Less-liquid asset classes should have a wider, not narrower, corridor width. Less-liquid assets should have a wider corridor to avoid frequent rebalancing costs. For taxable investors, transactions trigger capital gains in jurisdictions that tax them. For such investors, higher tax rates on capital gains should be associated with wider (not narrower) corridor widths.

3. A is correct. The original funding ratio is the market value of assets divided by the present value of liabilities. This plan's ratio is $205 million/$241 million = 0.8506. When the assets and liabilities both decrease by $25 million, the funding ratio will decrease to $180 million/$216 million = 0.8333.

4. B is correct. The objective function expected value is $U_m^{LR} = E\left(R_{s,m}\right) - 0.005\lambda\sigma^2\left(R_{s,m}\right)$. λ is equal to 1.5, and the expected value of the objective function is shown in the rightmost column below.

Portfolio	$E(R_s,m)$	$\sigma^2(R_{s,m})$	$U_m^{LR} = E(R_{s,m}) - 0.005(1.5)\sigma^2(R_{s,m})$
1	13.00	576	8.68
2	12.00	324	9.57
3	11.00	361	8.29

Portfolio 2 generates the highest value, or utility, in the objective function.

5. C is correct. The hedging/return-seeking portfolios approach is best for this client. Beade should construct two portfolios, one that includes riskless bonds that will pay off the fixed obligation in 10 years and the other a risky portfolio that earns a competitive risk-adjusted return. This approach is a simple two-step process of hedging the fixed obligation and then investing the balance of the assets in a return-seeking portfolio.

6. A is correct. Goal 1 requires a success rate of at least 95%, and Subportfolio A has the highest minimum expected return (2.05%) meeting this requirement. Goal 2 requires the highest minimum expected return that will be achieved 85% of the time. Subportfolio C meets this requirement (and has a minimum expected return of 3.26%).

7. C is correct. A risk parity asset allocation is based on the notion that each asset

class should contribute equally to the total risk of the portfolio. Bonds have the lowest risk level and must contribute 25% of the portfolio's total risk, so bonds must be overweighted (greater than 25%). The equal contribution of each asset class is calculated as:

$$w_i \times \text{Cov}\left(r_i, r_p\right) = \frac{1}{n}\sigma_p^2$$

where

w_i = weight of asset i

$\text{Cov}(r_i, r_p)$ = covariance of asset i with the portfolio

n = number of assets

σ_p^2 = variance of the portfolio

In this example, there are four asset classes, and the variance of the total portfolio is assumed to be 25%; therefore, using a risk parity approach, the allocation to each asset class is expected to contribute (1/4 × 25%) = 6.25% of the total variance. Because bonds have the lowest covariance, they must have a higher relative weight to achieve the same contribution to risk as the other asset classes.

8. A is correct. Comment 1 is correct because the "120 minus your age" rule reduces the equity allocation as the client ages, while the 60/40 rule makes no such adjustment. Comments 2 and 3 are not correct. The Yale model emphasizes investing in alternative assets (such as hedge funds, private equity, and real estate) as opposed to investing in traditional asset classes (such as stock and bonds). The 1/*N* rule allocates an equal weight to each asset without regard to its investment characteristics, treating all assets as indistinguishable in terms of mean returns, volatility, and correlations.

9. C is correct. The risk aversion coefficient (λ) for Mary Perkins is 8. The utility of each asset allocation is calculated as follows:

   Asset Allocation A:

   $$U_A = 10.0\% - 0.005(8)(12\%)^2$$
   $$= 4.24\%$$

   Asset Allocation B:

   $$U_B = 8.0\% - 0.005(8)(8\%)^2$$
   $$= 5.44\%$$

   Asset Allocation C:

   $$U_C = 6.0\% - 0.005(8)(2\%)^2$$
   $$= 5.84\%$$

   Therefore, the preferred strategic allocation is Asset Allocation C, which generates the highest utility given Perkins's level of risk aversion.

10. C is correct. Less liquid asset classes—such as direct real estate, infrastructure, and private equity—represent unique challenges when applying many of the common asset allocation techniques. Common illiquid asset classes cannot be readily diversified to eliminate idiosyncratic risk, so representing overall asset class performance is problematic. Furthermore, there are far fewer indexes that attempt to represent aggregate performance for these less liquid asset classes

than indexes of traditional highly liquid asset classes. Finally, the risk and return characteristics associated with actual investment vehicles—such as direct real estate funds, infrastructure funds, and private equity funds—are typically significantly different from the characteristics of the asset classes themselves.

11. B is correct. The goal of risk budgeting is to maximize return per unit of risk. A risk budget identifies the total amount of risk and attributes risk to its constituent parts. An optimum risk budget allocates risk efficiently.

12. A is correct. One common criticism of MVO is that the model outputs, the asset allocations, tend to be highly sensitive to changes in the model. Another common criticism of MVO is that the resulting asset allocations tend to be highly concentrated in a subset of the available asset classes.

13. A is correct. The factors commonly used in the factor-based approach generally have low correlations with the market and with each other. This results from the fact that the factors typically represent what is referred to as a zero (dollar) investment or self-financing investment, in which the underperforming attribute is sold short to finance an offsetting long position in the better-performing attribute. Constructing factors in this manner removes most market exposure from the factors (because of the offsetting short and long positions); as a result, the factors generally have low correlations with the market and with one another. Also, the factors commonly used in the factor-based approach are typically similar to the fundamental or structural factors used in multifactor models.

14.

Determine which allocation in Exhibit 1 Tomb should recommend to Youngmall. (circle one)

Allocation A	Allocation B

Justify your response.

- Tomb should recommend Allocation B.
- The expected utility of Allocation B is 1.89%, which is higher than Allocation A's expected utility of 1.74%.

MVO provides a framework to determine how much to allocate to each asset class or to create the optimal asset mix. The given objective function is:

$$U_m = E\left(R_m\right) - 0.005\lambda\sigma_m^2$$

Using the given objective function and the expected returns and expected standard deviations for Allocations A and B, the expected utilities (certainty-equivalent returns) for the two allocations are calculated as:

Allocation A: $6.7\% - 0.005\ (7)\ (11.9\%)^2 = 1.74\%$

Allocation B: $5.9\% - 0.005\ (7)\ (10.7\%)^2 = 1.89\%$

Therefore, Tomb should recommend Allocation B because it results in higher expected utility than Allocation A.

15. **Contrast,** using the information provided above, the results of a reverse optimization approach with that of the MVO approach for each of the following:

i. The asset allocation mix

- The asset allocation weights for the reverse optimization method are inputs into the optimization and are determined by the market capitalization weights of the global market portfolio.
- The asset allocation weights for the MVO method are outputs of the optimization with the expected returns, covariances, and a risk aversion coefficient used as inputs.
- The two methods result in significantly different asset allocation mixes.
- In contrast to MVO, the reverse optimization method results in a higher percentage point allocation to global bonds, US bonds, and global equities as well as a lower percentage point allocation to cash and US equities.

The reverse optimization method takes the asset allocation weights as its inputs that are assumed to be optimal. These weights are calculated as the market capitalization weights of a global market portfolio. In contrast, the outputs of an MVO are the asset allocation weights, which are based on (1) expected returns and covariances that are forecasted using historical data and (2) a risk aversion coefficient. The two methods result in significantly different asset allocation mixes. In contrast to MVO, the reverse optimization method results in a 4.9, 5.5, and 10.1 higher percentage point allocation to US bonds, global equities, and global bonds, respectively, and a 6.1 and 14.4 lower percentage point allocation to cash and US equities, respectively.

The asset allocation under the two methods is as follows:

		Asset Allocation Weights		
Asset Class	**Market Cap (trillions)**	**Reverse Optimization**	**MVO Approach**	**Difference**
Cash	$4.2	3.9%	10%	−6.1%
US bonds	$26.8	24.9%	20%	4.9%
US equities	$22.2	20.6%	35%	−14.4%
Global equities	$27.5	25.5%	20%	5.5%
Global bonds	$27.1	25.1%	15%	10.1%
Total	$107.8	100.0%	100.0%	

ii. The values of the expected returns for US equities and global bonds

- For the reverse optimization approach, the expected returns of asset classes are the outputs of optimization with the market capitalization weights, covariances, and the risk aversion coefficient used as inputs.
- In contrast, for the MVO approach, the expected returns of asset classes are inputs to the optimization, with the expected returns generally estimated using historical data.
- The computed values for the expected returns for global bonds and US equities using the reverse optimization method are 5.3% and 9.7%, respectively.
- In contrast, the expected return estimates used in the MVO approach from Exhibit 1 for global bonds and US equities are 4.7% and 8.6%, respectively.

The output of the reverse optimization method are optimized returns which are viewed as unobserved equilibrium or imputed returns. The equilibrium returns are essentially long-run capital market returns provided by each asset class and are strongly linked to CAPM. In contrast, the expected returns in the MVO approach are generally forecasted based on historical data and are used as inputs along with covariances and the risk aversion coefficient in the optimization. The reverse-optimized returns are calculated using a CAPM approach. The return on an asset class using the CAPM approach is calculated as follows:

Return on Asset Class = Risk-Free Rate + (Beta) (Market Risk Premium)

Therefore, the implied returns for global bonds and US equities are calculated as follows:

Return on Global Bonds = 2.0% + (0.6) (5.5%) = 5.3%

Return on US Equities = 2.0% + (1.4) (5.5%) = 9.7%

The implied equilibrium returns for global bonds and US equities are 5.3% and 9.7%, respectively. These implied returns are above the forecasted returns based on historical data (from Exhibit 1) used as inputs in the MVO approach for global bonds and US equities of 4.7% and 8.6%, respectively.

16.

Determine which asset allocation in Exhibit 1 would be *most appropriate* for Johansson given her recommendation.
(circle one)

Allocation 1	Allocation 2	Allocation 3

Justify your response.

- Allocation 3 is most appropriate.
- To fully hedge the fund's liabilities, 85% ($8.5 billion/$10.0 billion) of the fund's assets would be linked to index-linked government bonds.
- Residual $1.5 billion surplus would be invested into a return-seeking portfolio.

The pension fund currently has a surplus of $1.5 billion ($10.0 billion – $8.5 billion). To adopt a hedging/return-seeking portfolios approach, Johansson would first hedge the liabilities by allocating an amount equal to the present value of the fund's liabilities, $8.5 billion, to a hedging portfolio. The hedging portfolio must include assets whose returns are driven by the same factors that drive the returns of the liabilities, which in this case are the index-linked government bonds.

So, Johansson should allocate 85% ($8.5 billion/$10.0 billion) of the fund's assets to index-linked government bonds. The residual $1.5 billion surplus would then be invested into a return-seeking portfolio. Therefore, Allocation 3 would be the most appropriate asset allocation for the fund because it allocates 85% of the fund's assets to index-linked government bonds and the remainder to a return-seeking portfolio consisting of corporate bonds and equities.

17.

Select, for each of Armstrong's three goals, which sub-portfolio module from Exhibit 1 Abbott should choose in constructing a portfolio.
(circle one module for each goal)

Goal 1	Goal 2	Goal 3
Module A	Module A	Module A
Module B	Module B	Module B
Module C	Module C	Module C
Module D	Module D	Module D

Justify each selection.

- Module C should be chosen for Goal 1, Module B should be chosen for Goal 2, and Module D should be chosen for Goal 3.
- The module that should be selected for each goal is the one that offers the highest return given the time horizon and required probability of success.

The module that should be selected for each goal is the one that offers the highest return given the time horizon and required probability of success. For Goal 1, which has a time horizon of five years and a required probability of success of 85%, Module C should be chosen because its 4.4% expected return is higher than the expected returns of all the other modules. Similarly, for Goal 2, which has a time horizon of 10 years and a required probability of success of 99%, Module B should be chosen because its 2.2% expected return is higher than the expected returns of all the other modules. Finally, for Goal 3, which has a time horizon of 25 years and a required probability of success of 75%, Module D should be chosen because its 7.5% expected return is higher than the expected returns of all the other modules.

18. Guideline Answer:

- The module that should be selected for each goal is the one that offers the highest return given the time horizon and required probability of success.
- Approximately 16.4%, 12.7%, 50.4%, and 20.5% should be invested in Modules A, B, C, and D, respectively.

The appropriate goals based allocation for the Armstrongs is as follows:

	Goals			
	1	**2**	**3**	**Surplus**
Horizon (years)	5	10	25	
Probability of success	85%	99%	75%	
Selected module	**C**	**B**	**D**	**A**
Discount rate	4.4%	2.2%	7.5%	
Dollars invested (millions)	$4.03	$1.01	$1.64	$1.32
As a % of total	**50.4%**	**12.7%**	**20.5%**	**16.4%**

Supporting calculations:

For Goal 1, which has a time horizon of five years and a required probability of success of 85%, Module C should be chosen because its 4.4% expected return is higher than the expected returns of all the other modules. The present value of Goal 1 is calculated as follows:

N = 5, FV = –5,000,000, I/Y = 4.4%; CPT PV = \$4,031,508 (or \$4.03 million)

So, approximately 50.4% of the total assets of \$8 million (= \$4.03 million/\$8.00 million) should be allocated to Module C.

For Goal 2, which has a time horizon of 10 years and a required probability of success of 99%, Module B should be chosen because its 2.2% expected return is higher than the expected returns of all the other modules. The present value of Goal 2 is calculated as follows:

$$PV = \frac{\$100,000}{(1.022)^1} + \frac{\$100,000(1.03)^1}{(1.022)^2} + \frac{\$100,000(1.03)^2}{(1.022)^3} + \ldots + \frac{\$100,000(1.03)^9}{(1.022)^{10}}$$

PV = \$1,013,670 (or \$1.01 million)

So, approximately 12.7% of the total assets of \$8 million (= \$1.01 million/\$8.00 million) should be allocated to Module B.

For Goal 3, which has a time horizon of 25 years and a required probability of success of 75%, Module D should be chosen because its 7.5% expected return is higher than the expected returns of all the other modules. The present value of Goal 3 is calculated as follows:

N = 25, FV = –10,000,000, I/Y = 7.5%; CPT PV = \$1,639,791 (or \$1.64 million)

So, approximately 20.5% of the total assets of \$8 million (= \$1.64 million/\$8.00 million) should be allocated to Module D.

Finally, the surplus of \$1,315,032 (= \$8,000,000 – \$4,031,508 – \$1,013,670 – \$1,639,791), representing 16.4% (= \$1.32 million/\$8.00 million), should be invested in Module A following Abbott's suggestion.

LEARNING MODULE

5

Asset Allocation with Real-World Constraints

by Peter Mladina, Brian J. Murphy, CFA, and Mark Ruloff, FSA, EA, CERA.

Peter Mladina is at Northern Trust and UCLA (USA). Brian J. Murphy, CFA, is at Willis Towers Watson (USA). Mark Ruloff, FSA, EA, CERA, is at Aon (USA).

LEARNING OUTCOMES

Mastery	*The candidate should be able to:*
☐	discuss asset size, liquidity needs, time horizon, and regulatory or other considerations as constraints on asset allocation
☐	discuss tax considerations in asset allocation and rebalancing
☐	recommend and justify revisions to an asset allocation given change(s) in investment objectives and/or constraints
☐	discuss the use of short-term shifts in asset allocation
☐	identify behavioral biases that arise in asset allocation and recommend methods to overcome them

INTRODUCTION

1

This reading illustrates ways in which the asset allocation process must be adapted to accommodate specific asset owner circumstances and constraints. It addresses adaptations to the asset allocation inputs given an asset owner's asset size, liquidity, and time horizon as well as external constraints that may affect the asset allocation choice (Sections 2–5). We also discuss the ways in which taxes influence the asset allocation process for the taxable investor (Sections 6–7). In addition, we discuss the circumstances that should trigger a re-evaluation of the long-term strategic asset allocation (Section 8), when and how an asset owner might want to make short-term shifts in asset allocation (Section 9), and how innate investor behaviors can interfere with successful long-term planning for the investment portfolio (Section 10). Throughout the reading, we illustrate the application of these concepts using a series of hypothetical investors.

2 CONSTRAINTS IN ASSET ALLOCATION AND ASSET SIZE

☐ discuss asset size, liquidity needs, time horizon, and regulatory or other considerations as constraints on asset allocation

General asset allocation principles assume that all asset owners have equal ability to access the entirety of the investment opportunity set, and that it is merely a matter of finding that combination of asset classes that best meets the wants, needs, and obligations of the asset owner. In practice, however, it is not so simple. An asset owner must consider a number of constraints when modeling and choosing among asset allocation alternatives. Some of the most important are asset size, liquidity needs, taxes, and time horizon. Moreover, regulatory and other external considerations may influence the investment opportunity set or the optimal asset allocation decision.

Asset Size

The size of an asset owner's portfolio has implications for asset allocation. It may limit the opportunity set—the asset classes accessible to the asset owner—by virtue of the scale needed to invest successfully in certain asset classes or by the availability of investment vehicles necessary to implement the asset allocation.

Economies and diseconomies of scale are perhaps the most important factors relevant to understanding asset size as a constraint. The size of an asset owner's investment pool may be too small—or too large—to capture the returns of certain asset classes or strategies efficiently. Asset owners with larger portfolios can generally consider a broader set of asset classes and strategies. On the one hand, they are more likely to have sufficient governance capacity—sophistication and staff resources—to develop the required knowledge base for the more complex asset classes and investment vehicles. They also have sufficient size to build a diversified portfolio of investment strategies, many of which have substantial minimum investment requirements. On the other hand, some asset owners may have portfolios that are *too* large; their desired minimum investment may exhaust the capacity of active external investment managers in certain asset classes and strategies. Although "too large" and "too small" are not rigidly defined, the following example illustrates the difficulty of investing a very large portfolio. Consider an asset owner with an investment portfolio of US$25 billion who is seeking to make a 5% investment in global small-cap stocks:

- The median total market capitalization of the stocks in the S&P Global SmallCap is approximately US$860 million as of November 2021.
- Assume a small-cap manager operates a 50-stock portfolio and is willing to own 3% of the market cap of any one of its portfolio companies. Their average position size would be US$26 million, and an effective level of assets under management (AUM) would be on the order of US$1.3 billion. Beyond that level, the manager may be forced to expand the portfolio beyond 50 stocks or to hold position sizes greater than 3% of a company's market cap, which could then create liquidity issues for the manager.
- Now, our US$25 billion fund is looking to allocate US$1.25 billion to small-cap stocks (US$25 billion × 5%). They want to diversify this allocation across three or four active managers—a reasonable allocation of governance resources in the context of all of the fund's investment activities. The average allocation per manager is approximately US$300 to US$400 million,

which would constitute between 23% and 31% of each manager's AUM. This exposes both the asset owner and the investment manager to an undesirable level of operational risk.

Although many large asset owners have found effective ways to implement a small-cap allocation, this example illustrates some of the issues associated with managing a large asset pool. These include such practical considerations as the number of investment managers that might need to be hired to fulfill an investment allocation and the ability of the asset owner to identify and monitor the required number of managers.

Research has shown that investment managers tend to incur certain disadvantages from increasing scale: Growth in AUM leads to larger trade sizes, incurring greater price impact; capital inflows may cause active investment managers to pursue ideas outside of their core investment theses; and organizational hierarchies may slow down decision making and reduce incentives.[1] Asset *owners,* however, are found to have *increasing* returns to scale, as discussed below.

A study of pension plan size and performance (using data spanning 1990–2008) found that large defined benefit plans outperformed smaller ones by 45–50 basis points per year on a risk-adjusted basis.[2] The gains are derived from a combination of cost savings related to internal management, a greater ability to negotiate fees with external managers, and the ability to support larger allocations to private equity and real estate investments. As fund size increases, the "per participant" costs of a larger governance infrastructure decline and the plan sponsor can allocate resources away from such asset classes as small-cap stocks, which are sensitive to diseconomies of scale, to such other areas as private equity funds or co-investments where they are more likely to realize scale-related benefits.

Whereas owners of large asset pools may achieve these operating efficiencies, scale may also impose obstacles related to the liquidity and trading costs of the underlying asset. Above some size, it becomes difficult to deploy capital effectively in certain active investment strategies. As illustrated in Exhibit 1, owners of very large portfolios may face size constraints in allocating to active equity strategies. The studies referenced earlier noted that these asset owners frequently choose to invest passively in developed equity markets where their size inhibits alpha potential. The asset owner's finite resources can then be allocated instead toward such strategies as private equity, hedge funds, and infrastructure, where their scale and resources provide a competitive advantage.

Exhibit 1: Asset Size and Investor Constraints

Asset Class	Investor Constraints by Size
▪ Cash equivalents and money market funds	No size constraints.
▪ Large-cap developed market equity ▪ Small-cap developed market equity ▪ Emerging market equity	Generally accessible to large and small asset owners, although the very large asset owner may be constrained in the amount of assets allocated to certain active strategies and managers.

1 See Stein (2002); Chen, Hong, Huang, and Kubik (2004); and Pollet and Wilson (2008).

2 See Dyck and Pomorski (2011). The median plan in this study was just over US$2 billion. The 25th percentile plan was US$780 million, and the 75th percentile plan was US$6.375 billion.

Asset Class	Investor Constraints by Size
▪ Developed market sovereign bonds ▪ Investment-grade bonds ▪ Non-investment-grade bonds ▪ Private real estate equity	Generally accessible to large and small asset owners, although to achieve prudent diversification, smaller asset owners may need to implement via a commingled vehicle.
Alternative Investments ▪ Hedge funds ▪ Private debt ▪ Private equity ▪ Infrastructure ▪ Timberland and farmland	May be accessible to large and small asset owners, although if offered as private investment vehicles, there may be legal minimum qualifications that exclude smaller asset owners. The ability to successfully invest in these asset classes may also be limited by the asset owner's level of investment understanding/expertise. Prudent diversification may require that smaller asset owners implement via a commingled vehicle, such as a fund of funds, or an ancillary access channel, such as a liquid alternatives vehicle or an alternatives ETF. For very large funds, the allocation may be constrained by the number of funds available.

Even in these strategies, very large asset owners may be constrained by scale. In smaller or less liquid markets, can a large asset owner invest enough that the exposure contributes a material benefit to the broader portfolio? For example, a sovereign wealth fund or large public pension plan may not find enough attractive hedge fund managers to fulfill their desired allocation to hedge funds. True alpha is rare, limiting the opportunity set. Asset owners who find that they have to split their mandate into many smaller pieces may end up with an index-like portfolio but with high active management fees; one manager's active bets may cancel out those of another active manager. A manager mix with no true alpha becomes index-like because the uncompensated, idiosyncratic return variation is diversified away. A much smaller allocation may be achievable, but it may be too small to meaningfully affect the risk and return characteristics of the overall portfolio. More broadly, a very large size makes it more difficult to benefit from opportunistic investments in smaller niche markets or from skilled investment managers who have a small set of unique ideas or concentrated bets. No hard and fast rules exist to determine whether a particular asset owner is too small or too large to effectively access an asset class. Greater governance resources more commonly found among owners of larger asset pools create the capacity to pursue the more complex investment opportunities, but the asset owner may still need to find creative ways to implement the desired allocation. Each asset owner has a unique set of knowledge and constraints that will influence the opportunity set.

Smaller asset owners (typically institutions with less than US$500 million in assets and private wealth investors with less than US$25 million in assets) also find that their opportunity set may be constrained by the size of their investment portfolio. This is primarily a function of the more limited governance infrastructure typical of smaller asset owners: They may be too small to adequately diversify across the range of asset classes and investment managers or may have staffing constraints (insufficient asset size to justify a dedicated internal staff). Complex strategies may be beyond the reach of asset owners that have chosen not to develop investment expertise internally or where the oversight committee lacks individuals with sufficient investment understanding. In some asset classes and strategies, commingled investment vehicles can be used to achieve the needed diversification, provided the governing documents do not prohibit their use.

Access to other asset classes and strategies—private equity, private real estate, hedge funds, and infrastructure—may still be constrained for smaller asset owners. The commingled vehicles through which these strategies are offered typically require high minimum investments. For successful private equity and hedge fund managers, in particular, minimum investments can be in the tens of millions of (US) dollars, even for funds of funds.

Regulatory restrictions can also impose a size constraint. In the United Kingdom, for example, an asset owner in a private investment vehicle must qualify as an elective professional client, meaning they must meet two of the following three conditions:

1. The client has carried out transactions, in significant size, on the relevant market at an average frequency of 10 per quarter over the previous four quarters.
2. The size of the client's financial instrument portfolio exceeds €500,000.
3. The client works or has worked in the financial sector for at least one year in a professional position, which requires knowledge of the transactions or services envisaged.

In the United States, investors must be either accredited or qualified purchasers to invest in many private equity and hedge fund vehicles. To be a qualified purchaser, a natural person must have at least US$5 million in investments, a company must have at least US$25 million in investable assets, and an investment manager must have at least US$25 million under management. In Hong Kong SAR, the Securities and Futures Commission requires that an investor must meet the qualifications of a "Professional Investor" to invest in certain categories of assets. A Professional Investor is generally defined as a trust with total assets of not less than HK$40 million, an individual with a portfolio not less than HK$8 million, or a corporation or partnership with a portfolio not less than HK$8 million or total assets of not less than HK$40 million. The size constraints related to these asset classes suggest that smaller asset owners have real challenges achieving an effective private equity or hedge fund allocation.

Asset size as a constraint is often a more acute issue for individual investors than institutional asset owners. Wealthy families may pool assets through such vehicles as family limited partnerships, investment companies, fund of funds, or other forms of commingled vehicles to hold their assets. These pooled vehicles can then access investment vehicles, asset classes, and strategies that individual family members may not have portfolios large enough to access on their own.

WHERE ASSET SIZE CONSTRAINS INVESTMENT OPPORTUNITY

As of early 2021, the 10 largest sovereign wealth funds globally each exceed US$350 billion in assets. For a fund of this size, a 5% allocation to hedge funds (the average sovereign wealth fund allocation) would imply US$17.5 *billion* to be deployed. The global hedge fund industry manages approximately US$4.3 trillion in total as of the second quarter of 2021. With about 10,000 hedge funds globally, the average asset size of a hedge fund thus would be US$430 million. At the same time, approximately 60% of the funds manage less than US$100 million, and the remaining 40% of the funds have an average size of near US$1 billion. If we assume that the asset owner would want to be no more than 20% of a firm's AUM, we can infer that the average investment might be approximately US$86 million considering the full hedge fund universe or about US$200 million if we limit the choice to larger sized hedge funds. With US$17.5 billion to deploy, the fund would need to invest with nearly 90 (bigger size hedge funds universe) to 200 (total universe) funds to achieve a 5% allocation to hedge funds.

Sources: Sovereign Wealth Fund Institute, BarclayHedge, and Preqin.

EXAMPLE 1

Asset Size Constraints in Asset Allocation

Describe asset size constraints that Aromdee might encounter in implementing this asset allocation. Discuss possible means to address them.

Given the asset size of the fund, formulate a set of questions regarding the feasibility of this recommendation that you would like staff to address at the next Investment Committee meeting.

The new president of the University has stated that he feels the current policy is overly restrictive, and he would like to see a more diversified program that takes advantage of the types of investment strategies used by large endowment programs. Choosing from among the following asset classes, propose a set of asset classes to be considered in the revised asset allocation. Justify your response.

- Cash equivalents and money market funds
- Large-cap developed market equity
- Small-cap developed market equity
- Emerging market equity
- Developed market sovereign bonds
- Investment-grade bonds
- Non-investment-grade bonds
- Private real estate equity
- Hedge funds
- Private debt
- Private equity

1. Akkarat Aromdee is the recently retired President of Alpha Beverage, a producer and distributor of energy drinks throughout Southeast Asia. Upon retiring, the company provided a lump sum retirement payment of THB880,000,000 (equivalent to €20 million), which was rolled over to a tax-deferred individual retirement savings plan. Aside from these assets, Aromdee owns company stock worth about THB70,000,000. The stock is infrequently traded. He has consulted with an investment adviser, and they are reviewing the following asset allocation proposal:

Global equities	40%
Global high-yield bonds	15%
Domestic intermediate bonds	30%
Hedge funds	10%
Private equity	5%

Solution:

With a THB88 million (€2 million) allocation to hedge funds and a THB44 million (€1 million) allocation to private equity funds, Aromdee may encounter restrictions on his eligibility to invest in the private investment vehicles typically used for hedge fund and private equity investment. To the extent he is eligible to invest in hedge funds and/or private equity funds, a fund-of-funds or similar commingled arrangement would be essential to achieving an appropriate level of diversification. Additionally, it is essential that he and his adviser develop the necessary level of expertise to invest in these alternative assets. To achieve a prudent level of diversification, the allocation to global high-yield bonds would most likely need to be accomplished via a commingled investment vehicle.

2. The CAF$40 billion Government Petroleum Fund of Caflandia is overseen by a nine-member Investment Committee. The chief investment officer has

a staff with sector heads in global equities, global bonds, real estate, hedge funds, and derivatives. The majority of assets are managed by outside investment managers. The Investment Committee, of which you are a member, approves the asset allocation policy and makes manager selection decisions. Staff has recommended an increase in the private equity allocation from its current 0% to 15%, to be implemented over the next 12 to 36 months. The head of global equities will oversee the implementation of the private equity allocation.

Solution:

Questions regarding the feasibility of the recommendation include the following:

- How many private equity funds do you expect to invest in to achieve the 15% allocation to private equity?
- What is the anticipated average allocation to each fund?
- Are there a sufficient number of high-quality private equity funds willing to accept an allocation of that size?
- What expertise exists at the staff or board level to conduct due diligence on private equity investment funds?
- What resources does the staff have to oversee the increased allocation to private equity?

3. The Courneuve University Endowment has US$250 million in assets. The current allocation is 65% global large-capitalization stocks and 35% high-quality bonds, with a duration target of 5.0 years. The University has adopted a 5% spending policy. University enrollment is stable and expected to remain so. A capital spending initiative of US$100 million for new science buildings in the next three to seven years is being discussed, but it has not yet been approved. The University has no dedicated investment staff and makes limited use of external resources. Investment recommendations are formulated by the University's treasurer and approved by the Investment Committee, composed entirely of external board members.

Solution:

Asset size and limited governance resources are significant constraints on the investment opportunity set available to the Endowment. The asset allocation should emphasize large and liquid investments, such as cash equivalents, developed and emerging market equity, and sovereign and investment-grade bonds. Some small portion of assets, however, could be allocated to commingled investments in real estate, private equity, or hedge funds. Given the University's limited staff resources, it is necessary to ensure that the board members have the level of expertise necessary to select and monitor these more complex asset classes. The Endowment might also consider engaging an outside expert to advise on investment activities in these asset classes.

3 LIQUIDITY

☐ discuss asset size, liquidity needs, time horizon, and regulatory or other considerations as constraints on asset allocation

Two dimensions of liquidity must be considered when developing an asset appropriate allocation solution: the liquidity needs of the asset owner and the liquidity characteristics of the asset classes in the opportunity set. Integrating the two dimensions is an essential element of successful investment planning.

The need for liquidity in an investment portfolio will vary greatly by asset owner and by the goals the assets are set aside to achieve. For example, a bank will typically have a very large portfolio supporting its day-to-day operations. That portfolio is likely to experience very high turnover and a very high need for liquidity; therefore, the investment portfolio must hold high-quality, very short-term, and highly liquid assets.

The same bank may have another designated investment pool one level removed from operating assets. Although the liquidity requirements for this portfolio may be lower, the investments most likely feature a high degree of liquidity—a substantial allocation to investment-grade bonds, perhaps with a slight extension of maturity. For its longer-term investment portfolio, the bank may choose to allocate some portion of its portfolio to less liquid investments. The opportunity set for each portfolio will be constrained by applicable banking laws and regulations.

Long-term investors, such as sovereign wealth funds and endowment funds, can generally exploit illiquidity premiums available in such asset classes as private equity, real estate, and infrastructure investments. However, pension plans may be limited in the amount of illiquidity they can absorb. For example, a frozen pension plan may anticipate the possibility of eliminating its pension obligation completely by purchasing a group annuity and relinquishing the responsibility for making pension payments to an insurance company. If there is a significant probability that the company will take this step in the near term, liquidity of plan assets will become a primary concern; and if there is a substantial allocation to illiquid assets, the plan sponsor may be unable to execute the desired annuity purchase transaction.

Liquidity needs must also consider the particular circumstances and financial strength of the asset owner and what resources they may have beyond those held in the investment portfolio. The following examples illustrate this point:

- A university must consider its prospects for future enrollments and the extent to which it relies on tuition to meet operating needs. If the university experiences a significant drop in enrollment, perhaps because of a poor economic environment, or takes on a new capital improvement project, the asset allocation policy for the endowment should reflect the increased probability of higher outflows to support university operations.
- A foundation whose mission supports medical research in a field in which a breakthrough appears imminent may desire a higher level of liquidity to fund critical projects than would a foundation that supports ongoing community efforts.
- An insurance company whose business is predominantly life or auto insurance, where losses are actuarially predictable, can absorb more liquidity risk than a property/casualty reinsurer whose losses are subject to unpredictable events, such as natural disasters.
- A family with several children nearing college-age will have higher liquidity needs than a couple of the same age and circumstances with no children.

When assessing the appropriateness of any given asset class for a given asset owner, it is wise to evaluate potential liquidity needs in the context of an extreme market stress event. The market losses of the 2008–2009 global financial crisis were extreme. Simultaneously, other forces exacerbated investors' distress: Many university endowments were called upon to provide an increased level of operating support; insurers dipped into reserves to offset operating losses; community foundations found their beneficiaries in even greater need of financial support; and some individual investors experienced setbacks that caused them to move, if only temporarily, from being net contributors to net spenders of financial wealth. A successful asset allocation effort will stress the proposed allocation; it will anticipate, where possible, the likely behavior of other facets of the saving/spending equation during times of stress.

It is also important to consider the intersection of asset class and investor liquidity in the context of the asset owner's governance capacity. Although the mission of the organization or trust may allow for a certain level of illiquidity, if those responsible for the oversight of the investment program do not have the mental fortitude or discipline to maintain course through the crisis, illiquid and less liquid investments are unlikely to produce the rewards typically expected of these exposures. Although rates of return may be mean-reverting, wealth is not. Losses resulting from panic selling during times of stress become permanent losses; there are fewer assets left to earn returns in a post-crash recovery.

THE CASE OF VANISHING LIQUIDITY

In the global financial crisis of 2008–2009, many investors learned painful truths about liquidity. When most needed—whether to rebalance or to meet spending obligations—it can evaporate. As investors liquidated their most liquid assets to meet financial obligations (or to raise cash in fear of further market declines), the remaining less liquid assets in their portfolios became an ever-larger percentage of the portfolio. Many investors were forced to sell private partnership interests on the secondary market at steeply discounted prices. Others defaulted on outstanding private fund capital commitments by refusing to honor future obligations.

Similarly, illiquidity became a substantial problem during the Asian currency crisis of 1997–1998 and again with the Russian debt default and Long-Term Capital Management (LTCM) crisis of 1998. In the following paragraphs, we describe several "liquidity crises" that are often used in stress testing asset allocation choices.

The Asian Currency Crisis of 1997

In the spring of 1997, Thailand spent billions to defend the Thai baht against speculative attacks, finally capitulating and devaluing the baht in July 1997. This triggered a series of moves throughout the region to defend currencies against speculators. Ultimately, these efforts were unsuccessful and many countries abandoned the effort and allowed their currencies to float freely. The Philippines, Indonesia, and South Korea abandoned their pegs against the US dollar. On 27 October 1997, rattled by the currency crisis, Asian and European markets declined sharply in advance of the opening of the US markets. The S&P 500 declined nearly 7%, and trading on US stock markets was suspended.

The Russian Debt Default/LTCM Crisis of August 1998

On 17 August 1998, the Russian government defaulted on its short-term debt. This unprecedented default of a sovereign debtor roiled the global bond markets. A global flight-to-quality ensued, which caused credit spreads to widen and liquidity to evaporate. Highly levered investors experienced significant losses. Long-Term

Capital Management, with reported notional exposure of over US$125 billion (a 25-to-1 leverage ratio), exacerbated these price declines as they faced their own liquidity crisis and were forced to liquidate large relative value, distressed, convertible arbitrage, merger arbitrage, and equity positions. Ultimately, the magnitude of the liquidity squeeze for LTCM and the risk of potential disruption to global markets caused the New York branch of the Federal Reserve Bank to orchestrate a disciplined, structured bailout of the LTCM fund.

Financial markets are increasingly linked across borders and asset classes; as a result, changes in liquidity conditions in one country can directly affect liquidity conditions elsewhere. These linkages do improve access to financing and capital markets, but they also show that a liquidity problem in one part of the world can ripple across the globe—increasing volatility, creating higher execution costs for investors, and possibly leading to a reduction in credit availability and a decline in economic activity.

QUANTITATIVE EASING

While the lack of liquidity clearly hurts investors, can too much liquidity in the market place (overliquidity, excess liquidity) also cause problems? Overliquidity in the market, or too much cash, to put it simply, is certainly not an issue for frictionless trade executions. On the other hand, too much liquidity in the market may lead to too high asset valuations as investors are trying to invest their excess liquidity, eroding the expected future returns of various asset classes. Following the Great Financial Crisis, as well as the outbreak of the COVID-19 pandemic, central banks globally pumped extra cash into the economy through the asset purchase/quantitative easing (QE) programs to keep interest rates low and stimulate consumption. The impact of QE (measured by the size of the US Federal Reserve's balance sheet) on equity (S&P 500 Index) valuations and real interest rates (10-year Treasury real yield) are illustrated in Exhibit 2. With the increase of the Federal Reserve's balance sheet in early 2020, the overliquidity fueled a strong rebound of the equity market.

Exhibit 2: Federal Reserve Balance Sheet (QE) and Asset Valuations

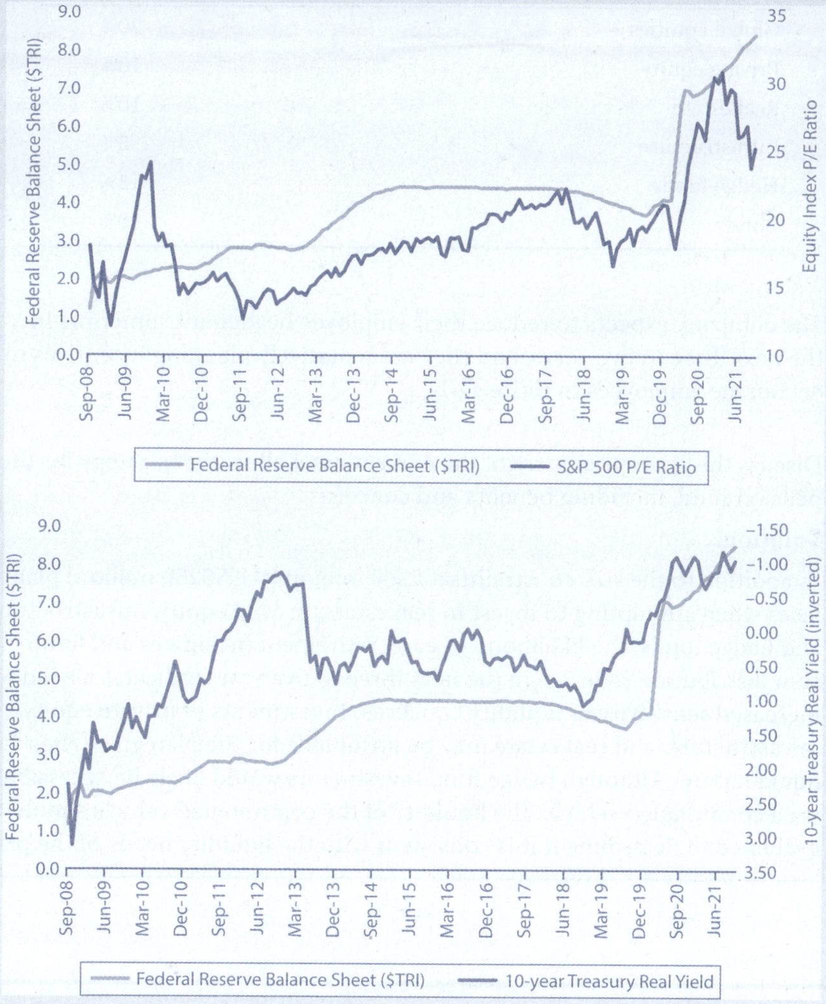

Similarly, the overliquidity pushed interest rates into the negative territory. Taken together, the impact of overliquidity created an environment that fueled the growth of the equity markets and consumption.

Source: Bloomberg.

EXAMPLE 2

Liquidity Constraints in Asset Allocation

1. The Frentel Furniture Pension Fund has £200 million frozen in a defined benefit pension plan that is 85% funded. The plan has a provision that allows employees to elect a lump sum distribution of their pension benefit at retirement. The company is strong financially and is committed to fully funding the pension obligations over time. However, they also want to minimize cash contributions to the plan. Few governance resources are allocated to

the pension fund, and there is no dedicated staff for pension investment activities. The current asset allocation is as shown:

Global equities	20%
Private equity	10%
Real estate	10%
Infrastructure	5%
Hedge funds	15%
Bonds	40%

The company expects to reduce their employee headcount sometime in the next three to five years, and they are tentatively planning incentives to encourage employees to retire early.

Discuss the appropriateness of the current asset allocation strategy for the pension fund, including benefits and concerns.

Solution:

In addition to the size constraints a £200 million (≈ US$250 million) plan faces when attempting to invest in real estate, private equity, infrastructure, and hedge funds, the likelihood of early retirement incentives and lump-sum distribution requests in the next three to five years indicates a need for increased sensitivity to liquidity concerns. Investments in private equity, infrastructure, and real estate may be unsuitable for the plan given their less liquid nature. Although hedge fund investments would likely be accessible via a commingled vehicle, the liquidity of the commingled vehicle should be evaluated to determine if it is consistent with the liquidity needs of the plan.

4 TIME HORIZON

☐ discuss asset size, liquidity needs, time horizon, and regulatory or other considerations as constraints on asset allocation

An asset owner's time horizon is a critical constraint that must be considered in any asset allocation exercise. A liability to be paid at a given point in the future or a goal to be funded by a specified date each define the asset owner's horizon, thus becoming a basic input to the asset allocation solution. The changing composition of the asset owner's assets and liabilities must also be considered. As time progresses, the character of both *assets* (human capital) and *liabilities* changes.

Changing Human Capital

When asset allocation considers such extended portfolio assets as human capital, the optimal allocation of financial capital can change through time (Bodie, Merton, and Samuelson 1992). Assuming no change in the investor's utility function, as human capital—with its predominately bond-like risk—declines over time, the asset allocation for financial capital would reflect an increasing allocation to bonds. This is a prime example of how time horizon can influence asset allocation.

Changing Character of Liabilities

The changing character of liabilities through time will also affect the asset allocation aligned to fund those liabilities.

As an example, the term structure of liabilities changes as they approach maturity. A pension benefit program is a simple way to illustrate this point. When the employee base is young and retirements are far into the future, the liability can be hedged with long-term bonds. As the employee base ages and prospective retirements are not so far into the future, the liability is more comparable to intermediate- or even short-term bonds. When retirements are imminent, the structure of the liabilities can be characterized as cash-like, and an optimal asset allocation would also have cash-like characteristics.

Similarly, the overall profile of an individual investor's liabilities changes with the progression of time, particularly for investors with finite investment horizons. Nearer-term goals and liabilities move from partially funded to fully funded, while other, longer-term goals and liabilities move progressively closer to funding. As the relative weights of the goals to be funded shift and the time horizon associated with certain goals shortens, the aggregate asset allocation must be adapted if it is to remain aligned with the individual's goals.

Time horizon is also likely to affect the manner in which an investor prioritizes certain goals and liabilities. This will influence the desired risk profile of the assets aligned to fund them. Consider a 75-year-old retired investor with two goals:

1. Fund consumption needs through age 95
2. Fund consumption needs from age 95 through age 105

He most likely assigns a much higher priority to funding goal 1, given the lower probability that he will live beyond age 95.[3] Let's also assume that he has sufficient assets to fund goal 1 and to partially fund goal 2. The higher priority assigned to goal 1 indicates he is less willing to take risk, and this sub-portfolio will be invested more conservatively. Now consider goal 2: Given the low probability of living past 95 and the fact that he does not currently have sufficient assets to fund that goal, the sub-portfolio assigned to goal 2 is likely to have a more growth-oriented asset allocation. The priority of a given goal can change as the investor's time horizon shortens—or lengthens.

Consider the hypothetical investors Ivy and Charles Lee from the reading "Introduction to Asset Allocation." Ivy is a 54-year-old life science entrepreneur. Charles is a 55-year-old orthopedic surgeon. They have two unmarried children aged 25 (Deborah) and 18 (David). Deborah has a daughter with physical limitations. Four goals have been identified for the Lees:

1. Lifestyle/future consumption needs
2. College education for son David, 18 years old
3. Charitable gift to a local art museum in 5 years
4. Special needs trust for their granddaughter, to be funded at the death of Charles

The lifestyle/consumption goal is split into three components: required minimum consumption requirements (a worst-case scenario of reduced lifestyle), baseline consumption needs (maintaining current standard of living), and aspirational consumption needs (an improved standard of living). At age 54, the risk preferences assigned to these goals might look something like the following:

3 A 75-year-old US American male has a life expectancy of 11.1 years, per the Social Security Administration's 2014 "Actuarial Life Tables," https://www.ssa.gov/oact/STATS/table4c6_2014.html (Accessed 22 Nov 2018).

Lifestyle Goals	Risk Preference	Asset Allocation	Sub-Portfolio as % of Total*
Required minimum	Conservative	100% bonds and cash	65%
Baseline	Moderate	60% equities/40% bonds	10%
Aspirational	Aggressive	100% equities	4%
College education	Conservative	100% bonds and cash	1%
Charitable gift (aspirational)	Aggressive	100% equities	5%
Special needs trust	Moderate	60% equities/40% bonds	15%
Aggregate portfolio		≈ 25% equities/75% bonds and cash	100%

* *The present value of each goal as a proportion of the total portfolio.*

The asset allocation for the total portfolio aggregates the asset allocations for each of the goal-aligned sub-portfolios, weighted by the present value of each goal. For the Lees, this is an overall asset allocation of about 25% equities and 75% bonds and cash. (Each goal is discounted to its present value by expected return of its respective goal-aligned sub-portfolio.)

Move forward 20 years. The Lees are now in their mid-70s, and their life expectancy is about 12 years. Their son has completed his college education and is successfully established in his own career. The charitable gift has been made. These two goals have been realized. The assets needed to fund the baseline consumption goal are significantly reduced because fewer future consumption years need to be funded. The special needs trust for their granddaughter remains a high priority. Although the Lee's risk preferences for these goals have not changed, the overall asset allocation *will* change because the total portfolio is an aggregated mix of the remaining goal-aligned sub-portfolios, weighted by their current present values:

Lifestyle Goals	Risk Preference	Asset Allocation	Sub-Portfolio as % of Total*
Required minimum	Conservative	100% bonds and cash	54%
Baseline	Moderate	60% equities/40% bonds	9%
Aspirational	Aggressive	100% equities	3%
Special needs trust	Moderate	60% equities/40% bonds	34%
Aggregate portfolio		≈ 30% equities/70% bonds and cash	100%

* *The present value of each goal as a proportion of the total portfolio. The implied assumption is that current assets are sufficient to fund all goals, provided the Lees adopt an aggressive asset allocation strategy for the aspirational and charitable gifting goals. If the value of current assets exceeds the present value of all goals, the Lees would have greater flexibility to adopt a lower risk preference for some or all goals.*

Although for ease of illustration our example assumed the Lee's risk preferences remained the same, this is not likely to be the case in the real world. Required minimum and baseline consumption goals would remain very important; there is less flexibility to withstand losses caused by either reduced earnings potential or lower likelihood of the market regaining lost ground within the shorter horizon. The aspirational lifestyle goal is likely to be a much lower priority, and it may have been eliminated altogether. The special needs trust may have a higher (or lower) priority as the needs of the granddaughter and the ability of her parents to provide for her needs after their death become more evident. The preferred asset allocation for each of these goals will shift over the course of the investor's lifetime.

As an investor's time horizon shifts, both human capital and financial market considerations, along with changes in the investor's priorities, will most likely lead to different asset allocation decisions.

EXAMPLE 3

Time Horizon Constraints in Asset Allocation

1. Akkarat Aromdee, the recently retired President of Alpha Beverage, is 67 years old with a remaining life expectancy of 15 years. Upon his retirement two years ago, he established a charitable foundation and funded it with THB600 million (≈ US$17.3 million). The remaining financial assets, THB350 million (≈ US$10 million), were transferred to a trust that will allow him to draw a lifetime income. The assets are invested 100% in fixed-income securities, consistent with Aromdee's desire for a high level of certainty in meeting his goals. He is a widower with no children. His consumption needs are estimated at THB20 million annually. Assets remaining in the trust at his death will pass to the charities named in the trust.

   While vacationing in Ko Samui, Aromdee met and later married a 45-year-old woman with two teenage children. She has limited financial assets of her own. Upon returning from his honeymoon, Aromdee meets with his investment adviser. He intends to pay the college expenses of his new stepchildren—THB2 million annually for eight years, beginning five years from now. He would also like to ensure that his portfolio can provide a modest lifetime income for his wife after his death.

   Discuss how these changed circumstances are likely to influence Aromdee's asset allocation.

   Solution:

   At the time Aromdee established the trust, the investment horizon was 15 years and his annual consumption expenditures could easily be funded from the trust. His desire to support his new family introduces two new horizons to be considered: In five years, the trust will begin making annual payments of THB2 million to fund college expenses, and the trust will continue to make distributions to his wife after his death, though at a reduced rate. When the trust needed to support only his consumption requirements, a conservative asset allocation was appropriate. However, the payment of college expenses will reduce his margin of safety and the lengthening of the investment horizon suggests that he should consider adding equity-oriented investments to the asset mix to provide for growth in assets over time.

TIME DIVERSIFICATION OF RISK

In practice, investors often align lower risk/lower return assets with short-term goals and liabilities and higher risk/higher return assets with long-term goals and liabilities. It is generally believed that longer-horizon goals can tolerate the higher volatility associated with higher risk/higher return assets as below average and above average returns even out over time. This is the notion of time diversification.

Mean–variance optimization, typically conducted using a multi-year time horizon, assumes that asset returns follow a random walk; returns in Year X are independent of returns in Year X – 1. Under this baseline assumption, there *is* no reduction in risk with longer time horizons.[4] Although the *probability* of reduced wealth or of a shortfall in funding a goal or liability (based on the mean of the distribution of possible outcomes) may be lower at longer time horizons, the dispersion of possible outcomes widens as the investment horizon expands. Thus, the *magnitude* of potential loss or shortfall can be greater.

Consider the choice of investing US$100,000 in a Global Equity Index ETF with a 7.0% expected return and 15% standard deviation versus a risk-free asset with a 1.5% annual return. The table below compares the return of the risk-free asset over various time horizons, with the range of predicted returns for the S&P 500 Index fund at a 95% confidence interval. Although the *mean* return of the distribution of S&P 500 returns exceeds that of the risk-free asset in each time period (thus the notion that the volatility of higher risk, higher return assets evens out over time), the lower boundary of expected S&P 500 returns is less than the initial investment for all periods less than 10 years! The lower boundary of the S&P 500 outcomes does not exceed the ending wealth of the risk-free investment until the investment horizon is extended to 30 years. If the confidence interval is expanded to 99%, the lower boundary of S&P 500 outcomes falls below the initial investment up until and through 20 years!

	Ending Wealth (US$)		
	S&P 500 95% Confidence Interval		
	Lower Boundary	Upper Boundary	Risk-Free Asset
1 year	77,601	136,399	101,500
5 years	72,815	250,369	107,728
10 years	79,265	452,566	116,054
15 years	91,494	771,352	125,023
20 years	108,876	1,275,182	134,686
30 years	162,543	3,305,454	156,308

Although one-year returns are largely independent, there is some evidence that risky asset returns can display mean-reverting tendencies over intermediate to longer time horizons. An assumption of mean-reverting risky asset returns would support the conventional arguments for funding long-term goals and liabilities with higher risk/higher return assets, and it would also support a reduction in the allocation to these riskier assets as the time horizon shortens.

4 See Samuelson (1963) and Samuelson (1969).

REGULATORY AND OTHER EXTERNAL CONSTRAINTS 5

☐ discuss asset size, liquidity needs, time horizon, and regulatory or other considerations as constraints on asset allocation

Just as an integrated asset/liability approach to asset allocation is likely to result in a different allocation decision than what might have been selected in an asset-only context, external considerations may also influence the asset allocation decision. Local laws and regulations can have a material effect on an investor's asset allocation decisions.

Pension funds, insurance companies, sovereign wealth funds, and endowments and foundations are each subject to externally imposed constraints that are likely to tilt their asset allocation decision away from what may have been selected in a pure asset/liability context.

Insurance Companies

Unlike pension fund or endowment assets—which are legally distinct from the assets of the sponsoring entity—insurance companies' investment activities are an integral part of their day-to-day operations. Although skilled underwriting may be the focus of the firm as the key to profitability, investment returns are often a material contributor to profits or losses. Regulatory requirements and accounting treatment vary from country to country, but insurers are most often highly focused on matching assets to the projected, probabilistic cash flows of the risks they are underwriting. Fixed-income assets, therefore, are typically the largest component of an insurance company's asset base, and investing with skill in this asset class is a key to competitive pricing and success. In some regions, the relevant accounting treatment may be a book value approach, rendering variability in the market pricing of assets to be a secondary consideration as long as an asset does not have to have its book value written down as "other than temporarily impaired" ("OTTI"). Risk considerations for an insurance company include the need for capital to pay policyholder benefits and other factors that directly influence the company's financial strength ratings. Some of the key considerations are risk-based capital measures, yield, liquidity, the potential for forced liquidation of assets to fund negative claims development, and credit ratings.

Additionally, allocations to certain asset classes are often constrained by a regulator. For example, the maximum limit on equity exposure is often 10%, but it ranges as high as 30% in Switzerland and 50% in Mexico. Israel and Korea impose a limit of 15% on real estate investments.[5] Restrictions on non-publicly traded securities might also limit the allocation to such assets as private equity, for example, and there may also be limits on the allocation to high-yield bonds. Insurance regulators generally set a minimum capital level for each insurer based on that insurer's mix of assets, liabilities, and risk. Many countries are moving to Solvency II regulatory standards designed to harmonize risk-based capital requirements for insurance companies across countries.[6] Asset classes are often treated differently for purposes of determining whether an insurer meets risk-based capital requirements.

5 https://www.oecd.org/finance/private-pensions/Regulation-of-Insurance-Company-and-Pension-Fund-Investment.pdf (September 2015)--accessed 23 November 2018).

6 Solvency II is an EU legislative program implemented in all 28 member states, including the United Kingdom, in January 2016. It introduces a new, harmonized EU-wide insurance regulatory regime.

Pension Funds

Pension fund asset allocation decisions may be constrained by regulation and influenced by tax rules.[7] Some countries regulate maximum or minimum percentages in certain asset classes. For example, Japanese pension funds must hold a certain minimum percentage of assets in Japanese bonds in order to maintain their tax-exempt status. Canada allows a maximum of 10% of market value invested in any one entity or related entities; Switzerland generally limits real estate investments to 30%; Estonia allows a maximum of 75% of assets invested in public equity with no limit on foreign investments; and Brazil allows a maximum of 70% in public equity with a maximum of 10% in foreign public equity.[8] Ukraine limits bond investments to no more than 40%.

Pension funds are also subject to a wide array of funding, accounting, reporting, and tax constraints that may influence the asset allocation decision. (For example, US public pension funding and public and corporate accounting rules favor equity investments—higher equity allocations support a higher discount rate—and thus lower pension cost. Loss recognition is deferred until later through the smoothing mechanism.) The plan sponsor's appetite for risk is defined in part by these constraints, and the choice among asset allocation alternatives is often influenced by funding and financial statement considerations, such as the anticipated contributions, the volatility of anticipated contributions, or the forecasted pension expense or income under a given asset allocation scenario. The specific constraints vary by jurisdiction, and companies with plans in multiple jurisdictions must satisfy the rules and regulations of each jurisdiction while making sound financial decisions for the organization as a whole.

Exhibit 3 illustrates how funding considerations may affect the asset allocation decision. In this chart, risk is defined as the probability of contributions exceeding some threshold amount. In this case, the risk threshold is specified as the 95th percentile of the present value of contributions—that point on the distribution of possible contributions (using Monte Carlo simulation) where the plan sponsor can be 95% certain that contributions will not exceed that amount.

Assume that an allocation of 70% equities/30% aggregate bonds represents the most efficient portfolio for the plan sponsor's desired level of risk in an asset optimization framework. In Exhibit 3, we can see that the 70% equity/30% aggregate bond mix (Portfolio A) is associated with a present value (PV) of expected contributions of approximately US$51 million (y-axis) and a 95% confidence level that contributions will not exceed approximately US$275 million (x-axis)—Portfolio A in Exhibit 3. If the plan sponsor were to maintain the 70/30 asset mix but shift to longer-duration bonds (from aggregate to long bonds) to better match the duration of liabilities—Portfolio D_1 on Exhibit 3—the PV of expected contributions declines by approximately US$5 million and the 95% confidence threshold improves to approximately US$265 million. In fact, Portfolio D_1 results in nearly the lowest PV of contributions for this plan sponsor. (Note that the vertical axis is ordered from highest contributions at the bottom and lowest contributions at the top, consistent with the notion of lower contributions as a better outcome.)

7 Information in this section is based on the OECD "Annual Survey of Investment Regulation of Pension Funds" (2017).

8 Foreign investment is restricted to MERCOSUR countries for equities (other asset classes are more flexible).

Exhibit 3: Efficient Frontiers Where Risk Is Defined as the Risk of Large Contributions

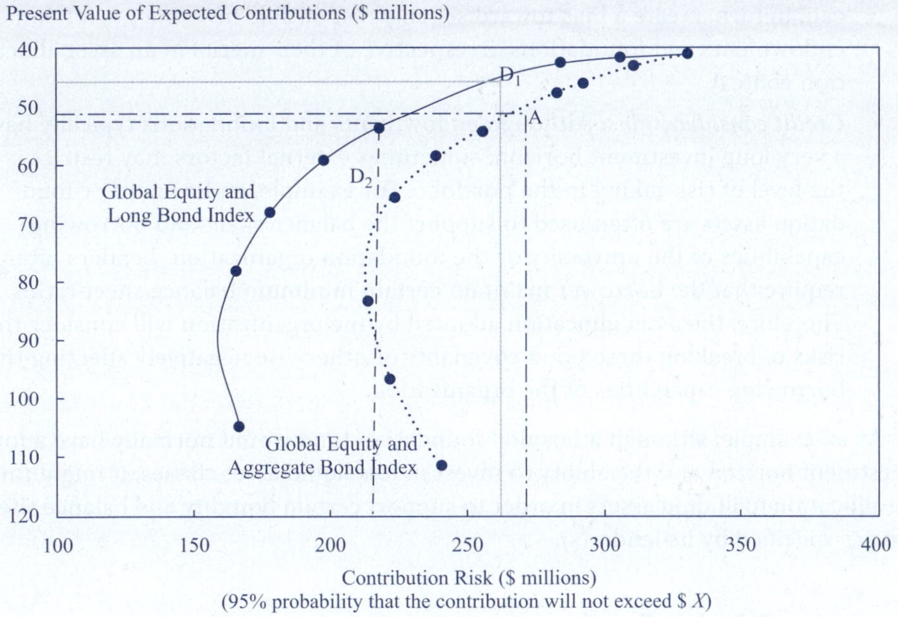

Now consider Portfolio D_2, 60% equities/40% long bonds. Reducing the equity exposure from 70% to 60% lowers the contribution risk significantly, with only marginally higher expected PV of contributions than Portfolio A. (A lower equity allocation implies a lower expected rate of return, which increases the PV of contributions. However, the lower equity allocation also reduces the probability that less-than-expected returns will lead to unexpectedly large contributions.) The sponsor that wishes to reduce contribution risk substantially is likely to give serious consideration to moving from Portfolio A to Portfolio D_2.

By iterating through various efficient frontiers using different definitions of risk, the sponsor is able to better understand the risk and reward trade-offs of alternative asset allocation choices. The regulatory or tax constraints on minimum and maximum contributions, or on minimum required funded levels, or other values that are important to the plan sponsor, can be factored into the simulations so the sponsor can better understand how these constraints might affect the risk and reward trade-offs.

Endowments and Foundations

Endowments and foundations are often established with the expectation that they will exist in perpetuity and thus can invest with a long investment horizon. In addition, the sponsoring entity often has more flexibility over payments from the fund than does a pension plan sponsor or insurance company. As a result, endowments and foundations generally can adopt a higher-risk asset allocation than other institutions. However, two categories of externally imposed constraints may influence the asset allocation decisions of an endowment or foundation: tax incentives and credit-worthiness considerations.

- *Tax incentives.* Although some endowments and foundations—US public foundations and some Austrian and Asian foundations, for example—are not required to make minimum distributions, many countries provide tax benefits tied to certain minimum spending requirements. For example, a private foundation may be subject to a requirement that it make charitable expenditures equal to at least 5% of the market value of its assets each year or risk losing its tax-favored status. These spending requirements may be relaxed if certain types of socially responsible investments are made, which can, in turn, create a bias toward socially responsible investments for some endowments and foundations, irrespective of their merits in an asset allocation context.

- *Credit considerations.* Although endowments and foundations typically have a very long investment horizon, sometimes external factors may restrict the level of risk-taking in the portfolio. For example, endowment or foundation assets are often used to support the balance sheet and borrowing capabilities of the university or the foundation organization. Lenders often require that the borrower maintain certain minimum balance sheet ratios. Therefore, the asset allocation adopted by the organization will consider the risks of breaking these bond covenants or otherwise negatively affecting the borrowing capabilities of the organization.

As an example, although a hospital foundation fund would normally have a long investment horizon and the ability to invest in less liquid asset classes, it might limit the allocation to illiquid assets in order to support certain liquidity and balance sheet metrics specified by its lender(s).

Sovereign Wealth Funds

Although every sovereign wealth fund (SWF) is unique with respect to its mission and objectives, some broad generalizations can be made with respect to the external constraints that may affect a fund's asset allocation choices. In general, SWFs are government-owned pools of capital invested on behalf of the peoples of their states or countries, investing with a long-term orientation. They are not generally seeking to defease a set of liabilities or known obligations as is common with pension funds and, to a lesser extent, endowment funds.

The governing entities adopt regulations that constrain the opportunity set for asset allocation. For example, the Korean SWF KIC cannot invest in Korean won-denominated domestic assets;[9] and the Norwegian SWF NBIM is not permitted to invest in any alternative asset class other than real estate, which is limited to no more than 7% of assets.[10] Furthermore, as publicly owned entities, SWFs are typically subject to broad public scrutiny and tend to adopt a lower-risk asset allocation than might otherwise be considered appropriate given their long-term investment horizon in order to avoid reputation risk.

In addition to the broad constraints of asset size, liquidity, time horizon, and regulations, there may be cultural or religious factors that also constrain the asset allocation choices. Environmental, social, and governance (ESG) considerations are becoming increasingly important to institutional and individual investors alike. Sharia law, for example, prohibits investment in any business that has links to pork, alcohol, tobacco, pornography, prostitution, gambling, or weaponry, and it constrains investments in most businesses that operate on interest payments (like major Western banks and mortgage providers) and in businesses that transfer risk (such as major Western insurers).[11]

---

9 https://mpra.ub.uni-muenchen.de/44028/1/MPRA_paper_44028.pdf (accessed 23 November 2018) Note: in principle, KIC must invest only in assets denominated in foreign currencies. If KIC manages KRW-denominated assets temporarily for an unavoidable reason, it must be either in the form of bank deposits or passively held public debt.

10 https://www.nbim.no/en/investments/investment-strategy/ (accessed 23 November 2018).

11 Islamic Investment Network (www.islamicinvestmentnetwork.com/sharialaw.php).

ESG goals are not typically modeled during the asset allocation decision process. Instead, these goals may be achieved through the implementation of the asset allocation, or the asset owner may choose to set aside a targeted portion of the assets for these missions. The asset allocation process would treat this "set-aside" in much the same way that a concentrated stock position might be handled: The risk, return, and correlation characteristics of this holding are specified; the "set aside" asset becomes an asset class in the investor's opportunity set; and the asset allocation constraints will designate a certain minimum investment in this asset class.

EXAMPLE 4

External Constraints and Asset Allocation

1. An insurance company has traditionally invested its pension plan using the asset allocation strategy adopted for its insurance assets: The pension assets are 95% invested in high-quality intermediate duration bonds and 5% in global equities. The duration of pension liabilities is approximately 25 years. Until now, the company has always made contributions sufficient to maintain a fully funded status. Although the company has a strong capability to fund the plan adequately and a relatively high tolerance for variability in asset returns, as part of a refinement in corporate strategy, management is now seeking to reduce long-term expected future cash contributions. Management is willing to accept more risk in the asset return, but they would like to limit contribution risk and the risk to the plan's funded status. The Investment Committee is considering three asset allocation proposals for the pension plan:

   A. Maintain the current asset allocation with the same bond portfolio duration.

   B. Increase the equity allocation and lengthen the bond portfolio duration to increase the hedge of the duration risk in the liabilities.

   C. Maintain the current asset allocation of 95% bonds and 5% global equities, but increase the duration of bond investments.

   Discuss the merits of each proposal.

   Solution:

   Given the intermediate duration bond allocation, Proposal A fails to consider the mismatch between pension assets and liabilities and risks a reduction in the funded status and *increased* contributions if bond yields decline. (If yields decline across the curve, the shorter duration bond portfolio will fail to hedge the increase in liabilities.) To meet the objective of lower future contributions, the asset allocation must include a higher allocation to equities. Proposal B has this higher allocation, and the extension of duration in the bond portfolio in Proposal B reduces balance sheet and surplus risk relative to the pension liabilities. The net effect could be a reduction in short-term contribution risk; moreover, if the greater expected return on equities is realized, it should result in reduced contributions to the plan over the long term. Proposal C improves the hedging of the liabilities, and it may result in a modest improvement in the expected return on assets if the yield curve is upward-sloping. However, the expected return on Proposal C is likely lower than the expected return of Proposal B and is therefore unlikely to achieve the same magnitude of reduction in future cash contributions. Proposal C would be appropriate if the goal was focused on reducing surplus risk rather than reducing long-term contributions.

2. A multinational corporation headquartered in Mexico has acquired a former competitor in the United States. It will maintain both the US pension plan with US$250 million in assets and the Mexican pension plan with MXN$18,600 million in assets (≈ US$1 billion). Both plans are 95% funded and have similar liability profiles. The Mexican pension trust has an asset allocation policy of 30% equities (10% invested in the Mexican equity market and 20% in equity markets outside Mexico), 10% hedge funds, 10% private equity, and 50% bonds. The treasurer has proposed that the company adopt a consistent asset allocation policy across all of the company's pension plans worldwide.

   Critique the treasurer's proposal.

   Solution:

   The treasurer's proposal fails to consider the relative asset size of the two pension plans as well as the likelihood that plans in different jurisdictions may be subject to different funding, regulatory, and financial reporting requirements. The US pension plan may be unable to effectively access certain alternative asset classes, such as private equity, infrastructure, and hedge funds. Although economies of scale may be realized if management of the pension assets is consolidated under one team, the legal and regulatory differences of the markets in which they operate mean that the asset allocation policy must be customized to each plan.

6 ASSET ALLOCATION FOR THE TAXABLE INVESTOR AND AFTER-TAX PORTFOLIO OPTIMIZATION

☐ discuss tax considerations in asset allocation and rebalancing

Portfolio theory developed in a frictionless world. But in the real world, taxes on income and capital gains can erode the returns achieved by taxable investors. The asset owner who ignores taxes during the asset allocation process is overlooking an economic variable that can materially alter the outcome. Although tax adjustments can be made after the asset allocation has been determined, this is a suboptimal approach because the pre-tax and after-tax risk and return characteristics of each asset class can be materially different.

Some assets are less tax efficient than others because of the character of their returns—the contribution of interest, dividends, and realized or unrealized capital gains to the total return. Interest income is usually taxed in the tax year it is received, and it often faces the highest tax rates. Therefore, assets that generate returns largely comprised of interest income tend to be less tax efficient in many countries.[12] Jurisdictional rules can also affect how the returns of certain assets are taxed. In the United States, for example, the interest income from state and local government bonds is generally exempt from federal income taxation. As a result, these bonds often constitute a large

12 See Deloitte's tax guides and country highlights: https://dits.deloitte.com/#TaxGuides.

portion of a US high-net-worth investor's bond allocation. Preferred stocks, often used in lieu of bonds as an income-producing asset, are also eligible for more favorable tax treatment in many jurisdictions, where the income from preferred shares may be taxed at more favorable dividend tax rates.

The tax environment is complex. Different countries have different tax rules and rates, and these rules and rates can change frequently. However, looking across the major economies, there are some high-level commonalities in how investment returns are taxed. Interest income is taxed typically (but not always) at progressively higher income tax rates. Dividend income and capital gains are taxed typically (but not always) at lower tax rates than those applied to interest income and earned income (wages and salaries, for example). Capital losses can be used to offset capital gains (and sometimes income). Generally, interest income incurs the highest tax rate, with dividend income taxed at a lower rate in some countries, and long-term capital gains receive the most favorable tax treatment in many jurisdictions. Once we move beyond these general commonalities, however, the details of tax treatment among countries quickly diverge.

Entities and accounts can be subject to different tax rules. For example, retirement savings accounts may be tax deferred or tax exempt, with implications for the optimal asset allocation solution. These rules provide opportunities for strategic asset *location*—placing less tax-efficient assets in tax-advantaged accounts.

We will provide a general framework for considering taxes in asset allocation. We will not survey global tax regimes or incorporate all potential tax complexities into the asset allocation solution. When considering taxes in asset allocation, the objective is to model material investment-related taxes, thereby providing a closer approximation to economic reality than is represented when ignoring taxes altogether.

For simplicity, we will assume a basic tax regime that represents no single country but includes the key elements of investment-related taxes that are roughly representative of what a typical taxable asset owner in the major developed economies must contend with.

After-Tax Portfolio Optimization

After-tax portfolio optimization requires adjusting each asset class's expected return and risk for expected tax. The expected after-tax return is defined in Equation 1:

$$r_{at} = r_{pt}(1 - t) \quad (1)$$

where

r_{at} = the expected after-tax return

r_{pt} = the expected pre-tax (gross) return

t = the expected tax rate

This can be straightforward for bonds in cases where the expected return is driven by interest income. Take, for example, an investment-grade par bond with a 3% coupon expected to be held to maturity. If interest income is subject to a 40% expected tax rate, the bond has an expected after-tax return of 1.80% [0.03(1 – 0.40) = 0.018].

The expected return for equity typically includes both dividend income and price appreciation (capital gains). Equation 2 expands Equation 1 accordingly:

$$r_{at} = p_d r_{pt}(1 - t_d) + p_a r_{pt}(1 - t_{cg}) \quad (2)$$

where

p_d = the proportion of r_{pt} attributed to dividend income

p_a = the proportion of r_{pt} attributed to price appreciation

t_d = the dividend tax rate

t_{cg} = the capital gains tax rate

The treatment of the capital gains portion of equity returns can be more complex. Assuming no dividend income, a stock with an 8% expected pre-tax return that is subject to a 25% capital gains tax rate has an expected after-tax return of 6% [0.08(1 – 0.25) = 0.06]. This is an approximation satisfactory for modeling purposes.[13]

Taxable assets may have existing unrealized capital gains or losses (i.e., the cost basis is below or above market value), which come with embedded tax liabilities (or tax assets). Although there is not a clear consensus on how best to deal with existing unrealized capital gains (losses), many approaches adjust the asset's current market value for the value of the embedded tax liability (asset) to create an after-tax value. Reichenstein (2006) approximates the after-tax value by subtracting the value of the embedded capital gains tax from the market value, as if the asset were sold today. Horan and Al Zaman (2008) assume the asset is sold in the future and discount the tax liability to its present value using the asset's after-tax return as the discount rate. Turvey, Basu, and Verhoeven (2013) argue that the after-tax risk-free rate is the more appropriate discount rate because the embedded tax liability is analogous to an interest-free loan from the government, where the tax liability can be arbitraged away by dynamically investing in the risk-free asset. We will discuss how to incorporate after-tax values into the portfolio optimization process in Section 7, where we address strategies to reduce the impact of taxes.

The ultimate purpose of an asset can be a consideration when modeling tax adjustments. In the preceding material on asset allocation, we discussed goals-based investing. If the purpose of a given pool of assets is to fund consumption in 10 years, then that 10-year holding period may influence the estimated implied annual capital gains tax rate. If the purpose of the specified pool of assets is to fund a future gift of appreciated stock to a tax-exempt charity, then capital gains tax may be ignored altogether. Through this alignment of goals with assets, goals-based investing facilitates more-precise tax adjustments.

Although correlation assumptions need not be adjusted when modeling asset allocation choices for the taxable asset owner (taxes are proportional to return, after-tax co-movements are the same as pre-tax co-movements), taxes do affect the standard deviation assumption for each asset class. The expected after-tax standard deviation is defined in Equation 3:

$$\sigma_{at} = \sigma_{pt}(1 - t) \tag{3}$$

where

σ_{at} = the expected after-tax standard deviation

σ_{pt} = the expected pre-tax standard deviation

Taxes alter the distribution of returns by both reducing the expected mean return and muting the dispersion of returns. Taxes truncate both the high and low ends of the distribution of returns, resulting in lower highs and higher lows. The effect of taxes is intuitive when considering a positive return, but the same economics apply

13 A more precise estimation of the expected after-tax return also takes into account the effect of the holding period on the capital gains tax. For those interested in a more detailed discussion of these issues, see Mladina (2011).

to a negative return: Losses are muted by the same $(1 - t)$ tax adjustment. The investor is not taxed on losses but instead receives the economic benefit of a capital loss, whether realized or not. In many countries, a realized capital loss can offset a current or future realized capital gain. An unrealized capital loss captures the economic benefit of a cost basis that is above the current market value, making a portion of expected future appreciation tax free.

How does the optimal asset allocation along a pre-tax efficient frontier compare with the optimal asset allocation along an after-tax efficient frontier? Let's assume all investment assets are taxable and that cost bases equal current market values. Assume also that interest income is taxed at 40%, and dividend income and capital gains are taxed at 25%.

The asset classes we will consider include investment-grade (IG) bonds, high-yield (HY) bonds, and equity. Exhibit 4 shows the expected pre-tax returns and standard deviations for each asset class as well as the correlation matrix. Note that for ease of illustration, we have assumed that the IG bonds and HY bond returns are comprised of 100% interest income. In practice, some portion of the expected return would be eligible for capital gains tax treatment.

Exhibit 4: Expected Pre-Tax Return and Risk

	Return	Std. Dev.
IG bonds	3.0%	4.0%
HY bonds	5.0%	10.0%
Equity	8.0%	20.0%

Correlations	IG Bonds	HY Bonds	Equity
IG bonds	1.0	0.2	0.0
HY bonds	0.2	1.0	0.7
Equity	0.0	0.7	1.0

Employing mean–variance portfolio optimization with these pre-tax inputs, we obtain the optimal asset allocations in Exhibit 5, which shows the allocations for portfolios P1 (lowest risk), P25, P50 (median risk), P75, and P100 (highest risk)—each on an efficient frontier comprised of 100 portfolios.

Exhibit 5: Optimal Pre-Tax Asset Mixes

	$P1_{pt}$	$P25_{pt}$	$P50_{pt}$	$P75_{pt}$	$P100_{pt}$
IG bonds	93%	52%	25%	0%	0%
HY bonds	5%	18%	26%	33%	0%
Equity	2%	30%	49%	67%	100%

Using Equation 1, Equation 2, and Equation 3, we calculate the expected after-tax returns and standard deviations displayed in Exhibit 6. No adjustments are made to correlations.

Exhibit 6: Expected After-Tax Return and Risk

	Return	Std. Dev.
IG bonds	1.8%	2.4%
HY bonds	3.0%	6.0%
Equity	6.0%	15.0%

Portfolio optimization using these after-tax inputs produces the optimal asset allocations shown in Exhibit 7.

Exhibit 7: Optimal After-Tax Asset Mixes

	$P1_{at}$	$P25_{at}$	$P50_{at}$	$P75_{at}$	$P100_{at}$
IG bonds	92%	60%	38%	16%	0%
HY bonds	7%	7%	7%	7%	0%
Equity	1%	33%	55%	77%	100%

In Exhibit 8, we compare the pre-tax and after-tax efficient frontiers from these previous exhibits. Note that the portfolios at either extreme (P1 and P100) are essentially unchanged after taxes are factored into the assumptions. In portfolios P25, P50, and P75, however, you can see a significant reduction in the allocation to high-yield bonds. This is because of the heavier tax burden imposed on high-yield bonds. Although investment-grade bonds receive the same tax treatment, they are less risky than high-yield bonds and demonstrate a lower correlation with equity, so they continue to play the important role of portfolio risk reduction.

Exhibit 8: Pre-Tax and After-Tax Asset Allocation Comparisons

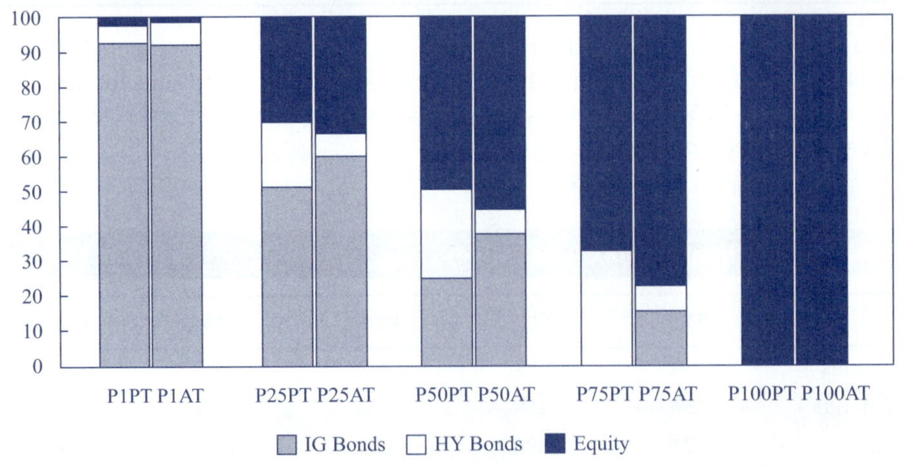

The optimal after-tax asset allocation depends on the interaction of after-tax returns, after-tax risk, and correlations. If an asset class or strategy is tax inefficient, it can still play a diversifying role in an optimal after-tax asset allocation if the asset or strategy offers sufficiently low correlations. After-tax portfolio optimization helps answer that question.

TAXES AND PORTFOLIO REBALANCING

7

☐ | discuss tax considerations in asset allocation and rebalancing

Among tax-exempt institutional asset owners, periodic portfolio rebalancing—reallocating assets to return the portfolio to its target strategic asset allocation—is an integral part of sound portfolio management. This is no less true for taxable asset owners, but with the important distinction that more frequent rebalancing exposes the taxable asset owner to realized taxes that could have otherwise been deferred or even avoided. Whereas the tax burden incurred by liquidating assets to fund-required consumption cannot be avoided, rebalancing is discretionary; thus, the taxable asset owner should consider the trade-off between the benefits of tax minimization and the merits of maintaining the targeted asset allocation by rebalancing. The decision to rebalance and incur taxes is driven by each asset owner's unique circumstances.

Because after-tax volatility is less than pre-tax volatility (Equation 3) and asset class correlations remain the same, it takes larger asset class movements to materially alter the risk profile of the taxable portfolio. This suggests that rebalancing ranges for a taxable portfolio can be wider than those of a tax-exempt portfolio with a similar risk profile.

For example, consider a portfolio with a 50% allocation to equity, where equity returns are subject to a 25% tax rate. A tax-exempt investor may establish a target allocation to equities of 50%, with an acceptable range of 40% to 60% (50% plus or minus 10%). A taxable investor with the same target equity allocation can achieve a similar risk constraint with a range of 37% to 63% (50% plus or minus 13%). The equivalent rebalancing range for the taxable investor is derived by adjusting the permitted 10% deviation (up or down) by the tax rate, as shown in Equation 4:

$$R_{at}=R_{pt}/(1-t) \tag{4}$$

where

R_{at} = the after-tax rebalancing range

R_{pt} = the pre-tax rebalancing range

In our example, the 10% rebalancing range for a tax-exempt investor becomes a 13.3% rebalancing range for a taxable investor (when ranges are viewed and monitored from the same gross return perspective):

$$0.10/(1-0.25)=13.3\%$$

Broader rebalancing ranges for the taxable investor reduce the frequency of trading and, consequently, the amount of taxable gains.

Strategies to Reduce Tax Impact

Additional strategies can be used to reduce taxes, including tax-loss harvesting and choices in the placement of certain types of assets in taxable or tax-exempt accounts (strategic asset location). Tax-loss harvesting is intentionally trading to realize a capital loss, which is then used to offset a current or future realized capital gain in another part of the portfolio, thereby reducing the taxes owned by the investor. It is discussed elsewhere in the curriculum, but we address strategic asset location strategies here.

Strategic asset location refers to placing (or locating) less tax-efficient assets in accounts with more favorable tax treatment, such as retirement savings accounts.

Aggregating assets across accounts with differing tax treatment requires modifying the asset value inputs to the portfolio optimization. Assets held in tax-*exempt* accounts require no tax adjustment to their market values. Assets in tax-*deferred* accounts grow tax free but are taxed upon distribution. Because these assets cannot be distributed (and consumed) without incurring the tax, the tax burden is inseparable from the economic value of the assets. Thus, the after-tax value of assets in a tax-deferred account is defined by Equation 5:

$$v_{at} = v_{pt}(1 - t_i) \quad (5)$$

where

v_{at} = the after-tax value of assets

v_{pt} = the pre-tax market value of assets

t_i = the expected income tax rate upon distribution

In our earlier example, we had three asset classes: investment-grade bonds, high-yield bonds, and equities. If we assume that each of these three asset classes can be held in either of two account types—taxable or tax-deferred—then our optimization uses six different after-tax asset classes (three asset classes times two account types). The three asset classes in taxable accounts use the after-tax return and risk inputs derived earlier. The three asset classes in tax-deferred accounts (which grow tax free) use expected pre-tax return and risk inputs. The optimization adds constraints based on the after-tax value of the assets currently available in each account type and derives the optimal after-tax asset allocation and asset location simultaneously.

As a general rule, the portion of a taxable asset owner's assets that are eligible for lower tax rates and deferred capital gains tax treatment should first be allocated to the investor's taxable accounts. For example, equities should generally be held in taxable accounts, while taxable bonds and high-turnover trading strategies should generally be located in tax-exempt and tax-deferred accounts to the extent possible.

One important exception to this general rule regarding asset location applies to assets held for near-term liquidity needs. Because tax-exempt and tax-deferred accounts may not be immediately accessible without tax penalty, a portion of the bond allocation may be held in taxable accounts if its role is to fund near-term consumption requirements.

EXAMPLE 5

Asset Allocation and the Taxable Investor

Sarah Moreau, 45 years old, is a mid-level manager at a consumer products company. Her investment portfolio consists entirely of tax-deferred retirement savings accounts. Through careful savings and investments, she is on track to accumulate sufficient assets to retire at age 60. Her portfolio is currently allocated as indicated below:

Investment-grade bonds	20%
High-yield bonds	20%
Common stock–dividend income strategy	30%
Common stock–total return (capital gain) strategy	30%
Total portfolio	100%

The common stock–dividend income strategy focuses on income-oriented, high-dividend-paying stocks; the common stock–total return strategy focuses on stocks that represent good, long-term opportunities but pay little to no dividend.

For the purposes of this example, we will assume that the expected long-term return is equivalent between the two strategies. Moreau has a high comfort level with this portfolio and the overall level of risk it entails.

Moreau has recently inherited additional monies, doubling her investable assets. She intends to use this new, taxable portfolio to support causes important to her personally over her lifetime. There is no change in her risk tolerance. She is interviewing prospective investment managers and has asked each to recommend an asset allocation strategy for the new portfolio using the same set of asset classes. She has received the following recommendations:

	Recommendation		
	A	B	C
Investment-grade bonds	20%	40%	30%
High-yield bonds	20%	0%	0%
Common stock–dividend income strategy	30%	30%	0%
Common stock–total return (capital gain) strategy	30%	30%	70%
Total portfolio	100%	100%	100%

1. Which asset allocation is *most* appropriate for the new portfolio? Justify your response.

   Solution:

   Recommendation C would be the most appropriate asset allocation for the new portfolio. The high-yield bond and common stock–dividend income strategies are tax disadvantaged in a taxable portfolio. (Although investment-grade bonds are also tax disadvantaged, they maintain the role of controlling portfolio risk to maintain Moreau's risk preference.) By shifting this equity-like risk to the total return common stock strategy, Moreau should achieve a greater after-tax return. Given the lower standard deviation characteristics of after-tax equity returns when held in the taxable portfolio, a higher allocation to common stocks may be justified without exceeding Moreau's desired risk level. Recommendations A and B do not consider the negative tax implications of holding the high-yield and/or common stock–dividend income strategies in a taxable portfolio. Recommendation B also fails to consider Moreau's overall risk tolerance: The volatility of the common stock–capital gain strategy is lower when held in a taxable portfolio, thus a higher allocation to this strategy can enhance returns while remaining within Moreau's overall risk tolerance.[14]

2. How should Moreau distribute these investments among her taxable and tax-exempt accounts?

   Solution:

   If Moreau is willing to think of her investable portfolio as a single portfolio, rather than as independent "retirement" and "important causes" portfolios, she should hold the allocation to high-yield bonds and dividend-paying stocks in her tax-exempt retirement portfolio. In addition, subject to the overall volatility of the individual tax-exempt and taxable portfolios, it

14 Investment-grade bonds also have lower after-tax volatility. The equivalent risk portfolios in pre-tax and after-tax environments are a function of a complex interaction of after-tax returns, standard deviations, and correlations.

would be sensible to bear any increased stock risk in the taxable portfolio. A new optimization for *all* of Moreau's assets—using pre-tax and after-tax risk and return assumptions and subject to the constraint that half of the assets are held in a taxable portfolio and half are held in the tax-exempt portfolio—would more precisely allocate investments across portfolio (account) types.

Asset Location for Optimal Tax Efficiency

	Tax Advantaged Retirement Account	Taxable Account
Investment-grade bonds	X	
High-yield bonds	X	
Common stock–dividend income strategy	X	
Common stock–total return (capital gain) strategy		X

3. You are a member of the Investment Committee for a multinational corporation, responsible for the supervision of two portfolios. Both portfolios were established to fund retirement benefits: One is a tax-exempt defined benefit pension fund, and the other is taxable, holding assets intended to fund non-exempt retirement benefits. The pension fund has a target allocation of 70% equities and 30% fixed income, with a +/– 5% rebalancing range. There is no formal asset allocation policy for the taxable portfolio; it has simply followed the same allocation adopted by the pension portfolio. Because of recent strong equity market returns, both portfolios are now allocated 77% to equities and 23% to bonds. Management expects that the equity markets will continue to produce strong returns in the near term. Staff has offered the following options for rebalancing the portfolios:

   Which recommendation is *most* appropriate? Justify your response.

   A. Do not rebalance.

   B. Rebalance both portfolios to the 70% equity/30% fixed-income target allocation.

   C. Rebalance the tax-exempt portfolio to the 70% equity/30% fixed-income target allocation, but expand the rebalancing range for the taxable portfolio.

   Solution:

   Recommendation C is the most appropriate course of action. Rebalancing of the tax-exempt portfolio is unencumbered by tax considerations, and rebalancing maintains the desired level of risk. The rebalancing range for the taxable portfolio can be wider than that of the tax-exempt portfolio based on the desire to minimize avoidable taxes and the lower volatility of after-tax equity returns. Recommendation A (no rebalancing) does not address the increased level of risk in the tax-exempt portfolio that results from the increase in the stock allocation. Recommendation B would create an unnecessary tax liability for the company, given that the portfolio is still operating in a reasonable range of risk when adjusted for taxes.

INCREASING ALLOCATIONS TO FIXED INCOME IN CORPORATE PENSION PLANS

Increasing allocations to fixed income by defined benefit pension funds worldwide have been driven largely by a desire to better hedge plan liabilities. In some countries, accounting standards discourage de-risking. De-risking, however, is not the only argument in favor of a higher fixed-income allocation.

De-risking

There has been much discussion globally of pension plans "de-risking"—moving toward larger fixed-income allocations to better hedge liabilities, thereby reducing contribution uncertainty. Some countries' accounting rules, however—most notably those in the United States—discourage companies from moving in that direction. Under US GAAP accounting rules, for example, a higher allocation to equities allows the plan sponsor to employ a higher return assumption, thereby reducing pension cost, a non-cash expense that directly affects reported income.

For underfunded pension plans, de-risking leads to higher pension contributions. If a company has a weak core business with a higher-than-average probability of going bankrupt and makes only the minimum required contribution, it might be argued that the asset allocation decision was contrary to the interests of plan participants. If the company were to go bankrupt, the participants would get only the benefits covered by any government guaranty program. Had the company taken equity risk in the plan, there would have been a possibility of closing the funding gap, resulting in higher benefit payments.

Efficient Allocation of Risk

A higher allocation to fixed income—and a lower allocation to equity—might also be driven by corporate governance considerations. Pension investment activities are not a core competency of many companies, especially non-financial companies. Assuming that the company has a limited appetite for risk, shareholders might prefer that management allocate its risk budget to the core business of the company where they are expected to have skill, rather than to the pension fund. The rewards per unit of risk should presumably be greater in the company's core business, and the improved profitability should offset the increase in pension contributions required as a result of the lower equity allocation.

A Holistic Approach to Asset Location

Finally, some have argued that an asset allocation of 100% fixed-income securities can be justified on the premise that the company is acting as an agent for the benefit of all stakeholders, including shareholders and plan participants. This argument centers on tax-efficient asset location. A taxable investor—the shareholder and plan participant—should prefer to take his long-term equity risk in that portion of his overall portfolio where he will receive the benefit of lower capital gains rates rather than in tax-deferred accounts, the proceeds of which will be taxed at income tax rates. Consider a small business owner with US$3 million in total assets. The assets are split between a pension fund of which he is the sole participant (US$1 million) and a taxable portfolio (US$2 million). Assume that the asset allocation that represents his preferred level of risk is 67% equities and 33% fixed income. Where should this individual hold his equity exposure? As discussed, the more favorable tax treatment of equity returns argues for holding the equity exposure in his taxable account, while the investments subject to the higher tax rate should be held in the tax-deferred account—the pension plan. Theoretically, this tax efficiency argument can be extended to pension funds operated by publicly traded companies.[15]

8 REVISING THE STRATEGIC ASSET ALLOCATION

☐ recommend and justify revisions to an asset allocation given change(s) in investment objectives and/or constraints

An asset owner's strategic asset allocation is not a static decision. Circumstances often arise that justify revisiting the original decision, either to confirm its appropriateness or to consider a change to the current allocation strategy. It is sound financial practice to periodically re-examine the asset allocation strategy even in the absence of one of the external factors discussed next. Many institutional asset owners typically re-visit the asset allocation policy at least once every five years through a formal asset allocation study, and all asset owners should affirm annually that the asset allocation remains appropriate given their needs and circumstances.

The circumstances that might trigger a special review of the asset allocation policy can generally be classified as relating to a change in *goals*, a change in *constraints*, or a change in *beliefs*. Among the reasons to review the strategic asset allocation are the following:

Goals

- Changes in business conditions affecting the organization supporting the fund and, therefore, expected changes in the cash flows
- A change in the investor's personal circumstances that may alter her risk appetite or risk capacity

Over an individual's lifespan, or throughout the course of an institutional fund's lifespan, it is unlikely that the investment goals and objectives will remain unchanged. An individual may get married, have children, or become disabled, for example, each of which may have implications for the asset allocation strategy.

Significant changes in the core business of an organization supporting or benefiting from the trust might prompt a re-examination of the asset allocation strategy. For example, an automobile manufacturer that has historically generated a significant portion of its revenues from its consumer finance activities may find that technology is disrupting this source of revenue as more online tools become available to car buyers. With greater uncertainty in its revenue stream, company management may move to reduce risk-taking in the pension fund in order to achieve a goal of reducing the variability in year-to-year contributions.

A university may embark on a long-term capital improvement plan that is reliant on the endowment fund for financial support. Or the university may be experiencing declining enrollments and must lean more heavily on the endowment fund to support

15 For those interested in a more detailed discussion of this concept, see "The Case against Stock in Public Pension Funds" (Bader and Gold 2007) or the UBS Q-Series article, "Pension Fund Asset Allocation" (Cooper and Bianco 2003).

its ongoing operational expenditures. The source of funds to a sovereign wealth fund may shrink considerably or even evaporate. When any of these, or similar, events occur or are anticipated, the existing asset allocation policy should be re-evaluated.

Constraints

A material change in any one of the constraints mentioned earlier—time horizon, liquidity needs, asset size, or regulatory or other external constraints—is also reason to re-examine the existing asset allocation policy. Some of these changes might include the following:

- Changes in the expected payments from the fund
- A significant cash inflow or unanticipated expenditure
- Changes in regulations governing donations or contributions to the fund
- Changes in time horizon resulting from the adoption of a lump sum distribution option at retirement
- Changes in asset size as a result of the merging of pension plans

Changes in the expected payments from the fund can materially affect the asset allocation strategy. For example, a university reduces its spending policy from 5% to 4% of assets annually; an individual retires early, perhaps for health reasons or an involuntary late-career layoff; or a US corporate pension sponsor reduces or freezes pension benefits because it can no longer afford increasing Pension Benefit Guaranty Corporation[16] premiums. Faced with lower payouts, the university endowment may have greater latitude to invest in less liquid segments of the market. Decisions as to how and where to invest given this greater flexibility should be made within the framework of an asset allocation study to ensure the resulting allocation achieves the optimal trade-off of risk and return.

Similarly, a significant cash inflow has the potential to materially affect the asset allocation strategy. If a university endowment fund with £500 million in assets receives a gift of £100 million, the new monies *could* be invested in parallel with the existing assets, but that fails to consider the increased earning potential of the fund and any spending requirements associated with the donation. Pausing to formally reassess the fund's goals, objectives, constraints, and opportunities through an asset allocation study allows the asset owner to consider more broadly how best to maximize this additional wealth.

A change in regulations may also give rise to a change in asset allocation policy. Examples of regulatory changes that could trigger a re-examination of the asset allocation include the following:

- Regulatory changes in the United States in 2006 mandated a change in the liability discount rate, which resulted in larger pension contributions. With higher required contributions, there was less need to reach for higher investment returns. Many US corporate pension plans began de-risking (adopting an asset allocation strategy focused on hedging the liabilities) to reduce contribution volatility.
- UK tax incentives (30% of social impact investment costs can be deducted from income tax) and relaxed regulations for institutional investors were instituted to encourage socially responsible (impact) investing.

Again, an asset allocation study to objectively evaluate the effect of these changes on the investment opportunity set can help ensure that any new investment strategies adopted are consistent with the fund's overarching goals and objectives.

16 The Pension Benefit Guaranty Corporation insures certain US pension plan benefits.

Beliefs

Investment beliefs are a set of guiding principles that govern the asset owner's investment activities. Beliefs are not static, however, and changes in the economic environment and capital market expectations or a change in trustees or committee members are two factors that may lead to an altering of the principles that guide investment activities.[17]

An integral aspect of any asset allocation exercise is the forecasting of expected returns, volatilities, and correlations of the asset classes in the opportunity set. It follows, then, that a material change in the outlook for one or more of the asset classes may heavily influence the asset allocation outcome.

Consider the 2015–2016 environment relative to the environment that prevailed in 1984–2014. The 1984–2014 investing environment was characterized by declining inflation and interest rates (from the extraordinarily high levels of the 1970s and early 1980s); strong global GDP growth, aided by favorable demographics; gains in productivity; and rapid growth in China. Corporate profit growth was extremely robust, reflecting revenue growth from new markets, declining corporate taxes over the period, and improved efficiencies. Despite increased market turbulence, returns on US and Western European equities and bonds during the past 30 years were considerably higher than the long-run trend.

The environment of 2015–2016 was much less favorable for investors. The dramatic decline in inflation and interest rates ended, and labor force expansion and productivity gains stalled, with negative implications for GDP growth. The largest developed-country companies that generated much of the profits of the past 30 years were faced with competitive pressures as emerging-market companies expanded and technology advances changed the competitive landscape. In April 2016, McKinsey Global Institute published a projection of stocks and bonds under two growth scenarios—a slow growth scenario and a moderate growth scenario (Exhibit 9). In neither instance do the expected returns of the next 30 years come close to the returns of the past 30 years.[18] Clearly, an asset allocation developed in 2010 built on return expectations based on the prior 26 years would look materially different than an asset allocation developed using more current, forward-looking return assumptions.

---

17 For an example of an investment belief statement, see www.uss.co.uk/how-uss-invests/investment-approach/investment-beliefs-and-principles.

18 McKinsey Global Institute, "Diminishing Returns: Why Investors May Need to Lower Their Expectations" (May 2016).

Exhibit 9: A Major Shift in Underlying Return Assumptions

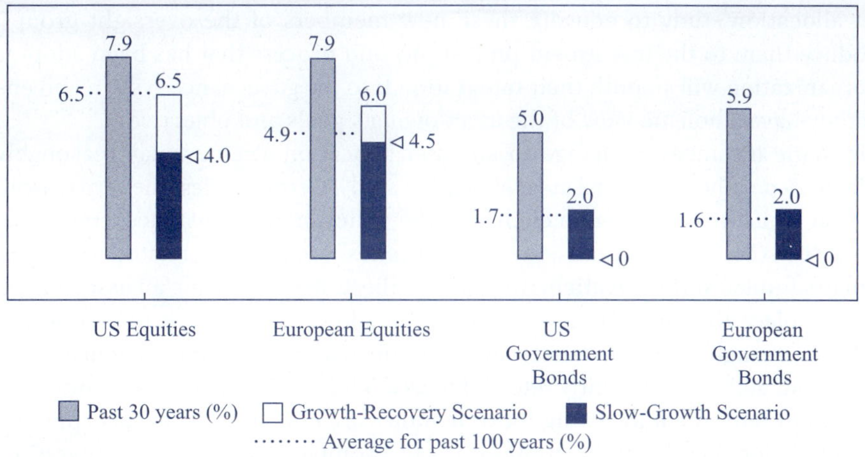

Notes:

Numbers for growth-recovery and slow-growth scenarios reflect the range between the low end of the slow-growth scenario and the high end of the growth-recovery scenario.

European equities: Weighted average real returns based on each year's Geary-Khamis purchasing power parity GDP for 14 countries in Western Europe.

US and European government bonds: Bond duration for United States is primarily 10 years; for Europe, duration varies by country but is typically 20 years.

Source: McKinsey Global Institute (www.mckinsey.com/industries/private-equity-and-principal-investors/our-insights/why-investors-may-need-to-lower-their-sights).

Asset returns and future return expectations shifted widely at the outbreak of the COVID-19 pandemic and during the following period. Unlike in the case of other economic and financial crises, the causes of the pandemic-related turmoil were outside of the economic and financial system; yet, lockdowns and the sudden stop of economic activities led to a recession. The unemployment rate in the United States jumped from 3.5% to 14.7% between February 2021 and April 2021, and the June 2020 annual real GDP growth was −9.1%—extreme numbers not observed since the Great Depression. Equity markets' peak to trough period lasted for about a month: From February through March 2020, the global equity (MSCI ACWI) index fell by 34%, high-yield bonds lost about 21%, and oil prices fell by more than 60%. At the same time, governments and central banks came to the rescue with unprecedented fiscal and monetary stimuli. The 10-year Treasury rate fluctuated around as low as 0.6% in the United States from March through August 2020, and equities posted a very strong recovery for the rest of the year (the MSCI ACWI global equity index was at +70.5% from 23 March 2020 to 31 December 2020).

While short-term market returns resembled a very wild roller coaster in 2020, long-term return expectations did not change that dramatically. Of course, bond return expectations became lower as a result of very low government yield levels due to the monetary stimulus, but it has been a general expectation that corporate earnings would recover as the disruptive impacts of the pandemic decline over time. Since the end of 2021, however, policymakers and market participants have been trying to get a better understanding of the long lasting impacts of the pandemic: Inflation, among others, is one of the most topical issues. The unprecedented fiscal and monetary stimuli, supply chain disruptions, and changes in many people's life style (working from home versus the office) may cause sticky price rises in certain segments of the economy.

Finally, as new advisers or members join the Investment Committee, they bring their own beliefs and biases regarding certain investment activities. Conducting an asset allocation study to educate these new members of the oversight group and introduce them to the investment philosophy and process that has been adopted by the organization will smooth their integration into the governance system and ensure that they have a holistic view of the asset owner's goals and objectives.

In some instances, a change to an asset allocation strategy may reasonably be implemented without a formal asset allocation study. Certain milestones are reasonable points at which to implement a change in the policy, in most instances, reducing the level of risk. (For pension funds, these "milestones" are typically related to changes in the plan's funded status.) Anticipating these milestones by putting an asset allocation policy in place that anticipates these changes allows the investor to respond more quickly to changing circumstances and in a non-reactive and objective manner. This rebalancing policy is frequently referred to as a "glide path." Target-date mutual funds common in retirement investing for individuals are one example of this approach to asset allocation. Exhibit 10 illustrates one fund company's approach to migrating the asset allocation away from equities and towards bonds as retirement approaches.

Exhibit 10: An Asset Allocation Glide Path

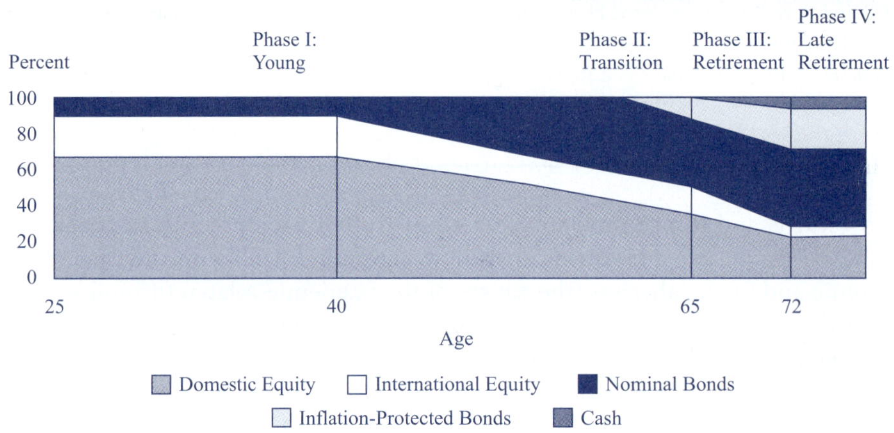

Source: Vanguard, "Target-Date Funds: A Solid Foundation for Retirement Investors" (May 2009): www.vanguard.com/jumppage/targetretirement/TRFCOMM.pdf.

In an institutional framework, the Investment Committee may specify certain funding levels it seeks to achieve. At the start of the period, an underfunded pension plan might adopt a higher equity allocation in an attempt to reduce the underfunding. If this is successful, the plan becomes better funded and there is less of a desire or need to take the higher level of equity risk. A pension fund may quickly implement "pre-programmed" asset allocation changes as the funded status of a pension plan improves. Typically, these planned reallocations are spelled out in an Investment Policy Statement.

EXAMPLE 6

Revising the Strategic Asset Allocation

Auldberg University Endowment Fund (AUE) has assets totaling CAF$200 million. The current asset allocation is as follows:

- CAF$100 million in domestic equities
- CAF$60 million in domestic government debt
- CAF$40 million in Class B office real estate

AUE has historically distributed to the University 5% of the 36-month moving average of net assets, contributing approximately CAF$10 million of Auldberg University's CAF$60 million annual operating budget. Real estate income (from the University's CAF$350 million direct investment in domestic commercial real estate assets, including office buildings and industrial parks, much of it near the campus) and provincial subsidies have been the main source of income to the University. Admission is free to all citizens who qualify academically.

Growth in the Caflandia economy has been fueled by low interest rates, encouraging excess real estate development. There is a strong probability that the economy will soon go into recession, negatively impacting both the property values and the income potential of the University's real estate holdings.

Gizi Horvath, a University alumna, has recently announced an irrevocable CAF$200 million gift to AUE, to be paid in equal installments over the next five years. AUE employs a well-qualified staff with substantial diverse experience in equities, fixed income, and real estate. Staff has recommended that the gift from Ms. Horvath be invested using the same asset allocation policy that the endowment has been following successfully for the past five years. They suggest that the asset allocation policy should be revisited once the final installment has been received.

1. Critique staff's recommendation, and identify the case facts that support your critique.

Solution:

The size of the anticipated contributions will double AUE's assets over the next five years, potentially increasing the opportunity set of asset classes suitable for their investment program. Given that a typical asset allocation study encompasses a long investment horizon—10 years, 20 years, or more—staff should begin to evaluate the opportunities available to them today in *anticipation* of the future cash flows. Given the material change in the economic balance sheet along with changes in the asset size, liquidity, and time horizon constraints, AUE should plan on a regular, more frequent, formal review of the asset allocation policy until the situation stabilizes. The asset allocation study should explore the feasibility of adding new asset classes as well as the ability to improve diversification within existing categories, perhaps by including non-domestic equities and bonds. Furthermore, the forecast economic environment may materially alter the outflows from the fund in support of the University's day-to-day operations. Cash flows from the University's real estate holdings are likely to decline, as are the values of those real estate assets. Given the outlook for real estate, a strong case can be made to limit or reduce the endowment's investment in real estate; moreover, consideration should be given to the effect of declining income from the current real estate investment.

2. The Government Petroleum Fund of Caflandia (GPFC) is operating under the following asset allocation policy, which was developed with a 20-year planning horizon. Target weights and actual weights are given:

	Target Asset Allocation	Current Asset Allocation
Global equities	30%	38%
Global high-yield bonds	10%	15%
Domestic intermediate bonds	30%	25%
Hedge funds	15%	15%
Private equity	15%	7%

When this asset allocation policy was adopted 5 years ago, the petroleum revenues that support the sovereign wealth fund were projected to continue to grow for at least the next 25 years and intergenerational distributions were expected to begin in 20 years. However, since the adoption of this policy, alternate fuel sources have eroded both the price and quantity of oil exports, the economy is undergoing significant restructuring, inflows to the fund have been suspended, and distributions are expected to begin within 5 years.

What are the implications of this change in the liquidity constraints for the current asset allocation policy?

Solution:

GPFC had adopted a long-range asset allocation policy under the expectation of continuing net cash inflows and no immediate liquidity constraints. With the change in circumstances, the need for liquidity in the fund has increased significantly. The current asset allocation policy allocates 40% of the fund's assets to less liquid asset classes—high-yield bonds, hedge funds, and private equity. Although the allocation to private equity has not been fully implemented, the fund is overweight high-yield bonds and at the target weight for hedge funds. These asset classes—or the size of the allocation to these asset classes—may no longer be appropriate for the fund given the change in circumstances.

3. O-Chem Corp has a defined benefit pension plan with US$1.0 billion in assets. The plan is closed, the liabilities are frozen, and the plan is currently 65% funded. The company intends to increase cash contributions to improve the funded status of the plan and then purchase annuities to fully address all of the plan's pension obligations. As part of an asset allocation analysis conducted every five years, the company has recently decided to allocate 80% of assets to liability-matching bonds and the remaining 20% to a mix of global equities and real estate. An existing private equity portfolio is in the midst of being liquidated. This allocation reflects a desired reduction in the level of investment risk.

O-Chem has just announced an ambitious US$15 billion capital investment program to build new plants for refining and production. The CFO informed the Pension Committee that the company will be contributing to the plan only the minimum funding required by regulations for the foreseeable future. It is estimated that achieving fully funded status for the pension plan under minimum funding requirements and using the current asset allocation approach will take at least 10 years.

What are the implications of this change in funding policy for the pension plan's asset allocation strategy?

Solution:

The Investment Committee should conduct a new asset allocation study to address the changes in cash flow forecasts. The lower contributions imply that the pension plan will need to rely more heavily on investment returns to reach its funding objectives. A higher allocation to return-seeking assets, such as public and private equities, is warranted. The company should suspend the current private equity liquidation plan until the new asset allocation study has been completed. A liability-matching bond portfolio is still appropriate, although less than the current 80% of assets should be allocated to this portfolio.

SHORT-TERM SHIFTS IN ASSET ALLOCATION 9

☐ discuss the use of short-term shifts in asset allocation

Strategic asset allocation (SAA), or policy asset allocation, represents long-term investment policy targets for asset class weights, whereas tactical asset allocation (TAA) allows short-term deviations from SAA targets.[19] TAA moves might be justified based on cyclical variations within a secular trend (e.g., stage of business or monetary cycle) or temporary price dislocations in capital markets. TAA has the objective of increasing return, or risk-adjusted return, by taking advantage of short-term economic and financial market conditions that appear more favorable to certain asset classes. In seeking to capture a short-term return opportunity, TAA decisions move the investor's risk away from the targeted risk profile. TAA is predicated on a belief that investment returns, in the short run, are predictable. (This contrasts with the random walk assumption more strongly embedded in most SAA processes.) Using either short-term views or signals, the investor actively re-weights broad asset classes, sectors, or risk factor premiums. TAA is not concerned with individual security selection. In other words, generating alpha through TAA decisions is dependent on successful market or factor timing rather than security selection. TAA is an asset-only approach. Although tactical asset allocation shifts must still conform to the risk constraints outlined in the investment policy statement, they do not expressly consider liabilities (or goals in goals-based investing).

The SAA policy portfolio is the benchmark against which TAA decisions are measured. Tactical views are developed and bets are sized relative to the asset class targets of the SAA policy portfolio. The sizes of these bets are typically subject to certain risk constraints. The most common risk constraint is a pre-established allowable range around each asset class's policy target. Other risk constraints may include either a predicted tracking error budget versus the SAA or a range of targeted risk (e.g., an allowable range of predicted volatility).

19 SAA and TAA are distinct from GTAA (global tactical asset allocation), an opportunistic investment strategy that seeks to take advantage of pricing or valuation anomalies across multiple asset classes, typically equities, fixed income, and currencies.

The success of TAA decisions can be evaluated in a number of ways. Three of the most common are

- a comparison of the Sharpe ratio realized under the TAA relative to the Sharpe ratio that would have been realized under the SAA;
- evaluating the information ratio or the *t*-statistic of the average excess return of the TAA portfolio relative to the SAA portfolio; and
- plotting the realized return and risk of the TAA portfolio versus the realized return and risk of portfolios along the SAA's efficient frontier. This approach is particularly useful in assessing the risk-adjusted TAA return. The TAA portfolio may have produced a higher return or a higher Sharpe ratio than the SAA portfolio, but it could be less optimal than other portfolios along the investor's efficient frontier of portfolio choices.

The composition of the portfolio's excess return over the SAA portfolio return can also be examined more closely using attribution analysis, evaluating the specific overweights and underweights that led to the performance differential.

Tactical investment decisions may incur additional costs—higher trading costs and taxes (in the case of taxable investors). Tactical investment decisions can also increase the concentration of risk relative to the policy portfolio. For example, if the tactical decision is to overweight equities, not only is the portfolio risk increased but also the diversification of risk contributions is reduced. This is particularly an issue when the SAA policy portfolio relies on uncorrelated asset classes. These costs should be weighed against the predictability of short-term returns.

There are two broad approaches to TAA. The first is discretionary, which relies on a qualitative interpretation of political, economic, and financial market conditions. The second is systematic, which relies on quantitative signals to capture documented return anomalies that may be inconsistent with market efficiency.

Discretionary TAA

Discretionary TAA is predicated on the existence of manager skill in predicting and timing short-term market moves away from the expected outcome for each asset class that is embedded in the SAA policy portfolio. In practice, discretionary TAA is typically used in an attempt to mitigate or hedge risk in distressed markets while enhancing return in positive return markets (i.e., an asymmetric return distribution).

Short-term forecasts consider a large number of data points that provide relevant information about current and expected political, economic, and financial market conditions that may affect short-term asset class returns. Data points might include valuations, term and credit spreads, central bank policy, GDP growth, earnings expectations, inflation expectations, and leading economic indicators. Price-to-earnings ratios, price-to-book ratios, and the dividend yield are commonly used valuation measures that can be compared to historical averages and across similar assets to inform short-to-intermediate-term tactical shifts. Term spreads provide information about the business cycle, inflation, and potential future interest rates. Credit spreads gauge default risk, borrowing conditions, and liquidity. Other data points are more directly related to current and expected GDP and earnings growth.

Short-term forecasts may also consider economic sentiment indicators. TAA often assumes a close relationship between the economy and capital market returns. Because consumer spending is a major driver of GDP in developed countries, consumer sentiment is a key consideration. Consumer confidence surveys provide insight as to the level of optimism regarding the economy and personal finances.

TAA also considers market sentiment—indicators of the optimism or pessimism of financial market participants. Data points considered in gauging market sentiment include margin borrowing, short interest, and a volatility index.

- Margin borrowing measures give an indication of the current level of bullishness, and the capacity for more or less margin borrowing has implications for future bullishness. Higher prices tend to inspire confidence and spur more buying; similarly, more buying on margin tends to spur higher prices. The aggregate level of margin can be an indicator that bullish sentiment is overdone, although the level of borrowing must be considered in the context of the rate of change in borrowing.
- Short interest measures give an indication of current bearish sentiment and also have implications for future bearishness. Although rising short interest indicates increasing negative sentiment, a high short interest ratio may be an indication of the extreme pessimism that often occurs at market lows.
- The volatility index, commonly known as the fear index, is a measure of market expectations of near-term volatility. VDAX-NEW in Germany, V2X in the United Kingdom, and VIX in the United States each measure the level of expected volatility of their respective indexes as implied by the bid/ask quotations of index options; it rises when put option buying increases and falls when call buying activity increases.

Different approaches to discretionary TAA may include different data points and relationships and also may prioritize and weight those data points differently depending on both the approach and the prevailing market environment. Despite the plethora of data inputs, the interpretation of this information is qualitative at its core.

Systematic TAA

Using signals, systematic TAA attempts to capture asset class level return anomalies that have been shown to have some predictability and persistence. Value and momentum, for example, are factors that have been determined to offer some level of predictability, both among securities within asset classes (for security selection) and at the asset class level (for asset class timing).

The value factor is the return of value stocks over the return of growth stocks. The momentum factor is the return of stocks with higher prior returns over the return of stocks with lower prior returns. Value and momentum (and size) factors have been determined to have some explanatory power regarding the relative returns of equity securities within the equity asset class. Value and momentum phenomena are also present at the asset class level and can be used in making tactical asset allocation decisions across asset classes.

Valuation ratios have been shown to have some explanatory power in predicting variation in future equity returns. Predictive measures for equities include dividend yield, cash flow yield, and Shiller's earnings yield (the inverse of Shiller's P/E[20]). Sometimes these yield measures are defined as the excess of the yield over the local risk-free rate or inflation.[21]

Other asset classes have their own value signals, such as yield and carry in currencies, commodities, and/or fixed income. Carry in currencies uses short-term interest rate differentials to determine which currencies (or currency-denominated assets) to overweight (or own) and which to underweight (or sell short). Carry in commodities

20 A price-to-earnings ratio based on the average inflation-adjusted earnings of the previous 10 years.

21 Return predictability for equity markets is driven by historical mean-reversion, which tends to occur over the intermediate-term. These valuation measures are often used as signals for TAA, but they can also be used to shape return expectations for SAA.

compares positive (backwardation) and negative (contango) roll yields to determine which commodities to own or short. And for bonds, yields-to-maturity and term premiums (yields in excess of the local risk-free rate) signal the relative attractiveness of different fixed-income markets.

Asset classes can trend positively or negatively for some time before changing course. Trend following is an investment or trading strategy based on the expectation that asset class (or asset) returns will continue in the same upward or downward trend that they have most recently exhibited.[22] A basic trend signal is the most recent 12-month return: The expectation is that the direction of the most recent 12-month returns can be expected to persist for the next 12 months. Shorter time frames and different weighting schemes can also be used. For example, another trend signal is the moving-average crossover, where the moving average price of a shorter time frame is compared with the moving average price of a longer time frame. This signals an upward (downward) trend when the moving average of the shorter time frame is above (below) the moving average of the longer time frame. Trend signals are widely used in systematic TAA. Asset classes may be ranked or categorized into positive or negative buckets based on their most recent prior 12-month performance and over- or underweighted accordingly. More-complex signals for both momentum/trend signals (such as those that use different lookback periods or momentum signals correlated with earnings momentum) and value/carry are also used.

EXAMPLE 7

Short-Term Shifts in Asset Allocation

Exhibit 11

Asset Class	Asset Allocation	Calendar Year Return
Investment-grade bonds	45%	3.45%
High-yield bonds	5%	−6.07%
Developed markets equity	45%	−0.32%
Emerging markets equity	5%	−14.60%

Exhibit 12

	Policy Portfolio	Realized Results
12-month return	−0.82%	0.38%
Risk-free rate	0.50%	0.50%
Standard deviation	5.80%	6.20%
Sharpe ratio	−0.23	−0.02

22 Trend following is also called time-series momentum. Cross-sectional momentum describes the relative momentum returns of securities within the same asset class.

Exhibit 13

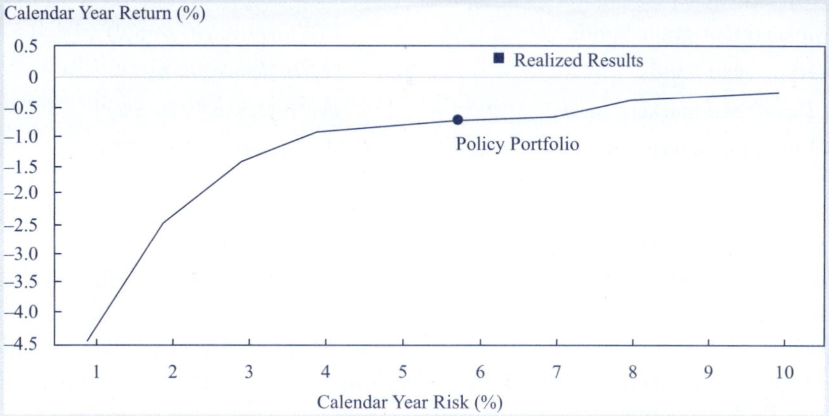

1. The investment policy for Alpha Beverage Corporation's pension fund allows staff to overweight or underweight asset classes, within pre-established bands, using a TAA model that has been approved by the Investment Committee. The asset allocation policy is reflected in Exhibit 14, and the output of the TAA model is given in Exhibit 15. Using the data presented in Exhibit 14 and Exhibit 15, recommend a TAA strategy for the pension fund and justify your response.

Exhibit 14: Strategic Asset Allocation Policy

SAA Policy	Current Weight	Target Allocation	Upper Policy Limit	Lower Policy Limit
Investment-grade bonds	45%	40%	45%	35%
High-yield bonds	10%	10%	15%	5%
Developed markets equity	35%	40%	45%	35%
Emerging markets equity	10%	10%	15%	5%

Exhibit 15: Trend Signal (the positive or negative trailing 12-month excess return)

	12-Month Return	Risk-Free Return	Excess Return	Signal
Investment-grade bonds	4%	1%	3%	Long
High-yield bonds	−2%	1%	−3%	Short
Developed markets equity	5%	1%	4%	Long
Emerging markets equity	−10%	1%	−11%	Short

Solution:

The TAA decision must be taken in the context of the SAA policy constraints. Thus, although the signals for high-yield bonds and emerging market equities are negative, the minimum permissible weight in each is 5%. Similarly, although the signals for investment-grade bonds and developed markets equities are positive, the maximum permissible weight in each is 45%. Asset classes can be over- or underweighted to the full extent of the policy limits. Based on the trend signals and the policy constraints, the recommended tactical asset allocation is as follows:

• Investment-grade bonds	45% *(overweight by 5%)*
• High-yield bonds	5% *(underweight by 5%)*
• Developed markets equity	45% *(overweight by 5%)*
• Emerging markets equity	5% *(underweight by 5%)*

2. One year later, the Investment Committee for Alpha Beverage Corporation is conducting its year-end review of pension plan performance. Staff has prepared the following exhibits regarding the tactical asset allocation decisions taken during the past year. Assume that all investments are implemented using passively managed index funds. Evaluate the effectiveness of the TAA decisions.

Solution:

The decision to overweight investment grade bonds and underweight emerging markets equity and high-yield bonds was a profitable one. The chosen asset allocation added approximately 120 basis points to portfolio return over the year. Although portfolio risk was elevated relative to the policy portfolio (standard deviation of 6.2% versus 5.8% for the policy portfolio), the portfolio positioning improved the fund's Sharpe ratio relative to allocations they might have selected along the efficient frontier.

A SILVER LINING TO THE 2008–2009 GLOBAL FINANCIAL CRISIS

Prior to 2008, corporate pension plans had begun to shift the fixed-income component of their policy portfolios from an intermediate maturity bond index to a long bond index. Despite the relatively low interest rates at the time, this move was made to better align the plans' assets with the long duration liability payment stream. The fixed-income portfolios were typically benchmarked against a long government and credit index that included both government and corporate bonds. Swaps or STRIPS* were sometimes used to extend duration.

During the global financial crisis that began in 2008, these heavier and longer-duration fixed-income positions performed well relative to equities (the long government and credit index was up 8%, whereas the S&P 500 Index was down 37% in 2008), providing plan sponsors with a level of investment protection that had not been anticipated. Additionally, with its exposure to higher-returning government bonds that benefited from investors' flight to safety, this fixed-income portfolio often outperformed the liabilities. (Recall from the earlier discussion on pension regulation that pension liabilities are typically measured using corporate bond yields. Thus, liabilities rose in the face of declining corporate bond yields while the liability-hedging asset rose even further given its overall higher credit quality.) This was an unintended asset/liability mismatch that had very positive results. Subsequent to this rally in bonds, some plan sponsors made a tactical asset allocation decision—to move out of swaps and government bonds and into physical corporate bonds (non-derivative fixed-income exposure)—locking in the gains and better hedging the liability.

* Treasury STRIPS are fixed-income securities with no interest payments that are sold at a discount to face value and mature at par. STRIPS is an acronym for Separate Trading of Registered Interest and Principal of Securities.

DEALING WITH BEHAVIORAL BIASES IN ASSET ALLOCATION

10

☐ identify behavioral biases that arise in asset allocation and recommend methods to overcome them

Although global capital markets are competitive pricing engines, human behavior can be less rational than most economic models assume. Behavioral finance—the hybrid study of financial economics and psychology—has documented a number of behavioral biases that commonly arise in investing. The CFA Program reading "The Behavioral Biases of Individuals" discusses 16 common behavioral biases. The biases most relevant in asset allocation include loss aversion, the illusion of control, mental accounting, representativeness bias, framing, and availability bias. An effective investment program will address these decision-making risks through a formal asset allocation process with its own objective framework, governance, and controls. An important first step toward mitigating the negative effects of behavioral biases is simply acknowledging that they exist; just being aware of them can reduce their influence on decision making. It is also possible to incorporate certain behavioral biases into the investment decision-making process to produce better outcomes. This is most commonly practiced in goals-based investing. We will discuss strategies that help deal with these common biases.

Loss Aversion

Loss-aversion bias is an emotional bias in which people tend to strongly prefer avoiding losses as opposed to achieving gains. A number of studies on loss aversion suggest that, psychologically, losses are significantly more powerful than gains. The utility derived from a gain is much lower than the utility given up with an equivalent loss. This behavior is related to the marginal utility of wealth, where each additional dollar of wealth is valued incrementally less with increasing levels of wealth.

A diversified multi-asset class portfolio is generally thought to offer an approximately symmetrical distribution of returns around a positive expected mean return. Financial market theory suggests that a rational investor would think about risk as the dispersion or uncertainty (variance) around the mean (expected) outcome. However, loss aversion suggests the investor assigns a greater weight to the negative outcomes than would be implied by the actual shape of the distribution. Looking at this another way, risk is not measured relative to the expected mean return but rather on an absolute basis, relative to a 0% return. The loss-aversion bias may interfere with an investor's ability to maintain his chosen asset allocation through periods of negative returns.

In goals-based investing, loss-aversion bias can be mitigated by framing risk in terms of shortfall probability or by funding high-priority goals with low-risk assets.

Shortfall probability is the probability that a portfolio will not achieve the return required to meet a stated goal. Where there are well-defined, discrete goals, sub-portfolios can be established for each goal and the asset allocation for that sub-portfolio would use shortfall probability as the definition of risk.

Similarly, by segregating assets into sub-portfolios aligned to goals designated by the client as high-priority and investing those assets in risk-free or low risk assets of similar duration, the adviser mitigates the loss-aversion bias associated with this particular goal—freeing up other assets to take on a more appropriate level of risk. Riskier assets can then be used to fund lower-priority and aspirational goals.

In institutional investing, loss aversion can be seen in the herding behavior among plan sponsors. Adopting an asset allocation not too different from the allocation of one's peers minimizes reputation risk.

Illusion of Control

The illusion of control is a cognitive bias—the tendency to overestimate one's ability to control events. It can be exacerbated by overconfidence, an emotional bias. If investors believe they have more or better information than what is reflected in the market, they have (excessive) confidence in their ability to generate better outcomes. They may perceive *information* in what are random price movements, which may lead to more frequent trading, greater concentration of portfolio positions, or a greater willingness to employ tactical shifts in their asset allocation. The following investor behaviors might be attributed to this illusion of control:

- Alpha-seeking behaviors, such as attempted market timing in the form of extreme tactical asset allocation shifts or all in/all out market calls—the investor who correctly anticipated a market reversal now believes he has superior insight on valuation levels.
- Alpha-seeking behaviors based on a belief of superior resources—the institutional investor who believes her internal resources give her an edge over other investors in active security selection and/or the selection of active investment managers.
- Excessive trading, use of leverage, or short selling—the long/short equity investor who moves from a normal exposure range of 65% long/20% short to 100% long/50% short.
- Reducing, eliminating, or even shorting asset classes that are a significant part of the global market portfolio based on non-consensus return and risk forecasts—the chair of a foundation's investment committee who calls for shortening the duration of the bond portfolio from six years to six months based on insights drawn from his position in the banking industry.
- Retaining a large, concentrated legacy asset that contributes diversifiable risk—the employee who fails to diversify her holding of company stock.

Hindsight bias—the tendency to perceive past investment outcomes as having been predictable—exacerbates the illusion of control.

In the asset allocation process, an investor who believes he or she has better information than others may use estimates of return and risk that produce asset allocation choices that are materially different from the market portfolio. This can result in undiversified portfolios with outsized exposures to just one or two minor asset classes, called extreme corner portfolios. Using such biased risk and return estimates results in a biased asset allocation decision—precisely what an objective asset allocation process seeks to avoid.

The illusion of control can be mitigated by using the global market portfolio as the starting point in developing the asset allocation. Building on the basic principles of CAPM, Markowitz's mean–variance theory, and efficient market theory, the global market portfolio offers a theoretically sound benchmark for asset allocation. Deviations from this baseline portfolio must be thoughtfully considered and rigorously vetted, ensuring the asset allocation process remains objective. A formal asset allocation process that employs long-term return and risk forecasts, optimization constraints anchored around asset class weights in the global market portfolio, and strict policy ranges will significantly mitigate the illusion of control bias in asset allocation.

Mental Accounting

Mental accounting is an information-processing bias in which people treat one sum of money differently from another sum based solely on the mental account the money is assigned to. Investors may separate assets or liabilities into buckets based on subjective criteria. For example, an investor may consider his retirement investment portfolio independent of the portfolio that funds his child's education, even if the combined asset allocation of the two portfolios is sub-optimal. Or an employee with significant exposure to her employer's stock through vested stock options may fail to consider this exposure alongside other assets when establishing a strategic asset allocation.

Goals-based investing incorporates mental accounting directly into the asset allocation solution. Each goal is aligned with a discrete sub-portfolio, and the investor can specify the acceptable level of risk for each goal. Provided each of the sub-portfolios lies along the same efficient frontier, the sum of the sub-portfolios will also be efficient.[23]

Concentrated stock positions also give rise to another common mental accounting issue that affects asset allocation. For example, the primary source of an entrepreneur's wealth may be a concentrated equity position in the publicly traded company he founded. The entrepreneur may prefer to retain a relatively large exposure to this one security within his broader investment portfolio despite the inherent risk. Although there may be rational reasons for this preference—including ownership control, an information advantage, and tax considerations—the desire to retain this riskier exposure is more often the result of a psychological loyalty to the asset that generated his wealth. This mental accounting bias is further reinforced by the endowment effect—the tendency to ascribe more value to an asset already owned rather than another asset one might purchase to replace it.

The concentrated stock/mental accounting bias can be accommodated in goals-based asset allocation by assigning the concentrated stock position to an aspirational goal—one that the client would *like* to achieve but to which he or she is willing to assign a lower probability of success. Whereas lifetime consumption tends to be a high-priority goal requiring a well-diversified portfolio to fund it with confidence, an aspirational goal such as a charitable gift may be an important but much less highly valued goal. It can reasonably be funded with the concentrated stock position. (This could have the additional benefit of avoiding capital gains tax altogether!)

Representativeness Bias

Representativeness, or recency, bias is the tendency to overweight the importance of the most recent observations and information relative to a longer-dated or more comprehensive set of long-term observations and information. Tactical shifts in asset allocation, those undertaken in response to recent returns or news—perhaps shifting the asset allocation toward the highest or lowest allowable ends of the policy ranges—are particularly susceptible to recency bias. Return chasing is a common manifestation of recency bias, and it results in overweighting asset classes with good recent performance.

It is believed that asset prices largely follow a random walk; past prices cannot be used to predict future returns. If this is true, then shifting the asset allocation in response to recent returns, or allowing recent returns to unduly influence the asset class assumptions used in the asset allocation process, will likely lead to sub-optimal results. *If*, however, asset class returns exhibit trending behavior, the recent past *may*

23 This condition holds when the asset allocation process is unconstrained. With a long-only constraint, some efficiency is lost but the effect is much less significant than the loss of efficiency from inaccurately specifying risk aversion (which goals-based approaches to asset allocation attempt to mitigate). See Das, Markowitz, Scheid, and Statman (2010) and Das et al. (2011).

contain information relevant to tactical shifts in asset allocation. And if asset class returns are mean-reverting, comparing current valuations to historical norms may signal the potential for a reversal or for above-average future returns.

Recency bias is not uniformly negative. Random walk, trending, and mean-reversion may be simultaneously relevant to the investment decision-making process, although their effect on asset prices will unfold over different time horizons. The strongest defenses against recency bias are an objective asset allocation process and a strong governance framework. It is important that the investor objectively evaluate the motivation underlying the response to recent market events. A formal asset allocation policy with pre-specified allowable ranges will constrain recency bias. A strong governance framework with the appropriate level of expertise and well-documented investment beliefs increases the likelihood that shifts in asset allocation are made objectively and in accordance with those beliefs.

Framing Bias

Framing bias is an information-processing bias in which a person may answer a question differently based solely on the way in which it is asked. One example of framing bias is common in committee-oriented decision-making processes. In instances where one individual frequently speaks first and speaks with great authority, the views of other committee members may be suppressed or biased toward this first position put on the table.

A more nuanced form of framing bias can be found in asset allocation. The investor's choice of an asset allocation may be influenced merely by the manner in which the risk-to-return trade-off is presented.

Risk can mean different things to different investors: volatility, tail risk, the permanent loss of capital, or a failure to meet financial goals. These definitions are all closely related, but the relative importance of each of these aspects can influence the investor's asset allocation choice. Further, the investor's perception of each of these risks can be influenced by the manner in which they are presented—gain and loss potential framed in money terms versus percentages, for example.

Investors are often asked to evaluate portfolio choices using expected return, with standard deviation as the sole measure of risk. Standard deviation measures the dispersion or volatility around the mean (expected) return. Other measures of risk may also be used. Value at risk (VaR) is a loss threshold: "If I choose this asset mix, I can be pretty sure that my losses will not exceed X, most of the time." More formally, VaR is the minimum loss that would be expected a certain percentage of the time over a certain period of time given the assumed market conditions. Conditional value at risk (CVaR) is the probability-weighted average of losses when the VaR threshold is breached. VaR and CVaR both measure downside or tail risk.

Exhibit 16 shows the expected return and risk for five portfolios that span an efficient frontier from P1 (lowest risk) to P100 (highest risk). A normal distribution of returns is assumed; therefore, the portfolio's VaR and CVaR are a direct function of the portfolio's expected return and standard deviation. In this case, standard deviation, VaR, and CVaR measure precisely the same risk but frame that risk differently. Standard deviation presents that risk as volatility, while VaR and CVaR present it as risk of loss. When dealing with a normal distribution, as this example presumes, the 5% VaR threshold is simply the point on the distribution 1.65 standard deviations below the expected mean return.

Exhibit 16: There's More Than One Way to Frame Risk

	P1	P25	P50	P75	P100
Return	3.2%	4.9%	6.0%	7.0%	8.0%
Std. Dev.	3.9%	7.8%	11.9%	15.9%	20.0%
VaR (5%)	−3.2%	−8.0%	−13.6%	−19.3%	−25.0%
CVaR (5%)	−4.8%	−11.2%	−18.5%	−25.8%	−33.2%

When viewing return and volatility alone, many investors may gravitate to P50 with its 6.0% expected return and 11.9% standard deviation. P50 represents the median risk portfolio that appeals to many investors in practice because it balances high-risk and low-risk choices with related diversification benefits. However, loss-aversion bias suggests that some investors who gravitate to the median choice might actually find the −18.5% CVaR of P50 indicative of a level of risk they find very uncomfortable. The CVaR frame intuitively communicates a different perspective of exactly the same risk that is already fully explained by standard deviation—namely, the downside or tail-risk aspects of the standard deviation and mean. With this example, you can see that how risk is framed and presented can affect the asset allocation decision.

The framing effect can be mitigated by presenting the possible asset allocation choices with multiple perspectives on the risk/reward trade-off. The most commonly used risk measure—standard deviation—can be supplemented with additional measures, such as **shortfall probability** (the probability of failing to meet a specific liability or goal)[24] and tail-risk measures (e.g., VaR and CVaR). Historical stress tests and Monte Carlo simulations can also be used to capture and communicate risk in a tangible way. These multiple perspectives of the risk and reward trade-offs among a set of asset allocation choices compel the investor to consider more carefully what outcomes are acceptable or unacceptable.

Availability Bias

Availability bias is an information-processing bias in which people take a mental shortcut when estimating the probability of an outcome based on how easily the outcome comes to mind. Easily recalled outcomes are often perceived as being more likely than those that are harder to recall or understand. For example, more recent events or events in which the investor has personally been affected are likely to be assigned a higher probability of occurring again, regardless of the objective odds of the event actually occurring. Availability bias in this context is termed the recency effect and is a subset of recency, or representativeness, bias.

As an example, many private equity investors experienced a liquidity squeeze during the financial crisis that began in 2008. Their equity portfolios had suffered large losses, and their private equity investments were illiquid. Worse yet, they were contractually committed to additional capital contributions to those private equity funds. At the same time, their financial obligations continued at the same or an even higher pace. Investors who personally experienced this confluence of negative events are likely to express a strong preference for liquid investments, assigning a higher probability to such an event occurring again than would an investor who had cash available to acquire the private equity interests that were sold at distressed prices.

24 Shortfall risk and shortfall probability are often used to refer to the same concept. This author prefers shortfall probability because the measure refers to the probability of shortfall, not the magnitude of the potential shortfall. For example, you may have a low probability of shortfall but the size of the shortfall could be significant. In this case, it could be misleading to say the shortfall risk is low.

Familiarity bias stems from availability bias: People tend to favor the familiar over the new or different because of the ease of recalling the familiar. In asset allocation, familiarity bias most commonly results in a **home bias**—a preference for securities listed on the exchanges of one's home country. However, concentrating portfolio exposure in home country securities, particularly if the home country capital markets are small, results in a less diversified, less efficient portfolio. Familiarity bias can be mitigated by using the global market portfolio as the starting point in developing the asset allocation, where deviations from this baseline portfolio must be thoughtfully considered and rigorously vetted.

Familiarity bias may also cause investors to fall into the trap of comparing their investment decisions (and performance) to others', without regard for the appropriateness of those decisions for their own specific facts and circumstances. By avoiding comparison of investment returns or asset allocation decisions with others, an organization is more capable of identifying the asset allocation that is best tailored to their needs.

Investment decision making is subject to a wide range of potential behavioral biases. This is true in both private wealth *and* institutional investing. Employing a formal asset allocation process using the global market portfolio as the starting point for asset allocation modeling is a key component of ensuring the asset allocation decision is as objective as possible.

A strong governance structure, such as that discussed in the overview reading on asset allocation, is a necessary first step to mitigating the effect that these behavioral biases may have on the long-term success of the investment program. Bringing a diverse set of views to the deliberation process brings more tools to the table to solve any problem and leads to better and more informed decision making. A clearly stated mission—a common goal—and a commitment from committee members and other stakeholders to that mission are critically important in constraining the influence of these biases on investment decisions.

EFFECTIVE INVESTMENT GOVERNANCE

Six critical elements of effective investment governance are

1. clearly articulated long- and short-term investment objectives of the investment program;
2. allocation of decision rights and responsibilities among the functional units in the governance hierarchy, taking account of their knowledge, capacity, time, and position in the governance hierarchy;
3. established processes for developing and approving the investment policy statement that will govern the day-to-day operation of the investment program;
4. specified processes for developing and approving the program's strategic asset allocation;
5. a reporting framework to monitor the program's progress toward the agreed-upon goals and objectives; and
6. periodic governance audits.

EXAMPLE 8

Mitigating Behavioral Biases in Asset Allocation

Ivy Lee, the retired founder of a publicly traded company, has two primary goals for her investment assets. The first goal is to fund lifetime consumption expenditures of US$1 million per year for herself and her husband; this is a goal the Lees want to achieve with a high degree of certainty. The second goal is to provide an end-of-life gift to Auldberg University. Ivy has a diversified portfolio of stocks and bonds totaling US$5 million and a sizable position in the stock of the company she founded. The following table summarizes the facts.

Investor Profile	
Annual consumption needs	US$1,000,000
Remaining years of life expectancy	40
Diversified stock holdings	US$3,000,000
Diversified bond holdings	US$2,000,000
Concentrated stock holdings	US$15,000,000
Total portfolio	US$20,000,000

Assume that a 60% equity/40% fixed-income portfolio represents the level of risk Ivy is willing to assume with respect to her consumption goal. This 60/40 portfolio offers an expected return of 6.0%. (For simplicity, this illustration ignores inflation and taxes.)

The present value of the expected consumption expenditures is US$15,949,075. This is the amount needed on hand today, which, if invested in a portfolio of 60% equities and 40% fixed income, would fully fund 40 annual cash distributions of US$1,000,000 each.[25]

The concentrated stock has a highly uncertain expected return and comes with significant idiosyncratic (stock-specific) risk. A preliminary mean–variance optimization using three "asset classes"—stocks, bonds, and the concentrated stock—results in a zero allocation to the concentrated stock position. But Ivy prefers to retain as much concentrated stock as possible because it represents her legacy and she has a strong psychological loyalty to it.

1. Describe the behavioral biases most relevant to developing an asset allocation recommendation for Ivy.

   Solution:

   Two behavioral biases that the adviser must be aware of in developing an asset allocation recommendation for Ivy are illusion of control and mental accounting. Because Ivy was the founder of the company whose stock comprises 75% of her investment portfolio, she may believe she has more or better information about the return prospects for this portion of the portfolio. The belief that she has superior information may lead to a risk assessment that is not reflective of the true risk in the holding. Using a goals-based approach to asset allocation may help Ivy more fully understand the risks inherent in the concentrated stock position. The riskier, concentrated stock position can be assigned to a lower-priority goal, such as the gift to Auldberg University.

25 Assumes cash distributions occur at the beginning of the year and the expected return is the geometric average.

2. Recommend and justify an asset allocation for Ivy given the facts presented above.

Solution:

	Beginning Asset Allocation	Recommended Asset Allocation
Diversified stocks	US$3,000,000	US$9,600,000
Diversified bonds	US$2,000,000	US$6,400,000
Funding of lifestyle goal		*US$16,000,000*
Concentrated stock	US$15,000,000	US$4,000,000
Total portfolio	US$20,000,000	US$20,000,000

It is recommended that Ivy fully fund her high-priority lifestyle consumption needs (US$15,949,075) with US$16 million in a diversified portfolio of stocks and bonds. To achieve this, US$11 million of the concentrated stock position should be sold and the proceeds added to the diversified portfolio that supports lifestyle consumption needs. The remaining US$4 million of concentrated stock can be retained to fund the aspirational goal of an end-of-life gift to Auldberg University. In this example, the adviser has employed the mental accounting bias to achieve a suitable outcome: By illustrating the dollar value needed to fund the high-priority lifetime consumption needs goal, the adviser was able to clarify for Ivy the risks in retaining the concentrated stock position. The adviser might also simulate portfolio returns and the associated probability of achieving Ivy's goals using a range of scenarios for the performance of the concentrated stock position. Framing the effect this one holding may have on the likelihood of achieving her goals may help Ivy agree to reduce the position size. Consideration of certain behavioral biases like mental accounting can improve investor outcomes when they are incorporated in an objective decision-making framework.

SUMMARY

- The primary constraints on an asset allocation decision are asset size, liquidity, time horizon, and other external considerations, such as taxes and regulation.
- The size of an asset owner's portfolio may limit the asset classes accessible to the asset owner. An asset owner's portfolio may be too small—or too large—to capture the returns of certain asset classes or strategies efficiently.
- Complex asset classes and investment vehicles require sufficient governance capacity.
- Large-scale asset owners may achieve operating efficiencies, but they may find it difficult to deploy capital effectively in certain active investment strategies given liquidity conditions and trading costs.
- Smaller portfolios may also be constrained by size. They may be too small to adequately diversify across the range of asset classes and investment managers, or they may have staffing constraints that prevent them from monitoring a complex investment program.

- Investors with smaller portfolios may be constrained in their ability to access private equity, private real estate, hedge funds, and infrastructure investments because of the high required minimum investments and regulatory restrictions associated with those asset classes. Wealthy families may pool assets to meet the required minimums.
- The liquidity needs of the asset owner and the liquidity characteristics of the asset classes each influence the available opportunity set.
- Liquidity needs must also take into consideration the financial strength of the investor and resources beyond those held in the investment portfolio.
- When assessing the appropriateness of any given asset class for a given investor, it is important to evaluate potential liquidity needs in the context of an extreme market stress event.
- An investor's time horizon must be considered in any asset allocation exercise. Changes in human capital and the changing character of liabilities are two important time-related constraints of asset allocation.
- External considerations—such as regulations, tax rules, funding, and financing needs—are also likely to influence the asset allocation decision.
- Taxes alter the distribution of returns by both reducing the expected mean return and muting the dispersion of returns. Asset values and asset risk and return inputs to asset allocation should be modified to reflect the tax status of the investor. Correlation assumptions do not need to be adjusted, but taxes do affect the return and the standard deviation assumptions for each asset class.
- Periodic portfolio rebalancing to return the portfolio to its target strategic asset allocation is an integral part of sound portfolio management. Taxable investors must consider the tax implications of rebalancing.
- Rebalancing thresholds may be wider for taxable portfolios because it takes larger asset class movements to materially alter the risk profile of the taxable portfolio.
- Strategic asset location is the placement of less tax-efficient assets in accounts with more-favorable tax treatment.
- An asset owner's strategic asset allocation should be re-examined periodically, even in the absence of a change in the asset owner's circumstances.
- A special review of the asset allocation policy may be triggered by a change in goals, constraints, or beliefs.
- In some situations, a change to an asset allocation strategy may be implemented without a formal asset allocation study. Anticipating key milestones that would alter the asset owner's risk appetite, and implementing pre-established changes to the asset allocation in response, is often referred to as a "glide path."
- Tactical asset allocation (TAA) allows short-term deviations from the strategic asset allocation (SAA) targets and are expected to increase risk-adjusted return. Using either short-term views or signals, the investor actively re-weights broad asset classes, sectors, or risk-factor premiums. The sizes of these deviations from the SAA are often constrained by the Investment Policy Statement.
- The success of TAA decisions is measured against the performance of the SAA policy portfolio by comparing Sharpe ratios, evaluating the information ratio or the *t*-statistic of the average excess return of the TAA portfolio relative to the SAA portfolio, or plotting outcomes versus the efficient frontier.

- TAA incurs trading and tax costs. Tactical trades can also increase the concentration of risk.
- Discretionary TAA relies on a qualitative interpretation of political, economic, and financial market conditions and is predicated on a belief of persistent manager skill in predicting and timing short-term market moves.
- Systematic TAA relies on quantitative signals to capture documented return anomalies that may be inconsistent with market efficiency.
- The behavioral biases most relevant in asset allocation include loss aversion, the illusion of control, mental accounting, recency bias, framing, and availability bias.
- An effective investment program will address behavioral biases through a formal asset allocation process with its own objective framework, governance, and controls.
- In goals-based investing, loss-aversion bias can be mitigated by framing risk in terms of shortfall probability or by funding high-priority goals with low-risk assets.
- The cognitive bias, illusion of control, and hindsight bias can all be mitigated by using a formal asset allocation process that uses long-term return and risk forecasts, optimization constraints anchored around asset class weights in the global market portfolio, and strict policy ranges.
- Goals-based investing incorporates the mental accounting bias directly into the asset allocation solution by aligning each goal with a discrete sub-portfolio.
- A formal asset allocation policy with pre-specified allowable ranges may constrain recency bias.
- The framing bias effect can be mitigated by presenting the possible asset allocation choices with multiple perspectives on the risk/reward trade-off.
- Familiarity bias, a form of availability bias, most commonly results in an overweight in home country securities and may also cause investors to inappropriately compare their investment decisions (and performance) to other organizations. Familiarity bias can be mitigated by using the global market portfolio as the starting point in developing the asset allocation and by carefully evaluating any potential deviations from this baseline portfolio.
- A strong governance framework with the appropriate level of expertise and well-documented investment beliefs increases the likelihood that shifts in asset allocation are made objectively and in accordance with those beliefs. This will help to mitigate the effect that behavioral biases may have on the long-term success of the investment program.

REFERENCES

Bader, Lawrence N. and Jeremy Gold. 2007. "The Case against Stock in Public Pension Funds." *Financial Analysts Journal* 63, vol. , no. 1 (January/February): 55–62. 10.2469/faj.v63.n1.4407

Bodie, Zvi, Robert C. Merton, and William F. Samuelson. 1992. "Labor Supply Flexibility and Portfolio Choice in a Life Cycle Model." *Journal of Economic Dynamics & Control* 16, vol. : 427–449. 10.1016/0165-1889(92)90044-F

Chen, Joseph, Harrison Hong, Ming Huang, and Jeffrey Kubik. 2004. "Does Fund Size Erode Mutual Fund Performance? The Role of Liquidity and Organization." *American Economic Review* 94, vol. , no. 5: 1276–1302. 10.1257/0002828043052277

Cooper, Stephen and David Bianco. 2003. "Q-Series™: Pension Fund Asset Allocation." UBS Investment Research (September).

Das, Sanjiv, Harry Markowitz, Jonathan Scheid, and Meir Statman. 2010. "Portfolio Optimization with Mental Accounts." *Journal of Financial and Quantitative Analysis* 45, vol. , no. 2: 311–334. 10.1017/S0022109010000141

Das, Sanjiv, Harry Markowitz, Jonathan Scheid, and Meir Statman. 2011. "Portfolios for Investors Who Want to Reach Their Goals While Staying on the Mean–Variance Efficient Frontier." *Journal of Wealth Management* 14, vol. , no. 2 (Fall): 25–31. 10.3905/jwm.2011.14.2.025

Dyck, Alexander and Lukasz Pomorski. 2011. "Is Bigger Better? Size and Performance in Pension Plan Management." Rotman School of Management Working Paper No. 1690724.

Horan, Stephen and Ashraf Al Zaman. 2008. "Tax-Adjusted Portfolio Optimization and Asset Location: Extensions and Synthesis." *Journal of Wealth Management* 11, vol. , no. 3: 56–73. 10.3905/JWM.2008.11.3.056

Kritzman, Mark. 2015. "What Practitioners Need to Know about Time Diversification (corrected March 2015)." *Financial Analysts Journal* 71, vol. , no. 1 (January/February): 29–34. 10.2469/faj.v71.n1.4

Mladina, Peter. 2011. "Portfolio Implications of Triple Net Returns." *Journal of Wealth Management* 13, vol. , no. 4 (Spring): 51–59. 10.3905/jwm.2011.13.4.051

Pollet, Joshua and Mungo Wilson. 2008. "How Does Size Affect Mutual Fund Behavior?" *Journal of Finance* 63, vol. , no. 6 (December): 2941–2969. 10.1111/j.1540-6261.2008.01417.x

Reichenstein, William. 2006. "After-Tax Asset Allocation." *Financial Analysts Journal* 62, vol. , no. 4 (July/August): 14–19. 10.2469/faj.v62.n4.4183

Samuelson, Paul A. 1963. "Risk and Uncertainty: A Fallacy of Large Numbers." *Scientia* 57, vol. , no. 98: 108–113.

Samuelson, Paul A. 1969. "Lifetime Portfolio Selection by Dynamic Stochastic Programming." *Review of Economics and Statistics* 51, vol. , no. 3: 239–246. 10.2307/1926559

Stein, Jeremy. 2002. "Information Production and Capital Allocation: Decentralized versus Hierarchical Firms." *Journal of Finance* 57, vol. , no. 5 (October): 1891–1921. 10.1111/0022-1082.00483

Turvey, Philip, Anup Basu, and Peter Verhoeven. 2013. "Embedded Tax Liabilities and Portfolio Choice." *Journal of Portfolio Management* 39, vol. , no. 3: 93–101. 10.3905/jpm.2013.39.3.093

PRACTICE PROBLEMS

The following information relates to questions 1-7

Elsbeth Quinn and Dean McCall are partners at Camel Asset Management (CAM). Quinn advises high-net-worth individuals, and McCall specializes in retirement plans for institutions.

Quinn meets with Neal and Karina Martin, both age 44. The Martins plan to retire at age 62. Twenty percent of the Martins' $600,000 in financial assets is held in cash and earmarked for funding their daughter Lara's university studies, which begin in one year. Lara's education and their own retirement are the Martins' highest-priority goals. Last week, the Martins learned that Lara was awarded a four-year full scholarship for university. Quinn reviews how the scholarship might affect the Martins' asset allocation strategy.

The Martins have assets in both taxable and tax-deferred accounts. For baseline retirement needs, Quinn recommends that the Martins maintain their current overall 60% equity/40% bonds (± 8% rebalancing range) strategic asset allocation. Quinn calculates that given current financial assets and expected future earnings, the Martins could reduce future retirement savings by 15% and still comfortably retire at 62. The Martins wish to allocate that 15% to a sub-portfolio with the goal of making a charitable gift to their alma mater from their estate. Although the gift is a low-priority goal, the Martins want the sub-portfolio to earn the highest return possible. Quinn promises to recommend an asset allocation strategy for the Martins' aspirational goal.

Next, Quinn discusses taxation of investments with the Martins. Their interest income is taxed at 35%, and capital gains and dividends are taxed at 20%. The Martins want to minimize taxes. Based on personal research, Neal makes the following two statements:

Statement 1	The after-tax return volatility of assets held in taxable accounts will be less than the pre-tax return volatility.
Statement 2	Assets that receive more favorable tax treatment should be held in tax-deferred accounts.

The equity portion of the Martins' portfolios produced an annualized return of 20% for the past three years. As a result, the Martins' equity allocation in both their taxable and tax-deferred portfolios has increased to 71%, with bonds falling to 29%. The Martins want to keep the strategic asset allocation risk levels the same in both types of retirement portfolios. Quinn discusses rebalancing; however, Neal is somewhat reluctant to take money out of stocks, expressing confidence that strong investment returns will continue.

Quinn's CAM associate, McCall, meets with Bruno Snead, the director of the Katt Company Pension Fund (KCPF). The strategic asset allocation for the fund is 65% stocks/35% bonds. Because of favorable returns during the past eight recession-free years, the KCPF is now overfunded. However, there are early signs of the economy weakening. Since Katt Company is in a cyclical industry, the Pension Committee is concerned about future market and economic risk and fears that the high-priority goal of maintaining a fully funded status may be adversely affected. McCall suggests to Snead that the KCPF might benefit from an updated IPS. Following a thorough review, McCall recommends a new IPS and strategic asset allocation.

The proposed IPS revisions include a plan for short-term deviations from strategic asset allocation targets. The goal is to benefit from equity market trends by automatically increasing (decreasing) the allocation to equities by 5% whenever the S&P 500 Index 50-day moving average crosses above (below) the 200-day moving average.

1. Given the change in funding of Lara's education, the Martins' strategic asset allocation would *most likely* decrease exposure to:

   A. cash.

   B. bonds.

   C. equities.

2. The *most* appropriate asset allocation for the Martins' new charitable gift sub-portfolio is:

   A. 40% equities/60% bonds.

   B. 70% equities/30% bonds.

   C. 100% equities/0% bonds.

3. Which of Neal's statements regarding the taxation of investments is correct?

   A. Statement 1 only

   B. Statement 2 only

   C. Both Statement 1 and Statement 2

4. Given the Martins' risk and tax preferences, the taxable portfolio should be rebalanced:

   A. less often than the tax-deferred portfolio.

   B. as often as the tax-deferred portfolio.

   C. more often than the tax-deferred portfolio.

5. During the rebalancing discussion, which behavioral bias does Neal exhibit?

   A. Framing bias

   B. Loss aversion

   C. Representativeness bias

6. Given McCall's IPS recommendation, the *most* appropriate new strategic asset allocation for the KCPF is:

   A. 40% stocks/60% bonds.

   B. 65% stocks/35% bonds.

   C. 75% stocks/25% bonds.

7. The proposal for short-term adjustments to the KCPF asset allocation strategy is

known as:

A. de-risking.

B. systematic tactical asset allocation.

C. discretionary tactical asset allocation.

The following information relates to questions 8-13

Rebecca Mayer is an asset management consultant for institutions and high-net-worth individuals. Mayer meets with Sebastian Capara, the newly appointed Investment Committee chairman for the Kinkardeen University Endowment (KUE), a very large tax-exempt fund.

Capara and Mayer review KUE's current and strategic asset allocations, which are presented in Exhibit 1. Capara informs Mayer that over the last few years, Kinkardeen University has financed its operations primarily from tuition, with minimal need of financial support from KUE. Enrollment at the University has been rising in recent years, and the Board of Trustees expects enrollment growth to continue for the next five years. Consequently, the board expects very modest endowment support to be needed during that time. These expectations led the Investment Committee to approve a decrease in the endowment's annual spending rate starting in the next fiscal year.

Exhibit 1: Kinkardeen University Endowment—Strategic Asset Allocation Policy

Asset Class	Current Weight	Target Allocation	Lower Policy Limit	Upper Policy Limit
Developed markets equity	30%	30%	25%	35%
Emerging markets equity	28%	30%	25%	35%
Investment-grade bonds	15%	20%	15%	25%
Private real estate equity	15%	10%	5%	15%
Infrastructure	12%	10%	5%	15%

As an additional source of alpha, Mayer proposes tactically adjusting KUE's asset-class weights to profit from short-term return opportunities. To confirm his understanding of tactical asset allocation (TAA), Capara tells Mayer the following:

Statement 1 The Sharpe ratio is suitable for measuring the success of TAA relative to SAA.

Statement 2 Discretionary TAA attempts to capture asset-class-level return anomalies that have been shown to have some predictability and persistence.

Statement 3 TAA allows a manager to deviate from the IPS asset-class upper and lower limits if the shift is expected to produce higher expected risk-adjusted returns.

Capara asks Mayer to recommend a TAA strategy based on excess return forecasts for the asset classes in KUE's portfolio, as shown in Exhibit 2.

Exhibit 2: Short-Term Excess Return Forecast

Asset Class	Expected Excess Return
Developed markets equity	2%
Emerging markets equity	5%
Investment-grade bonds	−3%
Private real estate equity	3%
Infrastructure	−1%

Following her consultation with Capara, Mayer meets with Roger Koval, a member of a wealthy family. Although Koval's baseline needs are secured by a family trust, Koval has a personal portfolio to fund his lifestyle goals.

In Koval's country, interest income is taxed at progressively higher income tax rates. Dividend income and long-term capital gains are taxed at lower tax rates relative to interest and earned income. In taxable accounts, realized capital losses can be used to offset current or future realized capital gains. Koval is in a high tax bracket, and his taxable account currently holds, in equal weights, high-yield bonds, investment-grade bonds, and domestic equities focused on long-term capital gains.

Koval asks Mayer about adding new asset classes to the taxable portfolio. Mayer suggests emerging markets equity given its positive short-term excess return forecast. However, Koval tells Mayer he is not interested in adding emerging markets equity to the account because he is convinced it is too risky. Koval justifies this belief by referring to significant losses the family trust suffered during the recent economic crisis.

Mayer also suggests using two mean–variance portfolio optimization scenarios for the taxable account to evaluate potential asset allocations. Mayer recommends running two optimizations: one on a pre-tax basis and another on an after-tax basis.

8. The change in the annual spending rate, in conjunction with the board's expectations regarding future enrollment and the need for endowment support, could justify that KUE's target weight for:

   A. infrastructure be increased.

   B. investment-grade bonds be increased.

   C. private real estate equity be decreased.

9. Which of Capara's statements regarding tactical asset allocation is correct?

   A. Statement 1

   B. Statement 2

   C. Statement 3

10. Based on Exhibits 1 and 2, to attempt to profit from the short-term excess return

forecast, Capara should increase KUE's portfolio allocation to:

A. developed markets equity and decrease its allocation to infrastructure.

B. emerging markets equity and decrease its allocation to investment-grade bonds.

C. developed markets equity and increase its allocation to private real estate equity.

11. Given Koval's current portfolio and the tax laws of the country in which he lives, Koval's portfolio would be more tax efficient if he reallocated his taxable account to hold more:

A. high-yield bonds.

B. investment-grade bonds.

C. domestic equities focused on long-term capital gain opportunities.

12. Koval's attitude toward emerging markets equity reflects which of the following behavioral biases?

A. Hindsight bias

B. Availability bias

C. Illusion of control

13. In both of Mayer's optimization scenarios, which of the following model inputs could be used without adjustment?

A. Expected returns

B. Correlation of returns

C. Standard deviations of returns

The following information relates to questions 14-18

Emma Young, a 47-year-old single mother of two daughters, ages 7 and 10, recently sold a business for $5.5 million net of taxes and put the proceeds into a money market account. Her other assets include a tax-deferred retirement account worth $3.0 million, a $500,000 after-tax account designated for her daughters' education, a $400,000 after-tax account for unexpected needs, and her home, which she owns outright.

Her living expenses are fully covered by her job. Young wants to retire in 15 years and to fund her retirement from existing assets. An orphan at eight who experienced childhood financial hardships, she places a high priority on retirement security and wants to avoid losing money in any of her three accounts.

14. **Identify** the behavioral biases Young is *most likely* exhibiting. **Justify** each

response.

Bias	Justification
Loss Aversion	
Illusion of Control	
Mental Accounting	
Representative Bias	
Framing Bias	
Availability Bias	

15. A broker proposes to Young three portfolios, shown in Exhibit 1. The broker also provides Young with asset class estimated returns and portfolio standard deviations in Exhibit 2 and Exhibit 3, respectively. The broker notes that there is a $500,000 minimum investment requirement for alternative assets. Finally, because the funds in the money market account are readily investible, the broker suggests using that account only for this initial investment round.

Exhibit 1: Proposed Portfolios

Asset Class	Portfolio 1	Portfolio 2	Portfolio 3
Municipal Bonds	5%	35%	30%
Small-Cap Equities	50%	10%	35%
Large-Cap Equities	35%	50%	35%
Private Equity	10%	5%	0%
Total	100%	100%	100%

Exhibit 2: Asset Class Pre-Tax Returns

Asset Class	Pre-Tax Return
Municipal Bonds	3%
Small-Cap Equities	12%
Large-Cap Equities	10%
Private Equity	25%

Exhibit 3: Portfolio Standard Deviations

Proposed Portfolio	Post-Tax Standard Deviation
Portfolio 1	28.2%
Portfolio 2	16.3%
Portfolio 3	15.5%

Young wants to earn at least 6.0% after tax per year, without taking on additional incremental risk. Young's capital gains and overall tax rate is 25%.

Determine which proposed portfolio *most closely* meets Young's desired objectives. **Justify** your response.

Portfolio 1	Portfolio 2	Portfolio 3
Justify your response.		

16. The broker suggests that Young rebalance her $5.5 million money market account and the $3.0 million tax-deferred retirement account periodically in order to maintain their targeted allocations. The broker proposes the same risk profile for the equity positions with two potential target equity allocations and rebalancing ranges for the two accounts as follows:

   - Alternative 1: 80% equities +/– 8.0% rebalancing range
   - Alternative 2: 75% equities +/– 10.7% rebalancing range

   Determine which alternative *best* fits each account. **Justify** each selection.

Account	Alternative	Justify each selection.
$5.5 Million Account	Alternative 1 Alternative 2	
$3.0 Million Account	Alternative 1 Alternative 2	

17. Ten years later, Young is considering an early-retirement package offer. The package would provide continuing salary and benefits for three years. The broker recommends a special review of Young's financial plan to assess potential changes to the existing allocation strategy.

   Identify the *primary* reason for the broker's reassessment of Young's circumstances. **Justify** your response.

Change in goals	Change in constraints	Change in beliefs
Justify your response.		

18. Young decides to accept the retirement offer. Having very low liquidity needs, she wants to save part of the retirement payout for unforeseen costs that might occur more than a decade in the future. The broker's view on long term stock market prospects is positive and recommends additional equity investment.

   Determine which of Young's accounts (education, retirement, reallocated money market, or unexpected needs) is *best* suited for implementing the broker's recommendation.

Account	Justification
Education	
Reallocated Money Market	

Retirement	
Unexpected Needs	

The following information relates to questions 19-20

Mark DuBord, a financial adviser, works with two university foundations, the Titan State Foundation (Titan) and the Fordhart University Foundation (Fordhart). He meets with each university foundation investment committee annually to review fund objectives and constraints.

Titan's portfolio has a market value of $10 million. After his annual meeting with its investment committee, DuBord notes the following points:

- Titan must spend 3% of its beginning-of-the-year asset value annually to meet legal obligations.
- The investment committee seeks exposure to private equity investments and requests DuBord's review of the Sun-Fin Private Equity Fund as a potential new investment.
- A recent declining trend in enrollment is expected to continue. This is a concern because it has led to a loss of operating revenue from tuition.
- Regulatory sanctions and penalties are likely to result in lower donations over the next five years.

DuBord supervises two junior analysts and instructs one to formulate new allocations for Titan. This analyst proposes the allocation presented in Exhibit 1.

Exhibit 1: Fund Information for Titan

Fund Name	Existing Allocation	Proposed Allocation	Fund Size in Billions (AUM)	Fund Minimum Investment
Global Equity Fund	70%	70%	$25	$500,000
Investment-Grade Bond Fund	27%	17%	$50	$250,000
Sun-Fin Private Equity Fund	0%	10%	$0.40	$1,000,000
Cash Equivalent Fund	3%	3%	$50	$100,000

19. **Discuss** *two* reasons why the proposed asset allocation is inappropriate for Titan.

20. The Fordhart portfolio has a market value of $2 billion. After his annual meeting with its investment committee, DuBord notes the following points:

- Fordhart must spend 3% of its beginning-of-the-year asset value annually to meet legal obligations.
- The investment committee seeks exposure to private equity investments and requests that DuBord review the CFQ Private Equity Fund as a potential new investment.

- Enrollment is strong and growing, leading to increased operating revenues from tuition.
- A recent legal settlement eliminated an annual obligation of $50 million from the portfolio to support a biodigester used in the university's Center for Renewable Energy.

DuBord instructs his second junior analyst to formulate new allocations for Fordhart. This analyst proposes the allocation presented in Exhibit 2.

Exhibit 2: Fund Information for Fordhart

Fund Name	Existing Allocation	Proposed Allocation	Fund Size in Billions (AUM)	Fund Minimum Investment
Large-Cap Equity Fund	49%	29%	$50	$250,000
Investment-Grade Bond Fund	49%	59%	$80	$500,000
CFQ Private Equity Fund	0%	10%	$0.5	$5,000,000
Cash Equivalent Fund	2%	2%	$50	$250,000

Discuss *two* reasons why the proposed asset allocation is inappropriate for Fordhart.

SOLUTIONS

1. A is correct. The changing character of liabilities through time affects the asset allocation to fund those liabilities. The Martins' investment horizon for some of their assets has changed. The amount of liquidity needed for Lara's near-term education has been greatly reduced owing to the receipt of the scholarship. The Martins will likely still have to pay for some university-related expenses; however, a large part of the $120,000 in cash that is earmarked for Lara's expenses can now be allocated to the Martins' long-term goal of early retirement. Retirement is 18 years away, much longer than the one- to five-year horizon for university expenses. Therefore, the Martins' allocation to cash would likely decrease.

2. C is correct. The Martins' sub-portfolio is aspirational and a low priority. Investors are usually willing to take more risk on lower-priority, aspirational portfolios. The charitable gift will be made from their estate, which indicates a long time horizon. In addition, the Martins want the highest return possible. Therefore, the highest allocation to equities is most appropriate.

3. A is correct. Taxes alter the distribution of returns by both reducing the expected mean return and muting the dispersion of returns. The portion of an owner's taxable assets that are eligible for lower tax rates and deferred capital gains tax treatment should first be allocated to the investor's taxable accounts.

4. A is correct. The Martins wish to maintain the same risk level for both retirement accounts based on their strategic asset allocation. However, more frequent rebalancing exposes the taxable asset owner to realized taxes that could have otherwise been deferred or even avoided. Rebalancing is discretionary, and the Martins' also wish to minimize taxes. Because after-tax return volatility is lower than pre-tax return volatility, it takes larger asset-class movements to materially alter the risk profile of a taxable portfolio. This suggests that rebalancing ranges for a taxable portfolio can be wider than those of a tax-exempt/tax-deferred portfolio with a similar risk profile; thus, rebalancing occurs less frequently.

5. C is correct. Representativeness, or recency, bias is the tendency to overweight the importance of the most recent observations and information relative to a longer-dated or more comprehensive set of long-term observations and information. Return chasing is a common result of this bias, and it results in overweighting asset classes with strong recent performance.

6. A is correct. McCall recommends a new IPS. Changes in the economic environment and capital market expectations or changes in the beliefs of committee members are factors that may lead to an altering of the principles that guide investment activities. Because the plan is now overfunded, there is less need to take a higher level of equity risk. The Pension Committee is concerned about the impact of future market and economic risks on the funding status of the plan. Katt Company operates in a cyclical industry and could have difficulty making pension contributions during a recession. Therefore, a substantial reduction in the allocation to stocks and an increase in bonds reduce risk. The 40% stocks/60% bonds alternative increases the allocation to bonds from 35% to 60%. Increasing the fixed-income allocation should moderate plan risk, provide a better hedge for liabilities, and reduce contribution uncertainty.

7. B is correct. Using rules-based, quantitative signals, systematic tactical asset allocation (TAA) attempts to capture asset-class-level return anomalies that have been shown to have some predictability and persistence. Trend signals are widely

used in systematic TAA. A moving-average crossover is a trend signal that indicates an upward (downward) trend when the moving average of the shorter time frame, 50 days, is above (below) the moving average of the longer time frame, 200 days.

8. A is correct. A lower annual spending rate, in addition to the board's expectations of rising enrollment and minimal need for endowment support over the next five years, indicates a decreased need for liquidity. Therefore, KUE could justify an increase in the strategic allocation to less liquid asset classes (such as private real estate equity and infrastructure) and a decrease in the strategic allocation to liquid assets (such as investment-grade bonds).

9. A is correct. The Sharpe ratio is suitable for measuring the success of TAA relative to SAA. Specifically, the success of TAA decisions can be evaluated by comparing the Sharpe ratio realized under the TAA with the Sharpe ratio that would have been realized under the SAA.

10. A is correct. The forecast for expected excess returns is positive for developed markets equity and negative for infrastructure. Therefore, to attempt to profit from the short-term excess return forecast, KUE can overweight developed markets equity and underweight infrastructure. These adjustments to the asset-class weights are within KUE's lower and upper policy limits.

11. C is correct. As a general rule, the portion of a taxable asset owner's assets that are eligible for lower tax rates and deferred capital gains tax treatment should first be allocated to the investor's taxable accounts. Assets that generate returns mainly from interest income tend to be less tax efficient and in Koval's country are taxed at progressively higher rates. Also, the standard deviation (volatility) of after-tax returns is lower when equities are held in a taxable account. Therefore, Koval's taxable account would become more tax efficient if it held more domestic equities focused on long-term capital gain opportunities.

12. B is correct. Availability bias is an information-processing bias in which people take a mental shortcut when estimating the probability of an outcome based on how easily the outcome comes to mind. On the basis of the losses incurred by his family trust during the recent economic crisis, Koval expresses a strong preference for avoiding the emerging markets equity asset class. Such behavior is consistent with availability bias, where investors who personally experience an adverse event are likely to assign a higher probability to such an event occurring again.

13. B is correct. After-tax portfolio optimization requires adjusting each asset class's expected return and risk for expected taxes. The correlation of returns is not affected by taxes and does not require an adjustment when performing after-tax portfolio optimization.

14. Of the six potential behavioral biases, Young is most likely exhibiting three as explained below.

Identify the behavioral biases Young is *most likely* exhibiting. (Circle the correct answers.) **Justify** each response.

Bias	Justification

Loss Aversion	Under loss-aversion bias, people strongly prefer avoiding losses as opposed to achieving gains and they assign a greater weight to potential negative outcomes than positive ones. Young's strong emphasis on retirement security and her desire to avoid losing money indicates that she has a loss-aversion bias. This bias could interfere with her willingness to maintain ideal asset allocations during times of negative returns.
Illusion of Control	
Mental Accounting	Under mental accounting bias, people treat one sum of money differently from another sum based solely on the mental account to which the money is assigned. Young is considering her \$3 million tax-deferred retirement account, her \$500,000 account for the girls' education, and the \$400,000 emergency account separately, rather than seeing them all as a combined investable total. In doing this, she sets herself up for the possibility of sub-optimal allocation.
Representative Bias	
Framing Bias	
Availability Bias	Under availability bias, people take a mental shortcut when estimating the probability of an outcome based on how easily the outcome comes to mind. Easily recalled outcomes are often perceived as being more likely than those that are harder to recall or understand. Young's strong emphasis on retirement security and her desire to avoid losing money both could be driven by her strong memories of her childhood financial hardships.

15.

Determine which proposed portfolio *most closely* meets Young's desired objectives. (Circle one.)

Portfolio 1	Portfolio 2	Portfolio 3

Justify your response.

Portfolio 3 comes closest to meeting Young's desire to earn at least 6% after tax per year without taking on additional incremental risk. Portfolio 3 offers a lower standard deviation than Portfolio 2, as summarized in Exhibit 3, while producing approximately the same return. Portfolio 1 achieves the highest returns but at a much greater level of volatility than Portfolio 3, not satisfying Young's risk criterion.

Given the \$500,000 minimum investment requirement for alternative assets, at Young's total portfolio size of \$5.5 million, the suggested 5% allocation to private equity in Portfolio 2 results in only a \$275,000 exposure, insufficient to invest in private equity. Thus, Portfolio 2, as presented, is not viable, whereas Portfolio 1, with a private equity investment of \$550,000, meets the minimum requirement for alternative investments. This minimum investment requirement is not an issue for Portfolio 3 because it has no private equity component.

Asset Class	Portfolio 3	Pre-Tax Return	Post-Tax Return	Resulting Return
Municipal Bonds	30%	3%	3.00%	0.90%
Small-Cap Equities	35%	12%	9.00%	3.15%
Large-Cap Equities	35%	10%	7.50%	2.63%

Asset Class	Portfolio 3	Pre-Tax Return	Post-Tax Return	Resulting Return
Private Equity	0%	25%	18.75%	0.00%
Total	100%			6.68%

16.

Determine which alternative (circle one) *best* fits each account.

Account	Alternative	**Justify** each selection.
$5.5 Million Account	Alternative 1 Alternative 2	The $5.5 million account is after tax. Because after-tax volatility is lower than pre-tax volatility, the rebalancing range for an after-tax account is wider. The range reflected for Alternative 2 is 10.7%, whereas the range for Alternative 1 is 8.0% (to achieve the same risk constraint), reflecting the impact of taxes on the $5.5 million account. In addition, asset sales in the after-tax account result in taxes due. A wider target range allows more price movement before the rebalancing range is exceeded (and a decision must be made to initiate an asset sale, incur associated tax payments, and rebalance back to the target equity allocation). The after-tax account range is calculated by adjusting the pre-tax range for taxes. After-tax rebalancing range = Pre-tax rebalancing range/(1 – Tax rate). 8.0%/(1 – 0.25) 10.67%
$3.0 Million Account	Alternative 1 Alternative 2	The $3.0 million is a tax-deferred retirement account. Because pre-tax volatility is higher than after-tax volatility, the rebalancing range for a pre-tax account is narrower. The range reflected for Alternative 1 is 8.0%, whereas the range for Alternative 2 is 10.7% (to achieve the same risk constraint), reflecting the impact of tax deferral on the $3.0 million account versus the effect of taxes on the $5.5 million account.

17.

Identify the *primary* reason for the broker's reassessment of Young's circumstances. (Circle one.)

Change in goals	Change in constraints	Change in beliefs

Justify your response.
A change in constraints relates to material changes in constraints, such as time horizon, liquidity needs, asset size, and regulatory or other external constraints. In this case, Young's circumstances have changed; she is considering accepting the offer and retiring five years sooner than she originally anticipated. A change in an investor's personal circumstances that may alter her risk appetite or risk capacity is considered to be a change in *goals*. In this circumstance, Young's risk appetite or risk capacity have not changed, whereas the time horizon associated with her goals has. A change in the investment beliefs or principles guiding an investor's investment activities is considered to be a change in *beliefs*. In this circumstance, Young's guiding principles have not changed.

Young decides to accept the retirement offer. Having very low liquidity needs, she wants to save part of the retirement payout for unforeseen costs that might occur more than a decade in the future. The broker's view on long-term stock market prospects is positive and recommends additional equity investment.

18.

Determine which of Young's accounts is *best* suited for implementing the broker's recommendation. (Circle one.)

Account	Justification
Education	
Reallocated Money Market	As a general rule, the portion of a taxable asset owner's assets that is eligible for lower tax rates and deferred capital gains tax treatment should first be allocated to the investor's taxable accounts. Equities should generally be held in taxable accounts, whereas taxable bonds and high turnover trading strategies should generally be located in tax-exempt and tax-deferred accounts. The reallocated money market account is a taxable account, whereas the retirement account is tax-deferred. The unexpected needs account requires liquidity (in case of unexpected needs), so it is better suited for shorter-term positions. Given the ages of Young's two daughters, now 17 and 20, the education account is most likely currently funding college expenses and will be for the next several years. Accordingly, it needs to be invested in highly liquid assets to cover these costs.
Retirement	
Unexpected Needs	

19. The proposed asset allocation for Titan is not appropriate because:

1. Given the shift in enrollment trends and declining donations resulting from the sanctions, Titan will likely need greater liquidity in the future because of the increased probability of higher outflows to support university operations. The proposed asset allocation shifts Titan's allocation into risky assets (increases the relative equity holdings and decreases the relative bond holdings), which would introduce greater uncertainty as to their future value.
2. Titan is relatively small for the proposed addition of private equity. Access to such an asset class as private equity may be constrained for smaller asset owners, such as Titan, who may lack the related internal investment expertise. Additionally, the Sun-Fin Private Equity Fund minimum investment level is \$1 million. This level of investment in private equity would be 10% of

Titan's total portfolio value. Given Titan's declining financial position due to declining enrollments and its resulting potential need for liquidity, private equity at this minimum level of investment is not appropriate for Titan.

20. The proposed asset allocation for Fordhart is inappropriate because:

1. Given the increasing enrollment trends and recent favorable legal settlement, Fordhart will likely require lower liquidity in the future. The proposed allocation shifts Fordhart's portfolio away from risky assets (decreases the relative equity holdings and increases the relative bond holdings).
2. The proposed 10% allocation to private equity creates an overly concentrated position in the underlying investment. A 10% allocation to the CFQ Private Equity Fund is $200 million (10% of Fordhart's $2 billion). The CFQ Private Equity Fund has assets under management (AUM) of $500 million. Hence, Fordhart would own 40% of the entire CFQ Private Equity Fund. This position exposes both Fordhart and the CFQ fund to an undesirable level of operational risk.

Glossary

Absolute return benchmark A minimum target return that an investment manager is expected to beat.

Accrual taxes Taxes levied and paid on a periodic basis.

Accumulation phase Phase where the government predominantly contributes to a sovereign wealth pension reserve fund.

Active management A portfolio management approach that allows risk factor mismatches relative to a benchmark index causing potentially significant return differences between the active portfolio and the underlying benchmark.

Active return The return on a portfolio minus the return on the portfolio's benchmark.

Active risk The standard deviation of active returns.

Active risk budgeting Risk budgeting that concerns active risk (risk relative to a portfolio's benchmark).

Active share A measure of how similar a portfolio is to its benchmark. A manager who precisely replicates the benchmark will have an active share of zero; a manager with no holdings in common with the benchmark will have an active share of one.

Aggregate wealth The total value of all assets owned, encompassing personal property, financial assets, real assets, and rights.

Arithmetic attribution An attribution approach which explains the arithmetic difference between the portfolio return and its benchmark return. The single-period attribution effects sum to the excess return, however, when combining multiple periods, the sub-period attribution effects will not sum to the excess return.

Ask price The price at which a trader will sell a specified quantity of a security. Also called *ask*, *offer price*, or *offer*.

Asset-only With respect to asset allocation, an approach that focuses directly on the characteristics of the assets without explicitly modeling the liabilities.

Authority bias A behavioral bias which involves groups deferring to a group member that is a subject matter expert or in a position of authority.

Aversion to complexity A behavioral phenomenon of groups in many professional contexts, in which disproportionate attention is given to trivial issues at the expense of important but harder-to-grasp or contested topics.

Back-fill bias The distortion in index or peer group data which results when returns are reported to a database only after they are known to be good returns.

Base With respect to a foreign exchange quotation of the price of one unit of a currency, the currency referred to in "one unit of a currency."

Basis risk The possibility that the expected value of a derivative differs unexpectedly from that of the underlying.

Bear spread An option strategy that becomes more valuable when the price of the underlying asset declines, so requires buying one option and writing another with a *lower* exercise price. A put bear spread involves buying a put with a higher exercise price and selling a put with a lower exercise price. A bear spread can also be executed with calls.

Best ask The offer to sell with the lowest ask price. Also called *best offer* or *inside ask*.

Best bid The highest bid in the market.

Best offer The lowest offer (ask price) in the market.

Best-in-class An ESG implementation approach that seeks to identify the most favorable companies and sectors based on ESG considerations. Also called *positive screening*.

Bid price In a price quotation, the price at which the party making the quotation is willing to buy a specified quantity of an asset or security.

Bid–ask spread The ask price minus the bid price.

Buffering Establishing ranges around breakpoints that define whether a stock belongs in one index or another.

Bull spread An option strategy that becomes more valuable when the price of the underlying asset rises, so requires buying one option and writing another with a *higher* exercise price. A call bull spread involves buying a call with a lower exercise price and selling a call with a higher exercise price. A bull spread can also be executed with puts.

Business cycle Fluctuations in GDP in relation to long-term trend growth, usually lasting 9-11 years.

Calendar rebalancing Rebalancing a portfolio to target weights on a periodic basis; for example, monthly, quarterly, semiannually, or annually.

Calendar spread A strategy in which one sells an option and buys the same type of option but with different expiration dates, on the same underlying asset and with the same strike. When the investor buys the more distant (near-term) call and sells the near-term (more distant) call, it is a long (short) calendar spread.

Canada model Characterized by a high allocation to alternatives. Unlike the endowment model, however, the Canada model relies more on internally managed assets. The innovative features of the Canada model are the: a) reference portfolio, b) total portfolio approach, and c) active management.

Capital market expectations (CME) Expectations concerning the risk and return prospects of asset classes.

Capital sufficiency analysis The process of evaluating whether a client has sufficient capital resources to achieve their financial goals and objectives; it considers the client's assets, liabilities, income, expenses, risk tolerance, time horizon, and other relevant factors.

Capture ratio A measure of the manager's gain or loss relative to the gain or loss of the benchmark.

Carhart model A four factor model used in performance attribution. The four factors are: market (RMRF), size (SMB), value (HML), and momentum (WML).

Carry trade A trading strategy that involves buying a security and financing it at a rate that is lower than the yield on that security.

Cash flow matching Immunization approach that attempts to ensure that all future liability payouts are matched precisely by cash flows from bonds or fixed-income derivatives.

Cash-secured put An option strategy involving the writing of a put option and simultaneously depositing an amount of money equal to the exercise price into a designated account (this strategy is also called a fiduciary put).

Collar An option position in which the investor is long shares of stock and then buys a put with an exercise price below the current stock price and writes a call with an exercise price above the current stock price. Collars allow a shareholder to acquire downside protection through a protective put but reduce the cash outlay by writing a covered call.

Contingent immunization Hybrid approach that combines immunization with an active management approach when the asset portfolio's value exceeds the present value of the liability portfolio.

Cost basis The initial cost of acquiring an investment including expenses incurred to acquire the investment. Also referred to as simply basis.

Covered call An option strategy in which a long position in an asset is combined with a short position in a call on that asset.

Cross hedge A hedge involving a hedging instrument that is imperfectly correlated with the asset being hedged; an example is hedging a bond investment with futures on a non-identical bond.

Cross-currency basis swap A swap in which notional principals are exchanged because the goal of the transaction is to issue at a more favorable funding rate and swap the amount back to the currency of choice.

Cross-sectional consistency A feature of expectations setting which means that estimates for all classes reflect the same underlying assumptions and are generated with methodologies that reflect or preserve important relationships among the asset classes, such as strong correlations. It is the internal consistency across asset classes.

Currency overlay programs A currency overlay program is a program to manage a portfolio's currency exposures for the case in which those exposures are managed separately from the management of the portfolio itself.

Custom security-based benchmark Benchmark that is custom built to accurately reflect the investment discipline of a particular investment manager. Also called a *strategy benchmark* because it reflects a manager's particular strategy.

Decision-reversal risk The risk of reversing a chosen course of action at the point of maximum loss.

Decumulation phase Phase where the government predominantly withdraws from a sovereign wealth pension reserve fund.

Deferred taxes Taxes postponed until some future date.

Defined benefit A retirement plan in which a plan sponsor commits to paying a specified retirement benefit.

Defined benefit plan Retirement plan that is funded by the employer that guarantees a retirement benefit based on factors such as years of service, salary, and age.

Defined contribution A retirement plan in which contributions are defined but the ultimate retirement benefit is not specified or guaranteed by the plan sponsor.

Defined contribution plan Retirement plan in which the employer, employee, or both contribute to an account in which the employee bears the investment risk.

Delay costs Implicit trading costs that arise from the inability to complete desired trades immediately. Also called *slippage.*

Delta The sensitivity of the derivative price to a small change in the value of the underlying asset.

Delta hedging Hedging that involves matching the price response of the position being hedged over a narrow range of prices.

Demand deposits Accounts that can be drawn upon regularly and without notice. This category includes checking accounts and certain savings accounts that are often accessible through online banks or automated teller machines (ATMs).

Diffusion index Reflects the proportion of the index's components that are moving in a pattern consistent with the overall index.

Dividend capture A trading strategy whereby an equity portfolio manager purchases stocks just before their ex-dividend dates, holds these stocks through the ex-dividend date to earn the right to receive the dividend, and subsequently sells the shares.

Domestic asset An asset that trades in the investor's domestic currency (or home currency).

Domestic currency The currency of the investor, i.e., the currency in which he or she typically makes consumption purchases, e.g., the Swiss franc for an investor domiciled in Switzerland.

Domestic-currency return A rate of return stated in domestic currency terms from the perspective of the investor; reflects both the foreign-currency return on an asset as well as percentage movement in the spot exchange rate between the domestic and foreign currencies.

Drawdown A percentage peak-to-trough reduction in net asset value.

Drawdown duration The total time from the start of the drawdown until the cumulative drawdown recovers to zero.

Due diligence Investigation and analysis in support of an investment action, decision, or recommendation.

Duration matching Immunization approach based on the duration of assets and liabilities. Ideally, the liabilities being matched (the liability portfolio) and the portfolio of assets (the bond portfolio) should be affected similarly by a change in interest rates.

Duration times spread Weighting of spread duration by credit spread in order to incorporate the empirical observation that spread changes for lower-rated bonds tend to be consistent on a percentage, rather than absolute, basis.

Dynamic asset allocation Dynamic asset allocation is an investment strategy premised on long-term asset allocation but employing short-term, tactical trading to maintain investment allocation targets.

Dynamic hedge A hedge requiring adjustment as the price of the hedged asset changes.

Econometrics The application of quantitative modeling and analysis grounded in economic theory to the analysis of economic data.

Economic balance sheet An extended balance sheet that includes the present values of both lifetime earnings and future consumption.

Economic indicators Economic statistics provided by government and established private organizations that contain information on an economy's recent past activity or its current or future position in the business cycle.

Effective federal funds (FFE) rate The fed funds rate actually transacted between depository institutions, not the Fed's target federal funds rate.

Effective spread Two times the difference between the execution price and the midpoint of the market quote at the time an order is entered.

Endowment model Characterized by a high allocation to alternative investments (private investments and hedge funds), significant active management, and externally managed assets.

Enhanced indexing approach Maintains a close link to the benchmark but attempts to generate a modest amount of outperformance relative to the benchmark.

Excess return Used in various senses appropriate to context: 1) The difference between the portfolio return and the benchmark return, which may be either positive or negative; 2) The return in excess of the risk-free rate, thus representing the return for bearing risk.

Exhaustive Covering or containing all possible outcomes.

Extended portfolio assets and liabilities Assets and liabilities beyond those shown on a conventional balance sheet that are relevant in making asset allocation decisions; an example of an extended asset is human capital.

Factor-model-based benchmarks Benchmarks constructed by examining a portfolio's sensitivity to a set of factors, such as the return for a broad market index, company earnings growth, industry, or financial leverage.

Family offices Private firms that offer a range of wealth management services tailored specifically for ultra-high-net-worth individuals.

Foreign assets Assets denominated in currencies other than the investor's home currency.

Foreign currency Currency that is not the currency in which an investor makes consumption purchases, e.g., the US dollar from the perspective of a Swiss investor.

Foreign-currency return The return of the foreign asset measured in foreign-currency terms.

Forward rate bias An empirically observed divergence from interest rate parity conditions that active investors seek to benefit from by borrowing in a lower-yield currency and investing in a higher-yield currency.

Funding currencies The low-yield currencies in which borrowing occurs in a carry trade.

Gamma A numerical measure of how sensitive an option's delta (the sensitivity of the derivative's price) is to a change in the value of the underlying.

General account Account holding assets to fund future liabilities from traditional life insurance and fixed annuities, the products in which the insurer bears all the risks—particularly mortality risk and longevity risk.

Gini coefficient A measure of inequality of wealth, or *i*, that ranges from 0 (perfect equality) to 1 (perfect inequality).

Goals-based With respect to asset allocation or investing, an approach that focuses on achieving an investor's goals (for example, related to supporting lifestyle needs or aspirations) based typically on constructing sub-portfolios aligned with those goals.

Goals-based investing An investment industry term for approaches to investing for individuals and families focused on aligning investments with goals (parallel to liability-driven investing for institutional investors).

Grinold–Kroner model An expression for the expected return on a share as the sum of an expected income return, an expected nominal earnings growth return, and an expected repricing return.

Groupthink A behavioral bias that occurs when a team minimizes conflict and dissent in reaching and maintaining a consensus.

Hedge ratio The proportion of an underlying that will offset the risk associated with a derivative position.

High-net-worth individuals (HNWIs) Individuals with investable assets exceeding a certain minimum level, often as low as USD1 million, but typically more.

High-water mark A measure that reflects the fund's maximum value as of a performance fee payment date net of fees.

Holdings-based attribution A "buy and hold" attribution approach which calculates the return of portfolio and benchmark components based upon the price and foreign exchange rate changes applied to daily snapshots of portfolio holdings.

Holdings-based style analysis A bottom-up style analysis that estimates the risk exposures from the actual securities held in the portfolio at a point in time.

Home bias A preference for securities listed on the exchanges of one's home country.

Home currency See *domestic currency.*

Home-country bias The favoring of domestic over non-domestic investments relative to global market value weights.

Human capital The present value of an individual's future expected labor income.

Impact investing Refers to investments made with the specific intent of generating positive, measurable social and environmental impact alongside a financial return (which differentiates it from philanthropy).

Implementation shortfall (IS) The difference between the return for a notional or paper portfolio, where all transactions are assumed to take place at the manager's decision price, and the portfolio's actual return, which reflects realized transactions, including all fees and costs.

Implied volatility The standard deviation that causes an option pricing model to give the current option price.

Implied volatility surface A three-dimensional plot, for put and call options on the same underlying asset, of days to expiration (*x*-axis), option strike prices (*y*-axis), and implied volatilities (*z*-axis). It simultaneously shows the volatility skew (or smile) and the term structure of implied volatility.

Inflation-linked bonds Debt instruments that link the principal and interest to inflation.

Input uncertainty Uncertainty concerning whether the inputs are correct.

Inside ask See *best ask.*

Inside bid See *best bid.*

Inside spread The spread between the best bid price and the best ask price. Also called the *market bid-ask spread, inside bid-ask spread,* or *market spread.*

Interaction effect The impact of overweighting and underweighting individual securities within sectors that are themselves overweighted or underweighted.

Intertemporal consistency A feature of expectations setting which means that estimates for an asset class over different horizons reflect the same assumptions with respect to the potential paths of returns over time. It is the internal consistency over various time horizons.

Intrinsic value The amount gained (per unit) by an option buyer if an option is exercised at any given point in time. May be referred to as the exercise value of the option.

Investable net worth The sum of liquid assets, such as savings and investment accounts, and less short-term liabilities such as credit card debt.

Investable wealth The sum of liquid assets such as savings and investment accounts.

Investment currencies The high-yielding currencies in a carry trade.

Investment policy statement (IPS) A description of a client's unique investment objectives, risk tolerance, investment time horizon, and other applicable constraints.

Investment style A natural grouping of investment disciplines that has some predictive power in explaining the future dispersion of returns across portfolios.

Key person risk The risk that results from over-reliance on an individual or individuals whose departure would negatively affect an investment manager.

Knock-in/knock-out Features of a vanilla option that is created (or ceases to exist) when the spot exchange rate touches a pre-specified level.

Latency The elapsed time between the occurrence of an event and a subsequent action that depends on that event.

Leading economic indicators Turning points that usually precede those of the overall economy; they are believed to have value for predicting the economy's future state, usually near-term.

Liability driven investing (LDI) model In the LDI model, the primary investment objective is to generate returns sufficient to cover liabilities, with a focus on maximizing expected surplus return (excess return of assets over liabilities) and managing surplus volatility.

Liability glide path A specification of desired proportions of liability-hedging assets and return-seeking assets and the duration of the liability hedge as funded status changes and contributions are made.

Liability-based mandates Mandates managed to match or cover expected liability payments (future cash outflows) with future projected cash inflows.

Liability-driven investing An investment industry term that generally encompasses asset allocation that is focused on funding an investor's liabilities in institutional contexts.

Liability-relative With respect to asset allocation, an approach that focuses directly only on funding liabilities as an investment objective.

Limit order book The book or list of limit orders to buy and sell that pertains to a security.

Limited-life foundations A type of foundation where founders seek to maintain control of spending while they (or their immediate heirs) are still alive.

Longevity risk The risk of exhausting an individual's financial resources before passing away, thereby leaving insufficient capital for living expenses and unmet needs.

Lorenz curve A measure of the cumulative percentage of wealth owned by each percentage of the population.

Macro attribution Attribution at the sponsor level.

Manager peer group See *manager universe.*

Manager universe A broad group of managers with similar investment disciplines. Also called *manager peer group.*

Marginal tax rate The highest rate of tax applied to taxable income.

Market fragmentation Trading the same instrument in multiple venues.

Market impact The effect of the trade on transaction prices. Also called *price impact.*

Micro attribution Attribution at the portfolio manager level.

Midquote price The average, or midpoint, of the prevailing bid and ask prices.

Minimum-variance hedge ratio A mathematical approach to determining the optimal cross hedging ratio.

Mission-related investing Investing aimed at causes promoting positive societal or environmental change.

Model uncertainty Uncertainty as to whether a selected model is correct.

Negative screening An ESG investment style that focuses on the exclusion of certain sectors, companies, or practices in a fund or portfolio on the basis of specific ESG criteria.

Net worth The difference between assets and liabilities.

Non-deliverable forwards Cash-settled forward contracts, used predominately with respect to foreign exchange forwards. Also called *contracts for differences.*

Nonstationarity A characteristic of series of data whose properties, such as mean and variance, are not constant through time. When analyzing historical data it means that different parts of a data series reflect different underlying statistical properties.

Norway model Characterized by an almost exclusive reliance on public equities and fixed income (the traditional 60/40 equity/bond model falls under the Norway model), with largely passively managed assets and with very little to no allocation to alternative investments.

Offer price The price at which a counterparty is willing to sell one unit of the base currency.

Opportunity cost Reflects the foregone opportunity of investing in a different asset. It is typically denoted by the risk-free rate of interest, *r*.

Optional stock dividends A type of dividend in which shareholders may elect to receive either cash or new shares.

Overbought A market condition in which market sentiment is thought to be unsustainably bullish.

Oversold A market condition in which market sentiment is thought to be unsustainably bearish.

Packeting Splitting stock positions into multiple parts.

Parameter uncertainty Uncertainty arising because a quantitative model's parameters are estimated with error.

Participant-switching life-cycle options Automatically switch DC plan members into a more conservative asset mix as their age increases. There may be several automatic de-risking switches at different age targets.

Participant/cohort option Pools the DC plan member with a cohort that has a similar target retirement date.

Passive management A buy-and-hold approach to investing in which an investor does not make portfolio changes based upon short-term expectations of changing market or security performance.

Percent-range rebalancing An approach to rebalancing that involves setting rebalancing thresholds or trigger points, stated as a percentage of the portfolio's value, around target values.

Performance attribution The process of disaggregating a portfolio's return to determine the drivers of its performance.

Personal assets Nonbusiness, on-investment assets including personal property and real property.

Personal property Property owned by individuals that are not real property and not considered investments.

Planned goals Financial objectives that can be reasonably estimated or quantified at the onset and can be achieved within an expected time horizon.

Position delta The overall or portfolio delta. For example, the position delta of a covered call, consisting of long 100 shares and short one at-the-money call, is +50 (= +100 for the shares and -50 for the short ATM call).

Positive screening An ESG implementation approach that seeks to identify the most favorable companies and sectors based on ESG considerations. Also called *best-in-class.*

Price improvement When trade execution prices are better than quoted prices.

Private wealth management Financial planning and investment management to help individual investors, particularly high-net-worth individuals (HNWIs) and ultra-high-net-worth individuals (UHNWIs), manage their wealth.

Protective put A strategy of purchasing an underlying asset and purchasing a put on the same asset.

Pure indexing Attempts to replicate a bond index as closely as possible, targeting zero active return and zero active risk.

Put spread A strategy used to reduce the upfront cost of buying a protective put, it involves buying a put option and writing another put option.

Re-base With reference to index construction, to change the time period used as the base of the index.

Realized volatility Historical volatility, the square root of the realized variance of returns, which is a measure of the range of past price outcomes for the underlying asset.

Rebalancing Adjusting the weights of the constituent securities in an index.

Rebalancing range A range of values for asset class weights defined by trigger points above and below target weights, such that if the portfolio value passes through a trigger point, rebalancing occurs. Also known as a corridor.

Rebate rate The portion of the collateral earnings rate that is repaid to the security borrower by the security lender.

Reduced form models Statistical credit models that solve for the probability of default over a specific time period, using observable company-specific and market-based variables.

Regime The governing set of relationships (between variables) that stem from technological, political, legal, and regulatory environments. Changes in such environments or policy stances can be described as changes in regime.

Relative value A concept that describes the selection of the most attractive individual securities to populate the portfolio with, using ranking and comparing.

Repo rate The interest rate on a repurchase agreement.

Repurchase agreements In repurchase agreements, or repos, a security owner agrees to sell a security for a specific cash amount while simultaneously agreeing to repurchase the security at a specified future date (typically one day later) and price.

Reserve portfolio The component of an insurer's general account that is subject to specific regulatory requirements and is intended to ensure the company's ability to meet its policy liabilities. The assets in the reserve portfolio are managed conservatively and must be highly liquid and low risk.

Resistance levels Price points on dealers' order boards where one would expect to see a clustering of offers.

Return attribution A set of techniques used to identify the sources of the excess return of a portfolio against its benchmark.

Returns-based attribution An attribution approach that uses only the total portfolio returns over a period to identify the components of the investment process that have generated the returns. The Brinson–Hood–Beebower approach is a returns-based attribution approach.

Returns-based benchmarks Benchmarks constructed by examining a portfolio's sensitivity to a set of factors, such as the returns for various style indexes (e.g., small-cap value, small-cap growth, large-cap value, and large-cap growth).

Returns-based style analysis A top-down style analysis that involves estimating the sensitivities of a portfolio to security market indexes.

Reverse repos Repurchase agreements from the standpoint of the lender.

Risk attribution The analysis of the sources of risk.

Risk aversion The dislike for risk such that compensation is required in terms of higher expected returns for assuming higher risk.

Risk budgeting The establishment of objectives for individuals, groups, or divisions of an organization that takes into account the allocation of an acceptable level of risk.

Risk capacity The ability to bear financial risk.

Risk premiums Extra returns expected by investors for bearing some specified risk.

Risk reversal A strategy used to profit from the existence of an implied volatility skew and from changes in its shape over time. A combination of long (short) calls and short (long) puts on the same underlying with the same expiration is a long (short) risk reversal.

Risk tolerance The level of risk an investor is willing and able to bear.

Seagull spread An extension of the risk reversal foreign exchange option strategy that limits downside risk.

Securities lending A form of collateralized lending that may be used to generate income for portfolios.

Selective An index construction methodology that targets only those securities with certain characteristics.

Separate accounts Accounts holding assets to fund future liabilities from variable life insurance and variable annuities, the products in which customers make investment decisions from a menu of options and themselves bear investment risk.

Sharpe ratio The ratio of mean excess return to standard deviation (excess return).

Shortfall probability The probability of failing to meet a specific liability or goal.

Shrinkage estimation Estimation that involves taking a weighted average of a historical estimate of a parameter and some other parameter estimate, where the weights reflect the analyst's relative belief in the estimates.

Special dividends Dividends paid by a company that does not pay dividends on a regular schedule, or dividends that supplement regular cash dividends with an extra payment.

Spread duration The change in bond price for a given change in yield spread. Also referred to as OAS duration when the option-adjusted spread (OAS) is the yield measure used.

Static hedge A hedge that is not sensitive to changes in the price of the asset hedged.

Stock lending Securities lending involving the transfer of equities.

Stops Stop-loss orders involve leaving bids or offers away from the current market price to be filled if the market reaches those levels.

Straddle An option combination in which one buys *both* puts and calls, with the same exercise price and same expiration date, on the same underlying asset. In contrast to this long straddle, if someone *writes* both options, it is a short straddle.

Strangle A variation on a straddle in which the put and call have different exercise prices; if the put and call are held long, it is a long strangle; if they are held short, it is a short strangle.

Strategic asset allocation A long-term strategy that establishes target allocations for various asset classes and aims to optimize the balance between risk and reward by diversifying investments.

Structural models Models that specify functional relationships among variables based on economic theory. The functional form and parameters of these models are derived from the underlying theory. They may include unobservable parameters.

Support levels Price points on dealers' order boards where one would expect to see a clustering of bids.

Surplus The difference between assets and liabilities, analogous to shareholders' equity on a corporate balance sheet.

Surplus portfolio The component of an insurer's general account that is intended to realize higher expected returns than the reserve portfolio and so can assume some liquidity risk. Surplus portfolio assets are often managed aggressively with exposure to alternative assets.

Survivorship bias Relates to the inclusion of only current investment funds in a database. As such, the returns of funds that are no longer available in the marketplace (have been liquidated) are excluded from the database. Also see *backfill bias*.

Synthetic long forward position The combination of a long call and a short put with identical strike price and expiration, traded at the same time on the same underlying.

Synthetic short forward position The combination of a short call and a long put at the same strike price and maturity (traded at the same time on the same underlying).

Tactical asset allocation A proactive strategy that adjusts asset class allocations within a portfolio based on short-term market trends, economic conditions, or valuation changes to capitalize on temporary market inefficiencies or opportunities to improve returns or manage risk more effectively.

Tax drag The negative effect of taxes on an investment's net returns.

Taylor rule A rule linking a central bank's target short-term interest rate to the rate of growth of the economy and inflation.

Term deposits Interest-bearing accounts that have a specified maturity date. This category includes savings accounts and certificates of deposit (CDs). Also see *time deposits*.

Term structure of volatility The plot of implied volatility (y-axis) against option maturity (x-axis) for options with the same strike price on the same underlying. Typically, implied volatility is not constant across different maturities – rather, it is often in contango, meaning that the implied volatilities for longer-term options are higher than for near-term ones.

Thematic investing An investment approach that focuses on companies in a specific sector or following a specific theme, such as energy efficiency or climate change.

Theta The change in a derivative instrument for a given small change in calendar time, holding everything else constant. Specifically, the theta calculation assumes nothing changes except calendar time. Theta also reflects the rate at which an option's time value decays.

Threshold-based rebalancing policy The manager rebalances the portfolio when asset class weights deviate from their target weights by a prespecified percentage regardless of timing and frequency.

Time deposits Interest-bearing accounts that have a specified maturity date. This category includes savings accounts and certificates of deposit (CDs). Also see *term deposits*.

Time value The difference between an option's premium and its intrinsic value.

Time-based rebalancing policy The manager rebalances the portfolio regularly, at a certain given time interval such as quarterly, semi-annually, or annually, regardless of any difference between prevailing asset class weights and target asset class weights.

Time-series estimation Estimators that are based on lagged values of the variable being forecast; often consist of lagged values of other selected variables.

Total factor productivity A scale factor that reflects the portion of growth unaccounted for by explicit factor inputs (e.g., capital and labor).

Total return payer Party responsible for paying the reference obligation cash flows and return to the receiver but that is also compensated by the receiver for any depreciation in the index or default losses incurred by the portfolio.

Total return receiver Receives both the cash flows from the underlying index and any appreciation in the index over the period in exchange for paying the MRR plus a predetermined spread.

Tracking risk The standard deviation of the differences between a portfolio's returns and its benchmarks returns. Also called *tracking error*.

Transactions-based attribution An attribution approach that captures the impact of intra-day trades and exogenous events such as a significant class action settlement.

Trigger points In the context of portfolio rebalancing, the endpoints of a rebalancing range (corridor).

Ultra-high-net-worth individuals (UHNWIs) Individuals with net worth usually exceeding USD30 million or more.

Unplanned goals Unforeseen financial needs that are difficult to quantify because either the funding need, the timing of the financial need, or both may not be estimated.

Unsmoothing An adjustment to the reported return series if serial correlation is detected. Various approaches are available to unsmooth a return series.

Variance notional The notional amount of a variance swap; it equals vega notional divided by two times the volatility strike price [i.e., (vega notional)/(2 × volatility strike)].

Vega A measure of the sensitivity of an option's price to changes in the underlying's volatility.

Vega notional The trade size for a variance swap, which represents the average profit and loss of the variance swap for a 1% change in volatility from the strike.

Vesting The process of an employee becoming unconditionally entitled to, and an employer becoming obligated to pay, compensation.

Volatility clustering The tendency for large (small) swings in prices to be followed by large (small) swings of random direction.

Volatility skew The skewed plot (of implied volatility (y-axis) against strike price (x-axis) for options on the same underlying with the same expiration) that occurs when the implied volatility increases for OTM puts and decreases for OTM calls, as the strike price moves away from the current price.

Volatility smile The U-shaped plot (of implied volatility (y-axis) against strike price (x-axis) for options on the same underlying with the same expiration) that occurs when the implied volatilities priced into both OTM puts and calls trade at a premium to implied volatilities of ATM options.

Wealth The value of all the assets owned by an individual.

Wealth life cycle Stages of an individual investor's wealth in terms of human capital, financial capital, and economic net worth.

CFA Institute®
CFA Program

PORTFOLIO CONSTRUCTION

CFA® Program Curriculum
2026 • LEVEL III CORE • VOLUME 2

WILEY

ISBN 978-1-39436-058-1

May 2025

Please visit our website at
www.WileyGlobalFinance.com.

WILEY

SKY30F854B3-B933-4220-80FD-13C0F5FCA3C2_022825

CONTENTS

How to Use the CFA Program Curriculum

The CFA® Program exams measure your mastery of the core knowledge, skills, and abilities required to succeed as an investment professional. These core competencies are the basis for the Candidate Body of Knowledge (CBOK™). The CBOK consists of four components:

A broad outline that lists the major CFA Program topic areas (www.cfainstitute.org/programs/cfa/curriculum/cbok/cbok)

Topic area weights that indicate the relative exam weightings of the top-level topic areas (www.cfainstitute.org/en/programs/cfa/curriculum)

Learning outcome statements (LOS) that tell you the specific knowledge, skills, and abilities you should gain from each curriculum topic area. You will find these statements at the start of each learning module and lesson. We encourage you to review the information about the LOS on our website (www.cfainstitute.org/programs/cfa/curriculum/study-sessions), including the descriptions of LOS "command words" on the candidate resources page at www.cfainstitute.org/-/media/documents/support/programs/cfa-and-cipm-los-command-words.ashx.

The CFA Program curriculum that candidates receive access to upon exam registration.

Therefore, the key to your success on the CFA exams is studying and understanding the CBOK. You can learn more about the CBOK on our website: www.cfainstitute.org/programs/cfa/curriculum/cbok.

The curriculum, including the practice questions, is the basis for all exam questions. The curriculum is selected/developed specifically to provide candidates with the knowledge, skills, and abilities reflected in the CBOK.

CFA INSTITUTE LEARNING ECOSYSTEM (LES)

Your exam registration fee includes access to the CFA Institute Learning Ecosystem (LES). This digital learning platform provides access to all the curriculum content and practice questions. The LES is organized as a series of learning modules consisting of short online lessons and associated practice questions. This tool is your source for all study materials, including practice questions and mock exams. The LES is the primary method by which CFA Institute delivers your curriculum experience. Here, you will find additional practice questions to test your knowledge, including some interactive questions.

DESIGNING YOUR PERSONAL STUDY PROGRAM

An orderly, systematic approach to exam preparation is critical. You should dedicate a consistent block of time every week to reading and studying. Review the LOS both before and after you study curriculum content to ensure you can demonstrate

the knowledge, skills, and abilities described by the LOS and the assigned learning module. Use the LOS as a self-check to track your progress and highlight areas of weakness for later review.

Successful candidates report an average of more than 300 hours preparing for each exam. Your preparation time will vary based on your prior education and experience, and you will likely spend more time on some topics than on others.

ERRATA

The curriculum development process is rigorous and involves multiple rounds of reviews by content experts. Despite our efforts to produce a curriculum that is free of errors, we must make corrections in some instances. Curriculum errata are periodically updated and posted by exam level and test date on the Curriculum Errata webpage (www.cfainstitute.org/en/programs/submit-errata). If you believe you have found an error in the curriculum, you can submit your concerns through our curriculum errata reporting process found at the bottom of the Curriculum Errata webpage.

OTHER FEEDBACK

Please send any comments or suggestions to info@cfainstitute.org, and we will review your feedback thoughtfully.

Portfolio Construction

LEARNING MODULE

1

Overview of Equity Portfolio Management

by James Clunie, PhD, CFA, and James Alan Finnegan, CAIA, RMA, CFA.

James Clunie, PhD, CFA, is at Jupiter Asset Management (United Kingdom). James Alan Finnegan, CAIA, RMA, CFA (USA).

LEARNING OUTCOMES

Mastery	*The candidate should be able to:*
☐	describe the roles of equities in the overall portfolio
☐	describe how an equity manager's investment universe can be segmented
☐	describe the types of income and costs associated with owning and managing an equity portfolio and their potential effects on portfolio performance
☐	describe the potential benefits of shareholder engagement and the role an equity manager might play in shareholder engagement
☐	describe rationales for equity investment across the active management spectrum
☐	discuss considerations in choosing a benchmark for an equity portfolio

INTRODUCTION

1

Equities represent a sizable portion of the global investment universe and are often a primary component of investors' portfolios. Rationales for investing in equities include potential participation in the growth and earnings prospects of an economy's corporate sector as well as an ownership interest in a range of business entities by size, economic activity, and geographical scope. Publicly traded equities are generally more liquid than other asset classes and thus enable investors to easily monitor price trends and trade securities at low costs.

This reading provides an overview of equity portfolio management. In the next section, we discuss the roles of equities in a portfolio. Then, we examine the equity investment universe, including several ways investors segment that universe. We will also cover the income and costs for an equity portfolio, as well as shareholder engagement between equity investors and investee companies. In addition, we will discuss equity investment across the active management spectrum and considerations for benchmark selection for equity strategies, including for index-based strategies. A summary of key points completes the learning module.

2 THE ROLES OF EQUITIES IN A PORTFOLIO

☐ describe the roles of equities in the overall portfolio

Equities play several roles in an overall portfolio, including providing such benefits as capital appreciation, dividend income, diversification with other asset classes, and a potential hedge against inflation. In addition to these benefits, client investment considerations play an important role for portfolio managers when deciding to include equities in portfolios.

Capital Appreciation

Long-term returns on equities, driven predominantly by capital appreciation, have historically been among the highest among major asset classes. Exhibit 1 shows geometric, annualized real returns on equities, bonds, and bills—both globally and in various regions—from 1900 to 2022. Equities outperformed both bonds and bills during this period across the world.

Exhibit 1: Real Returns on Equities, Bonds, and Bills (1900–2022)

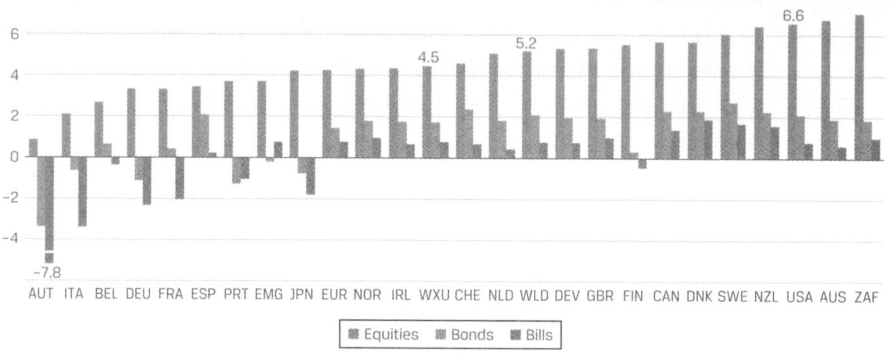

Source: Credit Suisse Global Investment Returns Yearbook 2023, Summary Edition.

Equities tend to outperform other asset classes during periods of strong economic growth, and they tend to underperform other asset classes during weaker economic periods. Capital (or price) appreciation of equities often occurs when investing in companies with growth in earnings, cash flows, and/or revenues—as well as in companies with competitive success. Capital appreciation can occur, for example, in growth-oriented companies, such as small technology companies, as well as in large, mature companies where management successfully maintains profitability.

Dividend Income

The most common source of income for an equity portfolio is dividends. Companies may choose to distribute free cash flows as dividends rather than reinvest in projects, particularly when suitable projects do not exist or do not have returns greater than investors' required rate of return. Large, well-established corporations often provide dividend payments that increase in value over time, although there are no assurances that dividend payments from these corporations will grow or even be maintained. In addition to dividends on common stock (common dividends), preferred dividends can provide dividend income to those shareholders owning preferred shares.

Dividends have represented a significant component of long-term total returns for equity investors. Over shorter periods of time, however, the proportion of equity returns from dividends (reflected as dividend yield) can vary considerably relative to capital gains or losses. Exhibit 2 illustrates this effect of dividend returns relative to annual total returns on the S&P 500 Index from 1930 through 2021. Since 1990, the dividend yield on the S&P 500 has been in the 1%–3% range; thus, the effect of dividends can clearly be significant during periods of weak equity market performance, such as during the first decade of the 21st century, when price returns were negative. Also note that the dividend yield may vary considerably by sector.

Exhibit 2: S&P 500 Dividend Contribution (1930–2022)

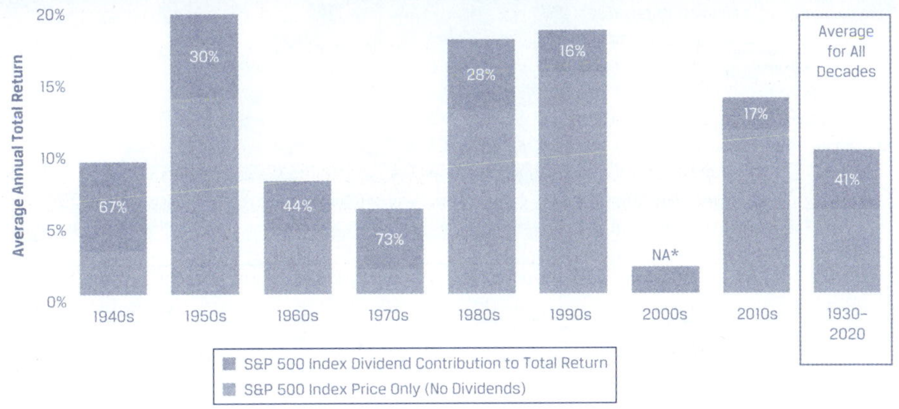

Sources: Morningstar and Hartford Funds.

Diversification with Other Asset Classes

Individual equities have unique characteristics, although the correlation of returns among equities is often high. In a portfolio context, however, equities can provide meaningful diversification benefits when combined with other asset classes (assuming less-than-perfect correlation). Recall that a major reason why portfolios can effectively reduce risk (typically expressed as standard deviation of returns) is that combining securities whose returns are less than perfectly correlated reduces the standard deviation of the diversified portfolio below the weighted average of the standard deviations of the individual investments. The challenge in diversifying risk is to find assets that have a correlation much lower than +1.0.

Exhibit 3 provides a correlation matrix across various global equity indexes and other asset classes using total monthly returns for the 20 years ended 31 October 2021. The correlation matrix shows that during this period, various broad equity indexes and, to a lesser extent, country equity indexes were highly correlated with each other. Conversely, both the broad and country equity indexes were considerably less correlated with indexes in other asset classes, notably Treasury bonds, investment-grade bonds, and gold. Overall, Exhibit 3 indicates that combining equities with other asset classes can result in portfolio diversification benefits.

It is important to note that correlations are not constant over time. During a long historical period, the correlation of returns between two asset classes may be low, but in any given period, the correlation can differ from the long term. Correlation estimates can vary based on the capital market dynamics during the period when the correlations are measured. During periods of market crisis, correlations across asset classes and among equities themselves often increase and reduce the benefit of diversification. As with correlations, volatility (standard deviation) of asset class returns may also vary over time.

Exhibit 3: Correlation Matrix, 20 Years Ended 31 October 2021

	1	2	3	4	5	6	7	8	9	10	11	12	13	14	15
1 MSCI World NR USD	1.00														
2 MSCI EM IMI NR USD	0.84	1.00													
3 MSCI EAFE NR USD	0.96	0.86	1.00												
4 S&P 500 TR USD	0.97	0.76	0.87	1.00											
5 MSCI China NR LCL	0.66	0.84	0.69	0.58	1.00										
6 MSCI Japan NR JPY	0.79	0.70	0.83	0.72	0.48	1.00									
7 EURO STOXX 50 NR EUR	0.84	0.70	0.91	0.74	0.50	0.46	1.00								
8 FTSE 100 TR GBP	0.88	0.75	0.92	0.78	0.52	0.53	0.87	1.00							
9 Bloomberg US Agg Bond TR USD	-0.02	0.06	0.03	-0.06	0.04	0.04	-0.01	-0.01	1.00						
10 Bloomberg Gbl Agg Ex USD TR USD	0.33	0.40	0.43	0.22	0.34	0.29	0.40	0.38	0.57	1.00					
11 Bloomberg Treasury 1-5 Yr TR USD	-0.36	-0.26	-0.30	-0.39	-0.19	-0.23	-0.29	-0.32	0.76	0.43	1.00				
12 Bloomberg Gbl HY Bond Composite TR USD	0.70	0.73	0.74	0.61	0.55	0.51	0.69	0.69	0.47	0.66	0.02	1.00			
13 S&P GSCI TR USD	0.45	0.48	0.48	0.38	0.39	0.35	0.41	0.54	-0.07	0.28	-0.22	0.44	1.00		
14 S&P GSCI Gold TR	0.12	0.29	0.16	0.05	0.24	0.11	0.10	0.14	0.37	0.52	0.30	0.40	0.23	1.00	
15 FTSE Nareit All Equity REITs TR USD	0.69	0.58	0.65	0.69	0.39	0.49	0.60	0.59	0.23	0.35	-0.12	0.60	0.25	0.13	1.00

0.76 to 1.00	0.51 to 0.75	0.26 to 0.50	0.01 to 0.25
-0.75 to -1.00	-0.50 to -0.74	-0.25 to -0.49	0.00 to -0.24

Source: Morningstar Direct.

Hedge against Inflation

Some individual equities or sectors can provide some protection against inflation, although the ability to do so varies. For example, certain companies may be successful at passing along higher input costs (such as raw materials, energy, or wages) to customers. This ability to pass along costs to customers can protect a company's or industry's profit margin and cash flow and can be reflected in its stock prices. As another example, companies in sectors that produce broad-based commodities (e.g., oil or industrial metals producers) can more directly benefit from increases in commodity prices. Although individual equities or sectors can protect against inflation, the success of equities as an asset class in hedging inflation has been mixed. Certain empirical studies have shown that real returns on equities and inflation have positive correlation over the long term, but the degree of correlation typically varies by country and is dependent on the time period assessed. For severe inflationary periods, such as periods with an annual inflation rate over 5%, studies have shown that real returns on equities and inflation have been *negatively* correlated. Therefore, the asset class's efficacy as an inflation hedge may fail when it is most needed.

Client Considerations for Equities in a Portfolio

The inclusion of equities in a client's portfolio is driven by their goals and needs. A client's investment considerations are typically described in an investment policy statement (IPS), which establishes, among other things, return objectives, risk tolerance, constraints, and unique circumstances. By understanding these client considerations, a financial adviser or wealth manager can determine whether—and what amount of—equities should be in a client's portfolio.

Equity investments are often characterized by such attributes as growth potential, income generation, risk and return volatility, and sensitivity to various macroeconomic variables (e.g., GDP growth, interest rates, and inflation). As a result, a portfolio manager can adapt such specific factors to an equity investor's investment goals and risk tolerance. For example, a risk-averse and conservative investor may prefer some exposure to well-established companies with strong and stable cash flow that pay meaningful dividends. Conversely, a growth-oriented investor with an aggressive risk tolerance may prefer smaller companies with greater growth potential.

Wealth managers and financial advisers often consider the following investment objectives and constraints when deciding to include equities (or asset classes in general, for that matter) in a client's portfolio:

- *Risk objective* addresses how risk is measured (e.g., in absolute or relative terms); the investor's willingness to take risk; the investor's ability to take risk; and the investor's specific risk objectives.
- *Return objective* addresses how returns are measured (e.g., in absolute or relative terms); this term refers to stated return objectives.
- *Liquidity requirement* is a constraint in which cash is needed for anticipated or unanticipated events.
- *Time horizon* is the time period associated with an investment objective (e.g., short term, long term, or some combination of the two).
- *Tax concerns* include tax policies that can affect investor returns; for example, dividends may be taxed at a different rate than capital gains.
- *Legal and regulatory factors* are external factors imposed by governmental, regulatory, or oversight authorities.
- *Unique circumstances* are an investor's considerations other than liquidity requirements, time horizon, or tax concerns that may constrain portfolio choices. These considerations may include environmental, social, and governance (ESG) issues or religious preferences.

Clients' interest in ESG and sustainable investing has grown. With regard to equities, these considerations often determine the suitability of certain sectors or individual company stocks for designated investor portfolios. Historically, ESG approaches used by portfolio managers have largely represented **negative screening** (or exclusionary screening) and **positive screening** or **best-in-class** approaches. Negative screening refers to the practice of excluding certain sectors or companies that deviate from accepted standards in such areas as human rights or environmental concerns. Positive screening attempts to identify companies or sectors that score most favorably with regard to ESG-related risks and/or opportunities. For example, a negative screening approach may involve excluding oil and gas producers from consideration for a client's portfolio strategy, while a positive screening approach may overweight companies and industries with strong governance practices, such as an independent board chair. Rather than screening, however, as of 2020, the largest sustainable investment strategy globally was ESG integration, which is the inclusion of ESG considerations in financial analysis and investment decisions (GSIA 2020).

The goals of ESG integration are to reduce financial risks and/or enhance financial returns by identifying and valuing risks or opportunities that are not typically identified and valued. ESG integration begins with identifying relevant ESG information for sector, industry, and company research and evaluating its financial materiality. Financially material ESG information is then used alongside traditional financial information to inform an analyst's valuation and recommendation to buy, hold, or sell a security. Just as with traditional equity analysis, a variety of tools and methods exist for integrating ESG information into the analytical process, and analysts must choose the ones they believe are most appropriate for their analysis.

GUIDANCE AND CASE STUDIES FOR ESG INTEGRATION

CFA Institute and the United Nations–supported Principles for Responsible Investment (PRI) initiative published a best practice report ("Guidance and Case Studies for ESG Integration: Equities and Fixed Income") and three regional reports—one for the Americas (AMER), one for Asia Pacific (APAC), and one for Europe, the Middle East, and Africa (EMEA)—to help investors understand how they can better integrate ESG factors into their equity, corporate bond, and sovereign debt portfolios. This report contains many case studies of ESG integration and introduces an ESG Integration Framework as a reference for practitioners. The following two cases are brief excerpts from that report.

Adjusting Revenue and Margins

In "Evaluating ESG Impact on Revenue and Margins," AGF Investments Inc. illustrates how ESG information can be used to adjust forecasted financials. In this case study, Company A is a global leader in specialty chemicals that has positioned itself to profit from trending consumer preferences for sustainable products. Company A recently shifted from purchasing petrochemicals for use as a product base to manufacturing its own product base using naturally sourced, renewable raw materials. AGF analysts project that the shift to in-house manufacturing and use of renewable materials will reduce costs from purchasing petrochemicals and managing hazardous waste materials. Analysts also project that consumers will pay a premium for Company A's sustainable products versus competitors' petrochemical-based products, which will increase annual revenue growth by 30 bps. Analysts estimate that the cost savings plus increased revenue over the next five years will result in a 100 bp improvement to EBIT (earnings before interest and taxes).

Adjusting the P/E Multiple

The case study "Valuation Adjustment According to Environmental Regulations" demonstrates the use of ESG information to adjust the P/E multiple.

In this example, analysts at E Fund Management Co., Limited, believed that new pollution regulations in China would be strictly enforced and developed a four-factor framework to score companies in affected industries on environmental protection factors. The case study compares the evaluation of Y Chemical and H Corporation. After scoring the companies, analysts concluded that H Corporation had a greater environmental risk than Y Chemical. Analysts were unable to estimate the projected environmental protection costs for the two companies, so they chose to discount the target P/E for H Corporation to a

P/E of 20 versus the industry average P/E of 23.7 (trailing 12 months). Analysts believed that H Corporation was overpriced due to its environmental risks not being recognized by the market and thus would have a negative return.

Source: CFA Institute and the PRI, "Guidance and Case Studies in ESG Integration: Equities and Fixed Income" (2018). www.cfainstitute.org/-/media/documents/survey/guidance-case-studies-esg-integration.pdf.

Two other approaches to ESG investing are **thematic investing** and **impact investing**. Thematic investing refers to investing in companies with positive exposure to ESG megatrends, such as clean energy, green technology, sustainable agriculture, gender diversity, or affordable housing. Global economic development has raised the demand for energy at the same time as increased greenhouse gas emissions are widely believed to negatively affect the earth's climate. Similarly, rising global living standards and industrial needs have created a greater demand for water along with the need to prevent drought or increase access to clean drinking water in certain regions of the world. While these themes are based on trends related to environmental issues, social issues—such as access to affordable health care and nutrition—are also of interest.

Impact investing is a related approach that seeks to achieve targeted social or environmental objectives along with measurable financial returns through engagement with a company or by direct investment in projects or companies. An example would include investing in products or services that help achieve 1 (or more) of the 17 Sustainable Development Goals (SDGs) launched by the United Nations in 2015, such as "SDG 6: Clean Water and Sanitation—Ensure availability and sustainable management of water and sanitation for all" and "SDG 11: Sustainable Cities and Communities—Make cities and human settlements inclusive, safe, resilient and sustainable." Impact investing is a relatively smaller segment of the broader sustainable and responsible investing market.

ROLES OF EQUITIES

1. Alex Chang, Lin Choi, and Frank Huber manage separate equity portfolios for the same investment firm. Chang's portfolio objective is conservative in nature, with a regular stream of income as the primary investment objective. Choi's portfolio is more aggressive in nature, with a long-term horizon and with growth as the primary objective. Finally, Huber's portfolio consists of wealthy entrepreneurs who are concerned about rising inflation and wish to preserve the purchasing power of their wealth.

   Discuss the investment approach that each portfolio manager would likely use to achieve his or her portfolio objectives.

   Solution

   Given that his portfolio is focused on a regular stream of income, Chang is likely to focus on companies with regular dividend income. More specifically, Chang is likely to invest in large, well-established companies with stable or growing dividend payments. With a long-term horizon, Choi is most interested in capital appreciation of her portfolio, so she is likely to focus on companies with earnings growth and competitive success. Finally, Huber's clients are concerned about the effects of inflation, so he will likely seek to invest in shares of companies that can provide an inflation hedge. Huber would likely seek companies that can successfully pass on higher input costs to their customers, and he may also seek commodity producers that may benefit from rising commodity prices.

3 EQUITY INVESTMENT UNIVERSE

☐ describe how an equity manager's investment universe can be segmented

Given the extensive range of companies in which an equity portfolio manager may invest and the range of clients' risk and return objectives, an important task for the manager is to segment the universe by grouping companies according to similar characteristics. This segmentation enables portfolio managers to better evaluate and analyze their equity investment universe, and it can help with portfolio diversification. Several approaches to segmenting the equity investment universe are discussed in the following sections.

Segmentation by Size and Style

A popular approach to segmenting the equity universe incorporates two factors: (1) size and (2) style. Size is typically measured by market capitalization and often categorized by large cap, mid cap, and small cap. Style is typically classified as value, growth, or a combination of value and growth (typically termed "blend" or "core"). In addition, style is often determined through a "scoring" system that incorporates multiple metrics or ratios, such as price-to-book ratios, price-to-earnings ratios, earnings growth, dividend yield, and book value growth. These metrics are then typically "scored" individually for each company, assigned certain weights, and then aggregated. The result is a composite score that determines where the company's stock is positioned along the value–growth spectrum. A combination of growth and value style is not uncommon, particularly for large corporations that have both mature and higher-growth business lines.

Exhibit 4 illustrates a common matrix that reflects size and style dimensions. Each category in the matrix can be represented by companies with considerably different business activities. For example, both a small, mature metal fabricating business and a small health care services provider may fall in the Small Cap Value category. An example of how several listed companies are categorized as of February 2023 is shown in Exhibit 5. In practice, individual stocks may not clearly fall into one of the size/style categories and classification is dynamic, so these are best thought of as guidelines rather than a strict taxonomy.

Exhibit 4: Equity Size and Style Matrix

	Style		
	Value	**Blend**	**Growth**
Large			
Mid			
Small			

Source: Morningstar.

Exhibit 5: Equity Size and Style, Example Classifications as of February 2023

	Style		
	Value	Blend	Growth
Large	Samsung Electronics Co. Ltd.	Tencent	Meituan
Mid	Schroders PLC	Gedeon Richter	Ocado PLC
Small	Hawaiian Airlines	National Beverage Corp.	WeWork Inc.

Source: Morningstar.

Segmentation by size/style can provide several advantages for portfolio managers. First, portfolio managers can construct an overall equity portfolio that reflects desired risk, return, and income characteristics in a relatively straightforward and manageable way. Second, given the broad range of companies in each segment, segmentation by size/style results in diversification across economic sectors or industries. Third, active equity managers—that is, those seeking to outperform a given benchmark portfolio—can construct performance benchmarks for specific size/style segments. Generally, large investment management firms may have sizable teams dedicated toward specific size/style categories, while small firms may specialize in a specific size/style category, particularly mid-cap and small-cap companies, seeking to outperform a standard benchmark or comparable peer group.

The final advantage of segmentation by size/style is that it allows a portfolio to reflect a company's maturity and potentially changing growth/value orientation. Specifically, many companies that undertake an IPO (initial public offering) are small and in a growth phase, and thus they may fall in the small-cap growth category. If these companies can successfully grow, their size may ultimately move to mid-cap or even large cap, while their style may conceivably shift from high growth to value or a combination of growth and value (e.g., a growth and income stock). Accordingly, over the life cycle of companies, investor preferences for these companies may shift increasingly from capital appreciation to dividend income. In addition, segmentation also helps fund managers adjust holdings over time—for example, when stocks that were previously considered to be in the growth category mature and possibly become value stocks. The key disadvantages of segmentation by size/style are that the categories may change over time and may be defined differently among investors.

Segmentation by Geography

Another common approach to equity universe segmentation is by geography. This approach is typically based on the stage of markets' macroeconomic development and wealth. Common geographic categories are *developed markets*, *emerging markets*, and *frontier markets*. Exhibit 6 demonstrates the commonly used geographic segmentation of international equity indexes according to MSCI. MSCI classifies countries as developed, emerging, or frontier according to a holistic framework that considers economic development, size and liquidity, and accessibility criteria, such as openness to foreign equity ownership. Other major index providers—such as FTSE, Standard & Poor's, and Russell—provide similar types of international equity indexes.

Geographic segmentation is useful to equity investors who have considerable exposure to their domestic market and want to diversify by investing in global equities. A key weakness of geographic segmentation is that investing in a specific market (e.g., market index) may provide lower-than-expected exposure to that market. As an example, Nestle, Roche, and Novartis together account for over half of the MSCI

Switzerland Index, but Switzerland accounts for less than 2% of each company's sales. Another key weakness of geographic segmentation is potential currency risk when investing in different global equity markets.

Exhibit 6: MSCI International Equity Indexes (as of January 2023)

Developed Markets

Americas	Europe and Middle East	Pacific
Canada	Austria	Australia
United States	Belgium	Hong Kong SAR
	Denmark	Japan
	Finland	New Zealand
	France	Singapore
	Germany	
	Ireland	
	Israel	
	Italy	
	Netherlands	
	Norway	
	Portugal	
	Spain	
	Sweden	
	Switzerland	
	United Kingdom	

Emerging Markets

Americas	Europe, Middle East, and Africa	Asia Pacific
Brazil	Czech Republic	Chinese mainland
Chile	Egypt	India
Colombia	Greece	Indonesia
Mexico	Hungary	South Korea
Peru	Kuwait	Malaysia
	Poland	Philippines
	Qatar	Taiwan region
	Saudi Arabia	Thailand
	South Africa	
	Turkey	
	United Arab Emirates	

Frontier Markets

Europe and CIS[1]	Africa	Middle East	Asia
Croatia	Kenya	Bahrain	Bangladesh
Estonia	Mauritius	Jordan	Pakistan
Iceland	Morocco	Oman	Sri Lanka
Lithuania	Nigeria		Vietnam
Kazakhstan	Tunisia		
Romania	WAEMU[2]		
Serbia			
Slovenia			

Notes: The following markets are not included in the developed, emerging, or MSCI frontier indexes but have their own market-specific indexes: Argentina, Jamaica, Panama, Trinidad and Tobago, Bosnia Herzegovina, Bulgaria, Malta, Russia, Ukraine, Botswana, Zimbabwe, Lebanon, and Palestine.
[1] *CIS:* Commonwealth of Independent States (formerly the USSR).
[2] *WAEMU:* West African Economic and Monetary Union, also known by its French acronym UEMOA,

which consists of the following countries: Benin, Burkina Faso, Ivory Coast, Guinea-Bissau, Mali, Niger, Senegal, and Togo.

Segmentation by Economic Activity

Economic activity is another characteristic that portfolio managers may use to segment the equity universe. Most equity classification systems group companies into industries/sectors using a *market-oriented* approach, grouping companies based on the markets they serve, the way revenue is earned, and the way customers use companies' products.

The four main commercial global classification systems, which were discussed earlier in the curriculum, are (1) the Global Industry Classification Standard (GICS); (2) the Industrial Classification Benchmark (ICB); (3) the Thomson Reuters Business Classification (TRBC); and (4) the Russell Global Sectors Classification (RGS). These classification systems help standardize industry definitions so that portfolio managers can compare and analyze companies and industries/sectors. In addition, the classification systems are useful in the creation of industry performance benchmarks.

Exhibit 7 compares the four primary classification systems. Each system is classified broadly and then increasingly more granularly to compare companies and their underlying businesses.

Exhibit 7: Primary Sector Classification Systems

Level/ System	GICS	ICB	TRBC	RGS
1st	11 Sectors	10 Industries	10 Economic Sectors	9 Economic Sectors
2nd	24 Industry Groups	19 Super Sectors	28 Business Sectors	33 Sub-Sectors
3rd	68 Industries	41 Sectors	54 Industry Groups	157 Industries
4th	157 Sub-Industries	114 Sub-Sectors	136 Industries	Not Applicable

Sources: Thomson Reuters, S&P/MSCI, FTSE/Dow Jones.

To illustrate how segmentation of the classification systems may be used in practice, Exhibit 8 demonstrates how GICS, perhaps the most prominent classification system, sub-divides selected sectors—in this case, Consumer Discretionary, Consumer Staples, and Information Technology—into certain industry group, industry, and sub-industry levels.

Exhibit 8: GICS Classification Examples

Sector	Consumer Discretionary	Consumer Staples	Information Technology
Industry Group Example	Automobiles and Components	Food, Beverage, and Tobacco	Technology Hardware and Equipment
Industry Example	Automobiles	Beverages	Electronic Equipment, Instruments, and Components
Sub-Industry Example	Motorcycle Manufacturers	Soft Drinks	Electronic Manufacturing Services

Source: MSCI.

As with other segmentation approaches mentioned previously, segmentation by economic activity enables equity portfolio managers to construct performance benchmarks for specific sectors or industries. Portfolio managers may also obtain better industry representation (diversification) by segmenting their equity universe according to economic activity. The key disadvantage of segmentation by economic activity is that the business activities of companies—particularly, large ones—may include more than one industry or sub-industry.

SEGMENTING THE EQUITY INVESTMENT UNIVERSE

1. A portfolio manager is initiating a new fund that seeks to invest in the Chinese robotics industry, which is experiencing rapidly accelerating earnings. To help identify appropriate company stocks, the portfolio manager wants to select an approach to segment the equity universe.

   Recommend which segmentation approach would be most appropriate for the portfolio manager.

   Solution

   Based on his desired strategy to invest in companies with rapidly accelerating (growing) earnings, the portfolio manager would most likely segment his equity universe by size/style. The portfolio manager would most likely use an investment style that reflects growth, with size (large cap, mid cap, or small cap) depending on the company being analyzed. Other segmentation approaches, including those according to geography and economic activity, would be less appropriate for the portfolio manager given the similar geographic and industry composition of the Chinese robotics industry.

Segmentation of Equity Indexes and Benchmarks

Segmentation of equity indexes or benchmarks reflects some of or all the approaches previously discussed in this section. For example, the MSCI Europe Large Cap Growth Index, the MSCI World Small Cap Value Index, the MSCI Emerging Markets Large Cap Growth Index, and the MSCI Latin America Midcap Index combine various geographic, size, and style dimensions. This combination of geography, size, and style also sometimes applies to individual countries—particularly those in large, developed markets.

A more focused approach to segmentation of equity indexes uses industries or sectors. Because many industries and sectors are global in scope, the most common types of these indexes are composed of companies in different countries. Examples include the following:

- Global Natural Resources—the *S&P Global Natural Resources Index* includes 90 of the largest publicly traded companies in natural resources and commodities businesses across three primary commodity-related sectors: agribusiness, energy, and metals and mining.
- Worldwide Oil and Natural Gas—the *MSCI World Energy Index* includes the large-cap and mid-cap segments of publicly traded oil and natural gas companies in the developed markets.
- Multinational Financials—the *Refinitiv Global Financials Index* includes the 100 largest publicly traded companies in the global financial services sector as defined by the TRBC classification system.

Finally, some indexes reflect specific investment approaches, such as ESG investing. Such ESG indexes are made up of companies that reflect certain considerations, such as sustainability or impact investing.

INCOME ASSOCIATED WITH OWNING AND MANAGING AN EQUITY PORTFOLIO

4

☐ describe the types of income and costs associated with owning and managing an equity portfolio and their potential effects on portfolio performance

Dividends are the primary source of income for equity portfolios. In addition, some portfolio managers may use securities lending or option-writing strategies to generate income. On the cost side, equity portfolios incur various fees and trading costs that adversely affect portfolio returns. The primary types of income and costs are discussed in this section.

Dividend Income

Investors requiring regular income may prefer to invest in stocks with large or frequent dividend payments, whereas growth-oriented investors may have little interest in dividends. Taxation is an important consideration for dividend income received, particularly for individuals. Depending on the country where the investor is domiciled, where dividends are issued, and the type of investor, dividends may be subject to withholding tax and/or income tax.

Beyond regular dividends, equity portfolios may receive **special dividends** from certain companies. Special dividends occur when companies decide to distribute excess cash to shareholders, but the payments may not be maintained over time. **Optional stock dividends** are another type of dividend in which shareholders may elect to receive either cash or new shares. When the share price used to calculate the number of stock dividend shares is established before the shareholder's election date, the choice between a cash or stock dividend may be important. This choice represents "optionality" for the shareholder, and the optionality has value. Some market participants, typically investment banks, may offer to purchase this "option," providing an additional, if modest, source of income to an equity investor.

Securities Lending Income

For some investors, **securities lending**—a form of collateralized lending—may be used to generate income for portfolios. Securities lending can facilitate short sales, which involve the sale of securities the seller does not own. When a securities lending transaction involves the transfer of equities, the transaction is generally known as **stock lending** and the securities are generally known as *stock loans.* Stock loans are collateralized with either cash or other high-quality securities to provide some financial protection to the lender. Stock loans are usually open-ended in duration, but the borrower must return the shares to the lender on demand.

Stock lenders generally receive a fee from the stock borrower as compensation for the loaned shares. Most stock loans in developed markets earn a modest fee, approximately 0.2%–0.5% on an annualized basis. In emerging markets, fees are typically higher, often 1%–2% annualized for large-cap stocks. In many equity markets, certain stocks—called "specials"—are in high demand for borrowing. These specials can earn fees that are substantially higher than average (typically 5%–15% annualized), and in cases of extreme demand, they could be as high as 25%–100% annually. However, such high fees do not normally persist for long periods of time.

In addition to fees earned, stock lenders can generate further income by reinvesting the cash collateral received (assuming a favorable interest rate environment). However, as with virtually any other investment, the collateral would be subject to market risk, credit risk, liquidity risk, and operational risk. The administrative costs of a securities lending program, in turn, will reduce the collateral income generated. Dividends on loaned stock are "manufactured" by the stock borrower for the stock lender; that is, the stock borrower ensures that the stock lender is compensated for any dividends that the lender would have received had the stock not been loaned.

Index funds are frequent stock lenders because of their large, long-term holdings in stocks. In addition, because index funds merely seek to replicate the performance of an index, portfolio managers of these funds are normally not concerned that borrowed stock used for short-selling purposes might decrease the prices of the corresponding equities. Large, actively managed pension funds, endowments, and institutional investors are also frequent stock lenders, although these investors are likely more concerned with the effect on their returns if the loaned shares are used to facilitate short selling. The evidence on the impact of stock lending on asset prices has, however, been mixed (see, for example, Kaplan, Moskowitz, and Sensoy 2013).

Ancillary Investment Strategies

Additional income can be generated for an equity portfolio through a trading strategy known as **dividend capture**. Under this strategy, an equity portfolio manager purchases stocks just before their ex-dividend dates, holds these stocks through the ex-dividend date to earn the right to receive the dividend, and subsequently sells the shares. Once a stock goes ex-dividend, the share price should, in theory, decrease by the value of the dividend. In this way, capturing dividends would increase portfolio income, although the portfolio would—again, in theory—experience capital losses of similar magnitude. However, the share price movement could vary from this theoretical assumption given income tax considerations, stock-specific supply/demand conditions, and general stock market moves around the ex-dividend date.

Selling (writing) options can also generate additional income for an equity portfolio. One such option strategy is writing a *covered call*, whereby the portfolio manager already owns the underlying stock and sells a call option on that stock. Another option strategy is writing a *cash-covered put* (also called a *cash-secured put*), whereby the portfolio manager writes a put option on a stock and simultaneously deposits money equal to the exercise price into a designated account. Under both covered calls and cash-covered puts, income is generated through the writing of options, but clearly the risk profile of the portfolio would be altered. For example, writing a covered call would limit the upside from share price appreciation of the underlying shares.

EQUITY PORTFOLIO INCOME

1. Isabel Cordova is an equity portfolio manager for a large multinational investment firm. Her portfolio consists of several dividend-paying stocks, and she is interested in generating additional income to enhance the

portfolio's total return. Describe potential sources of additional income for Cordova's equity portfolio.

Solution

Cordova's primary source of income for her portfolio would likely be "regular" and, in some cases, special dividends from those companies that pay them. Another potential source of income for Cordova is securities (stock) lending, whereby eligible equities in her portfolio can be loaned to other market participants, including those seeking to sell short securities. In this case, income would be generated from fees received from the stock borrower as well as from reinvesting the cash collateral received. Another potential income-generating strategy available to Cordova is dividend capture, which entails purchasing stocks just before their ex-dividend dates, holding the stocks through the ex-dividend date to earn the right to receive the dividend, and subsequently selling the shares. Selling (writing) options, including covered call and cash-covered put (cash-secured put) strategies, is another way Cordova can generate additional income for her equity portfolio.

COSTS ASSOCIATED WITH OWNING AND MANAGING AN EQUITY PORTFOLIO

5

☐ describe the types of income and costs associated with owning and managing an equity portfolio and their potential effects on portfolio performance

Management Fees

Management fees are typically determined as a percentage of the funds under management (an *ad-valorem* fee) at regular intervals. For actively managed portfolios, the level of management fees involves a balance between fees that are high enough to fund investment research but low enough to avoid detracting too much from investor returns. Management fees for actively managed portfolios include direct costs of research (e.g., remuneration and expenses for investment analysts and portfolio managers) and the direct costs of portfolio management (e.g., software, trade processing costs, and compliance). For index-based portfolios, management fees are typically low because of lower direct costs of research and portfolio management relative to actively managed portfolios.

Investment managers typically present a standard schedule of fees to a prospective client, although actual fees can be negotiated between the manager and investors. For a fund, fees are established in the prospectus, although investors could negotiate special terms (e.g., a discount for being an early investor in a fund).

Performance Fees

In addition to management fees, portfolio managers sometimes earn performance fees (also known as incentive fees) on their portfolios. Performance fees are generally associated with hedge funds and long/short equity portfolios, rather than long-only portfolios. These fees are an incentive for portfolio managers to achieve or outperform return objectives, to the benefit of both the manager and investors. As an example, a performance fee might represent 10%–20% of any capital appreciation in a portfolio that exceeds some stated annual absolute return threshold (e.g., 8%). Several performance fee structures exist, although performance fees tend to be "upwards only"; that is, fees are earned by the manager when performance objectives are met, but fund investors are not reimbursed when performance is negative. However, performance fees could be reduced following a period of poor performance. Fee calculations also reflect high-water marks. A **high-water mark** is the highest value, net of fees, that the fund has reached. The use of high-water marks protects clients from paying twice for the same performance. For example, if a fund performed well in a given year, it might earn a performance fee. If the value of the same fund fell the following year, no performance fee would be payable. Then, if the fund's value increased in the third year to a point just below the value achieved at the end of the first year, no performance fee would be earned because the fund's value did not exceed the high-water mark. This basic fee structure is used by many alternative investment funds and partnerships, including hedge funds.

Administration Fees

Equity portfolios are subject to administration fees. These fees include the processing of corporate actions, such as rights issues; the measurement of performance and risk of a portfolio; and voting at company meetings. Generally, these functions are provided by an investment management firm itself and are included as part of the management fee.

Some functions, however, are provided by external parties, with the fees charged to the client in addition to management fees. These externally provided functions include the following:

- *Custody fees* paid for the safekeeping of assets by a custodian (often a subsidiary of a large bank) that is independent of the investment manager
- *Depository fees* paid to help ensure that custodians segregate the assets of the portfolio and that the portfolio complies with any investment limits, leverage requirements, and limits on cash holdings
- *Registration fees* that are associated with the registration of ownership of units in a mutual fund

Marketing and Distribution Costs

Most investment management firms market and distribute their services to some degree. Marketing and distribution costs typically include the following:

- Costs of employing marketing, sales, and client servicing staff
- Advertising costs
- Sponsorship costs, including costs associated with sponsoring or presenting at conferences
- Costs of producing and distributing brochures or other communications to financial intermediaries or prospective clients
- "Platform" fees, which are costs incurred when an intermediary offers an investment management firm fund services on the intermediary's platform of funds (e.g., a "funds supermarket")
- Sales commissions paid to such financial intermediaries as financial planners, independent financial advisers, and brokers to facilitate the distribution of funds or investment services

When marketing and distribution services are performed by an investment management firm, the costs are likely included as part of the management fee. However, those marketing and distribution services that are performed by external parties (e.g., consultants) typically incur additional costs to the investor.

Trading Costs

Buying and selling equities incur a series of trading (or transaction) costs. Some of these trading costs are explicit, including brokerage commission costs, taxes, stamp duties, and stock exchange fees. In addition, many countries charge a modest regulatory fee for certain types of equity trading.

In contrast to explicit costs, some trading costs are implicit in nature. These implicit costs include the following:

- Bid–offer spread
- Market impact (also called price impact), which measures the effect of the trade on transaction prices
- Delay costs (also called slippage), which arise from the inability to complete desired trades immediately because of order size or lack of market liquidity

In an equity portfolio, total trading costs are a function of the size of trades, the frequency of trading, and the degree to which trades demand liquidity from the market. Unlike many other equity portfolio costs, such as management fees, the total cost of trading is generally not revealed to the investor. Rather, trading costs are incorporated into a portfolio's total return and presented as overall performance data. One final trading cost relates to stock lending transactions that were previously discussed. Equity portfolio managers who borrow shares in these transactions must pay fees on shares borrowed.

Investment Approaches and Effects on Costs

Equity portfolio costs tend to vary depending on their underlying strategy or approach. As mentioned previously, index-based strategies tend to charge lower management fees than active strategies primarily because of lower research costs. Index-based equity portfolios also tend to trade less frequently than actively managed equity portfolios, with trading in index-based portfolios typically involving rebalancing or changes to index constituents. Index funds, however, do face a "hidden" cost from potential predatory trading. As an illustration, a predatory trader may purchase (or sell short) shares prior to their effective inclusion (or deletion) from an index, resulting in price movement and potential profit for a predatory trader. Such predatory trading strategies can be regarded as a cost to investors in index funds, albeit a cost that is not necessarily evident to a portfolio manager or investor.

Some active investing approaches "demand liquidity" from the market. For example, in a momentum strategy, the investor seeks to buy shares that are already rising in price (or sell those that are already falling). In contrast, some active investing approaches are more likely to "provide liquidity" to the market, such as deep value strategies (i.e., those involving stocks that are deemed to be significantly undervalued). Investment strategies that involve frequent trading and demand liquidity are, unsurprisingly, likely to have higher trading costs than long-term, buy-and-hold investment strategies.

6 SHAREHOLDER ENGAGEMENT

☐ describe the potential benefits of shareholder engagement and the role an equity manager might play in shareholder engagement

Shareholder engagement refers to the process whereby investors actively interact with companies. Shareholder engagement often includes voting on corporate matters at general meetings as well as other forms of communication (e.g., quarterly investor calls or in-person meetings) between shareholders and representatives of a company. Generally, shareholder engagement concerns issues that can affect the value of a company and, by extension, an investor's shares.

When shareholders engage with companies, several issues may be discussed, including the following:

- *Strategy*—a company's strategic goals, resources, plans for growth, and constraints. Also of interest may be a company's research, product development, culture, sustainability and corporate responsibility, and industry and competitor developments. Shareholders may ask the company how it balances short-term requirements and long-term goals and how it prioritizes the interests of its various stakeholders.
- *Allocation of capital*—a company's process for selecting new projects as well as its mergers and acquisitions strategy. Shareholders may be interested to learn about policies on dividends, financial leverage, equity raising, and capital expenditures.
- *Corporate governance and regulatory and political risk*—including internal controls and the operation of the company's audit and risk committees.
- *Remuneration*—compensation structures for directors and senior management, incentives for certain behaviors, and alignment of interests between directors and shareholders.
- *Composition of the board of directors*—succession planning, director expertise and competence, culture, diversity, and board effectiveness.

Benefits of Shareholder Engagement

Shareholder engagement can provide benefits for both shareholders and companies. From a company's perspective, shareholder engagement can assist in developing a more effective corporate governance culture. In turn, shareholder engagement may lead to better company performance to the benefit of shareholders (as well as other stakeholders).

Investors may also benefit from engagement because they will have more information about companies or the sectors in which companies operate. Such information may include a company's strategy, culture, and competitive environment within an industry. Shareholder engagement is particularly relevant for active portfolio managers. By contrast, index-based fund managers are primarily focused on tracking a given benchmark or index while minimizing costs to do so. Any process, such as shareholder engagement, that takes up management time (and adds to cost) would detract from the primary goal of an index-based manager. This would be less of an issue for very large index-based portfolios, where any engagement costs could be spread over a sizable asset base.

Investors who do not pursue engagement can still benefit from the shareholder engagement of others as so-called free riders. Specifically, assume that a portfolio manager using an active strategy actively engages with a company to improve its operations and was successful in increasing the company's stock price. The manager's actions in this case improved the value of his portfolio and also benefited other investors who own the same stock in their portfolios. Investors who did not participate in shareholder engagement benefited from improved performance but without the costs necessary for engagement.

In addition to shareholders, other stakeholders of a company may also have an interest in the process and outcomes of shareholder engagement. These stakeholders may include creditors, customers, employees, regulators, governmental bodies, and certain other members of society (e.g., community organizations and citizen groups). These other stakeholders can gain or lose influence with companies depending on the outcomes of shareholder engagement. For example, employees can be affected by cost reduction programs requested by shareholders. Another example is when creditors of a company are affected by a change in a company's vendor payment terms, which can impact the company's working capital and cash flow. Such external forces as the media, the academic community, corporate governance consultants, and proxy voting advisers can also influence the process of shareholder engagement.

Shareholders that also have non-financial interests, such as ESG considerations, may also benefit from shareholder engagement. However, these benefits are difficult to quantify. Empirical evidence relating shareholder returns to a company's adherence to corporate governance and ESG practices is mixed. This mixed evidence could be partly attributable to the fact that a company's management quality and effective ESG practices may be correlated with one another. As a result, it is often difficult to isolate non-financial factors and measure the direct effects of shareholder engagement.

Disadvantages of Shareholder Engagement

Shareholder engagement is time consuming and can be costly for both shareholders and companies. Second, pressure on company management to meet near-term share price or earnings targets could be made at the expense of long-term corporate decisions. Third, engagement can result in selective disclosure of important information to a certain subset of shareholders, which could lead to a breach of insider trading rules while in possession of specific, material, non-public information about a company. Finally, conflicts of interest can result for a company. For example, a portfolio manager could engage with a company that also happens to be an investor in the manager's portfolio. In such a situation, a portfolio manager may be unduly influenced to support the company's management so as not to jeopardize the company's investment mandate with the portfolio manager.

The Role of an Equity Manager in Shareholder Engagement

Active managers of equity portfolios typically engage, to some degree, with companies in which they currently (or potentially) invest. In fact, investment firms in some countries have legal or regulatory responsibilities to establish written policies on stewardship and/or shareholder engagement. Engagement activities for equity portfolio managers often include regular meetings with company management or investor relations teams. Such meetings can occur at any time but are often held after annual, semi-annual, or quarterly company results have been published.

Larger investment firms may also employ an analyst (or team of analysts) that focus on ESG issues. They work in conjunction with traditional investment analysts on shareholder voting and other engagement topics.

Activist Investing

Activist investing is a distinct and specialized version of engagement. Activist investors (or activists) specialize in taking stakes in companies and creating change to generate a gain on their investment. Hedge funds are among the most common activists, possibly because of the potential for, in many cases, high performance fees. In addition, because hedge funds are subject to limited regulation, have fewer investment constraints, and can often leverage positions, these investors often have more flexibility as activists.

Engagement through activist investing can include meetings with management, shareholder resolutions, letters to management, presentations to other investors, and media campaigns. Activists may also seek representation on a company's board of directors as a way of exerting influence. Proxy contests are one method used to obtain board representation. These contests represent corporate takeover mechanisms in which shareholders are persuaded to vote for a group seeking a controlling position on a company's board of directors. Social media and other communication tools can help activists coordinate the actions of other shareholders.

Voting

The participation of shareholders in general meetings, also known as general assemblies, and the exercise of their voting rights are among the most influential tools available for shareholder engagement. General meetings enable shareholders to participate in discussions and to vote on major corporate matters and transactions that are not delegated to the board of directors. By engaging in general meetings, shareholders can exercise their voting rights on major corporate issues and better monitor the performance of the board and senior management.

Proxy voting enables shareholders who are unable to attend a meeting to authorize another individual (e.g., another shareholder or director) to vote on their behalf. Proxy voting is the most common form of investor participation in general meetings. Although most resolutions pass without controversy, sometimes minority shareholders attempt to strengthen their influence at companies via proxy voting. Occasionally, multiple shareholders may use this process to collectively vote their shares in favor of or in opposition to a certain resolution.

Some investors use external proxy advisory firms, such as Institutional Shareholder Services and Glass Lewis, that provide voting recommendations and reduce research efforts by investors. Portfolio managers need not follow the recommendations of proxy advisers, but these external parties can highlight potential controversial issues. An investor's voting instructions are typically processed electronically via third-party proxy voting agents.

When an investor loans shares, the transaction is technically an assignment of title with a repurchase option; that is, the voting rights are transferred to the borrower. The transfer of voting rights with stock lending could potentially result in the borrower having different voting opinions from the lending investor. To mitigate this problem, some stock lenders recall shares ahead of voting resolutions to enable exercise of their voting rights. The downside of this action would be the loss of stock lending revenue during the period of stock loan recall and potential reputation risk as an attractive lender. Investors, in some cases, may borrow shares explicitly to exercise the voting rights attached. This process is called *empty voting*, whereby no capital is invested in the voted shares.

SHAREHOLDER ENGAGEMENT

1. An investor manages a fund with a sizable concentration in the transportation sector and is interested in meeting with senior management of a small aircraft manufacturer. Discuss how the investor may benefit from

his or her shareholder engagement activities, as well as from the shareholder engagement of other investors, with this manufacturer.

Solution

The investor may benefit from information obtained about the aircraft manufacturer, such as its strategy, allocation of capital, corporate governance, remuneration of directors and senior management, culture, and competitive environment within the aerospace industry. The investor may also benefit as a "free rider," whereby other investors may improve the manufacturer's operating performance through shareholder engagement—to the benefit of all shareholders. Finally, if the investor has non-financial interests, such as ESG, he or she may address these considerations as part of shareholder engagement.

EQUITY INVESTMENT ACROSS THE ACTIVE MANAGEMENT SPECTRUM 7

☐ describe rationales for equity investment across the active management spectrum

The debate over index-based and active management of equity portfolios has been a longstanding one in the investment community. In reality, the decision between index-based and active management is not an "either/or" (binary) alternative. Instead, equity portfolios tend to exist on a spectrum, ranging from portfolios that closely track a broad, market-capitalization-weighted index to concentrated portfolios of a few equity securities. In some cases, portfolios may resemble a "closet index" in which the portfolio is advertised as actively managed but is essentially an index fund. For an equity manager (or investment firm), there are several considerations for positioning a portfolio along the spectrum.

Confidence to Outperform

An active investment manager typically needs to be confident that she can adequately outperform her benchmark. This determination requires an understanding of the manager's equity investment universe, a competitive analysis of other managers that have a similar investment universe, and appropriate resources (e.g., research staff and access to information).

Client Preference

For equity portfolio managers, client preference is a primary consideration when deciding between index-based or active management. Portfolio managers must assess whether their strategies will attract sufficient funds from clients to make the initiatives viable. Another consideration reflects investors' beliefs regarding the potential for active strategies to generate positive alpha. For example, in some equity market categories, such as large-cap/developed markets, companies are widely known and have considerable equity analyst coverage. For such categories, investors often believe that potential alpha is substantially reduced because all publicly available information is efficiently disseminated, analyzed, and reflected in stock prices.

Exhibit 9 illustrates the prevalence of index-based and active management in US open-end mutual funds and exchange-traded funds (ETFs) by Morningstar equity category. Nearly all assets under management (AUM) in some categories, such as foreign small/mid-cap growth, are managed on an active basis. Other categories, such as large-cap blend, are predominantly managed using an index-based approach.

Exhibit 9: Passive versus Active Equities in US Open-End Mutual Funds and ETFs

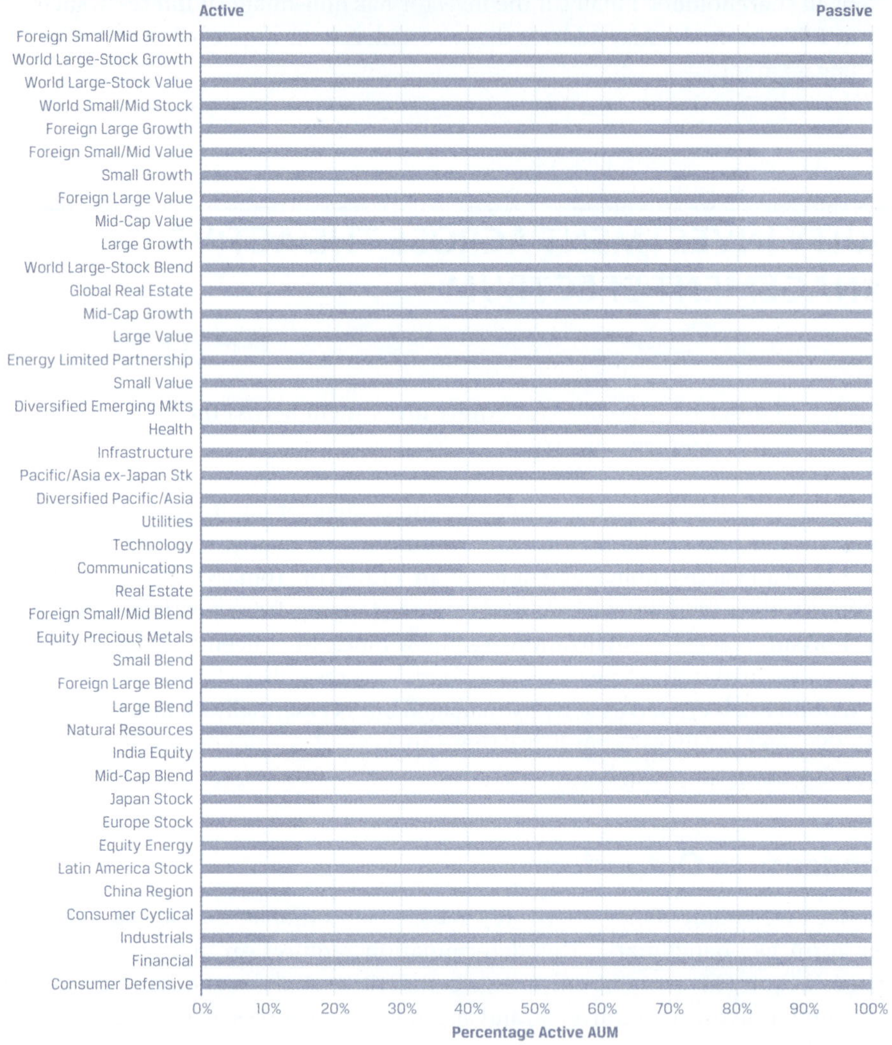

Source: Morningstar Direct. Data as of 31 October 2021.

Suitable Benchmark

An investor or equity manager's choice of benchmark can play a meaningful role in the ability to attract new funds. This choice is particularly relevant in the institutional equity market, where asset owners (and their consultants) regularly screen new managers in desired equity segments. As part of the selection process in desired equity segments, active managers normally must have benchmarks with sufficient liquidity of underlying securities (thus maintaining a reasonable cost of trading). In addition, the number of securities underlying the benchmark typically must be broad enough to generate sufficient alpha. For this reason, many country or sector-specific investment strategies (e.g., consumer defensive companies) are index based.

Client-Specific Mandates

Client-specific investment mandates, such as those related to ESG considerations, are typically managed actively. This active approach occurs because index-based management may not be particularly efficient or cost effective when managers must meet a client's desired holdings (or holdings to avoid). For example, a mandate to avoid investments in companies involved in certain "unacceptable" activities (e.g., the sale of military technology or weapons, tobacco/alcohol, or gambling) requires ongoing monitoring and management. As part of this *exclusionary* (or *negative*) *screening* process, managers need to determine those companies that are directly, as well as indirectly, involved in such "unacceptable" industries. Although ESG investing is typically active, there are a growing number of index-based ESG investment vehicles available.

Risks/Costs of Active Management

As mentioned previously, active equity management is typically more expensive to implement than index-based management. Additionally, "key person" risk is relevant for active managers if the success of an investment manager's firm is dependent on one or a few individuals ("star managers") who may potentially leave the firm.

Taxes

Compared with active strategies, index-based strategies generally have lower turnover and generate a higher percentage of long-term gains. An index fund that replicates its benchmark can have minimal rebalancing. In turn, active strategies can be designed to minimize tax consequences of gains/income at the expense of higher trading costs. One overall challenge is that tax legislation differs widely among countries.

ACTIVE MANAGEMENT SPECTRUM

1. James Drummond, an equity portfolio manager, is meeting with Marie Goudreaux, a wealthy client of his investment firm. Goudreaux is very cost conscious and believes that equity markets are highly efficient. Goudreaux also has a narrow investment focus, seeking stocks in specific country and industry sectors.

   Discuss where Goudreaux's portfolio is likely to be positioned along the active management spectrum.

   Solution

   Goudreaux's portfolio is likely to be managed using an index-based approach. Because she believes in market efficiency, Goudreaux likely believes that Drummond's ability to generate alpha is limited. Goudreaux's cost consciousness also supports index-based management, which is typically less expensive to implement than active management. Finally, Goudreaux's stated desire to invest in specific countries and sectors aligns with index-based approaches.

Advantages of Index-Based Equity Strategies

Many studies over decades support the use of index-based strategies for equities. Renshaw and Feldstein (1960) observed that the returns of professionally managed portfolios trailed the returns on the principal index of that time, the Dow Jones Industrial Average. They also concluded that the index would be a good basis for what they termed an "unmanaged investment company." French (2008) found that the cost of index-based investing is lower than the cost of active management.

Further motivation for index-based investing comes from studies that examine the return and risk consequences of security selection versus asset allocation. Brinson, Hood, and Beebower (1986) found a dominant role for asset allocation rather than security selection in explaining return variability. With index-based investing, portfolio managers eschew the idea of security selection, concluding that the benefits do not justify the costs.

The efficient market hypothesis gave credence to investors' interest in indexes by theorizing that stock prices incorporate all relevant information—implying that after costs, the majority of active investors could not consistently outperform the market. With this backdrop, investment managers began to offer strategies to replicate the returns of stock market indexes as early as 1971.

Index-based management requires substantially fewer personnel, fewer technological resources, and less time spent on analysis and management than active management. Consequently, index-based management fees are generally much lower than fees charged by active managers. This fee differential represents the most significant and enduring advantage of index-based management.

Another advantage is that managers seeking to track an index can generally achieve their objective. Index-based managers model their clients' portfolios to the benchmark's constituent securities and weights as reported by the index provider, in essence replicating the benchmark. The skill of an index-based manager is apparent in the ability to deliver risk-adjusted returns and explain their performance to clients. Gross-of-fees performance among index-based managers tends to be similar, so much of the industry views them as undifferentiated apart from their scope of offerings and client-servicing capabilities.

8 BENCHMARK SELECTION

☐ discuss considerations in choosing a benchmark for an equity portfolio

Successful investors choose their performance benchmarks with care. It is surprising that investors who spend countless hours analyzing the investment process and past performance of an active management strategy may accept a strategy based on a benchmark index without question. A comprehensive analysis of the creation methodology and performance of an index is just as important to investors as the analysis of an active strategy.

Indexes for Index-Based Strategies

For an index to become the basis for an equity investment strategy, it must meet three initial requirements. It must be rules based, transparent, and investable.

Examples of rules include criteria for including a constituent stock and the frequency with which weights are rebalanced. An active manager may use rules and guidelines, but it is often impossible for others to replicate the active manager's decision process. Index rules, in contrast, must be objective, consistent, and predictable.

Transparency may be the most important requirement because index-based managers expect to understand the rules underlying their investment choices. Benchmark providers disclose the rules used and constituents in creating their indexes without any black-box methodologies, which assures investors that indexes will continue to represent the intended strategy.

Equity index benchmarks are investable when their performance can be replicated in the market. For example, the FTSE 100 Index is an investable index because its constituent securities can be purchased easily on the London Stock Exchange. In contrast, most investors cannot track hedge fund-of-funds indexes, such as the HFRI series of indexes, because of the difficulty of buying the constituent hedge funds. Another example of a non-investable index is the Value Line Geometric Index, which is a multiplicative average price. The value of the index is obtained by multiplying the prices and taking a root corresponding to the number of stocks. This index is not useful for investing purposes because it cannot be replicated.

Certain features of individual securities make them non-investable as index constituents. Many stock indexes "free-float adjust" their shares outstanding, which means that they count only shares available for trade by the public, excluding those shares that are held by founders, governments, or other companies. When a company's shares that are floated in the market are a small fraction of the total shares outstanding, trading can result in disproportionate effects. Similarly, stocks for which trading volume is a small fraction of the total shares outstanding are likely to have low liquidity and commensurately high trading costs. Many indexes consequently require that stocks have float and average shares traded above a certain percentage of shares outstanding.

Equity index providers include CRSP, FTSE Russell, Morningstar, MSCI, and S&P Dow Jones. These index providers publicize the rules underlying their indexes, communicate changes in the constituent securities, and report performance. For a fee, they may also provide data to investors who want to replicate the underlying basket of securities.

Index providers have taken steps to make their indexes more investable. One key decision concerns when individual stocks will migrate from one index to another. As a stock increases in market capitalization over time, it might move from small-cap to mid-cap to large-cap status (or in the opposite direction if the stock decreases in market capitalization). Some index providers have adopted policies intended to limit stock migration problems and keep trading costs low for investors who replicate indexes. Among these policies are buffering and packeting. **Buffering** involves establishing ranges around breakpoints that define whether a stock belongs in one index or another. As long as stocks remain within the buffer zone, they stay in their current index. For example, the MSCI USA Large Cap Index contains the 300 largest companies in the US equity market. But a company currently in the MSCI USA Mid Cap Index must achieve a rank as the 200th largest stock to move up to the Large Cap Index. Similarly, a large-cap constituent must shrink and be the 451st largest stock to move down to the Mid Cap Index. Size rankings may change almost every day with market price movements, so buffering makes index transitions a more gradual and orderly process.

The effect of buffering is demonstrated with the MSCI USA Large Cap Index during the regularly scheduled May 2016 reconstitution. The MSCI USA Large Cap Index consists of stocks of US-based companies that meet the criterion to be considered for large cap. Further, the MSCI USA Large Cap Index is intended to represent the largest 70% of the market capitalization of the US equity market.

At each rebalance date, MSCI sets a cutoff value for the smallest company in the index and then sets the buffer value at 67% of the cutoff value. During the May 2016 rebalance, the cutoff market capitalization (market cap) of the smallest company in the index was USD15,707 million; so, the buffer value was USD10,524 million, or approximately USD10.5 billion.

Whole Foods Market, a grocery store operating primarily in the United States that was publicly traded before its acquisition by Amazon.com, had experienced a drop in market value from USD15.3 billion in May 2015 to USD10.4 billion in May 2016. The drop in value put the market cap of Whole Foods Market at a lower value than the acceptable buffer. That is, Whole Foods Market was valued at USD10.4 billion, which was below the buffer point of USD10.5 billion. Per the stated rules, Whole Foods Market was removed from the MSCI USA Large Cap Index and was added to the MSCI USA Mid Cap Index.

Packeting involves splitting stock positions into multiple parts. Let us say that a stock is currently in a mid-cap index. If its capitalization increases and breaches the breakpoint between mid-cap and large-cap indexes, a portion of the total holding is transferred to the large-cap index but the rest stays in the mid-cap index. On the next reconstitution date, if the stock value remains large cap and all other qualifications are met, the remainder of the shares are moved out of the mid-cap index and into the large-cap index. A policy of packeting can keep portfolio turnover and trading costs low. The Center for Research in Security Prices (CRSP) uses packeting in the creation of the CRSP family of indexes.

Considerations When Choosing a Benchmark Index

The first consideration when choosing a benchmark index is the desired factor exposures, which is driven by the objectives and constraints in the investor's investment policy statement (IPS). For equity portfolios, the choices to be made include the geographic market segment (broad versus sectors, domestic versus international), size (large, mid, or small market capitalization), style (value, growth, or blend/core), and other constituent characteristics (e.g., high or low momentum, low volatility, and quality) that are considered risk factors. These are the same factors discussed earlier in equity investment universe segmentation.

The choice of geographic market depends on the investor's circumstances. The investor's domicile, risk tolerance, liquidity needs, and legal considerations all influence the decision. For example, the decision will proceed differently for an Indian institutional investor than for a US-based individual investor. In India, while there are 7,000 listed equity securities, the domestic equity universe is less than one-tenth the size of the US equity market by market capitalization, making the Indian investor more likely to invest globally. But a domestic investment does not carry with it the complexities of cross-border transactions.

Market history and empirical studies show that small-cap stocks tend to be riskier and provide a higher long-term return than large-cap stocks, so size is an important consideration. To the extent that a benchmark's return is correlated with this risk factor, the benchmark has exposure to the size factor.

Size classifications range from mega-cap to micro-cap. Classifications are not limited to individual size categories. For example, many indexes seek to provide equity exposure to both small- and mid-cap companies ("smid-cap" indexes). Investors who desire exposure across the capitalization spectrum may use an "all-cap" index. Such indexes do not necessarily contain all stocks in the market; they usually just combine representative stocks from each of the size ranges. Note that a large-cap stock in an emerging market may have the same capitalization as a small-cap stock in a developed country. Accordingly, index providers usually classify company capitalizations in the context of the local market environment.

Equity benchmark selection also involves the investor's preference for exposure on the growth versus value style spectrum. Growth stocks exhibit such characteristics as high price momentum, high P/Es, and high EPS growth. Value stocks, however, may exhibit high dividend yields, low P/Es, and low price-to-book value ratios. Depending on their basic philosophy and market outlook, investors may have a strong preference for growth or value.

Exhibit 10 shows the number of available total-return equity indexes in various classifications available worldwide. Broad market exposure is provided by nearly 79% of all indexes. Developed market indexes are about four times as common as emerging market indexes. The majority of total-return global equity indexes cover the all-cap space or are otherwise focused on large-cap and mid-cap stocks. total-return global equity indexes cover the all-cap space or are otherwise focused on large-cap and mid-cap stocks.

Exhibit 10: Characteristics of Total-Return Global Equity Indexes

Total-return global equity indexes	14,650
Broad market indexes	11,559
Sector indexes	1,171
Not classified	1,920
Of the 14,650 total-return global equity market indexes:	
Developed markets	8,415
Emerging markets	2,210
Developed and emerging markets	4,006
Not classified	194
Of the 14,650 total-return global equity market indexes:	
All-cap stocks	6,806
Large-cap stocks	1,038
Large-cap and mid-cap stocks	5,766
Mid-cap stocks	216
Mid-cap and small-cap stocks	132
Small-cap stocks	682
Not classified	10

Source: Morningstar Direct, October 2021.

Once the investor has settled on the market, capitalization, and style of benchmark, the next step is to explore the method used in constructing and maintaining the benchmark index.

Index Construction Methodologies

Equity index providers differ in their stock inclusion methods, ranging from **exhaustive** to **selective** in their investment universes. Exhaustive stock inclusion strategies are those that select every constituent of a universe, while selective approaches target only those securities with certain characteristics. The FT Wilshire 5000 Index has perhaps the most exhaustive set of constituents in the US market. This market-cap-weighted index includes approximately 5,000 publicly traded stocks from across the market-cap spectrum. In contrast, the S&P 500 Index embodies a selective approach and aims to provide exposure to US large-cap stocks. Its constituent securities are selected using a committee process and are based on both size and broad industry affiliation.

The weighting method used in constructing an index influences its performance. One of the most common weighting methods is market-cap weighting. Each constituent company's weight in the index is calculated as its market capitalization divided by the total market capitalization of all constituents of the index. In the development of the capital asset pricing model, the capitalization-weighted market portfolio is mean–variance efficient, meaning that it offers the highest return for a given level of risk. To the extent a capitalization-weighted equity index is a reasonable proxy for the market portfolio, the tracking portfolio may be close to mean–variance efficient.

A further advantage of the capitalization-weighted approach is that it reflects a strategy's investment capacity. A cap-weighted index can be thought of as a liquidity-weighted index because the largest-cap stocks tend to have the highest liquidity and the greatest capacity to handle investor flows at a manageable cost. Many investor portfolios tend to be biased toward large-cap stocks and use benchmarks that reflect that bias.

The most common form of market-cap weighting is free-float weighting, which adjusts each constituent's shares outstanding for closely held shares that are not generally available to the investing public. The process to determine the free-float-adjusted shares outstanding relies on publicly available information to determine the holders of the shares and whether those shares would be available for purchase in the marketplace. One reason to adjust a company's share count is that strategic holdings by governments, affiliated companies, founders, and employees are seldom traded. Another less common reason is to account for limitations on foreign ownership of a company; these limitations typically represent rules that are generally set up by a governmental entity through regulation.

Adjusting a company's shares outstanding for float can be a complex task and often requires an index provider to work with the issuer's shareholder services unit or to rely on analytical judgements. Although all data used in determining a company's free-float-adjusted shares outstanding are public information, the various index providers often report a different number of float-adjusted shares outstanding for the same security based on methodological differences.

In a *price-weighted* index, the weight of each stock is its price per share divided by the sum of all share prices in the index. A price-weighted index can be interpreted as a portfolio that consists of one share of each constituent company. Although some price-weighted indexes, such as the Dow Jones Industrial Average and the Nikkei 225, have high visibility as indicators of day-to-day market movements, price-weighted investment approaches are not commonly used by portfolio managers. A stock split for any constituent of the index complicates the index calculation. The weight in the index of the stock that split decreases, and the index divisor decreases as well. With its divisor changed, the index ceases to be a simple average of the constituent stocks' prices. For price-weighted indexes, the assumption that the same number of shares is held in each component stock is a shortcoming, because very few market participants invest in that way.

Equally weighted indexes produce the least-concentrated portfolios. Such indexes have constituent weights of $1/n$, where n represents the number of stocks in the index. Equal weighting of stocks in an index can be considered a naive strategy because it does not show preference toward any single stock, but the reduction of single-stock concentration risk and slowly changing sector exposures make equal weighting attractive to many investors.

As noted by Zeng and Luo (2013), broad market equally weighted indexes are factor indifferent and the weighting randomizes factor mispricing. Equal weighting also produces higher volatility than cap weighting, one reason being that it imparts a small-cap bias to the portfolio. Equal weights deviate from market weights most dramatically for large-cap indexes, which contain mega-cap stocks. Constrained market-cap ranges, such as those of mid-cap indexes, even if market weighted, tend to have relatively uniform weights.

Equally weighted indexes require regular rebalancing because immediately after trading in the constituent stocks begins, the weights are no longer equal. Most index providers use a regular reweighting schedule. Standard & Poor's offers the S&P 500 Index in an equally weighted format and rebalances the index to equal weights once each quarter. Therein would appear to lie a misleading aspect of equally weighted indexes: For a 91-day quarter, the index is not equally weighted (albeit, modestly so) for 90/91 = 99% of the time.

Another drawback of equal weighting is its limited investment capacity. The smallest-cap constituents of an equally weighted index may have low liquidity, which means that investors cannot purchase a large number of shares without causing price changes. Zeng and Luo (2013) addressed this issue by assuming that 10% of shares in the cap-weighted S&P 100 and S&P 500 and 5% of shares in the cap-weighted S&P 400 and S&P 600 indexes are currently held in cap-weighted indexing strategies without any appreciable liquidity problems. They then focused on the smallest-cap constituent of each index as of December 2012, and they determined the value that 10% (5%) of its market capitalization represents. Finally, they multiplied this amount by the number of stocks in the index to estimate the total investment capacity for tracking each of the S&P equally weighted equity indexes. Zeng and Luo's estimates are shown in Exhibit 11.

Exhibit 11: Estimated Investment Capacity of Equally Weighted (EW) Equity Indexes

Index	Capitalization Category	Estimated Capacity
S&P 100 EW	Mega-cap	USD176 billion
S&P 500 EW	Large-cap	USD82 billion
S&P 400 EW	Mid-cap	USD8 billion
S&P 600 EW	Small-cap	USD2 billion

Source: Zeng and Luo (2013).

Qin and Singal (2015) showed that equally weighted portfolios have a natural advantage over cap-weighted portfolios. To the extent that any of the constituent stocks are mispriced, equally weighted portfolios will experience return superiority as the stock prices move up or down toward their correct intrinsic value. Because of the aforementioned need to rebalance back to equal weights, Qin and Singal found that the advantage largely vanishes when taxes and transaction costs are considered. However, based on their results, tax-exempt investors could experience superior returns from equal weighting.

Other non-cap-weighted indexes are weighted based on such attributes as a company's or stock's fundamental characteristics (e.g., sales, income, or dividends). Discussed in more detail later, fundamental weighting delinks a constituent stock's portfolio weight from its market value. The philosophy behind fundamental weighting is that although stock prices may become over- or undervalued, the market price will eventually converge to a level implied by the fundamental attributes.

Market-cap-weighted indexes and fundamentally weighted indexes share attractive characteristics, including low cost, rule-based construction, transparency, and investability. Their philosophies, however, are different. Market-cap-weighted portfolios are based on the efficient market hypothesis, while fundamentally weighted indexes look to exploit possible inefficiencies in market pricing.

An important concern in benchmark selection relates to how concentrated the index is. In this case, the concept of the effective number of stocks, which is an indication of portfolio concentration, can provide important information. An index that has a high degree of stock concentration or a low effective number of stocks may be relatively undiversified. Woerheide and Persson (1993) showed that the Herfindahl–Hirschman Index (HHI) is a valid measure of stock-concentration risk in a portfolio, and Hannam and Jamet (2017) demonstrated its use by practitioners. The HHI is calculated as the sum of the constituent weightings squared, as shown in Equation 1:

$$\text{HHI} = \sum_{i=1}^{n} w_i^2, \tag{1}$$

where w_i is the weight of stock i in the portfolio.

The HHI can range in value from $1/n$, where n is equal to the number of securities held, to 1.0. An HHI of $1/n$ would signify an equally weighted portfolio, and a value of 1.0 would signify portfolio concentration in a single security.

Using the HHI, one can estimate the effective (or equivalent) number of stocks, held in equal weights, that would mimic the concentration level of the chosen index. The effective number of stocks for a portfolio is calculated as the reciprocal of the HHI, as shown in Equation 2:

$$\text{Effective number of stocks} = \frac{1}{\sum_{i=1}^{n} w_i^2} = 1/\text{HHI}. \tag{2}$$

Malevergne, Santa-Clara, and Sornette (2009) demonstrated that cap-weighted indexes have a surprisingly low effective number of stocks. Consider the NASDAQ 100, a US-based market-cap-weighted index consisting of 100 stocks. If the index were weighted uniformly, each stock's weight would be 0.01 (1%). In May 2017, the constituent weights ranged from 0.123 for Apple, Inc., to 0.0016 for Liberty Global plc—a ratio of 77:1. Weights for the top five stocks totaled almost 0.38 (38%), a significant allocation to those securities. Across all stocks in the index, the median weight was 0.0039 (that is, 0.39%). The effective number of stocks can be estimated by squaring the weights for the stocks, summing the results, and calculating the reciprocal of that figure. The squared weights for the NASDAQ 100 stocks summed to 0.0404, the reciprocal of which is 1/0.0404 = 24.75, the effective number of stocks. Thus, the 100 stocks in the index had a concentration level that can be thought of as being equivalent to approximately 25 stocks held in equal weights.

EFFECTIVE NUMBER OF STOCKS

1. A market-cap-weighted index contains 50 stocks. The five largest-cap stocks have weights of 0.089, 0.080, 0.065, 0.059, and 0.053. The bottom 45 stocks represent the remaining weight of 0.654, and the sum of the squares of those weights is 0.01405. What are the portfolio's Herfindahl–Hirschman Index and effective number of stocks held?

Solution

The stocks, their weights, and their squared weights are shown in Exhibit 12.

Exhibit 12: Calculations for Effective Number of Stocks

Stock	Weight	Squared Weight
1	0.089	0.00792
2	0.080	0.00640
3	0.065	0.00423
4	0.059	0.00348
5	0.053	0.00281
Stocks 6–50	0.654	Sum of squared weights for Stocks 6–50: 0.01405
Total for Stocks 1–50	1.000	0.03889

The HHI is shown in the final row: 0.03889. The reciprocal of the HHI is 1/0.03889 = 25.71. Thus, the effective number of stocks is approximately 26. The fact that the portfolio weights are far from being a uniform 2% across the 50 stocks makes the effective number of stocks held in equal weights less than 26.

The stock market crises of 2000 and 2007 brought heightened attention to investment strategies that are defensive or volatility reducing. For example, some income-oriented investors are drawn to strategies that weight benchmark constituents based on the dividend yield of each stock. Volatility weighting calculates the volatility of each constituent stock and weights the index based on the inverse of each stock's relative volatility. A related method produces a minimum-variance index using mean–variance optimization.

Exhibit 13 shows the various methods for weighting the constituent securities of broad-based, non-industry-sector, total-return global equity indexes.

Exhibit 13: Equity Index Constituent Weighting Methods

Weighting Method	Number of Indexes
Market-cap, free-float adjusted	11,211
Market-cap weighted	1,362
Multi-factor weighted	442

Weighting Method	Number of Indexes
Equal weighted	715
Dividend weighted	357

Source: Morningstar Direct, October 2021.

Another consideration in how an index is constructed involves its periodic rebalancing and reconstitution schedule. Reconstitution of an index frequently involves the addition and deletion of index constituents, while rebalancing refers to the periodic reweighting of those constituents. Index reconstitution and rebalancing create turnover. The turnover for developed-market, large-cap indexes that are infrequently reconstituted tends to be low, while benchmarks constructed using stock selection rather than exhaustive inclusion have higher turnover. As seen in Exhibit 14, both rebalancing and reconstitution occur with varied frequency, although the former is slightly more frequent.

Exhibit 14: Index Rebalancing/Reconstitution Frequency for Broad Global Equity Market Total-Return Indexes

Frequency	Rebalancing	Reconstitution
Daily	18	25
Monthly	624	42
Quarterly	9,354	4,389
Semi-annually	1,328	6,235
Annually	2,925	3,102
As needed	147	33

Note: The totals for the Rebalancing and Reconstitution columns differ slightly, as does the index total in Exhibit 14.
Source: Morningstar Direct, October 2021.

The method of reconstitution may produce additional effects. When reconstitution occurs, index-tracking portfolios, mutual funds, and ETFs will want to hold the newly included names and sell the deleted names. The demand created by investors seeking to track an index can push up the stock prices of added companies while depressing the prices of the deleted ones. Research shows that this produces a significant price effect in each case. Depending on the reconstitution method used by index publishers, arbitrageurs may be able to anticipate the changes and front-run the trades that will be made by index-based managers. In some cases, the index rules are written such that the decision to add or remove an index constituent is voted on by a committee maintained by the index provider. Where a committee makes the final decision, the changes become difficult to guess ahead of time. In other cases, investors know the precise method used for reconstitution, so guessing is often successful.

Chen, Noronha, and Singal (2004) found that constituent changes for indexes that reconstitute using subjective criteria are often more difficult for arbitrageurs to predict than indexes that use objective criteria. Even indexes that use objective criteria for reconstitution often announce the changes several weeks before they are implemented. Stocks near the breakpoint between small-cap and large-cap indexes are especially vulnerable to reconstitution-induced price changes. The smallest-cap stocks in the Russell 1000 large-cap index have a low weight in that cap-weighted index. After any of those stocks are demoted to the Russell 2000 small-cap index, they are likely to have some of the highest weights. Petajisto (2010) showed that the process of moving in that direction tends to be associated with increases in stock prices, while movements into the large-cap index tend to have negative effects. He also concluded that transparency in reconstitution is a virtue rather than a drawback.

A final consideration is investability. As stated earlier, an effective benchmark must be investable in that its constituent stocks are available for timely purchase in a liquid trading environment. Indexes that represent the performance of a market segment that is not available for direct ownership by investors must be replicated through derivative strategies, which, for reasons explained later in the curriculum, may be sub-optimal for many investors.

SUMMARY

- Equities can play several roles in an overall portfolio, including providing such benefits as capital appreciation, dividend income, diversification with other asset classes, and a potential hedge against inflation.
- The inclusion of equities in a portfolio can be driven by a client's goals or needs. Portfolio managers often consider the following investment objectives and constraints when deciding to include equities (or asset classes in general, for that matter) in a client's portfolio: *risk objective*, *return objective*, *liquidity requirement*, *time horizon*, *tax concerns*, *legal and regulatory factors*, and *unique circumstances*.
- Investors often segment the equity universe according to (1) size and style, (2) geography, and (3) economic activity.
- Sources of equity portfolio income include dividends, securities lending fees and interest, dividend capture, covered calls, and cash-covered puts (or cash-secured puts).
- Sources of equity portfolio costs include management fees, performance fees, administration fees, marketing/distribution fees, and trading costs.
- Shareholder engagement is the process whereby companies engage with their shareholders. The process typically includes voting on corporate matters at general meetings and other forms of communication, such as quarterly investor calls or in-person meetings.
- Shareholder engagement can provide benefits for both shareholders and companies. From a company's perspective, shareholder engagement can assist in developing a more effective corporate governance culture. In turn, shareholder engagement may lead to better company performance to the benefit of shareholders (as well as other stakeholders).
- Disadvantages of shareholder engagement include costs and time involved, pressure on a company to meet near-term share price or earnings targets, possible selective disclosure of information, and potential conflicts of interest.
- Activist investors (or activists) specialize in taking stakes in companies and creating change to generate a gain on the investment.
- The participation of shareholders in general meetings, also known as general assemblies, and the exercise of their voting rights are among the most influential tools available for shareholder engagement.

- The choice of using active or index-based management is not an "either/or" (binary) decision. Investors may decide to position their portfolios across the active management spectrum based on their confidence in outperforming, client preference, suitable benchmarks, client-specific mandates, risks/costs of active management, and taxes.
- Many active equity portfolio managers are unsuccessful at beating benchmarks and have charged high management fees. Consequently, index-based strategies have increased in popularity.
- Selection of a benchmark is driven by the equity investor's objectives and constraints as presented in the investment policy statement. The benchmark index must be rule-based, transparent, and investable. Specific important characteristics include the domestic or foreign market covered, the market capitalization of the constituent stocks, where the index falls in the value–growth spectrum, and other risk factors.
- The equity benchmark index weighting scheme is another important consideration for investors. Weighting methods include market-cap weighting, price weighting, equal weighting, and fundamental weighting. Market-cap weighting has several advantages, including the fact that weights adjust automatically.
- Index rebalancing and reconstitution policies are important features. Rebalancing involves adjusting the portfolio's constituent weights after price changes, mergers, or other corporate events have caused those weights to deviate from the benchmark index. Reconstitution involves deleting names that are no longer in the index and adding names that have been approved as new index members.

REFERENCES

Brinson, Gary P., L. Randolph Hood, and Gilbert L. Beebower. 1986. "Determinants of Portfolio Performance." *Financial Analysts Journal* 42 (4): 39–44.

Chen, Honghui, Gregory Noronha, and Vijay Singal. 2004. "The Price Response to S&P 500 Index Additions and Deletions: Evidence of Asymmetry and a New Explanation." *Journal of Finance* 59 (4): 1901–30.

French, Kenneth R. 2008. "Presidential Address: The Cost of Active Investing." *Journal of Finance* 63 (4): 1537–1573.

GSIA. 2020. "*Global Sustainable Investment Review 2020.*" www.gsi-alliance.org/.

Hannam, Richard and Frédéric Jamet. 2017. "*IQ Insights: Equal Weighting and Other Forms of Size Tilting.*" SSGA white paper (January).

Kaplan, Steven, Tobias Moskowitz, and Berk Sensoy. 2013. "The Effects of Stock Lending on Security Prices: An Experiment." *Journal of Finance* 68 (5): 1891–936.

Malevergne, Yannick, Pedro Santa-Clara, and Didier Sornette. 2009. "Professor Zipf Goes to Wall Street." *Working Paper Series (National Bureau of Economic Research)* 15295 (August).

Petajisto, Antti. 2010. "*The Index Premium and Its Hidden Cost for Index Funds.*" Working paper, NYU Stern.

Qin, Nan and Vijay Singal. 2015. "*Investor Portfolios When Stocks Are Mispriced: Equally-Weighted or Value-Weighted?*" Working paper, Virginia Tech.

Renshaw, Edward F. and Paul J. Feldstein. 1960. "The Case for an Unmanaged Investment Company." *Financial Analysts Journal* 16 (1): 43–46.

Woerheide, Walt and Don Persson. 1993. "An Index of Portfolio Diversification." *Financial Services Review* 2 (2): 73–85.

Zeng, Liu and Frank Luo. 2013. "*10 Years Later: Where in the World Is Equal Weight Indexing Now?*" White paper, Standard & Poor's.

PRACTICE PROBLEMS

The following information relates to questions 1-8

Three years ago, the Albright Investment Management Company (Albright) added four new funds—the Barboa Fund, the Caribou Fund, the DoGood Fund, and the Elmer Fund—to its existing fund offering. Albright's new funds are described in Exhibit 1.

Exhibit 1: Albright Investment Management Company New Funds

Fund	Fund Description
Barboa Fund	Invests solely in the equity of companies in oil production and transportation industries in many countries.
Caribou Fund	Uses an aggressive strategy focusing on relatively new, fast-growing companies in emerging industries.
DoGood Fund	Investment universe includes all US companies and sectors that have favorable environmental, social, and governance (ESG) ratings and specifically excludes companies with products or services related to aerospace and defense.
Elmer Fund	Investments selected to track the S&P 500 Index. Minimizes trading based on the assumption that markets are efficient.

Hans Smith, an Albright portfolio manager, makes the following notes after examining these funds:

Note 1 The fee on the Caribou Fund is a 15% share of any capital appreciation above a 7% threshold and the use of a high-water mark.

Note 2 The DoGood Fund invests in Fleeker Corporation stock, which is highly rated in the ESG space, and Fleeker's pension fund has a significant investment in the DoGood Fund. This dynamic has the potential for a conflict of interest on the part of Fleeker Corporation but not for the DoGood Fund.

Note 3 The DoGood Fund's portfolio manager has written policies stating that the fund does not engage in shareholder activism. Therefore, the DoGood Fund may be a free rider on the activism by these shareholders.

Note 4 Of the four funds, the Elmer Fund is most likely to appeal to investors who want to minimize fees and believe that the market is efficient.

Note 5 Adding investment-grade bonds to the Elmer Fund will decrease the portfolio's short-term risk.

Smith discusses means of enhancing income for the three funds with the junior analyst, Kolton Frey, including engaging in securities lending or writing covered calls. Frey tells Smith the following:

Statement 1 Securities lending would increase income through reinvestment of the cash collateral but would require the fund to miss out on dividend income from the lent securities.

Statement 2 Writing covered calls would generate income, but doing so would limit the upside share price appreciation for the underlying shares.

1. The Barboa Fund can be *best* described as a fund segmented by:

   A. size/style.

   B. geography.

   C. economic activity.

2. The Caribou Fund is *most likely* classified as a:

   A. large-cap value fund.

   B. small-cap value fund.

   C. small-cap growth fund.

3. The DoGood Fund's approach to the aerospace and defense industry is *best* described as:

   A. positive screening.

   B. negative screening.

   C. thematic investing.

4. The Elmer fund's management strategy is:

   A. active.

   B. index.

   C. blended.

5. Based on Note 1, the fee on the Caribou Fund is *best* described as a:

   A. performance fee.

   B. management fee.

   C. administrative fee.

6. Which of the following notes about the DoGood Fund is correct?

   A. Only Note 2

   B. Only Note 3

   C. Both Note 2 and Note 3

7. Which of the notes regarding the Elmer Fund is correct?

   A. Only Note 4

B. Only Note 5

C. Both Note 4 and Note 5

8. Which of Frey's statements about securities lending and covered call writing is correct?

   A. Only Statement 1

   B. Only Statement 2

   C. Both Statement 1 and Statement 2

The following information relates to questions 9-11

Evan Winthrop, a senior officer of a US-based corporation, meets with Rebecca Tong, a portfolio manager at Cobalt Wealth Management. Winthrop recently moved his investments to Cobalt in response to his previous manager's relative underperformance and high expenses.

Winthrop resides in Canada and plans to retire there. His annual salary covers his current spending needs, and his vested defined benefit pension plan is sufficient to meet retirement income goals. Winthrop desires exposure to global equity markets with a focus on low management costs and minimal tracking error to any index benchmarks. The fixed-income portion of the portfolio may consist of laddered maturities with a home-country bias.

Tong proposes using an index-based equity strategy and reviews the most important requirements for an appropriate benchmark. With regard to investable indexes, Tong tells Winthrop the following:

Statement 1	A free-float adjustment to a market-capitalization-weighted index lowers its liquidity.
Statement 2	An index provider that incorporates a buffering policy makes the index more investable.

Winthrop asks Tong to select a benchmark for the equity allocation that holds all sectors of the Canadian equity market and to focus the portfolio on highly liquid, well-known companies. In addition, Winthrop specifies that any stock purchased should have a relatively low beta, a high dividend yield, a low P/E, and a low price-to-book ratio (P/B).

9. Which of Tong's statements regarding equity index benchmarks is correct?

   A. Only Statement 1

   B. Only Statement 2

   C. Both Statement 1 and Statement 2

10. To satisfy Winthrop's benchmark and security selection specifications, the equity index benchmark Tong selects should be:

    A. small capitalization with a core tilt.

    B. large capitalization with a value tilt.

C. mid-capitalization with a growth tilt.

11. What is a problem with Winthrop's benchmark preference?

    A. The geographic limitation to Canadian equities

    B. The exclusion of fixed-income securities given Winthrop's significant exposure

    C. The inclusion of all sectors

SOLUTIONS

1. C is correct. The Barboa Fund invests solely in the equity of companies in the oil production and transportation industries in many countries. The fund's description is consistent with the production-oriented approach, which groups companies that manufacture similar products or use similar inputs in their manufacturing processes.

   A is incorrect because the fund description does not mention the firms' size or style (i.e., value, growth, or blend). Size is typically measured by market capitalization and often categorized as large cap, mid-cap, or small cap. Style is typically classified as value, growth, or a blend of value and growth. In addition, style is often determined through a "scoring" system that incorporates multiple metrics or ratios, such as price-to-book ratios, price-to-earnings ratios, earnings growth, dividend yield, and book value growth. These metrics are then typically "scored" individually for each company, assigned certain weights, and then aggregated.

   B is incorrect because the fund is invested in many countries, which indicates that the fund is not segmented by geography. Segmentation by geography is typically based on the stage of countries' macroeconomic development and wealth. Common geographic categories are developed markets, emerging markets, and frontier markets.

2. C is correct because the fund focuses on new companies that are generally classified as small firms, and the fund has a style classified as aggressive. A widely used approach to segment the equity universe incorporates two factors: size and style. Size is typically measured by market capitalization and often categorized as large cap, mid-cap, or small cap. Style is typically classified as value, growth, or a blend of value and growth.

3. B is correct. The DoGood fund excludes companies based on specified activities (e.g., aerospace and defense), which is a process of negative screening. Negative, or exclusionary, screening refers to the practice of excluding certain sectors or companies that deviate from accepted standards in such areas as human rights or environmental concerns.

   A is incorrect because positive screening attempts to identify companies or sectors that score most favorably regarding ESG-related risks and/or opportunities. The restrictions on investing indicate that a negative screen is established.

   C is incorrect because thematic investing focuses on investing in companies in a specific sector or following a specific theme, such as energy efficiency or climate change. The DoGood Fund's investment universe includes all companies and sectors that have favorable ESG ratings (no specific sectors or screens) but with specific exclusions.

4. B is correct. The fund is managed under the assumption that the market is efficient, and investments are selected to mimic an index. Compared with active strategies, index strategies generally have lower turnover and generate a higher percentage of long-term gains. An index fund that replicates its benchmark can have minimal rebalancing.

5. A is correct. Performance fees serve as an incentive for portfolio managers to achieve or outperform return objectives, to the benefit of both the manager and investors. Several performance fee structures exist, although performance fees tend to be "upward only"; that is, fees are earned by the manager when performance objectives are met, but fund investors are not reimbursed when performance is negative. Performance fees could be reduced, however, following a

period of poor performance. Fee calculations also reflect high-water marks. As described in Note 1, the fee for the Caribou Fund is a 15% share of any capital appreciation above a 7% threshold, with the use of a high-water mark, and is therefore a performance fee.

B is incorrect because management fees include direct costs of research (such as remuneration and expenses for investment analysts and portfolio managers) and the direct costs of portfolio management (e.g., software, trade processing costs, and compliance). Management fees are typically determined as a percentage of the funds under management.

C is incorrect because administrative fees include the processing of corporate actions, such as rights issues and optional stock dividends; the measurement of performance and risk of a portfolio; and voting at company meetings. Generally, these functions are provided by an investment management firm itself and are included as part of the management fee.

6. B is correct because the fund becomes a free rider if it allows other shareholders to engage in actions that benefit the fund, and therefore Note 3 is correct. Investors benefit from the shareholder engagement of others under the so-called free-rider problem. Specifically, assume that a portfolio manager using an active strategy actively engages with a company to improve its operations and was successful in increasing the company's stock price. The manager's actions in this case improved the value of his portfolio and also benefited other investors that own the same stock in their portfolios. Those investors that did not participate in shareholder engagement benefit from improved performance but without the costs necessary for engagement.

   Note 2 is incorrect because a conflict of interest arises on the part of the DoGood Fund if it owns shares of a company that invests in the fund. Conflicts of interest can result for a company. For example, a portfolio manager could engage with a company that also happens to be an investor in the manager's portfolio. In such a situation, a portfolio manager may be unduly influenced to support the company's management so as not to jeopardize the company's investment mandate with the portfolio manager.

7. A is correct. For index-based portfolios, management fees are typically low because of lower direct costs of research and portfolio management relative to actively managed portfolios. Therefore, Note 4 is correct.

   Note 5 is incorrect because the predictability of correlations is uncertain.

8. B is correct. Writing covered calls also generates additional income for an equity portfolio, but doing so limits the upside from share price appreciation of the underlying shares. Therefore, Statement 2 is correct.

   A is incorrect because dividends on loaned stock are "manufactured" by the stock borrower for the stock lender; that is, the stock borrower ensures that the stock lender is compensated for any dividends that the lender would have received had the stock not been loaned. Therefore, Statement 1 is incorrect. Frey is incorrect in stating that the funds would miss out on dividend income on lent securities.

9. B is correct. The three requirements for an index to become the basis for an equity investment strategy are that the index be (a) rule based, (b) transparent, and (c) investable. Buffering makes index benchmarks more investable (Statement 2) by making index transitions a more gradual and orderly process.

   A is incorrect because basing the index weight of an individual security solely on the total number of shares outstanding without using a free-float adjustment may make the index less investable. If a stock market cap excludes shares held by founders, governments, or other companies, then the remaining shares more accurately reflect the stock's true liquidity. Thus a free-float adjustment (Statement 1) to a market index more accurately reflects its actual liquidity (it does not lower its liquidity). Many indexes require that individual stocks have float and average shares traded above a certain percentage of shares outstanding.

10. B is correct. To address Winthrop's concerns (sector diversification, liquidity, risk, dividend yield, P/E, and P/B), the benchmark should consist of large-capitalization stocks with a value tilt. A large-capitalization index contains the largest-cap stocks, which tend to have the highest liquidity. Value stocks tend to exhibit high dividend yields and low P/E and P/B ratios.

    A is incorrect because small-capitalization stocks tend to be riskier than large-capitalization stocks. Winthrop has a preference for low-beta (low-risk) stocks.

    C is incorrect because a growth index will not address Winthrop's preference for a low P/E. Growth stocks exhibit such characteristics as high price momentum, high P/Es, and high EPS growth.

11. A is correct. Winthrop desires exposure to global equity markets, so the equity benchmark should be global as well—for example, the MSCI All Country World Index.

    B is incorrect because Winthrop was stating a preference for the benchmark for his equity allocation. Including fixed income would be inappropriate.

    C is incorrect because including all sectors is appropriate because his investment strategy includes all sectors.

LEARNING MODULE

2

Overview of Fixed-Income Portfolio Management

by Bernd Hanke, PhD, CFA, and Brian J. Henderson, PhD, CFA.

Bernd Hanke, PhD, CFA, is at Global Systematic Investors LLP (United Kingdom). Brian J. Henderson, PhD, CFA, is at the George Washington University (USA).

LEARNING OUTCOMES

Mastery	The candidate should be able to:
□	discuss roles of fixed-income securities in portfolios and how fixed-income mandates may be classified
□	describe fixed-income portfolio measures of risk and return as well as correlation characteristics
□	describe bond market liquidity, including the differences among market sub-sectors, and discuss the effect of liquidity on fixed-income portfolio management
□	describe and interpret a model for fixed-income returns
□	discuss the use of leverage, alternative methods for leveraging, and risks that leverage creates in fixed-income portfolios
□	discuss differences in managing fixed-income portfolios for taxable and tax-exempt investors
□	describe liability-driven investing
□	describe the strategy of cash flow matching
□	describe construction, benefits, limitations, and risk–return characteristics of a laddered bond portfolio

INTRODUCTION

1

Investors often seek regular income from their investments as well as a predetermined date when their capital will be returned. Fixed-income investments offer both.

Fixed-income instruments include a broad range of publicly traded securities (such as commercial paper, notes, and bonds traded through exchanges as well as OTC) and non-publicly traded instruments (such as loans and private placements). Individual loans or fixed-income obligations may be bundled into a pool of assets supporting such instruments as asset-backed securities and covered bonds. Fixed-income portfolio managers combine these diverse instruments across issuers, maturities, and jurisdictions to meet the various needs of investors. We discuss the different roles of fixed-income securities in portfolios and explain the two main types of fixed-income mandates—liability-based mandates and total return mandates—as well as bond market liquidity. We also provide an overview of portfolio measures, instruments, and vehicles used in fixed-income portfolio management and introduce a model of how a bond position's total expected return can be decomposed.

We explain liability-driven investing in fixed-income investing by demonstrating how to best structure a fixed-income portfolio when considering both the asset and liability sides of the investor's balance sheet. We introduce the idea of structuring a bond portfolio to match the future cash liabilities that have bond-like characteristics. Asset–liability management (ALM) strategies are based on the concept that investors incorporate both rate-sensitive assets and liabilities into the portfolio decision-making process. When the liabilities are given and assets are managed, liability-driven investing (LDI), a common type of ALM strategy, may be used to ensure adequate funding for an insurance portfolio, a pension plan, or an individual's budget after retirement. The techniques and risks associated with LDI are introduced and then expanded to cover both cash flow and duration-matching techniques and multiple liabilities. This strategy, known as immunization, may be viewed simply as a special case of interest rate hedging.

2 ROLES OF FIXED-INCOME SECURITIES IN PORTFOLIOS

☐ discuss roles of fixed-income securities in portfolios and how fixed-income mandates may be classified

Fixed-income securities serve important roles in investment portfolios, including diversification, regular cash flows, and possible inflation hedging. We will briefly review the roles in turn.

Diversification Benefits

Fixed-income investments can provide diversification benefits when combined with other asset classes in a portfolio. Recall that a major reason portfolios can effectively reduce risk is that combining securities whose returns are not perfectly correlated (i.e., a correlation coefficient of less than +1.0) provides risk diversification. Lower correlations are associated with higher diversification benefits and lower risk. The challenge in diversifying risk is to find assets with correlations much lower than +1.0.

Correlations between fixed-income and equity securities vary, but adding fixed-income exposure to portfolios that include equity securities is usually an effective way to obtain diversification benefits. Fixed-income investments may also provide risk reduction because of their low correlations with other asset classes, such as real estate and commodities. Exhibit 1 shows the correlation between the S&P 500 Index and various fixed-income categories based on total returns (monthly) over a 20-year period ending in December 2019.

Exhibit 1: Total Return Correlations between US Fixed Income and Equities

	Fixed-Income Indexes						
	US Aggregate	10Y US Treasury	US Corporate Bonds	Global Aggregate	US TIPS	US High Yield	Emerging Market (USD)
S&P 500	−0.09	−0.30	0.20	0.15	0.02	0.63	0.51

Note: Bloomberg Barclays Indices are shown.
Source: Bloomberg.

Exhibit 2 shows the divergent performance of US equities and bonds from the end of 2019 to the end of March 2020. For example, bonds outperformed equities amid the fears over the global COVID-19 pandemic in Q1 2020.

Exhibit 2: Returns of S&P 500 vs. 10-Year Treasuries, 12 December 2019–31 March 2020

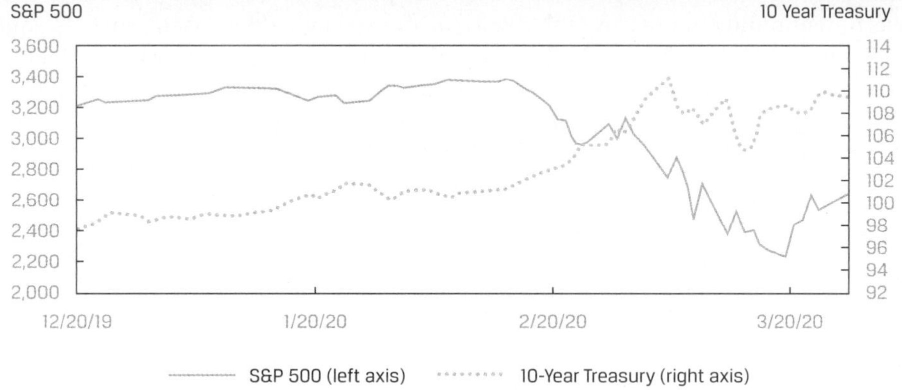

Note: Daily data; constant-maturity 10-year Treasuries used.

Within the fixed-income asset class, the correlation between fixed-income indexes will be driven largely by the interest rate component (i.e., duration) and by geography. Rate changes can explain a significant amount of movement in fixed-income securities prices. The credit component or credit spread will likely result in diversification given differences in sectors, credit quality, and geography. For example, investment-grade securities may exhibit less correlation with below-investment-grade securities and with emerging market securities and equities. The rate component of the return can be isolated by calculating correlations using excess returns (this is more meaningful when evaluating returns across fixed-income sectors). Exhibit 3 shows correlations on an excess return basis between various fixed-income indexes.

Exhibit 3: Excess Return Correlations of Barclays Bloomberg Indices over a 20-Year Period

	US Aggregate	US Corporate	Global Aggregate	US High Yield	Emerging Market (USD)
US Aggregate	1.00				
US Corporate	0.93	1.00			
Global Aggregate	0.88	0.86	1.00		
US High Yield	0.86	0.84	0.76	1.00	
Emerging Market (USD)	0.79	0.76	0.74	0.80	1.00

Notes: Bloomberg Barclays Indices shown. Based on monthly data over 20 years ending December 2019.
Source: Bloomberg.

Importantly, correlations are not constant over time. During a long historical period, the average correlation of returns between two asset classes may be low, but in any period, the correlation can differ from the average correlation. During periods of market stress, investors may exhibit a "flight to quality" by buying safer assets, such as government bonds (increasing their prices), and selling riskier assets, such as equity securities and high-yield bonds (lowering their prices). These actions may decrease the correlation between government bonds and equity securities, as well as between government bonds and high-yield bonds. At the same time, the correlation between riskier assets, such as equity securities and high-yield bonds, may increase.

Note that similar to correlations, volatility (standard deviation) of asset class returns may also vary over time. If interest rate volatility increases, bonds, particularly those with long maturities, can exhibit higher near-term volatility relative to the average volatility over a long historical period. The standard deviation of returns for lower-credit-quality (high-yield) bonds can rise significantly during times of financial stress because as credit quality declines and the probability of default increases, investors often view these bonds as being more similar to equities.

Exhibit 4 shows the annual returns of the S&P 500 versus the Bloomberg Barclays US Corporate High Yield Index over a 20-year period ending in December 2019. It illustrates how the fixed-income sector and equities can behave in a similar way. Recall that both asset classes are strongly linked to the issuer's business performance and fundamentals. Over the 20-year period, the average return was 7.96% and 6.26% for the high-yield index and the S&P 500, respectively, and the standard deviation was 15.54% and 17.02%, respectively. The correlation was 0.69.

Exhibit 4: Relationship between S&P 500 and High-Yield Returns

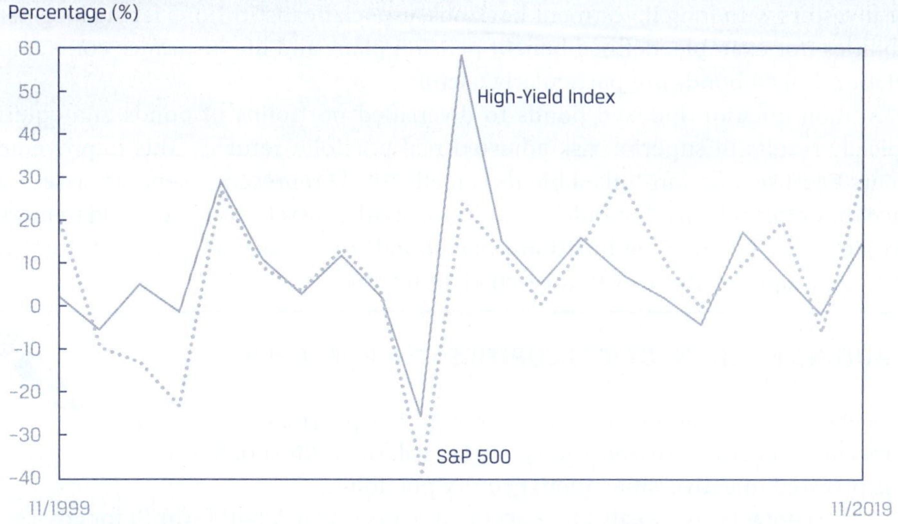

Benefits of Regular Cash Flows

Fixed-income investments typically produce regular cash flows for a portfolio. Regular cash flows allow investors—both individual and institutional—to meet known future obligations, such as tuition payments, pension obligations, and payouts on life insurance policies. In these cases, future liabilities can be estimated with some reasonable certainty. Fixed-income securities are often acquired and "dedicated" to funding those future liabilities. In dedicated portfolios, fixed-income securities are selected with cash flows matching the timing and magnitude of projected future liabilities.

It is important to note that reliance on regular cash flows assumes that no credit event (such as an issuer missing a scheduled interest or principal payment) or other market events (such as a decrease in interest rates that causes an increase in prepayments of mortgages underlying mortgage-backed securities) will occur. These events may cause actual cash flows of fixed-income securities to differ from expected cash flows. If any credit or market event occurs or is forecasted to occur, a portfolio manager may need to adjust the portfolio.

Inflation-Hedging Potential

Some fixed-income securities can provide a hedge for inflation. Bonds with floating-rate coupons can protect interest income from inflation because the market reference rate should adjust for inflation over time. The principal payment at maturity is unadjusted for inflation. Inflation-linked bonds provide investors with valuable inflation-hedging benefits by paying a return that is directly linked to an index of consumer prices and adjusting the principal for inflation. The return on inflation-linked bonds, therefore, includes a real return plus an additional component that is tied directly to the inflation rate. All else equal, inflation-linked bonds typically exhibit lower return volatility than conventional bonds and equities do because the volatility of the returns on inflation-linked bonds depends on the volatility of *real*, rather than *nominal*, interest rates. The volatility of real interest rates is typically lower than the volatility of nominal interest rates that drive the returns of conventional bonds and equities.

Many governments in developed countries and some in developing countries have issued inflation-linked bonds, as have financial and non-financial corporate issuers. For investors with long investment horizons, especially institutions facing long-term liabilities (for example, defined benefit pension plans and life insurance companies), inflation-linked bonds are particularly useful.

Adding inflation-indexed bonds to diversified portfolios of bonds and equities typically results in superior risk-adjusted real portfolio returns. This improvement occurs because inflation-linked bonds can effectively represent a separate asset class since they offer returns that differ from those of other asset classes and add to market completeness. Introducing inflation-linked bonds to an asset allocation strategy can result in a superior mean–variance-efficient frontier.

ADDING FIXED-INCOME SECURITIES TO A PORTFOLIO

Mary is anxious about the level of risk in her portfolio because of a recent period of increased equity market volatility. Most of her wealth is invested in a diversified global equity portfolio.

She contacts two wealth management firms (Firm A and Firm B) for advice. In her conversations with each adviser, she expresses her desire to reduce her portfolio's risk and to have a portfolio that generates a cash flow stream with consistent purchasing power over her 15-year investment horizon.

The correlation coefficient of Mary's diversified global equity portfolio with a diversified fixed-coupon bond portfolio is –0.10 and with a diversified inflation-linked bond portfolio is 0.10. The correlation coefficient between a diversified fixed-coupon bond portfolio and a diversified inflation-linked bond portfolio is 0.65.

The adviser from Firm A suggests diversifying half of her investment assets into nominal fixed-coupon bonds. The adviser from Firm B also suggests diversification but recommends that Mary invest 25% of her investment assets in fixed-coupon bonds and 25% in inflation-linked bonds.

1. Evaluate the advice given to Mary by each adviser based on her stated desires regarding portfolio risk reduction and cash flow stream. Recommend which advice Mary should follow, making sure to discuss the following concepts in your answer:

   a. Diversification benefits

   b. Cash flow benefits

   c. Inflation-hedging benefits

Solution

Advice from Firm A:

Diversifying into fixed-coupon bonds would offer substantial diversification benefits in lowering overall portfolio volatility (risk) given the negative correlation of –0.10. The portfolio's volatility, measured by standard deviation, would be lower than the weighted sum of standard deviations of the diversified global equity portfolio and the diversified fixed-coupon bond portfolio. The portfolio will generate regular cash flows because it includes fixed-coupon bonds. This advice, however, does not address Mary's desire to have the cash flows maintain purchasing power over time and thus serve as an inflation hedge.

Advice from Firm B:

Diversifying into both fixed-coupon bonds and inflation-linked bonds offers additional diversification benefits beyond that offered by fixed-coupon bonds only. The correlation between diversified global equities and inflation-linked bonds is only 0.10. The correlation between nominal fixed-coupon bonds and inflation-linked bonds is 0.65, which is also less than 1.0. The portfolio will generate regular cash flows because of the inclusion of fixed-coupon and inflation-linked bonds. Adding the inflation-linked bonds helps at least partially address Mary's desire for consistent purchasing power over her investment horizon.

Which Advice to Choose:

Based on her stated desires and the analysis given, Mary should follow the advice provided by Firm B.

Classifying Fixed-Income Mandates

The previous section covered the roles of fixed-income securities in portfolios and the benefits these securities provide. When investment mandates include an allocation to fixed income, investors need to decide how to add fixed-income securities to portfolios. Fixed-income mandates can be broadly classified into liability-based mandates and total return mandates. Exhibit 5 provides a broad overview of the different types of mandates, splitting the universe into two broad categories—liability-based mandates and total return mandates.

Exhibit 5: Fixed-Income Mandates

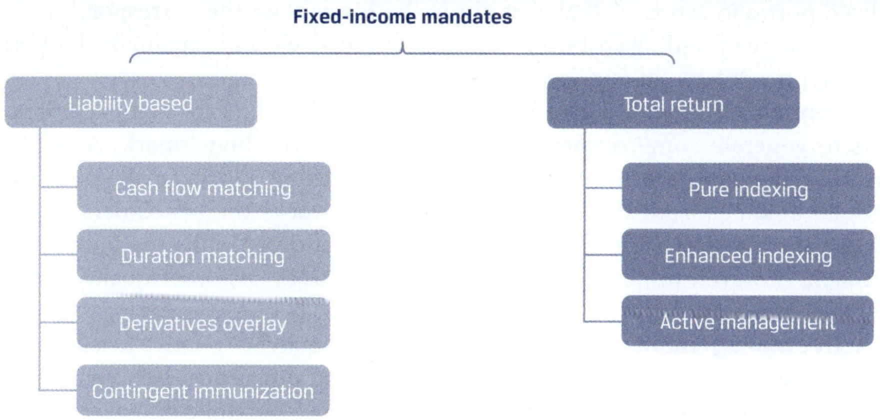

Liability-Based Mandates

Liability-based mandates are investments that take an investor's future obligations into consideration. Liability-based mandates are managed to match or cover expected liability payments (future cash outflows) with future projected cash inflows. As such, they are also referred to as asset/liability management (ALM) or mandates that use liability-driven investments (LDIs). These types of mandates are structured in a way to ensure that a liability or a stream of liabilities (e.g., a company's pension liabilities or those projected by insurance companies) can be covered and that any risk of shortfalls or deficient cash inflows is minimized. **Cash flow matching** is an immunization approach that attempts to ensure that all future liability payouts are matched precisely by cash flows from bonds or fixed-income derivatives. **Duration matching** is an immunization approach that is based on the duration of assets and liabilities. Ideally, the liabilities being matched (the liability portfolio) and the portfolio of assets (the bond portfolio) should be affected similarly by a change in interest rates. The mandates may use futures contracts (such as in a derivatives overlay) and, as in the case of **contingent immunization**—a hybrid approach that combines immunization with an active management approach when assets exceed the present value of liabilities—may allow for active bond portfolio management. Such liability-based mandates, which will be covered in detail later, are important because of their extensive use by such entities as pension plans and insurance companies.

Total Return Mandates

Total return mandates are generally managed to either track or outperform a market-weighted fixed-income benchmark, such as the Bloomberg Barclays Global Aggregate Bond Index. They are used by many types of investors, including individuals, foundations, endowments, sovereign wealth funds, and defined contribution retirement plans. Liability-based and total return mandates exhibit common features, such as the goal to achieve the highest risk-adjusted returns (or perhaps the highest yields to maturity) given a set of constraints. The two types of mandates, however, have fundamentally different objectives. A common total return approach is **pure indexing**. It attempts to replicate a bond index as closely as possible and is sometimes referred to as "full replication." Under this approach, the targeted **active return** (portfolio return minus benchmark return, also known as "tracking difference") and **active risk** (annualized standard deviation of active returns, also known as the benchmark **tracking risk** or tracking error) are both zero. In practice, even if the active risk is zero, the realized portfolio return will almost always be lower than the corresponding index return because of trading costs and management fees. We will explain the limitations of this approach later, in our coverage of index-based strategies.

An **enhanced indexing approach** maintains a close link to the benchmark but seeks to generate some outperformance relative to the benchmark. As with the pure indexing approach, in practice, enhanced indexing allows small deviations in portfolio holdings from the benchmark index but tracks the benchmark's primary risk factor exposures very closely (particularly duration). Unlike the pure indexing approach, however, minor risk factor mismatches (e.g., sector or quality bets) are used in enhanced indexing.

Active management allows larger risk factor mismatches relative to a benchmark index. These mismatches may cause significant return differences between the active portfolio and the underlying benchmark. Most notably, portfolio managers may take views on portfolio duration that differ markedly from the duration of the underlying benchmark. To take advantage of potential opportunities in changing market environments, active managers may incur significant portfolio turnover—often considerably higher than the underlying benchmark's turnover. Active portfolio managers normally charge higher management fees than pure or enhanced indexing managers charge.

Exhibit 6 summarizes the key features of the total return approaches.

Exhibit 6: Total Return Approaches: Key Features

	Pure Indexing	Enhanced Indexing	Active Management
Objective	Match benchmark return and risk as closely as possible	Modest outperformance (generally 20–30 bps) of benchmark while active risk is kept low (typically around 50 bps or lower)	Higher outperformance (generally around 50 bps or more) of benchmark and higher active risk levels
Portfolio weights	Ideally the same as benchmark or only slight mismatches	Small deviations from underlying benchmark	Significant deviations from underlying benchmark
Target risk factor profile	Aims to match risk factors exactly	Most primary risk factors are closely matched (in particular, duration)	Large risk factor deviations from benchmark (in particular, duration; note that some active strategies do not take large risk factor deviations and focus on high idiosyncratic risk)
Turnover	Similar to underlying benchmark	Slightly higher than underlying benchmark	Considerably higher than underlying benchmark

Fixed-Income Mandates with ESG Considerations

Some fixed-income mandates include a requirement that environmental, social, and governance (ESG) factors be considered during the investment process. When considering these factors, an analyst or portfolio manager may look for evidence of whether the portfolio contains companies whose operations are favorable or unfavorable in the context of ESG and whether such companies' actions and resource management practices reflect a sustainable business model. For example, the analyst or portfolio manager may consider whether a company's activities involved significant environmental damage, instances of unfair labor practices, or lapses in corporate governance integrity. For companies that do not fare favorably in an ESG analysis, investors may assume that these companies are more likely to encounter future ESG-related incidents that could cause serious reputational and financial damage to the company. Such incidents could impair a company's credit quality and result in a decline in both the price of the company's bonds and the performance of a portfolio containing those bonds.

THE CHARACTERISTICS OF DIFFERENT TOTAL RETURN APPROACHES

1. A consultant for a large corporate pension plan is looking at three funds (Funds X, Y, and Z) as part of the pension plan's global fixed-income allocation. All three funds use the Bloomberg Barclays Global Aggregate Bond Index as a benchmark. Exhibit 7 provides the characteristics of each fund and the index. Identify the approach (pure indexing, enhanced indexing, or

active management) that is *most likely* used by each fund and support your choices by referencing the information in Exhibit 7.

Exhibit 7: Characteristics of Funds X, Y, and Z and the Bloomberg Barclays Global Aggregate Bond Index

Risk and Return Characteristics	Fund X	Fund Y	Fund Z	Bloomberg Barclays Global Aggregate Bond Index
Average maturity (years)	8.61	8.35	9.45	8.34
Modified duration (years)	6.37	6.35	7.37	6.34
Average yield to maturity (%)	1.49	1.42	1.55	1.43
Convexity	0.65	0.60	0.72	0.60
Quality				
AAA	41.10	41.20	40.11	41.24
AA	15.32	15.13	14.15	15.05
A	28.01	28.51	29.32	28.78
BBB	14.53	14.51	15.23	14.55
BB	0.59	0.55	1.02	0.35
Not rated	0.45	0.10	0.17	0.05
Maturity Exposure				
0–3 years	21.43	21.67	19.20	21.80
3–5 years	23.01	24.17	22.21	24.23
5–10 years	32.23	31.55	35.21	31.67
10+ years	23.33	22.61	23.38	22.30
Country Exposure				
United States	42.55	39.44	35.11	39.56
Japan	11.43	18.33	13.33	18.36
France	7.10	6.11	6.01	6.08
United Kingdom	3.44	5.87	4.33	5.99
Germany	6.70	5.23	4.50	5.30
Italy	4.80	4.01	4.43	4.07
Canada	4.44	3.12	5.32	3.15
Other	19.54	17.89	26.97	17.49

Notes: Quality, maturity exposure, and country exposure are shown as a percentage of the total for each fund and the index. Weights do not always sum to 100 because of rounding. Historical data used as of February 2016.

Source: Barclays Research.

Solution

Fund X most likely uses an enhanced indexing approach. Fund X's modified duration and convexity are very close to those of the benchmark but still differ slightly. The average maturity of Fund X is slightly longer than that of the benchmark, whereas Fund X's average yield to maturity is slightly higher than that of the benchmark. Fund X also has deviations in quality, maturity exposure, and country exposure from the benchmark, providing further evidence of an enhanced indexing approach. Some of these deviations are meaningful; for example, Fund X has a relatively strong underweighting in Japan.

Fund Y most likely uses a pure indexing approach because it provides the closest match to the Bloomberg Barclays Global Aggregate Bond Index. The risk and return characteristics are almost identical for Fund Y and the benchmark. Furthermore, quality, maturity exposure, and country exposure deviations from the benchmark are very minor.

Fund Z most likely uses an active management approach because risk and return characteristics, quality, maturity exposure, and country exposure differ markedly from the index. The difference can be seen most notably with the mismatch in modified duration (7.37 for Fund Z versus 6.34 for the benchmark). Other differences between Fund Z and the index exist, but a sizable duration mismatch provides the strongest evidence of an active management approach.

FIXED-INCOME PORTFOLIO MEASURES 3

☐ describe fixed-income portfolio measures of risk and return as well as correlation characteristics

We first provide a brief review of fixed-income risk and return measures introduced in earlier lessons (Exhibit 8).

Exhibit 8: Bond Risk and Return Measures

Macaulay duration (MacDur)	Macaulay duration is a weighted average of the time to receipt of the bond's promised payments, where the weights are the shares of the full price that correspond to each of the bond's promised future payments.
Modified duration (ModDur)	The Macaulay duration statistic is divided by one plus the yield per period, which estimates the percentage price change (including accrued interest) for a bond given a change in its yield to maturity.
Effective duration (EffDur)	The sensitivity of the bond's price to a change in a benchmark yield curve (i.e., using a parallel shift in the benchmark yield curve (ΔCurve). Effective duration is essential to the measurement of the interest rate risk of a complex bond where future cash flows are uncertain.
Key rate duration (KeyRatDur, also called *partial duration*)	A measure of a bond's sensitivity to a change in the benchmark yield curve at a specific maturity point or segment. Key rate durations help identify "shaping risk" for a bond or a portfolio—that is, its sensitivity to changes in the shape of the benchmark yield curve (e.g., the yield curve becoming steeper or flatter or showing more or less curvature).

Empirical duration	A measure of interest rate sensitivity that is determined from market data—that is, run a regression of bond price returns on changes in a benchmark interest rate (for example, the price returns of a 10-year euro-denominated corporate bond could be regressed on changes in the 10-year German bund or the 10-year Euribor swap rate).
Money duration	A measure of the price change in units of the currency in which the bond is denominated. Money duration can be stated per 100 of par value or in terms of the bond's actual position size in the portfolio. Commonly called "dollar duration" in the United States.
Price value of a basis point (PVBP)	An estimate of the change in a bond's price given a 1 bp change in yield to maturity. PVBP "scales" money duration so that it can be interpreted as money gained or lost for each basis point change in the reference interest rate. Also referred to in North America as the "dollar value of an 0.01" (pronounced *oh-one*) and abbreviated as DV01. It is calibrated to a bond's par value of 100; for example, a DV01 of \$0.08 is equivalent to 8 cents per 100 points. (The terms PVBP and DV01 are used interchangeably; we will generally use PVBP, but DV01 has the same meaning). A related statistic to PVBP, sometimes called "basis point value" (or BPV), is the money duration times 0.0001 (1 bp).
Convexity	A second-order effect that describes a bond's price behavior for larger yield movements. It captures the extent to which the yield/price relationship deviates from a linear relationship. If a bond has positive convexity, the expected return of the bond will be higher than the return of an identical-duration, lower-convexity bond if interest rates change. This price behavior is valuable to investors, and therefore, a bond with higher convexity might be expected to have a lower yield to maturity than a similar-duration bond with less convexity. Nominal convexity calculations assume that the cash flows do not change when yields to maturity change.
Effective convexity (EffCon)	A curve convexity statistic that measures the secondary effect of a change in a benchmark yield curve. A pricing model is used to determine the new prices when the benchmark curve is shifted upward (PV+) and downward (PV−) by the same amount (ΔCurve), holding other factors constant.

Exhibit 8 provides a reminder of convexity and why it is valuable. It is likely to be even more valuable when interest rate volatility is expected to increase. This dynamic tends to drive changes in the shape of the yield curve: As convexity becomes more valuable, investors will bid up prices on the longer-maturity bonds (which have more convexity), and the long end of the curve may decline or even invert (or invert further), increasing the curvature of the yield curve. A helpful heuristic for understanding convexity is that for zero-coupon (option free) bonds, the following are true:

- Macaulay durations increase linearly with maturity: A 30-year zero-coupon bond has three times the duration of a 10-year zero-coupon bond. Convexity is approximately proportional to duration squared; therefore, a 30-year zero-coupon bond has about nine times the convexity of a 10-year zero-coupon bond.
- Coupon-paying bonds have more convexity than zero-coupon bonds: A 30-year coupon-paying bond with a duration of approximately 18 years has more convexity than an 18-year zero-coupon bond. The more widely dispersed a bond's cash flows are around the duration point, the more convexity it will exhibit. For this reason, a zero-coupon bond has the lowest convexity of all bonds of a given duration.

SCALING CONVENTIONS

Convexity statistics must always be interpreted carefully because there is no convention for how they should be presented. When calculating the impact of convexity in approximating returns, the proper accounting for the scaling of convexity is important. Note that some data vendors report the convexity statistic divided by 100, whereas other applications may use the "raw" number.

Portfolio Measures of Risk and Return

Building on the measures of risk and return that apply to individual fixed-income securities, we now provide an overview of measures of risk and return applicable to portfolios of fixed-income securities. We will then illustrate their use in fixed income in a portfolio management scenario and refer to them in the subsequent coverage of liability-driven investing and total return strategies.

Bond portfolio duration is the sensitivity of a portfolio of bonds to small changes in interest rates. Recall that it can be calculated as the weighted average of time to receipt of the aggregate cash flows or, more commonly, as the weighted average of the individual bond durations of the portfolio.

Modified duration of a bond portfolio indicates the percentage change in the market value given a change in yield to maturity. If the modified duration of a portfolio is 15, then for a 100 bp increase or decrease in yield to maturity, the market value of the portfolio is expected to decrease or increase by about 15%. Modified duration of a portfolio comprising *j* fixed-income securities can be estimated as

$$\text{AvgModDur} = \sum_{j=1}^{J} \text{ModDur}_j \left(\frac{MV_j}{MV}\right),$$

where MV stands for market value of the portfolio and MV_j is the market value of a specific bond.

Convexity of a bond portfolio can be a valuable tool when positioning a portfolio. Importantly, it is a second-order effect; it operates behind duration in importance and can largely be ignored for small yield changes. When convexity is added with the use of derivatives, however, it can be extremely important to returns. This effect will be demonstrated later. Negative convexity may also be an important factor in a bond's or a portfolio's returns. For bonds with short option positions embedded in their structures (such as mortgage-backed securities or callable bonds) or portfolios with short option positions, the convexity effect may be large. For a portfolio comprising *j* fixed-income securities, it can be estimated as

$$\text{AvgConvexity} = \sum_{j=1}^{J} \text{Convexity}_j \left(\frac{MV_j}{MV}\right).$$

Adding convexity to a portfolio is not costless. Portfolios with higher convexity are most often characterized by lower yields to maturity. Investors will be willing to pay for increased convexity when they expect yields to change by more than enough to cover the amount given up in yield to maturity. Convexity is more valuable when yields to maturity are more volatile. A portfolio's convexity can be altered by shifting the maturity/duration distribution of bonds in the portfolio, by adding individual bonds with the desired convexity properties, or by using derivatives.

Effective duration and convexity of a portfolio are the relevant summary statistics when future cash flows of bonds in a portfolio are contingent on interest rate changes.

$$\text{Effective Duration(EffDur)} = \frac{(\text{PV}_-) - (\text{PV}_+)}{2(\Delta\text{Curve})(\text{PV}_0)}.$$

$$\text{Effective Convexity(EffCon)} = \frac{(\text{PV}_-) + (\text{PV}_+) - 2(\text{PV}_0)}{(\Delta\text{Curve})^2(\text{PV}_0)}.$$

Spread duration is a useful measure for determining a portfolio's sensitivity to changes in credit spreads. Duration indicates the percentage price effect of an interest rate change on a bond, and spread duration measures the effect of a change in yield spread on a bond's price. Spread duration provides the approximate percentage increase (decrease) in bond price expected for a 1% decrease (increase) in credit spread.

Duration times spread (DTS) is a modification of the spread duration definition to incorporate the empirical observation that spread changes across the credit spectrum tend to occur on a *proportional percentage* basis rather than being based on *absolute* basis point changes. This measure, reviewed in detail in a later lesson, weights the spread duration by a factor equal to the current credit spread, increasing the magnitude of expected price changes for a given change in spread.

Portfolio dispersion captures the variance of the times to receipt of cash flows with respect to the duration. It is used in measuring interest rate immunization for liabilities. Whereas Macaulay duration is the weighted *average* of the times to receipt of cash flows, dispersion is the weighted *variance*. It measures the extent to which the payments are spread out around the duration. Convexity is affected by the dispersion of cash flows. Higher cash flow dispersion leads to an increase in convexity.

Correlations between Fixed-Income Sectors

Correlation characteristics refer to the interplay between benchmark rates, spreads, and such factors as currencies. Correlations between fixed-income sectors within a market are likely to be higher than those across markets given country-specific factors, such as central bank policy, economic growth, and inflation. In developed economies, investment-grade securities with a low probability of default are highly correlated with interest rate changes in the sovereign yield curve. Below-investment-grade securities are affected more by changes in spread than by changes in general interest rates and often exhibit stronger correlations with equity markets. Recall that correlations between interest rates and spreads can often be negative. As the economy worsens, interest rates fall and spreads widen, and the reverse occurs when the economy improves. Correlations for global government bonds will be partly driven by changes in interest rates but also by changes in local currency exchange rates.

Use of Measures of Risk and Return in Portfolio Management

We now provide an overview of how portfolio measures may be used by fund managers to reflect their views.

Portfolio Duration in Total Return Mandates

Total return mandates that are actively managed often use a top-down approach to establish the large risk factors in a portfolio combined with a bottom-up approach of individual security selection. The analytics discussed earlier can be used to measure and manage the macroeconomic risk factors in the portfolio. Portfolio managers develop or use a forecast of the direction of the economy and an assessment of the current business, political, and regulatory environment to develop themes that can be reflected in the portfolio. On the basis of expectations for changes in interest rates and the shape of the yield curve, portfolio managers can adjust the duration of a portfolio to reflect their view. For example, if the portfolio manager expects interest rates to rise and the yield curve to steepen, she would reduce the exposure of the portfolio to longer-dated bonds relative to the benchmark, which would reduce portfolio duration. If her view materialized as expected, all else equal, the fund would outperform the benchmark, resulting in active excess returns.

Managing Credit Exposure Using Spread Duration

Portfolio managers often use the spread duration measures introduced earlier to gauge the portfolio's sensitivity to changes in credit spreads. A portfolio manager expecting credit spreads to narrow may wish to increase the spread duration in an actively managed portfolio. The manager may face constraints, such as a target duration, rating-based restrictions, or limits to derivatives use, as part of the investment mandate. A second way to increase the portfolio credit exposure is to reduce the average credit rating of the portfolio; for example, reduce A rated names and increase BBB rated credits. In this case, the duration times spread measure may be a more appropriate measure of portfolio value changes. These active portfolio management tools are addressed in more detail in a later lesson on credit strategies.

The single bond risk and return measures discussed previously at an aggregate level will determine the large risk factors for the portfolio. The portfolio manager will select securities as part of the portfolio construction process to achieve a targeted level of tracking error or active risk relative to a benchmark. The contribution to duration, convexity, spread duration, and DTS of a single bond to the portfolio is weighted by the market value of the position relative to the total market value of the portfolio. The portfolio manager will select a diversified universe of holdings to construct the portfolio in the manner he believes will optimize expected return and risk.

Relative Value Concept

Relative value is a key concept in the active management of fixed-income portfolios that describes the selection of the most attractive individual securities to populate the portfolio with, using ranking and comparing. Portfolio managers analyze and rank securities based on such considerations as valuation, issuer fundamentals, and market technical conditions (supply and demand). This analysis is carried out across sectors, issuers, and individual securities to select securities with the most attractive risk and return profiles. The portfolio manager will establish a time horizon over which the relative value analysis is applied. The single bond characteristics can be used to express an active position relative to the benchmark. For example, each bond has a distinct key rate duration (KeyRateDur) profile. If the portfolio manager wants to establish a bullet or barbell position as part of the active risk decision, bonds with a specific KeyRateDur profile will be selected. Similarly, the portfolio manager can select securities that in aggregate have more/less DTS than the benchmark if she is bullish/bearish on corporate bond spreads. The selection of the most attractive individual securities to populate the portfolio will apply relative value analysis to compare and rank securities. In the context of the efficient frontier, those securities that offer the most expected return for a given level of risk would offer the best relative value.

The positioning of the portfolio reflects the portfolio manager's total return expectations for the market and relative returns versus the benchmark, given his views about both the direction of interest rates and credit spread changes. Diversification considerations ensure that idiosyncratic risks are within acceptable risk parameters.

KNOWLEDGE CHECK

1. Which of the following best describes a measure of sensitivity to changes in yields to maturity for a portfolio of bonds with cash flows contingent on interest rate changes?

   A. Portfolio dispersion

   B. Modified duration

   C. Effective duration

   Solution

   C is correct. Effective duration is particularly relevant in scenarios where the cash flows from the bonds held in a portfolio are contingent on changes in interest rates.

2. Which of the following is a true statement about portfolio dispersion?

   A. It can be described as the variance of time to the receipt of cash flows.

   B. The higher the dispersion, the lower the convexity of the portfolio.

   C. It determines the portfolio's sensitivity to changes in credit spreads.

   Solution

   A is correct. Dispersion measures the variance of the time to receive cash flows from the fixed-income securities held.

4 BOND MARKET LIQUIDITY

☐ describe bond market liquidity, including the differences among market sub-sectors, and discuss the effect of liquidity on fixed-income portfolio management

A liquid security is one that may be transacted quickly with little effect on the security's price. Fixed-income securities vary greatly in their liquidity.

Compared with equities, fixed-income markets are generally less liquid. The global fixed-income universe contains many individual bonds with varying features. Many issuers have multiple bonds outstanding with their own unique maturity dates, coupon rates, early redemption features, and other specific features.

An important structural feature affecting liquidity is that fixed-income markets are typically over-the-counter dealer markets. Search costs (the costs of finding a willing counterparty) exist in bond markets because investors may have to locate desired bonds. In addition, when either buying or selling, investors may have to obtain quotes from various dealers to obtain the most advantageous pricing. With limited, although improving, sources for transaction prices and quotes, bond markets are ordinarily less transparent than equity markets. Liquidity, search costs, and price transparency are closely related to the type of issuer and its credit quality. An investor is likely to find that bonds of a highly creditworthy government issuer are more liquid, have greater price transparency, and have lower search costs than bonds of, for example, a corporate issuer with lower credit quality.

Bond liquidity is typically highest immediately after issuance. For example, an on-the-run bond issue (the most recently issued bonds) of a highly creditworthy sovereign entity is typically more liquid than a bond with similar features—including maturity—that was issued previously (an off-the-run bond). On-the-run bonds also trade at narrow bid–ask spreads. This difference in liquidity is typically present even if the off-the-run bond was issued only one or two months earlier. One reason for this phenomenon is that soon after bonds are issued, dealers normally have a supply of the bonds in inventory, but as time goes by and bonds are traded, many are purchased by buy-and-hold investors. Once in the possession of such investors, those bonds are no longer available for trading.

Recall that liquidity typically affects bond yields to maturity. Bond investors require higher yields for investing in illiquid securities relative to otherwise identical securities that are more liquid. The higher yield to maturity compensates investors for the costs they may encounter if they try to sell illiquid bonds prior to maturity. These costs include the opportunity costs associated with the delays in finding trading counterparties as well as the bid–ask spread (which is a direct loss of wealth). The incremental yield to maturity investors require for holding illiquid bonds instead of liquid bonds is referred to as a *liquidity premium*. The magnitude of the liquidity premium normally varies depending on such factors as the issuer, the issue size, and time to maturity. For example, when a 10-year US Treasury bond shifts from on-the-run to off-the-run status, it typically trades at a yield to maturity several basis points above that of the new on-the-run bond.

Liquidity among Bond Market Sub-Sectors

Bond market liquidity varies across sub-sectors. These sub-sectors can be categorized by such key features as issuer type, credit quality, issue size, and maturity. The global bond market includes sovereign government bonds, non-sovereign government bonds, government-related bonds, corporate bonds, and securitized bonds (such as asset-backed securities and commercial mortgage-backed securities). Sovereign government bonds are typically more liquid than corporate and non-sovereign government bonds. Their superior liquidity relates to their large issuance size, use as benchmark bonds, acceptance as collateral in the repo market, and well-recognized issuers. Sovereign government bonds of countries with high credit quality and large issuance are typically more liquid than bonds of lower-credit-quality countries.

Corporate bonds are issued by many different companies and represent a wide spectrum of credit quality. For corporate bonds with low credit quality, it can be difficult to find a counterparty dealer with the securities in inventory or willing to take them into inventory. Bonds of infrequent issuers are often less liquid than the bonds of issuers with many outstanding issues because market participants are less familiar with companies that seldom issue debt. In addition, smaller issues are generally less liquid than larger issues because small bond issues are typically excluded from major bond indexes with minimum issue size requirements.

The Effects of Liquidity on Fixed-Income Portfolio Management

Liquidity concerns influence fixed-income portfolio management in multiple ways, including pricing, portfolio construction, and consideration of alternatives to bonds (such as derivatives).

Pricing

Sources for pricing of recent bond transactions—notably corporate bonds—are not always readily available. Note that price transparency is improving in some bond markets. In the United States, the Financial Industry Regulatory Authority's Trade Reporting and Compliance Engine (TRACE) and the Municipal Securities Rulemaking Board's Electronic Municipal Market Access (EMMA) are electronic systems that help increase transparency in corporate and municipal bond markets, and similar initiatives play a similar role elsewhere for corporate bonds traded on market exchanges, increasing pricing transparency. In most bond markets, however, the lack of transparency in corporate bond trading presents a challenge.

Because many bonds do not trade or trade infrequently, using recent transaction prices to represent current value is not practical. Reliance on last traded prices, which may be out of date and may not incorporate current market conditions, could result in costly trading decisions. The determinants of corporate bond value, including interest rates, credit spreads, and liquidity premiums, change frequently. One solution to the pricing problem is to use matrix pricing that makes use of observable liquid benchmark yields of similar maturity and duration as well as benchmark spreads of bonds with comparable times to maturity, credit quality, and sector or security type to estimate the current market yield and price.

Portfolio Construction

Investors' liquidity preferences directly influence portfolio construction. In constructing a portfolio, investors must consider the important trade-off between yield to maturity and liquidity. As mentioned previously, illiquid bonds typically have higher yields to maturity; a buy-and-hold investor seeking higher returns will often prefer less liquid bonds with higher yields to maturity. In contrast, investors who prefer greater liquidity will likely sacrifice returns and choose more liquid bonds with lower yields to maturity. Some investors may restrict their portfolio holdings to bonds within a certain maturity range. This restriction reduces the need to sell bonds to generate needed cash inflows. In such cases, the investors that anticipate their liquidity needs may give up the higher yield to maturity typically available to longer-term bonds. In addition to avoiding longer-term bonds, investors with liquidity concerns may also avoid small issues and private placements of corporate bonds.

A challenge in bond portfolio construction relates to the dealer market. Bond dealers often carry an inventory of bonds because buy and sell orders do not arrive simultaneously. A dealer is not certain how long bonds will remain in its inventory. Less liquid bonds are likely to remain in inventory longer than liquid bonds. A dealer provides bid–ask quotes (prices at which it will buy and sell) on bonds of its choice. Some illiquid bonds will not have quotes, particularly bid quotes, from any dealer. Several different factors determine the bid–ask spread. Riskier bonds often have higher bid–ask spreads because of dealers' aversion to hold those bonds in inventory. Because bond dealers must finance their inventories, the dealers incur costs in both obtaining funding and holding those bonds. Dealers seek to cover their costs and make a profit through the bid–ask spread, and therefore, the spread will be higher for illiquid bonds that are likely to remain in inventory longer.

A bond's bid–ask spread is also a function of the bond's complexity and how easily market participants can analyze the issuer's creditworthiness. Bid–ask spreads in government bonds are generally lower than spreads in corporate bonds or structured financial instruments, such as asset-backed securities. Conventional (plain vanilla) corporate bonds normally have lower spreads than corporate bonds with non-standard or complex features, such as embedded options. Bonds of large, high-credit-quality corporations that have many outstanding bond issues are the most liquid among corporate bonds, and thus they have relatively low bid–ask spreads compared with smaller, less creditworthy companies.

Illiquidity directly increases bid–ask spreads of bonds, which increases the cost of trading. Higher transaction costs reduce the benefits of active portfolio decisions and may decrease portfolio managers' willingness to adjust their portfolios to take advantage of opportunities that present themselves. As an example to quantify trading costs, if a corporate bond with a 15-year duration is being quoted by dealers with a 10 bp bid–ask spread, the cost impact to the portfolio is approximately 1.50% (0.0010 × 15 × 100 = 1.50%). The portfolio manager would buy the bond at $100, and when the portfolio is priced (typically at bid or the midpoint between the bid and the ask), the bond would have a value of $98.50, reducing the total portfolio return. This is the price that would be realized if the bond were sold, holding other factors constant. To mitigate trading costs, investors can participate in the primary or new issue market where bonds are typically issued at a discount to the price at which a similar issue trades in the secondary market.

KNOWLEDGE CHECK

1. Rank the following instruments from the usually most liquid to the least liquid:

   - Low-credit-quality corporate bond
   - Recently issued on-the-run sovereign bond issued by a high-credit-quality government
   - High-credit-quality corporate bond
   - Sovereign bond issued a year ago by a high-credit-quality government

   Solution

   - Recently issued on-the-run sovereign bond issued by a high-credit-quality government
   - Sovereign bond issued a year ago by a high-credit-quality government
   - High-credit-quality corporate bond
   - Low-credit-quality corporate bond

Alternatives to Direct Investment in Bonds

Because transacting in fixed-income securities may present challenges resulting from low liquidity in many segments of the fixed-income market, fund managers may use alternative methods to establish bond market exposures. The methods we outline are applicable across different fixed-income mandates. We will take a more in-depth look at the ones particularly relevant to passive and liability-driven mandates later as part of our coverage dedicated to such mandates. Next, we provide an overview of the most common methods—specifically, mutual funds, exchange-traded funds (ETFs), exchange-traded derivatives, and OTC derivatives. In considering direct versus indirect investments, the asset manager must weigh the ongoing fees associated with such instruments as mutual funds and ETFs against the bid–offer cost of direct investment in the underlying securities.

ETFs and mutual funds. These products provide an alternative to transacting in individual bonds. Mutual funds are pooled investment vehicles whose shares or units represent a proportional share in the ownership of the assets in an underlying portfolio. In the case of open-end mutual funds, new shares may be redeemed or issued at the fund's net asset value (NAV) established at the end of each trading day based on the fund's valuation of all existing assets minus liabilities, divided by the total number of shares outstanding. Bond mutual fund investors enjoy the advantage of being able to redeem holdings at the fund's NAV rather than needing to sell illiquid positions. The benefit from economies of scale is usually the overriding factor for smaller investors in their choice of a bond mutual fund over direct investment. Because bonds often trade at a minimum lot size of USD1 million or higher per bond, successful replication of a broad index or construction of a diversified actively managed portfolio could easily require hundreds of millions of dollars in investments. Therefore, the greater diversification across fixed-income markets achievable by a larger fund may be well worth the additional cost in terms of an upfront load in some instances and an annual management fee.

Although investors benefit from increased diversification, the fund must outline its stated investment objectives and periodic fees, but actual security holdings are available only on a retroactive basis. Unlike the underlying securities, bond mutual funds have no maturity date; the fund manager continuously purchases and sells bonds to track index performance, and monthly interest payments fluctuate based on fund holdings.

Exchange-traded funds share some mutual fund characteristics but have more tradability features. Investors benefit from greater bond ETF liquidity versus mutual funds given their availability to be purchased or sold throughout the trading day.

Exchange-traded derivatives. Futures and options on futures provide exposure to underlying bonds. Being exchange-traded, they involve financial instruments with standardized terms, documentation, and pricing traded on an organized exchange. Exchange-traded products also include interest rate products and options for interest rate–related ETFs.

OTC derivatives. Interest rate swaps are the most widely used OTC derivative worldwide and entail customized arrangements between two counterparties that reference an underlying market price or index. Some interest rate swaps are liquid, with multiple swap dealers posting competitive two-way quotes. In addition to interest rate swaps, fixed-income portfolio managers use inflation swaps, total return swaps, and credit swaps to alter their portfolio exposure. Because they trade over the counter, swaps may be tailored to an investor's specific needs.

A total return swap (TRS), a common over-the-counter portfolio derivative strategy, combines elements of interest rate swaps and credit derivatives. Similar to an interest rate swap, a total return swap involves the periodic exchange of cash flows between two parties for the life of the contract. Unlike an interest rate swap, in which counterparties exchange a stream of fixed cash flows versus a floating-rate benchmark such as the MRR (the market reference rate) to transform fixed assets or liabilities to a variable exposure, a TRS has a periodic exchange based on a reference obligation that is an underlying equity, commodity, or bond index. Exhibit 9 outlines the most basic TRS structure. The **total return receiver** receives both the cash flows from the underlying index and any appreciation in the index over the period in exchange for paying the MRR plus a predetermined spread. The **total return payer** is responsible for paying the reference obligation cash flows and return to the receiver but will also be compensated by the receiver for any depreciation in the index or default losses incurred by the portfolio.

Exhibit 9: Total Return Swap Mechanics

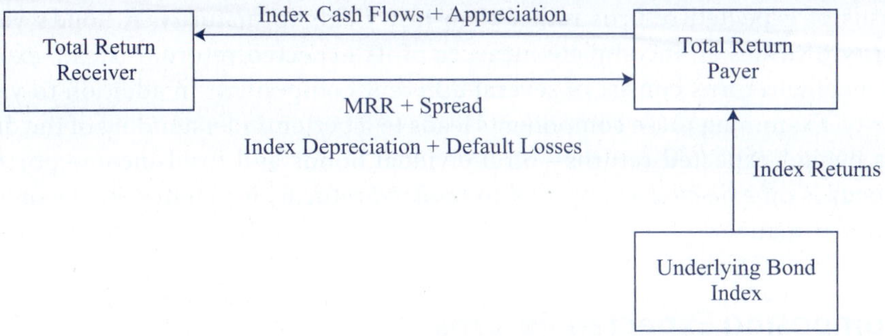

The TRS transaction is an over-the-counter derivative contract based on an ISDA (International Swaps and Derivatives Association) master agreement. This contract specifies a notional amount, periodic cash flows, and final maturity, as well as the credit and other legal provisions related to the transaction. The historical attractiveness of using TRS stemmed from the efficient risk transfer on the reference obligation from one counterparty to another on a confidential basis without requiring the full cash outlay associated with the mutual fund or ETF purchase. In fact, another way to think of the TRS is as a synthetic secured financing transaction in which the investor (the total return receiver) benefits from more-advantageous funding terms faced by a dealer (typically the total return payer) offering to facilitate the transaction.

The potential for both a smaller initial cash outlay and lower swap bid–offer costs compared with the transaction costs of direct purchase or use of a mutual fund or ETF are the most compelling reasons to consider a TRS to add fixed-income exposure. As a funding cost arbitrage transaction, the TRS can allow investors to gain particular access to subsets of the fixed-income markets, such as bank loans or high-yield instruments for which cash markets are relatively illiquid or the cost and administrative complexity of maintaining a portfolio of these instruments is prohibitive for the investor.

That said, several considerations may offset these benefits in a few instances:

- The investor does not legally own the underlying assets but, rather, has a combined synthetic long position in the market and the credit risk of the index that is contingent on the performance of the total return payer. The total return receiver must both perform the necessary credit due diligence on its counterparty and face the rollover risk at maturity of having the ability to renew the contract with reasonable pricing and business terms in the future.
- Structural changes to the market and greater regulatory oversight, particularly capital rules affecting dealers, have raised the cost and increased the operational burden of these transactions because of the need to collateralize mark-to-market positions frequently and within a shorter timeframe.

A MODEL FOR FIXED-INCOME RETURNS 5

☐ describe and interpret a model for fixed-income returns

Investors often have views on future changes in the yield curve and structure or restructure their portfolios accordingly. Investment strategies should be evaluated in terms of expected returns rather than just yields to maturity. A bond's yield to maturity provides an incomplete measure of its expected return. Instead, expected fixed-income returns consist of several different components in addition to yield to maturity. Examining these components leads to a better understanding of the driving forces behind expected returns—on individual bonds and fixed-income portfolios. The focus is on *expected* as opposed to *realized* returns, which may be decomposed in a similar manner.

Decomposing Expected Returns

Decomposing expected fixed-income returns allows an investor to differentiate among several important return components. At the most general level, expected returns, denoted as $E(R)$, can be decomposed (approximately) in the following manner:

$E(R) \approx$ Coupon income

+/– Rolldown return

+/– E(ΔPrice due to investor's view of benchmark yield)

+/– E(ΔPrice due to investor's view of yield spreads)

+/– E(ΔPrice due to investor's view of currency value changes),

where $E(\ldots)$ represents effects on expected returns based on expectations of the item in parentheses and Δ represents "change." The decomposition holds only approximately and ignores taxes (note that some of the material on decomposing expected returns has been adapted from Hanke and Seals (2010).

Coupon Income

Coupon income is the income that an investor receives from coupon payments relative to the bond's price and interest on reinvestment income. Assuming there is no reinvestment income, coupon income equals a bond's annual current yield.

Coupon income (or Current yield) = Annual coupon payment/Current bond price.

Rolldown Return

The rolldown return, sometimes referred to as "rolldown and carry return," results from the bond "rolling down" the yield curve as the time to maturity decreases (see Exhibit 10), assuming zero interest rate volatility. Bond prices change as time passes even if the market discount rate remains the same. As time passes, a bond's price typically moves closer to par. This price movement is illustrated by the constant-yield price trajectory, which shows the "pull to par" effect on the price of a bond trading at a premium or a discount to par value. If the issuer does not default, the price of a bond approaches par value as its time to maturity approaches zero.

Exhibit 10: Rolling down the Yield Curve Effect

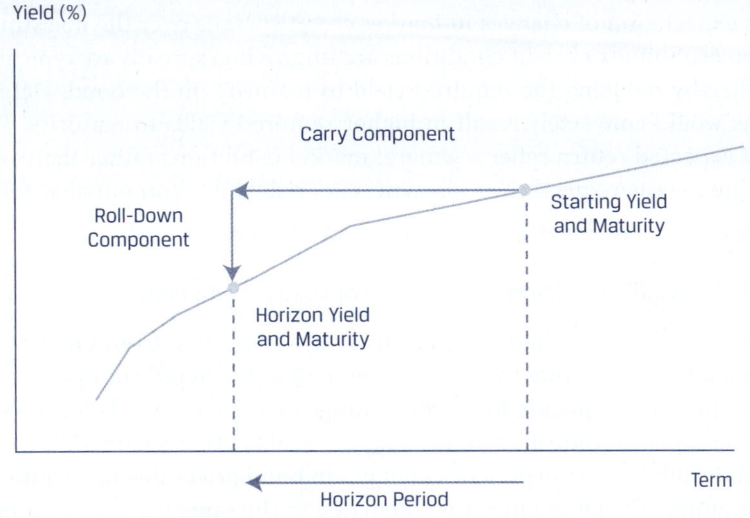

The rolldown return equals the bond's percentage price change assuming an unchanged yield curve over the strategy horizon. Bonds trading at a premium to their par value will experience capital losses during their remaining life, and bonds trading at a discount relative to their par value will experience capital gains during their remaining life.

To compute the rolldown return, the bond has to be revalued at the end of the strategy horizon assuming an unchanged yield curve. Then the rolldown return is as follows:

$$\text{Rolldown return} = \frac{\left(\text{Bond price}_{End\text{-}of\text{-}horizonperiod} - \text{Bond price}_{Beginning\text{-}of\text{-}horizonperiod}\right)}{\text{Bond price}_{Beginning\text{-}of\text{-}horizonperiod}}.$$

The sum of the coupon income and the rolldown return may be referred to as the bond's *rolling yield.*

Views of Benchmark Yields

The expected change in price based on investor's views of benchmark yields to maturity and the term structure of yield volatility reflects an investor's expectation of changes in yields to maturity and yield volatility over the investment horizon. This expected change is zero if the investor expects yield curves and yield volatility to remain unchanged. Assuming the investor does expect a change in the yield curve, this expected return component is computed as follows:

$$E(\Delta\text{Price based on investor's views of yields and yield volatility)}$$

$$= (-\text{ModDur} \times \Delta\text{Yield}) + [\tfrac{1}{2} \times \text{Convexity} \times (\Delta\text{Yield})^2\ ],$$

where ModDur is the modified duration of a bond, ΔYield is the expected change in yield to maturity, and Convexity reflects the second-order effect of the price–yield relationship. Note that for bonds with embedded options, the duration and convexity measures used should be effective duration and effective convexity. Also, in contrast to fixed-coupon bonds, floating-rate notes have a modified duration that is largely due to spread changes, as described in detail later.

Views of Yield Spreads

The expected change in price based on investor's views of yield spreads reflects an investor's expectation of changes in market credit spreads over the investment horizon. When economic or credit conditions are improving, spreads are typically said to tighten, thereby reducing the required yield to maturity on the bond. Deteriorating conditions would conversely result in higher required yields to maturity. This component of expected return reflects general market conditions rather than any spread changes due to issuer-specific (or idiosyncratic) risk and is computed as follows:

E(ΔPrice based on investor's views of yield spreads)

$$= (-\text{ModSpreadDur} \times \Delta\text{Spread}) + [\tfrac{1}{2} \times \text{Convexity} \times (\Delta\text{Yield})^2].$$

Yield spreads can also fluctuate because of idiosyncratic risk. Credit migration refers to credit quality changes that may result in an issuer downgrade or upgrade. This can result in either lower spreads for higher ratings or higher spreads for lower ratings affecting the expected return on bonds. Higher-quality credits tend to have low probabilities of default but can experience changes in bond prices due to an anticipated or actual migration. The price impact is calculated in the same way as noted previously for market changes in yield to maturity. Note that investors face price declines on non-defaulted bonds if spreads widen. Yearly default rates can vary significantly and are more severe for speculative-grade (high-yield) issues.

Views of Currency Value Changes

If an investor holds bonds denominated in a currency other than her home currency, she also needs to factor in any expected fluctuations in the currency exchange rate or expected currency gains or losses over the investment horizon. The magnitude and direction of the change in the exchange rate can be based on a variety of factors, including the manager's own view, results from surveys, or a quantitative model output. It can also be based on the exchange rate that can be locked in over the investment horizon using currency forwards.

Return measured in functional currency terms (domestic currency returns of foreign currency assets) can be shown as $R_{DC} = (1 + R_{FC})(1 + R_{FX}) - 1$ for a single asset or

$$R_{DC} = \sum_{i=1}^{n} \omega_i (1 + R_{FC,i})(1 + R_{FX,i}) - 1$$

for a portfolio, where R_{DC} and R_{FC} are the domestic and foreign currency returns expressed as a percentage, R_{FX} is the percentage change of the domestic currency versus the foreign currency, and ω_i is the respective portfolio weight of each foreign currency asset (in domestic currency terms), with the sum of ω_i equal to 1. In the context of the return decomposition framework, R_{DC} simply combines the third factor, E(ΔPrice due to investor's view of benchmark yield), and the fifth factor, (+/− E(ΔFunctional currency value), in the expected fixed-income return model.

DECOMPOSING EXPECTED RETURNS

1. Ann Smith works for a US investment firm in its London office. She manages the firm's British pound–denominated corporate bond portfolio. Her department head in New York City has asked Smith to make a presentation on next year's total expected return of her portfolio in US dollars and the components of this return. Exhibit 11 shows information on the portfolio and Smith's expectations for the next year. Expected return (for the bond portfolio) and its components are on an annualized basis, and any

potential coupons are assumed to be paid annually. Calculate the total expected return of Smith's bond portfolio, assuming no reinvestment income.

Exhibit 11: Portfolio Characteristics and Expectations

Notional principal of portfolio (in millions)	£100
Average bond coupon payment (per £100 par value)	£2.75
Coupon frequency	Annual
Investment horizon	1 year
Current average bond price	£97.12
Expected average bond price in one year (assuming an unchanged yield curve)	£97.285
Average bond convexity in one year	18
Average bond modified duration in one year	3.70
Expected average benchmark yield-to-maturity change	0.26%
Expected change in spread (spread expected to narrow in this scenario)	–0.10%
Expected currency losses (£ depreciation versus US$)	0.50%

Solution

The portfolio's coupon income is 2.83%. The portfolio has an average coupon of £2.75 on a £100 notional principal and currently trades at £97.12. The coupon income over a one-year horizon is 2.83% = £2.75/£97.12.

In one year's time, assuming an unchanged yield curve and zero interest rate volatility, the rolldown return is 0.15% = (£97.285 – £97.12)/£97.12.

The rolling yield, which is the sum of the coupon income and the rolldown return, is 3.00% = 2.98% + 0.15%.

The expected change in price based on Smith's views of benchmark yields to maturity is –0.96%, calculated as follows: The bond portfolio has a modified duration of 3.70 and a convexity statistic of 18. Smith expects an average benchmark yield-to-maturity change of 0.26%. Smith expects to incur a decrease in prices and a reduction in return based on her rate view. The expected change in price based on Smith's views of yields to maturity and yield spreads is thus $-0.0096 = (-3.70 \times 0.0026) + [\frac{1}{2} \times 18 \times (0.0026)^2]$. So, the expected reduction in return based on Smith's rate view is 0.96%.

Smith expects an impact from the 0.1% change (narrowing in this scenario) in spread in her well-diversified investment-grade bond portfolio. The impact on the expected return is, therefore, $0.37\% = [-3.70 \times (-0.0010)] + [1/2 \times 18 \times (-0.0010)^2]$.

Smith expects the British pound, the foreign currency in which her bond position is denominated, to depreciate by an annualized 50 bps (or 0.5%) over the investment horizon against the US dollar, the home country currency. The expected currency loss to the portfolio is thus 0.50%.

The total expected return on Smith's bond position is 1.91%, as summarized in Exhibit 12.

Exhibit 12: Return Component Calculations

Return Component	Formula	Calculation
Coupon income	Annual coupon payment/Current bond price	£2.75/£97.12 = 2.83%
+ Rolldown return	$\frac{(\text{Bond price}_{End\text{-}of\text{-}horizon\ period} - \text{Bond price}_{Beginning\text{-}of\text{-}horizon\ period})}{\text{Bond price}_{Beginning\text{-}of\text{-}horizon\ period}}$	(£97.285 – £97.12)/£97.12 = 0.17%
= Rolling yield	Coupon income + Rolldown return	2.83% + 0.17% = 3.00%
+/– *E*(ÄPrice* based on Smith's benchmark yield view)	(–ModDur × ΔYield) + [½ × Convexity × $(\Delta\text{Yield})^2$]	(–3.70 × 0.0026) + [½ × 18 × $(0.0026)^2$] = –0.96%
+/– *E*(ÄPrice due to investor's view of yield spreads)	(–ModDur × ΔSpread) + [½ × Convexity × $(\Delta\text{Spread})^2$]	(–3.70 × –0.0010) + [1/2 × 18 × $(-0.0010)^2$] = 0.37%
+/– *E*(Currency gains or losses)	Given	–0.50%
= Total expected return		**1.91%**

**Note that the change in price in the context of this example refers to the change in portfolio value.*

Estimation of the Inputs

In the model for fixed-income returns discussed earlier, some of the individual expected return components can be more easily estimated than others. The easiest component to estimate is the coupon income. The return model's most uncertain individual components are the investor's views of changes in benchmark yields and yield spreads and expected currency movements. These components are normally based on purely qualitative (subjective) criteria, a quantitative model (including surveys), or a mixture of the two. Although a quantitative approach may seem more objective, there are several quantitative models that can be used, each with different methodologies associated with the underlying calculations.

Limitations of the Expected Return Decomposition

The return decomposition just described is an approximation; only duration and convexity are used to summarize the price–yield relationship. In addition, the model implicitly assumes that all intermediate cash flows of the bond are reinvested at the yield to maturity, which results in different coupon reinvestment rates for different bonds.

The model also ignores other factors, such as local richness/cheapness effects and potential financing advantages. Local richness/cheapness effects are deviations of individual maturity segments from the fitted yield curve, which were obtained using a curve estimation technique. Yield curve estimation techniques produce relatively smooth curves, and there are likely slight deviations from the curve in practice. There may be financing advantages to certain maturity segments in the repo market. The repo market provides a form of short-term borrowing for dealers in government securities who sell government bonds to other market participants overnight and buy them back, typically on the following day. In most cases, local richness/cheapness effects and financing advantages tend to be relatively small and are thus not included in the expected return decomposition model.

COMPONENTS OF EXPECTED RETURN

Kevin Tucker manages a global bond portfolio. At a recent investment committee meeting, Tucker discussed his portfolio's domestic (very high-credit-quality) government bond allocation with another committee member. The other committee member argued that if the yield curve is expected to remain unchanged, the only determinants of a domestic government bond's expected return are its coupon payment and its price.

1. Explain why the other committee member is incorrect, including a description of the additional expected return components that need to be included.

Solution

A bond's coupon payment and its price allow only its coupon income to be computed. Coupon income is an incomplete measure of a bond's expected return. For domestic government bonds, in addition to coupon income, the rolldown return needs to be considered. The rolldown return results from the fact that bonds are pulled to par as the time to maturity decreases, even if the yield curve is expected to remain unchanged over the investment horizon. Currency gains and losses would also need to be considered in a global portfolio. Because the portfolio consists of government bonds with very high credit quality, the view on yield spreads is less relevant for Tucker's analysis. For government and corporate bonds with lower credit quality, however, yield spreads would also need to be considered as additional return components.

LEVERAGE 6

☐ discuss the use of leverage, alternative methods for leveraging, and risks that leverage creates in fixed-income portfolios

Leverage is the use of borrowed capital to increase the magnitude of portfolio positions, and it is an important tool for fixed-income portfolio managers. By using leverage, fixed-income portfolio managers may be able to increase portfolio returns relative to what they can achieve in unleveraged portfolios.

Managers often have mandates that place limits on the types of securities they may hold. Simultaneously, managers may have return objectives that are difficult to achieve, especially during low–interest rate environments. Through the use of leverage, a manager can increase his investment exposure and may be able to increase the returns to fixed-income asset classes that typically have low returns. The increased return potential, however, comes at the cost of increased risk: If losses occur, these would be higher than in unleveraged positions.

Using Leverage

Leverage increases portfolio returns if the securities in the portfolio have returns higher than the cost of borrowing. In an unleveraged portfolio, the return on the portfolio (r_p) equals the return on invested funds (r_I). When the manager uses leverage, however, the invested funds exceed the portfolio's equity by the amount that is borrowed.

The leveraged portfolio return, r_p, can be expressed as the total investment gains per unit of invested capital:

$$r_P = \frac{\text{Portfolio return}}{\text{Portfolio equity}} = \frac{r_I \times (V_E + V_B) - (V_B \times r_B)}{V_E},$$

where

V_E = Value of the portfolio's equity

V_B = Borrowed funds

r_B = Borrowing rate (cost of borrowing)

r_I = Return on the invested funds (investment returns)

r_p = Return on the levered portfolio

The numerator represents the total return on the portfolio assets, $r_I \times (V_E + V_B)$, minus the cost of borrowing, $V_B \times r_B$, divided by the portfolio's equity.

The leveraged portfolio return can be decomposed further to better identify the effect of leverage on returns:

$$\begin{aligned} r_P &= \frac{r_I \times (V_E + V_B) - (V_B \times r_B)}{V_E} \\ &= \frac{(r_I \times V_E) + [V_B \times (r_I - r_B)]}{V_E} \\ &= r_I + \frac{V_B}{V_E}(r_I - r_B). \end{aligned}$$

This expression decomposes the leveraged portfolio return into the return on invested funds and a portion that accounts for the effect of leverage. If $r_I > r_B$, then the second term is positive because the rate of return on invested funds exceeds the borrowing rate; in this case, leverage increases the portfolio's return. If $r_I < r_B$, then the second term is negative because the rate of return on invested funds is less than the borrowing rate; in this case, the use of leverage decreases the portfolio's return. The degree to which the leverage increases or decreases portfolio returns is proportional to the use of leverage (amount borrowed), V_B/V_E, and the amount by which investment return differs from the cost of borrowing, $r_I - r_B$.

Methods for Leveraging Fixed-Income Portfolios

Fixed-income portfolio managers have a variety of tools available to create leveraged portfolio exposures—notably, the use of financial derivatives and borrowing via collateralized money markets. Derivatives and borrowing are explicit forms of leverage. Other forms of leverage, such as the use of structured financial instruments, are more implicit. We provide a description of the most common ones.

Futures Contracts

Futures contracts embed significant leverage because they permit the counterparties to gain exposure to a large quantity of the underlying asset without having to transact in the underlying. Futures contracts can be obtained for a modest investment that comes in the form of a margin deposit. A futures contract's notional value equals the current value of the underlying asset multiplied by the multiplier, or the quantity of the underlying asset controlled by the contract.

The futures leverage is the ratio of the futures exposure (in excess of the margin deposit) normalized by the amount of margin required to control the notional amount. We can calculate the futures leverage using the following equation:

$$\text{Leverage}_{Futures} = \frac{\text{Notional value} - \text{Margin}}{\text{Margin}}.$$

Swap Agreements

An interest rate swap can be viewed as a portfolio of bonds. In an interest rate swap, the fixed-rate payer is effectively short a fixed-rate bond and long a floating-rate bond. When interest rates increase, the value of the swap to the fixed-rate payer increases because the present value of the fixed-rate liability decreases, and the floating-rate payments received increase. The fixed-rate receiver in the interest rate swap agreement effectively has a long position in a fixed-rate bond and a short position in a floating-rate bond. If interest rates decline, the value of the swap to the fixed-rate receiver increases because the present value of the fixed-rate asset increases, and the floating-rate payments made decrease.

Because interest rate swaps are economically equivalent to a long–short bond portfolio, they provide leveraged exposure to bonds; the only capital required to enter into swap agreements is collateral required by the counterparties. Collateral for interest rate swap agreements has historically occurred between the two (or more) counterparties in the transaction. Increasingly, collateral for interest rate and other swaps occurs through central clearinghouses.

Repurchase Agreements

Repurchase agreements (repos) are an important source of short-term financing for fixed-income security dealers and other financial institutions, as evidenced by the trillions of dollars of repo transactions that take place annually. In a repurchase agreement, a security owner agrees to sell a security for a specific cash amount while simultaneously agreeing to repurchase the security at a specified future date (typically one day later) and price. Repos are thus effectively collateralized loans. When discussing a repo, the transaction normally refers to the borrower's standpoint; from the standpoint of the lender (such as a money market fund), these agreements are referred to as **reverse repos**. Exhibit 13 illustrates the transaction.

The interest rate on a repurchase agreement, called the **repo rate**, is the difference between the security's selling price and its repurchase price. For example, consider a dealer wishing to finance a EUR15 million bond position with a repurchase agreement. The dealer enters an overnight repo at a repo rate of 5%. We can compute the price at which she agrees to repurchase this bond after one day as the EUR15 million value today plus one day of interest. The interest amount is computed as follows:

$$\text{Dollar interest} = \text{Principal amount} \times \text{Repo rate} \times (\text{Term of repo in days}/360).$$

Continuing with the example, the dollar interest is EUR2,083.33 = EUR15 million × 5% × (1/360). Thus, the dealer will repurchase the bond the next day for EUR15,002,083.33.

Exhibit 13: Repo and Reverse Repo

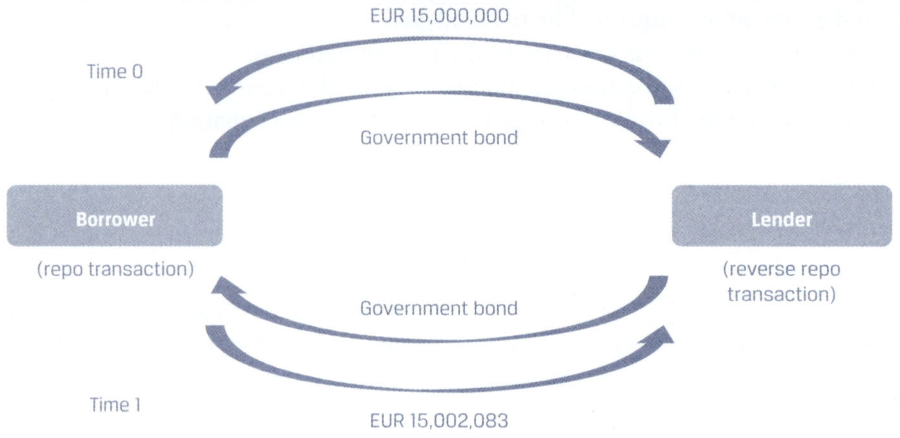

The term, or length, of a repurchase agreement is measured in days. Overnight repos are common, although they are often rolled over to create longer-term funding. A repo agreement may be cash driven or security driven. Cash-driven transactions feature one party that owns bonds and wants to borrow cash, as in the foregoing example. Cash-driven transactions usually feature "general collateral"—securities commonly accepted by investors and dealers, such as Treasury bonds. In a security-driven transaction, the lender typically seeks a particular security. The motives may be for hedging, arbitrage, or speculation.

Credit risk is a concern for the counterparty that lends capital in a repo agreement. Protection against a default by the borrower is provided by the underlying collateral bonds. Additional credit protection comes from the "haircut," the amount by which the collateral's value exceeds the repo principal amount. For example, haircuts for high-quality government bonds typically range from 1% to 3% and are higher for other types of bonds. The size of the haircut serves to not only protect the lender against a potential default by the borrower but also to limit the borrower's net leverage capacity. Generally, the size of the haircut increases as the price volatility of the underlying collateral increases.

Repos are categorized as bilateral repos or tri-party repos, depending on the way they are settled. Bilateral repos are conducted directly between two institutions, and settlement is typically conducted as "delivery versus payment," meaning that the exchanges of cash and collateral occur simultaneously through a central custodian (for example, the Depository Trust Company in the United States). Bilateral repos are usually used for security-driven transactions. Tri-party repo transactions involve a third party that provides settlement and collateral management services. Most cash-motivated repo transactions against general collateral are conducted as tri-party repo transactions.

Security Lending

Security lending is another form of collateralized lending and is closely linked to the repo market. The primary motive of security lending transactions is to facilitate short sales, which involve the sale of securities the seller does not own. A short seller must borrow the securities he has sold short to deliver them upon trade settlement. Another motive for security lending transactions is financing, or collateralized borrowing. In a financing-motivated security loan, a bond owner lends the bond to another investor in exchange for cash.

Security lending transactions are collateralized by cash or high-credit-quality bonds. In the United States, most transactions feature cash collateral, although in many other countries, highly rated bonds are used as collateral. Typically, security lenders require collateral valued more than the value of the borrowed securities when bonds are used as collateral. For example, if high-quality government bonds are used as collateral, the lender may require bonds valued at 102% of the value of the borrowed securities. The extra 2% functions in the same way as the haircut in the repo market, providing extra protection against borrower default. The collateral required will increase if lower-quality bonds are used as collateral.

In security lending transactions with cash collateral, the security borrower typically pays the security lender, typically a long-only investment fund, a fee equal to a percentage of the value of the securities loaned. For securities that are readily available for lending, that fee is small. The security lender earns an additional return by reinvesting the cash collateral. In cases where the security loan is initiated for financing purposes, the lending fee is typically negative, indicating that the security lender pays the security borrower a fee in exchange for its use of the cash.

When bonds are posted as collateral, the income earned on the collateral usually exceeds the security lending rate; the security lender (who is in possession of the bonds as collateral) usually repays the security borrower a portion of the interest earned on the bond collateral. The term **rebate rate** refers to the portion of the collateral earnings rate that is repaid to the security borrower by the security lender. This relationship can be expressed as follows:

Rebate rate = Collateral earnings rate – Security lending rate.

When securities are difficult to borrow, typically because there is high demand to short those securities, the rebate rate may be negative, which means the fee for borrowing the securities is greater than the return earned on the collateral. In this case, the security borrower pays a fee to the security lender in addition to foregoing the interest earned on the collateral.

There are important differences between repurchase agreements and security lending transactions. Unlike repurchase agreements, security lending transactions are typically open-ended. The security lender may recall the securities at any time, forcing the borrower to deliver the bonds by buying them back or borrowing from another lender. Similarly, the borrower may deliver the borrowed securities back to the lender at any time, forcing the lender, or its agent, to return the collateral (cash or bonds) and search for another borrower.

Risks of Leverage

Leverage alters the risk–return properties of an investment portfolio. A heavily leveraged portfolio may incur significant losses even when portfolio assets suffer only moderate valuation declines.

Leverage can lead to forced liquidations. If the value of the portfolio decreases, the portfolio's equity relative to borrowing levels is reduced and the portfolio's leverage increases. Portfolio assets may be sold to pay off borrowing and reduce leverage. If portfolio assets are not liquidated, then the overall leverage increases, corresponding to higher levels of risk. Decreases in portfolio value can lead to forced liquidations even if market conditions are unfavorable for selling—for example, during crisis periods. The term "fire sale" refers to forced liquidations at prices that are below fair value because of the seller's need for immediate liquidation. Reducing leverage, declining asset values, and forced sales have the potential to create spiraling effects that can result in severe declines in values and reduction in market liquidity.

Additionally, reassessments of counterparty risk typically occur during extreme market conditions, such as during the 2008–09 Global Financial Crisis. During periods of financial crisis, counterparties to short-term financing arrangements, such as credit lines, repurchase agreements, and security lending agreements, may withdraw their financing. These withdrawals undermine the ability of leveraged market participants to maintain their investment exposures. Thus, leveraged investors may be forced to reduce their investment exposure at exactly the worst time—that is, when prices are depressed.

USING LEVERAGE IN A FIXED-INCOME PORTFOLIO

1. Arturo manages a mutual fund that is benchmarked to the Global Aggregate Bond Index. He currently has a bullish view of the global economy and believes corporate bond spreads are attractive. He is bearish on US Treasury interest rates given his economic growth forecast and expects rates to increase. The fund's US corporate bond holdings have a duration of seven years. He believes the best opportunities are in emerging market securities, and he is bullish on Brazilian rates, expecting them to decrease. The fund has experienced strong inflows recently and is fully invested. Arturo is evaluating ways to potentially increase the fund's total return by creating leveraged fixed-income exposures.

   Given Arturo's plan to leverage exposures in his fund, discuss how he would achieve his objectives and identify the strategy risks.

   Solution

   The mutual fund is fully invested; therefore, Arturo needs to use leverage to potentially increase his returns. His bearish view on US Treasury interest rates would require that he reduce the fund's seven-year duration contributed by the US corporate bond holdings. He can sell the number of futures contracts on US Treasuries, whose notional value and associated duration would offset the duration of the corporate bonds to his new target duration. Doing so would allow him to retain exposure (spread duration) to the corporate bonds, whose spreads may contract as the economy grows while shedding the interest rate exposure, since he believes rates will rise, adversely affecting bond prices.

   Arturo's bullish view on Brazilian rates can be expressed by entering into a receive fixed-rate, pay floating-rate swap on Brazilian rates. The fund will effectively have the equivalent of a fixed-rate bond that will appreciate in price if his view that Brazilian interest rates will fall materializes.

   Both the short US Treasury futures and long Brazilian interest rate swap positions are leveraged since the only capital used is the collateral required by the counterparties. The risk to the leveraged strategy is that if Arturo's view on either position turns out to be incorrect, losses are magnified. This may also require positions to be closed and assets sold to cover the losses, which may occur at an inopportune time if the markets have sold off.

FIXED-INCOME PORTFOLIO TAXATION 7

☐ discuss differences in managing fixed-income portfolios for taxable and tax-exempt investors

A tax-exempt investor's objective is to achieve the highest possible risk-adjusted returns net of fees and transaction costs. A prudent taxable investor needs to also consider the effects of taxes on both expected and realized net investment returns.

The investment management industry has traditionally made investment decisions based on pretax returns as though investors are tax exempt (such as pension funds in many countries; see Rogers [2006]). Most of the world's investable assets, however, are owned by taxable investors, who are concerned with after-tax, rather than pretax, returns.

Taxes may differ among investor types, among countries, and based on income source, such as interest or capital gains. In many countries, pension funds are exempt from taxes, but corporations generally have to pay tax on their investments. Many countries make some allowance for tax-sheltered investments that individuals can use (up to certain limits). These types of tax shelters generally offer either an exemption from tax on investment income or a deferral of taxes until an investor draws money from the shelter (usually after retirement). Such shelters allow returns to accrue on a pretax basis until retirement, which can provide substantial benefits. In a fixed-income context for taxable investors, coupon payments (interest income) are typically taxed at the investor's normal income tax rate. Capital gains, however, may be taxed at a lower effective rate than an investor's normal income tax rate. In some countries, income from special types of fixed-income securities, such as bonds issued by a sovereign government, a non-sovereign government, or various government agencies, may be taxed at a lower effective rate, or even not taxed.

Specific tax rules vary among jurisdictions. Any discussion of the effect of taxes on investor returns—and, therefore, on how portfolios should optimally be managed for taxable investors—is especially challenging if it needs to apply on a global level. Although accounting standards have become more harmonized globally, any kind of tax harmonization among countries is not likely to occur anytime soon. An investor should consider how taxes affect investment income in the country where the income is earned and how the investment income is treated when it is repatriated to the investor's home country. Treaties between countries may affect tax treatment of investment income. Taxes are complicated and can make investment decisions difficult. Portfolio managers who manage assets for taxable individual investors, as opposed to tax-exempt investors, need to consider a few issues.

Principles of Fixed-Income Taxation

Although tax codes differ among jurisdictions, there are certain principles that most tax codes have in common regarding taxation of fixed-income investments:

- The two primary sources of investment income that affect taxes for fixed-income securities are coupon payments (interest income) and capital gains or losses.
- In general, tax is payable only on capital gains and interest income that have been received. In some countries, an exception to this rule applies to zero-coupon bonds. Imputed interest that is taxed throughout a

zero-coupon bond's life may be calculated. This method of taxation ensures that tax is paid over the bond's life and that the return on a zero-coupon bond is not taxed entirely as a capital gain.

- Capital gains are frequently taxed at a lower effective tax rate than interest income.
- Capital losses generally cannot be used to reduce sources of income other than capital gains. Capital losses reduce capital gains in the tax year in which they occur. If capital losses exceed capital gains in the year, they can often be "carried forward" and applied to gains in future years; in some countries, losses may also be "carried back" to reduce capital gains taxes paid in prior years. Limits on the number of years that capital losses can be carried forward or back typically exist.
- In some countries, short-term capital gains are taxed at a different (usually higher) rate than long-term capital gains.

An investor or portfolio manager generally has no control over the timing of when coupon income is received, and the related income tax must be paid. However, he or she can generally decide the timing of the sale of investments and, therefore, has some control over the timing of realized capital gains and losses. This control can be valuable for a taxable investor because it may be optimal to delay realizing gains and related tax payments and to realize losses as early as possible. This type of tax-driven strategic behavior is referred to as tax-loss harvesting.

Key points for managing taxable fixed-income portfolios include the following:

- Selectively offset capital gains and losses for tax purposes.
- If short-term capital gains tax rates are higher than long-term capital gains tax rates, then be judicious when realizing short-term gains.
- Realize losses considering tax consequences. They may be used to offset current or future capital gains for tax purposes.
- Control turnover in the fund. In general, the lower the turnover, the longer capital gains tax payments can be deferred.
- Consider the trade-off between capital gains and income for tax purposes.

Investment Vehicles and Taxes

The choice of investment vehicle often affects how investments are taxed at the final investor level. In a pooled investment vehicle (sometimes referred to as a *collective investment scheme*), such as a mutual fund, interest income is generally taxed at the final investor level when it occurs—regardless of whether the fund reinvests interest income or pays it out to investors. In other words, for tax purposes the fund is considered to have distributed interest income for tax purposes in the year it is received even if it does not actually pay it out to investors. Taxation of capital gains arising from the individual investments within a fund is often treated differently in different countries.

Some countries, such as the United States, use what is known as *pass-through treatment* of capital gains in mutual funds. Realized net capital gains in the underlying securities of a fund are treated as if distributed to investors in the year that they arise, and investors need to include the gains on their tax returns. Other countries, such as the United Kingdom, do not use pass-through treatment. Realized capital gains arising within a fund increase the net asset value of the fund shares that investors hold. Investors pay taxes on the net capital gain when they sell their fund shares. This tax treatment leads to a deferral in capital gains tax payments. A UK portfolio manager's decisions on when to realize capital gains or losses do not affect the timing of tax payments on capital gains by investors.

In a separately managed account, an investor typically pays tax on realized gains in the underlying securities at the time they occur. The investor holds the securities directly rather than through shares in a fund. For separately managed accounts, the portfolio manager needs to consider tax consequences for the investor when making investment decisions.

Tax-loss harvesting, which we defined earlier as deferring the realization of gains and realizing capital losses early, allows investors to accumulate gains on a pretax basis. The deferral of taxes increases the present value of investments for the investor.

MANAGING TAXABLE AND TAX-EXEMPT PORTFOLIOS

A bond portfolio manager needs to raise €10,000,000 in cash to cover outflows in the portfolio she manages. To satisfy her cash demands, she considers one of two corporate bond positions for potential liquidation: Position A and Position B. For tax purposes, capital gains receive pass-through treatment; realized net capital gains in the underlying securities of a fund are treated as if distributed to investors in the year that they arise. Assume that the capital gains tax rate is 28% and the income tax rate for interest is 45%. Exhibit 14 provides relevant data for the two bond positions.

Exhibit 14: Selected Data for Two Bonds

	Position A		Position B
Current market value	€10,000,000		€10,000,000
Capital gain/loss	€1,000,000		−€1,000,000
Coupon rate	5.00%		5.00%
Remaining maturity	10 years		10 years
Income tax rate		45%	
Capital gains tax rate		28%	

The portfolio manager considers Position A to be slightly overvalued and Position B to be slightly undervalued. Assume that the two bond positions are identical regarding all other relevant characteristics. How should the portfolio manager optimally liquidate bond positions if she manages the portfolio for the following investors?

1. How should the portfolio manager optimally liquidate bond positions if she manages the portfolio for tax-exempt investors?

   Solution

   The taxation of capital gains and capital losses has minimal consequences for tax-exempt investors. Consistent with the portfolio manager's investment views, the portfolio manager would likely liquidate Position A, which she considers slightly overvalued, rather than liquidating Position B, which she considers slightly undervalued.

2. How should the portfolio manager optimally liquidate bond positions if she manages the portfolio for taxable investors?

   Solution

   All else equal, portfolio managers for taxable investors should have an incentive to defer capital gains taxes and realize capital losses early (tax-loss harvesting) so that losses can be used to offset current or future capital gains. Despite the slight undervaluation of the position, the portfolio manager might want to liquidate Position B because of its embedded capital loss, which will result in a lower realized net capital gain being distributed to investors. This decision assumes that there are no other capital losses in the portfolio that can be used to offset other capital gains. Despite the slight overvaluation of Position A, its liquidation would be less desirable for a taxable investor because of the required capital gains tax.

8 LIABILITY-DRIVEN INVESTING

☐ describe liability-driven investing

Let us start with the example of a 45-year-old investor who plans to retire at age 65 and who would like to secure a stable stream of income thereafter. It is quite probable that he currently has a diversified portfolio that includes bonds, equities, and possibly other asset classes. Our focus here is on the fixed-income portion of his overall portfolio. We will assume that the investor builds the bond portfolio (immediately) and will add to it each year. Upon retirement, he plans to sell the bonds and buy an annuity that will pay a fixed benefit for his remaining lifetime. This investor's initial 20-year time horizon is critical to identifying and measuring the impact on retirement income arising from future interest rate volatility, and it forms the initial frame of reference for understanding and dealing with interest rate risk.

More generally, the frame of reference is in the form of a balance sheet of rate-sensitive assets and liabilities. In the example of the 45-year-old investor, the asset is the growing bond portfolio, and the liability is the present value of the annuity that the investor requires to satisfy the fixed lifetime benefit.

Liability-Driven Investing vs. Asset-Driven Liabilities

Liability-driven investing (LDI) and asset-driven liabilities (ADL) are special cases of ALM. The key difference is that with ADL, the assets are given, and the liabilities are structured to manage interest rate risk; whereas with LDI, which is much more common, the liabilities are given, and the assets are managed. As an example of LDI, a life insurance company acquires a liability portfolio based on the insurance policies underwritten by its sales force. Another example involves the future employee benefits promised by a defined benefit pension plan, which create a portfolio of rate-sensitive liabilities. In each circumstance, the liabilities are defined and result from routine business and financial management decisions. The present value of those liabilities depends on current interest rates (as well as other factors). A life insurance or pension manager will use the estimated interest rate sensitivity of plan liabilities as a starting point when making investment portfolio decisions. This process often requires building a model for the liabilities.

With ADL, the asset side of the balance sheet results from a company's underlying businesses, and the debt manager seeks a liability structure to reduce interest rate risk. One example might be a leasing company with short-term contracts that chooses to finance itself with short-term debt. The company is aiming to match the maturities of its assets and liabilities to minimize risk. Alternatively, a manufacturing company might identify that its operating revenues are highly correlated with the business cycle. Monetary policy is typically managed so there is positive correlation between interest rates and the business cycle. Central banks lower policy rates when the economy is weak and raise them when it is strong. Therefore, this company has a natural preference for variable-rate liabilities so that operating revenue and interest expense rise and fall together.

Types of Liabilities

An LDI strategy starts with analyzing the size and timing of the entity's liabilities. Exhibit 15 shows a classification scheme for this analysis.

Exhibit 15: Classification of Liabilities

Liability Type	Amount of Cash Outlay	Timing of Cash Outlay	Examples
Type I	Known	Known	Traditional fixed-income bond with no embedded options
Type II	Known	Uncertain	Callable and putable bonds Term life insurance policy (timing of death unkown)
Type III	Uncertain	Known	Floating-rate note-interest payments depend on future interest rates Inflation-protected securities-amounts of interest and principal payments tied to inflation
Type IV	Uncertain	Uncertain	Property and casualty insurance (weather events difficult to predict)

Type I: MacDur, ModDur, money duration, and the PVBP can be used to measure the interest rate sensitivity

Types II–IV: Effective duration needed to estimate interest rate sensitivity. Calculated using a model for:
- Uncertain amount and/or timing of the cash flows
- Initial assumption about the yield curve

Note that effective duration is needed with Types II, III, and IV liabilities, based on initial assumptions about the yield curve. Then, the yield curve is shifted up and down to obtain new estimates for the present value of the liabilities. We demonstrate this process later for the sponsor of a defined benefit pension plan, which is another example of an entity with Type IV liabilities.

EXAMPLE 1

Modern Mortgage, a savings bank, decides to establish an ALCO (asset–liability committee) to improve risk management and coordination of its loan and deposit rate–setting processes. Modern's primary assets are long-term, fixed-rate, monthly payment, fully amortizing residential mortgage loans. The mortgage loans are prime quality and have loan-to-value ratios that average 80%. The loans are pre-payable at par value by the homeowners at no fee. Modern also holds a portfolio of non-callable, fixed-income government bonds (considered free of default risk) of varying maturities to manage its liquidity needs. The primary liabilities are demand and time deposits that are fully guaranteed by a government deposit insurance fund. The demand deposits are redeemable by check or debit card. The time deposits have fixed rates and maturities ranging from 90 days to three years and are redeemable before maturity at a small fee. The banking-sector regulator in the country in which Modern operates has introduced a new capital requirement for savings banks. In accordance with the requirement, contingent convertible long-term bonds are issued by the savings bank and sold to institutional investors. The key feature is that if defaults on the mortgage loans reach a certain level or the savings bank's capital ratio drops below a certain level, as determined by the regulator, the bonds convert to equity at a specified price per share.

As a first step, the ALCO needs to identify the types of assets and liabilities that comprise its balance sheet using the classification scheme in Exhibit 15. Type I has certain amounts and dates for its cash flows; Type II has known amounts but uncertain dates; Type III has specified dates but unknown amounts; and Type IV has uncertain amounts and dates.

1. Specify and explain the classification scheme for residential mortgage loans

Solution

Residential mortgage loans are Type IV assets to the savings bank. The timing of interest and principal cash flows is uncertain because of the prepayment option held by the homeowner. This type of call option is complex. Homeowners might elect to prepay for many reasons, including sale of the property as well as the opportunity to refinance if interest rates come down. Therefore, a prepayment model is needed to project the timing of future cash flows. Default risk also affects the projected amount of the cash flow for each date. Even if the *average* loan-to-value ratio is 80%, indicating high-quality mortgages, some loans could have higher ratios and be more subject to default, especially if home prices decline.

2. Specify and explain the classification scheme for government bonds

Solution

Fixed-rate government bonds are Type I assets because the coupon and principal payment dates and amounts are determined at issuance.

3. Specify and explain the classification scheme for demand and time deposits

Solution

Demand and time deposits are Type II liabilities from the savings bank's perspective. The deposit amounts are known, but the depositor can redeem the deposits prior to maturity, creating uncertainty about timing.

4. Specify and explain the classification scheme for contingent convertible bonds

Solution

The contingent convertible bonds are Type IV liabilities. The presence of the conversion option makes both the amount and timing of cash flows uncertain.

MANAGING THE INTEREST RATE RISK OF MULTIPLE LIABILITIES

9

☐ describe the strategy of cash flow matching

The principle of interest rate immunization applies to multiple liabilities in addition to a single liability. For now, we continue to assume that these are Type I cash flows in that the scheduled amounts and payment dates are known to the asset manager. In this section, we discuss two approaches to manage these liabilities:

- *Cash flow matching,* which entails building a dedicated portfolio of zero-coupon or fixed-income bonds to ensure that there are sufficient cash inflows to pay the scheduled cash outflows (a related concept, the so-called "laddered portfolio," also falls into the cash flow matching category of approaches);
- *Duration matching,* which extends the ideas of the previous section to a portfolio of debt liabilities.

Cash Flow Matching

A classic strategy to eliminate the interest rate risk arising from multiple liabilities is to build a dedicated asset portfolio of high-quality fixed-income bonds that, as closely as possible, matches the amount and timing of the scheduled cash outflows. "Dedicated" means that the bonds are placed in a held-to-maturity portfolio. A natural question is, if the entity has enough cash to build the dedicated bond portfolio, why not just use that cash to buy back and retire the liabilities? The answer is that the buyback strategy is difficult and costly to implement if the bonds are widely held by buy-and-hold institutional and retail investors. Most corporate bonds are rather illiquid, so buying them back on the open market is likely to drive up the purchase price. Cash flow matching can be a better use of the available cash assets.

A corporate finance motivation for cash flow matching is to improve the company's credit rating. The entity has sufficient cash assets to retire the debt liabilities, and dedicating the bonds effectively accomplishes that objective. Under some circumstances, a corporation might even be able to remove both the dedicated asset portfolio and the debt liabilities from its balance sheet through the process of accounting defeasance. Also called in-substance defeasance, accounting defeasance is a way of extinguishing a debt obligation by setting aside sufficient high-quality securities, such as US Treasury notes, to repay the liability.

Panel A in Exhibit 16 illustrates the dedicated cash flow matching asset portfolio. These assets could be zero-coupon bonds or traditional fixed-income securities. Panel B represents the amount and timing of the debt liabilities. The amounts are the sum of the coupon and principal payments of debt securities on a hypothetical balance sheet.

Exhibit 16: Cash Flow Matching

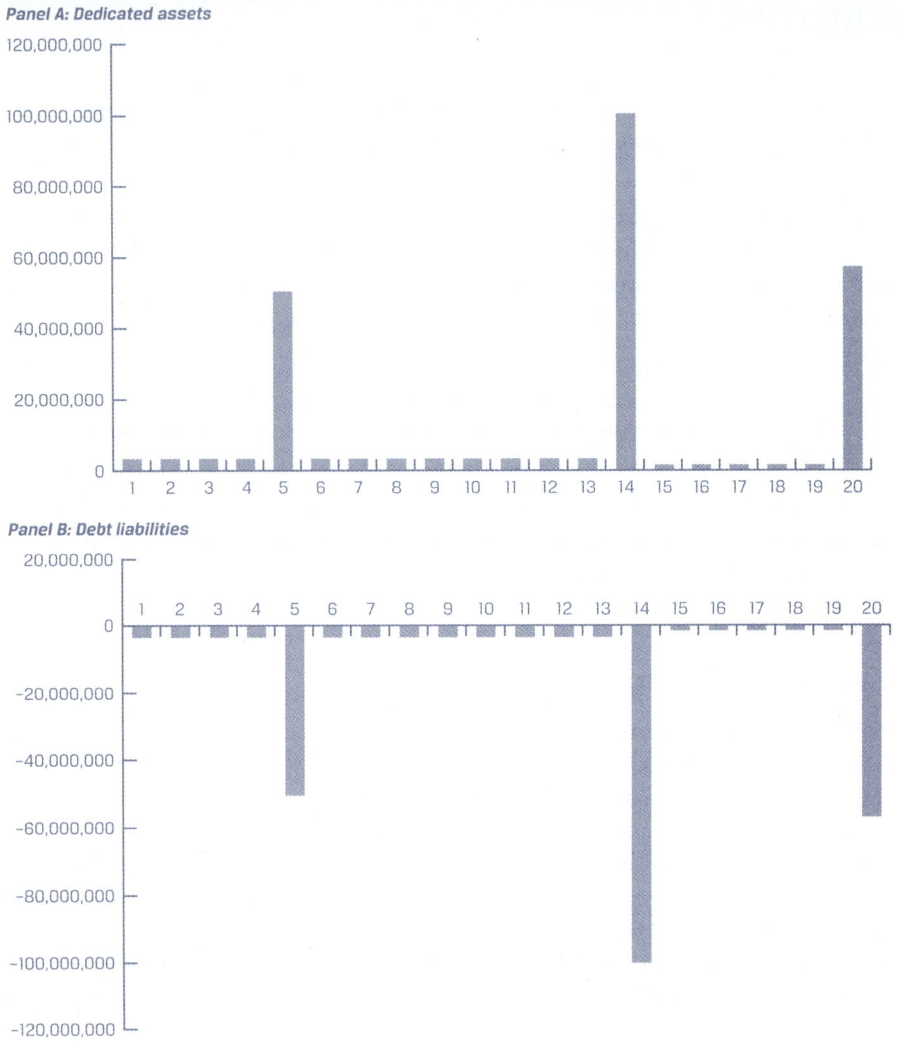

A concern when implementing this strategy is the *cash-in-advance constraint*. That means securities are not sold to meet obligations; instead, sufficient funds must be available on or before each liability payment date to meet the obligation. The design of traditional bonds—a fixed coupon rate and principal redemption at maturity—is a problem if the liability stream, unlike in Exhibit 16, is a level payment annuity. That scenario could lead to large cash holdings between payment dates and, therefore, cash flow reinvestment risk, especially if yields on high-quality, short-term investments are low (or worse, negative).

EXAMPLE 2

Alfred Simonsson is assistant treasurer at a Swedish lumber company. The company has sold a large tract of land and now has sufficient cash holdings to retire some of its debt liabilities. The company's accounting department assures Alfred that its external auditors will approve of a defeasement strategy if Swedish government bonds are purchased to match the interest and principal payments on the liabilities. Following is the schedule of payments due on the debt as of June Year 1 that the company plans to defease:

June Year 2	SEK3,710,000
June Year 3	SEK6,620,000
June Year 4	SEK4,410,000
June Year 5	SEK5,250,000

The following Swedish government bonds are available. Interest on the bonds is paid annually in May of each year.

Coupon Rate	Maturity Date
2.75%	May Year 2
3.50%	May Year 3
4.75%	May Year 4
5.50%	May Year 5

1. How much in par value for each government bond will Alfred need to buy to defease the debt liabilities, assuming that the minimum denomination in each security is SEK10,000?

Solution

The cash flow matching portfolio is built by starting with the last liability of SEK5,250,000 in June Year 5. If there were no minimum denomination, that liability could be funded with the 5.50% bonds due May Year 5 having a par value of SEK4,976,303 (= SEK5,250,000/1.0550). To deal with the constraint, however, Alfred buys SEK4,980,000 in par value. That bond pays SEK5,253,900 (= SEK4,980,000 × 1.0550) at maturity. This holding also pays SEK273,900 (= SEK4,980,000 × 0.0550) in coupon interest in May Year 2, 3, and 4.

Then move to the June Year 4 obligation, which is SEK4,136,100 after subtracting the SEK273,900 received on the 5.50% bond: SEK4,410,000 – SEK273,900 = SEK4,136,100. Alfred buys SEK3,950,000 in par value of the 4.75% bond due May Year 4. That bond pays SEK4,137,625 (= SEK3,950,000 × 1.0475) at maturity and SEK187,625 in interest in May Year 2 and Year 3.

The net obligation in June Year 3 is SEK6,158,475 (= SEK6,620,000 – SEK273,900 – SEK187,625) after subtracting the interest received on the longer-maturity bonds. The company can buy SEK5,950,000 in par value of the 3.50% bond due May Year 3. At maturity, this bond pays SEK6,158,250 (= SEK5,950,000 × 1.0350). The small shortfall of SEK225 (= SEK6,158,475 – SEK6,158,250) can be made up because the funds received in May are reinvested until June. This bond also pays SEK208,250 in interest in May Year 2.

Finally, Alfred needs to buy SEK2,960,000 in par value of the 2.75% bond due May Year 2. This bond pays SEK3,041,400 (= SEK2,960,000 × 1.0275) in May Year 2. The final coupon and principal, plus the interest on the 5.50%, 4.75%, and 3.50% bonds, total SEK3,711,175 (= SEK3,041,400 + SEK273,900 + SEK187,625 + SEK208,250). That amount is used to pay off the June Year 2 obligation of SEK3,710,000. Note that the excess could be kept in a bank account to cover the Year 3 shortfall.

In sum, Alfred buys the following portfolio:

Bond	Par Value
2.75% due May Year 2	SEK2,960,000
3.50% due May Year 3	SEK5,950,000

Bond	Par Value
4.75% due May Year 4	SEK3,950,000
5.50% due May Year 5	SEK4,980,000

The following chart illustrates the cash flow matching bond portfolio: Each bar represents the par amount of a bond maturing in that year plus coupon payments from bonds maturing in later years.

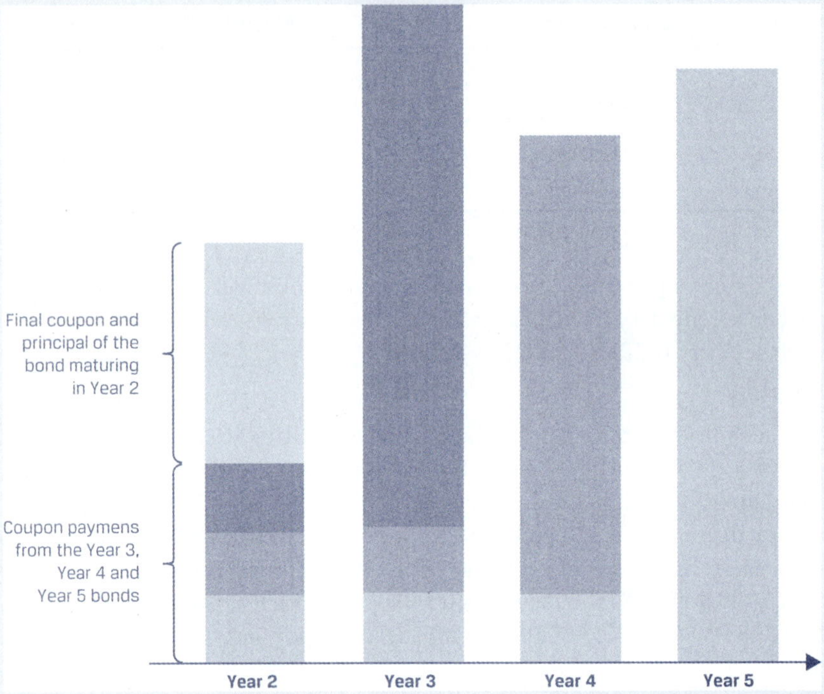

10 LADDERED PORTFOLIOS

☐ describe construction, benefits, limitations, and risk–return characteristics of a laddered bond portfolio

A popular fixed-income investment strategy in the wealth management industry is to build a "laddered" portfolio for clients. Exhibit 17 illustrates this approach, along with two other maturity-based strategies—a "bullet" portfolio and a "barbell" portfolio. The laddered portfolio spreads the bonds' maturities and par values evenly along the yield curve. The bullet portfolio concentrates the bonds at a particular point on the yield curve, whereas the barbell portfolio places the bonds at the short-term and long-term ends of the curve. In principle, each can have the same portfolio duration statistic and approximately the same change in value for a parallel shift in the yield curve. A non-parallel shift or a twist in the curve, however, leads to very different outcomes for the bullet and barbell structures. An obvious advantage to the laddered portfolio is protection from shifts and twists—the cash flows are essentially "diversified" across the time spectrum.

Exhibit 17: Laddered, Bullet, and Barbell Fixed-Income Portfolios

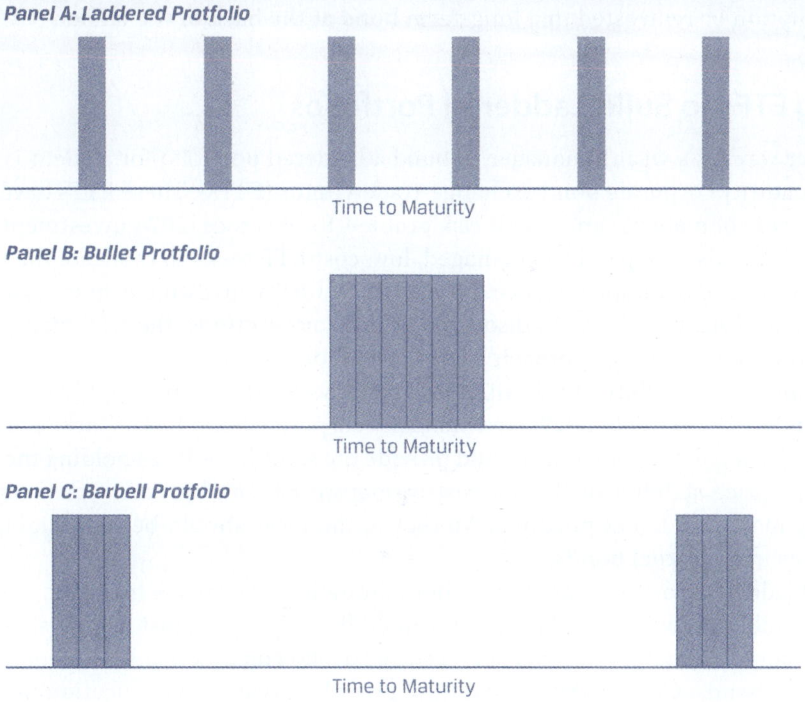

Benefits of Using Laddered Portfolios

This "diversification" over time provides the investor a balanced position between the two sources of interest rate risk—cash flow reinvestment and market price volatility. Bonds mature each year and are reinvested at the longer-term end of the ladder, typically at higher rates than short-term securities. Over time, the laddered portfolio likely includes bonds that were purchased at high interest rates as well as low interest rates. Investors familiar with "dollar cost averaging" will see the similarity. In addition, reinvesting funds as bonds mature maintains the duration of the overall portfolio.

Another attractive feature to the laddered portfolio apparent in Exhibit 17 is in convexity. Convexity, technically, is the second-order effect on the value of an asset or liability given a change in the yield to maturity. Importantly, it is affected by the dispersion of cash flows, as indicated in the following equation:

$$\text{Immunized Portfolio Convexity} = \frac{\text{MacDur}^2 + \text{MacDur} + \text{Dispersion}}{(1 + \text{Cash flow yield})^2}.$$

If the three portfolios have the same duration (and cash flow yield), then the barbell clearly has the highest convexity and the bullet the lowest. The laddered portfolio will tend to have relatively high convexity because its cash flows by design are spread over the timeline. Compared with the barbell, the laddered portfolio has much less cash flow reinvestment risk.

In practice, perhaps the most desirable aspect of the laddered portfolio is in liquidity management. This aspect is particularly relevant if the bonds are not actively traded, as is the case for many corporate securities. As time passes, there is always a bond that is close to redemption. Its duration will be low so that its price is fairly stable even in a time of interest rate volatility. If the client needs immediate cash, the soon-to-mature bond makes for high-quality collateral on a personal loan or, for an institution, a repo contract. As the bonds mature, the final coupon and principal can be deployed for consumption or reinvested in a long-term bond at the back of the ladder.

Using ETFs to Build Laddered Portfolios

Another way for a wealth manager to build a laddered portfolio for a client is to use fixed-maturity corporate bond exchange-traded funds (ETFs). These ETFs have a designated year of maturity and credit risk profile—for instance, 2024 investment-grade corporate bonds. The passively managed, low-cost ETF seeks to replicate the performance of an index of, for instance, 50 held-to-maturity investment-grade corporate bonds that mature in 2021. As discussed in previous sections, the ETF manager can use a stratified sampling approach to track the index.

Suppose that in 2021, the wealth manager buys for the client roughly equal positions in the 2022 through 2029 fixed-maturity corporate bond ETFs. These purchases create a laddered portfolio that should provide the same benefits as holding the bonds directly—price stability in the soonest-to-mature ETF and greater convexity than holding more of a bullet portfolio. Moreover, the ETFs should be more liquid than positions in the actual bonds.

But laddered portfolios are not without limitations. For many investors, the decision to build a laddered bond portfolio should be weighed against buying shares in a fixed-income mutual fund, especially if the portfolio consists of a limited number of corporate bonds. Clearly, the mutual fund provides greater diversification of default risk. Moreover, actual bonds can entail a much higher cost of acquisition. If the entire investment needs to be liquidated, the mutual fund shares can be redeemed more quickly than the bonds can be sold, and likely at a better price.

EXAMPLE 3

Mr. Zheng is a Shanghai-based wealth adviser. A major client of his, the Wang family, holds most of its assets in residential property and equity investments and relies on regular cash flows from those holdings. Zheng recommends that the Wang family also have a laddered portfolio of Chinese government bonds. He suggests the portfolio shown in Exhibit 18, priced for settlement on 1 January 2021.

Exhibit 18: Zheng's Suggested Portfolio

Coupon Rate	Payment Frequency	Maturity	Flat Price	Yield (s.a.)	Par Value (CNY)	Market Value (CNY)
3.22%	Annual	26-Mar-22	101.7493	1.758%	10 million	10,422,826
3.14%	Annual	8-Sept-24	102.1336	2.508%	10 million	10,312,292
3.05%	Annual	22-Oct-26	101.4045	2.764%	10 million	10,199,779
2.99%	Semi-annual	15-Oct-29	101.4454	2.803%	10 million	10,208,611
					40 million	41,143,508

The yields to maturity on the first three bonds have been converted from a periodicity of one to two in order to report them on a consistent semi-annual bond basis, as indicated by "(s.a.)." The total market value of the portfolio is CNY41,143,508. The cash flow yield for the portfolio is 2.661%, whereas the market value-weighted average yield is 2.455%.

Most important for his presentation to the senior members of the Wang family is the schedule for the 30 cash flows:

1	26-Mar-21	322,000	16	8-Sep-24	10,314,000
2	15-Apr-21	149,500	17	15-Oct-24	149,500
3	8-Sep-21	314,000	18	22-Oct-24	305,000
4	15-Oct-21	149,500	19	15-Apr-25	149,500
5	22-Oct-21	305,000	20	15-Oct-25	149,500
6	26-Mar-22	10,322,000	21	22-Oct-25	305,000
7	15-Apr-22	149,500	22	15-Apr-26	149,500
8	8-Sep-22	314,000	23	15-Oct-26	149,500
9	15-Oct-22	149,500	24	22-Oct-26	10,305,000
10	22-Oct-22	305,000	25	15-Apr-27	149,500
11	15-Apr-23	149,500	26	15-Oct-27	149,500
12	8-Sep-23	314,000	27	15-Apr-28	149,500
13	15-Oct-23	149,500	28	15-Oct-28	149,500
14	22-Oct-23	305,000	29	15-Apr-29	149,500
15	15-Apr-24	149,500	30	15-Oct-29	10,149,500

1. Indicate the main points that Zheng should emphasize in this presentation about the laddered portfolio to senior members of the Wang family.

Solution

Zheng should emphasize three features of the portfolio:

High credit quality. Given that the family already has substantial holdings in residential property and equity, which are subject to price volatility and risk, investments in government bonds provide the Wang family with holdings in a very low-risk asset class.

Liquidity. The schedule of payments shows that coupon payments are received each year. These funds can be used for any cash need, including household expenses. The large principal payments can be reinvested in longer-term government bonds at the back of the ladder.

Yield curve diversification. The bond investments are spread out along four segments of the government bond yield curve. If they were concentrated at a single point, the portfolio would have the risk of higher yields at that point. By spreading out the maturities in the ladder formation, the portfolio has the benefit of diversification.

SUMMARY

- Fixed-income investments provide diversification benefits in a portfolio context. These benefits arise from the generally low correlations of fixed-income investments with other major asset classes, such as equities.
- Floating-rate and inflation-linked bonds can be used to hedge inflation risk.
- Fixed-income investments have regular cash flows, which is beneficial for the purposes of funding future liabilities.

- For liability-based fixed-income mandates, portfolio construction follows two main approaches—cash flow matching and duration matching—to match fixed-income assets with future liabilities.
- Total return mandates are generally structured to either track or outperform a benchmark.
- Total return mandates can be classified into various approaches according to their target active return and active risk levels. Approaches range from pure indexing to enhanced indexing to active management.
- Bond portfolio duration is the sensitivity of a portfolio of bonds to small changes in interest rates. It can be calculated as the weighted average of time to receipt of the aggregate cash flows or, more commonly, as the weighted average of the individual bond durations that comprise the portfolio.
- Modified duration of a bond portfolio indicates the percentage change in the market value given a change in yield to maturity. Modified duration of a portfolio comprising *j* fixed-income securities can be estimated as

$$\text{AvgModDur} = \sum_{j=1}^{J} \text{ModDur}_j \left(\frac{\text{MV}_j}{\text{MV}}\right),$$

  where MV stands for market value of the portfolio and MV_j is the market value of a specific bond in the portfolio.
- Convexity of a bond portfolio is a second-order effect; it operates behind duration in importance and can largely be ignored for small yield changes. When convexity is added with the use of derivatives, however, it can be extremely important to returns.
- Effective duration and convexity of a portfolio are the relevant summary statistics when future cash flows of bonds in a portfolio are contingent on interest rate changes.
- Spread duration is a useful measure for determining a portfolio's sensitivity to changes in credit spreads. It provides the approximate percentage increase (decrease) in bond price expected for a 1% decrease (increase) in credit spread.
- Duration times spread is a modification of the spread duration definition to incorporate the empirical observation that spread changes across the credit spectrum tend to occur on a *proportional percentage* basis rather than being based on *absolute* basis point changes.
- Portfolio dispersion captures the variance of the times to receipt of cash flows around the duration. It is used in measuring interest rate immunization for liabilities.
- Duration management is the primary tool used by fixed-income portfolio managers.
- Convexity supplements duration as a measure of a bond's price sensitivity for larger movements in interest rates. Adjusting convexity can be an important portfolio management tool.
- For two portfolios with the same duration, the portfolio with higher convexity has higher sensitivity to large declines in yields to maturity and lower sensitivity to large increases in yields to maturity.
- Interest rate derivatives can be used effectively to increase or decrease duration and convexity in a bond portfolio.

- Liquidity is an important consideration in fixed-income portfolio management. Bonds are generally less liquid than equities, and liquidity varies greatly across sectors.
- Liquidity affects pricing in fixed-income markets because many bonds either do not trade or trade infrequently.
- Liquidity affects portfolio construction because there is a trade-off between liquidity and yield to maturity. Less liquid bonds have higher yields to maturity, all else being equal, and may be more desirable for buy-and-hold investors. Investors anticipating liquidity needs may forego higher yields to maturity for more liquid bonds.
- Investors can obtain exposure to the bond market using mutual funds and ETFs that track a bond index. Shares in mutual funds are redeemable at the net asset value with a one-day time lag. ETF shares have the advantage of trading on an exchange.
- A total return swap, an over-the-counter derivative, allows an institutional investor to transform an asset or liability from one asset category to another—for instance, from variable-rate cash flows referencing the market reference rate to the total return on a particular bond index.
- A total return swap (TRS) can have some advantages over a direct investment in a bond mutual fund or ETF. As a derivative, it requires less initial cash outlay than direct investment in the bond portfolio for similar performance but carries counterparty risk.
- As a customized over-the-counter product, a TRS can offer exposure to assets that are difficult to access directly, such as some high-yield and commercial loan investments.
- When evaluating fixed-income investment strategies, it is important to consider expected returns and to understand the various components of expected returns.
- Decomposing expected fixed-income returns allows investors to understand the different sources of returns given expected changes in bond market conditions.
- A model for expected fixed-income returns can decompose them into the following components: coupon income, rolldown return, expected change in price based on investor's views of yields to maturity and yield spreads, and expected currency gains or losses.
- Leverage is the use of borrowed capital to increase the magnitude of portfolio positions. By using leverage, fixed-income portfolio managers may be able to increase portfolio returns relative to what they can achieve in unleveraged portfolios. The potential for increased returns, however, comes with increased risk.
- Methods for leveraging fixed-income portfolios include the use of futures contracts, swap agreements, repurchase agreements, structured financial instruments, and security lending.
- Taxes can complicate investment decisions in fixed-income portfolio management. Complications result from the differences in taxation among investor types, countries, and income sources.
- The two primary sources of investment income that affect taxes for fixed-income securities are coupon payments (interest income) and capital gains or losses. Tax is usually payable only on capital gains and interest income that have actually been received.

- Capital gains are frequently taxed at a lower effective tax rate than interest income. If capital losses exceed capital gains in the year, they can often be "carried forward" and applied to gains in future years.
- Structured fixed-income investing requires a frame of reference, such as a balance sheet, to structure the bond portfolio. This frame of reference can be as simple as the time to retirement for an individual or as complex as a balance sheet of rate-sensitive assets and liabilities for a company.
- Assets and liabilities can be categorized by the degree of certainty surrounding the amount and timing of cash flows. Type I assets and liabilities, such as traditional fixed-rate bonds with no embedded options, have known amounts and payment dates. For Type I assets and liabilities, such yield duration statistics as Macaulay, modified, and money duration apply.
- Type II, III, and IV assets and liabilities have uncertain amounts and/or uncertain timing of payment. For Type II, III, and IV assets and liabilities, curve duration statistics, such as effective duration, are needed. A model is used to obtain the estimated values when the yield curve shifts up and down by the same amount.
- Structural risk to immunization arises from some non-parallel shifts and twists to the yield curve. This risk is reduced by minimizing the dispersion of cash flows in the portfolio, which can be accomplished by minimizing the convexity statistic for the portfolio.
- For multiple liabilities, one method of immunization is cash flow matching. A portfolio of high-quality zero-coupon or fixed-income bonds is purchased to match as closely as possible the amount and timing of the liabilities.
- A motive for cash flow matching can be accounting defeasance, whereby both the assets and liabilities are removed from the balance sheet.
- A laddered bond portfolio is a common investment strategy in the wealth management industry. The laddered portfolio offers "diversification" over the yield curve compared with "bullet" or "barbell" portfolios.
- A laddered portfolio offers an increase in convexity because the cash flows have greater dispersions than a more concentrated (bullet) portfolio.
- A laddered portfolio provides liquidity in that it always contains a soon-to-mature bond that could provide high-quality, low-duration collateral on a repo contract if needed.

REFERENCES

Hanke, B. and G. Seals. 2010. "*Fixed-Income Analysis: Yield Curve Construction, Trading Strategies, and Risk Analysis.*" CFA Institute online course.

Rogers, D. 2006. *Tax-Aware Investment Management: The Essential Guide.* New York: Bloomberg Press.

PRACTICE PROBLEMS

The following information relates to questions 1-6

Cécile is a junior analyst for an international wealth management firm. Her supervisor, Margit, asks Cécile to evaluate three fixed-income funds as part of the firm's global fixed-income offerings. Selected financial data for the funds Aschel, Permot, and Rosaiso are presented in Exhibit 1. In Cécile's initial review, she assumes that there is no reinvestment income and that the yield curve remains unchanged.

Exhibit 1: Selected Data on Fixed-Income Funds

	Aschel	Permot	Rosaiso
Current average bond price	\$117.00	\$91.50	\$94.60
Expected average bond price in one year (end of Year 1)	\$114.00	\$96.00	\$97.00
Average modified duration	7.07	7.38	6.99
Average annual coupon payment	\$3.63	\$6.07	\$6.36
Present value of portfolio's assets (millions)	\$136.33	\$68.50	\$74.38
*Bond type**			
Fixed-coupon bonds	95%	38%	62%
Floating-coupon bonds	2%	34%	17%
Inflation-linked bonds	3%	28%	21%
*Quality**			
AAA	65%	15%	20%
BBB	35%	65%	50%
B	0%	20%	20%
Not rated	0%	0%	10%
Value of portfolio's equity (millions)	\$94.33		
Value of borrowed funds (millions)	\$42.00		
Borrowing rate	2.80%		
Return on invested funds	6.20%		

**Bond type and quality are shown as a percentage of the total for each fund.*

After further review of the composition of each of the funds, Cécile makes the following notes:

Note 1 Aschel is the only fund of the three that uses leverage.

Note 2 Rosaiso is the only fund of the three that holds a significant number of bonds with embedded options.

Margit asks Cécile to analyze liability-based mandates for a meeting with Villash Foundation. Villash Foundation is a tax-exempt client. Prior to the meeting,

Cécile identifies what she considers to be two key features of a liability-based mandate.

Feature 1 It matches expected liability payments with future projected cash inflows.

Feature 2 It can minimize the risk of deficient cash inflows for a company.

Two years later, Margit learns that Villash Foundation needs $5 million in cash to meet liabilities. She asks Cécile to analyze two bonds for possible liquidation. Selected data on the two bonds are presented in Exhibit 2.

Exhibit 2: Selected Data for Bonds 1 and 2

	Bond 1		Bond 2
Current market value	$5,000,000		$5,000,000
Capital gain/loss	$400,000		–$400,000
Coupon rate	2.05%		2.05%
Remaining maturity	8 years		8 years
Investment view	Overvalued		Undervalued
Income tax rate		39%	
Capital gains tax rate		30%	

1. Based on Exhibit 1, which fund provides the highest level of protection against inflation for coupon payments?

   A. Aschel

   B. Permot

   C. Rosaiso

2. Based on Exhibit 1, the rolling yield of Aschel over a one-year investment horizon is *closest* to:

   A. 2.56%.

   B. 0.54%.

   C. 5.66%.

3. The leveraged portfolio return for Aschel is *closest* to:

   A. 7.25%.

   B. 7.71%.

   C. 8.96%.

4. Based on Note 2, Rosaiso is the only fund for which the expected change in price based on the investor's views of yields to maturity and yield spreads should be calculated using:

   A. convexity.

   B. modified duration.

C. effective duration.

5. Is Cécile correct with respect to key features of liability-based mandates?

   A. Yes.

   B. No, only Feature 1 is correct.

   C. No, only Feature 2 is correct.

6. Based on Exhibit 2, the optimal strategy to meet Villash Foundation's cash needs is the sale of:

   A. 100% of Bond 1.

   B. 100% of Bond 2.

   C. 50% of Bond 1 and 50% of Bond 2.

The following information relates to questions 7-12

Celia is chief investment officer for the Topanga Investors Fund, which invests in equities and fixed income. The clients in the fund are all taxable investors. The fixed-income allocation includes a domestic (US) bond portfolio and an externally managed global bond portfolio.

The domestic bond portfolio has a total return mandate, which specifies a long-term return objective of 25 basis points (bps) over the benchmark index. Relative to the benchmark, small deviations in sector weightings are permitted, such risk factors as duration must closely match, and tracking error is expected to be less than 50 bps per year. These features are typical of enhanced indexing.

The objectives for the domestic bond portfolio include the ability to fund future liabilities, protect interest income from short-term inflation, and minimize the correlation with the fund's equity portfolio. The correlation between the fund's domestic bond portfolio and equity portfolio is currently 0.14. Celia plans to reduce the fund's equity allocation and increase the allocation to the domestic bond portfolio. She reviews two possible investment strategies.

Strategy 1	Purchase AAA-rated fixed-coupon corporate bonds with a modified duration of two years and a correlation coefficient with the equity portfolio of –0.15.
Strategy 2	Purchase US government agency floating-coupon bonds with a modified duration of one month and a correlation coefficient with the equity portfolio of –0.10.

Celia realizes that the fund's return may decrease if the equity allocation of the fund is reduced. Celia decides to liquidate $20 million of US Treasuries that are currently owned and to invest the proceeds in the US corporate bond sector. To fulfill this strategy, Celia asks Dan, a newly hired analyst for the fund, to recommend specific Treasuries to sell and corporate bonds to purchase.

Dan recommends Treasuries from the existing portfolio that he believes are overvalued and will generate capital gains. Celia asks Dan why he chose only overvalued bonds with capital gains and did not include any bonds with capital losses.

Dan responds with two statements.

Statement 1 Taxable investors should prioritize selling overvalued bonds and always sell them before selling bonds that are viewed as fairly valued or undervalued.

Statement 2 Taxable investors should never intentionally realize capital losses.

Regarding the purchase of corporate bonds, Dan collects relevant data, which are presented in Exhibit 1.

Exhibit 1: Selected Data on Three US Corporate Bonds

Bond Characteristics	Bond 1	Bond 2	Bond 3
Credit quality	AA	AA	A
Issue size ($ millions)	100	75	75
Maturity (years)	5	7	7
Total issuance outstanding ($ millions)	1,000	1,500	1,000
Months since issuance	New issue	3	6

Celia and Dan review the total expected 12-month return (assuming no reinvestment income) for the global bond portfolio. Selected financial data are presented in Exhibit 2.

Exhibit 2: Selected Data on Global Bond Portfolio

Notional principal of portfolio (in millions)	€200
Average bond coupon payment (per €100 par value)	€2.25
Coupon frequency	Annual
Investment Horizon	1 year
Current average bond price	€98.45
Expected average bond price in one year (assuming an unchanged yield curve)	€98.62
Average bond convexity	22
Average bond modified duration	5.19
Expected average benchmark yield-to-maturity change	0.15%
Expected change in credit spread (widening)	0.13%
Expected currency gains (€ appreciation vs. $)	0.65%

Celia contemplates adding a new manager to the global bond portfolio. She reviews three proposals and determines that each manager uses the same index as its benchmark but pursues a different total return approach, as presented in Exhibit 3.

Exhibit 3: New Manager Proposals: Fixed-Income Portfolio Characteristics

Sector Weights (%)	Manager A	Manager B	Manager C	Index
Government	53.5	52.5	47.8	54.1
Agency/quasi-agency	16.2	16.4	13.4	16.0
Corporate	20.0	22.2	25.1	19.8
MBS	10.3	8.9	13.7	10.1

Risk and Return Characteristics	Manager A	Manager B	Manager C	Index
Average maturity (years)	7.63	7.84	8.55	7.56
Modified duration (years)	5.23	5.25	6.16	5.22
Average yield to maturity (%)	1.98	2.08	2.12	1.99
Turnover (%)	207	220	290	205

7. Which approach to its total return mandate is the fund's domestic bond portfolio *most likely* to use?

   A. Pure indexing

   B. Enhanced indexing

   C. Active management

8. Strategy 2 is *most likely* preferred to Strategy 1 for meeting the objective of:

   A. protecting against inflation.

   B. funding future liabilities.

   C. minimizing the correlation of the fund's domestic bond portfolio and equity portfolio.

9. Are Dan's statements to Celia that support Dan's choice of bonds to sell correct?

   A. Only Statement 1 is correct.

   B. Only Statement 2 is correct.

   C. Neither Statement 1 nor Statement 2 is correct.

10. Based on Exhibit 1, which bond *most likely* has the highest liquidity premium?

    A. Bond 1

    B. Bond 2

    C. Bond 3

11. Based on Exhibit 2, the total expected return of the fund's global bond portfolio is *closest* to:

    A. 0.90%.

    B. 1.66%.

    C. 3.76%.

12. Based on Exhibit 3, which manager is *most likely* to have an active management total return mandate?

    A. Manager A

    B. Manager B

    C. Manager C

SOLUTIONS

1. B is correct. Permot has the highest percentage of floating-coupon bonds and inflation-linked bonds. Bonds with floating coupons protect interest income from inflation because the reference rate should adjust for inflation. Inflation-linked bonds protect against inflation by paying a return that is directly linked to an index of consumer prices and adjusting the principal for inflation. Inflation-linked bonds protect both coupon and principal payments against inflation.

   The level of inflation protection for coupons equals the percentage of the portfolio in floating-coupon bonds plus the percentage of the portfolio in inflation-linked bonds:

   Aschel = 2% + 3% = 5%.

   Permot = 34% + 28% = 62%.

   Rosaiso = 17% + 21% = 38%.

   Thus, Permot has the highest level of inflation protection, with 62% of its portfolio in floating-coupon and inflation-linked bonds.

2. B is correct. The rolling yield is the sum of the coupon income and the rolldown return. Coupon income is the sum of the bond's annual current yield and interest on reinvestment income. Cécile assumes that there is no reinvestment income for any of the three funds, and the yield income for Aschel will be calculated as follows:

   Coupon income = Annual average coupon payment/Current bond price

   = \$3.63/\$117.00

   = 0.0310, or 3.10%.

   The rolldown return is equal to the bond's percentage price change assuming an unchanged yield curve over the horizon period. The rolldown return will be calculated as follows:

$$\text{Rolldown Returns} = \frac{\left(\text{Bond price}_{\textit{End-of-horizon period}} - \text{Bond price}_{\textit{Beginning-of-horizon period}}\right)}{\text{Bond price}_{\textit{Beginning-of-horizon period}}}$$

$$= \frac{(\$114.00 - \$117.00)}{\$117.00}$$

$$= -0.0256, \text{ or } -2.56\%.$$

   Rolling yield = Coupon income + Rolldown return = 3.10% – 2.56% = 0.54%.

3. B is correct. The return for Aschel is 7.71%, calculated as follows:

$$r_P = \frac{r_I \times (V_E + V_B) - V_B \times r_B}{V_E}.$$

$$= r_I + \frac{V_B}{V_E}(r_I - r_B)$$

$$= 6.20\% + \frac{\$42.00 \text{ million}}{\$94.33 \text{ million}}(6.20\% - 2.80\%)$$

$$= 7.71\%.$$

4. C is correct. Rosaiso is the only fund that holds bonds with embedded options. Effective duration should be used for bonds with embedded options. For bonds with embedded options, the duration and convexity measures used to calculate the expected change in price based on the investor's views of yields to maturity and yield spreads are effective duration and effective convexity. For bonds without embedded options, convexity and modified duration are used in this calculation.

5. A is correct. Liability-based mandates are investments that take an investor's future obligations into consideration. Liability-based mandates are managed to match expected liability payments with future projected cash inflows. These types of mandates are structured in a way to ensure that a liability or a stream of liabilities can be covered and that any risk of shortfalls or deficient cash inflows for a company are minimized.

6. A is correct. The optimal strategy for Villash is the sale of 100% of Bond 1, which Cécile considers to be overvalued. Because Villash is a tax-exempt foundation, tax considerations are not relevant and Cécile's investment views drive her trading recommendations.

7. B is correct. The domestic bond portfolio's return objective is to modestly outperform the benchmark. Its risk factors, such as duration, are to closely match the benchmark. Small deviations in sector weights are allowed, and tracking error should be less than 50 bps per year. These features are typical of enhanced indexing.

8. A is correct. Floating-coupon bonds provide inflation protection for the interest income because the reference rate should adjust for inflation. The purchase of fixed-coupon bonds as outlined in Strategy 1 provides no protection against inflation for either interest or principal. Strategy 1 would instead be superior to Strategy 2 in funding future liabilities (better predictability as to the amount of cash flows) and reducing the correlation between the fund's domestic bond portfolio and equity portfolio (better diversification).

9. C is correct. Since the fund's clients are taxable investors, there is value in harvesting tax losses. These losses can be used to offset capital gains within the fund that will otherwise be distributed to the clients and result in higher tax payments, which decreases the total value of the investment to clients. The fund has to consider the overall value of the investment to its clients, including taxes, which may result in the sale of bonds that are not viewed as overvalued. Tax-exempt investors' decisions are driven by their investment views without regard to offsetting gains and losses for tax purposes.

10. C is correct. Bond 3 is most likely to be the least liquid of the three bonds presented in Exhibit 1 and will thus most likely require the highest liquidity premium. Low credit ratings, longer time since issuance, smaller issuance size, smaller issuance outstanding, and longer time to maturity typically are associated with lower liquidity (and thus a higher liquidity premium). Bond 3 has the lowest credit quality and the longest time since issuance of the three bonds. Bond 3 also has a smaller issue size and a longer time to maturity than Bond 1. The total issuance outstanding for Bond 3 is smaller than that of Bond 2 and equal to that of Bond 1.

11. B is correct. The total expected return is calculated as follows:

Total expected return =

Rolling yield

+/– *E*(Change in price based on investor's benchmark yield view)

+/– *E*(Change in price due to investor's view of credit spread)

+/– *E*(Currency gains or losses),

where Rolling yield = Coupon income + Rolldown return.

Return Component	Formula	Calculation
Coupon income	Annual coupon payment/Current bond price	€2.25/€;98.45 = 2.29%
+ Rolldown return	(Bond price$_{End\text{-}of\text{-}horizon\ period}$ – Bond price$_{Beginning\text{-}of\text{-}horizon\ period}$)/Bond price$_{Beginning\text{-}of\text{-}horizon\ period}$	(€98.62 – €98.45)/€98.45 = 0.17%
= Rolling yield	Coupon income + Rolldown return	2.29% + 0.17% = 2.46%
+/– *E*(Change in price based on investor's benchmark yield view)	(–MD × ΔYield) + [½ × Convexity × (ΔYield)^2]	(–5.19 × 0.0015) + [½ × 22 × (0.0015)^2] = –0.78%
+/– *E*(Change in price due to investor's view of credit spread)	(–MD × ΔSpread) + [½ × Convexity × (ΔSpread)^2]	(–5.19 × 0.0013) + [½ × 22 × (0.0013)^2] = –0.67%
+/– *E*(Currency gains or losses)	Given	0.65%
= Total expected return		**1.66%**

12. C is correct. The sector weights, risk and return characteristics, and turnover for Manager C differ significantly from those of the index, which is typical of an active management mandate. In particular, Manager C's modified duration of 6.16 represents a much larger deviation from the benchmark index modified duration of 5.22 than that of the other managers, which is a characteristic unique to an active management mandate.

LEARNING MODULE

3

Asset Allocation to Alternative Investments

by Adam Kobor, PhD, CFA, and Mark D. Guinney, CFA.

Adam Kobor, PhD, CFA, is at New York University (USA). Mark D. Guinney, CFA (USA).

LEARNING OUTCOMES

Mastery	The candidate should be able to:
☐	explain the roles that alternative investments play in multi-asset portfolios
☐	compare alternative investments and bonds as risk mitigators in relation to a long equity position
☐	compare traditional and risk-based approaches to defining the investment opportunity set, including alternative investments
☐	discuss investment considerations that are important in allocating to different types of alternative investments
☐	discuss suitability considerations in allocating to alternative investments
☐	discuss approaches to asset allocation to alternative investments
☐	discuss the importance of liquidity planning in allocating to alternative investments
☐	discuss considerations in monitoring alternative investment programs

INTRODUCTION 1

☐	explain the roles that alternative investments play in multi-asset portfolios

Asset allocation is a critical decision in the investment process. The mathematical and analytical processes inherent in contemporary asset allocation techniques are complicated by the idiosyncrasies of alternative investments. Approaches to incorporating alternative assets into the strategic asset allocation have developed rapidly as allocations to assets other than stocks and bonds have accelerated in the aftermath of the 2008 Global Financial Crisis. The term "alternative" understates the prominence of alternative investment allocations in many investment programs, because institutional and private clients have been increasingly turning to these investments not just to supplement traditional long-only stocks and bonds but also sometimes to replace them altogether. For example, the Yale Endowment and the Canada Pension Plan Investment Board both have close to 50% of their assets allocated to alternatives.[1] Although these two funds are admittedly outliers, between 2008 and 2017 most of the pension funds around the world substantially expanded their allocations to alternative asset classes. On average, pension funds in developed markets increased their allocation from 7.2% to 11.8% of assets under management (AUM) in 2017, a 63% increase.[2]

"Alternative" investment has no universally accepted definition. For the purposes of this reading, alternative investments include private equity, hedge funds, real assets (including energy and commodity investments), commercial real estate, and private credit.

The reading begins with a discussion of the role alternative assets play in a multi-asset portfolio and explores how alternatives may serve to mitigate long-only equity risk, a role traditionally held by bonds. We then consider different ways investors may define the opportunity set—through the traditional asset class lens or, more recently, using a risk- or factor-based lens. An allocation to alternatives is not for all investors, so the reading describes issues that should be addressed when considering an allocation to alternatives. We then discuss approaches to asset allocation when incorporating alternatives in the opportunity set and the need for liquidity planning in private investment alternatives. Finally, the reading discusses the unique monitoring requirements for an alternatives portfolio.

The Role of Alternative Investments in a Multi-Asset Portfolio

Allocations to alternatives are playing an increasing role in investor portfolios largely driven by the belief that these investments increase the risk-adjusted return expectations for their programs. Some allocations are driven by expectations of higher returns, while others are driven by the expected diversification (risk-reduction) benefits. In the aggregate, the portfolio's *risk-adjusted* return is expected to improve. Exhibit 1 provides a framework for how the common alternative strategies are generally perceived to affect the risk/return profile of a "typical" 60/40 portfolio of public stocks and bonds.

1 Boston Consulting Group (BCG), "The Rise of Alternative Assets and Long-Term Investing (March 2017).

2 See Ivashina and Lerner 2018.

Exhibit 1: Alternative Investments in the Risk/Reward Continuum

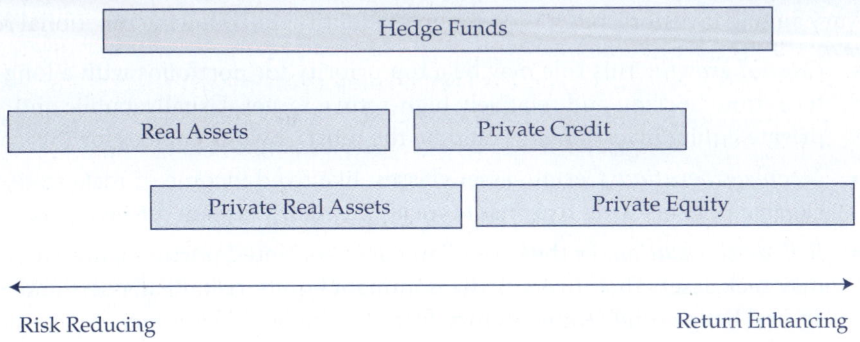

Although we present a simplified view, real assets are generally believed to mitigate the risks to the portfolio arising from unexpected inflation. At the other end of the spectrum, venture capital investments (private equity) are expected to provide a sufficient return premium over public equities to compensate for their illiquidity risk and heightened operational complexity. Hedge funds, the least homogenous of strategies, span the spectrum from "risk reducing" or diversifying (many arbitrage strategies) to "return enhancing" (e.g., an activist fund that takes significant positions in public companies with the goal of improving performance through management changes, capital allocation policies, and/or company strategy).

Risk reduction can mean different things to different investors. Institutions may choose to add non-correlated strategies to their portfolios to reduce the volatility of the overall investment program. Private clients are frequently concerned with reducing only downside volatility—the "left tail" risk associated with significant public equity market drawdowns. An insurance pool whose liabilities are sensitive to inflation might benefit from real assets that could reduce its asset–liability mismatch. Exhibit 2 provides some guidance as to how an allocator might view alternative assets vis-à-vis traditional asset classes.

Exhibit 2: Illustrative Capital Market Assumptions

	Traditional Assets				Alternative Assets					
	Public Equities	**Cash**	**Govt Bonds**	**Broad Fixed Income**	**Private Credit**	**Hedge Funds**	**Commodities**	**Public Real Estate**	**Private Real Estate**	**Private Equity**
Expected Return (Geometric Average)	6.5%	2.0%	2.3%	2.8%	6.5%	5.0%	4.5%	6.0%	5.5%	8.5%
Volatility	17.0%	1.1%	4.9%	3.4%	10.0%	8.1%	25.2%	20.4%	13.8%	15.7%
Correlation with Equities	1.00	−0.12	−0.60	−0.41	0.70	0.83	0.21	0.60	0.37	0.81
Equity Beta	1.00	−0.01	−0.17	−0.08	0.40	0.40	0.31	0.72	0.30	0.74

Source: Authors' own data.

In the context of asset allocation, investors may categorize an asset class based on the role it is expected to play in the overall portfolio. The roles and their relative importance will vary among investors, but it is common to identify the following functional roles:

- *Capital growth*: This role may be a top priority for portfolios with a long-term time horizon and relatively high-return target. Usually, public and private equity investments would be the most obvious choices for this role.
- *Income generation*: Certain asset classes, like fixed income or real estate, are capable of generating reasonably steady cash flow stream for investors.
- *Risk diversification*: In the case of an equity-oriented portfolio, investors may seek assets that diversify the dominant equity risk. Real assets and several hedge fund strategies may fit here. Similarly, fixed-income investors may be interested in diversifying pure yield curve risk via private credit.
- *Safety*: Certain asset classes may play the role of safe haven when most of the risky asset classes suffer. Government bonds or gold may potentially play such roles in a well-diversified portfolio.

Exhibit 3 illustrates how each of the alternative assets is generally perceived to fulfill these functional roles.

Exhibit 3: The Role of Asset Classes in a Multi-Asset Portfolio

		Role			
Asset Class		**Capital Growth**	**Income**	**Diversifying Public Equities**	**Safety**
Fixed Income and Credit	Governments		M	H	H
	Inflation-Linked		M	H	H/M
	Inv.-Grade Credit		M	H	M
	High-Yield Credit		H	M	
	Private Credit		H	M	
Equities	Public Equity	H	M		
	Private Equity	H	M	M	
Real Estate	Public Real Estate	M	H	M	
	Private Real Estate	M	H	M	
Real Assets	Public Real Assets (Energy, Metal, etc.)			H	
	Private Real Assets (Timber, etc.)	H	H	H	
Hedge Funds	Absolute Return		M	H	
	Equity Long/Short			M	

Notes: H = high/strong potential to fulfill the indicated role; M = moderate potential to fulfill the indicated role.

Exhibit 4 illustrates the potential contributions the various alternative strategies might make to a portfolio dominated by equity risk. Note that the graph illustrates the *average* investment characteristics of each asset class over some extended period of time. Some assets—gold, for example—may not consistently exhibit attractive *aggregate* characteristics compared to other strategies but may serve the portfolio well during many major market shocks.

Exhibit 4: Diversification Potential of Various Alternative Asset Classes

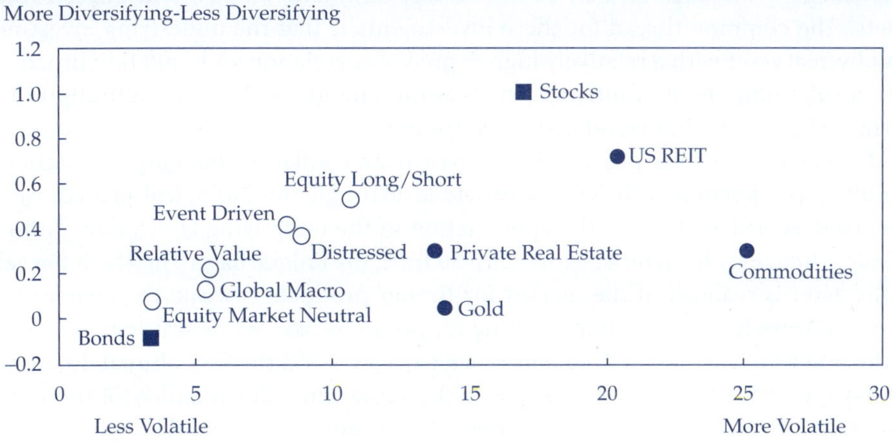

Sources: Bloomberg and authors' own data and calculations.

The Role of Private Equity in a Multi-Asset Portfolio

Private equity investments are generally viewed as a return enhancer in a portfolio of traditional assets. The expectation for a return premium over public equities stems from the illiquidity risk that comes with most forms of private equity investment. Because of the strong link between the fundamentals of private and public companies, there are limited diversification benefits when added to a portfolio that otherwise contains significant public equity exposure. Private equity volatility is not directly observable because holdings are not publicly traded. Assets tend to be valued at the lower of cost or the value at which the company raises additional capital or when ownership changes hands (e.g., through an initial public offering or a sale to a strategic buyer or to another private equity sponsor). Consequently, private equity indexes do not provide a true picture of the strategy's risk. For asset allocation exercises, volatility is often estimated using a public equity proxy with an adjustment to better represent the nature of the private equity program. For example, a proxy for early stage venture capital might be microcap technology companies. A proxy for buyout funds might start with the volatility of a geographically relevant large-cap equity index (e.g., S&P 500, Nikkei), which is then adjusted for relative financial leverage.

The Role of Hedge Funds in a Multi-Asset Portfolio

As illustrated in Exhibit 1, hedge funds span the spectrum from being risk reducers to return enhancers. Generally speaking, long/short equity strategies are believed to deliver equity-like returns with less than full exposure to the equity premium but with an additional source of return that might come from the manager's shorting of individual stocks. Short-biased equity strategies are expected to lower a portfolio's overall equity beta while producing some measure of alpha. Arbitrage and event-driven strategies, executed properly, look to exploit small inefficiencies in the public markets while exhibiting low to no correlation with traditional asset classes. However, most hedge fund arbitrage strategies involve some degree of "short volatility" risk. Because of this "short volatility" risk, the volatility in an arbitrage strategy is non-symmetrical; the aggregate volatility may look muted if the period from which the data are drawn does not include a market stress period. "Opportunistic" strategies (e.g., global macro and managed futures), although very volatile as stand-alone strategies, provide exposures not otherwise readily accessible in traditional stock and bond strategies.

The Role of Real Assets in a Multi-Asset Portfolio

This category includes timber, commodities, farmland, energy, and infrastructure assets. The common thread for these investments is that the underlying investment is a physical asset with a relatively high degree of correlation with inflation broadly or with a sub-component of inflation, such as oil (energy funds), agricultural products (farmland), or pulp and wood products (timber).

Timber investments provide both growth and inflation-hedging properties in a multi-asset portfolio. Growth is provided through the biological growth of the tree itself as well as through the appreciation in the underlying land value. Timber's inflation-hedging characteristics are derived from the unique nature in which the value of the asset is realized: If the market for timber products is weak, the owner of the asset can leave it "on the stump" waiting for prices to rise. While waiting, the volume of the asset increases—the tree continues to grow—and there is ultimately more of the asset to sell when prices recover. At the same time, the volatility of the timber asset rises; the market for more mature timber is more volatile, and the potential loss from pests and natural disasters rises.

Commodities investments (i.e., tradable commodities) fall into the following four categories:

- Metals (gold, silver, platinum, copper)
- Energy (crude oil, natural gas, heating oil, gasoline)
- Livestock and Meat (hogs, pork bellies, live cattle)
- Agricultural (corn, soybeans, wheat, rice, cocoa, coffee, cotton, sugar)

Although it is possible to own the commodity asset directly (e.g., corn, wheat, barrel of oil), most investors will invest in commodity derivatives (i.e., futures contracts) whose price is directly related to the price of the physical commodity. Investors generally own commodities as a hedge against a core constituent of inflation measures as well as a differentiated source of alpha. Gold and other precious metals are frequently owned directly because they are thought to be a good store of value in the face of a depreciating currency. Storage and insurance costs come with owning commodities directly.

Farmland investing involves two primary approaches. The higher return/risk strategy involves owning the farmland while providing the farmer a salary for tending and selling the crops. The investor retains the commodity risk and the execution risk. This approach requires a long time horizon and has high sensitivity to natural disasters and regulatory risk, such as trade disputes. In the other main approach, the investor owns the farmland but leases the property to the farmer. The farmer retains the risk for execution and commodity prices. If an investor pursues this second strategy, farmland is more like core commercial real estate investing than a real asset (commodity) strategy.

Energy investments consist of strategies that focus on the exploration, development, transportation, and delivery of energy (primarily oil and natural gas-based energy sources but also increasingly wind, hydroelectric, and solar) as well as all the ancillary services that facilitate energy production. Investors usually do not own the land that holds the minerals. Most energy investments are executed through call-down, private equity-style funds and are usually long-dated, illiquid holdings. Energy assets are generally considered real assets because the investor owns the mineral rights to certain commodities (e.g., natural gas, oil, methane) that can be correlated with certain inflationary factors. Master limited partnerships (MLPs) are another frequently used vehicle for energy investments. MLPs generally construct and own the pipelines that carry oil or natural gas from the wellhead to the storage facility. MLPs rarely take ownership of the energy assets. The companies charge a fee based on the volume of oil/natural gas they transport. This fee is often pegged to the Producer Price Index.

Infrastructure is a strategy that typically involves the construction and maintenance of public-use projects, such as building bridges, toll roads, or airports. Because of the illiquid nature of these assets, the holding period associated with these funds can be even longer than the typical illiquid strategy, with some lasting 20 years or longer. These assets tend to generate stable or modestly growing income, and the asset itself often requires minimal upkeep or capital expenditures once built. The revenue generated by the assets tends to have high correlation with overall inflation, though it is often subject to regulatory risks because governmental agencies may be involved in price setting with certain jurisdictions and assets.

The Role of Commercial Real Estate in a Multi-Asset Portfolio

Real estate investing involves the development, acquisition, management, and disposition of commercial properties, including retail, office, industrial, housing (including apartments), and hotels. Strategies range from *core,* the ownership of fully occupied properties and collecting rents, to *opportunistic,* ground-up property development (land acquisition, construction, and sale) and/or the purchase of distressed assets with the intent to rehabilitate them.

Real estate investments are believed to provide protection against unanticipated increases in inflation. Two fundamental attributes of real estate investment contribute to this inflation protection. Well-positioned properties frequently have the ability to increase rents in response to inflationary pressures, and the value of the physical buildings may increase with inflation (properties are often valued as a function of replacement cost). In this way, real estate contributes both income and capital gain potential to a portfolio. Building a diversified private commercial real estate program can be challenging for all but the largest and most sophisticated allocators. The public real estate market is a fraction of the size of the private real estate market, but it may be easier and cheaper to build a diversified real estate investment program in some geographies (e.g., United States, Europe) via the public markets. However, private real estate can offer exposures that are difficult if not impossible to achieve through publicly-traded real estate securities. Investing directly (or in a private fund) offers customization by geography, property type, and strategy (e.g., distressed, core, development).

The Role of Private Credit in a Multi-Asset Portfolio

Private credit includes distressed investment and direct lending. Although both strategies involve the ownership of fixed-income assets, their roles in an investment program are quite different. Direct-lending assets are income-producing, and the asset owner assumes any default or recovery risks. Direct-lending assets generally behave like their public market counterparts with similar credit profiles (i.e., high-quality, direct-lending assets behave like investment-grade bonds, and low-quality, direct-lending assets behave like high-yield bonds). Distressed debt assets have a more equity-like profile. The expected return is derived from the value of a company's assets relative to its debt. Illiquidity risks are high with both strategies. Direct-lending assets have no secondary market.

Direct-lending funds provide capital to individuals and small businesses that generally cannot access more traditional lending channels. Some loans are unsecured while others might be backed by an asset, such as a house or car. Direct lending is one of the least liquid debt strategies because there is typically no secondary market for these instruments. Investors in direct-lending strategies gain access to a high-yielding but riskier segment of the debt market that is not available via the traditional public markets.

Distressed funds typically purchase the securities of an entity that is under stress and where the stress is relieved through legal restructuring or bankruptcy. The investment can take the form of debt or equity, and in many strategies, the manager often takes an active role throughout the restructuring or bankruptcy. Because many investors are precluded from owning companies or entities that are in bankruptcy or default, managers of distressed funds are often able to purchase assets (usually the debt) at a significant discount. Experience with the bankruptcy process frequently distinguishes these managers from others. Although the asset is usually a bond, distressed investments typically have low sensitivity to traditional bond risks (i.e., interest rate changes or changes in spreads) because the idiosyncratic risk of the company itself dominates all other risks.

2 DIVERSIFYING EQUITY RISK

☐ compare alternative investments and bonds as risk mitigators in relation to a long equity position

In this section, we examine the claim that alternative assets may be better risk mitigators than government bonds. To address this question, we must agree on *which* risks alternatives are said to mitigate and on *what* time horizon is relevant. If your investment horizon is short term, volatility may be the most important risk measure. If you are a long-term investor, not achieving the long-horizon return objective may be the most relevant concern.

Volatility Reduction over the Short Time Horizon

Let's look first at the short horizon investor and consider how alternative asset classes compare to bonds as a volatility reducer in an equity-dominated portfolio. Advocates of alternative investments as risk reducers sometimes argue that alternative investments' volatilities calculated based on reported returns are significantly lower than the volatility of public equities. An immediate technical challenge is that reported returns of many alternative asset classes need an adjustment called **unsmoothing** for proper risk estimation. (Various approaches have been developed to unsmooth a return series that demonstrates serial correlation. The specifics of those approaches are beyond the scope of this reading.) In the case of private investments, reported returns are calculated from appraisal-based valuations that may result in volatility and correlation estimates that are too low. (The underlying assumptions in most appraisal models tend to lead to gradual and incremental changes in appraised value that may not accurately capture the asset's true price realized in an actual transaction. The low volatility of the return stream may also dampen the reported correlation between the appraisal-based asset and the more volatile market-based asset.) Other factors may also contribute to underestimated risk across alternatives. For example, **survivorship bias** and **back-fill bias** (reporting returns to a database only after they are known to be good returns) in hedge fund databases can potentially lead to an understatement of downside risk. Additionally, a hedge fund "index" includes many managers whose returns exhibit low correlation; in the same way that combining stocks and bonds in a portfolio can be expected to lower overall portfolio volatility, so too does combining several hedge funds into an "index."

As an example, we build a hypothetical, equally-weighted index of long/short equity hedge funds with volatilities ranging from 6% to 11%. As shown in Exhibit 5, given the less-than-perfect correlation among the constituents of our index, the index volatility is only 4.9%:

Exhibit 5: Volatility Is Less Than the Sum of Its Parts

	Fund 1	Fund 2	Fund 3	Fund 4	Fund 5	Combined
Volatility	10.9%	6.5%	8.5%	9.7%	8.1%	**4.9%**
Correlation						
Fund 1		−0.02	0.14	0.00	0.15	
Fund 2			0.27	0.39	0.29	
Fund 3				0.25	−0.03	
Fund 4					0.14	

Exhibit 6 shows the correlations of fixed-income and alternative asset classes to public equities based on observed market data over 1997–2017. We also show each asset class's estimated equity beta. To estimate correlations and betas, we used unsmoothed return data for alternative asset classes. We discuss unsmoothing of returns in more detail in a later section.

Exhibit 6: Fixed-Income's and Alternative's Equity Beta and Correlation with Equities

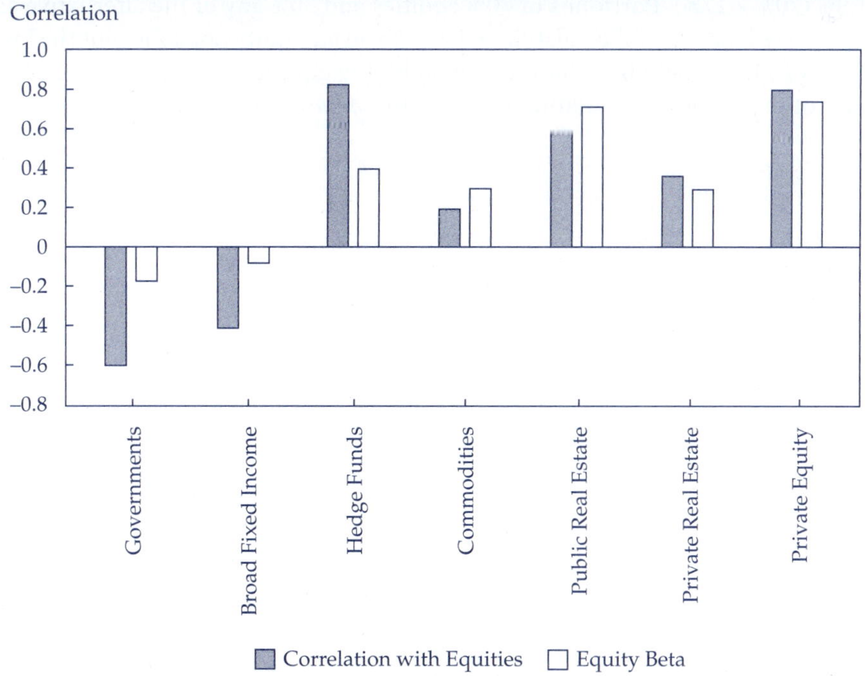

Sources: Bloomberg and authors' own data and calculations.

Most of the alternative investment categories had positive, but less than perfect, correlation with equities. Although certain alternatives (e.g., commodities, particularly gold) may rally during a public equity market downturn, other alternative investments—like hedge funds, private credit, or private equities—also experience drawdowns at the same time the equity market falls. Hedge funds and private equities have a correlation co-efficient with equities over +0.8, and this indicates a fairly strong positive relationship between public equities and these alternative investments.

Government bonds, however, have a −0.6 estimated correlation with equities, which indicates a negative relationship of moderate strength. This is consistent with the tendency for government bonds to serve as a risk haven during "risk-off" or "flight to quality" episodes.

Although correlation and beta have the same sign and are statistically interrelated, we have to remember that they quantify two different things. The correlation coefficient quantifies the strength of a linear relationship between two variables, thus playing a crucial role in portfolio diversification: The lower the correlation, the stronger the asset's diversification power. Beta, however, measures the response of an asset to a unit change in a reference index; for example, equity beta measures how various assets would respond to a 1% rise of public equities. Hedge funds' beta is estimated at around 0.4; thus, we would expect a 0.4% return (excluding manager alpha) from hedge funds if equities rose by 1%. Hedge funds' relatively low beta (0.4) and high correlation (+0.8) means that hedge funds' rise or fall is milder than those of public equities in magnitude, but this directional relationship is fairly strong in a statistical sense. Commodities also have an equity beta of similar positive magnitude (0.3), but their correlation with equities is much weaker (+0.2); so, we can expect that a much bigger portion of commodity price changes would be driven by factors unrelated to the equity markets.

In Exhibit 7, we compare the total return volatility of public equities (black bar) with volatilities of portfolios comprised of 70% equity and 30% other asset classes. Using 20 years of data, the volatility of public equities is estimated at approximately 17%. A portfolio allocated 70% to equity and 30% to cash would imply a portfolio volatility of 11.9% (70% × 17%). Portfolios of 70% equities and 30% any of the alternative asset classes also reduces portfolio volatility relative to an all-equity portfolio, but the lowest volatility of 11.1% could be achieved by combining equities with government bonds because of the negative correlation between these two asset classes.

Exhibit 7: Volatility of Portfolios Comprised of 70% Equities and 30% Other Asset Class

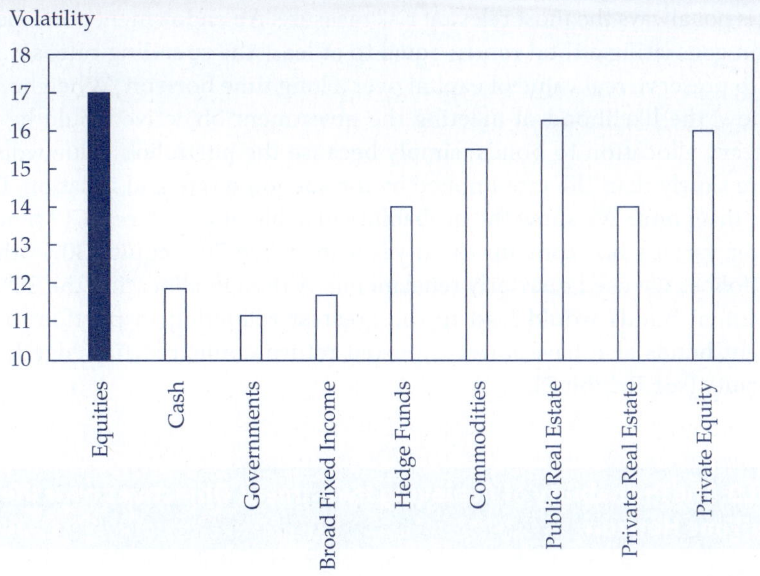

Sources: Bloomberg and authors' own data and calculations.

Bear in mind, however, that this analysis is based on 20 years of returns ending in 2017, a period that was characterized by a persistent negative equity–bond correlation. Because there was limited inflation in developed markets over this period, economic growth prospects were the dominant influence on asset prices. Positive growth surprises are good for equities (better earnings outlook) and negative for bonds (potential central bank rate increases). If inflation becomes a threat, bonds' risk mitigation power could erode. Exhibit 8 looks at the US equity–bond correlation since the 1950s. As the chart suggests, the correlation between US equities and government bonds was, in fact, positive in the 1970s through the 1990s when inflation was also more elevated.

Exhibit 8: Long-Term Historical Equity–Bond Correlation and Inflation

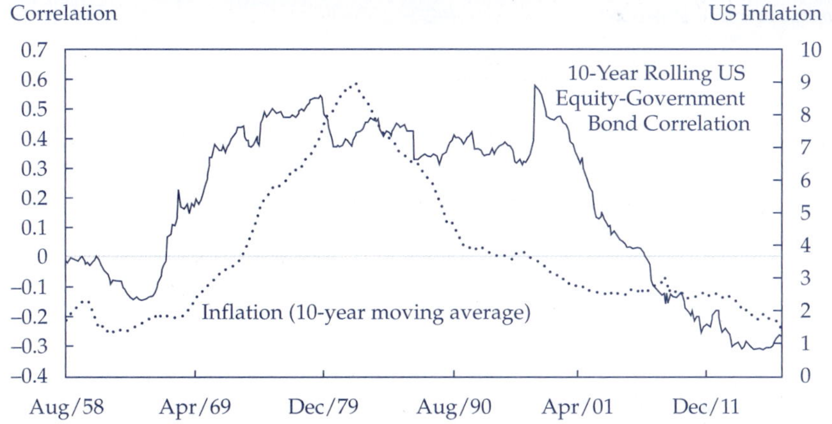

Sources: Bloomberg and the authors' own data and calculations.

Risk of Not Meeting the Investment Goals over the Long Time Horizon

Volatility is not always the most relevant risk measure. An endowment portfolio is often focused on generating a total return equal to at least the spending rate, say 5%, plus inflation to preserve real value of capital over a long time horizon. When bond yields are very low, the likelihood of meeting the investment objective would be reduced given a heavy allocation to bonds, simply because the portfolio's value would likely grow more slowly than the rate implied by the spending rate and inflation. Exhibit 9 illustrates this point: We show the probability of achieving a 5% real (7.1% nominal[3]) return over various horizons up to 10-years for three 70% equity/30% other asset class portfolios. We used quarterly rebalancing. Although allocating the 30% "other" to government bonds would lead to the greatest reduction in portfolio volatility, government bonds also have lower expected return compared to hedge funds and private equity (see Exhibit 2).

Exhibit 9: The Probability of Achieving Investment Objectives over the Longer Time Horizon

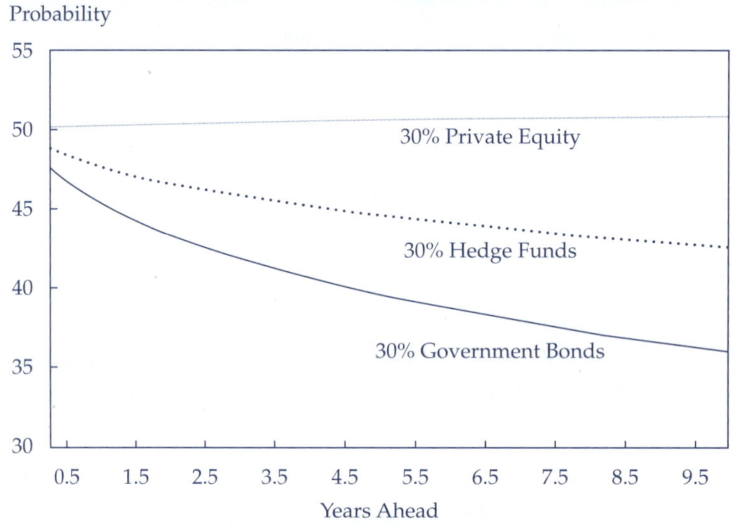

Note: Portfolios comprised of 70% equities and 30% other asset classes.

Source: Authors' calculations.

The 70% public equities/30% government bond portfolio has an expected return of 5.7%[4], below the nominal return target of 7.1%. The 70% public equities/30% private equities portfolio has an expected geometric return of 7.2%, slightly over the return target. Both portfolios' expected returns are 50th percentile returns; there is a 50% probability that this is the return that would be realized over time. Thus, the 70% public equities/30% private equities portfolio, with a nominal expected return of 7.2%, has slightly better than a 50% probability of meeting the 7.1% nominal return target. The 70% public equities/30% government bond portfolio, with an expected return less than the nominal return target, therefore has less than a 50% probability of meeting

3 By using the Fisher equation to combine the 5% real return and 2% inflation: $(1 + 5\%) * (1 + 2\%) - 1 = 7.1\%$.

4 Note that geometric expected return is approximated as the expected arithmetic return minus half of the investment's variance. Thus, portfolio expected geometric return is not simply the weighted average of the asset classes' expected geometric returns because portfolio variance benefits from diversification.

the required return. Why does the 70% public equities/30% private equities portfolio maintain its 50%+ probability of meeting the return target over time while the probability that the 70% public equities/30% government bond portfolio meets the return target declines over time? As the time horizon lengthens, return accumulation (compounding) becomes more and more important. In a simplified way, return accumulates proportionally with time, whereas volatility scales with the square root of time. Thus, as we lengthen the time horizon, the gap between the cumulative return target and the expected return accumulation widens faster than the range of possible portfolio return outcomes. As a result, the likelihood of a low-returning portfolio catching up to the target return declines over time.

To summarize, bonds have been a more effective volatility mitigator than alternatives over shorter time horizons, but over long horizons, a heavy allocation to bonds would reduce the probability of achieving the investment goal. It is important to emphasize that volatility and the probability of achieving the target return are two very different dimensions of risk. Volatility addresses interim fluctuations in portfolio return, whereas achieving a return target takes on increasing importance as we expand the time horizon over multiple years. Both risks are important, especially for a program that is distributing 7% of assets per year as in this example. Although the 30% allocation to private equity increases the chance of meeting the expected return, a severe and sustained short-term drawdown in the public equity markets could significantly handicap the fund's ability to achieve its long-term return objectives. This is why drawdowns (related to volatility) need to be considered and managed.

EXAMPLE 1

Mitigating Equity Risk by Allocating to Hedge Funds or Bonds

The investment committee of a major foundation is concerned about high equity valuations and would like to increase the allocation either to hedge funds or to high-grade, fixed-income assets to diversify equity risk. As the risk manager of this foundation:

1. Discuss the justifications and the limitations of using bonds to mitigate equity risk.

Solution:

- Supporting argument: Bonds have exhibited negative correlation and beta to equities in a low inflation environment, so as long as inflation stays at or below average historical levels, this negative equity–bond correlation should lead to the highest reduction in portfolio volatility.
- Limitations: The negative stock/bond correlation may be temporary, and amid high inflation the stock/bond correlation could turn positive. Furthermore, if bonds' expected return is low, a heavy allocation to bonds may reduce the probability of achieving the foundation's long-term return objectives.

2. Discuss the justifications and the limitations of using hedge funds to mitigate equity risk.

Solution:

- Supporting argument: With an equity beta of around 0.4 (see Exhibit 2), hedge funds would reduce an equity-dominated portfolio's overall beta. With higher expected returns than bonds, an allocation to hedge funds would make achieving the long-term return target more feasible.
- Limitations: Although a well-constructed hedge fund portfolio may reduce portfolio volatility and beta, hedge funds are often highly actively managed, levered investment strategies, and individual hedge funds may suffer significant and permanent losses during turbulent times.

3 TRADITIONAL APPROACHES TO ASSET CLASSIFICATION

☐ compare traditional and risk-based approaches to defining the investment opportunity set, including alternative investments

In this section, we consider how traditional approaches to asset allocation can be adapted to include alternative investments and how investors can apply risk-based approaches to incorporate alternatives in their asset allocation. This reading extends the asset allocation framework introduced in earlier readings on asset allocation. Although the ultimate goal of meeting the investment objectives subject to the relevant constraints remains the same, investors often face several analytical and operational challenges when introducing alternative asset classes.

Traditional Approaches to Asset Classification

When defining asset classes for the traditional approaches to asset allocation, investors may group and classify alternative assets along several dimensions. Two common approaches (in addition to the growth–income–diversification–safety roles described earlier) are with respect to the liquidity of the asset class and with respect to asset behavior under various economic conditions.

A Liquidity-Based Approach to Defining the Opportunity Set

Certain alternative investments, like REITs or commodity futures, are highly liquid and can be easily traded in public markets. Private investments, however, are highly illiquid and usually require long-term commitments (more than 10 years) from the investors. Of course, there are differences among various private asset classes in this respect as well: Private equity investments may require longer than a 10-year commitment, while the term of a private credit fund can be shorter, say 5 to 8 years. Although public equity and private equity may be similar asset classes from the fundamental economic point of view, they differ significantly in their liquidity characteristics.

The long investment horizon and the lack of liquidity in many of the alternative asset classes make it difficult to accurately characterize their risk characteristics for purposes of the asset allocation exercise. One approach to dealing with this issue is to make the initial asset allocation decision using only the broad, liquid asset classes in which the underlying data that drive risk, return, and correlation assumptions are robust (e.g., stocks, bonds, and real estate). A second iteration of the asset allocation exercise would break the equity/fixed-income/real estate asset allocation down further by using the asset groupings as shown in Exhibit 10, which illustrates a possible categorization of asset classes that incorporates their broad liquidity profile.

Exhibit 10: Major Asset Class Categories

	Equity & Equity-Like	Fixed Income & Fixed Income-Like	Real Estate
Marketable/Liquid	Public Equity Long/Short Equity Hedge Funds	Fixed Income Cash	Public Real Estate Commodities
Private/Illiquid	Private Equity	Private Credit	Private Real Estate Private Real Assets

An Approach Based on Expected Performance under Distinct Macroeconomic Regimes

Investors may also categorize asset classes based on how they are expected to behave under different macroeconomic environments, and investors may assign roles to them in a broad macroeconomic context:

- *Capital growth assets* would be expected to benefit from healthy economic growth. Public and private equities would belong to this category.
- *Inflation-hedging assets*—so-called "real assets" such as real estate, commodities, and natural resources but also inflation-linked bonds—would be expected to outperform other asset classes when inflation expectations rise or actual inflation exceeds expectations.
- *Deflation-hedging assets* (e.g., nominal government bonds) would be expected to outperform most of the other asset classes when the economy slows and inflation becomes very low or negative.

In Exhibit 11, we illustrate how investors may think about the expected performance of various asset classes in a broad macroeconomic context. Each asset class is positioned along the continuum to illustrate the macroeconomic environment in which we would expect it to generate strong performance. Such mapping is usually based on both historical experience and qualitative judgment. Considering the fundamental economic drivers of asset classes could help investors construct portfolios that are better diversified and more robust under various economic conditions and scenarios.

Exhibit 11: Asset Classes Grouped by the Macroeconomic Environment under Which They Would Be Expected to Generate Strong Performance

		Inflation Environment		
		Deflation	**Moderate Inflation**	**High Inflation**
Economic Environment	High Growth		Public Equity Private Equity High-Yield Bonds Private Credit	Real Estate Commodities
	Low Growth/ Recession	Government Bonds		Inflation-Linked Bonds Gold

Source: Authors' data.

Exhibit 12 illustrates the average quarterly total return of various asset classes and alternative strategies under stronger and weaker economic growth environments between 1997 and 2017, a period of low to moderate inflation in developed markets.

Exhibit 12: Historical Asset Class Performance under Stronger and Weaker Economic Growth Periods (1997–2017)

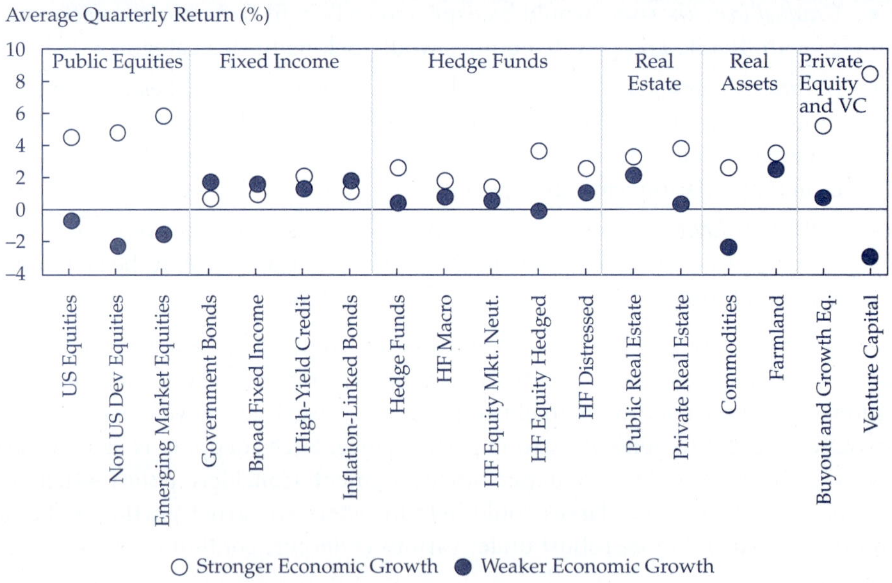

Notes: Strong and weak economic periods were determined using quarterly GDP data. Strong growth periods were those quarters when GDP growth exceeded the average GDP growth through the full historical sample.

Sources: The exhibit is based on the authors' calculations. Index data is based on the following. US Equities: Russell 3000; Non-US Developed Market Equities: MSCI EAFE USD Net unhedged; Emerging Market Equities: MSCI Emerging Markets Net USD unhedged; Governments: Bloomberg Barclays US Treasury Index; Broad Fixed Income: Bloomberg Barclays US Aggregate; High Yield: Bloomberg Barclays US Corporate High Yield; Inflation-Linked Bonds: Bloomberg Barclays US Government Inflation-Linked Bonds Index; Hedge Funds: HFRI; Public Real Estate: Dow Jones Equity REIT Index; Private Real Estate: NCREIF Property Index; Commodities: S&P GSCI Total Return Index; Farmland: NCREIF Farmland Index; Buyout and Growth Equities: Cambridge Associates US Private Equity Index; Venture Capital: Cambridge Associates US Venture Capital Index.

Public and private equities, hedge funds, and commodities posted strong returns amid strong economic growth conditions and weaker returns amid weaker economic conditions. Commodities exhibit a bigger disparity between returns in periods of stronger and weaker growth than does the hedge fund category.

Within fixed income, government bonds posted higher returns during periods of weaker economic growth—when investors likely reallocated from risky assets to safer assets. On the other hand, high-yield bonds (and potentially private credit, if we assume a behavior pattern similar to that of high-yield bonds) performed well during periods of stronger economic growth but posted lower returns during weaker economic periods, likely because of concerns about weakening credit quality.

Understanding how various asset classes behave under distinct macroeconomic regimes enables investors to tailor the asset allocation to align with their fundamental goals or to mitigate their fundamental risks. If the investment portfolio has a specific goal, such as hedging inflation risk, then it would be logical to build a portfolio that is dominated by asset classes that are expected to perform best amid rising inflation. Even if the portfolio's goal is to generate high return over the long run, combining "growth" asset classes with "inflation-hedging" or "deflation-hedging" asset classes could make the asset allocation more resilient to changing economic and market conditions. This approach can be extended to macroeconomic scenario analysis and stress testing when the analyst evaluates how various asset allocation options would perform under conditions of high or low economic growth and/or inflation, and it can identify which economic conditions would hurt the investment portfolio the most.

RISK-BASED APPROACHES TO ASSET CLASSIFICATION 4

☐ compare traditional and risk-based approaches to defining the investment opportunity set, including alternative investments

When we assign traditional and alternative asset classes to certain functional roles in the portfolio, or when we assess how different asset classes would perform under distinct macroeconomic regimes, we can also easily realize that many traditional and alternative asset classes share similar characteristics that can result in high correlations. We may put public equities in the same functional bucket as private equity, and we may expect elevated default rates from high-yield bonds and private credit during recessionary environments.

Exhibit 13 compares the betas of various traditional and alternative asset classes to global equities. The chart clearly shows that private equity and venture capital asset classes have global equity betas similar to public equites. On the other hand, betas of various hedge fund strategies differ significantly. Hedge fund returns, in aggregate, had a beta of 0.4. However, global macro or equity market-neutral strategies had betas as low as 0.1. The long/short "equity hedged" strategy's beta is estimated to be much higher, around 0.5, which is consistent with its long equity bias.

Exhibit 13: Global Equity Beta of Various Asset Classes, 1997–2017

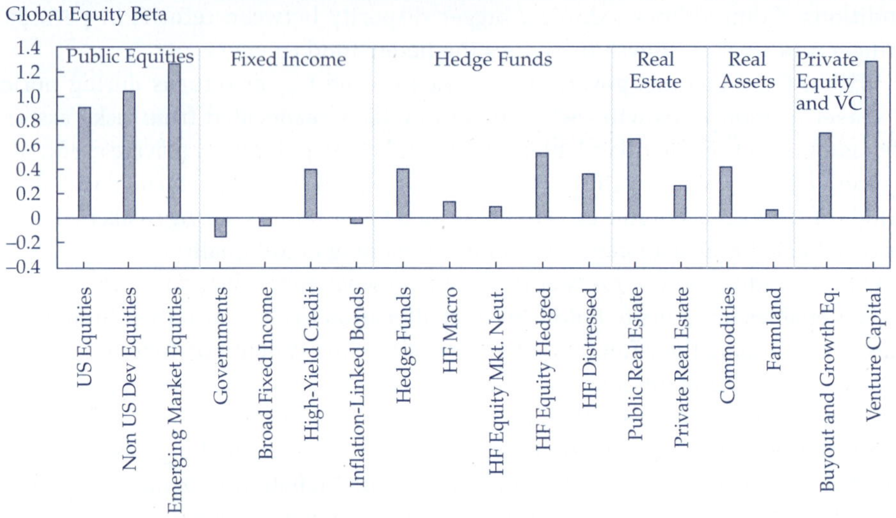

Note: Betas were estimated as a regression slope of representative index returns relative to the global equity return stream over the time period 1997–2017.

Sources: Authors' calculations; index data sources are the same as those in Exhibit 12.

Many investors have begun to view asset allocation through a risk factor lens to capture these similarities. In this section, we extend the risk factor asset allocation framework introduced in earlier readings to alternative investments using the following risk factors:

- *Equity market return*: representative of the general direction of global equity markets, and investors may also refer to this as the best market proxy for "growth."
- *Size*: excess return of small-cap equities over large-cap equities.
- *Value*: excess return of value versus growth stocks (*negative* factor sensitivity = *growth* bias.
- *Liquidity*: the Pastor–Stambaugh liquidity factor[5]—a market-wide liquidity measure based on the excess returns of stocks with large sensitivity to changes in aggregate liquidity (less-liquid stocks) versus stocks with less sensitivity to changing liquidity (more-liquid stocks).
- *Duration*: sensitivity to 10-year government yield changes.
- *Inflation*: sensitivity to 10-year breakeven inflation changes obtained from the inflation-linked bond markets.
- *Credit spread*: sensitivity to changes in high-yield spread.
- *Currency*: sensitivity to changes in the domestic currency versus a basket of foreign currencies.

This framework can easily be extended further to other risk factors, like momentum or volatility.

Exhibit 14 illustrates risk factor sensitivities of various traditional and alternative investment strategies using a construct as discussed by Naik, Devarajan, Nowobilski, Page, and Pedersen (2016). The parameters in the table are regression coefficients based on 20 years of historical data. Quarterly index returns representing each asset class were regressed on the risk factors listed previously. Note that for conventional

5 For more details on Pastor–Stambaugh liquidity factors, see Naik et al. (2016).

reasons we changed the signs of the "nominal duration" and "credit spread" sensitivities: The 4.2 duration of broad fixed income, for example, means that this asset class would experience an approximate 4.2% decline in response to a 100 bps increase in the nominal interest rates.

Exhibit 14: Factor Sensitivity Estimates across Various Asset Classes

Asset Classes	Equity	Size	Value	Liquidity	Nominal Duration	Inflation	Credit Spread	Currency	R-squared
US Equities	1.0								1.00
Non-US Dev Equities	0.9							0.7	0.86
Emerging Mkt Equities	1.1	0.5						0.5	0.66
Government Bonds					4.8				0.96
Broad Fixed Income					4.2		0.6		0.89
High-Yield Credit					4.1		4.2		0.95
Inflation-Linked Bonds					6.6	7.0			0.82
Hedge Funds	0.3	0.1					0.6		0.74
HF Macro	0.2	0.2			1.9	3.1	−0.9	0.1	0.28
HF Equity Mkt. Neut.	0.1								0.14
HF Equity Hedged	0.5								0.72
HF Distressed	0.1	0.2					1.8		0.72
Commodities						18.0		0.8	0.36
Public Real Estate	0.9				4.6	0.9			0.38
Private Real Estate	0.2			0.1		2.4			0.20
Buyout & Growth Equities	0.6	0.2	−0.3	0.1					0.70
Venture Capital	0.8	0.6	−1.8	0.2					0.38

Note: Only statistically significant slopes are displayed in the exhibit. Sources are the same as those for Exhibit 12.

In a risk factor-based asset allocation framework, the factors represent the systematic risks embedded in the selected asset classes and investment strategies. The primary systematic risk factors would fully, or almost fully, explain the behavior of broad, passive traditional public asset classes. There should be a relatively larger portion of unexplained risk in the alternative asset classes. This arises from such issues as the appraisal-based valuation in real estate, the idiosyncratic risks in the portfolio companies of private equity funds, or the idiosyncratic risks in hedge funds resulting from active management. (This last one is logically intuitive if you subscribe to the belief that returns generated by hedge fund strategies should be primarily driven by *alpha* rather than systematic risk factors.)

The extension of the risk factor framework to alternative asset classes allows every asset class to be described using the same framework. Investors can therefore more clearly understand their sources of investment risk and identify the intended and unintended tilts and biases they have in the portfolio. Furthermore, a risk factor framework enables investors to more efficiently allocate capital and risk in a multi-dimensional framework (i.e., a framework that seeks to do more than simply achieve the highest return at a given level of volatility). If an investor, for example, would like to increase the portfolio's inflation risk-mitigating exposure, decomposing this specific risk factor from inflation-linked bonds, real estate, or commodity asset classes could help the investor to identify the asset classes and exposures that are most likely to facilitate that goal.

Risk factor-based approaches improve upon the traditional approaches in identifying the investment opportunity set but do have certain limitations. As mentioned earlier, a small set of systematic risk factors is insufficient to describe the historical return stream of alternative asset classes. Note that all non-zero-risk factor coefficients displayed in the table are statistically significant based on their *t*-statistics. Although our eight illustrative factors fit the total return history of traditional asset classes with *r*-squared statistics of 0.8–1.0, the *r*-squared ratios for alternative investments are lower, ranging between 0.3 and 0.7. Increasing the number of risk factors would certainly improve the goodness of fit, but too many factors could make the risk factor-based asset allocation framework difficult to handle and interpret. In addition, certain risk factor sensitivities can be quite volatile, making a "point in time" factor-based definition of an asset class a poor descriptor of the class's expected behavior. For example, the aggregate hedge fund inflation beta typically fluctuates in the range of 0.3 to 0.4, while the inflation beta of commodities fluctuates much more widely.[6]

EXAMPLE 2

Applying Risk Factors for Inflation Hedging

1. The CIO (chief investment officer) of the United Retired Workers Plan would like to reduce inflation risk in the portfolio. Based on the data displayed in Exhibit 14, which asset classes would you recommend as potential inflation-hedging tools?

Solution:

Commodities and inflation-linked bonds have the highest factor sensitivity to inflation, so they are the most obvious candidates. Real estate (both public and private) also has some potential to protect against inflation. Based on the data presented, macro hedge fund strategies also exhibited a positive inflation beta, but given their active nature, further analysis may be needed before choosing them as inflation-hedging vehicles.

2. The CIO is not only concerned about inflation but also rising interest rates. Which alternative asset classes would you recommend for consideration?

Solution:

Commodities and private real estate would be the likely asset classes to hedge against rising interest rates, given their zero-factor sensitivity to nominal duration. Some of the hedge fund strategies also show zero-factor sensitivity to duration, but the relationship may not hold true in the future given the actively managed nature of hedge funds. Although Exhibit 14 indicates equity strategies (both public and private) also show little to no sensitivity to rising interest rates (duration) bonds and equities have been more highly correlated in the past.

6 For further detail on expanding asset allocation to risk allocation, we refer to Naik et al. (2016) and Cambridge Associates LLC (2013).

Illustration: Asset Allocation and Risk-Based Approaches

Let's look at an example of how a risk-based approach may enhance traditional asset allocation. In Exhibit 15, we show two investment portfolios, Portfolio A and Portfolio B, that have exactly the same high-level asset allocations. However, the underlying investments in the two portfolios are quite different. The fixed-income assets in Portfolio A are government bonds, while the fixed-income assets in Portfolio B are high-yield bonds. Hedge fund investments in Portfolio A are represented by very low equity beta market neutral strategies, while Portfolio B is invested in the higher beta long/short equity hedge funds. Similarly, Portfolio B's investments in real assets and private equity have higher risk than those in Portfolio A.

Exhibit 15: Traditional Asset Allocation and Risk Contribution Comparison

Broad Asset Classes	Asset Allocation		Underlying Investments		% Contribution to Risk	
	Portfolio A	Portfolio B	Portfolio A	Portfolio B	Portfolio A	Portfolio B
Fixed Income	20%	20%	Government Bonds	High-Yield Bonds	−6.5%	7.6%
Public Equities	20%	20%	US Equities	Non-US Developed Equities	51.4%	18.2%
Hedge Funds	20%	20%	Equity Market Neutral	Long/Short Equity	5.4%	11.1%
Real Assets	20%	20%	Inflation-linked bonds	REITs	0.7%	13.2%
Private Equity	20%	20%	Buyout	Venture Capital	48.9%	49.8%
Total	**100%**	**100%**				
				Expected Return	**5.3%**	**8.8%**
				Volatility	**5.9%**	**16.5%**
				Equity Beta	**0.30**	**0.79**

Notes: The percentage contribution to risk is a result of three components: the asset allocation to a specific asset, its volatility, and its correlation with the other assets. For fixed income, the contribution to total risk is negative in the case of Portfolio A because government bonds have negative correlations with other asset classes; however, it is positive in the case of Portfolio B because high-yield bonds have positive correlations with the other asset classes.

Source: Authors' calculations.

As a result of these major differences between nominally similar broad asset allocations, it is not surprising that Portfolio B has higher volatility, beta, and expected return compared to Portfolio A. Let's look more closely at the risk contribution of each of the asset classes:

Portfolio A.

The majority of the risk in Portfolio A comes from public and private equity. Hedge funds contribute approximately 5% to the total risk, and fixed income actually reduces risk because government bonds had negative correlations with public equities in our historical data sample.

Portfolio B.

Private equity explains about half of the total portfolio risk of Portfolio B. (In this portfolio, the private equity allocation is represented by the higher risk venture capital.) Public equities, hedge funds, and real assets each contribute roughly the same to the total risk of the portfolio. This is consistent with the equity-like characteristics of the underlying assets in the portfolio. The long/short equity hedged strategy has an equity beta of around 0.5, and REITs have an equity beta of 0.9. In Portfolio B, fixed income contributes positively to total risk, consistent with high-yield bonds' positive correlation with equities over the time series.

Although the nominal asset allocations of the two portfolios are the same, the risk profile and the risk allocation among asset classes are significantly different. Let's go one step further and apply the risk factor sensitivities of Exhibit 14 to our hypothetical portfolios. Exhibit 16 shows the absolute contribution to total portfolio risk by risk factor. This approach moves beyond the borders of asset classes and aggregates the equity risk factor embedded in public equities, private equities, venture capital, and REITs into a single-factor contribution. Both portfolios are highly dominated by exposure to equity risk. Portfolio A's total risk is almost fully explained by the exposure to the equity factor, while about 70% of Portfolio B's total risk comes from the equity risk factor alone. Portfolio B also has exposure to the size and value factors, driven by the allocation to venture capital. Finally, we can also see that although Portfolio B is not directly investing in government bonds, some risk mitigation benefit still arises from the low "duration" component of high-yield bonds and REITs.

Exhibit 16: Absolute Contribution to Total Risk by Risk Factors

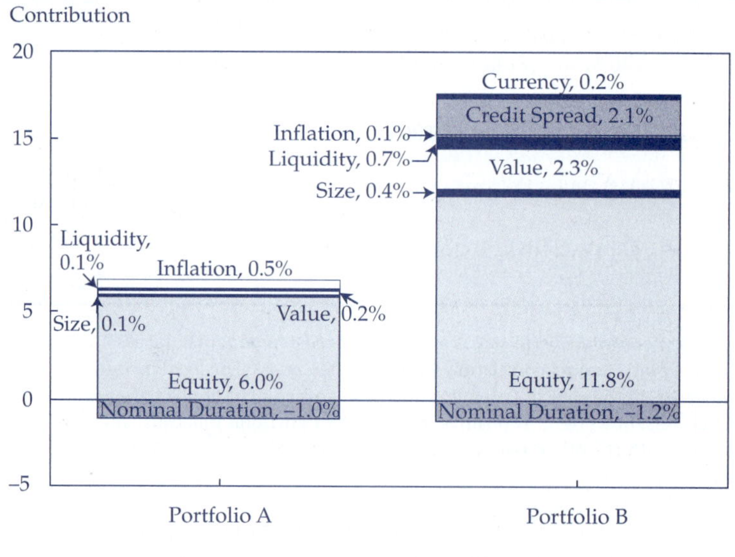

This is an extreme example (the two portfolios have vastly different expected returns), but it is useful to illustrate how factor sensitivities can be used to explore the underlying risk exposures in seemingly similar asset allocations.

Comparing Risk-Based and Traditional Approaches

Investors often employ multiple approaches in setting their asset allocation for a portfolio that includes alternative investments. When applying these various approaches, investors must consider their strengths and limitations.

Main strengths of traditional approaches:

- *Easy to communicate.* Listing the roles of various asset classes is intuitive and easy to explain to the decision makers, who often have familiarity with the traditional asset class-based approach. Scenario analyses based on historical or expected behavior of various asset classes under different macroeconomic conditions can help to introduce quantitative aspects of the portfolio's expected performance and risk and substantiate the asset allocation proposal.
- *Relevance for liquidity management and operational considerations.* Public and private asset class mandates have vastly distinct liquidity profiles. Thus, although private and public equity would have a lot of commonality in their risk factor exposures, they would be positioned very differently from a liquidity management perspective. Similarly, investors must implement the target asset allocation by allocating to investment managers. The traditional categorization of asset classes may be necessary to identify the relevant mandates—what portion of the equity portfolio she would like to allocate to equity-oriented hedge funds rather than to long-only equity managers.

Main limitations of traditional approaches:

- *Over-estimation of portfolio diversification.* Without a proper analytical framework for assessing risk, investors may have a false sense of diversification. An allocation spread across a large number of different asset classes may appear to be very well diversified, when, in fact, the underlying investments may be subject to the same underlying risks.
- *Obscured primary drivers of risk.* Investments with very different risk characteristics may be commingled under the same asset class category. For example, government bonds and high-yield bonds may both be classified as "fixed income," but each has distinct risk characteristics.

Risk-based approaches are designed to overcome some of these limitations.

Key benefits of risk-based approaches:

- *Common risk factor identification.* Investors are able to identify common risk factors across all investments, whether public or private, passive or active.
- *Integrated risk framework.* Investors are able to build an integrated risk management framework, leading to more reliable portfolio-level risk quantification.

Key limitations of risk-based approaches:

- *Sensitivity to the historical look-back period.* Empirical risk factor exposure estimations may be sensitive to the historical sample. For example, the duration of a bond portfolio or the beta of a diversified equity portfolio could be reasonably stable, but the estimated inflation sensitivity of real assets can change rapidly over time. Thus, the analyst has to be cautious when interpreting some of the risk factor sensitivities, such as the "inflation beta" of commodities.

- *Implementation hurdles.* Establishing a strategic target to different risk factors is a very important high-level decision, but converting these risk factor targets to actual investment mandates requires additional considerations, including liquidity planning, time and effort for manager selection, and rebalancing policy.
- *Determining which risk factors should be used and how to measure them in different asset classes.* One drawback with risk-based approaches is the decision on which risk factors to use is somewhat subjective and how these factors are measured can also be subjective. For example, if using a liquidity factor, should it be measured by the Pastor-Stambaugh metric or by some other metric?

  This issue is highlighted by noting that in Level III *Hedge Fund Strategies*, hedge fund returns are analyzed via a conditional factor model using just four risk factors: equities, credit, currencies, and volatility. These risk factors were selected as they are deemed to provide a reasonably broad cross-section of risk exposures for the typical hedge fund, and each of the factor returns can be realized through relatively liquid instruments.

  In sum, a limitation of risk-based approaches is the potential subjectivity embedded in their implementation.

5 RISK CONSIDERATIONS, RETURN EXPECTATIONS, AND INVESTMENT VEHICLE

☐ discuss investment considerations that are important in allocating to different types of alternative investments

In addition to the risk, return, and correlation characteristics relevant to the decision to invest in the alternative asset classes, many operational and practical complexities must be considered before finalizing a decision to invest. It is essential that the investor be fully aware of these complexities: Failure to grasp these differences between traditional and alternative investments can derail an investment program. The primary factors to consider include:

- properly defining risk characteristics;
- establishing return expectations;
- selection of the appropriate investment vehicle;
- operational liquidity issues;
- expense and fee considerations;
- tax considerations (applicable for taxable entities); and
- build vs. buy.

Risk Considerations

Mean–variance optimization (MVO), widely used in modeling asset allocation choices, cannot easily accommodate the characteristics of most alternative investments. MVO characterizes an asset's risk using standard deviation. Standard deviation is a one-dimensional view of risk and an especially poor representation of the risk characteristics of alternative investments—where assets suffer some degree of illiquidity, valuations may be subjective, and returns may be "chunky" and not normally distributed. The non-standard deviation risks are usually accommodated in an MVO framework by assigning a higher standard deviation than might be derived solely by looking at the historical returns of the asset class.

Most approaches to asset allocation assume that the portfolio's allocation to an asset class is always fully invested. Although this is not an assumption that is limited to alternatives, the problem is exaggerated with the private alternative strategies where it could take several years for capital to be invested and where capital is returned to the investor as investments are sold. Thus, it is rare that the *actual* asset allocation of a program with a significant exposure to alternatives will mirror the *modeled* asset allocation. This suggests that the investor must carefully (and continually) monitor the program's aggregate exposures to ensure that the risks are in line with the strategic asset allocation. A case in point: Some investors over-allocated to private equity, real-estate, and other call-down funds prior to 2008 in order to more quickly reach their asset allocation targets. Many of these investors then found themselves in a situation where they were receiving capital calls for these commitments during 2008 and 2009, a period where their public assets had lost considerable value and liquidity and cash were scarce. Some investors had to reduce distributions, sell illiquid investments in the secondary market at severely discounted prices, and/or walk away from their fund commitments, thereby forfeiting earlier investments.

Although every strategy (and, by extension, each individual fund) will have its own unique risk profile, we provide two examples of the complications that might be encountered when modelling an allocation to alternative investments.

Short-only strategy:

A short-biased fund can provide strong diversification benefits, lowering a portfolio's aggregate exposure to the equity risk factor; however, a short-only fund has a risk profile quite unlike a long-only equity fund. Most investors understand that a long-only equity fund has theoretically infinite upside potential and a downside loss bounded by zero (assuming no leverage). A short-biased or short-only fund has the opposite distribution. A short-selling strategy is capped on its upside but has unlimited downside risk.

Option payouts:

Some hedge fund strategies will structure their trades as call options either by owning call options outright or by synthetically replicating a call option (e.g., convertible bond arbitrage in which the manager goes long the convertible bond, short the equity for the same underlying, and hedges the interest rate risk). If executed properly, the fund would have limited downside but unlimited upside. It is difficult, if not impossible, to accurately model such a return profile by looking simply at a fund's historical standard deviation or other risk metrics, especially if the fund's track record does not encompass a full market cycle.

Return Expectations

Given the limited return history of alternative investments (relative to stocks and bonds) and the idiosyncratic nature of alternative investment returns, no single accepted approach to developing the return expectations required in an asset allocation exercise exists. One approach that can be applied with some consistency across asset classes is a "building blocks" approach: Begin with the risk-free rate, estimate the return associated with the factor exposures relevant to the asset class (e.g., credit spreads, level and shape of the yield curve, equity, leverage, liquidity), apply an assumption for manager alpha, and deduct appropriate fees (management and incentive) and taxes. Where the portfolio already contains an allocation to alternative investments, the underlying money managers can be helpful in estimating exposures and return potential. The portfolio's current positions can be characterized by their known exposures, rather than through a generic set of exposures that may not be truly representative of the program's objectives for the asset class exposure. Say, for example, that the investor's hedge fund program deliberately excludes long/short equity hedge funds because the investor chooses to take equity risk in the long-only portion of the portfolio. The return (and risk) characteristics of this hedge fund allocation would be very different from those of a broad-based allocation to hedge funds, which typically has a significant weight to long/short equity funds.

Investment Vehicle

Most alternative investments are implemented through a private (limited) partnership that is controlled by a general partner (GP), the organization and individuals that manage the investments. The asset owner becomes a limited partner (LP) in the private partnership. The main rationale for using the limited partnership format is that it limits the investor's liability to the amount of capital that she has contributed; she is not responsible for the actions of or the debts incurred by the GP. The investor may invest directly into a manager's fund or through a fund of funds, a private partnership that invests in multiple underlying partnerships. Larger investors may also consider making co-investments alongside a manager into a portfolio company, or they may make direct private equity investments on their own.

Private limited partnerships are the dominant investment vehicle for most alternative investments in private equity, real estate, private credit, and real assets. In the United States, hedge funds will tend to employ two structures: a limited partnership (typically Delaware-based) or an offshore corporation or feeder fund (possibly based in the Cayman Islands, Bermuda, or the British Virgin Islands) that usually feeds into an underlying limited partnership (i.e., feeder fund). European hedge funds tend to register their vehicles in Ireland or Luxembourg[7] as a public limited company, a partnership limited by shares, or a special limited partnership.

There are growing opportunities to invest in alternatives using mutual funds, undertakings for collective investment in transferable securities (UCITS), and/or separately managed accounts (SMAs), although the strategies implemented through these more-liquid vehicles are unlikely to have the same risk/return profile as their less-liquid counterparts. The requirements and demands of a broader investor base have made mutual funds, UCITS, and SMAs increasingly popular. We describe the structure, benefits, and drawbacks of each of these vehicles.

Direct investment in a limited partnership:

An investor with the necessary scale and expertise can purchase limited partnership interests directly from the GP. GPs have broad discretion to select and manage the underlying investments and will typically invest a portion of their capital in the fund alongside the limited partners. Because each limited partnership follows its own distinct investment strategy, the investor must often invest in multiple partnerships to diversify idiosyncratic risk. In order to maintain the limited liability shield afforded by the limited partnership structure, the investor must not become too involved in the operation of the fund itself.

7 See Eurekahedge, "2016 Key Trends in Global Hedge Funds" (August 2016).

Funds of funds (FOFs):

Many investors lack the necessary scale and investment/operational expertise to access, evaluate, and develop a diversified alternative investment program. An FOF pools the capital of these investors, allowing them to achieve an allocation to an asset class that would otherwise be unobtainable. An FOF manager will typically specialize in a certain alternative strategy, such as Asian private equity funds, and may invest in either many or just a handful of underlying funds. The FOF manager is responsible for sourcing, conducting due diligence on, and monitoring the underlying managers. Using an FOF simplifies the investor's accounting and reporting: Capital calls from the underlying funds are frequently consolidated into a single capital call by the FOF, and investors receive a single report consolidating the accounting and investment results of all the underlying funds. The FOF manager does charge additional fees for these services. Investors in an FOF also lose a degree of flexibility to customize their exposures.

SMAs/funds of one:

As large institutions and family offices increased capital allocated to the alternative investment space, many of them demanded more-favorable investment terms and conditions than those offered to smaller investors. Some alternative investment managers, interested in accessing these large pools of capital, have agreed to offer investment management services to these clients through a highly customizable SMA. SMAs have very high minimum investments and pose greater operational challenges for both the manager and the investor. In instances where an SMA is impractical, fund managers have created a "fund of one"—a limited partnership with a single client. These funds have many of the same benefits as an SMA but can be easier to implement. (For example, an SMA requires that the *investor* must be approved by each of the counterparties to any derivatives contracts. In a fund of one, GPs must obtain and maintain these approvals, which is something that they do in the ordinary course of running their investment businesses.)

SMAs and funds of one cannot generally avail themselves of the alignment of interests that arises from the investment of GP capital alongside that of the LPs. When other clients are invested in the GP's primary investment vehicles at the GP's standard fees and to which the GP has committed some of its own capital, there is a risk that the GP favors these other funds in allocating capital-constrained investment opportunities.

Mutual funds/UCITS/publicly traded funds:

A number of open-ended mutual funds and UCITS seek to replicate some alternative investment strategies, particularly hedge funds. Nominally, these allow smaller investors to access asset classes that would otherwise be unavailable to them. It should be noted, however, that these vehicles often operate with regulatory restrictions that limit the fund manager's ability to implement the investment strategy offered via their primary investment vehicle. Accordingly, the investor must be cautious in considering whether the track record achieved in the manager's primary investment vehicle is representative of what might be achieved in a mutual fund, UCIT, or other publicly-traded vehicle. For example, a mutual fund that offers daily liquidity is unlikely to be a suitable investment vehicle for a distressed or activist investment fund, where the time horizon to realize investment returns may be one to two years. This "liquid-alt" space grew significantly following the Global Financial Crisis.

6 LIQUIDITY

☐ discuss investment considerations that are important in allocating to different types of alternative investments

Traditional assets are generally highly liquid, and the vehicles that are typically used by investors to access the asset class (e.g., separate accounts or daily valued commingled funds, such as mutual funds and UCITS) typically do not impose additional liquidity constraints. That is not the case with many alternative assets, where both the vehicle and the underlying instruments may expose the investor to some degree of liquidity risk. We address liquidity risks at the fund and security level separately.

Liquidity Risks Associated with the Investment Vehicle

The most common vehicle employed by alternative asset managers is the private limited partnership previously described. (Some investors will invest via an offshore corporate structure used for certain tax and regulatory reasons. This offshore corporation is typically a "feeder" fund—a vehicle that channels investors' assets to the master limited partnership.) The private placement memorandum (PPM) details the subscription and redemption features of the partnership. Liquidity provisions differ across asset classes but are substantially similar within asset classes. Exhibit 17 details the typical liquidity considerations associated with investing in a private limited partnership. SMA liquidity provisions may be negotiated directly with the manager.

Exhibit 17: Typical Liquidity Provisions for Alternative Investment Vehicles

	Subscription	Redemption	Lock-Up
Hedge Funds	▪ Typically accept capital on a monthly or quarterly basis.	▪ Quarterly or annual redemptions with 30 to 90 days' notice required. ▪ May be subject to a gate limiting the amount of fund or investor assets that can be redeemed at any one redemption date. ▪ 10% holdback of the redemption amount pending completion of the annual audit.	▪ Typically one year in the US; shorter in Europe. ▪ Redemptions prior to the lock-up period may be permitted but are subject to a penalty, typically 10%.
Private Equity, Private Credit, Real Estate, and Real Asset Funds	▪ Funds typically have multiple "closes." The final close for new investors is usually one year after the first close. Committed capital is called for investment in stages over a 3-year investment period.	▪ No redemption provisions. Fund interests may be sold on the secondary market, subject to GP approval. ▪ Distributions paid as investments are realized over the life of the fund. Unrealized assets may be distributed in kind to the LP at fund termination.	▪ Typical 10-year life, with GP option to extend fund term 1 to 2 years.

Secondary markets:

Although fund terms may prevent investors from redeeming early, a small but growing secondary market for many alternative funds exists. Some brokers will match sellers and buyers of limited partnership interests, and some secondary funds' main objective is to buy limited partnership interests from the original investor. These transactions typically occur at a significant discount to the net asset value (NAV) of the fund and usually require the GP to approve the transaction.

Understanding a drawdown structure:

Private equity/credit, private real estate, and real asset funds typically call investors' capital in stages as fund investments are identified. This investment period is specified in the PPM and typically ranges from three to five years from the initial capital call. Thus, although an investor may have committed a specified percentage of the portfolio to an asset class, the allocation may not be fully funded until some point well into the future. We will illustrate the drawdown structure for a single fund using a hypothetical commitment to a real estate fund:

The Chan Family Partnership commits €5,000,000 to Uptown Real Estate LP. The fund has a three-year investment period. When fully invested, Uptown expects to hold 12 to 15 properties. The capital call schedule for Uptown may look something like this:

- Year 1: €1,500,000 of the €5,000,000 committed is called, covering three investments
- Year 2: €2,500,000 is called, covering six investments
- Year 3: €500,000 is called, covering two investments
- Year 6: €2,000,000 is distributed by Uptown Real Estate
- More distributions in subsequent years

Expanding on this example, Exhibit 18 shows how the cash flows for our hypothetical fund might operate throughout the fund's life.

Exhibit 18: Hypothetical Capital Call—Distribution Schedule

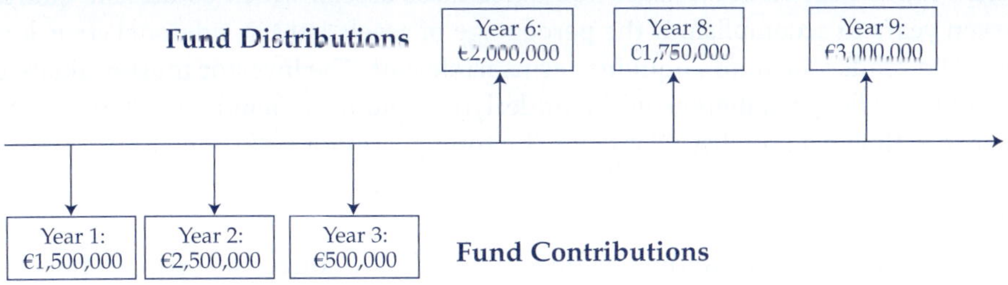

In reality, most funds will have several capital calls in a year. It is also possible that a fund may make a distribution before the final capital call occurs. Because of the highly uncertain liquidity profile of call down (or drawdown) funds (private equity/credit, real estate/real assets), it is incumbent on the investor to plan for multiple contingencies. Funds may end up calling significantly less capital than the investor assumed or may call capital at a faster pace than planned. Capital may be returned to the investor more quickly or more slowly than originally anticipated. Each of these scenarios could result in investors being under or over their target allocations. Critically, investors will want to verify that they have suitable liquidity, such that even under adverse conditions they are able to meet their capital calls. Investors who are unable to meet their capital calls may be required to forfeit their entire investment in the fund (or such other penalties as may be specified in the PPM).

The capital commitment/drawdown structure also presents potential opportunity costs for the investor. Returning to Exhibit 18, having committed €5,000,000 to Uptown Real Estate LP, the Chan Family Partnership is obligated to meet the GP's capital calls but must address the opportunity cost of having the committed capital invested in lower-returning liquid (cash) assets pending the capital call—or face the risk of having insufficient assets available to meet the capital call if the funds were invested in another asset class that has experienced a loss in the interim. Also note that only €4,500,000 of the €5,000,000 commitment was called before distributions began.

Liquidity Risks Associated with the Underlying Investments

The investor must be aware of any potential mismatch between the fund terms and the liquidity profile of the underlying instruments held by the fund. This is particularly important if the investor is negotiating fund terms or if other investors have terms that may be different from his own. Because the private market funds rarely offer interim liquidity, this problem most often arises in hedge funds. We provide a few examples of the issues an investor may encounter.

Equity-oriented hedge funds:

The majority of assets in a typical equity-oriented hedge fund are liquid, marketable securities compatible with monthly or quarterly fund-level liquidity terms. Short positions may be notably less liquid than long positions, so funds that make greater use of short selling will have correspondingly lower overall liquidity. This should be taken into consideration when evaluating the potential for a liquidity mismatch between the fund's terms and the underlying holdings. Some otherwise liquid hedge fund strategies may own a portion of their holdings in illiquid or relatively illiquid securities. The GP may designate these securities as being held in a "side pocket." Such "side-pocketed" securities are not subject to the fund's general liquidity terms. The redeeming investor's pro rata share of the side pocket would remain in the fund and be distributed at such time as the fund manager liquidates these assets, which could take quarters or even years to accomplish. If the percentage of assets held in side pockets is large, this could render the fund's liquidity terms irrelevant. The investor must evaluate the illiquidity challenges inherent in the underlying holdings, including side pockets, in order to estimate a liquidity profile for the total portfolio.

Event-driven hedge funds:

Event-driven strategies, by their nature, tend to have longer investment horizons. The underlying investments in a merger arbitrage strategy, for example, are generally liquid, but the nature of the strategy is such that returns are realized in "chunks." It is in the manager's and the investor's interests to ensure that the liquidity terms provide the necessary flexibility to execute the investment thesis. A hedge fund focused on distressed investing is dealing with both the "workout" horizon (the time frame over which the negotiations between the creditors and the company are being conducted) and the lesser liquidity of the distressed assets. The fund terms for a distressed strategy are likely to be much longer than other hedge fund strategies. (In fact, many distressed funds choose to organize in a private equity fund structure.)

Relative value hedge funds:

Many relative value hedge funds will invest in various forms of credit, convertibles, derivatives, or equities that have limited or at least uncertain liquidity characteristics. Many funds will include provisions in the fund documents to restrict redemptions under certain scenarios so that they are not forced to sell illiquid securities at inopportune moments. Without such provisions, the fund manager may be forced to sell what securities they *can* (i.e., the more liquid holdings) rather than the securities that they *want.* This could have the unfortunate consequence of leaving remaining investors in the fund holding a sub-optimally illiquid portfolio. On the other hand, funds that deal in managed futures or similar instruments may have very flexible terms (daily or weekly liquidity, only a few days notification, etc.). This was a scenario many hedge fund managers faced during the Global Financial Crisis as investors made significant redemption requests to meet their own cash needs. The liquid funds were disproportionately affected as investors sought to raise cash wherever they could find it.

Leverage:

A fund's use of leverage and its agreements with counterparties providing the leverage can also affect the alignment between fund terms and the investment strategy. If a strategy is levered, lenders have a first claim on the assets. The lenders' claims are superior to those of the LPs, and the lenders have preferential liquidity terms; most lenders can make a margin call on stocks, bonds, or derivatives positions with just two days' notice. Given that margin calls are most likely to happen when the markets (and/or the fund) are stressed, the LPs' liquidity can evaporate as the most-liquid positions in the portfolio are sold to meet margin calls. The need to de-lever and sell assets to meet margin calls will typically result in a lower return when the market eventually recovers.

FEES AND EXPENSES, TAX CONSIDERATIONS, AND OTHER CONSIDERATIONS 7

In addition to management fees of 0.5% to 2.5% of assets and incentive fees of 10% to 20% of returns, investments in alternative assets often entail higher expenses passed through to or paid directly by the investor. These fees can result in a significant variation between the gross and net of fee returns. Consider a hedge fund that was earning a 3% gross quarterly return (12.6% annualized). After deducting a 2% management and a 20% incentive fee, accrued quarterly, the net return at year-end is just 8.2%.

Fees can have a larger impact on the difference between gross and net returns for such call-down-type fund structures as private equity funds, where the management fee is charged on *committed* capital, not invested capital. If the manager is slow to deploy capital, there can be a pronounced J-curve effect (negative IRRs in the early years) that can be difficult to overcome (the adage 'it takes a 100% return to recover from a 50% loss').

In addition, most alternative investment funds will pass through normal fund expenses, including legal, custodial, audit, administration, and accounting fees. For smaller funds, these additional costs can add up to another 0.5%. Larger funds can spread these same costs out over the larger asset base, and the pass-through to investors is likely to be in the range of 0.05% to 0.20% of assets. Some of these expenses have a limited life (e.g., the capitalized organizational expenses), so the impact can vary over time. Funds may also pass through to investors costs associated with acquiring an asset, including the due diligence costs and any brokerage commissions paid. A careful evaluation of the fund's offering documents is essential to understanding the all-in cost of an investment in alternatives.

Tax Considerations

For taxable investors, the tax implications associated with many alternatives can have a significant impact on their relative attractiveness. In many instances, a tax inefficient strategy, one that generates substantial short-term gains or taxable income, can significantly erode the anticipated return benefits. This arises frequently with many hedge fund strategies, especially those funds and fund companies where tax-exempt investors dominate the client base and the fund manager may be insensitive to tax efficiency. Vehicle selection becomes an important tool to mitigate potential tax consequences. For example, certain Asia-based investors may use European or other offshore vehicles that feed into US strategies in order to mitigate US tax withholding. Conversely, some funds benefit from preferential tax treatment that might add to its relative attractiveness.

Here are a few examples of these tax considerations:

- The US tax code has provisions that favor real estate, timber, and energy investments. Timber sales, for example, are taxed at lower capital gains rates rather than as ordinary income and may benefit from a depletion deduction. Commercial and residential building assets can be depreciated according to various schedules, with the depreciation offsetting income received on those assets. Some oil and natural gas royalty owners may benefit from a depletion deduction, offsetting income generated from the sale of the oil or gas.
- Some alternative investment strategies can generate unrelated business income tax (UBIT). UBIT arises when a US tax-exempt organization engages in activities that are not related to the tax-exempt purpose of that organization. Since most tax-exempt entities seek to mitigate (if not avoid) taxes, they will want to verify whether such a fund might generate UBIT and, if so, whether the fund manager has an offshore vehicle that may shield the investor from such income.
- The taxable investor faces additional costs and operational hurdles because of the more complex tax filings. Some taxable investors must estimate their expected annual income, including income that is derived from investments. Deriving an accurate estimate can be a challenge. Unfortunately, if the misestimation is large enough it might result in tax penalties.

Tax considerations, like fees, will affect the return assumptions used in the asset allocation exercise.

Other Considerations

Although smaller investors seeking to build a diversified alternative investment program are generally constrained to use an intermediary, such as a fund of funds, large investors have the opportunity to build a program in-house and must decide whether this approach is appropriate given their governance structure. Key questions to explore in evaluating the options include the following:

- What is the likelihood that the investor can identify and gain access to the top-tier managers in the investment strategy?

  Truly differentiated strategies and top-tier managers are notoriously capacity constrained, which tends to limit the amount of assets they can reasonably manage without negatively affecting investment returns. Fund managers who recognize this problem frequently limit the number of investors that they allow into their fund and may close their doors to new clients or capital. This can make it extremely difficult for investors to find and access top-tier managers. Investors who are subject to public disclosure requirements may be rejected by a manager who believes that success is based on a proprietary informational edge that could be eroded through these required public disclosures. Many studies on alternative assets have concluded that it may not be worth the costs and resources required to be successful in this space if investors do not have access to top-tier funds.

- What is the likelihood that the investor will be accorded the access needed to conduct effective due diligence on an investment strategy?

  It is not enough to know when or if to invest with a fund manager; it is equally, if not more, important to be able to determine when to terminate the relationship. Having poor to no access to the key decision makers within the organization could make it difficult to ascertain if the conditions have changed such that a redemption is warranted. The situation could be even worse if other clients have good (or preferential) access to the fund manager, which might result in their redeeming early, leaving other, less-informed investors subject to gates or other more-restrictive redemption terms that could be triggered.

- What skills and resources does the investor have in-house to evaluate and monitor an alternative investment program?

  This question is evaluated through a consideration of the cost tradeoffs, the investment expertise of in-house staff, the desire to tailor an investment program to investor-specific wants and needs, and the degree of control.

  - Cost is typically the overriding factor in the decision to build a program in-house or buy an existing off-the-shelf product. The all-in costs of compensation, benefits, rent, technology, reporting, travel, overhead, and other miscellaneous expenses associated with managing an alternative investments program can far exceed the costs associated with running a traditional asset portfolio. However, very large organizations may be able to justify the costs of building in-house teams.
  - Investors seeking to leverage a manager's expertise through co-investments and other direct investment opportunities must build an in-house team with the expertise to evaluate specific securities and deals and must provide the infrastructure needed to support those efforts.
  - Investors who require highly customized investment programs might be poorly served by consultants or FOFs who typically gain scale and margin by providing solutions that can be broadly applied to a large number of clients. For example, an endowment that wants their alternative investment program to consider environmental, social, and governance (ESG) factors (i.e., socially responsible investing) may have a difficult time finding an investment consultant who can deliver on the client's specific ESG requirements. Or, a family office that wants to emphasize tax-efficient angel investments might need to hire in-house resources in order to find and supervise these more specialized investments.
  - Those investors who desire a high degree of control and/or influence over the implementation of the investment program are more likely to have this need met through an in-house program.

EXAMPLE 3

Considerations in Allocating to Alternative Investments

The investment committee (IC) for a small endowment has decided to invest in private equity for the first time and has agreed upon a 10% strategic target. The internal investment team comprises the CIO (chief investment officer) and two analysts. The IC asks the CIO to recommend an implementation plan at the next meeting.

1. What are the options the CIO should include in her report as it relates to vehicles, and what factors might influence the recommendation?

Solution:

The primary considerations for the CIO include the size of the private equity allocation, the team's expertise with private equity, and the available resources. Because this is a small endowment, it may be difficult to commit enough capital to achieve an adequate level of diversification. The size of the fund's investment team is also likely to be a concern. Unless there are financial resources to add a private equity specialist and/or employ an outside consultant, the fund-of-funds route would likely be the optimal vehicle(s) to implement a diversified private equity program.

2. The IC provided no guidance as to expectations for when the investment program should reach its 10% target weight. What additional information should the CIO gather before presenting her plan of action?

Solution:

The CIO should factor in the cash flows and anticipated liquidity profile of the overall endowment in considering the speed with which they would commit to a significant PE program. If, for example, the foundation is embarking on a capital campaign and anticipated distributions are small over the next few years, then commitments may be accelerated after factoring in an appropriate vintage year diversification. (Because private investment returns are very sensitive to the fund's vintage year, it is common for investors to build up to a full allocation over a period of years, called vintage year diversification.) However, if the rest of the investment program is heavily exposed to illiquid investments (e.g., real estate, certain hedge fund strategies) and anticipated distributions to fund operating expenses are high, the CIO may want to commit at a slower pace.

EXAMPLE 4

Considerations in Allocating to Alternative Investments

A $100 million client of a family office firm has requested that all public securities investments meet certain ESG criteria. The ESG ratings will be provided by an independent third-party firm that provides a rating for most public equities and some fixed-income issuers. Moreover, the family would like to dedicate a percentage of assets to support an "environmental sustainability" impact theme.

1. Which alternative investment strategies may not be suitable for this client given the ESG requirements?

Solution:

Because the ESG criteria apply to all public securities, most hedge fund strategies would be precluded because they are typically owned in a commingled vehicle, such as a limited partnership or a mutual fund where transparency of holdings is limited and the investor has no influence over the composition of the underlying portfolio. Separate account strategies are available for certain large portfolios, but it is unlikely that a $100 million client would be eligible for a custom portfolio that would be allocating only a small asset base to any particular fund.

2. What additional information might the family office firm require from the client in order to meet the environmental sustainability threshold?

Solution:

The client and the manager would need to agree on a clear definition of environmental sustainability and the types of investments that might qualify for this theme. It is unlikely that most hedge funds, private credit, energy, or infrastructure strategies would be considered to positively impact environmental sustainability. The most likely candidates for consideration could be timber, sustainable farmland, and clean-tech funds under the venture capital category.

SUITABILITY CONSIDERATIONS 8

☐ discuss suitability considerations in allocating to alternative investments

Alternative investments are not appropriate for all investors. We discuss briefly several *investor* characteristics that are important to a successful alternative investment program.

Investment Horizon

Investors with less than a 15-year investment horizon should generally avoid investments in private real estate, private real assets, and private equity funds. An alternative investment program in private markets may take 5 to 7 years to fully develop and another 10 to 12 years to unwind, assuming no new investments are made after the 7-year mark. Even a 10-year horizon may be too short to develop a robust private alternative investment program.

Other strategies can tolerate a shorter investment focus. Many hedge fund strategies that focus on public equities or managed futures have much shorter lock-ups (on the order of months or not at all). Some strategies can be entered and exited in shorter time frames, and the purchase or sale of limited partnership interests on the secondary market may be used to shorten the entry and exit phases of the process.

However, the alternative investment program has a higher likelihood of success if the investor adopts a long-horizon approach coupled with an understanding of the underlying investment processes.

Expertise

A successful alternative investment program requires that the investor understand the risks entailed and the market environments that drive success or failure of each of the strategies. Understanding the breadth of the alternative investment opportunities and the complexity of strategies within each alternative class requires a relatively high level of investment expertise. Even if the investor is highly experienced, the risk of information asymmetry between the limited partner (LP) and the general partner (GP) is always there. A pension fund without full-time investment staff, or an individual without the resources to hire an adviser with a dedicated alternative investments team, is unlikely to have the investment expertise necessary to implement a successful alternative investment program.

Additionally, the investment philosophy of the asset owner (or its overseers) must be consistent with the principles of alternative investments. An investor whose investment philosophy is rooted in a belief that markets are fundamentally efficient may struggle to embrace an alternative investment program, where success is predicated on active management. A mismatch in philosophy could very well be a set up for failure when the alternative investments underperform traditional asset classes.

Governance

A robust investment governance framework ensures that an alternative investment program is structured to meet the needs of the investor. The following are hallmarks of a strong governance framework suitable to an alternative investment program:

- The long- and short-term objectives of the investment program are clearly articulated.
- Decision rights and responsibilities are allocated to those individuals with the knowledge, capacity, and time required to critically evaluate possible courses of action.
- A formal investment policy has been adopted to govern the day-to-day operations of the investment program.
- A reporting framework is in place to monitor the program's progress toward the agreed-on goals and objectives.

Investors without a strong governance program are less likely to develop a successful alternative investment program.

Transparency

Investors must be comfortable with less than 100% transparency into the underlying holdings of their alternative investment managers. In real estate, private equity, and real asset funds, the investor is typically buying into a "blind pool"—committing capital for investment in a portfolio of as-yet-unidentified assets. During the course of investment due diligence, the investor may have looked at the assets acquired in the manager's previous funds, but there is no assurance that the new fund will look anything like the prior funds. Hedge fund managers are generally reluctant to disclose the full portfolio to investors on an ongoing basis. Even if you were to have access to the full underlying portfolio, it is rarely apparent where the true risk exposures lie without a detailed understanding of the investment themes the manager is pursuing.

Reporting for alternative funds is often less transparent than investors are accustomed to seeing on their stock and bond portfolios. Generally, no legal requirements mandate the frequency, timing, and details of fund reporting for private investment partnerships. For many illiquid strategies (real estate/assets, private equity/credit), reporting is often received well past month- or quarter-end deadlines that investors are accustomed to with their traditional investments.

A typical hedge fund report, usually available on a quarterly basis, may detail performance, top 10 holdings, and some general commentary on the capital markets as well as some factors that influenced fund performance. The hedge fund manager may also provide a risk report that broadly outlines the major risk exposures of the fund. There is no commonality among the risk reports provided from fund to fund. This hampers an investor's efforts to develop a picture of aggregate risk exposure. Clients with separately managed accounts have access to portfolio holdings and may be able to produce their own risk reporting with a common set of risk metrics.

Private equity funds will provide more transparency into portfolio holdings, but the private equity fund report is unlikely to "slice-and-dice" the exposures by geography, sector, or industry. The investor must gather the additional information needed to develop a fuller exposure of the portfolio's risk exposures and progress toward meeting expectations. Private equity managers typically provide an abbreviated quarterly report with a more detailed annual report following the completion of the fund's annual audit.

This lack of transparency can shield questionable actions by GPs. In 2014, the US Securities and Exchange Commission found that more than 50% of private equity firms had collected or misallocated fees without proper disclosure to their clients.[8] This study and subsequent lawsuits have increased transparency within the industry, although the industry remains opaque at many levels.

Reporting for private real estate funds commonly consists of a quarterly report with details on the fund's size, progress in drawdowns, realizations to date, and valuations of unrealized investments as well as market commentary relevant to the fund's strategy. Reports typically include details on each investment such as the original acquisition cost(s), square footage, borrowing details (e.g., cost of debt, leverage ratios, and debt maturity dates), and fundamental metrics regarding the health of the properties (e.g., occupancy rates and, if appropriate, the estimated credit health of tenants). Often there is qualitative commentary on the health of the property's submarket, on anticipated next steps, and on the timing of realization(s). Reports are typically issued with a one-quarter lag to allow sufficient time to update property valuations. Annual reports, which frequently require updated third-party appraisals, may not be available until the second quarter following year end.

Investors should ensure that funds use independent administrators to calculate the fund and LPs' NAV. These administrators are also responsible for processing cash flows, including contributions, fee payments, and distributions that are consistent with the fund documents. The use of independent administrators is common practice among hedge funds. It is relatively uncommon for a fund investing in illiquid strategies (e.g., private equity/credit, real estate/natural resources) to use an independent administrator. Funds that do not use third-party administrators have wide discretion in valuing assets. In the midst of the Great Financial Crisis, it was not uncommon for two different private equity firms with ownership interests in the same company to provide very different estimates of the company's value.

The lack of transparency common with many alternative investments can challenge risk management and performance evaluation. High-quality alternative investment managers will engage an independent and respected accounting firm to perform an annual audit of the fund; the audit report should be available to the LPs.

---

8 Andrew Ceresney, "Keynote Address: Private Equity Enforcement," Securities Enforcement Forum West (12 May 2016).

Regulatory requirements for mutual funds and UCITS funds require such standardized information as costs, expected risks, and performance data. Additional information may also be available on a periodic basis. Information provided to one investor should be available to all shareholders. These rules have been interpreted by some mutual fund/UCITS managers to mean that they cannot provide more-detailed, non-standardized information given the complexity of sharing it with a broad audience. This can possibly restrict the level of transparency certain shareholders can obtain for these vehicles.

EXAMPLE 5

Suitability Considerations in Allocating to Alternative Investments

The Christian family office is concerned with investor or manager fraud and so will invest only in separately managed accounts (SMAs).

1. What are the benefits and drawbacks to the use of SMAs?

Solution:

Although an SMA allows for greater transparency and control of capital flows (the manager does not generally have the authority to distribute capital from the client account), it has several potential disadvantages: 1) SMAs are not available or appropriate for many alternative strategies; thus, the requirement to invest via an SMA may limit the ability to develop an optimal alternative investment program. 2) A manager cannot invest alongside the client in the client's SMA. This may reduce the alignment of interest between the manager and the client and may give rise to conflicts of interest as trades are allocated between the SMA and the manager's other funds.

2. The 75-year-old patriarch of the Christian family would like to consider a significant private equity allocation in a trust that he oversees on behalf of his youngest daughter. This would be the first alternative investment commitment made with any of the family's assets. The daughter is 40 years old. She will receive one-half of the assets outright upon his death. The remainder of the assets will be held in trust subject to the terms of the trust agreement. List some of the reasons why private equity may or may not be appropriate for this trust.

Solution:

- Successful private equity investment requires a long time horizon. Given the patriarch's age, it is likely that half of the trust's assets will be distributed before the private equity program has had time to mature. This may lead to an unintended doubling in the size of the private equity allocation.
- The patriarch has no experience investing in alternative assets. Unless he is willing to commit the time, money, and effort and engage an outside adviser with the relevant expertise and access to top-tier funds, the likelihood of a successful private equity investment program would be low.

- Because the beneficiary of the trust is relatively young, the time horizon of the investment likely matches the profile of the underlying investor. It may be appropriate for the trust to invest in long-dated private equity assets, provided the investment is sized appropriately and the necessary expertise has been retained.

ASSET ALLOCATION APPROACHES AND STATISTICAL PROPERTIES AND CHALLENGES

9

☐ discuss approaches to asset allocation to alternative investments

We mentioned earlier that one approach to determining the desired allocation to the alternative asset classes is to make the initial asset allocation decision using only the broad, liquid asset classes and do a second iteration of the asset allocation exercise incorporating alternative assets. After first addressing the challenges in developing risk and return assumptions for alternative asset classes, we then discuss three primary approaches that investors use to approach this second iteration.

1. *Monte Carlo simulation.* We discuss how Monte Carlo simulation may be used to generate return scenarios that relax the assumption of normally distributed returns. We illustrate how simulation can be applied to estimate the long-term risk profile and return potential of various asset allocation alternatives, and, in particular, we evaluate whether various asset allocation alternatives would satisfy the investor's ultimate investment objectives.
2. *Optimization techniques.* Mean–variance optimization (MVO) typically over-allocates to alternative asset classes, partly because risk is underestimated because of stale or infrequent pricing and the underlying assumption that returns are normally distributed. Practitioners usually address this bias towards alternatives by establishing limits on the allocations to alternatives. Optimization methods that incorporate downside risk (mean–CVaR optimization) or take into account skew may be used to enhance the asset allocation process.
3. *Risk factor-based approaches.* Risk factor-based approaches to alternative asset allocation can be applied to develop more robust asset allocation proposals.

These analytical techniques complement each other, and investors frequently rely on all of them rather than just using one or the other. Monte Carlo simulation can provide simulated non-normal (fat-tailed) data for a mean–CVaR optimization, but simulation can also be applied to analyze the long-term behavior of various asset allocation alternatives that are the results of portfolio optimization.

Statistical Properties and Challenges of Asset Returns

Alternative investments present the modeler with a number of analytical challenges. These two are particularly relevant in the asset allocation process:

1. Appraisal-based valuations used in private alternative investments often lead to stale and/or artificially smoothed returns. Volatility and other risk measures estimated based on these smoothed time series would potentially understate the actual, fundamental risk.
2. Although even the public asset classes can exhibit non-normal return distributions, skewness and fat tails (excess kurtosis) are more pronounced with many of the alternative investment strategies. Leverage, sensitivity to the disappearance of liquidity, and even the asymmetric nature of performance fees all contribute to additional skewness and excess kurtosis among alternative investments. This option–payoff style quality can undermine a simplistic statistical approach.

Asset allocators use various analytical approaches to mitigate the impact of these challenges.

Stale Pricing and Unsmoothing

Appraisal-based valuation is common in private real estate and private equity. The valuation parameter assumptions in the appraisal process change quite slowly. This has a smoothing effect on reported returns and gives the illusion that illiquid assets' performance is much less volatile than that of public marketable assets with similar fundamental characteristics. This issue also affects hedge funds in which the manager invests in illiquid or less-liquid assets whose valuations are updated infrequently or are using models with static valuation assumptions. These artificially smoothed returns can be detected by testing the return stream for serial correlation. If serial correlation is detected and found statistically significant, the analyst needs to unsmooth the returns to get a more accurate representation of the risk and return characteristics of the asset class we are modelling.

To illustrate unsmoothing, we use a simple approach described by Ang (2014). Exhibit 19 illustrates the reported quarterly return history of the Cambridge Associates Private Equity Index, as well as the unsmoothed series.[9] The annualized volatility estimated using the reported quarterly return data and scaling using the square root of time convention is 9.5%.[10] The widely accepted rule of scaling by the square root of time, however, is based on the assumption of serially uncorrelated, normally-distributed returns. In our example, the serial correlation of the quarterly reported private equity returns is 0.38, which, given the number of observations, is significant with a *t*-statistic of 4.09. Because our returns are serially correlated, we want to unsmooth the returns to get a better estimate of volatility. The volatility calculated on the unsmoothed return series is 14.0%, significantly higher than the volatility estimated from the unsmoothed data.

---

9 We used the following formula to unsmooth the report total return time series:

$r_{t,\text{unsmoothed}} = (r_{t,\text{reported}} - s \times r_{t-1,\text{reported}})/(1 - s)$,

where s denotes the estimated serial correlation of the time series.

10 To scale volatility estimates to a longer (or shorter) time horizon, the volatility can be multiplied by the square root of time. For example, if we know the quarterly volatility and want an annual volatility estimate, we would multiply the quarterly volatility estimate by the square root of 4. (This scaling convention assumes price changes are independent and returns are not serially correlated over time.)

Exhibit 19: C|A Private Equity Index Quarterly Returns

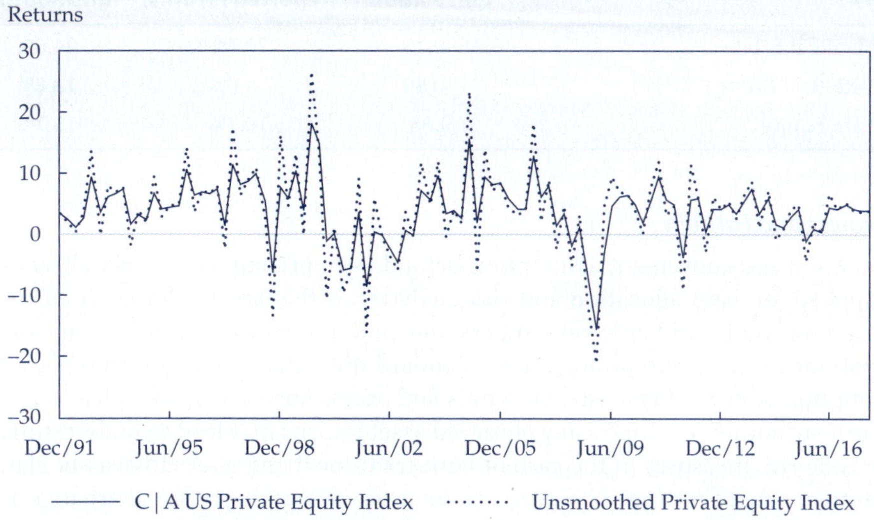

Exhibit 20 illustrates serial correlation and volatility estimates based on quarterly returns of a broad range of asset classes. Although the serial correlation of public marketable asset classes is generally low, private asset classes and some hedge fund strategies have higher serial correlations that indicate stronger smoothing effects. The higher the serial correlation in the reported return series, the larger the difference between the volatility based on the unsmoothed and reported (smoothed) return data. The impact of smoothing is the highest in the case of private investments, as suggested by the serial correlation for private real estate (0.85) and private equity (0.38). The unsmoothed volatility of private real estate is, in fact, three times the volatility that we would estimate based on the reported returns. Given the serial correlation evident in private alternative strategies, it is not surprising that the distressed hedge fund strategy exhibits higher serial correlation (0.36) than other hedge fund strategies.

Exhibit 20: The Effect of Serial Correlation on Volatility

Quarterly Data Dec. 1997–Sept. 2017	Serial Correlation	Volatility (reported returns)	Volatility (unsmoothed)
US Equities	0.03	17.0%	17.7%
Non-US Developed Market Equities	0.08	19.2%	20.8%
Emerging Market Equities	0.17	26.2%	30.8%
Governments	−0.01	4.9%	4.9%
Broad Fixed Income	0.02	3.4%	3.5%
High-Yield Credit	0.34	10.0%	14.3%
Inflation-Linked Bonds	0.12	5.0%	5.7%
Hedge Funds—Aggregate	0.15	8.1%	9.5%
HF Macro	0.08	5.4%	5.9%
HF Equity Market Neutral	0.17	3.5%	4.1%
HF Equity Hedged	0.19	10.7%	13.1%
HF Distressed	0.36	8.9%	13.0%
Commodities	0.14	25.2%	28.8%

Quarterly Data Dec. 1997–Sept. 2017	Serial Correlation	Volatility (reported returns)	Volatility (unsmoothed)
Public Real Estate	0.15	20.4%	24.0%
Private Real Estate	0.85	4.6%	13.8%
Private Equity	0.38	10.7%	15.7%

Skewness and Fat Tails

A common and convenient assumption behind asset pricing theory, as well as models applied for asset allocation and risk analytics, is that asset returns are normally distributed. Both academic researchers and practitioners are widely aware of the limitations of this assumption, but no standard quantitative method to replace this assumption of normality exists. Skewness and excess kurtosis, or so-called "fat tails," in the distributions of empirically observed asset returns may lead to underestimated downside risk measures in the case of both traditional and alternative asset classes. Non-normality of returns, however, can be more severe in private alternative asset class and certain hedge fund strategies than in most of the traditional asset classes.

In Exhibit 21, we show skewness and excess kurtosis parameters calculated based on 20 years of unsmoothed quarterly return data of various public and alternative asset classes. We also show 95% quarterly conditional value at risk (CVaR) estimates based on the assumption of normally distributed asset returns, as well as based on the observed (actual) distributions. Positive skewness indicates smaller downside risk potential, while negative skewness indicates greater downside risk potential. Excess kurtosis (i.e., a kurtosis parameter exceeding 3) similarly points toward greater downside risk than would be apparent from the numbers calculated using the assumption of normally-distributed returns. The observed (actual) CVaR estimates typically exceed the normal distribution-based CVaR figures when kurtosis is high and skewness is negative. Equity market-neutral hedge funds and private real estate have the biggest *relative* differences between the 95% normal distribution CVaR and the observed CVaR (columns C and D divided by column C). Both of these strategies have negative skewness and fairly high excess kurtosis. It's interesting to note that distressed hedge funds similarly have high kurtosis and negative skewness, but the difference in tail risk measures becomes mainly visible at the 99% confidence level, where the extreme but infrequent losses may occur.

Exhibit 21: Normal Distribution Assumption and Observed Downside Risk Measures

	(A)	(B)	(C)	(D)	(E)	(F)
Unsmoothed Quarterly Data Dec. 1997–Sept. 2017	Skewness	Excess Kurtosis	95% CVaR (Normal Distribution)	95% CVaR (Observed)	99% CVaR (Normal Distribution)	99% CVaR (Observed)
US Equities	−0.51	0.43	−15.3%	−17.7%	−20.3%	−23.9%
Non-US Dev Equities	−0.19	0.29	−18.9%	−19.8%	−24.8%	−20.7%
Emerging Mkt Equities	−0.23	−0.03	−28.2%	−25.4%	−37.0%	−27.7%
Governments	0.59	0.39	−3.5%	−3.2%	−4.9%	−4.0%
Broad Fixed Income	−0.05	−0.41	−2.1%	−2.4%	−3.1%	−3.1%
High-Yield Credit	0.18	6.14	−7.9%	−9.8%	−10.8%	−19.7%
Inflation-Linked Bonds	−0.32	1.08	−4.2%	−4.2%	−5.8%	−8.1%
Hedge Funds	−0.17	1.69	−7.6%	−8.6%	−10.3%	−9.7%

	(A)	(B)	(C)	(D)	(E)	(F)
Unsmoothed Quarterly Data Dec. 1997–Sept. 2017	Skewness	Excess Kurtosis	95% CVaR (Normal Distribution)	95% CVaR (Observed)	99% CVaR (Normal Distribution)	99% CVaR (Observed)
HF Macro	0.36	0.85	−4.3%	−4.1%	−6.0%	−5.1%
HF Equity Market Neutral	−1.17	3.55	−2.9%	−3.9%	−4.1%	−5.4%
HF Equity Hedged	0.08	2.24	−10.8%	−10.6%	−14.5%	−12.7%
HF Distressed	−1.25	3.52	−10.8%	−11.1%	−14.5%	−16.9%
Commodities	−0.71	1.62	−28.4%	−30.6%	−36.6%	−50.6%
Public Real Estate	−0.88	4.60	−20.9%	−24.5%	−27.7%	−40.2%
Private Real Estate	−2.80	9.62	−11.3%	−15.4%	−15.3%	−27.9%
Private Equity	−0.46	2.05	−12.2%	−15.7%	−16.7%	−22.6%

Source: Authors' calculations.

To further illustrate the impact of non-normality on the downside risk, in Exhibit 22 we compare the ratio of observed to normal CVaR measures with the skewness and excess kurtosis. Although the skewness or excess kurtosis alone doesn't fully explain the relative difference between observed and normal 95% CVaR (positive skewness may compensate high excess kurtosis or vice versa), we can see the evidence that higher kurtosis or more negative skewness usually increases the likely severity of any tail risk.

Exhibit 22: The Impact of Skewness and Kurtosis on Tail Risk

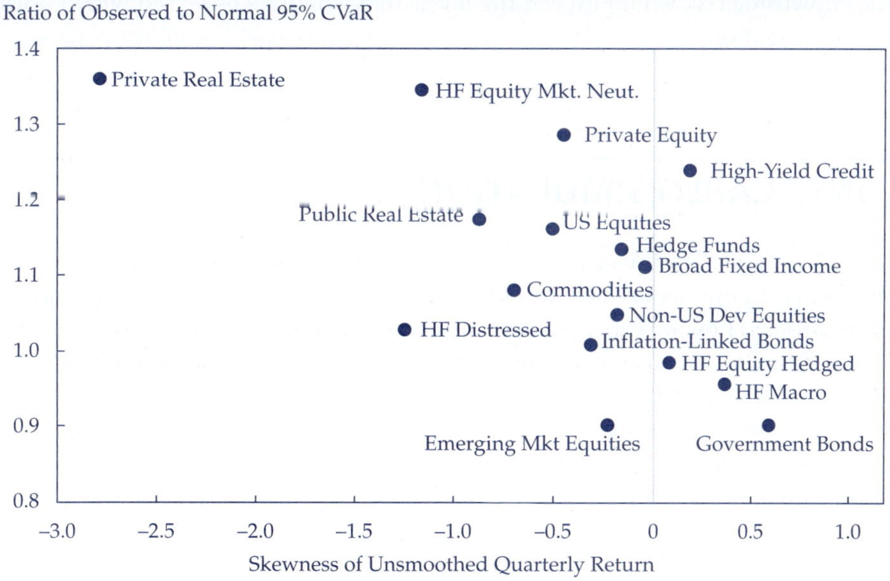

Source: Authors' calculations.

Analysts can choose to incorporate non-normality into their analyses in a few different ways. The most obvious and straightforward choice is to use empirically observed asset returns instead of working with the normal distribution. Still, in private investments where we typically have only quarterly return data, the analyses may be subject to serious limitations. Even with 20 years of quarterly return data, we have only 80 data points (and the industry has changed significantly over this time, further straining the validity of the data).

With sufficient data, analysts and researchers can capture the effects of fat tails by using advanced mathematical or statistical models:

- Time-varying volatility models (e.g., stochastic volatility), which assume that volatility is not constant over time but changes dynamically, can be used.
- Regime-switching models capture return, volatility, and correlation characteristics in different market environments (bull/bear or low volatility and moderate correlation vs. high volatility and elevated correlation). The combination of two or more normal distributions with different average returns, volatilities, and correlations could capture skewed and fat-tailed distributions.
- Extreme value theory and other fat-tailed distributions can be used when the analyst wants to focus on the behavior in the tails.

Although no single and uniformly accepted approach exists to address all of these quantitative challenges to the asset allocation exercise, a sound asset allocation process will do the following:

1. Adjust the observed asset class return data by unsmoothing the return series if the autocorrelation is significant.
2. Determine whether it is reasonable to accept an assumption of normal return distributions, in which case mean–variance optimization is appropriate to use.
3. Allow you to choose an optimization approach that takes the tail risk into account if the time series exhibits fat tails and skewness and if the potential downside risk would exceed the levels that would be observed with a normal distribution.

10 MONTE CARLO SIMULATION

Monte Carlo simulation can be a very useful tool in asset allocation to alternative investments. In this section, we discuss two applications of this modeling approach. First, we discuss how we can simulate risk factor or asset return scenarios that exhibit the skewness and kurtosis commonly seen in alternative investments. Second, we illustrate simulation-based risk and return analytics over a long time horizon in a broad asset allocation context.

At a very high level, we can summarize the model construction process in the following steps:

1. Identify those variables that we would like to randomly generate in our simulation. These variables may be asset class total returns directly, or risk factors, depending on the model.
2. Establish the quantitative framework to generate realistic random scenarios for the selected asset class returns or risk factors. Here, the analyst faces several choices, including the following:

    a. What kind of time-series model are we using? Will it be a random walk? Or will it incorporate serial correlations and mean-reversion-like characteristics?

   b. What kind of distribution should we assume for the shocks or innovations to the variables? Is normal distribution reasonable? Or, will we use some fat-tailed distribution model instead?

   c. Are volatilities and correlations stable over time? Or, do they vary across time?

3. If using a risk factor approach, convert the risk factors to asset or asset class returns using a factor-based model. In this reading, all our illustrations are based on linear factor models, but certain asset types with optionality need more-sophisticated models to incorporate non-linear characteristics as well.
4. Further translate realistic asset class return scenarios into meaningful indicators. We can simultaneously model, for example, the investment portfolio and the liability of a pension fund, enabling us to assess how the funding ratio is expected to evolve over time. Or, in the case of an endowment fund, we can assess whether certain asset allocation choices would improve the probability of meeting the spending rate target while preserving the purchasing power of the asset base.

Simulating Skewed and Fat-Tailed Financial Variables

A fairly intuitive way of incorporating non-normal returns into the analysis is to assume that there are two (or more) possible states of the world. Individually, each state can be described by using a normal distribution (*conditional normality*), but the combination of these two distributions will not be normally distributed.[11] Next, we show a fairly simplified application for the public equities and government bonds. Note that the same approach can be applied to more asset classes as well, or it can be applied to risk factor changes rather than asset class returns.

For this illustration, we assume that the capital markets can be described by two distinct regimes—a "quiet period" (Regime 1) and a high-volatility state (Regime 2). Exhibit 23 shows the quarterly return history of the US equities and government bonds as well as the model's more volatile regimes (the gray-shaded periods). It is easy to see that the Global Financial Crisis—and such earlier crisis periods as the 1997 Asian currency contagion, the 1998 Russian ruble crisis and LTCM meltdown, and the 2002 tech bubble burst—all belong to the high-volatility regimes. The mean return and volatility statistics for the full period as well as each of the two regimes can be found in Exhibit 24. Equities outperformed government bonds over the full observation period, and it's interesting to see how dynamics changed between the quiet to the volatile periods. In the quiet period (Regime 1), equities outperformed bonds by around 4.6% quarterly, whereas in the volatile period (Regime 2), government bonds outperformed equities by more than 5%. The total return volatilities also jumped dramatically when the market switched from quiet to volatile periods. In addition, the correlation between equities and bonds was near zero during the quiet period but turned significantly negative (about −0.6) during the volatile period. Finally, we estimate that the low-volatility Regime 1 prevailed 62% of the time and the high-volatility Regime 2 prevailed 38% of the time.

11 The estimation process of such models is beyond the scope of this reading. Readers interested in additional details are referred to Hamilton (1989) and Kim and Nelson (1999).

Exhibit 23: US Equities and Government Bonds Return History and Identification of High-Volatility Regimes

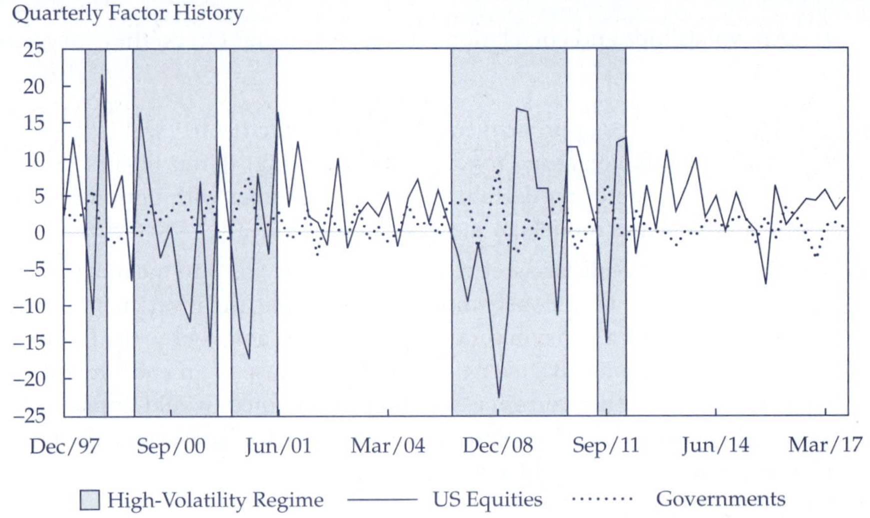

Source: Authors' calculations.

Exhibit 24: Return Statistics (1997–2017)

	Equities	Government Bonds
Quarterly Average Return	2.1%	1.2%
Quarterly Return Volatility	8.5%	4.5%
Skewness	–0.5	0.6
Kurtosis	0.4	0.4
Average Return in Regime 1	5.1%	0.5%
Average Return in Regime 2	–3.1%	2.4%
Volatility in Regime 1	5.5%	1.9%
Volatility in Regime 2	13.7%	3.8%
Correlation in Regime 1	0.0	
Correlation in Regime 2	–0.6	

If we want to capture only skewness and fat tails in a simulation framework, we just need the normal distribution parameters of the distinct regimes and the overall state probabilities of either Regime 1 or Regime 2. Then, the analyst would generate normally distributed random scenarios based on the different means and covariances estimated under the two (or more) regimes with the appropriate frequency of the estimated probability of being the quiet or hectic regimes. This mixture of high- and low-volatility normal distributions would lead to an altogether skewed and fat-tailed distribution of asset class return or risk factor changes. In practice, some may build a more dynamic, multi-step simulation model for a longer time horizon, in which case it's also important to estimate the probability of switching from one regime to another.

Exhibit 25 shows histograms of equity returns, overlaid with the fitted normal distribution and the combined distributions from our regime-switching model. As the chart illustrates, the combination of two normal distributions improves the distribution fit and introduces some degree of skewness and fat-tail characteristics.

Exhibit 25: Normal and Fat-Tailed Distribution Fit for US Equity Quarterly Returns

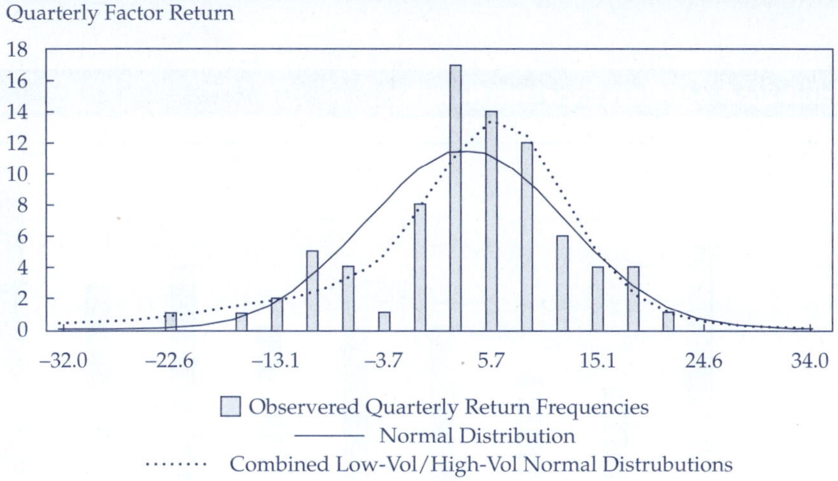

Source: Authors' calculations.

Several variations of regime-switching models are available. We have used a very basic set-up to illustrate the additional richness a regime-switching model can bring to the analysis. We could also apply a similar approach if we were to build asset classes using risk factors. We could overlay the non-normal distributions of the risk factors on the relevant asset class returns.[12]

Simulation for Long-Term Horizon Risk Assessment

We will now work through a practical application of Monte Carlo simulation in the context of asset allocation over a long time horizon. We simulate asset class returns in quarterly steps over a 10-year time horizon.[13] Such models exhibit some degree of mean-reversion and also capture dynamic interactions across risk factors or asset classes over multiple time periods.

The volatilities, correlations, and other parameters of the time series model are estimated based on the past 20 years of unsmoothed asset class return data. The expected returns for the selected asset classes (shown in Exhibit 26), however, are not based on historical average returns but are illustrative, forward-looking estimates. Note that these return expectations mostly assume passive investments in the specific asset class and don't include the possible value-added from (or lost through) active management. Hedge funds are the exception, of course, because by definition hedge

12 In this reading, we assume that various asset classes have constant risk factor sensitivities over time, an assumption that can be relaxed in practice. For example, Berkelaar, Kobor, and Kouwenberg (2009) present time-varying risk factors for various hedge fund strategies in a similar Monte Carlo simulation framework.
13 To ensure that we not only capture short-horizon risks but also properly assess long-term asset return behavior characteristics, we capture the linear interdependencies among multiple time series by working with a vector-autoregressive model.

funds are actively managed investment strategies rather than a true stand-alone asset class. The expected returns are also generally assumed to be net of fees to make them comparable across asset classes.

Asset class-level expected returns are critically important to an asset allocation exercise. Return expectations should be reflective of the current market conditions—including valuations, levels of interest rates, and spreads. Setting return expectations requires a combination of objective facts (e.g., the current yield and spread levels) and judgment (how risk factors and valuation ratios might change from the current levels over the relevant time horizon).

Exhibit 26: Asset Class Expected Returns

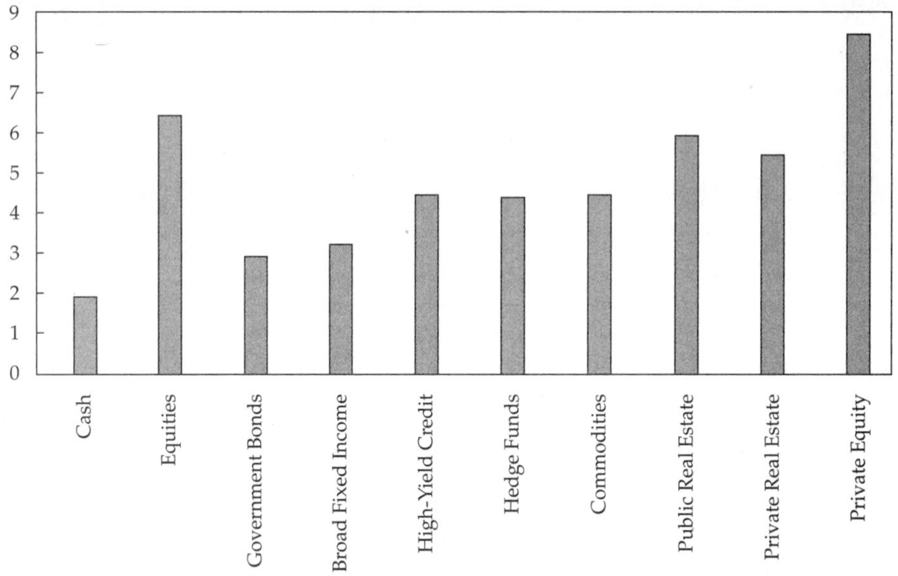

Source: Authors' data.

In this example, we compare three possible portfolios:

- A portfolio 100% invested in government bonds
- A portfolio allocated 50% to global public equities and 50% to broad fixed income
- A diversified "endowment portfolio" allocated 40% to global public equities, 15% to fixed income, 20% to broad hedge funds, 15% to private equity, 5% to private real estate, and 5% to commodities

Exhibit 27 shows the risk and return statistics for the three portfolios. VaR and CVaR downside risk measures focus over the shorter, quarterly, and 1-year time horizons. The worst drawdown and the cumulative annualized total return ranges are expressed over a 10-year time horizon.

Exhibit 27: Portfolio Risk and Return Estimates

	Government Bond Portfolio	50/50 Portfolio	Endowment Portfolio
Expected Geometric Return over 10 Years	2.3%	5.6%	7.0%
Annual Total Return Volatility	4.2%	6.6%	11.2%
95% VaR over Q/Q (quarter over quarter)	−3.1%	−2.9%	−4.6%
95% VaR over 1 Year	−5.2%	−4.2%	−9.1%
95% CVaR over Q/Q	−4.0%	−3.9%	−6.4%
95% CVaR over 1 Year	−6.9%	−6.6%	−13.1%
99% VaR over Q/Q	−4.5%	−4.6%	−7.5%
99% VaR over 1 Year	−7.9%	−8.1%	−15.6%
99% CVaR over Q/Q	−5.2%	−5.5%	−8.7%
99% CVaR over 1 Year	−9.2%	−10.3%	−18.7%
Worst Drawdown over 10 Years	−19.8%	−22.5%	−36.9%

10-Year Return Distribution	Government Bond Portfolio	50/50 Portfolio	Endowment Portfolio
5% Low	0.0%	2.3%	1.9%
25% Low	1.2%	4.2%	4.8%
50% (Median)	2.3%	5.6%	7.0%
75% High	3.1%	7.0%	9.1%
95% High	4.5%	9.0%	12.2%

From Exhibit 27, we see that the multi-asset endowment portfolio generates a significantly higher return than the portfolio exclusively invested in government bonds, albeit at much higher downside risk as measured by VaR, CVaR, or worst drawdown. This table alone, however, is insufficient to determine which investment alternative a particular investor should choose.

Consider the case of a university endowment fund. Let's assume that the investment objective is to support a 5% annual spending rate as well as to preserve the purchasing power of the asset base over the 10-year time horizon. We use the same simulation engine to generate the analytics of Exhibit 28. Here, we plot the expected cumulative total return within a +/− 1 standard deviation range together with the cumulative spending rate, as well as the spending rate augmented with inflation on a cumulative basis. The latter two variables represent the investment target, so we can meaningfully interpret the return potential of the two investment choices in the context of the investment objective. The 50% equities/50% government bond portfolio initially appeared to be a lower risk alternative in Exhibit 27, but Exhibit 28 shows that this choice is more likely to fall short of the return target, given that its median return of 5.6% is less than the nominal return target of approximately 7% (the 5% spending rate plus 2% inflation). At the same time, the endowment portfolio's 7% median return indicates that it would have a better chance of meeting the investment objective.

Exhibit 28: Cumulative Total Return Cones Simulated over a 10-Year Horizon

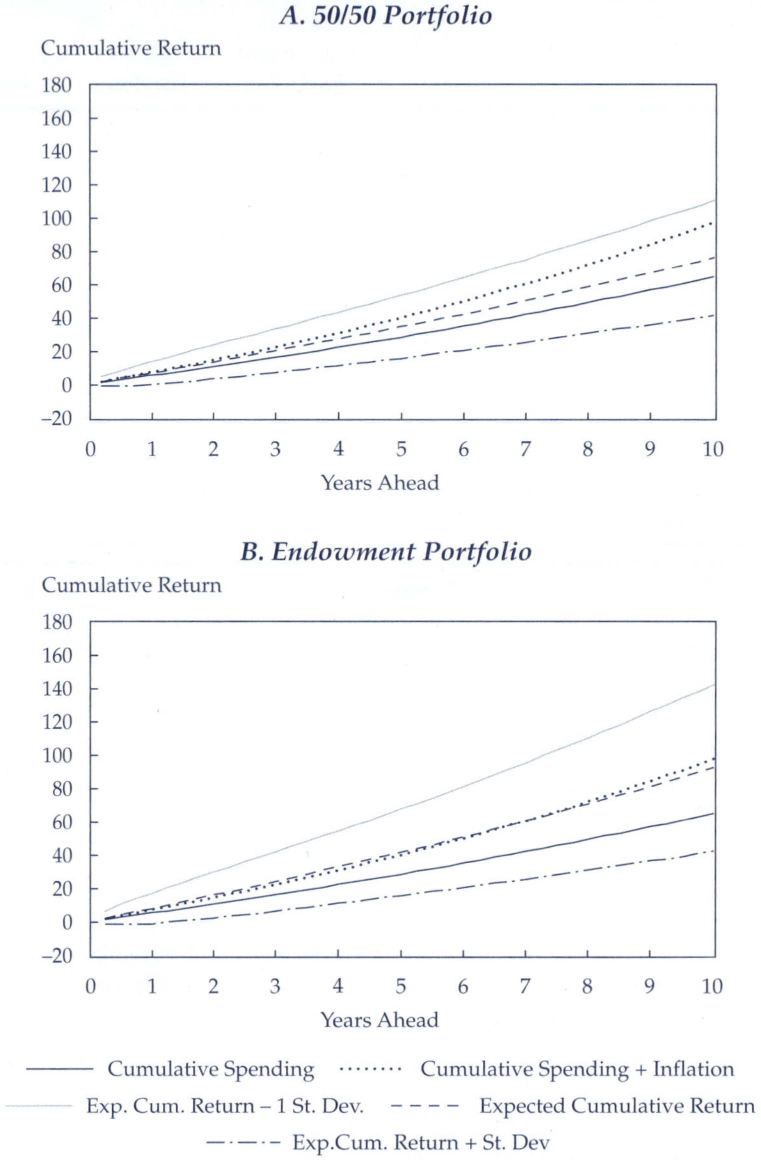

Exhibit 29 shows the probability of meeting the spending rate as well as the spending rate plus inflation at any point in time over the investment horizon. If risk is defined as the probability of falling short of meeting the return target (rather than the asset-only perspective of risk, volatility), the otherwise lower-risk 50% equities and 50% government bond portfolio becomes the higher risk alternative.

Exhibit 29: Estimated Probability of Achieving the Investment Goal

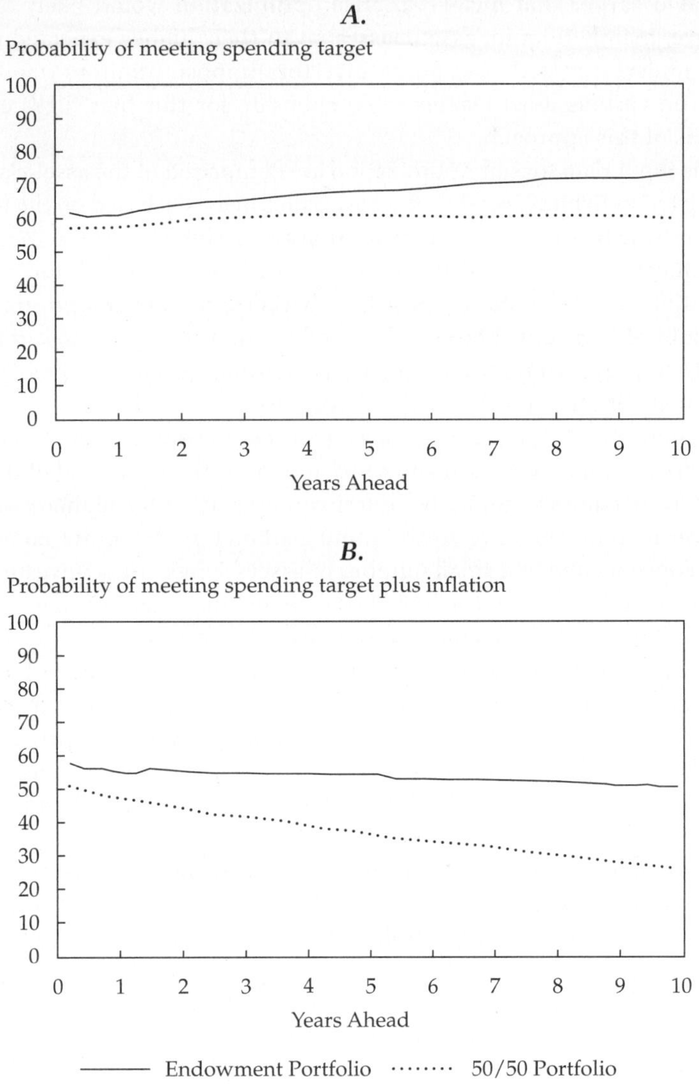

PORTFOLIO OPTIMIZATION

11

☐ discuss approaches to asset allocation to alternative investments

Portfolio optimization for asset allocation has been covered in great detail in earlier readings. Here we focus on some special considerations for optimization in the context of alternative investments.

Mean–Variance Optimization without and with Constraints

We mentioned earlier that mean–variance optimization would likely over-allocate to alternative, mainly illiquid, asset classes given their higher expected returns and potentially underestimated risk. Some investors impose minimum and maximum constraints on various asset classes to compensate for this bias. Let's consider the ramifications of this approach.

Here, the input data for our optimization are comprised of the asset class expected returns depicted in Exhibit 26, while the covariance matrix is based on the unsmoothed asset class return history over the past 20 years. Exhibit 30 shows the optimized portfolio allocations generated by the mean–variance optimization without and with constraints. Each column in these bar charts represents an optimized portfolio allocation subject to a return target. The exhibit progresses from low-return targets on the left to high-return targets on the right. In total, we show 20 possible portfolio allocations first without and then with constraints.

By reviewing Panel B of Exhibit 30, we can see that the unconstrained portfolio allocations are dominated by cash and fixed income at the lower end of the risk spectrum, and private equity becomes the dominant asset class for higher risk portfolios. Optimization is quite sensitive to the input parameters: It's quite common to see allocations concentrated in a small number of asset classes. Thus, investors shouldn't take the unconstrained output as the "best" allocation. Small changes in the input variables could lead to large changes in the asset allocations.

Because investors would potentially reject the raw, concentrated output of unconstrained mean–variance optimization, we also ran a constrained optimization where we capped private equity and hedge fund allocations at 30% each, private real estate at 15%, and major public asset classes at 50% each. The resulting constrained allocations, shown in the Panel A of Exhibit 30, are less concentrated and appear to be more diversified.

Exhibit 31 depicts the mean–variance efficient frontiers corresponding to the optimized portfolio allocations of Exhibit 30. Note that both frontiers contain 20 dots, each representing an optimized portfolio. The numbers under each bar in Exhibit 30 identify the allocation associated with each of the dots on the efficient frontiers in Exhibit 31 (e.g., the allocation associated with portfolio 20 on the efficient frontier in Exhibit 31 is the one shown at the rightmost edge of Exhibit 30).

Exhibit 30: Unconstrained and Constrained Asset Allocations

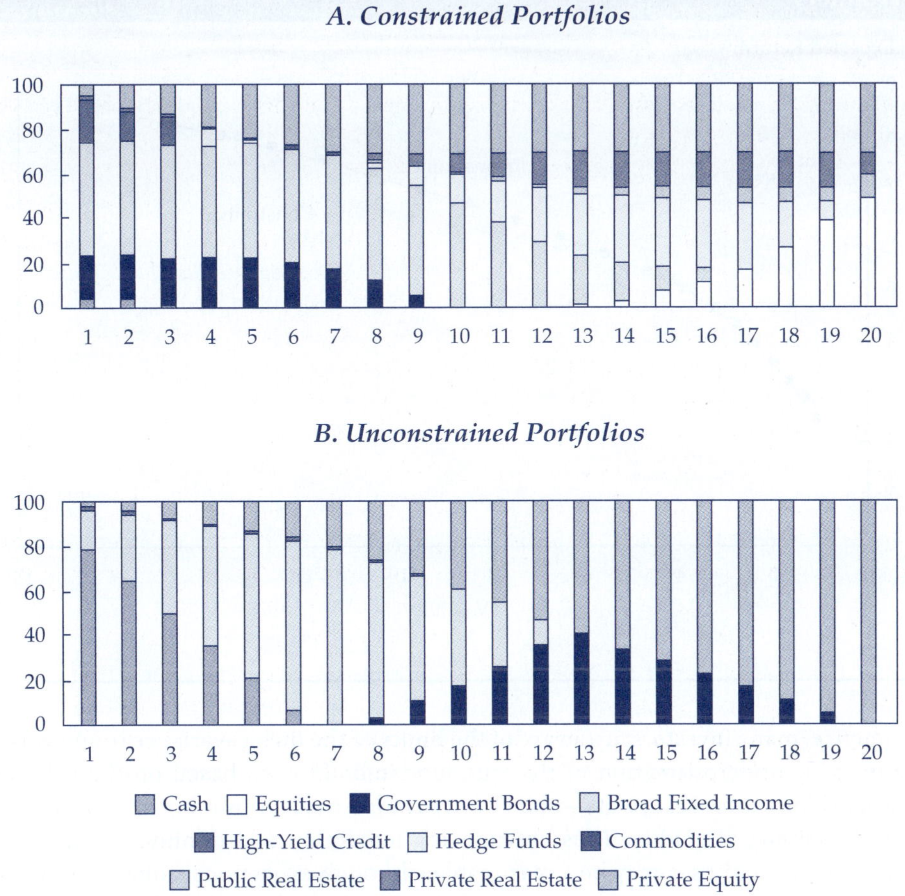

Note that the constrained efficient frontier runs below its unconstrained peer (Exhibit 31). This is not unexpected, as we artificially prohibited the optimization from selecting the most efficient allocation it could get based on the available quantitative data.

Exhibit 31: Unconstrained and Constrained Mean–Variance Efficient Frontiers

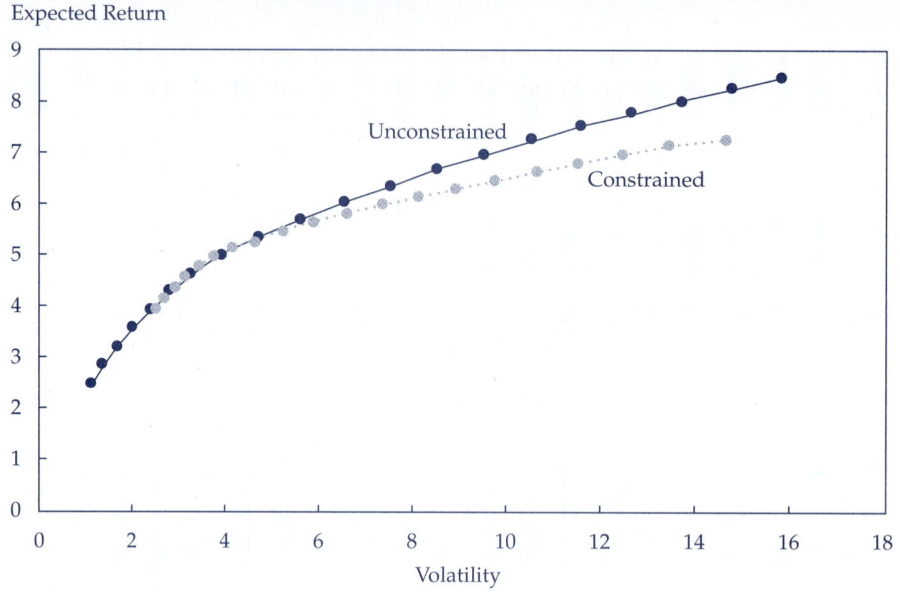

In practice, many investors are aware of the limits of the mean–variance framework—the possible underestimation of the true fundamental risks based on the reported returns of private investments—and they may also have in mind other constraints, such as capping illiquidity. Thus, introducing maximum and minimum constraints for certain asset classes may be a reasonable, although exogenous, adjustment to the quantitative optimization. However, not even constrained optimized allocations should be accepted without further scrutiny. In fact, similar volatility and expected return profiles can be achieved with a wide variety of asset allocations. So, although optimized portfolios may serve as analytical guidance, it's important to validate whether a change to an asset allocation policy results in a significant return increment and/or volatility reduction. Sometimes the results of a constrained optimization are largely driven by the constraints (especially if they are very tight). If that is the case, then the optimizer might not be able to perform its job due to the many (or very tight) constraints applied.

Mean–CVaR Optimization

Portfolio optimization can also improve the asset allocation decision through a risk management lens. An investor who is particularly concerned with the downside risk of a proposed asset allocation may choose to minimize the portfolio's CVaR rather than its volatility relative to a return target.[14] If the portfolio contains asset classes and investment strategies with negative skewness and long tails, the CVaR lens could materially alter the asset allocation decision. Minimizing CVaR subject to an expected return target is quantitatively much more complex than portfolio variance minimization: It requires a large number of historical or simulated return scenarios to properly incorporate potential tail risk into the optimization.[15]

14 Because we are optimizing allocation to asset classes, the CVaR tail risk measure quantifies *systematic* asset class level risks. Individual asset managers or securities may impose additional idiosyncratic risk when the asset allocation is implemented in practice.

15 Technical details are provided by Rockafellar and Uryasev (2000).

Our first illustration is applied to three hedge fund strategies: macro, equity market neutral, and long/short equity hedged. Our expected returns for the three strategies are 3.6%, 3.6%, and 6.0%, respectively. The observed return distribution for macro strategy is fairly normal, while equity market neutral exhibits negative skew and the highest kurtosis of these three strategies (see Exhibit 21).

Panels A and B of Exhibit 32 compare 20 possible portfolio allocations generated by the mean–variance and mean–CVaR optimizations, varying from low to high risk/return profiles. The allocation to long/short equity hedged (the black bar) is similar under both the MVO and CVaR approaches. The macro strategy receives a much higher allocation using the CVaR approach than it does using the MVO approach.

Exhibit 32: Hedge Fund Allocations

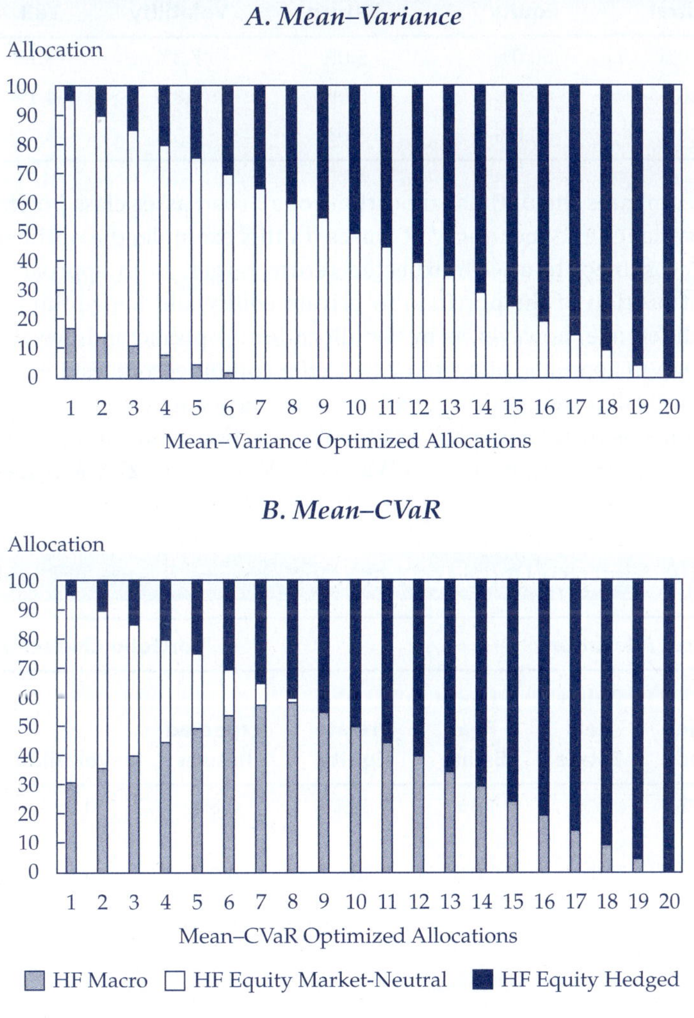

Exhibit 33 compares portfolio #12 from the mean–variance efficient frontier to portfolio #12 from the mean–CVaR efficient frontier. Both portfolios allocated 60% to the long/short equity strategy. Under the CVaR-optimization approach, the remaining 40% of the portfolio is invested in global macro. Under the MVO approach, the remaining 40% of the portfolio is invested in equity market-neutral.

Let's compare the portfolio volatilities and downside risk measures. The mean–CVaR portfolio has higher volatility (7.8% vs 7.3%) but lower tail risk (–6.8% vs –7.7%). Exhibit 33 also shows a third portfolio, which evenly *splits* the 40% not allocated to equity-hedged between global macro and equity market neutral. The volatility of this portfolio lies between the two optimal portfolios. Although nominally more diversified than either of the #12 portfolios from the optimization, its CVaR is worse than that of the mean–CVaR optimized portfolio (but still better than that of the MVO portfolio). An investor may have qualitative considerations that warrant including this more-diversified portfolio among the options to be evaluated.

Exhibit 33: Mean–Variance and Mean–CVaR Efficient Hedge Fund Allocations

	Asset Allocation			Portfolio Characteristics			
	Macro	Equity Market Neutral	Long/Short Equity	Expected Return	Volatility	95% VaR	95% CVaR
Mean–Variance Optimal	0.0%	40.0%	60.0%	5.0%	7.3%	–3.7%	–7.7%
Mean–CVaR Optimal	40.0%	0.0%	60.0%	5.0%	7.8%	–4.1%	–6.8%
Combination	20.0%	20.0%	60.0%	5.0%	7.5%	–3.7%	–7.3%

Exhibit 34 compares the optimal allocations of a broad asset class portfolio through the mean–variance and mean–CVaR lenses. In this example, the optimal allocations were selected subject to a 6.8% expected return target. Both approaches allocated a significant portion of the portfolio to private equity and hedge funds (30% each). A notable difference, however, is in the allocation to public and private real estate. Where the MVO approach allocated 22% to the combined real estate categories, the CVaR approach allocated nothing at all to either real estate category. We can identify the reason for this by referring back to Exhibit 21: The public and private real estate categories are characterized by 99% CVaRs of –40.2% and –27.9%, respectively.

Exhibit 34: Mean–Variance and Mean–CVaR Efficient Multi-Asset Portfolios

	Asset Allocation						Portfolio Characteristics		
	Equities	Govt Bonds	Hedge Funds	Public Real Estate	Private Real Estate	Private Equity	Expected Return	Volatility	99% CVaR
Mean–Variance Optimal	18%	0%	30%	7%	15%	30%	6.8%	11.5%	–20.7%
Mean–CVaR Optimal	34%	6%	30%	0%	0%	30%	6.8%	12.1%	–15.6%

EXAMPLE 6

Asset Allocation Recommendation

The CIO (chief investment officer) of the International University Endowment Fund (the Fund) is preparing for the upcoming investment committee (IC) meeting. The Fund's annual asset allocation review is on the agenda, and the CIO plans to propose a new strategic asset allocation for the Fund. Subject to prudent risk-taking, the recommended asset allocation should offer

- the highest expected return and

- the highest probability of achieving the long-term 5% real return target.

The inflation assumption is 2%.

In addition, the risk in the Fund is one factor that is considered when lenders assign a risk rating to the university. The university's primary lender has proposed a loan covenant that would trigger a re-evaluation of the university's creditworthiness if the Fund incurs a loss greater than 20% over any 1-year period.

The investment staff produced the following tables to help the CIO prepare for the meeting.

	Asset Allocation						
Alternative	Cash	Public Equity	Govt	Credit	Hedge Fund	Real Estate	Private Equity
A	5.0%	60.0%	30.0%	5.0%	0.0%	0.0%	0.0%
B	4.0%	50.0%	16.0%	5.0%	10.0%	5.0%	10.0%
C	2.0%	40.0%	8.0%	5.0%	18.0%	7.0%	20.0%
D	1.0%	30.0%	5.0%	4.0%	20.0%	10.0%	30.0%
E	2.0%	40.0%	3.0%	3.0%	15.0%	7.0%	30.0%
F	2.0%	50.0%	3.0%	0.0%	10.0%	5.0%	30.0%
G	1.0%	56.0%	3.0%	0.0%	10.0%	0.0%	30.0%

Portfolio Characteristics					10-Year Horizon:			
Alternative	Expected Return	Volatility	1-Year 99% VaR	1-Year 99% CVaR	5th Percentile Return	95th Percentile Return	Probability of Meeting 5% Real Return	Probability of Purchasing Power Impairment
A	6.0%	9.0%	−12.4%	−15.0%	1.6%	10.5%	37.0%	7.1%
B	6.7%	10.3%	−14.6%	−17.3%	2.0%	11.4%	46.1%	4.3%
C	7.1%	11.1%	−15.8%	−18.8%	2.2%	12.2%	52.1%	3.2%
D	7.4%	11.5%	−16.3%	−19.4%	2.4%	12.6%	56.1%	2.5%
E	7.7%	12.3%	−17.4%	−20.6%	2.4%	13.2%	58.8%	2.8%
F	7.8%	13.0%	−18.5%	−21.8%	2.2%	13.7%	60.8%	3.6%
G	7.9%	13.5%	−19.3%	−22.7%	2.1%	14.1%	61.0%	4.0%

Notes:

- 1-year horizon 99% VaR: the lowest return over any 1-year period at a 99% confidence level (i.e., only a 1% chance to experience a total return below this threshold).
- 1-year horizon 99% CVaR: the expected return if the return falls below the 99% VaR threshold.
- 5th and 95th percentile annualized returns over a 10-year time horizon: a 90% chance that the annualized 10-year total return will fall between these two figures

- probability of purchasing power impairment[16]: as defined by the IC, the probability of losing 40% of the endowment's purchasing power over 10 years after taking gifts to the endowment, spending from the endowment, and total return into account.

1. Which asset allocation is *most likely* to meet the committee's objective and constraints?

Solution:

Portfolio D. Portfolios E, F, and G have 1-year, 99% CVaRs, which, if realized, would trigger the loan covenant. Portfolio D has the next highest probability of meeting the 5% real return target and the lowest probability of purchasing power impairment. Portfolios A, B, and C have lower probabilities of meeting the return targets and higher probabilities of purchasing power impairment.

12 RISK FACTOR-BASED OPTIMIZATION

Increasingly, investors believe that viewing investment decisions through a risk factor lens (e.g., growth, inflation, credit risk) may improve the investment process. Separating fundamentally similar investments, like public and private equities, into distinct asset classes ignores the probability that both are exposed to the same risk factors. In this section, we will work through an asset allocation example using a risk factor lens.

Let's assume that an investor starts the asset allocation exercise by first allocating the overall risk budget across the main risk factors.[17] Instead of setting expectations for distinct asset classes, she may start thinking about the return expectations and correlation of the fundamental risk factors. Exhibit 35 shows her return expectations for the risk factors described in Exhibit 14. In this illustration, the global equity risk factor (a practical proxy for macroeconomic-oriented "growth") is expected to generate the highest return. She expects the duration and value factors to generate negative returns because stronger economic growth fueled by advances in technology would lead to rising rates and better returns for growth stocks. She is concerned about rising inflation, so she has assigned a positive expected return to the inflation factor.

16 Similar measures of risk are proposed by Swensen (2009) in the context of endowment funds.

17 Approaches to asset allocation and portfolio construction are expanding as the understanding of risk factors is increasing. A risk parity approach to asset allocation, for example, would allocate total risk in equal portion to the selected risk factors.

Exhibit 35: Expected Factor Returns

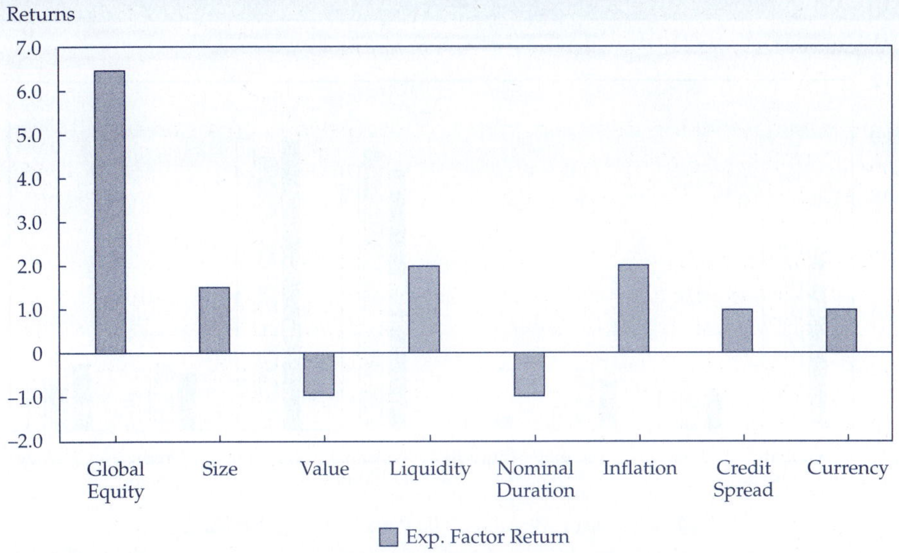

Using these returns and the historical factor volatilities and correlations, we can optimize the risk factor exposure by minimizing factor-implied risk subject to a total return target of 6.5%. The black bars in Exhibit 36 show these optimal factor exposures. Note that the target exposures of the value and nominal duration factors are positive, although the associated expected factor returns are negative. The model allocates to these factors for their diversification potential because they are negatively correlated with other risk factors. Duration and equity factors have a correlation of −0.6, whereas value and equity factors have a correlation of −0.3 based on the data used for this illustration.

We have established optimal risk factor exposures, so now we must implement this target using actual investments. Some investors may have access to only public market investments, while other investors may also have access to private illiquid investments. The gray and white bars in Exhibit 36 illustrate the two possible implementations of the target factor exposures. Portfolio 1 assumes the investor is limited to public market investments. Portfolio 2 uses both public market investments and private, illiquid investments. The portfolio allocation details are displayed in Exhibit 37.

Exhibit 36: Optimal Risk Factor Allocations and Associated Asset Class Portfolios

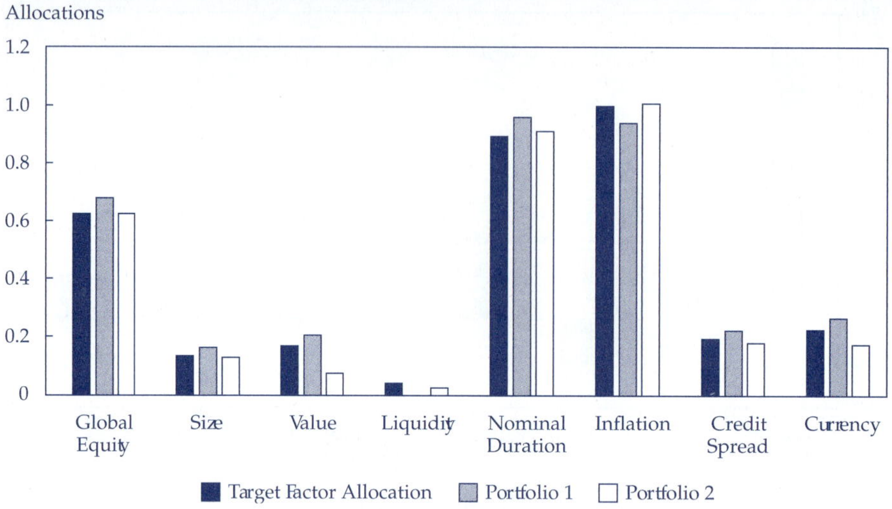

Exhibit 37: Asset Class Portfolios Designed Based on Optimal Risk Factor Allocations

	Portfolio 1	Portfolio 2
Domestic Equities; *Value Tilt*	21.0%	13.0%
Non-Domestic Developed Market Equities; *Value Tilt*	21.0%	13.0%
Foreign Emerging Market Equities	21.0%	12.0%
Government Bonds	0.0%	5.0%
Broad Fixed Income	10.0%	0.0%
High-Yield Credit	2.0%	3.0%
Inflation-Linked Bonds	7.0%	0.0%
Hedge Funds	15.0%	10.0%
Commodities	3.0%	4.0%
Public Real Estate	0.0%	12.0%
Private Real Estate	0.0%	13.0%
Private Equity	0.0%	15.0%
Total	**100.0%**	**100.0%**
Expected Return	6.2%	6.9%
Volatility	13.5%	13.2%

Even though they have similar factor exposures, you can see some significant differences in the asset class allocations of the two portfolios. Portfolio 1 allocates 63% to public equities, whereas Portfolio 2 allocates 35% to public equities plus 15% to private equity for its higher return potential. Portfolio 1 allocates 18% to alternatives (15% in hedge funds and 3% in commodities, two of the most liquid alternative asset classes), while Portfolio 2 has allocated 54% to alternatives (10% hedge funds, 4% commodities, 12% public real estate, 13% private real estate, and 15% private equity). Portfolio 1 achieves its inflation sensitivity by allocating to inflation-linked bonds and commodities. Portfolio 2 achieves its desired exposure to the inflation factor through a combined allocation to real estate and commodities. The volatility of the two portfolios is similar, but Portfolio 2 is able to achieve a higher expected return given its ability to allocate to private equity.

Although a risk factor-driven approach is conceptually very elegant, we must mention a few caveats:

- While generally accepted asset class definitions provide a common language among the investment community, risk factors may be defined quite differently investor-to-investor. It's important to establish a common understanding of factor definitions and factor return expectations among the parties to an asset allocation exercise. This includes an agreement as to what financial instruments can be used to best match the factor exposures if they are not directly investable.
- Correlations among risk factors, just like correlations across asset classes, may dramatically shift under changing market conditions; thus, careful testing needs to be applied to understand how changing market conditions will affect the asset allocation.
- Some factor sensitivities are stable (like the nominal interest rate sensitivity of government bonds), while others are very unstable (like the inflation sensitivity of commodities). Factor sensitivities also need to be very carefully tested to validate whether the invested portfolio would truly deliver the desired factor exposures and not deliver unintended factor returns.

EXAMPLE 7

Selecting an Asset Allocation Approach

1. You have a new client who has unexpectedly inherited a substantial sum of money. The client is in his early 30s and newly married. He has no children and no other investible assets. What asset allocation approach is most suitable for this client?

Solution:

Mean–variance optimization with Monte Carlo simulation is most appropriate for this client. He has limited investment expertise, so your first responsibility is to educate him with respect to such basic investment concepts as risk, return, and diversification. A simple MVO approach supplemented with Monte Carlo simulation to illustrate potential upside and downside of an asset allocation choice is mostly likely to serve the asset allocation and investment education needs.

2. Your client is a tax-exempt foundation that recently received a bequest doubling its assets to €200 million. There is an outside investment adviser but no dedicated investment staff; however, the six members of the investment committee (IC) are all wealthy, sophisticated investors in their own right. The IC conducts an asset allocation study every three years and reviews the asset allocation at its annual meeting. The current asset allocation is 30% equities, 20% fixed income, 25% private equity, and 25% real estate. Three percent of assets are paid out annually in grants; this expenditure is covered by an annuity purchased some years ago. The foundation's primary investment objective is to maximize returns subject to a maximum level of

volatility. A secondary consideration is the desire to avoid a permanent loss of capital. What asset allocation approach is most suitable for this client?

Solution:

Given the sophistication and investment objectives of the IC members, using a mean–CVaR optimization approach is appropriate to determine the asset allocation. This client has a more sophisticated understanding of risk and will appreciate the more nuanced view of risk offered by mean–CVaR optimization. Given the portfolio's exposure to alternative investments, the asset allocation decision will be enhanced by the more detailed picture of left-tail risk offered by CVaR optimization (the risk of permanent loss) relative to mean–variance optimization. The lack of permanent staff and a once-per-year meeting schedule suggest that a risk factor-based approach may not be appropriate.

13 LIQUIDITY PLANNING

☐ discuss the importance of liquidity planning in allocating to alternative investments

Earlier, we addressed various aspects of liquidity associated with investing in alternative asset classes. In this section, we focus on multi-year horizon liquidity planning for private investments.

When managing portfolios that contain allocations to alternative investments, managing liquidity risk takes on critical importance. We need to ensure sufficient liquidity to meet interim obligations or goals, which might include:

- periodic payments to beneficiaries (e.g., a pension fund's retirement benefit payments or an endowment fund's distributions to support operating expenses);
- portfolio rebalancing or funding new asset manager mandates; or
- fulfilling a commitment made to a private investment fund when the general partner makes the capital call.

Alternative investments pose unique liquidity challenges that must be explicitly addressed before committing to an alternative investment program. Private investments—including private equity, private real estate, private real assets, and private credit—represent the most illiquid components of an investment portfolio. Private investments usually require a long-term commitment over an 8- to 15-year time horizon. An investor contributes capital over the first few years (the investment period) and receives distributions in the later years. Combined with the call down (or drawdown) structure of a private investment fund, this creates a need to model a hypothetical path to achieving and maintaining a diversified, fully-invested allocation to private investments. Here we will explore the challenges with private investment liquidity planning with three primary considerations:

1. How to achieve and maintain the desired allocation.
2. How to handle capital calls.
3. How to plan for the unexpected.

Achieving and Maintaining the Strategic Asset Allocation

Strategic planning is required to determine the necessary annual commitments an investor should make to reach and maintain the long-term target asset allocation. Large private investors often use a liquidity forecasting model for their private investment programs. Here, we illustrate one such model based on work published by Takahashi and Alexander (2001). We also discuss private investment commitment pacing as an application of this model. This model is only one possible way to forecast private investment cash flows; investors may develop their own model using their own assumptions and experience.

We will illustrate this model with a hypothetical capital commitment (CC) of £100 million to a fund with a contractual term (L) of 12 years.

We begin by modeling the capital contributions (C) to the fund. Certain assumptions must be made regarding the rate of contribution (RC). We'll assume that 25% is contributed in the first year and that 50% of the remaining commitments are contributed in each of the subsequent years:

Year 1: £100 million × 25% = £25 million

Year 2: (£100 million − £25 million) × 50% = £37.5 million

Year 3: (£100 million − £25 million − £37.5 million) × 50% = £18.75 million

and so on.

The capital contribution (C) in year *t* can be expressed with the following formula:

$$C_t = RC_t \times (CC - PIC_t) \quad (1)$$

where PIC denotes the already paid-in capital.

Alternatively, we can express this in words:

Capital Contribution

= Rate of Contribution × (Capital Commitment − Paid-in-Capital)

In practice, the investment period is often limited to a defined number of years; also, not all of the committed capital may be called.

The next step is to estimate the periodic distribution paid to investors. Distributions (D) are a function of the net asset value (NAV). From one year to the next, the NAV rises as additional capital contributions are made and as underlying investments appreciate. NAV declines as distributions are made (or as assets are written down).

If the partnership investment develops as anticipated, then the fund's IRR would be equal to this rate.

To estimate the expected annual distribution payments, we need to make an assumption about the pattern of distributions. For example, an analyst may assume that the fund does not distribute any money in Year 1 or Year 2 but distributes 10% of the prevailing net asset value in Year 3, 20% in Year 4, 30% in Year 5, and 50% of the remaining balance in each of the remaining years. In the case of real estate funds, it is also possible that there is a pre-defined minimum annual distribution rate (called the "yield"). Once the annual rates of distribution are determined, the annual amount distributed is calculated by the following formula:

$$D_t = RD_t[NAV_{t-1} \times (1 + G)] \quad (2)$$

where

$$RD_t = (t/L)^B, \quad (3)$$

$$NAV_t = [NAV_{t-1} \times (1 + G)] + C_t - D_t \quad (4)$$

Again, in words:

Distributions at time t

= Rate of Distribution at time t × [NAV at time t-1 × (1 + Growth Rate)], and

NAV at time t

= prior NAV × (1 + Growth Rate) + Capital Contribution – Distributions

In Exhibit 38, we display the forecasted annual capital contributions, outstanding commitment forecast, distributions, NAV, and cumulative net cash flow for a private investment fund with a 12-year life. We assume that 25% of the committed capital is contributed in the first year and that 50% of the remaining commitments are contributed in each of the subsequent years. Using a bow (B) parameter of 2.5, we set the RD_t distribution rates such that the yearly distribution rates would increase fairly gradually. We assume a 13% growth rate from the investments in this fund.

Exhibit 38: Expected Annual Contribution, Outstanding Commitment, Rate of Distribution, Annual Distribution, NAV, and Net Cash Flow of a Hypothetical Private Investment Fund

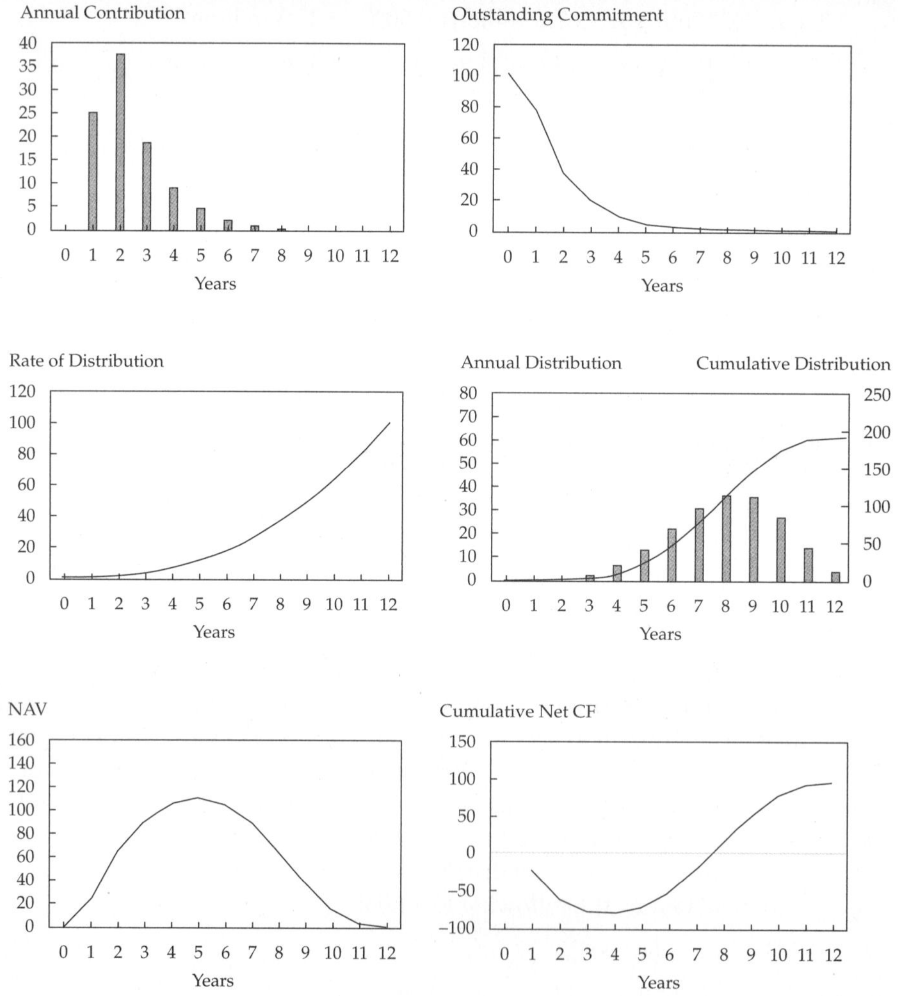

The corresponding annual RD_t rates are displayed in Exhibit 39.

Exhibit 39: Assumed Annual Distribution Rates (RD_t)

Year	1	2	3	4	5	6	7	8	9	10	11	12
Rate of Distribution	0%	1%	3%	6%	11%	18%	26%	36%	49%	63%	80%	100%

How does the shape of the expected rate of distribution influence NAV and the annual distribution amounts? For illustration purposes we can change our assumption of RD by setting the bow parameter (B) to 5.0, such that early year distribution rates are very low and start increasing in the second half of the fund's life. The new distribution rates are shown in Exhibit 40, and Exhibit 41 shows how distributions and the NAV would react to this change.

Exhibit 40: Alternative Assumed Annual Distribution Rates (RD_t)

Year	1	2	3	4	5	6	7	8	9	10	11	12
Rate of Distribution	0%	0%	0%	0%	1%	3%	7%	13%	24%	40%	65%	100%

Exhibit 41: Rate of Distribution, Expected Annual Distribution, NAV, and Cumulative Net Cash Flow with Back-Loaded Distributions

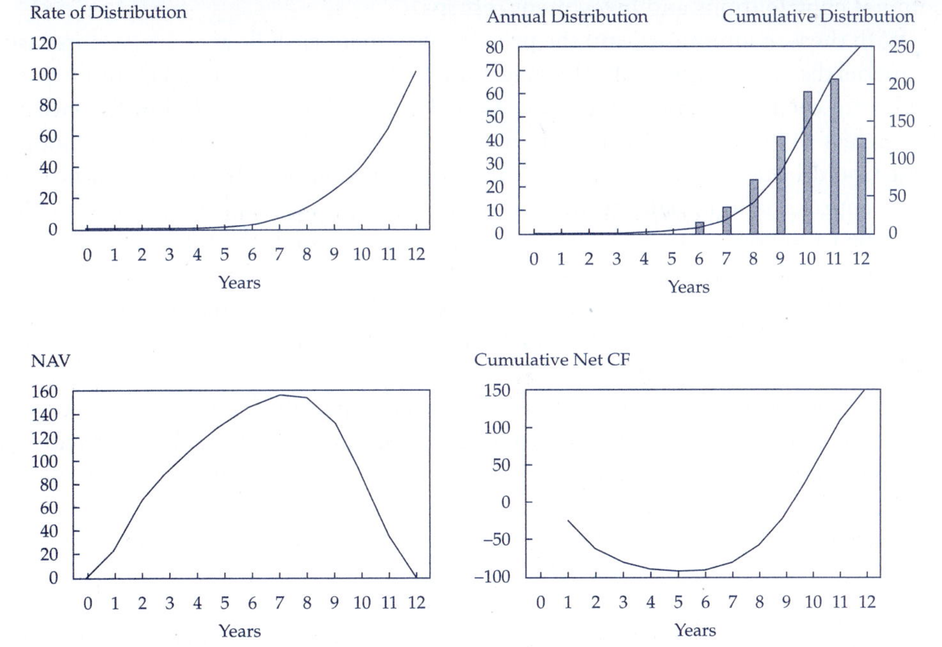

Although the annual capital contributions would not be affected, we can see that the lower distribution rate in the early years allows the NAV to grow higher. The cumulative net cash flow, however, would stay in the negative zone for a longer time.

EXAMPLE 8

Liquidity Planning for Private Investments

1. The NAV of an investor's share in a private renewable energy fund was €30 million at the end of 2020. All capital has been called. The investor expects a 20% distribution to be paid at the end of 2021. The expected growth rate is 12%. What is the expected NAV at year-end 2022?

Solution:

The expected NAV at year-end 2022 is €30,105,600. The expected distribution at the end of 2021 is €6.72 million [(€30 million x 1.12) x 20%]. The NAV at year-end 2022 is therefore (€30 million x 1.12) x (1 – 0.20) x 1.12 = €30,105,600.

An important practical application of such models is to help determine the size of the annual commitment an investor needs to make to reach the target allocation of an asset class over the coming years (i.e., investment commitment pacing).

Assume that we manage an investment portfolio of £1 billion and that our strategic asset allocation target for private equities is 20%. We currently do not have any private equity investment in the portfolio. We also must project the growth of the aggregate investment portfolio, because we want to achieve the 20% allocation based on the expected *future* value of the portfolio and of the private equity investment, not today's value. We assume an aggregate portfolio growth rate of 6% per year, including both net contributions and investment returns.

With these assumptions, and the private investment cash flow and NAV forecasting model discussed previously, the investor can determine the annual commitments needed to reach the overall target allocation. By using the same cash flow forecasting parameters as for the analysis in Exhibit 38, we can see that a £100 million commitment would lead the NAV to peak at around £110 million five years from now. A rough approximation could be the following: In five years, the total portfolio size would be £1 billion $\times$ $1.06^5 \approx$ £1.338 billion; so, at that point, the total private equity NAV should be approximately 20% $\times$ £1.338 billion=£268 million. Since we know that a £100 million commitment would lead to an NAV of £110 million in five years, we can extrapolate to arrive at the conclusion that a £243 million commitment today could achieve the goal.

However, this would result in a very concentrated private equity investment, with an NAV peaking in four to five years and then declining over the following years as distributions are made. A better practice is to spread commitments out over multiple years. A stable and disciplined multi-year commitment schedule leads to a more stable NAV size over time. It also achieves an important objective of diversifying exposure across vintage years. Thus, an investor can choose to commit a target amount of around £70 million per year over a period of four years (2017 through 2020) instead of concentrating the commitment in a single year. This schedule would bring the total private equity NAV to the target 20% level over five years. In Exhibit 42, we illustrate how the portfolio of private equity investments of different vintage years would build up over time. We also show how the total NAV would evolve beyond 2022 if no further capital commitment is made. As the chart suggests, the NAV would continue to grow through 2023 but would start to decline in later years as the 2017–2020 vintage private funds make distributions.

Exhibit 42: Commitment Pacing: Cumulative NAV of Private Equity Investments

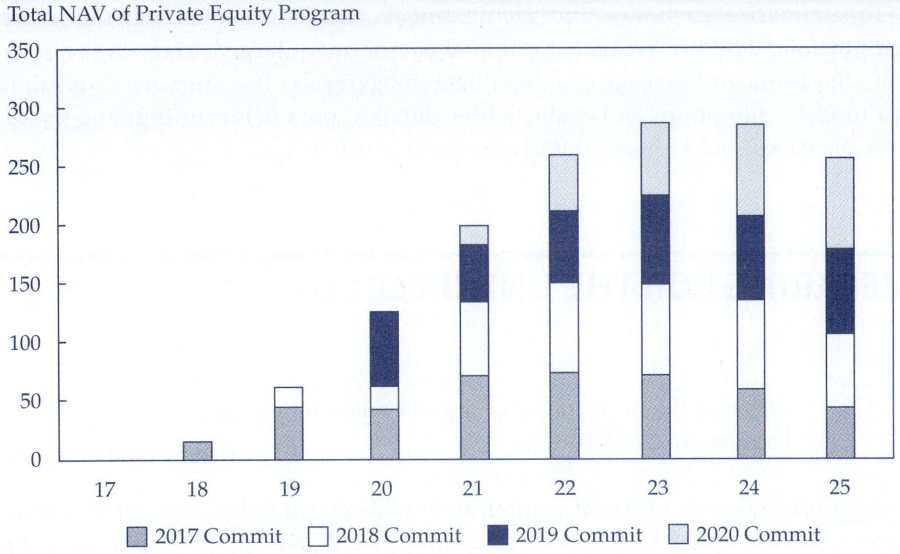

In Exhibit 43, we show how private equity investments would grow as a proportion of the overall investment portfolio. As in the previous chart, we extend the forecast beyond 2022 to show the proportion of private equity investments will start to decline without further capital commitments after 2020.

Exhibit 43: Commitment Pacing: Private Equity NAV as % of the Total Portfolio

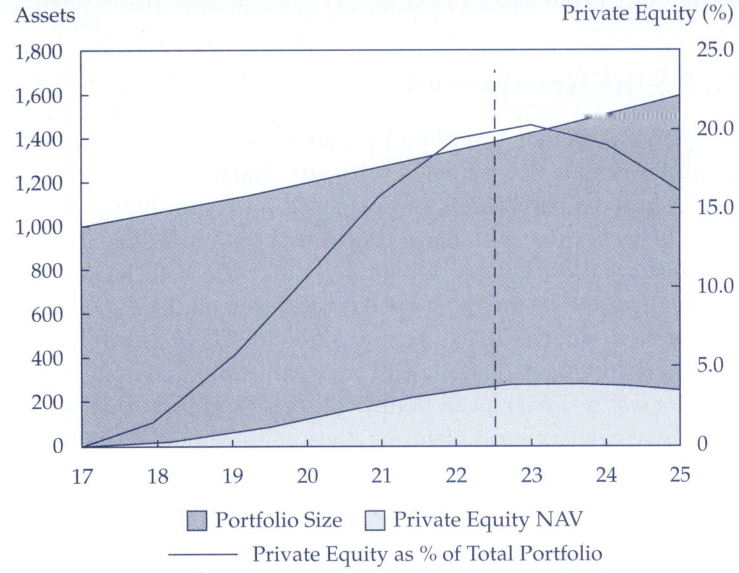

The investor must review her pacing model forecast periodically, updating it as needed based on the actual commitments and transactions that have occurred and refreshing the assumptions for the future. If the investor plans to maintain a 20% allocation to private equity investments over the long run, she will clearly have to make ongoing commitments in the future, although at a slower pace once private equity is an established asset class in the portfolio.

To summarize, cash flow and pacing models enable investors to better manage their portfolio liquidity, set realistic annual commitment targets to reach the desired asset allocation, and manage portfolio beta in aggregate. Investors need to validate their model assumptions and evaluate how different parameter settings and liquidity stress scenarios could impact their investment portfolios.

14 PREPARING FOR THE UNEXPECTED

☐ discuss the importance of liquidity planning in allocating to alternative investments

The investor makes an up-front commitment of a certain dollar amount to a private investment fund, and the funds will typically be called (paid in) over a period of three to four years. In many cases, the general partner (GP) will never call the full amount of the capital commitment. The limited partner (LP) is obligated to pay the capital call in accordance with the terms agreed to with the GP, often within 30 days of receiving the call notification. However, it is not practical to keep all the committed (but not yet called) capital in liquid reserves given the opportunity cost of being out of the markets during the investment phase. Investors must develop a strategy for maintaining the asset allocation while waiting for the fund to become fully invested. Capital pending investment in a private equity fund is often invested in public equities as a proxy for private equities. A similar approach may be followed in the case of other private asset classes: The investor may consider high yield as a placeholder for pending private credit investments, REITs as a placeholder for private real estate investments, and energy stocks or commodity futures as a proxy for private real asset investments.

Preparing for the Unexpected

The liquidity-planning model described here addresses the key components of cash inflows and outflows, but the model results are clearly heavily dependent on the assumptions. The model parameters can be based purely on judgment, but a better practice would be to verify estimates and forecasts with a sample of representative private funds' historical experience. Obviously, the realized cash flows in the future are likely to differ from what the model predicted based on the assumed parameters. Thus, it is advisable to run the analysis using different sets of assumptions and under different scenarios. In a bear market, GPs may call capital at a higher pace and/or make distributions at a slower pace than had been expected. This suggests that in addition to the base case scenario planning, the analyst should develop an additional set of assumptions with faster capital calls and lower distribution rates.

If the fund is scheduled to begin liquidation when the investor's public market portfolio is performing poorly (as it did in the 2007–2008 period), it is likely that the GP will exercise his option to extend the fund life. If this happens, investors may find themselves with an asset allocation significantly different from target or being unable to meet the capital calls that were intended to be funded from the distributions. These contingencies should be modeled as part of stress testing the asset allocation.

EXAMPLE 9

Private Investments, Asset Allocation, and Liquidity Planning

The Endowment Fund of the University of Guitan (the Fund) has $750 million in assets. The investment committee (IC) adopted the following strategic asset allocation four years ago. Private investments are at the lower end of the permitted range. To reach the target allocation among private investments, the investment team has made several new commitments recently, and they expect capital calls over the coming year equal to approximately about 20% of the current private asset net asset value.

	Strategic Asset Allocation Target	Permitted Range	Current Asset Allocation (%)	Current Asset Allocation ($mil)
Cash	2%	0 to 5%	3%	22.5
Public Equities (including long/short equity)	35%	30 to 40%	35%	262.5
Government Bonds	5%	4 to 10%	7%	52.5
High-Yield Credit	3%	2 to 5%	5%	37.5
Hedge Funds (excluding long/short equity)	20%	17 to 23%	23%	172.5
Private Real Estate	10%	7 to 13%	8%	60.0
Private Real Assets	5%	3 to 7%	4%	30.0
Private Equity	20%	15 to 22%	15%	112.5
Total				$750 mil
Expected Return	7.1%			
Expected Volatility	11.1%			
99% CVaR	−18.8%			
Assumed Inflation Rate	2%			

The strategic asset allocation has a 52% probability of meeting the 5% real return target (4% spend rate, 1% principal growth, and 2% inflation).

At its last meeting, the endowment committee of the board approved a temporary increase in the spending rate, raising it from 4% to 5% for the next five years to support the university's efforts to reposition itself in the face of declining enrollments. The spending rate is calculated as a percentage of the Fund's trailing 5-year average value.

The CIO (chief investment officer) has produced a capital market outlook that will guide the fund's tactical asset allocation strategy for the next several quarters. Key elements of the outlook are:

- accommodative central bank policies are ending;
- equity valuation metrics have recently set new highs;
- the economic cycle is at or near its peak (i.e., there is a meaningful probability of rising inflation and a weaker economic environment over the next several quarters); and
- returns will quite likely be lower than what has been experienced over the past five years.

She also developed the following stress scenario based on her capital market outlook:

Return Stress Scenario	
Cash	2%
Public Equities (including l/s equity)	−30%
Government Bonds	−3%
High-Yield Credit	−10%
Hedge Funds (excluding l/s equity)	−8%
Private Real Estate	0%
Private Real Assets	10%
Private Equity	−10%

1. Identify and discuss the liquidity factors that the CIO should consider as she develops her portfolio positioning strategy for the next 12 to 24 months.

Solution:

- Given the market outlook, it is reasonable to assume cash flows into the fund from existing private investments will be negligible.
- The fund has next-12-month liabilities as follows:
  - Approximately \$37.5 million to the university (\$750 million x 5%). This is a high (conservative) estimate based on an assumption that the trailing 5-year average Fund value is less than the current \$750 million.
  - Approximately \$40.5 million in capital calls from private investment commitments (equally allocated across private real estate, private real assets, and private equity

  [(\$60m + \$30m + \$112.5m) × 20%]

  - Total liabilities next 12 months = \$78 million
- Sources of immediate liquidity:
  - Cash = \$22.5 million
  - Government bonds are at the midpoint of the permitted range. The allocation could be reduced from 7% to 4% and remain within the permitted range. This would free up \$22.5 million (\$750 million x 3%) of immediate liquidity. However, if the return scenario is realized (government bonds down 3%), then the government bond allocation will fall below the 4% minimum and additional rebalancing will be required.
  - \$75.0 million in total (less than the \$78 million liability)
- Other liquidity:
  - Public equities are at the midpoint of the permitted range. The allocation could be reduced from 35% to 30% and remain within the permitted range. This would free up \$37.5 million (\$750 million x 5%) for reinvestment in more-defensive asset classes or to meet anticipated liquidity needs. However, if the return scenario is realized (equities down 30%), then the equity allocation will fall below the 30% minimum and additional rebalancing will be required.

- High-yield credit is at the upper end of the allowed range. The allocation could be reduced from the current 5% to 2% or 3%, freeing up an additional $15 to $22.5 million. The limited liquidity in high-yield bond markets may make this challenging.
- The hedge fund allocation is at the upper end of the allowed range. The allocation could be reduced from the current 23% to something in the range of 17% to 20% (between the lower end of the band and the target allocation). However, given the required redemption notice (generally 60 to 90 days in advance of the redemption date), if the market weakens the hedge funds might invoke any gates allowed for in their documents.

- Longer term, a temporary increase in the spending rate reduces the probability that the fund will meet its real return target. This objective would be further threatened if the inflation rate does rise as the CIO fears. The liquidity profile of the Fund's investments should prepare for the possibility that, in a bad year, they may be called upon to dip into capital to fund the spending obligation.

2. Recommend and justify a tactical asset allocation strategy for the Fund.

Solution:

- The Fund should target the upper end of the ranges for cash and government bonds in light of the current high equity valuations, weakening economic outlook, and threat of rising inflation. Given rising inflation and interest rate concerns, she may also consider shortening the duration of the government bond portfolio.
- The higher cash and bond allocation will also provide the liquidity buffer needed to meet the Fund's liabilities. Additional cash might be justified to fund the known payouts.
- A high allocation to real estate could also be considered a defensive positioning, but the current 8% allocation may rise toward its 13% maximum, even without additional allocations, given the expected decline in the balance of the portfolio. In addition, tactical tilts in private asset classes are difficult to implement because it would take an extended time period to make new commitments and invest the additional capital.
- The allocations to public equites and hedge funds could be reduced to fund the increases in cash and government bonds.

The following table summarizes the proposed allocation and looks at the likely end-of-year allocations if events unfold as forecast.

	Allowed Ranges			Proposed Allocation			Allocation 12 Months Forward	
	Lower Limit	Upper Limit	Current Allocation	%	$ (mil)	Expected Return Next 12 Months	%	$ (mil)
Cash	0%	5%	3%	10%	75	2%		0*
Public Equities	30%	40%	35%	30%	225	−30%	25%	157.50
Government Bonds	4%	10%	7%	10%	75	−3%	12%	72.75

	Allowed Ranges			Proposed Allocation			Allocation 12 Months Forward	
	Lower Limit	Upper Limit	Current Allocation	%	$ (mil)	Expected Return Next 12 Months	%	$ (mil)
High-Yield Credit	2%	5%	5%	5%	37.5	−10%	5%	33.75
Hedge Funds	17%	23%	23%	17%	127.5	−8%	19%	117.30
Private Real Estate	7%	13%	8%	8%	60	0%	12%	72.00
Private Real Assets	3%	7%	4%	5%	37.5	10%	8%	48.75
Private Equity	15%	22%	15%	15%	112.5	−10%	20%	123.75
Total				**100%**	**$750.0**		**100%**	**$625.80**

** Cash paid to fund liabilities ($37.5 million to the university and $40.5 million to fund private investment capital calls. Additional cash needs funded from government bond portfolio.*

15 MONITORING THE INVESTMENT PROGRAM

☐ discuss considerations in monitoring alternative investment programs

The monitoring of an alternative investment program is time and labor intensive. Data are hard to come by and are not standardized among managers or asset classes. The analyst must spend a good amount of time gathering data and ensuring that the analysis is comparable across managers and asset classes. It is incumbent on the investor to both monitor the managers *and* the alternative investment program's progress toward the goals that were the basis for the investment in these assets.

Overall Investment Program Monitoring

When an investor makes a strategic decision to invest in alternative assets, specific goals are typically associated with the alternative investment program—return enhancement, income, risk reduction, safety, or a combination of the four. The goals may vary by asset class. A real estate program, for example, might be undertaken with the objective of replacing a portion of the fixed-income allocation—providing yield or income but also providing some measure of growth and/or inflation protection. The real estate program should be monitored relative to those goals, not simply relative to a benchmark.

We know that an alternative investment program is likely to take a number of years to reach fully-invested status. Is it reasonable to defer an assessment of the program until that point? Probably not. The investor must monitor developments in the relevant markets to ensure that the fundamental thesis underlying the decision to invest remains intact. Continuing with our real estate analogy, if real estate cap rates[18] fall to never-before-seen lows, what are the implications for the real estate's ability to continue to fulfill its intended role in the portfolio? Or if the managers hired within the real estate allocation allocate more to commercial office properties than was anticipated, what are the implications for the ability of real estate to fulfill the income-oriented goal? Only by monitoring the development of the portfolio(s) will the investor be able to adjust course and ensure that the allocation remains on track to achieve the goals established at the outset.

We also know that investor goals and objectives are subject to change. Perhaps a university experiences a persistent decline in enrollments and the endowment fund will be called upon to provide greater support to the university while it transitions to the new reality; what are the implications for a private equity program? Or what if the primary wage-earner in a two-parent household becomes critically ill; how might this affect the asset allocation? These types of events cannot be predicted, but it is important to continuously monitor the linkages between the asset allocation and the investor's goals, objectives, and circumstances. Particularly in the private markets—where changing course requires a long lead time and abruptly terminating an investment program can radically alter the risk and return profile of the portfolio—an early warning of an impending change can greatly improve the investor's ability to maintain the integrity of the investment program.

Performance Evaluation

Properly benchmarking an alternative investment strategy is a challenge that has important implications for judging the effectiveness of the alternative investment program. Many investors resort to custom index proxies (e.g., a static return premium over cash or equity index) or rely on peer group comparisons (e.g., Hedge Fund Research, Inc., Eurekahedge, Cambridge Private Equity Index). Both approaches have significant limitations.

Consider a private equity program benchmarked to the MSCI World Index plus 3%. This custom index may help frame the return expectation the investment committee holds with regard to its private equity assets, but it is unlikely to match the realized risk, return, and liquidity characteristics of the actual private equity program.

It is similarly challenging to develop a peer group representative of a manager's strategy given the high level of idiosyncratic risk inherent in most alternative investment funds. Existing providers follow vastly different rules in constructing these "benchmarks." They all have their own set of definitions (e.g., whether a fund is a credit fund or an event-driven fund), weighting methodology (asset weighted or equal weighted), method for dealing with potential survivorship bias, and other rules for inclusion (e.g., whether the fund is currently open or closed to new capital).

Exhibit 44 shows the returns from three different hedge fund index providers. An event driven fund that generated a 6% return over the relevant 5-year period might look attractive if evaluated relative to the Credit Suisse index, whereas it might look subpar if evaluated relative to the Eurekahedge index. Additionally, a manager's ranking within the peer group is affected as much by what *other* managers do as by his own actions. Clearly, peer group ranking is, at best, one small part of the overall benchmarking exercise.

---

18 The ratio of net operating income (NOI) to property asset value (the inverse of price/earnings).

Exhibit 44: The Trouble with Peer Groups

Strategy	Provider	3-Year Annualized Return (%)	5-Year Annualized Return (%)
		ending December 31, 2017	
Equity Hedge	HFRI	5.7	6.6
	Credit Suisse	4.3	7.1
	Eurekahedge	6.5	7.8
Event-Driven	HFRI	3.8	5.9
	Credit Suisse	0.8	3.7
	Eurekahedge	6.8	7.2
Global Macro	HFRI	0.6	0.7
	Credit Suisse	2.0	2.7
	Eurekahedge	−0.1	1.2

The timing and nature of reported alternative investment returns also pose challenges to monitoring the performance of alternative investment managers. For call-down strategies such as private equity, private real estate, and real assets, tracking and calculating performance might require different systems and methodologies. Private equity, credit, and real estate returns are typically reported using internal rates of return (IRRs) rather than time-weighted returns (TWR) as is common in the liquid asset classes. IRRs are sensitive to the timing of cash flows into and out of the fund. Two managers may have similar portfolios but very different return profiles depending on their particular capital call and distribution schedule. Investors have to be wise to the ways in which a manager can bias their reported IRR. Alternative metrics, such as multiple on invested capital (MOIC) have been developed to provide an additional frame of reference. (MOIC is a private equity measure that divides the current value of the underlying companies plus any distributions received by the total invested capital.)

Pricing issues also complicate performance evaluation of most alternative strategies. Stale pricing common in many alternative strategies can distort reported returns and the associated risk metrics. Betas, correlations, Sharpe ratios, and other measures must be interpreted with a healthy degree of skepticism.

Although performance measurement has its challenges with all asset classes, relying exclusively on any single measure with alternative investments increases the likelihood of inaccurate or misleading conclusions. With respect to the more illiquid investment strategies, judgment as to whether a given fund is meeting its investment objectives should be reserved until most or even all of the investments have been monetized, and capital has been returned to the investor. If capital is returned quickly (thereby possibly producing extraordinarily high IRRs), the investor may want to put greater emphasis on the MOIC measure. Similarly, funds that return capital more slowly than expected might want to put greater weight on the IRR measure. Even a fund with both a weak MOIC and a weak IRR need the measures to be put into context. An appropriate peer group analysis can help ascertain whether the "poor" performance was common across all funds of similar vintage (perhaps suggesting a poor investment climate) or whether it was specific to that fund. Likewise, a fund that posts strong performance may simply have benefited from an ideal investment period.

Perhaps the best way to gain performance insight beyond the numbers is to develop a qualitative understanding of the underlying assets. What are the manager's expectations at the time of acquisition? How does the manager plan to add value to the investment over the holding period? What is the manager's exit strategy for the investment? The investor can monitor how the investment develops relative to the initial thesis. This type of qualitative assessment can lead to a better understanding of whether the manager did well for the right reasons, whether the manager was wrong but for the right reasons, or whether the manager was just wrong.

Monitoring the Firm and the Investment Process

In addition to monitoring the portfolio, monitoring of the investment process and the investment management firm itself are particularly important in alternative investment structures where the manager cannot be terminated easily, and the assets transferred to another manager in which the investor has more confidence. What follows is a non-exhaustive list of issues that the investor will want to monitor:

- *Key person risk*: Most alternative investment strategies depend to a large extent on the skill of a few key investment professionals. These are what are known as "key persons." Key persons are typically specified in the fund documents, with certain rights allocated to the limited partners in the event a key person leaves the firm. It is important to ensure that these investment professionals remain actively involved in the investment process. There are also other employees of the investment manager whose departure may negatively affect the operation of the business or signal an underlying problem. If, for example, the chief operating officer or chief compliance officer leaves the firm, it is important to understand why and what effect it may have on the business. Finally, it is important to note that for quantitatively oriented strategies, key person risk is often reduced because the quantitative investment process remains in place even if a key person leaves.
- *Alignment of interests*: Alignment of interest issues range from the complexity of the organization, structure of management fees, compensation of the investment professionals, growth in assets under management (AUM), and the amount of capital the key professionals have committed to the funds that they are managing. The investor will want to verify that the money manager's interests remain closely aligned with their own. Has the manager withdrawn a significant portion of her own capital that had been invested alongside the limited partners? If so, why? Is the manager raising a new fund? If so, what safeguards are in place to ensure that the investment professionals are not unduly distracted with fundraising, firm administration, or unfairly concentrated on managing other funds? Is the opportunity set deep enough to support the additional capital being raised? Will the funds have shared ownership interest in a given asset? If so, what conflicts of interest may arise (e.g., the manager may earn an incentive fee in one fund if the asset is sold, while it may be in the best interest of the second fund to sell the asset at a later date).
- *Style drift*: Fund documents often give managers wide latitude as to their investment options and parameters, but it is incumbent on the investor to understand where the fund manager has a competitive advantage and skill and confirm that the investments being made are consistent with the manager's edge.
- *Risk management*: The investor should understand the manager's risk management philosophy and processes and periodically confirm that the fund is abiding by them. Where a fund makes extensive use of leverage, a robust risk management framework is essential.
- *Client/asset turnover*: A critical part of the ongoing due diligence process should include a review of clients and assets. A significant gain or drop in either may be a sign of an underlying problem. An unusual gain in assets

could make it difficult for the investment professionals to invest in suitably attractive investments, potentially handicapping future performance. Conversely, significant client redemptions may force the money manager to sell attractive assets as he looks to raise cash. If this occurs during periods of market turmoil when liquidity in the market itself may be low, the manager may be forced to sell what he can rather than what he should in order to optimize performance. This could hurt the returns of non-redeeming clients and/or leave the remaining clients with illiquid holdings that might make it difficult for them to redeem in the future.

- *Client profile*: Investors will want to gauge the profile of the fund manager's other clients. Are the fund's other clients considered long-term investors, or do they have a history of redeeming at the first sign of trouble? Are they new to the alternative investment space and perhaps don't understand the nuances of the fund's strategy and risks? You may have a strong conviction in a money manager's skills, but the actions of others may affect your ability to reap the benefits of those skills. If too many of her other clients elect to redeem, the manager may invoke the gates allowed by the fund's documents or, at the extreme, liquidate the fund at what might be the worst possible moment. This was a common occurrence during 2008–2009, when investors sought to raise cash by redeeming from their more liquid fund managers. Even if a money manager weathers massive outflows, profitability and the ability to retain key talent may be at risk.
- *Service providers:* Investors will want to ensure that the fund manager has engaged independent and reputable third-party service providers, including administrators, custodians, and auditors. Although an investor may have performed extensive checks prior to investing, it is good practice to periodically verify that these relationships are intact and working well. If the service provider changes, the investor will want to understand *why*. Has the fund's AUM grown to a level that cannot be handled adequately by the current provider? Perhaps the service provider has chosen to terminate the relationship because of actions taken by the fund manager. Exploring the motivation behind a change in a service provider can uncover early warning flags deserving of further investigation.

EXAMPLE 10

Monitoring Alternative Investment Programs

1. The O'Hara family office determined that the illiquidity risk inherent in private investments is a risk that the family is ill-suited to bear. As a result, they decided several years ago to unwind their private equity program. There are still a few remaining assets in the portfolio. The CIO (chief investment officer) notices that the private equity portfolio has delivered outstanding performance lately, especially relative to other asset classes. He presents the data to his research staff and wants to revisit their decision to stop making new private equity investments. Explain why the investment results that prompted the CIO's comments should not be relied upon.

Solution:

With small, residual holdings, even a modest change in valuation can result in outsized returns; for example, a $2,000 investment that gets revalued to $3,000 would report a nominal return of 50%. The 50% return is not representative of private equity investment as a whole but is merely an artifact of the unwinding process. A more accurate picture of performance must consider the development of the fund IRR over time and consider other performance measures, such as the MOIC.

2. The ZeeZaw family office has been invested in the Warriors Fund, a relatively small distressed debt strategy, which has performed very well for a number of years. In a recent conversation with the portfolio manager, the CIO for ZeeZaw discovered that the Warriors fund will be receiving a significant investment from a large institution within the next few weeks. What are some of the risks that might develop with the Warriors Fund as a result of this new client? What are some other issues that the CIO might want to probe with the Warriors Fund?

Solution:

The CIO should investigate whether the fund manager is able to appropriately deploy this new capital consistent with the investment process and types of investments that contributed to the Warriors Fund success. Because the fund was relatively small, a very large influx of capital might force the portfolio manager to make larger investments than is optimal or more investments than they did before. Either change without the appropriate resources could undermine future success. Finally, a large influx of cash could dilute near-term performance, especially if the funds remain undeployed for a significant period of time.

SUMMARY

- Allocations to alternatives are believed to increase a portfolio's risk-adjusted return. An investment in alternatives typically fulfills one or more of four roles in an investor's portfolio: capital growth, income generation, risk diversification, and/or safety.
- Private equity investments are generally viewed as return enhancers in a portfolio of traditional assets.
- Long/short equity strategies are generally believed to deliver equity-like returns with less than full exposure to the equity premium. Short-biased equity strategies are expected to lower a portfolio's overall equity beta while producing some measure of alpha. Arbitrage and event-driven strategies are expected to provide equity-like returns with little to no correlation with traditional asset classes.
- Real assets (e.g., commodities, farmland, timber, energy, and infrastructure assets) are generally perceived to provide a hedge against inflation.
- Timber investments provide both growth and inflation-hedging properties.
- Commodities (e.g., metals, energy, livestock, and agricultural commodities) serve as a hedge against inflation and provide a differentiated source of alpha. Certain commodity investments serve as safe havens in times of crisis.
- Farmland investing may have a commodity-like profile or a commercial real-estate-like profile.

- Energy investments are generally considered a real asset as the investor owns the mineral rights to commodities that are correlated with inflation factors.
- Infrastructure investments tend to generate stable/modestly growing income and to have high correlation with overall inflation.
- Real estate strategies range from core to opportunistic and are believed to provide protection against unanticipated increases in inflation. Core real estate strategies are more income-oriented, while opportunistic strategies rely more heavily on capital appreciation.
- Bonds have been a more effective volatility mitigator than alternatives over shorter time horizons.
- The traditional approaches to defining asset classes are easy to communicate and implement. However, they tend to over-estimate portfolio diversification and obscure primary drivers of risk.
- Typical risk factors applied to alternative investments include equity, size, value, liquidity, duration, inflation, credit spread, and currency. A benefit of the risk factor approach is that every asset class can be described using the same framework.
- Risk factor-based approaches have certain limitations. A framework with too many factors is difficult to administer and interpret, but too small a set of risk factors may not accurately describe the characteristics of alternative asset classes. Risk factor sensitivities are highly sensitive to the historical look-back period.
- Investors with less than a 15-year investment horizon should generally avoid investments in private real estate, private real asset, and private equity funds.
- Investors must consider whether they have the necessary skills, expertise, and resources to build an alternative investment program internally. Investors without a strong governance program are less likely to develop a successful alternative investment program.
- Reporting for alternative funds is often less transparent than investors are accustomed to seeing on their stock and bond portfolios. For many illiquid strategies, reporting is often received well past typical monthly or quarter-end deadlines. Full, position-level transparency is rare in many alternative strategies.
- Three primary approaches are used to determine the desired allocation to the alternative asset classes:
  - Monte Carlo simulation may be used to generate return scenarios that relax the assumption of normally distributed returns.
  - Optimization techniques, which incorporate downside risk or take into account skew, may be used to enhance the asset allocation process.
  - Risk factor-based approaches to alternative asset allocation can be applied to develop more robust asset allocation proposals.
- Two key analytical challenges in modelling allocations to alternatives include stale and/or artificially smoothed returns and return distributions that exhibit significant skewness and fat tails (or excess kurtosis).
- Artificially smoothed returns can be detected by testing the return stream for serial correlation. The analyst needs to unsmooth the returns to get a more accurate representation of the risk and return characteristics of the asset class.

- Skewness and kurtosis can be dealt with by using empirically observed asset returns because they incorporate the actual distribution. Advanced mathematical or statistical models can also be used to capture the true behavior of alternative asset classes.
- Applications of Monte Carlo simulation in allocating to alternative investments include:
  1. simulating skewed and fat-tailed financial variables by estimating the behavior of factors and/or assets in low-volatility regimes and high-volatility regimes, then generating scenarios using the different means and covariances estimated under the different regimes; and
  2. simulating portfolio outcomes (+/− 1 standard deviation) to estimate the likelihood of falling short of the investment objectives.
- Unconstrained mean–variance optimization (MVO) often leads to portfolios dominated by cash and fixed income at the low-risk end of the spectrum and by private equity at the high-risk end of the spectrum. Some investors impose minimum and maximum constraints on asset classes. Slight changes in the input variables could lead to substantial changes in the asset allocations.
- Mean–CVaR optimization may be used to identify allocations that minimize downside risk rather than simply volatility.
- Investors may choose to optimize allocations to risk factors rather than asset classes. These allocations, however, must be implemented using asset classes. Portfolios with similar risk factor exposures can have vastly different asset allocations.
- Some caveats with respect to risk factor-based allocations are that investors may hold different definitions for a given risk factor, correlations among risk factors may shift under changing market conditions, and some factor sensitivities are very unstable.
- Cash flow and commitment-pacing models enable investors in private alternatives to better manage their portfolio liquidity and set realistic annual commitment targets to reach the desired asset allocation.
- An alternative investment program should be monitored relative to the goals established for the alternative investment program, not simply relative to a benchmark. The investor must monitor developments in the relevant markets to ensure that the fundamental thesis underlying the decision to invest remains intact.
- Two common benchmarking approaches to benchmarking alternative investments—custom index proxies and peer group comparisons—have significant limitations.
- IRRs are sensitive to the timing of cash flows into and out of the fund: Two managers may have similar portfolios but different return profiles depending on their capital call and distribution schedule.
- Pricing issues can distort reported returns and the associated risk metrics, such as betas, correlations, and Sharpe ratios.
- Monitoring of the firm and the investment process are particularly important in alternative investment structures where the manager cannot be terminated easily. Key elements to monitor include key person risk, alignment of interests, style drift, risk management, client/asset turnover, client profile, and service providers.

REFERENCES

Ang, A. 2014. *Asset Management: A Systematic Approach to Factor Investing*. New York: Oxford University Press. 10.1093/acprof:oso/9780199959327.001.0001

Berkelaar, A. B., A. Kobor, and R. R. P. Kouwenberg. 2009. "Asset Allocation for Hedge Fund Strategies: How to Better Manage Tail Risk." In *The VaR Modeling Handbook: Practical Applications in Alternative Investing, Banking, Insurance, and Portfolio Management*, ed. Gregoriou, Greg N. New York: McGraw-Hill.

Hamilton, J. D. 1989. "A New Approach to the Economic Analysis of Nonstationary Time Series and the Business Cycle." *Econometrica* 57 (2): 357–84. 10.2307/1912559

Ivashina, Victoria and Josh Lerner. 2018. "Looking for Alternatives: Pension Investments around the World, 2008 to 2017." Federal Reserve of Boston conference paper.

Kim, C. and C. R. Nelson. 1999. *State-Space Models with Regime Switching – Classical and Gibbs-Sampling Approaches and Applications*. Cambridge, MA: MIT Press.

Naik, V., M. Devarajan, A. Nowobilski, S. Page, and N. Pedersen. 2016. *Factor Investing and Asset Allocation – A Business Cycle Perspective*. Charlottesville, VA: CFA Institute Research Foundation.

Rockafellar, R. T. and S. Uryasev. 2000. "Optimization of Conditional Value at Risk." *Journal of Risk* 2 (3): 21–42. 10.21314/JOR.2000.038

Swensen, D. F. 2009. *Pioneering Portfolio Management: An Unconventional Approach to Institutional Investment*. New York: Free Press.

Takahashi, D. and S. Alexander. 2001. "*Illiquid Alternative Asset Fund Modeling*." Yale School of Management (January).

PRACTICE PROBLEMS

The following information relates to questions 1-8

Kevin Kroll is the chair of the investment committee responsible for the governance of the Shire Manufacturing Corporation (SMC) defined benefit pension plan. The pension fund is currently fully funded and has followed an asset mix of 60% public equities and 40% bonds since Kroll has been chair. Kroll meets with Mary Park, an actuarial and pension consultant, to discuss issues raised at the last committee meeting.

Kroll notes that the investment committee would like to explore the benefits of adding alternative investments to the pension plan's strategic asset allocation. Kroll states:

Statement 1 The committee would like to know which alternative asset would best mitigate the risks to the portfolio due to unexpected inflation and also have a relatively low correlation with public equities to provide diversification benefits.

The SMC pension plan has been able to fund the annual pension payments without any corporate contributions for a number of years. The committee is interested in potential changes to the asset mix that could increase the probability of achieving the long-term investment target return of 5.5% while maintaining the funded status of the plan. Park notes that fixed-income yields are expected to remain low for the foreseeable future. Kroll asks:

Statement 2 If the public equity allocation remains at 60%, is there a single asset class that could be used for the balance of the portfolio to achieve the greatest probability of maintaining the pension funding status over a long time horizon? Under this hypothetical scenario, the balance of the portfolio can be allocated to either bonds, hedge funds, or private equities.

Park confirms with Kroll that the committee has historically used a traditional approach to define the opportunity set based on distinct macroeconomic regimes, and she proposes that a risk-based approach might be a better method. Although the traditional approach is relatively powerful for its ability to handle liquidity and manager selection issues compared to a risk-based approach, they both acknowledge that a number of limitations are associated with the existing approach.

Park presents a report (Exhibit 1) that proposes a new strategic asset allocation for the pension plan. Kroll states that one of the concerns that the investment committee will have regarding the new allocation is that the pension fund needs to be able to fund an upcoming early retirement incentive program (ERIP) that SMC will be offering to its employees within the next two years. Employees who have reached the age of 55 and whose age added to the number of years of company service sum to 75 or more can retire 10 years early and receive the defined benefit pension normally payable at age 65.

Exhibit 1: Proposed Asset Allocation of SMC Defined Benefit Pension Plan

Asset Class	Public Equities	Broad Fixed Income	Private Equities	Hedge Funds	Public Real Estate	Total
Target	45%	25%	10%	10%	10%	100%
Range	35%–55%	15%–35%	0%–12%	0%–12%	0%–12%	–

Kroll and Park then discuss suitability considerations related to the allocation in Exhibit 1. Kroll understands that one of the drawbacks of including the proposed alternative asset classes is that daily reporting will no longer be available. Investment reports for alternatives will likely be received after monthly or quarter-end deadlines used for the plan's traditional investments. Park emphasizes that in a typical private equity structure, the pension fund makes a commitment of capital to a blind pool as part of the private investment partnership.

In order to explain the new strategic asset allocation to the investment committee, Kroll asks Park why a risk factor-based approach should be used rather than a mean–variance-optimization technique. Park makes the following statements:

Statement 3 Risk factor-based approaches to asset allocation produce more robust asset allocation proposals.

Statement 4 A mean–variance optimization typically overallocates to the private alternative asset classes due to stale pricing.

Park notes that the current macroeconomic environment could lead to a bear market within a few years. Kroll asks Park to discuss the potential impact on liquidity planning associated with the actions of the fund's general partners in the forecasted environment.

Kroll concludes the meeting by reviewing the information in Exhibit 2 pertaining to three potential private equity funds analyzed by Park. Park discloses the following due diligence findings from a recent manager search: Fund A retains administrators, custodians, and auditors with impeccable reputations; Fund B has achieved its performance in a manner that appears to conflict with its reported investment philosophy; and Fund C has recently experienced the loss of three key persons.

Exhibit 2: Potential Private Equity Funds, Internal Rate of Return (IRR)

Private Equity Fund	Fund A	Fund B	Fund C
5-year IRR	12.9%	13.2%	13.1%

1. Based on Statement 1, Park should recommend:

   A. hedge funds.

   B. private equities.

   C. commodity futures.

2. In answering the question raised in Statement 2, Park would *most likely* recommend:

   A. bonds.

B. hedge funds.

C. private equities.

3. A limitation of the existing approach used by the committee to define the opportunity set is that it:

   A. is difficult to communicate.

   B. overestimates the portfolio diversification.

   C. is sensitive to the historical look-back period.

4. Based on Exhibit 1 and the proposed asset allocation, the greatest risk associated with the ERIP is:

   A. liability.

   B. leverage.

   C. liquidity.

5. The suitability concern discussed by Kroll and Park *most likely* deals with:

   A. governance.

   B. transparency.

   C. investment horizon.

6. Which of Park's statements regarding the asset allocation approaches is correct?

   A. Only Statement 3

   B. Only Statement 4

   C. Both Statement 3 and Statement 4

7. Based on the forecasted environment, liquidity planning should take into account that general partners may:

   A. call capital at a slower pace.

   B. make distributions at a faster pace.

   C. exercise an option to extend the life of the fund.

8. Based on Exhibit 2 and Park's due diligence, the pension committee should consider investing in:

   A. Fund A.

   B. Fund B.

   C. Fund C.

The following information relates to questions 9-13

Eileen Gension is a portfolio manager for Zen-Alt Investment Consultants (Zen-Alt), which assists institutional investors with investing in alternative investments. Charles Smittand is an analyst at Zen-Alt and reports to Gension. Gension and Smittand discuss a new client, the Benziger University Endowment Fund (the fund), as well as a prospective client, the Opeptaja Pension Plan (the plan).

The fund's current portfolio is invested primarily in public equities, with the remainder invested in fixed income. The fund's investment objective is to support a 6% annual spending rate and to preserve the purchasing power of the asset base over a 10-year time horizon. The fund also wants to invest in assets that provide the highest amount of diversification against its dominant equity risk. Gension considers potential alternative investment options that would best meet the fund's diversification strategy.

In preparation for the first meeting between Zen-Alt and the fund, Gension and Smittand discuss implementing a short-biased equity strategy within the fund. Smittand makes the following three statements regarding short-biased equity strategies:

Statement 1	Short-biased equity strategies generally provide alpha when used to diversify public equities.
Statement 2	Short-biased equity strategies are expected to provide a higher reduction in volatility than bonds over a long time horizon.
Statement 3	Short-biased equity strategies are expected to mitigate the risk of public equities by reducing the overall portfolio beta of the fund.

Gension directs Smittand to prepare asset allocation and portfolio characteristics data on three alternative portfolios. The fund's risk profile is one factor that potential lenders consider when assigning a risk rating to the university. A loan covenant with the university's primary lender states that a re-evaluation of the university's creditworthiness is triggered if the fund incurs a loss greater than 20% over any one-year period. Smittand states that the recommended asset allocation should achieve the following three goals, in order of priority and importance:

- Minimize the probability of triggering the primary lender's loan covenant.
- Minimize the probability of purchasing power impairment over a 10-year horizon.
- Maximize the probability of achieving a real return target of 6% over a 10-year horizon.

Smittand provides data for three alternative portfolios, which are presented in Exhibits 1 and 2.

Exhibit 1: Asset Allocation

Alternative Portfolio	Cash	Public Equity	Gov't.	Credit	Hedge Fund	Real Estate	Private Equity
A	4.0%	35.0%	6.0%	5.0%	20.0%	10.0%	20.0%
B	2.0%	40.0%	8.0%	3.0%	15.0%	7.0%	25.0%
C	1.0%	50.0%	3.0%	6.0%	10.0%	0.0%	30.0%

Exhibit 2: Portfolio Characteristics

Alternative Portfolio	1-Year 99% VaR	1-Year 99% CVaR	Probability of Meeting 6% Real Return (10-Year Horizon)	Probability of Purchasing Power Impairment (10-Year Horizon)
A	−16.3%	−19.4%	56.1%	2.5%
B	−17.4%	−20.6%	58.8%	2.8%
C	−19.3%	−22.7%	61.0%	4.0%

Notes:

- One-year horizon 99% VaR: the lowest return over any one-year period at a 99% confidence level
- One-year horizon 99% CVaR: the expected return if the return falls below the 99% VaR threshold
- Probability of purchasing power impairment: the probability of losing 40% of the fund's purchasing power over 10 years, after consideration of new gifts received by the fund, spending from the fund, and total returns

Gension next meets with the investment committee (IC) of the Opeptaja Pension Plan to discuss new opportunities in alternative investments. The plan is a $1 billion public pension fund that is required to provide detailed reports to the public and operates under specific government guidelines. The plan's IC adopted a formal investment policy that specifies an investment horizon of 20 years. The plan has a team of in-house analysts with significant experience in alternative investments.

During the meeting, the IC indicates that it is interested in investing in private real estate. Gension recommends a real estate investment managed by an experienced team with a proven track record. The investment will require multiple capital calls over the next few years. The IC proceeds to commit to the new real estate investment and seeks advice on liquidity planning related to the future capital calls.

9. Which asset class would *best* satisfy the Fund's diversification strategy?

   A. Private equity

   B. Private real estate

   C. Absolute return hedge fund

10. Which of Smittand's statements regarding short-biased equity strategies is *incorrect?*

    A. Statement 1

    B. Statement 2

    C. Statement 3

11. Based on Exhibit 2, which alternative portfolio should Gension recommend for the fund given Smittand's stated three goals?

    A. Portfolio A

    B. Portfolio B

    C. Portfolio C

12. Which of the following investor characteristics would *most likely* be a primary-concern for the plan's IC with respect to investing in alternatives?

    A. Governance

    B. Transparency

    C. Investment horizon

13. With respect to liquidity planning relating to the plan's new real estate investment, Gension should recommend that the fund set aside appropriate funds and invest them in:

    A. 100% REITs.

    B. 100% cash equivalents.

    C. 80% cash equivalents and 20% REITs.

The following information relates to questions 14-15

Inge Greslo is an adviser with an investment management company and focuses on asset allocation for the company's high-net-worth investors. She prepares for a meeting with Maarten Pua, a new client who recently inherited a $10 million portfolio solely comprising public equities.

Greslo meets with Pua and proposes that she create a multi-asset portfolio by selling a portion of his equity holdings and investing the proceeds in another asset class. Greslo advises Pua that his investment objective should be to select an asset class that has a high potential to fulfill two functional roles: risk diversification and capital growth. Greslo suggests the following three asset classes:

- Public real estate
- Private real assets (timber)
- Equity long/short hedge funds

14. **Determine** which asset class is *most likely* to meet Pua's investment objective. **Justify** your response.

- Public real estate
- Private real assets (timber)
- Equity long/short hedge funds

15. Five years after her first meeting with Pua, Greslo monitors a private real estate investment that Pua has held for one year. Until recently, the investment had been managed by a local real estate specialist who had a competitive advantage in this market; the specialist's strategy was to purchase distressed local residential housing properties, make strategic property improvements, and then sell them. Pua is one of several clients who have invested in this opportunity.

Greslo learns that the specialist recently retired and the investment is now managed by a national real estate company. The company has told investors that it now plans to invest throughout the region in both distressed housing and commercial properties. The company also lengthened the holding period for each investment property from the date of the initial capital call because of the complexity of the property renovations, and it altered the interim profit distribution targets.

Discuss the qualitative risk issues that have *most likely* materialized over the past year.

The following information relates to questions 16-18

The Ælfheah Group is a US-based company with a relatively small pension plan. Ælfheah's investment committee (IC), whose members collectively have a relatively basic understanding of the investment process, has agreed that Ælfheah is willing to accept modest returns while the IC gains a better understanding of the process Two key investment considerations for the IC are maintaining low overhead costs and minimizing taxes in the portfolio. Ælfheah has not been willing to incur the costs of in-house investment resources.

Qauhtèmoc Ng is the investment adviser for Ælfheah. He discusses with the IC its goal of diversifying Ælfheah's portfolio to include alternative assets. Ng suggests considering the following potential investment vehicles:

- Publicly traded US REIT
- Relative value hedge fund
- Tax-efficient angel investment

Ng explains that for the relative value hedge fund alternative, Ælfheah would be investing alongside tax-exempt investors.

16. **Determine** which of the potential investment vehicles *best* meets the investment considerations for Ælfheah. **Justify** your response. **Explain** for *each* investment not selected why the investment considerations are not met.

- Publicly traded US REIT
- Relative value hedge fund
- Tax-efficient angel investment

17. Ng and the IC review the optimal approach to determine the asset allocation for Ælfheah, including the traditional and risk-based approaches to defining the investment opportunity set.

    Determine which approach to determine the asset allocation is *most appropriate* for Ælfheah. **Justify** your response.

    - Traditional
    - Risk based

18. The following year, Ng and the IC review the portfolio's performance. The IC has gained a better understanding of the investment process. The portfolio is meeting Ælfheah's liquidity needs, and Ng suggests that Ælfheah would benefit from diversifying into an additional alternative asset class. After discussing suitable investment vehicles for the proposed alternative asset class, Ng proposes the following three investment vehicles for further review:

    - Funds of funds (FOFs)
    - Separately managed accounts (SMAs)
    - Undertakings for collective investment in transferable securities (UCITS)

    Determine the investment vehicle that would be *most appropriate* for Ælfheah's proposed alternative asset class. **Justify** your response.

The following information relates to questions 19-20

Mbalenhle Calixto is a global institutional portfolio manager who prepares for an annual meeting with the investment committee (IC) of the Estevão University Endowment. The endowment has €450 million in assets, and the current asset allocation is 42% equities, 22% fixed income, 19% private equity, and 17% hedge funds.

The IC's primary investment objective is to maximize returns subject to a given level of volatility. A secondary objective is to avoid a permanent loss of capital, and the IC has indicated to Calixto its concern about left-tail risk. Calixto considers two asset allocation approaches for the endowment: mean–variance optimization (MVO) and mean–CVaR (conditional value at risk) optimization.

19. **Determine** the asset allocation approach that is *mostsuitable* for the Endowment. **Justify** your response.

    - MVO
    - Mean–CVaR optimization

20. Calixto reviews the endowment's future liquidity requirements and analyzes one of its holdings in a private distressed debt fund. She notes the following about the fund:

    - As of the most recent year end:
        - The NAV of the endowment's investment in the fund was €25,000,000.
        - All capital had been called.

- At the end of the current year, Calixto expects a distribution of 18% to be paid.
- Calixto estimates an expected growth rate of 11% for the fund.

Calculate the expected NAV of the fund at the end of the current year.

SOLUTIONS

1. C is correct. Real assets (which include energy, infrastructure, timber, commodities, and farmland) are generally believed to mitigate the risks to the portfolio arising from unexpected inflation. Commodities act as a hedge against a core constituent of inflation measures. Rather than investing directly in the actual commodities, commodity futures may be incorporated using a managed futures strategy. In addition, the committee is looking for an asset class that has a low correlation with public equities, which will provide diversification benefits. Commodities are regarded as having much lower correlation coefficients with public equities than with private equities and hedge funds. Therefore, commodities will provide the greatest potential to fulfill the indicated role and to diversify public equities.

2. C is correct. When projecting expected returns, the order of returns from highest to lowest is typically regarded as private equities, hedge funds, bonds. Therefore, the probability of achieving the highest portfolio return while maintaining the funded status of the plan would require the use of private equities in conjunction with public equities. In addition, private equities have a high/strong potential to fulfill the role of capital growth. Fixed-income investments are expected to have a high/strong potential to fulfill the role of safety.

3. B is correct. A traditional approach has been used to define the opportunity set based on different macroeconomic conditions. The primary limitations of traditional approaches are that they overestimate the portfolio diversification and obscure the primary drivers of risk.

4. C is correct. With the introduction of the early retirement incentive plan (ERIP), the defined benefit pension plan will likely be called upon to make pension payments earlier than originally scheduled. As a result, the near term liquidity of the plan is the greatest risk arising from the addition of the alternative asset classes (e.g., private equities, hedge funds, and real estate). Investments in alternatives, such as private equities, can take upwards of five years to reach a full commitment and potentially another decade to unwind.

5. B is correct. The pension plan's investment in private equities via a blind pool presents the prospect that less than perfect transparency will be associated with the underlying holdings of the alternative asset manager. Capital is committed for an investment in a portfolio of assets that are not specified in advance. In addition, reporting for alternative funds is often less transparent than investors are accustomed to seeing on their stock and bond portfolios.

6. C is correct. Statement 3 is correct because risk factor-based approaches to asset allocation can be applied to develop more robust asset allocations. Statement 4 is correct because a mean–variance optimization typically overallocates to the private alternative asset classes, partly because of underestimated risk due to stale pricing and the assumption that returns are normally distributed

7. C is correct. Park notes that the current macroeconomic environment could lead to a bear market within a few years. Liquidity planning should take into account that under a scenario in which public equities and fixed-income investments are expected to perform poorly, general partners may exercise an option to extend the life of the fund.

8. A is correct. Fund A should be selected based on both quantitative and quali-

tative factors. Fund A has a five-year IRR (12.9%) that is slightly lower than, but comparable to, both Fund B (13.2%) and Fund C (13.1%). Given the sensitivity to the timing of cash flows into and out of a fund associated with the IRR calculation, however, the final decision should not be based merely on quantitative returns. It is also important to monitor the investment process and the investment management firm itself, particularly in alternative investment structures. Considering the qualitative factors identified by Park, Fund A is the only fund with a strong, positive factor: It benefits from service providers (administrators, custodians, and auditors) with impeccable reputations. Fund B seems to be experiencing style drift, which suggests that the returns are not consistent with the manager's advertised investment edge (hence, a negative factor). Fund C has experienced the departure of key persons, which puts future fund returns in jeopardy (hence, a negative factor).

9. C is correct. An absolute return hedge fund has a greater potential to diversify the fund's dominant public equity risk than either private equity or private real estate. Absolute return hedge funds exhibit an equity beta that is often less than that of private equity or private real estate. Also, absolute return hedge funds tend to exhibit a high potential to diversify public equities, whereas equity long/short hedge funds exhibit a moderate potential to fulfill this role.

   A is incorrect because although private equity provides moderate diversification against public equity, an absolute return hedge fund has a greater potential to do so. The primary advantage of private equity is capital growth.

   B is incorrect because private real estate provides only moderate diversification against public equity, whereas absolute return hedge funds have a greater potential to do so. The primary advantage of private real estate is income generation.

10. B is correct. While bonds reduce the probability of achieving a target return over time, they have been more effective as a volatility mitigator than alternatives over an extended period of time.

    A is incorrect because Statement 1 is correct. Short-biased strategies are expected to provide some measure of alpha in addition to lowering a portfolio's overall equity beta.

    C is incorrect because Statement 3 is correct. Short-biased equity strategies help reduce an equity-dominated portfolio's overall beta. Short-biased strategies are believed to deliver equity-like returns with less-than-full exposure to the equity premium but with an additional source of return that might come from the manager's shorting of individual stocks.

11. A is correct. Among the three portfolios, Portfolio A minimizes the probability of triggering the primary lender's loan covenant, which is the highest-priority goal, because it has the lowest one-year 99% CVaR, –19.4%. Portfolio A also has the lowest probability of purchasing power impairment over a 10-year horizon (2.5%). While Portfolio A has the lowest probability of achieving a real return target of 6% over a 10-year horizon (56.1%), that is the least important goal to be met. Therefore, Gension should recommend Portfolio A for the fund.

    B is incorrect because Portfolio B has a one-year 99% CVaR of –20.6%, which crosses the loan covenant threshold of a 20% loss. Portfolio A is the only one that satisfies the most important goal and is the portfolio least likely to trigger the loan covenant. Since Portfolio B does not achieve the most important goal of minimizing the probability of triggering the primary lender's loan covenant, Portfolio B should not be the recommended portfolio.

    C is incorrect because despite the fact that Portfolio C has the highest probability of meeting the 6% real return over a 10-year horizon, 61.0%, it also has a one-year 99% CVaR of –22.7% and thus the highest probability of triggering the loan covenant. Portfolio A is the only one that satisfies the most important goal and is the portfolio least likely to trigger the loan covenant. Since Portfolio C does not achieve the most important goal of minimizing the probability of triggering the primary lender's loan covenant, Portfolio C should not be the recommended portfolio.

12. B is correct. As a public pension fund that is required to provide detailed reports to the public, a primary concern for the IC is transparency. Investors in alternative investments must be comfortable with less than 100% transparency in their holdings. Private equity funds often necessitate buying into a "blind pool." Although an investor can look at the assets acquired in a manager's previous funds, there is no assurance that future investments will exactly replicate the previous funds.

    A is incorrect because the IC has a formal investment policy, as well as an in-house team with experience in alternatives and the knowledge and capacity to critically evaluate alternative investments.

    C is incorrect because the IC has a long-term investment horizon. While investors with less than a 15-year horizon should generally avoid investing in alternatives, the IC has a 20-year investment horizon that should easily accommodate an investment in private equity.

13. A is correct. REITs are most appropriate for funds committed to private real estate investments since they will have the most similar return and risk characteristics and will help maintain the strategic asset allocation of the plan. Although cash equivalents have less volatility over a short-term horizon, they are less likely to meet the plan's long-term return objectives.

    B is incorrect because the opportunity cost of being out of the markets over the next few years during the capital call period makes cash equivalents an inappropriate investment. Although cash equivalents have lower volatility, which is often desirable over a short-term period, they will not help the plan meet its long-term return objectives.

    C is incorrect because, although REITs will have the return and risk characteristics most similar to private real estate, a 20% allocation is not large enough to achieve the plan's long-term return objectives. The 80% allocation to cash equivalents will greatly affect the return, making the plan less likely to meet the long-term return objectives.

14. Private real assets (timber) is *most likely* to meet Pua's investment objective.

    - Timber exhibits a low correlation with public equities and can fulfill the functional role of risk diversification.
    - Timber provides high long-term returns and can fulfill the functional role of capital growth.

      Private real assets (timber) is the asset class most likely to meet Pua's objective. Private real assets, such as timber, tend to exhibit a low correlation with public equities and therefore have a high potential to fulfill the functional role of risk diversification in Pua's current all-equity portfolio. In addition, timber has a high potential to fulfill the functional role of capital growth in the portfolio since growth is provided by the underlying biological growth of the tree as well as through appreciation in the underlying land value.

      Compared with timber, public real estate as an asset class would likely offer less opportunity for capital growth and lower diversification benefits. Also, equity long/short hedge funds as an asset class would provide a moderate degree of risk diversification in Pua's all-equity portfolio but do not carry significant capital growth potential.

15.

- Pua's investment has been affected by key person risk as shown by the effect of the management change.
- Style drift has occurred as shown by the change from a local to a regional investment strategy and the expansion of the investment strategy to include commercial properties.
- The risk of the investment has changed owing to the added complexity of the property renovations.
- The longer holding periods and the change in interim profit distribution targets will affect this investment.
- Client/asset turnover following the management change may now affect the performance of the investment.
- The management change may alter the client profile, which could have a negative effect on investment performance.

Qualitative considerations can lead to a better understanding of the revised strategy for the investment and whether this investment remains suitable for Pua. Pua's investment has been affected by key person risk as shown by the management change from the local manager to a national company. Style drift has occurred as shown by the change from a local to a regional investment strategy and the expansion of the strategy to include commercial properties.

The risk of the investment has changed because of the added complexity of the renovations, and monitoring the company's risk management will be important for Greslo as she manages Pua's portfolio. Monitoring of the private real estate investment has revealed discrepancies in the new management strategy of the national company relative to the initial investment strategy of the local manager, including the longer holding periods and the changed interim profit distribution targets. Client/asset turnover following the management change may now significantly affect the performance of the investment. Finally, the change in management may alter the client profile, which could have a negative effect on investment performance.

16. Publicly traded US REIT *best* meets the investment considerations for Ælfheah. The publicly traded US REIT offers tax advantages to Ælfheah from the depreciation of its US real estate assets. The depreciation would help offset income received on those assets. In addition, the REIT would not require an in-house management team; thus, Ælfheah can maintain low overhead costs.

The relative value hedge fund is unlikely to be a tax-efficient strategy for Ælfheah. This tax inefficiency is seen frequently with many hedge fund strategies, especially those funds and fund companies where tax-exempt investors dominate the client base. The fund manager may be insensitive to tax considerations for a taxable investor such as Ælfheah.

The tax-efficient angel investment is a specialized investment that will require a highly customized investment approach. Researching and managing this type of investment will require an in-house team to locate and supervise these more specialized investments. Adding these resources would increase overhead costs and violate the IC's investment consideration of maintaining low overhead costs.

17. The traditional approach to determine the asset allocation is *most appropriate* for Ælfheah.

- The traditional approach is more appropriate since describing the roles of various asset classes is intuitive.

- This approach will be easier for Ng to explain to the IC, whose members have only a basic understanding of the investment process.
- This approach will make it easier to identify relevant mandates for the portfolio's alternative investments.
- Since Ælfheah seeks to maintain low overhead costs, the risk-based approach would not be appropriate.

The traditional approach is more appropriate for Ælfheah. The IC is less sophisticated in its understanding of alternative investments but may have some familiarity with the traditional asset class-based approach. Listing the roles of various asset classes will be more intuitive and easy for Ng to explain to the IC.

The traditional approach has relevance for the IC's liquidity and operational considerations. This approach will make it easier to identify relevant mandates for the alternative investments in the portfolio. The traditional approach also will allow the IC to obtain a better understanding of how various asset classes behave so that Ng can tailor the asset allocation to address any concerns. The traditional approach will be easier to implement, and the IC does not want to add costly in-house resources, which would likely be necessary with the risk-based approach.

18. FOFs is the the investment vehicle that would be *most appropriate* for Ælfheah's proposed alternative asset class.

- An FOF would allow Ælfheah to co-invest with other investors in alternative investment opportunities for which Ælfheah might otherwise be too small to participate.
- An in-house team would not be necessary to review and maintain an FOF, which uses an outside manager.
- Ælfheah is unlikely to meet the very high minimum investment of an SMA, which may also require enhanced in-house investment resources.
- Ælfheah does not need the higher liquidity of UCITS, which have a less attractive risk/return profile for Ælfheah's relatively small-sized portfolio.

An FOF is the most appropriate investment vehicle for Ælfheah. This vehicle allows Ælfheah to co-invest alongside other investors in order to participate in alternative investment opportunities for which it would otherwise be too small to participate. An expert in-house team would not be necessary to review and maintain the types of investments in an FOF since this investment vehicle uses an outside manager.

SMAs are available for certain large portfolios, such as those of large family offices or foundations, but it is unlikely that Ælfheah would meet the very high minimum investment requirement. This type of investment poses greater operational challenges for the investor; thus, an SMA may require enhanced in-house investment resources. UCITS are less appropriate for Ælfheah since its liquidity needs are being met. Ælfheah should instead invest in a vehicle that offers lower liquidity with a more attractive risk/return profile. Also, UCITS have regulatory restrictions that can make them more difficult for a fund manager to implement the desired investment strategy.

19. Mean–CVaR optimization is the asset allocation approach that is *most suitable*

for the Endowment.

- Mean–CVaR will better address the IC's concern about left-tail risk (the risk of a permanent capital loss).
- If the portfolio contains asset classes and investment strategies with negative skewness and long tails, CVaR optimization could materially alter the asset allocation decision.

  Given the IC's investment objectives for the endowment, using a mean–CVaR optimization approach is more suitable for determining the asset allocation. The IC has 36% of its portfolio invested in alternative assets, 19% in private equity, and 17% in hedge funds. Thus, the IC has a more sophisticated understanding of risk and will appreciate the more nuanced view of risk offered by mean–CVaR optimization. The portfolio has exposure to alternative investments, and the IC is concerned about left-tail risk (the risk of a permanent loss of capital), as indicated to Calixto. Thus, the asset allocation decision will be enhanced by the more detailed understanding of left-tail risk offered by mean–CVaR optimization relative to MVO. MVO cannot easily accommodate the characteristics of most alternative investments. MVO characterizes an asset's risk using standard deviation. Standard deviation, a one-dimensional view of risk, is a poor representation of the risk characteristics of alternative investments for which asset returns may be not normally distributed. MVO typically over-allocates to alternative asset classes, partly because risk is underestimated because of stale or infrequent pricing and the underlying assumption that returns are normally distributed.

  An investor particularly concerned with the downside risk of a proposed asset allocation may choose to minimize the portfolio's CVaR rather than its volatility relative to a return target. If the portfolio contains asset classes and investment strategies with negative skewness and long tails, CVaR optimization could materially alter the asset allocation decision.

20. The expected NAV of the fund at the end of the current year is €22,755,000, calculated as follows:

    First, the expected distribution at the end of the current year is calculated as

    Expected distribution

    = [Prior-year NAV × (1 + Growth rate)] × (Distribution rate).

    Expected distribution = [(€25,000,000 × 1.11) × 18%] = €4,995,000.

    Therefore, the expected NAV of the fund at the end of the current year is

    Expected NAV

    = Prior-year NAV × (1 + Growth rate) + Capital contributions – Distributions.

    Expected NAV = (€25,000,000 × 1.11) + 0 – €4,995,000 = €22,755,000.

LEARNING MODULE

4

An Overview of Private Wealth Management

LEARNING OUTCOMES

Mastery	*The candidate should be able to:*
☐	discuss the different types of individual wealth and how wealth is created and distributed globally
☐	evaluate how changes in human capital, financial capital, and economic net worth across the financial stages of an individual's life influence their financial decision making
☐	justify how returns, risks, objectives, and constraints for individuals relate to their human and financial capital
☐	evaluate how various types of taxes imposed on individual investors and the impact of inflation influence investment decisions
☐	discuss the differences between private and institutional clients and formulate an appropriate Investment Policy Statement for private clients

INTRODUCTION 1

Private wealth management combines financial planning and investment management to help individual investors, particularly **high-net-worth individuals (HNWIs)** and **ultra-high-net-worth individuals (UHNWIs)**, manage their **wealth**. This service encompasses several interconnected processes including personalized financial planning, specialized investment and financial advice, portfolio management, and advising on wealth management, tax planning, and estate planning matters.

Over the past 40 years global wealth has increased significantly, and private wealth management has become an integral, vital service offered by financial institutions, banks, asset management firms, and specialized advisors. This reading uses terms like "private wealth managers," "wealth managers," "managers," and "advisors" interchangeably and refers to their individual investors as "private clients" or, simply, "clients."

Private wealth management is a highly tailored service and involves close collaboration between the wealth manager and the client to define, plan for, and achieve financial objectives. Wealth managers work with clients to understand their financial goals, risk tolerance, and investment preferences, typically focusing on one or more of the interconnected processes listed above. They establish a complete picture of the client's personal and financial circumstances including assets, liabilities, income, and expenses. In developing comprehensive financial plans, wealth managers are supported by tax advisory, estate planning, wealth transfer, and multigenerational planning expertise.

The primary objective of private wealth managers is to maximize after-tax wealth while considering the client's goals, risk tolerance, and portfolio constraints. Private wealth managers can add value in various ways, such as purchasing undervalued securities, selling overpriced securities, and improving asset allocations. Efficient tax management is essential, as taxes can significantly impact net performance for the taxable investor. Tax rates, especially for HNWIs, can greatly influence returns and typically have a more substantial effect than portfolio management costs. Moreover, private wealth managers can offer retirement strategies, charitable giving and philanthropic advising, and client education on various financial matters when needed. This underscores the comprehensive approach to private wealth management.

This reading presents a framework for private wealth management based on a life-cycle view of human capital. Section 1 introduces the concept of wealth in a global context. Section 2 discusses the life-cycle view of human capital and its influence on investment decision making. Section 3 examines individual investors' return and risk considerations, including their objectives and constraints. Section 4 addresses the impact of taxation and inflation on investment decision making. Finally, Section 5 concludes the reading by exploring the unique features of individual investors, their investment plans, and investment policy statements.

LEARNING MODULE OVERVIEW

- Net worth refers to the value of all assets owned by an individual, minus any liabilities or debts. Sources of wealth include accumulated after-tax income from personal and business assets and intergenerational wealth transfers.
- Following World War II, global growth was boosted by new technology, more competition, government policies that supported businesses, and, in some cases, privatization of public services. The growth of free market capitalism, fewer regulatory obstacles, easier access to investment capital, and an increase in entrepreneurship and new businesses greatly encouraged global economic growth and wealth creation. The increase in the value of assets and financial innovations also played a role.
- The global expansion of free markets in recent decades pushed global per capita wealth higher, especially in lower middle income and low income economies.
- However, wealth inequality measures indicate increasing levels of inequality across global populations, with greater disparities in developed markets. While there is more wealth, there is also more wealth inequality.
- Individual investors and institutional investors have different time horizons, tax structures, liquidity needs, investment knowledge and research capabilities, decision-making processes, access to investment opportunities, and roles in the market.

- Individual investors in developed and emerging markets have different levels of access to financial information, different investment opportunities available to them, different investment preferences, and different regulatory environments.
- The **wealth life cycle** of an individual investor typically consists of seven phases: the education phase, the early career phase, the career development phase, the peak accumulation phase, the preretirement phase, the early retirement phase, and the late retirement phase.
- Human capital is the net present value of an individual's future expected labor income. Economic balance sheets include the human capital of an individual and provide a more comprehensive view of an individual's wealth. Individual wealth and asset composition tend to evolve throughout their lifetime, with financial wealth typically increasing as the horizon to build human capital declines.
- Consequently, as individuals approach retirement, the value of their assets and investments tends become a more significant portion of their aggregate human capital.
- Individuals need to diversify their income and risk sources during the wealth accumulation phase to decouple it from their human capital.
- Wealthier individuals in retirement may focus less on covering costs and more on fulfilling philanthropic goals, transferring wealth, and achieving other long-term financial objectives.
- Models for quantifying wealth, such as human capital calculations, are useful but may not fully capture the complexities of real-life situations.
- The impact of inflation on investment returns can vary based on the investment horizon. Investors should focus on preserving their long-term purchasing power, not just nominal returns.
- Assessing a client's risk tolerance involves understanding their willingness and ability to bear financial risk. Risk tolerance questionnaires are commonly used, but they have limitations and should be supplemented with in-depth discussions that can yield valuable insights about the individual's risk tolerance and investment approach.
- Clients often have multiple financial goals, and their risk tolerance may vary for each. Goals can be either planned (like retirement or specific purchases) or unplanned (like unexpected expenses).
- In most jurisdictions, different tax rates apply to different types of investment returns: interest, dividends, and capital gains or losses. Some tax systems impose a wealth tax, which function similarly to income taxes by reducing after-tax returns and accumulations.
- Tax drag, or the negative effect of taxes on after-tax returns, increases with higher investment returns and longer investment horizons.
- Deferral of taxes, often applied to capital gains, helps accumulate returns without tax drag until they are realized. The benefit of tax deferral compounds over time and can outweigh a lower tax rate over time. Investments with deferred capital gains taxation can be more tax efficient than those with annually taxed returns.
- Tax-advantaged investment vehicles help mitigate the impact of taxes on investment returns by offering tax deferrals, reduced tax rates, or tax exemptions, enabling investors to retain more returns for reinvestment and growth over time.

- Portfolio returns originate from various sources and are subject to different tax rates, which must be considered for portfolio management.
- Inflation affects future purchasing power and can change consumption patterns throughout an individual's life cycle. Solely focusing on nominal returns can distort the perception of an investment's real, after-tax, long-term performance.
- By considering the joint effects of taxes and inflation, investors can make informed decisions and choose investments for the most favorable long-term outcomes.
- An investment policy statement (IPS) documents a client's specific investment goals, risk tolerance, investment time frame, and constraints and reflects the mutual understanding of the investment manager's mandate.
- The IPS defines the investment process, clarifies the advisor's fiduciary duty, and is updated regularly to accommodate changes in the client's situation or market conditions.
- The main components of an IPS are the client's background and investment objectives, investment program parameters, portfolio asset allocation ranges, portfolio management processes, and duties and responsibilities of the involved parties.

2 WEALTH IN A GLOBAL CONTEXT

☐ discuss the different types of individual wealth and how wealth is created and distributed globally

The first section focuses on the concept of wealth, sources of wealth and income, and the distribution of wealth across the world.

Defining Wealth

Typically, wealth refers to the value of all the assets owned by an individual less any liabilities or debts owed, as shown in Exhibit 1. There are various approaches to categorizing asset types, but the following offers a comprehensive view of different sources of wealth, excluding human capital, which we will discuss later.

Exhibit 1: Aggregate Wealth

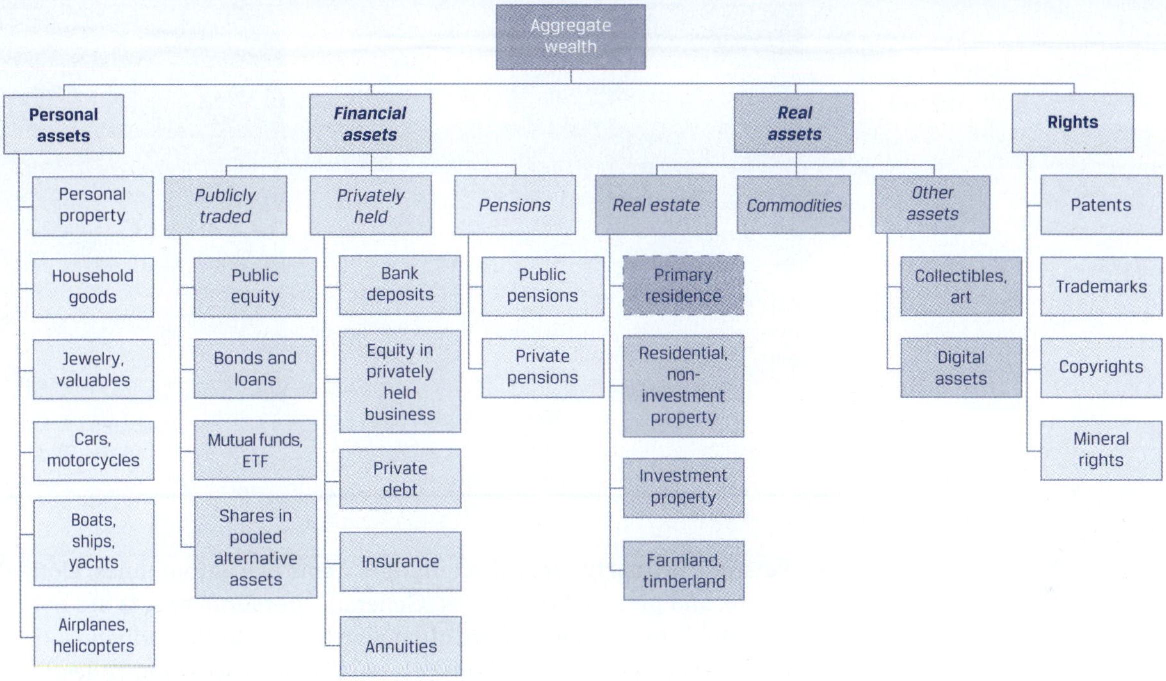

To determine someone's wealth, it is necessary to differentiate among various definitions of wealth. Exhibit 2 breaks down wealth into distinct components including personal, financial, real assets, and rights.

Exhibit 2: Components of Wealth

	Personal property	Financial assets			Real assets			Rights
		Publicly traded	Privately held	Pensions	Real estate	Commodities	Other assets	
Aggregate wealth	√	√	√	√	√	√	√	√
Financial wealth		√		√				
Real wealth					√	√	√	√
Productive wealth			√		√	√		√
Liquid wealth		√					√	
Investable wealth		√						

An individual's **aggregate wealth** is the total value of all assets owned, encompassing personal property, financial assets, real assets, and rights. **Net worth** is the difference between assets and liabilities whose values are relatively easy to measure, such as publicly traded investments, privately held assets, real estate, and debts, as illustrated in Exhibit 3.

This representation excludes intangible assets like copyrights, digital rights, and other nontangible assets, claims, or rights, which can be a significant part of wealth but are not included here because of their uncertain market value, complex valuation, and limited liquidity.

Exhibit 3: Net Worth

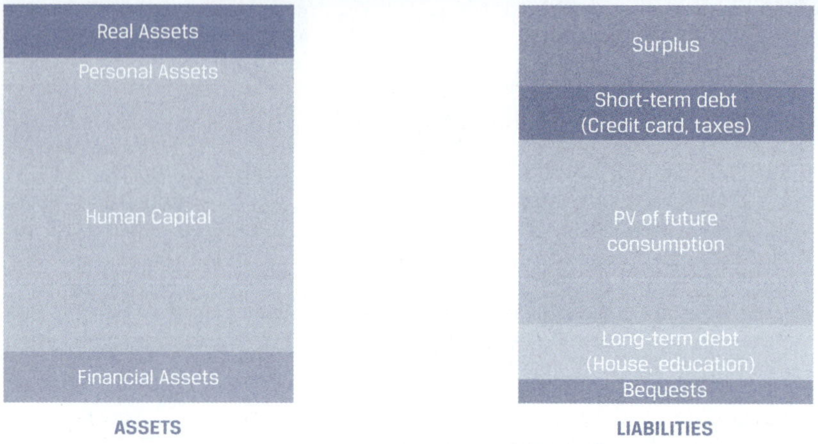

- ***Personal property*** typically comprises items like automobiles, clothes, furniture, and personal residences. Generally, **personal assets** are not expected to appreciate in value and are often worth more to the individual than their current fair market value. Some assets, like real estate and collectibles (jewelry, wine, stamps, and artwork), could be considered "mixed" assets with both personal and real asset characteristics. Some consider primary residential property as a personal property. Others would consider secondary residential properties as investments. For simplicity, we categorize primary residential property as a real asset.
- *Financial wealth* comprises all financial assets, such as publicly traded equity, debt, and investments in pooled vehicles like mutual funds, and alternative assets like hedge funds, private equity, and private debt investments. Financial wealth excludes direct ownership in non–publicly traded businesses like family businesses. Financial assets are often the easiest to identify and include both tangible investment assets and less tangible assets like accrued pensions. One criterion for subdividing financial assets is marketability: publicly traded, non–publicly traded, or privately held. Portfolio management has traditionally concentrated on publicly traded financial assets, overlooking privately held assets such as annuities, insurance, and business assets.
- *Real wealth* refers to tangible assets typically including real estate, commodities, and other owned assets and excluding both personal property and financial assets. Real assets, especially a primary residence, may be the largest asset owned by an individual. For example, in Germany, approximately half of households own a home, whereas in China, the number is closer to 90%. To purchase a home, most individuals obtain a mortgage, a loan secured by the property, which is frequently the largest fixed obligation of homeowners. The use of debt to purchase homes magnifies the impact of home value changes on homeowners' equity and net worth.
- *Productive wealth* reflects assets that can be used to generate income through production and business operations, such as a business directly owned by an individual or a family. For many wealthy individuals, productive wealth constitutes the largest portion of their aggregate wealth. Investing for business owners involves unique considerations, as their total capital may be closely tied to their business's overall performance (i.e., if

the business does poorly, it affects not only the value of the business but also the owner's earnings). The value of business assets may vary based on market conditions and will often correlate with other financial assets within a household portfolio.

- *Liquid, available, or cash wealth* refers to assets that can be easily converted into cash, typically including publicly traded equity and debt in addition to cash and cash equivalents, bank deposits, or ready cash held on hand.
- ***Investable wealth*** refers to financial and other assets that are readily available for investment and is typically a subset of financial assets. Private wealth management often focuses primarily on investable wealth.
- **Investable net worth** is the sum of liquid assets, such as savings and investment accounts, and less short-term liabilities such as credit card debt.
- *Economic net worth* extends net worth to include claims to future assets that can be used for consumption, such as the individual's human capital and pension benefits. **Human capital** is the present value of future income streams adjusted by the actuarial probability of survival, wage growth, and a discount rate that reflects occupational income risk. A large part of an individual's wealth may be attributable to pensions, different types of retirement plans offered across the globe. Pensions can be offered by employers or government programs. Forms of retirement plans vary. Common forms include employee-directed savings plans, in which the contribution amounts and investments are controlled by the individual, or traditional defined benefit pension plans that guarantee some level of retirement benefits typically based on past wages. Government pensions are like employer pension plans but are generally more secure (in countries with low inflation and a high degree of creditworthiness). Because pension benefits typically accrue over time, only their vested value should be recognized in current wealth calculations; moreover, because they are claims on future cash payments, their value can be hard to estimate, and they are not as liquid as other financial assets. When we refer to economic net worth in this reading, we refer to the more holistic accounting of resources that can be used to fund future consumption for the purpose of financial planning over the life cycle.

The simplest balance sheet for an individual includes recognizable marketable assets (investment portfolio, retirement portfolio, real estate, and other tangible and intangible items of value) and liabilities (mortgage debt, credit card debt, auto loans, business or other debts guaranteed by the individual, and student loans). Such a simple balance sheet or statement of net worth is depicted in the case study below.

Valuing publicly traded investments and homeowners' equity is relatively straightforward. For example, an individual with a home valued at EUR1 million and a EUR900,000 mortgage only has EUR100,000 in equity. However, the human capital of an individual is influenced by hard-to-quantify factors such as wage growth, income risk, and economic considerations. Two individuals with the same life expectancy, each earning EUR50,000 annually, may experience positive or negative events over time (unexpected wage growth, job loss, or other impacts to their income) that lead to significantly different wealth outcomes.

CASE STUDY

Taylor, Aiysha, and Chimwala: Traditional Balance Sheet

Assets for three clients across different wealth levels and asset distributions are:

- Taylor: Young professional with limited assets (age: 25)
- Aiysha: Established small business owner with substantial assets tied up in the business (age: 45)
- Chimwala: Entrepreneur who is about to sell a large private business (age: 55)

Balance Sheet as of 31 December 20X1 in Thousands of EUR

Assets and liabilities	Taylor Age 25	Aiysha Age 45	Chimwala Age 55
Liquid assets			
Checking account[a]	10	35	400
Savings account	20	100	500
Total liquid assets	**30**	**135**	**900**
Investment assets			
Taxable investment account	5	350	1,000
Retirement plan, private pension[b]	75	2,000	500
Tax advantaged investment account	75	750	1,500
Total investment assets	**155**	**3,100**	**3,000**
Personal property			
Apartment, house	-	1,000	300
Vacation home	-	500	250
Cars	-	500	100
House contents	10	150	200
Collectibles	-	300	50
Total personal property	**10**	**2,450**	**900**
Business assets			
Direct and / or indirect ownership in business or business interests[c]	-	5,000	25,000
Total assets (Aggregate worth)	***195***	***10,685***	***29,800***
Short-term liabilities			
Short-term debt, credit card debt	15	250	5
Total short-term liabilities	**15**	**250**	**5**
Long-term liabilities			
Education loans	300	500	-
Car loan	10	400	-
Home mortgage	-	500	-
Home equity loan	-	750	500
Business debt			

Assets and liabilities	Taylor Age 25	Aiysha Age 45	Chimwala Age 55
Business loans[d]	-	4,000	7,000
Total long-term liabilities	**310**	**6,150**	**7,500**
Total liabilities	***325***	***6,400***	***7,505***
Net worth	**(130)**	**4,285**	**22,295**
Investable net worth[e]	**100**	**1,200**	**3,000**
Investable net worth after the business is sold		2,200	21,000

[a] *As a transaction account, the checking account may not be considered as part of investable net worth*
[b] *Retirement plans may or may not be considered part of investable net worth, depending on the structure of the retirement plan*
[c] *The way assets are held can vary based on a company's structure, as they may be owned directly or indirectly through a suitable legal entity; valuation methods for privately held assets have been discussed earlier in the curriculum*
[d] *Corporate debt, as corporate equity, can be either direct or indirect, and it might be backed by the company's ultimate beneficial owner; valuing privately held liabilities can be simplified using the valuation adjustments previously explained*
[e] *Savings account and investment accounts, excluding pension*

This balance sheet presents the varied financial situations of three clients, each with different backgrounds and asset levels. A wealth manager can utilize this information to develop customized strategies for each client, addressing their distinct financial objectives and situations.

- Taylor, a young professional, has a limited amount of assets and liabilities. Most of the assets are liquid and investable, while the liabilities are short term. However, considering the significant educational debt load (which is not unusual for young professionals), Taylor currently has a negative net worth. Moreover, if Taylor's income grows as a result of the educational investment, then the negative net worth should disappear as the loans are repaid.
- Aiysha, a successful small business owner, has a higher net worth but also carries substantial debt, which consists of personal debt, mortgage debt, and business debt.
- Chimwala, an entrepreneur, boasts a remarkable net worth, but the assets are mostly locked up in business assets. Once the business is liquidated, Chimwala's assets will become liquid, realizing the value of the ownership as it is converted into investable assets.

For both Aiysha and Chimwala, the portion of total assets invested in their businesses is crucial, as equity and retained earnings constitute a significant part of their current wealth. The percentage of earnings they allocate as compensation influences their present consumption, while retaining earnings can enhance their businesses' cash flow, capital, and competitive standing.

Sources of Global Wealth

In the decades following World War II, economic growth around the world has been substantial, albeit geographically uneven and sometimes volatile. This history is described in the example box on global economic transformation below and illustrated in Exhibit 4.

This economic growth reflects fundamentally improved economic opportunities combining technological advances, increased economic and business competition, broad deregulation, business-friendly policies, privatization, and emphasis on entrepreneurship as an engine for growth, with changes in international trade that integrate different parts of the world. Other contributing factors to wealth creation have been positively trending asset price appreciation and the marginal but often anecdotally supported influx of accidental wealth through unexpected stardom. While we could consider windfalls from lottery earnings, gambling wins, inherited wealth, or court settlements as examples of such unforeseen wealth, it is critical to emphasize that these instances primarily involve wealth transfer rather than wealth generation.

Exhibit 4: GDP Growth for the World and Select Countries Measured by the Average Per Capita GDP between 1960 and 2022 in Constant 2010 USD

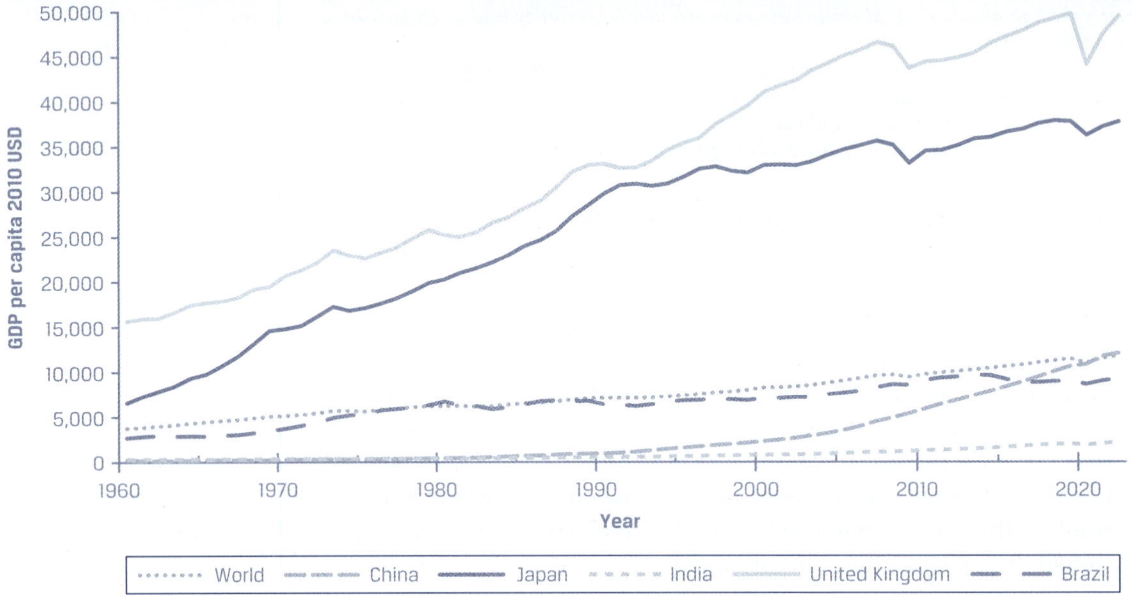

Source: Federal Reserve Bank of St. Louis, https://fred.stlouisfed.org.

THE GLOBAL ECONOMIC TRANSFORMATION

The global economic landscape fundamentally changed after World War II. The war brought about the collapse of the old colonial system, while technological breakthroughs spurred persistent productivity growth and increased international trade further accelerated economic growth. These political, economic, and commercial changes were transformative and led to a substantial rise in global wealth. Exhibit 5 shows the 10-year change in GDP per capita.

Exhibit 5: Decennial Change in GDP Per Capita in Selected Geographic Areas between 1950 and 2020

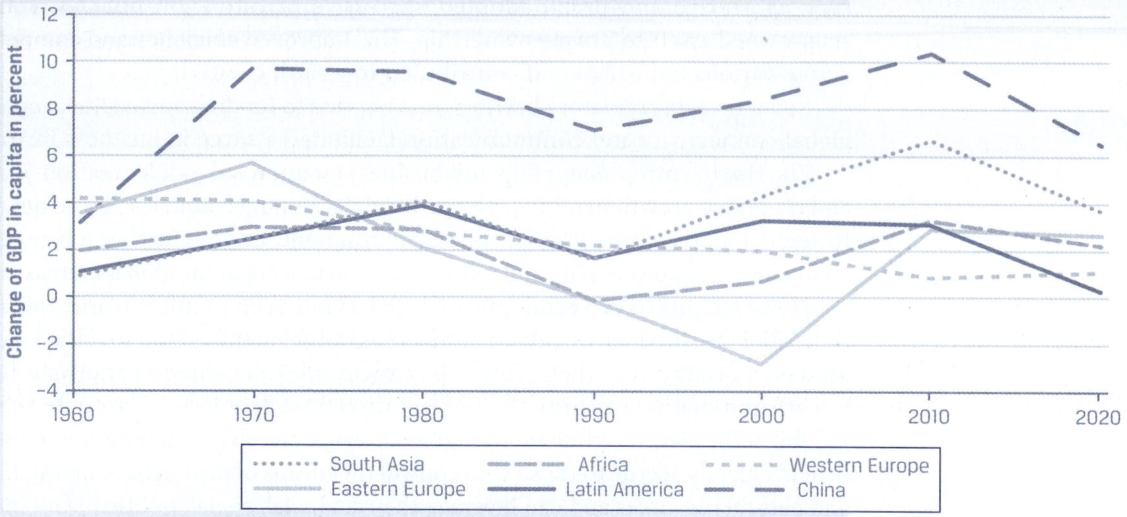

Source: World Bank Data, World Development Indicators (WDI), https://data.worldbank.org.

Decolonization played a key role in this transformation. European powers such as Britain and France could no longer maintain their colonial empires, leading to over 50 countries gaining independence from 1945 to 1960. Despite challenges such as political instability and social inequalities, this shift allowed new nations to control resources and industries, leading to economic expansion.

In South Asia, India and Bangladesh pursued economic strategies that led to both growth and challenges. India focused on developing heavy industries and infrastructure, achieving a 3.5% annual GDP growth rate from 1951 to 1980. Bangladesh, after initial struggles, saw wealth creation through the growth of its ready-made garment industry.

In Africa, countries faced different economic outcomes after decolonization. While nations like Botswana and Mauritius achieved significant economic growth through good governance and economic diversification, others, like Somalia and Nigeria, suffered because of various reasons including corruption and political instability.

Europe saw a division in economic paths, with Western Europe experiencing rapid growth through economic integration and Eastern Europe struggling under inefficient centrally planned economies. However, the fall of the Soviet Union in 1991 prompted market-oriented reforms leading to growth in Eastern Europe.

In Latin America, countries experienced varied economic outcomes based on state intervention, external influences, and policy effectiveness. While policies encouraging domestic market production initially led to growth, they eventually resulted in inefficiencies and hindered wealth creation. External actors and global economic shifts also significantly influenced the region's economic outcomes.

Economic opportunities are crucial in driving economic growth and wealth creation. After the fall of the Berlin Wall in 1989, market-oriented economic policies and increased cross-border competition boosted global economic capacity and spurred wealth creation. Advances in information technology and widespread adoption of many other new technologies led to unprecedented productivity growth. Increased trade flows between different parts of the world also contributed to growth.

The shift towards free market capitalism also played a significant role. Countries like the United Kingdom, former Soviet bloc nations, and Latin American countries such as Mexico and Brazil adopted aggressive privatization policies, transferring state-owned assets to private ownership. This improved efficiency and competitiveness across various industries and contributed to wealth creation.

Reductions in regulatory barriers, more access to funding and capital, and increased global connectivity and communication facilitated a surge in business formation.

The rise in entrepreneurship and business creation led to job creation, innovation, and economic growth in both developed and developing countries. These new ventures fostered a more competitive business environment, driving further advancements in technology and productivity and ultimately contributing to the global increase in wealth.

However, protracted economic growth has not been uniform worldwide nor has it translated into broader wealth creation across all segments of the society. A commonly advanced argument is that economic growth does not directly translate to income growth and that wealth growth does not directly reflect income growth, as shown in Exhibit 6. In fact, rapid economic growth can exacerbate income inequality, as the benefits mainly accrue to those who control the means of production, investable capital, and natural resources and can leverage their financial, social, political, and intellectual capital. High income concentration can reduce demand from the general population, further concentrating capital and wealth in the hands of the already wealthy. To counter these developments, policymakers can implement policies that promote competition, dismantle oligopolies and monopolies, and transfer wealth through taxation. Breaking up dominant market players reduces market entry barriers, fosters innovation, and provides opportunities for new businesses to grow. This process can stimulate job creation and promote a more equitable distribution of wealth.

Moreover, investing in education, building infrastructures, and improving both access to and the quality of healthcare can support long-term economic growth and benefit the broader population. This not only supports social mobility but also supports the workforce by giving individuals the skills necessary to compete globally. Both of these developments also support wealth creation and wealth accumulation. Nonetheless, almost all countries have benefited from economic growth.

Exhibit 6: Net National Wealth to Net National Income Per Capita between 1995 and 2020 in Constant 2021 PPP EUR

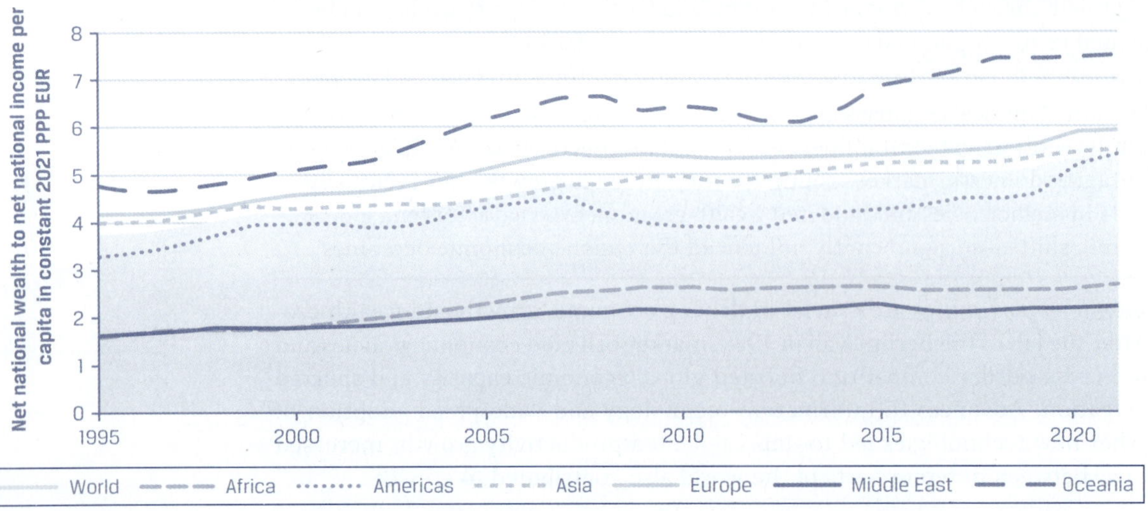

Note: Net national wealth to net national income per capita is calculated in constant 2021 PPP EUR.

Source: World Income Inequality Database – WIID, 30 June 2022. https://www.wider.unu.edu/database/world-income-inequality-database-wiid.

Gains from economic growth are reflected in Credit Suisse's Global Wealth Report 2022 (Exhibit 7), which shows that global per capita wealth has increased over the past 20 years, most notably in the lower middle income and low income economies that account for 75% of the world's population and one-third of global GDP.

MEASURING NET WORTH

The lack of a universally accepted definition of net worth leads to different organizations using their own methodologies when calculating it. For example, Credit Suisse defines net worth or "wealth" of households as the value of financial assets plus real assets (mainly housing) owned by households, minus their debts. This resembles a household's balance sheet, listing owned items and their net value if sold. Credit Suisse's definition excludes private pension fund assets but includes state pension entitlements. It does not consider human capital or an individual's share in state-owned assets and debts, which are difficult to assign to individuals.

This definition may differ from academic research on wealth and income inequality, which can use varying metrics, methodologies, and models leading to different wealth and income levels. Additionally, estimates for the ultra-wealthy may rely on statistical approximations rather than census data. As a result, comparisons between different studies on wealth and income should be made cautiously, considering the specific definitions and methodologies used.

According to the World Bank's classification, in 2021, lower middle income economies had a gross national income (GNI) per capita ranging from USD1,036 to USD4,045. The upper middle income economies had a GNI per capita between USD4,046 and USD12,535. According to the same classification, China is an upper middle income economy. India is identified as a lower middle income economy. This classification highlights the connection between economic opportunities and accelerated wealth growth in rapidly developing countries. There are no countries classified as low income in Europe or North America, and all North American countries are considered high income countries.

Exhibit 7: Average Per Capita Wealth Growth in USD between 2000 and 2021 across Different Regions and Income Levels

Region/country	High income	Upper middle income	Lower middle income	Low income	Average growth
Africa	164%	165%	190%	210%	194%
Asia Pacific	107%	186%	192%	123%	159%
China		289%			289%
Europe	127%	229%	302%		154%
India			177%		177%
Latin America	88%	125%	149%	–18%	112%

Region/country	High income	Upper middle income	Lower middle income	Low income	Average growth
North America	113%				113%
Average	117%	170%	193%	187%	160%

Source: Credit Suisse Research Institute, Global Wealth Databook 2022. https://www.credit-suisse.com/media/assets/corporate/docs/about-us/research/publications/global-wealth-databook-2022.pdf. Data as of December 31, 2021.

Since the 1980s, *entrepreneurship* and new business formation has grown across the world. Entrepreneurs create new markets, disrupt old industries, and create jobs by incorporating new technologies, increasing access to capital and information, engaging in global trade and investments, and shifting attitudes for risk taking and innovation. Many entrepreneurs build and sell their business, thereby transferring real wealth to financial wealth. Increasingly, entrepreneurs drive economic growth by creating new products, services, and markets using the latest technological advances.

Asset price appreciation, especially in the United States and other developed markets, drove wealth growth over the past decades. Exhibit 8 shows the relationship between global stock market capitalization and global GDP. Between 1970 and the end of 2021, both the global stock market capitalization and global GDP grew by around 7%. The graph shows that global stock market capitalization and global GDP are highly positively correlated over the time period.

Exhibit 8: The Growth of Global Stock Market Capitalization and Global GDP in Current USD between 1970 and 2021

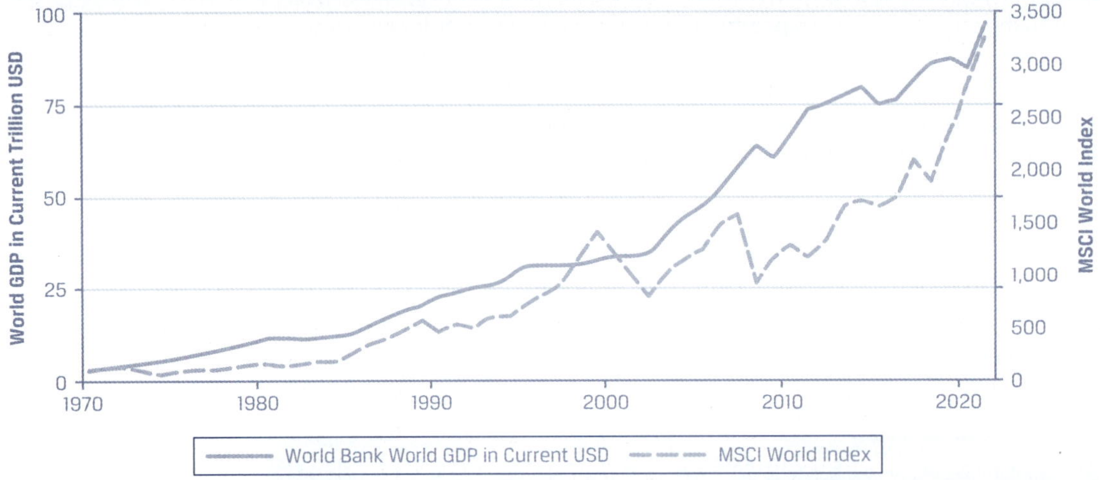

Source: Bloomberg. MXWO Index is the annual MSCI World Index and WGDPWRLD is the World Bank World GDP in Current USD.

Privatizing government assets, selling family-owned businesses, and initial public offerings contributed to this wealth increase. So did financial innovation and financial product development, which drove investments into commodity and real estate markets worldwide. Even though the public listing of a family-owned business reclassifies wealth (from privately held wealth to publicly held wealth, as the cash proceeds from sales can be invested in financial assets), wealth created through entrepreneurship and asset price appreciation remains the main source of wealth creation in most economies.

Furthermore, the significance of inheritance-related wealth transfers is predicted to increase in the future. However, this is not the creation of new riches, but rather the transfer of existing wealth between generations. In the coming decades, the Silent Generation (those born between 1925 and 1945) and the Baby Boomers (those born between 1946 and 1965) will transfer trillions of USD in wealth to subsequent generations through inheritances and gifts.

Finally, accidental wealth through large legal settlements and awards and lottery and gambling winnings is a small but anecdotally significant source of wealth. Gambling is not directly derived from productive work but can dramatically change an individual's financial status overnight. These sources of wealth may be less common, and they do not create new wealth, but they transfer existing wealth.

Much like lottery or gambling winnings, sudden fame can lead to a rapid accumulation of wealth for individuals who suddenly gain immense popularity or recognition in their respective fields such as entertainment, sports, or social media. However, unlike lottery winnings, sudden fame leads to wealth creation.

The global distribution of financial wealth, nonfinancial wealth, and indebtedness generally has remained stable over time across different regions. Here, nonfinancial wealth includes personal property and real assets but excludes human capital. Exhibit 9 shows the distribution of total wealth from 2000 and 2020. Although there are clear disparities among the drivers of wealth growth at the national level — reflecting, in part, differences in economic development, market structure, economic policy, and political preferences — there are some notable regional patterns.

Exhibit 9: Distribution of Total Wealth across the Globe

Region	Wealth type in percent	2000	2005	2010	2015	2020
Africa	Financial wealth	41	44	43	39	44
	Nonfinancial wealth	59	56	57	61	56
	Debts	9	11	11	8	7
Asia- Pacific	Financial wealth	50	52	50	50	50
	Nonfinancial wealth	50	48	50	51	50
	Debts	15	12	12	12	12
China	Financial wealth	36	37	41	43	44
	Nonfinancial wealth	64	63	59	57	56
	Debts	1	4	6	8	11
Europe	Financial wealth	49	43	41	45	45
	Nonfinancial wealth	52	57	59	56	55
	Debts	14	14	15	14	13
India	Financial wealth	24	24	24	22	24
	Nonfinancial wealth	76	76	76	78	76
	Debts	6	7	8	8	9
Latin America	Financial wealth	38	40	40	45	46
	Nonfinancial wealth	62	60	60	55	54
	Debts	10	9	12	11	11
North America	Financial wealth	67	62	68	71	72
	Nonfinancial wealth	33	38	32	29	29
	Debts	14	16	17	14	12
World	Financial wealth	55	51	51	53	54

Region	Wealth type in percent	2000	2005	2010	2015	2020
	Nonfinancial wealth	45	49	49	47	46
	Debts	14	14	14	12	12

Source: Credit Suisse Research Institute, Global Wealth Databook 2022. Data as of December 31, 2021. https://www.credit-suisse.com/media/assets/corporate/docs/about-us/research/publications/global-wealth-databook-2022.pdf.

Between 2000 and 2020, China experienced a significant increase in indebtedness, which may be due to its rapid economic growth and the need for credit to support that growth. In North America, financial wealth plays a crucial role, possibly because of a strong financial market performance, a widespread investment in financial assets, and an overall favorable investment and tax climate. Nonfinancial wealth is more important in India, consistently accounting for around 76% of total wealth from 2000 to 2020, which could be attributed to a cultural emphasis on holding tangible assets, such as real estate and gold, traditionally viewed as reliable stores of value in Indian culture. Finally, both Africa and India tend to accumulate relatively low levels of debt compared to other regions, with debts constituting 7% to 9% of total wealth in 2020. This may reflect limited access to credit financing, substantial underbanked populations, and a general cultural aversion to debt.

Exhibit 10 shows that global wealth is concentrated in North America and Europe, which in 2021 collectively accounted for close to 57% of total global wealth.

Exhibit 10: Wealth Distribution across Different Parts of the World at the End of 2021

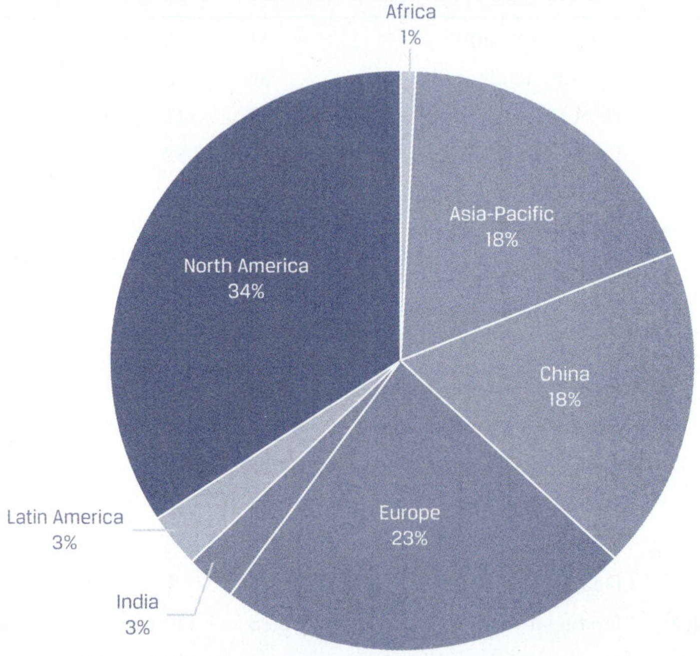

Source: Credit Suisse Research Institute, Global Wealth Databook 2022. Data as of December 31, 2021. https://www.credit-suisse.com/media/assets/corporate/docs/about-us/research/publications/global-wealth-databook-2022.pdf.

In *North America*, the primary drivers of wealth are economic growth, largely fueled by business formation and entrepreneurship. Steady economic and productivity growth, along with positive financial market returns, have led to increased wealth levels. However, this wealth distribution has been unequal, primarily benefiting the more affluent segments of society. A significant factor contributing to this inequality is the prevalence of equity-based compensation for employees in publicly traded companies, such as professionals and executives. Additionally, successful business owners who have commercialized their ideas and sold their businesses to investors contribute to wealth creation. Accomplished professionals, athletes, and artists also play a role in generating wealth in North America.

In *Europe*, as in North America, economic growth has been a main driver of wealth creation. But unlike private business formation or "new money" in North America, it is "old money" that dominates Western European wealth. There are a substantial number of family-controlled medium- to large-sized businesses in Western Europe that typically remain privately held. But the main source of wealth is inherited wealth, primarily real estate.

In the formerly Communist Central and Eastern European countries, the significant structural economic change and privatization that followed the fall of the Soviet Union spurred immense wealth creation, helped by their ascendancy into the European Union, increased direct foreign investment, and investments in education. As these countries transitioned from communist to market-based economies through waves of privatization, many opportunists became wealthy quickly. Example 1 describes the changing fortunes of Czechia/Czech Republic and Slovakia (formerly Czechoslovakia) during this time. In many other formerly Communist countries with large natural resources and commodity-driven economies, there has been significant wealth creation that mainly benefitted a group of politically well-connected individuals.

EXAMPLE 1

The Changing Fortunes of Czechoslovakia, Czechia, and Slovakia

Czechoslovakia was one of the most prosperous European countries before World War II, with an estimated GDP per capita of approximately USD1,800 in 1938, the highest in Central Europe. It had a developed, diverse, and competitive industrial sector.

After World War II Czechoslovakia became a Communist state. Its economy became centrally planned, with state ownership of most of its businesses. The overall economic growth in Communist Czechoslovakia was slow, and living standards remained low, even though both educational opportunities and health care improved.

After the fall of Communism in 1989, the new regime started broad market-oriented economic reforms. Privatization began in 1991 and led to substantial job losses, particularly in industries that were not internationally competitive. Additionally, it also led to a few well-connected oligarchs controlling most of its economy. Allegations of corruption and cronyism were rampant, but the economic changes and privatization revitalized the economy and increased its overall competitiveness. Overall, the Czechoslovakian privatization process is considered a success. After 1993, when Czechoslovakia peacefully split into two independent countries, the Czech Republic (Czechia) and Slovakia, economic growth continued.

The *Asia-Pacific* region has experienced significant economic growth because of high economic growth rates, integration into global commerce, and financial development, which has resulted in considerable wealth accumulation. This growth has been fueled by a transformation from agrarian-based economies to industrialized ones focusing on manufacturing and services. A combination of domestic policies and focus on international trade drove this transformation. For instance, Japan, South Korea, and Singapore adopted an export-oriented strategy, attracting foreign investment, and investing in education and training to develop a globally competitive and highly skilled workforce. Both India and China also created considerable wealth. The region also has intense entrepreneurship across broad sectors including manufacturing, trade, and real estate development. That entrepreneurship in several Asian countries, where small and medium-sized enterprises drive economic growth, has made many entrepreneurs rich. Moreover, real estate development has also played a noticeable role in wealth creation. Finally, the high savings rates, relatively young and educated population, and substantive foreign direct investments all contribute to wealth accumulation.

In *Latin America*, the rapid growth and modernization of stagnant economies have resulted in a significant increase in personal wealth; however, the wealth is distributed relatively unequally. Several Latin American countries have some of the largest wealth and income inequalities. Enterprises and small business owners are also a source of wealth. However, sustained economic growth and political stability remain elusive in many Latin American nations.

In the *Middle East*, petroleum remains the main economic driver, having generated tremendous affluence. However, this wealth is extremely concentrated among a small number of families who have inherited their riches over multiple generations and control significant portions of national economies. Example 2 discusses a shift away from oil dependence, as Saudi Arabia is seeking to diversify its economy by investing its wealth into sectors that can continue to propel its economic growth, albeit at a lower rate.

EXAMPLE 2

The Saudi 2030 Vision

Because up to 40% of Saudi Arabia's GDP comes directly from oil revenue, in 2016 the country launched the Vision 2030 plan to reduce the country's reliance on oil, diversify its economy, and improve the quality of life for its citizens. The plan focuses on three main pillars.

The first pillar aims to create a tolerant, cohesive society that is committed to Islamic and national values and can support the growth of the economy.

The second pillar aims to develop new industries, attract foreign investment, and reduce the country's dependence on oil exports. The plan is to raise non–oil-related export sources of Saudi Arabia's GDP by 2030, specifically to raise the share of non-oil GDP from 16% to 50%. Because a fall in oil prices negatively affects the economy, such diversification reduces Saudi Arabia's dependence on oil as the main driver of its economy. To further reduce its reliance on oil, this plan also aims to increase foreign direct investment inflows from approximately 4% of GDP in 2019 to close to 6% by 2030. Through economic diversification, Saudi Arabia intends to insulate its economy from secular changes in the demand for oil, as the demand for oil is expected to slow down. Finally, the plan also seeks to transform Saudi Arabia into one of the world's 15 largest economies.

The third pillar aims to improve the education system, develop the health care sector, and create a more efficient and effective government. Additionally, the goal is to increase the international competitiveness of the educational sector, aiming to have five Saudi universities among the top 200 universities in international rankings. Moreover, the plans call to increase Saudi Arabian life expectancy to 80 years from 74 years.

A successful implementation of Vision 2030 could increase Saudi Arabia's geopolitical influence in the Middle East.

In recent years, *Africa* has witnessed a rather robust increase in wealth driven by revenues from oil and other commodities, the acceleration in GDP growth, the increase in foreign direct investment, the comparatively robust performance of local economies, and the relative appreciations of local currencies. Still, wealth remains concentrated among the ruling elite, executives, and professionals, as well as small and family-owned enterprises. Wealth in Africa is highly concentrated, with inequality levels comparable to those found in Latin America. Many African countries, such as Botswana, are pursuing policies to reduce their reliance on their core industries and diversify their economies as discussed in Example 3.

EXAMPLE 3

Botswana's Economic Diversification: Moving Beyond Diamonds

Botswana, as the world's top producer of gem diamonds, generates around 40% of the global output, and diamonds contribute to around 35% to its GDP. Botswana now aims to expand other sectors and diversify its economy by focusing on tourism, agriculture, and manufacturing.

Capitalizing on Botswana's diverse wildlife and natural beauty, tourism has grown in significance. In 2000, tourism accounted for approximately 6% of GDP. In 2019, it represented 13%. Because agriculture amounts to 2% of its GDP and is important to subsistence farmers, the government in Botswana has been enhancing both farming productivity and crop diversity. Finally, Botswana is also promoting investments in industries such as manufacturing, services, and technology to create jobs and foster economic growth.

Understanding growth in real wealth, particularly in countries or regions that have suffered extreme economic changes or otherwise are prone to significant exchange rate volatility, requires explicitly accounting for the impacts of inflation and variable exchange rates, as Example 4 on Argentina explains.

EXAMPLE 4

The Deceptive Rise of Wealth: Understanding the Difference between Nominal and Real Growth in Times of Crisis

Argentina has experienced several economic crises including sharp currency devaluations and hyperinflation. In the late 1980s, its annual inflation rate was almost 500%. In 2002, the inflation rate peaked at 41%. Hyperinflationary periods have significantly decreased the real purchasing power of Argentinians. Although the nominal wealth of Argentinians appeared to increase because of hyperinflation, the devaluation of the currency decreased the foreign currency value of their assets. Consequently, the real wealth decreased due to the hyperinflation.

Inflation Rate and Relevant USD Exchange Rates in Argentina 1987–2022

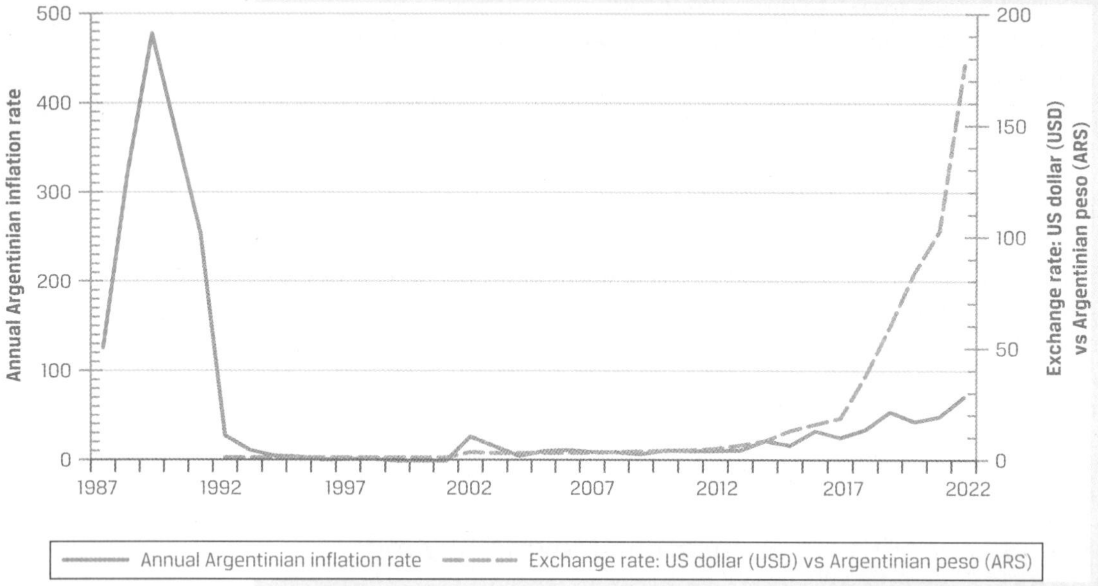

For instance, in 2001, the GDP per capita of Argentina was approximately USD7,100, but by 2002, it had fallen to approximately USD2,500 because of hyperinflation and currency devaluation. Moreover, the severe economic downturn that followed led to a negative real GDP growth rate of −11% in 2002, as depicted in the graph below. Furthermore, the poverty rate, measured by the proportion of the population living under USD5.50 per day, increased from 31% in 2001 to 44% in 2002.

GDP Per Capita in USD and GDP Growth in Argentina, 1986–2022

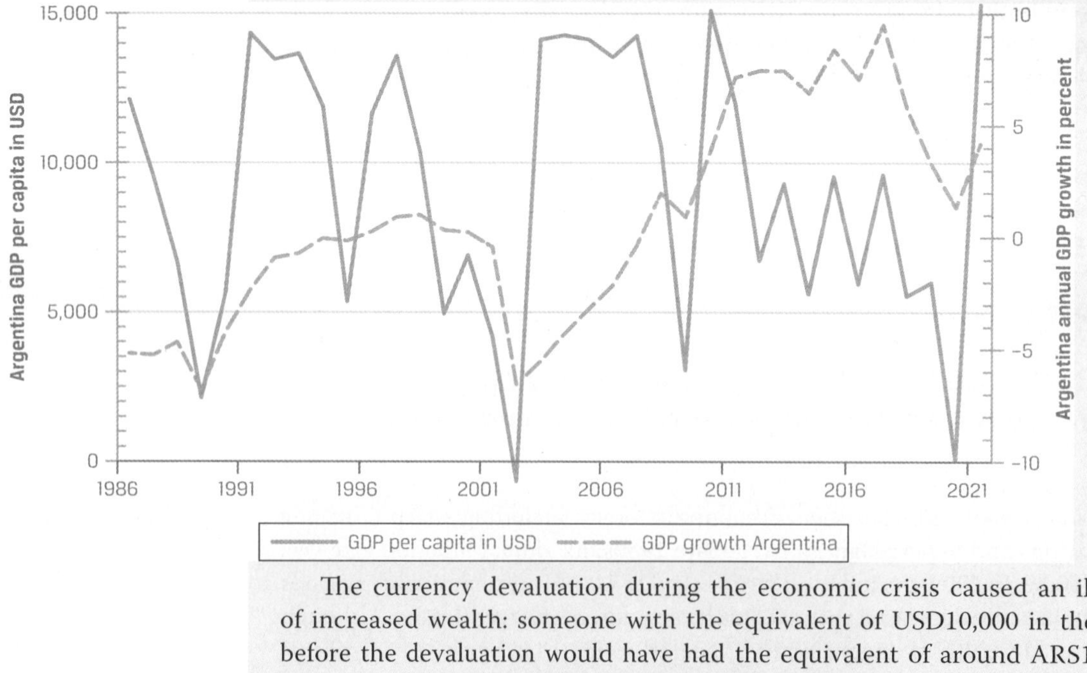

The currency devaluation during the economic crisis caused an illusion of increased wealth: someone with the equivalent of USD10,000 in the bank before the devaluation would have had the equivalent of around ARS10,000. After devaluation, the same dollar wealth would be worth around ARS30,000.

Although nominal wealth increased because of hyperinflation during the crisis, the real value of this wealth had actually decreased. The importance of factoring in inflation and exchange rates when analyzing wealth growth in markets or regions prone to extreme events or exchange rate volatility is underscored by this example.

Distribution of Global Wealth

Although the precise wealth levels across the world continuously evolve, driven by asset price, commodity price, and exchange rate dynamics, there are some persistent trends. First, wealth is unevenly distributed. Second, wealth is highly concentrated. Third, very few people hold large amounts of wealth. Fourth, the number of millionaires is increasing each year because the USD1 million cutoff point changes with economic growth rates, exchange rate fluctuations, and inflation. Understanding these trends helps wealth managers better serve their high-net-worth clients.

According to Credit Suisse, in 2021 the household wealth distribution across the global adult population of 5.3 billion shows that 2.8 billion people, or 53% of all adults, had wealth below USD10,000; 1% of the adults, or approximately 54 million people, had wealth exceeding USD1,000,000; see Exhibit 11.

Exhibit 11: Distribution of Global Wealth

	Africa	Asia Pacific	China	Europe	India	Latin America	North America	World
Number of adults in millions	690	1,257	1,111	589	916	453	282	5,299
Mean wealth per adult (in USD)	8,419	64,700	76,639	180,275	15,535	27,717	560,846	87,489
Median wealth per adult (in USD)	1,111	5,218	28,258	26,385	3,457	5,139	95,255	8,360
Distribution of adults by wealth range (USD) in percent								
Under 10,000	87	63	18	32	75	65	22	53
Between 10,000 and 100,000	12	26	67	36	23	30	29	34
Between 100,000 and 1,000,000	1	10	15	29	2	5	39	12
Over 1,000,000	0	1	1	3	0	0	10	1

Source: Credit Suisse Research Institute, Global Wealth Databook 2022. Data as of December 31, 2021. https://www.credit-suisse.com/media/assets/corporate/docs/about-us/research/publications/global-wealth-databook-2022.pdf.

Median global wealth is USD8,360, while the mean global wealth is USD87,489, as a few individuals with very high levels of wealth can greatly increase the average wealth while the median wealth remains relatively low. The global distribution of wealth can be shown by comparing the wealth of the top wealth groups compared to the average citizen and comparing the average citizen to those at the bottom of the wealth distribution. Exhibit 12 contains all wealth deciles to show the different distribution of wealth across different parts of the world. The top decile of individuals controls more wealth than the remaining 90% of the population. At the end of 2021, the bottom 50% of adults in the global wealth distribution controlled less than 1% of total global wealth.

Exhibit 12: Distribution of Global Wealth across Deciles

	Wealth share (%) per wealth population decile										Top percentile (1%)
Geographic areas	1	2	3	4	5	6	7	8	9	10	
Africa	−1	0	0	0	1	2	3	5	10	79	44
Asia Pacific	0	0	0	0	1	1	2	4	10	82	39
China	0	1	2	2	3	4	6	8	14	60	31
Europe	−1	0	0	1	1	2	5	9	16	68	30
India	−1	0	1	1	2	3	4	6	11	73	41
Latin America	−1	0	0	1	1	2	4	6	12	76	39
North America	−1	0	0	1	1	2	4	6	12	74	35
World	−1	0	0	0	1	1	2	4	10	82	46

Source: Credit Suisse Research Institute, Global Wealth Databook 2022. Data as of December 31, 2021. https://www.credit-suisse.com/media/assets/corporate/docs/about-us/research/publications/global-wealth-databook-2022.pdf.

The richest decile, the top 10% of the adults in the world, controls 82% of wealth, and the remaining 90% control 18%. For example, in the Asia-Pacific region, the top 1% of wealth holders have a wealth share of 39%, while the bottom 90% have a wealth share of 18%. In China, the top 10% of wealth holders have a wealth share of 60%, while the bottom 50% have a wealth share of 9%. Overall, the table shows that wealth is concentrated at the top decile, particularly in the top 1%, with the largest wealth share in most regions held by this group. The top 1% of the adult population controls 46% of the global wealth. In some regions, such as Africa and India, there are negative wealth shares in the lower wealth deciles, indicating that those groups have negative net worth.

The difference in entry points to different wealth deciles shows the regional differences in wealth and that, in many parts of the world, a notable number of individuals have negative net worth. In 2021, the minimum wealth to belong to the richest 10% of the world's adults was USD138,000, to belong to the richest 5%, USD296,000, and to the top 1%, USD1,147,000. There are notable regional and national differences for these cutoff points, as shown in Exhibit 13.

Exhibit 13: Minimum Wealth in USD to Qualify for a Wealth Decile

	Minimum wealth of deciles (USD per adult)								
Geographic area	2	3	4	5	6	7	8	9	10
Africa	−235	−14	172	576	1,111	1,988	3,323	5,978	12,692
Asia Pacific	−213	513	1,583	3,112	5,218	8,635	15,709	34,796	122,248
China	4,888	11,043	15,279	20,348	28,258	37,907	51,593	80,292	134,193
Europe	−266	3,386	8,929	15,044	26,385	57,074	114,292	200,285	397,553
India	−596	904	1,398	2,295	3,457	5,243	7,819	12,325	25,377
Latin America	−1,229	−541	580	2,576	5,139	8,015	13,122	22,055	48,597
North America	−13,302	8,563	22,428	58,948	95,255	156,896	255,099	468,151	909,331
World	−162	840	2,214	4,493	8,360	14,155	25,123	51,633	138,346

Source: Credit Suisse Research Institute, Global Wealth Databook 2022. https://www.credit-suisse.com/

media/assets/corporate/docs/about-us/research/publications/global-wealth-databook-2022.pdf.

These are threshold estimates to qualify for each of the deciles. Note that there are no estimates for the first decile.

The table shows that the minimum wealth of the different deciles varies greatly across regions. In Africa, for example, the poorest 10% have a maximum wealth of –USD235 per adult. This means that to be in the second-lowest wealth decile, one would have a maximum wealth of –USD235; they are net debtors, with their debts exceeding the value of their assets. In contrast, the wealthiest 10% in Africa have a minimum wealth of USD12,692 per adult.

The maximum wealth of the poorest 10% in North America, similarly, the entry threshold to the second decile of the wealth distribution, is –USD13,302 and is much lower than the maximum wealth of the poorest 10% in Asia Pacific, or –USD213. The minimum wealth of the wealthiest 10% is also much higher in North America than in other regions.

All the data demonstrates the extent of wealth inequality. All countries contain varying degrees of wealth inequality or income inequality. Wealth inequality is different from income inequality because income inequality looks at the distribution of income generated by society, and wealth inequality looks at the economic distribution of assets and their ownership and reinforces wide national wealth gaps.

The **Gini coefficient**, a more broad-based measure of inequality that focuses on the entirety of the wealth spectrum, confirms the skewness of the wealth distribution. It ranges from 0 to 1, where 0 represents perfect equality (everyone gets an equal share of the wealth) and 1 represents perfect inequality (one individual owns all the wealth). It compares the **Lorenz curve**, the cumulative percentage of wealth owned by each percentage of the population, with the line of perfect equality, where wealth is uniformly distributed across the population. Each percentage of the population owns an equal percentage of the wealth. Example 5 looks at how the Gini coefficient captures different types of wealth distribution.

EXAMPLE 5

Gini Coefficient

The Gini coefficient measures wealth inequality in a population. It ranges from 0 to 1, with 0 indicating a perfectly equal wealth distribution and 1 indicating maximum wealth inequality. Here are three examples:

	Cumulative percentage of wealth		
Cumulative percentage of households	**Example 1 Perfect wealth distribution Gini coefficient = 0**	**Example 2 Low degree of wealth inequality Gini coefficient = 0.27**	**Example 3 High degree of wealth inequality Gini coefficient = 0.69**
0%	0%	0%	0%
10%	10%	1%	1%
20%	20%	5%	2%
30%	30%	10%	3%
40%	40%	20%	4%
50%	50%	30%	6%
60%	60%	40%	7%
70%	70%	55%	10%
80%	80%	70%	20%

	Cumulative percentage of wealth		
Cumulative percentage of households	Example 1 Perfect wealth distribution Gini coefficient = 0	Example 2 Low degree of wealth inequality Gini coefficient = 0.27	Example 3 High degree of wealth inequality Gini coefficient = 0.69
90%	90%	85%	50%
100%	100%	100%	100%

Exhibit 14 shows these examples graphically.

Exhibit 14: Gini Coefficient and Wealth Distribution

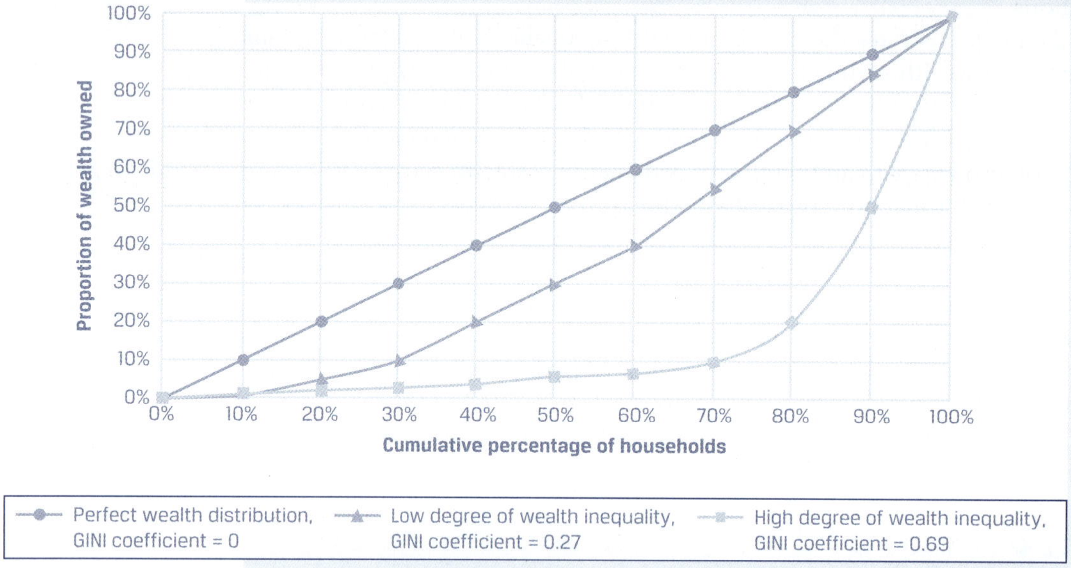

In the first example, the Gini coefficient is 0, which represents a perfectly equal wealth distribution. This means that every household in the population has the same amount of wealth. The area under the Lorenz curve is also 0, which indicates that the cumulative percentage of households and the cumulative percentage of wealth are the same. This can be an ideal situation for a society in terms of wealth equality.

In the second example, the Gini coefficient is 0.27, indicating a low degree of wealth inequality in the population. This means that the distribution of wealth is relatively even across the population, with a small percentage of households holding a disproportionate amount of wealth. The area under the Lorenz curve is also relatively small, indicating a smaller degree of inequality. In this situation, the mean wealth per household provides a more accurate representation of the economic status of the population, as there is less concentration of wealth in a small group of households.

In the third example, the Gini coefficient is 0.69, indicating a high degree of wealth inequality in the population. This means that a small percentage of households have a disproportionate amount of wealth compared to the rest of the population. The area under the Lorenz curve is also relatively large, indicating a large degree of inequality. In this situation, the mean wealth per household does not provide an accurate representation of the economic status of the population, as there is a significant concentration of wealth in a small group of households.

Long-term changes in Gini coefficients reveal trends in wealth inequality. When the Gini coefficients rise over time, wealth inequality worsens. Economic policies, technological advances, and demographic shifts can affect long-term change in Gini coefficients over time, as we can see in Exhibit 15. In a recession or depression, wealth becomes more concentrated among fewer people or households, raising the Gini coefficient. Looking at the global long-term changes between 2000 and 2020, the overall wealth distribution appears to have changed in several countries. Both the global financial crisis and the COVID-19 pandemic impacted wealth inequality. Many individuals in lower and middle income brackets experienced substantial financial hardships, job losses, and economic problems. Wealthier individuals, on average, fared better. The COVID-19 pandemic exacerbated this divide. Individuals in lower income brackets, usually employed in service-based industries, lost their jobs. Wealthier individuals, on the other hand, benefitted from surging stock markets and increased demand in certain technology-centric industries.

Although wealth inequality increased in both developed and developing markets, the gap is greater in the developed markets due to weaker social safety nets and greater income variability.

Exhibit 15: Trends in Gini Coefficients for Selected Countries between 2000 and 2020

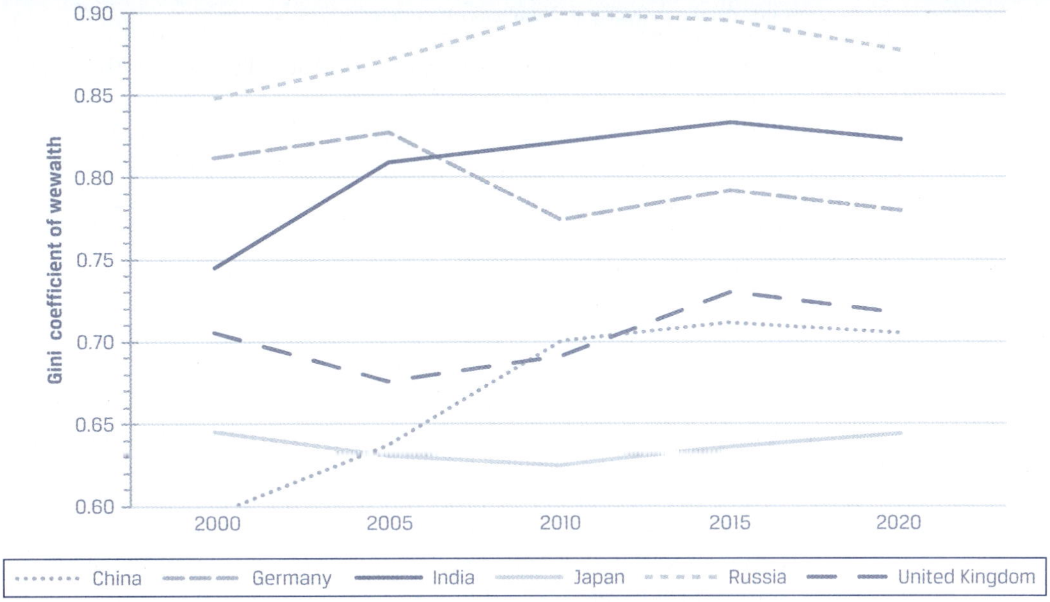

Source: Credit Suisse Research Institute, Global Wealth Databook 2022. Data as of December 31, 2021. https://www.credit-suisse.com/media/assets/corporate/docs/about-us/research/publications/global-wealth-databook-2022.pdf. Reported estimates.

Over time, changes in global wealth inequality reflect both shifts in the wealth inequality within countries and between countries. The rise of household wealth in many emerging markets has pushed overall global wealth inequality down. For instance, between 2000 and 2021, the average wealth in India increased by 9% annually and in China by 15%. At the same time, the average growth rate of wealth across the globe was 5%. The fact that average wealth levels in China are approaching global wealth levels suggests that global wealth distribution is becoming less unequal in aggregate.

Private wealth managers have traditionally categorized clients by wealth levels. Each wealth stratum presents unique demands, challenges, and opportunities from the wealth manager's perspective. These segments typically include mass-affluent and affluent clients in the top decile of the wealth pyramid, as well as wealthier clients such as HNWIs, very-high-net-worth individuals (VHNWIs), and UHNWIs, as shown in Exhibit 16.

Exhibit 16: Wealth Segments and the Number of Individuals (in Thousands) Belonging to Each of These Segments across the Globe

Wealth segment	Wealth range (in million USD)	North America	Europe	Asia Pacific	China	Latin America	India	Africa	World
High net worth (HNWI)	1–5	21,565	15,300	9,859	5,582	809	696	316	54,126
Very high net worth (VHNWI)	5–10	3,360	912	587	366	63	59	24	5,371
	10–50	1,706	442	279	210	38	37	11	2,723
Ultra-high net worth (UHNWI)	50–100	107	27	19	20	3	3	1	180
	100–500	38	14	10	11	2	2	1	77
	500+	2	2	1	1	1	-	-	7

Source: Credit Suisse Research Institute, Global Wealth Databook 2022. Data as of December 31, 2021. https://www.credit-suisse.com/media/assets/corporate/docs/about-us/research/publications/global-wealth-databook-2022.pdf. Numbers are rounded.

However, this segmentation method may not fully capture the sophistication and complexity of the guidance, investment planning, and financial, legal, and tax advice a client requires. Factors such as a client's legal and physical domicile, stage in their financial life cycle, demographics, income, wealth structure, asset class holdings, and values can influence service expectations, which may vary among clients with similar wealth levels.

Private wealth managers prioritize liquid or investable wealth over total wealth, as it provides an initial indication of a client's position in the wealth strata and their current and future service needs. For example, private wealth managers would offer different levels of services to a client with USD50 million that included an investment portfolio of USD3 million and a family business equity worth USD47 million, compared to a client with USD45 million in their investment portfolio and USD5 million in private real estate.

The UHNWI category typically consists of the upper half of decamillionaires, who have a net worth exceeding USD10 million, and includes the centimillionaires, with a net worth surpassing USD100 million. As per *Forbes*' 2022 calculations, there are around 2,300 billionaires worldwide, and to be among the top 500 richest individuals, an estimated net worth of USD5 billion is necessary.

Family offices play a vital role in managing UHNWIs' wealth. These private firms offer a range of wealth management services, including investment, tax, estate planning, and philanthropy management, tailored specifically to UHNWIs and their families' needs. The primary objective of family offices is to preserve and grow wealth across generations while tackling the unique challenges and opportunities associated with significant wealth. By possessing a deeper understanding of a family's values, goals, and legacy objectives, family offices can effectively address the complex financial needs of UHNWIs. This close relationship allows them to develop and execute long-term strategies aligned with the family's vision while navigating the complex legal, tax, and regulatory landscape linked to substantial wealth.

Furthermore, family offices often employ or collaborate with highly specialized professionals, such as legal advisors, accountants, and investment managers, to deliver a holistic wealth management approach. This comprehensive strategy ensures that all aspects of a family's wealth are considered and managed, encompassing investment management, risk mitigation, succession planning, and philanthropic activities. Exhibit 17 illustrates *Bloomberg*'s RICH <GO> function, displaying the richest individuals in the world.

Exhibit 17: RICH <GO> at *Bloomberg* as of October 31, 2023

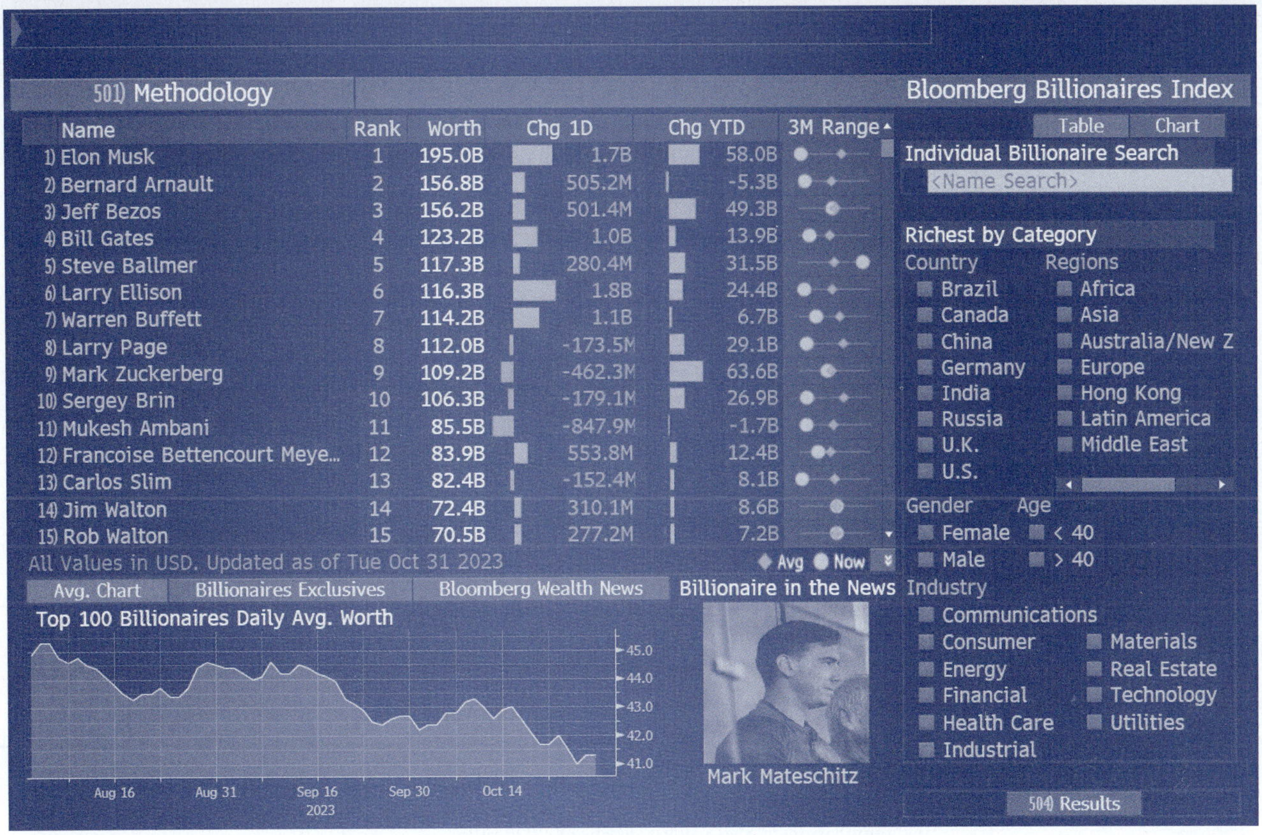

It is worth looking at the size of the global UHNWI market to assess the potential revenues that accumulated wealth can generate in the following case study.

CASE STUDY

Sizing the Global UHNWI Market

This example estimates the potential revenue for the global UHNWI wealth management market based on assets under management–based fees. For assets between USD50 million and USD100 million, revenue is around 5 bp; for USD100 million and USD500 million, around 1 bp; and for assets over USD500 million, around 0.1 bp.

Region Data as of 2021	Individuals with wealth between USD50 m and 100 m	Individuals with wealth between USD100 m and 500 m	Individuals with wealth above USD500 m	Total number of UHNWIs	% of the world
United States	103,669	35,740	1,726	141,135	53.4
China	20,013	11,411	1,282	32,706	12.4
Germany	6,052	3,354	318	9,724	3.7
Canada	3,472	1,912	123	5,507	2.1
India	3,024	1,750	210	4,984	1.9
Japan	3,373	1,411	88	4,872	1.8
France	3,237	1,314	85	4,636	1.8
Australia	2,947	1,576	109	4,632	1.8
United Kingdom	2,787	1,278	110	4,175	1.6
Italy	2,574	1,253	103	3,930	1.5
Korea	2,450	1,319	117	3,886	1.5
Russia	2,134	1,488	253	3,875	1.5
Switzerland	2,115	987	92	3,194	1.2
Hong Kong SAR	1,790	1,139	127	3,056	1.2
Sweden	1,866	1,019	76	2,961	1.1
Taiwan Region	1,874	912	93	2,879	1.1
Spain	1,509	666	51	2,226	0.8
Brazil	1,238	749	95	2,082	0.8
Singapore	974	570	73	1,617	0.6
Netherlands	1,100	471	28	1,599	0.6

Source: Credit Suisse Research Institute, Global Wealth Databook 2022. Data as of December 31, 2021. https://www.credit-suisse.com/media/assets/corporate/docs/about-us/research/publications/global-wealth-databook-2022.pdf.

To estimate the average wealth within each range, we will use the midpoint of the specified intervals. For the USD50 million to 100 million range, we will use USD75 million as the average, for the USD100 million to 500 million range, USD300 million will serve as the average, and for individuals with wealth exceeding USD500 million, the average wealth is conservatively estimated at USD1 billion. Based on these calculations, the estimated revenue for the top 10 countries is approximately USD7.5 billion, while the combined revenue for all the mentioned countries is around USD8.5 billion.

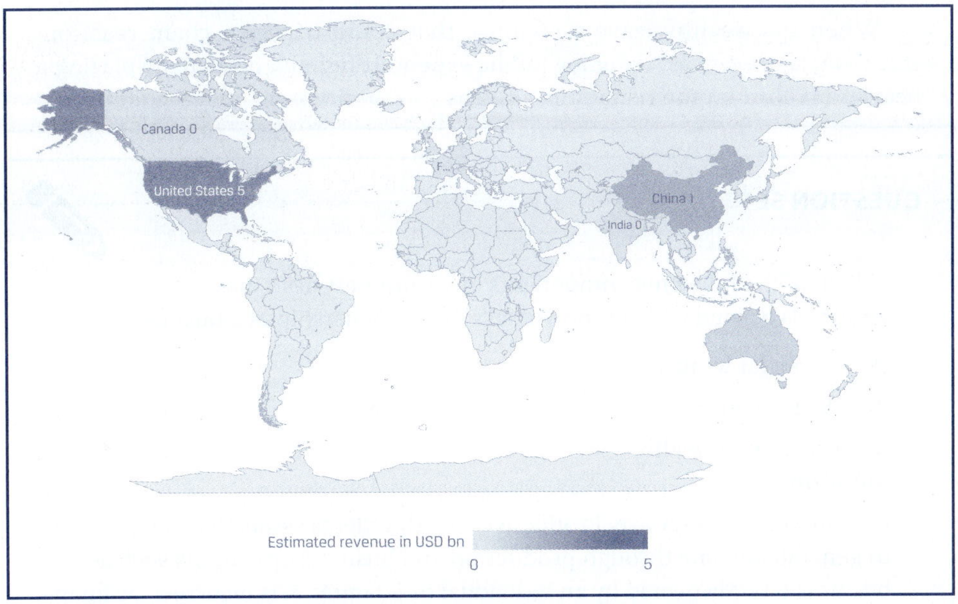

Wealth inequality is a critical issue in contemporary society. One particularly contentious point centers on the tax obligations of UHNWIs and the phenomenon of wealthy individuals considering the move to tax-friendly jurisdictions.

THE MOBILITY OF HNWIS

Decisions made by HNWIs and their financial advisors significantly impact not only their personal wealth but also the economic and social fabric of their home countries. As wealth mobility increases, balancing the legitimate need for wealth preservation and legal protection with an ethical responsibility of contributing to societal well-being can come to the forefront.

HNWIs might perceive high taxes as unfairly punitive or as diminishing the incentive for wealth creation and entrepreneurial activities, and, consequently, they often consider moving their assets, legal residence, or both to jurisdictions with more tax-friendly policies, "tax havens." However, taxes may not be the only motivator.

Political risk is a significant concern and goes beyond direct expropriations. It can include changes in regulations, legal frameworks, taxation regimes, and discriminatory practices. Deteriorating rule of law and instances of physical violence, such as kidnappings, can all be substantial threats to their wealth and business operations and could compel them to relocate to places offering more legal protection, political stability, and predictability. Moreover, political risk is not limited to developing countries, as populist governments are elected in developed countries, as well.

Investors must consider these factors in their decision-making processes when assessing the situation in their home country, the country where they plan to seek domicile, and the physical and legal locations of their wealth.

Besides legal, economic, and political factors, there may be a crucial aspect wealthy individuals should consider. The wealth many wealthy individuals accumulate is often deeply intertwined with the resources and benefits available in their country. Elements such as the legal framework, the education system, regulatory and political structures, public infrastructure, and educational systems are often funded by taxpayers and play a significant role in creating an environment where businesses and entrepreneurship can thrive and generate wealth. Thus, prosperity often depends directly on the infrastructure and public goods that taxpayers finance.

When the wealthy leave a country, that could trigger a chain reaction: shrinking tax revenues, reducing public expenditures, and potentially placing a heavier tax load on the remaining citizens.

QUESTION SET

1. Which of the following components of wealth best describes wealth associated with an individual's direct ownership of a business?

   A. Financial wealth

   B. Real wealth

   C. Productive wealth

   Solution:

   C is the correct response. Productive wealth reflects assets that can be used to generate income through production and business operations such as a business directly owned by an individual or a family. A is incorrect. as financial wealth comprises all financial assets but excludes direct ownership of businesses. B is incorrect, as real wealth refers to tangible assets such as real estate and commodities.

2. Contrast an individual's aggregate wealth and net worth.

   Solution:

   Aggregate wealth is the total value of all assets. Net worth reflects the value of assets minus the individual's liabilities. As such, an individual could conceivably have a very large value of assets versus a low net worth. This would happen if an individual were highly levered.

3. Discuss the factors that a private wealth management firm might consider with respect to identifying countries in which individuals are likely to have greater economic opportunities for income and wealth growth.

   Solution:

   Factors associated with greater economic opportunities and wealth growth within countries or regions include (1) technological advancements that contribute to productivity improvements; (2) shifts towards free market capitalism; (3) business privatization (transfers of state-owned assets to private ownership); (4) increases in business formation, especially entrepreneurial ventures that lead to job creation, innovation, and economic growth worldwide; and (5) economic and business deregulation. Additionally, asset price appreciation in real terms is a factor driving wealth growth in countries and regions.

4. Which of the following factors would typically result in a scenario where a region or country is experiencing economic growth, along with improvement in income and wealth inequality?

   A. The regional economy's growth is highly dependent on natural resources.

   B. Significant concentration of control of investable capital within a country.

C. Regulatory effort within a country to dismantle monopoly businesses.

Solution:

C is the correct response. A country with a regulatory focus on breaking up monopolies may help promote improvements in income and wealth inequality. Both responses A and B make statements that would be more consistent with higher levels of income and wealth inequality.

5. A country's Gini coefficient for income distribution is currently 0.35 and was 0.25 10 years earlier. Which of the following responses best describes the level and change of the country's income inequality?

A. Income inequality is relatively low currently and has decreased over the last 10 years.

B. Income inequality is relatively low currently and has increased over the last 10 years.

C. Income inequality is relatively high currently and has improved over the last 10 years.

Solution:

B is the correct response. Gini coefficients range from zero to one, with a value of zero reflecting income equality. Income inequality is greater as the Gini coefficient moves higher. With a value closer to zero, 0.35 likely reflects relatively low levels of income inequality. But, as the coefficient has moved higher over the last 10 years, it indicates an increase in income inequality or a decrease in income equality in the country.

3 LIFE-CYCLE VIEW OF HUMAN CAPITAL

☐ evaluate how changes in human capital, financial capital, and economic net worth across the financial stages of an individual's life influence their financial decision making

Large institutional investors, who typically invest capital on the behalf of their clients, differ from individual investors, who invest their own capital with some of the notable differences outlined in Exhibit 18.

Exhibit 18: Differences between Institutional and Individual Investors

Characteristics	Institutional	Individual
Purpose	Specific	Multiple
Investment objectives	Static	Dynamic
Number of liabilities	Many	Handful
Relative size of individual liabilities	Small	Variable
Time horizon	Long term/infinite	Multiple (for different objectives)
Asset size	Very large	Usually small

Characteristics	Institutional	Individual
Investment options	More access	Less access
Tax situation	Differing, often tax-exempt	Usually taxable and complex
Performance measurement	Index, benchmark	Shortfall meeting a goal or liability
Client sophistication	High	Low to average
Risk	Objective and quantifiable	Failing to meet a specific goal
Customization	Low to medium	High

Institutional investors, such as pension funds, endowments, insurance companies, hedge funds, and investment managers, actively allocate capital to generate returns aligned with their specific investment mandates. Sometimes these objectives are to meet their clients' financial obligations, who may be individual investors seeking long-term capital accumulation by investing with an investment manager.

Institutional investors secure, pool, and manage capital. Some institutional investors, such as pension funds and insurance companies, have long-term obligations towards their clients. These investors design and implement investment strategies to fulfill those obligations over long horizons, oftentimes decades. In executing their strategies, some institutional investors accumulate returns in a tax-aware manner, while others are tax exempt.

Institutional investors measure and evaluate their investment performance against defined indices or benchmarks and use risk measures, such as various measures of volatility, to quantify the risk that they take with client funds. Many large institutional investors have the resources to conduct extensive research and analysis to identify investment opportunities in various markets, sectors, and asset classes. Consequently, they invest across a diverse array of strategies. Here, because of their size, they benefit from economies of scale that reduces their expenses, which they can pass onto their clients. These lower expenses can benefit their clients, who do not have the same capital or professional research capabilities and who are willing to pay a fee to have their assets professionally managed by institutional investors.

Individual investors allocate their own, generally more limited capital to achieve multiple, sometimes conflicting, objectives: growing personal wealth, saving for retirement, buying a car or home, starting a business, or leaving a legacy for their heirs. Their time horizons combine short-, medium-, and long-term objectives. Some of their short-term financial goals may be only a few years away, while their longest-term objectives, such as funding retirement and enabling generational wealth transfer, are typically bookended by the natural human life span. Overall, individual investors manage multiple smaller liabilities, such as saving for a house or retirement, with different certainty throughout their lives. Additionally, these investment objectives (i.e., liabilities) are more likely to change or evolve over time as the family's situation changes. Because their resources are smaller, individuals typically have less access to various investment products or opportunities compared to institutional investors.

Because they are usually taxed on their investment income, capital gains, or dividends, individual investors' decisions may hinge on the tax implications of their investment choices. Since tax rates depend on their tax domicile, tax jurisdiction, and their level of income, individual investors may benefit from having some flexibility to manage the size and timing of their tax obligations. As a result, their tax situations can be more complex than those of institutions. Individual investors gauge their performance by their ability to meet their financial objectives. If they do not fulfill their financial goals or obligations, they have underperformed their objectives. It is worth emphasizing that, despite some of the additional complexities associated with private wealth management, clients are typically less sophisticated in a financial sense than institutional clients.

However, there are some individual investors, particularly UHNWIs, for whom investment strategies, objectives, and resources are more akin to those of a small or medium-size institution than those of an average individual investor. Most UHNWIs have large portions of their portfolios allocated to more complex investment strategies that require scale, such as tax-loss harvesting, and alternative investments such as private equity, infrastructure, and hedge funds that are normally not accessible to the average HNWI.

There are also differences between individual investors domiciled in developed markets and in emerging markets. Apart from the notable differences in wealth levels, distinctions in investment opportunities and market conditions also characterize the two groups. Many emerging market–domiciled investors seek to pursue wealth management services in developed markets to expand their investment alternatives. Conversely, investors domiciled in developed markets may seek out emerging market investment opportunities. Some pertinent differences in investment opportunities between developed and emerging markets are summarized in Exhibit 19.

Exhibit 19: Differences in Investment Opportunities

	Developed markets	Emerging markets
Markets	Large, active markets and multiple different investment alternatives	Smaller markets with limited investment alternatives
Access to information	High	Low
Regulation	Regulated market practices	Less regulated market practices

Compared to investors in emerging markets, individual investors in developed markets tend to have access to larger, active markets with more investment opportunities, have higher access to information, and benefit from more regulated market practices.

Developed markets offer large active financial markets with a range of different investment opportunities and investment alternatives. Their robust financial systems, mature capital markets, and enhanced transparency collectively promote long-term wealth accumulation. The established institutional structure in these markets, including access to premium financial information, grants investors a unique advantage for long-term wealth accumulation. Moreover, regulatory integrity in developed markets safeguards investors, fostering trust in the financial system.

Investors in emerging markets typically can only choose from a more limited array of investment alternatives, and the regulatory support for investments may not be as stringent as in developed markets. In many emerging markets, investors eschew investments in financial markets for familiar investment opportunities, such as private businesses owned by family members and friends, or in tangible assets such as real estate or gold for long-term wealth accumulation. Nonetheless, considering the size and development of emerging markets, there are more and more investors there who seek to diversify their investments.

The Wealth Life Cycle

Financial stages of life are a useful construct when thinking about financial goals, priorities, objectives, and constraints. The financial stages are often divided into seven periods, as Exhibit 20 shows.

Exhibit 20: The Seven Financial Stages of Life

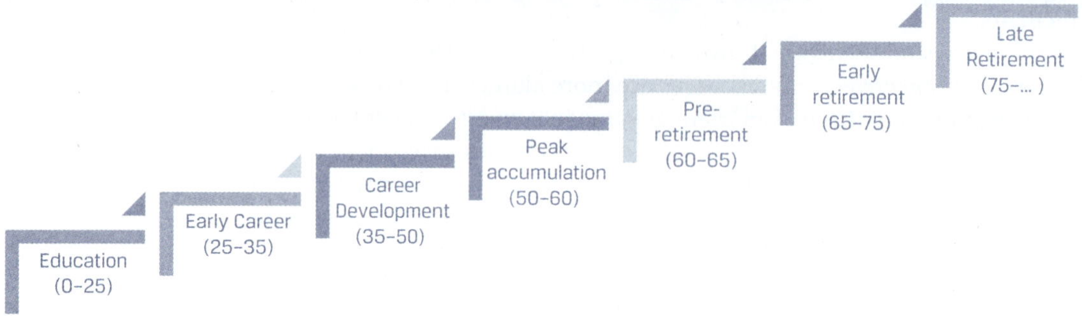

- The *education phase* occurs during the individual's education before entering the workforce. During this phase, individuals may be financially dependent on their parents or guardians and have little accumulated financial capital or focus on savings.
- The *early career phase* normally begins when an individual enters the workforce, usually in their late teens to early thirties. During this phase, individuals may marry, have young children, incur debt to purchase a home, and begin to save for their children's education expenses.
- The *career development phase* typically occurs during the ages of 35–50 and is a time of specific skill development, upward career mobility, and income growth. However, significant family and housing expenses during this phase may limit an individual's ability to save, with human capital representing a large proportion of total wealth.
- The *peak accumulation phase* typically begins during the ages of 50–60, when most people have reached maximum earnings and have the greatest opportunity for wealth accumulation. During this phase, individuals may accumulate funds for other goals and objectives, but retirement income planning and minimizing taxes are usually the primary focus.
- The *pre-retirement phase* consists of the few years preceding the planned retirement age, usually around 65 years of age. It is typically an individual's maximum career income and highest point of wealth accumulation. For those forced to retire due to injury or unemployment, this time may involve changing expectations and adapting to a lifestyle more commensurate with their wealth.
- The *early retirement phase* is the most active period of retirement and is when an individual is less likely to suffer from cognitive or mobility limitations. Even in retirement, it is important to continue taking an appropriate level of investment risk in portfolios to ensure asset growth.
- The *late retirement phase* is a complex phase because of its unknown duration. This uncertainty is known as **longevity risk**, the risk that an individual outlives their financial resources in retirement. Cognitive decline and physical activity and mobility limitations can present risks as well as concerns about the need for long-term health care and the need to care for disabled children.

The earlier part of the reading discussed the role of entrepreneurship in wealth creation. The case study below offers a perspective on how wealth managers can support social entrepreneurs throughout their professional and personal lives.

CASE STUDY

Saffron Threads: How Wealth Managers Support Entrepreneurs throughout Their Life Cycle

Arya is a 28-year-old social entrepreneur who decides to move to a Southeast Asian country to launch a sustainable clothing business, Saffron Threads. The business focuses on producing inclusive-size clothing that is environmentally conscious, while also empowering and educating rural women from marginalized communities.

To start her business, Arya receives initial seed capital from her family, as well as funds secured from the United Nations Development Programme (UNDP) and the International Finance Corporation (IFC). Arya's wealth manager, M.N. Thaler, a leading Swiss wealth management firm, through their network of specialized financial service providers helped her receive crucial financial advice on managing the seed capital, investing in the business, and mitigating risks.

As Arya's business grows, her wealth also increases, reaching CHF5 million. M.N. Thaler advises Arya to diversify her portfolio and raise additional capital for business expansion.

During Arya's peak accumulation phase in her early 50s, Saffron Threads employs hundreds of women, and Arya's wealth grows to CHF15 million. M.N. Thaler assists Arya with approaches that optimize her tax exposure and coordinates employee benefits with her investment and retirement plans.

As Arya enters the pre-retirement phase, her wealth has grown to CHF50 million. This is after selling her business to a private equity firm affiliated with M.N. Thaler. They ensure that the proceeds from the sale are invested wisely, considering Arya's long-term financial goals and retirement plans.

In the early retirement phase, Arya purchases a vineyard in Australia and runs it alongside a restaurant while supporting and empowering women and minorities through her new ventures. Together with M.N. Thaler, Arya explores various impact investing opportunities in Australia, identifying investments that not only generate returns but also make a positive impact on society and the environment.

In the late retirement phase, M.N. Thaler continues to manage Arya's financial resources. They consider the impact of cognitive decline and the potential need for long-term health care, adjusting Arya's investment portfolio and financial strategies accordingly.

Throughout Arya's entrepreneurial journey, M.N. Thaler has been a crucial partner in her financial life cycle, providing tailored services and advice at each stage of her wealth accumulation, business growth, and eventual retirement. Together, they demonstrate the power of impact investing in creating both financial and social returns, contributing to a more sustainable and equitable future.

Exhibit 21 shows the stylized relationship between the different stages of life and the economic wealth of the individual.

Exhibit 21: Wealth Accumulation across the Seven Financial Stages of Life

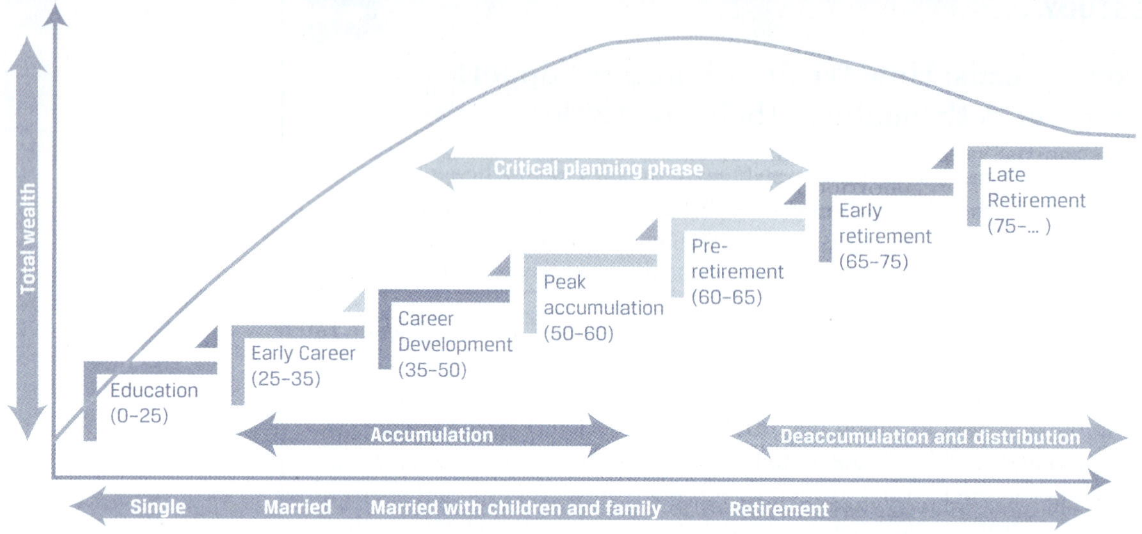

The wealth of an individual changes throughout one's lifetime, as does the underlying asset composition: financial wealth is accumulated as human capital declines. As human capital declines, consumption needs are increasingly met using accumulated financial, real, and personal assets.

The Economic Value of the Individual

Applying a traditional balance sheet view to quantify an individual's assets and liabilities fails to consider two important components: the value of human capital and the present value of future consumption needs.

An individual's **economic balance sheet**, or holistic extended family balance sheet, more comprehensively represents the assets available to fund life-cycle consumption, to preserve wealth, and to transfer wealth during their lifetime and at death. In this context, **surplus** replaces the concept of net worth in the economic balance sheet. It is the difference between the assets including human capital and liabilities including future consumption.

As Exhibit 22 shows, it supplements the traditional balance sheet with the net present value of an individual's expected future earnings and the present value of future consumption. This is particularly important when human capital is a significant share of the individual's overall wealth or when pension assets are considerable.

Exhibit 22: Economic Balance Sheet

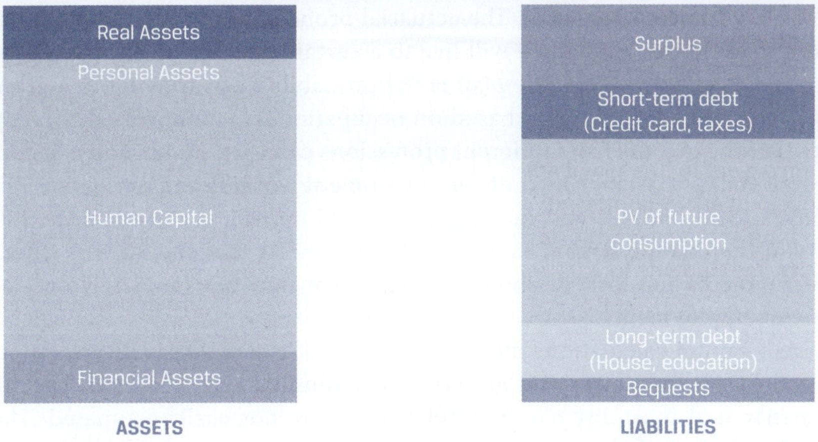

KNOWLEDGE CHECK: COMPARING FINANCIAL AND HUMAN CAPITAL

1. Describe human capital and financial capital.

   Solution:

   Human capital is an implied asset commonly defined as the mortality-weighted net present value of an individual's future expected labor income. Financial capital is explicit assets that include the tangible and intangible assets (outside of human capital) owned by an individual or household. For example, a home, a car, stocks, bonds, a vested retirement portfolio, and money in the bank are all examples of an individual's financial capital (or financial assets).

An economic balance sheet quantifies the optimal level of future consumption given nonconsumption goals and the individual's financial and other resources. This form of balance sheet allows an individual to anticipate how available resources can be used in the future to maximize the expected utility of future consumption. Human capital is calculated as the present value of future income streams adjusted by the actuarial probability of survival, wage growth, and a discount rate that reflects occupational income risk, as Equation 1 shows:

$$HC_0 = \sum_{t=1}^{N} \frac{p(s_t) w_{t-1}(1+g_t)}{(1+r_f+y)^t} \quad (1)$$

where

$p(s_t)$ = the probability of surviving to year (or age) t

$w_{t\text{-}1}$ = the income from employment in period $t\text{-}1$

g_t = the annual wage growth rate

r_f = the nominal risk-free rate

y = risk premium associated with occupational income volatility

N = the length of working life in years

Human capital calculations in Equation 1 quantify wealth from all future earnings, $w_{t-1}(1 + g_t)$, an individual is expected to receive over their working lifetime, discounted to its current value, $(1 + r_f + y)^t$. The actuarial probability of survival, $p(s_t)$, refers to the likelihood that an individual will live to a certain age, based on mortality tables and statistical models. Mortality $p(s_t)$ is the probability of surviving to a given year (or age). The risk adjustment, y, based on occupational income volatility recognizes the fact that the income from different professions can vary significantly. Specifically, the overall stability of labor income for government workers and teachers is different from investment bankers and race car drivers. Moreover, it considers the inherent stability of the income stream as well as the possibility that the income stream will be interrupted by job loss, disability, or death that may be completely unrelated to the type of employment.

Human capital calculations quantify wealth, but the reality is more complicated than models. Income levels and growth rates, nominal risk-free rates, specific risk adjustments, and mortality can be modeled but are not easily estimated. The case study below computes human capital for a young professional in the early days of employment.

CASE STUDY

Taylor: Estimating Human Capital

Taylor is the hypothetical example of an early career individual used in the first case study from this reading. This example will illustrate how the relative value of various household assets changes over a lifetime. Taylor is 25 years old and just entered the workforce.

Taylor's initial salary is EUR20,000, which is expected to increase by 1.5% annually in real terms (inflation assumption is 2%) over the planned trajectory of 40 years, making the nominal growth rate, g, equal to approximately 3.5%, or, more specifically, 3.53% (i.e., (1.015) x (1.02) – 1). Since the choice of the career path generates a stable income flow, the income volatility is expected to be 1%. Taylor has no initial financial capital but designates 5% of the annual income into investment and savings.

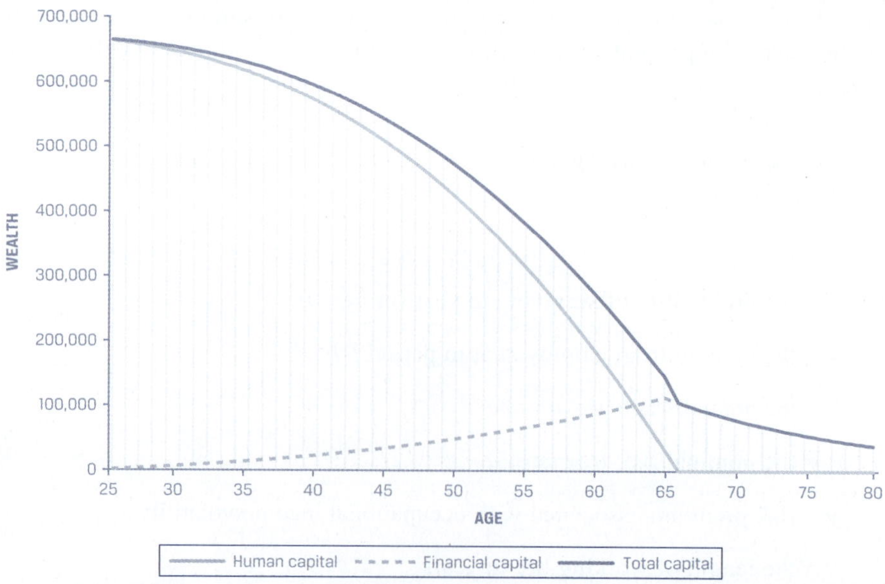

Considering a retirement age of 65 years and 15-year life expectancy beyond that (to 80) with an annual withdrawal of 10% of the available financial capital, the pattern of human capital used is calculated as:

Age	Human capital	Financial capital	Total capital
25	636,156	927	637,082
30	618,751	6,346	625,097
35	589,338	13,288	602,626
40	545,442	22,083	567,524
45	484,421	33,112	517,533
50	403,856	46,795	450,651
55	302,031	63,577	365,609
60	177,905	83,939	261,844
65	31,720	108,372	140,092
70	-	76,003	76,003
75	-	53,302	53,302
80	-	37,382	37,382

Human capital starts high and declines over time, while financial capital begins to accumulate during the working years. The table above provides annual estimates of human capital, financial capital, and total capital. At the start of the year when Taylor turns 25, the human capital is EUR636,156, financial capital amounts to EUR927, and the total capital equals EUR637,082. At the beginning of the year when Taylor turns 65 (or at the conclusion of Taylor's 64th year), the human capital value decreases to EUR31,720. However, the financial capital is EUR108,372, making the total capital amount to EUR140,092.

For the typical individual, the financial capital, or investment portfolio, represents a significant portion of wealth at the beginning of age 65, or retirement. The financial capital is often capital accumulated directly by the individual; a substantive proportion can be retirement savings, which may be self directed or secured through an employer or a government run pension system. Private wealth management focuses on managing this financial capital.

As individuals progress through their lives, the value of their financial and other investments becomes more significant, particularly as they approach retirement. At this point, people tend to rely more on their investment portfolio to provide them with income in retirement. However, once individuals retire, the relative importance of their investment portfolio typically decreases. Instead, the remaining mortality-weighted net present value of benefits, such as pension benefits and the value of real estate such as their personal residence, become more crucial factors in determining their financial situation in retirement.

The mortality-weighted net present value of benefits is the total expected value of future retirement benefits adjusted for the likelihood of surviving to each future year of receipt and the time value of money. This calculation reflects the probability that individuals will live long enough to receive their retirement benefits and the potential impact of inflation on the value of those benefits. Meanwhile, the value of real estate can be a significant determinant of financial stability in retirement. For example, individuals can use the value of their personal residence to generate additional income by downsizing to a less expensive home or borrowing against the capital built up over the years through reverse mortgages, equity release mortgages, or similar products.

The case study below provides an example in which Taylor's total capital accumulation is estimated with some more realistic conditions: it includes investment in a primary residence and the existence of a pension system. These two are often the greatest sources of an individual's total wealth.

CASE STUDY

Taylor: Estimating Total Capital with Investments and Pensions

Expanding on the previous example, Taylor's purchases a home at age 30 that equals twice the annual income at that age, putting 5% of the value of the home as equity and borrowing the balance over 30 years. The real estate increases in value by 1% annually in real terms. Additionally, Taylor is also the beneficiary of a simple defined benefit pension plan that accumulates each year at 10% of income paid by the employer. The pension payments vest after 10 years. The pension payments during the decumulation phase will be adjusted for inflation.

With these changes, the human wealth is changed as well; more specifically, the trajectory is impacted by the purchase of a home and the accumulation of pension wealth.

[redacted]

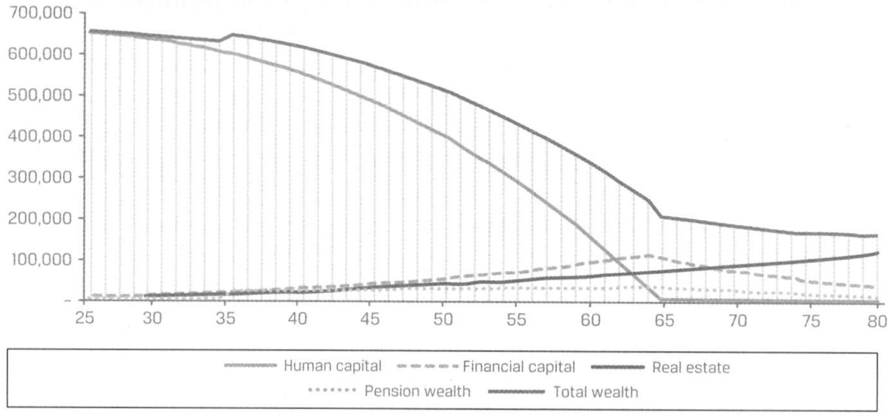

The change in relative wealth across the lifetime demonstrates the importance of real estate and pensions as a source of total wealth.

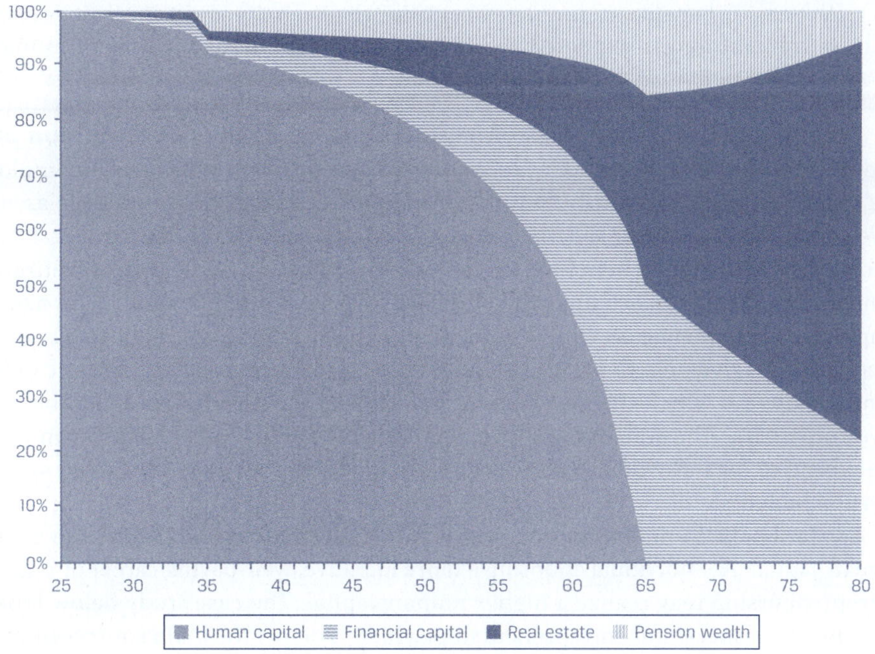

The table below provides annual estimates of human capital, financial capital, real estate value, pension wealth, and total capital.

Age	Human capital	Financial capital	Real estate	Pension wealth	Total wealth
25	636,156	927	0	0	637,082
30	618,751	6,346	2,032	0	627,129
35	589,338	13,288	8,897	20,158	631,681
40	545,442	22,083	16,458	22,095	606,077
45	484,421	33,112	24,767	24,186	566,486
50	403,856	46,795	33,880	26,363	510,894
55	302,031	63,577	43,860	28,473	437,941
60	177,905	83,939	54,768	30,333	346,945
65	31,720	108,372	66,676	31,722	238,490
70	0	76,003	79,656	24,859	180,518
75	0	53,302	93,787	17,487	164,576
80	0	37,382	109,152	9,692	156,226

Pension benefits and real estate investment do not impact Taylor's human capital at 25, which equals EUR637,082. The impact of the pension benefit increases Taylor's total capital when it vests after 10 years of work, at the age of 35. At the beginning of the year when Taylor turns 65 (or at the conclusion of Taylor's 64th year), the human capital value decreases to EUR31,720. However, the financial capital is EUR108,372, the real estate capital EUR66,676, and pension wealth EUR31,722, making the total capital amount to EUR238,490. By allocating some of the human capital income to residential real estate, the total capital at retirement has increased by the equity value of the residence.

As pension benefits accumulate over time, their relative share increases closer to retirement and is expected to compensate for some of the loss of human capital that comes with retirement.

There are generally two types of pension systems: **defined contribution plans** and **defined benefit plans**. In a defined contribution plan, typically the employee, the employer, or both contribute to the employee's account. The employee assumes investment risk, and the final benefit is based on the performance of their investments. In contrast, in a defined benefit plan, the employer guarantees a monthly retirement benefit based on factors such as the employee's years of service, salary, and age. The employer is responsible for funding the plan and bears the investment risk to ensure there are enough assets to pay the benefits. Most public pension systems are defined benefit plans for which the government determines the benefit levels and bears the investment risk. The stability and predictability of defined benefit plans can reduce the incentive for individuals to save for retirement, as they may rely solely on their pension benefits.

Educational attainment and choice of career alternatives determine the value of human capital. An individual choosing a more lucrative, well-paying career or choosing entrepreneurship may realize a higher human capital. The case study below looks at the benefits of successful entrepreneurship, which is one of the main sources of wealth that is being created, and human capital.

CASE STUDY

Taylor: Entrepreneurship and Human Capital

Expanding on the previous examples, let us assume that Taylor decides to pursue a different career path: entrepreneurship. In exchange for a lower and more stable income stream from full time employment, Taylor, as an entrepreneur, expects to accumulate greater wealth at the expense of greater certainty and income stability.

This higher expected value and income volatility influences the aggregate wealth accumulation through greater estimated cash flows and higher discount rates and thus influences the value of human capital. The business grows rapidly and steadily. And, instead of retiring at age 65, Taylor sells the business and rolls over the proceeds into financial capital to use together with other accumulated pension wealth to finance consumption during the remainder of life. With these changes, total wealth is changed, as well.

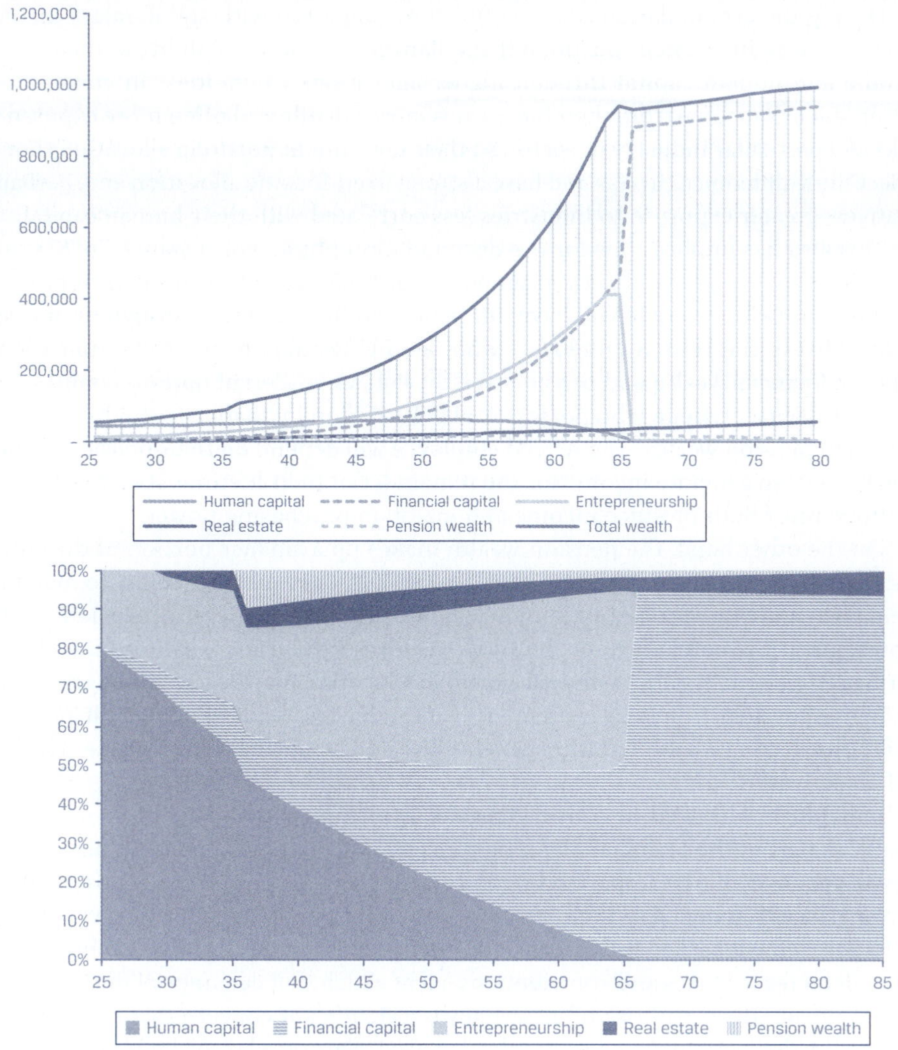

The proportion of pension wealth as a component of total wealth declines, and the considerable financial wealth that comes from the liquidation of the entrepreneurial activities continues to increase in value throughout the life.

For affluent individuals, pension wealth usually constitutes a small portion of their total wealth portfolio during retirement. The proportion of pension wealth in an individual's overall wealth portfolio depends on their unique circumstances. For instance, a 45-year-old full-time employee with EUR5 million in human capital, EUR1 million in pension benefits, and EUR1 million in financial assets will have different investment options compared to a 45-year-old entrepreneur with EUR10 million in human capital invested in their business, EUR1 million in pension benefits, and EUR1 million in financial assets.

The full-time employee's human capital is linked to their salary income, which is generally stable and predictable, while the entrepreneur's human capital is tied to their business, which has more uncertain and unpredictable cash flows. The volatility and growth of income in human capital calculations seeks to account for this difference. To diversify their human capital, pension benefits, and financial assets, individuals mainly have control over how their financial portfolios are invested and allocated. Consequently, during the accumulation phase, they should seek to allocate their investment portfolio to diversify their income and risk from human capital.

During the accumulation phase, a full-time employee with stable salary income should have an investment portfolio that balances the relative stability of their salary income and human capital through higher allocations to equities. In contrast, an entrepreneur's income from their business is more volatile and often more exposed to risks of a particular industry or sector, so their investment portfolio allocation should reflect these differences in risk and have a strong fixed-income allocation and, perhaps, relatively greater exposure to industries less correlated with their human capital.

This also has implications for the decumulation phase. For instance, in 20 years' time, the now 65-year-old retired employee and 65-year-old retired entrepreneur from the previous example will have different spending patterns throughout the rest of their lives. The retired employee, who has EUR4 million in wealth split evenly between financial wealth and pension wealth, will have different options compared to the retired entrepreneur, who possesses EUR40 million in financial wealth and EUR2 million in pension wealth. The retired employee will depend on their pension wealth, which needs to generate income for the remainder of their lifetime. As a result, their portfolio must both produce income and maintain purchasing power.

On the other hand, the pension wealth makes up a smaller portion of the entrepreneur's total wealth and therefore has limited influence on their ability to maintain their post-retirement spending for the rest of their life. Generally, pension wealth represents a low percentage of the total wealth portfolio for wealthier individuals during retirement. The focus of their portfolio allocation may be less about generating income to cover costs in their retirement years and more about fulfilling philanthropic goals, transferring wealth to future generations, and achieving other long-term financial objectives.

Individuals will need to consider means to safeguard the value of their pension wealth as part of the financial planning process. For example, a pension plan from a private employer may be impacted by company-specific risk, just like an entrepreneur's personal wealth is linked to their business. A private pension plan can be terminated, and a government backed public pension system can face shortfalls that cannot be met through increased taxes and contributions, all of which that can imperil the likelihood of repayment. The broad risk of insolvency is a significant concern that could lead to the loss of the benefits from an employer-based pension plan or an entrepreneur's financial wealth.

To reduce this risk from such equity-like or equity-linked sources of wealth, such as from a privately held business, investments in fixed-income instruments can be a viable option. However, this involves a trade-off between higher yet volatile returns and lower yet safer returns. Individuals need to determine whether this aligns with their financial objectives.

While the investment portfolio holds substantial importance for the typical individual at age 65 or retirement, it still represents less than 50% of the total economic wealth when considering other factors such as home equity, pension wealth, and human capital. As individuals move through retirement and spend their funds, the investment portfolio's relative share decreases. The remaining mortality-weighted net present value of benefits and real estate value, such as the individual's home, become the primary factors determining their financial situation during retirement.

While human capital calculations provide a framework for quantifying wealth, it is important to note that reality is more complex than models. For instance, estimating income levels and growth rates, nominal risk-free rates, specific risk adjustments, and mortality can be challenging. Particularly in the early stages of the life cycle, the potential loss of human capital is a significant risk factor.

QUESTION SET

1. Contrast performance measurement and the definition of risk for institutional investors and the typical individual investor.

Solution:

Institutional investors measure performance relative to defined indices or benchmarks, while individual investors assess performance based on the attainment of specific financial goals. For an institutional investor, a portfolio underperforms if its performance is less than the stated index or set benchmark. Institutional investors define risk with quantitative measures, such as volatility, beta, and so on. For an individual investor, a portfolio underperforms if the performance does not sufficiently meet a set goal. Individual investors define risk by the likelihood and consequences of failing to meet specific financial goals. Hence, risk and performance are closely linked.

2. Which of the following statements accurately characterizes the comparison between developed and emerging financial markets based on the given text?

   A. Both developed and emerging markets offer a similar array of investment opportunities and regulatory support for investments.

   B. Developed markets offer larger active financial markets and more stringent regulatory support compared to emerging markets.

   C. Emerging markets typically offer more diverse investment alternatives and better access to high quality financial information than developed markets.

Solution:

B is the correct response. Developed markets offer a wider range of investment alternatives and have a more stringent regulatory framework. This allows for a broader spectrum of investment choices and promotes trust in the financial system, offering investors a unique advantage for long-term wealth accumulation.

Both statements A and C are incorrect. Developed markets offer a larger variety of investment opportunities and more robust regulatory support than emerging markets. Developed markets also offer better access to high-quality financial information. Also, emerging markets are characterized by a more limited array of investment alternatives compared to developed markets.

3. At what stage of the wealth life cycle does accumulated or total wealth typically achieve its maximum level?

   A. Peak accumulation

   B. Pre-retirement

   C. Early retirement

Solution:

B is the correct response. Pre-retirement years (typically from age 60–65) should be the period in which wealth reaches its maximum. Answer A is not correct, as wealth continues to grow during the peak accumulation years, and answer C is not correct, as the period of wealth deaccumulation begins at early retirement.

4. Contrast the most appropriate portfolio allocations to equities and fixed-income securities for the following two individuals in the accumulation phase of their wealth life cycles: an individual who works in a government job with stable income characteristics, and an individual who is pursuing an entrepreneurial career.

Solution:

The individual working in a government job with stable income characteristics is likely to allocate more to risky equity securities in their portfolio allocation as compared to the individual pursuing an entrepreneurial career. The entrepreneur's riskier future income stream is likely to cause a larger allocation to fixed-income securities as compared to the individual pursuing a government career with a less risky future income stream.

4 INDIVIDUAL INVESTORS: RETURN, RISK, AND OTHER OBJECTIVES AND CONSTRAINTS

☐ justify how returns, risks, objectives, and constraints for individuals relate to their human and financial capital

Nominal and Inflation-Adjusted Returns

For long-term individual investors, especially those saving for retirement, safeguarding their long-term purchasing power is more crucial than focusing solely on nominal returns. By considering purchasing power–adjusted returns, investors can make well-informed decisions about their investments and ensure that their financial objectives are achieved. The influence of inflation on investment returns can differ based on the investment horizon, and neglecting it may result in inaccurate conclusions about an investment's performance.

The fact that inflation diminishes the purchasing power of capital has significant consequences for investment management, portfolio construction, and purchasing power adjusted wealth accumulation. In the short term, inflation reduces purchasing power, affecting the value of returns and principal investments. Rising inflation rates can hinder individual investors' ability to invest effectively. Over the long term, the impact of inflation compounds, potentially leading to a significant decrease in the real, purchasing power– adjusted value of investments and potentially impeding individuals' capacity to accumulate enough wealth to meet their long-term financial goals or needs. For those in the decumulation phase who depend on their accumulated capital as their primary income source, investment returns that do not outpace inflation will result in a decline in their purchasing power. To protect against inflation, investors usually consider assets such as equities, real estate, and commodities, which have historically produced returns that surpass long-term inflation rates.

It is important to distinguish between beating inflation and hedging against inflation. Assets like equities over long periods tend to provide a return that outpaces inflation: the average annual return of the stock market over the past several decades has generally outperformed inflation. Equities perform especially well in real terms when inflation is low. However, equities can be quite volatile in the short term, and their returns may not outpace increasing or persistent inflation. Additionally, commodities, such as oil and gold, can see their prices outperform during inflationary periods but can also be seen to contribute to increased inflation. Hence, investing in these assets could be, at least for shorter periods, considered as a hedge against inflation. However, they do not always outperform persistent inflation, and their prices can, at times, be quite volatile.

Inflation-protected bonds issued by governments link the return to inflation and are designed to keep pace with inflation. Despite the existence of such **inflation-linked bonds**, most fixed-income instruments are not inflation linked. Additionally, real estate can serve as a hedge against inflation because the value of properties tends to rise over time along with the general price level. As inflation leads to a general increase in prices, the price of real estate often increases, as landlords may increase rents over time to keep up with inflation. This increasing income stream can keep pace with rising prices, but that is not always the case. Real estate prices can sometimes stagnate or even decrease during inflationary periods because of factors such as general economic uncertainty.

Risks

Individual investors face different types of risks that can affect their investment outcomes such as asset price and return volatility, drawdown risk, and the risk of not achieving financial objectives.

- Return volatility refers to the fluctuations in the value and returns of an investment over time and captures the likelihood that an investment may decline in value because of changes in market conditions, economic factors, or company-specific events. It impacts all asset classes.
- Drawdown risk is the risk of experiencing losses because of a decline in the value of an investment over a specific period and is the difference between the investment's peak value and its lowest point during a market downturn. This can be material either when an investor benchmarks the portfolio against achieving a certain financial goal and objective, or when an investor is forced to realize a loss. An investor who buys an exchange-traded fund (ETF) for ZAR90,000 that subsequently increases in value to ZAR100,000 and then drops in value to ZAR80,000 experiences a drawdown of ZAR20,000. A drawdown is not a realized loss; rather, it is a decline in value, a paper loss. A realized loss would only occur if the investor sold the ETF or if the ETF were used as collateral for a loan and there were suddenly a collateral shortfall that the investor could not address. The investor would then be forced to liquidate the asset to remain compliant with the loan covenants.
- The risk of not achieving financial objectives refers to the possibility that an investor will not achieve their planned financial goals because of a combination of possible factors including return shortfalls, market environment, and economic conditions, or because the investor did not dedicate enough capital to meet the goals.

Investors can reduce the impact of volatility and drawdown risk by diversifying across a range of different asset classes. All investors should review and adjust their investment strategies, portfolios, and asset allocations regularly, but it is particularly important for individual investors for whom the inherent risk is not achieving set financial objectives. For individual investors, inflation is a critical factor to consider when assessing the risk of not achieving financial objectives — meeting income needs. Purchasing power–adjusted returns also affect the volatility of an investment, as changes in inflation rates can impact market conditions and asset values and may also affect drawdown risk, as inflation can reduce the inflation-adjusted value of an investment.

Evaluating a private client's risk tolerance is a key step in the information-gathering process. The term risk tolerance usually describes a set of risk-related concepts. The following are some key terms used in this context:

- **Risk tolerance** refers to the level of risk an individual is willing and able to bear. Differently put, risk tolerance is the willingness to engage in a risky behavior in which possible outcomes can be negative. Risk tolerance is related to **risk aversion**, which is the degree of an investor's *unwillingness* to take risk.
- **Risk capacity** is the ability to bear financial risk. The key difference between risk capacity and risk tolerance is that risk capacity is more objective in nature, while risk tolerance relates to an attitude. Risk capacity is determined by the client's wealth, income, investment time horizon, liquidity needs, and other relevant factors. Clients with greater risk capacity can tolerate greater financial losses without compromising current or future consumption goals.
- Risk perception is the subjective assessment of the risk involved in the outcome of an investment decision. Unlike risk tolerance, risk perception — how a client perceives the riskiness of an investment decision or the investment climate — depends on the circumstances involved. Consequently, a wealth manager can help shape a client's risk perception. Risk perception varies considerably across individuals.

In practice, wealth managers often utilize questionnaires to assess clients' risk tolerances. The result of a risk tolerance questionnaire, typically a numerical score, is often used as an input in the investment planning process. The questionnaire in Exhibit 23 provides some common types of questions that may be found on a risk tolerance questionnaire.

Exhibit 23: Sample Questions from a Risk Tolerance Questionnaire

1. When you make investment decisions, on which of the following do you tend to focus?
   a. Always on the potential for gain
   b. Usually on the potential for gain
   c. Always on the potential for loss
   d. Usually on the potential for loss
2. Compared to your friends and family, are you:
   a. less willing to take risk?
   b. equally willing to take risk?
   c. more willing to take risk?
3. What potential percentage decline in your investment portfolio value over a one-year period are you willing to experience?
   a. 5%
   b. 10%
   c. 20%
   d. 30%
   e. More than 30%
4. Which of the following statements best describes your attitude about the performance of your investment portfolio over the next year?

   a. I can tolerate a substantial loss.
   b. I can tolerate a loss.
   c. I can tolerate a small loss.
   d. I would have a hard time tolerating a loss of any magnitude.

5. Suppose that you have made an investment that, because of a sudden broad market decline, has declined in price by 25%. Which of the following actions would you take?
   a. Sell all of the investment
   b. Sell a portion of the investment
   c. Hold the investment (take no action)
   d. Buy more of the investment

6. Suppose that you have access to two types of investments: one investment with low risk and low expected return and one with high risk and high expected return. Which of the following portfolio mixes would you select?
   a. 100% low risk/low return
   b. 75% low risk/low return and 25% high risk/high return
   c. 50% low risk/low return and 50% high risk/high return
   d. 25% low risk/low return and 75% high risk/high return
   e. 100% high risk/high return

7. Suppose that you are offered employment that involves the choice of a fixed salary, variable compensation that could be higher or lower than the fixed salary, or some mix of the two. Which of the following would you choose?
   a. Entirely fixed salary
   b. Mostly fixed salary
   c. Entirely variable compensation
   d. Mostly variable compensation
   e. An equal mix of the two

8. Which of the following best characterizes the time horizon for your primary investment goal?
   a. Less than 3 years
   b. 3 to 8 years
   c. 9 to15 years
   d. 16 to 20 years
   e. Greater than 20 years

Risk tolerance questionnaires have limitations. It is also unclear if they can accurately predict investor behavior. Relying solely on the results of such questionnaires to recommend investments or asset allocations for a client demands significant judgment and inevitably involves some guesswork by wealth managers. Academic research suggests that client questionnaires are highly subjective, which can lead to the manager's own risk perceptions influencing investment decision making on behalf of clients. Furthermore, studies have shown that the sequence and structure of questions can directly affect the responses.

The way losses are presented, either as a percentage (relative loss) or a currency amount (absolute loss), can result in different responses from the same person. Moreover, a question involving a small absolute loss on a smaller portfolio might elicit a different reaction compared to a question involving a large absolute loss on a larger portfolio, even if the relative losses are identical.

Risk tolerance conversations, which are more difficult to conduct than administering questionnaires, are more suitable for higher net worth clients and can yield valuable insights into the individual's risk tolerance, such as

- How much are the client's financial decisions influenced by friends or family members?
- What financial experiences have shaped the client's perspective? Individuals who lived through deep recessions, even in childhood, may bring that perspective to present-day investment decisions.
- What are the client's past (notable) investment mistakes and (celebrated) successes?
- What are the sources of the client's investment wealth? Individuals could achieve wealth through saving, investments, speculation, inheritance, business activities, a liquidity event (such as selling a privately held business), substantial real estate holdings, other less liquid assets (such as collectibles), or a combination of these various sources.
- How does the client evaluate investment risk? Individuals can think about investment losses in absolute or percentage terms.

Risk tolerance discussions enable wealth managers to educate clients about investment risks. A wealth manager may present a client with an array of portfolio options, each having different expected returns and expected levels of volatility. The client's selection from these options offers insights into their risk tolerance. This process is dynamic, as educating the client and gathering their feedback can reveal valuable information about their investment approach that may not be apparent from a risk tolerance questionnaire or a personality type assessment. Additionally, the dynamic aspect of risk tolerance conversations offers the client opportunities to learn about the complexities of investing and the associated risks.

Objectives

To this point, we have discussed a client's overall risk tolerance. Because clients often have multiple goals or objectives, their risk tolerance may vary for different goals. For example, a client may have a low risk tolerance with respect to larger near-term goals but a higher risk tolerance when it comes to longer-term goals. A challenge for wealth managers in managing client relationships is to satisfactorily address potentially conflicting risk tolerance levels.

Wealth managers assist their customers in formulating, prioritizing, and implementing their financial objectives, which may span a range of needs and desires, through goal prioritization and the implementation of investment strategies. Rather than being a one-time exercise, identifying client goals is an ongoing communication between wealth manager and client.

- **Planned goals** are those financial objectives that can be reasonably estimated or quantified at the onset and can be achieved within an expected time horizon. Such planned goals typically include retirement, specific purchases such as a primary residence, vehicle, or luxury item, family events such as weddings, education such as college or professional education, wealth transfer through gifts and bequests, and philanthropy.

- **Unplanned goals** are those related to unforeseen financial needs, and as such they are more difficult to quantify than planned goals because either the funding need or the timing of the financial need or both may not be estimated. Such unplanned goals typically include unexpected expenses such as property repairs that insurance may not cover fully, medical expenses not covered by the health care system or medical insurance, and similar expenses.

Planning for goals is among the more challenging areas of a client's financial profile, as they are sometimes poorly articulated. By quantifying goals, prioritizing goals, and adjusting to changing goals, wealth managers directly assist clients in identifying these financial objectives. For instance, the manager may conclude that a client's clearly stated retirement goals are unfeasible based on their assessment. In this case, the manager has the chance to develop specific, more realistic, and achievable client goals, which can further help the client quantify each goal and develop appropriate plans.

Wealth managers also assist clients with setting priorities when they have multiple parallel and conflicting objectives, such as launching a new business, purchasing a second home, and retiring to Provence, as illustrated in the case study below. A wealth manager should conduct periodic reviews of the client's financial circumstances, including their financial goals, in order to modify an investment strategy if there is any significant change in the goals and circumstances.

CASE STUDY

C.Y. Lee: Client Goals

Mr. C.Y. Lee is a managing director for the investment firm Acme & Bass, which is located in the Asia-Pacific region. Lee is 40 years old, is married, and has two children, ages 12 and 10. He and his family reside in a home that they own in Singapore. In a conversation with his wealth manager, Lee states that he wishes to fund the undergraduate tuition for his children to study abroad. Lee expects the tuition cost to be approximately GBP40,000 per child per year and annual living expenses an additional GBP40,000, or approximately a total of GBP640,000. Lee also wishes to fund his children's weddings at some point in the future. Lee also wants to provide for his and his wife's elderly and infirm relatives. Additionally, Lee is also concerned about the future health care expenses of his wife's parents and to what degree he and his wife may need to support them financially.

Because the education costs will occur in the next 5–10 years, Mr. Lee states that they are his top priority. The secondary goal is to provide financially for the welfare of their elderly relatives.

Lee anticipates working until age 65 and does not know how much he and his wife will need to fund their retirement lifestyle. He mentions his desire to purchase a flat in London and let (rent) it as part of their retirement plan. The flat would cost approximately GBP5 million.

Questions:

1. Identify Lee's planned goals.

   Answer:

   Lee's planned goals are (a) funding his children's education, (b) funding his children's weddings, (c) funding his and his wife's retirement, (d) purchasing and subsequently letting (renting) a flat in London, and e) providing financially for the welfare of elderly relatives.

2. Identify Lee's unplanned goals.

Answer:

Lee's unplanned goals relate to the future health care expenses of his wife's parents, as well as possible uninsured property repairs for the Lee's Singapore residence and, if purchased, their London flat.

3. Discuss the issue of goal quantification for Lee.

Answer:

Lee has quantified the education funding goal and the flat purchase. He and his wealth manager should work to estimate the cost of the weddings for Lee's children, the anticipated retirement lifestyle needs for Lee and his wife, and the cost of providing for the welfare of their elderly relatives. Understandably, the health care cost quantification may be difficult to achieve.

4. Discuss the issue of goal prioritization for Lee.

Answer:

Lee states that his first priority is education funding for his children. However, the timing of a need should not be the sole determinant of goal priority. If funding their children's education costs will leave Lee and his wife unprepared for retirement, for example, they may wish to reevaluate their priorities.

QUESTION SET

1. What distinguishes risk tolerance from risk capacity?

Solution:

Risk tolerance focuses on the willingness of the investor to take on risk, and if risk is taken on, the appropriate level of compensation is expected for the level of risk. Risk capacity focuses on how much investors can put at risk without affecting their current or future consumption.

2. Which of the following asset classes is least likely to provide protection against inflation?

A. Equity securities

B. Inflation-linked bonds

C. Fixed-income securities

Solution:

C is the correct response. Fixed-income securities, except for inflation-linked bonds, are not considered as providing potential for inflation protections. The value of cash flows of fixed-income securities declines, in present value terms, as discount rates rise during periods of inflation. Because of this feature of fixed-income securities, they likely do not provide inflation protection.

A is incorrect because equities are noted specifically for their ability to not only provide some degree of inflation protection but also to potentially provide returns that outpace inflation over the long term.

B is incorrect because inflation-linked bonds are structured to provide incremental cash flows that adjust with the inflation rate, so they are likely to provide protection against inflation.

3. Differentiate between an asset used as an inflation hedge and an asset that outpaces inflation in an investment strategy.

Solution:

An asset used as an inflation hedge protects the purchasing power during periods of inflation as their value or returns increase in line with or close to the inflation rate. Inflation-linked bonds may protect against inflation, but they do not necessarily provide real growth in value. An asset that outpaces inflation is expected to not only maintain its value during inflationary periods but also increase in value at a rate higher than the rate of inflation. Typically, equities, or stocks, fall into this category; however, this may not always be the case. Individual companies and broader market indexes can exhibit different behaviors, as some companies can often pass increased costs on to consumers during inflationary periods, leading to increased profits and thus increased stock prices. However, the overall market performance can lag, particularly when inflation is persistently high.

4. An individual investor is assessing three different risky investment portfolios with the following expected characteristics:

- Portfolio A has an expected return of 8% with volatility of 20%.
- Portfolio B has an expected return of 9% with volatility of 25%.
- Portfolio C has an expected return of 10% with volatility of 30%.

The risk-free rate is 4%. This investor can take on the risk associated with the highest risk portfolio and has been assessed as having low risk aversion. The investor chooses Portfolio A. Which one of the following concepts can lead the investor to choose Portfolio A?

A. Risk tolerance

B. Risk capacity

C. Risk perception

Solution:

C is the correct response. Even though each of the portfolios offers the same return-to-risk trade-off (Sharpe ratio of each portfolio is 0.2), the investor has chosen the portfolio with the lowest risk. This choice implies that the investor has a subjective assessment (i.e., perception) that the higher risk portfolios are not attractive.

A is incorrect because low risk aversion reflects high risk tolerance. B is incorrect because the investor has the capacity to invest in the highest risk portfolio.

5. A 40-year-old individual investor meets with a financial advisor and discusses two specific goals: university education for her two children (ages 6 and 8) and her retirement at age 60. She is very specific with her advisor that her children have the financial means to attend a top-tier private university. On the other hand, she is willing to accept a wide range of acceptable income

levels during her retirement. Evaluate this investor's risk tolerance with respect to the two investment objectives discussed with the adviser.

Solution:

This investor is more likely to have lower risk tolerance with respect to meeting the goal of funding her children's future education expenses. Because she has a very specific type of institution in mind, her tolerance for not meeting this objective is likely low. On the other hand, she seems to be willing to accept a wide range of possible income levels in retirement, so her risk tolerance is likely to be high for this objective.

5 THE IMPACT OF TAXATION AND INFLATION

☐ evaluate how various types of taxes imposed on individual investors and the impact of inflation influence investment decisions

This section focuses on taxes that most directly affect tax planning for investments: specifically, taxes on investment income to individuals.

The tax systems in many countries are designed to encourage or discourage certain activities through tax incentives. Tax structures vary globally and can change as the needs and objectives of the governmental jurisdiction change. As the environment is dynamic, investment managers must comprehend the effects of various tax structures on investment returns and wealth. Instead of outlining specific country tax rules, this reading offers a framework to help managers understand and implement investment strategies in a changing environment where dissimilar tax situations may apply to different clients and clients' tax environments may shift over time.

In most tax jurisdictions, a tax rate structure is applied to ordinary income such as earnings from employment. Special categories of income, such as investment income (sometimes referred to as capital income for tax purposes), may be subject to other tax rates. Investment income (e.g., interest, dividends, distributions, or capital gains) is frequently taxed differently depending on the type of income and losses.

Exhibit 24 shows a simple and highly generalized schematic of how different components of investment returns can be taxed. Some components may be taxed as part of ordinary income, while others may be taxed at more advantageous rates. Certainly, investment income can also be taxed at a higher rate. Note that countries may choose to tax investment income separately from ordinary income and apply tax rates different from ordinary income tax rates. For example, as the right side of Exhibit 24 shows, dividends could be subject to a reduced tax rate or excluded from taxable income altogether.

Exhibit 24: Taxation of Investment Income

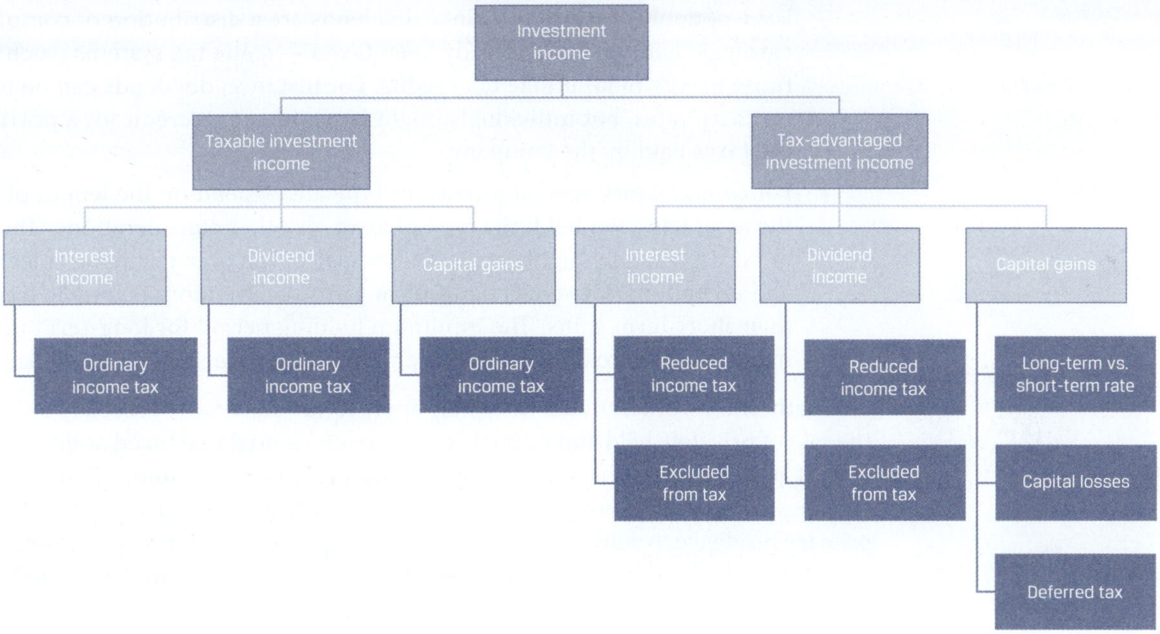

- *Investment income* is often taxed based on the nature of the income: interest, dividends, or realized capital gains and losses.
- *Interest income and dividends* are typically taxed in the year they are received or on an annual basis. Some jurisdictions exclude certain types of interest income from taxation; others tax dividend income more advantageously.
- *Capital gains tax* is typically triggered when the asset is sold at an appreciated value. Some systems recognize the impact of capital losses, which can be used to offset capital gains taxes. Additionally, many systems allow for deferring the payment of capital income tax until a later date, which is a valuable option for the investor.

Most countries and their tax systems build on a progressive tax rate structure, in which higher income levels are taxed at increasingly higher rates. There are some countries where the tax system is flat, in which all income is taxed at the same rate regardless of the total income earned.

Taxes on Investment Income

Some tax systems tax investment incomes at the tax rates applicable to ordinary income (ordinary rates) unless special provisions exist that reduce the tax liability on investment income. Other tax systems have separate tax rates for investment income and ordinary income.

- For *interest income*, special provisions typically include exemptions for specific types of interest income, favorable tax rates, or exclusion amounts that allow a limited amount of interest income to be tax free. In some jurisdictions, inflation adjustments for fixed-income instruments may not be subject to taxation.

- For *dividend income*, special provisions typically include exemptions, special tax rates, or exclusions as mentioned for interest income. To address the issue of double taxation — since dividends are a distribution of company earnings that may have already been taxed — some tax systems (such as those in Australia) utilize tax credits. For instance, dividends can be taxed at standard rates, but individuals might be entitled to a credit for a portion of the taxes paid by the company.
- For *capital gains*, special provisions typically depend on the length of time the asset has been held, the type of asset, or other considerations. This form of taxation can be highly complex because of the ever-changing rules, rates, and exceptions. Generally, long-term gains receive more favorable treatment than short-term gains. The minimum holding period for long-term investments varies across jurisdictions and may also differ among asset classes.

Furthermore, different tax rates may apply to various types of assets. For instance, the sale of privately held and publicly traded equities might be taxed at different rates even if both positions have identical holding periods. Real estate often has unique tax rates compared to other asset classes, especially if the property is the taxpayer's primary residence. Additionally, tax systems may provide lifetime capital gains exemptions for individuals or establish thresholds under which accumulated capital gains are not subject to taxation. Finally, capital gains can be offset by capital losses, and the rules recognizing capital losses can be quite complex.

The case study below, Nataliia Kozlowska: Tax Rates and Tax Calculations, shows the basics of tax calculations commonly applied to ordinary income based on a progressive tax system. In a progressive tax system, the different tax brackets are graduated, and the **marginal tax rate** is the rate at which the highest level of income is taxed.

CASE STUDY

Nataliia Kozlowska: Tax Rates and Tax Calculations

Ms. Nataliia Kozlowska, a new client living in a jurisdiction with a progressive tax rate structure, expects to earn a taxable ordinary income of EUR700,000 this year. She additionally expects to receive investment income: EUR10,000 in interest income and EUR5,000 in dividend income.

The graduated tax rate structure in her jurisdiction is:

Taxable income (EUR)		Tax on column 1	Percentage on excess over column 1
Over	Up to		
0	30,000	—	5
30,000	60,000	1,500	10
60,000	90,000	4,500	15
90,000	250,000	9,000	20
250,000	500,000	41,000	30
500,000	1,000,000	116,000	40
1,000,000		316,000	50

Questions:

1. What is Ms. Kozlowska's marginal tax rate on her ordinary income?

   Answer:

   The marginal tax rate is the rate applied to the last EUR of income, which is the rate applicable to the income level that immediately follows the taxable income. In this case, the taxable income is EUR700,000, which falls under the next to last income bracket. Therefore, the applicable marginal tax rate would be 40%. If the taxable income exceeds EUR1,000,000, the marginal tax is 50% (i.e., for each additional unit of income, 50% will be taxed away).

2. What is Ms. Kozlowska's tax liability and average tax rate on her ordinary income?

   Answer:

   For incomes between EUR500,000 and EUR1,000,000, the tax rate is 40%. For the first EUR500,000, the tax is EUR150,000, and for the next EUR200,000 the tax rate is 40% x (EUR700,000 – EUR500,000) = EUR80,000. The total tax payable is then EUR150,000 + EUR80,000 = EUR230,000, and the average tax rate is 32.86%.

3. What is Ms. Kozlowska's total tax liability and average tax rate if all her investment income is taxed at the same rate as her ordinary income?

   Answer:

   Considering the expected investment income of EUR10,000 in interest income and EUR5,000 in dividend income, the total income is EUR715,000. For the first EUR500,000 in ordinary income tax, the tax is EUR150,000, and for the next EUR215,000, the tax rate is 40% x (EUR715,000 – EUR500,000) = EUR86,000. The total tax payable is then EUR150,000 + EUR86,000 = EUR236,000. Thus, 33.01% of the total income of EUR715,000 is paid in taxes.

4. What is Ms. Kozlowska's total tax liability if the first EUR5,000 in interest income is excluded from taxation and the remainder is subject to the income tax rate and her dividend income is taxed at 15%?

   Answer:

   In this scenario, the investment income is taxed differently than ordinary tax rates, as part of the interest income is excluded from ordinary income tax rates and dividend income is taxed at a lower rate than the marginal tax rate. Of the total interest income of EUR10,000, EUR5,000 is excluded from taxation. This means that the taxable income is reduced from EUR715,000 to EUR710,000 after accounting for the interest income exclusion. Two different tax rates apply to this taxable income.

   i. The ordinary income, which comprises the regular income (EUR700,000) and the taxable portion of the interest income (EUR5,000), is taxed according to the table above. Meanwhile, the dividend income of EUR5,000 is subject to a flat tax of 15%.

> **ii.** The ordinary income tax amounts to EUR150,000 for the first EUR500,000 and EUR82,000 for the remaining EUR205,000 (including the taxed portion of her interest income). This is calculated as 40% x (EUR705,000 – EUR500,000) = EUR82,000, resulting in a total income tax of EUR232,000.
>
> For the dividend income of EUR5,000, there is a 15% tax, equating to EUR750. In total, she pays EUR232,000 in ordinary income tax and EUR750 in investment income tax on the dividends, with a total tax liability of EUR232,750. She pays 32.55% of her total income of EUR715,000 in taxes, and her taxable income is EUR710,000.

Additionally, there are other important dimensions in tax planning for investments. Some countries permit the use of tax deferred savings and retirement accounts that typically

- delay taxation on investment returns within the account to some later date;
- may permit a deduction for contributions to the account that reduce taxable income; and
- may occasionally permit tax free distributions under certain circumstances.

Finally, there are tax systems that impose a wealth tax on the accumulation of wealth. These wealth taxes are usually levied annually, and because they are often set as a percentage of the wealth, they function the same way as income taxes do, by reducing after-tax returns and accumulations.

The Impact of Accrual Taxes on Investment Returns

Estimating the taxes on investment alternatives allows taxable investors to compare returns and wealth accumulations for different types of investments subjected to different tax rates and methods of taxation. **Accrual taxes** are levied and paid on a periodic basis, usually annually. **Deferred taxes** can be postponed until some future date.

When investment returns are subject to accrual taxes, the after-tax return is equal to the pretax return, R, multiplied by $(1 - t_x)$, where t_x represents the tax rate applicable to investment income. For simplicity, the investment's return is entirely taxed at a single uniform rate. Then, the amount of money accumulated for each unit of currency, invested for T years, assuming that returns (after taxes at rate t_x are paid) are reinvested at the same rate of return, R, is simply

$$FVIF_T = [1 + \mathrm{R}(1 - t_x)]^{\mathrm{T}} \qquad (2)$$

Equation 2 is simply the future value interest factor (FVIF) based on an after-tax return. Comparing the accumulation with and without the impact of taxes gives the **tax drag**, the negative impact of taxes on an investment's net returns, reducing the overall performance and growth of an investment portfolio.

With accrual taxation, the tax drag on capital accumulation compounds over time. By contrast, when taxes on gains are deferred until the end of the investment horizon, the tax rate equals the tax drag on capital accumulation, as the case study involving Nataliia Kozlowska shows.

CASE STUDY

Nataliia Kozlowska: Accrual Taxes and Tax Drag

Ms. Nataliia Kozlowska is determining the impact of taxes on her expected investment returns and wealth accumulations. Ms. Kozlowska lives in a tax jurisdiction with a flat tax rate of 20%, which applies to all types of income and is taxed annually. Ms. Kozlowska expects to earn 7% per year on her investment over a 20-year time horizon and has an initial portfolio of EUR100,000.

Questions:

1. What is Ms. Kozlowska expected wealth at the end of 20 years?

   Answer:

   FV_t = EUR100,000 × $[1 + R(1 - t_x)]^T$ = EUR100,000 × $[1 + 0.07(1 - 0.20)]^{20}$ = EUR297,357.

2. What proportion of potential investment gains was consumed by taxes?

   Answer:

   Ignoring taxes, FV = EUR100,000 $[1 + 0.07]^{20}$ = EUR386,968. The difference between this and the after-tax amount accumulated from above is EUR89,611(EUR386,968 – EUR297,357). The proportion of potential investment gains consumed by taxes was EUR89,611/EUR286,968 = 31%, which is greater than the 20% tax rate. The negative impact of taxes on the investment's net returns reduced the overall performance and growth of an investment by 31%. This proportion of potential investment gains is a measure of "tax drag".

As long as taxes can be delayed, the compounding effect of the tax drag can be neutralized, which increases long term accumulation. Moreover, since longer-term capital gains can be taxed at a lower rate compared to shorter-term capital gains, the longer taxes can be delayed, the lower the loss of the accumulated increase in purchasing power.

The size of the tax drag is considerable enough to be a specific factor in making investment decisions. Exhibit 25 illustrates the impact of taxes on capital growth for various investment horizons and rates of return.

Exhibit 25: Proportion of Potential Investment Growth Consumed by Annual Taxes on Return

	Investment horizon in years (n)							
r(%)	5	10	15	20	25	30	35	40
1	0.30	0.31	0.31	0.32	0.33	0.33	0.34	0.34
2	0.31	0.32	0.33	0.34	0.35	0.36	0.37	0.38
5	0.32	0.35	0.37	0.40	0.43	0.46	0.48	0.51
10	0.34	0.39	0.45	0.50	0.55	0.60	0.64	0.68

	Investment horizon in years (n)							
r(%)	5	10	15	20	25	30	35	40
12	0.35	0.41	0.47	0.54	0.59	0.65	0.69	0.74
15	0.36	0.44	0.51	0.59	0.65	0.71	0.76	0.80
20	0.38	0.48	0.57	0.66	0.73	0.79	0.84	0.87

Note: The calculations assume a 30% annual tax rate assessed on investment returns.

According to Exhibit 25, tax drag has the following effects:

- When investment returns are taxed annually, the impact of taxes on capital growth is more significant than the nominal annual tax rate suggests.
- Over time, the negative consequences of taxes on capital growth compound, resulting in a growing gap between pretax and after-tax gains.
- As investment returns increase, tax drag also increases, assuming other factors remain constant.
- Both return and investment horizons have a multiplicative effect on tax drag related to future accumulations.

This implies that for fixed-income instruments, for which most or even all investment returns are subject to annual taxation, the effect of returns on tax drag is more substantial for longer investment periods. Moreover, the influence of investment horizon is more significant when dealing with higher returns.

The Impact of Deferral of Taxes on Investment Returns

Certain types of investment income, such as capital gains, are subject to deferred taxes. Capital gains taxes are typically incurred when an asset is sold, and they are applied to the realized gain, which is calculated as the difference between the selling price and the basis. In most cases, the basis refers to the initial investment made when acquiring the asset. Although it is uncommon for unrealized capital gains to be taxed, it happens in some tax jurisdictions. Additionally, tax-advantaged investment accounts can help defer capital gains taxes. In these cases, investment returns and income from capital gains accumulate for a time without tax drag and are only subject to taxation when they are withdrawn from the account.

If the tax on an investment's return is deferred until the end of its investment horizon T and taxed as a capital gain at rate t_{CG}, then the after-tax future accumulation can be represented as

$$FVIF_{CG} = (1 + R)^T - [(1 + R)^T - 1] \times t_{CG}$$

$$= (1 + R)^T (1 - t_{CG}) + t_{CG} \quad (3)$$

The term $(1 + R)^T$ represents the pretax accumulation. The $[(1 + R)^T - 1] \times t_{CG}$ term is the tax on the capital gain. Viewed differently, $(1 + R)^T(1 - t_{CG})$ represents the future accumulation if the entire amount was subjected to tax. Here, the t_{CG} term returns the tax of the untaxed cost associated with the initial investment; these calculations are explained in detail in the case study on Nataliia Kozlowska's deferral of tax liability.

CASE STUDY

Nataliia Kozlowska: Deferral of Tax Liability

Assume the same facts as in the previous case study. Ms. Kozlowska invests EUR100,000 at 7%. However, the return comes in the form of deferred capital gains that are not taxed until the investment is sold in 20 years' time.

Questions:

1. What is Ms. Kozlowska's expected wealth at the end of 20 years?

   Answer:

   $$FV_{CG} = 100,000\ (1+0.07)^{20} - \{[(1+0.07)^{20} - 1] \times 0.20\}$$

   $$= 100,000\ [3.8697 - (2.8697 \times 0.20)]$$

   $$= 100,000 \times 3.2958 = \text{EUR}329,576$$

2. What proportion of potential investment gains were consumed by taxes?

   Answer:

   Ignoring taxes, FV = EUR100,000 × $(1 + 0.07)^{20}$ = EUR386,968. The difference between this and the after-tax amount accumulated from above is EUR57,392 (EUR386,968 – EUR329,576). The proportion of potential investment gains consumed by taxes was EUR57,392/EUR286,968 = 20%. This result compares favorably to the potential investment gains consumed by taxes in the previous case study, in which 31% of investment gains were consumed by taxes.

The deferral of taxes demonstrates that when tax deferrals are available, the percentage of potential investment growth consumed by taxes is equal to the tax rate, which is lower than the impact of annual taxation. Essentially, the value of capital gain tax deferral offsets a portion of tax drag, and both increase with investment return and time horizon. For long-term taxable investors, maximizing tax deferrals is an essential investment consideration.

While tax drag on after-tax accumulations subject to annual taxes compounds over time, the tax drag from deferred capital gains remains a fixed percentage regardless of investment return or time horizon. The longer the tax deferral, the lower the present value of the tax liability, allowing more capital accumulation to be protected from the ravaging effects of taxation. The case study below expands on the example of Nataliia Kozlowska and provides a more detailed illustration, emphasizing that for long-term taxable investors, maximizing after-tax capital accumulation is a key investment consideration.

CASE STUDY

Nataliia Kozlowska: Comparing Taxable Investment Alternative with Tax-Deferred Investment Alternative

Assume the same facts as in the previous two case studies. Ms. Kozlowska has a choice between a taxable investment alternative (i.e., taxed annually) and tax-deferred investment alternative.

In the taxable alternative, at the end of the 20-year horizon the initial investment of EUR100,000 has grown to

$$FV_t = \text{EUR}100{,}000 \times [1 + 0.07 \times (1 - 0.20)]^{20}$$

$$= \text{EUR}100{,}000 \times [1 + 0.07 \times 0.80]^{20}$$

$$= \text{EUR}100{,}000 \times (1 + 0.056)^{20}$$

$$= \text{EUR}297{,}357$$

The proportion of potential investment gains consumed by taxes was EUR89,611/EUR286,968 = 31% (recall that, ignoring taxes, FV = EUR100,000 × $(1 + 0.07)^{20}$ = EUR386,968).

In the tax-advantaged alternative, at the end of the 20-year horizon the initial investment of EUR100,000 has grown to

$$FV_{CG} = \text{EUR}100{,}000\ \left[(1 + 0.07)^{20} - \left[(1 + 0.07)^{20} - 1\right] \times 0.20\right]$$

$$= \text{EUR}100{,}000\ \left[(1 + 0.07)^{20} \times 0.80 + 0.20\right]$$

$$= \text{EUR}100{,}000\ \left[(1.07)^{20} \times 0.80 + 0.20\right]$$

$$= \text{EUR}100{,}000\ [3.8697 \times 0.80 + 0.20]$$

$$= \text{EUR}100{,}000\ [3.0958 + 0.20]$$

$$= \text{EUR}329{,}576$$

The proportion of potential investment gains consumed by taxes was EUR57,394/EUR286,968 = 20%.

The benefit from the tax deferral leads to an additional EUR32,218 (EUR329,575 – EUR297,357) investment growth. The tax drag is reduced from 31% to 20%.

One crucial implication of tax deferral value is that investments with deferred capital gains taxation can be more tax efficient than those with annual taxed returns even if the marginal tax rates applied on both returns are the same. The advantage of tax deferral compounds over time. Furthermore, even if deferred capital gains or tax-advantaged investments have higher tax rates than annually taxed (accrual) investment income, the deferral value can outweigh a lower annually applied tax rate over time.

The relative accumulations can be significantly larger when gains can be deferred over long time horizons, particularly for high returns. These models assume investors earn a fair risk-adjusted return. The benefits of tax deferral, however, can be diminished or even completely extinguished if investments taxed on an accrual basis offer sufficiently large risk-adjusted returns (i.e., pretax alpha). In other words, purchasing securities sufficiently below their intrinsic value (or short selling securities sufficiently above intrinsic value) can overcome tax drag even if the investment is taxed heavily on an annual basis. For taxable investments with lower returns, there may not be benefits from delaying taxes.

Lastly, many tax systems have lower capital gains tax rates compared to other investment or ordinary income tax rates, providing a dual benefit for capital gains returns. First, there is the tax deferral advantage and a favorable tax rate upon realization of gains. Second, capital gains tax rates on longer holding periods may receive lower tax rates to encourage long-term investments over short-term ones.

The Impact of Basis on Capital Gains

Basis or **cost basis** is the original cost of an investment including any additional expenses incurred to acquire it and is used to calculate capital gains or losses when the asset is sold. In some circumstances, this basis may be increased or decreased. For calculating capital gain taxes, the selling price minus the calculated cost basis is multiplied with the applicable tax rate.

Often, an asset purchased earlier will have a cost basis differing from the current market value. If the asset's value has increased since its purchase, the cost basis might be less than the market value. This cost basis impacts after-tax accumulation, as it sets the taxable capital gain. An asset with a low cost basis has an embedded tax liability because of potential capital gains tax from selling it today even without considering future growth. In contrast, recent investments and cash do not carry this immediate tax liability.

If the cost basis is expressed as proportion B of the current market value of the investment, then the future after-tax accumulation value can be expressed by simply subtracting this additional tax liability from the expression in Equation 3, or

$$FVIF_{CG,B} = (1+R)^T(1-t_{CG}) + t_{CG} - (1-B) \times t_{CG}$$

$$= (1+R)^T(1-t_{CG}) + t_{CG}B \qquad (4)$$

This equation resembles Equation 3, $(1 + R)^T(1 - t_{CG}) + t_{CG}$, and the last term, $t_{CG}B$, represents the after-tax basis at the end of investment horizon.

An investment with an initial low cost basis has a greater current embedded tax liability than an investment with a higher cost basis because, if it were liquidated today, tax on the embedded gain would be due. Hence, when selling an appreciated asset, the potential tax liability must be weighed against the potential for return as the case study on Nataliia Kozlowska and the cost basis shows.

CASE STUDY

Nataliia Kozlowska: Cost Basis

Continuing with the facts in this series of case studies, Ms. Kozlowska has a current investment with a market value of EUR100,000 and cost basis of EUR80,000. The stock price grows at 7% per year for 20 years. The applicable tax rate is 20%.

Questions:

1. Express the cost basis as a percent of the current market value.

   Answer:

   Cost basis/Current market value = B = EUR80,000/ EUR100,000 = 0.80.

2. What is Ms. Kozlowska's expected wealth after 20 years?

   Answer:

   $$FVIF_{CB,\ G} = \text{EUR}100{,}000 \times [(1 + 0.07)^{20}(1 - 0.20) + 0.20(0.80)]$$

   $$= \text{EUR}325{,}575.$$

   This amount is EUR4,000 smaller than Ms. Kozlowska's expected wealth in the earlier example about deferral of tax liability (EUR329,575), in which it was assumed that the cost basis equaled the current market value.

Inflation

Inflation, which represents the rate at which the general price level for goods and services in an economy changes over time, diminishes the future purchasing power of money and can impact the composition of the consumption basket throughout an individual's life cycle. Factors such as changes in income, priorities, lifestyle, and family dynamics drive these shifts. For instance, younger adults tend to spend more on leisure, entertainment, and clothing, whereas retired individuals are more likely to allocate their funds towards health-related expenses, housing, and transportation. These variations in consumption patterns hold significant implications for long-term savings, including retirement planning.

By considering the joint effects of accrual taxes and inflation on long-term wealth accumulation, investors can make informed decisions and choose investments that offer the most favorable long-term outcomes. Concentrating solely on nominal returns can result in a distorted perception of an investment's real, after-tax, long-term performance.

As periodic taxes and inflation gradually erode accumulated capital, then the future after-tax inflation-adjusted accumulation on capital, $FVIF_{t,inf}$, can be calculated as in Equation 5:

$$FVIF_{t,infl} = \left[\frac{1 + R(1 - t_X)}{1 + infl}\right]^T \tag{5}$$

In this equation, the nominal after-tax returns from Equation 2 are reduced by the inflation rate. The nominator, $1 + R(1 - t_x)$, is the after-tax return, and the denominator, $1 + infl$, is the inflation adjustment. The case study on Nataliia Kozlowska's wealth accumulation considering taxes and inflation demonstrates the joint effects of tax and inflation.

CASE STUDY

Nataliia Kozlowska: The Effects of Tax and Inflation on Wealth Accumulation

Continuing with the facts in this series of case studies, Ms. Kozlowska is determining the impact of inflation and annual taxes on her wealth accumulations. Ms. Kozlowska expects to earn a nominal 7% per year on her investment over a 20-year time horizon and has an initial portfolio of EUR100,000. The anticipated inflation is 3% annually.

Questions:

1. What is Ms. Kozlowska's expected inflation adjusted wealth at the end of 20 years without the impact of taxes?

   Answer:

$$FV_{t=0,infl} = \text{EUR}100,000\left[\frac{1+0.07\,(1-0)}{(1+0.03)}\right]^T$$

$$= \text{EUR}100,000\left[\frac{1.07}{1.03}\right]^{20}$$

$$= \text{EUR}100,000 \times 1.0388^{20}$$

$$= \text{EUR}100,000 \times 2.1411$$

$$= \text{EUR}214,110$$

   Ms. Kozlowska's expected inflation-adjusted wealth at the end of 20 years without the impact of taxes is EUR214,110. The purchasing power of EUR386,968 in nominal terms and ignoring taxes equals the purchasing power of EUR214,110 in real terms ignoring taxes.

2. What is Ms. Kozlowska's expected inflation adjusted wealth at the end of 20 years with the impact of taxes?

   Answer:

$$FV_{t,infl} = \text{EUR}100,000\left[\frac{1+0.07\,(1-0.20)}{(1+0.03)}\right]^T$$

$$= \text{EUR}100,000\left[\frac{1.056}{1.03}\right]^{20}$$

$$= \text{EUR}100,000 \times 1.0252^{20}$$

$$= \text{EUR}100,000 \times 1.6450$$

$$= \text{EUR}164,500$$

   Ms. Kozlowska's expected after-tax inflation-adjusted wealth at the end of 20 years with the impact of annual taxes is EUR164,500.

3. How much purchasing power have taxes eroded?

Answer:

Taxes eroded the equivalent of EUR49,601 in purchasing power.

4. How much purchasing power would taxes erode if the return were 4% with no inflation (i.e., a similar real return to the 7% nominal return and 3% inflation presented earlier)?

Answer:

$$FV_{t=0,infl} = \text{EUR}100,000\left[\frac{1+0.04\,(1-0)}{(1+0)}\right]^{20} = \text{EUR}219,112$$

$$FV_{t=0.20,infl} = \text{EUR}100,000\left[\frac{1+0.04\,(1-0.20)}{(1+0)}\right]^{20} = \text{EUR}187,756$$

In this case, taxes eroded the equivalent of EUR31,356 in purchasing power. Although the erosion of purchasing power was less when the nominal returns were higher in the above example, the real returns are similar. This demonstrates that inflation, in conjunction with taxes, can decrease purchasing power even when there is no change in the real pretax returns.

Adapting Equation 3, where capital accumulates on a tax-advantaged basis with tax assessed on the accumulation upon sale or at liquidation (i.e., deferred capital gain), inflation can be incorporated, arriving at the relationship shown in Equation 6:

$$FVIF_{CG,\,B,\,infl} = \frac{(1+R)^T(1-t_{CG})+t_{CG}B}{(1+infl)^T} \tag{6}$$

The inflation adjustment reduces the after-tax value. Taxes are paid in nominal terms and not in purchasing power–adjusted values; however, it is the purchasing power of the after-tax wealth that is relevant from a wealth management perspective. The case study comparing increase in purchasing power of taxable accounts with tax-deferred accounts shows the effect of the time horizon, the inflation rate, and the return.

CASE STUDY

Nataliia Kozlowska: Comparing Increases in Purchasing Power of Taxable Accounts with Tax-Deferred Accounts

Continuing with the facts in this series of case studies, Ms. Kozlowska has a current investment with a market value of EUR100,000 and cost basis of EUR80,000. The stock price grows at 7% per year for 20 years. Inflation is 3%, and the applicable tax rate is 20%.

Questions:

1. What is Ms. Kozlowska's expected wealth in real, inflation-adjusted, and after-tax terms after 20 years?

Answer:

$$FV_{CG,\,B,\,infl} = \text{EUR}100,000\left[\frac{(1+R)^T\,(1-t_{CG})+t_{CG}B}{(1+infl)^T}\right]$$

$$= \text{EUR}100{,}000 \frac{(1+0.07)^{20}(1-0.20)+0.20\times 0.80}{(1+0.03)^{20}}$$

$$= \text{EUR}100{,}000 \frac{1.07^{20}\times 0.80+0.16}{1.03^{20}}$$

$$= \text{EUR}100{,}000 \times 1.8027$$

$$= \text{EUR}180{,}270.$$

This amount is EUR15,770 greater than Ms. Kozlowska's after-tax, purchasing power–adjusted wealth in the previous case study (EUR 164,500), where taxes were applied annually.

2. How would the answer change if the basis were EUR100,000?

Answer:

$$FV_{CG,\,B,\,infl} = \text{EUR}100{,}000\left[\frac{(1+R)^T(1-t_{CG})+t_{CG}B}{(1+infl)^T}\right]$$

$$= \text{EUR}100{,}000 \frac{(1+0.07)^{20}(1-0.20)+0.20\times 1}{(1+0.03)^{20}}$$

$$= \text{EUR}100{,}000 \frac{1.07^{20}\times 0.80+0.20}{1.03^{20}}$$

$$= \text{EUR}100{,}000 \times 1.8248 = \text{EUR}182{,}480.$$

This amount is EUR2,210 greater than Ms. Kozlowska's after-tax, purchasing power–adjusted wealth when the basis was EUR80,000, illustrating the additional tax liability associated with a lower cost basis.

An important insight is that tax liabilities are levied on nominal price appreciation rather than real price appreciation. As a result, inflation exacerbates the eroding impact of taxes on the long-term increase and preservation of real purchasing power.

The Impact of Different Sources of Returns with Taxes

The prior examples demonstrate the basic mechanics of tax calculations in a simplified manner, with a single constant return exposed to a single, uniform, unchanging tax rate. In reality, portfolio returns often originate from various sources and may be subject to different tax rates. These rate of return and tax rate issues have implications for portfolio management.

A more comprehensive return model incorporates annual income component, R_{INC}, taxed yearly at the tax rate, t_X, and capital appreciation, $R_{CAPITAL}$, taxed upon liquidation at the capital gains rate, t_{CG}. Incorporating the after-tax effects on annual returns and the capital gains tax upon investment liquidation on the capital gains portion of an investment's return, we arrive at Equation 7 below as a future value accumulation factor:

$$\begin{aligned} \text{FVIF}_{\text{INC,CAPITAL,TX,TCG}} &= \left[1+(R_{INC}\times(1-t_X))+R_{CAPITAL}\right]^T \\ &-\left[\frac{R_{CAPITAL}}{R_{INC}\times(1-t_X)+R_{CAPITAL}}\times\left[\left[1+(R_{INC}\times(1-t_X))+R_{CAPITAL}\right]^T-1\right]\times t_{CG}\right] \end{aligned} \quad (7)$$

Equation 7 may be explained as consisting of two primary elements as described below:

- The first bracketed term is the future value of the investment after incorporating the annual tax on income gains.

- The second term in brackets consists of three intermediate terms.
  - The first intermediate term is the ratio of the capital gain return to the total after-tax annual return on income and capital gains.
  - The second intermediate term is a computation of the total gain on the investment.
  - The third intermediate term is the tax rate on capital gains.
  - Multiplying the three intermediate terms comprising the second primary element provides the total capital gains tax which is deducted from the investment's future value after incorporating annual taxes on income gains.

An application of Equation 7 is demonstrated in the following case study.

CASE STUDY

Nataliia Kozlowska: Comparing After-Tax Returns on Different Return Sources and Tax Rates

Continuing with the facts in this series of case studies, Ms. Kozlowska's EUR100,000 investment in the stock expects to generate 5% in nominal annual price appreciation and 2% in nominal annual dividend income. The dividend income is taxed at 20% annually, while the price appreciation is also taxed at 20% upon investment liquidation. Ms. Kozlowska has an investment time horizon of 20 years. For purposes of this example, we assume no inflation.

Questions:

1. Calculate Ms. Kozlowska's expected wealth in after-tax terms after 20 years.

   Answer:

   Ms. Kozlowska's expected wealth is expected to equal EUR319,792.40 after 20 years as described below.

   Equation 7 is shown below and the solution process discusses the different components of the calculation.

$$\text{FVIF}_{\text{INC,CAPITAL,TX,TCG}} = \left[1 + (R_{INC} \times (1 - t_X)) + R_{CAPITAL}\right]^T$$

$$-\left[\frac{R_{CAPITAL}}{R_{INC} \times (1 - t_X) + R_{CAPITAL}} \times \left[\left[1 + (R_{INC} \times (1 - t_X)) + R_{CAPITAL}\right]^T - 1\right] \times t_{CG}\right]$$

   As a starting point, we compute that the after-tax annual rate of return implied by RINC and RCAPITAL is 6.6% per year.

$$\textit{Annual after tax rate of return} = 2\% \times (1 - 20\%) + 5\% = 6.6\%$$

   Thus, the future value accumulation factor for an investment generating 6.6% per year for 20 years is 3.5904104. This is the first bracketed term in the equation above.

$$[1 + (2\% \times (1 - 20\%) + 5\%]^{20} = 3.5904104$$

Next, we compute the amount of the capital gains tax by employing the three components of the second primary element of the equation.

- Ratio of the capital gain return to the total after-tax annual return on income and capital gains = 5% ÷ 6.6% = 75.76%
- Total gain on the investment = 2.5904104
- Capital gains tax rate = 20%

$$\textit{Total capital gains tax} = 0.7576\ x\ 2.59041\ x\ 0.20 = 0.3924864$$

$$FVIF_{INC,CAPITAL,TX,TCG} = 3.5904104 - 0.3924864 = 3.197924$$

Multiplying the above result by the initial investment of EUR100,000 provides Ms. Kozlowska's expected wealth in after-tax terms after 20 years of EUR319,792.40.

2. Suppose that Ms. Kozlowska has a different investment opportunity which expects to generate 2% in nominal annual price appreciation and 5% in nominal annual dividend income. Calculate Ms. Kozlowska's expected wealth in after-tax terms after 20 years.

Answer:

Following the same process as illustrated in the calculations to the prior scenario, we find that Ms. Kozlowska's expected after-tax wealth for this investment is EUR306,001 as shown below.

In this case, the after-tax annual rate of return implied by RINC and RCAPITAL is 6.0% per year.

$$\textit{Annual after tax rate of return} = 5\% \times (1 - 20\%) + 2\% = 6.0\%$$

The future value accumulation factor for an investment generating 6.0% per year for 20 years is 3.20713547.

$$[1 + (5\% \times (1 - 20\%) + 2\%]^{20} = 3.20713547$$

The three components of the second primary element of the equation are as follows:

- Ratio of the capital gain return to the total after-tax annual return on income and capital gains = 2% ÷ 6% = 33.33%
- Total gain on the investment = 2.20713547
- Capital gains tax rate = 20%

$$\textit{Total capital gains tax} = 0.3333\ x\ 2.20713547\ x\ 0.20 = 0.14712765$$

$$FVIF_{INC,CAPITAL,TX,TCG} = 3.20713547 - 0.14712765 = 3.06001$$

Multiplying the above result by the initial investment of EUR100,000 provides Ms. Kozlowska's expected wealth in after-tax terms after 20 years of EUR306,001.

3. Contrast the after-tax wealth implications of the two investments above by discussing the tax drag associated with the two investments considered in the two prior questions.

Answer:

To assess the tax drag of these two investments, we first note that, in the absence of taxes, both investments generate 7% in annual return. Without taxes, the after-tax wealth of EUR100,000 invested for 20 years at 7% is equal to EUR386,968.44 as shown below.

$$100,000 \times [1 + 0.07]^{20} = 386,968.44$$

The tax drag is reflected by the difference between the after-tax wealth compared to the wealth in the absence of taxes as a percentage of the total gain in the absence of taxes. Ms. Kozlowska is clearly better off from an after-tax perspective with the investment opportunity implied by the first question in which income taxed annually generates the lower return of 2% per year while the higher capital gains return of 5% is not taxed until the end of the 20-year investment horizon.

$$\textit{Tax drag of first scenario} = \frac{386,968.44 - 319,792.40}{286,968.44} = 23.4\%$$

$$\textit{Tax drag of second scenario} = \frac{386,968.44 - 306,001}{286,968.44} = 28.2\%$$

Effectively, the second scenario creates a larger total tax burden because more of each year's return is taxed. The first scenario featured 6.6% annual return after-tax while the second scenario only generated 6.0% annual return after-tax. Despite lower capital gains taxes in the second scenario, the compounding power of the additional 60 basis points of after-tax annual return sufficiently offsets the additional capital gains taxes paid in the first scenario.

Comparing Nominal and After-Tax Nominal with Real and After-Tax Real Returns

Examining long-term returns as represented by the S&P 500 Total Return, S&P 500 Price Return, and US inflation rates, we can illustrate the combined impact of taxes and inflation. The difference between S&P 500 Total Return and S&P 500 Price Return indicates the dividend yield, while the S&P 500 Price Return only reflects the capital appreciation. Both the dividend yield and the capital appreciation are taxed, but they are taxed at different rates. By applying different tax rates to these components and timing the realization of the capital appreciation that triggers capital gains taxation, we can demonstrate the impact of taxes on capital accumulation. Exhibit 26 below presents the wealth accumulation in nominal returns for four different investment alternatives:

- A tax-exempt investment alternative in which neither income nor capital accumulation is taxed
- A tax-advantaged investment alternative with a 25% tax rate on income but no tax on capital appreciation
- A taxable investment alternative in which both income and capital appreciation are taxed at 25%
- A high-tax taxable investment alternative with a 50% tax rate on both income and capital appreciation

To compute these returns, taxes were applied at the end of each month. While this example streamlines the calculations, it underscores that tax-advantaged investment options significantly reduce the impact of taxes on wealth accumulation over time. The process of accumulating USD1 million for each of the four investment alternatives is summarized below:

Exhibit 26: Accumulation of USD1 Million in Nominal Terms from 1988–2022

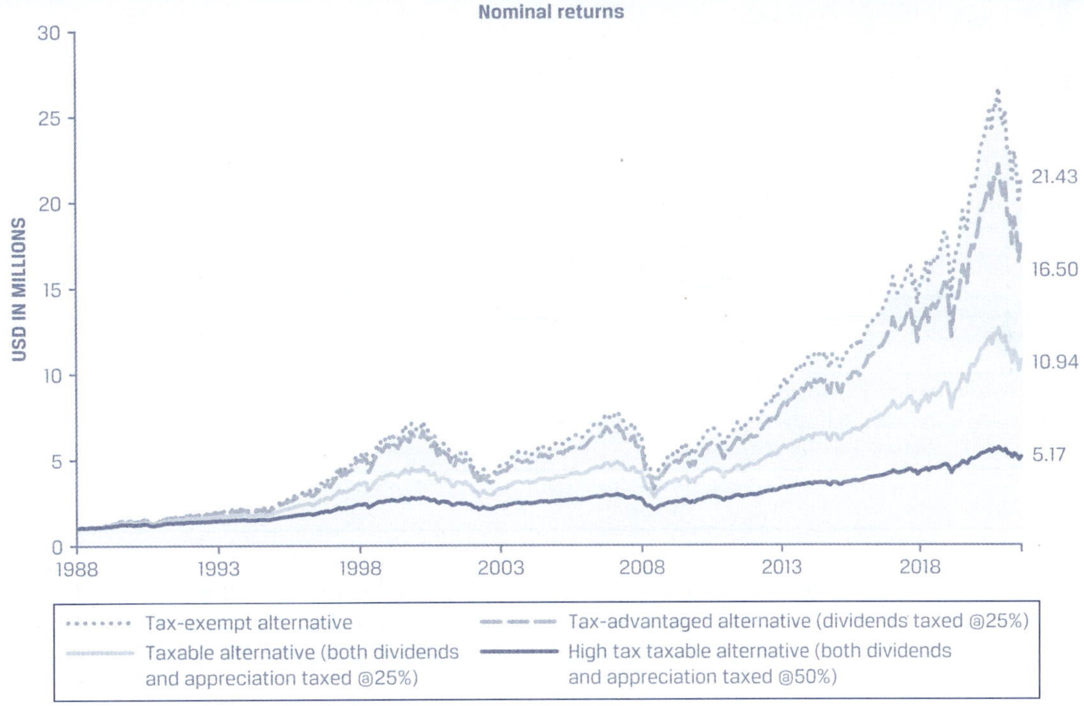

Considering the impact of the monthly consumer inflation rate, which is an important consideration for private wealth clients aiming to build wealth and enhance their purchasing power, the wealth accumulation results in Exhibit 27 are observed (illustrated on the same scale):

Exhibit 27: Accumulation of USD1 Million in Real Terms from 1988–2022

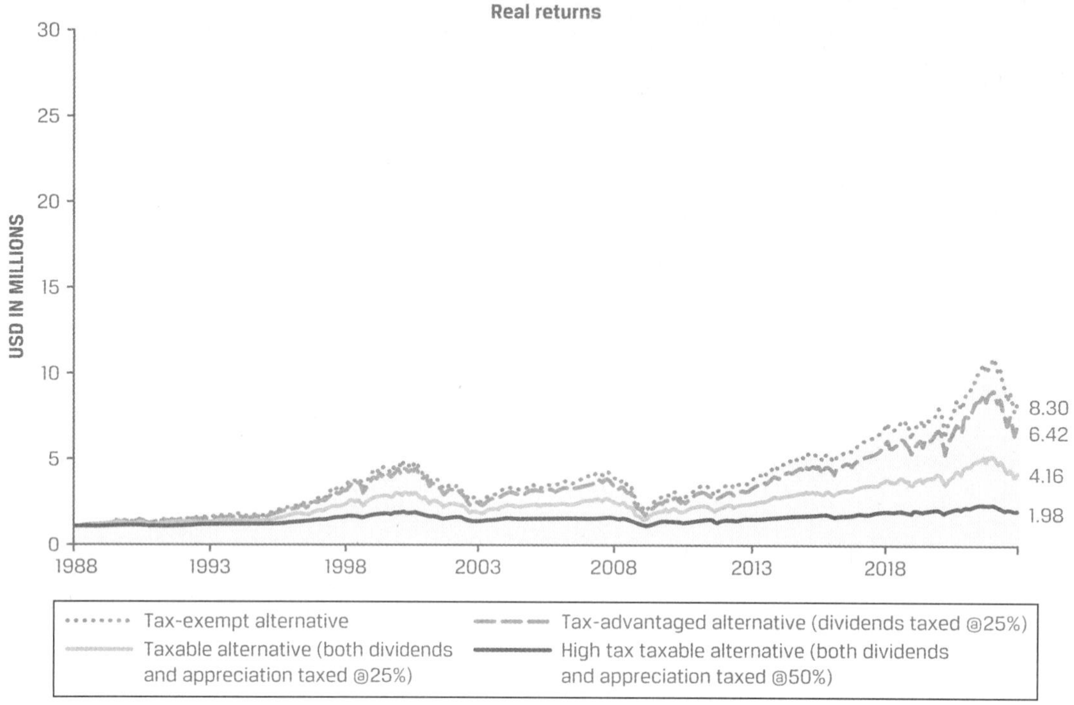

The growth in purchasing power is notably lower than in nominal terms. Exhibit 28 presents the real and nominal accumulation of an initial USD1 million invested in each of the four investment alternatives, highlighting the effects of both taxes and inflation:

Exhibit 28: The Accumulation of USD1 Million Invested

	Accumulation in millions of USD	
	Nominal terms	**Real terms**
Tax-exempt alternative	21.43	8.30
Tax-advantaged alternative (dividends taxed at 25%)	17.78	6.88
Taxable alternative (both dividends and appreciation taxed at 25%)	10.74	4.16
High-tax taxable alternative (both dividends and appreciation taxed at 50%)	5.12	1.98

A substantial portion of wealth accumulation can be lost to inflation, especially in long-term investments. Inflation can be particularly detrimental to fixed-income investments, as it devalues the returns on these investments in real terms. At the same time, tax-advantaged investment vehicles can help mitigate the impact of taxes on investment returns. By offering tax deferrals, reduced tax rates, or even tax exemptions, these investment alternatives enable investors to retain a larger portion of their returns, which can then be reinvested to compound and grow over time.

QUESTION SET

1. An investor plans to invest GBP25,000 in an investment opportunity expected to generate 6% in taxable income per year over the next 10 years. The appropriate tax rate is 40%, and taxes on the returns are paid annually. Demonstrate that the tax drag of this investment is greater than the tax rate.

   Solution:

   Using

   $$FV = \text{GBP}25,000 \times [1 + 0.06 \times (1 - 0.40)]^{10}$$

   $$= \text{GBP}25,000 \times (1 + 0.036)^{10} = \text{GBP}25,000 \times 1.4243 = \text{GBP}35,607$$

   Comparing the result with the no-tax alternative, the investment would have grown to

   $$FV = \text{GBP}25,000 \times (1 + 0.06)^{10} = \text{GBP}25,000 \times 1.06^{10}$$

   $$= \text{GBP}25,000 \times 1.7908 = \text{GBP}44,771$$

   The additional growth due to the absence of taxes, GBP44,771 – GBP35,607, is GBP9,164. The tax drag is

   $$\frac{\text{GBP}9,164}{\text{GBP}44,771 - \text{GBP}25,000} = 46\%,$$

   which is greater than the 40% tax rate. The negative impact of taxes on the investment's net returns reduced the overall performance and growth of an investment by 46%.

2. An investor plans to invest GBP50,000 in an investment opportunity expected to generate a return of 8% per year, which is taxed as a deferred capital gain only after 10 years. The tax rate is 20%. Compare the impact of taxes on the after-tax return relative to if taxes were paid annually at a 20% rate.

   Solution:

   The investment using deferred taxation grows to

   $$FV = \text{GBP}50,000\left[(1 + 0.08)^{10} - \left[(1 + 0.08)^{10} - 1\right] \times 0.20\right]$$

   $$= \text{GBP}50,000\left[(1 + 0.08)^{10}(1 - 0.20) + 0.20\right]$$

   $$= \text{GBP}50,000\left[(1 + 0.08)^{10} \times 0.80 + 0.20\right]$$

   $$= \text{GBP}50,000\left[(1.08)^{10} \times 0.80 + 0.20\right]$$

   $$= \text{GBP}50,000[2.1589 \times 0.80 + 0.20]$$

   $$= \text{GBP}50,000[1.7271 + 0.20] = \text{GBP}96,355.$$

   The investment using annual taxation grows to

   $$FV = \text{GBP}50,000 \times [1 + 0.08 \times (1 - 0.20)]^{10}$$

$$= \text{GBP}50,000 \times 1.064^{10} = \text{GBP}92,979.$$

The deferred taxation provides a higher accumulation of GBP3,376.

3. Discuss how the benefits of tax deferral can be overcome by finding mispriced investment opportunities.

Solution:

The benefits of tax deferral can be overwhelmed if investments taxed on an accrual basis offer sufficiently high risk-adjusted returns. That is, purchasing securities sufficiently below their intrinsic value (or short selling securities sufficiently above intrinsic value) can overcome tax drag even if the investment is taxed heavily on an annual basis.

6 INDIVIDUAL INVESTORS AND INVESTMENT POLICY STATEMENTS

☐ discuss the differences between private and institutional clients and formulate an appropriate Investment Policy Statement for private clients

An **investment policy statement (IPS)** outlines the client's unique investment objectives, risk tolerance, investment time horizon, and other applicable constraints and guides the wealth manager when constructing and implementing the client's portfolio and asset allocation. The IPS evolves through the conversation between the client and the wealth manager.

The IPS should be reviewed routinely as the client's circumstances or market conditions change. An IPS benefits both the client and the manager because it promotes discipline and commitment to the strategy, particularly during adverse or volatile market conditions, while describing the investment process and the advisor's fiduciary responsibility to the client. Additionally, an IPS focuses on achieving short-, medium-, and long-term financial goals rather than just short-term performance. By offering a clear, mutual understanding of the manager's mandate, an IPS helps ensure, but does not guarantee, that the client's financial objectives are met.

The IPS contains information about the client's investment objectives, asset base, and the overall asset allocation. Together with the wealth manager's capital market assumptions, these define the inputs needed for a capital sufficiency analysis. **Capital sufficiency analysis** is the process of evaluating whether a client has sufficient capital resources to achieve their financial goals and objectives, and it considers the client's assets, liabilities, income, expenses, risk tolerance, time horizon, and other relevant factors to determine if their current and future capital resources can adequately support their lifestyle, financial goals, and long-term financial stability. Whenever the capital sufficiency analysis does not support the investment objective, the manager must work with the client to revise objectives and create those that the manager judges to be achievable.

An IPS may further specify whether the assets are managed using strategic asset allocation, tactical asset allocation, or a combination of both.

- **Strategic asset allocation** is a long-term strategy that establishes target allocations for various asset classes and aims to optimize the balance between risk and reward by diversifying investments, considering an investor's financial objectives, risk tolerance, and investment timeline. The target allocation relies on historical data, projected returns, and correlations between asset classes.
- **Tactical asset allocation** is a more proactive strategy that adjusts asset class allocations within a portfolio based on short-term market trends, economic conditions, or valuation changes to capitalize on temporary market inefficiencies or opportunities to improve returns or manage risk more effectively. Unlike strategic asset allocation's long-term focus, tactical asset allocation allows for more frequent portfolio adjustments in response to market conditions and expectations. Consequently, this method entails higher trading costs and increased complexity and requires consistent monitoring of market conditions and asset performance. Additionally, tactical asset allocation demands a higher level of skill and experience.

The case study below provides a practical example of how these asset allocation strategies affect a portfolio's management.

CASE STUDY

C.Y. Lee: Combining Strategic and Tactical Asset Allocation

Mr. C.Y. Lee, the managing director for the investment firm Acme & Bass located in the Asia-Pacific region, is working with his wealth manager to combine strategic and tactical asset allocation in his IPS.

In establishing the portfolio asset allocation, the wealth manager considers Mr. Lee's assets, expected cash needs, risk tolerance, and financial goals. To achieve higher long-term risk-adjusted returns, the manager combines both strategic and tactical asset allocation approaches while incorporating rebalancing limits for the strategic allocation. A potential strategic asset allocation plan with target allocations and rebalancing limits for various asset classes can be as follows:

	Lower rebalancing limit	Strategic allocation	Upper rebalancing limit
Cash	3%	**5%**	7%
Cash and equivalents		5%	
Fixed income	25%	**30%**	35%
Short-term debt investments		20%	
Intermediate-term bonds		10%	
Equities	45%	**50%**	55%
Domestic, Singapore		10%	
International, Asia Pacific only		10%	

	Lower rebalancing limit	Strategic allocation	Upper rebalancing limit
International, ex-Asia Pacific		30%	
Alternatives	8%	**10%**	12%
Private equity	3%	**5%**	7%

The rebalancing limits ensure that the portfolio remains aligned with Mr. Lee's long-term financial goals, risk tolerance, and investment horizon. If any asset class allocation drifts beyond the specified limits, the portfolio manager will rebalance the portfolio, typically to bring it back in line with the target strategic allocations. As we shall see shortly, there are several methods for triggering portfolio rebalancing: one method is based on time, so the portfolio is rebalanced at set time intervals (i.e., quarterly or semi-annually, etc.), and the other method is based on thresholds, so the portfolio is rebalanced whenever specified limits are breached.

Additionally, the IPS allows for tactical asset allocation adjustments specifically in international equities to capitalize on short-term market trends or opportunities. For example, the wealth manager might have the discretion to temporarily increase the allocation to international equities by up to 10%, or a total of 50% of the portfolio, if they identify an attractive investment opportunity in a specific market or sector and by selling some of the domestic equity holdings. This tactical adjustment would be subject to the following conditions, such as the overall equities allocation should remain within the rebalancing limit (i.e., should not exceed 55% or fall below 45%).

The manager must provide a rationale for a tactical adjustment, including the anticipated duration and expected impact on the portfolio's risk and return profile.

The tactical allocation must be reviewed periodically, at least quarterly, to assess its ongoing appropriateness and potential need for further adjustment.

This hybrid approach allows Mr. Lee to benefit from the stability and diversification provided by strategic asset allocation while also leveraging tactical adjustments in international equities to enhance returns or manage risk more effectively.

Parts of an IPS

The IPS lays the foundation for the client–wealth manager relationship and details how the wealth manager will make investment decisions. As such, it guides the management of an investment portfolio by outlining the investment goals, risk tolerance, and constraints for an individual or an organization. It provides a framework for making investment decisions and helps ensure that the investment strategy aligns with the investor's objectives.

The IPS includes the client's background and investment objectives, the key parameters of the investment program, the portfolio asset allocation, and some discussion of the duties and responsibilities of relevant parties. It is developed by the wealth manager, reflects conversations and discussions with the client, and serves as a guidance document. An IPS is a dynamic document that should be reviewed regularly to capture changing conditions, preferences, goals, objectives, and time horizons. Exhibit 29 depicts the typical components of an IPS.

Exhibit 29: Components of an IPS

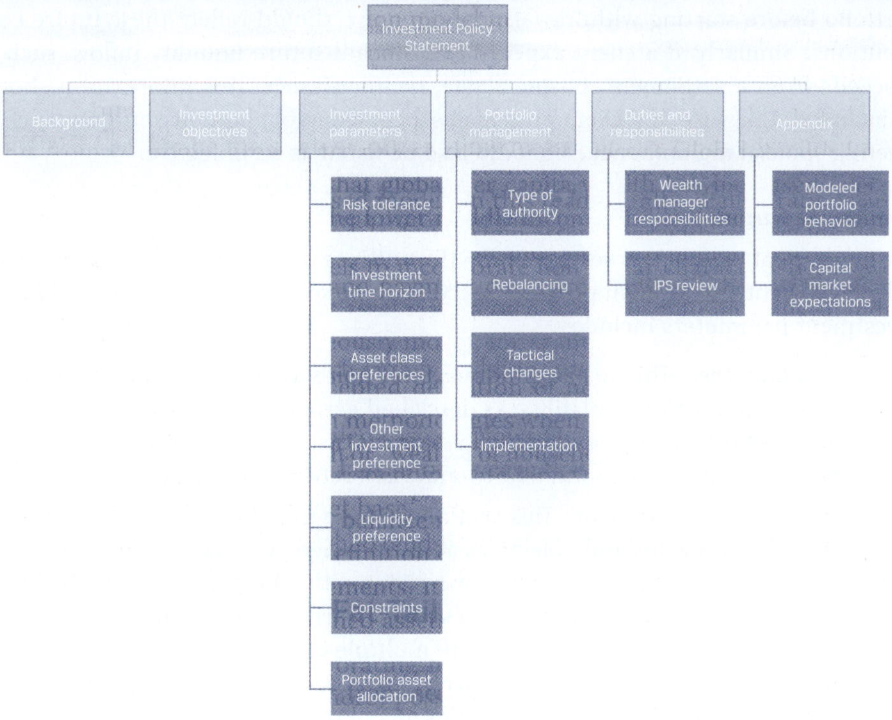

Background

The background section of the IPS usually contains the client's name, age, personal details, and pertinent financial information. This should include the portfolio's personal and business assets' market value and individual accounts within the portfolio, as well as the tax status of these accounts, and delineate substantial financial or nonfinancial assets not managed by the wealth manager. Such assets might encompass privately held business interests, real estate portfolios, and other valuable privately held assets. This section should also include a description of the family, its members, its sources of wealth (e.g., family business), and if appropriate, its core values. Specifics about tax jurisdictions where income and capital gains are taxed should be included here.

Investment objectives

The investment objectives section of the IPS typically outlines various short-term and long-term goals. Clients often have multiple, conflicting objectives they want to achieve with the same portfolio, which emerge during discussions between the client and the manager about financial matters.

Investment objectives should include overall portfolio return and risk objectives. Specific investment objectives should be detailed and quantifiable whenever possible. For example, a client might have specific amounts in mind for future bequests such as funds for their children or charitable donations. Investment objectives should avoid being oversimplified and vague. When dealing with multiple competing objectives, the manager should identify the primary goal, especially when the client has difficulty assigning specific amounts to future objectives. For instance, if a client wants to support their retirement lifestyle while preserving an inheritance for their children, the main objective would be retirement security, with the inheritance as a secondary consideration.

Investment objectives should also account for cash flows that affect capital sufficiency analysis. If a client plans to make regular contributions to the investment portfolio before starting withdrawals, the objective should reflect these future contributions. Similarly, if a client expects a significant future liquidity inflow, such as proceeds from a settlement, business sale, or inheritance, this information should be included. Likewise, if a client anticipates a considerable liquidity outflow, such as meeting spousal maintenance, it should also be listed as an objective.

Investment parameters

The investment parameters section of the IPS outlines preferences that influence each individual client's investment program and reflect the specific client's individual needs. Investment parameters include:

- *Risk tolerance*: This section outlines the client's ability and willingness to withstand portfolio volatility, as described earlier, and can reflect the score on a risk tolerance questionnaire as well as discussions that include risk preference, risk tolerance, and overall risk–return trade-offs.
- *Investment time horizon*: This section lists the time horizon for the agreed-upon goals and objectives across a range of years. It reflects discussions with the client. Typically, for a client with a long horizon, the IPS may state it as "exceeds 15 years"; for a shorter horizon, the IPS may state it as "less than 10 years." When there are multiple or parallel goals, each specific goal may be listed with its own time horizon, some of which, such as bequests and philanthropic activities, may exceed the client's lifetime.
- *Asset class preference*: This section lists the main asset classes included in the client's portfolio. These asset class preferences are often described in the context of risk, return, and income characteristics.
- *Liquidity preferences*: This section addresses liquidity considerations for clients who maintain cash in their portfolios and outlines a specific cash balance that the wealth manager must maintain. If a preference for cash constrains the asset class selection or implementation decisions, this should be discussed and then documented in the IPS. For instance, if a client's cash needs dictate that the entire portfolio should be held in relatively liquid assets, then there may be a cap on holding less liquid private equity and similarly illiquid asset classes.
- *Other investment preferences*: This section contains client-specific information such as specific "legacy" holdings that a client wishes to retain, like equity in a former employer, or an investment that the client wishes to make countering the wealth manager's advice. Some clients may hold a substantive proportion of their portfolio in their current or former employer's equity. This may create portfolio concentration risk, which can adversely impact the risk–return characteristics of the portfolio. Environmental, social, and governance (ESG)-related constraints should normally appear in this section. When a client expresses preferences for investments that meet socially responsible investing (SRI), ESG investment standards, or are otherwise acceptable or unacceptable due to religious, ethical, or personal preferences or beliefs, they should be noted here. Additionally, investment preferences may include portfolio turnover policy detailing how and when realization of potential gains should be conducted. Moreover, a preference for investing in actively or passively managed funds could also be added. Finally, any special tax or legal considerations should be noted. These might include issues of dual citizenship, legal residence in multiple countries, and the like.

- *Constraints*: This section lists investment constraints that may restrict the wealth manager from implementing certain investments or strategies. For example, a client may be constrained by an investment with large unrealized capital gains, which would create significant tax liabilities if sold. Such constraints should be clearly and unambiguously documented in the IPS, outlining the specific policy or programs for managing the effects of such a concentration. This may include a range of preferences from keeping to liquidating the investment over time. The choice of appropriate tax mitigation strategy should also be included here. For clients expressing preferences for SRI, ESG, religious, or ethical investment standards, the constraints imposed by these should be noted here. Finally, the process for client approval should also be unambiguously documented.
- *Portfolio asset allocation*: This section contains the target allocation or range for each asset class in the client's portfolio. Wealth managers who use a strategic asset allocation typically define a target allocation for each asset class as well as upper and lower bounds. Wealth managers who use a tactical asset allocation approach may list asset class target "ranges" rather than specific target allocation percentages.

Portfolio management

The portfolio management section of the IPS typically incorporates portfolio management topics such as the extent of any discretionary authority, the frequency and method of rebalancing, and, if relevant, changes to tactical asset allocation. The wealth manager may be granted discretionary authority to manage assets without explicit client approval. There are, however, different levels of such authority:

- A wealth manager *with full discretion* is free to implement rebalancing trades and replace fund managers without prior client approval.
- A wealth manager with less than full discretion has received authority to make certain specific changes such as rebalancing.
- A wealth manager *in a nondiscretionary capacity* makes recommendations to the client but is not able to take action without a client's consent.

Wealth managers may follow different methods of rebalancing a portfolio to realign the portfolio to the target allocation. Rebalancing may be included in the asset allocation section of an IPS. Expectations regarding the frequency of portfolio revisions may be stated a number of ways:

In a **time-based rebalancing policy**, the wealth manager rebalances client portfolios regularly, at a certain given time interval such as quarterly, semi-annually, or annually, regardless of any difference between prevailing asset class weights and target asset class weights.

Time-based rebalancing is a straightforward, simple, easy to understand and easy to implement policy. Its predictable rebalancing schedule ensures regular portfolio reassessment, keeping the strategic asset allocation on track, thereby reducing the risk of portfolio drift from their target allocations due to market fluctuations. Effectively, the systematic nature of rebalancing serves as an inherent risk management mechanism. However, the time-based rebalancing strategy is somewhat unresponsive to significant and sudden market changes, which may expose the portfolio to higher risks or cause missed investment opportunities between scheduled rebalancing times. Furthermore, it may lead to unnecessary transactions, which is particularly burdensome when the difference between prevailing asset class weights and target asset class weights is small (i.e., when the portfolio has not deviated much from its target allocations). Additionally, rebalancing transactions may incur extra costs both in terms of transaction fees and potential tax liabilities. Finally, the deterministic nature of time-based rebalancing means that buying or selling assets is dictated by the calendar rather than the prevailing market conditions. This could sometimes result in transacting at less than favorable prices.

In a **threshold-based rebalancing policy**, the wealth manager rebalances the portfolio when asset class weights deviate from their target weights by a prespecified percentage, for example, upper and lower rebalancing limits, regardless of timing and frequency.

Threshold-based rebalancing reacts to changing market conditions: the portfolio is rebalanced whenever there is a significant deviation from its target allocation, that is, whenever upper or lower rebalancing limits are breached. This strategy is sensitive to market volatility and sudden shifts. This approach could potentially be more efficient than the time-based rebalancing because it involves rebalancing only when necessary. This minimizes transaction costs and tax liabilities. Furthermore, because it allows for swift adjustments in response to volatile markets, it may offer better risk management, but at potentially higher cost.

However, threshold-based rebalancing is inherently complex, often requiring more sophisticated monitoring and automation systems to keep track of portfolio drift and execute rebalancing when needed. Also, the timing of rebalancing can be inconsistent. During stable markets, there may not be an adjustment for long periods. However, during periods of volatility, there may be frequent rebalancing in response to sudden periods of persistent volatility, which can create a more short-term focus. Because the rebalancing trigger is tied closely to market fluctuations, there is a risk of overreacting to short-term market events, potentially skewing away from long-term investment goals.

Both time-based rebalancing and threshold-based rebalancing require defining the target rebalancing weight, which is typically the strategic asset allocation. Exhibit 30 presents a comparison of time-based and threshold-based portfolio rebalancing.

Exhibit 30: Comparison of Time-Based and Threshold-Based Portfolio Rebalancing

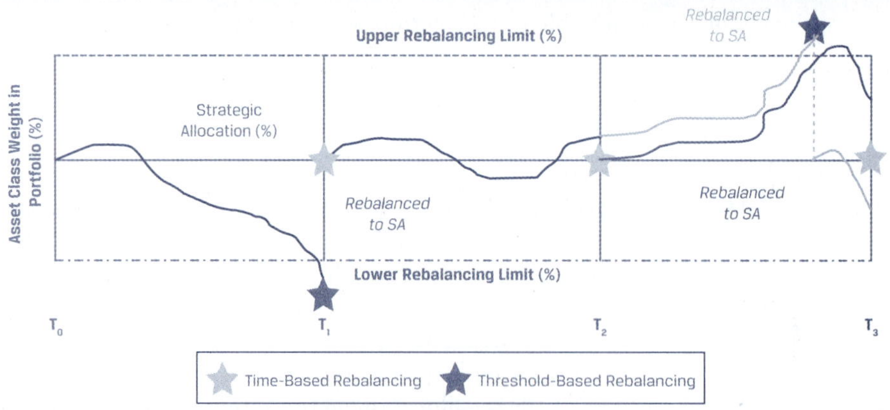

In a hypothetical portfolio, the asset class weights are initially set (at T_0) to those of the strategic allocation. At the end of period 1 (T_1), which could be a quarter, for example, portfolio rebalancing occurs both on a time and threshold basis to bring the asset class back to its strategic allocation. At the end of T_2, rebalancing would be performed on a time basis but not on a threshold basis because no threshold limit has been reached. During T_3, threshold-based rebalancing would be implemented when the upper rebalancing limit was breached. However, time-based rebalancing would only be performed at the end of period 3.

The section on tactical changes lists the specific parameters wealth managers must consider when making periodic adjustments, tactical changes, or other adjustments to a client's asset allocation. If target allocation ranges have been established in the earlier portfolio asset allocation section, this section of the IPS indicates whether, when, and how the manager can break those ranges when executing a tactical change.

This section includes information about the timeline over which the new portfolio will be created and the asset classes, investment alternatives, investment products, and derivatives the wealth manager anticipates using. Typically, it includes any specific third-party funds or money managers recommended by the wealth manager, the proprietary investment offerings managed by the wealth manager's firm, or some combination of these approaches. This section indicates whether the wealth manager prefers to invest in mutual funds, ETFs, private equity, hedge funds, or individual securities. When using third-party money managers, some additional relevant information includes the incremental costs, the specific selection and retention criteria the wealth manager uses to vet and pick third-party managers, and the extent, frequency, and steps included in the wealth manager's due diligence process to vet external managers.

Duties and responsibilities

The duties and responsibilities section of the IPS typically discusses the wealth manager's overall responsibilities, including expectations about the ongoing review of an IPS.

The wealth management responsibilities section helps the client in understanding how the wealth manager assists the client to reach their investment objectives and may include the following information:

- Developing an appropriate asset allocation
- Recommending or selecting investment options such as pooled investment vehicles or individual securities
- Monitoring the asset allocation and rebalancing
- Using derivatives, leverage, short sales, and repurchase agreements (repos) in an appropriate manner that is consistent with the client's investment and risk objectives
- Monitoring strategy implementation costs
- Monitoring the activities of third-party service providers (e.g., asset managers and/or custodians)
- Drafting and maintaining the IPS
- Reporting of performance, including an indication of the base currency
- Reporting of taxes and financial statements
- Voting proxies
- Assisting with the preparation of agreements associated with private fund offerings
- When the manager uses third-party providers, the IPS might also list their responsibilities. The distinct and important role of an asset custodian that maintains segregated client accounts, values the investment assets, collects income, and settles transactions is typically included.

The *IPS review* section sets expectations for how frequently the client and wealth manager will review the IPS and affirm that the investment objectives remain accurate and that the prevailing strategy is likely to meet those objectives.

IPS appendix

The appendix to the IPS often includes details that typically change more frequently than the main portion of the IPS, such as:

- *Modeled portfolio behavior*: This section describes a range of possible performance outcomes over various holding periods and can provide more value to the client than merely stating the return objective or the "expected compound return." The wealth manager may provide a modeled distribution of returns at various percentile ranges, which enables the wealth manager to quantify portfolio downside risk, particularly over short time periods. This can help to confirm what level of downside risk the client is able to accept.
- *Capital market expectations*: This section contains the modeled, simulated, or calculated portfolio statistics, including expected returns, standard deviations, and correlations. The section may also include historical returns both on a portfolio and individual asset class basis.

The case study below provides an example of how investment objectives are formulated for an HNWI.

CASE STUDY

Huang Zhuo Wei: Background and Investment Objectives

Huang Zhuo Wei, age 51, is a private investor in Singapore. Wei is an engineer by trade but has also been a successful real estate developer. His portfolio consists of SGD50 million in a liquid securities portfolio, including common stock positions in which he has large, embedded capital gains, and several real estate investments valued at approximately SGD90 million (combined). He expects to make additional real estate investments in the coming years. He estimates that he can invest approximately SGD1,000,000 per year, inflation-adjusted, in real estate until retirement.

He has a much higher than average risk tolerance and, historically, his liquid portfolio has consisted mostly of large-cap technology companies. He has stated that his time horizon is 10 years because he anticipates retiring in approximately 10 years. He estimates that he will need approximately SGD3 million per year, inflation-adjusted, to support his lifestyle in retirement. He wishes to grow his investment resources and create a significant inheritance for his children.

Questions:

1. Discuss how Wei's wealth manager should create the investment objectives section of Wei's IPS.

   Solution:

   The purpose of this portfolio is to support Wei's lifestyle in retirement and to provide an inheritance for his children. Aside from the investment assets in his portfolio, Wei has private real estate investments valued at approximately SGD90 million and is likely to add to this segment of his net worth over the next several years. Wei does not anticipate needing distributions from this portfolio for at least 10 years.

   Wei estimates an annual, inflation-adjusted lifestyle need of approximately SGD3 million per year beginning at his retirement in 10 years. His cash needs will be satisfied in part through portfolio distributions and in part from his real estate portfolio. The wealth manager will continue to work with Wei to quantify his bequest objective and ensure that his portfolio distribution rate is sustainable throughout his retirement.

2. Discuss how his wealth manager should reflect Wei's investment horizon in the IPS.

Solution:

Given his desire to create a significant inheritance for his children, Wei's true investment horizon is through retirement, a period that likely will be much longer than 10 years. His wealth manager should describe his time horizon as exceeding 10 years. The life expectancy in Singapore for a male is around 81 years; hence, the time in retirement can be approximately 20 years.

Sample Investment Policy Statement

The following case study demonstrates a sample IPS for a private client couple, David and Amelia King. The Kings' wealth manager does not use a tactical asset allocation approach for the couple, so the section on tactical changes is not relevant in this case.

CASE STUDY

David and Amelia King: Sample Investment Policy Statement

Background and Investment Objectives

This IPS is designed to assist David and Amelia in meeting their financial objectives. It contains a summation of their objectives and expectations, sets forth an investment structure for attaining these objectives, and outlines ongoing responsibilities.

The purpose of this portfolio is to support the continuation of David and Amelia's current lifestyle, provide for their family's needs, and fund their philanthropic objectives. Maintenance of their current lifestyle is their primary objective, followed by support for family members and charitable aspirations, in that order. To meet these objectives, they anticipate needing approximately USD350,000 per year in inflation-adjusted portfolio distributions. Furthermore, they intend to purchase a second residence within the next two years. They expect the purchase price for the second residence to be approximately USD1.5 million. David and Amelia have not articulated a specific dollar amount that they intend to leave to their children, nor a specific dollar amount that they wish to leave to charity at their death. These amounts must be quantified as soon as possible.

In establishing their asset allocation, David and Amelia have considered their total assets and expected cash needs. They are seeking to achieve a higher long-term rate of return and are willing to assume the associated portfolio volatility.

Portfolio accounts

1. Taxable joint account for David and Amelia
2. Tax-deferred account for David
3. Tax-deferred account for Amelia

Current combined market value = USD12,250,000

Investment Parameters

Risk tolerance

David and Amelia are able and willing to withstand short- and intermediate-term portfolio volatility. They recognize and acknowledge the anticipated level of portfolio volatility associated with their asset allocation (as illustrated in the Modeled Portfolio Behavior section of the Appendix).

Investment time horizon

David and Amelia have an investment time horizon that exceeds 15 years.

Asset class preferences

The following asset classes are selected:

- Short-term debt investments
- Intermediate-term bonds
- US stocks
- Non-US stocks
- Global real estate securities

Liquidity preferences

David and Amelia wish to maintain within their portfolio a minimum cash balance of USD50,000. They typically maintain a more sizable cash balance at their primary bank.

Other investment preferences

The Kings wish to maintain their positions in Acme Manufacturing, Inc., which Amelia received through inheritance, and Artful Publishing, Ltd., which is her former employer. Neither position represents significant concentration risk in the context of their broader portfolio.

David has an interest in a private real estate limited partnership that invests primarily in office buildings throughout Asia. This exposure has been taken into consideration in designing the asset allocation.

Constraints

Amelia's position in Artful Publishing, Ltd., has significant embedded capital gains.

Portfolio Asset Allocation

	Lower rebalancing limit	Strategic allocation	Upper rebalancing limit
Short-term debt investments	8%	10%	12%
Intermediate-term bonds	16%	20%	24%
US stocks	30%	35%	40%
Non-US stocks	20%	25%	30%
Global real estate securities	8%	10%	12%

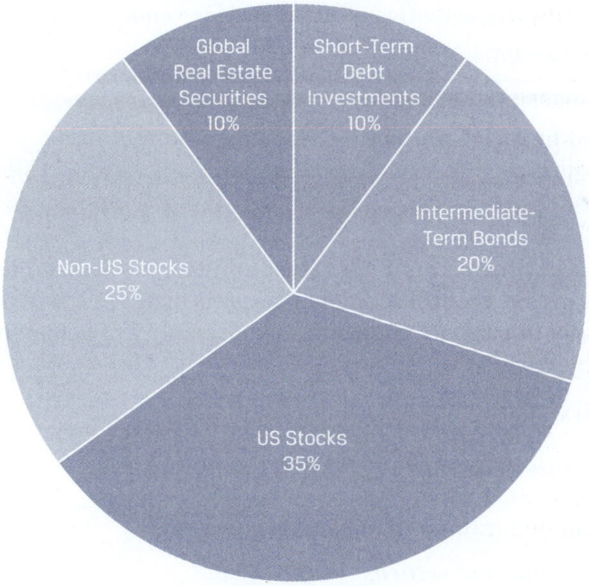

Portfolio Management

Discretionary authority

The wealth manager has full discretion to implement portfolio changes related to rebalancing the portfolio, investing new funds in existing positions, and generating liquidity to meet withdrawal requests from existing positions.

The wealth manager will receive approval prior to establishing new positions or eliminating existing positions.

Rebalancing

The wealth manager will review the portfolio on at least a monthly basis. Rebalancing will be determined by the lower and upper asset class limits set forth in the Portfolio Asset Allocation section of the IPS.

Implementation

The wealth manager will use third party money managers via mutual funds, ETFs, and separate accounts of individual securities to implement the investment strategy. The wealth manager conducts a quarterly due diligence process to evaluate recommended managers as well as the universe of other available managers. This process involves quantitative risk and return comparisons to appropriate indexes and peer groups, as well as qualitative assessments of other factors that may impact a manager's ability to perform in the future. More information about this process is available at the client's request.

Duties and Responsibilities

Wealth manager responsibilities

The wealth manager is responsible for the following:

- Developing an appropriate asset allocation
- Selecting investment options
- Implementing the agreed-upon strategy
- Monitoring the asset allocation and rebalancing when necessary
- Monitoring the costs associated with implementing the investment strategy

- Monitoring the activities of other service vendors (e.g., custodians)
- Drafting and maintaining the IPS
- Performance reporting
- Tax and financial accounting reporting
- Proxy voting
- IPS reviews

The client will review this IPS at least annually to determine whether the investment objectives are still accurate. The wealth manager will review this IPS at least annually to evaluate the continued feasibility of achieving the client's investment objectives.

IPS Appendix

Modeled portfolio behavior

Modeled compound (inflation-adjusted) return: 6.23%

Modeled distribution of returns

Year	10th percentile	25th percentile	50th percentile	75th percentile	90th percentile
1	−10.45	−2.89	6.23	16.21	26.01
3	−3.75	0.86	6.23	11.88	17.24
5	−1.58	2.05	6.23	10.58	14.66
10	0.64	3.25	6.23	9.29	12.12
15	1.65	3.79	6.23	8.72	11.02
25	2.66	4.34	6.23	8.15	9.92

Portfolio downside risk, 1-year horizon:

- 25% likelihood of a return less than −2.89%
- 10% likelihood of a return less than −10.45%

Portfolio downside risk, 15-year horizon:

- 25% likelihood of a compound annual return less than 3.79%
- 10% likelihood of a compound annual return less than 1.65%

Capital market assumptions

Modeled Portfolio Statistics

	Expected return (%) *	Standard deviation (%)	Modeled compound return (%) *
Short-term debt investments	2.5	2.0	2.5
Intermediate-term bonds	3.5	8.0	3.2
US stocks	8.5	22.0	6.1
Non-US stocks	10.0	26.0	6.6
Global real estate securities	7.5	23.0	4.9

* *Inflation-adjusted*

Modeled correlations

		(1)	(2)	(3)	(4)	(5)
1	Short-term debt investments	1.00				
2	Intermediate-term bonds	0.79	1.00			
3	US stocks	−0.08	−0.03	1.00		
4	Non-US stocks	−0.29	−0.27	0.76	1.00	
5	Global real estate securities	−0.15	0.08	0.42	0.39	1.00

QUESTION SET

1. Contrast strategic and tactical asset allocation in forming investment strategy.

   Solution:

   Strategic asset allocation focuses on target allocations across asset categories and is a long-term strategy, whereas tactical asset allocation is a proactive strategy to adjust asset allocations reflecting short-term market trends, economic conditions, or valuation changes.

2. A client's limited partnership stake in a venture that invests in office buildings throughout Asia has been revalued such that this stake is now worth 30% less than estimated at the time the IPS was written. Assume that, prior to the revaluation, this stake accounted for 10% of the total market value of the portfolio and was worth EUR10 million, the target strategic allocation for global real estate securities. The lower bound for rebalancing is 8%. The next annual review of the IPS is scheduled in nine months. Which response below best describes the next IPS review?

   A. The next IPS review should take place in nine months as scheduled.

   B. The next IPS review should be rescheduled as soon as possible with a focus on capital sufficiency analysis.

   C. The next IPS review should be rescheduled as soon as possible to review the asset allocation of the portfolio.

   Solution:

   C is the correct response.

   Given the assumption on the initial size of the limited partnership stake, the decline in the total portfolio value is just 3%, so a capital sufficiency analysis is unnecessary. Moreover, the allocation to Global Real Estate Securities declines to 7.2% (from 10%), so it is just below the 8% lower rebalancing limit for this asset class — see calculations below. Therefore, the next IPS review should be rescheduled as soon as possible to review the asset allocation of the portfolio with a view towards rebalancing.

   Decline in total portfolio value:

   $$\frac{USD10,000,000 - (0.10 \times 0.30 \times USD10,000,000) - USD10,000,000}{USD10,000,000}$$

   $$= -0.03 \ or - 3\%$$

   Allocation to global real estate securities:

$$\frac{0.10 \times 0.70 \times \text{USD}10,000,000}{\text{USD}10,000,000 - (0.10 \times 0.30 \times \text{USD}10,000,000)} = 0.072 \textit{ or } 7.2\%$$

A is incorrect because significant changes in market conditions, such as the revaluation of the limited partnership stake, can create the need for an IPS review earlier than a scheduled once per year review.

B is incorrect because the couple can tolerate portfolio volatility, and the decline in total portfolio value is just 3%, so a focus on the capital sufficiency analysis should not be a necessary aspect of the next IPS review.

3. A client of a private wealth manager has specifically stated a long-term time horizon. This client wants to achieve a goal of EUR4,000,000 to fund retirement in 20 years. Additionally, with no dependents of her own, the client would like to contribute towards her young niece's eventual university expenses. Which of the following best describes the priority of client goals within the investment objectives section of an IPS?

   A. Both goals reflect primary objectives.

   B. The educational funding goal is a primary objective, while the retirement goal is a secondary objective.

   C. The retirement goal is a primary objective, while the educational funding goal is a secondary objective.

Solution:

C is the correct response. Because the retirement goal is quantified and has a time frame that is consistent with the client's long-term time horizon, it is the primary objective. Funding the niece's education is a secondary objective since no amount or timing is specified for it.

A is incorrect because both goals cannot be primary objectives.

B is incorrect because the client's time horizon is for the long term, so individual retirement goals should take precedence over the funding of the niece's education, for which no amount or timing is specified.

PRACTICE PROBLEMS

The following information relates to questions 1-6

Henriette Zhao is a private wealth manager and is meeting with a new client, Nestor Cree, to plan a wealth management strategy. To begin this meeting, Zhao seeks additional background information from Cree necessary as part of preparing the IPS. Zhao learns that Cree is 45 years old and is married with three children (ages 8, 5, and 1). Cree is currently employed as an attorney with annual salary of EUR300,000. Cree has several specific financial goals that he wishes to achieve in the future but has no particular return objective for his portfolio currently valued at EUR2,500,000. Because he has been investing for 20 years, Cree is comfortable with moderate levels of market volatility. His employment provides for his current expenses, so Cree's liquidity requirements are minimal. Cree prefers to have his environmental and social concerns reflected in his investment choices.

Zhao then focuses on Cree's financial goals. Cree plans to retire in 17 years and expects to need EUR200,000 per year on an inflation-adjusted basis to fund a desired retirement lifestyle for himself and his spouse. However, he is also concerned about how increasing medical expenses might affect his portfolio's ability to fund their retirement. As a potential solution to this concern, Cree hopes to purchase an apartment building within the next three years and use the rental income from this investment property to help fund medical expenses during retirement. Cree wants to fund university expenses for his three children, with the first payment starting in 10 years and continuing for 12–15 years. Cree's wife enjoys donating to philanthropic causes. She currently donates EUR10,000 per year, but by the time Cree retires, she hopes to increase this amount to EUR30,000 per year. Cree collects antique furniture and budgets EUR15,000 per year for additions to his collection. He mentions that this year's antique purchase will be his next large expense and currently has the highest priority of all his goals.

Zhao continues the discussion with Cree in order to evaluate his degree of risk tolerance. Cree considers retirement a long-term goal and is willing to endure a 10% drop in expected retirement spending. However, he is very concerned with having sufficient funds to cover medical expenses and views purchasing an investment property as a source of stable income to cover these expenses, so it is very important to him to purchase the building.

1. Which of the following investment parameter categories of the IPS is *least likely* to include Cree's preference for investments that reflect his environmental and social concerns?

   A. Asset class preference

   B. Other investment preferences

   C. Constraints

2. Identify and discuss at least one important missing component of Cree's financial background necessary to preparing the IPS.

3. Which one of the following would most likely be described as an unplanned goal

for Cree?

A. Medical expenses

B. Apartment building purchase

C. University expenses

4. Identify and discuss two areas in which Cree needs to improve goal quantification.

5. Discuss how a capital sufficiency analysis may assist Zhao in helping Cree with goal prioritization across his identified goals.

6. Determine Cree's degree of risk tolerance (lower versus higher) with respect to his retirement goal. Justify your response.

The following information relates to questions 7-9

Sharl Zik, a private wealth manager, is meeting with a 60-year-old client, Edmundo Patel, in order to create an IPS for Patel's upcoming retirement in the next year. Patel estimates that he will require EUR200,000 per year, with annual increases for inflation, during retirement. Patel's primary spending goals during retirement are to provide for his family's needs and maintain his retirement lifestyle. His secondary goals are to fund his philanthropic activities and leave a significant inheritance to his children.

During his retirement, Patel will receive union pension payments of EUR50,000 per year with annual increases for inflation. In his spare time, Patel runs a small business that provides him with an annual income of EUR120,000 and is valued at EUR1 million. He will continue running his business during retirement.

Patel holds a portfolio of securities valued at approximately EUR4 million with a cost basis of EUR1 million. Patel expects an annual pretax capital gains return of 6.5% per year on his securities portfolio. The capital gains tax rate is 20%. The portfolio primarily contains dividend-paying stocks and interest-bearing bonds, and the yield on the portfolio is 2%. Both stock dividend and bond interest are taxed annually at a rate of 40%. In the past, Patel has reinvested all these distributions back into his portfolio but anticipates that after retirement he may need to use some of the distributions to fund his expenses.

Additionally, Patel plans to buy a vacation home to enjoy his early retirement years and expects to hold the home for 10 years. His budget for the vacation home is approximately EUR1.7 million. He expects an 8% annual pretax appreciation in the value of his vacation home and expects to pay capital gains tax of 20% on the sale of this vacation home. Patel is considering selling half of his securities portfolio to fund the vacation home purchase.

Patel is also worried about the effects of inflation. While his pension income will adjust for inflation, he is concerned that the income from his small business is unlikely to adjust with inflation. He asks Zik to do an analysis to assess whether his income sources are expected to be sufficient in 10 years to cover the effects of inflation of 5% per year.

7. Determine whether the distributions from Patel's portfolio are expected to be sufficient to cover the expected shortfall between his retirement needs and his

anticipated income.

8. Determine whether Patel should sell half of his securities portfolio to buy the vacation home.

9. Evaluate Patel's ability to generate his retirement needs in 10 years after accounting for the effects of inflation on his small business income and his securities portfolio value.

The following information relates to questions 10-14

Val Sili, age 22, has just graduated from university and begins making ambitious plans for her future. She has accepted a position as a data science analyst in a start-up company starting next month. Her starting annual salary is USD96,000 per year (after tax), and as part of her compensation, will also receive stock options in the company annually worth USD50,000. She expects to be able to set aside 25% of her after-tax salary into investments in a taxable account while also maximizing her investment contributions to a defined-contribution account.

Sili believes that by the age of 28, she will be earning several times more than her starting salary at the age of 22. She further believes that she will have realized a payoff from her company stock options of at least USD5 million and plans to use her option proceeds to purchase real estate and make selected investments in other start-up ventures. She expects the value of her financial assets to be approximately USD300,000.

By the age of 35, Sili is expecting to be a top executive at a technology firm, with personal investable net worth in excess of USD20 million and a net worth of at least USD100 million.

Between the ages of 35 and 40, Sili expects to have gained sufficient experience and access to financial capital to start her own technology company, with an initial public offering several years later that will generate a payoff of at least USD1 billion. After serving as chair and CEO of the company for two years while it transitions to being a public company, Sili plans to retire from life as a technology company senior executive. She plans to live a relatively minimalist lifestyle financially in retirement while using her vast wealth to invest in young technology startups and provide advisory services for startup managers. As her abilities to provide such services decline, she plans to gradually donate her wealth to fund endowments to nonprofit scientific organizations devoted to solving important world problems with a specific focus on targeted investments in countries with high Gini coefficients.

10. Which of the following investments would be most appropriate for Sili during the beginning years of her career?

    A. Technology equity funds

    B. Lower-risk equity funds and fixed-income funds

    C. Fixed-income funds

11. Discuss the expected roles of Sili's financial asset portfolio and her plan to purchase real estate at the age of 30 in terms of the value of her future wealth.

12. Explain the assumptions that Sili is making regarding the change in her wealth

between the ages of 28 and 35.

13. Discuss the implications of Sili's retirement plan with respect to the value of her human capital, financial capital, and total wealth, as well as with respect to the decumulation phase of her economic life cycle.

14. Which of the following is most likely considered investable wealth for an individual?

    A. Checking account used for day-to-day expenses

    B. Savings account representing funds not needed for day-to-day needs

    C. Defined benefit pension plan participation with payments only after reaching age 60

---

15. A client reports the following assets and liabilities in thousands:

Checking account	50
Savings account	100
Taxable investment account	200
Tax-advantaged investment account	150
Vehicles	80
Primary residence	500
Business assets	800
Short-term credit card debt	25
Business liabilities	250

The client's investable net worth in thousands is closest to:

A. 475

B. 975

C. 1,175

16. A Gini wealth coefficient of 0.50 most likely indicates that there is:

    A. perfect wealth equality.

    B. greater inequality compared to a Gini coefficient of 0.35.

    C. less inequality compared to a Gini coefficient of 0.35.

17. Longevity risk is most likely associated with which phase in the wealth life cycle?

    A. Preretirement

    B. Early retirement

    C. Later retirement

18. The estimation of the value of human capital, the future income, is discounted at the:

    A. real risk-free rate.

    B. nominal risk-free rate plus a premium for inflation.

C. nominal risk-free rate plus a premium associated with occupational income volatility.

19. The value of human capital tends to:

A. increase over time until retirement.

B. stay the same until retirement.

C. decrease over time until retirement.

20. Suppose a client has taxable income of EUR1,500,000. Based on the tax rate schedule, what is the client's average tax rate?

Taxable income (EUR)		Tax on	Percentage on excess
Over	**Up to**	**column 1**	**over column 1**
0	30,000	—	5
30,000	60,000	1,500	10
60,000	90,000	6,000	15
90,000	250,000	13,500	20
250,000	500,000	50,000	30
500,000	1,000,000	150,000	40
1,000,000		400,000	50

A. 27%

B. 43%

C. 50%

21. Deferred taxes on income, relative to accrual taxes,

A. decrease tax drag.

B. do not affect tax drag.

C. increase tax drag.

22. Which of the following investment parameters categories of an IPS is least likely to include a client's preferences for investments that reflect his environmental and social concerns?

A. Asset class preferences

B. Other investment preferences

C. Constraints

SOLUTIONS

1. The correct answer is B because this "Other investment preferences" category typically includes legacy holdings such as shares of stock of a former employer or an investment that the client wishes to make countering the wealth manager's advice.

   A is incorrect because it represents a category that may include a client's preference for environmental and socially oriented investments. C is incorrect because it represents a category that may include a client's preference for environmental and socially oriented investments. In fact, depending on the strength of Zhao's preference, it could potentially be included in investment objectives, as well.

2. Two potentially important missing pieces of Cree's financial background needed to prepare the IPS are the following:

   - The financial background omits the tax status (i.e., taxable versus tax deferred) of the portfolio. As the taxation of the portfolio will have a significant impact on the after-tax return performance necessary to conduct capital sufficiency analysis, this is a vitally important aspect that needs to be included in the IPS.
   - Another financial factor omitted from the financial background discussion is whether Cree's employment provides a pension and the expected amount of pension income. Future pension income may provide an important component with respect to Cree's financial background in the IPS.

3. The correct answer is A because medical expenses are more difficult to quantify, since either the funding need or the timing of the financial need, or both, may not be estimated. B is incorrect because the apartment building purchase can be reasonably estimated or quantified at the onset and can be achieved within an expected time horizon. C is incorrect because university expenses can be reasonably estimated or quantified at the onset and can be achieved within an expected time horizon.

4. Cree has neglected to quantify goals related to

   1. His children's university expenses, and
   2. The scope of the planned apartment building purchase.

   Given Cree's goal of funding university expenses for his three children beginning in 10 years, these amounts may compete for funds with his planned retirement in 17 years. By better quantifying amounts expected, Zhao can help determine whether the education-funding goal is consistent with the retirement-funding goal.

   The apartment building purchase presents a short-term financial need in that Cree must budget for how much he is willing to spend on the building, and furthermore, the amount of future rental income that will be available from the purchased building (along with budgeted expenses to maintain the building). A specific plan will assist Cree in assessing whether the building purchase will be consistent with the longer-term goals of funding retirement and his children's education.

5. Capital sufficiency analysis is the process of evaluating whether a client has sufficient capital resources to determine if their current and future capital resources can adequately support their lifestyle, financial goals, and long-term financial

stability. Whenever the capital sufficiency analysis does not support the investment objective, the wealth manager must work with the client to revise objectives and create those that the wealth manager judges to be achievable. After quantifying his children's education goals and the apartment building purchase goal, a capital sufficiency analysis would allow Cree to assess the likelihood of being able to achieve each of the stated quantified goals (retirement, children's education, apartment building purchase, philanthropy, and antique furniture collection). If his capital resources appear to be insufficient based on Zhao's capital sufficiency analysis, then Cree can choose to prioritize which goals should be adjusted downward or eliminated and which are most important to maintain.

6. Retirement goal: Higher risk tolerance.

   Retirement is a long-term goal with a very long time horizon given that his planned retirement date is in 17 years, so this time frame reflects the beginning of his financial needs for this goal. Cree is willing to incur a moderate drop in his planned expenses, so he likely has a higher risk tolerance for that goal. Cree is concerned about paying future medical expenses in retirement, and since his retirement is still 17 years in the future, he likely has a higher risk tolerance with the medical expenses goal, especially given that he views the planned investment property purchase as providing a stable income stream.

7. The solution below shows that the expected distributions of EUR48,000 are greater than the expected shortfall of EUR30,000. Thus, the distributions are expected to be more than sufficient to help Patel meet his annual income needs in retirement.

   The expected shortfall between Patel's retirement needs and his anticipated income is equal to EUR30,000 (=200,000 – 50,000 – 120,000).

   The expected after-tax distributions from his portfolio are EUR48,000, as shown below:

   $$FVA = B\ \{\ [1 + r\,(1 - t_x)]^T\ \} - 1 =$$

   $$4{,}000{,}000\ \{\ [1 + 0.02\ (1 - 0.40)\ ]^1 - 1\ \} = 48{,}000$$

   The current value of the portfolio or basis, B, is EUR4,000,000. The before-tax return, r, is the 2% yield from dividends and interest. The tax rate, t_x, is 40%, and T equals 1 to reflect the annual cash distributions to augment the shortfall. Note that this return ignores the after-tax return from capital appreciation, which would add to the excess of after-tax earnings over annual income needs.

8. To determine whether Patel should sell the securities, an analysis can be done to compare the expected after-tax value of the home purchase and the expected after-tax value of the securities portfolio at the end of the 10-year time horizon. To avoid additional complexity, the analysis may initially avoid considering the cash distributions of the securities portfolio.

   If half of the securities portfolio (i.e., EUR2,000,000) is sold, then Patel will realize a capital gain of EUR1,500,000 (i.e., half of the capital gain of the full portfolio). Thus, the tax on the sale of the securities will be EUR300,000 (=20% x 1,500,000), and Patel will have EUR1,700,000 (=2,000,000 – 300,000) to buy the house. Alternatively, Patel could choose to forego buying the vacation home and maintain his securities portfolio for another 10 years (i.e., continue to invest EUR2,000,000).

   For both alternatives, use the following equation to calculate the after-tax values:

   $$FVA_{cgb} = B\ [(1 + r)^T\ (1 - t_{cg}) + t_{cg}\ (B)]$$

   For the vacation home purchase alternative, the basis (B) is equal to EUR1,700,000 and the expected pretax rate of return r is equal to 8%. If the vacation home is foregone and the portfolio is fully reinvested, the basis is equal to EUR2,000,000 and the expected pretax rate of return is equal to 6.5%. In both cases, the time horizon (T) is 10 years and the capital gains tax rate (t_{cg}) is 20%.

After-tax value of vacation home =

$$1{,}700{,}000\ [(1 + 0.08)^{10}\ (1 - 0.20) + 0.20\ (1{,}700{,}000/1{,}700{,}000)] = 3{,}276{,}138$$

After-tax value of reinvesting =

$$2{,}000{,}000\ [(1 + 0.065)^{10}\ (1 - 0.20) + 0.20\ (2{,}000{,}000/2{,}000{,}000)] = 3{,}403{,}420$$

Thus, although the pretax investment return on the securities portfolio is lower than the pretax return on the vacation, the higher-value solution on an after-tax basis is to keep the securities portfolio in place. This is because a return can be earned on the capital gains tax amount that would have to be paid if the securities were liquidated. Patel should consider an alternative source of funding for the vacation home.

9. Patel requires EUR200,000 of real purchasing power throughout retirement. His pension income will adjust for inflation, so this amounts to EUR50,000 of real income. So, he needs EUR150,000 of real income from his securities portfolio and his small business income.

   The effects of inflation on his small business income are as follows if it remains at a nominal amount of EUR120,000 per year:

   Real business income in 10 years = 120,000 x $(1 - 0.05)^{10}$ = 71,848

   So, in 10 years, the inflation of 5% annually is expected to reduce the purchasing power of Patel's small business income to EUR71,848. Deducting this amount from EUR150,000 gives a subtotal of EUR78,152.

   Can the securities portfolio provide this amount of income in 10 years? Applying the following formula to the value of the securities portfolio:

   $$FVIF_{tx,inflation} = [1 + r\ (1 - t_x)]^T - (1 - \pi)^T$$

   Using the capital gains appreciation of 6.5% for r, 0% for the annual tax rate, 10 for T, and 5% for inflation (π), we can determine the future value of the securities portfolio in real purchasing power terms currently.

   $$FVIF_{tx,inflation} = [1 + r\ (1 - t_x)\ ]^T - (1 - \pi)\ ^T =$$

   $$[1 + 0.065\ (1 - 0)]^{10} - (1 - 0.05)^{10} = 1.27840$$

   Multiplying this amount by the current portfolio value of EUR4 million gives EUR5,113,600. The securities portfolio generates a 2% pretax cash distribution taxed annually at a 40% rate; thus, the after-tax distribution is 1.2% of the portfolio value.

   Cash distribution in real terms in 10 years = 0.012 x 5,113,600 = EUR61,363

   Thus, Patel faces an income shortfall in 10 years of EUR16,789 (= 78,152 – 61,363). To cover the shortfall, Patel may have to consider liquidating small portions of his securities portfolio to generate additional cash flow each year. Of course, such reductions will cause a decline in the value of his portfolio, thus also reducing future cash distributions from the portfolio, so these would have to be considered as well.

10. The correct answer is B. In her early career stage, the value of Sili's human capital is significant, and she plans to begin building financial capital. Her option position in her employer's stock creates an undiversified equity position, and her early-career stage in a high-income job suggests that she would benefit from additional equity exposure as long as it provides diversification relative to

her employer's stock. Because of the start-up nature of her new employer, her compensation is riskier, implying that she may benefit from some fixed-income exposure.

A is incorrect because this investment would ensure that Sili's financial capital is quite high risk, thus not providing much diversification to her employment compensation. C is incorrect because of her early career stage. The diversification benefit of fixed-income investments ignores the potential for adding some additional equity exposure, as the value of her human capital is very high and she is able to take reasonable amounts of investment risk.

11. As Sili progresses in her career, the value of her human capital is likely to begin declining. To help offset the decline in her human capital, the value of her financial assets and real estate is likely to increase over time. Thus, these assets help protect the value of her future total wealth.

12. The most important assumption that Sili is making reflects a belief that one or more of the start-up ventures in which she invests will become quite valuable, but these investments will not yet be liquid during this seven-year time frame. The value of these business interests will account for the USD80 million difference between Sili's net worth and investible net worth.

    A second assumption is that the value of Sili's financial assets will continue to grow significantly during the stated time period in order for investible net worth to reach USD20 million.

    A secondary assumption that Sili may be making is that the equity in her real estate assets increases in value significantly.

13. While Sili's human capital value likely declines in retirement as she ages, her ability to earn money from her investments and advisory work for start-ups may negate significant declines in the value of her human capital. However, eventually she may decide to make fewer investments and take on fewer advisory assignments, and at this stage, her human capital will decline in value more significantly.

    Sili's financial capital is likely to continue to increase as long as she remains effective at identifying good candidate start-ups in which to invest. As these companies succeed financially, Sili will continue to realize profits from these investments.

    Eventually, she will begin converting some of her financial capital into donations to her philanthropic interests during the decumulation phase of her economic life. At this point in time, her total wealth may finally begin to decline.

14. The correct answer is B. The savings account can be used for investments, especially if the checking account is sufficient to meet ordinary expenses.

    A is incorrect because this is a transactions account and may not be considered investable. C is incorrect because the individual does not make the investment decisions until payments begin, and the individual may then invest the payments once living expenses are covered.

15. The correct answer is A. The investable net worth in thousands is calculated as

    Investable net worth =100 + 200 + 150 – 25 = 475.

    B is incorrect because it includes the business assets and liabilities:

    Investable net worth = 100 + 200 + 150 + 800 – 25 – 250 = 975. C is incorrect because it includes a checking account and business assets and liabilities, as well as nonliquid personal assets: Investable net worth = 50 + 100 + 200 + 150 + 80 + 800 – 25 – 250 = 1,175

16. The correct answer is B. Gini coefficients range from 0 (perfect equality) to 1 (perfect inequality). Because 0.50 is greater than 0.35, this indicates that there is greater inequality for the situation with a coefficient of 0.50.

    A is incorrect because perfect equality would have a Gini coefficient equal to 0. C in incorrect because 0.50 is closer to perfect inequality (that is, a coefficient equal to 1.0) than a coefficient of 0.35.

17. The correct answer is C. Longevity risk is the risk of outliving one's financial resources. A is incorrect because longevity risk is the risk of outliving one's financial resources. B is incorrect because longevity risk is the risk of outliving one's financial resources.

18. C is correct. A premium associated with the occupational income is added to the nominal interest rate. The numerator in the human capital valuation is the anticipated income. A is incorrect because the income that is being discounted is in nominal terms. B is incorrect because the nominal risk-free rate includes an inflation premium.

19. The correct answer is C. The value of human capital diminishes over time because this value includes projected income, so as time progresses, there is less of this future income included in the valuation. B is incorrect. The value of human capital diminishes over time because this value includes projected income, so as time progresses, there is less of this future income included in the valuation. A is incorrect. The value of human capital diminishes over time because this value includes projected income, so as time progresses, there is less of this future income included in the valuation.

20. The correct answer is B. The tax is

    $$\text{Tax} = 400{,}000 + 0.50(1{,}500{,}000 - 1{,}000{,}000) = 650{,}000$$

    And the average tax rate is

    $$\text{Average tax rate} = \frac{650{,}000}{1{,}500{,}000} = 0.4333 \text{ or } 43.33\%$$

    A is incorrect because the income over 1,000,000 is not included in the tax: Average tax rate $= \frac{400{,}000}{1{,}500{,}000} =$ 02667 or 26.67%. C is incorrect because this is the marginal tax rate corresponding to the highest income bracket.

21. The correct answer is A. Deferred taxes, with taxes on gains, are deferred until the end of the investment horizon, and the tax rate equals the tax drag on capital accumulation. C is incorrect because with accrual taxation, the tax drag on capital accumulation compounds over time. B is incorrect because accrual taxes create more tax drag relative to deferred taxes.

22. The correct answer is B. The "Other investment preferences" category typically includes legacy holdings such as shares of stock of a former employer or an investment the client wishes to make countering the wealth manager's advice. A is incorrect because it represents a category that may include a client's preference for environmentally and socially oriented investments. C is incorrect because it represents a category that may include client's preferences for environmentally and socially oriented investments.

LEARNING MODULE

5

Portfolio Management for Institutional Investors

by Arjan Berkelaar, PhD, CFA, Kate Misic, CFA, and Peter C. Stimes, CFA.

Arjan Berkelaar, PhD, CFA, is at KAUST Investment Management Company (USA). Kate Misic, CFA, is at Telstra Super Pty Ltd (Australia). Peter C. Stimes, CFA, is a private investor in Fallbrook, California (USA).

LEARNING OUTCOMES

Mastery	*The candidate should be able to:*
☐	discuss common characteristics of institutional investors as a group
☐	discuss investment policy of institutional investors
☐	discuss the stakeholders in the portfolio, the liabilities, the investment time horizons, and the liquidity needs of different types of institutional investors
☐	describe the focus of legal, regulatory, and tax constraints affecting different types of institutional investors
☐	evaluate risk considerations of private defined benefit (DB) pension plans in relation to 1) plan funded status, 2) sponsor financial strength, 3) interactions between the sponsor's business and the fund's investments, 4) plan design, and 5) workforce characteristics
☐	evaluate the investment policy statement of an institutional investor
☐	evaluate the investment portfolio of a private DB plan, sovereign wealth fund, university endowment, and private foundation
☐	describe considerations affecting the balance sheet management of banks and insurers

CFA Institute would like to thank Karl Mergenthaler, CFA, for his contributions to earlier drafts of this reading.

1 INSTITUTIONAL INVESTORS: TYPES AND COMMON CHARACTERISTICS

☐ discuss common characteristics of institutional investors as a group

Institutional investors are corporations, trusts, or other legal entities that invest in financial markets on behalf of groups or individuals, including both current and future generations. On a global basis, the total value of assets under management (AUM) by the global asset management industry as of 2020 reached more than USD100 trillion, and, as such, wields significant influence over capital markets.

The universe of institutional investors includes, but is not limited to, defined benefit and defined contribution pension plans, sovereign wealth funds, endowments, foundations, banks, and insurance companies. Pension plans, which account for approximately US$57 trillion in investable assets or roughly half of global institutional assets under management, include both defined benefit plans, in which the sponsor (employer) assumes investment risk, and defined contribution plans, in which the individual makes investment decisions and assumes the investment risk. Sovereign wealth funds, which account for about US$8 trillion in assets as of the end of 2020, are government-owned investment funds that invest in financial and/or real assets. Endowments and foundations, which account for approximately US$1.6 trillion in assets, manage assets on behalf of educational institutions, hospitals, churches, museums, and other charitable organizations. Banks and insurance companies, comprising net financial assets on the order of US$9 trillion, are financial intermediaries that balance portfolios of securities, loans, and derivatives for the purposes of (i) meeting the claims of depositors, counterparties, policyholders, and creditors and (ii) providing adequate returns to their contractual capital holders. The universe of institutional investors is comprised of large, complex, and sophisticated investors that must contend with a multitude of investment challenges and constraints.

There has been an important shift in the asset allocation of institutional investors over the last half century. In the 1970s, most pensions and endowments invested almost exclusively in domestic, fixed-income instruments. In the 1980s, many institutional investors began to invest in equity markets and often pursued a long-term strategic allocation of 60% equities/40% fixed income. In the 1990s, investors recognized the benefits of diversification and many made their first forays into international equity markets. At the turn of the 21st century, many of the world's largest pension funds and endowments further diversified their portfolios and increased investments in alternative asset classes, including private equity, hedge funds, real estate, and other alternative or illiquid assets.

Meanwhile, institutional investors have seen broad shifts in their strategic investment behavior. The trend toward Liability Driven Investing (LDI), long a mainstay of banks and insurance companies, has taken hold among many defined benefit pension plans, particularly US corporate and public pension funds. Sovereign wealth funds have amassed significant assets over the past several decades, and many have implemented innovative investment approaches characterized by active management. Many endowments have adopted the "Endowment Model" of investing that involves significant exposure to alternative investments. Meanwhile, banks and insurers must navigate a complex and ever-changing economic and regulatory environment.

In this reading, we endeavor to put the numerous factors that affect investment by institutional investors into context. Section 1 discusses common characteristics of institutional investors as a group. Section 2 provides an overview of investment policies for institutional investors. Detailed coverage by institutional investor type begins with Sections 3–7, pension funds, where we discuss various factors that influence investments, including: stakeholders, liability streams, investment horizons, and liquidity needs; major legal, regulatory, accounting, and tax constraints; investment objectives and key components of Investment Policy Statements; and, finally, asset allocation and investment portfolios that emanate from the foregoing factors and constraints. Sections 8–10 follow the same approach for sovereign wealth funds, and Sections 11–15 do the same for university endowments and private foundations. Sections 16–19 covers banks and insurers and includes balance sheet management considerations. A summary of key points concludes the reading.

Institutional Investors: Common Characteristics

For the purposes of this reading, institutional investors include pension plans, sovereign wealth funds, endowments, foundations, banks, and insurance companies. As we will see in upcoming sections where we cover each of these six institutional types in detail, their objectives and constraints can vary widely. First, in this section we discuss important defining characteristics of institutional investors as a group, characteristics that set them apart from individual (retail and high-net-worth) investors. The common defining characteristics of institutional investors include the following:

1. **Scale (i.e., asset size):** The issue of scale is relevant for institutional investors because it may impact investment capabilities, access to investment strategies, liquidity, trading costs, and other key aspects of the investment process.
2. **Long-term investment horizon:** Institutional investors generally have a long-term investment horizon that is often determined by a specific liability stream, such as the benefit obligation of a pension plan, the spending policy of an endowment, or other obligations.
3. **Regulatory frameworks:** Institutional investors must contend with multiple regulatory frameworks that frequently vary by jurisdiction and complexity and are often evolving.
4. **Governance framework:** Institutional investors typically implement their investment programs through an investment office that often has a clearly defined governance model.
5. **Principal–Agent issues:** As institutional investors manage assets on behalf of others, principal–agent issues must be recognized and managed appropriately.

We discuss these five common characteristics in more detail next.

Scale

Institutional investors' assets under management can range from relatively small (e.g., less than US$25 million) to relatively large (e.g., more than US$10 billion). Smaller institutions may face challenges in building a diversified portfolio spanning public and private asset classes because they may be unable to access certain investments that have a high minimum investment size. For example, smaller institutions are less likely to be able to invest in private equity or real estate assets (i.e., property). Small institutional investors may also face challenges in hiring skilled investment professionals. As a result, they are more likely to outsource investments to external asset managers and rely on investment consultants. Larger institutional investors experience scale benefits that allow them access to a wider investment universe, and they can readily hire investment professionals. They may potentially manage part of their portfolios in-house if benefits outweigh costs. The largest institutional investors, however, may experience dis-economies of scale. For example, they might be unable to invest in certain niche investments like venture capital ("VC"). Given the huge asset size of investments under management, a small allocation to VC may not generate sufficient returns to justify the position (including due diligence costs). The largest institutional investors may also be unable to deploy as much capital as desired with some external managers as certain investment strategies are capacity constrained. External managers who want to avoid jeopardizing their ability to generate superior returns will close the strategy to new investors. To overcome these constraints, some of the largest institutions buy private companies, property, and infrastructure assets directly and manage their traditional asset-class portfolios in-house. Large institutional investors also face the costs of market impact given their sizable trading orders.

Rapidly growing institutional investors may experience high cash inflow relative to the size of their portfolios, which requires them to continuously invest inflows and to maintain the appropriate asset mix (strategic asset allocation). Ensuring access to investments capable of absorbing their growth in assets under management may be challenging when investing in capacity-constrained strategies, such as small-cap equity or venture capital.

Long-Term Investment Horizon

Pension funds, sovereign wealth funds, endowments, and foundations all typically have long investment horizons and relatively low liquidity needs. Cash outlays are relatively modest as a percent of assets under management, with net payouts typically around 5% or less. However, there are exceptions: For example, frozen defined benefit plans might be in a de-risking mode that increases their liquidity needs. Relatively low liquidity needs allow these institutions to invest in a broad range of alternative asset classes, including private equity, private real estate, natural resources, infrastructure, and hedge funds. Banks and insurance companies, however, tend to be much more asset/liability focused while operating within tight regulations designed to ensure adequacy of capital.

Regulatory Frameworks

Institutional investors are typically subject to different legal, regulatory, tax, and accounting frameworks than individual investors. These frameworks define the set of rules an institutional investor must follow to qualify for reduced tax rates or tax-exempt status. Importantly, these frameworks and rules typically differ by national jurisdiction in which the institutional investor operates. Some examples of important relevant legal, regulatory, taxation, and accounting frameworks and organizations include the following:

- United States:
  - Employee Retirement Income Security Act (ERISA)
  - Pension Protection Act (PPA)
  - Uniform Prudent Management of Institutional Funds Act (UPMIFA)
  - Uniform Prudent Investor Act (UPIA)
  - Freedom of Information Act (FOIA)
  - Governmental Accounting Standards Board (GASB)
  - Generally Accepted Accounting Principles (GAAP) set by the Financial Accounting Standards Board (FASB)
  - Statutory Accounting Principles (SAP) set by the National Association of Insurance Commissioners (NAIC)
- United Kingdom:
  - Pensions Act

  - Finance Acts (various)
- European Union:
  - Institutions for Occupational Retirement Provision (IORP) II
- South Korea:
  - Employee Retirement Benefit Security Act
- Australia:
  - Superannuation Industry (Supervision) Act (SIS Act)
- International:
  - International Financial Reporting Standards (IFRS) set by the International Accounting Standards Board (IASB)
  - International Organization of Securities Commissions (IOSCO)

Many relevant regulatory bodies govern and supervise institutional investors and their portfolios globally. The International Organization of Securities Commissions (IOSCO) is the international body that brings together the world's securities regulators, and it has 217 members. Ordinary members (127) include the national securities commissions or similar governmental bodies. Associate members (24) are supranational governmental regulators, subnational governmental regulators, intergovernmental international organizations, and other international standard-setting bodies. Affiliate members (66) include self-regulatory organizations, securities exchanges, and other financial market infrastructure and international regulatory bodies.

The key drivers of the legal and regulatory frameworks faced by institutional investors are investor protection, safety and soundness of financial institutions, and integrity of financial markets. Changes to these frameworks following the 2007–2009 global financial crisis focused on leverage limits, enhanced collateral requirements, increased liquidity requirements, central clearing, proprietary trading limits, private equity limits, trading tax implementation, brokerage fee limits, compensation limits, and requirements for more transparent reporting. Examples of regulations focusing on such reforms include the following:

- United States:
  - Dodd-Frank Wall Street Reform and Consumer Protection Act (Dodd-Frank)
  - Section 619 (12 U.S.C. Section 1851) of the Dodd-Frank Act (Volcker Rule)
  - Foreign Account Tax Compliance Act (FATCA), which has international implications
- United Kingdom:
  - Retail Distribution Review (RDR)
- European Union (with most adopted by the United Kingdom):
  - Undertakings for the Collective Investment of Transferable Securities V (UCITS V)
  - Alternative Investment Fund Managers Directive (AIFMD)
  - Solvency II Directive (Solvency II)
  - Markets in Financial Instruments Directive II (MIFID II)
  - European Market Infrastructure Regulation (EMIR)
  - Financial Transaction Tax (FTT)

  - Packaged Retail Investment and Insurance Products (PRIIPs)
- International:
  - Third Basel Accord / Capital Requirements Directive (Basel III / CRD IV)
  - Santiago Principles (Generally Accepted Principles and Practices for Sovereign Wealth Funds)
  - Principles of the Linaburg-Maduell Transparency Index (Sovereign Wealth Funds)

Governance Framework

Institutional investors typically operate under a formal governance structure. The governance structure generally includes a board of directors and an investment committee. The board may comprise company representative directors, employee representative directors, and independent directors. Independent directors are usually selected to increase the board's overall investment expertise. Investment committees can be sub-committees of the board with delegated authority to oversee investment policy. Alternatively, investment committees can be internal and consist of investment staff tasked with implementing the investment policy set by the board. The board and/or investment committee provide a key role in establishing the organization's investment policy, defining the risk appetite, setting the investment strategy, and monitoring the investment performance.

The board often sets the long-term strategic asset allocation and can delegate the setting of medium-term tactical asset allocation to its investment staff. It may also delegate manager selection to investment staff. Notably though, many institutional investor boards will seek to retain control through overseeing hiring and firing of managers. Best practice suggests, however, that it is better to delegate the hiring and firing of external managers to investment staff to ensure that the board focuses on such broader issues as governance, investment policy, and strategic asset allocation.

Institutional investors typically implement their investment strategy through an investment office. The investment office can be structured in different ways, but the most common model involves a Chief Investment Officer, who is supported by a team of asset-class specialists or a team of generalists working across asset classes. Institutional investors may manage investments in-house (e.g., some large Canadian pension plans and Australian superannuation funds) or outsource investment management partially or entirely to external assets managers. The factors affecting the decision to manage assets internally include the size of assets under management, capability of internal resources, or a desire to pursue custom strategies not readily offered by external managers. It can be costly to build the capability to manage assets internally, so in most cases asset owners need to achieve a certain threshold of assets under management before the benefits outweigh the costs of internalization.

For pension funds, sovereign wealth funds, endowments, and foundations, outsourcing elements of the investment function to external asset managers—or even outsourcing the entire investment operation to an outsourced chief investment officer (CIO) firm—is much more common than managing investments in-house. Such asset owners typically rely on specialized consultants to assist with asset allocation decisions and investment manager selection. These consultants often provide macro-economic forecasts and capital market assumptions for asset classes that are integral to determining the investor's optimal asset allocation. In addition, the consultant assists in monitoring the large universe of external asset managers. Finally, the consultant may provide independent performance attribution and reporting and may monitor any internally managed investments and benchmark them against the external asset manager universe.

In contrast, banks and insurance companies undertake most of their investing, risk budgeting, compliance, and balance sheet management activities internally.

Principal–Agent Issues

Institutional investors frequently experience conflicts of interest that stem from principal–agent issues. The principal–agent issue arises if one person, the agent, makes decisions on behalf of another person or institution, the principal, and their interests are not aligned. A dilemma exists for the agent when he/she may be motivated to act in his/her own best interests and not in the best interests of the principal. Because of operational and investment complexity, institutional investors generally rely on various parties (i.e., agents) to act on their behalf. Agents may be internal or external. Internal agents include investment committee members and investment staff. External agents include third-party asset managers, broker/dealers, consultants, and board members. A typical example of the principal–agent problem is where performance fee structures are designed by external fund managers to provide attractive compensation to them via a high base fee, which is due regardless of fund performance. This fee structure gives little incentive for the fund manager to produce superior performance. Such fee arrangements are common among hedge funds and have led to greater demand for fee transparency and alignment of interest between hedge fund managers and their clients. To manage principal–agent issues, institutional investors will typically have highly developed governance models and high levels of accountability with a board and/or investment committee typically overseeing the investment office. Such models should be designed to explicitly acknowledge and manage conflicts of interest and align the interests of all agents with those of the principals.

OVERVIEW OF INVESTMENT POLICY 2

☐ discuss investment policy of institutional investors

Institutional investors codify their mission, investment objectives, and guidelines in an Investment Policy Statement (IPS). The IPS establishes policies and procedures for the effective administration and management of the institutional assets. A well-crafted IPS can help minimize principal–agent challenges by providing clear guidance on day-to-day management of the assets. Besides mission and investment objectives (i.e., return and risk tolerance), the IPS should cover any constraints that affect the asset allocation, asset allocation policy with ranges and asset class benchmarks, rebalancing policy, guidelines affecting the implementation of the asset allocation policy, and reporting requirements. The IPS should be reviewed annually; however, revisions should be infrequent, such as when material changes occur in investor circumstances and/or the market environment, as the IPS serves as the foundation for the investment program. The asset allocation policy and investment guidelines are typically included in an appendix that can be modified more easily.

Investment objectives flow from the organization's overall mission. For banks and insurance companies, the investment objective is to maximize net present value by balancing (i) the expected returns on assets, (ii) the expected cost of liabilities, (iii) the overall risks of assets and liabilities, and (iv) the economic relationships between and among assets and liabilities.

The investment objectives are more straightforward for the other types of institutions covered in this reading. For example, the overall objective of a DB pension fund might be to maintain a funded ratio in excess of 100%; for an endowment, it may be to maintain long-term purchasing power while providing needed financial support to its university. Investment objectives are typically expressed as a desired return target over the medium-to-long term (which should be clearly specified) with an acceptable level of risk. This return target should be evaluated in the context of the organization's overall mission and should be tied to the evaluation of liabilities (e.g., discount rate used to value DB pension plan liabilities or spending rate for an endowment). When expressing the return target in real terms, the relevant inflation metric must be defined. For example, GIC—Singapore's sovereign wealth fund—uses global inflation defined as G3 (the US, Japan, and Eurozone) inflation, while some US endowments use the Higher Education Price Index (HEPI) published by Commonfund (an independent asset management firm serving non-profit organizations and promoting best practices among institutional investors).

Investment objectives and return targets must be consistent with an organization's risk tolerance and other constraints. Risk tolerance can be expressed in different ways, such as for:

- DB pension funds: surplus volatility (standard deviation of asset returns in excess of liability returns);
- Sovereign wealth funds (SWFs): probability of investment losses (or probability of not maintaining purchasing power) over a certain time period;
- Endowments and foundations: volatility of total returns (standard deviation of total returns); and
- Banks and insurance companies: value at risk (VaR) or conditional VaR (CVaR) and comprehensive, scenario-based stress tests.

Finally, constraints (legal, regulatory, tax, and accounting) have a bearing on investment objectives and should be incorporated into the design of an investment policy. For example, constraints might limit the scope of acceptable risk and available asset classes.

Once the investment objectives—the desired risk and return characteristics—have been established, a strategic asset allocation or policy portfolio is designed. The investment portfolio of an institutional investor is designed to meet its objectives and should reflect the appropriate risk and liquidity considerations addressed in the IPS. For example, a large allocation to private equity is probably not appropriate for institutions with a relatively short investment horizon and high liquidity requirements. Similarly, a large fixed-income allocation might not be appropriate for an institution with a long investment horizon and low liquidity requirements. While institutional investors each have unique liability characteristics, several investment approaches have emerged over the past couple of years. Broadly speaking, these can be grouped into four different approaches:

1. **Norway model** popularized by Norway's global pension fund, Government Pension Fund Global (GPFG). The Norway model is characterized by an almost exclusive reliance on public equities and fixed income (the traditional 60/40 equity/bond model falls under the Norway model), with largely passively managed assets and with very little to no allocation to alternative investments. Investments are usually managed with tight tracking error limits. The advantages of this approach are that investment costs/fees are low, investments are transparent, the risk of poor manager selection is low, and there is little complexity for a governing board. The disadvantage is that there is limited potential for value-added (i.e., alpha from security selection skills) above-market returns. However, Norway's GPFG has begun to seek additional value over market-capitalization benchmarks by attempting to capture systematic risk factors.

2. **Endowment model** popularized by the Yale Endowment. The endowment model is characterized by a high allocation to alternative investments (private investments and hedge funds), significant active management, and externally managed assets. This investment approach stands in almost direct contrast to the Norway model. Although labeled 'endowment model,' this investment approach is not only followed by many university endowments and foundations but also by several sovereign wealth funds and defined benefit pension funds. The endowment model is appropriate for institutional investors that have a long-term investment horizon, high risk tolerance, relatively small liquidity needs, and skill in sourcing alternative investments (the nature of alternative investments is such that there is large variation between the worst and best performing asset managers, and selecting the right manager is therefore critically important). The endowment model is difficult to implement for small institutional investors as they might not be able to access high quality managers. It might also be difficult to implement for very large institutional investors because of their very large footprint. The endowment model is more expensive in terms of costs/fees compared to the Norway model.
3. **Canada model** popularized by the Canada Pension Plan Investment Board (CPPIB). The Canada model, just like the endowment model, is characterized by a high allocation to alternatives. Unlike the endowment model, however, the Canada model relies more on internally managed assets. The innovative features of the Canada model are the: a) reference portfolio, b) total portfolio approach, and c) active management. The reference portfolio is a passive mix of public equities, fixed income, and cash that represents a cheap and easily implementable portfolio that is expected to achieve the long-term expected return consistent with the institution's investment objectives and risk appetite. The reference portfolio effectively defines a transparent, risk-equivalent benchmark for the investment portfolio, and serves as a low-cost alternative to the fund's actual portfolio. The reference portfolio might be different from the institution's strategic asset allocation or policy portfolio. Importantly, the reference portfolio is typically made up of only publicly traded securities (in the form of common public market indices in equities and fixed income) that can be more easily understood by the governing board, while the strategic asset allocation may include target allocations to private markets and hedge funds. The total portfolio approach is the method of constructing the portfolio to ensure that planned risk exposures at the total portfolio level are maintained as individual investments enter, leave or change in value. It is an approach that is aimed at minimizing the unintended exposures and uncompensated risks that may arise as added value is sought by extending investments beyond the reference portfolio. For example, if private equity is added, management considers that it is leveraged equity and as a result the exposure to public equities needs to be reduced by more than the proposed allocation to private equity and the allocation to fixed-income needs to be increased to offset the leverage. Although the Canada model starts with a passive reference portfolio, it is important to note that the Canada model employs active management from tilting asset allocation through to stock selection. A good example of a sovereign wealth fund that has embraced the concept of the reference portfolio is the New Zealand Superannuation Fund.
4. **Liability Driven Investing (LDI) Model** has gained significant importance, particularly among corporate defined benefit pension plans in the United States, although some of the European pension funds—particularly in Denmark and in the Netherlands—adopted the LDI concept even prior to

the 2007–2009 global financial crisis. In the LDI model, the primary investment objective is to generate returns sufficient to cover liabilities. As such, the investor's focus shifts away from operating in an asset-only context, to a focus on maximizing expected surplus return (excess return of assets over liabilities) and managing surplus volatility. Although the implementation and resultant asset allocation may vary significantly, LDI portfolios—other than for banks and insurance institutions—typically have a significant exposure to long duration fixed-income securities. In some LDI implementations, institutional investors separate their portfolios into a hedging portfolio (this portfolio usually hedges the main risk factor in the liabilities, which is interest rate risk) and a return-generating portfolio (this portfolio needs to generate sufficient returns to offset the growth rate of liabilities, other than changes in the discount rate). The hedging portfolio for defined benefit pension funds, sovereign wealth funds, and endowments/foundations usually consists of long duration fixed-income securities and may entail the use of derivatives, such as interest rate swaps, to extend the duration of the portfolio. The return-generating portfolio usually includes public equities and alternative investments.

Exhibit 1 summarizes these four investment approaches.

Exhibit 1: Common Investment Approaches Used by Institutional Investors

Investment Approach	Description
Norway Model	Traditional style characterized by 60%/40% equity/fixed-income allocation, few alternatives, largely passive investments, tight tracking error limits, and benchmark as a starting position. *Pros*: Low cost, transparent, suitable for large scale, easy for board to understand. *Cons*: Limited value-added potential.
Endowment Model	Characterized by high alternatives exposure, active management and outsourcing. *Pros*: High value-added potential. *Cons*: Expensive and difficult to implement for most sovereign wealth funds because of their large asset sizes.
Canada Model	Characterized by high alternatives exposure, active management, and insourcing. *Pros*: High value-added potential and development of internal capabilities. *Cons*: Potentially expensive and difficult to manage.
LDI Model	Characterized by focus on hedging liabilities and interest rate risk including via duration-matched, fixed-income exposure. A growth component in the return-generating portfolio is also typical (exceptions being bank and insurance company portfolios). *Pros*: Explicit recognition of liabilities as part of the investment process. *Cons*: Certain risks (e.g., longevity risk, inflation risk) may not be hedged.

3 PENSION FUNDS: TYPES AND STAKEHOLDERS

Pension funds are long-term saving and investment plans designed to accumulate sufficient assets to provide for the financial needs of retirees. There are two main types of pension plans: **defined benefit**, in which a plan sponsor commits to paying a specified retirement benefit, and **defined contribution**, in which contributions are defined but the ultimate retirement benefit is not specified or guaranteed by the plan sponsor. Globally, there are many variations and nuances of these two broad categories of pension plans. Exhibit 2 compares the key features of defined benefit and defined contribution pension plans.

Exhibit 2: Comparison of Defined Benefit and Defined Contribution Pension Plan Features

Characteristics/Features	Defined Benefit Pension Plan	Defined Contribution Pension Plan
Benefit payments	Benefit payouts are defined by a contract between the employee and the pension plan (payouts are often calculated as a percentage of salary).	Benefit payouts are determined by the performance of investments selected by the participant.
Contributions	The employer is the primary contributor, though the employee may contribute as well. The size of contributions is driven by several key factors, including performance of investments selected by the pension fund.	The employee is typically the primary contributor—although the employer may contribute as well or may have a legal obligation to contribute a percentage of the employee's salary.
Investment decision making	The pension fund determines how much to save and what to invest in to meet the plan objectives.	The employee determines how much to save and what to invest in to meet his/her objectives (from the available menu of investment vehicles selected by the plan sponsor).
Investment risk	The employer bears the risk that the liabilities are not met and may be required to make additional contributions to meet any shortfall.	The employee bears the risk of not meeting his/her objectives for this account in terms of funding retirement.
Mortality/Longevity risk	Mortality risk is pooled. If a beneficiary passes away early, he/she typically leaves a portion of unpaid benefits in the pool offsetting additional benefit payments required by beneficiaries that live longer than expected. As a result, the individual does not bear any of the risk of outliving his/her retirement benefits.	The employee bears the risk of not meeting his/her objectives for this account in terms of funding retirement. The employee bears longevity risk.

Source: World Economic Forum, "Alternative Investments 2020: The Future of Alternative Investments" (2015).

Pension funds are significant players in the global investment landscape. Over the past 20 years, there has been a move away from defined benefit (DB) plans (especially non-government DB plans) to defined contribution (DC) plans. Among drivers of this shift are DC plans' lower financial risk for plan sponsors, absence of risk of becoming underfunded, and ease of portability (simplifies job mobility). Willis Towers Watson reports in its "Global Pension Assets Study 2018" covering the seven largest pension markets, the "P7" (Australia, Canada, Japan, the Netherlands, Switzerland, the United Kingdom, and the United States) that during the past 20 years DC pension plans have risen from 33% to 49% of total plan assets.

The split between DB and DC plans can vary significantly from country to country. One of the challenges of classifying countries by this split is that many countries offer hybrid pension plans, such as that in Switzerland where defined contribution connotes a cash balance plan in which all assets are pooled and the plan sponsor shares the investment risk. There are basically no pure DC plans in Switzerland. Exhibit 3 presents the split between DB and DC plans for the P7 countries. Together these countries comprise more than 90% of worldwide pension assets. Note that a substantial difference exists between countries. Some countries (such as Australia) rely almost exclusively on DC plans, while others (such as Japan and the Netherlands) predominantly use DB plans.

Exhibit 3: Split Between DB or Hybrid Plans and DC Plans in Select Countries (2021)

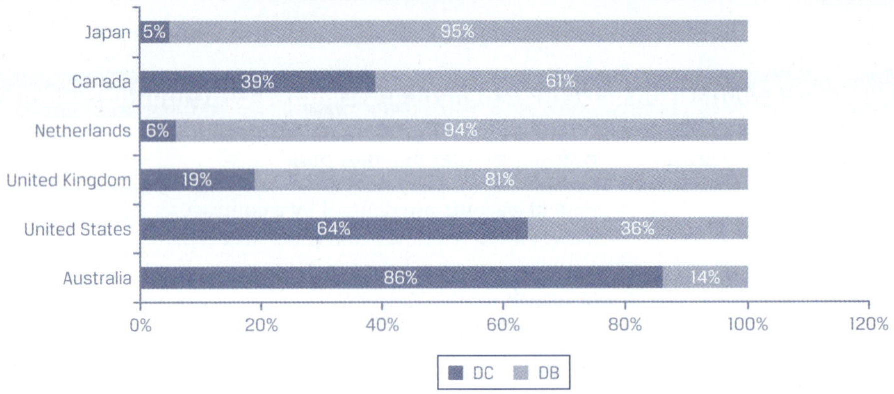

Source: Willis Towers Watson Thinking Ahead Institute (2021).

Stakeholders

Many entities are involved with institutional retirement plans. These include the employer, employees, retirees, unions, management, the investment committee and/or board, and shareholders. Governments have generally encouraged pension plans as a tool to assist individuals to build sufficient financial resources to fund their retirement needs. Government support typically comes in the form of favorable tax treatment for both companies and individuals who contribute to or manage pension plans, provided they operate according to local pension plan regulations. The government and taxpayers will bear some of the shortfall risks (in terms of added welfare or social security payments) in instances of employers failing to pay agreed on defined benefit payments and where individuals fail to accumulate sufficient wealth for retirement.

Defined Benefit Pension Plans

The stakeholders of a defined benefit pension plan are the employer [typically referred to as the plan sponsor and usually represented by management and the Chief Financial Officer (CFO)]; plan beneficiaries (employees and retirees); the Chief Investment Officer (CIO) and investment staff; the investment committee and/or board; and the government, unions, and shareholders in the case of corporate DB plans. Defined benefits promised to beneficiaries create liabilities for the plan sponsor. In operating the pension plan, the sponsor and investment staff must make investment decisions in the interest of the ultimate beneficiaries (employees and retirees). Defined benefit pension liabilities are typically funded from two sources: 1) employer and employee contributions and 2) investment returns on funded assets. Employee contributions can be fixed or variable, but employer contributions usually vary depending on the plan's funded status. Although each of the stakeholders has a strong interest in plan assets being invested appropriately, opinions might differ over the acceptable level of investment risk and the magnitude of employer contributions to the plan.

The plan sponsor may have an interest in 1) minimizing employer contributions due to budget constraints and/or 2) managing the volatility of employer contributions (by aiming for less volatility in investment returns). This allows management to plan future contributions with less uncertainty. Management and the CFO may also want to manage the impact of pension assets and liabilities on the sponsor's balance sheet. Employees and retirees, however, want to maximize the probability that plan liabilities are met and thus want the sponsor to make timely and sufficient plan contributions. Finally, the CIO and investment staff should be interested in meeting the investment objectives and constraints of the investment policy statement.

In a defined benefit pension plan, the sponsor bears the ultimate risk of the portfolio falling short of meeting liabilities. This risk manifests itself in the form of higher contributions from the plan sponsor when the plan becomes underfunded. In the extreme case of default, however—when the plan sponsor can no longer meet its legal obligations and cannot contribute further to the plan—the employee bears the ultimate risk and may need to find alternative means to meet financial needs in retirement. Some of this risk may be shared by taxpayers via additional social security or welfare payments, making the government a stakeholder in a defined benefit pension plan.[1]

The investment office of the DB pension plan is tasked with investing assets appropriately and may have variable compensation (bonuses) tied to investment performance. The investment committee or board will consider recommendations from investment staff, such as setting strategy and investment manager selection. In setting and executing strategy, all stakeholders' positions must be considered, including the sponsor's ability to make plan contributions. Ultimately, however, the board has a fiduciary duty to employees and retirees.

Finally, for corporate DB plans the company's shareholders are stakeholders. They are interested in the sustainability of the pension plan because if it is underfunded, any shortfall becomes a liability on the balance sheet, reducing the value of the company. Contributions to an underfunded plan also reduce net income. Underfunded status also increases financial risk, which may cause higher volatility in the stock price.

Defined Contribution Pension Plans

The main stakeholders of a defined contribution pension plan are the plan beneficiaries, the employer, the board, and the government.

A key stakeholder in a DC plan is the participant. Each participant has an individual account into which contributions are made on a regular basis—either by the employee, the employer, or both. Plan participants must ensure that 1) adequate contributions are made and 2) appropriate investment options are selected to generate sufficient investment returns. For a DC pension plan, the individual participant bears the investment risk of the portfolio failing to meet future liabilities (i.e., retirement needs). If plan participants outlive their savings, they will need to find other ways to meet their financial needs in retirement. In that case, the government (via taxpayers) may need to provide additional social welfare benefits, making the government another stakeholder in a DC plan.

Although DC plan participants control the investment decisions for their individual accounts, perhaps acting upon the advice of their financial adviser, the plan sponsor still has important fiduciary responsibilities, including overseeing the appropriate investment of plan assets (either by internal staff or by third-party asset managers or a combination thereof), offering suitable investment options, and selecting administrative providers. The plan sponsor, therefore, is an important stakeholder in a DC plan. The plan sponsor typically has an obligation to contribute to the DC plan on behalf of the employee as specified by the employment contract or through a government-mandated system. In some countries, a plan sponsor may also have an obligation to provide employees with a choice of different investment options within the employer-sponsored DC plan or even the choice of different DC plans. The sponsor typically must ensure that the investment options provide appropriate

1 Some risk is also shared by other plan sponsors through agencies as the Pension Benefit Guaranty Corporation (PBGC) in the United States. It is not funded by the government; rather, PBGC's funding comes primarily from insurance premiums paid by DB plan sponsors, the assets of failed pension plans that the PBGC takes over, and investment income.

levels of diversification. It may also need to provide investment education and communications so that employees can make well informed investment choices. Running DC plans can be more expensive than DB plans given their increased complexity of administration and meeting regulatory compliance, all of which may result in higher fees for DC plan participants.

The board of a DC plan sponsor must consider the differing levels of sophistication among participants and provide adequate disclosure in communications to ensure participants are well informed. The board may be required to select a default investment option when participants do not explicitly make an investment choice. In such cases, the board has a higher obligation because by entering the default option, the participant is indicating that he/she either does not have sufficient understanding to make an informed choice or that he/she trusts the board of the pension plan to make the best choice.

4 PENSION FUNDS: LIABILITIES, INVESTMENT HORIZON, AND LIQUIDITY NEEDS

☐ discuss the stakeholders in the portfolio, the liabilities, the investment time horizons, and the liquidity needs of different types of institutional investors

Liabilities and Investment Horizon

Defined Benefit Pension Plans

The liabilities of a DB pension plan are the present value of the future payments it will make to beneficiaries upon retirement, disability, or death. Calculating DB liabilities is complex and typically undertaken by actuaries employed by the plan sponsor or by external actuaries. Here we will highlight some key elements and focus on the discount rate used in calculating the present value of future benefit payments.

The first step in determining DB liabilities is to calculate the expected future cash flows (i.e., retirement benefits). These depend on the design and specifics of the pension plan. Some of the key elements common among DB plans in the calculation of expected cash flows are:

1. **Service/tenure:** The number of years the employee has been with the company or organization (or service years) determines the defined benefit the employee is expected to receive upon retirement. The higher the service years, the higher the retirement benefit. Sometimes a minimum number of service years is required before retirement benefits become vested (i.e., the employee becomes eligible to receive a pension).
2. **Salary/earnings:** The salary or earnings level of the employee affects the calculation of the defined benefit the employee is expected to receive upon retirement. The defined benefit may be a function of the average earnings over the entire career or the average earnings over the last several years prior to retirement (e.g., last three years).
3. **Mortality/longevity:** The length of time that retirement benefits are expected to be paid to plan participants is important in calculating expected cash flows. This requires assumptions about employees' and retirees' life

expectancies. Importantly, ever-increasing life expectancies is a key factor in making DB pension plans less affordable from the sponsor's perspective. Longevity risk is the risk to the plan sponsor that participants will live longer than assumed in the pension liabilities calculations.

In estimating future benefits, the plan sponsor must make several key assumptions, such as the growth rate of salaries, expected vesting, and mortality and disability assumptions. **Vesting** means that employees only become eligible to receive a pension after meeting certain criteria, typically a minimum number of years of service. In measuring defined benefit obligations, the plan sponsor must consider the likelihood that some employees may not satisfy the vesting requirements. Under both International Financial Reporting Standards (IFRS) and US generally accepted accounting principles (GAAP), pension obligations are determined as the present value of future benefits earned by employees for service provided to date. Assumptions about future salary increases, expected vesting, and life expectancy change over time and will change the estimated pension obligation. Given the importance of these factors, pension plans require periodic actuarial reviews to determine the value of the liabilities and the sponsor's annual required contribution rate.

Once expected future benefits are calculated, they must be discounted to determine their present value. Practices of marking-to-market liabilities using market discount rates can vary considerably based on country, or even within a country, between private and public pension plans. Typical discount rates include government bond yields or swap rates, corporate bond yields, and constant actuarial discount rates (long-term expected rate of return). Plan sponsors might be inclined to use a higher discount rate that will, all else equal, result in lower pension liabilities, a better funded status, and potentially lower contributions. Beneficiaries prefer to see a lower discount rate being used that will, all else equal, result in higher pension liabilities, a worse funded status, and potentially higher contributions. There is a delicate balance, however, because if contributions become unsustainable, the plan sponsor might decide to shut down its DB plan and substitute it with a less risky DC plan.

Over the past 15 years, a shift has occurred in many countries toward tying the discount rate to market rates. As a result, many pension plans have adopted a more liability-driven investment approach to partially or fully hedge the interest rate risk in their liabilities. Given the low interest rate environment since the 2007–2009 financial crisis, this has posed tremendous challenges for pension funds globally.

Discount Rates for Defined Benefit Plans in the US

In the United States, private and corporate DB pension plans may discount liabilities at rates based on high-grade bond yields averaged over 25 years. This was allowed under the 2012 update to the Pension Protection Act (PPA), part of broader legislation known as MAP-21. The change effectively raised the applicable discount rates (and reduced DB pension liabilities), providing some relief to defined benefit plans given what were perceived to be 'artificially' low interest rates. Prior to the PPA, corporate DB plans had to discount liabilities using current investment-grade corporate bond yields, not a historical average.

US public DB pension plans use actuarial discount rates which, as required by the US Governmental Accounting Standards Board (GASB), are based on the expected return of the pension plan asset portfolio. These are typically far higher than bond rates. The higher discount rates lower their liabilities and raise their funded status. However, this may cause such pension plans to potentially make inadequate plan contributions and take on excessive risk by investing heavily in equities and alternatives in hope of generating an expected rate of return that supports the high discount rate.

Exhibit 4 summarizes the key elements in the calculation of defined benefit pension plan liabilities.

Exhibit 4: Factors Affecting Calculation of Defined Benefit Liabilities

Factor	Impact on Liabilities
Service/tenure	Depending on plan design, often the longer the period of service or tenure, the larger the benefit payments.
Salary/earnings	The faster salaries or earnings grow, the larger the benefit payments.
Additional or matching contributions	Additional or matching contributions are often rewarded by a step change increase in benefit payments.
Mortality/Longevity assumptions	If life expectancy increases, the obligations or liabilities will increase.
Expected Vesting	If employee turnover decreases, expected vesting will increase.
Expected Investment Returns	In some cases, increases in expected returns will result in a higher discount rate being used—hence, lower obligations or liabilities.
Discount Rate	A higher (lower) discount rate results in lower (higher) liabilities.

The main objective of a DB plan is to have sufficient assets to cover future benefit payments. A common pension industry metric used to gauge asset sufficiency is the funded ratio, also known as the vested benefit index (VBI) in some countries. The funded ratio is defined as:

Funded ratio = Fair value of plan assets/PV of Defined benefit obligations

In some countries, if the funded ratio is less than 100%, the sponsor must increase contributions until it exceeds 100%. Improving the plan's funded ratio can transform the pension obligation from a liability to an asset on the plan sponsor's balance sheet. It is important to note that in some cases, underfunded pension plans may take more investment risk in the hope of achieving higher returns and growing assets sufficiently to return to fully funded status. In other cases, underfunded pension plans reduce investment risk and rely on other actions to improve their funded status, such as increasing contributions or reducing benefits.

Additional considerations in DB pension design are:

1. the size of the pension plan relative to the size of the sponsor's balance sheet; and
2. the cyclicality of the plan sponsor's core business.

If plan assets and liabilities are small relative to the sponsor's balance sheet, then there may be more flexibility in taking investment risk and more tolerance for volatility in employer contributions. If, on the other hand, plan asset and liabilities are large in relation to the sponsor's balance sheet, then there may be less appetite for volatility of employer contributions and hence a reduced desire for taking investment risk.

Another important factor is the core business of the plan sponsor. If the plan sponsor's revenues are highly cyclical, it will not want plan funded status to deteriorate when the core business suffers from a cyclical downturn. In such cases, the DB plan's asset allocation would be modified to ensure adequate diversification so as not to have significant exposure to assets highly correlated with the sponsor's core business or industry. In sum, it is desirable for plan assets to have low (high) correlations with the sponsor's operating assets (liabilities).

The plans sponsor's ability to tolerate volatility of contribution rates may impact the investment horizon, and hence the pension plan's appetite for such illiquid investments as private equity and venture capital. Another important factor determining the investment horizon is the mix of active plan participants (i.e., current employees) versus retirees. The higher the proportion of retirees (so the higher the liability associated with retirees only) relative to the proportion of active participants (or the liability associated with active participants), the more mature the plan—hence, the lower its risk tolerance. Some mature DB pension plans have been frozen (closed to new participants) as they typically experience negative cash flow where benefit payments exceed contributions. Generally, the more mature a pension fund, the shorter its investment horizon, which directly affects risk tolerance and the allocation between fixed-income assets and riskier assets.

Defined Contribution Pension Plans

In a DC plan, participants' pension benefits are based on amounts credited to their individual accounts in the form of contributions (from the employee and possibly the employer) and investment returns. Consequently, the liabilities of a DC pension plan sponsor are equal only to its required contributions. DC plan assets are typically pooled, and the sponsor invests according to the investment choices selected by plan participants. Often the DC plan may invest in a broadly diversified portfolio that may include investments not generally offered to retail investors, such as private equity and hedge funds. This is possible since pooling of assets gives rise to scale and the long-term horizon of the aggregate beneficiaries. In such case, the plan sponsor takes on the residual investment risk of its asset allocation. Once invested in such alternative asset types, the DC plan sponsor bears liquidity risk if any event occurs that causes a significant proportion of its participants to exit the plan. The asset allocation may be impacted to such an extent that the plan sponsor is unable to provide the asset allocation promised to its participants. Such a circumstance will have regulatory and reputational consequences for the DC plan sponsor.

Individuals in a DC plan are at different stages of their careers, so each has a different investment time horizon (the time period from his/her current age until expected death or expected death of a spouse, whichever is longer) as well as different risk tolerances. Therefore, key considerations for most DC plans are participants' ages and invested balances. If the plan has a larger proportion of older (younger) participants with large (small) invested balances, the investment options might reflect a shorter (longer) investment horizon. Many DC plans offer investment options that allow participants to select the investment horizon that best aligns with their own investment horizon. Examples are life-cycle options or target date options, which feature a glide path that manages the asset mix based on a desired retirement date. In the United States, most DC plans offer target-date options as default options; in Hong Kong SAR it is mandated that every default option plan have a life-cycle option.

There are two main types of life-cycle options. **Participant-switching life-cycle options** automatically switch members into a more conservative asset mix as their age increases. There may be several automatic de-risking switches at different age targets. A **participant/cohort option** pools the participant with a cohort that has a similar target retirement date. For example, if a participant is 40 years old in 2020 and plans to retire at the age of 65, he/she could invest in an option with a target date of 2045 and the fund would manage the appropriate asset mix over the next 25 years. In

2020, the assets might be 90% invested in equities and 10% in bonds. As time passes, however, the fund would gradually change the asset mix (less equities and more bonds) to reflect an appropriate allocation given the time to retirement.

Liquidity Needs

Although pension plans typically have long investment time horizons, they still must maintain sufficient liquidity relative to their projected liabilities. Liquidity needs are driven by:

- Proportion of active employees relative to retirees—The former contribute to the plan, while the latter receive benefit payments. More mature pension funds have higher liquidity needs. Frozen DB pension plans, often facing negative cash flow, must hold even more cash and other liquid investments compared to open mature plans.
- Age of workforce—Liquidity needs rise as the age of the workforce increases, since the closer participants are, on average, to retirement, the sooner they will switch from the contribution phase to benefit payment stage. This is true for both DB and DC plans.
- DB plan funded status—If the plan is well funded, the plan sponsor may reduce contributions, generating a need to hold higher balances of liquid assets to pay benefits.
- Ability of participants to switch/withdraw from plan—If pension plan participants can switch to another plan or withdraw on short notice, then higher balances of liquid assets must be held to facilitate these actions. This applies to DB and some DC plans.

A pension plan with lower liquidity needs can hold larger balances in private investments—such as real estate, infrastructure, private equity, and hedge funds—and can invest a higher proportion in equities and credit. A pension plan with higher liquidity needs, however, must invest a higher proportion of its assets in cash, government bonds, and highly liquid, investment-grade corporate bonds.

It is important for pension plans to regularly perform liquidity stress tests, which may include stressing the value of their assets and modelling reduced liquidity of certain asset classes in a market downturn. Such stress-testing may also help DC plans anticipate whether participants might switch out of more volatile investment options during market downturns.

EXAMPLE 1

Comparing Defined Benefit (DB) and Defined Contribution (DC) Pension Plans

1. Geoff Albright is 35 years old and has been working at Henley Consulting in Melbourne, Australia, for 10 years. Henley Consulting offers a defined benefit (DB) pension plan for its employees. The defined benefit plan is fully funded. Geoff Albright's benefit formula for monthly payments upon retirement is: final monthly salary × benefit percentage (=1.5%) × number of years of service, where final monthly salary equals his average monthly earnings for the last three financial years immediately prior to retirement date. Hav-

ing been at Henley Consulting for 10 years, his benefits have vested and can be transferred to another pension plan.

Geoff has been offered a job at rival Australian firm, Horizon Ventures Consulting, which is offering a similar salary; however, Horizon Ventures Consulting offers a defined contribution (DC) pension plan for its employees. Horizon Ventures Consulting will pay 15% of annual salary into the plan each year. Employees can choose to invest in one of three diversified portfolios offered by the plan sponsor—Horizon Growth, Horizon Balanced, and Horizon Conservative—based upon their risk appetite, and employees can elect to make additional contributions to the plan. The monthly pension payments will depend on what has accumulated in Geoff's account when he retires.

Discuss the features that Geoff should consider in evaluating the two plans. Please address benefit payments, contributions, shortfall risk, and mortality/longevity risks.

Solution:

- Geoff notes his benefits at Henley Consulting have vested and can be transferred to Horizon Ventures Consulting's DC plan.
- Henley Consulting's plan provides a defined benefit payment linked to years of service and final salary, whereas Horizon Ventures Consulting's plan provides an uncertain benefit payment linked to the company's and Geoff's contribution rates and investment performance of plan assets. The benefits he can achieve in Henley Consulting's DB plan increase both by time employed as well as by growth in his wages. Geoff considers his capacity to achieve wage growth and compares this to the return objectives of his chosen option in Horizon Ventures Consulting's DC plan. Geoff notes his risk appetite and time horizon are suited to the Horizon Growth option.
- Although Henley Consulting's contribution rate is not known, Geoff is aware that the plan is currently fully funded and that it is Henley Consulting's obligation to maintain a fully funded status. Horizon Ventures Consulting's contribution rate is known (15% of annual salary), and Geoff can also make additional contributions himself.
- Geoff notes that the shortfall risk of plan assets being insufficient to meet his retirement benefit payments falls to his employer in the case of Henley Consulting's DB plan. But, for Horizon Ventures Consulting's DC plan, the shortfall risk falls to Geoff and depends on the contribution rate (15% from the company plus any additional contributions he chooses to make) and the performance of his chosen investments.
- Henley's DB plan pools mortality risk such that those in the pool who die prematurely leave assets that help fund benefit payments for those who live longer than expected. Horizon Venture Consulting's DC plan pays out the amount accumulated in Geoff's account, and he bears the risk of outliving his savings.

5 PENSION FUNDS: EXTERNAL CONSTRAINTS

☐ describe the focus of legal, regulatory, and tax constraints affecting different types of institutional investors

In this section, we take a high-level view of some of the legal and regulatory constraints faced by pension funds. In the next section, we consider tax and accounting constraints that may affect investing by pension funds.

Legal and Regulatory Constraints

Regulatory bodies supervising pension funds typically cover financial services licensing and regulation, prudential supervision, capital adequacy, market integrity, and consumer protection. Breeching key regulations may result in loss of operating licenses and/or loss of tax benefits, where applicable, which provides a strong incentive to comply. Regulations do vary from country to country; for example, some countries specify minimum and maximum percentage allocations to certain asset classes, while other countries require a minimum contribution rate by employers, particularly if the plan's funded ratio falls below 100%. However, despite national differences, there are similar themes in regulation globally.

Reporting and transparency are heavily influenced by regulatory requirements, as some regulators now require extensive reporting, not only on direct investment fees and costs incurred by pension plans but also on indirect fees and costs of external commingled vehicles. Drivers of more detailed reporting and transparency are avoidance of corruption by government officials involved with public pension plans and increased consumer protection for private pension plans so participants and stakeholders make appropriate investment choices. Many countries have increased personal liability for pension trustees to ensure they act in the best interests of ultimate beneficiaries. For example, DC plan participants must choose their contribution rates and the investment risk they are willing to bear. However, regulators are aware that many DC plan participants have little understanding of how to invest for retirement. Although regulators may require the plan sponsor to provide investor education to their employees, DC plan trustees, as fiduciaries, are still required to operate with prudence and as if they were the asset owners.

In Australia, for example, most employees are covered by the DC Superannuation Guarantee, under which employers must contribute 9.5% of an employee's salary. Since many participants do not actively make investment decisions, the government applies strict licensing and other obligations for trustees when offering the default option (MySuper), including: providing a single diversified investment strategy as a default option suitable for the majority of participants; avoiding unnecessary or excessive fees; and delivering value for money (measured by long-term net returns). A similar default DC plan account exists in the United States (known as the Qualified Default Investment Alternative), which must also be diversified.

In Europe the updated Institutions for Occupational Retirement Provision (IORP II) will lead to regulatory changes for pension plans. Although each country will interpret the provisions slightly differently, the changes relate to governance, risk management, and disclosure. A number of key functions are defined, such as an internal audit, and standards are applied to those executing these key functions, including a requirement that such a person does not carry out a similar function for the plan sponsor. Many pension plans will need to document their risk management policies and procedures. For example, each fund must document its "own risk assessment" covering items such as the risk of not meeting benefit obligations and operational risk, including administrative error or fraud. For disclosure, there will also be greater harmonization of pension benefit statements with certain items required to be included.

US corporate pension plans are subject to significant regulatory oversight. The Employee Retirement Income Security Act of 1974 (ERISA) regulates vesting, funding requirements, and payouts. ERISA includes a fiduciary code of conduct and required disclosures. ERISA established the Pension Benefit Guaranty Corporation, a US government agency that collects premiums from pension plan sponsors and pays benefits to participants (approximately 630,000) in terminated plans. Although ERISA protects benefits that workers have earned, an employer may still terminate a plan, essentially freezing a worker's ability to earn additional benefits. Moreover, the US Pension Protection Act of 2006 established minimum funding standards for DB plans, while later revisions raised the rates corporations could use to discount their liabilities (high-grade bond yields averaged over 25 years). Importantly, a potential consequence of using higher discount rates is these DB plans must generate higher returns for their funding status to remain sustainable, which typically requires taking on greater investment risk.

Tax and Accounting Constraints

Governments around the world encourage citizens to save for retirement by typically providing favorable tax treatment to retirement savings. Favorable tax treatment may come in different forms: reduced taxes on retirement plan contributions, favorable tax rates on investment income and/or capital gains, and lower tax rates on benefit payments drawn throughout retirement (versus higher taxes on lump sum payments). Foregone tax revenues from such favorable tax treatment are costly, so to ensure pension plans actually reduce tax burdens for retirement savers, governments typically place restrictions on plan design, governance, and investment activities in order for plans to qualify for the favorable tax treatment.

In the United States, 401(k) plans are tax deferred as participants make pre-tax contributions and do not pay tax on investment earnings; benefit payments, however, are taxed as ordinary income. To encourage savings retention within the pension plan, early withdrawals before age 59½ are taxed an additional 10%. In the United Kingdom, private pension plans are also tax deferred, with no tax on contributions or on investment earnings. The first 25% of benefit payments are tax free, and the remaining 75% is taxed as ordinary income after a tax-free personal allowance. In China, companies providing occupational pensions (known as Enterprise Annuities) are given tax relief amounting to 4% of wages; however, there are taxation differences between regions.

Pension plans taxed on investment earnings must be aware of tax implications of their investment activities. For example, there may be favorable capital gains tax treatment for investments held over 1 year, which should incentivize investing in lower turnover strategies. Also, pension plans must consider tax implications when returns from investing via futures and other derivatives are treated as income and taxed at higher rates than returns from investing in the underlying securities, which are typically taxed at lower capital gains and dividend rates. When investing internationally, double taxation may occur when the same income or capital gain is taxed both by the jurisdiction in which it is earned *and* in the jurisdiction where the pension fund resides. To achieve tax efficiency, pension plans should invest via legal structures that provide access to double taxation treaties, whereby taxes paid in the country of residence are exempt in the country where they arise (alternatively, the plan receives a foreign tax credit in its country of residence to reflect taxes withheld in the country where the income/gain arose).

Accounting treatment is another important external factor that drives investment decision making by pension funds. These treatments may differ across countries, so it is important to be fully aware of them. Here we focus on the United States to illustrate how accounting treatment may influence investment choices. Corporate DB pension plans must follow generally accepted accounting principles—notably, Accounting Standards Codification (ASC) 715, Compensation—Retirement Benefits, which requires that an overfunded (underfunded) plan must appear as an asset (liability) on the balance sheet of the corporate sponsor. Such plan sponsor must also report gains, losses, and service costs as part of net income. This accounting treatment significantly increased the transparency of US plans' funded status, and it prompted many corporate plans to implement liability-driven investing techniques to reduce the effect of funded ratio volatility on their financial statements.

Public pension plans in the US must follow Governmental Accounting Standards Board (GASB) rules. Under GASB rules, public plan sponsors must report fair market values of plan assets and can use a blended approach to valuing plan liabilities. The latter involves discounting the funded portion of pension liabilities using the (higher) expected return on plan assets as well as discounting the unfunded portion of liabilities based on the (lower) yield on tax-exempt municipal bonds. Using a higher discount rate for the funded portion of liabilities skews the risk tolerance of public pension plans and incentivizes them to allocate relatively large proportions of assets to equities and alternative investments.

6 PENSION FUNDS: RISK CONSIDERATIONS

☐ evaluate risk considerations of private defined benefit (DB) pension plans in relation to 1) plan funded status, 2) sponsor financial strength, 3) interactions between the sponsor's business and the fund's investments, 4) plan design, and 5) workforce characteristics

Despite the long-term trend in the shift away from DB plans toward DC plans, as previously demonstrated, DB plans (and their hybrids) are still a key part of the pension landscape in several P7 countries, such as Canada, Japan, the Netherlands, and Switzerland. As such, it is important to review risk management considerations of private defined benefit pension plans—a topic that has intensified following the global financial crisis of 2007-2009. Key risk considerations of such plans must be measured and managed.

1. Plan funded status

   When a defined benefit pension plan is fully funded, the value of assets is greater than or equal to the present value of the liabilities. If the value of the assets falls below the present value of the liabilities, the pension plan is considered to be underfunded and the plan sponsor is left with a financial liability. The plan sponsor can take several approaches in order to minimize the risk of generating a financial liability:

   a. Seek to match assets to liabilities in terms of quantity, timing, and risk using a Liability Driven Investing (LDI) approach. Duration gap management or cash flow–matching suits plans that are close to fully funded and seek to maintain that status.

b. Seek to grow assets at a higher rate of return than the expected growth in liabilities—which typically involves taking on more investment risk. This form of investment suits plans that are underfunded and wishing to return to a fully funded status. It may also suit fully funded plans that are seeking to lower their contribution rate over time and are willing to endure the increased volatility in funded status that this approach entails.

c. Seek to invest in more defensive assets expected to deliver less volatile returns. This may suit defined benefit pension plans where the plan sponsor is willing to make higher contributions over time in exchange for less variability in the plan funded status.

In cases where a plan is adequately funded, the sponsoring corporation may seek to remove pension-driven balance sheet volatility by engaging pension risk transfer through such mechanisms as:

- offering lump sum payments to beneficiaries in exchange for voluntarily leaving the plan; or
- negotiating a transfer of the risk to an insurance provider.

2. Sponsor financial strength

When a defined benefit pension plan sponsor is not financially strong, there is a considerable risk that it may fail to make the necessary contributions to the plan. The plan sponsor may not be able to meet its defined benefit pension plan liabilities if there is a funding shortfall. If the plan sponsor files for bankruptcy protection, an underfunded pension plan is in the same difficult position as other creditors, having to join the queue claiming the firm's remaining assets.

The relative size of the plan also influences the sponsor's ability to assume risk. If the pension plan is small (large) relative to the size of the sponsor, then volatility in pension assets, liabilities, and/or contributions will have a smaller (larger) effect on the sponsoring company's balance sheet.

3. Interactions between the sponsor's business and the fund's investments

In the past, many private defined benefit pension plans have held significant stakes in the equity of the sponsor company. However, due to the risk involved, many regulators have restricted how much a plan may invest in the stock of the sponsor company. This risk materializes in circumstances in which the company performs poorly and its share price falls, thereby increasing the risk that pension plan assets fall below liabilities. This may coincide with a point in time when the sponsor's financial strength is poor, constraining its ability to make additional contributions necessary to address the developing funding shortfall. For this reason, it is advisable for the plan to diversify out of the sponsor company's stock. It is also prudent to diversify away from companies operating in the same industry, because their risk and return are expected to be highly correlated with those of the sponsor company's stock.

4. Plan design

Poor plan design can contribute many risks for the private defined benefit pension plan sponsor. When setting out the formula for calculation of defined benefit payments, the plan sponsor must balance adequacy (will the benefit payment be sufficient to meet income needs in retirement) and sustainability (what contribution rate is sustainable, and what investment return can realistically be achieved) within the context of its risk tolerance.

There is a significant risk that a company will be overly optimistic in predicting its ability to make contributions to its pension plan decades into the future.

The plan design is informed by its purpose as an employee retention tool to mitigate the risk of losing employees to a competitor. The company/sponsor may also wish to increase future defined benefit payments to address worker unrest, which may otherwise lead to strike action or lengthy negotiations with unions. If a company does not have immediate excess cash flow, it may prefer to increase future defined benefit payments instead of granting immediate pay raises.

5. Workforce characteristics

The nature of the workforce is an important risk consideration for companies because it impacts what the duration of the assets should be. The younger the workforce, the longer the duration of assets and the greater risk tolerance the plan will have. If a company's workforce has high turnover, it may have few employees whose entitlements to defined benefit payments will vest. On the other hand, if the average tenure of the workforce increases, then more liabilities will vest, thereby reducing the plan's funded status. If the workforce is older and nearer to retirement age, an important risk consideration is keeping sufficient liquidity so the plan can meet liabilities when they become due. Conversely, in a plan where the workforce is younger, on average, the sponsor may take on more liquidity risk. A workforce with a high level of vested benefits may constrain the company in terms of flexibility in managing its workforce. For example, a company may prefer to downsize its workforce, but doing so might require it to pay out excessive vested benefits.

Retired workers also influence the longevity risk of DB plans. Longevity risk is the risk that an individual will live longer than expected and draw more in benefit payments than the amount determined in the calculation of plan liabilities. In private DB pension plans, longevity risk is pooled such that if a participant dies earlier than expected, he/she leaves more assets in the pool that can then cover additional payments for those who live longer than expected. However, this pooling of longevity risk does not mitigate the effect of rising life expectancies, which implies, all else equal, an increase in total DB plan liabilities.

In setting a risk objective, plan sponsors must consider plan status, sponsor financial status and profitability, sponsor and pension fund common risk exposures, plan features, and workforce characteristics, as shown in Exhibit 5.

Exhibit 5: Factors Affecting Risk Tolerance and Risk Objectives of Defined Benefit Plans

Category	Variable	Explanation
Plan status	▪ Plan funded status (surplus or deficit)	▪ Higher pension surplus or higher funded status implies potentially greater risk tolerance.
Sponsor financial status and profitability	▪ Debt to total assets ▪ Current and expected profitability ▪ Size of plan compared to market capitalization of sponsor company	▪ Lower debt ratios and higher current and expected profitability imply greater risk tolerance. ▪ Large sponsor company size relative to pension plan size implies greater risk tolerance.

Category	Variable	Explanation
Sponsor and pension fund common risk exposures	▪ Correlation of sponsor operating results with pension asset returns	▪ The lower the correlation, the greater the risk tolerance, all else equal.
Plan features	▪ Provision for early retirement ▪ Provision for lump-sum distributions	▪ Such options tend to reduce the duration of plan liabilities, implying lower risk tolerance, all else equal.
Workforce characteristics	▪ Age of workforce ▪ Active lives relative to retired lives	▪ The younger the workforce and the greater the proportion of active lives, the greater the duration of plan liabilities and the greater the risk tolerance.

EXAMPLE 2

Andes Sports Equipment Corporation—Defined Benefit Plan

1. Frank Smit, CFA, is chief financial officer of Andes Sports Equipment Company (ADSE), a leading Dutch producer of winter and water sports gear. ADSE is a small company based in Amsterdam, and all of its revenues come from Europe. Product demand has been strong in the past few years, although it is highly cyclical. The company has rising earnings and a strong (low debt) balance sheet. ADSE is a relatively young company, and as such, its defined benefit pension plan has no retired employees. This essentially active-lives plan has €100 million in assets and an €8 million surplus in relation to the projected benefit obligation (PBO). Several facts concerning the plan follow:

   - The duration of the plan's liabilities (which are all Europe-based) is 20 years.
   - The discount rate applied to these liabilities is 6 percent.
   - The average age of ADSE's workforce is 39 years.

   Based on the information provided, discuss ADSE's risk tolerance.

Solution:

ADSE appears to have above average risk tolerance for the following reasons:

- **a.** The plan has a small surplus (8 percent of plan assets); that is, the plan is overfunded by €8 million.
- **b.** The company's balance sheet is strong (low use of debt).
- **c.** The company is profitable despite operating in a cyclical industry.
- **d.** The average age of its workforce is low.

2. Smit must set risk objectives for the ADSE pension plan. Because of excellent recent investment results, ADSE has not needed to make a contribution to the pension fund in the two most recent years. Smit considers it very important to maintain a plan surplus in relation to PBO. Because an €8 million surplus will be an increasingly small buffer as plan liabilities increase, Smit

decides that maintaining plan funded status, stated as a ratio of plan assets to PBO at 100 percent or greater, is his top priority.

Based on the information provided, state an appropriate risk objective for ADSE.

Solution:

Given Smit considered it very important to maintain a plan surplus in relation to PBO, an appropriate risk objective for ADSE relates to shortfall risk with respect to the plan's funded status falling below 100 percent. For example, ADSE may want to minimize the probability that funded status falls below 100 percent, or it may want the probability that funded status falls below 100 percent to be less than or equal to 10 percent. If a plan surplus is maintained, ADSE may experience more years in which it does not need to make a contribution. Indeed, a major motivation for maintaining a plan surplus is to reduce the contributions ADSE needs to make in the future. As such, another relevant type of risk objective would be to minimize the present value of expected cash contributions.

7 PENSION FUNDS: INVESTMENT OBJECTIVES AND ASSET ALLOCATION

- ☐ evaluate the investment policy statement of an institutional investor
- ☐ evaluate the investment portfolio of a private DB plan, sovereign wealth fund, university endowment, and private foundation

Investment Objectives

Defined Benefit Pension Plans

Defined benefit pension plans ultimately need to meet pension liabilities through a combination of investment returns and contributions. In practice, the investment objective of a DB pension plan is often to achieve a long-term rate of return on plan assets that exceeds the assumed rate of return used by the pension plan actuaries, typically the discount rate used in valuing pension liabilities. Importantly, targeting a long-term return based on the discount rate may be inappropriate in some cases. For example, when the discount rate is set using yields on government bonds, the target return is likely too low. In such a case, it may be preferable to fully hedge interest rate risk by adopting a liability-driven investing approach.

In determining an appropriate target return, it is worth noting that, ideally, the asset base should grow—through investment returns and contributions—in line with the growth of liabilities. If a plan is underfunded, the asset base must grow faster than liabilities. Because the growth of liabilities is met through investment returns and contributions (from the plan sponsor and/or employees), the DB plan's board and investment committee must consider the appropriate level of portfolio risk relative to the plan sponsor's willingness and ability to raise contribution rates should investment returns fall short of expectations.

In summary, the primary objective for DB pension plans is to achieve a long-term target return (usually defined in nominal terms) over a specified investment horizon (3–5 years or even as long as 10 or 25 years) with an appropriate level of risk that allows the plan to meet its contractual liabilities. The secondary objective could be to minimize the present value of expected cash contributions.

In setting overall investment strategy, many DB pension plans engage in detailed Asset Liability Management studies every 3–5 years. These studies include Monte Carlo simulations of thousands of scenarios for asset returns and factors driving pension liabilities (importantly, the discount rate) aimed at producing probability distributions for funded ratios and contribution rates at different horizons. These distributions are useful for determining key metrics, such as the expected funded ratio in 10 or 15 years, surplus volatility, surplus-at-risk, and volatility of contribution rates. Additionally, many pension funds engage in detailed liquidity modeling and stress testing that involve modeling contributions, benefit payments, capital calls for funding private equity investments, stressed asset values, and reduced liquidity of certain asset classes in market downturns. Besides providing an assessment of the appropriateness of the pension fund's liquidity profile, such stress testing provides insights into meeting liquidity needs during a financial crisis.

Defined Contribution Pension Plans

The main objective of defined contribution pension plans is to prudently grow assets that will support spending needs in retirement. Defined contribution plans usually offer a variety of investment options with differing investment objectives to suit participants of different ages, asset balances, and risk appetites. The investment options offered by the DC plan sponsor can be managed either in-house or externally as well as passively or actively. Most DC pension plans also provide a default option for disengaged participants. Plan trustees/boards must set an appropriate investment objective of the default option after reviewing the characteristics of existing default participants. Unsurprisingly, many DC plans end up with a balanced asset allocation mix as the default option—frequently in the form of a life-cycle fund. In cases where a DC plan provides participants a balanced asset allocation option with active management, a secondary objective may be to outperform the long-term policy benchmark consisting of the weighted average of individual asset class benchmarks and the policy weights defined by the strategic asset allocation. Finally, for some DC plans it is important their investment options outperform those of other DC pension plans, which is particularly relevant in countries where participants can voluntarily switch between DC plan providers.

Sample Investment Objectives of Different Pension Plans

Public DB Pension Plan:

1. The assets of Public Plan will be invested with the objective of achieving a long-term rate of return that meets or exceeds the Public Plan actuarial expected rate of return.
2. Public Plan will seek to maximize returns for the level of risk taken.
3. Public Plan will also seek to achieve a return that exceeds the Policy Index.
4. Public Plan will seek to achieve its objectives on an after fees basis.

Corporate DB Pension Plan:

The Trustee wishes to ensure that the Corporate Plan can meet its obligations to the beneficiaries while recognizing the cost implications to the Company of pursuing excessively conservative investment strategies. The objectives of the Plan are defined as: wishing to maximize the long-term return on investments subject to, in its opinion, an acceptably low likelihood of failing to achieve an ongoing 105% funding level.

Corporate DC Pension Plan:

The Fund currently offers a range of investment options to its participants and has adopted an age-based default strategy for participants who do not choose an investment option.

The investment strategy of the Fund is to put in place portfolios to achieve the objectives of its stakeholders over a reasonable period of time with a reasonable probability of success.

In establishing each option's investment objectives, the Trustee takes into account the average participant's age, account balance, and risk appetite. The participant's choice of investment option indicates his/her risk appetite.

For example, a participants selecting the growth option indicates a higher risk tolerance over a longer investment time horizon. The investment objective for the growth option is to build an investment portfolio to outperform inflation + 4% per annum over 7-year periods while accepting a high level of risk that is expected to generate 4–6 negative annual returns over any 20-year period.

Asset Allocation by Pension Plans

An examination of pension fund asset allocations shows very large differences in average asset allocations by country. Moreover, examining pension fund asset allocations within a country also typically shows large differences despite these plans seeking to achieve similar goals. Such inter- and intra-national differences are driven by many factors discussed earlier in this reading, including the differences in legal, regulatory, accounting, and tax constraints; the investment objectives, risk appetites, and investment beliefs of the stakeholders; the liabilities to and demographics of the ultimate beneficiaries; the availability of investment opportunities; and the expected cost of living in retirement.

Exhibit 6 presents the average asset allocation of pension funds in the world's largest pension fund markets. The data are an aggregation of both DB and DC plans as presented (the split between DB and DC plans for each of the P7 countries is shown in Exhibit 3).

Note the category 'Other' includes hedge funds, private equity funds, loans, structured products, other mutual funds (i.e., not invested in equities, bonds, or cash), land, buildings, and other miscellaneous investments.

Exhibit 6: Pension Asset Allocation for P7 Countries (2021)

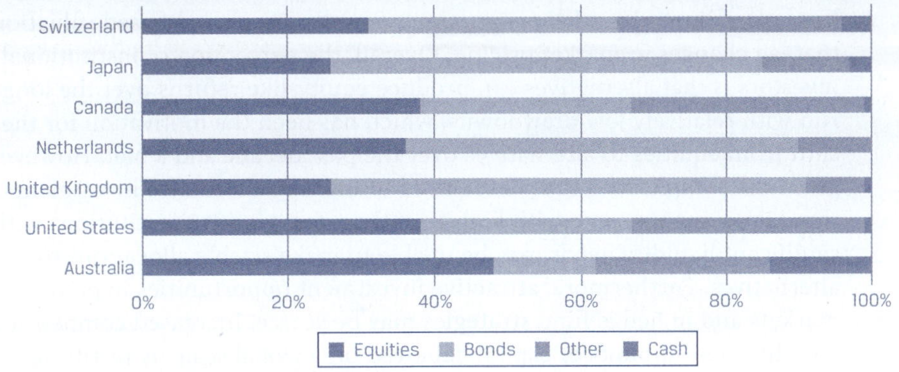

Source: Willis Towers Watson Thinking Ahead Institute (2021).

The key observations regarding the data presented in Exhibit 6 are as follows:

- *Equities*: Equities provide a long-term risk premium over bonds and cash and are typically viewed as the asset class of choice for long-term investors, like pension plans because of the higher expected returns they offer. Traditionally, equities are also viewed as an inflation hedge, as opposed to bonds that do not perform well in an inflationary environment. However, over the past decade, there has been a decrease in the equity allocation in several countries, particularly in Japan, Canada, and Australia. In aggregate, the resulting reallocation has been to the category 'Other,' which includes such alternatives as private equity and debt, real assets, and hedge funds, as well as to bonds (and fixed income, generally) as DB pension funds have reduced their risk appetite to lower the volatility of their funded ratios. Australia and the US have the largest proportions of DC pension assets and also the largest allocations to equities. Although not shown in Exhibit 6, it is worth noting that the United States, Australia, and the Netherlands have the highest proportions of their equities allocations invested in their local markets. Given the size of the domestic equities markets in Australia and the Netherlands, this implies significant home bias.
- *Fixed Income*: Fixed income plays a defensive role in pension fund portfolios, because during times of financial market stress, equity markets and interest rates tend to fall. Fixed-income investments also help DB pension plans hedge the interest rate risk relative to their pension liabilities. Many regulators, in fact, require DB pension plans to hold a minimum allocation in fixed-income investments. Over the last decade, US corporate pension plans have increased their allocations to fixed-income investments, despite low expected returns, driven by the desire to reduce their funded ratio volatility. Conversely, US public pension plans have reduced their fixed-income allocations overall while increasing their allocations in the fixed-income space to high yield (riskier) bonds. The reallocation and repositioning are driven by the large gap that has opened between their expected rate of return and the yield available on long-term government securities.
- *Alternatives (Other)*: This category includes private equity and debt markets, real estate, hedge funds, and real assets. As a group, these alternative assets tend to have low, or negative, correlations with traditional investments as well as lower drawdowns. In the case of hedge funds, this may be explained by the lower volatility of these strategies versus equity markets. Private asset

classes have historically also exhibited lower drawdowns compared to equities. This may be partially explained by a lack of fully marking-to-market because of limited market transactions as well as appraisal-based valuations that lag changes in market pricing. Overall, the perception of institutional investors is that alternatives can produce equity-like returns over the long run with relatively low drawdowns, which has been the motivation for the shift from equities to alternatives over the past decade and a half. However, given the complexity and skill required to manage alternative investments, these investments come with high fees; thus, fee-sensitive institutions with significant liquidity needs may be unable to make sizable allocations to alternatives. Furthermore, attractive investment opportunities in private markets and in hedge fund strategies may be scarce. Increased competition and the huge amounts of capital deployed on a global scale by institutional investors may put downward pressure on future returns. Although still a smaller part of most institutional portfolios, allocations to real assets have increased significantly because they are considered an attractive way to hedge inflation. Japan has been slowest among the select countries to increase allocations to alternatives; however, the transition is underway with the country's largest pension plan, Government Pension Investment Fund (GPIF), which is reducing its allocation to domestic bonds in favor of alternatives.

EXAMPLE 3

Asset Allocation by a Public Defined Benefit Plan

1. Susan Liew, CFA, is the chief investment officer of the Lorenza State Pension Plan (LSPP), a public DB plan. The plan maintains an asset allocation of 30% US equities, 30% international equities, 30% US fixed income, and 10% international fixed income. Liew's investment team developed the following long-term expected real returns for the asset classes in which the LSPP has traditionally invested. The outlook for US and international equities is slightly below long-term averages, while the outlook for US and international fixed income is well below long-term averages.

Asset Class	Expected Long-Term (10-Year) Annual Return
US equities	4.0%
International equities	5.0%
US fixed income	1.0%
International fixed income	–0.5%

Given the poor prospects for fixed income and the mediocre expectations for equities, Liew is exploring making allocations to various alternatives and has asked LSPP's asset consultant to provide comments on considerations for each alternative asset class, as shown here:

Asset Class	Comments
Alternative debt	Represents a diverse range of high yielding and floating-rate debt expected to return 300 bps annually over traditional fixed income (default-adjusted basis). The additional returns are compensation for increased liquidity risk in private debt, added credit risk in high yield and EM debt, and non-performing loans.
Infrastructure funds	Strong income-like characteristics given contracted cash flows for most underlying infrastructure projects. This asset class entails increased liquidity risk but offers some inflation protection (many contracted cash flows are linked to inflation).
Hedge funds	Provide access to various diversifying strategies, including those with potential to generate gains in both rising and falling markets. Expected to return 250 bps annually over traditional long-only equities. Careful manager selection and underlying strategy selection (especially exposure to equity market beta) are important factors.

Liew recommends to LSPP's Board of Trustees the following change in asset allocation:

Asset Class	Current Asset Allocation	Recommended Asset Allocation
US equities	30%	25%
International equities	30%	25%
US fixed income	30%	15%
International fixed income	10%	5%
Alternative debt	—	10%
Infrastructure funds	—	10%
Hedge funds	—	10%

How would the recommended change in asset allocation be expected to affect LSPP's funded status?

Solution:

The recommended changes in asset allocation would likely affect LSPP's funded status as follows:

- The changes would increase expected returns, implying higher expected asset values for LSPP over time.
- Given that both alternative debt and hedge funds have higher projected long-term returns than traditional debt and equities, respectively, the discount rate applied to LSPP's liabilities can be increased, thereby reducing their present value.

- On balance, LSPP's funded status would be expected to improve because of the recommended changes in asset allocation. In addition to generating higher asset values and lower present value of liabilities, the volatility of assets (and therefore the risk to funded status) should be reduced because of the lower correlation among asset returns.

Note that although these alternative investments entail reduced liquidity, this does not impact funded status; in fact, funded status improves because of the factors mentioned previously. However, the reduced liquidity must be considered to ensure sufficient coverage of prospective liabilities. Alternative investments entail greater manager selection risk and larger dispersion of returns around the policy benchmark relative to a passive allocation to public markets. Careful manager selection would likely require resources that would increase internal costs, and also require paying higher fees to access skilled alternative asset managers.

Exhibit 7 shows the evolution of pension fund asset allocation trends from 2000 –2020 for the P7 countries. It is apparent that the allocation to equities has decreased from about 60% in 2000 to about 43% in 2020, while allocations to the 'Other' category of alternatives has increased from about 7% to 26% over the same time period. This is consistent with the general trend among institutional investors of diversifying out of equities and into alternative investments, including private equity, natural resources, real estate, and hedge funds.

Exhibit 7: Evolution of Pension Asset Allocation from 2000 to 2020

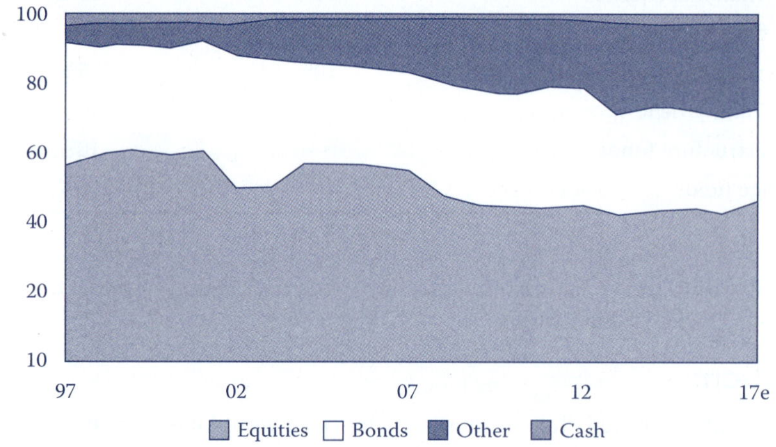

Source: Willis Towers Watson Thinking Ahead Institute (2021).

SOVEREIGN WEALTH FUNDS: TYPES AND STAKEHOLDERS

8

☐ discuss the stakeholders in the portfolio, the liabilities, the investment time horizons, and the liquidity needs of different types of institutional investors

Sovereign wealth funds (SWFs) are state-owned investment funds or entities that invest in financial or real assets. Sovereign wealth funds have increased significantly in number and size over the past two decades. Governments have established SWFs from budget surpluses to meet different objectives. The International Monetary Fund (IMF) has defined five broad types of sovereign wealth funds, and each pursues different investment objectives. Exhibit 8 summarizes these five types with their main objective and some notable examples.

Exhibit 8: Major Types of Sovereign Wealth Funds

Type	Objective	Examples
Budget stabilization funds	Set up to insulate the budget and economy from commodity price volatility and external shocks.	Economic and Social Stabilization Fund of Chile; Timor-Leste Petroleum Fund; Russia's Oil Stabilization Fund
Development funds	Established to allocate resources to priority socio-economic projects, usually infrastructure.	Mubadala (UAE); Iran's National Development Fund; Ireland Strategic Investment Fund; Temasek (Singapore)
Savings funds	Intended to share wealth across generations by transforming non-renewable assets into diversified financial assets.	Abu Dhabi Investment Authority; Kuwait Investment Authority; Qatar Investment Authority; Russia's National Wealth Fund
Reserve funds	Intended to reduce the negative carry costs of holding reserves or to earn higher return on ample reserves.	China Investment Corporation; Korea Investment Corporation; GIC Private Ltd. (Singapore)
Pension reserve funds	Set up to meet identified future outflows with respect to pension-related contingent-type liabilities on governments' balance sheets.	National Social Security Fund (China); New Zealand Superannuation Fund; Future Fund of Australia

Source: International Monetary Fund, "Sovereign Wealth Funds—A Work Agenda" (29 February 2008).

Exhibit 9 shows some of the largest sovereign wealth funds, which manage a total of about US$3.6 trillion in assets—close to 50% of all SWF assets (more than US$7.3 trillion).

Exhibit 9: Select Large Sovereign Wealth Funds

Fund	Inception Date	Country	Type
Kuwait Investment Authority	1953	Kuwait	Savings Fund
Abu Dhabi Investment Authority	1976	Abu Dhabi, United Arab Emirates	Savings Fund
Norway's Government Pension Fund—Global	1990	Norway	Budget Stabilization/ Savings/Pension Reserve
China Investment Corporation	2007	China	Reserve Fund

Source: SWF Institute (www.swfinstitute.org).

Stakeholders

SWF stakeholders include the citizens, the government, and external asset managers as well as the SWF management, investment committees, and boards.

The ultimate SWF stakeholders are the current and future citizens (or residents) of the country. Depending on the objectives of the SWF, these stakeholders either benefit directly in the form of payments (e.g., for pension reserve funds) or indirectly through stabilization of government budgets, lower taxes, or investments by the SWF in the domestic economy. If the SWF fails to meet its objectives, citizens/residents might be impacted through higher future taxes. Several SWFs are explicitly set up to benefit not only the current generation but also future generations. When such intergenerational wealth transfer is part of the objective, significant transparency and communication are required by the SWF and government to gain support from all stakeholders. This also requires long-term thinking by the government, which can be challenging when some governments have tenures of only a few years and when fiscal budgets vary significantly over the economic cycle.

The management or investment office of an SWF is tasked with investing its assets according to the investment policy and objectives of the fund. They monitor assets, make recommendations on investment strategy, and either select external asset managers or manage assets in-house. Appointment to an SWF's board, which oversees the management or investment office, is typically executed through a formal process that may include appointment by the current ruling government. In any case, the board has a fiduciary duty to the ultimate beneficiaries, the nation's current and future generations.

9 SOVEREIGN WEALTH FUNDS: OTHER CONSIDERATIONS

Liabilities and Investment Horizons

There is a wide variety in investment objectives, liabilities, investment horizons, and liquidity needs among the five types of SWFs, so we will discuss each type separately. As a group, however, SWFs are different from the other institutional investors covered in this reading when it comes to liabilities. The liabilities of DB pension funds, endowments and foundations, insurance companies, and banks are clearly defined, which facilitates asset/liability management (ALM) processes. SWFs, however, do not generally have clearly defined liabilities given their mission of intergenerational wealth transfer. It is also worth noting that SWFs do not necessarily fit neatly into one of the five different types discussed in this section. For example, Norway's Government Pension Fund Global (formerly known as Norway's Petroleum Fund) undertakes elements of stabilization and sterilization, accumulating pension reserves, and saving for future generations.

Budget Stabilization Funds

Budget stabilization funds are established to insulate the fiscal budget from commodity price volatility and other external shocks, particularly if a nation's revenue is tied to natural resource production or other cyclical industries. These funds have uncertain liabilities and relatively short investment horizons. Their main purpose is risk management because such funds may be needed on a short-term basis to help support the government budget. The investment objective is usually to deliver returns in excess of inflation with a low probability of a negative return in any year. Budget stabilization funds typically avoid assets that are highly correlated with the main sources of government revenue, and they may engage in hedging against declines in prices of commodities that are important revenue generators for the local economy. These funds mainly invest in government bonds and other debt securities. Examples of budget stabilization funds include the Economic and Social Stabilization Fund of Chile and Russia's Oil Stabilization Fund.

Development Funds

Development funds are established to support a nation's economic development through investing in essential infrastructure, innovation, or by supporting key industries. Liabilities are not clearly defined and typically uncertain for development funds, but their overall objective is to raise a country's economic growth or to diversify the economy. As such, these funds have an implicit real return target: to increase real domestic GDP growth and productivity. Some initiatives, such as infrastructure/industrial development, may be ongoing and long-term, while others may have a fixed, medium-term horizon, such as a medical research fund. Examples of development funds include Mubadala Development Corp. (UAE) and the National Development Fund of Iran.

Savings Funds

Savings funds are typically established to transform proceeds from the sale of non-renewable natural resources into long-term wealth and a diversified portfolio of financial assets. The mission of a savings fund is wealth transfer to future generations after the sources of natural wealth have been depleted. As such, their liabilities are long-term. Some savings funds have a real return objective or an explicit spending policy (like endowments). Norway's Government Pension Fund Global (GPFG) uses a fiscal spending rule whereby it intends to withdraw 3% of the fund's value annually with the goal of gradually phasing oil revenue into the Norwegian economy. This spending rate is linked to the expected real return earned by the GPFG. A special case of savings funds involves government investment holding companies, which are funded from the privatization proceeds of national companies (e.g., Singapore's Temasek Holdings). Because of their long-term horizons, savings funds invest in risky and illiquid assets, including equities and a wide range of alternative investments. Of course, savings funds should avoid investing in assets highly correlated with the non-renewable resources from which the government is trying to diversify.

Reserve Funds

Reserve investment funds are established from central bank excess foreign currency reserves. The objective is to achieve a return higher than that on FX reserves (usually invested in low-duration, high-grade debt instruments) and to reduce the negative cost-of-carry of holding FX reserves. Reserve funds are common in export-intensive economies that have built up large FX reserves. Central banks accumulate such reserves as they print local currency to buy FX (like US dollars or euros) from local firms selling export goods. The central banks then issue monetary stabilization bonds to absorb the excess local currency. So, the central banks typically end up with FX reserves invested in low-yielding US Treasury or other high-quality sovereign debt instruments, while their liabilities (monetary stabilization bonds) pay much higher yields that create the negative cost-of-carry. Countries mitigate this cost by creating sovereign wealth reserve funds, placing excess FX reserves in these funds, and investing them globally in higher yielding, risky assets. Although their true liabilities are the central bank's monetary stabilization bonds, in practice, reserve funds operate somewhat similarly to endowments and foundations by having either a nominal or real return target. Also, their investment horizons are very long, with typically no immediate or interim payout expectation. Consequently, reserve funds generally invest in diversified portfolios with significant exposure to equities and other high-yielding alternative investments. Examples of reserve funds include China Investment Corporation (CIC), Korea Investment Corporation (KIC), and GIC Private Limited (GIC), formerly known as Government of Singapore Investment Corporation.

Pension Reserve Funds

Pension reserve funds are established to help prefund contingent pension-related liabilities on the government's balance sheet. Pension reserve funds are usually funded from fiscal surpluses during economic booms. The goal is to help reduce the burden on future taxpayers by prefunding social security and health care costs arising from aging populations, so these funds generally have long-term investment horizons. There is usually an **accumulation phase** (**decumulation phase**) where the government predominantly contributes to (withdraws from) the fund. However, additional uncertainty also exists around expected cash flows, particularly in the case of funding health care because those costs are quite volatile. The investment objective of pension reserve funds is to earn returns sufficient to maximize the likelihood of meeting future pension, social security, and/or health care costs as they arise. Therefore, such funds will typically invest in a diversified portfolio with the majority in such equities and alternative investments as property, infrastructure, hedge funds, and private markets. An example of a pension reserve fund is Future Fund of Australia (FFA). Its goal is to meet unfunded pension liabilities (retirement payments or superannuation payments in Australia) that will be owed to former public employees starting in 2020. FFA was funded from budget surpluses and privatization proceeds of Telstra, an Australian telecommunications company that was formerly a state-owned enterprise. The investment mandate for FFA is to achieve an average annual return of at least the Consumer Price Index (CPI) + 4% to 5% per year over the long term with an acceptable level of risk.

Liquidity Needs

Budget Stabilization Funds

Stabilization funds must maintain a high level of liquidity and invest in assets that have a low risk of significant losses over short time periods. For example, in the event of a negative commodity price shock, the government might experience a significant budget deficit caused by lower commodity-based revenues. To stabilize the budget and meet spending needs, the stabilization fund's assets must be readily accessible. As a result, budget stabilization funds invest a significant portion of their portfolios in cash and high-grade, fixed-income instruments that are very liquid and carry little risk of significant drawdown.

Development Funds

A development fund supports national economic development. Liquidity needs depend on the particular strategic economic development initiatives the fund was created to support. For example, infrastructure investments are very long-term, so funds established to develop infrastructure would have low liquidity needs. Development funds designed to promote research and innovation may also require long time periods to see the fruits of investments in innovation and research and are likely to have low liquidity needs as well.

Savings Funds

Savings funds have a very long-term investment horizon and low liquidity needs. Their main objective is to grow wealth for future generations, so their liquidity needs, being long-term in nature, are comparable to those of endowments and foundations. In instances where the savings fund was established to transform the proceeds from the sale of non-renewable commodities into long-term wealth, the fund's liquidity needs may change once the nation's natural resources have been depleted because the government is more likely to begin withdrawing money from the fund to support its budgetary needs.

Reserve Funds

Reserve funds operate to offset negative carry effects of holding FX reserves, and consequently, excess reserves are invested in higher growth investments. The liquidity needs of reserve funds are lower than those of stabilization funds but higher than those of savings funds. Reserve funds typically hold 50%–70% in equity or equity-equivalent investments to achieve their return targets. The remainder, however, is likely to be invested in liquid fixed-income securities that could be readily sold should a dramatic change in the balance of trade require additional central bank reserves.

Pension Reserve Funds

Pension reserve funds need to meet future pension or health care liabilities when they come due. Depending on when significant fund withdrawals are expected, liquidity needs change over time. During the accumulation phase, reserve funds can hold a significant part of their portfolios in equities and relatively illiquid investments. Once the decumulation phase begins, the asset allocation will gradually shift toward more liquid, high-quality, fixed-income investments.

External Constraints Affecting Investment

In this section and the next, we briefly highlight some legal/regulatory and tax constraints, respectively, that sovereign wealth funds must consider when investing.

Legal and Regulatory Constraints

Sovereign wealth funds are typically established by national legislation that contains details on: the fund's mission; contributions to the fund; circumstances allowing withdrawals from the fund; and governance structure, including selection of board members, their roles, and the level of board independence. Some SWFs are set up with clear rules on asset allocation. For example, a technology development fund may be required to be 100% invested in offshore technology assets to provide diversification (versus local economic drivers) and eventual technology transfer. Alternatively, an industrial development fund may be required to invest 100% locally to support the development of key industries in the domestic economy. In any case, SWFs should operate in a transparent and accountable manner as they are ultimately established for the benefit of a nation's people and future generations. Sound governance, independence, transparency, and accountability are all essential to ensure that SWFs are protected from political influence.

The International Forum of SWFs (IFSWF) is a self-governing body established to promote best practices among SWFs. All IFSWF members have endorsed a set of generally accepted principles and practices (GAPP). Known as the "Santiago Principles" for the city where they were drafted, the GAPP provide a best practices framework by which SWFs should operate that addresses such key elements as sound legal framework, well-defined mission, independence, accountability, transparency, disclosure, ethics and professionalism, effective risk management, and regular review for compliance with the Santiago Principles.

Tax and Accounting Constraints

Typically, sovereign wealth funds are given tax-free status by the legislation that governs them. However, SWFs may be ineligible to claim withholding taxes or tax credits that are ordinarily available to taxable investors. As SWFs invest in offshore markets, they also need to consider any tax treaties that may exist between the countries in which they are investing and their own country. Some regulators allow SWFs to be exempt from domestic tax rules that have been put in place to deter tax avoidance by corporations and individuals. To prevent any international diplomatic issues, SWFs should be sensitive to ensuring they are not perceived as trying to avoid paying taxes in any offshore jurisdictions where they operate or invest.

10 SOVEREIGN WEALTH FUNDS: INVESTMENT OBJECTIVES AND ASSET ALLOCATION

- ☐ evaluate the investment policy statement of an institutional investor
- ☐ evaluate the investment portfolio of a private DB plan, sovereign wealth fund, university endowment, and private foundation

Investment Objectives

Budget Stabilization Funds

The investment objective of budget stabilization funds is capital preservation. This is achieved by endeavoring to deliver returns in excess of inflation with a low probability of a negative return in any given year. In addition, budget stabilization funds should avoid cyclical assets whose returns are highly correlated to the main sources of government revenue (such as natural resources industries). According to the stated investment objectives of Chile's Economic and Social Stabilization Fund, *"the main aim of its investment policy is to maximize the fund's accumulated value in order to partially cover cyclical reductions in fiscal revenues while maintaining a low level of risk. Its risk aversion is reflected by the choice of an investment portfolio with a high level of liquidity and low credit risk and volatility, thereby ensuring the availability of the resources to cover fiscal deficits and preventing significant losses in the fund's value."*

Development Funds

Development funds are established to support a nation's economic development with the ultimate goal of raising a country's long-term economic growth. The implicit investment objective of development funds is therefore to achieve a real rate of return in excess of real domestic GDP or productivity growth.Accordingly, Khazanah Nasional Berhard, the strategic investment fund of the government of Malaysia, *"strives to create sustainable value and cultivate a high-performance culture that helps contribute to Malaysia's economic competitiveness. Utilizing a proactive investment approach, we aim to build true value through management of our core investments, leveraging on our global footprint for new growth, as well as undertaking catalytic investments that strategically boost the country's economy. We also actively develop human, social and knowledge capital for the country."*

Savings Funds

The mission of savings funds is to ensure wealth transfer to future generations. Therefore, their primary objective is to maintain purchasing power of the assets in perpetuity while achieving investment returns sufficient to sustain the spending necessary to support ongoing governmental activities. According to Alaska Statutes 37.13.020, the Alaska Permanent Fund, *"should provide a means of conserving a portion of the state's revenue from mineral resources to benefit all generations of Alaskans; the fund's goal should be to maintain safety of principal while maximizing total return; the fund should be used as a savings device managed to allow the maximum use of disposable income from the fund for purposes designated by law."*

Reserve Funds

The investment objective of reserve funds is usually to achieve a rate of return above the return the government must pay on its monetary stabilization bonds, thereby eliminating the negative cost-of-carry of holding excess FX reserves (that are typically invested in low duration, high-grade, fixed-income instruments). For example, Singapore's Government Investment Corporation (GIC) has a clearly defined purpose: *"We aim to achieve good long-term returns for the Government—a reasonable risk-adjusted rate above global inflation over a 20-year investment horizon. By achieving these returns, we meet our responsibility to preserve and enhance the international purchasing power of Singapore's foreign reserves. The reserves provide a stream of income that can be spent or invested for the benefit of present and future generations."*

Pension Reserve Funds

The investment objective of pension reserve funds is to earn sufficient returns to maximize the likelihood of being able to meet future unfunded pension, social security, and/or health care liabilities of plan participants as they arise. Accordingly, among its mandates, the Australian government states that its Future Fund should *"maximise the return earned on the Fund over the long term; ... adopt an average return of at least the Consumer Price Index (CPI) +4 to +5 per cent per annum over the long term as the benchmark return on the Fund; [and] in targeting the benchmark return, the Board must determine an acceptable but not excessive level of risk for the Fund...."*

EXAMPLE 4

The People's Fund of Wigitania—A Pension Reserve Fund

The People's Fund is a pension reserve fund established by the government of Wigitania by setting aside current government surpluses. Its objective is to meet future unfunded social security payments caused by an aging population. The following is an extract from the People's Fund IPS.

Effective from 2030, the government will have the ability to withdraw assets to meet pension and social security liabilities falling due each year. Actuarial projections estimate annual payouts to be about 5% of the total fund value at that time. Given this level of cash flow, the Fund is expected to maintain most of its asset base for the foreseeable future. As such, 2030 does not represent an 'end date' for measurement purposes. A long-term investment horizon remains appropriate at present. However, the appropriate timeframe, risk tolerance, portfolio construction and liquidity profile may change.

1. What are the liquidity needs of the People's Fund?

Solution:

From the extract, we see that the unfunded pension and social security liabilities that the Fund is meant to cover are expected to be about 5% of total fund value per year, starting in 2030. Management of the fund will need to ensure that they have sufficient liquidity at that time to meet those ongoing liabilities. Until that time, liquidity needs are very low, which should allow the People's Fund to invest a significant part of its portfolio in less-liquid alternative asset classes.

2. What factors does the Board need to consider when reviewing the Fund's investment horizon?

Solution:

The Board should consider two separate phases when reviewing the Fund's investment horizon and investment policy: an accumulation phase and a decumulation phase. The accumulation phase lasts until 2030 and allows the Fund to invest with little to no liquidity needs and little concern for interim volatility. The decumulation phase starts after 2030, when the government expects to withdraw about 5% of the assets on an annual basis. The investment horizon, liquidity needs, and risk tolerance will need to be modified during the decumulation phase, which will affect the investment policy.

Asset Allocation by Sovereign Wealth Funds

Each of the five types of sovereign wealth funds have very different objectives and purposes. Not surprisingly then, these funds have very different asset allocations. Development funds usually have little flexibility with their asset allocations as they operate within a limited investment universe as part of their mandate (e.g., they are required to invest in local infrastructure development projects). Given that national development projects can be different in nature and purpose between countries, it would be difficult to envision a 'typical' asset allocation for a development fund. The other four types of sovereign wealth funds are more homogeneous within their respective groups, for which Exhibit 10 provides illustrative asset allocations.

Exhibit 10: Illustrative Asset Allocations for Different Types of Sovereign Wealth Funds

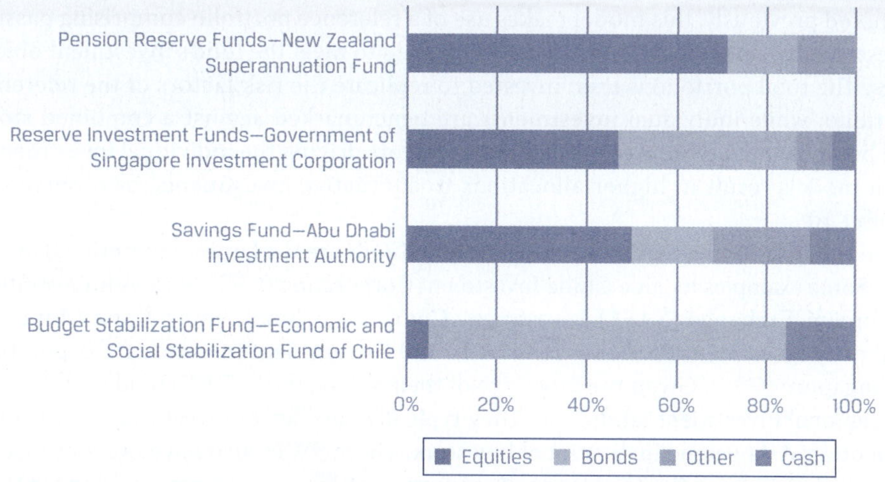

Sources: 1. Economic and Social Stabilization Fund of Chile website; 2. Abu Dhabi Investment Authority (ADIA), *2020 Review*; 3. Government Investment Corporation (GIC), *Report on the Management of the Government's Portfolio for the Year 2020/21*; 4. NZSUPERFUND, *New Zealand Superannuation Fund Annual Report2021*.

Several key points stand out from the data in Exhibit 10:

- The portfolios of budget stabilization funds are dominated by fixed-income investments because of their defensive nature, relatively stable investment returns, and diversification against cyclically sensitive factors (such as commodity prices) that drive government budget revenues in some countries. The conservative asset allocation may be partly explained by the fact that several major stabilization funds are managed by their countries' central bank or Ministry of Finance; these entities tend to be relatively risk averse.
- The portfolios of savings funds are shown to be tilted toward growth assets, equities, and alternatives (the "Other" category). Due to their very long investment horizons, these funds can take on more equity-related risks, and they consequently hold relatively high allocations to such alternative investments as real assets, private equity and debt (loans), and hedge funds.
- Reserve investment funds have a similar allocation to savings funds but they tend to allocate less to alternatives. This may be partially explained by reserve funds having potentially higher liquidity needs compared to savings funds because of central bank activities. Public equities are typically the most liquid growth asset available and help counter the negative carry generated by foreign exchange reserves, while bonds and other fixed-income investments help to reduce reserve funds' portfolio volatility.
- The portfolios of pension reserve funds are relatively heavily tilted toward equities with a significant allocation to alternative assets, such as real assets and infrastructure, private equity and debt markets, and hedge funds. Pension reserve funds generally have long-term investment horizons (but not necessarily inter-generational as with savings funds) and low liquidity needs during their accumulation phases, which can explain their high allocation to alternatives compared with other SWFs.

Sovereign wealth funds with savings or pension reserve objectives typically follow the endowment investment model. Some also adopt the Canada reference portfolio model. An example of the latter is the New Zealand Superannuation Fund (NZSF). As noted previously, this model makes use of a reference portfolio comprising passive investment in stocks and bonds that are expected to meet the fund's investment objectives. The total portfolio is then invested to replicate the risk factors of the reference portfolio, while individual investments are benchmarked against a combined stock and bond benchmark representing the risk factors driving the individual investments. Both models result in higher allocations to alternative investments, as observed in Exhibit 10.

In the Asia Pacific region, sovereign wealth funds are the largest institutional investors. Some examples include China Investment Corporation (CIC), State Administration of Foreign Exchange (SAFE) Investment Company (China), Hong Kong Monetary Authority Investment Portfolio (HKMAIP) and Government Investment Corporation of Singapore (GIC). Given the huge size of their assets, these SWFs tend to dominate the regional investment landscape. They typically have fewer investment constraints than other Asia Pacific institutional investors. These SWFs also have broader investment mandates, minimal investment management fee constraints, and longer time horizons as compared to (for example) pension funds. Such flexibility allows these SWFs to implement higher allocations to alternative assets.

11 UNIVERSITY ENDOWMENTS AND PRIVATE FOUNDATIONS

☐ describe the focus of legal, regulatory, and tax constraints affecting different types of institutional investors

This section introduces university endowments and private foundations. As will be seen shortly, these two types of institutional investors have some similarities but also important differences that affect their investing activities.

University Endowments

Many institutions have endowments, including universities, churches, museums, and hospitals. These endowments are typically funded through gifts and donations and are intended to help the institutions provide for some of their main services. Endowment funds invest in capital markets to provide a savings and growth mechanism that allows the institution to meet its mission in perpetuity. The main objective is to provide intergenerational equity. As James Tobin wrote in 1974: "The trustees of an endowed institution are the guardians of the future against the claims of the present. Their task is to preserve equity among generations."

Throughout this reading, for simplicity we will focus on university endowments. The investment objectives and philosophies of the endowments of other institutions are typically not very different from those of university endowments. Exhibit 11 shows some large (by assets) university endowments.

Exhibit 11: Select US University Endowments

University	Assets (US$ bn)
Harvard University	40.5
University of Texas System	31.9
Yale University	31.2
Stanford University	28.9
Princeton University	26.6

Source: TIAA and the National Association of College and University Business Officers (NACUBO), *2020 NACUBO–TIAA Study of Endowments (NCSE).*

Private Foundations

Foundations are nonprofit organizations that typically make grants to outside organizations and persons who carry out social, educational and other charitable activities. Many foundations are located in the United States, but some large foundations are outside the United States, such as the Wellcome Trust in the United Kingdom. Foundations are more common in the United States because of favorable tax treatment. Outside the United States, charitable giving is typically undertaken by family offices.

There are four different types of foundations:

1. *Community foundations*: These are charitable organizations that make social or educational grants for the benefit of a local community (e.g., the New York Community Trust). These foundations are usually funded by public donations.
2. *Operating foundations*: Organizations that exist to operate a not-for-profit business for charitable purposes. They are typically funded by individual donors or donor families.
3. *Corporate foundations*: These are established by businesses and funded from profits.
4. *Private grant-making foundations*: These are established by individual donors or donor families to support specific types of charities. Most of the largest foundations in the US fall into this category.

Community foundations are a type of public charity associated with such community organizations as hospitals, schools, and churches. They are funded by many relatively small donors, and they typically provide charitable support in the region or community where they are located. Private operating foundations are established to provide funding and support for related programs and activities (e.g., operating a museum) rather than giving grants to outside organizations or activities.

Private grant-making foundations (also called private non-operating foundations) are by far the largest group (in number of foundations and in total assets), so they are our primary focus. Private grant-making foundations support different types of charities and usually run a large grant-making operation in addition to an investment office. The main objective of most private grant-making foundations is to maintain purchasing power into perpetuity, so that the organization can continue making grants. In recent years, however, there has been a trend toward limited-life foundations as original donors seek to maintain control over foundation spending during their lives.

The focus of grants varies widely and includes issues such as health, education, environment, arts, and culture. Some foundations make large and targeted grants to very specific causes while others make many smaller grants to a wide variety of causes. Exhibit 12 shows some large US foundations and their missions.

Exhibit 12: Select US Foundations

Foundation	Mission
Bill & Melinda Gates Foundation	Focus on global health and poverty. In US focus on education.
Ford Foundation	Focus on inequality.
Robert Wood Johnson Foundation	Improve health and health care of all Americans.
Lilly Endowment Inc.	Support religion, education, community development.
William and Flora Hewlett Foundation	Help people build measurably better lives by focusing on education, the environment, global development, performing arts, philanthropy, and population. Also supports disadvantaged communities in San Francisco.

Source: Foundation Center (www.foundationcenter.org).

External Constraints Affecting Investment

In this section and the next we briefly touch on some legal/regulatory and tax constraints, respectively, that affect investing by university endowments and private foundations.

Legal and Regulatory Constraints

Charitable organizations, including endowments and foundations, are typically subject to rules and regulations in their country of domicile that: 1) require investment committees/officers/boards to invest on a total return basis and consider portfolio diversification when managing assets (i.e., follow the principles of modern portfolio theory, MPT); and 2) require investment committees/officers/boards to exercise a duty of care and prudence in overseeing the assets and making investment decisions (i.e., fiduciary duty).

In the United States, endowments and foundations are governed by the Uniform Prudent Management of Institutional Funds Act of 2006 (UPMIFA). Two important features of UPMIFA include:

1. Allowing charitable organizations flexibility in spending decisions, which could be adjusted for fluctuations in the market value of assets. Endowments, particularly, could meet the fiduciary standard of prudence by maintaining purchasing power of the fund.
2. Modernizing the standard of prudence for the management of charitable funds by adopting the principles of MPT established by the Uniform Prudent Investor Act (1994).

UK endowments and foundations are typically organized as trusts. Until 2000, UK trusts were limited to spending only income earned from investments (not capital gains). The Trustee Act (2000) changed that and, like UPMIFA in the United States, required trustees to manage trust assets based on MPT principles. The act also imposed a duty of care upon trustees. The shift toward managing portfolios using MPT principles has enabled endowments and foundations to embrace a broader range of asset classes compared to the traditional 60/40 equity/bond mix. It has also allowed them to focus on total return rather than solely on income return (high coupon bond and/or high-dividend-yield stocks).

Tax and Accounting Constraints

Endowments and foundations typically enjoy tax-exempt status. Tax-exempt status has three elements:

1. *Taxation of gifts and donations to endowments and foundations*: Gifts and donations to endowments and foundations are usually tax-deductible (up to a certain percentage of adjusted gross income) for the person or entity making the gift or donation.
2. *Taxation of income and capital gains on assets*: Income and capital gains on assets are usually tax-exempt in countries that have endowments and charitable organizations, which are tied to such non-profit, tax-exempt organizations as universities, religious organizations, or museums.
3. *Taxation on payouts from endowments and foundations*: Payouts are tax exempt if the receiving institution is exempt from income tax. If payouts are made to support the operating budget of a for-profit business, then that business is required to treat the payout as taxable income.

In the United States, private grant-making foundations enjoy the same tax-exempt status as endowments. But unlike endowments, such private foundations are subject to minimum payout (spending) requirements, whereby they must distribute a minimum of 5% of their asset value on an annual basis in grants that support their mission. Failing to meet this spending requirement subjects such foundations to 30% tax on undistributed income. Most tax-exempt private foundations also have an excise tax of 2% on their net investment income. In the United Kingdom, charitable organizations do not pay taxes on most of their income and gains if these are used for charitable purposes; however, taxes must be paid on funds that are not used for charitable purposes.

UNIVERSITY ENDOWMENTS: OTHER CONSIDERATIONS 12

☐ discuss the stakeholders in the portfolio, the liabilities, the investment time horizons, and the liquidity needs of different types of institutional investors

Stakeholders of a university endowment include current and future students, alumni, current and future university faculty and administrators, and the larger university community. Each of these stakeholders has a strong interest in seeing the endowment invested prudently. There is potential, however, for tension between increasing spending to meet current needs versus preserving sufficient funds to serve future generations. Endowment boards or investment committees, therefore, need to determine an appropriate balance.

University endowments are generally funded by gifts and donations from alumni. It is common that donors specify the handling and use of their gifts—for example, that only the income portion be spent or that only specific scholarships, programs, or departments benefit. Other gifts may be unrestricted and can be spent for general purposes. Alumni are concerned about current students and faculty and also future generations, so they expect endowment assets to be invested for the long-run. Endowment payouts support the university's operating budget and provide an important source of income. Endowments provide stability and continuity when other revenues sources, such as tuition and government funding, fluctuate. Endowments also allow universities to more readily undertake long-term capital projects, knowing required resources are available to meet those future commitments.

Stakeholders of a university endowment often have representation on the endowment's board or investment committee, including alumni who are investment professionals running or working for financial services organizations.

University Endowments—Liabilities and Investment Horizon

Although most endowments operate on an asset-only basis, their main purpose is to support the university's operating budget based on the principle of intergenerational equity. The investment horizon for endowments is thus perpetuity, and their main objective is to maintain long-term purchasing power. An endowment's liabilities are the future stream of payouts to the university, which are typically codified in an official spending policy. The spending policy serves two important purposes: 1) to ensure intergenerational equity; and 2) to smooth endowment payouts to partially insulate contributions to the university from capital market volatility.

Although the spending policy defines how much of the endowment's assets are paid out annually, several other liability characteristics should be considered when designing an appropriate investment policy, including:

a. What is the university's capacity for fund-raising: How much in gifts and donations are contributed (on average) each year?

b. What percentage of the university's operating budget is supported by the endowment?

c. Balance sheet health: Does the endowment or university have the ability to issue debt?

We first discuss different types of spending policies and then discuss other important liability-related characteristics. Broadly speaking, there are three different types of endowment spending policies:

1. *Constant Growth Rule*: The endowment provides a fixed amount annually to the university, typically adjusted for inflation (the growth rate). The inflation rate is usually based on the Higher Education Price Index (HEPI)[2] in the United States or a more general consumer price index elsewhere, possibly with an additional spread. A shortcoming of constant growth spending rules is that spending does not adjust based on the endowment's value. If the endowment experiences weak (strong) average returns, the spending amount expressed as a percentage of assets may become very high (low). This spending rule is therefore commonly complemented with caps and floors, typically between 4% and 6% of average assets under management (AUM) over one or three years.
2. *Market Value Rule*: The endowment pays a pre-specified percentage (the spending rate) of the moving average of asset values, typically between 4% and 6%. Asset values are usually smoothed using a 3- to 5-year moving average. A disadvantage of this spending rule is that it tends to be pro-cyclical; when markets have performed well (poorly), the overall payout increases (decreases).

2 The HEPI is calculated annually by Commonfund and tracks the most important components in the cost of higher education. More information can be found at https://www.commonfund.org/commonfund-institute/higher-education-price-index-hepi.

3. *Hybrid Rule*: Spending is calculated as a weighted average of the constant growth and market value rules. Commonly referred to as the Yale spending rule, weights can range from 30% to 70%. This spending rule was designed to strike a balance between the shortcomings of the respective spending rules.

All three spending rules can be summarized by the following formula:

Spending Amount in Year $t + 1$

$= w \times$ [Spending Amount in Year $t \times (1 + \text{Inflation Rate})] + (1 - w) \times$ Spending Rate $\times$ Average AUM,

where w denotes the weight put on the prior year's spending amount. When $w = 1$, the formula simplifies to a constant growth rule; when $w = 0$, it simplifies to a market value rule. For any other choice of w ($0 < w < 1$), the formula represents a hybrid spending rule. Most US endowments use a market value spending rule, but some of the larger ones use a hybrid rule. As noted, a market value spending rule is pro-cyclical: This may not be an issue for universities that receive only a small percentage of their operating budgets from their endowment, but this may be more problematic otherwise. The goal of providing intergenerational equity means university endowments aim to maintain their purchasing power. Therefore, endowments target a real rate of return (after inflation) equal to or greater than their spending rates. Given that endowments pay out (on average) between 4% and 6% of assets annually, they typically target a 5% to 5.5% real, long-term rate of return.

Other liability-related factors must be considered when managing an endowment. Universities regularly raise money from donors. Depending on the wealth of their alumni base, such fund-raising activity may be more or less successful. Because of gifts and donations, endowments' net spending rate tends to be lower than the headline spending of 4% to 6% of assets previously discussed. On average, net spending is closer to 2% to 4% of assets. Another important distinction between endowments is how much the university relies on its endowment to support the operating budget. Such support may be less than 5% for some universities, while in other cases, 40% to 50% of the university's operating budget is provided by its endowment. All else equal, endowments that support a smaller percentage of the overall budget should be able to tolerate more market, credit, and liquidity risk. In practice, however, this important distinguishing factor is typically insufficiently incorporated in the design of investment policies. It is common for university endowments to be benchmarked against each other, which creates herding behavior even though the organizations might have very different liability characteristics. A final consideration is the debt issuance capability of the endowment (or university). Some endowments access the public and private debt markets on a regular basis. The capability to access debt markets, especially during periods of market stress, affects the levels of risk and illiquidity endowments can accept in their investments.

University Endowments—Liquidity Needs

The liquidity needs of university endowments are relatively low (compared to foundations). On average, endowments' annual net spending is 2% to 4% of assets, after factoring in gifts and donations. Low liquidity needs combined with long investment horizons allow endowments to accept relatively high short-term volatility in pursuit of superior long-term returns. Consequently, many university endowments have relatively high allocations to equity markets and illiquid private asset classes and small allocations to fixed income. Having significant allocations to illiquid asset classes, such as private equity and private real estate, creates additional liquidity needs to meet annual net capital calls from general partners managing these assets. Finally, to the extent that endowments use derivatives for rebalancing or portable alpha strategies, there may be further liquidity needs—particularly during times of financial market stress—to meet margin calls or to cover higher collateral demands.

13 PRIVATE FOUNDATIONS

Stakeholders of a foundation include the founding family, donors, grant recipients, and the broader community that may benefit indirectly from the foundation's activities. Each has a strong interest in seeing the foundation's assets invested appropriately. As with university endowments, a tension may exist between increasing current grant spending versus preserving sufficient funds to serve future generations of grant recipients. The founding family and donors typically want their donations to support grant recipients in perpetuity. There is a trend, however, toward limited-life foundations as donors seek to maintain control over foundation spending during their lives. Finally, the government (Internal Revenue Service in the United States) may also be a stakeholder because of the favorable tax treatment that foundations enjoy. The government's main concern is that foundations remain engaged strictly in charitable work.

The boards of foundations tend to be different in terms of skill sets than the boards of endowments. University endowments typically have alumni sitting on their boards—people with a special relationship to the university and who may have significant financial market skills (for example, in private equity or hedge funds). Board members for foundations, however, are typically individuals involved with grant making and not necessarily investment professionals. This difference in skill sets may affect the quality of board oversight, the level of delegation of decision making to investment staff, and the quality of investment decisions.

Mission-related investing (also known as "**impact investing**"), which aims to direct a significant portion of assets in excess of annual grants into projects promoting the foundation's mission, is becoming increasingly important. For example, the Ford Foundation has allocated up to US$1.0 billion (more than 8% of assets) over 10 years to investments related to its mission of addressing global inequality. The challenge for foundations is to ensure that mission-related investments generate financial returns commensurate with risks assumed. As typically lower yielding mission-related investments are undertaken at the expense of higher return investment opportunities, portfolio returns (expected and realized) may decline, which could result in foundation assets being spent down sooner and annual grant-making activities being reduced.

Private Foundations—Liabilities and Investment Horizon

In practice, the investment philosophy of private foundations is typically similar to that of university endowments, despite important differences between them in terms of liabilities and liquidity needs. Foundations and endowments both typically have perpetual investment horizons (although, as noted shortly, some foundations may have finite lives) and both invest to maintain purchasing power; however, foundations generally have higher liquidity needs. In the United States, private grant-making foundations are legally required to pay out 5% of assets (on a trailing 12-month basis) plus investment expenses, while university endowments have more-flexible spending rules. In addition, foundations must spend any donations in the year received, known as flow-through (but this is not necessarily the case outside the United States). Foundations typically use a smoothing formula similar to that of university endowments to ensure payouts do not fluctuate with the market volatility of assets. The constant growth spending rule and the hybrid spending rule, discussed previously for university endowments, are rarely used by foundations.

Foundations sometimes issue bonds. The capability to access debt markets, especially during periods of market stress, is positively associated with the levels of investment risk and liquidity risk that foundations can accept in their investments. The Wellcome Foundation (United Kingdom), with a credit rating of AAA, has occasionally issued bonds. For example, in early 2018, it issued £750 million of century bonds (i.e., 100-year maturity) with a coupon of 2.517%.[3] Proceeds from such bonds have been used to support charitable work, and bondholders are repaid by the returns generated on the investment portfolio.

Spending Rate and Investment Expenses of Foundations

Costs of running a foundation are included in the 5% required payout, excluding investment expenses, which means the investment office is considered a cost center. Consequently, the investment office of a foundation will typically be much smaller compared to that of a similar-sized (by AUM) endowment, leading to potentially different investment behavior. For example, many small foundations have limited investment staff and therefore rely on an outsourced CIO model, whereby assets are managed by an external organization that assumes fiduciary duty and takes responsibility for the strategic asset allocation and investments across various asset classes. Although many outsourced CIOs do offer allocations to alternative asset classes, the result of such outsourcing may typically be a heavier allocation to public markets, more-intensive use of passive strategies, and a heavier reliance on beta as a driver of returns.

Many foundations typically receive a one-time gift from the founding family. Some foundations are allowed to raise money on an ongoing basis, but in the US, any such donations must be spent on a flow-through basis. Unlike universities that derive revenues from other sources besides their endowments, such as tuition and research grants, foundations rely almost exclusively on their investment portfolios to support operating budgets. This high dependency has important implications for risk tolerance, and as a result, foundations (on average) have more conservative, more-liquid investment portfolios compared to endowments.

Typically, the original gift must be maintained in perpetuity (principal protection). There is, however, a trend toward **limited-life foundations**, as some founders seek to maintain control of spending while they (or their immediate heirs) are still alive. For example, the Bill and Melinda Gates Foundation is mandated to spend down assets to zero within 30 years of the Gates' death. There is risk—and concern by some founding donors—that as the foundation's leadership changes over time, the mission may move away from the founder's vision. Thus, to minimize this risk, more limited-life foundations are being established. Importantly, a limited-life foundation faces a different investment problem than a perpetual foundation: As the investment horizon of a limited-life foundation shortens, its liquidity needs increase and risk tolerance decreases.

Real-Life Example of a Limited-Life Foundation

The Atlantic Philanthropies, set up by Chuck Feeney in 1982, is among the largest limited-life foundations to complete its grant-making activities. After giving a total of US$8 billion over 35 years to human rights, health care, and education

3 In late 2017, Oxford University issued a century bond with the same size and similar coupon.

causes, the last grant was made in 2016 and the Atlantic Philanthropies expects to close in 2020. All stakeholders have been informed of the spend-down process and critical challenges are being addressed, including: 1) choosing who will oversee the portfolio wind-down process with staff departing for other employment opportunities; and 2) deciding how best to liquidate private investments. As a limited-life foundation gives away its assets, liquidity needs increase and risk tolerance decreases, resulting in lower financial returns and thus limiting the size of the grants that can be made. The de-risking process requires a very "hands-on" investment approach and includes liquidating private portfolios by reducing/stopping commitments, selling private portfolios in the secondary markets, and reinvesting distributions. This becomes increasingly challenging as talented investment staff depart the organization. Actions taken and lessons learned by The Atlantic Philanthropies provide a great case study for other limited-life foundations.

Private Foundations—Liquidity Needs

The liquidity needs of foundations are relatively low but still higher than those of university endowments. US foundations are legally required to spend 5% of assets or face a tax penalty. They must set aside monies to pay one-year grants and to meet annual installments for longer-term (typically two- to five-year) grants. Having a significant allocation to such relatively illiquid asset classes as private equity and private real estate creates additional liquidity needs to meet general partners' annual net capital calls. Also, derivatives use for such activities as portfolio rebalancing or implementing portable alpha strategies may result in added liquidity demands to meet increased margin calls or to cover higher collateral demands (especially during times of financial market stress).

Exhibit 13 presents a summary comparison of foundations and endowments.

Exhibit 13: Comparison Between Private US Foundations and US University Endowments

	US Foundation	US University Endowment
Purpose	Grant-making for social, educational, and charitable purposes; principal preservation focus.	General support of institution or restricted support; principal preservation focus.
Stakeholders	Founding family, donors, grant recipients, and broader community that may benefit from foundation's activities.	Current/future students, alumni, university faculty and administration, and the larger university community.
Liabilities/Spending	Legally mandated to spend 5% of assets + investment expenses + 100% of donations (flow-through).	Flexible spending rules (headline spending rate between 4% and 6% of assets) with smoothing.
Other liability considerations	Future gifts and donations, or just one-time gift?	Gifts and donations, percentage of operating budget supported by endowment, and ability to issue debt.
Investment time horizon	Very long-term/perpetual (except limited-life foundations).	Perpetual
Risk	High risk tolerance with some short-term liquidity needs.	High risk tolerance with low liquidity needs.
Liquidity needs	Annual net spending is at least 5% of assets.	Annual net spending is typically 2% to 4% of assets, after alumni gifts and donations.

UNIVERSITY ENDOWMENTS: INVESTMENT OBJECTIVES AND ASSET ALLOCATION

14

- [ ] evaluate the investment policy statement of an institutional investor
- [ ] evaluate the investment portfolio of a private DB plan, sovereign wealth fund, university endowment, and private foundation

We now consider the investment objectives and investment policy statement for university endowments and the investment objectives of private foundations.

University Endowments

A university endowment's mission is to maintain the purchasing power of the assets into perpetuity while achieving investment returns sufficient to sustain the level of spending necessary to support the university budget. For a university endowment, investment policy and spending policy are intertwined, so the IPS should cover spending policy. As discussed previously, endowments use different spending rules. In general, endowments target a spending rate of about 5% of (average) assets. The effective spending rate will, however, be reduced after accounting for gifts and donations. An endowment's primary investment objective is typically to achieve a total real rate of return (after inflation) of X% with an expected volatility of Y% over the long term (K years). A common target for X% is 5%, with inflation being measured using the Higher Education Price Index (HEPI), to be achieved over 3 to 5 years (i.e., $K = 3$ or 5). The expected volatility of returns, Y%, is typically in the range of 10% to 15% annually. Note that the target rate of return may also be expressed as a nominal (as opposed to real) return.

Endowments sometimes have secondary and tertiary investment objectives. A secondary objective might be to outperform the long-term policy benchmark. A third objective might be to outperform a set of pre-defined peers (e.g., outperform the average of the 20 largest university endowments). Peer comparison can lead to herding behavior and be detrimental to long-term success if the focus moves away from managing investments based on each organization's unique liability characteristics to exploit their own comparative advantages. To achieve their objectives, endowments invest in a broad range of asset classes, including fixed income, public equities, hedge fund strategies, private equity, private real estate, and natural resources (e.g. energy and timber). Given that endowments aim to maintain the purchasing power of their assets, they tend to have significant allocations to real assets that are expected to generate returns commensurate with inflation.

The following box provides two examples of investment objectives found in IPSs for real-life endowments.

Investment Objectives of University Endowments

Oxford University Endowment: *"The specific investment objective of the Oxford Endowment Fund is to grow our investors' capital by an average of 5% per annum in real terms, and to achieve this at a lower volatility than would be experienced by investing solely in the public equity markets."*

Source: Oxford Endowment Fund, www.ouem.co.uk/the-oxford-endowment-fund/.

Note: The Oxford Endowment Fund defines its investors as the University of Oxford, including 23 of its colleges and five associated foundations and trusts.

Massachusetts Institute of Technology Endowment: *"Our primary long-term goal is to generate sufficient investment returns to maintain the purchasing power of the endowment after inflation and after MIT's annual spending. Assuming inflation will average around 3% over the long-term and MIT's spending rate will average around 5%, we need to earn approximately 8% to meet this goal. As a secondary check on the quality of our performance, we compare our returns to other endowments and to passive benchmark alternatives."*

Source: www.mitimco.org/wp-content/uploads/2017/03/MITIMCo-Alumni-Letter.pdf.

One of the lessons from the 2007–2009 global financial crisis is that liquidity risk must be managed carefully, particularly for institutions that invest heavily in illiquid assets. Most endowments now engage in detailed cash flow modeling for the illiquid portions of their portfolios, and some use a liquidity risk band as part of their overall risk profile. The liquidity risk band is defined as total NAV allocated to illiquid investments plus uncalled commitments to total fund AUM. If the liquidity band is violated (i.e., when the total allocation to illiquid investments exceeds a pre-specified upper bound), this may trigger a reduction (or even a stoppage) of commitments or possibly a sale of some illiquid investments in secondary markets to bring the overall illiquid allocation back to within the liquidity risk band.

EXAMPLE 5

Investment Objectives of the Ivy University Endowment

The hypothetical Ivy University Endowment was established in 1901 by Ivy University and supports up to 40% of the university's operating budget. Historically, the endowment has invested in a traditional 20% public US equities and 80% US Treasury portfolio, entirely implemented through passive investment vehicles. The investment staff at the endowment is relatively small. With the appointment of a new chief investment officer, the investment policy is being reviewed. Endowment assets are US$250 million, and the endowment has an annual spending policy of paying out 5% of the 3-year rolling asset value to the university.

An investment consultant hired by the new CIO to assist with the investment policy review has provided the following 10-year (nominal) expected return assumptions for various asset classes: US equities: 7%, Non-US equities: 8%, US Treasuries: 2%, hedge funds: 5%, and private equity: 10%. Additionally, the investment consultant believes the endowment could generate an extra 50 bps per year in alpha from active management in equities. Expected inflation for the next ten years is 2% annually.

1. Draft the investment objectives section of the IPS of the Ivy University Endowment.

Solution:

The mission of the Ivy University Endowment is to maintain purchasing power of its assets while financing up to 40% of Ivy University's operating budgeting in perpetuity. The investment objective, consistent with this mission, is to achieve a total real rate of return over the Higher Education Price Index (HEPI) of at least 5% with a reasonable level of risk; the volatility of returns should not to exceed 15% annually.

2. Discuss whether the current investment policy is appropriate given the investment objectives of Ivy University Endowment.

Solution:

Given the expected returns provided by the consultant, a portfolio of 80% fixed income and 20% public equities, invested passively, is expected to provide a nominal expected return of 3% per year (= 0.8 × 2% + 0.2 × 7%). Given, expected inflation of 2%, this implies a 1% real rate of return, which falls well short of the 5% spending rate and the stated objective of a 5% real rate of return. The endowment will see its purchasing power deteriorate over time if it continues with its current asset mix and spending rate.

3. What decisions could the CIO and board of the Ivy University Endowment take to align the investment policy and the spending policy?

Solution:

The CIO and board could either change the investment policy by adopting an asset mix that has a more reasonable probability of achieving a 5% real rate of return (an asset allocation including non-US equities and private equity); they could change the spending rate to more accurately reflect the expected real rate of return of the current investment policy; or the new CIO may want to recommend a combination of both.

Below is an example of a university endowment Investment Policy Statement. In this case the university endowment has clearly articulated primary and secondary investment objectives.

University Endowment Investment Policy Statement

A. Introduction

The hypothetical Ivy University Endowment Fund (the "Endowment") has been established to fund scholarships, fellowships, faculty salaries, programs, activities, and facilities designed to promote and advance the mission of Ivy University (the "University"). This investment policy statement (IPS) is established by the Investment Committee of the Board of Trustees (the "IC") for the guidance of the IC, the Investment Office, the Endowment's investment managers, and other fiduciaries in the course of investing the monies of the Endowment. This IPS establishes policies and procedures for the administration and investment of the Endowment's assets. This document formally defines the goals, objectives, and guidelines of the Endowment's investment program.

B. Mission and Investment Objectives

The Endowment provides financial support for the operations of the University. Investment and spending policies are designed to balance the current goals of the University with its future needs, in order to achieve parity in supporting both current and future generations of Ivy students. The goal for the Endowment is to provide a real total return that preserves the purchasing power of the Endowment's assets while generating an income stream to support the academic activities of the University.

The primary investment objective of the Endowment is to earn an average annual real total return (net of portfolio management fees) of at least 5% per year over the long term (rolling five-year periods), within prudent levels of risk. Attainment of this objective will be sufficient to maintain, in real terms, the purchasing power of the Endowment's assets and support the defined spending policy.

A secondary investment objective is to outperform, over the long term, a blended custom benchmark based on a current asset allocation policy of: 30% MSCI World Index, 20% Cambridge Associates LLC US Private Equity Index, 10% NCREIF Property Index, 10% Consumer Price Index for All Urban Consumers (annualized CPI-U) + 5%, 20% HFRI Fund of Funds Index, and 10% Citigroup US Treasury Index.

C. Spending Policy

The Endowment's spending policy was developed to meet several objectives, namely to: (a) provide a sustainable level of income to support current operations, (b) provide year-to-year budget stability, and (c) meet intergenerational needs by protecting the future purchasing power of the Endowment against the impact of inflation. Under this policy, spending for a given year equals 80% of spending in the previous year, adjusted for inflation (CPI within a range of 0% and 6%), plus 20% of the long-term spending rate (5.0%) applied to the 12-quarter rolling average of market values. This spending policy has two implications. First, by incorporating the previous year's spending, the policy eliminates large fluctuations and so enables the University to plan for operating budget needs. Second, by adjusting spending toward a long-term rate of 5.0%, the policy ensures that spending levels will be sensitive to fluctuating market value levels, thereby providing stability in long-term purchasing power.

D. Asset Allocation Policy, Allowable Ranges, and Benchmarks

The single most important investment decision is the allocation of the Endowment to various asset classes. The primary objective of the Endowment's asset allocation policy is to provide a strategic mix of asset classes that produces the highest expected investment return within a prudent risk framework. To achieve this, the Endowment will allocate among several asset classes with a bias toward equity and equity-like investments caused by their higher long-term return expectations. Other asset classes may be added to the Endowment to enhance returns, reduce volatility through diversification, and/or offer a broader investment opportunity set.

To ensure broad diversification among the major categories of investments, the Endowment has adopted the following capital allocation policy ranges for each asset class within the overall portfolio set forth in the Annex. This asset allocation framework is reviewed annually by the IC, but because of the long-term nature of the Endowment, changes to the framework are expected to be infrequent:

Asset Class	Policy Range	Benchmark
Global equity	20%–40%	MSCI World Index
Private equity & venture capital	15%–25%	Cambridge Associates LLC US Private Equity Index
Private real estate	5%–15%	NCREIF Property Index

Asset Class	Policy Range	Benchmark
Real assets	5%–15%	Consumer Price Index for All Urban Consumers (annualized CPI-U) + 5%
Absolute return strategies	15%–25%	HFRI Fund of Funds Index
Fixed income & cash	5%–15%	Citigroup US Treasury Index

The following core investment principles provide the foundation for the asset allocation policy:

- Equity dominance: Equities are expected to be the highest-performing asset class over the long term and thus will dominate the portfolio.
- Illiquid assets: In general, private illiquid investments are expected to outperform more-liquid public investments by exploiting market inefficiencies.
- Global orientation: The Endowment will consider the broadest possible set of investment opportunities in its search for attractive risk/return profiles.
- Diversification: Thoughtful diversification within and between asset classes by region, sector, and economic source of return can lower volatility and raise compound returns over the long term.

E. Rebalancing

The IPS establishes the long-term asset allocation targets for the endowment and policy ranges for the various asset classes approved by the IC. The role of the capital allocation ranges is to allow for short-term fluctuations caused by market volatility or near-term cash flows, to recognize the flexibility required in managing private investments, and to provide limits for tactical investing. The IC will rely on investment staff to determine allocations within the stated ranges and to regularly manage actual asset class allocations to be within the ranges where possible. In addition, the IC will review actual asset allocations relative to this asset allocation framework at each quarterly meeting.

F. Reporting

The Investment Team, with the oversight of management, must provide adequate reporting to the Board of Trustees, the IC, and other stakeholders. The reporting structure should include the following:

- Performance measurement and attribution for the quarter and trailing periods for the portfolio both in absolute terms and relative to the established benchmarks
- Asset allocation of the total portfolio
- Market value of the total portfolio

Asset Allocation

We now consider asset allocation, investment portfolios, and investment performance of university endowments. We follow with a similar discussion focusing on private foundations.

University Endowments

Most large endowments follow the endowment investment model and rely heavily on alternative investments to achieve their long-term investment objectives. This approach is not without risks. During the global financial crisis, several large endowments faced significant liquidity challenges and were forced to either sell portions of their private investment portfolios in the secondary markets, reduce payouts to their universities, or issue bonds to bridge their liquidity needs. The rapid post-crisis recovery arguably bailed out many endowments, but had the crisis lasted longer, the pain would have been substantially worse. David Swensen, the longtime CIO of the Yale Endowment, and his colleagues have regularly warned against a blanket application of the endowment model. Yale and some of the other large endowments have enjoyed a first-mover advantage in their private investments, and their alumni networks have provided access to investment opportunities that may not be as easily accessible to other institutions.

Exhibit 14 shows the average asset allocation for US endowments by size at the end of June 2020 using data from a study in which more than 800 colleges and universities participated. Here alternatives include private equity and venture capital, hedge funds and other marketable alternative strategies, private real estate, energy and natural resources (e.g., oil, gas, timber, commodities, and managed futures), and distressed debt.

These data reveal several important points. First, the larger endowments have a significantly higher allocation to alternatives. Larger endowments have achieved better returns over the past 10 years, and their larger allocation to alternatives has played an important role. Second, the larger endowments do not face the "home bias" issue that smaller endowments seem to suffer. The allocation of smaller endowments to US equities is significantly larger than their allocation to non-US equities. Finally, the larger endowments hold a significantly smaller amount of their assets in fixed-income securities. This might pose a challenge during liquidity crises—such as in the 2007–2009 global financial crisis when some larger endowments struggling to meet their liquidity needs pressured managers of private investment funds to delay any calls (i.e., demands) for additional capital. Some universities also issued bonds during the crisis to help relieve the liquidity pressures faced by their endowments.

Exhibit 14: Average Asset Allocation for US University Endowments, as of June 2020 [note: x-axis is in US$ and y-axis is Allocation (%)]

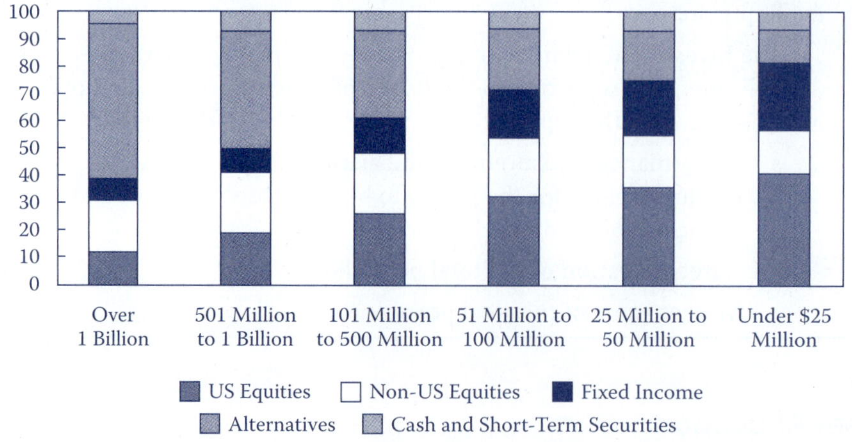

Source: TIAA and the National Association of College and University Business Officers (NACUBO), *2020 NACUBO–TIAA Study of Endowments*.

Exhibit 15 shows the average asset allocation at the end of June 2005 and June 2017 for university endowments of more than US$1 billion in size. During this period, the largest endowments significantly increased their allocation to alternatives from 39% to 60%. This increased allocation to alternatives has come at the expense of public equities (reduced from 45% to 30%) and fixed income (reduced from 14% to 11%).

Exhibit 15: Average Asset Allocation for the Largest (> US$1 billion) US Endowments: FY2005 versus FY2020 [note: y-axis is Allocation (%)]

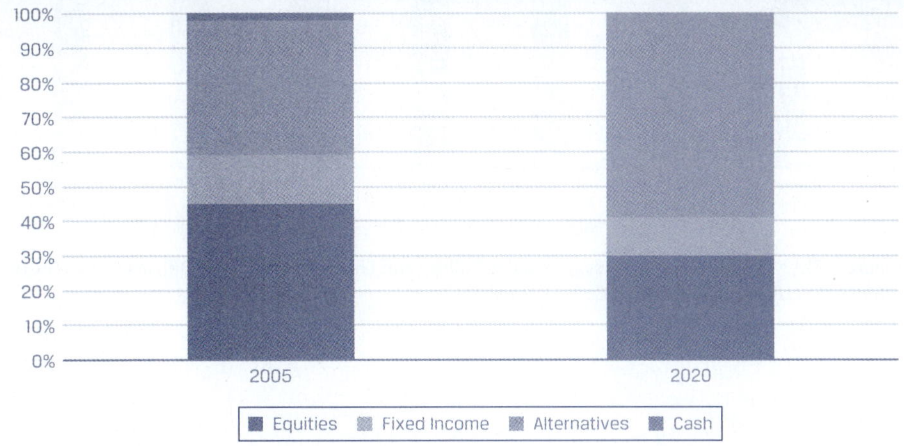

Sources: Commonfund and the National Association of College and University Business Officers (NACUBO), *2005 NACUBO–Commonfund Study of Endowments* and TIAA and the NACUBO, *2020 NACUBO–TIAA Study of Endowments.*

Given asset allocations that are tilted toward alternative investments, how have endowments fared over the past 10 years? Exhibit 16 shows the average annual 10-year return (net of fees) for US endowments by size as of end-June 2020. The mean US Consumer Price Index was about 1.8% over the same period, while the mean Higher Education Price Index (HEPI) was 2.0%. Note: Larger endowments have generally been able to generate higher returns during this period. Endowments of more than US$1 billion have generated anywhere between 50 bps to 60 bps higher returns (annually) compared to the smaller endowments (with less than US$500 million). This difference compounds to a significant gap over a 10-year period. These higher returns have allowed the larger endowments to pay out a larger part of their assets to support their universities. It is worth noting that the 10-year period ending 30 June 2020 is time-period specific. A different 10-year period might lead to a different conclusion. However, this 10-year period is reasonably representative of long-term asset class returns because capital markets have generally rewarded growth assets over the period.

Exhibit 16: Average Annual 10-Year Nominal Returns for US University Endowments as of June 2020 [note: x-axis is in US$ and y-axis is Nominal Return (%)]

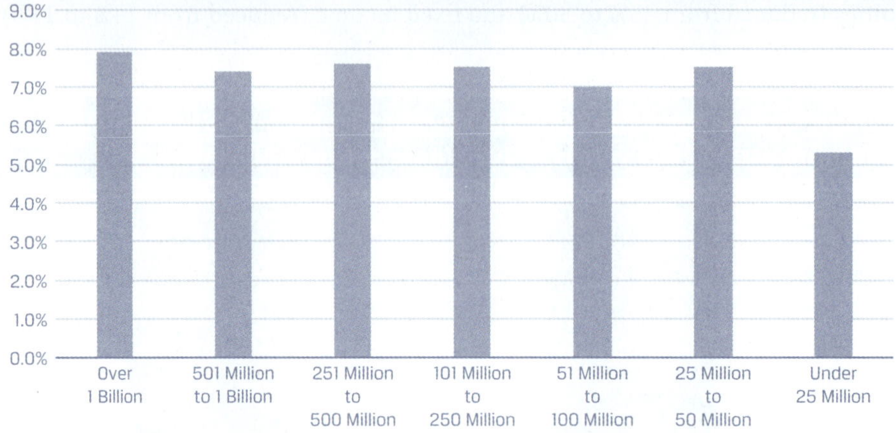

Source: TIAA and the National Association of College and University Business Officers (NACUBO), *2020 NACUBO–TIAA Study of Endowments.*

EXAMPLE 6

Investment Portfolio of the Ivy University Endowment

The hypothetical Ivy University Endowment was established in 1901 and supports Ivy University. The endowment supports about 40% of the university's operating budget. Historically, the endowment has invested in a traditional 20% public US equities, 80% US Treasury portfolio, and it is entirely implemented through passive investment vehicles. The investment staff at the endowment is relatively small. With the appointment of a new chief investment officer, the investment policy is being reviewed. Endowment assets are US$250 million, and the endowment has a spending policy of paying out 5% of the 3-year rolling asset value to the university.

The new CIO has engaged an investment consultant to assist her with the investment policy review. The investment consultant has provided the following 10-year (nominal) expected return assumptions for various asset classes: US equities: 7%, Non-US equities: 8%, US Treasuries: 2%, hedge funds: 5%, private equity: 10%. In addition, the investment consultant believes that the endowment could generate an additional 50 bps in alpha from active management in equities. Expected inflation for the next 10 years is 2%.

The new CIO was at a previous endowment that invested heavily in private investments and hedge funds and recommends a change in the investment policy to the board of Ivy University Endowment. She recommends investing 30% in private equity, 30% in hedge funds, 30% in public equities (15% US and 15% non-US with *active* management), and 10% in fixed income. This mix would have an expected real return of 5.1% based on the expected return assumptions provided by the investment consultant.

1. Given the expected return assumptions from the investment consultant, provide an asset mix that would be more appropriate for Ivy University Endowment?

Solution:

To achieve a 5% real rate of return, the endowment will need to accept significantly more equity risk, diversify its assets internationally, allocate some of its assets to hedge funds and private equity, and engage in active management. There are several possible combinations that could result in a portfolio with a 5% expected real rate of return. Here are two possible asset mixes:

I: 40% in US equities with active management (7.5% expected return), 40% in non-US equities with active management (8.5% expected return), 10% in US Treasuries (2% expected return), 10% in hedge funds (5% expected return). This asset mix would result in an expected nominal return of 7.1% or an expected real return of 5.1%.

II: 50% in US equities with passive management (7% expected return), 30% in non-US equities with active management (8.5% expected return), 10% in US Treasuries (2% expected return), 10% in private equity (10% expected return). This asset mix would result in an expected nominal return of 7.25% or an expected real return of 5.25%.

2. Should the board approve the new CIO's recommendation? Provide your reasoning.

Solution:

The board should reject the CIO's recommendation. This is a very significant departure from the current practice. The size of the investment team is small, and they have no prior experience in managing hedge fund and private equity portfolios (except for the new CIO). Additionally, given the size of the endowment, it is unlikely to have access to top quartile managers in the hedge fund and private equity spaces. The CIO should explain why the recommended asset mix with 60% in alternatives is preferable over asset mixes that deliver the same or higher expected real return (such as I and II in Solution 1).

PRIVATE FOUNDATIONS: INVESTMENT OBJECTIVES AND ASSET ALLOCATION 15

- [ ] evaluate the investment policy statement of an institutional investor
- [ ] evaluate the investment portfolio of a private DB plan, sovereign wealth fund, university endowment, and private foundation

As discussed previously, private foundations in the United States are legally required to pay out a minimum of 5% of assets annually to be eligible for tax-exempt status. Foundations strive to be capable of making grants that support their overall missions in perpetuity while meeting the minimum 5% payout requirement. The primary investment objective for foundations is typically to generate a total real return over consumer price inflation of 5%, plus investment expenses, with a reasonable expected volatility (approximately 10%–15% annual standard deviation) over a 3- to 5-year period. A secondary investment objective may include outperforming the policy benchmark with a specified tracking error budget. Monte Carlo-based modeling for generating expected returns and risk distributions as well as liquidity modeling and asset stress testing mentioned earlier for DB pension plans are also used by management and consultants to develop cogent investment objectives and policies for foundations and endowments. Foundations, like endowments, invest in a broad range of asset classes, including fixed income, public equities, hedge fund strategies, and private equity.

The following box provides two real-life examples of investment objectives for foundations.

Investment Objectives for Private Foundations

Wellcome Trust (UK):

"Our overall investment objective is to generate 4.5% real return over the long term. This is to provide for real increases in annual expenditure while preserving the Trust's capital base to balance the needs of current and future beneficiaries. We use this absolute return strategy because it aligns asset allocation with funding requirements and provides a competitive framework in which to judge individual investments."

Note: Wellcome Trust's IPS mentions that the real return is based on an average of US and UK consumer price inflation.

Source: Wellcome Trust, wellcome.ac.uk/about-us/investments.

Robert Wood Johnson Foundation:

"The Robert Wood Johnson Foundation is working to improve the health and well-being of everyone in America. Reflecting our Guiding Principles, 'we act as good stewards of private resources, using them to advance the public's interest with a focus on helping the most vulnerable.'... Achieving comprehensive and meaningful change in health and health care will require sustained attention over many years to come. The Foundation therefore seeks to earn an investment return that, over time, equals or exceeds the sum of its annual spending, as a percentage of the Foundation's assets plus the rate of inflation. This balance of investment return and spending is designed to spread risk and promote a steady, stable flow of support for our grantees."

Source: Robert Wood Johnson Foundation, www.rwjf.org/en/about-rwjf/financials.html.

The IPS of a private foundation is not very different from that of a university endowment and follows a similar format as outlined in the previous section. The mission statement would be framed slightly differently, but the IPS would cover the same elements.

Private Foundations

Foundations tend to follow a similar investment approach compared to endowments, despite important differences in their liability structures. Two of the most notable differences between foundations and endowments that should have a bearing on their asset allocation are that:

1. foundations support the entire budget of their organization, while universities have significant other sources of financing available besides the endowment; and
2. foundations (in the United States) are mandated to pay out at least 5% of their assets to maintain tax-exempt status and typically receive no additional inflows in the form of gifts and donations (or, if there are gifts/donations, these need to be spent in the same year that they are received and do not count against the 5% mandated payout), whereas university endowments typically have a net payout of less than 5%.

Exhibit 17 shows the average asset allocations for US foundations by size and type at year-end 2016. The underlying data cover 203 institutions (123 private foundations and 80 community foundations). Here, alternative investments include private equity and venture capital, hedge funds and other marketable alternative strategies, private real estate, energy and natural resources, and distressed debt.

Exhibit 17: Average Asset Allocation for US Foundations as of Year-End 2016 [note: x-axis is in US$ and y-axis is Allocation (%)]

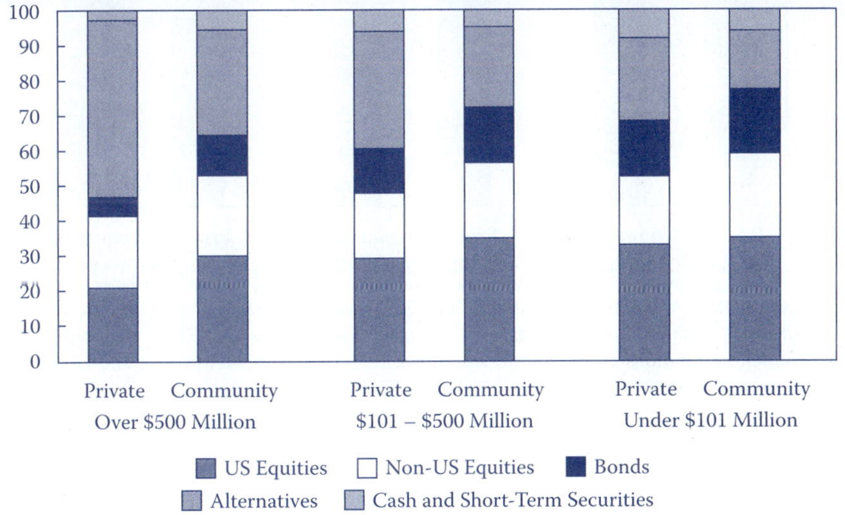

Source: Council on Foundations–Commonfund, *2016 Council on Foundations–Commonfund Study of Investment of Endowments for Private and Community Foundations (CCSF)*: www.cof.org/content/2016-council-foundations-commonfund-study-investment-endowments-private-and-community.

These data highlight several key points. The larger foundations have a significantly higher allocation to alternatives, and private foundations have higher allocations to alternatives compared to community foundations. The largest private foundations (more than US$500 million) have about half of their assets invested in alternatives. Although not shown, the largest private and community foundations have similar allocations to marketable alternatives (hedge funds), but the private foundations have significantly higher allocations to the higher-return-generating, illiquid alternatives—such as private equity, venture capital, private real estate, and distressed debt. Smaller foundations seem generally to have a higher allocation to US equities compared to the larger foundations. Finally, the larger private foundations hold a smaller amount of their assets in fixed-income securities.

Foundations must generate real (net of fee) returns above 5% to maintain their purchasing power. Exhibit 18 shows that over the 10-year period to year-end 2016 (when US CPI averaged 1.8%), US foundations have fallen well short of this minimum target. As a result, their purchasing power has deteriorated. However, during this period larger private foundations (more than US$500 million) have been able to generate higher returns—anywhere between 10 bps to 60 bps higher returns (annually)—compared to medium/small private foundations. Their larger allocation to alternatives likely played a key role in this outperformance. Note that the effective spending rate in 2016 was 5.8% for private foundations.

Exhibit 18: Average Annual 10-Year Nominal Return for US Foundations as of Year-End 2016 [note: x-axis is in US$ and y-axis is Nominal Return (%)]

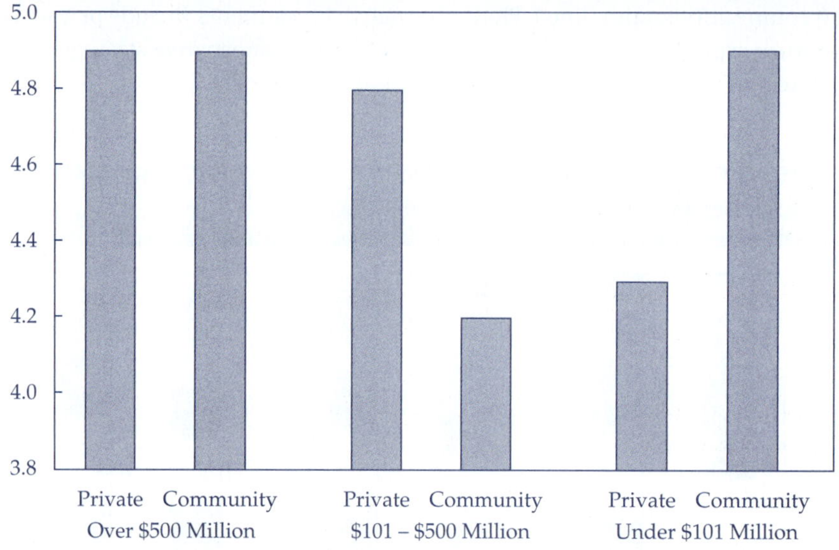

Source: Council on Foundations–Commonfund, *2016 Council on Foundations–Commonfund Study of Investment of Endowments for Private and Community Foundations (CCSF)*: www.cof.org/content/2016-council-foundations-commonfund-study-investment-endowments-private-and-community.

Real-Life Case Study: Wellcome Trust (UK)

Wellcome Trust ("the Trust") provides a historical example of how a foundation transformed its investment approach and asset allocation and, in the process, significantly improved its investment performance. The Wellcome Trust was founded in 1936 and managed about £23 billion in its investment portfolio (as of end-September 2017). The investment portfolio supported all of the charitable work of the Trust, which provides funding for scientific and medical research to improve health worldwide. During FY2016–17, charitable grants were more than £1 billion.

Between 1936 and 1986, the Trust was the sole owner of Burroughs Wellcome, the pharmaceutical company founded by Henry Wellcome. In 1986, the Trust began selling shares in the company and used the proceeds to diversify its assets. Over the two decades leading up to 2017, the portfolio generated an average annual (nominal) return of 14%. The overall investment objective was to generate a 4.5% real return over the long term. The Trust used to target a payout rate of 4.7% of the weighted average value of the portfolio over the previous three years. Historically, this resulted in an average annual payout of 4.3%.

Daniel Truell joined the Trust as CIO in 2005 and initiated radical changes to its investment approach and asset mix, shifting from short-term, liquid, and low-risk assets to longer-term, less-liquid, and higher risk assets. The most notable changes were an increase in the allocation to private equity (including buyout and venture capital funds) and hedge funds as well as reduced allocations to public equities and cash. In addition to radically changing its allocations, the decision was made to concentrate assets with fewer managers and in fewer, higher quality investments, such that by 2017 less than 100 investments represented nearly 85% of the portfolio's value. The Trust also shifted to more direct investments, and active management in public equities was brought predominantly in-house and conducted by an investment team of more than 30 professionals.

At end-September 2017, the Trust's investment portfolio consisted of 53% in public equities, 9% in hedge funds, 24% in private equity, 9% in property and infrastructure, 1% in commodity futures and options, and 4% in cash. The Trust has issued bonds totaling £2 billion—representing about 8% of total assets. Proceeds from the bond issuance are used for investments.

In 2017, the Trust adopted a new approach to determine how much to fund its charitable activities. According to the October 2017 IPS, the Trust "*targets an annual real cash spend in the Primary Fund (based on UK CPI) of £900 million in 2017 prices. This level of spending will be reviewed in 2022, or earlier in the event of declines in the investment portfolio below £20 billion in 2017 prices.*"

The Trust managed risk by ongoing monitoring of the following key risk factors: 1) 95% value-at-risk at a one-year horizon (if more than 20%, then this is highlighted to the Investment Committee), 2) foreign currency exposure (if more than 85%, then this is highlighted to the Investment Committee), 3) forecast of cash levels (unencumbered cash should exceed 2% of gross assets within a 5-year forecast period), and 4) estimated equity beta for the portfolio should be in the range of 0.4 to 0.8.

Sources: 1. Wellcome Trust, "Investment Policy" (October 2017): https://wellcome.ac.uk/sites/default/files/investment-policy-october-2017.pdf. 2. Wellcome Trust, *Annual Report and Financial Statements 2016* (https://wellcome.ac.uk/sites/default/files/WellcomeTrustAnnualReportFinancialStatements_160930.pdf). 3. Wellcome Trust, Annual Report and Financial Statements 2017 (https://wellcome.ac.uk/sites/default/files/wellcome-trust-annual-report-and-financial-statements-2017.pdf). 4. World Economic Forum, "Alternative Investments 2020: The Future of Alternative Investments" (2015). 5. Steve Johnson, "Uncovering Little Investment Gems among the Shrunken Heads," *Financial Times* (12 April 2014): www.ft.com/content/c49bb40c-be63-11e3-b44a-00144feabdc0.

BANKS AND INSURERS

16

This section focuses on institutional investors that are also financial intermediaries, namely banks and insurance companies.

Banks

Banks are financial intermediaries that take deposits, lend money, safeguard assets, execute transactions in securities and cash, act as counterparties in derivatives transactions, provide advisory services, and invest in securities. The universe of banks is quite large and diverse, ranging from small community banks to global diversified financial services institutions. A precise estimate of total worldwide banking assets is difficult to obtain; nevertheless, using publicly available data from such sources as the Bank for International Settlements (BIS), Reuters, and individual balance sheets for the largest public banks, an estimate of more than US$100 trillion seems reasonable.[4] An order-of-magnitude estimate for bank equity capitalization works out to US$7 trillion. Our focus here is on the largest, most globally important banks—the two to three dozen banks that account for the great majority of international commercial bank assets and liabilities. Exhibit 19 shows some of these banks, all of which are designated as global systemically important banks by the Financial Stability Board, an international body that monitors the global financial system.

Exhibit 19: Select Large Global Banks

Bank	Country/Region
Industrial & Commercial Bank of China	China
China Construction Bank Corp.	China
Agricultural Bank of China	China
Bank of China	China
HSBC Holdings Plc	Hong Kong SAR/United Kingdom
JPMorgan Chase & Co.	United States
Wells Fargo	United States
Mitsubishi UFJ Financial Group	Japan
Bank of America	United States
CitiGroup	United States

Source: Marie Kemplay, "Top 1000 World Banks 2021," *The Banker*, https://top1000worldbanks.com/ (20 October 2021).

Insurers

The universe of insurance companies can be divided into two broad categories:

- Life insurers
- Property and casualty (P&C) insurers

According to the OECD (Organisation for Economic Co-Operation and Development) data on 35 large countries (ex-China and India), aggregate direct-insurance assets for both types of insurers had combined totals of more than US$22 trillion, with equity capitalization of more than US$2.2 trillion.[5]

4 Inter-company and cross-border transactions, non-contemporaneous reporting dates, differing accounting treatment (IFRS vs. GAAP, for example), and currency exchange rate conversions are inescapable complications.

5 OECD (2016).

The life insurance product set includes traditional whole and term insurance, variable life insurance and annuity products, as well as health insurance. The P&C product suite encompasses insurance against a wide range of perils—covering commercial property and liability, homeowner's property and liability, and automotive as well as such multiple specialty coverage lines as marine, surety, and workers' compensation. Exhibit 20 lists some of the largest global insurance companies.

Exhibit 20: Select Large Global Insurance Companies

Entity	Country/Region
AXA	France
Zurich Insurance Group	Switzerland
China Life Insurance	China
Ping An Insurance	China
Berkshire Hathaway	United States
Prudential plc	United Kingdom
Nippon Life Insurance	Japan
Munich Re Group	Germany
Assicurazioni Generali S.p.A.	Italy
Japan Post Holding Co., Ltd.	Japan
Allianz SE	Germany

Source: "Commercial Insurance," Insurance Information Institute, www.iii.org/publications/commercial-insurance/rankings (accessed 20 October 2021).

External Constraints Affecting Investment

The legal and regulatory environments, as well as tax and accounting constraints, faced by banks and insurers are complex and may vary according to the national and local jurisdictions in which these institutional investors do business. In this section, we take a high-level view of some of the major legal and regulatory constraints within which banks and insurers must operate. In the following section, we consider tax and accounting constraints that affect investing by banks and insurers.

Legal and Regulatory Constraints

For banks and insurance companies, the liabilities to depositors, the claims of policyholders, and the amounts due to creditors are clearly and contractually defined. This is different from the other types of institutions discussed previously where there typically can be a great deal of discretion in the timing and amounts due and paid to stakeholders. Furthermore, banks and insurance companies carry out important functions with respect to the underlying economies in which they operate. These include facilitation of individual and commercial payments, extensions of credit, safeguarding of assets, and transfers of risk—to name the more important. The activities of companies in the financial industry not only are deeply intertwined with the non-financial, or *real*, economy, but their activities also are deeply intertwined with each other. Thus, a disturbance in the operation of individual banks and insurance companies can spread through the entire financial industry with great speed and with compounding damage; significant adverse effects can easily overflow into the real economy. Such negatives can include depositor runs on a banking system, credit crunches whereby companies or governments cannot obtain funding for maintaining operations, or the failure of insurance companies that undermine the viability of large sectors of the economy, such as residential housing or the health care markets. Consequently, banking and insurance regulators in most jurisdictions are intensely focused on capital adequacy, liquidity, and leverage to mitigate systemic or contagion risk.

Banks and insurance companies are primarily regulated at national and state levels and are increasingly overseen by supranational regulatory and advisory bodies. The need to regulate banks and insurance companies at high, rather than local, levels stems from the fact that financial institutions are mainly large and spread across many local and national jurisdictions. At its most essential, the regulation of financial institutions centers on making sure banks and insurance companies have adequate capitalization to absorb losses rather than allowing losses to be borne by the rest of the financial system or the real economy—including depositors, insurance policyholders, creditors, or taxpayers.

Lowering the risk of assets through regulation is the first way to lower the potential strains on bank and insurance company capitalization. This can be through requirements for diversification, asset quality (including adequate reserve provisioning for credit, market, and operational risk losses) and liquidity maintenance. Likewise, setting requirements on liabilities can lower potential stress on bank and insurance capital resources. Such regulation of liabilities may include requirements for funding sources to be diversified over time and among different groups of depositors and debtholders. In the case of insurance companies, potential losses from liabilities can be regulated through rules limiting the size and concentration of potential policy claims. In addition to limiting potential losses from assets and liabilities—or from other operational risks—regulators may mandate certain minimum required capitalization.

Turning to insurers, the US insurance industry is regulated by individual states, each having its own administrative agency; the federal government does not play a major role in oversight. The National Association of Insurance Commissioners (NAIC), of which every state is a member, provides a forum for industry issues and sets accounting policies and financial reporting standards for the industry. In Europe, regulators have developed the Solvency II framework to standardize insurance regulation across member states.

The size and diversity of financial institutions result from powerful economies of scale. These economies of scale arise because most activities of banks and insurance companies (such as extension of credit, underwriting health or property risks, or taking of deposits) are made in large numbers, where the successes and failures of individual transactions are not normally highly correlated among each other. By the law of large numbers, the volatility of the weighted sum of independent risks decreases as a function of the square root of the number of independent risks assumed. This diversification effect would be a benefit to a financial firm that grows larger than its competitors. In fact, it would represent increasing returns to scale because the largest institution could hold a portfolio of assets with less capital than its competitors, because asset and liability volatility would be much less and would result in a higher and less volatile return on capital for the largest institution. Of course, offsetting factors keep this effect from dominating. Other marginal costs of operation, communications, and management keep the industry from eventually evolving into one giant financial firm. Nevertheless, the powerful impacts of diversification in terms of credit defaults, deposit funding, casualty insurance claims, and life-and-health mortality/morbidity claims are very strong factors in contributing to the existence of a small number of large national and international financial firms that comprise most of the financial industry's assets and earnings.

These few large firms are regarded as systemically important financial institutions (SIFIs). Since the worldwide financial system meltdown of 2008–2009, legislators and regulators worldwide have moved in the direction of bolstering the financial system by raising capital requirements—directly, by requiring higher absolute amounts of primary capital, and indirectly, by (1) effectively increasing the amount of capital needed to support the holding of certain investments, (2) limiting the payout of dividends and repurchases of common equity, and (3) making subordinated debt and preferred shareholders less able to assert their claims in the event of bankruptcy or regulator-mandated restructuring. Furthermore, regulators' actions have resulted in tightening regulations on the use of derivatives, proprietary trading, and off-balance-sheet liabilities/guarantees. These actions require institutions through stress testing to show how they can survive severe economic and financial market turbulence, and they impose more stringent accounting/disclosure rules and reserving requirements. The consequences of a relatively small number of SIFIs dominating the financial industry and the existence of regulatory cycles mean that the management of a financial institution must take into account the actions of its SIFI competitors and must integrate its asset and liability portfolio decisions with a view to where the rules are today *and* where they are likely heading.

Accounting and Tax Considerations

Three different types of accounting systems apply for every financial institution. For the enterprise and its subsidiaries, the first is standard financial accounting, whether in the form of GAAP or IFRS, and which is used for communicating results to shareholders (or members), deposit or policyholders, and suppliers of debt capital. Regulators of banks and insurance companies, in addition, impose a second type of accounting in various forms and known as *statutory* accounting. Statutory accounting rules can be very different across different national and local regulatory jurisdictions. Although statutory results are normally available to the public, they mostly are utilized by regulators. Finally, the third type, true economic accounting, marks all assets and liabilities (net of imputed income taxes) to current market values.

Each accounting system is designed with a particular objective in mind, and it is incumbent upon financial institution managers and investment analysts to understand the purposes of all three. Economic or mark-to-market (MTM) accounting provides the best picture of an entity's assets, liabilities, and changes in economic well-being. MTM earnings are the most volatile of all because they reflect all value changes contemporaneously rather than being smoothed over time. The results of MTM reporting are likely to differ from those from financial reporting, where the reporting rules are consistently and conservatively applied over time (but where asset and liability values may depart from reported balance sheet amounts). Financial reporting has moved increasingly in the direction of MTM accounting over the past several decades, although changes in asset and liability values often are reported by way of balance sheet comprehensive income accounts rather than directly through an income statement. On balance, financial reporting will provide the smoothest reporting of income and asset/liability valuations.

Statutory accounting represents essentially a system of adjustments to standard financial accounting. For both bank and insurance regulators, this means most significantly the subtracting of intangible assets from asset and common equity accounts and/or the acceleration of certain expenses, such as policy underwriting and sales costs. In other cases, it is the recognition and assignment of additional reserves against losses on assets or unexpectedly large losses on guarantees or insurance claims. Statutory accounting usually results in lower earnings and lower common equity capital than in financial accounting. Capital requirements for both banks and insurance companies are predicated on one or another version of statutory reporting.

In terms of taxation, banks and insurance companies typically are taxable entities, and the industry-specific tax rules can be quite complicated. As taxable entities, banks and insurance companies must manage their investment programs with consideration of after-tax returns.

17 BANKS: OTHER CONSIDERATIONS

☐ describe considerations affecting the balance sheet management of banks and insurers

Bank stakeholders include external parties (such as shareholders, creditors, customers, credit rating agencies, regulators, and even the communities where they operate) as well as internal parties (such as employees, management, and boards of directors). A bank's investment program must meet the needs and expectations of multiple parties. Most large, international banks are typically companies with publicly issued securities, which are expected to maximize the net present value of shareholders' capital. As will be seen shortly in greater detail, this hinges importantly on the ability of banks to manage the volatility of the value of shareholders' capital.

On the liability side, bank customers are comprised of a variety of depositors, including individuals, corporations, and municipalities. Individuals deposit cash and depend on banks to safeguard their assets over time. Legal entities, ranging from small privately held companies to large publicly listed corporations, often have multiple banking relationships and depend on banks to provide financing throughout economic cycles. Similarly, municipalities and other public entities deposit funds and rely on banks' safekeeping and transaction services. In addition, both for their own account and for the benefit of customers, banks are important counterparties to both publicly traded and over-the-counter derivatives transactions. Finally, most global banking institutions are significant issuers of fixed-income securities, either directly or via such other means as asset-backed trusts.

On the asset side, bank customers include both retail and commercial borrowers. Individuals borrow money from banks to finance large purchases, such as houses that are often financed with mortgages. On the corporate side, real estate developers often require bank financing through commercial real estate loans. Additionally, large companies require commercial and industrial loans from banks in order to finance working capital, ongoing operations, or capital improvements.

Internal stakeholders include a bank's employees, management, and board of directors. Notably, the largest banks may each have more than 200,000 employees around the globe. At banks with a national or global presence, management teams are often highly visible in regulatory and economic affairs. At the regional and local level, bank management teams are often integrated within the local business community.

Banks—Liabilities and Investment Horizon

Banks are unique in that they originate assets (loans), liabilities (deposits, derivatives, fixed-income securities), and capital (preferred and common stock) in the normal course of business. The ability to originate and manage both assets and liabilities has implications for the management of a bank's interest rate risk exposure (i.e., asset/liability gap management) and the volatility of equity capitalization.

The largest component of bank assets is loans, typically comprising up to 50% or more of the assets of the large, international banks that dominate the sector. The next largest component of assets is debt securities, typically accounting for 25% or more of total assets. The largest remaining portion of assets consists of currency, deposits with central banks (e.g., Bank of Japan or Bank of England), receivables, and bullion.

Banks' liabilities are comprised of deposits and also include short-term funding, such as commercial paper, as well as longer term debt. Deposits are the largest component of liabilities, usually more than half of total liabilities. Bank deposits include the following:

- **Time deposits** or **term deposits** – These interest-bearing accounts have a specified maturity date. This category includes savings accounts and certificates of deposit (CDs). Banks have visibility on the duration of these deposits because they require advance notice prior to withdrawal.
- **Demand deposits** – These accounts can be drawn upon regularly and without notice. This category includes checking accounts and certain savings accounts that are often accessible through online banks or automated teller machines (ATMs). Consequently, banks have limited visibility on the expected lives of these accounts and tend to assume they are short-term in duration.

In addition to deposits, banks can access wholesale funding, sources of which include Federal Funds, public funds, and other government-supported, short-term vehicles. Banks must actively monitor the expected cash outlays and timing of their liabilities. For time deposits, the amount and timing of the cash outlay are known, while for demand deposits, the amount is known but the timing is uncertain. Other liabilities comprise (1) long-term debt, 10%–15% of total balance sheet; and (2) such items as trading/securities payables and repurchase finance payables, also on the order of 10%–20% of balance sheet liabilities.

The tactical investment horizon for a bank's investment portfolio is directly impacted by the nature and maturities of its asset base and liability structure.[6] Although commercial banks, as corporations, have a perpetual time horizon (possibly longer than the other institutions in this reading), the instruments held in a bank portfolio tend to have far shorter maturities than those held by other financial institutions.

SUSTAINABILITY LINKED LOANS: PROMOTING SUSTAINABLE DEVELOPMENT WHILE ALSO MANAGING RISK

As per the Sustainability Linked Loan Principles, "Sustainability linked loans are any types of loan instruments and/or contingent facilities (such as bonding lines, guarantee lines or letters of credit) which incentivize the borrower's achievement of ambitious, predetermined sustainability performance objectives." These loans aim to support environmentally and socially sustainable economic activity and growth and look to improve the borrower's sustainability profile by aligning loan terms to the borrower's performance against the relevant predetermined targets.

As some environmental and social issues such as carbon emissions, deforestation, water scarcity, and occupational health and safety become increasingly material for certain sectors, they could affect a company's ability to generate sustainable returns in the long term. Therefore, ensuring that corporates are managing such issues sufficiently well and avoiding any large negative impact on their ability to repay the loan is in the interest of providers of capital such as banks. In this context, a product such as a sustainability-linked loan provides the right incentive for corporates viz. a lower cost of capital, if they can manage the said risk(s) well. For banks, it is a way to manage and mitigate their credit risk exposure.

6 Its strategic horizon is perpetuity because of its corporate structure, which makes it as long, or longer, than many defined benefit plans, endowments, foundations, and sovereign wealth funds.

Example:

During Q1 2021, ING together with Santander coordinated one of the largest sustainability-linked revolving credit facilities ever issued. Anheuser-Busch InBev (AB InBev), a multinational drinks and brewing company, was provided a USD10.1 billion revolving credit facility with a five-year term by a consortium of 26 leading global financial institutions.

The pricing mechanism incentivizes AB InBev to address four key performance areas that are aligned with its sustainability goals:

1. Further improving water efficiency at AB InBev's breweries globally
2. Increasing PET recycled content in PET primary packaging
3. Sourcing purchased electricity from renewable sources as outlined in the RE100 commitment
4. Reducing greenhouse gas emissions as part of the science-based Climate Action Goal

The difference between the long time horizon of the institution and the much shorter maturity of most of its assets and liabilities may seem counterintuitive. Suppose that in the current market, the credit spreads on loans are narrow and the economy is nearing recession. The long-term horizon of the bank is evidenced by it: (1) cutting back new lending, (2) selling part of its existing loan portfolio, (3) increasing allocations to short-maturity, liquid securities, and (4) decreasing leverage through fewer large wholesale time deposits. The bank is sacrificing current earnings while looking forward to an uncertain time horizon when it can aggressively expand in the more favorable future environment. The long-term time horizon means that it expects to apply similar tactics—with medium to short-term maturity assets and liabilities—many more times over the indefinite future.

Banks—Liquidity Needs

Liquidity management is a core consideration in the management of bank portfolios. Given the short duration of deposits, as well as the potential need for increased liquidity in adverse market conditions, management and regulators have developed a robust framework around liquidity management for bank portfolios. Apart from asset or cash flow securitization, banks must have the ability to liquidate their investment portfolios within a certain period to generate adequate cash in the event of a crisis.

Bank liquidity needs have evolved since the global financial crisis of 2007–2009. Prior to that period, deficiencies in liquidity from deposits were made up with wholesale funding; banks would use their portfolios as a source of return so were invested in lower quality, less liquid securities. In the post-crisis environment, however, bank portfolios are increasingly comprised of higher quality, more liquid securities. This trend to more conservative management of investment portfolios has largely been driven by increased regulatory scrutiny on a global basis, most noticeably through the introduction of mandated liquidity coverage ratios (LCRs) and net stable funding ratios (NSFRs).[7]

7 LCRs require that highly liquid assets must constitute more than 100% of highly probable near-term expected cash outflows. NSFRs set minimum requirements for stable funding sources relative to assets; such stable sources include capital, long-term debt, and non-volatile deposits.

In general, contrasting commercial banks and retail-oriented banks, commercial banks have a higher cost of funds and lower liquidity because of wholesale funding of loan commitments and other contingent commitments. Conversely, retail banks have a lower cost of funds and better liquidity because their retail deposits are relatively low cost and tend to be more stable.

INSURERS

18

The stakeholders of insurers include such external parties as shareholders, derivatives counterparties, policyholders, creditors, regulators, and rating agencies as well as such internal parties as employees, management, and boards of directors. Insurance companies are organized as either companies with publicly listed securities or mutual companies.

In North America and Europe, most large insurers are companies with publicly issued securities, with the inherent shareholder concerns and pressures. As such, there is significant interest and scrutiny on quarterly investment performance, corporate earnings, and balance sheet strength. Within this context, as with banks, optimal management must focus on the long-term maximization of net present value of shareholders' capital. Concretely, this requires balancing expected returns on investments and policy writing in such a way that all insurance liabilities will be met. This requires a very strong focus by management and regulators on maintaining tight control over the volatility of the value of shareholder capital. Capital must be maintained at all investment horizons and under all scenarios so that the company will be able to honor its obligations, especially to policyholders.

Mutual companies are owned by policyholders. Mutual companies either retain profits as surplus or rebate excess cash to policyholders in the form of dividends or premium reductions.[8] Although mutual companies are free from the shareholder pressure for earnings performance, they have less access to capital markets than peers with publicly issued securities. Mutual companies remain quite prevalent in the United States, Canada, Japan, and many European countries. To provide certainty that policyholders are paid under all economic conditions, the need to control and maintain capital surplus is fundamentally the same as in the case of for-profit insurers.

Customers are primarily policyholders who have a need to protect themselves against specific risks. The main objective of any insurance company investment program is to fund policyholder benefits and claims.

Given the nature and requirements of their product suite, life insurers maintain both a **general account** and **separate accounts**. For traditional life insurance products and fixed annuities, insurers bear all the risks—particularly mortality risk and longevity risk, respectively—so they maintain a general account of assets to fund future liabilities from these products. However, in the case of variable life and variable annuity products, customers make investment decisions from a menu of options and themselves bear investment risk. Consequently, insurers invest the assets arising from these products within separate accounts. Exhibit 21 summarizes the main bearers of investment risk and the account structure for the major categories of insurance and annuity products.

8 Mutual companies can also increase the amount of "paid up insurance" for whole-life policies.

Exhibit 21: Main Investment Risk Bearers for Different Insurance Products

Products	Bearer of Investment Risk	Account
Whole and term life insurance	Company	General
Universal life insurance	Company	General
Fixed annuities	Company	General
Variable life insurance	Policyholder	Separate
Variable annuities	Policyholder	Separate

The insurance industry is tightly regulated in most countries, usually by state or national authorities. The regulatory environment, including constraints impacting insurance asset management, will be discussed shortly. The rating agencies—including A.M. Best, Standard & Poor's, Moody's, and Fitch—are stakeholders in the management of insurance investment portfolios because they monitor the financial stability of insurance companies and provide credit ratings and data on the industry to the investment community globally.

An insurance company's management team and employees are also direct stakeholders. The large global insurance companies may have thousands of employees spread over many countries. Their management teams are often highly visible in terms of regulatory and economic affairs. Clearly, the employees are impacted by the amount of risks taken on an insurance company's balance sheet.

Insurers—Liabilities and Investment Horizon

Insurance companies manage their investment portfolios with an intense focus on asset/liability management (ALM). Within the insurance industry, the business line is critical because it determines the nature and structure of the liabilities. Further, effective management of liabilities is crucial to the long-term viability of any insurance company.

Life Insurers

Broadly speaking, life insurers face a liability stream and time horizon with a long duration. Life insurance involves a range of products, including Individual Life, Group Life and Disability, Individual Annuity, and Retirement Plan products. Life insurance portfolios are comprised of asset accumulation products, with some nuances in the associated liability stream. The liability stream is driven by the predictability of claims, which can vary based on the specific product line. For example, Term Life products have a one-time payout and the predictability is relatively high using statistical and actuarial analyses on large portfolios with many policies. Meanwhile, annuity products involve an ongoing payout with shorter duration that is subject to longevity risk. The nature of the liability stream has important implications for the amount of investment risk that can be tolerated.

Within life insurance, product features and resulting liabilities as well as policyholder behavior are key determinants of the associated portfolios' investment horizons. Historically, life insurance companies set portfolio return objectives with long time horizons of 20 to 40 years.

Property & Casualty Insurers

In general, P&C insurers face a shorter duration liability stream and investment horizon than life insurers. Further, P&C insurance involves events with lower probability of occurrence and potentially higher cost (especially in the case of natural disasters), leading to highly volatile business claims. This results in a liability stream with short duration and high uncertainty.

For example, a P&C insurance company may initiate policies against catastrophic events, such as hurricanes or other natural disasters. By definition, this insurance involves unpredictable and infrequent events that are difficult to hedge against. Insurance companies utilize statistical and actuarial analyses to forecast liability cash flows on a probabilistic (scenario) basis. P&C insurers may benefit from developing global, diversified portfolios that are more applicable to statistical analysis because of the law of large numbers. In any case, P&C insurers face a liability stream with a shorter duration and more potential volatility than life insurers.

MEASURING AND MANAGING PHYSICAL CLIMATE RISKS

Environmental risks such as the physical impacts of climate change (e.g., floods, droughts, wildfires) are affecting our day-to-day lives both more frequently and on a larger scale than ever imagined. Physical risks might have financial implications for organizations, such as direct damage to assets and indirect impacts from supply chain disruption. Wildfires in California, the Amazon Forest, and Australia that caused billions of dollars in financial losses, in addition to the loss of life and to megacities such as Cape Town and Chennai almost running out of water, are just a few recent examples of how climate change and related global warming are accelerating the frequency and magnitude of such erratic weather patterns.

For insurance companies, this increase in frequency of the hitherto infrequent and low-probability events poses a new set of modeling challenges. AXA S.A., a French multinational insurance company, for example, states that as of the end of 2020, the annual average losses (AAL) for its real estate portfolio are estimated to be EUR4.3 million due to floods and EUR6.2 million due to windstorms. To manage these physical climate risks, AXA's models that assess the risk of natural hazards consider three components: the hazard (as defined by its severity and frequency), the exposure (as characterized by the building's physical properties), and the vulnerability (as defined by destruction rates, function of the hazard, and the exposure). These risk evaluation and management efforts would naturally evolve to consider potential financial impacts under various climate scenarios that are published by the Intergovernmental Panel on Climate Change, such as the Representative Concentration Pathways 2.6 and 8.5 scenarios, which make predictions of how concentrations of greenhouse gases in the atmosphere (and thus global temperature rise) will change in the future because of human activities.

As these physical climate risks become more and more material, insurance companies will have to better understand their exposure to physical risk and chart appropriate adaptation efforts to limit such exposures.

With both life and P&C insurers, as with banks, the nature and timing of expected policy claims strongly influence the time horizon and nature of investments held. Even so, the ultimate management time horizon is perpetuity. A natural and frequently occurring example for both types of insurers is the case of underwriting cycles. Such cycles relate to the pricing of newly issued policies relative both to then-existing expected security returns and to the actuarial outlook for life and casualty loss claims. Long-term strategic investment and balance-sheet management policies result in modifications to portfolios and overall company leverage at different points in time to adjust to the varying relative attractiveness of bearing investment risk versus bearing underwriting risk and/or financial (leverage) risk.

Insurers—Liquidity Needs

Insurance companies must actively manage and monitor the liquidity of their portfolios. The level of liquidity required has important implications across the portfolio management process, including the insurer's ability to utilize leverage. Further, liquidity needs can vary greatly based on the business line.

Both life and P&C insurers need a sound, two-part liquidity plan that includes internal and external components. An insurer's internal liquidity includes cash and cash equivalents maintained on the balance sheet. Insurers must actively manage cash from operations (including investment income) that involves steady inflows and outflows. Further, insurers manage and project the cash flows from investment portfolio income and principal repayments. An insurer's external liquidity includes the ability to issue bonds in the capital markets and to access credit lines through syndicated commercial bank credit lines or other lines of credit. Finally, insurers manage short-term liquidity by actively buying and selling repurchase agreements. In this way, insurers consistently manage both internal and external sources of liquidity.

The liquidity needs of life insurance companies must also be considered in the context of the interest rate environment. In periods of rising/high interest rates, insurance companies may face the risk of significant net cash outflow as policies are surrendered by customers searching for higher yields in other investments. P&C insurers face uncertainty regarding both the value and timing of the payment of benefits. This significant cash flow uncertainty necessitates maintaining ample liquidity and results in P&C portfolios comprised of high proportions of cash and cash substitutes as well as short-term fixed-income instruments.

Insurers segment general account investment portfolios into two major components: **reserve portfolio** and **surplus portfolio**. Insurance companies are typically subject to specific regulatory requirements to maintain a reserve portfolio that is intended to ensure the company's ability to meet its policy liabilities. The surplus portfolio is intended to realize higher expected returns. Insurance companies manage reserve assets relatively conservatively. The size of the reserve portfolio is typically dictated by statute, and assets must be highly liquid and low risk. Meanwhile, insurance companies have more of an ability to assume liquidity risk in the surplus portfolio. Insurance companies are often willing to manage these assets aggressively with exposure to alternative assets, including private equity, hedge funds, and non-security assets.

19 BANKS AND INSURERS: INVESTMENT OBJECTIVES

☐ describe considerations affecting the balance sheet management of banks and insurers

We now consider the investment objectives of banks followed by a discussion of investment objectives and an investment policy statement for insurers.

Banks

The investment securities portfolio of a bank is an integral component of the overall banking enterprise. The primary objective of a bank's securities investment portfolio is to manage the bank's liquidity and risk position relative to its non-securities assets, derivatives positions, liabilities, and shareholders' capitalization. Given the highly regulated nature of the industry, banks typically have formally documented investment policies as well as multiple levels of oversight in the form of internal committees and external regulators.

What follows provides a real-life example of how investment objectives are framed at banks.

Bank Investment Objective

JPMorgan Chase & Co., Treasury and Chief Investment Officer Overview

"Treasury and CIO is predominantly responsible for measuring, monitoring, reporting and managing the Firm's liquidity, funding, capital, structural interest rate and foreign exchange risks. The risks managed by Treasury and CIO arise from the activities undertaken by the Firm's four major reportable business segments to serve their respective client bases, which generate both on- and off-balance sheet assets and liabilities.

Treasury and CIO achieve the Firm's asset-liability management objectives generally by investing in high-quality securities that are managed for the longer-term as part of the Firm's investment securities portfolio. Treasury and CIO also use derivatives to meet the Firm's asset-liability management objectives."

Source: JPMorgan Chase & Co., *Annual Report 2020*, www.jpmorganchase.com/content/dam/jpmc/jpmorgan-chase-and-co/investor-relations/documents/annualreport-2020.pdf.

Banks establish an asset/liability management committee ("ALCo") that provides direction and oversight of the investment portfolio. The ALCo has significant visibility with the bank's management and board of directors, as well as with external regulators. This ALCo sets the investment policy statement (IPS), monitors performance on an ongoing basis, and has the ability to mandate adjustments on the asset and liability sides of the balance sheet. The ALCo also ensures that market (interest rate and FX), credit, liquidity, and solvency (capital adequacy) risk positions are within the limits of the bank's specified risk tolerances. Once the overall investment objectives and risk levels are set, the investment team establishes policy benchmarks. The investment team monitors performance and such portfolio characteristics as duration and convexity relative to the benchmark for each asset class. Further, the investment team may monitor performance relative to a set of peers with comparable business models and investment objectives. Finally, the investment team makes periodic presentations to senior management and the board of directors regarding performance and characteristics of the investment portfolio.

Insurers

Given the highly regulated nature of the insurance industry, a detailed and well-documented Investment Policy Statement is of paramount importance. It is a best practice for an IPS to take a holistic approach and include the parent company's strategic enterprise risk management framework. Similar to banks, insurers manage their investment portfolios with a focus on liquidity as well as interest rate, foreign exchange, credit, and other risk factors.

The investment oversight function is a critical part of an insurer's overall governance. Insurers typically have a committee on the board of directors that maintains oversight of all investment policies, procedures, strategies, and performance evaluation. Insurers provide significant transparency to their underlying portfolios—including showing the inherent duration, credit, and other risks to regulators and other external stakeholders.

The IPS should encompass the insurer's appetite for market risk, credit risk, and interest rate risk. An insurer's risk tolerance may vary relative to the competitive environment for various product lines, regulatory and tax changes, market conditions, and other factors. Moreover, the IPS should be a "living document" that evolves as market, regulatory, and business conditions change.

Hypothetical Life Insurance Company—Investment Policy Statement

i. Introduction

XYZ Life Insurance Company ("the Company") underwrites and markets life insurance and annuity products. The Company is licensed to provide insurance products in all 50 US states, as well as several foreign countries. This investment policy statement ("IPS") documents the policies and procedures that govern the Company's general account securities portfolio. There are detailed policy statements for each asset segment within the portfolio that provide a more granular breakdown of investment guidelines.

ii. Governance and Stakeholders

The Company's investment policies, including investment objectives and constraints, are the responsibility of the Investment and Finance Committee ("IFC") of the board of directors ("BoD"). The insurer's senior management team ("Mgmt") is responsible for implementation of the investment program consistent with this policy. In turn, the investment team ("InvTeam") manages the investment portfolio on a day-to-day basis.

The IFC will review the investment policy on an annual basis. The IFC must consider changes to the Company's strategic direction, regulatory changes, tax changes, financial market conditions, and any other relevant factors that may arise. The IFC proposes adjustments to the IPS to the BoD, and all material changes must be approved by the BoD in their entirety.

The IFC has responsibility to employ appropriate resources for the management of the investment portfolio. The IFC may retain or dismiss InvTeam personnel at its discretion. Further, the IFC may retain investment consultants or other advisers to manage specific asset classes or other sub-components of the portfolio. All consultant, external investment managers, and other advisers are required to comply with this IPS.

iii. Mission and Investment Objective

The core mission of the general account is twofold:

1. Provide liquidity for the payment of policyholder claims in the normal course of insurance operations.
2. Grow the Company's surplus over the long-term.

The investment objective must follow prudent investing practices and achieve an appropriate balance between maintaining short-term liquidity and contributing to long-term asset growth.

iv. Risk Tolerance and Constraints

The Company is subject to significant scrutiny from internal and external stakeholders, including shareholders, regulators, and others. The general account investment program must take into account the following key factors:

- **Liquidity.** The investment portfolio must maintain sufficient liquidity to meet all policyholder claims that may arise on a short-term and long-term basis. The InvTeam monitors investment cash flow to ensure the Company's ability to meet all obligations in a timely manner. Further, the InvTeam may liquidate publicly traded securities as a secondary source of liquidity.
- **Interest Rate Risk.** The InvTeam monitors the portfolio's exposure to changes in interest rates, including the relative exposure of both assets and liabilities.
- **Credit Risk.** The InvTeam monitors the credit (default) risk inherent in the portfolio and must continually monitor the financial health of key counterparties.
- **Foreign Exchange Risk.** The Company is subject to foreign exchange risk in the normal course of business. The InvTeam monitors the aggregate foreign exchange risk of the portfolio.
- **Regulatory Requirements.** All investments must adhere to the insurance code of the Company's state of domicile as well as all other applicable domestic and foreign guidelines. Further, the investment program must comply with risk-based capital considerations and rating agency requirements.
- **Tax Considerations.** Further, the securities portfolio must account for tax considerations, and all investment decisions should be evaluated on an after-tax basis. The income tax planning of the Company may impact the timing of realization of capital gains and losses.

v. Asset Allocation Policy, Allowable Ranges, and Benchmarks

The primary investment vehicles within the Company's investment portfolio will consist of highly liquid instruments, including US and foreign government obligations, corporate debt, and other fixed-income instruments. Further, the Company may invest in private placement bonds, commercial mortgage loans, and other less liquid instruments within the parameters specified. Further, the Company may invest in real estate and private equity in order to enhance long-term returns and contribute to the surplus growth of the company. However, strict guidelines apply for less liquid asset classes.

The IFC establishes the strategic asset allocation that is consistent with the long-term constraints of the Company. The IFC will review the strategic asset allocation annually and may make adjustments as appropriate. Further, the IFC sets out allowable ranges of allocation for each asset class. Further, the IFC approves appropriate benchmarks for each asset class upon consultation with the InvTeam.

vi. Investment Guidelines

The InvTeam should seek to diversify holdings in terms of economic exposure, counterparty, and other applicable attributes to the extent possible. Securities that are guaranteed by the US government or its agencies must constitute at least 25% of the portfolio.

vii. Reporting

The InvTeam, with the oversight of Mgmt, must provide adequate reporting to the BoD and other stakeholders. The reporting structure should include the following:

- Daily Flash Report: Summary of market values, yield, and interest rate position of entire portfolio
- Monthly Investment Performance Detail: Detailed investment performance by asset class, including market values, yields, and interest rate position
- Quarterly Investment Summary: Detailed analysis of market values, yield, and interest rate exposure, including long-term performance metrics and attribution

20 BANKS AND INSURERS: BALANCE SHEET MANAGEMENT AND INVESTMENT CONSIDERATIONS

☐ describe considerations affecting the balance sheet management of banks and insurers

We turn now to the portfolio investment strategy for banks and insurance companies. The objectives and constraints are very different from what we have seen with respect to pensions, sovereign wealth funds, endowments, and foundations. In the case of banks and insurance companies, the need is to fund deposits, policy claims, derivatives payoffs, and debtholders. A financial institution's fundamental purpose is to assure such contractual parties the full and timely payment of claims when they come due. A firm can only hope to earn a profit if it can provide counterparties assurance it will be able to meet all claims with extremely high probability.

The financial claims against banks and insurers may not always be known with certainty, but they are, at any point in time, measurable. Such measurement may require the use of probabilistic methods to account for such outcomes as: (1) the liquidation of bank deposits; (2) insurance policy claims and surrenders; (3) losses on derivatives, guarantees, or forward purchase commitments; and (4) returns on variable annuities, among other outcomes. Thus, in the case of banks and insurers, the well-defined, contractual nature of the financial claims, along with their measurability, imply that—unlike with defined benefit and defined contribution pension plans, sovereign wealth funds, endowments, and foundations—the underlying investment strategy is mainly liability driven investing (LDI as earlier defined).

We can obtain insight about both investment strategy and regulation of financial institutions by applying a fairly simple but intuitive economic model. The model's first two equations define the relationship between an institution's assets A, liabilities (claims) L, and residual equity of the institution's shareholders or members E:

$$A = L + E \qquad (1)$$

$$\Delta A = \Delta L + \Delta E \qquad (2)$$

Assets are equal to the sum of contractual claims and residual ownership. Likewise, all changes in assets must equal the sum of changes in the value of contractual claims and ownership interest (equity capitalization). These equations are set forth in terms of current market—or economic—values, which will not necessarily coincide with GAAP, IFRS, or regulatory/statutory values. However, using current market values will facilitate the subsequent application of these other accounting valuations.

These equations can be used to understand not just market value changes but also the impact of earnings, the consequences of adding or selling off assets in total, and changes in an institution's capital structure. All of these are relevant to investment strategy and are additional layers of complexity as compared with the other portfolio strategies in this reading.

By multiplying the various terms by 1 (i.e., $A \div A$ or $L \div L$), dividing both sides by E, and doing a little regrouping, we obtain a useful expression, namely:

$$\frac{\Delta A}{A}\left(\frac{A}{E}\right) = \frac{\Delta L}{L}\left(\frac{L}{E}\right) + \frac{\Delta E}{E} \qquad (3)$$

Using Equation 1 and moving liabilities and assets to the same side of the equation, we rewrite this as:

$$\frac{\Delta E}{E} = \frac{\Delta A}{A}\left(\frac{A}{E}\right) - \frac{\Delta L}{L}\left(\frac{A-E}{E}\right) = \frac{\Delta A}{A}\left(\frac{A}{E}\right) - \frac{\Delta L}{L}\left(\frac{A}{E} - 1\right) \qquad (4)$$

Equation 4 provides an easy way to see how percentage changes in market value of both assets and liabilities are magnified by the leverage factors.

To demonstrate this point, Exhibit 22 presents the effects on the market value of the institution's equity capital as a function of (i) declines in underlying asset value,[9] and (ii) beginning degree of leverage. Asset values can decline for several reasons, such as deterioration in credit quality and/or liquidity of loans or securities held. The value of assets can also be hurt by rising interest rates in the case of fixed-rate loans or securities.

Exhibit 22: Effects on Market Value of Equity Due to Change in Market Value of Assets (Given Beginning Degree of Leverage)

Beg. Equity to Assets Ratio	Leverage (x)	Percentage Change in Institution's Equity Value Due to Change in Asset Value of:			
(E÷A)	**(A÷E)**	**−0.5%**	**−1.0%**	**−1.5%**	**−2.0%**
20%	5.0	−2.5%	−5.0%	−7.5%	−10.0%
15%	6.7	−3.3%	−6.7%	−10.0%	−13.3%

9 Which, for our analysis, focuses on the investment portfolio assets. The net equity described here is net financial equity. The portion of an institution's equity associated with financing other assets, such as buildings and equipment, are not a focus of this reading.

Beg. Equity to Assets Ratio	Leverage (x)	Percentage Change in Institution's Equity Value Due to Change in Asset Value of:			
(E÷A)	**(A÷E)**	**−0.5%**	**−1.0%**	**−1.5%**	**−2.0%**
10%	10.0	−5.0%	−10.0%	−15.0%	−20.0%
5%	20.0	−10.0%	−20.0%	−30.0%	−40.0%

This analysis reveals that even small losses in the market value of assets can have a pronounced negative effect on the institution's equity capital account because of the leverage factor. Naturally, it works in reverse; Small gains in assets can have a very positive impact for equity capital holders. These relationships give rise to a conflict of interest: Because equity capital holders can only lose the value of their investment but also can make extremely large gains if assets perform well, liability holders require some form of protection against the potential inclination of the institution to take excessive risks. Contractual, regulatory, and reputational methods all come into play to provide such protection. In one form or another, they relate to limiting the volatility of assets and providing for a capital cushion so that equity capital holders, rather than liability holders, are expected to absorb unforeseen losses on assets.

Similarly, financial institutions face the possibility of loss from adverse changes in the market value of liabilities. In the case of insurance companies, unexpectedly high policy loss claims are the most notable cause of expanding liabilities. For banks, it could be having to make a forward-funding commitment to a struggling company, the exercise of a guarantee, or a loss on forward currency purchase contracts. Exhibit 23 uses Equation 4 to illustrate the effect on the market value of the institution's equity capital as a function of (i) increases in its liabilities and (ii) beginning degree of leverage.

Exhibit 23: Effects on Market Value of Equity Due to Change in Market Value of Liabilities (Given Beginning Degree of Leverage)

Beg. Equity to Assets Ratio	Leverage (x)	Percentage Change in Institution's Equity Value Due to Change in Liability Value of:			
(E÷A)	**[(A÷E) − 1]**	**+0.5%**	**+1.0%**	**+1.5%**	**+2.0%**
20%	4.0	−2.0%	−4.0%	−6.0%	−8.0%
15%	5.7	−2.8%	−5.7%	−8.5%	−11.3%
10%	9.0	−4.5%	−9.0%	−13.5%	−18.0%
5%	19.0	−9.5%	−19.0%	−28.5%	−38.0%

Exhibit 23 bolsters the conclusions reached in Exhibit 22. Mainly, liability holders, regulators, and owners (equity shareholders) of a financial institution all are motivated to limit the volatility and magnitude, relative to the base capital level, of market value changes in the institution's liabilities.

Now we must integrate the analysis of both sides of the balance sheet with the capital management strategy of the financial institution. To do this, we would like to have a framework for understanding various interactions in a more rigorous manner. A customary starting point is with an analysis of interest rate risk. Our framework comfortably accommodates the standard duration-based model of value changes with respect to interest rate changes. In order to find the percentage change in the value of the institution's equity capital associated with a change in the reference yield, y, on the asset holdings, we divide Equation 4 by the change in such yield, thereby obtaining:

$$\frac{\Delta E}{E\Delta y} = \frac{\Delta A}{A\Delta y}\left(\frac{A}{E}\right) - \frac{\Delta L}{L\Delta y}\left(\frac{A}{E} - 1\right) \tag{5}$$

Likewise, we want to understand how this relates to the change in the effective yield on the liabilities, i. Multiplying by $1 = \Delta i \div \Delta i$ in the appropriate location, we restate Equation 5 as:

$$\frac{\Delta E}{E\Delta y} = \frac{\Delta A}{A\Delta y}\left(\frac{A}{E}\right) - \frac{\Delta L}{L\Delta i}\left(\frac{\Delta i}{\Delta y}\right)\left(\frac{A}{E} - 1\right) \tag{6}$$

Recall that the modified duration of asset W with respect to its yield-to-maturity, r, (D_W^*) is defined as:

$$D_W^* = -\frac{\Delta W}{W\Delta r} \tag{7}$$

This allows us to revise Equation 6 to a practical and intuitive analytical tool, namely,

$$D_E^* = \left(\frac{A}{E}\right)D_A^* - \left(\frac{A}{E} - 1\right)D_L^*\left(\frac{\Delta i}{\Delta y}\right) \tag{8}$$

Over reasonably modest yield changes, Equation 8 provides a useful way to break down the volatility of a financial institution's equity capital as a function of degree of leverage, comparative (modified) duration of assets and liabilities, and correlation (or sensitivity) of changes in yields of assets and liabilities.

Exhibit 24 and Exhibit 25 show how sensitive the valuation of equity is to changes in the security portfolio yield for differing degrees of mismatching of asset and liability durations. In both these exhibits, the x-axis shows the duration of the financial institution's liabilities, the y-axis shows the duration of its security portfolio assets, and the z-axis (vertical axis) shows the resulting duration of the institution's shareholders' equity. The yields on liabilities are assumed to move only 90% as much as the yields on portfolio assets. That is,

$$\frac{di}{dy} = \frac{\Delta i}{\Delta y} = 0.90$$

Exhibit 24 and Exhibit 25 show results for differing initial degrees of leverage, as measured by the equity-to-assets ratio, which is 20% and 10%, respectively.

Exhibit 24: Duration of Shareholders' Equity as a Function of Asset and Liability Durations (Given Equity/Assets = 20% and Sensitivity of Yield Changes = 0.90)

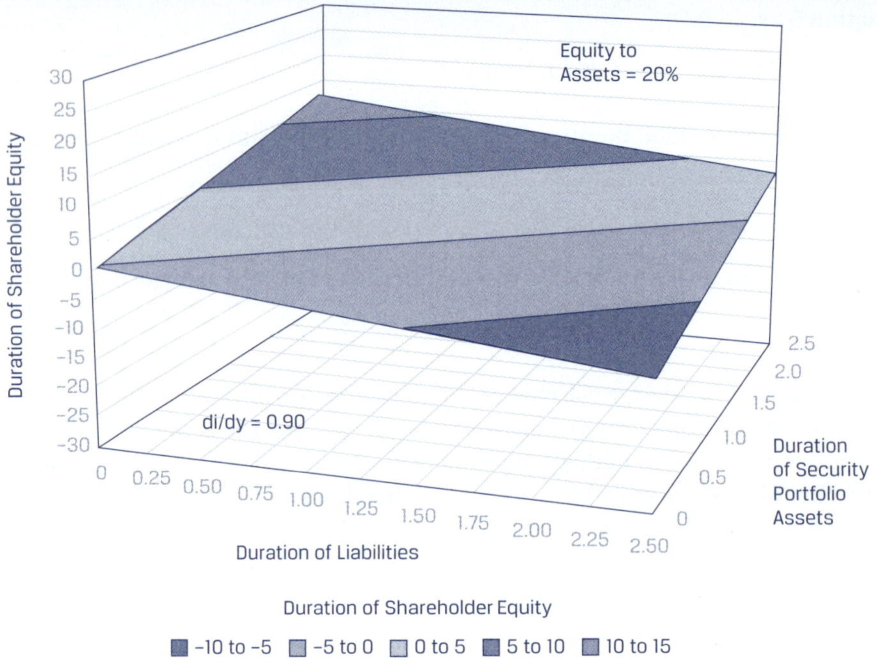

Exhibit 24 indicates that, even at relatively high capital ratios of 20%, moderate differences between asset and liability durations can imply durations for equity that can be sizable in either a positive or negative direction. Remember that, by definition, the modified duration of a zero-coupon bond is its final maturity divided by one plus its yield. Thus, by comparison, a 10-year zero coupon bond would have a modified duration around 9.75. Utilizing Equation 7, a +/− 100 basis point change in interest rates when multiplied by a modified duration of 9.75 implies an approximate +/− 10% change in value. It is highly unlikely that regulators would like to see large asset/liability duration mismatches, since regulators want equity capital to remain stable in periods of large adverse interest rate changes.

Exhibit 25: Duration of Shareholders' Equity as a Function of Asset and Liability Durations (Given Equity/Assets = 10% and Sensitivity of Yield Changes = 0.90)

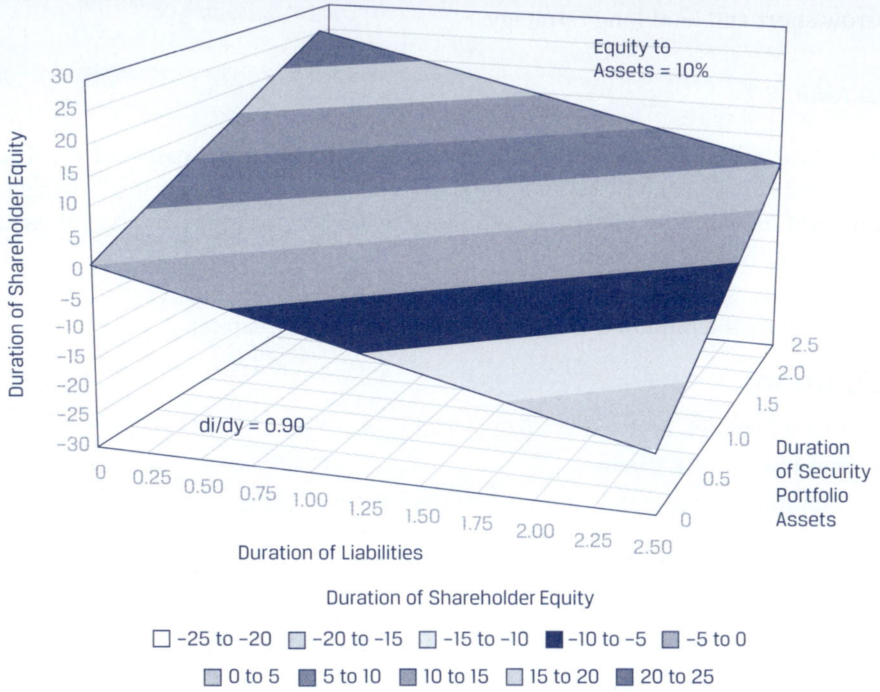

In Exhibit 25, we see that lowering the equity capital ratio to 10% means that in order to avoid very high durations for equity capitalization, it is all the more necessary to keep assets and liabilities from having large differences in duration. It is often mistakenly thought that banks (and to a lesser degree, insurance companies) climb the yield curve by raising capital through the issuance of short maturity deposits that they then invest in longer duration loans and securities. The foregoing exhibits indicate the potential dangers of such an asset/liability mismatch. In Exhibit 25, assuming a liability duration of close to zero (very short-term deposits and overnight borrowing), even if the security portfolio duration is only 2.5 years, the duration of shareholder's equity reaches 25 years (about the equivalent of a 26-year zero coupon bond). In such a case, a +/− 100 basis point change in asset yields would produce a +/− 25% change in shareholder equity value. The loss potential is a danger that neither deposit holders, creditors, stockholders, nor regulators would be keen to embrace.

In actuality, in order to lower asset duration, financial institutions hold cash, deposits at central banks, foreign currency reserves, and other highly liquid (zero duration) assets. Also, as a means of lowering effective asset durations, banks typically make business loans that float according to market reference rates, which are expected to move in line with the variable cost of deposits. Likewise, credit card and many real estate loans are tied to variable rate indexes in order to minimize the sensitivity of values to interest rates. Moreover, many fixed-rate mortgage loans are securitized and sold off to private investors. All these foregoing techniques are ways of limiting the duration of asset portfolios.

On the liability side, there are many ways in which the duration of liabilities can be extended far beyond the implicit zero duration of demand deposits. These include issuance of intermediate and longer-term debt instruments, deeply subordinated capital securities, and perpetual preferred stock. Finally, banks can and do utilize financial futures and interest rate swaps to alleviate asset/liability mismatches.

In the light of persistent low interest rates since the global financial crisis of 2007–2009, many large international banks have an asset/liability structure where earnings are poised to benefit from a rise in interest rates. In such cases, the duration of assets is actually shorter than the duration of liabilities. This is clearly not the naïve "borrow short and lend long" strategy.

EXAMPLE 7

MegaWorld Bancorp has an equity capital ratio for financial assets of 9%. The modified duration of its assets is 2.0 and of its liabilities is 1.5. Over small changes, the yield on liabilities is expected to move by 85 bps for every 100 bps of yield change in its asset portfolio.

1. Compute the modified duration of the bank's equity capital.

Solution:

Using Equation 8, $A \div E = 1/0.09 = 11.11$; $(A \div E) - 1 = 10.11$; $D_A^* = 2.0$; $D_L^* = 1.5$; and $\Delta i \div \Delta y = 0.85$.

Therefore, the modified duration of shareholders' capital is:

$$D_E^* = (11.11 \times 2) - (10.11 \times 1.50) \times 0.85 = 9.33$$

2. What would be the impact on the value of shareholder capital of a 50 basis point rise in the level of yields on its asset portfolio?

Solution:

Using the implications of Equation 7, the change in equity capitalization value is computed as:

$$0.5\% \times -9.33 = -4.67\%.$$

3. Management is considering issuing common stock, selling investment portfolio assets, and paying off some liabilities in order to achieve an equity capitalization ratio of 10%. Assuming no change in the durations of assets and liabilities and assuming no change in the sensitivity of liability yields to asset yields, what is the resulting modified duration of the bank's equity capital?

Solution:

With this less leveraged balance sheet, $A \div E = 1/0.1 = 10$; $(A \div E) - 1 = 9$; and the duration of shareholders' equity is:

$$D_E^* = (10\times 2) - (9 \times 1.50) \times 0.85 = 8.53$$

4. Using the facts in question 3 but assuming the bank rebalances its investment portfolio to achieve a modified duration of assets of 1.75, what happens to the duration of the bank's equity capital?

Solution:

The duration of shareholders' capital now declines to:

$$D_E^* = (10 \times 1.75) - (9 \times 1.50) \times 0.85 = 6.03$$

BANKS AND INSURERS: INVESTMENT STRATEGIES AND ASSET AND LIABILITY VOLATILITY

21

Our previous discussion has given us some insight into the effects of leverage and the volatility of underlying assets and liabilities on the value of a financial institution's equity. The degree of leverage was given; the sensitivity of changes in liability to asset yields (*di/dy*) was constant; and the durations of assets and liabilities varied. Although quite useful in many circumstances, such duration analysis captures the effects of only small changes in overall levels of interest rates and only over short time intervals.[10] Although of great significance, changes in the overall levels of interest rates are only one source of volatility. An expansion of Equation 4 is therefore necessary. A natural step is to extend it in a probabilistic way. We can thereby capture the volatility of the market value change in the financial institution's equity capital as shown in Equation 9. Volatility is defined here as standard deviation, where $\sigma_{\frac{\Delta E}{E}}$, $\sigma_{\frac{\Delta A}{A}}$, and $\sigma_{\frac{\Delta L}{L}}$ represent the standard deviations of the percentage changes in market value of equity capital, asset holdings, and liability claims, respectively.[11] Furthermore, $-1 \leq \rho \leq 1$ denotes the correlation between percentage value changes of assets and liability claims.[12]

$$\sigma^2_{\frac{\Delta E}{E}} = \left(\frac{A}{E}\right)^2 \sigma^2_{\frac{\Delta A}{A}} + \left(\frac{A}{E} - 1\right)^2 \sigma^2_{\frac{\Delta L}{L}} - 2\left(\frac{A}{E}\right)\left(\frac{A}{E} - 1\right)\rho\,\sigma_{\frac{\Delta A}{A}}\sigma_{\frac{\Delta L}{L}} \tag{9}$$

Equation 9 states the relationship in precise mathematical terms. It also incorporates the concept of correlation, which is an essential element of liability-driven investing. Exhibit 26 is a graphical representation of Equation 9 and illustrates the magnitude of the asset/liability correlation effect (ρ is measured on the x-axis) on the volatility of the financial institution's equity capital ($\sigma_{\frac{\Delta E}{E}}$ is measured on the y-axis) for various levels of leverage (the downward-sloping dotted lines). For purposes of this exhibit, the volatilities of asset and liability percentage value changes ($\sigma_{\frac{\Delta A}{A}}$, $\sigma_{\frac{\Delta L}{L}}$) are both assumed to be constant at 1.5%.

Exhibit 26 demonstrates that over the range of leverage shown (equity/assets ratios from 5% to 20%), the volatility of the financial institution's equity capital decreases as the correlation between asset and liability *value changes* (ρ) increases toward +1.0. This beneficial effect is most pronounced when the financial institution is highly leveraged.

For example, assuming leverage of 20% (assets/equity = 5x) and correlations (ρ) of 0.5 and then 0.9, the volatility of equity declines from 6.9% to 3.5%. However, if higher leverage is assumed, at 5% equity/assets, and ρ takes the same two values, then the decrease in volatility of equity from 29.3% to 13.2% is more dramatic.

If the correlation between assets and liabilities is 1.0, the volatility of shareholders' equity capital shrinks to minimal amounts, even for high leverage (equity to assets = 5.0%). However, the flip side is that any divergence in correlations—such as can often occur in turbulent markets—causes equity volatility to increase and especially dramatically when leverage is high.

10 Most notably, the duration model does not reflect well on non-linear factors, such as convexity and embedded options in many fixed-income securities and derivatives.

11 The variance of any random variable is equal to the square of the standard deviation of the variable.

12 Transforming Equation 4 into Equation 9 follows the basic statistical property that, for any random variable Z, which is a linear sum of two other random variables X and Y (specifically, $Z = AX + BY$), the variance of Z is $\sigma_Z^2 = A^2\sigma_X^2 + B^2\sigma_Y^2 + 2AB\rho\sigma_X\sigma_Y$. This expression does not depend on the nature and shape of the underlying probability distributions of either X or Y.

Exhibit 26: Volatility of Value of Shareholders' Equity as a Function of Correlation of Asset and Liability Value Changes and Beginning Leverage

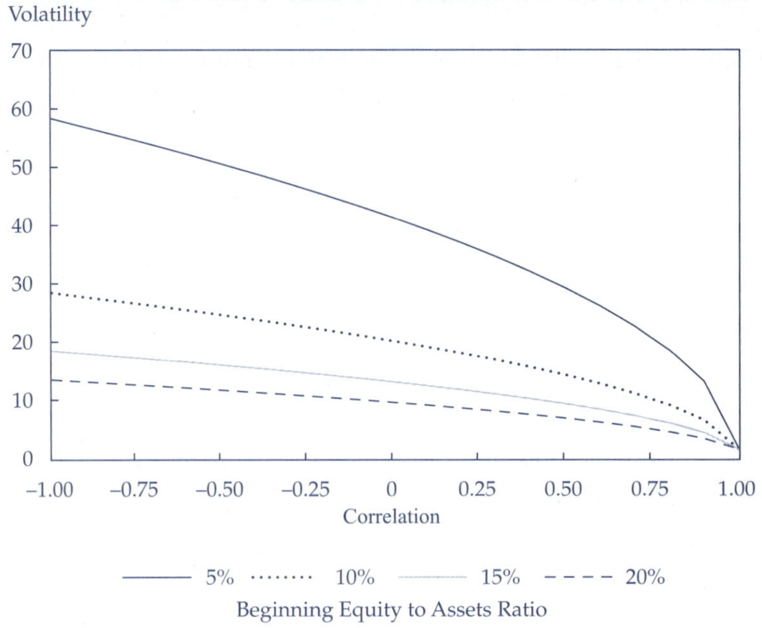

With the comprehensive framework provided by Equation 9, we next turn to a brief catalogue, shown in Exhibit 27, of how differing portfolio strategies and actions affect the inputs and thus the results of the volatility paradigm in Equation 9. Before doing so, however, it is important to note that hedging with derivatives, duration-based portfolio management and funding, and other techniques for raising the correlation between asset and liability values are not a cure-all. High correlations between assets and liabilities are not easy to achieve in practice, and often breakdown during periods of financial industry stress or stress in an individual institution. In the final analysis, techniques for raising correlations are not a pure substitute for maintaining adequate capitalization buffers.

Exhibit 27: Investment Strategies and Effects on Bank/Insurer Asset and Liability Volatility

Portfolio Strategy Considerations	Main Factors Affected	Explanation/Rationale	Additional Regulatory Concerns
Diversified fixed-income investments	Decreases $\frac{\sigma \Delta A}{A}$	Debt securities are less volatile than common equities, real estate, and other securities.	Effective diversification involves a multiplicity of issuers and industries, both domestic and foreign.
High-quality bond/debt investments	Decreases $\frac{\sigma \Delta A}{A}$	Overall, higher quality securities are less likely to be downgraded or default, thereby lessening the probability of significant loss of value through either losses or widening of credit spreads.	Regulatory structures and central banks favor sovereign issuers most for this reason.

Portfolio Strategy Considerations	Main Factors Affected	Explanation/Rationale	Additional Regulatory Concerns
Maintain reasonable balance between asset and liability durations, key rates durations, and sensitivity to embedded borrower and claimant options	Increases ρ	Requires more in-depth analysis than simple duration-matching strategy, because must account for convexity and asymmetric payoffs due to (i) defaults, (ii) principal payoffs prior to maturity, and (iii) annuity, life-insurance policy, and bank CD surrenders in high interest rate scenarios.	Regulatory structures penalize institutions with unjustifiable asset/liability mismatches.
Common Stock Investments	Increases $\sigma\frac{\Delta A}{A}$, typically decreases ρ	Equity and other high-volatility assets provide only slight diversification benefits while adding to volatility. Also, common stock returns do not correlate well with financial institution returns, which pushes correlation, ρ, away from 1.0 toward 0.0.	Most regulatory structures require 100% or more risk weighting for common stock investments thus, such investments are ineligible for backing financial liability issuance.
Derivatives transparency, collateralization	Decreases both $\sigma\frac{\Delta A}{A}$ and $\sigma\frac{\Delta L}{L}$ and increases ρ	Whether derivatives are used to hedge or synthesize (i) assets or (ii) liabilities, the more "plain vanilla" (and protected against counterparty default) they are, the less likely they will revalue in unexpected directions.	Transparency fosters regulatory "financial stress test" confidence. It also allows regulators and claimants to ascertain whether derivatives are being used in a justifiable manner.
Liquidity of portfolio investments	Decreases $\sigma\frac{\Delta A}{A}$	Includes short-maturity debt securities of highly rated issuers, currency reserves, access to credit lines, and access for banks to emergency central bank borrowing.	Problems occur for regulators when financial contagion extends beyond just a few institutions.
Surrender penalties	Decreases $\sigma\frac{\Delta L}{L}$	For typical life insurance, annuities, and bank deposits, such penalties cushion losses to financial institutions for having to pay back liabilities "at par" when rising interest rates would otherwise have reduced the discounted present value of the obligations.	Properly computed surrender penalties must account for interest rate volatility and slope of the yield curve. Typically, regulators/customers do not tolerate economically justified surrender penalties (they are usually priced too low to offset the institution's risk).
Prepayment penalties on debt investments	Increases ρ	When interest rates are declining, borrowers must incur a penalty to repay loans at par to refinance. Also, prepayment penalties help institutions offset rising values of their fixed-rate liabilities in falling rate environments.	None.
Catastrophic insurance risks	Increases $\sigma\frac{\Delta L}{L}$	By definition, these losses faced by insurance companies are less predictable and possibly very large.	Regulators and insurance customers usually expect (i) higher capital ratios, (ii) higher quality and liquid investment portfolios, and (iii) strong reinsurance agreements compared with typical home, health, auto, and fire insurance.

Portfolio Strategy Considerations	Main Factors Affected	Explanation/Rationale	Additional Regulatory Concerns
Predictability of underwriting losses	Decreases $\frac{\sigma \Delta L}{L}$	High frequency, low cost loss events caused by law of large numbers make total insurance liabilities less uncertain.	Adverse changes in legal or regulatory systems cannot be offset by actions on the asset side of the financial institution. These are risks borne by owners of the institution's equity capital.
Diversifying insurance business	Decreases $\frac{\sigma \Delta L}{L}$	Diversifying across several business lines increases aggregate risk-reduction potential (due to law of large numbers).	None.
Variable annuities	Increases ρ, and $\frac{\sigma \Delta A}{A}$, $\frac{\sigma \Delta L}{L}$ diminish in relevance	Where equity/bond market risks are fully borne by policyholders, the correlation between asset and liability returns approaches 1.0, independent of investment performance of the underlying, segregated account assets.	Assuming adequate risk disclosure to policyholders, and sufficient asset custody protections, regulators permit greater investment flexibility than in insurer's standard business lines.

The last key implication of the aggregate risk framework in Equation 9 relates to the importance of raising equity capitalization externally. The ability to raise capital is not just the key to expanding operations; more importantly, it is a way of buffering financial uncertainty. It diminishes both the probability of default to liability holders and the total volatility of equity capitalization values.[13] Over the past several decades, the financial industry has moved increasingly to publicly traded, for-profit, corporations, rather than mutual or membership co-ops. This is primarily because publicly traded companies can issue new common stock capital in cases of either opportunity or emergency. Mutual and membership co-ops (for example, credit unions) are restricted by the growth of their membership, which usually cannot change much over short periods of time.

EXAMPLE 8

Foresight International Assurance is an international multiline insurance conglomerate. Under its overall strategic financial plan, it computes the annualized standard deviation of returns on investment assets as 5.0% and on liabilities as 2.5%. The bulk of its liabilities are constituted by the net present value of expected claims payouts. The correlation between asset and liability returns is therefore a very low 0.25. Foresight's common equity to financial assets ratio is 20.0%.

13 Although raising equity ratios negatively impacts return on common equity (ROCE) and earnings per share of financial companies, the diminished volatility of earnings and economic value acts toward raising price-earnings and market-to-book ratios. Perhaps somewhat counterintuitively, the issuing of common stock by financial companies can be neutral or even a net benefit to pre-existing shareholders.

1. What is the standard deviation of changes in the value of Foresight's shareholder capitalization?

Solution:

We use Equation 9 recognizing that $A \div E = 1/0.20 = 5$; $(A \div E) - 1 = 4$; the standard deviation of asset returns ($\sigma_{\frac{\Delta A}{A}}$) = 0.05; the standard deviation of changes in liability values ($\sigma_{\frac{\Delta L}{L}}$) = 0.025; and the correlation between asset and liability value changes (ρ)= 0.25.

First, we compute the variance of shareholders' capital value changes:

$$\sigma^2_{\frac{\Delta E}{E}} = 5^2 \times 0.05^2 + 4^2 \times 0.025^2 - 2 \times 5 \times 4 \times 0.25 \times 0.05 \times 0.025 = 0.06.$$

The standard deviation of shareholder capital valuation change is the square root of the variance. Thus,

$$\sigma_{\frac{\Delta E}{E}} = \sqrt{\sigma^2_{\frac{\Delta E}{E}}} = \sqrt{0.06} = 0.245 = 24.5\% \text{ per year.}$$

2. Management believes the overall risk profile of the company is too high and desires to increase the common equity ratio by issuing additional shares of common equity and listing such shares on several international stock market exchanges. The new target equity ratio will be 25.0%. All other things being equal, how does this impact the volatility of value changes in shareholder capitalization?

Solution:

The new asset to equity ratio is $A \div E = 1/0.25 = 4$, and so $(A \div E) - 1 = 3$. Using the existing values of the other variables in Equation 9, we obtain

$$\sigma^2_{\frac{\Delta E}{E}} = 4^2 \times 0.05^2 + 3^2 \times 0.025^2 - 2 \times 4 \times 3 \times 0.25 \times 0.05 \times 0.025 = 0.038125.$$

from which we see $\sigma_{\frac{\Delta E}{E}} = \sqrt{\sigma^2_{\frac{\Delta E}{E}}} = \sqrt{0.038125} \approx 0.195 = 19.5\%$ per year.

3. Management believes it also needs to lower the volatility of its assets. It shifts out of low-quality bonds into higher quality, more liquid government securities and, by doing so, expects to lower the standard deviation of asset returns to 4.0% per year without having any impact on the correlation ratio between assets and liabilities. Along with the stronger capital ratios premised in question 2, what does this do to the volatility of shareholder equity value?

Solution:

Equation 9 now produces the following results:

$$\sigma^2_{\frac{\Delta E}{E}} = 4^2 \times 0.04^2 + 3^2 \times 0.025^2 - 2 \times 4 \times 3 \times 0.25 \times 0.04 \times 0.025 = 0.025225$$

from which we obtain $\sigma_{\frac{\Delta E}{E}} = \sqrt{\sigma^2_{\frac{\Delta E}{E}}} = \sqrt{0.025225} \approx 0.159 = 15.9\%$.

4. What is the impact of the various portfolio and capitalization changes on the value of Foresight's common shares outstanding? Explain your answer.

Solution:

We note that the proposed changes are likely to reduce earnings per share, first by having a greater number of shares outstanding and second by lowering the expected returns on assets (because there will now be a greater percentage of safer, lower yielding assets). All other things being equal, this would pressure the common stock price. However, Foresight is also lowering its overall equity risk exposure while strengthening its reputation as a more soundly operated and capitalized insurance company. The lower risk profile might well result in a higher credit rating and a lower discount rate at which the lower earnings per share trajectory is valued. Also, the improved long-term survivability and underwriting strength could result in a higher *long-term* growth outlook. In sum, the impact on common equity prices cannot be predicted merely by a change in capital structure and near-term reduction in earnings and portfolio expected returns.

22 BANKS AND INSURERS: IMPLEMENTATION OF PORTFOLIO DECISIONS

☐ describe considerations affecting the balance sheet management of banks and insurers

With sovereign wealth funds, endowments, foundations, and employee benefit plans (DB and DC), the investment adviser must primarily focus on the investment of assets. In the case of financial institutions, optimal management must simultaneously focus on liabilities, particularly the volatility and convexity of asset and liability payouts. Consequently, the investment strategy of financial institutions must also consider the appropriate degree of leverage and total amount of common equity capital. Returning to the basic framework of Equations 2 and 4, the proper way to maximize long-term economic earnings thus might be to raise (lower) leverage through: (a) the acquisition (disposal) of portfolio assets; (b) the underwriting (retirement) of liabilities; or (c) the repurchase (issuance) of capital stock.

The financial management of a bank or insurer has not only to deal with the level and direction of interest rates, credit spreads, derivatives markets, economic cycles, and stock markets as they impact the investment portfolio, but we also now see it needs to have a keen understanding of the valuation of its own common equity and debt capital securities. Financial management also requires a view on the actions of competitors. For example, will they create a housing bubble through excessive lending to low-quality borrowers? Will they drive down insurance policy premiums through overly aggressive underwriting? Finally, financial management must satisfy all existing regulations as well as the ones that may evolve with changes in global economic circumstances and other political pressures.

In sum, financial and portfolio management of banks and insurance companies is an attempt to create positive net present value for capital holders by solving simultaneously several different conditions with several different variables. Consequently, key decisions are typically made at the highest levels of the institution's management. Specific analysts and investment managers are typically assigned only to specialized subsets of the institution's varied assets and liabilities.

In such dynamically changing economic and regulatory environments, it is difficult to specify particular portfolio investment rules and policies. Therefore, the following mini-case studies are offered to provide illustrations of the types of high-level portfolio decisions that are required.

EXAMPLE 9

Mini-Case A:

A bank considers reducing its ownership of commercial loans in smaller businesses. These loans pay interest quarterly at various contractually pre-specified spreads above the floating market reference rate (MRR). The runoff of the loan portfolio through repayments, together with proceeds of outright sales and securitizations of other loans, are to be reinvested in a portfolio of fixed-rate government securities of comparable maturities. The securities will be hedged fully against general interest rate risk through the use of publicly traded options and futures on government securities. Additionally, hedging interest rate risk completely would create a synthetic variable rate asset. If interest rates rise, gains on hedges can be reinvested to raise overall portfolio income; if interest rates fall, losses on hedges will require some assets to pay counterparties, thereby lowering overall portfolio income.

1. How would this portfolio restructuring affect the asset/liability profile of the bank?
2. What is the expected impact on the volatility of bank shareholder equity valuation?
3. What is the likely impact on bank earnings?
4. What are reasons that argue in favor of this portfolio redeployment?

Solution to 1:

Switching from variable rate to fixed-rate assets of similar maturities increases the duration of the bank's overall portfolio. However, entering into hedging positions with futures and options on fixed-rate assets has the effect of shortening overall duration. As described, the net effect of the portfolio alteration likely should have little effect on the bank's existing asset/liability duration profile, because floating-rate corporate loans also have little price exposure in the event of rising or falling interest rates.

Solution to 2:

The overall volatility of assets and bank capitalization should decrease, because a hedged portfolio of government securities is more liquid than a portfolio of individual small business loans and also less subject to volatility arising from changes in credit default spreads on corporate loans.

Solution to 3:

Bank earnings would be expected to decline, independent of subsequent changes in the overall level of interest rates. This is because the yields on business loans, adjusting for expected default rates, are higher than on government securities, adjusting for the costs of hedging the government securities. Furthermore, if overall interest rates subsequently rise, the business loan portfolio would generate higher income to the bank. However, hedges on the government securities generate gains when interest rates rise—offsetting losses on the underlying securities and thus permitting more money to be reinvested in now higher yielding government securities. Similarly, a decline in interest rates would lead to a loss on the hedges and a sale of appreciated underlying government securities to cover these hedge losses. The portfolio value is approximately unchanged, but the (reduced) ability to generate income has tracked interest rates downward. In sum, *changes* in overall interest rates impact income-generating ability similarly for both the loan portfolio and the hedged securities portfolio. This is the flip side of the coin; in other words, the two portfolios have similar modified durations. In any environment, the net yields on the hedged government securities are lower than on the business loans. Thus, bank net income is unambiguously lower because of the portfolio rebalancing.

Solution to 4:

Although the proposed redeployment is expected to lower bank earnings, there are at least three good reasons for this action, any of which would justify the decision: (a) the bank believes it needs to have a more liquid investment portfolio because of the risk of unexpected claims against assets; (b) the bank needs to raise its regulatory "equity to risky assets" ratio (by substituting low credit-risk for high credit-risk assets); and (c), the bank believes it will be able to reverse the trade in the future after a recession has driven up the effective default-adjusted spreads (i.e., driven down the prices) on small business loans. In all three rationales, overall volatility is expected to decline and the reduction in volatility is expected to provide a benefit that more than offsets the anticipated reduction in earnings. That is, the risk-adjusted return is projected to rise.

Mini-Case B:

A medium size insurance company plans to sell a large portion of its diversified, fixed-rate, investment-grade-rated securities in order to redeploy proceeds into a special purpose trust holding a diversified portfolio of automobile loans with original loan lives of 5 years. The loans are collateralized by direct liens on the vehicles, and the underlying borrowers meet minimum consumer credit scores set by a national credit rating agency. The underlying loans were randomly selected for the trust, and the collateral constitutes a nationwide sample of automobiles of different foreign and domestic manufacturers.

1. What does this transaction reveal about the regulatory capital of this insurer?
2. What key information must the insurer know about the automobile loans held by the trust in order to manage its asset/liability duration profile?
3. What external factors might the insurer need to consider with respect to the duration of trust assets?
4. What is the expected impact from the proposed investment transaction on (a) the insurer's earnings, and (b), the overall volatility of the insurer's common equity capitalization?

Solution to 1:

The portfolio redeployment reduces the insurer's liquidity. Given that the insurer is able to undertake this action, the company has excess regulatory capital, because the underlying illiquid loans require more regulatory capital than high-quality/investment-grade, marketable, fixed-income securities.

Solution to 2:

The insurer must make actuarial projections of contractual cash flows from the auto loans, which must take into account full and partial pre-payments because of accidents, auto trade-ins, and loan defaults. The acceptable credit quality of the borrowers and the geographical and brand diversity contribute to the accuracy of such predictions. The overall asset/liability profile for the insurer might well change depending on how the projected modified duration of the auto loan receivables compares with the investment-grade marketable securities to be sold. A material difference might require management to undertake (a) changes in the modified duration of the insurance company's liabilities, such as by altering the maturities of future debt issuances; or (b), implementation of interest rate-hedging transactions.

Solution to 3:

The insurer must be concerned about an adverse change in the economic cycle, changes in technology, and/or energy prices—all of which could adversely impact the value of the auto loan receivables (as compared with the marketable securities portfolio to be sold) and which could undermine the cash flow assumptions made with respect to setting the company's overall asset/liability profile.

Solution to 4:

The portfolio redeployment is likely to raise the insurer's earnings, because the expected yield on the auto loans, net of credit losses, is higher than for investment-grade, liquid securities. However, the company is taking on more credit risk, which should translate into higher volatility of the value of assets and, thus, higher volatility of equity capitalization.

Mini-Case C:

Floating-rate securities, paying a fixed spread over the floating MRR, are trading at historically narrow yield spreads over MRR. In addition, issuers of these securities tend to be concentrated disproportionately in a small number of industries—notably in banks, insurers, and other financial services companies. A bank's investment manager considers selling the bank's portfolio holdings of these floating-rate securities, which have a 5-year maturity and trade at 0.1% over MRR. The proceeds will be used to buy more-diversified (by issuer type), investment-grade, fixed-rate securities that are selling at more normal spreads versus government bond yields of comparable duration (which trade at 1.0% over 5-year US Treasury bond yields). The fixed-rate securities portfolio is to be combined with pay-fixed/receive-floating interest rate swaps under standard mark-to-market collateralization terms. The 5-year interest rate swap terms permit one to receive MRR while paying 0.4% over Treasury yields.

1. What does the portfolio alteration do to required regulatory risk-based capital?
2. What might indicate that the bank's senior managers are more concerned about risks to equity capitalization than are regulators?
3. What is the expected effect on the bank's asset/liability profile?
4. What is the expected effect on expected earnings?
5. Summarize the rationale for the portfolio alteration.

Solution to 1:

To a first approximation, substituting one kind of marketable security for another should have little effect on regulatory risk-based capital requirements, because there is little apparent change in average credit quality. The new portfolio will have more issuer and industry diversification than the securities being sold. Thus, under robust scenario simulation testing, the new portfolio should be somewhat more resistant to loss than the more-concentrated portfolio assets being sold.

Solution to 2:

The bank's senior managers appear to be concerned about systemic risk in the financial sector, especially since the securities the bank plans to sell are concentrated in the financial sector and are trading at unusually high prices (narrow spreads to MRR). Apart from interest rate risk, the probability of underperformance for financial company securities is higher than for a diversified portfolio of fixed-rate securities. In the bank's view, the prospective volatility of floating-rate bank assets—and thus, the company's own equity capital—is higher than what is reflected in the regulatory risk-weight framework, because the latter does not take into account relative price risk. Thus, from the bank's perspective, the proposed trade lowers asset and equity volatility.

Solution to 3:

Substituting fixed-rate securities in place of variable-rate securities tends to increase the modified duration of the bank's assets. However, entering into a pay-fixed/receive-floating swap is equivalent to creating a synthetic liability, which becomes (i) smaller as interest rates rise and (ii) greater as interest rates fall. The interest rate swap can be tailored to offset the tendency of the newly acquired fixed-rate securities to lose value as interest rates rise and gain value as interest rates fall. Said differently, the synthetic liability increases the duration of the bank's liabilities to counterbalance the rise in asset duration from replacing variable-rate with fixed-rate debt securities.

Solution to 4:

Earnings are expected to rise. The securities sold pay a low spread over MRR. The new package (fixed-rate securities plus pay-fixed/receive-floating interest rate swap) pays a higher expected spread over MRR. The high yield received on the fixed-rate securities, net of the fixed-rate leg of the interest rate swap paid, represents the new built-in spread that is then added to the MRR received in the floating-leg of the interest rate swap. Specifically, the new portfolio will (i) receive 5-year Treasury yield plus 1.0% on the fixed-rate securities, (ii) pay 5-year Treasury yield plus 0.4% on the fixed leg of the interest rate swap, and (iii) receive MRR on the floating side of the interest rate swap. The net result is that the hedged, fixed-rate holdings will pay the bank the 5-year Treasury yield (T) + 1.0% – (T + 0.4%) + MRR = MRR + 0.6%. This synthetic floating-rate portfolio compares with the original floating-rate portfolio that paid just MRR + 0.1%.

Solution to 5:

A pay-fixed/receive-floating interest rate swap is "plain vanilla"; it is easy to value and unwind. The trade would thus not have any major adverse impact on the institution's liquidity. The bank, by selling securities in the banking and financial services industry, can lower its own exposure to systemic financial risk. In essence, the trade achieves better diversification while creating cheap (i.e., higher yielding) synthetic MRR floaters in place of true MRR floaters. The regulatory system in which the bank operates likely has a statistical system that penalizes excessive use of derivatives by deeming worst-case liabilities in a stress test. This should not be an issue assuming the proposed trade is small enough, relative to the institution's size, to have no significant impact on stress test results. Overall, the trade would be a duration-neutral trade, achieving higher net earnings and lower asset and equity risk without significantly impacting the bank's regulatory capital ratios.

Mini-Case D:

In the aftermath of prolonged financial turmoil and a recession, a large pan-European life insurance company believes that corporate debt securities and asset-based securities are now very attractive relative to more-liquid government securities. The yield spreads more than compensate for default and credit downgrade risk. Interest rates for government securities are near cyclical lows. The insurance company is concerned that rates may rise and that, as a result, many outstanding annuities might be surrendered. The insurer believes the probability of a large, adverse move in interest rates is much higher than is currently reflected by the implied volatility of traded options on government securities in the eurozone. The insurer's regulatory capital and reserves are deemed to be healthy.

1. What are the consequences of lowering allocations to government securities and raising allocations to corporate and asset-backed securities?
2. Are there steps that the insurer should take on the liability side?

Solution to 1:

These proposed asset reallocations have several implications. First, corporate debt securities have higher yields and thus shorter durations than government securities of similar maturity. Asset-backed securities tend to have lower effective durations than corporate and government bonds. Thus, the proposed rebalancing would likely lower the overall duration of the investment portfolio, which is consistent with the insurer's concerns about rising interest rates and the expected consequences. Second, the change in portfolio allocation would likely lower the company's overall liquidity and lower regulatory risk-based capital measures, because the new securities are treated less favorably for regulatory purposes (less liquid, higher credit risk corporate debt and asset-backed securities require a higher equity charge than liquid, low credit risk government securities, so regulatory "equity to risky assets" is reduced). Thus, the proposed portfolio moves make sense only if the regulatory capital position of the insurer is already ample and if the existing liquidity elsewhere in the portfolio is enough to fund an uptick of annuity surrenders in the case of rising interest rates. Finally, the reallocation would increase expected earnings (from higher interest income) and set the stage for price gains if credit spreads versus government securities contract to more normal levels.

Solution to 2:

Because overall interest rates are low, the company must also deal with an asymmetric risk separate and apart from the reallocation of its investment portfolio. In other words, the insurer must alter its liability profile in order to minimize potential adverse changes in its common equity capitalization. A spike up in interest rates could result in a rise in surrenders of annuities during a time when asset values are coming under pressure. Because the company is more concerned about higher interest rate volatility than is reflected in current option prices, the insurer might consider purchasing out-of-the-money puts on government securities and/or purchasing swaptions with the right to be a fixed-payer/floating-receiver. Sharp rises in rates would make both positions profitable[14] and offset some of the burden of premature annuity surrenders. If time passes without any substantial rise in interest rates, the cost of purchasing option protection would detract from the incremental benefits from the proposed switch into higher yielding securities.

SUMMARY

This reading has introduced the subject of managing institutional investor portfolios. The key points made in this reading are as follows:

- The main institutional investor types are pension plans, sovereign wealth funds, endowments, foundations, banks, and insurance companies. Common characteristics among these investors include a large scale (i.e., asset size), a long-term investment horizon, regulatory constraints, a clearly defined governance framework, and principal–agent issues.
- Institutional investors typically codify their mission, investment objectives, and guidelines in an Investment Policy Statement (IPS).
- Four common investment approaches to managing portfolios used by institutional investors are the Norway model, the Endowment model, the Canada model, and the Liability Driven Investing (LDI) model.
- There are two main types of pension plans: defined benefit (DB), in which a plan sponsor commits to paying a specified retirement benefit; and defined contribution (DC), in which contributions are defined but the ultimate retirement benefit is not specified or guaranteed by the plan sponsor.
- Pension plan stakeholders include the employer, employees, retirees, unions, management, the investment committee and/or board of directors, and shareholders.
- The key elements in the calculation of DB plan liabilities are as follows:
    - Service/tenure: The higher the service years, the higher the retirement benefit.
    - Salary/earnings: The higher the salary over the measurement period, the higher the retirement benefit.
    - Mortality/longevity: The longer the participant's expected life span, the higher the plan sponsor's liability.
    - Vesting: Lower turnover results in higher vesting, increasing the plan sponsor's liabilities.
    - Discount rate: A higher discount rate reduces the present value of the plan sponsor's liabilities.
- DB plan liquidity needs are driven by the following:
    - Proportion of active employees relative to retirees: More mature pension funds have higher liquidity needs.

14 A put option becomes valuable to the holder if prices of the underlying asset fall. A swaption with the right to enter a swap paying fixed and receiving floating is economically analogous to a put option on a bond. If rates rise, the swaption owner has the right to receive a rising stream of floating payments in exchange for what will have then become a stream of reasonably low fixed payments. The swaption contract will have gained in value.

    - Age of workforce: Liquidity needs rise as the age of the workforce increases.
    - Plan funded status: If the plan is well funded, the sponsor may reduce contributions, generating a need to hold higher balances of liquid assets to pay benefits.
    - Flexibility: Ability of participants to switch among the sponsor's plans or to withdraw from the plan.
- Pension plans are subject to significant and evolving regulatory constraints designed to ensure the integrity, adequacy, and sustainability of the pension system. Some incentives, such as tax exemption, are only granted to plans that meet these regulatory requirements. Notable differences in legal, regulatory, and tax considerations can lead to differences in plan design from one country to another or from one group to another (e.g., public plans vs. corporate plans).
- The following risk considerations affect the way DB plans are managed:
    - Plan funded status
    - Sponsor financial strength
    - Interactions between the sponsor's business and the fund's investments
    - Plan design
    - Workforce characteristics
- An examination of pension fund asset allocations shows very large differences in average asset allocations by country and within a country despite these plans seeking to achieve similar goals. Such inter- and intra-national differences are driven by many factors, including the differences in legal, regulatory, accounting, and tax constraints; the investment objectives, risk appetites, and investment views of the stakeholders; the liabilities to and demographics of the ultimate beneficiaries; the availability of suitable investment opportunities; and the expected cost of living in retirement.
- The major types of sovereign wealth funds (SWFs) follow:
    - Budget Stabilization funds: Set up to insulate the budget and economy from commodity price volatility and external shocks.
    - Development funds: Established to allocate resources to priority socioeconomic projects, usually infrastructure.
    - Savings funds: Intended to share wealth across generations by transforming non-renewable assets into diversified financial assets.
    - Reserve funds: Intended to reduce the negative carry costs of holding foreign currency reserves or to earn higher return on ample reserves.
    - Pension Reserve funds: Set up to meet identified future outflows with respect to pension-related, contingent-type liabilities on governments' balance sheets.
- Stakeholders of SWFs include the country's citizens, the government, external asset managers, and the SWF's management, investment committee and board of directors.
- Given their mission of intergenerational wealth transfer, SWFs do not generally have clearly defined liabilities, so do not typically pursue asset/liability matching strategies used by other institutional investor types.

- Sovereign wealth funds have differing liquidity needs. Budget stabilization funds require the most liquidity, followed by reserve funds. At the other end of the spectrum are savings funds with low liquidity needs, followed by pension reserve funds.
- The investment objectives of SWFs are often clearly articulated in the legislative instruments that create them. They are often tax free in their home country, though must take foreign taxation into consideration. Given their significant asset sizes and the nature of their stakeholders, SWFs have aimed to increase transparency regarding their investment activities. In this regard, the Santiago Principles are a form of self-regulation.
- The typical asset allocation by SWF type shows budget stabilization funds are invested mainly in bonds and cash given their liquidity needs. Reserve Funds invest in equities and alternatives but maintain a significant allocation of bonds for liquidity. Savings funds and pension reserve funds hold relatively higher allocations of equities and alternatives because of their longer-term liabilities.
- Endowments and foundations typically invest to maintain purchasing power while financing their supporting university (endowments) or making grants (foundations) in perpetuity—based on the notion of intergenerational equity. Endowments and foundations usually have a formal spending policy that determines how much is paid out annually to support their mission. This future stream of payouts represents their liabilities. For endowments, other liability-related factors to be considered when setting investment policy are: 1) the ability to raise additional funds from donors/alumni, 2) the percentage of the university's operating budget provided by the endowment, and 3) the ability to issue debt.
- Foundations and endowments typically enjoy tax-exempt status and face relatively little regulation compared to other types of institutional investors.
- Foundations face less flexible spending rules compared to endowments; foundations in the US are legally mandated to pay out 5% of their assets annually to maintain tax-exempt status. Endowments and foundations have relatively low liquidity needs. However, foundations have somewhat higher liquidity needs (vs. endowments), because they 1) typically pay out slightly more as a percentage of assets, and 2) finance the entire operating budget of the organization they support.
- Endowments and foundations typically have a long-term real return objective of about 5% consistent with their spending policies. This real return objective, and a desire to maintain purchasing power, results in endowments and foundations making significant allocations to real assets. In general, endowments and foundations invest heavily in private asset classes and hedge funds and have relatively small allocations to fixed income.
- Banking and insurance companies manage both portfolio assets and institutional liabilities to achieve an extremely high probability that obligations on deposits, guarantees, derivatives, policyholder claims, and other liabilities will be paid in full and on time.
- Banking and insurance companies have perpetual time horizons. Strategically, their goal is to maximize net present value to capital holders; tactically, this may be achieved by liability driven investing (LDI) over intermediate and shorter horizons.

- Financial institutions are highly regulated because of their importance to the non-financial, or real, sectors of the economy. Such institutions are also regulated in order to minimize contagion risk rippling throughout the financial and real sectors.
- The underlying premise of regulation is that an institution's capital must be adequate to absorb shocks to both asset and liability values. This implies limiting the volatility of value of the institution's shareholder capital.
- The volatility of shareholder capital can be managed by (a) reducing the price volatility of portfolio investments, loans, and derivatives; (b) lowering the volatility from unexpected shocks to claims, deposits, guarantees, and other liabilities; (c) limiting leverage; and (d) attempting to achieve positive correlation between changes in the value of assets and liabilities.
- Ample liquidity, diversification of portfolio and other assets, high investment quality, transparency, stable funding, duration management, diversification of insurance underwriting risks, and monetary limits on guarantees, funding commitments, and insurance claims are some of the ways management and regulators attempt to achieve low volatility of shareholder capital value.

REFERENCES

OECD. 2016. *OECD Insurance Statistics 2008–2016*. https://read.oecd-ilibrary.org/finance-and-investment/oecd-insurance-statistics-2016_ins_stats-2016-en#page1.

Willis Towers Watson Thinking Ahead Institute. 2021. "*Global Pension Assets Study 2021*" (February). https://www.thinkingaheadinstitute.org/research-papers/global-pension-assets-study-2021.

PRACTICE PROBLEMS

The following information relates to questions 1-5

Bern Zang is the recently hired chief investment officer of the Janson University Endowment Investment Office. The Janson University Endowment Fund (the Fund) is based in the United States and has current assets under management of $12 billion. It has a long-term investment horizon and relatively low liquidity needs. The Fund is overseen by an Investment Committee consisting of board members for the Fund. The Investment Office is responsible for implementing the investment policy set by the Fund's Investment Committee.

The Fund's current investment approach includes an internally managed fund that holds mostly equities and fixed-income securities. It is largely passively managed with tight tracking error limits. The target asset allocation is 55% equities, 40% fixed income, and 5% alternatives. The Fund currently holds private real estate investments to meet its alternative investment allocation.

1. **Identify** the investment approach currently being used by the Investment Committee for managing the Fund. **Justify** your response.

Identify the investment approach currently being used by the Investment Committee for managing the Fund.
(circle one)

Norway Model	Endowment Model	Canadian Model	LDI Model

Justify your response.

2. **Discuss** the advantages and the disadvantages of the investment approach currently being used by the Investment Committee.

	Discuss the advantages and the disadvantages of the investment approach currently being used by the Investment Committee.
Advantages	
Disadvantages	

3. **Describe** how *each* of the following common characteristics of institutional investors supports the Fund's allocation to private real estate:

   i. Scale
   ii. Investment horizon
   iii. Governance framework

	Describe how *each* of the following common characteristics of institutional investors supports the Fund's allocation to private real estate.
Scale	
Investment Horizon	
Governance Framework	

4. After a thorough internal review, Zang concludes that the current investment approach will result in a deterioration of the purchasing power of the Fund over time. He proposes a new, active management approach that will substantially decrease the allocation to publicly traded equities and fixed income in order to pursue a higher allocation to private investments. The management of the new investments will be outsourced.

   Identify the new investment approach proposed by Zang for managing the Fund. **Justify** your response.

Identify the new investment approach proposed by Zang for managing the Fund. (circle one)

Norway Model	Endowment Model	Canadian Model	LDI Model
Justify your response.			

5. After a thorough internal review, Zang concludes that the current investment approach will result in a deterioration of the purchasing power of the Fund over time. He proposes a new, active management approach that will substantially decrease the allocation to publicly traded equities and fixed income in order to pursue a higher allocation to private investments. The management of the new investments will be outsourced.

   Discuss the advantages and the disadvantages of the new investment approach proposed by Zang.

	Discuss the advantages and the disadvantages of the new investment approach proposed by Zang.
Advantages	
Disadvantages	

The following information relates to questions 6-12

William Azarov is a portfolio manager for Westcome Investments, an asset management firm. Azarov is preparing for meetings with two of Westcome's clients and obtains the help of Jason Boulder, a junior analyst. The first meeting is with Maglav Inc., a rapidly growing US-based technology firm with a young workforce and high employee turnover. Azarov directs Boulder to review the details of Maglav's defined benefit (DB) pension plan. The plan is overfunded and has assets under management of $25 million. Boulder makes the following two observations:

Observation 1	Maglav's shareholders benefit from the plan's overfunded status.
Observation 2	The funded ratio of Maglav's plan will decrease if employee turnover decreases.

Maglav outsources the management of the pension plan entirely to Westcome Investments. The fee structure requires Maglav to compensate Westcome with a high base fee regardless of performance. Boulder tells Azarov that outsourcing offers small institutional investors, such as Maglav's pension plan, the following three benefits:

Benefit 1: Regulatory requirements are reduced.

Benefit 2: Conflicts of interest are eliminated from principal–agent issues.

Benefit 3: Investors have access to a wider range of investment strategies through scale benefits.

In the meeting with Maglav, Azarov describes the investment approach used by Westcome in managing the pension plan. The approach is characterized by a high allocation to alternative investments, significant active management, and a reliance on outsourcing assets to other external asset managers. Azarov also explains that Maglav's operating results have a low correlation with pension asset returns and that the investment strategy is affected by the fact that the pension fund assets are a small portion of Maglav's market capitalization. Azarov states that the plan is subject to the Employee Retirement Income Security Act of 1974 (ERISA) and follows generally accepted accounting principles, including Accounting Standards Codification (ASC) 715, *Compensation—Retirement Benefits*.

Azarov's second meeting is with John Spintop, chief investment officer of the Wolf University Endowment Fund (the Fund). Spintop hired Westcome to assist in developing a new investment policy to present to the Fund's board of directors. The Fund, which has assets under management of $200 million, has an overall objective of maintaining long-term purchasing power while providing needed financial support to Wolf University. During the meeting, Spintop states that the Fund has an annual spending policy of paying out 4% of the Fund's three-year rolling asset value to Wolf University, and the Fund's risk tolerance should consider the following three liability characteristics:

Characteristic 1	The Fund has easy access to debt markets.
Characteristic 2	The Fund supports 10% of Wolf University's annual budget.
Characteristic 3	The Fund receives significant annual inflows from gifts and donations.

The Fund has a small investment staff with limited experience in managing alternative assets and currently uses the Norway model for its investment approach. Azarov suggests a change in investment approach by making an allocation to externally managed alternative assets—namely, hedge funds and private equity. Ten-year nominal expected return assumptions for various asset classes, as well as three proposed allocations that include some allocation to alternative assets, are presented in Exhibit 1.

Exhibit 1: 10-Year Nominal Expected Return Assumptions and Proposed Allocations

Asset Class	Expected Return	Allocation 1	Allocation 2	Allocation 3
US Treasuries	4.1%	45%	10%	13%
US Equities	6.3%	40%	15%	32%
Non-US Equities	7.5%	10%	15%	40%
Hedge Funds	5.0%	0%	30%	5%
Private Equity	9.1%	5%	30%	10%

Expected inflation for the next 10 years is 2.5% annually.

6. Which of Boulder's observations regarding Maglav's pension plan is correct?

   A. Only Observation 1

   B. Only Observation 2

   C. Both Observation 1 and Observation 2

7. Which of the benefits of outsourcing the management of the pension plan suggested by Boulder is correct?

   A. Benefit 1

   B. Benefit 2

   C. Benefit 3

8. Westcome's investment approach for Maglav's pension plan can be *best* characterized as the:

   A. Norway model.

   B. Canadian model.

   C. endowment model.

9. The risk tolerance of Maglav's pension plan can be *best* characterized as being:

   A. below average.

   B. average.

   C. above average.

10. Based on Azarov's statement concerning ERISA and ASC 715, which of the following statements is correct?

    A. Maglav is not allowed to terminate the plan.

    B. Maglav can exclude the plan's service costs from net income.

    C. Maglav's plan must appear as an asset on Maglav's balance sheet.

11. The risk tolerance of the Wolf University Endowment Fund can be *best* characterized as:

    A. below average.

B. average.

C. above average.

12. Which proposed allocation in Exhibit 1 would be *most appropriate* for the Fund given its characteristics?
    A. Allocation 1
    B. Allocation 2
    C. Allocation 3

The following information relates to questions 13-15

The Prometheo University Scholarship Endowment (the Endowment) was established in 1950 and supports scholarships for students attending Prometheo University. The Endowment's assets under management are relatively small, and it has an annual spending policy of 6% of the five-year rolling asset value.

13. **Formulate** the investment objectives section of the investment policy statement for the Endowment.

14. Prometheo University recently hired a new chief investment officer (CIO). The CIO directs her small staff of four people to implement an investment policy review. Historically, the endowment has invested 60% of the portfolio in US equities and 40% in US Treasuries. The CIO's expectation of annual inflation for the next 10 years is 2.5%.

    The CIO develops nominal 10-year return assumptions for US Treasuries and US equities, which are presented in Exhibit 1.

Exhibit 1: Asset Class Return Assumptions

Asset Class	10-Year Return Assumptions (Nominal)
US Treasuries	4.0%
US Equities	7.4%

Discuss whether the current investment policy is appropriate given the Endowment's annual spending policy.

15. Upon completion of the investment policy review by her four-person staff, the CIO makes some recommendations to the Endowment's board regarding the investment objectives and asset allocation. One of her recommendations is to adopt the endowment model as an investment approach. She recommends investing 20% in private equity, 40% in hedge funds, 25% in public equities, and 15% in fixed income.

    Determine whether the board should accept the CIO's recommendation. **Justify** your response.

Determine whether the board should accept the CIO's recommendation. (circle one)	Justify your response.
Accept	
Reject	

16. Fiona Heselwith is a 40-year-old US citizen who has accepted a job with Lyricul, LLC, a UK-based company. Her benefits package includes a retirement savings plan. The company offers both a defined benefit (DB) plan and a defined contribution (DC) plan but stipulates that employees must choose one plan and remain with that plan throughout their term of employment.

The DB plan is fully funded and provides full vesting after five years. The benefit formula for monthly payments upon retirement is calculated as follows:

- Final monthly salary × Benefit percentage of 2% × Number of years of service
- The final monthly salary is equal to average monthly earnings for the last five financial years immediately prior to the retirement date.

The DC plan contributes 12% of annual salary into the plan each year and is also fully vested after five years. Lyricul offers its DC plan participants a series of life-cycle funds as investment choices. Heselwith could choose a fund with a target date matching her planned retirement date. She would be able to make additional contributions from her salary if she chooses.

Discuss the features that Heselwith should consider in evaluating the two plans with respect to the following:

i. Benefit payments

ii. Contributions

iii. Shortfall risk

iv. Mortality/longevity risks

	Discuss the features that Heselwith should consider in evaluating the two plans with respect to the following:
Benefit Payments	
Contributions	
Shortfall Risk	
Mortality/ Longevity Risks	

17. Dianna Mark is the chief financial officer of Antiliaro, a relatively mature textile production company headquartered in Italy. All of its revenues come from Europe, but the company is losing sales to its Asian competitors. Earnings have been steady but not growing, and the balance sheet has taken on more debt in the past few years in order to maintain liquidity. Mark reviews the following facts concerning the company's defined benefit (DB) pension plan:

- The DB plan currently has €1 billion in assets and is underfunded by €100 million in relation to the projected benefit obligation (PBO) because of investment losses.

- The company to date has made regular contributions.
- The average employee age is 50 years, and the company has many retirees owing to its longevity.
- The duration of the plan's liabilities (which are all Europe based) is 10 years.
- The discount rate applied to these liabilities is 6%.
- There is a high correlation between the operating results of Antiliaro and pension asset returns.

Determine whether the risk tolerance of the DB plan is below average or above average. **Justify** your response with *two* reasons.

Determine whether the risk tolerance of the DB plan is below average or above average. (circle one)	Justify your response with *two* reasons.
Below Average	1.
Above Average	2.

18. Meura Bancorp, a US bank, has an equity capital ratio for financial assets of 12%. Meura's strategic plans include the incorporation of additional debt in order to leverage earnings since the current capital structure is relatively conservative. The bank plans to restructure the balance sheet so that the equity capitalization ratio drops to 10% and the modified duration of liabilities is 1.90. The bank also plans to rebalance its investment portfolio to achieve a modified duration of assets of 2.10. Given small changes in interest rates, the yield on liabilities is expected to move by 65 bps for every 100 bps of yield change in the asset portfolio.

    Calculate the modified duration of the bank's equity capital after restructuring. **Show** your calculations.

SOLUTIONS

1.

Identify the investment approach currently being used by the Investment Committee for managing the Fund.
(circle one)

Norway Model	Endowment Model	Canadian Model	LDI Model

Justify your response.

The investment approach currently used to manage the Fund's assets is the Norway model. This approach is characterized by a heavy allocation to public equities and fixed-income securities with little allocation to alternatives and largely passively managed assets with tight tracking error limits.

2.

	Discuss the advantages and the disadvantages of the investment approach currently being used by the Investment Committee.
Advantages	Advantages of using the Norway model are that investment costs/fees are low, investments are transparent, manager risk is low, and there is little complexity for a governing board (the model is easy to understand).
Disadvantages	The disadvantage of using the Norway model is that there is limited potential for value-added (i.e., alpha from security selection skills), above-market returns.

3.

	Describe how *each* of the following common characteristics of institutional investors supports the Fund's allocation to private real estate.
Scale	The Fund has $12 billion of assets under management. Its relatively large size allows it access to a broad investment universe and to investments that have a high minimum investment size, such as private real estate.
Investment Horizon	Alternative investments, such as private real estate, require a long-term investment horizon. Janson, like most university endowments, has a long-term investment horizon and relatively low liquidity needs. This makes private real estate an appropriate investment and also helps the endowment maintain long-term purchasing power.
Governance Framework	Institutional investors usually operate under a formal governance framework. Janson has a well-structured governance framework that includes an Investment Committee that is part of the board overseeing the endowment's investment portfolio. This framework also includes an Investment Office that implements the investment policy approved by the Investment Committee. The decision to invest in private real estate had to go through an approval process that is set and maintained by the governance structure in place.

4.

Identify the new investment approach proposed by Zang for managing the Fund. (circle one)			
Norway Model	Endowment Model	Canadian Model	LDI Model
Justify your response.			
The new investment approach proposed by Zang is the endowment model. This model is characterized by significant active management, a high allocation to alternative investments, and externally managed assets (which distinguishes it from the Canadian model, an approach that relies more on internally managed assets).			

5.

	Discuss the advantages and the disadvantages of the new investment approach proposed by Zang.
Advantages	The primary advantage of using the endowment model is a higher potential for value-added, above-market returns.
Disadvantages	The endowment model can be difficult to implement for small institutional investors because they might not be able to access high-quality managers. The endowment model may also be difficult to implement for a very large institutional investor because of the institutional investor's very large footprint. Furthermore, relative to the Norway model, the endowment model is more expensive in terms of costs/fees.

6. C is correct. Both observations are correct. For a corporate defined benefit plan, Maglav's shareholders are stakeholders. These stakeholders are interested in the sustainability of the pension plan, and the overfunded status is an asset on the balance sheet, potentially increasing the value of Maglav's stock. The overfunded status also allows management to potentially lower employer contributions to the plan and increase net income. It also lowers financial risk, which may reduce volatility in the stock price. In addition, decreasing employee turnover will increase plan liabilities and worsen the funded ratio. With high turnover, fewer workers will be vested and entitled to defined benefit payments. Conversely, if employee turnover decreases, expected vesting will increase, leading to higher plan liabilities and a lower funded ratio.

7. C is correct. Scale (asset size) is a defining characteristic for institutional investors since it affects key aspects of the investment process. Maglav's pension plan is small, with $25 million in assets under management. Smaller institutions may be unable to access certain investments that have a high minimum investment, such as private equity and real estate assets. These smaller institutions may also have difficulty in hiring skilled investment professionals. As a result, small institutional investors, such as Maglav's pension plan, are more likely to outsource all or most of the investment operations to external asset managers or investment consultants.

8. C is correct. The endowment model operates in an asset-only context and is characterized by a high allocation to alternative investments, including private investments and hedge funds; significant active management; and outsourcing to external managers. These characteristics describe the investment approach used by Westcome. The skill in sourcing alternative investments is critically important given the large variation in performance among asset managers, especially for alternative investments.

9. C is correct. The risk tolerance for Maglav's defined benefit plan is high and thus above average. Several factors influence the plan sponsor's ability to assume risk. For Maglav, the overfunded status of the pension fund allows the plan to withstand more volatility, and its small size relative to the company size implies greater risk tolerance. The low correlation of Maglav's operating results with pension asset returns also results in greater risk tolerance. Finally, the workforce characteristics imply greater risk tolerance. The younger workforce increases the duration of the plan liabilities and enables the sponsor to take on more liquidity risk. The high turnover of the workforce means fewer employees may be vested, reducing the number of employees entitled to receive defined benefit payments. All these factors contribute to an above average risk tolerance for Maglav's defined benefit plan.

10. C is correct. ASC 715, *Compensation—Retirement Benefits* requires that an overfunded (underfunded) plan appear as an asset (liability) on the balance sheet of the corporate sponsor. Maglav's plan is overfunded, so it appears as an asset on Maglav's balance sheet.

11. C is correct. The risk tolerance of the Wolf University Endowment Fund is above average since endowments that support a small percentage of the university's operating budget (10% in this case) should be able to tolerate more market, credit, and liquidity risk. In addition, the Fund's ability to access debt markets, especially during periods of market stress, increases the level of risk the endowment can accept in its investments. Finally, because of the significant inflows from gifts and donations, the effective spending rate will be lower than the annual spending policy of paying out 4% of the Fund's three-year rolling asset value. Thus, the Fund can rely less on investment returns to generate the income stream needed to support the university and can accept higher-risk investments.

12. C is correct. Allocation 3 is the most appropriate allocation for the Fund. The annual expected returns for the three allocations are as follows:

$$\text{Allocation 1 exp. return} = (0.45 \times 4.1\%) + (0.40 \times 6.3\%) + (0.10 \times 7.5\%) + (0.05 \times 9.1\%) = 5.57\%.$$

$$\text{Allocation 2 exp. return} = (0.10 \times 4.1\%) + (0.15 \times 6.3\%) + (0.15 \times 7.5\%) + (0.30 \times 5.0\%) + (0.30 \times 9.1\%) = 6.71\%.$$

$$\text{Allocation 3 exp. return} = (0.13 \times 4.1\%) + (0.32 \times 6.3\%) + (0.40 \times 7.5\%) + (0.05 \times 5.0\%) + (0.10 \times 9.1\%) = 6.71\%.$$

The real return for Allocation 1 is 3.07% (= 5.57% – 2.50%), and the real return for Allocation 2 and Allocation 3 is 4.21% (= 6.71% – 2.50%).

Therefore, Allocation 1 is not appropriate because the expected real rate of return is less than the annual spending rate of 4%. With expected spending at 4%, the purchasing power of the Fund would be expected to decline over time with Allocation 1.

Allocations 2 and 3 both offer an expected real rate of return greater than the annual spending rate of 4%. Thus, the purchasing power of the Fund would be expected to grow over time with either allocation. However, Allocation 3 is more appropriate than Allocation 2 because of its lower allocation to alternative assets (hedge funds and private equity). The total 60% allocation to alternative assets in Allocation 2 is well above the 15% allocation in Allocation 3 and is likely too high considering the Fund's small investment staff and its limited experience with managing alternative investments. Also, given the Fund's relatively small size of assets under management ($200 million), access to top hedge funds and private equity managers is likely to be limited.

13. The mission of the Prometheo University Scholarship Endowment is to provide scholarships for students attending the university. In order to achieve this mission, the Endowment must maintain the purchasing power of the assets in perpetuity while achieving investment returns sufficient to sustain the level of spending necessary to support the scholarship budget. Therefore, the investment objective of the endowment should be to achieve a total real rate of return (after inflation) of at least 6% with a reasonable level of risk.

14. GUIDELINE ANSWER:

- The policy is not appropriate.
- The expected real return of 3.54% is less than the spending policy rate of 6%.
- Therefore, the current allocation and investment objectives are not sustainable.

The nominal expected return on the current portfolio, according to the nominal return assumptions in Exhibit 1, is 6.04% per year (0.6 × 7.4% + 0.4 × 4.0% = 6.04%). The expected real return is approximately 3.54% (6.04% – 2.5% = 3.54%), which is below the 6% spending rate and the stated objective of a 6% real return. Therefore, this real return is not sufficient to meeting the spending policy, which makes the Endowment's goals unsustainable. The Endowment will need to change its asset allocation to earn higher returns and/or lower its spending policy rate.

15.

Determine whether the board should accept the CIO's recommendation. (circle one)	Justify your response
Accept Reject	The board should reject the CIO's recommendation. This recommendation is a significant departure from current practice and entails a much higher level of risk. The size of the investment team is small, with only four people, and it may not have adequate access to or experience in alternative investments. Given the relatively small size of the Endowment, it is unlikely that it has access to top managers in the hedge fund and private equity spaces.

16.

	Discuss the features that Heselwith should consider in evaluating the two plans with respect to the following:
Benefit Payments	Heselwith notes that the vesting schedule with regard to the company's contributions is the same in both plans, although her contributions in the DC plan are vested immediately. The DB plan provides a defined payment linked to final salary and years of service, whereas the DC plan provides an uncertain benefit based on Lyricul's and Heselwith's contributions as well as the investment performance of the plan assets.
Contributions	Lyricul's contribution rate to the DB plan is not known, but the plan is fully funded. However, there is no guarantee that it will remain fully funded or that Lyricul is committed to maintaining the DB plan's fully funded status. The rate for the DC plan is stated to be 12% of annual salary.
Shortfall Risk	Heselwith notes that the shortfall risk of plan assets being insufficient to meet her retirement benefit payments falls to her employer, Lyricul, with the DB plan. However, for the DC plan, the shortfall risk falls to her and depends on the 12% contribution rate from the company, plus any additional contributions she chooses to make, as well as the performance of the chosen investments.
Mortality/ Longevity Risks	The DB plan pools mortality risk such that those in the pool who die prematurely leave assets that help fund benefit payments for those who live longer than expected. Heselwith bears the risk of outliving her savings with the DC plan.

17.

Determine whether the risk tolerance of the DB Plan is below average or above average. (circle one)	Justify your response with *two* reasons.
Below Average	• The plan is underfunded, and the discount rate being used is fairly aggressive. 1. The DB plan already has a deficit, despite regular contributions, and is suffering from investment losses. The discount rate is already aggressive and should not be increased to lower the contribution. • The uncertain financial condition of the company. 2. The uncertain condition of Antiliaro may constrain its ability to make contributions to the DB plan. Lack of earnings growth and increasing debt on the balance sheet over the last few years imply below-average risk tolerance.

Determine whether the risk tolerance of the DB Plan is below average or above average. (circle one)	Justify your response with *two* reasons.
Above Average	• The plan suffers from investment losses. 3. Often, investment losses can lead a DB plan to take on more investment risk to achieve higher returns, but the other constraints, such as the plan's underfunded status and the company's financial condition, prevent this approach. • The older age of employees necessitates liquidity. 4. The average employee age is 50 years, and the company has many retirees because of its longevity. These characteristics generate a need for liquidity, which lowers the amount of risk the plan can assume. • The high correlation between the operating results of Antiliaro and pension asset returns lowers the risk tolerance of the pension plan. 5. The high correlation between the operating results of Antiliaro and the pension asset returns suggests a low risk tolerance. If Antiliaro is performing poorly as a company, this will constrain its ability to make additional contributions that may be necessary to address the shortfall in the pension's funding.

18. The modified duration of the bank's equity capital after restructuring is 9.89 years:

$$D_E^* = \left(\frac{A}{E}\right) D_A^* - \left(\frac{A}{E} - 1\right) D_L^* \left(\frac{\Delta i}{\Delta y}\right)$$

$$= \left(\frac{1}{0.10}\right) \times 2.10 - \left(\frac{1}{0.10} - 1\right) \times 1.90 \times 0.65$$

$$= 9.89 \text{ years}$$

LEARNING MODULE

6

Trading Costs and Electronic Markets

by Larry Harris, PhD, CFA.

Larry Harris, PhD, CFA, is at the USC Marshall School of Business (USA).

LEARNING OUTCOMES

Mastery	*The candidate should be able to:*
☐	explain the components of execution costs, including explicit and implicit costs
☐	calculate and interpret effective spreads and VWAP transaction cost estimates
☐	describe the implementation shortfall approach to transaction cost measurement
☐	describe factors driving the development of electronic trading systems
☐	describe market fragmentation
☐	identify and contrast the types of electronic traders
☐	describe characteristics and uses of electronic trading systems
☐	describe comparative advantages of low-latency traders
☐	describe the risks associated with electronic trading and how regulators mitigate them
☐	describe abusive trading practices that real-time surveillance of markets may detect

This reading draws from *Trading and Electronic Markets: What Investment Professionals Need to Know,* by Larry Harris, PhD, CFA, Research Foundation of CFA Institute.

1 COSTS OF TRADING

☐ explain the components of execution costs, including explicit and implicit costs

Securities research, portfolio management, and securities trading support the investment process. Of the three, trading is often the least understood and least appreciated function. Among the questions addressed in this reading are the following:

- What are explicit and implicit trading costs, and how are they measured?
- How is a limit order book interpreted?
- How have trading strategies adapted to market fragmentation?
- What types of electronic traders can be distinguished?

This reading is organized as follows: Section 2 discusses the direct and indirect costs of trading.[1] Section 3 discusses developments in electronic trading and the effects they had on transaction costs and market fragmentation. Section 4 identifies the most important types of electronic traders. Section 5 describes electronic trading facilities and some important ways traders use them. Section 6 discusses risks posed by electronic trading and how regulators control them. Finally, Section 7 summarizes the reading.

Costs of Trading

Understanding the costs of trading is critical for ensuring optimal execution and transaction cost management for portfolios. Because trading costs are a significant source of investment performance slippage, investment sponsors and their investment managers pay close attention to trading processes.

The costs of trading include fixed costs and variable costs. For buy-side institutions, fixed trading costs include the costs of employing buy-side traders, the costs of equipping them with proper trading tools (electronic systems and data), and the costs of office space (trading rooms or corners). Small buy-side institutions often avoid these costs by not employing buy-side traders. Their portfolio managers submit their orders directly to their brokers. Variable transaction costs arise from trading activity and consist of explicit and implicit costs.

Explicit costs are the direct costs of trading, such as broker commission costs, transaction taxes, stamp duties, and fees paid to exchanges. They are costs for which a trader could receive a receipt.

Implicit costs, by contrast, are indirect costs caused by the market impact of trading. Buyers often must raise prices to encourage sellers to trade with them, and sellers often must lower prices to encourage buyers. The price concessions that impatient traders make to complete their trades are called the market impacts of their trades. For small orders, market impact often is limited to buying at bid prices and selling at lower ask prices. Small market orders generally have small market impact because these orders often are immediately filled by traders willing to trade at quoted bid and offer prices, or even better prices. Larger orders have greater market impact when traders must move the market to fill their orders. In these cases, traders must accept larger price concessions (less attractive prices) to execute their orders in entirety. Although no receipt can be given for implicit costs, they are real nonetheless.

1 CFA Institute would like to thank Ananth Madhavan, PhD, at BlackRock (USA) for his contribution to this section, which includes material first written by him.

Implicit costs result from the following issues:

- The **bid–ask spread** is the ask price (the price at which a trader will sell a specified quantity of a security) minus the bid price (the price at which a trader will buy a specified quantity of a security). Traders who want to trade quickly buy at higher prices and sell at lower prices than those willing to wait for others to trade with them.
- **Market impact** (or price impact) is the effect of the trade on transaction prices. Traders who want to fill large orders often must move prices to encourage others to trade with them.
- **Delay costs** (also called slippage) arise from the inability to complete the desired trade immediately. Traders fail to profit when they fill their orders after prices move as they expect.
- **Opportunity costs** (or unrealized profit/loss) arise from the failure to execute a trade promptly. Traders fail to profit when their orders fail to trade and price move as they expect.

Dealer Quotes

Dealers provide liquidity to other traders when they allow traders to buy and sell when those traders want to trade. Those traders may be the clients known to the dealers, or they may be unknown traders whose orders exchanges assign to standing dealer orders and quotes.

Unlike brokers, dealers trade for their accounts when filling their customers' orders. When dealers buy or sell, they increase or reduce their inventories. Dealers profit by selling at ask prices that are higher than the bid prices at which they buy. If buying interest is greater than selling interest, dealers raise their ask prices to discourage buyers and raise their bid prices to encourage sellers. Likewise, if selling interest is greater than buying interest, dealers lower their ask prices to encourage buyers and lower their bid prices to discourage sellers.

Dealers help markets function well by being continuously available to take the other side of a trade when other traders want to trade. Dealers thus make markets more continuous. They are especially important in markets for infrequently traded securities in which buyers and sellers rarely are present at the same time. For example, most bond markets are overwhelmingly dealer markets because most bonds rarely trade. If an investor wants to sell a rarely traded bond, the investor might have a long wait before another investor interested in buying that bond arrives. Instead, a dealer generally will buy the bond and then try to market it to potential buyers. Practitioners say that dealers "make market" when they offer to trade.

Bid–Ask Spreads and Order Books

The prices at which dealers will buy or sell specified quantities of a security are, respectively, their **bid prices** and **ask prices**. (Ask prices are also known as offer prices.) The excess of the ask price over the bid price is the dealer's **bid–ask spread**.

When several dealers offer bid prices, the **best bid** is the offer to buy with the highest bid price. The best bid is also known as the **inside bid**. The **best ask**, also known as the **best offer** or **inside ask**, is the offer to sell with the lowest ask price.

The spread between the best bid price and the best ask price in a market is the market bid–ask spread, which is also known as the **inside spread**. It will be smaller (tighter or narrower) than the individual dealer spreads if the dealer with the highest bid price is not also the dealer with the lowest ask price.

For example, suppose that a portfolio manager gives the firm's trading desk an order to buy 1,000 shares of Economical Chemical Systems, Inc. (ECSI). Three dealers (coded A, B, and C) make a market in those shares. When the trader views the market in ECSI at 10:22 a.m. on his computer screen, the three dealers have put in the following limit orders to trade at an exchange market:

- Dealer A: *bid*: 98.85 for 600 shares; *ask*: 100.51 for 1,000 shares
- Dealer B: *bid*: 98.84 for 500 shares; *ask*: 100.55 for 500 shares
- Dealer C: *bid*: 98.82 for 700 shares; *ask*: 100.49 for 200 shares

The bid–ask spreads of Dealers A, B, and C are, respectively,

- 100.51 – 98.85 = 1.66
- 100.55 – 98.84 = 1.71
- 100.49 – 98.82 = 1.67

The best bid price, 98.85 by Dealer A, is lower than the best ask price, 100.49 by Dealer C. The market spread is thus 100.49 – 98.85 = 1.64, which is lower than any of the dealers' spreads.

The trader might see the quote information organized on his screen as shown in Exhibit 1. In this display, called a **limit order book**, the bids and asks are separately ordered from best to worst with the best at the top. The trader also notes that the **midquote price** (halfway between the market bid and ask prices) is (100.49 + 98.85)/2 = 99.67.

Exhibit 1: The Limit Order Book for Economical Chemical Systems, Inc.

Bids				Asks			
Dealer	Time Entered	Price	Size	Dealer	Time Entered	Price	Size
A	10:21 a.m.	98.85	600	C	10:21 a.m.	100.49	200
B	10:21 a.m.	98.84	500	A	10:21 a.m.	100.51	1,000
C	10:19 a.m.	98.82	700	B	10:19 a.m.	100.55	500

Note: The bids are ordered from highest to lowest, while the asks are ordered from lowest to highest. These orderings are from best bid or ask to worst bid or ask.

If the trader on the firm's trading desk submits a market buy order for 1,000 shares, the trader would purchase 200 shares from Dealer C at 100.49 per share and 800 shares from Dealer A at 100.51 per share.

Note that filling the second part of the order cost the trader 0.02 per share more than the first part because Dealer C's ask size was insufficient to fill the entire order. Large orders have price impact when they move down the book as they fill. The price impact of an order depends on its size and the available liquidity.

If this market were not an exchange market, the trader might choose to direct the buy order to a specific dealer—for example, to Dealer A. The trader may do so for many reasons. The trader may believe that Dealer A more likely will honor her quote than would Dealer C. Alternatively, the trader may believe that Dealer A more likely will settle the trade than Dealer C. Such considerations are especially important in markets for which no clearinghouse guarantees that all trades will settle—for example, most currency markets. Institutions active in such markets may screen counterparties on credit criteria. Finally, the trader might fear that Dealer A will cancel her quote when she (or a computer managing her quote) sees that a trade took place at 100.49. Sending the order first to Dealer A thus could produce a better average price.

Implicit Transaction Cost Estimates

Investment managers and traders measure transaction costs so that they can better predict the cost of filling orders and so that they can better manage the brokers and dealers who fill their orders. Buyers, of course, want to trade at low prices, while sellers want to trade at high prices. Expensive trades are purchases arranged at high prices or sales arranged at low prices.

To estimate transaction costs, analysts compare trade prices to a benchmark price. Commonly used price benchmarks include the midquote price at the time of the trade, the midquote price at the time of the order submission, and a volume-weighted average price around the time of the trade. These three benchmarks, respectively, correspond to the effective spread, implementation shortfall, and VWAP methods of transaction cost estimation.

EFFECTIVE SPREADS AND VOLUME-WEIGHTED COST ESTIMATES

2

- ☐ calculate and interpret effective spreads and VWAP transaction cost estimates
- ☐ describe the implementation shortfall approach to transaction cost measurement

The market spread is a measure of trade execution costs. It is how much traders would lose per quantity traded if they simultaneously submitted buy and sell market orders that respectively execute at the ask and bid prices. The loss is the cost of trading, because this strategy otherwise accomplishes nothing. Given that two trades generated the cost, the cost per trade is one half of the quoted spread.

The prices that traders receive when trading often differ from quoted prices. Smaller orders sometimes fill at better prices; larger orders often fill at worse prices. Standing orders offering liquidity fill at same-side prices (buy at bid, sell at ask), if they fill at all.

The effective spread provides a more general estimate of the cost of trading. It uses the midquote price (the average, or midpoint, of the bid and the ask prices at the time the order was entered) as the benchmark price:

Effective spread transaction cost estimate =

$$\text{Trade size} \times \begin{cases} \text{Trade price} - \left(\dfrac{\text{Bid} + \text{Ask}}{2}\right) & \text{for buy orders} \\ \left(\dfrac{\text{Bid} + \text{Ask}}{2}\right) - \text{Trade price} & \text{for sell orders} \end{cases}$$

For a buy order filled at the ask, the estimated implicit cost of trading is half the bid–ask spread, because Ask – [(Bid + Ask)/2] = [(Ask – Bid)/2]. Multiplying this midquote price benchmark transaction cost estimate by 2 produces a statistic called the **effective spread**. It is the spread that traders would have observed if the quoted ask (for a purchase) or the bid (for a sale) were equal to the trade price.

The effective spread is a sensible estimate of transaction costs when orders are filled in single trades. If an order fills at a price better than the quoted price (e.g., a buy order fills at a price below the ask price), the order is said to receive **price improvement** and the spread is effectively lower. Price improvement occurs when trade execution prices are better than quoted prices. An order that fills at a price outside the quoted spread has an effective spread that is larger than the quoted spread. Such results occur when trade execution prices are worse than quoted prices.

The effective spread is a poor estimate of transaction costs when traders split large orders into many parts to fill over time. Such orders often move the market and cause bid and ask prices to rise or fall. The impact of the order on market prices, called **market impact**, makes trading expensive—especially for the last parts to fill—but the effective spread will not fully identify this cost if it is computed separately for each trade.

For example, suppose that a buy order for 10,000 shares fills in two trades. The prices and sizes of these trades and the best bids and offers in the market when the trades occurred appear in the following table:

Trade	Trade Price	Trade Size	Prevailing Bid	Prevailing Offer
#1	10.21	4,000	10.19	10.21
#2	10.22	6,000	10.20	10.22

For this buy order, the effective spread transaction cost per share is 0.01, or [(10.21–10.19)/2] and [(10.22 – 10.20)/2], for both trades (the effective spreads are both 0.02). Thus, the total transaction cost estimate measured using the midquote price benchmark is 100 = 0.01 × 10,000. This estimate is problematic because it reflects the higher price of the second trade, which was likely caused by the market impact of the trader's first trade.

Effective spreads also do not measure **delay costs** (also called slippage) that arise from the inability to complete the desired trade immediately because of its size in relation to the available market liquidity. Delay costs also arise when portfolio managers or their traders fail to create and route orders quickly to the markets where they will fill most quickly. Analysts often measure delay costs on the portion of the order carried over from one day to the next. Delay is costly when price moves away from an order (up for a buy order, down for a sell order), often because information leaks into the market before or during the execution of the order.

When delays in execution cause a portion of the order to go unfilled, the associated cost is called **opportunity cost**. For example, suppose a futures trader places an order to buy 10 contracts with a limit price of 99.00, good for one day, when the market quote is 99.01 to 99.04. The order does not execute, and the contract closes at 99.80. If the order could have been filled at 99.04, the difference (99.80 – 99.04 = 0.76) reflects the opportunity cost per contract. By trading more aggressively, the trader might have avoided these costs. Opportunity costs are difficult to measure. In the example, the one-day time frame is arbitrary, and the assumption that the order could fill at 99.04 may be suspect. The estimate usually is sensitive to the time frame chosen for measurement and to assumptions about the prices at which orders could trade.

Implementation Shortfall

The implementation shortfall method of measuring trading costs addresses the problems associated with the effective spread method. Implementation shortfall is also attractive because it views trading from an investment management perspective and measures the total cost of implementing an investment decision by capturing all explicit and implicit costs. The implementation shortfall method includes the market impact costs and delay costs as well as opportunity costs, which are often significant for large orders.

Implementation shortfall compares the values of the actual portfolio with that of a paper portfolio constructed on the assumption that trades could be arranged at the prices that prevailed when the decision to trade is made. The prevailing price—also called the decision price, the arrival price, or the strike price—is generally taken to be the midquote price at the time of the trade decision. The excess of the paper value over the actual value is the **implementation shortfall**. The coverage of implementation shortfall is continued at Level III.

VWAP Transaction Cost Estimates

Volume-weighted average price (VWAP) is one of the most widely used benchmark prices that analysts use to estimate transaction costs. Analysts typically compute the VWAP using all trades that occurred from the start of the order until the order was completed, a measure that is often referred to as "interval VWAP." The VWAP is the sum of the total dollar value of the benchmark trades divided by the total quantity of the trades. The VWAP transaction cost estimate formula is as follows:

$$\text{VWAP transaction cost estimate} = \text{Trade size} \times \begin{cases} \text{Trade VWAP} - \text{VWAP benchmark} & \text{for buy orders} \\ \text{VWAP benchmark} - \text{Trade VWAP} & \text{for sell orders} \end{cases}$$

The VWAP transaction cost estimate is popular in part because it is easy to interpret. It answers this question: Did you get a better or worse average price than all traders trading when you were trading?

Interpreting VWAP transaction cost estimates is problematic when the trades being evaluated are a substantial fraction of all trades in the VWAP benchmark, or, more generally, when the trades took place at the same rate as other trades in the market. In both cases, the Trade VWAP and the VWAP benchmark will be nearly equal, which would suggest that the evaluated trades were not costly. But this conclusion would be misleading if the trade had substantial price impact. For example, if a large trader were the only buyer for a given trading period (or interval), the VWAP transaction cost estimate would be zero regardless of the market impact.

This bias toward zero helps explain why the measure is so popular. Investment managers like to show their investment sponsors transaction cost estimates that suggest that trading is not expensive.

EXAMPLE 1

Transaction Cost Analyses for an Illiquid Stock

Arapahoe Tanager, portfolio manager of a Canadian small-cap equity mutual fund, and his firm's chief trader, Lief Schrader, are reviewing the execution of a ticket to sell 12,000 shares of Alpha Company, limit C$9.95. The order was traded over the day.

Schrader split the ticket into three orders that executed that day as follows:

A. A market order to sell 2,000 shares executed at a price of C$10.15. Upon order submission, the market was C$10.12 bid for 3,000 shares, 2,000 shares offered at C$10.24.

B. A market order to sell 3,000 shares executed at a price of C$10.11. Upon order submission, the market was C$10.11 bid for 3,000 shares, 2,000 shares offered at C$10.22.

C. Toward the end of the trading day, Schrader submitted an order to sell the remaining 7,000 shares, limit C$9.95. The order executed in part, with 5,000 shares trading at an average price of C$10.01. Upon order submission, the market was C$10.05 bid for 3,000 shares, 2,000 shares offered at C$10.19. This order exceeded the quoted bid size and "walked down" the limit order book (i.e., after the market bid was filled, the order continued to sell at lower prices). After the market closed, Schrader allowed the order to cancel. Tanager did want to sell the 2,000 unfilled shares on the next trading day.

Only two other trades in Alpha Company occurred on this day: 2,000 shares at C$10.20 and 1,000 shares at C$10.15. The last trade price of the day was C$9.95; it was C$9.50 on the following day.

1. For each of the three fund trades, compute the quoted spread. Also, compute the average quoted spreads prevailing at the times of each trade.

Solution:

The quoted spread is the difference between the ask and bid prices. For the first order, the quoted spread is C$10.24 – C$10.12 = C$0.12. Similarly, the quoted spreads for the second and third orders are C$0.11 and C$0.14, respectively. The average quoted spread is (C$0.12 + C$0.11 + C$0.14)/3 = C$0.1233.

2. For each of the three fund trades, compute the effective spread (use the average fill price for the third trade). Also, compute the average effective spread.

Solution:

The effective spread for a sell order is 2 × (Midpoint of the market at the time of order entry – Trade price). For the first order, the midpoint of the market at the time of order entry is (C$10.12 + C$10.24)/2 = C$10.18, so that the effective spread is 2 × (C$10.18 – C$10.15) = C$0.06.

The effective spread for the second order is 2 × [(C$10.11 + C$10.22)/2 – C$10.11] = C$0.11.
The effective spread for the third order is 2 × [(C$10.05 + C$10.19)/2 – C$10.01] = C$0.22.
The average effective spread is (C$0.06 + C$0.11 + C$0.22)/3 = C$0.13.

3. Explain the relative magnitudes of quoted and effective spreads for each of the three fund trades.

Solution:

The first trade received price improvement because the shares sold at a price above the bid price. Therefore, the effective spread is less than the quoted spread. No price improvement occurred for the second trade because the shares sold at the bid price. Also, the second trade had no price impact beyond trading at the bid; the entire order traded at the quoted bid. Accordingly, the effective and quoted spreads are equal. The effective spread for the third trade is greater than the quoted spread because the large order size, which was greater than the bid size, caused the order to walk down the limit order book. The average sale price was less than the bid so that the effective spread was higher than the quoted spread.

4. Calculate the VWAP for all 13,000 Alpha Company shares that traded that day and for the 10,000 shares sold by the mutual fund. Compute the VWAP transaction cost estimate for the 10,000 shares sold.

Solution:

The VWAP for the day is the total dollar volume divided by the total number of shares traded. The dollar volume is 2,000 shares × C$10.15 + 3,000 shares × C$10.11 + 5,000 shares × C$10.01 + 2,000 shares × C$10.20 + 1,000 shares at C$10.15 = C$131,230. Dividing this by the 13,000-share total volume gives a VWAP of C$10.0946. A similar calculation using only the sales made by the mutual fund gives a trade VWAP of C$10.0680. The VWAP transaction cost estimate for the sale is the difference multiplied by the 10,000 shares sold: C$266.15 = 10,000 shares × (C$10.0946 – C$10.0680) [differences due to rounding].

DEVELOPMENT OF ELECTRONIC MARKETS

3

- ☐ describe factors driving the development of electronic trading systems
- ☐ describe market fragmentation

The application of new information technologies to trading processes produced radical changes in how investment managers trade. Automated trading systems and trading strategies replaced manual processes. New electronic exchanges, alternative trading systems, electronic traders, and securities dramatically changed trading in most markets. The resulting efficiencies generally improved market quality, but electronic trading also produced new regulatory concerns. High levels of fragmentation and electronification now characterize most global trading markets.

Electronic Trading

Trading at organized exchanges now depends critically on automated electronic systems used both by exchanges and by their trader clients. The exchanges use electronic systems to arrange trades by matching orders submitted by buyers with those submitted by sellers. Traders use electronic systems to generate the orders that the exchanges process. The most important electronic traders are dealers, arbitrageurs, and buy-side institutional traders who use algorithmic trading tools provided by their brokers to fill their large orders.

The two types of systems are co-dependent: Traders need high-speed order processing and communication systems to implement their electronic trading strategies, and the exchanges need electronic exchange systems to process the vast numbers of orders that these electronic traders produce. The adoption of electronic exchange systems led to huge growth in automated order creation and submission systems.

The widespread use of electronic trading systems significantly decreased trading costs for buy-side traders. Costs fell as exchanges obtained greater cost efficiencies from using electronic matching systems instead of floor-based, manual trading systems. These technologies also decreased costs and increased efficiencies for the dealers and arbitrageurs, who provide much of the liquidity offered at exchanges. Competition forced them to pass along many of the benefits of their new technologies to buy-side traders in the form of narrower spreads quoted for larger sizes. New electronic buy-side order management systems also decreased buy-side trading costs by allowing a smaller number of buy-side traders to process more orders and to process them more efficiently than manual traders.

Advantages of Electronic Trading Systems

Compared with floor-based trading systems, electronic order-matching systems enjoy many advantages:

- Most obviously, electronic systems are cheap to operate once built. Operating in server rooms, they require less physical space than trading floors. Also, in contrast to floor-based trading systems, electronic trading systems do not require exchange officials to record and report prices.
- Electronic exchange systems do exactly what they are programmed to do. When properly programmed, they precisely enforce the exchange's trading order precedence and pricing rules without error or exception.
- Electronic exchange systems can also keep perfect audit trails so that forensic investigators can determine the exact sequence and timing of events that may interest them.
- Electronic exchange systems that support hidden orders keep those orders perfectly hidden. Unlike floor brokers, they never inadvertently or fraudulently reveal their clients' hidden orders to others.
- In contrast to floor-based brokers and exchange officials, electronic order-matching systems can operate, for the most part, on a continuous, "around-the-clock" basis.
- Finally, electronic exchanges can operate when bad weather or other events would likely prevent workers from convening on a floor.

These efficiencies led to great growth. Electronic trading systems have largely displaced floor-based trading systems in all instruments for which order-driven markets are viable. Order-driven markets—markets in which orders submitted by traders are arranged based on a rules-based, order-matching system run by an exchange, a broker, or an alternative trading system (ATS)—are now organized by most exchanges and electronic communication networks (ECNs).

Additionally, computers have come to dominate the implementation of many trading strategies because they are so efficient and so unlike human traders:

- Computers have infinite attention spans and a very wide attention scope. They can continuously watch and respond to information from many instruments and many markets simultaneously and essentially forever.
- Their responses are extraordinarily fast.
- Computers are perfectly disciplined and do only what they are instructed (programmed) to do.
- Computers do not forget any information that their programmers want to save.

Electronification of Bond Markets

The electronic market structures of equity, futures, and options markets have attracted tremendous attention throughout the world. Much less attention has been given to the market structures of corporate and municipal bond markets, most of which, from the customer's point of view, have changed little since the late 19th century. Despite the efforts of many creative developers of electronic bond trading systems, most public investors in these markets still trade largely over the counter with dealers. The potential for electronic trading systems in these markets—and the attendant growth in electronic trading strategies—is quite large. Such systems undoubtedly will reflect the fact that bond issues—especially municipal bonds—vastly outnumber stock issues. Accordingly, except for the most actively traded bonds, limit order book trading systems will not be successful because buyers and sellers rarely will be present at the same time.

However, systems can be built that would allow public investors to trade with each other when both sides are present in the market. These systems would provide order display facilities, where public investors and proprietary traders could post limit orders so that all traders could see them. Like marketable orders, limit orders seek to obtain the best price immediately available; additionally, they instruct not to accept a price higher than a specified limit price when buying or a price lower than a specified limit price when selling. If these facilities also had automatic execution mechanisms and regulations or legal decisions to prevent dealers from trading through displayed orders when arranging their trades, bond transaction costs would drop substantially and bond trading would become much more active. Many such electronic bond order-matching systems already exist, but they primarily serve dealers and not public investors. Recent empirical research suggests that public investors would greatly benefit if their brokers provided them with direct access to these systems as they presently do in the equity markets. Instead, most broker/dealers commonly interpose themselves.

Market Fragmentation

Markets for many asset classes have become increasingly fragmented throughout the world because venues trading the same instruments have proliferated and trading in any given instrument now occurs in multiple venues. Available liquidity for an instrument on any one exchange now often represents just a small fraction of the aggregate liquidity for that instrument. **Market fragmentation**—trading the same instrument in multiple venues—increases the potential for price and liquidity disparities across venues because buyers and sellers often are not in the same venues at the same time.

For example, in the United States, order flow in exchange-listed equities is now divided among 11 exchanges, 40 alternative trading systems, and numerous dealers. In the late 20th century, however, trading mainly occurred on three primary exchanges, a few minor regional exchanges, and in the offices of some large institutional broker/dealers. Alternative trading systems (ATSs), also known as electronic communication networks (ECNs) or multilateral trading facilities (MTFs), are increasingly important trading venues. They function like exchanges but do not exercise regulatory authority over their subscribers except concerning the conduct of their trading in their trading systems.

With increasing market fragmentation, traders filling large orders now adapt their trading strategies to search for liquidity across multiple venues and across time to control the market impacts of their trades. Electronic algorithmic trading techniques, such as liquidity aggregation and smart order routing, help traders manage the challenges and opportunities presented by fragmentation. Liquidity aggregators create "super books" that present liquidity across markets for a given instrument. These tools offer global views of market depth (available liquidity) for each instrument regardless of which trading venue offers the liquidity. For example, the best bid, or highest price a buyer is willing to pay, for a Eurodollar future may be on the Chicago Mercantile Exchange (CME) and the second best on ELX Markets, a fully electronic futures exchange. Smart order-routing algorithms send orders to the markets that display the best-quoted prices and sizes.

Effects on Transaction Costs

Numerous studies show that transaction costs declined with the growth of electronic trading over time. Some studies also show that at a given point in time, lower transaction costs are found in those markets with the greatest intensity of electronic trading. These time-series and cross-sectional results are not surprising. They result from the greater cost efficiencies associated with electronic trading.

With the growth of electronic trading, bid–ask spreads decreased substantially. These decreases lowered transaction costs for retail traders and institutions trading small orders.

Overall transaction costs also decreased for large orders, many of which are now broken into smaller parts for execution. A study of the execution costs of tens of thousands of equity orders for US stocks involving tens of millions of dollars of principal value shows that the implementation shortfall cost of filling those orders dropped with the growth of electronic trading. This evidence suggests that any profits obtained by parasitic traders from front running orders are smaller than the cost savings obtained by buy-side traders from trading in electronic markets using algorithms.

4 TYPES OF ELECTRONIC TRADERS

☐ identify and contrast the types of electronic traders

The proliferation of electronic exchange trading systems has led to the adoption of electronic trading by proprietary traders, buy-side traders, and the electronic brokers that serve them. Proprietary traders include dealers, arbitrageurs, and various types of front runners—all of whom are profit-motivated traders. In contrast, buy-side traders trade to fill orders for investment and risk managers who use the markets to establish positions from which they derive various utilitarian and profit-motivated benefits. Electronic brokers serve both types of traders.

Electronic traders differ in how they send orders to markets. Those proprietary traders who are registered as broker/dealers usually send their orders directly to exchanges. Those who are not broker/dealers must send their orders to brokers, who then forward them to exchanges. These brokers are said to provide sponsored access to their proprietary electronic trader clients. Brokers who provide sponsored access have very fast electronic order processing systems that allow them to forward orders to exchanges as quickly as possible while still undertaking the regulatory functions necessary to protect the markets and themselves from various financial and operational risks associated with brokering orders for proprietary electronic traders.

Electronic trading strategies are most profitable or effective when they can act on new information quickly. Accordingly, proprietary traders and electronic brokers build automated trading systems that are extremely fast. These systems often can receive information of interest to the trader, process it, and place a trading instruction at an exchange in less than a few milliseconds—and sometimes much faster.

The events that interest electronic traders include:

- trade reports and quote changes in the securities or contracts that they trade;
- similar data for instruments that are correlated with the securities or contracts that they trade;

- indexes that summarize these data across markets and for various instrument classes;
- changes in limit order books; and
- news releases from companies, governments, and other producers and aggregators of information.

Electronic traders typically receive information about these events via high-speed electronic data feeds. Not all electronic traders analyze all these different information sources, but many do.

Electronic proprietary traders include high-frequency traders and low-latency traders. High-frequency and low-latency (i.e., extremely fast) traders must often trade very quickly in response to new information to be profitable. They are distinguished by how often they trade.

High-frequency traders (HFTs) generally complete round trips composed of a purchase followed by a sale (or a sale followed by a purchase) within a minute and often as quickly as a few milliseconds. During a day, they may trade in and out of an actively traded security or contract more than a thousand times—but usually only in small sizes.

Low-latency traders include news traders who trade on electronic news feeds and certain parasitic traders. Parasitic traders are speculators who base their predictions about future prices on information they obtain about orders that other traders intend, or will soon intend, to fill. Parasitic traders include front runners, who trade in front of traders who demand liquidity, and quote matchers, who trade in front of traders who supply liquidity. When trying to open or close positions, low-latency traders often need to send or cancel orders very quickly in response to new information. In contrast to HFTs, low-latency traders may hold their positions for as long as a day and sometimes longer.

The distinction between HFTs and low-latency traders is relatively new. Many commentators do not make any distinction, calling all electronic traders who need to trade quickly HFTs.

The Major Types of Electronic Traders

Electronic news traders subscribe to high-speed electronic news feeds that report news releases made by corporations, governments, and other aggregators of information. They then quickly analyze these releases to determine whether the information they contain will move the markets and, if so, in which direction. They trade on this information by sending marketable orders—instructions to fill the order at the best available price—to wherever they expect they may be filled. News traders profit when they can execute against stale orders—orders that do not yet reflect the new information.

For example, stock prices usually rise when a company announces earnings of 25 pence a share when the consensus forecast is only 10 pence. Electronic news traders who receive the initial press release will use their computers to parse the text of the release to find the earnings number. The computers then will compare that number with the consensus forecast, which they have stored in their memory rather than on disk to reduce access time. If the 15 pence difference is sufficiently large, news traders may send one or more marketable buy orders to exchanges for execution. News traders must be very quick to ensure that they get to the market before others do. If they are too late, the price may have changed already or liquidity suppliers may have canceled their quotes.

Some news traders also process news releases that do not contain quantitative data. Using natural language-processing techniques, they try to identify the importance of the information for market valuations. For example, a report stating that "our main pesticide plant shut down because of the accidental release of poisonous chemicals" might be marked as having strong negative implications for values. Electronic news traders would sell on this information. If they are correct, the market will drop as other, slower traders read, interpret, and act on the information. If they are wrong, the market will not react to the information. In that case, news traders will reverse their position and lose the transaction costs associated with their round-trip trades. (Note that these transaction costs could be high if many news traders made the same wrong inference.) Because round-trip transaction costs usually are lower than the profits that electronic news traders can occasionally make when significant news arrives, news traders often may trade with the expectation of being right only occasionally.

Electronic dealers, like all dealers, make markets by placing bids (prices at which they are willing to buy) and offers (prices at which they are willing to sell) with the expectation that they can profit from round trips at favorable net spreads. Those who trade at the highest frequencies tend to be very wary. On the first indication that prices may move against their inventory positions (i.e., price decreases if they are long or own the asset; price increases if they are short or sold an asset they do not own), they immediately take liquidity by executing on the opposite side to reduce their exposure. They generally will not hold large inventory positions in actively traded stocks. As soon as they reach their inventory limit on one side of the market or the other, they cease bidding or offering on that side. Electronic dealers often monitor electronic news feeds. They may immediately cancel all their orders in any security mentioned in a news report. If the news is material, they do not want to offer liquidity to news traders to whom they would lose. If the news is immaterial, they merely lose whatever opportunity to trade may have come their way while out of the market.

Electronic dealers, like all other dealers, also keep track of scheduled news releases. They cancel their orders just before releases to avoid offering liquidity to traders who can act faster than they can. They also may try to reduce their inventories before a scheduled release to avoid holding a risky position.

Electronic arbitrageurs look across markets for arbitrage opportunities in which they can buy an undervalued instrument and sell a similar overvalued one. The combination of these two positions is called an arbitrage portfolio, and the positions are called legs. Electronic arbitrageurs try to construct their arbitrage portfolios at minimum cost and risk.

Electronic front runners are low-latency traders who use artificial intelligence methods to identify when large traders, or many small traders, are trying to fill orders on the same side of the market. They will purchase when they believe that an imbalance of buy orders over sell orders will push the market up and sell when they believe the opposite. Their order anticipation strategies try to identify predictable patterns in order submission. They may search for patterns in order submissions, trades, or the relations between trades and other events.

In most jurisdictions, dealers and brokers cannot legally front run orders that their clients have submitted. These orders include large orders that they know their clients are breaking up to fill in small pieces. But dealers and brokers can study records of their clients' past orders to identify patterns in their behavior that would allow them to predict orders not yet submitted.

Some front runners also look for patterns in executed trades. For example, suppose that a trader sees that trades of a given size have been occurring at the offer every 10 minutes for an hour. If the trader has seen this pattern of trading before, the trader may suspect that the activity will continue. If so, the trader may buy on the assumption that a trader is in the market filling a large buy order by breaking it into smaller pieces.

Buy-side traders, and the brokers who provide them with algorithms to manage large orders, are aware of the efforts that electronic traders make to detect and front run their orders. Accordingly, they randomize their strategies to make them more difficult to detect. They submit orders at random times instead of at regular intervals, and they submit various sizes instead of the same size. Although these techniques make detection more difficult, hiding large, liquidity-demanding trades is always challenging because sophisticated traders can ultimately identify them by the inevitable relation between prices and volumes that they create. Electronic front runners look for these patterns, often using very advanced, automated data-mining tools.

Finally, some front runners examine the relation between trades and other events to predict future trades. Traders who identify these events quickly may be able to profit by buying ahead of retail or institutional traders. Because many traders initiate trades in response to common stimuli or in response to predictable situations, traders who can identify patterns in the relations between trades and events may profit from trading ahead. When the time between the stimulus and the response is short, electronic traders have a clear advantage.

Electronic quote matchers try to exploit the option values of standing orders. Standing orders are limit orders waiting to be filled. Options to trade are valuable to quote matchers because they allow them to take positions with potentially limited losses. Quote matchers buy when they believe they can rely on standing buy orders to get out of their positions, and they sell when they can do the same with standing sell orders. Traders say that quote matchers lean on these orders. If prices then move in the quote matchers' favor, they profit for as long as they stay in the security or contract. But if the quote matchers conclude that prices are moving against them, they immediately try to exit by trading with the standing orders and thereby limiting their losses.

For example, a fast quote matcher may buy when a slow trader is bidding at 20. If the price subsequently rises, the quote matcher will profit. If the quote matcher believes that the price will fall, the quote matcher will sell the position to the buyer at 20 and thereby limit his losses. The main risk of the quote-matching strategy is that the standing order may be unavailable when the quote matcher needs it. Standing orders disappear when filled by another trader or when canceled.

Most large buy-side traders use electronic order management systems (OMSs) to manage their trading. These systems keep track of the orders that their portfolio managers want to be filled, which orders have been sent out to be filled, and which fills have been obtained. Buy-side OMSs generally allow the buy-side trader to route orders to brokers for further handling, along with instructions for how the orders should be handled. These entities may include exchanges, brokers, dealers, and various alternative trading systems. The OMSs typically have dashboards that allow the buy-side trader to see summaries of all activity of interest so that the trader can better manage the trading process. Finally, the OMSs help the buy-side traders report and confirm the trades to all interested parties.

Buy-side traders often employ electronic brokers to arrange their trades. In addition to supporting standard order instructions, such as limit or market orders, these brokers often provide a full suite of advanced orders, trading tactics, and algorithms. The broker's electronic trading system generally manages these advanced orders, tactics, and algorithms, but in some cases, exchange computers may perform these functions.

ELECTRONIC TRADING SYSTEM: CHARACTERISTICS AND USES 5

- ☐ describe characteristics and uses of electronic trading systems
- ☐ describe comparative advantages of low-latency traders

Traders value speed because it allows them to act before other traders can act. This section identifies the three situations where speed is valuable, how exchanges and traders build and use fast trading systems, and some select examples of how electronic trading changed trading strategies.

Why Speed Matters

Electronic traders must be fast to trade effectively, regardless of whether they are proprietary traders or buy-side traders. Electronic traders have three needs for speed:

1. **Taking**. Electronic traders sometimes want to take a trading opportunity before others do. A new trading opportunity may attract many traders, and an existing trading opportunity may attract many traders when market events cause it to become more valuable (e.g., a standing limit order to sell becomes much more attractive when the prices of correlated securities rise). Often only the first trader to reach the attractive opportunity will benefit. Thus, electronic traders must be fast so they can beat other traders to attractive trading opportunities.
2. **Making**. Market events often create attractive opportunities to offer liquidity. For example, at most exchanges when prices rise, the first traders to place bids at improved prices acquire time precedence at those prices that may allow them to trade sooner or at better prices than they otherwise would be able to trade. Therefore, electronic traders must be fast so they can acquire priority when they want it and before other traders do.
3. **Canceling**. Frequently, traders must quickly cancel orders they no longer want to fill, often because market events have increased the option values of those orders. For example, if traders have limit buy orders standing at the best bid and large trades take place at other exchanges at the same price, these traders may reasonably conclude that prices may drop and that they may obtain better executions at a lower price. They must cancel their orders as quickly as possible to reduce the probability that they will trade.

Note that electronic traders do not simply need to be fast to trade effectively: They must be faster than their competitors. Little inherent value comes from being fast; the value lies in being faster. The reason electronic trading systems have such low latencies (i.e., are extremely fast) is because electronic traders have been trying for years to be faster than their competitors.

Electronic order-handling systems used by exchanges also have grown faster as exchanges compete for order flows from electronic traders. Electronic traders often will not send orders to exchanges where they cannot quickly cancel them, especially if other exchanges have faster trading systems. Accordingly, exchanges with slow order-handling systems have lost market share.

Latency is the elapsed time between the occurrence of an event and a subsequent action that depends on that event. For example, the event might be a trade at one exchange, and the action might be the receipt by another exchange of an instruction to cancel a standing order that a trader has sent upon learning of the trade. Electronic traders measure these latencies in milliseconds or microseconds (millionths of a second).

The latency of a linear multi-step process is the sum of the latencies of each step in the process. The submission of an order instruction by a trader in response to an event consists of three major steps, each of which involves many smaller steps beyond the scope of this discussion:

1. The trader must learn that the event took place.

2. The trader must respond to the new information with a new order instruction.
3. The trader must send, and the exchange must receive, the new instruction.

Traders must use very fast communication systems to minimize the latencies associated with steps 1 and 3 (communicating in and out), and they must use very fast computer systems to minimize the latency associated with step 2 (responding).

Fast Communications

Electronic traders and brokers use several strategies to minimize their communication times. These strategies involve minimizing communication distances and maximizing line speeds. Note that the relevant measure of communication distance is the total of two distances that signals must travel. The first distance is from where the event is reported (often an exchange but sometimes another type of news source) to the computer that will process the information. The second distance is from the computer to the exchange trading system where the trader wants to deliver an order instruction.

Electronic traders and brokers locate their computers as close as possible to the exchanges at which they trade to minimize latencies resulting from physics: No message can travel faster than the speed of light. At 300,000 kilometers (186,000 miles) per second in a vacuum, light travels 300 kilometers in a millisecond. Although the speed of light is incredibly fast, a fast computer with a clock speed of 5 GHz (billion cycles per second) can do 5 million operations in a millisecond—which often is more than required to receive information, process it, and send out an order instruction in response.

Communication latencies are particularly important when messages must travel significant distances. For example, the great circle (shortest) distances between Chicago and New York and between New York and London are, respectively, 1,146 kilometers and 5,576 kilometers. Thus, round-trip communications between these two pairs of cities have minimum latencies of approximately 8 and 37 milliseconds simply because of the speed of light. (The actual minimum latencies are longer because the speed of light in standard optical fiber is 31% slower than the speed of light in a vacuum.) Such delays illustrate that no electronic trader located at any significant distance from where information is created or must be delivered can effectively compete with traders who have minimized these combined distances.

Many exchanges allow electronic traders to place their servers in the rooms where the exchange servers operate, a practice called collocation. Exchanges charge substantial fees for collocation space and related services, such as air conditioning and power. Note that even within collocation centers, concerns about fairness dictate that the communication lines connecting proprietary servers to exchange servers all be of the same length for all customers buying the same class of collocation service.

Electronic traders and brokers also use the fastest communication technologies they can obtain to collect and transmit information when any distance separates the places where information events occur from the places where they act on those events. To that end, they use the fastest and most direct communication lines that are available. For example, they prefer line-of-sight microwave channels to fiber-optic and copper channels because of the differences in speed of electromagnetic wave propagation through these materials. (Microwaves travel through air at just slightly below the speed of light, whereas signals travel through fiber-optic channels and copper wires only two-thirds as quickly.) They also ensure that their communications pass through the fewest electronic routers and switches possible because passage through each of these devices adds its latency to the total latency of the line.

Finally, electronic traders and brokers subscribe to special high-speed data feeds directly from exchanges and other data vendors. The vendors charge premium prices for these services, which are delivered over very high-speed communication lines. Some exchanges provide multiple classes of data services that vary by speed to price-discriminate among their clients.

Fast Computations

Once electronic traders receive information about an event of interest, they must decide whether to act on that information and how. Those traders who can make decisions faster than their competitors will trade more profitably. Electronic traders minimize the latencies associated with their decision making by using several strategies.

First and most obviously, they use very fast computers. They overclock their processors (i.e., run them faster than the processor designers intended) and use liquid cooling systems to keep them from melting. They store all information in fast memory to avoid the latencies associated with physical disk drives, which cannot deliver information while their heads are seeking the right track and can only deliver information as fast as their disks spin once the right track is found. They sometimes use specialized processors designed to solve their specific trading problems quickly, and they may even use processors etched on gallium arsenide rather than silicon.

Electronic traders also must run very efficient software. They often use simple and specialized operating systems to avoid the overhead associated with supporting operating system functions they do not use. Remarkably, many electronic trading systems run under variants of the original MS-DOS operating system because of its simplicity.

Electronic traders optimize their computer code for speed. They often write important functions that they repeatedly use in assembler language to ensure that they run quickly. (Code written in high-level languages, such as C++, tends to be slower because their compilers are designed to handle all types of code, not just code written to solve trading problems.) And they avoid using such languages as Python because they are interpreter languages that compile (create executable machine code) as they run, rather than compiling only once when first written.

Some electronic trading problems change so frequently that speed of coding is more important than speed of execution. For example, some problems depend on ever-changing sets of conditions or exceptions that present or constrain profit opportunities. For such problems, traders use high-level languages (e.g., Python), because they can code faster and more accurately in these languages than in lower-level languages, such as C++. If they expect that the software will remain useful, they may later recode their routines in other languages to make them run faster.

Some electronic traders also reduce latency by creating contingency tables that contain prearranged action plans. For example, suppose that a bid rises in a market in which electronic traders are active. In response to the increased bid, traders may want to raise their bids or offers. The decision to do so may depend on their inventory positions and perhaps on many other factors as well. To decide what to do following an increased bid may require substantial analyses, which take time. Traders can reduce their decision latencies by doing these analyses before the bid increases instead of afterward. Seeing the increased bid, they can respond by simply looking up the optimal response in a contingency table stored in memory. To be most useful, the contingency tables must be kept up to date and must include responses for most-likely events. In this example, traders presumably would also have precomputed responses for a decrease in the bid, among many other contingencies.

EXAMPLE 2

Latency

1. Explain why low-latency is important to electronic traders.

Solution:

Electronic traders need a comparative speed advantage to 1) take advantage of market opportunities before others do, 2) receive time precedence that would allow them to trade sooner when offering liquidity to others, and 3) ensure order cancellation when they no longer want to fill the order. To gain a comparative advantage relative to others, electronic traders try to minimize latency—the time between an event occurring and a subsequent action, typically the submission of an order instruction, based upon that event. To minimize latency, electronic traders invest in very fast communication systems and very fast computer systems.

Advanced Orders, Tactics, and Algorithms

Buy-side traders often use electronic brokers and their systems for advanced orders, trading tactics, and algorithms provided by their electronic brokers to search for liquidity.

Advanced order types.

Advanced orders generally are limit orders with limit prices that change as market conditions change. An example would be a pegged limit order for which the trader would like to maintain a bid or an offer at a specified distance relative to some benchmark. Suppose that a trader wants to peg a limit buy order two ticks below the current ask. A broker who supports this instruction may forward it to an exchange that supports the instruction if the probability of the order's filling at that exchange is favorable compared with other exchanges. When the ask rises or falls, the exchange system will immediately cancel the order and replace it with a new limit order to keep the order at two ticks below the current ask. If the exchange does not support this instruction, the broker's computer will manage the order by submitting a limit order priced two ticks below the current ask and adjusting it as necessary to maintain the peg when the market moves. Effective management of a pegged limit order requires an electronic trading system with very low latency. If the order is not adjusted quickly enough, it risks being executed at an unfavorable price (in this example, if prices drop) or being resubmitted after other orders have been placed at the new price so the probability of execution at that price will be lower (if prices rise). Traders sometimes call pegged limit orders floating limit orders.

Trading tactics.

A trading tactic is a plan for executing a simple function that generally involves the submission of multiple orders. Note that the distinction between advanced orders and tactics can be arbitrary, and not all traders will use the same language to describe various trading functions. An example of a trading tactic is an instruction to sweep through every market at a given price to find hidden trading opportunities.

Suppose that the best exposed bid among all trading venues is 20.00 and the best exposed offer is 20.02. Because many trading systems permit traders to hide their orders, hidden buyers or sellers may be willing to trade at the 20.01 midpoint. Depending on the exchange, at least three types of orders could permit a trade at the midpoint. First, among exchanges that permit hidden orders, one or more exchanges may be holding a hidden limit order at 20.01. Second, among exchanges that permit discretionary limit orders, one or more exchanges may be holding a discretionary limit order that can be filled at the midpoint. For example, suppose that an exchange is holding a limit order to buy at 19.99 with 0.02 discretion. This order can be filled at 20.01 if a suitable sell limit order arrives at that price. Finally, among exchanges and dark pools that permit midspread orders, one or more exchanges or dark pools may be holding such an order. Dark pools are trading venues that do not publish their liquidity and are only available to selected clients. A midspread order is a limit order that is pegged to the midpoint of the quoted bid–ask spread.

To find such hidden liquidity, an electronic trading system may submit an immediate or cancel (IOC) order priced at 20.01 to the exchange that the trader expects will most likely have hidden liquidity on the needed side of the market. If such liquidity exists, the order will execute up to the minimum of the sizes of the two orders. If not, the exchange will immediately cancel the order and report the cancellation. If the order has any remaining unfilled size, the electronic trading system will search for liquidity at another exchange. This process will continue until the order is filled or until the trader decides that further search is probably futile. This sweeping tactic is most effective when the electronic trading system managing it has very low latency. A slow system may lose an opportunity to trade if someone else takes it first. Also, a slow system that obtains one or more partial fills may lose opportunities to trade at other exchanges if the proprietary electronic trading systems managing the standing orders that provide those opportunities cancel their standing orders when they suspect someone is sweeping the market, as they might if they see trade reports inside the quoted spread.

An example of another trading tactic is placing a limit order at some price with the hope that it will fill at that price. If the order does not fill after some time period (which might be random or based on information), the electronic trading system will cancel the order and resubmit it with an improved price (i.e., a higher price for a buy order or a lower price for a sell order). The process is repeated until the order fills.

Algorithms.

Algorithms ("algos" for short) are programmed strategies for filling orders. Algorithms may use combinations or sequences of simple orders, advanced orders, or multiple orders to achieve their objectives. Buy-side traders use algorithms, often provided by brokers, extensively to trade small orders and to reduce the price impacts of large trades. For example, many algorithms break up large orders and submit the pieces to various markets over time. Breaking up orders makes it difficult for other traders to infer that a trader is trying to fill a large order. The algorithms typically submit the orders at random times, in random sizes, and sometimes to randomly selected exchanges to hide their common origin.

The rates at which algorithms try to fill large orders may depend on market volumes or on elapsed time. For example, VWAP algorithms attempt to obtain a volume-weighted average fill price that is close to (or better than) the volume-weighted average price (VWAP) of all trades arranged within a prespecified time interval. To minimize the variation between the actual average fill price and the VWAP over the interval, these algorithms try to participate in an equal fraction of all trading volume throughout the interval. To do so, they forecast volumes based on the historical volume profile and on current volumes. The algorithm trades more during periods of historically high volume (e.g., around market open and close) and when the market has been more active than normal. It trades less during periods of relatively low volume. In practice, the execution rate will vary because volumes will differ from expectations. Buy-side traders use VWAP algorithms when spreading the order over time and when obtaining the average market price within an interval is acceptable to them or their portfolio managers.

Many algorithms use floating limit orders with the hope of obtaining cheap executions. If they fail to fill after some time period, they may switch to more-aggressively priced orders or to marketable orders to ensure that they fill. Large traders who use algorithms to manage their orders are especially concerned about hiding their intentions from front runners. Many electronic traders use artificial intelligence systems to detect when large traders are present in the market. In particular, they look for patterns that large traders may leave. For example, a poorly designed algorithm may submit orders exactly at the same millisecond within a second whenever it submits an order. A clever trader who is aware of this regularity may detect when a large trader is in the market and, equally important, when the trader has completed filling his order. To avoid these problems, algorithm designers often randomize order submission times and sizes to avoid producing patterns that might give them away. They also sometimes try to hide their orders among other orders so that front runners cannot easily identify their intentions.

Developing good algorithms requires extensive research into the origins of transaction costs. Algorithm authors must understand transaction costs well so that they can design algorithms that will trade effectively. To that end, algorithm providers build and estimate models of the costs of trading orders of various sizes, models of the impact trades of a given size or frequency will have on prices, and models of the probabilities that limit orders will fill under a variety of conditions. They must also predict volumes accurately. The most effective algorithms are based on the best research and implemented on the fastest and most capable electronic systems.

Good algorithms generally obtain low-cost executions by knowing when and where to offer liquidity via limit orders, when to use market orders, and how to most effectively keep the market from being aware of their efforts. They reduce the price impacts of large trades and greatly reduce the costs of managing many small trades.

EXAMPLE 3

Use of Electronic Brokers

1. You have recently been hired recently as a junior buy-side analyst. Part of your training (on-boarding) has been to sit with the trading desk to learn how the desk trades through its electronic brokers. In a meeting with your manager, she asks you to explain the use of electronic brokers for advanced orders, trading tactics, and algorithmic trading tools that your electronic brokers provide. What would you say?

Solution:

The use of electronic brokers and their systems is valuable for such advanced order types as pegged or floating limit orders, whose limit prices change as market conditions change. Traders use these order types to supply liquidity at a specified distance from the market. These orders require continuous real-time evaluation to determine if an order cancellation or replacement is needed as market conditions change. The use of electronic brokers relieves the need for the trader to continuously monitor the market to cancel and resubmit orders when prices change. An electronic broker is also valuable for orders placed a few ticks outside the best market that will be among the last orders to supply liquidity to a large trader, hopefully at a good price.

Electronic brokers also allow their clients to access order execution tactics (presented as another complex order type) that involve multiple submissions that may "sweep" through markets to uncover hidden liquidity. These tactics allow traders to submit multiple orders with a single instruction.

Finally, electronic brokers also provide algorithmic trading tools. Algorithms are automated (programmed trading strategies for combinations of simple and single, advanced, or multiple orders and various trading tactics) to fill small orders efficiently based on various criteria. They often break up large orders into smaller pieces to minimize the market impact of filling the order. They may route the orders to multiple venues at the same time or to the same venue at various times. For example, VWAP algorithms attempt to fill orders at the volume-weighted average price (or better) of all trades over a specified interval. The systems running algorithms that place standing limit orders must be very fast to cancel orders in trading. In these cases, low latency is critical to ensure order cancellation before unfavorable executions occur. Fast systems also help ensure that traders are first to respond when market conditions change and to maintain time precedence.

Select Examples of How Electronic Trading Changed Trading Strategies

The growth in electronic trading systems changed how traders interact with the market. Proprietary traders, buy-side traders, and brokers adapted their trading strategies to use new electronic tools and facilities. Select characteristics of electronic trading are described below.

Hidden orders.

Hidden orders are very common in electronic markets. Hidden orders are orders that are exposed (or shown) only to the brokers or exchanges who receive them. Traders—especially large traders—submit them when they do not want to reveal the existence of the trading options that their standing orders provide to the markets. Traders concerned about quote matchers can protect themselves to some extent by submitting hidden limit orders. Note that hidden limit orders are the electronic equivalent of giving orders to floor brokers to fill with the understanding that the floor brokers may expose the orders only if they can arrange trades. Such orders work better at electronic exchanges than at floor-based exchanges because computers never inadvertently or intentionally display these orders improperly. In electronic markets, the most common type of order by far is the immediate or cancel (IOC) limit order. Traders use these orders to discover hidden orders that may stand in the spread between a market's quoted bid and ask prices. Because they cancel immediately if they do not find liquidity, these orders are also hidden and thus do not reveal trade intentions.

Some electronic traders try to discover hidden orders by pinging the market: They submit a small IOC limit order for only a few shares at the price at which they are looking for hidden orders. If the pinging order trades, they know that a hidden order is present at that price; however, they do not know the full size of the order (which they can discover only by trading with it). Traders then may use this information to adjust their trading strategies.

All traders who subscribe to a complete trade feed that includes odd-lot transactions (substandard transaction sizes) can see the results of a ping that discovers liquidity. At almost all exchanges, however, only the pinger will know on which side of the market the hidden liquidity lies. Nonetheless, the information produced by someone else's successful ping can be useful to various traders. It indicates that someone in the market is concerned enough about liquidity conditions that pinging is worthwhile and that hidden liquidity is available on one side of the market.

Leapfrog.

When bid–ask spreads are wide, dealers often are willing to trade at better prices than they quote. They quote wide spreads because they hope to trade at more favorable prices. When another trader quotes a better price, dealers often immediately quote an even better price. For example, if the market is 20 bid, offered at 28, and a buy-side trader bids at 21, a dealer might instantly bid at 22. (The improved price might also come from a quote matcher.) This behavior frustrates buy-side traders, who then must quote a better price to maintain order precedence. If the spread is sufficiently wide, a game of leapfrog may ensue as the dealer jumps ahead again.

Flickering quotes.

Electronic markets often have flickering quotes, which are exposed limit orders that electronic traders submit and then cancel shortly thereafter, often within a second. Electronic dealers and algorithmic buy-side traders submit and repeatedly cancel and resubmit their orders when they do not want their orders to stand in the market; rather, they want other traders to see that they are willing to trade at the displayed price. Traders who wish to trade with a flickering quote can place a hidden limit order at the price where the quote is flickering. If the flickering order returns, it will hit their hidden limit order, and then they will trade with it.

Electronic arbitrage.

Electronic arbitrageurs use electronic trading systems to implement three types of arbitrage trading strategies:

1. **Take liquidity on both sides**. The costliest and least risky arbitrage trading strategy involves using marketable orders to fill both legs, or positions (i.e., buying an undervalued instrument and selling a similar overvalued instrument), of the arbitrage portfolio. This strategy is profitable only if the arbitrage spread is sufficiently large, but competition among arbitrageurs ensures that such large arbitrage spreads are quite rare. Arbitrageurs can seldom simultaneously take liquidity in two markets for identical instruments and make a profit. To effectively execute this strategy, arbitrageurs must use very fast trading systems so that they can lock in the arbitrage spread before prices in one or both markets change.
2. **Offer liquidity on one side**. In this strategy, arbitrageurs offer liquidity in one or both markets in which they trade. When they obtain a fill in one market, they immediately take liquidity in the other market to complete the construction of their arbitrage portfolio. This strategy produces lower-cost executions, but it is a bit riskier than the first strategy.

   For example, suppose that Markets A and B are both quoting 20 bid, offered at 21 for the same instrument. An arbitrageur may place a bid at 19 in Market A with the hope that a large seller will come along who takes all liquidity at 20 (i.e., fills all bids at 20) in Market A and then proceeds to fill the arbitrageur's order at 19. If so, the arbitrageur will immediately try to sell to the 20 bid in Market B. If the arbitrageur is quick enough, he may be able to fill his order before the bidder at 20 in Market B cancels that bid and before any other trader—particularly the large trader—takes it. If successful, the arbitrageur realizes a profit of 1. Of course, the arbitrageur will immediately cancel his 19 bid in Market A if the 20 bid in Market B disappears.

3. **Offer liquidity on both sides.** The final arbitrage strategy involves offering liquidity in both markets. In this strategy, after the first order to execute fills, the arbitrageur continues to offer liquidity to complete the second trade. This strategy is the riskiest strategy because arbitrageurs are exposed to substantial price risk when one leg is filled and the other is not. Moreover, if prices are moving because well-informed traders are on the same side in both markets—as they might be if the well-informed traders possess information about common risk factors—the leg providing liquidity to the informed traders will fill quickly, whereas the other leg probably will not fill.

   Arbitrageurs using this strategy trade much like dealers—switching from offering (supplying) liquidity to taking (demanding) liquidity when they believe that offering liquidity may be too risky. They may also often cancel and resubmit their orders when market conditions change. Thus, they are most effective when they use fast trading systems.

   When the arbitrage spread reverts, as the arbitrageurs expect, the arbitrageurs will reverse their trades, often using the same strategy they used to acquire their arbitrage portfolios. Of course, if the spread never reverts, arbitrageurs will lose regardless of how they trade. They will lose less, however, if they can trade their arbitrage portfolio by offering liquidity in one or both legs.

Machine learning.

Machine learning, also known as data mining, uses advanced statistical methods to characterize data structures, particularly relations among variables. These methods include neural nets, genetic algorithms, classifiers, and other methods designed to explain variables of interest using sparse data or data for which the number of potential explanatory variables far exceeds the number of observations.

Machine-learning methods produce models based on observed empirical regularities rather than on theoretical principles identified by analysts. These methods can be powerful when stable processes generate vast amounts of data, such as occurs in active financial markets.

Many trading problems are ideally suited for machine-learning analyses because the problems repeat regularly and often. For such problems, machine-based learning systems can be extraordinarily powerful.

However, these systems are often useless—or worse—when trading becomes extraordinary (e.g., when volatilities shoot up). Machine-learning systems frequently do not produce useful information during volatility episodes because these episodes have few precedents from which the machines can learn. Thus, traders often instruct their electronic trading systems to stop trading—and sometimes to close out their positions—whenever they recognize that they are entering uncharted territory. Many traders shut down when volatility spikes, both because high-volatility episodes are uncommon and thus not well understood and because even if such episodes were well understood, they represent periods of exceptionally high risk.

6 ELECTRONIC TRADING RISKS

☐ describe the risks associated with electronic trading and how regulators mitigate them

The advent of electronic trading affected securities markets in many ways. Investors now benefit from greater trade process efficiencies and reduced transaction costs, but electronic trading also creates new systemic risks for market participants.

The HFT Arms Race

The competition among high-frequency traders (HFTs) has created an "arms race" in which each trader tries to be faster than the next. Consequently, the state-of-the-art, high-frequency trading technologies necessary to compete successfully are now very expensive, making entry quite costly. These costs form barriers to entry that can create natural monopolies. Although substantial evidence suggests that electronic trading benefits the markets, these benefits may erode if only a few HFTs survive and can exploit their unique positions. Already, many HFTs are quitting the markets because they cannot compete effectively.

More generally, many commentators have observed that most of the costly technologies that high-frequency traders acquire do little to promote better or more-liquid markets. HFTs primarily incur these costs so they can beat their competitors. The utilitarian traders who demand liquidity ultimately pay these costs. Concerns about the costs of the HFT arms race have led to calls for changes in market structure that would diminish the advantages of being faster. Some commentators suggest that markets be slowed by running call markets once a second or more often instead of trading continuously. Others suggest that the order processing be delayed by random intervals to reduce the benefits of being fast and thus the incentives to invest in speed.

Systemic Risks of Electronic Trading

Electronic trading created new systemic risks that concern regulators and practitioners. A systemic risk is a risk that some failure will hurt more than just the entity responsible for the failure. Systemic risks are particularly problematic when the responsible entity is not required or is unable to compensate others for the costs its failure imposes on them. When people do not bear the full costs of their behaviors, they tend not to be as careful in avoiding damaging behaviors as they otherwise would be.

Systemic risks associated with fast trading may be caused by electronic exchange trading system failures or excessive orders submitted by electronic traders. Electronic exchange trading system failures occur when programmers make mistakes, exchange servers have insufficient capacity to handle traffic, or computer hardware or communication lines fail.

The 18 May 2012 Facebook IPO at NASDAQ is an example of a trading system failure caused by a programming error that unexpectedly high demands on capacity revealed. In this case, two software processes locked into an infinite loop as they took turns responding to each other.

Examples of systemic risks caused by excessive orders submitted by electronic traders include the following:

- *Runaway algorithms* produce streams of unintended orders that result from programming mistakes. The problems sometimes occur when programmers do not anticipate some contingency. The Knight Capital trading failure on 1 August 2012 may be the most extreme example of a runaway algorithm incident. Owing to a software programming mistake, Knight sent millions of orders to the markets over a 45-minute period when it intended only to fill 212 orders, some of which normally might have been broken up but none of which would have generated so many orders. These orders produced 4 million executions involving 397 stocks. Knight lost $400 million in the incident.

- *Fat finger errors* occur when a manual trader submits a larger order than intended. They are called fat finger errors because they sometimes occur when a trader hits the wrong key or hits a key more often than intended. These types of errors are not unique to electronic trading systems, but their consequences are often greater in electronic systems because of the speed at which they operate and because clerks often catch these errors in manual trading systems before they cause problems.
- *Overlarge orders* demand more liquidity than the market can provide. In these events, a trader—often inexperienced—will try to execute a marketable order that is too large for the market to handle without severely disrupting prices in the time given to fill the order. The 6 May 2010 Flash Crash occurred as a result of such an order. The crash was triggered when a large institutional trader tried to sell $4.1 billion in E-mini S&P 500 futures contracts using an algorithm over a short period. The algorithm was designed to participate in a fixed fraction of the market volume. When the initial trades depressed S&P 500 futures prices, trading volumes increased substantially as arbitrageurs and others started to trade. The increase in trading volumes caused the algorithm to increase the rate of its order submissions, which exacerbated the problem. The market reverted to its former levels after the Chicago Mercantile Exchange briefly halted trading in the E-mini S&P 500 futures contract, and the large order eventually was filled.
- *Malevolent order streams* are created deliberately to disrupt the markets. The perpetrators may be market manipulators; aggrieved employees, such as traders or software engineers; or terrorists. Traders conducting denial-of-service attacks designed to overwhelm their competitors' electronic trading systems with excessive quotes also may create malevolent order streams.

The solutions to the systemic risk problems associated with electronic trading systems are multifold:

- Most obviously, traders must test software thoroughly before using it in live trading. Exchanges often conduct mock trading sessions to allow developers to test their software.
- Rigorous market access controls must ensure that only those orders coming from approved sources enter electronic order-matching systems.
- Rigorous access controls on software developers must ensure that only authorized developers can change software. Best practice mandates that these controls also include the requirement that all software be read, understood, and vouched for by at least one developer besides its author.
- The electronic traders who generate orders and the electronic exchanges that receive orders must surveil their order flow in real time to ensure that it conforms to preset parameters that characterize its expected volume, size, and other characteristics. When the order flow is different than expected, automatic controls must shut it off immediately.
- Brokers must surveil all client orders that clients introduce into electronic trading systems to ensure that their clients' trading is appropriate. Brokers must not allow their clients to enter orders directly into exchange trading systems—a process called sponsored naked access—because it would allow clients to avoid broker oversight.
- Some exchanges have adopted price limits and trade halts to stop trading when prices move too quickly. These rules stop trading when excess demands for liquidity occur. They also prevent the extreme price changes

that can occur in electronic markets when market orders arrive and no liquidity is present. Most brokers now automatically convert market orders into marketable limit orders to ensure that they do not trade at unreasonable prices.

HISTORICAL EVENT: THE FLASH CRASH

The 6 May 2010 Flash Crash was the most notable market structure event in recent memory. During the crash, which started at about 2:42 p.m. ET, the E-mini S&P 500 futures contract dropped approximately 5% in 5 minutes and then recovered nearly fully in the next 10 minutes. The price volatility spilled from the equity futures market into the stock market, where some stocks traded down more than 99% or up more than 1,000%. In the immediate aftermath of the crash, regulators decided that more than 20,000 trades in more than 300 securities that occurred more than 60% away from earlier prices would be broken (canceled).

This extraordinary event raised many concerns about security market structure—in particular, how the adoption of electronic trading may have increased potential systemic risks. This subsection describes the events that led up to the crash, what happened during the crash, and the regulatory responses to the crash.

The Event and Its Causes

On Thursday, 6 May 2010, the stock market traded down throughout the day at an accelerating rate. By 2:30 p.m., it had lost about 4% from its previous close. Contemporaneous commentators attributed the fall to concerns about Greek sovereign debt and the implications of a Greek default for other markets. During the day, many traders who had been providing liquidity to the market were accumulating substantial long positions as people demanded to sell. As the day wore on, their willingness to continue to accumulate additional inventory decreased. Moreover, day traders, who do not normally carry inventory overnight, also were considering how and when they would sell their losing positions.

Presumably, in response to the European concerns and perhaps other concerns, portfolio managers at Waddell & Reed Financial Inc. (W&R) decided to reduce US equity exposure in their $27 billion Asset Strategy Fund by selling 75,000 June 2010 E-mini S&P 500 futures contracts with a nominal value of approximately $4.1 billion. They gave this order to their buy-side trader, who proceeded to fill it using an algorithm that split the order into small pieces for execution. Although the order was the largest single order submitted to the E-mini futures market that year, it was not without precedent. Two earlier orders in the previous year were of similar size or larger, one of which had been submitted by W&R. Those orders had been filled in more stable markets and over longer periods of time than W&R's 6 May order. The order started to execute at 2:32 p.m.

W&R's head trader, who normally would have handled such a large order, was out of the office that day. Instead, a less-senior trader in his office handled the order.

The trader set parameters on the algorithm to target an execution rate of 9% of the trading volume calculated over the previous minute without regard to price or time. This trading strategy was more aggressive than the one W&R had used to fill its large order from the previous year. The trader probably set an aggressive rate because he feared that the firm would obtain a worse execution if prices continued to fall. The more aggressive strategy contributed to the crash.

When the initial trades depressed S&P 500 futures prices, trading volumes increased substantially as arbitrageurs and others started to trade, many of them trading with each other as they normally did. The arbitrageurs bought the futures and sold equities and equity ETFs (exchange-traded funds), such as the SPDR S&P 500 Trust (ticker SPY). Some arbitrageurs also sold call option contracts and bought put option contracts. The increase in trading volumes caused the algorithm to increase the rate of its order submissions as it tried to keep up with its mandate to participate in 9% of the market volume. The increasing order submission rate exacerbated the problem.

Initially, high-frequency traders and other liquidity suppliers in the E-mini futures markets supplied liquidity to W&R's order and accumulated long positions. Between 2:41 p.m. and 2:44 p.m., these short-term traders sold these positions as the algorithm continued to pump more orders into the market. During this 4-minute period, the E-mini dropped 3%. By the end of this period, buy-side depth (total size of standing buy orders) in the E-mini contract dropped to only 1% of the average depth observed earlier in the day. The E-mini contract then dropped 1.7% in the next 15 seconds.

The arbitrage trades caused the equity markets to drop. In many securities—especially the ETFs—falling prices triggered stock loss market orders, which further depressed prices. The levered ETFs were particularly affected because their high volatilities make them popular with technical traders and retail traders, many of whom routinely place stop orders to protect their positions.

As the prices changed quickly, many traders who were providing liquidity in the futures and equity markets dropped out because they were unwilling to trade in the face of such extreme volatility. Many also had already accumulated large inventory positions from earlier in the day and did not want to buy more. Interestingly, researchers later discovered that the largest and most active high-frequency trading firms did not withdraw. Nonetheless, limit order books thinned out—especially on the buy side—as traders canceled standing orders and as sellers filled those buy orders still standing.

In some stocks, all standing buy orders were exhausted and trading stopped. In other stocks, all buy orders except those placed with a limit price of only a cent or two were exhausted. In these stocks, exchange trading systems blindly filled market sell orders at extraordinarily low prices. In a few other stocks, the withdrawal of liquidity suppliers from the market also removed essentially all liquidity from the sell side of the market. Some stocks then traded at prices as high as $100,000 when market buy orders were filled against sell orders placed at extraordinarily high prices.

The slide stopped at 2:45:28 p.m. when a Chicago Mercantile Exchange trading rule called Stop Logic Functionality caused the exchange's computers to halt trading briefly in the E-mini S&P 500 futures contract and to clear the limit order book of all standing limit orders. The rule is triggered when it becomes apparent that pending order executions would cause prices to jump too far. The futures contract dropped about 5% from when the algorithm started to trade at 2:32 p.m. to the market halt at 2:45 p.m. The algorithm sold about 35,000 contracts during this period.

When trading resumed 5 seconds later, the buy-side algorithm continued to trade, but many liquidity suppliers were now willing to provide liquidity. Prices rose quickly in orderly markets.

The episode largely ended when the big W&R order completed filling at around 2:51 p.m., about 20 minutes after it started. However, the market remained quite volatile during the remainder of the day as traders adjusted their positions and responded to the extreme volatility.

Following the crash, regulators broke all trades that had occurred more than 60% away from the previous close.

Implications for Traders

The Flash Crash provided three important lessons for observant traders:

- First, market orders are incompatible with electronic order-matching systems that do not curb trading when prices move too quickly. Had traders priced all their orders, no trades would have taken place at unreasonably high or low prices. Following the crash, many retail brokers adopted a policy of converting all customer market orders into marketable limit orders with limit prices set about 10% above the current ask for buy orders and 10% below the current bid for sell orders.
- Second, institutional traders using algorithms must be careful not to demand more liquidity than orderly markets can provide. Most buy-side investors probably immediately recognized that W&R lost a substantial amount of its clients' money owing to the extraordinarily high transaction costs associated with the trade. To obtain a crude estimate of this loss, assume that the algorithm traded all $4.1 billion of its order at a uniform rate throughout the 5% price reversal. The average market impact of the trade would have been 2.5%, which implies total transaction costs of about $100 million, or 0.37% of the $27 billion in assets of the W&R Asset Strategy Fund. Such significant losses attract attention. Within a week, many algorithm writers probably coded limits into their algorithms to help prevent them from being used irresponsibly.
- Finally, algorithm writers and the traders who use algorithms must pay much more attention to the dangers of using algorithms that can create destructive feedback loops. They particularly must understand how algorithms respond to market conditions that they may create themselves.

Regulatory Responses

Following the Flash Crash, regulators adopted new rules to prevent a similar crash from happening again. They placed curbs that halt trades in a stock for 5 minutes if prices move up or down by more than 10% for large stocks and 20% for smaller stocks. This rule ensures that prices cannot move too quickly, but it does not prevent traders from behaving foolishly. Had it been in effect during the Flash Crash, the rule would have stopped trades from occurring at ridiculously low or high prices, but it would not have stopped the W&R trader from submitting an unrealistically aggressive order.

Regulators also adopted rules to establish when and which trades will be broken in the event of another extreme price change. Such rules should help ensure that liquidity suppliers who are afraid that their trades may be broken do not withdraw from the market prematurely.

EXAMPLE 4

Electronic Trading and Transaction Costs

1. Describe the impact of electronic trading on transaction costs.

Solution:

Growth in electronic trading has resulted in greater trade process efficiencies and reduced transaction costs for investors. Electronic systems are much cheaper to operate than floor-based systems (requiring less physical space and fewer exchange personnel). These systems can operate on a close-to-continuous basis at far greater scale and scope and at much faster speeds than humans. Process efficiencies from electronic trading have led to significant decreases in bid–ask spreads, which have lowered transaction costs for investors.

7 DETECTING ABUSIVE TRADING PRACTICES

☐ describe abusive trading practices that real-time surveillance of markets may detect

Regulators around the world recognize that real-time market monitoring and surveillance systems allow faster responses to potential crises and market abuses with the potential for rapid intervention to prevent or minimize damages. Many trading venues have long used real-time surveillance technologies, but their use is not consistent across all markets. The goal of real-time market surveillance is to detect potential market abuse while it is happening. Real-time surveillance often can detect the following damaging behaviors:

Front running.

Front running involves buying in front of anticipated purchases and selling in front of anticipated sales. In most jurisdictions, front running is illegal if the front runners acquire their information about orders improperly—for example, by a tip from a broker handling a large order.

Some traders use electronic artificial intelligence systems to identify when traders are filling large orders over time by breaking them up into small pieces. When these traders suspect that buyers or sellers are working large orders, they will trade ahead on the same side with the hope of benefiting when the large traders move prices as they fill their orders. This front-running strategy is legal if the information on which it is based is properly obtained— for example, by watching a market data feed.

Front running increases transaction costs for the traders whose orders are front run because the front runners take liquidity that the front-run traders otherwise would have taken for themselves.

Market manipulation.

In general, market manipulation consists of any trading strategy whose purpose is to produce misleading or false market prices, quotes, or fundamental information to profit from distorting the normal operation of markets. Market manipulators are parasitic traders who attempt to fool or force others into making disadvantageous trades. Many market manipulation strategies exist—including bluffing, squeezing, cornering, and gunning.

In most jurisdictions, market manipulation strategies are illegal. Enforcement is often difficult, however, because the exact infractions can be hard to define and because prosecutors generally must prove scienter (a legal term meaning intent or knowledge of wrongdoing), which can be difficult when defendants suggest alternative explanations for their behavior.

Market manipulation strategies usually involve one or more of the following improper market activities:

- *Trading for market impact* involves trading to raise or lower prices deliberately. A market manipulator often is willing to incur substantial transaction costs to raise or lower the price of a security to influence other traders' perceptions of value.
- R*umormongering* is the dissemination of false information about fundamental values or about other traders' trading intentions to alter investors' value assessments. Financial analysts must be careful to ensure that they base their analyses on valid information and not on false information designed to fool them into making poor decisions. Note that although rumormongering is illegal in most jurisdictions, simply reporting one side of an issue is not illegal. Financial analysts, therefore, must also be careful to ensure that they base their analyses on balanced information and not on information that is true but selectively presented to them with the purpose of distorting their analyses.
- *Wash trading* consists of trades arranged among commonly controlled accounts to create the impression of market activity at a particular price. The purpose of wash trading is to fool investors into believing that a market is more liquid than it truly is and to thereby increase investors' confidence both in their ability to exit positions without substantial cost and in their assessments of security values. Manipulators also can achieve these purposes by falsely reporting trades that never occurred, which is essentially what happens when they arrange trades among commonly controlled accounts.
- *Spoofing*, also known as *layering*, is a trading practice in which traders place exposed standing limit orders to convey an impression to other traders that the market is more liquid than it is or to suggest to other traders that the security is under- or overvalued. For example, suppose that a spoofer wants to buy stock cheaply or quickly. The spoofer might place a hidden buy order in the market. The spoofer then places one or more exposed sell limit orders in the market to convey the impression that prices may soon fall. Seeing the spoofing sell orders, one or more traders may conclude that values may be lower than market prices suggest. On that basis, they may sell into the spoofer's buy order, enabling the spoofer to obtain a quick and possibly cheaper purchase than the spoofer otherwise would have obtained had the spoofer not placed the spoofing sell orders. Of course, immediately following the execution of the buy order, the spoofer will cancel the sell orders.

  Spoofing is risky because the spoofing orders that spoofers submit might execute before their intended orders execute. Spoofers can manage this risk by keeping track of the orders in the limit order book ahead of their spoofing orders. If these orders fill before the spoofers' intended orders fill, spoofers will cancel their spoofing orders to prevent them from executing. To effectively manage these processes, spoofers use electronic systems to monitor trading and to ensure that they can quickly cancel their orders as soon as they no longer want them to stand.

Market manipulators often use these improper market activities singly or in combination when they try to fool or force other traders into trades that will ultimately prove to be disadvantageous to them. Market manipulation strategies include:

- **Bluffing**. Bluffing involves submitting orders and arranging trades to influence other traders' perceptions of value. Bluffers often prey on momentum traders, who buy when prices are rising and sell when prices are falling. For example, consider typical "pump-and-dump" schemes in which bluffers buy stock to raise its price and thereby encourage momentum traders to buy. The bluffers then sell the stock to the momentum traders at higher prices. To further the scheme, bluffers may engage in such activities as rumormongering or wash trading. Note also that bluffers may time their purchases to immediately follow the release of valid positive information about the security and thereby fool traders into overvaluing the material significance of the new information.

In a pump-and-dump manipulation, the bluffer tries to raise prices. Similar manipulations can occur on the short side, though they are less common. In such manipulations, manipulators take short positions and then try to repurchase shares at lower prices. These manipulations are often called "short and distorts."

To avoid falling into these traps, financial analysts must ensure that they base their analyses on independent assessments of value. Their analyses must have a proper foundation as required by Standard V(A): Diligence and Reasonable Basis, of the CFA Institute Code of Ethics and Standards of Professional Conduct.

- **Gunning the market**. Gunning the market is a strategy used by market manipulators to force traders to do disadvantageous trades. A manipulator generally guns the market by selling quickly to push prices down with the hope of triggering stop-loss sell orders. A stop-loss (or stop) sell order becomes valid for execution once the specified stop price condition is met by a trade occurring at or below the stop price. For example, suppose that a market manipulator believes that traders have placed many stop-loss sell orders at 50. These sell orders would become valid upon a trade occurring at 50 or below. The manipulator may sell aggressively to push prices down from 51 to 50 and thereby trigger the stop-loss sell orders. The manipulator then may be able to profit by repurchasing at lower prices.
- **Squeezing and cornering**. Squeezing, cornering, and gunning the market are all schemes that market manipulators use to force traders to do disadvantageous trades. In a squeeze or corner, the manipulator obtains control over resources necessary to settle trading contracts. The manipulator then unexpectedly withdraws those resources from the market, which causes traders to default on their contracts, some of which the manipulator may hold. The manipulator profits by providing the resources at high prices or by closing the contracts at exceptionally high prices.

  For example, in short squeezes, manipulators obtain control of a substantial fraction of all available lendable stock shares or bonds. If the securities are overvalued, as they might be if the manipulators are also engaging in a pump and dump, many speculators may be short selling the securities by unknowingly borrowing them from the manipulators. The manipulators then will recall the security loans. If the short sellers ("shorts") cannot borrow the securities from others, they will be forced to buy securities in the market to cover their stock loans. Their purchases will raise prices and allow the manipulators to sell their securities at overvalued prices. Manipulators also may profit by raising the rates they charge to lend their securities. To avoid being caught in a short squeeze, short sellers must be sure that the market for lendable securities has many participants and is not concentrated in the hands of one or more entities acting in concert.

  In commodity market corners, manipulators buy many futures contracts while simultaneously buying in the spot markets much of the deliverable supply of the commodity. When the contract approaches expiration, the manipulators then demand delivery from the shorts, most of whom will not own the deliverable commodity. The shorts then must buy the deliverable supply from the manipulators at exceptionally high prices. Alternatively, they may repurchase their contracts from the manipulators, again at very high prices.

Corners can occur in commodity markets because most participants in commodity futures contracts do not demand to receive or make delivery when the contract expires. Instead, they close their positions by arranging offsetting trades in the futures market, either because they are simultaneously accepting or making delivery elsewhere or because they are rolling their positions into future contract months. Accordingly, most short sellers neither expect nor intend to make delivery. When forced to make delivery, they are caught short.

Corners are illegal in most jurisdictions, and they always violate the rules of the exchanges on which futures contracts trade. In general, long holders cannot demand delivery if they do not have a valid business reason for doing so. However, enforcement is complicated by the fact that manipulators may offer plausible reasons for requesting unexpected deliveries. Note also that sometimes, unexpected supply shortages coupled with unexpected legitimate demands for delivery can result in inadvertent short squeezes. Thus, short sellers who do not intend to make delivery should try to close their positions early to ensure that they are not caught in an intentional corner or an inadvertent squeeze.

SUMMARY

This reading explains the implicit and explicit costs of trading as well as widely used methods for estimating transaction costs. The reading also describes developments in electronic trading, the main types of electronic traders, their needs for speed and ways in which they trade. Electronic trading benefits investors through lower transaction costs and greater efficiencies but also introduces systemic risks and the need to closely monitor markets for abusive trading practices. Appropriate market governance and regulatory policies will help reduce the likelihood of events such as the 2010 Flash Crash. The reading's main points include:

- Dealers provide liquidity to buyers and sellers when they take the other side of a trade if no other willing traders are present.
- The bid–ask spread is the difference between the bid and the ask prices. The effective spread is two times the difference between the trade price and the midquote price before the trade occurred. The effective spread is a poor estimate of actual transaction costs when large orders have been filled in many parts over time or when small orders receive price improvement.
- Transaction costs include explicit costs and implicit costs. Explicit costs are the direct costs of trading. They include broker commissions, transaction taxes, stamp duties, and exchange fees. Implicit costs include indirect costs, such as the impact of the trade on the price received. The bid–ask spread, market impact, delay, and unfilled trades all contribute to implicit trading costs.

- The implementation shortfall method measures the total cost of implementing an investment decision by capturing all explicit and implicit trading costs. It includes the market impact costs, delay costs, as well as opportunity costs.
- The VWAP method of estimating transaction costs compares average fill prices to average market prices during a period surrounding the trade. It tends to produce lower transaction cost estimates than does implementation shortfall because it often does not measure the market impact of an order well.
- Markets have become increasingly fragmented as venues trading the same instruments have proliferated. Trading in any given instrument now occurs in multiple venues.
- The advantages of electronic trading systems include cost and operational efficiencies, lack of human bias, extraordinarily fast speed, and infinite span and scope of attention.
- Latency is the elapsed time between the occurrence of an event and a subsequent action that depends on that event. Traders use fast communication systems and fast computer systems to minimize latency to execute their strategies faster than others.
- Hidden orders, quote leapfrogging, flickering quotes, and the use of machine learning to support trading strategies commonly are found in electronic markets.
- Traders commonly use advanced order types, trading tactics, and algorithms in electronic markets.
- Electronic trading has benefited investors through greater trade process efficiencies and reduced transaction costs. At the same time, electronic trading has increased systemic risks.
- Examples of systemic risks posed by electronic traders include: runaway algorithms that produce streams of unintended orders caused by programming mistakes, fat finger errors that occur when a manual trader submits a larger order than intended, overlarge orders that demand more liquidity than the market can provide, and malevolent order streams created deliberately to disrupt the markets.
- Real-time surveillance of markets often can detect order front running and various market manipulation strategies.
- Market manipulators use such improper activities as trading for market impact, rumormongering, wash trading, and spoofing to further their schemes.
- Market manipulation strategies include bluffing, squeezing, cornering, and gunning.

PRACTICE PROBLEMS

The following information relates to questions 1-10

Brian Johnson is a senior manager at Star Asset Management (SAMN), a large asset management firm in the United States. Tim Martin has just earned his advanced degree in statistics and was hired to support the trading team at SAMN. Martin meets with Johnson to undergo a training relating to SAMN's trading activities.

Johnson begins the training with a review of the limit order book for Light Systems, Inc., which is presented in Exhibit 1. Three dealers make market for the shares of Light Systems. Based on these prices, SAMN's trading desk executes a market sell order for 1,100 shares of Light Systems.

Exhibit 1: Limit Order Book for Light Systems, Inc.

Bid				Ask			
Dealer	Time Entered	Price	Size	Dealer	Time Entered	Price	Size
B	10.10 a.m.	$17.15	900	C	10.11 a.m.	$17.19	1,200
C	10.11 a.m.	$17.14	1,500	B	10.10 a.m.	$17.20	800
A	10.11 a.m.	$17.12	1,100	A	10.12 a.m.	$17.22	1,100

Johnson then discusses a market buy order for 5,000 shares of an illiquid stock. The order was filled in three trades, and details about the three trades are presented in Exhibit 2.

Exhibit 2: Buy Trade Order Details

Trade #	Time	Trade Price	Trade Size	Bid Price	Ask Price
1	9.45 a.m.	$25.20	1,200	$25.17	$25.20
2	9.55 a.m.	$25.22	1,300	$25.19	$25.22
3	11.30 a.m.	$25.27	2,500	$25.22	$25.26

Johnson explains to Martin that the number of venues trading the same instruments has proliferated in recent years, and trading in any given instrument has now been distributed across these multiple venues. As a result, the available liquidity on any one of those exchanges represents just a small portion of the aggregate liquidity for that security. As a result, SAMN has had to adapt its trading strategies, particularly for large trades.

Johnson asks Martin about his views on how the introduction of electronic trading might have impacted SAMN. Martin tells Johnson:

Statement 1 Once built, electronic trading systems are more efficient and cheaper to operate than floor-based trading systems.

Statement 2 Electronic trading systems have attracted a lot of new buy-side traders, and the increased competition has resulted in narrower bid–ask spreads.

Statement 3 The introduction of electronic markets has had a much greater impact on the trading of corporate and municipal bonds than on the trading of equities.

Johnson tells Martin that communication speed is SAMN's current highest priority. All of SAMN's competitors have increased their communication speeds in recent months, and Johnson says management wants SAMN to be faster than its competitors. SAMN's trading desk is located in a residential area far from downtown where the exchanges it works with are located. SAMN's trading team is relatively large with experienced investment professionals, and the firm recently invested in fast computers with the latest algorithms.

At the end of the training, Johnson gives Martin his first assignment. The assignment is for Martin to use the vast amount of data that SAMN has collected to design a machine learning (ML) model using advanced statistical methods to characterize data structures and relations. Then he has to build a trading algorithm based on the same model. Since electronic trading has added systemic risk to the market, Johnson asks Martin to suggest ways to minimize the systemic risk introduced by his algorithm. Martin offers two suggestions:

Suggestion 1 Perform extensive testing of the algorithm before its launch.

Suggestion 2 Impose mandatory trading halts if prices change outside a threshold range.

A month into the job, Johnson sends Martin to an investment conference focused on abusive trading practices. Based on what he learned at the conference, Martin recommends to Johnson that SAMN incorporate a new rule that news be validated before a trade triggered by news is executed.

1. Based on Exhibit 1, the inside bid–ask spread for the limit order book for Light Systems is *closest* to:

   A. \$0.04.

   B. \$0.07.

   C. \$0.10.

2. Based on Exhibit 1, the total amount that SAMN will receive, on a per share basis, for executing the market sell order is *closest* to:

   A. \$17.14.

   B. \$17.15.

   C. \$17.22.

3. Based on Exhibit 2, the market impact relating to Trade 2, on a per share basis, is *closest* to:

   A. \$0.02.

   B. \$0.03.

   C. \$0.07.

4. Based on Exhibit 2, the average effective spread of the three trades is *closest to*:
   A. $0.0333.
   B. $0.0367.
   C. $0.0400.
5. The reason for SAMN having to adapt its trading strategies is a result of:
   A. latency.
   B. market fragmentation.
   C. high frequency trading.
6. Which of Martin's statements relating to the introduction of electronic markets is correct?
   A. Statement 1
   B. Statement 2
   C. Statement 3
7. Which of the following changes should SAMN make to address its key priority?
   A. Hire more investment professionals
   B. Upgrade to more complex operating systems
   C. Move the trading desk physically closer to the exchanges it works with
8. The model that Martin is tasked with designing will likely be *most* effective:
   A. for testing new markets.
   B. in a well-understood market environment.
   C. during periods of higher than normal market volatility.
9. Which of Martin's suggestions will *most likely* be effective in limiting the systemic risk introduced by his algorithm?
   A. Only Suggestion 1
   B. Only Suggestion 2
   C. Both Suggestion 1 and Suggestion 2
10. Which market manipulation strategy is *most likely* the target of the new rule suggested by Martin?
   A. Rumormongering
   B. Gunning the market
   C. Trading for market impact

The following information relates to questions 11-16

Michael Bloomfield is a trader at 2Fast Trading, a proprietary trading company that uses machine learning and algorithms to execute trades. He works with Amy Riley, a junior trader at the company. Bloomfield and Riley meet to review the company's trading systems and several trades in Bloomfield's trading account.

They discuss the increasing impact of market fragmentation on available liquidity for the company's trading strategies. Riley makes the following comments regarding market fragmentation:

Comment 1 Liquidity aggregation and smart order routing help traders manage the challenges and opportunities presented by fragmentation.

Comment 2 With increasing market fragmentation, traders who fill large orders now search for liquidity across multiple venues and across time to control market impact.

Bloomfield tells Riley that he noticed trades of 500 shares of BYYP stock were executed every 20 minutes for an hour. Bloomfield saw the same pattern of trading in the stock during the previous trading day. He instructs Riley to submit an order to purchase BYYP shares on the assumption that a trader seeks liquidity and is executing a large buy order by breaking it into pieces. The prices of these trades and the best bids and offers in the market when the BYYP trades occurred are presented in Exhibit 1.

Exhibit 1: BYYP Trade Details

Trade	Trade Price	Prevailing Bid	Prevailing Offer
1	41.50	41.45	41.50
2	41.75	41.73	41.75

Bloomfield shifts the conversation to AXZ Corp. Bloomfield notes that AXZ's bid–ask spread is narrow, even though AXZ's share price has been experiencing a period of high volatility. After extensive research, Bloomfield will purchase AXZ shares using a trading strategy that does not include standing orders.

Bloomfield then assesses the risks that 2Fast's electronic trading strategies introduce into the market. He is concerned that these risks may bring on more regulation. Bloomfield claims that the risks can be reduced by changing the structure of the market, and those structural changes can maintain 2Fast's primary competitive advantage, which is trading faster than competitors.

Bloomfield mentions that a regulatory body is investigating a competitor's trading practices. The investigation involves a tip that the competitor is manipulating markets by submitting orders and arranging trades to influence other traders' perceptions of value. Specifically, regulators were informed that the competitor has been buying stock to raise its price, thereby encouraging momentum traders to buy, and then selling the stock to them at higher prices. The regulator confirmed that the competitor did not use standing limit orders or commonly controlled accounts for the trades under investigation.

11. Which of Riley's comments related to market fragmentation is accurate?

A. Only Comment 1

B. Only Comment 2

C. Both Comment 1 and Comment 2

12. Bloomfield's strategy to purchase BYYP shares is *best* classified as electronic:

A. arbitrage.

B. front running.

C. quote matching.

13. Based on Exhibit 1, the average effective spread of the BYYP trades is *closest* to:

A. \$0.018.

B. \$0.035.

C. \$0.070.

14. Bloomfield's trading strategy for the purchase of AXZ shares *most likely* includes the use of:

A. flickering quotes.

B. machine learning.

C. leapfrogging quotes.

15. Which structural change for the market associated with electronic trading systems is *most* consistent with Bloomfield's claim?

A. Delaying order processing by random intervals

B. Exchanges using trade halts when prices move too quickly

C. Slowing markets by running call markets once a second or more often instead of trading continuously

16. The competitor company's trading is *best* described as:

A. bluffing.

B. spoofing.

C. wash trading.

SOLUTIONS

1. A is correct. The inside bid–ask spread, or market bid–ask spread, is the difference between the highest bid price and the lowest ask price. The highest bid price for Light Systems is \$17.15, and the lowest ask price is \$17.19. Therefore, the inside bid–ask spread = \$17.19 – \$17.15 = \$0.04.

2. B is correct. SAMN's trading desk executes a market sell order for 1,100 shares. Based on the limit order book, the trader would first sell 900 shares at \$17.15 (highest bid, Dealer B) and then sell the remaining 200 shares at \$17.14 (second highest bid, Dealer C). Therefore, the approximate price per share received by SAMN for selling the 1,100 shares is equal to [(900 × \$17.15) + (200 × \$17.14)] / 1,100 = \$17.1482 per share (\$17.15 rounded).

3. A is correct. Market impact, or price impact, is the effect of a trade on transaction prices. After the first trade (Trade 1) was executed at \$25.20, Trade 2 was executed at \$25.22, which is \$0.02 per share higher than the trade price of Trade 1. So, the execution of Trade 1 led to a price impact of \$0.02 per share on Trade 2.

4. C is correct. The effective bid–ask spread for buy orders is calculated as:

   Effective bid–ask spread (buy order) = 2 × {Trade price − [(Ask price + Bid price) / 2)]} or

   = 2 × (Trade price − Midpoint of the market at the time an order is entered).

   So, the effective bid–ask spreads for the three buy trades are calculated as:

   Effective spread of Trade 1 = 2 × {\$25.20 − [(\$25.20 + \$25.17)/2]} = \$0.0300.

   Effective spread of Trade 2 = 2 × {\$25.22 − [(\$25.22 + 25.19)/2]} = \$0.0300.

   Effective spread of Trade 3 = 2 × {\$25.27 − [(\$25.26 + \$25.22)/2]} = \$0.0600.

   The resulting average effective spread is then calculated as:

   Average effective spread

   = (Effective spread of Trade 1 + Effective spread of Trade 2 + Effective spread of Trade 3)/3.

   Average effective spread = (\$0.0300 + \$0.0300 + \$0.0600)/3 = \$0.0400.

5. B is correct. According to Johnson, markets have become increasingly fragmented as the number of venues trading the same instruments has proliferated and trading in any given instrument has been split (or fragmented) across these multiple venues. As a result, the available liquidity on any one exchange represents just a small portion of the aggregate liquidity for that instrument. This phenomenon is known as market fragmentation and creates the potential for price and liquidity disparities across venues. As a result, SAMN has had to adapt its trading strategies to this fragmented liquidity to avoid intensifying the market impact of a large trade.

6. A is correct. Once built, electronic systems are indeed cheaper to operate than floor-based trading systems. They require less physical space than do trading floors, and in contrast to floor-based trading systems, they do not require exchange officials to record and report prices. Furthermore, the widespread use

of electronic trading systems significantly decreased trading costs for buy-side traders. Costs fell as exchanges obtained greater cost efficiencies from using electronic matching systems instead of floor-based manual trading systems. These technologies also decreased costs and increased efficiencies for the dealers and arbitrageurs who provide much of the liquidity offered at exchanges. Competition forced them to pass along much of the benefits of their new technologies to buy-side traders in the form of narrower spreads quoted for larger sizes. New electronic buy-side order management systems also decreased buy-side trading costs by allowing a smaller number of buy-side traders to process more orders and to process them more efficiently than manual traders.

While electronic trading has had a significant effect on equity markets, it has not had as much of an effect on the markets for corporate and municipal bonds. The market structures of corporate and municipal bond markets have hardly changed since the late 19th century. Despite the efforts of many creative developers of electronic bond trading systems, most public investors in these markets still trade largely over the counter with dealers.

7. C is correct. The speed required by electronic traders is affected by fast communication and fast computations. The shorter the distance between the trader and the exchange, the faster the communication. Many exchanges allow electronic traders to place their servers in the rooms where the exchange servers operate, a practice called collocation.

8. B is correct. Many trading problems are ideally suited for machine learning analyses because the problems repeat regularly and often. For such problems, machine-based learning systems can be extraordinarily powerful. However, these systems are often useless—or worse—when trading becomes extraordinary, as when volatilities shoot up. Machine learning systems frequently do not produce useful information during volatility episodes because they have few precedents from which the machines can learn. Thus, traders often instruct their electronic trading systems to stop trading—and sometimes to close out their positions—whenever they recognize that they are entering uncharted territory. Many traders shut down when volatility spikes—both because high-volatility episodes are uncommon and thus not well understood and because even if such episodes were well understood, they represent periods of exceptionally high risk.

9. C is correct. Both suggestions will likely be effective in minimizing the systemic risk introduced by electronic trading. First, exhaustive testing of the algorithm prior to its launch can minimize risk relating to programming errors, which could result in an extreme market reaction that could trigger an even more extreme market reaction. Second, imposing mandatory trade halts in case of large price changes (outside a given threshold) would limit potential undesired results and help minimize systemic risk.

10. A is correct. Rumormongering is the dissemination of false information about fundamental values or about other traders' trading intentions in an attempt to alter investors' value assessments. Martin's suggested news validation rule would reduce the likelihood that SAMN would be adversely affected by this market manipulation strategy.

11. C is correct. Both of Riley's comments are correct. Electronic algorithmic trading techniques, such as liquidity aggregation and smart order routing, help traders manage the challenges and opportunities presented by fragmentation. Liquidity aggregators create "super books" that present liquidity across markets for a given instrument. These tools offer global views of market depth (available liquidity) for each instrument regardless of the trading venue that offers the liquidity. Smart

order-routing algorithms send orders to the markets that display the best quoted prices and sizes. Additionally, with increasing market fragmentation, traders filling large orders adapt their trading strategies to search for liquidity across multiple venues and across time to control the market impacts of their trades.

12. B is correct. Bloomfield noticed a pattern of trading in BYYP and decided to front run shares on the assumption that a trader is in the market filling a large buy order by breaking it into pieces. Electronic front runners trade in front of traders who demand liquidity. They identify when large traders or many small traders are trying to fill orders on the same side of the market. The order anticipation strategies of electronic front runners try to identify predictable patterns in order submission. They may search for patterns in order submissions, trades, or the relations between trades and other events.

    A is incorrect because electronic arbitrageurs look across markets for arbitrage opportunities in which they can buy an undervalued instrument and sell a similar overvalued one. His decision to purchase BYYP shares is based on the pattern of trading that Bloomfield observed.

    C is incorrect because quote matchers trade in front of traders who supply (not demand) liquidity. Bloomfield decides to purchase BYYP shares on the assumption that a trader is in the market seeking (not supplying) liquidity, which is consistent with front running (not quote matching). Quote matchers trade in front of traders who supply liquidity and try to exploit the option values of standing orders. Quote matchers buy when they believe they can rely on standing buy orders to get out of their positions, and they sell when they can do the same with standing sell orders.

13. B is correct. The effective spread is calculated as follows:

    $$\text{Effective spread} = 2 \times \left(\text{Trade price} - \text{Midpoint of market at time of order entry}\right)$$

    $$\text{Effective spread of Trade 1} = 2 \times (\$41.50 - \$41.475) = \$0.05$$

    $$\text{Effective spread of Trade 2} = 2 \times (\$41.75 - \$41.74) = \$0.02$$

    $$\text{Average Effective Spread} = (\$0.05 + \$0.02)/2 = \$0.035$$

14. A is correct. Flickering quotes are exposed limit orders that electronic traders submit and then cancel shortly thereafter, often within a second. Electronic dealers and algorithmic buy-side traders submit and repeatedly cancel and resubmit their orders when they do not want their orders to stand in the market; rather, they want other traders to see that they are willing to trade at the displayed price. Bloomfield does not want his orders to stand in the market; using flickering quotes to purchase AXZ shares would satisfy that objective.

    B is incorrect because AXZ shares are currently in a period of high volatility, so Bloomfield would not likely use machine learning to execute his trades. Machine-learning systems frequently do not produce useful information during volatility episodes because these episodes have few precedents from which the machines can learn. Machine-learning methods produce models based on observed empirical regularities rather than on theoretical principles identified by analysts. Many traders shut down when volatility spikes, both because high-volatility episodes are uncommon and thus not well understood and because even if such episodes were well understood, they represent periods of exceptionally high risk.

    C is incorrect because market participants use leapfrogging quotes when spreads are wide (not narrow), and Bloomfield noted that the bid–ask spread for AXZ shares is narrow. When bid–ask spreads are wide, dealers often are willing to trade at better prices than they quote. They quote wide spreads because they hope to trade at more favorable prices. When another trader quotes a better price, dealers often immediately quote an even better price. If the spread is sufficiently wide, a game of leapfrog may ensue as the dealer jumps ahead again.

15. B is correct. To reduce the systemic risks associated with fast trading, some exchanges have adopted trade halts when prices move too quickly. These rules stop trading when excess demand for liquidity occurs. They also prevent the extreme price changes that can occur in electronic markets when market orders arrive and no liquidity is present. 2Fast Trading's competitive advantage will be maintained despite exchange trading halts because the company will be free to trade faster than its competitors once trading resumes. Therefore, exchanges using trade halts to stop trading is the risk reduction strategy that most likely maintains 2Fast Trading's competitive advantage and is consistent with Bloomfield's claim that risks can be reduced by changing the structure of the market.

    A is incorrect because delaying order processing by random intervals reduces the benefits of high-frequency traders being faster than their competitors and investing in speed. Therefore, delaying order processing by random order intervals does not maintain 2Fast Trading's primary competitive advantage, which is trading faster than competitors, because that advantage will be reduced.

    C is incorrect because slowing markets by running call markets once a second or more often instead of trading continuously diminishes the benefits of high-frequency traders being faster than their competitors and investing with speed. Therefore, slowing markets once a second or more often instead of trading continuously does not maintain 2Fast Trading's primary competitive advantage, which is trading faster than competitors, because that advantage will be reduced.

16. A is correct. Bluffing involves submitting orders and arranging trades to influence other traders' perceptions of value. Bluffers often prey on momentum traders, who buy when prices are rising and sell when prices are falling. Similarly, Bloomfield mentioned that regulators were informed that 2Fast's competitor has been submitting orders and arranging trades to influence other traders' perceptions of value; regulators were informed the competitor has been buying stock to raise its price, thereby encouraging momentum traders to buy, and then selling the stock to them at higher prices.

    B is incorrect because the competitor did not use standing limit orders—those orders that are used in a spoofing strategy—for the trades the regulator is investigating. Spoofing is a trading practice in which traders place exposed standing limit orders to convey an impression to other traders that the market is more liquid than it is or to suggest to other traders that the security is under- or overvalued.

    C is incorrect because the competitor did not use commonly controlled accounts—those accounts that are used in a wash trading strategy—for the trades that regulators are investigating. Wash trading consists of trades arranged among commonly controlled accounts to create the impression of market activity at a particular price. The purpose of wash trading is to fool investors into believing that a market is more liquid than it truly is and to thereby increase investors' confidence both in their ability to exit positions without substantial cost and in their assessments of security values.

LEARNING MODULE

7

Case Study in Portfolio Management: Institutional (SWF)

by Steve Balaban, CFA, Arjan Berkelaar, PhD, CFA, Nasir Hasan, and Hardik Sanjay Shah, CFA.

Steve Balaban, CFA, is at Mink Capital Inc. (Canada). Arjan Berkelaar, PhD, CFA, is at KAUST Investment Management Company (USA). Nasir Hasan is at Ernst & Young (UAE). Hardik Sanjay Shah, CFA, is at GMO LLC (Singapore).

LEARNING OUTCOMES

Mastery	*The candidate should be able to:*
☐	discuss financial risks associated with the portfolio strategy of an institutional investor
☐	discuss environmental and social risks associated with the portfolio strategy of an institutional investor
☐	analyze and evaluate the financial and non-financial risk exposures in the portfolio strategy of an institutional investor
☐	discuss various methods to manage the risks that arise on long-term direct investments of an institutional investor
☐	evaluate strengths and weaknesses of an enterprise risk management system and recommend improvements

INTRODUCTION

1

The focus of this reading is a fictional "case study." The case itself will focus on the portfolio of a sovereign wealth fund (SWF) specifically looking at risk in terms of the SWF's long-term investments. There are three Learning Outcome Statements (LOS) within the case. Prior to the case, we provide two LOS outside the case. These LOS will provide some background information that will be helpful to the candidate in understanding the case.

2 FINANCIAL RISKS FACED BY INSTITUTIONAL INVESTORS

☐ discuss financial risks associated with the portfolio strategy of an institutional investor

Long-Term Perspective

Institutional investors (also referred to as *asset owners*) such as pension funds, sovereign wealth funds, endowments, and foundations are distinct from other institutional investors such as banks and insurance companies in terms of the time horizon over which they invest their assets. This long-term perspective allows these institutions to take on certain investment risks that other institutional investors simply cannot bear and to invest in in a broad range of alternative asset classes, including private equity, private real estate, natural resources, infrastructure, and hedge funds. This section will focus on the financial risks associated with the portfolio strategy of long-term institutional investors and in particular will focus on investments in illiquid asset classes. Banks and insurance companies are excluded from the discussion because they are typically much more asset/liability focused and face much tighter regulatory constraints to ensure capital adequacy.

This section will not cover the quantitative aspects of risk management or the mechanics behind various risk metrics, such as standard deviation and conditional value at risk, or risk management techniques, such as Monte Carlo simulation and factor modelling. Those topics are covered in other parts of the CFA Program curriculum. Instead, this reading will cover key risk considerations faced by long-term institutional investors as they invest in a range of traditional and alternative asset classes, including private equity and infrastructure. An important distinguishing feature of long-term institutional investors is their ability to invest in illiquid asset classes. Since the late 1990s, such asset classes have become an ever more important part of the investment portfolios of pension funds, sovereign wealth funds, endowments, and foundations. In this reading, we put particular emphasis on the financial risks that emanate from illiquid investments because these risks tend to be least well quantified but can pose an existential threat to long-term investors if not addressed and managed carefully. The focus is on how market and liquidity risk interact to create potential challenges at the overall portfolio level and affect the institutional investor's ability to meet its long-term objectives.

Section 2.2 briefly discusses the various lenses through which risk management can be viewed. Risk management is a very broad topic, and the goal is to simply provide the reader with a frame of reference. Section 2.3 focuses on the key financial risks that institutional investors face. The focus is on portfolio-level, top-down, long-term financial risk. Risk management for long-term institutional investors should primarily be concerned with events that may jeopardize the organization's ability to meet its long-term objectives. The interaction between market and liquidity risk plays a critical role. In Section 2.4 we discuss the challenges associated with investing in illiquid asset classes from a risk management perspective. We discuss two important aspects of illiquid asset classes: the uncertainty of cash flows and return-smoothing behavior in the return pattern. Section 2.5 describes how institutional investors address and manage liquidity risk at the overall portfolio level.

Dimensions of Financial Risk Management

The aim of risk management is to avoid an existential threat to the organization. In other words, risk management should focus on what types of events can jeopardize the organization's ability to meet its long-term objectives. Existential threats can arise from both financial risks (e.g., market losses and liquidity risk in the form of the inability to meet cash flows) and non-financial risks (e.g., reputational risks). In this reading, we solely focus on financial risk. Financial risk needs to be viewed through multiple lenses. There is no simple template to financial risk management. It is not simply a matter of calculating, for example, the value at risk of a portfolio. There are several dimensions to sound financial risk management, and we cover them briefly in the following subsections. Our goal is to simply provide a frame of reference for the reader because risk management is a very broad topic.

Top-down vs. bottom-up risk analysis

Risk management requires both a top-down and a bottom-up perspective. From a top-down perspective, the board and chief investment officer (CIO) set overall risk guidelines for the portfolio that serve as guardrails within which the investment team is expected to operate. Risk management involves measuring, monitoring, and reporting portfolio results versus the guidelines. The investment team is tasked with implementing the overall investment strategy either through hiring external asset managers or by directly purchasing and managing securities and assets. The investment team takes a more bottom-up, sub-portfolio approach to managing the risks of each individual portfolio or asset class, while assessing and monitoring their interaction and impact on the risk level of the overall portfolio.

Portfolio-level risk vs. asset-class-specific risk

Although risk management for an institutional investor is ultimately about controlling overall portfolio-level risk, risks also need to be managed and controlled at the asset-class or strategy level so that no particular asset class or strategy will have an undue adverse effect on the overall portfolio. Different asset classes require different risk management techniques. Some risk metrics and methods make sense for publicly traded asset classes, but they may not be meaningful when assessing the risk of, for example, illiquid asset classes or hedge fund investments. For some asset classes, such as public equities, detailed security-level information might be available, whereas for other asset classes, such as hedge funds, only monthly manager returns may be available. In the case of a public equity portfolio, risk analysis might be very granular and rely on sophisticated factor models, whereas risk analysis for hedge fund investments might simply involve calculating the historical volatility of observed returns. Because of differences in data transparency, data frequency, and risk methods used, it is difficult—if not impossible—to aggregate these results at the overall portfolio level. It is not uncommon for institutional investors to have an overall risk management system for portfolio-wide risk metrics in addition to asset-class-specific systems or approaches that provide a more in-depth risk view tailored to a particular asset class.

Return-based vs. holdings-based risk approaches

Financial risk management systems are typically described as being return based (risk estimation relies on the historical return streams of an external manager or a portfolio of securities) or holdings based (risk estimation relies on individual security holdings and the historical returns of those securities in the portfolio). Both approaches have their pros and cons, and they are not mutually exclusive. Return-based systems are relatively easy to implement but may produce risk estimates that are biased because they rely on past returns from a strategy that may be very different today compared with, for example, five years ago. Holdings-based risk systems, in contrast, tend to be more costly and time-consuming to implement. For many institutional investors that invest in hedge funds and illiquid asset classes, holdings-based risk systems for the entire portfolio are typically not feasible because of a lack of transparency on holdings and their related investment strategy (a multi-strategy fund may maintain a long position in a security within one strategy book and a short position in another strategy book), data being available with a one-month to three-month lag, and significant turnover in certain types of hedge fund investments.

Absolute vs. relative risk

Investors are interested in both absolute risk and relative risk. Absolute risk concerns the potential for overall losses and typically relies on overall portfolio-level metrics, such as standard deviation, conditional value at risk, and maximum drawdown. Relative risk concerns underperformance versus policy benchmarks and relies on such metrics as tracking error (the standard deviation of returns relative to a benchmark).

Long-term vs. short-term risk metrics

Modern risk systems used by institutional investors typically focus on calculating volatility, value at risk, and conditional value at risk using sophisticated risk factor techniques. Given the heavy reliance on the current portfolio composition and the granular modeling of each component in the portfolio, these risk systems are most useful in providing an estimate for the potential for near-term losses. Institutional investors are also interested in calculating longer-term risks, such as the probability of losses, the probability of not being able to meet cash flows, and the probability of maintaining purchasing power or meeting a certain return target over longer time periods, such as 5 years, 10 years, 20 years, and so forth.

These long-term risk metrics are typically calculated using Monte Carlo simulation, where asset-class returns are simulated on the basis of a set of forward-looking capital market assumptions (typically expected returns, volatilities, and correlations) and total assets are calculated including cash flows, such as benefit payments and contributions in the case of pension funds and payouts (spending amounts) in case of endowments and foundations. These methods, although typically much less granular than a risk management system, are better able to incorporate future portfolio changes, different rebalancing methods, and cash flows.

Quantitative vs. qualitative risks

At the end of the day, risk management is not simply a quantitative endeavor. Quantitative risk management techniques are backward looking by nature and typically parametric (i.e., they rely on historical data to estimate parameters). Although history can serve as a guide, it does not provide a prediction of the future. Risk management is about assessing the potential for future losses, and quantitative tools need to be complemented with qualitative assessments. However, with qualitative assessments, it is important for risk managers to be aware of their own biases because they are basing these assessments on their own past experience. Thus, it is important for risk managers to recognize and mitigate the backward-looking bias in both quantitative (explicit) and qualitative (implicit) risk analysis.

Pre- and post-investment risk assessment

Finally, although risk management efforts typically focus on measuring the risks of existing investments, a sound risk management philosophy ensures a proper assessment of financial risks prior to making investments. Institutional investors typically put a lot of effort into operational and investment due diligence prior to making investments. In addition to analyzing past investment performance, it is critical when hiring external managers to evaluate the character of the key decision makers, the business ethics of the firm, the investment experience of the team, the quality of operations (such as accounting and trade settlements), and the risk management practices of the external manager. As part of their investment due diligence, institutional investors also look at the quality of the non-executive directors of the fund, the integrity and independence of external auditors, fee structures, master fund and feeder fund structure, custodians, and safekeeping on assets. These considerations are even more important for illiquid investments because it is very difficult to exit from them (investors cannot easily change their mind). After investing, risk management might take on a more quantitative role, but continued due diligence and monitoring are of equal importance. In the case of external managers, this obligation resides with the team responsible for the hiring and firing of the managers. In the case of internal management, an in-house risk management team may be tasked with the ongoing due-diligence and monitoring responsibilities.

The various risk dimensions we have described should provide a sense of the wide-ranging nature of risk management as a discipline. For this reading, we focus exclusively on the key financial risks that long-term institutional investors face. We take a portfolio-level, top-down perspective and are primarily concerned with how illiquid asset classes and the interaction between market and liquidity risk affect an institutional investor's ability to meet its long-term objectives. This risk is unique to long-term institutional investors. The next section will provide a more in-depth description of this risk.

Risk Considerations for Long-Term Investors

Long-term institutional investors have the ability to invest a significant part of their portfolio in risky and illiquid assets because of their long-term investment horizon and relatively low liquidity needs. The past two decades have seen a steady increase in the allocation to illiquid asset classes, such private equity, private real estate, and infrastructure, by pension funds, sovereign wealth funds, endowments, and foundations. These asset classes create unique risk management challenges and can pose an existential threat if the risks are not addressed and managed carefully. As stated before, the ultimate objective of risk management is to ensure that the organization survives and can meet its long-term objectives.

We start with briefly describing and reviewing the main objectives of long-term institutional investors and their key risk considerations. Exhibit 1 provides an overview by institutional investor type. The ultimate risk consideration for each of these institutional investors is their ability to meet the payouts that they were set up to provide. This risk is largely affected by how the overall investment portfolio performs over time. On the one hand, a very low-risk portfolio that consists primarily of fixed-income investments is unlikely to cause a problem in providing the required payouts in the short run but will almost certainly jeopardize the organization's ability to provide the required payouts in the long run. On the other hand, a very risky and illiquid portfolio is expected to provide high expected returns in the long run but could cause significant pain in the short run during a significant market downturn or financial crisis. Long-term institutional investors aim to strike the right balance between these two extremes in designing their investment policy or strategic asset allocation.

Exhibit 1: Objectives and Risk Considerations by Institutional Investor Type

Institutional Investor	Main Objective	Key Risk Consideration
Pension funds	Provide retirement income to plan participants	Inability to meet pension payouts to beneficiaries
Sovereign wealth funds	Varies by type of SWF but most have been set up to provide some future financial support to the government	Inability to provide financial support to the government
Endowments and Foundations	Provide financial support in perpetuity while maintaining intergenerational equity	Inability to provide financial support to the institution or to the mission

This process usually involves a Monte Carlo simulation exercise where asset-class returns are simulated on the basis of a set of forward-looking capital market assumptions and total assets are calculated including cash flows, such as benefit payments and contributions in the case of pension funds and payouts (spending amounts) in the case of endowments and foundations. Monte Carlo simulation allows institutional investors to calculate such metrics as the probability of maintaining purchasing power and the probability of a certain loss or drawdown (e.g., 25%) over a specific time period (e.g., 5 or 10 years) and to determine the appropriate trade-off between two such metrics. What is often ignored in this type of analysis, however, is the important interaction between potential market losses and liquidity. Pension funds, SWFs, endowments, and foundations are unique in that they can often tolerate significantly more market and liquidity risk than other investors. Their long-term investment horizon allows them to survive a significant market correction and even operate in a counter-cyclical way during a market crisis. As institutional investors invest more in such illiquid asset classes as private equity, private real estate, and infrastructure, however, their ability to tolerate market losses may diminish.

Institutional investors need liquidity to meet payouts (retirement payments in the case of pension plans, payouts to the university or foundation in the case of endowments and foundations, etc.), meet capital calls on their illiquid investments, and rebalance their portfolios. During a significant market downturn, these needs can become stretched and impact the institution's ability to meet cash flows, particularly if a large part of the portfolio is invested in illiquid asset classes, such as private equity, real estate, and infrastructure. Exhibit 2 shows the main liquidity needs and the main sources of liquidity for long-term institutional investors. Each of these liquidity needs and sources may be adversely affected during a financial crisis.

Exhibit 2: Liquidity Needs and Sources for Institutional Investors

Liquidity Needs	Liquidity Sources
Outflows (e.g., pension payouts to beneficiaries, university payouts, and financial support to the government)	Inflows (e.g., pension contributions, gifts, donations, government savings)
Capital calls for illiquid investments	Distributions from illiquid investments
Portfolio rebalancing	Investment income and proceeds from selling liquid asset classes (cash, fixed income, public equities)

We first start with discussing how liquidity needs may increase during a crisis. First, payouts might increase as the beneficiary requires additional financial support. For example, a university may need additional funds from its endowment to support its operations as other sources of income dry up, or a government might require additional financial support from the sovereign wealth fund to mitigate the crisis situation. Second, there might be an acceleration of capital calls as attractive investment opportunities present themselves during a crisis. Finally, rebalancing flows will be more significant during a crisis because of significant market movements. Good governance and best practice suggest that investors rebalance their portfolios at regular intervals. Sticking to rebalancing practices is particularly important during a financial crisis because failure to rebalance may prevent investors from fully participating in the rebound after the crisis.

Having discussed how the needs for liquidity may increase during a significant market downturn, we next turn to how sources of liquidity might dry up under those circumstances. First, inflows might decrease in a crisis. For example, donors might be struggling financially and donate less to their alma mater, or plan sponsors might be faced with budgetary challenges and, therefore, less inclined to contribute to the pension fund. Second, distributions from illiquid investments might be reduced because there are no attractive exit points due to depressed prices or lower profitability. Finally, investments that are otherwise liquid might become less liquid or simply undesirable to exit from. The main sources of liquidity during a financial crisis are typically cash and fixed-income investments. And most long-term institutional investors hold relatively low allocations to cash and fixed income in their portfolios.

Illiquid asset classes (such as private equity, real estate, and infrastructure) are not available to meet liquidity needs during a crisis. These asset classes cannot be rebalanced or redeemed because they are long term in nature and the assets can be locked up for 5–10 years or even longer. Semi-liquid asset classes, such as hedge fund investments, should not be expected to be liquid and available to meet liquidity needs during a financial crisis because many of these managers might impose redemption gates or have lockups in place or their investments might turn out to be less liquid than anticipated. Finally, although public equity investments are technically liquid, investors may be reluctant to sell part of their public equity portfolio to meet liquidity needs because the market value of these investments may have gone down significantly in a crisis. In addition, investors might not want to redeem from certain active external managers, even if the investments are liquid, because it may impact the future relationship with that manager (particularly for high-demand active managers with limited available capacity).

In conclusion, the main risk that long-term institutional investors face is having insufficient liquidity during a significant market downturn to meet their obligations and rebalance their portfolios. Liquidity needs tend to increase in a crisis while sources of liquidity dry up. This risk increases as institutional investors allocate more to illiquid asset classes. The combination of financial losses and not being able to meet cash flows or rebalance the portfolio because of insufficient liquidity can become a matter of survival. Managing this risk is, therefore, very important for long-term institutional investors. In the next section, we will discuss in more detail the risks associated with illiquid asset classes. In Section 2.5, we will discuss the various ways in which institutional managers manage liquidity risk.

Risks Associated with Illiquid Asset Classes

Illiquid asset classes, such as private equity, real estate, and infrastructure, offer the potential for returns in excess of those on publicly traded asset classes, such as public equity and fixed income. The higher expected return of these asset classes comes at a cost to investors in the form of illiquidity. Illiquid asset classes are typically subject to a drawdown structure where committed capital is called at an unknown schedule and investors receive profits at an unknown schedule. As a result, investors need to hold sufficient liquid assets to meet capital calls from their private fund managers. The uncertain pattern of cash flows poses both a liquidity and a risk management challenge for investors in illiquid asset classes.

In addition to the importance of adequately managing liquidity needs when investing in illiquid assets, these asset classes tend to be subject to stale pricing, appraisal-based valuations, and a lagged response to movements in public markets. As a result, illiquid asset classes exhibit returns that are smooth, understating the true volatility and correlation with publicly traded asset classes. For example, the standard deviation of observed returns for private equity is often smaller than that of public equity. Although this feature may be appealing for institutional investors, it causes traditional asset allocation models, such as mean–variance optimization, to over-allocate to private asset classes because the Sharpe ratios of observed returns are superior to those of publicly traded asset classes.

Finally, illiquid asset classes cannot be rebalanced easily and costlessly. Although investors could potentially, for example, sell their private equity stakes in the secondary market, this cannot be done instantaneously and investors may have to accept a significantly lower price compared with the true market value.

Cash flow modeling

Illiquid asset classes are subject to a drawdown structure. The investor (typically the limited partner, or LP, in the partnership agreement) commits capital, and this capital gets drawn down over time at the discretion of the general partner, or GP. Investors need to figure out both the commitment strategy (i.e., how much to commit each year) to reach a certain target allocation to illiquid assets and the liquidity needs to meet capital calls when required. Committing too much can pose severe liquidity risk because the percentage allocation to illiquid asset classes may soar due to the so-called denominator effect (total assets under management, or AUM, falls by a larger amount than the repricing of illiquid asset classes). Committing too little may prevent the investor from reaching the target allocation and may result in falling short of return expectations.

In managing liquidity needs and determining the appropriate commitment strategy to illiquid asset classes, investors need to be able to predict future cash flows.

Addressing return smoothing behavior of illiquid asset classes

To calculate the true underlying economic risks of illiquid asset classes as part of their risk management efforts, institutional investors typically use one of two approaches: (1) Use public market proxies in place of private asset classes—for example, use small-cap public equities as a proxy for private equity—or (2) unsmooth observed returns of private asset classes. The objective of the latter is to remove the serial correlation structure of the original return series. The implicit assumption is that the serial correlations in reported returns are entirely due to the smoothing behavior funds engage in when reporting results. A common and simple technique to unsmooth the returns of illiquid asset classes and hedge funds is a method developed by Geltner (1993) to address appraisal-based valuations in real estate. The method proposed by Geltner removes only the first-order serial correlation in observed returns. Okunev and White (2003) extended the method of Geltner (1993) to include higher-order serial correlations. An alternative to the Geltner method is the GLM method proposed by Getmansky, Lo, and Makarov (2004). They assumed that observed returns for illiquid asset classes and hedge funds follow a moving-average process.

To show the effect of these different methods on the annualized volatility of various illiquid asset classes, we use quarterly historical returns for global buyouts, global venture capital, global private real estate, and global private natural resources for the period from Q1 1990 until Q4 2019. Exhibit 3 shows the annualized volatility of the observed returns and the volatility of adjusted returns using the three methods briefly discussed earlier. For the Okunev–White and GLM methods, we use up to four lags. Exhibit 4 shows the beta to global equity returns. For global equity returns, we use quarterly returns for the MSCI World Index from 1990 to 2019.

Exhibit 3: Impact of Unsmoothing on Annualized Volatility

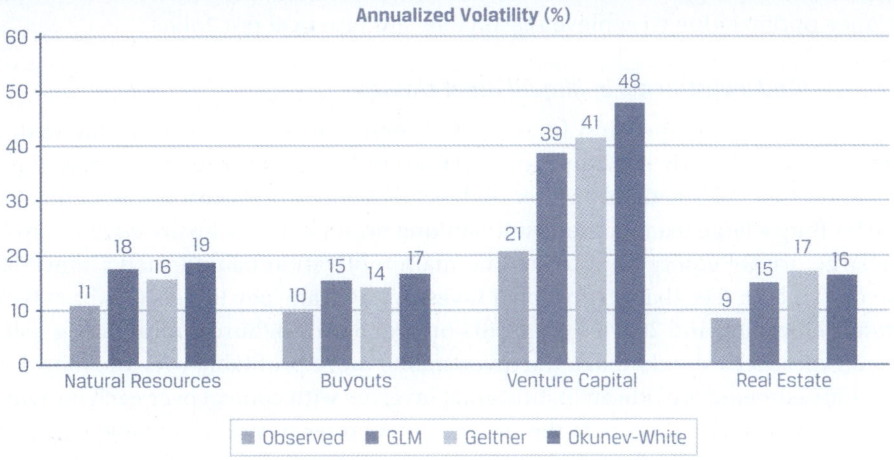

Source: Data is from Cambridge Associates.

Exhibit 4: Impact of Unsmoothing on Beta to Public Equities

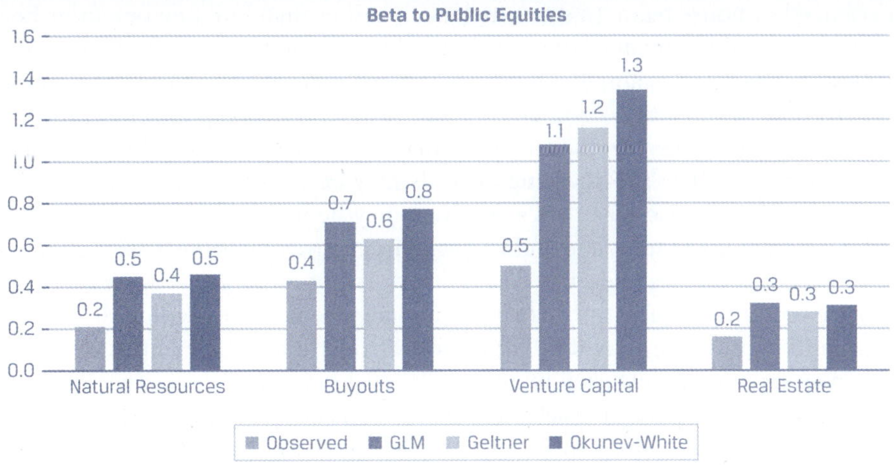

Source: Data is from Cambridge Associates.

As illustrated in Exhibit 3 and Exhibit 4, after applying unsmoothing techniques, the resulting returns exhibit higher volatility and are typically more correlated with public equity markets. These unsmoothed return series can then be used along with returns on publicly traded asset classes to determine the covariance matrix to be used in a mean–variance optimization exercise when determining the appropriate allocation to illiquid asset classes and hedge funds. Mean–variance optimization, however, still falls short as an adequate asset allocation tool for institutional investors because it is not able to take into account the illiquid nature of some asset classes. Illiquid asset classes cannot be rebalanced easily without a potential significant price concession. Single-period optimization methods, such as mean–variance optimization, fail when illiquid asset classes are introduced, because such techniques implicitly assume that investors keep portfolio weights constant over time (i.e., portfolio weights are rebalanced perfectly) and they ignore the drawdown structure of illiquid asset classes and the uncertainty of cash flows. Currently, there are not any widely accepted alternatives. Most investors simply constrain the allocations to illiquid asset classes in the mean–variance optimization to achieve reasonable and practical portfolios.

Direct vs. fund investments in illiquid asset classes

In recent years, large pension funds and sovereign wealth funds have increasingly opted to invest directly in illiquid asset classes rather than through the more typical limited partner (LP)–general partner (GP) setup. Some large pension funds and SWFs have built up a large team of merchant banking professionals who are equally capable as a large private equity fund team. The main motivation behind such a move is to save on the high fees that institutional investors typically pay to GPs (2% base fee on committed capital and 20% fee on profits or over a certain hurdle rate). Being able to save on these fees should make the investments more profitable over the long term. Direct investments provide an institutional investor with control over each individual investment. This situation puts the investor in a better position to manage liquidity. In the case of direct investments, there are no unfunded commitments, making it easier to manage capital. The investor also has full discretion over the decision when to exit investments and will not have to be forced to sell in a down market. As a result, direct investments partially alleviate some of the liquidity challenges typically associated with private asset classes and resolve some of the principal–agent issues associated with fund investing.

There are also disadvantages to direct investments in private asset classes. Direct investments in private equity, real estate, or infrastructure require a dedicated and experienced in-house team. In some instances, rather than building out an in-house team for private investments, large pension funds and sovereign wealth funds acquire a general partner. For example, Ontario Teachers' Pension Plan purchased Cadillac Fairview, a large operating company for real estate. Managing and assembling an in-house team adds several challenges compared with the more nimble setup in the case of fund investing. The sourcing of deals may be constrained by the talent and network of the in-house team. As a result, it may be more difficult to diversify the portfolio across geography and industries. Direct investment portfolios may have higher concentration risk because direct investors opt for larger investments due to staffing issues and scalability. This risk could adversely affect the liquidity of these investments because they might be harder to sell and, therefore, potentially less liquid. If the investor relies on external managers for deal sourcing or a partnership agreement, there is a risk of adverse selection. Finally, the governance structure is not set up as well in the case of direct investing compared with fund investments. In contrast to fund managers, employees of a pension fund or sovereign wealth fund may not be able to sit on the board of a private company. Institutional investors may not be able to afford the liability issues associated with direct investing. For fund investments, the investor is a limited partner and has limited liability, whereas with direct investments, the investor may be considered a general partner, with additional liability risks. Finally, institutional investors may find it difficult to adequately compensate internal staff to ensure that they hire and retain talent. This is usually a problem for public pension funds because there is public pressure to keep compensation down.

Managing Liquidity Risk

In this section, we discuss some of the tools used by institutional investors to manage overall liquidity risk in their portfolios.

Liquidity management steps:

1. **Establish liquidity risk parameters.**

   Institutional investors typically create liquidity guidelines regarding what percentage of assets needs to be liquid and available on a daily or monthly basis. In addition, given the drawdown structure of illiquid asset classes, institutional investors need to keep track of uncalled commitments, not simply invested capital. It is typical for institutional investors to have internal guidelines or bands around the sum of invested capital and uncalled commitments as a percentage of total assets. In addition to such bands, they may have automatic or semiautomatic escalation triggers, such as reducing commitments to illiquid asset classes or even actively seeking to reduce investments through secondary sales once the sum of invested capital plus uncalled commitments reaches a certain level (expressed as a percentage of total assets). These liquidity risk parameters can either be internal or be included in an investment policy statement approved by the board.

2. **Assess the liquidity of the current portfolio and how it evolves over time.**

   The second step in managing liquidity risk at the overall portfolio level is to have a clear sense of the liquidity of the portfolio and measure liquidity parameters versus guidelines. Most institutional investors have an internal report that shows what percentage of the portfolio can be liquidated within a day, within a week, within a month, within a quarter, and within a year and what percentage of the portfolio takes more than a year to be liquidated. It is important not only to have a snapshot of that report at a given point in time but also to understand how it evolves over time as the portfolio changes. A good starting point for developing these statistics is to simply look at the legal terms that are in place with external managers. This is particularly relevant for active managers and hedge funds that have redemption notices and lockups included in the investment agreement. In the case of internal management, an even more granular assessment can be made depending on the types of securities being held and using market liquidity measures to gauge how much of these securities can be sold over different time frames during a financial crisis. As discussed in Section 2.3, investors may also want to take into account how redeeming from certain external managers during a crisis may impact the future relationship with that manager (in other words, they may not want to redeem even if the investments are liquid and instead include these investments in a less liquid category).

3. **Develop a cash flow model and project future expected cash flows.**

   The third step is to understand and model the various cash flows. As discussed in Section 2.3, institutional investors make payouts (retirement payments, foundation spending, etc.), they receive inflows (gifts and donations for an endowment, pension contributions for a pension plan, etc.), they have to meet capital calls for illiquid asset classes and receive distributions, and they have to rebalance their portfolios. Most institutional investors model each of those cash flows and project future expected cash flows. Section 2.4 briefly discussed how capital calls and distributions are modeled for illiquid asset classes.

4. **Stress test liquidity needs and cash flow projections.**

The standard cash flow modeling and projections assume business as usual, but it is important to stress test these cash flow projections and liquidity needs. As discussed in Section 2.4, cash flows are affected by market movements. For example, donations might be lower in a crisis and payouts might be higher. Institutional investors stress test their cash flow projections and liquidity needs. It is important to point out that this process is more of an art than a science and there is no universally accepted method for stress testing (as there are universally accepted methods for market risk calculations).

5. **Put in place an emergency plan.**

   Finally, institutional investors should put in place an emergency action plan. Such an action plan should include what to liquidate—and in what order—in a crisis to meet cash flows and how to rebalance the portfolio in a crisis. Having such a plan in place can help avoid the risk of panicking in a crisis. Sharing the emergency action plan with the board to get buy-in can also help when a crisis occurs and mitigate the risk of board members pressuring the investment team to make sub-optimal short-term decisions.

Exhibit 5 summarizes the five steps in developing a liquidity management plan.

Exhibit 5: Liquidity Management Steps

1. Establish liquidity risk parameters.
2. Assess the liquidity of current portfolio, and monitor the evolution over time.
3. Develop a cash flow model and project future cash flows.
4. Stress test liquidity needs and cash flow projections.
5. Develop an emergency action plan.

Long-term institutional investors are able take on certain investment risks that other institutional investors simply cannot bear. Since the late 1990s, they have increasingly invested in a broad range of alternative asset classes, including private equity, private real estate, natural resources, infrastructure, and hedge funds. In this reading, we focus on the financial risks that emanate from illiquid investments because these risks tend to be less well quantified but can pose an existential threat to long-term investors if not addressed and managed carefully. The focus has been on how market and liquidity risk interact to create potential challenges at the overall portfolio level and affect the institutional investor's ability to meet its long-term objectives. We propose several steps institutional investors can take to better manage liquidity at the overall portfolio level.

Enterprise Risk Management for Institutional Investors

Exhibit 6 provides a high-level view of a risk management framework in an enterprise context:

Exhibit 6: Risk Management Framework in an Enterprise Context

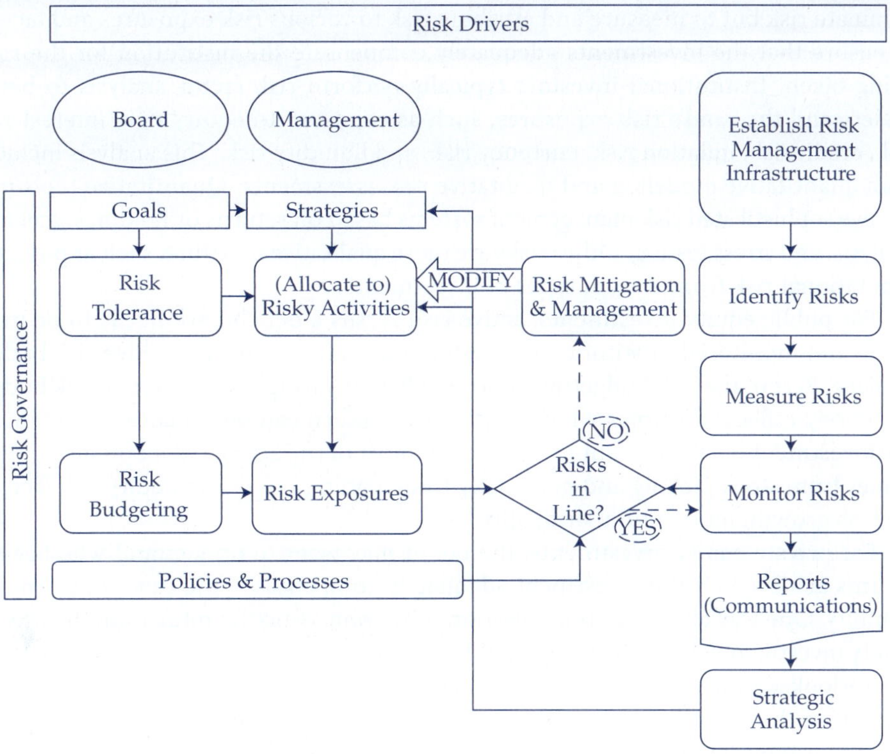

Source: "Risk Management: An Introduction," CFA Program Level I curriculum reading (2021).

We can apply this framework to the setting of an institutional investor in the following manner. The risk management process for an institutional investor starts with the board setting the overall risk tolerance for the organization that is consistent with its objectives and constraints. Risk tolerance should capture the amount of market risk that an institutional investor is willing and able to take in order to maximize expected returns, and it informs the most important investment decision that is made by the board—namely, the strategic asset allocation. Risk tolerance can be expressed in asset-only (for sovereign wealth funds, endowments, and foundations) or asset/liability terms (for pension funds and insurance companies). Typical risk measures used for setting the risk tolerance of institutional investors include volatility, maximum drawdown, and value at risk or conditional value at risk (sometimes referred to as *expected tail loss*, or *ETL*).

In addition to setting the overall risk tolerance (for market losses), the board usually approves additional risk parameters, limits, requirements, and guidelines (some quantitative and others procedural) that are codified in an investment policy statement (IPS). These may include liquidity risk parameters if the institutional investor has a significant allocation to illiquid asset classes, an active risk budget to limit and control the amount of active management pursued by investment staff, restrictions on leverage and the use of derivatives, ethical investment guidelines, and possibly credit risk parameters and constraints in the case of significant fixed-income investments (for example, for an insurance company). These additional guidelines and constraints are put in place to ensure that the investment activities are consistent with the board's risk tolerance and expectations (and with regulatory requirements if applicable).

Management (i.e., the investment team) is tasked with implementing the strategic asset allocation (SAA) and investing the assets either internally or through external managers across the various asset classes included in the SAA. The investment team is also responsible for managing and monitoring the risks associated with the implementation of the SAA and reporting to the board. The objective is not to minimize or eliminate risk but to measure and attribute risk to various risk exposures and factors to ensure that the investments adequately compensate the institution for the risks being taken. Institutional investors typically perform risk factor analysis to better understand the fund's risk exposures, such as exposure to equity risk, interest rate risk, credit risk, inflation risk, currency risk, and liquidity risk. This analysis includes both quantitative modeling and qualitative risk assessments. Quantitative tools may involve sophisticated risk management systems based on returns or holdings, scenario analysis, and stress testing. Other risks are more qualitative in nature, such as potential reputational risk from certain types of investments.

For public equity investments, active risk versus a benchmark needs to be measured and monitored. Institutional investors may have an explicit active risk budget in place. Part of the risk budgeting effort involves ensuring that the active risk budget accurately reflects the areas where most excess return can be expected. In addition, the investment team will want to ensure that most of the active risk in public equities comes from stock picking and not simply from loading on certain equity risk factors, such as growth, momentum, or quality.

For private equity investments, the board may want to understand whether the returns achieved on the investment adequately compensated the fund for giving up liquidity. One way to answer that question is by comparing the returns on the private equity investment with the return of public equities. Currency risk tends to sometimes be overlooked by institutional investors. This risk can have an outsized and unexpected impact on the overall return. Although currency risk can be hedged in some cases, doing so is typically costly or even impossible when investing in emerging and frontier markets. The risk of currency devaluation needs to be acknowledged and assessed prior to making investments. Another risk that gets overlooked is asset allocation drift. The investment portfolio should be rebalanced on a regular basis to bring it back in line with the strategic asset allocation that was approved by the board.

The risk management infrastructure of the institutional investor should be set up to identify and measure the aforementioned risks and monitor how they change over time and whether they are in line with the guidelines set up by the board in the IPS and with additional—more granular—internal guidelines set by the Chief Investment Officer and risk team. The risk team is usually tasked with risk reporting to the various stakeholders, which may include an internal investment committee and the board to ensure adequate risk oversight. The investment team should recognize when risk exposures are not aligned with the overall risk tolerance and guidelines and take action to bring them back into alignment. These actions may involve hedging, rebalancing, and secondary sales or in the case of illiquid investments, reducing commitments.

3 ENVIRONMENTAL AND SOCIAL RISKS FACED BY INSTITUTIONAL INVESTORS

☐ discuss environmental and social risks associated with the portfolio strategy of an institutional investor

Universal Ownership, Externalities, and Responsible Investing

In this section, we define universal owners as large institutional investors that effectively own a slice of the whole economy and hence are generally managing their total market exposure, instead of focusing on a subset of issuers. Institutional investors such as sovereign wealth funds and public pension funds usually have large portfolios that are highly diversified and built with a long-term focus. Such portfolios are representative of global capital markets, thereby making such investors "universal owners."

Investing long term in widely diversified holdings inevitably exposes such portfolios to increasing costs related to negative environmental and social externalities. An externality is an impact that an individual's or a corporation's activities have on a third party. If everyone acts in their own self-interest, it could lead to an overall negative outcome for society. Examples of negative environmental externalities include plastic pollution in the ocean, poor air quality due to industrial and vehicular emissions, and water toxicity due to improper effluent management.

Universal owners find it challenging to effectively diversify risks arising from negative environmental and social externalities. Costs that are externalized by one portfolio company can negatively affect the profitability of another portfolio company, thereby adversely affecting the overall portfolio return. For example, a sovereign wealth fund invests in a plastic manufacturer that is saving waste treatment and disposal costs by directly releasing waste pellets and other chemical residues into a nearby river. Water toxicity arising as a result of these actions causes reduced productivity in the agriculture operations downstream, which the asset owner is also invested in. In addition, strengthening regulations related to environmental protection, for example, may lead to monetary fines and penalties, thereby leading to financial risks for a company causing such negative externalities.

According to the UN-backed Principles for Responsible Investment (PRI), environmental costs for universal owners are reflected in portfolio impacts via insurance premiums, taxes, inflated input prices, and the physical costs associated with weather-related disasters (PRI Association 2017). Also, the cost of remediating environmental damage is often significantly higher than the cost of preventing it. Given these facts, it is imperative for large institutional investors to internalize the price of such negative externalities by considering the impact of their investments on society and future generations.

Exhibit 7 provides a non-exhaustive list of environmental and social issues that we have introduced in Level I of the CFA Program curriculum.

Exhibit 7: Examples of Environmental and Social Factors

Environmental Issues	Social Issues
Climate change and carbon emissions	Customer satisfaction and product responsibility
Air and water pollution	Data security and privacy
Biodiversity	Gender and diversity
Deforestation	Occupational health and safety
Energy efficiency	Community relations and charitable activities
Waste management	Human rights
Water scarcity	Labor standards

In the next section, we share examples of how some of these environmental and social issues could impact the portfolio strategy for large institutional investors that have a long-term focus toward their investments.

Systemic risks have the potential to destabilize capital markets and lead to serious negative consequences for financial institutions and the broader economy. The unpredictable nature of such megatrends as climate change and their related impacts, both environmental and socioeconomic, pose clear systemic risks to global financial markets. A study carried out by researchers at the Grantham Research Institute on Climate Change and the Environment (2016) at the London School of Economics and Political Science and Vivid Economics projected that climate change could reduce the value of global financial assets by as much as $24 trillion—resulting in permanent damage that would far eclipse that from the 2007–09 financial crisis.

Material Environmental Issues for an Institutional Investor

For an institutional investor, such as a sovereign wealth fund, such megatrends as climate change and their related risks—both physical and transition risks—have the potential to cause significant harm to a portfolio's value over the medium to long term, particularly for investments in real assets (real estate, infrastructure) and private equity, neither of which are easily divestible. Next, we will discuss the impact of climate-related risks on an institutional investor's portfolio from the perspective of private equity and real asset investments.

Physical climate risks

As we have observed since the beginning of the current century, climate change has profoundly affected the physical world we live in. Annual average temperatures across the globe are continuously rising, and 19 of the 20 warmest years have occurred since 2001 (NASA 2019). Erratic weather patterns, such as heavy precipitation, droughts, and hurricanes, are both more frequent and of higher magnitude. Similarly, wildfires are causing more and more devastation every year. In addition, the chronic issue of sea-level rise is causing coastal flooding. As shown in Exhibit 8, an increase in extreme weather events has occurred.

Exhibit 8: Extreme Weather Events on the Rise

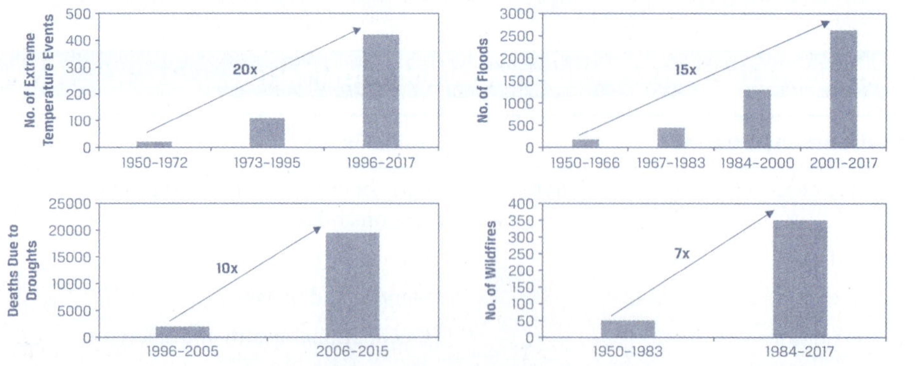

Source: Emergency Events Database (www.emdat.be).

With continued climate change, all these physical climate risks could become more severe in the future and, to a certain extent, become the new normal for the world. Depending on global responses to climate change in the coming decade, the degree of their impact on our economies and investments may be alleviated.

So, what does this mean for the portfolio strategy of large institutional investors with private equity and real asset investments?

Impact on real assets

Should these trends continue, the physical risks that we have discussed could create increased levels of stress on such assets as residential and commercial real estate and infrastructure, such as roads and railways. Rising sea levels that lead to flooding would impact both rents and property valuation for hitherto prime coastal properties. Prolonged exposure to extreme heat would negatively affect the useful life of roads and train tracks, which would lead to accelerated depreciation of such assets and, therefore, more frequent replacement costs for companies and governments (CFA Institute 2020).

Similarly, physical damage caused by frequent, large-scale weather-related events, such as hurricanes or even wildfires—once considered too irregular to insure against—could not only lead to large-scale drawdowns in the portfolio's asset value but also make it difficult or expensive to insure such assets. Most of the flooding-related losses around the world are uninsured, thereby causing additional stress on a country's economy and its people (see Exhibit 9).

Exhibit 9: Global Flood Losses and Insurance Levels

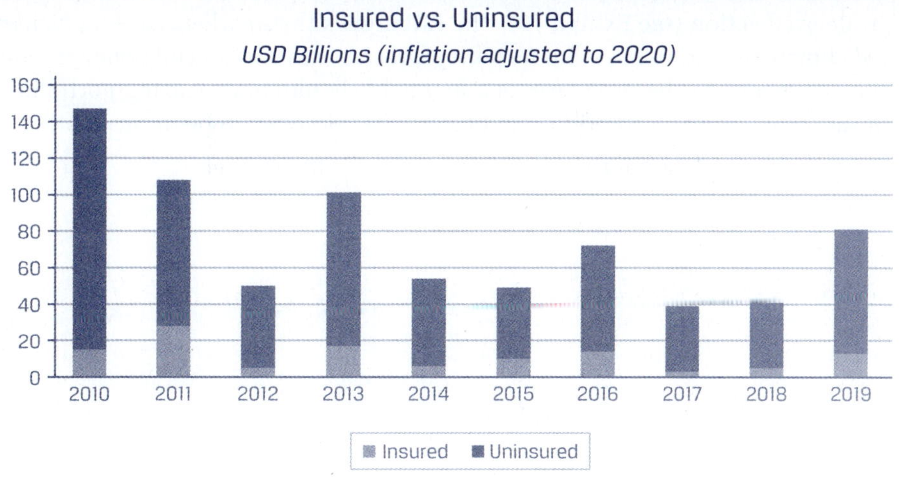

Source: Aon.

Because these physical climate-related risks continue to play out in a much larger and more frequent manner than previously anticipated, they will continue to bring down prices and rental yields of prime real estate, leading to permanent impairments of asset valuations. For a large institutional investor that is looking to preserve capital and provide growth benefits to multiple generations, it is imperative that these risks be factored into the portfolio construction strategies.

Climate transition risks

In line with the 2015 Paris Climate Agreement, countries and companies around the world are already making efforts to dramatically reduce or eliminate their CO_2 emissions in order to limit the global temperature increase in this century to 2 degrees Celsius above preindustrial levels. To keep global warming less than 2°C, scientists project that energy-related CO_2 emissions need to fall 25% by 2030 and reach "net zero" by 2070 (Intergovernmental Panel on Climate Change 2018; IEA 2020).

One of the most ambitious efforts to incentivize decarbonization is the European Union's sustainable finance taxonomy, which helps investors understand whether an economic activity is environmentally sustainable. As of October 2020, looking at the scientific evidence about the current and potential impacts of climate change, it has become clear that the world needs to move toward a low-carbon future if we are to cap global warming at less than 2°C and prevent the negative effects that not doing so would bring to our climate, our ecosystems, and human life. What is currently unclear is the pace at which this decarbonization will happen.

Rapid decarbonization will lead to restrictions on carbon emissions, implementation of some form of carbon pricing, introduction of new technologies, and changes in the consumer behavior. All these effects can create massive disruptions in certain sectors, such as electricity generation (with the increasing cost competitiveness of renewable energy sources as compared with coal) and automobiles (with the impending widespread switch from internal combustion engines to electric vehicles. The International Energy Agency has forecast that in order to reach carbon neutrality by 2050, half of all cars in the world should be electric by 2030 (Lo 2020).

The PRI's Inevitable Policy Response (IPR) project aims to prepare financial markets for climate-related policy risks that are likely to emerge in the short to medium term. The IPR forecast a response by 2025 that will be forceful, abrupt, and disorderly because of the delayed action (see Exhibit 10). The PRI argues that markets have inefficiently priced climate transition risks, but its policy forecast is that a forceful policy response to climate change in the near term is a highly likely outcome, leaving portfolios of institutional investors exposed to significant risks that need to be mitigated.

Exhibit 10: IPR Key Policy Forecasts

Coal phase-outs	Sales ban on Internal Combustion Engines (ICE)	Carbon Pricing (Emission Allowances)	Zero carbon power
Early coal phase-out for first mover countries by 2030	Early sales ban for first mover countries by 2035	US$40-80/t$CO_2$ prices by 2030 for first movers	Significant ramp-up of renewable energy globally
Steady retirement of coal-fired power generation after 2030 in lagging countries	Other countries follow suit as automotive industry reaches tipping point	Global convergence accelerated by Border Carbon Adjustment (BCA) to >=$100/t$CO_2$ by 2050	Policy support of nuclear capacity increase in a small set of countries, nuclear phased out elsewhere

Carbon Capture and Storage (CCS) & industry decarbonisation	Energy efficiency	Green House Gas (GHG) removal (Land use-based)	Agriculture
Limited CCS support in power,	Increase in coverage and stringency of performance standards	Improved forestry and nature-based solutions	Technical support to improve agricultural yields
Policy incentives primarily for industrial and bioenergy CCS	Utility obligation programs	Stronger enforcement of zero deforestation	Increasing public investment in irrigation and AgTech
Public support for demonstration, and then deployment of hydrogen clusters	Financial and behavioral incentives	Controlled expansion of bioenergy crops	Incremental behavioural incentives away from beef

Source: PRI IPR (www.unpri.org/the-inevitable-policy-response-policy-forecasts/4849.article).

Given the uncertainty around the precise timing and magnitude of the impact of climate change, organizations are increasingly using climate-related scenario analysis to better understand how their businesses might perform under a variety of global warming scenarios—for example, in a world that is 2°C, 3°C, or 4°C warmer. The Task force on Climate-Related Financial Disclosures (TCFD) recommends organizations, including banks, asset managers, and asset owners, use scenario analysis to estimate the implications of such risks and opportunities for their businesses over time and also to inform their strategic thinking. The International Energy Agency and the Intergovernmental Panel on Climate Change both publicly offer a set of climate-related scenarios that are widely used. To learn more about climate-related scenario analysis, refer to the technical supplement issued by the TCFD.

Climate opportunities

Although most of the investor focus in dealing with climate change has been on managing physical and transition risks, exciting investment opportunities are arising in companies focused on climate change mitigation and adaptation. These opportunities exist in secondary markets and, in some cases, investments in real assets and infrastructure projects, such as wind and solar farms and smart grids.

Because the levelized cost of energy for renewable energy generation technologies has considerably decreased since 2010, these have become cost competitive with some conventional generation technologies, such as coal-based power generation, as shown in Exhibit 11.

Exhibit 11: 2019 Levelized Cost of Energy, Unsubsidized

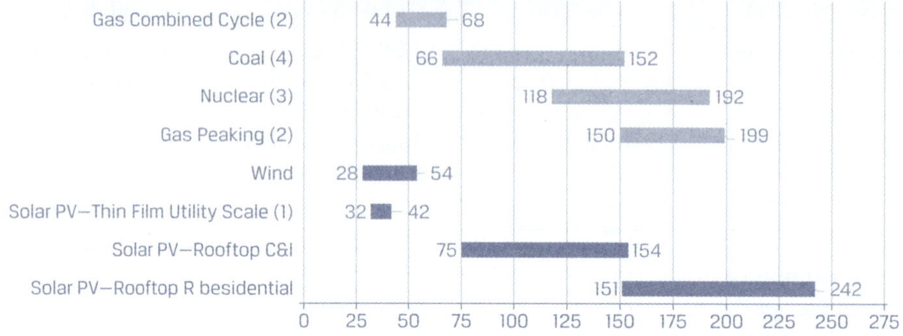

Note: Levelized cost of energy is a measure of the average net present cost of electricity generation for a power plant over its lifetime.

(1) Unless otherwise indicated herein, the low end represents a single-axis tracking system and the high end represents a fixed-tilt system.

(2) The fuel cost assumption for Lazard's global, unsubsidized analysis for gas-fired generation resources is $3.45/MMBTU.

(3) Unless otherwise indicated, the analysis herein does not reflect decommissioning costs, ongoing maintenance-related capital expenditures or the potential economic impacts of federal loan guarantees or other subsidies.

(4) High end incorporates 90% carbon capture and compression. Does not include cost of transportation and storage.

Sources: Data is from Lazard (www.lazard.com/perspective/lcoe2019).

This cost competitiveness, coupled with the urgency to decarbonize our economies to avoid the potentially catastrophic physical impacts of climate change, has created secular growth opportunity for such businesses and assets, thereby attracting increasingly large investor attention.

A summary of the business segments where such opportunities may lie follows.

Climate mitigation

This category includes companies that are positioned to benefit, directly or indirectly, from efforts to curb or mitigate the long-term effects of global climate change, to address the environmental challenges presented by global climate change, or to improve the efficiency of resource consumption.

Exhibit 12: Climate Mitigation Opportunity Examples

Business Segment	Description
Clean energy	Companies in this segment are involved in the generation of clean energy from such sources as wind, solar, and small hydro. This segment also includes manufacturers of such equipment as windmills and solar panels, as well as related service providers.
Energy efficiency	This segment comprises businesses that provide products and services to improve the efficiency of energy consumption in a variety of processes. Examples include energy efficient transportation and building solution providers and recycling technology.

Business Segment	Description
Batteries and storage	This segment includes companies that help improve battery storage capacity and efficiency. These improvements are critical, for instance, to sustainable growth and wider penetration of some of the previously mentioned technologies, such as clean energy generation and distribution and electric vehicles.
Smart grids	Smart grids are digitally enhanced versions of the conventional electricity grid, with a layer of communication network overlaying the traditional grid. They are a key enabler for energy security and reliability and integration of clean energy resources.
Materials	Such materials as copper and battery-grade lithium are key ingredients in the clean energy value chain because they are required in clean energy power generation, storage solutions, and electric vehicles, resulting in a projected demand rise as the world transitions toward a low-carbon future.

Climate adaptation

This category includes companies that would help better adjust to actual or expected future change in climate with an aim to reduce vulnerability to the harmful effects of climate change, such as food insecurity, sea-level rise, and frequent extreme weather events.

Exhibit 13: Climate Adaptation Opportunity Examples

Business Segment	Description
Sustainable agriculture	Companies in this segment are involved in providing products that improve agriculture productivity and reduce the resource consumption in the entire process. Sustainable fish farming and timber production are other activities included here.
Water	This This segment consists of businesses that provide products and services to improve the efficiency of water consumption in a variety of processes, including wastewater treatment and reuse.

Many institutional investors are increasing allocations to such sectors as part of their real-asset allocation or as a potential equity alpha opportunity with the expectation that companies in these sectors will outperform the broad equity market over a long period of time as the world transitions to a low carbon future. Evaluating and sufficiently managing both physical and transition climate risks in the portfolio and capturing some of the aforementioned secular growth opportunities could position large institutional investor portfolios to outperform and grow in value in the long term.

Material Social Issues for an Institutional Investor

Environmental issues, such as climate change and air pollution, are reasonably mature and quite well understood, making them easier to accommodate in discounted cash flow models. Social issues, such as community relation, occupational health and safety, privacy and data security, modern slavery and other human right violations in the supply chain, and inequality, however, are relatively challenging to quantify and integrate into financial models. Most social issues have largely qualitative data reported by companies, such as health and safety policies and initiatives, lists of product quality certifications, and human capital management policies, rather than metrics on which long-term performance can be judged. Nevertheless, these issues have the potential to cause reputational and financial damage to a company and its investors if not managed sufficiently well.

Managing community relations and the social license to operate

For large institutional investors, such as sovereign wealth funds and public pension funds, their investments may have positive social impacts, such as improving essential public infrastructure and services or providing better access to medicine and technology, or negative social impacts, via poor labor standards or forceful relocation and improper rehabilitation of communities by their portfolio companies. Good corporate behavior is usually well received by the community relations, leading to a sustainable and mutually beneficial long-term relationship. In many ways, these aspects are essential to keeping a company's social license to operate.

Let's take a hypothetical example of a sovereign wealth fund (SWF) that has invested in a dam-based hydroelectric power plant in an economically less developed part of its country. Although there will be a positive environmental impact of the project because it will generate electricity from a renewable source, the social impacts of the project could be mixed. On the positive side, rural electrification arising from this project will lead to economic development in the region, thereby improving the standard of living. Dam-based hydroelectric power plants require large-scale land acquisition, often leading to relocation and rehabilitation of indigenous communities. Some locals protest that they have not been sufficiently consulted by the government before issuing consent to establish this project. Moreover, there are allegations of acquisition of land for the project at unfair/poor valuations. In some instances, protesting locals were forcefully removed and relocated by local government authorities, leading to unrest. Eventually, the SWF decides to cease the project implementation owing to this wide variety of instances of pushback from the society.

This example highlights the importance of considering social risks when investing. Despite having the positive intent of supporting development of renewable power generation in a less economically developed part of the country, the SWF faced pushback and reputational damage for not holistically considering the interests of all the stakeholders involved, especially local communities that were the most affected by the project. Some of the best practices in community relation management include extensive stakeholder consultation meetings to better understand their needs and address their concerns, providing alternative employment opportunities to those affected, and ensuring fair land acquisition, rehabilitation, and resettlement practices.

Labor issues in the supply chain

Another increasingly important social topic is the one related to poor labor practices, especially in the supply chain. Driven by globalization, a consumption boom across developed and emerging markets, and the availability of cheap labor in certain parts of the world, a large portion of the manufacturing and assembling activities across such key sectors as technology and garments has been outsourced to developing and frontier markets, such as India, Vietnam, and Malaysia. Although access to cheap, semi-skilled labor has led to better bottom lines for multinational companies, it has also come at the cost of exploitation of workers in such supply chains. Labor rights are being compromised in the form of heavy reliance on temporary workers, excessive or forced overtime, and low wages. Moreover, lax regulations in many countries allow legal prevention of unionization or any form of collective bargaining, thereby making such workers more vulnerable.

Large brands in the apparel industry, such as Nike and Gap, and in the technology space, such as Apple and Samsung, have all been accused of various levels of lapses in their supply chain related to the aforementioned labor management issues. Apart from suffering significant damage to their brands and reputations, which could lead to consumer boycotts, such companies may also face additional costs and/or fines related to product recalls and ad hoc shifting of supply chains.

For SWFs with equity exposure to some of the largest apparel brands and branded tech hardware companies, considering such issues while making investments is of paramount importance because lack of transparency in the supply chain and lapses in labor management may weigh heavily on the resilience of such supply chains amid global-scale disruptions, such as that caused by the COVID-19 pandemic. In addition to the financial risks, reputational risks may also arise because of a view that the SWF implicitly supports such improper and unethical business practices.

The "just" transition

Sustainable development involves meeting the needs of the present generation without compromising the ability of future generations to meet their own needs. Sustainable development includes economic, social, and environmental dimensions, all of which are interrelated. In the transition to environmentally sustainable economies and societies, several challenges may arise—for example, displacement of workers and job losses in certain industries, such as coal mining, fossil fuel extraction/production, and fossil fuel-based power generation. Similarly, increased energy costs due to carbon taxes and higher costs of commodities partly resulting from sustainable production practices may have adverse effects on the incomes of poor households. Therefore, a "just" transition is necessary to ensure that there are limited negative social impacts in our pursuit of positive environmental impacts via avoiding fossil fuels and implementing sustainable agriculture and business practices. Although there is no fixed set of guidelines, the just transition encourages a dialogue between workers, industry, and governments influenced by geographical, political, cultural, and social contexts in order to tackle some of the aforementioned challenges.

CASE STUDY 4

- ☐ analyze and evaluate the financial and non-financial risk exposures in the portfolio strategy of an institutional investor
- ☐ discuss various methods to manage the risks that arise on long-term direct investments of an institutional investor
- ☐ evaluate strengths and weaknesses of an enterprise risk management system and recommend improvements

Case Study: Introduction

You are working as a Risk Analyst at a small sovereign wealth fund (SWF) and reporting to the Head of Risk. The SWF is considering making some new investments in direct private equity and direct infrastructure. You have been asked to review risk aspects of these investment opportunities, which will be discussed in an upcoming investment committee meeting. Assuming the investments will be made, you will also have the responsibility to monitor the risk of the investments as well as make recommended improvements to the SWF's risk management system. You are excited about these opportunities and look forward to putting your knowledge and skills learned from the CFA Program to work!

Case Study: Background

- Over 20 years ago, the "Republic of Ruritania" discovered an extremely large deposit of crucial rare earth metals that are key elements in the manufacturing of high-speed computers used in science and finance. The entire deposit was sold to various entities allowing Ruritania to secure its financial future. At the same time, the government of Ruritania "dollarized" the economy, moving from the domestic RRR currency to the USD.
- The government of Ruritania (R) decided to form a sovereign wealth fund, R-SWF, in order to grow the capital for future generations. This type of SWF is a "savings fund," intended to share wealth across generations by transforming non-renewable assets into diversified financial assets.
- R-SWF has built up a diversified portfolio of equities, fixed income, and alternative investments.
- In equities and fixed income, the SWF invests in developed markets, emerging markets, and frontier markets through both fund investing and direct investing.
- In alternatives, the SWF invests in private equity (PE), infrastructure, and real estate. Investment methods used include direct investing, making co-investments, and fund investing.
- The case study begins in Section 3 at an investment committee meeting to discuss two potential investments. The next scene, in Section 4, is set three years later, when the performance of the investments are discussed at another investment committee meeting. The final scene, in Section 5, is set five years later and provides additional information on investment performance.

R-SWF'S Investments: 1.0

Initial Case Facts (1.0)

Today, the investment committee of R-SWF is considering several new investments, including direct private equity and direct infrastructure investments. The investment committee will be discussing risk aspects of the investments, led by the Head of Risk and supported by *you*, a Risk Analyst.

- The investment committee meeting will open with an overview of asset allocation and a few basic discussions on the two proposed investments. However, the focus of the meeting is on the potential risks of the new investment proposals, not details on the investments themselves. (An in-depth investment committee meeting on the new investments was held last month.)
- The meeting will then move on to a discussion of the potential risks of the two specific direct investments being considered.

    1. Direct infrastructure investment in an airport
    2. Direct PE investment in a beverage manufacturer

- The investment committee meeting will discuss key risks that R-SWF should consider as it decides whether to make new direct investments in PE and infrastructure.

- All investment committee participants (and CFA Program Level III candidates) are provided with a background memo with the following information:

  Memo A: Background on R-SWF's asset allocation and performance

  Memo B: Details on the proposed direct infrastructure investment

  Memo C: Details on the proposed direct private equity investment

INVESTMENT COMMITTEE MEETING MEMO 1.0

To: R-SWF Investment Committee Members

From: R-SWF Chief Investment Officer

Re: Investment Committee Meeting Agenda

Distribution: Head of Risk, Head of PE, Head of Infrastructure, Head of Equities, and Level III Candidates in the CFA Program

An agenda for today's meeting is as follows:

Agenda

- Opening Remarks and Review of Asset Allocation: Chief Investment Officer
- Review of Infrastructure Investment Opportunity: Head of Infrastructure
- Review of Private Equity Investment Opportunity: Head of PE
- Discussion of Risk—Infrastructure Investment: Head of Risk + Everyone
- Discussion of Risk—PE Investment: Head of Risk + Everyone
- Closing Remarks: Chief Investment Officer

The investment committee meeting will discuss key risks that R-SWF should consider as it determines whether to make new direct investments in PE and infrastructure.

Memo 1A: Asset Allocation and Performance

- Since its inception, over a 25+ year period, R-SWF has built a diversified portfolio of investments. As of last month, the fund had AUM of $50 billion USD, with the fund outperforming its overall benchmark by 150 bps net of fees since inception. Of course, there have been short-term periods of underperformance as the fund pursued its long-term strategy.
- Asset allocation as of last month for the overall fund was as follows:

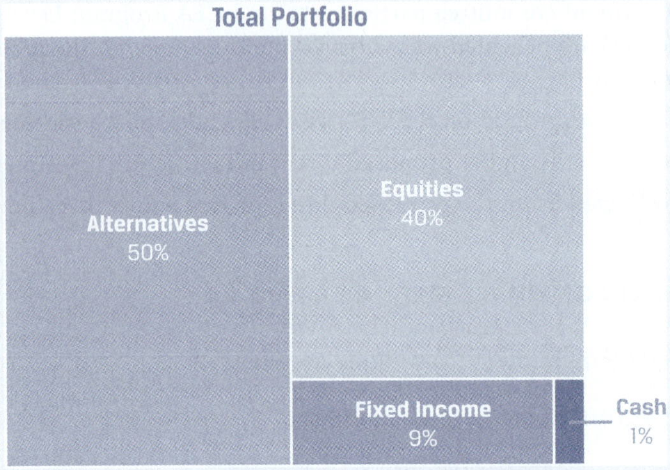

- As of last month, R-SWF had approximately 50% of assets invested in alternative investments, consistent with its long-term objectives.
- In today's investment committee meeting, R-SWF is considering two new investments in alternative investments—specifically, in direct private equity and direct infrastructure investments. *(Note: Funding for these two investments will come from a combination of cash, dividends, receivables, and fixed income. The mix will be determined by the Asset/Liability Committee, or ALCO).*
- Because today's investment committee meeting will focus on alternative investments, we will break the allocation of alternatives down further, as follows:

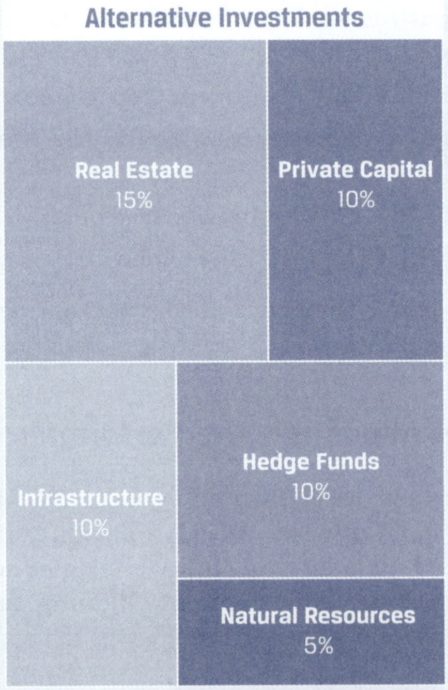

- As of last month, R-SWF had approximately 10% of assets invested in private capital and 10% of assets invested in Infrastructure.
- Next, we provide a breakdown of private capital and infrastructure:

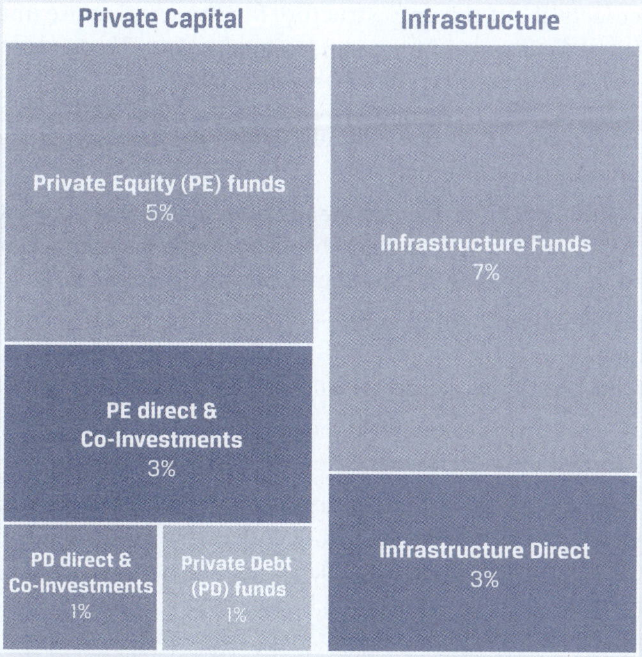

- As of last month, R-SWF had approximately 3% of assets invested in private equity direct and co-investment and 3% of assets invested in direct Infrastructure.
- The investment committee will be discussing risk aspects of the cases, led by the Head of Risk and supported by the Risk Analyst.
- Details on the proposed infrastructure investment are found in Memo 1B.
- Details on the proposed private equity investment are found in Memo 1C.

Memo 1B: Proposed Direct Infrastructure Investment

- The infrastructure direct investment opportunity is an investment in helping modernize an airport in the frontier market island nation of "Sunnyland."
- Sunnyland has beautiful beaches and several hotels, ranging from 3–star to 5–star. However, the Sunnyland Airport has only one small runway that can support airplanes of only up to 10 passengers.
- The Sunnyland government is keen on expanding the airport with a new terminal and new runway. Doing so will allow much larger aircraft to land (up to 150 passengers) and be a major boost to tourism.
- The airport is located about 2 km from the sea, providing scenic views on takeoff and landing. The new runway will be built 1 km from the sea, providing even nicer views.
- R-SWF has been approached by the Sunnyland Airport Authority (SAA) to consider a $100 million investment in a public–private partnership (PPP) on a build–operate–transfer (BOT) basis.
- For R-SWF (with assets of $50 billion), this is a small investment (0.2% of total assets). The investment will be about 2% of total infrastructure assets—$100 million/($100 million + $5,000 million)—which includes investments in funds and direct investments.

- Other facts about this infrastructure investment that are important for the investment committee to understand: *(Note: The focus of the case and investment committee discussion is risks.)*
  - Total project cost of $500 million for new 5 million passenger per annum (pax) terminal
  - $33 million investment to be provided by Airport Operating Group (AOG), which will operate the airport under a management agreement (with fixed fee plus/minus performance incentive)
  - $300 million funding to be provided through non-recourse project finance debt (i.e., approx. 70/30 debt/equity) with 15–year tenor following 3-year grace period
  - 2–year construction period, with fixed price construction contract awarded under tender
  - 25–year concession (including 2–year construction period), with investor consortium entitled to collect all regulated airport charges (e.g., passenger departure charge, landing charges) and commercial revenue (duty free, retail, F&B, car parking), subject to payment of quarterly concession fee of 35% of all revenue to SAA
  - Airport charges (70% of all revenue) are regulated by concession contract—that is, schedule of charges set and then subject to stated formula for future changes (e.g., CPI)
  - Concession agreement includes quality and performance standards to be met for design/construction/development (including timely delivery of new terminal) and operations, respectively
  - Expected IRR for full investment term of 25 years of 15%

Risk Discussion: Infrastructure Investment

The Head of Infrastructure believes the potential return on this project far outweighs the potential risk(s). However, she is happy to discuss potential risks with the investment committee.

Memo 1C: Proposed Direct Private Equity Investment

- The private equity direct investment opportunity is an investment in a local beverage company (Atsui Beverage Company Limited (ABC)) that manufactures and sells carbonated beverages. The investment will be used to modernize the plant.
- ABC is an unlisted beverage company located in the tropical, land-locked nation of "Atsui." Atsui has a developing economy and can be considered a frontier market.
- ABC is the only local manufacturer of carbonated beverages in Atsui. All other beverages are imported.
- ABC's factory is located near a river that allows for transport to the port. Also, the river is known for its unique biodiversity.
- R-SWF's Head of Private Equity has been on several vacations to Atsui and saw an investment opportunity.
- ABC is keen on modernizing its plant, but the founder is worried about giving up control. Thus, the founder is willing to sell only a minority stake of 35% in exchange for $25 million.

- For R-SWF (with assets of $50 billion), this is a small investment (0.05% of total assets). The investment will be about 0.4% of total PE assets—$25 million/($25 million + $6,000 million)—which includes investments in funds, co-investments, and direct investments.
- Other facts about this direct PE investment that are important for the investment committee to understand: *(Note: The focus of the case and investment committee discussion is risks.)*
  - R-SWF has been investing in PE for many years in funds. Over the years, R-SWF has developed direct investing capabilities through its co-investments and is now expanding its direct investing program.
  - Because of the increased direct investing capabilities of R-SWF and recent outperformance in returns, R-SWF is looking to increase its private equity allocation to direct investments over the next five years.
  - The government of Atsui has implemented tariffs on all soft drink imports. There is an upcoming election that could change this stance.
  - The cost to modernize the ABC plant is estimated to be $20 million.
  - Over the last 12 months, ABC had a revenue of $50 million. Revenue is expected to increase significantly over the next 10 years—with a modernized plant.
  - Over the last 12 months, ABC had an EBITDA of $7 million. This is an EBITDA margin of 14% and a 10× EBITDA multiple. The Head of PE feels that there is significant room for improvement.
  - With the new technology from the plant modernization, ABC will be able to expand into non-carbonated drinks, such as sports drinks and juices.
  - Once the plant is modernized, productivity will improve significantly, allowing ABC to reduce factory staff headcount by 40%, from 500 employees to 300 employees, which will drive a higher EBITDA margin in the future.
  - With a significant minority, R-SWF will be allowed to have two seats on the board of ABC. So, the board will expand from five members to seven members. R-SWF is planning to have the Head of PE join the board of ABC but hasn't decided on the other board seat.

Risk Discussion: Private Equity Investment

The Head of PE believes the potential return on this project far outweighs the potential risk(s). However, he is happy to discuss potential risks with the Investment Committee.

IN-TEXT QUESTION:

Please respond to the following question based on **Investment Committee Memo 1.0**.

As R-SWF's Risk Analyst, do you anticipate liquidity risk will likely be highlighted as a significant financial risk in the upcoming risk discussions for either investment? Explain your thinking.

Guideline Answer:

No. I do not anticipate the Head of Infrastructure or the Head of PE to highlight liquidity risk as a significant risk for either investment. Although liquidity risk is the main risk that long-term institutional investors face, particularly during a significant market decline, each of these investments represents a small portion of R-SWF's total assets. R-SWF does not have cash flow pressure, unlike many institutional investors that face pressure from the regular payment of liabilities. In addition, R-SWF has been growing over time and is making a concerted effort to expand its direct investment program.

Direct investments typically help mitigate some of the liquidity issues commonly experienced when investing in a fund because direct investment provides a greater amount of control and discretion over when to exit investments. Furthermore, as the direct investment program grows and the proportion of direct investments as part R-SWF's total assets increases, R-SWF's ability to manage capital should improve. I believe there are other financial risks that are more likely to be highlighted as a significant risk for each investment.

Investment Committee Meeting 1.0

Participants

Chief Investment Officer (CIO)

Head of Infrastructure

Head of PE

Head of Risk

Head of Equities

Analysts [no speaking role]

Chief Investment Officer:
Good morning, everyone. Welcome to today's investment committee meeting of the sovereign wealth fund of the Republic of Ruritania. After running this money on behalf of our citizens and future generations since its inception, the fund has outperformed our benchmark by 150 basis points, net of fees, and we've grown AUM to $50 billion over 25 years. We are very blessed.

At last month's investment committee meeting, our **Head of Infrastructure** and our **Head of PE** got together to discuss the financials and particulars of two investment opportunities. As they both deserve our attention, today we are joined by our **Head of Risk**, along with our **Head of Equities**, to review them through the lens of risk. Our esteemed junior analysts are in the room with us to observe and provide additional analysis as required.

For now, as we consider our opportunities, I'm mostly here as a facilitator, to pave the way for a robust discussion of investment risk.

Memo A shows us our asset allocation as of mid-June, and we've got 50% in alternatives. We believe in alternatives because our liabilities are negligible and we take a long-term view of things. About 40% of our allocation is in listed equities, with a large portion of that in emerging markets, which we're also big believers in. If we do fund one or both of the two investments on the table, we'll do it with a mix of cash, dividends receivable, and fixed income, but that's not for this committee to decide; the ALCO will go over that at a later date.

In any event, our focus here is private capital, the private equity side. We've got about 3% of our investments in direct private equity and co-investments and about 3% in direct infrastructure.

Again, this meeting is primarily about risk. Let's go to Memo B and ask our **Head of Infrastructure** to talk us through the first investment. It's usually the depth of her infrastructure experience that gives R-SWF the comfort to proceed in the face of risk.

Infrastructure Investment Discussion

Head of Infrastructure:

Thank you for the kind words, **CIO**. I'm glad everyone's here so we can apply the full breadth of the investment committee's expertise.

This is an airport BOT project, a PPP in the frontier island nation of Sunnyland, whose primary industry is tourism. The members of our hard-working analyst team who are new to infrastructure have been briefed on the build-operate-transfer models that private developers often adopt under private-public partnerships so they can operate the facilities they have designed and built for a number of years before handing them over to government agencies.

[**Head of Infrastructure** looks around the room to see a few polite nods from the assembled analysts.]

Funds are needed for an airport upgrade: A new terminal and a new, bigger runway will accommodate larger planes. Sunnyland needs to get rid of the passenger bottleneck to allow for an all-important boost in tourism. We're thinking $500 million and two years of construction time should be enough.

Ruritania is prepared to contribute $100 million, and we're insisting on bringing in AOG, a properly experienced airport operator, which will also be investing private equity—about $33 million. The rest of the capital will be no-recourse debt, about $300 million, and an equity injection from the government and other infrastructure investors for the remainder. The debt will be 15-year with a 3-year grace period.

With the BOT arrangements, of course, we take over the airport from the beginning under a 25-year concession agreement for all the cash flows from the terminal. So that's airport charges, like aircraft landing and passenger departure fees, as well as the commercial revenue from duty-free concessions, retail, and so forth, and we remit 35% of what we collect to the Sunnyland Airport Authority on a quarterly basis. If we want to charge more, any increases—say, for CPI adjustments—are worked out according to fixed formulas.

CIO has set the stage for this discussion of risk, and in that spirit, everyone should note the standards and conditions of our agreement with the government. You already know we've got a two-year development program—that's two years to see the revamped airport up and running—so if there are delays or shortfalls in quality, the concession agreement sets out the consequences.

Finally, our expected return for the full 25-year term given our fund's $100 million investment is a 15% IRR.

Chief Investment Officer:

Thank you, **Head of Infrastructure**. That's a sufficient return, to be sure, but let's also understand that our involvement can help our friends down in Sunnyland. If we execute this project carefully, it means a boost to the wealth of all Sunnylanders.

You've been there recently, right?

Head of Infrastructure:

I have. All indications are that it's an attractive tourist destination. Tourism is key to them now; they lack natural and other resources to diversify the economy. That's what they're depending on to build the economy.

Things are constrained because of the airport. The runway allows only for short, smaller aircraft, so just by increasing runway size and the associated facilities, you're paving a path for the whole nation to grow.

Chief Investment Officer:

I ask the assembled team to consider for a minute the responsibilities we have to ourselves, to Ruritania; we all feel partly responsible for its success. When we invest in another sovereign country, such as Sunnyland, we may carry over a similar sense of responsibility, and we take that seriously. While our proposed $100 million investment is just 0.2% of our AUM, this single investment in transportation infrastructure will have an outsized impact on our investees.

With that in mind, let's move to the other proposal on the table. Our **Head of PE** has recently returned from Atsui, the site of the proposed private equity investment outlined in Memo C. Over to you, **Head of PE**.

Private Equity Investment Discussion

Head of PE:

Yeah, I just got back. The company is called Atsui Beverage Company or ABC for short, and it was kind of "love at first sight"—or sip. I was on the beach, and a waiter brought me a drink and said it was called the "Mango Special." I thanked him but I was barely listening. You know how it is; my mind was elsewhere. But after the third sip, I was paying less attention to my leisure and more attention to just how good this drink was: refreshing, perfectly sweet, and unlike anything I'd tasted before. You know I'm always thinking about investments, ladies and gents, and I began to think I'd stumbled onto a winner.

I've been back to Atsui three times, and I introduced R-SWF to the team at the ABC plant that makes the Mango Special. I explained how sovereign wealth funds usually partner for the long term, and I built some trust while learning about their business. I know how small this is compared to the rest of our portfolio, but I'm still obsessed with this drink, so I figured out that we can invest $25 million for 35% of the business. They've got $50 million in revenue and $7 million in EBITDA. For those on the team who can't do math quickly like I can, that's a 14% EBITDA margin. And we're looking at a company valuation of roughly 10× EBITDA.

So, wait: Is this a good deal or not?

Well, let's think about it. ABC markets the only locally sourced carbonated beverage in Atsui, *and* tariffs are imposed on foreign competitors. That alone seems pretty great. And they'd use $20 million of our $25 million to modernize the plant. That way, they can turn out product way faster while also gearing up to make non-carbonated drinks like sports drinks and juices. We'd drive efficiency enough to cut headcount from 500 to 300, and that's even better for the EBITDA margin: new equipment, big changes.

I've got the most knowledge on the ground, so I could take a board seat along with someone else from our team. We've gotten pretty comfortable with co-investing, making some money, and developing our skills, and since we're expanding our direct investing effort anyway, this seems like a good fit. It's just $25 million out of our $50 billion pool, so it's a good way to learn, even if some of us think it's risky.

And, you know, sun, mango drinks, and the beach—I bet everyone wants to join the board!

Chief Investment Officer:
So, the plant modernization allows for both a meaningful expansion of the product line *and* significant cost savings. But you said that a cut of 200 people underpins those savings?

Head of PE:
Yeah.

Chief Investment Officer:
OK. Any further questions for **Head of PE**?

Head of Risk:
A question from me for **Head of PE**. You mentioned that these guys are the sole beverage manufacturer in Atsui and that there are entry barriers on foreign manufacturers coming in. You've been on the ground, so are local competitors raising their voices about giving ABC some competition?

Head of PE:
I've done a lot of local research, and I'm not seeing anyone. When ABC thinks about threats, they think of the big international drink players, who are still scared off by the government's import tariffs.

Chief Investment Officer:
A lot of senior officials are keen to grow the local industry. It's a small country, and there's a common emotional investment in ABC's success.

Head of Risk:
These do seem like heavy tariffs. **CIO** mentioned they're as high as 100% if you try to buy Coke or Pepsi. The memo says there's an election coming up. Surely there's a risk those entry barriers fall away?

Head of PE:
A mango drink is much better than cola, I promise!

Chief Investment Officer:
I've done a little outreach myself to people in the know. Combining that with **Head of PE**'s research, I'd say a relaxing of tariffs after the election is a fair assumption.

Head of Equities:
I have a question. Will this investment allow for ABC to start exports? Is that part of the expansion plan?

Head of PE:
The markets nearby are also tropical, frontier nations. Business relations are decent, and the plant is next to a river that connects to a big port.

Chief Investment Officer:
Head of PE has explained that the plant workers fish on the freshwater river during their lunch and during breaks, and the river does indeed connect to Atsui's major port. I see good potential for connecting to neighbouring buyers.

Head of Risk:
But let's remember that this is a frontier market with a developing economy.

Chief Investment Officer:
Quite right. Beverages are still somewhat of a luxury item. Nevertheless, there's plenty of growth potential for us and for them.

Head of Equities:
Sure, that's encouraging on exports, but **Head of PE** said that ABC sees its competition as the big international drink players, who are still scared off by the government's tariffs. If the election brings in a government keen on foreign investment, that could completely overturn the advantage this particular business has.

Let's apply a probability to a tariff reduction and to import markets opening up. Pepsi and Coca-Cola have much deeper pockets for waiting out a price war.

Head of PE:
I hear you, but maybe I went too far by saying ABC sees them as competitors. Products like the Mango Special and their other drinks don't actually exist in the Coke and Pepsi product lines, and the Mango Special recipe is so proprietary that if we protect it, it's a real competitive advantage. The other ABC beverages use tropical fruit the multinationals don't have supply chains for, and we believe—I mean, *ABC* believes they have a way of mixing things that no one else can figure out. If that's the case, a path to exports is still there.

With investment, they still have time to get into other juices and diversify. And we're always talking to government officials and to people who could make up the government, and everyone's pretty aligned.

Chief Investment Officer:
These risks are tied to the modernization program we're investing in, which means job cuts. In frontier markets, this is very sensitive: Unions may protest, and politicians may make it part of their election agenda, especially given that we're talking about one of the country's more popular companies. We're veering into reputational risk here.

Look, this is a rather small investment, of $25 million, but even a small investment can have an outsized negative impact on us if we don't manage the risk properly.

Thoughts?

Head of PE:
We're not just investing and then forgetting things, folks. We're going to be proactive. Before modernization starts, we're going to do some research that shows us what issues are in the minds of all the people of Atsui, not just our workers, and we're going to design new community programs around that. We'll try to make a positive impact first.

We know that cutting employees is sensitive. But by helping many more people than we let go and by giving employees proper training so they have the skills for whatever they're doing next, we're going to be part of a sensible transition.

Head of Equities:
That's going to be critical. Community relations is a key component of our social license to operate.

Chief Investment Officer:
My dialogue with the **Head of PE** on the ground in Atsui has been ongoing, and he wants us to do right by the community. It's almost an impact investment in and of itself.

Any other questions on the PE investment?

Head of Risk:
How comfortable are you with ABC's management? We'll only have a minority stake, and founders are sometimes not the best people to run a business.

So are these people reliable? Do they have the right skill set? The right education? Any worry about potential corruption?

Head of PE:
Our due diligence is thorough, and we don't think corruption is an issue. We're new to direct investing, and so we'll be tracking progress extra carefully. And also we're the ones implementing a lot of the modernization, so there'll be more monitoring built in than ever before.

Do we keep management or not? You always have this question in private equity. With all the co-investing we've done, the directors of the funds we partner with find management teams and then keep them and then work *with* them to help them grow.

I see your point that we'd only hold 35% of ABC, but we'll also hold two board seats. I can't predict the future, but we've done a lot of due diligence and we've done a lot of interviews with management, customers, and suppliers. We've interviewed a lot of people who know the management.

We're paying \$25 million, and \$20 million goes to modernizing the plant. Management will take a little money off the table, and we'll structure it so that they are incentivized in alignment with growth and good oversight. After all, they'll still hold 65%.

We think they'll see that working with us will create success and that willful mismanagement or corruption or taking too much money out of the business works against them in the long run. We're coming to them with our track record through the co-investments we've made, our expertise, and our channels to other markets.

There's always risk, but that's my point of view.

Head of Equities:
I support the PE investment. With management having this much skin in the game, their interests are aligned with ours.

Chief Investment Officer:
This is a \$25 million investment out of our \$50 billion fund, and there are impact elements as well that make it more interesting.

Head of PE:
Yeah, and to build our direct investment program, we must learn by doing. We've gotten really comfortable with co-investing, and that's great, but to me, it's the people who do this a lot on their own who tend to be really successful.

Yes, there's some risk with management and the government, but a lot of those are risks we're willing to take with one of our first direct investments, where we can get our hands dirty. It's a simple business, right? It's carbonated beverages, and then maybe we go into juices and non-carbonated stuff, right? We can really build the experience of working with management and the other skills that our direct program is going to need.

Hey, maybe our next committee meeting should be in Atsui!

General Discussion on Risk

Chief Investment Officer:
I won't argue, but let me ask the committee about a risk that applies to both of these investments. We're an open forum, and so I ask the entire room: What bears more scrutiny?

Head of Risk:
The first thing that comes to my mind when we're investing in frontier markets like these is, "How do we deal with the currency risk?" It's hard to hedge these currencies. Meanwhile, they can move wildly against the dollar, turning a really good investment into a really bad investment.

What's your read on this, **Head of PE**?

Head of PE:
I'm not stressed about it. When it comes to me and most other visitors to Atsui, we're using US dollars.

Head of Infrastructure:
I can speak to the currency risk in Sunnyland. When we're talking about the aviation industry and airports, a lot of revenues for infrastructure investors come in the form of regulated charges. Look at our own concession contract: 70% of the revenues are airport charges. It's typical with these arrangements to outsource the collection of these charges to international organizations like IATA. They collect the revenue from the airline, and almost all of that is paid in dollars, so we're comfortable there.

That leaves the 30% of our revenue coming from commercial sources—retail revenue in the terminal and past the gate and all that duty free and parking. In the big international airports, those transactions take place in the local currency, but we're in a locale that's expressly seeking international tourism. Pricing will be geared to international markets, so we'll have the freedom to price everything in dollars and benchmark the pricing against the affluent traveler.

Head of Risk:
I'm glad to hear that.

What about the borrowing side, though? To keep people happy and the logistics simple, I assume any borrowings will come from local banks that use their country's currency.

Head of Infrastructure:
It's a good thought, but no. The lenders are big international banks. The in-country banks may participate, but given the size of the loans and how long term these arrangements are—at least in Sunnyland—the local banks just don't have the capacity yet.

Whoever the lenders are, they'll be comfortable knowing the investors are getting their returns mostly in US dollars, which is what the $300 million of debt is denominated in.

Head of Risk:
Which brings me to defaults.

Head of Infrastructure:
Right, well, this is non-recourse financing, and the concession agreement outlines the terms of default and termination. These are matters that impinge on the direct arrangement between the government and the banks, so while it's something to be aware of, I don't see us getting dragged in.

Head of Risk:
Thanks.

Head of Equities:
I know the **Head of Risk** was coming to this, but the topic is coming up very often recently.

If you look at the World Economic Forum's "Global Risk Report" since 2017, climate risk and extreme weather feature in the top risks every time. Year over year, the weather gets more erratic. Sea-level rise may be gradual, but it doesn't stop. And while I understand the need to support Sunnyland's economy by expanding the airport, the memo says that the new runway is less than a kilometer from the sea.

Sure, you get a fantastic view when you take off and land, but the sea *is* rising, and the risk of flooding could become real even just during high tide. Running an airport in those conditions would not be possible.

It's a 25-year infrastructure investment. That's long enough for climate risks to materialize and impact operations. We've got to factor this in.

Head of Infrastructure
These points are well taken, but keep in mind that to even get as far as finding interested lenders for the airport, it means we've gone through the due diligence process. The big banks need environmental-impact statements before they jump on board, and even just in our role as equity investors, we had to satisfy ourselves that these kinds of issues were thought through.

Head of Risk:
Sure, and naming risks is necessary and commendable, but—

Head of Infrastructure:
—But that doesn't mean the risk goes away. Of course.

I'm obviously not an engineer or a contractor, but what I'd say to the committee is that the experts tells us, in the time frame we're looking at, environmental risks are unlikely to materialize, and even so, they're accounted for during the design process. The drainage systems are modified to handle increases in groundwater levels, and the engineers are building in once-in-50-years and once-in-100-years flood scenarios. Those are risks they're confident they can build for.

Chief Investment Officer:
None of us are experts here, but my perspective is that we can take comfort from the fact that these kinds of challenges have been around for decades. Consider Kansai International Airport in Japan: People are always saying that it's sinking—and it *has* gone down a tiny bit—but it's been around for over 25 years and it's been fine.

It's important to be aware of it, and I'm glad you brought it up, but indications are that there's nothing really stopping us on this front.

Head of Infrastructure:
That's right. We've come to rely on the reports from the technical adviser, and that's a fairly standard approach for us with these sorts of investments.

Head of PE:
Agreed.

Head of Risk:
What about previous foreign investment in Sunnyland? Did political risk come into play for other investments? What's the general feeling?

Head of PE:

Head of Infrastructure called me from Sunnyland when I was on the beach in Atsui planning the ABC upgrades, and he asked me to look into it. Investment in Sunnyland has mostly been on the tourism side. There's a mixture of three- and five-star hotels, so major international hotel operators are around. And they're still arriving, but they feel the transportation bottleneck. Those who are there and the ones who are thinking about coming in are happy about the airport project.

Head of Infrastructure:

And I haven't heard any horror stories about investors in Sunnyland getting burned because of unfair rule changes. Plus, relations are good. The Sunnyland authorities approached us as a fellow government institution, so we're comfortable on a sort of government-to-government basis.

Chief Investment Officer:

One nice thing about an island nation is that it *is* an island. There's less political interference from the neighbours. From what **Head of Infrastructure** was telling me, we can feel positive that our investment in the airport will help the economy and stabilize the local political situation more than the contrary.

Head of Risk:

Good to hear. Let's dig a little deeper on the modeling we've done for the airport investment. We expect a 15% IRR over 25 years. That is our base case. Have we done any stress tests to those baseline expectations? What if there are delays and we have to pay a penalty? What if construction costs overrun the budget? What if revenues fall short? Give us an idea of how bad the IRR could get if we don't achieve the base case.

Head of Infrastructure:

Sure. I like how you've framed the question, because it covers some key risks.

From our perspective, the biggest risk is traffic—comparing the actual number of visitors and tourists coming in and out of the airport against our projections. We're not experts here, either, but we hired an established traffic consultant who looks at the global tourism numbers and the particulars of our development to make a determination.

The consultant produced a low case and a high case based on different traffic forecasts. The low case is also of interest to the banks, of course, which want confidence that they'll be paid.

Our analysis of the reasonable low case puts IRR down to around 10% or 11%. The high case pushes the return out into the high teens.

There are some sensitivities around CapEx, and we're looking to manage this risk through a fixed-price contract, the language of which says that whatever penalties we'd face for delayed or subpar construction will be passed down to the contractor. We've applied a ±10% sensitivity around that, and it does impinge on the IRR a little bit but not as much as the low-traffic case. If we run into real cost overruns or delays, we're looking at about a 13% IRR.

Head of PE:

The airport's key source of revenue is tourist numbers, and we've got an exotic luxury destination on our hands, folks.

Head of Equities:

Agreed. And therefore, we need to consider the risk of a prolonged global recession when discretionary vacations and spending take a nosedive. For a small island like Sunnyland, this is a big risk. Some scenario analysis that considers the impact of a downturn that lasts for two or three or even four years seems necessary.

Head of Infrastructure:
We've done some work on those scenarios, and it's influenced by a specific responsibility of the government, which they have explicitly accepted, to aggressively promote tourism as soon as, if not before, a recession hits.

Think of the aviation industry, which has been through shocks again and again. With downtimes like the global financial crisis around 2009 and the few instances where travelers were spooked by crashes, the airlines came out with attractive deals and recovery was quick.

Sunnyland's government is used to adjusting and always reduces pricing to attract tourists when they need to. Our sense is that even a prolonged recession isn't a deal killer, because the authorities and the industry will react quickly.

Head of PE:
I like your optimism.

Chief Investment Officer
Well, beyond optimism, we're starting from a low base; there's enormous room for growth in Sunnyland.

Head of Risk:
If I may, **CIO**, just a follow-up question to the **Head of Equities**' point on the recession: We all experienced the coronavirus pandemic in 2020, and plenty of scientists have warned us that pandemics are going to be more likely—

Head of Equities:
—Helped along by climate change!

Head of Risk:
Yes, thank you, because of how we're damaging the environment, and again, this investment has a 25-year horizon. What if another pandemic causes rampant restrictions and people are simply not allowed to travel? Has that been factored into our scenario analysis?

Head of Infrastructure:
To a limited extent, yes. We pass through 35% of whatever revenue we take on, so our payments to the government are handled that way in the concession agreement. That leaves the crucial aspect of defaults to lenders and what would trigger them.

The built-in debt-service reserve covers us for a period of time, and if travel is on hold for too much longer, then we turn to restructuring or rescheduling the financing.

But let's understand that the COVID-19 pandemic in 2020 was a game-changer, and the language and dynamics of certain contractual agreements were adjusted to avoid straight defaults in these cases. And the concern here is about short-term impact, whereas over 25 years, we expect things to gradually recover, so our concerns are more about keeping the project going and avoiding default during the problem period.

Voting on Infrastructure Investment

Chief Investment Officer:
OK, I'm grateful for the expertise we have around this table. I think that's probably good for a committee vote. Let's start with our **Head of Infrastructure**: yes or no?

Head of Infrastructure:
Yes.

Chief Investment Officer:
How about our **Head of Risk**?

Head of Risk:
I have my doubts, but because it is a $100 million investment on AUM of $50 billion, we'll give it a shot. I'll say "yes."

Chief Investment Officer:
We have to take a little bit of risk, after all.

Head of PE, how about you?

Head of PE:
Before we ultimately pull the trigger, we should take another look at our other investments and similar memos to see if they're related to tourism and it would mean too much correlation. Besides that, I'm a "yes."

Chief Investment Officer:
OK. **Head of Equities**?

Head of Equities:
Yes from me as well. Given the size of the investment, I think it's worth taking the risk.

Chief Investment Officer:
And I vote "yes."

As a sovereign wealth fund, beyond our responsibility to manage risks and returns well, we want to give back, and where our participation helps nations develop, we feel a responsibility there as well.

Voting on Private Equity Investment

Chief Investment Officer:
All right, very good. Let's move on to our direct private equity investment in ABC. **Head of PE**, what say you?

Head of PE:
I'm in. Yes.

Chief Investment Officer:
Very good. How about you, **Head of Equities**?

Head of Equities:
I'm supportive of this. For one thing, it presents much less risk than the airport in Sunnyland. Yes.

Chief Investment Officer:
OK. And our resident infrastructure expert, what say you?

Head of Infrastructure:
Well, you might expect me to disagree with **Head of Equities** in terms of the risk—we have a minority position, for one thing. But the investment is small, so I'm fine. Yes.

Chief Investment Officer:
OK. And finally, **Head of Risk**?

Head of Risk:
Head of PE made some very good points. It *is* indeed a simple investment to understand and a chance to gain some experience in direct investment. Even if it doesn't work out financially, there's upside to building our experience and to having a positive impact on the wider community, to name but two areas of non-financial return. Yes from me.

Chief Investment Officer:
OK, we have two investments that I'm excited to proceed with. I'd like **Head of Infrastructure** and **Head of PE** to run with those and keep us posted, and now it's time—

Head of PE:
—To fight for the open board seat!

Head of Risk:
Sounds fun, but actually, let's do this the old-fashioned way by filling the other board seat on the basis of experience?

Head of PE:
One free Mango Special to our wise, risk-averse colleague!

Chief Investment Officer:
And with that, we'll see everyone for the next investment committee meeting, in a month's time.

—The End—

IN-TEXT QUESTIONS

Please respond to the following questions based on **Investment Committee Meeting 1.0**.

1. The Head of Infrastructure identified a key risk to the Sunnyland airport investment. Explain what analysis could be shared with you to increase your confidence that the key risk is properly managed prior to making the investment in the Sunnyland airport.
2. Explain how the upcoming election most likely exposes the R-SWF's investment in ABC to financial risk. Discuss whether or not you believe the Head of PE's approach to managing this particular risk is sufficient.

Guideline Answers:

1. During the investment committee meeting, the Head of Infrastructure identified traffic as the key risk to the Sunnyland airport investment. The island might not draw an increased number of tourists simply because the airport can accommodate larger planes and more passengers. Although the Head of Infrastructure alluded to the fact that he has quantified the financial risk should the level of tourists not meet expectations after the completion of the new airport, I would like to review his scenario analysis to feel comfortable with his assumptions. Scenario analysis would be the best way to manage this financial risk prior to making the investment in Sunnyland.
2. I do not think the Head of PE's approach to managing the financial risk due to the upcoming election is sufficient. My understanding is that the upcoming election will expose ABC to financial risk because the current government has imposed large tariffs on foreign competitors that would like to export their products to Atsui. In the event a different political party, specifically one that opposes such tariffs, wins

the upcoming election in Atsui, it could have a significant effect on the profitability of ABC because the company would need to compete for local customers.

Of course, a change in government is not something that ABC can control. Although I believe the steps the Head of PE has taken to manage this particular risk are good, including building rapport with the current government, it is not clear to me that he has conducted a thorough analysis to illustrate the potential financial impact on ABC should the tariffs be reduced or eliminated after the upcoming election. This analysis should be done using scenario analysis. Despite this being a relatively small investment for R-SWF, the financial risk of a change in the tariff policy should be thoroughly modeled and assessed prior to making the investment.

R-SWF'S Investments: 2.0

Extension of Case Facts (2.0)

After Investment Committee Meeting 1.0, the investment committee of the sovereign wealth fund of Ruritania, R-SWF, added two new significant investments to its portfolio. These investments were direct infrastructure and direct private equity investments—the investments in the airport in Sunnyland and the beverage manufacturer in Atsui, respectively.

- Three years have passed, and the investment committee of R-SWF has decided to conduct an investment review of the two projects.
- Note: The focus of the meeting is on the risks (current and potential) of the new investment proposals, not details on the financial performance of the investments. (An in-depth meeting on the financial performance of the investments was held in the previous month).
- All investment committee participants (and Level III candidates in the CFA Program) are provided with a background memo with the following information:
    - Memo A: Update on R-SWF's asset allocation and performance
    - Memo B: Update on the direct infrastructure investment (airport expansion in Sunnyland) and a list of risks for discussion
    - Memo C: Provides details on the proposed direct private equity investment (investment in ABC) and a list of risks for discussion.

INVESTMENT COMMITTEE MEETING MEMO 2.0

To: R-SWF Investment Committee Members

From: R-SWF Chief Investment Officer

Re: Investment Committee Meeting 2.0 Agenda

Distribution: Head of Risk, Head of PE, Head of Infrastructure, Head of Equities, and Junior Staff

Agenda

- Opening Remarks and Asset Allocation CIO—5 minutes
- Infrastructure Update CIO + Head of Infrastructure—5 minutes
- PE Update CIO + Head of PE—5 minutes
- Discussion of Risk—Infrastructure: Head of Infrastructure, Head of Risk, All—10 minutes
- Discussion of Risk—PE: Head of PE, Head of Risk, All—10 minutes
- Other Risks: Head of Equities + All—5–10 minutes
- Closing Remarks: CIO—5 minutes

Memo 2A: Asset Allocation and Performance

- Since its inception, R-SWF has built a diversified portfolio of investments. As of last month, the fund had AUM of $56 billion USD, with the fund outperforming its overall benchmark by 130 bps net of fees since inception. Of course, there have been short-term periods of underperformance as the fund pursued its long-term strategy.
- The asset allocation as of last month for the overall fund was as follows:

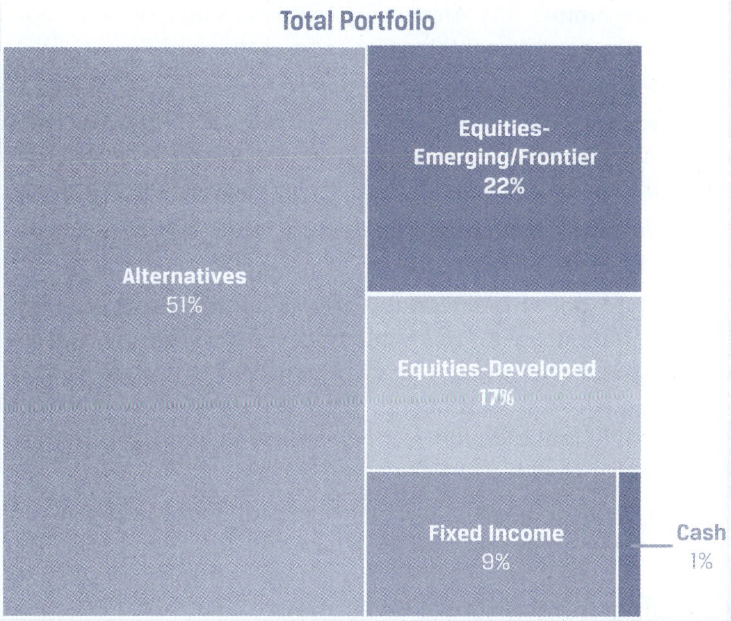

- R-SWF had approximately 51% of assets invested in alternative investments, consistent with its long-term objectives.
- Asset allocation was covered extensively in the prior month's investment committee meeting, so today's meeting will not provide any further breakdown.
- The investment committee will be discussing various points of view on risk aspects of the investments—including risk mitigation.
- The discussion will include "other risks" that were perhaps not covered well in the initial discussion. Discussion of environmental and social risks are challenging for long-term direct investing.

- Updates on the airport expansion in Sunnyland infrastructure investment are found in Memo 2B.
- Updates on the PE investment in ABC in Atsui are found in Memo 2C.

Memo 2B: Update on Infrastructure Investment in Sunnyland Airport

Investment Update

- Based on investment committee approval, the $100 million investment in Sunnyland has moved forward in accordance with agreed plans. This amount represents approximately 0.2% of total R-SWF assets.
- The Sunnyland government is happy with the progress of construction, which was completed recently. There was a delay in getting started, but that is Island life. Thankfully, there were no material cost overruns on the project.
- The new terminal is beautifully built and will be a great addition to the island nation as it further develops its tourism capabilities.
- We expect a grand opening of the new terminal in September, in time for the busy fall season. Tourist season is primarily from October through May, with the summer months being very hot (around 40°C) and humid.
- There are rumors that Airport Operating Group (AOG) is looking to renegotiate its contract for a higher fixed fee.
- One of the advantages of Sunnyland as a tourist attraction is its beautiful beaches with easy access to the airport, with the new runway, only 1 km from the sea, providing spectacular views.
- However, climate change has led to rising seas and more frequent storms. Storms are common in island nations; however, the rising seas are of concern.
- In addition, hotter temperatures are of additional concern. A few years ago, the tourist season was September through June, with only July and August being "too hot." However, in May this year, daytime highs were frequently 42°C or higher. There is a risk that the hotter temperatures lasting longer in the year will reduce tourism (and revenues for the airport project).
- Although this is a small investment in total, there are some risks we should focus on in today's discussion.

Risk Discussion: Infrastructure Investment

The following key risks are highlighted for discussion:

- Currency risk
- Expropriation risk by the Sunnyland government
- Risk that revenue from airport is less than expected
- Risk of project delays
- Risk of operating and maintenance costs being higher than projected
- Risk of default of AOG
- Risk that actual future (borrowing) interest rates will be higher than forecast

- Risk of underperformance regarding service quality–not meeting defined standards
- Other risks

Possible Mitigation of the Key Risks

- What should we do to mitigate the key risks?
- What should be our priorities? Action plan?

Memo 2C: Update on PE Investment in Atsui Beverage Company

Investment Update

- Based on investment committee approval, the $25 million investment in ABC has moved forward in accordance with agreed plans. This amount represents approximately 0.05% of total R-SWF assets.
- The modernization of the ABC plant went well, and the product expansion is starting to take shape. However, there several key updates that are unfortunately negative:
    - Atsui and surrounding nations went into a recession last year. Furthermore, a currency devaluation is anticipated. Beverages are considered a luxury item in Atsui.
    - A new government was elected in Atsui last year and took office in January. One of the first orders of business was to reduce tariffs on imported beverages from a 100% tariff to a 20% tariff. This change hurts our cost advantage over foreign brands. It is rumored that tariffs were reduced because Atsui wants to gain favor with foreign governments for potential loans.
    - Because the modern equipment will improve productivity, the original plan was to reduce headcount by 40%. In addition, due to slowing sales, management wanted to reduce staff by a total of 50%. However, labor laws are strict in Atsui. In order to terminate the employment of an Atsui citizen, significant notice (two years) is required. Plus, there is reputational risk for R-SWF for firing factory employees in a frontier market during a recession.
    - In order to make up for lower profits (due to the above reasons), plant management has started to cut corners to save on costs. Unfortunately, one way to do this was to dump waste into the nearby river rather than transport the waste for proper treatment. Although the waste is not toxic, it is starting to spoil the lovely fishing spot near the factory.
    - Another way ABC has tried to cut costs is by reducing employee breaks from one hour to 30 minutes and removing soap from the restrooms, requesting that employees bring their own.
- Although this is a small investment in total, there are some risks we should focus on in today's discussion.

Risk Discussion: Private Equity Investment

The following key risks are highlighted for discussion:

- Currency risk

- Expropriation risk by the Atsui government
- Quality control issues
- Challenges with local management (don't have a majority stake)
- Competitor pressure
- Growing trend of health foods that would result in avoidance of many carbonated beverages
- Elimination of tariffs protecting ABC from foreign-owned manufacturers
- Other risks

Possible Mitigation of the Key Risks

- What should we do to mitigate these risks?
- What should be our priorities? Action plan?

IN-TEXT QUESTIONS

Please respond to the following questions based on **Investment Committee Memo 2.0**.

The investment committee has identified several new risks that were not previously discussed (before Memos 2B and 2C). The CIO asks you to recommend how R-SWF can manage each of the following risks:

a. Risk of actual future (borrowing) interest rates will be higher than forecast (Memo 2B)

b. Growing trend of health foods that would result in avoidance of many carbonated beverages (Memo 2C)

Guideline Answers:

a: R-SWF can manage the risk that actual future (borrowing) interest rates will be higher than forecast by hedging its interest rate exposure for the Sunnyland airport project.

b: R-SWF can manage the risk of carbonated beverages falling out of favor due to an increasing preference for health foods by working to develop new healthy alternatives to carbonated, presumably sugar-filled drinks. As the production facility expands its ability to produce product, ABC could focus its new product development on healthy alternatives. The company can leverage its experience producing such beverages given the success of its natural mango drink in order to differentiate itself and increase market share.

Investment Committee Meeting 2.0

Participants

Chief Investment Officer (CIO)

Head of Infrastructure
Head of PE
Head of Risk
Head of Equities
Analysts [no speaking role]

Chief Investment Officer:
Good morning, everyone, and welcome to today's investment committee meeting of the sovereign wealth fund of the Republic of Ruritania. We're grateful for the opportunity to serve our constituents.

During last month's committee meeting, we reviewed the financial statements of the two projects in question—the airport in Sunnyland and the beverage manufacturer in Atsui. Our **Head of PE** provided the Mango Specials, so thank you for that!

It's been three years—wow, time really flies—since we unanimously approved proceeding with both investments. We'll go through some updates, but today's focus is risks and sensible mitigation measures.

First, though, the bigger picture: In those three years, AUM have grown by $6 billion. We're still outperforming our overall benchmark, but our outperformance has been dulled by difficulties with some assets, primarily real estate, because commercial real estate has underperformed. So that's hurt us a little bit, but as ever, we are long-term investors, and we may reap the benefits of those investments yet.

As we discuss risk mitigation, let's consider environmental and social risks. The greater pressure we've put on ourselves to invest responsibly and sustainably is matched by increased scrutiny from outside observers.

Whether we've decided to make an exit on our own or because of outside pressure, our rather long-term horizon doesn't make it any easier for us to step away from an investment when the time comes. As a contrast, our **Head of Equities** was telling me before the meeting started that he wasn't too happy about how much one of his portfolio companies was polluting, and so he just went ahead and sold the position. It was a liquid investment in a public market, and he was done within the hour. That's a contrast we have to keep in mind.

Allow me to read this comment about ABC from the minutes of the last meeting, as a sort of touchstone for us today: "This is a rather small investment, of $25 million, but even a small investment can have an outsized negative impact on us if we don't manage the risk properly."

But let's begin with Sunnyland airport. **Head of Infrastructure**, why don't you start us off?

Head of Infrastructure:
Thanks, **CIO**.

The good news is that the new terminal is pretty much complete and in line with specifications. We received some good reviews, both from locals and the international trade press. The downside is delays: At the outset, we expected a two-year construction program, but we're now well into the third year, unfortunately. There were noticeable cost overruns, and those were borne by the contractor, according to the contract, but there are some delay penalties that have yet to be settled.

The government, the contractor, and ourselves and AOG as investors—we're in discussions about these penalties, and the contractors are pointing to variations they say arose from our side. What they're calling "variations" we see as necessary design thinking for optimizing the commerciality of the retail outlets. The "variations" were pretty minimal, so let's see where our discussions end up. And some further disagreements center around the offices of customs and immigration within the terminal, which the contractor is laying at the foot of the government.

We should also highlight that as we're nearing the startup of terminal operations, the operator, AOG, has started complaining that the costs of training local staff are higher than expected. They haven't said anything formally yet, but I imagine they'll want to renegotiate their fixed-fee contract—nothing too serious.

Meanwhile, the grand opening of the terminal is a month away, in late August. It should be a good, high-profile event, and we should make a good showing. At least four Ruritania representatives, I think.

And then always swirling around our work is the focus of the press on the environmental movement and climate change, so we need to think about the impact on tourism. The main tourist season is September through June, historically, but it's just getting too hot, and so really the prime window for visitors will narrow to October through May.

The debate in the local press is frequently about the impact of so many tourists flying to Sunnyland, and AOG is in dialogue with the airlines about it. We have yet to see how that plays out in terms of impact on the airport operations down the road, but at the grand opening, we'll be able to celebrate the start of the upcoming season in September; bookings are in line with optimistic projections for the first year with the new terminal and runway.

Chief Investment Officer:
OK, thank you for that update.

And what can we say about ABC in Atsui?

Head of PE:
So, there are positives and negatives. A big positive is that this has been a fantastic learning experience for our direct investment program. But there's been a currency devaluation, and you could argue it's going to get worse because of the recession—the recession that started last year and that you all know so well because we're in the middle of it.

Still, is that good or bad? We do sell to tourists who bring their own currency, and we've got a lot of flexibility to shift our pricing so we can keep prices where they should be relative to our costs, which is positive.

But following the recent election, the new administration is talking about dropping all sorts of import tariffs, including the ones on food and drink. They've basically said, "For sure, we're going to cut them from 100% to 20%."

Obviously, this hurts our cost advantage over foreign brands, and the challenge here is that the new government wants to win favor with foreign governments before asking them for big loans, so the issue is about more than just carbonated drinks.

Chief Investment Officer:
There's a rumor that the new president likes Pepsi, so it's almost as if she doesn't want to pay double for a can, but 20% more is OK.

Head of PE:
ABC's new modernized equipment is ready to go, but here's the problem: Management is now saying they want to reduce headcount by 50%, instead of just 40%, because of the slowing sales. But labor laws in Atsui are strict, and to let someone go, you usually have to give as much as two years' notice.

Head of Risk:
Two years?

Head of PE:
Yeah, and the other issue is that for us as a sovereign wealth fund, there's reputational risk. Flying in from world cities and firing factory employees in frontier markets mean bad publicity, especially in Atsui and especially during the recession.

And here's another thing: In order to make up for lower profits, management has started cutting corners. They're dumping waste in the nearby river rather than paying to transport it to the treatment site. Do you remember how the plant is right next to the river and the employees fish in it during lunch? It's spoiling the fishing spot. This is a problem. And it gets worse: Scientists are saying that the plant site and the river overlap with the range of a rare reptile that is found here and only one other place on earth. So our site has attracted the attention of people with no interest in soda or mangoes.

Head of Risk:
This is a problem.

Head of PE:
Now here's another thing: ABC has tried to cut costs by reducing employee breaks from an hour to 30 minutes and—this is probably a little granular for our meeting, but risks are risks, they have removed soap from the restrooms! Everyone has to bring their own soap now.

Now, I know we're a $50 billion sovereign wealth fund—

Chief Investment Officer:
—$56 billion.

Head of PE:
I know we're a $56 billion sovereign wealth fund, and here we are talking about removing soap from a few bathrooms in the tropics where we have a $25 million direct investment, but stuff like this can have a reputational impact.

Head of Risk:
Agreed.

Chief Investment Officer:
Our focus right now is risk, and we should be talking about this. We haven't really faced any of these health and safety or social issues before at the individual investment level, and it's a learning opportunity as we expand our direct investing program. **Head of PE**, when you went to the restroom and found out there was no soap, you had to borrow some from the plant manager. Is that right? Did he give it to you for free, or did he charge you?

Head of PE:
He wanted to charge me, but I didn't need any soap because I had hand sanitizer with me. I got used to carrying hand sanitizer around with me everywhere back in the coronavirus days, so now I just do that when I'm in Atsui.

Chief Investment Officer:
OK, then let's discuss infrastructure.

Three years ago when we approved this investment, we talked potential risks, including climate, and we were comfortable with the position that the threat of rising seas was well into the future. We may have to re-evaluate that position.

Head of Risk:
Despite our comfort then, the fact is that storms have become more frequent and the sea level *has* risen measurably—in three short years.

Head of Infrastructure:

The lenders have also raised this point, as has our in-country political adviser. I still don't see any impact in the immediate term. If you remember three years ago, much of our comfort came from the environmental-impact assessments, which were required and were factored into the design. What has been constructed can deal with it sufficiently.

The bigger worry is the force of an unanticipated and rare storm that compounds the impact of some already bad flooding. Originally, the engineers planned for a once-in-50-years or once-in-100-years scenario, and it may be that the risk of those events has increased.

There's a discussion to be had with the government about architectural solutions—maybe some proper flood barriers. As for the cost of them, if they'll even work, and whose responsibility that is—those issues are unclear. It's not in anybody's interest for the airport to shut down.

Head of Equities:

My experience engaging with large public companies on climate risk tells me that a tiny island like Sunnyland can't have any meaningful impact on a global scale and hence they must focus on adaptation rather than worry too much about mitigation. **Head of Infrastructure** points to one of the more logical solutions: some sort of storm-surge barrier like the Netherlands has relied on for years.

As for who's going to pay for it, let's think beyond our own project for a minute. Rising seas aren't just going to have an impact on the airport; every five-star, beach-facing property will feel it too. The prime hotels feel it, and eventually the whole tourist ecosystem feels it, and with the country so dependent on tourism, my view is that this has to be a government-driven initiative. And a storm-surge barrier that successfully avoids damaging floods will be important enough to private interests, such as real estate and other infrastructure investors, that they'll form part of the funding circle.

Head of Infrastructure:

I think that's right. It's a question for the whole economy and for the government. Serious talks are taking place in Sunnyland about a new tax to cover the costs, a sort of climate tax that would go to a host of worsening climate issues.

How the authorities end up structuring that tax will inform whether we can avoid it.

Chief Investment Officer:

Understood, but as a sovereign institution, even if we could avoid such a tax to protect our investment value, from a reputational perspective, we should think twice.

Head of PE:

Head of Infrastructure said that AOG might be asking for a higher fixed fee to operate the new terminal. I'm not sure if this is a question for this point in the meeting, but is there anything we can do to proactively protect ourselves against a higher contract fee in the event AOG gets its renegotiation?

Head of Infrastructure:

We all signed a well-structured agreement, and that affords us some decent protection against any meddling in the fee structure, though there are break clauses if anything gets too out of line. Still, there are incentives built into the concession agreement to make sure everyone wins to a greater or lesser extent when traffic goes up.

Equally, we don't want a disgruntled operator. Happy employees, happy travelers, better experience, more traffic.

We haven't been formally approached about this, but let's not dismiss it out of hand just because we have a contract we can hide behind. AOG is a strong global operator. If they did activate a break clause in two or three years' time, that lands us with a responsibility we really don't want, which is finding a new operator. We're still satisfied with their cooperation. I recommend seeing how talks over the delays play out, and if we find that the government is liable for the delay, we'll request an extension to the concession and then sit down with AOG to positively collaborate on retooling the whole picture.

Chief Investment Officer:
OK, we've covered the environmental and reputational risks, the climate risk, and the AOG item as well. Are there any other risks we should examine at this point?

Head of Risk:
That covers the important ones. Currency risk and the risk of further delays are less of a concern. With climate change, we can't *solve* it; as **Head of Equities** insists, we have to adapt. It affects the entire nation, so hopefully the government will step in.

And I reinforce the idea of positive negotiations with AOG. We want a happy operator.

Chief Investment Officer:
Right. OK, very good.

Head of Risk, it looks like something is still on your mind.

Head of Risk:
Thanks for noticing. A little more scrutiny of ABC is warranted. I acknowledge its importance for boosting our direct investment know-how. It's been a great learning experience for **Head of PE** and his team, and it's a very small investment. Even if we lose money, it's not going to move the needle for our fund, but—and this is a substantial "but"—the reputational risk is a big concern.

We don't want to end up in the newspaper firing people during a recession, polluting the river, threatening endangered species, and being rather petty about soap.

Head of Infrastructure:
True on all counts.

Head of Risk:
Ladies and gentlemen, the writing is on the wall. I propose we exit this investment as soon as possible, if we can. Maybe we can't, and if that's the case, I would remain very concerned.

Head of PE:
No, I'm happy you mentioned it, and it's good that it's all coming out in this room. Let me tell you how we see things.

Before we jumped into this as one of our first direct investments, we co-invested and participated in many private equity funds that invest in all kinds of things, including special situations and distressed investments, and we've always gone in with third-party experts or used our own experts. Just because things get a little dicey, it doesn't mean we exit.

When we started, ABC was a conventional, if small, investment. If that's changed and it now is a problem business, we've got a team whose job it is to make lemonade out of lemons, so let's think about passing ABC over to the distressed-asset team before it becomes properly distressed. I'm not saying we keep it or some other team takes it. I'm saying let's at least see if it's a better fit for someone else.

What if we keep going? We've got risks around firing employees, dumping waste in the river, and pettiness around soap. And we're shifting our mindset, and the challenge is less about the return and more about the reputational risk.

So we really need to figure out: Can we change how this business functions to manage that risk? We have a 35% interest, we know that management has skin in the game. But in what game? With management incentivized to improve the bottom line, we're motivating them to cut employees instead of keeping employees happy and avoiding resentment.

So we're asking ourselves a new question: How do we motivate management to keep people inside and outside the plant happy? We have two board seats, and investing more money in modernization seems to make less sense now.

And we've got employees now who don't have much to do, but they're collecting a salary, so why would they leave? And if we can't fire them, it's an issue. Maybe we pay them a percentage—say, half their regular salary—while offering them good training and assistance for eight months to find another job. At the same time, we'd convince management to shift to a less profit-driven focus.

I don't know if any of that will work. Maybe we should have divested earlier, but that's our thinking if we keep holding on.

Head of Equities:
And what about the toxic stuff being released into the river?

Head of PE:
It's actually not toxic, technically, but we don't even want to be talking about whether it's toxic or not toxic. Ending that practice is an important piece of our talks with management, and so is removing incentives to cut corners.

Can we fundamentally change the way things are going? If we can't, then maybe this is an investment for someone else. Or perhaps we sell our 35% stake back to management?

Chief Investment Officer:
Thanks, **Head of PE**. We talked about this being a learning experience. We also talked about it displaying aspects of impact investment. Maybe part of the value is in education. In some less developed areas, they think it's maybe not a big deal to throw things into the river. Can we inform their thinking with the idea that wanting a beautiful river for fishing and enjoyment is a virtue and that it's not really that hard to dispose of waste properly? What can we intelligently say about impact?

Head of Equities:
This line of thinking makes sense to me. Our experience in other developing nations as well as developed nations tells us that you'll save some costs in the short term with actions like dumping waste directly into water bodies, but in the long run, regulations catch up to you and the cost of pre-treatment or appropriate handling of waste is much lower than the penalties you get for taking such shortcuts.

If we decide to stay, we have to paint the picture for management that there's a fatal flaw in our approach at the moment. Public perception is one issue, but eventually regulations will be introduced with penalties and obligations to clean up the river.

If we do try to salvage the situation and continue with our investment, there's a path that involves the government. Our pitch should be that if there are legal roadblocks for cutting 50% of the jobs, you might be putting 100% of the jobs at risk because the company won't survive if tariffs are reduced to 20%. The government doesn't want the factory to shut down because of *its* rigid labor laws, so there may well be room for a more, let's say, negotiated conclusion.

It's worth exploring, again, in consultation with the local management.

Chief Investment Officer:
Lobbying the government, reframing management's incentives—these are interesting ways to pivot. We should also consider as a committee the extent to which we want to maintain our direct investing/private equity approach or whether there is wisdom

in recasting our work as more of an impact program. The committee's analysis has highlighted the difficulties faced by a sovereign wealth fund in cutting staff. It ends up being a headline risk.

The conventional private equity houses can more easily cut jobs for purely financial reasons. However, as a sovereign wealth fund, it is more complicated for us. Imagine the headline: "Government of Ruritania Cuts Jobs in XYZ during a Recession."

Head of Infrastructure:
It's not a good look.

Chief Investment Officer:
It's not a good look. Right.

Head of Risk:
From my point of view, we've covered the main risks for ABC. I like the sequence: We engage with management to change the mindset, and we lobby government on how a two-year notice period and similar restrictions could jeopardize the whole business. We give it another year, and if we're not making progress, we look for an exit option, maybe handing things over to a team that is comfortable with these thorny issues.

Chief Investment Officer:
Well summarized. I'm grateful for the focus we are putting on the risks here.

And as for Sunnyland?

Head of Equities:
I'd submit to the team that while the world's major governments have *started* taking action on climate change, we're not going to "fix" these problems easily so the planet can just go back to the way it was 30 years ago. The impact will intensify, and we have to adapt.

In my mind, the focus should be on liaising with the government. They will have to drive things because of the scale of the investment required—

Chief Investment Officer:
—And because of how long term the investment horizon is.

Team, this is the sort of experienced scrutiny of risk we needed, so thank you very much. This was a highly worthwhile meeting, and let's keep a keen focus on the risks.

—The End—

IN-TEXT QUESTIONS

Please answer the following question based on **Investment Committee Meeting 2.0**.

1. In the template provided, state the primary environmental risk that has been identified by R-SWF's investment committee for each investment. Recommend how each risk can be managed in the future.

Investment	Primary Environmental Risk	Risk Management Recommendation
Sunnyland Airport		
Atsui Beverage Company		

2. Identify one significant social risk that both investments have in common and that was not originally identified by the investment committee. Discuss whether or not this risk is easily managed once recognized.

Guideline Answers

1. In the template provided, state the primary environmental risk that has been identified by R-SWF's investment committee for each investment. Recommend how each risk can be managed in the future.

Investment	Primary Environmental Risk	Risk Management Recommendation
Sunnyland Airport	Climate change due to rising sea levels	Given the uncertainty around the precise timing and magnitude of the impact of climate change and rising sea levels specifically, R-SWF should use climate-related scenario analysis to better understand how climate change will affect its investment in Sunnyland. In addition, since R-SWF cannot mitigate climate change, it must focus on adaptation strategies. In this case, a strategy to provide protection for the airport against a storm surge or higher sea levels is the most realistic option. An adaptation strategy is consistent with the development mandate of R-SWF's investment in Sunnyland.
Atsui Beverage Company	Waste management due to dumping waste into river	R-SWF must find a way to persuade the board and local management to stop dumping waste in the river in an effort to pursue sustainable development and a "just" transition. Although it might be a cost savings in the short run, in the long run, regulations will catch up. Cleanup of improperly disposed waste is far more costly than appropriately disposing of waste up front. One of the ways to encourage prioritization of protecting the river is to educate the local community about the importance of a healthy river. Community education, the pursuit of sustainable development, and a "just" transition are consistent with the impact investing element of this investment for R-SWF.

2. Reputational risk is very significant in the case of each investment and can have an outsized effect on the performance of the investments. Social issues, such as reputational risk, are generally quite difficult to manage even once identified and understood because they are relatively challenging to quantify and integrate into financial models. Furthermore, best practices include considering the interests of all the stakeholders involved, which is not easy.

In Sunnyland, R-SWF must contribute to any effort to raise funds to implement protection against rising seas. This project will likely be expensive. However, it is not in R-SWF's best interest to appear to be avoiding contributing to the project to accommodate climate change. Doing so could significantly damage R-SWF's reputation in Sunnyland and beyond given the international attention paid to the construction of the new airport. In theory, reputational risk in this case is relatively simple to manage in that R-SWF simply needs to be a contributor to the project and overall community by supporting efforts to adapt to climate change so as to not destroy Sunnyland's tourism industry. However, execution of such a strategy to mitigate R-SWF's reputational risk in Sunnyland will need to be closely monitored in order to effectively execute it. Managing this type of risk is not easy.

Reputational risk is also very significant in the case of ABC because of two major social issues: (1) occupational health and safety and (2) labor standards. Each of these issues could significantly damage R-SWF's reputation. Removing hand soap from the restrooms is an occupational health and safety issue that could cause reputational damage. Shortening employee breaks and firing people during a recession are social issues related to labor standards.

These types of choices indicate that local management is more concerned about profitability than reputational risk. In order to manage its reputational risk, R-SWF needs to persuade the board to adjust its incentive structure in order to encourage local management to reverse course on these short-sighted, destructive social issues, even if it is expensive. R-SWF does not want to be perceived as an investor that exploits its labor force. Soap should be provided for employees, breaks should be reasonable in length, and rather than firing employees, which can't be effectively executed because of the strict labor laws, ABC should focus on retraining employees for the future of the business. This is a complicated, multifaceted course especially as a minority owner. It isn't easily implemented but can be done. Any changes will need to be monitored to ensure they continue and have the desired outcome—a sustainable and mutually beneficial long-term relationship with the local community.

R-SWF'S Investments: 3.0

Second Extension of Case Facts (3.0)

You left R-SWF at the end of Year 3 and took a position as a Senior Risk Consultant at Kiken Consulting, a risk consulting firm.

In the summer of Year 5, you are reading the newspaper and notice some commentary on two of the R-SWF investments you had been involved with. You read the following excerpts with nostalgic interest.

Update on Infrastructure Investment

- The infrastructure investment continues to perform poorly because of a combination of the following:
    - lower revenue (fewer tourists) vs. forecast (50% lower than base case)
    - higher costs (mitigating flood damage) vs. forecast (50% higher than base case)
- The medium- and long-term forecast on this investment does not look promising.

Update on PE Investment

- The PE team was able to avoid a diplomatic crisis and reputational risk damage by finding a buyer for the 35% stake. They sold the full position at $27 million.
- The stake was sold to an international beverage company that had been exporting to Atsui. The company's sales had been adversely affected by a weaker Atsui currency. Thus, producing locally is advantageous because it provides a natural foreign exchange hedge.

You set the newspaper down and start thinking about Sunnyland and Atsui when your boss suddenly interrupts you with the following news:

Kiken Consulting has a new client! R-SWF has hired the firm for a risk analysis project. Because you have prior knowledge on R-SWF's approach, your boss has assigned you to the project with a lead role. You are expected to evaluate the strengths and weaknesses of R-SWF's enterprise risk management system and to make recommendations for improvements.

IN-TEXT QUESTION

Please respond to the following question.

1. Provide key facts/inputs from the R-SWF case, use them to evaluate the strengths and weaknesses of R-SWF's enterprise risk management processes, and make recommendations for improvements.

Guideline Answer

1. One of the main strengths of R-SWF's risk management process is that R-SWF dedicated an entire internal investment committee meeting to identifying and discussing the potential risks of two relatively small investment opportunities. Ample time was taken to allow senior management of R-SWF to express their concerns and discuss mitigation strategies to reduce potential risks. The investment committee was able to identify various potential risk factors, and senior management voted on both investment opportunities.

One of the weaknesses of R-SWF's risk management process is that too little effort was made in trying to quantify the various risks and agreeing on specific actions that could be taken if some of those risk materialized. The team, with the help of the Head of Risk, could have done a better job at performing scenario analysis for both investments and presented a base case, an optimistic case, and a pessimistic case. Although the team identified and discussed several risk factors, they should have put together an action plan for risk mitigation and potential hedging tools prior to making the investments. This action plan would be conditional on certain bad outcomes materializing. Finally, since both investments were quite small in the overall scheme and had limited financial and liquidity risk implications for the fund, more consideration could have been given to identifying potential reputational risks and ESG.

REFERENCES

Geltner, D. 1993. "Estimating Market Values from Appraised Values without Assuming an Efficient Market." *Journal of Real Estate Research* 8:325–45.

Getmansky, M., A. W. Lo, and I. Makarov. 2004. "An Econometric Model of Serial Correlation and Illiquidity in Hedge Fund Returns." *Journal of Financial Economics* 74:529–609. 10.1016/j.jfineco.2004.04.001

Grantham Research Institute on Climate Change and the Environment. "*New Study Estimates Global Warming of 2.5 Centigrade Degrees by 2100 Would Put at Risk Trillions of Dollars of World's Financial Assets.*" Press release (4 April 2016). www.lse.ac.uk/GranthamInstitute/news/us2-5-trillion-of-the-worlds-financial-assets-would-be-at-risk-from-the-impacts-of-climate-change-if-global-mean-surface-temperature-rises-by-2-5c.

IEA. 2020. "*World Energy Outlook 2020*" (October). www.iea.org/reports/world-energy-outlook-2020.

Intergovernmental Panel on Climate Change. 2018. "*Special Report: Global Warming of 1.5 °C*" (6 October). www.ipcc.ch/sr15/chapter/spm.

Lo, Joe. 2020. "*IEA Outlines How World Can Reach Net Zero Emissions by 2050.*" *Climate Home News* (13 October). www.climatechangenews.com/2020/10/13/iea-outlines-world-can-reach-net-zero-emissions-2050.

NASA. 2019. "*NASA Global Climate Change: Vital Signs of the Planet.*" https://climate.nasa.gov/vital-signs/global-temperature.

Okunev, J. and D. White. 2003. "*Hedge Fund Risk Factors and Value at Risk of Credit Trading Strategies.*" Working paper, University of New South Wales. 10.2139/ssrn.460641

Glossary

Absolute return benchmark A minimum target return that an investment manager is expected to beat.

Accrual taxes Taxes levied and paid on a periodic basis.

Accumulation phase Phase where the government predominantly contributes to a sovereign wealth pension reserve fund.

Active management A portfolio management approach that allows risk factor mismatches relative to a benchmark index causing potentially significant return differences between the active portfolio and the underlying benchmark.

Active return The return on a portfolio minus the return on the portfolio's benchmark.

Active risk The standard deviation of active returns.

Active risk budgeting Risk budgeting that concerns active risk (risk relative to a portfolio's benchmark).

Active share A measure of how similar a portfolio is to its benchmark. A manager who precisely replicates the benchmark will have an active share of zero; a manager with no holdings in common with the benchmark will have an active share of one.

Aggregate wealth The total value of all assets owned, encompassing personal property, financial assets, real assets, and rights.

Arithmetic attribution An attribution approach which explains the arithmetic difference between the portfolio return and its benchmark return. The single-period attribution effects sum to the excess return, however, when combining multiple periods, the sub-period attribution effects will not sum to the excess return.

Ask price The price at which a trader will sell a specified quantity of a security. Also called *ask*, *offer price*, or *offer*.

Asset-only With respect to asset allocation, an approach that focuses directly on the characteristics of the assets without explicitly modeling the liabilities.

Authority bias A behavioral bias which involves groups deferring to a group member that is a subject matter expert or in a position of authority.

Aversion to complexity A behavioral phenomenon of groups in many professional contexts, in which disproportionate attention is given to trivial issues at the expense of important but harder-to-grasp or contested topics.

Back-fill bias The distortion in index or peer group data which results when returns are reported to a database only after they are known to be good returns.

Base With respect to a foreign exchange quotation of the price of one unit of a currency, the currency referred to in "one unit of a currency."

Basis risk The possibility that the expected value of a derivative differs unexpectedly from that of the underlying.

Bear spread An option strategy that becomes more valuable when the price of the underlying asset declines, so requires buying one option and writing another with a *lower* exercise price. A put bear spread involves buying a put with a higher exercise price and selling a put with a lower exercise price. A bear spread can also be executed with calls.

Best ask The offer to sell with the lowest ask price. Also called *best offer* or *inside ask*.

Best bid The highest bid in the market.

Best offer The lowest offer (ask price) in the market.

Best-in-class An ESG implementation approach that seeks to identify the most favorable companies and sectors based on ESG considerations. Also called *positive screening*.

Bid price In a price quotation, the price at which the party making the quotation is willing to buy a specified quantity of an asset or security.

Bid–ask spread The ask price minus the bid price.

Buffering Establishing ranges around breakpoints that define whether a stock belongs in one index or another.

Bull spread An option strategy that becomes more valuable when the price of the underlying asset rises, so requires buying one option and writing another with a *higher* exercise price. A call bull spread involves buying a call with a lower exercise price and selling a call with a higher exercise price. A bull spread can also be executed with puts.

Business cycle Fluctuations in GDP in relation to long-term trend growth, usually lasting 9-11 years.

Calendar rebalancing Rebalancing a portfolio to target weights on a periodic basis; for example, monthly, quarterly, semi-annually, or annually.

Calendar spread A strategy in which one sells an option and buys the same type of option but with different expiration dates, on the same underlying asset and with the same strike. When the investor buys the more distant (near-term) call and sells the near-term (more distant) call, it is a long (short) calendar spread.

Canada model Characterized by a high allocation to alternatives. Unlike the endowment model, however, the Canada model relies more on internally managed assets. The innovative features of the Canada model are the: a) reference portfolio, b) total portfolio approach, and c) active management.

Capital market expectations (CME) Expectations concerning the risk and return prospects of asset classes.

Capital sufficiency analysis The process of evaluating whether a client has sufficient capital resources to achieve their financial goals and objectives; it considers the client's assets, liabilities, income, expenses, risk tolerance, time horizon, and other relevant factors.

Capture ratio A measure of the manager's gain or loss relative to the gain or loss of the benchmark.

Carhart model A four factor model used in performance attribution. The four factors are: market (RMRF), size (SMB), value (HML), and momentum (WML).

Carry trade A trading strategy that involves buying a security and financing it at a rate that is lower than the yield on that security.

Cash flow matching Immunization approach that attempts to ensure that all future liability payouts are matched precisely by cash flows from bonds or fixed-income derivatives.

Cash-secured put An option strategy involving the writing of a put option and simultaneously depositing an amount of money equal to the exercise price into a designated account (this strategy is also called a fiduciary put).

Collar An option position in which the investor is long shares of stock and then buys a put with an exercise price below the current stock price and writes a call with an exercise price above the current stock price. Collars allow a shareholder to acquire downside protection through a protective put but reduce the cash outlay by writing a covered call.

Contingent immunization Hybrid approach that combines immunization with an active management approach when the asset portfolio's value exceeds the present value of the liability portfolio.

Cost basis The initial cost of acquiring an investment including expenses incurred to acquire the investment. Also referred to as simply basis.

Covered call An option strategy in which a long position in an asset is combined with a short position in a call on that asset.

Cross hedge A hedge involving a hedging instrument that is imperfectly correlated with the asset being hedged; an example is hedging a bond investment with futures on a non-identical bond.

Cross-currency basis swap A swap in which notional principals are exchanged because the goal of the transaction is to issue at a more favorable funding rate and swap the amount back to the currency of choice.

Cross-sectional consistency A feature of expectations setting which means that estimates for all classes reflect the same underlying assumptions and are generated with methodologies that reflect or preserve important relationships among the asset classes, such as strong correlations. It is the internal consistency across asset classes.

Currency overlay programs A currency overlay program is a program to manage a portfolio's currency exposures for the case in which those exposures are managed separately from the management of the portfolio itself.

Custom security-based benchmark Benchmark that is custom built to accurately reflect the investment discipline of a particular investment manager. Also called a *strategy benchmark* because it reflects a manager's particular strategy.

Decision-reversal risk The risk of reversing a chosen course of action at the point of maximum loss.

Decumulation phase Phase where the government predominantly withdraws from a sovereign wealth pension reserve fund.

Deferred taxes Taxes postponed until some future date.

Defined benefit A retirement plan in which a plan sponsor commits to paying a specified retirement benefit.

Defined benefit plan Retirement plan that is funded by the employer that guarantees a retirement benefit based on factors such as years of service, salary, and age.

Defined contribution A retirement plan in which contributions are defined but the ultimate retirement benefit is not specified or guaranteed by the plan sponsor.

Defined contribution plan Retirement plan in which the employer, employee, or both contribute to an account in which the employee bears the investment risk.

Delay costs Implicit trading costs that arise from the inability to complete desired trades immediately. Also called *slippage.*

Delta The sensitivity of the derivative price to a small change in the value of the underlying asset.

Delta hedging Hedging that involves matching the price response of the position being hedged over a narrow range of prices.

Demand deposits Accounts that can be drawn upon regularly and without notice. This category includes checking accounts and certain savings accounts that are often accessible through online banks or automated teller machines (ATMs).

Diffusion index Reflects the proportion of the index's components that are moving in a pattern consistent with the overall index.

Dividend capture A trading strategy whereby an equity portfolio manager purchases stocks just before their ex-dividend dates, holds these stocks through the ex-dividend date to earn the right to receive the dividend, and subsequently sells the shares.

Domestic asset An asset that trades in the investor's domestic currency (or home currency).

Domestic currency The currency of the investor, i.e., the currency in which he or she typically makes consumption purchases, e.g., the Swiss franc for an investor domiciled in Switzerland.

Domestic-currency return A rate of return stated in domestic currency terms from the perspective of the investor; reflects both the foreign-currency return on an asset as well as percentage movement in the spot exchange rate between the domestic and foreign currencies.

Drawdown A percentage peak-to-trough reduction in net asset value.

Drawdown duration The total time from the start of the drawdown until the cumulative drawdown recovers to zero.

Due diligence Investigation and analysis in support of an investment action, decision, or recommendation.

Duration matching Immunization approach based on the duration of assets and liabilities. Ideally, the liabilities being matched (the liability portfolio) and the portfolio of assets (the bond portfolio) should be affected similarly by a change in interest rates.

Duration times spread Weighting of spread duration by credit spread in order to incorporate the empirical observation that spread changes for lower-rated bonds tend to be consistent on a percentage, rather than absolute, basis.

Dynamic asset allocation Dynamic asset allocation is an investment strategy premised on long-term asset allocation but employing short-term, tactical trading to maintain investment allocation targets.

Dynamic hedge A hedge requiring adjustment as the price of the hedged asset changes.

Econometrics The application of quantitative modeling and analysis grounded in economic theory to the analysis of economic data.

Economic balance sheet An extended balance sheet that includes the present values of both lifetime earnings and future consumption.

Economic indicators Economic statistics provided by government and established private organizations that contain information on an economy's recent past activity or its current or future position in the business cycle.

Effective federal funds (FFE) rate The fed funds rate actually transacted between depository institutions, not the Fed's target federal funds rate.

Effective spread Two times the difference between the execution price and the midpoint of the market quote at the time an order is entered.

Endowment model Characterized by a high allocation to alternative investments (private investments and hedge funds), significant active management, and externally managed assets.

Enhanced indexing approach Maintains a close link to the benchmark but attempts to generate a modest amount of outperformance relative to the benchmark.

Excess return Used in various senses appropriate to context: 1) The difference between the portfolio return and the benchmark return, which may be either positive or negative; 2) The return in excess of the risk-free rate, thus representing the return for bearing risk.

Exhaustive Covering or containing all possible outcomes.

Extended portfolio assets and liabilities Assets and liabilities beyond those shown on a conventional balance sheet that are relevant in making asset allocation decisions; an example of an extended asset is human capital.

Factor-model-based benchmarks Benchmarks constructed by examining a portfolio's sensitivity to a set of factors, such as the return for a broad market index, company earnings growth, industry, or financial leverage.

Family offices Private firms that offer a range of wealth management services tailored specifically for ultra-high-net-worth individuals.

Foreign assets Assets denominated in currencies other than the investor's home currency.

Foreign currency Currency that is not the currency in which an investor makes consumption purchases, e.g., the US dollar from the perspective of a Swiss investor.

Foreign-currency return The return of the foreign asset measured in foreign-currency terms.

Forward rate bias An empirically observed divergence from interest rate parity conditions that active investors seek to benefit from by borrowing in a lower-yield currency and investing in a higher-yield currency.

Funding currencies The low-yield currencies in which borrowing occurs in a carry trade.

Gamma A numerical measure of how sensitive an option's delta (the sensitivity of the derivative's price) is to a change in the value of the underlying.

General account Account holding assets to fund future liabilities from traditional life insurance and fixed annuities, the products in which the insurer bears all the risks—particularly mortality risk and longevity risk.

Gini coefficient A measure of inequality of wealth, or *i*, that ranges from 0 (perfect equality) to 1 (perfect inequality).

Goals-based With respect to asset allocation or investing, an approach that focuses on achieving an investor's goals (for example, related to supporting lifestyle needs or aspirations) based typically on constructing sub-portfolios aligned with those goals.

Goals-based investing An investment industry term for approaches to investing for individuals and families focused on aligning investments with goals (parallel to liability-driven investing for institutional investors).

Grinold–Kroner model An expression for the expected return on a share as the sum of an expected income return, an expected nominal earnings growth return, and an expected repricing return.

Groupthink A behavioral bias that occurs when a team minimizes conflict and dissent in reaching and maintaining a consensus.

Hedge ratio The proportion of an underlying that will offset the risk associated with a derivative position.

High-net-worth individuals (HNWIs) Individuals with investable assets exceeding a certain minimum level, often as low as USD1 million, but typically more.

High-water mark A measure that reflects the fund's maximum value as of a performance fee payment date net of fees.

Holdings-based attribution A "buy and hold" attribution approach which calculates the return of portfolio and benchmark components based upon the price and foreign exchange rate changes applied to daily snapshots of portfolio holdings.

Holdings-based style analysis A bottom-up style analysis that estimates the risk exposures from the actual securities held in the portfolio at a point in time.

Home bias A preference for securities listed on the exchanges of one's home country.

Home currency See *domestic currency*.

Home-country bias The favoring of domestic over non-domestic investments relative to global market value weights.

Human capital The present value of an individual's future expected labor income.

Impact investing Refers to investments made with the specific intent of generating positive, measurable social and environmental impact alongside a financial return (which differentiates it from philanthropy).

Implementation shortfall (IS) The difference between the return for a notional or paper portfolio, where all transactions are assumed to take place at the manager's decision price, and the portfolio's actual return, which reflects realized transactions, including all fees and costs.

Implied volatility The standard deviation that causes an option pricing model to give the current option price.

Implied volatility surface A three-dimensional plot, for put and call options on the same underlying asset, of days to expiration (*x*-axis), option strike prices (*y*-axis), and implied volatilities (*z*-axis). It simultaneously shows the volatility skew (or smile) and the term structure of implied volatility.

Inflation-linked bonds Debt instruments that link the principal and interest to inflation.

Input uncertainty Uncertainty concerning whether the inputs are correct.

Inside ask See *best ask*.

Inside bid See *best bid*.

Inside spread The spread between the best bid price and the best ask price. Also called the *market bid-ask spread, inside bid-ask spread*, or *market spread*.

Interaction effect The impact of overweighting and underweighting individual securities within sectors that are themselves overweighted or underweighted.

Intertemporal consistency A feature of expectations setting which means that estimates for an asset class over different horizons reflect the same assumptions with respect to the potential paths of returns over time. It is the internal consistency over various time horizons.

Intrinsic value The amount gained (per unit) by an option buyer if an option is exercised at any given point in time. May be referred to as the exercise value of the option.

Investable net worth The sum of liquid assets, such as savings and investment accounts, and less short-term liabilities such as credit card debt.

Investable wealth The sum of liquid assets such as savings and investment accounts.

Investment currencies The high-yielding currencies in a carry trade.

Investment policy statement (IPS) A description of a client's unique investment objectives, risk tolerance, investment time horizon, and other applicable constraints.

Investment style A natural grouping of investment disciplines that has some predictive power in explaining the future dispersion of returns across portfolios.

Key person risk The risk that results from over-reliance on an individual or individuals whose departure would negatively affect an investment manager.

Knock-in/knock-out Features of a vanilla option that is created (or ceases to exist) when the spot exchange rate touches a pre-specified level.

Latency The elapsed time between the occurrence of an event and a subsequent action that depends on that event.

Leading economic indicators Turning points that usually precede those of the overall economy; they are believed to have value for predicting the economy's future state, usually near-term.

Liability driven investing (LDI) model In the LDI model, the primary investment objective is to generate returns sufficient to cover liabilities, with a focus on maximizing expected surplus return (excess return of assets over liabilities) and managing surplus volatility.

Liability glide path A specification of desired proportions of liability-hedging assets and return-seeking assets and the duration of the liability hedge as funded status changes and contributions are made.

Liability-based mandates Mandates managed to match or cover expected liability payments (future cash outflows) with future projected cash inflows.

Liability-driven investing An investment industry term that generally encompasses asset allocation that is focused on funding an investor's liabilities in institutional contexts.

Liability-relative With respect to asset allocation, an approach that focuses directly only on funding liabilities as an investment objective.

Limit order book The book or list of limit orders to buy and sell that pertains to a security.

Limited-life foundations A type of foundation where founders seek to maintain control of spending while they (or their immediate heirs) are still alive.

Longevity risk The risk of exhausting an individual's financial resources before passing away, thereby leaving insufficient capital for living expenses and unmet needs.

Lorenz curve A measure of the cumulative percentage of wealth owned by each percentage of the population.

Macro attribution Attribution at the sponsor level.

Manager peer group See *manager universe*.

Manager universe A broad group of managers with similar investment disciplines. Also called *manager peer group*.

Marginal tax rate The highest rate of tax applied to taxable income.

Market fragmentation Trading the same instrument in multiple venues.

Market impact The effect of the trade on transaction prices. Also called *price impact*.

Micro attribution Attribution at the portfolio manager level.

Midquote price The average, or midpoint, of the prevailing bid and ask prices.

Minimum-variance hedge ratio A mathematical approach to determining the optimal cross hedging ratio.

Mission-related investing Investing aimed at causes promoting positive societal or environmental change.

Model uncertainty Uncertainty as to whether a selected model is correct.

Negative screening An ESG investment style that focuses on the exclusion of certain sectors, companies, or practices in a fund or portfolio on the basis of specific ESG criteria.

Net worth The difference between assets and liabilities.

Non-deliverable forwards Cash-settled forward contracts, used predominately with respect to foreign exchange forwards. Also called *contracts for differences*.

Nonstationarity A characteristic of series of data whose properties, such as mean and variance, are not constant through time. When analyzing historical data it means that different parts of a data series reflect different underlying statistical properties.

Norway model Characterized by an almost exclusive reliance on public equities and fixed income (the traditional 60/40 equity/bond model falls under the Norway model), with largely passively managed assets and with very little to no allocation to alternative investments.

Offer price The price at which a counterparty is willing to sell one unit of the base currency.

Opportunity cost Reflects the foregone opportunity of investing in a different asset. It is typically denoted by the risk-free rate of interest, *r*.

Optional stock dividends A type of dividend in which shareholders may elect to receive either cash or new shares.

Overbought A market condition in which market sentiment is thought to be unsustainably bullish.

Oversold A market condition in which market sentiment is thought to be unsustainably bearish.

Packeting Splitting stock positions into multiple parts.

Parameter uncertainty Uncertainty arising because a quantitative model's parameters are estimated with error.

Participant-switching life-cycle options Automatically switch DC plan members into a more conservative asset mix as their age increases. There may be several automatic de-risking switches at different age targets.

Participant/cohort option Pools the DC plan member with a cohort that has a similar target retirement date.

Passive management A buy-and-hold approach to investing in which an investor does not make portfolio changes based upon short-term expectations of changing market or security performance.

Percent-range rebalancing An approach to rebalancing that involves setting rebalancing thresholds or trigger points, stated as a percentage of the portfolio's value, around target values.

Performance attribution The process of disaggregating a portfolio's return to determine the drivers of its performance.

Personal assets Nonbusiness, on-investment assets including personal property and real property.

Personal property Property owned by individuals that are not real property and not considered investments.

Planned goals Financial objectives that can be reasonably estimated or quantified at the onset and can be achieved within an expected time horizon.

Position delta The overall or portfolio delta. For example, the position delta of a covered call, consisting of long 100 shares and short one at-the-money call, is +50 (= +100 for the shares and -50 for the short ATM call).

Positive screening An ESG implementation approach that seeks to identify the most favorable companies and sectors based on ESG considerations. Also called *best-in-class*.

Price improvement When trade execution prices are better than quoted prices.

Private wealth management Financial planning and investment management to help individual investors, particularly high-net-worth individuals (HNWIs) and ultra-high-net-worth individuals (UHNWIs), manage their wealth.

Protective put A strategy of purchasing an underlying asset and purchasing a put on the same asset.

Pure indexing Attempts to replicate a bond index as closely as possible, targeting zero active return and zero active risk.

Put spread A strategy used to reduce the upfront cost of buying a protective put, it involves buying a put option and writing another put option.

Re-base With reference to index construction, to change the time period used as the base of the index.

Realized volatility Historical volatility, the square root of the realized variance of returns, which is a measure of the range of past price outcomes for the underlying asset.

Rebalancing Adjusting the weights of the constituent securities in an index.

Rebalancing range A range of values for asset class weights defined by trigger points above and below target weights, such that if the portfolio value passes through a trigger point, rebalancing occurs. Also known as a corridor.

Rebate rate The portion of the collateral earnings rate that is repaid to the security borrower by the security lender.

Reduced form models Statistical credit models that solve for the probability of default over a specific time period, using observable company-specific and market-based variables.

Regime The governing set of relationships (between variables) that stem from technological, political, legal, and regulatory environments. Changes in such environments or policy stances can be described as changes in regime.

Relative value A concept that describes the selection of the most attractive individual securities to populate the portfolio with, using ranking and comparing.

Repo rate The interest rate on a repurchase agreement.

Repurchase agreements In repurchase agreements, or repos, a security owner agrees to sell a security for a specific cash amount while simultaneously agreeing to repurchase the security at a specified future date (typically one day later) and price.

Reserve portfolio The component of an insurer's general account that is subject to specific regulatory requirements and is intended to ensure the company's ability to meet its policy liabilities. The assets in the reserve portfolio are managed conservatively and must be highly liquid and low risk.

Resistance levels Price points on dealers' order boards where one would expect to see a clustering of offers.

Return attribution A set of techniques used to identify the sources of the excess return of a portfolio against its benchmark.

Returns-based attribution An attribution approach that uses only the total portfolio returns over a period to identify the components of the investment process that have generated the returns. The Brinson–Hood–Beebower approach is a returns-based attribution approach.

Returns-based benchmarks Benchmarks constructed by examining a portfolio's sensitivity to a set of factors, such as the returns for various style indexes (e.g., small-cap value, small-cap growth, large-cap value, and large-cap growth).

Returns-based style analysis A top-down style analysis that involves estimating the sensitivities of a portfolio to security market indexes.

Reverse repos Repurchase agreements from the standpoint of the lender.

Risk attribution The analysis of the sources of risk.

Risk aversion The dislike for risk such that compensation is required in terms of higher expected returns for assuming higher risk.

Risk budgeting The establishment of objectives for individuals, groups, or divisions of an organization that takes into account the allocation of an acceptable level of risk.

Risk capacity The ability to bear financial risk.

Risk premiums Extra returns expected by investors for bearing some specified risk.

Risk reversal A strategy used to profit from the existence of an implied volatility skew and from changes in its shape over time. A combination of long (short) calls and short (long) puts on the same underlying with the same expiration is a long (short) risk reversal.

Risk tolerance The level of risk an investor is willing and able to bear.

Seagull spread An extension of the risk reversal foreign exchange option strategy that limits downside risk.

Securities lending A form of collateralized lending that may be used to generate income for portfolios.

Selective An index construction methodology that targets only those securities with certain characteristics.

Separate accounts Accounts holding assets to fund future liabilities from variable life insurance and variable annuities, the products in which customers make investment decisions from a menu of options and themselves bear investment risk.

Sharpe ratio The ratio of mean excess return to standard deviation (excess return).

Shortfall probability The probability of failing to meet a specific liability or goal.

Shrinkage estimation Estimation that involves taking a weighted average of a historical estimate of a parameter and some other parameter estimate, where the weights reflect the analyst's relative belief in the estimates.

Special dividends Dividends paid by a company that does not pay dividends on a regular schedule, or dividends that supplement regular cash dividends with an extra payment.

Spread duration The change in bond price for a given change in yield spread. Also referred to as OAS duration when the option-adjusted spread (OAS) is the yield measure used.

Static hedge A hedge that is not sensitive to changes in the price of the asset hedged.

Stock lending Securities lending involving the transfer of equities.

Stops Stop-loss orders involve leaving bids or offers away from the current market price to be filled if the market reaches those levels.

Straddle An option combination in which one buys *both* puts and calls, with the same exercise price and same expiration date, on the same underlying asset. In contrast to this long straddle, if someone *writes* both options, it is a short straddle.

Strangle A variation on a straddle in which the put and call have different exercise prices; if the put and call are held long, it is a long strangle; if they are held short, it is a short strangle.

Strategic asset allocation A long-term strategy that establishes target allocations for various asset classes and aims to optimize the balance between risk and reward by diversifying investments.

Structural models Models that specify functional relationships among variables based on economic theory. The functional form and parameters of these models are derived from the underlying theory. They may include unobservable parameters.

Support levels Price points on dealers' order boards where one would expect to see a clustering of bids.

Surplus The difference between assets and liabilities, analogous to shareholders' equity on a corporate balance sheet.

Surplus portfolio The component of an insurer's general account that is intended to realize higher expected returns than the reserve portfolio and so can assume some liquidity risk. Surplus portfolio assets are often managed aggressively with exposure to alternative assets.

Survivorship bias Relates to the inclusion of only current investment funds in a database. As such, the returns of funds that are no longer available in the marketplace (have been liquidated) are excluded from the database. Also see *backfill bias.*

Synthetic long forward position The combination of a long call and a short put with identical strike price and expiration, traded at the same time on the same underlying.

Synthetic short forward position The combination of a short call and a long put at the same strike price and maturity (traded at the same time on the same underlying).

Tactical asset allocation A proactive strategy that adjusts asset class allocations within a portfolio based on short-term market trends, economic conditions, or valuation changes to capitalize on temporary market inefficiencies or opportunities to improve returns or manage risk more effectively.

Tax drag The negative effect of taxes on an investment's net returns.

Taylor rule A rule linking a central bank's target short-term interest rate to the rate of growth of the economy and inflation.

Term deposits Interest-bearing accounts that have a specified maturity date. This category includes savings accounts and certificates of deposit (CDs). Also see *time deposits.*

Term structure of volatility The plot of implied volatility (y-axis) against option maturity (x-axis) for options with the same strike price on the same underlying. Typically, implied volatility is not constant across different maturities – rather, it is often in contango, meaning that the implied volatilities for longer-term options are higher than for near-term ones.

Thematic investing An investment approach that focuses on companies in a specific sector or following a specific theme, such as energy efficiency or climate change.

Theta The change in a derivative instrument for a given small change in calendar time, holding everything else constant. Specifically, the theta calculation assumes nothing changes except calendar time. Theta also reflects the rate at which an option's time value decays.

Threshold-based rebalancing policy The manager rebalances the portfolio when asset class weights deviate from their target weights by a prespecified percentage regardless of timing and frequency.

Time deposits Interest-bearing accounts that have a specified maturity date. This category includes savings accounts and certificates of deposit (CDs). Also see *term deposits.*

Time value The difference between an option's premium and its intrinsic value.

Time-based rebalancing policy The manager rebalances the portfolio regularly, at a certain given time interval such as quarterly, semi-annually, or annually, regardless of any difference between prevailing asset class weights and target asset class weights.

Time-series estimation Estimators that are based on lagged values of the variable being forecast; often consist of lagged values of other selected variables.

Total factor productivity A scale factor that reflects the portion of growth unaccounted for by explicit factor inputs (e.g., capital and labor).

Total return payer Party responsible for paying the reference obligation cash flows and return to the receiver but that is also compensated by the receiver for any depreciation in the index or default losses incurred by the portfolio.

Total return receiver Receives both the cash flows from the underlying index and any appreciation in the index over the period in exchange for paying the MRR plus a predetermined spread.

Tracking risk The standard deviation of the differences between a portfolio's returns and its benchmarks returns. Also called *tracking error.*

Transactions-based attribution An attribution approach that captures the impact of intra-day trades and exogenous events such as a significant class action settlement.

Trigger points In the context of portfolio rebalancing, the endpoints of a rebalancing range (corridor).

Ultra-high-net-worth individuals (UHNWIs) Individuals with net worth usually exceeding USD30 million or more.

Unplanned goals Unforeseen financial needs that are difficult to quantify because either the funding need, the timing of the financial need, or both may not be estimated.

Unsmoothing An adjustment to the reported return series if serial correlation is detected. Various approaches are available to unsmooth a return series.

Variance notional The notional amount of a variance swap; it equals vega notional divided by two times the volatility strike price [i.e., (vega notional)/(2 × volatility strike)].

Vega A measure of the sensitivity of an option's price to changes in the underlying's volatility.

Vega notional The trade size for a variance swap, which represents the average profit and loss of the variance swap for a 1% change in volatility from the strike.

Vesting The process of an employee becoming unconditionally entitled to, and an employer becoming obligated to pay, compensation.

Volatility clustering The tendency for large (small) swings in prices to be followed by large (small) swings of random direction.

Volatility skew The skewed plot (of implied volatility (y-axis) against strike price (x-axis) for options on the same underlying with the same expiration) that occurs when the implied volatility increases for OTM puts and decreases for OTM calls, as the strike price moves away from the current price.

Volatility smile The U-shaped plot (of implied volatility (y-axis) against strike price (x-axis) for options on the same underlying with the same expiration) that occurs when the implied volatilities priced into both OTM puts and calls trade at a premium to implied volatilities of ATM options.

Wealth The value of all the assets owned by an individual.

Wealth life cycle Stages of an individual investor's wealth in terms of human capital, financial capital, and economic net worth.

CFA Institute®
CFA Program

PERFORMANCE MEASUREMENT

CFA® Program Curriculum
2026 • LEVEL III CORE • VOLUME 3

WILEY

ISBN 978-1-39436-059-8

May 2025

Please visit our website at
www.WileyGlobalFinance.com.

WILEY

SKYBF5A3ED3-62AF-4A31-B183-3BE73EB8AA76_022825

CONTENTS

How to Use the CFA Program Curriculum

The CFA® Program exams measure your mastery of the core knowledge, skills, and abilities required to succeed as an investment professional. These core competencies are the basis for the Candidate Body of Knowledge (CBOK™). The CBOK consists of four components:

A broad outline that lists the major CFA Program topic areas (www.cfainstitute.org/programs/cfa/curriculum/cbok/cbok)

Topic area weights that indicate the relative exam weightings of the top-level topic areas (www.cfainstitute.org/en/programs/cfa/curriculum)

Learning outcome statements (LOS) that tell you the specific knowledge, skills, and abilities you should gain from each curriculum topic area. You will find these statements at the start of each learning module and lesson. We encourage you to review the information about the LOS on our website (www.cfainstitute.org/programs/cfa/curriculum/study-sessions), including the descriptions of LOS "command words" on the candidate resources page at www.cfainstitute.org/-/media/documents/support/programs/cfa-and-cipm-los-command-words.ashx.

The CFA Program curriculum that candidates receive access to upon exam registration.

Therefore, the key to your success on the CFA exams is studying and understanding the CBOK. You can learn more about the CBOK on our website: www.cfainstitute.org/programs/cfa/curriculum/cbok.

The curriculum, including the practice questions, is the basis for all exam questions. The curriculum is selected/developed specifically to provide candidates with the knowledge, skills, and abilities reflected in the CBOK.

CFA INSTITUTE LEARNING ECOSYSTEM (LES)

Your exam registration fee includes access to the CFA Institute Learning Ecosystem (LES). This digital learning platform provides access to all the curriculum content and practice questions. The LES is organized as a series of learning modules consisting of short online lessons and associated practice questions. This tool is your source for all study materials, including practice questions and mock exams. The LES is the primary method by which CFA Institute delivers your curriculum experience. Here, you will find additional practice questions to test your knowledge, including some interactive questions.

DESIGNING YOUR PERSONAL STUDY PROGRAM

An orderly, systematic approach to exam preparation is critical. You should dedicate a consistent block of time every week to reading and studying. Review the LOS both before and after you study curriculum content to ensure you can demonstrate

the knowledge, skills, and abilities described by the LOS and the assigned learning module. Use the LOS as a self-check to track your progress and highlight areas of weakness for later review.

Successful candidates report an average of more than 300 hours preparing for each exam. Your preparation time will vary based on your prior education and experience, and you will likely spend more time on some topics than on others.

ERRATA

The curriculum development process is rigorous and involves multiple rounds of reviews by content experts. Despite our efforts to produce a curriculum that is free of errors, we must make corrections in some instances. Curriculum errata are periodically updated and posted by exam level and test date on the Curriculum Errata webpage (www.cfainstitute.org/en/programs/submit-errata). If you believe you have found an error in the curriculum, you can submit your concerns through our curriculum errata reporting process found at the bottom of the Curriculum Errata webpage.

OTHER FEEDBACK

Please send any comments or suggestions to info@cfainstitute.org, and we will review your feedback thoughtfully.

Performance Measurement

LEARNING MODULE

1

Portfolio Performance Evaluation

by Marc A. Wright, CFA, and Charles Mitchell Conover, CFA, CIPM.

Marc A. Wright, CFA, is at Russell Investments (USA). Charles Mitchell Conover, CFA, CIPM, is at the University of Richmond (USA).

LEARNING OUTCOMES

Mastery	*The candidate should be able to:*
☐	explain the following components of portfolio evaluation and their interrelationships: performance measurement, performance attribution, and performance appraisal
☐	describe attributes of an effective attribution process
☐	contrast return attribution and risk attribution; contrast macro and micro return attribution
☐	describe returns-based, holdings-based, and transactions-based performance attribution, including advantages and disadvantages of each
☐	interpret the sources of portfolio returns using a specified attribution approach
☐	interpret the output from fixed-income attribution analyses
☐	discuss considerations in selecting a risk attribution approach
☐	identify and interpret investment results attributable to the asset owner versus those attributable to the investment manager
☐	discuss uses of liability-based benchmarks
☐	describe types of asset-based benchmarks
☐	discuss tests of benchmark quality
☐	describe the impact of benchmark misspecification on attribution and appraisal analysis
☐	describe problems that arise in benchmarking alternative investments

LEARNING OUTCOMES

Mastery	The candidate should be able to:
☐	calculate and interpret the Sortino ratio, the appraisal ratio, upside/downside capture ratios, maximum drawdown, and drawdown duration
☐	describe limitations of appraisal measures and related metrics
☐	evaluate the skill of an investment manager

1 INTRODUCTION

Performance evaluation is one of the most critical areas of investment analysis. Performance results can be used to assess the quality of the investment approach and suggest changes that might improve it. They are also used to communicate the results of the investment process to other stakeholders and may even be used to compensate the investment managers. Therefore, it is of vital importance that practitioners who use these analyses understand how the results are generated. By gaining an understanding of the details of how these analyses work, practitioners will develop a greater understanding of the insights that might be gathered from the analysis and will also be cognizant of the limitations of those approaches, careful not to infer more than what is explicit or logically implicit in the results.

We will first consider the broad categories of performance measurement, attribution, and appraisal, differentiating between the three and explaining their interrelationships. Next, we will provide practitioners with tools to evaluate the effectiveness of those analyses as we summarize various approaches to performance evaluation. We will cover returns-based, holdings-based, and transactions-based attribution, addressing the merits and shortcomings of each approach and providing guidance on how to properly interpret attribution results. Again, by reviewing how each approach generates its results, we reveal strengths and weaknesses of the individual attribution approaches.

Next, we will turn to the subject of benchmarks and performance appraisal ratios. We will review the long-standing tests of benchmark quality and differentiate market indexes from benchmarks. We will also review different ratios used in performance appraisal, considering the benefits and limitations of each approach.

Lastly, we will provide advice on using these tools to collectively evaluate the skill of investment managers. This advice relies heavily on understanding the analysis tools, the limitations of the approaches, the importance of data to the quality of the analysis, and the pitfalls to avoid when making recommendations.

PERFORMANCE EVALUATION AND ATTRIBUTION 2

- ☐ explain the following components of portfolio evaluation and their interrelationships: performance measurement, performance attribution, and performance appraisal
- ☐ describe attributes of an effective attribution process
- ☐ contrast return attribution and risk attribution; contrast macro and micro return attribution
- ☐ describe returns-based, holdings-based, and transactions-based performance attribution, including advantages and disadvantages of each

Performance evaluation includes three primary components, each corresponding to a specific question we need to answer to evaluate a portfolio's performance:

- Performance measurement—what was the portfolio's performance?
- Performance attribution—how was the performance achieved?
- Performance appraisal—was the performance achieved through manager skill or luck?

We will consider each of these components on their own and the interrelationships between them.

Performance measurement provides an overall indication of the portfolio's performance, typically relative to a benchmark. In its simplest form, performance measurement is the calculation of investment returns for both the portfolio and its benchmark. This return calculation is a critical first step in the performance evaluation process, building the foundation on which performance evaluation is based. The investment return tells us what the portfolio achieved over a specific period, irrespective of peer or benchmark performance. For purposes of this reading, we will call this the *absolute return*. But it also provides the basis to understand the difference between the portfolio return and its benchmark return, the **excess return**.

In addition to return, performance measurement must consider the risk incurred to achieve that return. We measure risk using a variety of *ex post* (looking back in time) and *ex ante* (looking forward in time) techniques. For *ex post*, we might consider the volatility or standard deviation of the past returns, along with many other performance appraisal ratios considered later in this reading. The calculation of a portfolio's value at risk (VaR) at a point in time is an example of an *ex ante* measure. These measures of risk allow us to quantify the risk in a portfolio and better assess the performance.

Performance attribution then builds on the foundation of the investment returns and risk, helping us explain *how* that performance was achieved or that risk was incurred. Performance attribution can be used to explain either absolute returns or relative returns. It can be used to understand what portion of returns was driven by active manager decisions and what portion was a result of exposures not specifically targeted by the portfolio manager. Performance attribution can also be used to decompose the excess return into its component sources, where it is used to help explain why a manager over- or underperformed the target benchmark. Similarly, risk attribution can be used to decompose the risk incurred in the portfolio.

The third component of performance evaluation, performance appraisal, makes use of risk, return, and attribution analyses to draw conclusions regarding the *quality* of a portfolio's performance. Performance appraisal attempts to distinguish manager skill from luck. Did the portfolio manager's decisions help achieve a better outcome, or was the outcome due to market changes outside of the manager's control? If superior results can be attributed to skill, there is a higher likelihood that the manager will generate superior performance in the future. The analysis may affirm the management process or may contain insights for improving the process. This is a key feedback loop in the investment management process.

EXAMPLE 1

Performance Evaluation

1. Performance attribution:

   A. measures the excess performance of a portfolio.

   B. explains the proportion of returns due to manager skill.

   C. explains how the excess performance or risk was achieved.

Solution:

C is correct. Performance attribution identifies the drivers of investment returns. A is not correct because measuring the excess performance of a portfolio is the subject of performance measurement. B is not correct because it is performance appraisal that distinguishes skill from luck.

2. Performance appraisal:

   A. identifies the sources of under- or outperformance.

   B. decomposes a portfolio's risk and return into their constituent parts.

   C. uses the results of risk, return, and attribution analyses to assess the quality of a portfolio's performance.

Solution:

C is correct. Performance appraisal combines all the techniques of performance measurement and attribution to assess the quality of performance. Both A and B describe performance attribution.

Performance Attribution

As previously described, performance attribution is a critical component of the portfolio evaluation process. Used by senior management, client relationship specialists, risk controllers, operations staff, portfolio managers, and sales and marketing professionals, attribution analysis provides important insights to the investment decision-making process. Clients and prospects also use attribution analysis as part of their evaluation of that process. Effective performance attribution analysis requires a thorough understanding of the investment decision-making process and should reflect the active decisions of the portfolio manager.

An effective performance attribution process must

- account for *all* of the portfolio's return or risk exposure,
- reflect the investment decision-making process,
- quantify the active decisions of the portfolio manager, and
- provide a complete understanding of the excess return/risk of the portfolio.

If the return or risk quantified by the attribution analysis does not account for all the return or risk presented to the client, then at best the attribution is incomplete and at worst the quality of the attribution analysis is brought into doubt. If the attribution does not reflect the investment decision-making process, then the analysis will be of little value to either the portfolio manager or the client. For example, if the portfolio manager is a genuine bottom-up stock picker who ignores sector benchmark weights, then measuring the impact of sector allocation against these weights is not measuring decisions made as part of the investment process; sector effects are merely a byproduct of the manager's investment decisions.

Performance attribution includes return attribution and risk attribution (although in practice, "performance attribution" is often used to mean "return attribution"). **Return attribution** analyzes the impact of active investment decisions on *returns*; **risk attribution** analyzes the *risk* consequences of those decisions. Depending on the purpose of the analysis, risk may be viewed in absolute or benchmark-relative terms. For example, when risk relative to a benchmark is the focus, a risk attribution analysis might identify and evaluate a portfolio's deviations from a benchmark's exposures to risk factors.

Performance attribution provides a good starting point for a conversation with clients, explaining both positive and negative aspects of recent performance. Return attribution analysis is particularly important when performance is weak; portfolio managers must demonstrate an understanding of their performance, provide a rationale for their decisions, and generate confidence in their ability to add value in the future. When it accurately reflects the investment decision-making process, return attribution provides quality control for the investment process and provides senior management with a tool to manage a complex business with multiple investment strategies.

The attribution process described earlier—understanding the drivers of a manager's returns and whether those drivers are consistent with the stated investment process—is a common application of attribution analysis. But attribution can also be conducted to evaluate the asset owner's tactical asset allocation and manager selection decisions (called **macro attribution**) or to evaluate the impact of the portfolio manager's decisions on the performance of the asset owner's total fund (called **micro attribution**). A defined-benefit pension plan makes the decision to allocate a given percentage of the fund to each asset class and decides which manager(s) to hire for each asset class. Macro attribution measures the effect of the sponsor's choice to deviate from the strategic asset allocation, including the effect of "gaps" between the strategic asset allocation and its implementation (e.g., where the sum of the managers' benchmarks is equal to something other than the benchmark index).

Micro attribution measures the impact of portfolio managers' allocation and selection decisions on total fund performance.

Performance attribution may be either returns based, holdings based, or transactions based. The decision to use one set of inputs rather than another depends on the availability of data as well as the investment process being measured.

Returns-based attribution uses only the total portfolio returns over a period to identify the components of the investment process that have generated the returns. Returns-based attribution is most appropriate when the underlying portfolio holding information is not available with sufficient frequency at the required level of detail. For example, one might use returns-based attribution to evaluate hedge funds, because it can be difficult to obtain the underlying holdings of hedge funds. Returns-based attribution is the easiest method to implement, but because it does not use the underlying holdings, it is the least accurate of the three approaches and the most vulnerable to data manipulation.

Unlike returns-based attribution, **holdings-based attribution** references the beginning-of-period holdings of the portfolio. Calculated with monthly, weekly, or daily data, the accuracy of holdings-based attribution improves when using data with shorter time intervals. For longer evaluation periods, we link together the attribution results for the shorter measurement periods. Because holdings-based attribution fails to capture the impact of any transactions made during the measurement period, it may not reconcile to the actual portfolio return. For example, in a daily holdings-based attribution, securities are included at the end of the day they are purchased and excluded at the end of the day they are sold. If the transaction price is significantly different from the closing price, the attribution analysis can differ significantly from the actual performance.

The residual caused by ignoring transactions might be described as a timing or trading effect. Holdings-based analysis is most appropriate for investment strategies with little turnover (e.g., passive strategies). Holdings-based analysis may be improved by valuing the portfolio with the same prices used to calculate the underlying benchmark index, removing one potential difference between the portfolio and benchmark returns that is not a management effect.

The third approach, **transactions-based attribution**, uses both the holdings of the portfolio and the transactions (purchases and sales) that occurred during the evaluation period. For transaction-based attribution, both the weights and returns reflect *all transactions* during the period, including transaction costs. Transaction-based attribution is the most accurate type of attribution analysis but also the most difficult and time-consuming to implement. To obtain meaningful results, the underlying data must be complete, accurate, and reconciled from period to period. Because all the data are available, the entire excess return can be quantified and explained. The return used in the attribution analysis will reconcile with the return presented to the client, and attribution analysis can be used as a diagnostic tool to identify errors.

The choice of attribution approach depends on the availability and quality of the underlying data, the reporting requirements for the client, and the complexity of the investment decision-making process.

EXAMPLE 2

Performance Attribution

1. Effective attribution analysis must:

   A. use intraday transaction data.

   B. reconcile to the total portfolio return or risk exposure.

   C. measure the contribution of security and sector selection decisions.

Solution:

B is correct. An effective attribution process accounts for all of the portfolio's return or risk exposure. A is not correct; an attribution analysis is improved with intraday transaction data, but an effective attribution analysis can be produced with a returns- or holdings-based approach. C is not correct because an attribution process that measures the sector selection effects of a bottom-up stock-picker does not measure the effectiveness of the investment decision-making process.

2. Which of the following most accurately describes macro attribution?

   A. Attribution analysis at the portfolio level

   B. Attribution analysis of the fund sponsor decisions

   C. Attribution analysis of asset allocation decisions

Solution:

B is correct. Macro attribution measures the effect of the sponsor's choice to deviate from the strategic asset allocation and the sponsor's manager selection decisions. A is not correct because attribution analysis at the portfolio level may be either macro attribution or micro attribution. C is not correct because macro attribution measures both asset allocation and manager selection decisions of the asset owner.

3. Risk attribution differs from return attribution in that it:

   A. is not conducted relative to a benchmark.

   B. quantifies the risk consequences of the investment decisions.

   C. quantifies the investment decisions of the investment manager.

Solution:

B is correct. Risk attribution, unlike return attribution, attempts to quantify the risk consequences of the investment decisions. A is not correct because risk attribution may be conducted on either an absolute or a relative basis. C is not correct because risk attribution does not capture the return impact of a manager's investment decisions.

4. An analyst is *most likely* to use returns-based attribution when:

   A. the portfolio has a low turnover.

   B. the holdings for the portfolio are not available.

   C. she wants the analysis to be as accurate as possible.

Solution:

B is correct. Returns-based attribution is typically used when the holdings data are not available. Neither A nor C is correct because returns-based attribution is the least accurate of the three approaches.

RETURN ATTRIBUTION 3

☐ interpret the sources of portfolio returns using a specified attribution approach

Return attribution allows us to look across a specific time horizon and identify which investment decisions have either added value to or detracted value from the portfolio, relative to its benchmark. As feedback to the portfolio management process, return attribution quantifies the active decisions of portfolio managers and informs management and clients. In this way, return attribution can be thought of as "backward looking" or *ex post,* meaning that it is used to evaluate the investment decisions for some historical time horizon.

Return attribution is a set of techniques used to identify the sources of excess return of a portfolio against its benchmark, quantifying the consequences of active investment decisions.

Specific return attribution approaches have been designed to evaluate particular types of assets. In this section, we will consider two common approaches for equity attribution: Brinson–Fachler and factor-based attribution. We will also review the output and findings from a typical fixed-income attribution approach.

Practitioners may also encounter the concept of geometric attribution and arithmetic attribution, two approaches to measuring attribution effects over longer periods. **Arithmetic attribution** approaches are designed to explain the **excess return**, the arithmetic difference between the portfolio return, R, and its benchmark return, B.

When using an arithmetic attribution approach, the attribution effects will sum to the excess return. Arithmetic approaches are straightforward for a single period, for which there is no difference between the sum of the attribution effects and the excess return. However, when combining multiple periods, the sub-period attribution effects will *not* sum to the excess return. Because the excess return is calculated by *geometrically* linking the sub-period returns, adjustments must be made to "smooth" the *arithmetic* sub-period attribution effects over time. Multiple smoothing approaches exist in the industry, including algorithms suggested by David Cariño (1999) and Jose Menchero (2000).

Geometric attribution approaches extend the arithmetic approaches by attributing the geometric excess return (G), as defined below:

$$G = \frac{1+R}{1+B} - 1 = \frac{R-B}{1+B}$$

Note that the geometric excess return is simply the arithmetic excess return divided by the wealth ratio of the benchmark (1 plus the return on the benchmark during the period).

In a geometric attribution approach, the attribution effects will compound (multiply) together to total the geometric excess return. Because the attribution effects compound together to exactly equal the geometric excess return, the compounding works across multiple periods. Therefore, no smoothing is required to adjust the geometric attribution effects across multiple periods.

Practitioners typically choose arithmetic attribution approaches when they want to use the attribution analysis with non-practitioner clients or in marketing reports. With results that add up to the total excess return for all periods, arithmetic approaches are more intuitively understood. Geometric approaches tend to be limited to practitioners who understand the approach and who appreciate that they do not have to adjust the attribution effects over time.

A Simple Return Attribution Example

Suppose a portfolio's return for the past year was 5.24% and the portfolio's benchmark return for that same period was 3.24%. In this case, the portfolio achieved a positive arithmetic excess return of 2.00% (5.24% – 3.24% = 2.00%) over the past year.

To understand how the 2.00% was achieved, we apply return attribution. In this example, return attribution will quantify two typical sources of excess return: *security selection* and *asset allocation*. Security selection answers the question, Was the return achieved by selecting securities that performed well relative to the benchmark or by avoiding benchmark securities that performed relatively poorly? Asset allocation answers the question, Was the return achieved by choosing to overweight an asset category (e.g., economic sector or currency) that outperformed the total benchmark or to underweight an asset category that underperformed the total benchmark? (The term "allocation" is used somewhat differently here. It is not measuring the plan sponsor's asset allocation decision but, rather, the *manager's* decision to allocate among countries, sectors, or, in cases where the manager has a broad mandate, asset classes.)

Models of equity return attribution often attempt to separate the investment process into those two key decisions—selection and allocation—assigning each a magnitude and direction (plus or minus) for both decisions. For instance, for the portfolio referenced previously, we might calculate the return attribution results shown in Exhibit 1:

Exhibit 1: Total Portfolio Return Attribution Analysis (Time Period: Past 12 Months)

Portfolio Return	Benchmark Return	Excess Return	Allocation Effect	Selection Effect
5.24%	3.24%	2.00%	−0.50%	2.50%

As we noted, the investment decisions generated a positive excess return of 200 basis points (bps) relative to the benchmark. We use the "return attribution analysis" to see how this 200 bps was generated. First, note that the *negative* allocation effect indicates that the allocation decisions over the past 12 months, whatever they were, had a negative impact on the total portfolio performance. They *subtracted* 50 bps from the excess return. In contrast, the *positive* selection effect indicates that the security selection decisions—decisions to overweight or underweight securities relative to their benchmark weights—*added* 250 bps to the excess return. Our return attribution analysis implies that the portfolio manager's security selection decision was far superior to his or her asset allocation decision for the past 12 months.

Equity Return Attribution—The Brinson–Hood–Beebower Model

The foundations of return attribution were established in two articles, one written by Brinson and Fachler (1985) and the other by Brinson, Hood, and Beebower (1986). The Brinson–Fachler model is more widely used in performance attribution today, but we introduce the Brinson–Hood–Beebower (BHB) model first to lay an important foundation.

BHB is built on the assumption that the total portfolio and benchmark returns are calculated by summing the weights and returns of the sectors within the portfolio (Equation 1) and the benchmark (Equation 2):

$$\text{Portfolio return } R = \sum_{i=1}^{i=n} w_i R_i \tag{1}$$

$$\text{Benchmark return } B = \sum_{i=1}^{i=n} W_i B_i \tag{2}$$

where

w_i = weight of the *i*th sector in the portfolio

R_i = return of the portfolio assets in the *i*th sector

W_i = weight of the *i*th sector in the benchmark

B_i = return of the benchmark in the *i*th sector

n = number of sectors or securities

The sum of the weights in both the portfolio and the benchmark must equal 100%. The presence of leverage would require a position with a negative weight (borrowings or short positions) to balance to 100%.

Attribution analysis quantifies each of the portfolio manager's active decisions that explain the difference between the portfolio return, R, and the benchmark return, B. Note that for this example, we are concerned with only single-period, single-currency return attribution models.

Exhibit 2 provides data for a three-sector domestic equity portfolio, used to illustrate the BHB model.

Exhibit 2: BHB Model Illustration—Portfolio and Benchmark Data

Sector	Portfolio Weight	Benchmark Weight	Portfolio Return	Benchmark Return
Energy	50%	50%	18%	10%
Health care	30%	20%	−3%	−2%
Financials	20%	30%	10%	12%
Total	**100%**	**100%**	**10.1%**	**8.2%**

Total portfolio return $R = (50\% \times 18\%) + (30\% \times -3\%) + (20\% \times 10\%) = 10.1\%$

Total benchmark return $B = (50\% \times 10\%) + (20\% \times -2\%) + (30\% \times 12\%) = 8.2\%$

Thus, the excess return is 1.9% (10.1% – 8.2% = 1.9%), or 190 bps.

We will use the weights and returns data shown in Exhibit 2 to calculate the basic attribution effects using the BHB model, including the allocation effect, the security selection effect, and the interaction effect. The allocation effect refers to the value the portfolio manager adds (or subtracts) by having portfolio sector weights that are different from the benchmark sector weights. A sector weight in the portfolio greater than the benchmark sector weight would be described as *overweight*, and a sector weight less than the benchmark sector weight would be described as *underweight*.

To calculate allocation, we first calculate the contribution to allocation (A_i) for each sector. The contribution to allocation in the ith sector is equal to the portfolio's sector weight minus the benchmark's sector weight, times the benchmark sector return:

$$A_i = (w_i - W_i)B_i \tag{3}$$

Using the data from Exhibit 2, we calculate individual sector allocation effects as follows:

- Energy: (50% – 50%) × 10% = 0.0%
- Health care: (30% – 20%) × –2.0% = –0.2%
- Financials: (20% – 30%) × 12% = –1.2%

To find the total portfolio allocation effect, A, we sum the individual sector contributions to allocation:

$$A = \sum_{i=1}^{i=n} A_i \tag{4}$$

Total allocation effect = 0.0% − 0.2% − 1.2% = −1.4%

We can then use the results to state the following conclusions:

- The portfolio weight in the energy sector is equal to the benchmark weight; therefore, there is no contribution to allocation in energy.

- In health care, the portfolio manager held a higher weight than the benchmark (30% versus 20%), but the sector underperformed the aggregate benchmark (−2.0% versus 8.2%). Therefore, the decision to overweight health care lowered the overall excess return; the contribution to allocation is −0.2%.
- In financials, the portfolio manager chose to underweight versus the benchmark (20% versus 30%). But because financials outperformed the aggregate benchmark (12% versus 8.2%), the decision to underweight financials also lowered the overall excess return; the contribution to allocation is −1.2%.
- Overall, the combined allocation effect for this portfolio was −1.4%, demonstrating that the weighting decisions negatively contributed to the performance of the portfolio.

The other attribution effect in the BHB model is security selection—the value the portfolio manager adds by holding individual securities or instruments within the sector in different-from-benchmark weights.

To calculate selection, we first calculate the contribution to selection (S_i) for each sector. The contribution to selection in the *i*th sector is equal to the benchmark sector weight times the portfolio's sector return minus the benchmark's sector return.

$$S_i = W_i(R_i - B_i) \tag{5}$$

Using the data from Exhibit 2, we calculate individual sector selection effects as follows:

- Energy: 50% × (18% − 10%) = 4.0%
- Health care: 20% × (−3% − −2.0%) = −0.2%
- Financials: 30% × (10% − 12%) = −0.6%

To find the total portfolio selection effect, *S*, we sum the individual sector contributions to selection:

$$S = \sum_{i=1}^{i=n} S_i \tag{6}$$

Total selection effect = 4.0% + −0.2% + −0.6% = 3.2%

We can use the results to state the following conclusions:

- The portfolio's energy sector outperformed the benchmark's energy sector by 800 bps (18% − 10%); 800 bps times the benchmark weight of 50% for this sector results in a 4.0% contribution to selection.
- The portfolio's health care sector underperformed the benchmark's health care sector by 100 bps [(−3%) − (−2%)]; 100 bps times the benchmark weight of 20% for this sector results in a contribution of −0.2%.
- The portfolio's financials sector underperformed the benchmark's financials sector by 200 bps (10% − 12%); 200 bps times the benchmark weight of 30% to this sector results in a contribution of −0.6%.
- Overall, the combined selection effect for this portfolio was 3.2%.

In the BHB model, selection and allocation do not completely explain the arithmetic difference. For example, in the attribution analysis based on Exhibit 2, allocation (−1.4%) and selection (3.2%) together represent just 1.8% of the arithmetic difference between the portfolio return of 10.1% and the benchmark return of 8.2%; 0.1% is missing. To explain this remaining difference in the excess return, the BHB model uses a third attribution effect, called "interaction." The **interaction effect** is the effect resulting from the interaction of the allocation and selection decisions combined.

To calculate interaction, we first calculate the contribution to interaction for each sector. The contribution to interaction in the ith sector is equal to the portfolio sector weight minus the benchmark sector weight, times the portfolio sector return minus the benchmark sector return:

$$I_i = (w_i - W_i)(R_i - B_i) \quad (7)$$

Using the data from Exhibit 2, we calculate individual sector selection effects as follows:

- Energy: (50% – 50%) × (18% – 10%) = 0.0%
- Health care: (30% – 20%) × (–3% – –2.0%) = –0.1%
- Financials: (20% – 30%) × (10% – 12%) = 0.2%

To find the total portfolio interaction effect, we sum the individual sector contributions to interaction:

$$I = \sum_{i=1}^{i=n} I_i \quad (8)$$

Total interaction effect = 0.0% + –0.1% + 0.2% = 0.1%

We can use the results to state the following conclusions:

- For the energy sector, the portfolio weight equals the benchmark weight and thus there is no contribution to interaction.
- Because the manager had an overweight to a sector in which selection was negative, the contribution from interaction in health care was also negative, –0.1%.
- In the financials sector, the manager was underweight by 10% and selection was negative. The effect of being underweight in a sector in which the manager underperforms leads to a contribution from interaction of +0.2%.
- Total contribution from interaction is +0.1%, representing the combined effect of the interaction of the selection and allocation effects.

EXAMPLE 3

Interpreting the Results of a BHB Attribution

BHB Attribution Analysis Results Table

Region	Portfolio Return	Benchmark Return	Portfolio Weight	Benchmark Weight	Allocation	Selection	Inter-action	Total
Americas	2.80%	1.20%	30%	30%	0.00%	0.48%	0.00%	0.48%
APAC	–1.50%	–0.50%	20%	30%	0.05%	–0.30%	0.10%	–0.15%
EMEA	0.70%	1.50%	50%	40%	0.15%	–0.32%	–0.08%	–0.25%
Total	**0.89%**	**0.81%**	**100%**	**100%**	**0.20%**	**–0.14%**	**0.02%**	**0.08%**

Use the table above to answer the following questions.

1. Why is the contribution to selection for Europe, the Middle East, and Africa (EMEA) negative?

   A. The total benchmark return is less than the total portfolio return.

   B. The manager selected securities in EMEA that underperformed the benchmark.

C. The manager underweighted an outperforming sector.

Solution:

B is correct. The manager selected securities that underperformed the benchmark, with a portfolio return for EMEA of 0.7% versus a benchmark return for EMEA of 1.5%.

2. Why is the contribution to allocation for Asia Pacific (APAC) equal to +5 bps?

   A. The benchmark weight and the portfolio weight are equal.

   B. The manager has an overweight position in an overperforming region.

   C. The manager has an underweight position in an underperforming region.

Solution:

C is correct. The manager is underweight in APAC, 20% versus a benchmark weight of 30%. The APAC portion of the portfolio underperformed, with a –0.50% benchmark return versus the total benchmark return of 0.81%.

3. Which of the following conclusions from the above attribution analysis is *most* correct?

   A. The manager's security selection decisions were better in the Americas than in APAC.

   B. The manager's security selection decisions were better in EMEA than in APAC.

   C. The manager's allocation decisions were better in APAC than in EMEA.

Solution:

A is correct. As reflected in the contribution to selection, the manager's security selection decisions were better in the Americas (0.48%) than in APAC (–0.30%).

4. Which of the following conclusions from the above attribution analysis is *most* correct?

   A. Overall, the manager made better allocation decisions than selection decisions.

   B. Overall, the manager made better selection decisions than allocation decisions.

   C. Contribution from interaction was most noticeable in the Americas.

Solution:

A is correct. Overall, the manager made better allocation decisions (0.20%) than selection decisions (–0.14%).

Brinson–Fachler Model

The Brinson–Fachler (BF) model differs from the BHB model only in how individual sector allocation effects are calculated.

In the BHB model, all overweight positions in sectors with positive returns will generate positive allocation effects irrespective of the overall benchmark return, whereas all overweight positions in negative markets will generate negative allocation effects. Thus, overweighting a sector i that earns a positive return, $B_i > 0$, results in a positive allocation effect, $A_i = (w_i - W_i)B_i > 0$, even when the sector return is less than the overall benchmark return (i.e., $B_i < B$). When the sector return is negative, $0 > B_i$, overweighting produces a negative allocation effect, $A_i = (w_i - W_i)B_i < 0$.

Clearly, if the portfolio manager is overweight in a negative market that has outperformed the overall benchmark, the effect should be positive.

The BF model solves this problem by modifying the asset allocation factor to compare returns with the overall benchmark as follows:

$$B_S - B = \sum_{i=1}^{i=n} (w_i - W_i)\, B_i = \sum_{i=1}^{i=n} (w_i - W_i)\, (B_i - B) \tag{9}$$

Because $\sum_{i=1}^{i=n} w_i = \sum_{i=1}^{i=n} W_i = 1$, the constant B can be introduced. The contribution to asset allocation in the ith sector is now:

$$A_i = (w_i - W_i)\, (B_i - B) \tag{10}$$

Note that in Equation 10, the allocation effect at the portfolio level, $B_S - B$, is unchanged from the BHB model.

The contribution to arithmetic excess return from sector allocation for the portfolio data shown in Exhibit 2 is $B_S - B = 6.8\% - 8.2\% = -1.4\%$. Revised BF sector allocation effects are calculated for the portfolio data in Exhibit 2 as follows, using $A_i = (w_i - W_i)(B_i - B)$:

Energy	(50% − 50%) × (10% − 8.2%) = 0.0%
Health care	(30% − 20%) × (−2.0% − 8.2%) = −1.02%
Financials	(20% − 30%) × (12% − 8.2%) = −0.38%
Total	0.0% − 1.02% − 0.38% = −1.4%

The impact in health care is much greater. In addition to being overweight in a negative market, which costs −0.2%, the portfolio manager is correctly penalized the opportunity cost of not being invested in the overall market return of 8.2%, generating a further cost of 10% × −8.2% = −0.82% and resulting in a total impact of −1.02%. To describe it another way, the portfolio is 10% overweight in a market that is underperforming the overall market by −10.2% (i.e., −2.0% − 8.2%) and generating a loss of −1.02%

The impact in financials is much smaller. Although being underweight in a positive market cost −1.2%, we must add back the opportunity cost of being invested in the overall market return of 8.2%, generating a contribution of −10% × −8.2% = 0.82% and resulting in a total impact of −0.38%. To describe it another way, the portfolio is 10% underweight in an industry that is outperforming the overall market by 3.8% (i.e., 12.0% − 8.2%), generating a loss of −0.38%. As expected, at the portfolio level, the allocation effect of −1.4% remains the same as that calculated with the BHB model.

The revised attribution effects are summarized in Exhibit 3.

Exhibit 3: BF Return Attribution Results

	Portfolio Weight	Benchmark Weight	Portfolio Return	Benchmark Return	Allocation	Selection	Interaction
Energy	50%	50%	18%	10%	0.0%	4.0%	0.0%
Health care	30%	20%	−3%	−2%	−1.02%	−0.2%	−0.1%

	Portfolio Weight	Benchmark Weight	Portfolio Return	Benchmark Return	Allocation	Selection	Interaction
Financials	20%	30%	10%	12%	−0.38%	−0.6%	0.2%
Total	**100%**	**100%**	**10.1%**	**8.2%**	**−1.4%**	**3.2%**	**0.1%**

EXAMPLE 4

Allocation Using the BF Model

Exhibit 4: Sample Portfolio Data

	Portfolio Weight	Benchmark Weight	Portfolio Return	Benchmark Return
Technology	20%	30%	−11.0%	−10.0%
Telecommunications	30%	40%	−5.0%	−8.0%
Utilities	50%	30%	−8.0%	−5.0%
Total	**100%**	**100%**	**−7.7%**	**−7.7%**

1. Using the BF method, the allocation effect of utilities based on the portfolio data in Exhibit 4 is:

   A. −1.50%.

   B. 0.54%.

   C. 1.35%.

Solution:

B is correct: $(w_i - W_i)(B_i - B)$ = (50% − 30%)(−5.0% + 7.7%) = 0.54%. The portfolio is 20% overweight in a sector outperforming the overall benchmark by 2.7%, therefore contributing 0.54% to the overall allocation effect.

A is incorrect: W_iB_i = 30% × −5.0% = −1.5% is the contribution to the benchmark return from utilities.

C is incorrect: $w_i(B_i - B)$ = 50% × (−5.0% + 7.7%) = +1.35%. Only the portfolio weight of 50% has been used, not the overweight position of 20%.

FACTOR-BASED AND FIXED-INCOME RETURN ATTRIBUTION 4

- ☐ interpret the sources of portfolio returns using a specified attribution approach
- ☐ interpret the output from fixed-income attribution analyses

As we have seen, return attribution allows us to analyze a portfolio's excess return by comparing the accounting information (weights and returns) in the portfolio with the information in the benchmark. The Brinson–Fachler model focuses on security selection, asset allocation, and the interaction of selection and allocation. But what if we want to assess other decisions within the investment process?

Another type of return attribution uses fundamental factor models to decompose the contributions to excess return from *factors*. Fundamental factor analysis allows us to quantify the impact of specific active investment decisions within the portfolio, showing how they add or remove value relative to the benchmark. We want to remove the effects of the market to identify the excess return generated by the active investment decisions. To do that, we return to our definition of excess return: Excess return = $R - B$.

Many different factor models can be used to decompose excess returns. The choice of factor model is driven by which aspects of the investment process you want to measure. One of the factor models commonly used in equity attribution analyses is the Carhart four-factor model, or simply the **Carhart model**, given in Equation 11 (Carhart 1997). The Carhart model explains the excess return on the portfolio in terms of the portfolio's sensitivity to a market index (RMRF), a market-capitalization factor (SMB), a book-value-to-price factor (HML), and a momentum factor (WML).

$$R_p - R_f = a_p + b_{p1}\text{RMRF} + b_{p2}\text{SMB} + b_{p3}\text{HML} + b_{p4}\text{WML} + E_p \quad (11)$$

where

R_p and R_f = the return on the portfolio and the risk-free rate of return, respectively

a_p = "alpha" or return in excess of that expected given the portfolio's level of systematic risk (assuming the four factors capture all systematic risk)

b_p = the sensitivity of the portfolio to the given factor

RMRF = the return on a value-weighted equity index in excess of the one-month T-bill rate

SMB = small minus big, a size (market-capitalization) factor (SMB is the average return on three small-cap portfolios minus the average return on three large-cap portfolios)

HML = high minus low, a value factor (HML is the average return on two high-book-to-market portfolios minus the average return on two low-book-to-market portfolios)

WML = winners minus losers, a momentum factor (WML is the return on a portfolio of the past year's winners minus the return on a portfolio of the past year's losers)

E_p = an error term that represents the portion of the return to the portfolio, p, not explained by the model

By analyzing the results of a factor return attribution analysis, we can identify the investment approach and infer the relative strengths and/or weaknesses of the investment decisions. For example, using the Carhart factor model, we calculate the following results for a hypothetical manager.

Exhibit 5: Sample Carhart Factor Model Attribution

	Factor Sensitivity				Contribution to Active Return	
	Portfolio	Benchmark	Difference	Factor Return	Absolute	Proportion of Total
Factor	(1)	(2)	(3)	(4)	(3) × (4)	Active
RMRF	0.95	1.00	−0.05	5.52%	−0.28%	−13.30%
SMB	−1.05	−1.00	−0.05	−3.35%	0.17%	8.10%
HML	0.40	0.00	0.40	5.10%	2.04%	98.40%
WML	0.05	0.03	0.02	9.63%	0.19%	9.30%
				A. Factor tilts return =	2.12%	102.40%
				B. Security selection =	−0.05%	−2.40%
				C. Active return (A + B) =	2.07%	100.00%

This attribution analysis yields information about this portfolio's investment approach, how the manager generated excess return, and his or her ability to consistently add value relative to the benchmark.

Let's first look at the analysis of the benchmark (column 2). The sensitivity to RMRF of 1 indicates that the assigned benchmark has average market risk, consistent with it being a broad-based index. The benchmark's negative sensitivity to SMB indicates a large-cap orientation. Assuming, of course, that the benchmark is a good fit for the manager's stated strategy, we can describe the approach as large cap without a value/growth bias (HML is zero) or a momentum bias (WML is close to zero).

Let's now look at where the portfolio manager's approach differed from that of the benchmark. Based on the factor sensitivities shown in column 1 (positive sensitivity to HML of 0.40) and the differences relative to the benchmark shown in column 3, we can see that the manager likely had a value tilt but was otherwise relatively neutral to the benchmark. We would expect the portfolio to hold more value-oriented stocks than the benchmark, and we would want to evaluate the contribution of this tilt.

We can examine the effects of this decision by looking at the balance of the table. Positive active exposure to the HML factor—the bet on value stocks—contributed 204 bps to the realized active return, about 98% of the 207 bps of total realized active return. The manager's minor active exposures to small stocks and momentum also contributed positively to return, whereas the active exposure to RMRF was a drag on performance. However, because the magnitudes of the exposures to RMRF, SMB, and WML were relatively small, the effects of those bets were minor compared with the value tilt (HML).

What about the manager's ability to contribute return through stock selection? Again, assuming that the benchmark is a good fit for the manager's investment process, the overall active return from security selection is the portion of return not explained by factor sensitivities. In this period, the contribution from selection was slightly negative (−0.05%).

In the aggregate, the manager's positive active return was largely the result of the large active bet on HML (+0.40) and a high return to that factor during the period (+5.10%). Is this type of tilt consistent with the manager's stated investment process? If yes, the manager can be credited with an active decision that contributed positively to return. If no, then the excess return in the period is unlikely to result from manager skill but, rather, is a byproduct of luck. What does the manager's investment process say about the role of security selection? If the manager does not profess skill in security selection but instead focuses on sector or factor allocation, then the minimal contribution of security selection should not be perceived as a negative reflection on manager skill.

EXAMPLE 5

Factor-Based Attribution

Use the data from Exhibit 5 to answer the following questions.

1. Which of the following statements is *not* correct?

   A. The manager's slight small-cap tilt contributed positively to return.

   B. The manager's slight momentum tilt contributed positively to return.

   C. The manager's below-benchmark beta contributed negatively to return.

Solution:

A is the correct answer. The negative coefficient on SMB indicates that the manager had a slight large-cap bias relative to the benchmark. The slight tilt on WML (+0.02) combined with a positive return to the factor resulted in a positive contribution to return. The below-benchmark beta of RMRF (−0.05) combined with a positive return to the factor resulted in a negative contribution to return.

2. What investment approach, not taken by the portfolio manager, could have delivered more value to the portfolio during the investment period?

   A. A momentum-based approach

   B. A growth-oriented approach

   C. A small-cap-based approach

Solution:

A is correct. Had the manager overweighted momentum stocks during the period, the momentum factor (WML) return of 9.63% would have contributed significant positive performance to the portfolio.

Fixed-Income Return Attribution

Fixed-income portfolios are driven by decisions made with respect to credit risk and positioning along the yield curve. Building on work by Groupe de Reflexion en Attribution de Performance, or GRAP, outlined in Giguère (2005) and Murira and Sierra (2006), we will discuss three typical approaches to fixed-income attribution:

- Exposure decomposition—duration based
- Yield curve decomposition—duration based
- Yield curve decomposition—full repricing based

Candidates are not responsible for *calculating* fixed-income attribution but should be able to interpret the results of a fixed-income attribution analysis.

Exposure Decomposition—Duration Based

Exposure decomposition is a top-down attribution approach that seeks to explain the active management of a portfolio relative to its benchmark, typically working through a hierarchy of decisions from the top to the bottom. These decisions might include portfolio duration bets, yield curve positioning or sector bets, each relative to the benchmark. The term "exposure decomposition" relates to the decomposition of portfolio risk exposures by means of grouping a portfolio's component bonds by specified characteristics (e.g., duration, bond sector). The term "duration based" relates to the typical use of duration to represent interest rate exposure decisions.

Models that take an exposure decomposition approach are similar to Brinson-type equity attribution models, where we might group the portfolio by its market value weights in different economic sectors. In this case, however, we group the portfolio by its market value weights in duration buckets (i.e., exposure to different ranges of duration). This approach simplifies the data requirements and allows straightforward presentation of results relative to other fixed-income approaches. For these reasons, the exposure decomposition approach is used primarily for marketing and client reports, where an important benefit is that users can easily understand and articulate the results of active portfolio management.

Yield Curve Decomposition—Duration Based

The duration-based yield curve decomposition approach to fixed-income attribution can be either executed as a top-down approach or built bottom-up from the security level. This approach estimates the return of securities, sector buckets, or years-to-maturity buckets using the known relationship between duration and changes in yield to maturity (YTM), as follows:

$$\% \text{ Total return} = \% \text{ Income return} + \% \text{ Price return},$$

where % Price return ≈ –Duration × Change in YTM.

Duration measures the sensitivity of bond price to a change in the bond's yield to maturity. So, the percentage price return of a bond will be approximately equal to the negative of its duration for each 100 bp change in yields. The change in yield to maturity of the portfolio or instrument can be broken down into yield curve factors and spread factors to provide additional insights. These factors represent the changes in the risk-free government curve (e.g., changes in level, slope, and curvature) and in the premium required to hold riskier sectors and bonds. When they are combined and applied to the duration, we can determine a percentage price change for each factor.

For example, a manager may have a view as to how the yield curve factors will change over time. We can use the attribution analysis to determine the value of the yield curve views as they unfold over time.

This approach is applied to both the portfolio and the benchmark to identify contributions to total return from changes in the yield to maturity. Comparing the differences between the benchmark's return drivers and the portfolio's return drivers gives us the *effect of active portfolio management decisions.*

In this regard, this group of models is quite different from the exposure decomposition. One consequence of this difference is that we require more data points to calculate the separate absolute attribution analyses for the portfolio and the benchmark. Thus, the yield decomposition approach exchanges better transparency for more operational complexity. These models are typically used when preparing reports for analysts and portfolio managers, rather than in marketing or client reports.

Yield Curve Decomposition—Full Repricing

Instead of estimating price changes from changes in duration and yields to maturity, bonds can be repriced from zero-coupon curves (spot rates). Recall that a bond's price is the sum of its cash flows discounted at the appropriate spot rate for each cash flow's maturity. The discount rate to compute the present value depends on the yields offered on the market for comparable securities and represents the required yield an investor expects for holding that investment. Typically, we discount each cash flow at a rate from the spot curve that corresponds to the time the cash flow will be received.

As with the duration-based approaches, instruments can be repriced following incremental changes in spot rates, whether resulting from changes in overall interest rates, spreads, or bond-specific factors. This bottom-up security-level repricing can then be translated into a contribution to a security's return and aggregated for portfolios, benchmarks, and active management.

This full repricing attribution approach provides more precise pricing and allows for a broader range of instrument types and yield changes. It also supports a greater variety of quantitative modeling beyond fixed-income attribution (e.g., *ex ante* risk). This approach is better aligned with how portfolio managers typically view the instruments. However, it requires the full capability to reprice all financial instruments in the portfolio and the benchmark, including the rates and the characteristics of the instrument. Its complex nature can make it more difficult and costly to administer operationally and can make the results more difficult to understand, particularly for non-fixed-income professionals.

All three approaches can be applied to single-currency and multi-currency portfolios. We can most clearly demonstrate the principles of fixed-income attribution by using a single-currency domestic portfolio, without digressing into the relative merits of the various multi-currency approaches. Therefore, this example is a single-currency example.

Fixed-Income Attribution—Worked Example

Let's begin with an example of exposure decomposition analysis.

Exhibit 6 shows a breakdown of the portfolio and the benchmark by weights, duration, and each bucket's contribution to duration, aggregated by sector and duration buckets. For this example, the short-, mid-, and long-duration buckets are defined as follows:[1]

Bucket	Duration
Short	Less than or equal to 5
Mid	Greater than 5 and less than or equal to 10
Long	Greater than 10

1 Note that the practitioner should take care when selecting the upper and lower bands of each duration bucket. By grouping bonds of different durations in the same bucket, one is measuring the combined impact of those bonds relative to the combined impact of similar bonds in the benchmark. In this example (Exhibit 6 and the related discussion), for instance, a bond with a duration of 5.5 is treated the same as a bond with a duration of 9.5 in terms of its relative impact on the portfolio versus its benchmark.

Exhibit 6: Sample Exposure Decomposition: Relative Positions of Portfolio and Benchmark

	Portfolio Weights				Portfolio Duration				Portfolio Contribution to Duration			
	Short	Mid	Long	Total	Short	Mid	Long	Total	Short	Mid	Long	Total
Government	10.00%	10.00%	20.00%	40.00%	4.42	7.47	10.21	8.08	0.44	0.75	2.04	3.23
Corporate	10.00%	20.00%	30.00%	60.00%	4.40	7.40	10.06	8.23	0.44	1.48	3.02	4.94
Total	20.00%	30.00%	50.00%	100.00%	4.41	7.42	10.12	8.17	0.88	2.23	5.06	8.17

	Benchmark Weights				Benchmark Duration				Benchmark Contribution to Duration			
	Short	Mid	Long	Total	Short	Mid	Long	Total	Short	Mid	Long	Total
Government	20.00%	20.00%	15.00%	55.00%	4.42	7.47	10.21	7.11	0.88	1.49	1.53	3.91
Corporate	15.00%	15.00%	15.00%	45.00%	4.40	7.40	10.06	7.29	0.66	1.11	1.51	3.28
Total	35.00%	35.00%	30.00%	100.00%	4.41	7.44	10.14	7.19	1.54	2.60	3.04	7.19

	Portfolio Weights				Portfolio Returns				Portfolio Contribution to Return			
	Short	Mid	Long	Total	Short	Mid	Long	Total	Short	Mid	Long	Total
Government	10.00%	10.00%	20.00%	40.00%	−3.48%	−5.16%	−4.38%	−4.35%	−0.35%	−0.52%	−0.88%	−1.74%
Corporate	10.00%	20.00%	30.00%	60.00%	−4.33%	−6.14%	−5.42%	−5.48%	−0.43%	−1.23%	−1.63%	−3.29%
Total	20.00%	30.00%	50.00%	100.00%	−3.91%	−5.81%	−5.00%	−5.03%	−0.78%	−1.74%	−2.50%	−5.03%

	Benchmark Weights				Benchmark Returns				Benchmark Contribution to Return			
	Short	Mid	Long	Total	Short	Mid	Long	Total	Short	Mid	Long	Total
Government	20.00%	20.00%	15.00%	55.00%	−3.48%	−5.16%	−4.38%	−4.34%	−0.70%	−1.03%	−0.66%	−2.39%
Corporate	15.00%	15.00%	15.00%	45.00%	−4.33%	−6.14%	−5.86%	−5.44%	−0.65%	−0.92%	−0.88%	−2.45%
Total	35.00%	35.00%	30.00%	100.00%	−3.84%	−5.58%	−5.12%	−4.83%	−1.35%	−1.95%	−1.54%	−4.83%

From Exhibit 6, we can make the following inferences regarding the manager's investment decisions:

- With a higher duration than the benchmark (8.17 compared with 7.19 for the benchmark), the manager likely expected the rates to fall and took a bullish position on long-term bonds (interest rates) by increasing exposure to the long end of the interest rate curve (e.g., investing 50% of the portfolio in the longest-duration bucket versus 30% for the benchmark).
- Based on the overweight in the corporate sector (60% versus the 45% benchmark weight), the manager likely expected credit spreads to narrow.[2] Notice that this bet increases the 4.94 contribution to duration of the corporate sector in the portfolio compared with the 3.28 contribution to duration for the benchmark. This allocation makes the portfolio more exposed to market yield fluctuations in the corporate sector.
- The total portfolio return is −5.03%, relative to a total benchmark return of −4.83%, showing an underperformance of −0.20% over the period.

2 If corporate yields were at a historically large spread with respect to governments, the overweight to corporates might also have been a yield bet. Even if spreads do not narrow, the higher-yielding corporates are likely to outperform the government bonds in the portfolio.

We can then use the portfolio and benchmark information from Exhibit 6 to calculate the portfolio's attribution results. These results are summarized in Exhibit 7. (Note that candidates are expected to be able to interpret, but not calculate, these results.)

Total interest rate allocation is the contribution from active management resulting from the manager's active exposures to changes in the level and shape of the yield curve. This can be decomposed into the duration effect (the contribution to active management from taking a different-from-benchmark aggregate duration position) and the curve effect (the specific points along the yield curve at which the manager made his benchmark-relative duration bets).

Sector allocation measures the effect of the manager's decision to overweight corporate bonds, whereas the selection effect measures the impact of the manager's decision to hold non-benchmark bonds in the portfolio. The hypothetical portfolio underlying this example contains only one bond that is not in the benchmark—a long-duration corporate bond, Corp. (P). Accordingly, there is no selection effect in the other duration buckets.

Exhibit 7: Sample Exposure Decomposition: Attribution Results

Duration Bucket	Sector	Duration Effect	Curve Effect	Total Interest Rate Allocation	Sector Allocation	Bond Selection	Total
Short	Government					0.00%	0.00%
	Corporate				0.04%	0.00%	0.04%
	Total	*0.40%*	*0.12%*	*0.52%*	*0.04%*	*0.00%*	***0.56%***
Mid	Government					0.00%	0.00%
	Corporate				−0.05%	0.00%	−0.05%
	Total	*0.23%*	*0.03%*	*0.26%*	*−0.05%*	*0.00%*	***0.21%***
Long	Government					0.00%	0.00%
	Corporate				−0.22%	0.13%	−0.09%
	Total	*−1.25%*	*0.37%*	*−0.88%*	*−0.22%*	*0.13%*	***−0.97%***
Total		**−0.62%**	**0.52%**	**−0.10%**	**−0.23%**	**0.13%**	**−0.20%**

Using the results from Exhibit 7, we can draw the following conclusions about the investment decisions made by this manager:

- The portfolio underperformed its benchmark by 26 bps.
- 62 bps were lost by taking a long-duration position during a period when yields increased (benchmark returns were negative in each duration bucket).
- 52 bps were gained as a result of changes in the shape of the yield curve. Given the manager's overweighting in the long-duration bucket, we can infer that the yield curve flattened.
- 23 bps were lost because the manager overweighted the corporate sector during a period when credit spreads widened (the benchmark corporate returns in each duration bucket were less than the government returns in those same duration buckets).
- 7 bps were added through bond selection.

Exhibit 8 provides an example of a sample duration-based yield curve decomposition attribution analysis. Again, we do not include the calculations for this analysis but instead present the results and suggested interpretations.

Exhibit 8: Yield Curve Decomposition—Duration Based: Active Return Contribution

Bond	Yield	Roll	Shift	Slope	Curvature	Spread	Specific	Residual	Total
Gov't. 5% 30 June 21	–0.19%	–0.04%	0.43%	0.01%	0.15%	0.00%	0.00%	–0.01%	0.35%
Gov't. 7% 30 June 26	–0.22%	–0.03%	0.71%	0.04%	0.04%	0.00%	0.00%	–0.03%	0.52%
Gov't. 6% 30 June 31	0.12%	0.01%	–0.48%	0.05%	0.09%	0.00%	0.00%	–0.01%	–0.22%
Corp. 5% 30 June 21	–0.11%	–0.02%	0.21%	0.05%	0.05%	0.04%	0.02%	–0.02%	0.22%
Corp. 7% 30 June 26	0.12%	0.01%	–0.35%	–0.02%	–0.02%	–0.07%	0.00%	0.02%	–0.31%
Corp. (B) 6% 30 June 31	–0.39%	–0.03%	1.41%	–0.26%	–0.11%	0.30%	0.00%	–0.04%	0.88%
Corp. (P) 6% 30 June 31	0.78%	0.06%	–2.82%	0.52%	0.33%	–0.60%	0.15%	–0.05%	–1.63%
Total	0.11%	–0.04%	–0.89%	0.39%	0.53%	–0.33%	0.17%	–0.14%	–0.20%
	Time:	*0.08%*	*Curve Movement:*		*0.03%*				

Note: There may be minor differences due to rounding in this table.

Using the data from Exhibit 6 and Exhibit 8, we can infer the following about the portfolio investment process over this period:

- *Yield*: The portfolio overweighted corporate bonds and longer-term maturities relative to the benchmark (from Exhibit 6), which generally offer higher yield than government bonds and short-term maturities. This decision contributed 11 bps to the excess return (from Exhibit 8).
- *Roll*: The portfolio overweighted longer maturities (from Exhibit 6). Because of the shape of the yield curve, bonds with longer maturities generally sit on a flatter part of the yield curve, where the roll return is limited. The overweighting of the longer maturities reduced the portfolio roll return by 4 bps.
- *Shift*: The portfolio overall duration of 8.17 is greater than the benchmark duration of 7.19 (from Exhibit 6), which reduced the portfolio return by 89 bps.
- *Slope*: The slope flattening caused the long-term yields to increase less than yields on shorter terms to maturity. The overweight at the long end of the curve contributed 39 bps to the excess return.
- *Curvature*: The reshaping of the yield curve resulted in a larger yield increase at the five-year maturity point. The manager underweighted that part of the yield curve. This decision contributed 53 bps to the excess return.
- *Spread*: The manager overweighted the corporate sector, which resulted in a 33 bp reduction in return because corporate spreads widened.
- *Specific spread*: Looking at the bond-specific spreads in Exhibit 8, the corporate 5% 30 June 2021 bond added 2 bps of selection return and the corporate (P) 6% 30 June 2031 bond added 15 bps of selection return. These decisions added a total of 17 bps to active return.
- *Residual*: A residual of –0.14% is unaccounted for because duration and convexity can only *estimate* the percentage price variation. It is not an accurate measure of the true price variation. The residual becomes more important during large yield moves, which is the case here, with a +1% yield shift.

EXAMPLE 6

Fixed-Income Return Attribution

Use the data in Exhibit 7 and Exhibit 8 to answer the following questions.

1. Which decision had the most positive effect on the overall performance of the portfolio?

   A. Taking a long-duration position

   B. Security selection of bond issues

   C. Overweighting the long end of the yield curve

Solution:

C is correct: 52 bps were gained by overweighting the long end of the yield curve during a period when the slope of the yield curve flattened.

2. Explain the contribution of the long-duration bucket to overall portfolio performance.

Solution:

The long-duration bucket cost the portfolio 97 bps of relative return. From Exhibit 7, the curve and selection effects were positive (37 bps and 7 bps, respectively) whereas the duration and sector allocation effects were negative (−125 bps and −16 bps, respectively). The negative duration effect indicates that the manager took a longer-than-benchmark-duration position in the long-duration bucket, a decision that hurt performance because interest rates rose. The positive curve effect implies that the manager's specific positioning along the long end of the yield curve benefited from changes in the shape of the yield curve. This implication is further supported by the positive slope effect shown in Exhibit 8. Taken together, the duration and curve effects accounted for the majority of the manager's underperformance relative to the benchmark. In the long-duration bucket, the manager overweighted corporate bonds relative to the benchmark. This decision penalized returns because credit spreads widened, which can be inferred from the weaker performance of the long-duration corporate segment of the benchmark (−5.42%) relative to the long-duration government segment (−4.38%). The positive selection effect of 7 bps implies that the manager's specific bond selections added to return. This implication is supported by the specific spread contribution reflected in Exhibit 8.

5 RISK ATTRIBUTION

☐ discuss considerations in selecting a risk attribution approach

Performance attribution, on its own, is typically insufficient to evaluate the investment process. In addition to performance, we need to understand the impact of exposure to risk by including risk attribution.

Risk attribution identifies the sources of risk in the investment process. For absolute mandates, it identifies the sources of portfolio volatility. For benchmark-relative mandates, it identifies the sources of tracking risk. Managers seek opportunities for profit by taking specific exposures to risk (e.g., portfolio volatility or tracking risk). Risk attribution identifies these risks taken and, together with return attribution, quantifies the contributions to both the return and risk of the investment manager's active decisions.

Risk attribution should reflect the investment decision-making process. Exhibit 9 classifies investment decision-making processes and suggests appropriate risk attribution approaches. The columns indicate whether the focus is absolute risk or benchmark-relative risk. The rows categorize investment decision-making processes as bottom up, top down, or factor based. A bottom-up approach focuses on individual security selection. Top-down approaches focus first on macro decisions, such as allocations to economic sectors, and then on security selection within sectors. A factor-based approach looks for profits by taking different-from-benchmark exposures to the risk factors believed to drive asset returns.

Exhibit 9: Selecting the Appropriate Risk Attribution Approach

Investment Decision-Making Process	Type of Attribution Analysis: Relative (vs. Benchmark)	Type of Attribution Analysis: Absolute
Bottom up	Position's marginal contribution to tracking risk	Position's marginal contribution to total risk
Top down	Attribute tracking risk to relative allocation and selection decisions	Factor's marginal contribution to total risk and specific risk
Factor based	Factor's marginal contribution to tracking risk and active specific risk	

For portfolios that are managed against benchmarks, a common measure of risk is tracking risk (TR), also often called tracking error. The objective of an attribution model for a benchmark-relative portfolio is to quantify the contribution of active decisions to TR. For bottom-up benchmark-relative investment processes, each position's marginal contribution to TR multiplied by its active weight gives the position's contribution to TR. For benchmark-relative top-down investment processes, the active return is explained first by the allocation decisions. Risk attribution, accordingly, will identify the total contribution of allocation and selection to TR.

For absolute mandates, the risk of the portfolio is explained by exposures to the market, size and style factors, and the specific risk due to stock selections. The attribution model quantifies the contribution of each exposure and of specific risk. Suppose that the manager follows an absolute bottom-up process where the measure of risk is the volatility (standard deviation) of returns. In this case, we want to measure the contribution of selection decisions to overall portfolio risk. To do this, we need to know the marginal contribution of each asset to the portfolio risk—the increase or decrease in the portfolio standard deviation due to a slight increase in the holding of that asset. If we know the marginal contribution of a security to absolute portfolio risk, we can then calculate the overall risk contribution of the portfolio manager's selection decisions.

In all cases, risk attribution explains only where risk was introduced into the portfolio. It needs to be combined with return attribution to understand the full impact of those decisions. For example, if a manager has added to excess return through asset allocation (e.g., positive return attribution allocation effect), we use risk attribution to understand whether those allocation decisions introduced additional risk. As such, risk attribution complements the return attribution by evaluating the risk consequences of the investment decisions.

EXAMPLE 7

Risk Attribution

Manager A is a market-neutral manager following a systematic investment approach, scoring each security on a proprietary set of risk factors. He seeks to maximize the portfolio score on the basis of the factor characteristics of individual securities. He has a hurdle rate of T-bills plus 5%.

Manager B has a strong fundamental process based on a comprehensive understanding of the business model and competitive advantages of each firm. He also uses sophisticated models to make explicit three-year forecasts of the growth of free cash flow to determine the attractiveness of each security's current valuation. His objective is to outperform the MSCI World ex-US Index by 200 bps.

Manager C specializes in timing sector exposure and generally avoids idiosyncratic risks within sectors. Using technical analyses and econometric methodologies, she produces several types of forecasts. The manager uses this information to determine appropriate sector weights. The risk contribution from any single sector is limited to 30% of total portfolio risk. She hedges aggregate market risk and seeks to earn T-bills plus 300 bps.

1. Which risk attribution approach is most appropriate to evaluate Manager A?

   A. Marginal contribution to total risk

   B. Marginal contribution to tracking risk

   C. Factor's marginal contributions to total risk and specific risk

Solution:

A is correct. Manager A is a bottom-up manager with an absolute return target. B is incorrect because tracking risk is not relevant to an absolute return mandate. C is incorrect because, as a market-neutral manager, Manager A is not seeking to take different-from-market exposures.

2. Which risk attribution approach is most appropriate to evaluate Manager B?

   A. Marginal contribution to total risk

   B. Marginal contribution to tracking risk

   C. Factor's marginal contributions to total risk and specific risk

Solution:

B is correct. Manager B is a bottom-up manager with a relative return target. A and C are incorrect because they are best suited to absolute return mandates.

3. Which risk attribution approach is most appropriate to evaluate Manager C?

   A. Marginal contribution to total risk

   B. Marginal contribution to tracking risk

   C. Factor's marginal contributions to total risk and specific risk

Solution:

C is correct. Manager C is a top-down manager with an absolute return target. A factor-based attribution is best suited to evaluate the effectiveness of the manager's sector decisions and hedging of market risk.

RETURN ATTRIBUTION ANALYSIS AT MULTIPLE LEVELS

6

☐ identify and interpret investment results attributable to the asset owner versus those attributable to the investment manager

To this point, the return attribution presented in the Brinson examples focused on the bottom-up approach, where we calculated attribution effects at security and sector levels and summed those effects to determine their impact at the total portfolio and fund levels. We can use a similar return attribution approach at multiple levels of the decision process to evaluate the impact of different decisions.

Macro Attribution—An Example

Consider an example in which the top level is the fund sponsor (e.g., a university endowment or a defined-benefit pension plan sponsor). At the fund sponsor level, the first decision might be to allocate a certain weight to asset classes—the strategic asset allocation. If the fund sponsor does not manage funds internally, it would delegate a second investment decision to the investment managers to decide on any tactical deviations from the strategic asset allocation. The sponsor might also select multiple portfolio managers to manage against specific mandates within a given asset class.

The attribution analysis that we use to determine the impact of these fund sponsor decisions is sometimes called macro attribution. The attribution of the individual portfolio manager decisions is sometimes called micro attribution.

Assume our hypothetical fund sponsor has the following total equity benchmark:

- 50% large-cap value equities
- 25% small-cap value equities
- 25% large-cap growth equities

The fund sponsor hires two investment managers to manage the equity portion of the fund. Value Portfolio Manager manages the large-cap and small-cap value allocations, and Growth Portfolio Manager manages the growth equity allocation. The investment returns are shown in Exhibit 10.

Exhibit 10: Performance of Value and Growth Equity Managers

	Fund Weight	Fund Return	Benchmark Weight	Benchmark Return
Total	**100%**	**0.95**	**100%**	**−0.03**
Value Portfolio Manager	78%	0.99	75%	0.32
Small-cap value equities	20%	2.39	25%	1.52

	Fund Weight	Fund Return	Benchmark Weight	Benchmark Return
Large-cap value equities	58%	0.51	50%	−0.28
Growth Portfolio Manager	22%	0.82	25%	−1.08
Large-cap growth equities	22%	0.82	25%	−1.08

To evaluate the decisions of the fund sponsor, we perform a return Brinson–Fachler attribution analysis using the set of weight and return data in Exhibit 10. "Allocation" measures the tactical asset allocation decision of the sponsor against its own strategic benchmark. In this example, the fund sponsor overweighted value equities and underweighted growth equities. "Selection" measures the fund sponsor's manager selection decision: Did the selected managers add value relative to their assigned benchmarks?

For the decision to hire the Value Portfolio Manager, we would calculate the effects as follows:

$$\text{Allocation} = (78\% - 75\%)[0.32 - (-0.03)] = 0.01$$

- The fund sponsor overweighted value equities (78% – 75%).
- Value equities outperformed the fund's aggregate benchmark [0.32 – (−0.03)].
- The decision to overweight value equities added to portfolio return.

$$\text{Selection} + \text{Interaction} = [(75\%)(0.99 - 0.32)] + [(78\% - 75\%)(0.99 - 0.32)] = 0.52$$

- The value manager outperformed the value benchmark (0.99 – 0.32). Thus, the fund sponsor's manager selection decision, independent of the decision to overweight value equities, added value.
- The fund sponsor overweighted a manager who outperformed his benchmark [(78% – 75%)(0.99 – 0.32)]. This is the interaction effect. (For simplicity, we combine interaction with selection, rather than showing interaction separately. By combining with selection, we assume that the selection decisions include the interaction and leave the allocation decision separate.) The interaction effect was positive.

For the decision to hire the Growth Portfolio Manager, we would calculate the effects as follows:

$$\text{Allocation} = (22\% - 25\%)[-1.08 - (-0.03)] = 0.03$$

- The fund sponsor underweighted growth equities (22% – 25%)
- Growth equities underperformed the fund's aggregate benchmark (−1.08 versus −0.03)
- The decision to underweight growth equities added to portfolio return

$$\text{Selection} + \text{Interaction} = [(25\%)(0.82 - (-1.08)] + [(22\% - 25\%)(0.82 - (-1.08)] = 0.42$$

- The growth manager outperformed the growth benchmark (+0.82 versus −1.08). Thus, the fund sponsor's manager selection decision, independent of the decision to underweight growth equities, added value.
- The fund sponsor underweighted a manager who outperformed his benchmark [(– 3%)(0.82 – (– 1.08)]. The interaction effect was negative.

The results are summarized in Exhibit 11.

Exhibit 11: Macro Attribution

Return Attribution (Plan Sponsor Level)	Selection + Interaction	Allocation	Total
Total	0.94	0.04	0.98
Value Portfolio Manager	**0.52**	**0.01**	**0.53**
Growth Portfolio Manager	**0.42**	**0.03**	**0.45**

Return attribution analysis is most often calculated with reference to the portfolio's agreed-upon benchmark. But it is entirely possible to attribute one portfolio against another when both are using the same or a similar investment strategy. The purpose of such analysis might be to explain an unexpected difference in return between two portfolios managed by the same portfolio manager using the same investment decision-making process.

Micro Attribution—An Example

Using the same return data, we now move to the next level of the investment decision-making process and will evaluate the impact of the portfolio managers' decisions on total fund performance. We calculate the return attribution effects using the Brinson–Fachler approach at the segment level (i.e., small-cap value, large-cap value, and large-cap growth):

$$\text{Allocation} = (w_i - W_i)(B_i - B)$$

$$\text{Selection + Interaction} = W_i(R_i - B_i) + (w_i - W_i)(R_i - B_i)$$

We calculate the attribution effects for the small-cap value equities:

$$\text{Allocation} = (20\% - 25\%)[1.52 - (-0.03)] = -0.08$$

$$\text{Selection + Interaction} = [(25\%)(2.39 - 1.52)] + [(20\% - 25\%)(2.39 - 1.52)]$$
$$= 0.17$$

Using the same approach for large-cap value equities and large-cap growth equities yields the results shown in Exhibit 12. (Note that the numbers are rounded to two decimal places and may not sum because of this rounding.)

Exhibit 12: Segment-Level Return Attribution

Return Attribution (Segment Level)	Fund Weight	Selection + Interaction	Allocation	Total
Total	**100%**	**1.05**	**−0.07**	**0.98**
Value Portfolio Manager	78%	0.63	−0.10	0.53
Small-cap value equities	*20%*	*0.17*	*−0.08*	*0.10*
Large-cap value equities	*58%*	*0.46*	*−0.02*	*0.44*
Growth Portfolio Manager	22%	0.42	0.03	0.45
Large-cap growth equities	*22%*	*0.42*	*0.03*	*0.45*

In Exhibit 12, the attribution results in italics are calculated at the segment level. The attribution results at the next level above, the Value Portfolio Manager and Growth Portfolio Manager, are sums of the segment-level results. For example, the allocation effect for the Value Portfolio Manager is equal to the sum of the small-cap and large-cap segments: –0.08 + –0.02 = –0.10.

Summing up the segment-level results for each manager, we reach the following conclusions:

- The total outperformance at the overall fund level of 98 bps is almost entirely the result of positive security selection decisions (105 bps in total).
- The decision of the Value Portfolio Manager to underweight small cap in favor of large cap detracted from total fund performance because the small-cap value benchmark outperformed the total benchmark (1.52% versus –0.03%), leading to an allocation effect of –0.10.
- The large-cap growth benchmark underperformed the total benchmark (–1.08% versus –0.03%). Because the portfolio was underweight large-cap growth, this led to a positive allocation effect of 0.03.
- In total, allocation decisions contributed –7 bps.

Note that in using the total fund benchmark in this analysis, we are evaluating the *impact* of the Value Portfolio Manager's decision on the performance of the total fund.

We can extend the attribution analysis down another level and examine the investment manager's results relative to the investment process. The manager may have an investment process that specifically targets country allocations.[3] At this level of analysis, the same allocation formula will calculate the impact of country allocation decisions within the manager's portfolio and the selection formula will calculate the impact of selection decisions within each country.

If the portfolio manager has an investment process that specifically targets sector allocations within each country, the allocation formula can be used to calculate the impact of sector selection decisions within countries and the selection decisions within sectors.

Whatever the level of analysis, the return attribution must reflect the decision-making process of the portfolio manager. For example, a eurozone investment strategy might use a country allocation process with security selection within each country or a sector allocation process with security selection within each industrial sector. Exhibit 13 and Exhibit 14 illustrate the different results that might be reached from an analysis based on the investment process. In each case, an arithmetic Brinson approach has been used.

Exhibit 13: Country Allocation

	Portfolio Weight	Benchmark Weight	Portfolio Return	Benchmark Return	Allocation	Selection + Interaction
France	20%	30%	8.0%	6.0%	0.15%	0.40%
Germany	20%	35%	8.0%	7.0%	0.07%	0.20%
Holland	20%	10%	9.0%	15.0%	0.76%	–1.20%
Italy	30%	15%	10.0%	9.0%	0.23%	0.30%
Spain	10%	10%	3.0%	3.5%	0.00%	–0.05%
Total	**100%**	**100%**	**8.3%**	**7.45%**	**1.20%**	**–0.35%**

3 For some portfolios, the next level may be asset classes (as an example).

Exhibit 14: Industry Sector Allocation

	Portfolio Weight	Benchmark Weight	Portfolio Return	Benchmark Return	Allocation	Selection + Interaction
Energy	25%	30%	18.0%	12.0%	−0.23%	1.50%
Health care	30%	20%	−3.0%	−6.0%	−1.35%	0.90%
Financial	20%	30%	10.0%	12.0%	−0.46%	−0.40%
Transportation	10%	15%	12.0%	8.0%	−0.03%	0.40%
Metals and mining	15%	5%	10.0%	5.0%	−0.25%	0.75%
Total	**100%**	**100%**	**8.3%**	**7.45%**	**−2.30%**	**3.15%**

Exhibit 13 suggests that the manager demonstrated good country allocation but negative security selection within countries, whereas Exhibit 14 suggests that the manager demonstrated poor sector allocation but strongly positive security selection within industrial sectors. This apparent "contradiction" illustrates the importance of designing an attribution approach around the investment decision-making process used by the manager.

Drilling down to the lowest level, the same allocation and selection formulas can be used to calculate the contribution of individual security decisions within sectors. For example, the allocation formula can be used to determine the impact of over- or underweighting individual securities, whereas the selection formula can be used to determine the contribution arising from a difference in the return of a security in the portfolio and the return of the same security in the benchmark. If the pricing sources used in the portfolio and the benchmark are identical, then any difference in return will be caused by transaction activity. Transaction activity because of trading expenses and bid–offer spreads will negatively affect returns, but occasionally because of timing, the portfolio manager may be able to trade at advantageous prices during the day and recover all the transaction costs by the end of the day, resulting in a positive effect.

Exhibit 15 shows the security-level return attribution effects for a small portfolio of oil stocks against a customized benchmark consisting of the same oil stocks. This approach would be used by a pure stock picker, the only decisions in the portfolio being individual stock weighting and timing decisions.

Exhibit 15: Security-Level Return Attribution Effects of Pure Stock Picker

	Portfolio Weight	Benchmark Weight	Portfolio Return	Benchmark Return	Allocation	Transaction Costs and Timing Effects
Chevron	24%	30%	10%	10%	−0.18%	0.00%
ConocoPhillips	21%	25%	8%	8%	−0.04%	0.00%
ExxonMobil	41%	35%	5%	6%	−0.06%	−0.41%
Marathon Oil	6%	5%	4%	4%	−0.03%	0.00%
Newfield Expl.	8%	5%	−5%	−5%	−0.36%	0.00%
Total	**100%**	**100%**	**5.97%**	**7.05%**	**−0.67%**	**−0.41%**

The arithmetic allocation effects of each security using the Brinson approach are as follows:

Chevron	(24% − 30%) × (10% − 7.05%) = −0.18%
ConocoPhillips	(21% − 25%) × (8.0% − 7.05%) = −0.04%
ExxonMobil	(41% − 35%) × (6.0% − 7.05%) = −0.06%

Marathon Oil	(6% – 5%) × (4.0% – 7.05%) = –0.03%
Newfield Exploration	(8% – 5%) × (–5.0% – 7.05%) = –0.36%

Allocation in this context measures the value added from individual security selection. Transactions occur for only one security during the period—ExxonMobil. Therefore, the only selection effects (transaction costs and timing) occur for this security. The calculation is as follows:

ExxonMobil	41% × (5.0% – 6.0%) = –0.41%

EXAMPLE 8

Macro Attribution

1. AAA Asset Management runs a fixed-income fund of funds. The fund's benchmark is a blended benchmark comprising 80% Bloomberg Barclays Global Aggregate Index and 20% Bloomberg Barclays Global Treasury Index (both in US dollars, unhedged). Two internal investment teams have been selected to manage the fund's assets. The allocations to the two products are determined by the firm's chief fixed-income strategist. The fund has underperformed its benchmark in each of the last three years. You are a member of the board of directors, which is meeting to determine what action should be taken. Based solely on the data in the table below, which of the following courses of action would you recommend? Justify your response.

   A. Terminate the manager of Product A.

   B. Terminate the manager of Product B.

   C. Remove the chief fixed-income strategist as manager of the fund of funds.

Fund-of-Funds Return

	Year 1	Year 2	Year 3	Cumulative Return
Total Fund	3.72%	–3.00%	–0.13%	0.47%
Benchmark:	3.84%	–2.94%	0.07%	0.86%

Product Returns

	Year 1		Year 2		Year 3		
	Weight	**Return**	**Weight**	**Return**	**Weight**	**Return**	
Product A	0.7	4.45%	0.75	–2.50%	0.8	–0.10%	1.74%
Benchmark: Bloomberg Barclays Global Aggregate		4.32%		–2.60%		0.29%	1.90%
Product B	0.3	2.00%	0.25	–4.50%	0.2	–0.25%	–2.83%
Benchmark: Bloomberg Barclays Global Treasury		1.93%		–4.30%		–0.79%	–3.22%

Solution:

C is correct. Based solely on the information provided, the chief fixed-income strategist's allocation decision was the main driver of the fund's underperformance. Product A modestly underperformed its benchmark over the three-year period (−16 bps). Product B outperformed its benchmark (+39 bps). The strategist's allocation decisions were strongly negative in Years 1 and 2, when he overweighted the Treasury allocation and the Treasury index underperformed the aggregate fund benchmark. The results of the attribution analysis are shown below:

AAA Asset Management Fixed-Income Fund-of-Funds Attribution Analysis

	Year 1		Year 2		Year 3	
	Allocation	**Selection**	**Allocation**	**Selection**	**Allocation**	**Selection**
Product A	−0.05%	0.10%	−0.02%	0.08%	0.00%	−0.31%
Product B	−0.19%	0.01%	−0.07%	−0.04%	0.00%	0.11%
Total	−0.24%	0.12%	−0.09%	0.04%	0.00%	−0.20%

ASSET- AND LIABILITY-BASED BENCHMARKS

7

- ☐ discuss uses of liability-based benchmarks
- ☐ describe types of asset-based benchmarks

An investment benchmark is typically a collection of securities that represents the pool of assets available to the portfolio manager. For example, an investor in Japanese small-cap stocks might have a benchmark consisting of a broad portfolio of small-cap Japanese equities. A benchmark should reflect the investment process and the constraints that govern the construction of the portfolio. If the benchmark does not reflect the investment process, then the evaluation and analysis that flow from the comparison with the benchmark are flawed.

Benchmarks communicate information about the set of assets that may be considered for investment and the investment discipline. They provide investment managers with a guidepost for acceptable levels of risk and return and can be a powerful influence on investment decision making.

In investment practice, we use benchmarks as

- reference points for segments of the sponsor's portfolio,
- communication of instructions to the manager,
- communication with consultants and oversight groups (e.g., a board of directors),
- identification and evaluation of the current portfolio's risk exposures,
- interpretations of past performance and performance attribution,
- manager selection and appraisal,
- marketing of investment products, and

- demonstrations of compliance with regulations, laws, or standards.

Benchmarks help analysts measure the effectiveness of a manager's decisions to depart from benchmark weights.

When considering benchmarks, we need to understand the differences between a "benchmark" and a "market index." A market index represents the performance of a specific security market, market segment, or asset class. For example, the FTSE 100 Index is constructed to represent the broad performance of large-cap UK equities. The S&P US Aggregate Bond Index is designed to measure the performance of publicly issued US dollar-denominated investment-grade debt. The constituents of these indexes are selected for their appropriateness in representing the target market, market segment, or asset class.

A market index may be considered for use as a benchmark or a comparison point for an investment manager. Consider the case of passive managers, who typically invest in portfolios designed to closely track the performance of market indexes. For example, the iShares Core S&P 500 ETF seeks investment results, before fees and expenses, that correspond to the price and yield performance of US large-cap stocks as represented by the S&P 500 Index. Because the investment objective of the iShares Core S&P 500 ETF is to track the performance of the S&P 500, the S&P 500 is the appropriate benchmark for the iShares Core S&P 500 ETF.

However, the most appropriate benchmark for an investment manager is not necessarily a market index. Many active managers follow specific investment disciplines that cannot be adequately described by a security market index. For example, market-neutral long–short managers typically have absolute return benchmarks—a specific minimum rate of return or a specified spread over a risk-free rate. Benchmarks must be suitable to the specific needs of the asset owner and any investment manager hired to manage money; market indexes are typically meant to serve the general public's purposes and to have broad appeal. Nonetheless, indexes can sometimes serve as valid benchmarks.

Another category of benchmarks is liability-based benchmarks, which focus on the cash flows that the asset must generate. Liability-based benchmarks are most often used when the assets are required to pay a specific future liability (e.g., as in a defined benefit pension plan). They allow the asset owner to track the fund's progress toward fully funded status (assets greater than or equal to liabilities) or, if fully funded, to track the performance of assets relative to the changes in liabilities. The performance relative to liabilities is important because it would be possible for the portfolio to outperform a market index but still not meet its liabilities. Furthermore, a market-value-weighted index would likely be an inappropriate benchmark because the liability often has a targeted asset allocation and risk exposures that are different from those of the index.

As an example, consider the fixed-income portion of a pension fund. A cap-weighted index is typically not a suitable benchmark because the duration of the index is usually shorter than the duration of most pension plans' liabilities. Furthermore, many fixed-income indexes are heavily weighted toward corporate bonds in the short maturities, which may represent a greater degree of credit risk than the plan desires. As an alternative, a well-diversified portfolio of individual bonds that minimizes idiosyncratic risk could be used as the benchmark. A more recent innovation is liability-driven investment (LDI) indexes. The Bloomberg Barclays LDI Index Series is a series of six investible indexes designed specifically for portfolios intended to hedge pension liabilities. However, they may not describe a plan's liability structure as accurately as a benchmark constructed specifically for the plan.

To best determine how a liability-based benchmark should be constructed, the manager first needs to understand the nature of the plan's liabilities and the plan's projected future cash flows. Although each plan will have its own unique characteristics, the following plan features will influence the structure of the liability:

- the average number of years to retirement in the workforce,
- the percentage of the workforce that is retired,
- the average participant life expectancy,
- whether the benefits are indexed to inflation,
- whether the plan offers an early retirement option,
- whether the sponsor could increase its plan contributions (e.g., whether the sponsor is profitable and diversified),
- the correlation between plan assets and the sponsoring company's operating assets (a lower correlation is desired so that the sponsor can make contributions when the plan requires funds), and
- whether the plan is a going concern (e.g., plans will eventually terminate if the sponsor has exited its business).

These characteristics influence the composition of the pension plan portfolio and hence its liability-based benchmark. Nominal bonds, real return bonds, and common shares are the assets most commonly found in liability-driven portfolios. The allocation to each asset class is driven by the proportion of accrued versus future obligations, whether the benefits are inflation indexed, and whether the plan is growing. A younger workforce means that more is allocated to equities. Greater inflation indexing of the benefits would imply more inflation-indexed bonds. If the fund's managers outperform the benchmark constructed according to these principles, the pension obligations should be met. Risk and noise that cannot be modeled in the benchmark may require additional future contributions.

EXAMPLE 9

Liability-Based Benchmarks

1. Which of the following portfolios is most likely to use a liability-based benchmark?

   A. A portfolio managed for a private client with a goal of capital appreciation

   B. An intermediate-duration fixed-income portfolio managed for a defined benefit pension fund

   C. The total portfolio for a defined benefit pension fund with an asset allocation of 80% fixed income/20% equity

Solution:

C is correct. A liability-based benchmark is most likely to be used for the total pension fund portfolio as the plan sponsor tracks its funded status.

2. Which of the following most accurately describes a liability-based benchmark?

   A. It focuses on the cash flows that the benchmarked asset must generate.

   B. It represents the performance of a specific security market, market segment, or asset class.

C. It is a collection of securities that represents the pool of assets available to the portfolio manager.

Solution:

A is correct. A liability-based benchmark is constructed according to the cash flows that the benchmarked asset must generate.

Asset-Based Benchmarks

Benchmarks are an important part of the investment process for both institutional and private wealth clients. In the following discussion, we introduce the types of benchmarks based on the discussion in Bailey, Richards, and Tierney (2007). The seven types of benchmarks introduced in this section are

- absolute (including target) return benchmarks,
- broad market indexes,
- style indexes,
- factor-model-based benchmarks,
- returns-based (Sharpe style analysis) benchmarks,
- manager universes (peer groups), and
- custom security-based (strategy) benchmarks.

An **absolute return benchmark** is a minimum target return that the manager is expected to beat. The return may be a stated minimum (e.g., 9%), stated as a spread above a market index (e.g., the Euro Interbank Offered Rate + 4%), or determined from actuarial assumptions. An example of an absolute return benchmark is 20% per annum return for a private equity investment. Market-neutral long–short equity funds often have absolute return benchmarks. Such funds consist of long and short positions in perceived undervalued and overvalued equities. Overall, the portfolio is expected to be insensitive to broad equity market movements (i.e., market neutral with a market beta of zero). Therefore, market-neutral fund benchmarks may be specified as a three-month Treasury bill return; the investment objective is often to outperform the benchmark consistently by a given number of basis points.

Broad market indexes are measures of broad asset class performance, such as the JP Morgan Emerging Market Bond Index (EMBI) for emerging market bonds or the MSCI World Index for global developed market equities. Broad market indexes are well known, readily available, and easily understood. The performance of broad market indexes is widely reported in the popular media.

Market indexes have also been more narrowly defined to represent investment styles within asset classes, resulting in style indexes. An **investment style** is a natural grouping of investment disciplines that has some predictive power in explaining the future dispersion of returns across portfolios.[4] In the late 1970s, researchers found that stock valuation (e.g., the price-to-earnings ratio) and market capitalization explained much of stock return variation. In response, many index providers created various style versions of their broad market indexes (e.g., the Russell 2000 Value and Russell 1000 Growth Indexes).

Factor-model-based benchmarks can be constructed to more closely capture the investment decision-making process. Building a factor model identifies the relative explanatory powers of each factor in the portfolio return. Examples of factors include

4 Brown and Goetzmann (1997).

broad market index returns, industry exposure, and financial leverage. To determine the factor sensitivities, the portfolio's return is regressed against the factors believed to influence returns. The general form of a factor model is:

$$R_p = a_p + b_1F_1 + b_2F_2 \ldots b_kF_k + \varepsilon_p \quad (12)$$

where

R_p = the portfolio's periodic return

a_p = the "zero-factor" term, which is the expected portfolio return if all factor sensitivities are zero

b_k = the sensitivity of portfolio returns to the factor return

F_k = systematic factors responsible for asset returns

ε_p = residual return due to nonsystematic factors

The sensitivities (b_k) are then used to predict the return the portfolio should provide for given values of the systematic-risk factors. Earlier, we discussed the four-factor Carhart model, but any key element of the investment process can be considered for inclusion in a factor model. As an example, if the investment manager believes that interest rates are inversely related to security prices, then the model can incorporate an interest rate factor. If interest rates unexpectedly rise, then security returns can be expected to fall by an amount determined by the security's sensitivity (b_k) to interest rate changes.

Returns-based benchmarks (Sharpe style analysis) are like factor-model-based benchmarks in that portfolio returns are related to a set of factors that explain portfolio returns. With returns-based benchmarks, however, the factors are the returns for various style indexes (e.g., small-cap value, small-cap growth, large-cap value, and large-cap growth). The style analysis produces a benchmark of the weighted average of these asset class indexes that best explains or tracks the portfolio's returns. Unlike the investment-style indexes previously discussed, returns-based benchmarks *view style on a continuum*. For example, a portfolio may be characterized as 60% small-cap value and 40% small-cap growth. To create a returns-based benchmark using Sharpe style analysis, we use an optimization procedure to force the portfolio's sensitivities (analogous to the b_k's in factor-model-based benchmarks) to be non-negative and sum to 1.

A **manager universe**, or **manager peer group**, is a broad group of managers with similar investment disciplines. Although not a benchmark, per se, a manager universe allows investors to make comparisons with the performance of other managers following similar investment disciplines. Managers are typically expected to beat the universe's median return. Manager universes are typically formed by asset class and the investment approach within that class.

Peer groups as benchmarks suffer from some significant weaknesses. Although managers within a peer group may all nominally be classified as "large-cap value" or "small-cap growth," for example, they may not truly be substitutable for one another. Some may have tilts or constraints that create an investment product very different from that of the median manager. A manager's ranking within the peer group might change considerably with very small changes in performance, often in response to factors outside of the manager's control: A change in the ranking may be driven not by something he did but by the actions of others in the peer group (e.g., other managers in the peer group may have chosen to overweight a "hot" sector, whereas the target manager's investment discipline constrains him from making a similar bet).

Lastly, **custom security-based benchmarks** are built to more precisely reflect the investment discipline of an investment manager. Such benchmarks are developed through discussions with the manager and an analysis of past portfolio exposures.

After identifying the manager's investment process, the benchmark is constructed by selecting securities and weightings consistent with that process and client restrictions. If an allocation to cash is a key component of the investment process, an appropriate cash weight will be incorporated into the benchmark. The benchmark is rebalanced on a periodic basis to ensure that it stays consistent with the manager's investment practice. Custom security-based benchmarks are also referred to as *strategy benchmarks* because they should reflect the manager's strategy. Custom security-based benchmarks are particularly appropriate when the manager's strategy cannot be closely matched to a broad market index or style index. These benchmarks are costly to calculate and maintain.

8 BENCHMARK SELECTION

- ☐ discuss tests of benchmark quality
- ☐ describe the impact of benchmark misspecification on attribution and appraisal analysis

The choice of benchmark often has a significant effect on the assessment of manager performance. Investment managers should be compared only with benchmarks that reflect the universe of securities available to them. A valid benchmark must satisfy certain criteria. We examine the characteristics of a valid benchmark by using the definitive list from Bailey and Tierney (1998).

- *Unambiguous*—The individual securities and their weights in a benchmark should be clearly identifiable. For example, we should be able to identify whether Nestlé is included in a global equity benchmark and its weight.
- *Investable*—It must be possible to replicate and hold the benchmark to earn its return (at least gross of expenses). The sponsor should have the option of moving assets from active management to a passive benchmark. If the benchmark is not investable, it is not a viable investment alternative.
- *Measurable*—It must be possible to measure the benchmark's return on a reasonably frequent and timely basis.
- *Appropriate*—The benchmark must be consistent with the manager's investment style or area of expertise.
- *Reflective of current investment opinions*—The manager should be familiar with the securities that constitute the benchmark and their factor exposures. Managers should be able to develop an opinion regarding their attractiveness as investments; they should not be given a mandate of obscure securities.
- *Specified in advance*—The benchmark must be constructed prior to the evaluation period so that the manager is not judged against benchmarks created after the fact.
- *Accountable*—The manager should accept ownership of the benchmark and its securities and be willing to be held accountable to the benchmark. The benchmark should be fully consistent with the manager's investment process, and the manager should be able to demonstrate the validity of his or her benchmark. Through acceptance of the benchmark, the sponsor

assumes responsibility for any discrepancies between the targeted portfolio for the fund and the benchmark. The manager becomes responsible for differences between the benchmark and her performance.

The properties outlined by Bailey and Tierney help ensure that a benchmark will serve as a valid instrument for the purposes of evaluating the manager's performance. Although these qualities for a desirable benchmark may seem straightforward, we will show later that many commonly used benchmarks do not incorporate them.

EXAMPLE 10

Benchmarks

1. You have hired a bond manager to run an intermediate-duration government fixed-income portfolio. Which type of benchmark is most suitable for this portfolio?

   A. A broad market index

   B. A liability-based benchmark

   C. A factor-model-based benchmark

Solution:

A is correct. A broad market index is a suitable benchmark for a government bond portfolio provided the maturity and duration characteristics of the benchmark align with those of the investment mandate.

2. You have hired a top-down quantitative equity manager who has built a proprietary process based on timing the fund's exposures to systematic risks. Which type of benchmark is most suitable for this portfolio?

   A. A broad market index

   B. A liability-based benchmark

   C. A factor-model-based benchmark

Solution:

C is correct. Factors represent systematic risks. The manager's approach attempts to create alpha by timing the portfolio's exposure to factors. A factor-model-based benchmark can be constructed to represent the manager's investment approach.

3. You are on the board of a pension fund that is seeking to close the gap between its assets and its liabilities. What is the most appropriate benchmark against which to measure the performance of the plan's outsourced chief investment officer?

   A. A broad market index

   B. A liability-based benchmark

   C. A factor-model-based benchmark

Solution:

B is correct. The primary investment objective of the pension portfolio is to close the gap between assets and liabilities. The performance of the pension fund's manager should be evaluated relative to this objective.

4. You are a portfolio manager at JEMstone Capital. Your firm has been hired to run a global small-cap developed market equity portfolio. The agreement with the client sets a minimum market cap of US$500 million and a liquidity constraint that states that a portfolio holding is capped at 5 times its average daily liquidity over the past 12 months. Most portfolios managed by the firm are managed without constraint against the MSCI ACWI Small Cap Index, which has an average market cap of approximately $1.2 billion and a median market cap of approximately $650 million. A stock is eligible for inclusion in the index if the shares traded over the prior three months are equal to at least 20% of the security's free-float-adjusted market capitalization.[5] Your team is discussing the suitability of the MSCI ACWI Small Cap Index for this portfolio. Discuss the validity of this benchmark using the Richards and Tierney framework.

Solution:

- The benchmark meets the criteria of *unambiguous*. The individual securities and their weights are clearly identifiable.
- The benchmark most likely meets the criteria of *investable*. The shares in the index are freely tradeable.
- The benchmark meets the criteria of *measurable*. Index returns are published daily.
- The benchmark *does not* meet the criteria of *appropriate*. The liquidity and capitalization constraints imposed by the client are not consistent with the manner in which the manager runs other portfolios managed by the firm.
- The benchmark meets the criteria of *reflective of current investment opinions*. The benchmark was selected by the manager and is presumed to be representative of the manager's investment process.
- The benchmark meets the criteria of *specified in advance*. The benchmark is not created after the fact.
- The manager may choose to be *accountable* to this index if the liquidity and capitalization constraints are not expected to interfere with the ability to execute the investment strategy. The client should be made aware of the discrepancies between the portfolio constraints and the benchmark.

Evaluating Benchmark Quality: Analysis Based on a Decomposition of Portfolio Holdings and Returns

Once a benchmark is constructed, we can evaluate its quality using tests. To understand these tests, it helps to first decompose the benchmark's returns. Using the decomposition from Bailey et al. (2007), we can first state the identity where a portfolio's return (P) is equal to itself:

$$P = P \tag{13}$$

5 This is a very abbreviated representation of the liquidity constraint used in the construction of the MSCI indexes. For a more complete description of the liquidity requirements, refer to "MSCI Global Investable Market Indexes Methodology": www.msci.com/eqb/methodology/meth_docs/MSCI_GIMIMethodology_Nov2018.pdf (accessed 5 December 2019).

Then, add an appropriate benchmark (B) to, and subtract this benchmark from, the right-hand side of the equation:

$$P = B + (P - B) \quad (14)$$

The term P – B is the result of the manager's active management decisions, which we denote as A. Thus, we have

$$P = B + A \quad (15)$$

From Equations 13–15, we see that the portfolio return is a function of the benchmark and the manager's active decisions.

Next, add the market index return (M) to and subtract it from the right-hand side of the equation:

$$P = M + (B - M) + A \quad (16)$$

The difference between the benchmark return and the market index (B – M) is the manager's style return, which we denote as S:

$$P = M + S + A \quad (17)$$

Equation 17 states that the portfolio return (P) is a result of the market index return (M), a style return (S), and the active management return (A).

If the manager's portfolio is a broad market index where S = 0 and A = 0, then the portfolio earns the broad market return: P = M.

If the benchmark is a broad market index, then S is assumed to be zero and the prediction is that the manager earns the market return and a return to active management: P = M + A. However, if the benchmark is a broad market index and the manager *does* have style differences from the benchmark, the analysis using the broad market benchmark is incorrect. In this case, any style return (S) will be lumped together with the measured active management component (A), such that an analysis of a manager's true added value will be obscured.

We can use these benchmark building blocks to further search for systematic biases between the active management return and the style return, identified through correlation. For instance, if we measure the correlation between active management return, A = (P – B), and style return, S = (B – M), we can identify whether the manager's active selection decisions align with the style currently favored by the market. A good benchmark should not reflect these systematic biases, where the correlation between A and S should not be statistically different from zero. Likewise, we define the difference between the portfolio and the broad market index as E = (P – M). When a manager's style (S) is in (out of) favor relative to the market, we expect both the benchmark and the account to outperform (underperform) the market. Therefore, a good benchmark will have a statistically significant positive correlation coefficient between S and E.

EXAMPLE 11

Decomposition of Portfolio Return

1. Assume that the Courtland account has a return of –5.3% in a given month, during which the portfolio benchmark has a return of –5.5% and the market index has a return of –2.8%.

   A. Calculate the Courtland account's return due to the manager's style.

   B. Calculate the Courtland account's return due to active management.

Solution:

A. The return due to style is S = B − M = −5.5% − (−2.8%) = −2.7%.

B. The return due to active management is A = P − B = −5.3% − (−5.5%) = 0.2%.

2. Assume that Mr. Kuti's account has a return of 5.6% in a given month, during which the portfolio benchmark has a return of 5.1% and a market index has a return of 3.2%.

A. Calculate the return due to the manager's style for Mr. Kuti's account.

B. Calculate the return due to active management for Mr. Kuti's account.

Solution:

A. The return due to style is S = B − M = 5.1% − 3.2% = 1.9%.

B. The return due to active management is A = P − B = 5.6% − 5.1% = 0.5%.

3. An actively managed mid-cap value equity portfolio has a return of 9.24%. The portfolio is benchmarked to a mid-cap value index that has a return of 7.85%. A broad equity market index has a return of 8.92%. Calculate the return due to the portfolio manager's style.

Solution:

The return due to style is the style-specific benchmark return of 7.85% minus the broad market return of 8.92%: −1.07%.

4. A US large-cap value portfolio run by Anderson Investment Management returned 18.9% during the first three quarters of 2019. During the same time period, a US large-cap value index had a return of 21.7% and a broad US equity index returned 25.2%.

A. Calculate the return due to style.

B. Calculate the return due to active management.

C. Using your answers to A and B, discuss Anderson's performance relative to the benchmark and relative to the market.

Solution:

A. The return due to style is the difference between the benchmark and the market index, or S = (B − M) = (21.7% − 25.2%) = −3.5%.

B. The return due to active management is the difference between the portfolio and the benchmark, or A = (P − B) = (18.9% − 21.7%) = −2.8%.

C. Anderson's underperformance relative to the broad US equity index is partly a function of style and partly a function of the manager's weak performance within the style. Given that the US large-cap value index underperformed the US market index by 3.5%, we can infer that large-cap value was out of favor during the period measured. Provided the US large-cap value index is an appropriate benchmark for Anderson, the manager's underperformance bears further investigation. The client would want to understand the specific drivers of the underperformance and relate those decisions to the manager's stated investment process.

Importance of Choosing the Correct Benchmark

As we have described, performance evaluation and attribution require appropriate benchmarks. When benchmarks are misspecified, subsequent performance measurement will be incorrect; both the attribution and the appraisal analyses will be useless.

For example, consider a manager who invests in Japanese stocks. The sponsor uses the MSCI Pacific Index to evaluate the manager. Japanese stocks constitute most of the MSCI Pacific, but the index also includes four other developed markets (Australia, New Zealand, Hong Kong SAR, and Singapore). Thus, the MSCI Japan Index more closely represents the manager's normal portfolio. The returns were as follows:

- Manager return: 18.0%
- MSCI Pacific (investor's benchmark) return: 20.0%
- MSCI Japan (normal portfolio) return: 9.0%

Although the manager *underperformed* the investor's benchmark (18.0% for the manager versus 20.0% for the MSCI Pacific), the manager *outperformed* when correctly benchmarked against the normal portfolio (18.0% for the manager versus 9.0% for the normal portfolio). In summary,

- True Active Return = Mgr Return − Normal Portfolio Return = 18.0 − 9.0 = 9.0%
- Investor (Mismeasured) Active Return = Mgr Return − Investor Benchmark return = (Mgr Return - Normal portfolio Return) + (Normal Portfolio Return - Investor Benchmark return) = True Active Return + Misfit Active Return = 18.0 − 20.0 = 9.0 + (−11.0) = −2.0%

Measuring the manager's results against the normal portfolio instead of the investor's benchmark more accurately evaluates the manager's performance. The manager's negative "true" active return indicates that the manager outperformed the normal portfolio. Fundamentally, any further performance attribution against the investor's benchmark will also be useless. By using the incorrect benchmark, the attribution would attempt to explain an underperformance, rather than the true active return, which contributed positively to the investor's return.

Peer group benchmarking is particularly susceptible to selection problems. For example, practitioners must select the appropriate peers without suggesting to the portfolio managers that median peer group performance is the target. Peer group benchmarks provide an incentive not to underperform the peer group median, often leading to herding around the median return. As a result, the investment decisions of the fund manager can be biased by the structure of the benchmarks chosen.

Sometimes, benchmarks are chosen for the wrong reasons. Underperforming managers have been known to change benchmarks to improve their measured excess return, which is both inappropriate and unethical.

Benchmark misspecification can lead to mismeasurement of the value added by the portfolio managers. A "normal portfolio" or "normal benchmark" is the portfolio that most closely represents the manager's typical positions in his investment universe. The manager's "true" active return is equal to his return minus his normal portfolio return.

Most investors, however, tend to use a broad market benchmark for manager evaluation. The manager's active return is thus measured as the manager's return minus the investor's benchmark return. There is a mismatch between the broad market benchmark and the manager's "normal" portfolio or benchmark; this is not the manager's "true" active return but is more appropriately termed the "misfit active return" (see, e.g., Gastineau, Olma, and Zielinski 2007). Using a broad market index typically misses the manager's style (i.e., creates style bias). This decomposition is useful for understanding the impact of a misspecified benchmark on performance appraisal.

For example, consider a manager who invests in US value stocks. The sponsor uses the broad Russell 3000 equity index (the "investor's benchmark") to evaluate the manager. However, the manager's normal portfolio is better represented by his or her universe of value stocks. In this example, the manager returns 15%, the Russell 3000 (the investor's benchmark) return is 10%, and the manager's normal portfolio return is 18%. Although the manager has outperformed the investor's benchmark (15% versus 10%), the manager has underperformed when correctly benchmarked against the normal portfolio (15% versus 18%).

9 BENCHMARKING ALTERNATIVE INVESTMENTS

☐ describe problems that arise in benchmarking alternative investments

Performance evaluation for alternative asset classes presents many challenges. The selection of an appropriate benchmark is stymied by the lack of high-quality, investible market indexes, the frequent use of leverage in many strategies, the limited liquidity and lack of readily available market values for many underlying assets, and the use of internal rates of return rather than time-weighted rates of return.

In the following sections addressing each of the major alternative asset classes, we will consider how these challenges affect performance evaluation.

Benchmarking Hedge Fund Investments

Hedge funds do not represent an asset class, such as equities or fixed income. Rather, hedge funds encompass a broad range of possible strategies designed to exploit market inefficiencies. Hedge funds may have an unlimited investment universe, vary substantially from one to another, and can vary their asset allocations over time. Hedge funds also use leverage, sell assets short, take positions in derivatives, and may be opportunistic in their choice of strategy. These characteristics make it difficult to create a single standard against which hedge funds should be judged.

Some hedge funds lever many times their capital base, which increases their expected return and risk. Short positions and derivatives used in long–short strategies can increase return or reduce risk. A manager's use of style, leverage, short positions, and derivatives may change over time. Hedge funds also typically lack transparency, are difficult to monitor, and are often illiquid.

These characteristics of hedge funds make it clear that broad market indexes are unsuitable as hedge fund benchmarks.

The risk-free rate (e.g., Treasury yield) plus a spread (e.g., 3%–6%) is sometimes advocated as a hedge fund benchmark for arbitrage-based hedge fund strategies. The argument for using the risk-free rate is that investors desire a positive return and that arbitrage strategies are risk free, with the spread reflecting the active management return and management costs.

However, most funds, even those that target market-neutral strategies, are not completely free of systematic risk, and the use of leverage could magnify that systematic risk. In this case, the spread relative to the risk-free rate should be adjusted upward.

Both broad market indexes and the risk-free rate will be weakly correlated or uncorrelated with hedge fund returns, thus failing the benchmark quality test of Bailey et al. (2007) that states that portfolio and benchmark factor sensitivities should be similar.

Because of the shortcomings of broad market indexes and the risk-free rate, hedge fund manager universes from such providers as CSFB/Tremont are often used as hedge fund benchmarks. Hedge fund peer universes are subject to a number of limitations:

1. The risk and return characteristics of a strategy peer group is unlikely to be representative of the approach taken by a single fund.
2. Hedge fund peer groups suffer from survivorship and backfill bias. Backfill bias occurs when the index provider adds a manager to the index and imports the manager's entire return history.
3. Hedge fund performance data are often self-reported and typically not confirmed by the index provider. A fund's reported net asset value may be a managed value. Even if the manager has no intention to misreport the data, hedge funds hold illiquid assets that require some subjectivity in pricing. If the previous period's price is used as the current price or an appraisal is used, then the data will be smoothed. The presence of stale pricing will result in downward-biased standard deviations and temporal instability in correlations, with hedge funds potentially given larger portfolio allocations as a result.

Benchmarking Real Estate Investments

There are numerous private real estate indexes offered by industry associations, large and small index providers, investment consultants, and others who collect real estate data. There are indexes and sub-indexes for nearly all the major developed countries, major sectors, investment styles, and structures (open-end and closed-end funds). Choosing the appropriate real estate benchmark requires careful consideration and an understanding of the limitations of such benchmarks—and their relevance to the investment strategy under evaluation. The following are some limitations of the available real estate benchmarks:

1. The benchmarks are based on a subset of the real estate opportunity set and, therefore, are not fully representative of the asset class.
2. Index performance is likely to be highly correlated with the returns of the largest fund data contributors.
3. Benchmark returns are based on manager-reported performance and may be inherently biased.
4. Benchmarks weighted by fund or asset value may place a disproportionate emphasis on the most expensive cities and asset types.
5. Valuations of the underlying properties are typically based on appraisals because there are few transactions to measure. Appraisals are infrequent, they smooth changes in property values, and they can lag underlying property performance. Transaction-based indexes are becoming more readily available.
6. Some benchmark returns are unlevered, whereas others contain varying degrees of leverage based on the structure used by the investor that contributed the data.
7. Real estate indexes do not reflect the high transaction costs, limited transparency, and lack of liquidity that drive performance for actual real estate investments.

Further complicating the performance evaluation of real estate funds is the selection of the appropriate return measure. Open-end funds, for which the contributions and withdrawals are at the discretion of the investor, generally use time-weighted rates of return. Closed-end funds, however, for which the timing of the contributions and withdrawals is at the discretion of the fund manager, generally report using internal rates of return.

Benchmarking Private Equity

When measuring the performance of a private equity investment, investors typically calculate an internal rate of return (IRR) based on cash flows since inception of the investment and the ending valuation of the investment (the net asset value or residual value). Similarly, major venture capital benchmarks, such as those of Cambridge Associates, provide IRR estimates for private equity funds that are based on fund cash flows and valuations. Major indexes serving as benchmarks for US and European private equity include those provided by Cambridge Associates, Preqin, and LPX.

These benchmarks can be used to compare the managers' individual funds with an appropriate peer group, normally defined by subclass, geography, and vintage year of the underlying fund. Benchmarks commonly used for this purpose include ones prepared by Burgiss, Cambridge Associates, and the Institutional Limited Partners Association.

Although relative performance measures help an investor understand how a fund performs relative to peers or a relevant public index, there are several limitations to be aware of when comparing returns among managers:

1. The valuation methodology used by the managers may differ.
2. A fund's IRR can be meaningfully influenced by an early loss or an early win in the portfolio.
3. The data are from a specific point in time, and the companies in a fund can be at different stages of development.

The public market equivalent (PME) methodology has been developed to allow comparisons of private equity IRRs with returns of publicly traded equity indexes. The methodology uses cash flow data to replicate the general partner's capital calls and distributions, assuming these same cash flows were invested in the chosen equity index. Comparing the performance of the PME index with the net IRR of the fund reveals the extent of over- or underperformance of the PME index relative to the public index. Several PME methodologies exist, the most common being Long–Nickels PME, PME+, Kaplan and Schoar PME, and Direct Alpha PME. It is important to choose the appropriate PME for each private equity fund; a poorly chosen PME raises the risk of leading the investor to an incorrect conclusion.

Benchmarking Commodity Investments

Commodity benchmarks tend to use indexes based on the performance of futures-based commodity investments. These include the Reuters/Jefferies Commodity Research Bureau (RJ/CRB) Index, the S&P Goldman Sachs Commodity Index (GSCI), and the Bloomberg Commodity Index (BCOM). However, because the indexes use futures, rather than actual assets, they attempt to replicate the returns available to holding long positions in commodities. The S&P GSCI, the BCOM, and the RJ/CRB Index provide returns comparable to those of passive long positions in listed futures contracts. Because the cost-of-carry model ensures that the return on a fully margined position in a futures contract mimics the return on an underlying spot deliverable, futures contract returns are often used as a surrogate for cash market performance.

These indexes are considered investable. The major indexes contain some common groups of underlying assets. For example, the RJ/CRB Index, the BCOM, and the S&P GSCI all include energy (oil and gas), metals (industrial and precious), grains (corn, soybeans, and wheat), and soft commodities (cocoa, coffee, cotton, and sugar). However, beyond these basic groupings, they and other commodity indexes vary greatly in their composition and weighting schemes. A market-cap-weighting scheme, so common for equity and bond market indexes, cannot be carried over to indexes of commodity futures. Because every long futures position has a corresponding short futures position, the market capitalization of a futures contract is always zero.

Benchmarking of commodity investments presents similar challenges to other alternatives, including

1. the use of derivatives to represent actual commodity assets,
2. varying degrees of leverage among funds, and
3. the discretionary weighting of exposures within the index.

Benchmarking Managed Derivatives

Because market indexes do not exist for managed derivatives, the benchmarks are typically specific to a single investment strategy. For example, the Mount Lucas Management Index takes both long and short positions in many futures markets based on a technical (moving-average) trading rule that is, in effect, specific to an active momentum strategy.

Other derivative benchmarks are based on peer groups. For example, the BarclayHedge and CISDM CTA trading strategy benchmarks are based on peer groups of commodity trading advisers (CTAs). The CISDM CTA Equal Weighted Index reflects manager returns for all reporting managers in the CISDM CTA database. These indexes suffer from the known limitations of peer group–based benchmarks, including survivorship bias.

Benchmarking Distressed Securities

Distressed securities are illiquid and almost non-marketable at the time of purchase, making it very difficult to find suitable benchmarks. If the companies' prospects improve, the values of the distressed securities may go up gradually and liquidity may improve. Typically, it takes a relatively long time for this strategy to play out; thus, valuing the holdings may be a challenge. It is difficult to estimate the true market values of distressed securities, and stale pricing is almost inevitable.

One possible strategy is to use market indexes, such as the Barclay Distressed Securities Index. This index is constructed from fund managers who invest in distressed securities. Because this index is constructed from multiple strategies, however, it is difficult to discern whether the index is suitable for a given investment approach. In addition, because the valuations for the member funds are calculated at random intervals, it doesn't necessarily correct for the valuation issues noted previously.

PERFORMANCE APPRAISAL: RISK-BASED MEASURES 10

- ☐ calculate and interpret the Sortino ratio, the appraisal ratio, upside/downside capture ratios, maximum drawdown, and drawdown duration
- ☐ describe limitations of appraisal measures and related metrics

Investment performance appraisal identifies and measures investment skill, providing the information to assess how effectively money has been invested given the risks that were taken. (Risk-adjusted past performance is just one of many considerations when choosing investment managers. Qualitative considerations, although not within the scope of this reading, are also very important.)

Performance appraisal is most often concerned with ranking investment managers who follow similar investment disciplines. Return attribution provides information that can complement a performance appraisal analysis by providing more details about the consequences of managerial decisions. Performance attribution identifies and quantifies the sources of added value, whereas performance appraisal seeks to ascertain whether added value was a result of managerial skill.

Skill in any profession can be thought of as the ability to influence outcomes in desired directions. We define active investment management skill as the ability of a portfolio manager to add value on a risk-adjusted basis through investment analysis and insights. In everyday language, active investment skill is typically viewed as the ability to "beat the market" or an assigned benchmark with some consistency. The evaluation of active management skill is the focus of performance appraisal and this reading.

Distinguishing Investment Skill from Luck

An investment manager's record for any specific period will reflect good luck (unanticipated good developments) and bad luck (unanticipated bad developments). One reason that luck should be considered important when appraising investment performance is the paradox of skill. As people become more knowledgeable about an activity, the difference between the worst and the best performers becomes narrower. Thus, the ever-increasing aggregate skill level of investment managers, supplemented by massive computing power and access to "big data," may lead to narrower investment performance differentials and a greater likelihood that these differentials can be explained by luck.

Deciding whether a portfolio manager has or lacks active investment skill on the basis of past returns is difficult and always subject to error. Financial market returns have a large element of randomness. Some of this randomness reflects the impact of news and information that relate directly or indirectly to asset values. Trading motivated by liquidity needs and by the emotions of investors adds to return volatility.

When we observe the historical performance of an investment portfolio, we see only one out of a potentially unlimited number of outcomes for a manager applying the same investment discipline but with different luck. Perhaps we gain additional insight into skill by examining the consistency of performance over time. But the hypothesis that the manager's underlying mean return exceeds the benchmark's mean return may require many years of observations to confirm with a reasonably high degree of confidence.[6]

6 Can you be lucky once and correctly pick the flip of a fair coin? Of course! How about four times in a row? Yes, although this outcome is much less likely. Can a portfolio manager be lucky enough to generate 15 continuous years of superior investment performance? This outcome is very unlikely, but with hundreds or even thousands of portfolio managers, a few might succeed solely because of luck. One problem faced in investment performance appraisal is that many investment management performance records are only a few years long, making it difficult to distinguish between luck and skill.

Appraisal Measures

The academic and the professional investment literatures have developed several returns-based measures to assess the value of active management. Important measures include the following:

- Sharpe ratio
- Treynor ratio
- Information ratio
- Appraisal ratio
- Sortino ratio
- Capture ratios

The selection of an appropriate appraisal measure requires an understanding of which aspect of risk is most important given the role of the investment in the client's total portfolio. It is also important to understand the assumptions a measure makes about the probability distribution of possible returns and any assumptions regarding the underlying theoretical pricing model. The Sharpe, information, and Treynor ratios are covered elsewhere in the curriculum and are not covered in depth here. This section will focus primarily on the remaining measures.

The Sharpe Ratio

The **Sharpe ratio** measures the additional return for bearing risk above the risk-free rate, stated per unit of return volatility. In performance appraisal, this additional return is often referred to as **excess return**. This use contrasts with how "excess return" is used in return performance attribution—that is, as a return in excess of a benchmark's return.

The Sharpe ratio is commonly used on an *ex post* basis to evaluate historical risk-adjusted returns, as in

$$S_A = \frac{\overline{R}_A - \overline{r}_f}{\hat{\sigma}_A} \qquad (18)$$

One weakness of the Sharpe ratio is that the use of standard deviation as a measure of risk assumes investors are indifferent between upside and downside volatility. For example, for an investor looking for a potentially high-rewarding investment, volatility on the upside is not necessarily a negative. Similarly, risk-averse investors concerned about the preservation of capital are clearly most concerned with downside risk.

The Treynor Ratio

The Treynor ratio (Treynor 1965) measures the excess return per unit of systematic risk. With the Treynor ratio, as well as the systematic-risk-based appraisal measures that follow, we must carefully choose an efficient market benchmark against which to measure the systematic risk of the manager's fund. In contrast, the Sharpe ratio can be compared among different funds without the explicit choice of a market benchmark.

$$T_A = \frac{\overline{R}_A - \overline{r}_f}{\hat{\beta}_A} \qquad (19)$$

The usefulness of the Treynor ratio depends on whether systematic risk or total risk is most appropriate in evaluating performance. Because of its reliance on beta, the Treynor ratio shows how a fund has performed in relation not to its own volatility but to the volatility it would bring to a well-diversified portfolio. Thus, a ranking of portfolios based on the Treynor ratio is most useful if the portfolios whose performance is being evaluated are being combined in a broader, fully diversified portfolio. The ratio is most informative when the portfolios being evaluated are compared with the same benchmark index.

The Information Ratio

The information ratio (IR) is a simple measure that allows the evaluator to assess performance relative to the benchmark, scaled by risk. The implicit assumption is that the chosen benchmark is well matched to the risk of the investment strategy. The IR is calculated by dividing the portfolio's mean excess return relative to its benchmark by the variability of that excess return, as shown in Equation 18. The denominator of the information ratio, $\sigma(r_p - r_B)$, is the portfolio's tracking risk, a measure of how closely a portfolio follows the index to which it is benchmarked. (Many writers use "tracking error" in the sense of "tracking risk," although, confusingly, tracking error is also used to refer to simply the return difference between a passive portfolio and its benchmark.)

$$\text{IR} = \frac{E\left(r_p\right) - E\left(r_B\right)}{\sigma\left(r_p - r_B\right)} \tag{20}$$

The Appraisal Ratio

The appraisal ratio (AR) is a returns-based measure, like the IR. It is the annualized alpha divided by the annualized residual risk. In the appraisal ratio, both the alpha and the residual risk are computed from a factor regression. Although the AR can be computed using any factor model appropriate for the portfolio, the measure was first introduced by Treynor and Black (1973) using Jensen's alpha and the standard deviation of the portfolio's residual or non-systematic risk. Treynor and Black argued that security selection ability implies that deviations from benchmark portfolio weights can be profitable and showed that the optimal deviations from the benchmark holdings for securities depend on what they called an "appraisal ratio." The appraisal ratio is also referred to as the *Treynor–Black ratio* or the *Treynor–Black appraisal ratio.*

The appraisal ratio measures the reward of active management relative to the risk of active management (alpha from a factor model):

$$\text{AR} = \frac{\alpha}{\sigma_\varepsilon} \tag{21}$$

where σ_ε equals the standard deviation of ε_t, commonly denoted as the "standard error of regression," which is readily available from the output of commonly used statistical software.

The Sortino Ratio

The Sortino ratio is a modification of the Sharpe ratio that penalizes only those returns that are lower than a user-specified return. The Sharpe ratio penalizes both upside and downside volatility equally.

Equation 22 presents the *ex ante* Sortino ratio, where r_T is the minimum acceptable return (MAR), which is sometimes referred to as a *target rate of return.*[7] Instead of using standard deviation in the denominator, the Sortino ratio uses a measure of downside risk known as target semi-standard deviation or target semideviation, σ_D, as shown in Equation 23. By using this value, the Sortino ratio penalizes managers only for "harmful" volatility and is a measure of return per unit of downside risk.

7 The MAR is the lowest rate of return at which an investor will consider investing. For example, an MAR set equal to the expected rate of inflation would be associated with capital preservation in real terms. It is possible to use the benchmark return as the MAR. The MAR does not determine intrinsic value. Rather, it is a constraint or decision criterion that applies to all investment considerations.

$$\mathrm{SR}_D = \frac{E\left(r_p\right) - r_T}{\sigma_D} \tag{22}$$

$$\widehat{\mathrm{SR}}_D = \frac{\bar{r}_p - \bar{r}_T}{\hat{\sigma}_D} \tag{23}$$

$$\sigma_D = \left[\frac{\sum_{t=1}^{N} \min\left(r_t - r_T, 0\right)^2}{N}\right]^{1/2} \tag{24}$$

Assume a portfolio has an MAR of 4.0%. The portfolio's returns over a 10-year period are given in Exhibit 16. The numerator of the Sortino ratio is the average portfolio return minus the target return: $\bar{r}_p - \bar{r}_T = 6.0\% - 4.0\% = 2.0\%$. The calculation of target semi-standard deviation is reported in Exhibit 16. Based on the information in the table, the Sortino ratio is approximately 0.65.

Exhibit 16: Sortino Ratio Using Target Semi-Standard Deviation

		Target Return: $r_T = 4\%$
Year	**Rate of Return: r_t**	**$\min(r_t - r_T, 0)^2$**
1	6.0%	0
2	8.0%	0
3	−1.0%	0.0025
4	18.0%	0
5	12.0%	0
6	3.0%	0.0001
7	−4.0%	0.0064
8	5.0%	0
9	2.0%	0.0004
10	11.0%	0

$$\sum_{t=1}^{N} \min\left(r_t - r_T, 0\right)^2 = 0.0094$$

$$\sigma_D = \left[\frac{\sum_{t=1}^{N} \min\left(r_t - r_T, 0\right)^2}{N}\right]^{1/2} = \left(\frac{0.0094}{10}\right)^{1/2} = 3.07\%$$

More so than traditional performance measures, the Sortino ratio offers the ability to accurately assess performance when return distributions are not symmetrical. For example, because of its underlying assumption of normally distributed returns, the Sharpe ratio would not effectively distinguish between strategies with greater-than-normal upside volatility (positively skewed strategies, such as trend following) and strategies with greater-than-normal downside volatility (negatively skewed strategies, such as option writing). Both types of volatility are penalized equally in the Sharpe ratio. The Sortino ratio is arguably a better performance metric for such assets as hedge funds or commodity trading funds, whose return distributions are purposefully skewed away from the normal.

The Sortino ratio formula is not a risk premium. It is the return a portfolio manager generates that is greater than what is minimally acceptable to the investor. Essentially, the Sortino ratio penalizes a manager when portfolio return is lower than the MAR; it is most relevant when one of the investor's primary objectives is capital preservation.

Although there are arguments in favor of both the Sharpe ratio and the Sortino ratio, the Sharpe ratio has been much more widely used. In some cases, this preference may reflect a certain comfort level associated with the use of standard deviation, which is a more traditional measure of volatility. Also, cross-sectional comparisons of Sortino ratios are difficult to make applicable to every investor, because the MAR is investor-specific.

EXAMPLE 12

Performance Appraisal Measures

1. Portfolio B delivered 10.0% annual returns on average over the past 60 months. Its average annual volatility as measured by standard deviation was 14.0%, and its downside volatility as measured by target semi-standard deviation was 8.0%. Assuming the target rate of return is 3.0% per year, the Sortino ratio of portfolio B is closest to:

   A. 0.66.

   B. 0.77.

   C. 0.88.

Solution:

C is correct.

$$\widehat{SR}_D = \frac{\bar{r}_P - \bar{r}_T}{\hat{\sigma}_D} = \frac{0.10 - 0.03}{0.08} = 0.88$$

2. Why might a practitioner use the Sortino ratio, rather than the Sharpe ratio, to indicate performance?

   A. He is measuring option writing.

   B. The return distributions are not symmetrical.

   C. The investor's primary objective is capital preservation.

   D. All of the above

Solution:

D is correct, because the Sortino ratio is more relevant when return distributions are not symmetrical, as with option writing. The Sortino ratio is also preferable when one of the primary objectives is capital preservation.

3. Portfolio Y delivered an average annualized return of 9.0% over the past 60 months. The annualized standard deviation over this same time period was 20.0%. The market index returned 8.0% per year on average over the same time period, with an annualized standard deviation of 12.0%. Portfolio Y has an estimated beta of 1.40 versus the market index. Assuming the risk-free rate is 3.0% per year, the appraisal ratio is *closest* to:

   A. −0.8492.

   B. −0.0922.

   C. −0.0481.

Solution:

B is correct. Jensen's alpha is −1.0%: $\alpha_p = 9.0\% - [3.0\% + 1.40(8.0\% - 3.0\%)] = -1.0\% = -0.01$. Non-systematic risk is 0.011776: $\sigma_{\varepsilon_p}^2 = 0.20^2 - 1.40^2(0.12^2) = 0.011776$. The appraisal ratio is approximately −0.0922: $\widehat{AR} = \frac{-0.01}{\sqrt{0.011776}} = -0.0922$.

4. The appraisal ratio is the ratio of the portfolio's alpha to the standard deviation of its:

   A. total risk.

   B. systematic risk.

   C. non-systematic risk.

Solution:

C is correct. The appraisal ratio is the ratio of the portfolio's alpha to the standard deviation of the portfolio's non-systematic risk. Essentially, this ratio allows an investor to evaluate whether excess returns warrant the additional non-systematic risk in actively managed portfolios.

5. Assume a target return of 3.0%. Annual returns over the past four years have been 6.0%, −3.0%, 7.0%, and 1.0%. The target semi-standard deviation is *closest* to:

   A. 1.33%.

   B. 3.16%.

   C. 4.65%.

Solution:

B is correct.

		Target Return: $r_T = 3\%$
Year	**Rate of Return: r_t**	**$\min(r_t - r_T, 0)^2$**
1	6.0%	0
2	−3.0%	0.0036
3	7.0%	0
4	1.0%	0.0004
	$\sum_{t=1}^{N} \min(r_t - r_T, 0)^2 =$	0.004

$$\sigma_D = \left[\frac{\sum_{t=1}^{N} \min(r_t - r_T, 0)^2}{N}\right]^{1/2} = \left(\frac{0.004}{4}\right)^{1/2} \approx 0.0316 = 3.16\%$$

11 PERFORMANCE APPRAISAL: CAPTURE RATIOS AND DRAWDOWNS

- ☐ calculate and interpret the Sortino ratio, the appraisal ratio, upside/downside capture ratios, maximum drawdown, and drawdown duration
- ☐ describe limitations of appraisal measures and related metrics

In investing, we understand that large losses require proportionally greater gains to reverse or offset. Performance measures used to monitor this aspect of manager performance include capture ratios and drawdowns. Capture ratios have several variations that reflect various aspects of the manager's gain or loss relative to the gain or loss of the benchmark. Capture ratios also help assess manager suitability relative to the investor, especially in relation to the investor's time horizon and risk tolerance. **Drawdown** is the loss in value incurred in any continuous period of negative returns. A manager who experiences larger drawdowns may be less suitable for an investor with a shorter time horizon. This section reviews capture ratios and drawdowns, their implications for performance, and their use in evaluating manager performance and suitability.

Capture Ratios

Capture ratios measure the manager's participation in up and down markets—that is, the manager's percentage return relative to that of the benchmark. The upside capture ratio, or upside capture (UC), measures capture when the benchmark return is positive. The downside capture ratio, or downside capture (DC), measures capture when the benchmark return is negative. Upside capture greater (less) than 100% generally suggests outperformance (underperformance) relative to the benchmark, and downside capture less (greater) than 100% generally suggests outperformance (underperformance) relative to the benchmark. Practitioners should note that when the manager and benchmark returns are of the opposite sign, the ratio will be negative—for example, a manager with a 1% return when the market is down 1% will have a downside capture ratio of −100%.

The expressions for upside capture and downside capture are

$$\text{UC}(m,B,t) = \text{R}(m,t)/\text{R}(B,t) \text{ if } \text{R}(B,t) \geq 0$$

$$\text{DC}(m,B,t) = \text{R}(m,t)/\text{R}(B,t) \text{ if } \text{R}(B,t) < 0$$

where

$\text{UC}(m,B,t)$ = upside capture for manager m relative to benchmark B for time t

$\text{DC}(m,B,t)$ = downside capture for manager m relative to benchmark B for time t

$\text{R}(m,t)$ = return of manager m for time t

$\text{R}(B,t)$ = return of benchmark B for time t

The upside/downside capture, or simply the capture ratio (CR), is the upside capture divided by the downside capture. It measures the asymmetry of return and, as such, is like bond convexity and option gamma. A capture ratio greater than 1 indicates positive asymmetry, or a convex return profile, whereas a capture ratio less than 1 indicates negative asymmetry, or a concave return profile. Exhibit 17 illustrates what is meant by concave and convex return profiles. The dotted-line curve for a concave return profile resembles a downward-facing bowl, and the solid-line curve for a convex return profile resembles an upward-facing bowl. The horizontal and vertical axes are, respectively, benchmark returns [R(*B*)] and portfolio returns [R(*m*)]. As benchmark returns increase (i.e., moving to the right on the horizontal axis), portfolio returns increase—but at a *decreasing* rate for a concave return profile and at an *increasing* rate for a convex return profile. The expression for the capture ratio is

CR(*m*,*B*,*t*) = UC(*m*,*B*,*t*)/DC(*m*,*B*,*t*)

where

CR(*m*,*B*,*t*) = capture ratio for manager *m* relative to benchmark *B* for time *t*

Exhibit 17: Convex and Concave Return Profiles

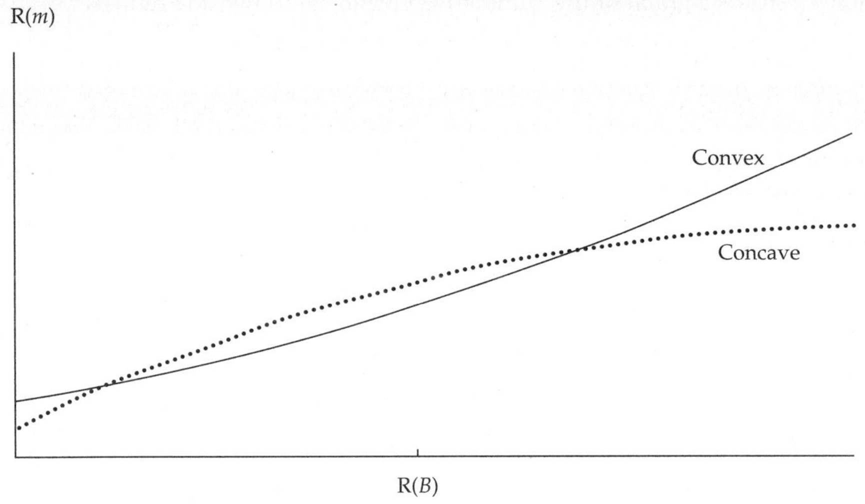

Consider the following return series for the manager, R(*m*), and the benchmark, R(*B*), shown in Exhibit 18. The upside columns calculate the cumulative return for the manager, Cum R(*m*), and the benchmark, Cum R(*B*), for those periods when the benchmark return is positive. The downside columns calculate the cumulative returns when the benchmark return is negative.

Exhibit 18: Capture Ratio

			Upside Return				Downside Return			
t	R(*m*)	R(*B*)	R(*m*)	R(*B*)	Cum R(*m*)	Cum R(*B*)	R(*m*)	R(*B*)	Cum R(*m*)	Cum R(*B*)
1	0.6%	1.0%	0.6%	1.0%	0.60%	1.00%			0.00%	0.00%
2	−0.3%	−0.5%			0.60%	1.00%	−0.3%	−0.5%	−0.30%	−0.50%
3	1.0%	1.5%	1.0%	1.5%	1.61%	2.52%			−0.30%	−0.50%
4	0.1%	0.2%	0.1%	0.2%	1.71%	2.72%			−0.30%	−0.50%
5	−1.0%	−2.0%			1.71%	2.72%	−1.0%	−2.0%	−1.30%	−2.49%
6	0.5%	0.6%	0.5%	0.6%	2.22%	3.34%			−1.30%	−2.49%
7	0.2%	0.1%	0.2%	0.1%	2.42%	3.44%			−1.30%	−2.49%
8	−0.8%	−1.0%			2.42%	3.44%	−0.8%	−1.0%	−2.09%	−3.47%

			Upside Return				Downside Return			
t	R(*m*)	R(*B*)	R(*m*)	R(*B*)	Cum R(*m*)	Cum R(*B*)	R(*m*)	R(*B*)	Cum R(*m*)	Cum R(*B*)
9	0.8%	1.0%	0.8%	1.0%	3.24%	4.47%			−2.09%	−3.47%
10	0.4%	0.5%	0.4%	0.5%	3.65%	5.00%			−2.09%	−3.47%
Geometric average			0.51%	0.70%			−0.70%	−1.17%		
Upside capture				0.51%/0.70% = 72.8%			Downside capture		−0.70%/−1.17% = 59.8%	
Capture ratio				72.8%/59.8% = 121.7%						

During up markets, the geometric average return is 0.51% for the manager and 0.70% for the benchmark, giving an upside capture of 72.8%. During down markets, the geometric average return is −0.70% for the manager and −1.17% for the benchmark, giving a downside capture of 59.8%. The manager's capture ratio is 1.217, or 121.7%. Exhibit 19 shows a graph of the cumulative upside and downside returns.

Exhibit 19: Cumulative Upside and Downside Returns

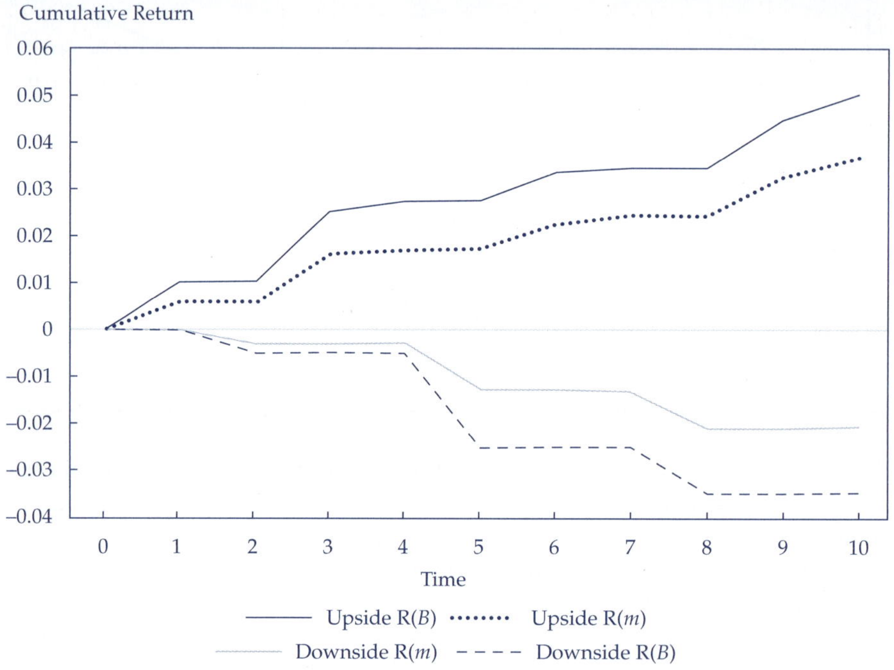

Drawdown

Drawdown is measured as the cumulative peak-to-trough loss during a continuous period. Drawdown duration is the total time from the start of the drawdown until the cumulative drawdown recovers to zero, which can be segmented into the drawdown phase (start to trough) and the recovery phase (trough-to-zero cumulative return).

$$\text{Maximum DD}(m,t) = \min([V(m,t) - V(m,t^*)]/V(m,t^*), 0)$$

where

$V(m,t)$ = portfolio value of manager m at time t

$V(m,t^*)$ = peak portfolio value of manager m

$t > t^*$

Consider the return on the S&P 500 Index at the start of the global COVID-19 outbreak (from November 2019 to February 2020, shown in Exhibit 20 and Exhibit 21. The drawdown is 0% until January 2020, when the return is –0.04% and the drawdown continues to worsen, reaching a maximum of –19.6% in March 2020. The strong positive returns from April to July 2020 reverse the drawdown. The total duration of the drawdown was 7 months, with a 4-month recovery period.

Exhibit 20: Drawdown

Month	R(*m*)	Cumulative R(*m*)	Drawdown	Cumulative Drawdown	
November 2019	3.63%	7.86%		0.00%	
December 2019	3.01%	11.10%		0.00%	
January 2020	-0.04%	11.05%	-0.04%	-0.04%	Drawdown begins
February 2020	-8.23%	1.91%	-8.23%	-8.27%	
March 2020	-12.35%	-10.67%	-12.35%	-19.60%	Maximum drawdown
April 2020	12.82%	0.78%		-9.30%	
May 2020	4.76%	5.58%		-4.98%	
June 2020	1.99%	7.67%		-3.09%	
July 2020	5.64%	13.75%		0.00%	Recovery begins

Exhibit 21: Drawdown

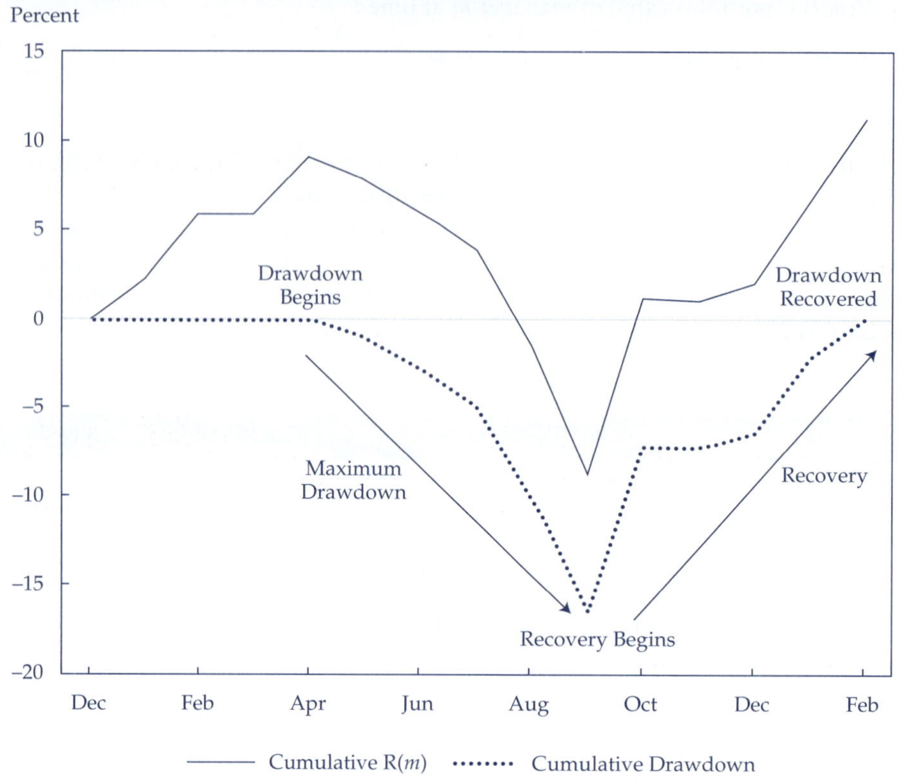

An asymmetrical return profile or avoiding large drawdowns, particularly during periods when the market is not trending strongly upward, can result in higher risk-adjusted returns. The reason is the all-too-familiar reality for investors that it takes proportionally larger gains to recover from increasingly large losses. This asymmetry arises from basis drift, from the change in the denominator when calculating returns, or from the practical problem of recovering from a smaller asset base after a large loss. For example, a portfolio decline of 50% must be followed by a gain of 100% to return to its previous value. Exhibit 22 illustrates this relationship.

Exhibit 22: Percentage Gain Necessary to Offset a Given Loss

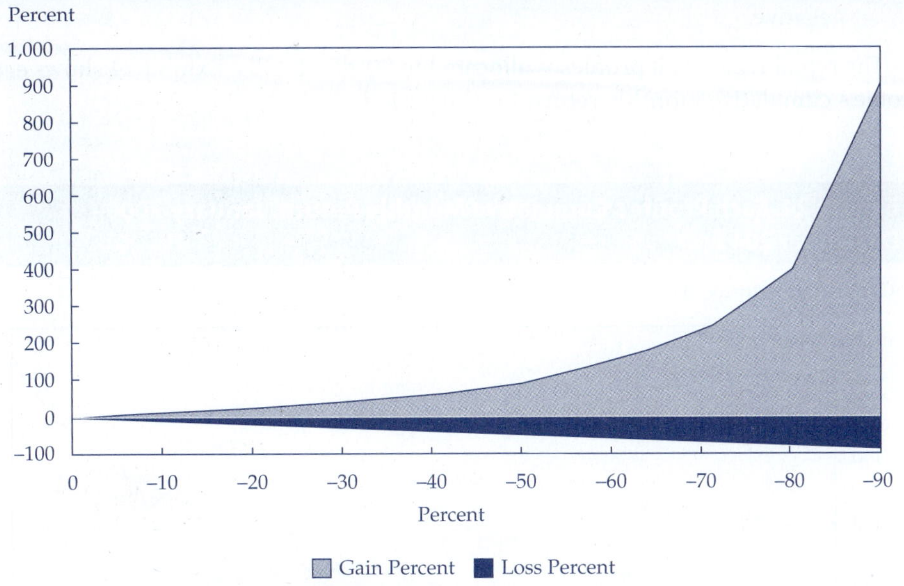

To further illustrate, consider the four return profiles with different upside and downside capture ratios shown in Exhibit 23.

Exhibit 23: Return Profile Summary

Profile	Upside Capture	Downside Capture	Ratio
Long only	100%	100%	1.0
Positive asymmetry	75%	25%	3.0
Low beta	50%	50%	1.0
Negative asymmetry	25%	75%	0.3

We designed these four trading strategies to illustrate the potential effects of the capture ratio and drawdown on return performance and to highlight why understanding the capture ratio and drawdown is important for manager selection.[8] Each strategy's allocation to the S&P 500 Total Return (TR) Index and to 90-day T-bills (assuming monthly rebalancing to simplify the calculations) is based on the realized monthly return from January 2000 to December 2013. (We chose this time period to illustrate the need to examine the asymmetry in a strategy's returns specifically because it encompasses the extreme drawdown of 2008–2009.)

- The long-only profile is 100% allocated to the S&P 500 throughout the period.
- The low-beta profile is allocated 50% to the S&P 500 throughout the period.
- The positive asymmetry profile is allocated 75% to the S&P 500 for months when the S&P 500 return is positive and 25% when the S&P 500 return is negative.

8 If the market return is known beforehand, the correct strategy is to allocate 100% to the S&P 500 Total Return (TR) Index in up months and 100% to 90-day T-bills in down months (or –100% S&P 500 TR Index if shorting is allowed).

- The negative asymmetry profile is allocated 25% to the S&P 500 for months when the S&P 500 return is positive and 75% when the S&P 500 return is negative.

The remainder for all profiles is allocated to 90-day T-bills. Exhibit 24 shows each profile's cumulative monthly return for the period.

Exhibit 24: Each Profile's Cumulative Monthly Return, January 2000–December 2013

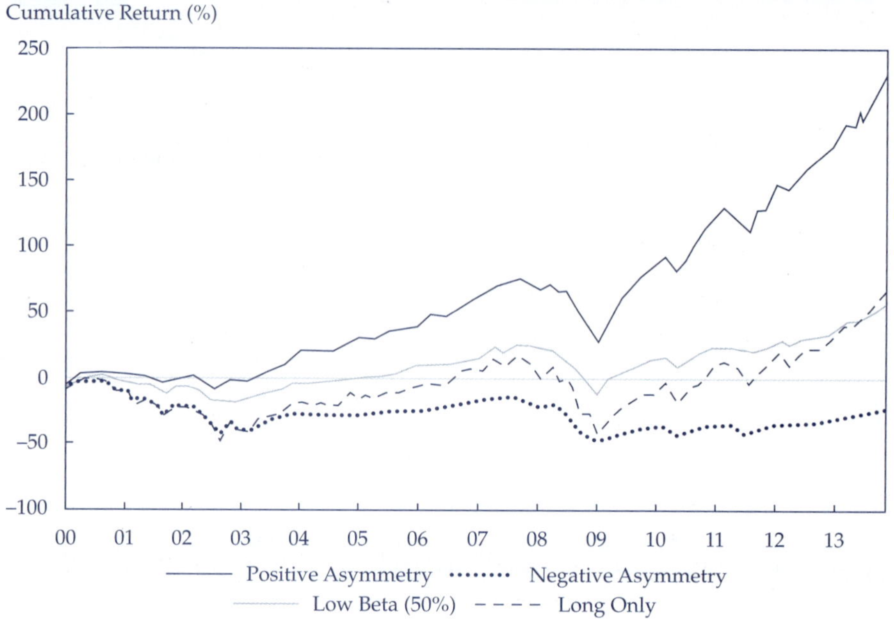

Exhibit 25 provides summary statistics for each profile based on monthly returns from January 2000 to December 2013. Although the long-only profile outperformed the low-beta profile, this outperformance resulted from the strong up market of 2013. The low-beta profile outperformed the long-only profile for most of the period, with lower realized volatility and higher risk-adjusted returns during the entire period. The low-beta profile declined only 18.8%, compared with the long-only decline of 42.5%, from January 2000 to September 2002. As a result, the low-beta profile had higher cumulative performance from January 2000 to October 2007 despite markedly lagging the long-only profile (56.0% to 108.4%) from October 2002 to October 2007.

Although a low-beta approach may sacrifice performance, it shows that limiting drawdowns can result in better absolute and risk-adjusted returns in certain markets. Not surprisingly, positive asymmetry results in better performance relative to long only, low beta, and negative asymmetry. Although the positive asymmetry profile lags in up markets, this lag is more than offset by the lower participation in down markets. Not surprisingly, the negative asymmetry profile lags, with lower participation in up markets insufficient to offset the greater participation in down markets.

Exhibit 25: Summary Statistics for Each Profile, January 2000–December 2013

Strategy	Long Only	Low Beta	Positive Asymmetry	Negative Asymmetry
Cumulative return	64.0%	54.2%	228.1%	−24.4%
Annualized return	3.60%	3.14%	8.86%	−1.98%
Annualized standard deviation	15.64%	7.79%	9.61%	10.01%
Sharpe ratio	0.10	0.14	0.71	−0.40
Beta	1.00	0.50	0.61	0.64
Drawdown (maximum)	−50.9%	−28.3%	−26.9%	−48.9%

Although positive asymmetry is a desirable trait, only some strategies are convex. We need to understand the strategy and how the return profile is created, particularly whether the strategy is inherently convex or whether convexity relies on manager skill. For example, a hedging strategy implemented by rolling forward out-of-the-money put options will typically return many small losses because more options expire worthless than are compensated for by the occasional large gain during a large market downturn. This strategy will likely exhibit consistent positive asymmetry because it depends more on the nature of the strategy than on investment skill.

We should also evaluate the consistency between the stated investment process and reported investment performance. An inconsistency could indicate issues with the strategy's repeatability and implementation or more serious reporting and compliance concerns. Capture ratios can be useful in evaluating consistency issues. We also need to understand the strategy's robustness and potential risks. For example, the expected benefits of diversification—in particular, mitigating downside capture—might not be realized in a crisis if correlations converge toward 1.

Manager responses to a large drawdown provide evidence of the robustness and repeatability of the investment, portfolio construction, and risk management processes, as well as insight into the people implementing the processes. This information requires an understanding of the source of the drawdown and the potential principal–agent risk, operational risk, and business risk that it entails. Drawdowns are stress tests of the investment process and provide a natural point to evaluate and improve processes, which is particularly true of firm-specific drawdowns.

As noted, practitioners should also consider investment horizon and its relationship with risk capacity. An investor closer to retirement, with less time to recover from losses, places more emphasis on absolute measures of risk. In addition, even if the manager maintains her discipline during a large drawdown, the investor may not. This dynamic arises if the investor's perception of risk is path dependent or the drawdown changes risk tolerance. If there has been no change to investment policy and no change in the view that the manager remains suitable, the temptation to exit should be resisted to avoid exiting at an inauspicious time. Investors with shorter horizons, with lower risk capacity, or who are prone to overreact to losses may bias selection toward managers with shallower and shorter expected drawdowns.

EXAMPLE 13

Capture Ratios and Drawdown

1. Do losses require proportionally greater gains to reverse or offset? Choose the best response.

   A. Yes, because in investing, it is easier to lose than to gain.

   B. No, gains should reflect losses.

   C. Yes, because we calculate percentage gains/losses on the basis of the starting amount of portfolio holdings.

Solution:

C is the correct response. If the denominator of the gain calculation is lower, a higher percentage gain is required to offset the loss. For example, if you lose 10% of $100, your new holding is $90. To earn back the $10 loss, you must earn 10/90, or 11%. A is not correct because the "ease" of gaining or losing is not relevant. B is not correct because proportionally higher gains are required.

t	R(*m*) (%)	R(*B*) (%)
1	−3.06	−3.60
2	6.32	3.10
3	6.00	6.03
4	3.21	1.58
5	−9.05	−7.99
6	−4.09	−5.23
7	4.34	7.01
8	−5.72	−4.51
9	12.76	8.92
10	5.38	3.81
11	0.33	0.01
12	5.68	6.68

2. Using the return information in the table above, what is the manager's downside capture ratio?

   A. 103%

   B. 108%

   C. 115%

Solution:

A is the correct answer. See the table below.

			Upside Return				Downside Return			
t	R(*m*)	R(*B*)	R(*m*)	R(*B*)	Cum R(*m*)	Cum R(*B*)	R(*m*)	R(*B*)	Cum R(*m*)	Cum R(*B*)
1	−3.06%	−3.60%			0.00%	0.00%	−3.06%	−3.60%	−3.06%	−3.60%
2	6.32%	3.10%	6.32%	3.10%	6.32%	3.10%			−3.06%	−3.60%
3	6.00%	6.03%	6.00%	6.03%	12.70%	9.32%			−3.06%	−3.60%
4	3.21%	1.58%	3.21%	1.58%	16.32%	11.04%			−3.06%	−3.60%

			Upside Return				Downside Return			
t	**R(*m*)**	**R(*B*)**	**R(*m*)**	**R(*B*)**	**Cum R(*m*)**	**Cum R(*B*)**	**R(*m*)**	**R(*B*)**	**Cum R(*m*)**	**Cum R(*B*)**
5	−9.05%	−7.99%			16.32%	11.04%	−9.05%	−7.99%	−11.83%	−11.30%
6	−4.09%	−5.23%			16.32%	11.04%	−4.09%	−5.23%	−15.44%	−15.94%
7	4.34%	7.01%	4.34%	7.01%	21.36%	18.83%			−15.44%	−15.94%
8	−5.72%	−4.51%			21.36%	18.83%	−5.72%	−4.51%	−20.28%	−19.73%
9	12.76%	8.92%	12.76%	8.92%	36.85%	29.43%			−20.28%	−19.73%
10	5.38%	3.81%	5.38%	3.81%	44.21%	34.36%			−20.28%	−19.73%
11	0.33%	0.01%	0.33%	0.01%	44.69%	34.37%			−20.28%	−19.73%
12	5.68%	6.68%	5.68%	6.68%	52.91%	43.35%			−20.28%	−19.73%
Geometric average			5.45%	4.60%			−5.51%	−5.35%		
Upside capture			5.45%/4.60% = 118%				**Downside capture**		**−5.51%/−5.35% = 103%**	
Capture ratio			118%/103% = 115%							

EVALUATION OF INVESTMENT MANAGER SKILL

12

☐ evaluate the skill of an investment manager

Using the tools and principles of performance evaluation presented in this reading, this section presents a specific case to use those tools in an evaluation of manager skill.

For this section, we will consider the case of Manager A, benchmarked against the MSCI Pacific Index. Drawing from the previous sections in this reading, we compiled sample data to evaluate the skill of Manager A. For simplicity of analysis and presentation, we exclude the impact from currency.

Over a five-year period, Manager A's performance is 9.42%, versus the benchmark performance of 9.25%. So, we know that the manager added 17 bps (9.42 – 9.25) of outperformance. But did the manager earn the 17 bps through skill, or was she the beneficiary of luck?

To further evaluate the outperformance, we turn to the tools presented throughout this reading. We include a sample attribution analysis to tell us how the outperformance was achieved. We then use appraisal ratio analysis to compare Manager A's performance to other managers during the same period. Combining the analyses helps present a more balanced assessment of the manager's skill.

Performance Attribution Analysis

Attribution analysis, as we have shown, is one of the most important tools for evaluating manager skill. Attribution will tell us how the outperformance was achieved, distinguishing the stock selection from country allocation. In the Exhibit 26, we present the sample attribution analysis (for simplicity, we have combined the interaction effect with stock selection).

Exhibit 26: Sample Attribution Analysis

	Manager A		MSCI Pacific		Attribution Effects		
Market	Weight	5-Year Return	Weight	5-Year Return	Allocation	Selection + Interaction	Total
Japan	51.0%	12.40%	60.5%	11.48%	−0.21%	0.47%	0.26%
Australia	30.0%	5.12%	25.4%	4.10%	−0.24%	0.31%	0.07%
Hong Kong SAR	15.0%	8.90%	10.0%	10.08%	0.04%	−0.18%	−0.14%
Singapore	3.5%	5.10%	3.0%	5.38%	−0.02%	−0.01%	−0.03%
New Zealand	0.5%	8.75%	1.0%	9.08%	0.00%	0.00%	0.00%
Total	**100%**	**9.42%**	**100%**	**9.25%**	**−0.43%**	**0.59%**	**0.17%**

Using this analysis, let us consider the impacts of country allocation weights versus the benchmark weights. Overall, the portfolio manager lost 43 bps of performance as a result of allocation decisions. Specifically, the manager's decision to overweight Australia (30% to 25%) lost 24 bps, because Australia underperformed the total MSCI Pacific benchmark (4.10% versus 9.25%). In addition, the decision to underweight Japan (51% to 60%) lost 21 bps, because Japan outperformed the total benchmark (12.4% versus 9.25%). With this attribution analysis, we can say the manager did not make good weighting decisions over the five-year period.

Now, let us consider the impact from the manager's stock selection decisions. Overall, the portfolio manager gained 59 bps of performance from stock selection decisions. Specifically, the manager added 47 bps through selecting Japanese stocks and 31 bps from selecting Australian stocks. Stock selection in Hong Kong SAR was not as successful, where the manager lost 18 bps.

Overall, we can conclude from the attribution analysis that the manager is a good stock picker, especially for Japanese and Australian stocks. But the manager has not been as successful in choosing the markets to allocate assets. We infer these conclusions on the basis of an analysis of the manager's performance attribution over a five-year period. To better evaluate the manager's performance, we need to understand the risk incurred to achieve that performance. For that risk assessment, we will consider Manager A relative to other managers, using a sample appraisal ratio analysis over the same five-year period.

Appraisal Measures

As described previously, appraisal analysis uses techniques to review past periods of performance and risk. Consider the sample results presented in Exhibit 27. For the same five-year period, we have calculated a set of performance appraisal measures for Manager A, presented previously, as well as two other managers with the same benchmark over the same period, Managers B and C.

Exhibit 27: Sample Analysis Using Various Appraisal Measures

	Appraisal Measures			
	Manager A	Manager B	Manager C	Benchmark
Annualized return	9.42	8.23	10.21	9.25
Annualized std. dev.	10.83	8.10	12.34	9.76
Sharpe ratio	0.68	0.76	0.66	0.73

	Appraisal Measures			
	Manager A	**Manager B**	**Manager C**	**Benchmark**
Treynor ratio	0.35	0.32	0.19	0.57
Information ratio	0.43	0.41	0.30	0.00
Sortino ratio (MAR = 3%)	0.82	0.51	1.03	0.97

In considering this historical analysis, note that Manager A has a higher volatility of returns than the benchmark (manager standard deviation of 10.83 versus benchmark standard deviation of 9.76). This volatility is greater than that for Manager B (8.10) but is less than that for Manager C (12.34). In general, Manager A's return is slightly more volatile—riskier—than the benchmark's and slightly more and less volatile than that of Managers B and C, respectively.

This consistency is demonstrated in the Sharpe ratio measurement as well. Recall that the Sharpe ratio indicates the amount of performance earned over a risk-free proxy per unit of risk. In this assessment, Manager A's Sharpe ratio is less than the benchmark's Sharpe ratio (0.68 versus 0.73) and less than Manager B's Sharpe ratio (0.76). Thus, for this period, we know Manager A certainly incurred more risk than the benchmark and Manager B did for the same amount of return generated. Is the manager incurring too much risk for the return generated? To answer this question, we should consider some of the other appraisal measures as well.

Unlike the Sharpe ratio, the Treynor ratio measures the return earned per unit of *systematic* risk. The information ratio indicates how well the manager has performed relative to the benchmark, *after accounting for the differences in the volatility of the portfolio and the benchmark.* Given that Manager A has the highest Treynor and information ratios for this period, she has been able to produce a higher return relative to systematic risk. In addition, consider her Sortino ratio of 0.82, not significantly higher than the Sharpe ratio, but again indicative of an ability to generate higher returns relative to downside risk (where the target is 3%).

Sample Evaluation of Skill

In summary, the analysis based on these appraisal measures supports the conclusion generated by the performance attribution analysis that Manager A has been able to generate excess return over the benchmark through stock selection. She has done so without incurring significant excess risk relative to the benchmark and two similar managers. Therefore, within the limits of these analyses, Manager A has exhibited some level of skill worthy of further analysis.

The analysis does not, however, help us evaluate the country allocation conclusions of our attribution analysis. We know that the manager made incorrect bets in Japan and Australia. What beliefs about country selection are embedded in her investment philosophy? Are country allocations an integral part of her investment approach, or are they a by-product of her stock selection? Answers to these questions will help us determine whether our assessment of skill should be penalized by the poor outcomes of the country selection decisions in this period.

It is important to recognize that our analysis encompasses only a small sample of the possible outcomes that are not necessarily indicative of future outcomes. A long track record is necessary to have any statistical certainty in a conclusion of skill or no skill. Practitioners will want to conduct additional analyses to increase their confidence in their conclusions. These additional studies could include some of the other tools presented in this reading, such as risk attribution or *ex ante* analyses. In addition, practitioners will want to include qualitative analyses of the manager (e.g., direct interviews with management to assess abilities), assessment of investment goals and management fees, and so on. In the end, we must understand and acknowledge the limits of all tools, being careful to qualify any conclusions regarding investment skill with the appropriate level of prudence.

EXAMPLE 14

Investment Manager Skill

Use the examples in Exhibit 26 and Exhibit 27 to help answer the following questions.

1. Which statement *best* describes Manager A's performance during this five-year period?

   A. On an absolute basis, Manager A performed better than either Manager B or Manager C.

   B. Relative to systematic risk, Manager A performed better than either Manager B or Manager C.

   C. Manager C incurred the least risk.

Solution:

B is correct. The Treynor ratio measures performance relative to systematic risk. Manager A's Treynor ratio was better than that of both Manager B and Manager C for the period. A is not correct because Manager A's return for the period was less than Manager C's return. C is not correct because Manager C's annualized standard deviation (volatility) was highest.

2. Which of the following *best* provides evidence of manager skill?

   A. Security selection attribution effect of 47 bps

   B. Annualized performance equal to 9.42%

   C. Annualized standard deviation equal to 12.34%

Solution:

A is correct. Performance attribution can be indicative of manager skill, especially over longer historical time periods. Neither B nor C is correct because neither performance nor standard deviation, on their own, is necessarily indicative of manager skill.

3. How can a practitioner *best* distinguish manager skill from luck?

   A. Run thousands of analyses of the same manager over an extended period.

   B. Avoid making broad-based judgments without statistical evidence.

   C. Use multiple analysis tools to jointly infer conclusions, sensitive to the limits of those tools.

Solution:

C is correct. Practitioners should use multiple analyses with different tools to find multiple sources that agree on evidence of skill. A is not correct, because thousands of analyses, especially the same types of analyses, may not necessarily lead to more conclusive results. B is not correct because it states best practice but not necessarily techniques to distinguish skill from luck.

SUMMARY

Performance evaluation is an essential tool for understanding the quality of the investment process. Practitioners must take care, however, to understand how performance results are generated. They need a good understanding of the performance methods used, the data inputs, and the limitations of those methods. They particularly need to be careful not to infer results beyond the capabilities of the methods or the accuracy of the data. In this reading, we have discussed the following:

- Performance measurement provides an overall indication of the portfolio's performance.
- Performance attribution builds on performance measurement to explain how the performance was achieved.
- Performance appraisal leverages both returns and attribution to infer the quality of the investment process.
- An effective attribution process must reconcile to the total portfolio return/risk, reflect the investment decision-making process, quantify the active portfolio management decisions, and provide a complete understanding of the excess return/risk of the portfolio.
- Return attribution analyzes the impact of investment decisions on the returns, whereas risk attribution analyzes the risk consequences of the investment decisions.
- Macro attribution considers the decisions of the fund sponsor, whereas micro attribution considers the decisions of the individual portfolio manager.
- Returns-based attribution uses returns to identify the factors that have generated those returns.
- Holdings-based attribution uses the holdings over time to evaluate the decisions that contributed to the returns.
- Transactions-based attribution uses both holdings and transactions to fully explain the performance over the evaluation period.
- There are various techniques for interpreting the sources of portfolio returns using a specified attribution approach.
- Fixed-income attribution considers the unique factors that drive bond returns, including interest rate risk and default risk.
- When selecting a risk attribution approach, practitioners should consider the investment decision-making process and the type of attribution analysis.
- Attribution is used to calculate and interpret the contribution to portfolio return and volatility from the asset allocation and within-asset-class active/passive decisions.
- Liability-based benchmarks focus on the cash flows that the assets are required to generate.
- Asset-based benchmarks contain a collection of assets to compare against the portfolio's assets.
- Valid benchmarks should be unambiguous, investable, measurable, appropriate, reflective of current investment opinions, specified in advance, and accountable.
- Benchmark misspecification creates subsequent incorrect performance measurement and invalidates the attribution and appraisal analyses.

- Alternative investments are difficult to benchmark because they are typically less liquid, have fewer available market benchmarks, and often lack transparency.
- Investment performance appraisal ratios—including the Sortino ratio, upside/downside capture ratios, maximum drawdown, and drawdown duration—measure investment skill.
- Appraisal ratios must be used with care, noting the assumptions of each ratio and affording the appropriateness to the measured investment process, risk tolerance, and investor time horizon.
- Although appraisal ratios help identify manager skill (as opposed to luck), they often are based on investment return data, which are often limited and subject to error.
- Evaluation of investment manager skill requires the use of a broad range of analysis tools, with fundamental understanding of how the tools work, how they complement each other, and their specific limitations.

REFERENCES

Bailey, Jeffery V., Thomas M. Richards, and David Tierney. 2007. "Evaluating Portfolio Performance." In *Managing Investment Portfolios: A Dynamic Process*. 3rd ed., ed. Maginn, John, Donald Tuttle, Dennis McLeavey, and Jerald Pinto. Hoboken, NJ: John Wiley & Sons.

Bailey, Jeffery V. and David E. Tierney. 1998. *Controlling Misfit Risk in Multiple-Manager Investment Programs*. Charlottesville, VA: Research Foundation of CFA Institute.

Brinson, Gary and Nimrod Fachler. 1985. "Measuring Non-US Equity Portfolio Performance." *Journal of Portfolio Management* 11 (5): 73–76. 10.3905/jpm.1985.409005

Brinson, Gary, Randolph Hood, and Gilbert Beebower. 1986. "Determinants of Portfolio Performance." *Financial Analysts Journal* 42 (4): 39–44. 10.2469/faj.v42.n4.39

Brown, Stephen and William Goetzmann. 1997. "Mutual Fund Styles." *Journal of Financial Economics* 43 (3): 373–99. 10.1016/S0304-405X(96)00898-7

Carhart, M. M. 1997. "On Persistence in Mutual Fund Performance." *Journal of Finance* 52 (1): 57–82. 10.1111/j.1540-6261.1997.tb03808.x

Cariño, David. 1999. "Combining Attribution Effects over Time." *Journal of Performance Measurement* (Summer).

Giguère, C. 2005. "Thinking through Fixed Income Attribution—Reflections from a Group of French Practitioners." *Journal of Performance Measurement* (Summer): 46–65.

Menchero, Jose. 2000. "An Optimized Approach to Linking Attribution Effects over Time." *Journal of Performance Measurement* (Fall).

Murira, Bernard and Hector Sierra. 2006. "Fixed Income Attribution: A United Framework—Part 1." *Journal of Performance Measurement* 11 (1): 23–35.

Treynor, J. 1965. "How to Rate Management of Investment Funds." *Harvard Business Review* 43 (1): 63–75.

Treynor, J. and F. Black. 1973. "How to Use Security Analysis to Improve Portfolio Selection." *Journal of Business* 46 (1): 66–86. 10.1086/295508

PRACTICE PROBLEMS

The following information relates to questions 1-5

Alexandra Jones, a senior adviser at Federalist Investors (FI), meets with Erin Bragg, a junior analyst. Bragg just completed a monthly performance evaluation for an FI fixed-income manager. Bragg's report addresses the three primary components of performance evaluation: measurement, attribution, and appraisal. Jones asks Bragg to describe an effective attribution process. Bragg responds as follows:

Response 1	Performance attribution draws conclusions regarding the quality of a portfolio manager's investment decisions.
Response 2	Performance attribution should help explain how performance was achieved by breaking apart the return or risk into different explanatory components.

Bragg notes that the fixed-income portfolio manager has strong views about the effects of macroeconomic factors on credit markets and follows a top-down investment process.

Jones reviews the monthly performance attribution and asks Bragg whether any risk-adjusted historical performance indicators are available. Bragg produces the following data:

Exhibit 1: 10-Year Trailing Risk-Adjusted Performance

Average annual return	8.20%
Minimum acceptable return (MAR)	5.00%
Sharpe ratio	0.95
Sortino ratio	0.87
Upside capture	0.66
Downside capture	0.50
Maximum drawdown	–24.00%
Drawdown duration	4 months

1. Which of Bragg's responses regarding effective performance attribution is correct?

   A. Only Response 1

   B. Only Response 2

   C. Both Response 1 and Response 2

2. The *most appropriate* risk attribution approach for the fixed-income manager is to:

   A. decompose historical returns into a top-down factor framework.

B. evaluate the marginal contribution to total risk for each position.

C. attribute tracking risk to relative allocation and selection decisions.

3. Based on Exhibit 1, the target semideviation for the portfolio is *closest to:*

   A. 2.78%.

   B. 3.68%.

   C. 4.35%.

4. Based on Exhibit 1, the capture ratios of the portfolio indicate:

   A. a concave return profile.

   B. positive asymmetry of returns.

   C. that the portfolio generates higher returns than the benchmark during all market conditions.

5. The maximum drawdown and drawdown duration in Exhibit 1 indicate that:

   A. the portfolio recovered quickly from its maximum loss.

   B. over the 10-year period, the average maximum loss was −24.00%.

   C. a significant loss once persisted for four months before the portfolio began to recover.

The following information relates to questions 6-14

Stephanie Tolmach is a consultant hired to create a performance attribution report on three funds held by a defined benefit pension plan (the Plan). Fund 1 is a domestic equity strategy, Fund 2 is a global equity strategy, and Fund 3 is a domestic fixed income strategy.

Tolmach uses three approaches to attribution analysis: the return-based, holdings-based, and transaction-based approaches. The Plan's investment committee asks Tolmach to (1) apply the attribution method that uses only each fund's total portfolio returns over the last 12 months to identify return-generating components of the investment process and (2) include the impact of specific active investment decisions and the attribution effects of allocation and security selection in the report.

Tolmach first evaluates the performance of Fund 1 by constructing a Carhart factor model; the results are presented in Exhibit 1.

Exhibit 1: Fund 1 Factor Model Attribution

	Factor Sensitivity				Contribution to Active Return	
Factor*	**Portfolio (1)**	**Benchmark (2)**	**Difference (3)**	**Factor Return (4)**	**Absolute (3) × (4)**	**Proportion of Active Return**
RMRF	1.22	0.91	0.31	16.32%	5.06%	−126.80%
SMB	0.59	0.68	−0.09	−3.25%	0.29%	−7.33%
HML	−0.17	0.04	−0.21	−9.60%	2.02%	−50.53%
WML	−0.05	0.07	−0.12	3.38%	−0.41%	10.17%
				A. Factor Tilt Return:	6.96%	−174.49%
				B. Security Selection:	−10.95%	274.49%
				C. Active Return (A + B):	−3.99%	100.00%

** RMRF is the return on a value-weighted equity index in excess of the one-month T-bill rate, SMB is the small minus big market capitalization factor, HML is the high minus low factor, and WML is the winners minus losers factor.*

Tolmach turns her attention to Fund 2, constructing a region-based, Brinson–Fachler micro attribution analysis to evaluate the active decisions of the portfolio manager. The results are presented in Exhibit 2.

Exhibit 2: Fund 2 Performance—Allocation by Region

Return Attribution (Region Level)	Portfolio Weight	Benchmark Weight	Portfolio Return	Benchmark Return
North America	10.84%	7.67%	16.50%	16.47%
Greater Europe	38.92%	42.35%	23.16%	25.43%
Developed Asia and Australasia	29.86%	31.16%	11.33%	12.85%
South America	20.38%	18.82%	20.00%	35.26%
Total	**100.00%**	**100.00%**	**18.26%**	**22.67%**

Next, Tolmach evaluates Fund 3 and the appropriateness of its benchmark. The benchmark is a cap-weighted bond index with daily reported performance; the index is rebalanced frequently, making it difficult to replicate. The benchmark has a meaningful investment in foreign bonds, whereas Fund 3 invests only in domestic bonds.

In the final section of the report, Tolmach reviews the entire Plan's characteristics, asset allocation, and benchmark. Tolmach observes that the Plan's benefits are no longer indexed to inflation and that the workforce is, on average, younger than it was when the current fund allocations were approved. Tolmach recommends a change in the Plan's asset allocation policy.

6. Of the three attribution approaches referenced by Tolmach, the method requested by the committee:

   A. is the least accurate.

   B. uses the underlying holdings of the actual portfolio.

C. is the most difficult and time consuming to implement.

7. Based on Exhibit 1 and relative to the benchmark, the manager of Fund 1 *most likely* used a:

   A. growth tilt.

   B. greater tilt toward small cap.

   C. momentum-based investing approach.

8. Based on Exhibit 1, which of the following factors contributed the *least* to active return?

   A. HML

   B. SMB

   C. RMRF

9. Based on Exhibit 1, the manager could have delivered more value to the portfolio during the investment period by weighting more toward:

   A. value stocks.

   B. small-cap stocks.

   C. momentum stocks.

10. Based on Exhibit 2, the allocation effect for South America is *closest* to:

    A. −0.04%.

    B. 0.03%.

    C. 0.20%.

11. Based on Exhibit 2, the decision to overweight or underweight which of the following regions contributed positively to performance at the overall fund level?

    A. North America

    B. Greater Europe

    C. Developed Asia and Australasia

12. Based on Exhibit 2, the underperformance at the overall fund level is predominantly the result of poor security selection decisions in:

    A. South America.

    B. greater Europe.

    C. developed Asia and Australasia.

13. The benchmark for Fund 3 has which of the following characteristics of a valid benchmark?

    A. Investable

    B. Measurable

C. Appropriate

14. Based on the final section of Tolmach's report, the Plan should use:

A. a liability-based benchmark.

B. an absolute return benchmark.

C. a manager universe benchmark.

SOLUTIONS

1. B is correct. Performance attribution helps explain how performance was achieved; it breaks apart the return or risk into different explanatory components. Effective performance attribution must account for all of the portfolio's return or risk exposure, reflect the investment decision-making process, quantify the active decisions of the portfolio manager, and provide a complete understanding of the excess return/risk of the portfolio.

2. C is correct. The portfolio is managed against a benchmark, which indicates a relative-risk type of risk attribution analysis. For a top-down investment approach, the analysis should attribute tracking risk to allocation and selection decisions relative to the benchmark.

3. B is correct. The target semi-standard deviation or target semideviation is the denominator of the Sortino ratio. The numerator of the Sortino ratio is the average portfolio return minus the target rate of return (minimum acceptable return, or MAR).

   $$\text{Sortino ratio} = \frac{(\text{Average portfolio return} - \text{MAR})}{\text{Target semideviation}}$$

   Substituting the values provided in Exhibit 3, the target semideviation is as follows:

   $$\text{Target semideviation} = \frac{8.20\% - 5.00\%}{0.87}$$
   $$= 3.678\% = 3.68\%$$

4. B is correct. The upside/downside capture, or simply the capture ratio (CR), is the upside capture ratio divided by the downside capture ratio.

   (Upside capture)/(Downside capture) = 0.66/0.50 = 1.32.

   A capture ratio greater than 1 indicates positive asymmetry of returns, or a convex return profile.

5. A is correct. Maximum drawdown is the cumulative peak-to-trough loss during a continuous period. Drawdown duration is the total time from the start of the drawdown until the cumulative drawdown recovers to zero, which can be segmented into the drawdown phase (start to trough) and the recovery phase (trough to zero cumulative return). The maximum drawdown was –24.00%, with a drawdown period of four months. Given the 10-year time frame, the portfolio recovered quickly from its maximum loss.

6. A is correct. The committee described a return-based attribution, which is the least accurate of the three approaches (the return-based, holdings-based, transaction-based approaches). Return-based attribution uses only the total portfolio returns over a period to identify the components of the investment process that have generated the returns.

7. A is correct. Based on the factor sensitivities in column 1 (negative sensitivity of –0.17 to HML) and the differences relative to the benchmark shown in column 3, the manager likely had a growth tilt.

8. B is correct. With an absolute return of 0.29% and with 7.33% of the contribution to return, SMB contributed far less than HML (2.02% and 50.53%, respectively) and RMRF (5.06% and 126.80%, respectively).

9. C is correct. Had the manager weighted more toward momentum stocks during the period, the momentum factor (WML) return of 3.38% would have contributed positively to the portfolio.

   A is incorrect because the HML factor return was –9.60%; thus, weighting more toward value stocks would have detracted from portfolio returns.

   B is incorrect because the SMB factor return was –3.25%; thus, weighting more toward small-cap stocks would have detracted from portfolio returns.

10. C is correct. The allocation effect for South America is 0.20%.

$$\text{Allocation} = (w_i - W_i)(B_i - B)$$
$$= (20.38\% - 18.82\%)(35.26 - 22.67\%)$$
$$= 0.1964\% = 0.20\%$$

11. C is correct. The decision to underweight developed Asia and Australasia was a good one because the benchmark for this region underperformed the total benchmark (12.85% versus 22.67%). Alternatively, the question can be answered by calculating the allocation effects for the three regions, as follows:

$$\text{Allocation} = (w_i - W_i)(B_i - B)$$
$$\text{North America} = (10.84\% - 7.67\%)(16.47\% - 22.67\%)$$
$$= -0.20\%$$
$$\text{Greater Europe} = (38.92\% - 42.35\%)(25.43\% - 22.67\%)$$
$$= -0.09\%$$
$$\text{Developed Asia and Australasia} = (29.86\% - 31.16\%)(12.85\% - 22.67\%)$$
$$= 0.13\%$$

   Developed Asia and Australasia is the only region of the three that had a positive allocation effect.

12. A is correct. The total –441 bps of underperformance from security selection and interaction at the overall fund level is predominantly the result of poor South American security selection decisions (–311 bps = 3.11%).

Return Attribution (Segment Level)	Allocation	Selection + Interaction	Total
North America	–0.1966%	0.0033%	–0.1934%
Greater Europe	–0.0946%	–0.8835%	–0.9781%
Developed Asia and Australasia	0.1277%	–0.4539%	–0.3262%

Return Attribution (Segment Level)	Allocation	Selection + Interaction	Total
South America	0.1964%	–3.1100%	–2.9136%
Total	0.0329%	–4.4441%	–4.4112%

$$\text{Allocation} = (w_i - W_i)(B_i - B)$$

$$\text{North America} = (10.84\% - 7.67\%)(16.47\% - 22.67\%)$$
$$= -0.20\%$$

$$\text{Greater Europe} = (38.92\% - 42.35\%)(25.43\% - 22.67\%)$$
$$= -0.09\%$$

$$\text{Developed Asia and Australasia} = (29.86\% - 31.16\%)(12.85\% - 22.67\%)$$
$$= 0.13\%$$

$$\text{South America} = (20.38\% - 18.82\%)(35.26\% - 22.67\%)$$
$$= 0.20\%$$

$$\text{Selection + Interaction} = W_i(R_i - B_i) + (w_i - W_i)(R_i - B_i)$$

$$\text{North America} = 7.67\%(16.50\% - 16.47\%) + (10.84\% - 7.67\%)(16.50\% - 16.47\%)$$
$$= 0.00\%$$

$$\text{Greater Europe} = 42.35\%(23.16\% - 25.43\%) + (38.92\% - 42.35\%)(23.16\% - 25.43\%)$$
$$= -0.88\%$$

$$\text{Developed Asia and Australasia} = 31.16\%(11.33\% - 12.85\%) + (29.86\% - 31.16\%)(11.33\% - 12.85\%)$$
$$= -0.45\%$$

$$\text{South America} = 18.82\%(20.00\% - 35.26\%) + (20.38\% - 18.82\%)(20.00\% - 35.26\%)$$
$$= -3.11\%$$

13. B is correct. Daily reported performance is available for the benchmark; thus, it is possible to measure the benchmark's return on a reasonably frequent and timely basis.

    A is incorrect because the benchmark is a cap-weighted bond index that is rebalanced frequently, making it difficult to replicate. For a benchmark to be investable, it must be possible to replicate and hold the benchmark to earn its return (at least gross of expenses). The sponsor should have the option of moving assets from active management to a passive benchmark. If the benchmark is not investable, it is not a viable investment alternative. Bond indexes are often not investable and are rebalanced frequently over time.

    C is incorrect because the index has a meaningful investment in foreign bonds, whereas Fund 3 invests only in domestic bonds, making the benchmark inappropriate. The benchmark must be consistent with the manager's investment style or area of expertise.

14. A is correct. Based on the Plan's type (defined benefit) and its characteristics as detailed in the final section of Tolmach's report, a liability-based benchmark is most appropriate. Liability-based benchmarks are used most frequently when assets are required to pay a specific future liability, as in a defined benefit pension plan.

LEARNING MODULE

2

Investment Manager Selection

by Jeffrey C. Heisler, PhD, CFA, and Donald W. Lindsey, CFA.

Jeffrey C. Heisler, PhD, CFA, is at TwinFocus Capital Partners (USA). Donald W. Lindsey, CFA (USA).

LEARNING OUTCOMES

Mastery	The candidate should be able to:
☐	describe the components of a manager selection process, including due diligence
☐	contrast Type I and Type II errors in manager hiring and continuation decisions
☐	describe uses of returns-based and holdings-based style analysis in investment manager selection
☐	describe uses of the upside capture ratio, downside capture ratio, maximum drawdown, drawdown duration, and up/down capture in evaluating managers
☐	evaluate a manager's investment philosophy and investment decision-making process
☐	discuss how behavioral factors affect investment team decision making, and recommend techniques for mitigating their effects
☐	evaluate the costs and benefits of pooled investment vehicles and separate accounts
☐	compare types of investment manager contracts, including their major provisions and advantages and disadvantages
☐	describe the three basic forms of performance-based fees
☐	analyze and interpret a sample performance-based fee schedule

INTRODUCTION

1

Most investors do not hold securities directly but rather invest using intermediaries. Whether the intermediary is a separately managed account or a pooled investment vehicle, such as a UCITS (undertakings for collective investment in transferable securities) fund, a hedge fund, a private equity fund, or an exchange-traded fund (ETF), a professional investment manager is entrusted with helping investors achieve their investment objectives. In all these cases, the selection of appropriate investment managers is a challenge with important financial consequences.

Evaluating an investment manager is a complex and detailed process that encompasses a great deal more than analyzing investment returns. The investigation and analysis in support of an investment action, decision, or recommendation is called **due diligence**. In conducting investment manager due diligence, the focus is on understanding how the investment results were achieved and on assessing the likelihood that the investment process that generated these returns will produce superior or at least satisfactory investment results going forward. Due diligence also entails an evaluation of a firm's integrity, operations, and personnel. As such, due diligence involves both quantitative and qualitative analysis.

This learning module provides a framework that introduces and describes the important elements of the manager selection process. Although it is important to have a well-defined methodology, this learning module is not intended to be a rigid checklist, a step-by-step guide, or an in-depth analysis but rather to present a structure from which the reader can develop their own approach.

We assume that the investment policy statement (IPS) has been drafted, the asset allocation determined, and the decision to use an outside adviser has been made. As a result, the focus is on determining which manager offers the "best" means to implement or express those decisions. The discussion has three broad topics:

- Outlining a framework for identifying, evaluating, and ultimately selecting investment managers.
- Quantitative considerations in manager selection.
- Qualitative considerations in manager selection.

The learning module concludes with a summary of selected important points.

2 A FRAMEWORK FOR INVESTMENT MANAGER SEARCH AND SELECTION

☐ describe the components of a manager selection process, including due diligence

An underlying assumption of investment manager due diligence is that a consistent, robust investment process will generate a similar return distribution relative to risk factors through time, assuming the underlying dynamics of the market have not dramatically changed. One important goal of manager due diligence is to understand whether the manager's investment process, people, and portfolio construction satisfy this assumption—that is, will the investment process generate the expected return from the expected sources? The manager search and selection process has three broad components: the universe, a quantitative analysis of the manager's performance track record, and a qualitative analysis of the manager's investment process. The qualitative analysis consists of investment due diligence, which evaluates the manager's investment process, and operational due diligence, which evaluates the manager's infrastructure and firm. Exhibit 1 details these components.

Exhibit 1: Manager Selection Process Overview

Key aspects	Key Question
Universe	
Defining the universe	What is the feasible set of managers that fit the portfolio need?
▪ Suitability	Which managers are suitable for the IPS?
▪ Style	Which have the appropriate style?
▪ Active vs. passive	Which fit the active versus passive decision?
Quantitative Analysis	
Quantitative	What has been the manager's return distribution?
▪ Attribution and Appraisal	Has the manager displayed skill?
▪ Capture ratio	How does the manager perform in "up" markets versus "down" markets?
▪ Drawdown	Does the return distribution exhibit large drawdowns?
Qualitative Analysis	
Investment due diligence	Which manager "best" fits the portfolio need?
Qualitative	Is the manager expected to continue to generate this return distribution?
▪ Philosophy	What market inefficiency does the manager seek to exploit?
▪ Process	Is the investment process capable of exploiting this inefficiency?
▪ People	Do the investment personnel possess the expertise and experience necessary to effectively implement the investment process?
▪ Portfolio	Is portfolio construction consistent with the stated investment philosophy and process?
Operational due diligence	Is the manager's track record accurate, and does it fully reflect risks?
▪ Process and procedure	Is the back office strong, safeguarding assets and able to issue accurate reports in a timely manner?
▪ Firm	Is the firm profitable, with a healthy culture, and likely to remain in business? Is the firm committed to delivering performance over gathering assets?
▪ Investment vehicle	Is the vehicle suitable for the portfolio need?
▪ Terms	Are the terms acceptable and appropriate for the strategy and vehicle?
▪ Monitoring	Does the manager continue to be the "best" fit for the portfolio need?

EXAMPLE 1

Components of the Manager Selection Process

1. Qualitative analysis of the manager selection process includes:

   A. attribution.

   B. setting ESG objectives.

C. investment and operational due diligence.

Solution

C is correct. Qualitative analysis consists of investment due diligence, which evaluates the manager's investment process, and operational due diligence, which evaluates the manager's infrastructure and firm.

2. Which of the following is considered a key aspect of operational due diligence?

   A. People

   B. Philosophy

   C. Procedures

Solution

C is correct. Process and procedures are key aspects of operational due diligence, whereas people and philosophy are key aspects of investment due diligence.

Defining the Manager Universe

The manager selection process begins by defining the universe of feasible managers, those managers that potentially satisfy the identified portfolio need. The objective is to reduce the manager universe to a manageable size relative to the resources and time available to evaluate it. This process also involves balancing the risks of too narrow a search, which potentially excludes interesting managers, and too broad a search, which leads to little gain in reducing the list of potential managers. Like many interesting problems, this step is a combination of art and science. In the initial screening process, the search parameters can be narrowed and widened to determine which managers enter and exit and to evaluate whether these additions or deletions improve the universe.

The IPS and the reason for the manager search largely determine the universe of managers considered and the benchmark against which they are compared. A new search based on a strategic or tactical view, such as adding a new strategy or risk exposure, will examine a broad universe of comparable managers and look to select the best within the universe. Adding a manager to increase capacity or diversification within a strategy already held will look for a complement to current holdings. Replacing a single manager in a particular strategy will look for the best manager within the strategy universe. The IPS in part determines what the relative terms "best," "complement," and "cost/benefit" mean.

Typically, a search starts with a benchmark that represents the manager's role within the portfolio. The benchmark also provides a reference for performance attribution and appraisal. There are several approaches to assigning a manager to a benchmark:

- *Third-party categorization.* Database or software providers and consultants typically assign managers to a strategy sector. This categorization provides an easy and efficient way to define the universe. The risk is that the provider's definition may differ from the desired portfolio role. As such, it is important to understand the criteria used by the provider.
- *Returns-based style analysis.* The risk exposures derived from the manager's actual return series has the advantage of being objective. The disadvantage is additional computational effort and the limitations of returns-based analysis.

- *Holdings-based style analysis.* This approach allows for the estimation of current factor exposures but adds to computational effort and depends on timing and amount of transparency.
- *Manager experience.* The assignment can be based on an evaluation of the manager and observations of portfolios and returns over time.

Not surprisingly, a hybrid strategy that combines elements of each approach is recommended. Using third-party categorizations is an efficient way to build an initial universe that can then be complemented and refined with quantitative methods and experience. The screening should avoid using performance at this point. The focus should be on understanding the manager's risk profile and identifying candidates to fill the desired role in the portfolio. Lastly, the universe of potential managers is not static—it will evolve through time not only as manager strategies evolve but also as a result of the entry and exit of managers.

TYPE I AND TYPE II ERRORS IN MANAGER SELECTION 3

☐ contrast Type I and Type II errors in manager hiring and continuation decisions

Certain concepts from hypothesis testing, discussed earlier in the curriculum, can be relevant to the decision to hire an investment manager or to retain or dismiss a manager previously hired.

The determination of whether a manager is skillful typically starts with the null hypothesis (the hypothesis assumed to be true until demonstrated otherwise) that the manager is not skillful. As a result, there are two types of potential error (see Exhibit 2):

- Type I: Hiring or retaining a manager who subsequently underperforms expectations. Rejecting the null hypothesis of no skill when it is correct; a false positive.
- Type II: Not hiring or firing a manager who subsequently outperforms, or performs in line with, expectations. Not rejecting the null hypothesis when it is incorrect; a false negative.

Exhibit 2: Type I and Type II Errors

		Realization	
		Below expectations (no skill)	**At or above expectations (skill)**
Decision	**Hire/Retain**	Type I	Correct
	Not Hire/Fire	Correct	Type II

Type I and Type II errors can occur anytime a decision is made regarding the hiring or firing of a manager. The decision maker must determine which error is preferred based on the expected benefits and costs of changing managers.

Qualitative Considerations in Type I and Type II Errors

Decision makers appear predisposed to worry more about Type I errors than Type II errors. Potential reasons for this focus on Type I errors are as follows:

- Psychologically, people seek to avoid feelings of regret. Type I errors are mistaken rejections, whereas Type II errors are failures to detect a true relationship. As a result, Type I errors create explicit costs, whereas Type II errors create opportunity costs. Because individuals appear to put less weight on opportunity costs, Type I errors are psychologically more painful than Type II errors.
- Type I errors are relatively straightforward to measure and are often directly linked to the decision maker's compensation. Portfolio holdings are regularly monitored, and managers' out- and underperformance expectations are clearly identified. Type II errors are less likely to be measured—what is the performance impact of not having selected a particular manager? As such, the link between compensation and Type II errors is less clear.
- Similarly, Type I errors are more transparent to investors, so they entail not only the regret of an incorrect decision but the pain of having to explain this decision to the investor. Type II errors, firing (or not hiring) a manager with skill, are less transparent to investors, unless the investor tracks fired managers or evaluates the universe themselves.

Although Type I errors are likely more familiar and more of a concern to most decision makers, a consistent pattern of Type II errors can highlight weaknesses in the manager selection process. One approach to examine this issue is to monitor not only managers currently held but also managers that were evaluated and not hired as well as managers that were fired. The goal of monitoring is to determine the following:

- Are there identifiable factors that differentiate managers hired and managers not hired?
- Are these factors consistent with the investment philosophy and process of the decision maker?
- Are there identifiable factors driving the decision to retain or fire managers?
- Are these factors consistent with the investment philosophy and process of the decision maker?
- What is the added value of the decision to retain or fire managers?

The objective is to avoid making decisions based on short-term performance (trend following) and to identify any evidence of behavioral biases (regret, loss aversion) in the evaluation of managers during the selection process.

Performance Implications of Type I and Type II Errors

The cost of Type I errors is holding a manager without skill, as opposed to the cost of Type II errors, which is not holding managers with skill. The cost is driven by the size, shape, mean, and dispersion of the return distributions of the skilled and unskilled managers within the universe. The smaller the difference in sample size and distribution mean and the wider the dispersion of the distributions, the smaller the expected cost of the Type I or Type II error. More efficient markets are likely to exhibit smaller differences in the distributions of skilled and unskilled managers, indicating a lower opportunity cost of retaining and the lower the cost of hiring an unskilled manager.

The extent to which a strategy is mean-reverting also has a bearing on the cost of Type I and Type II errors. If a strategy's performance is mean reverting, firing a poor performer (or hiring a strong performer) only to see a reversion in performance results is a Type I error. A Type II error would be trimming or not hiring strong performers and hiring managers with weaker track records. There is evidence that individual investors significantly underperform the average mutual fund because of poor timing and fund selection decisions. A study of institutional plan sponsor allocation decisions found that investment products receiving contributions subsequently underperformed products experiencing withdrawals. The study estimated that more than $170 billion was lost during the period examined (Stewart, Neumann, Knittel, and Heisler 2009).

EXAMPLE 2

Type I and Type II Errors

1. A Type I error is:

   A. hiring or retaining a manager that subsequently underperforms expectations.

   B. hiring or retaining a manager that subsequently outperforms, or performs in line with, expectations.

   C. not hiring or firing a manager who subsequently outperforms, or performs in line with, expectations.

   Solution

   A is correct. The error consists of rejecting the null hypothesis (no skill) when it is correct.

2. A Type II error is:

   A. hiring or retaining a manager that subsequently underperforms expectations.

   B. hiring or retaining a manager that subsequently outperforms, or performs in line with, expectations.

   C. not hiring or firing a manager who subsequently outperforms, or performs in line with, expectations.

   Solution

   C is correct. The error consists of not rejecting the null hypothesis (no skill) when it is incorrect.

3. The difference in expected cost between Type I and Type II errors is *most likely*:

   A. higher the smaller the perceived difference between the distribution of skilled and unskilled managers.

   B. lower the smaller the perceived difference between the distribution of skilled and unskilled managers.

   C. zero.

   Solution

   B is correct. The less distinct the distribution of skilled managers from unskilled managers, the lower the opportunity cost of retaining and cost of hiring an unskilled manager. That is, the smaller the perceived difference between the distribution of skilled and unskilled managers, the lower the cost and incentive to fire a manager.

4 QUANTITATIVE ELEMENTS OF MANAGER SEARCH AND SELECTION

☐ describe uses of returns-based and holdings-based style analysis in investment manager selection

Performance appraisal captures most aspects of quantitative analysis, evaluating a manager's strengths and weaknesses as measured by that manager's ability to add value to a stated benchmark. Although the determination of whether the manager possesses skill is important, it is equally important to understand the manager's risk profile. The manager has likely been selected to fill a particular role in the portfolio. As such, although it is important to select a skillful manager, the "best" manager may be one that delivers the desired exposures and is suitable for the investor's assumptions, expectations, and biases.

Style Analysis

An important component of performance appraisal and manager selection is understanding the manager's risk exposures relative to the benchmark and how they evolve over time. This understanding helps define the universe of potential managers and the monitoring of selected managers. The process is referred to as style analysis.

A manager's self-reported risk exposures, such as portfolio concentration, industry exposure, capitalization exposure, and other quantitative measures, are the starting point in style analysis. They provide a means to classify managers by style for defining the selection process, a point of reference for evaluating the returns-based and holdings-based style analysis, and an interesting operational check on the manager.

The results of the returns-based style analysis (RBSA) and the holdings-based style analysis (HBSA) should be consistent with the manager's philosophy and the investment process. If not, the process might not be repeatable or might be implemented inconsistently. It is essential to look at all portfolio construction and risk management issues.

The results of the returns-based style analysis and the holdings-based style analysis should be tracked over time in order to ascertain if the risk trends or exposures are out of line with expectations or the manager's stated style. Deviations may signal that issues, such as style drift, are developing.

Returns-based and holdings-based style analyses provide a means to determine the risks and sources of return for a particular strategy. To be useful, style analysis must be:

- *Meaningful.* The risks reported must represent the important sources of performance return and risk.
- *Accurate.* The reported values must reflect the manager's actual risk exposures.
- *Consistent.* The methodology must allow for comparison over time and across multiple managers.
- *Timely.* The report must be available in a timely manner so that it is useful for making informed investment decisions.

Style analysis is most useful with strategies that hold publicly traded securities where pricing is frequent. It can be applied to other strategies (hedge funds and private equity, for example), but the insights drawn from a style analysis of such strategies are more likely to be used for designing additional lines of inquiry in the course of due diligence rather than for confirmation of the investment process.

Returns-based style analysis (RBSA) is a top-down approach that involves estimating a portfolio's sensitivities to security market indexes representing a range of distinct factors. Although RBSA adds the additional analytical step of estimating the risk factors, as opposed to using a third-party or self-reported style categorization, the analysis is straightforward and typically does not require a large amount of additional, or difficult to acquire, data. RBSA should identify the important drivers of return and risk factors for the period analyzed and can be estimated even for complicated strategies. In addition, the process is comparable across managers and through time, and the use of returns data provides an objective style check that is not subject to window dressing. The analysis can be run immediately after the data are available, particularly in the case of publicly traded securities. As such, RBSA has many of the attributes of effective risk reporting.

The disadvantage is that RBSA is an imprecise tool. Although the additional computational effort required is not onerous, accuracy may be compromised, because RBSA effectively attributes performance to an unchanging average portfolio during the period. This attribution limits the ability to identify the impact of dynamic investment decisions and may distort the decomposition across sources of added value. Furthermore, the portfolio being analyzed might not reflect the current or future portfolio exposures. If the portfolio contains illiquid securities, stale prices may understate the risk exposure of the strategy. This is a particular problem for private equity (PE) and venture capital (VC) managers that hold illiquid or non-traded securities. VC and PE firms report performance based on the internal rate of return of cash distributions and appraisals of ongoing projects. As a result, reported performance can understate the volatility of return for shorter horizons or time periods with limited liquidity events. Longer periods generally provide more-accurate estimates of the manager's underlying standard deviation of return. The timeliness of any analysis depends on the securities that take the longest to price, which can be challenging for illiquid or non-traded securities.

Holdings-based style analysis (HBSA) is a bottom-up approach that estimates the risk exposures from the actual securities held in the portfolio at a point in time. This approach allows for estimation of current risk factors and offers several advantages. Similar to RBSA, HBSA should identify all important drivers of return and risk factors; be comparable across managers and through time; provide an accurate view of the manager's risk exposures, although potentially subject to window dressing; and be estimated immediately after the data become available.

Exhibit 3 presents a typical holdings-based style map. The manager being evaluated, along with the other managers in the universe, is placed along the size (y-axis) and style (x-axis) dimensions. The portfolio holdings of the manager being evaluated exhibit a large-cap value bias in what is otherwise a rather diverse universe.

Exhibit 3: Example of Holdings-Based Style Analysis

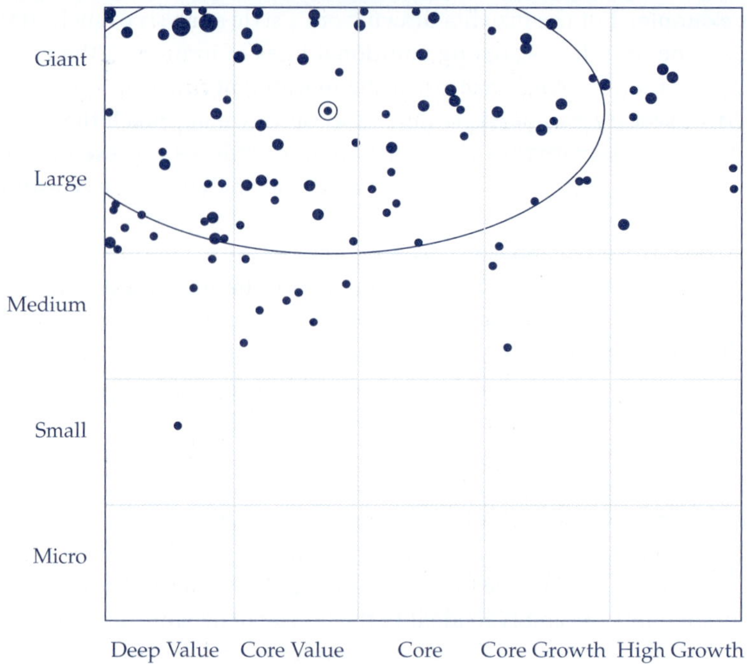

Source: Morningstar Direct, The Mutual Fund Research Center.

As with RBSA, HBSA has some disadvantages. The computational effort increases with the complexity of the strategy and depends on the timing and degree of the transparency provided by the manager. This extra effort can be challenging for hedge fund, private equity, and venture capital managers that may be averse to or unable to provide position-level pricing. Even with mutual funds, the necessary transparency may come with a time lag. The usefulness of the analysis may be compromised because the portfolio reflects a snapshot in time and might not reflect the portfolio going forward, particularly for high-turnover strategies. Some factors may be difficult to estimate if the strategy is complex because HBSA requires an understanding of the underlying strategy. In general, HBSA is typically easier with equity strategies, particularly for ETFs because holdings are published daily. If the portfolio has illiquid securities, stale pricing may underestimate the risk exposure of the strategy. The report's timeliness depends on the securities that take the longest to price, which can be challenging for illiquid or non-traded securities.

EXAMPLE 3

Style Analysis

1. Which of the following is an advantage of RBSA?

   A. It is a more precise tool than HBSA.

   B. It does not require potentially difficult to acquire data.

C. It is more accurate than HBSA when the portfolio contains illiquid securities.

Solution

B is correct. The data needed for RBSA are usually easier to obtain than the data required for HBSA. RBSA is not a precise tool, and it is not more accurate than HBSA when the portfolio holds illiquid securities.

2. Which of the following is an advantage of HBSA?

A. It works well for high-turnover strategies.

B. It can identify important drivers of return and risk factors and is comparable across managers and through time.

C. It effectively attributes performance to a snapshot of the portfolio at a particular time and thus is not subject to window dressing.

Solution

B is correct. Although HBSA allows for estimation of current risk factors and is comparable across managers and through time, the necessary computational effort increases with the strategy's complexity and depends on the timing and degree of the transparency provided by the manager. Some factors may be difficult to estimate if the strategy is complex because this approach requires an understanding of the underlying strategy. In general, HBSA is typically easier for equity strategies. If the portfolio has illiquid securities, stale pricing may underestimate the risk exposure of the strategy. Window dressing and high turnover can compromise the results because the results are attributed to a snapshot of the portfolio.

CAPTURE RATIOS AND DRAWDOWNS IN MANAGER EVALUATION 5

☐ describe uses of the upside capture ratio, downside capture ratio, maximum drawdown, drawdown duration, and up/down capture in evaluating managers

Because large losses require proportionally greater gains to reverse or offset, drawdowns and capture ratios can be important factors in investment manager evaluation. A manager that experiences larger drawdowns may be less suitable for an investor closer to the end of their investment horizon. The capture ratio helps assess manager suitability relative to the investor's IPS, especially in relation to the investor's time horizon and risk tolerance.

Recall the following: (1) Upside capture (UC) measures capture when the benchmark return is positive. UC greater than 100% suggests out-performance relative to the benchmark. (2) Downside capture (DC) measures capture when the benchmark return is negative. DC less than 100% generally suggests out-performance relative to the benchmark. (3) The **capture ratio** (CR)—upside capture divided by downside capture—measures the asymmetry of return. (4) **Drawdown** is the cumulative peak-to-trough loss during a particular continuous period and **drawdown duration** is the total time from the start of the drawdown until the cumulative drawdown recovers to zero.

Let's illustrate the use of capture ratios in the analysis of manager returns. Consider the four stylized return profiles in Exhibit 4.

Exhibit 4: Return Profile Summary

Profile	Upside Capture	Downside Capture	Ratio
Long only	100%	100%	1.0
Positive asymmetry	75%	25%	3.0
Low beta	50%	50%	1.0
Negative asymmetry	25%	75%	0.3

Each strategy's allocation to the S&P 500 Total Return (TR) Index and to 90-day T-bills (assuming monthly rebalancing to simplify the calculations) is based on the realized monthly return from January 2000 to December 2013. (This time period encompasses two significant drawdowns: the "tech bubble burst" of the early 2000s and the extreme drawdown of the Global Financial Crisis in 2008–2009.)

- The long-only profile is 100% allocated to the S&P 500 throughout the period.
- The low-beta profile is allocated 50% to the S&P 500 throughout the period.
- The positive asymmetry profile is allocated 75% to the S&P 500 for months when the S&P 500 return is positive and 25% when the S&P 500 return is negative.
- The negative asymmetry profile is allocated 25% to the S&P 500 for months when the S&P 500 return is positive and 75% when the S&P 500 return is negative.

The remainder for all profiles is allocated to 90-day T-bills. Exhibit 5 shows each profile's cumulative monthly return for the period.

Exhibit 5: Each Profile's Cumulative Monthly Return, January 2000–December 2013

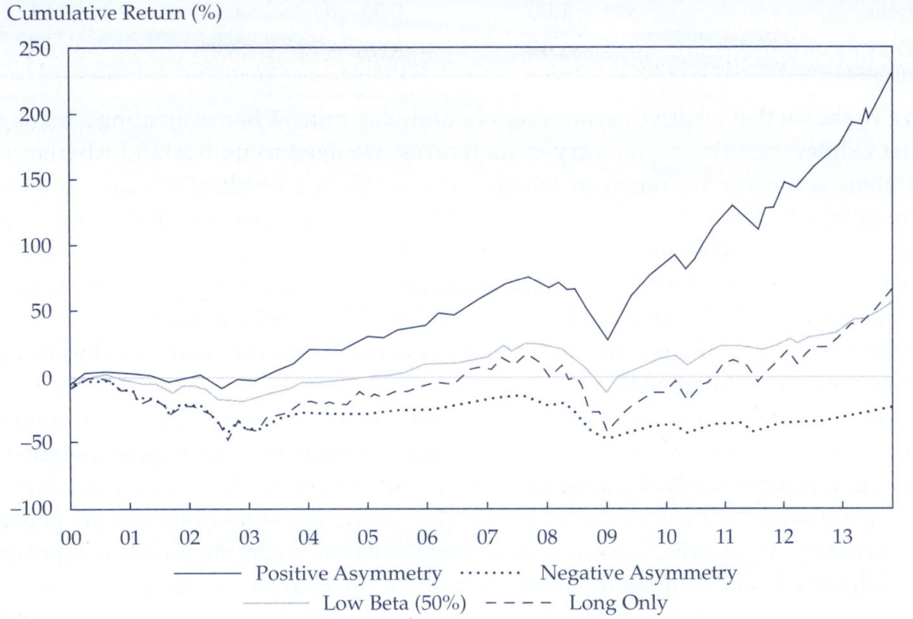

Exhibit 6 provides summary statistics for each profile based on monthly returns from January 2000 to December 2013. Although the long-only profile outperformed the low-beta profile over the full period, this outperformance resulted from the strong up market of 2013—the long-only profile lagged the low-beta profile for most of the period. The low beta profile achieved higher risk-adjusted returns and only half the volatility for the full period. The low-beta profile declined only 18.8% from January 2000 to September 2002, compared with the long-only decline of 42.5%. As a result, the low-beta profile had higher cumulative performance from January 2000 to October 2007 despite markedly lagging the long-only profile (56.0% to 108.4%) from October 2002 to October 2007.

Although a low-beta approach may sacrifice performance, it shows that limiting drawdowns can result in better absolute and risk-adjusted returns in certain markets.

Not surprisingly, positive asymmetry results in better performance relative to long only, low beta, and negative asymmetry. Although the positive asymmetry profile lags in up markets, this lag is more than offset by the lower participation in down markets. Not surprisingly, the negative asymmetry profile lags.

Exhibit 6: Summary Statistics for Each Profile, January 2000–December 2013

Strategy	Long Only	Low Beta	Positive Asymmetry	Negative Asymmetry
Cumulative return	64.0%	54.2%	228.1%	−24.4%
Annualized return	3.60%	3.14%	8.86%	−1.98%
Annualized standard deviation	15.64%	7.79%	9.61%	10.01%
Sharpe ratio	0.10	0.14	0.71	−0.40

Strategy	Long Only	Low Beta	Positive Asymmetry	Negative Asymmetry
Beta	1.00	0.50	0.61	0.64
Drawdown (maximum)	−50.9%	−28.3%	−26.9%	−48.9%

We've shown that positive asymmetry is a desirable trait. When evaluating a manager that exhibits positive asymmetry in its returns, we need to understand whether the strategy is inherently convex or whether the profile is a result of manager skill. For example, a hedging strategy implemented by rolling forward out-of-the-money put options will typically return many small losses because more options expire worthless than are compensated for by the occasional large gain during a large market downturn. A manager employing this strategy will likely exhibit consistent positive asymmetry in his returns, but the positive asymmetry is likely due to the nature of the strategy rather than investment skill.

Let's consider now the use of drawdowns in the analysis of manager returns. Drawdowns are stress tests of the investment process and can expose potentially flawed or inconsistently implemented investment processes, inadequate risk controls, or operational issues. Did the manager implement the stated investment process consistently? If yes, what lessons were learned and how might the investment process have been adapted as a result? If the drawdown resulted from a deviation from the stated investment process, why? During a large or long drawdown, a manager could start to worry more about business risk than investment risk and act in their own best interest rather than that of their investors. How a manager responds to a large drawdown as it occurs (and what lessons are learned) provides evidence of the robustness and repeatability of the investment, portfolio construction, and risk management processes, as well as insight into the people implementing the processes.

EVENTS OF AUGUST 2007

Starting on 7 August 2007, many quantitative equity long–short strategies began to experience large drawdowns. Many managers had never experienced such losses or market conditions and started to sell positions as stop-loss and risk management policies were triggered (Khandani and Lo 2011). This activity added to additional selling pressure, and the S&P 500 declined 13.4% by 8 August. Those managers that sold ended up locking in large losses because the underperforming stocks and market subsequently recovered, with the S&P 500 down only 5.7% for the month. In many cases, those funds that sold experienced redemptions or ended up closing.

As August 2007 demonstrated, distinguishing prudent risk management from a misalignment of interests is not always straightforward. Should a manager continue to actively trade a portfolio if the market environment no longer reflects their investment philosophy? In addition, traders will claim that it is better to cut losses because losses can signal that something has changed or that the timing of the trade is not right. Conversely, selling into a down market raises the risk of crystallizing losses and missing any subsequent reversal. The decision maker must assess whether the manager's behavior was a disciplined application of the investment process, reflected a misalignment of interests, or simply resulted from panic or overreaction by the manager.

One aspect of suitability for the IPS is the investment horizon and its relationship to risk capacity. An investor closer to retirement, with less time to recover from losses, places more emphasis on absolute measures of risk. If there has been no change to investment policy and no change in the view that the manager remains suitable, the temptation to exit should be resisted to avoid exiting at an inauspicious time. Investors with shorter horizons, with lower risk capacity, or those prone to overreacting to losses may be better served by allocating to managers with shallower and shorter expected drawdowns.

THE CONCEPT OF ACTIVE SHARE

Active share measures the difference in portfolio holdings relative to the benchmark. A manager that precisely replicates the benchmark will have an active share of zero; a manager with no holdings in common with the benchmark will have an active share of one.

Given a strategy with N securities ($i = 1, 2, \ldots, N$), active share is calculated as

$$\text{Active Share} = \frac{1}{2}\sum_{i=1}^{N} \left| \text{Strategy Weight}_i - \text{Benchmark Weight}_i \right|$$

Typically, managers are somewhere along the spectrum. The categorization of active share and tracking risk in Exhibit 7 has been suggested for active managers. It is clear that full replication will appear as a closet indexer. A manager that uses sampling techniques to build the portfolio may, however, appear as a diversified stock picker depending on the universe under consideration and the dispersion of active share of the constituents. Tracking risk will be low, but active share might not be because only a subset of constituents is held. One reason is that high and low are relative to the universe being examined and the category definitions used. As such, it is important to examine risk factors and portfolio construction techniques of both active and passive managers.

Exhibit 7: Active Share vs. Tracking Risk

		Active Share	
		Low	High
Tracking risk	High	Sector rotation	Concentrated stock pickers
	Low	Closet indexer	Diversified stock pickers

THE MANAGER'S INVESTMENT PHILOSOPHY

6

- ☐ evaluate a manager's investment philosophy and investment decision-making process
- ☐ discuss how behavioral factors affect investment team decision making, and recommend techniques for mitigating their effects

The goal of manager due diligence is to weigh the potential risks that may arise from entering into an investment management relationship and entrusting assets to a firm. Although it is impossible to eliminate all potential risks, the allocator must assess how the firm will manage the broad range of risks it is likely to face in the future. This lesson outlines the general aspects of manager due diligence and the particular questions the investor needs to answer.

Investment due diligence examines and evaluates the qualitative considerations that illustrate that the manager's investment process is repeatable and consistently implemented. The objective is to understand whether the investment philosophy, process, people, and portfolio construction satisfy the assumption that past performance provides some guidance for expected future performance. In other words, are the conclusions drawn from performance measurement, attribution, and appraisal reliable selection criteria? In addition, it is important to remember that investment managers are businesses. Regardless of the strength of the investment process or historical performance, investment management firms must be operated as successful businesses to ensure sustainability. Operational due diligence examines and evaluates the firm's policies and procedures, to identify potential risks that might not be captured in historical performance and to assess the firm's sustainability.

Investment Philosophy

The investment philosophy is the foundation of the investment process. Every investment strategy is based on a set of assumptions about the factors that drive performance and the manager's beliefs about their ability to successfully exploit these sources of return. The investment manager should have a clear and concise investment philosophy.

First, every manager makes assumptions about market efficiency, including the degree and the time frame. Index-based strategies assume markets are sufficiently efficient and that active management cannot add value after transaction costs and fees. As a result, these strategies seek to capture return through exposure to systematic **risk premiums**, such as equity risk, duration risk, or credit risk. These strategies can also look to capture alternative risk premiums such as liquidity risk, natural disaster risk (through, for example, catastrophe bonds and quota shares), volatility risk, or some combination of these premiums (e.g., distressed strategies seek to capture credit and liquidity risk premiums).

In contrast, active strategies assume markets are sufficiently inefficient that security mispricings can be identified and exploited. These opportunities typically arise when market behavior deviates from the manager's fundamental assumptions. Generally speaking, inefficiencies can be categorized as behavioral or structural.

- *Behavioral inefficiencies* are perceived mispricings created by the actions of other market participants, usually associated with biases, such as trend following or loss aversion. These inefficiencies are temporary, lasting long enough for the manager to identify and exploit them before the market price and perceived intrinsic value converge.
- *Structural inefficiencies* are perceived mispricings created by external or internal rules and regulations. These inefficiencies can be long lived and assume a continuation of the rules and regulations rather than a convergence.

Active strategies also typically make assumptions about the dynamics and structures of the market, such as the following: The correlation structure of the market is sufficiently stable over the investment horizon to make diversification useful for risk management; prices eventually converge to intrinsic value, which can be estimated by using a discounted cash flow model; or market prices are driven by predictable macroeconomic trends.

It is important to evaluate these assumptions and the role they play in the investment process to understand how the strategy will behave through time and across market environments.

- Can the manager clearly and consistently articulate their investment philosophy? It is hard to have confidence in the repeatability and efficacy of an investment process if the manager, and investment personnel, cannot explain the assumptions that underpin the process. This clarity also provides a consistency check that the investment process and personnel are appropriate for the stated philosophy.
- Are the assumptions credible and consistent? That is, does the decision maker agree with the assumptions underlying the strategy, and are these assumptions consistent with the investment process? A decision maker who believes a market is efficient would likely not find the assumptions of an active manager in that market credible. In the decision maker's judgment, the assumptions must support a repeatable and robust investment process.
- How has the philosophy developed over time? Ideally, the philosophy is unchanged through time, suggesting a repeatable process. If philosophy has evolved, it is preferred that changes are judged to be reasonable responses to changing market conditions rather than a series of ad hoc reactions to performance or investor flows. Such changes suggest a lack of repeatability and robustness.
- Are the return sources linked to credible and consistent inefficiencies? The decision maker must judge whether the investment philosophy is based on an inefficiency that is based on an informational advantage, or behavioral and structural inefficiencies that suggest the investment process is repeatable.

If the source of return is linked to a credible inefficiency, there is the additional issue of capacity. Capacity has several related aspects, such as the level of assets the strategy or opportunity can absorb without a dilution of returns, the number of opportunities or securities available, and the ability to transact in a timely manner at or near the market price—that is, liquidity. Overall, capacity is the level, repeatability, and sustainability of returns that the inefficiency is expected to support in the future.

- Does the inefficiency provide a sufficient frequency of opportunity and level of return to cover transaction costs and fees? If so, does this require leverage?
- Does the inefficiency provide a repeatable source of return? That is, can the opportunity be captured by a repeatable process, or is each opportunity unique, requiring a different process of skill set to exploit?
- Is the inefficiency sustainable? That is, at what asset level would the realized return from the inefficiency be unacceptably low? Sustainability will be a function of the market's depth and liquidity, as well as how much capital is allocated, either by the manager or competitors, to the inefficiency. All else equal, the more well-known an inefficiency, the more likely it is to be arbitraged away.

UNCOMMON WAYS OF PASSING THE INVESTMENT PHILOSOPHY TEST

1. Managers that measure the success of the steps of the process and not just the ultimate outcome.

For example, consider a bond manager that makes the claim that his or her credit research not only predicts upgrades and downgrades, but makes those predictions before the expectation of a rating change is reflected in the market price. This manager tracks every prediction to see if the market consensus (as reflected by price) and rating agencies come around to his or her view. Benefits of such an approach include (1) the manager knows their views only have value if they are not only correct but different than consensus, and (2) they track how prices eventually come to reflect, or not reflect, their views. Similarly, managers that evaluate their own performance with strategy benchmarks designed to replicate their selection universe demonstrate they understand the importance of attempting to differentiate alpha from noise (see Kuenzi 2003).

2. Managers that recognize that every strategy they come up with is potentially subject to being arbitraged away.

   For example, consider a quantitative equity manager that that plays many themes at once. Each theme is viewed as having a finite life, and the performance of each theme is isolated and monitored so as to observe the decay in the value of the theme. The manager considers his or her competitive advantage to be in the identification of new themes, and in the technology for measuring the contribution of each theme to performance. A similar idea is presented in the adaptive market hypothesis of Lo (2004), where the market is always tending toward efficiency, but the types of trades needed to move it towards efficiency rotate and evolve over time.

3. Managers that claim they exploit inefficiencies, and identify the specific inefficiency they are exploiting with every position they take.

   Most managers that say they exploit inefficiencies use this claim as a broad justification for their investment process, but are unable to identify the specific inefficiency they are exploiting in any given decision they make. Those that routinely specify how their information or point of view differs from that reflected in price are much more credible.

4. Managers that know their companies so well that they are quicker to interpret change, even though they have no explicit alpha thesis.

   There is always an exception to the rule. Sometimes a manager is simply talented and cannot articulate an alpha thesis.

Despite examples such as these, it remains frustratingly difficult to distinguish between true alpha-generators and alpha-pretenders. Investors should insist that alpha-generators explain their source of advantage.

This excerpt is from John R. Minahan, CFA, "The Role of Investment Philosophy in Evaluating Investment Managers: A Consultant's Perspective on Distinguishing Alpha from Noise," *Journal of Investing* 15 (May 2006): 6–11.

EXAMPLE 4

Investment Philosophy

1. Which of the following is *not* an important consideration when evaluating a manager's investment philosophy?

   A. What are the compensation arrangements of key employees?

B. Are the investment philosophy assumptions credible and consistent?

C. Can the manager clearly and consistently articulate their investment philosophy?

Solution

A is correct. Employee compensation is a legal and compliance issue considered as part of operational due diligence.

2. Generally speaking, inefficiencies can be *most usefully* categorized as:

A. large and small.

B. internal and external.

C. structural and behavioral.

Solution

C is correct. Behavioral inefficiencies are created by the actions of other participants in the market. These inefficiencies are temporary, lasting long enough for the manager to identify and exploit them before the market price and perceived intrinsic value converge. Structural inefficiencies are created by external or internal rules and regulations. These inefficiencies can be long lived and assume a continuation of the rules and regulations rather than a convergence.

3. Which of the following is *not* an important consideration when evaluating the capacity of an inefficiency?

A. Does the strategy rely on unique information?

B. Does the inefficiency provide a repeatable source of return?

C. Does the inefficiency provide a sufficient frequency of opportunity and level of return to cover transaction costs and fees?

Solution

A is correct. The uniqueness of information used by the manager is a consideration when evaluating the assumptions of the investment process.

Investment Personnel

An investment process can only be as good as the people who create and implement it, and even the best process can be compromised by poor execution by the people involved. This view is not a question of liking the manager or team but of trusting that they possess the expertise and experience to effectively implement the strategy.

- Does the investment team have sufficient expertise and experience to effectively execute the investment process? The need for expertise is self-evident. The greater the experience, particularly managing the current strategy across market environments, the greater the confidence in the manager's ability to effectively execute the investment process. As noted with drawdowns, it is especially instructive to see how the manager responded to stressed markets and poor performance.
- Does the investment team have sufficient depth to effectively execute the investment process? A strategy that focuses on a small universe of publicly traded stocks might not require a large investment team. A global macro or multi-strategy fund, which holds positions across numerous global markets, likely requires a large team with expertise and experience supporting the manager.

- What is the level of **key person risk**? A strategy that is overly dependent on the judgment or particular skills of an individual or small team of people faces key person risk, an overreliance on an individual or individuals whose departure would negatively affect the strategy's performance.
- What kinds of agreements (e.g., non-compete) and incentives (ownership, bonus, pay) exist to retain and attract key employees to join and stay at the firm?
- What has been the turnover of firm personnel? High personnel turnover risks the loss of institutional knowledge and experience within the team.

Behavioral Biases among Investment Teams

Investment decisions are often made by teams rather than individuals. In 2021, team-managed mutual funds accounted for 64% of all US active mutual funds (Karagiannidis and Booth 2022). The primary motivation for team management is the idea that "two heads are better than one." More formally, the application to a task of a number of individuals, each with different skills and experiences, can provide for more effective decision making. A secondary motivation for team investment management is to mitigate key person risk.

While teams can mitigate some individual behavioral biases, such as overconfidence in forecasting, teams also introduce new biases or exacerbate others. Indeed, research on the performance of team-managed versus individual-managed mutual funds is mixed. Several studies have found that team-managed funds underperform individual-managed funds (Chen, Harrison, Ming, and Kubik 2004; Baer, Kempf, and Ruenzi 2005; Bär, Ciccotello, and Ruenzi 2010; Goldman, Sun, and Zhou 2016). Several other studies have found the opposite (Patel and Sarkissian 2017; Karagiannidis 2010). And some studies have found there is no difference in performance between the two (Bliss, Potter, and Schwarz 2008; Wang 2016; Sargis and Chang 2017). The mixed performance record suggests that there is nothing magical about a team, so managers should focus on creating an effective structure and culture.

Three common behavioral biases that can adversely affect investment teams' performance are groupthink, authority bias, and aversion to complexity.

Groupthink occurs when a team minimizes conflict and dissent in reaching and maintaining a consensus. The pursuit of harmony overrides individual expression and may even encourage individuals to withhold information and their perspectives from the team. Common symptoms of groupthink are closed-mindedness and confirmation bias, where fresh sources of information, different interpretations, and dissent are ignored or minimized. A portfolio management team may become convinced that a recession is imminent based on an inverted yield curve and falling commodity prices and thus seek to position the portfolio defensively by decreasing exposure to cyclicals. While this may ultimately be the right decision, the team must remain open to the possibility that it isn't. For example, other leading economic indicators may suggest a different conclusion, and it may behoove the team to speak with an analyst who has made a different call. The team should also investigate its own historical track record of recession calls, as well as the reliability of calls made based on an inverted yield curve and falling commodity prices.

Authority bias involves groups deferring to a group member that is a subject matter expert or in a position of authority (e.g., the senior-most group member). For example, a research analyst may recommend a semiconductor equipment stock to a team of three portfolio managers. One of the portfolio managers is a former technology research analyst and votes to not buy the stock. The other two members vote the same way, deferring to the subject matter expertise of the other manager. While this may be the right call, it undermines the reason for a team in the first place: a synthesis of diverse perspectives and skills.

Aversion to complexity is a well-known phenomenon of groups in many professional contexts, in which disproportionate attention is given to trivial issues at the expense of important but harder-to-grasp or contested topics. This phenomenon is also known as Parkinson's law of triviality or, colloquially, "bike-shedding," named after C. Northcote Parkinson's 1957 memorable story of a hypothetical committee organized to approve plans for a nuclear power plant that spent more time discussing the design of a bicycle storage shed outside the plant than the design of the nuclear reactor.

Aversion to complexity can surface in numerous ways. For example, a portfolio management team may spend far more time scrutinizing a position in a consumer staples company that they have personal experience with but comparatively little time on a position in a semiconductor or biotechnology company, even if the latter position is larger in the portfolio.

Investment team meetings can also be sidetracked by immaterial business issues that are best left to other venues or personnel. A survey of more than 120 investment committees asked committee members to rank their tasks from most to least important and then asked the members to keep track of how they actually allocated their time. The survey revealed that the committees spent a great deal of time on issues they rated as unimportant, at the expense of important and more difficult issues, such as asset allocation, capital market expectations, and manager selection (Payne and Wood 2002).

Similar to how investment due diligence should inquire about a manager's personnel, it can also be useful to inquire about whether the manager has built team structures and processes to mitigate behavioral biases. Such an inquiry may include the following:

- How large is the investment decision-making team? Research suggests that a team size between three and five is optimal, with larger teams introducing too many coordination issues (Patel and Sarkissian 2017) and increasing the odds of groupthink.
- How are decisions made? While it may be awkward, using a secret ballot may be preferable to open deliberation because it reduces groupthink and authority bias.
- How are meetings conducted? What makes it on the agenda? To avoid complexity aversion, as well as availability bias, meeting agendas should be agreed on in advance, with the most important topics covered first and allotted the longest time for discussion.
- Is the investment team diverse? Research suggests that team diversity—in terms of social and cognitive categories—can reduce groupthink and errors (analogous to how combinations of uncorrelated assets reduce portfolio volatility) and that members of diverse teams may devote more effort to tasks because they are less concerned with socially "fitting in" and conflict avoidance, which is common in homogeneous groups. For these reasons and others, CFA Institute has long advocated for diversity, equity, and inclusion (DEI) in the investment industry. For more information on DEI and the CFA Institute DEI Code, visit https://rpc.cfainstitute.org/en/codes-and-standards/diversity-equity-inclusion-codes.

7 THE MANAGER'S INVESTMENT DECISION-MAKING PROCESS

☐ evaluate a manager's investment philosophy and investment decision-making process

The investment decision-making process has four elements: signal creation, signal capture, portfolio construction, and portfolio monitoring.

Signal Creation (Idea Generation)

An investment signal is a data point or fact that can be observed early enough to implement as an investment position. The basic question is, how are investment ideas generated? The efficient market hypothesis posits that the key to exploiting inefficiencies is to have information that is all of the following:

- *Unique.* Does the strategy rely on unique information? If so, how is this information collected, and how is the manager able to retain an informational edge, particularly in a regulatory environment that seeks to reduce informational asymmetries?
- *Timely.* Does the strategy possess an information timing advantage? If so, how is this information collected, and how is the manager able to retain a timing edge, particularly in a regulatory environment that seeks to reduce informational asymmetries?
- *Interpreted differently.* Interpretation is typically how managers seek to differentiate themselves. Does the manager possess a unique way of interpreting information? Or does the manager claim their strategy possesses a "secret sauce" component or that its team is simply smarter than other managers?

Signal Capture (Idea Implementation)

The second step is signal capture, translating the generated investment idea into an investment position.

- What is the process for translating investment ideas into investment positions?
- Is this process repeatable and consistent with the strategy assumptions?
- What is the process, and who is ultimately responsible for approving an investment position?

Portfolio Construction

The third element is portfolio construction; how investment positions are implemented within the portfolio. This element begins to capture the manager's risk management methodology. Good investment ideas need to be implemented properly to exploit opportunities and capture desired risk premiums. It is also important that portfolio construction is consistent with the investment philosophy and process as well as the expertise of the investment personnel.

- How are portfolio allocations set and adjusted? The allocation process should be consistent with investment philosophy and process. For example, if the portfolio is actively managed, its turnover should agree with the frequency of signals, the payoff horizon of the signals, and the securities' liquidity. The allocation process should be well defined and consistently applied, supporting the repeatability of the investment process. For example, are allocations made quantitatively or qualitatively?
- Do portfolio allocations incorporate the manager's conviction (besides just the securities' risks and correlations with other securities in the portfolio)?
- How have the portfolio characteristics changed with asset growth? Has the number and/or characteristics of the positions held changed to accommodate a larger amount of AUM?
- Does the portfolio use stop-losses to manage risk? If so, are they hard (positions are automatically sold when the loss threshold is reached) or soft (positions are evaluated when the loss threshold is reached)? Although stop-losses represent a clear risk management approach, the goal of protecting against large losses must be balanced with the risk of closing positions too frequently.
- What types of securities are used? Does the manager use derivatives to express investment ideas? What experience does the manager have investing in these securities? The manager should be sufficiently well-versed and experienced with the securities used to understand how they will behave in different market environments.
- How are hedges implemented? What security types are used? How are hedge ratios set? Consider a manager that focuses on stock selection to generate alpha and hedges to reduce or remove market risk. The hedges must be sized correctly, or they can be ineffective (underhedged) or they can overwhelm stock selection (overhedged), with performance driven more by beta than by alpha.
- How are long and short ideas expressed? A manager might target a certain long/short exposure that may or may not vary according to market conditions. If long and short positions are fully offset, with the idea of minimizing market risk but capturing alpha, the positions must be well matched and sized correctly. A manager can implement this by taking positions that are local-currency neutral (i.e., dollar neutral) and have an equal value of securities on both sides. However, to fully minimize any remaining market risk, the manager should also aim to be beta neutral so that aggregate long and short exposures net to zero.

Alternatively, a manager can pursue a pairs strategy to construct long and short exposures. Pairs trading is a relative value strategy where a manager selects two or more securities with similar characteristics that are correlated and whose price relationship is out of historical trading range. The manager generally establishes a short position in the overvalued securities and an equal-sized long position in the undervalued securities based on a view that their price relationship will converge to historical norms.

An important risk is liquidity. Strategies that are not intending to capture a liquidity risk premium must be aware of portfolio liquidity in terms of adapting to changing information, changing market conditions, and changing investor liquidity demands. An existing portfolio consisting of illiquid securities will be more costly to change, not only to take advantage of new opportunities but also to trade because of higher transaction costs. There is the additional cost of having to sell positions at inopportune times as a result of market events or investor liquidity demands. When assessing security liquidity, it is important to consider all of the assets under management for that particular manager and investment process.

- What percentage of the portfolio can be liquidated in five business days or less? What percentage requires more than 10 business days to liquidate? The less liquid the portfolio, the higher the transaction costs if the manager is forced to sell one or more positions. A more liquid portfolio offers flexibility if the manager faces unexpected investor liquidity demands or rapidly changing market conditions.
- What is the average daily volume weighted by portfolio position size?
- Have any of the portfolio holdings been suspended from trading? If so, what is the name of the company, and what are the circumstances pertaining to the suspension?
- Are there any holdings in which ownership by the firm across all portfolios collectively accounts for more than 5% of the market capitalization or float of the security?
- What is the firm's trading strategy? Does the investment manager tend to provide liquidity or demand it? Has the trading strategy changed in response to asset growth?

Monitoring the Portfolio

The investment decision-making process is a feedback loop that consists of ongoing monitoring of the portfolio in light of new information and analysis. This monitoring includes an assessment of both external and internal considerations. External considerations include the economic and financial market environments. Has anything meaningful occurred that might affect the manager's ability to exploit the market inefficiency that is the strategy's focus? Internal considerations include the portfolio's performance, risk profile, and construction. Has anything changed that might signal potential style drift or other deviations from the investment process? Ongoing monitoring and performance attribution help to ensure that the manager remains appropriate for the clients' mandates.

8 OPERATIONAL DUE DILIGENCE

- ☐ evaluate the costs and benefits of pooled investment vehicles and separate accounts
- ☐ compare types of investment manager contracts, including their major provisions and advantages and disadvantages

Performance appraisal assumes that reported returns are accurate and fully reflect the manager's risk profile. Unfortunately, as we have seen, this assumption is not always true. Although investment due diligence is one step toward understanding these risks, one must remember that investment management firms are *businesses*, and in many cases, they are small businesses with a high degree of business risk. Regardless of the strength of the investment process or the historical investment results, investment management firms must be operated as a successful business in order to ensure their sustainability. This requirement creates the potential for a misalignment of interests between the manager and the investor. Operational due diligence analyzes the integrity of the business and seeks to understand and evaluate these risks by examining and evaluating the firm's policies and procedures.

Weaknesses in the firm's infrastructure represent latent risks to the investor. A strong back office (support staff) is critical for safeguarding assets and ensuring that accurate reports are issued in a timely manner. The manager should have a robust trading process that seeks to avoid human error. A repeatable process requires consistent implementation. The allocator needs to understand the following:

- What is the firm's trading policy?
- Does the firm use soft dollar commissions? If so, is there a rigorous process for ensuring compliance?
- What is the process for protecting against unauthorized trading?
- How are fees calculated and collected?
- How are securities allocated across investor accounts, including both pooled and separately managed accounts? The allocation method should be objective (e.g., based on invested capital) to avoid the potential to benefit some investors at the expense of others.
- How many different strategies does the firm manage, and are any new strategies being contemplated? Is the firm's infrastructure capable of efficiently and accurately implementing the different strategies?
- What information technology offsite backup facilities are in place?
- Does the firm have processes, software, and hardware in place to handle cybersecurity issues?

An important constituent of the infrastructure is third-party service providers, including the firm's prime broker, administrator, auditor, and legal counsel. They provide an important independent verification of the firm's performance and reporting.

- Are the firm's third-party service providers known and respected?
- Has there been any change in third-party providers? If so, when and why? This information is particularly important with regard to the firm's auditor. Frequent changes of the auditor are a red flag and may mean the manager is trying to hide something.

The risk management function should be viewed as an integral part of the investment firm and not considered a peripheral function. The extent to which integration exists provides insight into the firm's culture and the alignment of interests between the manager and the investor. The manager should have a risk manual that is readily available for review:

- Does the portfolio have any hard/soft investment guidelines?
- How are these guidelines monitored?
- What is the procedure for curing breaches?
- Who is responsible for risk management?
- Is there an independent risk officer?

Firm

An investment management firm must operate as a successful business to ensure sustainability. A manager that goes out of business does not have a repeatable investment process. An important aspect of manager selection is assessing the level of business risk.

- What is the ownership structure of the firm?
- What are the total firm AUM and AUM by investment strategy?
- What is the firm's breakeven AUM (the asset base needed to generate enough fee revenue to cover total firm expenses)?
- Are any of the firm's strategies closed to new capital?
- How much capital would the firm like to raise?

A firm that is independently owned may have greater autonomy and flexibility than a firm owned by a larger organization, but it may have a higher cost structure and lack financial support during market events, raising potential business risks. Outside ownership could create a situation in which the outside owner has objectives that conflict with the investment strategy. For instance, the outside owner might want to increase the asset base to generate higher fee revenue, but this action could prevent the portfolio from holding lower-capitalization stocks. Ideally, ownership should be spread across as many employees as is feasible and practical. A firm managing a smaller asset base may be more nimble and less prone to dilution of returns but will likely have lower revenues to support infrastructure and compensate employees. At a minimum, the asset base needs to be sufficient to support the firm's current expenditures.

Last, and by no means least important, are legal and compliance issues. It is critical that the firm's interests are aligned with those of the investor.

- What are the compensation arrangements for key employees? For example, are any people compensated with stock in the firm, and if so, what happens to this stock when they leave the firm?
- Do employees invest personal assets in the firm's strategies? Investing their own money in the same products in which the firm's clients invest creates an alignment of interests, but too large a proportion of their own assets invested in this one product may create personal/business risk for the manager that overrides the alignment of interests.
- Does the firm foster a culture of compliance?
- What is covered in the compliance manual?
- Has the firm or any of its employees been involved with an investigation by any financial market regulator or self-regulatory organization?
- Has the firm been involved in any lawsuits?
- Are any of the firm's employees involved in legal actions or personal litigation that might affect their ability to continue to fulfill their fiduciary responsibilities?

Hiring a manager requires trust. A firm's culture as expressed by its compliance policies and procedures should provide a level of confidence that the manager's and investor's interests are aligned.

THE INVESTMENT PROCESS

Bernard "Bernie" L. Madoff ran one of the biggest frauds in Wall Street history. One of the first indications that something was amiss at Bernard L. Madoff Investment Securities arose when Harry Markopolos was unable to reconcile the return track record with the investment process. In addition to observing the unrealistically consistent nature of the claimed returns, Markopolos concluded that there was no way to generate the returns using the claimed investment process. Further analysis convinced him that Madoff's returns resulted not from front running—that is, taking positions to exploit knowledge of investor trade flows—but rather from fraud.

In hindsight, there were many red flags over the years that indicated there was something wrong with Madoff's investment management process. The firm claimed to generate steady returns in every market environment. Mr. Madoff was known to dismiss questions about his strategy, arguing that his business was too complicated for outsiders to understand. He also operated as a broker/dealer with an asset management division, profiting from trading commissions rather than the investment management fees that hedge funds charged. The structure seemed odd to other investment professionals, raising concerns about the firm's legitimacy. Another red flag was raised when it became known that the firm used a small, unknown auditor with only three employees. If, as Mr. Madoff claimed, the strategy was so complex that no one could understand it, a small, three-person audit firm would be unlikely to be able to effectively audit the financial statements (Zuckerman 2008).

SELF-REPORTED RISK FACTORS

Requesting and obtaining self-reported risk factors not only is important for understanding the manager's investment process but also provides an interesting operational check. A manager should readily comply with all requests for risk reporting. If not, it suggests a lack of transparency that may become challenging for monitoring the manager and strategy in the future. Additionally, it might indicate an inability to generate essential reports, which raises questions about the firm's policies and procedures.

All risk reporting should be meaningful, consistent, accurate, and timely. A lack of meaningful reporting indicates that the reports are not useful in monitoring the manager and that there is a lack of transparency. In the worst case, the manager does not understand the risk exposures or does not want to disclose them.

A lack of consistent reporting also reduces the usefulness of the reporting. Inconsistent reports preclude the ability to track levels and trends of important risk factors. The manager may be choosing to selectively report particular risks that they deem important or interesting. In the worst case, it may mean that the manager is selectively reporting in order to hide risks created by deviations from the stated investment process.

A lack of accuracy suggests that the manager cannot properly measure portfolio risks or is intentionally misreporting results. A lack of timeliness reduces the reports' usefulness and suggests either inefficient procedures or attempts to manipulate the flow of information. In all of these cases, poor risk reporting, at a minimum, suggests a reevaluation of the manager and, if issues are identified, potential termination.

Investment Vehicle

There are two broad options for implementing investment strategies: individual separate accounts and pooled (or commingled) vehicles. An additional operational consideration is the evaluation of the investment vehicle—its appropriateness to the investment strategy and its suitability for the investor. Separate accounts offer additional control, customization, tax efficiency, reporting, and transparency advantages, but these come at a higher cost.

In a pooled or commingled vehicle, the money from multiple investors is held as a single portfolio and managed without potential customization for any investor. Such vehicles include open-end funds, closed-end funds, exchange-traded funds, exchange-traded notes, and hedge funds.

Separately Managed Accounts

As the name implies, a separately managed account (SMA) vehicle holds assets in an investor's name separate from other investors. The assets are managed to a particular mandate with the potential to customize the strategy for each investor. The advantages of SMA vehicles include the following:

- *Ownership.* In an SMA, the investor owns the individual securities directly. This approach provides additional safety should a liquidity event occur. Although the manager continues to make investment decisions, these decisions will not be influenced by the redemption or liquidity demand of *other* investors in the strategy. An SMA also provides clear legal ownership for the recovery of assets resulting from unforeseen events, such as bankruptcy or mismanagement.
- *Customization.* SMAs allow the investor to potentially express individual constraints or preferences within the portfolio. SMAs can thus more closely address the investor's particular investment objectives.
- *Tax efficiency.* SMAs offer potentially improved tax efficiency—for example, in such jurisdictions as the United States, where investors pay taxes only on realized capital gains.
- *Transparency.* SMAs offer real-time, position-level detail to the investor, providing complete transparency and accurate attribution to the investor. Even if a pooled vehicle provides position-level detail, such information will likely be presented with a delay.

If the SMA is customized, additional investment due diligence may be required to account for differences in security selection or portfolio construction. In addition, there are operational due diligence considerations.

- *Cost.* Separate accounts represent an additional operational burden on the manager, which translates into potentially higher costs for the investor. SMAs do not scale as easily as pooled vehicles. Once a pooled investment is established and the fixed costs paid, the cost of each new investor is largely the incremental costs of custody, trading larger positions, and generating an additional report. With an SMA, a new account must be established for each investor. In addition, SMAs are likely to face higher transaction costs to the degree that trades cannot be aggregated to reduce trade volumes. These costs are a function of the extent to which the strategy is customized or traded differently to accommodate different investor needs.
- *Tracking risk.* Customization of the strategy creates tracking risk relative to the benchmark, which can confuse attribution because performance will reflect investor constraints rather than manager decisions.
- *Investor behavior.* Transparency, combined with control and customization, allows for potential micromanagement by the investor—that is, the investor attempting to manage the portfolio. Such an effort not only negates the benefit of hiring a manager but is particularly problematic if these changes

decrease the portfolio's value. Potential investor behaviors include performance chasing, familiarity bias (being overly averse to unfamiliar holdings), and loss aversion (a tendency to disaggregate the portfolio and not appreciate the value of hedging).

The allocator's goal is to evaluate the costs and benefits of the vehicle used and judge its suitability for the IPS:

- Is the vehicle structure consistent with the investment process?
- Does the manager have the operational infrastructure necessary to manage the SMA?
- Is there a benefit to holding the securities in a separate account? If so, are these benefits sufficient to compensate for additional costs?
- Is tax efficiency an important objective of the IPS?
- Are there concerns that the available transparency and ability to customize will result in decisions by the investor that do not add value?

EXAMPLE 5

Pooled Investments and Separate Accounts

1. Which of the following are advantages of separately managed accounts compared with pooled investments?

   A. Typically lower cost

   B. Potential management of the portfolio by the investor

   C. Ability to take close account of individual client constraints or preferences

Solution

C is correct. With SMAs, the investor owns the individual securities directly and can potentially express individual constraints or preferences within the portfolio. In particular, SMAs offer potentially improved tax efficiency in some jurisdictions, such as the United States because the investor pays taxes only on the capital gains realized and allows the implementation of tax-efficient investing and trading strategies.

Evaluation of the Investment's Terms

An additional and important aspect of manager selection is understanding the terms of the investment as presented in the prospectus, private placement memorandum, and/or limited partnership agreement. These documents are, in essence, the contract between the investor and the manager, outlining each party's rights and responsibilities. Although these documents cover numerous topics, this lesson focuses on liquidity and fees. The objective of the decision maker is to determine whether the liquidity and fee structure make the manager suitable for the investor's needs and the "best" manager for expressing a particular portfolio need.

Liquidity

Different vehicles provide different degrees of liquidity. Liquidity is defined as the timeliness with which a security or asset can be sold at or near the current price. The same criteria can be applied to managers.

The most liquid vehicles are closed-end funds and ETFs. As listed securities, they can be bought and sold intra-day, and the price received will depend on the trading volume and depth of the fund. The obvious advantage of these funds is ease of trading, although there can be some price uncertainty for less liquid funds, particularly when trying to buy or sell a large number of shares. Open-end funds are slightly less liquid, providing daily liquidity but also price certainty; shares are bought and sold at the end-of-day NAV.

Unlike open-end funds, ETFs, or closed-end funds, limited partnerships, such as hedge funds, venture capital funds, and private equity funds, typically require investors to invest their money for longer periods. Hedge fund liquidity has four basic features: redemption frequency, notification period, lockup, and gates. Redemption frequency indicates how often an investor can withdraw capital from the fund, and the notification period indicates how far in advance of the redemption investors must tell the fund of their intention to redeem. A lockup is the initial period, after making an investment, during which investors cannot redeem their holding. Lockups have two types: a hard lock, which allows for no redemptions, and a soft lock, which charges a fee, paid into the fund, for redemptions. A mutual fund redemption fee is equivalent to a hedge fund soft lock. Gates limit the amount of fund assets, or investor assets that can be redeemed at one redemption date.

Private equity and venture capital funds provide the least liquidity. Investors are contractually obligated to contribute specific amounts (capital calls) during the investment phase and then receive distributions and capital as investments are harvested during the remaining term of the fund. A typical investment phase is 5 years. The typical life of a fund is 10 years, with the option to extend the term for two 1-year periods.

The obvious disadvantage of partnership liquidity terms is the reduced flexibility to adjust portfolio allocations in light of changing market conditions or investor circumstances, as well as the reduced ability to meet unexpected liquidity needs. The advantage of such terms is that they do lock up capital for longer horizons, allowing funds to take long-term views and hold less liquid securities—such as start-up companies, buyouts, turnarounds, real estate, or natural resources—with reduced risk of having to sell portfolio holdings at inopportune times in response to redemption requests. An additional advantage, which was apparent during the 2008 financial crisis, is that limited liquidity imposes this long horizon view on investors, reducing or removing their ability to overreact.

Because SMA assets are held in the investor's name, the securities in the portfolio can be sold at any time. As a result, an SMA's liquidity will depend on the liquidity of the securities held. An SMA holding listed large-cap stocks will likely be highly liquid, whereas an investor in an SMA that holds unlisted or illiquid securities will have to accept a discount when selling.

9 MANAGEMENT FEES

- ☐ describe the three basic forms of performance-based fees
- ☐ analyze and interpret a sample performance-based fee schedule

Investors seek strong performance net of fees. Managers charge fees to cover operating costs and earn a return on their capital—primarily human capital. A manager's fixed costs are relatively small and primarily cover the costs of technology and the long-term lease of office space. Variable costs, which consist largely of payroll and marketing costs, dominate the income statements of asset management companies. Because a considerable portion of employee compensation comes in the form of bonuses, senior management can reduce bonus payouts as fee revenue declines in order to smooth a company's profitability.[1]

Investors are increasingly sensitive to management fees. Average asset-weighted expense ratios (management fees and fund expenses) incurred by mutual fund investors have fallen substantially. In 2000, equity mutual fund investors incurred expense ratios of 0.99%, on average, or 99 cents for every $100 invested. By 2021, that average had fallen to 0.47%, a decline of 53%. Hybrid and bond mutual fund expense ratios also have declined. The average hybrid mutual fund expense ratio fell from 0.89% in 2000 to 0.57% in 2021, a reduction of 36%. The average bond mutual fund expense ratio fell from 0.76% in 2000 to 0.39% in 2021, a decline of 49%. The decline is a function of several factors: the allocation of the fixed portion of expenses over a larger asset base, increasing investor preference for no-load share classes, and the increasing allocations to lower-cost index funds. Aside from these structural factors lowering average expense ratios, there has been more generalized downward pressure on fees—the average expense ratio of actively managed equity mutual funds declined from 1.06% in 2000 to 0.68% in 2021. Likewise, the average expense ratio of actively managed bond mutual funds declined from 0.77% in 2000 to 0.46% in 2021. Average expense ratios for index-based equity and bond funds declined from 27 bps and 21 bps in 2000, respectively, to 6 bps each in 2021.[2]

Investment firms charge fees in several different ways. In general, mutual fund managers charge fees based on a fund's assets under management.[3] Some classes of mutual funds, including those with reduced fees, require minimum balances. In contrast, institutional managers frequently offer declining percentage fees on increasing account sizes for separate or commingled pool accounts. Institutional accounts frequently specify minimum account sizes or minimum dollar fees. Fixed-percentage fees facilitate managers' and investors' planning for future cash flows, whereas dollar fees are subject to the variability of asset values.

Fee structures can influence which managers will be willing to accept a particular investment mandate. They can also strongly affect manager behavior. Economic theory suggests that the principal–agent problem is complicated by the fact that an agent's skills and actions are not fully visible to the principal. Although principals control asset availability, agents control both their expenditure of effort and portfolio risk. Moreover, the agent and principal may have different preferences; each might care about different time horizons and agents might not view losses the same way that principals do.[4] Finally, total performance is, to some extent, beyond the control of either party. As a result of these factors, the principal's and agent's interests may not be fully aligned. In reality, managers are motivated to work hard even without incentive fees because they want to retain current clients and expand their client base and pricing power. Incentives are useful, however, to help ensure that managers routinely act in their clients' best interest.

---

1 This lesson is based on Chapter 6 in *Essays on Manager Selection*, by Scott D. Stewart, PhD, CFA, Research Foundation of CFA Institute.

2 ICI Investment Company Fact Book (2022).

3 Although mutual funds may offer a declining management fee as fund assets increase, the individual investor does not benefit from investing more money unless the extra money qualifies the investor for a lower-fee fund class.

4 For a summary of theoretical research on investment compensation, see Stracca (2006).

Assets under Management Fees

Assets under management fees, also called "ad valorem fees" (from the Latin for "according to value"), result from applying stated percentage rates to assets under management. These fees reward managers who attract and retain assets, generate added value, and experience benefits from rising markets. Managers primarily grow their assets through skillful investing, hard work, and effective marketing. A manager's success, however, also results partly from luck, especially in the short term. Managers benefit from rising portfolio values, which are attributable to the combination of alpha and beta decisions, but are also, at least for long-only managers, greatly affected by market cycles beyond the manager's control. A decline in ad valorem percentages as assets grow helps reduce the fee impact on investors from rising markets, but does not eliminate it.

Once a manager's assets are large, he or she might not want to risk losing them. Assets are typically "sticky"—that is, once investors allocate their assets to a manager, the manager often does not need to generate the same level of returns to retain the assets as he or she did to attract them. Empirical evidence suggests this stickiness is the case, to some extent, for mutual fund assets. To motivate such managers to work harder or discourage them from closet indexing, an incentive fee determined by future performance may be useful.

Performance-Based Fees

Performance-based fees, common for hedge funds and less common for long-only strategies, are determined by portfolio returns and are designed to reward managers with a share of return for their skill in creating value. Performance can be calculated by using either total or relative return, and the return shared can be a percentage of total performance or performance net of a base or fixed fee. Performance-based fees are structured in one of three basic ways:

1. a symmetrical structure in which the manager is fully exposed to both the downside and upside (Computed fee = Base + Sharing of performance);
2. a bonus structure in which the manager is not fully exposed to the downside but is fully exposed to the upside (Computed fee = Higher of either [1] Base or [2] Base plus sharing of positive performance); or
3. a bonus structure in which the manager is not fully exposed to either the downside or the upside (Computed fee = Higher of [1] Base or [2] Base plus sharing of performance, to a limit).

Performance fees are paid annually or, in some cases, less frequently. These fees may include maximum and high-water mark (or clawback) features that protect investors from situations such as paying for current positive performance before the negative effects of prior underperformance have been offset. Private equity, hedge fund, and real estate partnerships commonly earn performance fees on total returns and typically do not limit the amount of the performance fee. Hedge funds commonly include high-water mark features.

Consider the example of private equity partnerships, in which base fees are commonly applied to committed (not just invested) capital. Performance fees are earned as profits are realized, and invested capital is returned to investors. A common provision that helps protect private equity limited partners (the investors) is a requirement that the limited partners receive their principal and share of profits before performance fees are distributed to the general partner (the manager).

Specific performance-based fee structures are designed by both clients and managers. A formula is agreed upon based on the anticipated distribution of returns and the perceived attractiveness of the investment strategy. Managers who can command attractive terms, such as real estate managers that are in high demand and have limited capacity, have the power to stipulate the highest base fees and profit sharing in their fee agreements. Fee schedules are typically designed by fund managers, included in marketing materials, and set forth in partnership agreements. Large investors may influence the terms of fee schedules or negotiate side letters for special treatment.

A simple performance-based fee, as illustrated in Exhibit 8, specifies a base fee below which the computed fee can never fall. In this case, the manager is protected against sharing for performance below 25 bps. To make the result symmetrical around the commonplace 50 bps fee, the manager does not share in active performance beyond 2.75%.

Exhibit 8: Sample Performance-Based Fee Schedule

Panel A. Sample Fee Structure

Standard fee	0.50%
Base fee	0.25%
Sharing*	20%
Breakeven active return	1.50%
Maximum annual fee	0.75%

Panel B. Numerical Examples for Annual Periods

	Active Return				
	≤ 0.25%	1.00%	1.50%	2.00%	≥ 2.75%
Billed fee	0.25%	0.40%	0.50%	0.60%	0.75%
Net active return	≤ 0.00%	0.60%	1.00%	1.40%	≥ 2.00%

**On active return, beyond base fee.*

If investment outcomes result from a mix of skill and luck (i.e., a probability distribution around a positive mean alpha), then performance fees constitute risk sharing. Fee structures must be designed carefully to avoid favoring one party over the other. Performance-based fees work to align the interests of managers and investors because both parties share in investment results. Investors benefit by paying performance-based fees, rather than standard fees, when active returns are low. Managers may work harder to earn performance-based fees, inspiring the term "incentive based." Empirical evidence suggests a correlation between performance-based fees and higher alphas (also, lower fees) for mutual funds and higher risk-adjusted returns for hedge funds.[5] Asset managers may consider performance-based fees attractive because such fees provide an opportunity to enhance profits on the upside and ensure guaranteed, although perhaps minimal, streams of revenue from base fees when performance is poor.

Performance-based fees can also create tensions between investors and managers. Investors must pay base fees even when managers underperform. Management firm revenues decline when cash is needed to invest in operations or retain talent. In fact, the failure rate for poor-performing and even zero-alpha managers may tend to be higher when performance-based rather than standard fees are used.[6]

Performance-based fee structures may also lead to misestimates of portfolio risk. Such fee structures convert symmetrical gross active return distributions into asymmetrical net active return distributions, reducing variability on the upside but not the

5 See Elton, Gruber, and Blake (2003) and Ackermann, McEnally, and Ravenscraft (1999).
6 See Grinold and Rudd (1987).

downside. As a result, a single standard deviation calculated on a return series that incorporates active returns, above and below the base fee, can lead to the underestimation of downside risk.[7]

Investors and managers may have different incentives when performance-based fees are used. For example, according to a utility maximization model, fully symmetric fees, in which the manager is fully exposed to the downside, tend to yield closer alignment in risk and effort than bonus-style fees.[8] Understandably, symmetrical fee structures are unpopular with managers because of their impact on bankruptcy risk.

Bonus-style fees are the close equivalent of a manager's call option on a share of active return, for which the base fee is the strike price. Consider Exhibit 9, which shows a familiar-looking option payoff pattern using the fee parameters defined in Exhibit 8. In this case, the option payoff is modified by a maximum fee feature. The graph illustrates three fee components: a 25 bps base fee, plus a long call option on active return with a strike price equal to the minimum (base) fee, minus another (less valuable) call option with a strike price equal to the maximum fee.

Exhibit 9: Payoff Line of Sample Performance-Based Fee Schedule

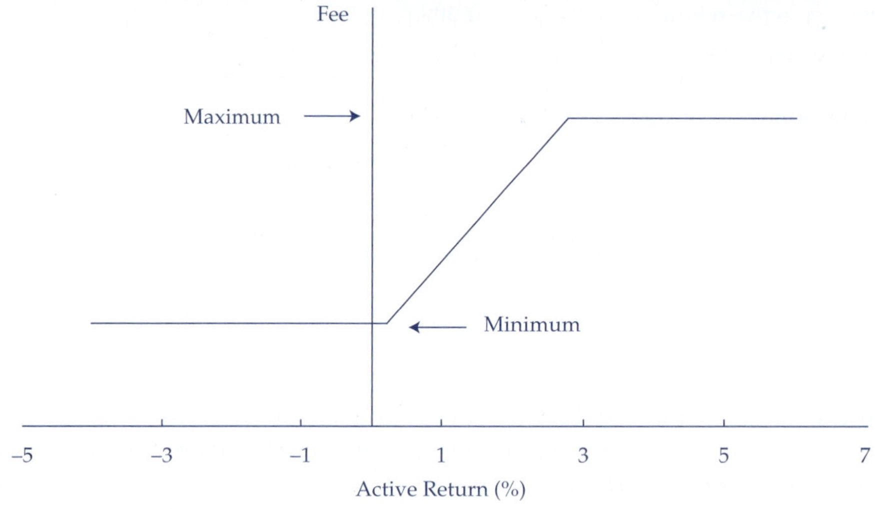

Managers must retain clients year to year, avoid poor performance, and not violate management guidelines. But managers also tend to have an interest in increasing risk, which may conflict with these goals. Based on option pricing theory,[9] higher volatility leads to higher option value, which encourages managers to assume higher portfolio risk. This behavior has been observed in the marketplace.[10] As a result, investors, when possible, should carefully select benchmarks and monitor risk in their portfolios.[11]

7 See Kritzman (2012).

8 See Starks (1987).

9 Margrabe (1978) notes that an incentive fee (without a maximum) consists of a call option on the portfolio and a put on the benchmark. As a result, the value depends on the volatility of the portfolio and the benchmark and the correlation between the two—in other words, the active risk.

10 See Elton et al. (2003).

11 Starks (1987) notes that an investor can simply set a fee schedule incorporating penalties for observed risk to align interests regarding risk levels.

Senior management at investment firms should also ensure that their compensation systems penalize portfolio managers for assuming excessive risk as well as reward them for earning superior returns.[12]

REAL STORY: THE CLIENT'S FREE OPTION IN A PERFORMANCE FEE AGREEMENT

Consider the case of an equity manager in the early 1990s offering a performance-based fee that consisted of a 10 bp base fee and a 20% share of active return in excess of the benchmark index (net of the 10 bps). The fee structure also included a maximum annual fee provision that reserved excess fees for subsequent years. Because there was no penalty for cancelling the fee agreement, clients could opt out of the performance-based fee in exchange for a standard flat fee when performance was particularly strong. This arrangement allowed them to avoid paying the manager's accrued, fully earned share, and is precisely what many clients did in the mid-1990s following a period of high active returns.

Other problems exist with performance-based fees. When managers have clients with varying fee structures, it is in their (short-term) interest to favor customers that have performance-based fees. Although doing so may be unethical or potentially illegal, managers can direct trades or deals (including initial public offerings) to performance-fee clients to their benefit and to the detriment of others. It may be difficult for clients to monitor this activity. Fortunately, most managers recognize that such actions, once discovered, could destroy their careers or lead to criminal charges. Here again, due diligence, including the review of internal compliance systems, will help limit an investor's exposure to unscrupulous managers.

When managers can control the timing of profit realization, as is often the case with private equity partnerships, they may have an incentive to hold on to assets until a profit can be realized. Managers may do so even when clients would benefit from selling assets at a loss and investing the proceeds outside of the partnership. In contrast, hedge fund managers have an incentive to return assets in poor-performing partnerships when the high-water mark is substantially above current value (i.e., the performance-fee option is considerably out of the money). This action results in the investor missing the opportunity to recoup previously paid fees based on future strong performance.

Funds of funds (FoFs) commonly charge fees in addition to the fees charged by the underlying funds.[13] These fees pay for the investor's access to the underlying funds and for the FoFs' due diligence, portfolio construction, and monitoring. In addition to these two sets of fees, investors are required to share the profits from well-performing underlying funds but incur the full loss from poorly performing funds.[14] To protect investors from paying overly high fees, hedge fund consortiums have recently begun to offer fee structures based on the total portfolio value of underlying funds, rather than the sum of fees computed at the individual fund level.

12 Although it adds a layer of complexity to the evaluation process, an active-risk-adjusted bonus formula can be specified.

13 When funds of funds were popular in the 2000s, it was common for them to charge a performance-based fee.

14 Kritzman (2012) calls this result an "asymmetry penalty."

THE IMPACT OF FEE STRUCTURE ON NET RETURNS

Consider four fee structures applied to the same 12-month return series gross of fees:

- 0.50% management fee, 0% performance fee
- 0.50% management fee, 15% performance fee
- 1.50% management fee, 0% performance fee
- 1.50% management fee, 15% performance fee

The fees are accrued at the end of each month. This example is a simplification but illustrates the important effects of fee level and structure on net performance. As Exhibit 10 shows, the average monthly gross return is 0.72% with a 1.37% monthly standard deviation. Not surprisingly, charging a management fee (MF) lowers the level of realized return without affecting the standard deviation of the series. The management fee is a constant shift in the level and thus does not affect volatility. The addition of a performance fee (PF) also lowers the level of realized returns but has the added effect of lowering the realized standard deviation. This dynamic occurs because in up months, the performance fee is accrued, and in down months, it is subtracted from the accrual balance to reflect the appropriate fee for the cumulative performance. This accounting has the effect of adjusting the monthly returns toward zero and lowering the measured volatility. The larger the performance fee, the more pronounced this effect. Exhibit 11 shows a graph of the cumulative returns for each fee structure.

Exhibit 10: Effects of Expense on Portfolio Performance

	Monthly Gross Return				
		MF = 0.5%		MF = 1.5%	
Month	MF = 0% PF = 0%	PF = 0%	PF = 15%	PF = 0%	PF = 15%
1	2.00%	1.96%	1.66%	1.88%	1.59%
2	3.00%	2.96%	2.51%	2.88%	2.44%
3	−0.20%	−0.24%	−0.21%	−0.32%	−0.28%
4	−0.50%	−0.54%	−0.46%	−0.62%	−0.53%
5	0.50%	0.46%	0.39%	0.37%	0.32%
6	0.90%	0.86%	0.73%	0.77%	0.66%
7	1.00%	0.96%	0.81%	0.88%	0.74%
8	−2.00%	−2.04%	−1.74%	−2.12%	−1.81%
9	1.50%	1.46%	1.24%	1.37%	1.17%
10	2.00%	1.96%	1.66%	1.88%	1.59%
11	−0.50%	−0.54%	−0.46%	−0.62%	−0.53%
12	1.00%	0.96%	0.81%	0.88%	0.74%
Average Return	0.72%	0.67%	0.57%	0.59%	0.50%
S.D.	1.37%	1.37%	1.16%	1.37%	1.16%

Exhibit 11: Cumulative Return

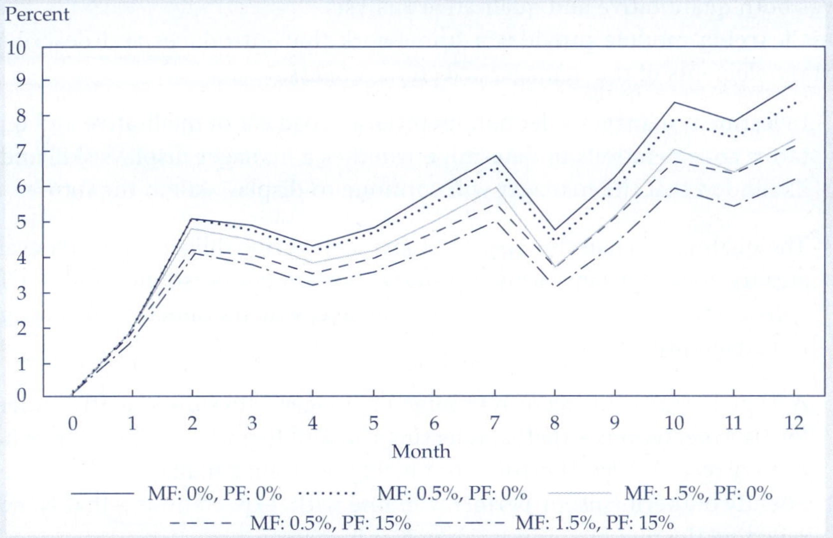

Given the potentially significant effect of expenses, a clear distinction must be drawn between performance analysis based on gross returns and net of expenses returns.

An additional consideration is the different degree of uncertainty between expenses and the potential added value of the active portfolio manager. Expenses are paid for certain, whereas the added value of the active strategy compared with the passive strategy is uncertain. For example, suppose an active strategy is expected to generate a gross return that is 2% greater than the passive strategy, but the cost of the active strategy is 2% greater than the passive strategy. A risk-averse investor would likely prefer the passive strategy; although the expected net return of the strategies is the same, the uncertainty of the outperformance would be unappealing. The riskier the active strategy, the greater the return volatility and the greater the volatility of the added value relative to the passive strategy. The significance is, the added value of the active strategy has to be sufficiently large and certain to justify the higher cost of the strategy.

In sum, the presence of positive significant average excess return is evidence for manager skill. This excess return, however, must be net of fees and expenses for the benefit of this skill to accrue to the investor.[15] The preference is for more linear compensation to the manager to reduce the incentives to change the portfolio's risk profile at inflection points.

SUMMARY

Evaluating an investment manager is a complex and detailed process. It encompasses a great deal more than analyzing investment returns. In conducting investment manager due diligence, the focus is on understanding how the investment results were achieved and assessing the likelihood that the manager will continue to follow the same investment process that generated these returns. This process also entails operational

15 Ultimately, the net return to the investor accounts not only for fees and expenses but also for taxes. This more complex issue is beyond the scope of this learning module.

due diligence, including an evaluation of the integrity of the firm, its operations, and personnel, as well as evaluating the vehicle structure and terms. As such, due diligence involves both quantitative and qualitative analysis.

This learning module provides a framework that introduces and describes the important elements of the manager selection process:

- Investment manager selection involves a broad set of qualitative and quantitative considerations to determine whether a manager displays skill and the likelihood that the manager will continue to display skill in the future.

- The qualitative analysis consists of investment due diligence, which evaluates the manager's investment process, investment personnel, and portfolio construction; and operational due diligence, which evaluates the manager's infrastructure.

- A Type I error is hiring or retaining a manager who subsequently underperforms expectations—that is, rejecting the null hypothesis of no skill when it is correct. A Type II error is not hiring or firing a manager who subsequently outperforms, or performs in line with, expectations—that is, not rejecting the null hypothesis when it is incorrect.

- The manager search and selection process has three broad components: the universe, a quantitative analysis of the manager's performance track record, and a qualitative analysis of the manager's investment process. The qualitative analysis includes both investment due diligence and operational due diligence.

- Capture ratio measures the asymmetry of returns, and a ratio greater than 1 indicates greater participation in rising versus falling markets. Drawdown is the loss incurred in any continuous period of negative returns.

- The investment philosophy is the foundation of the investment process. The philosophy outlines the set of assumptions about the factors that drive performance and the manager's beliefs about their ability to successfully exploit these sources of return. The investment manager should have a clear and concise investment philosophy. It is important to evaluate these assumptions and the role they play in the investment process to understand how the strategy will behave over time and across market environments. The investment process has to be consistent and appropriate for the philosophy, and the investment personnel need to possess sufficient expertise and experience to effectively execute the investment process.

- Investment teams, rather than individual investors, often have the responsibility for making investment decisions and are subject to behavioral biases. It is important for investment teams to implement procedures to alleviate the effect of behavioral biases and improve decision making. An investment due diligence process should inquire about an investment manager's team size, structure, and decision-making processes.

- Style analysis, understanding the manager's risk exposures relative to the benchmark, is an important component of performance appraisal and manager selection, helping to define the universe of suitable managers.

- Returns-based style analysis is a top-down approach that involves estimating the risk exposures from an actual return series for a given period. Although RBSA adds an additional analytical step, the analysis is straightforward and should identify the important drivers of return and risk factors for the period analyzed. It can be estimated even for complicated strategies and is comparable across managers and through time. The disadvantage is that RBSA is an imprecise tool, attributing performance to an unchanging average portfolio during the period that might not reflect the current or future portfolio exposures.

- Holdings-based style analysis is a bottom-up approach that estimates the risk exposures from the actual securities held in the portfolio at a point in time. HBSA allows for the estimation of current risk factors and should identify all important drivers of return and risk factors, be comparable across managers and through time, and provide an accurate view of the manager's risk exposures. The disadvantages are the additional computational effort, dependence on the degree of transparency provided by the manager, and the possibility that accuracy may be compromised by stale pricing and window dressing.

- The prospectus, private placement memorandum, and/or limited partnership agreement are, in essence, the contract between the investor and the manager, outlining each party's rights and responsibilities. The provisions are liquidity terms and fees. Limited liquidity reduces the investor's flexibility to adjust portfolio allocations in light of changing market conditions or investor circumstances. On the other hand, limited liquidity allows the funds to take long-term views and hold less liquid securities with reduced risk of having to divest assets at inopportune times in response to redemption requests. A management fee lowers the level of realized return without affecting the standard deviation, whereas a performance fee has the added effect of lowering the realized standard deviation. The preference is for more linear compensation to reduce the incentives to change the portfolio's risk profile at inflection points.

- The choice between individual separate accounts and pooled (or commingled) vehicles is dependent upon the consistency with the investment process, the suitability for the investor IPS, and whether the benefits outweigh the additional costs.

- Investment management fees take one of two forms: a fixed percentage fee based on assets under management or a performance-based fee which charges a percentage of the portfolio's total return or excess return over a benchmark or hurdle rate. Performance-based fees work to align the interests of managers and investors because both parties share in investment results. Most managers that charge a performance fee also charge some level of fixed percentage fee to aid business continuity efforts. Fee structures must be designed carefully to avoid favoring one party over the other.

REFERENCES

Ackermann, Carl, Richard McEnally, and David Ravenscraft. 1999. "The Performance of Hedge Funds: Risk, Return and Incentives." *Journal of Finance* 54 (3): 833–74. 10.1111/0022-1082.00129

Baer, M., A. Kempf, and S. Ruenzi. 2005. "*Team Management and Mutual Funds.*" Working paper, Centre for Financial Research. 10.2139/ssrn.809484

Bliss, R. T., M. E. Potter, and C. Schwarz. 2008. "Performance Characteristics of Individual-Managed versus Team-Managed Funds." *Journal of Portfolio Management* 34 (3): 110–19. 10.3905/jpm.2008.706248

Bär, M., C. S. Ciccotello, and S. Ruenzi. 2010. "Risk Management and Team-Managed Mutual Funds." *Journal of Risk Management and Financial Institutions* 4 (1): 57–73.

Chen, J., H. Harrison, H. Ming, and J. Kubik. 2004. "Does Fund Size Erode Mutual Fund Performance: The Role of Liquidity and Organization." *American Economic Review* 94 (5): 1276–302. 10.1257/0002828043052277

Elton, Edwin, Martin Gruber, and Christopher Blake. 2003. "Incentive Fees and Mutual Funds." *Journal of Finance* 58 (2): 779–804. 10.1111/1540-6261.00545

Goldman, E., Z. Sun, and X.(T.) Zhou. 2016. "The Effect of Management Design on the Portfolio Concentration and Performance of Mutual Funds." *Financial Analysts Journal* 72 (4): 49–61. 10.2469/faj.v72.n4.9

Grinold, Richard and Andrew Rudd. 1987. "Incentive Fees: Who Wins? Who Loses?" *Financial Analysts Journal* 43 (1): 27–38. 10.2469/faj.v43.n1.27

Karagiannidis, I. 2010. "Management Team Structure and Mutual Fund Performance." *Journal of Financial Markets, Institutions and Money* 20 (2): 197–211. 10.1016/j.intfin.2009.10.003

Karagiannidis, Iordanis and G. Geoffrey Booth. 2022. "The Influence of Management Design on Mutual Fund Performance." *Multinational Finance Journal* 26 (1/2): 1–26.

Khandani, Amir E. and Andrew W. Lo. 2011. "What Happened to the Quants in August 2007? Evidence from Factors and Transactions Data." *Journal of Financial Markets* 14 (1): 1–46. 10.1016/j.finmar.2010.07.005

Kritzman, Mark. 2012. "Two Things about Performance Fees." *Journal of Portfolio Management* 38 (2): 4–5. 10.3905/jpm.2012.38.2.004

Kuenzi, David E. 2003. "Strategy Benchmarks." *Journal of Portfolio Management* 29 (2): 46–56. 10.3905/jpm.2003.319872

Lo, Andrew W. 2004. "The Adaptive Markets Hypothesis: Market Efficiency from an Evolutionary Perspective." *Journal of Portfolio Management* 30 (5): 15–29. 10.3905/jpm.2004.442611

Margrabe, William. 1978. "The Value of an Option to Exchange One Asset for Another." *Journal of Finance* 33 (1): 177–86. 10.1111/j.1540-6261.1978.tb03397.x

Patel, S. and S. Sarkissian. 2017. "To Group or Not to Group? Evidence from Mutual Fund Databases." *Journal of Financial and Quantitative Analysis* 52 (5): 1989–2021. 10.1017/S0022109017000655

Payne, John and Arnold Wood. 2002. "Individual Decision Making and Group Decision Processes." *Journal of Psychology and Financial Markets* 3 (2): 94–101. 10.1207/S15327760JPFM0302_04

Sargis, M. and K. Chang. 2017. *The Aftermath of Fund Management Change*. Morningstar.

Starks, Laura. 1987. "Performance Incentive Fees: An Agency Theoretic Approach." *Journal of Financial and Quantitative Analysis* 22 (1): 17–32. 10.2307/2330867

Stewart, Scott D., John J. Neumann, Christopher R. Knittel, and Jeffrey Heisler. 2009. "Absence of Value: An Analysis of Investment Allocation Decisions by Institutional Plan Sponsors." *Financial Analysts Journal* 65 (6): 34–51. 10.2469/faj.v65.n6.4

Stracca, Livio. 2006. "Delegated Portfolio Management: A Survey of the Theoretical Literature." *Journal of Economic Surveys* 20 (5): 823–48. 10.1111/j.1467-6419.2006.00271.x

Wang, D. 2016. "What Does It Mean to Be a Team? Evidence from U.S. Mutual Fund Managers." 29th Australasian Finance and Banking Conference, Sydney, Australia. 10.2139/ssrn.2825534

Zuckerman, Gregory. 2008. "*Fees, Even Returns and Auditor All Raised Red Flags.*" *Wall Street Journal* (13 December).

PRACTICE PROBLEMS

1. Which of the following qualitative considerations is *most* associated with determining whether investment manager selection will result in superior repeatable performance?

   A. Transparency

   B. Investment process

   C. Operational process

2. The manager selection process begins by defining the universe of feasible managers. When defining this manager universe, the selection process should avoid:

   A. excluding managers based on historical risk-adjusted returns.

   B. identifying the benchmark against which managers will be evaluated.

   C. using third-party categorizations of managers to find those that might fill the desired role in the portfolio.

The following information relates to questions 3-5

John Connell inherited $700,000 at the beginning of the year and has been developing related investment goals and policies with a financial adviser. The adviser has identified three potential investment funds for consideration. All three have earned similar returns over the last five years and are expected to earn similar returns going forward. Publishing their investment results on a timely and routine basis, they include the following asset classes:

- US equities
- Global equities
- Venture capital
- Corporate bonds
- Government bonds
- Cash reserves

Exhibit 1 presents information about the funds.

Exhibit 1: Fund Characteristics

Characteristic	Zeta	Eta	Theta
Organization	Independent investment fund	Part of a medium-sized investment firm with multiple funds	Part of a large investment firm that rotates investment professionals among funds
Team Size	Small	Small	Small
Staff Turnover	High	Medium	Low

Characteristic	Zeta	Eta	Theta
Incentive Compensation	Salary adjustment when returns exceed benchmark	Annual salary adjustment	Annual salary adjustment and performance-based bonus
Key People	Founder directs all trades and investment decisions	Fund manager and assistant fund manager make investment decisions	Fund manager and assistant fund manager lead team in selecting investments
Longevity/Experience	Founder in the investment business for > 25 years	Fund manager in the investment business for > 15 years; assistant fund manager for > 12 years	Fund manager in the investment business for > 20 years; assistant fund manager for > 10 years. Fund family is more than 50 years old.

3. Based on the Exhibit 1 data, which fund is *most appropriate* for Connell's needs. Justify your selection with *two* reasons.

4. Connell elects to defer fund selection and places his inheritance in a short-term money market account. A year later, Connell reviews the one-year performance results of the three funds compared to the benchmark, as shown in Exhibit 2.

Exhibit 2: Fund Performance Compared to Benchmark*

Fund	Underperforms	In Line	Outperforms
Zeta		X	
Eta	X		
Theta			X

**Assume performance is mean reverting within this period.*

Connell believes he now has two main alternatives for fund investment:

Alternative 1 Keep his inheritance in the money market account to avoid the Eta fund.

Alternative 2 Place his inheritance in the Theta fund.

Identify the type of error Connell is at risk of committing and its associated cost for *each* alternative. Justify your selection.

5. Connell asks the adviser about the conditions under which any form of style analysis would be useful for understanding the funds he is considering.

Identify the conditions under which the adviser would find style analysis *most* useful.

The following information relates to questions 6-7

Donna Grimmett is working with a financial adviser to establish her investment goals for €850,000, which she recently earned as a bonus. She asks the adviser about how to best select a manager for her funds.

The adviser responds that both qualitative and quantitative components are involved in outlining a framework for identifying, evaluating, and ultimately selecting a manager.

6. Describe *two* considerations for *each* type of component recommended to Grimmett for her manager selection process.

7. Grimmett asks the adviser if any other preparatory steps should be taken before choosing the best investment manager(s). The adviser produces a checklist related to manager selection in response to Grimmett's question.

---

8. A decision-making investor is *most likely* to worry more about making a Type I error than a Type II error because:

   A. Type II errors are errors of mistaken rejection.

   B. Type I errors are more easily measured.

   C. Type II errors are more likely to have to be explained as to why a skilled manager was fired.

9. An investor is considering hiring three managers who have the following skill levels:

Manager	Large-cap skill level	Small-cap skill level
1	Skilled	Unskilled
2	Skilled	Skilled
3	Unskilled	Unskilled

   Type I and Type II errors both occur when the investor is:

   A. hiring Manager 1 for large-cap stocks and not hiring Manager 3 for small-cap stocks.

   B. hiring Manager 3 for large-cap stocks and not hiring Manager 2 for small-cap stocks.

   C. hiring Manager 3 for large-cap stocks and not hiring Manager 1 for small-cap stocks.

10. A return distribution of skilled managers that is highly distinct from the return distribution of unskilled managers, *most likely* implies a:

   A. highly efficient market.

   B. low opportunity cost of not hiring a skilled manager.

   C. high opportunity cost of not hiring a skilled manager.

11. Boinic Corporation introduced an employee pension plan and set aside $20 million to fund the plan. Assessing five investment management firms, A through E, and expecting all to perform in line with their benchmarks, Boinic selected three firms (A, D, and E) to manage part of the pension plan assets. Exhibit 1 shows the managers' performance compared to their benchmark in the one year after being

selected.

Exhibit 1: Year 1 Investment Firm Performance versus Benchmark

	Firm A	Firm B	Firm C	Firm D	Firm E
Year 1 performance versus benchmark	Above	Above	Below	Below	Above

On analyzing these results, Boinic determines that it has made both a Type I and Type II error.

Identify the firm associated with Boinic's Type I and Type II error. Justify your selection for *each* error type, discussing the psychological effects of its Year 1 performance on Boinic.

12. Suppose that the results of a style analysis for an investment manager are not consistent with the stated philosophy of the manager and the manager's stated investment process. These facts suggest the:

    A. absence of style drift.

    B. investment process may not be repeatable.

    C. manager should be included in the universe of potential managers.

13. Compared with holdings-based style analysis (HBSA), a returns-based style analysis (RBSA):

    A. is subject to window dressing.

    B. requires less effort to acquire data.

    C. is more accurate when illiquid securities are present.

14. A manager has a mandate to be fully invested with a benchmark that is a blend of large-cap stocks and investment-grade bonds. Which of the following is *not* an indication that style drift has occurred? The manager:

    A. initiates an allocation to small-cap stocks.

    B. decreases investments in investment-grade corporate bonds.

    C. increases allocation to cash in anticipation of a market decline.

15. An advantage of a returns-based style analysis is that such analysis:

    A. is comparable across managers.

    B. is suitable for portfolios that contain illiquid securities.

    C. can effectively profile a manager's risk exposures using a short return series.

16. Which of the following types of style analysis use(s) a bottom-up approach to estimate the risk exposures in a portfolio?

    A. Returns-based style analysis only

    B. Holdings-based style analysis only

C. Both return-based and holdings-based style analysis

17. A manager whose relative performance is worse during market downturns *most likely* has a capture ratio that is:

A. less than one.

B. equal to one.

C. greater than one.

18. In a quarter, an investment manager's upside capture is 75% and downside capture is 125%. We can conclude that the manager underperforms the benchmark:

A. only when the benchmark return is positive.

B. only when the benchmark return is negative.

C. when the benchmark return is either positive or negative.

The following information relates to questions 19-20

Cassandra Yang, age 59, is a manager at a large US manufacturing firm. Yang is single, owns a home, is debt free, and saves 20% of her pre-tax income in a company retirement plan and 15% of her after-tax income in a short-term money market account. Her accounts are self-directed; Yang makes all related decisions independently.

While Yang hates to suffer investment losses, she now seeks higher returns on 80% of the funds in her money market account. To help achieve her goal of retiring within three years, she is considering the actively managed investment funds listed in Exhibit 1.

Exhibit 1: Return Profile Summary

Fund	Upside Capture	Downside Capture	Most Recent Drawdown Loss	Most Recent Drawdown Duration
Alpha	80	20	57%	21 months
Beta	55	45	38%	15 months
Gamma	50	50	28%	12 months

19. Select the *best* fund for Yang, using only the information provided. Justify your selection.

20. Yang is also considering Aspen Investments (Aspen) for a portion of her money market funds. Aspen's investment philosophy states: "We pursue a passive investment strategy, which seeks to identify and exploit structural inefficiencies through identifying mispricings created by loss aversion. Our strategy and philosophy have evolved over time in response to fund and market performance."

Determine whether Yang is likely to judge that Aspen follows a consistent investment philosophy, using only the information provided. Justify your response with *two* reasons.

---

21. Which of the following is consistent with the expectation that exploiting a structural inefficiency is repeatable?

    A. The inefficiency is a unique event that occurs infrequently.

    B. The level of gross return is equal to the amount of transaction costs and expenses.

    C. The aggregate value of all assets affected by the inefficiency is larger than the AUM of the manager and its competitors.

22. Susan Patnode, age 66, was recently widowed and received £2,000,000 from a spousal life insurance policy. Patnode would like to invest the proceeds to generate predictable income to cover her ongoing living expenses.

    Patnode is considering three investment managers, Laurbær Partners, Alcanfor Limited, and Mylesten Management, to manage the insurance policy proceeds. All three take an active investment approach. Further information regarding each of the investment manager's investment philosophy and approach is provided in Exhibit 1.

Exhibit 1: Information on Investment Manager Philosophy/Approach

Investment Manager	Investment Philosophy/Approach
Laurbær Partners	Seeks to produce returns through investing in new investment themes and emphasizes measuring the contribution of each to performance.
Alcanfor Limited	Seeks to produce returns through investing in securities that appear to be mispriced in their industry sectors and tracks their ultimate performance against market benchmarks.
Mylesten Management	Seeks to produce returns through investing with maximum flexibility to the most popular investor sentiments worldwide

Identify which investment manager is *most* suitable for Patnode. Justify your response based solely on *each* manager's investment philosophy and approach.

23. Which of the following statements is consistent with the manager adhering to a stated investment philosophy and investment decision-making process?

    A. Senior investment team members have left to form their own firm.

    B. A senior employee has been cited by the SEC for violating insider trading regulations.

    C. A large drawdown occurs because of an unforeseen political event in a foreign country.

The following information relates to questions 24-25

Frances Lute is an investment manager for a large institutional investment management firm in London. His client, Parade University (Parade), has an endowment worth approximately GBP1.6 billion. Lute is considering three active investment managers in order to add one new style. Parade's investment policy statement (IPS) highlights the endowment's preference for low turnover and trading costs.

Lute is particularly concerned about portfolio construction and the prospective implementation of investments within the portfolio. All else equal, Lute has identified these distinguishing characteristics for the processes affecting portfolio construction by the three managers.

- Manager A uses hard-stop losses to manage risk.
- Manager B's portfolio can be liquidated within five business days or less.
- Manager C's portfolio turnover is greater than the frequency of signals generated.

24. Identify which manager is *most* appropriate for Parade. Justify your response.

25. Upon choosing a manager, Lute must allocate the funds either to a separately managed account (SMA) customized for Parade or a pooled vehicle called Diversified. In addition to low turnover and trading costs, Parade's IPS also prioritizes the following characteristics for its investment: transparency, investor behavior, cost, liquidity, and tracking risk. While each type of investment vehicle offers distinct advantages, Parade is unclear as to which advantage is applicable by type.

    Identify which investment vehicle *best* addresses *each* characteristic highlighted in Parade's IPS. Justify your response.

---

26. Brickridge Investment Consultants meets weekly to review the positives and negatives of investment managers being considered for client portfolios. In the latest meeting, analyst Brad Moore discusses investment manager Lyon Management (Lyon). His in-depth analysis of one of Lyon's investment strategies includes the following summary details:

    Detail 1: Long and short positions are paired.

    Detail 2: Investment strategy relies on unique information.

    Detail 3: AUM connected with the strategy have grown substantially, while the number and characteristics of positions have stayed the same.

    Asked about Lyon's regulatory context, Moore states, "The regulatory environment is strong and seeks to decrease information asymmetries."

    Identify whether each detail from Moore's summary is *most likely* a benefit or a drawback of the strategy. Justify your selection.

27. Which of the following is *most likely* a key consideration in investment due diligence?

    A. Suitability of the investment vehicle

    B. Back office processes and procedures

    C. Depth of expertise and experience of investment personnel

28. Which of the following is *not* a reason that an investor might favor a separately managed account rather than a pooled vehicle? The investor:

    A. is tax exempt.

    B. requires real-time details on investment positions.

    C. has expressed certain constraints and preferences for the portfolio.

29. Which of the following investment vehicles provide investors with the highest degree of liquidity?

    A. Open-end funds

    B. Private equity funds

    C. Limited partnerships

30. An investor should prefer a pooled investment vehicle to a separately managed account when she:

    A. is cost sensitive.

    B. focuses on tax efficiency.

    C. requires clear legal ownership of assets.

31. Which of the following investment types is the most liquid?

    A. ETFs

    B. Hedge funds

    C. Private equity funds

The following information relates to questions 32-34

Jack Porter and Melissa Smith are co-managers for the Circue Library Foundation (Circue) in Canada. Within the next six months, Porter and Smith will be replacing one of Circue's underperforming active managers. This choice will rely on the terms of investment management contracts—specifically, liquidity and management fee structure. Circue's IPS indicates some tolerance for lower liquidity, a moderate sensitivity to management fees, and a heightened sensitivity to closet indexing.

Circue is considering the following three investment vehicles with distinct fee structures:

- Hedge funds with a soft lock
- Open-end funds with an incentive fee
- Closed-end funds with no incentive fee

32. Determine which of the three investment vehicles is *most* appropriate for Circue's IPS. Justify your response.

33. Porter and Smith next consider how the performance-based fee structures of the

prospective managers may affect portfolio risk.

Porter states: "I've noticed more managers are applying a bonus structure in which the manager is not fully exposed to the downside but is fully exposed to the upside."

Smith states: "Circue's current market view is that there are increasing risks to the downside."

Discuss how Smith's stated expectation would be reflected in estimated portfolio risk under the fee structure identified by Porter.

34. After narrowing their choice to three managers with different fee structures, Porter and Smith analyze the effect of the performance-based fee structure for each manager. Exhibit 1 provides applicable data for one of the managers.

Exhibit 1: Selected Performance-Based Fee Data for a Prospective Manager

Fee Structure	Fee (%)
Standard Fee	0.35
Base Fee	0.20
Sharing*	0.25
Breakeven Active Return	1.25
Maximum Annual Fee	0.90

On active return, beyond base fee.

To understand the effect each fee structure has on its respective portfolio, Porter and Smith must estimate the net active return for several possible gross active returns, including less than or equal to 0.20%, 0.75%, 1.25%, and 1.75%.

Calculate the net active return based on each possible gross active return provided using the selected data in Exhibit 1. Show your calculations.

35. Institutional investment consultant Wilsot Consultants (Wilsot) is reviewing multiple investment managers within a prospective client's portfolio. Two of the managers, Vaudreuil Capital Management (Vaudreuil) and Pourtir Investments (Pourtir), have similar strategies that show comparable performance on a net-of-fees basis. Assessing the portfolio effects of management fees, a Wilsot analyst reviews both manager contracts to determine their advantages and disadvantages to the client. Checking client fee structures, the analyst notes Vaudreuil's fees are AUM-based while Pourtir's are performance-based.

Discuss *one* advantage and *one* disadvantage to the client of *each* manager's contracted fee structure.

36. Which of the following fee structures *most likely* decreases the volatility of a portfolio's net returns?

A. Incentive fees only

B. Management fees only

C. Neither incentive fees nor management fees

The following information relates to questions 37-42

The Tree Fallers Endowment plans to allocate part of its portfolio to alternative investment funds. The endowment has hired Kurt Summer, a consultant at Summer Brothers Consultants, to identify suitable alternative investment funds for its portfolio.

Summer has identified three funds for potential investment and will present the performance of these investments to the endowment's board of directors at their next quarterly meeting.

Summer is reviewing each of the fund's fee schedules and is concerned about the manager's incentive to take on excess risk in an attempt to generate a higher fee. Exhibit 1 presents the fee schedules of the three funds.

Exhibit 1: Fee Schedules

Fund	Computed Fee	Base Fee	Sharing	Maximum Annual Fee
Red Grass Fund	Higher of either (1) base or (2) base plus sharing of positive performance; sharing is based on return net of the base fee.	1.00%	20%	na
Blue Water Fund	Higher of either (1) base or (2) base plus sharing of positive performance, up to a maximum annual fee of 2.50%; sharing is based on active return.	0.50%	20%	2.50%
Yellow Wood Fund	Base plus sharing of both positive and negative performance; sharing is based on return net of the base fee.	1.50%	20%	na

Exhibit 2 presents the annual gross returns for each fund and its respective benchmark for the period of 2016–2018. All funds have an inception date of 1 January 2016. Summer intends to include in his report an explanation of the impact of the fee structures of the three funds on returns.

Exhibit 2: Fund and Benchmark Returns

	2016		2017		2018	
Fund	Gross Return (%)	Benchmark Return (%)	Gross Return (%)	Benchmark Return (%)	Gross Return (%)	Benchmark Return (%)
Red Grass Fund	8.00	8.00	−2.00	−10.00	5.00	4.50
Blue Water Fund	10.00	9.00	−4.00	−1.50	14.00	2.00
Yellow Wood Fund	15.00	14.00	−5.00	−6.50	7.00	9.50

The board of directors of the Tree Fallers Endowment asks Summer to recalculate the fees of the Red Grass Fund assuming a high-water mark feature whereby a sharing percentage could only be charged to the extent any losses had been recouped.

37. Based on Exhibit 1, which fund has a symmetrical fee structure?

A. Red Grass

B. Blue Water

C. Yellow Wood

38. Based on the fee schedules in Exhibit 1, the portfolio manager of which fund has the greatest incentive to assume additional risk to earn a higher investment management fee?

A. Red Grass

B. Blue Water

C. Yellow Wood

39. Based on Exhibit 1 and Exhibit 2, the Yellow Wood Fund's 2016 investment management fee is:

A. 3.00%.

B. 4.20%.

C. 4.50%.

40. Based on Exhibit 1 and Exhibit 2, the Red Grass Fund's 2017 investment management fee is:

A. 0.40%.

B. 1.00%.

C. 2.60%.

41. Based on Exhibit 1 and Exhibit 2, the Blue Water Fund's 2018 investment management fee is:

A. 2.40%

B. 2.50%.

C. 2.90%

42. In which year would the Red Grass Fund's investment management fee be affected by Summer's recalculation using the high-water mark?

A. 2016

B. 2017

C. 2018

---

43. At a meeting for the local municipal pension fund, a group of beneficiaries expressed concern about current investment management fees. The beneficiaries asked the Investment Committee for a fee summary of each manager in the

portfolio.

The next day, a pension fund staff member briefed the Committee on the managers' full contracted fee schedules. The Committee was surprised to hear that the managers work under numerous different fee structures and rates. A sample of these fee schedules for two managers is provided in Exhibit 1:

Exhibit 1: Fee Schedules for Selected Managers: Hidden Lake and Carpenter Management

Fee Type	Hidden Lake	Carpenter Management
Base Fee	0.30%	0.18%*
Sharing**	15%	20%
Maximum Annual Fee	N/A	0.80%

**Minimum fee.*
***On active return, beyond base fee.*

In explaining the differences, the staff member said that fee structures may lead to misestimates of portfolio risk. She also noted that performance-based fees sometimes are a close equivalent to a manager's call option on active return.

Identify which manager's fee structure is *most* similar to a call option on a share of active return. Justify your selection.

SOLUTIONS

1. B is correct. A critical element of manager selection is to assess if the investment process is superior, repeatable, and can be consistently applied.

2. A is correct. The focus of the initial screening process is on building a universe of managers that could potentially satisfy the identified portfolio need and should not focus on historical performance. Identifying a benchmark is a key component of defining the manager's role in the portfolio, and third-party categorizations are an efficient way to build an initial universe which can then be further refined.

3. The Theta fund, which is managed by an investment team rather than a single manager (as at Zeta) or by two managers (as at Eta), has lower key person risk. If the single manager at Zeta leaves or either manager at Eta leaves, the fund's performance could suffer.

   The Theta fund has the lowest level of staff turnover among the three funds. This higher level of personnel continuity limits the risk of the loss of institutional knowledge and experience within the investment team.

   The Theta fund offers a more attractive compensation package than Eta or Zeta. This incentivizes its investment professionals to stay at Theta, leading to greater longevity and experience over time. Additionally, Theta's package, unlike those of the other funds, will directly increase the rewards to its managers when performance exceeds benchmarks. This better aligns their interests with those of Connell.

4. *Alternative 1*

   If Connell avoids the Eta fund because of its recent underperformance, with performance reverting to the mean, he is at risk of making a Type II error (by not retaining managers with skill). A Type II error is an error of failing to detect a true relationship, or in this case, the opportunity cost associated with not hiring Eta and seeing its performance improve.

   Alternative 2

   If Connell selects the Theta fund because of its recent superior performance, with performance reverting to the mean, he is at risk of making a Type I error. A Type I error occurs when hiring or retaining a manager who subsequently underperforms expectations. The cost of a Type I error is explicit and relatively straightforward to measure.

   In deciding which fund to hire, the goal is to avoid making decisions based on short-term performance (trend following) and to identify evidence of behavioral biases in the evaluation of managers during the selection process.

5. The adviser would find style analysis most useful, whether it be returns-based (RBSA) or holdings-based (HBSA), when applied to strategies that hold publicly-traded securities where pricing is frequent. It can be applied to other strategies (hedge funds and private equity, for example), but the insights drawn from a style analysis of such strategies are more likely to be used for designing additional lines of inquiry in the course of due diligence rather than for confirmation of the investment process.

   In addition, style analysis, whether returns-based or holdings-based, must be meaningful, accurate, consistent, and timely in order to be useful. Accordingly, style analysis would be most useful to Connell in understanding most of the asset classes in the funds he is considering, including the equities and bonds. However, it would be less meaningful for evaluating the venture capital assets since they are not traded and are thus illiquid.

6. *Qualitative*

   Process and people: Evaluating the manager's investment process, including the manager's philosophy, process, people, and portfolio. This consideration is broadly described as part of "investment due diligence."

   Operational due diligence: Evaluating the manager's infrastructure and firm, including the accuracy of the manager's track record and whether the record fully reflects risks; the back office processes and procedures; the terms and if they are acceptable and appropriate for the strategy and vehicle; and the firm's profitability, its culture, and if it's likely to remain in business. This and the following bulleted considerations as a whole are broadly described as part of "operational due diligence":

   - Investment vehicle: Is the investment vehicle suitable for the portfolio need?
   - Terms: Are the terms acceptable and appropriate for the strategy and vehicle?
   - Monitoring: Does the manager continue to be the "best" fit for the portfolio need?

   Quantitative:

   Attribution and appraisal: To assess if the manager has displayed skill in investing.

   The capture ratio: How has the manager performed in "up" versus "down" markets?

   Drawdown: Does the return distribution exhibit large drawdowns?

7. Grimmett, with her adviser, would ensure the following tasks were performed prior to manager selection:

   - Decide that outside support is necessary.
   - Complete an investment policy statement (IPS).
   - Determine the appropriate asset allocation.

   Short of these key actions, Grimmett will be unable to identify the managers who fit her needs, confirm that the managers are suitable for her IPS, and be confident that they will act upon the appropriate asset allocation.

8. B is correct. Type I errors are more easily measured than Type II errors. In addition, Type I errors may be linked to the compensation of the decision maker. Type I errors are errors of mistaken rejection, whereas Type II are errors failing to detect a true relationship. Firing a skilled manager is less transparent to the investor.

9. B is correct. Hiring unskilled Manager 3 for large-cap stocks is an error of mistaken rejection or Type I error, whereas not hiring skilled Manager 2 for small-cap stocks is an error of failing to detect a true relationship or Type II error.

10. C is correct. When the two distributions are highly distinct, the unskilled managers are expected to significantly underperform the skilled managers, implying a high opportunity cost of not hiring the skilled managers. Efficient markets are likely to exhibit smaller differences of returns between skilled and unskilled managers.

11. *Type I:*

    Hiring Firm D, which later underperformed expectations, resulted in a Type I error. A Type I error occurs when a manager is hired or retained who subsequently underperforms expectations. This situation involves rejecting the null hypothesis of no skill when it is correct.

It is most likely Boinic will find its hiring of Firm D to be psychologically troubling.

Decision makers appear predisposed to worry more about Type I errors than Type II errors. Potential reasons for this focus are as follows:

- Psychologically, people seek to avoid feelings of regret. Type I errors are errors of mistaken rejection, active decisions that turn out to be incorrect, whereas Type II errors are errors of failing to detect a true relationship. Type I errors create explicit costs, whereas Type II errors create opportunity costs. Because individuals appear to put less weight on opportunity costs, Type I errors are psychologically more painful than Type II errors.
- Type I errors are more transparent to investors, so they entail not only the regret of an incorrect decision but the pain of having to explain this decision to the investor. Type II errors, such as firing (or not hiring) a manager with skill, are less transparent to investors—unless the investor tracks fired managers or evaluates the universe themselves.

Type II:

Not hiring Firm B, which later outperformed expectations, resulted in a Type II error. A Type II error occurs when a manager who subsequently outperforms, or performs in line with, expectations is not hired. This situation involves not rejecting an incorrect null hypothesis. As noted previously, a Type II error is typically less psychologically troubling than a Type I error.

The other three decisions did not result in either a Type I or Type II error.

12. B is correct. The results of the returns-based style analysis and the holdings-based style analysis should be consistent with the philosophy of the manager and the investment process. If this is not the case, it may suggest that the process is not repeatable or not consistently implemented. For these results, the manager should not be included in the universe of potential managers, whereas if the results track over time, they may suggest style drift.

13. B is correct. RBSA typically does not require a large amount of additional, or difficult to acquire, data. HBSA requires data on each security in the investment portfolio. HBSA is a snapshot of the portfolio at a single point of time and thus is subject to window dressing. Both HBSA and RBSA are subject to difficulties in interpreting returns when illiquid securities are present.

14. B is correct. In the normal course of business, the manager conforms to its style by reducing exposure to some class of investment grade bonds. Increasing allocation to cash and small-cap stocks is in violation of the mandate to be fully invested with equity exposure to large-cap stocks.

15. A is correct. Returns-based style analysis on portfolios of liquid assets is generally able to identify the important drivers of return and the relevant risk factors for the period analyzed, even for complicated strategies. In addition, the process is comparable across managers and through time. If the portfolio contains illiquid securities, the lack of current prices on those positions may lead to an underestimation of the portfolio's volatility in a returns-based style analysis. Longer return series generally provide a more accurate estimate of the manager's underlying standard deviation of return.

16. B is correct. Holdings-based style analysis estimates the portfolio's risk exposures using the securities held in the portfolio (a bottom-up approach), whereas returns-based style analysis uses portfolio returns to estimate a portfolio's sensitivities to security market indexes (a top-down approach).

17. A is correct. A capture ratio less than one indicates the downside capture is greater than upside capture and reflects greater participation in falling markets than in rising markets.

18. C is correct. Upside capture of 75% suggests that the manager only gained 75% of benchmark increase when the benchmark return was positive. Downside capture of 125% suggests that the manager lost 125% as much as the benchmark when the benchmark return was negative. Therefore, the manager underperformed the benchmark in both scenarios.

19. With Yang hoping to retire in three years and not wanting to suffer investment losses, she has less time to recover from losses than someone with a longer time horizon. Yang should seek a fund with a shallower and shorter expected drawdown. The Gamma fund has the smallest drawdown and the shortest drawdown duration.

20. Passive strategies seek to earn risk premiums, which are defined as the return in excess of a minimal risk ("risk-free") rate of return that accrues to bearing a risk that is not easily diversified away—so-called systematic risk. Active strategies, in contrast, assume markets are sufficiently inefficient that security mispricings can be identified and exploited.

    So, in assessing Aspen, Yang first would find its investment philosophy to be inconsistent because it states an active strategy but labels its strategy as a passive one. Aspen is unable to clearly and consistently articulate its investment philosophy.

    Yang would also note that Aspen has altered its investment philosophy over time in response to market performance. This suggests Aspen is reacting to markets, not pursuing a consistent philosophy. With this approach, Aspen's performance results may not be repeatable.

21. C is correct. Given the amount of inefficient assets compared with the AUM of managers likely to exploit them provides some assurance that the inefficiency is repeatable. It would likely take some time for the inefficiency to converge to efficient valuation. The infrequent nature of the inefficiency and the zero marginal return suggest that the inefficiency is probably not worthwhile to pursue.

22. Given Patnode's goal of predictably covering expenses and given the choice among these three active managers to invest her insurance policy proceeds, Laurbær is most suitable. Laurbær recognizes its strategy is exposed to potentially being arbitraged away and is more likely to evolve over time to deliver the ongoing returns desired by Patnode.

    Alcanfor and Mylesten, in contrast, are making more generic claims that have a weaker foundation for long-term results. Alcanfor is making its judgments based on performance in industry sectors but is judging effectiveness based on overall market benchmarks. This is not providing evidence related to success within its selection domain but instead gauging itself against a broader market standard. Mylesten is offering a more ad hoc reaction to changing market conditions and investment flows, suggesting a lack of repeatability and robustness. So, both of them would have greater uncertainty as to the production of the income Patnode needs.

23. C is correct. A large drawdown that results from an unforeseen event is explainable as a single isolated event that does not prohibit the manager from adhering to its investment philosophy and process. The events of senior team members leaving to form their own investment firm and an insider trading investigation by the SEC call into question the ability of the firm to adhere to its philosophy and

decision-making process.

24. All else equal, Manager B is most appropriate for Parade because the portfolio is liquid. That will reduce trading costs in comparison to a portfolio consisting of illiquid securities. Investment strategies not intending to capture a liquidity risk premium must be aware of portfolio liquidity. An existing portfolio consisting of illiquid securities will be more costly to change, not only to take advantage of new opportunities but also to trade because of higher transaction costs. Manager A is not the most appropriate choice because its use of hard-stop losses can risk closing positions too frequently. That, in turn, will increase turnover as well as trading costs. Manager C is problematic because in the case of an actively managed portfolio, the portfolio turnover should agree with (not be greater than) the frequency of signals generated and the securities' liquidity.

25. Transparency: SMA. Offering real-time, position-level detail to the investor, SMAs provide complete transparency and accurate attribution. Even if Diversified offers position-level detail, it is likely available with a delay.

    Investor Behavior: Diversified. Diversified is not as susceptible to investor micromanagement. Decisions are set by the manager, and portfolio value is determined by the related strategy without investor modification.

    Cost: Diversified. An SMA investor owns individual securities directly, which provides additional safety should a liquidity event occur. Although the manager continues to make investment decisions, those will not be influenced by the redemption or liquidity demands of other investors in the strategy.

    Liquidity: SMA. An SMA investor owns individual securities directly, which provides additional safety should a liquidity event occur. Although the manager continues to make investment decisions, those will not be influenced by the redemption or liquidity demands of other investors in the strategy.

    Tracking Risk: Diversified. Diversified would have lower tracking risk compared to SMAs, whose customization increases the chances of tracking risk relative to the benchmark. This can confuse attribution because performance will reflect investor constraints rather than manager decisions.

26. Detail 1. Benefit: This is a benefit if Lyon's positions are paired with the idea of capturing alpha as prices converge while offsetting market risk and are well-matched and sized correctly.

    Detail 2. Drawback: The reliance of Lyon's strategy on unique information is a drawback as it is difficult for Lyon to have an informational edge in a regulatory environment that seeks to reduce informational asymmetries.

    Detail 3. Drawback: This is a drawback because in a context of significant asset growth, Lyon should adjust the number and/or characteristics of the positions held to accommodate the increase in AUM.

27. C is correct. Experienced investment personnel is a key aspect of investment due diligence. A strong back office and suitable investment vehicles are key aspects of operational due diligence.

28. A is correct. The tax advantages to separately managed accounts do not accrue to a tax exempt investor. Choices B and C are considerations that reflect the investor's preferences and could be better satisfied using a separately managed account.

29. A is correct. Open-end funds provide daily liquidity; shares are bought and sold at the end-of-day NAV. Limited partnerships and private equity funds typically require investors to invest their money for longer periods.

30. A is correct. Pooled investment vehicles are typically operated at a lower cost than separately managed accounts because operational costs can be spread among multiple investors. An investor who is focused on tax efficiency would prefer a separately managed account because a separate account allows the implementation of tax-efficient investing and trading strategies, and the investor pays taxes only on capital gains realized. If the investor requires clear legal ownership, they would prefer a separately managed account in which the investor owns the individual security directly.

31. A is correct. ETFs, as listed securities that can be bought and sold intra-day, are the most liquid vehicles. Hedge fund liquidity features—such as redemption frequency, notification period, lockup, and gates—limit the liquidity of hedge funds. Private equity funds return capital and make profit distributions to investors only as investments are sold during the life of the fund, which is often 10 years and may be extended.

32. Open-end funds with an incentive fee. Open-end funds with an incentive fee are the most appropriate among the three investment vehicles being considered by Circue. Although slightly less liquid than closed-end funds, open-end funds still offer daily liquidity—with Circue indicating some tolerance for lower liquidity. An incentive fee is applicable in this case as mutual fund assets are often "sticky"; investors are reluctant to switch allocations once made and may accept lower returns. This outcome decreases manager motivation and leads to closet indexing, to which Circue has a heightened sensitivity among its active managers. Thus, the incentive fee can help motivate managers to work harder to improve performance. Closed-end funds are the most liquid of the three choices. Without an accompanying incentive fee, however, the closed-end fund manager may not have the same motivation to work harder than the open-end fund manager, who does have an incentive fee. Hedge funds are inappropriate here because they are the least liquid of the three options. A soft lock charges a redemption fee, paid into the fund, which is inconsistent with Circue's moderate sensitivity to fees.

33. Under the fee structure identified by Porter, Smith's stated expectation would be reflected in a misestimation of portfolio risk because performance-based fee structures may lead to such misestimates. Performance-based fee structures convert symmetrical gross active return distributions into asymmetrical net active return distributions, reducing variability on the upside but not the downside. As a result, a single standard deviation calculated on a return series that incorporates active returns, above and below the base fee, can lead to the underestimation of downside risk. In contrast, fully symmetric fees (fully exposing the manager to both upside and downside results) tend to yield closer alignment in risk and effort than bonus-style fees.

34. Gross Active Return ≤ 0.20%: Gross Active Return at or below the Base Fee – Base Fee = Net Active Return: 0.20 – 0.20 = 0.00, therefore Base Fee = Billed Fee (No Sharing Fee)0.20

    Gross Active Return = 0.75%: Active Return − Base Fee = Return Subject to Sharing Fee: 0.75 − 0.20

    = 0.55

    Return Subject to Sharing Fee × Sharing Fee = Additional Fee Due to Sharing Fee: 0.55 × 0.25

    = 0.1375

    Base Fee + Additional Fee Due to Sharing Fee = Billed Fee: 0.20 + 0.1375

    = 0.3375

Active Return − Billed Fee = Net Active Return: 0.75 − 0.3375

= 0.4125, rounded to 0.41%

Gross Active Return = 1.25% is the breakeven active return (No Sharing Fee): Gross Active Return − Standard Fee = Net Active Return: 1.25 – 0.35

= 0.90 or 0.90%

Standard Fee = Billed Fee (No Sharing Fee)0.35

Gross Active Return = 1.75%: Gross Active Return − Base Fee = Return Subject to Sharing Fee: 1.75 − 0.20

= 1.55

Return Subject to Sharing Fee × Sharing Fee = Additional Fee Due to Sharing Fee: 1.55 × 0.25

= 0.3875

Base Fee + Additional Fee Due to Sharing Fee = Billed Fee: 0.2 + 0.3875

= 0.5875

Gross Active Return − Billed Fee = Net Active Return: 1.75 − 0.5875

= 1.1625, rounded to 1.16%

35. Vaudreuil. The impact of Vaudreuil's fees on the client is lower as assets grow in a rising market. This is a benefit to the client. The client might not achieve the same level of returns as would be available under a different fee structure. Vaudreuil might not want to risk losing assets once they are large and may not work to generate the same level of returns to retain assets because they tend to be "sticky."

    Pourtir. Performance-based fees work to align the interests of Pourtir and the client because both parties share in the investment results.

    The client benefits by paying lower fees when active returns are low.

    Pourtir may work harder. Tension can be created between the client and Pourtir, as the client must pay base fees even if Pourtir underperforms.

    Pourtir's fee structure may lead to misestimates of portfolio risk and may incentivize Pourtir to assume higher portfolio risk.

    The client and Pourtir may have different incentives when performance-based fees are used, specifically in the case of bonus-style fees.

    Performance-based fees may incentivize Pourtir to hold on to assets until a profit can be realized even if the client would benefit from selling the assets at a loss and investing the proceeds elsewhere.

36. A is correct. Because incentive fees are fees charged as a percentage of returns (reducing net gains in positive months and reducing net losses in negative months), its use lowers the standard deviation of realized returns. Charging a management fee (a fixed percentage based on assets) lowers the level of realized return without affecting the standard deviation of the return series.

37. C is correct. A symmetrical fee structure is one in which the fees are affected by both positive and negative performance. Of the three funds in Exhibit 1, only Yellow Wood has a symmetrical structure. Yellow Wood's profit sharing component will be negative if its return is negative and positive if it is positive.

38. A is correct. Red Grass's fee arrangement allows for unlimited performance-based fees on the upside and no negative consequences on the

downside.

39. B is correct. The fund's fee schedule includes a base fee of 1.50% and a 20% performance-based fee. The performance-based fee is applied after the base fee is deducted. The total fee is calculated as follows:

    $1.5\% + [20\% \times (15\% - 1.5\%)] = 4.20\%$

40. B is correct. Red Grass Fund's fee schedule states that the fee will be the higher of either (1) the base fee or (2) the base fee plus the sharing of the positive performance. The 2017 return was negative and only the base fee should be applied.

41. B is correct. The fee schedule states that the fee will be the higher of either (1) the base fee or (2) the base fee plus sharing of the positive performance, with a maximum fee of 2.50%. Furthermore, it states that the performance-based fee is assessed on the active return. Without an upper limit, the fee would be 0.5% + [20% × (14% – 2%)] = 2.90%, which is greater than 2.50%; so, the 2.50% fee is assessed.

42. C is correct. The 2016 fee calculation would not be affected by the high-water mark provision because it is the first year of operation of the fund and the return is positive (no prior losses to be offset). The investment management fee in 2016 is calculated as follows:

    $\text{Investment management fee} = 1.00\% + [20\% \times (8.0\% - 1.00\%)] = 2.4\%.$

    The 2017 fee calculation would also not be affected by the high-water mark provision because the profit-sharing component of the fee is zero as a result of a negative return in that year. The investment management fee is calculated as follows:

    $\text{Investment management fee} = 1.00\% + 0.00\% = 1.00\%.$

    The 2018 fee would be affected by the high-water mark provision because the sharing fee percentage would now be part of the 2018 gain and will need to offset the prior year losses, and only the remaining gains will generate a fee. The performance-based fee would be based on only the gains in excess of the high-water mark. The actual investment management fee charged (percentage and dollar value) will depend on the specific feature of the calculation, which is beyond the scope of this learning module. Note that the correct answer can be identified by observing that 2018 is the only year in which a positive return follows a negative return in the prior year.

43. Carpenter Management. Carpenter Management has a bonus-style fee with a maximum fee feature. Bonus-style fees are the close equivalent of a manager's call option on a share of active return, for which the base fee is the strike price—for example, the 18 bps base fee, plus a long call option on active return with a strike price equal to the minimum (base) fee, minus another (less valuable call option) with a strike price equal to the maximum fee. Hidden Lake has a symmetrical fee structure in which the manager is fully exposed to both the downside and upside. So, of the two firms, Carpenter Management's fee structure is most similar to a call option.

LEARNING MODULE

3

Overview of the Global Investment Performance Standards

by Philip Lawton, PhD, CFA, CIPM.

Philip Lawton, PhD, CFA, CIPM (USA).

LEARNING OUTCOMES

Mastery	*The candidate should be able to:*
☐	discuss the objectives and scope of the GIPS standards and their benefits to prospective clients and investors, as well as investment managers
☐	explain the fundamentals of compliance with the GIPS standards, including the definition of the firm and the firm's definition of discretion
☐	discuss requirements of the GIPS standards with respect to return calculation methodologies, including the treatment of external cash flows, cash and cash equivalents, and expenses and fees
☐	explain the recommended valuation hierarchy of the GIPS standards
☐	explain requirements of the GIPS standards with respect to composite return calculations, including methods for asset weighting portfolio returns
☐	explain the meaning of "discretionary" in the context of composite construction and, given a description of the relevant facts, determine whether a portfolio is likely to be considered discretionary
☐	explain the role of investment mandates, objectives, or strategies in the construction of composites
☐	explain requirements of the GIPS standards with respect to composite construction, including switching portfolios among composites, the timing of the inclusion of new portfolios in composites, and the timing of the exclusion of terminated portfolios from composites

LEARNING OUTCOMES

Mastery	The candidate should be able to:
□	explain requirements of the GIPS standards with respect to presentation and reporting
□	explain the conditions under which the performance of a past firm or affiliation may be linked to or used to represent the historical performance of a new or acquiring firm
□	discuss the purpose, scope, and process of verification

1 OBJECTIVE AND SCOPE OF THE GIPS STANDARDS

□	discuss the objectives and scope of the GIPS standards and their benefits to prospective clients and investors, as well as investment managers

This reading explains the rationale and application of certain provisions of the 2020 edition of the Global Investment Performance Standards (GIPS®) for Firms. The 2020 edition of the GIPS standards contains three chapters: the GIPS Standards for Firms, the GIPS Standards for Asset Owners, and the GIPS Standards for Verifiers, each with its own glossary. ***Candidates are responsible not only for the material contained directly in this reading but also for the sections of the GIPS Standards for Firms specifically referenced within this reading.*** The entirety of the 2020 GIPS Standards for Firms can be found here:

https://www.cfainstitute.org/en/ethics/codes/gips-standards/firms

The GIPS standards fulfill an essential role in investment management around the world. They meet the need for globally accepted standards for investment management firms in calculating and presenting their investment returns to **prospective clients** and **prospective investors**. (In the context of the GIPS Standards for Firms, a prospective *client* is any person or entity that has expressed interest in one of the firm's strategies and qualifies to invest in that strategy via a segregated account, irrespective of whether the person or entity currently invests with the firm through another strategy that the firm offers. A prospective *investor* is any person or entity that has expressed interest in one of the firm's pooled funds and qualifies to invest in the pooled fund, again irrespective of any other current investments with the firm. These and other terms bolded in this reading are defined in the glossary of the GIPS Standards for Firms. For purposes of this reading, the terms *client* and *investor* may be used interchangeably.)

The GIPS standards are based on the ideals of fair representation and full disclosure of an investment management firm's performance history. Firms that claim compliance with the GIPS standards must adhere to rules governing not only return calculations but also the way in which returns are displayed in a **GIPS Report**. (A GIPS Report is a specific type of performance presentation that must be provided to *prospective* clients and investors when a firm claims compliance with the GIPS standards.) They are further required to make certain disclosures and are encouraged to make others in a GIPS Report, thereby assisting the user in interpreting and evaluating the reported returns. Prospective and current clients can have a high degree of confidence that the information shown in a GIPS Report reflects the results of the firm's past investment decisions. They can also be confident that the returns are calculated and presented on a consistent basis and are objectively comparable for a given strategy with those reported by other firms claiming compliance with the GIPS standards.

Objective and Scope of the GIPS Standards

The GIPS standards evolved from earlier efforts to improve the reliability of investment performance information and to standardize calculation methodologies and presentation standards. In this part of the reading, we explain the objectives and scope of the GIPS standards.

The Need for Global Investment Performance Standards

To appreciate the value of industry-wide performance presentation standards, consider some of the many ways in which unscrupulous employees might attempt to gather and retain assets by misrepresenting a firm's historical record. In communicating with a prospective client or investor, they could

- present returns only for the best-performing portfolios as though those returns fully represented the firm's expertise in a given strategy or style;
- base portfolio values on their own unsubstantiated estimates of asset prices;
- inflate returns by annualizing partial-period results;
- select the most favorable measurement period, calculating returns from a low point to a high point;
- present simulated returns as though they had actually been earned;
- choose as a benchmark the particular index the selected portfolios have outperformed by the greatest margin during the preferred measurement period;
- portray the growth of assets in the style or strategy of interest so as to mask the difference between investment returns and client contributions; or
- use the marketing department's expertise in graphic design to underplay unfavorable performance data and direct the prospect's attention to the most persuasive elements of the sales presentation.

Some of the foregoing examples are admittedly egregious abuses. They are not, however, farfetched. The investment management industry is highly competitive, and people whose careers and livelihoods depend on winning new business want to communicate their firm's performance in the most favorable light. The GIPS standards are ethical criteria designed to ensure that the firm's performance history is fairly represented and adequately disclosed. Indeed, employees who are pressured to misrepresent their firm's investment results can and should cite the GIPS standards.

Without established, well-formulated, and widely adopted standards for investment performance measurement and presentation, the prospective client's or investor's ability to make sound decisions in selecting investment managers would be impaired. Individual clients, investors, and their advisors, as well as pension plan sponsors, foundation trustees, and other institutional investors with fiduciary responsibility for asset pools, need reliable information. The GIPS standards increase their confidence that the returns shown fairly represent an investment firm's historical record. The GIPS standards also enable them to make reasonable comparisons among different investment management firms before hiring one of them. Evaluating past returns is only one dimension of the manager selection process, but it is an important one in fulfilling the due diligence responsibilities expected of fiduciaries.

Global standards for performance presentation, including a requirement to show a strategy's returns alongside the returns of an appropriate **benchmark**, can lead to an informative discussion about the firm's investment decision-making process. A prospective client might ask, for instance, why the strategy outperformed the benchmark in some periods and not in others, inviting the firm's spokespersons to explain past returns and to describe how the investment product is positioned for the future. The firm's representatives should be able to explain the sources of past returns reasonably, credibly, and insightfully in light of the firm's investment philosophy and investment decision-making process as well as the then-prevailing capital market environment.

(It must be stressed in this context that reviewing properly calculated, fully disclosed historical results does not exempt the prospective client from a thorough investigation of the candidate firm's background, resources, and capabilities for the mandate under consideration. Due diligence in selecting an investment manager includes, among many other important elements, examining a firm's regulatory history, the experience and professional credentials of its decision makers, the soundness of its investment philosophy, the nature of its investment and operational risk controls, and the independence of its service providers.)

The benefits of the GIPS standards to prospective and current clients are clear. What, if any, are the benefits to the investment management firms incurring the expenses required to achieve and maintain compliance with the GIPS standards?

There is, first, an immeasurable benefit to the investment management industry as a whole. The development of well-founded, thoughtfully defined performance presentation standards is a great credit not only to the vision of certain professionals and organizations but, above all, to the leadership of the investment management firms that adopted the standards early on. The GIPS standards may reassure investors about compliant firms' integrity in the area of investment performance reporting, especially if they have been verified. **Verification**, discussed later in this reading, refers to an investment firm's voluntarily engaging an independent third party to test the firm's design and implementation of certain performance measurement policies and procedures. Verification brings additional credibility to the firm's claim of compliance with the GIPS standards.

The practical benefits to individual firms facing the initial and ongoing expenses of GIPS compliance have increased over time. In some markets, the GIPS standards are so well accepted by plan sponsors and consultants that non-compliance is a serious competitive impediment to a firm's winning new institutional business. Requests for proposals (RFPs) in manager searches routinely ask if the responding firm is in compliance with the GIPS standards and if the firm has been independently verified. In addition, the global recognition the GIPS standards have gained helps the compliant firm to compete in international markets because prospective clients and investors value the ability to equitably compare its investment performance to that of local GIPS-compliant firms. Compliance with the GIPS standards has appropriately been characterized as the investment management firm's passport to the international marketplace.

Because the GIPS standards reflect best practices in the calculation and presentation of investment performance, firms may also realize internal benefits. In the course of implementing the GIPS standards, they might identify opportunities to strengthen managerial controls. The discipline of reviewing portfolio guidelines and defining, documenting, and adhering to internal policies in support of compliance with the GIPS standards typically improves the firm's oversight of investment operations and provides management with additional comfort in the accuracy of the firm's performance reporting and the quality of the presentations provided to prospective clients and investors. Similarly, technological enhancements designed to provide valid calculation input data and presentation elements, such as dispersion statistics, may improve the quality of information available to the firm.

The Scope of the GIPS Standards for Firms

Only investment management firms and asset owners that manage assets on a discretionary basis—and compete for business—may claim compliance with the GIPS Standards for Firms. (An asset owner that manages investments, directly and/or through the use of external managers, on behalf of participants, beneficiaries, or the organization itself—but does not compete for business—would comply with the GIPS Standards for Asset Owners.) Consultants, software houses, or third-party performance measurement providers such as custodians may not claim to be GIPS-compliant.

GIPS compliance cannot be claimed for only some of an investment firm's products, nor for specific **composites, pooled funds,** or **portfolios**; compliance can be achieved only on a firm-wide basis. A firm's claim of compliance signifies, among other things, that the firm's performance measurement data inputs, processes, and return calculation methodology conform to the prescribed guidelines; that all of the firm's fee-paying discretionary **segregated accounts** have been assigned to at least one composite; and that all **limited distribution pooled funds** meeting a **composite definition** are properly included in the appropriate composites.

UNDERSTANDING KEY TERMS

Here we pause for a brief detour to define a few terms that have very specific meaning in the context of the GIPS standards:

Composite. A composite is an aggregation of one or more portfolios that are managed according to a similar investment mandate, objective, or strategy.

Segregated Account. A segregated account is a portfolio owned by a single client, sometimes referred to in practice as a separately managed account (SMA).

Pooled Fund. A pooled fund is also a "portfolio," but we distinguish between a segregated account portfolio and a pooled fund portfolio in this reading because the requirements of the GIPS standards for pooled funds may differ from those that apply to segregated accounts. Pooled funds are further distinguished between limited distribution and broad distribution pooled funds. A broad distribution pooled fund is a pooled fund that is regulated under a framework that would permit the general public to purchase or hold the pooled fund's shares and is not exclusively offered in one-on-one presentations. Mutual fund and UCITs are examples of broad distribution pooled funds. A limited distribution pooled fund is any pooled fund that is not a broad distribution pooled fund. Examples of limited distribution pooled funds include many private equity or hedge funds.

This reading is based on the 2020 edition of the GIPS standards, which are effective as of 1 January 2020. **GIPS Reports** that include performance for periods ending on or after 31 December 2020 must be prepared in accordance with the 2020 edition of the GIPS standards.

Overview of the GIPS Standards

The Introduction to the GIPS standards articulates the mission and objectives of the GIPS standards and provides an overview of key concepts important to understanding the objectives and scope of the GIPS standards.

The mission of the GIPS standards is "to promote ethics and integrity and instill trust through the use of the GIPS standards by achieving universal demand for compliance by asset owners, adoption by asset managers, and support from regulators for the ultimate benefit of the global investment community."

The five objectives of the GIPS standards are to:

- promote investor interests and instill investor confidence;
- ensure accurate and consistent data;
- obtain worldwide acceptance of a single standard for calculating and presenting performance;
- promote fair, global competition among investment firms; and
- promote industry self-regulation on a global basis.

Key concepts of the GIPS Standards for Firms include the following:

- *Fair representation and full disclosure of investment performance is the key principle underlying the GIPS standards.* As ethical standards, the GIPS standards are voluntary.
- *Fair representation and full disclosure likely requires adherence to both the minimum requirements and the recommendations of the GIPS standards.* When appropriate, firms have the responsibility to include information in the GIPS Reports that is not specifically addressed by the GIPS standards.
- *Firms must comply with all applicable requirements of the GIPS standards, including any Guidance Statements, interpretations, and Questions & Answers (Q&As) published by CFA Institute and the GIPS standards governing bodies.* The GIPS standards consist of requirements which must be followed in order for a firm to claim compliance. The GIPS standards also include recommendations, which are optional but should be followed because they represent best practice in performance presentation.
- *The GIPS standards do not address every aspect of performance measurement and will continue to evolve over time to address additional areas of investment performance.* The GIPS standards will continue to evolve as the industry tackles additional areas of performance measurement and recognizes the implications of new investment strategies, instruments, and technologies.
- *Composites are required for all strategies managed on behalf of or marketed to segregated account clients to prevent firms from cherry-picking the performance presented to prospective clients.* To promote fair representations of performance, the GIPS standards require firms to include *all* actual fee-paying, discretionary segregated accounts in at least one composite. Composites are defined by investment mandate, objective, or strategy. Pooled funds must also be included in any composite if the pooled fund meets the composite definition.
- *The GIPS standards rely on the integrity of input data, including the valuations of portfolio holdings and the use of certain calculation methodologies.* Because the GIPS standards are global, **prospective clients** and **prospective investors** engaged in an evaluation of competing GIPS-compliant firms' historical performance know that rates of return have been calculated in accordance with a common set of valuation principles and methodological guidelines.

The GIPS standards require that firms must meet *all* the applicable requirements set forth in the GIPS standards. There can be no exceptions. As stated in the part of the Introduction headed "Claiming Compliance and Verification," firms must take all steps necessary to ensure that they have satisfied all of the applicable requirements before claiming compliance with the GIPS standards. Moreover, firms are strongly encouraged to perform periodic internal compliance checks to confirm the validity of compliance claims. Implementing adequate internal controls during all stages of the investment performance process will instill confidence in the performance presented and in the claim of compliance. The GIPS standards recommend that firms be verified.

When the GIPS standards conflict with laws and/or regulations regarding the calculation and presentation of performance, the GIPS standards obligate firms to comply with laws and regulations and to disclose the conflict in the GIPS Report. Firms are strongly encouraged to comply with the GIPS standards in addition to applicable regulatory requirements.

In the next sections, we discuss specific requirement of the GIPS standards. The GIPS Standards for Firms are divided into eight sections:

1. Fundamentals of Compliance
2. Input Data and Calculation Methodology
3. Composite and Pooled Fund Maintenance
4. Composite Time-Weighted Return Report
5. Composite Money-Weighted Return Report
6. Pooled Fund Time-Weighted Return Report
7. Pooled Fund Money-Weighted Return Report
8. GIPS Advertising Guidelines

Sections 4, 5, 6, and 7 detail the requirements and recommendations for the various report types specified by the GIPS standards: Composite Time-Weighted Return Reports, Composite Money-Weighted Return Reports, Pooled Fund Time-Weighted Return Reports, and Pooled Fund Money-Weighted Return Reports. Section 8 focuses on the GIPS Advertising Guidelines, outlining the conditions under which a firm that claims compliance with the GIPS standards can include such a claim in its advertising. The balance of this reading focuses primarily on the remaining sections of the GIPS standards: (1) Fundamentals of Compliance, (2) Input Data and Calculation Methodology, and (3) Composite and Pooled Fund Maintenance.

Exhibit 1 contains an excerpt from the GIPS standards introducing each of these topics.

Exhibit 1: Content of the Global Investment Performance Standards

1. **Fundamentals of Compliance:** Several core principles create the foundation for the GIPS standards, including properly defining the firm, providing GIPS Reports to all prospective clients and prospective pooled fund investors, adhering to applicable laws and regulations, and ensuring that information presented is not false or misleading. Two important issues that a firm must consider when becoming compliant with the GIPS standards are the definition of the firm and the firm's definition of discretion. The definition of the firm is the foundation for firm-wide compliance and creates defined boundaries whereby total firm assets can be determined. The firm's definition of discretion establishes criteria to judge which portfolios must be included in a composite and is based on the firm's ability to implement its investment strategies.
2. **Input Data and Calculation Methodology:** Consistency of input data used to calculate performance is critical to effective compliance with the GIPS standards and establishes the foundation for full, fair, and comparable investment performance presentations. Achieving comparability among investment management firms' performance

presentations requires uniformity in methods used to calculate returns. The GIPS standards mandate the use of certain calculation methodologies to facilitate comparability.

3. **Composite and Pooled Fund Maintenance:** A composite is an aggregation of one or more portfolios managed according to a similar investment mandate, objective, or strategy. The composite return is the asset-weighted average of the performance of all portfolios in the composite. Creating meaningful composites is essential to the fair presentation, consistency, and comparability of performance over time and among firms. A composite must include all portfolios that meet the composite definition.

In the next seventeen sections, we discuss select required provisions of Fundamentals of Compliance, Input Data and Calculation Methodology, and Composite and Pooled Fund Maintenance.

2 FUNDAMENTALS OF COMPLIANCE

☐ explain the fundamentals of compliance with the GIPS standards, including the definition of the firm and the firm's definition of discretion

Section 1 of the GIPS Standards for Firms, "Fundamentals of Compliance," contains 39 requirements and seven recommendations. For our purposes, we focus on selected *required* fundamentals of compliance, emphasizing the definition of the firm.

Candidates should read all of Section 1.A of the GIPS Standards for Firms for a complete understanding of the required fundamentals of compliance.

Although the concept of discretion, specifically the firm's definition of discretion, is not technically a part of the Fundamentals of Compliance, the concept is integral to developing an understanding of the applications of the GIPS standards and thus is covered prior to delving more deeply into the standards themselves.

Definition of the Firm

The **firm** must be defined as an investment firm, subsidiary, or division held out to the public as a **distinct business entity**. The Glossary defines a distinct business entity as a "unit, division, department, or office that is organizationally and functionally segregated from other units, divisions, departments, or offices and that retains discretion over the assets it manages and that should have autonomy over the investment decision-making process." Possible criteria for identifying a distinct business entity are the organization being a legal entity, having a distinct market or client type, or using a separate and distinct investment process.

The way in which the investment management organization is held out to the public is a key factor in defining the firm. For example, if a unit of a larger company specializes in providing investment management services to private clients, and it is marketed as a specialist in meeting the investment needs of high-net-worth individuals and family offices, then that organizational unit might qualify as a "firm" for the purpose of compliance with the GIPS standards. Certainly, however, the unit's entitlement to be considered a firm under the GIPS standards could be justified if it additionally were incorporated as a subsidiary and had its own dedicated financial analysts, portfolio managers, and traders located in a separate building or area of the company and reporting through a separate chain of command to the parent organization's senior management.

IMPLEMENTATION

Defining the Firm

For small investment management boutiques, defining the firm may be a relatively easy task, but it can prove challenging for large firms.

Consider the case of a super-regional bank whose wealth management department consists of two separate and distinct divisions: the private client division and the institutional client division. The private client division, called Eastern National Bank Wealth Management Services, offers investment management to private individuals and families. The institutional client division, called Eastern Institutional Asset Advisors, serves tax-exempt non-profit organizations including pension funds and charitable foundations; it does not solicit or handle non-institutional business. Each division has its own investment management team, traders, marketing department, administrative personnel, and accounting department. After a few years of operating in this manner, the institutional investment unit decides to achieve compliance with the GIPS standards, but the private client division makes a business decision not to implement the GIPS standards. The institutional client division may nonetheless be in position to become GIPS-compliant because it holds itself out to customers as a distinct business unit, with its own autonomous investment management, research, trading, and administrative team.

Based on the information provided, the institutional client division appears to satisfy the conditions for defining itself as a firm for the purpose of compliance with the GIPS standards. Sample language might be, "The firm is defined as Eastern Institutional Asset Advisors, the institutional asset management division of Eastern National Bank."

On the other hand, if both divisions were to use the same investment process, approved security list, style models, and so on, and they merely divided assets between personal and institutional portfolios, then neither division alone could compellingly claim compliance. If the senior investment personnel of the Private Client division had authority to dictate the Institutional Client division's investment strategy or tactical asset allocations, or to mandate the investment of institutional clients' funds in specific securities, then the Institutional Client division would likely not qualify as a distinct business unit having autonomy over the investment decision-making process and discretion over the assets it manages. If the two divisions were organizationally segregated but shared the same trading desk, the Institutional Client division would have to determine whether its decision-making autonomy is compromised by the trading arrangement. If the traders merely fill the portfolio manager's orders, then the Institutional Client division arguably remains autonomous, but if the traders actively participate in the identification of misvalued securities, a greater impediment to the autonomy argument would exist.

Defining the firm in such a situation calls for the scrupulous exercise of professional judgment, with due attention to the ethical objectives of the Global Investment Performance Standards.

In view of the complexity of modern organizational structures, it may require judgment to determine if a given unit properly meets the definition of a firm. The decision has immediate and lasting practical consequences, however. Because the

GIPS standards apply firm-wide, the definition of the firm will determine the extent of the initial implementation and ongoing compliance activities. It also establishes the boundaries for determining total firm assets. The phrase **total firm assets** refers to the aggregate **fair value** of all assets (whether or not discretionary or fee-paying) for which a firm has investment management responsibility. Total firm assets include assets managed by sub-advisors that the firm has authority to select but do not include **advisory-only assets** or uncalled **committed capital**.

A firm that has been defined for the purposes of the GIPS standards may very well undergo subsequent changes in its corporate structure or organizational design. Changes in a firm's organization are not permitted to lead to alteration of historical performance, however. Indeed, we may put it down as a general rule that, apart from correcting errors, historical performance is not to be altered.

Definition of Discretion

The GIPS Standards for Firms require that all discretionary, fee-paying segregated accounts must be included in at least one composite. Discretionary, fee-paying pooled funds must also be included in at least one composite if they meet a composite definition. A key term in this requirement is "discretionary," although the GIPS standards do not define the term itself. Generally speaking, a portfolio is discretionary if the manager is able to implement the intended investment strategy. For example, the manager of a discretionary domestic mid-cap value portfolio is free to purchase any stock issued in the investor's home country that meets the pertinent market capitalization and style criteria. The firm might define mid-cap stocks as those whose market capitalization falls within a certain range. Similarly, the firm might define value stocks in terms of their price-to-earnings multiple, price-to-book ratio, dividend yield, or other characteristics intended to distinguish them from growth stocks. In line with best practice, the firm and the client will agree in advance that the portfolio's investment objective is to outperform a specified benchmark that is an appropriate measure of success in the domestic mid-cap market. For instance, the firm might construct a custom benchmark that is acceptable to the client, or the firm and the client might agree to use a commercially available index that mirrors the domestic mid-cap market.

Although both discretionary and non-discretionary portfolios are included in total firm assets, only discretionary portfolios are included in composites. If the client imposes restrictions on the manager's freedom to make investment decisions to buy, hold, and sell securities so as to carry out the investment strategy and achieve the portfolio's financial objectives, then the manager must consider whether the portfolio is in fact discretionary. In general, restrictions that impede the investment process to such an extent that the strategy cannot be implemented as intended may be presumed to render the portfolio non-discretionary, and it should not be included in a composite.

Other Fundamentals of Compliance

Other requirements under Section 1, Fundamentals of Compliance, can be broadly characterized as relating to:

- the minimum number of years required in order to initially claim compliance with the GIPS standards;
- documenting policies and procedures related to compliance;
- complying with laws and regulations;
- avoiding false or misleading performance and performance-related information;

- the requirements concerning the distribution of GIPS Reports and lists of firm composites and pooled funds;
- the use of total return benchmarks reflective of the investment strategy;
- the requirement to correct **material errors** in a GIPS Report and the redistribution of the report to the appropriate parties;
- the maintenance of data and information necessary to support the elements of the GIPS Reports; and
- conditions under which performance may be used or linked to that of another firm.

TIME-WEIGHTED RETURN

3

☐ discuss requirements of the GIPS standards with respect to return calculation methodologies, including the treatment of external cash flows, cash and cash equivalents, and expenses and fees

Section 2.A of the GIPS Standards for Firms addresses, among other aspects, the requirements for calculating portfolio and composite returns. The GIPS standards mandate the use of a **time-weighted return** (TWR). **Money-weighted returns** (MWRs) may be used for portfolios meeting certain conditions (described later). In the following paragraphs, we address TWR, MWR, and the treatment of cash balances and fees and expenses.

Candidates should read Section 2.A, Provisions 2.A.1 through 2.A.39 of the GIPS Standards for Firms. Candidates are not responsible for the provisions in Section 2 related to Private Market Investments, Real Estate, Carve-Outs, Wrap Fees, and Side Pockets and Subscription Lines of Credit (Provisions 2.A.40 through 2.A.50).

Time-Weighted Return

TWR is a method of calculating period-by-period returns that reflects the change in value and negates the effects of **external cash flows**. Except for private market investment portfolios, portfolios using TWR must be valued monthly, and the TWR must be calculated at least monthly as of the calendar month end or last business day of the month. If returns are not calculated daily and the portfolio receives an intra-month **large cash flow**, the portfolio must be valued and a sub-period return must be calculated at the time of the large cash flow. Private market investment portfolios (e.g., real estate and infrastructure, private equity, and similar investments that are illiquid, not publicly traded, and not traded on an exchange) must be valued quarterly.

What constitutes a large cash flow is defined by the firm. It is usually an external cash flow of such size that it may distort the return if the portfolio is not valued and a sub-period return is not calculated at the time of the cash flow. A large cash flow may be defined either relative to an absolute monetary threshold or as a percentage of the portfolio or composite assets.

If the portfolio is a pooled fund (a fund whose ownership interests may be held by more than one investor), and the pooled fund is not included in one of the firm's composites, the fund must be valued and returns must be calculated at least annually.

Similar to the composite requirements presented above, the pooled fund must be valued at the time of any subscriptions or redemptions and a sub-period return calculated as of that date. The sub-period return is then linked with other sub-period returns.

In the simplest case, when no external cash flows (i.e., client-initiated additions to or withdrawals from invested assets) occur during the period, calculating the TWR is straightforward:

$$r_t = \frac{V_1 - V_0}{V_0} \quad (1)$$

where r_t is the TWR for period t; V_1 is the ending value of the portfolio, including cash and accrued income, at the end of the period; and V_0 is the portfolio's beginning value, including cash and accrued income, at the beginning of the specified period. Equation 1 assumes that there are no cash inflows or cash outflows and expresses return as the ratio of the change in value during the period to the value at the start of the period. Despite its simplicity, the TWR equation produces an accurate representation of investment results in a single period with no external cash flows. As we will see, this equation is also used to calculate sub-period results under the intra-period valuation method when external cash flows occur.

Most portfolios, of course, do have external cash flows. A segregated account for an institutional investor, for example, may routinely have contributions and withdrawals based on the institution's needs. The TWR methodology removes the effect of such contributions and withdrawals from the return calculation, allowing the performance evaluator to focus on the value added by investment decisions that are controlled by the investment management firm.

If the portfolio experiences a cash flow that is not a large cash flow, the GIPS Standards for Firms do not require that the portfolio be valued as of the date of the cash flow. Instead, firms must use a method that adjusts for daily weighted cash flows, which is an approximation of a true TWR.

The most accurate way to calculate a total return while eliminating the impact of external cash flows is to value the portfolio whenever an external cash flow occurs, compute a sub-period return, and geometrically link sub-period returns expressed in relative form according to Equation 2:

$$r_{twr} = (1 + r_{t,1}) \times (1 + r_{t,2}) \times \ldots \times (1 + r_{t,n}) - 1 \quad (2)$$

where r_{twr} is the time-weighted total return for the entire period and $r_{t,1}$ through $r_{t,n}$ are the sub-period returns. The GIPS standards require that the periodic returns be geometrically linked.

For example, consider a portfolio with a beginning value of $100,000 as of 31 May, a value of $109,000 on 5 June (which includes a cash contribution of $10,000 received that day), and an ending value of $110,550 on 30 June. Consider that the first sub-period ends and the second sub-period begins on the cash flow date, such that the ending value for Sub-period 1 is $99,000 ($109,000 less the contribution of $10,000) and the beginning value for Sub-period 2, including the $10,000 contribution, is $109,000. The portfolio's true time-weighted return using the intra-period valuation method is 0.41%, computed as follows:

$$r_{t,1} = \frac{V_1 - V_0}{V_0} = \frac{(109,000 - 10,000) - 100,000}{100,000} = \frac{99,000 - 100,000}{100,000} = -0.01$$

$$r_{t,2} = \frac{V_2 - V_1}{V_1} = \frac{110,550 - 109,000}{109,000} = 0.0142$$

$$r_{twr} = \left(1 + r_{t,1}\right) \times \left(1 + r_{t,2}\right) - 1 = [1 + (-0.01)] \times (1 + 0.0142) - 1$$
$$= 1.0041 - 1 = 0.0041 = 0.41\%$$

Geometric linking is used because returns are compounded and so are not additive but multiplicative.

If the portfolio experiences cash flows that are not large cash flows, and the firm does not calculate daily performance, portfolio returns must be calculated using a method that adjusts for daily weighted cash flows. Examples of acceptable approaches are the Modified Dietz method and the Modified Internal Rate of Return (Modified IRR) method, both of which weight each cash flow by the proportion of the measurement period it is held in the portfolio.

Equation 3 shows the formula for estimating the time-weighted rate of return using the Modified Dietz method:

$$r_{ModDietz} = \frac{V_1 - V_0 - CF}{V_0 + \sum_{i=1}^{n}(CF_i \times w_i)} \tag{3}$$

where $\sum_{i=1}^{n}(CF_i \times w_i)$ is the sum of each cash flow multiplied by its weight and $CF = \Sigma CF_i$. The weight (w_i) is simply the proportion of the measurement period, in days, that each cash flow has been in the portfolio, as shown in Equation 4:

$$w_i = \frac{CD - D_i}{CD} \tag{4}$$

where CD is the total number of calendar days in the period and D_i is the number of calendar days from the beginning of the period to the time cash flow CF_i occurs. (Note that this formula assumes that cash flows occur at the end of the day.[1]) In our example, a \$10,000 contribution occurs on 5 June, so $D_i = 5$, and there are 30 days in June, so $CD = 30$. The proportion of the measurement period for which the \$10,000 is in the portfolio is thus

$$w_i = \frac{CD - D_i}{CD} = \frac{30-5}{30} = \frac{25}{30} = 0.83$$

Applying the Modified Dietz formula to the same example gives a return of 0.51%:

$$r_{ModDietz} = \frac{V_1 - V_0 - CF}{V_0 + \sum_{i=1}^{n}(CF_i \times w_i)} = \frac{110,550 - 100,000 - 10,000}{100,000 + [10,000 \times (25/30)]} = 0.0051 = 0.51\%$$

Note that this formula as given assumes that the portfolio is not valued at the time of the external cash flow.

The Modified IRR method is another estimation approach. This method determines the internal rate of return (IRR) for the period, adjusted to take into account the timing of cash flows. The Modified IRR is the value of r that satisfies Equation 5:

$$\text{Ending Value} = V_1 = \sum_{i=1}^{n}\left[CF_i \times (1+r)^{w_i}\right] + V_0(1+r) \tag{5}$$

where the exponent, w_i, is as previously defined the ratio of the amount of time CF_i is in the portfolio to the total time in the measurement period. The equation is solved iteratively by a trial-and-error procedure, settling on the value of r that makes the series of cash flows equal to the ending fair value. The Modified IRR method is computationally intensive, but programs are available for solving the equation efficiently. (Some Modified IRR programs use the Modified Dietz return as an initial estimate or seed value.) Applying the Modified IRR method to the simple example used earlier in this section gives a result of 0.51%, the same as the rate of return found with the Modified Dietz method.

1 Cash flows can also be assumed to occur at the beginning of the day. In that case, the weight factor is adjusted to add another day to the period that the cash flow is in the portfolio: $w_i = (CD - D_i + 1)/CD$. It is incumbent upon the firm to establish and consistently apply a policy, for each composite or pooled fund, related to the weighting of cash flows.

TRUE VS. ESTIMATED TIME-WEIGHTED RETURNS

In the foregoing section, different methodologies for calculating a rate of return from a single set of input data gave different answers. To recapitulate:

Inputs:

Fair value on 31 May: $100,000

Cash flow on 5 June: + $10,000

Fair value on 5 June: $109,000 (after the cash flow)

Fair value on 30 June: $110,550

Solutions:

True time-weighted return: 0.41%

Modified Dietz method: 0.51%

Modified IRR method: 0.51%

In this particular example, the external cash flow causes the day-weighted estimates (0.51%) to vary by 10 basis points from the true time-weighted return (0.41%).

To appreciate the potentially distorting effect of external cash flows on estimated time-weighted rates of return, consider Exhibit 2 through Exhibit 4. The exhibits depict a "market index" with a value of 100 as of 31 May, and the data following each exhibit represent portfolios with a value of $100,000 on 31 May and contributions of $10,000 received on 5 June (on the left-hand side) and 15 June (on the right-hand side). In flat and steadily rising or falling markets (illustrated in Exhibit 2 and Exhibit 3), the timing of the cash flows has a relatively modest effect on the estimates' accuracy. We can observe this phenomenon by comparing the true time-weighted returns with those calculated using the Modified Dietz method. When markets are volatile, however, as illustrated in Exhibit 4, large external cash flows may have a material effect on the estimated return's accuracy. The reader should work through these examples using the formulas for the true time-weighted return and the Modified Dietz method. The calculations for the first example, on the left-hand side of Exhibit 2, were shown earlier.

Exhibit 2: Effect of Cash Flows in a Flat Market

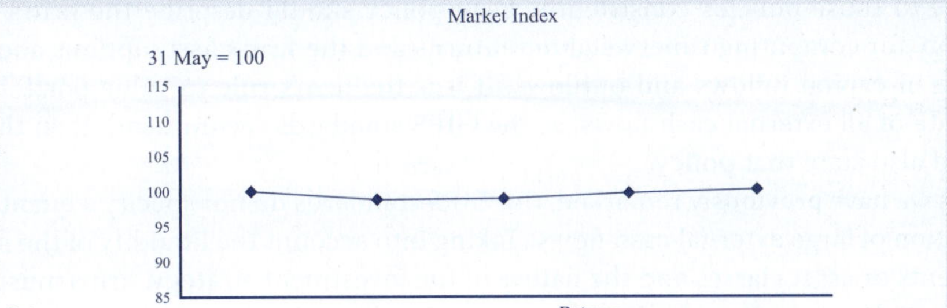

Returns			Returns		
	31-May Fair Value	$ 100,000		31-May Fair Value	$ 100,000
–1.00%	5-Jun Fair Value	$ 99,000	–0.93%	15-Jun Fair Value	$ 99,075
	Contribution	$ 10,000		Contribution	$ 10,000
	Total Fair Value	$ 109,000		Total Fair Value	$ 109,075
1.42%	30-Jun Fair Value	$ 110,550	1.35%	30-Jun Fair Value	$ 110,550
0.41%	Modified Dietz	0.51%	0.41%	Modified Dietz	0.52%

Source: Paula Gehr

Exhibit 3: Effect of Cash Flows in a Steadily Rising Market

Returns			Returns		
	31-May Fair Value	$ 100,000		31-May Fair Value	$ 100,000
2.00%	5-Jun Fair Value	$ 102,000	4.00%	15-Jun Fair Value	$ 104,000
	Contribution	$ 10,000		Contribution	$ 10,000
	Total Fair Value	$ 112,000		Total Fair Value	$ 114,000
5.88%	30-Jun Fair Value	$ 118,588	3.85%	30-Jun Fair Value	$ 118,385
8.00%	Modified Dietz	7.93%	8.00%	Modified Dietz	7.99%

Source: Paula Gehr

Exhibit 4: Effect of Cash Flows in a Volatile Market

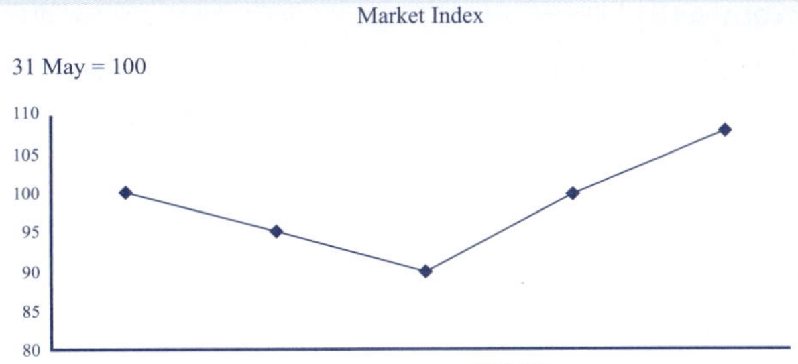

Returns			Returns		
	31-May Fair Value	$ 100,000		31-May Fair Value	$ 100,000
–5.00%	5-Jun Fair Value	$ 95,000	–10.00%	15-Jun Fair Value	$ 90,000
	Contribution	$ 10,000		Contribution	$ 10,000
	Total Fair Value	$ 105,000		Total Fair Value	$ 100,000
13.68%	30-Jun Fair Value	$ 119,364	20.00%	30-Jun Fair Value	$ 120,000
8.00%	Modified Dietz	8.64%	8.00%	Modified Dietz	9.52%

Source: Paula Gehr

The GIPS standards require firms to formulate and document composite-specific and pooled fund–specific policies for the treatment of external cash flows and to adhere to those policies consistently. Each policy should describe the firm's methodology for computing time-weighted returns and the firm's assumptions about the timing of capital inflows and outflows. If it is the firm's rule to value portfolios on the date of all external cash flows, as the GIPS standards recommend, then the firm should also state that policy.

As we have previously remarked, the GIPS standards do not specify a quantitative definition of large external cash flows. Taking into account the liquidity of the market segments or asset classes and the nature of the investment strategy, firms must make their own determinations for each composite. For example, a relatively high percentage of portfolio value might be easily deployed in a developed equity market, whereas a lower percentage of portfolio value might be deemed the appropriate criterion for a large external cash flow in a comparatively illiquid emerging debt market.

Whatever definition a firm adopts, it must document the policy and follow it without exception. If a portfolio receives a large external cash flow, as defined for the composite in which the portfolio is included, the firm is not at liberty to omit the valuation on the grounds that the market was not especially volatile during the measurement period. Inconsistent applications of firm policies constitute a breach of the GIPS standards.

IMPLEMENTATION

Return Calculation Policies

Firms must calculate time-weighted rates of return that adjust for external cash flows. Both periodic and sub-period returns must be geometrically linked. External cash flows must be treated according to the firm's composite-specific policy. These portfolios must be valued on the date of all large cash flows, and firms must define what constitutes a large cash flow for each composite in order to determine when the portfolios in that composite must be valued. Here are examples of internal policy statements addressing these elements:

Portfolio return calculation methodology: "Eastern Institutional Asset Advisors calculates each portfolio's time-weighted rate of return on a monthly basis. For periods beginning on or after 1 January 2010, portfolios are valued monthly and when large cash flows occur. In the event of a large cash flow, a sub-period return will be calculated using the Modified Dietz method and sub-period returns will be geometrically linked to calculate the monthly return. Returns for longer measurement periods are computed by geometrically linking the monthly returns."

Large external cash flows: "Eastern Institutional Asset Advisors revalues portfolios that belong to the Large-Cap Domestic Equity composite when capital equal to 10% or more of fair value as of the end of the most recent measurement period is contributed or withdrawn."

MISCELLANEOUS RETURN CALCULATION TOPICS

4

- ☐ discuss requirements of the GIPS standards with respect to return calculation methodologies, including the treatment of external cash flows, cash and cash equivalents, and expenses and fees
- ☐ explain the recommended valuation hierarchy of the GIPS standards

A firm may choose to present MWRs instead of TWRs if the firm has control over the external cash flows *and*: (1) the portfolios are **closed-end**, **fixed life**, or **fixed commitment** or (2) **illiquid investments** are a significant part of the investment strategy. Annualized, since-inception MWRs must be calculated at least annually. For periods beginning with the effective date of the 2020 GIPS Standards, daily external cash flows must be used. (External cash flows for periods prior to this date must be reflected on at least a quarterly basis.) Portfolios for which a money-weighted return is calculated must be valued at least annually and as of the period end for which performance is calculated.

Annualizing Returns

Returns for periods of less than one year must not be annualized. Extrapolating partial-year returns by annualizing them would amount to a prediction about investment results for the rest of the year.

Treatment of Cash Equivalents

Returns from cash and cash equivalents held in portfolios must be included in all total return calculations. A primary purpose of performance measurement is to enable prospective clients and, by extension, their consultants to evaluate an investment management firm's results. Within the constraints established by a client's investment policy statement (IPS), active managers often have discretion to decide what portion of a portfolio's assets to hold in cash or cash equivalents. The portfolio return will be affected by how much cash the manager elects to hold, and thus return calculations must reflect the contribution of the cash and cash equivalents to investment results. Even if the management of cash balances is handled by another firm (as is often the case in manager-of-manager arrangements), cash and cash equivalents must be included in the total return calculation.

Consider the case of an institutional investor such as a defined benefit pension plan sponsor. The structure of the sponsor's investment program is generally based on an asset/liability study identifying the optimal mix of asset classes to meet the pension fund's financial objectives at an acceptable level of risk. The sponsor retains investment management firms to invest the fund's assets in specific markets in accordance with the study results. For example, within the domestic equity allocation, the sponsor might hire one firm to invest a certain portion of the fund's assets in small-cap growth stocks and another firm to invest a portion in large-cap value stocks. The sponsor expects the managers to remain fully invested in their mandated market sectors at all times. The sponsor's IPS may, however, allow the managers to hold some amount (e.g., up to 5% of portfolio assets) in cash and cash equivalents, if only to accommodate the frictional cash that arises in the process of buying and selling securities. (The client will usually define "cash equivalents," for example, as money market instruments and fixed-income securities with less than one year to maturity.) In this case, the manager has discretion over the size of the cash position, up to 5% of assets.

Treatment of Expenses and Fees

The GIPS standards require that returns be calculated after the deduction of **transaction costs** incurred during the period. Transaction costs are the costs of buying or selling investments. These costs typically take the form of brokerage commissions, exchange fees and/or taxes, or spreads from either internal or external brokers. For private market investments, transaction costs include all legal, financial, advisory, and investment banking fees related to buying, selling, restructuring, and/or recapitalizing investments but do not include costs associated with investments that were considered but did not ultimately make it into the fund. **Custody fees** should not be considered transaction costs, even when they are charged on a per-transaction basis.

Commissions are explicit costs, generally a negotiated amount per share of common stock bought or sold, intended to compensate the broker, as the investor's agent, for arranging and settling trades. Bid–offer spreads are the difference between the price at which a dealer, acting for his firm's account, is willing to buy a security from a seller and the price at which he is willing to sell the security to a buyer. From the investor's perspective, the spread is the cost of immediacy or liquidity, and it compensates the dealer for both the cost of operations and the risk of adverse selection (the possibility that a well-informed trader has better information than the dealer has about the fundamental value of a security in the dealer's inventory). Transaction costs can be estimated for a specific portfolio only if actual transaction costs are not known.

Some portfolios may pay **bundled fees**, which can include any combination of **investment management fees**, transaction costs, custody fees, and/or **administrative fees**. **All-in fee** arrangements are common when a single company offers diverse services such as asset management, brokerage, and custody. If transaction costs cannot be identified (either actual transactions costs or estimated transactions costs based on a reasonable estimation method) and segregated from a bundle fee, composites for institutional investors must reduce the **gross-of-fees** return by the entire amount of the bundled fee or by that portion of the bundled fee that includes the transaction costs.

Valuation Requirements

Meaningful performance measurement presupposes the validity of beginning and ending asset values. Section 2 of the GIPS Standards for Firms also addresses asset valuation. Firms are required to apply a fair value methodology when valuing assets. The GIPS standards define **fair value** as the amount at which an investment could be sold in an orderly, arm's-length transaction between willing parties. The valuation must be determined using the objective, observable, unadjusted quoted market price for an identical investment in an active market on the measurement date, if available. Fair value must include any accrued income on fixed-income securities and all other investments that earn interest income (the firm may choose to recognize income on cash and cash equivalents on a cash basis rather than an accrual basis).

If objective, observable, unadjusted quoted market prices for identical investments in active markets on the measurement date are not available, the GIPS standards recommend the following alternatives, in declining order of preference:

1. quoted prices for similar investments in active markets. If such inputs are not available or appropriate, then investments should be valued based on:
2. quoted prices for identical or similar investments in markets that are not active (markets in which there are few transactions for the investment, the prices are not current, or price quotations vary substantially over time and/or between market makers). If such inputs are not available or appropriate, then investments should be valued based on:

3. market-based inputs, other than quoted prices, that are observable for the investment. If such inputs are not available or appropriate, then investments should be valued based on:
4. subjective, unobservable inputs.

IMPLEMENTATION

Valuation Policies and Procedures

Firms may enter transactions involving a wide range of financial instruments, including derivative securities, in many different markets. It is fitting, therefore, that the GIPS standards not only require firms to document their valuation policies, procedures, methodologies, and hierarchies but also recommend that the valuation hierarchies be composite-or pooled fund-specific. Normally, for investment strategies that employ plain-vanilla securities trading in robust markets, quoted prices are readily available. Other composites, however, may represent strategies that materially make use of securities that trade infrequently in relatively illiquid markets where values must be imputed or estimated. Real estate and private equity are obvious examples, but valuing investments in swaps, options, and other derivatives that are tied to underlying securities uniquely issued by specific companies may present difficulties, especially if the firm cannot refer to recent transactions in identical or similar assets. Implementing the GIPS standards offers firms an opportunity to re-examine their valuation policies, procedures, and methodologies and to define valuation hierarchies reflecting the characteristics of the securities held in each composite or pooled fund and the markets in which the strategy is executed. For assets valued using quantitative models, it is useful to list input factors such as discount rates and risk-adjusted cash flow projections and to review the basis for estimating them. Portfolio managers, security analysts, quantitative analysts, and traders should participate in these discussions. Once established, the valuation policies must be documented, followed consistently, and made available to prospective clients upon request.

COMPOSITE TIME-WEIGHTED RETURN CALCULATIONS 5

☐ explain requirements of the GIPS standards with respect to composite return calculations, including methods for asset-weighting portfolio returns

The notion of composites is central to the GIPS standards. The GIPS standards define a composite as an aggregation of one or more portfolios that are managed according to a similar investment mandate, objective, or strategy. Because composite returns convey the firm's investment results for a given investment mandate, objective, or strategy, proper composite construction is essential to achieving the ethical aims of the GIPS standards as well as the fair representation and full disclosure of the firm's performance. Provisions relating to the construction and maintenance of composites can be found in Section 3 of the GIPS standards.

Candidates should read Section 3.A, Provisions 3.A.1 through 3.A.14 of the GIPS Standards for Firms for more complete understanding of the requirements for composite and pooled fund maintenance. Candidates are not responsible for the required provisions in Section 3 related to Wrap Fee and Carve-Outs (Provisions 3.A.14 through 3.A.19).

To prevent firms from presenting only their best-performing portfolios to prospective clients, the GIPS standards require all actual, fee-paying, discretionary segregated accounts to be included in at least one composite. All actual, fee-paying, discretionary pooled funds must also be included in at least one composite if they meet a composite definition. Non-discretionary segregated accounts and pooled funds must not be included in composites. Non-fee-paying discretionary segregated accounts and pooled funds *may* be included in a composite, but additional disclosures may be required. (For example, in the interest of public service or community relations, a firm might waive the investment management fee on a charitable organization's portfolio, or a firm might use its own or its principals' capital to implement a new investment strategy.) If a strategy is offered as a pooled fund *and* a segregated account, the pooled fund must be included in a composite for that strategy. The firm does need not to create a composite for a strategy if it is offered only as a pooled fund.

Composite Time-Weighted Return Calculations

Time-weighted composite returns must be calculated in one of three ways: asset-weighting the individual portfolio returns using beginning-of-period values; using a method that reflects both beginning-of-period values and external cash flows; or using the Aggregate Return method. Exhibit 5 displays the beginning asset values of four portfolios that, taken together, constitute a composite. The exhibit also shows the external cash flows experienced by each portfolio during the month of June. For completeness, the exhibit also shows each portfolio's ending fair value.

Exhibit 5: A Composite Including Four Portfolios: Weighted External Cash Flows

	Cash Flow Weighting Factor	Portfolio ($ Thousands)				
		A	B	C	D	Total
Beginning assets (31 May)		100.00	97.40	112.94	124.47	434.81
External cash flows						
5 June	0.83	10.00	15.00			25.00
8 June	0.73				−15.00	−15.00
17 June	0.43		−5.00			−5.00
24 June	0.20				−6.50	−6.50
29 June	0.03		−2.50		−4.00	−6.50
Ending assets (30 June)		110.55	105.20	113.30	100.50	429.55
Beginning assets + Weighted cash flows		108.30	107.63	112.94	112.10	440.97
Percentage of total beginning assets		23.00%	22.40%	25.97%	28.63%	100.00%
Percentage of total beginning assets + Weighted cash flows		24.56%	24.41%	25.61%	25.42%	100.00%

Note: Weighted cash flows reflect two-decimal-place precision in the weighting factors.

Determining the relative weight of each portfolio in the composite at the beginning of the measurement period is straightforward. Portfolio A had a beginning fair value of \$100,000, and all four portfolios combined had a beginning fair value of approximately \$435,000, so the weight assigned to Portfolio A is 100/434.81 = 0.23 = 23%. As we will show in a moment, under a method reflecting only beginning-of-period values, we can calculate the composite return by multiplying the individual portfolio returns by the portfolio's beginning weight, then summing the products.

Determining a composite return when there are external cash flows is a little more complex. The cash flows must be weighted following the methodology introduced in our discussion of the Modified Dietz rate-of-return calculation. Each external cash flow is weighted in proportion to percentage of the time it is held in the portfolio during the measurement period as shown in Equation 4:

$$w_i = \frac{CD - D_i}{CD}$$

where CD is the total number of calendar days in the period and D_i is the number of calendar days since the beginning of the period until the time cash flow CF_i occurs. Exhibit 5 showed the weighting factor computed to two decimal places with this formula for each of the days in the measurement period (the month of June) on which external cash flows occur that affect any of the portfolios in the composite. It also showed the weighted external cash flows under the two methods discussed. For the method incorporating weighted external cash flows, the sum of beginning assets and weighted external cash flows, V_p, is calculated as shown in Equation 6:

$$V_p = V_0 + \sum_{i=1}^{n}(CF_i \times w_i) \tag{6}$$

where V_0 is the portfolio's beginning value and $\sum_{i=1}^{n}(CF_i \times w_i)$ is the sum of each portfolio's weighted external cash inflows and outflows. Note that the right-hand side in Equation 6 is the denominator of the Modified Dietz formula (see Equation 4).

The composite return is the weighted-average return of the individual portfolios that belong to that composite. Under the "beginning assets" weighting method, the composite return calculation is shown in Equation 7:

$$r_C = \sum\left[r_{pi} \times \frac{V_{0,pi}}{\sum_{pi=1}^{n} V_{0,pi}}\right] \tag{7}$$

where r_C is the composite return, r_{pi} is the return of an individual portfolio i, $V_{0,pi}$ is the beginning value of portfolio i, and $\sum_{pi=1}^{n} V_{0,pi}$ is the total beginning fair value of all the individual portfolios in the composite. In other words, the composite return is the sum of the individual portfolio returns weighted in proportion to their respective percentages of aggregate beginning assets.

Under the alternate "beginning assets plus weighted cash flows" method, shown in Equation 8, the return calculation uses the individual portfolios' V_P, computed earlier, in place of $V_{0,p}$:

$$r_C = \sum\left(r_{pi} \times \frac{V_{pi}}{\sum V_{pi}}\right) \tag{8}$$

Exhibit 6 supplies each individual portfolio's return for the month of June and presents the composite returns resulting from these two weighting methods.

Exhibit 6: Composite Returns

	Percentage of Beginning Assets	Percentage of Beginning Assets + Weighted Cash Flows	Return for Month of June
Portfolio A	23.00%	24.56%	0.51%
Portfolio B	22.40%	24.41%	0.28%
Portfolio C	25.97%	25.61%	0.32%
Portfolio D	28.63%	25.42%	1.36%
	100.00%	100.00%	
Composite Return:			
Based on beginning assets			0.65%
Based on beginning assets plus weighted cash flows			0.62%

Under the "beginning assets" weighting method, the composite return shown in Exhibit 6 is as follows:

$$r_C = (0.0051 \times 0.23) + (0.0028 \times 0.224) + (0.0032 \times 0.2597) + (0.0136 \times 0.2863)$$
$$= 0.0065$$
$$= 0.65\%$$

Similarly, the composite return under the "beginning assets plus weighted cash flows" method is as follows:

$$r_C = (0.0051 \times 0.2456) + (0.0028 \times 0.2441) + (0.0032 \times 0.2561)$$

$$+ (0.0136 \times 0.2542) = 0.0062 = 0.62\%$$

The Aggregate Return method combines all the composite assets and external cash flows to calculate returns as if the composite were one portfolio. Beginning assets and intra-period external cash flows can be summed and, treating the entire composite as though it were a single portfolio, the return can be computed directly with the Modified Dietz formula. This approach can be illustrated with data from Exhibit 5, using Equation 3:

$$r_{ModDietz} = \frac{V_1 - V_0 - CF}{V_0 + \sum_{i=1}^{n}(CF_i \times w_i)}$$

$$r_C = \frac{429.55 - 434.81 - 25 - (-15) - (-5) - (-6.5) - (-6.5)}{440.97}$$

$$= \frac{2.74}{440.97} = 0.0062 = 0.62\%$$

Composite time-weighted returns, except for private market investment composites, must be calculated at least monthly. The less frequently the asset-weighting exercise is conducted, the greater the likelihood that composite returns will inaccurately reflect the constituent portfolios' aggregate performance.

COMPOSITES: QUALIFYING PORTFOLIOS AND DEFINING INVESTMENT STRATEGIES

6

- ☐ explain the meaning of "discretionary" in the context of composite construction and, given a description of the relevant facts, determine whether a portfolio is likely to be considered discretionary
- ☐ explain the role of investment mandates, objectives, or strategies in the construction of composites

Investors commonly set forth investment restrictions in investment policy statements (IPSs). In addition to articulating the investor's overall financial objectives, an IPS normally expresses a number of constraints intended to limit the investment risks to which the assets are exposed. For example, the IPS may limit an individual equity portfolio's economic sector exposure to a certain percentage of portfolio assets or a certain relationship to the comparable benchmark weight: "No portfolio shall hold more than 15% of assets or 125% of the corresponding benchmark weight, whichever is greater, in any given sector, such as consumer discretionary stocks or information technology stocks." A fixed-income portfolio may be constrained to hold no securities rated below investment grade and to maintain the portfolio's weighted-average duration within a specified range, such as 75% to 125% of the benchmark duration. These restrictions are intended to preserve the portfolios from losses in value resulting from inadequate sector diversification, excessive credit quality risk, or unacceptable levels of interest rate risk.

Clearly, in addition to ensuring that the benchmark is appropriate, investors must be careful to formulate constraints that achieve their intended risk-control objectives without unduly impairing the portfolio managers' ability to act on their professional judgment regarding the relative attractiveness of sectors and securities. In other words, a well-written IPS meets the client's need for risk mitigation while respecting the portfolio manager's discretion. The manager is well advised to discuss with the client any restrictions that are incompatible with the intended investment strategy. Upon accepting the investment management assignment, however, the portfolio manager is ethically bound by the client's stated policies. Moreover, investment management agreements often incorporate the IPS, so the portfolio manager may also be legally required to comply with properly communicated client-specified constraints.

In some cases, the client's investment constraints may impinge on the portfolio manager's flexibility. Some clients may have environmental, social or governance (ESG) restrictions that prohibit investment in securities issued by companies operating in alcohol, tobacco, or gaming industries. Other clients might have restrictions that prohibit the sale of company stock. Additionally, legal restrictions may apply. For instance, a public fund might be statutorily precluded from investing in non-domestic securities. None of these constraints automatically renders a portfolio non-discretionary. Rather, in these and other cases, the portfolio manager must determine whether the client-imposed constraints are likely to materially affect her ability to execute the investment strategy. If the constraints are determined to not have a material effect, the manager could include the portfolio in a composite with portfolios that have no such restriction. If the constraint is material, the manager may include the portfolio in a composite with other, similarly constrained portfolios or classify it as non-discretionary and exclude the portfolio from all composites.

IMPLEMENTATION

Defining Discretion

The GIPS standards require that all actual fee-paying discretionary segregated accounts be included in at least one composite. (If a pooled fund meets the composite definition, it must be included in the composite.) Because discretion is a key variable that determines inclusion in or exclusion from a composite, a firm implementing the GIPS standards must have a clear, written definition of discretion. The firm must consistently apply its definition of discretion.

A client could insist that the manager retain specific holdings that might or might not otherwise be held in a portfolio. For example, the client could direct that legacy holdings with a low cost basis must not be sold because of the adverse tax consequences of realizing large gains. In such cases, retaining the asset in the portfolio may skew performance, and—whether the impact is favorable or unfavorable in any given measurement period—the outcome would not reflect the results of the manager's actual discretionary investment management. If holding the assets hinders the manager's ability to implement the intended strategy, either the entire portfolio should be considered non-discretionary and excluded from the firm's composites or the individual assets should be removed and the remaining assets for which the manager has full discretion should be included in the composite. Alternately, the firm might include a materiality threshold in its policy, enabling it to consider a portfolio discretionary if the non-discretionary assets consist of less than a certain percentage of portfolio assets.

Recognizing that degrees of discretion exist, the firm must consider the interactions among client-directed constraints, the portfolio's strategy or style, and the investment process, notably including the financial instruments used. For example, a client's investment policy might prohibit the use of derivative securities such as futures, swaps, and options. In this case, the firm must consider whether the restriction is pertinent. If a portfolio manager is managing a domestic mid-cap stock portfolio, the fact that the client prohibits the use of derivatives may be irrelevant if the manager's typical investment approach simply buys, holds, and sells common stocks. If the use of derivative securities is central to the firm's implementation of the investment mandate, however, then the client's policy may render the portfolio non-discretionary.

In some cases, the pattern of external cash flows might make a portfolio non-discretionary. For example, if a client frequently makes large withdrawals, perhaps on a regular schedule, a portfolio manager might have to maintain such a high level of liquidity that he cannot truly implement the investment strategy as he does for other portfolios with a similar stated investment mandate, objective, or strategy.

In the process of developing, testing, and refining new investment strategies, firms frequently construct model portfolios and use historical security prices to simulate hypothetical performance in past measurement periods. No model or hypothetical portfolios may be included in any composite. Firms may not link the **theoretical performance** of simulated or model portfolios with actual performance. (Model, hypothetical, backtested, or simulated returns are all considered theoretical performance. These returns can be shown as **supplemental information** but cannot be linked to actual composite or pooled fund returns.)

On the other hand, if the firm created a new strategy and managed portfolios in this strategy with its own assets—sometimes called seed money—it could include those portfolios from inception in appropriate composites (or, more likely, construct new composites reflecting the new strategies), subject to any presentation and reporting requirements related to the inclusion of non-fee-paying portfolios in composites.

To summarize the criteria for including portfolios in composites:

- All actual, fee-paying, discretionary segregated accounts must be included in at least one composite.
- Discretionary segregated accounts that are non–fee paying may be included in composites, but neither non-discretionary nor simulated or model portfolios may be included in any composite.
- Pooled funds must be included in any composite for which they meet the composite definition.
- A composite must include all portfolios that meet the composite definition.

Composites—Defining Investment Strategies

Defining and constructing meaningful composites constitute a vital step toward achieving the ideal of fair representation and the goal of providing prospective clients with useful comparative information. Under the GIPS standards, composites must be defined according to investment mandate, objective, or strategy; composites must include all portfolios that meet the composite definition; and the composite definition, including detailed criteria that determine the assignment of portfolios to the composite, must be documented in the firm's policies and procedures. Well-defined composites will be objectively representative of the firm's products and consistent with the firm's marketing strategy.

One possible hierarchy that may be helpful for the firm considering how to define composites is outlined as follows.

Investment Mandate
  Asset Classes
    Style or Strategy
      Benchmarks
        Risk/Return Characteristics

A composite based on the investment mandate bears a summary product or strategy description, such as "Global Equities." This summary description may be an entirely acceptable composite definition as long as no significant strategic differences exist among the portfolios included in the composite. It is a guiding principle of composite definition that firms are not permitted to include portfolios with different investment mandates, objectives, or strategies in the same composite.

A composite based on the constituent portfolios' asset class, such as "equity" or "fixed income," may also be acceptable; however, asset classes are broadly inclusive, and because generic descriptions are not very informative, asset class composites should be offered only if they are legitimately and meaningfully representative of the firm's products.

To afford investors a better understanding of the nature of a composite, the firm may use an asset-class modifier indicating the composite's investment style or strategy. For example, equity portfolios may be restricted to a specific economic sector, such as telecommunication services. Stocks issued by corporations competing in the same economic sector are presumably affected more or less the same way by exogenous factors such as changes in raw material prices, consumer demand, or the general level of interest rates.

Portfolios might also be classified according to a defined style. An equity style matrix that classifies portfolios by capitalization (large cap, mid-cap, and small cap) and by style (value; core, also called neutral, market oriented, or blend; and growth) might be the starting point for defining a set of composites. Fixed-income portfolios may be classified by a combination of duration and/or market segment that generally aligns with the major fixed-income indexes.

A portfolio may be assigned to one of the style categories based on the money-weighted averages of pertinent characteristics of the portfolio's holdings. For example, a portfolio holding stocks with an average market capitalization of $5 billion along with a relatively high price-to-earnings multiple, a relatively high price-to-book ratio, and a relatively low dividend yield, would likely be identified as a mid-cap growth portfolio. Alternately, the portfolio's historical monthly or quarterly returns might be regressed against the returns of pertinent capital market indexes to determine which style-specific benchmarks best explain the portfolio's performance. Evaluating the comparative merits of these approaches falls outside the scope of this reading. Suffice it to say that, given the widespread acceptance of these categories, a firm may meaningfully and usefully define composites with reference to the capitalization range and the style in which the constituent portfolios are managed.

IMPLEMENTATION

Defining Composites

One of the greatest challenges in implementing the GIPS standards is devising the set of composites that will most meaningfully represent the firm's products. A firm must create composites for the firm's strategies that are managed for or offered as a segregated account. Composites must be defined according to investment mandate, objective, or strategy. What appears to be a straightforward exercise—defining composites and assigning portfolios to them—may prove rather difficult in practice.

A useful guideline is to build a set of composites that will accurately represent the firm's distinct investment strategies. With too few composites, a firm risks overlooking significant differences and grouping diverse portfolios together into a single, overly broad composite subject to a wide dispersion of portfolio returns. With too many composites, in addition to incurring unnecessary costs, the firm runs the risk of creating narrowly defined groupings that are too much alike in investment strategy, contain too few portfolios or assets to be useful, or compromise client confidentiality.

Assuming that the definitions of the "firm" and "discretion" have been agreed upon and that a master list of portfolios has been compiled, here is a common-sense strategy a firm might follow to reach agreement on composite definitions.

1. Review the firm's organizational structure and investment process to see if distinctive strategies can be readily identified. For instance, an equity advisor might have units specializing in one or more active management strategies as well as index fund construction and quantitatively driven enhanced indexing.
2. Review the firm's existing marketing materials to determine which strategies are offered as a segregated account. If possible, review marketing materials from competitors and recently received requests for proposals (RFPs) to determine how the industry defines products similar to those the firm offers.
3. Construct a provisional framework using descriptive captions to identify possible composites.

4. Taking into consideration the clients' investment policies, test how well the firm's fee-paying, discretionary portfolios would fit the provisional framework. The inevitable identification of exceptions—that is, the discovery that some segregated accounts do not really fit any composite defined in the provisional framework—will lead to the redefinition of proposed composites or the creation of new composites. Several iterations may be needed.
5. Review the proposed set of composites to ensure that, in the aggregate, the composites are likely to satisfy the requirements of the GIPS standards.
6. Document the composite definitions in detail and circulate the definitions for final review by all affected parties within the firm.

Of course, the most effective process for defining composites may differ from one firm to another in view of variables such as organizational structure, culture, and investment strategies, among other factors. Nonetheless, composite definitions have lasting consequences, and it is highly desirable to have a plan for reaching consensus.

Firms may also define composites based on the portfolios' benchmarks, as long as the benchmarks reflect the investment strategy and the firm has no other composites with the same characteristics. This approach is particularly appropriate if the portfolios are limited to holding stocks that are held in the index.

Finally, portfolios sharing distinctive risk/return profiles may reasonably be grouped together. For example, enhanced index funds with benchmark-specific targeted excess returns and tracking error tolerances might fall into natural groups.

Fixed-income composites can likewise be meaningfully and usefully defined in many dimensions. For example, composites might conform to asset classes or market segments such as government debt, mortgage-backed securities, convertible bonds, or high-yield bonds; investment strategies such as fundamental credit analysis, sector rotation, or interest rate anticipation; or investment styles such as indexing or core-plus. However a firm chooses to define the composites representing its investment products, those composites must consist of portfolios managed in accordance with similar investment strategies or objectives.

COMPOSITES: INCLUDING AND EXCLUDING PORTFOLIOS 7

- [ ] explain requirements of the GIPS standards with respect to composite construction, including switching portfolios among composites, the timing of the inclusion of new portfolios in composites, and the timing of the exclusion of terminated portfolios from composites

The GIPS standards governing composite construction require that composites include new portfolios on a timely and consistent basis after the portfolio comes under management. Firms are required to establish, document, and consistently apply a policy of including new portfolios in the appropriate composites on a timely basis. For many strategies, new portfolios should be included as of the beginning of the next full performance measurement period after the firm receives the funds. If composite returns are calculated monthly and a portfolio is funded on 20 May, the composite should include the new portfolio as of the beginning of June. It may take time to invest the assets of a new portfolio in accordance with the desired investment strategy, however, particularly when the portfolio is funded in kind (that is, with securities other than cash and cash equivalents) and the assets have to be redeployed, or when the securities to be purchased are relatively illiquid (e.g., in emerging markets). Accordingly, the GIPS standards give firms some discretion to determine when to add the new portfolio to a composite. In such cases, the firm must establish a policy on a composite-by-composite basis and apply it consistently to all new portfolios.

In addition to winning new business, firms routinely lose relationships. Under the GIPS standards, a firm must include a terminated portfolio in the historical performance of the appropriate composite through the last full measurement period in which the firm had the discretion to manage the portfolio to the strategy. In many cases, the firm loses its discretion over the portfolio upon being notified of a pending termination. For instance, the client may instruct the firm to stop buying securities immediately and to commence the liquidation of holdings in preparation for an outbound cash transfer on a specified date. Alternately, the client may halt trading and transfer control of the portfolio to a transition management organization to facilitate moving assets to a new firm. When the firm being terminated loses its discretion over the portfolio, it should include the portfolio in the composite through the last full measurement period prior to notification of termination. To use the same example, if a firm that calculates performance monthly is informed on 20 May that its management contract is being terminated effective 31 May and is instructed to stop trading forthwith, then the firm should include the portfolio in its composite only through 30 April. In any event, it is incumbent upon the GIPS-compliant firm to have defined and documented its policies governing the removal of terminated portfolios from composites and, of course, to apply those policies consistently.

IMPLEMENTATION

Adding, Removing, and Switching Portfolios

GIPS-compliant firms must have written policies setting forth when portfolios may be added to or removed from composites. These policies should be composite-specific. For a firm that reports composite performance monthly, a policy statement could read as follows:

> "All new portfolios funded with cash or securities on or before the 15th day of the month shall be added to the appropriate composite at the beginning of the following month. All new portfolios funded with cash or securities after the 15th day of the month shall be added to the appropriate composite at the beginning of the second month after funding. All terminating portfolios will be removed from the composite at the end of the last full month for which the firm has full discretion. The historical performance of terminated portfolios shall remain in the appropriate composite."

Policies like the foregoing sample allow firms a reasonable amount of time to implement the strategy without delaying inclusion of the portfolio in the appropriate composite. Each firm must develop a policy that conforms to its own investment process while meeting the GIPS standards requirement to include portfolios in composites on a timely basis. Here is a sample statement for a policy:

> "Portfolios shall not be moved from one composite to another unless the composite is redefined or documented changes in the client's guidelines require restructuring the portfolio in such a way that another composite becomes more appropriate. The portfolio shall be removed from the original composite at the end of the last calendar month before the event

causing the removal occurred and shall be added to the appropriate new composite at the beginning of the calendar month following the date on which the portfolio is substantially invested. The historical performance of the portfolio shall remain in the original composite."

The firm's policy for adding portfolios to or removing portfolios from a composite must also include language outlining conditions under which a portfolio may be switched from one composite to another. The GIPS standards stipulate that portfolios cannot be switched from one composite to another unless documented changes in the portfolio's investment mandate, objective, or strategy or the redefinition of the composite make it appropriate. The historical performance of the portfolio must remain with the original composite. This is an important requirement; if the GIPS standards permitted firms to transfer portfolios from one composite to another at will, an unethical firm might identify and exploit opportunities to improve the reported performance of selected composites by re-populating them with the portfolios whose investment results were most advantageous during the measurement period.

The GIPS standards describe two conditions under which portfolios can be reassigned. First, a portfolio can be switched from one composite to another if the client revises the mandate, objective, or strategy governing the investment of portfolio assets and the guideline changes are documented. For instance, a client might decide to modify the portfolio mandate from mid-cap value to large-cap value, or from domestic equity to global equity, with a corresponding change in the benchmark, while retaining the same investment advisor to restructure and manage the "same" portfolio in accordance with the new strategy. Or perhaps a client might decide to allow the use of derivative securities, previously prohibited, triggering a change in the investment strategy and making it suitable to assign the portfolio to a composite made up of portfolios that use derivatives.

Second, a portfolio can be reassigned to another composite if the original composite is redefined in such a way that the portfolio no longer fits it. Generally, if a strategy changes over time, it is most appropriate to create a new composite; accordingly, the redefinition of an existing composite should be a highly unusual event.

In the event of **significant cash flows**, a portfolio may be temporarily removed from the composite.

A significant cash flow is a client-directed cash flow sufficiently large that it may temporarily prevent the firm from implementing the strategy. Significant cash flows are more likely to be an issue for strategies such as fixed income and emerging markets, wherein the liquidity of the underlying securities inhibits the ability to quickly invest the incoming cash or to conduct an orderly sale of portfolio securities to meet a cash outflow. Firms must define "significant" on an *ex ante*, composite-specific basis and must consistently follow the composite-specific significant cash flow policy.

Alternatively, firms may use **temporary new accounts** to remove the effect of a significant cash flow. Firms adopting this approach place client-initiated incoming cash and securities into a temporary account that is not included in any composite until the external cash flows have been invested in accordance with the portfolio's investment mandate, objective, or strategy, at which time they would be transferred into the main portfolio and treated as an external cash flow. Relatedly, when the client initiates a large capital withdrawal, the firm transfers cash and securities in the desired amount to a temporary account until it liquidates the securities and the funds are distributed. The transfer is treated as an external cash outflow when calculating the portfolio's time-weighted total return.

The provisions governing composite construction additionally address the issue of minimum asset levels. A firm might decide that a particular composite will not include any portfolios whose value is below a specified level, on the grounds, for instance, that the investment strategy can be fully implemented only for portfolios above a certain size. Portfolios below the minimum asset level would be considered non-discretionary with respect to that composite. If a firm establishes a minimum asset level for a composite, it must document policies addressing how portfolios will be treated if they fall below the minimum. As an example, a firm may elect to remove portfolios the month after they fall below the minimum. As another example, the firm may determine that the minimum asset level required to *add* a portfolio to a composite is $1 million but that a portfolio will not be *removed* from a composite unless its assets fall below $900,000. The GIPS standards further state that any changes to a composite-specific minimum asset level must not be applied retroactively.

If a portfolio is removed from a composite because it fell below the minimum, its prior performance must remain in the composite. The firm must determine if the portfolio that has been removed meets any other composite definition and include it in the appropriate composite in a timely and consistent manner.

8 PRESENTATION AND REPORTING REQUIREMENTS FOR COMPOSITES

- ☐ explain requirements of the GIPS standards with respect to presentation and reporting
- ☐ explain the conditions under which the performance of a past firm or affiliation may be linked to or used to represent the historical performance of a new or acquiring firm

Firms claiming compliance with the GIPS standards must make every reasonable effort to provide a GIPS Report to all prospective clients and limited distribution pooled fund investors. The GIPS Report must be one that represents the strategy being marketed to the prospect.

There are two types of GIPS Reports: a **GIPS Composite Report** and a **GIPS Pooled Fund Report**. A GIPS Composite Report includes all of the information required by the GIPS standards for a specific composite. A GIPS Pooled Fund Report includes all of the information required by the GIPS standards for a specific pooled fund. Sections 4 and 5 of the 2020 GIPS Standards for Firms address the requirements and recommendations for GIPS Composite Time-Weighted and Money-Weighted Return Reports, respectively. In this section, we will focus on certain required elements of the time-weighted return reports.

Candidates should read Provisions 4.A.1 through 4.A.12 and 4.A.18 of the GIPS Standards for Firms for a more complete understanding of the requirements relating to Composite Time-Weighted Return Reports. Candidates are not responsible for Provisions 4.A.13 through 4.A.17 relating to carve-outs and overlay strategy and wrap fee composites.

Minimum Years of Performance

For each GIPS Composite Report that includes time-weighted returns, the GIPS standards require that firms show at least 5 years of annual performance (unless the composite has been in existence for less than 5 years) and that the GIPS-compliant performance record must then be extended each year until at least 10 years of performance have been presented. If the composite has been in existence for less than 5 years, the firm may present returns since inception and build over time to the 10 years of required returns.

Required Elements of a GIPS Composite Report

The core elements of a GIPS Composite Report that presents a time-weighted return include the following:

- composite and benchmark annual returns for all years;
- the number of portfolios (if six or more) in the composite at each period end;
- the amount of assets in the composite;
- the amount of total firm assets at the end of each period;
- a measure of **internal dispersion** of individual portfolio returns for each annual period if the composite contains six or more portfolios for the full year; and
- if monthly composite returns are available, a three-year annualized *ex post* standard deviation of the composite and benchmark returns as of each annual period end.

Dispersion Measures

The GIPS standards require that for each annual period a measure of internal dispersion of the returns earned by individual portfolios in the composite be presented. This important requirement is intended to allow users to see how consistently the firm implemented its strategy across individual portfolios. A wide range of results should prompt the recipient of the performance presentation to inquire about possible causes of the variability of returns to portfolios that are purportedly managed in accordance with the same strategy. It may suggest, among many other possibilities, that the composite is defined too broadly to provide meaningful information.

The dispersion of annual returns for individual portfolios within a composite can be measured in various ways. The GIPS Glossary entry for internal dispersion mentions several acceptable methods. Let us refer to the data in Exhibit 7, showing the beginning values (in euros) and the annual rates of return earned by the 14 portfolios that were in a German equity composite for the full year 20XX. (Note that only those portfolios in the composite for the entire year are included in the calculation of this dispersion measure.) The portfolios presented in Exhibit 7 are arrayed in descending order of returns.

Exhibit 7: Data for Calculation of Dispersion

Portfolio	Beginning Value	20XX Return
A	€118,493	2.66%
B	€79,854	2.64%
C	€121,562	2.53%
D	€86,973	2.49%
E	€105,491	2.47%
F	€112,075	2.42%
G	€98,667	2.38%

Portfolio	Beginning Value	20XX Return
H	€92,518	2.33%
I	€107,768	2.28%
J	€96,572	2.21%
K	€75,400	2.17%
L	€77,384	2.07%
M	€31,264	1.96%
N	€84,535	1.93%

The Glossary in the GIPS Standards for Firms defines **internal dispersion** as "a measure of the spread of the annual returns of individual portfolios within a composite" and indicates that acceptable measures include, but are not limited to, high/low, range, and the equal-weighted or asset-weighted standard deviation of portfolio returns. Using the data in Exhibit 7, we will consider each of these measures.

The simplest method of expressing internal dispersion for an annual period is to disclose the highest and lowest returns earned by portfolios that were in the composite for the full year. In the case of the German equity composite, the highest return was 2.66% and the lowest was 1.93%. As an alternative, the high/low range—the arithmetic difference between the highest and the lowest return—might also be presented. In this case it was 0.73%, or 73 bps. In either form, the high/low disclosure is easy to understand. It has a potential disadvantage, however. In any annual period, an outlier—that is, one portfolio with an abnormally high or low return—may be present, resulting in a measure of dispersion that is not entirely representative of the distribution of returns. Although they are more difficult to calculate and to interpret, other dispersion measures may convey better information.

The standard deviation of returns for portfolios included in the composite is another acceptable measure of internal dispersion. As applied to composites, standard deviation measures the cross-sectional dispersion of returns for portfolios included in the composite for the full year. The standard deviation for a composite in which the constituent portfolios are equally weighted is calculated using Equation 9:

$$S_c = \sqrt{\frac{\sum_{i=1}^{n}\left(r_i - \bar{r}_c\right)^2}{n}} \tag{9}$$

where r_i is the return of each individual portfolio, $\bar{r}_c$ is the equal-weighted mean or arithmetic mean return to the portfolios in the composite, and n is the number of portfolios in the composite. Applying Equation 9 to the portfolio data given in Exhibit 7, assuming equal weighting, the mean return is 2.32% and the standard deviation is 22 bps (0.22%). If the individual portfolio returns are normally distributed around the mean return, then approximately two-thirds of the portfolios will have returns falling between the mean plus the standard deviation (2.32% + 0.22% = 2.54%) and the mean minus the standard deviation (2.32% – 0.22% = 2.10%).

Some firms prefer to present the asset-weighted standard deviation rather than the equal-weighted standard deviation. The asset-weighted standard deviation of individual portfolio returns within a composite can be calculated using Equation 10:

$$S_{C_{aw}} = \sqrt{\sum_{i=1}^{n}\left[\left(r_i - \bar{r}_{proxy}\right)^2 \times w_i\right]} \tag{10}$$

where $\bar{r}_{proxy}$ is the asset-weighted mean return of portfolios 1 through n (see Equation 9); w_i is the weight of portfolio i, calculated as the ratio of the beginning value of portfolio i to the total beginning value of the assets of portfolios 1 through n, that is, $w_i = \frac{V_{0,i}}{V_{0,\,Total}}$; and the sum of the weights w_1 through w_n is 1.

$$\bar{r}_{proxy} = \sum_{i=1}^{n}(w_i \times r_i) \qquad (11)$$

Applying Equation 11 and 12 to the data given in Exhibit 7, we find that the asset-weighted standard deviation is 21 bps (0.21%).

Note that the GIPS standards do not limit firms to using one of the measures of internal dispersion described here. A firm may prefer another way of expressing composite dispersion. The method chosen should, however, fairly represent the range of returns for each annual period.

The 2020 GIPS Standards for Firms also require that firms present information about the historical variability of composite and benchmark returns. Specifically, the GIPS standards state that, where monthly composite returns are available, firms must present, as of each annual period end, the three-year annualized *ex post* standard deviation of the monthly returns of both the composite and the benchmark. The rationale is to give prospective clients an indication of the risk of an investment strategy as executed by the firms under consideration. Because all GIPS Composite Reports include the same risk measure, and that measure is based on historical experience rather than subjective inputs, the GIPS standards allow for some degree of comparability among firms that claim compliance.

Portability

The "portability" of past performance is a complex and sometimes contentious subject. Performance from a past firm or affiliation may be linked to the performance of the new or acquiring firm if the new or acquiring firm meets certain requirements. The requirements, which apply on a composite-specific basis, are that (1) substantially all the investment decision makers are employed by the new or acquiring firm, (2) the decision-making process remains substantially intact and independent within the new or acquiring firm, (3) the new or acquiring firm has records that document and support the reported performance, and (4) there must be no break in the track record between the past firm or affiliation and the new or acquiring firm. If there is a break in the track record between the past firm and the new or acquiring firm, and if the first three portability tests are met, then the performance from the past firm or affiliation may be used to represent the historical performance of the new or acquiring firm—but the two performance records may not be linked. If a GIPS-compliant firm acquires another firm or affiliation, the firm is given a one-year "grace period" to bring any non-compliant assets into compliance for future reporting periods.

Sample Reports

Appendices A and B of the 2020 GIPS Standards for Firms contain several sample GIPS Composite and Pooled Fund Reports. We have included Sample 1 in Exhibit 8.

Exhibit 8: Composite with Time-Weighted Returns

Spinning Top Investments Large-Cap Growth Composite, 1 February 2011–31 December 2020

Year	Composite Gross Return TWR (%)	Composite Net Return TWR (%)	Benchmark Return (%)	3-Year Std Deviation		Number of Portfolios	Internal Dispersion (%)	Composite Assets ($ M)	Firm Assets[b] ($ M)
				Composite Gross (%)	Benchmark (%)				
2011[a]	2.18	1.25	1.17			31	n/a	165	n/a
2012	18.66	17.49	15.48			34	2	235	n/a
2013	41.16	39.90	33.36			39	5.7	344	n/a
2014	14.50	13.37	13.03	11.30	9.59	45	2.8	445	1,032
2015	6.52	5.47	5.67	12.51	10.68	48	3.1	520	1,056
2016	8.22	7.15	7.09	12.95	11.15	49	2.8	505	1,185
2017	33.78	32.48	30.18	12.29	10.53	44	2.9	475	1,269
2018	-0.84	-1.83	-0.65	13.26	11.91	47	3.1	493	1,091
2019	33.08	31.78	29.76	12.81	11.71	51	3.5	549	1,252
2020	7.51	6.44	6.30	13.74	12.37	54	2.5	575	1,414

[a] *Returns are for the period 1 February 2011 to 31 December 2011.*
[b] *Spinning Top investments acquired the composite through an acquisition of ABC Capital in May 2014. Firm assets prior to 2014 are not presented because the composite was not part of the firm.*

Disclosures

1. Spinning Top Investments claims compliance with the Global Investment Performance Standards (GIPS®) and has prepared and presented this report in compliance with the GIPS standards. Spinning Top Investments has been independently verified for the periods 1 January 2011 to 31 December 2020. The verification report is available upon request. A firm that claims compliance with the GIPS standards must establish policies and procedures for complying with all the applicable requirements of the GIPS standards. Verification provides assurance on whether the firm's policies and procedures related to composite and pooled fund maintenance, as well as the calculation, presentation, and distribution of performance, have been designed in compliance with the GIPS standards and have been implemented on a firm-wide basis. Verification does not provide assurance on the accuracy of any specific performance report.
2. Spinning Top Investments is an equity investment manager that invests solely in US-based securities. Spinning Top Investments is defined as an independent investment management firm that is not affiliated with any parent organization. Spinning Top Investments acquired ABC Capital in May 2014.
3. The Large Cap Growth Composite includes all institutional portfolios that invest in large-cap US stocks that are considered to have growth in earnings prospects that are superior to that of the average company within the XYZ Large Cap Growth Index. Key material risks include the risks that stock prices will decline and that the composite will underperform its benchmark. The account minimum for the

composite is $5 million. Prior to July 2016, the account minimum was $2 million. Prior to March 2020, the name of the composite was the Growth Composite.

4. Performance prior to May 2014 occurred while the investment management team was affiliated with another firm. The investment management team has managed the composite since its inception, and the investment process has not changed. The historical performance has been linked to performance earned at Spinning Top Investments.
5. The benchmark is the XYZ Large Cap Growth Index, a market-capitalization-weighted equity index of all US stocks with a market cap greater than $10 billion and a growth tilt.
6. Returns presented are time-weighted returns. Valuations are computed and performance is reported in US dollars.
7. Gross-of-fees returns are presented before management and custodial fees but after all trading expenses. Composite and benchmark returns are presented gross of non-reclaimable withholding taxes. Net-of-fees returns are calculated by deducting a model management fee of 0.083%, 1/12th of the highest management fee of 1.00%, from the monthly gross composite return. The management fee schedule for separate accounts is as follows: 1.00% on the first $25 million; 0.60% thereafter. The management fee schedule and total expense ratio for the Large Cap Collective Fund, which is included in the composite, are 0.65% on all assets and 0.93%, respectively.
8. Policies for valuing investments, calculating performance, and preparing GIPS reports are available upon request.
9. A list of composite descriptions and a list of broad distribution pooled funds are available upon request.
10. The composite was created in November 2011, and the inception date is 1 February 2011.
11. As of 1 January 2014, internal dispersion is calculated using the equal-weighted standard deviation of annual gross returns of those portfolios that were included in the composite for the entire year. Prior to 2014, internal dispersion was calculated using asset-weighted standard deviation.
12. The three-year annualized standard deviation measures the variability of the composite gross returns and the benchmark returns over the preceding 36-month period.
13. Effective 1 November 2011, portfolios are removed from the composite if they have a significant cash flow. A significant cash flow is defined as a contribution or withdrawal greater than 25% of the beginning market value of a portfolio. The portfolio is removed from the composite for the month in which the significant cash flow occurred.
14. GIPS® is a registered trademark of CFA Institute. CFA Institute does not endorse or promote this organization, nor does it warrant the accuracy or quality of the content contained herein.

9 VERIFICATION

☐ discuss the purpose, scope, and process of verification

Verification may be informally and unofficially characterized as a process in which an independent expert assesses a firm's policies and procedures for constructing composites and calculating and presenting performance in light of the requirements of the GIPS standards. Verification is intended to provide the firm and the users of its GIPS Reports greater confidence in its claim of compliance with the GIPS standards. Verification does not provide assurance as to the accuracy of any particular composite or pooled fund presentation. In addition to making the claim of compliance on a firm-wide basis more credible, however, the verification process may benefit the firm in other ways: increased knowledge in the performance measurement team, consistently higher quality of performance presentations, improved internal processes and procedures, and potential marketing advantages. Above all, verification supports the guiding principles of fair representation and full disclosure of investment performance.

The GIPS standards recommend that firms undergo verification.

IMPLEMENTATION

Selecting a Verification Firm

Verification is a major undertaking, and it is crucial for the investment management firm to choose an independent verifier whose resources match the firm's needs. At the outset of the selection process, the investment management firm approaching verification should consider the scope of its operations and the nature of its products. The requirements of a large investment management organization with a presence in markets around the world will differ from those of a firm operating in only a single country. Similarly, a hedge fund manager, a manager who engages in real estate or private equity investing, a quantitatively oriented manager whose investment strategies rely heavily on the use of derivative securities, or a manager who manages tax-aware portfolios for individuals may have more specialized requirements than a manager who manages funds for tax-exempt institutions such as pension plans and charitable foundations. These factors should be communicated to potential verifiers and reflected in the selection criteria.

Some organizations have standard RFP templates that can be adapted for specific purposes. The RFP should include a description of the issuing organization and a statement on the scope of the project. Firms investigating verifiers' qualifications might consider conducting an internet search and initially asking RFP respondents for the following information:

- a description of the verification firm, including its history, ownership, and organizational structure; a description of the performance-related services it offers; and a representative list of verification assignments completed indicating the nature of the investment management firm verified (e.g., "institutional client division of a regional bank");
- an explanation of the firm's approach to project management, sampling, and testing;
- the roles and biographies, including professional designations, of the verifiers who will be assigned to this project;

- client references, including contact details, and information about the number of clients added and lost over a specific period (for instance, the last three years);
- the verification firm's fees; and
- a preliminary project plan setting forth the major tasks and estimated timeframes for completion of the verification.

Scope of Verification

Verification, which must be performed by a qualified and independent third party, provides assurance on whether the firm's policies and procedures related to composite and pooled fund maintenance, as well as the calculation, presentation, and distribution of performance have been designed in compliance with the GIPS standards and have been implemented on a firm-wide basis. A verifier must conduct the verification in accordance with the GIPS Standards for Verifiers.

A single verification report is issued only with respect to the whole firm; verification cannot be carried out on a single composite or pooled fund. If a firm does not meet *all* the requirements of the GIPS standards, it may not state or in any other way represent that it is in compliance with the GIPS standards—a firm cannot claim that a single composite is "in compliance," or that all the equity strategies are "in compliance."

A firm that is verified may choose to have a detailed **performance examination** conducted on one or more specific composites or pooled funds, and it may state that a composite has been examined *if* a performance examination report has been issued for the specific composite.

Verification Process

The GIPS Standards for Verifiers outlines various procedures that verifiers must follow in the course of conducting a verification. We will focus here on the requirements for planning, sample selection and testing, as these elements will help the reader understand the scope and process of verification.

Verifiers must learn about the firm, including its corporate structure and how it operates, and they must understand the firm's policies and procedures for complying with all applicable requirements and adopted recommendations of the GIPS standards. Verifiers must not only obtain a copy of the firm's GIPS-related policies and procedures but also ensure that all applicable policies and procedures are properly included and adequately documented. Finally, verifiers must understand the policies, procedures, and methodologies the firm uses to value portfolios and compute investment performance.

Although verification is conducted on a firm-wide basis, verifiers may use a sampling methodology to conduct the required testing. When selecting sample portfolios, verifiers must take into consideration the number of composites and pooled funds at the firm and the number of portfolios in each composite. In addition, verifiers must also take into account the total assets under management, the internal control structure at the firm, the number of years being verified, the systems used in the construction and maintenance of composites, the method of calculating performance, and whether the firm uses external performance measurement services. The selection of sample accounts for testing is a critical step in the verification process. If the verifier encounters errors or discovers that the firm's record-keeping is deficient, a larger sample or additional verification procedures may be warranted.

IMPLEMENTATION

Preparing for Verification

The investment management firm undertaking verification should gather the following information. The verifiers may use this information to prepare a fee estimate and a project plan, and they will need it in the course of the review.

- information about the firm, including its corporate structure and the types of investment product it manages;
- sample GIPS Reports and marketing materials;
- *all* of the firm's policies and procedures used to establish and maintain compliance with the GIPS standards, such as the firm's definition of discretion, the sources, methods, and review procedures for asset valuations, the time-weighted rate-of-return calculation methodology, the treatment of external cash flows, the computation of composite returns, the correction of errors, etc.;
- the complete list of composite and limited distribution pooled fund descriptions and a list of all broad distribution pooled funds (descriptions are not required for broad distribution pooled funds);
- composite definitions, including benchmarks and the criteria for including portfolios;
- a list of all portfolios under management, with each portfolio's value;
- a list of all the portfolios that have been in each composite during the verification period, the dates they were in the composites, and documentation supporting any changes to the portfolios in the composites; and
- a list of all portfolios excluded from all composites.

The verifiers will require the investment management agreements and investment policy statements for selected portfolios and historical portfolio- and composite-level performance data for sampling and testing. Although the items listed here represent a good starting point for initiating a verification, other information requirements will likely surface during the course of the verification.

Verifiers must perform sufficient testing procedures to determine that the firm satisfies certain fundamental requirements with respect to recordkeeping, policies and procedures (including error correction policies), the definition of the firm, the completeness of the list of composite and limited distribution pooled fund descriptions, and the calculation of total firm assets. Verifiers must conduct a series of tests to determine that portfolios are properly assigned to composites and that portfolios not included in composites have been properly excluded. They must evaluate outlier returns within a sample of the firm's composites for possible indications of errors in return calculation and/or mis-assignment of a portfolio to the composite.

Verifiers must review selected portfolios to determine that the treatment of certain input data is consistent with the firm's policies and the requirements of the GIPS standards. The GIPS standards specifically identify the classification of portfolio flows (for example, receipts, disbursements, dividends, interest, fees, and taxes) as one such item. Other items to evaluate include the treatment of: dividend and interest income; taxes, tax reclaims, and tax accruals; fees and expenses; and the accounting treatment and valuation methodologies for investments.

The verifier must determine that portfolio holdings, income, and cash flows used in calculating returns are supported by documentation from independent third parties, such as custodial or brokerage statements, as applicable.

We have already stressed that verification does not provide assurance that specific composite or pooled fund returns are correctly calculated and presented. Nonetheless, testing the firm's performance-related calculations is an important element of the verification process. Verifiers must determine that the firm has calculated and presented performance in accordance with the requirements of the GIPS standards as well as with the firm's policies and procedures. In so doing, they must recalculate rates of return for selected portfolios and composites to confirm that a return formula that meets the requirements of the GIPS standards is used and that fees and expenses have been treated in conformity with both the GIPS standards and the firm's policies and procedures.

Testing the construction and maintenance of composites is central to the verification process. Verifiers must obtain a list of all portfolios in the composite, including closed portfolios; select a sampling of new, existing, and closed portfolios for review; and perform sufficient procedures to determine that the selected portfolios are appropriately classified as discretionary or non-discretionary. In making this determination, verifiers will refer to the firm's policies and procedures related to investment discretion and the selected portfolios' investment management agreements and/or investment guidelines.

Verifiers must determine that portfolios sharing the same investment mandate, objective, or strategy are included in the same composite and that the timing of portfolios' inclusion in and exclusion from composites is in accordance with the firm's policies and procedures. Finally, verifiers must determine that portfolios' movements from one composite to another are appropriate and consistent with the redefinition of the composite or documented changes to the investment mandate, objective, or strategy.

Finally, verifiers must test a sample of GIPS Reports to ensure that the calculations are accurate and that the report includes all the required information and disclosures. Moreover, the information and disclosures must be consistent with the firm's documented policies and procedures and the firm's records. The verifier must also evaluate a sample of the firm's marketing materials to ensure that when an advertisement references the GIPS standards, the reference to the GIPS standards is proper, calculations in the advertisement are correct, and the advertisement includes all the required information and disclosures.

We have remarked that verification alone, without a specifically focused performance examination, does not ensure that any particular presentation of composite or pooled fund performance meets the requirements of the GIPS standards or represents investment results fairly, completely, and accurately. A verification report issued by a verifier who meets or exceeds the required verification procedures, as summarized here, lends additional credibility to the firm's claim of compliance with the GIPS standards.

SUMMARY

The Global Investment Performance Standards for Firms meet the need for globally accepted standards for investment management firms in calculating and presenting their results to clients and prospective clients. The GIPS standards will continue to evolve to address additional aspects of performance presentation. Firms that claim compliance must meet all applicable requirements, including not only the provisions of the GIPS standards but also any Guidance Statements, interpretations, and Questions & Answers published by CFA Institute and the GIPS standards governing bodies. Practitioners should register for the GIPS Newsletter to stay informed about existing and new requirements and recommended best practices. CFA Institute and other organizations offer publications and conduct conferences and workshops designed to help practitioners implement and maintain compliance with the GIPS standards.

This reading has made the following points:

- Only investment management firms and asset owners that manage assets on a discretionary basis—and compete for business—may claim compliance with the GIPS Standards for Firms.
- The objectives of the GIPS standards are as follows: (1) Promote investor interests and instill investor confidence; (2) ensure accurate and consistent data; (3) obtain worldwide acceptance of a single standard for calculating and presenting performance; (4) promote fair, global competition among investment firms; and (5) promote industry self-regulation on a global basis.
- When the GIPS standards conflict with law and/or regulations regarding the calculation and presentation of performance, firms must comply with the law or regulations and disclose the conflict in the GIPS Report.
- Required fundamentals of compliance with the GIPS standards include properly defining the firm, providing GIPS Reports to all prospective clients/investors, adhering to applicable laws and regulations, and ensuring that information presented is not false or misleading.
- A "firm" is an investment firm, subsidiary, or division held out to the public as a distinct business entity.
- A composite is an aggregation of one or more portfolios managed according to a similar investment mandate, objective, or strategy. The composite return is the weighted average of the return of all portfolios in the composite.
- All discretionary, fee-paying, segregated accounts must be included in at least one composite. All discretionary, fee-paying pooled funds must be included in any composite for which they meet the composite definition. A portfolio is discretionary if the firm is able to implement the intended investment strategy.
- Firms must formulate, document, and adhere to composite- and pooled fund–specific policies for the treatment of external cash flows and to adhere to those policies consistently.
- The GIPS standards mandate the use of certain calculation methodologies to facilitate comparability of results among firms. Time-weighted returns are required for all portfolios except portfolios meeting certain criteria.
- Money-weighted returns may be presented instead of time-weighted returns if the firm has control over the external cash flows into the portfolios in the composite or the pooled fund and at least one of the following conditions is met: the portfolios in the composite are (or the pooled fund is): 1) closed-end; 2) fixed life; 3) fixed commitment; or 4) have illiquid investments as a significant part of the investment strategy.
- Returns for periods of less than one year must not be annualized.
- Returns from cash and cash equivalents must be included in all total return calculations.
- Returns must be calculated after the deduction of transaction costs.
- Assets must be valued using a fair value methodology. If objective, observable, unadjusted quoted market prices for identical investments in active markets on the measurement date are available, they must be used. If they are not available, firms may use, in this order: (1) quoted prices for similar investments in markets that are active; (2) quoted prices for identical or similar investments in markets that are not active; (3) market-based inputs, other than quoted prices, that are observable for the investment; or (4) subjective, unobservable inputs.

- A firm must have a clear, written definition of discretion that is consistently applied.
- Firms may not link the theoretical performance of simulated or model portfolios with actual performance.
- GIPS Composite Reports that present TWRs must include the following key items:
    - at least five years of annual performance (unless the composite has been in existence for a shorter period), building to a minimum of 10 years of returns;
    - composite and benchmark annual returns for all years;
    - the number of portfolios (if six or more) in the composite at each period end;
    - the amount of assets in the composite;
    - the amount of total firm assets at the end of each period;
    - a measure of internal dispersion of individual portfolio returns for each annual period and, where monthly returns are available; and
    - the three-year annualized *ex post* standard deviation of the composite and of the benchmark as of each annual period end.
- Performance from a past firm or affiliation may be linked to the performance of the new or acquiring firm if (1) substantially all the investment decision makers are employed by the new or acquiring firm, (2) the decision-making process remains substantially intact and independent within the new or acquiring firm, (3) the new or acquiring firm has records that document and support the reported performance, and (4) there is no break in the track record between the past firm or affiliation and the new or acquiring firm.
- Verification provides assurance on whether the firm's policies and procedures related to composite and pooled fund maintenance, as well as the calculation, presentation, and distribution of performance have been designed in compliance with the GIPS standards and have been implemented on a firm-wide basis.
- Verifiers must determine if the firm satisfies the GIPS standards requirements with respect to recordkeeping, policies and procedures, the definition of the firm, the completeness of the list of composites and limited distribution pooled fund descriptions, and the calculation of total firm assets.
- A verification report may be issued only with respect to the whole firm.

PRACTICE PROBLEMS

1. Company C manages money for both retail and institutional clients. There are two autonomous groups within the company: "Company C Institutional Investment Management," which manages institutional assets, and "Company C Retail Investors," which manages retail assets. How should Company C define itself as a firm to comply with the GIPS standards?

2. Firm A is a multinational investment firm with offices around the world, including Japan, Australia, the United Kingdom, and the United States. Although all of its offices are part of the global parent firm, each office is registered with the appropriate national regulatory authority and each is held out to clients and prospective clients as a distinct business entity. Firm A (United States) claims compliance with the GIPS standards. Can the US entity claim compliance with the GIPS standards?

3. Which statement *most accurately* expresses a requirement of the GIPS standards?

   A. Non-fee-paying portfolios must not be included in composites.

   B. All actual fee-paying discretionary segregated accounts must be included in at least one composite.

   C. All actual fee-paying discretionary segregated accounts must be included in only one composite.

4. Use the information in the following table to answer this question (amounts in €):

Date	Fair Value	External Cash Flow	Fair Value Post Cash Flow
31 December 2018	200,000		
31 January 2019	208,000		
16 February 2019	217,000	+40,000	257,000
28 February 2019	263,000		
22 March 2019	270,000	–30,000	240,000
31 March 2019	245,000		

   Calculate the rate of return for this portfolio for January, February, March, and the first quarter of 2019 using revaluing for large cash flows methodology (assume "large" is defined as greater than 5%).

5. The GIPS standards do **not** require firms to value portfolios in accordance with:

   A. the definition of fair value.

   B. composite-specific valuation policies.

   C. generally accepted principles of financial accounting.

6. Convenable Capital Management manages an equity portfolio for the Flender Company. Cash held in the portfolio is invested by Flender's existing custodial bank. Must Convenable include cash and cash equivalents in the portfolio return calculations?

   A. Yes

B. No, the cash is not invested by Convenable

C. No, Convenable does not have discretion over the selection of the custodian

7. Under the GIPS standards, the *most* accurate statement is that transaction costs do **not** include:

   A. spreads from internal brokers.

   B. brokerage commissions.

   C. custody fees charged per transaction.

The following information relates to questions 8-10

A European equity composite contains three portfolios whose cash flow weighting factors are as follows.

	Cash Flow Weighting Factor	Portfolio (€ millions)		
		A	B	C
Fair value as of 31 July		74.9	127.6	110.4
External cash flows:				
8 August	0.742		−15	
12 August	0.613	7.5		
19 August	0.387		−5	15
Fair value as of 31 August		85.3	109.8	128.4

8. Calculate the returns of Portfolio A, Portfolio B, and Portfolio C for the month of August using the Modified Dietz formula.

9. Calculate the August composite return by asset-weighting the individual portfolio returns using beginning-of-period values.

10. Calculate the August composite return by asset-weighting the individual portfolio returns using a method that reflects both beginning-of-period values and external cash flows.

11. Can a firm include a single portfolio in more than one of the firm's composites?

12. In March 2016, Tan/Lim Asset Management, a GIPS-compliant firm, introduced a new technical analysis model that management believed would be a powerful tool in tactical asset allocation. After extensive backtesting, Tan/Lim began to use the model to manage actual "live" portfolios in June 2016, and managers constructed a composite composed of actual, fee-paying, discretionary portfolios managed in accordance with the model. In 2019, after three very successful years of managing client funds in this way, management decided that because the actual performance of live portfolios validated the model's performance, the firm should present the simulated performance of the model through the backtesting period to prospective clients. Tan/Lim proceeded to link the backtested returns to the actual performance of the composite and to present 3-, 5- and 10-year

performance as a continuous record in GIPS Reports. Does this practice comply with the GIPS standards?

13. Midwest National Bank manages a domestic equity portfolio for the Springfield Municipal Employees' Retirement Fund (SMERF), a mature defined benefit pension plan. The SMERF portfolio is included in Midwest's Institutional Equity composite. The composite description states, "Portfolios included in the Institutional Equity composite are actively managed for long-term capital appreciation." SMERF's investment policy statement includes the following provisions:

    All security transactions must be approved in advance by the SMERF Investment Committee. SMERF anticipates making regular net withdrawals in substantial amounts from the portfolio to meet pension liabilities. SMERF staff will prepare a schedule of withdrawals at the beginning of each fiscal year. The portfolio manager must manage liquidity so as to disburse funds in accordance with the withdrawal schedule.

    In view of these restrictions, discuss whether Midwest National Bank can justify including the SMERF portfolio in the composite.

14. A fixed-income portfolio is *most likely* to be considered non-discretionary if the client's investment policy states that:

    A. securities held at a gain must not be sold.

    B. the average credit quality must be investment grade.

    C. securities held in the portfolio must be issued in developed markets.

15. A charitable foundation transfers securities in kind to Taurus Asset Management Ltd. to fund a new bank loan portfolio. Taurus estimates that after liquidating the transferred securities, it will take five months to invest the foundation's assets in bank loans. Which statement *best* describes a requirement of the GIPS standards? Taurus must include the foundation's portfolio in the appropriate composite:

    A. on a timely and consistent basis.

    B. when the assets are substantially invested.

    C. as of the beginning of the next full measurement period.

16. Ord Capital Management, an investment management firm that claims compliance with the GIPS standards, manages a global equity portfolio for a pension plan sponsored by Chimie Bio-Industrielle. On 15 April, the plan sponsor notifies Ord that the firm will be terminated as of the end of the month and instructs the manager to stop trading immediately. Assuming Ord calculates composites using monthly portfolio returns, Ord must include the Chimie portfolio in the historical returns of the composite to which it belongs up to:

    A. 31 March.

    B. 15 April.

    C. 30 April.

17. Southwest Capital Advisors LLC manages a fixed-income composite in accordance with an enhanced indexing strategy that makes strategic use of high-yield and emerging market bonds in addition to investment grade bonds issued in developed markets. The Merrimack Company, a family office, has a portfolio that is

included in the firm's fixed-income enhanced indexing composite. Merrimack informs Southwest in writing that, because of changes in its investment policy, the portfolio can no longer hold high-yield or emerging market bonds. In accordance with the GIPS standards, Southwest decides to switch the Merrimack portfolio to another composite. The historical performance of the portfolio must be:

A. reflected in both composites.

B. switched to the new composite.

C. retained in the enhanced indexing composite.

The following information relates to questions 18-20

Bamako Investment Management defines its core-plus fixed-income composite as containing all discretionary portfolios of more than $10 million that are invested in accordance with a strategy that includes domestic high-yield debt in addition to US government and agency securities and investment-grade bonds issued by US corporations. The composite benchmark is 75% Bloomberg Barclays Capital US Government/Credit Index and 25% Bloomberg Barclays Capital US High Yield Index, rebalanced monthly.

18. The core-plus fixed-income composite includes a portfolio managed on behalf of the Bida Academy endowment fund. The trustees of Bida inform Bamako in writing that because of a change in investment policy, the endowment fund is no longer permitted to hold below-investment-grade securities. Bamako determines that henceforth, the Bida portfolio should be included in the core fixed-income composite rather than the core-plus fixed-income composite. The historical record of the portfolio must be:

    A. included in both composites.

    B. kept in the core-plus fixed-income composite.

    C. excluded from the core-plus fixed-income composite.

19. After an extended period of rising interest rates, the value of Bouwa Special Equipment Company's core-plus fixed-income portfolio falls below the composite minimum of $10 million. The Bouwa portfolio remains below the composite-specific minimum asset level for nine months, at which point the client makes an additional contribution that brings it back above $10 million in assets. During the nine months the portfolio is below the composite minimum asset level, Bamako must:

    A. temporarily switch the Bouwa portfolio to the firm's miscellaneous composite.

    B. include the Bouwa portfolio in the core-plus fixed-income composite in all measurement periods.

    C. exclude the Bouwa portfolio from the core-plus fixed-income composite for the period it was below the minimum asset level.

20. Mahe Manufacturing Company, a core-plus fixed-income client, informs Bamako in writing that, in the future, all security transactions must be approved in

advance by Mahe's controller. The *most likely* consequence is that Bamako must prospectively exclude the Mahe portfolio from:

A. all composites.

B. total firm assets.

C. the core-plus fixed-income composite only.

---

21. What is the minimum number of portfolios that a composite must contain to comply with the GIPS standards? Must a firm disclose the number of portfolios in a composite?

22. Macondo Institutional Asset Management has been managing equity, fixed-income, and balanced accounts since 2007. The firm became GIPS-compliant on 1 January 2012 and has prepared GIPS Composite Reports using time-weighted returns for the 2007–2019 period. Fixed-income performance was poor prior to 2015, when a new team of managers was brought on board. When Jorge Garcia joins Macondo as marketing director in June 2020, he suggests showing performance starting with calendar 2015, the first year that performance started to improve. He proposes to show composites with returns for the five calendar years 2015 through 2019. Does this course of action comply with the GIPS standards?

23. Dylan O'Connor is a portfolio manager at JEMStone Asset Management. He makes all the investment decisions for the portfolios in the firm's Emerging Market composite, supported by JEMStone's research department and trading desk. Acella Investment Advisors is seeking to establish an emerging market investment strategy and hires O'Connor to join Acella. Can Acella link O'Connor's historical performance while at JEMStone to the performance of its new strategy and comply with the GIPS standards?

24. It is *most* accurate to say that verification:

    A. makes the claim of compliance more credible.

    B. certifies that the firm has adequate internal controls.

    C. ensures the accuracy of specific composite presentations.

25. Renner, Williams & Woods decides to have its equity and balanced composites verified. Because the firm has only a handful of fixed-income accounts and does not present fixed-income management results in marketing materials shown to prospects, management decides that it would be a waste of time and money to hire a verification firm to verify such a small composite. Is it possible for Renner, Williams & Woods to obtain a firm-wide verification that covers only the equity and balanced composites?

SOLUTIONS

1. The GIPS standards encourage firms to adopt the broadest, most meaningful definition of a firm. Company C should consider defining itself to include the assets managed by both the institutional entity and the retail entity for the purposes of claiming compliance with the GIPS standards. Company C could define the two autonomous entities as separate firms, however, if each subsidiary is held out to clients and prospective clients as a distinct business unit.

2. Yes, the US entity is a distinct business entity and thus meets the definition of a firm under the GIPS standards.

3. B is correct. The GIPS standards require that all actual, fee-paying, discretionary segregated accounts must be included in at least one composite. Although non-fee-paying discretionary accounts may be included in a composite (with appropriate disclosure), non-discretionary segregated accounts must not be included in a firm's composites.

4. January:

   $R_{\text{Jan}} = (208{,}000 - 200{,}000)/200{,}000 = \mathbf{4.00\%}$

   February:

   $R_{\text{Feb1-15}} = (217{,}000 - 208{,}000)/208{,}000 = 4.33\%$

   $R_{\text{Feb16-28}} = (263{,}000 - 257{,}000)/257{,}000 = 2.33\%$

   $R_{\text{Feb1-28}} = [(1 + 0.0433) \times (1 + 0.0233)] - 1 = \mathbf{6.76\%}$

   March:

   $R_{\text{Mar1-21}} = (270{,}000 - 263{,}000)/263{,}000 = 2.66\%$

   $R_{\text{Mar22-31}} = (245{,}000 - 240{,}000)/240{,}000 = 2.08\%$

   $R_{\text{Mar1-31}} = [(1 + 0.0266) \times (1 + 0.0208)] - 1 = \mathbf{4.80\%}$

   Quarter 1:

   $R_{\text{QT1}} = [(1 + 0.0400) \times (1 + 0.0676) \times (1 + 0.0480)] - 1 = \mathbf{16.36\%}$

5. C is correct. The GIPS standards state that portfolios must be valued in accordance with the definition of fair value, and that firms must value portfolios in accordance with the composite-specific valuation policy. The GIPS standards do not require firms to adhere to the principles of financial accounting.

6. A is correct. The GIPS standards state, "Returns from cash and cash equivalents must be included in all return calculations, even if the firm does not control the specific cash investment(s)."

7. C is correct. The GIPS Glossary defines transaction costs as "the costs of buying or selling investments" and states, "These costs typically take the form of brokerage commissions, exchange fees and/or taxes, and/or bid–offer spreads from either internal or external brokers. Custodial fees charged per transaction should be considered custody fees and not transaction costs."

8. Portfolio returns:

$$r_A = \frac{85.3 - 74.9 - 7.5}{74.9 + (7.5 \times 0.613)} = \frac{2.9}{79.5} = 0.0365 = 3.65\%$$

$$r_B = \frac{109.8 - 127.6 - (-15) - (-5)}{127.6 + (-15 \times 0.742) + (-5 \times 0.387)} = \frac{2.2}{114.535} = 0.0192 = 1.92\%$$

$$r_C = \frac{128.4 - 110.4 - 15}{110.4 + (15 \times 0.387)} = \frac{3}{116.205} = 0.0258 = 2.58\%$$

9. To calculate the composite return based on beginning assets, first determine the percentage of beginning composite assets represented by each portfolio; then determine the weighted-average return for the month:

   Beginning composite assets = 74.9 + 127.6 + 110.4 = 312.9

   Portfolio A = 74.9/312.9 = 0.239 = 23.9%

   Portfolio B = 127.6/312.9 = 0.408 = 40.8%

   Portfolio C = 110.4/312.9 = 0.353 = 35.3%

   $r_{Comp} = (0.0365 \times 0.239) + (0.0192 \times 0.408) + (0.0258 \times 0.353)$

   $= 0.0257 = 2.57\%$

10. To calculate the composite return based on beginning assets plus cash flows, first use the denominator of the Modified Dietz formula to determine the percentage of total beginning assets plus weighted cash flows represented by each portfolio, and then calculate the weighted-average return:

    Beginning composite assets + Weighted cash flows = [74.9 + (7.5 × 0.613)] + [127.6 + (−15 × 0.742) + (−5 × 0.387)] + [110.4 + (15 × 0.387)] = 79.5 + 114.535 + 116.205

    = 310.24

    Portfolio A = 79.5/310.24 = 0.256 = 25.6%

    Portfolio B = 114.535/310.24 = 0.369 = 36.9%

    Portfolio C = 116.205/310.24 = 0.375 = 37.5%

    $r_{Comp} = (0.0365 \times 0.256) + (0.0192 \times 0.369) + (0.0258 \times 0.375)$

    $= 0.0261 = 2.61\%$

    The Aggregate Return method is calculated by summing beginning assets and intra-period external cash flows, treating the entire composite as though it were a single portfolio and then computing the return directly with the Modified Dietz formula.

    $$r_{Comp} = \frac{323.5 - 312.9 - (-15 + 7.5 + 10)}{312.9 + [(-15) \times 0.742 + 7.5 \times 0.613 + 10 \times 0.387]}$$
    $$= 0.0261 = 2.61\%$$

11. Yes. The GIPS standards state that firms must include all actual, discretionary, fee-paying segregated accounts in at least one of the firm's composites. If the segregated account meets the defined criteria for inclusion in more than one composite, the firm must include the account in all the firm's appropriate composites. For example, a firm may have a large-cap composite and a large-cap growth composite. If the firm manages a segregated account that meets the criteria for inclusion in the large-cap composite as well as the large-cap growth composite,

the firm must include the account in both composites.

12. No, Tan/Lim may not claim compliance with the GIPS standards if model performance is linked to actual performance. The GIPS standards state that composites must include only actual assets under management within the defined firm, and they expressly prohibit linking the performance of simulated or model portfolios with actual performance.

13. The GIPS standards prohibit including non-discretionary portfolios in composites. IPS restrictions do not necessarily render a portfolio non-discretionary. It is up to the investment management firm to define discretion and to determine whether it has the discretion to implement the investment strategy, given the restrictions of the IPS. In this case, however, it appears likely that SMERF's policy requiring transactions to be approved in advance by the Investment Committee and the pension plan's liquidity needs prevent Midwest National Bank from fully implementing the investment objective of achieving long-term capital appreciation through active management. If so, Midwest National Bank must classify the SMERF portfolio as non-discretionary and exclude it from all composites.

14. A is correct. Such a restriction would most likely lead to the composition of this portfolio differing materially from other fixed-income portfolios run by the firm and, as such, the manager could reasonably classify this portfolio as non-discretionary. The restrictions stated in answers B and C are constraints that are likely to be specified as part of a fixed-income strategy.

15. A is correct. The GIPS standards state, "Composites must include new portfolios on a timely and consistent basis after each portfolio comes under management." In this case, it is expected to take an extended period to invest the new client's assets in accordance with the composite strategy. Assuming Taurus complies with the GIPS standards, its documented policy would provide for the inclusion of new bank loan portfolios in the composite on a timely basis. For example, Taurus's policy may require new portfolios to be included in the composite as of the first full measurement period that the assets are fully invested. Taurus must apply its policy consistently.

16. A is correct. Terminated portfolios must be included in the historical performance of the composite through the last full measurement during which the firm had discretion. The last full measurement period during which the Chimie Bio-Industrielle portfolio was under the management of Ord Capital Management was the month of March.

17. C is correct. The portfolio's historical performance must remain with the original composite. Portfolios must not be switched from one composite to another unless either documented changes to a portfolio's investment mandate, objective, or strategy or the redefinition of the composite make it appropriate.

18. B is correct. The portfolio's historical performance must remain with the original composite. Portfolios must not be switched from one composite to another unless either documented changes to a portfolio's investment mandate, objective, or strategy or the redefinition of the composite make it appropriate.

19. C is correct. The GIPS standards state, "If the firm sets a minimum asset level for portfolios to be included in a composite, the firm must not include portfolios below the minimum asset level in that composite." However, a firm may set one minimum asset level at which to *add* a portfolio to a composite and another level at which a portfolio must be *removed* from a composite. Unless Bamako's policies specify different minimum asset levels for adding and removing portfolios

from composites, Bamako must remove the Bouwa portfolio from the core-plus fixed-income composite when the portfolio's assets fall below the minimum and return it to the composite when it once again qualifies for inclusion. A is incorrect because composites must be defined according to similar investment mandates, objectives, and/or strategies; there should be no "miscellaneous" composite.

20. A is correct. The client's prior approval authority for security transactions most likely renders the portfolio non-discretionary. The GIPS standards state "non-discretionary portfolios must not be included in composites." B is incorrect because total firm assets must include all discretionary and non-discretionary assets managed by the firm.

21. Under the GIPS standards, there is no minimum or maximum number of portfolios that a composite may include. The GIPS standards require that firms disclose the number of portfolios in each composite as of the end of each annual period presented, unless there are five or fewer portfolios.

22. The GIPS standards require that when a firm initially claims compliance with the GIPS standards, it must present at least five years of GIPS-compliant performance (or for the period since the composite inception date if the composite has been in existence less than five years). After presenting a minimum of five years of GIPS-compliant performance (or for the period since the composite inception date if the composite has been in existence less than five years), the firm must present an additional year of performance each year, building up to a minimum of 10 years of GIPS-compliant performance. In 2020, Macondo must present performance from 2010 through 2019. Macondo Institutional Asset Management thus cannot drop the years prior to 2015 at the time Garcia suggests it do so. In addition to violating a specific requirement, Garcia's suggestion was not in the spirit of fair representation and full disclosure of performance. The firm may eliminate returns from more than 10 years ago from its GIPS Report, as long as it continues to show at least the most recent 10 years. It is recommended, however, that Macondo show its entire GIPS-compliant performance record.

23. Acella must determine if O'Connor's performance track record meets all of the portability requirements. Acella must have records supporting the performance of portfolios currently in the composite and those that were previously managed to the strategy but have since terminated. The firm must also be comfortable that Mr. O'Connor was the primary decision maker for the strategy while at JEM-Stone and that the strategy will remain substantially intact and independent once at Acella. If these requirements are met, Acella may port the track record, but the ported composite must pass one more test if the firm wishes to link performance: There must not be a break in the track record between the past firm and Acella. For example, if O'Connor left his prior firm at the end of February 2019 and did not start with Acella until 1 May 2019, there will be a break in the track record and Acella must not link to the prior performance.

24. A is correct. Verification brings additional credibility to the claim of compliance, but it "does not provide assurance on the accuracy of any specific performance report." Verification also does not provide assurance on the adequacy of a firm's internal controls.

25. No, a firm may not choose to have only a portion of the firm verified. A firm that has been verified may choose to have a detailed performance *examination* conducted on one or more specific composites, but verification cannot be carried out on only select composites, pooled funds, or portfolios. Firms must not state that a particular composite has been "verified."

Glossary

Absolute return benchmark A minimum target return that an investment manager is expected to beat.

Accrual taxes Taxes levied and paid on a periodic basis.

Accumulation phase Phase where the government predominantly contributes to a sovereign wealth pension reserve fund.

Active management A portfolio management approach that allows risk factor mismatches relative to a benchmark index causing potentially significant return differences between the active portfolio and the underlying benchmark.

Active return The return on a portfolio minus the return on the portfolio's benchmark.

Active risk The standard deviation of active returns.

Active risk budgeting Risk budgeting that concerns active risk (risk relative to a portfolio's benchmark).

Active share A measure of how similar a portfolio is to its benchmark. A manager who precisely replicates the benchmark will have an active share of zero; a manager with no holdings in common with the benchmark will have an active share of one.

Aggregate wealth The total value of all assets owned, encompassing personal property, financial assets, real assets, and rights.

Arithmetic attribution An attribution approach which explains the arithmetic difference between the portfolio return and its benchmark return. The single-period attribution effects sum to the excess return, however, when combining multiple periods, the sub-period attribution effects will not sum to the excess return.

Ask price The price at which a trader will sell a specified quantity of a security. Also called *ask*, *offer price*, or *offer*.

Asset-only With respect to asset allocation, an approach that focuses directly on the characteristics of the assets without explicitly modeling the liabilities.

Authority bias A behavioral bias which involves groups deferring to a group member that is a subject matter expert or in a position of authority.

Aversion to complexity A behavioral phenomenon of groups in many professional contexts, in which disproportionate attention is given to trivial issues at the expense of important but harder-to-grasp or contested topics.

Back-fill bias The distortion in index or peer group data which results when returns are reported to a database only after they are known to be good returns.

Base With respect to a foreign exchange quotation of the price of one unit of a currency, the currency referred to in "one unit of a currency."

Basis risk The possibility that the expected value of a derivative differs unexpectedly from that of the underlying.

Bear spread An option strategy that becomes more valuable when the price of the underlying asset declines, so requires buying one option and writing another with a *lower* exercise price. A put bear spread involves buying a put with a higher exercise price and selling a put with a lower exercise price. A bear spread can also be executed with calls.

Best ask The offer to sell with the lowest ask price. Also called *best offer* or *inside ask*.

Best bid The highest bid in the market.

Best offer The lowest offer (ask price) in the market.

Best-in-class An ESG implementation approach that seeks to identify the most favorable companies and sectors based on ESG considerations. Also called *positive screening*.

Bid price In a price quotation, the price at which the party making the quotation is willing to buy a specified quantity of an asset or security.

Bid–ask spread The ask price minus the bid price.

Buffering Establishing ranges around breakpoints that define whether a stock belongs in one index or another.

Bull spread An option strategy that becomes more valuable when the price of the underlying asset rises, so requires buying one option and writing another with a *higher* exercise price. A call bull spread involves buying a call with a lower exercise price and selling a call with a higher exercise price. A bull spread can also be executed with puts.

Business cycle Fluctuations in GDP in relation to long-term trend growth, usually lasting 9-11 years.

Calendar rebalancing Rebalancing a portfolio to target weights on a periodic basis; for example, monthly, quarterly, semiannually, or annually.

Calendar spread A strategy in which one sells an option and buys the same type of option but with different expiration dates, on the same underlying asset and with the same strike. When the investor buys the more distant (near-term) call and sells the near-term (more distant) call, it is a long (short) calendar spread.

Canada model Characterized by a high allocation to alternatives. Unlike the endowment model, however, the Canada model relies more on internally managed assets. The innovative features of the Canada model are the: a) reference portfolio, b) total portfolio approach, and c) active management.

Capital market expectations (CME) Expectations concerning the risk and return prospects of asset classes.

Capital sufficiency analysis The process of evaluating whether a client has sufficient capital resources to achieve their financial goals and objectives; it considers the client's assets, liabilities, income, expenses, risk tolerance, time horizon, and other relevant factors.

Capture ratio A measure of the manager's gain or loss relative to the gain or loss of the benchmark.

Carhart model A four factor model used in performance attribution. The four factors are: market (RMRF), size (SMB), value (HML), and momentum (WML).

Carry trade A trading strategy that involves buying a security and financing it at a rate that is lower than the yield on that security.

Cash flow matching Immunization approach that attempts to ensure that all future liability payouts are matched precisely by cash flows from bonds or fixed-income derivatives.

Cash-secured put An option strategy involving the writing of a put option and simultaneously depositing an amount of money equal to the exercise price into a designated account (this strategy is also called a fiduciary put).

Collar An option position in which the investor is long shares of stock and then buys a put with an exercise price below the current stock price and writes a call with an exercise price above the current stock price. Collars allow a shareholder to acquire downside protection through a protective put but reduce the cash outlay by writing a covered call.

Contingent immunization Hybrid approach that combines immunization with an active management approach when the asset portfolio's value exceeds the present value of the liability portfolio.

Cost basis The initial cost of acquiring an investment including expenses incurred to acquire the investment. Also referred to as simply basis.

Covered call An option strategy in which a long position in an asset is combined with a short position in a call on that asset.

Cross hedge A hedge involving a hedging instrument that is imperfectly correlated with the asset being hedged; an example is hedging a bond investment with futures on a non-identical bond.

Cross-currency basis swap A swap in which notional principals are exchanged because the goal of the transaction is to issue at a more favorable funding rate and swap the amount back to the currency of choice.

Cross-sectional consistency A feature of expectations setting which means that estimates for all classes reflect the same underlying assumptions and are generated with methodologies that reflect or preserve important relationships among the asset classes, such as strong correlations. It is the internal consistency across asset classes.

Currency overlay programs A currency overlay program is a program to manage a portfolio's currency exposures for the case in which those exposures are managed separately from the management of the portfolio itself.

Custom security-based benchmark Benchmark that is custom built to accurately reflect the investment discipline of a particular investment manager. Also called a *strategy benchmark* because it reflects a manager's particular strategy.

Decision-reversal risk The risk of reversing a chosen course of action at the point of maximum loss.

Decumulation phase Phase where the government predominantly withdraws from a sovereign wealth pension reserve fund.

Deferred taxes Taxes postponed until some future date.

Defined benefit A retirement plan in which a plan sponsor commits to paying a specified retirement benefit.

Defined benefit plan Retirement plan that is funded by the employer that guarantees a retirement benefit based on factors such as years of service, salary, and age.

Defined contribution A retirement plan in which contributions are defined but the ultimate retirement benefit is not specified or guaranteed by the plan sponsor.

Defined contribution plan Retirement plan in which the employer, employee, or both contribute to an account in which the employee bears the investment risk.

Delay costs Implicit trading costs that arise from the inability to complete desired trades immediately. Also called *slippage*.

Delta The sensitivity of the derivative price to a small change in the value of the underlying asset.

Delta hedging Hedging that involves matching the price response of the position being hedged over a narrow range of prices.

Demand deposits Accounts that can be drawn upon regularly and without notice. This category includes checking accounts and certain savings accounts that are often accessible through online banks or automated teller machines (ATMs).

Diffusion index Reflects the proportion of the index's components that are moving in a pattern consistent with the overall index.

Dividend capture A trading strategy whereby an equity portfolio manager purchases stocks just before their ex-dividend dates, holds these stocks through the ex-dividend date to earn the right to receive the dividend, and subsequently sells the shares.

Domestic asset An asset that trades in the investor's domestic currency (or home currency).

Domestic currency The currency of the investor, i.e., the currency in which he or she typically makes consumption purchases, e.g., the Swiss franc for an investor domiciled in Switzerland.

Domestic-currency return A rate of return stated in domestic currency terms from the perspective of the investor; reflects both the foreign-currency return on an asset as well as percentage movement in the spot exchange rate between the domestic and foreign currencies.

Drawdown A percentage peak-to-trough reduction in net asset value.

Drawdown duration The total time from the start of the drawdown until the cumulative drawdown recovers to zero.

Due diligence Investigation and analysis in support of an investment action, decision, or recommendation.

Duration matching Immunization approach based on the duration of assets and liabilities. Ideally, the liabilities being matched (the liability portfolio) and the portfolio of assets (the bond portfolio) should be affected similarly by a change in interest rates.

Duration times spread Weighting of spread duration by credit spread in order to incorporate the empirical observation that spread changes for lower-rated bonds tend to be consistent on a percentage, rather than absolute, basis.

Dynamic asset allocation Dynamic asset allocation is an investment strategy premised on long-term asset allocation but employing short-term, tactical trading to maintain investment allocation targets.

Dynamic hedge A hedge requiring adjustment as the price of the hedged asset changes.

Econometrics The application of quantitative modeling and analysis grounded in economic theory to the analysis of economic data.

Economic balance sheet An extended balance sheet that includes the present values of both lifetime earnings and future consumption.

Economic indicators Economic statistics provided by government and established private organizations that contain information on an economy's recent past activity or its current or future position in the business cycle.

Effective federal funds (FFE) rate The fed funds rate actually transacted between depository institutions, not the Fed's target federal funds rate.

Effective spread Two times the difference between the execution price and the midpoint of the market quote at the time an order is entered.

Endowment model Characterized by a high allocation to alternative investments (private investments and hedge funds), significant active management, and externally managed assets.

Enhanced indexing approach Maintains a close link to the benchmark but attempts to generate a modest amount of outperformance relative to the benchmark.

Excess return Used in various senses appropriate to context: 1) The difference between the portfolio return and the benchmark return, which may be either positive or negative; 2) The return in excess of the risk-free rate, thus representing the return for bearing risk.

Exhaustive Covering or containing all possible outcomes.

Extended portfolio assets and liabilities Assets and liabilities beyond those shown on a conventional balance sheet that are relevant in making asset allocation decisions; an example of an extended asset is human capital.

Factor-model-based benchmarks Benchmarks constructed by examining a portfolio's sensitivity to a set of factors, such as the return for a broad market index, company earnings growth, industry, or financial leverage.

Family offices Private firms that offer a range of wealth management services tailored specifically for ultra-high-net-worth individuals.

Foreign assets Assets denominated in currencies other than the investor's home currency.

Foreign currency Currency that is not the currency in which an investor makes consumption purchases, e.g., the US dollar from the perspective of a Swiss investor.

Foreign-currency return The return of the foreign asset measured in foreign-currency terms.

Forward rate bias An empirically observed divergence from interest rate parity conditions that active investors seek to benefit from by borrowing in a lower-yield currency and investing in a higher-yield currency.

Funding currencies The low-yield currencies in which borrowing occurs in a carry trade.

Gamma A numerical measure of how sensitive an option's delta (the sensitivity of the derivative's price) is to a change in the value of the underlying.

General account Account holding assets to fund future liabilities from traditional life insurance and fixed annuities, the products in which the insurer bears all the risks—particularly mortality risk and longevity risk.

Gini coefficient A measure of inequality of wealth, or *i*, that ranges from 0 (perfect equality) to 1 (perfect inequality).

Goals-based With respect to asset allocation or investing, an approach that focuses on achieving an investor's goals (for example, related to supporting lifestyle needs or aspirations) based typically on constructing sub-portfolios aligned with those goals.

Goals-based investing An investment industry term for approaches to investing for individuals and families focused on aligning investments with goals (parallel to liability-driven investing for institutional investors).

Grinold–Kroner model An expression for the expected return on a share as the sum of an expected income return, an expected nominal earnings growth return, and an expected repricing return.

Groupthink A behavioral bias that occurs when a team minimizes conflict and dissent in reaching and maintaining a consensus.

Hedge ratio The proportion of an underlying that will offset the risk associated with a derivative position.

High-net-worth individuals (HNWIs) Individuals with investable assets exceeding a certain minimum level, often as low as USD1 million, but typically more.

High-water mark A measure that reflects the fund's maximum value as of a performance fee payment date net of fees.

Holdings-based attribution A "buy and hold" attribution approach which calculates the return of portfolio and benchmark components based upon the price and foreign exchange rate changes applied to daily snapshots of portfolio holdings.

Holdings-based style analysis A bottom-up style analysis that estimates the risk exposures from the actual securities held in the portfolio at a point in time.

Home bias A preference for securities listed on the exchanges of one's home country.

Home currency See *domestic currency*.

Home-country bias The favoring of domestic over non-domestic investments relative to global market value weights.

Human capital The present value of an individual's future expected labor income.

Impact investing Refers to investments made with the specific intent of generating positive, measurable social and environmental impact alongside a financial return (which differentiates it from philanthropy).

Implementation shortfall (IS) The difference between the return for a notional or paper portfolio, where all transactions are assumed to take place at the manager's decision price, and the portfolio's actual return, which reflects realized transactions, including all fees and costs.

Implied volatility The standard deviation that causes an option pricing model to give the current option price.

Implied volatility surface A three-dimensional plot, for put and call options on the same underlying asset, of days to expiration (*x*-axis), option strike prices (*y*-axis), and implied volatilities (*z*-axis). It simultaneously shows the volatility skew (or smile) and the term structure of implied volatility.

Inflation-linked bonds Debt instruments that link the principal and interest to inflation.

Input uncertainty Uncertainty concerning whether the inputs are correct.

Inside ask See *best ask*.

Inside bid See *best bid*.

Inside spread The spread between the best bid price and the best ask price. Also called the *market bid-ask spread*, *inside bid-ask spread*, or *market spread*.

Interaction effect The impact of overweighting and underweighting individual securities within sectors that are themselves overweighted or underweighted.

Intertemporal consistency A feature of expectations setting which means that estimates for an asset class over different horizons reflect the same assumptions with respect to the potential paths of returns over time. It is the internal consistency over various time horizons.

Intrinsic value The amount gained (per unit) by an option buyer if an option is exercised at any given point in time. May be referred to as the exercise value of the option.

Investable net worth The sum of liquid assets, such as savings and investment accounts, and less short-term liabilities such as credit card debt.

Investable wealth The sum of liquid assets such as savings and investment accounts.

Investment currencies The high-yielding currencies in a carry trade.

Investment policy statement (IPS) A description of a client's unique investment objectives, risk tolerance, investment time horizon, and other applicable constraints.

Investment style A natural grouping of investment disciplines that has some predictive power in explaining the future dispersion of returns across portfolios.

Key person risk The risk that results from over-reliance on an individual or individuals whose departure would negatively affect an investment manager.

Knock-in/knock-out Features of a vanilla option that is created (or ceases to exist) when the spot exchange rate touches a pre-specified level.

Latency The elapsed time between the occurrence of an event and a subsequent action that depends on that event.

Leading economic indicators Turning points that usually precede those of the overall economy; they are believed to have value for predicting the economy's future state, usually near-term.

Liability driven investing (LDI) model In the LDI model, the primary investment objective is to generate returns sufficient to cover liabilities, with a focus on maximizing expected surplus return (excess return of assets over liabilities) and managing surplus volatility.

Liability glide path A specification of desired proportions of liability-hedging assets and return-seeking assets and the duration of the liability hedge as funded status changes and contributions are made.

Liability-based mandates Mandates managed to match or cover expected liability payments (future cash outflows) with future projected cash inflows.

Liability-driven investing An investment industry term that generally encompasses asset allocation that is focused on funding an investor's liabilities in institutional contexts.

Liability-relative With respect to asset allocation, an approach that focuses directly only on funding liabilities as an investment objective.

Limit order book The book or list of limit orders to buy and sell that pertains to a security.

Limited-life foundations A type of foundation where founders seek to maintain control of spending while they (or their immediate heirs) are still alive.

Longevity risk The risk of exhausting an individual's financial resources before passing away, thereby leaving insufficient capital for living expenses and unmet needs.

Lorenz curve A measure of the cumulative percentage of wealth owned by each percentage of the population.

Macro attribution Attribution at the sponsor level.

Manager peer group See *manager universe*.

Manager universe A broad group of managers with similar investment disciplines. Also called *manager peer group*.

Marginal tax rate The highest rate of tax applied to taxable income.

Market fragmentation Trading the same instrument in multiple venues.

Market impact The effect of the trade on transaction prices. Also called *price impact.*

Micro attribution Attribution at the portfolio manager level.

Midquote price The average, or midpoint, of the prevailing bid and ask prices.

Minimum-variance hedge ratio A mathematical approach to determining the optimal cross hedging ratio.

Mission-related investing Investing aimed at causes promoting positive societal or environmental change.

Model uncertainty Uncertainty as to whether a selected model is correct.

Negative screening An ESG investment style that focuses on the exclusion of certain sectors, companies, or practices in a fund or portfolio on the basis of specific ESG criteria.

Net worth The difference between assets and liabilities.

Non-deliverable forwards Cash-settled forward contracts, used predominately with respect to foreign exchange forwards. Also called *contracts for differences*.

Nonstationarity A characteristic of series of data whose properties, such as mean and variance, are not constant through time. When analyzing historical data it means that different parts of a data series reflect different underlying statistical properties.

Norway model Characterized by an almost exclusive reliance on public equities and fixed income (the traditional 60/40 equity/bond model falls under the Norway model), with largely passively managed assets and with very little to no allocation to alternative investments.

Offer price The price at which a counterparty is willing to sell one unit of the base currency.

Opportunity cost Reflects the foregone opportunity of investing in a different asset. It is typically denoted by the risk-free rate of interest, r.

Optional stock dividends A type of dividend in which shareholders may elect to receive either cash or new shares.

Overbought A market condition in which market sentiment is thought to be unsustainably bullish.

Oversold A market condition in which market sentiment is thought to be unsustainably bearish.

Packeting Splitting stock positions into multiple parts.

Parameter uncertainty Uncertainty arising because a quantitative model's parameters are estimated with error.

Participant-switching life-cycle options Automatically switch DC plan members into a more conservative asset mix as their age increases. There may be several automatic de-risking switches at different age targets.

Participant/cohort option Pools the DC plan member with a cohort that has a similar target retirement date.

Passive management A buy-and-hold approach to investing in which an investor does not make portfolio changes based upon short-term expectations of changing market or security performance.

Percent-range rebalancing An approach to rebalancing that involves setting rebalancing thresholds or trigger points, stated as a percentage of the portfolio's value, around target values.

Performance attribution The process of disaggregating a portfolio's return to determine the drivers of its performance.

Personal assets Nonbusiness, on-investment assets including personal property and real property.

Personal property Property owned by individuals that are not real property and not considered investments.

Planned goals Financial objectives that can be reasonably estimated or quantified at the onset and can be achieved within an expected time horizon.

Position delta The overall or portfolio delta. For example, the position delta of a covered call, consisting of long 100 shares and short one at-the-money call, is +50 (= +100 for the shares and -50 for the short ATM call).

Positive screening An ESG implementation approach that seeks to identify the most favorable companies and sectors based on ESG considerations. Also called *best-in-class*.

Price improvement When trade execution prices are better than quoted prices.

Private wealth management Financial planning and investment management to help individual investors, particularly high-net-worth individuals (HNWIs) and ultra-high-net-worth individuals (UHNWIs), manage their wealth.

Protective put A strategy of purchasing an underlying asset and purchasing a put on the same asset.

Pure indexing Attempts to replicate a bond index as closely as possible, targeting zero active return and zero active risk.

Put spread A strategy used to reduce the upfront cost of buying a protective put, it involves buying a put option and writing another put option.

Re-base With reference to index construction, to change the time period used as the base of the index.

Realized volatility Historical volatility, the square root of the realized variance of returns, which is a measure of the range of past price outcomes for the underlying asset.

Rebalancing Adjusting the weights of the constituent securities in an index.

Rebalancing range A range of values for asset class weights defined by trigger points above and below target weights, such that if the portfolio value passes through a trigger point, rebalancing occurs. Also known as a corridor.

Rebate rate The portion of the collateral earnings rate that is repaid to the security borrower by the security lender.

Reduced form models Statistical credit models that solve for the probability of default over a specific time period, using observable company-specific and market-based variables.

Regime The governing set of relationships (between variables) that stem from technological, political, legal, and regulatory environments. Changes in such environments or policy stances can be described as changes in regime.

Relative value A concept that describes the selection of the most attractive individual securities to populate the portfolio with, using ranking and comparing.

Repo rate The interest rate on a repurchase agreement.

Repurchase agreements In repurchase agreements, or repos, a security owner agrees to sell a security for a specific cash amount while simultaneously agreeing to repurchase the security at a specified future date (typically one day later) and price.

Reserve portfolio The component of an insurer's general account that is subject to specific regulatory requirements and is intended to ensure the company's ability to meet its policy liabilities. The assets in the reserve portfolio are managed conservatively and must be highly liquid and low risk.

Resistance levels Price points on dealers' order boards where one would expect to see a clustering of offers.

Return attribution A set of techniques used to identify the sources of the excess return of a portfolio against its benchmark.

Returns-based attribution An attribution approach that uses only the total portfolio returns over a period to identify the components of the investment process that have generated the returns. The Brinson–Hood–Beebower approach is a returns-based attribution approach.

Returns-based benchmarks Benchmarks constructed by examining a portfolio's sensitivity to a set of factors, such as the returns for various style indexes (e.g., small-cap value, small-cap growth, large-cap value, and large-cap growth).

Returns-based style analysis A top-down style analysis that involves estimating the sensitivities of a portfolio to security market indexes.

Reverse repos Repurchase agreements from the standpoint of the lender.

Risk attribution The analysis of the sources of risk.

Risk aversion The dislike for risk such that compensation is required in terms of higher expected returns for assuming higher risk.

Risk budgeting The establishment of objectives for individuals, groups, or divisions of an organization that takes into account the allocation of an acceptable level of risk.

Risk capacity The ability to bear financial risk.

Risk premiums Extra returns expected by investors for bearing some specified risk.

Risk reversal A strategy used to profit from the existence of an implied volatility skew and from changes in its shape over time. A combination of long (short) calls and short (long) puts on the same underlying with the same expiration is a long (short) risk reversal.

Risk tolerance The level of risk an investor is willing and able to bear.

Seagull spread An extension of the risk reversal foreign exchange option strategy that limits downside risk.

Securities lending A form of collateralized lending that may be used to generate income for portfolios.

Selective An index construction methodology that targets only those securities with certain characteristics.

Separate accounts Accounts holding assets to fund future liabilities from variable life insurance and variable annuities, the products in which customers make investment decisions from a menu of options and themselves bear investment risk.

Sharpe ratio The ratio of mean excess return to standard deviation (excess return).

Shortfall probability The probability of failing to meet a specific liability or goal.

Shrinkage estimation Estimation that involves taking a weighted average of a historical estimate of a parameter and some other parameter estimate, where the weights reflect the analyst's relative belief in the estimates.

Special dividends Dividends paid by a company that does not pay dividends on a regular schedule, or dividends that supplement regular cash dividends with an extra payment.

Spread duration The change in bond price for a given change in yield spread. Also referred to as OAS duration when the option-adjusted spread (OAS) is the yield measure used.

Static hedge A hedge that is not sensitive to changes in the price of the asset hedged.

Stock lending Securities lending involving the transfer of equities.

Stops Stop-loss orders involve leaving bids or offers away from the current market price to be filled if the market reaches those levels.

Straddle An option combination in which one buys *both* puts and calls, with the same exercise price and same expiration date, on the same underlying asset. In contrast to this long straddle, if someone *writes* both options, it is a short straddle.

Strangle A variation on a straddle in which the put and call have different exercise prices; if the put and call are held long, it is a long strangle; if they are held short, it is a short strangle.

Strategic asset allocation A long-term strategy that establishes target allocations for various asset classes and aims to optimize the balance between risk and reward by diversifying investments.

Structural models Models that specify functional relationships among variables based on economic theory. The functional form and parameters of these models are derived from the underlying theory. They may include unobservable parameters.

Support levels Price points on dealers' order boards where one would expect to see a clustering of bids.

Surplus The difference between assets and liabilities, analogous to shareholders' equity on a corporate balance sheet.

Surplus portfolio The component of an insurer's general account that is intended to realize higher expected returns than the reserve portfolio and so can assume some liquidity risk. Surplus portfolio assets are often managed aggressively with exposure to alternative assets.

Survivorship bias Relates to the inclusion of only current investment funds in a database. As such, the returns of funds that are no longer available in the marketplace (have been liquidated) are excluded from the database. Also see *backfill bias*.

Synthetic long forward position The combination of a long call and a short put with identical strike price and expiration, traded at the same time on the same underlying.

Synthetic short forward position The combination of a short call and a long put at the same strike price and maturity (traded at the same time on the same underlying).

Tactical asset allocation A proactive strategy that adjusts asset class allocations within a portfolio based on short-term market trends, economic conditions, or valuation changes to capitalize on temporary market inefficiencies or opportunities to improve returns or manage risk more effectively.

Tax drag The negative effect of taxes on an investment's net returns.

Taylor rule A rule linking a central bank's target short-term interest rate to the rate of growth of the economy and inflation.

Term deposits Interest-bearing accounts that have a specified maturity date. This category includes savings accounts and certificates of deposit (CDs). Also see *time deposits*.

Term structure of volatility The plot of implied volatility (y-axis) against option maturity (x-axis) for options with the same strike price on the same underlying. Typically, implied volatility is not constant across different maturities – rather, it is often in contango, meaning that the implied volatilities for longer-term options are higher than for near-term ones.

Thematic investing An investment approach that focuses on companies in a specific sector or following a specific theme, such as energy efficiency or climate change.

Theta The change in a derivative instrument for a given small change in calendar time, holding everything else constant. Specifically, the theta calculation assumes nothing changes except calendar time. Theta also reflects the rate at which an option's time value decays.

Threshold-based rebalancing policy The manager rebalances the portfolio when asset class weights deviate from their target weights by a prespecified percentage regardless of timing and frequency.

Time deposits Interest-bearing accounts that have a specified maturity date. This category includes savings accounts and certificates of deposit (CDs). Also see *term deposits*.

Time value The difference between an option's premium and its intrinsic value.

Time-based rebalancing policy The manager rebalances the portfolio regularly, at a certain given time interval such as quarterly, semi-annually, or annually, regardless of any difference between prevailing asset class weights and target asset class weights.

Time-series estimation Estimators that are based on lagged values of the variable being forecast; often consist of lagged values of other selected variables.

Total factor productivity A scale factor that reflects the portion of growth unaccounted for by explicit factor inputs (e.g., capital and labor).

Total return payer Party responsible for paying the reference obligation cash flows and return to the receiver but that is also compensated by the receiver for any depreciation in the index or default losses incurred by the portfolio.

Total return receiver Receives both the cash flows from the underlying index and any appreciation in the index over the period in exchange for paying the MRR plus a predetermined spread.

Tracking risk The standard deviation of the differences between a portfolio's returns and its benchmarks returns. Also called *tracking error*.

Transactions-based attribution An attribution approach that captures the impact of intra-day trades and exogenous events such as a significant class action settlement.

Trigger points In the context of portfolio rebalancing, the endpoints of a rebalancing range (corridor).

Ultra-high-net-worth individuals (UHNWIs) Individuals with net worth usually exceeding USD30 million or more.

Unplanned goals Unforeseen financial needs that are difficult to quantify because either the funding need, the timing of the financial need, or both may not be estimated.

Unsmoothing An adjustment to the reported return series if serial correlation is detected. Various approaches are available to unsmooth a return series.

Variance notional The notional amount of a variance swap; it equals vega notional divided by two times the volatility strike price [i.e., (vega notional)/(2 × volatility strike)].

Vega A measure of the sensitivity of an option's price to changes in the underlying's volatility.

Vega notional The trade size for a variance swap, which represents the average profit and loss of the variance swap for a 1% change in volatility from the strike.

Vesting The process of an employee becoming unconditionally entitled to, and an employer becoming obligated to pay, compensation.

Volatility clustering The tendency for large (small) swings in prices to be followed by large (small) swings of random direction.

Volatility skew The skewed plot (of implied volatility (y-axis) against strike price (x-axis) for options on the same underlying with the same expiration) that occurs when the implied volatility increases for OTM puts and decreases for OTM calls, as the strike price moves away from the current price.

Volatility smile The U-shaped plot (of implied volatility (y-axis) against strike price (x-axis) for options on the same underlying with the same expiration) that occurs when the implied volatilities priced into both OTM puts and calls trade at a premium to implied volatilities of ATM options.

Wealth The value of all the assets owned by an individual.

Wealth life cycle Stages of an individual investor's wealth in terms of human capital, financial capital, and economic net worth.

CFA Institute®
CFA Program

DERIVATIVES AND RISK MANAGEMENT

CFA® Program Curriculum
2026 • LEVEL III CORE • VOLUME 4

WILEY

ISBN 978-1-39436-060-4

May 2025

Please visit our website at
www.WileyGlobalFinance.com.

WILEY

SKY98BB00E7-84ED-4B2D-A7E2-A4E817811369_022825

CONTENTS

How to Use the CFA Program Curriculum

The CFA® Program exams measure your mastery of the core knowledge, skills, and abilities required to succeed as an investment professional. These core competencies are the basis for the Candidate Body of Knowledge (CBOK™). The CBOK consists of four components:

A broad outline that lists the major CFA Program topic areas (www.cfainstitute.org/programs/cfa/curriculum/cbok/cbok)

Topic area weights that indicate the relative exam weightings of the top-level topic areas (www.cfainstitute.org/en/programs/cfa/curriculum)

Learning outcome statements (LOS) that tell you the specific knowledge, skills, and abilities you should gain from each curriculum topic area. You will find these statements at the start of each learning module and lesson. We encourage you to review the information about the LOS on our website (www.cfainstitute.org/programs/cfa/curriculum/study-sessions), including the descriptions of LOS "command words" on the candidate resources page at www.cfainstitute.org/-/media/documents/support/programs/cfa-and-cipm-los-command-words.ashx.

The CFA Program curriculum that candidates receive access to upon exam registration.

Therefore, the key to your success on the CFA exams is studying and understanding the CBOK. You can learn more about the CBOK on our website: www.cfainstitute.org/programs/cfa/curriculum/cbok.

The curriculum, including the practice questions, is the basis for all exam questions. The curriculum is selected/developed specifically to provide candidates with the knowledge, skills, and abilities reflected in the CBOK.

CFA INSTITUTE LEARNING ECOSYSTEM (LES)

Your exam registration fee includes access to the CFA Institute Learning Ecosystem (LES). This digital learning platform provides access to all the curriculum content and practice questions. The LES is organized as a series of learning modules consisting of short online lessons and associated practice questions. This tool is your source for all study materials, including practice questions and mock exams. The LES is the primary method by which CFA Institute delivers your curriculum experience. Here, you will find additional practice questions to test your knowledge, including some interactive questions.

DESIGNING YOUR PERSONAL STUDY PROGRAM

An orderly, systematic approach to exam preparation is critical. You should dedicate a consistent block of time every week to reading and studying. Review the LOS both before and after you study curriculum content to ensure you can demonstrate

the knowledge, skills, and abilities described by the LOS and the assigned learning module. Use the LOS as a self-check to track your progress and highlight areas of weakness for later review.

Successful candidates report an average of more than 300 hours preparing for each exam. Your preparation time will vary based on your prior education and experience, and you will likely spend more time on some topics than on others.

ERRATA

The curriculum development process is rigorous and involves multiple rounds of reviews by content experts. Despite our efforts to produce a curriculum that is free of errors, we must make corrections in some instances. Curriculum errata are periodically updated and posted by exam level and test date on the Curriculum Errata webpage (www.cfainstitute.org/en/programs/submit-errata). If you believe you have found an error in the curriculum, you can submit your concerns through our curriculum errata reporting process found at the bottom of the Curriculum Errata webpage.

OTHER FEEDBACK

Please send any comments or suggestions to info@cfainstitute.org, and we will review your feedback thoughtfully.

Derivatives and Risk Management

LEARNING MODULE

1

Options Strategies

by Adam Schwartz, PhD, CFA, and Barbara Valbuzzi, CFA.

Adam Schwartz, PhD, CFA, is at Bucknell University (USA). Barbara Valbuzzi, CFA (Italy).

LEARNING OUTCOMES

Mastery	The candidate should be able to:
☐	demonstrate how an asset's returns may be replicated by using options
☐	discuss the investment objective(s), structure, payoff, risk(s), value at expiration, profit, maximum profit, maximum loss, and breakeven underlying price at expiration of a covered call position
☐	discuss the investment objective(s), structure, payoff, risk(s), value at expiration, profit, maximum profit, maximum loss, and breakeven underlying price at expiration of a protective put position
☐	compare the delta of covered call and protective put positions with the position of being long an asset and short a forward on the underlying asset
☐	compare the effect of buying a call on a short underlying position with the effect of selling a put on a short underlying position
☐	discuss the investment objective(s), structure, payoffs, risk(s), value at expiration, profit, maximum profit, maximum loss, and breakeven underlying price at expiration of the following option strategies: bull spread, bear spread, straddle, and collar
☐	describe uses of calendar spreads
☐	discuss volatility skew and smile
☐	identify and evaluate appropriate option strategies consistent with given investment objectives
☐	demonstrate the use of options to achieve targeted equity risk exposures

CFA Institute would like to thank Robert Strong, PhD, CFA, and Russell Rhoads, CFA, for their work on previous versions of this reading.

1 INTRODUCTION

Derivatives are financial instruments through which counterparties agree to exchange economic cash flows based on the movement of underlying securities, indexes, currencies, or other instruments or factors. A derivative's value is thus *derived* from the economic performance of the underlying. Derivatives may be created directly by counterparties or may be facilitated through established, regulated market exchanges. Direct creation between counterparties has the benefit of tailoring to the counterparties' specific needs but also the disadvantage of potentially low liquidity. Exchange-traded derivatives often do not match counterparties' specific needs but do facilitate early termination of the position, and, importantly, mitigate counterparty risk. Derivatives facilitate the exchange of economic risks and benefits where trades in the underlying securities might be less advantageous because of poor liquidity, transaction costs, regulatory impediments, tax or accounting considerations, or other factors.

Options are an important type of contingent-claim derivative that provide their owner with the right but not an obligation to a payoff determined by the future price of the underlying asset. Unlike other types of derivatives (i.e., swaps, forwards, and futures), options have nonlinear payoffs that enable their owners to benefit from movements in the underlying in one direction without being hurt by movements in the opposite direction. The cost of this opportunity, however, is the upfront cash payment required to enter the options position.

Options can be combined with the underlying and with other options in a variety of different ways to modify investment positions, to implement investment strategies, or even to infer market expectations. Therefore, investment managers routinely use option strategies for hedging risk exposures, for seeking to profit from anticipated market moves, and for implementing desired risk exposures in a cost-effective manner.

The main purpose of this reading is to illustrate how options strategies are used in typical investment situations and to show the risk–return trade-offs associated with their use. Importantly, an informed investment professional should have such a basic understanding of options strategies to competently serve his investment clients.

Section 2 of this reading shows how certain combinations of securities (i.e., options, underlying) are equivalent to others. Sections 3–6 discuss two of the most widely used options strategies, covered calls and protective puts. In Sections 7 and 8, we look at popular spread and combination option strategies used by investors. The focus of Section 9 is implied volatility embedded in option prices and related volatility skew and surface. Section 10 discusses option strategy selection. Sections 11 and 12 demonstrate a series of applications showing ways in which an investment manager might solve an investment problem with options. The reading concludes with a summary.

2 POSITION EQUIVALENCIES

- [ ] demonstrate how an asset's returns may be replicated by using options

It is useful to think of derivatives as building blocks that can be combined to create a specific payoff with the desired risk exposure. A synthetic position can be created for any option or stock strategy. Most of the time, market participants use synthetic positions to transform the payoff profile of their positions when their market views change. We cover a few of these relationships in the following pages. First, a brief recap of put–call parity and put–call–forward parity will help readers to understand such synthetic positions.

As you may remember, put–call parity shows the equivalence (or parity) of a portfolio of a call and a risk-free bond with a portfolio of a put and the underlying, which leads to the relationship between put and call prices. Put–call parity can be expressed in the following formula, where S_0 is the price of the underlying; p_0 and c_0 are the prices (i.e., premiums) of the put and call options, respectively; and $X/(1 + r)^T$ is the present value of the risk-free bond: $S_0 + p_0 = c_0 + X/(1 + r)^T$.

A closely related concept is put–call–forward parity, which identifies the equivalence between buying a fiduciary call, given by the purchase of a call and the risk-free bond, and a synthetic protective put. The latter involves the purchase of a put option and a forward contract on the underlying that expires at the same time as the put option. In the put–call–forward parity formula, S_0 is replaced with a forward contract to buy the underlying, where the forward price is given by $F_0(T) = S_0(1 + r)^T$. Therefore, put–call–forward parity is: $F_0(T)/(1 + r)^T + p_0 = c_0 + X/(1 + r)^T$.

Synthetic Forward Position

The combination of a long call and a short put with identical strike price and expiration, traded at the same time on the same underlying, is equivalent to a **synthetic long forward position**. In fact, the long call creates the upside and the short put creates the downside on the underlying.

Consider an investor who buys an at-the-money (ATM) call and simultaneously sells a put with the same strike and the same expiration date. Whatever the stock price at expiration, one of the two options will be in the money. If the contract has a physical settlement, the investor will buy the underlying stock by paying the strike price. In fact, on the expiration date, the investor will exercise the call she owns if the stock price is above the strike price. Otherwise, if the underlying price is below the strike price, the put owner will exercise his right to deliver the stock and the investor (who sold the put) must buy it for the strike price. Exhibit 1 shows the values of the two options and the combined position at expiration, compared with the value of the stock purchase at that same time. The stock in this case does not pay dividends.

Exhibit 1: Synthetic Long Forward Position at Expiration

Stock price at expiration:	40	50	60
Alternative 1:			
Long 50-strike call payoff	0	0	10
Short 50-strike put payoff	−10	0	0
Total value	−10	0	10
Alternative 2:			
Long stock at 50	−10	0	10
Total value	−10	0	10

We now compare the same option strategy with the payoff of a forward or futures contract in Exhibit 2. The motivation to create a synthetic long forward position could be to exploit an arbitrage opportunity presented by the actual forward price or the need for an alternative to the outright purchase of a long forward position. Frequently, a forward contract is used instead of futures to acquire a stock position because it allows for contract customization.

Exhibit 2: Synthetic Long Forward Position vs. Long Forward/Futures

Stock price at expiration:	40	50	60
Alternative 1:			
Long 50-strike call payoff	0	0	10
Short 50-strike put payoff	−10	0	0
Total value	−10	0	10
Alternative 3:			
Long forward/futures at 50			
Value	−10	0	10

EXAMPLE 1

Synthetic Long Forward Position vs. Long Forward/Futures

A market maker has sold a three-month forward contract on Vodafone that allows the client (counterparty) to buy 10,000 shares at 200.35 pence (100p = £1) at expiration. The current stock price (S_0) is 200p, and the stock does not pay dividends until after the contract matures. The annualized interest rate is 0.70%. The cost (i.e., premium) of puts and calls on Vodafone is identical.

1. Discuss (a) how the market maker can hedge her short forward position upon the sale of the forward contract and (b) the market maker's position upon expiration of the forward contract.

Solution:

a. To offset the short forward contract position, the market maker can borrow £20,000 (= 10,000 × S_0/100) and buy 10,000 Vodafone shares at 200p. There is no upfront cost because the stock purchase is 100% financed.

b. At the expiry of the forward contract, the market maker delivers the 10,000 Vodafone shares she owns to the client that is long the forward, and then the market maker repays her loan. The net outflow for the market maker is zero because the following two transactions offset each other:

Amount received for the delivery of shares: 10,000 × 200.35p = £20,035

Repayment of loan: 10,000 × 200p [1 + 0.700% × (90/360)] = £20,035

2. Discuss how the market maker can hedge her short forward contract position using a synthetic long forward position, and explain what happens at expiry if the Vodafone share price is above or below 200.35p.

Solution:

To hedge her short forward position, the market maker creates a synthetic long forward position. She purchases a call and sells a put, both with a strike price of 200.35p and expiring in three months.

At the expiry of the forward contract, if the stock price is above 200.35p, the market maker exercises her call, pays £20,035 (=10,000 × 200.35p), and receives 10,000 Vodafone shares. She then delivers these shares to the client and receives £20,035.

At the expiry of the forward contract, if the stock price is below 200.35p, the owner of the long put will exercise his option, and the market maker receives the 10,000 Vodafone shares for £20,035. She then delivers these shares to the client and receives £20,035.

Consider now a trader who wants to short a stock over a specified period. He needs to borrow the stock from the market and then sell the borrowed shares. Instead, the trader can create a **synthetic short forward position** by selling a call and buying a put at the same strike price and maturity. When using options to replicate a short stock position, it is important to be aware of early assignment risk that could arise with American-style options. As Exhibit 3 shows, the payoff is the exact opposite of the synthetic long forward position.

The same outcome can be achieved be selling forwards or futures contracts (as seen in Exhibit 3). These instruments are also commonly used to eliminate future price risk. Consider an investor who owns a stock and wants to lock in a future sales price. The investor might enter into a forward or futures contract (as seller) requiring her to deliver the shares at a future date in exchange for a cash amount determined today. Because the initial and final stock prices are known, this investment should pay the risk-free rate. For a dividend-paying stock, the dividends expected to be paid on the stock during the term of the contract will decrease the price of the forward or futures.

Exhibit 3: Synthetic Short Forward Position

Stock price at expiration:	40	50	60
Alternative 1:			
Short 50-strike call payoff	0	0	−10
Long 50-strike put payoff	10	0	0
Total value	10	0	−10
Alternative 2:			
Short stock at 50	10	0	−10
Value	10	0	−10
Alternative 3:			
Short forward/futures at 50	10	0	−10
Value	10	0	−10

Synthetic forwards on stocks and equity indexes are often used by market makers that have sold a forward contract to customers—to hedge the risk, the market-maker would implement a synthetic long forward position—or by investment banks wishing to hedge forward exposure arising from structured products.

Synthetic Put and Call

As already described, market participants can use synthetic positions to transform the payoff and risk profile of their positions. The symmetrical payoffs of long and short stock, forward, and futures positions can be altered by implementing synthetic options positions. For example, the symmetric payoff of a short stock position can become asymmetrical if the investor transforms it into a synthetic long put position by buying a call.

Exhibit 4 shows the payoffs of a synthetic long put position that consists of short stock at 50 and a long call with an exercise price of 50. It can be seen that the payoffs from this synthetic put position at various stock prices at option expiration are identical to those of a long put with a 50-strike price. Of course, all positions are assumed to expire at the same time. Note that the same transformation of payoff and risk profile for a position of short forwards or futures can also be accomplished using long call options.

Exhibit 4: Synthetic Long Put

Stock price at expiration:	40	50	60
Alternative 1:			
Short stock at 50	10	0	−10
Long 50-strike call payoff	0	0	+10
Total value	10	0	0
Alternative 2			
Long 50-strike put payoff	10	0	0
Value	10	0	0

EXAMPLE 2

Synthetic Long Put

Three months ago, Wing Tan, a hedge fund manager, entered into a short forward contract that requires him to deliver 50,000 Generali shares, which the fund does not currently own, at €18/share in one month from now. The stock price is currently €16/share. The hedge fund's research analyst, Gisele Rossi, has a non-consensus expectation that the company will report an earnings "beat" next month. The stock does not pay dividends.

1. Under the assumption that Tan maintains the payoff profile of his current short forward position, discuss the conditions for profit or loss at contract expiration.

Solution:

If Tan decides to keep the current payoff profile of his position, at the expiry date, given a stock price of S_T, the profit or loss on the short forward will be 50,000 × (€18 − S_T). The position will be profitable only if S_T is below €18; otherwise the manager will incur in a loss.

2. After discussing with Rossi her earnings outlook, Tan remains bearish on Generali. He decides to hedge his risk, however, in case the stock does

report a positive earnings surprise. Discuss how Tan can modify his existing position to produce an asymmetrical, risk-reducing payoff.

Solution:

Tan decides to modify the payoff profile on his short forward position so that, at expiration, it will benefit from any stock price decrease below €16 while avoiding losses if the stock rises above that price. He purchases a call option with a strike price €16 and one month to maturity at a cost (premium) of €0.50. At expiration, the payoffs are as follows:

- On the short forward contract: 50,000 × (€18 – S_T)
- On the long call: 50,000 × {Max[0,(S_T – €16)] – €0.50}
- On the combined position: 50,000 × {(€18 – S_T) + [Max[0,(S_T – €16)] – €0.50]}

If $S_T \leq$ €16, the call will expire worthless and the profit will amount to 50,000 × (€18 – S_T + 0 – €0.50).
If $S_T >$ €16, the call is exercised and the Generali shares delivered for a maximum profit of 50,000 × (€18 – €16 – €0.50) = €75,000.

In similar fashion, an investor with a long stock position can change his payoff and risk profile into that of a long call by purchasing a put ("protective put" strategy). The long put eliminates the downside risk, whereas the long stock leaves the profit potential unlimited. As shown in Exhibit 5, the strategy has a payoff profile resembling that of a long call. Again, all positions are assumed to expire at the same time. We will have much more to say about the protective put strategy later in this reading. Finally, the payoff profile of a long call can also be achieved by adding a long put to a long forward or futures position, all with the same expiration dates and the same strike and forward (or futures) prices.

Exhibit 5: Synthetic Long Call

Stock price at expiration:	40	50	60
Alternative 1:			
Long stock at 50	−10	0	10
Long 50-strike put payoff	10	0	0
Total value	0	0	10
Alternative 2			
Long 50-strike call payoff	0	0	10
Value	0	0	10

COVERED CALLS AND PROTECTIVE PUTS 3

☐ discuss the investment objective(s), structure, payoff, risk(s), value at expiration, profit, maximum profit, maximum loss, and breakeven underlying price at expiration of a covered call position

Writing a **covered call** is a very common option strategy used by both individual and institutional investors. In this strategy, a party that already owns shares sells a call option, giving another party the right to buy their shares at the exercise price.[1] The investor owns the shares and has taken on the potential obligation to deliver the shares to the call option buyer and accept the exercise price as the price at which she sells the shares. For her willingness to do this, the investor receives the premium on the option.

When someone simultaneously holds a long position in an asset and a long position in a put option on that asset, the put is often called a **protective put**. The name comes from the fact that the put protects against losses in the value of the underlying asset.

The examples that follow use the convention of identifying an option by the underlying asset, expiration, exercise price, and option type. For example, in Exhibit 6, the PBR October 16 call option sells for 1.42. The underlying asset is Petróleo Brasileiro (PBR) common stock, the expiration is October, the exercise price is 16, the option is a call, and the call premium is 1.42. It is important to note that even though we will refer to this as the October 16 option, it does not expire on 16 October. Rather, 16 reflects the price at which the call owner has the right to buy, otherwise known as the exercise price or strike.

Petróleo Brasileiro (PBR)	October	16	Call
Underlying asset	*Expiration*	*Exercise price*	*Option type*

On some exchanges, certain options may have weekly expirations in addition to a monthly expiration, which means investors need to be careful in specifying the option of interest. For a given underlying asset and exercise price, there may be several weekly and one monthly option expiring in October. The examples that follow all assume a single monthly expiration.

Investment Objectives of Covered Calls

Consider the option data in Exhibit 6. Suppose there is one month until the September expiration. By convention, option listings show data for a single call or put, but in practice, the most common trading unit for an exchange-traded option is one contract covering 100 shares. Besides call and put premiums for various strike (i.e., exercise) prices and monthly expirations, the option data also shows implied volatilities as well as the "Greeks" (variables so named because most of the common ones are denoted by Greek letters). Implied volatility is the value of the unobservable volatility variable that equates the result of an option pricing model—such as the Black–Scholes–Merton (BSM) model—to the market price of an option, using all other required (and observable) input variables, including the option's strike price, the price of the underlying, the time to option expiration, and the risk-free interest. Before proceeding further, we provide a brief review of the Greeks because they will be an integral part of the discussion of the various option strategies to be presented.

- **Delta** (Δ) is the change in an option's price in response to a change in price of the underlying, all else equal. Delta provides a good approximation of how an option's price will change for a small change in the underlying's price. Delta for long calls is always positive; delta for long puts is always negative. *Delta* (Δ) $\approx$ *Change in value of option/Change in value of underlying.*

1 When someone creates (writes) a call without owning the underlying asset, it is known as a "naked" call.

- **Gamma (Γ)** is the change in an option's delta for a change in price of the underlying, all else equal. Gamma is a measure of the curvature in the option price in relationship to the underlying price. Gamma for long calls and long puts is always positive. *Gamma (Γ) ≈ Change in delta/Change in value of underlying.*
- **Vega (ν)** is the change in an option's price for a change in volatility of the underlying, all else equal. Vega measures the sensitivity of the underlying to volatility. Vega for long calls and long puts is always positive. *Vega (ν) ≈ Change in value of option/Change in volatility of underlying.*
- **Theta (Θ)** is the daily change in an option's price, all else equal. Theta measures the sensitivity of the option's price to the passage of time, known as time decay. Theta for long calls and long puts is generally negative.

Assume the current PBR share price is 15.84 and the risk-free rate is 4%. Now let us consider three different market participants who might logically use covered calls.

Exhibit 6: PBR Option Prices, Implied Volatilities, and Greeks

Call Prices			Exercise Price	Put Prices		
SEP	OCT	NOV		SEP	OCT	NOV
1.64	1.95	2.44	15	0.65	0.99	1.46
0.97	1.42	1.90	16	1.14	1.48	1.96
0.51	1.02	1.44	17	1.76	2.09	2.59

Call Implied Volatility				Put Implied Volatility		
SEP	OCT	NOV		SEP	OCT	NOV
64.42%	57.33%	62.50%	15	58.44%	56.48%	62.81%
55.92%	56.11%	60.37%	16	59.40%	56.35%	62.27%
51.07%	55.87%	58.36%	17	59.59%	56.77%	63.40%

Delta: change in option price per change of +1 in stock price, all else equal

Call Deltas				Put Deltas		
SEP	OCT	NOV		SEP	OCT	NOV
0.657	0.647	0.642	15	−0.335	−0.352	−0.359
0.516	0.540	0.560	16	−0.481	−0.460	−0.438
0.351	0.434	0.475	17	−0.620	−0.564	−0.513

Gamma: change in delta per change of +1 in stock price, all else equal

Call Gammas				Put Gammas		
SEP	OCT	NOV		SEP	OCT	NOV
0.125	0.100	0.075	15	0.136	0.102	0.075
0.156	0.109	0.082	16	0.147	0.109	0.080
0.159	0.109	0.086	17	0.140	0.107	0.079

Theta: daily change in option price, all else equal

Call Thetas (daily)				Put Thetas (daily)		
SEP	OCT	NOV		SEP	OCT	NOV
−0.019	−0.012	−0.011	15	−0.015	−0.010	−0.009
−0.018	−0.013	−0.011	16	−0.017	−0.011	−0.010
−0.015	−0.012	−0.011	17	−0.016	−0.011	−0.010

Vega: change in option price per 1% increase in volatility, all else equal

Call Vegas (per %)				Put Vegas (per %)		
SEP	OCT	NOV		SEP	OCT	NOV
0.017	0.024	0.030	15	0.017	0.024	0.030
0.018	0.026	0.031	16	0.018	0.026	0.031
0.017	0.025	0.032	17	0.017	0.025	0.032

Market Participant #1: Yield Enhancement

The most common motivation for writing covered calls is cash generation in anticipation of limited upside moves in the underlying. The call option writer keeps the premium regardless of what happens in the future. Some covered call writers view the premium they receive as an additional source of income in the same way they view cash dividends. For a covered call, a long position in 100 shares of the underlying is required for each short call contract. No additional cash margin is needed if the long position in the underlying is maintained. If the stock price exceeds the strike price at expiry, the underlying shares will be "called away" from the covered call writer and then delivered to satisfy the option holder's right to buy shares at the strike price. It is important to recognize, however, that when someone writes a call option, he is essentially giving up the returns above the strike price to the call holder.

Consider an individual investor who owns PBR and believes the stock price is likely to remain relatively flat over the next few months. With the stock currently trading at just under 16, the investor might think it unlikely that the stock will rise above 17. Exhibit 6 shows that the premium for a call option expiring in September with an exercise price of 17, referred to as the SEP 17 call, is 0.51. She could write that call and receive this premium. Alternatively, she could write a different call, say the NOV 17 call, and receive 1.44. There is a clear trade-off between the size of the option premium and the likelihood of option exercise. The option writer would get more cash from writing the longer-term option (because of a larger time premium), but there is a greater chance that the option would move in the money, resulting in the option being exercised by the buyer and, therefore, the stock being called away from the writer. The view of the covered call writer can be understood in terms of the call option's implied volatility. Essentially, writing the call expresses the view that the volatility of the underlying asset will be lower than the pricing of the option suggests. As shown in Exhibit 6, the implied volatility of the NOV 17 options is 58.36%. By writing the NOV 17 call for 1.44, the covered call investor believes that the volatility of the underlying asset will be less than the option's implied volatility of 58.36%. The call buyer believes the stock will move far enough above the strike price of 17 to provide a payoff greater than the 1.44 cost of the call.

Although it may be acceptable to think of the option premium as income, it is important to remember that the call writer has given up an important benefit of stock ownership: capital gains above the strike price. This dynamic can be seen in Exhibit 7. Consider an investor with a long position in PBR stock (with delta of +1) and a short position in a PBR NOV 17 call. The investor enjoys the benefit of the call premium of 1.44. This cushions the value of the position (Stock – Call, or S – C) as the PBR share price drops. If the PBR stock price drops to 5, the call option will drop to essentially 0. The portfolio will be worth about 6.44, as shown in Exhibit 7. As the stock price increases, however, the short call position begins to limit portfolio gains. If the price of PBR shares rises to 30, the call option delta approaches 1, so the delta of the portfolio (S – C) approaches 0. The portfolio gains from the long PBR stock position will be reduced by losses on the short call position. As the in-the-money option expires, the maximum value of the portfolio will approach 18.44, the exercise price of 17 plus the 1.44 premium, as in Exhibit 7.

Exhibit 7: Covered Call Portfolio Value: Long PBR Stock—NOV 17 Call

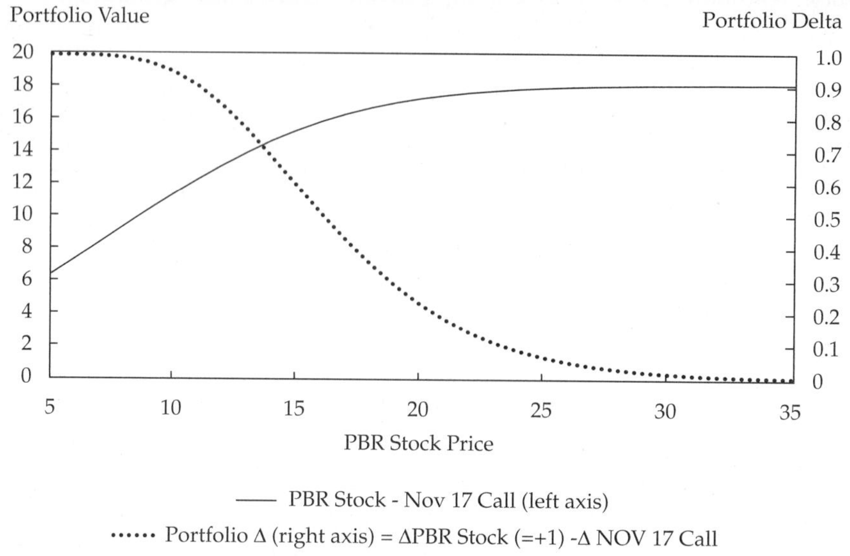

Market Participant #2: Reducing a Position at a Favorable Price

Next, consider Sofia Porto, a retail portfolio manager with a portfolio that has become overweighted in energy companies. She wants to reduce this imbalance. Porto holds 5,000 shares of PBR, an energy company, and she expects the price of this stock to remain relatively stable over the next month. She may decide to sell 1,000 shares for 15.84 each. As an alternative, Porto might decide to write 10 exchange-traded PBR SEP 15 call contracts. This means she is creating 10 option contracts, each of which covers 100 shares. In exchange for this contingent claim, she receives the option premium of 1.64/call × 100 calls/contract × 10 contracts = 1,640. Because the current PBR stock price (15.84) is above the exercise price of 15, the options she writes are in the money. Given her expectation that the stock price will be stable over the next month, it is likely that the option will be exercised. Because Porto wants to reduce the overweighting in energy stocks, this outcome is desirable. If the option is exercised, she has effectively sold the stock at 16.64. She receives 1.64 when she writes the option, and she receives 15 when the option is exercised. Porto could have simply sold the shares at their original price of 15.84, but in this specific situation, the option strategy resulted in a price improvement of 0.80 ([15 + 1.64] − 15.84) per share, or 5.05% (0.80/15.84), in a month's time.[2] By maintaining the stock position and selling a 15 call, she still risks the possibility of a stock price decline during the coming month resulting in a realized price lower than the current market price of 15.84. For example, if the PBR share price declined to 10 over the next month, Porto would realize only 10 + 1.64 =11.64 on her covered call position.

An American option premium can be viewed as having two parts: exercise value (also called intrinsic value) and time value.[3]

$$\text{Call Premium} = \text{Time Value} + \text{Intrinsic Value} = \text{Time Value} + \text{Max}(0, S - X)$$

2 Porto's effective selling price of 16.64 is 0.80 higher than the original price of 15.84: 0.80/15.84 = 5.05%.
3 In addition to exercise value, some use the term "economic value" for intrinsic value because it is the value of the option if the investor were to exercise it at this very moment and trade out of the stock position.

In this case, the right to buy at 15 when the stock price is 15.84 has an exercise (or intrinsic) value of 0.84. The option premium is 1.64, which is 0.80 more than the exercise value. This difference of 0.80 is called time value.

$$1.64 = \text{Time Value} + (15.84 - 15)$$

Someone who writes covered calls to improve on the market is capturing the time value, which augments the stock selling price. Remember, though, that giving up part of the return distribution would result in an opportunity loss if the underlying goes up.

Market Participant #3: Target Price Realization

A third popular use of options is really a hybrid of the first two objectives. This strategy involves writing calls with an exercise price near the target price for the stock. Suppose a bank trust department holds PBR in many of its accounts and that its research team believes the stock would be properly priced at 16 per share, which is only slightly higher than its current price. In those accounts for which the investment policy statement permits option activity, the manager might choose to write near-term calls with an exercise price near the target price, 16 in this case. Suppose an account holds 500 shares of PBR. Writing 5 SEP 16 call contracts at 0.97 brings in 485 in cash. If the stock is above 16 in a month, the stock will be called away at the strike price (target price), with the option premium adding an additional 6% positive return to the account.[4] If PBR fails to rise to 16, the manager might write a new OCT expiration call with the same objective in mind.

Although this strategy is popular, the investor should not view it as a source of free money. The stock is currently very close to the target price, and the manager could simply sell it and be satisfied. Although the covered call writing program potentially adds to the return, there is also the chance that the stock could experience bad news or the overall market might pull back, resulting in an opportunity loss relative to the outright sale of the stock. The investor also would have an opportunity loss if the stock rose sharply above the exercise price and it was called away at a lower-than-market price.

The exposure from the short position in the PBR SEP 16 call can be understood in terms of the Greeks in Exhibit 6. Delta measures how the option price changes as the underlying asset price changes, and gamma measures the rate of change in delta.[5] A PBR SEP 16 call has a delta = 0.516 and a gamma of 0.156. A short call will reduce the delta of the portfolio (S – C) from +1 to +0.484 (= +1[Share] – 0.516[Short Call]). The lower portfolio delta will reduce the upside opportunity. A share price increase of 1 will result in a portfolio gain of approximately 0.484.[6] The delta of the portfolio is not constant. By selling the PBR 16 call, the portfolio is now "short gamma". Remember, gamma is the rate of change of delta. Although the underlying PBR share has a gamma of 0, the short call will make the gamma of the portfolio −0.156. As the price of PBR shares increases above 16, the delta of the PBR call position will change, at a rate of gamma. Gamma is greatest for a near-the-money option and becomes progressively smaller as the option moves either into or out of the money (as seen in Exhibit 8).

Gamma of an ATM option can increase dramatically as the time to expiration approaches. Traders with large gamma exposure (especially large negative gamma) should be aware of the speed with which the position values can change. The change in portfolio delta and gamma for a PBR SEP 16 covered call as a function of share price can be seen in Exhibit 8. As the price of PBR shares increase, the portfolio delta

4 Relative to a stock price of 16, the option premium of 0.97 is 0.97/16 = 6.06%.

5 Delta is the calculus first derivative of the option price with respect to the underlying asset price. Gamma is the second derivative of the option price with respect to the underlying asset price.

6 The delta approximates the portfolio price change for very small changes in the underlying price. The delta itself is changing at a rate of gamma. For a change as large as 1%, the actual portfolio value will increase at a rate of less than 0.484 because it is short gamma.

changes at a rate of gamma. As the share price moves above the exercise price of 16, the portfolio (S – C) delta drops at a rate gamma towards its eventual limit of 0, effectively eliminating any remaining upside in the position.

Exhibit 8: Delta vs. Gamma for PBR 16 Covered Call Portfolio

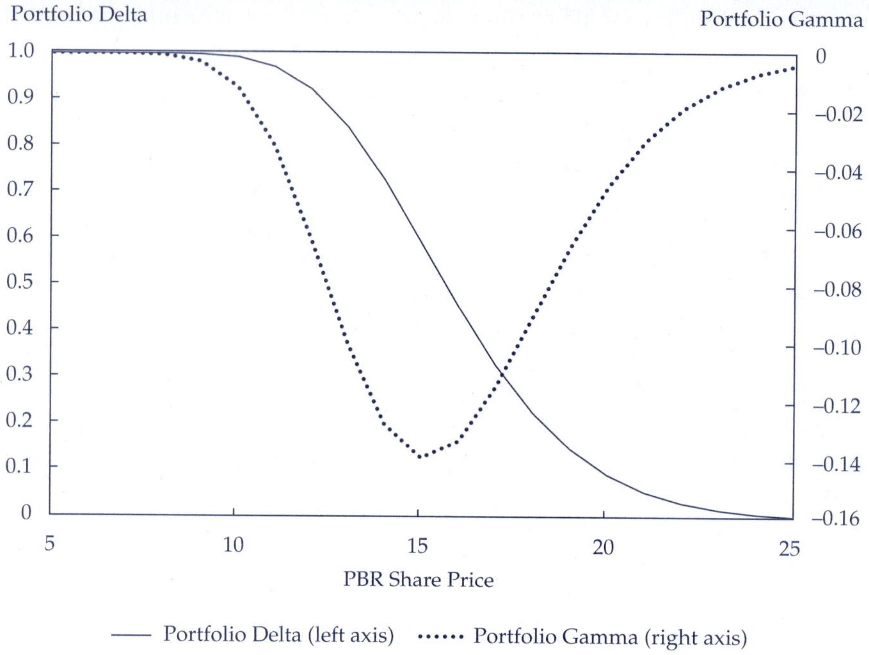

Profit and Loss at Expiration

In the process of learning option strategies, it is always helpful to look at a graphical display of the profit and loss possibilities at the option expiration. Suppose an investor owns PBR, currently trading at 15.84. The investor believes gains may be limited above a price of 17 and decides to write a call against the long share position. The 17 strike calls will have no intrinsic value because the share price is currently 15.84. The investor must now consider the available option maturities (SEP, OCT, and NOV) as shown in Exhibit 6. In deciding which option to write, the investor may consider the option premiums and implied volatilities. Based on the investor's view that volatility will remain low over the next three months, the investor chooses to write the NOV call. At 58.36%, the NOV 17 call has highest implied volatility of the available 17 strike options, so it would be the most overvalued assuming low volatility. The option premium of 1.44 is completely explained by the time value of the NOV option, because the NOV 17 option has no exercise value (Option premium = Time value + Intrinsic value; 1.44 = Time value + Max[0,15.84 – 17]). If the stock is above 17 at expiration, the option holder will exercise the call option and the investor will deliver the shares in exchange for the exercise price of 17. The maximum gain with a covered call is the appreciation to the exercise price plus the option premium.[7]

7 If someone writes an in-the-money covered call, there is "depreciation" to the exercise price, so the difference would be subtracted. For instance, if the stock price is 50 and a 45 call sells for 7, the maximum gain is –(50 – 45) + 7 = 2.

Some symbols will be helpful in learning these relationships:

S_0 = Stock price when option position opened

S_T = Stock price at option expiration

X = Option exercise price

c_0 = Call premium received or paid

The maximum gain is $(X - S_0) + c_0$. With a starting price of 15.84, a sale price of 17 results in 1.16 of price appreciation. The option writer would keep the option premium of 1.44 for a total gain of 1.16 + 1.44 = 2.60. This is the maximum gain from this strategy because all price appreciation above 17 belongs to the call holder. The call writer keeps the option premium regardless of what the stock does, so if it were to drop, the overall loss is reduced by the option premium received. Exhibit 9 shows the situation. The breakeven price for a covered call is the stock price minus the premium, or $S_0 - c_0$. In other words, the breakeven point occurs when the stock falls by the premium received—in this example, 15.84 – 1.44 = 14.40. The maximum loss would occur if the stock became worthless; it equals the original stock price minus the option premium received, or $S_0 - c_0$.[8] In this single unlikely scenario, the investor would lose 15.84 on the stock position but still keep the premium of 1.44, for a total loss of 14.40.

At option expiration, the *value* of the covered call position is the stock price minus the exercise value of the call. Any appreciation beyond the exercise price belongs to the option buyer, so the covered call writer does not earn any gains beyond that point. Symbolically,

$$\text{Covered Call Expiration Value} = S_T - \text{Max}[(S_T - X),0]. \quad (1)$$

The *profit* at option expiration is the covered call value plus the option premium received minus the original price of the stock:

$$\text{Covered Call Profit at Expiration} = S_T - \text{Max}[(S_T - X),0] + c_0 - S_0. \quad (2)$$

In summary:

Maximum gain = $(X - S_0) + c_0$

Maximum loss = $S_0 - c_0$

Breakeven price = $S_0 - c_0$

Expiration value = $S_T - \text{Max}[(S_T - X),0]$

Profit at expiration = $S_T - \text{Max}[(S_T - X),0] + c_0 - S_0$

8 Note that with a covered call, the breakeven price and the maximum loss are the same value.

Exhibit 9: Covered Call P&L Diagram: Stock at 15.84, Write 17 Call at 1.44

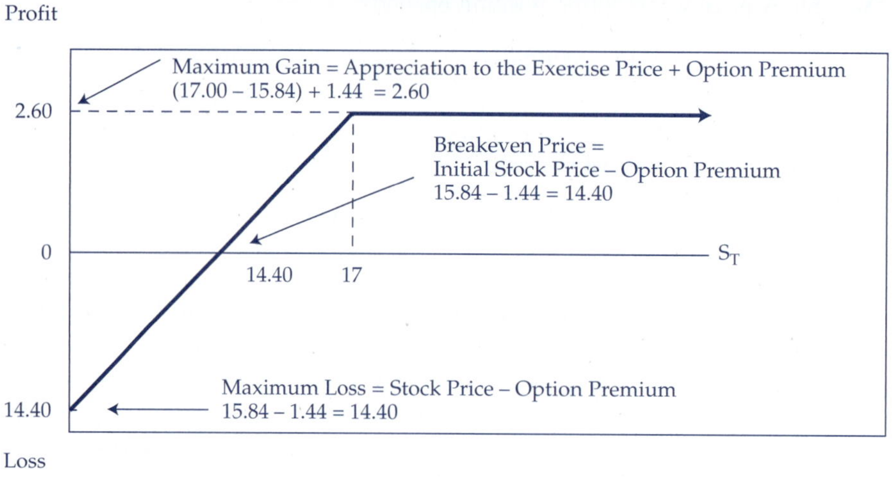

It is important to remember that these profit and loss diagrams depict the situation only at the end of the option's life.[9] Most equity covered call writing occurs with exchange-traded options, so the call writer always has the ability to buy back the option before expiration. If, for instance, the PBR stock price were to decline by 1 shortly after writing the covered call, the call value would most likely also decline. If this investor correctly believed the decline was temporary, he might buy the call back at the new lower option premium, making a profit on that trade, and then write the option again after the share price recovered.

EXAMPLE 3

Characteristics of Covered Calls

S_0 = Stock price when option position opened = 25.00

X = Option exercise price = 30.00

S_T = Stock price at option expiration = 31.33

c_0 = Call premium received = 1.55

1. Which of the following correctly calculates the maximum gain from writing a covered call?

   A. $(S_T - X) + c_0 = 31.33 - 30.00 + 1.55 = 2.88$

   B. $(S_T - S_0) - c_0 = 31.33 - 25.00 - 1.55 = 4.78$

   C. $(X - S_0) + c_0 = 30.00 - 25.00 + 1.55 = 6.55$

Solution:

C is correct. The covered call writer participates in gains up to the exercise price, after which further appreciation is lost to the call buyer. That is, $X - S_0 = 30.00 - 25.00 = 5.00$. The call writer also keeps c_0, the option premium, which is 1.55. So, the total maximum gain is 5.00 + 1.55 = 6.55.

9 It is also important to note that the general shape of the profit and loss diagram for a covered call is the same as that of writing a put. Covered call writing is the most common use of options by individual investors, whereas writing puts is the least common.

2. Which of the following correctly calculates the breakeven stock price from writing a covered call?

A. $S_0 - c_0 = 25.00 - 1.55 = 23.45$

B. $S_T - c_0 = 31.33 - 1.55 = 29.78$

C. $X + c_0 = 30.00 + 1.55 = 31.55$

Solution:

A is correct. The call premium of 1.55 offsets a decline in the stock price by the amount of the premium received: 25.00 – 1.55 = 23.45.

3. Which of the following correctly calculates the maximum loss from writing a covered call?

A. $S_0 - c_0 = 25.00 - 1.55 = 23.45$

B. $S_T - c_0 = 31.33 - 1.55 = 29.78$

C. $S_T - X + c_0 = 31.33 - 30.00 + 1.55 = 2.88$

Solution:

A is correct. The stock price can fall to zero, causing a loss of the entire investment, but the option writer still keeps the option premium received: 25.00 – 1.55 = 23.45

INVESTMENT OBJECTIVES OF PROTECTIVE PUTS 4

☐ discuss the investment objective(s), structure, payoff, risk(s), value at expiration, profit, maximum profit, maximum loss, and breakeven underlying price at expiration of a protective put position

The protective put is often viewed as a classic example of buying insurance. The investor holds a risky asset and wants protection against a loss in value. He then buys insurance in the form of the put, paying a premium to the seller of the insurance, the put writer. The exercise price of the put is similar to the coverage amount for an insurance policy. The insurance policy deductible is similar to the difference between the current asset price and the strike price of the put. A protective put with a low exercise price is like an insurance policy with a high deductible. Although less expensive, a low strike put involves greater price exposure before the payoff function goes into the money. For an insurance policy, a higher deductible is less expensive and reflects the increased risk borne by the insured party. For a protective put, a lower exercise price is less costly and has a greater risk of loss in the position.

Like traditional term insurance, this form of insurance provides coverage for a period of time. At the end of the period, the insurance expires and either pays off or not. The buyer of the insurance may or may not choose to renew the insurance by buying another put. A protective put can appear to be a great transaction with no drawbacks, because it provides downside protection with upside potential, but let us take a closer look.

Loss Protection/Upside Preservation

Suppose a portfolio manager has a client with a 50,000 share position in PBR. Her research suggests there may be a negative shock to the stock price in the next four to six weeks, and he wants to guard against a price decline. Consider the put prices shown in Exhibit 6; the purchase of a protective put presents the manager with some choices. Puts represent a right to sell at the strike price, so higher-strike puts will be more expensive. For this reason, the put buyer may select the 15-strike PBR put. Longer-term American puts are more expensive than their equivalent (same strike price) shorter-maturity puts. The put buyer must be sure the put will not expire before the expected price shock has occurred. The portfolio manager could buy a one-month (SEP) 15-strike put for 0.65. This put insures against the portion of the underlying return distribution that is below 15, but it will not protect against a price shock occurring after the SEP expiration.

Alternatively, the portfolio manager could buy a two-month option, paying 0.99 for an OCT 15 put, or she could buy a three-month option, paying 1.46 for a NOV 15 put. Note that there is not a linear relationship between the put value and its time until expiration. A two-month option does not sell for twice the price of a one-month option, nor does a three-month option sell for three times the price of a one-month option. The portfolio manager can also reduce the cost of insurance by increasing the size of the deductible (i.e., the current stock price minus the put exercise price), perhaps by using a put option with a 14 exercise price. A put option with an exercise price of 14 would have a lower premium but would not protect against losses in the stock until it falls to 14.00 per share. The option price is cheaper, but on a 50,000 share position, the deductible would be 50,000 more than if the exercise price of 15 were selected.[10]

Because of the uncertainty about the timing of the "shock event" she anticipates, the manager might consider the characteristics of the available option maturities. Given our assumptions, three of the BSM model inputs for the available 15 strike options are the same (PBR stock price 15.84, the strike price 15 and the risk-free rate of interest 4%). The difference in the cost of the SEP, OCT, and NOV options will be explained by the differences in time and the term structure of volatility. The BSM model assumes option volatility does not change over time or with strike price. In practice, volatility can vary across time and strike prices. For the 15 puts, the implied volatility is slightly greater for the NOV option, perhaps reflecting other traders' concerns about a shock event before expiration. Because the PBR stock price is 15.84 and the put options are all 15 strike, all three maturities have no intrinsic value.

The cost of each PBR 15 strike option is entirely explained by the remaining time value. If the stock price does not fall below 15, the SEP, OCT, and NOV put option values will erode to 0 as they approach their expiration dates. The erosion of the options value with time is approximated by the theta. The daily thetas (Theta/365) for the PBR puts and calls are given in Exhibit 6. Notice, all the theta values in the table are negative. These values approximate the daily losses on the option positions as time passes, all else equal. The NOV 15 put (90 days) has a theta of –0.009 and the SEP 15 put (30 days) has a theta of –0.015. If the NOV 15 option is held for one day, and the price and volatility of the underlying do not change, the put value will decline by approximately 0.009 to approximately 1.45 (= 1.46 – 0.009).

The graph of the BSM theta function for the PBR NOV 15 option as it approaches maturity is shown in Exhibit 10. Notice how the rate of decline changes as maturity approaches. If the PBR price does not drop below 15, the NOV 15 put will expire out-of-the-money and the option price will gradually fall to 0. All else equal, the sum of the daily losses approximated by theta will explain the entire loss of 1.46

10 The deductible is 50,000 × (15.84 – 15.00) with a strike price of 15. With a strike price of 14, the deductible would be 50,000 × (15.84 – 14.00), or 50,000 more.

in option value over that time. The complex shape of the theta graph in Exhibit 10 results from the nature of the BSM theta formula, which includes terms to reflect the probability that the stock price will fall below the strike price during the remaining time. Note that if the price of PBR remains at 15.84 for the last 10 days to maturity, the BSM put option value will erode to 0 at varying rates averaging about −0.03/day. Assumptions of the BSM model explain the negative peak in theta around three days prior to maturity as the remaining time value rapidly decays to 0. Theta values might help the investor decide which maturity to choose. If he were to buy the cheaper SEP put, the daily erosion of value (−0.015) would be greater than for the more expensive NOV put (−0.009).

Exhibit 10: PBR 15 Put Theta over Time

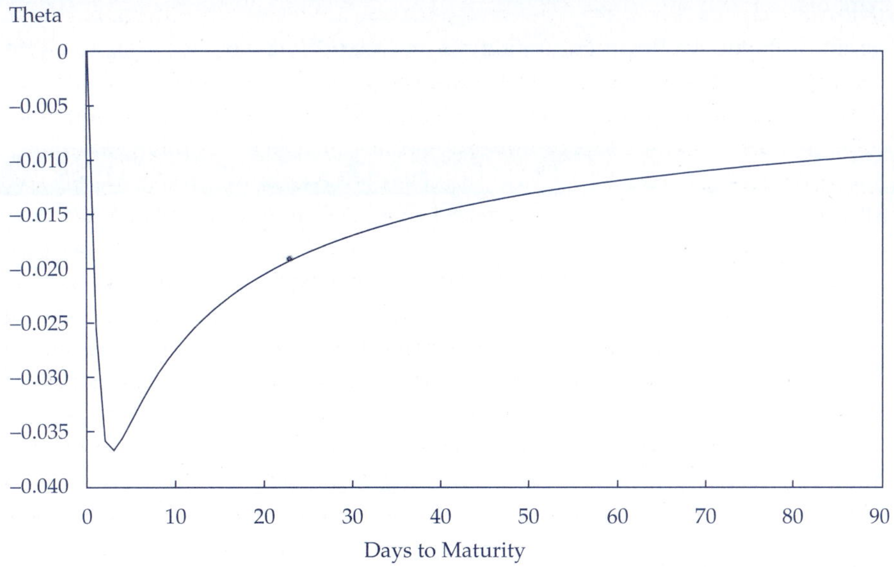

Given the four- to six-week time horizon for the shock event anticipated by the portfolio manager, the OCT put seems appropriate, but there is still the potential to lose the premium without realizing any benefit. With a 0.99 premium for the OCT 15 put and 50,000 shares to protect, the cost to the account would be almost 50,000. One advantage of the NOV option is that although it is more expensive, it has the smallest daily loss of value, as captured by theta. This option also has a greater likelihood of not having expired before the news hits. Also, although the portfolio manager could hold onto the put position until its expiration, she might find it preferable to close out the option prior to maturity and recover some of the premium paid.[11]

11 A price shock to the underlying asset might increase the market's expectations of future volatility, thereby likely increasing the put premium. By selling the option early, the investor would capture this increase. Also, once the adverse event occurred, there may be no reason to continue to hold the insurance. If the investor no longer needs it, he should cancel it and get part of the purchase price back. In other words, he should sell the put and recapture some of its cost.

Profit and Loss at Expiration

Exhibit 11 shows the profit and loss diagram for the protective put.[12] The stock can rise to any level, and the position would benefit fully from the appreciation; the maximum gain is unlimited. On the downside, losses are "cut off" once the stock price falls to the exercise price. With a protective put, the maximum loss is the depreciation to the exercise price plus the premium paid, or $S_0 - X + p_0$. At the option expiration, the value of the protective put is the greater of the stock price or the exercise price. The reason is because the stock can rise to any level but has a floor value of the put exercise price. In symbols,

$$\text{Value of Protective Put at Expiration} = S_T + \text{Max}[(X - S_T),0]. \quad (3)$$

The profit or loss at expiration is the ending value minus the beginning value. The initial value of the protective put is the starting stock price minus the put premium. In symbols,

$$\text{Profit of Protective Put at Expiration} = S_T + \text{Max}[(X - S_T),0] - S_0 - p_0. \quad (4)$$

Exhibit 11: Protective Put P&L Diagram: Stock at 15.84, Buy 15 Put at 1.46

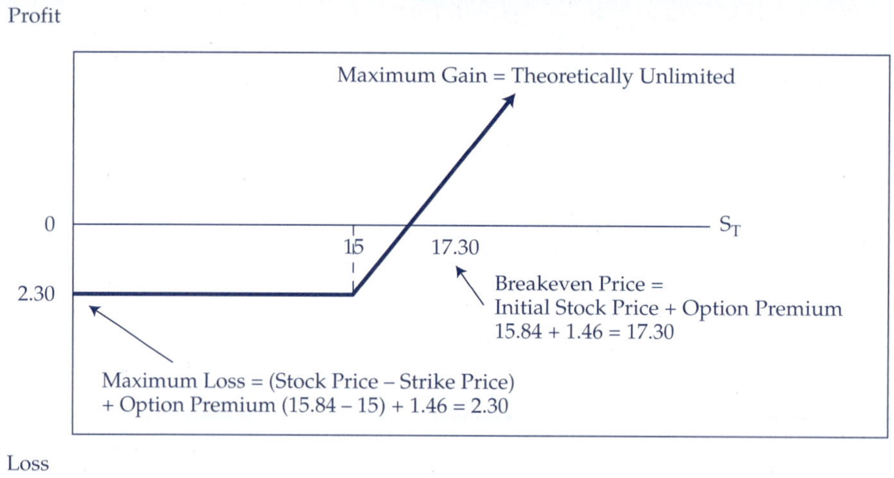

To break even, the underlying asset must rise by enough to offset the price of the put that was purchased. The breakeven point is the initial stock price plus the option premium. In symbols, Breakeven Price = $S_0 + p_0$.

In summary:

$$\text{Maximum gain} = S_T - S_0 - p_0 = \text{Unlimited}$$

$$\text{Maximum loss} = S_0 - X + p_0$$

$$\text{Breakeven price} = S_0 + p_0$$

$$\text{Expiration value} = S_T + \text{Max}[(X - S_T),0]$$

$$\text{Profit at expiration} = S_T + \text{Max}[(X - S_T),0] - S_0 - p_0$$

12 Note that the profit and loss diagram for a protective put has a shape similar to a long call position, which is the result of put–call parity. Long the asset and long the put is equivalent to long a call plus long a risk-free bond.

EXAMPLE 4

Characteristics of Protective Puts

S_0 = Stock price when option position opened = 25.00

X = Option exercise price = 20.00

$S_{T=}$ Stock price at option expiration = 31.33

p_0 = Put premium paid = 1.15

1. Which of the following correctly calculates the gain with the protective put?

   A. $S_T - S_0 - p_0 = 31.33 - 25.00 - 1.15 = 5.18$

   B. $S_T - S_0 + p_0 = 31.33 - 25.00 + 1.15 = 7.48$

   C. $S_T - X - p_0 = 31.33 - 20.00 - 1.15 = 10.18$

Solution:

A is correct. If the stock price is above the put exercise price at expiration, the put will expire worthless. The profit is the gain on the stock ($S_T - S_0$) minus the cost of the put. Note that the maximum profit with a protective put is theoretically unlimited, because the stock can rise to any level and the entire profit is earned by the stockholder.

2. Which of the following correctly calculates the breakeven stock price with the protective put?

   A. $S_0 - p_0 = 25.00 - 1.15 = 23.85$

   B. $S_0 + p_0 = 25.00 + 1.15 = 26.15$

   C. $S_T + p_0 = 31.33 + 1.15 = 32.48$

Solution:

B is correct. Because the option buyer pays the put premium, she does not begin to make money until the stock rises by enough to recover the premium paid.

3. Which of the following correctly calculates the maximum loss with the protective put?

   A. $S_0 - X + p_0 = 25.00 - 20.00 + 1.15 = 6.15$

   B. $S_T - X - p_0 = 31.33 - 20.00 - 1.15 = 10.18$

   C. $S_0 - p_0 = 25.00 - 1.15 = 23.85$

Solution:

A is correct. Once the stock falls to the put exercise price, further losses are eliminated. The investor paid the option premium, so the total loss is the "deductible" plus the cost of the insurance.

5 EQUIVALENCE TO LONG ASSET/SHORT FORWARD POSITION

☐ compare the delta of covered call and protective put positions with the position of being long an asset and short a forward on the underlying asset

All investors who consider option strategies should understand that some options are more sensitive to changes in the underlying asset than others. As we have seen, this relationship is measured by delta, an indispensable tool to an options user. Because a long call increases in value and a long put decreases in value as the underlying asset increases in price, call deltas range from 0 to 1 and put deltas range from 0 to −1. (Naturally, the signs are reversed for short positions in these options.) A long position in the underlying asset has a delta of 1.0, whereas a short position has a delta of −1.0. When the share price is close to the strike price, a rough approximation is that a long ATM option will have a delta that is approximately 0.5 (for a call) or −0.5 (for a put). Exhibit 12 shows the delta for the PBR SEP 16 put and call versus share price. As the stock price moves toward 16 (the strike price), the call option delta is approximately 0.52 and the put delta is −0.48. In general, Call Delta − Put Delta = 1 for options on the same underlying with the same BSM model inputs.

Exhibit 12: Delta of PBR Options vs. Stock Price

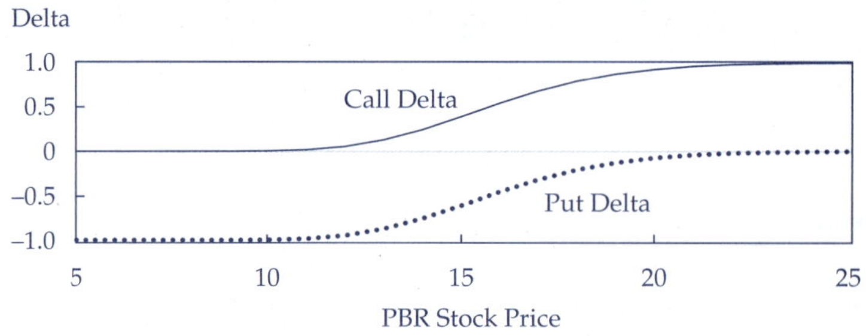

Delta can be applied to a portfolio as well. Suppose on the Tokyo Stock Exchange, Honda Motor Company stock sells for ¥3,500. A portfolio contains 100 shares, and the manager writes one exchange-traded covered call contract with a ¥3,500 strike. The delta of the 100-share position will be 100 × +1 = +100. Because the call is at the money, meaning that the stock price and exercise price are equal, it will have a delta of approximately 0.5. The portfolio, however, is short one call contract. From the perspective of the portfolio, the delta of the short call contract is −0.5 × 100 = −50. A short call *loses* money as the underlying price rises. So, this covered call has a **position delta** (which is an overall or portfolio delta) of 50, consisting of +100 points for the stock and −50 points for the short call. Compare this call with a protective put, in which someone buys 100 shares of stock and one contract of an ATM put. Its position delta would also be 50: +100 points for the stock and −50 points for the long put.

Finally, consider a long stock position of 100 shares and a short forward position of 50 shares. Because futures and forwards on non-dividend-paying stocks are essentially proxies for the stock, their deltas are also 1.0 for a long position and −1.0 for a short position. In this example, the short forward position "cancels" half the long stock position, so the position delta is also 50. These examples show three different positions: an ATM covered call, an ATM protective put, and a long stock/short forward position that all have the same delta. For small movements in the price of the underlying asset, these positions will show very similar gains and losses.

Writing Puts

If someone writes a put option and simultaneously deposits an amount of money equal to the exercise price into a designated account, it is called writing a **cash-secured put.**[13] This strategy is appropriate for someone who is bullish on a stock or who wants to acquire shares at a particular price. The fact that the option exercise price is escrowed provides assurance that the put writer will be able to purchase the stock if the option holder chooses to exercise. Think of the cash in a cash-secured put as being similar to the stock part of a covered call. When an investor sells a covered call, she takes on the obligation to sell a stock, and this obligation is covered by ownership in the shares. When a put option is sold to create a new position, the obligation that accompanies this position is to purchase shares. In order to cover the obligation to purchase shares, the portfolio should have enough cash in the account to make good on this obligation. The short put position is covered or secured by cash in the account.

Now consider two slightly different scenarios using the price data from Exhibit 6. In the first scenario, one investor might be bullish on PBR and is interested in buying the stock at a cheaper price. With the stock at 15.84, she writes the SEP 15 put for 0.65, which is purchased by another investor who is bearish on PBR stock. The option writer will keep the option premium regardless of what the stock price does. If the stock is below 15 at expiration, however, the put would be exercised and the option writer would be obliged to purchase shares from the option holder at the exercise price of 15.

Possible small (and independent) changes to the variables from Exhibit 6 are simulated in Exhibit 13 for the *long* PBR SEP 15 put position. The long put is illustrated here for simplicity—these statistics for the long put position should also help the put writer to understand the risks and returns for her position, because a short position is simply the mirror image of the long position. The initial values are 15.84 for the stock and 0.65 for the put, and the put buyer has acquired a delta of −0.335 and a gamma of 0.136.[14]

As demonstrated in change #1, if the stock price rises by 0.10 from 15.84 to 15.94, the long (short) put will lose (gain) approximately $-0.335 \times 0.10 = -0.0335$ (+0.0335), as the put value drops from 0.65 to approximately 0.617 ($\approx 0.6165 = 0.65 - 0.0335$). Remember, this approximation is good for only a small change in the underlying share price. As the stock price rises, the long put's initial delta, −0.335, will change at a rate of gamma, 0.136, so the delta then becomes −0.321.

13 This strategy is also called a *fiduciary put*. Note that for a European option, the amount deposited would equal the present value of the exercise price. When someone writes a put but does not escrow the exercise price, it is sometimes called a *nakedput*. Note that this is a slightly different use of the adjective "naked" than with a naked call. When writing a naked call, the call writer does not have the underlying *asset* to deliver if the call is exercised. When an investor writes a naked put, he has not set aside the *cash* necessary to buy the asset if the put is exercised.

14 The put writer (short position) will have a delta of $-(-0.335) = +0.335$.

Exhibit 13: Long PBR SEP 15 PUT, Greeks and Put Price Changes for Small, Independent Changes in Inputs

	Stock Price (S)	Delta (Δ)	Gamma (Γ)	Option Price (p)
Initial Values	15.84	−0.335	0.136	0.65
Change #1: Stock Price Increases by 0.10, from 15.84 to 15.94				
ΔS =+0.10 Δt = 0 ΔVol = 0	**15.94**	Δ changes at rate of Γ, so: $\Delta_1 \approx \Delta_0 + (\Gamma \times \Delta S)$ **−0.321 ≈** **−0.335 + (0.136 × 0.10)**	Γ changes slightly to 0.133	$p_1 \approx p_0 + (\Delta_0 \times \Delta S)$ ***0.617* ≈** **0.65 + (−0.335 × 0.10)**
Change #2: Time to Expiration Changes by 1 Day, from 30 to 29 Days				
ΔS = 0 **Δt = 1 day (to 29 Days)** ΔVol = 0	15.84	−0.335	0.136	$p_1 \approx p_0 + (\Theta \times \Delta t)$ ***0.635* ≈** **0.65 + (−0.015 × 1)**
Change #3: Implied Volatility Increases by 1 Percentage Point, from 58.44% to 59.44%				
ΔS = 0 Δt = 0 **ΔVol = +1% (to 59.44%)**	15.84	−0.335	0.136	$p_1 \approx p_0 + (\nu \times \Delta Vol)$ ***0.667* ≈** **0.65 + (0.017 × 1)**

The long SEP 15 put position also has a theta of −0.015 and a vega of +0.017.[15] As time decays, the long (short) put option will lose (gain) value at a rate of theta, so the value of long (short) position will decrease (increase) by approximately 0.015/per day. As demonstrated in change #2 (which is separate and independent from change #1), all else equal, the long put value would drop from about 0.65 to 0.635 as the put moves one day closer to expiration (from 30 to 29 days). If the implied volatility of the SEP 15 put were to increase by 1% (from 58.44% to 59.44%), all else equal, the option price would increase by 0.017 to approximately 0.667, as demonstrated in change #3. The increase in volatility would benefit the put holder at the expense of the writer, because the short put position would lose 0.017.

If the stock is above 15 at expiration, the put option will expire unexercised. At the expiration date, the put writer will either keep the premium or have PBR shares put to her at 15. Because the put writer was bullish on PBR and wanted to purchase it at a cheaper price, she may be happy with this result. Netting out the option premium received by the put writer would make her effective purchase price 15.00 − 0.65 = 14.35.

In another scenario, an institutional investor might be interested in purchasing PBR. Suppose the investor wrote the SEP 17 put for 1.76. This strategy will have slightly different values for the Greeks compared with the previous strategy. The delta of the SEP 17 short put position will be +0.62, gamma will be −0.140, and theta will equal +0.016. This position will be more sensitive to changes in the stock price than the SEP 15 put. If the PBR share price increases 0.10 from 15.84 to 15.94, the put writer will now profit by approximately +0.62 × 0.10 = 0.062. The higher strike price makes the short SEP 17 put a more bullish position than the SEP 15 put. This dynamic is reflected in the larger delta for the short SEP 17 put at +0.620 (versus +0.335 for the short SEP 15 put).

If the stock is below 17 at expiration, the SEP 17 puts will be exercised and the investor (i.e., put writer) will pay 17 for the shares, resulting in a net price of 17.00 − 1.76 = 15.24. Anytime someone writes an option, the maximum gain is the option premium received, so in this case, the maximum gain is 1.76. The maximum loss

15 All else equal, a long put loses time value as it approaches expiration (negative theta). All else equal, a long put increases in value as the volatility is increased (positive vega). In the case of a short put, the signs are reversed.

when writing a put occurs when the stock falls to zero. The option writer pays the exercise price for worthless stock but still keeps the premium. In this example, the maximum loss would be 17.00 − 1.76 = 15.24. Exhibit 14 shows the corresponding profit and loss diagram.

Exhibit 14: Short Put P&L Diagram: Write SEP 17 Put at 1.76

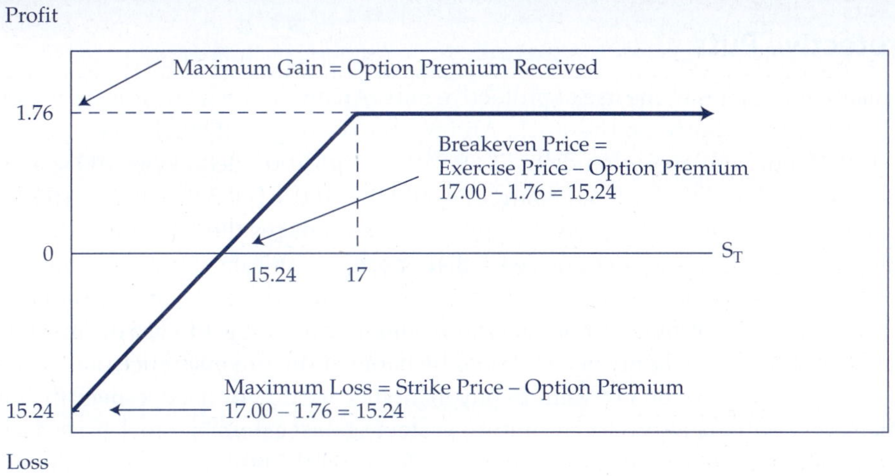

Note the similar shape of the covered call position in Exhibit 9 and the short put in Exhibit 14. Writing a covered call and writing a put are very similar with regard to their risk and reward characteristics.[16]

RISK REDUCTION USING COVERED CALLS AND PROTECTIVE PUTS

6

☐ compare the effect of buying a call on a short underlying position with the effect of selling a put on a short underlying position

Covered calls and protective puts may both be viewed as risk-reducing or hedging strategies. In the case of a covered call, some price uncertainty is eliminated for price increases. For a protective put, the price uncertainty is eliminated for price decreases. The risk reduction can be understood by considering hedge statistics.

Covered Calls

Consider the individual who owns 100 shares of a PBR stock at 15.84. The long position has a delta of +100. Suppose the investor now writes a NOV 17 call contract against this entire position. These options have a delta of 0.475. This covered call position has a position delta of (100 × +1.0) − (100 × 0.475) = +52.5. A position delta of 52.5 is equivalent (for small changes) to owning 52.5 shares of the underlying asset. An

16 The two strategies are very similar due to put–call parity. Recall that P = C − S + PV of X, implying that −P ≈ −C + S (ignoring PV of X), thus showing that a short put payoff profile is similar to that of a covered call.

investor can lose more money on a 100-share position than on a 52.5-share position. Even if the stock declines to nearly zero, the loss is reduced only by the amount of the option premium received. Viewed this way, the covered call position is less risky than the underlying asset held alone. The lower position delta will work against the investor if the share price increases. A PBR share price above 17 would result in the shares getting called away, and portfolio gains per share are limited to $2.60 = (X - S_0) + c_0 = (17 - 15.84) + 1.44$.

Protective Puts

Similar logic applies to the use of protective puts. An investor who buys a put is essentially buying insurance on the stock. An investor owning PBR stock could purchase a NOV 15 put with an option delta of −0.359. The position delta from 100 shares of PBR stock and one NOV 15 put contract would be $+100 + (-0.359 \times 100) = +64.1$ For small changes in price, the protective put portfolio reduces the risk of the 100-share PBR position to the equivalent of a 64.1 share position. This insurance lasts only until NOV. One buys insurance to protect against a risk, and the policyholder should not feel bad if the risk event does not materialize and he does not get to use the insurance. Stated another way, a homeowner should be happy if the fire insurance on his house goes unused. Still, we do not want to buy insurance we do not need, especially if it is expensive. Continually purchasing puts to protect against a possible stock price decline will result in lower volatility in the overall portfolio, but the trade-off between premium cost and risk reduction must be carefully considered. Such continuous purchasing of puts to protect against a possible stock price decline is an expensive strategy that would wipe out most of the long-term gain on an otherwise good investment. The occasional purchase of a protective put to manage a temporary situation, however, can be a sensible risk-reducing activity.

Buying Calls and Writing Puts on a Short Position

The discussion on protective puts (Stock + Put) and covered calls (Stock − Call) describes risk-reduction strategies for investors with long positions in the underlying asset. How can investors reduce risk when they are short the underlying asset? The short investor is worried the underlying stock will go up and profits if the underlying stock goes down. To offset the risks of a short position, an investor may purchase a call. The new portfolio will be (Call − Stock). The long call will offset portfolio losses when the share price increases.

To generate income from option premiums, the investor may also sell a put. As the stock drops in value, the investor profits from the short stock position, but the portfolio (− Put − Stock) gains will be reduced by the short put. When the share price increases, the short position loses money. The put expires worthless, meaning the investor will keep the put premium. The loss on the short position can still be substantial but is somewhat reduced by the put option premium.

Let us consider these two scenarios using the price data from Exhibit 6. In both cases, the investor is bearish on PBR and shorts the stock at 15.84. In the first case, she purchases the SEP 16 call for 0.97. As the share price increases above 16, the payoff from the call will act to offset losses in the short position. Exhibit 15 illustrates this dynamic. As the share price increases, portfolio losses never exceed 1.13. The profit on the short stock position plus the profit from the in-the-money call equals $(15.84 - S) + [(S - 16) - 0.97] = -1.13$. If the share price decreases, the investor profits from the short but loses the call premium of 0.97. The delta from the short PBR shares is −1. The SEP 16 call delta is 0.516. The overall portfolio delta is still negative at −0.484, making this a bearish strategy. The investor is also long vega from purchasing the call,

0.018, and the position is exposed to time decay, because theta is −0.018 per day. So, she is hoping to profit from increased downside volatility from the short PBR shares while the long call cushions losses from increased upside volatility.

Exhibit 15: P&L of Long PBR SEP 16 Call and Short PBR Stock

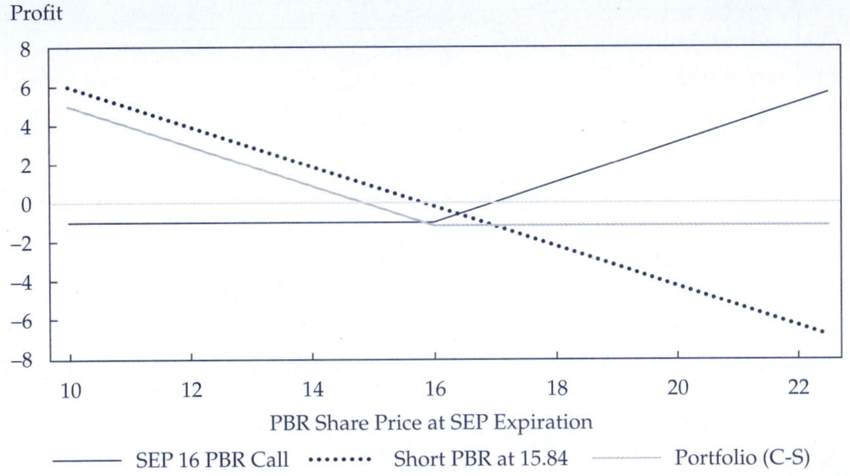

In the second scenario, the investor writes the SEP 15 put for 0.65 and collects the put premium. The upside protection from the long call in the first scenario is not provided by writing a put. The short stock position can have potentially unlimited losses. As shown in Exhibit 16, the potential gain from a falling PBR price now belongs to the put owner. The maximum gain from this strategy is given by the profit on the short stock position plus the profit from the out-of-the-money short put, which equals (15.84 − S) − [(15 − S) − 0.65] = 1.49. Losses from the short stock position will be cushioned only by the 0.65 premium collected from writing the put. The delta of the short PBR shares is −1, and the delta of the short put is − (−0.335), so the position delta is −1 + 0.335 = −0.665. The investor is bearish and hoping to profit from a downward price move. She is also short vega from writing the put, (−0.017), and benefits from time decay, as theta of the short put is +0.015 (= − [−0.015]). So, she is hoping for reduced volatility to give her an opportunity to collect the put premium without losing from the short on PBR shares.

Exhibit 16: P&L of Short PBR SEP 15 Put and Short PBR Stock

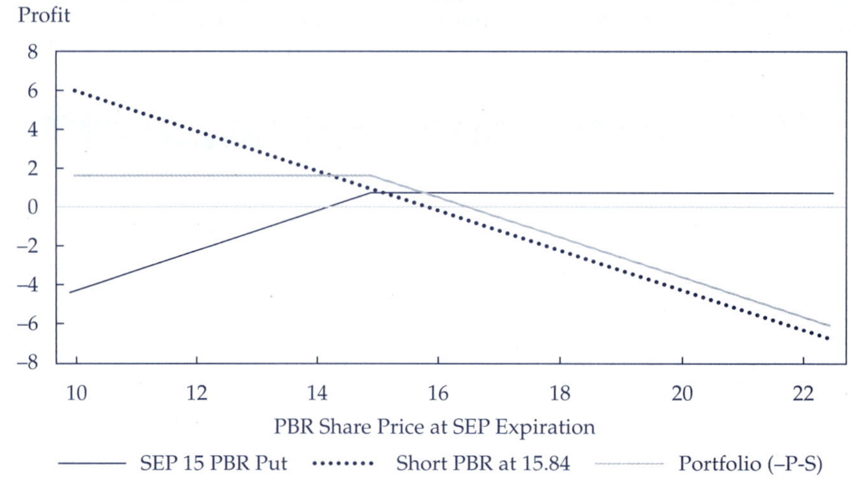

EXAMPLE 5

Risk-Reduction Strategies

Janet Reiter is a US-based investor who holds a limited partnership investment in a French private equity firm. She has received notice from the firm's general partner of an upcoming capital call. Reiter plans to purchase €1,000,000 in three months to meet the capital call due at that time. The current exchange rate is US$1.20/€1, but Reiter is concerned the euro will strengthen against the US dollar. She considers the following instruments to reduce the risk of the planned purchase:

- A three-month USD/EUR call option (to buy euros) with a strike rate X = US$1.25/€1 and costing US$0.02/€1
- A three-month EUR/USD put option (to sell dollars) with a strike rate X = €0.8080/US$1 priced at €0.0134/US$1
- A three-month USD/EUR futures contract (to buy euros) with f_0 = US$1.2052/€1

1. Discuss the position required in each instrument to reduce the risk of the planned purchase.

Solution:

Reiter could purchase a €1,000,000 call option struck at US$1.25/€1 for US$20,000. If the EUR price were to increase above US$1.25, she would exercise her right to buy EUR for US$1.25. She would also benefit from being able to purchase EUR at a cheaper price should the exchange rate weaken. A call on the euro is like a put on the US dollar. So, a put to sell dollars struck at an exchange rate of X = €0.8000/US$1 can be viewed as a call to buy Euro at an exchange rate of US$1/€0.8000 = US$1.25/€1. Reiter could also buy a put option on USD struck at X = €0.8080/US$1 which would allow her to sell US$1,237,624 (= €1,000,000/[€0.8080/$1]) to receive the €1,000,000 should the dollar weaken below that level. This would cost her €0.0134/

US$1 × US$1,237,624 = €16,584 or US$19,901 upfront. If USD appreciated against the EUR, Reiter would still be able to benefit from the lower cost to purchase the EUR. She could instead enter a long position in a three-month futures contract at US$1.2052. Reiter would have the obligation to purchase €1,000,000 at US$1.2052 regardless of the exchange rate in three months. The futures position requires a margin deposit, but no premium is paid.

2. Reiter purchases call options for US$20,000, and the exchange rate increases to US$1.29/€1 (EUR currency strengthens) over the next three months. The effective price Reiter pays for her 1,000,000 EUR purchase is closest to:

   A. US$1,270,000.

   B. US$1,290,000.

   C. US$1,310,000.

Solution:

A is correct. At an exchange rate of US$1.29/€1, the call with strike of X = US$1.25/€1 will be exercised. Including the call premium (US$0.02/€1), the price effectively paid for the euros is US$1.27/€1 × €1,000,000 = US$1,270,000.

3. Calculate the price Reiter will pay for the EUR using the three instruments if the exchange rate in three months falls to US$1.10/€1 (EUR currency weakens).

Solution:

Both the call and the put options will expire unexercised and Reiter benefits from the lower rate by purchasing €1,000,000 for US$1,100,000. However, she will lose the premiums she paid for the options. For the futures contract, she pays US$1.2052/€1 or US$1,205,200 for €1,000,000 regardless of the more favorable rate.

SPREADS AND COMBINATIONS 7

☐ discuss the investment objective(s), structure, payoffs, risk(s), value at expiration, profit, maximum profit, maximum loss, and breakeven underlying price at expiration of the following option strategies: bull spread, bear spread, straddle, and collar

Option spreads and combinations can be useful option strategies. We first consider money spreads, in which the two options differ only by exercise price. The investor buys an option with a given expiration and exercise price and sells an option with the same expiration but a different exercise price. Of course, the options are on the same underlying asset. The term *spread* is used here because the payoff is based on the difference, or spread, between option exercise prices. For a bull or bear spread, the investor buys one call and writes another call option with a different exercise price, or the investor buys one put and writes another put with a different exercise price.[17] Someone might, for instance, buy a NOV 16 call and simultaneously write a NOV 17 call, or one might buy a SEP 17 put and write a SEP 15 put. An option combination typically uses both puts and calls. The most important option combination is the straddle, on which we focus in this reading. We will investigate spreads first.

Bull Spreads and Bear Spreads

Spreads are classified in two ways: by market sentiment and by the direction of the initial cash flows. A spread that becomes more valuable when the price of the underlying asset rises is a **bull spread**; a spread that becomes more valuable when the price of the underlying asset declines is a **bear spread**. Because the investor buys one option and sells another, there is typically an initial net cash outflow or inflow. If establishing the spread requires a cash payment by the investor, it is referred to as a debit spread. Debit spreads are effectively long because the long option value exceeds the short option value. If the spread initially results in a cash inflow to the investor, it is referred to as a credit spread. Credit spreads[18] are effectively short because the short option value exceeds the long option value. Any of these strategies can be created with puts or calls. The motivation for a spread is usually to place a directional bet, giving up part of the profit potential in exchange for a lower cost of the position. Some examples will help make this clear.

Bull Spread

Regardless of whether someone constructs a bull spread with puts or with calls, the strategy requires buying one option and writing another with a *higher* exercise price. Because the higher exercise price call is less expensive than the lower strike, a call bull spread involves an initial cash outflow (debit spread). A bull spread created from puts also requires the investor to write the higher-strike option and buy the lower-strike one. Because the higher-strike put is more expensive, a put bull spread involves an initial cash inflow (credit spread).

Let's consider a call bull spread. Suppose, for instance, an investor thought it likely that by the September option expiration, PBR would rise to around 17 from its current level of 15.84. Based on the price data in Exhibit 6, what option strategy would capitalize on this anticipated price movement? If he were to buy the SEP 15 call for 1.64 and the stock rose to 17 at expiration, the call would be worth $S_T - X = 17 - 15 = 2$. If the price of the option was 1.64, the profit is 0.36. The maximum loss is the price paid for the option, or 1.64. If, instead, an investor bought the SEP 16 call for 0.97, at an expiration stock price of 17, the call would be worth 1.00 for a gain of 0.03. A spread could make more sense with the following option values. If he believes the stock will not rise above 17 by September expiration, it may make sense to "sell off" the part of the return distribution above that price. The investor would receive 0.51 for each SEP 17 call sold.

The value of the spread at expiration (V_T) depends on the stock price at expiration S_T. For a bull spread, the investor buys the low strike option (struck at X_L) and sells the high strike option (struck at X_H), so that:

$$V_T = \text{Max}(0, S_T - X_L) - \text{Max}(0, S_T - X_H). \quad (5)$$

17 One important exception to the typical option spread is a *butterfly spread*, which is essentially two simultaneous spreads and can be done using only calls or only puts.

18 The use of the term credit spread has a different interpretation than in fixed income investing. For bond investors, the credit spread is a measure of compensation for the bond's default risk.

Therefore, the value depends on the terminal stock price S_T:

$V_T = 0 - 0 = 0 \quad \text{if } S_T \le X_L$

$V_T = S_T - X_L - 0 = S_T - X_L \ \text{ if } X_L < S_T < X_H$

$V_T = S_T - X_L - (S_T - X_H) = X_H - X_L \text{ if } S_T \ge X_H$

The profit is obtained by subtracting the initial outlay for the spread from the foregoing value of the spread at expiration. To determine the initial outlay, recall that a call option with a lower exercise price will be more expensive than a call option with a higher exercise price. Because we are buying the call with the lower exercise price (for c_L) and selling the call with the higher exercise price (for c_H), the call we buy will cost more than the call we sell ($c_L > c_H$). Hence, the spread will require a net outlay of funds. This net outlay is the initial value of the position, $V_0 = c_L - c_H$, which we call the net premium. The profit is:

$$\Pi = \text{Max}(0,S_T - X_L) - \text{Max}(0,S_T - X_H) - (c_L - c_H). \quad (6)$$

In this manner, we see that the profit is the profit from the long call, $\text{Max}(0,S_T - X_L) - c_L$, plus the profit from the short call, $-\text{Max}(0,S_T - X_H) + c_H$. Broken down into ranges, the profit is as follows:

$\Pi = -c_L + c_H \text{ if } S_T \le X_L$

$\Pi = S_T - X_L - c_L + c_H \text{ if } X_L < S_T < X_H$

$\Pi = X_H - X_L - c_L + c_H \text{ if } S_T \ge X_H$

If S_T is below X_L, the strategy will lose a limited amount of money. When both options expire out of the money, the investor loses the net premium, $c_L - c_H$. The profit on the upside, if S_T is at least X_H, is also limited to the difference in strike prices minus the net premium.

Consider two alternatives for the call purchase leg of the bull spread: 1) buy the SEP 15 call or 2) buy the SEP 16 call instead. Which is preferred? With Alternative 1, the SEP 15 call costs 1.64. Writing the SEP 17 call brings in 0.51, so the net cost is 1.64 – 0.51 = 1.13. Traders would refer to this position as a PBR SEP 15/17 bull call spread. The maximum profit would occur at or above the exercise price of 17 because all gains above this level belong to the owner of the PBR SEP 17 call. At an underlying price of 17 or higher, from the trader's perspective, the position is worth 2, which represents the price appreciation from 15 to 17 (i.e., the difference in strikes). The maximum profit is

$\Pi = X_H - X_L - c_L + c_H = 17 - 15 - 1.64 + 0.51 = 0.87.$

Another way to look at it is that at a price above 17, the trader exercises the long call, buying the stock at 15, and is forced to sell the stock at 17 to the holder of his short call.

With Alternative 2, the investor buys the SEP 16 call and pays 0.97 for it. Writing the SEP 17 call brings in 0.51, so the net cost would be 0.97 – 0.51 = 0.46. At an underlying price of 17 or higher, the spread would be worth 1.00, so the maximum profit is

$\Pi = X_H - X_L - c_L + c_H = 17 - 16 - 0.97 + 0.51 = 0.54.$

Exhibit 17 compares the profit and loss diagrams for these two alternatives.

To determine the breakeven price with a spread, find the underlying asset price that will cause the exercise value of the two options combined to equal the initial cost of the spread. A spread has two exercise prices. There are also two option premiums. Mathematically, the breakeven price for a call bull spread can be derived from $\Pi = S_T^* - X_L - c_L + c_H = 0$ and is

$S_T^* = X_L + c_L - c_H,$

which represents the lower exercise price plus the cost of the spread. In the examples here, Alternative 1 costs 1.13 (= 1.64 – 0.51). The breakeven $S_T^* = X_L + c_L - c_H = 15 + 1.64 - 0.51 = 16.13$. If at option expiration the stock is 16.13, the 15-strike option would be worth 1.13 and the 17-strike call would be worthless. The breakeven price S_T^* is 15.00 + 1.13 = 16.13, as Exhibit 17 shows.

Exhibit 17: Bull Spreads: Current PBR Stock Price = 15.84

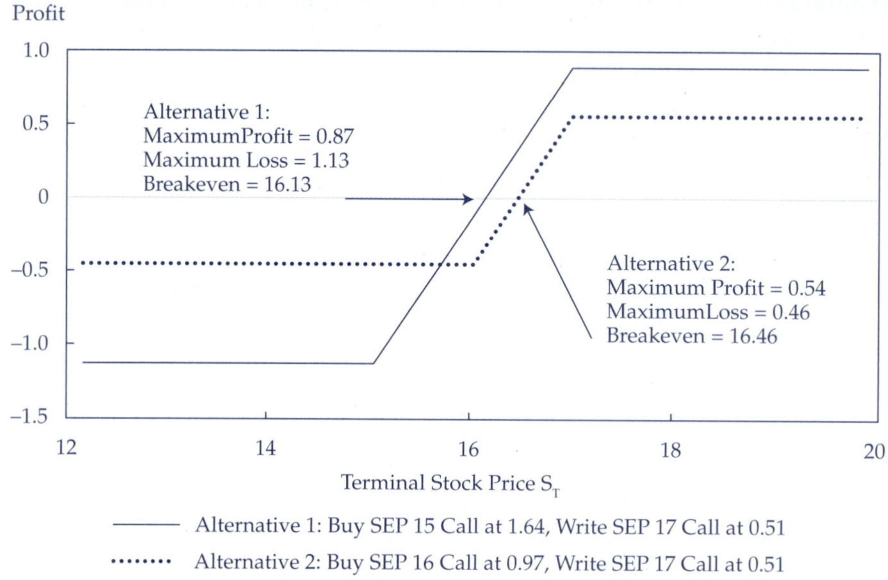

Which of the alternatives is preferable? There is no clear-cut answer. As Exhibit 17 shows, the maximum loss for alternative 1 is 1.64 – 0.51= 1.13, compared with a maximum loss of 0.97 – 0.51 = 0.46 for Alternative 2. However, Alternative 1 is potentially more profitable for a move above 17 and has a lower breakeven price.

With Alternative 1, the breakeven point of 16.13 is less than 2% above the current level of 15.84, whereas with Alternative 2, reaching the breakeven point requires almost a 4% rise in the stock price. There is some additional information in Exhibit 6 the investor may wish to consider. The SEP 15/17 spread involves buying the SEP15 call with implied volatility of 64.42% and selling the SEP 17 call option with implied volatility of 51.07%. The investor may believe the SEP 15 call being purchased is relatively expensive compared with the SEP 17 call being sold. The PBR SEP 16/17 involves buying a SEP 16 call at a cost of 0.97 with an implied volatility of 55.92%. The investor may believe the SEP 16 call represents a better value than the SEP 15 call and so may choose the PBR SEP 16/17 spread.

We can calculate the Greek values for the spread. For example, using Exhibit 6, we see the theta of the PBR SEP 15/17 spread is –0.004 = –0.019 – (–0.015), and the theta of the PBR SEP 16/17 is –0.003 = –0.018 – (–0.015). Therefore, the SEP 16/17 should experience slightly less erosion of value resulting from time decay. The investor may also consider the delta and gamma that each spread would add to her PBR position. The delta of the PBR SEP 15/17 spread is +0.306 = 0.657 – 0.351, and the delta of the PBR SEP 16/17 spread is +0.165 = 0.516 – 0.351. From the current PBR price of 15.84, the long position in the PBR 15 call will make the SEP 15/17 PBR spread slightly more sensitive to an increase in share price than the SEP 16/17 spread. For the SEP 15/17, we have gamma = –0.034 = 0.125 – 0.159 and for the SEP 16/17 gamma = –0.003 = 0.156 – 0.159. The more negative gamma value for the SEP 15/17 spread means that the position delta will decrease at a faster rate than the SEP 16/17 spread as the price of PBR shares increase. By carefully selecting the expiration and exercise prices for the options for the spread, an investor can choose the risk–return mix that most closely matches her investment outlook.

Bear Spread

With a bull spread, the investor buys the lower exercise price and writes the higher exercise price. It is the opposite with a bear spread: buy the higher exercise price and sell the lower. Because puts with higher exercise prices are (all else equal) more expensive, a put bear spread will result in an initial cash outflow (be a debit spread). For a call bear spread, the investor buys a higher exercise price call and sells the lower exercise price call. Because the higher exercise price call being purchased is less expensive than the lower strike being sold, a call bear spread will result in an initial cash inflow (credit spread).

If a trader believed PBR stock would be below 15 by the November expiration, one strategy would be to buy the PBR NOV 16 put at 1.96 and write the NOV 15 put at 1.46. This spread has a net cost of 0.50; this amount is the maximum loss, and it occurs at a PBR stock price of 16 or higher. The maximum gain is also 0.50, which occurs at a stock price of 15 or lower. (A useful way to see this result is to realize that reversing the signs of the trades leaves the horizontal axes in a diagram like Exhibit 17 intact, but it flips the profit/loss and cost lines vertically! A debit from buying a spread must be consistent with the seller of the same spread receiving a credit.) Finding the breakeven price uses the same logic as with a bull spread: find the underlying asset price at which the exercise value equals the initial cost. Let p_L represent the lower-strike put premium and p_H the higher-strike put premium. Mathematically, the value of this bear spread position at expiration is:

$$V_T = \text{Max}(0,X_H - S_T) - \text{Max}(0,X_L - S_T). \tag{7}$$

Broken down into ranges, we have the following relations:

$$V_T = X_H - S_T - (X_L - S_T) = X_H - X_L \text{ if } S_T \leq X_L$$

$$V_T = X_H - S_T - 0 = X_H - S_T \text{ if } X_L < S_T < X_H$$

$$V_T = 0 - 0 = 0 \quad \text{if } S_T \geq X_H$$

To obtain the profit, we subtract the initial outlay. Because we are buying the put with the higher exercise price and selling the put with the lower exercise price, the put we are buying is more expensive than the put we are selling. The initial value of the bear spread is $V_0 = p_H - p_L$. The profit is, therefore, $V_T - V_0$, which is:

$$\Pi = \text{Max}(0,X_H - S_T) - \text{Max}(0,X_L - S_T) - (p_H - p_L). \tag{8}$$

We see that the profit is that on the long put, $\text{Max}(0,X_H - S_T) - p_H$, plus the profit from the short put, $-\text{Max}(0,X_L - S_T) + p_L$. Broken down into ranges, the profit is as follows:

$$\Pi = X_H - X_L - p_H + p_L \text{ if } S_T \leq X_L$$

$$\Pi = X_H - S_T - p_H + p_L \text{ if } X_L < S_T < X_H$$

$$\Pi = -p_H + p_L \quad \text{if } S_T \geq X_H$$

The breakeven point, $S_T^* = X_H - p_H + p_L$, sets the profit equal to zero between the strike prices. In this example, 16 – 1.96 + 1.46 = 15.50. That is, at a stock price of 15.50 on the expiration day, the 16-strike put would be worth 0.50 and the 15-strike put would be worthless. Exhibit 18 shows the profit and loss for a NOV 15/16 bear spread.[19]

Exhibit 18: Bear Spread: Current PBR Stock Price = 15.84

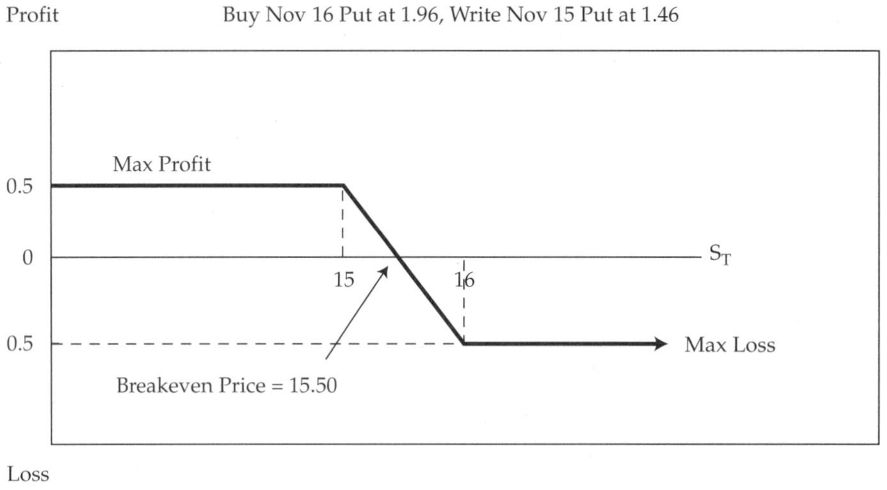

Refining Spreads

It is not necessary that both legs of a spread be established at the same time or maintained for the same period. Options are very versatile, and positions can typically be quickly adjusted as market conditions change. Here are a few examples of different tactical adjustments an option trader might consider.

Adding a Short Leg to a Long Position

Consider Carlos Aguila, a trader who in September paid a premium of 1.50 for a NOV 40 call when the underlying stock was selling for 37. A month later, in October, the stock has risen to 48. He observes the following premiums for one-month call options.

Strike	Premium
40	8.30
45	4.42
50	1.91

19 Bull spreads can also be created with puts, and bear spreads can also be created with calls. In both cases, the result is a credit spread with an initial cash inflow. Recall that American exercise–style options may be exercised at any time prior to expiration. Bull spreads with American puts have an additional risk, which is that the short put could be exercised early when the long put is not yet in the money. If the bull spread uses American calls and the short call is exercised, the long call is deeper in the money, which offsets that risk. A similar point can be applied to bear spreads using calls. Bear spreads with American calls have increased risk, because the short call may be exercised early when the long call may not yet be in the money. Thus, with American options, bull spreads with calls and bear spreads with puts are generally preferred but, of course, not required.

This position has become very profitable. The call he bought is now worth 8.30. He paid 1.50, so his profit at this point is 8.30 – 1.50 = 6.80. He thinks the stock is likely to stabilize around its new level and doubts that it will go much higher. Aguila is considering writing a call option with an exercise price of either 45 or 50, thereby converting his long call position into a bull spread. Looking first at the NOV 50 call, he notes that the 1.91 premium would more than cover the initial cost of the NOV 40 call. If he were to write this call, the new profit and loss diagram would look like Exhibit 19. To review, consider the following points:

- At stock prices of 50 or higher, the exercise value of the spread is 10.00. The reason is because both options would be in the money, and a call with an exercise price of 40 would always be worth 10 more at exercise than a call with an exercise price of 50. The initial cost of the call with an exercise price of 40 was 1.50, and there would be a 1.91 cash inflow after writing the call with an exercise price of 50. The profit is 10.00 – 1.50 + 1.91 = 10.41.
- At stock prices of 40 or lower, the exercise value of the spread is zero; both options would be out of the money. The initial cost of the call with an exercise price of 40 was 1.50, and there would be a 1.91 cash inflow after writing the call with an exercise price of 50. The profit is 0 – 1.50 + 1.91 = 0.41.
- Between the two strike prices (40 and 50), the exercise value of the spread rises steadily as the stock price increases. For every unit increase up to the higher strike price, the exercise value of this spread increases by 1.0.

For instance, if the stock price remains unchanged at 48, the exercise value of the spread is 8.00. The reason is because the call with an exercise price of 40 would be worth 8.00 and the call with an exercise price of 50 would be worthless. The initial cost of the 40-strike call was 1.50, and there would be a 1.91 cash inflow when the 50-strike call was written. The profit is 8.00 – 1.50 + 1.91 = 8.41.

Now assume that he has written the NOV 50 call. Aguila needs to be careful how he views this new situation. No matter what happens to the stock price between now and expiration, the position is profitable, relative to his purchase price of the calls with an exercise price of 40. If the stock were to fall by any amount from its current level, however, he would have an opportunity loss. His profit would decrease progressively if the price trended back to 40. Aguila would be correct in saying that the bull spread will make a profit of at least 0.41. But, writing the NOV 50 call only partially hedges against a decline in the value of his new strategy. The position can still lose about 96% of its maximum profit, because only about 4% (0.41/10.41) has been hedged.

Exhibit 19: Spread Creation: Buy a Call with Exercise Price of 40 at 1.50; Write a Call Later with Exercise Price of 50 at 1.91

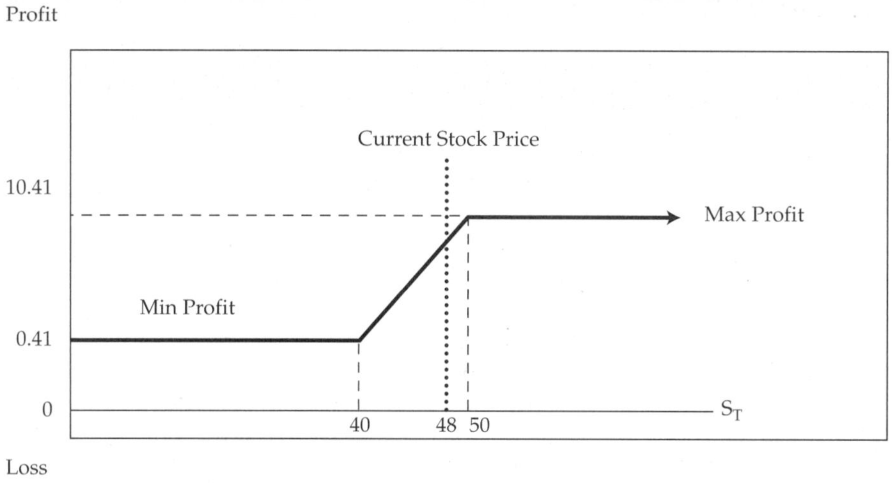

Spreads and Delta

A spread strategy may be adapted to a changing market view. Suppose the market has been rising, and Lars Clive, an options trader, expects this trend to continue. Hypothetical company ZKQ currently sells for $44. Suppose Clive buys a NOV 45 call for 5.25. He computes the delta of this call as +0.55 and gamma as +0.028. Initially, Clive will profit at a rate of 0.55 for an increase of $1 in the price of ZKQ stock. For small changes, the delta of his position will increase at a rate of 0.028 for an increase of $1 in the price of ZKQ shares.

Three days later, the stock price has risen to $49, the value of the NOV 45 call has increased to 8.18, and the call delta has increased to +0.68. For the NOV 45 call, the option price increased by 2.93 (= 8.18 – 5.25) instead of by 2.75 (= 5 × 0.55, the stock price change multiplied by the initial delta value). Because delta is changing at a rate gamma, the approximation works best for small changes in share prices. With the stock at $49, a higher-strike NOV 50 call sells for 5.74 and has a delta of +0.55. Now Clive establishes a 45/50 bull call spread by writing the NOV 50 call. Clive is less bullish at the price of 49, and his 45/50 spread portfolio now has a delta of +0.13 = +0.68 – 0.55.

Now suppose another five days pass and the stock price falls to 45. The new option values would be 5.41 for the NOV 45 call and 3.55 for the NOV 50 call. Clive closes out the NOV 50 short call by buying it back. He sold the call for 5.74 and bought it back for 3.55, so he makes 5.74 – 3.55 = 2.19, or 2.19 per contract. He still holds the long position in the NOV 45 call, and his portfolio delta increases to +0.57.

Another four days pass, and ZKQ has risen to 48. The new price for the NOV 50 call is 4.71 with a delta of 0.51. Clive owns the NOV 45 with a price of 7.10 and a delta of 0.66. He then decides to write a NOV 50 call and lower his position delta to 0.15 (= 0.66 – 0.51).

At this point, Clive has had two cash outflows totaling 8.80: the initial 5.25 plus the 3.55 to buy back the NOV 50 call. He has two cash inflows totaling 10.45: the premium income of 5.74 and then 4.71 from the two instances of writing the NOV 50 calls. Exhibit 20 provides a summary of the results of Clive's trades. Because the inflows of 10.45 exceed the outflows of 8.80, he has a resulting profit and loss diagram similar to the plot in Exhibit 19 that we saw in the previous example. Clive's timing was excellent—in each case, he increased his portfolio delta prior to an increase in

ZKQ stock and decreased delta before the share price decreased. The important point is that increasing portfolio delta will result in greater profits (losses) when the underlying asset value increases (decreases).

Exhibit 20: Spreads and Deltas: A Summary of Results of Clive's Trades

Day	ZKQ Price	Activity	Portfolio Delta	Cash Out	Cash In
1	44	Buy NOV 45 call	0.55	5.25	—
4	49	Sell NOV 50 call	0.13 (= 0.68 – 0.55)	—	5.74
9	45	Buy NOV 50 call	0.57	3.55	—
13	48	Sell NOV 50 call	0.15 (= 0.66 – 0.51)	—	4.71
Total				**8.80**	**10.45**
Net Inflow					**1.65**

Spreads are primarily a directional play on the underlying asset's spot price (and also potentially on its volatility); still, spread traders can attempt to take advantage of changes in price, and it is easy to create a hypothetical example like this one. There obviously is no guarantee that any assumed price trend will continue. In fact, in actual practice, the excellent results shown in Exhibit 20 are exceedingly difficult to achieve. Still, the experienced option user knows to look for opportunistic plays that arise from price swings.

EXAMPLE 6

Spreads

Use the following information to answer questions 1 to 3 on spreads.

$S_0 = 44.50$

OCT 45 call = 2.55, OCT 45 put = 2.92

OCT 50 call = 1.45, OCT 50 put = 6.80

1. What is the maximum gain with an OCT 45/50 bull call spread?

   A. 1.10

   B. 3.05

   C. 3.90

Solution:

C is correct. With a bull spread, the maximum gain occurs at the high exercise price. At an underlying price of 50 or higher, the spread is worth the difference in the strike prices, or 50 – 45 = 5. The cost of establishing the spread is the price paid for the lower-strike option minus the price received for the higher-strike option: 2.55 – 1.45 = 1.10. The maximum gain is 5.00 – 1.10 = 3.90.

2. What is the maximum loss with an OCT 45/50 bear put spread?

   A. 1.12

   B. 3.88

   C. 4.38

Solution:

B is correct. With a bear spread, an investor buys the higher exercise price and writes the lower exercise price. When this strategy is done with puts, the higher exercise price option costs more than the lower exercise price option. Thus, the investor has a debit spread with an initial cash outlay, which is the most he can lose. The initial cash outlay is the cost of the OCT 50 put minus the premium received from writing the OCT 45 put: 6.80 – 2.92 = 3.88.

3. What is the breakeven price with an OCT 45/50 bull call spread?

   A. 46.10

   B. 47.50

   C. 48.88

Solution:

A is correct. An investor buys the OCT 45 call for 2.55 and sells the OCT 50 call for 1.45, for a net cost of 1.10. She breaks even when the position is worth the price she paid. The long call is worth 1.10 at a stock price of 46.10, and the OCT 50 call will expire out of the money and thus be worthless. The breakeven price is the lower exercise price of 45 plus the 1.10 cost of the spread, or 46.10.

8 STRADDLE

☐ discuss the investment objective(s), structure, payoffs, risk(s), value at expiration, profit, maximum profit, maximum loss, and breakeven underlying price at expiration of the following option strategies: bull spread, bear spread, straddle, and collar

☐ describe uses of calendar spreads

A long **straddle** is an option combination in which one buys *both* puts and calls, with the same exercise price and same expiration date, on the same underlying asset.[20] If someone *writes* both options, it is a short straddle. Because a long call is bullish and a long put is bearish, this strategy may seem illogical. When the Greeks are considered, the trader's position becomes clearer. The classic example is in anticipation of some event in which the outcome is uncertain but likely to significantly affect the price of the underlying asset, regardless of how the event is resolved.

A straddle is an example of a directional play on the underlying volatility, expressing the view that volatility will either increase, for a long straddle, or decrease, for a short straddle, from its current level. A profitable outcome from a long straddle, however, usually requires a significant price movement in the underlying asset. The straddle buyer pays the premium for two options, so to make a profit, the underlying asset must move either above or below the option exercise price by at least the total amount spent on the straddle. As an example, suppose in the next few days there is a verdict expected in a liability lawsuit against an automobile manufacturer. An investor expects

20 If someone buys puts and calls with different exercise prices, the position is called a *strangle*.

the stock to move sharply one way or the other once the verdict is revealed. When the exercise price is chosen close to the current stock price, the straddle is neither a bullish nor a bearish strategy—the delta of the straddle is close to zero. With any other exercise price, there may be a directional bias (non-zero delta) because one of the options will be in the money and one will be out of the money. If the price increases (decreases) significantly, the delta of the call will approach +1 (0), and the put delta will approach 0 (−1), making the delta of the position approximately +1 (−1).

Experienced option traders know that it is difficult to make money with a straddle. In the example, other people will also be watching the court proceedings. The market consensus will predict higher volatility once the verdict is announced, and option prices rise when volatility expectations rise. This increased volatility means that both the puts and the calls become expensive well before the verdict is revealed, and the long straddle requires the purchase of both options. To make money, the straddle buyer must be correct in his view that the "true" underlying volatility is higher than the market consensus. Essentially, the bet is that the straddle buyer is right and the other market participants, on average, are wrong by underestimating volatility.

Suppose the underlying stock sells for 50, and an investor selects 30-day options with an exercise price of 50. The call sells for 2.29 and the put for 2.28, for a total investment of 4.57. At prices above 50, the call is in the money. At prices below 50, the put is in the money. For the straddle to be profitable, one of these two options must be profitable enough to pay for the costs of both the put and call. To recover this cost, the underlying asset must either rise or fall by at least 4.57, as shown by the breakeven points in Exhibit 21.

Exhibit 21: Long Straddle: Current Stock Price = 50; Buy 50-Strike Call at 2.29, Buy 50-Strike Put at 2.28

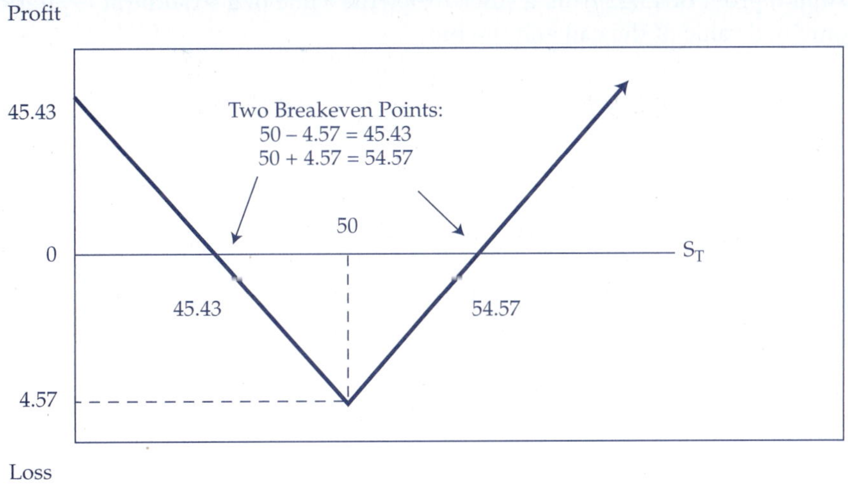

The straddle portfolio and Greeks are shown in Exhibit 22. The long straddle initially has a very low delta (+0.069 for this example) with a high gamma (0.139). The trader does not initially favor an increase or a decrease in the share price but knows the delta may quickly change. Once a direction (increase or decrease in the underlying price) asserts itself, the trader's position will take on a non-zero delta value. The trader's view can be better understood from a vega perspective. The long straddle will be profitable only if the stock price moves enough to recover both premiums. The short straddle writer collects the put and call premiums but will lose if the stock price moves more than 4.57 away from the strike price. The long (short) straddle trade is said to be long (short) volatility. The long straddle is a bet that increased volatility will move the stock price strongly above or below the strike price. The sensitivity of the straddle to changes in volatility is measured by vega. As shown in Exhibit 22, vega for our long straddle is +0.114, meaning the portfolio will profit by approximately 0.114 from increased volatility of 1% in the underlying. A stock price change large enough to cause the price of one option to exceed the cost of the combined premiums is needed to make the straddle trade profitable. A large increase in the underlying price will cause the delta of the call option to approach +1 and the delta of the put to approach 0. A large decrease in the underlying price will cause the delta of the call to drop to 0 and the put delta to approach −1.

Exhibit 22: Long and Short Straddle Greeks

	Call	Put	Long Straddle = Call + Put	Short Straddle = −Call + −Put
Cost	2.29	2.28	4.570	−4.570
Delta	0.534	−0.465	0.069	−0.069
Gamma	0.072	0.067	0.139	−0.139
Vega	0.057	0.057	0.114	−0.114
Theta	−0.039	−0.036	−0.075	0.075
Implied Volatility	38%	41%	—	—

Theoretically, the stock can rise to any level, so the maximum profit with the long call is unlimited. If the stock declines, it can fall to no lower than zero. If that happens, the long put would be worth 50. Subtracting the 4.57 cost of the straddle gives a maximum profit of 45.43 from a stock drop. The value of a straddle at expiration is the combined value of the call and the put:

$$V_T = \text{Max}(0,S_T - X) + \text{Max}(0,X - S_T). \quad (9)$$

Broken down into ranges,

$V_T = X - S_T$ if $S_T < X$, and

$V_T = S_T - X$ if $S_T > X$.

The profit is $V_T - V_0$, or $\Pi = \text{Max}(0,S_T - X) + \text{Max}(0,X - S_T) - c_0 - p_0$. (10)

Broken down into ranges,

$\Pi = X - S_T - c_0 - p_0$ if $S_T < X$, and

$\Pi = S_T - X - c_0 - p_0$ if $S_T > X$.

As can be seen in Exhibit 21, the straddle has two breakeven points. The lower breakeven for the straddle is $S_{TL}^* = X - c_0 - p_0$, and the upper breakeven is $S_{TH}^* = X + c_0 + p_0$.

For the straddle buyer, the worst outcome is if the stock closes exactly at 50, meaning both the put and the call would expire worthless. At any other price, one of the options will have a positive exercise value. Note that at expiration, the straddle is not profitable if the stock price is in the range 45.43 to 54.57. The long straddle shown in Exhibit 21 requires more than a 9% price move in one month to be profitable. A trader who believed such a move was unlikely might be inclined to *write* the straddle, in which case the profit and loss diagram in Exhibit 21 is reversed, with a maximum gain of 4.57 and a theoretically unlimited loss if prices rise. The risk of a long straddle is limited to the amount paid for the two option positions. The straddle can also be understood in terms of theta. As shown in Exhibit 22, theta of the long straddle is –0.075. All else equal, the long put and call positions will lose their time value as expiration approaches. The long straddle buyer is betting on a large price move in the underlying prior to expiration. If the stock price does not change significantly, the short straddle, which has a positive theta, will benefit from the erosion of time value of the short put and call positions.

Collars

A **collar** is an option position in which the investor is long shares of stock and then buys a put with an exercise price below the current stock price and writes a call with an exercise price above the current stock price.[21] Collars allow a shareholder to acquire downside protection through a protective put but reduce the cash outlay by writing a covered call. By carefully selecting the options, an investor can often offset most of the put premium paid by the call premium received. Using a collar, the profit and loss on the equity position is limited by the option positions.

For equity investors, the collar typically entails ownership of the underlying asset and the purchase of a put, which is financed with the sale of a call. In a typical investment or corporate finance setting, an interest rate collar may be used to hedge interest rate risk on floating-rate assets or liabilities. For example, a philanthropic foundation funds the grants it makes from income generated by its investment portfolio of floating-rate securities. The foundation's chief investment officer (CIO) wants to hedge interest rate risk (the risk of rates falling on its floating securities) by buying an interest rate floor (a portfolio of interest rate puts) and paying for it by writing a cap (a portfolio of interest rate calls). Should the rates on the portfolio fall, the long floor will provide a lower limit for the income generated by the portfolio. To finance the floor purchase, the foundation sells a cap. The cap will limit the income generated from the floating rate portfolio in the event the floating rate rises. The CIO is still holding a floating-rate securities portfolio but has restricted the returns using the collar. By setting both a minimum and a maximum portfolio return, the CIO may be better able to plan funding requests.

Collars on an Existing Holding

A zero-cost collar involves the purchase of a put and sale of a call with the same premium. In Exhibit 6, for instance, the NOV 15 put costs 1.46 and the NOV 17 call is 1.44, very nearly the same. A collar written in the over-the-counter market can be easily structured to provide a precise offset of the put premium with the call premium.[22]

The value of the collar at expiration is the sum of the value of the underlying asset, the value of the long put (struck at X_1), and the value of the short call (struck at X_2):

$$V_T = S_T + \text{Max}(0, X_1 - S_T) - \text{Max}(0, S_T - X_2), \text{ where } X_2 > X_1. \quad (11)$$

The profit is the profit on the underlying share plus the profit on the long put and the short call so that:

$$\Pi = S_T + \text{Max}(0, X_1 - S_T) - \text{Max}(0, S_T - X_2) - S_0 - p_0 + c_0. \quad (12)$$

21 A collar is also called a *fence* or a *hedge wrapper*.

22 Most collars are structured so that the call and put premiums completely offset each other. If the investor starts with the put at a specific exercise price, he then sells a call that has the same premium. There is one specific call with the same premium, and it has a particular exercise price, which is above the exercise price of the put. An algorithm can be used to search for the exercise price on the call that has the same premium as that of the put, which is then the call that the investor should sell. Most collars are structured and transacted in the over-the-counter market because the exercise price on the call must be a specific one. Exchange-traded options have standardized exercise prices, whereas the exercise prices of over-the-counter options can be set at whatever the investor wants.

Broken down into ranges, the total profit on the portfolio is as follows:

$\Pi = X_1 - S_0 - p_0 + c_0$ if $S_T \leq X_1$

$\Pi = S_T - S_0 - p_0 + c_0$ if $X_1 < S_T < X_2$

$\Pi = X_2 - S_0 - p_0 + c_0$ if $S_T \geq X_2$

Consider the risk–return trade-off for a shareholder who previously bought PBR stock at 12 and now buys the NOV 15 put for 1.46 and simultaneously writes the NOV 17 covered call for 1.44. Exhibit 23 shows a profit and loss worksheet for the three positions. Exhibit 24 shows the profit and loss diagram.

Exhibit 23: Collar P&L: Stock Purchased at 12, NOV 15 Put Purchased at 1.46, NOV 17 Call Written at 1.44

Stock price at expiration	5	10	15	16	17	20
Profit/loss from long stock	−7.00	−2.00	3.00	4.00	5.00	8.00
Profit/loss from long 15 put	8.54	3.54	−1.46	−1.46	−1.46	−1.46
Profit/loss from short 17 call	1.44	1.44	1.44	1.44	1.44	−1.56
Total	2.98	2.98	2.98	3.98	4.98	4.98

At or below the put exercise price of 15, the collar realizes a profit of $X_1 - S_0 - p_0 + c_0 = 15 - 12 - 1.46 + 1.44 = 2.98$. At or above the call exercise price of 17, the profit is constant at $X_2 - S_0 - p_0 + c_0 = 17 - 12 - 1.46 + 1.44 = 4.98$.

In this example, because the stock price had appreciated before establishing the collar, the position has a minimum gain of at least 2.98 as shown in Exhibit 24. Investors typically establish a collar on a position that is already outstanding.

Exhibit 24: Collar P&L Diagram: Stock Purchased at 12, NOV 15 Put Purchased at 1.46, NOV 17 Call Written at 1.44

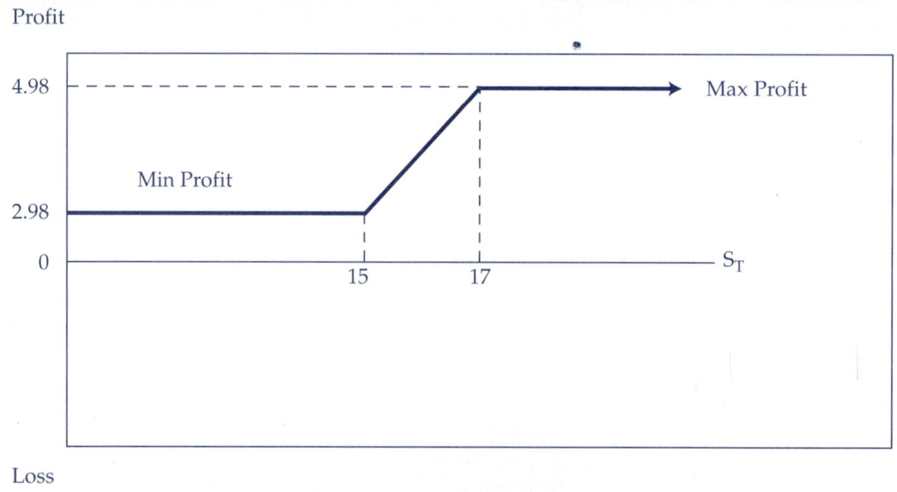

The Risk of a Collar

We have already discussed the risks of covered calls and protective puts. The collar is essentially the simultaneous holding of both of these positions. See Exhibit 25 for the return distribution of a collar. A collar sacrifices the positive part of the return distribution in exchange for the removal of the adverse portion. With the short call option, the option writer sold the right side of the return distribution, which includes the most desirable outcomes. With the long put, the investor is protected against the left side of the distribution and the associated losses. The option premium paid for the put is largely and, often precisely, offset by the option premium received from writing the call. The collar dramatically narrows the distribution of possible investment outcomes, which is risk reducing. In exchange for the risk reduction, the return potential is limited.

The risks of the collar can be understood in terms of the Greeks from Exhibit 6. For example, with a long share the delta of the portfolio = +1. With a collar, the portfolio delta is equal to the delta of the share plus the delta of the long NOV 15 put (−0.359) and short NOV 17 call (−0.475), so the portfolio delta = +1 + (−0.359) + (−0.475) = +0.166. Portfolio gamma, which equals put gamma minus call gamma, will be close to zero, −0.011 (= 0.075 − 0.086). By writing a call and buying a put, the investor reduces the portfolio's delta at a price of 15.84 from +1 to +0.166 and the gamma is very close to zero. If the stock price moves outside the range depicted in Exhibit 25, the delta of the position will approach zero over time. If the share price moves above 17, the NOV 17 call approaches a delta of +1, and the put will approach a delta of 0. The collar is short the call, so above 17 the portfolio delta (long stock with delta = +1 plus a short call with delta = −1) will approach zero. At prices below 15, the NOV 17 call will have a delta approaching 0, but the long put approaches a delta of −1, so the portfolio delta will again approach zero (long stock with delta = +1 plus the long put with delta = −1). The portfolio's sensitivity to changes in the stock price will be limited, as shown in Exhibit 25.

Exhibit 25: Collars and Return Distribution: Stock at 15.84, Write NOV 17 Call and Buy NOV 15 Put

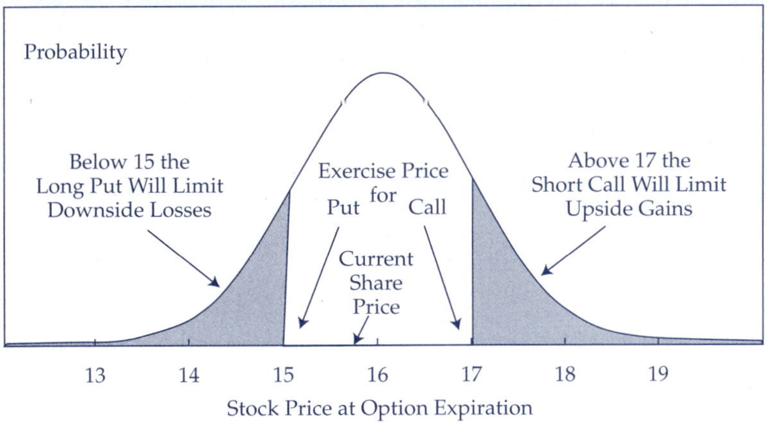

As the chosen put and call exercise prices move successively farther in opposite directions from the current price, the combined collar position begins to replicate the underlying gain/loss pattern of a long position in the underlying security. Conversely, as the chosen strike prices approach and meet each other, the expected returns and volatility become less and less equity-like and eventually converge on those of a risk-free, fixed income return to the time horizon. Thus, a collar position is, economically, intermediate between pure equity and fixed-income exposure.

The Risk of Spreads

Note that the shape of the profit and loss diagram for the bull spread in Exhibit 17 is similar to that of the collar in Exhibit 24. The upside return potential is limited, but so is the maximum loss. As with the risk–return tradeoff with the collar, an option spread takes the tails of the distribution out of play and leaves only price uncertainty between the option exercise prices. Looking at this scenario another way, if someone were to simply buy a long call, the maximum gain would be unlimited and the maximum loss would be the option premium paid. If someone decides to convert this to a spread, doing so limits the maximum gain while simultaneously reducing the total cost.

Calendar Spread

A strategy in which one sells an option and buys the same type of option but with different expiration dates, on the same underlying asset and with the same strike, is commonly referred to as a **calendar spread**. When the investor buys the more distant call and sells the near-term call, it is a long calendar spread. The investor could also buy a near-term call and sell a longer-dated one, known as a short calendar spread. Calendar spreads can also be done with puts; the investor would still buy a long-maturity put and sell a near-term put with the same strike and underlying to create a long calendar spread. As discussed previously, a portion of the option premium is time value. Time value decays over time and approaches zero as the option expiration date nears. Taking advantage of this time decay is a primary motivation behind a calendar spread. Time decay is more pronounced for a short-term option than for one with a long time until expiration. A calendar spread trade seeks to exploit this characteristic by purchasing a longer-term option and writing a shorter-term option.

Here is an example of how someone might use a calendar spread. Suppose XYZ stock is trading at 45 a share in August. XYZ has a new product to be introduced to the public early the following year. A trader believes this new product introduction will have a positive effect on the share price. Until the excitement associated with this announcement starts to affect the stock price, the trader believes that the stock will languish around the current level. See the option prices, deltas and thetas in Exhibit 26. Based on the bullish outlook for the stock going into January, the trader purchases the XYZ JAN 45 call with a theta (indicator of daily price erosion) of −0.014 for a price of 3.81. Noting that the near-term price forecast is neutral, the trader also decides to sell the XYZ SEP 45 call for 1.55. The theta for the XYZ SEP 45 Call is −0.029. The position costs 2.26 (= 3.81 − 1.55) to create and has an initial theta of +0.015 (= −0.014 − (−0.029)). If the stock price of XYZ remains constant over the next 30 days, the XYZ SEP 45 call will lose time value more rapidly than the JAN 45 call. The delta of calendar spread equals the delta of the JAN 45 call less the delta of the SEP 45 call and will be very low (Delta = +0.041 = 0.572 − 0.531).

Now move forward to the September expiration and assume that XYZ is trading at 45. The September option will now expire with no value, which is a good outcome for the calendar spread trader. The value of the position (now just the XYZ JAN 45 call) is 3.48, a gain of 1.22 over the position cost of 2.26. If the trader still believes that XYZ will stay around 45 into October before starting to move higher, the trader may continue to execute this strategy. An XYZ OCT 45 call might be sold for 1.55 with the hope that it also expires with no value.

Exhibit 26: Calendar Spread Call Option Prices, Deltas, and Thetas

150 days until January option expiration. Underlying stock price = 45

Exercise Price	SEP	OCT	JAN
40	5.15	5.47	6.63
45	1.55	2.19	3.81
50	0.22	0.62	1.99
		Delta	
40	0.975	0.902	0.800
45	0.531	0.545	0.572
50	0.121	0.217	0.363
		Theta (daily)	
40	−0.007	−0.011	−0.011
45	−0.029	−0.020	−0.014
50	−0.014	−0.014	−0.013

Just before September option expiration. Underlying stock price = 45

Exercise Price	SEP	OCT	JAN
40	5.00	5.15	6.39
45	0	1.55	3.48
50	0	0.22	1.69

In this example, the calendar spread trader has a directional opinion on the stock but does not believe that the price movement is imminent. Rather, the trader sees an opportunity to capture time value in one or more shorter-lived options that are expected to expire worthless.

A short calendar spread is created by purchasing the near-term option and selling a longer-dated option. Thetas for in-the-money calls may provide motivation for a short calendar spread. For in-the-money calls, note the near dated SEP option has a lower rate of theta decay (−0.007) than the far dated OCT decay rate (−0.011). This is the opposite of the relationship we observerd in at-the-money calls. Assume a trader purchases the XYZ SEP 40 call with a theta of −0.007 for a price of 5.15. The trader sells the OCT 40 call with a theta of −0.011 for 5.47 to offset the cost of the SEP 40 call. The position nets the trader a cash inflow of 0.32 (= 5.47 – 5.15), and the initial position theta is slightly positive −0.007 – (−0.011) = +0.004.

If the stock price of XYZ remains at 45 (above the strike of 40) at the SEP expiration, the XYZ OCT 40 call will lose time value more rapidly than the SEP 40 call. The trader may close the position at the SEP expiration and make a profit of 0.17 = 0.32 + (5 – 5.15). Note that the profit consists of the 0.32 initial inflow plus the net cost of selling the SEP 40 call (at 5.00) and buying the OCT 40 call (at 5.15). In the event of a larger move, the position values will vary. For a large down move, for example an extreme case in which XYZ loses all of its value (so $S = 0$ at expiration), the long and the short call positions will be approximately worthless and the profit on the spread will be around 0.32 (= 0.32 + [0 – 0])). For a smaller down move to the strike price ($S = 40$ at expiration), the short calendar spread may result in a loss. If the XYZ stock price were to fall to 40 at the SEP expiration, the long position in the SEP 40 call would expire worthless but the OCT 40 call would still have a BSM model value of about 1.00 (not shown in Exhibit 26). This scenario would result in a loss of 0.68 = 0.32 + (0 – 1) to close the position. The writer of a calendar spread would typically be looking for a large move away from the strike price in either direction.

In sum, a big move in the underlying market or a decrease in implied volatility will help a short calendar spread, whereas a stable market or an increase in implied volatility will help a long calendar spread. Thus, calendar spreads are sensitive to movement of the underlying but also sensitive to changes in implied volatility.

9 IMPLIED VOLATILITY AND VOLATILITY SKEW

☐ discuss volatility skew and smile

An important factor in the current price of an option is the outlook for the future volatility of the underlying asset's returns, the **implied volatility**. Implied volatility is not observable per se, but it is derived from an option pricing model—such as the Black–Scholes–Merton (BSM) model—and it is value that equates the model price of an option to its market price. Note that all other input variables to the BSM model, including the option's strike price, the price of the underlying, the time to option expiration, and the risk-free interest rate, are observable. Implied volatilities incorporate investors' expectations about the future course of financial asset returns and the level of market uncertainty associated with them.

Implied volatilities for options on a specific asset may differ with strike price (i.e., moneyness), side (i.e., put or call), and time to expiration. In particular, out-of-the-money (OTM) puts typically command higher implied volatilities than ATM or OTM calls. This phenomenon is attributed to investors' reassessments of the probabilities of negative "fat-tailed" market events such as the 2007–2009 global financial crisis.

Implied volatility is often compared with **realized volatility** (i.e., historical volatility), which is the square root of the realized variance of returns and measures the range of past returns for the underlying asset. To calculate the historical volatility for the given option, stock, or equity index, a series of past prices is needed. For example, to calculate the volatility of the S&P 500 Index over the past month (i.e., 21 trading days), it is necessary to first calculate the daily percentage change for each day's index closing price. This is done using the following formula, where P_t is the closing price and P_{t-1} is the prior day's closing price: $(P_t - P_{t-1})/P_{t-1}$. The next step is to apply the standard deviation formula you learned in Level I Quantitative Methods to the daily percentage change data to calculate the standard deviation (i.e., volatility) of the S&P 500 for the selected period, which in this case is the past month.

The standard deviation over the past month is then annualized by multiplying by the square root of the number of periods in a year. Because we assume the average number of trading days in a year and in a month are 252 and 21 (excluding weekends and holidays), respectively, the formula is:

$$\sigma_{Annual}(\%) = \sigma_{Monthly}(\%)\sqrt{\frac{252}{21}}. \tag{13}$$

Note that this example uses one month of daily return data, but the process is equally applicable to any other period.

Obviously, we cannot use the previous formula for realized volatility, which is based on past prices, to obtain implied volatility, which is the expected volatility of future returns of the underlying asset. Instead, the one-month annualized implied volatility can be derived from the current price of an option maturing in one month by using the BSM model. Once the one-month annualized implied volatility is obtained, it can then be converted into an estimate of the volatility expected on the underlying asset over the 21-day life of the option. This expected monthly volatility is given by the one-month annualized implied volatility divided by the square root of the number of 21-day periods in a 252-day trading year, as follows:

$$\sigma_{Monthly}(\%) = \sigma_{Annual}(\%) / \sqrt{\frac{252}{21}} \tag{14}$$

When option prices are compared within or across asset classes or relative to their historical values, they are assessed by their implied volatility. Exhibit 27 shows a comparison of the one-month annualized (ATM) implied volatility at a given point in time for options across three European equity indexes (Euro Stoxx 50, FTSE MIB, and DAX). The DAX shows the lowest implied volatility among the three indexes.

Exhibit 27: One-Month Annualized Implied Volatility

Underlying Index	Implied Volatility	Three-Year Low	Three-Year High
Euro Stoxx 50	9.56	9.0	17.9
FTSE MIB	14.22	11.0	21.7
DAX	9.29	7.3	13.9

Using the one-month annualized implied volatility for DAX index options of 9.29%, the volatility expected to materialize in the DAX index over the next month (21 trading days) can be calculated as follows:

$$\sigma_{Monthly}(\%) = 9.29\% / \sqrt{\frac{252}{21}} = 2.68\%$$

So, for example, if an investor buys an ATM one-month (21-day) straddle using puts and calls on the DAX, in order for the strategy to be profitable at expiration, the index must move up or down by at least 2.68%. The investor can compare this price movement needed to reach breakeven with the DAX's realized volatility over similar time horizons in the past. If such a price change is considered reasonable, then the investor can elect to implement the strategy.

The implied volatility of ATM options, calculated from the options' market prices using the BSM model, remains the simplest way to measure the prevailing volatility level. The BSM model assumes that volatility is constant, and notably, before the 1987 stock market crash, there was little volatility skew in equity index markets. Today, however, options prices on several asset classes display persistent volatility skew and, in some circumstances, volatility smile. The implied volatilities of options of a given expiration are thus dependent on their strike prices.

Exhibit 28 plots implied volatility (y-axis) against strike price (x-axis) for options on the same underlying, the FTSE MIB (trading at 19,000), with the same expiration. When the implied volatilities priced into both OTM puts and calls trade at a premium to implied volatilities of ATM options (those with strike price at 19,000), the curve is U-shaped and is called a **volatility smile**, because it resembles the shape of a smile. The more common shape of the implied volatility curve, however, is a **volatility skew**, where the implied volatility increases for OTM puts and decreases for OTM calls, as the strike price moves away from the current price. This shape persists across asset classes and over time because investors have generally less interest in OTM calls whereas OTM put options have found universal demand as portfolio insurance against a market sell-off.

Exhibit 28: Implied Volatility Curves for Three-Month Options on FTSE MIB

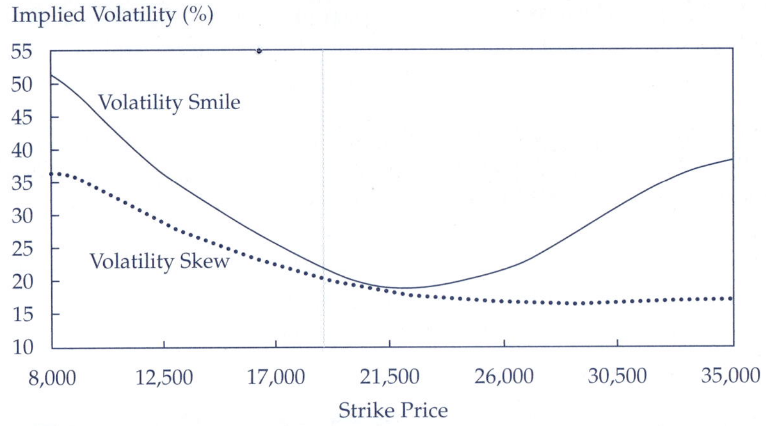

The extent of the skew depends on several factors, including investor sentiment and the relative supply/demand for puts and calls, among others. Several theoretical models try to use these factors to forecast skew variation. However, these models do not lead to unique predictions. In general, we can say that when the implied volatility is significantly higher (relative to historical levels) for puts with strike prices below the underlying asset's price, it means that there is an imbalance in the supply and demand for options. In fact, when investors are looking to hedge the underlying asset, the demand for put options exceeds that for call options. Option traders, who meet this excess demand by selling puts, increase the relative price of these options, thereby raising the implied volatility. A sharp increase in the level of the skew, accompanied with a surge in the absolute level of implied volatility, is an indicator that market sentiment is turning bearish. In contrast, higher implied volatilities (relative to historical levels) for calls with strike prices above the underlying asset's price indicate that investors are bullish and the demand for OTM calls to take on upside exposure is strong.

To better understand how to measure the volatility skew, consider Exhibit 29, which shows the levels of implied volatility at different degrees of moneyness for options expiring in three months on equity indexes where liquid derivatives markets exist. The 90% moneyness option is a put with strike (X) equal to 90% of the current underlying price (S); thus X/S = 90%. The 110% moneyness of the call is calculated similarly. Also shown is the skew, calculated as the difference between the implied volatilities of the 90% put and the 110% call.

Exhibit 29: Implied Volatilities and Skew for Three-Month Options

	Implied Volatility by Moneyness			90%–110%
Index	**ATM**	**Put: 90%**	**Call: 110%**	**Volatility Skew**
Nikkei 225	12.9	18.9	12.4	6.5
S&P 500	10.3	17.7	9.4	8.3
Euro Stoxx 50	12.3	17.8	9.3	8.5
DAX	14.5	20.0	11.0	9.0

For most asset classes, the level of option skew varies over time. Exhibit 30 presents the skew on the S&P 500, measured as the difference between the implied volatilities of options with 90% (puts) and 110% (calls) moneyness, and with three months to expiration.

Exhibit 30: 90% Put–110% Call Implied Volatility Skew for Three-Month Options on S&P 500

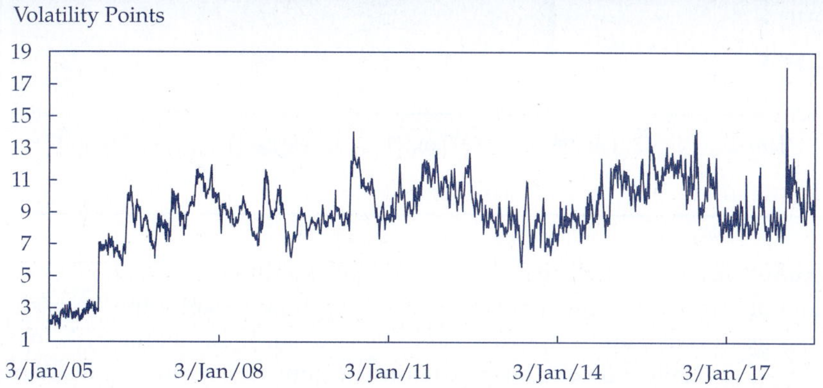

There are trading strategies that attempt to profit from the existence of an implied volatility skew and from changes in its shape over time. A common strategy is to take a long or short position in a **risk reversal**, which is then delta hedged. Using OTM options, a combination of long (short) calls and short (long) puts on the same underlying with the same expiration is a long (short) risk reversal. In particular, when a trader thinks that the put implied volatility is too high relative to the call implied volatility, she creates a long risk reversal, by selling the OTM put and buying the same expiration OTM call. The options position is then delta-hedged by selling the underlying asset. The trader is not aiming to profit from the movement in the overall level in implied volatility. In fact, depending on the strikes of the put and the call, the trade could be vega-neutral. For the trade to be profitable, the trader expects that the call will rise more (or decrease less) in implied volatility terms relative to the put.

Typically, implied volatility is not constant across different maturities, which means that options with the same strike price but with different maturities display different implied volatilities. This determines the **term structure of volatility**, which is often in contango, meaning that the implied volatilities for longer-term options are higher than for near-term ones. When markets are in stress and de-risking sentiment prevails, however, market participants demand short-term options, pushing up their prices and causing the term structure of volatility to invert. Exhibit 31 shows, for options on the S&P 500, a common indicator watched by market participants: the spread between the implied volatilities of 12-month and 3-month ATM options. Values below zero indicate that the term structure is inverted with 3-month options having a higher implied volatility than the 12-month options. In periods when equity markets experience large sell-offs, such as during the 2007–2009 global financial crisis, the term structure of implied volatility typically shows significant inversion. In such periods, the general level of equity volatility and skew also remain high.

Exhibit 31: 12M–3M Implied Volatility Term Structure of S&P 500 Options

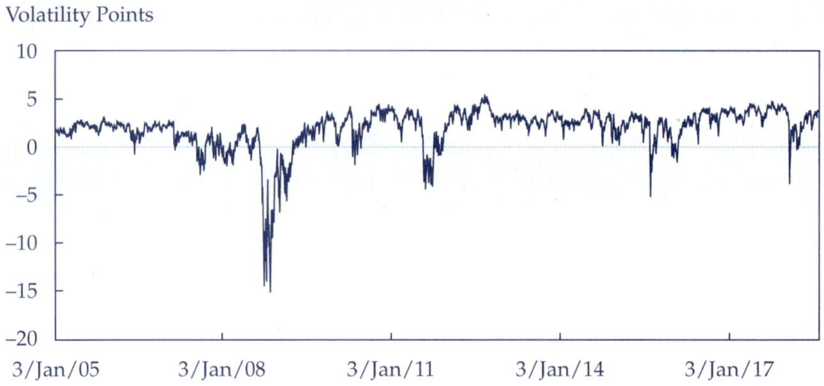

The **implied volatility surface** can be thought of as a three-dimensional plot, for put and call options on the same underlying asset, of days to expiration (x-axis), option strike prices (y-axis), and implied volatilities (z-axis). It simultaneously shows the volatility skew (smile) and the term structure of implied volatility. Considering that implied volatility varies across different option maturities and displays skew, the implied volatility surface is typically not flat as the BSM model may suggest. By observing the implied volatility surface, one can infer changes in market expectations. Several studies have focused on ways to extract information embedded in option market prices. The skew can provide insight into market participants' perceptions about the price movement of the underlying asset over a specified horizon. The general interpretation is that the shape of the volatility skew reflects varying degrees of market participants' fear about future market stress.

10 INVESTMENT OBJECTIVES AND STRATEGY SELECTION

☐ identify and evaluate appropriate option strategies consistent with given investment objectives

The Necessity of Setting an Objective

Every trade is based on an outlook on the market. With stocks and most assets, one thinks about the direction of the market: Is it going up or down, or is it stable? When dealing with options, it is not enough to think about the market *direction*; it is also important to think about the Greeks beyond delta: gamma, theta, and vega. Where option valuation is concerned, what matters is not only the direction in which the asset underlying the derivative contract is headed but also the volatility of the underlying and even other investors' perception of that volatility. The investor's investment objective may not be achieved if one of these factors moves in an undesired direction. Gamma could lead to a faster loss or gain, depending on whether the investor is short or long the option, whereas theta could lead to a loss despite the underlying asset moving in the right direction. Vega could rise or fall if market expectations of implied volatility change, leading to a loss or profit for the options position. Furthermore, the option premium paid (if long) or received (if short) must be considered when calculating a position's total profit and loss at maturity. For example, in a simple call option purchase, the underlying asset must go up enough so that the call option reaches breakeven by overcoming the premium paid for the call.

Moreover, with the introduction of volatility-based derivatives, investors increasingly view these investments as a way to protect their portfolios against downside risk and also as a method to improve their portfolios' efficiency. When considering hedging strategies, it is important to differentiate between situations in which the investor's goal is to benefit from rising volatility (long volatility)—for example, in hedging a long stock position—and situations in which the investor wants to benefit from falling volatility (short volatility)—for example, by writing a short straddle position.

Derivatives are used by portfolio managers, traders, and corporations to adjust their risk exposures, to achieve a specific investment objective, or even to infer market expectations in the short term (for example, inferring market expectations for central banks' interest rate decisions). The main advantage of derivatives is that they allow two parties with differing needs and market views to adjust quickly without having to enter into potentially costly and difficult trades in the underlying. Another advantage of using derivatives instead of investing in the physical underlying securities is leverage. The fact that investors can take on a large exposure to the underlying asset by putting up only a fraction of the amount of risk capital is an important feature of derivatives. Liquidity is another key aspect favoring derivatives usage in many markets—for example, the ability to buy or sell credit protection using index credit derivatives (CDS) instead of trading the actual underlying, and likely less liquid, bonds provides a huge liquidity advantage to traders and investors. In sum, given an actual or anticipated portfolio of equities, bonds, rates, currencies, or other assets; a market outlook and a timeframe; and an understanding of the benefits and limitations of derivatives, it is important to set realistic investment objectives, be they for hedging, for taking direction bets, or for capturing arbitrage opportunities.

Criteria for Identifying Appropriate Option Strategies

Investors use derivatives to achieve a target exposure based on their outlook for the underlying asset. Exhibit 32 shows one way of looking at the interplay of direction and volatility. The strategies identified are most profitable given the expected change in implied volatility and the outlook for the direction of movement of the underlying asset.

Exhibit 32: Choosing Options Strategies Based on Direction and Volatility of the Underlying Asset

		Outlook on the Trend of Underlying Asset		
		Bearish	**Trading Range/ Neutral View**	**Bullish**
Expected Move in Implied Volatility	**Decrease**	*Write calls*	*Write straddle*	*Write puts*
	Remain Unchanged	*Write calls and buy puts*	*Calendar spread*	*Buy calls and write puts*
	Increase	*Buy puts*	*Buy straddle*	*Buy calls*

Consider an investor who is bearish about a market. If he expects that implied volatility will increase as the market sells off, then he will buy a put to protect his investments. If instead he believes that volatilities are expected to fall, writing a call would likely be a profitable strategy. Investors need to keep in mind, however, that the two strategies have two different payoffs and risk management implications. As we have seen previously, a position in which the investor writes the call and buys the put is a collar, and it is often associated with holding a long position in the underlying asset. Investors use collars against a long stock position to hedge risk and smooth volatility. In fact, by selling a covered call while purchasing a protective put, the investor establishes a combined position with fixed downside protection while still providing some opportunity for profits.

Now consider an investor who has a bullish view. Buying calls is an option strategy that will allow the investor to benefit if her outlook is correct and implied volatility increases. When implied volatilities are expected to fall, writing a put represents an alternative strategy to take advantage of a bullish market view with declining volatility. If this happens, the position will likely be profitable, because as the stock rises and implied volatility decreases, the short put moves farther out of the money and its price will decrease. The combined position in which the investor is long calls and short puts (i.e., a long risk reversal) is used to implement a bullish view (the investor buys the calls) while lowering the cost (the investor sells the puts) of the long position in the underlying asset that will be established upon exercising the options.

Investors can also decide to sell puts when they want to buy a stock only if the price declines below a determined target price (the strike price of the puts will be the same as this target price). In this case, by selling the put options when implied volatilities are elevated (and the puts are expensive), the investor can realize an effective stock purchase price that is less than the target (strike) price by the size of the premium received.

The purchase of call or put spreads tends to be most appropriate when the investor has a bullish view (call bull spread) or a bearish view (put bear spread) but the underlying market is not clearly trending upward or downward. Furthermore, such spreads are a way to reduce the total cost, given that the spread is normally constructed by buying one option and writing another. Importantly, if the implied volatility curve is skewed, with the implied volatility of OTM puts relatively higher than for nearer-to-the-money options, the cost of a bearish spread is even lower. This is because in the put bear spread, the lower exercise price, more OTM (but relatively more expensive) put is sold and the higher exercise price, nearer-to-the-money (but relatively less expensive) put is purchased.

Now suppose that the market is expected to trade in range. Again, the investor should consider volatility. Suppose he believes the current consensus estimate of volatility implied in option prices is too low and the rate of the change in underlying prices will increase—that is, vega will increase. If the investor is neutral on market direction, the appropriate strategy will be a long straddle, because this strategy takes advantage of an increase in the long call or long put option prices in response to realization of the expected surge in volatility, vega, and gamma. At expiry, the long straddle will be profitable if the price of the call (put) is greater (less) than the upper (lower) breakeven price. In contrast, an investor who expects the market to trade in range and volatility to fall may want to write the straddle instead.

We now consider a strategy that combines a longer-term bullish/bearish outlook on the underlying asset with a near-term neutral outlook. This approach is the calendar spread (or time spread), a strategy using two options of the same type (puts or calls) and same strike price but with different maturity dates. Typically, a long calendar spread—wherein the shorter-maturity option is sold and the longer-maturity option is purchased—is a long volatility trading strategy because the longer-term option has a higher vega than the shorter-term option. The maximum profit is obtained when the short-term option expires worthless, then implied volatility surges, increasing the price of the remaining long-term option. Although the delta for a calendar spread is approximately zero, gamma is not, so the main risk for the calendar strategy is that the underlying stock price moves too fast and too far from the strike prices. For this reason, the calendar spread is typically implemented in option markets characterized by low implied volatility when the underlying stock is expected to remain in a trading range, but only until the maturity of the short-term option.

OPTIONS IN PORTFOLIO MANAGEMENT 11

☐ demonstrate the use of options to achieve targeted equity risk exposures

This section uses "mini cases" to illustrate some of the ways in which different market participants use derivative products to solve a problem or to alter a risk exposure. Note that with the wide variety of derivatives available, there are almost always multiple ways in which derivatives might logically be used in a particular situation. These mini cases cover only a few of them.

Covered Call Writing

Carlos Rivera is a portfolio manager in a small asset management firm focusing on high-net-worth clients. In mid-April, he is preparing for an upcoming meeting with Parker, a client whose daughter is about to marry. Parker and her husband have just decided to pay for their daughter's honeymoon and need to raise $30,000 relatively quickly. The client's portfolio is 70% invested in equities and 30% in fixed income and is by policy slightly aggressive. Currently the Parkers are "asset rich and cash poor," having largely depleted their cash reserves prior to the wedding expenses. The recently revised investment policy statement permits most option activity except the writing of naked calls.

Parker's account contains 5,000 shares of Manzana (MNZA) stock, a stock that she is considering selling in the near future. Rivera's firm has a bearish market outlook for MNZA shares over the next six months. Rivera reviews information on the 44-day exchange-listed options, which expire in May (shown in Exhibit 33). He is considering writing MNZA calls, which will accomplish two objectives. First, the sale of calls will generate the required cash for his client. Secondly, the sale will reduce the delta of Parker's account in line with his firm's bearish short-term outlook for MNZA shares. The current delta of Parker's MNZA position is 5,000(+1) or +5,000. Exhibit 33 contains call and put price information for May MNZA options with strike prices close to the current market price of MNZA shares (S_0 = $169).

Exhibit 33: Manzana Inc. May Options With 44 Days to Expiration, MNZA Stock = $169

Call Premium	Call Delta	Exercise Price	Put Premium	Put Delta	Put or Call Vega
12.55	0.721	160	3.75	−0.289	0.199
9.10	0.620	165	5.30	−0.384	0.224
6.45	0.504	170	7.69	−0.494	0.234

Call Premium	Call Delta	Exercise Price	Put Premium	Put Delta	Put or Call Vega
4.03	0.381	175	10.58	−0.604	0.225
2.50	0.271	180	14.10	−0.702	0.199

Discuss the factors that Rivera should consider and the strategy he should recommend to Parker.

Solution:

To generate cash, Rivera will want to write options. The account permits the writing of covered calls. Manzana options trade on an organized exchange with a standard contract size of 100 shares per contract. With 5,000 shares in the account, 50 call contracts would be covered.

If Rivera were to write the MAY 180 calls, doing so would not generate the required cash, $2.50 × 100 × 50 = $12,500. Writing the MAY 165 calls would generate more than enough income: $9.10 × 100 × 50 = $45,500. However, the May 165 call is in the money. Although the firm's outlook is bearish for the shares, Rivera feels there is a high likelihood of Parker's MNZA shares being called away at expiration. Writing the May 175 call would generate only $4.03 × 100 × 50 = $20,150. Although Rivera believes the 175 call would not be exercised, the cash generated would be only about two-thirds of the client's projected need. The May 170 call would generate $6.45 × 100 × 50 = $32,250, which looks good from a cash-generation perspective. The current price of MNZA shares is 169, so there is a considerable risk that MNZA shares will sell above that level at expiration. If MNZA stock trades above the strike price at the May expiration, then Parker would be exposed to having her shares called at 170. Given the firm's bearish outlook for MNZA shares and, as stated previously, "Parker is considering selling the stock in the near future," this risk might be acceptable. Using the May 170 call option data from Exhibit 33, the delta of Parker's MNZA position would be reduced from +5,000 to 5,000 × (+1 − 0.504) = +2,480.[23] The profit graph for the recommended sale of 50 May 170 call contracts against Parker's 5,000 share long position at 169 is shown in Exhibit 34.

23 Delta for the short calls will approach −1 if the stock price moves strongly above 170 close to maturity. The likelihood of the shares being called away in that scenario would push the position delta to 0 (= +5000 from the shares, −5000 for the short ITM calls).

Exhibit 34: Profit and Loss for MNZA May 170 Covered Call (S_0 = 169, c_0 = 6.45)

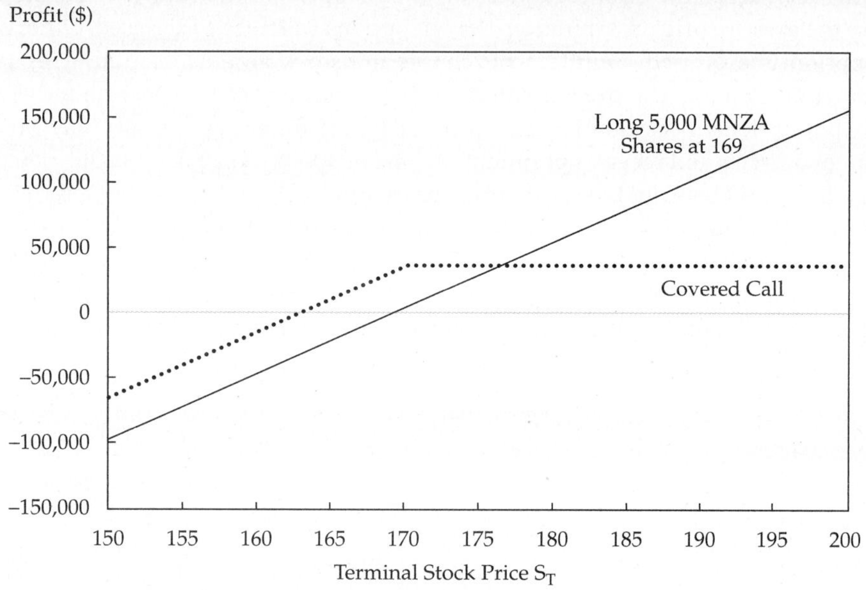

The $32,250 generated by the call option sales is Parker's to keep. There are two risks, however, that Rivera should point out to Parker using Exhibit 34. The first risk is that his outlook for MNZA shares might be incorrect. The reduced delta may cost his client a potential gain on the long position. If MNZA shares increase above 170, the profits will go to the call owner. Parker's MNZA shares may be called away at 170, limiting her profit to the option premium of $32,250 plus the $5,000 from selling her MNZA shares at a profit of $1 (= $170 – $169) as shown in Exhibit 34.[24] The second risk is that to write the covered call, Parker must continue to hold 5,000 MNZA shares. If the firm's bearish outlook is correct, the shares may drop in value during the next month, resulting in a loss on the long stock position. The loss would be cushioned somewhat by the 6.45 call premium, but a drop of more than 3.8% (below 162.55 = 169 – 6.45; 6.45/169 = 3.8%) results in an overall loss on the position. After Rivera explains the risks to Parker, she elects to write the MNZA 170 calls.

Put Writing

Oscar Quintera is the chief financial officer for Tres Jotas, a private investment firm in Buenos Aires. He wants to purchase 50,000 MNZA shares for the firm, but at the current price he considers MNZA shares to be a bit expensive. The current share price is $169, and Quintera is willing to buy the stock at a price not higher than $165. Quintera decides to write out-of-the-money puts on MNZA shares.

Discuss the outcome of the transaction, a short position in MNZA May 165 puts, assuming two scenarios:

- Scenario A: MNZA is $163 per share on the option expiration day.
- Scenario B: MNZA is $177 per share on the option expiration day.

24 Note that if the shares are called away at 170, there may also be tax consequences for Parker.

Solution:

Quintera can write OTM puts to effectively "get paid" to buy the stock. He sells puts and the firm keeps the cash regardless of what happens in the future. If the stock is above the exercise price at expiration, the put options will not be exercised. Otherwise, the option is exercised, Quintera purchases the stock and, as desired, Tres Jotas becomes an owner of the stock. Exhibit 33 shows the options information for 44-day MAY put options. Because his target price is 165, Quintera writes 500 May MNZA 165 put contracts and receives premium income of 500 × 100 × \$5.30 = \$265,000. The company keeps these funds regardless of future stock price movements. But, the firm is obligated to buy stock at \$165 if the put holder chooses to exercise. By writing the puts, Quintera has established a bullish position in MNZA stock. The delta of this MNZA position is −500 × 100 × −0.384 = +19,200, the equivalent of a long position in 19,200 MNZA shares. The portfolio profit on the short put is shown in Exhibit 35.

Exhibit 35: Short Position Profit for 500 MNZA May 165 Put Contracts

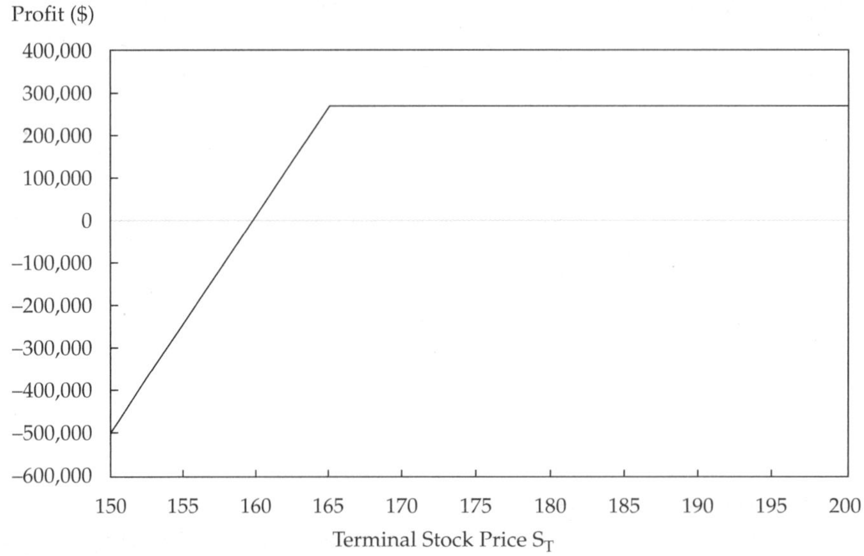

Scenario A:

The stock is \$163 per share on the option expiration day. With an exercise price of 165, the put is in the money and will be exercised. Quintera will be assigned to buy 50,000 shares at the exercise price of 165. The cost is 50,000 × \$165 = \$8,250,000. Quintera is satisfied with the outcome, because the firm keeps the premium income of \$265,000, so the net cost of purchase is \$8,250,000 – \$265,000 = \$7,985,000. On 50,000 shares, this means the *effective purchase price* is \$7,985,000/50,000 = \$159.70, which is below the maximum \$165 price Quintera was willing to pay. If the price of MNZA shares drops below 165, the effective purchase price will always be $X - p$ = 165 – 5.30 = \$159.70. This is the breakeven point for the short put position. At prices below the breakeven amount, Quintera would have been better off not writing the put and just buying MNZA shares outright. For example, if the MNZA price fell to \$150, Quintera would have been obligated to buy shares at 165, \$15 more than the market price. When the \$5.30 premium is considered, the \$15 difference would amount to a loss of \$9.70 per share or \$485,000 which can be seen in Exhibit 35.

Scenario B:

The stock price is $177 on the option expiration day. With an exercise price of 165.00, the MNZA puts are out of the money and would not be exercised. Tres Jotas keeps the $265,000 premium received from writing the option. This approach adds to the company's profitability, but Tres Jotas did not acquire the MNZA shares and experienced an opportunity cost relative to an outright purchase of the stock at $169. Any price above 165, will result in earning the premium of $265,000, as can be seen in Exhibit 35.

Long Straddle

Katrina Hamlet has been following Manzana stock for the past year. She anticipates the announcement of a major new product soon, but she is not sure how the critics will react to it. If the new product is praised, she believes the stock price will increase dramatically. If the product does not impress, she believes the share price will fall substantially. Hamlet has been considering trading around the event with a straddle. The stock is currently priced at $169.00, and she is focused on close-to-the-money (170) calls and puts selling for 6.45 and 7.69, respectively. Her initial strategy is presented as Exhibit 36.

Hamlet expects that the stock will move at least 10% either way once the product announcement is made, making the straddle strategy potentially appropriate. The vega of her position would be 0.234 + 0.234= +0.468, meaning a 1% move in the options' volatility would result in a gain of about $0.468 in the value of the straddle. The straddle's delta would be approximately zero, at +0.01 (Call Delta + Put Delta = (0.504 + [−0.494]). This strategy is long volatility. After the market close, Hamlet hears a news story indicating that the product will be unveiled at a trade show in two weeks. The following morning after the market opens, she goes to place her trade and finds that although the stock price remains at $169.00, the option prices have adjusted upward to $10.20 for the call and $10.89 for the put.

Discuss whether the new option premiums have any implications for Hamlet's intended straddle strategy.

Exhibit 36: Long Manzana Straddle

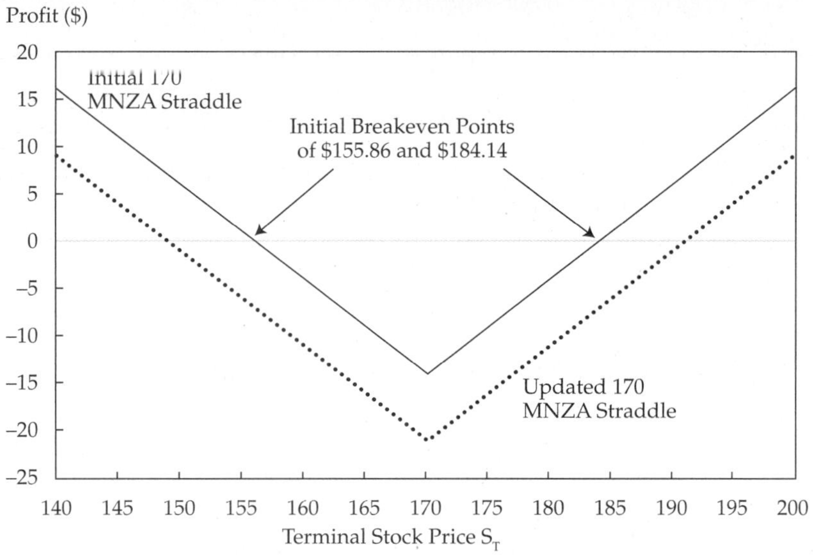

Solution:

Hamlet is betting on a substantial price movement in the underlying MNZA shares to make money with this trade. That price movement, up or down, must be large enough to recover the two premiums paid. In her earlier planning, that total was \$6.45 + \$7.69 = \$14.14. She expects at least a 10% price movement, which on a stock selling for \$169.00 would be an increase of \$16.90. This price movement would be sufficient to recover the \$14.14 cost of the straddle and make her strategy profitable. The breakeven points were \$155.86 and \$184.14, as shown in Exhibit 36.

The news report about the imminent product unveiling, however, has increased the implied volatility in the options, from about 30% to about 45%, raising their prices and making it more difficult to achieve the new breakeven points. After the news report, Hamlet finds the MAY 170 call now costs \$10.20 and the MAY 170 put is trading for \$10.89, so the MAY 170 straddle costs \$21.09 (\$10.20 + \$10.89) to implement. Relating back to the vega she calculated the day before, Hamlet computed an initial vega (pre-announcement) of +0.468 for the straddle. Now she sees the approximate 15 percentage point rise in implied volatility (to 45%) in both the put and call. According to her initial vega calculation, she would expect an increase of 15 × 0.468 = \$7.02 in her straddle value after the announcement. The announcement increased the price of the straddle by \$6.95 (= 21.09 – 14.14), which is very close to the \$7.02 increase predicted by the vega calculation. To reach the new breakeven points (170 ± 21.09), she now needs the stock to move by more than 12%, a larger move than 10% from the current level of 169. Given that Hamlet expects only a 10% price movement, she decides against executing this straddle trade.

EXAMPLE 7

Straddle Analytics

Use the following information to answer Questions 1 to 3 on straddles.

XYZ stock price = 100.00

100-strike call premium = 8.00

100-strike put premium = 7.50

Options expire in three months

1. If Yelena Strelnikov, a portfolio manager, buys a straddle on XYZ stock, she is *best* described as expecting a:

   A. higher volatility market.

   B. lower volatility market.

   C. stable volatility market.

Solution:

A is correct. A straddle is directionally neutral in terms of price; it is neither bullish nor bearish. The straddle buyer wants higher volatility and wants it quickly but does not care in which direction the price of the underlying moves. The worst outcome is for the underlying asset to remain stable.

2. This strategy will break even at expiration stock prices of:

   A. 92.50 and 108.50.

   B. 92.00 and 108.00.

C. 84.50 and 115.50.

Solution:

C is correct. To break even, the stock price must move enough to recover the cost of both the put and the call. These premiums total to $15.50, so the stock must move up at least to $115.50 or down to $84.50.

3. Reaching an upside breakeven point implies an annualized rate of return on XYZ stock *closest* to:

   A. 16%.

   B. 31%.

   C. 62%.

Solution:

C is correct. The price change to a breakeven point is 15.50 points, or 15.5% on a 100 stock. This is for three months. Ignoring compounding, this outcome is equivalent to an annualized rate of 62% on XYZ stock, found by multiplying by 12/3 (15.5% × 4 = 62%).

Collar

Bernhard Steinbacher has a client with a holding of 100,000 shares in Tundra Corporation, currently trading for €14 per share. The client has owned the shares for many years and thus has a very low tax basis on this stock. Steinbacher wants to safeguard the position's value because the client does not want to sell the shares. He does not find exchange-traded options on the stock. Steinbacher wants to present a way in which the client could protect the investment portfolio from a decline in Tundra's stock price.

Discuss an option strategy that Steinbacher might recommend to his client.

Solution:

In the over-the-counter market, Steinbacher might buy a put and then write an out-of-the money call. This strategy is a collar. The put provides downside protection below the put exercise price, and the call generates income to help offset the cost of the put. The investor decides the strike prices of the put and the call to achieve a specific level of downside protection, while still keeping some benefit from an increase in the stock price. When the strike of the call is set so that the call premium (to be received) exactly offsets the put premium (to be paid), then the position is called a "zero-cost collar." Recalling Exhibit 25 and the underlying return distribution, this strategy effectively sells the right tail of the distribution, which represents potential large gains, in exchange for eliminating the left tail, which represents potential large losses.

Calendar Spread

Ivanka Dubois is a professional advisor to high-net-worth investors. She expects little price movement in the Euro Stoxx 50 in the next three months but has a bearish long-term outlook. The consensus sentiment favoring a flat market shows no signs of changing over the next few months, and the Euro Stoxx 50 is currently trading at 3500. Exhibit 37 shows prices for two put options with strike price of 3500 that are available on the index. Both options have the same implied volatility.

Exhibit 37: 3,500 Strike Put Options on Euro Stoxx 50

	Option A	Option B
Current Price	€119	€173
Time to Maturity	3 months	6 months

1. Discuss how can Dubois take advantage of her out-of-consensus view.
2. Analyze four scenarios that Dubois might likely face for the Stoxx 50 index at the expiry of the three-month option (these scenarios are provided at the beginning of the Solution to 2).

Solution to 1:

Dubois's view is best implemented with a long position in a calendar spread that combines a longer-term bearish outlook on the underlying asset with a near-term neutral outlook. She is bearish long-term and so would buy a calendar put spread. A long calendar spread is a long volatility trading strategy whereby the maximum profit is obtained when the short-term at the money option expires worthless with the underlying almost unchanged.

Dubois can implement a put calendar spread trade by selling the three-month put option (A) for €119 and buying the six-month same strike put option (B) at the price for €173. Therefore, the cost of establishing this strategy is a net debit of €54 per contract (given by €173 – €119). Remember, Dubois has a bearish long-term outlook. If the put calendar spread is not profitable at the expiry of the three-month put, the short option expires worthless and then she owns the longer-term option free and clear. Thus, Dubois has managed to lower the cost of purchasing a longer-term put option, which could be kept for hedging her portfolio's downside risk.

Solution to 2:

If the put calendar spread position is held until the expiry of the three-month put, then Dubois might likely face one of the four following scenarios for the Euro Stoxx 50. In the first three scenarios, the implied volatility is assumed to remain constant:

Scenario 1	The index is still trading at 3500 as expected.
Scenario 2	The index has increased and is trading at 4200.
Scenario 3	The index has decreased and is trading at 3000.
Scenario 4	The index has decreased and is trading at 3000, but the implied volatility has significantly increased.

Scenario 1:

The Euro Stoxx 50 is still trading at 3500 as expected. The three-month put option expires worthless, and the original longer-term six-month option, which now has three months remaining to expiration, is worth €119 (because the implied volatility has remained constant). The total cost of the calendar spread was €54, and Dubois can sell the remaining put to a dealer for a profit of €65 (given by €119 – €54). As can be seen in Exhibit 38, which shows the profit and loss diagram for the calendar spread at the time of the expiration of the three-month put, this corresponds to the level of maximum payoff for this strategy.

Exhibit 38: P&L for 3,500 Strike Calendar Spread at Expiration of Three-Month Put

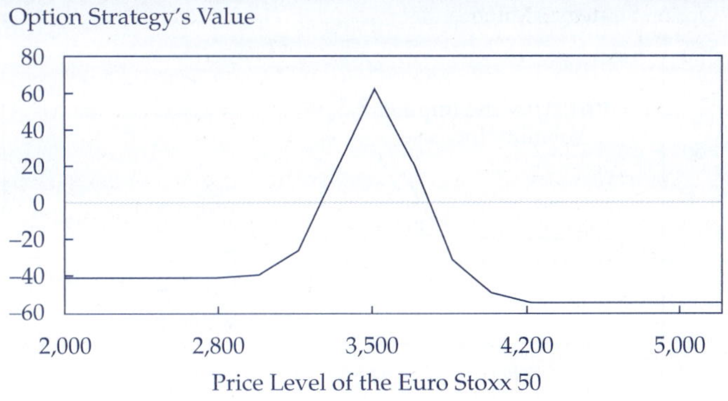

Scenario 2:

The Euro Stoxx 50 has increased and is trading at 4200. The three-month put option expires worthless. Also, the value of the six-month put is near zero, and if Dubois unwinds her (long) put option position she will lose all €54 (given by €173 – €119), the cost of the put calendar spread.

Scenario 3:

The Euro Stoxx 50 index has decreased and is trading at 3000. Dubois must pay €500 (€3,500 – €3,000) to settle the (short) three-month put option at expiration. The (long) put option with three months remaining to expiration is deep in the money and, assuming volatility is still unchanged and €15 of Time Value, it is worth €515 (given by Intrinsic Value of €500 + €15 of Time Value). If Dubois sells this put to a dealer, she will lose €39 (= €515 – €500 – €54) on the put calendar spread.

Scenario 4:

The Euro Stoxx 50 has decreased and is trading at 3000, and the implied volatility has significantly increased. Dubois must pay €500 (€3,500 – €3,000) to settle the (short) three-month put option at expiration. The (long) put option with three months remaining to expiration is deep in the money and, assuming volatility has increased and €30 of Time Value, it is worth €530 (given by Intrinsic Value of €500 + €30 of Time Value). If Dubois sells this put to a dealer, she will realize a loss of €24 (= €530 – €500 – €54) on the put calendar spread. Exhibit 39 adds the profit and loss diagram for the calendar spread at the time of the expiration of the three-month put, assuming that implied volatility of the six-month put has significantly increased.

Exhibit 39: P&L for 3,500 Strike Calendar Spread at Expiration of Three-Month Put Assuming an Increase in Implied Volatility

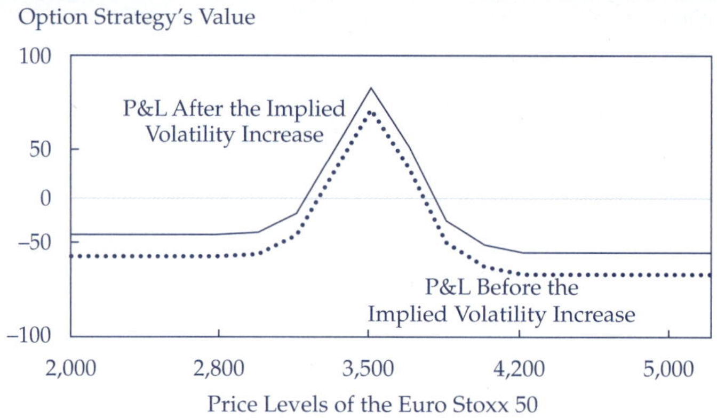

12 HEDGING AN EXPECTED INCREASE IN EQUITY MARKET VOLATILITY

☐ demonstrate the use of options to achieve targeted equity risk exposures

Jack Wu is a fund manager who oversees a stock portfolio valued at US$50 million that is benchmarked to the S&P 500. He expects an imminent significant correction in the US stock market and wants to profit from an anticipated jump in short-term volatility to hedge his portfolio's tail risk.

The VIX Index is currently at 14.87, and the front-month VIX futures trades at 15.60. Wu observes the quotes shown in Exhibit 40 for options on the VIX (these options have same implied volatility). It is important to note that VIX option prices reflect the VIX futures prices. Given that the VIX futures trade at 15.60 while the spot VIX is 14.87, the call is at the money while the put is out of the money by 5.45% (= [14.75 – 15.60]/15.60).

At maturity, the options' payoffs will depend on the settlement price of the relevant VIX futures contracts. The options will expire one month from now, and the contract size is 100.

Exhibit 40: Options on VIX Index

	Call Option	Put Option
Option Strike	15.60	14.75
Option Price	2.00	1.55

Discuss the following:

1. A strategy Wu can implement to hedge tail risk in his equity portfolio, by taking advantage of his expected increase in volatility while lowering his hedging cost
2. Profit and loss on the strategy at options expiration
3. Relevant issues and advantages of this strategy

Solution to 1:

Wu decides to purchase the 15.60 call on the VIX and, to partially finance the purchase, he sells an equal number of the 14.75 VIX puts. The total cost of the options strategy is 0.45 (= 2.00 – 1.55) per contract.

Solution to 2:

At maturity, the options' payoffs will depend on the settlement price of the relevant VIX futures. Exhibit 41 shows the profit and loss diagram for the option strategy at the time of the options' expiration. In particular, the horizontal axis shows the values corresponding to the relevant VIX futures contracts.

Exhibit 41: Profit and Loss of the VIX Options Strategy

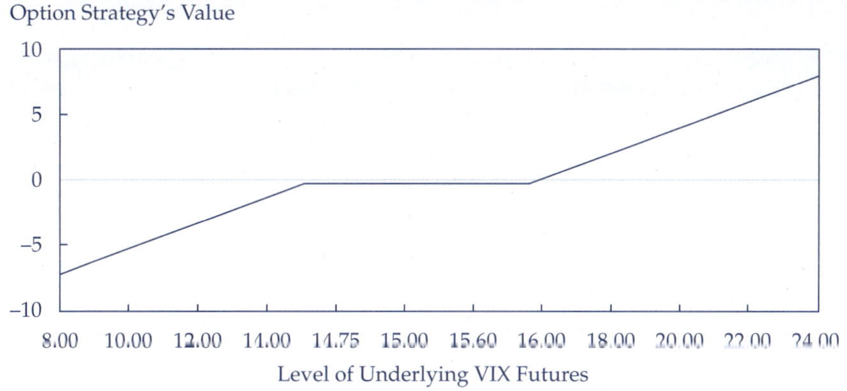

In this case, at the expiry the strategy will be profitable if volatility spikes up (as anticipated) and the VIX futures increase above 16.05. This is calculated as the call strike of 15.60 plus the net cost of the options (15.60 + 0.45). Above this level, the strategy will gain proportionally. In contrast, Wu's option strategy will lose proportionally to its exposure to the short puts if the VIX futures' settlement price is below 14.75 (put strike).

Solution to 3:

The hedge ratio that determines the number of calls to buy could be determined based on regression and scenario analysis on the portfolio's profit and loss versus rates of increase in implied volatility during significant stock market sell-offs in the past. Of course, a risk is that past correlations may not be indicative of future correlations. Importantly, the relative advantage of implementing this long volatility hedging strategy by purchasing calls on the VIX over buying VIX futures depends on the difference in leverage available, the difference in payoff profiles (asymmetrical for options and symmetrical for futures), and the shape of the volatility futures term structure, as well as the cost of the options compared with the cost of the index futures.

Establishing or Modifying Equity Risk Exposure

In this section, we examine some examples in which investors use derivatives for establishing an equity risk exposure, for risk management, or for implementing tactical asset allocation decisions. The choice of derivative that will satisfy the investment goal depends on the outlook for the underlying asset, the investment horizon, and expectations for implied volatility over that horizon.

Long Call

Armando Sanchez is a private wealth advisor working in London. He expects the shares of Markle Co. Ltd. will move from the current price of £60 a share to £70 a share over the next three months, thanks to an increase of positive news flows regarding the company's new fintech services. He also expects that the implied volatilities of options on Markle's stock will stay almost unchanged over the same period. Prices for three-month call options on the stock are shown in Exhibit 42 (note that each call contract represents one share). For his high-net-worth clients whose investment policy statements allow the use of derivatives, Sanchez plans to recommend that they purchase the call option that, based on the budget they intend to spend for implementing the strategy, would maximize profits if the stock price increases to £70 a share or more over the next three months.

Exhibit 42: Three-Month Call Options on Markle Co. Ltd.

	Option A	Option B	Option C
Strike	£58.00	£60.00	£70.00
Price	£4.00	£3.00	£0.40
Delta	0.6295	0.5227	0.1184
Gamma	0.0304	0.0322	0.0160

Discuss the option strategy that Sanchez should recommend to his clients.

Solution:

Sanchez has a bullish view because he anticipates a nearly 17% price increase in Markle shares over the next three months, from the current price of £60. He expects that implied volatilities of the options on Markle shares will stay unchanged, making the purchase of options a profitable strategy if his outlook materializes within the given timeframe.

The best strategy would be a long position in the £60 strike calls (option B). The breakeven price of the position is £63 (£60 + £3), so at option expiry, the overall position would profitable at any stock price above £63. In contrast, the breakeven price of the 58-strike call (option A) is £62 (£58 + £4) and for the 70-strike call (option C) the breakeven is £70.40 (£70 + £0.40). Therefore, Sanchez would not use option C to implement his strategy because the breakeven price is above his target price of £70/share.

Given the £60 strike call has a lower price (premium) than the £58 strike call, Sanchez's clients can purchase more of these lower-priced options for a given investment size. Moreover, the 60-strike call offers the largest profit potential per unit of premium paid if the stock price increases to £70 (as expected).

Call strike £58: (£70 − £62)/£4 = 2.0

Call strike £60: (£70 − £63)/£3 = 2.3

Purchasing the £60 strike call (option B) is the most profitable strategy given that Sanchez's expectations are realized. A position in the £60 strike call has a lower delta (= 0.5227) compared with the £58 strike call (delta = 0.6295), so at current prices of the underlying, the change in value of the £60 strike call is lower. If Markle's stock reaches £70 per share during the life of the option, however, the £60 strike call will benefit from having a larger gamma (= 0.0322) compared with the £58 strike call (gamma = 0.0304).

Risk Management: Protective Put Position

Investors use protective puts, collars, and equity swaps against a long stock position to hedge market risk. Here we turn to a practical application of protective puts.

Eliot McLaire manages a Glasgow-based hedge fund that holds 100,000 shares of Relais Corporation, currently trading at €42.00.

Situation A: Before Relais Corporation's quarterly earnings release:

Relais has a quarterly earnings announcement scheduled in one week. Although McLaire expects an earnings increase, he believes the company will miss the consensus earnings estimate, in which case he expects that the maximum drawdown from the current price of €42.00 would be 10%. He would like to protect the fund's position in the company for several days around the earnings announcement while keeping the cost of the protection to a minimum. Exhibit 43 provides information on options prices for Relais Corporation. Note that each put contract represents one share.

Exhibit 43: One-Month Put Options on Relais Corporation

	Option A	Option B	Option C
Strike	€40.00	€42.50	€45.00
Price	€1.45	€1.72	€3.46
Delta	−0.4838	−0.5385	−0.7762
Gamma	0.0462	0.0460	0.0346

1. Discuss an options strategy that McLaire can implement to hedge his fund's portfolio against a short-term decline in the share price of Relais Corp.

Solution to 1:

McLaire can purchase a protective put with the intent of selling it soon after the earnings announcement. He expects that the maximum drawdown from the current price of €42.00 will be 10%, to €37.80. This expectation narrows the choice of put options based on the following breakeven prices:

Put strike 40.0 (option A): €40.00 − €1.45 = €38.55

Put strike 42.5 (option B): €42.50 − €1.72 = €40.78

Put strike 45.0 (option C): €45.00 − €3.46 = €41.54

The put with strike price of 42.50 (option B) best fits the objective of keeping the cost of adequate protection to a minimum. This is because the 40-strike put (option A) offers limited protection because it is profitable only below €38.55, offering a profit of just €0.75 if the stock falls to €37.80. Furthermore, the 42.50-strike put offers a larger profit per unit of premium paid than the 45.00-strike put if the stock price decreases to €37.80.

Put strike 42.5: (€40.78 − €37.80)/€1.72 = 1.73

Put strike 45.0: (€41.54 − €37.80)/€3.46 = 1.08

The 42.50 strike put has a lower delta (= −0.5385) in absolute value terms than the 45.0 strike put (delta = −0.7762), but it has more gamma. If Relais Corporation's stock falls to €37.80 per share during the life of the option, a position in the 42.50 strike put will benefit from having a larger gamma (= 0.0460) compared with the 45.0 strike put (gamma = 0.0346).

Therefore, McLaire purchases 100,000 of the 42.50-strike puts at €1.72 for a total cost of €172,000.

If Relais Corporation's soon-to-be announced earnings miss the market's expectations, the stock is likely to fall, thereby increasing the long put value and partially offsetting the loss on the stock. If the earnings meet market expectations, then the put may be sold at a price near its purchase price. If the earnings are better than expected and the stock price rises, then the put will decline in value. McLaire would no longer need the "insurance," and he would sell the put position, thereby recovering part of the purchase price.

Situation B: One week later, just after Relais Corporation's earnings release:
McLaire holds the 100,000 puts with the exercise price of €42.50. Seven days have passed since the options' purchase; Relais has just released its earnings, and they turn out to be surprisingly good. Earnings beat the consensus estimate, and immediately after the announcement the stock price rises by 5% to €44.10. Exhibit 44 shows the options' prices on the day of the announcement, after the stock price has increased to €44.10 (the implied volatility remains unchanged).

Exhibit 44: 23-Day Put Options on Relais

	Option A	Option B	Option C
Strike	€40.00	€42.50	€45.00
Price	€0.15	€0.66	€1.85
Delta	−0.0923	−0.3000	−0.5916
Gamma	0.0218	0.0460	0.0514
Price Change	−90%	−62%	−47%
Loss on 100,000 Puts from Price Change	€130,000	€106,000	€161,000

2. Discuss how the strategy fared and how McLaire should proceed, assuming earnings beat the consensus estimate and Relais's stock price rises by 5% to €44.10.

Solution to 2:
The 42.50-strike put held by McLaire has 23 days to expiration. The price has declined from €1.72 to €0.66 (−62%), for a total loss of €106,000 (= [€1.72 – €0.66] × 100,000). This is less than the loss McLaire would have incurred if he had purchased the other

options. At the same time the value of the 100,000 Relais shares held by the fund has increased by €210,000 (= ($44.10 – $42.00) × 100,000). Now that the earnings announcement has been made, McLaire no longer needs the protection from the put options, so he should sell them and recover €66,000 from the original €172,000 put purchase price.

SUMMARY

This reading on options strategies shows a number of ways in which market participants might use options to enhance returns or to reduce risk to better meet portfolio objectives. The following are the key points.

- Buying a call and writing a put on the same underlying with the same strike price and expiration creates a synthetic long position (i.e., a synthetic long forward position).
- Writing a call and buying a put on the same underlying with the same strike price and expiration creates a synthetic short position (i.e., a synthetic short forward position).
- A synthetic long put position consists of a short stock and long call position in which the call strike price equals the price at which the stock is shorted.
- A synthetic long call position consists of a long stock and long put position in which the put strike price equals the price at which the stock is purchased.
- Delta is the change in an option's price for a change in price of the underlying, all else equal.
- Gamma is the change in an option's delta for a change in price of the underlying, all else equal.
- Vega is the change in an option's price for a change in volatility of the underlying, all else equal.
- Theta is the daily change in an option's price, all else equal.
- A covered call, in which the holder of a stock writes a call giving someone the right to buy the shares, is one of the most common uses of options by individual investors.
- Covered calls can be used to change an investment's risk–reward profile by effectively enhancing yield or reducing/exiting a position when the shares hit a target price.
- A covered call position has a limited maximum return because of the transfer of the right tail of the return distribution to the option buyer.
- The maximum loss of a covered call position is less than the maximum loss of the underlying shares alone, but the covered call carries the potential for an opportunity loss if the underlying shares rise sharply.
- A protective put is the simultaneous holding of a long stock position and a long put on the same asset. The put provides protection or insurance against a price decline.
- The continuous purchase of protective puts maintains the upside potential of the portfolio, while limiting downside volatility. The cost of the puts must be carefully considered, however, because this activity may be expensive. Conversely, the occasional purchase of a protective put to deal with a bearish short-term outlook can be a reasonable risk-reducing strategy.

- The maximum loss with a protective put is limited because the downside risk is transferred to the option writer in exchange for the payment of the option premium.
- With an option spread, an investor buys one option and writes another of the same type. This approach reduces the position cost but caps the maximum payoff.
- A bull spread expresses a bullish view on the underlying and is normally constructed by buying a call option and writing another call option with a higher exercise price (both options have same underlying and same expiry).
- A bear spread expresses a bearish view on the underlying and is normally constructed by buying a put option and writing another put option with a lower exercise price (both options have same underlying and same expiry).
- With either a bull spread or a bear spread, both the maximum gain and the maximum loss are known and limited.
- A long (short) straddle is an option combination in which the investor buys (sells) puts and calls with the same exercise price and expiration date. The long (short) straddle investor expects increased (stable/decreased) volatility and typically requires a large (small/no) price movement in the underlying asset in order to make a profit.
- A collar is an option position in which the investor is long shares of stock and simultaneously writes a call with an exercise price above the current stock price and buys a put with an exercise price below the current stock price. A collar limits the range of investment outcomes by sacrificing upside gain in exchange for providing downside protection.
- A long (short) calendar spread involves buying (selling) a long-dated option and writing (buying) a shorter-dated option of the same type with the same exercise price. A long (short) calendar spread is used when the investment outlook is flat (volatile) in the near term but greater (lesser) return movements are expected in the future.
- Implied volatility is the expected volatility an underlying asset's return and is derived from an option pricing model (i.e., the Black–Scholes–Merton model) as the value that equates the model price of an option to its market price.
- When implied volatilities of OTM options exceed those of ATM options, the implied volatility curve is a volatility smile. The more common shape is a volatility skew, in which implied volatility increases for OTM puts and decreases for OTM calls, as the strike price moves away from the current price.
- The implied volatility surface is a 3-D plot, for put and call options on the same underlying, showing expiration time (x-axis), strike prices (y-axis), and implied volatilities (z-axis). It simultaneously displays volatility skew and the term structure of implied volatility.
- Options, like all derivatives, should always be used in connection with a well-defined investment objective. When using options strategies, it is important to have a view on the expected change in implied volatility and the direction of movement of the underlying asset.

PRACTICE PROBLEMS

The following information relates to questions 1-10

Aline Nuñes, a junior analyst, works in the derivatives research division of an international securities firm. Nuñes's supervisor, Cátia Pereira, asks her to conduct an analysis of various option trading strategies relating to shares of three companies: IZD, QWY, and XDF. On 1 February, Nuñes gathers selected option premium data on the companies, presented in Exhibit 1.

Exhibit 1: Share Price and Option Premiums as of 1 February (share prices and option premiums in €)

Company	Share Price	Call Premium	Option Date/Strike	Put Premium
		9.45	April/87.50	1.67
IZD	93.93	2.67	April/95.00	4.49
		1.68	April/97.50	5.78
		4.77	April/24.00	0.35
QWY	28.49	3.96	April/25.00	0.50
		0.32	April/31.00	3.00
		0.23	February/80.00	5.52
XDF	74.98	2.54	April/75.00	3.22
		2.47	December/80.00	9.73

Nuñes considers the following option strategies relating to IZD:

Strategy 1: Constructing a synthetic long put position in IZD

Strategy 2: Buying 100 shares of IZD and writing the April €95.00 strike call option on IZD

Strategy 3: Implementing a covered call position in IZD using the April €97.50 strike option

Nuñes next reviews the following option strategies relating to QWY:

Strategy 4: Implementing a protective put position in QWY using the April €25.00 strike option

Strategy 5: Buying 100 shares of QWY, buying the April €24.00 strike put option, and writing the April €31.00 strike call option

Strategy 6: Implementing a bear spread in QWY using the April €25.00 and April €31.00 strike options

Finally, Nuñes considers two option strategies relating to XDF:

Strategy 7: Writing both the April €75.00 strike call option and the April €75.00 strike put option on XDF

Strategy 8: Writing the February €80.00 strike call option and buying the December €80.00 strike call option on XDF

1. Strategy 1 would require Nuñes to buy:

   A. shares of IZD.

   B. a put option on IZD.

   C. a call option on IZD.

2. Based on Exhibit 1, Nuñes should expect Strategy 2 to be *least* profitable if the share price of IZD at option expiration is:

   A. less than €91.26.

   B. between €91.26 and €95.00.

   C. more than €95.00.

3. Based on Exhibit 1, the breakeven share price of Strategy 3 is *closest* to:

   A. €92.25.

   B. €95.61.

   C. €95.82.

4. Based on Exhibit 1, the maximum loss per share that would be incurred by implementing Strategy 4 is:

   A. €2.99.

   B. €3.99.

   C. unlimited.

5. Strategy 5 is *best* described as a:

   A. collar.

   B. straddle.

   C. bear spread.

6. Based on Exhibit 1, Strategy 5 offers:

   A. unlimited upside.

   B. a maximum profit of €2.48 per share.

   C. protection against losses if QWY's share price falls below €28.14.

7. Based on Exhibit 1, the breakeven share price for Strategy 6 is *closest* to:

   A. €22.50.

   B. €28.50.

C. €33.50.

8. Based on Exhibit 1, the maximum gain per share that could be earned if Strategy 7 is implemented is:

   A. €5.74.

   B. €5.76.

   C. unlimited.

9. Based on Exhibit 1, the *best* explanation for Nuñes to implement Strategy 8 would be that, between the February and December expiration dates, she expects the share price of XDF to:

   A. decrease.

   B. remain unchanged.

   C. increase.

10. Over the past few months, Nuñes and Pereira have followed news reports on a proposed merger between XDF and one of its competitors. A government antitrust committee is currently reviewing the potential merger. Pereira expects the share price to move sharply upward or downward depending on whether the committee decides to approve or reject the merger next week. Pereira asks Nuñes to recommend an option trade that might allow the firm to benefit from a significant move in the XDF share price regardless of the direction of the move.

    The option trade that Nuñes should recommend relating to the government committee's decision is a:

    A. collar.

    B. bull spread.

    C. long straddle.

The following information relates to questions 11-16

Stanley Kumar Singh, CFA, is the risk manager at SKS Asset Management. He works with individual clients to manage their investment portfolios. One client, Sherman Hopewell, is worried about how short-term market fluctuations over the next three months might impact his equity position in Walnut Corporation. Although Hopewell is concerned about short-term downside price movements, he wants to remain invested in Walnut shares because he remains positive about its long-term performance. Hopewell has asked Singh to recommend an option strategy that will keep him invested in Walnut shares while protecting against a short-term price decline. Singh gathers the information in Exhibit 1 to explore various strategies to address Hopewell's concerns.

Another client, Nigel French, is a trader who does not currently own shares of Walnut Corporation. French has told Singh that he believes that Walnut shares will experience a large move in price after the upcoming quarterly earnings release in two weeks. French also tells Singh, however, that he is unsure which direction the stock will move. French asks Singh to recommend an option strategy that would allow him to profit should the share price move in either direction.

A third client, Wanda Tills, does not currently own Walnut shares and has asked Singh to explain the profit potential of three strategies using options in Walnut: a long straddle, a bull call spread, and a bear put spread. In addition, Tills asks Singh to explain the gamma of a call option. In response, Singh prepares a memo to be shared with Tills that provides a discussion of gamma and presents his analysis on three option strategies:

Strategy 1: A long straddle position at the $67.50 strike option

Strategy 2: A bull call spread using the $65 and $70 strike options

Strategy 3: A bear put spread using the $65 and $70 strike options

Exhibit 1: Walnut Corporation Current Stock Price: $67.79
Walnut Corporation European Options

Exercise Price	Market Call Price	Call Delta	Market Put Price	Put Delta
$55.00	$12.83	1.00	$0.24	–0.05
$65.00	$3.65	0.91	$1.34	–0.29
$67.50	$1.99	0.63	$2.26	–0.42
$70.00	$0.91	0.37	$3.70	–0.55
$80.00	$0.03	0.02	$12.95	–0.76

Note: Each option has 106 days remaining until expiration.

11. The option strategy Singh is *most likely* to recommend to Hopewell is a:

    A. collar.

    B. covered call.

    C. protective put.

12. The option strategy that Singh is *most likely* to recommend to French is a:

    A. straddle.

    B. bull spread.

    C. collar.

13. Based on Exhibit 1, Strategy 1 is profitable when the share price at expiration is *closest* to:

    A. $63.00.

    B. $65.24.

    C. $69.49.

14. Based on Exhibit 1, the maximum profit, on a per share basis, from investing in

Strategy 2, is *closest* to:

A. \$2.26.

B. \$2.74.

C. \$5.00.

15. Based on Exhibit 1, and assuming the market price of Walnut's shares at expiration is \$66, the profit or loss, on a per share basis, from investing in Strategy 3, is *closest* to:

A. \$2.36.

B. \$1.64.

C. \$2.64.

16. Based on the data in Exhibit 1, Singh would advise Tills that the call option with the *largest* gamma would have a strike price *closest* to:

A. \$ 55.00.

B. \$ 67.50.

C. \$ 80.00.

The following information relates to questions 17-23

Anneke Ngoc is an analyst who works for an international bank, where she advises high-net-worth clients on option strategies. Ngoc prepares for a meeting with a US-based client, Mani Ahlim.

Ngoc notes that Ahlim recently inherited an account containing a large Brazilian real (BRL) cash balance. Ahlim intends to use the inherited funds to purchase a vacation home in the United States with an expected purchase price of US\$750,000 in six months. Ahlim is concerned that the Brazilian real will weaken against the US dollar over the next six months. Ngoc considers potential hedge strategies to reduce the risk of a possible adverse currency movement over this time period.

Ahlim holds shares of Pselftarô Ltd. (PSÔL), which has a current share price of \$37.41. Ahlim is bullish on PSÔL in the long term. He would like to add to his long position but is concerned about a moderate price decline after the quarterly earnings announcement next month, in April. Ngoc recommends a protective put position with a strike price of \$35 using May options and a \$40/\$50 bull call spread using December options. Ngoc gathers selected PSÔL option prices for May and December, which are presented in Exhibit 1.

Exhibit 1: Selected PSÔL Option Prices (all prices in US dollars)

Exercise Price	Expiration Month	Call Price	Put Price
35	May	3.00	1.81
40	December	6.50	10.25
50	December	4.25	20.50

Ahlim also expresses interest in trading options on India's NIFTY 50 (National Stock Exchange Fifty) Index. Ngoc gathers selected one-month option prices and implied volatility data, which are presented in Exhibit 2. India's NIFTY 50 Index is currently trading at a level of 11,610.

Exhibit 2: Selected One-Month Option Prices and Implied Volatility Data: NIFTY 50 Index (all prices in Indian rupees)

Exercise Price	Market Call Price	Market Put Price	Implied Call Volatility	Implied Put Volatility
11,200	526.00	61.90	5.87	17.72
11,400	365.45	102.60	10.80	17.01
11,600	240.00	165.80	12.26	16.44
11,800	135.00	213.00	12.14	16.39
12,000	65.80	370.00	11.98	16.56

Ngoc reviews a research report that includes a one-month forecast of the NIFTY 50 Index. The report's conclusions are presented in Exhibit 3.

Exhibit 3: Research Report Conclusions: NIFTY 50 Index

One-month forecast:

- We have a neutral view on the direction of the index's move over the next month.
- The rate of the change in underlying prices (vega) is expected to increase.
- The implied volatility of index options is expected to be above the consensus forecast.

Based on these conclusions, Ngoc considers various NIFTY 50 Index option strategies for Ahlim.

17. Which of the following positions would best mitigate Ahlim's concern regarding the purchase of his vacation home in six months?

    A. Sell an at-the-money six-month BRL/USD call option.

    B. Purchase an at-the-money six-month USD/BRL put option.

    C. Take a short position in a six-month BRL/USD futures contract.

18. Based on Exhibit 1, the maximum loss per share of Ngoc's recommended PSÔL

protective put position is:

A. $0.60.

B. $2.41.

C. $4.22.

19. Based on Exhibit 1, the breakeven price per share of Ngoc's recommended PSÔL protective put position is:

A. $35.60.

B. $36.81.

C. $39.22.

20. Based on Exhibit 1, the maximum profit per share of Ngoc's recommended PSÔL bull call spread is:

A. $2.25.

B. $7.75.

C. $12.25.

21. Based on Exhibit 1, the breakeven price per share of Ngoc's recommended PSÔL bull call spread is:

A. $42.25.

B. $47.75.

C. $52.25.

22. Based on Exhibit 2, the NIFTY 50 Index implied volatility data *most likely* indicate a:

A. risk reversal.

B. volatility skew.

C. volatility smile.

23. Based on Exhibit 3, which of the following NIFTY 50 Index option strategies should Ngoc recommend to Ahlim?

A. Buy a straddle.

B. Buy a call option.

C. Buy a calendar spread.

SOLUTIONS

1. C is correct. To construct a synthetic long put position, Nuñes would buy a call option on IZD. Of course, she would also need to sell (short) IZD shares to complete the synthetic long put position.

2. A is correct. Strategy 2 is a covered call, which is a combination of a long position in shares and a short call option. The breakeven point of Strategy 2 is €91.26, which representsthe price per share of €93.93 minus the call premium received of €2.67 per share ($S_0 - c_0$). So, at any share price less than €91.26 at option expiration, Strategy 2 incurs a loss. If the share price of IZD at option expiration is greater than €91.26, Strategy 2 generates a gain.

3. A is correct. Strategy 3 is a covered call strategy, which is a combination of a long position in shares and a short call option. The breakeven share price for a covered call is the share price minus the call premium received, or $S_0 - c_0$. The current share price of IZD is €93.93, and the IZD April €97.50 call premium is €1.68. Thus, the breakeven underlying share price for Strategy 3 is $S_0 - c_0$ = €93.93 – €1.68 = €92.25.

4. B is correct. Strategy 4 is a protective put position, which is a combination of a long position in shares and a long put option. By purchasing the €25.00 strike put option, Nuñes would be protected from losses at QWY share prices of €25.00 or lower. Thus, the maximum loss per share from Strategy 4 would be the loss of share value from €28.49 to €25.00 (or €3.49) plus the put premium paid for the put option of €0.50: $S_0 - X + p_0$ = €28.49 – €25.00 + €0.50 = €3.99.

5. A is correct. Strategy 5 describes a collar, which is a combination of a long position in shares, a long put option with an exercise price below the current stock price, and a short call option with an exercise price above the current stock price.

6. B is correct. Strategy 5 describes a collar, which is a combination of a long position in shares, a long put option, and a short call option. Strategy 5 would require Nuñes to buy 100 QWY shares at the current market price of €28.49 per share. In addition, she would purchase a QWY April €24.00 strike put option contract for €0.35 per share and collect €0.32 per share from writing a QWY April €31.00 strike call option. The collar offers protection against losses on the shares below the put strike price of €24.00 per share, but it also limits upside to the call strike price of €31.00 per share. Thus, the maximum gain on the trade, which occurs at prices of €31.00 per share or higher, is calculated as $(X_2 - S_0) - p_0 + c_0$, or (€31.00 – €28.49) – €0.35 + €0.32 = €2.48 per share.

7. B is correct. Strategy 6 is a bear spread, which is a combination of a long put option and a short put option on the same underlying, where the long put has a higher strike price than the short put. In the case of Strategy 6, the April €31.00 put option would be purchased and the April €25.00 put option would be sold. The long put premium is €3.00 and the short put premium is €0.50, for a net cost of €2.50. The breakeven share price is €28.50, calculated as $X_H - (p_H - p_L)$ = €31.00 – (€3.00 – €0.50) = €28.50.

8. B is correct. Strategy 7 describes a short straddle, which is a combination of a short put option and a short call option, both with the same strike price. The maximum gain is €5.76 per share, which represents the sum of the two option premiums, or $c_0 + p_0$ = €2.54 + €3.22 = €5.76. The maximum gain per share is realized if both options expire worthless, which would happen if the share price

of XDF at expiration is €75.00.

9. C is correct. Nuñes would implement Strategy 8, which is a long calendar spread, if she expects the XDF share price to increase between the February and December expiration dates. This strategy provides a benefit from the February short call premium to partially offset the cost of the December long call option. Nuñes likely expects the XDF share price to remain relatively flat between the current price €74.98 and €80 until the February call option expires, after which time she expects the share price to increase above €80. If such expectations come to fruition, the February call would expire worthless and Nuñes would realize gains on the December call option.

10. C is correct. Nuñes should recommend a long straddle, which is a combination of a long call option and a long put option, both with the same strike price. The committee's announcement is expected to cause a significant move in XDF's share price. A long straddle is appropriate because the share price is expected to move sharply up or down depending on the committee's decision. If the merger is approved, the share price will likely increase, leading to a gain in the long call option. If the merger is rejected, then the share price will likely decrease, leading to a gain in the long put option.

11. C is correct. A protective put accomplishes Hopewell's goal of short-term price protection. A protective put provides downside protection while retaining the upside potential. Although Hopewell is concerned about the downside in the short term, he wants to remain invested in Walnut shares because he is positive on the stock in the long term.

12. A is correct. The long straddle strategy is based on expectations of volatility in the underlying stock being higher than the market consensus. The straddle strategy consists of simultaneously buying a call option and a put option at the same strike price. Singh could recommend that French buy a straddle using near at-the-money options ($67.50 strike). This allows French to profit should the Walnut stock price experience a large move in either direction after the earnings release.

13. A is correct. The straddle strategy consists of simultaneously buying a call option and buying a put option at the same strike price. The market price for the $67.50 call option is $1.99, and the market price for the $67.50 put option is $2.26, for an initial net cost of $4.25 per share. Thus, this straddle position requires a move greater than $4.25 in either direction from the strike price of $67.50 to become profitable. So, the straddle becomes profitable at $67.50 – $4.26 = $63.24 or lower, or $67.50 + $4.26 = $71.76 or higher. At $63.00, the profit on the straddle is positive.

14. A is correct. The bull call strategy consists of buying the lower-strike option and selling the higher-strike option. The purchase of the $65 strike call option costs $3.65 per share, and selling the $70 strike call option generates an inflow of $0.91 per share, for an initial net cost of $2.74 per share. At expiration, the maximum profit occurs when the stock price is $70 or higher, which yields a $5.00 per share payoff ($70 – $65) on the long call position. After deduction of the $2.74 per share cost required to initiate the bull call spread, the profit is $2.26 ($5.00 – $2.74).

15. B is correct. The bear put spread consists of buying a put option with a high strike price ($70) and selling another put option with a lower strike price ($65). The market price for the $70 strike put option is $3.70, and the market price for the $65 strike put option is $1.34 per share. Thus, the initial net cost of the bear

spread position is \$3.70 – \$1.34 = \$2.36 per share. If Walnut shares are \$66 at expiration, the \$70 strike put option is in the money by \$4.00, and the short position in the \$65 strike put expires worthless. After deducting the cost of \$2.36 to initiate the bear spread position, the net profit is \$1.64 per contract.

16. B is correct. The \$67.50 call option is approximately at the money because the Walnut share price is currently \$67.79. Gamma measures the sensitivity of an option's delta to a change in the underlying. The largest gamma occurs when options are trading at the money or near expiration, when the deltas of such options move quickly toward 1.0 or 0.0. Under these conditions, the gammas tend to be largest and delta hedges are hardest to maintain.

17. B is correct. Ahlim could mitigate the risk of the Brazilian real weakening against the US dollar over the next six months by (1) purchasing an at-the-money six-month BRL/USD call option (to buy US dollars), (2) purchasing an at-the-money six-month USD/BRL put option (to sell Brazilian reals), or (3) taking a long position in a six-month BRL/USD futures contract (to buy US dollars).
    Purchasing an at-the-money six-month USD/BRL put option (to sell Brazilian reals) would mitigate the risk of a weakening Brazilian real. If the Brazilian real should weaken against the US dollar over the next six months, Ahlim could exercise the put option and sell his Brazilian reals at the contract's strike rate (which would have been the prevailing market exchange rate at the time of purchase, since the option is at the money).
    A is incorrect because purchasing (not selling) an at-the-money six-month BRL/USD call option (to buy US dollars) would mitigate the risk of the Brazilian real weakening against the US dollar over the next six months. The long call position would give Ahlim the right to buy US dollars (and sell Brazilian reals). A call on US dollars is similar to a put on Brazilian reals. So, a put to sell Brazilian reals at a given strike rate can be viewed as a call to buy US dollars.
    C is incorrect because going long (not short) a six-month BRL/USD futures contract (to buy US dollars) would mitigate the risk of the Brazilian real weakening against the US dollar over the next six months. A long futures position would obligate Ahlim to buy US dollars (and sell Brazilian reals) at the futures contract rate.

18. C is correct. Ngoc recommends a protective put position with a strike price of \$35 using May options. The maximum loss per share on the protective put is calculated as

    Maximum loss per share of protective put = $S_0 - X + p_0$.

    Maximum loss per share of protective put = \$37.41 − \$35.00 + \$1.81 = \$4.22.

    In summary, with the protective put in place, Ahlim is protected against losses below \$35.00. Thus, taking into account the put option purchase price of \$1.81, Ahlim's maximum loss occurs at the share price of \$33.19, resulting in a maximum loss of \$4.22 per share (= \$37.41 – \$33.19).
    A is incorrect because \$0.60 reflects incorrectly subtracting (rather than adding) the put premium in the calculation of the maximum loss of protective put (i.e., \$37.41 – \$35.00 – \$1.81 = \$0.60).
    B is incorrect because \$2.41 does not include the put premium in the calculation but only reflects the difference between the current share price (\$37.41) and the put exercise price (\$35.00).

19. C is correct. Ngoc recommends a protective put position with a strike price of \$35 using May options. The breakeven price per share on the protective put is

calculated as

Breakeven price per share of protective put = $S_0 + p_0$.

Breakeven price per share of protective put = \$37.41 + \$1.81 = \$39.22.

In summary, Ahlim would need PSÔL's share price to rise by the price of the put option (\$1.81) from the current price of \$37.41 to reach the breakeven share price—the price at which the gain from the increase in the value of the stock offsets the purchase price of the put option.

A is incorrect because \$35.60 represents incorrectly subtracting (rather than adding) the put premium in the calculation of the protective put breakeven price: \$37.41 – \$1.81 = \$35.60.

B is incorrect because \$36.81 represents incorrectly adding the put premium to the strike price (not the current share price): \$35.00 + \$1.81 = \$36.81.

20. B is correct. Ngoc recommends a \$40/\$50 bull call spread using December options. To construct this spread, Ahlim would buy the \$40 call, paying the \$6.50 premium, and simultaneously sell the \$50 call, receiving a premium of \$4.25. The maximum gain or profit of a bull call spread occurs when the stock price reaches the high exercise price (\$50) or higher at expiration. Thus, the maximum profit per share of a bull call spread is the spread difference between the strike prices less the net premium paid, calculated as

    Maximum profit per share of bull call spread = $(X_H - X_L) - (c_L - c_H)$.

    Maximum profit per share of bull call spread = (\$50 – \$40) – (\$6.50 – \$4.25).

    Maximum profit per share of bull call spread = \$7.75.

    A is incorrect because \$2.25 represents only the net premium and does not include the spread difference.

    C is incorrect because \$12.25 represents the net premium being incorrectly added (rather than subtracted) from the spread difference.

21. A is correct. Ngoc recommends a \$40/\$50 bull call spread using December options. To construct this spread, Ahlim would buy the \$40 call, paying a \$6.50 premium, and simultaneously sell the \$50 call, receiving a \$4.25 premium. The breakeven price per share of a bull call spread is calculated as

    Breakeven price per share of bull call spread = $X_L + (c_L - c_H)$.

    Breakeven price per share of bull call spread = \$40 + (\$6.50 – \$4.25).

    Breakeven price per share of bull call spread = \$42.25.

    In summary, in order to break even, the PSÔL stock price must rise above \$40 by the amount of the net premium paid of \$2.25 to enter into the bull call spread. At the price of \$42.25, the lower \$40 call option would have an exercise value of \$2.25, exactly offsetting the \$2.25 cost of entering the trade.

    B is incorrect because \$47.75 represents the net premium being incorrectly subtracted from the high exercise price (rather than being added to the low exercise price): \$50 – (\$6.50 – \$4.25) = \$47.75.

    C is incorrect because \$52.25 represents the net premium being added to the high exercise price (rather than the low exercise price): \$50 + (\$6.50 – \$4.25) = \$52.25.

22. B is correct. When the implied volatility decreases for OTM (out-of-the-money) calls relative to ATM (at-the-money) calls and increases for OTM puts relative

to ATM puts, a volatility skew exists. Put volatility is higher, rising from 16.44 ATM to 17.72 OTM, likely because of the higher demand for puts to hedge positions in the index against downside risk. Call volatility decreases from 12.26 for ATM calls to 11.98 for OTM calls since calls do not offer this valuable portfolio insurance.

A is incorrect because a risk reversal is a delta-hedged trading strategy seeking to profit from a change in the relative volatility of calls and puts.

C is incorrect because a volatility smile exists when both call and put volatilities, not just put volatilities, are higher OTM than ATM.

23. A is correct. The research report concludes that the consensus forecast of the implied volatility of index options is too low and anticipates greater-than-expected volatility over the next month. Given the neutral market direction forecast, Ngoc should recommend a long straddle, which entails buying a one-month 11,600 call and buying a one-month put with the same exercise price. If the future NIFTY 50 Index level rises above its current level plus the combined cost of the call and put premiums, Ahlim would exercise the call option and realize a profit. Similarly, if the index level falls below the current index level minus the combined cost of the call and put premiums, Ahlim would exercise the put option and realize a profit. Thus, Ahlim profits if the index moves either up or down enough to pay for the call and put premiums.

    B is incorrect because the strategy to buy a call option would be reasonable given an increase in expected implied volatility with a bullish NIFTY 50 Index forecast, not a neutral trading range.

    C is incorrect because a long calendar spread is based on the expectation that implied volatility will remain unchanged, not increase, until the expiry of the shorter-term option.

LEARNING MODULE

2

Swaps, Forwards, and Futures Strategies

by Barbara Valbuzzi, CFA.

Barbara Valbuzzi, CFA (Italy).

LEARNING OUTCOMES

Mastery	*The candidate should be able to:*
☐	demonstrate how interest rate swaps, forwards, and futures can be used to modify a portfolio's risk and return
☐	demonstrate how currency swaps, forwards, and futures can be used to modify a portfolio's risk and return
☐	demonstrate how equity swaps, forwards, and futures can be used to modify a portfolio's risk and return
☐	demonstrate the use of volatility derivatives and variance swaps
☐	demonstrate the use of derivatives to achieve targeted equity and interest rate risk exposures
☐	demonstrate the use of derivatives in asset allocation, rebalancing, and inferring market expectations

MANAGING INTEREST RATE RISK WITH SWAPS 1

☐	demonstrate how interest rate swaps, forwards, and futures can be used to modify a portfolio's risk and return

There are many ways in which investment managers and investors can use swaps, forwards, futures, and volatility derivatives. The typical applications of these derivatives involve modifying investment positions for hedging purposes or for taking directional bets, creating or replicating desired payoffs, implementing asset allocation and portfolio rebalancing decisions, and even inferring current market expectations. The following table shows some common uses of these derivatives in portfolio management and the types of derivatives used by investors and portfolio managers.

Common Uses of Swaps, Forwards, and Futures	Typical Derivatives Used
Modifying Portfolio Returns and Risk Exposures (Hedging and Directional Bets)	Interest Rate, Currency, and Equity Swaps and Futures; Fixed-Income Futures; Variance Swaps
Creating Desired Payoffs	Forwards, Futures, Total Return Swaps
Performing Asset Allocation and Portfolio Rebalancing	Equity Index Futures, Government Bond Futures, Index Swaps
Inferring Market Expectations for Interest Rates, Inflation, and Volatility	Fed Funds Futures, Inflation Swaps, VIX Futures

It is important for an informed investment professional to understand how swaps, forwards, futures, and volatility derivatives can be used and their associated risk–return trade-offs. Therefore, the purpose of this reading is to illustrate ways in which these derivatives might be used in typical investment situations. Sections 2–4 of this reading show how swaps, forwards, and futures can be used to modify the risk exposure of an existing position. Sections 5–6 provide a discussion on derivatives on volatility. Sections 7–9 demonstrate a series of applications showing ways in which a portfolio manager might solve an investment problem with these derivatives. The reading concludes with a summary.

Changing Risk Exposures with Swaps, Futures, and Forwards

Financial managers can use swaps, forwards, and futures markets to quickly and efficiently alter the underlying risk exposure of their asset portfolios or anticipated investment transactions. This section covers a variety of common examples that use swaps, futures, and forwards.

Managing Interest Rate Risk

Interest Rate Swaps

An interest rate swap is an over-the-counter (OTC) contract between two parties that agree to exchange cash flows on specified payment dates—one based on a *variable* (floating) interest rate and the other based on a *fixed* rate (the "swap rate")—determined at the time the swap is initiated. The swap tenor is when the swap is agreed to expire. Both interest rates are applied to the swap's notional value to determine the size of each payment. Normally, the resulting two payments (one fixed, one floating) are in the same currency but will not be equal, so they are typically netted, with the party owing the greater amount paying the difference to the other party. In this manner, a party that currently has a fixed (floating) risk or other obligation can effectively convert it into a floating (fixed) one.

Interest rate swaps are among the most widely used instruments to manage interest rate risk. In particular, they are designed to manage the risk on cash flows arising from investors' assets and liabilities. Interest rate swaps and futures can also be used to modify the risk and return profile of a portfolio. This is associated with managing a portfolio of bonds that generally involves controlling the portfolio's duration. Although futures are commonly used to make duration changes, swaps can also be used, and we shall see how in this reading. Finally, interest rate swaps are used by financial institutions to hedge the interest rate risk exposure deriving from the issuance of financial instruments sold to clients. Example 1 shows how an interest rate swap is used to convert floating-rate securities into fixed-rate securities. Here the firm initially expects continuing low interest rates, so it issues floating-rate bonds. But after concluding that rates are likely to increase, the firm seeks to convert its interest rate risk to a fixed obligation, even though doing so means making higher payments up front.

EXAMPLE 1

Using an Interest Rate Swap to Convert Floating-Rate Securities into Fixed-Rate Securities

An investment firm has sold £20 million of three-year floating-rate bonds that pay a semiannual coupon equal to the six-month market reference rate plus 50 bps. A few days later, the firm's outlook changes substantially, and it now expects higher rates in the future. The firm enters into an interest rate swap with a tenor of approximately three years and semiannual payments, where the firm pays a fixed par swap rate of 1.25% and receives the six-month reference rate. The swap settlement dates are the same as the coupon payment dates on the floating-rate bonds. At the first swap settlement date, the six-month reference rate is 0.75%.

Analysis:

At the first coupon payment and swap settlement date, the six-month reference rate is 0.75% (annualized). This means that on the swap the investment firm will make a net payment of £50,000 as follows:

- Receive based on the reference rate: 0.75% × £20 million × (180/360) = £75,000.
- Pay based on the fixed rate: 1.25% × £20 million × (180/360) = £125,000.
- Net payment *made* by the firm to swap dealer: £125,000 − £75,000 = £50,000.

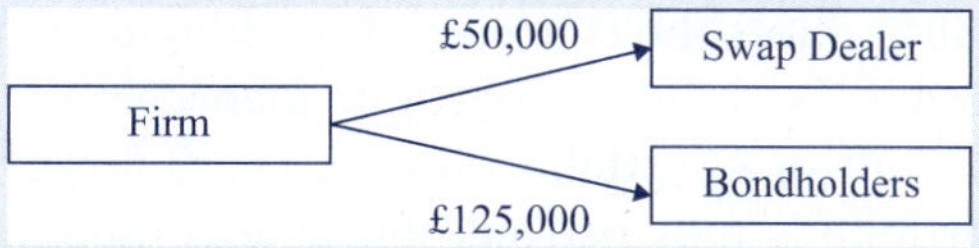

At the same time, the first semiannual coupon payment on the securities will be (0.75% + 0.50%) × £20 million × (180/360) = £125,000.

The total payment made by the investment firm on the securities and the swap is £175,000 (= £125,000 + £50,000).

Now assume that as we move forward to the second coupon payment and swap settlement date, interest rates have increased and the six-month reference rate is 1.50%.

On the swap, the investment firm will receive a net payment of £25,000 as follows:

- Receive based on the new reference rate: 1.50% × £20 million × (180/360) = £150,000.
- Pay based on the fixed rate: 1.25% × £20 million × (180/360) = £125,000.
- Net payment *received* by the firm: £150,000 − £125,000 = £25,000.

The coupon payment on the securities will be (1.50% + 0.50%) × £20 million × (180/360) = £200,000.

The total payment made by the investment firm on the securities and the swap is again £175,000 (= £200,000 − £25,000).

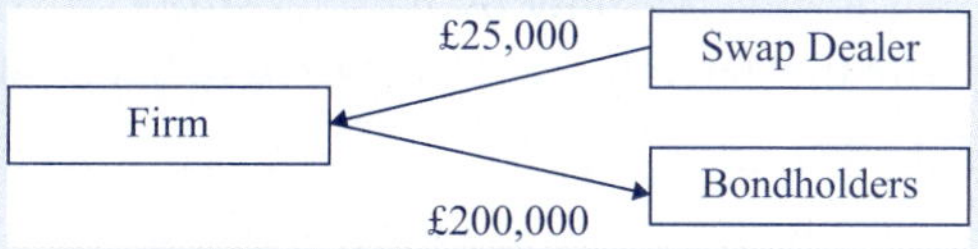

The investment firm has effectively fixed its all-in borrowing costs. Since this fixed cost is synthesized by a combination of the underlying debt position and the derivative contract, it can be described as a synthetic fixed security.

Why should the investment firm decide to pay a fixed rate of 1.25%, on a semiannual basis, for the remaining life of the securities when the reference rate is only 0.75% today? The reason is that the firm's outlook is now for higher rates in the future, as expressed by market participants in the upward-sloping yield curve. An upward-sloping yield curve reflects that investors require higher risk premium compensation for holding longer-term securities.

The agreed-on fixed rate on the swap is based on the term structure of rates at the time the deal is initiated. If the term structure changes, the new fixed rate agreed on by the counterparties on a swap with the same residual time to maturity as the original one will be different from the original rate. This means that the market value of the swap will become positive or negative. In particular, the investment firm in Example 1 has managed to fix the interest rate on future payments but has given away the opportunity to benefit from possible lower interest rates in the future. If the term structure of interest rates has a parallel shift downward, meaning that all rates across tenors decrease, the value of the swap will become negative from the perspective of the fixed-rate payer, depending on the new swap market fixed rate. The investment firm has managed to achieve the desired fixed profile of future cash flows, but it might incur a loss if the firm wants to unwind the interest rate swap before maturity. Alternatively, if rates rise, as now expected, the swap can be unwound at a profit by the same reasoning in reverse: The value of the swap becomes positive from the fixed-rate payer's view; fixed-rate payment paid is less than floating-rate payment received.

This explanation introduces the concepts of marking to market of the swap and how swaps can be used in fixed-income portfolio management with the objective to hedge the changes in value of a portfolio with fixed cash flows.

When a bond portfolio is fully hedged, its value is immunized with respect to changes in yields. This can be stated as $\Delta P = (N_S)(\Delta S)$, where ΔP is the change in the value of the bond portfolio and ΔS is the change in the value of the swap for a given change in interest rates. The notional principal of the swap (N_S) will be determined as $N_S = \Delta P / \Delta S$. To reduce changes in value of a fixed-rate portfolio, the manager will want to lower the overall duration by exchanging part of this fixed-rate income stream for a floating-rate stream. This can be done by entering an interest rate swap where the portfolio manager will pay the fixed rate and receive the floating rate.

It is important to keep in mind that most of the time, the hedging instrument and the asset or portfolio to be hedged are imperfect substitutes. The result is a market risk, called *basis risk* or *spread risk*—the difference between the market performance of the asset and the derivative instrument used to hedge it. When using an interest rate swap to hedge, it is possible that the changes in the underlying rate of the derivative contract, and thus in the value of the swap, do not perfectly mirror changes in the value of the bond portfolio.

Furthermore, the composition of the bond portfolio could bear additional market risks other than interest rate risk. For instance, suppose a portfolio of corporate bonds is hedged with an interest rate swap. In this case, even if interest rate risk is hedged, the investor is still exposed to credit spread risk.

The main underlying assumptions we will use are that the change in value of the bond portfolio can be approximated by using the concept of modified duration,[1] the yield curve is flat, and it is affected only by parallel shifts. Furthermore, we assume here that the portfolio and the derivative contract used to hedge are perfect substitutes.

1 Although there are various duration measures, we are concerned here with modified duration, which is an approximate measure of how a bond price changes given a small change in the level of interest rates.

A measure for the change in the value of the bond portfolio (ΔP) for a change in interest rates is given by the portfolio's modified duration, $MDUR_P$. The same measure calculated for the interest rate swap, $MDUR_S$, is used to determine the change in the value of the swap, ΔS. The target modified duration for the combined portfolio is $MDUR_T$, and MV_P is the market value of the bond portfolio.

By properly choosing the notional value and the tenor of the swap, the portfolio manager can achieve a combination of the existing portfolio and the interest rate swap that sets the overall portfolio duration to the target duration: $(MV_P)(MDUR_P) + (N_S)(MDUR_S) = (MV_P)(MDUR_T)$.

The equivalence $\Delta P = (N_S)(\Delta S)$ becomes $(MV_P)(MDUR_T - MDUR_P) = (N_S)(MDUR_S)$. To find the swap notional principal, N_S, we need to solve for the following formula:

$$N_S = \left(\frac{MDUR_T - MDUR_P}{MDUR_S}\right)(MV_P) \quad (1)$$

The modified duration of a swap ($MDUR_S$) is the net of the modified durations of the equivalent positions in fixed- and floating-rate bonds. Thus, the position of the pay-fixed party in a pay-fixed, receive-floating swap has the modified duration of a floating-rate bond minus the modified duration of a fixed-rate bond, where the floating- and fixed-rate bonds have cash flows equivalent to the corresponding cash flows of the swap. A pay-fixed, receive-floating swap has a negative (positive) duration from the perspective of a fixed-rate payer (receiver), because the duration of a fixed-rate bond is positive and larger than the duration of a floating-rate bond, which is near zero. Moreover, the negative duration of this position to the fixed-rate payer/floating-rate receiver makes sense in that the position would be expected to benefit from rising interest rates.

EXAMPLE 2

Using an Interest Rate Swap to Achieve a Target Duration

1. Consider a portfolio manager with an investment portfolio of €50 million of fixed-rate German bonds with an average modified duration of 5.5. Because he fears that interest rates will rise, he wants to reduce the modified duration of the portfolio to 4.5, but he does not want to sell any of the securities. One way to do this would be to add a negative-duration position by entering into an interest rate swap where he pays the fixed rate and receives the floating rate. A two-year interest rate swap has an estimated modified duration of –2.00 from the perspective of the fixed-rate payer.

   Demonstrate how the manager can use this interest rate swap to achieve the target modified duration.

Solution:

The portfolio manager's goal is for the bonds and the swap to combine to create a portfolio with a market value of €50 million and a target modified duration of 4.5. This relationship can be expressed as follows:

$$€50,000,000(5.50) + (N_S)(MDUR_S) = €50,000,000(4.50),$$

where

N_S = Interest rate swap's notional principal

$MDUR_S$ = Interest rate swap's modified duration, set equal to −2.00

So, the notional principal of this interest rate swap that the manager should use is determined using Equation 1, as follows:

$$N_S = [(4.50 - 5.50)/(-2.00)] \times €50,000,000 = €25,000,000.$$

2 MANAGING INTEREST RATE RISK WITH FORWARDS AND FUTURES

☐ demonstrate how interest rate swaps, forwards, and futures can be used to modify a portfolio's risk and return

The market in short-term interest rate derivatives is large and liquid, and the instruments involved are forward rate agreements (FRAs) and interest rate futures. A forward rate agreement is an OTC derivative instrument that is used mainly to hedge a loan expected to be taken out in the near future or to hedge against changes in the level of interest rates in the future. In fact, with advanced settled at maturity, an FRA will settle only the discounted difference between the interest rate agreed on in the contract and the actual rate prevailing at the time of settlement, applied on the notional amount of the contract. In general, managing short-term interest rate risk with an interest rate forward contract can also be done with an interest rate futures contract. Forwards, like swaps, are OTC instruments and are especially useful because they can be customized, but they do have counterparty risk. In contrast, exchange-traded interest rate futures contracts are standardized and guaranteed by a clearinghouse, so counterparty risk is virtually zero.[2]

Forward rate agreements and interest rate futures are widely used to hedge the risk associated with interest rates changing from the time a loan or a deposit is anticipated until it is actually implemented. Example 3 demonstrates how interest rate futures are used to lock in an interest rate.

EXAMPLE 3

Using Interest Rate Futures to Lock in an Interest Rate

Amanda Wright, the chief investment officer (CIO) of a US-based philanthropic foundation is expecting a donation of $30 million in two months' time from a member of the foundation's founding family. This significant donation will then be invested for three months and subsequently will be divided into smaller grants

2 Regulatory changes in global markets are moving both over-the-counter swaps and forward contracts toward a clearing process as well. The clearing process reduces the risk that one counterparty will default on its obligations (by requiring collateral for trades and by daily marking to market of open positions), and for this reason, the counterparty risk associated with each single trade is virtually zero. However, there is still the risk that a major counterparty will fail to carry out its obligations (e.g., Lehman Brothers), causing operational risks for investors.

to be made to medical and educational institutions supported by the foundation. The current (i.e., spot) three-month reference rate is 2.40% (annualized). The CIO expects interest rates to fall, and she decides to hedge the rate on the deposit with Eurodollar futures.

To provide background information, Eurodollar futures are cash settled on the basis of the market reference rate for an offshore deposit having a principal value of $1 million and a three-month maturity. These contracts are quoted in terms of the "IMM index"[3] that is equal to 100 less the annualized yield on the security. A 1 bp (0.01% or 0.0001) change in the value of the futures contract equates to a $25.00 movement in the contract value. Thus, the basis point value (BPV) of a $1 million face value, 90-day money market instrument is given by

$$BPV = \text{Face value} \times \left(\frac{\text{Days}}{360}\right) \times 0.01\,\% = \$1{,}000{,}000 \times \left(\frac{90}{360}\right) \times 0.01\,\%$$
$$= \$25$$

Analysis:

Wright buys 30 of the Eurodollar futures contracts at 97.60, locking in a forward rate of 2.40%. After two months, the donation is received and the CIO initiates the deposit at the then-lower spot rate of 2.10%. She unwinds the hedge at a futures price of 97.90, which is 30 bps higher than where the position was initiated.

The foundation will receive $180,000 from the deposit plus the hedge, as follows:

1. Interest obtained on the deposit: 2.10% × $30 million × (90/360) = $157,500.
2. Profit on the hedge is 30 bps (30 × $25 = $750), which for 30 contracts corresponds to $22,500 (= $750 × 30).

This corresponds to the return on an investment at the initial three-month reference rate of 2.40%, or 2.40% × $30 million × (90/360) = $180,000. This calculation demonstrates that by buying the Eurodollar futures, Wright did indeed lock in a forward rate of 2.40%.

Institutional investors and bond traders can decide to use interest rate futures or fixed-income futures (also referred to as "bond futures") contracts, which are longer dated, to hedge interest rate risk exposure. The choice will depend on the maturity of the bond or portfolio to be hedged. Since they are listed, interest rate futures have a limited number of maturities. Furthermore, the nearest months' contracts have higher liquidity than the longer tenors. For these reasons, interest rate futures (e.g., Eurodollar futures) are commonly used to hedge short-term bonds, with up to two to three years remaining to maturity. When using interest rate futures to hedge a short-term bond, an effective and widely adopted technique to construct the hedge is to use a strip of futures contracts. Having measured the responsiveness of the bond to an interest rate change, it is now necessary to measure the sensitivity of each cash flow to changes in the relevant forward rate. Then, one can calculate the number of futures contracts needed to hedge the interest rate exposure for each cash flow. Fixed-income futures contracts remain, however, the preferred instrument to hedge bond positions, given that their liquidity is very high. This is especially true for US Treasury bond futures.

3 The IMM, or International Monetary Market, was established as a division of CME many years ago. The distinction is seldom made today because CME operates as a unified entity, but references to IMM persist today.

Fixed-Income Futures

Portfolio managers that want to hedge the duration risk of their bond portfolios usually use fixed-income futures. They are standardized forward contracts listed on an exchange that have as underlying a basket of deliverable bonds with remaining maturities within a predefined range. The most liquid contracts include T-note and T-bond futures listed on the Chicago Board of Trade or the Chicago Mercantile Exchange. Contracts expire in March, June, September, and December, and the underlying assets include Treasury bills, notes, and bonds. In Europe, the most liquid and most heavily traded fixed-income futures are traded on the Eurex, and these are the Euro-Bund (FGBL), Euro-Bobl (FGBM), and Euro-Schatz (FCBS).[4] These futures contracts have German federal government–issued bonds with different maturities as underlying. The Schatz is also known as the short bund futures contract because the maturities of the underlying bonds range from 21 to 27 months. In contrast, maturities of underlying bonds range from 4.5 years to 5.5 years for the Bobl futures contract and are even longer (between 10 years and 30 years) for the Bund futures contract.

Bond futures are used by hedgers to protect an existing bond portfolio against adverse interest rate movements and by arbitrageurs to gain from price differences in equivalent instruments.

A fixed-income futures contract has as its underlying reference assets a basket of deliverable bonds with a range of different coupon levels and maturity dates. Most futures contracts are closed before delivery or rolled into the next contract month. However, in the case of delivery, the futures contract seller has the obligation to deliver and the right to choose which security to deliver. For this reason, the duration of a futures contract is usually consistent with the forward behavior of the cheapest underlying deliverable bond. This is called the cheapest-to-deliver (CTD) bond, the eligible bond that the seller will most likely choose to deliver under the futures contract if he decides to deliver (rather than close out the futures position). The price sensitivity of the bond futures will, therefore, reflect the duration of the CTD bond.

Within the underlying basket of bonds, the seller will deliver the CTD bond, the one that presents the greatest profit or smallest loss at delivery. To provide a guide for choosing the CTD bond, the concept of the conversion factor (CF) has been introduced. Given that the short side has the option of delivering any eligible security, a conversion factor invoicing system that allows for a less biased comparison in choosing among deliverable bonds has been established. In fact, the amount the futures contract seller receives at delivery will depend on the conversion factor that, when multiplied by the futures settlement price, will generate a price at which the deliverable bond would trade if its coupon were the notional coupon of the futures contract specification (e.g., 6% coupon and 20 years to maturity). The principal invoice amount at maturity is given in the following equation:[5]

$$\text{Principal invoice amount} = (\text{Futures settlement price}/100) \times CF \times \text{Contract size}. \quad (2)$$

4 "Bobl" comes from the German term "Bundesobligation," which corresponds to a federal government bond. "Schatz" is the English word for "Bundesschatzanweisungen," or "Schätze," which is two-year debt issued by the German federal government, whereas "Bunds" represent long-term obligations.

5 If there is accrued interest due on the CTD bond, the futures contract seller will receive the following at delivery: Total invoice amount = Principal invoice amount + Accrued interest.

The cheapest-to-deliver bond is determined on the basis of duration, relative bond prices, and yield levels. In particular, a bond with a low (high) coupon rate, a long (short) maturity, and thus a long (short) duration will most likely be the CTD bond if the market yield is above (below) the notional yield of the fixed-income futures contract. The notional yield is usually in line with the prevailing interest rate.

The pricing discrepancy between the price of the cash security and that of the fixed-income futures is the basis. It is determined by the spot cash price less the futures price multiplied by the conversion factor. The possibility of physical delivery of the underlying asset guarantees convergence of futures and spot prices on the delivery date. In fact, the no-arbitrage condition requires the basis to be zero on the delivery date; otherwise, substantial arbitrage profits can be made. However, basis traders look for arbitrage opportunities by capitalizing on relatively small pricing differences. If the basis is negative, a trader would make a profit by "buying the basis"—that is, purchasing the bond and shorting the futures. In contrast, the trader would make a profit by "selling the basis" when the basis is positive; in this case, she would sell the bond and buy the futures. Example 4 demonstrates how to determine the CTD bond for delivery under a Treasury bond futures contract.

EXAMPLE 4

Delivery on a Fixed-Income Futures Contract

A trader has sold 10-year US Treasury bond futures contracts expiring in June and now has the obligation to deliver and the right to choose which security to deliver (the CTD bond). The futures contract reference security is a US Treasury bond with 20 years to maturity and a coupon of 6%. The T-bond futures contract size is $100,000. The futures contract settlement price is $143.47. The trader now needs to determine which of the two bonds in the following table is cheapest to deliver.

	Bond A	Bond B
Cash Bond	T 4½ 02/15/36	T 5 05/15/37
Cash Dirty Price	$120.75	$128.50
Bond Purchase Value	$120,750	$128,500
Futures Settlement Price	143.47	143.47
Conversion Factor	0.8388	0.8883
Contract Size	$100,000	$100,000
Principal Invoice Amount	$120,342.64	$127,444.40
Delivery Gain/Loss	–$407.36 = $120,342.64 – $120,750	–$1,055.60 = $127,444.40 – $128,500

Analysis:

The trader will try to maximize the difference between the amount received upon delivery, given by the futures contract settlement price (divided by 100) times the conversion factor times $100,000, and the cost of acquiring the bond for delivery, given by its market price plus any accrued interest (i.e., the dirty price). Note that this example assumes no accrued interest.

The conversion factors for both bonds are less than 1 since both bonds have a coupon lower than 6%, the coupon for the futures contract standard. Bond A can be purchased for $120,750 and Bond B for $128,500, both per $100,000 face value. These purchase prices are compared with the amounts received upon delivery. Principal invoice amounts are calculated using Equation 2, as follows:

$$\text{Principal invoice amount} = (\text{Futures settlement price}/100) \times CF \times \$100{,}000.$$

Bond A: 143.47/100 × 0.8388 × \$100,000 = \$120,342.64.

Bond B: 143.47/100 × 0.8883 × \$100,000 = \$127,444.40.

The cheapest to deliver is Bond A, the 4½% T-bond with a maturity date of 02/15/36, since the loss on delivering Bond A (\$407.36) is less than the loss on delivering Bond B (\$1,055.60).

Continuing with the previous analysis where we hedged a portfolio of fixed-rate securities, we now determine the hedge ratio (HR) expressed as the number of fixed-income futures contracts to be sold or purchased. The relation $\Delta P = (HR)(\Delta F)$ is still valid; note that we saw it previously in the context of swaps as $\Delta P = (N_S)(\Delta S)$, where ΔP is the change in the value of the bond portfolio and ΔF is the change in the value of the fixed-income futures. The "ideal" hedge balances any change in value in the cash securities with an equal and opposite-sign change in the futures' value.

With futures, however, we have to consider the cheapest-to-deliver bond price and the conversion factor. Because the basis of the CTD bond is generally closest to zero, any change in the futures price level (ΔF) will be a reflection of the change in the value of the CTD bond adjusted by its conversion factor. By considering the relative price movement of the bond futures contract to the cheapest-to-deliver bond, we have $\Delta F = \Delta CTD/CF$. By substituting into the equation $\Delta P = (HR)(\Delta F)$, the hedge ratio becomes

$$HR = \frac{\Delta P}{\Delta CTD}(CF) \tag{3}$$

In the case where the bond to hedge is the CTD, then a hedge ratio based on the conversion factor is likely to be quite effective (given that the price of a fixed-income futures contract tends to track closely with that of the cheapest-to-deliver bond).

However, for other securities with different coupons and maturities, the number of bond futures that are used to hedge against price changes of a fixed-rate bond is calculated on the basis of a duration-based hedge ratio. Moreover, the relationship between the bond's price and its yield can also be stated in terms of basis point value and the portfolio's target modified duration, $MDUR_T$, such that the portfolio's target basis point value (BPV_T) is

$$BPV_T = MDUR_T \times 0.01\% \times MV_P \tag{4}$$

In the special case where the objective is to completely hedge the portfolio, $BPV_T = 0$. The effect of the basis point value hedge ratio ($BPVHR$) is then conceptualized as $BPV_P + BPVHR \times BPV_F = 0$. Thus, $BPVHR = -BPV_P/BPV_F$, which uses the basis point value of the portfolio to be hedged (BPV_P) and that of the futures contract (BPV_F), where

$$BPV_P = MDUR_P \times 0.01\% \times MV_P \tag{5}$$

and

$$BPV_F = BPV_{CTD}/CF \tag{6}$$

In Equation 6, the numerator is BPV_{CTD}, the basis point value of the cheapest-to-deliver bond under the futures contract, and the denominator is CF, its conversion factor. The basis point value of the cheapest-to-deliver bond is determined, in a manner analogous to Equation 4 and Equation 5, as

$$BPV_{CTD} = MDUR_{CTD} \times 0.01\% \times MV_{CTD} \tag{7}$$

where MV_{CTD} = (CTD price/100) × Futures contract size.

Finally, for small changes in yield, by substituting into the equation $BPVHR = -BPV_P/BPV_F$, where BPV_F becomes BPV_{CTD}/CF, in the special case of complete hedging, $BPVHR$ in terms of number of futures contracts is

$$BPVHR = \frac{-BPV_P}{BPV_{CTD}} \times \text{Conversion factor} \tag{8}$$

EXAMPLE 5

Hedging Bond Holdings with Fixed-Income Futures

A portfolio manager is holding €50 million (principal) in German bunds (DBRs) and wants to fully hedge the value of the bond investment against a rise in interest rates. The portfolio has a modified duration of 9.50 and a market value of €49,531,000. Moreover, the manager wishes to fully hedge the bond portfolio (so, $BPV_T = 0$) with a short position in Euro-Bund futures with a price of 158.33. The cheapest-to-deliver bond is the DBR 0.25% 02/15/27 that has a price of 98.14, modified duration of 8.623, and conversion factor of 0.619489. The size of the futures contract is €100,000.

Determine the following:

1. The BPV_P of the portfolio to be hedged

Solution:

The basis point value of the portfolio (BPV_P), stated in terms of the change in value for a 1 bp (0.01%) change in yield, is calculated using Equation 5, as follows:

$$BPV_P = MDUR_P \times 0.01\% \times MV_P$$

Portfolio Principal	€50,000,000
Portfolio Market Value	€49,531,000
Modified Duration	9.50

$$BPV_P = 9.50 \times 0.0001 \times €49{,}531{,}000 = €47{,}054.45.$$

Thus, the portfolio to be hedged has a BPV_P of €47,054.45 per €50 million notional.

2. The BPV_{CTD} of the futures contract hedging instrument

Solution:

The basis point value of the CTD bond underlying the futures contract (BPV_{CTD}) is calculated using Equation 7, as follows:

$$BPV_{CTD} = MDUR_{CTD} \times 0.01\% \times MV_{CTD}$$

Futures Hedge	
Euro-Bund Futures Price	158.33
Contract Size	€100,000

Cheapest-To-Deliver Bond	
DBR 0¼ 02/15/27 Gov't.	
Modified Duration	8.623
Bond Price	98.14
Conversion Factor	0.619489

$$BPV_{CTD} = 8.623 \times 0.0001 \times [(98.14/100) \times €100{,}000] = €84.63.$$

So, the BPV of the CTD bond (BPV_{CTD}) is €84.63.

3. The number of Euro-Bund futures contracts to sell to fully hedge the portfolio

Solution:

Using Equation 8 and the Solutions to 1 and 2, we have:

$$BPVHR = \frac{-BPV_P}{BPV_{CTD}} \times CF = \frac{-€47,054.45}{€84.63} \times 0.619489 = -344.437 \approx -344$$

Therefore, the number of Euro-Bund futures to *sell* to fully hedge the portfolio is 344 contracts.

In the real world, however, the hedging results are imperfect because (1) the hedge is done with the cheapest-to-deliver bond, and since the CTD bond can change over the holding period, the duration of the futures contract can also change; (2) the relationship between interest rates and bond prices is not linear, owing to convexity; and (3) the term structure of interest rates often changes via non-parallel moves.

Reconsidering Example 2 from before, in which the manager whose portfolio has a modified duration of 5.5 years wants to lower the duration to 4.5 years, the general principle is the same. What needs to be determined is the number of futures contracts that are required to reduce the portfolio's modified duration to the target level. In this more general case, where $MDUR_T$ (and BPV_T) is non-zero, stated in terms of basis point value and $BPVHR$, we have $BPV_P + BPVHR \times BPV_F = BPV_T$.

Solving for $BPVHR$ and substituting for BPV_F, we have the more general version of Equation 8:

$$\begin{aligned} BPVHR &= \left(\frac{BPV_T - BPV_P}{BPV_F}\right) \\ &= \left(\frac{BPV_T - BPV_P}{BPV_{CTD}/CF}\right) \\ &= \left(\frac{BPV_T - BPV_P}{BPV_{CTD}}\right) \times CF \end{aligned} \tag{9}$$

EXAMPLE 6

Decreasing Portfolio Duration with Futures

Consider the portfolio manager from Example 5 who now decides to decrease the portfolio's modified duration from 9.50 to 8.50. The yield curve is flat. Additionally, we have already demonstrated that given the portfolio's market value of €49,531,000, the BPV_P is €47,054.50. Finally, assume the CTD bond underlying the Euro-Bund futures is the same as before, DBR 0.25% 02/15/27, with a BPV_{CTD} of €84.63 and a conversion factor of 0.619489.

Determine the following:

1. The BPV_T of the portfolio to be hedged

Solution:

Using Equation 4 with a $MDUR_T$ of 8.50, the portfolio's target basis point value (BPV_T) will be

$$BPV_T = 8.50 \times 0.0001 \times €49,531,000 = €42,101.35.$$

2. The number of Euro-Bund futures contracts to sell to reduce the portfolio's modified duration to 8.50

Solution:

To achieve the target modified duration of 8.50, the portfolio manager must implement a short position in Euro-Bund futures. Using the same cheapest-to-deliver bond with a BPV_{CTD} of €84.63 and a conversion factor of 0.619489, the number of Euro-Bund futures to sell to decrease the portfolio's duration is calculated using Equation 9:

$$BPVHR = \left(\frac{€42,101.35 - €47,054.50}{€84.63}\right) \times 0.619489$$

$$= -36.26 \approx -36 \text{ futures contracts}$$

Therefore, the number of Euro-Bund futures to *sell* to achieve the target portfolio duration of 8.50 is 36 contracts.

MANAGING CURRENCY EXPOSURE 3

☐ demonstrate how currency swaps, forwards, and futures can be used to modify a portfolio's risk and return

Currency swaps, forwards, and futures can be used to effectively alter currency risk exposures. Currency risk is the risk that the value of a current or future asset (liability) in a foreign currency will decrease (increase) when converted into the domestic currency.

Currency Swaps

A currency swap is similar to an interest rate swap, but it is different in two ways: (1) The interest rates are associated with different currencies, and (2) the notional principal amounts may or may not be exchanged at the beginning and end of the swap's life.[6]

Currency swaps help the parties in the swap to hedge against the risk of exchange rate fluctuations and to achieve better rate outcomes. In particular, a **cross-currency basis swap** exchanges notional principals because the goal of the transaction is to issue at a more favorable funding rate and swap the amount back to the currency of choice. Firms that need foreign-denominated cash can obtain the funding in their local currency and then swap the local currency for the required foreign currency using a cross-currency basis swap. The swap periodically sets interest rate payments, mostly floating for floating, separately in two different currencies. The net effect is to use a loan in a local currency to take out a loan in a foreign currency while avoiding any foreign exchange risk. In fact, the exchange rate is fixed, as illustrated in Example 7.

6 Although an exchange of notional principals often occurs, the parties may agree not to do this. Some types of hedge transactions are designed to hedge only foreign interest cash flows and not principal payments, so a principal exchange on a currency swap would not be necessary.

EXAMPLE 7

Cross-Currency Basis Swap

Consider a Canadian private equity (PE) firm that is executing a leveraged buy-out (LBO) of a small, struggling US-based electronics manufacturer. The goal is to turn around the company by implementing new robotics technology for making servers and infrastructure devices for "bitcoin mining." Exit from the LBO via initial public offering is expected in three years. To execute the LBO and provide working capital for US operations, the PE firm needs USD40 million. The rate on a US dollar loan is the semiannual US dollar reference floating rate plus 100 bps. The PE firm discovers that it can borrow more cheaply in the local Canadian market and decides to fund the LBO in Canadian dollars (CAD) by borrowing CAD50 million for three years at the semiannual Canadian dollar reference floating rate plus 65 bps. Then it contacts a New York–based dealer and requests a quote for a three-year cross-currency basis swap with semiannual interest payments to exchange the CAD50 million into US dollars. The three-year CAD–USD cross-currency basis swap is quoted at −15 bps at a rate of USD/CAD 0.8000 (expressed as US dollars per 1 Canadian dollar). The swap agreement provides that both parties pay the semiannual reference floating rate, but the Canadian dollar rate also includes a "basis." Here the basis is the difference between interest rates in the cross-currency basis swap and those used to determine the forward exchange rates. If covered interest rate parity holds, a forward exchange rate is determined by the spot exchange rate and the interest rate differential between foreign and domestic currencies over the term of the forward rate. However, usually covered interest rate parity does not hold and thus gives rise to the basis.

The basis is quoted on the non-USD leg of the swap. "Paying" the basis would mean borrowing the other currency versus lending US dollars, whereas "receiving" the basis implies lending the other currency versus borrowing US dollars. The three-year CAD–USD cross-currency swap in this case is quoted at −15 bps. This means that the Canadian PE firm, the "lender" of the Canadian dollars in the swap, will receive the Canadian dollar reference rate, assumed to be 1.95%, minus 15 bps every six months in exchange for paying the US dollar reference rate for the US dollars it has "borrowed." Given that the PE firm pays the Canadian dollar floating rate plus 65 bps on its bank loan, the effective spread paid becomes 80 bps (= 65bps + 15 bps). This compares with a spread of 100 bps if instead it borrowed in US dollars.

Analysis:

We now examine the cash flows in the cross-currency basis swap, where N is the notional principal of the Canadian dollar leg of the swap and S_0, agreed at the start, is the spot exchange rate for all payments (at inception, on interest payment dates, and at maturity). For the Canadian PE firm, this means that

N = CAD50 million and S_0= USD/CAD 0.8000.

Flows at the inception of the swap.

At inception, the Canadian PE firm delivers Canadian dollars (N) in exchange for US dollars (at a rate of $N \times S_0$).

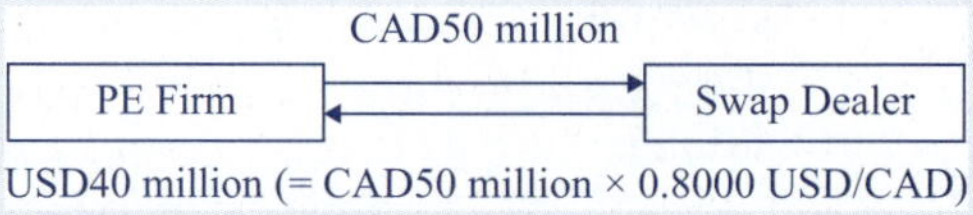

At each payment date, the PE firm makes a floating-rate payment in US dollars and receives a floating-rate payment in Canadian dollars that is passed on to the local Canadian lender. At maturity, the PE firm returns the USD40 million to the dealer and in return receives the CAD50 million, which it uses to pay off its lender.

Periodic payments.

At each swap payment date, the Canadian PE firm receives interest on Canadian dollars (N) in exchange for paying interest on US dollars ($N \times S_0$). Importantly, the "basis" component (of –15 bps) will be included along with the semiannual Canadian dollar reference floating rate.

Suppose that on the first settlement date the semiannual reference floating rate in Canadian dollars is 1.95% and the basis is –15 bps. Therefore, the Canadian dollar rate on the swap is 1.80% (= 1.95% – 15 bps), and we assume the US dollar rate is 2.50% (the semiannual reference floating rate). For the PE firm, the first of a sequence of periodic cash flows resulting from the swap amounts to:

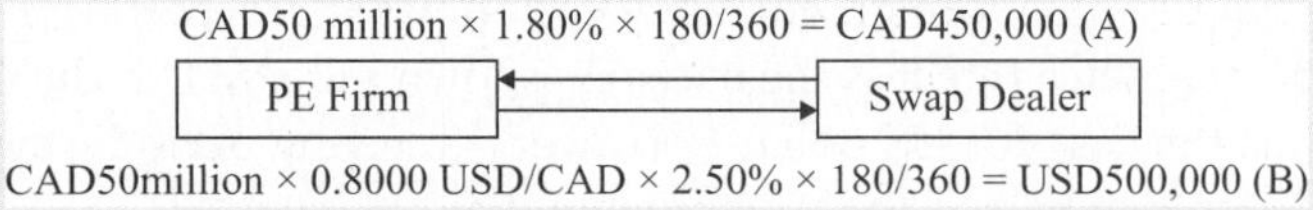

The interest rate payment on the PE firm's loan is CAD50 million × (1.95% + 0.65%) × (180/360) = CAD650,000. Considering the CAD450,000 received on the swap (A), the PE firm's net payment is CAD200,000.

At USD/CAD 0.8000, this net payment of CAD200,000 corresponds to a payment of USD160,000, which when added to the USD500,000 paid on the swap (B) totals USD660,000. Importantly, note that had the Canadian PE firm taken out the US loan instead, it would have paid periodically USD700,000 (= USD40 million × [2.50% + 1.0%] × [180/360]).

Flows at maturity.

At the maturity of the swap (and after a successful exit from the LBO via a US IPO), the Canadian PE firm swaps back US dollars in exchange for Canadian dollars (USD × $1/S_0$).

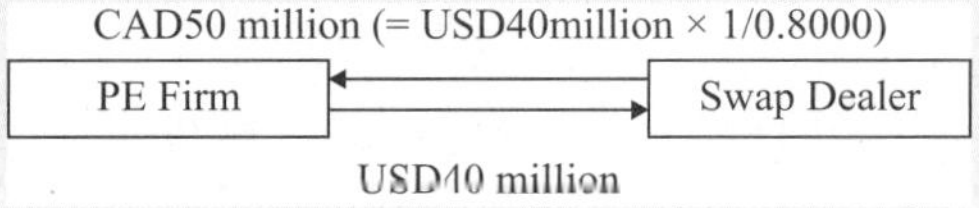

In this specific example, it is worth noting that the exchange rate was assumed not to change.

A common use of currency swaps by investors is in transactions meant to earn extra yield by investing in a foreign bond market and swapping the proceeds into the domestic currency. Given that the investment is hedged against the risk of exchange rate fluctuations, this corresponds to a synthetic domestic yield, but the repackaging allows the investor to earn a higher yield compared with the yield from direct purchase of the domestic asset, because of the level of the basis on the cross-currency swap. For example, during periods when demand for US dollars is strong relative to demand for Japanese yen (JPY), the US–Japan interest rate differential implied by the currency markets may be significantly wider than the actual interest rate differential. During such a period, a US investor might choose among the following two options: (1) Invest in short-term US Treasury bonds, or (2) use a cross-currency swap to lend an equivalent amount of US dollars and buy yen; buy short-term Japanese government debt; each period pay yen and receive US dollars on the swap; and at maturity swap an equivalent amount of yen back into US dollars. When the basis is largely negative, due to relatively weak (strong) demand for yen (US dollars) from swap market participants, the borrowing costs in yen (US dollars) are low (high), making the return from lending US dollars via a cross-currency swap particularly attractive. By choosing Option 2, the investor can earn more than he could from the investment in short-term US Treasury debt.

The rates on the cross-currency basis swaps will depend on the demand for US dollar funding, because when the US dollar reference floating rate is elevated, the counterparty receiving US dollars at initiation of the swap will be willing to receive a lower interest rate on the non-dollar currency periodic payments. Exhibit 1 shows the levels of the basis for one-year cross-currency swaps from May 2016 to April 2018 in the Australian dollar (AUD), the Canadian dollar (CAD), the euro (EUR), and the British pound (GBP) versus USD Libor (quoted as six-month USD Libor versus six-month AUD bank bills, six-month CAD Libor, six-month Euribor, and six-month GBP Libor, respectively). Cross-currency basis spreads vary over time and are driven by credit and liquidity factors, and supply and demand for cross-currency financing. As noted previously, relatively strong demand for US dollar financing against the foreign currency would require the US dollar "borrower" in the swap to accept a lower rate on the periodic foreign currency cash flows it receives—for example, the foreign periodic reference rate less the basis. As shown in Exhibit 1, during the period covered this was the case for US dollar borrowers receiving periodic swap payments in all currencies shown except the Australian dollar.

Exhibit 1: Historical Levels for One-Year Cross-Currency Swap Spreads (Basis) vs. Major Currencies (Six-Month Settlement)

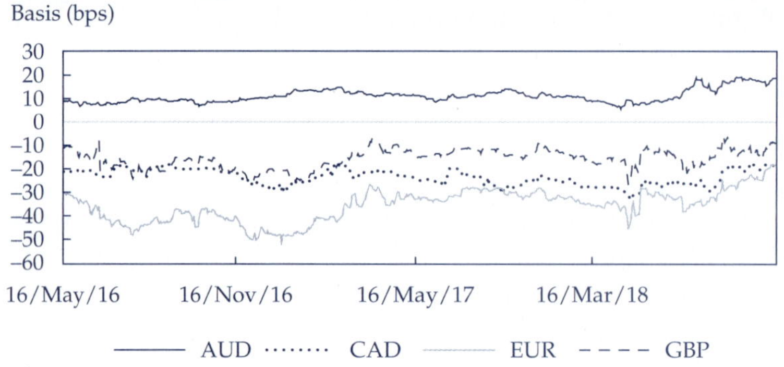

Currency Forwards and Futures

Currency forwards and futures are actively used to manage currency risk. These two financial instruments are used to hedge against undesired moves in the exchange rate by buying or selling a specified amount of foreign currency, at a defined time in the future and at an agreed-on price at contract initiation. Futures contracts are standardized and best meet dealers' and investors' needs to manage their portfolios' currency risk. Corporations often use customized forward contracts to manage the risk of cash flows in foreign currencies because they can be customized according to their needs.

For example, consider the general partner of a US-based venture capital (VC) firm that is calling down capital commitments for investment in "fintech" startups in Silicon Valley. It will receive in 30 days a payment of CAD50 million from a limited partner residing in Vancouver, British Columbia, and will immediately transfer the funds to its US dollar account. If the Canadian dollar were to depreciate versus the US dollar before the payment date, the US VC firm will receive fewer US dollars in exchange for the CAD50 million. To eliminate the foreign exchange risk associated with receiving this capital commitment, the firm can fix the price of the US dollars now via a forward contract in which it promises to sell CAD50 million for an agreed-on number of US dollars, based on the forward exchange rate, in 30 days.

EXAMPLE 8

Hedging Currency Risk with Futures

1. Consider the same US-based VC firm that is calling down capital commitments and will receive CAD50 million in 30 days. The general partner now decides to sell futures contracts to lock in the current USD/CAD rate. The hedge ratio is assumed to be equal to 1. The firm hedges its risk by selling Canadian dollar futures contracts with the closest expiry to the future Canadian dollar inflow.

   Given a price for the Canadian dollar futures contract of USD/CAD 0.7838 (number of US dollars for 1 Canadian dollar) and a contract size of CAD100,000, determine how many Canadian dollar futures contracts the VC firm must sell to hedge its risk.

Solution:

To hedge the risk of the Canadian dollar depreciating against the US dollar, the VC firm must sell 500 futures contracts:

$$\frac{\text{CAD50,000,000}}{\text{CAD100,000}} = 500 \text{ contracts}$$

When the futures contracts expire, the VC firm will receive (pay) any depreciation (appreciation) in the Canadian dollar versus the US dollar compared with the futures contract price of USD0.7838/CAD.[7] If the changes in futures and spot prices are equal during the life of the futures contract, the hedge will be fully effective. A basis risk arises when the differential given by Futures price_t – Spot price_t is either positive or negative. In the absence of arbitrage, between the time when a hedging position is initiated and the time when it is liquidated, this spread may either widen or narrow to zero.

MANAGING EQUITY RISK

4

☐ demonstrate how equity swaps, forwards, and futures can be used to modify a portfolio's risk and return

Investors can achieve or modify their equity risk exposures using equity swaps and equity forwards and futures. The asset underlying these financial instruments could be an equity index, a single stock, or a basket of stocks.

7 Remember that, assuming covered interest rate parity holds, the forward rate $\left(F_{f/d}\right)$—expressed as units of foreign currency (*f*) for 1 unit of domestic currency (*d*)—is calculated from the exchange spot rate $\left(S_{f/d}\right)$ and the differential between the foreign (i_f) and domestic (i_d) interest rates. The forward rate is calculated on the basis of the following formula: $F_{f/d} = S_{f/d} \times \left[\left(1 + i_f \times ACT/360\right) / \left(1 + i_d \times ACT/360\right)\right]$.

Equity Swaps

An equity swap is a derivative contract in which two parties agree to exchange a series of cash flows whereby one party pays a variable series that will be determined by a single stock, a basket of stocks, or an equity index and the other party pays either (1) a variable series determined by a different equity or rate or (2) a fixed series. An equity swap is used to convert the returns from an equity investment into another series of returns, which either can be derived from another equity series or can be a fixed rate. There are three main types of equity swaps:

- receive-equity return, pay-fixed;
- receive-equity return, pay-floating; and
- receive-equity return, pay-another equity return.

Because they are an OTC derivative instrument, each counterparty in the equity swap bears credit risk exposure to the other. For this reason, equity swaps are usually collateralized in order to reduce the credit risk exposure. At the same time, as equity swaps are created in the OTC market, they can be customized as desired by the counterparties.

A total return swap is a slightly modified equity swap; it also includes in the performance any dividends paid by the underlying stocks or index during the period until the swap maturity. The swap has a fixed tenor and may provide for one single payment at the end of the swap's life, although more typically a series of periodic payments would be arranged instead. In another variation, at the time of each periodic payment, the notional amount could be reset or remain unchanged.

Equity swaps provide synthetic exposure to physical stocks. They are preferred by some investors over ownership of shares when access to a specific market is limited, when taxes are levied for owning physical stocks (e.g., stamp duty) but are not levied on swaps, the custodian fees are high, or the cost of monitoring the stock position is elevated (e.g., because of corporate actions). However, it is important to note that equity swaps require putting up collateral, are relatively illiquid contracts, and do not confer voting rights.

Example 9 shows how an equity swap might be used by an institutional investor with a portfolio indexed to the performance of the S&P 500 Index. He believes the stock market will decline over the next six months and would like to temporarily hedge part of the market exposure of his portfolio. He can do this by entering into a six-month equity swap with one payment at termination, exchanging the total return on the S&P 500 for a floating rate. We will consider two scenarios: In the first scenario, in six months the underlying portfolio is up 5%; in the second, it is down 5%.

EXAMPLE 9

Six-Month Equity Swap

An institutional investor holds a $100 million portfolio of US stocks indexed to the S&P 500. He expects the index will fall in the next six months and wants to reduce his market exposure by 30%. He enters into an equity swap with notional principal of $30 million whereby he agrees to pay the return on the index and to receive the floating reference interest rate, assumed to be 2.25%, minus 25 bps—so, 2.00% per annum.

Scenario 1:

In the first scenario, the stock market has increased by 5%. Thus, at swap settlement the institutional investor has an obligation to pay 5% × $30 million, or $1.5 million, and would receive 2% × 180/360 × $30 million, or $300,000. The two parties would net the payments and provide for a single payment of $1.2 million, which the institutional investor would pay. Because the portfolio has gained $5 million in this scenario, the profit and loss (P&L) on the combined position (including the original portfolio and the swap) is positive and equal to $3.8 million.

Scenario 1 Equity Portfolio Rises 5%

US equity portfolio: $100 million × 5% =	+$5,000,000
P&L on the stock portfolio:	+$5,000,000
Swap settlement:	
Pay: $30 million × 5% =	−$1,500,000
Receive: $30 million × 2% × 180/360 =	+$300,000
Net payment on the swap:	−$1,200,000
P&L on the net position (70% of original exposure and 30% hedged): $5,000,000 − $1,200,000 =	+$3,800,000

Scenario 2:

In the second scenario, the stock market has decreased by 5%. So, it is slightly more complicated because the equity return that the institutional investor must pay is *negative*, which means he will receive money. He would receive $1.5 million because the S&P 500 had a negative performance in addition to receiving the $300,000. Because the portfolio has lost $5 million in this case, the P&L on the combined position is −$3.2 million. When the swap ends, the institutional investor returns to the same position in which he started, with the equity portfolio fully invested, and it is thereafter subject to full market risk once again.

Scenario 2 Equity Portfolio Declines 5%

US equity portfolio: $100 million × −5% =	−$5,000,000
P&L on the stock portfolio:	−$5,000,000
Swap settlement: *Receive (Pay negative return): $30 million × 5% =*	+$1,500,000
Receive: $30 million × 2% × 180/360 =	+$300,000
Net payment on the swap:	+$1,800,000
P&L on the net position (70% of original exposure and 30% hedged): −$5,000,000 + $1,800,000 =	−$3,200,000

To test the reasonableness of the result, a portfolio comprising 70% equities and 30% money market instruments assumed to earn 2% (1% over the six months) would achieve a return of 3.8% (= 0.7 × 5% + 0.3 × [2%/2]) or $3.8 million on $100 million in the bullish scenario (Scenario 1). In the bearish scenario (Scenario 2), the return would be −3.2% (= 0.7 × −5% + 0.3 × [2%/2]) or −$3.2 million on the initial $100 million portfolio. The total return swap effectively removes the risk associated with 30% of the equity portfolio allocation and converts it into money market equivalent returns.

Consider now a private high-net-worth investor who holds a large, concentrated position in a particular company's stock that pays dividends on a regular basis. She expects that in the next six months the total return from the stock, including the dividends received, will be negative, so she wants to temporarily neutralize her long exposure. At the same time, she does not wish to lose ownership and her voting rights by selling the stock on an exchange.

This investor can enter into a total return swap requiring her to transfer the total performance of the stock (i.e., total return) to the counterparty of the swap, at prespecified dates for an agreed-on fee. Under the terms of the swap, she will pay to the counterparty the share price appreciation plus the dividends received over the life of the contract. If the stock price decreases, she will receive the share price depreciation but net of the dividends. At the same prespecified dates, the investor will receive in exchange from the counterparty an agreed-on floating-rate interest payment based on the swap notional.

Equity swaps that have a single stock as underlying can be cash settled or physically settled. If the swap is cash settled, on the termination date of the contract the equity swap receiver will receive (pay) the equity appreciation (depreciation) in cash. If the swap is physically settled, on the termination date the equity swap receiver will receive the quantity of single stock specified in the contract and pay the notional amount. Let us assume for example that a portfolio manager is the receiver in a six-month equity swap with notional principal of €4.5 million and no interim cash flows that requires physical settlement, at maturity, of 300,000 shares of the Italian insurer Generali. At maturity of the swap, the portfolio manager will receive 300,000 shares of Generali and will pay €4.5 million, which corresponds to a purchase price per share of €15 (= €4.5 million/300,000). He will also pay the interest on the swap based on the agreed-on rate. Now let us also assume that at the swap's maturity the price of Generali is €16. This price implies a gain of €300,000 (= [€16 – €15] × 300,000) for the portfolio manager, assuming he sells the shares received in the swap at €16. If the same swap had cash settlement, instead of physical settlement, at maturity the portfolio manager would have received €300,000—given by €16 (the swap settlement price) less €15 (the agreed price on the swap) and multiplied by 300,000—against the payment of the interest on the swap.

Equity Forwards and Futures

Equity index futures are an indispensable tool for many investment managers: They are a low-cost instrument to implement tactical allocation decisions, achieve portfolio diversification, and attain international exposure. They are standardized contracts listed on an exchange, and when the underlying is a stock index, only cash settlement is available at contract expiration.

Single stock futures are also available to investors to acquire the desired exposure to a specific stock. This exposure is also achievable with equity forwards, which are OTC contracts that are used when the counterparties need a customized agreement. The underlying of a single stock futures contract is one specified stock, and the investor can receive or pay its performance. At expiration, the contract could require cash settlement or physical settlement using the stock.

In Example 9, rather than using an equity swap, the institutional investor could temporarily remove part of the market risk by selling S&P 500 Index futures. In the practical implementation of a stock index futures trade, we need to remember that the actual futures contract price is the quoted futures price times a designated multiplier. In determining the hedge ratio, the stock index futures price should be quoted on the same order of magnitude as the stock index.

For example, assume that a one-month futures contract on the S&P 500 is quoted at 2,700. Given the multiplier of \$250, the actual futures price is equal to \$675,000 (= 2,700 × \$250). We also assume that the portfolio to be hedged carries average market risk, meaning a beta of 1.0.[8] To hedge 30% of the \$100 million portfolio, the portfolio manager would want to sell 44 S&P 500 futures contracts, determined as follows:

$$\frac{\$30\text{ million}}{2,700(\$250)} = 44.444 \approx 44\text{ contracts}$$

Suppose the institutional investor sold the 44 futures at 2,700 and at expiration the S&P 500 *rises* by 0.5%. The cash settlement of the contract is at 2,713.5. Because the futures position is short and the index rose, there is a "loss" of 13.5 index points—each point being worth \$250—on 44 contracts, for a total cash outflow, paid by the institutional investor, of \$148,500:

−13.5 points per contract × \$250 per point × 44 contracts = −\$148,500 (a loss).

If the S&P 500 Index rose by 0.5%, the 30% of the portfolio that has been hedged would also be expected to rise by the same amount, but there is a small difference due to rounding the number of futures contracts used for the hedge:

\$30,000,000 × 0.5% = \$150,000.

If instead the S&P 500 *fell* by 0.5%, the numbers would be the same, but the signs would change. The institutional investor would receive the "gain" because he had a short stock index futures position when the index fell, which would offset the loss on the hedged portion of his stock portfolio. In sum, the equity market risk is hedged away.

In the previous example, the beta of the portfolio was the same as the beta of the equity index futures. This situation usually does not occur, and in most hedging strategies, it is necessary to determine the exact "hedge ratio" in terms of the number of futures contracts. Consider that the investment manager wishes to change the beta of the equity portfolio, β_S, to a target beta of β_T. Because the value of the futures contract begins each day at zero, the dollar beta of the combination of stocks and futures, assuming the target beta is achieved, is $\beta_T S$, where S is the market value of the stock portfolio.[9] The number of futures contracts we shall use is N_f, which can be determined by setting the target dollar beta equal to the dollar beta of the stock portfolio ($\beta_S S$) and the dollar beta of N_f futures ($N_f \beta_f F$), where β_f is the beta of the futures and F is the value per futures contract:

$$\beta_T S = \beta_S S + N_f \beta_f F$$

We then solve for N_f and obtain

$$N_f = \left(\frac{\beta_T - \beta_S}{\beta_f}\right)\left(\frac{S}{F}\right) \tag{10}$$

Note that if the investor wants to increase the portfolio's beta, β_T will exceed β_S and the sign of N_f will be positive, which means that she must buy futures. If she wants to decrease the beta, β_T will be less than β_S, the sign of N_f will be negative, and she must sell futures. This relationship should make sense: Selling futures will offset some of the risk of holding the stock, whereas buying futures will add risk.

In the special case in which the goal is to eliminate market risk, β_T would be set to zero and the formula would reduce to

8 If the portfolio carried above-market risk—say, with a beta of 1.10—the number of contracts needed to hedge would increase by this factor. Similarly, a lower-risk portfolio would require proportionately fewer contracts.

9 Recall that the market value of the portfolio will still be the same as the market value of the stock, because the value of the futures is zero. The futures value becomes zero whenever it is marked to market, which takes place at the end of each day. In other words, the target beta does not appear to be applied to the value of the futures in the preceding analysis because the value of the futures is zero.

$$N_f = -\left(\frac{\beta_S}{\beta_f}\right)\left(\frac{S}{F}\right)$$

In this case, the sign of N_f will always be negative, which makes sense, because in order to hedge away all the market risk, futures must be sold.

EXAMPLE 10

Increasing the Beta of a Portfolio with Futures

Paulo Bianchi is the manager of a fund that invests in UK defensive stocks, such as consumer staples producers and utilities. His firm's market outlook for the next quarter has become more positive, so Bianchi decides to increase the beta on the £40 million portfolio he manages from its current level of β_S = 0.85 to β_T = 1.10 for the next three months. He will execute this increase in equity market risk exposure using futures on the FTSE 100 Index. The futures contract price is currently £7,300, the contract's multiplier is £10 per index point (so each futures contract is worth £73,000), and its beta, β_f, is 1.00.

At the end of the three-month period, the UK stock market has increased by 2%. The stock portfolio has increased in value to £40,680,000, calculated as £40,000,000 × [1 + (0.02 × 0.85)]. The FTSE 100 futures contract has risen to £74,460.

1. Determine the appropriate number of FTSE 100 Index futures Bianchi should buy to increase the portfolio's beta to 1.10.

Solution:

Using Equation 10 and the preceding data, the appropriate number of futures contracts to buy to increase the portfolio's beta to 1.10 would be 137.

$$N_f = \left(\frac{\beta_T - \beta_S}{\beta_f}\right)\left(\frac{S}{F}\right) = \left(\frac{1.10 - 0.85}{1.00}\right)\left(\frac{£40,000,000}{£73,000}\right)$$

$$= 136.99 \text{ (rounded to 137)}$$

2. Demonstrate how the effective beta of the portfolio of stocks and the FTSE 100 Index futures matched Bianchi's target beta of 1.10.

Solution:

The profit on the futures contracts is 137 × (£74,460 – £73,000) = £200,020. Adding the profit from the futures to the value of the stock portfolio gives a total market value of £40,680,000 + £200,020 = £40,880,020. The rate of return for the combined position is

$$\frac{£40,880,020}{£40,000,000} - 1 = 0.0220, \text{ or } 2.2\%$$

Because the market went up by 2% and the overall gain was 2.2%, the effective beta of the portfolio was

$$\frac{0.0220}{0.020} = 1.10$$

Thus, the effective beta matched the target beta of 1.10.

Cash Equitization

Cash securitization (also known as "cash equitization" or "cash overlay") is a strategy designed to boost returns by finding ways to "equitize" unintended cash holdings. By purchasing futures contracts, fund managers attempt to replicate the performance of the underlying market in which the cash would have been invested. Given the liquidity of the futures market, doing so would be relatively easy. An alternative solution could be to purchase calls and sell puts on the underlying asset with the same exercise price and expiry date.

In this case, we have a cash holding, implying $\beta_S = 0$, so the number of futures (with beta of β_f) that would need to be purchased in a cash equitization transaction is given by

$$N_f = \left(\frac{\beta_T}{\beta_f}\right)\left(\frac{S}{F}\right) \tag{11}$$

EXAMPLE 11

Cash Equitization

1. Akari Fujiwara manages a large equity fund denominated in Japanese yen that is indexed to the Nikkei 225 stock index. She determines that the current level of excess cash that has built up in the portfolio amounts to JPY140 million. She decides to purchase futures contracts to replicate the return on her fund's target index. Nikkei 225 index futures currently trade at a price of JPY23,000 per contract, the contract multiplier is JPY1,000 per index point (so each futures contract is worth JPY23 million), and the beta, β_f, is 1.00.

   Determine the appropriate number of futures Fujiwara must buy to equitize her portfolio's excess cash position.

Solution:

Using Equation 11, which assumes $\beta_S = 0$, the answer is found as follows:

$$N_f = \left(\frac{\beta_T}{\beta_f}\right)\left(\frac{S}{F}\right) = \left(\frac{1.00}{1.00}\right)\left(\frac{\text{JPY}140,000,000}{\text{JPY}23,000,000}\right) = 6.087 \text{ (rounded to 6)}$$

The appropriate number of futures to buy to equitize the portfolio's excess cash position, based on the data provided, would be six contracts.

VOLATILITY DERIVATIVES: FUTURES AND OPTIONS 5

☐ demonstrate the use of volatility derivatives and variance swaps

With the introduction of volatility futures and variance swaps, many investors now consider volatility an asset class in itself. In particular, long volatility exposure can be an effective hedge against a sell-off in a long equity portfolio, notably during periods of extreme market movements. Empirical studies have identified a negative correlation between volatility and stock index returns that becomes pronounced during stock market downturns. Importantly, variance swaps, which will be discussed in this section, have a valuable convexity feature—as realized volatility increases (decreases), the positive (negative) swap payoffs increase (decrease)—that makes them particularly attractive for hedging long equity portfolios. For example, some investors use strategies that systematically allocate to volatility futures or variance swaps to hedge the "tail" risk of their portfolios. Naturally, the counterparties are selling a kind of insurance; they expect such return tails will not materialize. The effectiveness of such hedges should be compared against more traditional "long volatility" hedging methods, such as implementing a rolling series of out-of-the-money put options or futures. The roll aspect affects portfolio returns, so the term structure should be carefully considered. For example, if futures prices are in backwardation (contango), then overall returns to an investor with a long position in the futures would be enhanced (diminished) owing to positive (negative) roll return. The results are necessarily reversed for the holder of the short futures position. In sum, all these derivatives strategies should be assessed on the basis of their ability to reduce portfolio risk and improve returns. In contrast, a common investment strategy implemented by opportunistic investors involves being systematically short volatility, thereby attempting to capture the risk premium embedded in option prices. This strategy is most profitable under stable market conditions, but it can lead to large losses if market volatility rises unexpectedly.

Volatility Futures and Options

The CBOE Volatility Index, known as the VIX or the "fear index," is a measure of investors' expectations of volatility in the S&P 500 over the next 30 days. It is calculated and published by the Chicago Board Options Exchange (CBOE) and is based on the prices of S&P 500 Index options. The CBOE began publishing real-time VIX data in 1993, and in 2004, VIX futures were introduced. Investors cannot invest directly in the VIX but instead must use VIX futures contracts that offer investors a pure play on the level of expected stock market volatility, regardless of the direction of the S&P 500. Volatility futures allow investors to implement their views depending on their expectations about the timing and magnitude of a change in implied volatility. For example, in order for a long VIX futures position to protect an equity portfolio during a downturn, the stock market's implied volatility, as derived from S&P 500 Index options, must increase by more than the consensus expectation of implied volatility prior to the sell-off.

A family of volatility indexes has also been introduced for European equity markets, and they are designed to reflect market expectations of near-term to long-term volatility. The most well known of these is the VSTOXX index, based on real-time option prices on the EURO STOXX 50 index. The family of volatility indexes also includes the VDAX-NEW Index, based on DAX stock index options.

Next, we discuss various shapes of the VIX futures term structure. The CBOE Futures Exchange (CFE) lists nine standard (monthly) VIX index futures contracts and six weekly expirations in VIX futures. Each weekly and monthly contract settles 30 calendar days prior to the subsequent standard S&P 500 Index option's expiration. The weekly futures have lower volumes and open interest than the monthly futures contracts have. Exhibit 2 presents the first six monthly VIX futures contracts at three different fixed points in time for all expires; these are not consecutive days but, rather, are at intervals of about two months apart.

Exhibit 2: VIX Futures Contracts

CBOE VIX Futures Expiry	Day 1	Day 60	Day 120
April	16.68	33.46	9.77
May	17.00	19.85	14.05
June	17.00	19.10	14.55
July	17.35	18.50	15.25
August	17.51	18.75	15.60
September	17.80	18.90	16.10

Exhibit 3 shows the shape of the VIX futures term structure corresponding to the data in Exhibit 2. The vertical axis shows the futures prices, and the horizontal scale indicates the month of expiration.

Exhibit 3: Shapes of the VIX Futures Term Structure

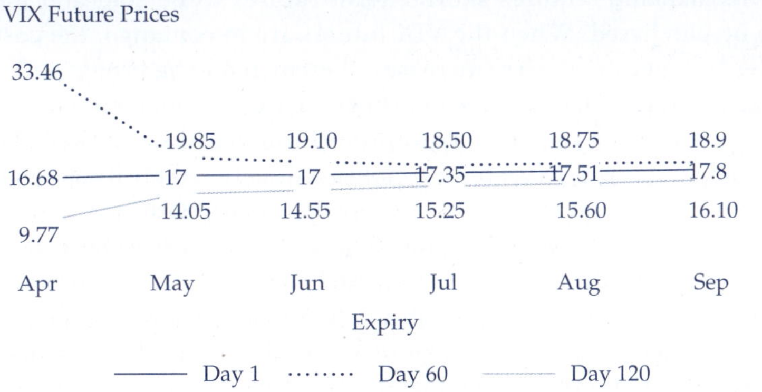

The shape of the VIX futures curve is always changing, reflecting the current volatility environment, investors' expectations regarding the future level of volatility, and the buying and selling activity in VIX futures contracts by market participants. Depending on the mix of these factors, the VIX futures term structure can change from being positively sloped to flat or inverted in just a few months' time.

Day 1 illustrates what happens when volatility is expected to remain stable over the near to long term: The term structure of VIX futures is flat. Day 60 shows the VIX futures in backwardation. This situation typically is a signal that investors expect more volatility in the short term and thus require higher prices for shorter-term contracts than for longer-term ones. In contrast, Day 120 is an example of the VIX futures being in contango. The curve is upward sloped, and it is steep for VIX buyers, with nearly 4.3 volatility points between the April and May expiries. Higher longer-term VIX futures prices are interpreted as an expectation that the VIX will rise because of increasing long-term volatility.

The VIX futures converge to the spot VIX as expiration approaches, so the two must be equal at expiration. When the VIX futures curve is in contango (backwardation) and assuming volatility expectations remain unchanged, the VIX futures price will get "pulled" closer to the VIX spot price, and they will decrease (increase) in price as they approach expiration. Traders calculate the daily roll as the difference between the front-month VIX futures price and the VIX spot price, divided by the number of business days until the VIX futures contract settles. Assuming that the basis declines linearly until settlement, when the term structure is in contango (backwardation), the trader who is long in back-month VIX futures would realize roll-down losses (profits).

Importantly, VIX futures may not reflect the index, especially when the VIX experiences large spikes, because longer-maturity futures contracts are less sensitive to short-term VIX movements. Furthermore, establishing long positions in VIX futures can be very expensive over time. When the short end of the VIX futures curve is much steeper than the long end of the curve, the carrying costs created from the contract roll down are elevated.

This phenomenon is particularly evident for investors who cannot invest directly in futures but must invest in volatility funds that attempt to track the VIX. These funds have attracted interest and substantial money flows because they are easily accessed in the form of exchange-traded products (ETPs) and, in particular, exchange-traded notes (ETNs) that provide exposure to short- and medium-term VIX futures. Some of these products also provide leveraged exposure. When using these investment products to hedge against a rise in the VIX, the VIX futures term structure should be taken into in consideration because volatility ETPs typically hold a mix of VIX futures that is adjusted daily to keep the average time to expiration of the portfolio constant. The daily rebalancing requires shorter-term futures to be sold and longer-dated futures to be purchased. When the VIX futures are in contango, the cost of rolling over hedges (i.e., negative carry) increases, thereby reducing profits and causing the ETP to underperform relative to the movement in the VIX. In contrast, "inverse" VIX ETPs offer investors the opportunity to profit from decreases in S&P 500 volatility. However, the purchase of these funds implies a directional positioning on volatility, and investors must accept the risk of large losses when volatility increases sharply.

In 2006, VIX options were introduced, providing an asymmetrical exposure to potential increases or decreases in anticipated volatility. VIX options are European style, and their prices depend on the prices of VIX futures with similar expirations because the market makers of VIX options typically hedge the risk of their option positions using VIX futures. To understand the use of VIX calls and puts, it is very important to recognize that the increases in the VIX (and VIX futures) are negatively correlated with the prices of equity assets. In particular, a trader or investor would purchase VIX call options when he expects that volatility will increase owing to a significant sell-off in the equity market. In contrast, VIX put options would be bought to profit from an expectation that volatility will decrease because of stable equity market conditions. Options on the VSTOXX index also exist, but they have lower volumes and open interest than those on the VIX.

6 VOLATILITY DERIVATIVES: VARIANCE SWAPS

☐ demonstrate the use of volatility derivatives and variance swaps

Variance swaps are instruments used by investors for taking directional bets on implied versus realized volatility for speculative or hedging purposes. The term "variance swap" refers to the fact that these instruments have a payoff analogous to that of a swap. In a variance swap, the buyer of the contract will pay the difference between the fixed *variance strike* agreed on in the contract and the *realized variance* (annualized) on the underlying over the period specified and applied to a variance notional. In variance swaps, there is no exchange of cash at the contract inception or during the life of the swap. The payoff at expiration of a long variance position will be positive (negative) when realized variance is greater (less) than the swap's variance strike. If the payment amount is positive (negative), the swap seller (buyer) pays the swap buyer (seller). The payoff at settlement is found as follows:

$$\text{Settlement amount}_T = (\text{Variance notional})(\text{Realized variance} - \text{Variance strike}) \qquad (12)$$

The realized variance is calculated as follows, where $R_i = \ln(P_{i+1}/P_i)$ and N is the number of days observed:

$$\text{Realized variance} = 252 \times \left[\sum_{i=1}^{N-1} R_i^2 / (N-1)\right] \qquad (13)$$

Since most market participants are accustomed to thinking in terms of volatility, variance swap traders typically agree on the following two things: (1) a variance swap trade size expressed in **vega notional**, N_{Vega} (not in variance notional), and (2) the strike (X), which represents the expected future variance of the underlying, expressed as volatility (not variance). This approach is intuitive because the vega notional represents the average profit and loss of the variance swap for a 1% change in volatility from the strike. For example, when the vega notional is \$50,000, the profit and loss for one volatility point of difference between the realized volatility and the strike will be close to \$50,000.

We must bear in mind that this is an approximation because the variance swap payoff is convex and the profit and loss is not linear for changes in the realized volatility. Specifically, to calculate the exact payoff, the variance strike is the strike squared and the **variance notional**, $N_{variance}$, is defined and calculated as

$$\text{Variance notional} = \frac{\text{Vega notional}}{2 \times \text{Strike price}} \qquad (14)$$

Thus, given the realized volatility (σ), we have the following equivalence:

$$\text{Settlement amount}_T = N_{Vega}\left(\frac{\sigma^2 - X^2}{2 \times \text{Strike price}}\right) = N_{variance}(\sigma^2 - X^2) \qquad (15)$$

The strike on a variance swap is calculated on the basis of the implied volatility skew for a specific expiration, derived from calls and puts quoted in the market. As discussed previously, volatility skew is a plot of the differences in implied volatilities of a basket of options with the same maturity and underlying asset but with different strikes (and thus moneyness). As a rule of thumb, the strike of a variance swap typically corresponds to the implied volatility of the put that has 90% moneyness (calculated as the option's strike divided by the current level of the underlying).

The mark-to-market valuation of a variance swap at time t (VarSwap_t) will depend on realized volatility from the swap's initiation to t, RealizedVol(0,t), and implied volatility at t, ImpliedVol(t,T), over the remaining life of the swap ($T - t$). $PV_t(T)$ is the present value at time t of \$1 received at maturity T. The value of a variance swap at time t is given by the following formula:[10]

$$\text{Var Swap}_t = \text{Variance notional} \times PV_t(T) \times \left\{\frac{t}{T} \times \left[\text{RealizedVol}(0,t)\right]^2 + \frac{T-t}{T} \times \left[\text{ImpliedVol}(t,T)\right]^2 - \text{Strike}^2\right\} \qquad (16)$$

Importantly, the sensitivity of a variance swap to changes in implied volatility diminishes over time.

10 Note that the terms in the braces—RealizedVol, ImpliedVol, and Strike—are all expressed in volatility units. They are squared so that they are expressed in variance units for determining the value of a variance swap.

A feature of variance swaps that makes them particularly interesting to investors is that their payoffs are convex in volatility, as seen Exhibit 4. This convexity occurs because being long a variance swap is equivalent to be long a basket of options and short the underlying asset (typically by selling a futures contract). A long position in a variance swap is thus long gamma and has a convex payoff. This characteristic allows volatility sellers to sell variance swaps at a higher price than at-the-money options because the swap's convex payoff profile is attractive to investors who desire a long volatility position as a tail risk hedge.

Exhibit 4: The Payoff of a Variance Swap Is Convex in Volatility

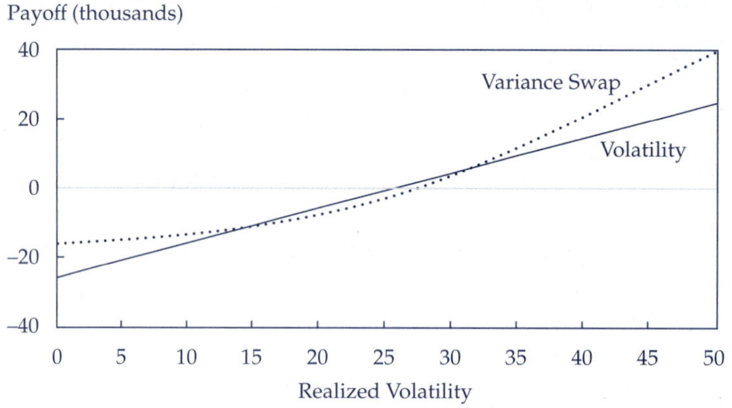

EXAMPLE 12

Variance Swap Valuation and Settlement

Olivia Santos trades strategies that systematically sell volatility on the S&P 500 Index. She sells $50,000 vega notional of a one-year variance swap on the S&P 500 at a strike of 20% (quoted as annual volatility).

Now six months have passed, and the S&P 500 has experienced a realized volatility of 16% (annualized). On the same day, the fair strike of a new six-month variance swap on the S&P 500 is 19%.

Determine the following:

1. The current value of the variance swap sold by Santos (note that the annual interest rate is 2.5%)

Solution:

Santos sold $50,000 vega notional of a one-year variance swap on the S&P 500 with a strike (in volatility terms) of 20%. The value of the variance swap sold by Santos is found using Equation 16:

$$\text{VarSwap}_t = \text{Variance notional} \times PV_t(T) \times \left\{\frac{t}{T} \times \left[\text{RealizedVol}(0,t)\right]^2 + \frac{T-t}{T} \times \left[\text{ImpliedVol}(t,T)\right]^2 - \text{Strike}^2\right\}$$

Values for the inputs are as follows:

Volatility strike on existing swap = 20.

Variance strike on existing swap = $20^2 = 400$.

From Equation 14, Variance notional $= \frac{\text{Vega notional}}{2 \times \text{Strike}} = \frac{\$50{,}000}{2 \times 20} = 1{,}250$.

$\text{RealizedVol}(0,t)^2 = 16^2 = 256$.

$\text{ImpliedVol}(t,T)^2 = 19^2 = 361$.

t = 6 months.

T = 12 months.

$PV_t(T) = 1/[1 + (2.5\% \times 6/12)] = 0.987654$ (= Present Value Interest Factor for six months, where the annual rate is 2.5%).

The current value of the swap is

$\text{VarSwap}_t = 1{,}250 \times (0.987654) \times [(6/12) \times 256 + (6/12) \times 361 - 400]$

$= -\$112{,}962.9263$.

Given that Santos is short the variance swap, the mark-to-market value is positive for her, and it equals $112,963.

2. The settlement amount at expiration of the swap if the one-year realized volatility is 18%

Solution:

The settlement amount is calculated using Equation 12 as follows:

$\text{Settlement}_T = \text{Variance notional} \times (\text{Realized variance} - \text{Variance strike}) = 1{,}250 \times (18^2 - 20^2)$

$= -\$95{,}000$

If the payment amount is positive (negative), the swap seller (buyer) pays the swap buyer (seller). So, in this case, Santos would receive $95,000 from the swap buyer.

USING DERIVATIVES IN ASSET ALLOCATION, PART 1 — 7

☐ demonstrate the use of derivatives to achieve targeted equity and interest rate risk exposures

Bernhard Steinbacher has a client with a holding of 100,000 shares in Tundra Corporation, currently trading for €14 per share. The client has owned the shares for many years and thus has a very low tax basis on this stock. Steinbacher wants to safeguard the value of the position since the client does not want to sell the shares. He cannot find exchange-traded options on the stock. Steinbacher wants to present a way in which the client could protect the investment portfolio from a decline in Tundra's stock price.

Discuss a swap strategy that Steinbacher might recommend to his client.

Solution:

A possible solution is to enter into an equity swap trading the Tundra stock return for the floating reference interest rate. Given Tundra's current share price of €14, the position is worth €1.4 million. Steinbacher can agree to exchange the *total return* on the shares (which includes the price performance and the dividends received) for the reference rate return on this sum of money. Now he needs to determine the time over which the protection is needed and must match the swap tenor to this period. After consulting with his client, Steinbacher decides on six months. The floating reference rate is 0.34%, expressed as an annual rate.

Scenario A:

Over the six months, Tundra pays a €0.10 dividend and the share price rises 1%.

The total return on the stock is

$$\frac{(14 \times 1.01) - 14 + 0.10}{14} = 1.71\%.$$

For a six-month period, the reference rate return would be half the annual rate, or 0.17%. Tundra's total return *exceeds* the six-month reference rate return: (1.71% – 0.17%) × €1.4 million = €21,620, which is a positive amount, so Steinbacher's client would need to *pay* the swap counterparty.

Scenario B:

Over the six months, Tundra pays a €0.10 dividend and the share price falls 1%.

The total return on the stock is

$$\frac{(14 \times 0.99) - 14 + 0.10}{14} = -0.29\%.$$

Tundra's total return is less than the six-month reference rate return: (–0.29% – 0.17%) × €1.4 million = –€6,380, which is a negative amount, so Steinbacher's client would *receive* the negative return and the reference rate return from the swap counterparty (meaning the client will receive a positive cash inflow of €6,380).

Cash Equitization

Georgia McMillian manages a fund invested in UK stocks that is indexed to the FTSE 100 Index. The fund has £250 million of total assets under management, including £20 million of cash reserves invested at the three-month British pound floating rate of 0.63% (annualized). McMillian does not have an expectation on the direction of UK stocks over the next quarter. However, she is keen to minimize tracking error risk, so she implements a cash equitization strategy attempting to replicate the performance of the FTSE 100 on the cash reserves. Futures on the FTSE 100 settling in three months currently trade at a price of £7,900, the contract's value is £10 per index point (so each futures contract is worth £79,000), and its beta, β_f, is 1.0.

McMillian engages in a synthetic index strategy to gain exposure on a notional amount of £20 million to the FTSE 100 by purchasing equity index futures. The number of futures she must purchase is given by the following:

$$N_f = \left(\frac{\beta_T}{\beta_f}\right)\left(\frac{S}{F}\right) = \left(\frac{1.0}{1.0}\right)\left(\frac{20{,}000{,}000}{79{,}000}\right) = 253.16 \approx 253$$

where the beta of the futures contract, β_f, and the target beta, β_T, are both equal to 1.0.

Scenario: Three months later, the FTSE 100 Index has increased by 5%.

Three months later, the FTSE 100 has increased by 5%, and the original value of £230 million invested in UK stocks has increased to £241.5 million. The price of the FTSE 100 Index futures contract has increased to £8,282.5. Interest on the cash invested at the three-month floating rate amounts to £31,500 (£20,000,000 × 0.63% × 90/360). McMillian bought the futures at £7,900, and the cash settlement of the contract at is £8,282.5. So, there is a "gain" of 382.5 index points, each point being worth £10, on 253 contracts for a total cash inflow of £967,725 (382.5 points per contract × £10 per point × 253 contracts). Adding to the portfolio the profit from the futures and the cash reserves plus the interest earned on the cash gives a total market value for McMillian's portfolio of £262,499,225 (= £241,500,000 + £20,000,000 + £967,725 + £31,500). The rate of return for the combined position is:

$$\frac{£262,499,225}{£250,000,000} - 1 = 0.05, \text{ or } 5\%$$

Importantly, without implementing this strategy, McMillian's return would have been slightly over 4.6%, calculated as (£230 million/£250 million) × 5.0% + (£20 million/£250 million) × 0.63% × (90/360). So, she accomplished her goal of minimizing tracking error by following this strategy.

USING DERIVATIVES IN ASSET ALLOCATION, PART 2

8

☐ demonstrate the use of derivatives in asset allocation, rebalancing, and inferring market expectations

Changing Allocations between Asset Classes Using Futures

Mario Rossi manages a €500 million portfolio that is allocated 70% to stocks and 30% to bonds. Over the next three-month horizon, he is bearish on eurozone stocks, except for German shares, and is bullish on Italian bonds. So, Rossi wants to reduce the overall allocation to stocks by 10%, to 60%, and achieve the same weight (30%) in Italian stocks (which have a beta of 1.1 with respect to the FTSE MIB Index) and German stocks (which have a beta of 0.9 with respect to the DAX index). He also wants to increase the overall allocation to Italian government bonds (BTPs) by 10%, to 40%. The bond portion of his portfolio has a modified duration of 6.45. In summary, as shown in Exhibit 5, Rossi needs to remove €100 million of exposure to Italian stocks, add €50 million of exposure to German stocks, and add €50 million of exposure to Italian bonds in his portfolio.

Exhibit 5: Summary of Rossi's Original and New Asset Allocation

Stock Index	Original (€350 Million, 70%)	New (€300 Million, 60%)	Transaction
FTSE MIB	€250 million (50%)	€150 million (30%)	Sell €100 million
DAX	€100 million (20%)	€150 million (30%)	Buy €50 million

Bonds	Original (€150 Million, 30%)	New (€200 Million, 40%)	Transaction
Italian BTPs	€150 million (30%)	€200 million (40%)	Buy €50 million

Rossi uses stock index futures and bond futures to achieve this objective. Once the notional values to be traded are known, Rossi determines how many futures contracts should be purchased or sold to achieve the desired asset allocation. The FTSE MIB Index futures contract has a price of 23,100 and a multiplier of €5, for a value of €115,500. The DAX index futures contract has a price of 13,000 and a multiplier of €25, for a value of €325,000. Both futures contracts have a beta of 1. The BTP futures contract has a price of 132.50 and a contract size of €100,000. The cheapest-to-deliver bond has a price of €121; a modified duration of 8.19; a BPV_{CTD} (from Equation 7) of €99.10, calculated as 8.19 × 0.0001 × [(121/100) × €100,000)]; and a conversion factor of 0.913292.

1. Determine how many stock index and bond futures contracts Rossi should use to implement the desired asset allocation and whether he should go long or short.
2. At the horizon date (three months later), the value of the Italian stock portfolio has fallen 5% whereas that of the German stock portfolio has increased 1%. The FTSE MIB futures price is 22,000, and the DAX futures price is 13,100. Determine the change in market value of the equity portfolio assuming the futures transactions specified in Part 1 have been carried out (note that you can ignore transaction costs).
3. At the horizon date, the Italian bond yield curve has a parallel shift downward of 25 bps. Determine the change in market value of the bond portfolio assuming the transactions specified in Part 1 have been carried out (note that you can ignore transactions costs).

Solution to 1:

The market value of the Italian stocks is 0.50(€500,000,000) = €250,000,000, and Rossi wants to reduce the exposure to this market by 0.20(€500,000,000) = €100,000,000. The market value of the German stocks is 0.20(€500,000,000) = €100,000,000, and he wants to increase the exposure to this market by 0.10(€500,000,000) = €50,000,000. He decides to sell enough futures contracts on the FTSE MIB to reduce the exposure to Italian stocks by €100 million and to purchase enough futures on the DAX index to increase the exposure to German stocks by €50 million.

The number of stock index futures, N_f, is

$$N_f = \left(\frac{\beta_T - \beta_S}{\beta_f}\right)\left(\frac{S}{F}\right)$$

where β_T is the target beta of zero, β_S is the stock beta of 1.1, β_f is the futures beta of 1.0, S is the market value of the stocks involved in the transaction, and F is the value of the futures contract.

To achieve the desired reduction in exposure to Italian stocks, the market value of the stocks involved in the transaction will be S = €100,000,000. The Italian stocks' beta (β_S) is 1.1, and the target beta is $\beta_T = 0$. The FTSE MIB Index futures have a contract value of €115,500 and a beta (β_f) of 1.0:

$$N_f = \left(\frac{\beta_T - \beta_S}{\beta_f}\right)\left(\frac{S}{F}\right) = \left(\frac{0.0 - 1.1}{1.0}\right)\left(\frac{€100,000,000}{€115,500}\right) = -952.38$$

Rossi sells 952 futures contracts (after rounding).

To achieve the desired exposure to German stocks (which have a beta of 0.9), the market value of the stocks involved in the transaction will be S = €50,000,000. In this case, $\beta_S = 0.0$ because Rossi is starting with a notional "cash" position from the reduction in Italian stock exposure, and the target beta is now $\beta_T = 0.9$. Given the value of the DAX index futures contract of €325,000 and a beta (β_f) of 1.0, we obtain

$$N_f = \left(\frac{\beta_T - \beta_S}{\beta_f}\right)\left(\frac{S}{F}\right) = \left(\frac{0.9 - 0.0}{1.0}\right)\left(\frac{€50,000,000}{€325,000}\right) = 138.46$$

Rossi buys 138 futures contracts (after rounding).

The market value of the Italian bonds is 0.30(€500,000,000) = €150,000,000, and Rossi wants to increase the exposure to this market by 0.10(€500,000,000) = €50,000,000. He decides to purchase enough Euro-BTP futures so that €50 million exposure in Italian bonds is added to the portfolio. The target basis point value exposure (BPV_T) is determined using Equation 4:

$$BPV_T = MDUR_T \times 0.01\% \times MV_P = 6.45 \times 0.0001 \times €50,000,000 = €32,250$$

The cheapest-to-deliver bond is the BTP 4¾ 09/01/28, which has a conversion factor of 0.913292 and BPV_{CTD} of €99.10. The number of Euro-BTP futures to buy to convert the €50 million in notional cash ($BPV_P = 0$) to the desired exposure in Italian bonds is found using Equation 9:

$$BPVHR = \left(\frac{BPV_T - BPV_P}{BPV_{CTD}}\right) \times CF = [(€32,250 - 0)/€99.10] \times 0.913292$$

$$= 297.21$$

Rossi buys 297 Euro-BTP futures contracts (after rounding).

Solution to 2:

The value of the Italian stock portfolio decreases by €7,264,000. This outcome is the net effect of the following:

- The original Italian stock portfolio decreases by €12,500,000 (= €250 million × –5%).
- The short position in 952 FTSE MIB futures gains €5,236,000, calculated as

– (22,000 – 23,100) × 952 × €5.

The value of the German stock portfolio increases by €1,345,000. This outcome is the net effect of the following:

- The original German stock portfolio increases by €1,000,000 (= €100 million × 1%).
- The long position in 138 DAX futures gains €345,000, calculated as (13,100 – 13,000) × 138 × €25.

The total value of the stock position has decreased by €5,919,000 or –1.691% (= –5,919,000/350,000,000).

Had Rossi sold the Italian stocks and then converted the proceeds into German stocks, the equity portfolio would have decreased by €6,000,000 or −1.71% (= −6,000,000/350,000,000). This outcome would have been the net effect of the following:

- A decrease in the new Italian stock portfolio of €7,500,000 (= €150 million × −5%)
- An increase in the new German stock portfolio of €1,500,000 (= €150 million × 1%)

Solution to 3:

The Italian bond yield curve had a parallel shift downward of 25 bps. The value of the Italian bond portfolio increases by €3,224,426. This outcome is the net effect of the following:

- The €150 million portfolio's BPV_P, per Equation 5, is €96,750 (= 6.45 × 0.0001 × €150,000,000). Thus, for a 25 bp decrease in rates, the portfolio value increases by €2,418,750 (= €96,750 × 25).
- The long position in 297 BTP futures has a BPV_{CTD} of €99.10, and the CF is 0.913292. So, using Equation 6, BPV_F is €108.51 (= €99.10/0.913292). Thus, for a 25 bp decrease in rates, the futures position increases in value by €805,676, calculated as follows: BPV_F × Change in yield × Number of futures contracts = €108.51 × 25 × 297.

Had Rossi bought the Italian bonds, the new €200 million bond portfolio would have increased by €3,225,000. The portfolio has a BPV_P of 6.45 × 0.0001 × €200,000,000 = €129,000. Thus, for a 25 bp decrease in rates, the portfolio value increases by €3,225,000 (= €129,000 × 25).

Rebalancing an Asset Allocation Using Futures

Yolanda Grant manages a portfolio with a target allocation of 40% in stocks and 60% in bonds. Over the last month, the value of the portfolio has increased from €100 million to €106 million, and Grant wants to rebalance it back to the target allocation (40% stocks/60% bonds). As shown in Exhibit 6, the current portfolio has €46 million (43.4%) in European stocks (with beta of 1.2 with respect to the EURO STOXX 50 index) and €60 million (56.6%) in German bunds. The bonds have a modified duration of 9.5.

Exhibit 6: Summary of Grant's Current and Rebalanced Allocation

Stocks	Current	Rebalanced	Transaction
European stocks	€46 million (43.4%)	€42.4 million (40%)	Sell €3.6 million

Bonds	Current	Rebalanced	Transaction
German bunds	€60 million (56.6%)	€63.6 million (60%)	Buy €3.6 million

Grant will use stock index futures and bond futures to achieve this objective. Once the notional values to be traded are known, she determines how many futures contracts should be purchased or sold to achieve the desired asset allocation.

The EURO STOXX 50 index futures contract has a price of 3,500 and a multiplier of €10, for a value of €35,000. The Euro-Bund futures contract has a contract size of €100,000. The cheapest-to-deliver bond has a modified duration of 8.623 and a price of 98.14, so (per Equation 7) its BPV_{CTD} is €84.63, calculated as 8.623 × 0.0001 × [(98.14/100) × €100,000)]. Its conversion factor is 0.619489.

Determine how many stock index and bond futures contracts Grant should use to implement the desired asset allocation and whether she should go long or short.

Solution:

The market value of the European stocks is €46,000,000, and Grant wants to reduce the exposure to this market to 40% or 0.40(€106,000,000) = €42,400,000. She decides to sell enough futures contracts on the EURO STOXX 50 to reduce the allocation to European stocks by 0.034(€106,000,000) = €3,604,000.

To achieve the desired reduction in exposure to European stocks, the market value of the stocks involved in the transaction (*S*) will be €3,604,000. The European stocks' beta (β_S) is 1.2, and the target beta is $\beta_T = 0$. The EURO STOXX 50 index futures have a contract value (*F*) of €35,000, with a beta (β_f) of 1.0, so

$$N_f = \left(\frac{\beta_T - \beta_S}{\beta_f}\right)\left(\frac{S}{F}\right) = \left(\frac{0.0 - 1.2}{1.0}\right)\left(\frac{€3,604,000}{€35,000}\right) = -123.57$$

Grant sells 124 futures contracts (after rounding).

The market value of the German bunds is €60,000,000, and Grant wants to increase the exposure to this market to 0.60(€106,000,000) = €63,600,000. She decides to purchase enough Euro-Bund futures so that €3,604,000 (= 0.034 × €106,000,000) of exposure to German bonds is added to the portfolio. The target basis point value (BPV_T) is given by Equation 4, as follows:

$$BPV_T = MDUR_T \times 0.01\% \times MV_P = 9.5 \times 0.0001 \times €3,604,000 = €3,424$$

The cheapest-to-deliver bond has a BPV_{CTD} of €84.63 and a conversion factor of 0.619489. The number of Euro-Bund futures to buy to convert the €3.6 million in notional cash ($BPV_P = 0$) to the desired exposure in German bonds is found using Equation 9:

$$BPVHR = \left(\frac{BPV_T - BPV_P}{BPV_{CTD}}\right) \times CF$$
$$= [(€3,424 - 0)/€84.63] \times 0.619489 = 25.06 \approx 25 \text{ contracts}$$

So, Grant should buy 25 Euro-Bund futures contracts.

Changing Allocations between Asset Classes Using Swaps

Tactical Money Management Inc. (TMM) is interested in changing the asset allocation on a $200 million segment of its portfolio. This money is invested 75% in US stocks and 25% in US bonds. Within the stock allocation, the funds are invested 60% in large cap, 30% in mid-cap, and 10% percent in small cap. Within the bond sector, the funds are invested 80% in US government bonds and 20% in investment-grade corporate bonds.

Given that it is bullish on equities, especially large-cap stocks, over the next year, TMM would like to change the overall allocation to 90% stocks and 10% bonds. Specifically, TMM would like to split the stock allocation into 65% large cap, 25% mid-cap, and 10% small cap. It also wants to change the bond allocation to 75% US government and 25% investment-grade corporate. The current position, the desired new position, and the necessary transactions to get from the current position to the new position are shown in Exhibit 7.

Exhibit 7: Summary of TMM's Current and New Asset Allocation

Stock	Current ($150 Million, 75%)	New ($180 Million, 90%)	Transaction
Large cap	$90 million (60%)	$117 million (65%)	Buy $27 million
Mid-cap	$45 million (30%)	$45 million (25%)	None
Small cap	$15 million (10%)	$18 million (10%)	Buy $3 million

Bonds	Current ($50 Million, 25%)	New ($20 Million, 10%)	Transaction
Government	$40 million (80%)	$15 million (75%)	Sell $25 million
Corporate	$10 million (20%)	$5 million (25%)	Sell $5 million

TMM knows these changes would entail a considerable amount of trading in stocks and bonds. So, TMM decides to execute a series of swaps that would enable it to change its position temporarily but more easily and less expensively than by executing the physical transactions. TMM engages Dynamic Dealers Inc. to perform the swaps.

TMM decides to increase the allocation in the large-cap sector by investing in the S&P 500 Index and to increase that in the small-cap sector by investing in the S&P SmallCap 600 Index (SPSC). To reduce the allocation in the overall fixed-income sector, TMM decides to replicate the performance of the Bloomberg Barclays US Treasury Index (BBT) for the government bond sector and the BofA Merrill Lynch US Corporate Index (BAMLC) for the corporate bond sector.

Discuss how TMM can use a combination of equity and fixed-income swaps to synthetically implement its desired asset allocation.

Solution:

To achieve the desired asset allocation, TMM takes the following exposures:

- A long position of $27 million in the S&P 500
- A long position of $3 million in the SPSC
- A short position of $25 million in the BBT
- A short position of $5 million in the BAMLC

The mid-cap exposure of $45 million does not change, so TMM does not need to incorporate a mid-cap index into the swap. TMM uses a combination of equity and fixed-income swaps to achieve its target allocation and structures the swap to have all payments occur on the same dates six months apart. TMM also decides that the swap should mature in one year. If it wishes to extend this period, TMM would need to renegotiate the swap at expiration. Likewise, TMM could decide to unwind the position before one year elapses, which it could do by executing a new swap with opposite payments for the remainder of the life of the original swap.

Every six months and at maturity, each of the equity swaps involves the settlement of the following cash flows:

- *Equity swap 1:* TMM receives the total return of the S&P 500 and makes a floating payment tied to the market reference rate (MRR) minus the agreed-on spread, both on a notional principal of $27 million.
- *Equity swap 2:* TMM receives the total return of the SPSC and makes a floating payment tied to the MRR minus the agreed-on spread, both on a notional principal of $3 million.

The fixed-income swaps will require the following cash flow settlements every six months and at maturity:

- *Fixed-income swap 1:* TMM pays the total return of the BBT and receives floating payments tied to the MRR minus the agreed-on spread, both on notional principal of $25 million.
- *Fixed-income swap 2:* TMM pays the total return of the BAMLC and receives floating payments tied to the MRR minus the agreed-on spread, both on a notional principal of $5 million.

It is important to recognize that this transaction will not perfectly replicate the performance of TMM's equity and fixed-income portfolios, unless they are indexed to the indexes selected as underlying of the swaps. In addition, TMM could encounter a cash flow problem if its fixed-income payments exceed its equity receipts and its portfolio does not generate enough cash to fund its net obligation. The stock and bond portfolio will generate cash only from dividends and interest. Capital gains will not be received in cash unless a portion of the portfolio is sold. But avoiding selling a portion of the portfolio is the very reason why TMM wants to use swaps.

USING DERIVATIVES TO INFER MARKET EXPECTATIONS

9

☐ demonstrate the use of derivatives in asset allocation, rebalancing, and inferring market expectations

As mentioned at the beginning of this reading, an important use of derivatives by market participants is for inferring market expectations. These expectations can be for changes in interest rates; for changes in prices for the whole economy (i.e., inflation), individual stocks, or other assets; or even for changes in key factors, such as implied volatility. Exhibit 8 provides a brief list of some of the myriad applications by which information embedded in derivatives prices is used to infer current market expectations. It is important to emphasize that these inferences relate to *current expectations* of future events—they do not foretell what will actually happen which can change with the arrival of new information.

Exhibit 8: Some Typical Applications of Derivatives for Inferring Market Expectations

Use Cases/Applications	Derivative Type
1. Inferring expectations for FOMC moves	Fed funds futures
2. Inferring expectations for inflation rates	CPI (inflation) swaps
3. Inferring expectations for market volatility	VIX futures

The first application in Exhibit 8, using fed funds futures to infer expectations of federal funds rate changes by the Federal Open Market Committee (FOMC), is likely the most common and well-publicized use of derivatives for inferring market expectations, so it is the focus of the following discussion.

Using Fed Funds Futures to Infer the Expected Average Federal Funds Rate

Market participants are interested in knowing the probabilities of various interest rate level outcomes, deriving from central banks' future decisions, as implied by the pricing of financial instruments. This provides them with an indication about the extent to which markets are "pricing in" future monetary policy changes. Note that such implied probabilities represent the market's view and may diverge from the guidance provided by central banks in their regular communications about the likely future course of monetary policy actions. Furthermore, especially for the longer-term horizon, these inferred probabilities usually do not have strong predictive power. Most information providers and the business media report current implied probability data for selected interest rates and historical analysis charts that show how the implied probabilities of policy rate settings have changed over time.

A commonly followed metric is the probability of a change in the federal funds rate at upcoming FOMC meetings that is implied by the prices of fed funds futures contracts. When the US central bank began its rate hiking cycle in 2015, it declared an intention to maintain a 25 bp "target range" (lower and upper bounds) for the federal funds rate. The Fed regularly communicates its "forward guidance" along with the so-called dot plot, which shows where each FOMC meeting participant believes the federal funds rate should be at the end of the year, for the next few years, and in the longer run.

To derive probabilities of potential upcoming Fed interest rate actions, market participants look at the pricing of fed funds futures, which are tied to the **effective federal funds (FFE) rate**—the rate actually transacted between depository institutions—not the Fed's target federal funds rate. The underlying assumption is that the implied futures market rates are predicting the value of the monthly average effective federal funds rate. As shown in Exhibit 9, where the dots represent forecasts of the federal funds rate by each FOMC member, implied market expectations (dotted line) can diverge significantly from the Fed's forward guidance (solid line, the median of the dots).

Exhibit 9: Hypothetical Example of Market's Implied Forecast vs. FOMC Forecast of Federal Funds Rate

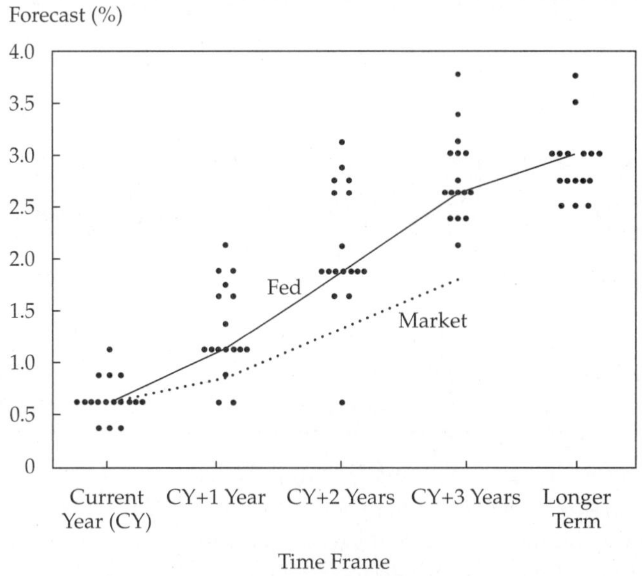

Fed funds futures are traded on the Chicago Board of Trade, and the contract price is quoted as 100 minus the market's expectation for the FFE rate, as follows:

$$\text{Fed funds futures contract price} = 100 - \text{Expected FFE rate.} \qquad (17)$$

At expiration, the contract is cash settled to the simple average (overnight) effective federal funds rate for the delivery month. The overnight rate is calculated and reported daily by the Federal Reserve Bank of New York.

To determine the probability of a change in the federal funds rate, the following formula is used, where the current federal funds rate is the midpoint of the current target range:

$$\frac{\text{Effective federal funds rate implied by futures contract} - \text{Current federal funds rate}}{\text{Federal funds rate assuming a rate hike} - \text{Current federal funds rate}} \qquad (18)$$

Inferring Market Expectations

Andrew Okyung manages a portfolio of short-term floating-rate corporate debt, and he is interested in understanding current market expectations for any Fed rate actions at the upcoming FOMC meeting. He observes that the current price for the fed funds futures contract expiring after the next FOMC meeting is 97.90. The current federal funds rate target range is set between 1.75% and 2.00%.

Demonstrate how Okyung can use the information provided to determine the following:

1. The expected average FFE rate
2. The probability of a 25 bp interest rate hike at the next FOMC meeting

Solution to 1:

The FFE rate implied by the futures contract price is 2.10% (= 100 – 97.90). Okyung understands that this is the rate that market participants expect to be the average federal funds rate for that month.

Solution to 2:

Okyung knows that given that the FFE rate embedded in the fed funds futures price is 2.10%, there is a high probability that the FOMC will increase rates by 25 bps from its current target range of 1.75%–2.00% to the new target range of 2.00%–2.25%. Given the Fed's declared incremental move size of 25 bps, he calculates the probability of a rate hike as

$$\frac{2.100\% - 1.875\%}{2.125\% - 1.875\%} = 0.90, \text{ or } 90\%$$

where 1.875% is the midpoint of the current target range (1.75%–2.00%) and 2.125% is the midpoint of the new target range (2.00%–2.25%) assuming a rate hike.

Exhibit 10 displays, as a hypothetical example, the trends in implied probabilities (y-axis) derived from fed funds futures prices of an FOMC rate action—either a 25 bp rate hike, a 25 bp rate cut, or no change—at the next FOMC meeting date. Note that the probability of a rate hike or cut is represented as the probability of a move from the current target range at the specified meeting date, and of course, the probabilities of all three actions at a particular meeting date sum to 1.

Exhibit 10: Hypothetical Example of Trends of Probabilities for Federal Funds Rate Actions by the FOMC

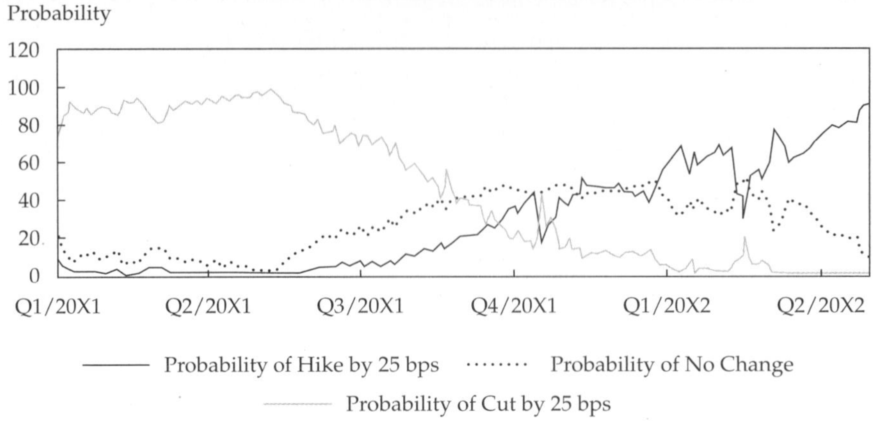

Importantly, typical end-of-month (EOM) activity by large financial and banking institutions often induces "dips" in the FFE rate that create bias issues when using the rate as the basis for probability calculations of potential FOMC rate moves. For example, if such activity increased the price for the relevant fed funds futures contract to 98.05, then the FFE rate would decline to 1.95% (= 100 – 98.05). In this case, using the same equation as before, the probability of an FOMC rate hike decreases from 90% to just 30%:

$$\frac{1.950 - 1.875}{0.25} = 0.30, \text{ or } 30\%$$

To overcome this end-of-month bias, data providers have implemented various methods of "smoothing" the EOM dips. One prominent data provider uses a method that builds a forward rate structure based on where the market believes interest rates will settle in non-FOMC meeting months and then uses these forward rates to make appropriate adjustments. For each FOMC meeting month, it is assumed that an effective rate prevails until the meeting date, and then some rate prevails after the meeting, with the average effective rate over the month being implied by the futures price.

SUMMARY

This reading on swap, forward, and futures strategies shows a number of ways in which market participants might use these derivatives to enhance returns or to reduce risk to better meet portfolio objectives. Following are the key points.

- Interest rate, currency, and equity swaps, forwards, and futures can be used to modify risk and return by altering the characteristics of the cash flows of an investment portfolio.
- An interest rate swap is an OTC contract in which two parties agree to exchange cash flows on specified dates, one based on a floating interest rate and the other based on a fixed rate (swap rate), determined at swap initiation. Both rates are applied to the swap's notional value to determine the size of the payments, which are typically netted. Interest rate swaps enable a party with a fixed (floating) risk or obligation to effectively convert it into a floating (fixed) one.

- Investors can use short-dated interest rate futures and forward rate agreements or longer-dated fixed-income (bond) futures contracts to modify their portfolios' interest rate risk exposure.
- When hedging interest rate risk with bond futures, one must determine the basis point value of the portfolio to be hedged, the target basis point value, and the basis point value of the futures, which itself is determined by the basis point value of the cheapest-to-deliver bond and its conversion factor. The number of bond futures to buy or sell to reach the target basis point value is then determined by the basis point value hedge ratio:

$$BPVHR = \left(\frac{BPV_T - BPV_P}{BPV_{CTD}}\right) \times CF.$$

- Cross-currency basis swaps help parties in the swap to hedge against the risk of exchange rate fluctuations and to achieve better rate outcomes. Firms that need foreign-denominated cash can obtain funding in their local currency (likely at a more favorable rate) and then swap the local currency for the required foreign currency using a cross-currency basis swap.
- Equity risk in a portfolio can be managed using equity swaps and total return swaps. There are three main types of equity swap: (1) receive-equity return, pay-fixed; (2) receive-equity return, pay-floating; and (3) receive-equity return, pay-another equity return. A total return swap is a modified equity swap; it also includes in the performance any dividends paid by the underlying stocks or index during the period until the swap maturity.
- Equity risk in a portfolio can also be managed using equity futures and forwards. Equity futures are standardized, exchange-listed contracts, and when the underlying is a stock index, only cash settlement is available at contract expiration. The number of equity futures contracts to buy or sell is determined by

$$N_f = \left(\frac{\beta_T - \beta_S}{\beta_f}\right)\left(\frac{S}{F}\right).$$

- Cash equitization is a strategy designed to boost returns by finding ways to "equitize" unintended cash holdings. It is typically done using stock index futures and interest rate futures.
- Derivatives on volatility include VIX futures and options and variance swaps. Importantly, VIX option prices are determined from VIX futures, and both instruments allow an investor to implement a view depending on her expectations about the timing and magnitude of a change in implied volatility.
- In a variance swap, the buyer of the contract will pay the difference between the fixed variance strike specified in the contract and the realized variance (annualized) on the underlying over the period specified and applied to a variance notional. Thus, variance swaps allow directional bets on implied versus realized volatility.
- Derivatives can be used to infer market participants' current expectations for changes over the short term in inflation (e.g., CPI swaps) and market volatility (e.g., VIX futures). Another common application is using fed funds futures prices to derive the probability of a central bank move in the federal funds rate target at the FOMC's next meeting.

PRACTICE PROBLEMS

1. A European bond portfolio manager wants to increase the modified duration of his €30 million portfolio from 3 to 5. She would *most likely* enter a receive-fixed interest rate swap that has principal notional of €20 million and:

   A. a modified duration of 2.

   B. a modified duration of 3.

   C. a modified duration of 4.

The following information relates to questions 2-8

Global Mega (Global) is a diversified financial services firm. Yasuko Regan, senior trader, and Marcus Whitacre, junior trader, both work on the firm's derivatives desk. Regan and Whitacre assist in structuring and implementing trades for clients in the financial services industry that have limited derivatives expertise. Regan and Whitacre are currently assisting one of Global's clients—Monatize, an asset management firm—with two of its portfolios: Portfolio A and Portfolio B.

Portfolio A is a bond portfolio composed solely of US Treasury bonds. Monatize has asked Global to quote the number of Treasury futures contracts necessary to fully hedge this bond portfolio against a rise in interest rates. Exhibit 1 presents selected data on Portfolio A, the relevant Treasury futures contract, and the cheapest-to-deliver (CTD) bond.

Exhibit 1: Selected Data on Portfolio A, the Treasury Futures Contract, and the CTD Bond

Portfolio A		Futures Contract and CTD Bond	
Market value	$143,234,000	Price	145.20
Modified duration	9.10	Modified duration	8.75
Basis point value	$130,342.94	Basis point value	$127.05
		Conversion factor	0.72382
		Contract size	$100,000

After an internal discussion, Monatize elects to not hedge Portfolio A but rather decrease the portfolio's modified duration to 3.10. Regan asks Whitacre to compute the number of Treasury futures contracts to sell in order to achieve this objective. Regan tells Whitacre to assume the yield curve is flat.

Portfolio B is a $100,000,000 equity portfolio indexed to the S&P 500 Index, with excess cash of $4,800,000. Monatize is required to equitize its excess cash to be fully invested, and the firm directs Global to purchase futures contracts to do so. To replicate the return of Portfolio B's target index, Whitacre purchases S&P 500 futures contracts, at a price of 3,300 per contract, that have a multiplier of $250 per index point and a beta of 1.00.

Monatize's CFO and Regan discuss two potential hedging strategies for Portfolio B to protect against a hypothetical extreme sell-off in equities. Regan first suggests that Monatize could enter into a total return equity swap, whereby Monatize agrees to pay the return on the S&P 500 and receive a fixed interest rate at pre-specified dates in exchange for a fee.

Regan next suggests that Monatize could alternatively hedge Portfolio B using variance swaps. Monatize's CFO asks Regan to calculate what the gain would be in five months on a purchase of $1,000,000 vega notional of a one-year variance swap on the S&P 500 at a strike of 15% (quoted as annual volatility), assuming the following:

- Over the next five months, the S&P 500 experiences a realized volatility of 20%;
- At the end of the five-month period, the fair strike of a new seven-month variance swap on the S&P 500 will be 18%; and
- The annual interest rate is 1.50%.

Regan and Whitacre discuss the use of federal funds futures contracts to infer probabilities of future monetary policy changes. Whitacre makes the following three statements about fed funds futures contracts:

Statement 1	Typical end-of-month activity by large financial and banking institutions often induces "dips" in the effective fed funds rate.
Statement 2	Especially for the longer-term horizon, the probabilities inferred from the pricing of fed funds futures usually have strong predictive power.
Statement 3	To derive probabilities of Federal Reserve interest rate actions, market participants look at the pricing of fed funds futures, which are tied to the Federal Reserve's target fed funds rate.

Whitacre then proposes to Regan that Global explore opportunities in bond futures arbitrage. Whitacre makes the following two statements:

Statement 4	If the basis is positive, a trader would make a profit by "selling the basis."
Statement 5	If the basis is negative, a trader would make a profit by selling the bond and buying the futures.

2. Based on Exhibit 1, the number of Treasury futures contracts Whitacre should sell to fully hedge Portfolio A is *closest* to:

   A. 650.

   B. 743.

   C. 1,026.

3. Based on Exhibit 1, the number of Treasury futures contracts Whitacre should sell to achieve Monetize's objective with respect to Portfolio A is *closest* to:

   A. 490.

   B. 518.

   C. 676.

4. The number of S&P 500 futures contracts that Whitacre should buy to equitize

Portfolio B's excess cash position is *closest* to:

A. 6.

B. 121.

C. 1,455.

5. The derivative product first suggested by Regan as a potential hedge strategy for Portfolio B:

A. is a relatively liquid contract.

B. eliminates counterparty credit risk.

C. allows Monatize to keep voting rights on its equity portfolio.

6. Based on the CFO's set of assumptions, the gain on the purchase of the variance swap on the S&P 500 in five months would be *closest* to:

A. $4,317,775.

B. $4,355,556.

C. $4,736,334.

7. Which of Whitacre's three statements about fed funds futures is correct?

A. Statement 1

B. Statement 2

C. Statement 3

8. Which of Whitacre's two statements regarding bond futures arbitrage is correct?

A. Only Statement 4

B. Only Statement 5

C. Both Statement 4 and Statement 5

---

9. A US bond portfolio manager wants to hedge a long position in a 10-year Treasury bond against a potential rise in domestic interest rates. He would *most likely:*

A. sell fixed-income (bond) futures.

B. enter a receive-fixed 10-year interest rate swap.

C. sell a strip of 90-day Eurodollar futures contracts.

10. The CIO of a Canadian private equity company wants to lock in the interest on a three-month "bridge" loan his firm will take out in six months to complete an LBO deal. He sells the relevant interest rate futures contracts at 98.05. In six-months' time, he initiates the loan at 2.70% and unwinds the hedge at 97.30. The effective interest rate on the loan is:

A. 0.75%.

B. 1.95%.

C. 2.70%.

The following information relates to questions 11-13

Nisqually Uff is the portfolio manager for the Chehalis Fund (the Fund), which holds equities and bonds in its portfolio. Uff focuses on tactical portfolio strategies and uses derivatives to implement his strategies.

Uff has a positive short-term outlook for equities relative to bonds and decides to temporarily increase the beta of the portfolio's equity allocation from 0.9 to 1.2. He will use three-month equity index futures contracts to adjust the beta. Exhibit 1 displays selected data for the Fund's current equity allocation and the relevant futures contract.

Exhibit 1: Selected Data for the Fund's Current Equity Allocation and Futures Contract

Current value of the Fund's equity allocation	**€168,300,000**
Current portfolio beta	0.9
Target portfolio beta	1.2
Index futures contract value	€45,000
Beta of futures contract	1.0

11. Determine the appropriate number of equity index futures contracts that Uff should use to achieve the target portfolio beta. Identify whether the equity index futures contracts should be bought or sold.

12. One month later, Uff expects interest rates to rise. He decides to reduce the modified duration of the bond allocation of the Fund's portfolio without selling any of its existing bonds. To do so, Uff adds a negative-duration position by entering into an interest rate swap in which he pays the fixed rate and receives the floating rate. Exhibit 2 presents selected data for the Fund's bond allocation and the relevant swap contract.

Exhibit 2: Selected Data for the Fund's Bond Allocation and Swap Contract

Current value of the Fund's bond allocation	**€90,100,000**
Current portfolio average modified duration	7.8000
Target portfolio modified duration	5.0000
Swap modified duration for fixed-rate payer	–2.4848

Determine the required notional principal for the interest rate swap in order to achieve the target modified duration for the portfolio.

13. Six months later, Uff has since closed out both the equity index futures contract

position and the interest rate swap position. In response to market movements, he now wants to implement a tactical rebalancing of the Fund's portfolio. Exhibit 3 presents the current and target asset allocations for the Fund's portfolio.

Exhibit 3: Current and Target Asset Allocations for the Fund's Portfolio

Asset Class	Current	Target
Equities	€201,384,000 (69.56%)	€188,181,500 (65.0%)
Bonds	€88,126,000 (30.44%)	€101,328,500 (35.0%)
Total	**€289,510,000**	**€289,510,000**

Uff decides to use equity index and bond futures contracts to rebalance the portfolio. Exhibit 4 shows selected data on the Fund's portfolio and the relevant futures contracts.

Exhibit 4: Selected Data on Fund's Portfolio and Relevant Futures Contracts

Beta of the Fund's equities relative to index	1.28
Modified duration of the Fund's bonds	4.59
Equity index futures contract value	€35,000
Beta of equity index futures contract	1.00
Basis point value of cheapest-to-deliver (CTD) bond	€91.26
Conversion factor (CF) for CTD bond	0.733194

Determine how many equity index and bond futures contracts Uff should use to rebalance the Fund's portfolio to the target allocation. Identify whether the futures contracts should be bought or sold.

The following information relates to questions 14-15

Canawacta Tioga is the CFO for Wyalusing Corporation, a multinational manufacturing company based in Canada. One year ago, Wyalusing issued fixed-rate coupon bonds in Canada. Tioga now expects Canadian interest rates to fall and remain low for three years. During this three-year period, Tioga wants to use a par interest rate swap to effectively convert the fixed-rate bond coupon payments into floating-rate payments.

14. Explain how to construct the swap that Tioga wants to use with regard to the swap:

    i. tenor

    ii. cash flows

    iii. notional value

    iv. settlement dates

15. Wyalusing will soon be building a new manufacturing plant in the United States. To fund construction of the plant, the company will borrow in its home currency of CAD because of favorable interest rates. Tioga plans to use a cross-currency basis swap so that Wyalusing will borrow in CAD but make interest payments in USD.

    Describe how the swap will function, from the perspective of Wyalusing, in terms of the:

    i. cash flows at inception.

    ii. periodic cash flows.

    iii. cash flows at maturity.

---

16. A US institutional investor in search of yield decides to buy Italian government bonds for her portfolio but wants to hedge against the risk of exchange rate fluctuations. She enters a cross-currency basis swap, with the same payment dates as the bonds, where at inception she delivers US dollars in exchange for euros for use in purchasing the Italian bonds. The notional principals on the swap are *most likely* exchanged:

    A. at inception only.

    B. at maturity only.

    C. both at inception and at maturity.

17. Continuing from the previous question, assume demand for US dollars is strong relative to demand for euros, so there is a positive basis for "lending" US dollars. By hedging the position in Italian government bonds with the currency basis swap, the US investor will *most likely* increase the periodic net interest payments received from the swap counterparty in:

    A. euros only.

    B. US dollars only.

    C. both euros and US dollars.

The following information relates to questions 18-19

Southern Sloth Sanctuary (Sanctuary) is a charitable organization that cares for orphaned and injured sloths from the rain forest in the country of Lushland. The organization is supported by both domestic and international contributions. The Sanctuary's CFO typically invests any funds that are not immediately needed for short-term operational expenses into a domestic index fund that tracks the Lushland 100 stock index, which is denominated in Lushland dollars (LLD).

The Sanctuary just received a large contribution from a local benefactor in the amount of LLD1,000,000. These funds are not needed for short-term operational expenses. The CFO intends to equitize this excess cash position using futures contracts to replicate the return on the Lushland 100 stock index. Exhibit 1 shows selected data for the Lushland 100 Index futures contract.

Exhibit 1: Selected Data for Lushland 100 Index Futures Contract

Quoted price of futures contract	1,247
Contract multiplier	LLD 200
Contract beta	1.00

18. Determine the appropriate number of futures contracts that the CFO should buy to equitize the excess cash position.

19. A Japanese benefactor recently donated a plot of land in Japan to the Sanctuary. Ownership of the land has been transferred to the Sanctuary, which has a binding contract to sell the property for JPY500,000,000. The property sale will be completed in 30 days. The Sanctuary's CFO wants to hedge the risk of JPY depreciation using futures contracts. The CFO assumes a hedge ratio of 1.

    Describe a strategy to implement the CFO's desired hedge.

---

20. An equity portfolio manager is invested 100% in US large-cap stocks, but he wants to reduce the current allocation by 20%, to 80%, and allocate 20% to US small caps. He decides not to sell the stocks because of the high transaction costs. Rather, he will use S&P 500 Index futures and Russell 2000 Index futures for achieving the desired exposure in, respectively, US large caps and small caps. To achieve the new allocation, he will for an equivalent of 20% of the portfolio value:

    A. purchase Russell 2000 futures only.

    B. purchase Russell 2000 futures and sell S&P 500 futures.

    C. sell Russell 2000 futures and purchase S&P 500 futures.

21. A volatility trader observes that the VIX term structure is upward sloping. In particular, the VIX is at 13.50, the front-month futures contract trades at 14.10, and the second-month futures contract trades at 15.40. Assuming the shape of the VIX term structure will remain constant over the next three-month period, the trader decides to implement a trade that would profit from the VIX carry roll down. She will *most likely* purchase the:

    A. VIX and sell the VIX second-month futures.

    B. VIX and sell the VIX front-month futures.

    C. VIX front-month futures and sell the VIX second-month futures.

22. The CEO of a corporation owns 100 million shares of his company's stock, which is currently priced at €30 a share. Given the huge exposure of his personal wealth to this one company, he has decided to sell 10% of his position and invest the funds in a floating interest rate instrument. A derivatives dealer suggests that he do so using an equity swap.

    Explain how to structure such a swap.

23. A $30 million investment account of a bank trust fund is allocated one-third to stocks and two-thirds to bonds. The portfolio manager wants to change the overall allocation to 50% stock and 50% bonds and the allocation within the stock fund from 70% domestic stock and 30% foreign stock to 60% domestic and 40% foreign. The bond allocation will remain entirely invested in domestic corporate

issues.

Explain how swaps can be used to implement this adjustment. The market reference rate is assumed to be flat for all swaps, and you do not need to refer to specific stock and bond indexes.

24. Sarah Ko, a private wealth adviser in Singapore, is developing a short-term interest rate forecast for her private wealth clients who have holdings in the US fixed-income markets. Ko needs to understand current market expectations for possible upcoming central bank (i.e., US Federal Reserve Board) rate actions. The current price for the fed funds futures contract expiring after the next FOMC meeting is 97.175. The current federal funds rate target range is set between 2.50% and 2.75%.

    Explain how Ko can use this information to understand potential movements in the federal funds rate. Calculate the probability of an increase of 25 bps in the target range.

SOLUTIONS

1. B is correct. The portfolio manager's goal is to use the receive-fixed, pay-floating swap such that the €30 million of bonds, with modified duration of 3, and the €20 million swap will combine to make up a portfolio with a market value of €30 million and modified duration of 5. This relationship can be expressed as follows:

   $€30{,}000{,}000(3) + (N_S \times MDUR_S) = €30{,}000{,}000(5).$

   Given the swap's notional (N_S) of €20,000,000, its required modified duration can be obtained as:

   $MDUR_S = [(5 - 3)€30{,}000{,}000]/€20{,}000{,}000 = 3.$

2. B is correct. The basis point value of Portfolio A (BPV_P) is $130,342.94, and the basis point value of the cheapest-to-deliver bond (BPV_{CTD}) is $127.05 with a conversion factor of 0.72382. The basis point value hedge ratio ($BPVHR$), in the special case of complete hedging, provides the number of futures contracts needed, calculated as follows:

   $$BPVHR = \frac{-BPV_P}{BPV_{CTD}} \times CF = \frac{-\$130,342.94}{\$127.05} \times 0.72382 = -742.58$$

   Therefore, Whitacre should sell 743 Treasury bond futures to fully hedge Portfolio A.

   A is incorrect because it incorrectly uses the price of the cheapest-to-deliver bond (rather than its basis point value, BPV_{CTD}) in the denominator of the $BPVHR$ calculation:

   $$BPVHR = \frac{-BPV_P}{CTD\,Bond\,Price} \times CF = \frac{-\$130,342.94}{\$145.20} \times 0.72382 = -649.76$$

   C is incorrect because it does not include the conversion factor for the cheapest-to-deliver bond when calculating $BPVHR$:

   $$BPVHR = \frac{-BPV_P}{BPV_{CTD}} = \frac{-\$130,342.94}{\$127.05} = -1,025.92$$

3. A is correct. Monetize wants to reduce Portfolio A's modified duration to a target of 3.10. BPV_T is calculated as follows:

   $$BPV_T = MDUR_T \times 0.01\% \times MV_P$$

   $$BPV_T = (3.10) \times 0.0001 \times \$143,234,000 = \$44,402.54$$

   The basis point value of Portfolio A (BPV_P) is $130,342.94, and the basis point value of the cheapest-to-deliver bond (BPV_{CTD}) is $127.05 with a conversion factor of 0.72382. The basis point value hedge ratio ($BPVHR$), which provides the number of futures contracts needed, is then calculated as follows:

   $$BPVHR = \frac{BPV_T - BPV_P}{BPV_{CTD}} \times CF$$

   $$BPVHR = \frac{\$44,402.54 - \$130,342.94}{\$127.05} \times 0.72382 = -489.6134$$

   Thus, to decrease the modified duration of Portfolio A to 3.10, Whitacre should sell 490 Treasury bond futures contracts.

   B is incorrect because it incorrectly subtracts 6.00 from the modified duration (equal to 9.10 – 3.10, or the change in the modified duration for Portfolio A) of the cheapest-to-deliver bond, rather than from the modified duration of the bond portfolio, in computing BPV_T.

$$BPV_T = (8.75 - 6.00) \times 0.0001 \times \$143{,}234{,}000 = \$39{,}389.35$$

This error results in an incorrect calculation of *BPVHR*:

$$BPVHR = \frac{\$39{,}389.35 - \$130{,}342.94}{\$127.05} \times 0.72382 = -518.1741$$

C is incorrect because it does not include the conversion factor for the cheapest-to-deliver bond when calculating *BPVHR*:

$$BPVHR = \frac{\$44{,}402.54 - \$130{,}342.94}{\$127.05} = -676.4298$$

4. A is correct. The number of equity index futures contracts to purchase in order to equitize Monatize's excess cash position is calculated as follows:

$$N_f = \left(\frac{\beta_T}{\beta_f}\right)\left(\frac{S}{F}\right) = \left(\frac{1.00}{1.00}\right)\left(\frac{\$4{,}800{,}000}{\$825{,}000}\right) = 5.82, \text{ or } 6 \text{ contracts}$$

The actual futures contract purchase value of \$825,000 is the product of the quoted S&P 500 futures price of 3,300 and the designated multiplier of \$250 per index point.

B is incorrect because \$100,000,000, the total value of Portfolio B, is incorrectly used as the market value of the stock portfolio to equitize (*S*), instead of Portfolio B's excess cash position:

$$N_f = \left(\frac{\beta_T}{\beta_f}\right)\left(\frac{S}{F}\right) = \left(\frac{1.00}{1.00}\right)\left(\frac{\$100{,}000{,}000}{\$825{,}000}\right) = 121.21, \text{ or } 121 \text{ contracts}$$

C is incorrect because 3,300, the quoted S&P 500 futures price, is incorrectly used as the actual futures contract price, instead of calculating the actual futures contract price of \$825,000:

$$N_f = \left(\frac{\beta_T}{\beta_f}\right)\left(\frac{S}{F}\right) = \left(\frac{1.00}{1.00}\right)\left(\frac{\$4{,}800{,}000}{\$3{,}300}\right) = 1{,}454.54, \text{ or } 1{,}455 \text{ contracts}$$

5. C is correct. The first hedging strategy suggested by Regan is entering into a total return equity swap in exchange for a fee. Equity swaps, which are relatively illiquid contracts and are OTC derivative instruments in which each party bears counterparty risk, do not confer voting rights to the counterparty receiving the performance of the underlying. Under the terms of the total return equity swap, at pre-specified dates, the counterparties will net the index total return (increase/decrease plus dividends) against the fixed interest payment. If the index total return exceeds the fixed interest payment, Monatize will pay the counterparty the net payment. If the index total return is less than the fixed interest payment, then Monatize will receive the net payment from the counterparty.

A is incorrect because equity swaps are relatively illiquid contracts.

B is incorrect because equity swaps are OTC derivative instruments, and each counterparty in the equity swap bears the risk exposure to the other counterparty. For this reason, equity swaps are usually collateralized in order to reduce credit risk exposure.

6. A is correct. The gain on the variance swap is calculated as:

$$VarSwap_t = Variance\ Notional \times PV_t(T)$$
$$\times \left\{\frac{t}{T} \times \left[RealizedVol(0,t)\right]^2 + \frac{T-t}{T} \times \left[ImpliedVol(t,T)\right]^2 - Strike^2\right\}$$

Values for the inputs are as follows:

Volatility strike on existing swap = 15

Variance strike on existing swap = $15^2 = 225$

$$Variance\ Notional = \frac{Vega\ Notional}{2 \times Strike} = \frac{\$1,000,000}{2 \times 15} = \$33,333.33$$

$$\text{RealizedVol}(0,t)^2 = 20^2 = 400$$

$$\text{ImpliedVol}(t,T)^2 = 18^2 = 324$$

$t = 5$

$T = 12$

$$PV_t(T) = \frac{1}{1 + \left[1.50\% \left(\frac{7}{12}\right)\right]} = 0.991326,$$

which is the present value interest factor after five months (i.e., discounting for seven remaining months, from t to T), where the annual interest rate is 1.50%.

Thus, the value of the swap in five months is calculated as follows:

$$VarSwap_t = \$33,333.33 \times 0.991326 \times \left\{\frac{5}{12} \times 400 + \frac{12-5}{12} \times 324 - 225\right\}$$
$$= \$4,317,774.59$$

Given that Monatize would be long the swap, the mark-to-market value would be positive (i.e., a gain) for Monatize, equal to \$4,317,775.

B is incorrect because the value of the variance swap in five months incorrectly omits the present value interest factor of 0.991326.

The value of the swap in five months, incorrectly omitting the present value interest factor, is calculated as follows:

$$VarSwap_t = \$33,333.33 \times \left\{\frac{5}{12} \times 400 + \frac{12-5}{12} \times 324 - 225\right\} = \$4,355,555.56$$

C is incorrect because the values of $[RealizedVol(0,t)]^2$ and $[ImpliedVol(t,T)]^2$ are incorrectly switched.

The value of the swap in five months, incorrectly switching the values of $[RealizedVol(0,t)]^2$ and $[ImpliedVol(t,T)]^2$, is calculated as follows:

$$VarSwap_t = \$33,333.33 \times 0.991326 \times \left(\frac{5}{12} \times 324 + \frac{12-5}{12} \times 400 - 225\right)$$
$$= \$4,736,334.37$$

7. A is correct. Typical end-of-month (EOM) activity by large financial and banking institutions often induces “dips” in the effective federal funds (FFE) rate that create bias issues when using the rate as the basis for probability calculations of potential Federal Open Market Committee rate moves. If EOM activity increases the price for the relevant fed funds contract, the FFE rate would decline. A decline in the FFE rate would decrease the probability of a change in the fed funds rate. To overcome this EOM bias, data providers have implemented various methods of “smoothing” EOM dips.

   Statement 2 is incorrect because the probabilities inferred from the pricing of fed funds futures usually do not have strong predictive power, especially for the longer-term horizon.

   Statement 3 is incorrect because, to derive probabilities of Fed interest rate actions, market participants look at the pricing of fed funds futures, which are tied to the FFE rate—that is, the rate used in actual transactions between depository institutions, not the Fed’s target fed funds rate.

B is incorrect because the probabilities inferred from the pricing of fed funds futures usually do not have strong predictive power, especially for the longer-term horizon.

C is incorrect because, to derive probabilities of Fed interest rate actions, market participants look at the pricing of fed funds futures, which are tied to the FFE rate—that is, the rate that depository institutions actually use for lending to each other, not the Fed's target federal funds rate. The underlying assumption is that the implied futures market rates are predicting the value of the monthly average FFE rate.

8. A is correct. If the basis is positive, a trader would make a profit by "selling the basis"—that is, selling the bond and buying the futures. In contrast, when the basis is negative, the trader would make a profit by "buying the basis," in which the trader would purchase the bond and short the futures.

   B is incorrect because Statement 5 is incorrect. If the basis is negative, a trader would make a profit by "buying the basis"—that is, purchasing (not selling) the bond and shorting (not buying) the futures.

   C is incorrect because Statement 5 is incorrect. If the basis is negative, a trader would make a profit by "buying the basis"—that is, purchasing (not selling) the bond and shorting (not buying) the futures.

9. A is correct. The portfolio manager would *most likely* use a longer-dated fixed-income (bond) futures contract to hedge his interest rate risk exposure. The choice of the hedging instrument, in fact, will depend on the maturity of the bond being hedged. Interest rate futures, like 90-day Eurodollar futures, have a limited number of maturities and can be used to hedge short-term bonds. The mark-to-market value of a receive-fixed 10-year interest rate swap will become negative if interest rates rises, and thus the swap cannot be used as a hedge in this case.

10. B is correct. The CIO sells the relevant interest rate future contracts at 98.05. After six months, the CIO initiates the bridge loan at a rate of 2.70%, but he unwinds the hedge at the lower futures price of 97.30, thus gaining 75 bps (= 98.05 – 97.30). The effective interest rate on the loan is 1.95% (= 2.70% – 0.75%).

11. The number of equity index futures contracts required to achieve the target portfolio beta of 1.2 is calculated as follows:

$$N_f = \left(\frac{\beta_T - \beta_S}{\beta_f}\right)\left(\frac{S}{F}\right)$$

$$N_f = \left(\frac{1.2 - 0.9}{1.0}\right)\left(\frac{€168,300,000}{€45,000}\right)$$

$$N_f = 1,122$$

Because the number of futures contracts (N_f) is positive, Uff should buy 1,122 equity index futures contracts.

12. The swap notional principal required to achieve the target portfolio modified duration is calculated as follows:

$$N_S = \left(\frac{MDUR_T - MDUR_P}{MDUR_S}\right)(MV_P)$$

$$N_S = \left(\frac{5.0000 - 7.8000}{-2.4848}\right)(€90,100,000)$$

$$N_S = €101,529,298.13$$

Therefore, Uff should enter into the selected three-year par pay-fixed, receive-floating interest rate swap with a notional principal of approximately

€101,529,298.

13. Uff needs to reduce the equity allocation by €13,202,500 (= €201,384,000 – €188,181,500).

    The number of equity index futures contracts required to rebalance the Fund's portfolio to the target allocation is calculated as follows:

$$N_f = \left(\frac{\beta_T - \beta_S}{\beta_f}\right)\left(\frac{S}{F}\right)$$

    Uff needs to move to a notional "cash" position ($\beta_T = 0$) to reduce equity exposure, and the portfolio beta is $\beta_S = 1.28$. The beta of the equity index futures contract (β_f) is 1.00, so the number of equity index futures contracts required is calculated as follows:

$$N_f = \left(\frac{0.00 - 1.28}{1.00}\right)\left(\frac{€13,202,500}{€35,000}\right)$$
$$N_f = -482.83$$

    Because the number of futures contracts (N_f) is negative, Uff should sell 483 equity index futures contracts (after rounding).

    Uff needs to increase the bond allocation by €13,202,500 (= €101,328,500 – €88,126,000).

    The number of bond futures contracts required to rebalance the Fund's portfolio to the target allocation is calculated as follows:

$$BPVHR = \left(\frac{BPV_T - BPV_P}{BPV_{CTD}}\right) \times CF,$$

    where

$$BPV_T = MDUR_T \times 0.01\% \times MV_P$$
$$BPV_T = 4.59 \times 0.0001 \times €13,202,500$$
$$BPV_T = €6,059.95$$

    Now, starting with a notional "cash" position ($BPV_P = 0$) provided by the reduction in equity exposure above, and noting that BPV_{CTD} = €91.26 and CF = 0.733194, the number of bond futures contracts is calculated as follows:

$$BPVHR = \left(\frac{€6,059.95 - €0.00}{€91.26}\right) \times 0.733194$$
$$BPVHR = 48.69$$

    Because the BPVHR is positive, Uff should buy 49 bond futures contracts (after rounding).

14. Explain how to construct the swap that Tioga wants to use with regard to the swap:

    i. The swap tenor will be three years, consistent with the length of time for which Tioga expects interest rates to remain low.

    ii. Tioga will establish an interest rate swap in which Wyalusing will make payments based on a floating reference rate and will receive payments based on a fixed rate. The source of the reference rate and the value of the fixed rate will be set at the time of the swap's inception. The net effect for Wyalusing of the combination of making fixed payments on its coupon bond, receiving fixed payments on the swap, and making floating payments on the swap is to convert the fixed obligations of its bond coupon payments into floating-rate-based obligations. This scenario will allow Wyalusing to benefit if Tioga's expectation of low interest rates is realized.

iii. The notional value of the swap should be set such that the fixed payments that Wyalusing receives will equal the fixed coupon payments that Wyalusing must make on its fixed-rate bond obligations.

iv. Swap settlement dates should be set on the same days as the fixed-rate bond's coupon payment dates.

15. Describe how the swap will function, from the perspective of Wyalusing, in terms of the:

i. At inception, Wyalusing will pay the notional principal of CAD and will receive an amount of USD according to the USD/CAD exchange rate, agreed to at inception.

ii. At each swap payment date, Wyalusing will receive interest in CAD and will pay interest in USD. Both payments are based on floating reference rates for their respective currencies. The CAD rate will also include a basis rate that is quoted separately. On each settlement date, Wyalusing will receive an amount of CAD based on the CAD floating rate minus the basis rate applied to the swap notional value, and it will pay an amount of USD based on the USD floating rate and the USD/CAD exchange rate that was set at inception.

iii. At maturity, Wyalusing will receive the notional principal of CAD and will pay an amount of USD according to the USD/CAD exchange rate that was set at inception, applied to the CAD notional principal. The cash flows at maturity are the inverses of the cash flows at inception.

16. C is correct. In a cross-currency basis swap, the goals of the transaction are to achieve favorable funding and exchange rates and to swap the foreign currency amounts back to the currency of choice—in this case, the US dollar—at maturity. There is one exchange rate specified in the swap that is used to determine the notional principals in the two currencies, exchanged at inception and at maturity.

17. B is correct. By hedging the position in Italian government bonds with the cross-currency basis swap, the US investor will most likely increase the periodic net interest she receives in US dollars. The reason is that the periodic net interest payments made by the swap counterparty to the investor will include the positive basis resulting from the relatively strong demand for US dollars versus euros.

18. The Lushland 100 Index futures contract value is calculated as the quoted futures price multiplied by the designated contract multiplier:

$$F = 1{,}247 \times LLD200$$
$$F = LLD249{,}400$$

The target beta is the index beta, which equals 1.00. The number of Lushland 100 Index futures contracts that the Sanctuary must buy to equitize its excess cash position is calculated as follows:

$$N_f = \left(\frac{\beta_T}{\beta_f}\right)\left(\frac{S}{F}\right)$$
$$N_f = \left(\frac{1}{1}\right)\left(\frac{LLD1{,}000{,}000}{LLD249{,}400}\right)$$
$$N_f = 4.01 \text{ (rounded to 4)}$$

Therefore, the CFO should buy four Lushland 100 Index futures contracts to equitize the excess cash position.

19. The Sanctuary's CFO can use currency futures contracts to lock in the current LLD/JPY exchange rate. The CFO can hedge the Sanctuary's exchange rate risk by selling JPY futures contracts with the closest expiry to the expected future JPY inflow. When the futures contracts expire, the Sanctuary will receive (pay) any depreciation (appreciation) in JPY relative to LLD (when compared with the original LLD/JPY futures contract price). The CFO can determine the number of contracts needed by dividing the property's sale price of JPY500,000,000 by the JPY futures contract value. Because the hedge ratio is assumed to equal 1, the changes in futures and spot prices will be equal during the life of the futures contract, and so the hedge will be fully effective.

20. B is correct. To reduce the current allocation by 20%, to 80%, in US large-cap stocks, the portfolio manager will sell S&P 500 futures. At the same time, to allocate this 20% to US small caps, he will purchase Russell 2000 futures for the same notional amount.

21. C is correct. VIX futures converge to the spot VIX as expiration approaches, and the two must be equal at expiration. When the VIX futures curve is in contango and assuming volatility remains stable, the VIX futures will get "pulled" closer to the spot VIX, and they will decrease in price as they approach expiration. Traders calculate the difference between the front-month VIX futures price and the VIX as 0.60, and the spread between the front-month and the second-month futures is 1.30. Assuming that the spread declines linearly until settlement, the trader would realize roll-down gains as the spread decreases from 1.30 to 0.60 as the front-month futures approaches its expiration. At expiration, VIX futures are equal to the VIX, and the spread with the old second-month (and now the front-month) futures contract will be 0.60. Finally, since one cannot directly invest in the VIX, trades focusing on the VIX term structure must be implemented using either VIX futures or VIX options, so Answers A and B are not feasible.

22. The swap is structured such that the executive pays the return on 10 million shares of the company's stock, which is 10% of his holdings, and he receives the return based on a floating interest rate, such as the market reference rate, on a notional principal of €300 million (= €30/share × 10 million shares).

23. Currently the allocation is $10 million in stocks and $20 million in bonds. Within the stock category, the current allocation is $7 million domestic and $3 million foreign. The desired allocation is $15 million in stocks and $15 million in bonds. Thus, the allocation must change by moving $5 million into stocks and out of bonds. The desired stock allocation is $9 million domestic and $6 million foreign. The desired bond allocation is $15 million, all domestic corporate.

    To make the changes with swaps, the manager must enter into swaps against the market reference rate, which is assumed to be flat for all swaps in this example. Using the swaps, the bank trust fund portfolio manager needs to (1) receive the returns on $2 million based on a domestic equity index and on $3 million based on a foreign equity index and (2) pay the return on $5 million based on a domestic corporate bond index. The market reference rate outflows from the swaps in (1) and the inflows from the swap in (2) will cancel out through summation.

24. First, Ko knows that the FFE rate implied by the futures contract price of 97.175 is 2.825% (= 100 – 97.175). This is the rate that market participants expect to be the average federal funds rate for that month.

    Second, Ko should determine the probability of a rate change. She knows the 2.825% FFE rate implied by the futures signals a fairly high chance that the FOMC will increase rates by 25 bps from its current target range of 2.50%–2.75% to the new target range of 2.75%–3.00%. She calculates the probability of a rate hike as follows:

$$\frac{2.825\% - 2.625\%}{2.875\% - 2.625\%} = 0.80, \text{ or } 80\%$$

Ko can now incorporate this probability of a Fed rate hike into her forecast of short-term US interest rates.

LEARNING MODULE

3

Currency Management: An Introduction

by William A. Barker, PhD, CFA.

William A. Barker, PhD, CFA (Canada).

LEARNING OUTCOMES

Mastery	*The candidate should be able to:*
☐	analyze the effects of currency movements on portfolio risk and return
☐	discuss strategic choices in currency management
☐	formulate an appropriate currency management program given financial market conditions and portfolio objectives and constraints
☐	compare active currency trading strategies based on economic fundamentals, technical analysis, carry-trade, and volatility trading
☐	describe how changes in factors underlying active trading strategies affect tactical trading decisions
☐	describe how forward contracts and FX (foreign exchange) swaps are used to adjust hedge ratios
☐	describe trading strategies used to reduce hedging costs and modify the risk–return characteristics of a foreign currency portfolio
☐	describe the use of cross-hedges, macro-hedges, and minimum-variance-hedge ratios in portfolios exposed to multiple foreign currencies
☐	discuss challenges for managing emerging market currency exposures

INTRODUCTION 1

Globalization has been one of the most persistent themes in recent history, and this theme applies equally to the world of finance. New investment products, deregulation, worldwide financial system integration, and better communication and information networks have opened new global investment opportunities. At the same time, investors have increasingly shed their "home bias" and sought investment alternatives beyond their own borders.

The benefits of this trend for portfolio managers have been clear, both in terms of the broader availability of higher-expected-return investments as well as portfolio diversification opportunities. Nonetheless, investments denominated in foreign currencies also bring a unique set of challenges: measuring and managing foreign exchange risk. Buying foreign-currency denominated assets means bringing currency risk into the portfolio. Exchange rates are volatile and, at least in the short to medium term, can have a marked impact on investment returns and risks—*currency matters.* The key to the superior performance of global portfolios is the effective management of this currency risk.

This reading explores basic concepts and tools of currency management. Section 2 reviews some of the basic concepts of foreign exchange (FX) markets. The material in subsequent sections presumes an understanding of these concepts. Section 3 examines some of the basic mathematics involved in measuring the effects of foreign-currency investments on portfolio return and risk. Sections 4–6 discuss the *strategic* decisions portfolio managers face in setting the target currency exposures of the portfolio. The currency exposures that the portfolio can accept range from a fully hedged position to active management of currency risk. Sections 7–8 discuss some of the *tactical* considerations involving active currency management if the investment policy statement (IPS) extends some latitude for active currency management. A requisite to any active currency management is having a market view; so these sections includes various methodologies by which a manager can form directional views on future exchange rate movements and volatility. Sections 9–12 cover a variety of trading tools available to implement both hedging and active currency management strategies. Although the generic types of FX derivatives tools are relatively limited—spot, forward, option, and swap contracts—the number of variations within each and the number of combinations in which they can be used is vast. Section 13 examines some of the issues involved in managing the currency exposures of emerging market currencies—that is, those that are less liquid than the major currencies.

2 FOREIGN EXCHANGE CONCEPTS

We begin with a review of the basic trading tools of the foreign exchange market: spot, forward, FX swap, and currency option transactions. The concepts introduced in this section will be used extensively in our discussion of currency management techniques in subsequent sections.

Most people think only of spot transactions when they think of the foreign exchange market, but in fact the spot market accounts for less than 40% of the average daily turnover in currencies.[1] Although cross-border *business* may be transacted in the spot market (making and receiving foreign currency payments), the *risk management* of these flows takes place in FX derivatives markets (i.e., using forwards, FX swaps, and currency options). So does the hedging of foreign currency assets and liabilities. It is unusual for market participants to engage in any foreign currency transactions without also managing the currency risk they create. Spot transactions typically generate derivative transactions. As a result, understanding these FX derivatives markets, and their relation to the spot market, is critical for understanding the currency risk management issues examined in this reading.

1 2013 Triennial Survey, Bank for International Settlements (2013).

Spot Markets

In professional FX markets, exchange rate quotes are described in terms of the three-letter currency codes used to identify individual currencies. Exhibit 1 shows a list of some of the more common currency codes.

Exhibit 1: Currency Codes

USD	US dollar
EUR	Euro
GBP	British pound
JPY	Japanese yen
MXN	Mexican peso
CHF	Swiss franc
CAD	Canadian dollar
SEK	Swedish krona
AUD	Australian dollar
KRW	Korean won
NZD	New Zealand dollar
BRL	Brazilian real
RUB	Russian ruble
CNY	Chinese yuan
INR	Indian rupee
ZAR	South African rand

An exchange rate is the number of units of one currency (called the *price currency*) that one unit of another currency (called the *base currency*) will buy. For example, in the notation we will use a USD/EUR rate of 1.1650 which means that one euro buys \$1.1650; equivalently, the price of one euro is 1.1650 US dollars. Thus, the euro here is the base currency and the US dollar is the price currency. The exact notation used to represent exchange rates can vary widely between sources, and occasionally the same exchange rate notation will be used by different sources to mean completely different things. The reader should be aware that the notation used here may not be the same as that encountered elsewhere. To avoid confusion, this reading will identify exchange rates using the convention of "P/B," which refers to the price of one unit of the base currency "B" expressed in terms of the price currency "P."

How the professional FX market quotes exchange rates—which is the base currency, and which is the price currency, in any currency pair—is not arbitrary but follows conventions that are broadly agreed on throughout the market. Generally, there is a hierarchy as to which currency will be quoted as the base currency in any given P/B currency pair:

1. Currency pairs involving the EUR will use the EUR as the base currency (for example, GBP/EUR).
2. Currency pairs involving the GBP, other than those involving the EUR, will use the GBP as the base currency (for example, CHF/GBP).
3. Currency pairs involving either the AUD or NZD, other than those involving either the EUR or GBP, will use these currencies as the base currency (for example, USD/AUD and NZD/AUD). The market convention between these two currencies is for a NZD/AUD quote.

4. All other currency quotes involving the USD will use USD as the base currency (for example, MXN/USD).

Readers are encouraged to familiarize themselves with the quoting conventions used in the professional FX market because they are the currency quotes that will be experienced in practice. Exhibit 2 lists some of the most commonly traded currency pairs in global FX markets and their market-standard quoting conventions. These market-standard conventions will be used for the balance of this reading.

Exhibit 2: Select Market-Standard Currency Pair Quotes

Quote convention	Market name
USD/EUR	Euro-dollar
GBP/EUR	Euro-sterling
USD/GBP	Sterling-dollar
JPY/USD	Dollar-yen
USD/AUD	Aussie-dollar
CHF/USD	Dollar-Swiss
CAD/USD	Dollar-Canada
JPY/EUR	Euro-yen
CHF/EUR	Euro-Swiss
JPY/GBP	Sterling-yen

Another convention used in professional FX markets is that most spot currency quotes are priced out to four decimal places: for example, a typical USD/EUR quote would be 1.1500 and not 1.15. The price point at the fourth decimal place is commonly referred to as a "pip." Professional FX traders also refer to what is called the "big figure" or the "handle," which is the integer to the left side of the decimal place as well as the first two decimal places of the quote. For example, for a USD/EUR quote of 1.1568, 1.15 is the handle and there are 68 pips.

There are exceptions to this four decimal place rule. First, forward quotes—discussed later—will often be quoted out to five and sometimes six decimal places. Second, because of the relative magnitude of some currency values, some currency quotes will only be quoted out to two decimal places. For example, because it takes many Japanese yen to buy one US dollar, the typical spot quote for JPY/USD is priced out to only two decimal places (for example, 111.35 and not 111.3500).[2]

The spot exchange rate is usually for settlement on the second business day after the trade date, referred to as $T + 2$ settlement.[3] In foreign exchange markets—as in other financial markets—market participants confront a two-sided price in the form of a bid price and an offer price (also called an ask price) being quoted by potential counterparties. The **bid price** is the price, defined in terms of the price currency, at which the counterparty providing a two-sided price quote is willing to buy one unit of the **base** currency. Similarly, **offer price** is the price, in terms of the price currency, at which that counterparty is willing to sell one unit of the base currency. For example, given a price request from a client, a dealer might quote a two-sided price on the spot USD/EUR exchange rate of 1.1648/1.1652. This quote means that the dealer is willing to pay USD1.1648 to buy one euro (bid) and that the dealer will sell one euro

2 Many electronic dealing platforms in the FX market are moving to five decimal place pricing for spot quotes, using what are referred to as "deci-pips." In this case, for example, a USD/EUR spot quote might be shown as 1.37645. Spot quotes for JPY/USD on these systems will be given out to three decimal places.

3 The exception among the major currencies is CAD/USD, for which standard spot settlement is $T + 1$.

(offer) for USD1.1652. The market width, usually referred to as dealer's spread or the bid–offer spread, is the difference between the bid and the offer. When transacting on a dealer's bid-offer two-sided price quote, a client is said to either "hit the bid" (selling the base currency) or "pay the offer" (buying the base currency).

An easy check to see whether the bid or offer should be used for a specific transaction is that the party *asking* the dealer for a price should be on the more expensive side of the market. For example, if one wants to buy 1 EUR, 1.1652 is more USD per EUR than 1.1648. Hence, paying the offer involves paying more USD. Similarly, when selling 1 EUR, hitting the bid at 1.1648 means less USD received than 1.1652.

Forward Markets

Forward contracts are agreements to exchange one currency for another on a future date at an exchange rate agreed on today.[4] In contrast to spot rates, forward contracts are any exchange rate transactions that occur with settlement longer than the usual $T + 2$ settlement for spot delivery.

In professional FX markets, forward exchange rates are typically quoted in terms of "points." The points on a forward rate quote are simply the difference between the forward exchange rate quote and the spot exchange rate quote; that is, the forward premium or discount, with the points scaled so that they can be related to the last decimal place in the spot quote. Forward points are adjustments to the spot price of the base currency, using our standard price/base (P/B) currency notation.

This means that forward rate quotes in professional FX markets are typically shown as the bid–offer on the spot rate and the number of forward points at each maturity.[5] For illustration purposes, assume that the bid–offer for the spot and forward points for the USD/EUR exchange rate are as shown in Exhibit 3.

Exhibit 3: Sample Spot and Forward Quotes (Bid–Offer)

Maturity	Spot Rate or Forward Points
Spot (USD/EUR)	1.1649/1.651
One month	5.1/5.6
Three months	25.3/25.9
Six months	46.0/46.7
Twelve months	92.3/93.8

To convert any of these quoted forward points into a forward rate, one would divide the number of points by 10,000 (to scale down to the fourth decimal place, the last decimal place in the USD/EUR spot quote) and then add the result to the spot exchange rate quote.[6] But one must be careful about which side of the market (bid or offer) is being quoted. For example, suppose a market participant was *selling* the EUR forward against the USD. Given the USD/EUR quoting convention, the EUR is the base currency. This means the market participant must use the *bid* rates (i.e., the market participant will "hit the bid") given the USD/EUR quoting convention. Using the data in Exhibit 3, the three-month forward *bid* rate in this case would be based on the bid for both the spot and the forward points, and hence would be:

4 These are sometimes called outright forwards to distinguish them from FX swaps, which are discussed later.

5 Maturity is defined in terms of the time between spot settlement, usually $T + 2$, and the settlement of the forward contract.

6 Because the JPY/USD exchange rate is only quoted to two decimal places, forward points for the dollar/yen currency pair are divided by 100.

$$1.1649 + \left(\frac{25.3}{10,000}\right) = 1.16743$$

This result means that the market participant would be selling EUR three months forward at a price of USD1.1674 per EUR. Note that the quoted points are already scaled to each maturity—they are not annualized—so there is no need to adjust them.

Although there is no cash flow on a forward contract until settlement date, it is often useful to do a mark-to-market valuation on a forward position before then to (1) judge the effectiveness of a hedge based on forward contracts (i.e., by comparing the change in the mark-to-market of the underlying asset with the change in the mark-to-market of the forward), and (2) to measure the profitability of speculative currency positions at points before contract maturity.

As with other financial instruments, the mark-to-market value of forward contracts reflects the profit (or loss) that would be realized from closing out the position at current market prices. To close out a forward position, it must be offset with an equal and opposite forward position using the spot exchange rate and forward points available in the market when the offsetting position is created. When a forward contract is initiated, the forward rate is such that no cash changes hands (i.e., the mark-to-market value of the contract at initiation is zero). From that moment onward, however, the mark-to-market value of the forward contract will change as the spot exchange rate changes as well as when interest rates change in either of the two currencies.

Consider an example. Suppose that a market participant bought GBP10,000,000 for delivery against the AUD in six months at an "all-in" forward rate of 1.8600 AUD/GBP. (The all-in forward rate is simply the sum of the spot rate and the forward points, appropriately scaled to size.) Three months later, the market participant wants to close out this forward contract. To do that would require selling GBP10,000,000 three months forward using the AUD/GBP spot exchange rate and forward points in effect at that time. Assume the bid–offer for spot and forward points three months prior to the settlement date are as follows:

Spot rate (AUD/GBP)	1.8810/1.8815
Three-month points	−4/−2

To sell GBP (the base currency in the AUD/GBP quote) means calculating the *bid* side of the market. Hence, the appropriate all-in three-month forward rate to use is

$$1.8810 + -4/10,000 = 1.8806$$

Thus, the market participant originally bought GBP10,000,000 at an AUD/GBP rate of 1.8600 and subsequently sold them at a rate of 1.8806. These GBP amounts will net to zero at settlement date (GBP10 million both bought and sold), but the AUD amounts will not net to zero because the forward rate has changed. The AUD cash flow at settlement date will be equal to

$$(1.8806 - 1.8600) \times 10,000,000 = \text{AUD}206,000$$

This amount is a cash *inflow* because the market participant was long the GBP with the original forward position and the GBP subsequently appreciated (the AUD/GBP rate increased).

This cash flow is paid at settlement day, which is still three months away. To calculate the mark-to-market value on the dealer's position, this cash flow must be discounted to the present. The present value of this amount is found by discounting the settlement day cash flow by the three-month discount rate. Because it is an AUD amount, the three-month AUD discount rate is used, proxied by the market reference rate (MRR). The rate enters the equation in annualized terms, 0.10%, and the present value of this future AUD cash flow is

$$\frac{\text{AUD}206,000}{1 + 0.0010\left[\frac{90}{360}\right]} = \text{AUD}205,949$$

This is the mark-to-market value of the original long GBP10 million six-month forward contract when it is closed out three months prior to settlement.

To summarize, the process for marking-to-market a forward position is relatively straightforward:

1. Create an equal and offsetting forward position to the original forward position. (In the example earlier, the market participant is long GBP10 million forward, so the offsetting forward contract would be to sell GBP10 million.)
2. Determine the appropriate all-in forward rate for this new, offsetting forward position. If the base currency of the exchange rate quote is being sold (bought), then use the bid (offer) side of the market.
3. Calculate the cash flow at settlement day. This calculation will be based on the original contract size times the difference between the original forward rate and the rate calculated in Step 2. If the currency the market participant was originally long (short) subsequently appreciated (depreciated), then there will be a cash *inflow*. Otherwise, there will be a cash outflow. (In the earlier example, the market participant was long the GBP and it subsequently appreciated; this appreciation led to a cash inflow at the settlement day.)
4. Calculate the present value of this cash flow at the future settlement date. The currency of the cash flow and the discount rate must match. (In the example earlier, the cash flow at the settlement date is in AUD, so the market reference rate (MRR) is used to calculate the present value.)

Finally, we note that in the example, the mark-to-market value is given in AUD. It would be possible to translate this AUD amount into any other currency value using the current spot rate for the relevant currency pair. In the example above, this would be done by redenominating the mark-to-market in USD, by selling 206,000 AUD 90-days forward against the USD at the prevailing USD/AUD 90-day forward bid rate. This will produce a USD cash flow in 90 days. This USD amount can then be present-valued at the 90-day US rate to get the USD mark-to-market value of the AUD/GBP forward position. The day-count convention used here is an "actual/360" basis.

FX Swap Markets

An FX swap transaction consists of offsetting and simultaneous spot and forward transactions, in which the base currency is being bought (sold) spot and sold (bought) forward. These two transactions are often referred to as the "legs" of the swap. The two legs of the swap can either be of equal size (a "matched" swap) or one can be larger than the other (a "mismatched" swap). FX swaps are distinct from currency swaps. Similar to currency swaps, FX swaps involve an exchange of principal amounts in different currencies at swap initiation that is reversed at swap maturity. Unlike currency swaps, FX swaps have no interim interest payments and are nearly always of much shorter term than currency swaps.

FX swaps are important for managing currency risk because they are used to "roll" forward contracts forward as they mature. For example, consider the case of a trader who *bought* GBP1,000,000 one month forward against the CHF in order to set up a currency hedge. One month later, the forward contract will expire. To maintain this long position in the GBP against the CHF, two days prior to contract maturity, given $T + 2$ settlement, the trader must (1) sell GBP1,000,000 against the CHF spot, to settle the maturing forward contract; and (2) buy GBP1,000,000 against the CHF forward. That is, the trader is engaging in an FX swap (a matched swap in this case because the GBP currency amounts are equal).

If a trader wanted to adjust the size of the currency hedge (i.e., the size of the outstanding forward position), the forward leg of the FX swap can be of a different size than the spot transaction when the hedge is rolled. Continuing the previous example, if the trader wanted to increase the size of the long-GBP position by GBP500,000 as the outstanding forward contract expires, the transactions required would be to (1) sell GBP1,000,000 against the CHF spot, to settle the maturing forward contract; and (2) buy GBP1,500,000 against the CHF forward. This would be a mismatched swap.

The pricing of swaps will differ slightly depending on whether they are matched or mismatched swaps. If the amount of the base currency involved for the spot and forward legs of the swap are equal (a matched swap), then these are exactly offsetting transactions; one is a buy, the other a sell, and both are for the same amount. Because of this equality, a common *spot* exchange rate is typically applied to both legs of the swap transaction; it is standard practice to use the mid-market spot exchange rate for a matched swap transaction. However, the *forward* points will still be based on either the bid or offer, depending on whether the market participant is buying or selling the base currency forward. In the earlier example, the trader is *buying* the GBP (the base currency) forward and would hence pay the *offer* side of the market for forward points.

If the FX swap is mismatched, then pricing will need to reflect the difference in trade sizes between the two legs of the transaction. Continuing the example in which the trader increased the size of the long-GBP position by GBP500,000, this mismatched swap is equivalent to (1) a matched swap for a size of GBP1,000,000, and (2) an outright forward contract buying GBP500,000. Pricing for the mismatched swap must reflect this net GBP purchase amount. Because the matched swap would already price the forward points on the offer side of the market, typically this mismatched size adjustment would be reflected in the *spot* rate quoted as the base for the FX swap. Because a net amount of GBP is being *bought*, the spot quote would now be on the *offer* side of the CHF/GBP spot rate quote. (In addition, the trader would still pay the offer side of the market for the forward points.)

We will return to these topics later in the reading when discussing in more depth the use of forward contracts and FX swaps to adjust hedge ratios. (A **hedge ratio** is the ratio of the nominal value of the derivatives contract used as a hedge to the market value of the hedged asset.)

Currency Options

The final product type within FX markets is currency options. The market for currency options is, in many ways, similar to option markets for other asset classes, such as bonds and equities. As in other markets, the most common options in FX markets are call and put options, which are widely used for both risk management and speculative purposes. However, in addition to these vanilla options, the FX market is also characterized by active trading in exotic options. ("Exotic" options have a variety of features that make them exceptionally flexible risk management tools, compared with vanilla options.)

The risk management uses of both vanilla and exotic currency options will be examined in subsequent sections. Although daily turnover in FX options market is small in *relative* terms compared with the overall daily flow in global spot currency markets, because the overall currency market is so large, the *absolute* size of the FX options market is still very considerable.

CURRENCY RISK AND PORTFOLIO RISK AND RETURN

3

☐ analyze the effects of currency movements on portfolio risk and return

In this section, we examine the effect of currency movements on asset returns and portfolio risk. We then turn to how these effects help determine construction of a foreign asset portfolio.

Return Decomposition

In this section, we examine how international exposure affects a portfolio's return. A **domestic asset** is an asset that trades in the investor's **domestic currency** (or **home currency**). From a portfolio manager's perspective, the domestic currency is the one in which portfolio valuation and returns are reported. *Domestic* refers to a relation between the currency denomination of the asset and the investor; it is not an inherent property of either the asset or the currency. An example of a domestic asset is a USD-denominated bond portfolio from the perspective of a US-domiciled investor. The return on a domestic asset is not affected by exchange rate movements of the domestic currency.

Foreign assets are assets denominated in currencies other than the investor's home currency. An example of a foreign asset is a USD-denominated bond portfolio from the perspective of a eurozone-domiciled investor (and for whom the euro is the home currency). The return on a foreign asset will be affected by exchange rate movements in the home currency against the **foreign currency**. Continuing with our example, the return to the eurozone-domiciled investor will be affected by the USD return on the USD-denominated bond as well as movements in the exchange rate between the home currency and the foreign currency, the EUR and USD respectively.

The return of the foreign asset measured in foreign-currency terms is known as the **foreign-currency return**. Extending the example, if the value of the USD-denominated bond increased by 10%, measured in USD, that increase is the foreign-currency return to the eurozone-domiciled investor. The **domestic-currency return** on a foreign asset will reflect both the foreign-currency return on that asset as well as percentage movements in the spot exchange rate between the home and foreign currencies. The domestic-currency return is multiplicative with respect to these two factors:

$$R_{DC} = (1 + R_{FC})(1 + R_{FX}) - 1 \tag{1}$$

where R_{DC} is the domestic-currency return (in percent), R_{FC} is the foreign-currency return, and R_{FX} is the percentage change of the foreign currency against the domestic currency.

Returning to the example, the domestic-currency return for the eurozone-domiciled investor on the USD-denominated bond will reflect both the bond's USD-denominated return as well as movements in the exchange rate between the USD and the EUR. Suppose that the foreign-currency return on the USD-denominated bond is 10% and the USD appreciates by 5% against the EUR. In this case, the domestic-currency return to the eurozone investor will be:

$$(1 + 10\%)(1 + 5\%) - 1 = (1.10)(1.05) - 1 = 0.155 = 15.5\%$$

Although the concept is seemingly straightforward, the reader should be aware that Equation 1 hides a subtlety that must be recognized. The term R_{FX} is defined as the percentage change in the foreign currency against the domestic currency. However, this change is *not* always the same thing as the percentage change in the spot rate using market standard P/B quotes (for example, as shown in Exhibit 2). Specifically, it is not always the case that $R_{FX} = \%\Delta S_{P/B}$, where the term on the right side of the equal sign is defined in standard FX market convention (note that %Δ is percentage change).

In other words, R_{FX} is calculated as the change in the directly quoted exchange rate, where the domestic currency is defined as the investor's home currency. Because market quotes are not always in direct terms, analysts will need to convert to direct quotes before calculating percentage changes.

With this nuance in mind, what holds for the domestic-currency return of a single foreign asset also holds for the returns on a multi-currency portfolio of foreign assets, except now the portfolio weights must be considered. More generally, the domestic-currency return on a portfolio of multiple foreign assets will be equal to

$$R_{DC} = \sum_{i=1}^{n} \omega_i \left(1 + R_{FC,i}\right)\left(1 + R_{FX,i}\right) - 1 \quad (2)$$

where $R_{FC,i}$ is the foreign-currency return on the i-th foreign asset, $R_{FX,i}$ is the appreciation of the i-th foreign currency against the domestic currency, and ω_i are the portfolio weights of the foreign-currency assets (defined as the percentage of the aggregate domestic-currency value of the portfolio) and $\sum_{i=1}^{n} \omega_i = 1$. (Note that if short selling is allowed in the portfolio, some of the ω_i can be less than zero.) Again, it is important that the exchange rate notation in this expression (used to calculate $R_{FX,i}$) must be consistently defined with the domestic currency as the price currency.

Assume the following information for a portfolio held by an investor in India. Performance is measured in terms of the Indian rupee (INR) and the weights of the two assets in the portfolio, at the beginning of the period, are 80% for the GBP-denominated asset and 20% for the EUR-denominated asset, respectively. (Note that the portfolio weights are measured in terms of a common currency, the INR, which is the investor's domestic currency in this case.)

	One Year Ago	**Today***
INR/GBP spot rate	95.80	101.60
INR/EUR spot rate	86.95	86.45
GBP-denominated asset value, in GBP millions	43.80	50.70
EUR-denominated asset value, in EUR millions	14.08	12.17
GBP-denominated asset value, in INR millions	4,196.04	5,151.12
EUR-denominated asset value, in INR millions	1,224.26	1,052.10
GBP-denominated assets, portfolio weight (INR)	80%	
EUR-denominated assets, portfolio weight (INR)	20%	

* *Today's asset values are prior to rebalancing.*

The domestic-currency return (R_{DC}) is calculated as follows:

$$R_{DC} = 0.80(1 + R_{FC,GBP})(1 + R_{FX,GBP}) + 0.20(1 + R_{FC,EUR})(1 + R_{FX,EUR}) - 1$$

Note that given the exchange rate quoting convention, the INR is the price currency in the P/B quote for both currency pairs. Adding the data from the table leads to:

$$R_{DC} = 0.80\left(\frac{50.70}{43.80}\right)\left(\frac{101.60}{95.80}\right) + 0.20\left(\frac{12.17}{14.08}\right)\left(\frac{86.45}{86.95}\right) - 1$$

This solves to 0.154 or 15.4%.

To get the *expected* future return on a foreign-currency asset portfolio, based on Equation 2, the portfolio manager would need a market opinion for the expected price movement in each of the foreign assets ($R_{A,i}$) and exchange rates ($R_{FX,i}$) in the portfolio. There are typically correlations between all of these variables—correlations between the foreign asset price movements across countries, correlations between movements among various currency pairs, and correlations between exchange rate movements and foreign-currency asset returns. The portfolio manager would need to account for these correlations when forming expectations about future asset price and exchange rate movements.

Volatility Decomposition

Now we will turn to examining the effect of currency movements on the volatility of domestic-currency returns. Equation 1 can be rearranged as

$$R_{DC} = (1 + R_{FC})(1 + R_{FX}) - 1 = R_{FC} + R_{FX} + R_{FC}R_{FX}$$

When R_{FC} and R_{FX} are small, then the cross-term ($R_{FC}R_{FX}$) is small, and as a result this equation can be approximated as

$$R_{DC} \approx R_{FC} + R_{FX} \quad (3)$$

We return to the example in which the foreign-currency return on the USD-denominated bond was 10% and the USD appreciated by 5% against the EUR. In this example, the domestic-currency return for the Eurozone investor's holding in the USD-denominated bond was approximately equal to 10% + 5% = 15% (which is close to the exact value of 15.5%). We can combine the approximation of Equation 3 with the statistical rule that:

$$\sigma^2\left(\omega_x X + \omega_y Y\right) = \omega_x^2 \sigma^2(X) + \omega_y^2 \sigma^2(Y) + 2\omega_x \omega_y \sigma(X)\sigma(Y)\rho(X, Y) \quad (4)$$

where X and Y are random variables, ω are weights attached to X and Y, σ^2 is variance of a random variable, σ is the corresponding standard deviation, and ρ represents the correlation between two random variables. Applying this result to the domestic-currency return approximation of Equation 3 leads to:

$$\sigma^2(R_{DC}) \approx \sigma^2(R_{FC}) + \sigma^2(R_{FX}) + 2\sigma(R_{FC})\sigma(R_{FX})\rho(R_{FC},R_{FX}) \quad (5)$$

This equation is for the variance of the domestic-currency returns (R_{DC}), but risk is more typically defined in terms of standard deviation because mean and standard deviation are measured in the same units (percent, in this case). Hence, the total risk for domestic-currency returns—that is, $\sigma(R_{DC})$—is the square root of the results calculated in Equation 5.

Note as well that because Equation 5 is based on the addition of all three terms on the right side of the equal sign, exchange rate exposure will generally cause the variance of domestic-currency returns, $\sigma^2(R_{DC})$, to increase to more than that of the foreign-currency returns, $\sigma^2(R_{FC})$, considered on their own. That is, if there was no exchange rate risk, then it would be the case that $\sigma^2(R_{DC}) = \sigma^2(R_{FC})$. Using this as our base-case scenario, adding exchange rate risk exposure to the portfolio usually adds to domestic-currency return variance (the effect is indeterminate if exchange rate movements are negatively correlated with foreign asset returns).

These results on the variance of domestic-currency return can be generalized to a portfolio of foreign-currency assets. If we define the random variables X and Y in Equation 4 in terms of the domestic-currency return (R_{DC}) of two different foreign-currency investments, and the ω_i as portfolio weights that sum to one, then the result is the variance of the domestic-currency returns for the overall foreign asset portfolio:

$$\begin{aligned}&\sigma^2(\omega_1 R_1 + \omega_2 R_2)\\ &\approx \omega_1^2 \sigma^2(R_1) + \omega_2^2 \sigma^2(R_2) + 2\omega_1\omega_2\sigma(R_1)\sigma(R_2)\rho(R_1, R_2)\end{aligned} \quad (6)$$

where R_i is the domestic-currency return of the i-th foreign-currency asset. But as shown in Equation 3, the domestic-currency return of a foreign-currency asset (R_{DC}) is itself based on the sum of two random variables: R_{FC} and R_{FX}. This means that we would have to embed the variance expression shown in Equation 5 in *each* of the $\sigma^2(R_i)$ shown in Equation 6 to get the complete solution for the domestic-currency return variance of the overall portfolio. (We would also have to calculate the correlations between *all* of the R_i.) These requirements would lead to a very cumbersome mathematical expression for even a portfolio of only two foreign-currency assets; the expression would be far more complicated for a portfolio with many foreign currencies involved.

Thus, rather than attempt to give the complete mathematical formula for the variance of domestic-currency returns for a multi-currency portfolio, we will instead focus on the key intuition behind this expression. Namely, that the domestic-currency risk exposure of the overall portfolio—that is, $\sigma(R_{DC})$—will depend not only on the variances of *each* of the foreign-currency returns (R_{FC}) and exchange rate movements (R_{FX}) but also on how each of these *interacts* with the others. Generally speaking, negative correlations among these variables will help reduce the overall portfolio's risk through diversification effects.

Note as well that the overall portfolio's risk exposure will depend on the portfolio weights (ω_i) used. If short-selling is allowed in the portfolio, some of these ω_i can be negative as long as the total portfolio weights sum to one. So, for two foreign assets with a strong positive return correlation, short selling one can create considerable diversification benefits for the portfolio. (This approach is equivalent to trading movements in the price spread between these two assets.)

As before with the difference between realized and expected domestic-currency portfolio returns (R_{DC}), there is a difference between realized and expected domestic-currency portfolio risk, $\sigma(R_{DC})$. For Equation 6 to apply to the expected future volatility of the domestic-currency return of a multi-currency foreign asset portfolio, we would need to replace the observed, historical values of the variances and covariances in Equation 6 with their expected future values. This can be challenging, not only because it potentially involves a large number of variables but also because historical price patterns are not always a good guide to future price behavior. Variance and correlation measures are sensitive to the time period used to estimate them and can also vary over time. These variance and correlation measures can either drift randomly with time, or they can be subject to abrupt movements in times of market stress. It should also be clear that these observed, historical volatility and correlation measures need not be the same as the forward-looking *implied* volatility (and correlation) derived from option prices. Although sometimes various survey or consensus forecasts can be used, these too can be sensitive to sample size and composition and are not always available on a timely basis or with a consistent starting point. As with any forecast, they are also not necessarily an accurate guide to future developments; judgment must be used.

Hence, to calculate the expected future risk of the foreign asset portfolio, the portfolio manager would need a market opinion—however derived—on the variance of each of the foreign-currency asset returns (R_{FC}) over the investment horizon as well the variance of future exchange rate movements (R_{FX}) for each currency pair. The portfolio manager would also need a market opinion of how each of these future variables would interact with each other (i.e., their expected correlations). Historical price patterns can serve as a guide, and with computers and large databases, this modeling problem is daunting but not intractable. But the portfolio manager must always be mindful that historical risk patterns may not repeat going forward.

EXAMPLE 1

Portfolio Risk and Return Calculations

The following table shows current and future expected asset prices, measured in their domestic currencies, for both eurozone and Canadian assets (these can be considered "total return" indexes). The table also has the corresponding data for the CAD/EUR spot rate.

	Eurozone		Canada	
	Today	**Expected**	**Today**	**Expected**
Asset price	100.69	101.50	101.00	99.80
CAD/EUR	1.4500	1.4700		

1. What is the expected domestic-currency return for a eurozone investor holding the Canadian asset?

Solution:

For the eurozone investor, the R_{FC} = (99.80/101.00) − 1 = −1.19%. Note that, given we are considering the eurozone to be "domestic" for this investor and given the way the R_{FX} expression is defined, we will need to convert the CAD/EUR exchange rate quote so that the EUR is the *price* currency. This leads to R_{FX} = [(1/1.4700)/(1/1.4500)] − 1 = −1.364%. Hence, for the eurozone investor, R_{DC} = (1 − 1.19%)(1 − 1.364%) − 1 = −2.53%.

2. What is the expected domestic-currency return for a Canadian investor holding the eurozone asset?

Solution:

For the Canadian investor, the R_{FC} = (101.50/100.69) − 1 = +0.80%. Given that in the CAD/EUR quote the CAD is the price currency, for this investor the R_{FX} = (1.4700/1.4500) − 1 = +1.38%. Hence, for the Canadian investor the R_{DC} = (1 + 0.80%)(1 + 1.38%) − 1 = 2.19%.

3. From the perspective of the Canadian investor, assume that $\sigma(R_{FC})$ = 3% (the expected risk for the foreign-currency asset is 3%) and the $\sigma(R_{FX})$ = 2% (the expected risk of exchange rate movements is 2%). Furthermore, the expected correlation between movements in foreign-currency asset returns and movements in the CAD/EUR rate is +0.5. What is the expected risk of the domestic-currency return [$\sigma(R_{DC})$]?

Solution:

Because this is a single foreign-currency asset we are considering (not a portfolio of such assets), we can use Equation 5:

$$\sigma^2(R_{DC}) \approx \sigma^2(R_{FC}) + \sigma^2(R_{FX}) + 2\sigma(R_{FC})\sigma(R_{FX})\rho(R_{FC},R_{FX})$$

Inserting the relevant data leads to

$$\sigma^2(R_{DC}) \approx (3\%)^2 + (2\%)^2 + 2(3\%)(2\%)(0.50) = 0.0019$$

Taking the square root of this leads to $\sigma(R_{DC}) \approx 4.36\%$. (Note that the units in these expressions are all in percent, so in this case 3% is equivalent to 0.03 for calculation purposes.)

4 STRATEGIC DECISIONS IN CURRENCY MANAGEMENT

☐ discuss strategic choices in currency management

There are a variety of approaches to currency management, ranging from trying to avoid all currency risk in a portfolio to actively seeking foreign exchange risk in order to manage it and enhance portfolio returns.

There is no firm consensus—either among academics or practitioners—about the most effective way to manage currency risk. Some investment managers try to hedge all currency risk, some leave their portfolios unhedged, and others see currency risk as a potential source of incremental return to the portfolio and will actively trade foreign exchange. These widely varying management practices reflect a variety of factors including investment objectives, investment constraints, and beliefs about currency markets.

Concerning beliefs, one camp of thought holds that in the long run currency effects cancel out to zero as exchange rates revert to historical means or their fundamental values. Moreover, an efficient currency market is a zero-sum game (currency "A" cannot appreciate against currency "B" without currency "B" depreciating against currency "A"), so there should not be any long-run gains overall to speculating in currencies, especially after netting out management and transaction costs. Therefore, both currency hedging and actively trading currencies represent a cost to a portfolio with little prospect of consistently positive active returns.

At the other extreme, another camp of thought notes that currency movements can have a dramatic impact on short-run returns and return volatility and holds that there are pricing inefficiencies in currency markets. They note that much of the flow in currency markets is related to international trade or capital flows in which FX trading is being done on a need-to-do basis and these currency trades are just a spinoff of the other transactions. Moreover, some market participants are either not in the market on a purely profit-oriented basis (e.g., central banks, government agencies) or are believed to be "uninformed traders" (primarily retail accounts). Conversely, speculative capital seeking to arbitrage inefficiencies is finite. In short, marketplace diversity is believed to present the potential for "harvesting alpha" through active currency trading.

This ongoing debate does not make foreign-currency risk in portfolios go away; it still needs to managed, or at least, recognized. Ultimately, each portfolio manager or investment oversight committee will have to reach their own decisions about how to manage risk and whether to seek return enhancement through actively trading currency exposures.

Fortunately, there are a well-developed set of financial products and portfolio management techniques that help investors manage currency risk no matter what their individual objectives, views, and constraints. Indeed, the potential combinations of trading tools and strategies are almost infinite, and can shape currency exposures to custom-fit individual circumstance and market opinion. In this section, we explore various points on a spectrum reflecting currency exposure choices (a risk spectrum) and the guidance that portfolio managers use in making strategic decisions about where to locate their portfolios on this continuum. First, however, the implication of investment objectives and constraints as set forth in the investment policy statement must be recognized.

The Investment Policy Statement

The Investment Policy Statement (IPS) mandates the degree of discretionary currency management that will be allowed in the portfolio, how it will be benchmarked, and the limits on the type of trading polices and tools (e.g., such as leverage) than can be used.

The starting point for organizing the investment plan for any portfolio is the IPS, which is a statement that outlines the broad objectives and constraints of the beneficial owners of the assets. Most IPS specify many of the following points:

- the general objectives of the investment portfolio;
- the risk tolerance of the portfolio and its capacity for bearing risk;
- the time horizon over which the portfolio is to be invested;
- the ongoing income/liquidity needs (if any) of the portfolio; and
- the benchmark against which the portfolio will measure overall investment returns.

The IPS sets the guiding parameters within which more specific portfolio management policies are set, including the target asset mix; whether and to what extent leverage, short positions, and derivatives can be used; and how actively the portfolio will be allowed to trade its various risk exposures.

For most portfolios, currency management can be considered a sub-set of these more specific portfolio management policies within the IPS. The currency risk management policy will usually address such issues as the

- target proportion of currency exposure to be passively hedged;
- latitude for active currency management around this target;
- frequency of hedge rebalancing;
- currency hedge performance benchmark to be used; and
- hedging tools permitted (types of forward and option contracts, etc.).

Currency management should be conducted within these IPS-mandated parameters.

The Portfolio Optimization Problem

Having described the IPS as the guiding framework for currency management, we now examine the strategic choices that have to be made in deciding the benchmark currency exposures for the portfolio, and the degree of discretion that will be allowed around this benchmark. This process starts with a decision on the optimal foreign-currency asset and FX exposures.

Optimization of a multi-currency portfolio of foreign assets involves selecting portfolio weights that locate the portfolio on the efficient frontier of the trade-off between risk and expected return defined in terms of the investor's domestic currency. As a simplification of this process, consider the portfolio manager examining the expected return and risk of the multi-currency portfolio of foreign assets by using different combinations of portfolio weights (ω_i) that were shown in Equations 2 and 6, respectively, which are repeated here:

$$R_{DC} = \sum_{i=1}^{n} \omega_i \left(1 + R_{FC,i}\right)\left(1 + R_{FX,i}\right) - 1$$

$$\sigma^2\left(\omega_1 R_1 + \omega_2 R_2\right) \approx \omega_1^2 \sigma^2\left(R_1\right) + \omega_2^2 \sigma^2\left(R_2\right) + 2\omega_1 \sigma\left(R_1\right) \omega_2 \sigma\left(R_2\right) \rho\left(R_1, R_2\right)$$

Recall that the R_i in the equation for variance are the R_{DC} for each of the foreign-currency assets. Likewise, recall that the R_{FX} term is defined such that the investor's "domestic" currency is the price currency in the P/B exchange rate quote. In other words, this calculation may require using the algebraic reciprocal of the standard market quote convention. These two equations together show the domestic-currency return and risk for a multi-currency portfolio of foreign assets.

When deciding on an optimal investment position, these equations would be based on the *expected* returns and risks for each of the foreign-currency assets; and hence, including the *expected* returns and risks for each of the foreign-currency exposures. As we have seen earlier, the number of market parameters for which the portfolio manager would need to have a market opinion grows geometrically with the complexity (number of foreign-currency exposures) in the portfolio. That is, to calculate the expected efficient frontier, the portfolio manager must have a market opinion for *each* of the $R_{FC,i}$, $R_{FX,i}$, $\sigma(R_{FC,i})$, $\sigma(R_{FX,i})$, and $\rho(R_{FC,i}\ R_{FX,i})$, as well as for each of the $\rho(R_{FC,i}\ R_{FC,j})$ and $\rho(R_{FX,i}\ R_{FX,j})$. This would be a daunting task for even the most well-informed portfolio manager.

In a perfect world with complete (and costless) information, it would likely be optimal to *jointly* optimize all of the portfolio's exposures—over all currencies and all foreign-currency assets—simultaneously. In the real world, however, this can be a much more difficult task. Confronted with these difficulties, many portfolio managers handle asset allocation with currency risk as a two-step process: (1) portfolio optimization over fully hedged returns; and (2) selection of active currency exposure, if any. Derivative strategies can allow the various risk exposures in a portfolio to be "unbundled" from each other and managed separately. The same applies for currency risks. Because the use of derivatives allows the price risk ($R_{FC,i}$) and exchange rate risk ($R_{FX,j}$) of foreign-currency assets to be unbundled and managed separately, a starting point for the selection process of portfolio weights would be to assume a complete currency hedge. That is, the portfolio manager will choose the exposures to the foreign-currency assets first, and then decide on the appropriate currency exposures afterward (i.e., decide whether to relax the full currency hedge). These decisions are made to simplify the portfolio construction process.

If the currency exposures of foreign assets could be perfectly and costlessly hedged, the hedge would completely neutralize the effect of currency movements on the portfolio's domestic-currency return (R_{DC}).[7] In Equation 2, this would set R_{FX} = 0, meaning that the domestic-currency return is then equal to the foreign-currency return ($R_{DC} = R_{FC}$). In Equation 5, this would set $\sigma^2(R_{DC}) = \sigma^2(R_{FC})$, meaning that the domestic-currency return risk is equal to the foreign-currency return risk.

Removing the currency effects leads to a simpler, two-step process for portfolio optimization. First the portfolio manager could pick the set of portfolio weights (ω_i) for the foreign-currency assets that optimize the expected foreign-currency asset risk–return trade-off (assuming there is no currency risk). Then the portfolio manager could choose the desired currency exposures for the portfolio and decide whether and by how far to relax the constraint to a full currency hedge for each currency pair.

Choice of Currency Exposures

A natural starting point for the strategic decisions is the "currency-neutral" portfolio resulting from the two-step process described earlier. The question then becomes, How far along the risk spectrum between being fully hedged and actively trading currencies should the portfolio be positioned?

7 A "costless" hedge in this sense would not only mean zero transaction costs, but also no "roll yield."

Diversification Considerations

The time horizon of the IPS is important. Many investment practitioners believe that in the long run, adding unhedged foreign-currency exposure to a portfolio does not affect expected long-run portfolio returns; hence in the long run, it would not matter if the portfolio was hedged. (Indeed, portfolio management costs would be reduced without a hedging process.) This belief is based on the view that in the long run, currencies "mean revert" to either some fair value equilibrium level or a historical average; that is, that the *expected* $\%\Delta S = 0$ for a sufficiently long time period. This view typically draws on the expectation that purchasing power parity (PPP) and the other international parity conditions that link movements in exchange rates, interest rates, and inflation rates will eventually hold over the long run.

Supporting this view, some studies argue that in the long-run currencies will in fact mean revert, and hence that currency risk is lower in the long run than in the short run (an early example is Froot 1993). Although much depends on how long run is defined, an investor (IPS) with a very long investment horizon and few immediate liquidity needs—which could potentially require the liquidation of foreign-currency assets at disadvantageous exchange rates—might choose to forgo currency hedging and its associated costs. Logically, this would require a portfolio benchmark index that is also unhedged against currency risk.

Although the international parity conditions may hold in the long run, it can be a *very* long time—possibly decades. Indeed, currencies can continue to drift away from the fair value mean reversion level for much longer than the time period used to judge portfolio performance. Such time periods are also typically longer than the patience of the portfolio manager's oversight committee when portfolio performance is lagging the benchmark. If this very long-run view perspective is not the case, then the IPS will likely impose some form of currency hedging.

Diversification considerations will also depend on the *asset composition* of the foreign-currency asset portfolio. The reason is because the foreign-currency asset returns (R_{FC}) of different asset classes have different correlation patterns with foreign-currency returns (R_{FX}). If there is a negative correlation between these two sets of returns, having at least some currency exposure may help portfolio diversification and moderate the domestic-currency return risk, $\sigma(R_{DC})$. (Refer to Equation 5 in Section 3.)

It is often asserted that the correlation between foreign-currency returns and foreign-currency asset returns tends to be greater for fixed-income portfolios than for equity portfolios. This assertion makes intuitive sense: both bonds and currencies react strongly to movements in interest rates, whereas equities respond more to expected earnings. As a result, the implication is that currency exposures provide little diversification benefit to fixed-income portfolios and that the currency risk should be hedged. In contrast, a better argument can be made for carrying currency exposures in global equity portfolios.

To some degree, various studies have corroborated this relative advantage to currency hedging for fixed income portfolios. But the evidence seems somewhat mixed and depends on which markets are involved. One study found that the hedging advantage for fixed-income portfolios is not always large or consistent (Darnell 2004). Other studies (Campbell 2010; Martini 2010) found that the optimal hedge ratio for foreign-currency equity portfolios depended critically on the investor's domestic currency. (Recall that the hedge ratio is defined as the ratio of the nominal value of the hedge to the market value of the underlying.) For some currencies, there was no risk-reduction advantage to hedging foreign equities (the optimal hedge ratio was close to 0%), whereas for other currencies, the optimal hedge ratio for foreign equities was close to 100%.

Other studies indicate that the optimal hedge ratio also seems to depend on *market conditions* and longer-term trends in currency pairs. For example, Campbell, Serfaty-de Medeiros, and Viceira (2007) found that there were no diversification benefits from currency exposures in foreign-currency bond portfolios, and hence to minimize the risk to domestic-currency returns these positions should be fully hedged. The authors also found, however, that during the time of their study (their data spanned 1975 to 2005), the US dollar seemed to be an exception in terms of its correlations with foreign-currency asset returns. Their study found that the US dollar tended to appreciate against foreign currencies when global bond prices fell (for example, in times of global financial stress there is a tendency for investors to shift investments into the perceived safety of reserve currencies). This finding would suggest that keeping some exposure to the US dollar in a global bond portfolio would be beneficial. For non-US investors, this would mean under-hedging the currency exposure to the USD (i.e., a hedge ratio less than 100%), whereas for US investors it would mean over-hedging their foreign-currency exposures back into the USD. Note that some currencies—the USD, JPY, and CHF in particular—seem to act as a safe haven and appreciate in times of market stress. Keeping some of these currency exposures in the portfolio—having hedge ratios that are not set at 100%--can help hedge losses on riskier assets, especially for foreign currency equity portfolios (which are more risk exposed than bond portfolios).

Given this diversity of opinions and empirical findings, it is not surprising to see actual hedge ratios vary widely in practice among different investors. Nonetheless, it is still more likely to see currency hedging for fixed-income portfolios rather than equity portfolios, although actual hedge ratios will often vary between individual managers.

Cost Considerations

The costs of currency hedging also guide the strategic positioning of the portfolio. Currency hedges are not a "free good" and they come with a variety of expenses that must be borne by the overall portfolio. Optimal hedging decisions will need to balance the benefits of hedging against these costs.

Hedging costs come mainly in two forms: trading costs and opportunity costs. The most immediate costs of hedging involve trading expenses, and these come in several forms:

- Trading involves dealing on the bid–offer spread offered by banks. Their profit margin is based on these spreads, and the more the client trades and "pays away the spread," the more profit is generated by the dealer. Maintaining a 100% hedge and rebalancing frequently with every minor change in market conditions would be expensive. Although the bid–offer spreads on many FX-related products (especially the spot exchange rate) are quite narrow, "churning" the hedge portfolio would progressively add to hedging costs and detract from the hedge's benefits.
- Some hedges involve currency options; a long position in currency options requires the payment of up-front premiums. If the options expire out of the money (OTM), this cost is unrecoverable.
- Although forward contracts do not require the payment of up-front premiums, they do eventually mature and have to be "rolled" forward with an FX swap transaction to maintain the hedge. Rolling hedges will typically generate cash inflows or outflows. These cash flows will have to be monitored, and as necessary, cash will have to be raised to settle hedging transactions. In other words, even though the currency hedge may *reduce* the volatility of the domestic mark-to-market value of the foreign-currency asset portfolio, it will typically *increase* the volatility in the organization's cash accounts.

Managing these cash flow costs can accumulate to become a significant portion of the portfolio's value, and they become more expensive (for cash outflows) the higher interest rates go.

- One of the most important trading costs is the need to maintain an administrative infrastructure for trading. Front-, middle-, and back-office operations will have to be set up, staffed with trained personnel, and provided with specialized technology systems. Settlement of foreign exchange transactions in a variety of currencies means having to maintain cash accounts in these currencies to make and receive these foreign-currency payments. Together all of these various overhead costs can form a significant portion of the overall costs of currency trading.

A second form of costs associated with hedging are the opportunity cost of the hedge. To be 100% hedged is to forgo any possibility of favorable currency rate moves. If skillfully handled, accepting and managing currency risk—or any financial risk—can potentially add value to the portfolio, even net of management fees. (We discuss the methods by which this might be done in Sections 7–8.)

These opportunity costs lead to another motivation for having a strategic hedge ratio of less than 100%: regret minimization. Although it is not possible to accurately predict foreign exchange movements in advance, it is certainly possible to judge after the fact the results of the decision to hedge or not. Missing out on an advantageous currency movement because of a currency hedge can cause *ex post* regret in the portfolio manager or client; so too can having a foreign-currency loss if the foreign-currency asset position was unhedged. Confronted with this *ex ante* dilemma of whether to hedge, many portfolio managers decide simply to "split the difference" and have a 50% hedge ratio (or some other rule-of-thumb number). Both survey evidence and anecdotal evidence show that there is a wide variety of hedge ratios actually used in practice by managers, and that these variations cannot be explained by more "fundamental" factors alone. Instead, many managers appear to incorporate some degree of regret minimization into hedging decisions (for example, see Michenaud and Solnik 2008).

All of these various hedging expenses—both trading and opportunity costs—will need to be managed. Hedging is a form of insurance against risk, and in purchasing any form of insurance the buyer matches their needs and budgets with the policy selected. For example, although it may be possible to buy an insurance policy with full, unlimited coverage, a zero deductible, and no co-pay arrangements, such a policy would likely be prohibitively expensive. Most insurance buyers decide that it is not necessary to insure against every outcome, no matter how minor. Some minor risks can be accepted and "self-insured" through the deductible; some major risks may be considered so unlikely that they are not seen as worth paying the extra premium. (For example, most ordinary people would likely not consider buying insurance against being kidnapped.)

These same principles apply to currency hedging. The portfolio manager (and IPS) would likely not try to hedge every minor, daily change in exchange rates or asset values, but only the larger adverse movements that can materially affect the overall domestic-currency returns (R_{DC}) of the foreign-currency asset portfolio. The portfolio manager will need to balance the benefits and costs of hedging in determining both strategic positioning of the portfolio as well as any latitude for active currency management. However, around whatever strategic positioning decision taken by the IPS in terms of the benchmark level of currency exposure, hedging cost considerations alone will often dictate a *range* of permissible exposures instead of a single point. (This discretionary range is similar to the deductible in an insurance policy.)

5 SPECTRUM OF CURRENCY RISK MANAGEMENT STRATEGIES

- [ ] discuss strategic choices in currency management

The strategic decisions encoded in the IPS with regard to the trade-off between the benefits and costs of hedging, as well as the potential for incremental return to the portfolio from active currency management, are the foundation for determining specific currency management strategies. These strategies are arrayed along a spectrum from very risk-averse passive hedging, to actively seeking out currency risk in order to manage it for profit. We examine each in turn.

Passive Hedging

In this approach, the goal is to keep the portfolio's currency exposures close, if not equal to, those of a benchmark portfolio used to evaluate performance. Note that the benchmark portfolio often has no foreign exchange exposure, particularly for fixed-income assets; the benchmark index is a "local currency" index based only on the foreign-currency asset return (R_{FC}). However, benchmark indexes that have some foreign exchange risk are also possible.

Passive hedging is a rules-based approach that removes almost all discretion from the portfolio manager, regardless of the manager's market opinion on future movements in exchange rates or other financial prices. In this case, the manager's job is to keep portfolio exposures as close to "neutral" as possible and to minimize tracking errors against the benchmark portfolio's performance. This approach reflects the belief that currency exposures that differ from the benchmark portfolio inject risk (return volatility) into the portfolio without any sufficiently compensatory return. Active currency management—taking positional views on future exchange rate movements—is viewed as being incapable of consistently adding incremental return to the portfolio.

But the hedge ratio has a tendency to "drift" with changes in market conditions, and even passive hedges need periodic rebalancing to realign them with investment objectives. Often the management guidance given to the portfolio manager will specify the rebalancing period—for example, monthly. There may also be allowance for intra-period rebalancing if there have been large exchange rate movements.

Discretionary Hedging

This approach is similar to passive hedging in that there is a "neutral" benchmark portfolio against which actual portfolio performance will be measured. However, in contrast to a strictly rules-based approach, the portfolio manager now has some limited discretion on how far to allow actual portfolio risk exposures to vary from the neutral position. Usually this discretion is defined in terms of percentage of foreign-currency market value (the portfolio's currency exposures are allowed to vary plus or minus x% from the benchmark). For example, a eurozone-domiciled investor may have a US Treasury bond portfolio with a mandate to keep the hedge ratio within 95% to 105%. Assuming no change in the foreign-currency return (R_{FC}), but allowing exchange rates (R_{FX}) to vary, this means the portfolio can tolerate exchange rate movements between the EUR and USD of up to 5% before the exchange rate exposures in the portfolio are considered excessive. The manager is allowed to manage currency exposures within these limits without being considered in violation of the IPS.

This discretion allows the portfolio manager at least some limited ability to express directional opinions about future currency movements—to accept risk in an attempt to earn reward—in order to add value to the portfolio performance. Of course, the portfolio manager's actual performance will be compared with that of the benchmark portfolio.

Active Currency Management

Further along the spectrum between extreme risk aversion and purely speculative trading is active currency management. In principle, this approach is really just an extension of discretionary hedging: the portfolio manager is allowed to express directional opinions on exchange rates, but is nonetheless kept within mandated risk limits. The performance of the manager—the choices of risk exposures assumed—is benchmarked against a "neutral" portfolio. But for all forms of active management (i.e., having the discretion to express directional market views), there is no allowance for unlimited speculation; there are risk management systems in place for even the most speculative investment vehicles, such as hedge funds. These controls are designed to prevent traders from taking unusually large currency exposures and risking the solvency of the firm or fund.

In many cases, the difference between discretionary hedging and active currency management is one of emphasis more than degree. The primary duty of the discretionary hedger is to protect the portfolio from currency risk. As a secondary goal, within limited bounds, there is some scope for directional opinion in an attempt to enhance overall portfolio returns. If the manager lacks any firm market conviction, the natural neutral position for the discretionary hedger is to be flat—that is, to have no meaningful currency exposures. In contrast, the active currency manager is supposed to take currency risks and manage them for profit. The primary goal is to add alpha to the portfolio through successful trading. Leaving actual portfolio exposures near zero for extended periods is typically not a viable option.

Currency Overlay

Active management of currency exposures can extend beyond limited managerial discretion within hedging boundaries. Sometimes accepting and managing currency risk for profit can be considered a portfolio objective. Active currency management is often associated with what are called **currency overlay programs**, although this term is used differently by different sources.

- In the most limited sense of the term, currency overlay simply means that the portfolio manager has outsourced managing currency exposures to a firm specializing in FX management. This could imply something as limited as merely having the external party implement a fully passive approach to currency hedges. If dealing with FX markets and managing currency hedges is beyond the professional competence of the investment manager, whose focus is on managing foreign equities or some other asset class, then hiring such external professional help is an option. Note that typically currency overlay programs involve external managers. However, some large, sophisticated institutional investors may have in-house currency overlay programs managed by a separate group of specialists within the firm.
- A broader view of currency overlay allows the externally hired currency overlay manager to take directional views on future currency movements (again, with the caveat that these be kept within predefined bounds). Sometimes a distinction is made between currency overlay and "foreign exchange as an asset class." In this classification, currency overlay is limited

to the currency exposures already in the foreign asset portfolio. For example, if a eurozone-domiciled investor has GBP- and CHF-denominated assets, currency overlay risks are allowed only for these currencies.

- In contrast, the concept of foreign exchange as an asset class does not restrict the currency overlay manager, who is free to take FX exposures in any currency pair where there is value-added to be harvested, regardless of the underlying portfolio. In this sense, the currency overlay manager is very similar to an FX-based hedge fund. To implement this form of active currency management, the currency overlay manager would have a *joint* opinion on a range of currencies, and have market views not only on the expected movements in the spot rates but also the likelihood of these movements (the variance of the expected future spot rate distribution) as well as the expected correlation between future spot rate movements. Basically, the entire portfolio of currencies is actively managed and optimized over all of the expected returns, risks, and correlations among all of the currencies in the portfolio.

We will focus on this latter form of currency overlay in this reading: active currency management conducted by external, FX-specialized sub-advisors to the portfolio.

It is quite possible to have the foreign-currency asset portfolio fully hedged (or allow some discretionary hedging internally) but then also to add an external currency overlay manager to the portfolio. This approach separates the hedging and alpha function mandates of the portfolio. Different organizations have different areas of expertise; it often makes sense to allocate managing the hedge (currency "beta") and managing the active FX exposures (currency "alpha") to those individuals with a comparative advantage in that function.

Adding this form of currency overlay to the portfolio (FX as an asset class) is similar in principle to adding any type of alternative asset class, such as private equity funds or farmland. In each case, the goal is the search for alpha. But to be most effective in adding value to the portfolio, the currency overlay program should add incremental returns (alpha) and/or greater diversification opportunities to improve the portfolio's risk–return profile. To do this, the currency alpha mandate should have minimum correlation with both the major asset classes and the other alpha sources in the portfolio.

Once this FX as an asset class approach is taken, it is not necessary to restrict the portfolio to a single overlay manager any more than it is necessary to restrict the portfolio to a single private equity fund. Different overlay managers follow different strategies (these are described in more detail in Sections 7–8). Within the overall portfolio allocation to "currency as an alternative asset class", it may be beneficial to diversify across a range of active management styles, either by engaging several currency overlay managers with different styles or by applying a fund-of-funds approach, in which the hiring and management of individual currency overlay managers is delegated to a specialized external investment vehicle.

Whether managed internally or externally (via a fund of funds) it will be necessary to monitor, or benchmark, the performance of the currency overlay manager: Do they generate the returns expected from their stated trading strategy? Many major investment banks as well as specialized market-information firms provide a wide range of proprietary indexes that track the performance of the investible universe of currency overlay managers; sometimes they also offer sub-indexes that focus on specific trading strategies (for example, currency positioning based on macroeconomic fundamentals). However, the methodologies used to calculate these various indexes vary between suppliers. In addition, different indexes show different aspects of active currency management. Given these differences between indexes, there is no simple answer for which index is most suitable as a benchmark; much depends on the specifics of the active currency strategy.

EXAMPLE 2

Currency Overlay

Windhoek Capital Management is a South Africa-based investment manager that runs the Conservative Value Fund, which has a mandate to avoid all currency risk in the portfolio. The firm is considering engaging a currency overlay manager to help with managing the foreign exchange exposures of this investment vehicle. Windhoek does not consider itself to have the in-house expertise to manage FX risk.

Brixworth & St. Ives Asset Management is a UK-based investment manager, and runs the Aggressive Growth Fund. This fund is heavily weighted toward emerging market equities, but also has a mandate to seek out inefficiencies in the global foreign exchange market and exploit these for profit. Although Brixworth & St. Ives manages the currency hedges for all of its investment funds in-house, it is also considering engaging a currency overlay manager.

1. Using a currency overlay manager for the Conservative Value Fund is *most likely* to involve:

   A. joining the alpha and hedging mandates.

   B. a more active approach to managing currency risks.

   C. using this manager to passively hedge their foreign exchange exposures.

Solution:

C is correct. The Conservative Value Fund wants to avoid all currency exposures in the portfolio and Windhoek believes that it lacks the currency management expertise to do this.

2. Using a currency overlay manager for the Aggressive Growth Fund is *most likely* to involve:

   A. separating the alpha and hedging mandates.

   B. a less discretionary approach to managing currency hedges.

   C. an IPS that limits active management to emerging market currencies.

Solution:

A is correct. Brixworth & St. Ives already does the FX hedging in house, so a currency overlay is more likely to be a pure alpha mandate. This should not change the way that Brixworth & St. Ives manages its hedges, and the fund's mandate to seek out inefficiencies in the global FX market is unlikely to lead to a restriction to actively manage only emerging market currencies.

3. Brixworth & St. Ives is *more likely* to engage multiple currency overlay managers if:

   A. their returns are correlated with asset returns in the fund.

   B. the currency managers' returns are correlated with each other.

   C. the currency managers' use different active management strategies.

Solution:

C is correct. Different active management strategies may lead to a more diversified source of alpha generation, and hence reduced portfolio risk. Choices A and B are incorrect because a higher correlation with foreign-currency assets in the portfolio or among overlay manager returns is likely to lead to less diversification.

6 FORMULATING A CURRENCY MANAGEMENT PROGRAM

☐ formulate an appropriate currency management program given financial market conditions and portfolio objectives and constraints

We now try to bring all of these previous considerations together in describing how to formulate an appropriate currency management program given client objectives and constraints, as well as overall financial market conditions. Generally speaking, the *strategic* currency positioning of the portfolio, as encoded in the IPS, should be biased toward a more-fully hedged currency management program the more

- short term the investment objectives of the portfolio;
- risk averse the beneficial owners of the portfolio are (and impervious to *ex post* regret over missed opportunities);
- immediate the income and/or liquidity needs of the portfolio;
- fixed-income assets are held in a foreign-currency portfolio;
- cheaply a hedging program can be implemented;
- volatile (i.e., risky) financial markets are;[8] and
- skeptical the beneficial owners and/or management oversight committee are of the expected benefits of active currency management.

The relaxation of any of these conditions creates latitude to allow a more proactive currency risk posture in the portfolio, either through wider tolerance bands for discretionary hedging, or by introducing foreign currencies as a separate asset class (using currency overlay programs as an alternative asset class in the overall portfolio). In the latter case, the more currency overlay is expected to generate alpha that is uncorrelated with other asset or alpha-generation programs in the portfolio, the more it is likely to be allowed in terms of strategic portfolio positioning.

INVESTMENT POLICY STATEMENT

Kailua Kona Advisors runs a Hawaii-based hedge fund that focuses on developed market equities located outside of North America. Its investor base consists of local high-net-worth individuals who are all considered to have a long investment horizon, a high tolerance for risk, and no immediate income needs. In its prospectus to investors, Kailua Kona indicates that it actively manages both the fund's equity and foreign-currency exposures, and that the fund uses leverage through the use of loans as well as short-selling.

Exhibit 4 presents the hedge fund's currency management policy included in the IPS for this hedge fund.

8 As we will see, this also increases hedging costs when currency options are used.

Exhibit 4: Hedge Fund Currency Management Policy: An Example

Overall Portfolio Benchmark:	MSCI EAFE Index (local currency)
Currency Exposure Ranges:	Foreign-currency exposures, based on the USD market value of the equities actually held by the fund at the beginning of each month, will be hedged back into USD within the following tolerance ranges of plus or minus: ▪ EUR: 20% ▪ GBP: 15% ▪ JPY: 10% ▪ CHF: 10% ▪ AUD: 10% ▪ SEK: 10% Other currency exposures shall be left unhedged.
Rebalancing:	The currency hedges will be rebalanced at least monthly, to reflect changes in the USD-denominated market value of portfolio equity holdings.
Hedging Instruments:	▪ Forward contracts up to 12 months maturity; ▪ European put and call options can be bought or written, for maturities up to 12 months; and ▪ Exotic options of up to 12 months maturity can be bought or sold.
Reporting:	Management will present quarterly reports to the board detailing net foreign-currency exposures and speculative trading results. Speculative trading results will be benchmarked against a 100% hedged currency exposure.

With this policy, Kailua Kona Advisors is indicating that it is willing to accept foreign-currency exposures within the portfolio but that these exposures must be kept within pre-defined limits. For example, suppose that at the beginning of the month the portfolio held EUR10 million of EUR-denominated assets. Also suppose that this EUR10 million exposure, combined with all the other foreign-currency exposures in the portfolio, matches Kailua Kona Advisors' desired portfolio weights by currency (as a US-based fund, these desired percentage portfolio allocations across all currencies will be based in USD).

The currency-hedging guidelines indicate that the hedge (for example, using a short position in a USD/EUR forward contract) should be between EUR8 million and EUR12 million, giving some discretion to the portfolio manager on the size of the net exposure to the EUR. At the beginning of the next month, the USD values of the foreign assets in the portfolio are measured again, and the process repeats. If there has been either a large move in the foreign-currency value of the EUR-denominated assets and/or a large move in the USD/EUR exchange rate, it is possible that Kailua Kona Advisors' portfolio exposure to EUR-denominated assets will be too far away from the desired percentage allocation.[9] Kailua Kona Advisors will then need to either buy or sell EUR-denominated assets. If movements in the EUR-denominated value of the assets or in the USD/EUR exchange rate are large enough, this asset rebalancing may have to be done before month's end. Either way, once the asset rebalancing is done, it establishes the new EUR-denominated asset value on which the currency hedge will be based (i.e., plus or minus 20% of this new EUR amount).

If the portfolio is not 100% hedged—for example, continuing the Kailua Kona illustration, if the portfolio manager only hedges EUR9 million of the exposure and has a residual exposure of being long EUR1 million—the success or failure of the manager's tactical decision will be compared with a "neutral" benchmark. In this case, the comparison would be against the performance of a 100% fully hedged portfolio—that is, with a EUR10 million hedge.

7 ECONOMIC FUNDAMENTALS, TECHNICAL ANALYSIS AND THE CARRY TRADE

- ☐ compare active currency trading strategies based on economic fundamentals, technical analysis, carry-trade, and volatility trading
- ☐ describe how changes in factors underlying active trading strategies affect tactical trading decisions

The previous section discussed the *strategic* decisions made by the IPS on locating the currency management practices of the portfolio along a risk spectrum ranging from a very conservative approach to currency risk to very active currency management. In this section, we consider the case in which the IPS has given the portfolio manager (or currency overlay manager) at least some limited discretion for actively managing currency risk within these mandated strategic bounds. This then leads to *tactical* decisions: which FX exposures to accept and manage within these discretionary limits. In other words, tactical decisions involve active currency management.

A market view is a prerequisite to any form of active management. At the heart of the trading decision in FX (and other) markets, lies a view on future market prices and conditions. This market opinion guides all decisions with respect to currency risk exposures, including whether currency hedges should be implemented and, if so, how they should be managed.

In what follows, we will explore some of the methods used to form directional views about the FX market. However, a word of caution that cannot be emphasized enough: *There is no simple formula, model, or approach that will allow market participants to precisely forecast exchange rates (or any other financial prices) or to be able to be confident that any trading decision will be profitable.*

9 The overall portfolio percentage allocations by currency will also depend on the price moves of all *other* foreign-currency assets and exchange rates as well, but we will simplify our example by ignoring this nuance.

Active Currency Management Based on Economic Fundamentals

This section sets out a broad framework for developing a view about future exchange rate movements based on underlying fundamentals. In contrast to other methods for developing a market view (which are discussed in subsequent sections), at the heart of this approach is the assumption that, in a flexible exchange rate system, exchange rates are determined by logical economic relationships and that these relationships can be modeled.

The simple economic framework is based on the assumption that in the long run, the real exchange rate will converge to its "fair value," but short- to medium-term factors will shape the convergence path to this equilibrium.[10]

Recall that the real exchange rate reflects the ratio of the real purchasing power between two countries; that is, the once nominal purchasing power in each country is adjusted by its respective price level as well as the spot exchange rate between the two countries. The long-run equilibrium level for the real exchange rate is determined by purchasing power parity or some other model of an exchange rate's fair value, and serves as the anchor for longer-term movements in exchange rates.

Over shorter time frames, movements in real exchange rates will also reflect movements in the real interest rate differential between countries. Recall that the real interest rate (r) is the nominal interest rate adjusted by the expected inflation rate, or $r = i - \pi^{\varepsilon}$, where i is the nominal interest rate and π^{ε} is the expected inflation rate over the same term as the nominal and real interest rates. Movements in risk premiums will also affect exchange rate movements over shorter-term horizons. The riskier a country's assets are perceived to be by investors, the more likely they are to move their investments out of that country, thereby depressing the exchange rate. Finally, the framework recognizes that there are two currencies involved in an exchange rate quote (the price and base currencies) and hence movements in exchange rates will reflect movements in the *differentials* between these various factors.

As a result, all else equal, the base currency's real exchange rate should appreciate if there is an upward movement in

- its long-run equilibrium real exchange rate;
- either its real or nominal interest rates, which should attract foreign capital;
- expected foreign inflation, which should cause the foreign currency to depreciate; and
- the foreign risk premium, which should make foreign assets less attractive compared with the base currency nation's domestic assets.

The real exchange rate should also increase if it is currently below its long-term equilibrium value. All of this makes intuitive sense.

In summary, the exchange rate forecast is a mix of long-term, medium-term, and short-term factors. The long-run equilibrium real exchange rate is the anchor for exchange rates and the point of long-run convergence for exchange rate movements. Movements in the short- to medium-term factors (nominal interest rates, expected inflation) affect the timing and path of convergence to this long-run equilibrium. A stylized depiction of the price dynamics generated by this interaction between short-, medium-, and longer-term pricing factors is shown in Exhibit 5.

10 This model was derived and explained by Rosenberg and Barker (2017).

Exhibit 5: Interaction of Long-term and Short-term Factors in Exchange Rates

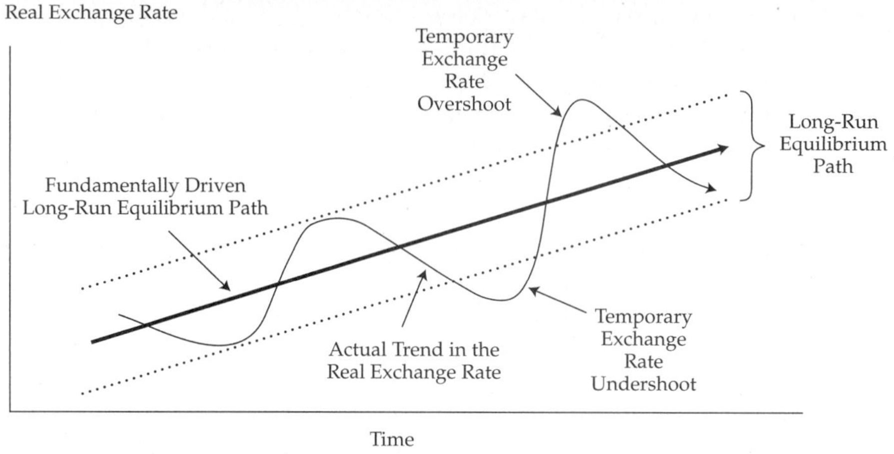

Source: Based on Rosenberg (2002), page 32.

It needs to be stressed that it can be very demanding to model how each of these separate effects—nominal interest rate, expected inflation, and risk premium differentials—change over time and affect exchange rates. It can also be challenging to model movements in the long-term equilibrium real exchange rate. A broad variety of factors, such as fiscal and monetary policy, will affect all of these variables in our simple economic model.[11]

Active Currency Management Based on Technical Analysis

Another approach to forming a market view is based on technical analysis. This approach is based on quite different assumptions compared with modeling based on economic fundamentals. Whereas classical exchange rate economics tends to view market participants as rational, markets as efficient, and exchange rates as driven by underlying economic factors, technical analysis ignores economic analysis. Instead, technical analysis is based on three broad themes.[12]

First, market technicians believe that in a liquid, freely traded market the historical price data can be helpful in projecting future price movements.[13] The reason is because many traders have already used any useful data external to the market to generate their trading positions, so this information is already reflected in current prices. Therefore, it is not necessary to look outside of the market to form an opinion on future price movements. This means it is not necessary to examine interest rates, inflation rates, or risk premium differentials (the factors in our fundamentally based model) because exchange rates already incorporate these factors.

Second, market technicians believe that historical patterns in the price data have a tendency to repeat, and that this repetition provides profitable trade opportunities. These price patterns repeat because market prices reflect human behavior and human beings have a tendency to react in similar ways to similar situations, even if this repetitive behavior is not always fully rational. For example, when confronted with an

11 A broader discussion of exchange rate economics can be found in Rosenberg and Barker (2017).
12 Some material in this section is based on Sine and Strong (2012).
13 In many other asset classes, technical analysis is based on trade volume data as well as price data. But there are no reliable, timely, and high-frequency trade volume data that are publicly available for over-the-counter (OTC) FX markets.

upward price trend, many market participants eventually come to believe that it will extrapolate (an attitude of "irrational exuberance" or "this time it is different"). When the trend eventually breaks, a panicked position exit can cause a sharp overshoot of fair value to the downside. Broadly speaking, technical analysis can be seen as the study of market psychology and how market participant emotions—primarily greed and fear—can be read from the price data and used to predict future price moves.

Third, technical analysis does not attempt to determine where market prices *should* trade (fair value, as in fundamental analysis) but where they *will* trade. Because these price patterns reflect trader emotions, they need not reflect—at least immediately—any cool, rational assessment of the underlying economic or fundamental situation. Although market prices may eventually converge to fair value in the long run, the long run can be a very long time indeed. In the meanwhile, there are shorter-term trading opportunities available in trading the technical patterns in the price data.

Combined, these three principles of technical analysis define a discipline dedicated to identifying patterns in the historical price data, especially as it relates to identifying market trends and market turning points. (Technical analysis is less useful in a trendless market.) Technical analysis tries to identify when markets have become **overbought** or **oversold**, meaning that they have trended too far in one direction and are vulnerable to a trend reversal, or correction. Technical analysis also tries to identify what are called **support levels** and **resistance levels**, either within ongoing price trends or at their extremities (i.e., turning points). These support and resistance levels are price points on dealers' order boards where one would except to see clustering of bids and offers, respectively. At these exchange rate levels, the price action is expected to get "sticky" because it will take more order flow to pierce the wall of either bids or offers. But once these price points are breached, the price action can be expected to accelerate as **stops** are triggered. (Stops, in this sense, refer to stop-loss orders, in which traders leave resting bids or offers away from the current market price to be filled if the market reaches those levels. A stop-loss order is triggered when the price action has gone against a trader's position, and it gets the trader out of that position to limit further losses.)

Technical analysis uses visual cues for market patterns as well as more quantitative technical indicators. There is a wide variety of technical indexes based on market prices that are used in this context. Some technical indicators are as simple as using moving averages of past price points. The 200-day moving average of daily exchange rates is often seen as an important indicator of likely support and resistance. Sometimes two moving averages are used to establish when a price trend is building momentum. For example, when the 50-day moving average crosses the 200-day moving average, this is sometimes seen as a price "break out" point.

Other technical indicators are based on more complex mathematical formulae. There is an extremely wide variety of these more mathematical indicators, some of them very esoteric and hard to connect intuitively with the behavior of real world financial market participants.

In summary, many FX active managers routinely use technical analysis—either alone or in conjunction with other approaches—to form a market opinion or to time position entry and exit points. Even though many technical indicators lack the intellectual underpinnings provided by formal economic modeling, they nonetheless remain a prominent feature of FX markets.

Active Currency Management Based on the Carry Trade

The **carry trade** is a trading strategy of borrowing in low-yield currencies and investing in high-yield currencies. The term "carry" is related to what is known as the cost of carry—that is, of carrying or holding an investment. This investment has either an implicit or explicit cost (borrowing cost) but may also produce income. The net cost of carry is the difference between these two return rates.

If technical analysis is based on ignoring economic fundamentals, then the carry trade is based on exploiting a well-recognized violation of one of the international parity conditions often used to describe these economic fundamentals: uncovered interest rate parity. Recall that uncovered interest rate parity asserts that, *on a longer-term average*, the return on an unhedged foreign-currency asset investment will be the same as a domestic-currency investment. Assuming that the base currency in the P/B quote is the low-yield currency, stated algebraically uncovered interest rate parity asserts that

$$\%\Delta S_{H/L} \approx i_H - i_L$$

where $\%\Delta S_{H/L}$ is the percentage change in the $S_{H/L}$ spot exchange rate (the low-yield currency is the base currency), i_H is the interest rate on the high-yield currency and i_L is the interest rate on the low-yield currency. If uncovered interest rate parity holds, the yield spread *advantage* for the high-yielding currency (the right side of the equation) will, on average, be matched by the *depreciation* of the high-yield currency (the left side of the equation; the low-yield currency is the base currency and hence a positive value for $\%\Delta S_{H/L}$ means a depreciation of the high-yield currency). According to the uncovered interest rate parity theorem, it is this offset between (1) the yield advantage and (2) the currency depreciation that equates, on average, the unhedged currency returns.

But in reality, the historical data show that there are persistent deviations from uncovered interest rate parity in FX markets, at least in the short to medium term. Indeed, high-yield countries often see their currencies *appreciate*, not depreciate, for extended periods of time. The positive returns from a combination of a favorable yield differential plus an appreciating currency can remain in place long enough to present attractive investment opportunities.

This persistent violation of uncovered interest rate parity described by the carry trade is often referred to as the **forward rate bias**. An implication of uncovered interest rate parity is that the forward rate should be an unbiased predictor of future spot rates. The historical data, however, show that the forward rate is not the center of the distribution for future spot rates; in fact, it is a *biased* predictor (for example, see Kritzman 1999). Hence the name "forward rate bias." With the forward rate premium or discount defined as $F_{P/B} - S_{P/B}$ the "bias" in the forward rate bias is that the premium typically overstates the amount of appreciation of the base currency, and the discount overstates the amount of depreciation. Indeed, the forward discount or premium often gets even the *direction* of future spot rate movements wrong.

The carry trade strategy (borrowing in low-yield currencies, investing in high-yield currencies) is equivalent to a strategy based on trading the forward rate bias. Trading the forward rate bias involves buying currencies trading at a forward discount, and selling currencies trading at a forward premium. This makes intuitive sense: It is desirable to buy low and sell high.

To show the equivalence of the carry trade and trading the forward rate bias, recall that covered interest rate parity (which is enforced by arbitrage) is stated as

$$\frac{F_{P/B} - S_{P/B}}{S_{P/B}} = \frac{\left(i_P - i_B\right)\left(\frac{t}{360}\right)}{1 + i_B\left(\frac{t}{360}\right)}$$

This equation shows that when the base currency has a lower interest rate than the price currency (i.e., the right side of the equality is positive) the base currency will trade at a forward premium (the left side of the equality is positive). That is, being low-yield currency and trading at a forward premium is synonymous. Similarly, being a high-yield currency means trading at a forward discount. Borrowing in the low-yield currency and investing in the high-yield currency (the carry trade) is hence equivalent to selling currencies that have a forward premium and buying currencies that have a forward discount (trading the forward rate bias). We will return to these concepts in Section 9 when we discuss the roll yield in hedging with forward contracts. Exhibit 6 summarizes several key points about the carry trade.

Exhibit 6: The Carry Trade: A Summary

	Buy/Invest	Sell/Borrow
Implementing the carry trade	High-yield currency	Low-yield currency
Trading the forward rate bias	Forward discount currency	Forward premium currency

The gains that one can earn through the carry trade (or equivalently, through trading the forward rate bias) can be seen as the risk premiums earned for carrying an unhedged position—that is, for absorbing currency risk. (In efficient markets, there is no extra reward without extra risk.) Long periods of market stability can make these extra returns enticing to many investors, and the longer the yield differential persists between high-yield and low-yield currencies, the more carry trade positions will have a tendency to build up. But these high-yield currency advantages can be erased quickly, particularly if global financial markets are subject to sudden bouts of stress. This is especially true because the carry trade is a *leveraged* position: borrowing in the low-yielding currency and investing in the high-yielding currency. These occasional large losses mean that the return distribution for the carry trade has a pronounced negative skew.

This negative skew derives from the fact that the **funding currencies** of the carry trade (the low-yield currencies in which borrowing occurs) are typically the safe haven currencies, such as the EUR, CHF, and JPY. In contrast, the **investment currencies** (the high-yielding currencies) are typically currencies perceived to be higher risk, such as several emerging market currencies. Any time global financial markets are under stress there is a flight to safety that causes rapid movements in exchange rates, and usually a panicked unwinding of carry trades. As a result, traders running carry trades often get caught in losing positions, with the leverage involved magnifying their losses. Because of the tendency for long periods of relatively small gains in the carry trade to be followed by brief periods of large losses, the carry trade is sometimes characterized as "picking up nickels in front of a steamroller." One guide to the riskiness of the carry trade is the volatility of spot rate movements for the currency pair; all else equal, lower volatility is better for a carry trade position.

We close this section by noting that although the carry trade can be based on borrowing in a single funding currency and investing in a single high-yield currency, it is more common for carry trades to use multiple funding and investment currencies. The number of funding currencies and investment currencies need not be equal: for example, there could be five of one and three of the other. Sometimes the portfolio weighting of exposures between the various funding and investment currencies are simply set equal to each other. But the weights can also be optimized to reflect the trader's market view of the expected movements in each of the exchange rates, as well as their individual risks ($\sigma[\%\Delta S]$) and the expected correlations between movements in the currency pairs. These trades can be dynamically rebalanced, with the relative weights among both funding and investment currencies shifting with market conditions.

8 VOLATILITY TRADING

- ☐ compare active currency trading strategies based on economic fundamentals, technical analysis, carry-trade, and volatility trading
- ☐ describe how changes in factors underlying active trading strategies affect tactical trading decisions

Another type of active trading style is unique to option markets and is known as volatility trading (or simply "vol trading").[14] To explain this trading style, we will start with a quick review of some option basics.

The derivatives of the option pricing model show the sensitivity of the option's premium to changes in the factors that determine option value. These derivatives are often referred to as the "Greeks" of option pricing. There is a very large number of first, second, third, and cross-derivatives that can be taken of an option pricing formula, but the two most important Greeks that we will consider here are the following:

- **Delta:** The sensitivity of the option premium to a small change in the price of the underlying[15] of the option, typically a financial asset. This sensitivity is an indication of *price* risk.
- **Vega:** The sensitivity of the option premium to a small change in implied volatility. This sensitivity is an indication of *volatility* risk.

The most important concept to grasp in terms of volatility trading is that the use of options allows the trader, through a variety of trading strategies, to *unbundle* and isolate all of the various risk factors (the Greeks) and trade them separately. Once an initial option position is taken (either long or short), the trader has exposure to *all* of the various Greeks/risk factors. The unwanted risk exposures, however, can then be hedged away, leaving *only* the desired risk exposure to express that specific directional view.

Delta hedging is the act of hedging away the option position's exposure to delta, the price risk of the underlying (the FX spot rate, in this case). Because delta shows the sensitivity of the option price to changes in the spot exchange rate, it thus defines the option's hedge ratio: The size of the offsetting hedge position that will set the *net* delta of the combined position (option plus delta hedge) to zero. Typically implementing this delta hedge is done using either forward contracts or a spot transaction (spot, by definition, has a delta of one, and no exposure to any other of the Greeks; forward contracts are highly correlated with the spot rate). For example, if a trader was long a call option on USD/EUR with a nominal value of EUR1 million and a delta of +0.5, the delta hedge would involve a short forward position in USD/EUR of EUR0.5 million. That is, the size of the delta hedge is equal to the option's delta times the nominal size of the contract. This hedge size would set the net delta of the overall position (option

14 In principle, this trading style can be applied to all asset classes with options, not just FX trading. But FX options are the most liquid and widely traded options in the world, so it is in FX where most of volatility trading likely takes place in global financial markets.

15 The underlying asset of a derivative is typically referred to simply as the "underlying."

and forward) to zero.[16] Once the delta hedge has set the net delta of the position to zero, the trader then has exposure *only* to the other Greeks, and can use various trading strategies to position in these (long or short) depending on directional views.

Although one could theoretically trade *any* of the other Greeks, the most important one traded is vega; that is, the trader is expressing a view on the future movements in implied volatility, or in other words, is engaged in volatility trading. Implied volatility is not the same as realized, or observed, historical volatility, although it is heavily influenced by it. By engaging in volatility trading, the trader is expressing a view about the future volatility of exchange rates *but not their direction* (the delta hedge set the net delta of the position to zero).

One simple option strategy that implements a volatility trade is a **straddle**, which is a combination of both an at-the-money (ATM) put and an ATM call. A long straddle buys both of these options. Because their deltas are −0.5 and +0.5, respectively, the net delta of the position is zero; that is, the long straddle is delta neutral. This position is profitable in more volatile markets, when either the put or the call go sufficiently in the money to cover the upfront cost of the two option premiums paid. Similarly, a short straddle is a bet that the spot rate will stay relatively stable. In this case, the payout on any option exercise will be less than the twin premiums the seller has collected; the rest is net profit for the option seller. A similar option structure is a **strangle** position for which a long position is buying out-of-the-money (OTM) puts and calls with the same expiry date and the same degree of being out of the money (we elaborate more on this subject later). Because OTM options are being bought, the cost of the position is cheaper—but conversely, it also does not pay off until the spot rate passes the OTM strike levels. As a result, the risk–reward for a strangle is more moderate than that for a straddle.

The interesting thing to note is that by using delta-neutral trading strategies, volatility is turned into a product that can be actively traded like any other financial product or asset class, such as equities, commodities, fixed-income products, and so on. Volatility is not constant nor are its movements completely random. Instead volatility is determined by a wide variety of underlying factors—both fundamental and technical—that the trader can express an opinion on. Movements in volatility are cyclical, and typically subject to long periods of relative stability punctuated by sharp upward spikes in volatility as markets come under periodic bouts of stress (usually the result of some dramatic event, financial or otherwise). Speculative vol traders—for example, among currency overlay managers—often want to be net-short volatility. The reason is because most options expire out of the money, and the option writer then gets to keep the option premium without delivery of the underlying currency pair. The amount of the option premium can be considered the risk premium, or payment, earned by the option writer for absorbing volatility risk. It is a steady source of income under "normal" market conditions. Ideally, these traders would want to "flip" their position and be long volatility ahead of volatility spikes, but these episodes can be notoriously difficult to time. Most hedgers typically run options positions that are net-long volatility because they are buying protection from unanticipated price volatility. (Being long the option means being exposed to the time decay of the option's time value; that is similar to paying insurance premiums for the protection against exchange rate volatility.)

We can also note that just as there are *currency overlay* programs for actively trading the portfolio's currency exposures (as discussed in Section 5) there can also be *volatility overlay* programs for actively trading the portfolio's exposures to movements in currencies' implied volatility. Just as currency overlay programs manage the

16 Strictly speaking, the net delta would be *approximately* equal to zero because forward contracts do not have identical price properties to those of the spot exchange rate. But it is close enough for our purposes here, and we will ignore this small difference.

portfolio's exposure to currency delta (movements in spot exchange rates), volatility overlay programs manage the portfolio's exposure to currency vega. These volatility overlay programs can be focused on earning speculative profits, but can also be used to hedge the portfolio against risk (we will return to this concept in the discussion of macro hedges in Section 11.).

Enumerating all the potential strategies for trading foreign exchange volatility is beyond the scope of this reading. Instead, the reader should be aware that this dimension of trading FX volatility (not price) exists and sees a large amount of active trading. Moreover, the best traders are able to think and trade in both dimensions simultaneously. Movements in volatility are often correlated with directional movements in the price of the underlying. For example, when there is a flight to safety as carry trades unwind, there is typically a spike in volatility (and options prices) at the same time. Although pure vol trading is based on a zero-delta position, this need not always be the case; a trader can express a market opinion on volatility (vega exposure) and still have a directional exposure to the underlying spot exchange rate as well (delta exposure). That is, the overall trading position has net vega and delta exposures that reflect the *joint* market view.

We end this section by explaining how currency options are quoted in professional FX markets. (This information will be used in Sections 9–12 when we discuss other option trading strategies.) Unlike exchanged-traded options, such as those used in equity markets, OTC options for currencies are not described in terms of specific strike levels (i.e., exchange rate levels). Instead, in the interdealer market, options are described in terms of their "delta." Deltas for puts can range from a minimum of −1 to a maximum of 0, with a delta of −0.5 being the point at which the put option is ATM; OTM puts have deltas between 0 and −0.5. For call options, delta ranges from 0 to +1, with 0.5 being the ATM point. In FX markets, these delta values are quoted both in *absolute* terms (i.e., in positive rather than negative values) and as percentages, with standard FX option quotes usually in terms of 25-delta and 10-delta options (i.e., a delta of 0.25 and 0.10, respectively; the 10-delta option is deeper OTM and hence cheaper than the 25-delta option). The FX options market is the most liquid around these standard delta quoting points (ATM, 25-delta, 10-delta), but of course, as a flexible OTC market, options of any delta/strike price can be traded. The 25-delta put option (for example) will still go in the money if the spot price dips below a *specific* exchange rate level; this *implied* strike price is *backed out* of an option pricing model once all the other pricing factors, including the current spot rate and the 25-delta of the option, are put into the option pricing model. (The specific option pricing model used is agreed on by both parties to the trade.)

These standard delta price points are often used to define option trading strategies. For example, a 25-delta strangle would be based on 25-delta put and call options. Similarly, a 10-delta strangle would be based on 10-delta options (and would cost less and have a more moderate payoff structure than a 25-delta strangle). Labeling option structures by their delta is common in FX markets.

EXAMPLE 3

Active Strategies

Annie McYelland works as an analyst at Scotland-based Kilmarnock Advisors, an investment firm that offers several investment vehicles for its clients. McYelland has been put in charge of formulating the firm's market views for some of the foreign currencies that these vehicles have exposures to. Her market views will be used to guide the hedging and discretionary positioning for some of the actively managed portfolios.

McYelland begins by examining yield spreads between various countries and the implied volatility extracted from the option pricing for several currency pairs. She collects the following data:

One-Year Yield Levels	
Switzerland	−0.80%
United States	0.30%
Poland	1.26%
Mexico	5.98%

One-Year Implied Volatility	
PLN/CHF	7.58%
MXN/CHF	12.7%
MXN/PLN	11.8%
MXN/USD	9.81%

Note: PLN = Polish zloty; the Swiss yields are negative because of Swiss policy actions.

McYelland is also examining various economic indicators to shape her market views. After studying the economic prospects for both Japan and New Zealand, she expects that the inflation rate for New Zealand is about to accelerate over the next few years, whereas the inflation rate for Japan should remain relatively stable. Turning her attention to the economic situation in India, McYelland believes that the Indian authorities are about to tighten monetary policy, and that this change has not been fully priced into the market. She reconsiders her short-term view for the Indian rupee (i.e., the INR/USD spot rate) after conducting this analysis.

McYelland also examines the exchange rate volatility for several currency pairs to which the investment trusts are exposed. Based on her analysis of the situation, she believes that the exchange rate between Chilean peso and the US dollar (CLP/USD) is about to become much more volatile than usual, although she has no strong views about whether the CLP will appreciate or depreciate.

One of McYelland's colleagues, Catalina Ortega, is a market technician and offers to help McYelland time her various market position entry and exit points based on chart patterns. While examining the JPY/NZD price chart, Ortega notices that the 200-day moving average is at 77.5035 and the current spot rate is 77.1905.

1. Based on the data she collected, all else equal, McYelland's *best* option for implementing a carry trade position would be to fund in:

   A. USD and invest in MXN.

   B. CHF and invest in MXN.

   C. CHF and invest in PLN.

Solution:

A is correct. The tradeoff between the yield spread between the funding and investment currencies and the implied volatility (risk) is the most attractive. The other choices have a narrower yield spread and higher risk (implied volatility).

2. Based on McYelland's inflation forecasts, all else equal, she would be *more likely* to expect a(n):

   A. depreciation in the JPY/NZD.

   B. increase in capital flows from Japan to New Zealand.

   C. more accommodative monetary policy by the Reserve Bank of New Zealand.

Solution:

A is correct. All else equal, an increase in New Zealand's inflation rate will decrease its real interest rate and lead to the real interest rate differential favoring Japan over New Zealand. This would likely result in a depreciation of the JPY/NZD rate over time. The shift in the relative real returns should lead to reduced capital flows from Japan to New Zealand (so Choice B is incorrect) and the RBNZ—New Zealand's central bank—is more likely to tighten monetary policy than loosen it as inflation picks up (so Choice C is incorrect).

3. Given her analysis for India, McYelland's short-term market view for the INR/USD spot rate is now *most likely* to be:

   A. biased toward appreciation.

   B. biased toward depreciation.

   C. unchanged because it is only a short-run view.

Solution:

B is correct. Tighter monetary policy in India should lead to higher real interest rates (at least in the short run). This increase will cause the INR to appreciate against the USD, but because the USD is the base currency, this will be represented as depreciation in the INR/USD rate. Choice C is incorrect because a tightening of monetary policy that is not fully priced-in to market pricing is likely to move bond yields and hence the exchange rate in the short run (given the simple economic model in Section 7).

4. Using CLP/USD options, what would be the *cheapest* way for McYelland to implement her market view for the CLP?

   A. Buy a straddle

   B. Buy a 25-delta strangle

   C. Sell a 40-delta strangle

Solution:

B is correct. Either a long straddle or a long strangle will profit from a marked increase in volatility in the spot rate, but a 25-delta strangle would be cheaper (because it is based on OTM options). Writing a strangle—particularly one that is close to being ATM, which is what a 40-delta structure is—is likely to be exercised in favor of the counterparty if McYelland's market view is correct.

5. Based on Ortega's analysis, she would *most likely* expect:

   A. support near 77.5035.

   B. resistance near 77.1095.

   C. resistance near 77.5035.

Solution:

C is correct. The 200-day moving average has not been crossed yet, and it is higher than the current spot rate. Hence this technical indicator suggests that resistance lies above the current spot rate level, likely in the 77.5035 area. Choice A is incorrect because the currency has not yet appreciated to 77.5035, so it cannot be considered a "support" level. Given that the currency pair has already traded through 77.1905 and is still at least 90 pips away from the 200-day moving average, it is more likely to suspect that resistance still lies above the current spot rate.

FORWARD CONTRACTS, FX SWAPS, AND CURRENCY OPTIONS

9

☐ describe how forward contracts and FX (foreign exchange) swaps are used to adjust hedge ratios

In this section, we focus on how the portfolio manager uses financial derivatives to implement both the *strategic* positioning of the portfolio along the risk spectrum (i.e., the performance benchmark) as well as the *tactical* decisions made in regard to variations around this "neutral" position. The manager's market view—whether based on carry, fundamental, currency volatility, or technical considerations—leads to this active management of risk positioning around the strategic benchmark point. Implementing both strategic and tactical viewpoints requires the use of trading tools, which we discuss in this section.

The balance of this reading will assume that the portfolio's strategic foreign-currency asset exposures and the maximum amount of currency risk desired have already been determined by the portfolio's IPS. We begin at the conservative end of the risk spectrum by describing a passive hedge for a single currency (with a 100% hedge ratio). After discussing the costs and limitations of this approach, we move out further along the risk spectrum by describing strategies in which the basic "building blocks" of financial derivatives can be combined to implement the manager's tactical positioning and construct much more customized risk–return profiles. Not surprisingly, the basic trading tools themselves—forwards, options, FX swaps—are used for both strategic and tactical risk management and by both hedgers and speculators alike (although for different ends). Note that the instruments covered as tools of currency management are not nearly an exhaustive list. For example, exchange-traded funds for currencies are a vehicle that can be useful in managing currency risk.

Forward Contracts

In this section, we consider the most basic form of hedging: a 100% hedge ratio for a single foreign-currency exposure. Futures or forward contracts on currencies can be used to obtain full currency hedges, although most institutional investors prefer to use forward contracts for the following reasons:

1. Futures contracts are standardized in terms of settlement dates and contract sizes. These may not correspond to the portfolio's investment parameters.

2. Futures contracts may not always be available in the currency pair that the portfolio manager wants to hedge. For example, the most liquid currency futures contracts trade on the Chicago Mercantile Exchange (CME). Although there are CME futures contracts for all major exchange rates (e.g., USD/EUR, USD/GBP) and many cross rates (e.g., CAD/EUR, JPY/CHF), there are not contracts available for all possible currency pairs. Trading these cross rates would need multiple futures contracts, adding to portfolio management costs. In addition, many of the "second tier" emerging market currencies may not have liquid futures contracts available against any currency, let alone the currency pair in which the portfolio manager is interested.
3. Futures contracts require up-front margin (initial margin). They also have intra-period cash flow implications, in that the exchange will require the investor to post additional variation margin when the spot exchange rate moves against the investor's position. These initial and ongoing margin requirements tie up the investor's capital and require careful monitoring through time, adding to the portfolio management expense. Likewise, margin flows can go in the investor's favor, requiring monitoring and reinvestment.

In contrast, forward contracts do not suffer from any of these drawbacks. Major global investment dealers (such as Deutsche Bank, Royal Bank of Scotland, UBS, etc.) will quote prices on forward contracts for practically every possible currency pair, settlement date, and transaction amount. They typically do not require margin to be posted or maintained.

Moreover, the daily trade volume globally for OTC currency forward and swap contracts dwarfs that for exchange-traded currency futures contracts; that is, forward contracts are more liquid than futures for trading in large sizes. Reflecting this liquidity, forward contracts are the predominant hedging instrument in use globally. For the balance of this section, we will focus only on currency forward contracts. However, separate side boxes discuss exchange-traded currency futures contracts and currency-based exchange-traded funds (ETFs).

Hedge Ratios with Forward Contracts

In principle, setting up a full currency hedge is relatively straight forward: match the current market value of the foreign-currency exposure in the portfolio with an equal and offsetting position in a forward contract. In practice, of course, it is not that simple because the market value of the foreign-currency assets will change with market conditions. This means that the actual hedge ratio will typically *drift* away from the desired hedge ratio as market conditions change. A **static hedge** (i.e., unchanging hedge) will avoid transaction costs, but will also tend to accumulate unwanted currency exposures as the value of the foreign-currency assets change. This characteristic will cause a mismatch between the market value of the foreign-currency asset portfolio and the nominal size of the forward contract used for the currency hedge; this is pure currency risk. For this reason, the portfolio manager will typically need to implement a **dynamic hedge** by rebalancing the portfolio periodically. This hedge rebalancing will mean adjusting some combination of the size, number, and maturities of the forward currency contracts.

A simple example will illustrate this rebalancing process. Suppose that an investor domiciled in Switzerland has a EUR-denominated portfolio that, at the start of the period, is worth EUR1,000,000. Assume a monthly hedge-rebalancing cycle. To hedge this portfolio, the investor would sell EUR1,000,000 one month forward against the CHF. Assume that one month later, the EUR-denominated investment portfolio is then actually worth only EUR950,000. To roll the hedge forward for the next month, the investor will engage in a mismatched FX swap. (Recall that a "matched" swap means that both the spot and forward transactions—the near and far "legs" of the swap, respectively—are of equal size). For the near leg of the swap, EUR1 million will be bought at spot to settle the expiring forward contract. (The euro amounts will then net to zero, but a Swiss franc cash flow will be generated, either a loss or a gain for the investor, depending on how the CHF/EUR rate has changed over the month). For the far leg of the swap, the investor will sell EUR950,000 forward for one month.

Another way to view this rebalancing process is to consider the case in which the original short forward contract has a three-month maturity. In this case, rebalancing after one month would mean that the manager would have to *buy* 50,000 CHF/EUR two months forward. There is no cash flow at the time this second forward contract is entered, but the *net* amount of euro for delivery at contract settlement two months into the future is now the euro hedge amount desired (i.e., EUR950,000). There will be a net cash flow (denominated in CHF) calculated over these two forward contracts on the settlement date two months hence.

Although rebalancing a dynamic hedge will keep the actual hedge ratio close to the target hedge ratio, it will also lead to increased transaction costs compared with a static hedge. The manager will have to assess the cost–benefit trade-offs of how frequently to dynamically rebalance the hedge. These will depend on a variety of idiosyncratic factors (manager risk aversion, market view, IPS guidelines, etc.), and so there is no single "correct" answer—different managers will likely make different decisions.

However, we can observe that the higher the degree of risk aversion, the more frequently the hedge is likely to be rebalanced back to the "neutral" hedge ratio. Similarly, the greater the tolerance for active trading, and the stronger the commitment to a particular market view, the more likely it is that the actual hedge ratio will be allowed to vary from a "neutral" setting, possibly through entering into new forward contracts. (For example, if the P/B spot rate was seen to be oversold and likely to rebound higher, an actively traded portfolio might buy the base currency through forward contracts to lock in this perceived low price—and thus change the actual hedge ratio accordingly.) The sidebar on executing a hedge illustrates the concepts of rolling hedges, FX swaps and their pricing (bid–offer), and adjusting hedges for market views and changes in market values.

EXECUTING A HEDGE

Jiao Yang works at Hong Kong SAR-based Kwun Tong Investment Advisors; its reporting currency is the Hong Kong Dollar (HKD). She has been put in charge of managing the firm's foreign-currency hedges. Forward contracts for two of these hedges are coming due for settlement, and Yang will need to use FX swaps to roll these hedges forward three months.

Hedge #1: Kwun Tong has a short position of JPY800,000,000 coming due on a JPY/HKD forward contract. The market value of the underlying foreign-currency assets has not changed over the life of the contract, and Yang does not have a firm opinion on the expected future movement in the JPY/HKD spot rate.

Hedge #2: Kwun Tong has a short position of EUR8,000,000 coming due on a HKD/EUR forward contract. The market value of the EUR-denominated assets has increased (measured in EUR). Yang expects the HKD/EUR spot rate to decrease.

The following spot exchange rates and three-month forward points are in effect when Yang transacts the FX swaps necessary to roll the hedges forward:

	Spot Rate	Three-Month Forward Points
JPY/HKD	14.4/14.42	−1.2/−1.1
HKD/EUR	9.0200/9.0210	173/176

Note: The JPY/HKD forward points will be scaled by 100; the HKD/EUR forward points will be scaled by 10,000

As a result, Yang undertakes the following transactions:

For **Hedge #1**, the foreign-currency value of the underlying assets has not changed, and she does not have a market view that would lead her to want to either over- or under-hedge the foreign-currency exposure. Therefore, to roll these hedges forward, she uses a matched swap. For matched swaps (see Section 2), the convention is to base pricing on the mid-market spot exchange rate. Thus, the spot leg of the swap would be to buy JPY800,000,000 at the mid-market rate of 10.81 JPY/HKD. The forward leg of the swap would require selling JPY800,000,000 forward three months. Selling JPY (the price currency in the JPY/HKD quote) is equivalent to buying HKD (the base currency). Therefore, she uses the offer-side forward points, and the all-in forward rate for the forward leg of the swap is as follows:

$$14.41 + \frac{-1.1}{100} = 14.40$$

For **Hedge #2**, the foreign-currency value of the underlying assets has increased; Yang recognizes that this implies that she should increase the size of the hedge greater than EUR8,000,000. She also believes that the HKD/EUR spot rate will decrease, and recognizes that this implies a hedge ratio of more than 100% (Kwun Tong Advisors has given her discretion to over- or under-hedge based on her market views). This too means that the size of the hedge should be increased more than EUR8,000,000, because Yang will want a larger short position in the EUR to take advantage of its expected depreciation. Hence, Yang uses a mismatched swap, buying EUR8,000,000 at spot rate against the HKD, to settle the maturing forward contract and then *selling* an amount *more* than EUR8,000,000 forward to increase the hedge size. Because the EUR is the base currency in the HKD/EUR quote, this means using the *bid* side for both the spot rate and the forward points when calculating the all-in forward rate:

$$9.0200 + \frac{173}{10,000} = 9.0373$$

The spot leg of the swap—buying back EUR8,000,000 to settle the outstanding forward transaction—is also based on the bid rate of 9.0200. This is because Yang is selling an amount larger than EUR8,000,000 forward, and the all-in forward rate of the swap is already using the bid side of the market (as it would for a matched swap). Hence, to pick up the net increase in forward EUR sales, the dealer Yang is transacting with would price the swap so that Yang also has to use bid side of the *spot* quote for the spot transaction used to settle the maturing forward contract.

Roll Yield

The roll yield (also called the roll return) on a hedge results from the fact that forward contracts are priced at the spot rate adjusted for the number of forward points at that maturity (see the example shown in Exhibit 3). This forward point adjustment can either benefit or detract from portfolio returns (positive and negative roll yield, respectively) depending on whether the forward points are at a premium or discount, and what side of the market (buying or selling) the portfolio manager is on.

The concept of roll yield is illustrated with the simplified example shown in Exhibit 7.

Exhibit 7: The Forward Curve and Roll Yield

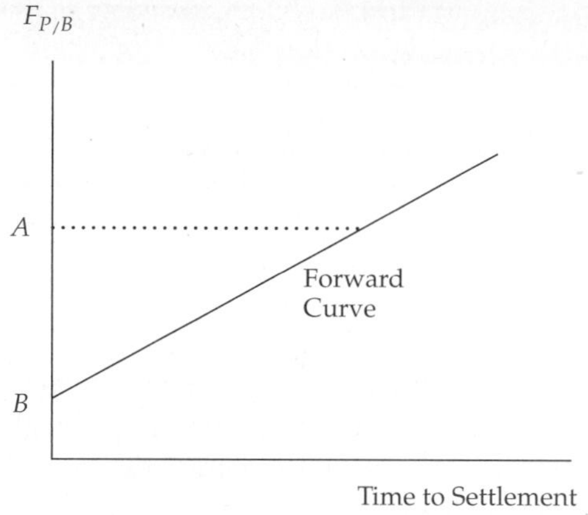

The magnitude of roll yield is given by $|(F_{P/B} - S_{P/B})/S_{P/B}|$ where "||" indicates absolute value. The sign depends on whether the investor needs to buy or to sell the base currency forward in order to maintain the hedge. A *positive* roll yield results from buying the base currency at a forward discount or selling it at a forward premium (the intuition here is that it is profitable to "buy low and sell high"). Otherwise, the roll yield is negative (i.e., a positive cost). Examining the case of negative roll yield, assume that to implement the hedge requires buying the base currency in the P/B quote, and that the base currency is trading at a forward premium (as shown in Exhibit 7). By using a long position in a forward contract to implement this hedge, it means paying the forward price of A. All else equal, as time passes the price of the forward contract will "roll down the curve" toward Price B as the forward contract's settlement date approaches. (Note that in reality the curve is not always linear.) At the settlement date of the forward contract, it is necessary to roll the hedging position forward to extend the currency hedge. This rolling forward will involve selling the base currency at the then-current spot exchange rate to settle the forward contract, and then going long another far-dated forward contract (i.e., an FX swap transaction). Note that the portfolio manager originally bought the base currency at Price A and then subsequently sold it at a lower Price B—and that buying high and selling low will be a cost to the portfolio. Or put differently, all else equal, the roll yield would be negative in this case. Note that the "all else equal" caveat refers to the fact that the all-in price of the forward contract consists of the spot rate and forward points, and both are likely to change over the life of the forward contract. It is possible that at the settlement date the spot rate would have moved higher than A, in which case the roll yield would be positive. But the larger the gap between A and B at contract initiation, the less likely this is to occur.

The concept of roll yield is very similar to the concept of forward rate bias (and the carry trade) introduced in Sections 7–8. Indeed, a negative roll yield typically indicates that the hedger was trading *against* the forward rate bias by buying a currency at a forward premium (as in Exhibit 7) or selling a currency at a forward discount. This is the exact opposite of trading the forward rate bias, which is to buy at a discount and sell at a premium. Given the equivalence between the forward rate bias and the carry trade, by trading against the forward rate bias the hedger with a negative roll yield is also essentially entering into *negative* carry trade, in effect borrowing at high rates and investing at low rates. On average, this will not be a winning strategy. Given the equivalence between implementing a carry trade, trading the forward rate bias, and earning positive roll yield, we can now complete Exhibit 6 introduced in Section 7 on the carry trade:

Exhibit 8: The Carry Trade and Roll Yield

<table>
<tr><th></th><th>Buy/Invest</th><th>Sell/Borrow</th><th></th></tr>
<tr><td>Implementing the carry trade</td><td>High-yield currency</td><td>Low-yield currency</td><td rowspan="2">Earning a positive roll yield</td></tr>
<tr><td>Trading the forward rate bias</td><td>Forward discount currency</td><td>Forward premium currency</td></tr>
</table>

Note as well that this concept of roll yield applies to forward and futures contracts used to trade *any* asset class, not just currencies: It applies equally well to forwards and futures on equities, fixed-income securities, commodities, and indeed, any financial product. For example, consider the case of a commodity processor that hedges the costs of its production process by going long corn futures contracts. If the futures curve for corn futures contracts is in contango (upward sloping, as in Exhibit 7), then this hedging position will also face the potential for negative roll yield.

To be fair, it is also possible for the level of, and movement in, forward points to be in the portfolio manager's favor. Extending our previous example, consider the case of a portfolio manager that has to *sell* the base currency to implement the currency hedge. In this case, the manager would be selling the base currency forward at Price A in Exhibit 7 and, all else equal and through entering an FX swap at settlement date, buying the currency back at the lower Price B—essentially, short selling a financial product with a declining price. In this case, the roll yield is positive.

Because the level of and movements in forward points can either enhance or reduce currency-hedged returns, it explains an observed tendency in foreign exchange markets for the amount of currency hedging to generally vary with movements in forward points. As forward points move against the hedger, the amount of hedging activity typically declines as the cost/benefit ratio of the currency hedge deteriorates. The opposite occurs when movements in forward points reduce hedging costs. Essentially the tendency to hedge will vary depending on whether implementing the hedge happens to be trading in the same direction of the forward rate bias strategy or against it. It is easier to sell a currency forward if there is a "cushion" when it is selling at a forward premium. Likewise, it is more attractive to buy a currency when it is trading at a forward discount. This swings the forward rate bias (and carry trade advantage) in favor of the hedge.

Combined with the manager's market view of future spot rate movements, what this concept implies is that, when setting the hedge ratio, the portfolio manager must balance the effect of expected future exchange rate movements on portfolio returns against the expected effect of the roll yield (i.e., the expected cost of the hedge).

A simple example can illustrate this effect. Consider a portfolio manager that needs to sell forward the base currency of a currency pair (P/B) to implement a currency hedge. Clearly, the manager would prefer to sell this currency at as high a price as possible. Assume that given the forward points for this currency pair and the time horizon for the hedge, the expected roll yield (cost of the hedge) is –3%. Suppose the portfolio manager had a market view that the base currency would depreciate by 4%. In this case, the hedge makes sense: It is better to pay 3% for the hedge to avoid an expected 4% loss.

Now, suppose that with a movement in forward points the new forward discount on the base currency is 6% away from the current spot rate. If the manager's market view is unchanged (an expected depreciation of the base currency of 4%), then now the use of the hedge is less clear: Does it make sense to pay 6% for the hedge to avoid an expected 4% loss? A *risk-neutral* manager would not hedge under these circumstances because the net expected value of the hedge is negative. But a *risk-averse* manager might still implement the hedge regardless of the negative net expected value. The reason is because it is possible that the market forecast is wrong and that the *actual* depreciation of the base currency (and realized loss to the portfolio) may be higher than the 6% cost of the hedge. The risk-averse manager must then weigh the *certainty* of a hedge that costs 6% against the *risk* that actual unhedged currency losses might be much higher than that.

Clearly, the cost/benefit analysis has shifted against hedging in this case, but many risk-averse investors would still undertake the hedge anyway. The risk-averse manager would likely only take an unhedged currency position if the difference between the expected cost of the hedge and the expected return on an unhedged position was so great as to make the risk acceptable. Balancing these two considerations would depend on the type of market view the manager held and the degree of conviction in it, as well as the manager's degree of risk aversion. The decision taken will vary among investors, so no definitive answer can be given as to what would be the appropriate hedging choice (different portfolio managers will make different choices given the same opportunity set). But hedging costs will vary with market conditions and the higher the expected cost of the hedge (negative roll yield) the more the cost/benefit calculation moves against using a fully hedged position. Or put another way, if setting up the hedge involves selling the low-yield currency and buying the high-yield currency in the P/B pair (i.e., an implicit carry position), then the more likely the portfolio will be fully hedged or even over-hedged. The opposite is also true: Trading against the forward rate bias is likely to lead to lower hedge ratios, all else equal.

EXAMPLE 4

The Hedging Decision

The reporting currency of Hong Kong SAR-based Kwun Tong Investment Advisors is the Hong Kong dollar (HKD). The investment committee is examining whether it should implement a currency hedge for the firm's exposures to the GBP and the ZAR (the firm has long exposures to both of these foreign currencies). The hedge would use forward contracts. The following data relevant to assessing the expected cost of the hedge and the expected move in the spot exchange rate has been developed by the firm's market strategist.

	Current Spot Rate	Six-Month Forward Rate	Six-Month Forecast Spot Rate
HKD/GBP	10.6000	10.5895	10.2000
HKD/ZAR	0.5210	0.5082	0.5100

1. Recommend whether to hedge the firm's long GBP exposure. Justify your recommendation.

Solution:

Kwun Tong is long the GBP against the HKD, and HKD/GBP is selling at a small forward discount of 0.099% compared with the current spot rate. All else equal, this is the expected roll yield—which is not in the firm's favor, in this case, because to implement the hedge Kwun Tong would be *selling* GBP, the base currency in the quote, at a price *lower* than the current spot rate. However, the firm's market strategist expects the GBP to *depreciate* by 3.77% against the HKD. Thus, the negative carry of hedging is small in comparison to the potential loss. Both of these considerations argue for hedging this exposure.

2. Discuss the trade-offs in hedging the firm's long ZAR exposure.

Solution:

Kwun Tong is long the ZAR against the HKD, and HKD/ZAR is selling at a forward discount of −2.5% compared with the current spot rate. Implementing the hedge would require the firm to *sell* the base currency in the quote, the ZAR, at a price *lower* than the current spot rate. This would imply that, all else equal, the roll yield would go against the firm; that is, the expected cost of the hedge would be 2.5%. But the firm's strategist also forecasts that the ZAR will depreciate against the HKD by 2.11%. This makes the decision to hedge less certain. A risk-neutral investor would not hedge because the expected cost of the hedge is more than the expected depreciation of the ZAR. But this is only a point forecast and comes with a degree of uncertainty—there is a risk that the HKD/ZAR spot rate might depreciate by more than the 2.5% cost of the hedge. In this case, the decision to hedge the currency risk would depend on the trade-offs between (1) the level of risk aversion of the firm; and (2) the conviction the firm held in the currency forecast—that is, the level of certainty that the ZAR would not depreciate by more than 2.5%.

Currency Options

One of the costs of forward contracts is the opportunity cost. Once fully hedged, the portfolio manager forgoes any upside potential for future currency moves in the portfolio's favor. Currency options remove this opportunity cost because they provide the manager the right, but not the obligation, to buy or sell foreign exchange at a future date at a rate agreed on today. The manager will only exercise the option at the expiry date if it is favorable to do so.[17]

Consider the case of a portfolio manager who is long the base currency in the P/B quote and needs to sell this currency to implement the hedge. One approach is to simply buy an at-the-money put option on the P/B currency pair. Matching a long position in the underlying with a put option is known as a **protective put** strategy. Suppose the current spot rate is 1.3650 and the strike price on the put option bought is 1.3650. If the P/B rate subsequently goes down (P appreciates and B depreciates) by the expiry date, the manager can exercise the option, implement the hedge, and

17 Almost all options in the FX market are European-style options, which only allow for exercise at the expiry date.

guarantee a selling price of 1.3650. But if the P/B rate increases (P depreciates and B appreciates), the manager can simply let the option expire and collect the currency gains.

Unfortunately, like forward contracts, currency options are not "free goods" and, like any form of insurance, there is always a price to be paid for it. Buying an option means paying an upfront premium. This premium is determined, first, by its **intrinsic value**, which is the difference between the spot exchange rate and the strike price of the option (i.e., whether the option is in the money, at the money, or out of the money, respectively). ATM options are more expensive than OTM options, and frequently these relatively expensive options expire without being exercised.

The second determinant of an option's premium is its **time value**, which in turn is heavily influenced by the volatility in exchange rates. Regardless of exchange rate volatility, however, options are always moving toward expiry. In general, the time value of the option is always declining. This is the time decay of the option's value (theta, one of the "Greeks" of option prices, describes this effect) and is similar in concept to that of negative roll yield on forward contracts described earlier. Time decay always works against the owner of an option.

As with forward contracts, a portfolio manager will have to make judgments about the cost/benefit trade-offs of options-based strategies. Although options do allow the portfolio upside potential from favorable currency movements, options can also be a very expensive form of insurance. The manager will have to balance any market view of potential currency gains against hedging costs and the degree of risk aversion. There is no "right" answer; different managers will make different decisions about the cost/benefit trade-offs when given the same opportunity set.

EXAMPLE 5

Hedging Problems

Brixworth & St. Ives Asset Management is a UK-based firm managing a dynamic hedging program for the currency exposures in its Aggressive Growth Fund. One of the fund's foreign-currency asset holdings is denominated in the Mexican peso (MXN), and one month ago Brixworth & St. Ives fully hedged this exposure using a two-month MXN/GBP forward contract. The following table provides the relevant information.

	One Month Ago	Today
Value of assets (in MXN)	10,000,000	9,500,000
MXN/GBP spot rate (bid–offer)	29.0500/29.0580	27.5985/28.0065
One-month forward points (bid–offer)	1,475/1,510	1,500/1,536
Two-month forward points (bid–offer)	2,590/2,650	2,640/2,700

The Aggressive Growth Fund also has an unhedged foreign-currency asset exposure denominated in the South African rand (ZAR). The current mid-market spot rate in the ZAR/GBP currency pair is 20.1050.

1. One month ago, Brixworth & St. Ives *most likely* sold:

   A. MXN9,500,000 forward at an all-in forward rate of MXN/GBP 19.6635.

   B. MXN10,000,000 forward at an all-in forward rate of MXN/GBP 29.3090.

   C. MXN10,000,000 forward at an all-in forward rate of MXN/GBP 29.3230.

Solution:

C is correct. Brixworth & St. Ives is long the MXN and hence must sell the MXN forward against the GBP. Selling MXN against the GBP means buying GBP, the base currency in the MXN/GBP quote. Therefore, the offer side of the market must be used. This means the all-in rate used one month ago would have been 29.058 + 2,650/10,000, which equals 29.3230. Choice A is incorrect because it uses today's asset value and the incorrect forward quotes and Choice B is incorrect because it uses the wrong side of the market (the bid side).

2. To rebalance the hedge today, the firm would *most likely* need to:

   A. buy MXN500,000 spot.

   B. buy MXN500,000 forward.

   C. sell MXN500,000 forward.

Solution:

B is correct. The foreign investment went down in value in MXN terms. Therefore Brixworth & St. Ives must reduce the size of the hedge. Previously it had sold MXN10,000,000 forward against the GBP, and this amount must be reduced to MXN9,500,000 by buying MXN500,000 forward. Choice A is incorrect because hedging is done with forward contracts not spot deals. Choice C is incorrect because selling MXN forward would increase the size of the hedge, not decrease it.

3. Given the data in the table, the roll yield on this hedge at the forward contracts' maturity date is *most likely* to be:

   A. zero.

   B. negative.

   C. positive.

Solution:

B is correct. To implement the hedge, Brixworth & St. Ives must sell MXN against the GBP, or equivalently, buy GBP (the base currency in the P/B quote) against the MXN. The base currency is selling forward at a premium, and—all else equal—its price would "roll down the curve" as contract maturity approached. Having to settle the forward contract means then selling the GBP spot at a lower price. Buying high and selling low will define a negative roll yield. Moreover, the GBP has depreciated against the MXN, because the MXN/GBP spot rate declined between one month ago and now, which will also add to the negative roll yield.

4. Assuming that all ZAR/GBP options considered have the same notional amount and maturity, the *most* expensive hedge that Brixworth & St. Ives could use to hedge its ZAR exposure is a long position in a(n):

   A. ATM GBP call.

   B. 25-delta GBP call.

   C. GBP put with a strike of 20.1050.

Solution:

A is correct. The Aggressive Growth Fund is long the ZAR through its foreign-currency assets, and to hedge this exposure it must sell the ZAR against the GBP, or equivalently, buy GBP—the base currency in the P/B quote—against the ZAR. Hedging a required purchase means a long position in a call option (not a put, which is used to hedge a required sale of the base currency in the P/B quote). An ATM call option is more expensive than a 25-delta call option.

CURRENCY MANAGEMENT STRATEGIES 10

☐ describe trading strategies used to reduce hedging costs and modify the risk–return characteristics of a foreign-currency portfolio

In the previous sections, we showed that completely hedging currency risk is possible—but can also be expensive. It can be even more expensive when trying to avoid all downside risk while keeping the full upside potential for favorable currency movements (i.e., a protective put strategy with ATM options). Hedging can be seen as a form of insurance, but it is possible to overpay for insurance. Judgments have to be made to determine at what point the costs outweigh the benefits.

As with any form of insurance, there are always steps that can be taken to reduce hedging costs. For most typical insurance products, these cost-reduction measures include such things as higher deductibles, co-pay arrangements, and lower maximum payouts. The same sorts of measures exist in the FX derivatives market; we will explore these various alterative measures in this section. The key point to keep in mind is that all of these various cost-reduction measures invariably involve some combination of *less downside protection* and/or *less upside potential* for the hedge. In efficient markets, lower insurance premiums mean lower insurance.

These cost-reduction measures also start moving the portfolio away from a passively managed 100% hedge ratio toward discretionary hedging in which the manager is allowed to take directional positions. Once the possibility of accepting some downside risk, and some upside potential, is introduced into the portfolio, the manager is moving away from a rules-based approach to hedging toward a more active style of trading. The portfolio manager can then use the trading tools and strategies described in the following sections to express a market view and/or cut hedging costs.

The variety of trading strategies—involving various combinations of forwards, options, and swaps—that can be deployed to this end is almost infinite. We will not attempt to explore all of them in this reading, but rather to give a sense of the range of trading tools and strategies available for managing currency risk. We begin with Exhibit 9, which gives a high-level description of some of these various trading strategies that will then be explained in more detail in subsequent sections. Note that as this section progresses, we will be describing strategies at different points along the risk spectrum described in Sections 4–6, moving in turn from passive hedge-based approaches to strategies used in more active currency management schemes.

Exhibit 9: Select Currency Management Strategies

Forward Contracts	Over-/under-hedging	Profit from market view
Option Contracts	OTM options	Cheaper than ATM
	Risk reversals	Write options to earn premiums

	Put/call spreads	Write options to earn premiums
	Seagull spreads	Write options to earn premiums
Exotic Options	Knock-in/out features	Reduced downside/upside exposure
	Digital options	Extreme payoff strategies

We will make one simplifying assumption for the following sections. Currency management strategies will differ fundamentally depending on whether the base currency of the P/B price quote must be bought or sold to decrease the foreign-currency exposure. To simplify the material and impose consistency on the discussions that follow, we will assume that the portfolio manager must sell the base currency in the P/B quote to reduce currency risk. In addition, unless otherwise noted, the notional amounts and expiration dates on all forward and options contracts are the same.[18]

Over-/Under-Hedging Using Forward Contracts

When the IPS gives the manager discretion either to over- or under-hedge the portfolio, relative to the "neutral" benchmark, there is the possibility to add incremental value based on the manager's market view. Profits from successful tactical positioning help reduce net hedging costs. For example, if the neutral benchmark hedge ratio is 100% for the base currency being hedged, and the portfolio manager has a market opinion that the base currency is likely to depreciate, then *over*-hedging through a short position in P/B forward contracts might be implemented—that is, the manager might use a hedge ratio higher than 100%. Similarly, if the manager's market opinion is that the base currency is likely to appreciate, the currency exposure might be *under*-hedged.

A variant of this approach would be to adjust the hedge ratio based on exchange rate movements: to increase the hedge ratio if the base currency depreciated, but decrease the hedge ratio if the base currency appreciated. Essentially, this approach is a form of "delta hedging" that tries to mimic the payoff function of a put option on the base currency. That is, this form of dynamic hedging with forward contracts tries to increasingly participate in any upside moves of the base currency, but increasingly hedge any downside moves. Doing so adds "convexity" to the portfolio, meaning that the hedge's payoff function will be a convex curve when this function is graphed with profit on the vertical axis and the spot rate on the horizontal axis. (Note that this concept of convexity is identical in intent to the concept of convexity describing bonds; as convexity increases the price of a bond rises more quickly in a declining yield environment and drops more slowly in a rising yield environment. Convexity is a desirable characteristic in both the fixed-income and currency-hedging contexts.)

Protective Put Using OTM Options

In the previous section, we examined a dynamic hedging strategy using forward contracts that tries to mimic the payoff function of an option and put convexity into the hedge's payoff function. The payoff functions for options are naturally convex to begin with. However, this can be a costly form of convexity (relatively high option premiums), and fully hedging a currency position with a protective put strategy using an ATM option is the most expensive means of all to buy convexity.

One way to reduce the cost of using options is to accept some downside risk by using an OTM option, such as a 25- or 10-delta option. These options will be less costly, but also do not fully protect the portfolio from adverse currency movements. Conversely, it makes sense to insure against larger risks but accept some smaller

18 Examples of implementing a hedge by *buying* the base currency will be provided in some of the practice examples.

day-to-day price movements in currencies. As an analogy, it may be possible to buy a home or car insurance policy with a zero deductible—but the premiums would be exorbitant. It may be more rational to have a cheaper insurance policy and accept responsibility for minor events, but insure against extreme damage.

Risk Reversal (or Collar)

Another set of option strategies involves *selling* options (also known as writing options) to earn income that can be used to offset the cost of buying a put option, which forms the "core" of the hedge. Recall that in this section, we are using the simplifying convention that the manager is long the base currency in the P/B quote; hence puts and not calls would be used for hedging in this case.

One strategy to obtain downside protection at a lower cost than a straight protective put position is to *buy* an OTM put option and *write* an OTM call option. Essentially, the portfolio manager is selling some of the upside potential for movements in the base currency (writing a call) and using the option's premiums to help pay the cost of the long put option being purchased. This approach is similar to creating a collar in fixed-income markets. The portfolio is protected against downside movements, but its upside is limited to the strike price on the OTM call option; the exchange rate risk is confined to a corridor or "collar."

In professional FX markets, having a long position in a call option and a short position in a put option is called a **risk reversal**. For example, buying a 25-delta call and writing a 25-delta put is referred to as a *long* position in a 25-delta risk reversal. The position used to create the collar position we just described (buying a put, writing a call) would be a *short* position in a risk reversal.

The majority of currency hedging for foreign-currency asset portfolios and corporate accounts is based on the use of forward contracts and simple option strategies (protective puts/covered calls and risk reversals/collars). We now begin to transition to more active trading strategies that are designed to express market views for speculative profit.

Put Spread

A variation of the short risk reversal position is a **put spread**, which is also used to reduce the upfront cost of buying a protective put. The short risk reversal is structured by buying a put option and writing a call option: the premiums received by writing the call help cover the cost of the put. Similarly, the put spread position involves buying a put option and writing another put option to help cover the cost of the long put's premiums. This position is typically structured by buying an OTM put, and writing a deeper-OTM put to gain income from premiums; both options involved have the same maturity.

To continue our previous example, with the current spot rate at 1.3550, the portfolio manager might set up the following put spread: buy a put with a strike of 1.3500 and write a put with a strike of 1.3450. The payoff on the put spread position will then be as follows: there is no hedge protection between 1.3550 and 1.3500; the portfolio is hedged from 1.3500 down to 1.3450; at spot rates below 1.3450, the portfolio becomes unhedged again. The put spread reduces the cost of the hedge, but at the cost of more limited downside protection. The portfolio manager would then use this spread only for cases in which a modest decline in the spot exchange rate was expected, and this position would have to be closely monitored against adverse exchange rate movements.

Note that the put spread structure will not be zero-cost because the deeper-OTM put (1.3450) being written will be cheaper than the less-OTM put (1.3500) being bought. However, there are approaches that will make the put spread (or almost any other option spread position) cheaper or possibly zero-cost: the manager could alter: (a) the strike prices of the options; (b) the notional amounts of the options; or (c) some combination of these two measures.

Altering the strike prices of the put options would mean moving them closer together (and hence more equal in cost). However, this would reduce the downside protection on the hedge. Instead, the portfolio manager could write a larger notional amount for the deeper-OTM option; for example, the ratio for the notionals for the options written versus bought might be 1:2. (In standard FX market notation, this would be a 1 × 2 put spread—the option with exercise price closest to being ATM is given first. However, to avoid confusion it is good practice to specify explicitly in the price quote which is the long and short positions, and what their deltas/strike prices are.) Although this structure may now be (approximately) zero-cost it is not without risks: for spot rates below 1.3450 the portfolio has now seen its exposure to the base currency double-up (because of the 1:2 proportion of notionals) and at a worse spot exchange rate for the portfolio on top of it. Creating a zero-cost structure with a 1 × 2 put spread is equivalent to adding leverage to the options position, because you are selling more options than you are buying. This means that this put spread position will have to be carefully managed. For example, the portfolio manager might choose to close out the short position in the deep-OTM put (by going long/buying an equivalent put option) before the base currency depreciates to the 1.3450 strike level. This may be a costly position exit, however, as the market moves against the manager's original positioning. Because of this, this sort of 1 × 2 structure may be more appropriate for expressing directional opinions rather than as a pure hedging strategy.

Seagull Spread

An alternative, and somewhat safer approach, would be to combine the original put spread position (1:1 proportion of notionals) with a covered call position. This is simply an extension of the concept behind risk reversals and put spreads. The "core" of the hedge (for a manager long the base currency) is the long position in a put option. This is expensive. To reduce the cost, a short risk reversal position writes a call option while a put spread writes a deep-OTM put option. Of course, the manager can always do both: that is, be long a protective put and then write *both* a call and a deep-OTM put. This option structure is sometimes referred to as a **seagull spread**.

As with the names for other option strategies based on winged creatures, the "seagull" indicates an option structure with at least three individual options, and in which the options at the most distant strikes—the wings—are on the opposite side of the market from the middle strike(s)—the body. For example, if the current spot price is 1.3550, a seagull could be constructed by going *long* an ATM put at 1.3550 (the middle strike is the "body"), *short* an OTM put at 1.3500, and *short* an OTM call at 1.3600 (the latter two options are the "wings"). Because the options in the "wings" are being written (sold) this is called a *short* seagull position. The risk/return profile of this structure gives full downside protection from 1.3550 to 1.3500 (at which point the short put position neutralizes the hedge) and participation in the upside potential in spot rate movements to 1.3600 (the strike level for the short call option).

Note that because *two* options are now being written to gain premiums instead of one, this approach allows the strike price of the long put position to be ATM, increasing the downside protection. The various strikes and/or notional sizes of these options (and hence their premiums) can always be adjusted up or down until a zero-cost structure is obtained. However, note that this particular seagull structure gives away some upside potential (the short call position) as well as takes on some downside risk (if the short put position is triggered, it will disable the hedge coverage coming from the long put position). As always, lower structure costs come with some combination of lower downside protection and/or less upside potential.

There are many variants of these seagull strategies, each of which provides a different risk–reward profile (and net cost). For example, for the portfolio manager wishing to hedge a long position in the base currency in the P/B quote when the current spot rate is 1.3550, another seagull structure would be to write an ATM call at 1.3550 and use the proceeds to buy an OTM put option at 1.3500 and an OTM call option at 1.3600. Note that in this seagull structure, the "body" is now a *short* option position, not a long position as in the previous example, and the "wings" are the long position. Hence, it is a *long* seagull spread. This option structure provides cheap downside protection (the hedge kicks in at the put's 1.3500 strike) while providing the portfolio manager with unlimited participation in any rally in the base currency beyond the 1.3600 strike of the OTM call option. As before, the various option strikes and/or notional sizes on the options bought and written can be adjusted so that a zero-cost structure is obtained.

Exotic Options

In this section, we move even further away from derivatives and trading strategies used mainly for hedging, and toward the more speculative end of the risk spectrum dominated by active currency management. Exotic options are often used by more sophisticated players in the professional trading market—for example, currency overlay managers—and are less frequently used by institutional investors, investment funds, or corporations for hedging purposes. There are several reasons for this relatively light usage of "exotics" for hedging purposes, some related to the fact that many smaller entities lack familiarity with these products. Another reason involves the difficulty of getting hedge accounting treatment in many jurisdictions, which is more advantageous for financial reporting reasons. Finally, the specialized terms of such instruments make them difficult to value for regulatory and accounting purposes.

In general, the term "exotic" refers to all options that are not "vanilla." In FX, vanilla refers essentially to European-style put and call options. The full range of exotic options is both very broad and constantly evolving; many are extraordinarily complex both to price and even to understand. However, all exotics, no matter how complex, typically share one defining feature in common: They are designed to customize the risk exposures desired by the client and provide them at the lowest possible price.[19] Much like the trading strategies described previously, they usually involve some combination of lower downside protection and/or lower upside potential while providing the client with the specific risk exposures they are prepared to manage, and to do so at what is generally a lower cost than vanilla options.

The two most common type of exotic options encountered in foreign exchange markets are those with **knock-in/knock-out** features and digital options.

An option with a knock-in feature is essentially a vanilla option that is created only when the spot exchange rate touches a pre-specified level (this trigger level, called the "barrier," is not the same as the strike price). Similarly a knock-out option is a vanilla option that ceases to exist when the spot exchange rate touches some pre-specified barrier level. Because these options only exist (i.e., get knocked-in or knocked-out) under certain circumstances, they are more restrictive than vanilla options and hence are cheaper. But again, the knock-in/out features provide less upside potential and/or downside protection.

Digital options are also called binary options, or all-or-nothing options. The expiry value of an in-the-money vanilla option varies based on the amount of difference between the expiry level and strike price. In contrast, digital options pay out a fixed amount if they are determined to be in-the-money. For example, American digital options pay a *fixed* amount if they "touch" their exercise level at any time before

19 Although the price is low for the client compared with vanilla options, exotics are typically nonetheless high profit margin items for investment dealers.

expiry (even if by a single pip). This characteristic of "extreme payoff" options makes them almost akin to a lottery ticket. Because of these large payoffs, digital options usually cost more than vanilla options with the same strike price. But digitals also provide highly leveraged exposure to movements in the spot rate. This makes these exotic products more appropriate as trading tools for active currency management, rather than as hedging tools. In practice, digital options are typically used by more sophisticated speculative accounts in the FX market to express directional views on exchange rates.

A full exposition of exotic options is beyond the scope of this reading, but the reader should be aware of their existence and why they exist.

Section Summary

Clearly, loosening the constraint of a fully hedged portfolio begins to introduce complicated active currency management decisions. The following steps can be helpful to sort things out:

a. First, identify the *base* currency in the P/B quote (currency pair) you are dealing with. Derivatives are typically quoted in terms of either buying or selling the *base* currency when the option is exercised. A move upward in the P/B quote is an appreciation of the base currency.

b. Then, identify whether the base currency must be *bought* or *sold* to establish the hedge. These are the price movements you will be protecting against.

c. If *buying* the base currency is required to implement the hedge, then the core hedge structure will be based on some combination of a long call option and/or a long forward contract. The cost of this core hedge can be reduced by buying an OTM call option or writing options to earn premiums. (But keep in mind, lower hedging costs equate to less downside protection and/or upside potential.)

d. If *selling* the base currency is required to implement the hedge, then the core hedge structure will be based on some combination of a long put option and/or a short forward contract. The cost of this core hedge can be reduced by buying an OTM put option or writing options to earn premiums.

e. The higher the allowed discretion for active management, the lower the risk aversion; and the firmer a particular market view is held, the more the hedge is likely to be structured to allow risk exposures in the portfolio. This approach involves positioning in derivatives that "lean the same way" as the market view. (For example, a market view that the base currency will depreciate would use some combination of short forward contracts, writing call options, buying put options, and using "bearish" exotic strategies.) This directional bias to the trading position would be superimposed on the core hedge position described in steps "c" and "d," creating an active-trading "tilt" in the portfolio.

f. For these active strategies, varying the strike prices and notional amounts of the options involved can move the trading position toward a zero-cost structure. But as with hedges, keep in mind that lower cost implies less downside protection and/or upside potential for the portfolio.

A lot of different hedging tools and strategies have been named and covered in this section. Rather than attempting to absorb all of them by rote memorization (a put spread is "X" and a seagull is "Y"), the reader is encouraged instead to focus on the intuition behind a hedge, and how and why it is constructed. It matters less what name (if any) is given to any specific approach; what is important is understanding how all the moving parts fit together. The reader should focus on a "building blocks" approach in understanding how and why the parts of the currency hedge are assembled in a given manner.

EXAMPLE 6

Alternative Hedging Strategies

Brixworth & St. Ives Asset Management, the UK-based investment firm, has hedged the exposure of its Aggressive Growth Fund to the MXN with a long position in a MXN/GBP forward contract. The fund's foreign-currency asset exposure to the ZAR is hedged by buying an ATM call option on the ZAR/GBP currency pair. The portfolio managers at Brixworth & St. Ives are looking at ways to modify the risk–reward trade-offs and net costs of their currency hedges.

Jasmine Khan, one of the analysts at Brixworth & St. Ives, proposes an option-based hedge structure for the long-ZAR exposure that would replace the hedge based on the ATM call option with either long or short positions in the following three options on ZAR/GBP:

a. ATM put option
b. 25-delta put option
c. 25-delta call option

Khan argues that these three options can be combined into a hedge structure that will have some limited downside risk, but provide complete hedge protection starting at the relevant 25-delta strike level. The structure will also have upside potential, although this will not start until the ZAR/GBP exchange rate moves to the relevant 25-delta strike level. Finally, this structure can be created at a relatively low cost because it involves option writing.

1. The *best* method for Brixworth & St. Ives to gain some upside potential for the hedge on the Aggressive Growth Fund's MXN exposure using MXN/GBP options is to replace the forward contract with a:

   A. long position in an OTM put.
   B. short position in an ATM call.
   C. long position in a 25-delta risk reversal.

Solution:

C is correct. The Aggressive Growth Fund has a long foreign-currency exposure to the MXN in its asset portfolio, which is hedged by selling the MXN against the GBP, or equivalently, buying the GBP—the base currency in the P/B quote—against the MXN. This need to protect against an *appreciation* in the GBP is why the hedge is using a *long* position in the forward contract. To set a collar around the MXN/GBP rate, Brixworth & St. Ives would want a long call option position with a strike greater than the current spot rate (this gives upside potential to the hedge) and a short put position with a strike less than the current spot rate (this reduces net cost of the hedge). A long call and a short put defines a long position in a risk reversal.

Choice A is incorrect because, if exercised, buying a put option would increase the fund's exposure to the MXN (sell GBP, buy MXN). Similarly, Choice B is incorrect because, if exercised, the ATM call option would increase the MXN exposure (the GBP is "called" away from the fund at the strike price with MXN delivered). Moreover, although writing the ATM call option would gain some income from premiums, writing options (on their own) is never considered the "best" hedge because the premium income earned is fixed but the potential losses on adverse currency moves are potentially unlimited.

2. While keeping the ATM call option in the ZAR/GBP, the method that would lead to *greatest* cost reduction on the hedge would be to:

   A. buy a 25-delta put.

   B. write a 10-delta call.

   C. write a 25-delta call.

Solution:

C is correct. As before, the hedge is implemented in protecting against an *appreciation* of the base currency of the P/B quote, the GBP. The hedge is established with an ATM call option (a long position in the GBP). Writing an OTM call option (i.e., with a strike that is more than the current spot rate of 20.1050) establishes a call spread (although hedge protection is lost if ZAR/GBP expires at or above the strike level). Writing a 25-delta call earns more income from premiums than a deeper-OTM 10-delta call (although the 25-delta call has less hedge protection). Buying an option would increase the cost of the hedge, and a put option on the ZAR/GBP would increase the fund's ZAR exposure if exercised (the GBP is "put" to the counterparty at the strike price and ZAR received).

3. Setting up Khan's proposed hedge structure would *most likely* involve being:

   A. long the 25-delta options and short the ATM option.

   B. long the 25-delta call, and short both the ATM and 25-delta put options.

   C. short the 25-delta call, and long both the ATM and 25-delta put options.

Solution:

A is correct. Once again, the hedge is based on hedging the need to sell ZAR/buy GBP, and GBP is the base currency in the ZAR/GBP quote. This means the hedge needs to protect against an *appreciation* of the GBP (an appreciation of the ZAR/GBP rate). Based on Khan's description, the hedge provides protection after a certain loss point, which would be a long 25-delta call. Upside potential after favorable (i.e., down) moves in the ZAR/GBP past a certain level means a long 25-delta put. Getting the low net cost that Khan refers to means that the cost of these two long positions is financed by selling the ATM option. (Together these three positions define a long seagull spread). Choice B is incorrect because although the first two legs of the position are right, a short position in the put does not provide upside potential (from a down-move in ZAR/GBP). Choice C is incorrect because any option-based hedge, given the need to hedge against an up-move in the ZAR/GBP rate, is going to be based on a long call position. C does not contain any of these.

HEDGING MULTIPLE FOREIGN CURRENCIES

11

- ☐ describe the use of cross-hedges, macro-hedges, and minimum-variance-hedge ratios in portfolios exposed to multiple foreign currencies

We now expand our discussion to hedging a portfolio with multiple foreign-currency assets. The hedging tools and strategies are very similar to those discussed for hedging a single foreign-currency asset, except now the currency hedge must consider the *correlation* between the various foreign-currency risk exposures.

For example, consider the case of a US-domiciled investor who has exposures to foreign-currency assets in Australia and New Zealand. These two economies are roughly similar in that they are resource-based and closely tied to the regional economy of the Western Pacific, especially the large emerging markets in Asia. As a result, the movements in their currencies are often closely correlated; the USD/AUD and USD/NZD currency pairs will tend to move together. If the portfolio manager has the discretion to take short positions, the portfolio may (for example) possibly have a net long position in the Australian foreign-currency asset and a net short position in the New Zealand foreign-currency asset. In this case, there may be less need to hedge away the AUD and NZD currency exposures separately because the portfolio's long exposure to the AUD is diversified by the short position on the NZD.

Cross Hedges and Macro Hedges

A **cross hedge** occurs when a position in one asset (or a derivative based on the asset) is used to hedge the risk exposures of a different asset (or a derivative based on it). Normally, cross hedges are not needed because, as we mentioned earlier, forward contracts and other derivatives are widely available in almost every conceivable currency pair. However, if the portfolio already has "natural" cross hedges in the form of negatively correlated residual currency exposures—as in the long-AUD/short-NZD example in Section 11—this helps moderate portfolio risk ($\sigma[R_{DC}]$) without having to use a direct hedge on the currency exposure.

Sometimes a distinction is made between a "proxy" hedge and a "cross" hedge. When this distinction is made, a *proxy hedge* removes the foreign currency risk by hedging it back to the investor's domestic currency—such as in the example with USD/AUD and USD/NZD discussed in the text. In contrast, a *cross hedge* moves the currency risk from one foreign currency to another foreign currency. For example, a US-domiciled investor may have an exposure to both the Indonesian rupiah (IDR) and the Thai baht (THB), but based on a certain market view, may only want exposure to the THB. In this context, the manager might use currency derivatives as a cross hedge to convert the IDR/USD exposure to a THB/USD exposure. But not all market participants make this sharp of a distinction between proxy hedges and cross hedges, and these terms are often used interchangeably. The most common term found among practitioners in most asset classes is simply a cross hedge, as we are using the term here: hedging an exposure with a closely correlated product (i.e., a proxy hedge when this distinction is made). The cross hedge of moving currency exposures between various *foreign* currencies is more of a special-case application of this concept. In our example, a US investor wanting to shift currency exposures between the IDR and THB would only need to shift the relative size of the IDR/USD and THB/USD forward contracts *already* being used. As mentioned earlier, forwards are available on almost every currency pair, so a cross hedge from foreign currency "A" to foreign currency "B" would be a special case when derivatives on one of the currencies are not available.

EXAMPLE 7

Cross Hedges

Mai Nguyen works at Cape Henlopen Advisors, which runs a US-domiciled fund that invests in foreign-currency assets of Australia and New Zealand. The fund currently has equally weighted exposure to one-year Australian and New Zealand treasury bills (i.e., both of the portfolio weights, $\omega_i = 0.5$). Because the foreign-currency return on these treasury bill assets is risk-free and known in advance, their expected $\sigma(R_{FC})$ is equal to zero.

Nguyen wants to calculate the USD-denominated returns on this portfolio as well as the cross hedging effects of these investments. She collects the following information:

Expected Values	Australia	New Zealand
Foreign-currency asset return R_{FC}	4.0%	6.0%
Foreign-currency return R_{FX}	5.0%	5.0%
Asset risk $\sigma(R_{FC})$	0%	0%
Currency risk $\sigma(R_{FX})$	8.0%	10.0%
Correlation (USD/AUD; USD/NZD)	+0.85	

Using Equation 1, Nguyen calculates that the expected domestic-currency return for the Australian asset is

$$(1.04)\ (1.05) - 1 = 0.092$$

or 9.2%. Likewise, she determines that the expected domestic-currency return for the New Zealand asset is

$$(1.06)\ (1.05) - 1 = 0.113$$

or 11.3%. Together, the result is that the expected domestic-currency return (R_{DC}) on the equally weighted foreign-currency asset portfolio is the weighted average of these two individual country returns, or

$$R_{DC} = 0.5(9.2\%) + 0.5(11.3\%) = 10.3\%$$

Nguyen now turns her attention to calculating the portfolio's investment risk [$\sigma(R_{DC})$]. To calculate the expected risk for the domestic-currency return, the currency risk of R_{FX} needs to be multiplied by the *known* return on the treasury bills. The portfolio's investment risk, $\sigma(R_{DC})$, is found by calculating the standard deviation of the right-hand-side of:

$$R_{DC} = (1 + R_{FC})(1 + R_{FX}) - 1$$

Although R_{FX} is a random variable—it is not known in advance—the R_{FC} term is in fact known in advance because the asset return is risk-free. Because of this Nguyen can make use of the statistical rules that, first, $\sigma(kX) = k\sigma(X)$, where X is a random variable and k is a constant; and second, that the correlation between a random variable and a constant is zero. These results greatly simplify the calculations because, in this case, she does not need to consider the correlation between exchange rate movements and foreign-currency asset returns. Instead, Nguyen needs to calculate the risk only on the currency side. Applying these statistical rules to the above formula leads to the following results:

A. The expected risk (i.e., standard deviation) of the domestic-currency return for the Australian asset is equal to (1.04) × 8% = 8.3%.

B. The expected risk (i.e., standard deviation) of the domestic-currency return for the New Zealand asset is equal to (1.06) × 10% = 10.6%.

Adding all of these numerical values into Equation 4 leads Nguyen to calculate:

$$\sigma^2(R_{DC}) = (0.5)^2(8.3\%)^2 + (0.5)^2(10.6\%)^2 + [(2)0.5(8.3\%)0.5(10.6\%)0.85]$$
$$= 0.8\%$$

The standard deviation of this amount—that is, $\sigma(R_{DC})$—is 9.1%. Note that in the expression, all of the units are in percent, so for example, 8.3% is equivalent to 0.083 for calculation purposes. The careful reader may also note that Nguyen is able to use an exact expression for calculating the variance of the portfolio returns, rather than the approximate expressions shown in Equations 3 and 5. This is because, with risk-free foreign-currency assets, the variance of these foreign-currency returns $\sigma^2(R_{FC})$ is equal to zero.

Nguyen now considers an alternative scenario in which, instead of an equally weighted portfolio (where the $\omega_i = 0.5$), the fund has a long exposure to the New Zealand asset and a short exposure to the Australian asset (i.e., the ω_i are +1 and −1, respectively; this is similar to a highly leveraged carry trade position). Putting these weights into Equations 2 and 4 leads to

$$R_{DC} = -1.0(9.2\%) + 1.0(11.3\%) = 2.1\%$$

$$\sigma^2(R_{DC}) = (1.0)^2(8.3\%)^2 + (1.0)^2(10.6\%)^2 + [-2.0(8.3\%)(10.6\%)0.85]$$
$$= 0.3\%$$

The standard deviation—that is, $\sigma(R_{DC})$—is now 5.6%, less than either of the expected risks for foreign-currency asset returns (results A and B). Nguyen concludes that having long and short positions in positively correlated currencies can lead to much lower portfolio risk, through the benefits of cross hedging. (Nguyen goes on to calculate that if the expected correlation between USD/AUD and USD/NZD increases to 0.95, with all else equal, the expected domestic-currency return risk on the long–short portfolio drops to 3.8%.)

Some types of cross hedges are often referred to as macro hedges. The reason is because the hedge is more focused on the entire portfolio, particularly when individual asset price movements are highly correlated, rather than on individual assets or currency pairs. Another way of viewing a macro hedge is to see the portfolio not just as a collection of financial assets, but as a collection of risk exposures. These various risk exposures are typically defined in categories, such as term risk, credit risk, and liquidity risk. These risks can also be defined in terms of the potential financial scenarios the portfolio is exposed to, such as recession, financial sector stress, or inflation. Often macro hedges are defined in terms of the financial scenario they are designed to protect the portfolio from.

Putting gold in the portfolio sometimes serves this purpose by helping to provide broad portfolio protection against extreme market events. Using a volatility overlay program can also hedge the portfolio against such risks because financial stress is typically associated with a spike in exchange rates' implied volatility. Using a derivative product based on an index, rather than specific assets or currencies, can also define a macro hedge. One macro hedge specific to foreign exchange markets uses derivatives based on fixed-weight baskets of currencies (such derivatives are available in both exchange-traded and OTC form). In a multi-currency portfolio, it may not always be cost efficient to hedge each single currency separately, and in these situations a macro hedge using currency basket derivatives is an alternative approach.

Minimum-Variance Hedge Ratio

A mathematical approach to determining the optimal cross hedging ratio is known as the **minimum-variance hedge ratio**. Recall that regression analysis based on ordinary least squares (OLS) is used to minimize the variance of $\hat{\varepsilon}$, the residual between actual and fitted values of the regression

$$y_t = \alpha + \beta x_t + \varepsilon_t \text{ where } \hat{\varepsilon}_t = y_t - \left(\hat{\alpha} + \hat{\beta} x_t\right)$$

This same principle can be used to minimize the tracking error between the value of the hedged asset and the hedging instrument. In the regression formula, we substitute the percentage change in the value of the asset to be hedged for y_t, and the percentage change in value of the hedging instrument for x_t (both of these values are measured in terms of the investor's domestic currency). The calculated coefficient in this regression ($\hat{\beta}$) gives the optimal hedging ratio, which means it minimizes the variance of $\hat{\varepsilon}$ and minimizes the tracking error between changes in the value of the hedge and changes in the value of the asset it is hedging. It can be shown that the formula for the minimum-variance hedge ratio—the formula for calculating the $\hat{\beta}$ coefficient in the regression—is mathematically equal to:

$$\frac{\text{covariance }(y,x)}{\text{variance }(x)} = \text{correlation }(y,x) \times \left[\frac{\text{std. dev. }(y)}{\text{std. dev. }(x)}\right]$$

where y and x are defined as before, the change in the domestic-currency value of the asset and the hedge, respectively.

Calculating the minimum-variance hedge ratio typically applies only for "indirect" hedges based on cross hedging or macro hedges; it is not typically applied to a "direct" hedge in which exposure to a spot rate is hedged with a forward contract in that same currency pair. This is because the correlation between movements in the spot rate and its forward contract is likely to be very close to +1. Likewise, the variance in spot price movements and movements in the price of the forward contract are also likely to be approximately equal. Therefore, calculating the minimum-variance hedge ratio by regressing changes in the spot exchange rate against changes in the forward rate will almost always result is a $\hat{\beta}$ regression estimate very close to 1, and hence a minimum-variance hedge ratio close to 100%. So, undertaking the regression analysis is superfluous.

But the minimum-variance hedge ratio can be quite different from 100% when the hedge is *jointly* optimized over *both* exchange rate movements R_{FX} and changes in the foreign-currency value of the asset R_{FC}. A sidebar discusses this case.

There can also be cases when the optimal hedge ratio may not be 100% because of the market characteristics of a specific currency pair. For example, a currency pair may not have a (liquid) forward contract available and hence an alternative cross hedging instrument or a macro hedge must be used instead. We examine when such situations might come up in Section 13.

Basis Risk

The portfolio manager must be aware that any time a direct currency hedge (i.e., a spot rate hedged against its own forward contract) is replaced with an indirect hedge (cross hedge, macro hedge), **basis risk** is brought into the portfolio. This risk reflects the fact that the price movements in the exposure being hedged and the price movements in the cross hedge instrument are not perfectly correlated, and that the correlation will change with time—and sometimes both dramatically and unexpectedly. For a minimum-variance hedge ratio, this risk is expressed as instability in the $\hat{\beta}$ coefficient estimate as more data become available.

For an example of basis risk, return to the illustration earlier of the foreign-currency asset portfolio that cross hedged a long USD/AUD exposure with a short USD/NZD exposure. It is not only possible, but highly likely, that the correlation between movements in the USD/AUD and the USD/NZD spot rates will vary with time. This varying correlation would reflect movements in the NZD/AUD spot rate. Another example of basis risk would be that the correlation between a multi-currency portfolio's domestic-currency market value and the value of currency basket derivatives being used as a macro hedge will neither be perfect nor constant.

At a minimum, this means that all cross hedges and macro hedges will have to be carefully monitored and, as needed, rebalanced to account for the drift in correlations. It also means that minimum-variance hedge ratios will have to be re-estimated as more data become available. The portfolio manager should beware that sudden, unexpected spikes in basis risk can sometimes turn what was once a minimum-variance hedge or an effective cross hedge into a position that is highly correlated with the underlying assets being hedged—the opposite of a hedge.

Basis risk is also used in the context of forward and futures contracts because the price movements of these derivatives products do not always correspond exactly with those of the underlying currency. This is because the price of the forward contract also reflects the interest rate differential between the two countries in the currency pair as well as the term to contract maturity. But with futures and forwards, the derivatives price converges to the price of the underlying as maturity approaches, which is enforced by arbitrage. This convergence is not the case with cross hedges, which potentially can go disastrously wrong with sudden movements in market risk (price correlations), credit risk, or liquidity risk.

OPTIMAL MINIMUM-VARIANCE HEDGES

For simple foreign-currency asset portfolios, it may be possible to use the single-variable OLS regression technique to do a *joint* optimization of the hedge over both the foreign-currency value of the asset R_{FC} and the foreign-currency risk exposure R_{FX}. This approach will reduce the variance of the all-in domestic-currency return R_{DC}, which is the risk that matters most to the investor, not just reducing the variance of the foreign exchange risk R_{FX}.

Calculating the minimum-variance hedge for the foreign exchange risk R_{FX} proceeds by regressing changes in the spot rate against changes in the value of the hedging instrument (i.e., the forward contract). But as indicated in the text, performing this regression is typically unnecessary; for all intents and purposes, the minimum-variance hedge for a spot exchange rate using a forward contract will be close to 100%.

But when there is only a *single* foreign-currency asset involved, one can perform a joint optimization over both of the foreign-currency risks (i.e., both R_{FC} and R_{FX}) by regressing changes in the domestic-currency return (R_{DC}) against percentage changes in the value of the hedging instrument. Basing the optimal hedge ratio on the OLS estimate for β in this regression will minimize the variance of the domestic-currency return $\sigma^2(R_{DC})$. The result will be a better hedge ratio than just basing the regression on R_{FX} alone because this joint approach will also pick up any *correlations* between R_{FX} and R_{FC}. (Recall from Section 4 that the asset mix in the portfolio, and hence the correlations between R_{FX} and R_{FC}, can affect the optimal hedge ratio.) This single-variable OLS approach, however, will only work if there is a single foreign-currency asset in the portfolio.

Work by Campbell (2010) has shown that the optimal hedge ratio based jointly on movements in R_{FC} and R_{FX} for international *bond* portfolios is almost always close to 100%. However, the optimal hedge ratio for single-country foreign *equity* portfolios varies widely between currencies, and will depend on *both* the investor's domestic currency and the currency of the foreign investment. For example, the optimal hedge ratio for a US equity portfolio will be different for UK and eurozone-based investors; and for eurozone investors, the optimal hedge ratio for a US equity portfolio can be different from that of a Canadian equity portfolio. The study found that the optimal hedge ratio for foreign equity exposures can vary widely from 100% between countries. But as the author cautions, these optimal hedge ratios are calculated on historical data that may not be representative of future price dynamics.

Minimum-Variance Hedge Ratio Example

Annie McYelland is an analyst at Scotland- based Kilmarnock Capital. Her firm is considering an investment in an equity index fund based on the Swiss Stock Market Index (SMI). The SMI is a market-cap weighted average of the twenty largest and most liquid Swiss companies, and captures about 85% of the overall market capitalization of the Swiss equity market.

McYelland is asked to formulate a currency-hedging strategy. Because this investment involves only one currency pair and one investment (the SMI), she decides to calculate the minimum-variance hedge ratio for the entire risk exposure, not just the currency exposure. McYelland collects 10 years of monthly data on the CHF/GBP spot exchange rate and movements in the Swiss Market Index.

McYelland notes that the GBP is the base currency in the CHF/GBP quote and that the formula for domestic-currency returns (R_{DC}) shown in Equation 1 requires that the domestic currency be the price currency. Accordingly, she starts by inverting the CHF/GBP quote to a GBP/CHF quote ($S_{GBP/CHF}$). Then she calculates the monthly percentage changes for this adjusted currency series ($\%\Delta S_{GBP/CHF}$) as well as for the SMI (%ΔSMI). This allows her to calculate the monthly returns of an unhedged investment in the SMI with these unhedged returns measured in the "domestic" currency, the GBP:

$$R_{DC} = (1 + R_{FC})(1 + R_{FX}) - 1$$

where R_{FC} = %ΔSMI and $R_{FX} = \%\Delta S_{GBP/CHF}$. Because McYelland wants to minimize the variance of these unhedged domestic-currency returns, she calculates the minimum-variance hedge ratio with the following OLS regression:

$$R_{DC} = \alpha + \beta(\%\Delta S_{GBP/CHF}) + \varepsilon$$

The calculated regression coefficients show that $\hat{\alpha} = -0.21$ and $\hat{\beta} = 1.35$. McYelland interprets these results to mean that the estimated $\hat{\beta}$-coefficient is the minimum-variance hedge ratio. This conclusion makes sense because $\hat{\beta}$ represents the sensitivity of the domestic-currency return on the portfolio to percentage changes in the spot rate. In this case, the return on the SMI seems very sensitive to the appreciation of the CHF. Indeed, over the 10 years of data she collected, McYelland notices that the correlation between %ΔSMI and $\%\Delta S_{GBP/CHF}$ is equal to +0.6.

On the basis of these calculations, she recommends that the minimum-variance hedge ratio for Kilmarnock Capital's exposure to the SMI be set at approximately 135%. This recommendation means that a *long* CHF1,000,000 exposure to the SMI should be hedged with a *short* position in CHF against the GBP of approximately CHF1,350,000. Because forward contracts in professional FX markets are quoted in terms of CHF/GBP for this currency pair, this would mean a *long* position in the forward contract ($F_{CHF/GBP}$)—that is, *selling* the CHF means *buying* the base currency GBP.

McYelland cautions the Investment Committee at Kilmarnock Capital that this minimum-variance hedge ratio is only approximate and must be closely monitored because it is estimated over historical data that may not be representative of future price dynamics. For example, the +0.6 correlation estimated between %ΔSMI and $\%\Delta S_{GBP/CHF}$ is the 10-year *average* correlation; future market conditions may not correspond to this historical average.

CURRENCY MANAGEMENT TOOLS AND STRATEGIES: A SUMMARY

12

- ☐ describe how forward contracts and FX (foreign exchange) swaps are used to adjust hedge ratios
- ☐ describe trading strategies used to reduce hedging costs and modify the risk–return characteristics of a foreign-currency portfolio
- ☐ describe the use of cross-hedges, macro-hedges, and minimum-variance-hedge ratios in portfolios exposed to multiple foreign currencies

This section has covered only some of the most common currency management tools and strategies used in FX markets—there are a great many other derivatives products and strategies that have not been covered. The key points are that there are *many* different hedging and active trading strategies, there are many possible *variations* within each of these strategies, and these strategies can be used in *combination* with each other. There is no need to cover all of what would be a very large number of possible permutations and combinations. Instead, we will close this section with a key thought: Each of these many approaches to either hedging or expressing a directional view on currency movements has its advantages and disadvantages, its risks, and its costs.

As a result, there is no single "correct" approach to initiating and managing currency exposures. Instead, at the strategic level, the IPS of the portfolio sets guidelines for risk exposures, permissible hedging tools, and strategies, which will vary among investors. At the tactical level, at which the portfolio manager has discretion on risk exposures, currency strategy will depend on the manager's management style, market view, and risk tolerance. It will also depend on the manager's perceptions of the relative costs and benefit of any given strategy. Market conditions will affect the cost/benefit calculations behind the hedging decision, as movements in forward points (expected roll yield) or exchange rate volatility (option premiums) affect the expected cost of the hedge; the same hedge structure can be "rich" or "cheap" depending on current market conditions.

Reflecting all of these considerations, different managers will likely make different decisions when confronted with the same opportunity set; and each manager will likely have a good reason for their individual decision. The most important point is that the portfolio manager be aware of all the benefits, costs, and risks of the chosen strategy and be comfortable that any remaining residual currency risks in the hedge are acceptable.

To summarize the key insights of Sections 9–12—and continuing our example of a portfolio manager who is long the base currency in the P/B quote and wants to hedge that price risk—the manager needs to understand the following:

1. Because the portfolio has a *long* exposure to base currency, to neutralize this risk the hedge will attempt to build a *short* exposure out of that currency's derivatives using some combination of forward and/or option contracts.
2. A currency hedge is not a free good, particularly a complete hedge. The hedge cost, real or implied, will consist of some combination of lost upside potential, potentially negative roll yield (forward points at a discount or time decay on long option positions), and upfront payments of option premiums.
3. The cost of any given hedge structure will vary depending on market conditions (i.e., forward points and implied volatility).
4. The cost of the hedge is focused on its "core." For a manager with a long exposure to a currency, the cost of this "core" hedge will be the implicit costs of a short position in a forward contract (no upside potential, possible negative roll yield) or the upfront premium on a long position in a put option. Either of these two forms of insurance can be expensive. However, there are various cost mitigation methods that can be used alone or in combination to reduce these core hedging costs:

    a. Writing options to gain upfront premiums.

    b. Varying the strike prices of the options written or bought.

    c. Varying the notional amounts of the derivative contracts.

    d. Using various "exotic" features, such as knock-ins or knock-outs.

5. There is nothing inherently wrong with any of these cost mitigation approaches—but the manager *must* understand that these invariably involve some combination of reduced upside potential and/or reduced downside protection. A reduced cost (or even a zero-cost) hedge structure is perfectly acceptable, but only as long as the portfolio manager fully understands all of the residual risks in the hedge structure and is prepared to accept and manage them.
6. There are often "natural" hedges within the portfolio, in which some residual risk exposures are uncorrelated with each other and offer portfolio diversification effects. Cross hedges and macro hedges bring basis risk into the portfolio, which will have to be monitored and managed.
7. There is no single or "best" way to hedge currency risk. The portfolio manager will have to perform a due diligence examination of potential hedge structures and make a rational decision on a cost/benefit basis.

EXAMPLE 8

Hedging Strategies

Ireland-based Old Galway Capital runs several investment trusts for its clients. Fiona Doyle has just finished rebalancing the dynamic currency hedge for Overseas Investment Trust III, which has an IPS mandate to be fully hedged using forward contracts. Shortly after the rebalancing, Old Galway receives notice that one of its largest investors in the Overseas Investment Trust III has served notice of a large withdrawal from the fund.

Padma Bhattathiri works at Malabar Coast Capital, an India-based investment company. Her mandate is to seek out any alpha opportunities in global FX markets and aggressively manage these for speculative profit. The Reserve Bank of New Zealand (RBNZ) is New Zealand's central bank, and is scheduled to announce its policy rate decision within the week. The consensus forecast among economists is that the RBNZ will leave rates unchanged, but Bhattathiri believes that the RBNZ will surprise the markets with a rate hike.

Jasmine Khan, analyst at UK-based Brixworth & St. Ives Asset Management, has been instructed by the management team to reduce hedging costs for the firm's Aggressive Growth Fund, and that more currency exposure—both downside risk and upside potential—will have to be accepted and managed. Currently, the fund's ZAR-denominated foreign-currency asset exposures are being hedged with a 25-delta risk reversal (on the ZAR/GBP cross rate). The current ZAR/GBP spot rate is 20.1350.

Bao Zhang is a market analyst at South Korea–based Kwangju Capital, an investment firm that offers several actively managed investment trusts for its clients. She notices that the exchange rate for the Philippines Peso (PHP/USD) is increasing (PHP is depreciating) toward its 200-day moving average located in the 50.2500 area (the current spot rate is 50.2475). She mentions this to Akiko Takahashi, a portfolio manager for one of the firm's investment vehicles. Takahashi's view, based on studying economic fundamentals, is that the PHP/USD rate should continue to increase, but after speaking with Zhang she is less sure. After further conversation, Zhang and Takahashi come to the view that the PHP/USD spot rate will either break through the 50.2500 level and gain upward momentum through the 50.2600 level, or stall at the 50.2500 level and then drop down through the 50.2400 level as frustrated long positions exit the market. They decide that either scenario has equal probability over the next month.

Annie McYelland is an analyst at Scotland-based Kilmarnock Capital. The firm is considering a USD10,000,000 investment in an S&P 500 Index fund. McYelland is asked to calculate the minimum-variance hedge ratio. She collects the following statistics based on 10 years of monthly data:

$\sigma(\%\Delta S_{GBP/USD})$	$\sigma(R_{DC})$	$\rho(R_{DC};\%\Delta S_{GBP/USD})$
2.7%	4.4%	0.2

Source: Data are from Bloomberg.

1. Given the sudden liquidity need announced, Doyle's *best* course of action with regard to the currency hedge is to:

   A. do nothing.

   B. reduce the hedge ratio.

   C. over-hedge by using currency options.

Solution:

A is correct. After rebalancing, the Overseas Investment Trust III is fully hedged; currency risk is at a minimum, which is desirable if liquidity needs have increased. Choices B and C are incorrect because they increase the currency risk exposures.

2. Given her market view, Bhattathiri would *most likely* choose which of the following long positions?

   A. 5-delta put option on NZD/AUD

B. 10-delta put option on USD/NZD

C. Put spread on JPY/NZD using 10-delta and 25-delta options

Solution:

A is correct. The surprise rate hike should cause the NZD to appreciate against most currencies. This appreciation would mean a depreciation of the NZD/AUD rate, which a put option can profit from. A 5-delta option is deep-OTM, but the price reaction on the option premiums will be more extreme than a higher-delta option. That is to say, the *percentage* change in the premiums for a 5-delta option for a given percentage change in the spot exchange rate will be higher than the percentage change in premiums for a 25-delta option. In a sense, a very low delta option is like a highly leveraged lottery ticket on the event occurring. With a surprise rate hike, the odds would swing in Bhattathiri's favor. Choice B is incorrect because the price reaction in the USD/NZD spot rate after the surprise rate hike would likely cause the NZD to appreciate; so Bhattathiri would want a call option on the USD/NZD currency pair. Choice C is incorrect because an appreciation of the NZD after the surprise rate hike would best be captured by a call spread on the JPY/NZD rate, which will likely increase (the NZD is the base currency).

3. Among the following, replacing the current risk reversal hedge with a long position in which of the following would *best* meet Khan's instructions? (All use the ZAR/GBP.)

A. 10-delta risk reversal

B. Put option with a 20.1300 strike

C. Call option with a 20.1350 strike

Solution:

A is correct. Moving to a 10-delta risk reversal will be cheaper (these options are deeper-OTM than 25-delta options) and widen the bands in the corridor being created for the ZAR/GBP rate. Choice B is incorrect because a long put provides no protection against an upside movement in the ZAR/GBP rate, which Brixworth & St. Ives is trying to hedge (recall that the fund is long ZAR in its foreign-currency asset exposure and hence needs to sell ZAR/buy GBP to hedge). Also, if Brixworth & St. Ives exercises the option, they would "put" GBP to the counterparty at the strike price and receive ZAR in return. Although this option position may be considered profitable in its own right, it nonetheless causes the firm to double-up its ZAR exposure. Choice C is incorrect because although an ATM call option on ZAR/GBP will provide complete hedge protection, it will be expensive and clearly more expensive than the current 25-delta risk reversal.

4. Which of the following positions would *best* implement Zhang's and Takahashi's market view?

A. Long a 50.2450 put and long a 50.2550 call

B. Long a 50.2450 put and short a 50.2400 put

C. Long a 50.2450 put and short a 50.2550 call

Solution:

A is correct. Zhang's and Takahashi's market view is that, over the next month, a move in PHP/USD to either 50.2400 or 50.2600 is equally likely. A strangle would express this view of heightened volatility but without a directional bias, and would require a long put and a long call positions. Choice B is incorrect because it is a put spread; it will profit by a move in PHP/USD between 50.2450 and 50.2400. If it moves below 50.2400 the short put gets exercised by the counterparty and neutralizes the long put. Although less costly than an outright long put position, this structure is not positioned to profit from a move higher in PHP/USD. Choice C is incorrect because it is a short risk reversal position. It provides relatively cheap protection for a down-move in PHP/USD but is not positioned to profit from an up-move in PHP/USD.

5. Which of the following positions would *best* implement Kilmarnock Capital's minimum-variance hedge?

A. Long a USD/GBP forward contract with a notional size of USD1.2 million

B. Long a USD/GBP forward contract with a notional size of USD3.3 million

C. Short a USD/GBP forward contract with a notional size of USD2.0 million

Solution:

B is correct. The formula for the minimum-variance hedge ratio (h) is:

$$h = \rho\left(R_{DC};R_{FX}\right) \times \left[\frac{\sigma\left(R_{DC}\right)}{\sigma\left(R_{FX}\right)}\right]$$

After inputting the data from the table, this equation solves to 0.33. This means that for a USD10 million investment in the S&P 500 (long position), Kilmarnock Capital would want to be *short* approximately USD3.3 million in a forward contract. Because the standard market quote for this currency pair is USD/GBP, to be short the USD means one would have to buy the GBP; that is, a *long* position in a USD/GBP forward contract. Choice A is incorrect because it inverts the ratio in the formula. Choice C is incorrect because it shows a short position in the USD/GBP forward, and because it only uses the correlation to set the contract size.

13 CURRENCY MANAGEMENT FOR EMERGING MARKET CURRENCIES

☐ discuss challenges for managing emerging market currency exposures

Most of the material in this reading has focused on what might be described as the major currencies, such as the EUR, GBP, or JPY. This focus is not a coincidence: The vast majority of daily flow in global FX markets is accounted for by the top half dozen currencies. Moreover, the vast majority of investable assets globally, as measured by market capitalization, are denominated in the major currencies. Nonetheless, more investors are looking at emerging markets, as well as "frontier markets," for potential investment opportunities. And many developing economies are beginning to emerge as major forces in the global economy. In the following sections, we survey the challenges for currency management and the use of non-deliverable forwards as one tool to address them.

Special Considerations in Managing Emerging Market Currency Exposures

Managing emerging market currency exposure involves unique challenges. Perhaps the two most important considerations are (1) higher trading costs than the major currencies under "normal" market conditions, and (2) the increased likelihood of extreme market events and severe illiquidity under stressed market conditions.

Many emerging market currencies are thinly traded, causing higher transaction costs (bid–offer spreads). There may also be fewer derivatives products to choose from, especially exchange-traded products. Although many global investment banks will quote spot rates and OTC derivatives for almost any conceivable currency pair, many of these are often seen as "specialty" products and often come with relatively high mark-ups. This mark-up increases trading and hedging costs. (In addition, the underlying foreign-currency asset in emerging markets can be illiquid and lack the full array of derivatives products.)

These higher currency trading costs would especially be the case for "crosses" in these currency pairs. For example, there is no reason why an investor in Chile (which uses the Chilean peso, currency code CLP) could not have an investment in assets denominated in the Thai baht (THB). But the CLP/THB cross is likely to be very thinly traded; there simply are not enough trade or capital flows between these two countries. Typically, any trade between these two currencies would go through a major intermediary currency, usually the USD. Hence, the trade would be broken into two legs: a trade in the CLP/USD pair and another in the THB/USD pair. These trades might go through different traders or trading desks at the same bank; or perhaps one leg of the trade would be done at one bank and the other leg through a different bank. There may also be time zone issues affecting liquidity; one leg of the trade may be relatively liquid at the same time as the other leg of the trade may be more thinly traded. The reason is because liquidity in most emerging market currencies is typically deepest in their domestic time zones. In any event, there are two bid–offer spreads—one for each leg of the trade—to be covered. This is often the case for many of the cross-rate currency pairs among developed market currencies as well. However, the bid–offer spreads are usually tighter for major currency pairs.

The liquidity issue is especially important when trades in these less-liquid currencies get "crowded," for example, through an excessive build-up of carry trades or through a fad-like popularity among investors for investing in a particular region or trading theme. Trades can be much easier to gradually enter into than to quickly exit, particularly under stressed market conditions. For example, after a long period of slow build-up, carry trades into these currencies can occasionally be subject to panicked unwinds as market conditions suddenly turn. This situation typically causes market liquidity to evaporate and leaves traders locked into positions that continue to accumulate losses.

The investment return probability distributions for currency (and other) trades subject to such relatively frequent extreme events have fatter tails than the normal distribution as well as a pronounced negative skew. Risk measurement and control tools (such as value at risk, or VaR) that depend on normal distributions can be misleading under these circumstances and greatly understate the risks the portfolio is actually exposed to. Many investment performance measures are also based on the normal distribution. Historical investment performance measured by such indexes as the Sharpe ratio can look very attractive during times of relative tranquility; but this seeming outperformance can disappear into deep losses faster than most investors can react (investors typically do a poor job of timing crises). As mentioned in the prior section on volatility trading, price volatility in financial markets is very cyclical and implied volatility can be subject to sharp spikes. These volatility spikes can severely affect both option prices and hedging strategies based on options. Even if the initial option protection is in place, it will eventually have to be rolled as options expire—but then at much higher prices for the option buyer.

The occurrence of currency crises can also affect hedging strategies based on forward contracts. Recall that hedging a long exposure to a foreign currency typically involves selling the foreign currency forward. However, when currencies are under severe downward pressure, central banks often react by hiking the policy rate to support the domestic currency. But recall that the higher interest rates go in a country, then, all else equal, the deeper the forward discount for its currency (enforced by the arbitrage conditions of covered interest rate parity). Having to sell the currency forward at increasingly deep discounts will cause losses through negative roll yield and undermine the cost effectiveness of the hedging program.

Extreme price movements in financial markets can also undermine many hedging strategies based on presumed diversification. Crises not only affect the volatility in asset prices but also their correlations, primarily through "contagion" effects. The history of financial markets (circa 2012) has been characterized by a "risk-on, risk-off" environment dominated by swings in investor sentiment between speculative enthusiasm and pronounced flight-to-safety flows. In the process, there is often little differentiation between individual currencies, which tend to get traded together in broader baskets (such as "haven currencies"—USD, JPY, and CHF—and "commodity currencies"—AUD, NZD, and ZAR). Investors who may have believed that they had diversified their portfolio through a broad array of exposures in emerging markets may find instead in crises that they doubled-up their currency exposures. (Likewise, there can be correlated and extreme movements in the underlying assets of these foreign-currency exposures.)

Another potential factor affecting currency management in these "exotic" markets is government involvement in setting the exchange rate through such measures as foreign exchange market intervention, capital controls, and pegged (or at least tightly managed) exchange rates. These measures too can lead to occasional extreme events in markets; for example, when central banks intervene or when currency pegs change or get broken. Short-term stability in these government-influenced markets can lull traders into a false sense of overconfidence and over-positioning. When currency pegs break, the break can happen quickly. Assuming that investment returns will be normally distributed according to parameters estimated on recent historical data, or that correlation factors and liquidity will not change suddenly, can be lethal.

It bears noting that currency crises and government involvement in FX markets is not limited to emerging market currencies, but often occur among the major currencies as well. The central banks of major currencies will, on occasion, intervene in their own currencies or use other polices (such as sharp movements in policy rates) to influence exchange rate levels. These too can lead to extreme events in currency markets.

Non-Deliverable Forwards

Currencies of many emerging market countries trade with some form of capital controls. Where capital controls exist and delivery in the controlled currency is limited by the local government, it is often possible to use what are known as **non-deliverable forwards** (NDFs). These are similar to regular forward contracts, but they are cash settled (in the non-controlled currency of the currency pair) rather than physically settled (the controlled currency is neither delivered nor received). The non-controlled currency for NDFs is usually the USD or some other major currency. A partial list of some of the most important currencies with NDFs would include the Chinese yuan (CNY), Korean won (KRW), Russian ruble (RUB), Indian rupee (INR), and Brazilian real (BRL). The NDF is essentially a cash-settled "bet" on the movement in the spot rate of these currencies.

For example, a trader could enter into a long position in a three-month NDF for the BRL/USD. Note that the BRL—the currency with capital controls—is the price currency and the base currency, the USD, is the currency that settlement of the NDF will be made in. Assume that the current all-in rate for the NDF is 5.5180 and the trader uses an NDF with a notional size of USD1,000,000. Suppose that three months later the BRL/USD spot rate is 5.5300 and the trader closes out the existing NDF contract with an equal and offsetting spot transaction at this rate. Settlement proceeds by noting that the USD amounts net to zero (USD1,000,000 both bought and sold on settlement date), so the net cash flow generated would normally be in BRL if this was an ordinary forward contract. The net cash flow to the long position in this case would be calculated as

$$(5.5300 - 5.5180) \times 1{,}000{,}000 = \text{BRL}12{,}000$$

But with an NDF, there is no delivery in the controlled currency (hence the name *non-deliverable* forward). Settlement must be in USD, so this BRL amount is converted to USD at the then-current spot rate of 5.5300. This leads to a USD cash inflow for the long position in the NDF of

$$\text{BRL}12{,}000 \div 5.5300 \text{ BRL/USD} = \text{USD}2{,}169.98$$

The credit risk of an NDF is typically lower than for the outright forward because the principal sums in the NDF do not move, unlike with an outright "vanilla" forward contract. For example, in the illustration the cash pay-off to the "bet" was the relatively small amount of USD2,169.98—there was no delivery of USD1,000,000 against receipt of BR5,518,000. Conversely, as noted previously, NDFs exist because of some form of government involvement in foreign exchange markets. Sudden changes in government policy can lead to sharp movements in spot and NDF rates, often reversing any investment gains earned during long periods of seeming (but artificial) market calm. The implicit market risk of the NDF embodies an element of "tail risk."

Finally, we note that when capital controls exist, the free cross-border flow of capital that enforces the arbitrage condition underlying covered interest rate parity no longer functions consistently. Therefore, the pricing on NDFs need not be exactly in accord with the covered interest rate parity theorem. Instead, NDF pricing will reflect the individual supply and demand conditions (and risk premia) in the offshore market, which need not be the same as the onshore market of the specific emerging market country. Some of the most active participants in the NDF market are offshore hedge funds and proprietary traders making directional bets on the emerging market currency, rather than corporate or institutional portfolio managers hedging currency exposures. Volatility in the net speculative demand for emerging market exposure can affect the level of forward points. We also note that the type and strictness of capital controls can vary among emerging markets; hence, the need for knowledge of local market regulations is another factor influencing currency risk management in these markets.

SUMMARY

In this reading, we have examined the basic principles of managing foreign exchange risk within the broader investment process. International financial markets create a wide range of opportunities for investors, but they also create the need to recognize, measure, and control exchange rate risk. The management of this risk starts with setting the overall mandate for the portfolio, encoding the investors' investment objectives and constraints into the investment policy statement and providing strategic guidance on how currency risk will be managed in the portfolio. It extends to tactical positioning when portfolio managers translate market views into specific trading strategies within the overall risk management guidelines set by the IPS. We have examined some of these trading strategies, and how a range of portfolio management tools—positions in spot, forward, option, and FX swap contracts—can be used either to hedge away currency risk, or to express a market opinion on future exchange rate movements.

What we have emphasized throughout this reading is that there is no simple or single answer for the "best" currency management strategies. Different investors will have different strategic mandates (IPS), and different portfolio managers will have different market opinions and risk tolerances. There is a near-infinite number of possible currency trading strategies, each with its own benefits, costs, and risks. Currency risk management—both at the strategic and tactical levels—means having to manage the trade-offs between all of these various considerations.

Some of the main points covered in this reading are as follows:

- In professional FX markets, currencies are identified by standard three-letter codes, and quoted in terms of a price and a base currency (P/B).
- The spot exchange rate is typically for $T + 2$ delivery, and forward rates are for delivery for later periods. Both spot and forward rates are quoted in terms of a bid–offer price. Forward rates are quoted in terms of the spot rate plus forward points.
- An FX swap is a simultaneous spot and forward transaction; one leg of the swap is buying the base currency and the other is selling it. FX swaps are used to renew outstanding forward contracts once they mature, to "roll them forward."
- The domestic-currency return on foreign-currency assets can be broken into the foreign-currency asset return and the return on the foreign currency (the percentage appreciation or depreciation of the foreign currency against the domestic currency). These two components of the domestic-currency return are multiplicative.
- When there are several foreign-currency assets, the portfolio domestic-currency return is the weighted average of the individual domestic-currency returns (i.e., using the portfolio weights, which should sum to one)
- The risk of domestic-currency returns (its standard deviation) can be approximated by using a variance formula that recognizes the individual variances and covariances (correlations) among the foreign-currency asset returns and exchange rate movements.
- The calculation of the domestic-currency risk involves a large number of variables that must be estimated: the risks and correlations between all of the foreign-currency asset returns and their exchange rate risks.
- Guidance on where to target the portfolio along the risk spectrum is part of the IPS, which makes this a *strategic* decision based on the investment goals and constraints of the beneficial owners of the portfolio.
- If the IPS allows currency risk in the portfolio, the amount of desired currency exposure will depend on both portfolio diversification considerations and cost considerations.

- Views on the diversifying effects of foreign-currency exposures depend on the time horizon involved, the type of foreign-currency asset, and market conditions.
- Cost considerations also affect the hedging decision. Hedging is not free: It has both direct transactional costs as well as opportunity costs (the potential for favorable outcomes is foregone). Cost considerations make a perfect hedge difficult to maintain.

- Currency management strategies can be located along a spectrum stretching from:

  - passive, rules-based, complete hedging of currency exposures;
  - discretionary hedging, which allows the portfolio manager some latitude on managing currency exposures;
  - active currency management, which seeks out currency risk in order to manage it for profit; and to
  - currency overlay programs that aggressively manage currency "alpha."

- There are a variety of methods for forming market views.

  - The use of macroeconomic fundamentals to predict future currency movements is based on estimating the "fair value" for a currency with the expectation that spot rates will eventually converge on this equilibrium value.
  - Technical market indicators assume that, based on market psychology, historical price patterns in the data have a tendency to repeat. Technical indicators can be used to predict support and resistance levels in the market, as well as to confirm market trends and turning points.
  - The carry trade is based on violations of uncovered interest rate parity, and is also based on selling low-yield currencies in order to invest in high-yield currencies. This approach is equivalent to trading the forward rate bias, which means selling currencies trading at a forward premium and buying currencies trading at a forward discount.
  - Volatility trading uses the option market to express views on the distribution of future exchange rates, not their levels.

- Passive hedging will typically use forward contracts (rather than futures contracts) because they are more flexible. However, currency futures contracts are an option for smaller trading sizes and are frequently used in private wealth management.
- Forward contracts have the possibility of negative roll yield (the forward points embedded in the forward price can work for or against the hedge). The portfolio manager will have to balance the advantages and costs of hedging with forward contracts.
- Foreign-currency options can reduce opportunity costs (they allow the upside potential for favorable foreign-currency movements). However, the upfront option premiums must be paid.
- There are a variety of means to reduce the cost of the hedging with either forward or option contracts, but these cost-reduction measures always involve some combination of less downside protection and/or less upside potential.
- Hedging multiple foreign currencies uses the same tools and strategies used in hedging a single foreign-currency exposure; except now the correlation between residual currency exposures in the portfolio should be considered.

- Cross hedges introduce basis risk into the portfolio, which is the risk that the correlation between exposure and its cross hedging instrument may change in unexpected ways. Forward contracts typically have very little basis risk compared with movements in the underlying spot rate.
- The number of trading strategies that can be used, for hedging or speculative purposes, either for a single foreign currency or multiple foreign currencies, is near infinite. The manager must assess the costs, benefits, and risks of each in the context of the investment goals and constraints of the portfolio. There is no single "correct" approach.

REFERENCES

Bank for International Settlements. 2013. "Triennial Central Bank Survey of Foreign Exchange and Derivatives Market Activity."

Campbell, John Y., Karine Serfaty-de Medeiros, and Luis. M. Viceira. 2007. "Global Currency Hedging," NBER Working Paper 13088 (May).

Campbell, John Y. 2010. "Global Currency Hedging: What Role Should Foreign Currency Play in a Diversified Investment Portfolio?" *CFA Institute Conference Proceedings Quarterly* 27 (4):8–18. 10.2469/cp.v27.n4.2

Darnell, R. Max. 2004. "Currency Strategies to Enhance Returns." In *Fixed-Income Tools for Enhancing Return and Meeting Client Objectives*. Charlottesville, VA: Association for Investment Management and Research.

Froot, Kenneth A. 1993. "Currency Hedging Over Long Horizons." NBER Working Paper 4355 (April): www.people.hbs.edu/kfroot/oldwebsite/cvpaperlinks/currency_hedging.pdf.

Kritzman, Mark P. 1999. "The Forward-Rate Bias." In *Currency Risk in Investment Portfolios*. Charlottesville, VA: Association for Investment Management and Research.

Martini, Giulio. 2010. "The Continuum from Passive to Active Currency Management." *CFA Institute Conference Proceedings Quarterly* 27(1):1–11. 10.2469/cp.v27.n1.1

Michenaud, Sébastien and Bruno Solnik. 2008. "Applying Regret Theory to Investment Choices: Currency Hedging Decisions." *Journal of International Money and Finance* 27 (5):677–694.

Rosenberg, Michael R. and William A. Barker. 2017. "Currency Exchange Rates: Understanding Equilibrium Value." CFA Program Curriculum, Level II.

Rosenberg, Michael R. 2002. *Deutsche Bank Guide to Exchange-Rate Determination*. London: Irwin Professional Publishing (May).

Sine, Barry M. and Robert A. Strong. 2012. "Technical Analysis." CFA Program Curriculum, Level I.

PRACTICE PROBLEMS

The following information relates to questions 1-6

Kamala Gupta, a currency management consultant, is hired to evaluate the performance of two portfolios. Portfolio A and Portfolio B are managed in the United States and performance is measured in terms of the US dollar (USD). Portfolio A consists of British pound (GBP) denominated bonds and Portfolio B holds euro (EUR) denominated bonds.

Gupta calculates a 19.5% domestic-currency return for Portfolio A and 0% domestic-currency return for Portfolio B.

1. **Analyze** the movement of the USD against the foreign currency for Portfolio A. **Justify** your choice.

Template for Question 1

Asset	Foreign-Currency Portfolio Return	USD Relative to Foreign-Currency (circle one)
Portfolio A	15%	appreciated depreciated

Justification

2. **Analyze** the foreign-currency return for Portfolio B. **Justify** your choice.

Template for Question 2

Asset	Percentage Movement in the Spot Exchange Rate	Foreign-Currency Portfolio Return (circle one)
Portfolio B	EUR appreciated 5% against the USD	positive negative

Justification

3. The fund manager of Portfolio B is evaluating an internally-managed 100% foreign-currency hedged strategy.

   Discuss *two* forms of trading costs associated with this currency management strategy.

4. Gupta tells the fund manager of Portfolio B:

   > "We need to seriously consider the potential costs associated with favorable currency rate movements, given that a 100% hedge-ratio strategy is being applied to this portfolio."

   Explain Gupta's statement in light of the strategic choices in currency management available to the portfolio manager.

5. The investment policy statement (IPS) for Portfolio A provides the manager with discretionary authority to take directional views on future currency movements. The fund manager believes the foreign currency assets of the portfolio could be fully hedged internally. However, the manager also believes existing firm personnel lack the expertise to actively manage foreign-currency movements to generate currency alpha.

   Recommend a solution that will provide the fund manager the opportunity to earn currency alpha through active foreign exchange management.

6. Gupta and the fund manager of Portfolio A discuss the differences among several active currency management methods.

   Evaluate each statement independently and select the active currency approach it *best* describes. **Justify** each choice.

Template for Question 6

Gupta's Statements	Active Currency Approach (circle one)	Justification
"Many traders believe that it is not necessary to examine factors like the current account deficit, inflation, and interest rates because current exchange rates already reflect the market view on how these factors will affect future exchange rates."	carry trade technical analysis economic fundamental	
"The six-month interest rate in India is 8% compared to 1% in the United States. This presents a yield pick-up opportunity."	carry trade technical analysis economic fundamental	
"The currency overlay manager will estimate the fair value of the currencies with the expectation that observed spot rates will converge to long-run equilibrium values described by parity conditions."	carry trade technical analysis economic fundamental	

The following information relates to questions 7-12

Guten Investments GmbH, based in Germany and using the EUR as its reporting currency, is an asset management firm providing investment services for local high net worth and institutional investors seeking international exposures. The firm invests in the Swiss, UK, and US markets, after conducting fundamental research in order to select individual investments. Exhibit 1 presents recent information for exchange rates in these foreign markets.

Exhibit 1: Exchange Rate Data

	One Year Ago	Today
Euro-dollar (USD/EUR)*	1.1330	1.1550
Euro-sterling (GBP/EUR)	0.8445	0.8550
Euro-Swiss (CHF/EUR)	1.0875	1.0780

* *The amount of USD required to buy one EUR*

In prior years, the correlation between movements in the foreign-currency asset returns for the USD-denominated assets and movements in the exchange rate was estimated to be +0.50. After analyzing global financial markets, Konstanze Ostermann, a portfolio manager at Guten Investments, now expects that this correlation will increase to +0.80, although her forecast for foreign-currency asset returns is unchanged.

Ostermann believes that currency markets are efficient and hence that long-run gains cannot be achieved from active currency management, especially after netting out management and transaction costs. She uses this philosophy to guide hedging decisions for her discretionary accounts, unless instructed otherwise by the client.

Ostermann is aware, however, that some investors hold an alternative view on the merits of active currency management. Accordingly, their portfolios have different investment guidelines. For these accounts, Guten Investments employs a currency specialist firm, Umlauf Management, to provide currency overlay programs specific to each client's investment objectives. For most hedging strategies, Umlauf Management develops a market view based on underlying fundamentals in exchange rates. However, when directed by clients, Umlauf Management uses options and a variety of trading strategies to unbundle all of the various risk factors (the "Greeks") and trade them separately.

Ostermann conducts an annual review for three of her clients and gathers the summary information presented in Exhibit 2.

Exhibit 2: Select Clients at Guten Investments

Client	Currency Management Objectives
Adele Kastner – A high net worth individual with a low risk tolerance.	Keep the portfolio's currency exposures close, if not equal to, the benchmark so that the domestic-currency return is equal to the foreign-currency return.

Client	Currency Management Objectives
Braunt Pensionskasse – A large private-company pension fund with a moderate risk tolerance.	Limited discretion which allows the actual portfolio currency risk exposures to vary plus-or-minus 5% from the neutral position.
Franz Trading GmbH – An exporting company with a high risk tolerance.	Discretion with respect to currency exposure is allowed in order to add alpha to the portfolio.

7. Based on Exhibit 1, the domestic-currency return over the last year (measured in EUR terms) was *higher* than the foreign-currency return for:

   A. USD-denominated assets.

   B. GBP-denominated assets.

   C. CHF-denominated assets.

8. Based on Ostermann's correlation forecast, the expected domestic-currency return (measured in EUR terms) on USD-denominated assets will *most* likely:

   A. increase.

   B. decrease.

   C. remain unchanged.

9. Based on Ostermann's views regarding active currency management, the percentage of currency exposure in her discretionary accounts that is hedged is *most likely:*

   A. 0%.

   B. 50%.

   C. 100%.

10. The active currency management approach that Umlauf Management is *least* likely to employ is based on:

    A. volatility trading.

    B. technical analysis.

    C. economic fundamentals.

11. Based on Exhibit 2, the currency overlay program *most* appropriate for Braunt Pensionskasse would:

    A. be fully passive.

    B. allow limited directional views.

    C. actively manage foreign exchange as an asset class.

12. Based on Exhibit 2, the client *most likely* to benefit from the introduction of an

additional overlay manager is:

A. Adele Kastner.

B. Braunt Pensionskasse.

C. Franz Trading GmbH.

The following information relates to questions 13-15

Mason Darden is an adviser at Colgate & McIntire (C&M), managing large-cap global equity separate accounts. C&M's investment process restricts portfolio positions to companies based in the United States, Japan, and the eurozone. All C&M clients are US-domiciled, with client reporting in US dollars.

Darden manages Ravi Bhatt's account, which had a total (US dollar) return of 7.0% last year. Darden must assess the contribution of foreign currency to the account's total return. Exhibit 1 summarizes the account's geographic portfolio weights, asset returns, and currency returns for last year.

Exhibit 1: Performance Data for Bhatt's Portfolio Last Year

Geography	Portfolio Weight	Asset Return	Currency Return
United States	50%	10.0%	NA
Eurozone	25%	5.0%	2.0%
Japan	25%	–3.0%	4.0%
Total	100%		

13. **Calculate** the contribution of foreign currency to the Bhatt account's total return. **Show** your calculations.

14. Darden meets with Bhatt and learns that Bhatt will be moving back to his home country of India next month to resume working as a commodity trader. Bhatt is concerned about a possible US recession. His investment policy statement (IPS) allows for flexibility in managing currency risk. Overall returns can be enhanced by capturing opportunities between the US dollar and the Indian rupee (INR) within a range of plus or minus 25% from the neutral position consisting of 100% of the portfolio as valued in USD. C&M has a currency overlay team that can appropriately manage currency risk for Bhatt's portfolio.

    Determine the *most appropriate* currency management strategy for Bhatt. **Justify** your response.

Determine the *most appropriate* currency management strategy for Bhatt. (Circle one.)

Passive hedging	Discretionary hedging	Active currency management

Justify your response.

15. Following analysis of Indian economic fundamentals, C&M's currency team expects continued stability in interest rate and inflation rate differentials between the United States and India. C&M's currency team strongly believes the US dollar will appreciate relative to the Indian rupee.

    C&M would like to exploit the perceived alpha opportunity using forward contracts on the USD10,000,000 Bhatt portfolio.

    Recommend the trading strategy C&M should implement. **Justify** your response.

The following information relates to questions 16-17

Wilson Manufacturing (Wilson) is an Australian institutional client of Ethan Lee, who manages a variety of portfolios across asset classes. Wilson prefers a neutral benchmark over a rules-based approach, with its investment policy statement (IPS) requiring a currency hedge ratio between 97% and 103% to protect against currency risk. Lee has assessed various currency management strategies for Wilson's US dollar-denominated fixed-income portfolio to optimally locate it along the currency risk spectrum. The portfolio is currently in its flat natural neutral position because of Lee's lack of market conviction.

16. **Identify** the *most likely* approach for Lee to optimally locate Wilson's portfolio on the currency risk spectrum, consistent with the IPS. **Justify** your response with *two* reasons supporting the approach.

Identify the *most likely* approach for Lee to optimally locate Wilson's portfolio on the currency risk spectrum, consistent with IPS. (Circle one.)

Passive Hedging	Discretionary Hedging	Active Currency Management	Currency Overlay

Justify your response with *two* reasons supporting the approach.

1.	2.

17. Lee and Wilson recently completed the annual portfolio review and determined the IPS is too short-term focused and excessively risk averse. Accordingly, the IPS is revised and foreign currency is introduced as a separate asset class. Lee hires an external foreign exchange sub-adviser to implement a currency overlay program, emphasizing that it is important to structure the program so that the

currency overlay is allowed in terms of strategic portfolio positioning.

Discuss a key attribute of the currency overlay that would *increase* the likelihood it would be allowed in terms of strategic portfolio positioning.

---

18. Kalila Al-Khalili has been hired as a consultant to a Middle Eastern sovereign wealth fund. The fund's oversight committee has asked her to examine the fund's financial characteristics and recommend an appropriate currency management strategy given the fund's Investment Policy Statement. After a thorough study of the fund and its finances, Al-Khalili reaches the following conclusions:

- The fund's mandate is focused on the long-term development of the country, and the royal family (who are very influential on the fund's oversight committee) are prepared to take a long-term perspective on the fund's investments.
- The fund's strategic asset allocation is tilted towards equity rather than fixed-income assets.
- Both its fixed-income and equity portfolios have a sizeable exposure to emerging market assets.
- Currently, about 90% of exchange rate exposures are hedged although the IPS allows a range of hedge ratios.
- Liquidity needs of the fund are minimal, since the government is running a balanced budget and is unlikely to need to dip into the fund in the near term to cover fiscal deficits. Indeed, the expected lifetime of country's large oil reserves has been greatly extended by recent discoveries, and substantial oil royalties are expected to persist into the future.

Based on her investigation, Al-Khalili would *most* likely recommend:

A. active currency management.

B. a hedging ratio closer to 100%.

C. a narrow discretionary band for currency exposures.

The following information relates to questions 19-22

Li Jiang is an international economist operating a subscription website through which she offers financial advice on currency issues to retail investors. One morning she receives four subscriber e-mails seeking guidance.

Subscriber 1 "As a French national now working in the United States, I hold US dollar-denominated assets currently valued at USD 700,000. The USD/EUR exchange rate has been quite volatile and now appears oversold based on historical price trends. With my American job ending soon, I will return to Europe. I want to protect the value of my USD holdings, measured in EUR terms, before I repatriate these funds back to France. To reduce my currency exposure I am going to use currency futures contracts. Can you explain the factors most relevant to implementing this strategy?"

Subscriber 2	"I have observed that many of the overseas markets for Korean export goods are slowing, while the United States is experiencing a rise in exports. Both trends can combine to possibly affect the value of the won (KRW) relative to the US dollar. As a result, I am considering a speculative currency trade on the KRW/USD exchange rate. I also expect the volatility in this exchange rate to increase."
Subscriber 3	"India has relatively high interest rates compared to the United States and my market view is that this situation is likely to persist. As a retail investor actively trading currencies, I am considering borrowing in USD and converting to the Indian rupee (INR). I then intend to invest these funds in INR-denominated bonds, but without using a currency hedge."
Subscriber 4	"I was wondering if trading in emerging market currencies provides the more opportunities for superior returns through active management than trading in Developed Market currencies."

19. For Subscriber 1, the *most* significant factor to consider would be:

    A. margin requirements.

    B. transaction costs of using futures contracts.

    C. different quoting conventions for future contracts.

20. For Subscriber 2, and assuming all of the choices relate to the KRW/USD exchange rate, the *best* way to implement the trading strategy would be to:

    A. write a straddle.

    B. buy a put option.

    C. use a long NDF position.

21. Which of the following market developments would be *most* favorable for Subscriber 3's trading plan?

    A. A narrower interest rate differential.

    B. A higher forward premium for INR/USD.

    C. Higher volatility in INR/USD spot rate movements.

22. Jiang's *best* response to Subscriber 4 would be that active trading in trading in emerging market currencies:

    A. typically leads to return distributions that are positively skewed.

    B. should not lead to higher returns because FX markets are efficient.

    C. often leads to higher returns through carry trades, but comes with higher risks and trading costs.

---

23. Gupta interviews a currency overlay manager on behalf of Portfolio A. The foreign currency overlay manager describes volatility-based trading, compares

volatility-based trading strategies and explains how the firm uses currency options to establish positions in the foreign exchange market. The overlay manager states:

Statement 1 "Given the current stability in financial markets, several traders at our firm take advantage of the fact that most options expire out-of-the money and therefore are net-short volatility."

Statement 2 "Traders that want to minimize the impact of unanticipated price volatility are net-long volatility."

Compare Statement 1 and Statement 2 and **identify** which *best* explains the view of a speculative volatility trader and which best explains the view of a hedger of volatility. **Justify** your response.

The following information relates to questions 24-25

Renita Murimi is a currency overlay manager and market technician who serves institutional investors seeking to address currency-specific risks associated with investing in international assets. Her firm also provides volatility overlay programs. She is developing a volatility-based strategy for Emil Konev, a hedge fund manager focused on option trading. Konev seeks to implement an "FX as an asset class" approach distinct to his portfolio to realize speculative gains and believes the long-term strength of the US dollar is peaking.

24. **Describe** how a volatility-based strategy for Konev would *most likely* contrast with Murimi's other institutional investors. **Justify** your response.

25. **Discuss** how Murimi can use her technical skills to devise the strategy.

The following information relates to questions 26-27

The fund manager of Portfolio B believes that setting up a full currency hedge requires a simple matching of the *current* market value of the foreign-currency exposure in the portfolio with an equal and offsetting position in a forward contract.

26. **Explain** how the hedge, as described by the fund manager, will eventually expose the portfolio to currency risk.

27. **Recommend** an alternative hedging strategy that will keep the hedge ratio close to the target hedge ratio. **Identify** the main disadvantage of implementing such a strategy.

The following information relates to questions 28-31

Rika Björk runs the currency overlay program at a large Scandinavian investment fund, which uses the Swedish krona (SEK) as its reporting currency. She is managing the fund's exposure to GBP-denominated assets, which are currently hedged with a GBP 100,000,000 forward contract (on the SEK/GBP cross rate, which is currently at 10.6875 spot). The maturity for the forward contract is December 1, which is still several months away. However, since the contract was initiated the value of the fund's assets has declined by GBP 7,000,000. As a result, Björk wants to rebalance the hedge immediately.

Next Björk turns her attention to the fund's Swiss franc (CHF) exposures. In order to maintain some profit potential Björk wants to hedge the exposure using a currency option, but at the same time, she wants to reduce hedging costs. She believes that there is limited upside for the SEK/CHF cross rate.

Björk then examines the fund's EUR-denominated exposures. Due to recent monetary tightening by the Riksbank (the Swedish central bank) forward points for the SEK/EUR rate have swung to a premium. The fund's EUR-denominated exposures are hedged with forward contracts.

Finally Björk turns her attention to the fund's currency exposures in several emerging markets. The fund has large positions in several Latin American bond markets, but Björk does not feel that there is sufficient liquidity in the related foreign exchange derivatives to easily hedge the fund's Latin American bond markets exposures. However, the exchange rates for these countries, measured against the SEK, are correlated with the MXN/SEK exchange rate. (The MXN is the Mexican peso, which is considered to be among the most liquid Latin American currencies). Björk considers using forward positions in the MXN to cross-hedge the fund's Latin American currency exposures.

28. To rebalance the SEK/GBP hedge, and assuming all instruments are based on SEK/GBP, Björk would buy:

    A. GBP 7,000,000 spot.

    B. GBP 7,000,000 forward to December 1.

    C. SEK 74,812,500 forward to December 1.

29. Given her investment goals and market view, and assuming all options are based on SEK/CHF, the *best* strategy for Björk to manage the fund's CHF exposure would be to buy an:

    A. ATM call option.

    B. ITM call option and write an OTM call option.

    C. OTM put option and write an OTM call option.

30. Given the recent movement in the forward premium for the SEK/EUR rate, Björk can expect that the hedge will experience higher:

    A. basis risk.

    B. roll yield.

    C. premia income.

31. The *most* important risk to Björk's Latin American currency hedge would be changes in:

A. forward points.

B. exchange rate volatility.

C. cross-currency correlations.

The following information relates to questions 32-34

Rosario Delgado is an investment manager in Spain. Delgado's client, Max Rivera, seeks assistance with his well-diversified investment portfolio denominated in US dollars.

Rivera's reporting currency is the euro, and he is concerned about his US dollar exposure. His portfolio IPS requires monthly rebalancing, at a minimum. The portfolio's market value is USD2.5 million. Given Rivera's risk aversion, Delgado is considering a monthly hedge using either a one-month forward contract or one-month futures contract.

32. **Determine** which type of hedge instrument combination is *most* appropriate for Rivera's situation. **Justify** your selection.

Determine which type of hedge instrument combination is *most* appropriate for Rivera's situation. (Circle one.)

Static Forward	Static Futures	Dynamic Forward	Dynamic Futures

Justify your selection.

33. Assume Rivera's portfolio was perfectly hedged. It is now time to rebalance the portfolio and roll the currency hedge forward one month. The relevant data for rebalancing are provided in Exhibit 1.

Exhibit 1: Portfolio and Relevant Market Data

	One Month Ago	Today
Portfolio value of assets (USD)	2,500,000	2,650,000
USD/EUR spot rate (bid–offer)	1.1713/1.1714	1.1575/1.1576
One-month forward points (bid–offer)	9/10	6/7

Calculate the net cash flow (in euros) as of today to maintain the desired hedge. **Show** your calculations.

34. With the US dollar currently trading at a forward premium and US interest rates lower than Spanish rates, Delgado recommends trading against the forward rate bias to earn additional return from a positive roll yield.

    Identify *two* strategies Delgado should use to earn a positive roll yield. **Describe** the specific steps needed to execute each strategy.

Identify *two* strategies Delgado should use to earn a positive roll yield.	**Describe** the specific steps needed to execute *each* strategy.
1.	
2.	

35. Carnoustie Capital Management, Ltd. (CCM), a UK-based global investment advisory firm, is considering adding an emerging market currency product to its offerings. CCM has for the past three years managed a "model" portfolio of emerging market currencies using the same investment approach as its developed economy currency products. The risk and return measures of the "model" portfolio compare favorably with the one- and three-year emerging market benchmark performance net of CCM's customary advisory fee and estimated trading costs. Mindful of the higher volatility of emerging market currencies, CCM management is particularly pleased with the "model" portfolio's standard deviation, Sharpe ratio, and value at risk (VAR) in comparison to those of its developed economy products.

    Recognizing that market conditions have been stable since the "model" portfolio's inception, CCM management is sensitive to the consequences of extreme market events for emerging market risk and return.

    Evaluate the application of emerging market and developed market investment return probability distributions for CCM's potential new product.

SOLUTIONS

1.

Template for Question 1

Asset	Foreign-Currency Portfolio Return	USD Relative to Foreign-Currency (circle one)
Portfolio A	**15%**	appreciated depreciated

Justification

The 19.5% domestic-currency return for Portfolio A is higher than the 15% foreign-currency portfolio return in GBP; therefore, the USD necessarily depreciated relative to the GBP.

The domestic-currency return on a foreign portfolio will reflect both the foreign-currency return on the portfolio and the percentage movements in the spot exchange rate between the domestic and foreign currency. The domestic-currency return is multiplicative with respect to these two factors:

$$R_{DC} = (1 + R_{FC})(1 + R_{FX}) - 1$$

where R_{DC} is the domestic-currency return (in percent), R_{FC} is the foreign-currency return of the asset (portfolio), and R_{FX} is the percentage change of the foreign currency against the domestic currency. (Note that in the R_{FX} expression the domestic currency—the USD in this case—is the price currency.)

Solving for R_{FX}: $(1 + 15\%)(1 + R_{FX}) - 1 = 19.50\%$; $R_{FX} = 3.91\%$

Thus, the USD depreciated relative to the GBP. That is, the GBP appreciated against the USD because R_{FX} is quoted in terms of USD/GBP, with the USD as the price currency and GBP as the base currency, and in this example R_{FX} is a positive number (3.91%).

2.

Template for Question 2

Asset	Percentage Movement in the Spot Exchange Rate	Foreign-Currency Portfolio Return (circle one)
Portfolio B	EUR appreciated 5% against the USD	positive negative

Justification

The domestic-currency return for Portfolio B is 0%, and the EUR appreciated 5% against the USD; therefore, the foreign-currency return for Portfolio B is necessarily negative.

The domestic-currency return on a foreign portfolio will reflect both the foreign-currency return on the portfolio and the percentage movements in the spot exchange rate between the domestic and foreign currency. The domestic-currency return is multiplicative with respect to these two factors:

$$R_{DC} = (1 + R_{FC})(1 + R_{FX}) - 1$$

where R_{DC} is the domestic-currency return (in percent), R_{FC} is the foreign-currency return of the asset (portfolio), and R_{FX} is the percentage change of the foreign currency against the domestic currency. (Note that once again, the domestic currency—the USD—is the price currency in the USD/EUR quote for R_{FX}.)

Solving for R_{FC}: $(1 + R_{FC})(1 + 5\%) - 1 = 0\%$; $R_{FC} = -4.76\%$

3. Any *two* of the following four points is acceptable:

   - Trading requires dealing on the bid/offer spread offered by dealers. Dealer profit margin is based on these spreads. Maintaining a 100% hedge will require frequent rebalancing of minor changes in currency movements and could prove to be expensive. "Churning" the hedge portfolio would progressively add to hedging costs and reduce the hedge's benefits.
   - A long position in currency options involves an upfront payment. If the options expire out-of-the-money, this is an unrecoverable cost.
   - Forward contracts have a maturity date and need to be "rolled" forward with an FX swap transaction to maintain the hedge. Rolling hedges typically generate cash inflows and outflows, based on movements in the spot rate as well as roll yield. Cash may have to be raised to settle the hedging transactions (increases the volatility in the organization's cash accounts). The management of these cash flow costs can accumulate and become a large portion of the portfolio's value, and they become more expensive for cash outflows as interest rates increase.
   - Hedging requires maintaining the necessary administrative infrastructure for trading (personnel and technology systems). These overhead costs can become a significant portion of the overall costs of currency trading.

4. Optimal hedging decisions require balancing the benefits of hedging against the costs of hedging. Hedging costs come mainly in two forms: trading costs and opportunity costs. Gupta is referring to the opportunity cost of the 100% hedge strategy. The opportunity cost of the 100% hedge strategy for Portfolio B is the forgone opportunity of benefiting from favorable currency rate movements. Gupta is implying that accepting some currency risk has the potential to enhance portfolio return. A complete hedge eliminates this possibility.

5. A solution is to put in place a currency overlay program for active currency management. Because internal resources for active management are lacking, the fund manager would outsource currency exposure management to a sub-advisor that specializes in foreign exchange management. This approach would allow the fund manager of Portfolio A to separate the currency hedging function (currency beta), which can be done effectively internally, and the active currency management function (currency alpha) which can be managed externally by a foreign currency specialist.

6.

Template for Question 6

Gupta's Statements	Active Currency Approach (circle one)	Justification
"Many traders believe that it is not necessary to examine factors like the current account deficit, inflation, and interest rates because current exchange rates already reflect the market view on how these factors will affect future exchange rates."	carry trade **technical analysis** economic fundamentals	Gupta is describing active currency management based on market technicals. Market technicians believe that in a liquid, freely-traded market the historical price data already incorporates all relevant information on future price movements. Technicians believe that it is not necessary to look outside the market at data like the current account deficit, inflation and interest rates because current exchange rates already reflect the market consensus view on how these factors will affect future exchange rates.
"The six-month interest rate in India is 8% compared to 1% in the United States. This presents a yield pick-up opportunity."	**carry trade** technical analysis economic fundamentals	Gupta is describing active currency management based on the carry trade. This strategy is implemented by borrowing in low-yield currencies (USD at 1%) and investing in high-yield currencies (INR at 8%).
"The currency overlay manager will estimate the fair value of the currencies with the expectation that observed spot rates will converge to long-run equilibrium values described by parity conditions."	carry trade technical analysis economic fundamentals	Gupta is describing active currency management based on economic fundamentals. This approach assumes that, in free markets, exchange rates are determined by logical economic relationships that can be modeled. A fundamentals-based approach estimates the "fair value" of the currency, with the expectation that observed spot rates will converge to long-run equilibrium values described by parity conditions.

7. C is correct. The domestic-currency return is a function of the foreign-currency return and the percentage change of the foreign currency against the domestic currency. Mathematically, the domestic-currency return is expressed as:

$$R_{DC} = (1 + R_{FC})(1 + R_{FX}) - 1$$

where R_{DC} is the domestic-currency return (in percent), R_{FC} is the foreign-currency return, and R_{FX} is the percentage change of the foreign currency against the domestic currency. Note that this R_{FX} expression is calculated using the investor's domestic currency (the EUR in this case) as the *price* currency in the P/B quote. This is different than the market-standard currency quotes in Exhibit 1, where the EUR is the *base* currency in each of these quotes. Therefore, for the foreign currency (USD, GBP, or CHF) to *appreciate* against the EUR, the market-standard quote (USD/EUR, GBP/EUR, or CHF/EUR, respectively) must *decrease*; i.e. the EUR must depreciate.

The Euro-Swiss (CHF/EUR) is the only spot rate with a negative change (from 1.0875 to 1.0780), meaning the EUR depreciated against the CHF (the CHF/EUR rate decreased). Or put differently, the CHF appreciated against the EUR, adding to the EUR-denominated return for the German investor holding CHF-denominated assets. This would result in a higher domestic-currency return (R_{DC}), for the German investor, relative to the foreign-currency return (R_{FC}) for the CHF-denominated assets. Both the Euro-dollar (USD/EUR) and Euro-sterling (GBP/EUR) experienced a positive change in the spot rate, meaning the EUR appreciated against these two currencies (the USD/EUR rate and the GBP/EUR rate both increased). This would result in a lower domestic-currency return (R_{DC}) for the German investor relative to the foreign-currency return (R_{FC}) for the USD- and GBP-denominated assets.

A is incorrect because the Euro-dollar (USD/EUR) experienced a positive change in the spot rate, meaning the EUR appreciated against the USD (the USD/EUR rate increased). This would result in a lower domestic-currency (i.e. EUR-denominated) return relative to the foreign-currency return for the USD-denominated assets, since the USD has depreciated against the EUR.

B is incorrect because the Euro-sterling (GBP/EUR) experienced a positive change in the spot rate, meaning the EUR appreciated against the GPB (the GBP/EUR rate increased). This would result in a lower domestic-currency (i.e. EUR-denominated) return relative to the foreign-currency return for the GBP-denominated assets, since the GBP has depreciated against the EUR.

8. C is correct. An increase in the expected correlation between movements in the foreign-currency asset returns and movements in the spot exchange rates from 0.50 to 0.80 would increase the domestic-currency return *risk* but would not change the *level* of expected domestic-currency return. The domestic-currency return risk is a function of the foreign-currency return risk [$\sigma(R_{FC})$] the exchange rate risk [$\sigma(R_{FX})$] and the correlation between the foreign-currency returns and exchange rate movements. Mathematically, this is expressed as:

$$\sigma^2(R_{DC}) \approx \sigma^2(R_{FC}) + \sigma^2(R_{FX}) + 2\sigma(R_{FC})\sigma(R_{FX})\rho(R_{FC}R_{FX})$$

If the correlation increases from +0.50 to +0.80, then the *variance* of the expected domestic-currency return will increase—but this will not affect the *level* of the expected domestic-currency return (R_{DC}). Refer to the equation shown for the answer in Question 1 and note that Ostermann's expected R_{FC} has not changed. (Once again, note as well that R_{FX} is defined with the domestic currency as the price currency.)

A and B are incorrect. An increase in the expected correlation between movements in the foreign-currency asset returns and movements in the spot rates from 0.50 to 0.80 would increase the domestic-currency return risk but would not impact the expected domestic-currency return.

9. A is correct. Guten believes that, due to efficient currency markets, there should not be any long-run gains for speculating (or active management) in currencies, especially after netting out management and transaction costs. Therefore, both currency hedging and actively trading currencies represent a cost to the portfolio with little prospect of consistently positive active returns. Given a long investment horizon and few immediate liquidity needs, Guten is most likely to choose to forgo currency hedging and its associated costs.

B and C are incorrect because given a long investment horizon and little immediate liquidity needs, Guten is most likely to choose to forgo currency hedging and its associated costs. Guten believes that due to efficient currency markets there should not be any long-run gains when speculating in currencies, especially after netting out management and transaction costs.

10. B is correct. Umlauf develops a market view based on underlying fundamentals in exchange rates (an economic fundamental approach). When directed by clients, Umlauf uses options and a variety of trading strategies to *unbundle* all of the various risk factors and trades them separately (a volatility trading approach). A market technical approach would entail forming a market view based on technical analysis (i.e., a belief that historical prices incorporate all relevant information on future price movements and that such movements have a tendency to repeat).

A is incorrect because, in using options and a variety of trading strategies to *unbundle* all of the various risk factors and trade them separately, Umlauf is likely to periodically employ volatility trading-based currency strategies.

C is incorrect because, in developing a market view based on underlying fundamentals in exchange rates, Umlauf does utilize an economic fundamentals approach.

11. B is correct. Braunt Pensionskasse provides the manager with limited discretion in managing the portfolio's currency risk exposures. This would be most consistent with allowing the currency overlay manager to take directional views on future currency movements (within predefined bounds) where the currency overlay is limited to the currency exposures already in the foreign asset portfolio. It would not be appropriate to use a fully-passive hedging approach since it would eliminate any alpha from currency movements. Further, a currency overlay program, which considers "foreign exchange as an asset class", would likely expose Braunt's portfolio to more currency risk than desired given the given primary performance objectives.

    A is incorrect because a directional view currency overlay program is most appropriate given the limited discretion Braunt Pensionskasse has given the manager. A fully passive currency overlay program is more likely to be used when a client seeks to hedge all the currency risk.

    C is incorrect because a directional view currency overlay program is most appropriate given the limited discretion Braunt Pensionskasse has given the manager. In contrast, the concept of "foreign exchange as an asset class" allows the currency overlay manager to take currency exposure positions in any currency pair where there is value-added to be harvested.

12. C is correct. The primary performance objective of Franz Trading GmbH is to add alpha to the portfolio, and thus has given the manager discretion in trading currencies. This is essentially a "foreign exchange as an asset class" approach. Braunt Pensionskasse and Kastner have more conservative currency strategies, and thus are less likely to benefit from the different strategies that a new overlay manager might employ.

    A is incorrect because Franz Trading GmbH is more likely to benefit from the introduction of an additional overlay manager. Kastner is more likely to have a fully passive currency overlay program.

    B is incorrect because Franz Trading GmbH is more likely to benefit from the introduction of an additional overlay manager. Braunt is more likely to have a currency overlay program where the manager takes a directional view on future currency movements.

13. Currency movements contributed 1.5% to the account's 7.0% total (US dollar) return, calculated as follows:

    The domestic-currency return (R_{DC}) on a portfolio of multiple foreign assets is

$$R_{DC} = \sum_{i=1}^{n} \omega_i (1 + R_{FC,i})(1 + R_{FX,i}) - 1$$

    Where $R_{FC,i}$ is the foreign-currency return on the ith foreign asset, $R_{FX,i}$ is the appreciation of the ith foreign currency against the domestic currency, and ω_i is the weight of the asset as a percentage of the aggregate domestic-currency value of the portfolio. This equation can be rearranged as

$$R_{DC} = \sum_{i=1}^{n} \omega_i [R_{FC,i} + R_{FX,i} + (R_{FC,i} \times R_{FX,i})]$$

    Therefore, the domestic-currency return is equal to the sum of the weighted asset return, the weighted currency return, and the weighted cross-product of the asset return and the currency return. The latter two terms explain the effects of foreign-currency movements on the Bhatt account's total (US dollar) return of 7.0%.

The weighted asset return is equal to 5.5%, calculated as follows:

(0.50 × 10.0%) + (0.25 × 5.0%) + [0.25 × (–3.0%)] = 5.5%.

The weighted currency return is equal to 1.5% calculated as follows:

(0.50 × 0.0%) + (0.25 × 2.0%) + (0.25 × 4.0%) = 1.5%.

The weighted cross-product is equal to –0.005%, calculated as follows:

[0.50 × (10.0% × 0.0%)] + [0.25 × (5.0% × 2.0%)] + [0.25 × (–3.0% × 4.0%)]
= –0.005%.

Therefore, the contribution of foreign currency equals 1.5%, calculated as the 7.0% total (US dollar) return less the 5.5% weighted asset return. Alternatively, the contribution of foreign currency to the total return can be calculated as the sum of the weighted currency return of 1.5% and the weighted cross-product of –0.005%:

1.5% + (–0.005%) = 1.495%, which rounds to 1.5%.

14.

Determine the *most appropriate* currency management strategy for Bhatt. (Circle one.)

Passive hedging	Discretionary hedging	Active currency management

Justify your response.

Active currency management is the most appropriate currency management strategy because with this approach, the portfolio manager is supposed to take currency risks and manage them for profit with the primary goal of adding alpha to the portfolio through successful trading. This primary goal differs from the discretionary hedging approach in which the manager's primary duty is to protect the portfolio from currency risk and secondarily seek alpha within limited bounds. While the difference between active currency management and discretionary hedging is one of emphasis more than degree, the bounded discretion that Bhatt has granted Darden (plus or minus 25% from the neutral position) strongly suggests that Darden is expected to take currency risk and seek alpha with priority over portfolio protection from currency risk.

Passive hedging is not appropriate because with this approach, the goal is to keep the portfolio's currency exposures close, if not equal to, those of a benchmark portfolio used to evaluate performance. Passive hedging is a rules-based approach that removes all discretion from the portfolio manager, regardless of the manager's market opinion on future movements in exchange rates. In this case, Bhatt has granted Darden the discretion to manage currency exposures within a range of plus or minus 25% from the neutral benchmark position.

A discretionary hedging approach is not appropriate because Bhatt has granted Darden more than limited discretion (plus or minus 25% from the neutral position), indicative of an active currency management approach. The discretion granted suggests that Darden's primary goal is to take currency risks and manage them for profit with a secondary goal of protecting the portfolio from currency risk. The primary goal of a discretionary hedging approach is to protect the portfolio from currency risk while secondarily seeking alpha within limited bounds.

15. Given C&M's research conclusion and the IPS constraints, the currency team should under-hedge Bhatt's portfolio by selling the US dollar forward against the Indian rupee in a forward contract (or contracts) at no less than a 75% hedge ratio of the portfolio's USD10,000,000 market value. By under-hedging the portfolio relative to the "neutral" (100% hedge ratio) benchmark, the team seeks to add incremental value on the basis of its view that the US dollar will appreciate against

the Indian rupee while maintaining compliance with the IPS.

Since the Indian rupee is assumed to depreciate against the US dollar, a 100% hedge ratio would largely eliminate any alpha opportunity. However, a hedge ratio greater than 75% but less than 100% (as dictated by the plus or minus 25% versus neutral IPS constraint) provides the opportunity to capture currency return in the expected US dollar appreciation against the Indian rupee.

16.

Identify the *most likely* approach for Lee to optimally locate Wilson's portfolio on the currency risk spectrum, consistent with IPS.
(Circle one.)

Passive Hedging	Discretionary Hedging	Active Currency Management	Currency Overlay

Justify your response with *two* reasons supporting the approach.

1. The portfolio is said to be in its flat natural neutral position because Lee does not have market conviction, which is consistent with a discretionary hedging approach.	2. The currency hedge ratio requirement reflects some discretion with actual portfolio currency risk exposures allowed to vary from the neutral position within a 3% band.

Passive hedging is not likely because the IPS allows the 3% band around the neutral position. In addition, passive hedging is a rules-based approach, which is contrary to Wilson's preference.

Active currency management is not likely because the 3% band around the neutral position is too limited for that approach. In many cases, the difference between discretionary hedging and active currency management is more of emphasis than degree. The primary duty of the discretionary hedger is to protect the portfolio from currency risk. Active currency management is supposed to take currency risks and manage them for profit. Leaving actual portfolio exposures near zero for extended periods is typically not a viable option.

Currency overlay is not likely because the 3% band is too small to indicate active currency management in a currency overlay program. In addition, currency overlay programs are often conducted by external, FX-specialized sub-advisers to a portfolio, whereas Lee is a generalist managing a variety of portfolios across asset classes. Finally, currency overlay allows for taking directional views on future currency movements, and a lack of market conviction is noted here.

17. The IPS revision allows for a more proactive currency risk approach in the portfolio because it was determined Wilson was too short-term focused and risk averse. Lee should structure the currency overlay so that it is as uncorrelated as possible with other asset or alpha-generation programs in the portfolio. By introducing foreign currencies as a separate asset class, the more currency overlay is expected to generate alpha that is uncorrelated with the other programs in the portfolio, the more likely it is to be allowed in terms of strategic portfolio positioning.

18. A is correct. The fund has a long-term perspective, few immediate liquidity needs, and a lower weight in fixed income that in equities (bond portfolios are typically associated with hedge ratios closer to 100% than equity portfolios). The emerging market exposure would also support active management, given these countries' typically higher yields (carry trade) and often volatile exchange rates.

B is incorrect because the characteristics of the fund and the beneficial investor (in this case, the royal family) do not argue for a conservative currency strategy.

C is incorrect because a more active currency management strategy would be more suitable for this fund.

19. A is correct. Exchange-traded futures contract not only have initial margin requirements, they also have daily mark-to-market and, as a result, can be subject to daily margin calls. Market participants must have sufficient liquidity to meet margin calls, or have their positions involuntarily liquidated by their brokers. Note that the risk of daily margin calls is not a feature of most forwards contracts; nor is initial margin. (However, this is changing among the largest institutional players in FX markets as many forward contracts now come with what are known as Collateral Support Annexes—CSAs—in which margin can be posted. Posting additional margin would typically not be a daily event, however, except in the case of extreme market moves.)

    B is incorrect because futures contracts have low transactions costs. C is incorrect because whether the EUR is the price or the base currency in the quote will not affect the hedging process. In fact, on the CME the quote would be the market-standard USD/EUR quote, with the EUR as the base currency.

20. C is correct. Based on predicted export trends, Subscriber 2 most likely expects the KRW/USD rate to increase (i.e., the won—the price currency—to depreciate relative to the USD). This would require a long forward position in a forward contract, but as a country with capital controls, a NDF would be used instead. (Note: While forward contracts offered by banks are generally an institutional product, not retail, the retail version of a non-deliverable forward contract is known as a "contract for differences" (CFD) and is available at several retail FX brokers.)

    A is incorrect because Subscriber 2 expects the KRW/USD rate to increase. A short straddle position would be used when the direction of exchange rate movement is unknown and volatility is expected to remain low.

    B is incorrect because a put option would profit from a decrease of the KRW/USD rate, not an increase (as expected). Higher volatility would also make buying a put option more expensive.

21. B is correct. Subscriber 3's carry trade strategy is equivalent to trading the forward rate bias, based on the historical evidence that the forward rate is not the center of the distribution for the spot rate. Applying this bias involves buying currencies trading at a forward discount and selling currencies trading at a forward premium. So a higher forward premium on the lower yielding currency—the USD, the base currency in the INR/USD quote—would effectively reflect a more profitable trading opportunity. That is, a higher premium for buying or selling the USD forward is associated with a lower US interest rate compared to India. This would mean a wider interest rate differential in favor of Indian instruments, and hence potentially more carry trade profits.

    A is incorrect because Subscriber 3's carry trade strategy depends on a wide interest rate differential between the high-yield country (India) and the low-yield country (the United States). The differential should be wide enough to compensate for the unhedged currency risk exposure.

    C is incorrect because a guide to the carry trade's riskiness is the volatility of spot rates on the involved currencies, with rapid movements in exchange rates often associated with a panicked unwinding of carry trades. All things being equal, higher volatility is worse for carry trades.

22. C is correct. Emerging market currencies are often the investment currencies in the carry trade. This reflects the higher yields often available in their money markets compared to Developed Market economies (funding currencies are typically low-yield currencies such as the JPY). This can lead to higher holding returns, but these higher returns can also come with higher risks: carry trades are occasional-

ly subject to panicked unwinds in stressed market conditions. When this occurs, position exit can be made more difficult by market illiquidity and higher trading costs (wider bid/offer spreads). The leverage involved in the carry trade can magnify trading losses under these circumstances.

A is incorrect because return distributions are often *negatively* skewed, reflecting the higher event risk (panicked carry trade unwinds, currency pegs being re-set, etc.) associated with the carry trade.

B is incorrect because although FX markets are typically efficient (or very close thereto) this does not mean that higher returns are not available. The key question is whether these are abnormally high *risk-adjusted* returns. Higher return in an efficient market comes with higher risk. The higher (short-term) return in the carry trade reflects the risk premia for holding unhedged currency risk, in the context of a favorable interest rate differential.

23. Statements 1 and 2 compare differences between speculative volatility traders and hedgers of volatility. Statement 1 best explains the view of a speculative volatility trader. Speculative volatility traders often want to be net-short volatility, if they believe that market conditions will remains stable. The reason for this is that most options expire out-of-the money, and the option writer can then keep the option premium as a payment earned for accepting volatility risk. (Speculative volatility traders would want to be long volatility if they thought volatility was likely to increase.) Statement 2 best describes the view of a hedger of volatility. Most hedgers are net-long volatility since they want to buy protection from unanticipated price volatility. Buying currency risk protection generally means a long option position. This can be thought of as paying an insurance premium for protection against exchange rate volatility.

24. In currency markets, volatility is not constant, nor are its movements completely random. Instead, volatility is determined by a wide variety of underlying factors, both fundamental and technical, for which a trader can express an opinion. Movements in volatility are cyclical and typically subject to long periods of relative stability punctuated by sharp upward spikes in volatility as markets come under stress. Speculative volatility traders among overlay managers often want to be net short volatility because most options expire out of the money and the option writer then gets to keep the premium without delivery of the underlying currency pair. Ideally these traders would want to flip their position and be long volatility ahead of the volatility spikes, but these episodes can be notoriously difficult to time. Most hedgers, in contrast, typically run option positions that are net long volatility because they are buying protection from the unanticipated price volatility.

    In this case, Konev would most likely be interested in speculative gains on US dollar weakness, while the other institutional clients would be hedgers seeking to minimize trading risks. The concept of foreign exchange as an asset class for Konev will most likely permit Murimi to take foreign exchange exposure in any currency pair where there is additional value to capture. A volatility-based strategy for Konev would typically be net short, as opposed to net long, volatility to earn the related risk premium for absorbing volatility risk. In contrast, the institutional investors, as hedgers in managing net long volatility positions, would be exposed to the time decay of an option's time value.

25. In forming a market view on such turning points in future exchange rate movements (e.g., peaking in the US dollar) or timing-related position entry and exit points, market technicians follow three principles: (1) Historical price data can be helpful in projecting future movements, (2) historical price patterns have a tendency to repeat and identify profitable trade opportunities, and (3) technical analysis attempts to determine not where market prices *should* trade but where

they *will* trade.

Thus, when devising a volatility strategy, Murimi can use her technical skills to time entry and exit points of positions. She can identify patterns in the historical price data on the US dollar, such as when it was overbought or oversold, meaning it has trended too far in one direction and is vulnerable to a trend reversal. She would appropriately position US dollar trades to maximize potential returns from volatility shifts that could be associated with US dollar exchange rate movements.

26. In practice, matching the *current* market value of the foreign-currency exposure in the portfolio with an equal and offsetting position in a forward contract is likely to be ineffective over time because the market value of foreign-currency assets will change with market conditions. A static hedge (i.e., an unchanging hedge) will tend to accumulate unwanted currency exposures as the value of the foreign-currency assets change. This will result in a mismatch between the market value of the foreign-currency asset portfolio and the nominal size of the forward contract used for the currency hedge (resulting in currency risk). For this reason, the portfolio manager will generally need to implement a dynamic hedge by rebalancing the portfolio periodically.

27. The fund manager should implement a dynamic hedging approach. Dynamic hedging requires rebalancing the portfolio periodically. The rebalancing would require adjusting some combination of the size, number, and maturities of the foreign-currency contracts.

    Although rebalancing a dynamic hedge will keep the actual hedge ratio close to the target hedge ratio, it has the disadvantage of increased transaction costs compared to a static hedge.

28. B is correct. The GBP value of the assets has declined, and hence the hedge needs to be *reduced* by GBP 7,000,000. This would require buying the GBP forward to net the outstanding (short) forward contract to an amount less than GBP 100,000,000.

    A is incorrect because to rebalance the hedge (reduce the net size of the short forward position) the GBP must be bought *forward*, not with a spot transaction.

    C is incorrect because the GBP must be bought, not sold. Buying SEK against the GBP is equivalent to selling GBP. Moreover, the amount of SEK that would be sold forward (to buy GBP 7,000,000 forward) would be determined by the *forward* rate, not the spot rate (7,000,000 × 10.6875 = 74,812,500).

29. C is correct. The fund holds CHF-denominated assets and hence Björk wants to protect against a depreciation of the CHF against the SEK, which would be a down-move in the SEK/CHF cross rate. An OTM put option provides some downside protection against such a move, while writing an OTM call option helps reduce the cost of this option structure. Note that Björk does not expect that the SEK/CHF rate will increase, so this option (in her view) will likely expire OTM and allow her to keep the premia. This hedging structure is known as a short risk reversal (or a collar) and is a popular hedging strategy.

    A is incorrect because the ATM call option will not protect against a decrease in the SEK/CHF rate. An ATM option is also expensive (compared to an OTM option). Note that Björk does not expect the SEK/CHF rate to increase, so would not want a long call option position for this rate.

    B is incorrect because this structure is expensive (via the long ITM call option) and does not protect against a decrease in the SEK/CHF rate.

30. B is correct. To hedge the EUR-denominated assets Björk will be selling forward contracts on the SEK/EUR cross rate. A higher forward premium will result in higher roll return as Björk is selling the EUR forward at a higher all-in forward

rate, and closing out the contract at a lower rate (all else equal), given that the forward curve is in contango.

A is incorrect because Björk is hedging EUR-denominated assets with a EUR-denominated forward contract. While it is true that the gap between spot and forward rates will be higher the higher the interest rate differential between countries, this gap (basis) converges to zero near maturity date, when the forward contracts would be rolled.

C is incorrect because forward contracts do not generate premia income; writing options does.

31. C is correct. A cross hedge exposes the fund to basis risk; that is, the risk that the hedge fails to protect against adverse currency movements because the correlations between the value of the assets being hedged and the hedging instrument change.

A is incorrect because movements in forward points (and hence roll yield) would be of secondary importance compared to the basis risk of a cross hedge.

B is incorrect because exchange rate volatility would not necessarily affect a hedge based on forward contracts, as long as the correlations between the underlying assets and the hedge remained stable. Although relevant, volatility in itself is not the "most" important risk to consider for a cross-hedge. (However, movements in volatility would affect hedges based on currency options.)

32.

Determine which type of hedge instrument combination is *most* appropriate for Rivera's situation. (Circle one.)

Static Forward	Static Futures	Dynamic Forward	Dynamic Futures

Justify your selection.

Static vs. Dynamic Justifications:
1. Both Rivera and Delgado are risk averse.
2. The portfolio's IPS requires monthly rebalancing.

Forward vs. Futures Justifications:
1. A forward contract is less expensive.
2. A forward contract has greater liquidity.

The hedge instrument combination most appropriate for Rivera's portfolio is a dynamic forward hedge for the reasons noted below.

First, a dynamic hedge is most appropriate here. A static hedge (i.e., unchanging hedge) will avoid transaction costs but will also tend to accumulate unwanted currency exposures as the value of the foreign-currency assets change. This characteristic will cause a mismatch between the market value of the foreign-currency asset portfolio and the nominal size of the forward contract used for the currency hedge; this is pure currency risk. Given this potential mismatch and because both Rivera and Delgado are risk averse, Delgado should implement a dynamic hedge by rebalancing the portfolio at least on a monthly basis.

Delgado must assess the cost–benefit trade-offs of how frequently to dynamically rebalance the hedge. This depends on a variety of factors (manager risk aversion, market view, IPS guidelines). The higher the degree of risk aversion, the more frequently the hedge is likely to be rebalanced back to the "neutral" hedge ratio.

A forward contract is more suitable because in comparison to a futures contract, a forward contract is more flexible in terms of currency pair, settlement date, and transaction amount. Forward contracts are also simpler than futures contracts from an administrative standpoint owing to the absence of margin requirements, reducing portfolio management expense. Finally, forward contracts are more liquid than futures for trading in large sizes because the daily trade volume for OTC currency forward contracts dwarfs those for exchange-traded futures contracts.

33. When hedging one month ago, Delgado would have sold USD2,500,000 one month forward against the euro.

To calculate the net cash flow (in euros) today, the following steps are necessary:

1. Sell USD2,500,000 at the one-month forward rate stated in the forward contract. Selling US dollars against the euro means buying euros, which is the base currency in the USD/EUR forward rate. Therefore, the offer side of the market must be used to calculate the inflow in euros.

All-in forward rate = 0.8914 + (30/10,000) = 0.8944

USD2,500,000 / 0.8944 = EUR2,795,169.95.

2. Buy USD2,500,000 at the spot rate to offset the USD sold in Step 1 above. Buying the US dollar against the euro means selling euros, which is the base currency in the USD/EUR spot rate. Therefore, the bid side of the market must be used to calculate the inflow in euros.

USD2,500,000 / 0.8875 = EUR2,816,901.41.

3. Therefore, the net cash flow is equal to EUR2,795,169.95 – EUR2,816,901.41, which is equal to a net outflow of EUR21,731.46.

   To maintain the desired hedge, Delgado will then enter into a new forward contract to sell the USD2,650,000. There will be no additional cash flow today arising from the new forward contract.

34.

Identify *two* strategies Delgado should use to earn a positive roll yield.	**Describe** the specific steps needed to execute *each* strategy.
1. Implement the carry trade.	Buy (invest in) the high-yield currency and sell (borrow) the low-yield currency.
2. Trade the forward rate bias.	Buy (invest in) the forward discount currency and sell (borrow) the forward premium currency.

Given that the base currency (the US dollar) is trading at a forward premium, the hedge requires the sale of US dollar forward, resulting in a positive roll yield. The concept of roll yield is very similar to forward rate bias and the carry trade. Here, Delgado is suggesting a strategy to pursue when there is a negative roll yield, because a hedger trading against the forward bias would be buying US dollars at a forward premium instead of selling them. The carry trade strategy of borrowing in low-yield currencies and investing in high-yield currencies is equivalent to trading the forward rate bias, not against it.

35. Emerging market currency trades are subject to relatively frequent extreme events and market stresses. Thus, return probability distributions for emerging market investments exhibit fatter tails than the normal distributions that are customarily used to evaluate developed market investment performance. Additionally, emerging market return probability distributions also have a pronounced negative skew when compared with developed market (normal) distributions.

Given these differences, risk management and control tools (such as VAR) that depend on normal distributions can be misleading under extreme market conditions and greatly understate the risks to which the portfolio is exposed. Likewise, many investment performance measures used to evaluate performance are also based on the normal distribution. As a result, historical performance evaluated by such measures as the Sharpe ratio can look very attractive when market conditions are stable, but this apparent outperformance can disappear into deep losses faster than most investors can react.

Short-term stability in emerging markets can give investors a false sense of overconfidence and thereby encourage over-positioning based on the illusion of normally distributed returns. Thus, CCM should not assume a normal distribution for its "model" emerging market portfolio. CCM should assume a fatter-tailed, negatively skewed return probability distribution better reflecting the risk exposure to extreme events.

Glossary

Absolute return benchmark A minimum target return that an investment manager is expected to beat.
Accrual taxes Taxes levied and paid on a periodic basis.
Accumulation phase Phase where the government predominantly contributes to a sovereign wealth pension reserve fund.
Active management A portfolio management approach that allows risk factor mismatches relative to a benchmark index causing potentially significant return differences between the active portfolio and the underlying benchmark.
Active return The return on a portfolio minus the return on the portfolio's benchmark.
Active risk The standard deviation of active returns.
Active risk budgeting Risk budgeting that concerns active risk (risk relative to a portfolio's benchmark).
Active share A measure of how similar a portfolio is to its benchmark. A manager who precisely replicates the benchmark will have an active share of zero; a manager with no holdings in common with the benchmark will have an active share of one.
Aggregate wealth The total value of all assets owned, encompassing personal property, financial assets, real assets, and rights.
Arithmetic attribution An attribution approach which explains the arithmetic difference between the portfolio return and its benchmark return. The single-period attribution effects sum to the excess return, however, when combining multiple periods, the sub-period attribution effects will not sum to the excess return.
Ask price The price at which a trader will sell a specified quantity of a security. Also called *ask*, *offer price*, or *offer*.
Asset-only With respect to asset allocation, an approach that focuses directly on the characteristics of the assets without explicitly modeling the liabilities.
Authority bias A behavioral bias which involves groups deferring to a group member that is a subject matter expert or in a position of authority.
Aversion to complexity A behavioral phenomenon of groups in many professional contexts, in which disproportionate attention is given to trivial issues at the expense of important but harder-to-grasp or contested topics.
Back-fill bias The distortion in index or peer group data which results when returns are reported to a database only after they are known to be good returns.
Base With respect to a foreign exchange quotation of the price of one unit of a currency, the currency referred to in "one unit of a currency."
Basis risk The possibility that the expected value of a derivative differs unexpectedly from that of the underlying.
Bear spread An option strategy that becomes more valuable when the price of the underlying asset declines, so requires buying one option and writing another with a *lower* exercise price. A put bear spread involves buying a put with a higher exercise price and selling a put with a lower exercise price. A bear spread can also be executed with calls.
Best ask The offer to sell with the lowest ask price. Also called *best offer* or *inside ask*.
Best bid The highest bid in the market.
Best offer The lowest offer (ask price) in the market.
Best-in-class An ESG implementation approach that seeks to identify the most favorable companies and sectors based on ESG considerations. Also called *positive screening*.
Bid price In a price quotation, the price at which the party making the quotation is willing to buy a specified quantity of an asset or security.
Bid–ask spread The ask price minus the bid price.
Buffering Establishing ranges around breakpoints that define whether a stock belongs in one index or another.
Bull spread An option strategy that becomes more valuable when the price of the underlying asset rises, so requires buying one option and writing another with a *higher* exercise price. A call bull spread involves buying a call with a lower exercise price and selling a call with a higher exercise price. A bull spread can also be executed with puts.
Business cycle Fluctuations in GDP in relation to long-term trend growth, usually lasting 9-11 years.
Calendar rebalancing Rebalancing a portfolio to target weights on a periodic basis; for example, monthly, quarterly, semiannually, or annually.
Calendar spread A strategy in which one sells an option and buys the same type of option but with different expiration dates, on the same underlying asset and with the same strike. When the investor buys the more distant (near-term) call and sells the near-term (more distant) call, it is a long (short) calendar spread.
Canada model Characterized by a high allocation to alternatives. Unlike the endowment model, however, the Canada model relies more on internally managed assets. The innovative features of the Canada model are the: a) reference portfolio, b) total portfolio approach, and c) active management.
Capital market expectations (CME) Expectations concerning the risk and return prospects of asset classes.
Capital sufficiency analysis The process of evaluating whether a client has sufficient capital resources to achieve their financial goals and objectives; it considers the client's assets, liabilities, income, expenses, risk tolerance, time horizon, and other relevant factors.
Capture ratio A measure of the manager's gain or loss relative to the gain or loss of the benchmark.
Carhart model A four factor model used in performance attribution. The four factors are: market (RMRF), size (SMB), value (HML), and momentum (WML).
Carry trade A trading strategy that involves buying a security and financing it at a rate that is lower than the yield on that security.
Cash flow matching Immunization approach that attempts to ensure that all future liability payouts are matched precisely by cash flows from bonds or fixed-income derivatives.

Cash-secured put An option strategy involving the writing of a put option and simultaneously depositing an amount of money equal to the exercise price into a designated account (this strategy is also called a fiduciary put).

Collar An option position in which the investor is long shares of stock and then buys a put with an exercise price below the current stock price and writes a call with an exercise price above the current stock price. Collars allow a shareholder to acquire downside protection through a protective put but reduce the cash outlay by writing a covered call.

Contingent immunization Hybrid approach that combines immunization with an active management approach when the asset portfolio's value exceeds the present value of the liability portfolio.

Cost basis The initial cost of acquiring an investment including expenses incurred to acquire the investment. Also referred to as simply basis.

Covered call An option strategy in which a long position in an asset is combined with a short position in a call on that asset.

Cross hedge A hedge involving a hedging instrument that is imperfectly correlated with the asset being hedged; an example is hedging a bond investment with futures on a non-identical bond.

Cross-currency basis swap A swap in which notional principals are exchanged because the goal of the transaction is to issue at a more favorable funding rate and swap the amount back to the currency of choice.

Cross-sectional consistency A feature of expectations setting which means that estimates for all classes reflect the same underlying assumptions and are generated with methodologies that reflect or preserve important relationships among the asset classes, such as strong correlations. It is the internal consistency across asset classes.

Currency overlay programs A currency overlay program is a program to manage a portfolio's currency exposures for the case in which those exposures are managed separately from the management of the portfolio itself.

Custom security-based benchmark Benchmark that is custom built to accurately reflect the investment discipline of a particular investment manager. Also called a *strategy benchmark* because it reflects a manager's particular strategy.

Decision-reversal risk The risk of reversing a chosen course of action at the point of maximum loss.

Decumulation phase Phase where the government predominantly withdraws from a sovereign wealth pension reserve fund.

Deferred taxes Taxes postponed until some future date.

Defined benefit A retirement plan in which a plan sponsor commits to paying a specified retirement benefit.

Defined benefit plan Retirement plan that is funded by the employer that guarantees a retirement benefit based on factors such as years of service, salary, and age.

Defined contribution A retirement plan in which contributions are defined but the ultimate retirement benefit is not specified or guaranteed by the plan sponsor.

Defined contribution plan Retirement plan in which the employer, employee, or both contribute to an account in which the employee bears the investment risk.

Delay costs Implicit trading costs that arise from the inability to complete desired trades immediately. Also called *slippage*.

Delta The sensitivity of the derivative price to a small change in the value of the underlying asset.

Delta hedging Hedging that involves matching the price response of the position being hedged over a narrow range of prices.

Demand deposits Accounts that can be drawn upon regularly and without notice. This category includes checking accounts and certain savings accounts that are often accessible through online banks or automated teller machines (ATMs).

Diffusion index Reflects the proportion of the index's components that are moving in a pattern consistent with the overall index.

Dividend capture A trading strategy whereby an equity portfolio manager purchases stocks just before their ex-dividend dates, holds these stocks through the ex-dividend date to earn the right to receive the dividend, and subsequently sells the shares.

Domestic asset An asset that trades in the investor's domestic currency (or home currency).

Domestic currency The currency of the investor, i.e., the currency in which he or she typically makes consumption purchases, e.g., the Swiss franc for an investor domiciled in Switzerland.

Domestic-currency return A rate of return stated in domestic currency terms from the perspective of the investor; reflects both the foreign-currency return on an asset as well as percentage movement in the spot exchange rate between the domestic and foreign currencies.

Drawdown A percentage peak-to-trough reduction in net asset value.

Drawdown duration The total time from the start of the drawdown until the cumulative drawdown recovers to zero.

Due diligence Investigation and analysis in support of an investment action, decision, or recommendation.

Duration matching Immunization approach based on the duration of assets and liabilities. Ideally, the liabilities being matched (the liability portfolio) and the portfolio of assets (the bond portfolio) should be affected similarly by a change in interest rates.

Duration times spread Weighting of spread duration by credit spread in order to incorporate the empirical observation that spread changes for lower-rated bonds tend to be consistent on a percentage, rather than absolute, basis.

Dynamic asset allocation Dynamic asset allocation is an investment strategy premised on long-term asset allocation but employing short-term, tactical trading to maintain investment allocation targets.

Dynamic hedge A hedge requiring adjustment as the price of the hedged asset changes.

Econometrics The application of quantitative modeling and analysis grounded in economic theory to the analysis of economic data.

Economic balance sheet An extended balance sheet that includes the present values of both lifetime earnings and future consumption.

Economic indicators Economic statistics provided by government and established private organizations that contain information on an economy's recent past activity or its current or future position in the business cycle.

Effective federal funds (FFE) rate The fed funds rate actually transacted between depository institutions, not the Fed's target federal funds rate.

Effective spread Two times the difference between the execution price and the midpoint of the market quote at the time an order is entered.

Endowment model Characterized by a high allocation to alternative investments (private investments and hedge funds), significant active management, and externally managed assets.

Enhanced indexing approach Maintains a close link to the benchmark but attempts to generate a modest amount of outperformance relative to the benchmark.

Excess return Used in various senses appropriate to context: 1) The difference between the portfolio return and the benchmark return, which may be either positive or negative; 2) The return in excess of the risk-free rate, thus representing the return for bearing risk.

Exhaustive Covering or containing all possible outcomes.

Extended portfolio assets and liabilities Assets and liabilities beyond those shown on a conventional balance sheet that are relevant in making asset allocation decisions; an example of an extended asset is human capital.

Factor-model-based benchmarks Benchmarks constructed by examining a portfolio's sensitivity to a set of factors, such as the return for a broad market index, company earnings growth, industry, or financial leverage.

Family offices Private firms that offer a range of wealth management services tailored specifically for ultra-high-net-worth individuals.

Foreign assets Assets denominated in currencies other than the investor's home currency.

Foreign currency Currency that is not the currency in which an investor makes consumption purchases, e.g., the US dollar from the perspective of a Swiss investor.

Foreign-currency return The return of the foreign asset measured in foreign-currency terms.

Forward rate bias An empirically observed divergence from interest rate parity conditions that active investors seek to benefit from by borrowing in a lower-yield currency and investing in a higher-yield currency.

Funding currencies The low-yield currencies in which borrowing occurs in a carry trade.

Gamma A numerical measure of how sensitive an option's delta (the sensitivity of the derivative's price) is to a change in the value of the underlying.

General account Account holding assets to fund future liabilities from traditional life insurance and fixed annuities, the products in which the insurer bears all the risks—particularly mortality risk and longevity risk.

Gini coefficient A measure of inequality of wealth, or *i*, that ranges from 0 (perfect equality) to 1 (perfect inequality).

Goals-based With respect to asset allocation or investing, an approach that focuses on achieving an investor's goals (for example, related to supporting lifestyle needs or aspirations) based typically on constructing sub-portfolios aligned with those goals.

Goals-based investing An investment industry term for approaches to investing for individuals and families focused on aligning investments with goals (parallel to liability-driven investing for institutional investors).

Grinold–Kroner model An expression for the expected return on a share as the sum of an expected income return, an expected nominal earnings growth return, and an expected repricing return.

Groupthink A behavioral bias that occurs when a team minimizes conflict and dissent in reaching and maintaining a consensus.

Hedge ratio The proportion of an underlying that will offset the risk associated with a derivative position.

High-net-worth individuals (HNWIs) Individuals with investable assets exceeding a certain minimum level, often as low as USD1 million, but typically more.

High-water mark A measure that reflects the fund's maximum value as of a performance fee payment date net of fees.

Holdings-based attribution A "buy and hold" attribution approach which calculates the return of portfolio and benchmark components based upon the price and foreign exchange rate changes applied to daily snapshots of portfolio holdings.

Holdings-based style analysis A bottom-up style analysis that estimates the risk exposures from the actual securities held in the portfolio at a point in time.

Home bias A preference for securities listed on the exchanges of one's home country.

Home currency See *domestic currency*.

Home-country bias The favoring of domestic over non-domestic investments relative to global market value weights.

Human capital The present value of an individual's future expected labor income.

Impact investing Refers to investments made with the specific intent of generating positive, measurable social and environmental impact alongside a financial return (which differentiates it from philanthropy).

Implementation shortfall (IS) The difference between the return for a notional or paper portfolio, where all transactions are assumed to take place at the manager's decision price, and the portfolio's actual return, which reflects realized transactions, including all fees and costs.

Implied volatility The standard deviation that causes an option pricing model to give the current option price.

Implied volatility surface A three-dimensional plot, for put and call options on the same underlying asset, of days to expiration (*x*-axis), option strike prices (*y*-axis), and implied volatilities (*z*-axis). It simultaneously shows the volatility skew (or smile) and the term structure of implied volatility.

Inflation-linked bonds Debt instruments that link the principal and interest to inflation.

Input uncertainty Uncertainty concerning whether the inputs are correct.

Inside ask See *best ask*.

Inside bid See *best bid*.

Inside spread The spread between the best bid price and the best ask price. Also called the *market bid-ask spread*, *inside bid-ask spread*, or *market spread*.

Interaction effect The impact of overweighting and underweighting individual securities within sectors that are themselves overweighted or underweighted.

Intertemporal consistency A feature of expectations setting which means that estimates for an asset class over different horizons reflect the same assumptions with respect to the potential paths of returns over time. It is the internal consistency over various time horizons.

Intrinsic value The amount gained (per unit) by an option buyer if an option is exercised at any given point in time. May be referred to as the exercise value of the option.

Investable net worth The sum of liquid assets, such as savings and investment accounts, and less short-term liabilities such as credit card debt.

Investable wealth The sum of liquid assets such as savings and investment accounts.

Investment currencies The high-yielding currencies in a carry trade.

Investment policy statement (IPS) A description of a client's unique investment objectives, risk tolerance, investment time horizon, and other applicable constraints.

Investment style A natural grouping of investment disciplines that has some predictive power in explaining the future dispersion of returns across portfolios.

Key person risk The risk that results from over-reliance on an individual or individuals whose departure would negatively affect an investment manager.

Knock-in/knock-out Features of a vanilla option that is created (or ceases to exist) when the spot exchange rate touches a pre-specified level.

Latency The elapsed time between the occurrence of an event and a subsequent action that depends on that event.

Leading economic indicators Turning points that usually precede those of the overall economy; they are believed to have value for predicting the economy's future state, usually near-term.

Liability driven investing (LDI) model In the LDI model, the primary investment objective is to generate returns sufficient to cover liabilities, with a focus on maximizing expected surplus return (excess return of assets over liabilities) and managing surplus volatility.

Liability glide path A specification of desired proportions of liability-hedging assets and return-seeking assets and the duration of the liability hedge as funded status changes and contributions are made.

Liability-based mandates Mandates managed to match or cover expected liability payments (future cash outflows) with future projected cash inflows.

Liability-driven investing An investment industry term that generally encompasses asset allocation that is focused on funding an investor's liabilities in institutional contexts.

Liability-relative With respect to asset allocation, an approach that focuses directly only on funding liabilities as an investment objective.

Limit order book The book or list of limit orders to buy and sell that pertains to a security.

Limited-life foundations A type of foundation where founders seek to maintain control of spending while they (or their immediate heirs) are still alive.

Longevity risk The risk of exhausting an individual's financial resources before passing away, thereby leaving insufficient capital for living expenses and unmet needs.

Lorenz curve A measure of the cumulative percentage of wealth owned by each percentage of the population.

Macro attribution Attribution at the sponsor level.

Manager peer group See *manager universe*.

Manager universe A broad group of managers with similar investment disciplines. Also called *manager peer group*.

Marginal tax rate The highest rate of tax applied to taxable income.

Market fragmentation Trading the same instrument in multiple venues.

Market impact The effect of the trade on transaction prices. Also called *price impact*.

Micro attribution Attribution at the portfolio manager level.

Midquote price The average, or midpoint, of the prevailing bid and ask prices.

Minimum-variance hedge ratio A mathematical approach to determining the optimal cross hedging ratio.

Mission-related investing Investing aimed at causes promoting positive societal or environmental change.

Model uncertainty Uncertainty as to whether a selected model is correct.

Negative screening An ESG investment style that focuses on the exclusion of certain sectors, companies, or practices in a fund or portfolio on the basis of specific ESG criteria.

Net worth The difference between assets and liabilities.

Non-deliverable forwards Cash-settled forward contracts, used predominately with respect to foreign exchange forwards. Also called *contracts for differences*.

Nonstationarity A characteristic of series of data whose properties, such as mean and variance, are not constant through time. When analyzing historical data it means that different parts of a data series reflect different underlying statistical properties.

Norway model Characterized by an almost exclusive reliance on public equities and fixed income (the traditional 60/40 equity/bond model falls under the Norway model), with largely passively managed assets and with very little to no allocation to alternative investments.

Offer price The price at which a counterparty is willing to sell one unit of the base currency.

Opportunity cost Reflects the foregone opportunity of investing in a different asset. It is typically denoted by the risk-free rate of interest, r.

Optional stock dividends A type of dividend in which shareholders may elect to receive either cash or new shares.

Overbought A market condition in which market sentiment is thought to be unsustainably bullish.

Oversold A market condition in which market sentiment is thought to be unsustainably bearish.

Packeting Splitting stock positions into multiple parts.

Parameter uncertainty Uncertainty arising because a quantitative model's parameters are estimated with error.

Participant-switching life-cycle options Automatically switch DC plan members into a more conservative asset mix as their age increases. There may be several automatic de-risking switches at different age targets.

Participant/cohort option Pools the DC plan member with a cohort that has a similar target retirement date.

Passive management A buy-and-hold approach to investing in which an investor does not make portfolio changes based upon short-term expectations of changing market or security performance.

Percent-range rebalancing An approach to rebalancing that involves setting rebalancing thresholds or trigger points, stated as a percentage of the portfolio's value, around target values.

Performance attribution The process of disaggregating a portfolio's return to determine the drivers of its performance.

Personal assets Nonbusiness, on-investment assets including personal property and real property.

Personal property Property owned by individuals that are not real property and not considered investments.

Planned goals Financial objectives that can be reasonably estimated or quantified at the onset and can be achieved within an expected time horizon.

Position delta The overall or portfolio delta. For example, the position delta of a covered call, consisting of long 100 shares and short one at-the-money call, is +50 (= +100 for the shares and -50 for the short ATM call).

Positive screening An ESG implementation approach that seeks to identify the most favorable companies and sectors based on ESG considerations. Also called *best-in-class*.

Price improvement When trade execution prices are better than quoted prices.

Private wealth management Financial planning and investment management to help individual investors, particularly high-net-worth individuals (HNWIs) and ultra-high-net-worth individuals (UHNWIs), manage their wealth.

Protective put A strategy of purchasing an underlying asset and purchasing a put on the same asset.

Pure indexing Attempts to replicate a bond index as closely as possible, targeting zero active return and zero active risk.

Put spread A strategy used to reduce the upfront cost of buying a protective put, it involves buying a put option and writing another put option.

Re-base With reference to index construction, to change the time period used as the base of the index.

Realized volatility Historical volatility, the square root of the realized variance of returns, which is a measure of the range of past price outcomes for the underlying asset.

Rebalancing Adjusting the weights of the constituent securities in an index.

Rebalancing range A range of values for asset class weights defined by trigger points above and below target weights, such that if the portfolio value passes through a trigger point, rebalancing occurs. Also known as a corridor.

Rebate rate The portion of the collateral earnings rate that is repaid to the security borrower by the security lender.

Reduced form models Statistical credit models that solve for the probability of default over a specific time period, using observable company-specific and market-based variables.

Regime The governing set of relationships (between variables) that stem from technological, political, legal, and regulatory environments. Changes in such environments or policy stances can be described as changes in regime.

Relative value A concept that describes the selection of the most attractive individual securities to populate the portfolio with, using ranking and comparing.

Repo rate The interest rate on a repurchase agreement.

Repurchase agreements In repurchase agreements, or repos, a security owner agrees to sell a security for a specific cash amount while simultaneously agreeing to repurchase the security at a specified future date (typically one day later) and price.

Reserve portfolio The component of an insurer's general account that is subject to specific regulatory requirements and is intended to ensure the company's ability to meet its policy liabilities. The assets in the reserve portfolio are managed conservatively and must be highly liquid and low risk.

Resistance levels Price points on dealers' order boards where one would expect to see a clustering of offers.

Return attribution A set of techniques used to identify the sources of the excess return of a portfolio against its benchmark.

Returns-based attribution An attribution approach that uses only the total portfolio returns over a period to identify the components of the investment process that have generated the returns. The Brinson–Hood–Beebower approach is a returns-based attribution approach.

Returns-based benchmarks Benchmarks constructed by examining a portfolio's sensitivity to a set of factors, such as the returns for various style indexes (e.g., small-cap value, small-cap growth, large-cap value, and large-cap growth).

Returns-based style analysis A top-down style analysis that involves estimating the sensitivities of a portfolio to security market indexes.

Reverse repos Repurchase agreements from the standpoint of the lender.

Risk attribution The analysis of the sources of risk.

Risk aversion The dislike for risk such that compensation is required in terms of higher expected returns for assuming higher risk.

Risk budgeting The establishment of objectives for individuals, groups, or divisions of an organization that takes into account the allocation of an acceptable level of risk.

Risk capacity The ability to bear financial risk.

Risk premiums Extra returns expected by investors for bearing some specified risk.

Risk reversal A strategy used to profit from the existence of an implied volatility skew and from changes in its shape over time. A combination of long (short) calls and short (long) puts on the same underlying with the same expiration is a long (short) risk reversal.

Risk tolerance The level of risk an investor is willing and able to bear.

Seagull spread An extension of the risk reversal foreign exchange option strategy that limits downside risk.

Securities lending A form of collateralized lending that may be used to generate income for portfolios.

Selective An index construction methodology that targets only those securities with certain characteristics.

Separate accounts Accounts holding assets to fund future liabilities from variable life insurance and variable annuities, the products in which customers make investment decisions from a menu of options and themselves bear investment risk.

Sharpe ratio The ratio of mean excess return to standard deviation (excess return).

Shortfall probability The probability of failing to meet a specific liability or goal.

Shrinkage estimation Estimation that involves taking a weighted average of a historical estimate of a parameter and some other parameter estimate, where the weights reflect the analyst's relative belief in the estimates.

Special dividends Dividends paid by a company that does not pay dividends on a regular schedule, or dividends that supplement regular cash dividends with an extra payment.

Spread duration The change in bond price for a given change in yield spread. Also referred to as OAS duration when the option-adjusted spread (OAS) is the yield measure used.

Static hedge A hedge that is not sensitive to changes in the price of the asset hedged.

Stock lending Securities lending involving the transfer of equities.

Stops Stop-loss orders involve leaving bids or offers away from the current market price to be filled if the market reaches those levels.

Straddle An option combination in which one buys *both* puts and calls, with the same exercise price and same expiration date, on the same underlying asset. In contrast to this long straddle, if someone *writes* both options, it is a short straddle.

Strangle A variation on a straddle in which the put and call have different exercise prices; if the put and call are held long, it is a long strangle; if they are held short, it is a short strangle.

Strategic asset allocation A long-term strategy that establishes target allocations for various asset classes and aims to optimize the balance between risk and reward by diversifying investments.

Structural models Models that specify functional relationships among variables based on economic theory. The functional form and parameters of these models are derived from the underlying theory. They may include unobservable parameters.

Support levels Price points on dealers' order boards where one would expect to see a clustering of bids.

Surplus The difference between assets and liabilities, analogous to shareholders' equity on a corporate balance sheet.

Surplus portfolio The component of an insurer's general account that is intended to realize higher expected returns than the reserve portfolio and so can assume some liquidity risk. Surplus portfolio assets are often managed aggressively with exposure to alternative assets.

Survivorship bias Relates to the inclusion of only current investment funds in a database. As such, the returns of funds that are no longer available in the marketplace (have been liquidated) are excluded from the database. Also see *backfill bias*.

Synthetic long forward position The combination of a long call and a short put with identical strike price and expiration, traded at the same time on the same underlying.

Synthetic short forward position The combination of a short call and a long put at the same strike price and maturity (traded at the same time on the same underlying).

Tactical asset allocation A proactive strategy that adjusts asset class allocations within a portfolio based on short-term market trends, economic conditions, or valuation changes to capitalize on temporary market inefficiencies or opportunities to improve returns or manage risk more effectively.

Tax drag The negative effect of taxes on an investment's net returns.

Taylor rule A rule linking a central bank's target short-term interest rate to the rate of growth of the economy and inflation.

Term deposits Interest-bearing accounts that have a specified maturity date. This category includes savings accounts and certificates of deposit (CDs). Also see *time deposits*.

Term structure of volatility The plot of implied volatility (y-axis) against option maturity (x-axis) for options with the same strike price on the same underlying. Typically, implied volatility is not constant across different maturities – rather, it is often in contango, meaning that the implied volatilities for longer-term options are higher than for near-term ones.

Thematic investing An investment approach that focuses on companies in a specific sector or following a specific theme, such as energy efficiency or climate change.

Theta The change in a derivative instrument for a given small change in calendar time, holding everything else constant. Specifically, the theta calculation assumes nothing changes except calendar time. Theta also reflects the rate at which an option's time value decays.

Threshold-based rebalancing policy The manager rebalances the portfolio when asset class weights deviate from their target weights by a prespecified percentage regardless of timing and frequency.

Time deposits Interest-bearing accounts that have a specified maturity date. This category includes savings accounts and certificates of deposit (CDs). Also see *term deposits*.

Time value The difference between an option's premium and its intrinsic value.

Time-based rebalancing policy The manager rebalances the portfolio regularly, at a certain given time interval such as quarterly, semi-annually, or annually, regardless of any difference between prevailing asset class weights and target asset class weights.

Time-series estimation Estimators that are based on lagged values of the variable being forecast; often consist of lagged values of other selected variables.

Total factor productivity A scale factor that reflects the portion of growth unaccounted for by explicit factor inputs (e.g., capital and labor).

Total return payer Party responsible for paying the reference obligation cash flows and return to the receiver but that is also compensated by the receiver for any depreciation in the index or default losses incurred by the portfolio.

Total return receiver Receives both the cash flows from the underlying index and any appreciation in the index over the period in exchange for paying the MRR plus a predetermined spread.

Tracking risk The standard deviation of the differences between a portfolio's returns and its benchmarks returns. Also called *tracking error*.

Transactions-based attribution An attribution approach that captures the impact of intra-day trades and exogenous events such as a significant class action settlement.

Trigger points In the context of portfolio rebalancing, the endpoints of a rebalancing range (corridor).

Ultra-high-net-worth individuals (UHNWIs) Individuals with net worth usually exceeding USD30 million or more.

Unplanned goals Unforeseen financial needs that are difficult to quantify because either the funding need, the timing of the financial need, or both may not be estimated.

Unsmoothing An adjustment to the reported return series if serial correlation is detected. Various approaches are available to unsmooth a return series.

Variance notional The notional amount of a variance swap; it equals vega notional divided by two times the volatility strike price [i.e., (vega notional)/(2 × volatility strike)].

Vega A measure of the sensitivity of an option's price to changes in the underlying's volatility.

Vega notional The trade size for a variance swap, which represents the average profit and loss of the variance swap for a 1% change in volatility from the strike.

Vesting The process of an employee becoming unconditionally entitled to, and an employer becoming obligated to pay, compensation.

Volatility clustering The tendency for large (small) swings in prices to be followed by large (small) swings of random direction.

Volatility skew The skewed plot (of implied volatility (y-axis) against strike price (x-axis) for options on the same underlying with the same expiration) that occurs when the implied volatility increases for OTM puts and decreases for OTM calls, as the strike price moves away from the current price.

Volatility smile The U-shaped plot (of implied volatility (y-axis) against strike price (x-axis) for options on the same underlying with the same expiration) that occurs when the implied volatilities priced into both OTM puts and calls trade at a premium to implied volatilities of ATM options.

Wealth The value of all the assets owned by an individual.

Wealth life cycle Stages of an individual investor's wealth in terms of human capital, financial capital, and economic net worth.

CFA Institute®
CFA Program

ETHICAL AND PROFESSIONAL STANDARDS

CFA® Program Curriculum

2026 • LEVEL III CORE • VOLUME 5

WILEY

ISBN 978-1-39436-061-1

May 2025

Please visit our website at
www.WileyGlobalFinance.com.

WILEY

SKY6818B242-3935-4DE0-97BF-48F8225F9E8C_022825

CONTENTS

How to Use the CFA Program Curriculum

The CFA® Program exams measure your mastery of the core knowledge, skills, and abilities required to succeed as an investment professional. These core competencies are the basis for the Candidate Body of Knowledge (CBOK™). The CBOK consists of four components:

A broad outline that lists the major CFA Program topic areas (www.cfainstitute.org/programs/cfa/curriculum/cbok/cbok)

Topic area weights that indicate the relative exam weightings of the top-level topic areas (www.cfainstitute.org/en/programs/cfa/curriculum)

Learning outcome statements (LOS) that tell you the specific knowledge, skills, and abilities you should gain from each curriculum topic area. You will find these statements at the start of each learning module and lesson. We encourage you to review the information about the LOS on our website (www.cfainstitute.org/programs/cfa/curriculum/study-sessions), including the descriptions of LOS "command words" on the candidate resources page at www.cfainstitute.org/-/media/documents/support/programs/cfa-and-cipm-los-command-words.ashx.

The CFA Program curriculum that candidates receive access to upon exam registration.

Therefore, the key to your success on the CFA exams is studying and understanding the CBOK. You can learn more about the CBOK on our website: www.cfainstitute.org/programs/cfa/curriculum/cbok.

The curriculum, including the practice questions, is the basis for all exam questions. The curriculum is selected/developed specifically to provide candidates with the knowledge, skills, and abilities reflected in the CBOK.

CFA INSTITUTE LEARNING ECOSYSTEM (LES)

Your exam registration fee includes access to the CFA Institute Learning Ecosystem (LES). This digital learning platform provides access to all the curriculum content and practice questions. The LES is organized as a series of learning modules consisting of short online lessons and associated practice questions. This tool is your source for all study materials, including practice questions and mock exams. The LES is the primary method by which CFA Institute delivers your curriculum experience. Here, you will find additional practice questions to test your knowledge, including some interactive questions.

DESIGNING YOUR PERSONAL STUDY PROGRAM

An orderly, systematic approach to exam preparation is critical. You should dedicate a consistent block of time every week to reading and studying. Review the LOS both before and after you study curriculum content to ensure you can demonstrate

the knowledge, skills, and abilities described by the LOS and the assigned learning module. Use the LOS as a self-check to track your progress and highlight areas of weakness for later review.

Successful candidates report an average of more than 300 hours preparing for each exam. Your preparation time will vary based on your prior education and experience, and you will likely spend more time on some topics than on others.

ERRATA

The curriculum development process is rigorous and involves multiple rounds of reviews by content experts. Despite our efforts to produce a curriculum that is free of errors, we must make corrections in some instances. Curriculum errata are periodically updated and posted by exam level and test date on the Curriculum Errata webpage (www.cfainstitute.org/en/programs/submit-errata). If you believe you have found an error in the curriculum, you can submit your concerns through our curriculum errata reporting process found at the bottom of the Curriculum Errata webpage.

OTHER FEEDBACK

Please send any comments or suggestions to info@cfainstitute.org, and we will review your feedback thoughtfully.

Ethical and Professional Standards

LEARNING MODULE

1

Code of Ethics and Standards of Professional Conduct

LEARNING OUTCOMES

Mastery	*The candidate should be able to:*
☐	describe the structure of the CFA Institute Professional Conduct Program and the disciplinary review process for the enforcement of the CFA Institute Code of Ethics and Standards of Professional Conduct
☐	explain the ethical responsibilities required by the Code and Standards, including the subsections of each standard

PREFACE

1

☐	describe the structure of the CFA Institute Professional Conduct Program and the disciplinary review process for the enforcement of the CFA Institute Code of Ethics and Standards of Professional Conduct
☐	explain the ethical responsibilities required by the Code and Standards, including the subsections of each standard

The *Standards of Practice Handbook* (*Handbook*) provides guidance to the people who grapple with real ethical dilemmas in the investment profession on a daily basis; the *Handbook* addresses the professional intersection where theory meets practice and where the concept of ethical behavior crosses from the abstract to the concrete. The *Handbook* is intended for a diverse and global audience: CFA Institute members navigating ambiguous ethical situations; supervisors and direct/indirect reports determining the nature of their responsibilities to each other, to existing and potential clients, and to the broader financial markets; and candidates preparing for the Chartered Financial Analyst (CFA) examinations.

Events in global financial markets test the ethical mettle of financial market participants, including CFA Institute members and candidates. The standards taught in the CFA Program and by which CFA Institute members and candidates must abide represent timeless ethical principles and professional conduct for all market conditions. Through adherence to these standards, which continue to serve as the model for ethical behavior in the investment profession globally, each market participant does his or her part to improve the integrity and efficient operations of the financial markets.

The *Handbook* provides guidance for understanding the interconnectedness of the aspirational and practical principles and provisions of the Code of Ethics and Standards of Professional Conduct (Code and Standards). The Code contains high-level aspirational ethical principles that drive members and candidates to create a positive and reputable investment profession. The Standards contain practical ethical principles of conduct that members and candidates must follow to achieve the broader industry expectations. However, applying the principles individually may not capture the complexity of ethical requirements related to the investment industry. The Code and Standards should be viewed and interpreted as an interwoven tapestry of ethical requirements. Through members' and candidates' adherence to these principles as a whole, the integrity of and trust in the capital markets are improved.

Evolution of the CFA Institute Code of Ethics and Standards of Professional Conduct

The Code and Standards are regularly reviewed and updated so that they remain effective and continue to represent the highest ethical standards in the global investment industry. CFA Institute strongly believes that revisions of the Code and Standards are undertaken not for cosmetic purposes but to add value by addressing legitimate concerns and improving comprehension. In 2023, the CFA Institute Board of Governors approved revisions to the Code and Standards that are fully described below.

Changes to the Code and Standards have far-reaching implications for the CFA Institute membership, the CFA Program, and the investment industry as a whole. CFA Institute members and candidates are *required* to adhere to the Code and Standards. In addition, the Code and Standards are often adopted, in whole or in part, by firms and regulatory authorities. Their relevance goes well beyond CFA Institute members and candidates.

Standards of Practice Handbook

The periodic revisions of the *Standards of Practice Handbook* have come in conjunction with updates of the Code and Standards. The *Handbook* is the fundamental element of the ethics education effort of CFA Institute and the primary resource for guidance in interpreting and implementing the Code and Standards. The *Handbook* seeks to educate members and candidates on how to apply the Code and Standards to their professional lives and thereby benefit their clients, employers, and the investing public in general. The *Handbook* explains the purpose of the Code and Standards and how they apply in a variety of situations. The sections discuss and amplify each standard and suggest procedures for compliance.

Examples in the "Application of the Standard" sections are meant to illustrate how the standard applies to hypothetical but factual situations. The names contained in the examples are fictional and are not meant to refer to any actual person or entity. Unless otherwise stated (e.g., one or more people specifically identified), individuals in each example are subject to the requirements of the Code and Standards. Because factual circumstances vary so widely and often involve gray areas, the explanatory material and examples are not intended to be all inclusive. Many examples set forth in the application sections involve standards that have legal counterparts; *members are strongly urged to discuss with their supervisors and legal and compliance departments the content of the Code and Standards and the members' general obligations under the Code and Standards.*

CFA Institute recognizes that the presence of any set of ethical standards may create a false sense of security unless the documents are fully understood, enforced, and made a meaningful part of everyday professional activities. The *Handbook* is intended to provide a useful frame of reference that outlines ethical professional conduct for the organization's members and candidates. The *Handbook* cannot cover every contingency or circumstance however, and it does not attempt to do so. The development and interpretation of the Code and Standards are evolving processes; the Code and Standards will be subject to continuing refinement.

Summary of the 2023 Revisions to the Code and Standards

In 2023, the CFA Institute Board of Governors revised the Standards of Professional Conduct in three areas, resulting in the inclusion of one new standard and revisions to two existing standards. The following is a summary of the changes:

1. Within Standard I: Professionalism, the Board approved a new standard requiring members to act with and maintain the competence necessary to fulfill their professional responsibilities, so reinforcing the principle set forth in the Code of Ethics.
2. Within Standard V: Investment Analysis, Recommendations, and Actions, the Board revised Standard V(B) Communication with Clients and Prospective Clients to require disclosures about the nature of the services provided by members and candidates and the costs to the client associated with those services.
3. Within Standard VI Conflicts of Interest, the Board changed the name of Standard VI(A) to "Standard VI(A) Avoid or Disclose Conflicts" and revised the standard to require members and candidates to either avoid conflicts of interest or disclose those conflicts. Previously there was no mention of avoiding conflicts of interest in the standard.

New guidance and examples have been added to the *Handbook* to fully explain these new requirements.

New and Revised Standards of Professional Conduct

Competence Standard

I. PROFESSIONALISM

E. Competence

Members and Candidates must:

1. Act with and maintain the competence necessary to fulfill their professional responsibilities.

Given the diverse range of professional services engaged in by members and candidates, the knowledge, skills, and abilities necessary to successfully fulfill their role will vary according to the nature of their professional duties. Over time, a member's role may expand, requiring new or different knowledge, skills, and abilities. Members will develop and refine their skills and abilities throughout their professional careers.

Requiring members and candidates to act with and maintain appropriate levels of competence will help ensure they provide a high standard of professional service for their clients and employers.

Currently, the Code of Ethics requires members and candidates to "act with integrity, competence, and diligence" and to "maintain and improve their professional competence and strive to improve the competence of other investment professionals." This new standard is consistent with and directly supports the requirements of the Code of Ethics. Standard I(E) makes these requirements of the Code of Ethics more explicit and emphasizes the need for members and candidates to continuously maintain or improve the competence required by their professional position.

The skills and abilities necessary for members and candidates to successfully fulfill their role vary according to the nature and complexity of their professional duties. As a result, there will be different criteria for competence for different members. An examination of the facts and circumstances of each member or candidate will dictate their expected conduct under this standard.

Finally, Standard I(E) does not require members and candidates to engage in any specific program of professional development or continuing education. There are a variety of ways members and candidates can demonstrate and maintain competence when engaging in their professional responsibilities.

Disclosure of Nature of Services and Costs to Client

V. INVESTMENT ANALYSIS, RECOMMENDATIONS, AND ACTIONS

B. Communication with Clients and Prospective Clients

Members and Candidates must:

1. Disclose to clients and prospective clients the nature of the services provided, along with information about the costs to the client associated with those services.

A fundamental goal of the Code and Standards is to protect client interests and allow clients to make fully informed decisions about their investments and financial well-being. Providing clients with information about the nature of the services they can expect from investment professionals and the financial impact they can expect from those services is critical to achieving this goal. The disclosures required by this new standard will permit clients to make informed decisions as to whether to engage with the member or candidate and his or her firm.

Standard V(B) Communication with Clients and Prospective Clients also requires members to disclose the basic format and general principles of the investment processes they use to analyze investments, select securities, and construct portfolios and to promptly disclose any material changes to these processes. The associated financial impact is an important part of the investment process but, until now, was not explicitly addressed as part of this disclosure. The revision to Standard V(B) fills this gap.

Revised Standard Relating to Conflicts

VI. CONFLICTS OF INTEREST

A. Avoid or Disclose Conflicts

Members and Candidates must:

1. Avoid or make full and fair disclosure of all matters that could reasonably be expected to impair their independence and objectivity and interfere with respective duties to their clients, prospective clients, and employer.
2. Ensure that such disclosures are prominent, are delivered in plain language, and communicate the relevant information effectively.

Standard VI(A) has always required members and candidates to disclose conflicts, but previously, the language of the standard made no mention of avoiding conflicts. Nevertheless, the guidance for Standard VI: Conflicts of Interest has long stated that best practice is to avoid conflicts or the appearance of conflicts. Including the option to avoid versus simply disclosing conflicts in the language of the standard emphasizes that members and candidates should avoid conflicts of interest whenever reasonably possible. While avoiding conflicts altogether is preferred, often in the investment industry it may not be reasonable for members and candidates to avoid a conflict or the perception of a conflict. When it is not reasonable for members and candidates to avoid a conflict, Standard VI(A) continues to require clear and complete disclosure of the conflict.

CFA Institute Professional Conduct Program

All CFA Institute members and candidates enrolled in the CFA Program are required to comply with the Code and Standards. The CFA Institute Board of Governors maintains oversight and responsibility for the Professional Conduct Program (PCP), which, in conjunction with the Disciplinary Review Committee (DRC), is responsible for enforcement of the Code and Standards. The DRC is a volunteer committee of CFA charterholders who serve on panels to review conduct and partner with Professional Conduct staff to establish and review professional conduct policies. The CFA Institute Bylaws and Rules of Procedure for Professional Conduct (Rules of Procedure) form the basic structure for enforcing the Code and Standards. The Professional Conduct division is also responsible for enforcing testing policies of other CFA Institute education programs, as well as the professional conduct of Certificate in Investment Performance Measurement (CIPM) certificants.

Professional Conduct inquiries come from a number of sources. First, members and candidates must self-disclose on the annual Professional Conduct Statement all matters that question their professional conduct, such as involvement in civil litigation or a criminal investigation or being the subject of a written complaint. Second, written complaints received by Professional Conduct staff can bring about an investigation. Third, CFA Institute staff may become aware of questionable conduct by a member or candidate through the media, regulatory notices, or another public source. Fourth, candidate conduct is monitored by proctors who complete reports on candidates suspected to have violated testing rules on exam day. Lastly, CFA Institute may also conduct analyses of scores and exam materials after the exam, as well as monitor online and social media to detect disclosure of confidential exam information.

When an inquiry is initiated, the Professional Conduct staff conducts an investigation that may include requesting a written explanation from the member or candidate; interviewing the member or candidate, complaining parties, and third parties; and collecting documents and records relevant to the investigation. Upon reviewing the material obtained during the investigation, the Professional Conduct staff may conclude the inquiry with no disciplinary sanction, issue a cautionary letter, or continue proceedings to discipline the member or candidate. If the Professional Conduct staff believes a violation of the Code and Standards or testing policies has occurred, the member or candidate has the opportunity to reject or accept any charges and the proposed sanctions.

If the member or candidate does not accept the charges and proposed sanction, the matter is referred to a panel composed of DRC members. Panels review materials and presentations from Professional Conduct staff and from the member or candidate. The panel's task is to determine whether a violation of the Code and Standards or testing policies occurred and, if so, what sanction should be imposed.

Sanctions imposed by CFA Institute may have significant consequences; they include public censure, suspension of membership and use of the CFA designation, and revocation of the CFA charter. Candidates enrolled in the CFA Program who have violated the Code and Standards or testing policies may be suspended or prohibited from further participation in the CFA Program.

Adoption of the Code and Standards

The Code and Standards apply to individual members of CFA Institute and candidates in the CFA Program. CFA Institute does encourage firms to adopt the Code and Standards, however, as part of their code of ethics. Those who claim compliance should fully understand the requirements of each of the principles of the Code and Standards.

Once a party—nonmember or firm—ensures its code of ethics meets the principles of the Code and Standards, that party should make the following statement whenever claiming compliance:

> [Insert name of party] claims compliance with the CFA Institute Code of Ethics and Standards of Professional Conduct. This claim has not been verified by CFA Institute.

CFA Institute welcomes public acknowledgement, when appropriate, that firms are complying with the CFA Institute Code of Ethics and Standards of Professional Conduct. For firms that would like to distribute the Code and Standards to clients and potential clients, attractive one-page copies of the Code and Standards, including translations, are available on the CFA Institute website (www.cfainstitute.org).

CFA Institute has also published the Asset Manager Code, which is designed, in part, to help asset managers comply with regulations mandating codes of ethics for investment advisers. Whereas the Code and Standards are aimed at individual investment professionals who are members of CFA Institute or candidates in the CFA Program, the Asset Manager Code applies to firms. The Asset Manager Code provides specific, practical guidelines for asset managers in six areas: loyalty to clients, the investment process, trading, compliance, performance, and disclosure. The Asset Manager Code and the appropriate steps to acknowledge compliance can be found on the CFA Institute website (www.cfainstitute.org).

Acknowledgments

CFA Institute is a not-for-profit organization that is heavily dependent on the expertise and intellectual contributions of member volunteers. Members devote their time because they share a mutual interest in the organization's mission to promote and achieve ethical practice in the investment profession. CFA Institute owes much to the volunteers' abundant generosity and energy in extending ethical integrity.

The CFA Institute Standards of Practice Council (SPC), a group consisting of CFA charterholder volunteers from many different countries, is charged with maintaining and interpreting the Code and Standards and ensuring that they are effective. The SPC draws its membership from a broad spectrum of organizations in the securities field, including brokers, investment advisers, banks, and insurance companies.

The SPC continually evaluates the Code and Standards, as well as the guidance in the *Handbook*, to ensure that they are

- representative of high standards of professional conduct,
- relevant to the changing nature of the investment profession,
- globally applicable,
- sufficiently comprehensive, practical, and specific,
- enforceable, and
- testable for the CFA Program.

Over the years, many volunteer members of the SPC have spent countless hours reviewing and discussing revisions to the Code and Standards and updates to the guidance that make up the *Handbook*. CFA Institute would like to thank all the current and former members of the SPC who generously donated their time and energy to this effort.

ETHICS AND THE INVESTMENT INDUSTRY

2

Society ultimately benefits from efficient markets where capital can freely flow to the most productive or innovative destination. Well-functioning capital markets efficiently match those needing capital with those seeking to invest their assets in revenue generating ventures. In order for capital markets to be efficient, investors must be able to trust that the markets are fair and transparent and offer them the opportunity to be rewarded for the risk they choose to take. Laws, regulations, and enforcement play a vital role but are insufficient alone to guarantee fair and transparent markets. The markets depend on an ethical foundation to guide participants' judgment and behavior. CFA Institute maintains and promotes the Code of Ethics and Standards of Professional Conduct in order to create a culture of ethics for the ultimate benefit of society.

Why Ethics Matters

Ethics can be defined as a set of moral principles or rules of conduct that provide guidance for our behavior when it affects others. Widely acknowledged fundamental ethical principles include honesty, fairness, diligence, and care and respect for others. Ethical conduct follows those principles and balances self-interest with both the direct and the indirect consequences of that behavior for other people.

Not only does unethical behavior by individuals have serious personal consequences—ranging from job loss and reputational damage to fines and even jail—but unethical conduct from market participants, investment professionals, and those who service investors can damage investor trust and thereby impair the sustainability of the global capital markets as a whole. Unfortunately, there seems to be an unending parade of stories bringing to light accounting frauds and manipulations, Ponzi schemes, insider-trading scandals, and other misdeeds. Not surprisingly, this has led to erosion in public confidence in investment professionals. Empirical evidence from numerous surveys documents the low standing in the eyes of the investing public of banks and financial services firms—the very institutions that are entrusted with the economic well-being and retirement security of society.

Governments and regulators have historically tried to combat misconduct in the industry through regulatory reform, with various levels of success. Global capital markets are highly regulated to protect investors and other market participants. However, compliance with regulation alone is insufficient to fully earn investor trust. Individuals and firms must develop a "culture of integrity" that permeates all levels of operations and promotes the ethical principles of stewardship of investor assets and working in the best interests of clients, above and beyond strict compliance with the law. A strong ethical culture that helps honest, ethical people engage in ethical behavior will foster the trust of investors, lead to robust global capital markets, and ultimately benefit society. That is why ethics matters.

Ethics, Society, and the Capital Markets

CFA Institute includes the concept "for the ultimate benefit of society" as part of its mission. The premise is that we want to live in a socially, politically, and financially stable society that fosters individual well-being and welfare of the public. A key ingredient for this goal is global capital markets that facilitate the efficient allocation of resources so that the available capital finds its way to places where it most benefits that society. These investments are then used to produce goods and services, to fund innovation and jobs, and to promote improvements in standards of living. Indeed, such a function serves the interests of the society. Efficient capital markets, in turn, provide a host of benefits to those providing the investment capital. Investors are provided the opportunity to transfer and transform risk because the capital markets serve as an information exchange, create investment products, provide liquidity, and limit transaction costs.

However, a well-functioning and efficient capital market system is dependent on trust of the participants. If investors believe that capital market participants—investment professionals and firms—cannot be trusted with their financial assets or that the capital markets are unfair such that only insiders can be successful, they will be unlikely to invest or, at the very least, will require a higher risk premium. Decreased investment capital can reduce innovation and job creation and hurt the economy and society as a whole. Reduced trust in capital markets can also result in a less vibrant, if not smaller, investment industry.

Ethics for a global investment industry should be universal and ultimately support trust and integrity above acceptable local or regional customs and culture. Universal ethics for a global industry strongly supports the efficiency, values, and mission of the industry as a whole. Different countries may be at different stages of development in establishing standards of practice, but the end goal must be to achieve rules, regulations, and standards that support and promote fundamental ethical principles on a global basis.

Capital Market Sustainability and the Actions of One

Individuals and firms also have to look at the indirect impacts of their actions on the broader investment community. The increasingly interconnected nature of global finance brings to the fore an added consideration of market sustainability that was, perhaps, less appreciated in years past. In addition to committing to the highest levels of ethical behavior, today's investment professionals and their employers should consider the long-term health of the market as a whole.

Apparently isolated and unrelated decisions, however innocuous when considered on an individual basis, in aggregate can precipitate a market crisis. In an interconnected global economy and marketplace, each participant should strive to be aware of how his or her actions or the products he or she distributes may have an impact on capital market participants in other regions or countries.

Investment professionals should consider how their investment decision-making processes affect the global financial markets in the broader context of how they apply their ethical and professional obligations. Those in positions of authority have a special responsibility to consider the broader context of market sustainability in their development and approval of corporate policies, particularly those involving risk management and product development. In addition, corporate compensation strategies should not encourage otherwise ethically sound individuals to engage in unethical or questionable conduct for financial gain. Ethics, sustainability, and properly functioning capital markets are components of the same concept of protecting the best interests of all. To always place the interests of clients ahead of both investment professionals' own interests and those of their employer remains a key ethos.

The Relationship between Ethics and Regulations

Some equate ethical behavior with legal behavior: If you are following the law, you must be acting appropriately. Ethical principles, like laws and regulations, prescribe appropriate constraints on our natural tendency to pursue self-interest that could harm the interests of others. Laws and regulations often attempt to guide people toward ethical behavior, but they do not cover all unethical behavior. Ethical behavior is often distinguished from legal conduct by describing legal behavior as what is required and ethical behavior as conduct that is morally correct. Ethical principles go beyond that which is legally sufficient and encompass what is the right thing to do.

Given many regulators' lack of sufficient resources to enforce well-conceived rules and regulations, relying on a regulatory framework to lead the charge in establishing ethical behavior has its challenges. Therefore, reliance on compliance with laws and regulation alone is insufficient to ensure ethical behavior of investment professionals or to create a truly ethical culture in the industry.

Inevitably, some individuals will succeed at circumventing the regulatory rules for their personal gain. Only the application of strong ethical principles, at both the individual level and the firm level, will limit abuses. Knowing the rules or regulations to apply in a particular situation, although important, may not be sufficient to ensure ethical conduct. Individuals must be able both to recognize areas that are prone to ethical pitfalls and to identify and process those circumstances and influences that can impair ethical judgment.

Applying an Ethical Framework

Laws, regulations, professional standards, and codes of ethics can guide ethical behavior, but individual judgment is a critical ingredient in making principled choices and engaging in appropriate conduct. When faced with an ethical dilemma, individuals must have a well-developed set of principles; otherwise, their thought processes can lead to, at best, equivocation and indecision and, at worst, fraudulent conduct and destruction of the public trust. Establishing an ethical framework for an internal thought process prior to deciding to act is a crucial step in engaging in ethical conduct.

Most investment professionals are used to making decisions from a business (profit/loss) outlook. But given the importance of ethical behavior in carrying out professional responsibilities, it is critical to also analyze decisions and potential conduct from an ethical perspective. Utilizing a framework for ethical decision making will help investment professionals effectively examine their conduct in the context of conflicting interests common to their professional obligations (e.g., researching and gathering information, developing investment recommendations, and managing money for others). Such a framework will allow investment professionals to analyze their conduct in a way that meets high standards of ethical behavior.

An ethical decision-making framework can come in many forms but should provide investment professionals with a tool for following the principles of the firm's code of ethics. Through analyzing the particular circumstances of each decision, investment professionals are able to determine the best course of action to fulfill their responsibilities in an ethical manner.

Commitment to Ethics by Firms

A firm's code of ethics risks becoming a largely ignored, dusty compilation if it is not truly integrated into the fabric of the business. The ability to relate an ethical decision-making framework to a firm's code of ethics allows investment professionals to bring the aspirations and principles of the code of ethics to life—transforming it from a compliance exercise to something that is at the heart of a firm's culture.

An investment professional's natural desire to "do the right thing" must be reinforced by building a culture of integrity in the workplace. Development, maintenance, and demonstration of a strong culture of integrity within the firm by senior management may be the single most important factor in promoting ethical behavior among the firm's employees. Adopting a code of ethics that clearly lays out the ethical principles that guide the thought processes and conduct the firm expects from its employees is a critical first step. But a code of ethics, while necessary, is insufficient.

Simply nurturing an inclination to do right is no match for the multitude of daily decisions that investment managers make. We need to exercise ethical decision-making skills to develop the muscle memory necessary for fundamentally ethical people to make good decisions despite the reality of conflicts of interest. Just as coaching and practice transform our natural ability to run across a field into the technique and endurance required to run a race, teaching, reinforcing, and practicing ethical decision-making skills prepare us to confront the hard issues effectively. It is good for business, individuals, firms, the industry, and the markets, as well as society as a whole, to engage in the investment management profession in a highly ethical manner.

Ethical Commitment of CFA Institute

An important goal of CFA Institute is to ensure that the organization and its members and candidates develop, promote, and follow the highest ethical standards in the investment industry. The CFA Institute Code of Ethics (Code) and Standards of Professional Conduct (Standards) are the foundation supporting the organization's quest to uphold the industry's highest standards of individual and corporate practice and to help serve the greater good. The Code is a set of principles that define the overarching conduct CFA Institute expects from its members and CFA Program candidates. The Code works in tandem with the Standards, which outline professional conduct that constitutes fair and ethical business practices.

For more than 60 years, CFA Institute members and candidates have been required to abide by the organization's Code and Standards. Periodically, CFA Institute has revised and updated its Code and Standards to ensure that they remain relevant to the changing nature of the investment profession and representative of the highest standard of professional conduct. Within the *Standards of Practice Handbook*, CFA Institute addresses ethical principles for the profession, including individual professionalism; responsibilities to capital markets, clients, and employers; ethics involved in investment analysis, recommendations, and actions; and possible conflicts of interest.

Although the investment world has become a far more complex place since the first publication of the *Standards of Practice Handbook*, distinguishing right from wrong remains the paramount principle of the Code and Standards.

New challenges will continually arise for members and candidates in applying the Code and Standards because many decisions are not unambiguously right or wrong. The dilemma exists because the choice between right and wrong is not always clear. Even well-intentioned investment professionals can find themselves in circumstances that may tempt them to cut corners. Situational influences can overpower the best of intentions.

CFA Institute has made a significant commitment to providing members and candidates with the resources to extend and deepen their understanding of how to appropriately apply the principles of the Code and Standards. The product offerings from CFA Institute offer a wealth of material. Through publications, conferences, webcasts, and podcasts, the ethical challenges of investment professionals are brought to light. Archived issues of these items are available on the CFA Institute website (www.cfainstitute.org).

By reviewing these resources and discussing with their peers, market participants can further enhance their abilities to apply an effective ethical decision-making framework. In time, this should promote the trust of clients, investors, and market participants.

Markets function to an important extent on trust. Investment professionals should remain mindful of the long-term health of financial markets and incorporate this concern for the market's sustainability in their investment decision making. CFA Institute and the Standards of Practice Council hope the *Handbook* will assist and guide investment professionals in meeting the ethical demands of the highly interconnected global capital markets for the ultimate benefit of society.

CFA INSTITUTE CODE OF ETHICS AND STANDARDS OF PROFESSIONAL CONDUCT

3

Preamble

The CFA Institute Code of Ethics and Standards of Professional Conduct are fundamental to the values of CFA Institute and essential to achieving its mission to continue to lead the investment profession globally by promoting the highest standards of ethics, education, and professional excellence for the ultimate benefit of society. High ethical standards are critical to maintaining the public's trust in financial markets and in the investment profession. Since their creation in the 1960s, the Code and Standards have promoted the integrity of CFA Institute members and served as a model for measuring the ethics of investment professionals globally, regardless of job function, cultural differences, or local laws and regulations. All CFA Institute members (including holders of the Chartered Financial Analyst [CFA] designation) and CFA candidates have the personal responsibility to embrace and uphold the provisions of the Code and Standards and are encouraged to notify their employer of this responsibility. Violations may result in disciplinary sanctions by CFA Institute. Sanctions can include revocation of membership, revocation of candidacy in the CFA Program, and revocation of the right to use the CFA designation.

The Code of Ethics

Members of CFA Institute (including CFA charterholders) and candidates for the CFA designation ("Members and Candidates") must:

- Act with integrity, competence, diligence, and respect and in an ethical manner with the public, clients, prospective clients, employers, employees, colleagues in the investment profession, and other participants in the global capital markets.
- Place the integrity of the investment profession and the interests of clients above their own personal interests.
- Use reasonable care and exercise independent professional judgment when conducting investment analysis, making investment recommendations, taking investment actions, and engaging in other professional activities.
- Practice and encourage others to practice in a professional and ethical manner that will reflect credit on themselves and the profession.
- Promote the integrity and viability of the global capital markets for the ultimate benefit of society.
- Maintain and improve their professional competence and strive to maintain and improve the competence of other investment professionals.

Standards of Professional Conduct

i. PROFESSIONALISM

A. Knowledge of the Law

Members and Candidates must understand and comply with all applicable laws, rules, and regulations (including the CFA Institute Code of Ethics and Standards of Professional Conduct) of any government, regulatory organization, licensing agency, or professional association governing their professional activities. In the event of conflict, Members and Candidates must comply with the more strict law, rule, or regulation. Members and Candidates must not knowingly participate or assist in and must dissociate from any violation of such laws, rules, or regulations.

B. Independence and Objectivity

Members and Candidates must use reasonable care and judgment to achieve and maintain independence and objectivity in their professional activities. Members and Candidates must not offer, solicit, or accept any gift, benefit, compensation, or consideration that reasonably could be expected to compromise their own or another's independence and objectivity.

C. Misrepresentation

Members and Candidates must not knowingly make any misrepresentations relating to investment analysis, recommendations, actions, or other professional activities.

D. Misconduct

Members and Candidates must not engage in any professional conduct involving dishonesty, fraud, or deceit or commit any act that reflects adversely on their professional reputation, integrity, or competence.

E. Competence

Members and Candidates must act with and maintain the competence necessary to fulfill their professional responsibilities.

ii. INTEGRITY OF CAPITAL MARKETS

A. Material Nonpublic Information

Members and Candidates who possess material nonpublic information that could affect the value of an investment must not act or cause others to act on the information.

B. Market Manipulation

Members and Candidates must not engage in practices that distort prices or artificially inflate trading volume with the intent to mislead market participants.

iii. DUTIES TO CLIENTS

A. Loyalty, Prudence, and Care

Members and Candidates have a duty of loyalty to their clients and must act with reasonable care and exercise prudent judgment. Members and Candidates must act for the benefit of their clients and place their clients' interests before their employer's or their own interests.

B. Fair Dealing

Members and Candidates must deal fairly and objectively with all clients when providing investment analysis, making investment recommendations, taking investment action, or engaging in other professional activities.

C. Suitability

1. When Members and Candidates are in an advisory relationship with a client, they must:

   a. Make a reasonable inquiry into a client's or prospective client's investment experience, risk and return objectives, and financial constraints prior to making any investment recommendation or taking investment action and must reassess and update this information regularly.

   b. Determine that an investment is suitable to the client's financial situation and consistent with the client's written objectives, mandates, and constraints before making an investment recommendation or taking investment action.

   c. Judge the suitability of investments in the context of the client's total portfolio.

2. When Members and Candidates are responsible for managing a portfolio to a specific mandate, strategy, or style, they must make only investment recommendations or take only investment actions that are consistent with the stated objectives and constraints of the portfolio.

D. Performance Presentation

When communicating investment performance information, Members and Candidates must make reasonable efforts to ensure that it is fair, accurate, and complete.

E. Preservation of Confidentiality

Members and Candidates must keep information about current, former, and prospective clients confidential unless:

1. The information concerns illegal activities on the part of the client or prospective client,

2. Disclosure is required by law, or

3. The client or prospective client permits disclosure of the information.

iv. DUTIES TO EMPLOYERS

A. Loyalty

In matters related to their employment, Members and Candidates must act for the benefit of their employer and not deprive their employer of the advantage of their skills and abilities, divulge confidential information, or otherwise cause harm to their employer.

B. Additional Compensation Arrangements

Members and Candidates must not accept gifts, benefits, compensation, or consideration that competes with or might reasonably be expected to create a conflict of interest with their employer's interest unless they obtain written consent from all parties involved.

C. Responsibilities of Supervisors

Members and Candidates must make reasonable efforts to ensure that anyone subject to their supervision or authority complies with applicable laws, rules, regulations, and the Code and Standards.

v. INVESTMENT ANALYSIS, RECOMMENDATIONS, AND ACTIONS

A. Diligence and Reasonable Basis

Members and Candidates must:

1. Exercise diligence, independence, and thoroughness in analyzing investments, making investment recommendations, and taking investment actions.

2. Have a reasonable and adequate basis, supported by appropriate research and investigation, for any investment analysis, recommendation, or action.

B. Communication with Clients and Prospective Clients

Members and Candidates must:

1. Disclose to clients and prospective clients the nature of the services provided, along with information about the costs to the client associated with those services.

2. Disclose to clients and prospective clients the basic format and general principles of the investment processes they use to analyze investments, select securities, and construct portfolios and must promptly disclose any changes that might materially affect those processes.

3. Disclose to clients and prospective clients significant limitations and risks associated with the investment process.

4. Use reasonable judgment in identifying which factors are important to their investment analyses, recommendations, or actions and include those factors in communications with clients and prospective clients.

5. Distinguish between fact and opinion in the presentation of investment analysis and recommendations.

C. Record Retention

Members and Candidates must develop and maintain appropriate records to support their investment analyses, recommendations, actions, and other investment-related communications with clients and prospective clients.

vi. CONFLICTS OF INTEREST

A. Avoid or Disclose Conflicts

Members and Candidates must avoid or make full and fair disclosure of all matters that could reasonably be expected to impair their independence and objectivity and interfere with respective duties to their clients, prospective clients, and employer. Members and Candidates must ensure that such disclosures are prominent, are delivered in plain language, and communicate the relevant information effectively.

B. Priority of Transactions

Investment transactions for clients and employers must have priority over investment transactions in which a Member or Candidate is the beneficial owner.

C. Referral Fees

Members and Candidates must disclose to their employer, clients, and prospective clients, as appropriate, any compensation, consideration, or benefit received from or paid to others for the recommendation of products or services.

vii. RESPONSIBILITIES AS A CFA INSTITUTE MEMBER OR CFA CANDIDATE

A. Conduct as Participants in CFA Institute Programs

Members and Candidates must not engage in any conduct that compromises the reputation or integrity of CFA Institute or the CFA designation or the integrity, validity, or security of CFA Institute programs.

B. Reference to CFA Institute, the CFA Designation, and the CFA Program

When referring to CFA Institute, CFA Institute membership, the CFA designation, or candidacy in the CFA Program, Members and Candidates must not misrepresent or exaggerate the meaning or implications of membership in CFA Institute, holding the CFA designation, or candidacy in the CFA Program.

PRACTICE PROBLEMS

1. Which of the following statements *best* describes an aspect of the Professional Conduct Program process?
   A. Inquiries are not initiated in response to information provided by the media.
   B. Investigations result in Disciplinary Review Committee panels for each case.
   C. Investigations may include requesting a written explanation from the member or candidate.

2. A current Code of Ethics principle reads in full, "Promote the integrity:
   A. and viability of the global capital markets."
   B. of and uphold the rules governing capital markets."
   C. and viability of the global capital markets for the ultimate benefit of society."

3. Which of the following is correct with regard to the Standards of Professional Conduct?
   A. They require supervisors to focus only on the detection and prevention of violations.
   B. They set ethical conduct requirements for members and candidates that have remained unchanged since their creation.
   C. They address the risks and limitations of recommendations being made to clients.

4. Which of the following statements *best* describes an aspect of the Standards of Professional Conduct? Members and candidates are required to:
   A. ensure a portfolio mandate is suitable for all investors.
   B. promptly disclose changes that might materially affect investment processes.
   C. have a reasonable and adequate basis for decisions about client confidentiality.

5. A CFA Institute member or candidate violates Standard II(A) Material Nonpublic Information by:
   A. conducting price distortion practices.
   B. inappropriately causing others to act.
   C. inadequately maintaining investment records.

6. Standard III(C) Suitability requires members and candidates in an advisory relationship with a client to:
   A. place their client's interests before their own interests.
   B. consider investments in the context of the client's total portfolio.
   C. not knowingly make misrepresentations relating to recommendations.

7. Standard III: Duties to Clients states that members and candidates must:

   A. document client financial constraints after an initial investment action.

   B. maintain an equal balance of interests owed to their clients and employers.

   C. deal fairly and objectively with all clients when engaging in professional activities.

8. Standard IV: Duties to Employers states that members and candidates must not:

   A. accept any gifts that might compromise their independence and objectivity.

   B. deprive their employer of their skills and abilities as related to their employment.

   C. accept compensation competing with their employer's interest without the written consent of their employer only.

9. Standard V: Investment Analysis, Recommendations, and Actions states that members and candidates must:

   A. find an investment suitable for their client before making a recommendation.

   B. make reasonable efforts to ensure that performance presentation is fair, accurate, and complete.

   C. distinguish between fact and opinion in the presentation of investment analysis and recommendations.

10. Standard VII: Responsibilities as a CFA Institute Member or CFA Candidate explicitly states a requirement regarding:

    A. loyalty.

    B. responsibility of supervisors.

    C. reference to the CFA Program.

SOLUTIONS

1. C is correct. When an inquiry is initiated, the Professional Conduct staff conducts an investigation that may include requesting a written explanation from the member or candidate.

   A is incorrect because Professional Conduct inquiries can be initiated in response to information provided by the media. CFA Institute staff may become aware of questionable conduct by a member or candidate through the media, regulatory notices, or other public sources.

   B is incorrect because although the Disciplinary Review Committee (DRC) is responsible for enforcement of the Code and Standards in conjunction with the Professional Conduct Program (PCP), only in the event that a member or candidate does not accept the charges and proposed sanction is the matter referred to a panel composed of DRC members.

2. C is correct. One of the principles in the Code of Ethics reflects the role that the capital markets have in society as a whole.

   A is incorrect because it is incomplete, missing the additional language to reflect the role that the capital markets have in society as a whole.

   B is incorrect because the principle as written in the Code of Ethics reflects the role of the capital markets in society as a whole.

3. C is correct. Given the constant development of new and exotic financial instruments and strategies, the standard regarding communicating with clients includes an implicit requirement to disclose to clients the risks and limitations of recommendations being made to clients.

   A is incorrect because the standard for members and candidates with supervision or authority over others within their firms stresses broader compliance expectations beyond the detection and prevention aspects of violations.

   B is incorrect because the standards have evolved over time to remain representative of the highest standards of professional conduct and relevant to the changing nature of the investment profession.

4. B is correct. The Standards of Professional Conduct require members and candidates to promptly disclose any changes that might materially affect investment processes.

   A is incorrect because under Standard III(C) Suitability, when members and candidates are responsible for managing a portfolio according to a specific mandate, they must take only investment actions that are consistent with the stated objectives of the portfolio and not be concerned with whether the mandate is suitable for all investors.

   C is incorrect because under Standard III(E) Preservation of Confidentiality, members and candidates must keep information about current clients confidential unless the information concerns illegal activities on the part of the client, disclosure is required by law, or the client permits disclosure. No decisions on confidentiality are required, with the "reasonable and adequate basis" criterion related to Standard V(A) Diligence and Reasonable Basis.

5. B is correct. Under Standard II(A) Material Nonpublic Information, members who possess material nonpublic information that could affect the value of an investment must not cause others to act on the information.

   A is incorrect because price distortion is mentioned in Standard II(B) Market Manipulation, not Standard II(A) Material Nonpublic Information.

C is incorrect because the maintenance of appropriate records to support investment analyses is noted in Standard V(C) Record Retention, not Standard II(A) Material Nonpublic Information.

6. B is correct. Standard III(C) Suitability states that when members and candidates are in an advisory relationship with a client, they must judge the suitability of investments in the context of the client's total portfolio.

   A is incorrect because this requirement is addressed under Standard III(A) Loyalty, Prudence, and Care, not Standard III(C) Suitability.

   C is incorrect because this requirement is addressed under Standard I(C) Misrepresentation, not Standard III(C) Suitability.

7. C is correct. Under Standard III(B) Fair Dealing, members and candidates must deal fairly and objectively with all clients when providing investment analysis, making investment recommendations, taking investment action, or engaging in other professional activities.

   A is incorrect because under Standard III(C) Suitability, members and candidates in an advisory relationship must make a reasonable inquiry into a client's financial constraints prior to (not after) taking investment action and must reassess and update this regularly.

   B is incorrect because under Standard III(A) Loyalty, Prudence, and Care, members and candidates must act for the benefit of their clients and place their clients' interests before (not maintain an equal balance with) their employer's or their own interests.

8. B is correct. Standard IV(A) Loyalty states that members and candidates cannot deprive their employer of the advantage of their skills and abilities in matters related to their employment.

   A is incorrect because accepting gifts that might compromise a member's or candidate's independence and objectivity is addressed by Standard I: Professionalism, not Standard IV: Duties to Employers.

   C is incorrect because Standard IV(B) Additional Compensation Arrangements permits members and candidates to accept compensation that competes with their employer's interest if they obtain written consent from all parties involved.

9. C is correct. Standard V(B) Communication with Clients and Prospective Clients states that members and candidates must distinguish between fact and opinion in the presentation of investment analysis and recommendations.

   A is incorrect because this standard is discussed in Standard III: Duties to Clients.

   B is incorrect because performance presentation is discussed in Standard III: Duties to Clients.

10. C is correct. Standard VII(B) Reference to CFA Institute, the CFA Designation, and the CFA Program explicitly states the appropriate manner to make reference to CFA Institute, CFA Institute membership, the CFA designation, or candidacy in the CFA Program.

    A is incorrect because Standard VII: Responsibilities as a CFA Institute Member or CFA Candidate does not refer to loyalty. Loyalty is addressed in two other standards, Standard III(A) Loyalty, Prudence, and Care and as part of Standard IV: Duties to Employers.

    B is incorrect because Standard VII does not refer to the responsibility of supervisors. The responsibility of supervisors is addressed in Standard IV(C) Responsibility of Supervisors.

LEARNING MODULE

2

Guidance for Standards I–VII

LEARNING OUTCOMES	
Mastery	*The candidate should be able to:*
☐	demonstrate a thorough knowledge of the CFA Institute Code of Ethics and Standards of Professional Conduct by interpreting the Code and Standards in various situations involving issues of professional integrity
☐	recommend practices and procedures designed to prevent violations of the Code and Standards

STANDARD I: PROFESSIONALISM

1

☐	demonstrate a thorough knowledge of the CFA Institute Code of Ethics and Standards of Professional Conduct by interpreting the Code and Standards in various situations involving issues of professional integrity
☐	recommend practices and procedures designed to prevent violations of the Code and Standards

Standard I(A) Knowledge of the Law

Members and Candidates must understand and comply with all applicable laws, rules, and regulations (including the CFA Institute Code of Ethics and Standards of Professional Conduct) of any government, regulatory organization, licensing agency, or professional association governing their professional activities. In the event of conflict, Members and Candidates must comply with the more strict law, rule, or regulation. Members and Candidates must not knowingly participate or assist in and must dissociate from any violation of such laws, rules, or regulations.

Guidance

Highlights:

- *Relationship between the Code and Standards and Applicable Law*
- *Participation in or Association with Violations by Others*
- *Investment Products and Applicable Laws*

Members and candidates must understand the applicable laws and regulations of the countries and jurisdictions where they engage in professional activities. These activities may include, but are not limited to, trading of securities or other financial instruments, providing investment advice, conducting research, or performing other investment services. On the basis of their reasonable and good faith understanding, members and candidates must comply with the laws and regulations that directly govern their professional activities and resulting outcomes and that protect the interests of the clients.

When questions arise, members and candidates should know their firm's policies and procedures for accessing compliance guidance. This standard does not require members and candidates to become experts, however, in compliance. Additionally, members and candidates are not required to have detailed knowledge of or be experts on all the laws that could potentially govern their activities.

During times of changing regulations, members and candidates must remain vigilant in maintaining their knowledge of the requirements for their professional activities. New financial products and processes, along with uncovered ethical missteps, create an environment for recurring and potentially wide-ranging regulatory changes. Members and candidates are also continually provided improved and enhanced methods of communicating with both clients and potential clients, such as mobile applications and web-based social networking platforms. As new local, regional, and global requirements are updated to address these and other changes, members, candidates, and their firms must adjust their procedures and practices to remain in compliance.

Relationship between the Code and Standards and Applicable Law

Some members or candidates may live, work, or provide investment services to clients living in a country that has no law or regulation governing a particular action or that has laws or regulations that differ from the requirements of the Code and Standards. When applicable law and the Code and Standards require different conduct, members and candidates must follow the more strict of the applicable law or the Code and Standards.

"Applicable law" is the law that governs the member's or candidate's conduct. Which law applies will depend on the particular facts and circumstances of each case. The "more strict" law or regulation is the law or regulation that imposes greater restrictions on the action of the member or candidate or calls for the member or candidate to exert a greater degree of action that protects the interests of investors. For example, applicable law or regulation may not require members and candidates to disclose referral fees received from or paid to others for the recommendation of investment products or services. Because the Code and Standards impose this obligation, however, members and candidates must disclose the existence of such fees.

Members and candidates must adhere to the following principles:

- Members and candidates must comply with applicable laws or regulations related to their professional activities.
- Members and candidates must not engage in conduct that constitutes a violation of the Code and Standards, even though it may otherwise be legal.

- In the absence of any applicable law or regulation or when the Code and Standards impose a higher degree of responsibility than applicable laws and regulations, members and candidates must adhere to the Code and Standards. Applications of these principles are outlined in Exhibit 1.

The applicable laws governing the responsibilities of a member or candidate should be viewed as the minimal threshold of acceptable actions. When members and candidates take actions that exceed the minimal requirements, they further support the conduct required of Standard I(A).

CFA Institute members are obligated to abide by the CFA Institute Articles of Incorporation, Bylaws, Code of Ethics, Standards of Professional Conduct, Rules of Procedure, Membership Agreement, and other applicable rules promulgated by CFA Institute, all as amended periodically. CFA candidates who are not members must also abide by these documents (except for the Membership Agreement) as well as rules and regulations related to the administration of the CFA® exam, the Candidate Responsibility Statement, and the Candidate Pledge.

Participation in or Association with Violations by Others

Members and candidates are responsible for violations in which they *knowingly* participate or assist. Although members and candidates are presumed to have knowledge of all applicable laws, rules, and regulations, CFA Institute acknowledges that members may not recognize violations if they are not aware of all the facts giving rise to the violations. Standard I(A) applies when members and candidates know or should know that their conduct may contribute to a violation of applicable laws, rules, or regulations or the Code and Standards.

If a member or candidate has reasonable grounds to believe that imminent or ongoing client or employer activities are illegal or unethical, the member or candidate must dissociate, or separate, from the activity. In extreme cases, dissociation may require a member or candidate to leave his or her employment. Members and candidates may take the following intermediate steps to dissociate from ethical violations of others when direct discussions with the person or persons committing the violation are unsuccessful. The first step should be to attempt to stop the behavior by bringing it to the attention of the employer through a supervisor or the firm's compliance department. If this attempt is unsuccessful, then members and candidates have a responsibility to step away and dissociate from the activity. Dissociation practices will differ on the basis of the member's or candidate's role in the investment industry. It may include removing one's name from written reports or recommendations, asking for a different assignment, or refusing to accept a new client or continue to advise a current client. Inaction combined with continuing association with those involved in illegal or unethical conduct may be construed as participation or assistance in the illegal or unethical conduct.

CFA Institute strongly encourages members and candidates to report potential violations of the Code and Standards committed by fellow members and candidates. Although a failure to report is less likely to be construed as a violation than a failure to dissociate from unethical conduct, the impact of inactivity on the integrity of capital markets can be significant. Although the Code and Standards do not compel members and candidates to report violations to their governmental or regulatory organizations unless such disclosure is mandatory under applicable law (voluntary reporting is often referred to as whistleblowing), such disclosure may be prudent under certain circumstances. Members and candidates should consult their legal and compliance advisers for guidance.

Additionally, CFA Institute encourages members, nonmembers, clients, and the investing public to report violations of the Code and Standards by CFA Institute members or CFA candidates by submitting a complaint in writing to the CFA Institute Professional Conduct Program via e-mail (pcprogram@cfainstitute.org) or the CFA Institute website (www.cfainstitute.org).

Investment Products and Applicable Laws

Members and candidates involved in creating or maintaining investment services or investment products or packages of securities and/or derivatives should be mindful of where these products or packages will be sold as well as their places of origination. The applicable laws and regulations of the countries or regions of origination and expected sale should be understood by those responsible for the supervision of the services or creation and maintenance of the products or packages. Members or candidates should make reasonable efforts to review whether associated firms that are distributing products or services developed by their employing firm also abide by the laws and regulations of the countries and regions of distribution. Members and candidates should undertake the necessary due diligence when transacting cross-border business to understand the multiple applicable laws and regulations in order to protect the reputation of their firm and themselves.

Given the complexity that can arise with business transactions in today's market, there may be some uncertainty surrounding which laws or regulations are considered applicable when activities are being conducted in multiple jurisdictions. Members and candidates should seek the appropriate guidance, potentially including the firm's compliance or legal departments and legal counsel outside the organization, to gain a reasonable understanding of their responsibilities and how to implement them appropriately.

Exhibit 1: Global Application of the Code and Standards

Members and candidates who practice in multiple jurisdictions may be subject to varied securities laws and regulations. If applicable law is stricter than the requirements of the Code and Standards, members and candidates must adhere to applicable law; otherwise, they must adhere to the Code and Standards. The following chart provides illustrations involving a member who may be subject to the securities laws and regulations of three different types of countries:

NS: country with no securities laws or regulations

LS: country with *less* strict securities laws and regulations than the Code and Standards

MS: country with *more* strict securities laws and regulations than the Code and Standards

Applicable Law	Duties	Explanation
Member resides in NS country, does business in LS country; LS law applies.	Member must adhere to the Code and Standards.	Because applicable law is less strict than the Code and Standards, the member must adhere to the Code and Standards.
Member resides in NS country, does business in MS country; MS law applies.	Member must adhere to the law of MS country.	Because applicable law is stricter than the Code and Standards, member must adhere to the more strict applicable law.

Applicable Law	Duties	Explanation
Member resides in LS country, does business in NS country; LS law applies.	Member must adhere to the Code and Standards.	Because applicable law is less strict than the Code and Standards, member must adhere to the Code and Standards.
Member resides in LS country, does business in MS country; MS law applies.	Member must adhere to the law of MS country.	Because applicable law is stricter than the Code and Standards, member must adhere to the more strict applicable law.
Member resides in LS country, does business in NS country; LS law applies, but it states that law of locality where business is conducted governs.	Member must adhere to the Code and Standards.	Because applicable law states that the law of the locality where the business is conducted governs and there is no local law, the member must adhere to the Code and Standards.
Member resides in LS country, does business in MS country; LS law applies, but it states that law of locality where business is conducted governs.	Member must adhere to the law of MS country.	Because applicable law of the locality where the business is conducted governs and local law is stricter than the Code and Standards, member must adhere to the more strict applicable law.
Member resides in MS country, does business in LS country; MS law applies.	Member must adhere to the law of MS country.	Because applicable law is stricter than the Code and Standards, member must adhere to the more strict applicable law.
Member resides in MS country, does business in LS country; MS law applies, but it states that law of locality where business is conducted governs.	Member must adhere to the Code and Standards.	Because applicable law states that the law of the locality where the business is conducted governs and local law is less strict than the Code and Standards, member must adhere to the Code and Standards.
Member resides in MS country, does business in LS country with a client who is a citizen of LS country; MS law applies, but it states that the law of the client's home country governs.	Member must adhere to the Code and Standards.	Because applicable law states that the law of the client's home country governs (which is less strict than the Code and Standards), member must adhere to the Code and Standards.
Member resides in MS country, does business in LS country with a client who is a citizen of MS country; MS law applies, but it states that the law of the client's home country governs.	Member must adhere to the law of MS country.	Because applicable law states that the law of the client's home country governs and the law of the client's home country is stricter than the Code and Standards, the member must adhere to the more strict applicable law.

2 STANDARD I(A): RECOMMENDED PROCEDURES

Members and Candidates

Suggested methods by which members and candidates can acquire and maintain understanding of applicable laws, rules, and regulations include the following:

- *Stay informed*: Members and candidates should establish or encourage their employers to establish a procedure by which employees are regularly informed about changes in applicable laws, rules, regulations, and case law. In many instances, the employer's compliance department or legal counsel can provide such information in the form of memorandums distributed to employees in the organization. Also, participation in an internal or external continuing education program is a practical method of staying current.
- *Review procedures*: Members and candidates should review, or encourage their employers to review, the firm's written compliance procedures on a regular basis to ensure that the procedures reflect current law and provide adequate guidance to employees about what is permissible conduct under the law and/or the Code and Standards. Recommended compliance procedures for specific items of the Code and Standards are discussed in this *Handbook* in the "Guidance" sections associated with each standard.
- *Maintain current files*: Members and candidates should maintain or encourage their employers to maintain readily accessible current reference copies of applicable statutes, rules, regulations, and important cases.

Distribution Area Laws

Members and candidates should make reasonable efforts to understand the applicable laws—both country and regional—for the countries and regions where their investment products are developed and are most likely to be distributed to clients.

Legal Counsel

When in doubt about the appropriate action to undertake, it is recommended that a member or candidate seek the advice of compliance personnel or legal counsel concerning legal requirements. If a potential violation is being committed by a fellow employee, it may also be prudent for the member or candidate to seek the advice of the firm's compliance department or legal counsel.

Dissociation

When dissociating from an activity that violates the Code and Standards, members and candidates should document the violation and urge their firms to attempt to persuade the perpetrator(s) to cease such conduct. To dissociate from the conduct, a member or candidate may have to resign his or her employment.

Firms

The formality and complexity of compliance procedures for firms depend on the nature and size of the organization and the nature of its investment operations. Members and candidates should encourage their firms to consider the following policies and procedures to support the principles of Standard I(A):

- *Develop and/or adopt a code of ethics*: The ethical culture of an organization starts at the top. Members and candidates should encourage their supervisors or managers to adopt a code of ethics. Adhering to a code of ethics facilitates solutions when people face ethical dilemmas and can prevent the need for employees to resort to a "whistleblowing" solution publicly alleging concealed misconduct. CFA Institute has published the *Asset Manager Code of Professional Conduct*, which firms may adopt or use as the basis for their codes (visit www.cfainstitute.org).
- *Provide information on applicable laws*: Pertinent information that highlights applicable laws and regulations might be distributed to employees or made available in a central location. Information sources might include primary information developed by the relevant government, governmental agencies, regulatory organizations, licensing agencies, and professional associations (e.g., from their websites); law firm memorandums or newsletters; and association memorandums or publications (e.g., *CFA Institute Magazine*).
- *Establish procedures for reporting violations*: Firms might provide written protocols for reporting suspected violations of laws, regulations, or company policies.

STANDARD I(A): APPLICATION OF THE STANDARD

3

Example 1 (Notification of Known Violations):

Michael Allen works for a brokerage firm and is responsible for an underwriting of securities. A company official gives Allen information indicating that the financial statements Allen filed with the regulator overstate the issuer's earnings. Allen seeks the advice of the brokerage firm's general counsel, who states that it would be difficult for the regulator to prove that Allen has been involved in any wrongdoing.

> *Comment*: Although it is recommended that members and candidates seek the advice of legal counsel, the reliance on such advice does not absolve a member or candidate from the requirement to comply with the law or regulation. Allen should report this situation to his supervisor, seek an independent legal opinion, and determine whether the regulator should be notified of the error.

Example 2 (Dissociating from a Violation):

Lawrence Brown's employer, an investment banking firm, is the principal underwriter for an issue of convertible debentures by the Courtney Company. Brown discovers that the Courtney Company has concealed severe third-quarter losses in its foreign operations. The preliminary prospectus has already been distributed.

Comment: Knowing that the preliminary prospectus is misleading, Brown should report his findings to the appropriate supervisory persons in his firm. If the matter is not remedied and Brown's employer does not dissociate from the underwriting, Brown should sever all his connections with the underwriting. Brown should also seek legal advice to determine whether additional reporting or other action should be taken.

Example 3 (Dissociating from a Violation):

Kamisha Washington's firm advertises its past performance record by showing the 10-year return of a composite of its client accounts. Washington discovers, however, that the composite omits the performance of accounts that have left the firm during the 10-year period, whereas the description of the composite indicates the inclusion of all firm accounts. This omission has led to an inflated performance figure. Washington is asked to use promotional material that includes the erroneous performance number when soliciting business for the firm.

Comment: Misrepresenting performance is a violation of the Code and Standards. Although she did not calculate the performance herself, Washington would be assisting in violating Standard I(A) if she were to use the inflated performance number when soliciting clients. She must dissociate herself from the activity. If discussing the misleading number with the person responsible is not an option for correcting the problem, she can bring the situation to the attention of her supervisor or the compliance department at her firm. If her firm is unwilling to recalculate performance, she must refrain from using the misleading promotional material and should notify the firm of her reasons. If the firm insists that she use the material, she should consider whether her obligation to dissociate from the activity requires her to seek other employment.

Example 4 (Following the Highest Requirements):

James Collins is an investment analyst for a major Wall Street brokerage firm. He works in a developing country with a rapidly modernizing economy and a growing capital market. Local securities laws are minimal—in form and content—and include no punitive prohibitions against insider trading.

Comment: Collins must abide by the requirements of the Code and Standards, which might be more strict than the rules of the developing country. He should be aware of the risks that a small market and the absence of a fairly regulated flow of information to the market represent to his ability to obtain information and make timely judgments. He should include this factor in formulating his advice to clients. In handling material nonpublic information that accidentally comes into his possession, he must follow Standard II(A) Material Nonpublic Information.

Example 5 (Following the Highest Requirements):

Laura Jameson works for a multinational investment adviser based in the United States. Jameson lives and works as a registered investment adviser in the tiny, but wealthy, island nation of Karramba. Karramba's securities laws state that no investment adviser registered and working in that country can participate in initial public offerings (IPOs) for the adviser's personal account. Jameson, believing that, as a US citizen working for a US-based company, she should comply only with US law, has ignored this Karrambian law. In addition, Jameson believes that as a charterholder, as long as she adheres to the Code and Standards requirement that she disclose her participation in any IPO to her employer and clients when such ownership creates a conflict of interest, she is meeting the highest ethical requirements.

> *Comment*: Jameson is in violation of Standard I(A). As a registered investment adviser in Karramba, Jameson is prevented by Karrambian securities law from participating in IPOs regardless of the law of her home country. In addition, because the law of the country where she is working is stricter than the Code and Standards, she must follow the stricter requirements of the local law rather than the requirements of the Code and Standards.

Example 6 (Laws and Regulations Based on Religious Tenets):

Amanda Janney is employed as a fixed-income portfolio manager for a large international firm. She is on a team within her firm that is responsible for creating and managing a fixed-income hedge fund to be sold throughout the firm's distribution centers to high-net-worth clients. Her firm receives expressions of interest from potential clients from the Middle East who are seeking investments that comply with Islamic law. The marketing and promotional materials for the fixed-income hedge fund do not specify whether or not the fund is a suitable investment for an investor seeking compliance with Islamic law. Because the fund is being distributed globally, Janney is concerned about the reputation of the fund and the firm and believes disclosure of whether or not the fund complies with Islamic law could help minimize potential mistakes with placing this investment.

> *Comment*: As the financial market continues to become globalized, members and candidates will need to be aware of the differences between cultural and religious laws and requirements as well as the different governmental laws and regulations. Janney and the firm could be proactive in their efforts to acknowledge areas where the new fund may not be suitable for clients.

Example 7 (Reporting Potential Unethical Actions):

Krista Blume is a junior portfolio manager for high net worth portfolios at a large global investment manager. She observes a number of new portfolios and relationships coming from a country in Europe where the firm did not have previous business and is told that a broker in that country is responsible for this new business. At a meeting on allocation of research resources to third-party research firms, Blume notes that this broker has been added to the list and is allocated payments for research. However, she knows the portfolios do not invest in securities in the broker's country, and she has not seen any research come from this broker. Blume asks her supervisor about the name being on the list and is told that someone in marketing is receiving the research and that the name being on the list is OK. She believes that what may be going on is that the broker is being paid for new business through the inappropriate research payments, and she wishes to dissociate from the misconduct.

> *Comment*: Blume should follow the firm's policies and procedures for reporting potential unethical activity, which may include discussions with her supervisor or someone in a designated compliance department. She should communicate her concerns appropriately while advocating for disclosure between the new broker relationship and the research payments.

Example 8 (Failure to Maintain Knowledge of the Law):

Colleen White is excited to use new technology to communicate with clients and potential clients. She recently began posting investment information, including performance reports and investment opinions and recommendations, to her Facebook page. In addition, she sends out brief announcements, opinions, and thoughts via her X account (for example, "Prospects for future growth of XYZ company look good! #makingmoney4U"). Prior to White's use of these social media platforms, the local regulator had issued new requirements and guidance governing online electronic communication. White's communications appear to conflict with the recent regulatory announcements.

> *Comment*: White is in violation of Standard I(A) because her communications do not comply with the existing guidance and regulation governing use of social media. White must be aware of the evolving legal requirements pertaining to new and dynamic areas of the financial services industry that are applicable to her. She should seek guidance from appropriate, knowledgeable, and reliable sources, such as her firm's compliance department, external service providers, or outside counsel, unless she diligently follows legal and regulatory trends affecting her professional responsibilities.

4 STANDARD I(B) INDEPENDENCE AND OBJECTIVITY

> Members and Candidates must use reasonable care and judgment to achieve and maintain independence and objectivity in their professional activities. Members and Candidates must not offer, solicit, or accept any gift, benefit, compensation, or consideration that reasonably could be expected to compromise their own or another's independence and objectivity.

Guidance

Highlights:

- *Buy-Side Clients*
- *Fund Manager and Custodial Relationships*
- *Investment Banking Relationships*
- *Performance Measurement and Attribution*
- *Public Companies*
- *Credit Rating Agency Opinions*
- *Influence during the Manager Selection/Procurement Process*
- *Issuer-Paid Research*
- *Travel Funding*

Standard I(B) states the responsibility of CFA Institute members and candidates in the CFA Program to maintain independence and objectivity so that their clients will have the benefit of their work and opinions unaffected by any potential conflict of interest or other circumstance adversely affecting their judgment. Every member and candidate should endeavor to avoid situations that could cause or be perceived to cause a loss of independence or objectivity in recommending investments or taking investment action.

External sources may try to influence the investment process by offering analysts and portfolio managers a variety of benefits. Corporations may seek expanded research coverage, issuers and underwriters may wish to promote new securities offerings, brokers may want to increase commission business, and independent rating agencies may be influenced by the company requesting the rating. Benefits may include gifts, invitations to lavish functions, tickets, favors, or job referrals. One type of benefit is the allocation of shares in oversubscribed IPOs to investment managers for their personal accounts. This practice affords managers the opportunity to make quick profits that may not be available to their clients. Such a practice is prohibited under Standard I(B). Modest gifts and entertainment are acceptable, but special care must be taken by members and candidates to resist subtle and not-so-subtle pressures to act in conflict with the interests of their clients. Best practice dictates that members and candidates reject any offer of gift or entertainment that could be expected to threaten their independence and objectivity.

Receiving a gift, benefit, or consideration from a *client* can be distinguished from gifts given by entities seeking to influence a member or candidate to the detriment of other clients. In a client relationship, the client has already entered some type of compensation arrangement with the member, candidate, or his or her firm. A gift from a client could be considered supplementary compensation. The potential for obtaining influence to the detriment of other clients, although present, is not as great as in situations where no compensation arrangement exists. When possible, prior to accepting "bonuses" or gifts from clients, members and candidates should disclose to their employers such benefits offered by clients. If notification is not possible prior to acceptance, members and candidates must disclose to their employer benefits previously accepted from clients. Disclosure allows the employer of a member or candidate to make an independent determination about the extent to which the gift may affect the member's or candidate's independence and objectivity.

Members and candidates may also come under pressure from their own firms to, for example, issue favorable research reports or recommendations for certain companies with potential or continuing business relationships with the firm. The situation may be aggravated if an executive of the company sits on the bank or investment firm's board and attempts to interfere in investment decision making. Members and candidates acting in a sales or marketing capacity must be especially mindful of their objectivity in promoting appropriate investments for their clients.

Left unmanaged, pressures that threaten independence place research analysts in a difficult position and may jeopardize their ability to act independently and objectively. One of the ways that research analysts have coped with these pressures in the past is to use subtle and ambiguous language in their recommendations or to temper the tone of their research reports. Such subtleties are lost on some investors, however, who reasonably expect research reports and recommendations to be straightforward and transparent and to communicate clearly an analyst's views based on unbiased analysis and independent judgment.

Members and candidates are personally responsible for maintaining independence and objectivity when preparing research reports, making investment recommendations, and taking investment action on behalf of clients. Recommendations must convey the member's or candidate's true opinions, free of bias from internal or external pressures, and be stated in clear and unambiguous language.

Members and candidates also should be aware that some of their professional or social activities within CFA Institute or its member societies may subtly threaten their independence or objectivity. When seeking corporate financial support for conventions, seminars, or even weekly society luncheons, the members or candidates responsible for the activities should evaluate both the actual effect of such solicitations on their independence and whether their objectivity might be perceived to be compromised in the eyes of their clients.

Buy-Side Clients

One source of pressure on sell-side analysts is buy-side clients. Institutional clients are traditionally the primary users of sell-side research, either directly or with soft dollar brokerage. Portfolio managers may have significant positions in the security of a company under review. A rating downgrade may adversely affect the portfolio's performance, particularly in the short term, because the sensitivity of stock prices to ratings changes has increased in recent years. A downgrade may also affect the manager's compensation, which is usually tied to portfolio performance. Moreover, portfolio performance is subject to media and public scrutiny, which may affect the manager's professional reputation. Consequently, some portfolio managers implicitly or explicitly support sell-side ratings inflation.

Portfolio managers have a responsibility to respect and foster the intellectual honesty of sell-side research. Therefore, it is improper for portfolio managers to threaten or engage in retaliatory practices, such as reporting sell-side analysts to the covered company in order to instigate negative corporate reactions. Although most portfolio managers do not engage in such practices, the perception by the research analyst that a reprisal is possible may cause concern and make it difficult for the analyst to maintain independence and objectivity.

Fund Manager and Custodial Relationships

Research analysts are not the only people who must be concerned with maintaining their independence. Members and candidates who are responsible for hiring and retaining outside managers and third-party custodians should not accepts gifts, entertainment, or travel funding that may be perceived as impairing their decisions. The use of secondary fund managers has evolved into a common practice to manage specific asset allocations. The use of third-party custodians is common practice for independent investment advisory firms and helps them with trading capabilities and reporting requirements. Primary and secondary fund managers, as well as third-party custodians, often arrange educational and marketing events to inform others about their business strategies, investment process, or custodial services. Members and candidates must review the merits of each offer individually in determining whether they may attend yet maintain their independence.

Investment Banking Relationships

Some sell-side firms may exert pressure on their analysts to issue favorable research reports on current or prospective investment banking clients. For many of these firms, income from investment banking has become increasingly important to overall firm profitability because brokerage income has declined as a result of price competition. Consequently, firms offering investment banking services work hard to develop and maintain relationships with investment banking clients and prospects. These companies are often covered by the firm's research analysts because companies often select their investment banks on the basis of the reputation of their research analysts, the quality of their work, and their standing in the industry.

In some countries, research analysts frequently work closely with their investment banking colleagues to help evaluate prospective investment banking clients. In other countries, because of past abuses in managing the obvious conflicts of interest, regulators have established clear rules prohibiting the interaction of these groups. Although collaboration between research analysts and investment banking colleagues may benefit the firm and enhance market efficiency (e.g., by allowing firms to assess risks more accurately and make better pricing assumptions), it requires firms to carefully balance the conflicts of interest inherent in the collaboration. Having analysts work with investment bankers is appropriate only when the conflicts are adequately and effectively managed and disclosed. Firm managers have a responsibility to provide an environment in which analysts are neither coerced nor enticed into issuing research that does not reflect their true opinions. Firms should require public disclosure of actual conflicts of interest to investors.

Members, candidates, and their firms must adopt and follow perceived best practices in maintaining independence and objectivity in the corporate culture and protecting analysts from undue pressure by their investment banking colleagues. The "firewalls" traditionally built between these two functions must be managed to minimize conflicts of interest; indeed, enhanced firewall policies may go as far as prohibiting all communications between these groups. A key element of an enhanced firewall is separate reporting structures for personnel on the research side and personnel on the investment banking side. For example, investment banking personnel should not have any authority to approve, disapprove, or make changes to research reports or recommendations. Another element should be a compensation arrangement that minimizes the pressures on research analysts and rewards objectivity and accuracy. Compensation arrangements should not link analyst remuneration directly to investment banking assignments in which the analyst may participate as a team member. Firms should also regularly review their policies and procedures to determine whether analysts are adequately safeguarded and to improve the transparency of disclosures relating to conflicts of interest. The highest level of transparency is achieved when disclosures are prominent and specific rather than marginalized and generic.

Performance Measurement and Attribution

Members and candidates working within a firm's investment performance measurement department may also be presented with situations that challenge their independence and objectivity. As performance analysts, their analyses may reveal instances where managers may appear to have strayed from their mandate. Additionally, the performance analyst may receive requests to alter the construction of composite indexes owing to negative results for a selected account or fund. The member or candidate must not allow internal or external influences to affect their independence and objectivity as they faithfully complete their performance calculation and analysis-related responsibilities.

Public Companies

Analysts may be pressured to issue favorable reports and recommendations by the companies they follow. Not every stock is a "buy," and not every research report is favorable—for many reasons, including the cyclical nature of many business activities and market fluctuations. For instance, a "good company" does not always translate into a "good stock" rating if the current stock price is fully valued. In making an investment recommendation, the analyst is responsible for anticipating, interpreting, and assessing a company's prospects and stock price performance in a factual manner. Many company managers, however, believe that their company's stock is undervalued, and these managers may find it difficult to accept critical research reports or ratings downgrades. Company managers' compensation may also be dependent on stock performance.

Due diligence in financial research and analysis involves gathering information from a wide variety of sources, including public disclosure documents (such as proxy statements, annual reports, and other regulatory filings) and also company management and investor-relations personnel, suppliers, customers, competitors, and other relevant sources. Research analysts may justifiably fear that companies will limit their ability to conduct thorough research by denying analysts who have "negative" views direct access to company managers and/or barring them from conference calls and other communication venues. Retaliatory practices include companies bringing legal action against analysts personally and/or their firms to seek monetary damages for the economic effects of negative reports and recommendations. Although few companies engage in such behavior, the perception that a reprisal is possible is a reasonable concern for analysts. This concern may make it difficult for them to conduct the comprehensive research needed to make objective recommendations. For further information and guidance, members and candidates should refer to the CFA Institute publication *Best Practice Guidelines Governing Analyst/Corporate Issuer Relations* (www.cfainstitute.org).

Credit Rating Agency Opinions

Credit rating agencies provide a service by grading the fixed-income products offered by companies. Analysts face challenges related to incentives and compensation schemes that may be tied to the final rating and successful placement of the product. Members and candidates employed at rating agencies should ensure that procedures and processes at the agencies prevent undue influences from a sponsoring company during the analysis. Members and candidates should abide by their agencies' and the industry's standards of conduct regarding the analytical process and the distribution of their reports.

The work of credit rating agencies also raises concerns similar to those inherent in investment banking relationships. Analysts may face pressure to issue ratings at a specific level because of other services the agency offers companies—namely, advising on the development of structured products. The rating agencies need to develop the necessary firewalls and protections to allow the independent operations of their different business lines.

When using information provided by credit rating agencies, members and candidates should be mindful of the potential conflicts of interest. And because of the potential conflicts, members and candidates may need to independently validate the rating granted.

Influence during the Manager Selection/Procurement Process

Members and candidates may find themselves on either side of the manager selection process. An individual may be on the hiring side as a representative of a pension organization or an investment committee member of an endowment or a charitable organization. Additionally, other members may be representing their organizations in attempts to earn new investment allocation mandates. The responsibility of members and candidates to maintain their independence and objectivity extends to the hiring or firing of those who provide business services beyond investment management.

When serving in a hiring capacity, members and candidates should not solicit gifts, contributions, or other compensation that may affect their independence and objectivity. Solicitations do not have to benefit members and candidates personally to conflict with Standard I(B). Requesting contributions to a favorite charity or political organization may also be perceived as an attempt to influence the decision-making process. Additionally, members and candidates serving in a hiring capacity should refuse gifts, donations, and other offered compensation that may be perceived to influence their decision-making process.

When working to earn a new investment allocation, members and candidates should not offer gifts, contributions, or other compensation to influence the decision of the hiring representative. The offering of these items with the intent to impair the independence and objectivity of another person would not comply with Standard I(B). Such prohibited actions may include offering donations to a charitable organization or political candidate referred by the hiring representative.

A clear example of improperly influencing hiring representatives was displayed in the "pay-to-play" scandal involving government-sponsored pension funds in the United States. Managers looking to gain lucrative allocations from the large funds made requested donations to the political campaigns of individuals directly responsible for the hiring decisions. This scandal and other similar events have led to new laws requiring additional reporting concerning political contributions and bans on hiring—or hiring delays for—managers that made campaign contributions to representatives associated with the decision-making process.

Issuer-Paid Research

In light of the recent reduction of sell-side research coverage, many companies, seeking to increase visibility both in the financial markets and with potential investors, have hired analysts to produce research reports analyzing their companies. These reports bridge the gap created by the lack of coverage and can be an effective method of communicating with investors.

Issuer-paid research conducted by independent analysts, however, is fraught with potential conflicts. Depending on how the research is written and distributed, investors may be misled into believing that the research is from an independent source when, in reality, it has been paid for by the subject company.

Members and candidates must adhere to strict standards of conduct that govern how the research is to be conducted and what disclosures must be made in the report. Analysts must engage in thorough, independent, and unbiased analysis and must fully disclose potential conflicts of interest, including the nature of their compensation. Otherwise, analysts risk misleading investors.

Investors need clear, credible, and thorough information about companies, and they need research based on independent thought. At a minimum, issuer-paid research should include a thorough analysis of the company's financial statements based on publicly disclosed information, benchmarking within a peer group, and industry analysis. Analysts must exercise diligence, independence, and thoroughness in conducting their research in an objective manner. Analysts must distinguish between fact and opinion in their reports. Conclusions must have a reasonable and adequate basis and must be supported by appropriate research.

Independent analysts must also strictly limit the type of compensation that they accept for conducting issuer-paid research. Otherwise, the content and conclusions of the reports could reasonably be expected to be determined or affected by compensation from the sponsoring companies. Compensation that might influence the research report could be direct, such as payment based on the conclusions of the report, or indirect, such as stock warrants or other equity instruments that could increase in value on the basis of positive coverage in the report. In such instances, the independent analyst has an incentive to avoid including negative information or making negative conclusions. Best practice is for independent analysts, prior to writing their reports, to negotiate only a flat fee for their work that is not linked to their conclusions or recommendations.

Travel Funding

The benefits related to accepting paid travel extend beyond the cost savings to the member or candidate and his firm, such as the chance to talk exclusively with the executives of a company or learning more about the investment options provided by an investment organization. Acceptance also comes with potential concerns; for example, members and candidates may be influenced by these discussions when flying on a corporate or chartered jet or attending sponsored conferences where many expenses, including airfare and lodging, are covered. To avoid the appearance of compromising their independence and objectivity, best practice dictates that members and candidates always use commercial transportation at their expense or at the expense of their firm rather than accept paid travel arrangements from an outside company. Should commercial transportation be unavailable, members and candidates may accept modestly arranged travel to participate in appropriate information-gathering events, such as a property tour.

5

STANDARD I(B): RECOMMENDED PROCEDURES

Members and candidates should adhere to the following practices and should encourage their firms to establish procedures to avoid violations of Standard I(B):

- *Protect the integrity of opinions*: Members, candidates, and their firms should establish policies stating that every research report concerning the securities of a corporate client should reflect the unbiased opinion of the analyst. Firms should also design compensation systems that protect the integrity of the investment decision process by maintaining the independence and objectivity of analysts.
- *Create a restricted list*: If the firm is unwilling to permit dissemination of adverse opinions about a corporate client, members and candidates should encourage the firm to remove the controversial company from the research universe and put it on a restricted list so that the firm disseminates only factual information about the company.
- *Restrict special cost arrangements*: When attending meetings at an issuer's headquarters, members and candidates should pay for commercial transportation and hotel charges. No corporate issuer should reimburse members or candidates for air transportation. Members and candidates should encourage issuers to limit the use of corporate aircraft to situations in which commercial transportation is not available or in which efficient movement could not otherwise be arranged. Members and candidates should take particular care that when frequent meetings are held between an individual issuer and an individual member or candidate, the issuer should not always host the member or candidate.
- *Limit gifts*: Members and candidates must limit the acceptance of gratuities and/or gifts to token items. Standard I(B) does not preclude customary, ordinary business-related entertainment as long as its purpose is not to influence or reward members or candidates. Firms should consider a strict value limit for acceptable gifts that is based on the local or regional customs and should address whether the limit is per gift or an aggregate annual value.
- *Restrict investments*: Members and candidates should encourage their investment firms to develop formal policies related to employee purchases of equity or equity-related IPOs. Firms should require prior approval for employee participation in IPOs, with prompt disclosure of investment actions taken following the offering. Strict limits should be imposed on investment personnel acquiring securities in private placements.
- *Review procedures*: Members and candidates should encourage their firms to implement effective supervisory and review procedures to ensure that analysts and portfolio managers comply with policies relating to their personal investment activities.
- *Independence policy*: Members, candidates, and their firms should establish a formal written policy on the independence and objectivity of research and implement reporting structures and review procedures to ensure that

research analysts do not report to and are not supervised or controlled by any department of the firm that could compromise the independence of the analyst. More detailed recommendations related to a firm's policies regarding research objectivity are set forth in the CFA Institute statement *Research Objectivity Standards* (www.cfainstitute.org).

- *Appointed officer*: Firms should appoint a senior officer with oversight responsibilities for compliance with the firm's code of ethics and all regulations concerning its business. Firms should provide every employee with the procedures and policies for reporting potentially unethical behavior, violations of regulations, or other activities that may harm the firm's reputation.

STANDARD I(B): APPLICATION OF THE STANDARD

6

Example 1 (Travel Expenses):

Steven Taylor, a mining analyst with Bronson Brokers, is invited by Precision Metals to join a group of his peers in a tour of mining facilities in several western US states. The company arranges for chartered group flights from site to site and for accommodations in Spartan Motels, the only chain with accommodations near the mines, for three nights. Taylor allows Precision Metals to pick up his tab, as do the other analysts, with one exception—John Adams, an employee of a large trust company who insists on following his company's policy and paying for his hotel room himself.

> *Comment*: The policy of the company where Adams works complies closely with Standard I(B) by avoiding even the appearance of a conflict of interest, but Taylor and the other analysts were not necessarily violating Standard I(B). In general, when allowing companies to pay for travel and/or accommodations in these circumstances, members and candidates must use their judgment. They must be on guard that such arrangements not impinge on a member's or candidate's independence and objectivity. In this example, the trip was strictly for business and Taylor was not accepting irrelevant or lavish hospitality. The itinerary required chartered flights, for which analysts were not expected to pay. The accommodations were modest. These arrangements are not unusual and did not violate Standard I(B) as long as Taylor's independence and objectivity were not compromised. In the final analysis, members and candidates should consider both whether they can remain objective and whether their integrity might be perceived by their clients to have been compromised.

Example 2 (Research Independence):

Susan Dillon, an analyst in the corporate finance department of an investment services firm, is making a presentation to a potential new business client that includes the promise that her firm will provide full research coverage of the potential client.

> *Comment*: Dillon may agree to provide research coverage, but she must not commit her firm's research department to providing a favorable recommendation. The firm's recommendation (favorable, neutral, or unfavorable) must be based on an independent and objective investigation and analysis of the company and its securities.

Example 3 (Research Independence and Intrafirm Pressure):

Walter Fritz is an equity analyst with Hilton Brokerage who covers the mining industry. He has concluded that the stock of Metals & Mining is overpriced at its current level, but he is concerned that a negative research report will hurt the good relationship between Metals & Mining and the investment banking division of his firm. In fact, a senior manager of Hilton Brokerage has just sent him a copy of a proposal his firm has made to Metals & Mining to underwrite a debt offering. Fritz needs to produce a report right away and is concerned about issuing a less-than-favorable rating.

> *Comment*: Fritz's analysis of Metals & Mining must be objective and based solely on consideration of company fundamentals. Any pressure from other divisions of his firm is inappropriate. This conflict could have been eliminated if, in anticipation of the offering, Hilton Brokerage had placed Metals & Mining on a restricted list for its sales force.

Example 4 (Research Independence and Issuer Relationship Pressure):

As in Example 3, Walter Fritz has concluded that Metals & Mining stock is overvalued at its current level, but he is concerned that a negative research report might jeopardize a close rapport that he has nurtured over the years with Metals & Mining's CEO, chief finance officer, and investment relations officer. Fritz is concerned that a negative report might result also in management retaliation—for instance, cutting him off from participating in conference calls when a quarterly earnings release is made, denying him the ability to ask questions on such calls, and/or denying him access to top management for arranging group meetings between Hilton Brokerage clients and top Metals & Mining managers.

> *Comment*: As in Example 3, Fritz's analysis must be objective and based solely on consideration of company fundamentals. Any pressure from Metals & Mining is inappropriate. Fritz should reinforce the integrity of his conclusions by stressing that his investment recommendation is based on relative valuation, which may include qualitative issues with respect to Metals & Mining's management.

Example 5 (Research Independence and Sales Pressure):

As support for the sales effort of her corporate bond department, Lindsey Warner offers credit guidance to purchasers of fixed-income securities. Her compensation is closely linked to the performance of the corporate bond department. Near the quarter's end, Warner's firm has a large inventory position in the bonds of Milton, Ltd., and has been unable to sell the bonds because of Milton's recent announcement of an operating problem. Salespeople have asked her to contact large clients to push the bonds.

> *Comment*: Unethical sales practices create significant potential violations of the Code and Standards. Warner's opinion of the Milton bonds must not be affected by internal pressure or compensation. In this case, Warner must refuse to push the Milton bonds unless she is able to justify that the market price has already adjusted for the operating problem.

Example 6 (Research Independence and Prior Coverage):

Jill Jorund is a securities analyst following airline stocks and a rising star at her firm. Her boss has been carrying a "buy" recommendation on International Airlines and asks Jorund to take over coverage of that airline. He tells Jorund that under no circumstances should the prevailing buy recommendation be changed.

> *Comment*: Jorund must be independent and objective in her analysis of International Airlines. If she believes that her boss's instructions have compromised her, she has two options: She can tell her boss that she cannot cover the company under these constraints, or she can take over coverage of the company, reach her own independent conclusions, and if they conflict with her boss's opinion, share the conclusions with her boss or other supervisors in the firm so that they can make appropriate recommendations. Jorund must issue only recommendations that reflect her independent and objective opinion.

Example 7 (Gifts and Entertainment from Related Party):

Edward Grant directs a large amount of his commission business to a New York–based brokerage house. In appreciation for all the business, the brokerage house gives Grant two tickets to the World Cup in South Africa, two nights at a nearby resort, several meals, and transportation via limousine to the game. Grant fails to disclose receiving this package to his supervisor.

> *Comment*: Grant has violated Standard I(B) because accepting these substantial gifts may impede his independence and objectivity. Every member and candidate should endeavor to avoid situations that might cause or be perceived to cause a loss of independence or objectivity in recommending investments or taking investment action. By accepting the trip, Grant has opened himself up to the accusation that he may give the broker favored treatment in return.

Example 8 (Gifts and Entertainment from Client):

Theresa Green manages the portfolio of Ian Knowlden, a client of Tisbury Investments. Green achieves an annual return for Knowlden that is consistently better than that of the benchmark she and the client previously agreed to. As a reward, Knowlden offers Green two tickets to Wimbledon and the use of Knowlden's flat in London for a week. Green discloses this gift to her supervisor at Tisbury.

> *Comment*: Green is in compliance with Standard I(B) because she disclosed the gift from one of her clients in accordance with the firm's policies. Members and candidates may accept bonuses or gifts from clients as long as they disclose them to their employer because gifts in a client relationship are deemed less likely to affect a member's or candidate's objectivity and independence than gifts in other situations. Disclosure is required, however, so that supervisors can monitor such situations to guard against employees favoring a gift-giving client to the detriment of other fee-paying clients (such as by allocating a greater proportion of IPO stock to the gift-giving client's portfolio).
>
> Best practices for monitoring include comparing the transaction costs of the Knowlden account with the costs of other accounts managed by Green and other similar accounts within Tisbury. The supervisor could also compare the performance returns with the returns of other clients with

the same mandate. This comparison will assist in determining whether a pattern of favoritism by Green is disadvantaging other Tisbury clients or the possibility that this favoritism could affect her future behavior.

Example 9 (Travel Expenses from External Manager):

Tom Wayne is the investment manager of the Franklin City Employees Pension Plan. He recently completed a successful search for a firm to manage the foreign equity allocation of the plan's diversified portfolio. He followed the plan's standard procedure of seeking presentations from a number of qualified firms and recommended that his board select Penguin Advisors because of its experience, well-defined investment strategy, and performance record. The firm claims compliance with the Global Investment Performance Standards (GIPS®) and has been verified. Following the selection of Penguin, a reporter from the *Franklin City Record* calls to ask if there was any connection between this action and the fact that Penguin was one of the sponsors of an "investment fact-finding trip to Asia" that Wayne made earlier in the year. The trip was one of several conducted by the Pension Investment Academy, which had arranged the itinerary of meetings with economic, government, and corporate officials in major cities in several Asian countries. The Pension Investment Academy obtains support for the cost of these trips from a number of investment managers, including Penguin Advisors; the Academy then pays the travel expenses of the various pension plan managers on the trip and provides all meals and accommodations. The president of Penguin Advisors was also one of the travelers on the trip.

> *Comment*: Although Wayne can probably put to good use the knowledge he gained from the trip in selecting portfolio managers and in other areas of managing the pension plan, his recommendation of Penguin Advisors may be tainted by the possible conflict incurred when he participated in a trip partly paid for by Penguin Advisors and when he was in the daily company of the president of Penguin Advisors. To avoid violating Standard I(B), Wayne's basic expenses for travel and accommodations should have been paid by his employer or the pension plan; contact with the president of Penguin Advisors should have been limited to informational or educational events only; and the trip, the organizer, and the sponsor should have been made a matter of public record. Even if his actions were not in violation of Standard I(B), Wayne should have been sensitive to the public perception of the trip when reported in the newspaper and the extent to which the subjective elements of his decision might have been affected by the familiarity that the daily contact of such a trip would encourage. This advantage would probably not be shared by firms competing with Penguin Advisors.

Example 10 (Research Independence and Compensation Arrangements):

Javier Herrero recently left his job as a research analyst for a large investment adviser. While looking for a new position, he was hired by an investor-relations firm to write a research report on one of its clients, a small educational software company. The investor-relations firm hopes to generate investor interest in the technology company. The firm will pay Herrero a flat fee plus a bonus if any new investors buy stock in the company as a result of Herrero's report.

> *Comment*: If Herrero accepts this payment arrangement, he will be in violation of Standard I(B) because the compensation arrangement can reasonably be expected to compromise his independence and objectivity.

Herrero will receive a bonus for attracting investors, which provides an incentive to draft a positive report regardless of the facts and to ignore or play down any negative information about the company. Herrero should accept only a flat fee that is not tied to the conclusions or recommendations of the report. Issuer-paid research that is objective and unbiased can be done under the right circumstances as long as the analyst takes steps to maintain his or her objectivity and includes in the report proper disclosures regarding potential conflicts of interest.

Example 11 (Recommendation Objectivity and Service Fees):

Two years ago, Bob Wade, trust manager for Central Midas Bank, was approached by Western Funds about promoting its family of funds, with special interest in the service-fee class of funds. To entice Central to promote this class, Western Funds offered to pay the bank a service fee of 0.25%. Without disclosing the fee being offered to the bank, Wade asked one of the investment managers to review Western's funds to determine whether they were suitable for clients of Central Midas Bank. The manager completed the normal due diligence review and determined that the new funds were fairly valued in the market with fee structures on a par with competitors. Wade decided to accept Western's offer and instructed the team of portfolio managers to exclusively promote these funds and the service-fee class to clients seeking to invest new funds or transfer from their current investments.

Now, two years later, the funds managed by Western begin to underperform their peers. Wade is counting on the fees to reach his profitability targets and continues to push these funds as acceptable investments for Central's clients.

Comment: Wade is violating Standard I(B) because the fee arrangement has affected the objectivity of his recommendations. Wade is relying on the fee as a component of the department's profitability and is unwilling to offer other products that may affect the fees received.

See also Standard VI(A) Disclosure of Conflicts.

Example 12 (Recommendation Objectivity):

Bob Thompson has been doing research for the portfolio manager of the fixed-income department. His assignment is to do sensitivity analysis on securitized subprime mortgages. He has discussed with the manager possible scenarios to use to calculate expected returns. A key assumption in such calculations is housing price appreciation (HPA) because it drives "prepays" (prepayments of mortgages) and losses. Thompson is concerned with the significant appreciation experienced over the previous five years as a result of the increased availability of funds from subprime mortgages. Thompson insists that the analysis should include a scenario run with –10% for Year 1, –5% for Year 2, and then (to project a worst-case scenario) 0% for Years 3 through 5. The manager replies that these assumptions are too dire because there has never been a time in their available database when HPA was negative.

Thompson conducts his research to better understand the risks inherent in these securities and evaluates these securities in the worst-case scenario, an unlikely but possible environment. Based on the results of the enhanced scenarios, Thompson does not recommend the purchase of the securitization. Against the general market trends, the manager follows Thompson's recommendation and does not invest. The following year, the housing market collapses. In avoiding the subprime investments, the manager's portfolio outperforms its peer group that year.

Comment: Thompson's actions in running the worst-case scenario against the protests of the portfolio manager are in alignment with the principles of Standard I(B). Thompson did not allow his research to be pressured by the general trends of the market or the manager's desire to limit the research to historical norms.

See also Standard V(A) Diligence and Reasonable Basis.

Example 13 (Influencing Manager Selection Decisions):

Adrian Mandel, CFA, is a senior portfolio manager for ZZYY Capital Management who oversees a team of investment professionals who manage labor union pension funds. A few years ago, ZZYY sought to win a competitive asset manager search to manage a significant allocation of the pension fund of the United Doughnut and Pretzel Bakers Union (UDPBU). UDPBU's investment board is chaired by a recognized key decision maker and long-time leader of the union, Ernesto Gomez. To improve ZZYY's chances of winning the competition, Mandel made significant monetary contributions to Gomez's union reelection campaign fund. Even after ZZYY was hired as a primary manager of the pension, Mandel believed that his firm's position was not secure. Mandel continued to contribute to Gomez's reelection campaign chest as well as to entertain lavishly the union leader and his family at top restaurants on a regular basis. All of Mandel's outlays were routinely handled as marketing expenses reimbursed by ZZYY's expense accounts and were disclosed to his senior management as being instrumental in maintaining a strong close relationship with an important client.

Comment: Mandel not only offered but actually gave monetary gifts, benefits, and other considerations that reasonably could be expected to compromise Gomez's objectivity. Therefore, Mandel was in violation of Standard I(B).

Example 14 (Influencing Manager Selection Decisions):

Adrian Mandel, CFA, had heard about the manager search competition for the UDPBU Pension Fund through a broker/dealer contact. The contact told him that a well-known retired professional golfer, Bobby "The Bear" Finlay, who had become a licensed broker/dealer serving as a pension consultant, was orchestrating the UDPBU manager search. Finlay had gained celebrity status with several labor union pension fund boards by entertaining their respective board members and regaling them with colorful stories of fellow pro golfers' antics in clubhouses around the world. Mandel decided to improve ZZYY's chances of being invited to participate in the search competition by befriending Finlay to curry his favor. Knowing Finlay's love of entertainment, Mandel wined and dined Finlay at high-profile bistros where Finlay could glow in the fan recognition lavished on him by all the other patrons. Mandel's endeavors paid off handsomely when Finlay recommended to the UDPBU board that ZZYY be entered as one of three finalist asset management firms in its search.

Comment: Similar to Example 13, Mandel lavished gifts, benefits, and other considerations in the form of expensive entertainment that could reasonably be expected to influence the consultant to recommend the hiring of his firm. Therefore, Mandel was in violation of Standard I(B).

Example 15 (Fund Manager Relationships):

Amie Scott is a performance analyst within her firm with responsibilities for analyzing the performance of external managers. While completing her quarterly analysis, Scott notices a change in one manager's reported composite construction. The change concealed the bad performance of a particularly large account by placing that account into a new residual composite. This change allowed the manager to remain at the top of the list of manager performance. Scott knows her firm has a large allocation to this manager, and the fund's manager is a close personal friend of the CEO. She needs to deliver her final report but is concerned with pointing out the composite change.

> *Comment*: Scott would be in violation of Standard I(B) if she did not disclose the change in her final report. The analysis of managers' performance should not be influenced by personal relationships or the size of the allocation to the outside managers. By not including the change, Scott would not be providing an independent analysis of the performance metrics for her firm.

Example 16 (Intrafirm Pressure):

Jill Stein is head of performance measurement for her firm. During the last quarter, many members of the organization's research department were removed because of the poor quality of their recommendations. The subpar research caused one larger account holder to experience significant underperformance, which resulted in the client withdrawing his money after the end of the quarter. The head of sales requests that Stein remove this account from the firm's performance composite because the performance decline can be attributed to the departed research team and not the client's adviser.

> *Comment*: Pressure from other internal departments can create situations that cause a member or candidate to violate the Code and Standards. Stein must maintain her independence and objectivity and refuse to exclude specific accounts from the firm's performance composites to which they belong. As long as the client invested under a strategy similar to that of the defined composite, it cannot be excluded because of the poor stock selections that led to the underperformance and asset withdrawal.

STANDARD I(C) MISREPRESENTATION

7

- ☐ demonstrate a thorough knowledge of the CFA Institute Code of Ethics and Standards of Professional Conduct by interpreting the Code and Standards in various situations involving issues of professional integrity
- ☐ recommend practices and procedures designed to prevent violations of the Code and Standards

> Members and Candidates must not knowingly make any misrepresentations relating to investment analysis, recommendations, actions, or other professional activities.

Guidance

Highlights:

- *Impact on Investment Practice*
- *Performance Reporting*
- *Social Media*
- *Omissions*
- *Plagiarism*
- *Work Completed for Employer*

Trust is the foundation of the investment profession. Investors must be able to rely on the statements and information provided to them by those with whom the investors have trusted their financial well-being. Investment professionals who make false or misleading statements not only harm investors but also reduce the level of investor confidence in the investment profession and threaten the integrity of capital markets as a whole.

A misrepresentation is any untrue statement or omission of a fact or any statement that is otherwise false or misleading. A member or candidate must not knowingly omit or misrepresent information or give a false impression of a firm, organization, or security in the member's or candidate's oral representations, advertising (whether in the press or through brochures), electronic communications, or written materials (whether publicly disseminated or not). In this context, "knowingly" means that the member or candidate either knows or should have known that the misrepresentation was being made or that omitted information could alter the investment decision-making process.

Written materials include, but are not limited to, research reports, underwriting documents, company financial reports, market letters, newspaper columns, and books. Electronic communications include, but are not limited to, internet communications, webpages, mobile applications, and e-mails. Members and candidates who use webpages should regularly monitor materials posted on these sites to ensure that they contain current information. Members and candidates should also ensure that all reasonable precautions have been taken to protect the site's integrity and security and that the site does not misrepresent any information and does provide full disclosure.

Standard I(C) prohibits members and candidates from guaranteeing clients any specific return on volatile investments. Most investments contain some element of risk that makes their return inherently unpredictable. For such investments, guaranteeing either a particular rate of return or preservation of investment capital (e.g., "I can guarantee that you will earn 8% on equities this year" or "I can guarantee that you will not lose money on this investment") is misleading to investors. Standard I(C) does not prohibit members and candidates from providing clients with information on investment products that have guarantees built into the structure of the products themselves or for which an institution has agreed to cover any losses.

Impact on Investment Practice

Members and candidates must not misrepresent any aspect of their practice, including (but not limited to) their qualifications or credentials, the qualifications or services provided by their firm, their performance record and the record of their firm, and the characteristics of an investment. Any misrepresentation made by a member or candidate relating to the member's or candidate's professional activities is a breach of this standard.

Members and candidates should exercise care and diligence when incorporating third-party information. Misrepresentations resulting from the use of the credit ratings, research, testimonials, or marketing materials of outside parties become the responsibility of the investment professional when it affects that professional's business practices.

Investing through outside managers continues to expand as an acceptable method of investing in areas outside a firm's core competencies. Members and candidates must disclose their intended use of external managers and must not represent those managers' investment practices as their own. Although the level of involvement of outside managers may change over time, appropriate disclosures by members and candidates are important in avoiding misrepresentations, especially if the primary activity is to invest directly with a single external manager. Standard V(B)–Communication with Clients and Prospective Clients discusses in further detail communicating the firm's investment practices.

Performance Reporting

The performance benchmark selection process is another area where misrepresentations may occur. Members and candidates may misrepresent the success of their performance record through presenting benchmarks that are not comparable to their strategies. Further, clients can be misled if the benchmark's results are not reported on a basis comparable to that of the fund's or client's results. Best practice is selecting the most appropriate available benchmark from a universe of available options. The transparent presentation of appropriate performance benchmarks is an important aspect in providing clients with information that is useful in making investment decisions.

However, Standard I(C) does not require that a benchmark always be provided in order to comply. Some investment strategies may not lend themselves to displaying an appropriate benchmark because of the complexity or diversity of the investments included. Furthermore, some investment strategies may use reference indexes that do not reflect the opportunity set of the invested assets—for example, a hedge fund comparing its performance with a "cash plus" basis. When such a benchmark is used, members and candidates should make reasonable efforts to ensure that they disclose the reasons behind the use of this reference index to avoid misrepresentations of their performance. Members and candidates should discuss with clients on a continuous basis the appropriate benchmark to be used for performance evaluations and related fee calculations.

Reporting misrepresentations may also occur when valuations for illiquid or non-traded securities are available from more than one source. When different options are available, members and candidates may be tempted to switch providers to obtain higher security valuations. The process of shopping for values may misrepresent a security's worth, lead to misinformed decisions to sell or hold an investment, and result in overcharging clients advisory fees.

Members and candidates should take reasonable steps to provide accurate and reliable security pricing information to clients on a consistent basis. Changing pricing providers should not be based solely on the justification that the new provider reports a higher current value of a security. Consistency in the reported information will improve the perception of the valuation process for illiquid securities. Clients will likely have additional confidence that they were able to make an informed decision about continuing to hold these securities in their portfolios.

Social Media

The advancement of online discussion forums and communication platforms, commonly referred to as "social media," is placing additional responsibilities on members and candidates. When communicating through social media channels, members and candidates should provide only the same information they are allowed to distribute to clients and potential clients through other traditional forms of communication. The online or interactive aspects of social media do not remove the need to be open and honest about the information being distributed.

Along with understanding and following existing and newly developing rules and regulations regarding the allowed use of social media, members and candidates should also ensure that all communications in this format adhere to the requirements of the Code and Standards. The perceived anonymity granted through these platforms may entice individuals to misrepresent their qualifications or abilities or those of their employer. Actions undertaken through social media that knowingly misrepresent investment recommendations or professional activities are considered a violation of Standard I(C).

Omissions

The omission of a fact or outcome can be misleading, especially given the growing use of models and technical analysis processes. Many members and candidates rely on such models and processes to scan for new investment opportunities, to develop investment vehicles, and to produce investment recommendations and ratings. When inputs are knowingly omitted, the resulting outcomes may provide misleading information to those who rely on it for making investment decisions. Additionally, the outcomes from models shall not be presented as fact because they represent the expected results based on the inputs and analysis process incorporated.

Omissions in the performance measurement and attribution process can also misrepresent a manager's performance and skill. Members and candidates should encourage their firms to develop strict policies for composite development to prevent cherry picking—situations in which selected accounts are presented as representative of the firm's abilities. The omission of any accounts appropriate for the defined composite may misrepresent to clients the success of the manager's implementation of its strategy.

Plagiarism

Standard I(C) also prohibits plagiarism in the preparation of material for distribution to employers, associates, clients, prospects, or the general public. Plagiarism is defined as copying or using in substantially the same form materials prepared by others without acknowledging the source of the material or identifying the author and publisher of such material. Members and candidates must not copy (or represent as their own) original ideas or material without permission and must acknowledge and identify the source of ideas or material that is not their own.

The investment profession uses a myriad of financial, economic, and statistical data in the investment decision-making process. Through various publications and presentations, the investment professional is constantly exposed to the work of others and to the temptation to use that work without proper acknowledgment.

Misrepresentation through plagiarism in investment management can take various forms. The simplest and most flagrant example is to take a research report or study done by another firm or person, change the names, and release the material as one's own original analysis. This action is a clear violation of Standard I(C). Other practices include (1) using excerpts from articles or reports prepared by others either verbatim or with only slight changes in wording without acknowledgment, (2) citing specific quotations as attributable to "leading analysts" and "investment experts" without naming the specific references, (3) presenting statistical estimates of forecasts prepared by others and identifying the sources but without including the qualifying statements or caveats that may have been used, (4) using charts and graphs without stating their sources, and (5) copying proprietary computerized spreadsheets or algorithms without seeking the cooperation or authorization of their creators.

In the case of distributing third-party, outsourced research, members and candidates may use and distribute such reports as long as they do not represent themselves as the report's authors. Indeed, the member or candidate may add value for the client by sifting through research and repackaging it for clients. In such cases, clients should be fully informed that they are paying for the ability of the member or candidate to find the best research from a wide variety of sources. Members and candidates must not misrepresent their abilities, the extent of their expertise, or the extent of their work in a way that would mislead their clients or prospective clients. Members and candidates should disclose whether the research being presented to clients comes from another source—from either within or outside the member's or candidate's firm. This allows clients to understand who has the expertise behind the report or whether the work is being done by the analyst, other members of the firm, or an outside party.

Standard I(C) also applies to plagiarism in oral communications, such as through group meetings; visits with associates, clients, and customers; use of audio/video media (which is rapidly increasing); and telecommunications, including electronic data transfer and the outright copying of electronic media.

One of the most egregious practices in violation of this standard is the preparation of research reports based on multiple sources of information without acknowledging the sources. Examples of information from such sources include ideas, statistical compilations, and forecasts combined to give the appearance of original work. Although there is no monopoly on ideas, members and candidates must give credit where it is clearly due. Analysts should not use undocumented forecasts, earnings projections, asset values, and so on. Sources must be revealed to bring the responsibility directly back to the author of the report or the firm involved.

Work Completed for Employer

The preceding paragraphs address actions that would constitute a violation of Standard I(C). In some situations, however, members or candidates may use research conducted or models developed by others within the same firm without committing a violation. The most common example relates to the situation in which one (or more) of the original analysts is no longer with the firm. Research and models developed while employed by a firm are the property of the firm. The firm retains the right to continue using the work completed after a member or candidate has left the organization. The firm may issue future reports without providing attribution to the prior analysts. A member or candidate cannot, however, reissue a previously released report solely under his or her name.

STANDARD I(C): RECOMMENDED PROCEDURES

8

Factual Presentations

Members and candidates can prevent unintentional misrepresentations of their qualifications or the services they or their firms provide if each member and candidate understands the limit of the firm's or individual's capabilities and the need to be accurate and complete in presentations. Firms can provide guidance for employees who make written or oral presentations to clients or potential clients by providing a written list of the firm's available services and a description of the firm's qualifications. This list should suggest ways of describing the firm's services, qualifications, and compensation that are both accurate and suitable for client or customer presentations. Firms can also help prevent misrepresentation by specifically designating which employees are authorized to speak on behalf of the firm. Regardless of whether the firm provides guidance, members and candidates should make certain that they understand the services the firm can perform and its qualifications.

Qualification Summary

In addition, to ensure accurate presentations to clients, each member and candidate should prepare a summary of his or her own qualifications and experience and a list of the services the member or candidate is capable of performing. Firms can assist member and candidate compliance by periodically reviewing employee correspondence and documents that contain representations of individual or firm qualifications.

Verify Outside Information

When providing information to clients from a third party, members and candidates share a responsibility for the accuracy of the marketing and distribution materials that pertain to the third party's capabilities, services, and products. Misrepresentation by third parties can damage the member's or candidate's reputation, the reputation of the firm, and the integrity of the capital markets. Members and candidates should encourage their employers to develop procedures for verifying information of third-party firms.

Maintain Webpages

Members and candidates who publish a webpage should regularly monitor materials posted on the site to ensure that the site contains current information. Members and candidates should also ensure that all reasonable precautions have been taken to protect the site's integrity, confidentiality, and security and that the site does not misrepresent any information and provides full disclosure.

Plagiarism Policy

To avoid plagiarism in preparing research reports or conclusions of analysis, members and candidates should take the following steps:

- *Maintain copies*: Keep copies of all research reports, articles containing research ideas, material with new statistical methodologies, and other materials that were relied on in preparing the research report.
- *Attribute quotations*: Attribute to their sources any direct quotations, including projections, tables, statistics, model/product ideas, and new methodologies prepared by persons other than recognized financial and statistical reporting services or similar sources.
- *Attribute summaries*: Attribute to their sources any paraphrases or summaries of material prepared by others. For example, to support his analysis of Brown Company's competitive position, the author of a research report on Brown might summarize another analyst's report on Brown's chief competitor, but the author of the Brown report must acknowledge in his own report the reliance on the other analyst's report.

STANDARD I(C): APPLICATION OF THE STANDARD

9

Example 1 (Disclosure of Issuer-Paid Research):

Anthony McGuire is an issuer-paid analyst hired by publicly traded companies to electronically promote their stocks. McGuire creates a website that promotes his research efforts as a seemingly independent analyst. McGuire posts a profile and a strong buy recommendation for each company on the website indicating that the stock is expected to increase in value. He does not disclose the contractual relationships with the companies he covers on his website, in the research reports he issues, or in the statements he makes about the companies in internet chat rooms.

> *Comment*: McGuire has violated Standard I(C) because the website is misleading to potential investors. Even if the recommendations are valid and supported with thorough research, his omissions regarding the true relationship between himself and the companies he covers constitute a misrepresentation. McGuire has also violated Standard VI(A)–Disclosure of Conflicts by not disclosing the existence of an arrangement with the companies through which he receives compensation in exchange for his services.

Example 2 (Correction of Unintentional Errors):

Hijan Yao is responsible for the creation and distribution of the marketing materials for his firm, which claims compliance with the GIPS standards. Yao creates and distributes a presentation of performance by the firm's Asian equity composite that states the composite has ¥350 billion in assets. In fact, the composite has only ¥35 billion in assets, and the higher figure on the presentation is a result of a typographical error. Nevertheless, the erroneous material is distributed to a number of clients before Yao catches the mistake.

> *Comment*: Once the error is discovered, Yao must take steps to cease distribution of the incorrect material and correct the error by informing those who have received the erroneous information. Because Yao did not knowingly make the misrepresentation, however, he did not violate Standard I(C). Because his firm claims compliance with the GIPS standards, it must also comply with the GIPS Guidance Statement on Error Correction in relation to the error.

Example 3 (Noncorrection of Known Errors):

Syed Muhammad is the president of an investment management firm. The promotional material for the firm, created by the firm's marketing department, incorrectly claims that Muhammad has an advanced degree in finance from a prestigious business school in addition to the CFA designation. Although Muhammad attended the school for a short period of time, he did not receive a degree. Over the years, Muhammad and others in the firm have distributed this material to numerous prospective clients and consultants.

Comment: Even though Muhammad may not have been directly responsible for the misrepresentation of his credentials in the firm's promotional material, he used this material numerous times over an extended period and should have known of the misrepresentation. Thus, Muhammad has violated Standard I(C).

Example 4 (Plagiarism):

Cindy Grant, a research analyst for a Canadian brokerage firm, has specialized in the Canadian mining industry for the past 10 years. She recently read an extensive research report on Jefferson Mining, Ltd., by Jeremy Barton, another analyst. Barton provided extensive statistics on the mineral reserves, production capacity, selling rates, and marketing factors affecting Jefferson's operations. He also noted that initial drilling results on a new ore body, which had not been made public, might show the existence of mineral zones that could increase the life of Jefferson's main mines, but Barton cited no specific data as to the initial drilling results. Grant called an officer of Jefferson, who gave her the initial drilling results over the telephone. The data indicated that the expected life of the main mines would be tripled. Grant added these statistics to Barton's report and circulated it within her firm as her own report.

Comment: Grant plagiarized Barton's report by reproducing large parts of it in her own report without acknowledgment.

Example 5 (Misrepresentation of Information):

When Ricki Marks sells mortgage-backed derivatives called "interest-only strips" (IOs) to public pension plan clients, she describes them as "guaranteed by the US government." Purchasers of the IOs are entitled only to the interest stream generated by the mortgages, however, not the notional principal itself. One particular municipality's investment policies and local law require that securities purchased by its public pension plans be guaranteed by the US government. Although the underlying mortgages are guaranteed, neither the investor's investment nor the interest stream on the IOs is guaranteed. When interest rates decline, causing an increase in prepayment of mortgages, interest payments to the IOs' investors decline, and these investors lose a portion of their investment.

Comment: Marks violated Standard I(C) by misrepresenting the terms and character of the investment.

Example 6 (Potential Information Misrepresentation):

Khalouck Abdrabbo manages the investments of several high-net-worth individuals in the United States who are approaching retirement. Abdrabbo advises these individuals that a portion of their investments be moved from equity to bank-sponsored certificates of deposit and money market accounts so that the principal will be "guaranteed" up to a certain amount. The interest is not guaranteed.

Comment: Although there is risk that the institution offering the certificates of deposits and money market accounts could go bankrupt, in the United States, these accounts are insured by the US government through the Federal Deposit Insurance Corporation. Therefore, using the term "guaranteed" in this context is not inappropriate as long as the amount is within the government-insured limit. Abdrabbo should explain these facts to the clients.

Example 7 (Plagiarism):

Steve Swanson is a senior analyst in the investment research department of Ballard and Company. Apex Corporation has asked Ballard to assist in acquiring the majority ownership of stock in the Campbell Company, a financial consulting firm, and to prepare a report recommending that stockholders of Campbell agree to the acquisition. Another investment firm, Davis and Company, had already prepared a report for Apex analyzing both Apex and Campbell and recommending an exchange ratio. Apex has given the Davis report to Ballard officers, who have passed it on to Swanson. Swanson reviews the Davis report and other available material on Apex and Campbell. From his analysis, he concludes that the common stocks of Campbell and Apex represent good value at their current prices; he believes, however, that the Davis report does not consider all the factors a Campbell stockholder would need to know to make a decision. Swanson reports his conclusions to the partner in charge, who tells him to "use the Davis report, change a few words, sign your name, and get it out."

> *Comment*: If Swanson does as requested, he will violate Standard I(C). He could refer to those portions of the Davis report that he agrees with if he identifies Davis as the source; he could then add his own analysis and conclusions to the report before signing and distributing it.

Example 8 (Plagiarism):

Claude Browning, a quantitative analyst for Double Alpha, Inc., returns from a seminar in great excitement. At that seminar, Jack Jorrely, a well-known quantitative analyst at a national brokerage firm, discussed one of his new models in great detail, and Browning is intrigued by the new concepts. He proceeds to test the model, making some minor mechanical changes but retaining the concepts, until he produces some very positive results. Browning quickly announces to his supervisors at Double Alpha that he has discovered a new model and that clients and prospective clients should be informed of this positive finding as ongoing proof of Double Alpha's continuing innovation and ability to add value.

> *Comment*: Although Browning tested Jorrely's model on his own and even slightly modified it, he must still acknowledge the original source of the idea. Browning can certainly take credit for the final, practical results; he can also support his conclusions with his own test. The credit for the innovative thinking, however, must be awarded to Jorrely.

Example 9 (Plagiarism):

Fernando Zubia would like to include in his firm's marketing materials some "plain-language" descriptions of various concepts, such as the price-to-earnings (P/E) multiple and why standard deviation is used as a measure of risk. The descriptions come from other sources, but Zubia wishes to use them without reference to the original authors. Would this use of material be a violation of Standard I(C)?

> *Comment*: Copying verbatim any material without acknowledgement, including plain-language descriptions of the P/E multiple and standard deviation, violates Standard I(C). Even though these concepts are general, best practice would be for Zubia to describe them in his own words or cite the sources from which the descriptions are quoted. Members and candidates would be violating Standard I(C) if they either were responsible for creating marketing materials without attribution or knowingly use plagiarized materials.

Example 10 (Plagiarism):

Through a mainstream media outlet, Erika Schneider learns about a study that she would like to cite in her research. Should she cite both the mainstream intermediary source as well as the author of the study itself when using that information?

> *Comment*: In all instances, a member or candidate must cite the actual source of the information. Best practice for Schneider would be to obtain the information directly from the author and review it before citing it in a report. In that case, Schneider would not need to report how she found out about the information. For example, suppose Schneider read in the *Financial Times* about a study issued by CFA Institute; best practice for Schneider would be to obtain a copy of the study from CFA Institute, review it, and then cite it in her report. If she does not use any interpretation of the report from the *Financial Times* and the newspaper does not add value to the report itself, the newspaper is merely a conduit of the original information and does not need to be cited. If she does not obtain the report and review the information, Schneider runs the risk of relying on second-hand information that may misstate facts. If, for example, the *Financial Times* erroneously reported some information from the original CFA Institute study and Schneider copied that erroneous information without acknowledging CFA Institute, she could be the object of complaints. Best practice would be either to obtain the complete study from its original author and cite only that author or to use the information provided by the intermediary and cite both sources.

Example 11 (Misrepresentation of Information):

Paul Ostrowski runs a two-person investment management firm. Ostrowski's firm subscribes to a service from a large investment research firm that provides research reports that can be repackaged by smaller firms for those firms' clients. Ostrowski's firm distributes these reports to clients as its own work.

> *Comment*: Ostrowski can rely on third-party research that has a reasonable and adequate basis, but he cannot imply that he is the author of such research. If he does, Ostrowski is misrepresenting the extent of his work in a way that misleads the firm's clients or prospective clients.

Example 12 (Misrepresentation of Information):

Tom Stafford is part of a team within Appleton Investment Management responsible for managing a pool of assets for Open Air Bank, which distributes structured securities to offshore clients. He becomes aware that Open Air is promoting the structured securities as a much less risky investment than the investment management policy followed by him and the team to manage the original pool of assets. Also, Open Air has procured an independent rating for the pool that significantly overstates the quality of the investments. Stafford communicates his concerns to his supervisor, who responds that Open Air owns the product and is responsible for all marketing and distribution. Stafford's supervisor goes on to say that the product is outside of the US regulatory regime that Appleton follows and that all risks of the product are disclosed at the bottom of page 184 of the prospectus.

> *Comment*: As a member of the investment team, Stafford is qualified to recognize the degree of accuracy of the materials that characterize the portfolio, and he is correct to be worried about Appleton's responsibility

for a misrepresentation of the risks. Thus, he should continue to pursue the issue of Open Air's inaccurate promotion of the portfolio according to the firm's policies and procedures.

The Code and Standards stress protecting the reputation of the firm and the sustainability and integrity of the capital markets. Misrepresenting the quality and risks associated with the investment pool may lead to negative consequences for others well beyond the direct investors.

Example 13 (Avoiding a Misrepresentation):

Trina Smith is a fixed-income portfolio manager at a pension fund. She has observed that the market for highly structured mortgages is the focus of salespeople she meets and that these products represent a significant number of trading opportunities. In discussions about this topic with her team, Smith learns that calculating yields on changing cash flows within the deal structure requires very specialized vendor software. After more research, they find out that each deal is unique and that deals can have more than a dozen layers and changing cash flow priorities. Smith comes to the conclusion that, because of the complexity of these securities, the team cannot effectively distinguish between potentially good and bad investment options. To avoid misrepresenting their understanding, the team decides that the highly structured mortgage segment of the securitized market should not become part of the core of the fund's portfolio; they will allow some of the less complex securities to be part of the core.

Comment: Smith is in compliance with Standard I(C) by not investing in securities that she and her team cannot effectively understand. Because she is not able to describe the risk and return profile of the securities to the pension fund beneficiaries and trustees, she appropriately limits the fund's exposure to this sector.

Example 14 (Misrepresenting Composite Construction):

Robert Palmer is head of performance for a fund manager. When asked to provide performance numbers to fund rating agencies, he avoids mentioning that the fund manager is quite liberal in composite construction. The reason accounts are included/excluded is not fully explained. The performance values reported to the rating agencies for the composites, although accurate for the accounts shown each period, may not present a true representation of the fund manager's ability.

Comment: "Cherry picking" accounts to include in either published reports or information provided to rating agencies conflicts with Standard I(C). Moving accounts into or out of a composite to influence the overall performance results materially misrepresents the reported values over time. Palmer should work with his firm to strengthen its reporting practices concerning composite construction to avoid misrepresenting the firm's track record or the quality of the information being provided.

Example 15 (Presenting Out-of-Date Information):

David Finch is a sales director at a commercial bank, where he directs the bank's client advisers in the sale of third-party mutual funds. Each quarter, he holds a division-wide training session where he provides fact sheets on investment funds the bank is allowed to offer to clients. These fact sheets, which can be redistributed to potential clients, are created by the fund firms and contain information about the funds, including investment strategy and target distribution rates.

Finch knows that some of the fact sheets are out of date; for example, one long-only fund approved the use of significant leverage last quarter as a method to enhance returns. He continues to provide the sheets to the sales team without updates because the bank has no control over the marketing material released by the mutual fund firms.

> *Comment*: Finch is violating Standard I(C) by providing information that misrepresents aspects of the funds. By not providing the sales team and, ultimately, the clients with the updated information, he is misrepresenting the potential risks associated with the funds with outdated fact sheets. Finch can instruct the sales team to clarify the deficiencies in the fact sheets with clients and ensure they have the most recent fund prospectus document before accepting orders for investing in any fund.

Example 16 (Overemphasis of Firm Results):

Bob Anderson is chief compliance officer for Optima Asset Management Company, a firm currently offering eight funds to clients. Seven of the eight had 10-year returns below the median for their respective sectors. Anderson approves a recent advertisement, which includes this statement: "Optima Asset Management is achieving excellent returns for its investors. The Optima Emerging Markets Equity fund, for example, has 10-year returns that exceed the sector median by more than 10%."

> *Comment*: From the information provided it is difficult to determine whether a violation has occurred as long as the sector outperformance is correct. Anderson may be attempting to mislead potential clients by citing the performance of the sole fund that achieved such results. Past performance is often used to demonstrate a firm's skill and abilities in comparison to funds in the same sectors.
>
> However, if all the funds outperformed their respective benchmarks, then Anderson's assertion that the company "is achieving excellent returns" may be factual. Funds may exhibit positive returns for investors, exceed benchmarks, and yet have returns below the median in their sectors.
>
> Members and candidates need to ensure that their marketing efforts do not include statements that misrepresent their skills and abilities to remain compliant with Standard I(C). Unless the returns of a single fund reflect the performance of a firm as a whole, the use of a singular fund for performance comparisons should be avoided.

10 STANDARD I(D) MISCONDUCT

- ☐ demonstrate a thorough knowledge of the CFA Institute Code of Ethics and Standards of Professional Conduct by interpreting the Code and Standards in various situations involving issues of professional integrity
- ☐ recommend practices and procedures designed to prevent violations of the Code and Standards

Members and Candidates must not engage in any professional conduct involving dishonesty, fraud, or deceit or commit any act that reflects adversely on their professional reputation, integrity, or competence.

Guidance

Whereas Standard I(A) addresses the obligation of members and candidates to comply with applicable law that governs their professional activities, Standard I(D) addresses *all* conduct that reflects poorly on the professional integrity, good reputation, or competence of members and candidates. Any act that involves lying, cheating, stealing, or other dishonest conduct is a violation of this standard if the offense reflects adversely on a member's or candidate's professional activities. Although CFA Institute discourages any sort of unethical behavior by members and candidates, the Code and Standards are primarily aimed at conduct and actions related to a member's or candidate's professional life.

Conduct that damages trustworthiness or competence may include behavior that, although not illegal, nevertheless negatively affects a member's or candidate's ability to perform his or her responsibilities. For example, abusing alcohol during business hours might constitute a violation of this standard because it could have a detrimental effect on the member's or candidate's ability to fulfill his or her professional responsibilities. Personal bankruptcy may not reflect on the integrity or trustworthiness of the person declaring bankruptcy, but if the circumstances of the bankruptcy involve fraudulent or deceitful business conduct, the bankruptcy may be a violation of this standard.

In some cases, the absence of appropriate conduct or the lack of sufficient effort may be a violation of Standard I(D). The integrity of the investment profession is built on trust. A member or candidate—whether an investment banker, rating or research analyst, or portfolio manager—is expected to conduct the necessary due diligence to properly understand the nature and risks of an investment before making an investment recommendation. By not taking these steps and, instead, relying on someone else in the process to perform them, members or candidates may violate the trust their clients have placed in them. This loss of trust may have a significant impact on the reputation of the member or candidate and the operations of the financial market as a whole.

Individuals may attempt to abuse the CFA Institute Professional Conduct Program by actively seeking CFA Institute enforcement of the Code and Standards, and Standard I(D) in particular, as a method of settling personal, political, or other disputes unrelated to professional ethics. CFA Institute is aware of this issue, and appropriate disciplinary policies, procedures, and enforcement mechanisms are in place to address misuse of the Code and Standards and the Professional Conduct Program in this way.

STANDARD I(D): RECOMMENDED PROCEDURES

11

In addition to ensuring that their own behavior is consistent with Standard I(D), to prevent general misconduct, members and candidates should encourage their firms to adopt the following policies and procedures to support the principles of Standard I(D):

- *Code of ethics*: Develop and/or adopt a code of ethics to which every employee must subscribe, and make clear that any personal behavior that reflects poorly on the individual involved, the institution as a whole, or the investment industry will not be tolerated.

- *List of violations*: Disseminate to all employees a list of potential violations and associated disciplinary sanctions, up to and including dismissal from the firm.
- *Employee references*: Check references of potential employees to ensure that they are of good character and not ineligible to work in the investment industry because of past infractions of the law.

12 STANDARD I(D): APPLICATION OF THE STANDARD

Example 1 (Professionalism and Competence):

Simon Sasserman is a trust investment officer at a bank in a small affluent town. He enjoys lunching every day with friends at the country club, where his clients have observed him having numerous drinks. Back at work after lunch, he clearly is intoxicated while making investment decisions. His colleagues make a point of handling any business with Sasserman in the morning because they distrust his judgment after lunch.

> *Comment*: Sasserman's excessive drinking at lunch and subsequent intoxication at work constitute a violation of Standard I(D) because this conduct has raised questions about his professionalism and competence. His behavior reflects poorly on him, his employer, and the investment industry.

Example 2 (Fraud and Deceit):

Howard Hoffman, a security analyst at ATZ Brothers, Inc., a large brokerage house, submits reimbursement forms over a two-year period to ATZ's self-funded health insurance program for more than two dozen bills, most of which have been altered to increase the amount due. An investigation by the firm's director of employee benefits uncovers the inappropriate conduct. ATZ subsequently terminates Hoffman's employment and notifies CFA Institute.

> *Comment*: Hoffman violated Standard I(D) because he engaged in intentional conduct involving fraud and deceit in the workplace that adversely reflected on his integrity.

Example 3 (Fraud and Deceit):

Jody Brink, an analyst covering the automotive industry, volunteers much of her spare time to local charities. The board of one of the charitable institutions decides to buy five new vans to deliver hot lunches to low-income elderly people. Brink offers to donate her time to handle purchasing agreements. To pay a long-standing debt to a friend who operates an automobile dealership—and to compensate herself for her trouble—she agrees to a price 20% higher than normal and splits the surcharge with her friend. The director of the charity ultimately discovers the scheme and tells Brink that her services, donated or otherwise, are no longer required.

> *Comment*: Brink engaged in conduct involving dishonesty, fraud, and misrepresentation and has violated Standard I(D).

Example 4 (Personal Actions and Integrity):

Carmen Garcia manages a mutual fund dedicated to socially responsible investing. She is also an environmental activist. As the result of her participation in nonviolent protests, Garcia has been arrested on numerous occasions for trespassing on the property of a large petrochemical plant that is accused of damaging the environment.

> *Comment*: Generally, Standard I(D) is not meant to cover legal transgressions resulting from acts of civil disobedience in support of personal beliefs because such conduct does not reflect poorly on the member's or candidate's professional reputation, integrity, or competence.

Example 5 (Professional Misconduct):

Meredith Rasmussen works on a buy-side trading desk of an investment management firm and concentrates on in-house trades for a hedge fund subsidiary managed by a team at the investment management firm. The hedge fund has been very successful and is marketed globally by the firm. From her experience as the trader for much of the activity of the fund, Rasmussen has become quite knowledgeable about the hedge fund's strategy, tactics, and performance. When a distinct break in the market occurs and many of the securities involved in the hedge fund's strategy decline markedly in value, Rasmussen observes that the reported performance of the hedge fund does not reflect this decline. In her experience, the lack of effect is a very unlikely occurrence. She approaches the head of trading about her concern and is told that she should not ask any questions and that the fund is big and successful and is not her concern. She is fairly sure something is not right, so she contacts the compliance officer, who also tells her to stay away from the issue of the hedge fund's reporting.

> *Comment*: Rasmussen has clearly come across an error in policies, procedures, and compliance practices within the firm's operations. According to the firm's procedures for reporting potentially unethical activity, she should pursue the issue by gathering some proof of her reason for doubt. Should all internal communications within the firm not satisfy her concerns, Rasmussen should consider reporting the potential unethical activity to the appropriate regulator.
>
> See also Standard IV(A) for guidance on whistleblowing and Standard IV(C) for the duties of a supervisor.

STANDARD I(E) COMPETENCE 13

- ☐ demonstrate a thorough knowledge of the CFA Institute Code of Ethics and Standards of Professional Conduct by interpreting the Code and Standards in various situations involving issues of professional integrity
- ☐ recommend practices and procedures designed to prevent violations of the Code and Standards

> Members and Candidates must act with and maintain the competence necessary to fulfill their professional responsibilities.

Guidance

Standard I(E) requires members and candidates to act with and maintain appropriate knowledge, skills, and diligence when they carry out their professional responsibilities so that they provide a high standard of professional service for their clients and employers. The Code of Ethics requires members and candidates to "act with integrity, competence, and diligence" and to "maintain and improve their professional competence and strive to improve the competence of other investment professionals." Standard I(E) directly supports these requirements of the Code of Ethics.

Given the diverse range of professional services members and candidates engage in, the knowledge, skills, and abilities necessary to successfully fulfill their roles will vary according to the nature of their professional duties. Determining what conduct specifically constitutes competence will differ for each role and will depend on the facts and circumstances applicable to each member or candidate.

While the specific conduct that leads to competence may be different for each member or candidate, the underlying principle of competence is straightforward. To be competent in your role and meet your duties under this standard means having sufficient knowledge, skills, and abilities suitable for a professional to work in that specific role with success. These attributes govern the expertise, experience, and accomplishments that professionals need to perform at the highest level.

- Knowledge is the body of information applied directly to the performance of a function and how effectively it is applied.
- Skills are capabilities to perform a role-specific act or function to complete specific tasks and achieve professional goals.
- Abilities are capabilities and attitudes that support behaviors that result in observable outcomes.

While competence allows members and candidates the opportunity to undertake an activity successfully, lack of competence cannot necessarily be determined by an unsuccessful or a negative outcome. Many competent investment professionals have experienced failure or loss in their professional lives. For example, a competent investment manager may not always make profitable investment decisions. A competent securities analyst may not accurately predict the future prospects of an investment, despite diligent and thorough analysis.

Competence is not limited to an examination of the education level of a member or candidate. A highly educated investment consultant may not have the experience to undertake consulting activities in an unfamiliar area of practice. An accounting professional supremely competent in providing financial statement audits may not be competent in assessing compliance with performance presentation standards, such as the GIPS standards. Or an investment consultant hired to conduct a search for an investment manager focused on sustainable investing may not have the skills needed to competently evaluate managers with that focus.

Over time, the professional responsibilities of members and candidates may change or expand, requiring new or different knowledge, skills, and abilities. Members and candidates will develop and refine their skills and abilities as their careers progress. Standard I(E) imposes the duty to not simply achieve but also maintain competence, emphasizing the need for members to continuously maintain or improve the competence required of their professional position. Although Standard I(E) contemplates ongoing professional development to maintain proficiency and competence, this standard does not mandate participation in a particular continuing education program or professional development plan. Members and candidates can attain and maintain the competence needed to fulfill their professional responsibilities in a variety of ways.

STANDARD I(E): RECOMMENDED PROCEDURES

14

To achieve and maintain competence, members and candidates should consider the following activities:

- Regularly engaging in a professional development or continuing education program
- Studying for or earning professional certifications or designations
- Attending conferences, seminars, or webinars
- Regularly participating in training offered by their employer
- Diligently engaging in informal continuing education or self-study, such as through outside reading of subject matter articles, treatises, and publications
- Participating in expert groups or organizations
- Becoming proficient with any new skill or knowledge, as necessary, when their professional responsibilities change

STANDARD I(E): APPLICATION OF THE STANDARD

15

Example 1 (Maintaining Competence):

Michelle Lee runs a geopolitical consulting firm where she analyzes international political, social, and economic issues and developments to produce research reports for her clients, many of which are investment management firms. Lee has been closely monitoring news regarding a new multinational trade deal that has the potential to significantly boost commercial activity among countries in a certain region of the world. As soon as the trade deal was officially ratified and announced, she quickly downloaded a copy of the agreement and read it to understand its terms and impact. She also consulted with experts in the field to obtain their opinions on the impacts of the trade deal and confirm her understanding of its terms and implications.

> *Comment*: Lee satisfied the requirement of Standard I(E). Lee was able to write a knowledgeable and informative research report for her clients by keeping abreast of developments in her field through news reports, consulting with experts, and studying the trade deal itself to ensure that her knowledge was up to date.

Example 2 (Improving Competence):

Chris Choe is the director of research at a large sell-side firm. Several of Choe's clients have asked her to incorporate environmental, social, and governance (ESG) ratings into the research reports the firm produces. Until now, the firm's research reports have been based only on traditional quantitative metrics. Choe hires an experienced ESG analyst for her team, and she requires all research analysts, including herself, to attend ESG-focused seminars and obtain an ESG investment specialist certificate. In due time, Choe and her team begin to incorporate ESG considerations into their research reports.

Comment: Choe extended her competence in her field by educating herself on new considerations relevant to her industry and by hiring someone with ESG expertise to fill a knowledge and skills gap before she and her team incorporated ESG considerations into the firm's research reports. As such, Choe satisfied the requirement of Standard I(E).

Example 3 (Change in Role):

Gerhardt Glusker is a regulatory attorney for a hedge fund who sought to transition to a sales role after impressing senior management with his strong business acumen. There is a licensing requirement involving an examination that an individual must first pass before being qualified to serve in a sales function. Among other things, the examination covers technical rules and regulations designed to ensure fairness when dealing with clients and prospects. Glusker was not familiar with these rules and regulations because he was never asked to provide guidance on them as a regulatory attorney. Glusker did not learn the materials or study for the examination and instead relied on his industry knowledge to receive a passing score.

Comment: Glusker failed to satisfy the requirement of Standard I(E). He did receive a passing score on a licensing examination, but passing the examination, by itself, is not adequate to demonstrate competency. Glusker's failure to learn the applicable rules and regulations relating to fairness when dealing with clients and prospects means that he does not possess the required knowledge to serve in his new role, despite passing the licensing examination.

Example 4 (Supervisory Responsibility):

Linda Evans is one member of a five-person team of analysts at a boutique research firm providing independent research to buy-side firms. Evans primarily covers the energy and transportation sectors. Evans's boss leaves the firm to return to academia. Firm management promotes Evans to director of research and hires two junior analysts to replace her. Evans now has supervisory responsibility for four analysts and is responsible for all research produced by the firm. Prior to her promotion date, Evans spends a great deal of time and effort getting up to speed on the research projects of the firm that she was not involved in. Although she has never directly managed others in the past, Evans does not spend any time becoming familiar with effectively managing employees, leading teams, or compliance requirements relating to subordinates.

Comment: Evans's new position demands competence in other skills, abilities, and knowledge beyond those needed for her previous position. Evans must ensure she extends her competence to cover all responsibilities of her new role. She also must now obtain the skills and knowledge needed for fulfilling her supervisory responsibility of the other analysts. This could include attending conferences or taking professional development courses on management, earning compliance credentials, and internal training on supervisory responsibility.

Example 5 (Choosing Investments):

Kwame Mifune is a financial planner for over 150 retail investors. Based on the investment objectives, financial circumstances, and risk tolerance of 40 of his clients, he suggests they purchase life insurance products from Vouchsafe Insurance Company.

Mifune researched Vouchsafe and recommended it because it has a high credit rating, strong financials, and a decade-long history of providing affordable, safe insurance products. Within 18 months, as the result of previously unknown financial impropriety and fraud by the company's chief financial officer, Vouchsafe goes bankrupt and the insurance contracts for thousands of policyholders become worthless. Mifune's clients claim that he was incompetent in recommending the Vouchsafe policies.

> *Comment*: Assuming that Mifune's research of Vouchsafe was thorough and appropriate, his failure to uncover the fraudulent practices of the company he recommended, which had misled the investment industry as whole, does not, by itself, indicate that Mifune is an incompetent financial planner.

Example 6 (Understanding New Investment Products):

Alex Halsey is a portfolio manager for a number of high-net-worth individuals. Several of his clients are impressed by the significant gains in a short time frame that they believe can be achieved by investing in cryptocurrency. They urge Halsey to include cryptocurrency products as part of their portfolios. Although Halsey is generally aware of cryptocurrency and has read several articles about the cryptocurrency investment trend in reputable newspapers, Halsey is unfamiliar with the nature of the asset or the difference between the many cryptocurrency products. Not wanting to seem out of touch with current developments in the market, lose clients, or miss out on a hot market trend by delaying an investment decision until he completes research into the asset, Halsey purchases a cryptocurrency product that has been heavily promoted through social media and online advertising for several of his clients.

> *Comment*: Given his limited knowledge, Halsey is not competent to invest in cryptocurrency for his clients. By hastily investing in cryptocurrency products without understanding the nature of the investment or the suitability of the investment for his clients, Halsey has violated Standard I(E).

STANDARD II: INTEGRITY OF CAPITAL MARKETS

16

- ☐ demonstrate a thorough knowledge of the CFA Institute Code of Ethics and Standards of Professional Conduct by interpreting the Code and Standards in various situations involving issues of professional integrity
- ☐ recommend practices and procedures designed to prevent violations of the Code and Standards

Standard II(A) Material Nonpublic Information

> Members and Candidates who possess material nonpublic information that could affect the value of an investment must not act or cause others to act on the information.

Guidance

Highlights:

- *What Is "Material" Information?*
- *What Constitutes "Nonpublic" Information?*
- *Mosaic Theory*
- *Social Media*
- *Using Industry Experts*
- *Investment Research Reports*

Trading or inducing others to trade on material nonpublic information erodes confidence in capital markets, institutions, and investment professionals by supporting the idea that those with inside information and special access can take unfair advantage of the general investing public. Although trading on inside information may lead to short-term profits, in the long run, individuals and the profession as a whole suffer from such trading. These actions have caused and will continue to cause investors to avoid capital markets because the markets are perceived to be "rigged" in favor of the knowledgeable insider. When the investing public avoids capital markets, the markets and capital allocation become less efficient and less supportive of strong and vibrant economies. Standard II(A) promotes and maintains a high level of confidence in market integrity, which is one of the foundations of the investment profession.

The prohibition on using this information goes beyond the direct buying and selling of individual securities or bonds. Members and candidates must not use material nonpublic information to influence their investment actions related to derivatives (e.g., swaps or option contracts), mutual funds, or other alternative investments. *Any* trading based on material nonpublic information constitutes a violation of Standard II(A). The expansion of financial products and the increasing interconnectivity of financial markets globally have resulted in new potential opportunities for trading on material nonpublic information.

What Is "Material" Information?

Information is "material" if its disclosure would probably have an impact on the price of a security or if reasonable investors would want to know the information before making an investment decision. In other words, information is material if it would significantly alter the total mix of information currently available about a security in such a way that the price of the security would be affected.

The specificity of the information, the extent of its difference from public information, its nature, and its reliability are key factors in determining whether a particular piece of information fits the definition of material. For example, material information may include, but is not limited to, information on the following:

- earnings;
- mergers, acquisitions, tender offers, or joint ventures;
- changes in assets or asset quality;
- innovative products, processes, or discoveries (e.g., new product trials or research efforts);
- new licenses, patents, registered trademarks, or regulatory approval/rejection of a product;
- developments regarding customers or suppliers (e.g., the acquisition or loss of a contract);
- changes in management;

- change in auditor notification or the fact that the issuer may no longer rely on an auditor's report or qualified opinion;
- events regarding the issuer's securities (e.g., defaults on senior securities, calls of securities for redemption, repurchase plans, stock splits, changes in dividends, changes to the rights of security holders, and public or private sales of additional securities);
- bankruptcies;
- significant legal disputes;
- government reports of economic trends (employment, housing starts, currency information, etc.);
- orders for large trades before they are executed; and
- new or changing equity or debt ratings issued by a third party (e.g., sell-side recommendations and credit ratings).

In addition to the substance and specificity of the information, the source or relative reliability of the information also determines materiality. The less reliable a source, the less likely the information provided would be considered material. For example, factual information from a corporate insider regarding a significant new contract for a company is likely to be material, whereas an assumption based on speculation by a competitor about the same contract is likely to be less reliable and, therefore, not material. Additionally, information about trials of a new drug, product, or service under development from qualified personnel involved in the trials is likely to be material, whereas educated conjecture by subject experts not connected to the trials is unlikely to be material.

Also, the more ambiguous the effect of the information on price, the less material that information is considered. If it is unclear whether and to what extent the information will affect the price of a security, the information may not be considered material. The passage of time may also render information that was once important immaterial.

What Constitutes "Nonpublic" Information?

Information is "nonpublic" until it has been disseminated or is available to the marketplace in general (as opposed to a select group of investors). "Disseminated" can be defined as "made known." For example, a company report of profits that is posted on the internet and distributed widely through a press release or accompanied by a filing has been effectively disseminated to the marketplace. Members and candidates must have a reasonable expectation that people have received the information before it can be considered public. It is not necessary, however, to wait for the slowest method of delivery. Once the information is disseminated to the market, it is public information that is no longer covered by this standard.

Members and candidates must be particularly aware of information that is selectively disclosed by corporations to a small group of investors, analysts, or other market participants. Information that is made available to analysts remains nonpublic until it is made available to investors in general. Corporations that disclose information on a limited basis create the potential for insider-trading violations.

Issues of selective disclosure often arise when a corporate insider provides material information to analysts in a briefing or conference call before that information is released to the public. Analysts must be aware that a disclosure made to a room full of analysts does not necessarily make the disclosed information "public." Analysts should also be alert to the possibility that they are selectively receiving material nonpublic information when a company provides them with guidance or interpretation of such publicly available information as financial statements or regulatory filings.

A member or candidate may use insider information provided legitimately by the source company for the specific purpose of conducting due diligence according to the business agreement between the parties for such activities as mergers, loan underwriting, credit ratings, and offering engagements. In such instances, the investment professional would not be considered in violation of Standard II(A) by using the material information. However, the use of insider information provided by the source company for other purposes, especially to trade or entice others to trade the securities of the firm, conflicts with this standard.

Mosaic Theory

A financial analyst gathers and interprets large quantities of information from many sources. The analyst may use significant conclusions derived from the analysis of public and nonmaterial nonpublic information as the basis for investment recommendations and decisions even if those conclusions would have been material inside information had they been communicated directly to the analyst by a company. Under the "mosaic theory," financial analysts are free to act on this collection, or mosaic, of information without risking violation.

The practice of financial analysis depends on the free flow of information. For the fair and efficient operation of the capital markets, analysts and investors must have the greatest amount of information possible to facilitate making well-informed investment decisions about how and where to invest capital. Accurate, timely, and intelligible communication is essential if analysts and investors are to obtain the data needed to make informed decisions about how and where to invest capital. These disclosures must go beyond the information mandated by the reporting requirements of the securities laws and should include specific business information about items used to guide a company's future growth, such as new products, capital projects, and the competitive environment. Analysts seek and use such information to compare and contrast investment alternatives.

Much of the information used by analysts comes directly from companies. Analysts often receive such information through contacts with corporate insiders, especially investor-relations staff and financial officers. Information may be disseminated in the form of press releases, through oral presentations by company executives in analysts' meetings or conference calls, or during analysts' visits to company premises. In seeking to develop the most accurate and complete picture of a company, analysts should also reach beyond contacts with companies themselves and collect information from other sources, such as customers, contractors, suppliers, and the companies' competitors.

Analysts are in the business of formulating opinions and insights that are not obvious to the general investing public about the attractiveness of particular securities. In the course of their work, analysts actively seek out corporate information not generally known to the market for the express purpose of analyzing that information, forming an opinion on its significance, and informing their clients, who can be expected to trade on the basis of the recommendation. Analysts' initiatives to discover and analyze information and communicate their findings to their clients significantly enhance market efficiency, thus benefiting all investors (see *Dirks v. Securities and Exchange Commission*). Accordingly, violations of Standard II(A) will *not* result when a perceptive analyst reaches a conclusion about a corporate action or event through an analysis of public information and items of nonmaterial nonpublic information.

Investment professionals should note, however, that although analysts are free to use mosaic information in their research reports, they should save and document all their research [see Standard V(C) Record Retention]. Evidence of the analyst's knowledge of public and nonmaterial nonpublic information about a corporation strengthens the assertion that the analyst reached his or her conclusions solely through appropriate methods rather than through the use of material nonpublic information.

Social Media

The continuing advancement in technology allows members, candidates, and the industry at large to exchange information at rates not previously available. It is important for investment professionals to understand the implications of using information from the internet and social media platforms because all such information may not actually be considered public.

Some social media platforms require membership in specific groups in order to access the published content. Members and candidates participating in groups with membership limitations should verify that material information obtained from these sources can also be accessed from a source that would be considered available to the public (e.g., company filings, webpages, and press releases).

Members and candidates may use social media platforms to communicate with clients or investors without conflicting with this standard. As long as the information reaches all clients or is open to the investing public, the use of these platforms would be comparable with other traditional forms of communications, such as e-mails and press releases. Members and candidates, as required by Standard I(A), should also complete all appropriate regulatory filings related to information distributed through social media platforms.

Using Industry Experts

The increased demand for insights for understanding the complexities of some industries has led to an expansion of engagement with outside experts. As the level of engagement increased, new businesses formed to connect analysts and investors with individuals who have specialized knowledge of their industry (e.g., technology or pharmaceuticals). These networks offer investors the opportunity to reach beyond their usual business circles to speak with experts regarding economic conditions, industry trends, and technical issues relating to specific products and services.

Members and candidates may provide compensation to individuals for their insights without violating this standard. However, members and candidates are ultimately responsible for ensuring that they are not requesting or acting on confidential information received from external experts, which is in violation of security regulations and laws or duties to others. As the recent string of insider-trading cases displayed, some experts are willing to provide confidential and protected information for the right incentive.

Firms connecting experts with members or candidates often require both parties to sign agreements concerning the disclosure of material nonpublic information. Even with the protections from such compliance practices, if an expert provides material nonpublic information, members and candidates would be prohibited from taking investment actions on the associated firm until the information became publicly known to the market.

Investment Research Reports

When a particularly well-known or respected analyst issues a report or makes changes to his or her recommendation, that information alone may have an effect on the market and thus may be considered material. Theoretically, under Standard II(A), such a report would have to be made public at the time it was distributed to clients. The analyst is not a company insider, however, and does not have access to inside information. Presumably, the analyst created the report from information available to the public (mosaic theory) and by using his or her expertise to interpret the information. The analyst's hard work, paid for by the client, generated the conclusions.

Simply because the public in general would find the conclusions material does not require that the analyst make his or her work public. Investors who are not clients of the analyst can either do the work themselves or become clients of the analyst to gain access to the analyst's expertise.

17 STANDARD II(A): RECOMMENDED PROCEDURES

Achieve Public Dissemination

If a member or candidate determines that information is material, the member or candidate should make reasonable efforts to achieve public dissemination of the information. These efforts usually entail encouraging the issuing company to make the information public. If public dissemination is not possible, the member or candidate must communicate the information only to the designated supervisory and compliance personnel within the member's or candidate's firm and must not take investment action or alter current investment recommendations on the basis of the information. Moreover, members and candidates must not knowingly engage in any conduct that may induce company insiders to privately disclose material nonpublic information.

Adopt Compliance Procedures

Members and candidates should encourage their firms to adopt compliance procedures to prevent the misuse of material nonpublic information. Particularly important is improving compliance in such areas as the review of employee and proprietary trading, the review of investment recommendations, documentation of firm procedures, and the supervision of interdepartmental communications in multiservice firms. Compliance procedures should suit the particular characteristics of a firm, including its size and the nature of its business.

Members and candidates are encouraged to inform their supervisor and compliance personnel of suspected inappropriate use of material nonpublic information as the basis for security trading activities or recommendations being made within their firm.

Adopt Disclosure Procedures

Members and candidates should encourage their firms to develop and follow disclosure policies designed to ensure that information is disseminated to the marketplace in an equitable manner. For example, analysts from small firms should receive the same information and attention from a company as analysts from large firms receive. Similarly, companies should not provide certain information to buy-side analysts but not to sell-side analysts, or vice versa. Furthermore, a company should not discriminate among analysts in the provision of information or "blackball" particular analysts who have given negative reports on the company in the past.

Within investment and research firms, members and candidates should encourage the development of and compliance with procedures for distributing new and updated investment opinions to clients. Recommendations of this nature may represent material market-moving information that needs to be communicated to all clients fairly.

Issue Press Releases

Companies should consider issuing press releases prior to analyst meetings and conference calls and scripting those meetings and calls to decrease the chance that further information will be disclosed. If material nonpublic information is disclosed for the first time in an analyst meeting or call, the company should promptly issue a press release or otherwise make the information publicly available.

Firewall Elements

An information barrier commonly referred to as a "firewall" is the most widely used approach for preventing the communication of material nonpublic information within firms. It restricts the flow of confidential information to those who need to know the information to perform their jobs effectively. The minimum elements of such a system include, but are not limited to, the following:

- substantial control of relevant interdepartmental communications, preferably through a clearance area within the firm in either the compliance or legal department;
- review of employee trading through the maintenance of "watch," "restricted," and "rumor" lists;
- documentation of the procedures designed to limit the flow of information between departments and of the actions taken to enforce those procedures; and
- heightened review or restriction of proprietary trading while a firm is in possession of material nonpublic information.

Appropriate Interdepartmental Communications

Although documentation requirements must, for practical reasons, take into account the differences between the activities of small firms and those of large, multiservice firms, firms of all sizes and types benefit by improving the documentation of their internal enforcement of firewall procedures. Therefore, even at small firms, procedures concerning interdepartmental communication, the review of trading activity, and the investigation of possible violations should be compiled and formalized.

Physical Separation of Departments

As a practical matter, to the greatest extent possible, firms should consider the physical separation of departments and files to prevent the communication of sensitive information that should not be shared. For example, the investment banking and corporate finance areas of a brokerage firm should be separated from the sales and research departments, and a bank's commercial lending department should be segregated from its trust and research departments.

Prevention of Personnel Overlap

There should be no overlap of personnel between the investment banking and corporate finance areas of a brokerage firm and the sales and research departments or between a bank's commercial lending department and its trust and research departments. For a firewall to be effective in a multiservice firm, an employee should be on only one side of the firewall at any time. Inside knowledge may not be limited to information about a specific offering or the current financial condition of a company. Analysts may be exposed to much information about the company, including new product developments or future budget projections that clearly constitute inside knowledge and thus preclude the analyst from returning to his or her research function. For example, an analyst who follows a particular company may provide limited assistance to the investment bankers under carefully controlled circumstances when the firm's investment banking department is involved in a deal with the company. That analyst must then be treated as though he or she were an investment banker; the analyst must remain on the investment banking side of the wall until any information he or she learns is publicly disclosed. In short, the analyst cannot use any information learned in the course of the project for research purposes and cannot share that information with colleagues in the research department.

A Reporting System

A primary objective of an effective firewall procedure is to establish a reporting system in which authorized people review and approve communications between departments. If an employee behind a firewall believes that he or she needs to share confidential information with someone on the other side of the wall, the employee should consult a designated compliance officer to determine whether sharing the information is necessary and how much information should be shared. If the sharing is necessary, the compliance officer should coordinate the process of "looking over the wall" so that the necessary information will be shared and the integrity of the procedure will be maintained.

A single supervisor or compliance officer should have the specific authority and responsibility of deciding whether information is material and whether it is sufficiently public to be used as the basis for investment decisions. Ideally, the supervisor or compliance officer responsible for communicating information to a firm's research or brokerage area would not be a member of that area.

Personal Trading Limitations

Firms should consider restrictions or prohibitions on personal trading by employees and should carefully monitor both proprietary trading and personal trading by employees. Firms should require employees to make periodic reports (to the extent that such reporting is not already required by securities laws) of their own transactions and transactions made for the benefit of family members. Securities should be placed on a restricted list when a firm has or may have material nonpublic information. The broad distribution of a restricted list often triggers the sort of trading the list was developed to avoid. Therefore, a watch list shown to only the few people responsible for compliance should be used to monitor transactions in specified securities. The use of a watch list in combination with a restricted list is an increasingly common means of ensuring effective control of personal trading.

Record Maintenance

Multiservice firms should maintain written records of the communications between various departments. Firms should place a high priority on training and should consider instituting comprehensive training programs, particularly for employees in sensitive areas.

Proprietary Trading Procedures

Procedures concerning the restriction or review of a firm's proprietary trading while the firm possesses material nonpublic information will necessarily depend on the types of proprietary trading in which the firm may engage. A prohibition on all types of proprietary activity when a firm comes into possession of material nonpublic information is *not* appropriate. For example, when a firm acts as a market maker, a prohibition on proprietary trading may be counterproductive to the goals of maintaining the confidentiality of information and market liquidity. This concern is particularly important in the relationships between small, regional broker/dealers and small issuers. In many situations, a firm will take a small issuer public with the understanding that the firm will continue to be a market maker in the stock. In such instances, a withdrawal by the firm from market-making activities would be a clear tip to outsiders. Firms that continue market-making activity while in the possession of material nonpublic information should, however, instruct their market makers to remain passive with respect to the market—that is, to take only the contra side of unsolicited customer trades.

In risk-arbitrage trading, the case for a trading prohibition is more compelling than it is in the case of market making. The impetus for arbitrage trading is neither passive nor reactive, and the potential for illegal profits is greater than in market making. The most prudent course for firms is to suspend arbitrage activity when a security is placed on the watch list. Those firms that continue arbitrage activity face a high hurdle in proving the adequacy of their internal procedures for preventing trading on material nonpublic information and must demonstrate a stringent review and documentation of firm trades.

Communication to All Employees

Members and candidates should encourage their employers to circulate written compliance policies and guidelines to all employees. Policies and guidelines should be used in conjunction with training programs aimed at enabling employees to recognize material nonpublic information. Such information is not always clearly identifiable.

Employees must be given sufficient training to either make an informed decision or to realize they need to consult a supervisor or compliance officer before engaging in questionable transactions. Appropriate policies reinforce that using material nonpublic information is illegal in many countries. Such trading activities based on material nonpublic information undermine the integrity of the individual, the firm, and the capital markets.

STANDARD II(A): APPLICATION OF THE STANDARD

18

Example 1 (Acting on Nonpublic Information):

Frank Barnes, the president and controlling shareholder of the SmartTown clothing chain, decides to accept a tender offer and sell the family business at a price almost double the market price of its shares. He describes this decision to his sister (SmartTown's treasurer), who conveys it to her daughter (who owns no stock in the family company at present), who tells her husband, Staple. Staple, however, tells his stockbroker, Alex Halsey, who immediately buys SmartTown stock for himself.

> *Comment*: The information regarding the pending sale is both material and nonpublic. Staple has violated Standard II(A) by communicating the inside information to his broker. Halsey also has violated the standard by buying the shares on the basis of material nonpublic information.

Example 2 (Controlling Nonpublic Information):

Samuel Peter, an analyst with Scotland and Pierce Incorporated, is assisting his firm with a secondary offering for Bright Ideas Lamp Company. Peter participates, via telephone conference call, in a meeting with Scotland and Pierce investment banking employees and Bright Ideas' CEO. Peter is advised that the company's earnings projections for the next year have significantly dropped. Throughout the telephone conference call, several Scotland and Pierce salespeople and portfolio managers walk in and out of Peter's office, where the telephone call is taking place. As a result, they are aware of the drop in projected earnings for Bright Ideas. Before the conference call is concluded, the salespeople trade the stock of the company on behalf of the firm's clients and other firm personnel trade the stock in a firm proprietary account and in employees' personal accounts.

> *Comment*: Peter has violated Standard II(A) because he failed to prevent the transfer and misuse of material nonpublic information to others in his firm. Peter's firm should have adopted information barriers to prevent the communication of nonpublic information between departments of the firm. The salespeople and portfolio managers who traded on the information have also violated Standard II(A) by trading on inside information.

Example 3 (Selective Disclosure of Material Information):

Elizabeth Levenson is based in Hanoi and covers the Vietnamese market for her firm, which is based in Singapore. She is invited, together with the other 10 largest shareholders of a manufacturing company, to meet the finance director of that company. During the meeting, the finance director states that the company expects its workforce to strike next Friday, which will cripple productivity and distribution. Can Levenson use this information as a basis to change her rating on the company from "buy" to "sell"?

> *Comment*: Levenson must first determine whether the material information is public. According to Standard II(A), if the company has not made this information public (a small group forum does not qualify as a method of public dissemination), she cannot use the information.

Example 4 (Determining Materiality):

Leah Fechtman is trying to decide whether to hold or sell shares of an oil-and-gas exploration company that she owns in several of the funds she manages. Although the company has underperformed the index for some time already, the trends in the industry sector signal that companies of this type might become takeover targets. While she is considering her decision, her doctor, who casually follows the markets, mentions that she thinks that the company in question will soon be bought out by a large multinational conglomerate and that it would be a good idea to buy the stock right now. After talking to various investment professionals and checking their opinions on the company as well as checking industry trends, Fechtman decides the next day to accumulate more stock in the oil-and-gas exploration company.

> *Comment*: Although information on an expected takeover bid may be of the type that is generally material and nonpublic, in this case, the source of information is unreliable, so the information cannot be considered material. Therefore, Fechtman is not prohibited from trading the stock on the basis of this information.

Example 5 (Applying the Mosaic Theory):

Jagdish Teja is a buy-side analyst covering the furniture industry. Looking for an attractive company to recommend as a buy, he analyzes several furniture makers by studying their financial reports and visiting their operations. He also talks to some designers and retailers to find out which furniture styles are trendy and popular. Although none of the companies that he analyzes are a clear buy, he discovers that one of them, Swan Furniture Company (SFC), may be in financial trouble. SFC's extravagant new designs have been introduced at substantial cost. Even though these designs initially attracted attention, the public is now buying more conservative furniture from other makers. Based on this information and on a profit-and-loss analysis, Teja believes that SFC's next-quarter earnings will drop substantially. He issues a sell recommendation for SFC. Immediately after receiving that recommendation, investment managers start reducing the SFC stock in their portfolios.

> *Comment*: Information on quarterly earnings data is material and nonpublic. Teja arrived at his conclusion about the earnings drop on the basis of public information and pieces of nonmaterial nonpublic information (such as opinions of designers and retailers). Therefore, trading based on Teja's correct conclusion is not prohibited by Standard II(A).

Example 6 (Applying the Mosaic Theory):

Roger Clement is a senior financial analyst who specializes in the European automobile sector at Rivoli Capital. Because he has been repeatedly nominated by many leading industry magazines and newsletters as a "best analyst" for the automobile industry, he is widely regarded as an authority on the sector. After speaking with representatives of Turgot Chariots—a European auto manufacturer with sales primarily in South Korea—and after conducting interviews with salespeople, labor leaders, his firm's South Korean currency analysts, and banking officials, Clement analyzed Turgot Chariots and concluded that (1) its newly introduced model will probably not meet sales expectations, (2) its corporate restructuring strategy may well face serious opposition from unions, (3) the depreciation of the South Korean won should lead to pressure on margins for the industry in general and Turgot's market segment in particular, and (4) banks could take a tougher-than-expected stance in the upcoming round of credit renegotiations with the company. For these reasons, he changes his conclusion about the company from "market outperform" to "market underperform." Clement retains the support material used to reach his conclusion in case questions later arise.

> *Comment*: To reach a conclusion about the value of the company, Clement has pieced together a number of nonmaterial or public bits of information that affect Turgot Chariots. Therefore, under the mosaic theory, Clement has not violated Standard II(A) in drafting the report.

Example 7 (Analyst Recommendations as Material Nonpublic Information):

The next day, Clement is preparing to be interviewed on a global financial news television program where he will discuss his changed recommendation on Turgot Chariots for the first time in public. While preparing for the program, he mentions to the show's producers and Mary Zito, the journalist who will be interviewing him, the information he will be discussing. Just prior to going on the air, Zito sells her holdings in Turgot Chariots. She also phones her father with the information because she knows that he and other family members have investments in Turgot Chariots.

Comment: When Zito receives advance notice of Clement's change of opinion, she knows it will have a material impact on the stock price, even if she is not totally aware of Clement's underlying reasoning. She is not a client of Clement but obtains early access to the material nonpublic information prior to publication. Her trades are thus based on material nonpublic information and violate Standard II(A).

Zito further violates the Standard by relaying the information to her father. It would not matter if he or any other family member traded; the act of providing the information violates Standard II(A). The fact that the information is provided to a family member does not absolve someone of the prohibition of using or communicating material nonpublic information.

Example 8 (Acting on Nonpublic Information):

Ashton Kellogg is a retired investment professional who manages his own portfolio. He owns shares in National Savings, a large local bank. A close friend and golfing buddy, John Mayfield, is a senior executive at National. National has seen its stock price drop considerably, and the news and outlook are not good. In a conversation about the economy and the banking industry on the golf course, Mayfield relays the information that National will surprise the investment community in a few days when it announces excellent earnings for the quarter. Kellogg is pleasantly surprised by this information, and thinking that Mayfield, as a senior executive, knows the law and would not disclose inside information, he doubles his position in the bank. Subsequently, National announces that it had good operating earnings but had to set aside reserves for anticipated significant losses on its loan portfolio. The combined news causes the stock to go down 60%.

Comment: Even though Kellogg believes that Mayfield would not break the law by disclosing inside information and money was lost on the purchase, Kellogg should not have purchased additional shares of National. It is the member's or candidate's responsibility to make sure, before executing investment actions, that comments about earnings are not material nonpublic information. Kellogg has violated Standard II(A).

Example 9 (Mosaic Theory):

John Doll is a research analyst for a hedge fund that also sells its research to a select group of paying-client investment firms. Doll's focus is medical technology companies and products, and he has been in the business long enough and has been successful enough to build up a very credible network of friends and experts in the business. Doll has been working on a major research report recommending Boyce Health, a medical device manufacturer. He recently ran into an old acquaintance at a wedding who is a senior executive at Boyce, and Doll asked about the business. Doll was drawn to a statement that the executive, who has responsibilities in the new products area, made about a product: "I would not get too excited about the medium-term prospects; we have a lot of work to do first." Doll incorporated this and other information about the new Boyce product in his long-term recommendation of Boyce.

Comment: Doll's conversation with the senior executive is part of the mosaic of information used in recommending Boyce. When holding discussions with a firm executive, Doll would need to guard against soliciting or obtaining material nonpublic information. Before issuing the report, the executive's statement about the continuing development of the product would need to be weighed against the other known public facts to determine whether it would be considered material.

Example 10 (Materiality Determination):

Larry Nadler, a trader for a mutual fund, gets a text message from another firm's trader, whom he has known for years. The message indicates a software company is going to report strong earnings when the firm publicly announces in two days. Nadler has a buy order from a portfolio manager within his firm to purchase several hundred thousand shares of the stock. Nadler is aggressive in placing the portfolio manager's order and completes the purchases by the following morning, a day ahead of the firm's planned earnings announcement.

Comment: There are often rumors and whisper numbers before a release of any kind. The text message from the other trader would most likely be considered market noise. Unless Nadler knew that the trader had an ongoing business relationship with the public firm, he had no reason to suspect he was receiving material nonpublic information that would prevent him from completing the trading request of the portfolio manager.

Example 11 (Using an Expert Network):

Mary McCoy is the senior drug analyst at a mutual fund. Her firm hires a service that connects her to experts in the treatment of cancer. Through various phone conversations, McCoy enhances her understanding of the latest therapies for successful treatment. This information is critical to Mary making informed recommendations of the companies producing these drugs.

Comment: McCoy is appropriately using the expert networks to enhance her evaluation process. She has neither asked for nor received information that may be considered material and nonpublic, such as preliminary trial results. McCoy is allowed to seek advice from professionals within the industry that she follows.

Example 12 (Using an Expert Network):

Tom Watson is a research analyst working for a hedge fund. To stay informed, Watson relies on outside experts for information on such industries as technology and pharmaceuticals, where new advancements occur frequently. The meetings with the industry experts often are arranged through networks or placement agents that have specific policies and procedures in place to deter the exchange of material nonpublic information.

Watson arranges a call to discuss future prospects for one of the fund's existing technology company holdings, a company that was testing a new semiconductor product. The scientist leading the tests indicates his disappointment with the performance of the new semiconductor. Following the call, Watson relays the insights he received to others at the fund. The fund sells its current position in the company and buys many put options because the market is anticipating the success of the new semiconductor and the share price reflects the market's optimism.

Comment: Watson has violated Standard II(A) by passing along material nonpublic information concerning the ongoing product tests, which the fund used to trade in the securities and options of the related company. Watson cannot simply rely on the agreements signed by individuals who participate in expert networks that state that he has not received information that would prohibit his trading activity. He must make his own determination whether information he received through these arrangements reaches a materiality threshold that would affect his trading abilities.

19 STANDARD II(B) MARKET MANIPULATION

- ☐ demonstrate a thorough knowledge of the CFA Institute Code of Ethics and Standards of Professional Conduct by interpreting the Code and Standards in various situations involving issues of professional integrity
- ☐ recommend practices and procedures designed to prevent violations of the Code and Standards

Members and Candidates must not engage in practices that distort prices or artificially inflate trading volume with the intent to mislead market participants.

Guidance

Highlights:

- *Information-Based Manipulation*
- *Transaction-Based Manipulation*

Standard II(B) requires that members and candidates uphold market integrity by prohibiting market manipulation. Market manipulation includes practices that distort security prices or trading volume with the intent to deceive people or entities that rely on information in the market. Market manipulation damages the interests of all investors by disrupting the smooth functioning of financial markets and lowering investor confidence.

Market manipulation may lead to a lack of trust in the fairness of the capital markets, resulting in higher risk premiums and reduced investor participation. A reduction in the efficiency of a local capital market may negatively affect the growth and economic health of the country and may also influence the operations of the globally interconnected capital markets. Although market manipulation may be less likely to occur in mature financial markets than in emerging markets, cross-border investing increasingly exposes all global investors to the potential for such practices.

Market manipulation includes (1) the dissemination of false or misleading information and (2) transactions that deceive or would be likely to mislead market participants by distorting the price-setting mechanism of financial instruments. The development of new products and technologies increases the incentives, means, and opportunities for market manipulation. Additionally, the increasing complexity and sophistication of the technologies used for communicating with market participants have created new avenues for manipulation.

Information-Based Manipulation

Information-based manipulation includes, but is not limited to, spreading false rumors to induce trading by others. For example, members and candidates must refrain from "pumping up" the price of an investment by issuing misleading positive information or overly optimistic projections of a security's worth only to later "dump" the investment (i.e., sell it) once the price, fueled by the misleading information's effect on other market participants, reaches an artificially high level.

Transaction-Based Manipulation

Transaction-based manipulation involves instances where a member or candidate knew or should have known that his or her actions could affect the pricing of a security. This type of manipulation includes, but is not limited to, the following:

- transactions that artificially affect prices or volume to give the impression of activity or price movement in a financial instrument, which represent a diversion from the expectations of a fair and efficient market, and
- securing a controlling, dominant position in a financial instrument to exploit and manipulate the price of a related derivative and/or the underlying asset.

Standard II(B) is not intended to preclude transactions undertaken on legitimate trading strategies based on perceived market inefficiencies. The intent of the action is critical to determining whether it is a violation of this standard.

STANDARD II(B): APPLICATION OF THE STANDARD 20

Example 1 (Independent Analysis and Company Promotion):

The principal owner of Financial Information Services (FIS) entered into an agreement with two microcap companies to promote the companies' stock in exchange for stock and cash compensation. The principal owner caused FIS to disseminate e-mails, design and maintain several websites, and distribute an online investment newsletter—all of which recommended investment in the two companies. The systematic publication of purportedly independent analyses and recommendations containing inaccurate and highly promotional and speculative statements increased public investment in the companies and led to dramatically higher stock prices.

> *Comment*: The principal owner of FIS violated Standard II(B) by using inaccurate reporting and misleading information under the guise of independent analysis to artificially increase the stock price of the companies. Furthermore, the principal owner violated Standard V(A) Diligence and Reasonable Basis by not having a reasonable and adequate basis for recommending the two companies and violated Standard VI(A) Disclosure of Conflicts by not disclosing to investors the compensation agreements (which constituted a conflict of interest).

Example 2 (Personal Trading Practices and Price):

John Gray is a private investor in Belgium who bought a large position several years ago in Fame Pharmaceuticals, a German small-cap security with limited average trading volume. He has now decided to significantly reduce his holdings owing to the poor price performance. Gray is worried that the low trading volume for the stock may cause the price to decline further as he attempts to sell his large position.

Gray devises a plan to divide his holdings into multiple accounts in different brokerage firms and private banks in the names of family members, friends, and even a private religious institution. He then creates a rumor campaign on various blogs and social media outlets promoting the company.

Gray begins to buy and sell the stock using the accounts in hopes of raising the trading volume and the price. He conducts the trades through multiple brokers, selling slightly larger positions than he bought on a tactical schedule, and over time, he is able to reduce his holding as desired without negatively affecting the sale price.

> *Comment*: John violated Standard II(B) by fraudulently creating the appearance that there was a greater investor interest in the stock through the online rumors. Additionally, through his trading strategy, he created the appearance that there was greater liquidity in the stock than actually existed. He was able to manipulate the price through both misinformation and trading practices.

Example 3 (Creating Artificial Price Volatility):

Matthew Murphy is an analyst at Divisadero Securities & Co., which has a significant number of hedge funds among its most important brokerage clients. Some of the hedge funds hold short positions on Wirewolf Semiconductor. Two trading days before the publication of a quarter-end report, Murphy alerts his sales force that he is about to issue a research report on Wirewolf that will include the following opinions:

- quarterly revenues are likely to fall short of management's guidance,
- earnings will be as much as 5 cents per share (or more than 10%) below consensus, and
- Wirewolf's highly respected chief financial officer may be about to join another company.

Knowing that Wirewolf has already entered its declared quarter-end "quiet period" before reporting earnings (and thus would be reluctant to respond to rumors), Murphy times the release of his research report specifically to sensationalize the negative aspects of the message in order to create significant downward pressure on Wirewolf's stock—to the distinct advantage of Divisadero's hedge fund clients. The report's conclusions are based on speculation, not on fact. The next day, the research report is broadcast to all of Divisadero's clients and to the usual newswire services.

Before Wirewolf's investor-relations department can assess the damage on the final trading day of the quarter and refute Murphy's report, its stock opens trading sharply lower, allowing Divisadero's clients to cover their short positions at substantial gains.

> *Comment*: Murphy violated Standard II(B) by aiming to create artificial price volatility designed to have a material impact on the price of an issuer's stock. Moreover, by lacking an adequate basis for the recommendation, Murphy also violated Standard V(A) Diligence and Reasonable Basis.

Example 4 (Personal Trading and Volume):

Rajesh Sekar manages two funds—an equity fund and a balanced fund—whose equity components are supposed to be managed in accordance with the same model. According to that model, the funds' holdings in stock of Digital Design Inc. (DD) are excessive. Reduction of the DD holdings would not be easy, however, because the stock has low liquidity in the stock market. Sekar decides to start trading larger portions of DD stock back and forth between his two funds to slowly increase the price; he believes market participants will see growing volume and increasing price and become interested in the stock. If other investors are willing to buy the DD stock because of such interest, then Sekar will be able to get rid of at least some of his overweight position without inducing price decreases. In this way, the whole transaction will be for the benefit of fund participants, even if additional brokers' commissions are incurred.

> *Comment*: Sekar's plan would be beneficial for his funds' participants but is based on artificial distortion of both trading volume and the price of the DD stock and thus constitutes a violation of Standard II(B).

Example 5 ("Pump-Priming" Strategy):

ACME Futures Exchange is launching a new bond futures contract. To convince investors, traders, arbitrageurs, hedgers, and so on, to use its contract, the exchange attempts to demonstrate that it has the best liquidity. To do so, it enters into agreements with members in which they commit to a substantial minimum trading volume on the new contract over a specific period in exchange for substantial reductions of their regular commissions.

> *Comment*: The formal liquidity of a market is determined by the obligations set on market makers, but the actual liquidity of a market is better estimated by the actual trading volume and bid–ask spreads. Attempts to mislead participants about the actual liquidity of the market constitute a violation of Standard II(B). In this example, investors have been intentionally misled to believe they chose the most liquid instrument for some specific purpose, but they could eventually see the actual liquidity of the contract significantly reduced after the term of the agreement expires. If the ACME Futures Exchange fully discloses its agreement with members to boost transactions over some initial launch period, it will not violate Standard II(B). ACME's intent is not to harm investors but, on the contrary, to give them a better service. For that purpose, it may engage in a liquidity-pumping strategy, but the strategy must be disclosed.

Example 6 (Creating Artificial Price Volatility):

Emily Gordon, an analyst of household products companies, is employed by a research boutique, Picador & Co. Based on information that she has gathered during a trip through Latin America, she believes that Hygene, Inc., a major marketer of personal care products, has generated better-than-expected sales from its new product initiatives in South America. After modestly boosting her projections for revenue and for gross profit margin in her worksheet models for Hygene, Gordon estimates that her earnings projection of US$2.00 per diluted share for the current year may be as much as 5% too low. She contacts the chief financial officer (CFO) of Hygene to try to gain confirmation of her findings from her trip and to get some feedback regarding her revised models. The CFO declines to comment and reiterates management's most recent guidance of US$1.95–US$2.05 for the year.

Gordon decides to try to force a comment from the company by telling Picador & Co. clients who follow a momentum investment style that consensus earnings projections for Hygene are much too low; she explains that she is considering raising her published estimate by an ambitious US$0.15 to US$2.15 per share. She believes that when word of an unrealistically high earnings projection filters back to Hygene's investor-relations department, the company will feel compelled to update its earnings guidance. Meanwhile, Gordon hopes that she is at least correct with respect to the earnings direction and that she will help clients who act on her insights to profit from a quick gain by trading on her advice.

Comment: By exaggerating her earnings projections in order to try to fuel a quick gain in Hygene's stock price, Gordon is in violation of Standard II(B). Furthermore, by virtue of previewing her intentions of revising upward her earnings projections to only a select group of clients, she is in violation of Standard III(B) Fair Dealing. However, it would have been acceptable for Gordon to write a report that

- framed her earnings projection in a range of possible outcomes,
- outlined clearly the assumptions used in her Hygene models that took into consideration the findings from her trip through Latin America, and
- was distributed to all Picador & Co. clients in an equitable manner.

Example 7 (Pump and Dump Strategy):

In an effort to pump up the price of his holdings in Moosehead & Belfast Railroad Company, Steve Weinberg logs on to several investor chat rooms on the internet to start rumors that the company is about to expand its rail network in anticipation of receiving a large contract for shipping lumber.

Comment: Weinberg has violated Standard II(B) by disseminating false information about Moosehead & Belfast with the intent to mislead market participants.

Example 8 (Manipulating Model Inputs):

Bill Mandeville supervises a structured financing team for Superior Investment Bank. His responsibilities include packaging new structured investment products and managing Superior's relationship with relevant rating agencies. To achieve the best rating possible, Mandeville uses mostly positive scenarios as model inputs—scenarios that reflect minimal downside risk in the assets underlying the structured products. The resulting output statistics in the rating request and underwriting prospectus support the idea that the new structured products have minimal potential downside risk. Additionally, Mandeville's compensation from Superior is partially based on both the level of the rating assigned and the successful sale of new structured investment products but does not have a link to the long-term performance of the instruments.

Mandeville is extremely successful and leads Superior as the top originator of structured investment products for the next two years. In the third year, the economy experiences difficulties and the values of the assets underlying structured products significantly decline. The subsequent defaults lead to major turmoil in the capital markets, the demise of Superior Investment Bank, and the loss of Mandeville's employment.

Comment: Mandeville manipulates the inputs of a model to minimize associated risk to achieve higher ratings. His understanding of structured products allows him to skillfully decide which inputs to include in support of the desired rating and price. This information manipulation for short-term gain, which is in violation of Standard II(B), ultimately causes significant damage to many parties and the capital markets as a whole. Mandeville should have realized that promoting a rating and price with inaccurate information could cause not only a loss of price confidence in the particular structured product but also a loss of investor trust in the system. Such loss of confidence affects the ability of the capital markets to operate efficiently.

Example 9 (Information Manipulation):

Allen King is a performance analyst for Torrey Investment Funds. King believes that the portfolio manager for the firm's small- and microcap equity fund dislikes him because the manager never offers him tickets to the local baseball team's games but does offer tickets to other employees. To incite a potential regulatory review of the manager, King creates user profiles on several online forums under the portfolio manager's name and starts rumors about potential mergers for several of the smaller companies in the portfolio. As the prices of these companies' stocks increase, the portfolio manager sells the position, which leads to an investigation by the regulator as King desired.

Comment: King has violated Standard II(B) even though he did not personally profit from the market's reaction to the rumor. In posting the false information, King misleads others into believing the companies were likely to be acquired. Although his intent was to create trouble for the portfolio manager, his actions clearly manipulated the factual information that was available to the market.

STANDARD III: DUTIES TO CLIENTS

21

- ☐ demonstrate a thorough knowledge of the CFA Institute Code of Ethics and Standards of Professional Conduct by interpreting the Code and Standards in various situations involving issues of professional integrity
- ☐ recommend practices and procedures designed to prevent violations of the Code and Standards

Standard III(A) Loyalty, Prudence, and Care

Members and Candidates have a duty of loyalty to their clients and must act with reasonable care and exercise prudent judgment. Members and Candidates must act for the benefit of their clients and place their clients' interests before their employer's or their own interests.

Guidance

Highlights:

- *Understanding the Application of Loyalty, Prudence, and Care*
- *Identifying the Actual Investment Client*
- *Developing the Client's Portfolio*
- *Soft Commission Policies*
- *Proxy Voting Policies*

Standard III(A) clarifies that client interests are paramount. A member's or candidate's responsibility to a client includes a duty of loyalty and a duty to exercise reasonable care. Investment actions must be carried out for the sole benefit of the client and in a manner the member or candidate believes, given the known facts and circumstances, to be in the best interest of the client. Members and candidates must exercise the same level of prudence, judgment, and care that they would apply in the management and disposition of their own interests in similar circumstances.

Prudence requires caution and discretion. The exercise of prudence by investment professionals requires that they act with the care, skill, and diligence that a reasonable person acting in a like capacity and familiar with such matters would use. In the context of managing a client's portfolio, prudence requires following the investment parameters set forth by the client and balancing risk and return. Acting with care requires members and candidates to act in a prudent and judicious manner in avoiding harm to clients.

Standard III(A) sets minimum expectations for members and candidates when fulfilling their responsibilities to their clients. Regulatory and legal requirements for such duties can vary across the investment industry depending on a variety of factors, including job function of the investment professional, the existence of an adviser/client relationship, and the nature of the recommendations being offered. From the perspective of the end user of financial services, these different standards can be arcane and confusing, leaving investors unsure of what level of service to expect from investment professionals they employ. The single standard of conduct described in Standard III(A) benefits investors by establishing a benchmark for the duties of loyalty, prudence, and care and clarifies that all CFA Institute members and candidates, regardless of job title, local laws, or cultural differences, are required to comply with these fundamental responsibilities. Investors hiring members or candidates who must adhere to the duty of loyalty, prudence, and care set forth in this standard can be confident that these responsibilities are a requirement regardless of any legally imposed fiduciary duties.

Standard III(A), however, is not a substitute for a member's or candidate's legal or regulatory obligations. As stated in Standard I(A), members and candidates must abide by the most strict requirements imposed on them by regulators or the Code and Standards, including any legally imposed fiduciary duty. Members and candidates must also be aware of whether they have "custody" or effective control of client assets. If so, a heightened level of responsibility arises. Members and candidates are considered to have custody if they have any direct or indirect access to client funds. Members and candidates must manage any pool of assets in their control in accordance with the terms of the governing documents (such as trust documents and investment management agreements), which are the primary determinant of the manager's powers and duties. Whenever their actions are contrary to provisions of those instruments or applicable law, members and candidates are at risk of violating Standard III(A).

Understanding the Application of Loyalty, Prudence, and Care

Standard III(A) establishes a minimum benchmark for the duties of loyalty, prudence, and care that are required of all members and candidates regardless of whether a legal fiduciary duty applies. Although fiduciary duty often encompasses the principles of loyalty, prudence, and care, Standard III(A) does not render all members and candidates fiduciaries. The responsibilities of members and candidates for fulfilling their obligations under this standard depend greatly on the nature of their professional responsibilities and the relationships they have with clients. The conduct of members and candidates may or may not rise to the level of being a fiduciary, depending on the type of client, whether the member or candidate is giving investment advice, and the many facts and circumstances surrounding a particular transaction or client relationship.

Fiduciary duties are often imposed by law or regulation when an individual or institution is charged with the duty of acting for the benefit of another party, such as managing investment assets. The duty required in fiduciary relationships exceeds what is acceptable in many other business relationships because a fiduciary is in an enhanced position of trust. Although members and candidates must comply with any legally imposed fiduciary duty, the Code and Standards neither impose such a legal responsibility nor require all members or candidates to act as fiduciaries. However, Standard III(A) requires members and candidates to work in the client's best interest no matter what the job function.

A member or candidate who does not provide advisory services to a client but who acts only as a trade execution professional must prudently work in the client's interest when completing requested trades. Acting in the client's best interest requires these professionals to use their skills and diligence to execute trades in the most favorable terms that can be achieved. Members and candidates operating in such positions must use care to operate within the parameters set by the client's trading instructions.

Members and candidates may also operate in a blended environment where they execute client trades and offer advice on a limited set of investment options. The extent of the advisory arrangement and limitations should be outlined in the agreement with the client at the outset of the relationship. For instance, members and candidates should inform clients that the advice provided will be limited to the propriety products of the firm and not include other products available on the market. Clients who want access to a wider range of investment products would have the information necessary to decide not to engage with members or candidates working under these restrictions.

Members and candidates operating in this blended context would comply with their obligations by recommending the allowable products that are consistent with the client's objectives and risk tolerance. They would exercise care through diligently aligning the client's needs with the attributes of the products being recommended. Members and candidates should place the client's interests first by disregarding any firm or personal interest in motivating a recommended transaction.

There is a large variety of professional relationships that members and candidates have with their clients. Standard III(A) requires them to fulfill the obligations outlined explicitly or implicitly in the client agreements to the best of their abilities and with loyalty, prudence, and care. Whether a member or candidate is structuring a new securitization transaction, completing a credit rating analysis, or leading a public company, he or she must work with prudence and care in delivering the agreed-on services.

Identifying the Actual Investment Client

The first step for members and candidates in fulfilling their duty of loyalty to clients is to determine the identity of the "client" to whom the duty of loyalty is owed. In the context of an investment manager managing the personal assets of an individual, the client is easily identified. When the manager is responsible for the portfolios of pension plans or trusts, however, the client is not the person or entity who hires the manager but, rather, the beneficiaries of the plan or trust. The duty of loyalty is owed to the ultimate beneficiaries.

In some situations, an actual client or group of beneficiaries may not exist. Members and candidates managing a fund to an index or an expected mandate owe the duty of loyalty, prudence, and care to invest in a manner consistent with the stated mandate. The decisions of a fund's manager, although benefiting all fund investors, do not have to be based on an individual investor's requirements and risk profile. Client loyalty and care for those investing in the fund are the responsibility of members and candidates who have an advisory relationship with those individuals.

Situations involving potential conflicts of interest with respect to responsibilities to clients may be extremely complex because they may involve a number of competing interests. The duty of loyalty, prudence, and care applies to a large number of persons in varying capacities, but the exact duties may differ in many respects in accord with the relationship with each client or each type of account in which the assets are managed. Members and candidates must not only put their obligations to clients first in all dealings but also endeavor to avoid all real or potential conflicts of interest.

Members and candidates with positions whose responsibilities do not include direct investment management also have "clients" that must be considered. Just as there are various types of advisory relationships, members and candidates must look at their roles and responsibilities when making a determination of who their clients are. Sometimes the client is easily identifiable; such is the case in the relationship between a company executive and the firm's public shareholders. At other times, the client may be the investing public as a whole, in which case the goals of independence and objectivity of research surpass the goal of loyalty to a single organization.

Developing the Client's Portfolio

The duty of loyalty, prudence, and care owed to the individual client is especially important because the professional investment manager typically possesses greater knowledge in the investment arena than the client does. This disparity places the individual client in a vulnerable position; the client must trust the manager. The manager in these situations should ensure that the client's objectives and expectations for the performance of the account are realistic and suitable to the client's circumstances and that the risks involved are appropriate. In most circumstances, recommended investment strategies should relate to the long-term objectives and circumstances of the client.

Particular care must be taken to detect whether the goals of the investment manager or the firm in conducting business, selling products, and executing security transactions potentially conflict with the best interests and objectives of the client. When members and candidates cannot avoid potential conflicts between their firm and clients' interests, they must provide clear and factual disclosures of the circumstances to the clients.

Members and candidates must follow any guidelines set by their clients for the management of their assets. Some clients, such as charitable organizations and pension plans, have strict investment policies that limit investment options to certain types or classes of investment or prohibit investment in certain securities. Other organizations have aggressive policies that do not prohibit investments by type but, instead, set criteria on the basis of the portfolio's total risk and return.

Investment decisions must be judged in the context of the total portfolio rather than by individual investment within the portfolio. The member's or candidate's duty is satisfied with respect to a particular investment if the individual has thoroughly considered the investment's place in the overall portfolio, the risk of loss and opportunity for gains, tax implications, and the diversification, liquidity, cash flow, and overall return requirements of the assets or the portion of the assets for which the manager is responsible.

Soft Commission Policies

An investment manager often has discretion over the selection of brokers executing transactions. Conflicts may arise when an investment manager uses client brokerage to purchase research services, a practice commonly called "soft dollars" or "soft commissions." A member or candidate who pays a higher brokerage commission than he or she would normally pay to allow for the purchase of goods or services, without corresponding benefit to the client, violates the duty of loyalty to the client.

From time to time, a client will direct a manager to use the client's brokerage to purchase goods or services for the client, a practice that is commonly called "directed brokerage." Because brokerage commission is an asset of the client and is used to benefit that client, not the manager, such a practice does not violate any duty of loyalty. However, a member or candidate is obligated to seek "best price" and "best execution" and be assured by the client that the goods or services purchased from the brokerage will benefit the account beneficiaries. "Best execution" refers to a trading process that seeks to maximize the value of the client's portfolio within the client's stated investment objectives and constraints. In addition, the member or candidate should disclose to the client that the client may not be getting best execution from the directed brokerage.

Proxy Voting Policies

The duty of loyalty, prudence, and care may apply in a number of situations facing the investment professional besides those related directly to investing assets.

Part of a member's or candidate's duty of loyalty includes voting proxies in an informed and responsible manner. Proxies have economic value to a client, and members and candidates must ensure that they properly safeguard and maximize this value. An investment manager who fails to vote, casts a vote without considering the impact of the question, or votes blindly with management on nonroutine governance issues (e.g., a change in company capitalization) may violate this standard. Voting of proxies is an integral part of the management of investments.

A cost–benefit analysis may show that voting all proxies may not benefit the client, so voting proxies may not be necessary in all instances. Members and candidates should disclose to clients their proxy voting policies.

STANDARD III(A): RECOMMENDED PROCEDURES

22

Regular Account Information

Members and candidates with control of client assets (1) should submit to each client, at least quarterly, an itemized statement showing the funds and securities in the custody or possession of the member or candidate plus all debits, credits, and transactions that occurred during the period, (2) should disclose to the client where the assets are to be maintained, as well as where or when they are moved, and (3) should separate the client's assets from any other party's assets, including the member's or candidate's own assets.

Client Approval

If a member or candidate is uncertain about the appropriate course of action with respect to a client, the member or candidate should consider what he or she would expect or demand if the member or candidate were the client. If in doubt, a member or candidate should disclose the questionable matter in writing to the client and obtain client approval.

Firm Policies

Members and candidates should address and encourage their firms to address the following topics when drafting the statements or manuals containing their policies and procedures regarding responsibilities to clients:

- *Follow all applicable rules and laws*: Members and candidates must follow all legal requirements and applicable provisions of the Code and Standards.
- *Establish the investment objectives of the client*: Make a reasonable inquiry into a client's investment experience, risk and return objectives, and financial constraints prior to making investment recommendations or taking investment actions.
- *Consider all the information when taking actions*: When taking investment actions, members and candidates must consider the appropriateness and suitability of the investment relative to (1) the client's needs and circumstances, (2) the investment's basic characteristics, and (3) the basic characteristics of the total portfolio.
- *Diversify*: Members and candidates should diversify investments to reduce the risk of loss, unless diversification is not consistent with plan guidelines or is contrary to the account objectives.
- *Carry out regular reviews*: Members and candidates should establish regular review schedules to ensure that the investments held in the account adhere to the terms of the governing documents.
- *Deal fairly with all clients with respect to investment actions*: Members and candidates must not favor some clients over others and should establish policies for allocating trades and disseminating investment recommendations.
- *Disclose conflicts of interest*: Members and candidates must disclose all actual and potential conflicts of interest so that clients can evaluate those conflicts.
- *Disclose compensation arrangements*: Members and candidates should make their clients aware of all forms of manager compensation.
- *Vote proxies*: In most cases, members and candidates should determine who is authorized to vote shares and vote proxies in the best interests of the clients and ultimate beneficiaries.
- *Maintain confidentiality*: Members and candidates must preserve the confidentiality of client information.
- *Seek best execution*: Unless directed by the client as ultimate beneficiary, members and candidates must seek best execution for their clients. (Best execution is defined in the preceding text.)
- *Place client interests first*: Members and candidates must serve the best interests of clients.

STANDARD III(A): APPLICATION OF THE STANDARD

23

Example 1 (Identifying the Client—Plan Participants):

First Country Bank serves as trustee for the Miller Company's pension plan. Miller is the target of a hostile takeover attempt by Newton, Inc. In attempting to ward off Newton, Miller's managers persuade Julian Wiley, an investment manager at First Country Bank, to purchase Miller common stock in the open market for the employee pension plan. Miller's officials indicate that such action would be favorably received and would probably result in other accounts being placed with the bank. Although Wiley believes the stock is overvalued and would not ordinarily buy it, he purchases the stock to support Miller's managers, to maintain Miller's good favor toward the bank, and to realize additional new business. The heavy stock purchases cause Miller's market price to rise to such a level that Newton retracts its takeover bid.

> *Comment*: Standard III(A) requires that a member or candidate, in evaluating a takeover bid, act prudently and solely in the interests of plan participants and beneficiaries. To meet this requirement, a member or candidate must carefully evaluate the long-term prospects of the company against the short-term prospects presented by the takeover offer and by the ability to invest elsewhere. In this instance, Wiley, acting on behalf of his employer, which was the trustee for a pension plan, clearly violated Standard III(A). He used the pension plan to perpetuate existing management, perhaps to the detriment of plan participants and the company's shareholders, and to benefit himself. Wiley's responsibilities to the plan participants and beneficiaries should have taken precedence over any ties of his bank to corporate managers and over his self-interest. Wiley had a duty to examine the takeover offer on its own merits and to make an independent decision. The guiding principle is the appropriateness of the investment decision to the pension plan, not whether the decision benefited Wiley or the company that hired him.

Example 2 (Client Commission Practices):

JNI, a successful investment counseling firm, serves as investment manager for the pension plans of several large regionally based companies. Its trading activities generate a significant amount of commission-related business. JNI uses the brokerage and research services of many firms, but most of its trading activity is handled through a large brokerage company, Thompson, Inc., because the executives of the two firms have a close friendship. Thompson's commission structure is high in comparison with charges for similar brokerage services from other firms. JNI considers Thompson's research services and execution capabilities average. In exchange for JNI directing its brokerage to Thompson, Thompson absorbs a number of JNI overhead expenses, including those for rent.

> *Comment*: JNI executives are breaching their responsibilities by using client brokerage for services that do not benefit JNI clients and by not obtaining best price and best execution for their clients. Because JNI executives are not upholding their duty of loyalty, they are violating Standard III(A).

Example 3 (Brokerage Arrangements):

Charlotte Everett, a struggling independent investment adviser, serves as investment manager for the pension plans of several companies. One of her brokers, Scott Company, is close to consummating management agreements with prospective new clients whereby Everett would manage the new client accounts and trade the accounts exclusively through Scott. One of Everett's existing clients, Crayton Corporation, has directed Everett to place securities transactions for Crayton's account exclusively through Scott. But to induce Scott to exert efforts to send more new accounts to her, Everett also directs transactions to Scott from other clients without their knowledge.

> *Comment*: Everett has an obligation at all times to seek best price and best execution on all trades. Everett may direct new client trades exclusively through Scott Company as long as Everett receives best price and execution on the trades or receives a written statement from new clients that she is *not* to seek best price and execution and that they are aware of the consequence for their accounts. Everett may trade other accounts through Scott as a reward for directing clients to Everett only if the accounts receive best price and execution and the practice is disclosed to the accounts. Because Everett does not disclose the directed trading, Everett has violated Standard III(A).

Example 4 (Brokerage Arrangements):

Emilie Rome is a trust officer for Paget Trust Company. Rome's supervisor is responsible for reviewing Rome's trust account transactions and her monthly reports of personal stock transactions. Rome has been using Nathan Gray, a broker, almost exclusively for trust account brokerage transactions. When Gray makes a market in stocks, he has been giving Rome a lower price for personal purchases and a higher price for sales than he gives to Rome's trust accounts and other investors.

> *Comment*: Rome is violating her duty of loyalty to the bank's trust accounts by using Gray for brokerage transactions simply because Gray trades Rome's personal account on favorable terms. Rome is placing her own interests before those of her clients.

Example 5 (Client Commission Practices):

Lauren Parker, an analyst with Provo Advisors, covers South American equities for her firm. She likes to travel to the markets for which she is responsible and decides to go on a trip to Chile, Argentina, and Brazil. The trip is sponsored by SouthAM, Inc., a research firm with a small broker/dealer affiliate that uses the clearing facilities of a larger New York brokerage house. SouthAM specializes in arranging South American trips for analysts during which they can meet with central bank officials, government ministers, local economists, and senior executives of corporations. SouthAM accepts commission dollars at a ratio of 2 to 1 against the hard-dollar costs of the research fee for the trip. Parker is not sure that SouthAM's execution is competitive, but without informing her supervisor, she directs the trading desk at Provo to start giving commission business to SouthAM so she can take the trip. SouthAM has conveniently timed the briefing trip to coincide with the beginning of Carnival season, so Parker also decides to spend five days of vacation in Rio de Janeiro at the end of the trip. Parker uses commission dollars to pay for the five days of hotel expenses.

> *Comment*: Parker is violating Standard III(A) by not exercising her duty of loyalty to her clients. She should have determined whether the commissions charged by SouthAM are reasonable in relation to the benefit of the

research provided by the trip. She also should have determined whether best execution and prices could be received from SouthAM. In addition, the five extra days are not part of the research effort because they do not assist in the investment decision making. Thus, the hotel expenses for the five days should not be paid for with client assets.

Example 6 (Excessive Trading):

Vida Knauss manages the portfolios of a number of high-net-worth individuals. A major part of her investment management fee is based on trading commissions. Knauss engages in extensive trading for each of her clients to ensure that she attains the minimum commission level set by her firm. Although the securities purchased and sold for the clients are appropriate and fall within the acceptable asset classes for the clients, the amount of trading for each account exceeds what is necessary to accomplish the client's investment objectives.

Comment: Knauss has violated Standard III(A) because she is using the assets of her clients to benefit her firm and herself.

Example 7 (Managing Family Accounts):

Adam Dill recently joined New Investments Asset Managers. To assist Dill in building a book of clients, both his father and brother opened new fee-paying accounts. Dill followed all the firm's procedures in noting his relationships with these clients and in developing their investment policy statements.

After several years, the number of Dill's clients has grown, but he still manages the original accounts of his family members. An IPO is coming to market that is a suitable investment for many of his clients, including his brother. Dill does not receive the amount of stock he requested, so to avoid any appearance of a conflict of interest, he does not allocate any shares to his brother's account.

Comment: Dill has violated Standard III(A) because he is not acting for the benefit of his brother's account as well as his other accounts. The brother's account is a regular fee-paying account comparable to the accounts of his other clients. By not allocating the shares proportionately across *all* accounts for which he thought the IPO was suitable, Dill is disadvantaging specific clients.

Dill would have been correct in not allocating shares to his brother's account if that account was being managed outside the normal fee structure of the firm.

Example 8 (Identifying the Client):

Donna Hensley has been hired by a law firm to testify as an expert witness. Although the testimony is intended to represent impartial advice, she is concerned that her work may have negative consequences for the law firm. If the law firm is Hensley's client, how does she ensure that her testimony will not violate the required duty of loyalty, prudence, and care to one's client?

Comment: In this situation, the law firm represents Hensley's employer and the aspect of "who is the client" is not well defined. When acting as an expert witness, Hensley is bound by the standard of independence and objectivity in the same manner as an independent research analyst would be bound. Hensley must not let the law firm influence the testimony she provides in the legal proceedings.

Example 9 (Identifying the Client):

Jon Miller is a mutual fund portfolio manager. The fund is focused on the global financial services sector. Wanda Spears is a private wealth manager in the same city as Miller and is a friend of Miller. At a local CFA Institute society meeting, Spears mentions to Miller that her new client is an investor in Miller's fund. She states that the two of them now share a responsibility to this client.

> *Comment*: Spears' statement is not totally correct. Because she provides the advisory services to her new client, she alone is bound by the duty of loyalty to this client. Miller's responsibility is to manage the fund according to the investment policy statement of the fund. His actions should not be influenced by the needs of any particular fund investor.

Example 10 (Client Loyalty):

After providing client account investment performance to the external-facing departments but prior to it being finalized for release to clients, Teresa Nguyen, an investment performance analyst, notices the reporting system missed a trade. Correcting the omission resulted in a large loss for a client that had previously placed the firm on "watch" for potential termination owing to underperformance in prior periods. Nguyen knows this news is unpleasant but informs the appropriate individuals that the report needs to be updated before releasing it to the client.

> *Comment*: Nguyen's actions align with the requirements of Standard III(A). Even though the correction may lead to the firm's termination by the client, withholding information on errors would not be in the best interest of the client.

Example 11 (Execution-Only Responsibilities):

Baftija Sulejman recently became a candidate in the CFA Program. He is a broker who executes client-directed trades for several high-net-worth individuals. Sulejman does not provide any investment advice and only executes the trading decisions made by clients. He is concerned that the Code and Standards impose a fiduciary duty on him in his dealing with clients and sends an e-mail to the CFA Ethics Helpdesk (ethics@cfainstitute.org) to seek guidance on this issue.

> *Comment*: In this instance, Sulejman serves in an execution-only capacity and his duty of loyalty, prudence, and care is centered on the skill and diligence used when executing trades—namely, by seeking best execution and making trades within the parameters set by the clients (instructions on quantity, price, timing, etc.). Acting in the best interests of the client dictates that trades are executed on the most favorable terms that can be achieved for the client. Given this job function, the requirements of the Code and Standards for loyalty, prudence, and care clearly do not impose a fiduciary duty.

STANDARD III(B) FAIR DEALING

24

- [ ] demonstrate a thorough knowledge of the CFA Institute Code of Ethics and Standards of Professional Conduct by interpreting the Code and Standards in various situations involving issues of professional integrity
- [ ] recommend practices and procedures designed to prevent violations of the Code and Standards

Members and Candidates must deal fairly and objectively with all clients when providing investment analysis, making investment recommendations, taking investment action, or engaging in other professional activities.

Guidance

Highlights:

- *Investment Recommendations*
- *Investment Action*

Standard III(B) requires members and candidates to treat all clients fairly when disseminating investment recommendations or making material changes to prior investment recommendations or when taking investment action with regard to general purchases, new issues, or secondary offerings. Only through the fair treatment of all parties can the investment management profession maintain the confidence of the investing public.

When an investment adviser has multiple clients, the potential exists for the adviser to favor one client over another. This favoritism may take various forms—from the quality and timing of services provided to the allocation of investment opportunities.

The term "fairly" implies that the member or candidate must take care not to discriminate against any clients when disseminating investment recommendations or taking investment action. Standard III(B) does not state "equally" because members and candidates could not possibly reach all clients at exactly the same time—whether by printed mail, telephone (including text messaging), computer (including internet updates and e-mail distribution), facsimile (fax), or wire. Each client has unique needs, investment criteria, and investment objectives, so not all investment opportunities are suitable for all clients. In addition, members and candidates may provide more personal, specialized, or in-depth service to clients who are willing to pay for premium services through higher management fees or higher levels of brokerage. Members and candidates may differentiate their services to clients, but different levels of service must not disadvantage or negatively affect clients. In addition, the different service levels should be disclosed to clients and prospective clients and should be available to everyone (i.e., different service levels should not be offered selectively).

Standard III(B) covers conduct in two broadly defined categories—investment recommendations and investment action.

Investment Recommendations

The first category of conduct involves members and candidates whose primary function is the preparation of investment recommendations to be disseminated either to the public or within a firm for the use of others in making investment decisions. This group includes members and candidates employed by investment counseling, advisory, or consulting firms as well as banks, brokerage firms, and insurance companies. The criterion is that the member's or candidate's primary responsibility is the preparation of recommendations to be acted on by others, including those in the member's or candidate's organization.

An investment recommendation is any opinion expressed by a member or candidate in regard to purchasing, selling, or holding a given security or other investment. The opinion may be disseminated to customers or clients through an initial detailed research report, through a brief update report, by addition to or deletion from a list of recommended securities, or simply by oral communication. A recommendation that is distributed to anyone outside the organization is considered a communication for general distribution under Standard III(B).

Standard III(B) addresses the manner in which investment recommendations or changes in prior recommendations are disseminated to clients. Each member or candidate is obligated to ensure that information is disseminated in such a manner that all clients have a fair opportunity to act on every recommendation. Communicating with all clients on a uniform basis presents practical problems for members and candidates because of differences in timing and methods of communication with various types of customers and clients. Members and candidates should encourage their firms to design an equitable system to prevent selective or discriminatory disclosure and should inform clients about what kind of communications they will receive.

The duty to clients imposed by Standard III(B) may be more critical when members or candidates change their recommendations than when they make initial recommendations. Material changes in a member's or candidate's prior investment recommendations because of subsequent research should be communicated to all current clients; particular care should be taken that the information reaches those clients who the member or candidate knows have acted on or been affected by the earlier advice. Clients who do not know that the member or candidate has changed a recommendation and who, therefore, place orders contrary to a current recommendation should be advised of the changed recommendation before the order is accepted.

Investment Action

The second category of conduct includes those members and candidates whose primary function is taking investment action (portfolio management) on the basis of recommendations prepared internally or received from external sources. Investment action, like investment recommendations, can affect market value. Consequently, Standard III(B) requires that members or candidates treat all clients fairly in light of their investment objectives and circumstances. For example, when making investments in new offerings or in secondary financings, members and candidates should distribute the issues to all customers for whom the investments are appropriate in a manner consistent with the policies of the firm for allocating blocks of stock. If the issue is oversubscribed, then the issue should be prorated to all subscribers. This action should be taken on a round-lot basis to avoid odd-lot distributions. In addition, if the issue is oversubscribed, members and candidates should forgo any sales to themselves or their immediate families in order to free up additional shares for clients. If the investment professional's family-member accounts are managed similarly to the accounts of other clients of the firm, however, the family-member accounts should not be excluded from buying such shares.

Members and candidates must make every effort to treat all individual and institutional clients in a fair and impartial manner. A member or candidate may have multiple relationships with an institution; for example, the member or candidate may be a corporate trustee, pension fund manager, manager of funds for individuals employed by the customer, loan originator, or creditor. A member or candidate must exercise care to treat all clients fairly.

Members and candidates should disclose to clients and prospective clients the documented allocation procedures they or their firms have in place and how the procedures would affect the client or prospect. The disclosure should be clear and complete so that the client can make an informed investment decision. Even when complete disclosure is made, however, members and candidates must put client interests ahead of their own. A member's or candidate's duty of fairness and loyalty to clients can never be overridden by client consent to patently unfair allocation procedures.

Treating clients fairly also means that members and candidates should not take advantage of their position in the industry to the detriment of clients. For instance, in the context of IPOs, members and candidates must make bona fide public distributions of "hot issue" securities (defined as securities of a public offering that are trading at a premium in the secondary market whenever such trading commences because of the great demand for the securities). Members and candidates are prohibited from withholding such securities for their own benefit and must not use such securities as a reward or incentive to gain benefit.

STANDARD III(B): RECOMMENDED PROCEDURES 25

Develop Firm Policies

Although Standard III(B) refers to a member's or candidate's responsibility to deal fairly and objectively with clients, members and candidates should also encourage their firms to establish compliance procedures requiring all employees who disseminate investment recommendations or take investment actions to treat customers and clients fairly. At the very least, a member or candidate should recommend appropriate procedures to management if none are in place. And the member or candidate should make management aware of possible violations of fair-dealing practices within the firm when they come to the attention of the member or candidate.

The extent of the formality and complexity of such compliance procedures depends on the nature and size of the organization and the type of securities involved. An investment adviser who is a sole proprietor and handles only discretionary accounts might not disseminate recommendations to the public, but that adviser should have formal written procedures to ensure that all clients receive fair investment action.

Good business practice dictates that initial recommendations be made available to all customers who indicate an interest. Although a member or candidate need not communicate a recommendation to all customers, the selection process by which customers receive information should be based on suitability and known interest, not on any preferred or favored status. A common practice to assure fair dealing is to communicate recommendations simultaneously within the firm and to customers.

Members and candidates should consider the following points when establishing fair-dealing compliance procedures:

- *Limit the number of people involved*: Members and candidates should make reasonable efforts to limit the number of people who are privy to the fact that a recommendation is going to be disseminated.

- *Shorten the time frame between decision and dissemination*: Members and candidates should make reasonable efforts to limit the amount of time that elapses between the decision to make an investment recommendation and the time the actual recommendation is disseminated. If a detailed institutional recommendation that might take two or three weeks to publish is in preparation, a short summary report including the conclusion might be published in advance. In an organization where both a research committee and an investment policy committee must approve a recommendation, the meetings should be held on the same day if possible. The process of reviewing reports and printing and mailing them, faxing them, or distributing them by e-mail necessarily involves the passage of time, sometimes long periods of time. In large firms with extensive review processes, the time factor is usually not within the control of the analyst who prepares the report. Thus, many firms and their analysts communicate to customers and firm personnel the new or changed recommendations by an update or "flash" report. The communication technique might be fax, e-mail, wire, or short written report.
- *Publish guidelines for pre-dissemination behavior*: Members and candidates should encourage firms to develop guidelines that prohibit personnel who have prior knowledge of an investment recommendation from discussing or taking any action on the pending recommendation.
- *Simultaneous dissemination*: Members and candidates should establish procedures for the timing of dissemination of investment recommendations so that all clients are treated fairly—that is, are informed at approximately the same time. For example, if a firm is going to announce a new recommendation, supervisory personnel should time the announcement to avoid placing any client or group of clients at an unfair advantage relative to other clients. A communication to all branch offices should be sent at the time of the general announcement. (When appropriate, the firm should accompany the announcement of a new recommendation with a statement that trading restrictions for the firm's employees are now in effect. The trading restrictions should stay in effect until the recommendation is widely distributed to all relevant clients.) Once this distribution has occurred, the member or candidate may follow up separately with individual clients, but members and candidates should not give favored clients advance information when such advance notification may disadvantage other clients.
- *Maintain a list of clients and their holdings*: Members and candidates should maintain a list of all clients and the securities or other investments each client holds in order to facilitate notification of customers or clients of a change in an investment recommendation. If a particular security or other investment is to be sold, such a list can be used to ensure that all holders are treated fairly in the liquidation of that particular investment.
- *Develop and document trade allocation procedures*: When formulating procedures for allocating trades, members and candidates should develop a set of guiding principles that ensure

  - fairness to advisory clients, both in priority of execution of orders and in the allocation of the price obtained in execution of block orders or trades,
  - timeliness and efficiency in the execution of orders, and
  - accuracy of the member's or candidate's records as to trade orders and client account positions.

With these principles in mind, members and candidates should develop or encourage their firm to develop written allocation procedures, with particular attention to procedures for block trades and new issues. Procedures to consider are as follows:

- requiring orders and modifications or cancellations of orders to be documented and time stamped;
- processing and executing orders on a first-in, first-out basis with consideration of bundling orders for efficiency as appropriate for the asset class or the security;
- developing a policy to address such issues as calculating execution prices and "partial fills" when trades are grouped, or in a block, for efficiency;
- giving all client accounts participating in a block trade the same execution price and charging the same commission;
- when the full amount of the block order is not executed, allocating partially executed orders among the participating client accounts pro rata on the basis of order size while not going below an established minimum lot size for some securities (e.g., bonds); and
- when allocating trades for new issues, obtaining advance indications of interest, allocating securities by client (rather than portfolio manager), and providing a method for calculating allocations.

Disclose Trade Allocation Procedures

Members and candidates should disclose to clients and prospective clients how they select accounts to participate in an order and how they determine the amount of securities each account will buy or sell. Trade allocation procedures must be fair and equitable, and disclosure of inequitable allocation methods does not relieve the member or candidate of this obligation.

Establish Systematic Account Review

Member and candidate supervisors should review each account on a regular basis to ensure that no client or customer is being given preferential treatment and that the investment actions taken for each account are suitable for each account's objectives. Because investments should be based on individual needs and circumstances, an investment manager may have good reasons for placing a given security or other investment in one account while selling it from another account and should fully document the reasons behind both sides of the transaction. Members and candidates should encourage firms to establish review procedures, however, to detect whether trading in one account is being used to benefit a favored client.

Disclose Levels of Service

Members and candidates should disclose to all clients whether the organization offers different levels of service to clients for the same fee or different fees. Different levels of service should not be offered to clients selectively.

26 STANDARD III(B): APPLICATION OF THE STANDARD

Example 1 (Selective Disclosure):

Bradley Ames, a well-known and respected analyst, follows the computer industry. In the course of his research, he finds that a small, relatively unknown company whose shares are traded over the counter has just signed significant contracts with some of the companies he follows. After a considerable amount of investigation, Ames decides to write a research report on the small company and recommend purchase of its shares. While the report is being reviewed by the company for factual accuracy, Ames schedules a luncheon with several of his best clients to discuss the company. At the luncheon, he mentions the purchase recommendation scheduled to be sent early the following week to all the firm's clients.

> *Comment*: Ames has violated Standard III(B) by disseminating the purchase recommendation to the clients with whom he has lunch a week before the recommendation is sent to all clients.

Example 2 (Fair Dealing between Funds):

Spencer Rivers, president of XYZ Corporation, moves his company's growth-oriented pension fund to a particular bank primarily because of the excellent investment performance achieved by the bank's commingled fund for the prior five-year period. Later, Rivers compares the results of his pension fund with those of the bank's commingled fund. He is startled to learn that, even though the two accounts have the same investment objectives and similar portfolios, his company's pension fund has significantly underperformed the bank's commingled fund. Questioning this result at his next meeting with the pension fund's manager, Rivers is told that, as a matter of policy, when a new security is placed on the recommended list, Morgan Jackson, the pension fund manager, first purchases the security for the commingled account and then purchases it on a pro rata basis for all other pension fund accounts. Similarly, when a sale is recommended, the security is sold first from the commingled account and then sold on a pro rata basis from all other accounts. Rivers also learns that if the bank cannot get enough shares (especially of hot issues) to be meaningful to all the accounts, its policy is to place the new issues only in the commingled account.

Seeing that Rivers is neither satisfied nor pleased by the explanation, Jackson quickly adds that nondiscretionary pension accounts and personal trust accounts have a lower priority on purchase and sale recommendations than discretionary pension fund accounts. Furthermore, Jackson states, the company's pension fund had the opportunity to invest up to 5% in the commingled fund.

> *Comment*: The bank's policy does not treat all customers fairly, and Jackson has violated her duty to her clients by giving priority to the growth-oriented commingled fund over all other funds and to discretionary accounts over nondiscretionary accounts. Jackson must execute orders on a systematic basis that is fair to all clients. In addition, trade allocation procedures should be disclosed to all clients when they become clients. Of course, in this case, disclosure of the bank's policy would not change the fact that the policy is unfair.

Example 3 (Fair Dealing and IPO Distribution):

Dominic Morris works for a small regional securities firm. His work consists of corporate finance activities and investing for institutional clients. Arena, Ltd., is planning to go public. The partners have secured rights to buy an arena football league franchise and are planning to use the funds from the issue to complete the purchase. Because arena football is the current rage, Morris believes he has a hot issue on his hands. He has quietly negotiated some options for himself for helping convince Arena to do the financing through his securities firm. When he seeks expressions of interest, the institutional buyers oversubscribe the issue. Morris, assuming that the institutions have the financial clout to drive the stock up, then fills all orders (including his own) and decreases the institutional blocks.

> *Comment*: Morris has violated Standard III(B) by not treating all customers fairly. He should not have taken any shares himself and should have prorated the shares offered among all clients. In addition, he should have disclosed to his firm and to his clients that he received options as part of the deal [see Standard VI(A) Disclosure of Conflicts].

Example 4 (Fair Dealing and Transaction Allocation):

Eleanor Preston, the chief investment officer of Porter Williams Investments (PWI), a medium-size money management firm, has been trying to retain a client, Colby Company. Management at Colby, which accounts for almost half of PWI's revenues, recently told Preston that if the performance of its account did not improve, it would find a new money manager. Shortly after this threat, Preston purchases mortgage-backed securities (MBSs) for several accounts, including Colby's. Preston is busy with a number of transactions that day, so she fails to allocate the trades immediately or write up the trade tickets. A few days later, when Preston is allocating trades, she notes that some of the MBSs have significantly increased in price and some have dropped. Preston decides to allocate the profitable trades to Colby and spread the losing trades among several other PWI accounts.

> *Comment*: Preston has violated Standard III(B) by failing to deal fairly with her clients in taking these investment actions. Preston should have allocated the trades prior to executing the orders, or she should have had a systematic approach to allocating the trades, such as pro rata, as soon as practical after they were executed. Among other things, Preston must disclose to the client that the adviser may act as broker for, receive commissions from, and have a potential conflict of interest regarding both parties in agency cross-transactions. After the disclosure, she should obtain from the client consent authorizing such transactions in advance.

Example 5 (Selective Disclosure):

Saunders Industrial Waste Management (SIWM) publicly indicates to analysts that it is comfortable with the somewhat disappointing earnings-per-share projection of US$1.16 for the quarter. Bernard Roberts, an analyst at Coffey Investments, is confident that SIWM management has understated the forecasted earnings so that the real announcement will cause an "upside surprise" and boost the price of SIWM stock. The "whisper number" (rumored) estimate based on extensive research and discussed among knowledgeable analysts is higher than US$1.16. Roberts repeats the US$1.16 figure in his research report to all Coffey clients but informally tells his large clients that he expects the earnings per share to be higher, making SIWM a good buy.

Comment: By not sharing his opinion regarding the potential for a significant upside earnings surprise with all clients, Roberts is not treating all clients fairly and has violated Standard III(B).

Example 6 (Additional Services for Select Clients):

Jenpin Weng uses e-mail to issue a new recommendation to all his clients. He then calls his three largest institutional clients to discuss the recommendation in detail.

Comment: Weng has not violated Standard III(B) because he widely disseminated the recommendation and provided the information to all his clients prior to discussing it with a select few. Weng's largest clients received additional personal service because they presumably pay higher fees or because they have a large amount of assets under Weng's management. If Weng had discussed the report with a select group of clients prior to distributing it to all his clients, he would have violated Standard III(B).

Example 7 (Minimum Lot Allocations):

Lynn Hampton is a well-respected private wealth manager in her community with a diversified client base. She determines that a new 10-year bond being offered by Healthy Pharmaceuticals is appropriate for five of her clients. Three clients request to purchase US$10,000 each, and the other two request US$50,000 each. The minimum lot size is established at US$5,000, and the issue is oversubscribed at the time of placement. Her firm's policy is that odd-lot allocations, especially those below the minimum, should be avoided because they may affect the liquidity of the security at the time of sale.

Hampton is informed she will receive only US$55,000 of the offering for all accounts. Hampton distributes the bond investments as follows: The three accounts that requested US$10,000 are allocated US$5,000 each, and the two accounts that requested US$50,000 are allocated US$20,000 each.

Comment: Hampton has not violated Standard III(B), even though the distribution is not on a completely pro rata basis because of the required minimum lot size. With the total allocation being significantly below the amount requested, Hampton ensured that each client received at least the minimum lot size of the issue. This approach allowed the clients to efficiently sell the bond later if necessary.

Example 8 (Excessive Trading):

Ling Chan manages the accounts for many pension plans, including the plan of his father's employer. Chan developed similar but not identical investment policies for each client, so the investment portfolios are rarely the same. To minimize the cost to his father's pension plan, he intentionally trades more frequently in the accounts of other clients to ensure the required brokerage is incurred to continue receiving free research for use by all the pensions.

Comment: Chan is violating Standard III(B) because his trading actions are disadvantaging his clients to enhance a relationship with a preferred client. All clients are benefiting from the research being provided and should incur their fair portion of the costs. This does not mean that additional trading should occur if a client has not paid an equal portion of the commission; trading should occur only as required by the strategy.

Example 9 (Limited Social Media Disclosures):

Mary Burdette was recently hired by Fundamental Investment Management (FIM) as a junior auto industry analyst. Burdette is expected to expand the social media presence of the firm because she is active with various networks, including Facebook, LinkedIn, and X. Although Burdette's supervisor, Joe Graf, has never used social media, he encourages Burdette to explore opportunities to increase FIM's online presence and ability to share content, communicate, and broadcast information to clients. In response to Graf's encouragement, Burdette is working on a proposal detailing the advantages of getting FIM onto X in addition to launching a company Facebook page.

As part of her auto industry research for FIM, Burdette is completing a report on the financial impact of Sun Drive Auto Ltd.'s new solar technology for compact automobiles. This research report will be her first for FIM, and she believes Sun Drive's technology could revolutionize the auto industry. In her excitement, Burdette sends a quick post to FIM X followers summarizing her "buy" recommendation for Sun Drive Auto stock.

> *Comment*: Burdette has violated Standard III(B) by sending an investment recommendation to a select group of contacts prior to distributing it to all clients. Burdette must make sure she has received the appropriate training about FIM's policies and procedures, including the appropriate business use of personal social media networks before engaging in such activities.
>
> See Standard IV(C) for guidance related to the duties of the supervisor.

Example 10 (Fair Dealing between Clients):

Paul Rove, performance analyst for Alpha-Beta Investment Management, is describing to the firm's chief investment officer (CIO) two new reports he would like to develop to assist the firm in meeting its obligations to treat clients fairly. Because many of the firm's clients have similar investment objectives and portfolios, Rove suggests a report detailing securities owned across several clients and the percentage of the portfolio the security represents. The second report would compare the monthly performance of portfolios with similar strategies. The outliers within each report would be submitted to the CIO for review.

> *Comment*: As a performance analyst, Rove likely has little direct contact with clients and thus has limited opportunity to treat clients differently. The recommended reports comply with Standard III(B) while helping the firm conduct after-the-fact reviews of how effectively the firm's advisers are dealing with their clients' portfolios. Reports that monitor the fair treatment of clients are an important oversight tool to ensure that clients are treated fairly.

27 STANDARD III(C) SUITABILITY

- ☐ demonstrate a thorough knowledge of the CFA Institute Code of Ethics and Standards of Professional Conduct by interpreting the Code and Standards in various situations involving issues of professional integrity
- ☐ recommend practices and procedures designed to prevent violations of the Code and Standards

1. When Members and Candidates are in an advisory relationship with a client, they must:
   a. Make a reasonable inquiry into a client's or prospective client's investment experience, risk and return objectives, and financial constraints prior to making any investment recommendation or taking investment action and must reassess and update this information regularly.
   b. Determine that an investment is suitable to the client's financial situation and consistent with the client's written objectives, mandates, and constraints before making an investment recommendation or taking investment action.
   c. Judge the suitability of investments in the context of the client's total portfolio.
2. When Members and Candidates are responsible for managing a portfolio to a specific mandate, strategy, or style, they must make only investment recommendations or take only investment actions that are consistent with the stated objectives and constraints of the portfolio.

Guidance

Highlights:

- *Developing an Investment Policy*
- *Understanding the Client's Risk Profile*
- *Updating an Investment Policy*
- *The Need for Diversification*
- *Addressing Unsolicited Trading Requests*
- *Managing to an Index or Mandate*

Standard III(C) requires that members and candidates who are in an investment advisory relationship with clients consider carefully the needs, circumstances, and objectives of the clients when determining the appropriateness and suitability of a given investment or course of investment action. An appropriate suitability determination will not, however, prevent some investments or investment actions from losing value.

In judging the suitability of a potential investment, the member or candidate should review many aspects of the client's knowledge, experience related to investing, and financial situation. These aspects include, but are not limited to, the risk profile of the investment as compared with the constraints of the client, the impact of the investment on the diversity of the portfolio, and whether the client has the means or net worth to assume the associated risk. The investment professional's determination of suitability should reflect only the investment recommendations or actions that a prudent person would be willing to undertake. Not every investment opportunity will be suitable for every portfolio, regardless of the potential return being offered.

The responsibilities of members and candidates to gather information and make a suitability analysis prior to making a recommendation or taking investment action fall on those members and candidates who provide investment advice in the course of an advisory relationship with a client. Other members and candidates may be simply executing specific instructions for retail clients when buying or selling securities, such as shares in mutual funds. These members and candidates and some others, such as sell-side analysts, may not have the opportunity to judge the suitability of a particular investment for the ultimate client.

Developing an Investment Policy

When an advisory relationship exists, members and candidates must gather client information at the inception of the relationship. Such information includes the client's financial circumstances, personal data (such as age and occupation) that are relevant to investment decisions, attitudes toward risk, and objectives in investing. This information should be incorporated into a written investment policy statement (IPS) that addresses the client's risk tolerance, return requirements, and all investment constraints (including time horizon, liquidity needs, tax concerns, legal and regulatory factors, and unique circumstances). Without identifying such client factors, members and candidates cannot judge whether a particular investment or strategy is suitable for a particular client. The IPS also should identify and describe the roles and responsibilities of the parties to the advisory relationship and investment process, as well as schedules for review and evaluation of the IPS. After formulating long-term capital market expectations, members and candidates can assist in developing an appropriate strategic asset allocation and investment program for the client, whether these are presented in separate documents or incorporated in the IPS or in appendices to the IPS.

Understanding the Client's Risk Profile

One of the most important factors to be considered in matching appropriateness and suitability of an investment with a client's needs and circumstances is measuring that client's tolerance for risk. The investment professional must consider the possibilities of rapidly changing investment environments and their likely impact on a client's holdings, both individual securities and the collective portfolio. The risk of many investment strategies can and should be analyzed and quantified in advance.

The use of synthetic investment vehicles and derivative investment products has introduced particular issues of risk. Members and candidates should pay careful attention to the leverage inherent in many of these vehicles or products when considering them for use in a client's investment program. Such leverage and limited liquidity, depending on the degree to which they are hedged, bear directly on the issue of suitability for the client.

Updating an Investment Policy

Updating the IPS should be repeated at least annually and also prior to material changes to any specific investment recommendations or decisions on behalf of the client. The effort to determine the needs and circumstances of each client is not a one-time occurrence. Investment recommendations or decisions are usually part of an ongoing process that takes into account the diversity and changing nature of portfolio and client characteristics. The passage of time is bound to produce changes that are important with respect to investment objectives.

For an individual client, important changes might include the number of dependents, personal tax status, health, liquidity needs, risk tolerance, amount of wealth beyond that represented in the portfolio, and extent to which compensation and other income provide for current income needs. With respect to an institutional client, such changes might relate to the magnitude of unfunded liabilities in a pension fund, the withdrawal privileges in an employee savings plan, or the distribution requirements of a charitable foundation. Without efforts to update information concerning client factors, one or more factors could change without the investment manager's knowledge.

Suitability review can be done most effectively when the client fully discloses his or her complete financial portfolio, including those portions not managed by the member or candidate. If clients withhold information about their financial portfolios, the suitability analysis conducted by members and candidates cannot be expected to be complete; it must be based on the information provided.

The Need for Diversification

The investment profession has long recognized that combining several different investments is likely to provide a more acceptable level of risk exposure than having all assets in a single investment. The unique characteristics (or risks) of an individual investment may become partially or entirely neutralized when it is combined with other individual investments within a portfolio. Some reasonable amount of diversification is thus the norm for many portfolios, especially those managed by individuals or institutions that have some degree of legal fiduciary responsibility.

An investment with high relative risk on its own may be a suitable investment in the context of the entire portfolio or when the client's stated objectives contemplate speculative or risky investments. The manager may be responsible for only a portion of the client's total portfolio, or the client may not have provided a full financial picture. Members and candidates can be responsible for assessing the suitability of an investment only on the basis of the information and criteria actually provided by the client.

Addressing Unsolicited Trading Requests

Members and candidates may receive requests from a client for trades that do not properly align with the risk and return objectives outlined in the client's investment policy statement. These transaction requests may be based on the client's individual biases or professional experience. Members and candidates will need to make reasonable efforts to balance their clients' trading requests with their responsibilities to follow the agreed-on investment policy statement.

In cases of unsolicited trade requests that a member or candidate knows are unsuitable for a client, the member or candidate should refrain from making the trade until he or she discusses the concerns with the client. The discussions and resulting actions may encompass a variety of scenarios depending on how the requested unsuitable investment relates to the client's full portfolio.

Many times, an unsolicited request may be expected to have only a minimum impact on the entire portfolio because the size of the requested trade is small or the trade would result in a limited change to the portfolio's risk profile. In discussing the trade, the member or candidate should focus on educating the investor on how the request deviates from the current policy statement. Following the discussion, the member or candidate may follow his or her firm's policies regarding the necessary client approval for executing unsuitable trades. At a minimum, the client should acknowledge the discussion and accept the conditions that make the recommendation unsuitable.

Should the unsolicited request be expected to have a material impact on the portfolio, the member or candidate should use this opportunity to update the investment policy statement. Doing so would allow the client to fully understand the potential effect of the requested trade on his or her current goals or risk levels.

Members and candidates may have some clients who decline to modify their policy statements while insisting an unsolicited trade be made. In such instances, members or candidates will need to evaluate the effectiveness of their services to the client. The options available to the members or candidates will depend on the services provided by their employer. Some firms may allow for the trade to be executed in a new unmanaged account. If alternative options are not available, members and candidates ultimately will need to determine whether they should continue the advisory arrangement with the client.

Managing to an Index or Mandate

Some members and candidates do not manage money for individuals but are responsible for managing a fund to an index or an expected mandate. The responsibility of these members and candidates is to invest in a manner consistent with the stated mandate. For example, a member or candidate who serves as the fund manager for a large-cap income fund would not be following the fund mandate by investing heavily in small-cap or start-up companies whose stock is speculative in nature. Members and candidates who manage pooled assets to a specific mandate are not responsible for determining the suitability of the *fund* as an investment for investors who may be purchasing shares in the fund. The responsibility for determining the suitability of an investment for clients can be conferred only on members and candidates who have an advisory relationship with clients.

STANDARD III(C): RECOMMENDED PROCEDURES

28

Investment Policy Statement

To fulfill the basic provisions of Standard III(C), a member or candidate should put the needs and circumstances of each client and the client's investment objectives into a written investment policy statement. In formulating an investment policy for the client, the member or candidate should take the following into consideration:

- client identification—(1) type and nature of client, (2) the existence of separate beneficiaries, and (3) approximate portion of total client assets that the member or candidate is managing;
- investor objectives—(1) return objectives (income, growth in principal, maintenance of purchasing power) and (2) risk tolerance (suitability, stability of values);
- investor constraints—(1) liquidity needs, (2) expected cash flows (patterns of additions and/or withdrawals), (3) investable funds (assets and liabilities or other commitments), (4) time horizon, (5) tax considerations, (6) regulatory and legal circumstances, (7) investor preferences, prohibitions, circumstances, and unique needs, and (8) proxy voting responsibilities and guidance; and
- performance measurement benchmarks.

Regular Updates

The investor's objectives and constraints should be maintained and reviewed periodically to reflect any changes in the client's circumstances. Members and candidates should regularly compare client constraints with capital market expectations to arrive at an appropriate asset allocation. Changes in either factor may result in a fundamental change in asset allocation. Annual review is reasonable unless business or other reasons, such as a major change in market conditions, dictate more frequent review. Members and candidates should document attempts to carry out such a review if circumstances prevent it.

Suitability Test Policies

With the increase in regulatory required suitability tests, members and candidates should encourage their firms to develop related policies and procedures. The procedures will differ according to the size of the firm and the scope of the services offered to its clients.

The test procedures should require the investment professional to look beyond the potential return of the investment and include the following:

- an analysis of the impact on the portfolio's diversification,
- a comparison of the investment risks with the client's assessed risk tolerance, and
- the fit of the investment with the required investment strategy.

29 STANDARD III(C): APPLICATION OF THE STANDARD

Example 1 (Investment Suitability—Risk Profile):

Caleb Smith, an investment adviser, has two clients: Larry Robertson, 60 years old, and Gabriel Lanai, 40 years old. Both clients earn roughly the same salary, but Robertson has a much higher risk tolerance because he has a large asset base. Robertson is willing to invest part of his assets very aggressively; Lanai wants only to achieve a steady rate of return with low volatility to pay for his children's education. Smith recommends investing 20% of both portfolios in zero-yield, small-cap, high-technology equity issues.

> *Comment*: In Robertson's case, the investment may be appropriate because of his financial circumstances and aggressive investment position, but this investment is not suitable for Lanai. Smith is violating Standard III(C) by applying Robertson's investment strategy to Lanai because the two clients' financial circumstances and objectives differ.

Example 2 (Investment Suitability—Entire Portfolio):

Jessica McDowell, an investment adviser, suggests to Brian Crosby, a risk-averse client, that covered call options be used in his equity portfolio. The purpose would be to enhance Crosby's income and partially offset any untimely depreciation in the portfolio's value should the stock market or other circumstances affect his holdings unfavorably. McDowell educates Crosby about all possible outcomes, including the risk of incurring an added tax liability if a stock rises in price and is called away and, conversely, the risk of his holdings losing protection on the downside if prices drop sharply.

Comment: When determining suitability of an investment, the primary focus should be the characteristics of the client's entire portfolio, not the characteristics of single securities on an issue-by-issue basis. The basic characteristics of the entire portfolio will largely determine whether investment recommendations are taking client factors into account. Therefore, the most important aspects of a particular investment are those that will affect the characteristics of the total portfolio. In this case, McDowell properly considers the investment in the context of the entire portfolio and thoroughly explains the investment to the client.

Example 3 (IPS Updating):

In a regular meeting with client Seth Jones, the portfolio managers at Blue Chip Investment Advisors are careful to allow some time to review his current needs and circumstances. In doing so, they learn that some significant changes have recently taken place in his life. A wealthy uncle left Jones an inheritance that increased his net worth fourfold, to US$1 million.

Comment: The inheritance has significantly increased Jones's ability (and possibly his willingness) to assume risk and has diminished the average yield required to meet his current income needs. Jones's financial circumstances have definitely changed, so Blue Chip managers must update Jones's investment policy statement to reflect how his investment objectives have changed. Accordingly, the Blue Chip portfolio managers should consider a somewhat higher equity ratio for his portfolio than was called for by the previous circumstances, and the managers' specific common stock recommendations might be heavily tilted toward low-yield, growth-oriented issues.

Example 4 (Following an Investment Mandate):

Louis Perkowski manages a high-income mutual fund. He purchases zero-dividend stock in a financial services company because he believes the stock is undervalued and is in a potential growth industry, which makes it an attractive investment.

Comment: A zero-dividend stock does not seem to fit the mandate of the fund that Perkowski is managing. Unless Perkowski's investment fits within the mandate or is within the realm of allowable investments the fund has made clear in its disclosures, Perkowski has violated Standard III(C).

Example 5 (IPS Requirements and Limitations):

Max Gubler, chief investment officer of a property/casualty insurance subsidiary of a large financial conglomerate, wants to improve the diversification of the subsidiary's investment portfolio and increase its returns. The subsidiary's investment policy statement provides for highly liquid investments, such as large-cap equities and government, supranational, and corporate bonds with a minimum credit rating of AA and maturity of no more than five years. In a recent presentation, a venture capital group offered very attractive prospective returns on some of its private equity funds that provide seed capital to ventures. An exit strategy was already contemplated, but investors would have to observe a minimum three-year lockup period and a subsequent laddered exit option for a maximum of one-third of their shares per year. Gubler does not want to miss this opportunity. After extensive analysis, with the intent to optimize the return on the equity assets within the subsidiary's current portfolio, he invests 4% in this seed fund, leaving the portfolio's total equity exposure still well below its upper limit.

Comment: Gubler is violating Standard III(A) Loyalty, Prudence, and Care as well as Standard III(C). His new investment locks up part of the subsidiary's assets for at least three years and up to as many as five years and possibly beyond. The IPS requires investments in highly liquid investments and describes accepted asset classes; private equity investments with a lockup period certainly do not qualify. Even without a lockup period, an asset class with only an occasional, and thus implicitly illiquid, market may not be suitable for the portfolio. Although an IPS typically describes objectives and constraints in great detail, the manager must also make every effort to understand the client's business and circumstances. Doing so should enable the manager to recognize, understand, and discuss with the client other factors that may be or may become material in the investment management process.

Example 6 (Submanager and IPS Reviews):

Paul Ostrowski's investment management business has grown significantly over the past couple of years, and some clients want to diversify internationally. Ostrowski decides to find a submanager to handle the expected international investments. Because this will be his first subadviser, Ostrowski uses the CFA Institute model "request for proposal" to design a questionnaire for his search. By his deadline, he receives seven completed questionnaires from a variety of domestic and international firms trying to gain his business. Ostrowski reviews all the applications in detail and decides to select the firm that charges the lowest fees because doing so will have the least impact on his firm's bottom line.

Comment: When selecting an external manager or subadviser, Ostrowski needs to ensure that the new manager's services are appropriate for his clients. This due diligence includes comparing the risk profile of the clients with the investment strategy of the manager. In basing the decision on the fee structure alone, Ostrowski may be violating Standard III(C).

When clients ask to diversify into international products, it is an appropriate time to review and update the clients' IPSs. Ostrowski's review may determine that the risk of international investments modifies the risk profiles of the clients or does not represent an appropriate investment.

See also Standard V(A) Diligence and Reasonable Basis for further discussion of the review process needed in selecting appropriate submanagers.

Example 7 (Investment Suitability—Risk Profile):

Samantha Snead, a portfolio manager for Thomas Investment Counsel, Inc., specializes in managing public retirement funds and defined benefit pension plan accounts, all of which have long-term investment objectives. A year ago, Snead's employer, in an attempt to motivate and retain key investment professionals, introduced a bonus compensation system that rewards portfolio managers on the basis of quarterly performance relative to their peers and to certain benchmark indexes. In an attempt to improve the short-term performance of her accounts, Snead changes her investment strategy and purchases several high-beta stocks for client portfolios. These purchases are seemingly contrary to the clients' investment policy statements. Following their purchase, an officer of Griffin Corporation, one of Snead's pension fund clients, asks why Griffin Corporation's portfolio seems to be dominated by high-beta stocks of companies that often appear among the most actively traded issues. No change in objective or strategy has been recommended by Snead during the year.

Comment: Snead violated Standard III(C) by investing the clients' assets in high-beta stocks. These high-risk investments are contrary to the long-term risk profile established in the clients' IPSs. Snead has changed the investment strategy of the clients in an attempt to reap short-term rewards offered by her firm's new compensation arrangement, not in response to changes in clients' investment policy statements.

See also Standard VI(A) Disclosure of Conflicts.

Example 8 (Investment Suitability):

Andre Shrub owns and operates Conduit, an investment advisory firm. Prior to opening Conduit, Shrub was an account manager with Elite Investment, a hedge fund managed by his good friend Adam Reed. To attract clients to a new Conduit fund, Shrub offers lower-than-normal management fees. He can do so because the fund consists of two top-performing funds managed by Reed. Given his personal friendship with Reed and the prior performance record of these two funds, Shrub believes this new fund is a winning combination for all parties. Clients quickly invest with Conduit to gain access to the Elite funds. No one is turned away because Conduit is seeking to expand its assets under management.

Comment: Shrub has violated Standard III(C) because the risk profile of the new fund may not be suitable for every client. As an investment adviser, Shrub needs to establish an investment policy statement for each client and recommend only investments that match each client's risk and return profile in the IPS. Shrub is required to act as more than a simple sales agent for Elite.

Although Shrub cannot disobey the direct request of a client to purchase a specific security, he should fully discuss the risks of a planned purchase and provide reasons why it might not be suitable for a client. This requirement may lead members and candidates to decline new customers if those customers' requested investment decisions are significantly out of line with their stated requirements.

See also Standard V(A) Diligence and Reasonable Basis.

STANDARD III(D) PERFORMANCE PRESENTATION 30

- ☐ demonstrate a thorough knowledge of the CFA Institute Code of Ethics and Standards of Professional Conduct by interpreting the Code and Standards in various situations involving issues of professional integrity
- ☐ recommend practices and procedures designed to prevent violations of the Code and Standards

When communicating investment performance information, Members and Candidates must make reasonable efforts to ensure that it is fair, accurate, and complete.

Guidance

Standard III(D) requires members and candidates to provide credible performance information to clients and prospective clients and to avoid misstating performance or misleading clients and prospective clients about the investment performance of members or candidates or their firms. This standard encourages full disclosure of investment performance data to clients and prospective clients.

Standard III(D) covers any practice that would lead to misrepresentation of a member's or candidate's performance record, whether the practice involves performance presentation or performance measurement. This standard prohibits misrepresentations of past performance or reasonably expected performance. A member or candidate must give a fair and complete presentation of performance information whenever communicating data with respect to the performance history of individual accounts, composites or groups of accounts, or composites of an analyst's or firm's performance results. Furthermore, members and candidates should not state or imply that clients will obtain or benefit from a rate of return that was generated in the past.

The requirements of this standard are not limited to members and candidates managing separate accounts. Whenever a member or candidate provides performance information for which the manager is claiming responsibility, such as for pooled funds, the history must be accurate. Research analysts promoting the success or accuracy of their recommendations must ensure that their claims are fair, accurate, and complete.

If the presentation is brief, the member or candidate must make available to clients and prospects, on request, the detailed information supporting that communication. Best practice dictates that brief presentations include a reference to the limited nature of the information provided.

31 STANDARD III(D): RECOMMENDED PROCEDURES

Apply the GIPS Standards

For members and candidates who are showing the performance history of the assets they manage, compliance with the GIPS standards is the best method to meet their obligations under Standard III(D). Members and candidates should encourage their firms to comply with the GIPS standards.

Compliance without Applying GIPS Standards

Members and candidates can also meet their obligations under Standard III(D) by

- considering the knowledge and sophistication of the audience to whom a performance presentation is addressed,
- presenting the performance of the weighted composite of similar portfolios rather than using a single representative account,
- including terminated accounts as part of performance history with a clear indication of when the accounts were terminated,

- including disclosures that fully explain the performance results being reported (for example, stating, when appropriate, that results are simulated when model results are used, clearly indicating when the performance record is that of a prior entity, or disclosing whether the performance is gross of fees, net of fees, or after tax), and
- maintaining the data and records used to calculate the performance being presented.

STANDARD III(D): APPLICATION OF THE STANDARD

32

Example 1 (Performance Calculation and Length of Time):

Kyle Taylor of Taylor Trust Company, noting the performance of Taylor's common trust fund for the past two years, states in a brochure sent to his potential clients, "You can expect steady 25% annual compound growth of the value of your investments over the year." Taylor Trust's common trust fund did increase at the rate of 25% per year for the past year, which mirrored the increase of the entire market. The fund has never averaged that growth for more than one year, however, and the average rate of growth of all of its trust accounts for five years is 5% per year.

> *Comment*: Taylor's brochure is in violation of Standard III(D). Taylor should have disclosed that the 25% growth occurred only in one year. Additionally, Taylor did not include client accounts other than those in the firm's common trust fund. A general claim of firm performance should take into account the performance of all categories of accounts. Finally, by stating that clients can expect a steady 25% annual compound growth rate, Taylor is also violating Standard I(C) Misrepresentation, which prohibits assurances or guarantees regarding an investment.

Example 2 (Performance Calculation and Asset Weighting):

Anna Judd, a senior partner of Alexander Capital Management, circulates a performance report for the capital appreciation accounts for the years 1988 through 2004. The firm claims compliance with the GIPS standards. Returns are not calculated in accordance with the requirements of the GIPS standards, however, because the composites are not asset weighted.

> *Comment*: Judd is in violation of Standard III(D). When claiming compliance with the GIPS standards, firms must meet *all* of the requirements, make mandatory disclosures, and meet any other requirements that apply to that firm's specific situation. Judd's violation is not from any misuse of the data but from a false claim of GIPS compliance.

Example 3 (Performance Presentation and Prior Fund/Employer):

Aaron McCoy is vice president and managing partner of the equity investment group of Mastermind Financial Advisors, a new business. Mastermind recruited McCoy because he had a proven six-year track record with G&P Financial. In developing

Mastermind's advertising and marketing campaign, McCoy prepares an advertisement that includes the equity investment performance he achieved at G&P Financial. The advertisement for Mastermind does not identify the equity performance as being earned while at G&P. The advertisement is distributed to existing clients and prospective clients of Mastermind.

> *Comment*: McCoy has violated Standard III(D) by distributing an advertisement that contains material misrepresentations about the historical performance of Mastermind. Standard III(D) requires that members and candidates make every reasonable effort to ensure that performance information is a fair, accurate, and complete representation of an individual's or firm's performance. As a general matter, this standard does not prohibit showing past performance of funds managed at a prior firm as part of a performance track record as long as showing that record is accompanied by appropriate disclosures about where the performance took place and the person's specific role in achieving that performance. If McCoy chooses to use his past performance from G&P in Mastermind's advertising, he should make full disclosure of the source of the historical performance.

Example 4 (Performance Presentation and Simulated Results):

Jed Davis has developed a mutual fund selection product based on historical information from the 1990–95 period. Davis tested his methodology by applying it retroactively to data from the 1996–2003 period, thus producing simulated performance results for those years. In January 2004, Davis's employer decided to offer the product and Davis began promoting it through trade journal advertisements and direct dissemination to clients. The advertisements included the performance results for the 1996–2003 period but did not indicate that the results were simulated.

> *Comment*: Davis violated Standard III(D) by failing to clearly identify simulated performance results. Standard III(D) prohibits members and candidates from making any statements that misrepresent the performance achieved by them or their firms and requires members and candidates to make every reasonable effort to ensure that performance information presented to clients is fair, accurate, and complete. Use of simulated results should be accompanied by full disclosure as to the source of the performance data, including the fact that the results from 1995 through 2003 were the result of applying the model retroactively to that time period.

Example 5 (Performance Calculation and Selected Accounts Only):

In a presentation prepared for prospective clients, William Kilmer shows the rates of return realized over a five-year period by a "composite" of his firm's discretionary accounts that have a "balanced" objective. This composite, however, consisted of only a few of the accounts that met the balanced criterion set by the firm, excluded accounts under a certain asset level without disclosing the fact of their exclusion, and included accounts that did not have the balanced mandate because those accounts would boost the investment results. In addition, to achieve better results, Kilmer manipulated the narrow range of accounts included in the composite by changing the accounts that made up the composite over time.

Comment: Kilmer violated Standard III(D) by misrepresenting the facts in the promotional material sent to prospective clients, distorting his firm's performance record, and failing to include disclosures that would have clarified the presentation.

Example 6 (Performance Attribution Changes):

Art Purell is reviewing the quarterly performance attribution reports for distribution to clients. Purell works for an investment management firm with a bottom-up, fundamentals-driven investment process that seeks to add value through stock selection. The attribution methodology currently compares each stock with its sector. The attribution report indicates that the value added this quarter came from asset allocation and that stock selection contributed negatively to the calculated return.

Through running several different scenarios, Purell discovers that calculating attribution by comparing each stock with its industry and then rolling the effect to the sector level improves the appearance of the manager's stock selection activities. Because the firm defines the attribution terms and the results better reflect the stated strategy, Purell recommends that the client reports should use the revised methodology.

Comment: Modifying the attribution methodology without proper notifications to clients would fail to meet the requirements of Standard III(D). Purell's recommendation is being done solely for the interest of the firm to improve its perceived ability to meet the stated investment strategy. Such changes are unfair to clients and obscure the facts regarding the firm's abilities.

Had Purell believed the new methodology offered improvements to the original model, then he would have needed to report the results of both calculations to the client. The report should also include the reasons why the new methodology is preferred, which would allow the client to make a meaningful comparison to prior results and provide a basis for comparing future attributions.

Example 7 (Performance Calculation Methodology Disclosure):

While developing a new reporting package for existing clients, Alisha Singh, a performance analyst, discovers that her company's new system automatically calculates both time-weighted and money-weighted returns. She asks the head of client services and retention which value would be preferred given that the firm has various investment strategies that include bonds, equities, securities without leverage, and alternatives. Singh is told not to label the return value so that the firm may show whichever value is greatest for the period.

Comment: Following these instructions would lead to Singh violating Standard III(D). In reporting inconsistent return values, Singh would not be providing complete information to the firm's clients. Full information is provided when clients have sufficient information to judge the performance generated by the firm.

Example 8 (Performance Calculation Methodology Disclosure):

Richmond Equity Investors manages a long–short equity fund in which clients can trade once a week (on Fridays). For transparency reasons, a daily net asset value of the fund is calculated by Richmond. The monthly fact sheets of the fund report month-to-date and year-to-date performance. Richmond publishes the performance based on the higher of the last trading day of the month (typically, not the last business day) or the last business day of the month as determined by Richmond. The fact sheet mentions only that the data are as of the end of the month, without giving the exact date. Maggie Clark, the investment performance analyst in charge of the calculations, is concerned about the frequent changes and asks her supervisor whether they are appropriate.

> *Comment*: Clark's actions in questioning the changing performance metric comply with Standard III(D). She has shown concern that these changes are not presenting an accurate and complete picture of the performance generated.

33 STANDARD III(E) PRESERVATION OF CONFIDENTIALITY

- ☐ demonstrate a thorough knowledge of the CFA Institute Code of Ethics and Standards of Professional Conduct by interpreting the Code and Standards in various situations involving issues of professional integrity
- ☐ recommend practices and procedures designed to prevent violations of the Code and Standards

Members and Candidates must keep information about current, former, and prospective clients confidential unless:

1. The information concerns illegal activities on the part of the client;
2. Disclosure is required by law; or
3. The client or prospective client permits disclosure of the information.

Guidance

Highlights:

- *Status of Client*
- *Compliance with Laws*
- *Electronic Information and Security*
- *Professional Conduct Investigations by CFA Institute*

Standard III(E) requires that members and candidates preserve the confidentiality of information communicated to them by their clients, prospective clients, and former clients. This standard is applicable when (1) the member or candidate receives information because of his or her special ability to conduct a portion of the client's business or personal affairs and (2) the member or candidate receives information that arises from or is relevant to that portion of the client's business that is the subject of the special or confidential relationship. If disclosure of the information is required by law or the information concerns illegal activities by the client, however, the member or candidate may have an obligation to report the activities to the appropriate authorities.

Status of Client

This standard protects the confidentiality of client information even if the person or entity is no longer a client of the member or candidate. Therefore, members and candidates must continue to maintain the confidentiality of client records even after the client relationship has ended. If a client or former client expressly authorizes the member or candidate to disclose information, however, the member or candidate may follow the terms of the authorization and provide the information.

Compliance with Laws

As a general matter, members and candidates must comply with applicable law. If applicable law requires disclosure of client information in certain circumstances, members and candidates must comply with the law. Similarly, if applicable law requires members and candidates to maintain confidentiality, even if the information concerns illegal activities on the part of the client, members and candidates should not disclose such information. Additionally, applicable laws, such as inter-departmental communication restrictions within financial institutions, can impose limitations on information flow about a client within an entity that may lead to a violation of confidentiality. When in doubt, members and candidates should consult with their employer's compliance personnel or legal counsel before disclosing confidential information about clients.

Electronic Information and Security

Because of the ever-increasing volume of electronically stored information, members and candidates need to be particularly aware of possible accidental disclosures. Many employers have strict policies about how to electronically communicate sensitive client information and store client information on personal laptops, mobile devices, or portable disk/flash drives. In recent years, regulatory authorities have imposed stricter data security laws applying to the use of mobile remote digital communication, including the use of social media, that must be considered. Standard III(E) does not require members or candidates to become experts in information security technology, but they should have a thorough understanding of the policies of their employer. The size and operations of the firm will lead to differing policies for ensuring the security of confidential information maintained within the firm. Members and candidates should encourage their firm to conduct regular periodic training on confidentiality procedures for all firm personnel, including portfolio associates, receptionists, and other non-investment staff who have routine direct contact with clients and their records.

Professional Conduct Investigations by CFA Institute

The requirements of Standard III(E) are not intended to prevent members and candidates from cooperating with an investigation by the CFA Institute Professional Conduct Program (PCP). When permissible under applicable law, members and candidates shall consider the PCP an extension of themselves when requested to provide information about a client in support of a PCP investigation into their own conduct. Members and candidates are encouraged to cooperate with investigations into the conduct of others. Any information turned over to the PCP is kept in the strictest confidence. Members and candidates will not be considered in violation of this standard by forwarding confidential information to the PCP.

34 STANDARD III(E): RECOMMENDED PROCEDURES

The simplest, most conservative, and most effective way to comply with Standard III(E) is to avoid disclosing any information received from a client except to authorized fellow employees who are also working for the client. In some instances, however, a member or candidate may want to disclose information received from clients that is outside the scope of the confidential relationship and does not involve illegal activities. Before making such a disclosure, a member or candidate should ask the following:

- In what context was the information disclosed? If disclosed in a discussion of work being performed for the client, is the information relevant to the work?
- Is the information background material that, if disclosed, will enable the member or candidate to improve service to the client?

Members and candidates need to understand and follow their firm's electronic information communication and storage procedures. If the firm does not have procedures in place, members and candidates should encourage the development of procedures that appropriately reflect the firm's size and business operations.

Communicating with Clients

Technological changes are constantly enhancing the methods that are used to communicate with clients and prospective clients. Members and candidates should make reasonable efforts to ensure that firm-supported communication methods and compliance procedures follow practices designed for preventing accidental distribution of confidential information. Given the rate at which technology changes, a regular review of privacy protection measures is encouraged.

Members and candidates should be diligent in discussing with clients the appropriate methods for providing confidential information. It is important to convey to clients that not all firm-sponsored resources may be appropriate for such communications.

35 STANDARD III(E): APPLICATION OF THE STANDARD

Example 1 (Possessing Confidential Information):

Sarah Connor, a financial analyst employed by Johnson Investment Counselors, Inc., provides investment advice to the trustees of City Medical Center. The trustees have given her a number of internal reports concerning City Medical's needs for physical plant renovation and expansion. They have asked Connor to recommend investments that would generate capital appreciation in endowment funds to meet projected capital expenditures. Connor is approached by a local businessman, Thomas Kasey, who is considering a substantial contribution either to City Medical Center or to another local hospital. Kasey wants to find out the building plans of both institutions before making a decision, but he does not want to speak to the trustees.

> *Comment*: The trustees gave Connor the internal reports so she could advise them on how to manage their endowment funds. Because the information in the reports is clearly both confidential and within the scope of the confidential relationship, Standard III(E) requires that Connor refuse to divulge information to Kasey.

Example 2 (Disclosing Confidential Information):

Lynn Moody is an investment officer at the Lester Trust Company. She has an advisory customer who has talked to her about giving approximately US$50,000 to charity to reduce her income taxes. Moody is also treasurer of the Home for Indigent Widows (HIW), which is planning its annual giving campaign. HIW hopes to expand its list of prospects, particularly those capable of substantial gifts. Moody recommends that HIW's vice president for corporate gifts call on her customer and ask for a donation in the US$50,000 range.

> *Comment*: Even though the attempt to help the Home for Indigent Widows was well intended, Moody violated Standard III(E) by revealing confidential information about her client.

Example 3 (Disclosing Possible Illegal Activity):

Government officials approach Casey Samuel, the portfolio manager for Garcia Company's pension plan, to examine pension fund records. They tell her that Garcia's corporate tax returns are being audited and the pension fund is being reviewed. Two days earlier, Samuel had learned in a regular investment review with Garcia officers that potentially excessive and improper charges were being made to the pension plan by Garcia. Samuel consults her employer's general counsel and is advised that Garcia has probably violated tax and fiduciary regulations and laws.

> *Comment*: Samuel should inform her supervisor of these activities, and her employer should take steps, with Garcia, to remedy the violations. If that approach is not successful, Samuel and her employer should seek advice of legal counsel to determine the appropriate steps to be taken. Samuel may well have a duty to disclose the evidence she has of the continuing legal violations and to resign as asset manager for Garcia.

Example 4 (Disclosing Possible Illegal Activity):

David Bradford manages money for a family-owned real estate development corporation. He also manages the individual portfolios of several of the family members and officers of the corporation, including the chief financial officer (CFO). Based on the financial records of the corporation and some questionable practices of the CFO that Bradford has observed, Bradford believes that the CFO is embezzling money from the corporation and putting it into his personal investment account.

> *Comment*: Bradford should check with his firm's compliance department or appropriate legal counsel to determine whether applicable securities regulations require reporting the CFO's financial records.

Example 5 (Accidental Disclosure of Confidential Information):

Lynn Moody is an investment officer at the Lester Trust Company (LTC). She has stewardship of a significant number of individually managed taxable accounts. In addition to receiving quarterly written reports, about a dozen high-net-worth individuals have indicated to Moody a willingness to receive communications about overall economic and financial market outlooks directly from her by way of a social media platform. Under the direction of her firm's technology and compliance departments, she established a new group page on an existing social media platform specifically for her clients. In the instructions provided to clients, Moody asked them to "join" the group so they may be granted access to the posted content. The instructions also advised clients that all comments posted would be available to the public and thus the platform was not an appropriate method for communicating personal or confidential information.

Six months later, in early January, Moody posted LTC's year-end "Market Outlook." The report outlined a new asset allocation strategy that the firm is adding to its recommendations in the new year. Moody introduced the publication with a note informing her clients that she would be discussing the changes with them individually in their upcoming meetings.

One of Moody's clients responded directly on the group page that his family recently experienced a major change in their financial profile. The client described highly personal and confidential details of the event. Unfortunately, all clients that were part of the group were also able to read the detailed posting until Moody was able to have the comment removed.

> *Comment*: Moody has taken reasonable steps for protecting the confidentiality of client information while using the social media platform. She provided instructions clarifying that all information posted to the site would be publicly viewable to all group members and warned against using this method for communicating confidential information. The accidental disclosure of confidential information by a client is not under Moody's control. Her actions to remove the information promptly once she became aware further align with Standard III(E).
>
> In understanding the potential sensitivity clients express surrounding the confidentiality of personal information, this event highlights a need for further training. Moody might advocate for additional warnings or controls for clients when they consider using social media platforms for two-way communications.

36 STANDARD IV: DUTIES TO EMPLOYERS

- ☐ demonstrate a thorough knowledge of the CFA Institute Code of Ethics and Standards of Professional Conduct by interpreting the Code and Standards in various situations involving issues of professional integrity
- ☐ recommend practices and procedures designed to prevent violations of the Code and Standards

Standard IV(A) Loyalty

> In matters related to their employment, Members and Candidates must act for the benefit of their employer and not deprive their employer of the advantage of their skills and abilities, divulge confidential information, or otherwise cause harm to their employer.

Guidance

Highlights:

- *Employer Responsibilities*
- *Independent Practice*
- *Leaving an Employer*
- *Use of Social Media*
- *Whistleblowing*
- *Nature of Employment*

Standard IV(A) requires members and candidates to protect the interests of their firm by refraining from any conduct that would injure the firm, deprive it of profit, or deprive it of the member's or candidate's skills and ability. Members and candidates must always place the interests of clients above the interests of their employer but should also consider the effects of their conduct on the sustainability and integrity of the employer firm. In matters related to their employment, members and candidates must not engage in conduct that harms the interests of their employer. Implicit in this standard is the obligation of members and candidates to comply with the policies and procedures established by their employers that govern the employer–employee relationship—to the extent that such policies and procedures do not conflict with applicable laws, rules, or regulations or the Code and Standards.

This standard is not meant to be a blanket requirement to place employer interests ahead of personal interests in all matters. The standard does not require members and candidates to subordinate important personal and family obligations to their work. Members and candidates should enter into a dialogue with their employer about balancing personal and employment obligations when personal matters may interfere with their work on a regular or significant basis.

Employer Responsibilities

The employer–employee relationship imposes duties and responsibilities on both parties. Employers must recognize the duties and responsibilities that they owe to their employees if they expect to have content and productive employees.

Members and candidates are encouraged to provide their employer with a copy of the Code and Standards. These materials will inform the employer of the responsibilities of a CFA Institute member or a candidate in the CFA Program. The Code and Standards also serve as a basis for questioning employer policies and practices that conflict with these responsibilities.

Employers are not obligated to adhere to the Code and Standards. In expecting to retain competent employees who are members and candidates, however, they should not develop conflicting policies and procedures. The employer is responsible for a positive working environment, which includes an ethical workplace. Senior management has the additional responsibility to devise compensation structures and incentive arrangements that do not encourage unethical behavior.

Independent Practice

Included in Standard IV(A) is the requirement that members and candidates abstain from independent competitive activity that could conflict with the interests of their employer. Although Standard IV(A) does not preclude members or candidates from entering into an independent business while still employed, members and candidates who plan to engage in independent practice for compensation must notify their employer and describe the types of services they will render to prospective independent clients, the expected duration of the services, and the compensation for the services.

Members and candidates should not render services until they receive consent from their employer to all of the terms of the arrangement. "Practice" means any service that the employer currently makes available for remuneration. "Undertaking independent practice" means engaging in competitive business, as opposed to making preparations to begin such practice.

Leaving an Employer

When members and candidates are planning to leave their current employer, they must continue to act in the employer's best interest. They must not engage in any activities that would conflict with this duty until their resignation becomes effective. It is difficult to define specific guidelines for those members and candidates who are planning to compete with their employer as part of a new venture. The circumstances of each situation must be reviewed to distinguish permissible preparations from violations of duty. Activities that might constitute a violation, especially in combination, include the following:

- misappropriation of trade secrets,
- misuse of confidential information,
- solicitation of the employer's clients prior to cessation of employment,
- self-dealing (appropriating for one's own property a business opportunity or information belonging to one's employer), and
- misappropriation of clients or client lists.

A departing employee is generally free to make arrangements or preparations to go into a competitive business before terminating the relationship with his or her employer as long as such preparations do not breach the employee's duty of loyalty. A member or candidate who is contemplating seeking other employment must not contact existing clients or potential clients prior to leaving his or her employer for purposes of soliciting their business for the new employer. Once notice is provided to the employer of the intent to resign, the member or candidate must follow the employer's policies and procedures related to notifying clients of his or her planned departure. In addition, the member or candidate must not take records or files to a new employer without the written permission of the previous employer.

Once an employee has left the firm, the skills and experience that an employee obtained while employed are not "confidential" or "privileged" information. Similarly, simple knowledge of the names and existence of former clients is generally not confidential information unless deemed such by an agreement or by law. Standard IV(A) does not prohibit experience or knowledge gained at one employer from being used at another employer. Firm records or work performed on behalf of the firm that is stored in paper copy or electronically for the member's or candidate's convenience while employed, however, should be erased or returned to the employer unless the firm gives permission to keep those records after employment ends.

The standard does not prohibit former employees from contacting clients of their previous firm as long as the contact information does not come from the records of the former employer or violate an applicable "noncompete agreement." Members and candidates are free to use public information after departing to contact former clients without violating Standard IV(A) as long as there is no specific agreement not to do so.

Employers often require employees to sign noncompete agreements that preclude a departing employee from engaging in certain conduct. Members and candidates should take care to review the terms of any such agreement when leaving their employer to determine what, if any, conduct those agreements may prohibit.

In some markets, there are agreements between employers within an industry that outline information that departing employees are permitted to take upon resignation, such as the "Protocol for Broker Recruiting" in the United States. These agreements ease individuals' transition between firms that have agreed to follow the outlined procedures. Members and candidates who move between firms that sign such agreements may rely on the protections provided as long as they faithfully adhere to all the procedures outlined.

For example, under the agreement between many US brokers, individuals are allowed to take some general client contact information when departing. To be protected, a copy of the information the individual is taking must be provided to the local management team for review. Additionally, the specific client information may only be used by the departing employee and not others employed by the new firm.

Use of Social Media

The growth in various online networking platforms, such as LinkedIn, X, and Facebook (commonly referred to as social media platforms), is providing new opportunities and challenges for businesses. Members and candidates should understand and abide by all applicable firm policies and regulations as to the acceptable use of social media platforms to interact with clients and prospective clients. This is especially important when a member or candidate is planning to leave an employer.

Social media use makes determining how and when departure notification is delivered to clients more complex. Members and candidates may have developed profiles on these platforms that include connections with individuals who are clients of the firm, as well as individuals unrelated to their employer. Communications through social media platforms that potentially reach current clients should adhere to the employer's policies and procedures regarding notification of departing employees.

Social media connections with clients are also raising questions concerning the differences between public information and firm property. Specific accounts and user profiles of members and candidates may be created for solely professional reasons, including firm-approved accounts for client engagements. Such firm-approved business-related accounts would be considered part of the firm's assets, thus requiring members and candidates to transfer or delete the accounts as directed by their firm's policies and procedures. Best practice for members and candidates is to maintain separate accounts for their personal and professional social media activities. Members and candidates should discuss with their employers how profiles should be treated when a single account includes personal connections and also is used to conduct aspects of their professional activities.

Whistleblowing

A member's or candidate's personal interests, as well as the interests of his or her employer, are secondary to protecting the integrity of capital markets and the interests of clients. Therefore, circumstances may arise (e.g., when an employer is engaged in illegal or unethical activity) in which members and candidates must act contrary to their employer's interests in order to comply with their duties to the market and clients. In such instances, activities that would normally violate a member's or candidate's duty to his or her employer (such as contradicting employer instructions, violating certain policies and procedures, or preserving a record by copying employer records) may be justified. Such action would be permitted only if the intent is clearly aimed at protecting clients or the integrity of the market, not for personal gain.

Nature of Employment

A wide variety of business relationships exists within the investment industry. For instance, a member or candidate may be an employee or an independent contractor. Members and candidates must determine whether they are employees or independent contractors in order to determine the applicability of Standard IV(A). This issue will be decided largely by the degree of control exercised by the employing entity over the member or candidate. Factors determining control include whether the member's or candidate's hours, work location, and other parameters of the job are set; whether facilities are provided to the member or candidate; whether the member's or candidate's expenses are reimbursed; whether the member or candidate seeks work from other employers; and the number of clients or employers the member or candidate works for.

A member's or candidate's duties within an independent contractor relationship are governed by the oral or written agreement between the member and the client. Members and candidates should take care to define clearly the scope of their responsibilities and the expectations of each client within the context of each relationship. Once a member or candidate establishes a relationship with a client, the member or candidate has a duty to abide by the terms of the agreement.

37 STANDARD IV(A): RECOMMENDED PROCEDURES

Employers may establish codes of conduct and operating procedures for their employees to follow. Members and candidates should fully understand the policies to ensure that they are not in conflict with the Code and Standards. The following topics identify policies that members and candidates should encourage their firms to adopt if the policies are not currently in place.

Competition Policy

A member or candidate must understand any restrictions placed by the employer on offering similar services outside the firm while employed by the firm. The policy may outline the procedures for requesting approval to undertake the outside service or may be a strict prohibition of such service. If a member's or candidate's employer elects to have its employees sign a noncompete agreement as part of the employment agreement, the member or candidate should ensure that the details are clear and fully explained prior to signing the agreement.

Termination Policy

Members and candidates should clearly understand the termination policies of their employer. Termination policies should establish clear procedures regarding the resignation process, including addressing how the termination will be disclosed to clients and staff and whether updates posted through social media platforms will be allowed. The firm's policy may also outline the procedures for transferring ongoing research and account management responsibilities. Finally, the procedures should address agreements that allow departing employees to remove specific client-related information upon resignation.

Incident-Reporting Procedures

Members and candidates should be aware of their firm's policies related to whistleblowing and encourage their firm to adopt industry best practices in this area. Many firms are required by regulatory mandates to establish confidential and anonymous reporting procedures that allow employees to report potentially unethical and illegal activities in the firm.

Employee Classification

Members and candidates should understand their status within their employer firm. Firms are encouraged to adopt a standardized classification structure (e.g., part time, full time, outside contractor) for their employees and indicate how each of the firm's policies applies to each employee class.

STANDARD IV(A): APPLICATION OF THE STANDARD

38

- ☐ demonstrate a thorough knowledge of the CFA Institute Code of Ethics and Standards of Professional Conduct by interpreting the Code and Standards in various situations involving issues of professional integrity
- ☐ recommend practices and procedures designed to prevent violations of the Code and Standards

Example 1 (Soliciting Former Clients):

Samuel Magee manages pension accounts for Trust Assets, Inc., but has become frustrated with the working environment and has been offered a position with Fiduciary Management. Before resigning from Trust Assets, Magee asks four big accounts to leave that firm and open accounts with Fiduciary. Magee also persuades several prospective clients to sign agreements with Fiduciary Management. Magee had previously made presentations to these prospects on behalf of Trust Assets.

> *Comment*: Magee violated the employee–employer principle requiring him to act solely for his employer's benefit. Magee's duty is to Trust Assets as long as he is employed there. The solicitation of Trust Assets' current clients and prospective clients is unethical and violates Standard IV(A).

Example 2 (Former Employer's Documents and Files):

James Hightower has been employed by Jason Investment Management Corporation for 15 years. He began as an analyst but assumed increasing responsibilities and is now a senior portfolio manager and a member of the firm's investment policy committee. Hightower has decided to leave Jason Investment and start his own investment management business. He has been careful not to tell any of Jason's clients that he is leaving; he does not want to be accused of breaching his duty to Jason by soliciting Jason's clients before his departure. Hightower is planning to copy and take with him the following documents and information he developed or worked on while at Jason: (1) the client list, with addresses, telephone numbers, and other pertinent client information; (2) client account statements; (3) sample marketing presentations to prospective clients containing Jason's performance record; (4) Jason's recommended list of securities; (5) computer models to determine asset allocations for accounts with various objectives; (6) computer models for stock selection; and (7) personal computer spreadsheets for Hightower's major corporate recommendations, which he developed when he was an analyst.

> *Comment*: Except with the consent of their employer, departing members and candidates may not take employer property, which includes books, records, reports, and other materials, because taking such materials may interfere with their employer's business opportunities. Taking any employer records, even those the member or candidate prepared, violates Standard IV(A). Employer records include items stored in hard copy or any other medium (e.g., home computers, portable storage devices, cell phones).

Example 3 (Addressing Rumors):

Reuben Winston manages all-equity portfolios at Target Asset Management (TAM), a large, established investment counselor. Ten years previously, Philpott & Company, which manages a family of global bond mutual funds, acquired TAM in a diversification move. After the merger, the combined operations prospered in the fixed-income business but the equity management business at TAM languished. Lately, a few of the equity pension accounts that had been with TAM before the merger have terminated their relationships with TAM. One day, Winston finds on his voice mail the following message from a concerned client: "Hey! I just heard that Philpott is close to announcing the sale of your firm's equity management business to Rugged Life. What is going on?" Not being aware of any such deal, Winston and his associates are stunned. Their internal inquiries are met with denials from Philpott management, but the rumors persist. Feeling left in the dark, Winston contemplates leading an employee buyout of TAM's equity management business.

> *Comment*: An employee-led buyout of TAM's equity asset management business would be consistent with Standard IV(A) because it would rest on the permission of the employer and, ultimately, the clients. In this case, however, in which employees suspect the senior managers or principals are not truthful or forthcoming, Winston should consult legal counsel to determine appropriate action.

Example 4 (Ownership of Completed Prior Work):

Laura Clay, who is unemployed, wants part-time consulting work while seeking a full-time analyst position. During an interview at Bradley Associates, a large institutional asset manager, Clay is told that the firm has no immediate research openings but would be willing to pay her a flat fee to complete a study of the wireless communications industry within a given period of time. Clay would be allowed unlimited access to Bradley's research files and would be welcome to come to the offices and use whatever support facilities are available during normal working hours. Bradley's research director does not seek any exclusivity for Clay's output, and the two agree to the arrangement on a handshake. As Clay nears completion of the study, she is offered an analyst job in the research department of Winston & Company, a brokerage firm, and she is pondering submitting the draft of her wireless study for publication by Winston.

> *Comment*: Although she is under no written contractual obligation to Bradley, Clay has an obligation to let Bradley act on the output of her study before Winston & Company or Clay uses the information to their advantage. That is, unless Bradley gives permission to Clay and waives its rights to her wireless report, Clay would be in violation of Standard IV(A) if she were to immediately recommend to Winston the same transactions recommended in the report to Bradley. Furthermore, Clay must not take from Bradley any research file material or other property that she may have used.

Example 5 (Ownership of Completed Prior Work):

Emma Madeline, a recent college graduate and a candidate in the CFA Program, spends her summer as an unpaid intern at Murdoch and Lowell. The senior managers at Murdoch are attempting to bring the firm into compliance with the GIPS standards, and Madeline is assigned to assist in its efforts. Two months into her internship, Madeline applies for a job at McMillan & Company, which has plans to become GIPS compliant. Madeline accepts the job with McMillan. Before leaving Murdoch, she copies the firm's software that she helped develop because she believes this software will assist her in her new position.

Comment: Even though Madeline does not receive monetary compensation for her services at Murdoch, she has used firm resources in creating the software and is considered an employee because she receives compensation and benefits in the form of work experience and knowledge. By copying the software, Madeline violated Standard IV(A) because she misappropriated Murdoch's property without permission.

Example 6 (Soliciting Former Clients):

Dennis Elliot has hired Sam Chisolm, who previously worked for a competing firm. Chisolm left his former firm after 18 years of employment. When Chisolm begins working for Elliot, he wants to contact his former clients because he knows them well and is certain that many will follow him to his new employer. Is Chisolm in violation of Standard IV(A) if he contacts his former clients?

Comment: Because client records are the property of the firm, contacting former clients for any reason through the use of client lists or other information taken from a former employer without permission would be a violation of Standard IV(A). In addition, the nature and extent of the contact with former clients may be governed by the terms of any noncompete agreement signed by the employee and the former employer that covers contact with former clients after employment.

Simple knowledge of the names and existence of former clients is not confidential information, just as skills or experience that an employee obtains while employed are not "confidential" or "privileged" information. The Code and Standards do not impose a prohibition on the use of experience or knowledge gained at one employer from being used at another employer. The Code and Standards also do not prohibit former employees from contacting clients of their previous firm, in the absence of a noncompete agreement. Members and candidates are free to use public information about their former firm after departing to contact former clients without violating Standard IV(A).

In the absence of a noncompete agreement, as long as Chisolm maintains his duty of loyalty to his employer before joining Elliot's firm, does not take steps to solicit clients until he has left his former firm, and does not use material from his former employer without its permission after he has left, he is not in violation of the Code and Standards.

Example 7 (Starting a New Firm):

Geraldine Allen currently works at a registered investment company as an equity analyst. Without notice to her employer, she registers with government authorities to start an investment company that will compete with her employer, but she does not actively seek clients. Does registration of this competing company with the appropriate regulatory authorities constitute a violation of Standard IV(A)?

> *Comment*: Allen's preparation for the new business by registering with the regulatory authorities does not conflict with the work for her employer if the preparations have been done on Allen's own time outside the office and if Allen will not be soliciting clients for the business or otherwise operating the new company until she has left her current employer.

Example 8 (Competing with Current Employer):

Several employees are planning to depart their current employer within a few weeks and have been careful to not engage in any activities that would conflict with their duty to their current employer. They have just learned that one of their employer's clients has undertaken a request for proposal (RFP) to review and possibly hire a new investment consultant. The RFP has been sent to the employer and all of its competitors. The group believes that the new entity to be formed would be qualified to respond to the RFP and be eligible for the business. The RFP submission period is likely to conclude before the employees' resignations are effective. Is it permissible for the group of departing employees to respond to the RFP for their anticipated new firm?

> *Comment*: A group of employees responding to an RFP that their employer is also responding to would lead to direct competition between the employees and the employer. Such conduct violates Standard IV(A) unless the group of employees receives permission from their employer as well as the entity sending out the RFP.

Example 9 (Externally Compensated Assignments):

Alfonso Mota is a research analyst with Tyson Investments. He works part time as a mayor for his hometown, a position for which he receives compensation. Must Mota seek permission from Tyson to serve as mayor?

> *Comment*: If Mota's mayoral duties are so extensive and time-consuming that they might detract from his ability to fulfill his responsibilities at Tyson, he should discuss his outside activities with his employer and come to a mutual agreement regarding how to manage his personal commitments with his responsibilities to his employer.

Example 10 (Soliciting Former Clients):

After leaving her employer, Shawna McQuillen establishes her own money management business. While with her former employer, she did not sign a noncompete agreement that would have prevented her from soliciting former clients. Upon her departure, she does not take any of her client lists or contact information and she clears her personal computer of any employer records, including client contact information. She obtains the phone numbers of her former clients through public records and contacts them to solicit their business.

Comment: McQuillen is not in violation of Standard IV(A) because she has not used information or records from her former employer and is not prevented by an agreement with her former employer from soliciting her former clients.

Example 11 (Whistleblowing Actions):

Meredith Rasmussen works on a buy-side trading desk and concentrates on in-house trades for a hedge fund subsidiary managed by a team at the investment management firm. The hedge fund has been very successful and is marketed globally by the firm. From her experience as the trader for much of the activity of the fund, Rasmussen has become quite knowledgeable about the hedge fund's strategy, tactics, and performance. When a distinct break in the market occurs, however, and many of the securities involved in the hedge fund's strategy decline markedly in value, Rasmussen observes that the reported performance of the hedge fund does not reflect this decline. In her experience, the lack of any effect is a very unlikely occurrence. She approaches the head of trading about her concern and is told that she should not ask any questions and that the fund is big and successful and is not her concern. She is fairly sure something is not right, so she contacts the compliance officer, who also tells her to stay away from the issue of this hedge fund's reporting.

Comment: Rasmussen has clearly come upon an error in policies, procedures, and compliance practices in the firm's operations. Having been unsuccessful in finding a resolution with her supervisor and the compliance officer, Rasmussen should consult the firm's whistleblowing policy to determine the appropriate next step toward informing management of her concerns. The potentially unethical actions of the investment management division are appropriate grounds for further disclosure, so Rasmussen's whistleblowing would not represent a violation of Standard IV(A).

See also Standard I(D) Misconduct and Standard IV(C) Responsibilities of Supervisors.

Example 12 (Soliciting Former Clients):

Angel Crome has been a private banker for YBSafe Bank for the past eight years. She has been very successful and built a considerable client portfolio during that time but is extremely frustrated by the recent loss of reputation by her current employer and subsequent client insecurity. A locally renowned headhunter contacted Crome a few days ago and offered her an interesting job with a competing private bank. This bank offers a substantial signing bonus for advisers with their own client portfolios. Crome figures that she can solicit at least 70% of her clients to follow her and gladly enters into the new employment contract.

Comment: Crome may contact former clients upon termination of her employment with YBSafe Bank, but she is prohibited from using client records built by and kept with her in her capacity as an employee of YBSafe Bank. Client lists are proprietary information of her former employer and must not be used for her or her new employer's benefit. The use of written, electronic, or any other form of records other than publicly available information to contact her former clients at YBSafe Bank will be a violation of Standard IV(A).

Example 13 (Notification of Code and Standards):

Krista Smith is a relatively new assistant trader for the fixed-income desk of a major investment bank. She is on a team responsible for structuring collateralized debt obligations (CDOs) made up of securities in the inventory of the trading desk. At a meeting of the team, senior executives explain the opportunity to eventually separate the CDO into various risk-rated tranches to be sold to the clients of the firm. After the senior executives leave the meeting, the head trader announces various responsibilities of each member of the team and then says, "This is a good time to unload some of the junk we have been stuck with for a while and disguise it with ratings and a thick, unreadable prospectus, so don't be shy in putting this CDO together. Just kidding." Smith is worried by this remark and asks some of her colleagues what the head trader meant. They all respond that he was just kidding but that there is some truth in the remark because the CDO is seen by management as an opportunity to improve the quality of the securities in the firm's inventory.

Concerned about the ethical environment of the workplace, Smith decides to talk to her supervisor about her concerns and provides the head trader with a copy of the Code and Standards. Smith discusses the principle of placing the client above the interest of the firm and the possibility that the development of the new CDO will not adhere to this responsibility. The head trader assures Smith that the appropriate analysis will be conducted when determining the appropriate securities for collateral. Furthermore, the ratings are assigned by an independent firm and the prospectus will include full and factual disclosures. Smith is reassured by the meeting, but she also reviews the company's procedures and requirements for reporting potential violations of company policy and securities laws.

> *Comment*: Smith's review of the company policies and procedures for reporting violations allows her to be prepared to report through the appropriate whistleblower process if she decides that the CDO development process involves unethical actions by others. Smith's actions comply with the Code and Standards principles of placing the client's interests first and being loyal to her employer. In providing her supervisor with a copy of the Code and Standards, Smith is highlighting the high level of ethical conduct she is required to adhere to in her professional activities.

Example 14 (Leaving an Employer):

Laura Webb just left her position as portfolio analyst at Research Systems, Inc. (RSI). Her employment contract included a non-solicitation agreement that requires her to wait two years before soliciting RSI clients for any investment-related services. Upon leaving, Webb was informed that RSI would contact clients immediately about her departure and introduce her replacement.

While working at RSI, Webb connected with clients, other industry associates, and friends through her LinkedIn network. Her business and personal relationships were intermingled because she considered many of her clients to be personal friends. Realizing that her LinkedIn network would be a valuable resource for new employment opportunities, she updated her profile several days following her departure from RSI. LinkedIn automatically sent a notification to Webb's entire network that her employment status had been changed in her profile.

> *Comment*: Prior to her departure, Webb should have discussed any client information contained in her social media networks. By updating her LinkedIn profile after RSI notified clients and after her employment ended, she has appropriately placed her employer's interests ahead of her own

personal interests. In addition, she has not violated the non-solicitation agreement with RSI, unless it prohibited any contact with clients during the two-year period.

Example 15 (Confidential Firm Information):

Sanjay Gupta is a research analyst at Naram Investment Management (NIM). NIM uses a team-based research process to develop recommendations on investment opportunities covered by the team members. Gupta, like others, provides commentary for NIM's clients through the company blog, which is posted weekly on the NIM password-protected website. According to NIM's policy, every contribution to the website must be approved by the company's compliance department before posting. Any opinions expressed on the website are disclosed as representing the perspective of NIM.

Gupta also writes a personal blog to share his experiences with friends and family. As with most blogs, Gupta's personal blog is widely available to interested readers through various internet search engines. Occasionally, when he disagrees with the team-based research opinions of NIM, Gupta uses his personal blog to express his own opinions as a counterpoint to the commentary posted on the NIM website. Gupta believes this provides his readers with a more complete perspective on these investment opportunities.

Comment: Gupta is in violation of Standard IV(A) for disclosing confidential firm information through his personal blog. The recommendations on the firm's blog to clients are not freely available across the internet, but his personal blog post indirectly provides the firm's recommendations.

Additionally, by posting research commentary on his personal blog, Gupta is using firm resources for his personal advantage. To comply with Standard IV(A), members and candidates must receive consent from their employer prior to using company resources.

STANDARD IV(B) ADDITIONAL COMPENSATION ARRANGEMENTS 39

Members and Candidates must not accept gifts, benefits, compensation, or consideration that competes with or might reasonably be expected to create a conflict of interest with their employer's interest unless they obtain written consent from all parties involved.

Guidance

Standard IV(B) requires members and candidates to obtain permission from their employer before accepting compensation or other benefits from third parties for the services rendered to the employer or for any services that might create a conflict with their employer's interest. Compensation and benefits include direct compensation by the client and any indirect compensation or other benefits received from third parties. "Written consent" includes any form of communication that can be documented (for example, communication via e-mail that can be retrieved and documented).

Members and candidates must obtain permission for additional compensation/benefits because such arrangements may affect loyalties and objectivity and create potential conflicts of interest. Disclosure allows an employer to consider the outside arrangements when evaluating the actions and motivations of members and candidates. Moreover, the employer is entitled to have full knowledge of all compensation/benefit arrangements so as to be able to assess the true cost of the services members or candidates are providing.

There may be instances in which a member or candidate is hired by an employer on a "part-time" basis. "Part-time" status applies to employees who do not commit the full number of hours required for a normal work week. Members and candidates should discuss possible limitations to their abilities to provide services that may be competitive with their employer during the negotiation and hiring process. The requirements of Standard IV(B) would be applicable to limitations identified at that time.

40

STANDARD IV(B): RECOMMENDED PROCEDURES

Members and candidates should make an immediate written report to their supervisor and compliance officer specifying any compensation they propose to receive for services in addition to the compensation or benefits received from their employer. The details of the report should be confirmed by the party offering the additional compensation, including performance incentives offered by clients. This written report should state the terms of any agreement under which a member or candidate will receive additional compensation; "terms" include the nature of the compensation, the approximate amount of compensation, and the duration of the agreement.

41

STANDARD IV(B): APPLICATION OF THE STANDARD

Example 1 (Notification of Client Bonus Compensation):

Geoff Whitman, a portfolio analyst for Adams Trust Company, manages the account of Carol Cochran, a client. Whitman is paid a salary by his employer, and Cochran pays the trust company a standard fee based on the market value of assets in her portfolio. Cochran proposes to Whitman that "any year that my portfolio achieves at least a 15% return before taxes, you and your wife can fly to Monaco at my expense and use my condominium during the third week of January." Whitman does not inform his employer of the arrangement and vacations in Monaco the following January as Cochran's guest.

> *Comment*: Whitman violated Standard IV(B) by failing to inform his employer in writing of this supplemental, contingent compensation arrangement. The nature of the arrangement could have resulted in partiality to Cochran's account, which could have detracted from Whitman's performance with respect to other accounts he handles for Adams Trust. Whitman must obtain the consent of his employer to accept such a supplemental benefit.

Example 2 (Notification of Outside Compensation):

Terry Jones sits on the board of directors of Exercise Unlimited, Inc. In return for his services on the board, Jones receives unlimited membership privileges for his family at all Exercise Unlimited facilities. Jones purchases Exercise Unlimited stock for the client accounts for which it is appropriate. Jones does not disclose this arrangement to his employer because he does not receive monetary compensation for his services to the board.

> *Comment*: Jones has violated Standard IV(B) by failing to disclose to his employer benefits received in exchange for his services on the board of directors. The nonmonetary compensation may create a conflict of interest in the same manner as being paid to serve as a director.

Example 3 (Prior Approval for Outside Compensation):

Jonathan Hollis is an analyst of oil-and-gas companies for Specialty Investment Management. He is currently recommending the purchase of ABC Oil Company shares and has published a long, well-thought-out research report to substantiate his recommendation. Several weeks after publishing the report, Hollis receives a call from the investor-relations office of ABC Oil saying that Thomas Andrews, CEO of the company, saw the report and really liked the analyst's grasp of the business and his company. The investor-relations officer invites Hollis to visit ABC Oil to discuss the industry further. ABC Oil offers to send a company plane to pick Hollis up and arrange for his accommodations while visiting. Hollis, after gaining the appropriate approvals, accepts the meeting with the CEO but declines the offered travel arrangements.

Several weeks later, Andrews and Hollis meet to discuss the oil business and Hollis's report. Following the meeting, Hollis joins Andrews and the investment relations officer for dinner at an upscale restaurant near ABC Oil's headquarters.

Upon returning to Specialty Investment Management, Hollis provides a full review of the meeting to the director of research, including a disclosure of the dinner attended.

> *Comment*: Hollis's actions did not violate Standard IV(B). Through gaining approval before accepting the meeting and declining the offered travel arrangements, Hollis sought to avoid any potential conflicts of interest between his company and ABC Oil. Because the location of the dinner was not available prior to arrival and Hollis notified his company of the dinner upon his return, accepting the dinner should not impair his objectivity. By disclosing the dinner, Hollis has enabled Specialty Investment Management to assess whether it has any impact on future reports and recommendations by Hollis related to ABC Oil.

STANDARD IV(C) RESPONSIBILITIES OF SUPERVISORS 42

- ☐ demonstrate a thorough knowledge of the CFA Institute Code of Ethics and Standards of Professional Conduct by interpreting the Code and Standards in various situations involving issues of professional integrity
- ☐ recommend practices and procedures designed to prevent violations of the Code and Standards

Members and Candidates must make reasonable efforts to ensure that anyone subject to their supervision or authority complies with applicable laws, rules, regulations, and the Code and Standards.

Guidance

Highlights:

- *System for Supervision*
- *Supervision Includes Detection*

Standard IV(C) states that members and candidates must promote actions by all employees under their supervision and authority to comply with applicable laws, rules, regulations, and firm policies and the Code and Standards.

Any investment professional who has employees subject to her or his control or influence—whether or not the employees are CFA Institute members, CFA charterholders, or candidates in the CFA Program—exercises supervisory responsibility. Members and candidates acting as supervisors must also have in-depth knowledge of the Code and Standards so that they can apply this knowledge in discharging their supervisory responsibilities.

The conduct that constitutes reasonable supervision in a particular case depends on the number of employees supervised and the work performed by those employees. Members and candidates with oversight responsibilities for large numbers of employees may not be able to personally evaluate the conduct of these employees on a continuing basis. These members and candidates may delegate supervisory duties to subordinates who directly oversee the other employees. A member's or candidate's responsibilities under Standard IV(C) include instructing those subordinates to whom supervision is delegated about methods to promote compliance, including preventing and detecting violations of laws, rules, regulations, firm policies, and the Code and Standards.

At a minimum, Standard IV(C) requires that members and candidates with supervisory responsibility make reasonable efforts to prevent and detect violations by ensuring the establishment of effective compliance systems. However, an effective compliance system goes beyond enacting a code of ethics, establishing policies and procedures to achieve compliance with the code and applicable law, and reviewing employee actions to determine whether they are following the rules.

To be effective supervisors, members and candidates should implement education and training programs on a recurring or regular basis for employees under their supervision. Such programs will assist the employees with meeting their professional obligations to practice in an ethical manner within the applicable legal system. Further, establishing incentives—monetary or otherwise—for employees not only to meet business goals but also to reward ethical behavior offers supervisors another way to assist employees in complying with their legal and ethical obligations.

Often, especially in large organizations, members and candidates may have supervisory responsibility but not the authority to establish or modify firm-wide compliance policies and procedures or incentive structures. Such limitations should not prevent a member or candidate from working with his or her own superiors and within the firm structure to develop and implement effective compliance tools, including but not limited to:

- a code of ethics,
- compliance policies and procedures,
- education and training programs,

- an incentive structure that rewards ethical conduct, and
- adoption of firm-wide best practice standards (e.g., the GIPS standards, the CFA Institute Asset Manager Code of Professional Conduct).

A member or candidate with supervisory responsibility should bring an inadequate compliance system to the attention of the firm's senior managers and recommend corrective action. If the member or candidate clearly cannot discharge supervisory responsibilities because of the absence of a compliance system or because of an inadequate compliance system, the member or candidate should decline in writing to accept supervisory responsibility until the firm adopts reasonable procedures to allow adequate exercise of supervisory responsibility.

System for Supervision

Members and candidates with supervisory responsibility must understand what constitutes an adequate compliance system for their firms and make reasonable efforts to see that appropriate compliance procedures are established, documented, communicated to covered personnel, and followed. "Adequate" procedures are those designed to meet industry standards, regulatory requirements, the requirements of the Code and Standards, and the circumstances of the firm. Once compliance procedures are established, the supervisor must also make reasonable efforts to ensure that the procedures are monitored and enforced.

To be effective, compliance procedures must be in place prior to the occurrence of a violation of the law or the Code and Standards. Although compliance procedures cannot be designed to anticipate every potential violation, they should be designed to anticipate the activities most likely to result in misconduct. Compliance programs must be appropriate for the size and nature of the organization. The member or candidate should review model compliance procedures or other industry programs to ensure that the firm's procedures meet the minimum industry standards.

Once a supervisor learns that an employee has violated or may have violated the law or the Code and Standards, the supervisor must promptly initiate an assessment to determine the extent of the wrongdoing. Relying on an employee's statements about the extent of the violation or assurances that the wrongdoing will not reoccur is not enough. Reporting the misconduct up the chain of command and warning the employee to cease the activity are also not enough. Pending the outcome of the investigation, a supervisor should take steps to ensure that the violation will not be repeated, such as placing limits on the employee's activities or increasing the monitoring of the employee's activities.

Supervision Includes Detection

Members and candidates with supervisory responsibility must also make reasonable efforts to detect violations of laws, rules, regulations, firm policies, and the Code and Standards. The supervisors exercise reasonable supervision by establishing and implementing written compliance procedures and ensuring that those procedures are followed through periodic review. If a member or candidate has adopted reasonable procedures and taken steps to institute an effective compliance program, then the member or candidate may not be in violation of Standard IV(C) if he or she does not detect violations that occur despite these efforts. The fact that violations do occur may indicate, however, that the compliance procedures are inadequate. In addition, in some cases, merely enacting such procedures may not be sufficient to fulfill the duty required by Standard IV(C). A member or candidate may be in violation of Standard IV(C) if he or she knows or should know that the procedures designed to promote compliance, including detecting and preventing violations, are not being followed.

43 STANDARD IV(C): RECOMMENDED PROCEDURES

Codes of Ethics or Compliance Procedures

Members and candidates are encouraged to recommend that their employers adopt a code of ethics. Adoption of a code of ethics is critical to establishing a strong ethical foundation for investment advisory firms and their employees. Codes of ethics formally emphasize and reinforce the client loyalty responsibilities of investment firm personnel, protect investing clients by deterring misconduct, and protect the firm's reputation for integrity.

There is a distinction, however, between codes of ethics and the specific policies and procedures needed to ensure compliance with the codes and with securities laws and regulations. Although both are important, codes of ethics should consist of fundamental, principle-based ethical and fiduciary concepts that are applicable to all of the firm's employees. In this way, firms can best convey to employees and clients the ethical ideals that investment advisers strive to achieve. These concepts need to be implemented, however, by detailed, firm-wide compliance policies and procedures. Compliance procedures assist the firm's personnel in fulfilling the responsibilities enumerated in the code of ethics and make probable that the ideals expressed in the code of ethics will be adhered to in the day-to-day operation of the firm.

Stand-alone codes of ethics should be written in plain language and should address general fiduciary concepts. They should be unencumbered by numerous detailed procedures. Codes presented in this way are the most effective in stressing to employees that they are in positions of trust and must act with integrity at all times. Mingling compliance procedures in the firm's code of ethics goes against the goal of reinforcing the ethical obligations of employees.

Separating the code of ethics from compliance procedures will also reduce, if not eliminate, the legal terminology and "boilerplate" language that can make the underlying ethical principles incomprehensible to the average person. Above all, to ensure the creation of a culture of ethics and integrity rather than one that merely focuses on following the rules, the principles in the code of ethics must be stated in a way that is accessible and understandable to everyone in the firm.

Members and candidates should encourage their employers to provide their codes of ethics to clients. In this case also, a simple, straightforward code of ethics will be best understood by clients. Unencumbered by the compliance procedures, the code of ethics will be effective in conveying that the firm is committed to conducting business in an ethical manner and in the best interests of the clients.

Adequate Compliance Procedures

A supervisor complies with Standard IV(C) by identifying situations in which legal violations or violations of the Code and Standards are likely to occur and by establishing and enforcing compliance procedures to prevent such violations. Adequate compliance procedures should

- be contained in a clearly written and accessible manual that is tailored to the firm's operations,
- be drafted so that the procedures are easy to understand,
- designate a compliance officer whose authority and responsibility are clearly defined and who has the necessary resources and authority to implement the firm's compliance procedures,
- describe the hierarchy of supervision and assign duties among supervisors,

- implement a system of checks and balances,
- outline the scope of the procedures,
- outline procedures to document the monitoring and testing of compliance procedures,
- outline permissible conduct, and
- delineate procedures for reporting violations and sanctions.

Once a compliance program is in place, a supervisor should

- disseminate the contents of the program to appropriate personnel,
- periodically update procedures to ensure that the measures are adequate under the law,
- continually educate personnel regarding the compliance procedures,
- issue periodic reminders of the procedures to appropriate personnel,
- incorporate a professional conduct evaluation as part of an employee's performance review,
- review the actions of employees to ensure compliance and identify violators, and
- take the necessary steps to enforce the procedures once a violation has occurred.

Once a violation is discovered, a supervisor should

- respond promptly,
- conduct a thorough investigation of the activities to determine the scope of the wrongdoing,
- increase supervision or place appropriate limitations on the wrongdoer pending the outcome of the investigation, and
- review procedures for potential changes necessary to prevent future violations from occurring.

Implementation of Compliance Education and Training

No amount of ethics education and awareness will deter someone determined to commit fraud for personal enrichment. But the vast majority of investment professionals strive to achieve personal success with dedicated service to their clients and employers.

Regular ethics and compliance training, in conjunction with adoption of a code of ethics, is critical to investment firms seeking to establish a strong culture of integrity and to provide an environment in which employees routinely engage in ethical conduct in compliance with the law. Training and education assist individuals in both recognizing areas that are prone to ethical and legal pitfalls and identifying those circumstances and influences that can impair ethical judgment.

By implementing educational programs, supervisors can train their subordinates to put into practice what the firm's code of ethics requires. Education helps employees make the link between legal and ethical conduct and the long-term success of the business; a strong culture of compliance signals to clients and potential clients that the firm has truly embraced ethical conduct as fundamental to the firm's mission to serve its clients.

Establish an Appropriate Incentive Structure

Even if individuals want to make the right choices and follow an ethical course of conduct and are aware of the obstacles that may trip them up, they can still be influenced to act improperly by a corporate culture that embraces a "succeed at all costs" mentality, stresses results regardless of the methods used to achieve those results, and does not reward ethical behavior. Supervisors can reinforce an individual's natural desire to "do the right thing" by building a culture of integrity in the workplace.

Supervisors and firms must look closely at their incentive structure to determine whether the structure encourages profits and returns at the expense of ethically appropriate conduct. Reward structures may turn a blind eye to how desired outcomes are achieved and encourage dysfunctional or counterproductive behavior. Only when compensation and incentives are firmly tied to client interests and *how* outcomes are achieved, rather than *how much* is generated for the firm, will employees work to achieve a culture of integrity.

44 STANDARD IV(C): APPLICATION OF THE STANDARD

Example 1 (Supervising Research Activities):

Jane Mattock, senior vice president and head of the research department of H&V, Inc., a regional brokerage firm, has decided to change her recommendation for Timber Products from buy to sell. In line with H&V's procedures, she orally advises certain other H&V executives of her proposed actions before the report is prepared for publication. As a result of Mattock's conversation with Dieter Frampton, one of the H&V executives accountable to Mattock, Frampton immediately sells Timber's stock from his own account and from certain discretionary client accounts. In addition, other personnel inform certain institutional customers of the changed recommendation before it is printed and disseminated to all H&V customers who have received previous Timber reports.

> *Comment*: Mattock has violated Standard IV(C) by failing to reasonably and adequately supervise the actions of those accountable to her. She did not prevent or establish reasonable procedures designed to prevent dissemination of or trading on the information by those who knew of her changed recommendation. She must ensure that her firm has procedures for reviewing or recording any trading in the stock of a corporation that has been the subject of an unpublished change in recommendation. Adequate procedures would have informed the subordinates of their duties and detected sales by Frampton and selected customers.

Example 2 (Supervising Research Activities):

Deion Miller is the research director for Jamestown Investment Programs. The portfolio managers have become critical of Miller and his staff because the Jamestown portfolios do not include any stock that has been the subject of a merger or tender offer. Georgia Ginn, a member of Miller's staff, tells Miller that she has been studying a local company, Excelsior, Inc., and recommends its purchase. Ginn adds that the company has been widely rumored to be the subject of a merger study by a well-known conglomerate and discussions between them are under way. At Miller's request, Ginn prepares a memo recommending the stock. Miller passes along Ginn's memo to the portfolio managers prior to leaving for vacation, and he notes that he has not reviewed the memo. As a result of the memo, the portfolio managers buy Excelsior stock immediately. The day Miller returns to the office, he learns that Ginn's only sources for the report were her brother, who is an acquisitions analyst with Acme Industries, the "well-known conglomerate," and that the merger discussions were planned but not held.

> *Comment*: Miller violated Standard IV(C) by not exercising reasonable supervision when he disseminated the memo without checking to ensure that Ginn had a reasonable and adequate basis for her recommendations and that Ginn was not relying on material nonpublic information.

Example 3 (Supervising Trading Activities):

David Edwards, a trainee trader at Wheeler & Company, a major national brokerage firm, assists a customer in paying for the securities of Highland, Inc., by using anticipated profits from the immediate sale of the same securities. Despite the fact that Highland is not on Wheeler's recommended list, a large volume of its stock is traded through Wheeler in this manner. Roberta Ann Mason is a Wheeler vice president responsible for supervising compliance with the securities laws in the trading department. Part of her compensation from Wheeler is based on commission revenues from the trading department. Although she notices the increased trading activity, she does nothing to investigate or halt it.

> *Comment*: Mason's failure to adequately review and investigate purchase orders in Highland stock executed by Edwards and her failure to supervise the trainee's activities violate Standard IV(C). Supervisors should be especially sensitive to actual or potential conflicts between their own self-interests and their supervisory responsibilities.

Example 4 (Supervising Trading Activities and Record Keeping):

Samantha Tabbing is senior vice president and portfolio manager for Crozet, Inc., a registered investment advisory and registered broker/dealer firm. She reports to Charles Henry, the president of Crozet. Crozet serves as the investment adviser and principal underwriter for ABC and XYZ public mutual funds. The two funds' prospectuses allow Crozet to trade financial futures for the funds for the limited purpose of hedging against market risks. Henry, extremely impressed by Tabbing's performance in the past two years, directs Tabbing to act as portfolio manager for the funds. For the benefit of its employees, Crozet has also organized the Crozet Employee Profit-Sharing Plan (CEPSP), a defined contribution retirement plan. Henry assigns Tabbing to manage 20% of the assets of CEPSP. Tabbing's investment objective for her portion of CEPSP's assets is aggressive growth. Unbeknownst to Henry, Tabbing frequently places S&P 500 Index purchase and sale orders for the funds and the CEPSP without providing the futures commission merchants (FCMs) who take the orders with any prior or simultaneous designation of the account for which the trade has been placed. Frequently, neither Tabbing nor anyone else at Crozet completes an internal trade ticket to record the time an order was placed or the specific account for which the order was intended. FCMs often designate a specific account only after the trade, when Tabbing provides such designation. Crozet has no written operating procedures or compliance manual concerning its futures trading, and its compliance department does not review such trading. After observing the market's movement, Tabbing assigns to CEPSP the S&P 500 positions with more favorable execution prices and assigns positions with less favorable execution prices to the funds.

Comment: Henry violated Standard IV(C) by failing to adequately supervise Tabbing with respect to her S&P 500 trading. Henry further violated Standard IV(C) by failing to establish record-keeping and reporting procedures to prevent or detect Tabbing's violations. Henry must make a reasonable effort to determine that adequate compliance procedures covering all employee trading activity are established, documented, communicated, and followed.

Example 5 (Accepting Responsibility):

Meredith Rasmussen works on a buy-side trading desk and concentrates on in-house trades for a hedge fund subsidiary managed by a team at the investment management firm. The hedge fund has been very successful and is marketed globally by the firm. From her experience as the trader for much of the activity of the fund, Rasmussen has become quite knowledgeable about the hedge fund's strategy, tactics, and performance. When a distinct break in the market occurs and many of the securities involved in the hedge fund's strategy decline markedly in value, however, Rasmussen observes that the reported performance of the hedge fund does not at all reflect this decline. From her experience, this lack of an effect is a very unlikely occurrence. She approaches the head of trading about her concern and is told that she should not ask any questions and that the fund is too big and successful and is not her concern. She is fairly sure something is not right, so she contacts the compliance officer and is again told to stay away from the hedge fund reporting issue.

Comment: Rasmussen has clearly come upon an error in policies, procedures, and compliance practices within the firm's operations. According to Standard IV(C), the supervisor and the compliance officer have the responsibility to review the concerns brought forth by Rasmussen. Supervisors have the responsibility of establishing and encouraging an ethical culture in the firm. The dismissal of Rasmussen's question violates Standard IV(C) and undermines the firm's ethical operations.

See also Standard I(D) Misconduct and, for guidance on whistleblowing, Standard IV(A) Loyalty.

Example 6 (Inadequate Procedures):

Brendan Witt, a former junior sell-side technology analyst, decided to return to school to earn an MBA. To keep his research skills and industry knowledge sharp, Witt accepted a position with On-line and Informed, an independent internet-based research company. The position requires the publication of a recommendation and report on a different company every month. Initially, Witt is a regular contributor of new research and a participant in the associated discussion boards that generally have positive comments on the technology sector. Over time, his ability to manage his educational requirements and his work requirements begin to conflict with one another. Knowing a recommendation is due the next day for On-line, Witt creates a report based on a few news articles and what the conventional wisdom of the markets has deemed the "hot" security of the day.

Comment: Allowing the report submitted by Witt to be posted highlights a lack of compliance procedures by the research firm. Witt's supervisor needs to work with the management of On-line to develop an appropriate review process to ensure that all contracted analysts comply with the requirements.

See also Standard V(A) Diligence and Reasonable Basis because it relates to Witt's responsibility for substantiating a recommendation.

Example 7 (Inadequate Supervision):

Michael Papis is the chief investment officer of his state's retirement fund. The fund has always used outside advisers for the real estate allocation, and this information is clearly presented in all fund communications. Thomas Nagle, a recognized sell-side research analyst and Papis's business school classmate, recently left the investment bank he worked for to start his own asset management firm, Accessible Real Estate. Nagle is trying to build his assets under management and contacts Papis about gaining some of the retirement fund's allocation. In the previous few years, the performance of the retirement fund's real estate investments was in line with the fund's benchmark but was not extraordinary. Papis decides to help out his old friend and also to seek better returns by moving the real estate allocation to Accessible. The only notice of the change in adviser appears in the next annual report in the listing of associated advisers.

Comment: Papis's actions highlight the need for supervision and review at all levels in an organization. His responsibilities may include the selection of external advisers, but the decision to change advisers appears arbitrary. Members and candidates should ensure that their firm has appropriate policies and procedures in place to detect inappropriate actions, such as the action taken by Papis.

See also Standard V(A) Diligence and Reasonable Basis, Standard V(B) Communication with Clients and Prospective Clients, and Standard VI(A) Disclosure of Conflicts.

Example 8 (Supervising Research Activities):

Mary Burdette was recently hired by Fundamental Investment Management (FIM) as a junior auto industry analyst. Burdette is expected to expand the social media presence of the firm because she is active with various networks, including Facebook, LinkedIn, and X. Although Burdette's supervisor, Joe Graf, has never used social media, he encourages Burdette to explore opportunities to increase FIM's online presence and ability to share content, communicate, and broadcast information to clients. In response to Graf's encouragement, Burdette is working on a proposal detailing the advantages of getting FIM onto X in addition to launching a company Facebook page.

As part of her auto industry research for FIM, Burdette is completing a report on the financial impact of Sun Drive Auto Ltd.'s new solar technology for compact automobiles. This research report will be her first for FIM, and she believes Sun Drive's technology could revolutionize the auto industry. In her excitement, Burdette sends a quick post to FIM X followers summarizing her "buy" recommendation for Sun Drive Auto stock.

Comment: Graf has violated Standard IV(C) by failing to reasonably supervise Burdette with respect to the contents of her post. He did not establish reasonable procedures to prevent the unauthorized dissemination of company research through social media networks. Graf must make sure all employees receive regular training about FIM's policies and procedures, including the appropriate business use of personal social media networks.

See Standard III(B) for additional guidance.

Example 9 (Supervising Research Activities):

Chen Wang leads the research department at YYRA Retirement Planning Specialists. Chen supervises a team of 10 analysts in a fast-paced and understaffed organization. He is responsible for coordinating the firm's approved process to review all reports before they are provided to the portfolio management team for use in rebalancing client portfolios.

One of Chen's direct reports, Huang Mei, covers the banking industry. Chen must submit the latest updates to the portfolio management team tomorrow morning. Huang has yet to submit her research report on ZYX Bank because she is uncomfortable providing a "buy" or "sell" opinion of ZYX on the basis of the completed analysis. Pressed for time and concerned that Chen will reject a "hold" recommendation, she researches various websites and blogs on the banking sector for whatever she can find on ZYX. One independent blogger provides a new interpretation of the recently reported data Huang has analyzed and concludes with a strong "sell" recommendation for ZYX. She is impressed by the originality and resourcefulness of this blogger's report.

Very late in the evening, Huang submits her report and "sell" recommendation to Chen without any reference to the independent blogger's report. Given the late time of the submission and the competence of Huang's prior work, Chen compiles this report with the recommendations from each of the other analysts and meets with the portfolio managers to discuss implementation.

> *Comment*: Chen has violated Standard IV(C) by neglecting to reasonably and adequately follow the firm's approved review process for Huang's research report. The delayed submission and the quality of prior work do not remove Chen's requirement to uphold the designated review process. A member or candidate with supervisory responsibility must make reasonable efforts to see that appropriate procedures are established, documented, communicated to covered personnel, and followed.

45 STANDARD V: INVESTMENT ANALYSIS, RECOMMENDATIONS, AND ACTIONS

- ☐ demonstrate a thorough knowledge of the CFA Institute Code of Ethics and Standards of Professional Conduct by interpreting the Code and Standards in various situations involving issues of professional integrity
- ☐ recommend practices and procedures designed to prevent violations of the Code and Standards

Standard V(A) Diligence and Reasonable Basis

Members and Candidates must:

1. Exercise diligence, independence, and thoroughness in analyzing investments, making investment recommendations, and taking investment actions.

2. Have a reasonable and adequate basis, supported by appropriate research and investigation, for any investment analysis, recommendation, or action.

Guidance

Highlights:

- *Defining Diligence and Reasonable Basis*
- *Using Secondary or Third-Party Research*
- *Using Quantitatively Oriented Research*
- *Developing Quantitatively Oriented Techniques*
- *Selecting External Advisers and Subadvisers*
- *Group Research and Decision Making*

The application of Standard V(A) depends on the investment philosophy the member, candidate, or firm is following, the role of the member or candidate in the investment decision-making process, and the support and resources provided by the member's or candidate's employer. These factors will dictate the nature of the diligence and thoroughness of the research and the level of investigation required by Standard V(A).

The requirements for issuing conclusions based on research will vary in relation to the member's or candidate's role in the investment decision-making process, but the member or candidate must make reasonable efforts to cover all pertinent issues when arriving at a recommendation. Members and candidates enhance transparency by providing or offering to provide supporting information to clients when recommending a purchase or sale or when changing a recommendation.

Defining Diligence and Reasonable Basis

Every investment decision is based on a set of facts known and understood at the time. Clients turn to members and candidates for advice and expect these advisers to have more information and knowledge than they do. This information and knowledge is the basis from which members and candidates apply their professional judgment in taking investment actions and making recommendations.

At a basic level, clients want assurance that members and candidates are putting forth the necessary effort to support the recommendations they are making. Communicating the level and thoroughness of the information reviewed before the member or candidate makes a judgment allows clients to understand the reasonableness of the recommended investment actions.

As with determining the suitability of an investment for the client, the necessary level of research and analysis will differ with the product, security, or service being offered. In providing an investment service, members and candidates typically use a variety of resources, including company reports, third-party research, and results from quantitative models. A reasonable basis is formed through a balance of these resources appropriate for the security or decision being analyzed.

The following list provides some, but definitely not all, examples of attributes to consider while forming the basis for a recommendation:

- global, regional, and country macroeconomic conditions,
- a company's operating and financial history,
- the industry's and sector's current conditions and the stage of the business cycle,

- a mutual fund's fee structure and management history,
- the output and potential limitations of quantitative models,
- the quality of the assets included in a securitization, and
- the appropriateness of selected peer-group comparisons.

Even though an investment recommendation may be well informed, downside risk remains for any investment. Members and candidates can base their decisions only on the information available at the time decisions are made. The steps taken in developing a diligent and reasonable recommendation should minimize unexpected downside events.

Using Secondary or Third-Party Research

If members and candidates rely on secondary or third-party research, they must make reasonable and diligent efforts to determine whether such research is sound. Secondary research is defined as research conducted by someone else in the member's or candidate's firm. Third-party research is research conducted by entities outside the member's or candidate's firm, such as a brokerage firm, bank, or research firm. If a member or candidate has reason to suspect that either secondary or third-party research or information comes from a source that lacks a sound basis, the member or candidate must not rely on that information.

Members and candidates should make reasonable enquiries into the source and accuracy of all data used in completing their investment analysis and recommendations. The sources of the information and data will influence the level of the review a member or candidate must undertake. Information and data taken from internet sources, such as personal blogs, independent research aggregation websites, or social media websites, likely require a greater level of review than information from more established research organizations.

Criteria that a member or candidate can use in forming an opinion on whether research is sound include the following:

- assumptions used,
- rigor of the analysis performed,
- date/timeliness of the research, and
- evaluation of the objectivity and independence of the recommendations.

A member or candidate may rely on others in his or her firm to determine whether secondary or third-party research is sound and use the information in good faith unless the member or candidate has reason to question its validity or the processes and procedures used by those responsible for the research. For example, a portfolio manager may not have a choice of a data source because the firm's senior managers conducted due diligence to determine which vendor would provide services; the member or candidate can use the information in good faith assuming the due diligence process was deemed adequate.

A member or candidate should verify that the firm has a policy about the timely and consistent review of approved research providers to ensure that the quality of the research continues to meet the necessary standards. If such a policy is not in place at the firm, the member or candidate should encourage the development and adoption of a formal review practice.

Using Quantitatively Oriented Research

Standard V(A) applies to the rapidly expanding use of quantitatively oriented research models and processes, such as computer-generated modeling, screening, and ranking of investment securities; the creation or valuation of derivative instruments; and quantitative portfolio construction techniques. These models and processes are being used for much more than the back testing of investment strategies, especially with continually advancing technology and techniques. The continued broad development of quantitative methods and models is an important part of capital market developments.

Members and candidates need to have an understanding of the parameters used in models and quantitative research that are incorporated into their investment recommendations. Although they are not required to become experts in every technical aspect of the models, they must understand the assumptions and limitations inherent in any model and how the results were used in the decision-making process.

The reliance on and potential limitations of financial models became clear through the investment crisis that unfolded in 2007 and 2008. In some cases, the financial models used to value specific securities and related derivative products did not adequately demonstrate the level of associated risks. Members and candidates should make reasonable efforts to test the output of investment models and other pre-programed analytical tools they use. Such validation should occur before incorporating the process into their methods, models, or analyses.

Although not every model can test for every factor or outcome, members and candidates should ensure that their analyses incorporate a broad range of assumptions sufficient to capture the underlying characteristics of investments. The omission from the analysis of potentially negative outcomes or of levels of risk outside the norm may misrepresent the true economic value of an investment. The possible scenarios for analysis should include factors that are likely to have a substantial influence on the investment value and may include extremely positive and negative scenarios.

Developing Quantitatively Oriented Techniques

Individuals who create new quantitative models and services must exhibit a higher level of diligence in reviewing new products than the individuals who ultimately use the analytical output. Members and candidates involved in the development and oversight of quantitatively oriented models, methods, and algorithms must understand the technical aspects of the products they provide to clients. A thorough testing of the model and resulting analysis should be completed prior to product distribution.

Members and candidates need to consider the source and time horizon of the data used as inputs in financial models. The information from many commercially available databases may not effectively incorporate both positive and negative market cycles. In the development of a recommendation, the member or candidate may need to test the models by using volatility and performance expectations that represent scenarios outside the observable databases. In reviewing the computer models or the resulting output, members and candidates need to pay particular attention to the assumptions used in the analysis and the rigor of the analysis to ensure that the model incorporates a wide range of possible input expectations, including negative market events.

Selecting External Advisers and Subadvisers

Financial instruments and asset allocation techniques continue to develop and evolve. This progression has led to the use of specialized managers to invest in specific asset classes or diversification strategies that complement a firm's in-house expertise. Standard V(A) applies to the level of review necessary in selecting an external adviser or subadviser to manage a specifically mandated allocation. Members and candidates must review managers as diligently as they review individual funds and securities.

Members and candidates who are directly involved with the use of external advisers need to ensure that their firms have standardized criteria for reviewing these selected external advisers and managers. Such criteria would include, but would not be limited to, the following:

- reviewing the adviser's established code of ethics,
- understanding the adviser's compliance and internal control procedures,

- assessing the quality of the published return information, and
- reviewing the adviser's investment process and adherence to its stated strategy.

Codes, standards, and guides to best practice published by CFA Institute provide members and candidates with examples of acceptable practices for external advisers and advice in selecting a new adviser. The following guides are available at the CFA Institute website (www.cfainstitute.org): Asset Manager Code of Professional Conduct, Global Investment Performance Standards, and Model Request for Proposal (for equity, credit, or real estate managers).

Group Research and Decision Making

Commonly, members and candidates are part of a group or team that is collectively responsible for producing investment analysis or research. The conclusions or recommendations of the group report represent the consensus of the group and are not necessarily the views of the member or candidate, even though the name of the member or candidate is included on the report. In some instances, a member or candidate will not agree with the view of the group. If, however, the member or candidate believes that the consensus opinion has a reasonable and adequate basis and is independent and objective, the member or candidate need not decline to be identified with the report. If the member or candidate is confident in the process, the member or candidate does not need to dissociate from the report even if it does not reflect his or her opinion.

46 STANDARD V(A): RECOMMENDED PROCEDURES

Members and candidates should encourage their firms to consider the following policies and procedures to support the principles of Standard V(A):

- Establish a policy requiring that research reports, credit ratings, and investment recommendations have a basis that can be substantiated as reasonable and adequate. An individual employee (a supervisory analyst) or a group of employees (a review committee) should be appointed to review and approve such items prior to external circulation to determine whether the criteria established in the policy have been met.
- Develop detailed, written guidance for analysts (research, investment, or credit), supervisory analysts, and review committees that establishes the due diligence procedures for judging whether a particular recommendation has a reasonable and adequate basis.
- Develop measurable criteria for assessing the quality of research, the reasonableness and adequacy of the basis for any recommendation or rating, and the accuracy of recommendations over time. In some cases, firms may consider implementing compensation arrangements that depend on these measurable criteria and that are applied consistently to all related analysts.
- Develop detailed, written guidance that establishes minimum levels of scenario testing of all computer-based models used in developing, rating, and evaluating financial instruments. The policy should contain criteria related to the breadth of the scenarios tested, the accuracy of the output over time, and the analysis of cash flow sensitivity to inputs.

- Develop measurable criteria for assessing outside providers, including the quality of information being provided, the reasonableness and adequacy of the provider's collection practices, and the accuracy of the information over time. The established policy should outline how often the provider's products are reviewed.
- Adopt a standardized set of criteria for evaluating the adequacy of external advisers. The policy should include how often and on what basis the allocation of funds to the adviser will be reviewed.

STANDARD V(A): APPLICATION OF THE STANDARD

47

- ☐ demonstrate a thorough knowledge of the CFA Institute Code of Ethics and Standards of Professional Conduct by interpreting the Code and Standards in various situations involving issues of professional integrity
- ☐ recommend practices and procedures designed to prevent violations of the Code and Standards

Example 1 (Sufficient Due Diligence):

Helen Hawke manages the corporate finance department of Sarkozi Securities, Ltd. The firm is anticipating that the government will soon close a tax loophole that currently allows oil-and-gas exploration companies to pass on drilling expenses to holders of a certain class of shares. Because market demand for this tax-advantaged class of stock is currently high, Sarkozi convinces several companies to undertake new equity financings at once, before the loophole closes. Time is of the essence, but Sarkozi lacks sufficient resources to conduct adequate research on all the prospective issuing companies. Hawke decides to estimate the IPO prices on the basis of the relative size of each company and to justify the pricing later when her staff has time.

> *Comment*: Sarkozi should have taken on only the work that it could adequately handle. By categorizing the issuers by general size, Hawke has bypassed researching all the other relevant aspects that should be considered when pricing new issues and thus has not performed sufficient due diligence. Such an omission can result in investors purchasing shares at prices that have no actual basis. Hawke has violated Standard V(A).

Example 2 (Sufficient Scenario Testing):

Babu Dhaliwal works for Heinrich Brokerage in the corporate finance group. He has just persuaded Feggans Resources, Ltd., to allow his firm to do a secondary equity financing at Feggans Resources' current stock price. Because the stock has been trading at higher multiples than similar companies with equivalent production, Dhaliwal presses the Feggans Resources managers to project what would be the maximum production they could achieve in an optimal scenario. Based on these numbers, he is able to justify the price his firm will be asking for the secondary issue. During a sales pitch to the brokers, Dhaliwal then uses these numbers as the base-case production levels that Feggans Resources will achieve.

Comment: When presenting information to the brokers, Dhaliwal should have given a range of production scenarios and the probability of Feggans Resources achieving each level. By giving the maximum production level as the likely level of production, he has misrepresented the chances of achieving that production level and seriously misled the brokers. Dhaliwal has violated Standard V(A).

Example 3 (Developing a Reasonable Basis):

Brendan Witt, a former junior sell-side technology analyst, decided to return to school to earn an MBA. To keep his research skills and industry knowledge sharp, Witt accepted a position with On-line and Informed, an independent internet-based research company. The position requires the publication of a recommendation and report on a different company every month. Initially, Witt is a regular contributor of new research and a participant in the associated discussion boards that generally have positive comments on the technology sector. Over time, his ability to manage his educational requirements and his work requirements begin to conflict with one another. Knowing a recommendation is due the next day for On-line, Witt creates a report based on a few news articles and what the conventional wisdom of the markets has deemed the "hot" security of the day.

Comment: Witt's knowledge of and exuberance for technology stocks, a few news articles, and the conventional wisdom of the markets do not constitute, without more information, a reasonable and adequate basis for a stock recommendation that is supported by appropriate research and investigation. Therefore, Witt has violated Standard V(A).

See also Standard IV(C) Responsibilities of Supervisors because it relates to the firm's inadequate procedures.

Example 4 (Timely Client Updates):

Kristen Chandler is an investment consultant in the London office of Dalton Securities, a major global investment consultant firm. One of her UK pension funds has decided to appoint a specialist US equity manager. Dalton's global manager of research relies on local consultants to cover managers within their regions and, after conducting thorough due diligence, puts their views and ratings in Dalton's manager database. Chandler accesses Dalton's global manager research database and conducts a screen of all US equity managers on the basis of a match with the client's desired philosophy/style, performance, and tracking-error targets. She selects the five managers that meet these criteria and puts them in a briefing report that is delivered to the client 10 days later. Between the time of Chandler's database search and the delivery of the report to the client, Chandler is told that Dalton has updated the database with the information that one of the firms that Chandler has recommended for consideration lost its chief investment officer, the head of its US equity research, and the majority of its portfolio managers on the US equity product—all of whom have left to establish their own firm. Chandler does not revise her report with this updated information.

Comment: Chandler has failed to satisfy the requirement of Standard V(A). Although Dalton updated the manager ratings to reflect the personnel turnover at one of the firms, Chandler did not update her report to reflect the new information.

Example 5 (Group Research Opinions):

Evelyn Mastakis is a junior analyst who has been asked by her firm to write a research report predicting the expected interest rate for residential mortgages over the next six months. Mastakis submits her report to the fixed-income investment committee of her firm for review, as required by firm procedures. Although some committee members support Mastakis's conclusion, the majority of the committee disagrees with her conclusion, and the report is significantly changed to indicate that interest rates are likely to increase more than originally predicted by Mastakis. Should Mastakis ask that her name be taken off the report when it is disseminated?

> *Comment*: The results of research are not always clear, and different people may have different opinions based on the same factual evidence. In this case, the committee may have valid reasons for issuing a report that differs from the analyst's original research. The firm can issue a report that is different from the original report of an analyst as long as there is a reasonable and adequate basis for its conclusions.
>
> Generally, analysts must write research reports that reflect their own opinion and can ask the firm not to put their name on reports that ultimately differ from that opinion. When the work is a group effort, however, not all members of the team may agree with all aspects of the report. Ultimately, members and candidates can ask to have their names removed from the report, but if they are satisfied that the process has produced results or conclusions that have a reasonable and adequate basis, members and candidates do not have to dissociate from the report even when they do not agree with its contents. If Mastakis is confident in the process, she does not need to dissociate from the report even if it does not reflect her opinion.

Example 6 (Reliance on Third-Party Research):

Gary McDermott runs a two-person investment management firm. McDermott's firm subscribes to a service from a large investment research firm that provides research reports. McDermott's firm makes investment recommendations on the basis of these reports.

> *Comment*: Members and candidates can rely on third-party research but must make reasonable and diligent efforts to determine that such research is sound. If McDermott undertakes due diligence efforts on a regular basis to ensure that the research produced by the large firm is objective and reasonably based, McDermott can rely on that research when making investment recommendations to clients.

Example 7 (Due Diligence in Submanager Selection):

Paul Ostrowski's business has grown significantly over the past couple of years, and some clients want to diversify internationally. Ostrowski decides to find a submanager to handle the expected international investments. Because this will be his first subadviser, Ostrowski uses the CFA Institute model "request for proposal" to design a questionnaire for his search. By his deadline, he receives seven completed questionnaires from a variety of domestic and international firms trying to gain his business. Ostrowski reviews all the applications in detail and decides to select the firm that charges the lowest fees because doing so will have the least impact on his firm's bottom line.

Comment: The selection of an external adviser or subadviser should be based on a full and complete review of the adviser's services, performance history, and cost structure. In basing the decision on the fee structure alone, Ostrowski may be violating Standard V(A).

See also Standard III(C) Suitability because it relates to the ability of the selected adviser to meet the needs of the clients.

Example 8 (Sufficient Due Diligence):

Michael Papis is the chief investment officer of his state's retirement fund. The fund has always used outside advisers for the real estate allocation, and this information is clearly presented in all fund communications. Thomas Nagle, a recognized sell-side research analyst and Papis's business school classmate, recently left the investment bank he worked for to start his own asset management firm, Accessible Real Estate. Nagle is trying to build his assets under management and contacts Papis about gaining some of the retirement fund's allocation. In the previous few years, the performance of the retirement fund's real estate investments was in line with the fund's benchmark but was not extraordinary. Papis decides to help out his old friend and also to seek better returns by moving the real estate allocation to Accessible. The only notice of the change in adviser appears in the next annual report in the listing of associated advisers.

Comment: Papis violated Standard V(A). His responsibilities may include the selection of the external advisers, but the decision to change advisers appears to have been arbitrary. If Papis was dissatisfied with the current real estate adviser, he should have conducted a proper solicitation to select the most appropriate adviser.

See also Standard IV(C) Responsibilities of Supervisors, Standard V(B) Communication with Clients and Prospective Clients, and Standard VI(A) Disclosure of Conflicts.

Example 9 (Sufficient Due Diligence):

Andre Shrub owns and operates Conduit, an investment advisory firm. Prior to opening Conduit, Shrub was an account manager with Elite Investment, a hedge fund managed by his good friend Adam Reed. To attract clients to a new Conduit fund, Shrub offers lower-than-normal management fees. He can do so because the fund consists of two top-performing funds managed by Reed. Given his personal friendship with Reed and the prior performance record of these two funds, Shrub believes this new fund is a winning combination for all parties. Clients quickly invest with Conduit to gain access to the Elite funds. No one is turned away because Conduit is seeking to expand its assets under management.

Comment: Shrub violated Standard V(A) by not conducting a thorough analysis of the funds managed by Reed before developing the new Conduit fund. Shrub's reliance on his personal relationship with Reed and his prior knowledge of Elite are insufficient justification for the investments. The funds may be appropriately considered, but a full review of their operating procedures, reporting practices, and transparency are some elements of the necessary due diligence.

See also Standard III(C) Suitability.

Example 10 (Sufficient Due Diligence):

Bob Thompson has been doing research for the portfolio manager of the fixed-income department. His assignment is to do sensitivity analysis on securitized subprime mortgages. He has discussed with the manager possible scenarios to use to calculate expected returns. A key assumption in such calculations is housing price appreciation (HPA) because it drives "prepays" (prepayments of mortgages) and losses. Thompson is concerned with the significant appreciation experienced over the previous five years as a result of the increased availability of funds from subprime mortgages. Thompson insists that the analysis should include a scenario run with –10% for Year 1, –5% for Year 2, and then (to project a worst-case scenario) 0% for Years 3 through 5. The manager replies that these assumptions are too dire because there has never been a time in their available database when HPA was negative.

Thompson conducts his research to better understand the risks inherent in these securities and evaluates these securities in the worst-case scenario, a less likely but possible environment. Based on the results of the enhanced scenarios, Thompson does not recommend the purchase of the securitization. Against the general market trends, the manager follows Thompson's recommendation and does not invest. The following year, the housing market collapses. In avoiding the subprime investments, the manager's portfolio outperforms its peer group that year.

> *Comment*: Thompson's actions in running the scenario test with inputs beyond the historical trends available in the firm's databases adhere to the principles of Standard V(A). His concerns over recent trends provide a sound basis for further analysis. Thompson understands the limitations of his model, when combined with the limited available historical information, to accurately predict the performance of the funds if market conditions change negatively.
>
> See also Standard I(B) Independence and Objectivity.

Example 11 (Use of Quantitatively Oriented Models):

Espacia Liakos works in sales for Hellenica Securities, a firm specializing in developing intricate derivative strategies to profit from particular views on market expectations. One of her clients is Eugenie Carapalis, who has become convinced that commodity prices will become more volatile over the coming months. Carapalis asks Liakos to quickly engineer a strategy that will benefit from this expectation. Liakos turns to Hellenica's modeling group to fulfill this request. Because of the tight deadline, the modeling group outsources parts of the work to several trusted third parties. Liakos implements the disparate components of the strategy as the firms complete them.

Within a month, Carapalis is proven correct: Volatility across a range of commodities increases sharply. But her derivatives position with Hellenica returns huge losses, and the losses increase daily. Liakos investigates and realizes that although each of the various components of the strategy had been validated, they had never been evaluated as an integrated whole. In extreme conditions, portions of the model worked at cross-purposes with other portions, causing the overall strategy to fail dramatically.

> *Comment*: Liakos violated Standard V(A). Members and candidates must understand the statistical significance of the results of the models they recommend and must be able to explain them to clients. Liakos did not take adequate care to ensure a thorough review of the whole model; its components were evaluated only individually. Because Carapalis clearly intended to implement the strategy as a whole rather than as separate parts, Liakos should have tested how the components of the strategy interacted as well as how they performed individually.

Example 12 (Successful Due Diligence/Failed Investment):

Alton Newbury is an investment adviser to high-net-worth clients. A client with an aggressive risk profile in his investment policy statement asks about investing in the Top Shelf hedge fund. This fund, based in Calgary, Alberta, Canada, has reported 20% returns for the first three years. The fund prospectus states that its strategy involves long and short positions in the energy sector and extensive leverage. Based on his analysis of the fund's track record, the principals involved in managing the fund, the fees charged, and the fund's risk profile, Newbury recommends the fund to the client and secures a position in it. The next week, the fund announces that it has suffered a loss of 60% of its value and is suspending operations and redemptions until after a regulatory review. Newbury's client calls him in a panic and asks for an explanation.

> *Comment*: Newbury's actions were consistent with Standard V(A). Analysis of an investment that results in a reasonable basis for recommendation does not guarantee that the investment has no downside risk. Newbury should discuss the analysis process with the client while reminding him or her that past performance does not lead to guaranteed future gains and that losses in an aggressive investment portfolio should be expected.

Example 13 (Quantitative Model Diligence):

Barry Cannon is the lead quantitative analyst at CityCenter Hedge Fund. He is responsible for the development, maintenance, and enhancement of the proprietary models the fund uses to manage its investors' assets. Cannon reads several high-level mathematical publications and blogs to stay informed of current developments. One blog, run by "Expert CFA," presents some intriguing research that may benefit one of CityCenter's current models. Cannon is under pressure from firm executives to improve the model's predictive abilities, and he incorporates the factors discussed in the online research. The updated output recommends several new investments to the fund's portfolio managers.

> *Comment*: Cannon has violated Standard V(A) by failing to have a reasonable basis for the new recommendations made to the portfolio managers. He needed to diligently research the effect of incorporating the new factors before offering the output recommendations. Cannon may use the blog for ideas, but it is his responsibility to determine the effect on the firm's proprietary models.
>
> See Standard VII(B) regarding the violation by "Expert CFA" in the use of the CFA designation.

Example 14 (Selecting a Service Provider):

Ellen Smith is a performance analyst at Artic Global Advisors, a firm that manages global equity mandates for institutional clients. She was asked by her supervisor to review five new performance attribution systems and recommend one that would more appropriately explain the firm's investment strategy to clients. On the list was a system she recalled learning about when visiting an exhibitor booth at a recent conference. The system is highly quantitative and something of a "black box" in how it calculates the attribution values. Smith recommended this option without researching the others because the sheer complexity of the process was sure to impress the clients.

> *Comment*: Smith's actions do not demonstrate a sufficient level of diligence in reviewing this product to make a recommendation for selecting the service. Besides not reviewing or considering the other four potential

systems, she did not determine whether the "black box" attribution process aligns with the investment practices of the firm, including its investments in different countries and currencies. Smith must review and understand the process of any software or system before recommending its use as the firm's attribution system.

Example 15 (Subadviser Selection):

Craig Jackson is working for Adams Partners, Inc., and has been assigned to select a hedge fund subadviser to improve the diversification of the firm's large fund-of-funds product. The allocation must be in place before the start of the next quarter. Jackson uses a consultant database to find a list of suitable firms that claim compliance with the GIPS standards. He calls more than 20 firms on the list to confirm their potential interest and to determine their most recent quarterly and annual total return values. Because of the short turnaround, Jackson recommends the firm with the greatest total return values for selection.

Comment: By considering only performance and GIPS compliance, Jackson has not conducted sufficient review of potential firms to satisfy the requirements of Standard V(A). A thorough investigation of the firms and their operations should be conducted to ensure that their addition would increase the diversity of clients' portfolios and that they are suitable for the fund-of-funds product.

Example 16 (Manager Selection):

Timothy Green works for Peach Asset Management, where he creates proprietary models that analyze data from the firm request for proposal questionnaires to identify managers for possible inclusion in the firm's fund-of-funds investment platform. Various criteria must be met to be accepted to the platform. Because of the number of respondents to the questionnaires, Green uses only the data submitted to make a recommendation for adding a new manager.

Comment: By failing to conduct any additional outside review of the information to verify what was submitted through the request for proposal, Green has likely not satisfied the requirements of Standard V(A). The amount of information requested from outside managers varies among firms. Although the requested information may be comprehensive, Green should ensure sufficient effort is undertaken to verify the submitted information before recommending a firm for inclusion. This requires that he goes beyond the information provided by the manager on the request for proposal questionnaire and may include interviews with interested managers, reviews of regulatory filings, and discussions with the managers' custodian or auditor.

Example 17 (Technical Model Requirements):

Jérôme Dupont works for the credit research group of XYZ Asset Management, where he is in charge of developing and updating credit risk models. In order to perform accurately, his models need to be regularly updated with the latest market data.

Dupont does not interact with or manage money for any of the firm's clients. He is in contact with the firm's US corporate bond fund manager, John Smith, who has only very superficial knowledge of the model and who from time to time asks very basic questions regarding the output recommendations. Smith does not consult Dupont with respect to finalizing his clients' investment strategies.

Dupont's recently assigned objective is to develop a new emerging market corporate credit risk model. The firm is planning to expand into emerging credit, and the development of such a model is a critical step in this process. Because Smith seems to follow the model's recommendations without much concern for its quality as he develops his clients' investment strategies, Dupont decides to focus his time on the development of the new emerging market model and neglects to update the US model.

After several months without regular updates, Dupont's diagnostic statistics start to show alarming signs with respect to the quality of the US credit model. Instead of conducting the long and complicated data update, Dupont introduces new codes into his model with some limited new data as a quick "fix." He thinks this change will address the issue without needing to complete the full data update, so he continues working on the new emerging market model.

Several months following the quick "fix," another set of diagnostic statistics reveals nonsensical results and Dupont realizes that his earlier change contained an error. He quickly corrects the error and alerts Smith. Smith realizes that some of the prior trades he performed were due to erroneous model results. Smith rebalances the portfolio to remove the securities purchased on the basis of the questionable results without reporting the issue to anyone else.

Comment: Smith violated Standard V(A) because exercising "diligence, independence, and thoroughness in analyzing investments, making investment recommendations, and taking investment actions" means that members and candidates must understand the technical aspects of the products they provide to clients. Smith does not understand the model he is relying on to manage money. Members and candidates should also make reasonable enquiries into the source and accuracy of all data used in completing their investment analysis and recommendations.

Dupont violated Standard V(A) even if he does not trade securities or make investment decisions. Dupont's models give investment recommendations, and Dupont is accountable for the quality of those recommendations. Members and candidates should make reasonable efforts to test the output of pre-programmed analytical tools they use. Such validation should occur before incorporating the tools into their decision-making process.

See also Standard V(B) Communication with Clients and Prospective Clients.

STANDARD V(B) COMMUNICATION WITH CLIENTS AND PROSPECTIVE CLIENTS

48

- [ ] demonstrate a thorough knowledge of the CFA Institute Code of Ethics and Standards of Professional Conduct by interpreting the Code and Standards in various situations involving issues of professional integrity
- [ ] recommend practices and procedures designed to prevent violations of the Code and Standards

Members and Candidates must:

1. Disclose to clients and prospective clients the nature of the services provided, along with information about the cost to the client associated with those services.
2. Disclose to clients and prospective clients the basic format and general principles of the investment processes they use to analyze investments, select securities, and construct portfolios and must promptly disclose any changes that might materially affect those processes.
3. Disclose to clients and prospective clients significant limitations and risks associated with the investment process.
4. Use reasonable judgment in identifying which factors are important to their investment analyses, recommendations, or actions and include those factors in communications with clients and prospective clients.
5. Distinguish between fact and opinion in the presentation of investment analyses and recommendations.

Guidance

Highlights:

- *Nature of Services and Information on Cost*
- *Informing Clients of the Investment Process*
- *Different Forms of Communication*
- *Identifying Risk and Limitations*
- *Report Presentation*
- *Distinction between Facts and Opinions in Reports*

Standard V(B) addresses member and candidate conduct with respect to communicating with clients. Developing and maintaining clear, frequent, and thorough communication practices is critical to providing high-quality financial services to clients. When clients understand the information communicated to them, they also can understand exactly how members and candidates are acting on their behalf, which gives clients the opportunity to make well-informed decisions about their investments. Such understanding can be accomplished only through clear communication.

Disclosing Nature of Services and Information about Costs to Clients and Prospective Clients

A fundamental goal of the Code and Standards is to protect client interests and allow clients to make fully informed decisions about their investments and financial well-being. Providing clients with a description of the nature of the services they can expect from investment professionals and information about the costs to the client for those services is critical to achieving this goal. The disclosures required by Standard V(B) will permit clients to make informed decisions as to whether to engage in professional services with members or candidates or their firms.

Full and fair disclosure builds trust with clients, and the disclosure of information about costs benefits clients and protects their interests. Standard V(B) makes clear that required disclosures cover all professional services provided by members and candidates. A clear understanding of the services that members and candidates provide is a foundational element of the client relationship. Clients must understand what services the member or candidate will provide and, critically, what services will not be provided so that members and candidates can set appropriate expectations. It is best practice for members and candidates with client-facing responsibilities to clearly set out in written form at the outset of the engagement a description of the nature and parameters of the professional services as part of the engagement agreement, contract, or other documents memorializing the terms of the client relationship.

In addition to understanding the nature of the services, clients must understand the cost they will be expected to pay for those services so they can make informed decisions about the professional services being provided. This standard requires members and candidates to inform their clients and prospective clients about the services they will receive and the associated costs. Disclosures regarding the cost of the services to clients mandated by Standard V(B) are those expected to be charged to and paid for by the client. Members and candidates should provide a reasonable amount of detail regarding the costs incurred by clients. The standard, however, does not require members and candidates to provide specific dollar amounts. For example, a firm that charges clients a quarterly fee based on the market value of assets under management will be unable to specify a dollar amount in advance. Members and candidates are also not required to disclose a description of the costs to the firm of providing those services. Again, best practice is for members and candidates with client-facing responsibilities to disclose information about the nature of the services and the related costs at the outset of the relationship as part of the client agreement.

The disclosure responsibilities of members and candidates under this standard are ongoing. Initial disclosures at the outset of the relationship alone may not meet the requirements of the standard. If the services or costs change, members and candidates must update the disclosures and provide the updated information to all impacted clients and prospective clients on a timely basis.

In addition, the scope of the disclosures is not limited to only those costs charged by the entity with which the client is in a direct relationship. Members and candidates with client-facing responsibilities must provide disclosures about all of the costs that are associated with the investment services and products that are provided to the client. This includes information on costs arising out of services provided by affiliates, related entities, or third parties for products and services utilized by members, candidates, or their firms in providing their services to clients. Members and candidates may not rely on the sophistication of clients and their supposed understanding of the nature and details of the investment process as a reason for not providing the information required by this standard. However, the information may be tailored to the knowledge and sophistication of each individual client.

The manner in which members and candidates provide the disclosures required by Standard V(B) is at their individual discretion so long as the disclosures are appropriate, accurate, timely, and complete. Best practice dictates that such disclosures be made in written form. Often, in large firms, disclosures about charges to and payments expected by clients are dictated by firm policy and practice. However, this does not relieve members or candidates of their responsibility to provide this information when that is part of their professional responsibilities. While members and candidates rely on and can be directed to use firm-generated disclosures, members and candidates should ensure that these disclosures meet the requirements of the Code and Standards. They have the responsibility to call to their firm's attention when the communication is lacking, flawed, or insufficient to meet the members' and candidates' responsibilities under the Code and Standards. In such a case, members and candidates should, when possible, supplement disclosures from the firm that they consider insufficient to meet the requirements of this standard. Ultimately, if members or candidates cannot rectify or supplement inadequate disclosures mandated by the firm, they should document their objections and take steps to dissociate from the activity.

Generally, this standard affects only client-facing members. While CFA Institute encourages all investment professionals to help ensure that clients receive sufficient disclosures, the standard does not impose a duty on members and candidates who do not interact with clients to ensure that others, not subject to the Code and Standards, comply with Standard V(B). As with other standards that may not be applicable to the professional responsibilities of all members and candidates (e.g., investment performance, suitability), those members and candidates who are part of a team of investment professionals providing services to clients but who do not have client-facing responsibilities need not expand their realm of responsibility to ensure appropriate disclosures to clients are made regarding the nature of services and the associated costs.

Informing Clients of the Investment Process

Members and candidates must adequately describe to clients and prospective clients the manner in which they conduct the investment decision-making process. Such disclosure should address factors that have positive and negative influences on the recommendations, including significant risks and limitations of the investment process used. The member or candidate must keep clients and other interested parties informed on an ongoing basis about changes to the investment process, especially newly identified significant risks and limitations. Only by thoroughly understanding the nature of the investment product or service can a client determine whether changes to that product or service could materially affect his or her investment objectives.

Understanding the basic characteristics of an investment is of great importance in judging the suitability of that investment on a standalone basis, but it is especially important in determining the impact each investment will have on the characteristics of a portfolio. Although the risk and return characteristics of a common stock might seem to be essentially the same for any investor when the stock is viewed in isolation, the effects of those characteristics greatly depend on the other investments held. For instance, if the particular stock will represent 90% of an individual's investments, the stock's importance in the portfolio is vastly different from what it would be to an investor with a highly diversified portfolio for whom the stock will represent only 2% of the holdings.

A firm's investment policy may include the use of outside advisers to manage various portions of clients' assets under management. Members and candidates should inform the clients about the specialization or diversification expertise provided by the external adviser(s). This information allows clients to understand the full mix of products and strategies being applied that may affect their investment objectives.

Different Forms of Communication

For purposes of Standard V(B), communication is not confined to a written report of the type traditionally generated by an analyst researching a security, company, or industry. A presentation of information can be made via any means of communication, including in-person recommendation or description, telephone conversation, media broadcast, or transmission by computer (e.g., on the internet).

Computer and mobile device communications have rapidly evolved over the past few years. Members and candidates using any social media service to communicate business information must be diligent in their efforts to avoid unintended problems because these services may not be available to all clients. When providing information to clients through new technologies, members and candidates should take reasonable steps to ensure that such delivery would treat all clients fairly and, if necessary, be considered publicly disseminated.

The nature of client communications is highly diverse—from one word ("buy" or "sell") to in-depth reports of more than 100 pages. A communication may contain a general recommendation about the market, asset allocations, or classes of investments (e.g., stocks, bonds, real estate) or may relate to a specific security. If recommendations are contained in capsule form (such as a recommended stock list), members and candidates should notify clients that additional information and analyses are available from the producer of the report.

Identifying Risks and Limitations

Members and candidates must outline to clients and prospective clients significant risks and limitations of the analysis contained in their investment products or recommendations. The type and nature of significant risks will depend on the investment process that members and candidates are following and on the personal circumstances of the client. In general, the use of leverage constitutes a significant risk and should be disclosed.

Members and candidates must adequately disclose the general market-related risks and the risks associated with the use of complex financial instruments that are deemed significant. Other types of risks that members and candidates may consider disclosing include, but are not limited to, counterparty risk, country risk, sector or industry risk, security-specific risk, and credit risk.

Investment securities and vehicles may have limiting factors that influence a client's or potential client's investment decision. Members and candidates must report to clients and prospective clients the existence of limitations significant to the decision-making process. Examples of such factors and attributes include, but are not limited to, investment liquidity and capacity. Liquidity is the ability to liquidate an investment on a timely basis at a reasonable cost. Capacity is the investment amount beyond which returns will be negatively affected by new investments.

The appropriateness of risk disclosure should be assessed on the basis of what was known at the time the investment action was taken (often called an *ex ante* basis). Members and candidates must disclose significant risks known to them at the time of the disclosure. Members and candidates cannot be expected to disclose risks they are unaware of at the time recommendations or investment actions are made. In assessing compliance with Standard V(B), it is important to establish knowledge of a purported significant risk or limitation. A one-time investment loss that occurs after the disclosure does not constitute a pertinent factor in assessing whether significant risks and limitations were properly disclosed. Having no knowledge of a risk or limitation that subsequently triggers a loss may reveal a deficiency in the diligence and reasonable basis of the research of the member or candidate but may not reveal a breach of Standard V(B).

Report Presentation

Once the analytical process has been completed, the member or candidate who prepares the report must include those elements that are important to the analysis and conclusions of the report so that the reader can follow and challenge the report's reasoning. A report writer who has done adequate investigation may emphasize certain areas, touch briefly on others, and omit certain aspects deemed unimportant. For instance, a report may dwell on a quarterly earnings release or new-product introduction and omit other matters as long as the analyst clearly stipulates the limits to the scope of the report.

Investment advice based on quantitative research and analysis must be supported by readily available reference material and should be applied in a manner consistent with previously applied methodology. If changes in methodology are made, they should be highlighted.

Distinction between Facts and Opinions in Reports

Standard V(B) requires that opinion be separated from fact. Violations often occur when reports fail to separate the past from the future by not indicating that earnings estimates, changes in the outlook for dividends, or future market price information are *opinions* subject to future circumstances.

In the case of complex quantitative analyses, members and candidates must clearly separate fact from statistical conjecture and should identify the known limitations of an analysis. Members and candidates may violate Standard V(B) by failing to identify the limits of statistically developed projections because such omission leaves readers unaware of the limits of the published projections.

Members and candidates should explicitly discuss with clients and prospective clients the assumptions used in the investment models and processes to generate the analysis. Caution should be used in promoting the perceived accuracy of any model or process to clients because the ultimate output is merely an estimate of future results and not a certainty.

STANDARD V(B): RECOMMENDED PROCEDURES

49

Because the selection of relevant factors is an analytical skill, determination of whether a member or candidate has used reasonable judgment in excluding and including information in research reports depends heavily on case-by-case review rather than a specific checklist.

Members and candidates should encourage their firms to have a rigorous methodology for reviewing research that is created for publication and dissemination to clients.

To assist in the after-the-fact review of a report, the member or candidate must maintain records indicating the nature of the research and should, if asked, be able to supply additional information to the client (or any user of the report) covering factors not included in the report.

50 STANDARD V(B): APPLICATION OF THE STANDARD

Example 1 (Costs of Services to Clients):

The nature of ABC Capital Private Equity Fund III's investments requires ABC Capital to routinely provide structuring advice to the companies in which the fund invests, for which ABC Capital charges a fee to those companies. It is the policy of ABC Capital to remit the fees it earns for restructuring advice to the fund if the investment in the underlying company decreases in value, but it retains the fees if the investment in the underlying company increases in value. The private placement memorandum does not disclose this arrangement because the firm's CEO, Alex Alphonso, views this as a common industry practice and that it provides a "win-win" for investors. ABC Capital's services contribute significantly to the returns enjoyed by investors in the ABC Capital Private Equity Fund III, and ABC Capital earns a substantial fee.

> *Comment*: Alphonso is in violation of Standard V(B) because the compensation received by ABC Capital has not been disclosed to clients who are investors in the fund. Alphonso may not rely on the sophistication of clients and their assumed understanding of the nature and details of the fee arrangements with underlying companies in which ABC Capital invests in as a reason for not providing the information required by this standard. This is true even though investors in ABC Private Equity Fund III benefit from the arrangement.

Example 2 (Costs of Services to Clients):

January James is an investment adviser tasked with completing a manager search for a client's portfolio. The search mandate is to identify a shortlist of investment managers who offer core fixed-income strategies managed to the benchmark identified in the client's investment policy statement. James begins her search with a set of criteria defined by her firm's manager research process policy. She identifies three candidates who fulfill these criteria but notices that her top-ranked manager has significantly higher fees than the other candidates on her list. Her firm's search criteria list fees as less important relative to the other criteria for ranking investment managers. To present investment performance for uniform comparison, James creates a fee comparison chart that lists each manager's performance on a gross-of-fee basis. She presents gross-of-fee performance over the same time periods and relative to the same benchmark. She also calculates the total amount of fees that would have been paid during each of the performance time periods presented. Finally, she lists each manager's fee schedule and any additional fees that may be charged outside the published fees. She explains to her client that prior to final selection, the investment managers will be required to present their final fee proposal.

> *Comment*: James's presentation of manager fees is appropriate because she provided a uniform comparison of manager services. Her presentation adheres to Standard V(B) Communication with Clients and Prospective Clients, which requires disclosure about the nature of services provided, along with information about the cost associated with those services.

Example 3 (Disclosure of Changed Fee Calculation Methodology):

Marc Maalouf works in a branch office for a large wealth management firm. The firm's fees are based on a percentage of the value of the assets managed in each client account. The firm has a standard method for valuing assets and calculating fees for all of its clients, which is disclosed to each client at the outset of the relationship. Maalouf becomes aware that, over time, the firm has transitioned to (1) using the market value of client assets at the end of the billing cycle instead of the average daily balance of the account and (2) including cash and cash equivalents in the fee calculation, which were previously excluded.

> *Comment*: Advisory fees are critical information that a client needs to know. Developing and maintaining clear, frequent, and thorough communication with clients about costs for the investment adviser's services allows them to make well-informed decisions about their investments, including about whether to engage or retain an investment adviser. Maalouf and his firm may change the advisory fee calculation methodology and policies over time for existing accounts, but Maalouf must make clients aware of any such changes. It is improper to change fee calculation methodology without disclosure, even if it results in lower fees.

Example 4 (Sufficient Disclosure of Investment System):

Sarah Williamson, director of marketing for Country Technicians, Inc., is convinced that she has found the perfect formula for increasing Country Technicians' income and diversifying its product base. Williamson plans to build on Country Technicians' reputation as a leading money manager by marketing an exclusive and expensive investment advice letter to high-net-worth individuals. One hitch in the plan is the complexity of Country Technicians' investment system—a combination of technical trading rules (based on historical price and volume fluctuations) and portfolio construction rules designed to minimize risk. To simplify the newsletter, she decides to include only each week's top five "buy" and "sell" recommendations and to leave out details of the valuation models and the portfolio structuring scheme.

> *Comment*: Williamson's plans for the newsletter violate Standard V(B). Williamson need not describe the investment system in detail in order to implement the advice effectively, but she must inform clients of Country Technicians' basic process and logic. Without understanding the basis for a recommendation, clients cannot possibly understand its limitations or its inherent risks.

Example 5 (Providing Opinions as Facts):

Richard Dox is a mining analyst for East Bank Securities. He has just finished his report on Boisy Bay Minerals. Included in his report is his own assessment of the geological extent of mineral reserves likely to be found on the company's land. Dox completed this calculation on the basis of the core samples from the company's latest drilling. According to Dox's calculations, the company has more than 500,000 ounces of gold on the property. Dox concludes his research report as follows: "Based on the fact that the company has 500,000 ounces of gold to be mined, I recommend a strong *buy*."

Comment: If Dox issues the report as written, he will violate Standard V(B). His calculation of the total gold reserves for the property based on the company's recent sample drilling is a quantitative opinion, not a fact. Opinion must be distinguished from fact in research reports.

Example 6 (Proper Description of a Security):

Olivia Thomas, an analyst at Government Brokers, Inc., which is a brokerage firm specializing in government bond trading, has produced a report that describes an investment strategy designed to benefit from an expected decline in U.S. interest rates. The firm's derivative products group has designed a structured product that will allow the firm's clients to benefit from this strategy. Thomas's report describing the strategy indicates that high returns are possible if various scenarios for declining interest rates are assumed. Citing the proprietary nature of the structured product underlying the strategy, the report does not describe in detail how the firm is able to offer such returns or the related risks in the scenarios, nor does the report address the likely returns of the strategy if, contrary to expectations, interest rates rise.

Comment: Thomas has violated Standard V(B) because her report fails to describe properly the basic characteristics of the actual and implied risks of the investment strategy, including how the structure was created and the degree to which leverage was embedded in the structure. The report should include a balanced discussion of how the strategy would perform in the case of rising as well as falling interest rates, preferably illustrating how the strategies might be expected to perform in the event of a reasonable variety of interest rate- and credit risk-spread scenarios. If liquidity issues are relevant with regard to the valuation of either the derivatives or the underlying securities, provisions the firm has made to address those risks should also be disclosed.

Example 7 (Notification of Fund Mandate Change):

May & Associates is an aggressive growth manager that has represented itself since its inception as a specialist at investing in small-cap U.S. stocks. One of May's selection criteria is a maximum capitalization of US$250 million for any given company. After a string of successful years of superior performance relative to its peers, May has expanded its client base significantly, to the point at which assets under management now exceed US$3 billion. For liquidity purposes, May's chief investment officer (CIO) decides to lift the maximum permissible market-cap ceiling to US$500 million and change the firm's sales and marketing literature accordingly to inform prospective clients and third-party consultants.

Comment: Although May's CIO is correct about informing potentially interested parties as to the change in investment process, he must also notify May's existing clients. Among the latter group might be a number of clients who not only retained May as a small-cap manager but also retained mid-cap and large-cap specialists in a multiple-manager approach. Such clients could regard May's change of criteria as a style change that distorts their overall asset allocations.

Example 8 (Notification of Fund Mandate Change):

Rather than lifting the ceiling for its universe from US$250 million to US$500 million, May & Associates extends its small-cap universe to include a number of non-US companies.

> *Comment*: Standard V(B) requires that May's CIO advise May's clients of this change because the firm may have been retained by some clients specifically for its prowess at investing in U.S. small-cap stocks. Other changes that require client notification are introducing derivatives to emulate a certain market sector or relaxing various other constraints, such as portfolio beta. In all such cases, members and candidates must disclose changes to all interested parties.

Example 9 (Notification of Changes to the Investment Process):

RJZ Capital Management is an active value style equity manager that selects stocks by using a combination of four multifactor models. The firm has found favorable results when back testing the most recent 10 years of available market data in a new dividend discount model (DDM) designed by the firm. This model is based on projected inflation rates, earnings growth rates, and interest rates. The president of RJZ decides to replace its simple model that uses price to trailing 12-month earnings with the new DDM.

> *Comment*: Because the introduction of a new and different valuation model represents a material change in the investment process, RJZ's president must communicate the change to the firm's clients. RJZ is moving away from a model based on hard data toward a new model that is at least partly dependent on the firm's forecasting skills. Clients would likely view such a model as a significant change rather than a mere refinement of RJZ's process.

Example 10 (Notification of Changes to the Investment Process):

RJZ Capital Management loses the chief architect of its multifactor valuation system. Without informing its clients, the president of RJZ decides to redirect the firm's talents and resources toward developing a product for passive equity management—a product that will emulate the performance of a major market index.

> *Comment:* By failing to disclose to clients a substantial change to its investment process, the president of RJZ has violated Standard V(B).

Example 11 (Notification of Changes to the Investment Process):

At Fundamental Asset Management, Inc., the responsibility for selecting stocks for addition to the firm's "approved" list has just shifted from individual security analysts to a committee consisting of the research director and three senior portfolio managers. Eleanor Morales, a portfolio manager with Fundamental Asset Management, thinks this change is not important enough to communicate to her clients.

Comment: Morales must disclose the process change to all her clients. Some of Fundamental's clients might be concerned about the morale and motivation among the firm's best research analysts after such a change. Moreover, clients might challenge the stock-picking track record of the portfolio managers and might even want to monitor the situation closely.

Example 12 (Sufficient Disclosure of Investment System):

Amanda Chinn is the investment director for Diversified Asset Management, which manages the endowment of a charitable organization. Because of recent staff departures, Diversified has decided to limit its direct investment focus to large-cap securities and supplement the needs for small-cap and mid-cap management by hiring outside fund managers. In describing the planned strategy change to the charity, Chinn's update letter states, "As investment director, I will directly oversee the investment team managing the endowment's large-capitalization allocation. I will coordinate the selection and ongoing review of external managers responsible for allocations to classes." The letter also describes the reasons for the change and the characteristics external managers must have to be considered.

Comment: Standard V(B) requires the disclosure of the investment process used to construct the portfolio of the fund. Changing the investment process from managing all classes of investments within the firm to the use of external managers is one example of information that needs to be communicated to clients. Chinn and her firm have embraced the principles of Standard V(B) by providing their client with relevant information. The charity can now make a reasonable decision about whether Diversified Asset Management remains the appropriate manager for its fund.

Example 13 (Notification of Changes to the Investment Process):

Michael Papis is the chief investment officer of his state's retirement fund. The fund has always used outside advisers for the real estate allocation, and this information is clearly presented in all fund communications. Thomas Nagle, a recognized sell-side research analyst and Papis's business school classmate, recently left the investment bank he worked for to start his own asset management firm, Accessible Real Estate. Nagle is trying to build his assets under management and contacts Papis about gaining some of the retirement fund's allocation. In the previous few years, the performance of the retirement fund's real estate investments was in line with the fund's benchmark but was not extraordinary. Papis decides to help out his old friend and also to seek better returns by moving the real estate allocation to Accessible. The only notice of the change in adviser appears in the next annual report in the listing of associated advisers.

Comment: Papis has violated Standard V(B). He attempted to hide the nature of his decision to change external managers by making only a limited disclosure. The plan recipients and the fund's trustees need to be aware when changes are made to ensure that operational procedures are being followed.

See also Standard IV(C) Responsibilities of Supervisors, Standard V(A) Diligence and Reasonable Basis, and Standard VI(A) Disclosure of Conflicts.

Example 14 (Notification of Errors):

Jérôme Dupont works for the credit research group of XYZ Asset Management, where he is in charge of developing and updating credit risk models. In order to perform accurately, his models need to be regularly updated with the latest market data.

Dupont does not interact with or manage money for any of the firm's clients. He is in contact with the firm's US corporate bond fund manager, John Smith, who has only very superficial knowledge of the model and who from time to time asks very basic questions regarding the output recommendations. Smith does not consult Dupont with respect to finalizing his clients' investment strategies.

Dupont's recently assigned objective is to develop a new emerging market corporate credit risk model. The firm is planning to expand into emerging credit, and the development of such a model is a critical step in this process. Because Smith seems to follow the model's recommendations without much concern for its quality as he develops his clients' investment strategies, Dupont decides to focus his time on the development of the new emerging market model and neglects to update the US model.

After several months without regular updates, Dupont's diagnostic statistics start to show alarming signs with respect to the quality of the US credit model. Instead of conducting the long and complicated data update, Dupont introduces new codes into his model with some limited new data as a quick "fix." He thinks this change will address the issue without needing to complete the full data update, so he continues working on the new emerging market model.

Several months following the quick "fix," another set of diagnostic statistics reveals nonsensical results and Dupont realizes that his earlier change contained an error. He quickly corrects the error and alerts Smith. Smith realizes that some of the prior trades he performed were due to erroneous model results. Smith rebalances the portfolio to remove the securities purchased based on the questionable results without reporting the issue to anyone else.

> *Comment*: Smith violated V(B) by not disclosing a material error in the investment process. Clients should have been informed about the error and the corrective actions the firm was undertaking on their behalf.
>
> See also Standard V(A) Diligence and Reasonable Basis

Example 15 (Notification of Risks and Limitations):

Quantitative analyst Yuri Yakovlev, has developed an investment strategy that selects small-cap stocks on the basis of quantitative signals. Yakovlev's strategy typically identifies only a small number of stocks (10–20) that tend to be illiquid, but according to his backtests, the strategy generates significant risk-adjusted returns. The partners at Yakovlev's firm, QSC Capital, are impressed by these results. After a thorough examination of the strategy's risks, stress testing, historical backtesting, and scenario analysis, QSC decides to seed the strategy with US$10 million of internal capital in order for Yakovlev to create a track record for the strategy.

After two years, the strategy has generated performance returns greater than the appropriate benchmark and the Sharpe ratio of the fund is close to 1.0. On the basis of these results, QSC decides to actively market the fund to large institutional investors. While creating the offering materials, Yakovlev informs the marketing team that the capacity of the strategy is limited. The extent of the limitation is difficult to ascertain with precision; it depends on market liquidity and other factors in his model that can evolve over time. Yakovlev indicates that given the current market conditions, investments in the fund beyond US$100 million of capital could become more difficult and negatively affect expected fund returns.

Alan Wellard, the manager of the marketing team, is a partner with 30 years of marketing experience and explains to Yakovlev that these are complex technical issues that will muddy the marketing message. According to Wellard the offering material should focus solely on the great track record of the fund. Yakovlev does not object because the fund, with US$12 million of capital, is very far from the US$100 million threshold.

Comment: Yakovlev and Wellard have not appropriately disclosed a significant limitation associated with the investment product. Yakovlev believes this limitation, once reached, will materially affect the returns of the fund. While the fund is currently far from the US$100 million mark, current and prospective investors must be made aware of this capacity issue. If significant limitations are complicated to grasp and clients do not have the technical background required to understand them, Yakovlev and Wellard should either educate the clients or ascertain whether the fund is suitable for each client.

Example 16 (Notification of Risks and Limitations):

Brickell Advisers offers investment advisory services mainly to South American clients. Julietta Ramon, a risk analyst at Brickell, describes to clients how the firm uses value at risk (VaR) analysis to track the risk of its strategies. Ramon assures clients that calculating a VaR at a 99% confidence level, using a 20-day holding period, and applying a methodology based on an ex-ante Monte Carlo simulation is extremely effective. The firm has never had losses greater than those predicted by this VaR analysis.

Comment: Ramon has not sufficiently communicated the risks associated with the investment process to satisfy the requirements of Standard V(B). The losses predicted by a VaR analysis depend greatly on the inputs used in the model. The size and probability of losses can differ significantly from what an individual model predicts. Ramon must disclose how the inputs were selected and the potential limitations and risks associated with the investment strategy.

Example 17 (Notification of Risks and Limitations):

Lily Smith attended an industry conference and noticed that John Baker, an investment manager with Baker Associates, attracted a great deal of attention from the conference participants. On the basis of her knowledge of Baker's reputation and the interest he received at the conference, Smith recommends adding Baker Associates to the approved manager platform. Her recommendation to the approval committee included the statement "John Baker is well respected in the industry, and his insights are consistently sought after by investors. Our clients are sure to benefit from investing with Baker Associates."

Comment: Smith is not appropriately separating facts from opinions in her recommendation to include the manager within the platform. Her actions conflict with the requirements of Standard V(B). Smith is relying on her opinions about Baker's reputation and the fact that many attendees were talking with him at the conference. Smith should also review the requirements of Standard V(A) regarding reasonable basis to determine the level of review necessary to recommend Baker Associates.

STANDARD V(C) RECORD RETENTION

51

- [ ] demonstrate a thorough knowledge of the CFA Institute Code of Ethics and Standards of Professional Conduct by interpreting the Code and Standards in various situations involving issues of professional integrity
- [ ] recommend practices and procedures designed to prevent violations of the Code and Standards

Members and Candidates must develop and maintain appropriate records to support their investment analyses, recommendations, actions, and other investment-related communications with clients and prospective clients.

Guidance

Highlights:

- *New Media Records*
- *Records Are Property of the Firm*
- *Local Requirements*

Members and candidates must retain records that substantiate the scope of their research and reasons for their actions or conclusions. The retention requirement applies to decisions to buy or sell a security as well as reviews undertaken that do not lead to a change in position. Which records are required to support recommendations or investment actions depends on the role of the member or candidate in the investment decision-making process. Records may be maintained either in hard copy or electronic form.

Some examples of supporting documentation that assists the member or candidate in meeting the requirements for retention are as follows:

- personal notes from meetings with the covered company,
- press releases or presentations issued by the covered company,
- computer-based model outputs and analyses,
- computer-based model input parameters,
- risk analyses of securities' impacts on a portfolio,
- selection criteria for external advisers,
- notes from clients from meetings to review investment policy statements, and
- outside research reports.

New Media Records

The increased use of new and evolving technological formats (e.g., social media) for gathering and sharing information creates new challenges in maintaining the appropriate records and files. The nature or format of the information does not remove a member's or candidate's responsibility to maintain a record of information used in his or her analysis or communicated to clients.

Members and candidates should understand that although employers and local regulators are developing digital media retention policies, these policies may lag behind the advent of new communication channels. Such lag places greater responsibility on the individual for ensuring that all relevant information is retained. Examples of non-print media formats that should be retained include, but are not limited to,

- e-mails,
- text messages,
- blog posts, and
- social media posts.

Records Are Property of the Firm

As a general matter, records created as part of a member's or candidate's professional activity on behalf of his or her employer are the property of the firm. When a member or candidate leaves a firm to seek other employment, the member or candidate cannot take the property of the firm, including original forms or copies of supporting records of the member's or candidate's work, to the new employer without the express consent of the previous employer. The member or candidate cannot use historical recommendations or research reports created at the previous firm because the supporting documentation is unavailable. For future use, the member or candidate must re-create the supporting records at the new firm with information gathered through public sources or directly from the covered company and not from memory or sources obtained at the previous employer.

Local Requirements

Local regulators often impose requirements on members, candidates, and their firms related to record retention that must be followed. Firms may also implement policies detailing the applicable time frame for retaining research and client communication records. Fulfilling such regulatory and firm requirements satisfies the requirements of Standard V(C). In the absence of regulatory guidance or firm policies, CFA Institute recommends maintaining records for at least seven years.

52 STANDARD V(C): RECOMMENDED PROCEDURES

The responsibility to maintain records that support investment action generally falls with the firm rather than individuals. Members and candidates must, however, archive research notes and other documents, either electronically or in hard copy, that support their current investment-related communications. Doing so will assist their firms in complying with requirements for preservation of internal or external records.

STANDARD V(C): APPLICATION OF THE STANDARD

53

Example 1 (Record Retention and IPS Objectives and Recommendations):

One of Nikolas Lindstrom's clients is upset by the negative investment returns of his equity portfolio. The investment policy statement for the client requires that the portfolio manager follow a benchmark-oriented approach. The benchmark for the client includes a 35% investment allocation in the technology sector. The client acknowledges that this allocation was appropriate, but over the past three years, technology stocks have suffered severe losses. The client complains to the investment manager for allocating so much money to this sector.

> *Comment*: For Lindstrom, having appropriate records is important to show that over the past three years, the portion of technology stocks in the benchmark index was 35%, as called for in the IPS. Lindstrom should also have the client's IPS stating that the benchmark was appropriate for the client's investment objectives. He should also have records indicating that the investment has been explained appropriately to the client and that the IPS was updated on a regular basis. Taking these actions, Lindstrom would be in compliance with Standard V(C).

Example 2 (Record Retention and Research Process):

Malcolm Young is a research analyst who writes numerous reports rating companies in the luxury retail industry. His reports are based on a variety of sources, including interviews with company managers, manufacturers, and economists; on-site company visits; customer surveys; and secondary research from analysts covering related industries.

> *Comment*: Young must carefully document and keep copies of all the information that goes into his reports, including the secondary or third-party research of other analysts. Failure to maintain such files would violate Standard V(C).

Example 3 (Records as Firm, Not Employee, Property):

Martin Blank develops an analytical model while he is employed by Green Partners Investment Management, LLP (GPIM). While at the firm, he systematically documents the assumptions that make up the model as well as his reasoning behind the assumptions. As a result of the success of his model, Blank is hired to be the head of the research department of one of GPIM's competitors. Blank takes copies of the records supporting his model to his new firm.

> *Comment*: The records created by Blank supporting the research model he developed at GPIM are the records of GPIM. Taking the documents with him to his new employer without GPIM's permission violates Standard V(C). To use the model in the future, Blank must re-create the records supporting his model at the new firm.

54 STANDARD VI: CONFLICTS OF INTEREST

- [ ] demonstrate a thorough knowledge of the CFA Institute Code of Ethics and Standards of Professional Conduct by interpreting the Code and Standards in various situations involving issues of professional integrity
- [ ] recommend practices and procedures designed to prevent violations of the Code and Standards

Standard VI(A) Avoid or Disclose Conflicts

Members and Candidates must avoid or make full and fair disclosure of all matters that could reasonably be expected to impair their independence and objectivity or interfere with respective duties to their clients, prospective clients, and employer. Members and Candidates must ensure that such disclosures are prominent, are delivered in plain language, and communicate the relevant information effectively.

Guidance

Highlights:

- *Disclosure of Conflicts to Employers*
- *Disclosure of Conflicts to Clients*
- *Cross-Departmental Conflicts*
- *Conflicts with Stock Ownership*
- *Conflicts as a Board Member or Director*

A conflict of interest is any matter that could reasonably be expected to impair independence and objectivity or raise a question about whether actions, judgment, or decision making is free from bias. Conflicts of interest occur when there is a personal or professional interest that may impair a member's or candidate's ability to perform his or her professional responsibilities in an independent and objective manner. Conflicts of interest often arise in the investment profession. Conflicts can occur between the interests of clients, the interests of employers, and the member's or candidate's own personal interests. Common sources for conflict are compensation structures, especially incentive and bonus structures that provide immediate returns for members and candidates with little or no consideration of long-term value creation. Identifying and managing conflicts of interest is critically important to engaging in ethical conduct.

Best practice is to avoid actual conflicts or the appearance of conflicts of interest. When it is not reasonable for members and candidates to avoid a conflict, clear and complete disclosure to mitigate the conflict is necessary.

Standard VI(A) protects investors and employers by requiring members and candidates to avoid or fully disclose to clients, potential clients, and employers all actual and potential conflicts of interest. When a member or candidate has made full disclosure of an unavoidable conflict, the member's or candidate's employer, clients, and prospective clients will have the information needed to evaluate the objectivity of the investment advice or action taken on their behalf.

To be effective, disclosures must be prominent and must be made in plain language and in a manner designed to effectively communicate the information. Members and candidates are responsible for determining how often, in what manner, and in what particular circumstances the disclosure of conflicts must be made. Best practice dictates updating disclosures when the nature of a conflict of interest changes materially—for example, if the nature of a conflict of interest worsens through the introduction of bonuses based on each quarter's profits as opposed to annual profits. In making and updating disclosures of conflicts of interest, members and candidates should err on the side of caution to ensure that conflicts are effectively communicated.

Disclosure of Conflicts to Employers

Disclosure of conflicts to employers may be appropriate in many instances. When reporting conflicts of interest to employers, members and candidates must give their employers enough information to assess the impact of the conflict. By complying with employer guidelines, members and candidates allow their employers to avoid potentially embarrassing and costly ethical or regulatory violations.

Reportable situations include conflicts that would interfere with rendering unbiased investment advice and conflicts that would cause a member or candidate to act not in the employer's best interest. The same circumstances that generate conflicts to be reported to clients and prospective clients also dictate reporting to employers. Ownership of stocks analyzed or recommended, participation on outside boards, and financial or other pressures that could influence a decision are to be promptly reported to the employer so that their impact can be assessed and a decision on how to resolve the conflict can be made.

The mere appearance of a conflict of interest may create problems for members, candidates, and their employers. Therefore, many of the conflicts previously mentioned may be explicitly prohibited by an employer in order to avoid those conflicts altogether. For example, many employers restrict personal trading, outside board membership, and related activities to prevent situations that might not normally be considered problematic from a conflict-of-interest point of view but that could give the appearance of a conflict of interest. Members and candidates must comply with these employer restrictions. Members and candidates should take reasonable steps to avoid conflicts. However, if the conflicts are not resolved, they must report conflicts promptly.

Standard VI(A) also deals with a member's or candidate's conflicts of interest that might be detrimental to the employer's business. Any potential conflict situation that could prevent clear judgment about or full commitment to the execution of a member's or candidate's duties to the employer should be avoided. If the member or candidate does not avoid the conflict, it must be reported to the member's or candidate's employer.

Disclosure of Conflicts to Clients

Members and candidates must maintain their objectivity when rendering investment advice or taking investment action. Investment advice or actions may be perceived to be tainted in numerous situations. For instance, a member or candidate may not be objective if he or she owns stock in the company that is the subject of an investment recommendation or if the member or candidate has a close personal relationship with the company managers. Requiring members and candidates to disclose all matters that reasonably could be expected to impair the member's or candidate's objectivity when a conflict exists mitigates the conflict and allows clients and prospective clients to judge motives and possible biases for themselves.

While avoiding conflicts altogether is preferred, often in the investment industry, a conflict or the perception of a conflict is not reasonably avoidable. The most obvious conflicts of interest, which must always be avoided or disclosed, are relationships between an issuer and the member, the candidate, or his or her firm (such as a directorship or consultancy by a member; investment banking, underwriting, and financial relationships; broker/dealer market-making activities; and material beneficial ownership of stock). For the purposes of Standard VI(A), members and candidates beneficially own securities or other investments if they have a direct or indirect pecuniary interest in the securities, have the power to vote or direct the voting of the shares of the securities or investments, or have the power to dispose or direct the disposition of the security or investment.

A member or candidate must take reasonable steps to determine whether a conflict of interest exists and disclose to clients any known conflicts of the member's or candidate's firm. As an example, disclosure of broker/dealer market-making activities alerts clients that a purchase or sale might be made from or to the firm's proprietary account and that the firm has a special interest in the price of the stock.

Additionally, disclosures must be made to clients regarding conflicts that may arise in fee arrangements, subadvisory agreements, or other situations involving nonstandard fee structures. Equally important is the disclosure of arrangements in which the firm benefits directly from investment recommendations. An obvious conflict of interest is the rebate of a portion of the service fee some classes of mutual funds charge to investors. Members and candidates must disclose such relationships so clients can fully understand such conflicts.

Cross-Departmental Conflicts

Other circumstances may give rise to actual or potential conflicts of interest. For instance, a sell-side analyst working for a broker/dealer may be encouraged, not only by members of her or his own firm but also by corporate issuers themselves, to write research reports about particular companies. The buy-side analyst is likely to be faced with similar conflicts as banks exercise their underwriting and security-dealing powers. The marketing division may ask an analyst to recommend the stock of a certain company in order to obtain business from that company.

The potential for conflicts of interest also exists with broker-sponsored limited partnerships formed to invest venture capital. Members and candidates may be expected not only to follow issues from these partnerships once they are offered to the public but also to promote the issues in the secondary market after public offerings. Members and candidates must resolve situations presenting potential conflicts of interest or disclose them in accordance with the principles set forth in Standard VI(A).

Conflicts with Stock Ownership

The most prevalent conflict requiring disclosure under Standard VI(A) is a member's or candidate's ownership of stock in companies that he or she recommends to clients or that clients hold. The simplest method for preventing a conflict is to avoid the conflict by prohibiting members and candidates from owning any such securities, but this approach may be overly burdensome and too restrictive. Members and candidates must disclose any beneficial ownership interest in a security or other investment that the member or candidate is recommending. Conflicts arising from personal investing are discussed more fully in the guidance for Standard VI(B).

Conflicts as a Board Member or Director

Service as a board member or director poses three basic conflicts of interest. First, a conflict may exist between the duties owed to clients and the duties owed to shareholders of the company. Second, investment personnel who serve as directors may receive securities or options to purchase securities of the company as compensation for serving on the board, which could raise questions about trading actions that might increase the value of those securities. Third, board service creates the opportunity to receive material nonpublic information involving the company. Even though the information is confidential, the perception could be that information not available to the public is being communicated to a director's firm—whether a broker, investment adviser, or other type of organization. When members or candidates providing investment services also serve as directors, they should be isolated from those making investment decisions by the use of firewalls or similar restrictions.

STANDARD VI(A): APPLICATION OF THE STANDARD

55

Example 1 (Conflict of Interest and Business Relationships):

Henry Weiss is a research analyst with Williamsburg Company, a broker and investment banking firm. Williamsburg's merger and acquisition department has represented Jimco, a conglomerate, in all of Jimco's acquisitions for 20 years. From time to time, Williamsburg officers sit on the boards of directors of various Jimco subsidiaries. Weiss is writing a research report on Jimco.

> *Comment*: Weiss must disclose in his research report Williamsburg's special relationship with Jimco. Broker/dealer management of and participation in public offerings must be disclosed in research reports. Because the position of underwriter to a company entails a special past and potential future relationship with a company that is the subject of investment advice, it threatens the independence and objectivity of the report writer and must be disclosed.

Example 2 (Conflict of Interest and Business Stock Ownership):

The investment management firm of Dover & Roe sells a 25% interest in its partnership to a multinational bank holding company, First of New York. Immediately after the sale, Roy Hobbs, president of Dover & Roe, changes her recommendation for First of New York's common stock from "sell" to "buy" and adds First of New York's commercial paper to Dover & Roe's approved list for purchase.

> *Comment*: Best practice would be for Hobbs to discontinue research coverage of First of New York because the new ownership interest in this company creates a conflict of interest. At minimum, Hobbs must disclose the new relationship with First of New York to all Dover & Roe clients. Hobbs must also require the ownership interest to be disclosed to clients by the firm's portfolio managers when they make specific investment recommendations or take investment actions with respect to First of New York's securities.

Example 3 (Conflict of Interest and Personal Stock Ownership):

Karl Fargmon, a research analyst who follows firms producing office equipment, has been recommending purchase of Kincaid Printing because of its innovative new line of copiers. After his initial report on the company, Fargmon's wife inherits from a distant relative US$3 million of Kincaid stock. One year after his initial report on the company, Fargmon is asked to write a follow-up report on Kincaid.

> *Comment*: At minimum, Fargmon must disclose his wife's ownership of the Kincaid stock to his employer and in his follow-up report. Best practice is to avoid the conflict by asking his employer to assign another analyst to draft the follow-up report.

Example 4 (Conflict of Interest and Personal Stock Ownership):

Julie Roberts is speculating in penny stocks for her own account and purchases 100,000 shares of Drew Mining, Inc., for US$0.30 a share. She intends to sell these shares at the sign of any substantial upward price movement of the stock. A week later, her employer asks her to write a report on penny stocks in the mining industry to be published in two weeks. Even without owning the Drew stock, Roberts would recommend it in her report as a "buy." A surge in the price of the stock to the US$2 range is likely to result once the report is issued.

> *Comment*: Roberts must disclose the conflict to her employer and should consider declining the research assignment on Drew Mining. If Roberts's employer has her write the report despite the conflict, Roberts must disclose the conflict in her report.

Example 5 (Conflict of Interest and Compensation Arrangements):

Sarah Snead, a portfolio manager for Thomas Investment Counsel, LLC, specializes in managing public retirement funds and defined benefit pension plan accounts, all of which have long-term investment objectives. A year ago, Snead's employer, in an attempt to motivate and retain key investment professionals, introduced a bonus compensation system that rewards portfolio managers on the basis of quarterly performance relative to their peers and to certain benchmark indexes. In an attempt to improve the short-term performance of her accounts, Snead changes her investment strategy and purchases several high-beta stocks for client portfolios. These purchases are seemingly contrary to the clients' investment policy statements (IPSs). No change in objective or strategy has been recommended by Snead during the year.

> *Comment*: Snead has violated Standard VI(A) by failing to inform her clients of the changes in her compensation arrangement with her employer, which created a conflict of interest between her compensation and her clients' IPSs. Firms may pay employees on the basis of performance, but pressure by Thomas Investment Counsel to achieve short-term performance goals conflicts with the requirement to take only investment actions that are consistent with the objectives of Snead's accounts.

Example 6 (Conflict of Interest and Compensation Arrangements):

Kevin Carter is a representative with Bengal International, a registered broker/dealer. Carter is approached by a stock promoter for Badger Company, who offers to pay Carter additional compensation for sales of Badger Company's stock to Carter's clients. Carter accepts the stock promoter's offer but does not disclose the arrangement to his clients or to his employer. Carter sells shares of the stock to his clients.

> *Comment*: Carter has violated Standard VI(A) by failing to disclose to clients that he is receiving additional compensation for recommending and selling Badger stock. At minimum, Carter must disclose the arrangement with Badger to his clients so they may evaluate whether Carter's recommendations to buy Badger were affected by this arrangement. Best practice is for Carter to avoid this conflict of interest altogether by declining the offer of additional compensation from Badger Company.

Example 7 (Conflict of Interest and Requested Favors):

Henri Papis is the chief investment officer of his state's retirement fund. The fund has always used external managers for the real estate allocation, and this information is clearly presented in all fund communications. Eric Nagle, a recognized sell-side research analyst and Papis's business school classmate, recently left the investment bank he worked for to start his own asset management firm, Accessible Real Estate. Nagle is trying to build his assets under management, and he contacts Papis about gaining some of the retirement fund's real estate allocation. In the previous few years, the performance of the retirement fund's real estate investments was in line with the fund's benchmark but was not extraordinary. Papis decides to help out his old friend and also to seek better returns by moving the real estate allocation to Accessible. The only notice of the change in managers appears in the next annual report in the listing of external managers.

> *Comment*: Papis has violated Standard VI(A) by not disclosing to his employer his personal relationship with Nagle. Disclosure of his past history with Nagle would allow his firm to determine whether the conflict may have impaired Papis's independence in deciding to change external managers.

STANDARD VI(B) PRIORITY OF TRANSACTIONS

56

- ☐ demonstrate a thorough knowledge of the CFA Institute Code of Ethics and Standards of Professional Conduct by interpreting the Code and Standards in various situations involving issues of professional integrity
- ☐ recommend practices and procedures designed to prevent violations of the Code and Standards

> Investment transactions for clients and employers must have priority over investment transactions in which a Member or Candidate is the beneficial owner.

Guidance

Highlights:

- *Avoiding Potential Conflicts*
- *Personal Trading Secondary to Trading for Clients*
- *Standards for Nonpublic Information*
- *Impact on All Accounts with Beneficial Ownership*

Standard VI(B) reinforces the responsibility of members and candidates to give the interests of their clients and employers priority over their personal financial interests. This standard is designed to prevent any potential conflict of interest or the appearance of a conflict of interest with respect to personal transactions. Client interests have priority. Client transactions must take precedence over transactions made on behalf of the member's or candidate's firm or personal transactions.

Avoiding Potential Conflicts

Conflicts between the client's interest and an investment professional's personal interest may occur. Although conflicts of interest exist, nothing is inherently unethical about individual managers, advisers, or mutual fund employees making money from personal investments as long as (1) the client is not disadvantaged by the trade, (2) the investment professional does not benefit personally from trades undertaken for clients, and (3) the investment professional complies with applicable regulatory requirements.

Some situations occur where a member or candidate may need to enter a personal transaction that runs counter to current recommendations or what the portfolio manager is doing for client portfolios. For example, a member or candidate may be required at some point to sell an asset to make a college tuition payment or a down payment on a home, to meet a margin call, or so on. The sale may be contrary to the long-term advice the member or candidate is currently providing to clients. In these situations, the same three criteria given in the preceding paragraph should be applied in the transaction so as to not violate Standard VI(B).

Personal Trading Secondary to Trading for Clients

Standard VI(B) states that transactions for clients and employers must have priority over transactions in securities or other investments for which a member or candidate is the beneficial owner. The objective of the standard is to prevent personal transactions from adversely affecting the interests of clients or employers. A member or candidate having the same investment positions or being co-invested with clients does not always create a conflict. Some clients in certain investment situations require members or candidates to have aligned interests. Personal investment positions or transactions of members or candidates or their firm should never, however, adversely affect client investments.

Standards for Nonpublic Information

Standard VI(B) covers the activities of members and candidates who have knowledge of pending transactions that may be made on behalf of their clients or employers, who have access to nonpublic information during the normal preparation of research recommendations, or who take investment actions. Members and candidates are prohibited from conveying nonpublic information to any person whose relationship to the member or candidate makes the member or candidate a beneficial owner of the person's securities. Members and candidates must not convey this information to any other person if the nonpublic information can be deemed material.

Impact on All Accounts with Beneficial Ownership

Members or candidates may undertake transactions in accounts for which they are a beneficial owner only after their clients and employers have had adequate opportunity to act on a recommendation. Personal transactions include those made for the member's or candidate's own account, for family (including spouse, children, and other immediate family members) accounts, and for accounts in which the member or candidate has a direct or indirect pecuniary interest, such as a trust or retirement account. Family accounts that are client accounts should be treated like any other firm account and should neither be given special treatment nor be disadvantaged because of the family relationship. If a member or candidate has a beneficial ownership in the account, however, the member or candidate may be subject to preclearance or reporting requirements of the employer or applicable law.

STANDARD VI(B): RECOMMENDED PROCEDURES

57

Policies and procedures designed to prevent potential conflicts of interest, and even the appearance of a conflict of interest, with respect to personal transactions are critical to establishing investor confidence in the securities industry. Therefore, members and candidates should urge their firms to establish such policies and procedures. Because investment firms vary greatly in assets under management, types of clients, number of employees, and so on, each firm should have policies regarding personal investing that are best suited to the firm. Members and candidates should then prominently disclose these policies to clients and prospective clients.

The specific provisions of each firm's standards will vary, but all firms should adopt certain basic procedures to address the conflict areas created by personal investing. These procedures include the following:

- *Limited participation in equity IPOs*: Some eagerly awaited IPOs rise significantly in value shortly after the issue is brought to market. Because the new issue may be highly attractive and sought after, the opportunity to participate in the IPO may be limited. Therefore, purchases of IPOs by investment personnel create conflicts of interest in two principal ways. First, participation in an IPO may have the appearance of taking away an attractive investment opportunity from clients for personal gain—a clear breach of the duty of loyalty to clients. Second, personal purchases in IPOs may have the appearance that the investment opportunity is being bestowed as an incentive to make future investment decisions for the benefit of the party providing the opportunity. Members and candidates can avoid these conflicts or appearances of conflicts of interest by not participating in IPOs.

Reliable and systematic review procedures should be established to ensure that conflicts relating to IPOs are identified and appropriately dealt with by supervisors. Members and candidates should preclear their participation in IPOs, even in situations without any conflict of interest between a member's or candidate's participation in an IPO and the client's interests. Members and candidates should not benefit from the position that their clients occupy in the marketplace—through preferred trading, the allocation of limited offerings, or oversubscription.

- *Restrictions on private placements*: Strict limits should be placed on investment personnel acquiring securities in private placements, and appropriate supervisory and review procedures should be established to prevent noncompliance.

Firms do not routinely use private placements for clients (e.g., venture capital deals) because of the high risk associated with them. Conflicts related to private placements are more significant to members and candidates who manage large pools of assets or act as plan sponsors because these managers may be offered special opportunities, such as private placements, as a reward or an enticement for continuing to do business with a particular broker.

Participation in private placements raises conflict-of-interest issues that are similar to issues surrounding IPOs. Investment personnel should not be involved in transactions, including (but not limited to) private placements, that could be perceived as favors or gifts that seem designed to influence future judgment or to reward past business deals.

Whether the venture eventually proves to be good or bad, managers have an immediate conflict concerning private placement opportunities. If and when the investments go public, participants in private placements have an incentive to recommend the investments to clients regardless of the suitability of the investments for their clients. Doing so increases the value of the participants' personal portfolios.

- *Establish blackout/restricted periods*: Investment personnel involved in the investment decision-making process should establish blackout periods prior to trades for clients so that managers cannot take advantage of their knowledge of client activity by "front-running" client trades (trading for one's personal account before trading for client accounts).

Individual firms must decide who within the firm should be required to comply with the trading restrictions. At a minimum, all individuals who are involved in the investment decision-making process should be subject to the same restricted period. Each firm must determine specific requirements related to blackout and restricted periods that are most relevant to the firm while ensuring that the procedures are governed by the guiding principles set forth in the Code and Standards. Size of firm and type of securities purchased are relevant factors. For example, in a large firm, a blackout requirement is, in effect, a total trading ban because the firm is continually trading in most securities. In a small firm, the blackout period is more likely to prevent the investment manager from front-running.

- *Reporting requirements*: Supervisors should establish reporting procedures for investment personnel, including disclosure of personal holdings/beneficial ownerships, confirmations of trades to the firm and the employee, and preclearance procedures. Once trading restrictions are in place, they must be enforced. The best method for monitoring and enforcing procedures to eliminate conflicts of interest in personal trading is through reporting requirements, including the following:

    - *Disclosure of holdings in which the employee has a beneficial interest*: Disclosure by investment personnel to the firm should be made upon commencement of the employment relationship and at least annually thereafter. To address privacy considerations, disclosure of personal holdings should be handled in a confidential manner by the firm.
    - *Providing duplicate confirmations of transactions*: Investment personnel should be required to direct their brokers to supply to firms duplicate copies or confirmations of all their personal securities transactions and copies of periodic statements for all securities accounts. The duplicate confirmation requirement has two purposes: (1) The requirement sends a message that there is independent verification, which reduces the likelihood of unethical behavior, and (2) it enables verification of the accounting of the flow of personal investments that cannot be determined from merely looking at holdings.
    - *Preclearance procedures*: Investment personnel should examine all planned personal trades to identify possible conflicts prior to the execution of the trades. Preclearance procedures are designed to identify possible conflicts before a problem arises.

- *Disclosure of policies*: Members and candidates should fully disclose to investors their firm's policies regarding personal investing. The information about employees' personal investment activities and policies will foster an atmosphere of full and complete disclosure and calm the public's legitimate concerns about the conflicts of interest posed by investment personnel's personal trading. The disclosure must provide helpful information to investors; it should not be simply boilerplate language, such as "investment personnel are subject to policies and procedures regarding their personal trading."

STANDARD VI(B): APPLICATION OF THE STANDARD

58

Example 1 (Personal Trading):

Research analyst Marlon Long does not recommend purchase of a common stock for his employer's account because he wants to purchase the stock personally and does not want to wait until the recommendation is approved and the stock is purchased by his employer.

> *Comment*: Long has violated Standard VI(B) by taking advantage of his knowledge of the stock's value before allowing his employer to benefit from that information.

Example 2 (Trading for Family Member Account):

Carol Baker, the portfolio manager of an aggressive growth mutual fund, maintains an account in her husband's name at several brokerage firms with which the fund and a number of Baker's other individual clients do a substantial amount of business. Whenever a hot issue becomes available, she instructs the brokers to buy it for her husband's account. Because such issues normally are scarce, Baker often acquires shares in hot issues but her clients are not able to participate in them.

> *Comment*: To avoid violating Standard VI(B), Baker must acquire shares for her mutual fund first and acquire them for her husband's account only after doing so, even though she might miss out on participating in new issues via her husband's account. She also must disclose the trading for her husband's account to her employer because this activity creates a conflict between her personal interests and her employer's interests.

Example 3 (Family Accounts as Equals):

Erin Toffler, a portfolio manager at Esposito Investments, manages the retirement account established with the firm by her parents. Whenever IPOs become available, she first allocates shares to all her other clients for whom the investment is appropriate; only then does she place any remaining portion in her parents' account, if the issue is appropriate for them. She has adopted this procedure so that no one can accuse her of favoring her parents.

> *Comment*: Toffler has violated Standard VI(B) by breaching her duty to her parents by treating them differently from her other accounts simply because of the family relationship. As fee-paying clients of Esposito Investments, Toffler's parents are entitled to the same treatment as any other client of the firm. If Toffler has beneficial ownership in the account, however, and Esposito Investments has preclearance and reporting requirements for personal transactions, she may have to preclear the trades and report the transactions to Esposito.

Example 4 (Personal Trading and Disclosure):

Gary Michaels is an entry-level employee who holds a low-paying job serving both the research department and the investment management department of an active investment management firm. He purchases a sports car and begins to wear expensive clothes after only a year of employment with the firm. The director of the investment management department, who has responsibility for monitoring the personal stock transactions of all employees, investigates and discovers that Michaels has made substantial investment gains by purchasing stocks just before they were put on the firm's recommended "buy" list. Michaels was regularly given the firm's quarterly personal transaction form but declined to complete it.

> *Comment*: Michaels violated Standard VI(B) by placing personal transactions ahead of client transactions. In addition, his supervisor violated Standard IV(C) Responsibilities of Supervisors by permitting Michaels to continue to perform his assigned tasks without having signed the quarterly personal transaction form. Note also that if Michaels had communicated information about the firm's recommendations to a person who traded the security, that action would be a misappropriation of the information and a violation of Standard II(A) Material Nonpublic Information.

Example 5 (Trading Prior to Report Dissemination):

A brokerage's insurance analyst, Denise Wilson, makes a closed-circuit TV report to her firm's branches around the country. During the broadcast, she includes negative comments about a major company in the insurance industry. The following day, Wilson's report is printed and distributed to the sales force and public customers. The report recommends that both short-term traders and intermediate investors take profits by selling that insurance company's stock. Seven minutes after the broadcast, however, Ellen Riley, head of the firm's trading department, had closed out a long "call" position in the stock. Shortly thereafter, Riley established a sizable "put" position in the stock. When asked about her activities, Riley claimed she took the actions to facilitate anticipated sales by institutional clients.

> *Comment*: Riley did not give customers an opportunity to buy or sell in the options market before the firm itself did. By taking action before the report was disseminated, Riley's firm may have depressed the price of the calls and increased the price of the puts. The firm could have avoided a conflict of interest if it had waited to trade for its own account until its clients had an opportunity to receive and assimilate Wilson's recommendations. As it is, Riley's actions violated Standard VI(B).

59 STANDARD VI(C) REFERRAL FEES

- ☐ demonstrate a thorough knowledge of the CFA Institute Code of Ethics and Standards of Professional Conduct by interpreting the Code and Standards in various situations involving issues of professional integrity
- ☐ recommend practices and procedures designed to prevent violations of the Code and Standards

> Members and Candidates must disclose to their employer, clients, and prospective clients, as appropriate, any compensation, consideration, or benefit received from or paid to others for the recommendation of products or services.

Guidance

Standard VI(C) states the responsibility of members and candidates to inform their employer, clients, and prospective clients of any benefit received for referrals of customers and clients. Such disclosures allow clients or employers to evaluate (1) any partiality shown in any recommendation of services and (2) the full cost of the services. Members and candidates must disclose when they pay a fee or provide compensation to others who have referred prospective clients to the member or candidate.

Appropriate disclosure means that members and candidates must advise the client or prospective client, before entry into any formal agreement for services, of any benefit given or received for the recommendation of any services provided by the member or candidate. In addition, the member or candidate must disclose the nature of the consideration or benefit—for example, flat fee or percentage basis, one-time or continuing benefit, based on performance, benefit in the form of provision of research, or other noncash benefit—together with the estimated dollar value. Consideration includes all fees, whether paid in cash, in soft dollars, or in kind.

STANDARD VI(C): RECOMMENDED PROCEDURES

60

Members and candidates should encourage their employers to develop procedures related to referral fees. The firm may completely restrict such fees. If the firm does not adopt a strict prohibition of such fees, the procedures should indicate the appropriate steps for requesting approval.

Employers should have investment professionals provide to the clients notification of approved referral fee programs and provide the employer regular (at least quarterly) updates on the amount and nature of compensation received.

STANDARD VI(C): APPLICATION OF THE STANDARD

61

Example 1 (Disclosure of Referral Arrangements and Outside Parties):

Brady Securities, Inc., a broker/dealer, has established a referral arrangement with Lewis Brothers, Ltd., an investment counseling firm. In this arrangement, Brady Securities refers all prospective tax-exempt accounts, including pension, profit-sharing, and endowment accounts, to Lewis Brothers. In return, Lewis Brothers makes available to Brady Securities on a regular basis the security recommendations and reports of its research staff, which registered representatives of Brady Securities use in serving customers. In addition, Lewis Brothers conducts monthly economic and market reviews for Brady Securities personnel and directs all stock commission business generated by referral accounts to Brady Securities.

Willard White, a partner in Lewis Brothers, calculates that the incremental costs involved in functioning as the research department of Brady Securities are US$20,000 annually.

Referrals from Brady Securities last year resulted in fee income of US$200,000 for Lewis Brothers, and directing all stock trades through Brady Securities resulted in additional costs to Lewis Brothers' clients of US$10,000.

Diane Branch, the chief financial officer of Maxwell Inc., contacts White and says that she is seeking an investment manager for Maxwell's profit-sharing plan. She adds, "My friend Harold Hill at Brady Securities recommended your firm without qualification, and that's good enough for me. Do we have a deal?" White accepts the new account but does not disclose his firm's referral arrangement with Brady Securities.

> *Comment*: White has violated Standard VI(C) by failing to inform the prospective customer of the referral fee payable in services and commissions for an indefinite period to Brady Securities. Such disclosure could have caused Branch to reassess Hill's recommendation and make a more critical evaluation of Lewis Brothers' services.

Example 2 (Disclosure of Interdepartmental Referral Arrangements):

James Handley works for the trust department of Central Trust Bank. He receives compensation for each referral he makes to Central Trust's brokerage department and personal financial management department that results in a sale. He refers several of his clients to the personal financial management department but does not disclose the arrangement within Central Trust to his clients.

> *Comment*: Handley has violated Standard VI(C) by not disclosing the referral arrangement at Central Trust Bank to his clients. Standard VI(C) does not distinguish between referral payments paid by a third party for referring clients to the third party and internal payments paid within the firm to attract new business to a subsidiary. Members and candidates must disclose all such referral fees. Therefore, Handley is required to disclose, at the time of referral, any referral fee agreement in place among Central Trust Bank's departments. The disclosure should include the nature and the value of the benefit and should be made in writing.

Example 3 (Disclosure of Referral Arrangements and Informing Firm):

Katherine Roberts is a portfolio manager at Katama Investments, an advisory firm specializing in managing assets for high-net-worth individuals. Katama's trading desk uses a variety of brokerage houses to execute trades on behalf of its clients. Roberts asks the trading desk to direct a large portion of its commissions to Naushon, Inc., a small broker/dealer run by one of Roberts' business school classmates. Katama's traders have found that Naushon is not very competitive on pricing, and although Naushon generates some research for its trading clients, Katama's other analysts have found most of Naushon's research to be not especially useful. Nevertheless, the traders do as Roberts asks, and in return for receiving a large portion of Katama's business, Naushon recommends the investment services of Roberts and Katama to its wealthiest clients. This arrangement is not disclosed to either Katama or the clients referred by Naushon.

> *Comment*: Roberts is violating Standard VI(C) by failing to inform her employer of the referral arrangement.

Example 4 (Disclosure of Referral Arrangements and Outside Organizations):

Alex Burl is a portfolio manager at Helpful Investments, a local investment advisory firm. Burl is on the advisory board of his child's school, which is looking for ways to raise money to purchase new playground equipment for the school. Burl discusses a plan with his supervisor in which he will donate to the school a portion of his service fee from new clients referred by the parents of students at the school. Upon getting the approval from Helpful, Burl presents the idea to the school's advisory board and directors. The school agrees to announce the program at the next parent event and asks Burl to provide the appropriate written materials to be distributed. A week following the distribution of the flyers, Burl receives the first school-related referral. In establishing the client's investment policy statement, Burl clearly discusses the school's referral and outlines the plans for distributing the donation back to the school.

> *Comment*: Burl has not violated Standard VI(C) because he secured the permission of his employer, Helpful Investments, and the school prior to beginning the program and because he discussed the arrangement with the client at the time the investment policy statement was designed.

Example 5 (Disclosure of Referral Arrangements and Outside Parties):

The sponsor of a state employee pension is seeking to hire a firm to manage the pension plan's emerging market allocation. To assist in the review process, the sponsor has hired Thomas Arrow as a consultant to solicit proposals from various advisers. Arrow is contracted by the sponsor to represent its best interest in selecting the most appropriate new manager. The process runs smoothly, and Overseas Investments is selected as the new manager.

The following year, news breaks that Arrow is under investigation by the local regulator for accepting kickbacks from investment managers after they are awarded new pension allocations. Overseas Investments is included in the list of firms allegedly making these payments. Although the sponsor is happy with the performance of Overseas since it has been managing the pension plan's emerging market funds, the sponsor still decides to have an independent review of the proposals and the selection process to ensure that Overseas was the appropriate firm for its needs. This review confirms that, even though Arrow was being paid by both parties, the recommendation of Overseas appeared to be objective and appropriate.

> *Comment*: Arrow has violated Standard VI(C) because he did not disclose the fee being paid by Overseas. Withholding this information raises the question of a potential lack of objectivity in the recommendation of Overseas by Arrow; this aspect is in addition to questions about the legality of having firms pay to be considered for an allocation.
>
> Regulators and governmental agencies may adopt requirements concerning allowable consultant activities. Local regulations sometimes include having a consultant register with the regulatory agency's ethics board. Regulator policies may include a prohibition on acceptance of payments from investment managers receiving allocations and require regular reporting of contributions made to political organizations and candidates. Arrow would have to adhere to these requirements as well as the Code and Standards.

62 STANDARD VII: RESPONSIBILITIES AS A CFA INSTITUTE MEMBER OR CFA CANDIDATE

- [ ] demonstrate a thorough knowledge of the CFA Institute Code of Ethics and Standards of Professional Conduct by interpreting the Code and Standards in various situations involving issues of professional integrity
- [ ] recommend practices and procedures designed to prevent violations of the Code and Standards

Standard VII(A) Conduct as Participants in CFA Institute Programs

Members and Candidates must not engage in any conduct that compromises the reputation or integrity of CFA Institute or the CFA designation or the integrity, validity, or security of CFA Institute programs.

Guidance

Highlights:

- *Confidential Program Information*
- *Additional CFA Program Restrictions*
- *Expressing an Opinion*

Standard VII(A) covers the conduct of CFA Institute members and candidates involved with the CFA Program and prohibits any conduct that undermines the public's confidence that the CFA charter represents a level of achievement based on merit and ethical conduct. There is an array of CFA Institute programs beyond the CFA Program that provide additional educational and credentialing opportunities, including the Certificate in Investment Performance Measurement (CIPM®) Program and the CFA Institute Investment Foundations® Program. The standard's function is to hold members and candidates to a high ethical criterion while they are participating in or involved with any CFA Institute program. Conduct covered includes but is not limited to

- giving or receiving assistance (cheating) on any CFA Institute examinations;
- violating the rules, regulations, and testing policies of CFA Institute programs;
- providing confidential program or exam information to candidates or the public;
- disregarding or attempting to circumvent security measures established for any CFA Institute examinations;
- improperly using an association with CFA Institute to further personal or professional goals; and
- misrepresenting information on the Professional Conduct Statement or in the CFA Institute Continuing Education Program.

Confidential Program Information

CFA Institute is vigilant about protecting the integrity of CFA Institute programs' content and examination processes. CFA Institute program rules, regulations, and policies prohibit candidates from disclosing confidential material gained during the exam process.

Examples of information that cannot be disclosed by candidates sitting for an exam include but are not limited to

- specific details of questions appearing on the exam and
- broad topical areas and formulas tested or not tested on the exam.

All aspects of the exam, including questions, broad topical areas, and formulas, tested or not tested, are considered confidential until such time as CFA Institute elects to release them publicly. This confidentiality requirement allows CFA Institute to maintain the integrity and rigor of exams for future candidates. Standard VII(A) does not prohibit candidates from discussing nonconfidential information or curriculum material with others or in study groups in preparation for the exam.

Candidates increasingly use online forums and new technology as part of their exam preparations. CFA Institute actively polices blogs, forums, and related social networking groups for information considered confidential. The organization works with both individual candidates and the sponsors of online or offline services to promptly remove any and all violations. As noted in the discussion of Standard I(A)–Knowledge of the Law, candidates, members, and the public are encouraged to report suspected violations to CFA Institute.

Additional CFA Program Restrictions

The CFA Program rules, regulations, and policies define additional allowed and disallowed actions concerning the exams. Violating any of the testing policies, such as the calculator policy, personal belongings policy, or the Candidate Pledge, constitutes a violation of Standard VII(A). Candidates will find all of these policies on the CFA Program portion of the CFA Institute website (www.cfainstitute.org). Exhibit 2 provides the Candidate Pledge, which highlights the respect candidates must have for the integrity, validity, and security of the CFA exam.

Members may participate as volunteers in various aspects of the CFA Program. Standard VII(A) prohibits members from disclosing and/or soliciting confidential material gained prior to or during the exam and grading processes with those outside the CFA exam development process.

Examples of information that cannot be shared by members involved in developing, administering, or grading the exams include but are not limited to

- questions appearing on the exam or under consideration,
- deliberation related to the exam process, and
- information related to the scoring of questions.

Members may also be asked to offer assistance with other CFA Institute programs, including but not limited to the CIPM and Investment Foundations programs. Members participating in any CFA Institute program should do so with the same level of integrity and confidentiality as is required of participation in the CFA Program.

Expressing an Opinion

Standard VII(A) does *not* cover expressing opinions regarding CFA Institute, the CFA Program, or other CFA Institute programs. Members and candidates are free to disagree and express their disagreement with CFA Institute on its policies, its procedures, or any advocacy positions taken by the organization. When expressing a personal opinion, a candidate is prohibited from disclosing content-specific information, including any actual exam question and the information as to subject matter covered or not covered in the exam.

Exhibit 2: Sample of CFA Program Testing Policies

Candidate Pledge	As a candidate in the CFA Program, I am obligated to follow Standard VII(A) of the CFA Institute Standards of Professional Conduct, which states that members and candidates must not engage in any conduct that compromises the reputation or integrity of CFA Institute or the CFA designation or the integrity, validity, or security of the CFA exam. ▪ Prior to this exam, I have not given or received information regarding the content of this exam. During this exam, I will not give or receive any information regarding the content of this exam. ▪ After this exam, I will not disclose **ANY** portion of this exam and I will not remove **ANY** exam materials from the testing room in original or copied form. I understand that all exam materials, including my answers, are the property of CFA Institute and will not be returned to me in any form. ▪ I will follow **ALL** rules of the CFA Program as stated on the CFA Institute website and the back cover of the exam book. My violation of any rules of the CFA Program will result in CFA Institute voiding my exam results and may lead to suspension or termination of my candidacy in the CFA Program.

63 STANDARD VII(A): APPLICATION OF THE STANDARD

Example 1 (Sharing Exam Questions):

Travis Nero serves as a proctor for the administration of the CFA examination in his city. In the course of his service, he reviews a copy of the Level II CFA exam on the evening prior to the exam's administration and provides information concerning the exam questions to two candidates who use it to prepare for the exam.

> *Comment*: Nero and the two candidates have violated Standard VII(A). By giving information about the exam questions to two candidates, Nero provided an unfair advantage to the two candidates and undermined the integrity and validity of the Level II CFA exam as an accurate measure of the knowledge, skills, and abilities necessary to earn the right to use the CFA designation. By accepting the information, the candidates also compromised the integrity and validity of the Level II CFA exam and undermined the ethical framework that is a key part of the designation.

Example 2 (Bringing Written Material into Exam Room):

Loren Sullivan is enrolled to take the Level II CFA exam. He has been having difficulty remembering a particular formula, so prior to entering the exam room, he writes the formula on the palm of his hand. During the afternoon section of the exam, a proctor notices Sullivan looking at the palm of his hand. She asks to see his hand and finds the formula.

> *Comment*: Because Sullivan wrote down information from the Candidate Body of Knowledge (CBOK) and took that written information into the exam room, his conduct compromised the validity of his exam performance and violated Standard VII(A). Sullivan's conduct was also in direct contradiction with the rules and regulations of the CFA Program, the Candidate Pledge, and the CFA Institute Code and Standards.

Example 3 (Writing after Exam Period End):

At the conclusion of the morning section of the Level I CFA exam, the proctors announce, "Stop writing now." John Davis has not completed the exam, so he continues to randomly fill in ovals on his answer sheet. A proctor approaches Davis's desk and reminds him that he should stop writing immediately. Davis, however, continues to complete the answer sheet. After the proctor asks him to stop writing two additional times, Davis finally puts down his pencil.

> *Comment*: By continuing to complete his exam after time was called, Davis has violated Standard VII(A). By continuing to write, Davis took an unfair advantage over other candidates, and his conduct compromised the validity of his exam performance. Additionally, by not heeding the proctor's repeated instructions, Davis violated the rules and regulations of the CFA Program.

Example 4 (Sharing Exam Content):

After completing the Level II CFA exam, Annabelle Rossi posts on her blog about her experience. She posts the following: "Level II is complete! I think I did fairly well on the exam. It was really difficult, but fair. I think I did especially well on the derivatives questions. And there were tons of them! I think I counted 18! The ethics questions were really hard. I'm glad I spent so much time on the Code and Standards. I was surprised to see there were no questions at all about IPO allocations. I expected there to be a couple. Well, off to celebrate getting through it. See you tonight?"

> *Comment*: Rossi did not violate Standard VII(A) when she wrote about how difficult she found the exam or how well she thinks she may have done. By revealing portions of the CBOK covered on the exam and areas not covered, however, she did violate Standard VII(A) and the Candidate Pledge. Depending on the time frame in which the comments were posted, Rossi not only may have assisted future candidates but also may have provided an unfair advantage to candidates yet to sit for the same exam, thereby undermining the integrity and validity of the Level II CFA exam.

Example 5 (Sharing Exam Content):

Level I candidate Etienne Gagne has been a frequent visitor to an internet forum designed specifically for CFA Program candidates. The week after completing the Level I CFA exam, Gagne and several others begin a discussion thread on the forum about the most challenging questions and attempt to determine the correct answers.

> *Comment*: Gagne has violated Standard VII(A) by providing and soliciting confidential exam information, which compromises the integrity of the exam process and violates the Candidate Pledge. In trying to determine correct answers to specific questions, the group's discussion included question-specific details considered to be confidential to the CFA Program.

Example 6 (Sharing Exam Content):

CFA4Sure is a company that produces test-preparation materials for CFA Program candidates. Many candidates register for and use the company's products. The day after the CFA exam, CFA4Sure sends an e-mail to all its customers asking them to share with the company the hardest questions from the exam so that CFA4Sure can better prepare its customers for the next exam administration. Marisol Pena e-mails a summary of the questions she found most difficult on the exam.

> *Comment*: Pena has violated Standard VII(A) by disclosing a portion of the exam questions. The information provided is considered confidential until publicly released by CFA Institute. CFA4Sure is likely to use such feedback to refine its review materials for future candidates. Pena's sharing of the specific questions undermines the integrity of the exam while potentially making the exam easier for future candidates.
>
> If the CFA4Sure employees who participated in the solicitation of confidential CFA Program information are CFA Institute members or candidates, they also have violated Standard VII(A).

Example 7 (Discussion of Exam Grading Guidelines and Results):

Prior to participating in grading CFA exams, Wesley Whitcomb is required to sign a CFA Institute Grader Agreement. As part of the Grader Agreement, Whitcomb agrees not to reveal or discuss the exam materials with anyone except CFA Institute staff or other graders. Several weeks after the conclusion of the CFA exam grading, Whitcomb tells several colleagues who are candidates in the CFA Program which question he graded. He also discusses the guideline answer and adds that few candidates scored well on the question.

> *Comment*: Whitcomb violated Standard VII(A) by breaking the Grader Agreement and disclosing information related to a specific question on the exam, which compromised the integrity of the exam process.

Example 8 (Compromising CFA Institute Integrity as a Volunteer):

Jose Ramirez is an investor-relations consultant for several small companies that are seeking greater exposure to investors. He is also the program chair for the CFA Institute society in the city where he works. Ramirez schedules only companies that are his clients to make presentations to the society and excludes other companies.

> *Comment*: Ramirez, by using his volunteer position at CFA Institute to benefit himself and his clients, compromises the reputation and integrity of CFA Institute and thus violates Standard VII(A).

Example 9 (Compromising CFA Institute Integrity as a Volunteer):

Marguerite Warrenski is a member of the CFA Institute GIPS Executive Committee, which oversees the creation, implementation, and revision of the GIPS standards. As a member of the Executive Committee, she has advance knowledge of confidential information regarding the GIPS standards, including any new or revised standards the committee is considering. She tells her clients that her Executive Committee membership will allow her to better assist her clients in keeping up with changes to the Standards and facilitating their compliance with the changes.

> *Comment*: Warrenski is using her association with the GIPS Executive Committee to promote her firm's services to clients and potential clients. In defining her volunteer position at CFA Institute as a strategic business advantage over competing firms and implying to clients that she would use confidential information to further their interests, Warrenski is compromising the reputation and integrity of CFA Institute and thus violating Standard VII(A). She may factually state her involvement with the Executive Committee but cannot infer any special advantage to her clients from such participation.

STANDARD VII(B) REFERENCE TO CFA INSTITUTE, THE CFA DESIGNATION, AND THE CFA PROGRAM

64

- ☐ demonstrate a thorough knowledge of the CFA Institute Code of Ethics and Standards of Professional Conduct by interpreting the Code and Standards in various situations involving issues of professional integrity
- ☐ recommend practices and procedures designed to prevent violations of the Code and Standards

> When referring to CFA Institute, CFA Institute membership, the CFA designation, or candidacy in the CFA Program, Members and Candidates must not misrepresent or exaggerate the meaning or implications of membership in CFA Institute, holding the CFA designation, or candidacy in the CFA Program.

Guidance

Highlights:

- *CFA Institute Membership*
- *Using the CFA Designation*
- *Referring to Candidacy in the CFA Program*

Standard VII(B) is intended to prevent promotional efforts that make promises or guarantees that are tied to the CFA designation. Individuals must not exaggerate the meaning or implications of membership in CFA Institute, holding the CFA designation, or candidacy in the CFA Program.

Standard VII(B) is not intended to prohibit factual statements related to the positive benefit of earning the CFA designation. However, statements referring to CFA Institute, the CFA designation, or the CFA Program that overstate the competency of an individual or imply, either directly or indirectly, that superior performance can be expected from someone with the CFA designation are not allowed under the standard.

Statements that highlight or emphasize the commitment of CFA Institute members, CFA charterholders, and CFA candidates to ethical and professional conduct or mention the thoroughness and rigor of the CFA Program are appropriate. Members and candidates may make claims about the relative merits of CFA Institute, the CFA Program, or the Code and Standards as long as those statements are implicitly or explicitly stated as the opinion of the speaker. Statements that do not express opinions have to be supported by facts.

Standard VII(B) applies to any form of communication, including but not limited to communications made in electronic or written form (such as on firm letterhead, business cards, professional biographies, directory listings, printed advertising, firm brochures, or personal resumes) and oral statements made to the public, clients, or prospects.

CFA Institute Membership

The term "CFA Institute member" refers to "regular" and "affiliate" members of CFA Institute who have met the membership requirements as defined in the CFA Institute Bylaws. Once accepted as a CFA Institute member, the member must satisfy the following requirements to maintain his or her status:

- remit annually to CFA Institute a completed Professional Conduct Statement, which renews the commitment to abide by the requirements of the Code and Standards and the CFA Institute Professional Conduct Program, and
- pay applicable CFA Institute membership dues on an annual basis.

If a CFA Institute member fails to meet any of these requirements, the individual is no longer considered an active member. Until membership is reactivated, individuals must not present themselves to others as active members. They may state, however, that they were CFA Institute members in the past or refer to the years when their membership was active.

Using the CFA Designation

Those who have earned the right to use the Chartered Financial Analyst® designation are encouraged to do so but only in a manner that does not misrepresent or exaggerate the meaning or implications of the designation. The use of the designation may be accompanied by an accurate explanation of the requirements that have been met to earn the right to use the designation.

"CFA charterholders" are those individuals who have earned the right to use the CFA designation granted by CFA Institute. These people have satisfied certain requirements, including completion of the CFA Program and required years of acceptable work experience. Once granted the right to use the designation, individuals must also satisfy the CFA Institute membership requirements (see above) to maintain their right to use the designation.

If a CFA charterholder fails to meet any of the membership requirements, he or she forfeits the right to use the CFA designation. Until membership is reactivated, individuals must not present themselves to others as CFA charterholders. They may state, however, that they were charterholders in the past.

Given the growing popularity of social media, where individuals may anonymously express their opinions, pseudonyms or online profile names created to hide a member's identity should not be tagged with the CFA designation.

Use of the CFA designation by a CFA charterholder is governed by the terms and conditions of the annual Professional Conduct Statement Agreement, entered into between CFA Institute and its membership prior to commencement of use of the CFA designation and reaffirmed annually.

Referring to Candidacy in the CFA Program

Candidates in the CFA Program may refer to their participation in the CFA Program, but such references must clearly state that an individual is a *candidate* in the CFA Program and must not imply that the candidate has achieved any type of partial designation. A person is a candidate in the CFA Program if

- the person's application for registration in the CFA Program has been accepted by CFA Institute, as evidenced by issuance of a notice of acceptance, and the person is enrolled to sit for a specified examination or
- the registered person has sat for a specified examination but exam results have not yet been received.

If an individual is registered for the CFA Program but declines to sit for an exam or otherwise does not meet the definition of a candidate as described in the CFA Institute Bylaws, then that individual is no longer considered an active candidate. Once the person is enrolled to sit for a future examination, his or her CFA Program candidacy resumes.

CFA Program candidates must never state or imply that they have a partial designation as a result of passing one or more levels or cite an expected completion date of any level of the CFA Program. Final award of the charter is subject to meeting the CFA Program requirements and approval by the CFA Institute Board of Governors.

If a candidate passes each level of the exam in consecutive years and wants to state that he or she did so, that is not a violation of Standard VII(B) because it is a statement of fact. If the candidate then goes on to claim or imply superior ability by obtaining the designation in only three years, however, he or she is in violation of Standard VII(B).

Exhibit 3 provides examples of proper and improper references to the CFA designation.

Exhibit 3: Proper and Improper References to the CFA Designation

Proper References	Improper References
"Completion of the CFA Program has enhanced my portfolio management skills."	"CFA charterholders achieve better performance results."
"John Smith passed all three CFA Program exams in three consecutive years."	"John Smith is among the elite, having passed all three CFA exams in three consecutive attempts."
"The CFA designation is globally recognized and attests to a charterholder's success in a rigorous and comprehensive study program in the field of investment management and research analysis."	"As a CFA charterholder, I am the most qualified to manage client investments."
"The credibility that the CFA designation affords and the skills the CFA Program cultivates are key assets for my future career development."	"As a CFA charterholder, Jane White provides the best value in trade execution."
"I enrolled in the CFA Program to obtain the highest set of credentials in the global investment management industry."	"Enrolling as a candidate in the CFA Program ensures one of becoming better at valuing debt securities."
"I passed Level I of the CFA Program."	"CFA, Level II"
"I am a 2010 Level III candidate in the CFA Program."	"CFA, Expected 2011"
"I passed all three levels of the CFA Program and may be eligible for the CFA charter upon completion of the required work experience."	"CFA, Expected 2011" "John Smith, Charter Pending"

65 STANDARD VII(B): RECOMMENDED PROCEDURES

Misuse of a member's CFA designation or CFA candidacy or improper reference to it is common by those in a member's or candidate's firm who do not possess knowledge of the requirements of Standard VII(B). As an appropriate step to reduce this risk, members and candidates should disseminate written information about Standard VII(B) and the accompanying guidance to their firm's legal, compliance, public relations, and marketing departments (see www.cfainstitute.org).

For materials that refer to employees' affiliation with CFA Institute, members and candidates should encourage their firms to create templates that are approved by a central authority (such as the compliance department) as being consistent with Standard VII(B). This practice promotes consistency and accuracy in the firm of references to CFA Institute membership, the CFA designation, and CFA candidacy.

STANDARD VII(B): APPLICATION OF THE STANDARD

66

Example 1 (Passing Exams in Consecutive Years):

An advertisement for AZ Investment Advisors states that all the firm's principals are CFA charterholders and all passed the three exams on their first attempt. The advertisement prominently links this fact to the notion that AZ's mutual funds have achieved superior performance.

> *Comment*: AZ may state that all principals passed the three exams on the first try as long as this statement is true, but it must not be linked to performance or imply superior ability. Implying that (1) CFA charterholders achieve better investment results and (2) those who pass the exams on the first try may be more successful than those who do not violates Standard VII(B).

Example 2 (Right to Use CFA Designation):

Five years after receiving his CFA charter, Louis Vasseur resigns his position as an investment analyst and spends the next two years traveling abroad. Because he is not actively engaged in the investment profession, he does not file a completed Professional Conduct Statement with CFA Institute and does not pay his CFA Institute membership dues. At the conclusion of his travels, Vasseur becomes a self-employed analyst accepting assignments as an independent contractor. Without reinstating his CFA Institute membership by filing his Professional Conduct Statement and paying his dues, he prints business cards that display "CFA" after his name.

> *Comment*: Vasseur has violated Standard VII(B) because his right to use the CFA designation was suspended when he failed to file his Professional Conduct Statement and stopped paying dues. Therefore, he no longer is able to state or imply that he is an active CFA charterholder. When Vasseur files his Professional Conduct Statement, resumes paying CFA Institute dues to activate his membership, and completes the CFA Institute reinstatement procedures, he will be eligible to use the CFA designation.

Example 3 ("Retired" CFA Institute Membership Status):

After a 25-year career, James Simpson retires from his firm. Because he is not actively engaged in the investment profession, he does not file a completed Professional Conduct Statement with CFA Institute and does not pay his CFA Institute membership dues. Simpson designs a plain business card (without a corporate logo) to hand out to friends with his new contact details, and he continues to put "CFA" after his name.

> *Comment*: Simpson has violated Standard VII(B). Because he failed to file his Professional Conduct Statement and ceased paying dues, his membership has been suspended and he has given up the right to use the CFA designation. CFA Institute has procedures, however, for reclassifying a member and charterholder as "retired" and reducing the annual dues. If he wants to obtain retired status, he needs to file the appropriate paperwork with CFA Institute. When Simpson receives his notification from CFA Institute

that his membership has been reclassified as retired and he resumes paying reduced dues, his membership will be reactivated and his right to use the CFA designation will be reinstated.

Example 4 (Stating Facts about CFA Designation and Program):

Rhonda Reese has been a CFA charterholder since 2000. In a conversation with a friend who is considering enrolling in the CFA Program, she states that she has learned a great deal from the CFA Program and that many firms require their employees to be CFA charterholders. She would recommend the CFA Program to anyone pursuing a career in investment management.

Comment: Reese's comments comply with Standard VII(B). Her statements refer to facts: The CFA Program enhanced her knowledge, and many firms require the CFA designation for their investment professionals.

Example 5 (Order of Professional and Academic Designations):

Tatiana Prittima has earned both her CFA designation and a PhD in finance. She would like to cite both her accomplishments on her business card but is unsure of the proper method for doing so.

Comment: The order of designations cited on such items as resumes and business cards is a matter of personal preference. Prittima is free to cite the CFA designation either before or after citing her PhD. Multiple designations must be separated by a comma.

Example 6 (Use of Fictitious Name):

Barry Glass is the lead quantitative analyst at CityCenter Hedge Fund. Glass is responsible for the development, maintenance, and enhancement of the proprietary models the fund uses to manage its investors' assets. Glass reads several high-level mathematical publications and blogs to stay informed on current developments. One blog, run by "Expert CFA," presents some intriguing research that may benefit one of CityCenter's current models. Glass is under pressure from firm executives to improve the model's predictive abilities, and he incorporates the factors discussed in the online research. The updated output recommends several new investments to the fund's portfolio managers.

Comment: "Expert CFA" has violated Standard VII(B) by using the CFA designation inappropriately. As with any research report, authorship of online comments must include the charterholder's full name along with any reference to the CFA designation.

See also Standard V(A), which Glass has violated for guidance on diligence and reasonable basis.

PRACTICE PROBLEMS

1. Which of the following is a correct statement of a member's or candidate's duty under the Code and Standards?

   A. In the absence of specific applicable law or other regulatory requirements, the Code and Standards govern the member's or candidate's actions.

   B. A member or candidate is required to comply only with applicable local laws, rules, regulations, or customs, even though the Code and Standards may impose a higher degree of responsibility or a higher duty on the member or candidate.

   C. A member or candidate who trades securities in a securities market where no applicable local laws or stock exchange rules regulate the use of material nonpublic information may take investment action based on material nonpublic information.

2. Ward is scheduled to visit the corporate headquarters of Evans Industries. Ward expects to use the information he obtains there to complete his research report on Evans stock. Ward learns that Evans plans to pay all of Ward's expenses for the trip, including costs of meals, hotel room, and air transportation. Which of the following actions would be the *best* course for Ward to take under the Code and Standards?

   A. Accept the expense-paid trip and write an objective report.

   B. Pay for all travel expenses, including costs of meals and incidental items.

   C. Accept the expense-paid trip but disclose the value of the services accepted in the report.

3. An investment management firm has been hired by ETV Corporation to work on an additional public offering for the company. The firm's brokerage unit now has a "sell" recommendation on ETV, but the head of the investment banking department has asked the head of the brokerage unit to change the recommendation from "sell" to "buy." According to the Standards, the head of the brokerage unit would be permitted to:

   A. increase the recommendation by no more than one increment (in this case, to a "hold" recommendation).

   B. place the company on a restricted list and give only factual information about the company.

   C. assign a new analyst to decide whether the stock deserves a higher rating.

4. Long has been asked to be the keynote speaker at an upcoming investment conference. The event is being hosted by one of the third-party investment managers currently used by his pension fund. The manager offers to cover all conference and travel costs for Long and make the conference registrations free for three additional members of his investment management team. To ensure that the conference obtains the best speakers, the host firm has arranged for an exclusive golf outing for the day following the conference on a local championship-caliber

course. Which of the following is *least likely* to violate Standard I(B)?

A. Long may accept only the offer to have his conference-related expenses paid by the host firm.

B. Long may accept the offer to have his conference-related expenses paid and may attend the exclusive golf outing at the expense of the hosting firm.

C. Long may accept the entire package of incentives offered to speak at this conference.

5. Grey recommends the purchase of a mutual fund that invests solely in long-term US Treasury bonds. He makes the following statements to his clients:
I. "The payment of the bonds is guaranteed by the US government; therefore, the default risk of the bonds is virtually zero."
II. "If you invest in the mutual fund, you will earn a 10% rate of return each year for the next several years based on historical performance of the market."
Did Grey's statements violate the CFA Institute Code and Standards?

A. Neither statement violated the Code and Standards.

B. Only Statement I violated the Code and Standards.

C. Only Statement II violated the Code and Standards.

6. Michelieu tells a prospective client, "I may not have a long-term track record yet, but I'm sure that you'll be very pleased with my recommendations and service. In the three years that I've been in the business, my equity-oriented clients have averaged a total return of more than 26% a year." The statement is true, but Michelieu only has a few clients, and one of his clients took a large position in a penny stock (against Michelieu's advice) and realized a huge gain. This large return caused the average of all of Michelieu's clients to exceed 26% a year. Without this one investment, the average gain would have been 8% a year. Has Michelieu violated the Standards?

A. No, because Michelieu is not promising that he can earn a 26% return in the future

B. No, because the statement is a true and accurate description of Michelieu's track record

C. Yes, because the statement misrepresents Michelieu's track record

7. Anderb, a portfolio manager for XYZ Investment Management Company—a registered investment organization that advises investment firms and private accounts—was promoted to that position three years ago. Bates, her supervisor, is responsible for reviewing Anderb's portfolio account transactions and her required monthly reports of personal stock transactions. Anderb has been using Jonelli, a broker, almost exclusively for brokerage transactions for the portfolio account. For securities in which Jonelli's firm makes a market, Jonelli has been giving Anderb lower prices for personal purchases and higher prices for personal sales than Jonelli gives to Anderb's portfolio accounts and other investors. Anderb has been filing monthly reports with Bates only for those months in which she has no personal transactions, which is about every fourth month. Which of the following is *most likely* to be a violation of the Code and Standards?

A. Anderb failed to disclose to her employer her personal transactions.

B. Anderb owned the same securities as those of her clients.

C. Bates allowed Anderb to use Jonelli as her broker for personal trades.

8. The mosaic theory holds that an analyst:

   A. violates the Code and Standards if the analyst fails to have knowledge of and comply with applicable laws.

   B. can use material public information and nonmaterial nonpublic information in the analyst's analysis.

   C. should use all available and relevant information in support of an investment recommendation.

9. An investment banking department of a brokerage firm often receives material nonpublic information that could have considerable value if used in advising the firm's brokerage clients. In order to conform to the Code and Standards, which one of the following is the best policy for the brokerage firm?

   A. Permanently prohibit both "buy" and "sell" recommendations of the stocks of clients of the investment banking department.

   B. Establish physical and informational barriers within the firm to prevent the exchange of information between the investment banking and brokerage operations.

   C. Monitor the exchange of information between the investment banking department and the brokerage operation.

10. Andrews, a private wealth manager, is conducting interviews for a new research analyst for his firm. One of the candidates is Wright, an analyst with a local investment bank. During the interview, while Wright is describing his analytical skills, he mentions a current merger in which his firm is acting as the adviser. Andrews has heard rumors of a possible merger between the two companies, but no releases have been made by the companies concerned. Which of the following actions by Andrews is *least likely* a violation of the Code and Standards?

    A. Waiting until the next day before trading on the information to allow time for it to become public

    B. Notifying all investment managers in his firm of the new information so none of their clients are disadvantaged

    C. Placing the securities mentioned as part of the merger on the firm's restricted trading list

11. During a round of golf, Rodriguez, chief financial officer of Mega Retail, mentions to Hart, a local investment adviser and long-time personal friend, that Mega is having an exceptional sales quarter. Rodriguez expects the results to be almost 10% above the current estimates. The next day, Hart initiates the purchase of a large stake in the local exchange-traded retail fund for her personal account.

    A. Hart violated the Code and Standards by investing in the exchange-traded fund that included Mega Retail.

    B. Hart did not violate the Code and Standards because she did not invest directly in securities of Mega Retail.

C. Rodriguez did not violate the Code and Standards because the comments made to Hart were not intended to solicit an investment in Mega Retail.

12. Pietro, president of Local Bank, has hired the bank's market maker, Vogt, to seek a merger partner. Local is currently listed on a stock exchange and has not reported that it is seeking strategic alternatives. Vogt has discussed the possibility of a merger with several firms, but they have all decided to wait until after the next period's financial data are available. The potential buyers believe the results will be worse than the results of prior periods and will allow them to pay less for Local Bank. Pietro wants to increase the likelihood of structuring a merger deal quickly. Which of the following actions would *most likely* be a violation of the Code and Standards?

    A. Pietro could instruct Local Bank to issue a press release announcing that it has retained Vogt to find a merger partner.

    B. Pietro could place a buy order for 2,000 shares (or four times the average weekly volume) through Vogt for his personal account.

    C. After confirming with Local's chief financial officer, Pietro could instruct Local to issue a press release reaffirming the firm's prior announced earnings guidance for the full fiscal year.

13. Stewart has been hired by Goodner Industries, Inc., to manage its pension fund. Stewart's duty of loyalty, prudence, and care is owed to:

    A. the management of Goodner.

    B. the participants and beneficiaries of Goodner's pension plan.

    C. the shareholders of Goodner.

14. One of the discretionary accounts managed by Farnsworth is the Jones Corporation employee profit-sharing plan. Jones, the company president, recently asked Farnsworth to vote the shares in the profit-sharing plan in favor of the slate of directors nominated by Jones Corporation and against the directors sponsored by a dissident stockholder group. Farnsworth does not want to lose this account, because he directs all the account's trades to a brokerage firm that provides Farnsworth with useful information about tax-free investments. Although this information is not of value in managing the Jones Corporation account, it does help in managing several other accounts. The brokerage firm providing this information also offers the lowest commissions for trades and provides best execution. Farnsworth investigates the director issue, concludes that the management-nominated slate is better for the long-run performance of the company than the dissident group's slate, and votes accordingly. Farnsworth:

    A. violated the Standards in voting the shares in the manner requested by Jones but not in directing trades to the brokerage firm.

    B. did not violate the Standards in voting the shares in the manner requested by Jones or in directing trades to the brokerage firm.

    C. violated the Standards in directing trades to the brokerage firm but not in voting the shares as requested by Jones.

15. Carter works for Invest Today, a local asset management firm. A broker that provides Carter with proprietary research through client brokerage arrangements is offering a new trading service. The broker is offering low-fee, execution-only

trades to complement its traditional full-service, execution-and-research trades. To entice Carter and other asset managers to send additional business its way, the broker will apply the commissions paid on the new service toward satisfying the brokerage commitment of the prior full-service arrangements. Carter has always been satisfied with the execution provided on the full-service trades, and the new, low-fee trades are comparable to the fees of other brokers currently used for the accounts that prohibit soft dollar arrangements.

A. Carter can trade for his accounts that prohibit soft dollar arrangements under the new, low-fee trading scheme.

B. Carter cannot use the new trading scheme because the commissions are prohibited by the soft dollar restrictions of the accounts.

C. Carter should trade only through the new, low-fee scheme and should increase his trading volume to meet his required commission commitment.

16. Which statement about a manager's use of client brokerage commissions violates the Code and Standards?

A. A client may direct a manager to use that client's brokerage commissions to purchase goods and services for that client.

B. Client brokerage commissions should be used to benefit the client and should be commensurate with the value of the brokerage and research services received.

C. Client brokerage commissions may be directed to pay for the investment manager's operating expenses.

17. Stafford is a portfolio manager for a specialized real estate mutual fund. Her firm clearly describes in the fund's prospectus its soft dollar policies. Stafford decides that entering the CFA Program will enhance her investment decision-making skill and decides to use the fund's soft dollar account to pay the registration and exam fees for the CFA Program. Which of the following statements is *most likely* correct?

A. Stafford did not violate the Code and Standards, because the prospectus informed investors of the fund's soft dollar policies.

B. Stafford violated the Code and Standards because improving her investment skills is not a reasonable use of the soft dollar account.

C. Stafford violated the Code and Standards because the CFA Program does not meet the definition of research allowed to be purchased with brokerage commissions.

18. Which one of the following actions will help ensure the fair treatment of brokerage firm clients when a new investment recommendation is made?

A. Informing all people in the firm in advance that a recommendation is to be disseminated.

B. Distributing recommendations to institutional clients prior to individual accounts.

C. Minimizing the time between the decision and the dissemination of a recommendation.

19. Smith, a research analyst with a brokerage firm, decides to change his recommendation for the common stock of Green Company, Inc., from a "buy" to a "sell." He mails this change in investment advice to all the firm's clients on Wednesday. The day after the mailing, a client calls with a buy order for 500 shares of Green Company. In this circumstance, Smith should:

    A. accept the order.

    B. advise the customer of the change in recommendation before accepting the order.

    C. not accept the order, because it is contrary to the firm's recommendation.

20. Brown works for an investment counseling firm. Green, a new client of the firm, is meeting with Brown for the first time. Green used another counseling firm for financial advice for years, but she has switched her account to Brown's firm. After spending a few minutes getting acquainted, Brown explains to Green that she has discovered a highly undervalued stock that offers large potential gains. She recommends that Green purchase the stock. Brown has committed a violation of the Standards. What should she have done differently?

    A. Brown should have determined Green's needs, objectives, and tolerance for risk before making a recommendation of any type of security.

    B. Brown should have thoroughly explained the characteristics of the company to Green, including the characteristics of the industry in which the company operates.

    C. Brown should have explained her qualifications, including her education, training, and experience and the meaning of the CFA designation.

21. ABC Investment Management acquires a new, very large account with two concentrated positions. The firm's current policy is to add new accounts for the purpose of performance calculation after the first full month of management. Cupp is responsible for calculating the firm's performance returns. Before the end of the initial month, Cupp notices that one of the significant holdings of the new accounts is acquired by another company, causing the value of the investment to double. Because of this holding, Cupp decides to account for the new portfolio as of the date of transfer, thereby allowing ABC Investment to reap the positive impact of that month's portfolio return.

    A. Cupp did not violate the Code and Standards, because the GIPS standards allow composites to be updated on the date of large external cash flows.

    B. Cupp did not violate the Code and Standards, because companies are allowed to determine when to incorporate new accounts into their composite calculation.

    C. Cupp violated the Code and Standards because the inclusion of the new account produces an inaccurate calculation of the monthly results according to the firm's stated policies.

22. Paper was recently terminated as one of a team of five managers of an equity fund. The fund had two value-focused managers and terminated one of them to reduce costs. In a letter sent to prospective employers, Paper presents, with written permission of the firm, the performance history of the fund to demonstrate

his past success.

A. Paper did not violate the Code and Standards.

B. Paper violated the Code and Standards by claiming the performance of the entire fund as his own.

C. Paper violated the Code and Standards by including the historical results of his prior employer.

23. Bronson provides investment advice to the board of trustees of a private university endowment fund. The trustees have provided Bronson with the fund's financial information, including planned expenditures. Bronson receives a phone call on Friday afternoon from Murdock, a prominent alumnus, requesting that Bronson fax him comprehensive financial information about the fund. According to Murdock, he has a potential contributor but needs the information that day to close the deal and cannot contact any of the trustees. According to the Standards, Bronson should:

A. send Murdock the information because disclosure would benefit the client.

B. not send Murdock the information to preserve confidentiality.

C. send Murdock the information, provided Bronson promptly notifies the trustees.

24. Townsend was recently appointed to the board of directors of a youth golf program that is the local chapter of a national not-for-profit organization. The program is beginning a new fundraising campaign to expand the number of annual scholarships it provides. Townsend believes many of her clients make annual donations to charity. The next week in her regular newsletter to all clients, she includes a small section discussing the fundraising campaign and her position on the organization's board.

A. Townsend did not violate the Code and Standards.

B. Townsend violated the Code and Standards by soliciting donations from her clients through the newsletter.

C. Townsend violated the Code and Standards by not getting approval of the organization before soliciting her clients.

25. Which of the following statements is *correct* under the Code and Standards?

A. CFA Institute members and candidates are prohibited from undertaking independent practice in competition with their employer.

B. Written consent from the employer is necessary to permit independent practice that could result in compensation or other benefits in competition with a member's or candidate's employer.

C. Members and candidates are prohibited from making arrangements or preparations to go into a competitive business before terminating their relationship with their employer.

26. A former hedge fund manager, Jackman, has decided to launch a new private wealth management firm. From his prior experiences, he believes the new firm needs to achieve US$1 million in assets under management in the first year. Jackman offers a US$10,000 incentive to any adviser who joins his firm with a

minimum of US$200,000 in committed investments. Jackman places notice of the opening on several industry web portals and career search sites. Which of the following is *correct* according to the Code and Standards?

A. A member or candidate is eligible for the new position and incentive if he or she can arrange for enough current clients to switch to the new firm and if the member or candidate discloses the incentive fee.

B. A member or candidate may not accept employment with the new firm because Jackman's incentive offer violates the Code and Standards.

C. A member or candidate is not eligible for the new position unless he or she is currently unemployed because soliciting the clients of the member's or candidate's current employer is prohibited.

27. Jurgen is a portfolio manager. One of her firm's clients told Jurgen that he will compensate her beyond the compensation provided by her firm on the basis of the capital appreciation of his portfolio each year. Jurgen should:

A. turn down the additional compensation because it will result in conflicts with the interests of other clients' accounts.

B. turn down the additional compensation because it will create undue pressure on her to achieve strong short-term performance.

C. obtain permission from her employer prior to accepting the compensation arrangement.

28. Willier is the research analyst responsible for following Company X. All the information he has accumulated and documented suggests that the outlook for the company's new products is poor, so the stock should be rated a weak "hold." During lunch, however, Willier overhears a financial analyst from another firm whom he respects offer opinions that conflict with Willier's forecasts and expectations. Upon returning to his office, Willier releases a strong "buy" recommendation to the public. Willier:

A. violated the Standards by failing to distinguish between facts and opinions in his recommendation.

B. violated the Standards because he did not have a reasonable and adequate basis for his recommendation.

C. was in full compliance with the Standards.

29. Scott works for a regional brokerage firm. He estimates that Walkton Industries will increase its dividend by US$1.50 a share during the next year. He realizes that this increase is contingent on pending legislation that would, if enacted, give Walkton a substantial tax break. The US representative for Walkton's home district has told Scott that although she is lobbying hard for the bill and prospects for its passage are favorable, concern of the US Congress over the federal deficit could cause the tax bill to be voted down. Walkton Industries has not made any statements about a change in dividend policy. Scott writes in his research report, "We expect Walkton's stock price to rise by at least US$8.00 a share by the end of the year because the dividend will increase by US$1.50 a share. Investors buying the stock at the current time should expect to realize a total return of at least 15% on the stock." Which of the following statements is true?

A. Scott violated the Standards because he used material inside information.

B. Scott violated the Standards because he failed to separate opinion from fact.

C. Scott violated the Standards by basing his research on uncertain predictions of future government action.

30. Cannan has been working from home on weekends and occasionally saves correspondence with clients and completed work on her home computer. Because of worsening market conditions, Cannan is one of several employees released by her firm. While Cannan is looking for a new job, she uses the files she saved at home to request letters of recommendation from former clients. She also provides to prospective clients some of the reports as examples of her abilities.

A. Cannan violated the Code and Standards because she did not receive permission from her former employer to keep or use the files after her employment ended.

B. Cannan did not violate the Code and Standards because the files were created and saved on her own time and computer.

C. Cannan violated the Code and Standards because she is prohibited from saving files on her home computer.

31. Smith is a financial analyst with XYZ Brokerage Firm. She is preparing a purchase recommendation on JNI Corporation. Which of the following situations is *most likely* to represent a conflict of interest for Smith that would have to be avoided or disclosed?

A. Smith frequently purchases items produced by JNI.

B. XYZ holds for its own account a substantial common stock position in JNI.

C. Smith's brother-in-law is a supplier to JNI.

32. Jamison is a junior research analyst at Howard & Howard, a brokerage and investment banking firm. Howard & Howard's mergers and acquisitions department has represented the Britland Company in all its acquisitions for the past 20 years. Two of Howard & Howard's senior officers are directors of various Britland subsidiaries. Jamison has been asked to write a research report on Britland. What is the best course of action for her to follow?

A. Jamison may write the report but must refrain from expressing any opinions because of the special relationships between the two companies.

B. Jamison should not write the report, because the two Howard & Howard officers serve as directors for subsidiaries of Britland.

C. Jamison may write the report if she discloses the director relationship between the two companies.

33. Which of the following statements clearly *conflicts* with the recommended procedures for compliance presented in the CFA Institute *Standards of Practice Handbook*?

A. Firms should disclose to clients the personal investing policies and procedures established for their employees.

B. Prior approval must be obtained for the personal investment transactions of all employees.

C. For confidentiality reasons, personal transactions and holdings should not be reported to employers unless mandated by regulatory organizations.

34. Rose, a portfolio manager for a local investment advisory firm, is planning to sell a portion of his personal investment portfolio to cover the costs of his child's tuition. Rose wants to sell a portion of his holdings in Household Products, but his firm recently upgraded the stock to "strong buy." Which of the following describes Rose's options under the Code and Standards?

A. Based on his firm's "buy" recommendation, Rose cannot sell the shares, because he would be improperly prospering from the inflated recommendation.

B. Rose is free to sell his personal holdings once his firm is properly informed of his intentions.

C. Rose can sell his personal holdings but only when a client of the firm places an order to buy shares of Household.

35. Which of the following statements is a stated purpose of disclosure in Standard VI(C) Referral Fees?

A. Disclosure will allow the client to request discounted service fees.

B. Disclosure will help the client evaluate any possible partiality shown in the recommendation of services.

C. Disclosure means advising a prospective client about the referral arrangement once a formal client relationship has been established.

36. Park is very frustrated after taking the Level II CFA exam. While she was studying for the exam, to supplement the curriculum provided, she ordered and used study material from a third-party provider. Park believes the additional material focused her attention on specific topic areas that were not tested while ignoring other areas. She posts the following statement on the provider's discussion board: "I am very dissatisfied with your firm's CFA Program Level II material. I found the exam extremely difficult and myself unprepared for specific questions after using your product. How could your service provide such limited instructional resources on the analysis of inventories and taxes when the exam had multiple questions about them? I will not recommend your products to other candidates." Which of the following statements is true?

A. Park violated the Code and Standards by purchasing third-party review material.

B. Park violated the Code and Standards by providing her opinion on the difficulty of the exam.

C. Park violated the Code and Standards by providing specific information on topics tested on the exam.

37. Albert and Tye, who recently started their own investment advisory business, have registered to take the Level III CFA examination. Albert's business card reads, "Judy Albert, CFA Level II." Tye has not put anything about the CFA designation on his business card, but promotional material that he designed for the business describes the CFA requirements and indicates that Tye participates in the CFA Program and has completed Levels I and II. Which of the following

statements is true?

A. Albert violated the Standards, but Tye did not.

B. Tye violated the Standards, but Albert did not.

C. Both Albert and Tye violated the Standards.

38. Rule has worked as a portfolio manager for a large investment management firm for the past 10 years. Rule earned his CFA charter last year and has decided to open his own investment management firm. After leaving his current employer, Rule creates some marketing material for his new firm. He states in the material, "In earning the CFA charter, a highly regarded credential in the investment management industry, I further enhanced the portfolio management skills learned during my professional career. While completing the examination process in three consecutive years, I consistently received the highest possible scores on the topics of ethics, alternative investments, and portfolio management." Did Rule violate Standard VII(B) Reference to CFA Institute, the CFA Designation, and the CFA Program in his marketing material?

A. Rule violated Standard VII(B) in stating that he completed the exams in three consecutive years.

B. Rule violated Standard VII(B) in stating that he received the highest scores in the topics of ethics, alternative investments, and portfolio management.

C. Rule did not violate Standard VII(B).

39. Quinn sat for the Level III CFA exam this past weekend. He updates his resume with the following statement: "In finishing the CFA Program, I improved my skills related to researching investments and managing portfolios. I will be eligible for the CFA charter upon completion of the required work experience."

A. Quinn violated the Code and Standards by claiming he improved his skills through the CFA Program.

B. Quinn violated the Code and Standards by incorrectly stating that he is eligible for the CFA charter.

C. Quinn did not violate the Code and Standards with his resume update.

SOLUTIONS

1. The correct answer is A because this question relates to Standard I(A) Knowledge of the Law—specifically, global application of the Code and Standards. Members and candidates who practice in multiple jurisdictions may be subject to various securities laws and regulations. If applicable law is more strict than the requirements of the Code and Standards, members and candidates must adhere to applicable law; otherwise, members and candidates must adhere to the Code and Standards. Therefore, answer A is correct. Answer B is incorrect because members and candidates must adhere to the higher standard set by the Code and Standards if local applicable law is less strict. Answer C is incorrect because when no applicable law exists, members and candidates are required to adhere to the Code and Standards, and the Code and Standards prohibit the use of material nonpublic information.

2. The correct answer is B. The best course of action under Standard I(B) Independence and Objectivity is to avoid a conflict of interest whenever possible. Therefore, for Ward to pay for all his expenses is the correct answer. Answer C details a course of action in which the conflict would be disclosed, but this solution is not as appropriate as avoiding the conflict of interest. Answer A would not be the best course because it would not remove the appearance of a conflict of interest; even though the report would not be affected by the reimbursement of expenses, it could appear to be.

3. The correct answer is B. This question relates to Standard I(B) Independence and Objectivity. When asked to change a recommendation on a company stock to gain business for the firm, the head of the brokerage unit must refuse in order to maintain his independence and objectivity in making recommendations. He must not yield to pressure by the firm's investment banking department. To avoid the appearance of a conflict of interest, the firm should discontinue issuing recommendations about the company. Answer A is incorrect; changing the recommendation in any manner that is contrary to the analyst's opinion violates the duty to maintain independence and objectivity. Answer C is incorrect because merely assigning a new analyst to decide whether the stock deserves a higher rating will not address the conflict of interest.

4. Answer A is correct. Standard I(B) Independence and Objectivity emphasizes the need for members and candidates to maintain their independence and objectivity. Best practices dictate that firms adopt a strict policy not to accept compensation for travel arrangements. At times, however, accepting paid travel would not compromise one's independence and objectivity. Answers B and C are incorrect because the added benefits—free conference admission for additional staff members and an exclusive golf retreat for the speaker—could be viewed as inducements related to the firm's working arrangements and not solely related to the speaking engagement. Should Long wish to bring other team members or participate in the golf outing, he or his firm should be responsible for the associated fees.

5. The correct answer is C. This question involves Standard I(C) Misrepresentation. Statement I is a factual statement that discloses to clients and prospects accurate information about the terms of the investment instrument. Statement II, which guarantees a specific rate of return for a mutual fund, is an opinion stated as a fact and, therefore, violates Standard I(C). If Statement II were rephrased to include a qualifying statement, such as "in my opinion, investors may earn . . . ," it would not be in violation of the Standards.

6. The correct answer is C. This question relates to Standard I(C) Misrepresentation. Although Michelieu's statement about the total return of his clients' accounts on average may be technically true, it is misleading because the majority of the gain resulted from one client's large position taken against Michelieu's advice. Therefore, this statement misrepresents the investment performance the member is responsible for. He has not taken steps to present a fair, accurate, and complete presentation of performance. Answer B is thus incorrect. Answer A is incorrect because although Michelieu is not guaranteeing future results, his words are still a misrepresentation of his performance history.

7. The correct answer is A. This question involves three of the Standards. Anderb, the portfolio manager, has been obtaining more favorable prices for her personal securities transactions than she gets for her clients, which is a breach of Standard III(A) Loyalty, Prudence, and Care. In addition, she violated Standard I(D) Misconduct by failing to adhere to company policy and by hiding her personal transactions from her firm. Anderb's supervisor, Bates, violated Standard IV(C) Responsibilities of Supervisors; although the company had requirements for reporting personal trading, Bates failed to adequately enforce those requirements. Answer B does not represent a violation because Standard VI(B) Priority of Transactions requires that personal trading in a security be conducted after the trading in that security of clients and the employer. The Code and Standards do not prohibit owning such investments, although firms may establish policies that limit the investment opportunities of members and candidates. Answer C does not represent a violation because the Code and Standards do not contain a prohibition against employees using the same broker for their personal accounts that they use for their client accounts. This arrangement should be disclosed to the employer so that the employer may determine whether a conflict of interest exists.

8. The correct answer is B. This question deals with Standard II(A) Material Nonpublic Information. The mosaic theory states that an analyst may use material public information and nonmaterial nonpublic information in creating a larger picture than shown by any individual piece of information and the conclusions the analyst reaches become material only after the pieces are assembled. Answers A and C are accurate statements relating to the Code and Standards but do not describe the mosaic theory.

9. The correct answer is B. The best policy to prevent violation of Standard II(A) Material Nonpublic Information is the establishment of firewalls in a firm to prevent exchange of insider information. The physical and informational barrier of a firewall between the investment banking department and the brokerage operation prevents the investment banking department from providing information to analysts on the brokerage side who may be writing recommendations on a company stock. Prohibiting recommendations of the stock of companies that are clients of the investment banking department is an alternative, but answer A states that this prohibition would be permanent, which is not the best answer. Once an offering is complete and the material nonpublic information obtained by the investment banking department becomes public, resuming publishing recommendations on the stock is not a violation of the Code and Standards, because the information of the investment banking department no longer gives the brokerage operation an advantage in writing the report. Answer C is incorrect because no exchange of information should be occurring between the investment banking department and the brokerage operation, so monitoring of such exchanges is not an effective compliance procedure for preventing the use of material nonpublic information.

10. Answer C is correct. The guidance for Standard II(A) Material Nonpublic Information recommends adding securities to the firm's restricted list when the firm has or may have material nonpublic information. By adding these securities to this list, Andrews would uphold this standard. Because waiting until the next day will not ensure that news of the merger is made public, answer A is incorrect. Negotiations between the two companies may take much longer, and the merger may never happen. Andrews must wait until the information is disseminated to the market before he trades on that information. Answer B is incorrect because Andrews should not disclose the information to other managers; no trading is allowed on material nonpublic information.

11. Answer A is correct. Hart's decision to invest in the retail fund appears directly correlated with Rodriguez's statement about the successful quarter of Mega Retail and thus violates Standard II(A) Material Nonpublic Information. Rodriguez's information would be considered material because it would influence the share price of Mega Retail and probably influence the price of the entire exchange-traded retail fund. Thus, answer B is incorrect. Answer C is also incorrect because Rodriguez shared information that was both material and nonpublic. Company officers regularly have such knowledge about their firms, which is not a violation. The sharing of such information, however, even in a conversation between friends, does violate Standard II(A).

12. Answer B is correct. Through placing a personal purchase order that is significantly greater than the average volume, Pietro is violating Standard II(B) Market Manipulation. He is attempting to manipulate an increase in the share price and thus bring a buyer to the negotiating table. The news of a possible merger and confirmation of the firm's earnings guidance may also have positive effects on the price of Local Bank, but Pietro's actions in instructing the release of the information does not represent a violation through market manipulation. Announcements of this nature are common and practical to keep investors informed. Thus, answers A and C are incorrect.

13. The correct answer is B. Under Standard III(A) Loyalty, Prudence, and Care, members and candidates who manage a company's pension fund owe these duties to the participants and beneficiaries of the pension plan, not the management of the company or the company's shareholders.

14. The correct answer is B. This question relates to Standard III(A) Loyalty, Prudence, and Care—specifically, a member's or candidate's responsibility for voting proxies and the use of client brokerage. According to the facts stated in the question, Farnsworth did not violate Standard III(A). Although the company president asked Farnsworth to vote the shares of the Jones Corporation profit-sharing plan a certain way, Farnsworth investigated the issue and concluded, independently, the best way to vote. Therefore, even though his decision coincided with the wishes of the company president, Farnsworth is not in violation of his responsibility to be loyal and to provide care to his clients. In this case, the participants and the beneficiaries of the profit-sharing plan are the clients, not the company's management. Had Farnsworth not investigated the issue or had he yielded to the president's wishes and voted for a slate of directors that he had determined was not in the best interest of the company, Farnsworth would have violated his responsibilities to the beneficiaries of the plan. In addition, because the brokerage firm provides the lowest commissions and best execution for securities transactions, Farnsworth has met his obligations to the client in using this brokerage firm. It does not matter that the brokerage firm also provides research information that is not useful for the account generating the commission, because Farnsworth is not paying extra client money for that information.

15. Answer A is correct. The question relates to Standard III(A) Loyalty, Prudence, and Care. Carter believes the broker offers effective execution at a fee that is comparable with those of other brokers, so he is free to use the broker for all accounts. Answer B is incorrect because the accounts that prohibit soft dollar arrangements do not want to fund the purchase of research by Carter. The new trading scheme does not incur additional commissions from clients, so it would not go against the prohibitions. Answer C is incorrect because Carter should not incur unnecessary or excessive "churning" of the portfolios (excessive trading) for the purpose of meeting the brokerage commitments of soft dollar arrangements.

16. The correct answer is C. This question involves Standard III(A) Loyalty, Prudence, and Care and the specific topic of soft dollars or soft commissions. Answer C is the correct choice because client brokerage commissions may not be directed to pay for the investment manager's operating expenses. Answer B describes how members and candidates should determine how to use brokerage commissions—that is, if the use is in the best interests of clients and is commensurate with the value of the services provided. Answer A describes a practice that is commonly referred to as "directed brokerage." Because brokerage is an asset of the client and is used to benefit the client, not the manager, such practice does not violate a duty of loyalty to the client. Members and candidates are obligated in all situations to disclose to clients their practices in the use of client brokerage commissions.

17. Answer C is correct. According to Standard III(A) Loyalty, Prudence, and Care, the CFA Program would be considered a personal or firm expense and should not be paid for with the fund's brokerage commissions. Soft dollar accounts should be used only to purchase research services that directly assist the investment manager in the investment decision-making process, not to assist the management of the firm or to further education. Thus, answer A is incorrect. Answer B is incorrect because the reasonableness of how the money is used is not an issue; the issue is that educational expense is not research.

18. The correct answer is C. This question, which relates to Standard III(B) Fair Dealing, tests the knowledge of the procedures that will assist members and candidates in treating clients fairly when making investment recommendations. The step listed in answer C will help ensure the fair treatment of clients. Answer A may have negative effects on the fair treatment of clients. The more people who know about a pending change, the greater the chance that someone will inform some clients before the information's release. The firm should establish policies that limit the number of people who are aware in advance that a recommendation is to be disseminated. Answer B, distributing recommendations to institutional clients before distributing them to individual accounts, discriminates among clients on the basis of size and class of assets and is a violation of Standard III(B).

19. The correct answer is B. This question involves Standard III(B) Fair Dealing. Smith disseminated a change in the stock recommendation to his clients but then received a request contrary to that recommendation from a client who probably had not yet received the recommendation. Prior to executing the order, Smith should take additional steps to ensure that the customer received the change of recommendation. Answer A is incorrect because the client placed the order prior to receiving the recommendation and, therefore, does not have the benefit of Smith's most recent recommendation. Answer C is also incorrect; simply because the client request is contrary to the firm's recommendation does not mean a member can override a direct request by a client. After Smith contacts the client to ensure that the client received the changed recommendation, if the client still

wants to place a buy order for the shares, Smith is obligated to comply with the client's directive.

20. The correct answer is A. In this question, Brown is providing investment recommendations before making inquiries about the client's financial situation, investment experience, or investment objectives. Brown is thus violating Standard III(C) Suitability. Answers B and C provide examples of information members and candidates should discuss with their clients at the outset of the relationship, but these answers do not constitute a complete list of those factors. Answer A is the best answer.

21. Answer C is correct. Cupp violated Standard III(D) Performance Presentations when he deviated from the firm's stated policies solely to capture the gain from the holding being acquired. Answer A is incorrect because the firm does not claim GIPS compliance and the GIPS standards require external cash flows to be treated in a consistent manner with the firm's documented policies. Answer B is incorrect because the firm does not state that it is updating its composite policies. If such a change were to occur, all cash flows for the month would have to be reviewed to ensure their consistent treatment under the new policy.

22. Answer B is correct. Paper violated Standard III(D) Performance Presentation by not disclosing that he was part of a team of managers that achieved the results shown. If he had also included the return of the portion he directly managed, he would not have violated the standard. Thus, answer A is incorrect. Answer C is incorrect because Paper received written permission from his prior employer to include the results.

23. The correct answer is B. This question relates to Standard III(A) Loyalty, Prudence, and Care and Standard III(E) Preservation of Confidentiality. In this case, the member manages funds of a private endowment. Clients, who are, in this case, the trustees of the fund, must place trust in members and candidates. Bronson cannot disclose confidential financial information to anyone without the permission of the fund, regardless of whether the disclosure may benefit the fund. Therefore, answer A is incorrect. Answer C is incorrect because Bronson must notify the fund and obtain the fund's permission before publicizing the information.

24. Answer A is correct. Townsend has not provided any information about her clients to the leaders or managers of the golf program; thus, she has not violated Standard III(E) Preservation of Confidentiality. Providing contact information about her clients for a direct-mail solicitation would have been a violation. Answer B is incorrect because the notice in the newsletter does not violate Standard III(E). Answer C is incorrect because the golf program's fundraising campaign had already begun, so discussing the opportunity to donate was appropriate.

25. The correct answer is B. Under Standard IV(A) Loyalty, members and candidates may undertake independent practice that may result in compensation or other benefit in competition with their employer as long as they obtain consent from their employer. Answer C is not consistent with the Standards, because the Standards allow members and candidates to make arrangements or preparations to go into competitive business as long as those arrangements do not interfere with their duty to their current employer. Answer A is not consistent with the Standards, because the Standards do not include a complete prohibition against undertaking independent practice.

26. Answer C is correct. Standard IV(A) Loyalty discusses activities permissible to members and candidates when they are leaving their current employer; soliciting

clients is strictly prohibited. Thus, answer A is inconsistent with the Code and Standards, even with the required disclosure. Answer B is incorrect because the offer does not directly violate the Code and Standards. There may be out-of-work members and candidates who can arrange the necessary commitments without violating the Code and Standards.

27. The correct answer is C. This question involves Standard IV(B) Additional Compensation Arrangements. The arrangement described in the question—whereby Jurgen would be compensated beyond the compensation provided by her firm, on the basis of an account's performance—is not a violation of the Standards as long as Jurgen discloses the arrangement in writing to her employer and obtains permission from her employer prior to entering into the arrangement. Answers A and B are incorrect; although the private compensation arrangement could conflict with the interests of other clients and lead to short-term performance pressures, members and candidates may enter into such agreements as long as they have disclosed the arrangements to their employer and obtained permission for the arrangement from their employer.

28. The correct answer is B. This question relates to Standard V(A) Diligence and Reasonable Basis. The opinion of another financial analyst is not an adequate basis for Willier's action in changing the recommendation. Answer C is thus incorrect. So is answer A because, although it is true that members and candidates must distinguish between facts and opinions in recommendations, the question does not illustrate a violation of that nature. If the opinion overheard by Willier had sparked him to conduct additional research and investigation that justified a change of opinion, then a changed recommendation would be appropriate.

29. The correct answer is B. This question relates to Standard V(B) Communication with Clients and Prospective Clients. Scott issued a research report stating that he expects the price of Walkton Industries stock to rise by US$8 a share "because the dividend will increase" by US$1.50 per share. He made this statement knowing that the dividend will increase only if Congress enacts certain legislation, an uncertain prospect. By stating that the dividend will increase, Scott failed to separate fact from opinion. The information regarding passage of legislation is not material nonpublic information, because it is conjecture, and the question does not state whether the US representative gave Scott her opinion on the passage of the legislation in confidence. She could have been offering this opinion to anyone who asked. Therefore, statement A is incorrect. It may be acceptable to base a recommendation, in part, on an expectation of future events, even though they may be uncertain. Therefore, answer C is incorrect.

30. Answer A is correct. According to Standard V(C) Record Retention, Cannan needed the permission of her employer to maintain the files at home after her employment ended. Without that permission, she should have deleted the files. All files created as part of a member's or candidate's professional activity are the property of the firm, even those created outside normal work hours. Thus, answer B is incorrect. Answer C is incorrect because the Code and Standards do not prohibit using one's personal computer to complete work for one's employer.

31. The correct answer is B. This question involves Standard VI(A) Avoid or Disclose Conflicts—specifically, the holdings of an analyst's employer in company stock. XYZ ownership of the stock of the company that is the subject of the research report creates a conflict of interest that must be disclosed in the research report. XYZ could avoid the conflict by not having Smith prepare a recommendation for JNI or any other company in which XYZ has an ownership interest. Answers A and C do not describe conflicts of interest that Smith would have to avoid or disclose. Answer A describes the use of a firm's products, which would not be a re-

quired disclosure, because it will likely not create a conflict of interest. In answer C, the relationship between the analyst and the company through a relative is so tangential that it does not create a conflict of interest necessitating disclosure.

32. The correct answer is B. This question involves Standard VI(A) Avoid or Disclose Conflicts. The question establishes a conflict of interest in which an analyst, Jamison, is asked to write a research report on a company that is a client of her employer. In addition, two directors of the company are senior officers of Jamison's employer. Best practice would be to avoid the conflicts of interest by not providing a research report on companies that are clients of or have a director relationship with Howard & Howard. If the conflicts are not avoided, both the client relationship and director relationship must be disclosed by Jamison in her research report. Answer C is incorrect because Jamison would be disclosing only one of the conflicts. Answer A is incorrect because whether Jamison expresses any opinions in the report is irrelevant to her duty to disclose all conflicts of interest. Not expressing opinions does not relieve the analyst of the responsibility to disclose the special relationships between the two companies.

33. The correct answer is C. This question asks about compliance procedures relating to personal investments of members and candidates. The statement in answer C clearly conflicts with the recommended procedures in the *Standards of Practice Handbook*. Employers should compare personal transactions of employees with those of clients on a regular basis regardless of the existence of a requirement by any regulatory organization. Such comparisons ensure that employees' personal trades do not conflict with their duty to their clients, and the comparisons can be conducted in a confidential manner. The statement in answer A does not conflict with the procedures in the *Handbook*. Disclosure of such policies will give full information to clients regarding potential conflicts of interest on the part of those entrusted to manage their money. Answer B is incorrect because firms are encouraged to establish policies whereby employees clear their personal holdings and transactions with their employers.

34. The correct answer is B. Standard VI(B) Priority of Transactions does not limit transactions of company employees that differ from current recommendations as long as the sale does not disadvantage current clients. Thus, answer A is incorrect. Answer C is incorrect because the Standard does not require the matching of personal and client trades.

35. The correct answer is B. Answer B gives one of the two primary reasons listed in the *Handbook* for disclosing referral fees to clients under Standard VI(C) Referral Fees. (The other is to allow clients and employers to evaluate the full cost of the services.) Answer A is incorrect because Standard VI(C) does not require members or candidates to discount their fees when they receive referral fees. Answer C is inconsistent with Standard VI(C) because disclosure of referral fees, to be effective, should be made to prospective clients before entering into a formal client relationship with them.

36. Answer C is correct. Standard VII(A) Conduct as Members and Candidates in the CFA Program prohibits providing information to candidates or the public that is considered confidential to the CFA Program. In revealing that questions related to the analysis of inventories and analysis of taxes were on the exam, Park violated this standard. Answer B is incorrect because the guidance for the standard explicitly acknowledges that members and candidates are allowed to offer their opinions about the CFA Program. Answer A is incorrect because candidates are not prohibited from using outside resources.

37. The correct answer is A. Standard VII(B) Reference to CFA Institute, the CFA

Designation, and the CFA Program is the subject of this question. The reference on Albert's business card implies that there is a "CFA Level II" designation; Tye merely indicates in promotional material that he is participating in the CFA Program and has completed Levels I and II. Candidates may not imply that there is some sort of partial designation earned after passing a level of the CFA exam. Therefore, Albert violated Standard VII(B). Candidates may communicate that they are participating in the CFA Program, however, and may state the levels that they have completed. Therefore, Tye has not violated Standard VII(B).

38. Answer B is correct, according to Standard VII(B) Reference to CFA Institute, the CFA Designation, and the CFA Program. CFA Program candidates do not receive their actual scores on the exam. Topic and subtopic results are grouped into three broad categories, and the exam is graded only as "pass" or "fail." Although candidates may achieve a topical score of "above 70%," they cannot factually state that they received the highest possible score, because that information is not reported. Thus, answer C is incorrect. Answer A is incorrect as long as the member or candidate actually completed the exams consecutively. Standard VII(B) does not prohibit the communication of factual information about completing the CFA Program in three consecutive years.

39. Answer B is correct. According to Standard VII(B) Reference to CFA Institute, the CFA Designation, and the CFA Program, Quinn cannot claim to have finished the CFA Program or be eligible for the CFA charter until he officially learns that he passed the Level III CFA exam. Until the results for the most recent exam are released, those who sat for the exam should continue to refer to themselves as "candidates." Thus, answer C is incorrect. Answer A is incorrect because members and candidates may discuss areas of practice in which they believe the CFA Program improved their personal skills.

LEARNING MODULE

3

Application of the Code and Standards: Level III

LEARNING OUTCOMES

Mastery	The candidate should be able to:
☐	evaluate practices, policies, and conduct relative to the CFA Institute Code of Ethics and Standards of Professional Conduct
☐	explain how the practices, policies, or conduct does or does not violate the CFA Institute Code of Ethics and Standards of Professional Conduct

INTRODUCTION

1

The purpose of this learning module is to provide examples of how the CFA Institute Code of Ethics and Standards of Professional Conduct (Code and Standards) can be applied in situations requiring professional and ethical judgment. Exhibit 1 presents a useful framework to help navigate the ethical decision-making process and apply the Code and Standards. The framework's components do not need to be addressed in the sequence shown, but a review of the outcome should conclude the process. This review provides insights for improved decision making in the future.

Exhibit 1: A Framework for Ethical Decision Making

- Identify: Relevant facts, stakeholders and duties owed, ethical principles, conflicts of interest
- Consider: Situational influences, additional guidance, alternative actions
- Decide and act
- Reflect: Was the outcome as anticipated? Why or why not?

These cases involve individuals in private wealth and institutional asset management settings and discussion as to whether actions, taken or not taken, are in violation of the Code and Standards. As you work through these cases, think about how applying the ethical decision-making framework might have changed the decisions and actions

Note: The quoted material that follows is from the most recent edition of the Standards of Practice Handbook, 11th edition (2014), which includes the Standards themselves, as well as the guidance for them.

of those in the scenarios. Referencing the Code and Standards will help in identifying applicable ethical principles upon which sound decisions and appropriate behavior can be based. The learning module concludes with practice problems in item-set format.

2 SOVEREIGN INVESTMENT CORPORATION

- [ ] evaluate practices, policies, and conduct relative to the CFA Institute Code of Ethics and Standards of Professional Conduct
- [ ] explain how the practices, policies, or conduct does or does not violate the CFA Institute Code of Ethics and Standards of Professional Conduct

Anthony Corrales and Victoria Adebayo worked together at a UK hedge fund (HFI) that specializes in making alternative investments in developing markets.[1] Recently, Adebayo decided to return to her home country and accept a position as chief financial officer and chief investment officer at her country's Sovereign Investment Corporation (SIC). SIC's mandate is to benefit the country's developing economy by financing local projects that generate positive investment returns and attract global partners to co-invest with SIC. A secondary goal for SIC is to develop the country's capital markets by promoting more activity and growth in the local stock market. To achieve these objectives, SIC has an investment company called National Investments (NI). In exchange for investment proceeds, investors are issued shares in NI that are listed on the country's sole national exchange. By bringing in outside investors, the capital invested by NI has a leverage effect on the local economy and society. Adebayo is excited about the opportunity to work for SIC and lead NI's investing activities. She makes appropriate arrangements for the move home.

Soon after Adebayo starts in her new role, one of the country's regional governors, who also leads the country's opposing political party, strenuously advocates for SIC to make a sizable investment in a complex mining project in an underpopulated, remote area of the nation. The project is expected to bring economic benefits to the governor's region but requires a major capital commitment. The country's minister of finance, who hired Adebayo, has different priorities. He wants SIC to fund a moderately sized urban infrastructure project. Although less capital intensive than the mining project, this project is expected to create hundreds of jobs for supporters of the political party currently in power.

Adebayo knows that although both projects are potentially important to the country, investing in both simultaneously would strain the team's resources. She quickly decides that NI should invest in the urban infrastructure project before investing in the mining project. Adebayo thinks this sequencing of investment by NI offers the benefit of supporting the current political party in power while postponing investment in the mining project until a time when the opposition party gains control of the government in a future election. She also believes the urban infrastructure project may be more profitable in the short term, thus helping to attract new investment partners. With more capital from outside investors and the extra time, Adebayo believes NI would then have sufficient funding and expertise to invest in the second, more capital intensive and complex project.

1 This case is by Jon Stokes, JD, and is based on cases from *Ethics in Practice: Ethics in Investment Management Casebook*. Consistent with the 11th edition of the *Standards of Practice Handbook*.

KNOWLEDGE CHECK

1. Did Adebayo's decision to invest in the urban infrastructure project rather than the mining project most likely violate the CFA Institute Code and Standards?

   A. No

   B. Yes, with regard to diligence and reasonable basis

   C. Yes, with regard to suitability

   Solution:

   B is correct. Standard V(A) Diligence and Reasonable Basis requires members to exercise diligence, independence, and thoroughness, as well as to have a reasonable and adequate basis to support investment action. Adebayo's decision to invest "quickly" without apparent analysis is made based on political, not investment or financial, considerations. Adebayo is facing political pressures from senior governmental supporters of each project. She must thoroughly and independently investigate each potential investment and be resolute in maintaining her independence and objectivity to act in the best interests of NI and its investors. In addition, Adebayo must not be swayed or influenced by conflicts of interest resulting from outside situational influences or pressures.

   A is incorrect because Adebayo's decision to invest "quickly" without apparent analysis is made based on political, not investment, considerations and violates her responsibilities to exercise diligence, independence, and thoroughness in analyzing investments and taking investment action. She does not have a reasonable and adequate basis, supported by appropriate research and investigation, for any investment analysis, recommendation, or action.

   C is incorrect. Both investments are suitable in meeting the goals of NI and may be justified on their merit in having a positive socioeconomic impact for the country. The mining project is likely to increase the country's wealth through increased economic activity and at the same time deliver a potentially attractive ROI. The infrastructure project will similarly enhance the local economy by providing long-term employment for hundreds of workers.

2. Which of the following would most likely mitigate any political bias influencing Adebayo's decisions regarding how to invest NI assets?

   A. Requiring all investments be approved by a higher governmental authority

   B. Developing a rigorous governance framework for investment decisions

   C. Requiring Adebayo to disclose conflicts of interest

   Solution:

   B is correct. NI should have a robust and rigorous governance framework for making investment decisions that supports an appropriate level of due diligence undertaken and facilitates Adebayo's duty to make independent and objective investment decisions free of bias, as required by Standard I(B) Independence and Objectivity. NI's development orientation does not justify taking a less-than-rigorous investment approach. If NI is to originate deals locally and bring in co-investors, it must demonstrate that it is acting in investors' best interests and is not subject to political pressures or other situational influences.

A is incorrect because deferring the decision to a higher governmental authority would not mitigate and may in fact enhance political influence on the investment decision rather than ensure each project is objectively considered for its individual investment merit.

C is incorrect because disclosing outside negative situational influences or conflicts of interest does not replace the need to act with independent and objective judgement when analyzing and selecting investment opportunities.

Anthony Corrales, CFA, Partner, Hedge Fund Investors

Anthony Corrales, CFA, Adebayo's former colleague and partner at the hedge fund HFI, contacts Adebayo and expresses interest in making a significant investment in NI. Corrales asks Adebayo for detailed information regarding NI's current financial condition, future projections, and projects. She gives him the standard investor disclosure package. After closely examining the material, Corrales decides it is an excellent investment for the hedge fund. He is confident Adebayo will deliver a strong ROI for NI, which in turn will generate strong performance for HFI.

To demonstrate his conviction and convince his hedge fund partners of the opportunity, Corrales immediately invests 25% of his personal portfolio in NI in return for shares. After several days of deliberation, the hedge fund partners decide to invest HFI assets in NI but seek assurances that NI will maintain its aggressive investment strategy and commitment to high returns. Adebayo assures Corrales and the other hedge fund partners that NI is committed to providing its investors with high rates of return. Corrales asks Adebayo to provide him directly with regular updates on NI's investment performance, financial health, future funding plans, and project status. After the hedge fund's investment with SIC is made public, shares in NI trade higher on the exchange.

Corrales is also interested in making private market investments directly for HFI. To help in this endeavor, the hedge fund uses local subadvisers to identify promising investment opportunities and navigate local laws and regulations. For their role, the subadvisers are paid from assets of the hedge fund, and although they have minimal or no experience as financial consultants or advisers, all subadvisers have close connections with local high-ranking government officials. Payments are made by the subadvisers on behalf of the hedge fund to cover substantial "deal fees" and other expenses to facilitate governmental support for each investment. Corrales does not require the local business partners to provide details of their activities or to identify what specific expenses the fees cover. Corrales views these expenditures as necessary to the fund's investment success and reports them as operating expenses to the fund's investors.

KNOWLEDGE CHECK

1. Which of Adebayo's interactions with Corrales most likely violates the CFA Institute Code and Standards?

   A. Sharing information about NI's current investments and financial condition

   B. Promising to provide updates directly to Corrales and the hedge fund partners

C. Committing that she will maximize return on investment for NI's investors

Solution:

C is correct. Standard III(C) Suitability requires CFA Institute members responsible for managing assets to a specific mandate, strategy, or style to take only investment actions that are consistent with that mandate. In the case of NI, Adebayo has a dual mandate to invest in projects that have both a beneficial socioeconomic impact and a positive expected investment return. This dual mandate is in contrast to traditional investment mandates that focus only on ROI regardless of outside or other impact. NI's investors are informed up front that investment return is not the single determining factor for NI's investment decisions. Any assurances by Adebayo to the hedge fund or other investors that promise a set rate of return or prioritize return maximization would be contrary to NI's mandate.

A is incorrect. Transparency is a fundamental principle in the Code and Standards. It would be appropriate and reasonable for Adebayo to provide detailed information about NI to potential investors, such as her former hedge fund partners, so they can conduct appropriate due diligence on NI. Although Adebayo must be careful to avoid improperly disclosing confidential information or material nonpublic information to potential investors, the facts make clear that Adebayo shares the information she is regularly disclosing to other potential investors. Adebayo can develop trust with the investment community, for NI's benefit, by providing ongoing transparency and accountability regarding her investment actions.

B is incorrect. Although Adebayo must be careful that she treats NI investors fairly, it may be acceptable in some circumstances to regularly communicate directly with a particular investor. This holds true as long as all investors of NI are treated fairly and receive the same disclosures about the financial prospects and other information about NI, with no preference for those investors with whom Adebayo has a close relationship. There is no indication from the facts that Adebayo is not also providing this same "hands on" service to other NI investors.

2. Did Corrales's investment for his own portfolio most likely violate the CFA Institute Code and Standards?

A. No

B. Yes, with regard to conflicts of interest

C. Yes, with regard to priority of transactions

Solution:

C is correct. In this instance, Corrales engaged in the unethical and often illegal practice of front-running, or trading in advance for one's personal account prior to trading for client accounts for economic advantage. Standard VI(B) Priority of Transactions states that investment transactions for clients must have priority over investment transactions for personal benefit. After the hedge fund invests in NI, the value of NI shares increases, benefiting Corrales through an increase in the value of his personal investment. This practice is unethical and violates Standard VI(B) even if his personal investment does not disadvantage the hedge fund in any way. Corrales should have waited to invest in NI until after the hedge fund had completed its investment in NI.

A is incorrect because Corrales is violating Standard VI(B) Priority of Transactions.

B is incorrect. Purchasing the same investments as your employer or investing in the same assets as your clients does not necessarily create a conflict of interest, although best practice recommends that such "co-investing" be disclosed.

3. By hiring subadvisers in a developing country to source investment opportunities, Corrales is most likely violating the Standard of Professional Conduct relating to:

   A. misrepresentation.

   B. diligence and reasonable basis.

   C. independence and objectivity.

Solution:

A is correct. By reporting subadvisory payments as legitimate hedge fund "operating expenses," Corrales is misrepresenting the nature of the payments to hide illegal activity and is in violation of Standard I(C) Misrepresentation. Although it is acceptable to hire subadvisers to assist in sourcing investment opportunities, Corrales is not hiring a subadviser to assist in the investment decision-making process but is essentially engaged in bribery and facilitating local corruption.

Such conduct would violate multiple standards. To ensure inside access to investment opportunities for the hedge fund, Corrales pays locally connected individuals with minimal or no financial experience to influence government officials and secure access to investment deals. The "deal fees" are corrupt transactions and are not supported by any documentation that details legitimate investment expenses. Corrales very likely violates Standard I(A) Knowledge of the Law because his conduct would most likely violate applicable anti-bribery laws.

B is incorrect. To better serve clients, investment professionals may choose to delegate to third parties work that requires specialization, knowledge, or expertise. For example, an investment adviser may hire subadvisers to handle a particular strategy or investment style outside the scope of the adviser's ability or experience. An adviser can hire a subadviser to manage an asset allocation invested in a particular market, and the payments to the subadviser would be legitimate investment expenses that could properly be passed on to investors in the hedge fund. Under Standard V(A) Diligence and Reasonable Basis, investment advisers who hire subadvisers must ensure they have the necessary knowledge or expertise to meet the need for diligence and thoroughness in using subadvisers in the investment decision-making process.

C is incorrect. Investment professionals may rely on the recommendations of subadvisers who have a particular specialization or specific knowledge or expertise when selecting investment opportunities without having separate or objective reasons for choosing those investments independent from the subadviser's recommendation.

Ani Mehrotra, CFA, Junior Analyst, National Investments

Back at NI, Adebayo hires Ani Mehrotra, a young analyst and recent CFA® charterholder who serves on the board of the CFA Institute local society. Mehrotra's responsibilities include globally promoting NI to potential investors. He is excited about his new role and is looking forward to working with Adebayo. Mehrotra asks Adebayo why she has not been participating in events held by the local society, given how active she was with CFA Society of the UK. Adebayo tells him that since taking her new role, she has not paid her CFA Institute membership dues or had the time to engage actively with the society. Mehrotra notices that Adebayo continues to use the CFA designation on her business card and on all marketing materials. When Mehrotra asks Adebayo about her use of the designation, she tells him that because she passed the exams and earned the charter, the credential is like a university degree that cannot be taken away.

During a sales presentation by Mehrotra and Adebayo, the potential client notes that his firm considers only investment opportunities that have CFA charterholders in senior investment positions. He asks Adebayo if all of NI's senior investment professionals are CFA charterholders. Adebayo responds, "Yes, that is correct." Mehrotra defers to Adebayo, his supervisor, and says nothing.

In serving as a board member in the CFA Institute local society, Mehrotra seeks to "give back" to the CFA Program by mentoring local candidates. He volunteers to lead the exam preparation course given by his local society for candidates in the CFA Program. After the exam, the society hosts a celebration for the students. During the celebration, a number of Mehrotra's students describe their experiences sitting for the exam. Most give their opinion on the relative difficulty of the exam, and some describe their surprise about areas of the curriculum that were not tested. Mehrotra asks the students their opinion on the most difficult exam questions. He hopes to use this information to help ensure his future students are better prepared.

KNOWLEDGE CHECK

1. With regard to communicating information to a potential investor about the qualifications of NI's investment team, who violated the CFA Institute Code and Standards?

   A. Only Adebayo

   B. Both Adebayo and Mehrotra

   C. Neither Adebayo or Mehrotra

   Solution:

   B is correct. Standard VII(B) Reference to CFA Institute, the CFA Designation, and the CFA Program states that when referring to the CFA designation, CFA Institute members and candidates "must not misrepresent . . . holding the designation." The CFA designation is not like a degree from a university in that once granted the right to use the designation, individuals must also satisfy CFA Institute membership requirements (including paying dues and submitting a Professional Conduct Statement annually) to maintain the right to refer to themselves as CFA charterholders. Although Adebayo earned her charter, her membership is considered lapsed because she has not been paying her CFA Institute dues. Until her membership is reactivated, she must not use the CFA designation or present herself as a charterholder to potential investors, although she may state she was previously a CFA Institute member.

   Mehrotra hears Adebayo refer to herself as a charterholder, but he knows that because Adebayo has not paid her dues, her CFA Institute membership has lapsed. Standard I(A) Knowledge of the Law prohibits members from knowingly participating or assisting in the violations of others and requires members to dissociate from any unethical or illegal conduct. Mehrotra's acquiescence and silence during Adebayo's misrepresentation to the client, at minimum, assists Adebayo's violation of the standard. By keeping silent about false information given to a potential investor, when doing so is potentially harmful to that investor, Mehrotra's behavior constitutes assisting in the violations of those who provide that false information even if there is no active conduct by Mehrotra. Best practice, although difficult, would be for Mehrotra to address Adebayo directly about her conduct and ask her to reinstate her membership or correct the statement made to the potential investor. If Adebayo refuses to take corrective action, Mehrotra could bring this conduct to the attention of the SIC's compliance department for them to address. Mehrotra should dissociate from the activity by not participating in any future sales meetings with Adebayo.

A is incorrect because Mehrotra violated Standard I(A) Knowledge of the Law, as outlined earlier.

C is incorrect because Adebayo violated Standard VII(B) Reference to CFA Institute, the CFA Designation, and the CFA Program and Mehrotra violated Standard I(A) Knowledge of the Law, as outlined earlier.

2. Which of Mehrotra's actions with respect to the local society's preparatory course least likely violates the CFA Institute Code and Standards?

   A. Soliciting information about the exam questions from students in an effort to improve the course for future preparatory classes

   B. Relating information about the exam to candidates in future preparatory classes to help prepare them for the exam

   C. Sharing his students' opinions about the difficulty of the exam to candidates in future preparatory classes to emphasize the need to thoroughly prepare

Solution:

C is correct. CFA Institute Standard VII(A) Conduct as Participants in CFA Institute Programs states that candidates must not engage in any conduct that compromises the integrity, validity, or security of CFA Institute programs. This standard is designed to protect the integrity and security of future exams. The standard includes giving or receiving assistance on any CFA exams and providing confidential program or exam information to candidates or the public. Candidates may generally disclose whether they believed the CFA exam was difficult relative to their expectations. It is acceptable for Mehrotra to advise future preparatory classes that his previous students found the CFA exam to be more difficult than expected and thus students should study the curriculum and prepare as much as possible.

A is incorrect. Candidates cannot provide specific information about the exam regarding the questions or the subjects tested within a topic area. Mehrotra violated Standard VII(A) by soliciting information about specific exam questions.

B is incorrect. Candidates can discuss their exam experience in general terms. However, they cannot provide specific information about the exam questions or curriculum subjects that are or are not tested on the exam. Mehrotra cannot pass such information to future candidates without violating Standard VII(A). For example, although CFA Institute makes known to candidates that ethics is one of 10 topic areas tested on the exam, there may not be an exam question on the subject of material nonpublic information. A candidate saying the ethics topic in the exam was difficult is not in violation of Standard VII(A), but a candidate saying there were no exam questions on insider information would violate Standard VII(A).

Marcia Lopez

June 2017 was a life-changing month for Marcia Lopez.[2] She earned a master's degree in finance from a top national university, sat for the Level I CFA exam, and accepted a job offer in her hometown as an associate in the wealth management division of BankGlobal, a multinational financial services firm.

In August, Lopez finds out that she passed Level I and begins working for BankGlobal. On her first day at BankGlobal, Lopez meets with her supervisor, David Hockett, CFA. Hockett has worked in the wealth management industry for almost 25 years and has been with BankGlobal for the past 10 years. He is eager to share his expertise with Lopez, which will enable her to assume greater client management responsibilities under his supervision. During their meeting, Hockett reviews BankGlobal's code of ethics, the specific policies and procedures needed to ensure compliance with their code, the CFA Institute Code and Standards, and all applicable securities laws and regulations. At the end of the meeting, Lopez asks him to approve her Business Card Request form, on which she describes herself as a "CFA, Level I." Hockett tells her that she should also put on her business card the year she expects to receive her CFA designation so clients can track her success in the program.

KNOWLEDGE CHECK

1. Did Lopez violate the Code and Standards in her description of herself on the Business Card Request form?

   A. Yes

   B. No, because she found out in August that she passed Level I

   C. No, because she knows the year that she expects to receive her CFA designation

Solution:

A is correct. Putting on her business card "CFA, Level I" and the year in which she expects to receive the CFA designation is a violation of Standard VII(B) Reference to CFA Institute, the CFA Designation, and the CFA Program. "Candidates in the CFA Program may refer to their participation in the CFA Program, but such references must clearly state that an individual is a *candidate* in the CFA Program and must not imply that the candidate has achieved any type of partial designation." Moreover, CFA candidates must never "cite an expected completion date of any level of the CFA Program."

B is incorrect. The fact that she found out she passed Level I is irrelevant to the standard. By putting "CFA, Level I" and the year she expects to receive her designation, Lopez violated Standard VII(B) Reference to CFA Institute, the CFA Designation, and the CFA Program.

C is incorrect. Lopez cannot know the year she expects to receive the designation because she needs to pass Levels II and III and gain sufficient relevant work experience—all of which involve future uncertainty. Even if knowing the date were possible, putting the year she expects to receive her designation violates Standard VII(B) Reference to CFA Institute, the CFA Designation, and the CFA Program.

2 This case is by Charles H. Kard, CFA, CFP, and Michael G. McMillan, PhD, CFA, in *Ethics Cases*. Consistent with the 11th edition of the *Standards of Practice Handbook*.

David Hockett and Team

Later that day, Hockett introduces Lopez to the four other members of his wealth management team. The team manages $900 million in assets for 150 high-net-worth clients. Almost 80% of the team's assets are managed in discretionary accounts, with the balance managed in non-discretionary accounts. For the past two years, the portfolios managed by Hockett's team have outperformed their benchmarks and most other wealth management teams at BankGlobal. This is partly due to the close relationships that the team has developed with the securities analysts in BankGlobal's research department. Because of bottlenecks in BankGlobal's information technology (IT) department, it generally takes about 45 minutes for changes in the analysts' recommendations to be published on the firm's website and emailed to clients. As a result, the analysts often call Hockett's team about changes in their recommendations before IT has published the information on BankGlobal's website. After receiving these calls, the team immediately acts on any analyst changes for their discretionary accounts to prevent their clients' portfolios from being adversely impacted when the recommendations are posted or to take advantage of better-than-expected reports.

KNOWLEDGE CHECK

1. By acting on the analysts' recommendations for their discretionary accounts, are members of Hockett's team violating the Code and Standards?

   A. No

   B. Yes, because they are not dealing fairly with all clients

   C. Yes, because they are acting on material nonpublic information

   Solution:

   B is correct. By acting on the analysts' recommendation changes for their discretionary accounts before the changes are publicly disseminated, the team is violating Standard III(B) Fair Dealing. Standard III(B) requires members and candidates to "deal fairly and objectively with all clients when providing investment analysis, making investment recommendations, taking investment action, or engaging in other professional activities." The guidance to Standard III(B) states, "Members and candidates must make every effort to treat all individual and institutional clients in a fair and impartial manner. A member or candidate may have multiple relationships with an institution; for example, the member or candidate may be a corporate trustee, pension fund manager, manager of funds for individuals employed by the customer, loan originator, or creditor. A member or candidate must exercise care to treat all clients fairly."

   A is incorrect. By acting on the analysts' recommendation changes for only some clients before the investment recommendations are publicly disseminated to all clients, Hockett's team is not treating all BankGlobal clients in a fair and impartial manner. Hockett is giving preferential treatment to his discretionary accounts at the expense of other clients, such as the non-discretionary accounts managed by Hockett's team and clients of other BankGlobal wealth teams.

   C is incorrect. The research team develops their recommendations for management of all BankGlobal's client accounts. These clients pay BankGlobal for its research. If other investors would like to access BankGlobal research, they can do so by becoming clients of the bank. The guidance to Standard II(A) Material Nonpublic Information states, "Information is material if it would significantly alter the total mix of information currently available about a security." To be considered material, there would need to be a clear indication that the general investing public relies on the information of BankGlobal. There is no indication in the material that BankGlobal recommendations are distributed to or highly valued by the general investing public.

The Kochanskis

After several months of learning about the wealth management division's operations and products, Hockett believes Lopez is ready to meet with prospective clients. Next week, Hockett is meeting with Marty and Mary Kochanski for the first time. The Kochanskis were referred to Hockett by Gary White, their business banker at BankGlobal. The Kochanskis are both 61 years of age, and they recently retired after Mary sold her medical insurance consulting business for $7.4 million. Hockett invites Lopez to participate in the meeting with the couple and asks her to prepare a presentation on BankGlobal's wealth management capabilities. Hockett also asks her to create a model "balanced portfolio" that he intends to recommend to the Kochanskis at the meeting.

Lopez is excited and immediately begins work on the presentation. To develop the Kochanskis' "balanced portfolio," Lopez prepares a list of fixed-income funds, equity mutual funds, and exchange-traded funds (ETFs). The list includes mutual funds and ETFs from BankGlobal's proprietary offerings, as well as those from other firms. Lopez then selects the top two performing equity and fixed-income funds with the highest five-year returns. To create a balanced portfolio, she gives an equal weight to each fund. Unsure how to present the model portfolio's past performance, Lopez uses an average of the four funds' five-year annualized rates of return and labels it "total portfolio return." For comparison purposes, Lopez shows the annual rates of return realized over a five-year period for a "composite portfolio" consisting of the team's discretionary accounts of similar size to the Kochanskis' that also have a balanced objective. To simplify the presentation, she excludes terminated accounts.

The day before they are to meet with the Kochanskis, Hockett reviews Lopez's presentation. Although he is impressed with the quality of her work, he asks her why she did not use only BankGlobal's proprietary mutual funds to create the Kochanskis' balanced portfolio. Hockett tells Lopez that, whenever possible, she should always use BankGlobal's products since they are "as good as any other firm's" and that the team receives a higher fee by using them. In addition, he states that "as employees and shareholders of BankGlobal, we have a fiduciary duty to maximize our shareholders' wealth." Before leaving to go home that evening, Lopez changes the funds in the Kochanskis' model portfolio to include only BankGlobal's proprietary funds and then updates the presentation.

The next morning, Hockett and Lopez meet with the Kochanskis. At the time White referred them to Hockett, White told Hockett only how much the Kochanskis wanted to invest, their ages, and their employment status. At the face-to-face meeting, the Kochanskis share that while they have a solid understanding of the health care and medical insurance businesses, they don't know enough about financial markets and securities to manage their own investments. Instead, they would prefer to have an investment professional manage their money, allowing them more time to travel and enjoy their grandchildren. During the 30-minute meeting with the Kochanskis, Hockett and Lopez go through Lopez's presentation and explain why a balanced portfolio is best suited for them.

KNOWLEDGE CHECK

1. Did Hockett and Lopez violate the Code and Standards in their recommendation of a balanced portfolio to the Kochanskis?

   A. Yes

   B. No, because they know the Kochanskis' investment objectives and risk tolerance

   C. No, because the balanced portfolio is most suitable for the Kochanskis given their age and wealth

   Solution:

   A is correct. Hockett and Lopez violated the Code and Standards. By developing and recommending a balanced portfolio for the Kochanskis without knowing their clients' investment objectives, risk tolerance, horizon, and so on, Hockett and Lopez violated Standard III(C) Suitability: "When Members and Candidates are in an advisory relationship with a client, they must:

   - Make a reasonable inquiry into a client's or prospective client's investment experience, risk and return objectives, and financial constraints prior to making any investment recommendation or taking investment action and must reassess and update this information regularly.
   - Determine that an investment is suitable to the client's financial situation and consistent with the client's written objectives, mandates, and constraints before making an investment recommendation or taking investment action.
   - Judge the suitability of investments in the context of the client's total portfolio."

   Hockett and Lopez should have developed an investment policy statement for the Kochanskis *before* they recommended any investments.

   B is incorrect. Hockett and Lopez violated Standard III(C) Suitability because they did not know their clients' investment objectives, risk tolerance, horizon, and so on, when they developed and recommended the balanced portfolio. Hockett and Lopez should have developed an investment policy statement for the Kochanskis before they recommended any investments.

   C is incorrect. Without knowing the Kochanskis' investment objectives, risk tolerance, horizon, and so on, it is simply not possible to know that the balanced portfolio as constructed is most suitable for the Kochanskis. Thus, the actions of Hockett and Lopez are in violation of Standard III(C) Suitability.

2. Which one of the following caused Lopez to violate the Code and Standards in her presentation of past performance information?

   A. Exclusion of terminated accounts

   B. Using an average return for the model portfolio's performance

   C. Using discretionary accounts of similar size to the Kochanskis' account

   Solution:

   A is correct. Lopez violated Standard III(D) Performance Presentation in her use and presentation of the composite portfolio's performance because she did not include the performance of terminated accounts. In addition, she included only the team's discretionary accounts of similar size to the Kochanskis'. Lopez should have included terminated and current discretionary accounts that were similar in her composite portfolio's performance. There is no need to include non-discretionary accounts because clients make their own investment decisions for such accounts.

B is incorrect. Using an average of the four funds' performance to present the model portfolio's performance is acceptable since the Kochanskis' knowledge of investments is unknown to Lopez. This easy-to-understand approach is appropriate for sharing information with novice investors. According to the guidance for Standard III(D), "Members and candidates can also meet their obligations under Standard III(D) by considering the knowledge and sophistication of the audience to whom a performance presentation is addressed."

C is incorrect. Lopez presented a composite based on accounts similar in nature to the one being recommended. According to the guidance for Standard III(D), "Members and candidates can also meet their obligations under Standard III(D) by presenting the performance of the weighted composite of similar portfolios rather than using a single representative account."

The Kochanskis are impressed with Lopez's presentation and BankGlobal's broad array of products and services, its commitment to clients, and its long-term view of the markets. As a result, they decide to open an account and invest their $7.4 million in the balanced portfolio.

Following the meeting with the Kochanskis, Hockett calls White to thank him for the referral. White replies, "Glad to do it. The new incentive referral program implemented in the corporate banking division in January of this year has been very rewarding for me. I receive a $250 gift certificate each time I refer one of my banking clients to the wealth management division. Because our referral program is internal and uses gift certificates, I do not have to disclose this to clients."

Hockett replies, "In January of this year, the wealth management division also established a new incentive program in order to motivate and retain key people, like myself and my team. All portfolio managers are now paid a quarterly bonus based on the performance of client accounts relative to certain benchmark indexes. Although 90% of our client accounts are conservative, with long-term investment objectives, we have been able to generate short-term 'alpha' in these accounts by investing 15%–20% of their portfolios in high-beta stocks that appear to have low risk. As a result, we have not had to change client investment objectives or their investment policy statements. Our returns have been great, and clients are pleased with our performance. Until that changes, I don't see a need to mention the incentive program to clients."

After work, Lopez posts the following message to her old high school friends on social media: "Just opened an account for Mr. Kochanski and his wife."

KNOWLEDGE CHECK

1. Is Hockett violating the Code and Standards by generating "alpha" for conservative client accounts?

   A. Yes

   B. No, because the stocks are high-beta, low-risk securities

   C. No, because client investment objectives and investment policy statements are unchanged

Solution:

A is correct. Hockett is violating Standard III(C) Suitability by investing in high-beta stocks for client accounts with long-term objectives in order to achieve his short-term quarterly performance bonus. According to Standard III(C), "When Members and Candidates are responsible for managing a portfolio to a specific mandate, strategy, or style, they must make only investment recommendations or take only investment actions that are consistent with the stated objectives and constraints of the portfolio." High-beta stocks by their very nature have risk.

Hockett is also violating Standard III(C) by investing 15%–20% of his clients' portfolios in high-beta stocks that "appear low risk." These high-beta stocks are contrary to the long-term risk profile established in the clients' investment policy statements (IPSs). Hockett changed the investment strategy for his clients in an attempt to gain short-term rewards offered by his firm's new compensation arrangement and not in response to changes in their investment needs and corresponding investment policy statements.

B is incorrect. High-beta stocks are not low risk. Hockett's statement is incorrect, and he is violating Standard III(C) by investing 15%–20% of clients' portfolios in high-beta stocks that are contrary to the long-term risk profile established in the clients' IPSs. Hockett has changed the investment strategy of his clients in an attempt to reap short-term rewards offered by his firm's new compensation arrangement.

C is incorrect. The fact that client investment objectives and investment policy statements are unchanged is irrelevant. Hockett violated Standard III(C) by investing 15%–20% of clients' portfolios in high-beta stocks that are contrary to the long-term risk profile established in the clients' IPSs. Hockett has changed the investment strategy of his clients in an attempt to reap short-term rewards offered by his firm's new compensation arrangement.

2. Did Lopez violate the Code and Standards in her use of social media?

   A. Yes

   B. No, because Lopez did not provide any specific information on the investments or dollar amounts

   C. No, because Lopez posted a message only to her old high school friends, not to people in the industry

Solution:

A is correct. Lopez violated Standard III(E) Preservation of Confidentiality by posting about the Kochanskis' opening of an account. According to Standard III(E), "Members and Candidates must keep information about current, former, and prospective clients confidential unless: 1. The information concerns illegal activities on the part of the client or prospective client, 2. Disclosure is required by law, or 3. The client or prospective client permits disclosure of the information." Standard III(E) requires that even the presence of a client account be kept confidentially within the firm unless the client has been informed and has consented to the disclosure of the information.

B is incorrect. Standard III(E) requires all information about current, former, or prospective clients be kept confidential, not just information about their investments or dollar amounts. Posting the name of the Kochanskis as new clients violated the required confidentiality.

C is incorrect. Standard III(E) requires all information about current, former, or prospective clients be kept confidential. This confidentiality extends beyond the investment industry to the population as a whole. By posting the name of the Kochanskis as new clients in a message to her high school friends, Lopez violated the confidentiality required under Standard III(E).

CASTLE BIOTECHNOLOGY CASE: DAVID PLUME, PHD, CFA

3

- ☐ evaluate practices, policies, and conduct relative to the CFA Institute Code of Ethics and Standards of Professional Conduct
- ☐ explain how the practices, policies, or conduct does or does not violate the CFA Institute Code of Ethics and Standards of Professional Conduct

Castle Biotechnology (CB) is a biopharmaceutical company dedicated to acquiring, developing, and commercializing pharmaceutical and biotechnology products.[3] These products are developed within CB and through the nine biopharmaceutical companies it controls. Fifteen months ago, CB purchased a controlling interest in Global Capital Management (Global), a full-service investment banking and asset management firm that provides a range of services that include underwriting, institutional sales, trading, equity research, and retail brokerage.

Shakira Chung, CFA, is CB's president, and Yusef Anders, CFA, is CB's chief executive. This morning, they are meeting to discuss the latest financial results of CB and its subsidiaries.

Anders says, "Shakira, your idea to purchase Global was brilliant. Global gives CB an in-house underwriter and a private sales force of 700 brokers to raise money to finance the research and development activities of the nine companies in our portfolio. Since acquiring Global, its brokers and research analysts have raised more than $75 million from investors around the world. Currently, Global has deals in progress to raise an additional $45 million."

Chung replies, "Yusef, we have built a unique model that inherently aligns CB's business objectives with the financial interests of Global's clients. We should be proud of the deals we have completed and the large amount of capital we have raised for our subsidiaries since we acquired Global."

Two of the biopharmaceutical companies in CB's portfolio that Global has recently taken public are Street Pharmaceuticals (STRX) and Appaloosa Biotech (APBX). Even though each company issued 75% of its shares to the public, CB stills retains voting control of each company. CB also has the right to receive a significant grant of each company's common stock each year.

David Plume, PhD, CFA

David Plume, PhD, CFA, follows the biopharmaceutical industry for Global. Prior to joining Global, Plume worked as a biochemist at CB for 15 years. During that time, he developed close professional and personal relationships with Chung and Anders. As a result, they encouraged him to become an equity analyst at Global after CB acquired it. Chung and Anders felt Plume's extensive, in-depth knowledge of the biotechnology

3 This case is by Michael G. McMillan, PhD, CFA, in *Ethics Cases*. Consistent with the 11th edition of the *Standards of Practice Handbook*.

and pharmaceutical industries would be a great help to Global. He would not only be able to write "perceptive" research reports on the companies in CB's portfolio, but he also would be able to help Global's corporate finance department identify which of its companies should be taken public. As part of his compensation package at Global, Plume receives an annual bonus equal to 0.10% of the gross proceeds raised for each initial public offering (IPO) he works on.

Prior to STRX and APBX going public with their IPOs, Plume spent a good deal of time with Global's investment bankers explaining the products each company was developing, their market potential, and the regulatory process required before their drugs could be approved for patient use by government regulators. On their first day of trading, the stock prices of STRX and APBX increased by 70% and 65%, respectively. Since then, however, their stock prices have declined 36% and 54%, respectively.

Shortly after STRX and APBX went public with their IPOs, Plume published positive research reports for both companies. In a note published on Global's website, Plume wrote that "STRX and APBX are the biopharmaceutical companies of the future. Although both are small and have no revenues to date, each company is developing a 'life-changing drug' currently undergoing clinical trials. As a result, I rate their stocks a 'buy' and predict their share prices will more than double in 9–12 months."

In his research reports, Plume does not mention that Global is owned by Castle, the same company that controls STRX and APBX, because this information is disclosed in each company's offering prospectus. He does state, however, that "one or more directors, officers, and/or employees of Global Capital and its affiliated companies or independent contractors affiliated with Global may be a director of the issuer of the securities mentioned herein." Plume also does not disclose that he owns Class A preferred shares of CB and options on CB's common stock, which were given/granted to him while he was a CB employee.

Three months after issuing his research report with a "buy" rating on APBX, Plume sells APBX short in his personal portfolio. He does not disclose the sale, because he was never a beneficial owner of APBX's stock.

KNOWLEDGE CHECK

1. Did Plume violate the Code and Standards by not disclosing in his research report that Global is owned by Castle?

   A. Yes

   B. No, because this does not affect his duty to Global or his duty to clients

   C. No, because this information is disclosed in each company's offering prospectus

   Solution:

   A is correct. By not disclosing that Global is owned by Castle in his research report, Plume is in violation of Standard VI(A) Avoid or Disclose Conflicts, which states that "Members and Candidates must avoid or make full and fair disclosure of all matters that could reasonably be expected to impair their independence and objectivity or interfere with respective duties to their clients, prospective clients, and employer. Members and Candidates must ensure that such disclosures are prominent, are delivered in plain language, and communicate the relevant information effectively."

   By not disclosing in his research reports the relationships between Castle, its nine subsidiaries, and Global, Plume is in violation of Standard VI(A). CB's ownership of Global and Plume's close relationships with CB's management raise questions about Plume's ability to remain independent and objective.

B is incorrect. Plume must disclose to his clients that Global is owned by Castle. Thus, the non-disclosure means he failed in his duty of full and fair disclosure of any conflicts of interest that may affect his clients.

C is incorrect. The fact that the relationships between Plume, CB, its subsidiaries, and Global are disclosed in the offering prospectus is necessary but not sufficient to meet Standard VI(A) because they may not communicate the information effectively or in a prominent manner.

2. Did Plume violate the Code and Standards by not disclosing his ownership of CB's Class A preferred shares and common stock options in his research report?

   A. Yes

   B. No, because he does not own shares of STRX and APBX

   C. No, because he does not have a beneficial interest in STRX and APBX

Solution:

A is correct. By not disclosing his ownership of CB's preferred shares and stock options in his research report, Plume is in violation of Standard VI(A) Avoid or Disclose Conflicts. Because of this ownership in CB, Plume has a beneficial ownership interest in the securities of STRX and APBX, both of which he recommended as "buys." The most obvious conflict that must always be disclosed involves relationships between an issuer and the member, the candidate, or his or her firm. For the purposes of Standard VI(A), members and candidates beneficially own securities or other investments if they have a direct or indirect pecuniary interest in the securities, have the power to direct the voting of the shares of the securities or investments, or have the power to dispose of or direct the disposition of the security or investment.

B is incorrect. Plume does not need to own shares in STRX and APBX directly to have a beneficial interest in the two companies. His ownership of CB's preferred shares and its common stock options, along with CB's voting control of each company, gives him a beneficial ownership interest in STRX and APBX. This situation creates a conflict of interest that requires disclosure.

C is incorrect. Plume's ownership of CB's preferred shares and its common stock options give him a beneficial ownership interest in STRX and APBX. This beneficial interest leads to the conflict of interest that requires disclosure of his holding of CB's Class A preferred shares and options on CB common stock.

3. Did Plume violate the Code and Standards by not disclosing in his research report his annual bonus based on his IPO work?

   A. Yes

   B. No, because it does not represent an additional compensation arrangement

   C. No, because it does not affect his duty of loyalty, prudence, and care to clients

Solution:

A is correct. By not disclosing his annual bonus in his research report, Plume is in violation of Standard I(B) Independence and Objectivity, which states, "Members and Candidates must use reasonable care and judgment to achieve and maintain independence and objectivity in their professional activities. Members and Candidates must not offer, solicit, or accept any gift, benefit, compensation, or consideration that reasonably could be expected to compromise their own or another's independence and objectivity."

Plume's annual bonus is equal to 0.10% of the gross proceeds for each IPO he works on with the corporate finance department. Can a member or candidate remain objective if on behalf of the firm, the member or candidate obtains or assists in obtaining fees for service? As a sell-side analyst, Plume may be encouraged by Global or CB to write potentially biased research reports about particular companies (i.e., the ones in CB's portfolio) to the exclusion of covering companies that may be more suitable for Global's clients. The guidance for Standard I(B) states, "Compensation arrangements should not link analyst remuneration directly to investment banking assignments in which the analysts may participate as a team member." The guidance also states, "Having analysts work with investment bankers is appropriate only when the conflicts are adequately and effectively managed and disclosed. Firm managers have a responsibility to provide an environment in which analysts are neither coerced nor enticed into issuing research that does not reflect their true opinions. Firms should require public disclosure of actual conflicts of interest to investors." Global can avoid the conflict by removing this incentive from Plume's compensation package.

B is incorrect. Plume's bonus is based on the gross proceeds of each IPO he works on, and so it does constitute an additional compensation arrangement. The compensation arrangement creates a conflict of interest that must be disclosed.

C is incorrect. Because Plume's bonus is based on the gross proceeds of each IPO he works on, it is reasonable to expect that his independence and objectivity may be compromised. This arrangement links his compensation directly to his participation in his investment banking assignments and thus creates a conflict of interest.

4. Did Plume violate the Code and Standards by selling APBX short in his personal portfolio?

   A. Yes

   B. No, because he was not a beneficial owner of APBX

   C. No, because he sold the shares short after issuing his research report

Solution:

A is correct. By selling ABPX short in his personal portfolio, Plume is in violation of Standard VI(A) Avoid or Disclose Conflicts, which states that "Members and Candidates must avoid or make full and fair disclosure of all matters that could reasonably be expected to impair their independence and objectivity or interfere with respective duties to their clients, prospective clients, and employer. Members and Candidates must ensure that such disclosures are prominent, are delivered in plain language, and communicate the relevant information effectively." Selling APBX short in his personal portfolio while having a "buy" recommendation on the stock is a conflict of interest that Plume needs to disclose. Global could avoid this conflict by prohibiting such transactions by its employees.

B is incorrect. Plume's ownership of CB's preferred shares and its common stock options, along with CB's voting control of each company, gives him a beneficial ownership interest in STRX and APBX. Selling APBX short after he issues a "buy" recommendation creates a conflict of interest that Plume must disclose to clients.

C is incorrect. Selling APBX short after he issues a "buy" recommendation creates a conflict of interest that Plume must disclose to clients.

CASTLE BIOTECHNOLOGY CASE 2: SANDRA BENNING, CFA, AND CLARIS DEACON

4

- ☐ evaluate practices, policies, and conduct relative to the CFA Institute Code of Ethics and Standards of Professional Conduct
- ☐ explain how the practices, policies, or conduct does or does not violate the CFA Institute Code of Ethics and Standards of Professional Conduct

Sandra Benning, CFA, is an investment adviser (broker) at Global and a rising star because of her exceptional skill in brokering stocks and developing relationships. Her clients include corporations, their senior executives, pension plans, and high-net worth individuals. Benning recently joined Global after working as an investment adviser at Kodiak Securities. While at Kodiak, she used her personal social media platforms, such as LinkedIn, X, and Facebook, as well as "old fashioned" email, to communicate with her clients. After she resigned from Kodiak, she immediately used her social media accounts to inform her clients of her departure and solicited them to follow her to Global. Global paid her a signing bonus of $250,000 based on the percentage of her Kodiak clients who moved their accounts to Global. One of the reasons Benning joined Global was to give her clients greater access to Global's initial public offerings. Global pays its investment advisers an annual year-end bonus based on the level of their clients' IPO participation. Benning does not disclose either bonus to clients.

KNOWLEDGE CHECK

1. Did Benning violate the Code and Standards in her use of social media and email to solicit former clients?

   A. No

   B. Yes, because Benning has a duty of loyalty to Kodiak

   C. Yes, because Benning is not preserving her clients' confidentiality

   Solution:

   A is correct. Benning's solicitation of former clients via social media does not violate the Code and Standards. Standard IV(A) Loyalty states, "The Code and Standards also do not prohibit former employees from contacting clients of their previous firm, in the absence of a noncompete agreement." In the absence of a noncompete agreement, as long as Benning maintains her duty of loyalty to Kodiak before joining Global, does not take steps to solicit clients until she has left Kodiak, and does not use material from Kodiak without the firm's permission after she has left the firm, she is not in violation of the Code and Standards.

   B is incorrect. In this case, Benning did not solicit clients until after she resigned from Kodiak. Benning used her personal social media platforms to connect with her clients, and she did not contact them until after she resigned from Kodiak. She did not use material from Kodiak without the firm's permission.

C is incorrect. Benning did not reveal confidential client information in her use of social medial to solicit former clients.

2. Did Benning violate the Code and Standards by not disclosing to clients the signing bonus received from Global to bring clients over from Kodiak?

   A. Yes

   B. No, because the bonus is not a referral fee

   C. No, because the bonus represents additional compensation

Solution:

A is correct. By not disclosing to her Kodiak clients the signing bonus she received from Global, Benning is in violation of Standard VI(A) Avoid or Disclose Conflicts. Benning's decision to solicit her Kodiak clients to move to Global could have been influenced by the fact that her signing bonus from Global was based on the percentage of her Kodiak clients who moved their accounts to Global. This creates an actual or potential conflict of interest that she must disclose to her former Kodiak clients. Global can avoid this conflict by not compensating Benning in this way.

According to Standard VI(A) Avoid or Disclose Conflicts, "Members and Candidates must avoid or make full and fair disclosure of all matters that could reasonably be expected to impair their independence and objectivity or interfere with respective duties to their clients, prospective clients, and employer." Standard VI(A) protects investors and employers by requiring members and candidates to avoid or fully disclose to clients, potential clients, and employers all actual and potential conflicts of interest.

B is incorrect. It is true that the bonus paid by Global represents compensation paid by the employer to the employee for services provided and is not a referral fee. It is also true, however, that the signing bonus could reasonably be expected to impair Benning's independence and objectivity or interfere with her respective duties to her clients, prospective clients, and her employer, which is in violation of Standard I(B). If such a potential conflict of interest exists, Standard VI(A) requires Benning to fully and fairly disclose it. Referral fees are defined in Standard VI(C) Referral Fees as "any compensation, consideration, or benefit received from or paid to others for the recommendation of products or services." Members and candidates must disclose referral fees to their employers, clients, and prospective clients, as appropriate.

C is incorrect. Additional compensation is defined in Standard IV(B) Additional Compensation Arrangements as "gifts, benefits, compensation, or consideration that competes with or might reasonably be expected to create a conflict of interest with their employer's interest unless they obtain written consent from all parties involved." Additional compensation arrangements generally refer to conflicts of interest the member or candidate has with their employer, not clients and prospects. The bonus does not represent additional compensation. It does, however, create an actual/potential conflict of interest.

3. Does Benning's non-disclosure of her year-end bonus that is based on the level of her clients' IPO participation place her in violation of the Code and Standards?

   A. No

   B. Yes, because the bonus represents a conflict of interest

   C. Yes, because the bonus represents additional compensation

   Solution:

   B is correct. Benning's year-end bonus is based on the level of her clients' participation in IPOs. This situation creates a conflict of interest between Benning and her clients. Is she recommending IPOs to clients based on their best interest or hers? Benning is in violation of Standard VI(A) Avoid or Disclose of Conflicts, which states that "Members and Candidates must avoid or make full and fair disclosure of all matters that could reasonably be expected to impair their independence and objectivity or interfere with respective duties to their clients, prospective clients, and employer. Members and Candidates must ensure that such disclosures are prominent, are delivered in plain language, and communicate the relevant information effectively." Global can avoid this conflict by not compensating Benning in this way.

   A is incorrect. Benning's year-end bonus is based on the level of her clients' participation in IPOs, which creates a conflict of interest between Benning and her clients that must be avoided or disclosed under Standard VI(A). Global can avoid this conflict by not compensating Benning in this way.

   C is incorrect. The bonus is not additional compensation, which is defined in Standard IV(B) as "gifts, benefits, compensation, or consideration that competes with or might reasonably be expected to create a conflict of interest with their employer's interest." In this case, the bonus is between the employer and the employee and does not create a conflict of interest between Global and Benning. The year-end bonus does, however, create a conflict of interest between Benning and her clients that must be disclosed under Standard VI(A). Global can avoid this conflict by not compensating Benning in this way.

Currently, Global is planning a highly anticipated initial public offering for Frontier Therapeutics (FTSX), a company in CB's portfolio. To determine interest in this IPO, Benning contacts her clients via social media and email and invites them to submit an application to participate in the FTSX public offering. In the invitation, she cautions her clients that "confirming your indication of interest does not guarantee an allocation of shares in the offering." She also warns that "depending on client demand, clients requesting IPO shares might receive all, some, or none of the shares they requested." On highly anticipated (oversubscribed) IPOs, Global's policy is to allocate the IPO shares to institutional clients who plan on purchasing additional shares on the first day of trading. Following Global's policy, Benning calls her institutional clients who expressed an interest in FTSX to ask if they plan on purchasing additional shares of FTSX on its first day of trading. For clients who indicate they plan on buying additional shares, Benning will allocate shares of FTSX to them in the IPO.

Once all client indications of interest have been submitted, Global then uses this information to determine an offering price for FTSX and the "basis of allotment" (i.e., the number of shares to be allocated) to each adviser/broker for their clients.

Global uses the following criteria to make its IPO allocation decisions:

- The level of business a client has conducted with the firm
- The long- or short-term interest of a client in the issuer

- The size of a client's anticipated long-term investment
- The client's track record of investment in similar issues
- The client's apparent interest in the issuer, as evidenced by attendance at road shows
- The size of the client's account
- The existing or potential business relationships between the client and Global

The day before FTSX's first day of trading (public listing), Benning emails her high-net-worth individual clients who were allocated shares of FTSX and warns them not to flip (sell) their shares when FTSX begins trading or else they will be excluded from future IPO allocations. She then phones her corporate clients (those with an existing investment banking relationship with Global) and tells them they are free to sell their shares of FTSX at the end of its first trading day. The following day, at the end of trading, FTSX's stock price closes down, at 65% of its initial offering price.

KNOWLEDGE CHECK

1. Does Benning violate the Code and Standards by allocating FTSX shares to institutional clients who plan on purchasing additional shares when it begins trading?

   A. Yes

   B. No, because Benning is following her employer's policy

   C. No, because Benning is treating all her clients fairly

   Solution:

   A is correct. This is an example of a tie-in agreement, where the underwriter requires the investor to buy more shares of a new issue in the secondary market as a condition of buying shares in the IPO. It is intended to artificially increase demand and support a higher share price. Tie-in agreements are a violation of Standard II(B) Market Manipulation: "Members and Candidates must not engage in practices that distort prices or artificially inflate trading volume with the intent to mislead market participants." By allocating shares of FTSX to institutional clients who agree to purchase additional shares on the first day of trading, Global and Benning may be distorting security prices or trading volume on the first day of trading by deceiving investors that rely on information in the market. The guidance for Standard II(B) states, "Transaction-based manipulation involves instances where a member or candidate knew or should have known that his or her actions could affect the pricing of a security." It appears that Benning and Global are artificially creating demand for FTSX shares (and increasing its price on the first day of trading) by allocating IPO shares only to clients who plan to purchase additional shares on the first day of trading.

   This practice also violates Standard III(B) Fair Dealing: "Members and Candidates must deal fairly and objectively with all clients when providing investment analysis, making investment recommendations, taking investment action, or engaging in other professional activities." In this case, Benning is not treating all her institutional clients fairly, because she is allocating IPO shares only to those clients who agree to purchase additional shares after FTSX begins trading on the first day. The overall criteria and policy used by Global to determine client allocations also are in violation of Standard III(B).

B is incorrect. Irrespective of whether she followed her employer's policy, Benning's actions are in violation of Standard II(B) Market Manipulation and Standard III(B) Fair Dealing.

C is incorrect. In this case, Benning is not treating all her institutional clients fairly because she is only allocating IPO shares to those clients who agree to purchase additional shares after FTSX begins trading on the first day. Benning's allocation to institutional investors violates Standard III(B) Fair Dealing: "Members and Candidates must deal fairly and objectively with all clients when providing investment analysis, making investment recommendations, taking investment action, or engaging in other professional activities."

Claris Deacon

Benning's newest client is Claris Deacon, a long-time family friend. To date, Deacon has made three visits to Benning's office to set up her investment account and portfolio. During her first visit, she completed and signed a New Account Agreement and a Limited Trade Authorization form, giving Benning discretion to transact securities in Deacon's account. During Deacon's second visit, she opened a cash management account that linked her brokerage account to an in-house checking (transaction) account. In her third visit, Deacon completed and signed an Option Account Application and Agreement, authorizing Benning to transact equity options in her account. After the third visit, Benning changed some of the language in the Option Account Application and Agreement pertaining to Deacon's suitability for the options she would be recommending. To save Deacon from having to make yet another trip to her office to initial the changes on the form, Benning initials the form on Deacon's behalf.

While traveling with her husband a week later, Deacon calls Benning because she is unable to transfer money from her brokerage account to her checking account. Upon further investigation, Benning discovers that the link between the accounts had not been activated. Proud of the superior customer service she provides to her clients, Benning immediately calls her client and obtains Deacon's authorization to sign the Account Linking form on Deacon's behalf. Within 24 hours, Deacon has access to her account.

A month later, Benning receives a phone call from Deacon's husband, Steve, who informs her that his wife is having serious health issues. He asks Benning to redeem $15,000 worth of mutual fund shares and send the proceeds as soon as possible. Over the next few weeks, Benning completes several redemptions and withdrawals from Deacon's account at Steve's request. Benning makes a note on the trade form each time a redemption is processed, indicating she has spoken with Steve, who is acting on Deacon's behalf.

KNOWLEDGE CHECK

1. In opening and servicing Deacon's account, does Benning violate the Code and Standards?

   A. Yes

   B. No, because Benning was acting in Deacon's best interest

C. No, because Benning was exercising prudent judgment, loyalty, and reasonable care

Solution:

A is correct. By changing the language on the Option Account Application and Agreement and initialing the form on behalf of Deacon, Benning is in violation of Standard I(D) Misconduct. Signing the Account Linking form on behalf of Deacon is also a violation of Standard I(D). According to Standard I(D) Misconduct, "Members and Candidates must not engage in any professional conduct involving dishonesty, fraud, or deceit or commit any act that reflects adversely on their professional reputation, integrity, or competence." The approval Benning received over the telephone to sign the Account Linking form is insufficient. Benning needs Deacon to personally sign the authorization.

By redeeming shares and transacting (withdrawals) in Deacon's account at her husband's request, Benning is in violation of Standard III(A) Loyalty, Prudence, and Care. Benning has no authority or authorization from Deacon, the account holder, allowing Deacon's husband, Steve, to redeem shares and approve withdrawals from her account. To transact in the account, Steve would need to be a cosigner on all the account documents or have a "power of attorney" written authorization signed by Deacon granting him the right to act on Deacon's behalf. According to Standard III(A), "Members and Candidates have a duty of loyalty to their clients and must act with reasonable care and exercise prudent judgment." Members and candidates must also be aware of whether they have "custody" or effective control of client assets. If so, a heightened level of responsibility arises.

B is incorrect. Even if Benning was acting in Deacon's best interests by making and initialing the changes on the Option Account Application and Agreement form and signing the Account Linking form, these changes cannot be implemented without Deacon's own written approval and thus are in violation of the Standards. In addition, she should not have transacted in Deacon's account at her husband's request without Deacon's authorization.

C is incorrect. Benning is *not* showing loyalty, prudence, or care by taking actions that violate Standard III(A). These actions include making and initialing the changes on the Option Account Application and Agreement form and signing the Account Linking form. These changes cannot be effected without Deacon's own written approval and are in violation of the Standards. In addition, Benning should not have transacted in Deacon's account at her husband's request without Deacon's authorization.

5 LIONSGATE LIMITED & BANK OF AUSTRALIA CASE 1

- ☐ evaluate practices, policies, and conduct relative to the CFA Institute Code of Ethics and Standards of Professional Conduct
- ☐ explain how the practices, policies, or conduct does or does not violate the CFA Institute Code of Ethics and Standards of Professional Conduct

Lionsgate Limited (LL) is a publicly listed Australian fund manager.[4] The firm has benefited greatly from the Superannuation Guarantee program that was created in 1992. This program requires all the country's employees aged 18–70 to contribute a percentage of their earnings to a tax-advantaged retirement account or superannuation fund. In addition, legislation enacted in 2005 gives all employees the right to select a superannuation fund administered by a retail financial services company, such as LL. LL offers a range of mutual funds.

Tony Hill and Team

LL's flagship fund is the Lionsgate Victory Capital Fund (VCF), an equity mutual fund that is managed by Tony Hill and his team of 16 analysts. In LL's marketing material, Hill states, "For the period ending 31 December 2018, the Victory Capital Fund is the best-performing fund in Australian equities over the 10-year period. The VCF has delivered returns of 28.7%, gross of fees over the 1-year period, and 13.2% annually since inception in 2005. During this time, assets under management (AUM) in Australian dollars increased from $18 million to $14 billion."

Hill has become the main media engagement person for the VCF and LL. He has a half-hour show on Sky News Business Channel, writes a weekly financial column for the *Australian Financial Review*, and regularly appears on daytime and evening talk shows, where he talks about the VCF and its holdings. Like the other guests on these shows, Hill does not receive financial compensation for his appearances. Instead, the shows' sponsors provide him with "thank you gift bags," containing wine, retail gift cards, restaurant gift certificates, and travel discounts on hotels and airfare. Hill does not disclose the receipt of these gift bags to LL.

In 2006, Nicole Martin, CFA, was hired as an intern at LL to cover the paper, chemical, and publishing industries. After graduating at the top of her class from a prestigious university, Nicole accepted a full-time position on Hill's team, covering the metals, mining, and energy industries. As Hill's outside activities increased, Martin assumed more responsibility for security selection and investment decision making for the VCF. For the past three years, the performance of the VCF has been directly attributable to her and the other analysts, although both she and Hill still state publicly that he is in charge of all investment decision making for the VCF.

As the VCF's "star stock picker," Hill is often invited to provide a fund update at LL's quarterly board meetings. Hill uses the most recent board meeting to announce his resignation and to notify the board he is starting his own fund management firm. Recognizing Hill's departure could have a negative impact on LL's stock price as well as cash flows into the VCF, the board asks Hill to keep his plans to resign confidential until the end of LL's fiscal year (in two weeks) to give it time to find his replacement. Hill agrees. After the board meeting, Hill has a "closed door" meeting with his team and announces his plan to resign and start his own firm. He then asks the team if they want to join him. Ten of the analysts agree to resign with him and work in his new firm. Martin and the five remaining analysts tell him they will remain at LL, and they leave the meeting. Hill tells the analysts who will join him, "Team, we have a lot of work to do over the next two weeks. We'll need to use time after work and on weekends to lease office space and to individually register with the government authorities in the name of our new firm. Since we have not signed a noncompete agreement with LL, we can begin soliciting former clients the day we open our new firm."

4 This case is by Susan Morey and Michael G. McMillan, PhD, CFA, in *Ethics Cases*. Consistent with the 11th Edition of the *Standards of Practice Handbook*.

KNOWLEDGE CHECK

1. Do Hill's statements in the Lionsgate Limited marketing materials violate the Code and Standards?

   A. No

   B. Yes, because he stated the Victory Capital Fund's returns gross of fees

   C. Yes, because he is not distinguishing between fact and opinion in discussing the fund's performance

   Solution:

   A is correct. There is no evidence to suggest Hill's statements are false or opinion based. In speaking about the fund's performance, Hill is stating facts. In addition, Hill states the performance is gross of fees or "pre-fees." According to Standard III(D) Performance Presentation, "When communicating investment performance information, Members and Candidates must make reasonable efforts to ensure that it is fair, accurate, and complete." The guidance for Standard III(D) states, "Members and candidates can also meet their obligations under Standard III(D) by including disclosures that fully explain the performance results being reported (for example, stating, when appropriate, that results are simulated when model results are used, clearly indicating when the performance record is that of a prior entity, or disclosing whether the performance is gross of fees, net of fees, or after tax)."

   B is incorrect. Hill states the performance is gross of fees or "pre-fees." The guidance for Standard III(D) states, "Members . . . can also meet their obligations under Standard III(D) by including disclosures that fully explain the performance results being reported (for example, . . . disclosing whether the performance is gross of fees, net of fees, or after tax)."

   C is incorrect. It is clear in this case that in speaking about the fund's performance, Hill is stating facts, not opinions.

2. Does Hill violate the Code and Standards by accepting "thank you gift bags" from the talk show sponsors?

   A. No

   B. Yes, because he does not disclose this to his employer

   C. Yes, because his independence and objectivity are being compromised

   Solution:

   A is correct. According to Standard IV(B) Additional Compensation Arrangements, "Members and Candidates must not accept gifts, benefits, compensation, or consideration that competes with or might reasonably be expected to create a conflict of interest with their employer's interest unless they obtain written consent from all parties involved." Hill's appearance on these shows does not create a conflict of interest with the interests of LL or the VCF.

   B is incorrect. No conflict of interest is created in this situation. By not disclosing his receipt of the "thank you gift bags," Hill is not in violation of the Code and Standards.

   C is incorrect. Hill's acceptance of the "thank you gift bags" does not create a conflict of interest between Hill and his employer or between Hill and his clients. Therefore, Hill's independence and objectivity are not compromised. Hill is not in violation of Standard I(B) Independence and Objectivity.

3. Has Martin or Hill violated the Code and Standards by publicly stating that Hill is in charge of investment decision making for the VCF?

A. Yes

B. No, because Hill still works for the VCF

C. No, because Martin and Hill both publicly state that Hill is in charge of investment decision making

Solution:

A is correct. Martin and Hill have failed to disclose to clients and prospective clients that Martin has assumed more responsibility for security selection and investment decision making at the fund and that she and the other analysts—not Hill—are primarily responsible for the fund's performance. Martin and Hill both violated Standard V(B) Communication with Clients and Prospective Clients: "Members and Candidates must: 1. Disclose to clients and prospective clients the basic format and general principles of the investment processes they use to analyze investments, select securities, and construct portfolios and must promptly disclose any changes that might materially affect those processes."

B is incorrect. Although Hill still works for the VCF, Martin has assumed more responsibility for security selection and investment decision making at the VCF, such that she and the other analysts are primarily responsible for the fund's performance.

C is incorrect. While Martin and Hill both publicly state Hill is in charge, it is not true. Martin—not Hill—is now primarily responsible for security selection and investment decision making at the VCF.

4. Did Hill violate the Code and Standards with respect to announcing his resignation in the "closed door" meeting with his team?

A. No

B. Yes, he should not have announced his plan to resign to his team.

C. Yes, he should have publicly announced his resignation immediately after the board meeting.

Solution:

B is correct. Hill violated the Code and Standards by telling his team about his planned resignation after the board's request that he keep this information strictly confidential until fiscal year end (in two weeks). Despite the board's request, Hill informed his team the same day. Hill's conduct violates Standard IV(A): Duties to Employers, Loyalty. While the board's request may be considered as an outward-facing directive, it can also be considered an internally-facing directive. By telling his team about his resignation after the board's request that he keep this information confidential until fiscal year end, Hill is not honoring the board's request and is being disloyal to his employer. Hill would have been free to discuss his resignation with his team prior to his informing the board of his plans and prior to the board's request for confidentiality.

A is incorrect. Hill did violate Standard IV(A): Loyalty. By telling his team about his resignation after the board's request that he keep this information confidential until fiscal year end, Hill is not honoring the board's request and is being disloyal to his employer.

C is incorrect. There is no duty under the Code and Standards for Hill to announce his resignation immediately after the board meeting.

5. Did Hill violate the Code and Standards by asking his team to join him at his new firm?

   A. No

   B. Yes, because Hill was the supervisor of the team

   C. Yes, because Hill owed a duty of loyalty to his current employer

Solution:

A is correct. It is not a violation for Hill to ask his team to join him at his new firm. The Guidance to Standard IV(A): Duties to Employers, Loyalty states, "A departing employee is generally free to make arrangements or preparations to go into a competitive business before terminating the relationship with his or her employer as long as such preparations do not breach the employee's duty of loyalty." Asking his team to join him at his new firm does not breach the duty of loyalty. However, any planning and activity on behalf of the new firm (such as the leasing of office space and individual registration) must be done by Hill and the individuals joining him on their own time.

B is incorrect. The fact that Hill was the supervisor of the team does not change his responsibility to his employer under Standard IV(A). Thus, he was not in violation of this Standard for the reasons given in the answer to A.

C is incorrect. Hill does owe a duty to his employer under Standard IV(A); however, asking his team to join him at his new firm does not breach the duty of loyalty under the criteria of this standard. Thus, Hill is not in violation of the Code and Standards.

6. Did Hill and his team violate the Code and Standards by leasing office space for the new firm and registering with the government authorities before resigning from Lionsgate?

   A. No

   B. Yes, because Hill and his team owe a duty of loyalty to Lionsgate

   C. Yes, because Hill and his team owe a duty of loyalty to Lionsgate's clients

Solution:

A is correct. It is not a violation for Hill and the team to lease office space and register with the government authorities before resigning from Lionsgate. According to Standard IV(A): Duties to Employers, Loyalty, "In matters related to their employment, Members and Candidates must act for the benefit of their employer and not ... cause harm to their employer." Moreover, Guidance to Standard IV(A) states, "A departing employee is generally free to make arrangements or preparations to go into a competitive business before terminating the relationship with his or her employer as long as such preparations do not breach the employee's duty of loyalty." Hill and the team are making preparations outside of work and on weekends; their actions to start a new business do not occur during hours when their employer would expect them to be at work. Thus, they are not in violation of the standard. Hill and the team are also not violating Standard III(A): Duties to Clients, Loyalty, Prudence, and Care because their actions are taking place during non-work hours, not when they should be working for the benefit of their clients.

B is incorrect. Hill and the individuals joining him at the new firm are using their time outside of work and on weekends to lease office space and to individually register with government authorities. Because they are not using work time, they are not breaching their duty of loyalty to Lionsgate, as defined in Standard IV(A): Duties to Employers, Loyalty.

C is incorrect. In using their time outside of work and on weekends to plan for the new firm, Hill and his team are not placing their own interests ahead of their clients' interests. They are not in violation of Standard III(A): Duties to Clients, Loyalty, Prudence, and Care.

7. Did Hill violate the Code and Standards by telling his team to begin soliciting former clients the day they open the new firm?

A. No

B. Yes, because Hill owes a duty of loyalty to Lionsgate

C. Yes, because Hill has a responsibility as their supervisor

Solution:

A is correct. Hill is not in violation of the Code and Standards. The Guidance to Standard IV(A): Duties to Employers, Loyalty states, "When members and candidates are planning to leave their current employer, they must continue to act in the employer's best interest. They must not engage in any activities that would conflict with this duty until their resignation becomes effective." The Guidance also states, "A member or candidate who is contemplating seeking other employment must not contact existing clients or potential clients prior to leaving his or her employer for purposes of soliciting their business for the new employer." By telling his team to begin solicitation on the new firm's opening day—not prior to its opening—there is no conflict of interest or violation of loyalty.

B is incorrect. The Guidance to Standard IV(A): Duties to Employers, Loyalty states, "When members and candidates are planning to leave their current employer, they must continue to act in the employer's best interest. They must not engage in any activities that would conflict with this duty until their resignation becomes effective." The Guidance also states, "A member or candidate who is contemplating seeking other employment must not contact existing clients or potential clients prior to leaving his or her employer for purposes of soliciting their business for the new employer." Hill tells his team to begin client solicitation on the new firm's opening day, not prior to its opening. At that time, Hill and his team will no longer work for Lionsgate.

C is incorrect. Hill is not violating Standard IV(C): Duties to Employers, Responsibilities of Supervisors. According to this standard, "Members and Candidates must make reasonable efforts to ensure that anyone subject to their supervision or authority complies with applicable laws, rules, regulations, and the Code and Standards." Hill did not ask anyone under his supervision to violate any of the Standards.

6 LIONSGATE LIMITED & BANK OF AUSTRALIA CASE 2

- [ ] evaluate practices, policies, and conduct relative to the CFA Institute Code of Ethics and Standards of Professional Conduct
- [ ] explain how the practices, policies, or conduct does or does not violate the CFA Institute Code of Ethics and Standards of Professional Conduct

Rob Portman, CFA, is a salesperson at LL who oversees the sales of the VCF to institutions and high-net-worth individuals. For each of the past five years, Portman has achieved his annual sales goal and has received a sizable bonus as a result. Portman is hoping this year will be no different. With two weeks remaining in LL's fiscal year, Portman is planning a big event next week for prospective clients that he hopes will enable him to achieve his sales goal.

Portman knows how much "prestige" institutional clients and high-net-worth individuals place on having Hill manage their money. To make the fund more attractive to prospective and current clients, Portman always discusses Hill's stock-picking acumen and Hill's success as the key investment decision maker for the VCF. In addition, he always invites Hill to meetings with important clients. However, when clients have investment-related questions about the fund's purchases and sales, he always refers them to Martin, who he refers to as Hill's "assistant."

Tonight is Portman's big event. Since LL's board meeting, Portman has heard rumors about Hill and members of his team leaving the firm. To clarify Hill's situation, Portman meets with LL's chief investment officer (CIO), who attended the recent board meeting. The CIO tells Portman to ignore the rumors about Hill and proceed with his planned event. Later that day, Portman learns from Sky News Business Channel that the CIO and two board members have sold shares in LL and the VCF. As a result, Portman sells his shares in LL and the VCF.

KNOWLEDGE CHECK

1. Did Portman violate the Code and Standards by inviting Hill to important client meetings and discussing Hill's stock-picking acumen?

   A. No

   B. Yes, because Portman is misrepresenting Hill's role in the investment process to clients

   C. Yes, because Portman is misrepresenting the VCF investment strategy and its limitations and risks

   Solution:

   B is correct. By inviting Hill to client meetings and referring to Martin as Hill's "assistant," Portman is giving clients the impression that Hill is responsible for stock selection and investment decision making at the fund. Portman is in violation of Standard I(C) Misrepresentation: "Members and Candidates must not knowingly make any misrepresentations relating to investment analysis, recommendations, actions, or other professional activities."

   A is incorrect. Portman is in violation of Standard I(C) Misrepresentation. By inviting Hill to client meetings and referring to Martin as Hill's "assistant," Portman is giving clients the impression that Hill is responsible for stock selection and investment decision making at the fund.

C is incorrect. Although Portman is misrepresenting Hill's role in executing the VCF's investment strategy, he is not misrepresenting the investment strategy itself.

2. Did Lionsgate's CIO and the two board members violate the Code and Standards by selling their shares in LL and the VCF?

   A. No

   B. Yes, because they owe a duty of loyalty to Lionsgate

   C. Yes, because they acted on material nonpublic information

Solution:

C is correct. By selling their shares before Hill's resignation was announced, they acted on material nonpublic information. According to Standard II(A) Material Nonpublic Information, "Members and Candidates who possess material nonpublic information that could affect the value of an investment must not act or cause others to act on the information." Information is "material" if its disclosure would probably have an impact on the price of a security or if reasonable investors would want to know the information before making an investment decision.

A is incorrect. They are clearly in violation of Standard II(A) Material Nonpublic Information.

B is incorrect. Although the CIO and two board members do owe a duty of loyalty to Lionsgate, they are not in violation of Standard IV(A) Loyalty by selling their shares in LL and the VCF. Instead, they are in violation of Standard II(A) Material Nonpublic Information.

3. Did Portman violate the Code and Standards by selling his shares in LL and the VCF?

   A. No

   B. Yes, because he owes a duty of loyalty to Lionsgate

   C. Yes, because he is acting on material nonpublic information

Solution:

A is correct. In this case, Portman does not know definitively whether Hill is resigning. In addition to the rumors he heard, Portman's sell decision is based on learning from Sky News Business Channel that the CIO and two board members sold their shares. Portman's decision to sell is not based on material nonpublic information, because this information was publicly reported. He is not in violation of Standard II(A) Material Nonpublic Information.

B is incorrect. Although Portman does owe a duty to his employer, Lionsgate, he is not in violation of Standard IV(A) Loyalty by selling his shares in LL and the VCF.

C is incorrect. In selling his shares in LL and the VCF, Portman is not acting on material nonpublic information and therefore is not in violation of Standard II(A) Material Nonpublic Information.

Kirk Graeme, CFA

Lionsgate Limited is partially owned by the Bank of Australia Financial Group (BOA). BOA consists of a retail bank, a capital market division (investment and corporate banking), and a wealth management division. Kirk Graeme, CFA, is a financial adviser in BOA's wealth management division. He is regarded as a subject matter expert at the firm because of the well-supported research he does on new issues and his experience in buying and selling them.

Although all accounts that Graeme manages are fee based, he does receive additional commissions (paid by the issuer) for new issue purchases.

BOA (through its capital market group) is a member of the syndicate for new issues purchased by Graeme. As a syndicate member, BOA also shares in fees and commissions paid by the issuer. BOA's policy does not require commission disclosure on new issues since clients receive prospectuses for new issue purchases that disclose commissions paid to the syndicate member. Graeme, however, does disclose his new issue commissions to clients who ask for this information.

In 2016 and 2017, Graeme earned a total of $477,000 in commissions from new issues, while BOA earned fees and commissions of $1,908,900 on the same transactions. From 2016 to 2017, Graeme's assets under management remained relatively unchanged; however, Graeme more than doubled the dollar value of new issue purchases relative to his AUM. Unfortunately, many of these new issues performed poorly. By the end of 2017, Graeme had sold—often significantly below purchase price—many of the issues he purchased in 2016. Despite the underperformance, Graeme continues to research and recommend new issues following the same process he has always used.

KNOWLEDGE CHECK

1. Did Graeme violate the Code and Standards with respect to his disclosure of new issue commissions earned on sales only to those clients who ask for the information?

   A. No, he does not need to disclose the commissions, because BOA's policy does not require it.

   B. No, he does not need to disclose the commissions, because clients receive this disclosure in the prospectuses for the new issues.

   C. Yes, he does need to disclose the commissions.

   Solution:

   C is correct. Graeme is in violation of Standard VI(A) Avoid or Disclose Conflicts, which states that "Members and Candidates must avoid or make full and fair disclosure of all matters that could reasonably be expected to impair their independence and objectivity or interfere with respective duties to clients, prospective clients, and employer. Members and Candidates must ensure that such disclosures are prominent, are delivered in plain language, and communicate the relevant information effectively." Graeme can avoid the conflict by not accepting commissions from new issues. If he does not avoid the conflict, Graeme must inform all clients, not just those who ask, of the commissions he receives on new issues so that his clients have the information necessary to evaluate the objectivity of the investment advice or action taken by him on their behalf.

   A is incorrect. There is a violation because the commissions could reasonably be expected to impair Graeme's objectivity. Standard VI(A) requires Graeme to disclose the conflict of interest that these commissions create to all his clients regardless of BOA's policy in this regard.

B is incorrect. There is a violation because the commissions could reasonably be expected to impair Graeme's objectivity. Graeme can avoid the conflict by not accepting the commissions. If he accepts the commissions, Standard VI(A) requires Graeme to disclose the conflict created by these commissions to all his clients regardless of what appears in the prospectuses of the new issues.

The Delaneys

In January 2017, Graeme opened a $250,000 joint account for Melissa and Rodney Delaney. During their initial conversation, the Delaneys stated that the account represented the majority of their investable assets, that their investment time horizon was 15–20 years, and that they had a low tolerance for risk. After this conversation, approximately half of Graeme's recommended purchases to the Delaneys were new issues; new issues represented approximately three-quarters of the dollar value of all purchases in their account. Between January and October 2017, the longest period of time that a new issue was held in their account was five months. Since opening the Delaneys' account, the majority of purchases were new issues. During this period, Graeme also made new issue purchases for the majority of his other client accounts.

At the end of 2017, Graeme met with his supervisor, Jane Balmer. During the meeting, Balmer raised concerns about the turnover in Graeme's accounts and his use of new issues. Balmer also escalated her concerns by reporting them to BOA's director of compliance. After his meeting with Balmer, Graeme significantly reduced his new issue purchases and turnover in his "book of business."

KNOWLEDGE CHECK

1. Did Graeme violate the Code and Standards in managing the Delaneys' account?

   A. No

   B. Yes, because their risk tolerance is low

   C. Yes, because their time horizon is 15–20 years

Solution:

B is correct. The Delaneys stated that their risk tolerance is low, which means they were unwilling to accept high levels of volatility in their portfolio. By purchasing new issues in their account and holding them for less than five months, Graeme's actions are unsuitable for the Delaneys' risk tolerance. As stated, the majority of the purchases Graeme made for the Delaneys were new issue purchases. Graeme violated Standard III(C) Suitability: "When Members and Candidates are in an advisory relationship with a client, they must: . . . b. determine that an investment is suitable to the client's financial situation and consistent with the client's written objectives, mandates, and constraints before making an investment recommendation or taking investment action." In addition, members and candidates must "judge the suitability of investments in the context of the client's total portfolio."

A is incorrect. Graeme violated Standard III(C) by purchasing new issues for the Delaneys' account that were unsuitable for the Delaneys' risk tolerance.

C is incorrect. It is the Delaneys' low risk tolerance—not their long time horizon—that makes the purchase of new issues unsuitable. Graeme violated Standard III(C).

2. Did Balmer follow the Code and Standards in addressing her concerns about Graeme's use of new issues?

   A. No

   B. Yes, because she escalated her concerns to the director of compliance

   C. Yes, because she raised her concerns with Graeme, who responded accordingly

   Solution:

   A is correct. Balmer violated Standard IV(C) Responsibilities of Supervisors, which states that "Members and Candidates must make reasonable efforts to ensure that anyone subject to their supervision or authority complies with applicable laws, rules, regulations, and the Code and Standards." Moreover, the guidance for this standard states, "Once a supervisor learns that an employee has violated or may have violated the law or the Code and Standards, the supervisor must promptly initiate an assessment to determine the extent of the wrongdoing. Relying on an employee's statements about the extent of the violation or assurances that the wrongdoing will not reoccur is not enough." Balmer should have initiated an investigation to ascertain the extent of Graeme's wrongdoing.

   B is incorrect. Rather than just escalating her concerns to the director of compliance, Balmer should have initiated an investigation to ascertain the extent of Graeme's wrongdoing.

   C is incorrect. Rather than just raising her concerns with Graeme, Balmer should have initiated an investigation to ascertain the extent of Graeme's wrongdoing.

David Milgram

Five years ago, Graeme opened an account for David Milgram, a 67-year-old retired chemical engineer. At that time, Graeme worked with Milgram to set Milgram's investment policy statement, which has remained in place ever since. Last month, Milgram sent a written complaint to Graeme's supervisor, Jane Balmer, titled "Request for an Urgent Review of My Account." In the complaint letter, Milgram stated, "I am concerned about the dismal performance of my account. The decrease in value is causing me considerable alarm. As a result, I would like to meet with you and Graeme. I am wondering about setting a new direction and getting a second opinion on the suitability of my holdings. At this point, however, I want to hear Graeme's side of the story and make a plan to stop the decline in my account value and get out of this mess."

After receiving the letter, Balmer calls Graham into her office to discuss the complaint and Milgram's account. However, she does not report Graeme or the complaint to BOA's director of compliance. The next day, Graeme meets with Balmer and Milgram at BOA's office. During the meeting, Graeme reviews Milgram's portfolio and updates the investment policy statement that he created when Milgram opened his account. Graeme also discusses the quality of the securities in Milgram's portfolio and advises him that he should not focus on the portfolio value alone. Satisfied with Graeme's explanation, Milgram leaves BOA's office.

KNOWLEDGE CHECK

1. Did Graeme violate the Code and Standards in the handling of Milgram's account?

   A. Yes

   B. No, because he updates Milgram's investment policy statement

   C. No, because he reviews Milgram's portfolio and the quality of security holdings with him

   Solution:

   A is correct. Graeme did not update Milgram's IPS for five years after it was first put in place. Graeme violated Standard III(C) Suitability. The guidance for Standard III(C) states that "updating the IPS should be repeated at least annually and also prior to material changes to any specific investment recommendations or decisions on behalf of the client."

   B is incorrect. Graeme has not updated Milgram's IPS since it was first put in place five years ago, which places him in violation of Standard III(C).

   C is incorrect. Graeme has not updated Milgram's IPS since it was first put in place, which places him in violation of Standard III(C).

2. Did Balmer violate the Code and Standards in the handling of Milgram's complaint?

   A. No

   B. Yes, because she did not report the complaint to BOA's department of compliance

   C. Yes, because she did not initiate an investigation of the complaint

   Solution:

   A is correct. Balmer did not violate the Code and Standards. As soon as she was made aware of the complaint, she initiated an investigation by calling Graeme into her office. She sat in on the meeting, where Graeme reviewed Milgram's account and IPS. According to Standard IV(C) Responsibilities of Supervisors, "Members and Candidates must make reasonable efforts to ensure that anyone subject to their supervision or authority complies with applicable laws, rules, regulations, and the Code and Standards." According to the guidance for this standard, "Once a supervisor learns that an employee has violated or may have violated the law or the Code and Standards, the supervisor must promptly initiate an assessment to determine the extent of the wrongdoing. Relying on an employee's statements about the extent of the violation or assurances that the wrongdoing will not reoccur is not enough."

   B is incorrect. Reporting the misconduct up the chain of command and warning the employee to cease the activity are not enough to meet Standard IV(C). Instead, as soon as Balmer received the complaint, she initiated an investigation by calling Graeme into her office to discuss and review Milgram's account. This is the requirement of Standard IV(C).

   C is incorrect. Balmer did initiate an investigation by summoning Graeme into her office to discuss the complaint. Balmer continued her investigation by attending the meeting with Milgram when Graeme reviewed Milgram's account and IPS.

7 GABBY SIM

- ☐ evaluate practices, policies, and conduct relative to the CFA Institute Code of Ethics and Standards of Professional Conduct
- ☐ explain how the practices, policies, or conduct does or does not violate the CFA Institute Code of Ethics and Standards of Professional Conduct

Global Harvest Bank (GHB) is an independent private bank that offers clients a range of services, including advisory lending and banking solutions, investment management, succession planning, tax reporting, and custody services.[5] GHB is headquartered in Singapore and has offices in Hong Kong SAR, Luxembourg, Zurich, and the Cayman Islands.

Gabby Sim was hired by GHB after graduating with first-class honors in finance from an international two-year MBA program. On her first day at the bank, Sim meets with her supervisor and the chief investment officer of GHB, Ahmad Yousoff, CFA, who oversees her onboarding experience.

After meeting with Sim, Yousoff meets with the president of GHB, Irene Wong, and two board members, David Tan and Audrey Chuong, CFA, to discuss the memorandum of understanding (MOU) that was recently signed by MGM2, a new institutional client. MGM2 is a strategic investment and development company that is wholly owned by the government of Saspara through its Ministry of Finance. The mission of MGM2 is to promote Sasparian economic development through global partnerships and foreign direct investment. Tan and Chuong have worked tirelessly over the past year to build a relationship with MGM2 on behalf of GHB. As a reward for their hard work, Yousoff and Wong decided to pay Tan and Chuong a portion of the annual investment advisory fees generated by MGM2. Yousoff did not disclose this fee-sharing arrangement in the MOU he provided to MGM2. During the meeting, Chuong asks Yousoff to meet with Bo Hie, a Sasparian businessman who helped found MGM2 and also played an instrumental role in developing relations between GHB and MGM2. Chuong, however, does not tell Yousoff that Hie recently hired her son in an executive role in his company.

KNOWLEDGE CHECK

1. Did Yousoff violate the Code and Standards by not disclosing the fee-sharing arrangement in the MOU?

   A. Yes

   B. No, because it is a fee-sharing arrangement and not a referral fee

5 This case is by Laurel Teo, CFA, and Michael G. McMillan, PhD, CFA, in *Ethics Cases*. Consistent with the 11th edition of the *Standards of Practice Handbook*.

C. No, because the referral fee arrangement was decided after the relationship with MGM2 had been established

Solution:

B is correct. Yousoff is not in violation of the Code and Standards. The fee-sharing arrangement is a reward paid to Tan and Chuong for their efforts to bring MGM2 on as a client. The fee arrangement is not a referral fee. Tan and Chuong did not refer MGM2 to GHB. A referral fee is compensation, consideration, or benefit received from or paid to others for the recommendation of products or services.

For referral fees, Standard VI(C) Referral Fees applies: "Members and Candidates must disclose to their employer, clients, and prospective clients, as appropriate, any compensation, consideration, or benefit received from or paid to others for the recommendation of products or services." The guidance for this standard explains, "Appropriate disclosure means that members and candidates must advise the client or prospective client, before entry into any formal agreement for services, of any benefit given or received for the recommendation of any services provided by the member or candidate."

A is incorrect. The fee-sharing arrangement is a reward paid to Tan and Chuong for their efforts to bring MGM2 on as a client. It is not a referral fee, so they are not in violation of Standard VI(C) Referral Fees.

C is incorrect. The fee-sharing arrangement is not a referral fee, so Yousoff does not have to disclose this arrangement in the MOU. Yousoff would need to disclose the arrangement if payment represented a conflict of interest. However, the case facts provide no evidence that a conflict of interest is present.

2. Did Chuong violate the Code and Standards by not disclosing information about her son to Yousoff?

   A. No

   B. Yes, because this situation represents a conflict of interest

   C. Yes, because Chuong is misrepresenting her relationship with Hie

Solution:

B is correct. Hie's hiring of Chuong's son in an executive position at Hie's firm could reasonably be expected to impair Chuong's independence and objectivity with respect to interactions between MGM2 and GHB. Standard VI(A) Avoid or Disclose Conflicts requires Chuong to disclose this conflict.

A is incorrect. A conflict of interest exists, and Chuong violated the Code and Standards by not disclosing the hiring of her son by Hie.

C is incorrect. This situation is not a violation of Standard I(C) Misrepresentation. By not disclosing information about her son, Chuong did not knowingly make any misrepresentation relating to investment analysis, recommendations, actions, or other professional activities.

Busy setting up the MGM2 account, Yousoff asks Sim to meet with Hie. During their meeting, Hie tells Sim that he wants to open an account in the name of his firm, Bad Moon Rising, Ltd. Sim has Hie complete and sign the Application for Opening an Account/Custody Account for Legal Entities and the Establishment of the Beneficial Owner's Identity form, which identifies him as the sole beneficial owner of the Bad Moon Rising account. Hie also completes and signs the Resolutions form, which lists Hie as the sole authorized signatory on the account. Included in the account opening documents is a copy of a page from Hie's Sasparian passport, which includes his photograph. Hie then presents Sim with a check for $15 million that is drawn on one of his personal bank accounts located in the Cayman Islands. When Sim begins to ask the firm's required questions for new clients on investment experience, objectives, and risk tolerance, Hie interrupts her and states, "I am a very busy man and do not have time to answer all these questions. Initially, I only plan to invest in short-term US government (risk-free) securities in this account, so your questions are irrelevant. Later, I plan to invest in securities in other asset classes. In addition, because of the confidential nature of my business relationships, please destroy all notes you have made during this meeting and use the following fact sheet to document our conversation":

Occupation:	Consultant
Employer:	Self-employed
Net Worth:	$110 million
Investment Objective:	Long term
Return Goal:	5%–10% per year
Risk Profile:	Conservative

Before leaving the meeting, Hie tells Sim, "You can expect a number of large deposits into my account from MGM2 over the next few months. Some of these deposits will then be wired to other accounts that I have set up around the world. If you process these transactions in a timely manner, I will pay you a bonus at the end of the year. In addition, since you are fluent in English, Mandarin Chinese, and a number of Chinese dialects, such as Hokkien and Cantonese, I will be referring a number of my elderly Chinese relatives to you. Many of them live in Singapore and either do not understand English or have little knowledge of the language. To this end, please meet with my mother-in-law, Madam Tan Swee Neo."

Hie continues, "Lastly, because of the sensitive nature of my work with MGM2 and the large sums of money involved, do not talk to anyone about this account or its transactions. Please do not email or correspond in writing to me concerning the Bad Moon Rising account. Instead, call me on my cell phone or instant message me to notify me whenever a deposit is received and a withdrawal has been executed." Sim agrees, and Hie concludes the meeting by telling Sim, "If you need any more information, please talk with GHB board members Tan and Chuong, who I am sure can answer any additional questions that you may have." Later that day, Sim uses the fact sheet that Hie provided to prepare his investment policy statement and destroys the other notes she took during their meeting. When she meets with Yousoff to tell him about her meeting with Hie, she does not mention the bonus that Hie has promised to pay her at the end of the year. Sim opens the account for Hie.

KNOWLEDGE CHECK

1. Did Sim violate the Code and Standards by fulfilling Hie's request to destroy documentation of their conversation?

   A. Yes

   B. No, because Sim is preserving Hie's confidentiality

   C. No, because Sim is exercising her duty of loyalty, prudence, and care

Solution:

A is correct. Sim violated Standard V(C) Record Retention: "Members and Candidates must develop and maintain appropriate records to support their investment analyses, recommendations, actions, and other investment-related communications with clients and prospective clients." The guidance for Standard V(C) states, "Members and candidates must retain records that substantiate the scope of their research and reasons for their actions or conclusions." Some examples of supporting documentation include "notes from clients from meetings to review investment policy statements." By destroying all notes from their meeting, Sim is not maintaining appropriate records to support her investment actions.

B is incorrect. Sim has a duty to her firm to retain records supporting her recommendations to and actions for clients of the firm. Keeping these records in no way compromises her duty of confidentiality to Hie under Standard III(E) Preservation of Confidentiality.

C is incorrect. The destruction of the documentation is not directly related to the actions considered necessary under Standard III(A) Loyalty, Prudence, and Care.

2. Did Sim violate the Code and Standards by not disclosing her bonus arrangement with Hie to Yousoff?

A. Yes

B. No, because the bonus will not create a conflict of interest

C. No, because the bonus does not represent additional compensation

Solution:

A is correct. By not disclosing her bonus arrangement with Hie, Sim violated the Code and Standards. According to Standard IV(B) Additional Compensation Arrangements, "Members and Candidates must not accept gifts, benefits, compensation, or consideration that competes with or might reasonably be expected to create a conflict of interest with their employer's interest unless they obtain written consent from all parties involved." Hie's promise of a bonus if Sim processes his transactions in a timely manner could conflict with Sim's responsibilities to her other clients or other clients of GHB.

Sim also violated Standard I(B) Independence and Objectivity. Per the guidance for the standard, "Members and candidates may accept bonuses or gifts from clients as long as they disclose them to their employer. . . . Disclosure is required, however, so that supervisors can monitor such situations to guard against employees favoring a gift-giving client to the detriment of other fee-paying clients."

B is incorrect. Hie's bonus has the potential to create a conflict of interest for Sim, thus jeopardizing her independence and objectivity. At a minimum, Sim must disclose the bonus arrangement to Yousoff, her employer.

C is incorrect. Hie's bonus is additional compensation to Sim. At a minimum, Sim must disclose the bonus arrangement to Yousoff, her employer.

3. In opening Hie's account, did Sim violate the Code and Standards?

A. Yes

B. No, because Hie plans to invest in risk-free securities

C. No, because Hie signed the required forms and provided Sim with a fact sheet with all the necessary information

Solution:

A is correct. Sim did not complete the required section on Hie's investment experience, objectives, and risk tolerance of new clients; the information Hie provided was not sufficient for Sim to develop an appropriate IPS. Sim violated Standard III(C) Suitability. The guidance for the standard states, "When an advisory relationship exists, members and candidates must gather client information at the inception of the relationship. Such information includes the client's financial circumstances, personal data (such as age and occupation) that are relevant to investment decisions, attitudes toward risk, and objectives in investing. This information should be incorporated into a written investment policy statement (IPS) that addresses the client's risk tolerance, return requirements, and all investment constraints (including time horizon, liquidity needs, tax concerns, legal and regulatory factors, and unique circumstances)."

B is incorrect. A client's statement regarding his or her desired investment strategy, especially without a fully formed IPS, does not meet the requirements of Standard III(C) Suitability.

C is incorrect. The fact sheet does not provide enough information for Sim to develop an investment policy statement for Hie; therefore, Sim's actions violate the requirements of Standard III(C) Suitability.

Two days after the Bad Moon Rising account is opened, $70 million is wired into it from an MGM2 account in Saspara. When Sim calls Hie to notify him about this deposit and ask what he wants to do with it, Hie tells her that a portion of the money will be used "to purchase real estate for MGM2 in the United States." He then faxes her a copy of an investment agreement between MGM2, as the client, and Bad Moon Rising, as the investment manager. According to this agreement, MGM2 was a "founding investor in Bad Moon Rising that wishes to support and assist Bad Moon Rising in realizing its purpose by providing an initial capital contribution of $70 million."

Sim, however, has concerns about the deposit size and justification for the $70 million deposit since it is from a state-owned entity, so she discusses it with Yousoff. Sim's plan is to set up another meeting with Hie and an official from MGM2, who can confirm the deposit and further explain the source and use of the deposit. Yousoff, however, tells her not to do this since Hie already provided documentation from MGM2 in the form of the investment agreement. Instead, Yousoff suggests to Sim that she speak with Tan and Chuong. That afternoon, Sim calls the two GHB board members to tell them about the $70 million deposit in Hie's account and faxes them a copy of the investment agreement Hie provided. After reviewing this information, Tan and Chuong confirm its validity and Hie's role with MGM2.

KNOWLEDGE CHECK

1. Did Yousoff violate the Code and Standards by instructing Sim to speak with Tan and Chuong?

   A. Yes

   B. No, because Tan and Chuong know and have worked with Hie

   C. No, because Hie already submitted documentation confirming the source and purpose of the $70 million deposit

Solution:

A is correct. Suggesting that Sim speak with Tan and Chuong does not absolve Yousoff of his responsibilities as a supervisor. Yousoff violated Standard IV(C) Responsibilities of Supervisors: "Members and Candidates must make reasonable efforts to ensure that anyone subject to their supervision or authority complies with applicable laws, rules, regulations, and the Code and Standards." In this case, Yousoff should have encouraged Sim to arrange a meeting with Hie and an official of MGM2 to confirm the source and purpose of the funds.

B is incorrect. A reasonable effort would have involved Sim arranging a meeting with Hie and an official of MGM2 (and ideally Yousoff also) to confirm the source and purpose of the funds. Neither Tan nor Chuong have firsthand knowledge of the actual transaction under scrutiny.

C is incorrect. Sim has expressed concern about the documentation of the transaction (its size and justification). Under Standard IV(C), Yousoff is required to make a reasonable effort to detect violations of the laws, rules, and the Code and Standards. Accepting the existing documentation violates this duty.

2. Did Sim violate client confidentiality by talking to Tan and Chuong about Hie's account?

A. Yes

B. No, because Hie instructed Sim to speak with Tan and Chuong

C. No, because Tan, Chuong, and Hie worked together to develop the relationship between GHB and MGM2

Solution:

B is correct. Hie has given specific permission to Sim to seek information from Tan and Chuong when he tells her as they conclude their meeting together, "If you need any more information, please talk with GHB board members, Tan and Chuong, who I am sure can answer any additional questions that you may have." As a result, Sim did not violate the Code and Standards in her disclosure of confidential information regarding her client, Hie.

According to the guidance for Standard III(E) Preservation of Confidentiality, the standard "requires that members and candidates preserve the confidentiality of information communicated to them by their clients, prospective clients, and former clients. This standard is applicable when (1) the member or candidate receives information because of his or her special ability to conduct a portion of the client's business or personal affairs and (2) the member or candidate receives information that arises from or is relevant to that portion of the client's business that is the subject of the special or confidential relationship."

According to the standard, then, a member or candidate can break confidence when permission is granted by the client. In this case, Hie has given his permission to Sim by telling her to seek information as needed from board members Tan and Chuong, so Sim is not in violation of the Code and Standards.

A is incorrect. Hie gave her permission to speak with Tan and Chuong, so Sim did not violate Standard III(E) Preservation of Confidentiality by disclosing confidential information about Hie.

C is incorrect. The fact that Tan, Chuong, and Hie worked together to develop the relationship between GHB and MGM2 does not allow Sim to discuss Hie's information with Tan and Chuong. Sim did not violate Standard III(E), however, because Hie gave her permission to speak with Tan and Chuong.

Over the next few months, MGM2 wires a total of $100 million into the Bad Moon Rising account in four separate transactions. Each transfer is a foreign exchange transaction completed through financial institutions in Saspara and processed through different US correspondent bank accounts. To justify these substantial fund transfers from MGM2, Hie tells Sim that MGM2 has entered into a number of real estate purchase agreements that he will be handling for them. He also provides her with copies of several agreements that are signed by Yousoff, GHB's CIO. Hie later transfers most of the $100 million to his bank accounts in Switzerland, Luxembourg, and the Cayman Islands.

Sim, however, remains suspicious about the size and frequency of the activity in Hie's account, so she meets with Yousoff to discuss her concerns. During the meeting, Sim tells Yousoff, "Hie recently transferred $50 million into and out of his account in less than a week. I can't find any reason or motivation for why this transaction had to pass through his GHB account and not come directly from the MGM2 account to its real estate partners. I believe that Hie may be using this account to launder money." In response, Yousoff tells her, "As Hie's investment adviser, your job should be to focus on processing these transactions in a timely manner. Remember, the president and the board of directors are watching you. Given that two of our board members established this relationship with MGM2, we have to assume that these board members represented the will of the bank's owners as far as these relationships and transactions are concerned. Therefore, we have to be very careful about how we handle their transactions and ensure they are handled smoothly, efficiently, and quickly. I have reviewed the large number of deposits and withdrawals in Hie's account, and my only concern is the speed with which they are processed."

KNOWLEDGE CHECK

1. Based on Yousoff's response to Sim about the transactions in Hie's account, what is the first course of action for Sim to take?

   A. Contact GHB's compliance department.

   B. Contact the regulator in her jurisdiction.

   C. Take no action since she has informed Yousoff of her concerns.

   Solution:

   A is correct. The guidance for Standard I(A) Knowledge of the Law states, "When in doubt about the appropriate action to undertake, it is recommended that a member or candidate seek the advice of compliance personnel or legal counsel concerning legal requirements. If a potential violation is being committed by a fellow employee, it may also be prudent for the member or candidate to seek the advice of the firm's compliance department or legal counsel."

   B is incorrect. Informing Yousoff produced no action toward resolving the concerns Sim has, and so according to Standard I(A), the next step for Sim is to seek the advice of compliance personnel or legal counsel regarding her concerns. The guidance for Standard I(A) states, "Although the Code and Standards do not compel members and candidates to report violations to their governmental or regulatory organizations unless such disclosure is mandatory under applicable law, . . . such disclosure may be prudent under certain circumstances."

   C is incorrect. Informing Yousoff produced no action toward resolving the concerns Sim has regarding these transactions. According to Standard I(A), Sim's responsibility is to take the next step and seek the advice of compliance personnel or legal counsel regarding her concerns.

Per Hie's request, Sim meets with Madam Tan Swee Neo for the first time. Madam Tan is a 70-year-old retired seamstress who has made her fortune buying and selling real estate. Since retiring from her job, Madam Tan has put most of her life savings in fixed deposits (certificates of deposit). Periodically, she invests the balance in the equities of lower-risk energy utility companies when she receives tips from her friends and relatives. Recently, however, her goals changed. She now wants to invest even more of her portfolio in conservative equities so that she can pay for her grandchildren's private school and college expenses.

Madam Tan tells Sim that she heard from her friends about an oil-linked structured note sold by GHB. "My friends tell me that these notes pay 10% a year, which is much higher than what I can get from fixed deposits. My energy stocks have been doing so badly; I need something new," Madam Tan adds. Sim offers Madam Tan a brochure on the structured note; however, the brochure is in English, which Madam Tan does not read. Sim provides a verbal summary of the product overview in Mandarin, explaining to Madam Tan that the product's return is linked to the performance of a basket of oil futures indexes. Although Sim does not translate the note's full terms and conditions in fine print, she does caution Madam Tan that the 10% annual coupon payment is not guaranteed and that while there is full principal protection if held to maturity, there will be a penalty for early redemption of the note, which matures in seven years. She also tells Madam Tan that since the product was launched three years ago, the conditions for coupon payment have been met every year. Madam Tan is not sure what oil futures are or how they work. Nevertheless, she decides to put $50,000 into the notes. Sim executes the transaction at Madam Tan's request.

KNOWLEDGE CHECK

1. Did Sim violate the Code and Standards by purchasing oil-linked structured notes for Madam Tan?

   A. Yes

   B. No, because Madam Tan asked her to purchase the notes

   C. No, because she warned Madam Tan that the 10% annual coupon payment is not guaranteed

   Solution:

   A is correct. Sim violated Standard III(C) Suitability. The structured notes are unsuitable for Madam Tan. Although Madam Tan has previously invested in real estate, since retiring, she has invested in fixed deposits and lower-risk energy utility stocks. She now wishes to invest more of her portfolio in conservative equites. In addition, Madam Tan shares that she is unsure what oil futures are or how they work.

   The guidance for Standard III(C) states that it "requires that members and candidates who are in an investment advisory relationship with clients consider carefully the needs, circumstances, and objectives of the clients when determining the appropriateness and suitability of a given investment or course of investment action. . . . Members and candidates may receive requests from a client for trades that do not properly align with the risk and return objectives outlined in the client's investment policy statement. These transaction requests may be based on the client's individual biases or professional experience. Members and candidates will need to make reasonable efforts to balance their clients' trading requests with their responsibilities to follow the agreed-on investment policy statement."

   B is incorrect. In this case, Sim violated Standard III(C) Suitability because the structured notes are not suitable for Madam Tan given her investment needs and objectives. The guidance for the standard states, "Members and candidates will need to make reasonable efforts to balance their clients' trading requests with their responsibilities to follow the agreed-on investment policy statement." When the transaction may have a material impact on the portfolio, the client's IPS should be updated to ensure the client understands the potential effect of the requested trade on his or her risk/return targets.

C is incorrect. Simply warning Madam Tan that the annual coupon is not guaranteed is insufficient to show Madam Tan that structured notes are not suitable for her investment needs and objectives. Handing Madam Tan a brochure written in English on the structured note has little value if she doesn't understand English and therefore is insufficient to meet Standard III(C).

A year later, Madam Tan is upset when she does not receive any payments from the structured notes. While visiting with her relatives in a neighboring country, she hears from her nephew who works at the state oil company that oil prices are likely to continue to slide over the next several years. Alarmed that this will worsen her investment, Madam Tan phones Sim. She tells Sim to immediately redeem the structured notes and switch the funds into a three-month fixed deposit. Sim suggests that Madam Tan consider the full costs and risks involved in redeeming before proceeding further, but Madam Tan says she cannot spend too much time on expensive international calls and instructs Sim to just "act on it right away." Because Madam Tan called Sim on her mobile phone rather than her office phone, Sim is not able to record the conversation. Sim completes the transactions because of the urgency of the request.

When Madam Tan returns home from her travel, she is shocked to find that her original $50,000 investment has shrunk to $30,000 upon redemption. She calls Sim and demands an explanation. Sim reminds her that she warned Madam Tan about the early redemption penalty a year ago when Madam Tan was considering the product. Madam Tan exclaims, "Yes, but I didn't realize the penalty would be so high! And I thought the product would be low risk since you told me there have been payments in each of the last three years." Outraged at the 40% loss in what had been half of her life savings, Madam Tan files a complaint against Sim.

KNOWLEDGE CHECK

1. In redeeming Madam Tan's structured notes and switching her funds to a fixed deposit, did Sim violate the Code and Standards?

   A. Yes

   B. No, because Sim followed Madam Tan's request to redeem the structured notes immediately

   C. No, because Sim has acted with reasonable care and prudent judgment

   Solution:

   A is correct. Sim violated Standard III(A) Loyalty, Prudence, and Care by redeeming the structured notes. Sim did not act with reasonable care or prudent judgment in executing the redemption immediately without fully explaining the associated costs to Madam Tan and investigating how the economic environment might impact the risk of the structured notes. It can also be argued that she violated Standard III(C) Suitability. According to the guidance for this standard, it "requires that members and candidates who are in an investment advisory relationship with clients consider carefully the needs, circumstances, and objectives of the clients when determining the appropriateness and suitability of a given investment or course of investment action. . . . Members and candidates may receive requests from a client for trades that do not properly align with the risk and return objectives outlined in the client's investment policy statement. These transaction requests may be based on the client's individual biases or professional experience. Members and candidates will need to make reasonable efforts to balance their clients' trading requests with their responsibilities to follow the agreed-on investment policy statement."

B is incorrect. Madam Tan's request to immediately redeem the structured notes was not in alignment with her IPS and reflected her lack of experience. In this circumstance, Standard III(C) requires Sim to make a reasonable effort to balance Madam Tan's request with her stated IPS objectives of investing in conservative equities so that she can pay for her grandchildren's private school and college expenses.

C is incorrect. Sim did not act with reasonable care or prudent judgment by immediately executing the redemption of the structured notes without first ensuring she fully explained the associated costs to Madam Tan. Sim also should have investigated whether Madam Tan's fears regarding the economic environment and its impact on the risk of the structured notes had any justification before she executed the redemption. Sim violated Standard III(A) Loyalty, Prudence, and Care.

PRACTICE PROBLEMS

The following information relates to questions 1-6

Jason Locke, CFA, has recently been hired as the chief investment officer of the Escarpment Regional Government Employees' Pension Fund (the Fund). Currently, he is conducting evaluations of all external managers employed by the Fund to ensure that they are providing the highest possible returns for their mandates while complying with all applicable laws and regulations.

Locke is evaluating the activity of Niagara Growth Managers (NGM), a local money manager with an allocation of 10% of the Fund's assets. He realizes that any reduction in the allocation to this local manager will be met with considerable political pressure. The investment policy statement for NGM's portion of the Fund's assets states that NGM is to actively manage an equity portfolio of local small-cap, high-tech companies.

Upon his review of NGM's activity, Locke is concerned about two items that he would like to have explained. At a meeting with NGM's portfolio manager, Emma Black, CFA, Locke asks her to comment on each item:

Commodity Positions

> **Locke:** "Over the last year, several large positions in commodities have been taken by the Fund's portfolio. This is inconsistent with the IPS."
>
> **Black:** "Commodities have significantly outperformed high-tech equities recently. I added commodities to larger clients' portfolios on a temporary basis. Clients were not informed, because the positions will be sold once market sentiment shifts. I have not managed commodities before, but I am getting good returns."
>
> **Locke:** "I am uncomfortable with these investments in this portfolio."

IPO Share Allocation

> **Locke:** "The Fund's portfolio received 50,000 shares of an initial public offering on 1 April. On 15 May, 30,000 shares were removed at the current market price."
>
> **Black:** "There was a problem with NGM's IPO allocation algorithm. Initially, you were overallocated. When we discovered the error, your account was adjusted."
>
> **Locke:** "Short-term interest should have been credited to the Fund for use of its cash to cover the trade. In any case, this was an IPO of a large international high-tech company. It was not an appropriate investment for the portfolio."

After the meeting, Locke is not satisfied with Black's comments and decides that further action is required. He also decides that he will allow NGM to continue to manage Fund assets until he finishes his evaluation. This decision is based on the superior returns of the NGM-managed assets, the significant diversification this portfolio adds to the Fund, and the political implications of firing the local money manager.

The next week, Locke calls Black and outlines several conditions that must be fulfilled for NGM to continue as a manager for the Fund. One of the conditions outlined relates to trade allocation.

Trade Allocation

> **Locke:** "Provide written trade allocation procedures consistent with the CFA Institute Standards of Professional Conduct."
>
> **Black:** "I will mail you a copy of our new procedures stating that trade allocations must be reviewed at the end of each month against the client's IPS. They also say that interest will be credited to accounts that have been incorrectly allocated shares and debited from those accounts that should have received shares."

With his evaluation complete, Locke must now consider whether to retain NGM as one of the Fund's asset managers.

1. According to the CFA Institute Standards of Professional Conduct, Locke owes his primary duty of loyalty in managing the Fund to:

   A. the plan trustees.

   B. all the pension plan beneficiaries.

   C. the Escarpment regional government.

2. With respect to the commodity positions, which of the following actions *best* describes Black's violation of the CFA Institute Standards of Professional Conduct? Black violated the Standards by:

   A. buying an asset class in which she has no prior management experience.

   B. buying assets that are inconsistent with the portfolio's investment policy statement.

   C. failing to notify the client that she would temporarily deviate from the client's investment policy statement.

3. With regard to the IPO share allocation, are NGM's method of trade correction on 15 May and Locke's demand for a short-term interest credit consistent with the CFA Institute Standards of Professional Conduct?

   A. Yes

   B. No, only the method of trade correction is consistent.

   C. No, only the demand for a short-term interest credit is consistent.

4. After his initial meeting with Black, does Locke's decision to allow NGM to continue managing the portfolio violate the CFA Institute Standards of Professional Conduct?

   A. No

   B. Yes, because he allowed political factors to influence his decision

   C. Yes, because he is obligated to immediately suspend NGM until he finishes his evaluation

5. With regard to Locke's condition regarding trade allocation, does Black's response violate the Standards of Professional Conduct with respect to allocation

reviews *and* interest adjustments?

A. Yes

B. No, it violates the Standards only with respect to allocation reviews.

C. No, it violates the Standards only with respect to interest adjustments.

6. Based on his complete evaluation, what is Locke's *best* course of action with respect to NGM's management of the Fund's assets?

A. Reduce NGM's allocation of the Fund's assets until NGM has demonstrated its compliance with Locke's conditions.

B. Eliminate NGM as a manager since Locke cannot be sure that NGM will act fairly and in accordance with the Fund's IPS.

C. Maintain NGM's allocation of the Fund's assets, and concentrate on evaluating managers with larger proportions of the Fund's assets or with substandard performance.

The following information relates to questions 7-12

Elias Nano, a recent MBA graduate and a Level II candidate in the CFA Program, is an unpaid summer intern with Patriarch Investment Counsel and expects to be offered a full-time paid position in the fall. Through his efforts, he is able to convince some family members and friends to become clients of the firm, and he now assists with the management of their accounts. His supervisor congratulates him and states, "These clients are the foundation from which you will be able to build your career as an investment adviser." After working hard all summer, Nano is told that Patriarch will not be able to offer him a paid position.

Nano interviews with a number of firms and tells each one about the accounts that he is managing and expects to be able to bring with him. Because he was merely an intern at Patriarch, he does not believe he owes any particular loyalty to Patriarch. He also believes that he can keep the clients because his former supervisor implied that these were Nano's clients.

Nano subsequently joins Markoe Advisers as an assistant director with supervisory responsibilities. Markoe Advisers is an investment management firm that advertises that it provides customized portfolio solutions for individual and institutional clients. As a matter of policy, Markoe Advisers does not reject as a client any individual meeting the account minimum size. Markoe Advisers has two strategies—aggressive growth equity and growth equity—and is always fully invested. Nano asks his family and friends to transfer their accounts from Patriarch to Markoe Advisers.

As the first CFA candidate to be employed by Markoe Advisers, Nano has been asked to head a team that is reviewing the firm's compliance policies and procedures, which Nano considers inadequate and incomplete. He states his concerns to the firm's president, Mr. Markoe: "Although Markoe Advisers, as a firm, cannot adopt the CFA Institute Code of Ethics and Standards of Professional Conduct, the firm can adopt the CFA Institute Asset Manager Code." Mr. Markoe tells Nano that the firm is considering acquiring another advisory firm that has similar compliance policies and procedures. Mr. Markoe says, "We are not going to consider any compliance changes at this time."

Nano decides to draft a model compliance document to guide discussions about future compliance issues at the firm. Nano's initial draft includes the following components of a compliance policy statement:

- **Performance Presentation**

  Performance data must be documented for each of Markoe Advisers' active accounts, be disclosed upon request, and be compared with the firm's composite, which is composed of active accounts only. Performance data must be presented on a before-tax basis to all clients, with the disclosure that all performance data are presented gross of fees.

- **Suitability of Investments**

  Markoe Advisers, to maintain consistency of performance, will assign each client to one of the firm's two portfolios. Both of these portfolios will be sufficiently broadly diversified to meet the investment objectives of all our clients.

- **Disclosures of Conflicts**

  Markoe Advisers encourages its staff to be involved in the business and civic community. Only business or civic interests that relate to current portfolio holdings need to be reported to the firm.

- **Violations**

  Any violation of the Markoe Advisers compliance policy statement will be reported to the president, and employees will receive an official warning.

- **Compensation**

  All staff members of Markoe Advisers will discuss with their supervisor all outside compensation that they are receiving or may receive.

7. Does Nano comply with the CFA Institute Standards of Professional Conduct when he asks his clients to transfer their accounts to Markoe Advisers?

   A. No

   B. Yes, because he contacted the clients after leaving Patriarch

   C. Yes, because he was an intern and not a paid employee of Patriarch

8. Is Nano's statement with respect to adoption of the CFA Institute Code of Ethics and Standards of Professional Conduct and the CFA Institute Asset Manager Code, respectively, correct?

	CFA Institute Code and Standards	CFA Institute Asset Manager Code
A	No	No
B	No	Yes
C	Yes	No

9. According to the CFA Institute Code and Standards, what action should Nano take after discussing the firm's compliance policy with Mr. Markoe? Nano should:

   A. resign from the firm.

   B. notify the board of directors.

C. decline to accept supervisory responsibilities.

10. Does Nano's draft compliance policy statement conform to the Code and Standards with respect to performance presentation?

    A. No, because terminated accounts are excluded

    B. No, because performance is reported to all clients gross of fees

    C. No, because performance data are presented on a before-tax basis

11. Does Nano's draft compliance policy statement conform to the CFA Institute Code and Standards with respect to suitability of investments and disclosures of conflicts?

	Suitability of investments	Disclosures of conflicts
A	No	No
B	No	Yes
C	Yes	No

12. Does Nano's draft compliance policy statement conform to the CFA Institute Code and Standards with respect to violations and compensation?

	Violations	Compensation
A	No	No
B	No	Yes
C	Yes	No

The following information relates to questions 13-18

Patricia Jollie, CFA, is the fixed-income analyst and portfolio manager at Mahsud Financial Corporation, a small investment firm.

On 5 April, a friend who works for a bond-rating agency mentions to Jollie that a bond the agency is analyzing will experience a rating change. That bond also happens to be in Mahsud Financial's portfolios. Not wanting to trade ahead of the rating change announcement, Jollie decides to wait for distribution of the information through her friend's scheduled interview on a business television program on the afternoon of 8 April. On the morning of 8 April, the information is released on a worldwide financial news service. Jollie immediately changes her mind about waiting for the interview and trades the bonds in Mahsud Financial's portfolios.

On 8 April, Jollie also trades a second bond to rebalance one of Mahsud Financial's portfolios. Jollie knows before executing her transaction that the bond is thinly traded. Although Jollie's trade will materially affect the bond's market price, it is not her intention to create price movement. A colleague witnesses the trade and large bond price change and says, "What a market overreaction; the bond price appears to be distorted now!" The colleague also points out to Jollie that Mahsud Financial's policy on market manipulation states, "Mahsud Financial employees must refrain from making transactions that distort security prices or volume with the intent to mislead market participants."

In conducting fixed-income research, Jollie believes that insight into prospective corporate bond returns can be derived from information that is also relevant to a company's stock. She spends several hours a week in equity investment chat rooms on the internet, and she pays particular attention to the research reports posted by Jill Dean, CFA, a self-employed analyst, on www.Jill_Dean_the_Independent_Analyst.com. Prior to writing each report, Dean is paid a flat fee by the companies whose stocks she researches, but she does not reveal this fact to readers of her reports. She produces reports only for those companies whose stocks she can legitimately give "buy" recommendations after conducting a thorough analysis. Otherwise, she returns the flat fee. Investors have come to recognize all her "buy" ratings as having a sound and reasonable basis.

Jollie considers Dean's summaries and forecasts to be very well crafted. Dean has given Jollie written permission to use her summaries and forecasts, word for word and without attribution, in her own bond analysis reports. On occasion, Jollie has done so. In Dean's other internet postings, she reports the results of relevant academic finance studies. Once Jollie learns of a study by reading Dean's postings, she often reads the original study and mentions the results in her own reports. Jollie always cites the original study only and does not reveal that she learned of the study through Dean.

Mahsud Financial occasionally sponsors seminars on ethics. In the most recent seminar, the main speaker made statements about the relationship between ethics and the law and also about potential conflict of interest sources for research analysts. The seminar speaker's statements were as follows:

Statement 1	An illegal action is unethical, and actions that are legal are ethically sound.
Statement 2	For analysts, a major source of conflict of interest is potential profit resulting from a weak barrier between the employer's research department and investment banking department.
Statement 3	For situations in which conflicts of interest cannot be avoided, Mahsud Financial's written compliance policy should include the following component: "For unavoidable conflicts of interest that the employee judges to be material, employees must disclose the conflicts of interest to clients prominently and in plain language."
Statement 4	On the matter of gifts that might impair employees' objectivity, Mahsud Financial's written compliance policy should also include the following component: "Employees must disclose to Mahsud Financial all client gifts regardless of value."

13. Did Jollie violate the CFA Institute Standards of Professional Conduct by trading on the news of the bond-rating change?

    A. No

    B. Yes, only because she possessed material nonpublic information

    C. Yes, only because she should have waited to trade until after her friend's television interview took place

14. Are Jollie's 8 April trade of the second bond and Mahsud Financial's policy on market manipulation consistent with the Standards with respect to market

manipulation?

A. Both Jollie's 8 April trade of the second bond and Mahsud Financial's policy on market manipulation are consistent with the Standards.

B. Jollie's 8 April trade of the second bond is inconsistent and Mahsud Financial's policy on market manipulation is consistent with the Standards.

C. Jollie's 8 April trade of the second bond is consistent and Mahsud Financial's policy on market manipulation is inconsistent with the Standards.

15. Did Dean violate the Standards in preparing and disseminating her equity reports?

A. No

B. Yes, only by misrepresenting her recommendations as independent

C. Yes, only by accepting payment from the companies on which she produces reports

16. In preparing investment reports, did Jollie violate the Standards with respect to her use of Dean's summaries and forecasts and citation of studies found in Dean's internet postings?

	Use of Dean's summaries and forecasts?	Citation of studies found in Dean's internet postings?
A	No	Yes
B	Yes	No
C	Yes	Yes

17. Are the seminar speaker's Statements 1 and 2 correct?

	Statement 1	Statement 2
A	No	No
B	No	Yes
C	Yes	No

18. Are the seminar speaker's Statements 3 and 4 sufficient to meet the requirements of the related Standards?

	Statement 3	Statement 4
A	No	No
B	No	Yes
C	Yes	No

The following information relates to questions 19-23

Stacia Finnegan, CFA, manages a regional office of Harvest Financial's brokerage business. Her responsibilities include training all personnel in compliance with the firm's standards, policies, procedures, and applicable laws and regulations.

Finnegan is currently providing training on the firm's new PlusAccount, a comprehensive, fee-based brokerage account. "PlusAccounts," she tells the brokers, "are an excellent way to ensure that the financial adviser does not recommend trades for the purpose of generating commissions. Adviser and client interests are aligned." She continues, "You will find that many clients will benefit from converting a traditional brokerage account to a PlusAccount. Be aware, however, that PlusAccounts are not appropriate for all categories of investors, including buy-and-hold clients and certain clients with assets less than $50,000."

Finnegan distributes written compliance procedures for establishing and maintaining PlusAccounts. She carefully explains that regulatory rules "require that we have reasonable grounds for believing that the PlusAccount is appropriate for a particular customer. Additionally, we must review each account on an annual basis to determine whether PlusAccount status remains appropriate. The policies outlined in these documents are designed to ensure compliance with industry standards and regulatory requirements. You must follow these compliance procedures exactly."

Finnegan then distributes and explains the sales and disclosure materials for clients. The materials include the following fee structure:

PlusAccount Annual Fee (as a percentage of assets)*

Account Asset Level	Equity (%)	Mutual Fund/Fixed Income (%)
$0–$250,000	2.00	1.00
Next $250,000	1.50	1.00
Next $250,000	1.25	1.00
Next $250,000	1.00	1.00
More than $1 million	0.75	0.75

**Minimum annual fee of $1,000, billed quarterly.*

Finnegan spends the rest of the afternoon training the staff on detailed procedures and answering their questions.

Chris Klein is a registered broker and financial adviser with Harvest. He is also a Level II candidate in the CFA Program. Klein is excited about the new PlusAccounts and believes they will be attractive for many clients.

One of Klein's clients is Elaine Vanderon, who contributes weekly to her brokerage account. Under Vanderon's directions, Klein invests the weekly contributions in actively managed mutual funds (unit trusts). The funds have below-average management fees and average returns. Commissions for Vanderon average $35 per transaction.

When Vanderon's account reaches $50,000 in assets, Klein recommends conversion to a PlusAccount. He carefully explains that in a PlusAccount, both the cost of investment advice and many implementation costs are wrapped into the management fee billed on a quarterly basis. Stock and bond commissions, he tells Vanderon, are discounted by 70%. Klein informs Vanderon that in a PlusAccount, she can buy or sell thousands of mutual funds or unit trusts (including those in which she invests) for no commissions or transaction charges. He explains that PlusAccounts are ideal for clients who trade often—or as part of a periodic investment program, such as hers. Vanderon reads through the disclosure material provided by Klein and accepts his recommendation.

Klein routinely informs clients about the benefits of PlusAccount status and presents them with all the disclosure materials. Another client Klein encourages to open a PlusAccount is Lee Brown. Brown has accumulated stock holdings of $300,000 and trades equities almost daily. His annual commissions for the previous 12 months equal $9,100. His portfolio is well diversified. He has a high risk tolerance and prefers growth stocks. After explaining the fee structure, Klein tells Brown, "The PlusAccount is ideal for an active trader like you."

One year later, Finnegan is promoted. She delegates supervisory responsibility for Klein and 15 other brokers to her assistant branch manager.

The same month, Klein meets with Vanderon and Brown to review their portfolios and financial situations. Both clients are happy with their PlusAccounts. Vanderon's commission costs have declined to zero. Her account continues to grow in line with her plans and expectations. Brown is also happy with his account. His annual commission costs have declined 70%, to $2,700.

Two months later, Vanderon receives a $1 million inheritance and places it in her PlusAccount. Although he conducted a full review two months earlier, Klein meets with Vanderon to review her financial situation and discuss potential changes to her investment policy. During their meeting, Klein mentions that he has completed the Level III CFA exam. He informs Vanderon, "Completion of the CFA Program has enhanced my portfolio management skills." He tells Vanderon, "As a CFA charterholder, I am the best qualified to manage your investments." Vanderon congratulates Klein on his accomplishment and agrees to consider any changes he recommends to her PlusAccount.

The following month, Klein telephones Vanderon to recommend a highly rated mutual fund. Klein states, "The fund has an excellent performance history and is ranked in the top decile of comparable funds. For the past three- and five-year periods, its average annual return has exceeded the benchmark by 90 bps. Of course, past performance is no guarantee of future returns, but several of my clients hold this fund and are very happy with it. One of them invested $50,000 five years ago. That investment is worth more than $100,000 today." When Vanderon asks about fees, Klein explains that the fund's management fees are 25 bps higher than those of her existing investments. He adds, "Because of your PlusAccount status, you won't incur a brokerage commission for this transaction even though I will receive a referral fee if you invest in the fund."

Six months later, Brown suffers serious medical and financial problems and stops trading. Klein telephones him to review his financial situation. Brown insists that he will make a full recovery and that he will be trading again shortly. During the next 12 months, Brown is too ill to trade. His growing expenses force him to withdraw large amounts from his PlusAccount. Within another 18 months, his PlusAccount value is less than $50,000.

19. When recommending that Vanderon convert to a PlusAccount, did Klein violate any of the Standards?

    A. No

    B. Yes, because he did not have a reasonable basis

    C. Yes, because the account is unsuitable for Vanderon

20. When recommending that Brown convert to a PlusAccount, did Klein violate any

of the Standards?

A. No

B. Yes, relating to suitability

C. Yes, relating to reasonable basis

21. When meeting with Vanderon, did Klein violate any of the Standards?

A. No

B. Yes, because he improperly referenced the CFA designation

C. Yes, because he claimed enhanced portfolio management skills

22. When recommending the mutual fund to Vanderon, did Klein violate any of the Standards?

A. No

B. Yes, relating to suitability

C. Yes, relating to referral fees

23. In her supervisory duties, did Finnegan violate any of the Standards?

A. No

B. Yes, because she failed to ensure that compliance procedures are enforced

C. Yes, because she delegated supervisory authority to her assistant branch manager

The following information relates to questions 24-29

A. J. Vinken, CFA, manages the Stonebridge Fund at Silk Road Capital Management. He develops a growth-stock selection model that produces highly favorable simulated performance results. He would like to use the model in managing the Stonebridge Fund, a large-capitalization equity fund. He drafts a letter for distribution to all shareholders. In it, he discusses in detail his approach to equity selection using the model. He includes both the actual and simulated performance results of the Stonebridge Fund for the past three years, as shown in Exhibit 1.

Exhibit 1: Stonebridge Fund Annual Returns

Year	Stonebridge Fund (Simulated)	Stonebridge Fund (Actual)
1	10.71%	9.22%
2	2.83%	–4.13%

Year	Stonebridge Fund (Simulated)	Stonebridge Fund (Actual)
3	22.23%	22.23%
Average annual return	11.92%	9.11%

Vinken writes, "Using the proprietary selection model for the past three years, the Stonebridge Fund would have earned an average annual return of almost 300 bps in excess of the fund's actual return. Based on these simulated results, I am confident that using the model will yield better performance results in the future; however, Silk Road Capital Management can make no statement of assurance or guarantee regarding future investment returns."

D. S. Khadri, CFA, is also a portfolio manager at Silk Road. She recently assumed management of the small-cap Westlake Fund from Vinken.

Khadri implements an electronic record-retention policy when she becomes the Westlake manager. In accordance with her policy, all records for the fund—including investment analyses, transactions, and investment-related communications with clients and prospective clients—are scanned and electronically stored. Vinken maintained the same records in hard copy format for the five years that he managed the Westlake Fund. Khadri has begun the process of scanning all the past records of the Westlake Fund; however, Vinken complains that Khadri is wasting company resources by scanning old records. Vinken insists that he will continue to maintain only hard copy records for the Stonebridge Fund for the five years required by regulators.

Khadri writes a performance review of the Westlake Fund for its quarterly newsletter. She reports that Silk Road Capital Management is moving toward compliance with the Global Investment Performance Standards (GIPS®). She states, "The Westlake Fund is already partially GIPS compliant. We expect to be fully compliant with the GIPS standards within the next 12 months."

In the quarterly newsletter, Khadri makes the following statements:

Statement 1 China's pegging of the yuan to the US dollar will end within the next 12 months, which will lead to the yuan increasing in value by more than 40%, supporting our overweighting of Chinese-related stocks in the Westlake Fund.

Statement 2 Increased geopolitical uncertainty around the globe should keep oil prices above three-year levels, which supports our recommendation for an overweighting of equities in the small-cap energy sector.

Khadri also reports the following:

"The quarterly return of the Westlake Fund was 4.07%. The quarterly return exceeded the performance of its benchmark, the Russell 2000 Index, by 0.16%. Investors should not expect this type of performance to continue into the foreseeable future.*

*Additional detailed information available upon request."

After the quarterly newsletter is distributed, a client contacts Khadri claiming that the Westlake Fund actually underperformed the benchmark during the quarter. After researching the issue, Khadri confirms that the client is correct and sends him a letter in which she provides the corrected results. In her letter to the client, she blames the discrepancy—which was the result of a human typographical error—on a computer programming error.

24. In his letter regarding the stock selection model, did Vinken violate any of the

Standards?

A. No

B. Yes, because he used simulated performance results

C. Yes, because he claimed that the new model will yield better performance results

25. Are the record-retention policies of both Khadri and Vinken consistent with the Standards?

A. Yes

B. No, Khadri's policy is not consistent.

C. No, Vinken's policy is not consistent.

26. Are Khadri's statements regarding compliance with the GIPS standards consistent with the Standards of Professional Conduct?

A. Yes

B. No, because Khadri may not claim partial compliance

C. No, because Khadri failed to disclose the areas of noncompliance

27. Are Khadri's statements in the quarterly newsletter consistent with the Standards of Professional Conduct?

A. Yes

B. No, because Statement 1 is opinion, not fact

C. No, because Statement 2 is opinion, not fact

28. Are Khadri's newsletter comments regarding returns consistent with the Standards?

A. Yes

B. No, because Khadri used an inappropriate benchmark

C. No, because Khadri did not disclose whether the performance results are before or after fees

29. When responding to the client complaint regarding Westlake's performance, Khadri *least likely* violated the standard relating to:

A. misconduct.

B. misrepresentation.

C. performance presentation.

The following information relates to questions 30-35

Omega Financial, a large financial services firm, makes a market in more than 500 stocks. As a market maker, the firm executes institutional orders, as well as retail orders placed by its private wealth unit, its broker/dealer affiliate, and other third-party broker/dealers.

A page in Omega's compliance manual, which adheres to all legal and regulatory requirements, includes the following information:

OTC Stocks in Which Omega Is a Market Maker

Definitions:

Riskless principal transaction: an order in which a firm, after receiving a customer's order, executes the order on a principal basis from another market center

Net trade/trade on a net basis: a principal transaction in which a market maker, after having received an order, executes the order at one price with another broker/dealer or another customer and then sells to (buys from) the customer at a different price

Compliance Policies:

Institutional Orders	*Retail Orders*
Riskless principal transactions may be traded on a net basis.	Riskless principal transactions may not be traded on a net basis. They receive the same execution price without markup, markdown, commissions, or fees.

Consistent with regulatory requirements, Omega discloses the information about riskless principal transactions to all clients and third-party broker/dealers. In addition, Omega informs third-party broker/dealers that it will seek best execution on retail orders.

Omega is developing an automated order-handling system to improve efficiencies in order flow. Anticipated benefits of the new system include much faster execution speeds. Additionally, the system design includes a trading mechanism that will execute portions of certain large orders to reduce market impact. The trading mechanism delays some orders to allow the firm to obtain a better overall price.

Xavier Brown, CFA, is responsible for overseeing the project to ensure its timely completion. Brown enlists the compliance department to review the programming during the initial development phase and identify any potential problems. The compliance department compares the order-handling function of the new system to the third-party software currently in use. They identify several potential problems, including delays in execution of certain large market orders and embedded markups and markdowns on stocks in which the firm makes a market. According to the compliance department, changes are necessary to comply with regulatory requirements.

Brown directs the programmers to correct the problems and run tests and simulations. The programmers spend the next few months making changes to the system and adding comments throughout the code that clearly explain the purpose of particular functions. After several months, the programmers report that they have corrected all the identified problems and run the necessary tests and simulations. The following month, the firm switches to the automated order-handling system as planned.

Joy Chen, CFA, trades Xydeo stock for Omega. One month following the switch to the new order-handling system, Chen is able to execute a number of principal riskless transactions for both institutional and retail clients at $25.00 per share. When processing the customer buy orders totaling 500,000 shares, the new system automatically uses the best-publicized price, $25.01, and then the firm issues client confirmations showing a purchase price of $25.01.

Stephen Smith, CFA, works across from Chen at the trading desk at Omega. His seat is close to a speaker for the company's squawk box, which is used to broadcast information about current analyst recommendations, news about market events, and information about pending block trades.

Smith's young brother-in-law, Adolfo Garcia, recently accepted a position as a broker at a third-party broker/dealer that trades with Omega. Garcia has a modest income and little savings. He is enthusiastic about investments and has enrolled as a CFA candidate. Smith calls Garcia early each morning to talk about the previous day's events. At the end of their conversation, Smith places the call on speakerphone and resumes his work.

In his office, Garcia can hear Omega's squawk box over the speakerphone. Garcia enjoys listening as Omega analysts discuss changes in ratings, economic forecasts, and capital market developments. He is careful not to trade in stocks mentioned explicitly on the squawk box. Rather, he sometimes researches competitors and other firms operating in the same industry. In one case, he immediately shorts the stock of Tefla Corporation after an Omega analyst downgrades a firm in the same industry.

Garcia frequently places large block orders for low-priced, small-capitalization stocks at the market price. Once the new system is operational, Smith processes the orders through the new trading system mechanism, which delays execution of portions of the orders and allows the firm to obtain a better price for Garcia.

30. For a CFA charterholder, would adhering to Omega's policies regarding riskless principal transactions result in a violation of the CFA Institute Standards of Professional Conduct?

    A. No

    B. Yes, because Omega disadvantages institutional clients

    C. Yes, because disclosure of the policy does not relieve Omega of its obligation to treat clients equally

31. When overseeing the development of the automated trading system, did Brown violate any of the Standards?

    A. No

    B. Yes, because he accepted an assignment for which he was inadequately trained and skilled

    C. Yes, because he did not ensure that the final system complied with regulatory requirements

32. With regard to Chen's trades in Xydeo, do both the institutional and retail trades comply with the Standards?

    A. Only the retail trades comply.

    B. Only the institutional trades comply.

    C. Neither the retail nor the institutional trades comply.

33. When placing the morning phone call on speakerphone, did Smith violate any of

the Standards?

A. No

B. Yes, his duty to Omega

C. Yes, his duty to clients and to Omega

34. When listening to the Omega squawk box, did Garcia violate any of the Standards?

A. No

B. Yes, the standard regarding professionalism

C. Yes, the standard regarding material nonpublic information

35. When shorting Tefla stock, did Garcia violate any of the Standards?

A. No

B. Yes, because he did not have a reasonable basis for the trade

C. Yes, because he was in possession of material nonpublic information

---

The following information relates to questions 36-41

Sebastian Riser, CFA, works as a portfolio manager for Swibank, a small private bank in Switzerland. Riser manages the accounts of his clients according to best practices, keeping clients' interests before those of the bank and his own. He allocates investments in a fair manner when he deems them consistent with the stated objectives and constraints of clients.

Swibank has a Luxembourg subsidiary, which distributes fund-of-funds products. Riser recently received a request to serve on the board of directors for the subsidiary. In this role, Riser would advise management on business strategies, market opportunities, potential clients, and current and prospective fund managers. For his role on the board, Riser would receive an annual payment directly from the subsidiary equivalent to 5% of his total portfolio manager salary in Switzerland.

The following month, Riser accepts the position on the board. The subsidiary registers each new fund-of-funds product with regulatory authorities in Luxembourg and discloses Riser's role as a board member in the required filings, which are public and readily available.

Riser serves as the contact person for the subsidiary's institutional clients in Switzerland and participates in the subsidiary's road shows in Switzerland. His role during these road shows varies. On some occasions, he simply attends the presentations while the operating management sells the products; on other occasions, he gives the actual presentation promoting the products. Riser's name does not appear in the promotional material distributed at the road shows.

Alexander Komm, a long-time colleague of Riser, is the founder of Komm Private Management, which provides asset management, advisory, and trust services to high-net-worth individuals. The firm has several well-managed proprietary funds. Komm offers Riser a position with the firm as managing partner. Riser is flattered but declines the offer, explaining that he is very happy working at

Swibank.

That same week, the subsidiary informs Riser that it needs an experienced fund manager to manage a new publicly traded Japanese equity product. Riser is convinced that Komm Private Management would be qualified and recommends the firm for the new product. After a thorough search process, the subsidiary hires Komm Private Management for the new product.

Six months later, after numerous discussions, Komm finally convinces Riser to join Komm Private Management as a managing partner. The following week, Riser submits his resignation to Swibank. His position on the board of the subsidiary is not dependent on his employment at the bank, and he agrees to serve the remaining three years of his term.

After signing and submitting his employment contract to Komm, Riser takes three weeks of vacation before starting his new position. During this time, he purchases 2,000 shares of the new Japanese equity product for his private account. When he begins working at Komm Private Management, he purchases a large block of shares in the Japanese equity product, which he allocates according to internal procedures to all accounts for which it is suitable.

36. According to the CFA Institute Standards of Professional Conduct, before accepting the position on the board of the subsidiary, Riser should:

   A. receive verbal consent from Swibank.

   B. receive verbal consent from his clients.

   C. disclose to his employer the financial compensation proposed by the subsidiary.

37. When participating in the road shows in Switzerland, Riser *least likely* violated the standard relating to:

   A. avoiding or disclosing conflicts.

   B. independence and objectivity.

   C. additional compensation arrangements.

38. When recommending Komm Private Management, did Riser violate any of the Standards?

   A. No

   B. Yes, relating to duties to employers

   C. Yes, relating to avoiding or disclosing conflicts

39. When resigning from Swibank, did Riser violate any of the Standards?

   A. No

   B. Yes, because he breached his duty of loyalty to his employer

   C. Yes, because he did not resign his position with the Luxembourg subsidiary

40. In his original purchase of 2,000 shares of the Japanese equity product, Riser *least likely* violated the standard relating to:

   A. suitability.

B. priority of transactions.

C. integrity of capital markets.

41. According to the Standards, Riser is not required to disclose to clients his:

A. holdings of the Japanese equity product.

B. relationship with the Swibank subsidiary.

C. compensation from the Swibank subsidiary.

The following information relates to questions 42-47

Prudent Investment Associates (PIA) is a small-cap equity investment management company that uses fundamental equity analysis in its investment decision-making process. All portfolio managers at PIA manage both discretionary and non-discretionary accounts. Kevin Danko, CFA, is PIA's owner and chief investment officer and supervises May Chau, a recently hired portfolio manager. PIA has adopted the CFA Institute Code of Ethics and Standards of Professional Conduct.

Chau is enrolled to sit for the Level III CFA exam. In its marketing brochure, PIA states, "May Chau is a Level III candidate in the CFA Program." A colleague tells Chau this statement may be incorrect according to the CFA Institute Code and Standards and suggests the following change: "May Chau has passed the Level II CFA exam."

PIA has established a relationship with Fair Trading Incorporated (FTI), a regional investment bank and broker/dealer. FTI provides clients with access to research and analysts' recommendations via a user-registered website. This access is available on the condition that clients not forward any of the research and recommendations to any other parties. In exchange for this access and after concluding that FTI provides best execution, Danko directs to FTI most of his trade orders.

FTI also provides to a select group of brokerage clients, including PIA, information regarding several of its investment banking customers. This information includes the customers' own earnings projections. FTI instructs this select group of brokerage clients not to disseminate these earnings projections to the public until released by the investment banking customers.

On a regular basis, Danko reviews the list of "strong buys" on FTI's website to see if there have been any new "buy" recommendations. Danko quickly places orders for discretionary client accounts to purchase shares of any company for which the investment recommendation has been changed to a "strong buy." He takes this action so discretionary account clients do not miss any price appreciation. After each purchase, he instructs Chau to perform the appropriate fundamental analysis on these companies within five business days so the research file is adequately documented.

From time to time, PIA receives initial public offering allocations from FTI. Danko allocates these IPOs to those discretionary accounts that normally participate in IPOs. If the IPO is oversubscribed, he excludes his wife's discretionary non-fee-paying account so that he is not accused of bias when allocating the oversubscribed IPOs.

During a recent presentation, Danko and Chau are asked what procedures PIA uses to ensure employees do not benefit from information prior to executing trades in client accounts. Danko responds that PIA has the following trading procedures:

Procedure 1	Investment personnel are not permitted to trade securities for five business days prior to trades executed in discretionary client accounts.
Procedure 2	Each quarter, a randomly selected group of investment personnel must provide duplicate trade confirmations to the PIA compliance officer.
Procedure 3	Investment personnel must receive prior approval for personal trades only for trades greater than $5,000.

42. Does the reference to Chau's participation in the CFA Program as presented in the marketing brochure or in the suggested change violate the Standards?

    A. No, it does not.

    B. The marketing brochure is a violation, but the suggested change is not a violation.

    C. The suggested change is a violation, but the marketing brochure is not a violation.

43. Did Danko violate the Standards when he directed trades to FTI?

    A. No

    B. Yes, because by trading with FTI, Danko put PIA's interests ahead of his clients

    C. Yes, because Danko has a duty to provide FTI's research to PIA's clients before executing trades

44. According to the Standards, which of the following actions is the *most* appropriate for Danko to take with respect to the use of the earnings projections? Danko should.

    A. disclose the information to the public.

    B. terminate PIA's relationship with FTI.

    C. keep the information confidential and not use it in his analysis.

45. Did Danko's decision to purchase shares that are recommended as a "strong buy" violate the Standards?

    A. No

    B. Yes, because Danko must have a reasonable and adequate basis prior to purchasing the shares

    C. Yes, because Danko must give non-discretionary accounts the opportunity to purchase equities at the same time he purchases equities in the discretionary accounts

46. Did Danko violate the Standards when he allocated oversubscribed IPO issues?

    A. No

    B. Yes, because he should have allocated the oversubscribed IPOs across all discretionary accounts

    C. Yes, because he should have treated his wife's account the same as other discretionary accounts and included it in the oversubscribed IPO allocations

47. Which of PIA's trading procedures is *most* consistent with the Standards?

    A. Procedure 1

    B. Procedure 2

    C. Procedure 3

SOLUTIONS

1. B is correct. Locke's primary duty is to his clients. In the case of a pension plan, the clients are all the ultimate beneficiaries.

2. B is correct. Under no circumstances should a manager take investment action that is inconsistent with the client's IPS.

3. C is correct. Locke's interest claim is legitimate since the Fund's cash was used to purchase equities that were later removed from the account. Therefore, the Fund is owed interest for the period in question.

4. A is correct. Until Locke's investigation is complete, he has no obligation to suspend the manager or take any other action. He believes the manager can and does add value through superior returns and diversification, and thus it may be reasonable to retain NGM if Locke can be satisfied that the manager can act within the constraints of the IPS and the Standards of Professional Conduct. Until the analysis is complete, suspending the manager and leaving the assets unmanaged or temporarily moving them to another manager for safekeeping would not be practical and Locke would be violating his duty to act in his clients' best interests.

5. A is correct. Client suitability for an investment must be reviewed prior to allocation, not afterward. With respect to interest adjustments, clients who were incorrectly allocated shares must be paid for the use of their cash; however, in no instance should clients suffer a loss because of an allocation error by the manager (that is, have interest removed from their portfolio even though shares are put in their account on a backdated basis).

6. B is correct. Locke has a duty to the pension plan beneficiaries to act in their best interests. He would be violating that duty if he continues to employ a manager who does not manage its mandate or demonstrate that it is aware of and complies with its own duties to clients. He must demonstrate his own professional competence by firing the manager.

7. B is correct. Standard IV(A) prohibits employees from soliciting the clients of employers prior to—but not subsequent to—their departure.

8. B is correct. The Code and Standards apply to individual members and candidates of CFA Institute, but firms are encouraged to adopt the Code and Standards as part of their firm code of ethics. The CFA Institute Asset Manager Code has been drafted specifically for firms.

9. C is correct. Standard IV(C) states that members and candidates should decline in writing to accept supervisory responsibilities until a firm adopts reasonable procedures to allow them to adequately exercise such responsibility.

10. A is correct. Standard III(D) states that both terminated and active accounts must be included as part of the performance history.

11. A is correct. By placing all clients in one of the two specialized portfolios it operates, Markoe Advisers is not giving adequate consideration to the individual needs, circumstances, and objectives of each client as required by the Standards. In addition, the Standards require that members and candidates avoid or disclose all actual and potential conflicts of interest, not just those that relate to current portfolio holdings.

12. A is correct. The Standards require that the supervisor promptly initiate an investigation to ascertain the extent of the violation and should take steps to ensure that violations will not be repeated by limiting or monitoring the employees' activities. The Standards also require that members and candidates obtain written permission from their employer before accepting any compensation or benefits from third parties that may create a conflict of interest.

13. A is correct. Jollie did not act on the material nonpublic information she possessed but waited until it became public. According to the *Standards of Practice Handbook*, "It is not necessary . . . to wait for the slowest method of delivery."

14. A is correct. Jollie's transaction is a legitimate market order in a thinly traded security, and Mahsud Financial's policy statement is consistent with the Standards with respect to the integrity of capital markets.

15. B is correct. It is not a violation to accept compensation from an issuer in exchange for research, but such arrangements must be disclosed prominently and in plain language.

16. B is correct. Receiving Dean's written permission does not absolve Jollie of her responsibility to provide attribution. Because Jollie uses the results of the research studies and does not use Dean's interpretation of the studies, it is appropriate to cite the original authors only.

17. B is correct. The first statement is incorrect, and the second statement is correct. What is legal is not necessarily ethical. A weak barrier between the employer's research department and investment banking department is a potential source of conflict.

18. B is correct. Statement 3 is incorrect. Conflicts must be avoided or disclosed. If not avoided, a conflict must be disclosed—prominently and in plain language—regardless of whether the member views the conflict as material. Statement 4 is in compliance with the Standards. The Mahsud Financial disclosure requirement complies with the Standards. Gifts from clients must be disclosed so the employer can determine whether the gift could affect the employee's independence and objectivity.

19. A is correct. Klein did not violate the Standards when recommending a PlusAccount to Vanderon. His actions comply with Standard III(A) Loyalty, Prudence, and Care; Standard III(C) Suitability; and Standard V(A) Diligence and Reasonable Basis. As required, Klein disclosed the fee structure associated with the PlusAccount. Based on the fee structure and Vanderon's trading activity, the PlusAccount appears to be a suitable investment vehicle. By converting to PlusAccount status, Vanderon will incur an annual fee of $1,000 and eliminate approximately $1,800 in annual brokerage commissions. The potential savings of approximately $800 provides a reasonable basis for recommending PlusAccount status.

20. A is correct. Klein did not violate the Standards when recommending a PlusAccount to Brown. His actions comply with Standard III(A) Loyalty, Prudence, and Care; Standard III(C) Suitability; and Standard V(A) Diligence and Reasonable Basis. As required, he disclosed the fee structure. Based on the fee structure and Brown's annual commissions, the PlusAccount appears to be a suitable investment vehicle. By converting to PlusAccount status, Brown will incur an annual fee of $5,750 and save approximately $6,370 in annual brokerage commissions. The potential savings of approximately $620 provides a reasonable basis for recommending PlusAccount status.

21. B is correct. Klein improperly referenced the CFA designation when he stated, "As a CFA charterholder, I am the best qualified to manage your investments." He is in violation of Standard VII(B) Reference to CFA Institute, the CFA Designation, and the CFA Program.

22. C is correct. Klein violated Standard VI(C) Referral Fees because he failed to provide appropriate disclosure. Standard VI(C) states that members must disclose the nature of the consideration or benefit—for example, whether on a flat fee or percentage basis, a one-time or continuing benefit, or based on performance—together with the estimated monetary value. Although Klein acknowledged receipt of referral fees from the fund, he did not disclose an estimated dollar value or the nature of the consideration.

23. B is correct. Finnegan violated Standard IV(C) Responsibilities of Supervisors by failing to ensure that compliance procedures are enforced. As she informed her staff, Harvest "must review each account on an annual basis to determine whether PlusAccount status remains appropriate." Had Vanderon's and Brown's accounts been reviewed annually in accordance with compliance procedures, it would have been clear that the PlusAccount was no longer suitable for either. Delegating supervisory authority to another individual does not violate the Standards.

24. A is correct. Vinken did not violate any of the Standards in his letter. In accordance with Standard III(D) Performance Presentation, he presented fair, accurate, and complete information when he identified actual and simulated performance results. Also in accordance with the standard, he did not guarantee superior future investment returns. In accordance with Standard V(B) Communication with Clients and Prospective Clients, Vinken described to his clients and prospective clients the process and logic of the new investment model. By providing the basic details of the model, Vinken provided his clients the basis for understanding the limitations or inherent risks of the investment strategy.

25. A is correct. The policies of both Khadri and Vinken are consistent with Standard V(C) Record Retention, which states that "Members and Candidates must develop and maintain appropriate records to support their investment analyses, recommendations, actions, and other investment-related communications with clients and prospective clients." The records required to support recommendations and/or investment actions depend on the role of the member or candidate in the investment decision-making process. Records can be maintained in either hard copy or electronic form. Even though they use different methods, Khadri and Vinken each maintain the appropriate records and have adequate systems of record control.

26. B is correct. Khadri is in violation of Standard III(D) Performance Presentation. When claiming compliance with the GIPS standards, firms must meet all the requirements. The GIPS standards, while voluntary, apply only on a firmwide basis. Neither a firm nor a fund can claim partial compliance with the GIPS standards.

27. B is correct. Standard V(B) Communication with Clients and Prospective Clients requires the member or candidate to separate and distinguish "facts from opinions" in the presentation of analyses and investment recommendations. Statement 1 in the newsletter says, "China's pegging of the yuan to the US dollar *will* end within the next 12 months which *will* lead to the yuan increasing in value by more than 40%, supporting our overweighting of Chinese-related stocks in the Westlake Fund." Khadri did not clearly differentiate between opinion and fact. The statement about the future of oil pricing is not as questionable, because Khadri used the term "should," which helps clients understand that this is an

opinion and not a certainty. Members may communicate opinions, estimates, and assumptions about future values and possible events, but they must take care to differentiate fact from opinion.

28. C is correct. Khadri violated Standard III(D) Performance Presentation because he did not disclose whether the performance results are before or after fees. Standard III(D) requires that members and candidates make reasonable efforts to ensure that investment performance information is "fair, accurate, and complete." According to the guidance provided in the *Standards of Practice Handbook*, members should include disclosures that fully explain the performance results (for example, whether the performance is gross of fees, net of fees, or after tax).

29. C is correct. Because Khadri provided the corrected information in her letter to the client, she is least likely to have violated Standard III(D) Performance Presentation. She is more likely to have violated the Standards relating to misconduct and misrepresentation because she knowingly misrepresented the cause of the error. Standard I(D) Misconduct requires that members "not engage in any professional conduct involving dishonesty." Standard I(C) Misrepresentation prohibits members from knowingly making any misrepresentations relating to investment actions and professional activities.

30. A is correct. Markups and markdowns in net trades are considered fees paid by clients. Standard III(B) Fair Dealing requires that members treat all clients fairly in light of their investment objectives and circumstances. Treating institutional and retail investors differently is not a violation. According to the Standards, members can differentiate their services to clients, but different levels of service must be disclosed and should not negatively affect clients. Omega has made the appropriate disclosures to its clients in compliance with legal and regulatory requirements and the Standards.

31. C is correct. Brown is in violation of Standard IV(C) Responsibilities of Supervisors because he did not ensure that the final system complied with regulatory requirements. According to Standard IV(C), Brown has a responsibility to make reasonable efforts to detect and prevent violations of applicable laws, rules, and regulations. Alerted to potential problems by the compliance department, he had a responsibility to ensure that the modifications corrected the potential problems without introducing new problems.

32. B is correct. Only the institutional trades comply with the Standards. All the trades were processed on a net basis. Because the firm disclosed that institutional orders may be executed on a net basis, the institutional trades did not result in a violation. The firm disclosed to clients that in riskless principal trades, retail clients will receive the same execution price without markup. Executing the retail orders on a net basis with a $0.01 markup resulted in a violation of Standard I(C) Misrepresentation and Standard III(B) Fair Dealing.

33. C is correct. Smith violated his duties to both clients and Omega by not protecting confidential information. By providing Garcia access to confidential information, such as changes in recommendations and information regarding block trades, Smith provided Garcia the opportunity to front-run, which could cause harm to both Omega and its clients. Thus, Smith's actions violated his duty of loyalty, prudence, and care to his clients and his duty of loyalty to his employer, Standards III(A) and IV(A), respectively.

34. B is correct. Garcia violated Standard I: Professionalism by engaging in eavesdropping on confidential information, including changes in analyst recommendations and pending block trades. According to Standard I(D) Misconduct,

members must not engage in professional conduct involving dishonesty, deceit, or fraud or commit any act that reflects adversely on their professional reputation, integrity, or competence. Garcia engaged in deceitful conduct in obtaining information from the squawk box. His actions reflect adversely on his professional reputation and integrity and thus violated Standard I(D). Although he listened to the material nonpublic information on pending block trades, Garcia is not in violation of Standard II(A) Material Nonpublic Information because he did not act on it. Possession of such material nonpublic information is not a violation of the standard, but acting on the information is.

35. C is correct. Garcia was in possession of material nonpublic information and acted on it, in violation of Standard II(A). After the analyst's recommendation has been issued and/or distributed publicly, Garcia would be free to make the trade. Because this is a personal purchase, the standard relating to diligence and reasonable basis is not applicable.

36. C is correct. According to Standard IV(B) Additional Compensation Arrangements, members must not accept compensation that competes with their employer's interest unless they obtain written consent from all parties involved. Thus, Riser must receive written, not verbal, consent from his employer before accepting the position on the subsidiary's board. According to the recommended procedures for compliance, Riser should make an immediate written report to his employer specifying the terms of the agreement, the nature of the compensation, the approximate amount of the compensation, and the duration of the agreement. The Standards do not require that members receive permission from clients before accepting board positions.

37. C is correct. Riser least likely violated Standard IV(B) Additional Compensation Arrangements when participating in the road shows. Standard IV(B) provides guidance regarding the acceptance and disclosure of compensation that might conflict with an employer's interests. Participating in the road shows and receiving compensation from the subsidiary do not appear to conflict with his employer's interests.

    When participating in the road shows, Riser may have violated Standard I(B) Independence and Objectivity and Standard VI(A) Avoid or Disclose Conflicts. Standard I(B) requires that members use reasonable care and judgment to achieve and maintain independence and objectivity in their professional activities. Riser's role as board member could jeopardize his objectivity and create a conflict of interest. Standard VI(A) requires that members avoid or make full and fair disclosure of all matters that could reasonably be expected to impair their independence and objectivity or interfere with respective duties to their clients, prospective clients, and employer. Full disclosure allows clients to judge motives and possible biases for themselves. Since Riser did not avoid the conflict, Standard VI(A) requires disclosure and Riser does not appear to have made adequate disclosure.

38. C is correct. Standard VI(A) requires all conflicts to be avoided or disclosed. Although Riser's recommendation may be based solely on his knowledge of the firm's track record, his prior relationship with Komm, including the job offer, is a conflict and must be disclosed so the subsidiary will have all the information needed to evaluate the objectivity of his recommendation.

39. A is correct. No violation occurred. Riser is not required to resign his position with the subsidiary. Riser did not engage in any activities that would conflict with his employer's interest before his resignation became effective.

40. A is correct. Riser least likely violated Standard III(C) Suitability when purchas-

ing shares for his own account. Riser may, however, have violated Standard II(A) Material Nonpublic Information and Standard VI(B) Priority of Transactions when making the purchase. If, when trading for his own account, Riser knew that he will place a large block trade for Komm Private Management clients, he may have been in possession of material nonpublic information. Standard VI(B) covers the activities of all members who have knowledge of pending transactions that may be made on behalf of their clients or employers. Riser has accepted the position of managing partner, has recommended the manager for the product, and knew or should have known that he will purchase the product for at least some Komm Private Management clients once he begins work at Komm. His purchase ahead of Komm Private Management's clients might be front-running. Best practice would be to delay his private account purchase until after he purchases shares for clients.

41. C is correct. Standard VI(A) Avoid or Disclose Conflicts states that "Members and Candidates must avoid or make full and fair disclosure of all matters that could reasonably be expected to impair their independence and objectivity or interfere with respective duties to their clients, prospective clients, and employer." Riser's holdings of the Japanese equity product and his position on the board of the subsidiary could impair his objectivity. Each conflict must be avoided or disclosed to clients. He need not disclose his compensation from the subsidiary, because it is not a referral fee.

42. A is correct. Both the first and second presentations are consistent with the CFA Institute Code and Standards. According to the Standards, candidates may reference their participation in the CFA Program as long as they are active, but they cannot imply a partial designation. A statement about the level of the exam successfully passed or a level of the exam upcoming is appropriate, whereas indicating or implying a partial designation or citing a future date of expected completion of a level in the CFA Program is prohibited.

43. A is correct. Danko directed his trading with FTI only after taking into account FTI's ability to provide best execution. There is no indication that FTI requires a certain amount of trading for access to the website, only that access is provided in exchange for orders. This arrangement for trading in return for research services is discussed in the guidance for Standard III(A) Loyalty, Prudence, and Care.

44. C is correct. The information that Danko received is material nonpublic information. Disclosing the information to the public is not his role. Further, earning gains for his clients does not excuse the violation and is not a justifiable reason for taking action on the material nonpublic information. The only entities that should release the information are the corporations or another entity with their permission, perhaps FTI.

45. B is correct. Investment decision making based on speed or on third-party research alone is insufficient for meeting Standard V(A) Diligence and Reasonable Basis.

46. A is correct. When an issue is oversubscribed, allocations cannot be made to accounts where members and candidates have beneficial interest; client orders must be filled first.

47. A is correct. A blackout period is appropriate for investment decision-making personnel so that managers do not take advantage of their knowledge of trading activity and "front-run" the trade. The actual detail of the blackout period is not specified in the Standards, only that one should exist.

LEARNING MODULE

4

Asset Manager Code of Professional Conduct

by Kurt N. Schacht, JD, CFA, Jonathan J. Stokes, JD, and Glenn Doggett, CFA.

Kurt N. Schacht, JD, CFA, is at CFA Institute (USA). Jonathan J. Stokes, JD, is at CFA Institute (USA). Glenn Doggett, CFA, is at CFA Institute (USA).

LEARNING OUTCOMES

Mastery	*The candidate should be able to:*
☐	explain the purpose of the Asset Manager Code and the benefits that may accrue to a firm that adopts the Code
☐	explain the ethical and professional responsibilities required by the six General Principles of Conduct of the Asset Manager Code
☐	determine whether an asset manager's practices and procedures are consistent with the Asset Manager Code
☐	recommend practices and procedures designed to prevent violations of the Asset Manager Code

INTRODUCTION, ADOPTING THE CODE AND CLAIMING COMPLIANCE

1

☐	explain the purpose of the Asset Manager Code and the benefits that may accrue to a firm that adopts the Code

Asset managers hold a unique place of trust in the lives of millions of investors. Investment professionals and firms that undertake and perform their responsibilities with honesty and integrity are critical to maintaining investors' trust and confidence and to upholding the client covenant of trust, loyalty, prudence, and care. CFA Institute and its members are committed to reinforcing those principles. The CFA Institute mission is to lead the investment profession globally by setting the highest standards of ethics, education, and professional excellence. To foster this culture of ethics and professionalism, CFA Institute offers this voluntary code of conduct. It is designed to be broadly adopted within the industry as a template and guidepost for investors seeking managers who adhere to sound ethical practice.

The Asset Manager Code of Professional Conduct outlines the ethical and professional responsibilities of firms that manage assets on behalf of clients. Whereas the CFA Institute Code of Ethics and Standards of Professional Conduct address individual conduct, this Code is meant to apply, on a global basis, to firms that manage client assets as separate accounts or pooled funds (including collective investment schemes, mutual funds, and fund of funds organizations); we refer to such firms as "Managers." In part, this document responds to requests from Managers to extend the scope of the Code and Standards to the firm level. Although many institutional asset managers, particularly those in well-regulated jurisdictions, already have such a code in place, they should use this Code to evaluate their own code and ensure that all of this Code's principles have been included. This Code also has been developed for use by asset managers, including hedge fund managers, who may not already have such a code in place. This second edition of the Code includes provisions relating to risk management as well as guidance for Managers seeking to claim compliance.

Ethical leadership begins at the highest level of an organization; therefore, the Code should be adopted by the Manager's senior management, board of directors, and similar oversight bodies. Such adoption sends a strong message regarding the importance of ethical behavior at the firm. Rather than creating rules that apply only to certain people or groups, this Code is intended to cover all employees of the firm. Although not every employee is actively involved in conduct covered in the Code, a code that is broadly applied reinforces the need for all employees to understand the ethical issues involved in the asset management business. By adopting and enforcing a code of conduct for their organizations, Managers demonstrate their commitment to ethical behavior and the protection of investors' interests. In doing so, the Managers also protect and enhance the reputation of their organizations.

The Code sets forth minimum ethical standards for providing asset management services for clients. It is meant to be general in nature and allows flexibility for asset managers of various sizes and structures to develop the particular policies and procedures necessary to implement the Code. The goal of this Code is to set forth a useful framework for all asset managers to provide services in a fair and professional manner and to fully disclose key elements of those services to clients, regardless of whether individual Managers are required to register or comply with applicable securities laws or regulations. Unregistered hedge fund managers, in particular, are encouraged to adopt the Code and implement its provisions to ensure fair dealing and integrity and to promote self-regulation in this dynamic sector.

We recognize that in the highly regulated and complex business of investment management, the adoption of a code of ethics by itself is not sufficient to ensure ethical conduct. To be implemented effectively, the principles and standards embodied in the Code must be supported by appropriate compliance procedures. The specific procedures that translate principle into practice will depend on a variety of factors, including the business of the Manager, the type of clients, the size of the Manager (based on assets under management and on number of employees), the regulatory régime with which the Manager must comply, and other factors.

Managers must adhere to all applicable laws and regulations governing their activities. Thus, the provisions of this Code may need to be supplemented with additional provisions to meet the requirements of applicable security regulation in markets around the world. Inevitably, in some markets, the Code will closely reflect or be aligned with existing regulation or accepted best practice and in other markets, the Code will expand on the existing work of regulatory authorities or may even break new ground. Furthermore, Managers operate in different types of market structures, which may affect the manner in which the Code can be applied. Despite these differences, the Code provides a universal set of principles and standards relevant to all asset managers.

Clients have a responsibility to be aware of, understand, and monitor how their assets are invested. Yet, to fulfill this responsibility, clients must be able to count on full and fair disclosure from their Managers. Providing clients with a code of ethics that sets a framework for how the Manager conducts business is an important step toward developing the trust and confidence necessary for a successful investment management relationship.

Adopting the Code and Claiming Compliance

Adoption of or compliance with the Asset Manager Code of Professional Conduct requires firms to adhere to all the principles of conduct and provisions set forth in the Code. Many asset management firms already have codes of ethics and other policies and procedures that address or go beyond the principles and provisions of the Code. Adoption of or compliance with the Code does not require a firm to amend its existing code of ethics or other policies and procedures as long as they are at least consistent with the principles and provisions set forth in the Code. Managers are strongly encouraged to review and consider the material in the Appendix when developing and reviewing their codes and other policies and procedures, although because of the many variables in size and complexity among asset management firms, compliance with the Code does not require strict adherence to this guidance.

If the Manager has not complied with each of the principles of conduct and provisions of the Code, the Manager cannot represent that it is in compliance with the Code. Statements referring to partial or incomplete compliance (e.g., "the firm complies with the Asset Manager Code *except for* . . ." or "the firm complies with parts A, B, and C of the Asset Manager Code") are prohibited.

Once a Manager has met each of the required elements of the Code, the firm must make the following statement whenever the firm claims compliance with the Code:

> "[Insert name of Firm] claims compliance with the CFA Institute Asset Manager Code of Professional Conduct. This claim has not been verified by CFA Institute."

Acknowledgement of Claim of Compliance to CFA Institute

Managers also must notify CFA Institute of their claim of compliance with the Asset Manager Code of Professional Conduct through the CFA Institute online notification process at www.cfainstitute.org/assetcode. This acknowledgement form is for communication and information-gathering purposes only and does not represent that CFA Institute engages in enforcement or quality control of an organization's claim of compliance. CFA Institute does not verify either the Manager's claim of compliance or actual compliance with the Code.

2 GENERAL PRINCIPLES OF CONDUCT AND ASSET MANAGER CODE OF PROFESSIONAL CONDUCT

☐ explain the ethical and professional responsibilities required by the six General Principles of Conduct of the Asset Manager Code

Managers have the following responsibilities to their clients. Managers must:

1. Act in a professional and ethical manner at all times.
2. Act for the benefit of clients.
3. Act with independence and objectivity.
4. Act with skill, competence, and diligence.
5. Communicate with clients in a timely and accurate manner.
6. Uphold the applicable rules governing capital markets.

Asset Manager Code of Professional Conduct

A. Loyalty to Clients

Managers must:

1. Place client interests before their own.
2. Preserve the confidentiality of information communicated by clients within the scope of the Manager–client relationship.
3. Refuse to participate in any business relationship or accept any gift that could reasonably be expected to affect their independence, objectivity, or loyalty to clients.

B. Investment Process and Actions

Managers must:

1. Use reasonable care and prudent judgment when managing client assets.
2. Not engage in practices designed to distort prices or artificially inflate trading volume with the intent to mislead market participants.
3. Deal fairly and objectively with all clients when providing investment information, making investment recommendations, or taking investment action.
4. Have a reasonable and adequate basis for investment decisions.
5. When managing a portfolio or pooled fund according to a specific mandate, strategy, or style:

   a. Take only investment actions that are consistent with the stated objectives and constraints of that portfolio or fund.

   b. Provide adequate disclosures and information so investors can consider whether any proposed changes in the investment style or strategy meet their investment needs.

6. When managing separate accounts and before providing investment advice or taking investment action on behalf of the client:

   a. Evaluate and understand the client's investment objectives, tolerance for risk, time horizon, liquidity needs, financial constraints, any unique circumstances (including tax considerations, legal or regulatory constraints, etc.) and any other relevant information that would affect investment policy.

   b. Determine that an investment is suitable to a client's financial situation.

C. Trading

Managers must:

1. Not act or cause others to act on material nonpublic information that could affect the value of a publicly traded investment.
2. Give priority to investments made on behalf of the client over those that benefit the Managers' own interests.
3. Use commissions generated from client trades to pay for only investment-related products or services that directly assist the Manager in its investment decision making process, and not in the management of the firm.
4. Maximize client portfolio value by seeking best execution for all client transactions.
5. Establish policies to ensure fair and equitable trade allocation among client accounts.

D. Risk Management, Compliance, and Support

Managers must:

1. Develop and maintain policies and procedures to ensure that their activities comply with the provisions of this Code and all applicable legal and regulatory requirements.
2. Appoint a compliance officer responsible for administering the policies and procedures and for investigating complaints regarding the conduct of the Manager or its personnel.
3. Ensure that portfolio information provided to clients by the Manager is accurate and complete and arrange for independent third-party confirmation or review of such information.
4. Maintain records for an appropriate period of time in an easily accessible format.
5. Employ qualified staff and sufficient human and technological resources to thoroughly investigate, analyze, implement, and monitor investment decisions and actions.
6. Establish a business-continuity plan to address disaster recovery or periodic disruptions of the financial markets.
7. Establish a firmwide risk management process that identifies, measures, and manages the risk position of the Manager and its investments, including the sources, nature, and degree of risk exposure.

E. Performance and Valuation

Managers must:

1. Present performance information that is fair, accurate, relevant, timely, and complete. Managers must not misrepresent the performance of individual portfolios or of their firm.
2. Use fair-market prices to value client holdings and apply, in good faith, methods to determine the fair value of any securities for which no independent, third-party market quotation is readily available.

F. Disclosures

Managers must:

1. Communicate with clients on an ongoing and timely basis.
2. Ensure that disclosures are truthful, accurate, complete, and understandable and are presented in a format that communicates the information effectively.
3. Include any material facts when making disclosures or providing information to clients regarding themselves, their personnel, investments, or the investment process.
4. Disclose the following:

    a. Conflicts of interests generated by any relationships with brokers or other entities, other client accounts, fee structures, or other matters.

    b. Regulatory or disciplinary action taken against the Manager or its personnel related to professional conduct.

    c. The investment process, including information regarding lock-up periods, strategies, risk factors, and use of derivatives and leverage.

    d. Management fees and other investment costs charged to investors, including what costs are included in the fees and the methodologies for determining fees and costs.

    e. The amount of any soft or bundled commissions, the goods and/or services received in return, and how those goods and/or services benefit the client.

    f. The performance of clients' investments on a regular and timely basis.

    g. Valuation methods used to make investment decisions and value client holdings.

    h. Shareholder voting policies.

    i. Trade allocation policies.

    j. Results of the review or audit of the fund or account.

    k. Significant personnel or organizational changes that have occurred at the Manager.

    l. Risk management processes.

APPENDIX 6: A. LOYALTY TO CLIENTS

- ☐ determine whether an asset manager's practices and procedures are consistent with the Asset Manager Code
- ☐ recommend practices and procedures designed to prevent violations of the Asset Manager Code

Appendix 6—Recommendations and Guidance

Adoption of the Code is insufficient by itself for a Manager to meet its ethical and regulatory responsibilities. Managers must adopt detailed policies and procedures to effectively implement the Code. This section provides guidance explaining the Code and includes recommendations and illustrative examples to assist Managers that are seeking to implement the Code. These examples are not meant to be exhaustive, and the policies and procedures needed to support the Code will depend on the particular circumstances of each organization and the legal and regulatory environment in which the Manager operates.

The following guidance highlights particular issues that Managers should consider when developing their internal policies and procedures that accompany the Code. The guidance is not intended to cover all issues or aspects of a Manager's operations that would have to be included in such policies and procedures to fully implement and support the Code.

A. Loyalty to Clients

Managers must:

1. **Place client interests before their own.**

   Client interests are paramount. Managers should institute policies and procedures to ensure that client interests supersede Manager interests in all aspects of the Manager–client relationship, including (but not limited to) investment selection, transactions, monitoring, and custody. Managers should take reasonable steps to avoid situations in which the Manager's interests and client interests conflict and should institute operational safeguards to protect client interests. Managers should implement compensation arrangements that align the financial interests of clients and Managers and avoid incentives that could result in Managers taking action in conflict with client interests.

2. **Preserve the confidentiality of information communicated by clients within the scope of the Manager–client relationship.**

   As part of their ethical duties, Managers must hold information communicated to them by clients or other sources within the context of the Manager–client relationship strictly confidential and must take all reasonable measures to preserve that confidentiality. This duty applies when Managers obtain information on the basis of their confidential relationship with the client or their special ability to conduct a portion of the client's business or personal affairs. Managers should create a privacy policy that addresses how confidential client information will be collected, stored, protected, and used.

The duty to maintain confidentiality does not supersede a duty (and in some cases the legal requirement) to report suspected illegal activities involving client accounts to the appropriate authorities. Where appropriate, Managers should consider creating and implementing a written anti-money-laundering policy to prevent their organizations from being used for money laundering or the financing of any illegal activities.

3. **Refuse to participate in any business relationship or accept any gift that could reasonably be expected to affect their independence, objectivity, or loyalty to clients.**

   As part of holding clients' interests paramount, Managers must establish policies for accepting gifts or entertainment in a variety of contexts. To avoid the appearance of a conflict, Managers must refuse to accept gifts or entertainment from service providers, potential investment targets, or other business partners of more than a minimal value. Managers should define what the minimum value is and should confer with local regulations which may also establish limits.

   Managers should establish a written policy limiting the acceptance of gifts and entertainment to items of minimal value. Managers should consider creating specific limits for accepting gifts (e.g., amount per time period per vendor) and prohibit the acceptance of any cash gifts. Employees should be required to document and disclose to the Manager, through their supervisor, the firm's compliance office, or senior management, the acceptance of any gift or entertainment.

   This provision is not meant to preclude Managers from maintaining multiple business relationships with a client as long as potential conflicts of interest are managed and disclosed.

4 APPENDIX 6: B. INVESTMENT PROCESS AND ACTIONS

- ☐ determine whether an asset manager's practices and procedures are consistent with the Asset Manager Code
- ☐ recommend practices and procedures designed to prevent violations of the Asset Manager Code

Managers must:

1. **Use reasonable care and prudent judgment when managing client assets.**

   Managers must exhibit the care and prudence necessary to meet their obligations to clients. Prudence requires caution and discretion. The exercise of prudence requires acting with the care, skill, and diligence that a person acting in a like capacity and familiar with such matters would use under the same circumstances. In the context of managing a client's portfolio, prudence requires following the investment parameters set forth by the client and balancing risk and return. Acting with care requires Managers to act in a prudent and judicious manner in avoiding harm to clients.

2. **Not engage in practices designed to distort prices or artificially inflate trading volume with the intent to mislead market participants.**

   Market manipulation is illegal in most jurisdictions and damages the interests of all investors by disrupting the efficient functioning of financial markets and causing deterioration in investor confidence.

   Market manipulation includes practices that distort security prices or values or artificially inflate trading volumes with the intent to deceive persons or entities that rely on information in the market. Such practices may involve, for example, transactions that deceive market participants by distorting the price-setting mechanism of financial instruments and the dissemination of false or misleading information. Transaction-based manipulation includes, but is not limited to, transactions that artificially distort prices or volume to give the impression of activity or price movement in a financial instrument (e.g., trading in illiquid stocks at the end of a measurement period to drive up the price and improve Manager performance) and securing a large position with the intent to exploit and manipulate the price of an asset and/or a related derivative. Information-based manipulation includes, but is not limited to, spreading knowingly false rumors to induce trading by others and pressuring sell-side analysts to rate or recommend a security in such a way that benefits the Manager or the Manager's clients.

3. **Deal fairly and objectively with all clients when providing investment information, making investment recommendations, or taking investment action.**

   To maintain the trust that clients place in them, Managers must deal with all clients in a fair and objective manner. Managers must not give preferential treatment to favored clients to the detriment of other clients. In some cases, clients may pay for a higher level of service or certain services and certain products may only be made available to certain qualifying clients (e.g., certain funds may be open only to clients with assets above a certain level). These practices are permitted as long as they are disclosed and made available to all clients.

   This provision is not intended to prevent Managers from engaging in secondary investment opportunities—referred to in some jurisdictions as "side-letter," "sidecar," or "tag-along" arrangements—with certain clients as long as such opportunities are fairly allocated among similarly situated clients for whom the opportunity is suitable.

4. **Have a reasonable and adequate basis for investment decisions.**

   Managers must act with prudence and make sure their decisions have a reasonable and adequate basis. Prior to taking action on behalf of their clients, Managers must analyze the investment opportunities in question and should act only after undertaking due diligence to ensure there is sufficient knowledge about specific investments or strategies. Such analysis will depend on the style and strategy being used. For example, a Manager implementing a passive strategy will have a very different basis for investment actions from that of a Manager that uses an active strategy.

   Managers can rely on external third-party research as long as Managers have made reasonable and diligent efforts to determine that such research has a reasonable basis. When evaluating investment research, Managers should consider the assumptions used, the thoroughness of the analysis performed, the timeliness of the information, and the objectivity and independence of the source.

Managers should have a thorough understanding of the securities in which they invest and the strategies they use on behalf of clients. Managers should understand the structure and function of the securities, how they are traded, their liquidity, and any other risks (including counterparty risk).

Managers who implement complex and sophisticated investment strategies should understand the structure and potential vulnerabilities of such strategies and communicate these in an understandable manner to their clients. For example, when implementing complex derivative strategies, Managers should understand the various risks and conduct statistical analysis (i.e., stress testing) to determine how the strategy will perform under different conditions. By undertaking adequate due diligence, Managers can better judge the suitability of investments for their clients.

5. **When managing a portfolio or pooled fund according to a specific mandate, strategy, or style:**

   a. **Take only investment actions that are consistent with the stated objectives and constraints of that portfolio or fund.**

   When Managers are given a specific mandate by clients or offer a product, such as a pooled fund for which the Managers do not know the specific financial situation of each client, the Managers must manage the funds or portfolios within the stated mandates or strategies. Clients need to be able to evaluate the suitability of the investment funds or strategies for themselves. Subsequently, they must be able to trust that Managers will not diverge from the stated or agreed-on mandates or strategies. When market events or opportunities change to such a degree that Managers wish to have flexibility to take advantage of those occurrences, such flexibility is not improper but should be expressly understood and agreed to by Managers and clients. Best practice is for Managers to disclose such events to clients when they occur or, at the very least, in the course of normal client reporting.

   b. **Provide adequate disclosures and information so investors can consider whether any proposed changes in the investment style or strategy meet their investment needs.**

   To give clients an opportunity to evaluate the suitability of investments, Managers need to provide adequate information to them about any proposed material changes to their investment strategies or styles. They must provide this information well in advance of such changes. Clients should be given enough time to consider the proposed changes and take any actions that may be necessary. If the Manager decides to make a material change in the investment strategy or style, clients should be permitted to redeem their investment, if desired, without incurring any undue penalties.

6. **When managing separate accounts and before providing investment advice or taking investment action on behalf of the client:**

   a. **Evaluate and understand the client's investment objectives, tolerance for risk, time horizon, liquidity needs, financial constraints, any unique circumstances (including tax considerations, legal or regulatory constraints, etc.) and any other relevant information that would affect investment policy.**

Prior to taking any investment actions for clients, Managers must take the necessary steps to understand and evaluate the client's financial situation, constraints, and other relevant factors. Without understanding the client's situation, the Manager cannot select and implement an appropriate investment strategy. Ideally, each client will have an investment policy statement (IPS) that includes a discussion of risk tolerances (both the ability and willingness of the client to bear risk), return objectives, time horizon, liquidity requirements, liabilities, tax considerations, and any legal, regulatory, or other unique circumstances.

The purpose of the IPS is to provide Managers with written strategic plans to direct investment decisions for each client. The Manager should take an opportunity to review the IPS for each client, offer any suggestions on clarifying the IPS, and discuss with the client the various techniques and strategies to be used to meet the client's investment goals. Managers should review each client's IPS with the client at least annually and whenever circumstances suggest changes may be needed.

The information contained in an IPS allows Managers to assess whether a particular strategy or security is suitable for a client (in the context of the rest of the client's portfolio), and the IPS serves as the basis for establishing the client's strategic asset allocation. (Note: In some cases, the client will determine the strategic asset allocation; in other cases, that duty will be delegated to the Manager). The IPS should also specify the Manager's role and responsibilities in managing the client's assets and establish schedules for review and evaluation. The Manager should reach agreement with the client as to an appropriate benchmark or benchmarks by which the Manager's performance will be measured and any other details of the performance evaluation process (e.g., when performance measurement should begin).

b. Determine that an investment is suitable to a client's financial situation.

Managers must evaluate investment actions and strategies in light of each client's circumstances. Not all investments are suitable for every client, and Managers have a responsibility to ensure that only appropriate investments and investment strategies are included in a client's portfolio. Ideally, individual investments should be evaluated in the context of clients' total assets and liabilities, which may include assets held outside of the Manager's account, to the extent that such information is made available to the Manager and is explicitly included in the context of the client's IPS.

APPENDIX 6: C. TRADING

5

- ☐ determine whether an asset manager's practices and procedures are consistent with the Asset Manager Code
- ☐ recommend practices and procedures designed to prevent violations of the Asset Manager Code

Managers must:

1. **Not act or cause others to act on material nonpublic information that could affect the value of a publicly traded investment.**

   Trading on material nonpublic information, which is illegal in most jurisdictions, erodes confidence in capital markets, institutions, and investment professionals and promotes the perception that those with inside and special access can take unfair advantage of the general investing public. Although trading on such information may lead to short-term profitability, over time, individuals and the profession as a whole suffer if investors avoid capital markets because they perceive them to be unfair by favoring the knowledgeable insider.

   Different jurisdictions and regulatory regimes may define materiality differently, but in general, information is "material" if it is likely that a reasonable investor would consider it important and if it would be viewed as significantly altering the total mix of information available. Information is "nonpublic" until it has been widely disseminated to the marketplace (as opposed to a select group of investors).

   Managers must adopt compliance procedures, such as establishing information barriers (e.g., fire walls), to prevent the disclosure and misuse of material nonpublic information. In many cases, pending trades or client or fund holdings may be considered material nonpublic information, and Managers must be sure to keep such information confidential. In addition, merger and acquisition information, prior to its public disclosure, is generally considered material nonpublic information. Managers should evaluate company-specific information that they may receive and determine whether it meets the definition of material nonpublic information.

   This provision is not meant to prevent Managers from using the mosaic theory to draw conclusions—that is, combine pieces of material public information with pieces of nonmaterial nonpublic information to draw conclusions that are actionable.

2. **Give priority to investments made on behalf of the client over those that benefit the Managers' own interests.**

   Managers must not execute their own trades in a security prior to client transactions in the same security. Investment activities that benefit the Manager must not adversely affect client interests. Managers must not engage in trading activities that work to the disadvantage of clients (e.g., front-running client trades).

   In some investment arrangements, such as limited partnerships or pooled funds, Managers put their own capital at risk alongside that of their clients to align their interests with the interests of their clients. These arrangements are permissible only if clients are not disadvantaged.

   Managers should develop policies and procedures to monitor and, where appropriate, limit the personal trading of their employees. In particular, Managers should require employees to receive approval prior to any personal investments in initial public offerings or private placements. Managers should develop policies and processes designed to ensure that client transactions take precedence over employee or firm transactions. One method is to create a restricted list and/or watch list of securities that are owned in client accounts or may be bought or sold on behalf of clients in the near future; prior to trading securities on such a list, employees would be required to seek approval. In addition, Managers could require employees to provide the compliance officer with copies of trade confirmations each quarter and annual statements of personal holdings.

3. **Use commissions generated from client trades to pay for only investment-related products or services that directly assist the Manager in its investment decision-making process, and not in the management of the firm.**

   Managers must recognize that commissions paid (and any benefits received in return for commissions paid) are the property of the client. Consequently, any benefits offered in return for commissions must benefit the Manager's clients.

   To determine whether a benefit generated from client commissions is appropriate, Managers must determine whether it will directly assist in the Manager's investment decision-making process. The investment decision-making process can be considered the qualitative and quantitative process and the related tools used by the Manager in rendering investment advice to clients. The process includes financial analysis, trading and risk analysis, securities selection, broker selection, asset allocation, and suitability analysis.

   Some Managers have chosen to eliminate the use of soft commissions (also known as soft dollars) to avoid any conflicts of interest that may exist. Managers should disclose their policy on how benefits are evaluated and used for the client's benefit. If Managers choose to use a soft commission or bundled brokerage arrangement, they should disclose this use to their clients. Managers should consider complying with industry best practices regarding the use and reporting of such an arrangement, which can be found in the CFA Institute Soft Dollar Standards.

4. **Maximize client portfolio value by seeking best execution for all client transactions.**

   When placing client trades, Managers have a duty to seek terms that secure best execution for and maximize the value of each client's portfolio (i.e., ensure the best possible result overall). Managers must seek the most favorable terms for client trades within each trades' particular circumstances (such as transaction size, market characteristics, liquidity of security, and security type). Managers also must decide which brokers or venues provide best execution while considering, among other things, commission rates, timeliness of trade executions, and the ability to maintain anonymity, minimize incomplete trades, and minimize market impact.

   When a client directs the Manager to place trades through a specific broker or through a particular type of broker, Managers should alert the client that by limiting the Manager's ability to select the broker, the client may not be receiving best execution. The Manager should seek written acknowledgment from the client of receiving this information.

5. **Establish policies to ensure fair and equitable trade allocation among client accounts.**

   When placing trades for client accounts, Managers must allocate trades fairly so that some client accounts are not routinely traded first or receive preferential treatment. Where possible, Managers should use block trades and allocate shares on a pro-rata basis by using an average price or some other method that ensures fair and equitable allocations. When allocating shares of an initial or secondary offering, Managers should strive to ensure that all clients for whom the security is suitable are given opportunities to participate. When Managers do not receive a large enough allocation to allow all eligible clients to participate fully in a particular offering, they must ensure that certain clients are not given preferential treatment and should establish a system to ensure that new issues are allocated fairly (e.g., pro rata). Manager's trade allocation policies should specifically address how initial public offerings and private placements are to be handled.

6 APPENDIX 6: D. RISK MANAGEMENT, COMPLIANCE AND SUPPORT

- ☐ determine whether an asset manager's practices and procedures are consistent with the Asset Manager Code
- ☐ recommend practices and procedures designed to prevent violations of the Asset Manager Code

Managers must:

1. **Develop and maintain policies and procedures to ensure that their activities comply with the provisions of this Code and all applicable legal and regulatory requirements.**

   Detailed and firmwide compliance policies and procedures are critical tools to ensure that Managers meet their legal requirements when managing client assets. In addition, the fundamental, principle-based, ethical concepts embodied in the Code should be put into operation by the implementation of specific policies and procedures.

   Documented compliance procedures assist Managers in fulfilling the responsibilities enumerated in the Code and ensure that the standards expressed in the Code are adhered to in the day-to-day operation of the firms. The appropriate compliance programs, internal controls, and self-assessment tools for each Manager will depend on such factors as the size of the firm and the nature of its investment management business.

2. **Appoint a compliance officer responsible for administering the policies and procedures and for investigating complaints regarding the conduct of the Manager or its personnel.**

   Effective compliance programs require Managers to appoint a compliance officer who is competent, knowledgeable, and credible and is empowered to carry out his or her duties. Depending on the size and complexity of the Manager's operations, Managers may designate an existing employee to also serve as the compliance officer, may hire a separate individual for that role, or may establish an entire compliance department. Where possible, the compliance officer should be independent from the investment and operations personnel and should report directly to the CEO or board of directors.

   The compliance officer and senior management should regularly make clear to all employees that adherence to compliance policies and procedures is crucial and that anyone who violates them will be held liable. Managers should consider requiring all employees to acknowledge that they have received a copy of the Code (as well as any subsequent material amendments), that they understand and agree to comply with it, and that they will report any suspected violations of the Code to the designated compliance officer. Compliance officers should take steps to implement appropriate employee training and conduct continuing self-evaluation of the Manager's compliance practices to assess the effectiveness of the practices.

Among other things, the compliance officer should be charged with reviewing firm and employee transactions to ensure the priority of client interests. Because personnel, regulations, business practices, and products constantly change, the role of the compliance officer (particularly the role of keeping the firm up to date on such matters) is particularly important.

The compliance officer should document and act expeditiously to address any compliance breaches and work with management to take appropriate disciplinary action.

3. **Ensure that portfolio information provided to clients by the Manager is accurate and complete and arrange for independent third-party confirmation or review of such information.**

   Managers have a responsibility to ensure that the information they provide to clients is accurate and complete. By receiving an independent third-party confirmation or review of that information, clients have an additional level of confidence that the information is correct, which may enhance the Manager's credibility. Such verification is also good business practice because it may serve as a risk management tool to help the Manager identify potential problems. The confirmation of portfolio information may take the form of an audit or review, as is the case with most pooled vehicles, or may take the form of copies of account statements and trade confirmations from the custodian bank where the client assets are held.

4. **Maintain records for an appropriate period of time in an easily accessible format.**

   Managers must retain records that substantiate their investment activities, the scope of their research, the basis for their conclusions, and the reasons for actions taken on behalf of their clients. Managers should also retain copies of other compliance-related records that support and substantiate the implementation of the Code and related policies and procedures, as well as records of any violations and resulting actions taken. Records can be maintained either in hard copy or electronic form.

   Regulators often impose requirements related to record retention. In the absence of such regulation, Managers must determine the appropriate minimum time frame for keeping the organization's records. Unless otherwise required by local law or regulation Managers should keep records for at least seven years.

5. **Employ qualified staff and sufficient human and technological resources to thoroughly investigate, analyze, implement, and monitor investment decisions and actions.**

   To safeguard the Manager–client relationship, Managers need to allocate all the resources necessary to ensure that client interests are not compromised. Clients pay significant sums to Managers for professional asset management services, and client assets should be handled with the greatest possible care.

   Managers of all sizes and investment styles struggle with issues of cost and efficiency and tend to be cautious about adding staff in important operational areas. Nevertheless, adequate protection of client assets requires appropriate administrative, back-office, and compliance support. Managers should ensure that adequate internal controls are in place to prevent fraudulent behavior.

A critical consideration is employing only *qualified* staff. Managers must ensure that client assets are invested, administered, and protected by qualified and experienced staff. Employing qualified staff reflects a client-first attitude and helps ensure that Managers are applying the care and prudence necessary to meet their obligations to clients. This provision is not meant to prohibit the outsourcing of certain functions, but the Manager retains the liability and responsibility for any outsourced work.

Managers have a responsibility to clients to deliver the actual services they claim to offer. Managers must use adequate resources to carry out the necessary research and analysis to implement their investment strategies with due diligence and care. Also, Managers must have adequate resources to monitor the portfolio holdings and investment strategies. As investment strategies and instruments become increasingly sophisticated, the need for sufficient resources to analyze and monitor them becomes ever more important.

6. **Establish a business-continuity plan to address disaster recovery or periodic disruptions of the financial markets.**

   Part of safeguarding client interests is establishing procedures for handling client accounts and inquiries in situations of national, regional, or local emergency or market disruption. Commonly referred to as business-continuity or disaster-recovery planning, such preparation is increasingly important in an industry and world highly susceptible to a wide variety of disasters and disruptions.

   The level and complexity of business-continuity planning depends on the size, nature, and complexity of the organization. At a minimum, Managers should consider having the following:

   - adequate backup, preferably off-site, for all account information;
   - alternative plans for monitoring, analyzing, and trading investments if primary systems become unavailable;
   - plans for communicating with critical vendors and suppliers;
   - plans for employee communication and coverage of critical business functions in the event of a facility or communication disruption; and
   - plans for contacting and communicating with clients during a period of extended disruption.

   Numerous other factors may need to be considered when creating the plan. According to the needs of the organization, these factors may include establishing backup office and operational space in the event of an extended disruption and dealing with key employee deaths or departures.

   As with any important business planning, Managers should ensure that employees and staff are knowledgeable about the plan and are specifically trained in areas of responsibility. Plans should be tested on a firmwide basis at intervals to promote employee understanding and identify any needed adjustments.

7. **Establish a firmwide risk management process that identifies, measures, and manages the risk position of the Manager and its investments, including the sources, nature, and degree of risk exposure.**

Many investors, including those investing in hedge funds and alternative investments or leveraged strategies, invest specifically to increase their risk-adjusted returns. Assuming some risk is a necessary part of that process. The key to sound risk management by Managers is seeking to ensure that the risk profile desired by clients matches the risk profile of their investments. Risk management should complement rather than compete with the investment management process. Investment managers must implement risk management techniques that are consistent with their investment style and philosophy.

The types of risks faced by Managers include, but are not limited to, market risk, credit risk, liquidity risk, counterparty risk, concentration risk, and various types of operational risk. Such types of risks should be analyzed by Managers as part of a comprehensive risk management process for portfolios, investment strategies, and the firm. These examples are illustrative only and may not be applicable to all investment organizations.

Although portfolio managers consider risk issues as part of formulating an investment strategy, the firm's risk management process must be objective, independent, and insulated from influence of portfolio managers. Managers may wish to describe to clients how the risk management framework complements the portfolio management process while remaining separate from that process. Managers should consider outsourcing risk management activities if a separate risk management function is not appropriate or feasible because of the size of the organization.

An effective risk management process will identify risk factors for individual portfolios as well as for the Manager's activities as whole. It will often be appropriate for managers to perform stress tests, scenario tests, and backtests as part of developing risk models that comprehensively capture the full range of their actual and contingent risk exposures. The goal of such models is to determine how various changes in market and investment conditions could affect investments. The risk models should be continuously evaluated and challenged, and Managers should be prepared to describe the models to clients. Despite the importance of risk models, however, effective risk management ultimately depends on the experience, judgment, and ability of the Managers in analyzing their risk metrics.

APPENDIX 6: E. PERFORMANCE AND EVALUATION 7

- ☐ determine whether an asset manager's practices and procedures are consistent with the Asset Manager Code
- ☐ recommend practices and procedures designed to prevent violations of the Asset Manager Code

Managers must:

1. **Present performance information that is fair, accurate, relevant, timely, and complete. Managers must not misrepresent the performance of individual portfolios or of their firm.**

Although past performance is not necessarily indicative of future performance, historical performance records are often used by prospective clients as part of the evaluation process when hiring asset managers. Managers have a duty to present performance information that is a fair representation of their record and includes all relevant factors. In particular, Managers should be certain not to misrepresent their track records by taking credit for performance that is not their own (i.e., when they were not managing a particular portfolio or product) or by selectively presenting certain time periods or investments (i.e., cherry picking). Any hypothetical or backtested performance must be clearly identified as such. Managers should provide as much additional portfolio transparency as feasibly possible. Any forward-looking information provided to clients must also be fair, accurate, and complete.

A model for fair, accurate, and complete performance reporting is embodied in the Global Investment Performance Standards (GIPS®), which are based on the principles of fair representation and full disclosure and are designed to meet the needs of a broad range of global markets. By adhering to these standards for reporting investment performance, Managers help assure investors that the performance information being provided is both complete and fairly presented. When Managers comply with the GIPS standards, both prospective and existing clients benefit because they can have a high degree of confidence in the reliability of the performance numbers the Managers are presenting. This confidence may, in turn, enhance clients' sense of trust in their Managers.

2. **Use fair-market prices to value client holdings and apply, in good faith, methods to determine the fair value of any securities for which no independent, third-party market quotation is readily available.**

   In general, fund Managers' fees are calculated as a percentage of assets under management. In some cases, an additional fee is calculated as a percentage of the annual returns earned on the assets. Consequently, a conflict of interest may arise where the portfolio Manager has the additional responsibility of determining end-of-period valuations and returns on the assets.

   These conflicts may be overcome by transferring responsibility for the valuation of assets (including foreign currencies) to an independent third party. For pooled funds that have boards of directors comprising independent members, the independent members should have the responsibility of approving the asset valuation policies and procedures and reviewing the valuations. For pooled funds without independent directors, we recommend that this function be undertaken by independent third parties who are expert in providing such valuations.

   Managers should use widely accepted valuation methods and techniques to appraise portfolio holdings of securities and other investments and should apply these methods on a consistent basis.

APPENDIX 6: F. DISCLOSURES

- ☐ determine whether an asset manager's practices and procedures are consistent with the Asset Manager Code
- ☐ recommend practices and procedures designed to prevent violations of the Asset Manager Code

Managers must:

1. **Communicate with clients on an ongoing and timely basis.**

   Developing and maintaining clear, frequent, and thorough communication practices is critical to providing high-quality financial services to clients. Understanding the information communicated to them allows clients to know how Managers are acting on their behalf and gives clients the opportunity to make well-informed decisions regarding their investments. Managers must determine how best to establish lines of communication that fit their circumstances and that enable clients to evaluate their financial status.

2. **Ensure that disclosures are truthful, accurate, complete, and understandable and are presented in a format that communicates the information effectively.**

   Managers must not misrepresent any aspect of their services or activities, including (but not limited to) their qualifications or credentials, the services they provide, their performance records, and characteristics of the investments or strategies they use. A misrepresentation is any untrue statement or omission of fact or any statement that is otherwise false or misleading. Managers must ensure that misrepresentation does not occur in oral representations, marketing (whether through mass media or printed brochures), electronic communications, or written materials (whether publicly disseminated or not).

   To be effective, disclosures must be made in plain language and in a manner designed to effectively communicate the information to clients and prospective clients. Managers must determine how often, in what manner, and under what particular circumstances disclosures must be made.

3. **Include any material facts when making disclosures or providing information to clients regarding themselves, their personnel, investments, or the investment process.**

   Clients must have full and complete information to judge the abilities of Managers and their actions in investing client assets. "Material" information is information that reasonable investors would want to know relative to whether or not they would choose to use or continue to use the Manager.

4. **Disclose the following:**

   a. **Conflicts of interests generated by any relationships with brokers or other entities, other client accounts, fee structures, or other matters.**

      Conflicts of interests often arise in the investment management profession and can take many forms. Best practice is to avoid such conflicts if possible. When Managers cannot reasonably avoid conflicts, they must carefully manage them and disclose them to clients. Disclosure of conflicts of interests protects investors by providing them with the information they need to evaluate the objectivity of their Managers' investment advice and actions taken on behalf of clients and by giving them the information to judge the circumstances, motives, and possible Manager bias for themselves. Examples of some of the types of activities that can constitute actual or potential conflicts of interest are the use of soft dollars or bundled commissions, referral and placement fees, trailing commissions, sales incentives, directed brokerage arrangements, allocation of investment opportunities among similar portfolios, Manager or employee holdings in the same securities as clients, whether the Manager co-invests alongside clients, and use of affiliated brokers.

b. Regulatory or disciplinary action taken against the Manager or its personnel related to professional conduct.

Past professional conduct records are an important factor in an investor's selection of a Manager. Such records include actions taken against a Manager by any regulator or other organization. Managers must fully disclose any significant instances in which the Manager or an employee was found to have violated standards of conduct or other standards in such a way that reflects badly on the integrity, ethics, or competence of the organization or the individual.

c. The investment process, including information regarding lock-up periods, strategies, risk factors, and use of derivatives and leverage.

Managers must disclose to clients and prospects the manner in which investment decisions are made and implemented. Such disclosures should address the overall investment strategy and should include a discussion of the specific risk factors inherent in such a strategy.

Understanding the basic characteristics of an investment is an important factor in judging the suitability of each investment on a stand-alone basis, but it is especially important in determining the effect each investment will have on the characteristics of the client's portfolio. Only by thoroughly understanding the nature of the investment product or service can a client determine whether changes to that product or service could materially affect his or her investment objectives.

d. Management fees and other investment costs charged to investors, including what costs are included in the fees and the methodologies for determining fees and costs.

Investors are entitled to full and fair disclosures of costs associated with the investment management services provided. Material that should be disclosed includes information relating to any fees to be paid to the Managers on an ongoing basis and periodic costs that are known to the Managers and that will affect investors' overall investment expenses. At a minimum, Managers should provide clients with gross- and net-of-fees returns and disclose any unusual expenses.

A general statement that certain fees and other costs will be assessed to investors may not adequately communicate the total amount of expenses that investors may incur as a result of investing. Therefore, Managers must not only use plain language in presenting this information but must clearly explain the methods for determining all fixed and contingent fees and costs that will be borne by investors and also must explain the transactions that will trigger the imposition of these expenses.

Managers should also retrospectively disclose to each client the actual fees and other costs charged to the clients, together with itemizations of such charges when requested by clients. This disclosure should include the specific management fee, any incentive fee, and the amount of commissions Managers paid on behalf of clients during the period. In addition, Managers must disclose to prospective clients the average or expected expenses or fees clients are likely to incur.

e. The amount of any soft or bundled commissions, the goods and/or services received in return, and how those goods and/or services benefit the client.

Commissions belong to the client and should be used in their best interests. Any soft or bundled commissions should be used only to benefit the client. Clients deserve to know how their commissions are spent, what is received in return for them, and how those goods and/or services benefit them.

f. The performance of clients' investments on a regular and timely basis.

Clients may reasonably expect to receive regular performance reporting about their accounts. Without such performance information, even for investment vehicles with lock-up periods, clients cannot evaluate their overall asset allocations (i.e., including assets not held or managed by the Managers) and determine whether rebalancing is necessary. Accordingly, unless otherwise specified by the client, Managers must provide regular, ongoing performance reporting. Managers should report to clients at least quarterly, and when possible, such reporting should be provided within 30 days after the end of the quarter.

g. Valuation methods used to make investment decisions and value client holdings.

Clients deserve to know whether the assets in their portfolios are valued on the basis of closing market values, third-party valuations, internal valuation models, or other methods. This type of disclosure allows clients to compare performance results and determine whether different valuation sources and methods may explain differences in performance results. This disclosure should be made by asset class and must be meaningful (i.e., not general or boilerplate) so that clients can understand how the securities are valued.

h. Shareholder voting policies.

As part of their fiduciary duties, Managers that exercise voting authority over client shares must vote them in an informed and responsible manner. This obligation includes the paramount duty to vote shares in the best interests of clients.

To fulfill their duties, Managers must adopt policies and procedures for the voting of shares and disclose those policies and procedures to clients. These disclosures should specify, among other things, guidelines for instituting regular reviews for new or controversial issues, mechanisms for reviewing unusual proposals, guidance in deciding whether additional actions are warranted when votes are against corporate management, and systems to monitor any delegation of share-voting responsibilities to others. Managers also must disclose to clients how to obtain information on the manner in which their shares were voted.

i. **Trade allocation policies.**

By disclosing their trade allocation policies, Managers give clients a clear understanding of how trades are allocated and provide realistic expectations of what priority they will receive in the investment allocation process. Managers must disclose to clients any changes in the trade allocation policies. By establishing and disclosing trade allocation policies that treat clients fairly, Managers foster an atmosphere of openness and trust with their clients.

j. **Results of the review or audit of the fund or account.**

If a Manager submits its funds or accounts (generally pooled or mutual funds) for an annual review or audit, it must disclose the results to clients. Such disclosure enables clients to hold Managers accountable and alerts them to any potential problems.

k. **Significant personnel or organizational changes that have occurred at the Manager.**

Clients should be made aware of significant changes at the Manager in a timely manner. "Significant" changes would include personnel turnover, merger and acquisition activities of the Manager, and similar actions.

l. **Risk management processes.**

Managers must disclose their risk management processes to clients. Material changes to the risk management process also must be disclosed. Managers should further consider regularly disclosing specific risk information and specific information regarding investment strategies related to each client. Managers must provide clients information detailing what relevant risk metrics they can expect to receive at the individual product/portfolio level.

PRACTICE PROBLEMS

The following information relates to questions 1-6

Henry Schmidt, David Zane, and Andrew Ronoldo founded SZR LLC (SZR), an investment advisory firm managing portfolios for individuals. Although none of the founders holds the CFA charter, SZR has adopted the CFA Institute Asset Manager Code of Professional Conduct.

SZR's client portfolios average $50,000 and are entirely invested in SZR's commingled fund, managed by Ronoldo. Ronoldo implements a quantitative enhanced index process in SZR's fund and has consistently added moderate performance (alpha) over the fund's mid-cap benchmark index. After five years of strong performance, Ronoldo worries that the mid-cap fund will lag broad market indexes, so he decides to broaden the fund's strategy. After doing research, he adds micro-cap, foreign, and convertible preferred stocks to the fund and doubles some holdings so that their weights are much larger than they are in the benchmark index. Since the fund achieves even stronger performance, both against the benchmark mid-cap index and major market indexes, Ronoldo plans to describe the new strategy in the company's next annual newsletter, due to be sent to clients in three months.

As a prominent member of the community, Schmidt has just joined the board of a local company, Trezeguet Baking Company, which recently went public. Trezeguet's shares are in most micro-capitalization (cap) indexes. As a board member, Schmidt receives a small annual stipend of $2,000; however, he is granted several thousand stock options, which he can exercise after 24 months' board service. Since his stipend is insignificant and he will not exercise his options for at least 24 months, Schmidt does not disclose his Trezeguet board service to SZR clients.

One of SZR's clients is president of Sastre International. Because of SZR's success, this client hires SZR to manage $800 million of Sastre International's corporate cash in a separate account, but asks that its hiring of SZR not be made public. Sastre's board asks Ronoldo to direct all of the Sastre account trades through a local financial advisor, to thank the advisor for selecting SZR. Ronoldo is concerned that this direction may limit SZR's ability to achieve best execution, but after Sastre acknowledges in writing that this is their preference, Ronoldo agrees to follow Sastre's direction.

As head of operations, Zane wishes to simplify trading and implements a new trade policy: first place trades for the Sastre account through the local financial advisor and then submit the commingled fund's trades through national brokerage houses and electronic networks. The local financial advisor is pleased with this arrangement, as he is able to buy securities before other clients; he informs Zane that he'll recommend SZR to additional clients.

Schmidt, SZR's sales director, sends the commingled fund's stellar performance track record to several investment consultants, who serve as "gatekeepers" for large institutional clients, but he is told that SZR is too small to be considered by their clients. After Schmidt reveals that Sastre has recently hired SZR, and offers to negotiate the same special fee discount that has been given to Sastre, one consultant agrees to consider SZR for its clients. The consultant indicates that if SZR agrees to sponsor the consulting firm's annual conference, Schmidt will meet many potential clients. Schmidt considers this conference sponsorship, but decides that it is too costly for SZR's budget, so he declines the offer.

As SZR grows, Zane hires his brother-in-law, John Karna (top salesman for a local auto parts company) as Compliance Officer. Karna is tasked with writing SZR's Code of Ethics and its Investment Policies and Procedures Manual. Karna is also put in charge of the firm's Business Continuity Plan. The plan consists of his taking home, each evening, the computer records of SZR's daily trades.

1. Does Ronoldo violate the CFA Institute Asset Manager Code of Professional Conduct with respect to his broader investment strategy?

   A. No.

   B. Yes, with respect to client disclosure only.

   C. Yes, with respect to reasonable and adequate basis only.

2. Does Schmidt violate the CFA Institute Asset Manager Code of Professional Conduct with respect to his current Trezeguet board service?

   A. No.

   B. Yes, with respect to priority of client interests only.

   C. Yes, with respect to priority of client interests and participation in business relationships.

3. By agreeing to Sastre's direction, does Ronoldo violate the CFA Institute Asset Manager Code of Professional Conduct?

   A. No.

   B. Yes, only with respect to best execution.

   C. Yes, only with respect to fair and equitable trade allocation.

4. Does Zane's revision of SZR's trading process violate the CFA Institute Asset Manager Code of Professional Conduct?

   A. No.

   B. Yes, only with respect to best execution.

   C. Yes, with respect to best execution and fair, equitable trade allocation.

5. Does Schmidt violate the CFA Institute Asset Manager Code of Professional Conduct in his interaction with consultants?

   A. No.

   B. Yes, only with respect to confidentiality.

   C. Yes, only with respect to business relationships that could affect independence.

6. Does Karna's role as Chief Compliance Officer, and the process of SZR's Business Continuity Plan, respectively, conform to the requirements and recommendations of the CFA Institute Asset Manager Code of Professional Conduct?

   A. Neither Karna's role nor the Business Continuity Plan conforms.

   B. Karna's role conforms, but the Business Continuity Plan does not conform.

C. Karna's role does not conform, but the Business Continuity Plan does conform.

The following information relates to questions 7-12

Bornelli Asset Management offers traditional long-only funds as well as a variety of hedge funds for both private and institutional clients. Bornelli is a well-managed firm of more than 100 employees. Its board of directors has voted to adopt the Asset Manager Code of Professional Conduct (the Code).

Bornelli has hired Ava Campanelli as chief compliance officer with responsibility for implementing the Code. Campanelli develops a plan to evaluate the firm's current policies and procedures for compliance with the Code. Campanelli begins by reviewing three of the firm's compliance procedures:

Portfolio review	Portfolio information provided to clients is reviewed by an independent third-party.
Record retention	The firm retains records to substantiate all investment decisions for seven years. In compliance with regulatory requirements, the firm also retains copies of all emails for the same period. The firm retains its records in a combination of both hard-copy and electronic formats.
Investigation of complaints	The chief compliance officer (CCO) is responsible for investigating and documenting all complaints. The CCO reports to the chief investment officer and works with management to take appropriate disciplinary action in cases of compliance breaches.

Campanelli then evaluates the firm's business-continuity plan. Under the current plan, the technology division backs up all of the firm's computer systems and client records twice daily. The back-ups are stored in a fireproof storage facility offsite. Bornelli outsources certain emergency plans to a disaster recovery firm. The disaster recovery firm is responsible for developing and implementing plans to communicate with employees and mission-critical vendors and suppliers in the event of a facility or communication disruption. The same firm also provides plans for contacting and communicating with clients in event of an extended disruption.

For her next project, Campanelli reviews the disclosures provided to both prospective and current clients. The disclosures regarding management fees state:

Bornelli charges a 2% asset-based management fee. In addition to the management fee, clients may pay an incentive fee at the end of each year. The incentive fee is equal to 20% of the account's net investment income and net realized and unrealized capital gains for the year.

No incentive fee will be paid unless the Fund has offset all prior net realized capital losses and net investment losses with realized capital gains, unrealized appreciation, and net investment income from all securities held by the Fund.

Campanelli's evaluation of the management fee disclosures is interrupted by a more urgent matter involving a client. The client has requested monthly performance reporting of his investment in a long-short equity hedge fund. The fund's administrator argues "Our procedures call for us to provide clients with both gross- and net-of-fees returns within 30 days of the end of the quarter." He adds "Quarterly reporting is the industry standard."

The administrator complains "This client, Rossi, is overly demanding. He telephoned yesterday and requested an itemization of the fees and other costs charged to him for the past three years. He wants to know the specific management fee, the incentive fee, and the amount of commissions paid. The more time we spend answering his requests, the less time we have to research investments." Campanelli promises to look into the matter for the administrator.

The following week, Campanelli meets with Lee Bruno, manager of the firm's alternative assets fund. Bruno informs Campanelli, "The fund has a three-year lock-up period. We disclosed to all the prospective clients in writing before they invested that this is a long-term investment and that they should not focus on short-term performance results. During the lock-up period, we provide semiannual reporting. After the lock-up, we report quarterly."

Bruno informs Campanelli that whenever possible, the firm uses fair market prices to value client holdings. He adds "Of course, our fund invests in alternative assets—some of which are very difficult to value. They aren't like public equities with independent, third-party market quotations available, so we use an internal model to value client holdings." He continues, "We disclose the use of internal models for valuation purposes on all our reports."

Following her conversation with Bruno, Campanelli researches a complaint from a new client regarding the valuations of his fund's holdings. The client complains that another management firm reported much lower valuations on similar instruments. Campanelli researches the methodologies Bornelli uses for valuing fund holdings. She determines the following:

- All publicly traded US and foreign equities, including large-, mid-, small-, and micro-cap shares are valued at the last available closing price.
- The value of certain securities such as swaps are based on quotes collected from broker-dealers.
- When prices are not available from either of the above sources, valuations are based on internal models.

7. Are the three compliance procedures reviewed by Campanelli consistent with both the required and recommended standards of the CFA Institute Asset Manager Code of Professional Conduct?

   A. No, the procedures regarding record retention are inconsistent.

   B. No, the procedures regarding portfolio review are inconsistent.

   C. No, the procedures regarding investigation of complaints are inconsistent.

8. Is Bornelli's disaster recovery plan consistent with both the required and recommended standards of the Asset Manager Code?

   A. Yes.

   B. No, because the plan lacks a backup plan for monitoring, analyzing, and trading investments.

   C. No, because the plan only provides for contacting and communicating with clients during periods of extended disruption.

9. Are the firm's disclosures regarding management fees consistent with the required and recommended standards of the Asset Manager Code?

   A. Yes.

B. No, because they do not use plain language.

C. No, because they do not include the average or expected expenses or fees clients are likely to incur.

10. Are the performance reporting procedures described by the fund's administrator consistent with the required disclosure standards of the Asset Manager Code?

A. Yes.

B. No, because the AMC requires firms to report performance to all clients on a monthly basis.

C. No, because the AMC requires firms to provide performance on a monthly basis when requested by clients.

11. To comply with both the required and recommended standards of the Asset Manager Code, must Bornelli honor Rossi's telephone request regarding an itemization of fees?

A. Yes.

B. No, because the firm is not required to disclose the amount of incentive fee charged to an individual client.

C. No, because unless the firm claims compliance with the Soft Dollar Standards, it is not required to disclose the amount of commissions paid on clients' behalf.

12. Are the policies of the alternative assets fund consistent with the required and recommended standards of the Asset Manager Code?

A. Yes.

B. No, the frequency of reporting is inconsistent with the AMC.

C. No, the use of internal valuation models is inconsistent with the AMC.

SOLUTIONS

1. B is correct. Ronoldo should have disclosed his change in investment strategy to clients, allowing them to move their accounts if not in agreement. Until he disclosed a planned change in strategy, he should have continued to manage in the manner for which clients had hired him.

2. C is correct. Schmidt is on the board of a company whose stock is in microcap indexes. This is a conflict of interest, as Ronoldo's widened investment guidelines allow purchase of Trezeguet stock for the fund. As Schmidt is an insider for the company and received options that can be sold (after 24 months), this relationship should be terminated.

3. A is correct. The Sastre board requests directed trading for its discretionary account and acknowledges, in writing, that trading through the local financial advisor may limit best execution. As this is a discretionary (not pension) account, the client has the right to direct to a less-than-optimal trading venue.

4. C is correct. Zane should have pursued best execution for all clients in the fund (which is not accomplished by placing trades with the local financial advisor first versus with national brokers or electronic networks), and fairly traded for all clients. While Sastre is welcome to direct trades, Zane's change in procedures harms other clients.

5. B is correct. Schmidt violated Code A-2 by revealing Sastre's hiring of SZR and its special fee discount.

6. A is correct. Karna's qualification as compliance officer is inadequate (D-2, D-5), and taking tapes home each night is inadequate business continuity for a firm of $1.5 billion (D-6).

7. C is correct. According to the recommendations of Section D(2) of the Asset Manager Code, where possible, the CCO should be independent from the investment and operations personnel and should report directly to the CEO or the board of directors.

8. B is correct. According to the guidance provided in Section D(6) of the Asset Manager Code, the level and complexity of business-continuity planning depends on the size, nature, and complexity of the organization involved. Bornelli is a large firm with hedge fund investments and it should have alternative plans for monitoring, analyzing, and trading investments if primary systems become unavailable.

9. C is correct. According to the recommendations and guidance of Section F(4d) of the Asset Manager Code, managers must disclose to prospective clients the average or expected expenses or fees clients are likely to incur, and to existing clients the actual fees and other costs charged to them.

10. A is correct. The performance reporting procedures described by the administrator are consistent with the Asset Manager Code (AMC) which requires disclosing the "performance of clients' investments on a regular and timely basis." The AMC recommends that "managers should report to clients at least quarterly, and when possible, such reporting should be provided within 30 days after the end of the quarter." The AMC also states that "at a minimum, Managers should provide clients with gross- and net-of-fees returns." Because quarterly reporting is the

recommended minimum, managers may choose to provide more timely performance to clients.

11. A is correct. According to the recommendations of Section F(4d) of the Asset Manager Code, managers should disclose to each client the actual fees and other costs charged to them, together with itemizations of such charges, when requested by clients. The disclosure should include the specific management fee, incentive fee, and the amount of commissions paid on clients' behalf during the period.

12. B is correct. Clients must have regular performance information to evaluate their overall asset allocations and to determine whether rebalancing is necessary. This concept applies even to investment vehicles with lock-up periods. According to the Asset Manager Code, unless otherwise specified by the client, managers should report to clients at least quarterly, and when possible, within 30 days of the end of the period.

Glossary

Absolute return benchmark A minimum target return that an investment manager is expected to beat.

Accrual taxes Taxes levied and paid on a periodic basis.

Accumulation phase Phase where the government predominantly contributes to a sovereign wealth pension reserve fund.

Active management A portfolio management approach that allows risk factor mismatches relative to a benchmark index causing potentially significant return differences between the active portfolio and the underlying benchmark.

Active return The return on a portfolio minus the return on the portfolio's benchmark.

Active risk The standard deviation of active returns.

Active risk budgeting Risk budgeting that concerns active risk (risk relative to a portfolio's benchmark).

Active share A measure of how similar a portfolio is to its benchmark. A manager who precisely replicates the benchmark will have an active share of zero; a manager with no holdings in common with the benchmark will have an active share of one.

Aggregate wealth The total value of all assets owned, encompassing personal property, financial assets, real assets, and rights.

Arithmetic attribution An attribution approach which explains the arithmetic difference between the portfolio return and its benchmark return. The single-period attribution effects sum to the excess return, however, when combining multiple periods, the sub-period attribution effects will not sum to the excess return.

Ask price The price at which a trader will sell a specified quantity of a security. Also called *ask*, *offer price*, or *offer*.

Asset-only With respect to asset allocation, an approach that focuses directly on the characteristics of the assets without explicitly modeling the liabilities.

Authority bias A behavioral bias which involves groups deferring to a group member that is a subject matter expert or in a position of authority.

Aversion to complexity A behavioral phenomenon of groups in many professional contexts, in which disproportionate attention is given to trivial issues at the expense of important but harder-to-grasp or contested topics.

Back-fill bias The distortion in index or peer group data which results when returns are reported to a database only after they are known to be good returns.

Base With respect to a foreign exchange quotation of the price of one unit of a currency, the currency referred to in "one unit of a currency."

Basis risk The possibility that the expected value of a derivative differs unexpectedly from that of the underlying.

Bear spread An option strategy that becomes more valuable when the price of the underlying asset declines, so requires buying one option and writing another with a *lower* exercise price. A put bear spread involves buying a put with a higher exercise price and selling a put with a lower exercise price. A bear spread can also be executed with calls.

Best ask The offer to sell with the lowest ask price. Also called *best offer* or *inside ask*.

Best bid The highest bid in the market.

Best offer The lowest offer (ask price) in the market.

Best-in-class An ESG implementation approach that seeks to identify the most favorable companies and sectors based on ESG considerations. Also called *positive screening*.

Bid price In a price quotation, the price at which the party making the quotation is willing to buy a specified quantity of an asset or security.

Bid–ask spread The ask price minus the bid price.

Buffering Establishing ranges around breakpoints that define whether a stock belongs in one index or another.

Bull spread An option strategy that becomes more valuable when the price of the underlying asset rises, so requires buying one option and writing another with a *higher* exercise price. A call bull spread involves buying a call with a lower exercise price and selling a call with a higher exercise price. A bull spread can also be executed with puts.

Business cycle Fluctuations in GDP in relation to long-term trend growth, usually lasting 9-11 years.

Calendar rebalancing Rebalancing a portfolio to target weights on a periodic basis; for example, monthly, quarterly, semiannually, or annually.

Calendar spread A strategy in which one sells an option and buys the same type of option but with different expiration dates, on the same underlying asset and with the same strike. When the investor buys the more distant (near-term) call and sells the near-term (more distant) call, it is a long (short) calendar spread.

Canada model Characterized by a high allocation to alternatives. Unlike the endowment model, however, the Canada model relies more on internally managed assets. The innovative features of the Canada model are the: a) reference portfolio, b) total portfolio approach, and c) active management.

Capital market expectations (CME) Expectations concerning the risk and return prospects of asset classes.

Capital sufficiency analysis The process of evaluating whether a client has sufficient capital resources to achieve their financial goals and objectives; it considers the client's assets, liabilities, income, expenses, risk tolerance, time horizon, and other relevant factors.

Capture ratio A measure of the manager's gain or loss relative to the gain or loss of the benchmark.

Carhart model A four factor model used in performance attribution. The four factors are: market (RMRF), size (SMB), value (HML), and momentum (WML).

Carry trade A trading strategy that involves buying a security and financing it at a rate that is lower than the yield on that security.

Cash flow matching Immunization approach that attempts to ensure that all future liability payouts are matched precisely by cash flows from bonds or fixed-income derivatives.

Cash-secured put An option strategy involving the writing of a put option and simultaneously depositing an amount of money equal to the exercise price into a designated account (this strategy is also called a fiduciary put).

Collar An option position in which the investor is long shares of stock and then buys a put with an exercise price below the current stock price and writes a call with an exercise price above the current stock price. Collars allow a shareholder to acquire downside protection through a protective put but reduce the cash outlay by writing a covered call.

Contingent immunization Hybrid approach that combines immunization with an active management approach when the asset portfolio's value exceeds the present value of the liability portfolio.

Cost basis The initial cost of acquiring an investment including expenses incurred to acquire the investment. Also referred to as simply basis.

Covered call An option strategy in which a long position in an asset is combined with a short position in a call on that asset.

Cross hedge A hedge involving a hedging instrument that is imperfectly correlated with the asset being hedged; an example is hedging a bond investment with futures on a non-identical bond.

Cross-currency basis swap A swap in which notional principals are exchanged because the goal of the transaction is to issue at a more favorable funding rate and swap the amount back to the currency of choice.

Cross-sectional consistency A feature of expectations setting which means that estimates for all classes reflect the same underlying assumptions and are generated with methodologies that reflect or preserve important relationships among the asset classes, such as strong correlations. It is the internal consistency across asset classes.

Currency overlay programs A currency overlay program is a program to manage a portfolio's currency exposures for the case in which those exposures are managed separately from the management of the portfolio itself.

Custom security-based benchmark Benchmark that is custom built to accurately reflect the investment discipline of a particular investment manager. Also called a *strategy benchmark* because it reflects a manager's particular strategy.

Decision-reversal risk The risk of reversing a chosen course of action at the point of maximum loss.

Decumulation phase Phase where the government predominantly withdraws from a sovereign wealth pension reserve fund.

Deferred taxes Taxes postponed until some future date.

Defined benefit A retirement plan in which a plan sponsor commits to paying a specified retirement benefit.

Defined benefit plan Retirement plan that is funded by the employer that guarantees a retirement benefit based on factors such as years of service, salary, and age.

Defined contribution A retirement plan in which contributions are defined but the ultimate retirement benefit is not specified or guaranteed by the plan sponsor.

Defined contribution plan Retirement plan in which the employer, employee, or both contribute to an account in which the employee bears the investment risk.

Delay costs Implicit trading costs that arise from the inability to complete desired trades immediately. Also called *slippage*.

Delta The sensitivity of the derivative price to a small change in the value of the underlying asset.

Delta hedging Hedging that involves matching the price response of the position being hedged over a narrow range of prices.

Demand deposits Accounts that can be drawn upon regularly and without notice. This category includes checking accounts and certain savings accounts that are often accessible through online banks or automated teller machines (ATMs).

Diffusion index Reflects the proportion of the index's components that are moving in a pattern consistent with the overall index.

Dividend capture A trading strategy whereby an equity portfolio manager purchases stocks just before their ex-dividend dates, holds these stocks through the ex-dividend date to earn the right to receive the dividend, and subsequently sells the shares.

Domestic asset An asset that trades in the investor's domestic currency (or home currency).

Domestic currency The currency of the investor, i.e., the currency in which he or she typically makes consumption purchases, e.g., the Swiss franc for an investor domiciled in Switzerland.

Domestic-currency return A rate of return stated in domestic currency terms from the perspective of the investor; reflects both the foreign-currency return on an asset as well as percentage movement in the spot exchange rate between the domestic and foreign currencies.

Drawdown A percentage peak-to-trough reduction in net asset value.

Drawdown duration The total time from the start of the drawdown until the cumulative drawdown recovers to zero.

Due diligence Investigation and analysis in support of an investment action, decision, or recommendation.

Duration matching Immunization approach based on the duration of assets and liabilities. Ideally, the liabilities being matched (the liability portfolio) and the portfolio of assets (the bond portfolio) should be affected similarly by a change in interest rates.

Duration times spread Weighting of spread duration by credit spread in order to incorporate the empirical observation that spread changes for lower-rated bonds tend to be consistent on a percentage, rather than absolute, basis.

Dynamic asset allocation Dynamic asset allocation is an investment strategy premised on long-term asset allocation but employing short-term, tactical trading to maintain investment allocation targets.

Dynamic hedge A hedge requiring adjustment as the price of the hedged asset changes.

Econometrics The application of quantitative modeling and analysis grounded in economic theory to the analysis of economic data.

Economic balance sheet An extended balance sheet that includes the present values of both lifetime earnings and future consumption.

Economic indicators Economic statistics provided by government and established private organizations that contain information on an economy's recent past activity or its current or future position in the business cycle.

Effective federal funds (FFE) rate The fed funds rate actually transacted between depository institutions, not the Fed's target federal funds rate.

Effective spread Two times the difference between the execution price and the midpoint of the market quote at the time an order is entered.

Endowment model Characterized by a high allocation to alternative investments (private investments and hedge funds), significant active management, and externally managed assets.

Enhanced indexing approach Maintains a close link to the benchmark but attempts to generate a modest amount of outperformance relative to the benchmark.

Excess return Used in various senses appropriate to context: 1) The difference between the portfolio return and the benchmark return, which may be either positive or negative; 2) The return in excess of the risk-free rate, thus representing the return for bearing risk.

Exhaustive Covering or containing all possible outcomes.

Extended portfolio assets and liabilities Assets and liabilities beyond those shown on a conventional balance sheet that are relevant in making asset allocation decisions; an example of an extended asset is human capital.

Factor-model-based benchmarks Benchmarks constructed by examining a portfolio's sensitivity to a set of factors, such as the return for a broad market index, company earnings growth, industry, or financial leverage.

Family offices Private firms that offer a range of wealth management services tailored specifically for ultra-high-net-worth individuals.

Foreign assets Assets denominated in currencies other than the investor's home currency.

Foreign currency Currency that is not the currency in which an investor makes consumption purchases, e.g., the US dollar from the perspective of a Swiss investor.

Foreign-currency return The return of the foreign asset measured in foreign-currency terms.

Forward rate bias An empirically observed divergence from interest rate parity conditions that active investors seek to benefit from by borrowing in a lower-yield currency and investing in a higher-yield currency.

Funding currencies The low-yield currencies in which borrowing occurs in a carry trade.

Gamma A numerical measure of how sensitive an option's delta (the sensitivity of the derivative's price) is to a change in the value of the underlying.

General account Account holding assets to fund future liabilities from traditional life insurance and fixed annuities, the products in which the insurer bears all the risks—particularly mortality risk and longevity risk.

Gini coefficient A measure of inequality of wealth, or *i*, that ranges from 0 (perfect equality) to 1 (perfect inequality).

Goals-based With respect to asset allocation or investing, an approach that focuses on achieving an investor's goals (for example, related to supporting lifestyle needs or aspirations) based typically on constructing sub-portfolios aligned with those goals.

Goals-based investing An investment industry term for approaches to investing for individuals and families focused on aligning investments with goals (parallel to liability-driven investing for institutional investors).

Grinold–Kroner model An expression for the expected return on a share as the sum of an expected income return, an expected nominal earnings growth return, and an expected repricing return.

Groupthink A behavioral bias that occurs when a team minimizes conflict and dissent in reaching and maintaining a consensus.

Hedge ratio The proportion of an underlying that will offset the risk associated with a derivative position.

High-net-worth individuals (HNWIs) Individuals with investable assets exceeding a certain minimum level, often as low as USD1 million, but typically more.

High-water mark A measure that reflects the fund's maximum value as of a performance fee payment date net of fees.

Holdings-based attribution A "buy and hold" attribution approach which calculates the return of portfolio and benchmark components based upon the price and foreign exchange rate changes applied to daily snapshots of portfolio holdings.

Holdings-based style analysis A bottom-up style analysis that estimates the risk exposures from the actual securities held in the portfolio at a point in time.

Home bias A preference for securities listed on the exchanges of one's home country.

Home currency See *domestic currency.*

Home-country bias The favoring of domestic over non-domestic investments relative to global market value weights.

Human capital The present value of an individual's future expected labor income.

Impact investing Refers to investments made with the specific intent of generating positive, measurable social and environmental impact alongside a financial return (which differentiates it from philanthropy).

Implementation shortfall (IS) The difference between the return for a notional or paper portfolio, where all transactions are assumed to take place at the manager's decision price, and the portfolio's actual return, which reflects realized transactions, including all fees and costs.

Implied volatility The standard deviation that causes an option pricing model to give the current option price.

Implied volatility surface A three-dimensional plot, for put and call options on the same underlying asset, of days to expiration (*x*-axis), option strike prices (*y*-axis), and implied volatilities (*z*-axis). It simultaneously shows the volatility skew (or smile) and the term structure of implied volatility.

Inflation-linked bonds Debt instruments that link the principal and interest to inflation.

Input uncertainty Uncertainty concerning whether the inputs are correct.

Inside ask See *best ask.*

Inside bid See *best bid.*

Inside spread The spread between the best bid price and the best ask price. Also called the *market bid-ask spread, inside bid-ask spread,* or *market spread.*

Interaction effect The impact of overweighting and underweighting individual securities within sectors that are themselves overweighted or underweighted.

Intertemporal consistency A feature of expectations setting which means that estimates for an asset class over different horizons reflect the same assumptions with respect to the potential paths of returns over time. It is the internal consistency over various time horizons.

Intrinsic value The amount gained (per unit) by an option buyer if an option is exercised at any given point in time. May be referred to as the exercise value of the option.

Investable net worth The sum of liquid assets, such as savings and investment accounts, and less short-term liabilities such as credit card debt.

Investable wealth The sum of liquid assets such as savings and investment accounts.

Investment currencies The high-yielding currencies in a carry trade.

Investment policy statement (IPS) A description of a client's unique investment objectives, risk tolerance, investment time horizon, and other applicable constraints.

Investment style A natural grouping of investment disciplines that has some predictive power in explaining the future dispersion of returns across portfolios.

Key person risk The risk that results from over-reliance on an individual or individuals whose departure would negatively affect an investment manager.

Knock-in/knock-out Features of a vanilla option that is created (or ceases to exist) when the spot exchange rate touches a pre-specified level.

Latency The elapsed time between the occurrence of an event and a subsequent action that depends on that event.

Leading economic indicators Turning points that usually precede those of the overall economy; they are believed to have value for predicting the economy's future state, usually near-term.

Liability driven investing (LDI) model In the LDI model, the primary investment objective is to generate returns sufficient to cover liabilities, with a focus on maximizing expected surplus return (excess return of assets over liabilities) and managing surplus volatility.

Liability glide path A specification of desired proportions of liability-hedging assets and return-seeking assets and the duration of the liability hedge as funded status changes and contributions are made.

Liability-based mandates Mandates managed to match or cover expected liability payments (future cash outflows) with future projected cash inflows.

Liability-driven investing An investment industry term that generally encompasses asset allocation that is focused on funding an investor's liabilities in institutional contexts.

Liability-relative With respect to asset allocation, an approach that focuses directly only on funding liabilities as an investment objective.

Limit order book The book or list of limit orders to buy and sell that pertains to a security.

Limited-life foundations A type of foundation where founders seek to maintain control of spending while they (or their immediate heirs) are still alive.

Longevity risk The risk of exhausting an individual's financial resources before passing away, thereby leaving insufficient capital for living expenses and unmet needs.

Lorenz curve A measure of the cumulative percentage of wealth owned by each percentage of the population.

Macro attribution Attribution at the sponsor level.

Manager peer group See *manager universe.*

Manager universe A broad group of managers with similar investment disciplines. Also called *manager peer group.*

Marginal tax rate The highest rate of tax applied to taxable income.

Market fragmentation Trading the same instrument in multiple venues.

Market impact The effect of the trade on transaction prices. Also called *price impact.*

Micro attribution Attribution at the portfolio manager level.

Midquote price The average, or midpoint, of the prevailing bid and ask prices.

Minimum-variance hedge ratio A mathematical approach to determining the optimal cross hedging ratio.

Mission-related investing Investing aimed at causes promoting positive societal or environmental change.

Model uncertainty Uncertainty as to whether a selected model is correct.

Negative screening An ESG investment style that focuses on the exclusion of certain sectors, companies, or practices in a fund or portfolio on the basis of specific ESG criteria.

Net worth The difference between assets and liabilities.

Non-deliverable forwards Cash-settled forward contracts, used predominately with respect to foreign exchange forwards. Also called *contracts for differences.*

Nonstationarity A characteristic of series of data whose properties, such as mean and variance, are not constant through time. When analyzing historical data it means that different parts of a data series reflect different underlying statistical properties.

Norway model Characterized by an almost exclusive reliance on public equities and fixed income (the traditional 60/40 equity/bond model falls under the Norway model), with largely passively managed assets and with very little to no allocation to alternative investments.

Offer price The price at which a counterparty is willing to sell one unit of the base currency.

Opportunity cost Reflects the foregone opportunity of investing in a different asset. It is typically denoted by the risk-free rate of interest, r.

Optional stock dividends A type of dividend in which shareholders may elect to receive either cash or new shares.

Overbought A market condition in which market sentiment is thought to be unsustainably bullish.

Oversold A market condition in which market sentiment is thought to be unsustainably bearish.

Packeting Splitting stock positions into multiple parts.

Parameter uncertainty Uncertainty arising because a quantitative model's parameters are estimated with error.

Participant-switching life-cycle options Automatically switch DC plan members into a more conservative asset mix as their age increases. There may be several automatic de-risking switches at different age targets.

Participant/cohort option Pools the DC plan member with a cohort that has a similar target retirement date.

Passive management A buy-and-hold approach to investing in which an investor does not make portfolio changes based upon short-term expectations of changing market or security performance.

Percent-range rebalancing An approach to rebalancing that involves setting rebalancing thresholds or trigger points, stated as a percentage of the portfolio's value, around target values.

Performance attribution The process of disaggregating a portfolio's return to determine the drivers of its performance.

Personal assets Nonbusiness, on-investment assets including personal property and real property.

Personal property Property owned by individuals that are not real property and not considered investments.

Planned goals Financial objectives that can be reasonably estimated or quantified at the onset and can be achieved within an expected time horizon.

Position delta The overall or portfolio delta. For example, the position delta of a covered call, consisting of long 100 shares and short one at-the-money call, is +50 (= +100 for the shares and -50 for the short ATM call).

Positive screening An ESG implementation approach that seeks to identify the most favorable companies and sectors based on ESG considerations. Also called *best-in-class.*

Price improvement When trade execution prices are better than quoted prices.

Private wealth management Financial planning and investment management to help individual investors, particularly high-net-worth individuals (HNWIs) and ultra-high-net-worth individuals (UHNWIs), manage their wealth.

Protective put A strategy of purchasing an underlying asset and purchasing a put on the same asset.

Pure indexing Attempts to replicate a bond index as closely as possible, targeting zero active return and zero active risk.

Put spread A strategy used to reduce the upfront cost of buying a protective put, it involves buying a put option and writing another put option.

Re-base With reference to index construction, to change the time period used as the base of the index.

Realized volatility Historical volatility, the square root of the realized variance of returns, which is a measure of the range of past price outcomes for the underlying asset.

Rebalancing Adjusting the weights of the constituent securities in an index.

Rebalancing range A range of values for asset class weights defined by trigger points above and below target weights, such that if the portfolio value passes through a trigger point, rebalancing occurs. Also known as a corridor.

Rebate rate The portion of the collateral earnings rate that is repaid to the security borrower by the security lender.

Reduced form models Statistical credit models that solve for the probability of default over a specific time period, using observable company-specific and market-based variables.

Regime The governing set of relationships (between variables) that stem from technological, political, legal, and regulatory environments. Changes in such environments or policy stances can be described as changes in regime.

Relative value A concept that describes the selection of the most attractive individual securities to populate the portfolio with, using ranking and comparing.

Repo rate The interest rate on a repurchase agreement.

Repurchase agreements In repurchase agreements, or repos, a security owner agrees to sell a security for a specific cash amount while simultaneously agreeing to repurchase the security at a specified future date (typically one day later) and price.

Reserve portfolio The component of an insurer's general account that is subject to specific regulatory requirements and is intended to ensure the company's ability to meet its policy liabilities. The assets in the reserve portfolio are managed conservatively and must be highly liquid and low risk.

Resistance levels Price points on dealers' order boards where one would expect to see a clustering of offers.

Return attribution A set of techniques used to identify the sources of the excess return of a portfolio against its benchmark.

Returns-based attribution An attribution approach that uses only the total portfolio returns over a period to identify the components of the investment process that have generated the returns. The Brinson–Hood–Beebower approach is a returns-based attribution approach.

Returns-based benchmarks Benchmarks constructed by examining a portfolio's sensitivity to a set of factors, such as the returns for various style indexes (e.g., small-cap value, small-cap growth, large-cap value, and large-cap growth).

Returns-based style analysis A top-down style analysis that involves estimating the sensitivities of a portfolio to security market indexes.

Reverse repos Repurchase agreements from the standpoint of the lender.

Risk attribution The analysis of the sources of risk.

Risk aversion The dislike for risk such that compensation is required in terms of higher expected returns for assuming higher risk.

Risk budgeting The establishment of objectives for individuals, groups, or divisions of an organization that takes into account the allocation of an acceptable level of risk.

Risk capacity The ability to bear financial risk.

Risk premiums Extra returns expected by investors for bearing some specified risk.

Risk reversal A strategy used to profit from the existence of an implied volatility skew and from changes in its shape over time. A combination of long (short) calls and short (long) puts on the same underlying with the same expiration is a long (short) risk reversal.

Risk tolerance The level of risk an investor is willing and able to bear.

Seagull spread An extension of the risk reversal foreign exchange option strategy that limits downside risk.

Securities lending A form of collateralized lending that may be used to generate income for portfolios.

Selective An index construction methodology that targets only those securities with certain characteristics.

Separate accounts Accounts holding assets to fund future liabilities from variable life insurance and variable annuities, the products in which customers make investment decisions from a menu of options and themselves bear investment risk.

Sharpe ratio The ratio of mean excess return to standard deviation (excess return).

Shortfall probability The probability of failing to meet a specific liability or goal.

Shrinkage estimation Estimation that involves taking a weighted average of a historical estimate of a parameter and some other parameter estimate, where the weights reflect the analyst's relative belief in the estimates.

Special dividends Dividends paid by a company that does not pay dividends on a regular schedule, or dividends that supplement regular cash dividends with an extra payment.

Spread duration The change in bond price for a given change in yield spread. Also referred to as OAS duration when the option-adjusted spread (OAS) is the yield measure used.

Static hedge A hedge that is not sensitive to changes in the price of the asset hedged.

Stock lending Securities lending involving the transfer of equities.

Stops Stop-loss orders involve leaving bids or offers away from the current market price to be filled if the market reaches those levels.

Straddle An option combination in which one buys *both* puts and calls, with the same exercise price and same expiration date, on the same underlying asset. In contrast to this long straddle, if someone *writes* both options, it is a short straddle.

Strangle A variation on a straddle in which the put and call have different exercise prices; if the put and call are held long, it is a long strangle; if they are held short, it is a short strangle.

Strategic asset allocation A long-term strategy that establishes target allocations for various asset classes and aims to optimize the balance between risk and reward by diversifying investments.

Structural models Models that specify functional relationships among variables based on economic theory. The functional form and parameters of these models are derived from the underlying theory. They may include unobservable parameters.

Support levels Price points on dealers' order boards where one would expect to see a clustering of bids.

Surplus The difference between assets and liabilities, analogous to shareholders' equity on a corporate balance sheet.

Surplus portfolio The component of an insurer's general account that is intended to realize higher expected returns than the reserve portfolio and so can assume some liquidity risk. Surplus portfolio assets are often managed aggressively with exposure to alternative assets.

Survivorship bias Relates to the inclusion of only current investment funds in a database. As such, the returns of funds that are no longer available in the marketplace (have been liquidated) are excluded from the database. Also see *backfill bias*.

Synthetic long forward position The combination of a long call and a short put with identical strike price and expiration, traded at the same time on the same underlying.

Synthetic short forward position The combination of a short call and a long put at the same strike price and maturity (traded at the same time on the same underlying).

Tactical asset allocation A proactive strategy that adjusts asset class allocations within a portfolio based on short-term market trends, economic conditions, or valuation changes to capitalize on temporary market inefficiencies or opportunities to improve returns or manage risk more effectively.

Tax drag The negative effect of taxes on an investment's net returns.

Taylor rule A rule linking a central bank's target short-term interest rate to the rate of growth of the economy and inflation.

Term deposits Interest-bearing accounts that have a specified maturity date. This category includes savings accounts and certificates of deposit (CDs). Also see *time deposits*.

Term structure of volatility The plot of implied volatility (y-axis) against option maturity (x-axis) for options with the same strike price on the same underlying. Typically, implied volatility is not constant across different maturities – rather, it is often in contango, meaning that the implied volatilities for longer-term options are higher than for near-term ones.

Thematic investing An investment approach that focuses on companies in a specific sector or following a specific theme, such as energy efficiency or climate change.

Theta The change in a derivative instrument for a given small change in calendar time, holding everything else constant. Specifically, the theta calculation assumes nothing changes except calendar time. Theta also reflects the rate at which an option's time value decays.

Threshold-based rebalancing policy The manager rebalances the portfolio when asset class weights deviate from their target weights by a prespecified percentage regardless of timing and frequency.

Time deposits Interest-bearing accounts that have a specified maturity date. This category includes savings accounts and certificates of deposit (CDs). Also see *term deposits*.

Time value The difference between an option's premium and its intrinsic value.

Time-based rebalancing policy The manager rebalances the portfolio regularly, at a certain given time interval such as quarterly, semi-annually, or annually, regardless of any difference between prevailing asset class weights and target asset class weights.

Time-series estimation Estimators that are based on lagged values of the variable being forecast; often consist of lagged values of other selected variables.

Total factor productivity A scale factor that reflects the portion of growth unaccounted for by explicit factor inputs (e.g., capital and labor).

Total return payer Party responsible for paying the reference obligation cash flows and return to the receiver but that is also compensated by the receiver for any depreciation in the index or default losses incurred by the portfolio.

Total return receiver Receives both the cash flows from the underlying index and any appreciation in the index over the period in exchange for paying the MRR plus a predetermined spread.

Tracking risk The standard deviation of the differences between a portfolio's returns and its benchmarks returns. Also called *tracking error*.

Transactions-based attribution An attribution approach that captures the impact of intra-day trades and exogenous events such as a significant class action settlement.

Trigger points In the context of portfolio rebalancing, the endpoints of a rebalancing range (corridor).

Ultra-high-net-worth individuals (UHNWIs) Individuals with net worth usually exceeding USD30 million or more.

Unplanned goals Unforeseen financial needs that are difficult to quantify because either the funding need, the timing of the financial need, or both may not be estimated.

Unsmoothing An adjustment to the reported return series if serial correlation is detected. Various approaches are available to unsmooth a return series.

Variance notional The notional amount of a variance swap; it equals vega notional divided by two times the volatility strike price [i.e., (vega notional)/(2 × volatility strike)].

Vega A measure of the sensitivity of an option's price to changes in the underlying's volatility.

Vega notional The trade size for a variance swap, which represents the average profit and loss of the variance swap for a 1% change in volatility from the strike.

Vesting The process of an employee becoming unconditionally entitled to, and an employer becoming obligated to pay, compensation.

Volatility clustering The tendency for large (small) swings in prices to be followed by large (small) swings of random direction.

Volatility skew The skewed plot (of implied volatility (y-axis) against strike price (x-axis) for options on the same underlying with the same expiration) that occurs when the implied volatility increases for OTM puts and decreases for OTM calls, as the strike price moves away from the current price.

Volatility smile The U-shaped plot (of implied volatility (y-axis) against strike price (x-axis) for options on the same underlying with the same expiration) that occurs when the implied volatilities priced into both OTM puts and calls trade at a premium to implied volatilities of ATM options.

Wealth The value of all the assets owned by an individual.

Wealth life cycle Stages of an individual investor's wealth in terms of human capital, financial capital, and economic net worth.

CFA Institute®
CFA Program

PRIVATE MARKETS PATHWAY

CFA® Program Curriculum
2026 • LEVEL III PRIVATE MARKETS PATHWAY

WILEY

ISBN 978-1-39436-063-5

SKY348DA160-B826-4993-95F3-2DFDDD8F1DB5_022825

Please visit our website at
www.WileyGlobalFinance.com.

WILEY

CONTENTS

How to Use the CFA Program Curriculum

The CFA® Program exams measure your mastery of the core knowledge, skills, and abilities required to succeed as an investment professional. These core competencies are the basis for the Candidate Body of Knowledge (CBOK™). The CBOK consists of four components:

A broad outline that lists the major CFA Program topic areas (www.cfainstitute.org/programs/cfa/curriculum/cbok/cbok)

Topic area weights that indicate the relative exam weightings of the top-level topic areas (www.cfainstitute.org/en/programs/cfa/curriculum)

Learning outcome statements (LOS) that tell you the specific knowledge, skills, and abilities you should gain from each curriculum topic area. You will find these statements at the start of each learning module and lesson. We encourage you to review the information about the LOS on our website (www.cfainstitute.org/programs/cfa/curriculum/study-sessions), including the descriptions of LOS "command words" on the candidate resources page at www.cfainstitute.org/-/media/documents/support/programs/cfa-and-cipm-los-command-words.ashx.

The CFA Program curriculum that candidates receive access to upon exam registration.

Therefore, the key to your success on the CFA exams is studying and understanding the CBOK. You can learn more about the CBOK on our website: www.cfainstitute.org/programs/cfa/curriculum/cbok.

The curriculum, including the practice questions, is the basis for all exam questions. The curriculum is selected/developed specifically to provide candidates with the knowledge, skills, and abilities reflected in the CBOK.

CFA INSTITUTE LEARNING ECOSYSTEM (LES)

Your exam registration fee includes access to the CFA Institute Learning Ecosystem (LES). This digital learning platform provides access to all the curriculum content and practice questions. The LES is organized as a series of learning modules consisting of short online lessons and associated practice questions. This tool is your source for all study materials, including practice questions and mock exams. The LES is the primary method by which CFA Institute delivers your curriculum experience. Here, you will find additional practice questions to test your knowledge, including some interactive questions.

DESIGNING YOUR PERSONAL STUDY PROGRAM

An orderly, systematic approach to exam preparation is critical. You should dedicate a consistent block of time every week to reading and studying. Review the LOS both before and after you study curriculum content to ensure you can demonstrate

the knowledge, skills, and abilities described by the LOS and the assigned learning module. Use the LOS as a self-check to track your progress and highlight areas of weakness for later review.

Successful candidates report an average of more than 300 hours preparing for each exam. Your preparation time will vary based on your prior education and experience, and you will likely spend more time on some topics than on others.

ERRATA

The curriculum development process is rigorous and involves multiple rounds of reviews by content experts. Despite our efforts to produce a curriculum that is free of errors, we must make corrections in some instances. Curriculum errata are periodically updated and posted by exam level and test date on the Curriculum Errata webpage (www.cfainstitute.org/en/programs/submit-errata). If you believe you have found an error in the curriculum, you can submit your concerns through our curriculum errata reporting process found at the bottom of the Curriculum Errata webpage.

OTHER FEEDBACK

Please send any comments or suggestions to info@cfainstitute.org, and we will review your feedback thoughtfully.

Private Markets Pathway

LEARNING MODULE

1

Private Investments and Structures

LEARNING OUTCOMES

Mastery	The candidate should be able to:
☐	contrast the features of private and public investments, and discuss characteristics of private and public markets
☐	discuss private investment methods and structures and their uses
☐	discuss the difference between public and private market performance, and calculate, interpret, and discuss the use of performance metrics including distributed to paid-in, residual value to paid-in, and total value to paid-in
☐	compare the risk and return of investing in private markets and public markets as part of a strategic asset allocation

INTRODUCTION

1

A major trend among institutional investors over the past few decades is the initiation of or significant increase in private market asset allocations to complement existing public market portfolios of listed equities, fixed-income securities, and cash. According to Preqin, an alternative data provider, private market assets under management (AUM) among global investors rose from under USD1 trillion in 2000 to nearly USD12 trillion in 2022. Historically dominated by the largest institutional investors (such as sovereign wealth funds and endowments), private market investments consisting of large direct purchases of entire companies or real estate properties have evolved over the past few decades to include professionally managed private investment portfolios. For example, private market funds in the form of closed-end limited partnerships have greatly expanded private market access among small institutional investors and high-net-worth individuals.

To better prepare candidates to identify, target, evaluate, and manage private market investments throughout their financial industry careers, CFA Institute has introduced a series of Level III Private Markets Pathway learning modules, the first of which focuses on private market investments and structures.

While public markets usually involve more standardized, liquid securities of mature issuers with price transparency, private investments are characterized by unique, illiquid investments across a broader range of company life cycle stages or project development phases held for longer periods. The distinct features of private markets also lead to different investment methods and structures, which vary based on investment size, asset type, and the internal resources an investor is willing and able to commit to managing the private asset over the investment holding period. Given a greater focus on asset price appreciation over an investment life cycle among private market investments, private market performance is measured using compounded return over a multiyear period, as opposed to periodic measures more common among public market securities. These distinct features of private market investments contribute to their complementary role when combined with more traditional public equity and fixed-income securities in a strategic asset allocation.

LEARNING MODULE OVERVIEW

- Public investments typically include non-controlling positions in debt or equity claims of mature issuers. Private investments, in contrast, often include controlling or large minority stakes in firms across the entire company life cycle, as well as private real estate or infrastructure. Public markets are characterized by the ability to readily buy or sell positions, while private markets are illiquid and trade on a negotiated basis.
- Private investment methods include a direct approach for the largest investors with sufficient expertise to manage positions over an investment period and indirect approaches, such as a closed-end limited partnership. Unlike security-based public investments, private investment structures are often created and tailored to a specific use, such as an acquisition company used for buyout equity or a special purpose entity formed to manage a project among investors and stakeholders in private real estate or infrastructure.
- While public markets typically use periodic income and asset appreciation performance measures based on observed prices, the relative illiquidity, uneven cash flows, and longer investment periods for private markets lead to the use of compounded return measures to gauge returns. For example, return multiples are often used to measure the proportion of realized and unrealized returns to a private fund investor relative to funds invested.
- The greater potential return and portfolio diversification often attributed to private market investments stems from both a longer, less liquid investment life cycle with greater uncertainty and a broader investment opportunity set across both the company life cycle and various asset types.

2 FEATURES OF PRIVATE AND PUBLIC INVESTMENTS AND MARKETS

☐ contrast the features of private and public investments, and discuss characteristics of private and public markets

Public investments generally involve listed securities representing debt or equity claims that are regularly traded on an exchange or among dealers in an over-the-counter market. Public fund managers invest in non-controlling debt and equity positions of more mature issuers typically with stable cash flows. Public investments are characterized by an investor's ability to readily buy or sell positions and to observe current and historical prices for securities and relevant benchmarks, such as indexes.

Private investments are unlisted assets for which no organized exchange or over-the-counter market exists or involve companies that choose not to or cannot access public markets due to their size, stage of development, limited financial disclosure, or concentrated ownership. Private funds often acquire controlling or significant minority stakes held for longer periods over which value creation occurs, resulting in cash flow improvements, which are a primary driver of investor returns. Private debt and private equity claims are usually non-standardized contracts that are negotiated rather than exchanged on a regular basis. While private activities span a wide range of investments, including sole proprietorships, our focus here is limited to private investments of relevance to institutional investors. It is also important to distinguish between *alternative* investments and *private* investments, terms that are often used interchangeably. Alternative investments are those other than ownership of traditional public equity, public fixed-income, and cash instruments. While alternatives include most private markets, some alternative investments, such as exchange-traded commodities and hedge funds, use strategies involving public securities, which were addressed in detail in the Level II curriculum.

Some alternative investments are held in both public and private forms. For example, real estate investment trusts (REITs) hold income-producing properties and most often have publicly traded shares, while private real estate includes major refurbishment and development of commercial and residential properties, as well as timberland and farmland, which are covered in detail in a later learning module. In addition, some private companies issue public debt securities, such as high-yield bonds. The Private Markets Pathway covered in the following learning modules focuses on the following asset types:

- Private equity
- Private debt
- Private special situations
- Private real estate
- Private infrastructure

Key features that distinguish public and private investments are summarized in Exhibit 1 and are subsequently outlined in detail.

Exhibit 1: Features of Public vs. Private Investments

Feature	Public	Private
Asset prices	Traded, observable	Negotiated, estimated
Performance measurement	Periodic	Compounded over holding period
Liquidity	Mostly liquid, with few trading restrictions	Illiquid, with sale prohibited or restricted
Investment process	Open-end, security selection	Closed-end, with due diligence, value creation, and exit

Feature	Public	Private
Investment manager skills	Industry, company, and financial analysis	Industry, management, and technical experience and expertise, legal and financial analysis
Portfolio diversification potential	Based on correlations of observed periodic returns	Based on different company and investment life cycle phases, as well as unique asset types

Asset Prices and Performance Measurement

Immediate access to current and historical price data for individual securities and relevant benchmarks supports a variety of public market investment approaches. For example, investors can easily measure returns, volatility, and correlations across time and construct portfolios with an efficient risk–return trade-off. Public market data are a critical input in judgement-based investment approaches seeking to capitalize on a market view, rule-based strategies using factor analysis, and index-based investment strategies.

Private market investors, in contrast, have little or no price transparency for prospective, existing, or comparable investments. As a result, investors rely on relative valuation techniques, discounted cash flow methods, and recent transactions among other approaches to estimate prices. Fund managers provide valuation estimates to investors with delays and at less frequent, often quarterly, time intervals, limiting the usefulness of such data for asset allocation purposes.

Periodic public market performance measures generally assume an initial cash outflow upon asset purchase and periodic inflows, including bond coupons, stock dividends, and net operating income for real estate. In contrast, private market investments involve far less predictable cash flows, with multiple cash outflows and inflows of uncertain timing. Performance metrics for private investments will be addressed in detail later in this reading.

Liquidity and Investment Process

Active trading of listed securities in public markets offers a high degree of liquidity and relatively low transaction costs. The purchase and sale of listed securities can be as simple as executing a market order, and short-term market developments may prompt a public fund manager to sell securities whose observed price exceeds what a manager considers to be fair market value or to purchase undervalued securities based on public market developments. Issuers of public equity and debt are usually in a mature phase of development with predictable, stable cash flows.

Privately held controlling or minority stakes in a firm, a project, or a real asset are inherently illiquid. Fund managers usually seek a larger capital commitment from investors and require a far longer investment time horizon than for public funds, sometimes up to 10 years or more. Private purchases and sales are often negotiated between two or very few potential buyers and sellers, leading private fund managers to prohibit or severely restrict investors from selling fund positions to avoid the need for early liquidation.

The different features of public and private investments also give rise to distinct investment processes. For example, the greater liquidity and price transparency of public investments allow for a more open-end investment approach and structure. Investments in illiquid private assets held for longer periods benefit from a closed-end approach in which investors align manager compensation with investment performance.

We refer to the development or transformation of private assets over this longer investment holding period as the **private asset investment life cycle**, whose distinct phases are shown in Exhibit 2.

Exhibit 2: Private Asset Investment Life Cycle

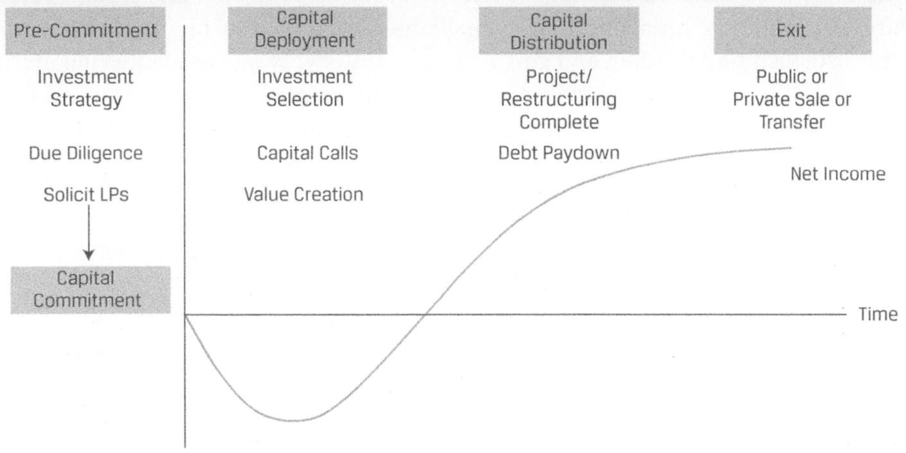

The private asset investment life cycle common among investment types consists of capital commitment, deployment, distribution, and exit phases, which will be addressed in detail in later learning modules. The private asset investment life cycle is characterized by negative returns in early phases followed by cash flow and income growth in later phases, referred to as the **J-curve effect**.

Public market investors with non-controlling stakes have little influence over issuers beyond the exercise of voting rights. Private investment managers, in contrast, are actively engaged in managing and controlling assets throughout the investment life cycle. Tasks range from identifying ideal targets, conducting due diligence, and creating detailed business and financing plans to managing the value creation process from capital deployment until an investment is ultimately sold or exited and capital is returned to investors.

Manager Skills

Distinct investment processes, as well as roles and responsibilities, among public and private fund managers give rise to different skill sets required for success in managing portfolios in these respective markets. As public fund managers largely delegate the value creation process to company managers, much of the underlying investment research is conducted across securities, companies, and industries. For example, publicly available corporate financial statements and other data sources are used to create and compare financial ratios and other relevant metrics as a basis for investment analysis.

Private market investments often lack the market price transparency of public market securities and include investment opportunities ranging from new real estate developments to mature firms in financial distress to startup companies with little more than a business idea. The manager skill set required to successfully shepherd these investments from selection through exit goes well beyond security analysis. In the case of real estate, local market knowledge and project development and management experience are critical. Private equity fund managers often bring significant operational experience and industry expertise. In addition, they bring industry relationships and management experience in founding, growing, or restructuring businesses, as well as legal, accounting, tax, and other qualifications, to their role in managing such investments. Given the prevalence of less standardized contracts in private markets, both investors and managers must be prepared to conduct additional legal analysis when considering such investments.

Early-stage companies with little or no revenue often solicit private equity investments known as **venture capital**, which involve both high risk and a high rate of failure. A company's initial success is usually measured by non-financial milestones, such as establishing a product and go-to-market strategy, as well as identifying market potential well before the company generates revenue or profits. Therefore, in addition to capital, startup investors often bring relevant experience, contacts, and partnerships to young companies to help establish a successful business as demonstrated in the following example.

EXAMPLE 1

CRISPR Therapeutics AG's Startup Phase

In 2013, French professor and researcher Emmanuelle Charpentier co-founded CRISPR Therapeutics AG, together with Rodger Novak and Shaun Foy. Using genome editing and engineering discoveries for which Charpentier and Jennifer Doudna were later awarded the Nobel Prize in Chemistry, CRISPR Therapeutics was established in order to use these new gene-editing tools in biotechnology and biomedical applications.

In the following year, CRISPR Therapeutics raised USD25 million in Series A equity from Versant Ventures, a US-based venture capital firm focused on the health care and biotechnology industries. Given Versant's multidisciplinary team of scientists and researchers, the company announced a broader team of leading experts in various fields of science to capitalize on this new technology at the time of financing.

According to Crunchbase, a startup and early-stage financing data provider, CRISPR Therapeutics conducted three additional equity financing rounds with 16 investors, including established pharmaceutical companies, such as Celgene and Bayer AG, as well as other venture capital firms, such as New Enterprise Associates (NEA).

NEA is a US-based private investment firm focused on the technology and health care industries and one of the world's largest venture capital funds, with over USD25 billion in committed capital. NEA's health care industry team members include physicians, research scientists, pharmacists, and other experts with extensive experience in the areas of biotechnology, pharmaceutical drug trials and medical devices. NEA partner Ali Behbahani, MD, MBA was appointed to CRISPR Therapeutics AG's board of directors at the time of NEA's investment.

In October 2016, CRISPR Therapeutics became public in an IPO on the NASDAQ exchange, which valued the company at USD590 million. The company has since reached a market capitalization over five times that of its IPO valuation, establishing many partnerships and developing several drugs for blood diseases, cancer, diabetes, and other illnesses.

As the example suggests, both the equity capital and industry expertise provided by private fund managers often contribute to a startup's success. For example, NEA's board membership and its involvement, along with other investors, in establishing partnerships and helping establish drug trials were key factors in expanding CRISPR's business at an early stage.

Portfolio Diversification Potential

The distinct features of private markets and investments are commonly assumed to result in relatively low correlations between private market returns and those of public market securities. While a public market security's correlation may be estimated easily relative to the existing public market portfolio because of observed market prices, private market illiquidity and longer investment periods preclude such a comparison. The diversification potential of private market investments is assessed differently. The following are key sources of potential diversification in private markets:

- Private company debt and equity exposures in life cycle phases, which are unavailable to public market investors, such as exposures to rapid growth or restructuring opportunities
- Private company debt and equity return dynamics over an investment life cycle, which vary from those of mature public companies
- Exposures other than private company debt or equity that exhibit return dynamics different from those of public securities

Successful firms emerge from a startup period via rapid expansion, with cash flows and profitability rising until they reach a mature, stable phase and subsequently facing decline, as shown in Exhibit 3.

Exhibit 3: Company Life Cycle Stages

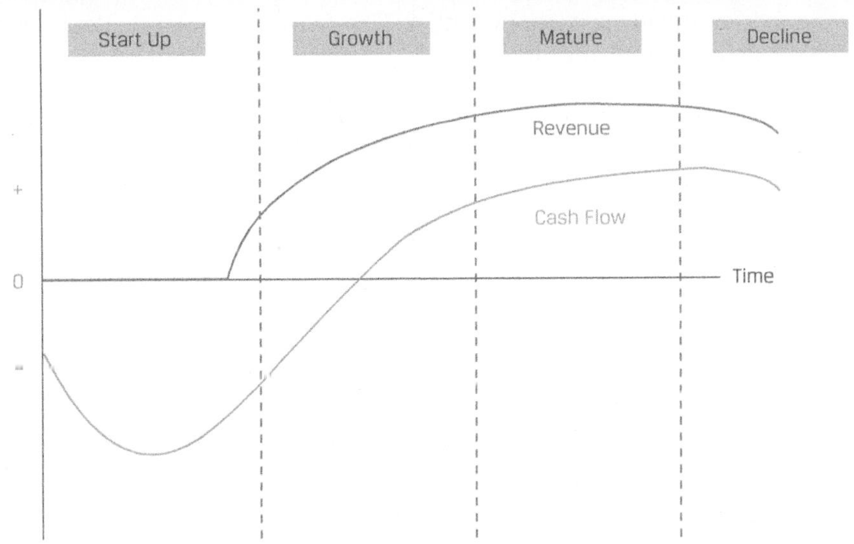

While public markets and investments are concentrated among mature companies, private investments span the entire company life cycle.

The CRISPR example illustrates the first of these diversification sources. Startup and early-stage companies usually fail to meet public equity listing criteria, nor do they reach minimum profitability or interest coverage requirements of traditional debt providers. While startups such as CRISPR Therapeutics have a very high return potential, they also have a high failure rate. If successful, early-stage and young companies in an expansion phase tend to exhibit above-trend growth that is less driven by the business cycle, which generally impacts more established firms. Private investors play a role in the success of these companies by applying industry-specific and other skills in selecting and managing investments, as discussed in detail in later learning modules.

A second potential source of diversification is more common among so-called **buyout equity** investments in existing public companies. Private equity buyouts often involve taking a mature public company private using debt and equity with the intent to transform, divest, or acquire businesses and sell the reorganized firm at a higher price. Given these steps taken by private fund managers over the investment life cycle, buyout company performance may diverge significantly from that of public equities. In some cases, private manager skill in selecting, acquiring, financing, restructuring, and selling companies may result in relative outperformance, while in other cases, timing differences of otherwise similar trends in private and public equity may result in reduced correlation.

A third area of potential variation among private and public market returns involves alternative asset classes, such as real estate or infrastructure. Private real estate often involves major refurbishment or new construction as opposed to more stable income-producing properties held by public REITs. Publicly traded infrastructure companies issue debt and equity securities with diversified exposure to a changing project portfolio as opposed to the large, single-use illiquid assets that characterize private infrastructure. Private real estate and private infrastructure are characterized by an investment life cycle, which distinguishes their risk and return features from those of public markets.

Many of the characteristics of private markets and investments that offer the possibility of attractive risk-adjusted and less correlated returns also historically represented barriers to entry for many institutional investors. For example, the relative lack of price transparency, illiquidity, large minimum investment size, and specialized knowledge necessary prevented all but the largest asset owners from taking advantage of private market investment opportunities. The following example describes one sovereign wealth fund's journey in investing in private market strategies.

EXAMPLE 2

GIC's Private Markets Investment Strategy

Government of Singapore Investment Corporation (GIC) is among the world's largest sovereign wealth funds, with an estimated USD700 billion in AUM. Established in 1981 with a mission to preserve and grow the global purchasing power of Singapore's strategic reserves, GIC gradually shifted from a conservative policy of 70% developed market bonds and cash to a greater equity and private market allocation similar to those of major endowments.

In conjunction with these changes, GIC disclosed a new investment framework in 2013:

- *Reference Portfolio:* A 65% global equity, 35% global bond benchmark representing the Government of Singapore's overall risk tolerance
- *Policy Portfolio:* GIC's asset allocation across six asset classes, which include real estate and private equity
- *Active Portfolio:* GIC has the flexibility to pursue what it refers to as skills-based and opportunistic investments within each asset class, as well as across and outside of the six primary asset class distinctions, within a predetermined risk budget set by the GIC board.

GIC rapidly adapted to this more active investment approach over the following decade, with a reported private equity allocation of 17% and real estate allocation of 13% as of 2022–2023. Despite its lack of disclosures of private investments outside of private equity, GIC's active role in private markets is evidenced by the growth in its investment team and in the number and size of private market transactions in which it participates. For example, GIC now employs over 2,000 investment professionals, 70 of whom are solely dedicated to infrastructure investments, in 11 global offices. According to a survey by Global SWF, a research firm, GIC participated in the largest number of private market transactions among state-owned investors in 2022, with 72 private market deals totaling USD39 billion.

Given its size, scope, and skilled management team, GIC can invest through private market funds, as well as acting as a direct investor or co-investor, to build a diversified private portfolio across vintage years, industries, and geographies. For example, in early 2023, GIC partnered with Oak Street, a US-based real estate private equity firm, to acquire STORE Capital Corporation, a publicly traded commercial REIT specializing in single-tenant operational real estate, for USD15 billion.

While most investors lack the size, scope, and in-house professional expertise of the sovereign wealth fund described in the previous case study, private market investments have evolved to become more widely accessible to a broad range of institutional investors and high-net-worth individuals. In what follows, we will review the various structures, forms of ownership, and investment methods that have made this situation possible.

QUESTION SET

1. Which one of the following skills is more essential to private market investment relative to public market investment?

   A. Company analysis

   B. Legal analysis

   C. Industry analysis

   Solution

   B is the correct response. While company and industry analyses are common in all investment analyses, both private and public, private investments involve taking large stakes in a company or asset. As such, a private investor should have the ability to conduct legal analysis as part of the due diligence process.

2. Which one of the following statements best describes a source of portfolio diversification potential from private market assets?

   A. Private markets offer potential access to higher-risk investments compared to public markets.

   B. Private markets offer potential access to investments in different company life cycle stages compared to public markets.

   C. Private markets offer the potential to invest in lower-risk companies in the mature phase of the company life cycle.

   Solution

   B is the correct response. Private company debt and equity investments create exposures in company life cycle phases that are unavailable to public market investors. A is not correct, because higher risk can always be achieved in public market investments by increasing leverage. C is not correct, because public markets also offer investors the potential to invest in lower-risk companies in their mature phase. The diversification benefits of private market investments stem from the fund manager's efforts to transform a mature business during the investment life cycle.

3. Discuss an important contrast between private and public market investments related to ownership stakes.

Solution

Private funds acquire controlling or significant minority stakes in companies or assets and hold these for longer periods. In contrast, public fund managers invest in non-controlling debt and equity positions of companies or assets and can readily liquidate them in traded markets.

3 PRIVATE VS. PUBLIC INVESTMENT STRUCTURES

☐ discuss private investment methods and structures and their uses

Public market investors typically face a relatively simple choice between direct selection of individual securities and an indirect approach in which security selection is delegated to a public fund manager. The longer investment holding period and more active manager engagement over the investment life cycle of private market investments give rise to more complex investment methods, including closed-end fund structures based on a **limited partnership** structure, as shown in Exhibit 4.

Exhibit 4: Limited Partnership Structure

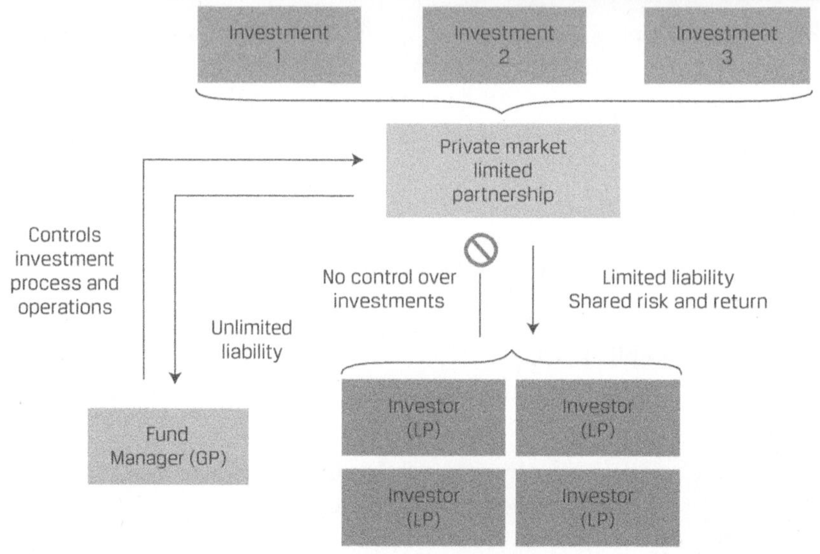

These partnerships are used to align the interests of private market fund managers, or **general partners (GPs)**, and private market fund investors, or **limited partners (LPs)**, as described in greater detail later.

Private Investment Methods

In private markets, the choice of a direct or indirect investment method depends on the investor's commitment size and the ability and willingness to commit the necessary resources to actively manage the position over the investment life cycle. Three common private market investment methods are shown in Exhibit 5.

Exhibit 5: Direct Investment, Co-Investment and Fund Investment Alternatives

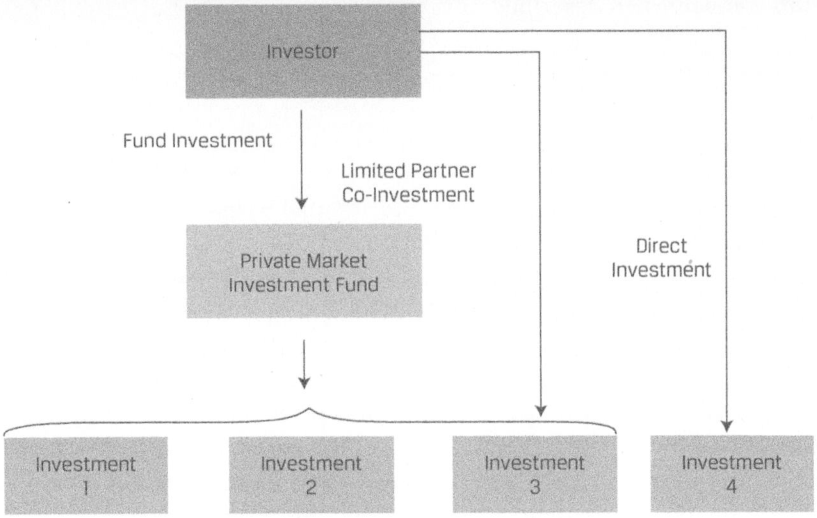

Direct Investment

Direct investment involves the purchase of an equity ownership stake or private debt investment *without* the use of a partner or an investment intermediary. This investment method may, for example, involve a controlling stake in a buyout equity transaction. If acquiring a majority equity stake, a direct investor must not only negotiate the purchase price but also establish and execute a successful business plan to create value over the investment holding period. For this reason, as well as due to the potential portfolio concentration risk of large-scale acquisitions or projects, the largest asset owners, such as GIC in the earlier example, tend to be the primary users of the direct investment approach. With 17% of its roughly USD700 billion in investments committed to private equity, a new USD1 billion buyout investment would represent less than 1% of GIC's exposure to this asset class.

Co-investment occurs either as a **direct co-investment** or as a **limited partner co-investment**, as shown in Exhibit 5. Direct co-investment involves the *direct* purchase of an ownership stake or private debt investment with the use of one or more partners, one or more of whom may be a private fund manager. The earlier example described GIC's acquisition of STORE Capital with Oak Street, an example of an Asian sovereign wealth fund co-investing with a private equity firm with a focus on US real estate. Direct co-investment offers investors the opportunity to reduce the size of their private market portfolio positions, benefit from the expertise of investment partners, and reduce fees as compared to indirect investment approaches. A limited partner co-investment, in contrast, involves the purchase of an ownership stake or private debt investment in a single investment that is managed by a private fund manager. In some cases, LP investors with established GP relationships who are willing to invest large amounts in a fund may receive co-investment rights. Such co-investment rights provide investors the option to co-invest in an opportunity before it is offered more widely.

In the case of minority stakes in startup firms, founder-managed businesses often seek investments of less than USD10 million. While relatively accessible to smaller investors, investments of this size are often not large enough to meaningfully impact the portfolios of the largest investors. The very high failure rate of such firms underscores the necessity of industry expertise and experience in evaluating prospective investments. It is quite common for high-net-worth individuals who are also often successful entrepreneurs known as **angel investors** to provide early-stage financing to startup companies, as described next.

ANUPAM MITTAL, ANGEL INVESTOR

Anupam Mittal is an Indian angel investor who began his career as an entrepreneur in 1997 by founding an online wedding service for non-resident Indians, which became Shaadi.com, a leading matrimonial website for Asians that has since expanded to retail outlets providing related services.

After raising capital for his own startup in Silicon Valley, given the lack of venture capital firms in India at the time, Mittal became one of the leading angel investors in Indian startups, investing in over 200 early-stage companies, including such successful firms as the ridesharing business Ola Cabs and the leading online grocer BigBasket. In 2021, Mittal became one of the original panelists on Shark Tank India, an Indian franchise of the successful US business reality television series, in which startup companies present to a panel of investors or "sharks" who decide whether to invest in each business.

Indirect Investment

Indirect forms of private market investment include co-investment and fund-based alternatives. In the case of a so-called limited partner co-investment, an LP purchases an equity ownership stake or private debt investment in a single investment that is managed by a GP. This form of indirect investment allows LPs to take a larger stake in specific assets of interest in a portfolio under the direction of a more experienced private fund manager. LPs who are offered co-investments are able to gain deeper insight into their GPs because they are given access to a substantial amount of the GPs' due diligence materials and investment memos related to the investments. Such material is not available to typical LP private fund investors. In addition to tailoring a private portfolio beyond a set of fund stakes, this approach gives LPs the opportunity to engage in the investment process more actively in exchange for fee reductions. General partners, in contrast, use the co-investment method to share investment risk, expand access to investor capital, and in some cases attract new investors outside an existing partnership.

As described earlier and shown in Exhibit 4, indirect investments in private market funds are often organized as limited partnerships. In contrast to highly liquid public investment funds, which offer price transparency, limited partners face long and illiquid investment holding periods. LPs must also commit capital in advance of investment selection and face uncertain timing of both capital calls and the distribution of returns over time. (The effect of this key feature of limited partnerships on investment portfolios and returns is addressed later.) As a result, limited partnerships typically involve performance-based incentive compensation among other features designed to manage information asymmetry and align manager and investor interests. The next reading will address these GP and LP perspectives and the investment process in greater detail.

Private Investment Structures

Whether a private market participant is acting as a direct investor or investing indirectly via a limited partnership, the underlying structures of individual private investments are less standardized than public security–based investments. Corporate governance for private corporations and other legal entities often deviates from the simple one-vote-per-share and majority rule more common among public companies and is subject to negotiation. For example, an influential minority investor may negotiate such provisions as a seat on a private company's board of directors or a supermajority vote requirement for key business decisions, which can grant a minority owner an effective veto right on certain strategic decisions. New legal entities are frequently created for and tailored to a specific use, such as the management of roles, responsibilities, risks, and return over a project's investment life cycle or the purchase of a public company by private investors, referred to as a **take-private transaction**, after which the target company's shares are no longer publicly traded, as in the following case study.

CASE STUDY

Straploc Industries Acquisition

Glidestone Capital Partners, a private equity buyout firm general partner, has targeted Straploc Industries for a take-private transaction because of its recent underperformance versus industry peers. Straploc is a manufacturer and distributor of specialty fasteners, adhesives, and seals used in numerous industrial applications that is publicly traded on the Toronto Stock Exchange. Glidestone intends to restructure Straploc's operations and sell the company in several years.

Since Glidestone plans to fund 70% of the expected CAD1.25 billion purchase price with debt and the remainder with committed equity capital, it has asked a group of banks also serving in an advisory role on the acquisition to arrange a temporary acquisition financing of CAD875 million to support its bid, pledging the Straploc shares it will acquire as loan collateral to the lenders.

In a take-private transaction such as the one in the prior case study, also referred to as a **leveraged buyout (LBO)** because of the high proportion of debt financing used to make the acquisition, a new legal entity is often created to facilitate the process. For example, as shown in Exhibit 6, a separately funded new acquisition company (AcquisitionCo) is often created for the sole purpose of acquiring a specific target company (TargetCo). If the bid is successful, its assets will consist of TargetCo shares and its liabilities will be short-term acquisition debt, with the equity contributed by the buyout firm.

Exhibit 6: Take-Private Acquisition Structure—Initial Phase

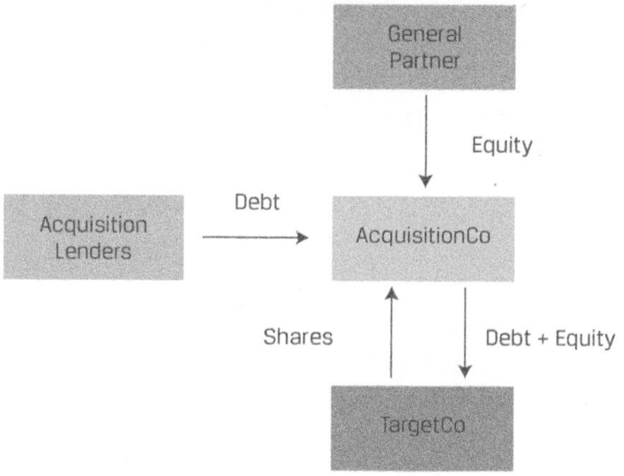

Take-private transactions, as well as other mergers and acquisitions, typically trigger the refinancing of a target company's existing debt. This situation occurs because existing lenders and bondholders are commonly protected by a **change of control clause**, a provision requiring the issuer to offer to repurchase outstanding debt if certain changes occur in a company's ownership or management.

In the second stage of the buyout, long-term financing is negotiated as the deal is closed. In some cases, an acquiror may have arranged to simultaneously sell certain divisions of TargetCo or combine the target with another company it already owns. In other cases, such actions may take place in a later restructuring phase. At this time, AcquisitionCo and TargetCo are combined in a merger (MergeCo), and the acquisition financing is replaced with medium- and long-term debt issued by the new legal entity, as shown in Exhibit 7.

Exhibit 7: Take-Private Acquisition Structure—Second Phase

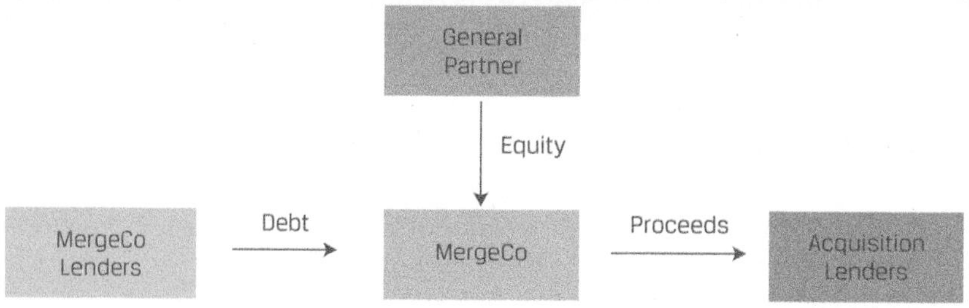

Private market strategies often involve debt structures that are less standardized than the non-callable fixed-coupon bonds common in public investment-grade debt markets. For example, the debt profile of leveraged buyouts typically involves a flexible structure to meet evolving issuer needs and the lender demands as illustrated in the following Straploc Industries case study.

CASE STUDY

Straploc Industries' New Debt Profile

Straploc Industries' management would like the ability to repay debt early as it restructures, balance both fixed and floating interest rate exposure, stagger debt maturities, and use its fixed assets as security to reduce borrowing costs.

The underwriting banks for Glidestone's acquisition loan have offered to arrange a **leveraged loan** for Straploc. This type of senior secured loan has a floating-rate coupon based on market reference rates, includes several restrictive debt covenants, and is prepayable.

As the buyout equity financial sponsor, Glidestone has directly solicited private investors to purchase Straploc debt and found the greatest investor interest in a **mezzanine loan**, or a debt claim serviced after senior debt claims but before common shares. This subordinated debt has a longer tenor and a higher fixed coupon than the floating coupon on a leveraged loan, is not prepayable, and has fewer restrictive covenants.

After considering both its goals and the associated trade-offs of different debt structures, Straploc management chooses to borrow using a larger (CAD600 million) leveraged loan tranche and a smaller (CAD275 million) mezzanine facility.

As in the case of equity, private debt investors may directly contract with a borrower or invest indirectly as a limited partner in a private credit fund to gain exposure to the senior secured debt or the mezzanine loans created in this transaction. Exhibit 8 shows the post-acquisition structure from the previous case study.

Exhibit 8: Post-Acquisition Private Debt Structure

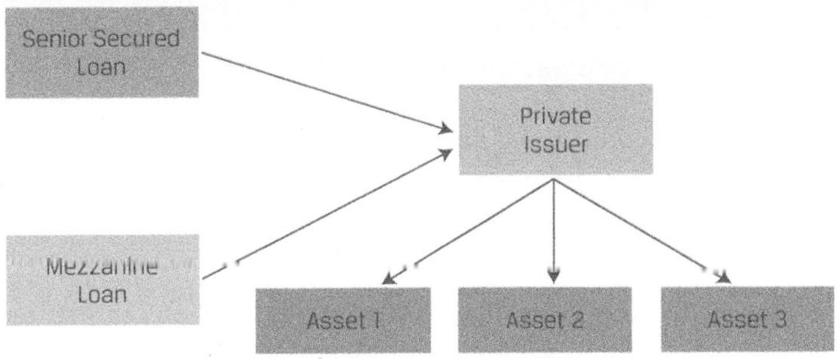

As in the case of the buyout equity transactions, project-based private investments in the areas of real estate or infrastructure also often involve the establishment of what is often referred to as a **special purpose entity (SPE)** or special purpose vehicle.

In the case of a project SPE, the entity's sole purpose is to facilitate the construction, operation, and financing of a real estate or infrastructure asset. Use of a separate, new legal entity isolates the assets, liabilities, cash flows, and income, as well as associated contractual obligations, from the balance sheets of investors and other stakeholders. This structure serves to segregate the claims and obligations of a project's sponsor from the project itself. For example, a new private real estate development usually involves the establishment of a project company. This company receives an equity contribution from a private real estate GP, purchasing undeveloped land, which is financed using this equity and debt secured by the property.

In the case of private infrastructure investment, an SPE structure is often used among various public and private entities as parties to a **concession agreement**, or a contractual arrangement under which an entity's terms and conditions are established with a developer or operator to plan, build, operate, finance, and maintain an infrastructure asset for a finite period (see Exhibit 9).

Exhibit 9: Infrastructure Special Purpose Entity

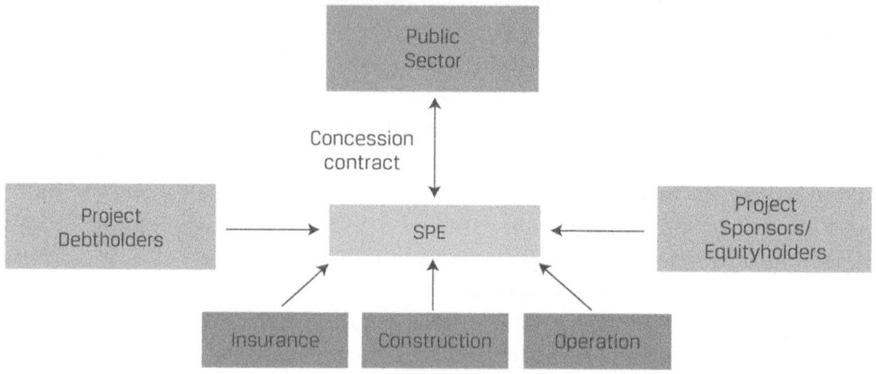

As shown in Exhibit 9, the SPE or in some cases a fully owned operating company is the focal point and often the contracting entity for many stakeholders, including regulators, debtholders, and equityholders.

QUESTION SET

1. Which of the following investment methods applies to private market investment but not public market investment?

   A. Direct investment

   B. Co-investment

   C. Fund investment

   Solution

   B is the correct response. Co-investment refers to either a direct investment in private equity or debt with one or more partners or an indirect investment as a single investment in private equity or debt with a fund general partner managing the investment. Both A and C are incorrect because direct investment and fund investment are approaches in either public or private market investment.

2. Discuss two reasons why direct investment in private market investments is typically limited to very large investors, such as sovereign wealth funds.

   Solution

   First, investors must control sufficient assets such that they can adequately manage the potential for portfolio concentration risk associated with large-scale acquisitions or project investments.

   Second, a direct investor must not only negotiate the purchase price and legal terms of an investment but also establish and execute on a successful business plan to create value over the investment holding period. Thus, the investor needs to have access to sufficient resources to have a team with the necessary expertise, which is likely only for very large investors.

3. Which one of the following private market investments is structured to address a change of control clause?

   A. Leveraged buyout

   B. Venture debt

   C. Leveraged loan

Solution

A is the correct response. Leveraged buyouts, as well as other mergers and acquisitions, typically trigger the refinancing of a target company's existing debt. This situation occurs because existing lenders and bondholders are commonly protected by a change of control clause, a provision requiring the issuer to offer to repurchase outstanding debt if certain changes occur in a company's ownership or management. B is incorrect because venture debt does not create any change of control issues. C is incorrect for the same reason, although a leveraged loan is likely part of the longer-term financing that is an outcome of the change of control clause in an LBO.

4. Which of the following is the most correct statement as to why private real estate and infrastructure projects are typically governed through a SPE?

   A. To limit the liability of investors for assumption of risks to those associated with the project

   B. To ensure that investors capture their share of returns from the project

   C. To protect the value of the investment at the end of the concession agreement

Solution

A is the correct response. An SPE creates a separate, new legal entity, which isolates the assets, liabilities, cash flows, and income of the project, as well as its associated contractual obligations, from the balance sheets of investors and other stakeholders. In this way, the SPE limits investor liability to only risks associated with the project. B is incorrect because the SPE does not govern the specific allocation of cash flows. Rather, the equity and debt investments specify these terms. C is incorrect because the value (if any) of the project reverts to the grantor at the end of the project.

PRIVATE VS. PUBLIC INVESTMENTS AND RETURN METRICS 4

☐ discuss the difference between public and private market performance, and calculate, interpret, and discuss the use of performance metrics including distributed to paid-in, residual value to paid-in, and total value to paid-in

The distinct features of public and private markets lead not only to differences in liquidity and price transparency but also to different performance dynamics and approaches to performance measurement.

Public vs. Private Market Performance

Public markets include listed equity and debt securities from mature issuers with stable cash flows. While most large public equity issuers pay periodic dividends to shareholders, public debt securities are usually non-callable bonds that pay periodic fixed coupons to debtholders. As a result, public security analysts typically rely on measures of income and asset appreciation calculated on a consistent periodic basis as the most appropriate measure to compare returns and performance. Exhibit 10 illustrates the comparison of return over different periods as shown in the CFA Program Level I fixed-income curriculum for the case of bonds.

Exhibit 10: Periodic Yield Measures for Fixed-Rate Bonds

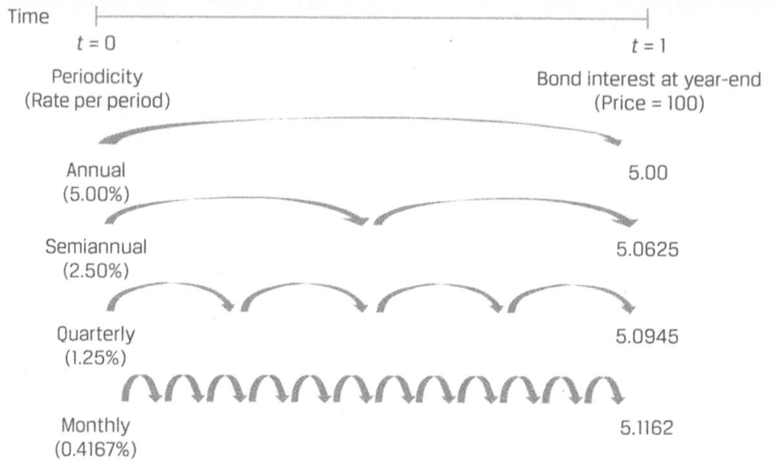

It is important to note that a high degree of price transparency and liquidity that is present in many public markets is necessary for such measures to be calculated, compared, and acted on in the case of arbitrage opportunities.

Private market investments, including private equity and debt from various stages over the company life cycle, as well as private real estate and infrastructure, face valuation challenges that complicate performance measurement. Their illiquidity, lack of price transparency, and dissimilarity among investments in the same private asset class preclude analysts from applying the same periodic and relative performance measures as for public markets.

In contrast to the stable cash flows of public market investments, the private asset investment life cycle shown in Exhibit 2, combining periods of positive and negative cash flow, implies that private market performance is best measured over a multiyear holding period. A common measure applied in such a case is the **internal rate of return (IRR)**, or the uniform discount rate for a series of cash flows (CF) over n periods that returns a net present value (NPV) of zero, as shown in Equation 1 and Exhibit 11:

$$\text{NPV} = 0 = \frac{\text{CF}_1}{(1+\text{IRR})^1} + \frac{\text{CF}_2}{(1+\text{IRR})^2} + \ldots + \frac{\text{CF}_n}{(1+\text{IRR})^n}. \quad (1)$$

Exhibit 11: IRR over the Private Asset Investment Life Cycle

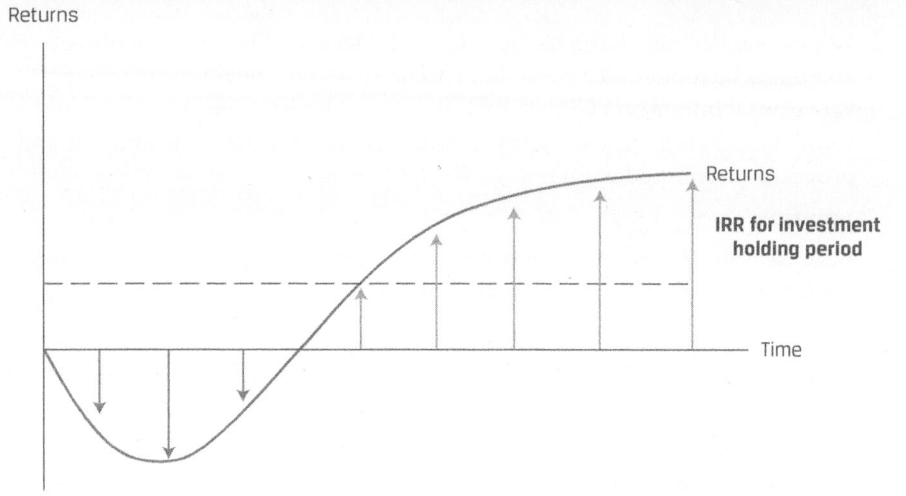

An important consideration when using IRR is that this calculation assumes interim cash flows may be invested at the IRR rate. While this assumption may hold in highly liquid public fixed-income markets, it is less realistic in the case of private market cash flows. For example, lower reinvestment rates of interim cash flows will reduce an investment's return.

Another cash flow–based performance measure commonly applied in private markets is the **return on investment (ROI)**, equal to the ratio or multiple of cash flows received versus those invested:

$$\mathrm{ROI} = \frac{\sum(\text{Cash flows received})}{\sum(\text{Cash flows invested})}. \quad (2)$$

Although simple to apply and widely used, note that the ROI measure ignores the time value of money and the investment holding period.

In the special case in which a single investment (cash outflow) occurs at the beginning of an investment holding period and a one-time payoff occurs at the end, we may convert the ROI over an investment time horizon to an equivalent IRR of an n-year investment holding period, as follows:

$$\mathrm{ROI} = (1 + \mathrm{IRR})^n. \quad (3)$$

These performance measures are shown using the prior case study.

CASE STUDY

Straploc Industries' ROI and IRR

After a five-year restructuring period, assume that Glidestone Partners can sell its initial CAD375 million (equal to 30% of the original CAD1.25 billion purchase price) equity stake in Straploc Industries for CAD1.45 billion.

1. If we assume that Glidestone makes a single initial investment and received no dividends or distributions over the five years prior to sale, calculate the ROI on the Straploc equity position.

   Solution

   Using Equation 2, we can solve for ROI using the initial purchase price in the denominator and the sales price in the numerator:

$$\text{ROI} = 3.867\times = \frac{\text{CAD1.45 billion}}{\text{CAD375 million}}.$$

2. Glidestone Partners has a target return of 30% over a five-year holding horizon on its buyout equity portfolio. Discuss whether the Straploc take-private transaction meets Glidestone's target and how the investment return would be affected if the investment were realized for the same amount and proceeds distributed earlier.

Solution

Because a single cash outflow occurs upon purchase and a single cash inflow occurs at the end, we can use Equation 3 to convert the ROI from Question 1 to an equivalent IRR over five years:

$$3.867\times = (1 + \text{IRR})^5.$$

$$\text{IRR} = 31.06\%.$$

The IRR of 31.06% exceeds Glidestone's return target of 30%. An earlier distribution of proceeds is a benefit to Glidestone's return. For example, a sale of Straploc at the end of four years results in an IRR of 40.23%. However, it is worth noting that this higher IRR assumes that the sale proceeds can be reinvested at 40.23% for an additional year. The earlier receipt results in the same five-year return of 31.06% only if these cash flows are not reinvested at all.

The private market investment life cycle involves the added complexity of extended upfront capital commitments, which do not exist in public markets. Investors must typically commit funds to a limited partnership months or years in advance of capital deployment, with little certainty regarding the timing or magnitude of capital calls. As a result, investors must often hold these commitments in more liquid public investments with possibly lower expected returns.

This feature adds to the challenge of assessing private market performance across all LPs in two ways: (1) the comparability of the return horizon between private and public markets and (2) the effects of public market conditions on capital call timing. The following example illustrates the comparison of public and private market performance.

CASE STUDY

Public vs. Private Market Return over an Investment Holding Period

Claire Thompson is an investment management consultant leading a conference workshop for public pension fund investment managers on comparing public and private market performance. She introduces a purely hypothetical example of a public pension manager with the following investment opportunities:

- Purchase shares in a public company for USD500,000 today, or
- Commit USD500,000 to a private equity fund today to be invested in a similar company in two years.

The manager expects public and private equity investment values to generate ROI of 2× over seven years, with the private company taken public at that time. Neither equity investment is expected to make interim distributions, and all calculations ignore investment fees and any other costs.

1. Calculate the IRR of the public investment opportunity over the seven-year holding period.

Solution

Given the doubling of investment value (ROI = 2×) with no interim cash flows, use Equation 3 to calculate the IRR:

$2\times = (1 + IRR)^7$; IRR = 10.41% [= $2^{(1/7)} - 1$].

2. Assume the private equity fund makes a single capital call in two years—that is, the USD500,000 will be deployed in the second year. Discuss why an investor cannot simply solve for expected private investment return using a five-year time horizon, an initial cash outflow of USD500,000, and a future inflow of USD1,000,000.

Solution

The assumption that the private market company will double in value over seven years might mistakenly lead a manager to believe that she will pay USD500,000 in two years and receive USD1,000,000 in seven years, resulting in an IRR of 14.87% [= $2^{(1/5)} - 1$]. However, this approach ignores the opportunity cost of committed capital, which is not invested for the first two years. If we instead assume the private investment generates the same 10.41% IRR as the public investment with *no* return on committed capital for the first two years, then USD500,000 in capital committed today and deployed in two years will return just USD820,374 [= USD500,000 × $(1 + 0.1041)^5$] at the end of seven years, or an ROI of 1.641× (= USD820,374/USD500,000). We may substitute this ROI into Equation 3 for seven years to solve for private equity IRR of 7.33%:

$1.641\times = (1 + IRR)^7$; IRR = 7.33% [= $1.641^{(1/7)} - 1$].

3. Given the uncertainty surrounding the timing and magnitude of capital calls for the private equity fund, the manager decides to invest committed capital in a liquid short-term fixed-income fund that returns 3.00% per annum. Discuss the effect of this decision on the IRR of the private equity fund allocation over the seven-year time horizon.

Solution

The manager's decision to invest committed capital in a short-term fixed-income fund will *reduce* but not fully offset the opportunity cost of committed capital that is eventually invested in private equity in two years. We would therefore expect the IRR of this allocation to be *above* the 7.33% in Question 2 given the assumption of zero return on committed capital but *below* the 10.41% IRR of the public investment that is fully deployed in shares for seven years.

We may demonstrate this outcome by calculating the revised IRR of the private equity fund under this assumption based on the following three steps:

Step 1 Solve for the future value of today's USD500,000 commitment.

The future value of USD500,000 at a 3% rate of return in two years can be determined using a simple time-value-of-money calculation:

USD530,450 = USD500,000 × $(1 + 0.03)^2$.

Step 2 Use the result to solve for investment value in seven years.

The same approach applies for the future value of USD530,450 at a 10.41% rate of return for five years:

$$USD870{,}355 = USD530{,}450 \times (1 + 0.1041)^5.$$

Step 3 Calculate ROI over the full seven years, and solve for IRR.

ROI is simply the ratio of the USD870,355 future value and the USD500,000 original value, or 1.741×. Solve for IRR using Equation 3:

$$1.741\times = (1 + IRR)^7 \quad IRR = 8.24\% \; [= 1.741^{(1/7)} - 1].$$

The prior example highlights the challenges associated with private market performance and public market comparisons when capital is not immediately deployed. Delayed cash *outflows* in the form of committed capital invested in more liquid investments with lower expected return will reduce IRR. Greater uncertainty surrounding the timing of capital calls makes the comparison of expected returns more challenging. Key factors affecting the timing of capital calls include the economic outlook and public market conditions, among other factors. For example, private buyout GPs deploy capital more rapidly in an environment where borrowing costs are low and expectations of solid economic growth support numerous restructuring opportunities. Under adverse market conditions, such as rising interest rates and greater risk aversion, capital deployment slows or pauses until GPs can find investment opportunities expected to meet or exceed target rates of return. For this reason, the **vintage year**, or year in which capital is initially deployed to a specific investment or project or more generally by a private market fund, is an important private investment characteristic that is closely tracked for comparing similar investments made at the same time and for seeking diversification over time across investment life cycles within a private market allocation.

Cash Flow and J-Curve Effects in Private Market Portfolios

The timing and return dynamics of individual private investments are also important drivers of private market *fund* performance. The J-curve effect shown in Exhibit 2 applies not only to individual investments but also to investment portfolios in private closed-end limited partnerships. As a fund is initiated, GPs solicit investors and obtain capital commitments. Once investment targets are identified, cash outflows occur successively as capital is deployed with no offsetting inflows. The negative cash flows of a fund's early years are expected to be offset by inflows from early investments as the fund becomes closer to fully invested. Once commitments are fully deployed, cash inflows from investments include exit values from specific investments. The following case study illustrates this process and its effect on performance.

CASE STUDY

Tenderledge Investment Fund VIII Performance

Tenderledge Partners, a private equity firm, has successfully generated capital commitments of USD100 million for its new private market investment fund. The fund's GP plans to deploy capital among four assets in three years, with an immediate USD20 million invested, followed by investments of USD40 million, USD30 million, and USD10 million at the end of each of the next three years. Each investment produces three years of uniform cash inflows in the years following investment with a sale four years after initial investment. The following table shows the expected cash flows (in millions of US dollars) and IRRs for each investment asset over their respective four-year time frames.

Cash flows by asset	Initial investment	First cash inflow	Second cash inflow	Third cash inflow	Final cash inflow	Asset IRR
Asset 1	−20	5	5	5	30	29.1%
Asset 2	−40	8	8	8	45	18.6%
Asset 3	−30	3	3	3	42	15.9%
Asset 4	−10	2	2	2	20	32.5%

Tenderledge is screening candidates for an analyst position and shows the previous table along with the previous description of the fund as part of its process for eliminating applicants. In addition to the information about the asset cash flows and IRRs, the following statements are shown:

Statement 1 The arithmetic average of the project IRRs is 24.0%.

Statement 2 The weighted average of the project IRRs is 21.3%.

Statement 3 The sum of the four project cash flows produces an IRR of 21.5%.

1. Discuss one reason why each statement is incorrect regarding the Tenderledge fund IRR.

Solution

Arithmetically averaging across project IRRs shown or simply adding the project cash flows by the year following investment is not a correct methodology. The cash flows of the four projects do not occur within the same time horizons. Thus, neither individual project IRRs nor project cash flows should be aggregated, because doing so ignores the time value of money. Instead, each year's cash flow must be calculated from the individual projects. For example, in Year 3, the sum of the cash flows is USD6 million, consisting of the asset's initial USD10 million cash outflow and cash inflows from the first three assets of USD5 million, USD8 million, and USD3 million, respectively.

The following shows the expected net cash flows for the Tenderledge fund.

USD millions	CF_0	CF_1	CF_2	CF_3	CF_4	CF_5	CF_6	CF_7	Asset IRR
Asset 1	−20	5	5	5	30				29.1%
Asset 2		−40	8	8	8	45			18.6%
Asset 3			−30	3	3	3	42		15.9%
Asset 4				−10	2	2	2	20	32.5%
Net cash flow	**−20**	**−35**	**−17**	**6**	**43**	**50**	**44**	**20**	**21.7%**

Negative net cash flows associated with initial investments dominate through the second year, while cash inflows from exiting investments and asset sale proceeds dominate in Years 4–6. The resulting IRR may be calculated using the IRR spreadsheet function, IRR({*values*},*guess*), as 21.7% [= IRR({−20,−35,−17,6,43,50,44,20},0)].

Private market fund investment IRRs reflect uneven timing of cash flows across the private asset investment life cycle. This timing issue creates challenges for benchmarking IRRs relative to public market returns measured over specific time periods. **Public market equivalent** (PME) methodologies are therefore commonly used to compare returns of private market fund returns with those of public market returns. This approach seeks to translate the uneven cash flows generated by private market funds into comparable public market returns. A basic PME methodology creates a theoretical public market investment in which private fund cash outflows are invested in a public market index while cash inflows are sold from a public market index. A terminal value is calculated from this hypothetical cash flow stream at the end of the private fund's life. The PME IRR is calculated based on the private fund's cash flows, with the PME terminal value replacing the fund's exit value. The following case study illustrates the PME approach.

CASE STUDY

Glidestone Partners Public Market Equivalent

Glidestone Partners recently closed a CAD70 million private equity fund with a four-year life. The fund's year-end cash flows, a comparable public market index, and its annual returns are shown in the following table.

Year	Glidestone Fund Cash Flow (CAD millions)	Public Market Index	Public Market Return
0	–40	100	NA
1	–30	120	20.00%
2	0	105	–12.50%
3	20	140	33.33%
4	78	150	7.14%

The fund's IRR is 10.50%, and the public market index compound annual return is 10.67%.

1. Discuss why Glidestone should not benchmark its fund's IRR against the public market index compound annual return of 10.67% to assess fund performance.

Solution

The public market return is computed as an annual return that ignores the uneven cash flow timing of Glidestone's fund. As a result, Glidestone cannot make a proper comparison to a public benchmark by simply using compound annual return.

2. The following table shows the year-end asset values of a PME for Glidestone's fund. Demonstrate how these amounts are derived using fund cash flows and the annual public market index returns. (Consider any beginning-of-year flows to be received at the end of the previous year.)

Year	Glidestone Fund PME Asset Values (CAD millions)
0	40
1	78
2	68.25
3	71
4	76.07

Solution

In Year 0, Glidestone invests CAD40 million in the public market index. During Year 1, Glidestone earns 20% on its CAD40 million initial investment for a return of CAD8 million (8 = 0.2 × 40).

At the beginning of Year 2, Glidestone invests CAD30 million, bringing total portfolio value to CAD78 million (78 = 48 + 30). In Year 2, public market return of –12.5% causes Glidestone's portfolio value to fall to CAD68.25 million [68.25 = 78 × (1 – 0.125)].

In Year 3, Glidestone has no cash inflow, with a 33.33% public market return and a CAD20 million cash outflow to investors at year-end. Thus, its asset value at the end of Year 3 is CAD71 million (= 68.25 × 1.33 – 20).

In Year 4, Glidestone has no cash inflow, and its asset value is assumed to earn the public market return of 7.14%, leading to a PME terminal value of CAD76.07 million (76.07 = 71 × 1.0714).

3. Evaluate whether Glidestone's fund exceeds its benchmark.

Solution

The IRR of the PME based on Glidestone's fund cash flows in Years 0–3 and the PME Year 4 asset value is 9.86% [= IRR({–40,–30,0,20,76.07},0)]. Thus, Glidestone's fund IRR of 10.50% exceeds the PME IRR of 9.86%. By accounting for the timing of Glidestone's cash flows in the context of public market returns, we find the opposite result of the earlier comparison against the public market's compound annual return.

Using a PME methodology provides a theoretically correct mechanism to account for the timing differences when comparing private and public market returns. The PME methodology has evolved over time to account for a variety of difficulties that can occur using the simple approach demonstrated previously. A more significant issue is associated with the choice of public market index. The previous Glidestone case study does not consider whether the public market index chosen reflects a proper public market comparable. For example, the best comparable public market index for a buyout equity fund might be a mid-cap or small-cap index rather than a large-cap index if the fund targets portfolio companies of smaller size. Furthermore, other factors may need to be considered in index selection, such as value versus growth, leverage differences, and other possible differences.

The cash flow stream from the previous case study example illustrates the importance of estimating overall fund returns based on *net* cash outflows and inflows over the life of the fund. The longer investment holding periods associated with investment selection, capital deployment, distribution of returns, and the investment exit processes can vary widely among GPs and private asset classes. As such, fund manager return calculations for limited partners at the overall fund level always incorporate cash flows across the time horizon. However, individual investments made by the fund manager can be assessed by their project IRR, which in some cases may only be computed using initial investments and exit values. For example, venture capital investments typically involve early-stage equity stakes in firms with little or no revenue that are usually sold before any distribution to shareholders takes place. Infrastructure investments, in contrast, frequently include an asset transfer to a public entity at the end of an operating period, where all shareholder returns are in the form of distributions prior to the end of the investment period.

To capture these and other differences in capital deployment, as well as returns over time and across investments, GPs commonly provide several return multiples to LPs to quantify and compare performance, which are introduced next.

Private Market Fund Multiples

In addition to IRR, GPs communicate performance to LPs using various return multiples, which offer more detail than the simple return on investment measure over the entire investment life cycle. Although these multiples also ignore the time value of money and the investment holding period, their ease of calculation and ability to differentiate between realized proceeds and the unrealized portfolio, as well as different types of return, make these ratios popular among limited partners.

The first of these multiples, **paid-in capital (PIC)**, addresses the proportion of total capital committed that has been deployed to date, as shown in Exhibit 12 and Equation 4.

Exhibit 12: Paid-In Capital

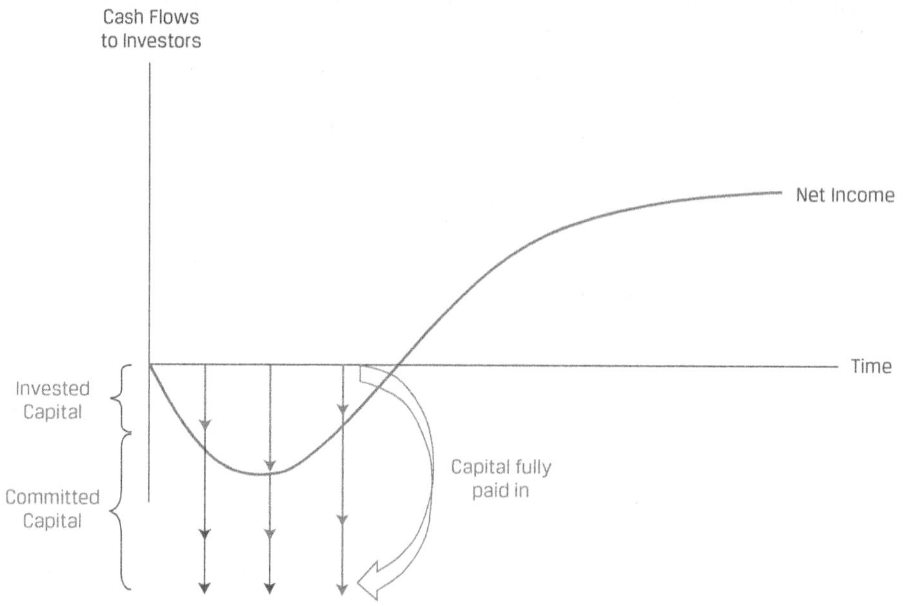

$$\text{PIC} = \frac{\text{Capital invested}}{\text{Total capital committed}}. \tag{4}$$

As Exhibit 12 suggests, PIC measures the degree to which the drawdown phase of the investment life cycle is complete, allowing LPs to compare similar investments across both GPs and vintage years, as well as across private asset classes. For example, an LP may expect an initial lower PIC for vintage years with adverse market conditions, as GPs become more selective and find fewer attractive investment opportunities. PIC is also used as an indicator for when the GP may return to market to raise a new fund. For example, GPs may raise a new fund when PIC reaches 75%.

The remaining multiples evaluate investor returns in the form of realized distributions and the net asset value, or *unrealized* value of investment, as compared to capital invested. Exhibit 13 illustrates these realized and unrealized returns in the context of the investment life cycle shown earlier.

Exhibit 13: Distributed, Residual, and Total Value to Capital Invested

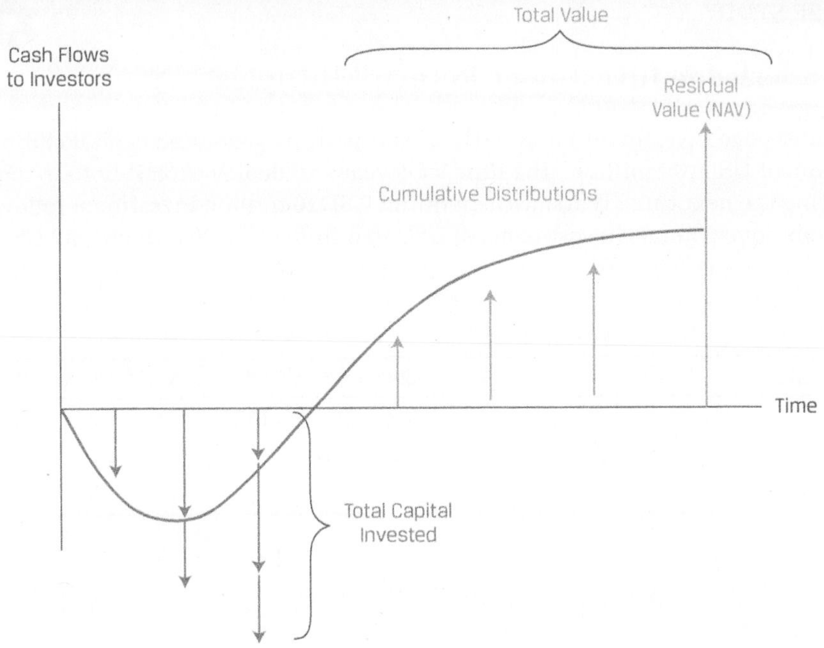

The first return measure is **distributed to paid-in (DPI)**, or the ratio of cumulative distributions to LPs to the capital invested. This measure indicates an investor's realized return on investment, often called the cash-on-cash return:

$$DPI = \frac{\text{Cumulative distributions}}{\text{Total capital invested}}. \quad (5)$$

Residual value to paid-in (RVPI) is the fund's net asset value (NAV) as a proportion of the total invested capital. Because the NAV reflects the value of the fund's remaining portfolio, this ratio is a measure of the investor's unrealized return on investment.

$$RVPI = \frac{\text{Net asset value}}{\text{Total capital invested}}. \quad (6)$$

The overall investment value to the LP, **total value to paid-in (TVPI)**, incorporates both the cumulative distributions received and the NAV as a proportion of invested capital. TVPI is the sum of DPI and RVPI.

$$TVPI = \frac{\text{Cumulative distributions} + \text{Net asset value}}{\text{Total capital invested}}. \quad (7)$$

$$TVPI = DPI + RVPI. \quad (8)$$

Average TVPIs of close to 3× are common in emerging, high-growth industries, such as information technology, and TVPIs near 2× are common in more mature industries, such as consumer goods. When considered gross of fees, which are addressed later, the TVPI is sometimes referred to as the **multiple of invested capital (MOIC)** or **multiple of money (MOM)**.

CASE STUDY

Tenderledge Investment Return Multiples

Tenderledge Investment Fund VIII has successfully generated capital commitments of USD100 million. The fund's GP plans to deploy capital in four stages during the next three years, with an initial USD20 million investment followed by subsequent annual investments of USD40 million, USD30 million, and USD10 million, respectively. Based on the expected cash inflows from the four capital deployments, Tenderledge has created the following table showing fund NAV, capital called, and distributions to LPs over the next seven years.

Years	0	1	2	3	4	5	6	7
Net asset value		65	108	134	147	132	106	56
Capital called	−20	−40	−30	−10				
Distributed capital		0	0	0	10	25	40	60

1. Calculate the fund's PIC as of the end of Year 2.

Solution

Using Equation 4, we can show the fund's paid-in capital to be 90% at the end of Year 2:

PIC = 0.9 = (20,000,000 + 30,000,000 + 40,000,000)/100,000,000.

By the end of Year 2, Tenderledge called USD90 million of capital in three stages. This amount represents 90% of the USD100 million of capital committed, an indication that it is near the end of the drawdown phase.

2. Calculate and interpret the fund's DPI as of the end of Year 7.

Solution

Using Equation 5, we can show distributed to paid-in as follows:

DPI = 1.35

= (10,000,000 + 25,000,000 + 40,000,000 + 60,000,000)/100,000,000.

The fund's DPI is 135% at the end of Year 7. This result implies that LPs have realized cash distributions 35% greater than the cash invested in the fund.

3. Calculate and interpret the fund's TVPI as of the end of Year 4.

Solution

Use Equation 7 to solve for fund TVPI at the end of Year 4 with USD10 million in cumulative distributions and a year-end fund NAV of USD147 million:

$$\text{TVPI} = \frac{10,000,000 + 147,000,000}{100,000,000}.$$

This result implies that the sum of the realized and unrealized returns to LPs is 57% above the initial amount invested into the fund. Note that this implies a DPI of 10% (= USD10 million/USD100 million) and an RVPI of 147% (= USD147 million/USD100 million), indicating that most of the fund's value is unrealized.

The previous Tenderledge case study shows how the return multiples introduced earlier can be used to gauge drawdown progress and the proportion of realized and unrealized returns to an LP's original investment over time.

QUESTION SET

1. Which of the following statements is most correct?

   Private market performance is best measured:

   A. over consistent time periods to benchmark against public market performance.

   B. over a multiyear holding period to assess the periodic effects of price appreciation.

   C. over a multiyear holding period because of periods of negative and positive cash flows.

   Solution

   C is correct. In contrast to the stable cash flows of public market investments, the investment life cycle of private market investments, which combines periods of positive and negative cash flows, implies that private market performance is best measured over a multiyear holding period. A is not correct, because the lack of traded market prices or stable cash flows negates the ability to estimate returns over shorter time periods that are common for public market investments. B is not correct, because the lack of traded market prices or other reliable estimates of asset values negates the ability to estimate price appreciation over shorter time periods.

2. Discuss why the vintage year is an important characteristic of a private market fund.

   Solution

   A private market fund's vintage year, or the first year in which the fund deploys capital, is an important private investment characteristic that is closely tracked for comparing similar investments made at the same time and seeking diversification over time across investment life cycles within a private market allocation. Managers of funds of the same vintage year with similar strategies faced the same economic outlook and public market conditions, so performance may be more easily compared.

3. In private market investing, the J-curve effect applies to:

   A. both individual investments and funds.

   B. only individual investment.

   C. only funds.

   Solution

   A is correct. The J-curve effect applies not only to individual investments but also to investment portfolios in private closed-end limited partnerships. As a fund is initiated, GPs solicit investors and obtain capital commitments. Once investment targets are identified, cash outflows occur successively as capital is deployed with no offsetting inflows. The negative cash flows of a fund's early years are eventually offset by inflows from early investments as the fund becomes closer to fully invested. Once commitments are fully deployed, cash inflows from investments include exit values from specific investments.

4. Which of the following ratios is a measure of the investor's unrealized return on investment?

   A. TVPI

   B. RVPI

   C. DPI

Solution

B is correct. Residual value to paid-in is the fund's NAV as a proportion of the total invested capital. Because the NAV reflects the value of the fund's remaining portfolio, this ratio is a measure of the investor's unrealized return on investment. A is not correct, because total value to paid-in incorporates both unrealized and realized gains on the fund. C is not correct, because distributed to paid-in includes only the cash distributions to the fund's investors.

5 PRIVATE VS. PUBLIC RISK AND RETURN

☐ compare the risk and return of investing in private markets and public markets as part of a strategic asset allocation

Given the favorable market conditions over the decade following the Global Financial Crisis (GFC) of 2008–2009, including very low interest rates and rising valuations and risk appetite, private markets outpaced their public counterparts both in generating returns and in attracting capital.

For example, according to McKinsey, a global management consulting firm, median net IRR for global private equity funds with vintage years from 2009 to 2019 averaged 20.1% from inception through late 2022, while the S&P 500 Index returned an annual average of 11.8% over roughly the same period. Global private market fundraising reached an annual high of over USD1.35 trillion in 2021, approximately double the amount raised in 2007, the year prior to the GFC.

In addition to rising allocations by institutional investors to private market asset classes, such as private equity, debt, real estate, and infrastructure, policymakers in Europe and North America have taken steps to facilitate private market access for smaller investors. Subsequent Private Markets Pathway learning modules will address the performance characteristics of specific private market asset classes; here, we focus on an investor's overall allocation to private versus public markets.

The specialized manager skills and broader range of investments and life cycle phases give rise to a high degree of variability among private market returns. For example, private equity returns are not only volatile over time but also much more variable among fund managers as compared to both public markets and other private market categories. For the private equity funds with vintage years from 2009 to 2019 from inception through late 2022, the manager performance differential between the top (29.8%) and bottom (11.4%) quartiles was 18.4%, implying that managers in the bottom quartile slightly underperformed the S&P 500 on average over the period. Other private asset classes, such as private debt, reflected smaller performance differences among managers.

Effects of Private Market Features on Risk and Return

As investors consider expanding their asset allocation to private markets, it is important to consider how the features of private markets affect risk and expected returns.

A key distinction between public and private markets is the longer investment holding period and associated J-curve effects in private markets shown in the investment life cycle in Exhibit 2. While the prior section addressed compound measures of return over the *full* investment cycle, Exhibit 14 highlights three key drivers of *periodic* return over the investment period.

Exhibit 14: Capital Calls, Deployment, and Returns over the Private Asset Investment Life Cycle

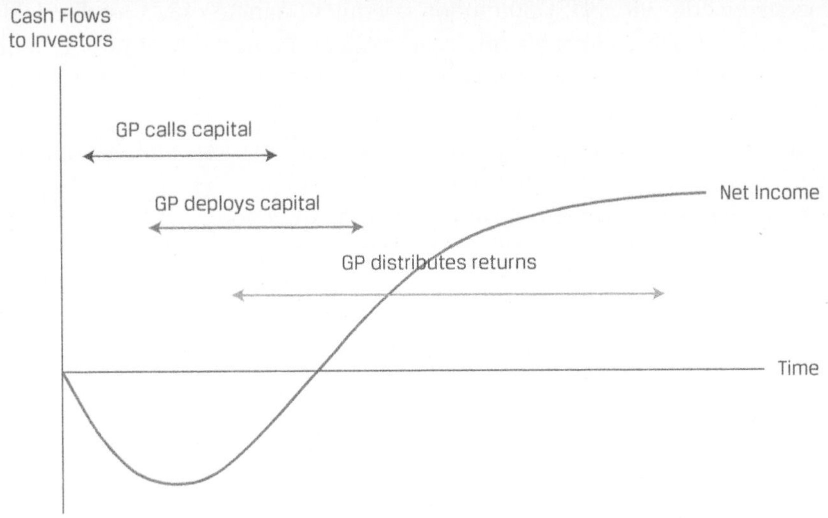

- *Commitment.* capital that is *committed* but not yet *called* is not yet invested in private market assets. Investors often hold these commitments in liquid public investments with lower expected returns.
- *Deployment.* In the early years of capital drawdown, committed funds are contributed before any returns are realized while being assessed fees, resulting in *negative* periodic returns. Over this period, GPs provide periodic fund valuations to investors. Prior to the distribution of returns, these valuations often include illiquid and unrealized capital gains that will only be received upon exit.
- *Return distribution.* Once returns reach the amount of capital contributed, the fund reaches an IRR of zero. Over time, the IRR converges to the true compounded return at the end of its life.

The combination of the long investment horizon and J-curve effects causes private market returns to be more reliant on price appreciation over the investment life cycle versus returns for public market investments, which are more likely to involve companies or assets that generate consistent, stable cash flow streams. Investors expect greater return in exchange for both the greater uncertainty and the illiquidity associated with private market strategies.

Private market debt and equity investments also provide investors access to a broader range of companies that expand the risk and return potential beyond available public investments. For example, early-stage venture capital investments target companies with exponential growth potential in emerging industries. These startup firms have a very high risk of failure but when successful also have a very high return potential, as shown in the following example.

THE STORY OF NUTANIX'S IPO

In 2009, Nutanix was founded by Dheeraj Pandey and Mohit Aron. As an early entrant in the rapidly growing area of cloud computing, the company was able to attract venture capital (VC) investor interest shortly after it was established, attracting such VCs as Khosla Ventures and Lightspeed Venture Partners. The company continued to expand and filed for an IPO in late 2015, finally going public in September 2016.

Lightspeed initially invested USD10 million in Nutanix and subsequently provided an additional USD30 million in equity financing for a total of USD40 million. When the company's stock rose 66% on its first day of public trading, Lightspeed's interest in the company was valued at USD1.035 billion, or more than 25× its initial investment.

Although Nutanix has continued to grow, with a market capitalization nearly quadruple that of its IPO price seven years later, public investors in Nutanix have not been able to match the returns of the company's pre-IPO private investors.

While well above the 20%–30% IRR commonly targeted by venture capital investors, the previous example is consistent with potential exit returns for startups with exponential growth potential. The exclusion of such very small or pregrowth companies from public listings reduces the potential return but also the risk associated with public equities. Venture capital investments in startup companies with little or no revenue and negative cash flow have a very high failure risk, as will be shown in a later learning module.

Risk and Return across Asset Classes

As investors consider strategic allocations to private market asset classes, it is instructive to contrast the relative risk and return of each type of investment with its more standardized, liquid equivalent in the public markets. Exhibit 15 provides a summary of these public and private asset class counterparts, which are expanded on in detail in later learning modules.

Exhibit 15: Public vs. Private Market Investments

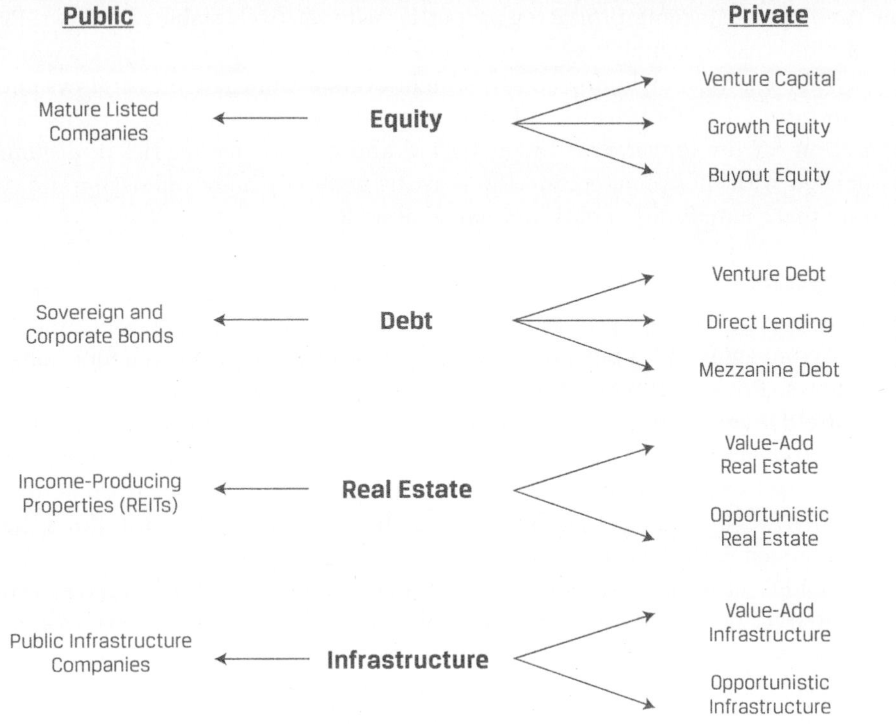

Equity

Whereas public equities involve larger companies in a mature life cycle phase with stable cash flows, private equity funds typically invest in early-stage venture capital or **growth equity** opportunities, as well as mature buyout opportunities whose investment thesis consists of purchasing a controlling stake in a firm to improve operations and target a higher exit price. Growth equity is a minority investment in a young company with a business model and rising revenue seeking to rapidly scale its operations.

Private equity strategies seek to achieve high risk-adjusted returns and portfolio diversification relative to public equities by targeting earlier company life cycle phases than those prevalent among listed companies and using high leverage over a restructuring period in the case of LBOs. Early-stage private investments are concentrated in emerging industries, such as information technology or biotechnology, or have new business models whose growth is often fueled by innovation rather than the economic cycle. Although private market investments may outperform listed equities in some periods, linkages between these markets remain in the form of entry and exit prices, market-based valuation multiples, and the cost of debt.

Debt

Public fixed-income investments consist largely of non-callable sovereign or investment-grade bonds from mature issuers with stable cash flows and little default risk. In contrast, private debt may involve early-stage startup borrowers with greater default risk, as in the case of **venture debt**; be sourced from non-bank lenders in the form of **direct lending**; or involve subordinated mezzanine debt with equity-like or other contingency features. Private debt return and risk dynamics often diverge from those of public debt due to different issuer life cycle stages, default risk, distinctive debt features, and a high degree of illiquidity.

Real Estate

Publicly traded securities typically involve real estate investment trusts, which directly own and operate income-producing properties with relatively stable cash flows. Private investments usually entail major renovations or new development projects with more equity-like features, including an investment cycle with negative cash flows and less certain future income prospects. Investors typically expect greater returns as compensation for the longer investment period and greater market risk and illiquidity associated with these strategies, as well as the generally higher idiosyncratic risk of private real estate funds versus more diversified REITS.

Infrastructure

Publicly traded corporations active in infrastructure are typically well-established, mature companies with a pipeline of projects at various stages that generate consistent cash flows. Private infrastructure investments, in contrast, often involve so-called **greenfield investments**, or new "to-be-built" projects with a long investment period and a high degree of execution risk. While private investors expect greater compensation in exchange for assuming these risks, they may also realize portfolio diversification benefits during a project's operating phase in the form of cash flows that are less correlated with the economic cycle.

An additional private market strategy that does not directly correspond to a similar public market asset class involves **special situations**. These investments target returns by investing in stressed, distressed, or event-driven opportunities, which may involve either public securities or private assets. The prevalence of greater financial distress in an economic downturn gives rise to the opportunity to generate high returns using these strategies under otherwise adverse market conditions.

Asset Allocation with Private Markets

Given the more complex investments and structures associated with private market strategies versus public markets, limited partners must appropriately plan and stage their private investments and engage with GPs at regular intervals to maximize the risk-adjusted return potential of a private market allocation.

First, the need to commit uncalled capital for an extended period and hold investments over a multiyear investment cycle with uncertain distribution size and timing gives rise to an enhanced need for liquidity planning. For example, investors must establish a plan for investing committed, uncalled capital and factor this plan into portfolio return expectations. Given the limited pricing transparency and high degree of illiquidity over an investment holding period, limited partners must factor the lagged performance reporting for these assets into their governance framework and maintain sufficient portfolio liquidity to minimize the potential of incurring secondary market costs associated with early liquidation.

As investors expand beyond an initial allocation to private markets, it is important to consider a pacing strategy to commit a certain proportion of assets to an asset class or strategy each period, regardless of market performance. In some instances, limited partners may establish limited discretion to accelerate or decelerate the pace of investment depending on relative market conditions. In cases where specific vintage years or strategies are more challenging to access, the investor must weigh the diversification benefit with the cost. Finally, it is important to maintain and develop relationships with GPs as private capital commitments are deployed and distributions begin, to roll a consistent proportion of uncommitted capital into new funds each period. The following case study addresses these considerations faced by an institutional investor seeking to increase its allocation to private markets.

CASE STUDY

Mid States University Endowment Strategic Asset Allocation Review

Mid States University is a growing regional university with a USD400 million endowment managed by Mid States University Management Company (MSUMC). Mid States University uses its endowment as a perpetual asset designed to provide for a real 4% rate of annual spending to support a variety of academic programs across the institution. Mid States University hired a new president who has introduced ambitious growth plans. In an effort to provide improved financial support to its programs, MSUMC launched a fundraising effort a year ago with a goal to grow the endowment to USD1 billion in three years. After its first year, the endowment growth plan is on track to meet its goal. The board of trustees of MSUMC is now reviewing the endowment's asset allocation to assess whether they should authorize material changes to the portfolio's strategic allocation.

Audrey Lake, CFA, serves as MSUMC's chief investment officer and compiles the following asset allocation information in preparation for a board meeting.

Asset class	Large university (>USD1,000 million) endowment allocations	MSUMC current allocation
Public equity	25%	45%
Public debt	20%	30%
Cash	4%	4%
Private equity	33%	15%
Private debt	1%	0%
Private RE	5%	3%
Private infra.	5%	0%
Other assets	7%	3%

As she begins to make her key points, Lake first highlights that MSUMC has 75% of its portfolio allocated to traditional public market assets, while the typical large endowment's public market allocation is only 45%. Private market assets constitute only 18% of MSUMC's portfolio, compared to 44% of large endowment portfolios. Lake argues that MSUMC should strive to reallocate its investments as the endowment grows to better match the allocation targets observed for large endowments.

One of the board members notes that MSUMC's total allocation of 60% to equity investments is not particularly different from the typical large endowment's 58% total allocation to equity investments. Lake uses this comment to discuss MSUMC's current private equity allocation to funds focused solely on buyout equity strategies. She mentions that MSUMC's allocation to this strategy is like that of large endowments. The major difference is that large endowments also allocate significant amounts to private equity funds investing in venture capital and growth equity strategies while MSUMC has no such allocations. As a result, the equity portfolio lacks exposure to startup and high-growth companies, sacrificing the higher expected returns and any potential diversification effects associated with these strategies.

QUESTION SET

1. Which of the following is the most correct statement about returns over a private market investment life cycle?

   A. Private market returns are typically less reliant on price appreciation over the investment life cycle versus public market returns.

   B. Once a fund's investment returns reach the amount of capital contributed, the fund reaches an IRR of zero.

   C. Fund returns are typically positive during a fund's capital deployment phase.

   Solution

   B is correct. Once fund returns reach the amount of capital contributed, cash inflows equal cash outflows. Mathematically, this leads to an IRR equal to zero. Any additional returns beyond this point then result in positive IRR for the fund. A is incorrect because private market returns are typically more reliant on asset price appreciation compared to public market returns. C is incorrect because the negative cash outflow occurring during capital deployment is consistent with negative periodic returns.

2. Discuss two factors for why a private market investor should typically expect higher returns than a public market investor in the same asset class, such as private equity versus public equity.

   Solution

   One factor is greater uncertainty associated with private market investments because of less stable cash flows and greater reliance on price appreciation. Another factor is the greater illiquidity associated with private market investments compared to public markets.

3. Discuss one fundamental asset characteristic that cause private real estate and infrastructure investments to usually be riskier than public investments in these asset classes.

   Solution

   Private investments in both real estate and infrastructure are likely to be new or significant redevelopments, which contrasts with public investments in these asset classes, which tend to reflect portfolios of already-built assets that generate stable cash flow. As a result, private investments have long investment life cycles with uncertain cash flows and high illiquidity.

PRACTICE PROBLEMS

The following information relates to questions 1-4

YYR Public Fund (YYRPF) is a large sovereign wealth fund managing a Southeast Asian country's monetary reserves with a long-term goal of maintaining and growing purchasing power through the fund's investment program. Earlier in its existence, YYRPF's strategic allocation was heavily weighted toward publicly traded government and corporate bonds generating fixed-coupon income with a secondary focus on publicly traded international equities along with a minor allocation toward domestic real estate. Over time, YYRPF has evolved its strategic asset allocation to be widely diversified across private asset classes in addition to continuing to allocate to publicly traded asset classes.

As part of its goal to maximize return performance while mitigating risk, YYRPF currently allocates approximately 20% of its portfolio to private equity investments and 25% to public equities. The fund diversifies across a range of private equity strategies, including venture capital, growth equity, and buyout equity. Its public equity strategy focuses on maintaining balanced allocations across global equity markets.

YYRPF has been expanding its internal private equity team over the years to build its expertise in this private market asset class. YYRPF plans to use direct investment for 100% of its private equity portfolio investments in the next five years. The resulting fee reduction from direct investing in private equity is expected to add a non-trivial amount to the fund's performance.

YYRPF includes allocations to private real estate and private infrastructure that amount to less than 10% of its total portfolio. As a result, YYRPF plans to invest in these asset classes strictly through limited partnerships. The available performance data suggest that YYRPF can expect returns of 10%–12% annually from investing in these asset classes. In conversations with a GP of a private real estate fund invested in by YYRPF, she specifically states that attractive investment opportunities appear infrequently, resulting in capital deployment periods possibly being as long as four years.

1. Discuss how YYRPF's approach to investment process and liquidity have likely changed as its strategic asset allocation has changed.

2. Discuss how YYRPF likely assesses diversification potential when adding a new public equity position versus a new private equity position to its equity portfolio.

3. Which of the following private market investment methods is most likely to be used by YYRPF to help the fund move toward pursuing its private investment goals?

   A. Limited partner co-investment

   B. Direct co-investment

   C. Angel investment

4. Discuss how YYRPF may consider incorporating potentially long capital deployment periods in private asset classes such as real estate and infrastructure into its

expectations of return performance for these types of investments.

The following information relates to questions 5-8

Mid States University Management Company (MSUMC), which manages a USD400 million endowment for Mid States University, is evaluating the potential for investment with Glidestone Partners, a firm running a variety of private market funds. As part of its due diligence process on Glidestone, MSUMC examines historical performance records of Glidestone's funds and selected investments made by these funds.

MSUMC notes the following basic facts about Glidestone's Fund 1. The fund invested EUR15 million per year at the beginning of each of Years 1–4, followed by cash inflows of EUR30 million per year at the ends of each of Years 4–7.

Glidestone's Fund 1 distributed EUR100 million to its investors during the last four years of the fund, as shown in the following table, which also shows net asset values at the end of each of the last five years of the fund's existence.

Years	3	4	5	6	7
Net asset value	60	65	50	35	20
Distributed capital	0	10	30	30	30

MSUMC personnel note that Fund 1 distributed EUR100 million to its investors over time while the fund generated EUR120 million of cash inflows.

During its due diligence, MSUMC discovers that Fund 1's portfolio consisted of four distinct asset investments of EUR15 million per year. Fund 1's IRR over the seven-year investment cycle was 300 bps greater than a public market benchmark with risk similar to that of Fund 1's investments.

5. Which of the following most closely approximates the ROI and IRR of Glidestone's Fund 1 over its seven-year life?

   A. ROI = 2×; IRR = 10.4%.

   B. ROI = 2×; IRR = 18.9%.

   C. ROI = 3×; IRR = 18.9%.

6. Which of the following most closely approximates Fund 1's TVPI at the end of the fund's life?

   A. 0.83

   B. 1.67

   C. 2.00

7. Discuss why Glidestone's NAV increases by EUR5 million between the ends of Years 3 and 4 using observations about fund distributions.

8. Which of the following statements most likely reflects the return earned by Fund 1 investors?

   A. Fund 1's ROI

B. Fund 1's IRR

C. A blend of Fund 1's IRR and the public market benchmark return

The following information relates to questions 9-12

Mid States University's USD400 million endowment is managed by Mid States University Management Company (MSUMC). The endowment targets real annual spending of 4% to support its programs. MSUMC is considering material changes to the portfolio's strategic asset allocation.

Audrey Lake, CFA, serves as MSUMC's chief investment officer and compiles the following information for a board meeting.

Asset class	Large university (>USD1,000 million) endowment allocations	MSUF current allocation
Public equity	25%	45%
Public debt	20%	30%
Cash	4%	4%
Private equity	33%	15%
Private debt	1%	0%
Private RE	5%	3%
Private infra.	5%	0%
Other assets	7%	3%

Lake first highlights that MSUMC has 75% of its portfolio allocated to traditional public market assets while the typical large endowment's public market allocation is only 45%. Private market assets are just 18% of MSUMC's portfolio, compared to 44% of large endowment portfolios. Lake argues that MSUMC should strive to reallocate its investments to better match the targets observed for large endowments.

One board member notes that MSUMC's total allocation of 60% to equity investments is not far from the average large endowment's equity allocation of 58%. Lake responds that MSUMC's current private equity allocation is solely focused on buyout equity strategies. She mentions that MSUMC's allocation to this type of strategy is similar to that of large endowments. However, other endowments also invest in venture capital and growth equity strategies while MSUMC does not, forgoing exposure to startup and high-growth phase companies.

Another board member questions Lake about her strategy for allocating to venture capital investments because it will effectively be a new asset class for the endowment. Lake's response focuses on a number of issues learned in working with buyout equity funds: (1) Identify VC general partners with top-quartile return histories, build relationships, and commit capital as opportunities develop; (2) have a well-defined plan for investing committed funds in liquid equities from industries similar to those of VC investments while awaiting capital calls; (3) accept the realities associated with lagged performance feedback from the fund; and (4) plan ahead in order to bear the illiquidity risk associated with the 7- to 10-year holding period of the fund.

The final question posed relates to the proposed roles for smaller asset classes, such as private debt. Lake mentions opportunities to improve returns from the debt portion of the portfolio by reallocating up to 5% from the public debt allocation. Specifically, Lake mentions the ability to invest in senior floating-rate notes as one way to gain yield along with inflation protection while ensuring high degrees of capital preservation from that portion of the portfolio.

9. Discuss why Lake believes that MSUMC should reallocate such that its portfolio is weighted more toward private market investments.

10. Contrast how the features of the MSUMC endowment portfolio likely differ from those of large endowments with a focus on risk and diversification.

11. Evaluate Lake's plan to invest VC committed capital in public equities from industries similar to those included in VC investments.

12. Identify and discuss a spending-related reason why Lake may be attracted to investing 5% of the endowment's portfolio in private debt.

SOLUTIONS

1. As YYRPF has shifted from public market to private market investments, its investment process has likely changed from identifying underpriced and overpriced liquid securities to buy or sell over a short- to medium-term horizon. The private investment process involves identifying and committing capital over a private asset investment life cycle in which illiquid closed-end investments are purchased and held for as long as 7–10 years.

2. Public equity positions have easily measured correlations with other public equity positions. As such, a lower correlation of a new public equity position may be viewed as providing better diversification potential. In contrast, the lack of observable market prices at regular intervals for private equity positions makes using correlations less plausible. Rather, the diversification potential of a private equity position may be a function of adding a company life cycle stage that is not typically available to public market equity investors, such as startup companies. Alternatively, private equity investments in buyout equity provide investors with the potential for benefiting from the transformation of a company's business model over a longer investment life cycle, thus providing a return stream that is different from what may be available from mature public market investments.

3. B is the correct response. YYRPF is attempting to build its expertise in private equity investing to achieve 100% direct investment in a quest to improve its net-of-fee performance. As it pursue this goal, it can best achieve expertise improvements along with lower fees by direct co-investment. YYRPF does not incur fees from a GP on its direct co-investments. A is incorrect because limited partner co-investment allows for expertise improvement, but the GP still collects a reduced fee from YYRPF. C is incorrect because angel investing is unlikely to provide the access to improved expertise across private equity since this method covers only the startup investing environment.

4. YYRPF must commit funds to a GP months or years in advance of capital deployment, with little certainty regarding the timing or magnitude of capital calls. As a result, investors must often hold these commitments in more liquid public investments possibly with lower expected returns. Therefore, YYRPF's overall return from the time of capital commitment through the investment life cycle will reflect a blended rate of return that includes both public and private market investment returns. If capital commitments are invested in lower-yielding public securities while waiting for capital to be deployed, the 10%–12% return estimates should be adjusted to reflect this situation.

5. B is correct. Glidestone's Fund 1 invested EUR60 (= 15 × 4 years) million and received EUR120 (= 30 × 4 years) million, so ROI is 2× (= 120 ÷ 60). The IRR is solved using either a spreadsheet or financial calculator IRR function as =IRR({–15,–15,–15,–15,30,30,30,30},0), which yields a solution of 18.9%. A is incorrect because the IRR of 10.4% assumes that all the cash outflows of EUR60 million occur at the beginning of the investment life cycle and that all the cash inflows of EUR120 million occur at the end of the investment life cycle. C is incorrect because ROI of 3× is incorrect.

6. C is correct. TVPI is equal to the sum of DPI and RVPI. DPI is the cumulative distributions paid divided by the total investment. Cumulative distributions are EUR100 million, and total investment is EUR60 million, so DPI is 1.67 (= 100 ÷ 60). RVPI is equal to net asset value divided by total investment, or 0.33 (= 20 ÷ 60). Thus, TVPI is equal to 2.00 (= 1.67 + 0.33). A is incorrect because it assumes

DPI of 0.5 (= 30 ÷ 60) plus the correct RVPI. B is incorrect because it assumes RVPI of 1.0, which implies NAV of EUR60 at the end of Year 7, plus the correct DPI.

7. Because Glidestone distributes only EUR10 million in Year 4 rather than the EUR30 million of cash flow generated, the extra EUR20 million is added to the fund's NAV. However, the exit of the original EUR15 million investment reduces the NAV such that the overall value increases by EUR5 million.

8. C is correct. Because of the time lag between the dates of LP's capital commitment and GP's capital call, the LP should not expect to earn the rate of return of the private market fund. Rather, the LP invests capital in a liquid public market investment until capital is called. Thus, the LP's overall return is a blended rate that reflects both the private market fund's IRR and the return earned from the liquid public market investment. A is incorrect because the ROI multiple does not account for time value of money or the time lag between capital commitment and call. B is incorrect because the fund's IRR does not account for the time lag between capital commitment and call.

9. Private market investments typically are expected to earn higher rates of return than their public market counterparts. Lake believes that the endowment, as a portfolio with a perpetual time horizon, is in a position to incur the higher risks posed by private market investments, such as illiquidity, as long as these extra risks generate sufficient additional returns to support the spending needs of the university.

10. With respect to risk differences, MSUMC's total equity portfolio is likely less risky compared to a large endowment portfolio. While both MSUMC and large endowments invest similar percentages of their overall portfolios in equities, MSUMC's equity portfolio is more heavily weighted toward public equities compared to those of large endowments. As a result, MSUMC has less exposure to riskier equity assets in private equity, especially given its lack of exposure to startup company equity.

    With respect to diversification differences, as mentioned for the risk differences, MSUMC may be lacking equity diversification across company life cycles in its equity portfolio. Additionally, MSUMC is more heavily weighted in public debt securities relative to large endowments that spread the non-equity portion of their portfolio across not only public but also private debt, as well as private real estate and infrastructure.

11. Lake is seeking to create a liquid portfolio with risk to that of the eventual VC investment by matching its industry exposure to target a similar return during the capital commitment period. Favorable market conditions may create more investment opportunities for the GP to call capital, and these may coincide with favorable returns on Lake's liquid equity portfolio. However, less favorable market conditions may cause declines in the value of this liquid portfolio during the time lag between capital commitment and call, thus creating a risk of being unable to meet a capital call in an extreme market downturn.

12. Private debt investments typically provide higher expected returns compared to those usually available in public debt investments and may provide inflation protection to assist MSUMC in its annual spending needs. MSUMC's spending needs are at a real rate of 4%, so the endowment's annual nominal spending reflects the effects of inflation. The discussion of private debt specifically mentions investing in floating-rate notes that provide potential for inflation protection.

LEARNING MODULE

2

General Partner and Investor Perspectives and the Investment Process

LEARNING OUTCOMES

Mastery	The candidate should be able to:
☐	discuss a general partner's roles and responsibilities in managing private investment funds
☐	discuss how private investment firms align their interests with those of their investors, and calculate, interpret, and discuss private market fund performance from an investor perspective, including management fees and carried interest
☐	discuss favorable characteristics of private investment targets and sources of value creation in private markets
☐	discuss the role of conducting due diligence and establishing a business plan in the private investment process
☐	discuss alternative exit routes in private investments and their impact on value

1 INTRODUCTION

Traditional fund managers analyze investments based on publicly available information, readily buy and sell publicly traded securities in a portfolio, and are usually compensated by investors based on a fixed percentage of assets under management (AUM). Public fund investors can easily compare relative risk and return among similar fund choices and trade these positions with few transaction costs. In private markets, underlying investments, as well as the methods and structures used to attract capital, manage assets, and distribute returns, give rise to very different interactions between private fund managers or general partners (GPs) and private market investors or limited partners (LPs). This reading addresses the unique relationship between GPs and LPs over the investment life cycle and the private market investment process.

According to Preqin, an alternative data provider, private market AUM globally are expected to rise to USD18 trillion by 2027, or more than triple their level from a decade earlier, due to higher potential returns and diversification opportunities. Private markets, such as private equity, private real estate, and unlisted infrastructure, are characterized by an investment life cycle with negative cash flows and/or high leverage during an initial period of development or transformation. This process requires more active manager engagement and specialized knowledge to evaluate cash flows and risks. Investors often must commit capital well in advance of deployment, hold investments for several years, and receive returns with distributions of uncertain magnitude and timing over a multiyear holding period.

In this reading, we first examine how the features of private markets define the roles and responsibilities of general partners of private funds. Differences in private manager compensation approaches and risk and return measures are two important investor considerations addressed in the following section. We then focus our attention for the remainder of the reading on the private investment process itself, including the following elements:

- Alignment of GP and LP interests over the investment life cycle and private market fund performance from an investor perspective
- Features of attractive private investment targets, economic value drivers, and sources of value creation in private markets
- Key components of due diligence and the business plan applicable over the period of development or transformation of a new or existing property, asset, or privately held company
- Determining the appropriate exit timing and method of a private investment to maximize return to investors over the holding period

The private market features and structures from the first reading combined with the GP and LP perspectives and investment process from this second reading create the foundation for a more detailed survey of individual private market asset classes and their role in strategic asset allocation in subsequent Private Markets Pathway readings.

LEARNING MODULE OVERVIEW

- As controlling or significant minority shareholders, general partners of private market funds are actively engaged throughout the investment life cycle in analyzing targets, acquiring firms or assets, and creating and implementing value creation strategies.
- GPs seek to align their interests with LPs by combining management fees levied on committed capital with performance-based compensation in the form of carried interest.
- Attractive characteristics of private investment targets involve the potential for value creation over the investment period, such as establishing a product and market for early-stage companies or improving the profitability of mature firms. GPs apply value drivers in the form of strategic, operational, organizational, and financial changes to companies or projects to achieve targeted returns.
- Due diligence activities in the private investment process involve a more in-depth and detailed analysis of a company or project than in public markets given the long holding period over which value creation takes place. GPs use this analysis to establish an action plan prioritizing investments and other changes needed to reach targeted returns.
- Private fund exit strategies include a public sale via an initial public offering (IPO), a private sale to a strategic or financial buyer, or liquidation. While a public sale achieves the broadest distribution and

access to capital, its impact on value is highly dependent on public market conditions. A private sale may be executed more quickly and flexibly, with value highly dependent on the competitive nature of the bidding process and types of potential buyers involved.

GENERAL PARTNER ROLES AND RESPONSIBILITIES

2

☐ discuss a general partner's roles and responsibilities in managing private investment funds

The nature of private market investments gives rise to specific roles and responsibilities for the general partners of closed-end private market funds. Public market fund managers primarily engage in security or index selection across or within markets based on public information, as either non-controlling shareholders with management decisions limited to voting rights for public shares or bondholders who lack the power to renegotiate terms of outstanding bonds prior to maturity. These public funds are generally open-ended, with an indefinite life and continuous inflows and outflows of investor capital. Public investments are in standardized equity or debt contracts for mature companies or ownership of income-producing assets, as in the case of listed real estate investment trusts (REITs).

Private funds, in contrast, are usually closed-end, illiquid limited partnerships with a fixed contractual term. These partnerships usually require an upfront capital commitment from investors. This capital is deployed over time in longer-term, illiquid investments that mature in the case of debt or are exited near the end of the partnership's contractual life. Examples include early-stage or mature companies with high potential and undervalued or undeveloped assets. Private investments focus on adding value and generating returns over the life cycle shown in Exhibit 1.

Exhibit 1: Private Asset Investment Life Cycle

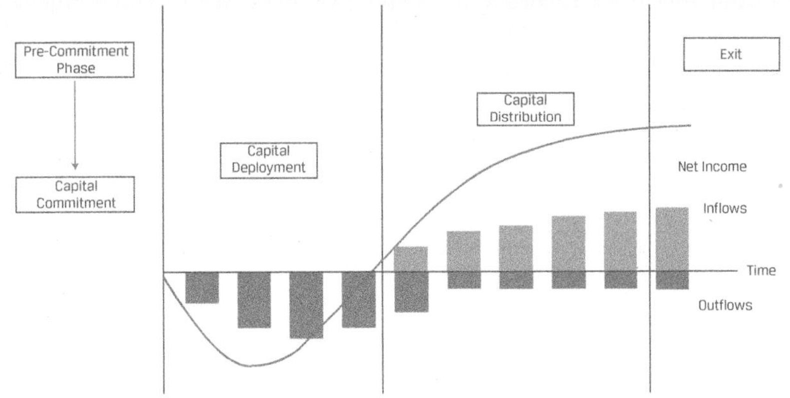

An earlier reading distinguished between private fund GPs more actively engaged in value creation strategies with fewer targeted investments held over a longer, multiyear private asset investment life cycle and public fund managers buying and selling fractional, non-controlling positions in numerous debt and equity securities with greater frequency. Public fund managers use financial statement analysis among other means as a basis for these decisions. Public markets also allow fund performance comparisons with available benchmarks. GPs operating in private markets, in contrast, typically have either control of or significant influence over fewer investments, with little or no price transparency or reliable benchmarking available during the life of an investment.

These differences in the public and private markets give rise to distinct roles and responsibilities among private market GPs. The following subsections discuss the duties of a private market GP over the private asset investment life cycle.

Pre-Commitment

In advance of seeking capital commitments from investors, private fund GPs establish an investment strategy or thesis reflecting the fund's focus. Specialized GP knowledge and experience are primary determinants of private market fund strategy given the greater degree of control exercised for these investments. For example, biotech venture capital fund GPs are often led and staffed by researchers and scientists with extensive experience and expertise in conducting basic research and clinical trials and bringing new drugs to market. A Southeast Asia–based real estate GP focused on new development, in contrast, will usually involve local expertise and experience in construction, contracting, and operations as important prerequisites for taking on opportunistic new development projects.

Identifying areas of investment focus prior to conducting and completing due diligence on a select few candidates is an important pre-commitment step. Potential for value creation over the investment life cycle is a common feature among prospective private investments, which occurs in different ways over the company life cycle. For venture capital, this may involve a new product going to market or targeting exponential growth, while for buyout equity, it often entails restructuring and streamlining established operations. Each of these areas is expanded on later.

Capital Commitment

Once a private fund GP has identified its area of primary focus and is ready to dedicate resources to initiate due diligence and create business and financing plans for targeted investments, it solicits unfunded capital commitments from limited partners. Prospective LPs engage in manager selection by conducting due diligence and analysis of the GP's track record and prospective investment opportunities, making unfunded debt or equity capital commitments to a fund by entering into a limited partnership agreement. The limited partnership agreement is a negotiated document that specifies fees, rights, terms, and conditions of the partnership. These fees, rights, terms, and conditions may vary among individual LPs based on the timing and size of commitment to a fund. The following case study further contrasts public and private fund commitments.

CASE STUDY

Private Real Estate Investment in Malaysia

Investors seeking to gain exposure to commercial real estate in Malaysia must choose between a publicly traded REIT or a private real estate fund. One possible area of private development focus might involve multifamily residential real estate projects near planned mass transit lines in urban areas such as Kuala Lumpur. This type of development follows a multiyear investment cycle starting with GPs seeking commitments from LPs. The GP then identifies an appropriate parcel of land for purchase, conducts necessary due diligence, and establishes the feasibility of the site to support the planned development, including proper permits and zoning requirements. Next, the GP forms a special purpose company to purchase the property using committed equity and debt in the form of acquisition and construction loans secured by the property. Once the property is completed and generates sufficient lease income upon completion, the GP often sells the property and distributes proceeds to LP equity investors.

Capital Deployment

Private fund GPs finalize due diligence on top targets, creating both a detailed business plan as a blueprint for new managers and a comprehensive financing plan to achieve expected returns prior to bidding on investments. Once a public or private company bid or project proposal is accepted, private market GPs draw down equity and debt capital pledged by investors to purchase individual portfolio investments. Additional drawdowns may be needed to fund successive investment stages for an existing project or asset. The initial year in which capital is deployed in a private market transaction is referred to as a fund's **vintage year**, an important benchmarking statistic that facilitates performance comparisons among investments made in different periods. A GP deploying capital over multiple years for a single fund has one vintage year, defined as the first year in which capital is deployed.

In the case of private equity, a GP may deploy buyout capital by purchasing a business for restructuring purposes. This may be an acquisition of a public company in a **take-private transaction**, which involves the purchase of the entire company, after which the target firm's shares cease trading; the purchase of a public company division; or an acquisition of a private firm. The initial phase of a buyout equity transaction, also referred to as a **leveraged buyout (LBO)**, and the roles of GPs and LPs in the transaction are shown in Exhibit 2.

Exhibit 2: GP and LP Roles in the Initial Take-Private Transaction Phase

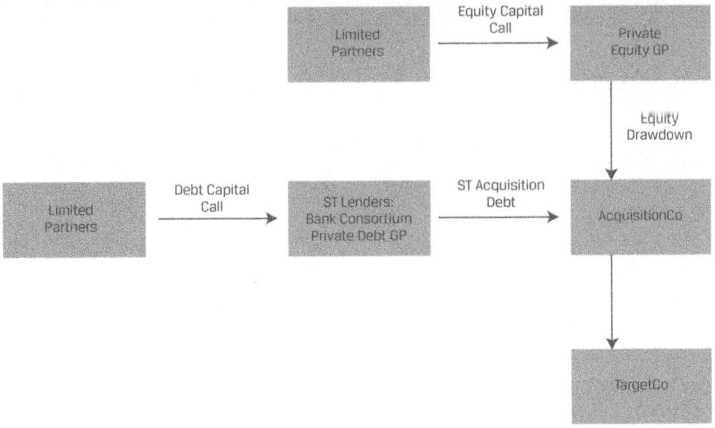

Both the initial financing phase shown in Exhibit 2 and subsequent refinancing stages are the primary responsibility of a general partner, which includes the following actions:

- Negotiate the target company (TargetCo) purchase price.
- Negotiate legal terms of the acquisition.
- Establish an acquiring entity (AcquisitionCo).
- Arrange short-term debt financing to complete the TargetCo purchase.

- Combine AcquisitionCo and TargetCo into a merged company.
- Raise an optimal combination of medium- and long-term debt instruments for the new entity.

While GPs retain primary responsibility for these and associated steps and in some cases also place the debt with private debt GPs, they often employ advisers in financing, legal, tax, and other areas to complete a transaction.

Once an acquisition and associated initial financing are in place, GPs play a critical role in initiating management changes, spinning off non-strategic business divisions, or combining entities to create potential synergies and driving the value creation process by monitoring progress as set out in the business plan. Because the timing and size of capital drawdowns is uncertain, in some cases GPs take advantage of credit facilities known as **subscription lines**, which are short-term lines of credit secured by investor fund commitments rather than the underlying assets themselves.

In the case of real estate or infrastructure development projects, the deployment phase often involves managing and monitoring progress over phases, including land or property acquisition, land improvement, and construction. Periodic drawdown of additional debt and equity are contingent on meeting specific milestones, as shown in the following case study.

CASE STUDY

Malaysian Real Estate Capital Deployment Based on Project Milestones

Private market investments in new real estate or infrastructure development are usually financed in phases corresponding to project completion. As an example, consider the Malaysian real estate case introduced earlier. A developer establishes a project plan to build 1,200 new residential units on vacant land near Kuala Lumpur near a proposed new mass transit hub. The project is expected to cost MYR275 million and take 24 months to complete.

Line Item	MYR
Land	25,000,000
On-site land improvements	10,000,000
Construction costs	240,000,000
Project cost	**275,000,000**

The private real estate GP developer determines that the project will be 75% (or MYR206,250,000) debt financed with the remainder (MYR68,750,000) financed in the form of equity. Equity is drawn in three phases with the following milestones:

Milestone	Month	Equity Drawn (MYR)	Equity Outstanding (MYR)
Land purchase	0	25,000,000	25,000,000
Certification of structural completion	12	25,000,000	50,000,000
Certificate of occupancy issued	24	18,750,000	68,750,000

Construction debt is slated to be drawn monthly based on more detailed milestones to purchase materials, lease equipment, and cover other contractor and construction costs. The proposed capital deployment schedule for the project is summarized in Exhibit 3.

Exhibit 3: Real Estate Capital Deployment

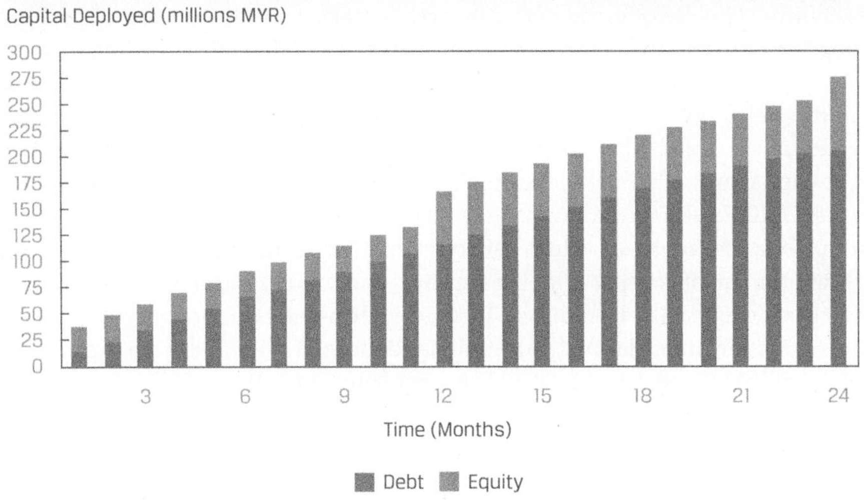

Capital Distribution and Exit

In contrast to more stable dividend and interest cash flows from listed securities in public funds, the timing and magnitude of private market fund distributions are uncertain, leading to the use of compound versus periodic measures of return, as shown in an earlier reading. These distributions consist of both dividends and divestments in the case of private equity funds and interest and principal payments in the case of private debt funds. GPs often exercise control over portfolio company dividend policies and divestments. As for private debt, issuer contingencies, such as debt prepayability, callability, or interest paid in kind or accrued with an increase in principal outstanding and repaid at maturity, contribute to greater cash flow uncertainty of private debt.

Despite the long-term contractual nature of limited partnerships, private market GPs also frequently play a role in offering LPs the ability to purchase or sell existing partnership stakes in the secondary market, which are referred to as **secondaries**. Secondaries trade at much wider spreads as a percentage of net asset value (NAV) than public securities exchanged at a bid–offer spread of a few basis points. Private market secondary spreads vary widely among private asset types and in different market conditions. For example, while buyout equity stakes have historically traded near 95% of NAV, venture capital stakes often trade closer to 80% of NAV.

The secondary market provides new investors the opportunity to purchase seasoned, mid-cycle investments, allowing diversification across managers, partnerships, and vintage years and granting LPs access to transactions in which they may not have had an opportunity to invest at inception. A secondary purchase of mid-cycle investments also avoids investment delays given the lack of a commitment phase. LPs selling secondaries, however, may also wish to reduce exposure to an existing investment and free up capital for new partnerships. By acting as an intermediary in secondary market transactions, GPs can provide investors the chance to buy or sell otherwise illiquid positions, offer a broader array of opportunities at different stages for varying periods, and expand and diversify their investor base for future transactions.

Private fund GPs are also primarily responsible for the sale or exit of an investment, asset, or project at the end of a holding period and return of capital to investors. In the case of private equity, this may involve the sale of a company to a private buyer or an initial public offering to public market investors. GP skills in executing a business plan that creates value and then identifying potential buyer synergies or preparing and executing a public offering under favorable market conditions are critical factors affecting LP returns. The alternative exit routes available within and across private investment classes and their impact on investment value will be addressed in detail later in this reading.

In addition to monitoring investments closely over the entire life of a fund to protect investor capital and maximize returns, GPs also provide periodic fund valuations to investors. Unlike public fund investments whose net asset value is based on observed market prices, private asset values rely on valuation techniques, such as discounted cash flows, the use of comparable transactions, and market-based multiples, as shown for each asset class in later readings. These private asset valuations are far less transparent, with their potential realization dependent on a GP's ability to realize illiquid capital gains in the company, project, or asset since inception.

QUESTION SET

1. Which one of the following is most likely to be conducted by a GP during the pre-commitment phase of the private market fund investment life cycle?

   A. Implementing a strategic financing plan

   B. Identifying target investments

   C. Deployment of capital.

   Solution

   B is the correct response. Along with establishing an investment strategy, a GP is most likely to begin identifying target investments fitting the strategy prior to soliciting capital commitments from LPs. A is not correct, because the fund's financing plan may be formulated in the pre-commitment stage but not implemented until the commitment or deployment stage. C is not correct, because capital is deployed later in the investment process.

2. Which one of the following statements is most accurate about vintage years in private market funds?

   A. A GP deploying capital over multiple years for a single fund has multiple vintage years for the fund.

   B. A GP deploying capital over multiple years for a single fund has one vintage year, defined as the final year in which capital is deployed.

   C. A GP deploying capital over multiple years for a single fund has one vintage year, defined as the first year in which capital is deployed.

   Solution

   C is the correct response. The initial year in which fund capital is deployed in a private market transaction is referred to as a fund's vintage year. A is not correct, because this statement implies that a single fund has multiple vintage years. B is not correct, because it identifies the last year of capital deployment rather than the first.

3. Identify two benefits of secondaries for buyers in private markets.

Solution

Secondaries provide new investors the opportunity to purchase seasoned, mid-cycle private market investments, providing such benefits as

- allowing diversification across managers, partnerships, and vintage years and
- granting LPs access to transactions in which they may not have had an opportunity to invest at inception.

INVESTOR (LP) PERSPECTIVES, FEES AND PERFORMANCE MEASUREMENT

3

☐ discuss how private investment firms align their interests with those of their investors, and calculate, interpret, and discuss private market fund performance from an investor perspective, including management fees and carried interest

Private fund GPs exercise greater control over illiquid investments for a longer holding period than public fund managers. These investments in unlisted assets with little or no publicly available information about portfolio investments or comparable funds offer investors little transparency. This information asymmetry limits an LP's ability to independently assess and benchmark private market GP performance, while long required holding periods prevent LPs from selling partnerships of underperforming managers without incurring significant bid–offer costs in the secondary market.

Private investment firms seek to bridge the information gap and align GP and LP interests by levying a combination of fees that include management fees to cover operating costs and performance-based incentive fees (referred to as **carried interest**) to incentivize and reward successful GPs.

Management Fees

Private fund GPs usually charge a higher management fee than public funds charge to cover operational costs, with average fees of around 1% for private debt and 2% for private equity. However, management fees can vary depending on the type and nature of the fund. In contrast to public fund fees levied as a percentage of AUM, private fund management fees are most often calculated as a percentage of total *committed* capital, which includes both drawn and undrawn portions. Once capital is fully deployed, these fees are levied on the amount of committed capital less the cumulative cost basis of investments exited and written off during the fund's life.

In some cases, additional transaction fees are paid to GPs when they provide advisory services for transactions such as mergers, acquisitions, or IPOs that benefit the fund. These fees may be split with LPs, and if such fee-sharing agreements apply, they are generally deducted from management fees and such deductions may be full or partial.

CASE STUDY

Management Fees for the Estragon SA Fund

Estragon SA, a French venture capital fund, seeks a EUR10 million equity commitment from Straddleton, a local UK government pension scheme, as a limited partner. Over a seven-year time span, Estragon draws down equity from Straddleton over the first two years, half each in Years 1 and 2; writes off two investments with a cost basis of 10% of committed capital each in Years 3 and 4; and exits investments with a cost basis of 20%, 25%, and 35% of committed capital in Years 5, 6, and 7, respectively.

1. Calculate Straddleton's annual management fee based on the assumptions provided.

   Solution

   Straddleton pays fees on the full capital commitment starting in Year 1 despite a delayed drawdown, which decline as the cost basis of investments is written off in Years 3 and 4 and exited in Years 5–7. Management fees over the seven-year period are shown in the last row of the table below:

Management Fees

Year/ Amount (EUR)	Year 1	Year 2	Year 3	Year 4	Year 5	Year 6	Year 7
Invested capital	5,000,000	5,000,000					
Cost basis of exits + write-offs			1,000,000	1,000,000	2,000,000	2,500,000	3,500,000
Committed capital minus exits and write-offs	10,000,000	10,000,000	9,000,000	8,000,000	6,000,000	3,500,000	0
Management fee (2%)	200,000	200,000	180,000	160,000	120,000	70,000	0

2. Discuss how Straddleton's management fees would change if drawdown were delayed.

   Solution

   Management fees are charged on the basis of the total amount of committed capital until capital is fully deployed. Thus, a delay in capital drawdowns will not change management fees.

The use of committed, rather than invested, capital as the calculation basis for management fees serves two primary purposes. It both compensates GPs for the significant upfront cost of due diligence and other GP responsibilities prior to capital deployment and reduces the incentive to deploy capital as quickly as possible in less attractive investments simply to generate fees. Also, the use of the cost basis reduces the potential conflict of interest associated with fund valuations, as GPs may otherwise have an incentive to inflate values over the life of a private investment to generate higher management fees.

Carried Interest

Carried interest is a critical component of private market fund compensation. Sharing in investment returns directly aligns GP and LP interests over a long holding period, although several terms and related contractual contingencies are subject to negotiation in a limited partner agreement that may benefit either GPs or LPs. In the case of highly sought-after, new closed-end private investments by managers with a strong performance record, GPs have a great deal of bargaining power to set terms. LPs who commit significant capital early to a new fund, however, may also be able to extract more favorable terms than those of LP investors who commit smaller amounts later to the same fund.

Carried interest is usually applied to investment returns above a **hurdle rate**, or a predetermined minimum target rate of return per period. GPs usually receive a 15%–20% share of returns above the hurdle. Limited partner agreements sometimes specify this threshold as being a **hard hurdle rate**, which means the GP earns incentive fees only on annual returns that exceed the hurdle rate. As an example, assume we exclude management fees and designate the one-period fund rate of return as r, with a hard hurdle rate of r_h and a GP performance fee percentage (p) of total return. The GP rate of return (r_{GP}) is

$$r_{GP} = \max[0, p(r - r_h)]. \tag{1}$$

While some alternative investment fund general partners charge performance fees annually, common practice in private market funds is to defer payment of carried interest until 100% of committed capital has been returned to limited partners through distributions or in some cases until the end of the fund's term, as in the following case study.

CASE STUDY

Bardstown Partners Carried Interest

Bardstown Partners is a general partner of a USD300 million private market fund focused on buyout equity transactions. As part of its fund terms, Bardstown includes carried interest to be paid by limited partners at the end of the fund's term in 10 years. Bardstown receives 20% of fund returns above a hard hurdle rate of 8% annually with no compounding. Over the fund's life, its investments return USD360 million in addition to the USD300 million of invested capital.

1. Calculate the amount of carried interest to be paid by limited partners to Bardstown after 10 years?

   Solution

   Carried interest will be paid only if total fund returns exceed USD240 million (= 8% × 10 years × USD300 million). Because the fund's returns exceed this amount, carried interest is calculated as USD24 million [= 20% × (USD360 million – USD240 million)].

While hard hurdle rates are a satisfactory approach when returns follow a steady path over an investment holding period or if performance fees are paid at the end of the fund's life, as in the previous example, both GPs and LPs seek to protect their interests for cases of expected volatile or uneven returns when carried interest is paid over multiple years of a fund's life.

One such approach is the use of a **soft hurdle rate**, or a return threshold above which the entire return is subject to an incentive fee once the hurdle is exceeded. Soft hurdle arrangements benefit GPs by ensuring their performance compensation "catches up" once a hurdle threshold is exceeded. Under a so-called **catch-up clause**, once the hurdle is exceeded, the GP often earns 100% of distributions (or a catch-up return of r_{cu}) until total return reaches a share of p for the GP and $(1 - p)$ for the LP. Remaining distributions are split on the same basis. As a result, the GP's performance fee (r_{GP}) from Equation 1 with a catch-up clause becomes

$$r_{GP} = \max[0, r_{cu} + p(r - r_h - r_{cu})]. \quad (2)$$

The incorporation of a soft hurdle rate may result in a higher carried interest *amount* earned by a private fund general partner even in the case of a lower carried interest *rate*, as discussed next.

CASE STUDY

Bardstown Partners' Use of a Soft vs. Hard Hurdle Rate

Bardstown Partners is reviewing its fund policies regarding carried interest. Rather than incorporating an 8% hard hurdle rate with a carried interest percentage of 20%, Bardstown is considering changing fund terms to include a soft hurdle rate of 9% and a carried interest percentage of 10%.

1. Assuming Bardstown's USD300 million fund generates USD360 million in returns over a 10-year fund life, discuss how the proposed new carried interest policy compares to the original carried interest approach using a hard hurdle rate.

   Solution

   Bardstown receives 10% (= USD36 million ÷ USD360 million) of the fund's total returns as carried interest under the new soft hurdle policy, compared to only 6.7% (= USD24 million ÷ USD360 million) in the hard hurdle rate scenario.

   With the soft hurdle rate of 9%, Bardstown's fund must generate more than USD270 million (= 9% × USD300 million × 10 years) in total return before carried interest may be paid. Bardstown Partners receives the next USD30 million from the fund's returns after the USD270 million return threshold is reached as the "catch-up" to reach its 10% carried interest percentage. The remaining USD60 million (= USD360 million – USD300 million) in returns is split between Bardstown and its limited partners according to a 10% versus 90% split, so Bardstown receives USD6 million in additional carried interest. Overall, Bardstown earns USD36 million in carried interest, or 10% of the fund's total returns. This represents a USD12 million improvement compared to the USD24 million from the 8% hard hurdle rate.

2. Discuss the potential downside risk to Bardstown of changing its carried interest compensation structure from the hard hurdle rate of 8% and carried interest rate of 20% to a higher soft hurdle rate and lower carried interest rate.

   Solution

   Under the new soft hurdle policy, Bardstown faces the potential downside risk of forgoing additional carried interest if the fund generates significantly higher returns. While carried interest is lower at the current return projection of USD360 million with the higher carry rate, carried interest increases by USD10 million for each additional USD50 million in fund return. With the 10% carried interest rate, Bardstown receives only an additional USD5 million for each additional USD50 million in fund return.

As shown in the prior example, the use of a soft hurdle rate, instead of a hard hurdle rate, makes the carried interest rate a reasonable approximation of the GP's ultimate share of total fund returns if the hurdle is cleared.

LPs also seek to limit or recoup fees paid to GPs for performance that fluctuates or declines over time. Earlier in the curriculum, a common strategy among hedge funds applied to some limited partnerships was described; it involves the use of a **high-water mark**, a measure that reflects the fund's maximum value as of a performance fee payment date net of fees. For example, if a private fund's value subsequently declines below its peak since inception adjusted by the hurdle rate over time, the GP may not levy performance fees until the fund value exceeds the previous high-water mark. High-water marks are generally applicable to investment vehicles that mark to market for purposes of calculating fees, such as hedge funds, rather than other private investment structures. **Clawback provisions**, in contrast, involve a return of GP performance fees to LPs in cases where returns from successful transactions earlier in a fund's life are offset by weaker returns later.

CASE STUDY

Tenderledge Investment Fund Fees and Performance

Tenderledge Investment Fund VIII has successfully exited its USD100 million private fund investments after seven years. The fund made one investment per year at the beginning of each of the first four years and exited each investment four years after capital deployment. The following table provides a summary of the fund's committed capital, capital deployment, cost basis of exited investments, and cash inflows by year over the fund's life.

USD millions	Year 0	Year 1	Year 2	Year 3	Year 4	Year 5	Year 6	Year 7
Committed capital	100	100	100	100				
Capital drawdown	−20	−40	−30	−10				
Cost basis of exits returned					20	40	30	10
Additional cash inflows from investments	0	5	13	16	23	10	14	10
Net cash flows	−20	−35	−17	6	43	50	44	20

Tenderledge assessed LP fees as follows:

Management fee:

- 2% of committed capital during the period in which the fund deployed capital (Years 1–3)
- 2% of committed capital less the cumulative cost basis of exited investments following the capital deployment phase (Years 4–7)

Carried interest:

- 20% of return net of management fees, over an 8% hard hurdle rate payable at the end of the fund's life. The annual hurdle rate is applied to each individual investment, so the total hurdle is based on a four-year investment horizon. Assume no compounding of returns.

1. Calculate the fund's management fees over its seven-year life.

Solution

Total management fees over the fund's life equal USD8.6 million:

- Years 1–3: USD2 million per year, for a total of USD6 million
  - USD2 million = 2% × USD100 million of committed capital.
- Years 4–7: USD2.6 million total
  - Multiply 2% by year-end committed capital minus cumulative cost basis of exited investments for each year:
    - Year 4: USD1.6 million = 2% × USD80 million.
    - Year 5: USD0.8 million = 2% × USD40 million.
    - Year 6: USD0.2 million = 2% × USD10 million.
    - Year 7: USD0 million = 2% × USD0 million.

USD2.6 million = 1.6 million + 0.8 million + 0.2 million + 0 million.

2. Contrast the fund's internal rate of return (IRR) *gross* of management fees with the IRR *net* of management fees.

Solution

Cash flow streams by year before fees and after payment of the management fees previously listed are as follows:

USD millions	Year 0	Year 1	Year 2	Year 3	Year 4	Year 5	Year 6	Year 7
Net cash flows before fees	−20	−35	−17	6	43	50	44	20
Net cash flows after management fees	−20	−37	−19	4	41.4	49.2	43.8	20

Using the IRR function in a spreadsheet or financial calculator gives a *gross* IRR of 21.7% and a 19.2% IRR *net* of management fees. The payment of USD8.6 million in fees spread over time reduces the estimated rate of return to LPs by approximately 250 bps.

3. Estimate the carried interest received by Tenderledge, and discuss the relative size of this performance fee as compared to management fees in terms of its effect on fund performance net of all fees.

Solution

Based on no compounding, an estimate of Tenderledge's carried interest payable at the end of the fund's life is USD10.08 million, calculated using the following simplified process.

The fund's return with no compounding is estimated as the sum of its yearly cash inflows plus the return of cash from exited investments less the original capital totaling USD91 million [= (5 + 13 + 16 + 43 + 50 + 44 + 20 – 100) × 1 million]. Total fund returns of USD91 million less management fees of USD8.6 million (calculated previously) give us returns after management fees of USD82.4 million (= USD91 million – USD8.6 million).

The 8% hurdle rate with no compounding implies annual required cash inflows of USD8 million per year. Multiplying this amount by four years gives USD32 million as the return hurdle. Finally, we calculate the carried interest by applying Equation 1:

USD10.08 million = max[0, 0.2 × (USD82.4 million – USD32 million)].

The total magnitude of the performance fee of USD10.08 million is somewhat higher than the total management fee of USD8.6 million. However, we have assumed the carried interest is paid entirely at the end of the fund's life, so its effect on the fund's IRR is much less significant. Tenderledge's net cash flow stream by year after deduction of performance fees and management fees is as follows:

USD millions	Year 0	Year 1	Year 2	Year 3	Year 4	Year 5	Year 6	Year 7
After-fee cash flows	−20	−37	−19	4	41.4	49.2	43.8	9.92

Using the IRR function in a spreadsheet or financial calculator on this yearly cash flow stream gives a result of 17.8%. The effect of carried interest on IRR to LPs is an additional reduction of approximately 140 bps.

4. Estimate the revised carried interest received by Tenderledge if we change our assumption to a soft hurdle rate of 10% and a carried interest rate of 15%, and discuss the revised carried interest amount relative to the earlier estimate.

Solution

Tenderledge earns USD12.36 million as carried interest in this scenario, and this amount equals 15% of the fund's returns net of management fees of USD82.4 million. The solution process can be described as follows.

Changing the hurdle rate to a soft hurdle of 10% implies that the fund must reach at least USD40 million of returns, or USD10 million per year over four years, in return for Tenderledge to receive any carried interest.

The first USD40 million of returns is paid to LPs given the soft hurdle rate of 10%. Tenderledge then earns catch-up carried interest on the returns above USD40 million until it has earned 15% of total returns; thus it receives all returns earned between USD40 million and USD47.06 million (i.e., USD7.06 million) as catch-up carried interest. USD47.06 million can be computed by dividing the USD40 million hurdle by 1 minus the carried interest rate (i.e., 47.06 = 40 ÷ 0.85).

After achieving USD47.06 million in returns, all additional returns are shared between Tenderledge and its LPs based on a 15%/85% split. Thus, Tenderledge's additional carried interest is USD5.30 million [= (82.4 – 47.06) × 0.15]. Tenderledge's total carried interest is the sum of the catch-up carried interest of USD7.06 million and the USD5.30 million calculated previously.

Tenderledge's carried interest is 15% of its total returns net of management fees of USD82.4 million. Despite the higher soft hurdle rate and the lower carried interest rate, Tenderledge earns a greater carried interest amount in this scenario compared to the earlier hard hurdle rate scenario.

The prior case study demonstrates the significant impact of management fees and carried interest on investor returns. In addition, carried interest structure and terms can provide considerable advantages to either GPs or LPs depending on fund performance. Finally, in contrast to the simplified case study, carried interest is typically structured such that the GP can begin receiving performance fees years before the end of the fund's life, provided that committed capital has been distributed in full. In such instances, clauses and provisions such as clawbacks may become important elements of the limited partnership agreement with LPs to ensure that the GP's share of returns over time does not become biased upward due to the timing of returns, as in the following case study.

CASE STUDY

Estragon SA Fund's Clawback Provision

Estragon SA, a French venture capital fund manager, recently exited its latest EUR100 million fund after seven years. The fund consisted of four investments of EUR25 million made at the beginning of the first four years of the fund's life. At the end of Year 4, Estragon exited its first investment, selling its stake for EUR200 million. Unfortunately, Estragon's subsequent three investments all failed, with exit values of zero. Estragon collected a carried interest charge from its LPs of 20% on returns in excess of a hurdle amount of EUR60 million at the end of Year 4. Estragon's LPs negotiated a clawback provision in the limited partnership agreement that total carried interest over the life of the fund could not exceed 20% of returns over a hurdle of EUR105 million.

1. Discuss how Estragon's LPs benefited from the inclusion of a clawback provision in the fund's terms.

Solution

The fund's excess returns in Year 4 were EUR140 million (= EUR200 million – EUR60 million), and Estragon collected EUR28 million (= EUR140 million × 0.20) in carried interest at the end of Year 4. However, the fund earned no additional return in the three subsequent years. The total carried interest at the end of fund's life could be no more than EUR19 million [= 0.20 × (EUR200 million – EUR105 million)]. So, the clawback provision mandates that Estragon must return EUR9 million (= EUR28 million – EUR19 million) to its LPs given the overpayment of carried interest early in the fund's life, since one highly successful investment was followed by three failures.

In addition to the attraction of unlimited upside potential, the relatively favorable tax attributes of carried interest, given both its deferral until the end of an investment period and its treatment as a long-term capital gain as opposed to ordinary income in some jurisdictions, provide an added incentive for GPs receiving this form of compensation.

TAX TREATMENT OF CARRIED INTEREST

Carried interest helps align incentives between GPs and LPs through efficient sharing of returns. That said, treatment of GP carried interest from a tax perspective can vary by jurisdiction and is a frequently debated topic. Does carried interest reflect a payment to GPs for services or a tax on gains for capital at risk on an investment? Because the distinction is not always clear, it is not surprising to observe that tax policies differ across jurisdictions as to whether carried interest should be taxed at a higher ordinary income rate or at a lower capital gains income rate.

The US and UK tax jurisdictions are examples in which carried interest is typically treated as capital gains income and are therefore more tax friendly for private fund managers. Nevertheless, the tax treatment of carried interest is often subject to change. For example, the United States has applied longer holding periods for carried interest to be eligible for capital gains income tax treatment. In the United Kingdom, there is considerable concern about double taxation issues associated with carried interest received in other jurisdictions with differing tax treatments. So, while the United Kingdom provides capital gains treatment on domestic carried interest, GPs also must monitor other relevant tax jurisdictions to avoid being taxed twice on the same return.

Germany offers a different historical perspective on its tax treatment of carried interest. Prior to 2004, German tax law viewed carried interest as capital gains income and its effective tax rate on carried interest was effectively zero. In 2004, Germany reversed its view on carried interest and began interpreting these payments as ordinary income to fund GPs. However, recognizing that such tax treatment could create a private capital exodus, a compromise was struck to tax 50% of the carried interest as ordinary income, with the remainder exempt from income tax. This hybrid approach to taxation prevented German GPs from immediately seeking more desirable tax jurisdictions. In 2009, Germany increased the 50% taxable portion to 60%, along with other new conditions. Overall, the German experience and legislative initiatives elsewhere to change tax treatment highlights the uncertainty regarding carried interest taxation.

Beyond the carried interest and management fees outlined previously, limited partnerships often face additional fees and potential conflicts of interest that must be considered when investing in a private fund. For example, general partners may receive fee payments from firms whose boards they control. While these fees are rebated in many cases, in other instances, restrictions or other complications reduce the rebated amount. Management service agreements may allow GPs to claim a wide range of discretionary expenses and in some cases may allow them to withhold fees to lenders, such as arrangement fees. Also, a GP's fee arrangements with the suppliers to portfolio companies represent an additional potential for conflicts of interest to arise.

In addition to fees, the performance of private market funds from an investor perspective must also take into consideration the liquidity risk associated with future capital calls of uncertain size and timing. Investors may incur an opportunity cost by holding committed capital in relatively liquid assets with return below that of private markets with higher correlation with public markets.

CASE STUDY

Northern States' Public vs. Private Investment Performance

Northern States, a large US state pension fund, commits USD50 million to Bardstown Partners' latest buyout equity fund with a term of 10 years. Based on its experience in private equity investing, Northern States believes that its capital will not be called for two years. During this period, Northern States invests in a public equity index. Northern States expects compound annual private equity returns of 16% and public equity returns of 10%, while US Treasury securities are expected to return 5% per year.

1. Discuss the extent to which Northern States' expectations of investment performance over 10 years may differ from the forecast private equity expectations of 16%.

Solution

If we assume that Bardstown calls capital in exactly two years and Northern States invests in public equities, Northern States expects to earn 10% per year during the first two years of the fund's life and 16% for the remaining eight years. The overall expected compounded return over 10 years is therefore approximately 14.8%:

$$14.8\% = [(1.10)^2 \times (1.16)^8]^{(1/10)} - 1.$$

As a result, assuming no volatility in returns and capital call timing certainty, the inability to earn private equity returns during the first two years of the fund's life is expected to cost Northern States 120 bps of expected return.

2. Discuss how Northern States might address the shortfall risk associated with its capital commitment.

Solution

Northern States has committed to investing USD50 million at an unknown future time. As mentioned earlier, Northern States may earn equity returns during the time lag between commitment and call by investing in liquid public equities. However, because of the uncertainty of public equity returns, this strategy creates substantial risk that Northern States may suffer a loss of principal, resulting in a capital shortfall when required to meet its commitment to Bardstown Partners. To reduce this risk, Bardstown may choose investments with lower volatility, reducing its overall return over the fund's life below the 14.8% calculated in the prior question. In an extreme case, Northern States may consider investing in securities with 5% expected annual return and no risk of loss of principal. The effect of such a strategy on the expected compounded return for Northern States over the 10-year horizon would be a further reduction to 13.7%:

$$13.7\% = [(1.05)^2 \times (1.16)^8]^{(1/10)} - 1.$$

The ability to benchmark and adequately diversify private market portfolios is an additional consideration when evaluating performance from an LP perspective. While public equity fund investors have a wide array of investible index-based alternatives, private market LPs face several barriers in matching the aggregate reported returns for a particular private asset class. First, the need to hold liquid investments for committed capital that is not yet deployed creates a drag on returns, as shown earlier. Second, an investor's ability to diversify across specific GPs is limited, and a high dispersion of realized returns often exists between the top and bottom quartiles of performance for private asset classes. Third, given the illiquidity of private investments and limited secondary markets, vintage year diversification is also difficult to achieve for investors seeking to increase private market allocations.

QUESTION SET

1. Discuss two reasons why private market investment fund management fees are typically paid to the GP by LPs based on committed capital as opposed to invested capital.

   Solution

   First, payment based on committed rather than invested capital compensates GPs for the significant upfront cost of due diligence and other GP responsibilities performed prior to capital deployment (because committed capital is greater than or equal to invested capital). Second, payment based on committed capital reduces the incentive to deploy capital as quickly as possible in less attractive investments simply to generate management fees.

2. Which of the following fund returns and carried interest structures is most likely to generate the highest amount of performance fees for a GP?

   A. Fund 1: 20% return after management fees, 20% carried interest rate, 8% hard hurdle rate

   B. Fund 2: 14% return after management fees, 20% carried interest rate, 10% soft hurdle rate

   C. Fund 3: 18% return after management fees, 15% carried interest rate, 8% soft hurdle rate

   Solution

   B is the correct response. Given that the 14% return exceeds the 10% soft hurdle rate, the GP receives 2.8% as carried interest (= 20% × 14%). This amount includes 2.5% of catch-up and 0.3% as the 20% share of the final 1.5% of return. The LP earns 11.2% (= 80% × 14%). Response A is not correct, because this return and structure generate only 2.4% as carried interest [= 20% × (20% – 8%)]. Response C is not correct, because this return and structure generate 2.7% carried interest (= 15% × 18%).

3. The LPs of a venture capital fund with high expected volatility of exit values of its portfolio companies following 100% distribution are most likely to seek which one of the following elements in the agreement with the fund's GP?

   A. Soft hurdle rate

   B. Clawback provision

   C. High-water mark

   Solution

   B is the correct response. The imposition of a clawback provision prevents LPs from paying performance fees on volatile returns that are not sustained over the full investment life cycle. A is not correct, because a soft hurdle rate benefits the GP by ensuring that volatile returns allow for the GP's carried interest to catch up whenever the fund return exceeds the soft hurdle rate. Response C is not correct, because high-water mark provisions are commonly used by hedge funds that mark to market transactions for purposes of calculating fees but are less likely to be observed in other private market structures.

4 PRIVATE INVESTMENT SELECTION AND VALUE CREATION

☐ discuss favorable characteristics of private investment targets and sources of value creation in private markets

Prioritizing private investment targets is a process that extends beyond the domain of security selection common among public fund managers. The active engagement of GPs over the investment life cycle requires not only the identification of companies and assets that may be undervalued but also narrowing of investment targets to those in which a controlling stake or significant minority position may be used to drive significant value creation over a longer investment period.

Potential for value creation over the investment life cycle is a common feature among prospective investments, which occurs in different ways among startup, growth, and mature companies in the company life cycle shown in Exhibit 4.

Exhibit 4: Company Life-Cycle Stages

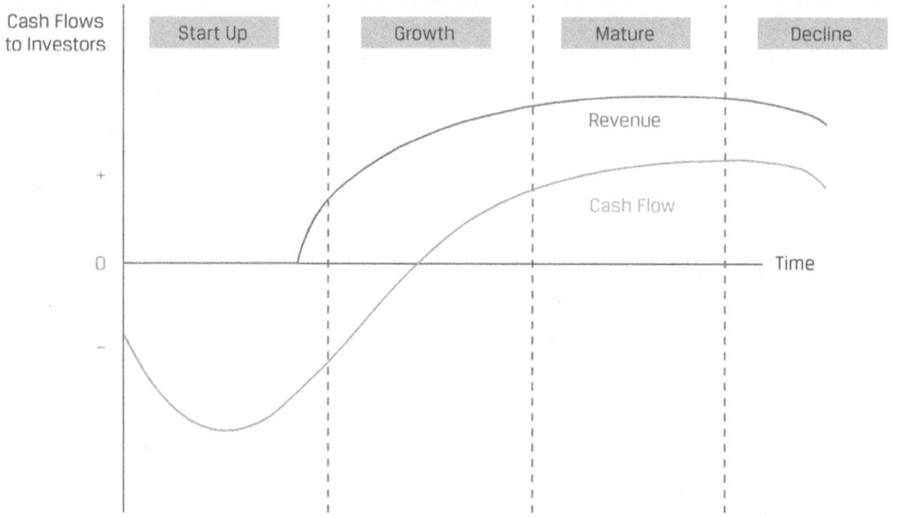

Among startup companies without an established product or revenue base, investors target firms with high growth potential in a new or emerging industry or one that seeks to disrupt an established industry with a new product or business model. Companies whose founders have patents, other intellectual property, or business ideas and industry expertise and/or a successful record of creating new companies represent the most sought-after investments. Value creation for startups involves non-financial milestones, such as new product prototypes and testing, validating a business concept, and setting a go-to-market strategy, as described in the following case study.

CASE STUDY

Kumartest LLP Venture Capital Funding

A biomedical engineering research group at a major Indian research university developed a revolutionary process to conduct instantaneous testing of complex assays (or laboratory analysis to determine the presence of substances) using mobile technology under laboratory conditions. The lead researcher, Dr. Sana Kumar, believes that this new technology has significant potential in the fields of mining, environmental protection, and medicine and establishes a new limited liability company (Kumartest LLP) to commercialize this technology. Dr. Kumar's first investors are herself and several family members, and the funds are used to develop prototypes to demonstrate the commercial applications to additional investors.

Growth companies are those with an existing product, customer base, and business model that have the potential for above-trend growth as measured by a firm's revenue relative to its **total addressable market**, or total revenue opportunity for a product. Optimal investment targets include well-managed young firms that have experienced initial success with a product in high demand but face capacity constraints in attaining their potential future size and level of profitability. Capital investments at this stage are needed to create the scale necessary to realize this opportunity for rapid growth.

Mature companies, in contrast, are often targeted by **buyout equity** investors, or those seeking to unlock an established firm's growth and profitability potential by acquiring a business to transform or streamline its existing operations. Targets include large firms with strong market share, consistent cash flows, and a substantial fixed asset base in a less competitive industry due to regulation or entry barriers. Firms meeting these criteria that face lagging performance or management issues are likely to reap the greatest benefit from a buyout transaction. In this case, value creation involves the use of debt financing to acquire and transform operations by adding management talent, increasing efficiency, and shedding non-strategic businesses. Subsequent debt reduction and higher profitability are the key elements necessary for reaching a higher market valuation upon exit that represents the bulk of buyout equity returns.

CASE STUDY

Bardstown Partners Chemical Industry Targets

Bardstown Partners, a private equity firm specializing in buyout equity, is considering a target company in the chemical industry to take private in a leveraged buyout transaction. Bardstown has a track record of success in taking industrial companies private and has built up considerable expertise and a strong network in the chemicals sector. Bardstown has identified the three following possible candidates for further due diligence:

- Blanckton Incorporated is the second-largest global company in chemicals, with approximately USD40 billion in revenue. Blanckton operates in a wide array of product markets and is geographically diversified with a significant number of joint ventures and other strategic partnerships. The company has consistently generated the best returns on capital in the chemicals industry.
- Maudville Corporation is a mature participant in the chemicals industry with approximately USD5 billion in revenues and USD1 billion in EBITDA. The company has carved out a competitive niche in a

specialized area of the industry. Despite its ability to generate stable cash flows, its margins and returns on capital are mediocre in comparison to its peers in the chemicals industry. The company has a long-time CEO, with no clear successor identified.

- Zbornak Incorporated is an emerging company in the industry with approximately USD500 million in revenues. Zbornak has been growing more rapidly than its more mature industry peers. The company has achieved success in identifying revenue opportunities with double-digit growth rates but has not yet found the scale necessary to realize consistent profitability.

After considering these three companies, Bardstown concludes that Maudville is the most appropriate choice to consider further in its due diligence process. The company exhibits several attributes of a promising buyout candidate, including its mature stage in the company life cycle, generation of stable cash flows, and potential for improvements by increasing efficiencies. Furthermore, because of the company's potential need for management succession, Bardstown may be able to find new leadership to drive change in the organization through its network of contacts.

Private equity targets and their value creation potential are affected by company- and industry-specific forces, as well as macroeconomic conditions, in different ways. Exhibit 5 summarizes some of the key sources of value creation used by private equity firms.

Exhibit 5: Sources of Value Creation in Private Equity

The application of strategic, operational, organizational, and financial value drivers shown in Exhibit 5 varies greatly among targeted investments based on a company's stage in the life cycle, its industry and competitive position. For example, a buyout equity firm targeting a mature manufacturing company with high operational leverage and significant fixed assets is most likely to focus on operational areas for improvement; however, a retailer with high financial leverage may find balance sheet optimization and inventory management of greater importance when seeking areas of improvement. The prospective future trajectory of an industry as well as the overall economic outlook are important factors affecting the performance of private equity strategies.

For example, rapid technological change in such industries as biotechnology and information technology often fuel startup growth, which is less sensitive to the economic cycle, while buyout targets in mature, cyclical industries with value creation strategies that rely on the availability of less costly debt financing face a greater adverse impact from rising interest rates or a cyclical downturn.

For private markets, such as real estate and infrastructure, which are usually project based, GPs follow capital commitment, deployment, and distribution phases over a common development life cycle, as shown in Exhibit 6.

Exhibit 6: Real Estate Development Life Cycle

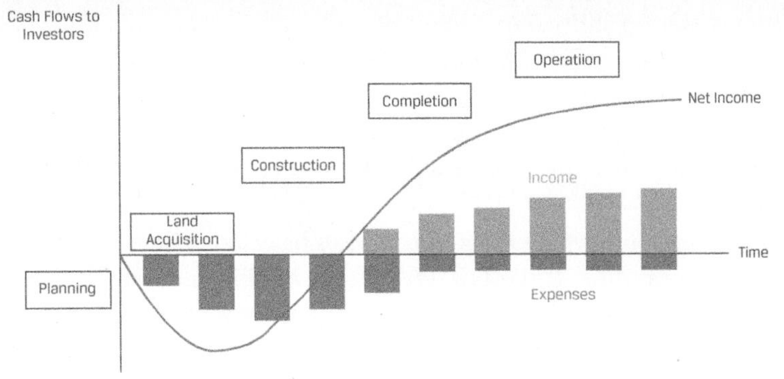

Exhibit 6 shows the phases involved in a newly developed real estate project or so-called **greenfield investment**, which involves "to be built" projects and assets earmarked to provide an essential service or public good.

Real estate investment values stem from a property's current and expected future economic use. Opportunistic private real estate projects are like startup companies in that they face cash outflows in an initial capital deployment phase. The real estate equivalent of mature companies with stable cash flows are existing, well-leased income-producing properties usually held in publicly traded REITs, although these types of core properties are also available in private markets through what are known as **open-end diversified core equity (ODCE) funds**.

Real estate development targets typically involve raw or developed land parcels, with a relative attractiveness for opportunistic investment driven by

- location and suitability for the proposed project versus other uses,
- existing supply and expected future nearby development, and
- local, regional, and global economic conditions.

Underlying property use is the most important feature to consider when evaluating target investments. As an example, while local industry conditions, transport links, and the proximity of customers and suppliers are key priorities in selecting an industrial warehouse location, a strong local job market and local educational and recreational opportunities are far more important when selecting among residential rental and owner-occupied housing projects.

The value creation process in real estate development hinges on a developer's ability to complete a project on time, reach full occupancy, and generate a stable future income stream whose expected terminal value exceeds project cost plus a required rate of return. In addition to such risks as project delays, changing economic conditions, and real estate cycle timing, real estate investors are exposed to technological change and other structural factors that can have a significant and lasting impact on real estate demand, as described in the following example.

HYBRID WORK AND THE COMMERCIAL REAL ESTATE MARKET

The trend toward hybrid office work, referring to the practice of combining in-office with remote work, took hold following the COVID-19 pandemic. The changing behaviors associated with this trend have profound structural implications for the commercial real estate market globally. With office workers spending less time in urban centers, visitors to urban retail stores near office-dense regions have declined.

These behavioral shifts have negative implications for demand for office and retail space in urban centers. As fewer workers are in the office, increasing office vacancy rates internationally are typically accompanied by declines in the asking price for rents. According to global management consulting firm McKinsey, demand for retail space in "superstar" global cities is projected to be 9% lower than pre-pandemic levels by 2030.

Market values of office and retail properties have fallen because of the remote work trend. Lower office and retail rents and declining occupancy reduce operating income for commercial investors, creating downward pressure on property values. An additional negative valuation factor comes from upward pressure on property discount rates. Cap rates, the common metric for discount rates in commercial real estate, increase as potential buyers see more risk associated with future cash flows in these property types. The value declines in urban office and retail properties are likely to make investments in such properties less attractive in the near to medium term.

While commercial real estate developers and owners of existing assets have some flexibility to adapt projects and properties to changing real estate demand, this is not true for most single-use, long-lived infrastructure assets.

In contrast to real estate, infrastructure assets derive their value from underlying long-term contracts known as **concession agreements**, or regulations that govern their economic use and income generation potential. Under a concession agreement, a granting entity, such as a public authority, contracts with a developer or operator on a long-term basis to build, operate, and eventually transfer asset ownership back to the so-called **grantor** at the end of a prespecified period. The final transfer of ownership under this **build–operate–transfer (BOT) project** requires GPs to generate all investor returns prior to the transfer of asset ownership to the grantor at zero terminal value. Attractive opportunistic infrastructure projects include those that provide essential services with relatively inelastic demand, less exposure to market cyclicality or economic shocks, and the ability to increase user fees along with inflation.

As in the case of real estate, the underlying economic use, industry, and business model under which a proposed new infrastructure project will operate are of primary importance in prioritizing target investments. For example, many developed countries have introduced subsidies and regulation-based payment schemes, among other incentives, to promote investment in renewable energy. GPs must factor the economic impact of these schemes across jurisdictions into their decision-making process when evaluating target investments.

WIND FARM SUBSIDIES IN EUROPE

Nine northern European countries expect to spend approximately EUR800 billion to dramatically expand offshore wind farm capacity in the North Sea to 300 gigawatts (1 GW equals 1,000 MW) by the year 2050. This comes as part of an urgent global push to reduce fossil fuel use as part of climate change initiatives and in response to regional energy security concerns—for example, following the outbreak of war in Ukraine in 2022.

While European policymakers seek to coordinate efforts to increase renewable energy generation, individual countries are taking the initiative to improve their capacity. For example, France plans to contribute over 13% of the 2050 goal with emphasis on offshore wind farms, while Great Britain aims to approximately triple offshore wind farm capacity by 2030. According to a consulting report commissioned by a variety of stakeholders, Norway alone has the potential to develop over 300 GW of offshore wind farm capacity, which is 10 times greater than the country's 2040 target.

One example of a government-supported program to support low-carbon electricity production is the United Kingdom's Contracts for Difference (CfD) scheme. These contracts are structured as swaps in which a renewable energy developer exchanges periodic payments with the Low Carbon Contracts Company, a UK government-owned entity, which effectively lock in a fixed unit price on a specific volume of a developer's electricity production for 15 years. As more renewable electricity comes to market, developers face the risk that future CfD price opportunities will reflect lower electricity prices and reduce the longer-term value of renewable energy generation projects.

As for other private market assets, GPs in private infrastructure seek to create value over a transformational life cycle. However, the greater size and illiquidity and a general inability to repurpose investments impose additional constraints on managers in pursuing this objective. With a development cycle involving sizable sunk costs and a finite holding period, which sometimes involves an asset transfer with no exit value, as in the case of BOT projects, GPs often focus on mitigating project risks, maximizing operating efficiency when facing fixed-price contracts (or extracting inflation-adjusted payments over time), and capitalizing on ancillary commercial opportunities when evaluating target infrastructure investments as described below.

AIRPORT PROJECT COMMERCIAL REVENUE OPPORTUNITY

Airport development is an infrastructure project example in which commercial payments from the concession contract associated with the build–operate–transfer plan may be augmented by other sources of return. While an airport concession typically provides for revenue on a per-passenger basis for travel-related services, the inclusion of duty-free and other shopping opportunities, restaurants, airport hotels, and other passenger amenities, such as parking, expands the potential for GPs to diversify and expand cash flow over the concession period.

The approximately USD30 billion global airport retailing market, dominated by the Asia-Pacific region, is expected to grow by over 12% annually through 2030, concentrated among mid-sized airports. As a result, a key driver of potential returns for infrastructure funds with airport development opportunities in the Asia-Pacific region involves maximizing the retailing potential within an airport over the concession period.

In what follows, we turn our attention to the remaining investment cycle phases of deployment, distribution, and exit; detailed evaluation of target investments; and the preparation and execution of the value creation process through the end of the partnership investment period when an asset is sold, exited, or transferred to a granting entity.

QUESTION SET

1. A primary value creation focus of private equity managers investing in companies in the startup phase of the company life cycle is most likely to be:

   A. achievement of non-financial outcomes, such as validating a business concept.

   B. achievement of company revenue growth greater than growth in the company's total addressable market.

   C. achievement of company efficiency gains.

   Solution

   A is the correct response. Value creation for startups involves non-financial milestones, such as new product prototypes and testing, validating a business concept, and setting a go-to-market strategy, as the first steps on a growth trajectory. B is not correct, because this sort of revenue growth focus is most likely in the growth phase of the life cycle. C is not correct, because this goal is more likely for companies in the mature phase.

2. Which of the following is a unique valuation component of the build–operate–transfer project model that is typically not used to value other categories of private market assets?

   A. BOT projects rely on a significant amount of debt financing.

   B. BOT projects have zero terminal value at the end of the concession agreement.

   C. BOT projects are valued based on the economic use of the asset.

   Solution

   B is the correct response. A unique component of valuing infrastructure assets operating with a BOT model is that the asset has zero terminal value at the time of transfer back to the concession grantor. A is not correct, because significant amounts of debt financing are also used in private real estate and buyout equity transactions. C is not correct, because private real estate value is also determined based on its economic use.

3. Which of the following is likely not a critical value creation strategy of a private real estate general partner?

   A. Ability to complete projects on schedule

   B. Ability to ensure that a new building is (close to) fully occupied on schedule

   C. Ability to anticipate changing economic conditions in development plans

   Solution

   C is the correct response. While private real estate fund general partners should be cognizant of the real estate cycle in their development plans, the ability to anticipate changes in economic conditions is not a critical part of the GP's value creation strategy. A and B reflect items that the GP can better manage in terms of generating value through real estate development. Finishing projects on schedule and ensuring that a building has paying tenants are both directly related to the cash inflows being reflective of the business plan.

DUE DILIGENCE AND STRATEGY EXECUTION

5

☐ discuss the role of conducting due diligence and establishing a business plan in the private investment process

GPs considering an illiquid, long-term investment in private equity, private debt, or a private asset or project in real estate or infrastructure conduct very thorough due diligence on targeted investments. The purpose of this process in private markets goes beyond identifying intrinsic versus fair market value or potential growth opportunities for a specific asset or investment as in public markets; it also extends to establishing a business and financing plan to meet or exceed targeted return over a multiyear investment life cycle.

The information available to GPs conducting due diligence for private market strategies varies when pursuing *company* due diligence versus *project* or *asset* due diligence. In the case of the former, early-stage companies have little more than a business idea or prototype with few customers, minimal revenue, and no profits, while mature buyout targets involve both business and accounting due diligence to evaluate a firm's prospective performance in established products and markets. The latter form of due diligence often involves initial construction and development phases, creating a real estate or infrastructure asset that produces future income. Private real estate GPs consider real estate market conditions upon project completion when assessing future income, while infrastructure investors focus attention on market and regulatory factors related to the provision of contractual, essential services as a primary future revenue source.

Given the lack of transparent performance benchmarking, upfront capital commitment, and long illiquid investment period of a typical limited partnership, LP due diligence on prospective fund managers differs from that in public markets, as described later in this learning module.

Company Due Diligence and Business Plans

The industry and competitive analysis tools and approaches introduced in Level I of the CFA Program curriculum also apply when conducting due diligence on private equity or private debt opportunities. Past and future company performance is driven by macroeconomic or industry-wide factors, such as economic growth, and company-specific factors, such as increased market share.

As non-controlling investors in established, mature companies, public fund managers rely on economic and industry analysis, publicly available information, and the financial statements of a company and its competitors, clients, and suppliers to forecast financial statements and assess a firm's intrinsic value versus its recently traded price.

Private fund GPs seeking significant minority or controlling stakes include these techniques in their analysis of investment targets but usually conduct a more exploratory, in-depth, dynamic process that varies greatly based on a company's life-cycle stage.

For example, prospective analysis of early-stage companies by potential investors often focuses on technical aspects of a prospective product or service and a founder's ability to rapidly go to market and reach scale, as shown in the following example.

CASE STUDY

Estragon SA's Kumartest LLP Due Diligence

Upon learning of Dr. Sana Kumar's research and new process to rapidly test complex assays using mobile technology, partners in the French venture capital firm Estragon SA initiate due diligence to consider a minority stake in her firm. Estragon's health care team is specifically focused on the new device's commercialization potential among European medical providers.

Estragon starts with an independent scientific verification of the new approach, believing it to be potentially far faster and more accurate than existing methods. In addition to its technical superiority, the team also draws the preliminary conclusion that the use of Kumartest's new technology could dramatically improve patient outcomes for several common diseases. Estragon uses this information as a basis to assess Kumartest's potential market size and identifies several major European medical centers as early adopters for its use. Finally, Estragon confers with experts on the time and resources required to clear the European Union's stringent conformity assessment process, ensuring Kumartest's new product meets safety and performance guidelines. Once Estragon has satisfied these preliminary criteria, it moves on to weigh the financial terms and timing of an investment, as well as possible partners and co-investors with similar expertise in entering the US health care market.

Note the importance of scientific and technical factors in the due diligence process for the previous startup example. The non-financial aspects of a company's initial development phase are more important than traditional financial statement analysis in evaluating prospective investments.

Private equity buyout investors in mature companies, in contrast, can conduct more thorough due diligence on the operating history of established companies, which includes but is not limited to financial statement analysis. Private equity GPs typically seek access to far more detailed non-public company information when bidding to purchase a public or private company. GPs usually must sign a **non-disclosure agreement**, or a legal contract specifying that confidential information received is only for the purposes of evaluating a possible transaction. Potential buyers are typically granted access to what is referred to as a **data room**, or a repository for confidential company documents and data that usually include the following areas:

- Legal and organizational: Key legal commitments, partnerships, and joint ventures, as well as company entities and organizational structure
- Commercial: Key client data, sales projections, new product pipelines, and existing pricing and supply arrangements with clients and suppliers
- Financial: Company cash flow projections, cost analyses, loan and other financing agreements, and the status of owned and leased real estate, fixed assets, equipment, and facilities
- Human resources: Organizational chart, employee biographical information, compensation levels and history, policies, and benefits
- Intellectual property: Trademark, patent, and copyright ownership and licensing

- Information technology: Creation, use, and licensing of software used to manage operations, sales, and other firm activities
- Compliance and litigation: Company records and data on meeting health and safety requirements, regulations, or privacy rules and on past or existing pending litigation or sanctions
- Environmental, social, and governance (ESG) issues
- Taxation: Tax history, tax liens, policies, and losses carried forward

THE RISE OF VIRTUAL DATA ROOMS

As part of the due diligence process, potential company investors or acquirers typically access privileged target company information from a secure data room. The data room used to be a physical repository, but it has increasingly become a virtual solution in recent years to address cost, efficiency, and security concerns. The digitization of business records combined with the advent of cloud computing created natural conditions for growth in virtual data rooms, and this trend accelerated because of the COVID-19 pandemic.

Firms raising private capital can gain insights by tracking permissioned user views of specific documents, demonstrate a commitment to data security to prospective investors, and contribute to a more efficient due diligence process. The rise in virtual data rooms has expanded the ability for private market GPs to evaluate target companies and collaborate across investment teams. As a result, the global revenue of virtual data room firms had a compound average growth rate in excess of 10% compounded annually, with global revenue forecasted to approach USD5 billion by 2028.

Private market due diligence is often an exploratory process in which GPs seek to both assess a company's prospects versus competitors and prioritize opportunities for improvement over a multiyear investment period that form the basis for a business plan.

CASE STUDY

Bardstown's Due Diligence Process for Maudville Corporation

As Bardstown searches for a take-private opportunity in the chemicals industry, it has narrowed its focus to conducting detailed due diligence on Maudville Corporation and comparing it to several industry peers in the commodity chemicals industry. Growth in commodity chemicals is relatively slow and highly exposed to the economic cycle, with the greatest potential opportunities for improved performance in the areas of greater asset efficiency and expense management. Although the basic technology used and underlying production costs among firms appear to be similar, the Bardstown team takes a deep dive into the supply chain, logistics, and distribution of the firm's products. As is common in the industry, Maudville is heavily reliant on freight rail to transport raw petroleum and natural gas material inputs, as well as outputs to intermediaries and customers. However, in contrast to most industry competitors, Maudville continues to own and operate many of its own rail tanker cars, whose average age exceeds the industry average of 20 years by roughly a decade. In addition to the aging cars' shorter remaining useful life, Maudville faces the prospective cost of retrofitting them in the near future to meet new environmental standards.

Maudville's top competitors have gradually outsourced their rail tanker fleets over the past several years. With long-term lease contracts and service agreements in place with existing logistics providers, most competitors have little or no opportunity for cost improvements in this area.

The Bardstown team sees an opportunity to increase Maudville's asset efficiency by selling its existing railcars and redeploying capital to upgrade and expand its production capacity to improve margins and return on capital.

Once private equity GPs have identified opportunities for value creation, they must take further steps to craft a plan of action when deploying investor capital to achieve targeted returns over an investment holding period. An important first step in devising a business plan is to define an industry, its barriers to entry, the competitive forces, and the sources of return, as well as the target company's existing and potential position in the industry sector. For example, as a new entrant in the established health care devices industry, the startup firm Kumartest introduced earlier must overcome regulatory and other barriers to entry to disrupt existing market providers and capture significant market share.

As a next step, it is important to quantify the potential of a new or existing market and the target company's potential given the gap between current and potential future performance. Once the size of an opportunity is established, GPs must prioritize the strategies, investments, and other changes necessary to reach the target's potential size, scale, and level of profitability. In the earlier case of Maudville, the GP pinpointed a shift from owned to leased fixed assets (in this case, railcars) common among competitors as a catalyst for unlocking the opportunity to increase asset efficiency and reduce costs.

Finally, it is important to put any proposed business plan into a market context to understand key risk factors and the performance sensitivity to changes in primary drivers. For example, while the health care industry tends to face less cyclicality, with inelastic demand for diagnostic testing, regulatory or technological changes may have a significant effect on performance.

Project Due Diligence

In contrast to private *company* analysis, *project* or *asset* due diligence in such areas as real estate and infrastructure usually makes a clear distinction between the construction and development phase over which an asset is built and the operational phase upon completion over which returns are generated.

The initial property and project plan review addresses the risks and mitigants associated with whether a project can be built on time, within its expected budget, and to the specifications necessary for its expected future economic use. Due diligence for this initial phase involves both the location and physical attributes of the land or property itself, as well as architects, developers, contractors, and suppliers involved in the construction phase.

Analysis of the post-completion operational phase seeks to ensure that expected payments from an asset's economic use adequately compensate investors for bearing the associated risks over the investment holding period. The nature and level of future asset income depend on the strategy and property type, as well as any contractual commitments in place upon completion. For example, a real estate development may be initiated on a purely speculative basis without prior commitments or built to suit a specific commercial tenant based on pre-agreed terms and a multiyear lease. Infrastructure assets, in contrast, often rely on concession agreement details as to whether future cash flows are fixed or inflation adjusted or depend on commercial or regulatory factors. For example, the earlier case study on European wind power subsidies underscored the potential impact of national regulatory schemes on the relative performance of energy infrastructure projects, whether powered by renewables or traditional energy sources.

As is true for private companies, project due diligence also incorporates different economic and market scenarios to evaluate key drivers of return. The following example of a major property refurbishment project addressed in further detail in a later reading illustrates several considerations that may arise during project due diligence.

CASE STUDY

Due Diligence for Kingston Tower

Kingston Tower is an old office building outside Toronto with few amenities and declining occupancy. A private real estate fund manager is considering a purchase of the tower to complete a major refurbishment project. Given the expected persistence of remote work following the COVID-19 pandemic, the prospective project involves a more costly conversion from full office usage to a mixed-use, amenity-rich coworking and luxury apartment complex.

The GP's initial property and project plan review considers both the location and physical attributes of the existing structure. The manager assesses the attractiveness of the location for residential use, including proximity to amenities and recreational opportunities, as well as the building's suitability for conversion in terms of access, floor plan layouts, and the reconfiguration of plumbing, heating, and electricity, among other changes. The GP confers with developers and architects with major refurbishment experience to reach the preliminary conclusion that the project is technically feasible and could be completed over a three-year period. As a next step, the GP also assesses how the project could be sequenced to retain existing office tenants and cash flow over as much of the renovation phase as possible.

The fund partners then turn their attention to the economic feasibility of the project, which depends on the building's net operating income once it becomes fully operational and leased to both commercial and residential tenants. While the project appears to exceed the GP's expected hurdle rate of return under a base-case scenario, she notes that the more costly coworking rental market tends to be more cyclical than the residential real estate market is and, therefore, decides to analyze the project using a downside case in which coworking rents and occupancy face a greater decline than the residential market faces.

As the prior case study suggests, a *project* business plan often differs in that the explicit development steps and associated milestones drive success in reaching the operational, income-producing phase that generates returns for investors. While the business plan of a private real estate project often involves the sale of a property once it is completed and fully occupied, in the case of infrastructure, a project or concession may have a finite life and be turned over to a public authority at the end at a price of zero or a low terminal value.

LP Due Diligence

Extended capital commitments, illiquidity, and lengthy investment periods compel limited partners to conduct a thorough investigation of GPs prior to committing to a new fund. Whereas detailed portfolio comparisons and frequent performance benchmarking versus other fund managers and indexes are common among public fund investors, private market investors use a combination of qualitative and quantitative factors to assess private fund GPs. The following case study illustrates the approach taken by a public pension fund to evaluate private equity GPs prior to committing capital.

CASE STUDY

Northern States Due Diligence of Tenderledge Investment Fund X

Northern States Pension Plan is a large US-based public pension fund with a 15% allocation target to private equity. Strategic objectives in growing its allocation include diversification across strategies and engagement to promote sound environmental practices.

Northern States is considering a USD25 million allocation to Tenderledge Investment's new Fund X. Northern States has previously invested with Tenderledge in both its recently completed Fund VIII and its existing Fund IX. Fund X is a growth equity fund seeking to raise capital of USD200 million with a cap of USD225 million, a source of potential diversification given Northern States' current allocation focused on venture capital and LBO investments.

Tenderledge has a track record of transforming small- and mid-cap companies through innovations in process improvements. Fund X will target similar companies to grow revenue and reduce costs via enhanced environmental processes.

Tenderledge was founded 25 years ago by Miranda Tender and Johan Ledge after 10 years in merger and acquisition advisory, and both remain senior partners. The firm has three other partners, with a total of 50 years in investment experience, and 10 additional staff with combined experience of 90 years.

Tenderledge has solid historical returns, generating an average net IRR after fees across all closed Funds I–VIII of 12.5%. For example, Fund VIII generated net total value to paid-in (TVPI) of 2.03 and a net IRR of 13.5%. Fund IX currently has a gross TVPI of 1.30, gross IRR of 15.0%, and an expected exit in four years. To date, Fund IX has made only small distributions to investors, with a distributed to paid-in of 0.20.

While Northern States views Tenderledge's strengths to be its experienced and growing team and continued focus on process improvements, it has two areas of concern related to Fund X. First, because of the growing popularity of ESG strategies, Northern States investigates whether Fund X's targets may attract many bidders, forcing it to overpay. However, its due diligence suggests that Tenderledge's plan to target smaller companies is unlikely to attract excessive bidding interest from other funds. Second, Northern States investigates whether the delays in Fund IX distributions are a sign that Tenderledge may fail to deliver expected returns by the fund's exit date. After careful analysis of Tenderledge's track record from completed funds, it becomes clear that distribution delays do not correlate with lower fund performance.

Finally, Northern States examines the firm's legal, ESG, and workplace diversity track record. Tenderledge has no pending or past lawsuits and recently became a signatory to the UN Principles of Responsible Investment. The firm has a robust due diligence and investment process that incorporates ESG considerations. Tenderledge's diversity statement includes statistics regarding current employment and its efforts to improve diversity among its management and employee ranks.

After evaluating all this evidence, Northern States concludes that Tenderledge Investment Fund X meets all its due diligence requirements.

QUESTION SET

1. An early-stage company is seeking private capital to provide sufficient funding for hiring a team to get its product to market. Which one aspect of company due diligence is likely to be least heavily weighted by the private market fund?

   A. Thorough examination and analysis of technical aspects of the company's product

   B. Thorough examination and analysis of the company's financial statements

   C. Thorough assessment of the company's founder and his or her ability to guide the new product to market

   Solution

   B is the correct response. The non-financial aspects of a company's initial development phase are more important than traditional financial statement analysis in evaluating prospective investments in early-stage companies. A is not correct, because analyzing technical aspects of an early-stage company's product is a critical part of company due diligence. C is not correct, because thorough assessment of the company's founder is also a critical component of company due diligence for early-stage companies.

2. Identify two resources used by companies that are potential acquisition targets of private equity firms, and briefly explain why these resources are used.

   Solution

   Non-disclosure agreements and data rooms are two resources used by companies that are potential targets of private equity firms or any other possible acquiror. Both resources help ensure that confidential information accessed by the potential buyer can be used only for the purpose of a possible transaction. A non-disclosure agreement is a legal document protecting confidentiality, and data rooms provide a secure location for confidential information to be stored.

3. Identify the next step for a private market fund following a positive due diligence process on a company target.

   Solution

   The next step following a positive due diligence process is to formulate a business plan to create value. Private market due diligence is an exploratory process in which GPs seek to both assess a company's prospects versus competitors and prioritize opportunities for improvement over a multiyear investment period that form the basis for a business plan or a plan for value creation.

4. Which one of the following most correctly reflects a contrast between project due diligence and company due diligence?

   A. Technical factors are more important for project due diligence than for company due diligence.

   B. A clear distinction in asset life-cycle phases (e.g., greenfield versus brownfield) creates distinct focus for project due diligence.

C. A financial outcome from a project due diligence process includes a cash flow forecast.

Solution

B is the correct response. In contrast to private company analysis, project or asset due diligence in such areas as real estate and infrastructure usually makes a clear distinction between the construction and development phase over which an asset is built and the operational phase upon completion over which returns are generated. A is incorrect because technical factors are also important in company due diligence for early-stage companies. C is incorrect because a cash flow forecast is an outcome of all due diligence processes, regardless of whether the due diligence is for a company or project.

6 PRIVATE INVESTMENT EXIT STRATEGIES

☐ discuss alternative exit routes in private investments and their impact on value

The final stage of the private investment life cycle is the eventual sale or exit of the investment, as shown in Exhibit 1. For many private investments, the sale price is a key driver of LP returns and GP performance-related compensation in the form of carried interest over the investment holding period. In other cases, such as private debt or an equity stake in a BOT infrastructure project, the maturity or transfer date is predetermined or contractual, with minimal impact on return. We will, therefore, focus attention on the impact of exit alternatives on value in private equity and real estate.

Whether investing in early-stage companies or buyout opportunities, private equity GPs conduct due diligence and establish a business plan fully intending to eventually sell the investment in several years' time. Broadly speaking, private funds exit investments by selling to the public via an IPO, selling to one or more private buyers through different approaches, or liquidating the firm, as shown in Exhibit 7.

Exhibit 7: Typical Venture Capital, Buyout, and Growth Exit Strategies

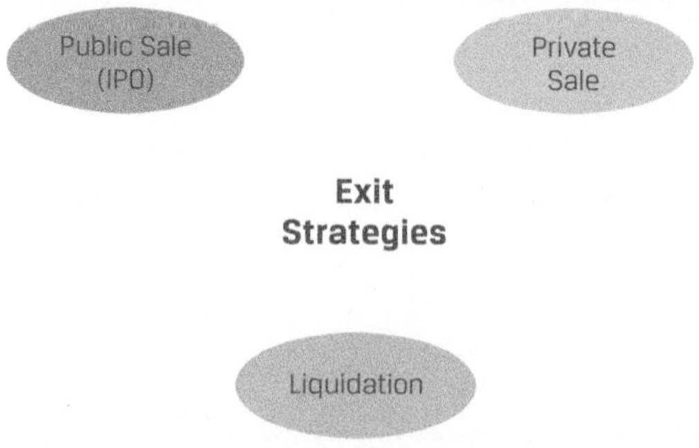

Most private equity firms consider their exit options well in advance of a planned exit, frequently engaging external advisers, such as investment banks, merger and acquisition advisory firms, and other consultants, in the process. These firms are often engaged to source interested buyers, prepare materials for public or private sales, and assist in negotiations.

Private market GPs generally select an exit route that maximizes LP returns and GP performance fees, and the choice of a particular approach is highly dependent on both top-down macroeconomic and market conditions and industry- and company-specific dynamics.

Public Sale

Going public via an initial public offering involves the issuance of publicly traded shares on an exchange, which greatly increases the liquidity of ownership and access to large amounts of capital from the broadest possible range of investors. A private company's initial share issuance may represent the reintroduction of a restructured firm that was taken private or the first opportunity to access the investment, as in the case of a successful startup company in the following example.

EXAMPLE 1

Tencent's IPO

Tencent, the Chinese technology giant behind WeChat, was founded in 1998. The company had early success with a communication application but quickly encountered cash flow and legal challenges as the company's user base grew rapidly. After failing to find a buyer for the company, Tencent was able to raise USD2.2 million from two Chinese venture capital funds in exchange for a 40% stake in the startup company in April 2000.

About one year later, Naspers, a South African technology investor, purchased a 46.5% stake in Tencent for approximately USD32 million. One of Tencent's early venture investors exited its initial investment at a return on investment (ROI) of 11×.

In June 2004, Tencent issued public shares on the Hong Kong Stock Exchange at a price valuing the company at approximately USD800 million, representing a 10× ROI for Nasper over a three-year holding period. After the IPO, Nasper retained a sizable stake in Tencent, and by February 2021, its 29% stake was worth approximately USD200 billion. Nasper's Tencent investment produced not only a sizable pre-IPO return but also an ROI of approximately 875× over the 17-year period on its continued holdings in the company.

The primary advantages of an IPO include the ability to maximize valuation multiples under favorable public equity market conditions and stage a controlled exit process in multiple phases with continuity of management and business strategy. For example, a primary issuer may capitalize on strong market conditions and growth following an IPO by executing one or more secondary share offerings. While this route is not available to all private companies, the ideal IPO candidate involves larger companies with an established operating history and excellent growth prospects.

That said, the IPO process is cumbersome, time consuming, and costly, with an outcome that is highly dependent on public market conditions. For example, smaller companies may pay as much as 7% of gross IPO proceeds in fees. The value upon exit from the IPO process to private investors depends not only on the initial price achieved in the primary offering but also on continued strong share performance, for two key reasons. First, GPs often sell their controlling stake in a firm in stages and, therefore, rely on continued strong market demand for shares. Second, private equity firms are typically subject to a **lockup agreement**, or sale restriction, at the time of issuance that prevents the GP from fully liquidating its interest in newly issued stock for a predetermined period, often up to 180 days. IPO markets have also shut down during periods of financial stress, such as the Global Financial Crisis of 2008–2009 and the COVID-19 pandemic.

For these reasons, IPOs are generally not the most common exit route, although this alternative often factors into a GP's preparation for monetizing an investment as a negotiating strategy. Given that the IPO process also involves the preparation of materials that support potential purchaser due diligence, in many instances, the prospect of a future IPO may accelerate the private sale of the company to an interested buyer without incurring underwriting fees.

Private Sale

The monetization of an existing investment via a sale to another private buyer can involve different parties and take multiple forms, as shown in Exhibit 8.

Exhibit 8: Private Sale Strategies

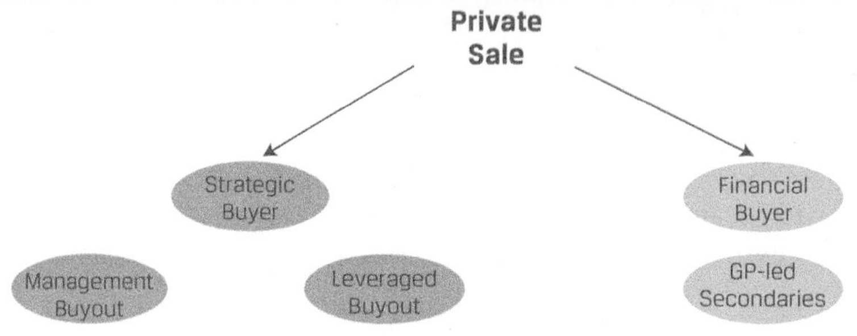

Key advantages of private sale include the relative speed and flexibility with which a transaction may take place, typically with fewer restrictions and at a lower cost compared with a public sale. Also, private sale prices do not directly depend on favorable public equity market prices, although such factors as the cost of debt, investor risk appetite, and the public market valuation multiples of comparable public companies used by buyers and sellers in negotiations have an indirect effect on the value a GP is able to realize upon sale.

In some instances, private sale dynamics involve a buyer willing to pay far more than what might be achieved in a public sale due to a unique strategic opportunity, and in other cases, a private buyer may be available despite unfavorable market conditions that preclude a public sale. The most common forms of private sale are outlined next.

Private Sale to a Strategic Buyer

In many cases, the highest bidder for a company is likely to be a **strategic buyer**, as described in a Level II CFA Program learning module on private company valuation. A strategic buyer is a buyer that seeks to capitalize on synergies by extending the value creation process initiated by the GP, combine the business with another portfolio company, or take other actions as a controlling investor to increase the firm's value. Strategic investors often see the greatest potential and are also able and willing to assume associated execution risk. A strategic buyer is often another private equity fund manager, but in some cases, such as in the following case study, the strategic buyer is a publicly traded company.

EXAMPLE 2

Facebook's Acquisition of WhatsApp

In October 2014, Facebook, now known as Meta Platforms, completed its USD19 billion acquisition of WhatsApp. The deal had been announced eight months earlier and was the largest acquisition of a venture-backed company at the time.

WhatsApp was founded in 2009 by two former Yahoo! employees as an instant messaging service for smartphones. WhatsApp's initial venture funding source was Sequoia Capital, which provided USD8 million of Series A financing in 2011. Sequoia made subsequent investments in WhatsApp, and its total investment before the Facebook acquisition grew to USD60 million. Sequoia's estimated ROI on its WhatsApp investment was close to 50×.

Given WhatsApp's minimal revenue at the time of purchase, Facebook's acquisition price suggested that the company saw huge potential in the company's technology, its user base, and their data, as well as a perceived threat to its own platform. WhatsApp had a user base of 600 million monthly active users, with significant growth in developing markets.

The strategic acquisition in the previous case study was paid for using the publicly traded shares of the acquiror, but in other cases, these transactions are conducted in the form of a leveraged buyout, where a public or private company acquires the target using a combination of debt and equity.

A special case of the private sale to a strategic buyer is the situation in which the acquiror involves the company's existing management in what is referred to as a **management buyout**. In a management buyout, the existing leadership team commits its own equity capital as an incentive to grow the firm's cash flows and value together with one or more private equity GPs. Management buyouts are frequently structured as an LBO, with debt forming a significant proportion of the purchase price.

Private Sale to a Financial Buyer

A **financial buyer**, in contrast, may in some cases be the highest bidder for a controlling interest for a private firm. A financial buyer is an owner that seeks to earn investment returns from an existing company without identifying or capitalizing on synergies from a controlling interest. A financial buyer may involve an investor seeking a strategic buyer or a private equity GP planning to hold the company in a limited partnership structure. Given the finite life of closed-end partnerships and growing demand for private market investments, GPs are increasingly selling assets from an existing portfolio into a new fund in what is referred to as the **GP-led secondary** market.

EXAMPLE 3

The Rise of GP-Led Secondaries

GP-led secondaries, also referred to as **continuation funds** or fund recapitalizations, have become common exit strategies for private fund sponsors. GP-led secondaries involve a private fund manager sale of assets from an existing fund to a new fund. This continuation fund is led by the same GP with capital from secondary investors. Pricing and terms are often negotiated with secondary investors, while existing fund investors are granted the opportunity to sell underlying assets, retain an investment interest in the new fund with similar terms as the existing fund, or re-invest in the continuation fund based on new terms.

According to Preqin, an alternative investment data company, the market for GP-led secondary transactions rose from just under a quarter of all secondaries in 2016 to over half the volume of secondaries five years later, with single-asset continuation funds experiencing the highest growth among secondaries.

The exit strategy of a private real estate fund GP is typically the sale of a property to a REIT once it has established consistent occupancy and cash flows. A private real estate fund GP may choose to retain stable income-producing properties if the fund's investment strategy provides latitude for inclusion of these types of assets. Additionally, real estate market conditions are an important factor in the exit timing of property investments.

Liquidation

Controlling shareholders have the power to sell the assets of a company if it is no longer viable as a going concern. In the case of startup companies funded by venture capital equity investments, the failure rate is extremely high, although these companies have very few fixed assets and little liquidation value.

For large, established companies in a declining phase of the company life cycle facing financial distress, the market value of the firm's fixed assets, real estate, inventory, and intellectual property may well exceed the value of its liabilities. In some cases, the firm may be able to receive protection from its creditors, restructure its assets and obligations, and maintain solvency, but in other cases, bankruptcy and liquidation are the best approach. In this case, while equityholders will typically face a loss of their entire investment, asset sales offer debtholders the highest recovery for their fixed claims. This topic will be addressed in greater detail in a subsequent reading on special situations.

QUESTION SET

1. Exit value realized from the sale of an operating property is a key driver of investor returns for which one of the following private market investments?

   A. Private debt

   B. Private infrastructure

   C. Private real estate

   Solution

   C is the correct response. The return to private real estate investments is largely a function of the sale of the operating property at the end of the fund's life. A and B are incorrect. For private debt investments or an equity investment in a BOT infrastructure project, the maturity or transfer date is predetermined or contractual, with minimal impact on return.

2. Identify and discuss three reasons why volatility of public equity prices may cause IPOs to not be more commonly used as an exit strategy for private equity investments.

   Solution

   - Unfavorable public market conditions at the time of IPO

- The existence of lockup agreements
- The need for a continued period of strong demand for company shares

Public market conditions may be unfavorable at any given point in the future, so it becomes difficult to plan for an IPO, especially given the long process required to prepare IPO filing materials.

Lockup agreements delay the date at which shares can be sold after an IPO, so any price declines after the IPO date become costly to the GP in terms of its exit value.

GPs often sell their controlling stake in a firm in stages and, therefore, rely on continued strong market demand for shares. Because post-IPO returns on individual company stocks may fall below equity benchmarks over longer time horizons, this may be an impediment to using an IPO as an exit strategy.

3. Which one of the following least likely describes a management buyout transaction?

A. Private sale by a financial buyer

B. Leveraged buyout

C. Private sale by a strategic buyer

Solution

A is the correct response because the company's management is not a financial buyer. A special case of the private sale to a strategic buyer is the situation in which the acquiror involves the company's existing management in what is referred to as a management buyout. In a management buyout, the existing leadership team commits its own equity capital as an incentive to grow the firm's cash flows and value together with one or more private equity GPs. Management buyouts are frequently structured as an LBO. Thus, both B and C are incorrect.

PRACTICE PROBLEMS

The following information relates to questions 1-4

Estragon SA is a growing French venture capital firm with five completed funds, with another fund nearing 100% capital deployment, and in planning stages for its seventh fund. As a result of its success and the growing capital base of each successive fund, the firm is seeking to hire a new associate. Suzette Dubois, senior partner of Estragon, is interviewing several candidates for the position. To introduce candidates to the fee structure of the firm's funds, Dubois makes the following statement to the job candidates to start a conversation:

Statement 1 The firm's management fees are typically calculated as 2% of the firm's valuation of total fund stakes in portfolio companies.

Following the discussion of management fees, Dubois asks candidates about carried interest. She discusses the common approach of a carried interest rate on fund returns with hurdle rates once 100% of committed capital has been returned to LPs. She comments that Estragon has been experiencing very strong interest from investors and that some continuing investors from its earlier funds are willing to commit large proportions of the fund's target upon the fund's opening to commitments. Estragon reserves some space to accommodate a limited amount of committed capital from LPs with no prior history investing in Estragon funds, but only later in the commitment phase.

Dubois continues a discussion of aspects of Estragon's fee structure. For earlier funds, Estragon included a clawback provision as part of its carried interest terms, but it recently changed its carried interest terms to no longer include this provision.

Dubois finishes the interview process with some discussion of how Estragon handles investment exit strategy. Estragon has been able to successfully take a small portion of its portfolio companies public; however, its preferred exit strategy is to find a strategic buyer for successful portfolio companies.

1. Evaluate the accuracy of Dubois' Statement 1.

2. Discuss Estragon's possible approaches to setting carried interest terms with continuing investors and new investors.

3. Which one of the following statements most accurately describes a reason for LPs to desire a clawback provision in carried interest terms?

   A. Clawback provisions prevent LPs from overpaying performance fees because of volatile returns that are not sustained over the full investment life cycle.

   B. Clawback provisions protect LPs from overpaying performance fees when early fund investments are exited successfully followed by much less successful investment exits.

   C. Clawback provisions protect LPs from overpaying performance fees when carried interest is fully paid at the end of the fund's life.

4. Identify and briefly discuss the most likely investment exit strategies used by

Estragon.

The following information relates to questions 5-8

Bardstown Partners is a global private equity firm based in the United States with a focus on take-private transactions. Jack Spear is a managing director at Bardstown and specializes in deals in consumer-oriented businesses. His most recent investment transaction for Bardstown was a EUR1.5 billion purchase of E and F Grocery financed with EUR900 million of debt.

Spear is currently researching opportunities in food retailing industries as potential investment targets. He has settled on three possible companies in the quick-service restaurant industry. Each of the three targets exhibits strong market share, consistent cash flows, and valuable assets. Other attributes are as follows:

Target 1: Returns on capital over the last three years below industry average and a CEO with majority ownership of company shares

Target 2: Returns on capital over the last three years below industry average and significant senior management turnover

Target 3: Returns on capital over the last three years above industry average and strong management team

Bardstown negotiated a EUR900 million purchase of Target 2 as a new fund investment. As part of its plans to transform the company, Bardstown plans to sell one non-core division of the company, focus on improving labor efficiency, and use more technology in the company's retail outlets.

During a recent Bardstown Partners investment committee meeting, a discussion about the possibility of moving the partnership's location occurred. Increasingly, Bardstown is finding a greater proportion of its investments in Europe, and as a result, more of its senior employees reside in Europe. However, all the partners reside in the United States.

5. Explain the two-part sequence of financing for Bardstown's purchase of E and F Grocery.

6. Which one of the target companies is likely the best opportunity for a take-private transaction?

   A. Target 1

   B. Target 2

   C. Target 3

7. Which one of the following categories of value creation sources is Bardstown least likely pursuing in its transformation plan?

   A. Operational

   B. Organizational

   C. Strategic

8. Discuss one potential area of concern related to taxation that Bardstown would want to research before proceeding with any plans for moving from the United States to a European country.

The following information relates to questions 9-12

Asiastruct is a private real estate firm based in Singapore. Its latest fund recently purchased a parcel of land in Thailand outside Bangkok for THB6 million, on which it plans to construct a residential development with planned completion in two years. The expected total cost of the development is THB54 million, to be drawn down from both debt and equity sources over the next 24 months.

Asiastruct's new development location was the result of careful due diligence regarding site selection. Specifically, the new property is located adjacent to a new section of a mass transit line with direct access to Bangkok and its airport. The region's economy is currently doing well, with strong job projections and other favorable developments to support residential housing development. Asiastruct believes that the returns on the project will be excellent because of its value creation abilities in residential real estate development and operations.

Asiastruct's investors are primarily pension plans, sovereign wealth funds, and ultra-high-net-worth investors who commit capital to the fund as limited partners at the beginning of the fund's life of about 10 years, and these investors are attracted to returns that are up to 400 bps greater than typical returns on liquid public real estate securities, such as REITs, which expect to yield approximately 6% annually. Asiastruct's capital deployment phase usually lasts four years, and the typical lag between capital commitment and deployment is two years.

Asiastruct is exploring the possibility of starting a private infrastructure fund. The fund's partners believe there are potential opportunities in certain types of Asian infrastructure projects, such as airport development, in which the firm may be able to capitalize on its construction network throughout the region. It has begun reaching out to certain individuals who may be good candidates to help start an infrastructure fund. During discussions with a few candidates, Asiastruct discovers a variety of commonalities and differences between private real estate and infrastructure investments, especially with respect to build–operate–transfer projects.

9. Which of the following most likely describes the capital drawdown during the initial two-year capital deployment phase of Asiastruct's Bangkok residential project?

   A. Drawdown is contingent on meeting defined project milestones.

   B. Drawdown occurs evenly over the 24 months.

   C. Drawdown occurs at the time of land purchase.

10. Identify three goals that Asiastruct should ideally aim to achieve as part of the value creation process on the Bangkok project.

11. Which of the following is closest to the LPs' annual expected rate of return over the 10-year fund cycle?

    A. 8.4%

B. 9.2%

C. 10%

12. Discuss one important exit strategy difference between private real estate and private BOT infrastructure investments.

SOLUTIONS

1. While 2% may be a typical rate for management fees, the portion of the statement that suggests the fee is calculated based on the firm's valuation of its portfolio companies is not correct. Such a fee scheme would provide incentives for the firm to inflate its valuations of its portfolio companies. Rather, management fees typically use the fund's committed capital during the capital deployment phase and committed capital less cost basis of exits during years following full capital deployment.

2. Estragon is in a strong bargaining position because the firm has a strong performance record and its funds are highly sought after. As a result, the firm is likely to set terms more in its favor. However, it may provide the least generous term to new investors committing late in the phase, whereas continuing LPs making larger and earlier commitments may receive somewhat more generous terms.

3. B is the correct response. In the case of a venture capital fund, successful exits of early investments could create distributions to LPs such that 100% of capital commitment has been distributed. Failure of later investments may reduce the fund's overall returns such that carried interest paid early in the fund's life cycle may reflect overpayments to the GP. A clawback provision allows for the excess carried interest to be returned to LPs. A is not correct, because this response describes a high-water mark. Response C is not correct, because carried interest paid entirely at the end of the fund's life will reflect the fund's final return. Clawbacks apply only if carried interest is paid prior to the end of the fund's life.

4. Estragon's most likely exit strategy for its portfolio companies is liquidation or private sale at a loss. Estragon is a venture capital fund investing in startup companies, and these companies are extremely likely to fail. As such, only a minority of Estragon's investments are likely to go public or be sold in a profitable private sale.

5. First, Bardstown contributes EUR600 million of equity to form a new acquiring business entity (AcquisitionCo) and arranges EUR900 million of short-term financing to purchase the target, E and F (TargetCo).

   Second, AcquisitionCo and TargetCo are merged into a new combined business entity, and this new entity arranges for longer-term debt financing of EUR900 million to refinance the short-term financing from the first stage.

6. B is the correct response. All three targets have attractive attributes noted, but companies facing lagging performance or management issues are likely to reap the greatest benefit from a buyout transaction, and Target 2 most closely aligns with this description. A is not correct, because Target 1 has lagging performance, but the CEO with majority ownership is likely to demand a high selling price. C is not correct, because Target 3 has neither lagging performance nor management issues.

7. B is the correct response. Bardstown does not seem to be focusing on any organizational sources of value creation, such as replacing management or improving processes. A is not correct, because both improving labor efficiency and using more technology are operational sources of value creation. C is not correct, because selling a non-core division is a strategic source of value creation.

8. Carried interest is a key component of the income generated by a private market fund partnership. Currently, the United States provides favorable tax treatment

to carried interest given both its deferral until the end of an investment period and its treatment as a long-term capital gain as opposed to ordinary income. Bardstown should research tax treatment of carried interest in other possible locations and continue to monitor the US tax environment for the possibility of future changes to the tax treatment of carried interest.

9. A is the correct response. Asiastruct draws down enough equity initially to pay for the land purchase, and later equity drawdowns occur at specific milestones in the development process, such as certifications of completion of the structure and occupancy. Debt capital is drawn down according to construction and development needs throughout the development process. B is not correct, because the development process cash flow needs are unlikely to occur evenly over the 24 months. C is not correct, because Asiastruct does not require the full amount of capital at the time of land purchase.

10.

- Complete the project on its planned two-year schedule.
- As the project is completed, ensure that the building is occupied at rates that are consistent with or greater than those planned.
- Ensure that the building's units are rented at prices consistent with or greater than those planned.

11. B is the correct response. An LP loses approximately 40 (= 400/10) bps per year during time lag between capital commitment and deployment if funds are invested in liquid REITs. The time lag is two years, so the loss compared to the private real estate return expectation is 80 bps. Thus, the approximate rate of return is 9.2% (= 10% – 0.8%). A is not correct; it would be true if the time lag were four years. C is not correct, because the LP does not earn the 10% private market return for 10 years.

12. Private real estate investments are likely to generate significant value from a GP's ability to sell the developed project at a price consistent with or greater than expectations when the project was initially developed. Thus, the exit strategy is an important consideration for a private real estate GP, such as Asiastruct. In contrast, a private BOT infrastructure project is transferred to the concession grantor at the end of the contract term at zero or minimal terminal value. Thus, the exit strategy for this type of project is predetermined by the contract.

LEARNING MODULE

3

Private Equity

LEARNING OUTCOMES

Mastery	The candidate should be able to:
☐	discuss private equity strategies over the company life cycle
☐	discuss characteristics of venture capital and growth equity investments
☐	discuss characteristics of buyout equity investments
☐	estimate and interpret key inputs and calculate the value of a private equity investment for venture capital, growth equity, and buyout situations
☐	discuss the risk and return among private equity investments as well as versus other investments as part of a strategic asset allocation

INTRODUCTION

1

Private equity remains the dominant form of private market investment. According to the global management consultant firm McKinsey, nearly two-thirds of the almost USD12 trillion in private market assets under management globally are held in private equity. While the classification of private equity investments varies among markets and participants, our focus will be on three distinct areas across the company life cycle, namely, venture capital used to launch high-potential startups, growth equity to assist young companies during periods of rapid growth, and buyouts in which investors take control of and restructure mature underperforming companies, which are also referred to as leveraged buyouts (or LBOs). Later readings address the use of debt financing in private market strategies and special situations such as distressed debt investing.

This reading first addresses different private equity strategies across the company life cycle, from new firms attracting minority shareholders to develop a business idea to the full takeover of an established firm seeking to add value by streamlining operations for an eventual sale. We address the distinct characteristics of these three private equity areas, including forms of investment and economic drivers as well as common features and differences in valuation methods applied to venture capital, growth, and buyout situations. Differences among private equity investments and with other markets contribute to distinctive risk and return features that influence their role in strategic asset allocation.

LEARNING MODULE OVERVIEW

- Private equity strategies over the company life cycle include venture capital for startups and their initial development, growth equity to expand operations, and buyout equity, which is used to acquire, control, and transform mature companies later sold to private or public investors.
- Venture capital is deployed in a company's initial, pre-revenue phase when cash flow is usually negative to launch a business, create a product, and establish a market.
- Growth equity is used by later-stage firms with a proven market to fund expansion with established products.
- Buyout equity investments, or leveraged buyouts, involve the purchase of a controlling stake in a mature company by investors who see an opportunity to increase valuation and improve cash flow. A company is usually purchased with equity and debt and then restructured with incremental cash flow used to repay debt, followed by a sale to generate returns.
- Investment valuation across private equity uses entry and exit values to determine return on investment (ROI) and internal rate of return (IRR). The venture capital (VC) method uses the exit value of equity and ROI to determine firm value before new equity is sold, whereas the growth equity method includes cash flow projections for profitable growth over an investment horizon. LBO model inputs, on the other hand, are derived from financial statement analysis for both the entry and exit value of equity with significant debt usage over the investment period, which is paid down over time.
- The role of private equity in a strategic asset allocation is to achieve high-risk-adjusted returns and diversification benefits relative to holding public market equities among other investments that more than adequately compensate investors for the added risks and costs of venture capital, growth equity, and buyout equity investments.

2 PRIVATE EQUITY STRATEGIES

☐ discuss private equity strategies over the company life cycle

In Level I of the CFA Program, we described how a successful company evolves from a startup period to a phase of rapid expansion with rising cash flows and profitability, followed by a more stable, mature development period, after which the company may enter a phase of decline as seen in Exhibit 1.

Exhibit 1: Company Life Cycle Stages

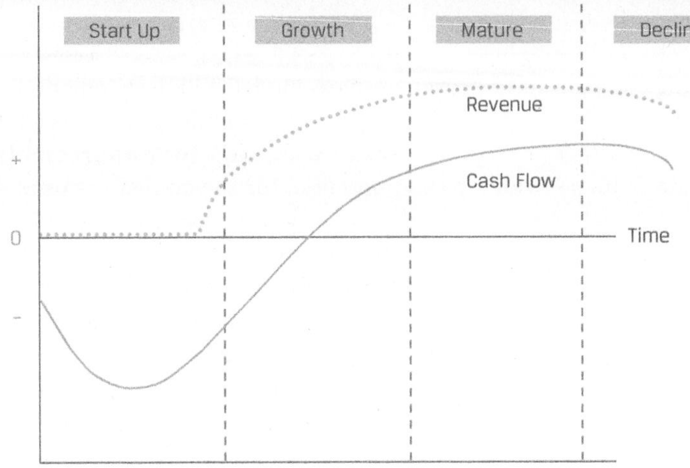

Standardized public stock exchanges impose listing rules such as a minimum number of shareholders, asset size, and net worth, and they mandate the periodic release of audited financial reports. Many companies unable or unwilling to meet these and other public market requirements choose instead to access private capital for various reasons at different stages in their life cycle. For many small- and medium-sized private firms, personal or family capital contributions prove sufficient to sustain business capital needs throughout their life cycles. However, institutional private equity investors can and often do play a critical role for companies at both earlier and later life cycle stages.

Startup companies have little to no revenue, negative cash flow, and few assets and are typically established with an equity contribution from a founding owner, friends, or family. As the new company develops, founders often seek active institutional investors willing to assume very high risk as it validates a business concept, determines market size and fit for its product, and initiates and grows operations. These **venture capital** investments typically involve minority equity positions held by more than one investor and often occur in stages. Venture capital investors are highly selective, targeting firms with the highest growth potential and seeking some form of control, such as a board or advisory role in a new company. While many well-known, large global firms such as Apple, Starbucks, and Tesla were successful beneficiaries of venture capital funding at their earliest stage of development, many more startup firms eventually fail, as in the following example.

ANATOMY OF A STARTUP FAILURE: AIRWARE

Founded in 2011, Airware was established as a pioneer in enterprise drone analytics, seeking to deliver high-quality data to enterprise clients in the insurance, mining, and construction industries. The company raised a total of nearly USD120 million over several financing rounds, starting in 2013 from top VC investors including Andreessen Horowitz and Kleiner Perkins.

As the commercial drone market rapidly evolved, Airware grew to over 100 employees and initially sought to create an enterprise operating system for drones. Later, the company began to manufacture its own hardware but found itself unable to compete with industry giants such as Shenzhen-based DJI, which at the time produced over two-thirds of drones sold globally. As competition forced Airware out of the hardware business, it shifted toward providing software for drone data collection and analysis, receiving an investment from Caterpillar

Ventures, whose parent sought to offer drone services to its heavy equipment customers. However, Airware's new strategy was not sufficient to provide enough cash flow to survive, and it ceased operations in late 2018.

Once a young company has a proven business model, initial customer relationships, and rising revenue—often despite low or negative profitability—it enters an expansion phase during which it seeks to capitalize on the company's **total addressable market**, a measure of the industry-wide revenue potential for the company's product or service. In some cases, the firm is acquired or seeks public investors via an initial public offering (IPO). If the company chooses to remain private instead, private investors contribute what is referred to as **growth equity** during this life cycle phase.

Growth equity provides capital specifically targeting profitable expansion well above the rate of growth of a particular industry and the overall economy by increasing the company's scale of production, marketing, and distribution. This growth may also occur via acquisition, new distribution channels, or new markets. In most cases, this new equity reduces the ownership concentration of founders and initial investors. Private firms in the expansion phase usually rely primarily on a minority equity capital stake as a source of funding, avoiding the periodic interest expense associated with debt funding due to the uncertain trajectory of cash flow and profitability growth. Firms are more likely to use hybrid instruments such as preferred shares or convertible instruments at this stage of development.

The majority of firms that are listed on global public equity exchanges and issue widely held fixed-income securities are in a more mature phase of the life cycle. Mature public firms tend to offer investors more stability than startup or growth companies, are more likely to pay periodic dividends to shareholders, and can support debt service payments from steady cash flows.

However, mature companies operating in dynamic markets are also subject to structural changes that impact growth, contraction, and enhanced profitability, as shown below in Exhibit 2.

Exhibit 2: Corporate Structural Changes

Investment *Grow*	Divestment *Shrink*	Restructuring *Enhance*
Business Acquisition	*Business Sale for Cash*	*Take Action to Increase Productivity, Lower Cost*

Earlier in the curriculum, it was shown that corporate restructuring is usually driven by company-specific factors, competitive industry pressures, or macroeconomic changes. In many cases, public company managers initiate such changes in response to declining market share or a falling share price.

Listed companies with widely dispersed ownership are often slower to restructure in response to competitive pressures or opportunities than closely held firms managed by private owners due in large part to the **agency cost of equity**. The agency cost of equity is a type of principal-agent problem arising when company managers have more information about the firm than its shareholders, limiting the owners' ability to assess performance and dismiss ineffective managers. In contrast to public companies, private equity ownership and management allows for more direct control over strategic decisions. In the case of so-called **buyout equity** investments, private equity firms acquire a controlling equity stake in underperforming public companies to transform, divest, or acquire businesses. These investors take steps to improve cash flow and profitability with the intent to sell the reorganized firm at a higher price to a private investor, existing public company, or the public via an IPO. Buyout equity transactions are also referred to as **leveraged buyouts** due to the high proportion of debt financing used to make the acquisition. The interaction between private and public sources of equity capital is typically not a one-time event but rather reflects a constant dynamic in many industries, such as the following example in the health care industry.

THE EVOLUTION OF WALGREENS BOOTS ALLIANCE

In mid-2007, private equity firm Kohlberg Kravis Roberts & Co. (KKR) partnered with a group of co-investors on a GBP11.1 billion deal to acquire European pharmacy chain Alliance Boots in a leveraged buyout funded with GBP9 billion of debt. KKR's equity stake in the LBO was equivalent to approximately GBP1.2 billion. The Alliance Boots LBO was the largest in Europe at the time and one of the last large leveraged buyouts closed during the boom years preceding the Global Financial Crisis of 2008–2009.

In August 2012, Walgreens, a leading US pharmacy chain, agreed to buy a 45% equity stake in Alliance Boots with an option to buy the remaining 55% of the equity within three years. As part of the first stage of the deal, KKR received cash along with seven million Walgreens shares. By the end of 2014, Walgreen completed the second stage of its Alliance Boots purchase. Between the two stages of the transaction, KKR had received GBP4.7 billion on its initial investment of GBP1.2 billion. The combined company, now known as Walgreens Boots Alliance, became a global health care giant with over 12,800 retail stores and 340 pharmaceutical distribution centers. After the sale, KKR retained a 4.6% public equity stake in Walgreens Boots Alliance.

While its stock performed exceptionally well between 2012 and 2015, Walgreens Boots Alliance's share price peaked in mid-2015 at over USD90 per share. As the stock price fell more than 30% from its peak during the latter half of the decade, discussions of a new LBO managed by KKR surrounded Walgreens Boots Alliance. However, no new buyout came to fruition.

In the 2020s, Walgreens Boots Alliance shares continued to languish. By late 2021, the company was exploring options to potentially spin off its Boots pharmacy business with a greater focus on its US operations. However, in mid-2022, Walgreens Boots Alliance decided to retain the Boots pharmacy business.

At some point, most companies eventually enter a phase of decline as competitive pressures, technological change, or other factors cause a firm's revenues and cash flow to fall, and this may result in financial distress. Private market investors often play a role in these so-called **special situations**—areas of investment that seek to generate return through investments in stressed, distressed, or event-driven opportunities—which are covered in detail in a later reading. Exhibit 3 summarizes these uses of private equity over the life cycle.

Exhibit 3: Uses of Private Equity Over the Company Life Cycle

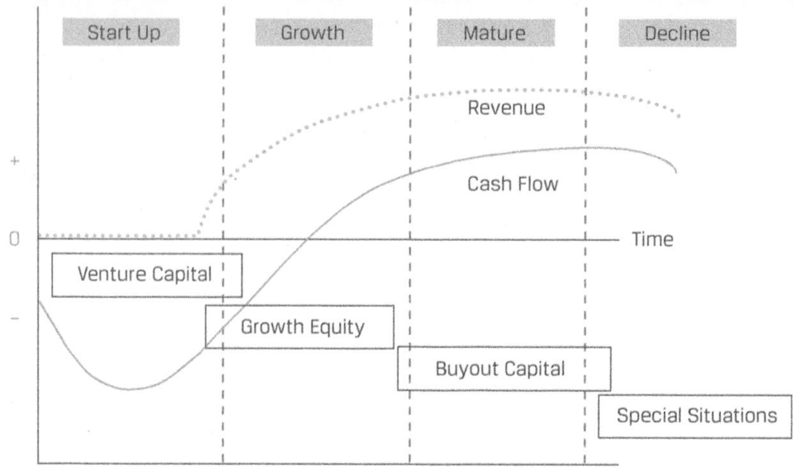

Note that these uses vary widely by company, industry, and market conditions, among other factors, as will be demonstrated as we examine the characteristics of these private equity investment forms in more detail in the following sections.

QUESTION SET

1. Which of the following characteristics most correctly reflects a company seeking growth equity?

   A. A company that has recently gone public via an IPO

   B. A private company seeking to enter new markets to increase revenues and profits

   C. A mature public company seeking to enter new markets to increase revenues and profits

   Solution

   Response B is correct. Growth equity is a form of private equity focused on private companies seeking profitable earning growth by entering new markets, increasing sales and distribution efforts, or pursuing a variety of other possible earnings growth strategies. Response A is not correct as a recent IPO company will seek new funding sources in the public equity and debt markets. Response C is not correct as a mature public company will most likely tap public markets rather than private equity funding to achieve these goals.

2. A typical portfolio of venture capital investments is characterized by which of the following?

   A. Financial investments with no governance or advisory role

   B. A diversified set of companies with varying growth prospects

   C. Companies receiving funding only after a highly selective process

   Solution

   Response C is correct. Venture capital investors are highly selective. Response A is not correct as the general partner takes on either board or advisory roles to assist the portfolio company. Response B is not correct as venture capital funds focus only on companies in specific industries in which the highest growth potential is possible.

3. Which form of private equity capital does the most to mitigate the problem of agency costs of equity?

   A. Buyout equity

   B. Growth equity

   C. Venture capital

Solution

Response A is correct. The agency costs of equity are a problem for mature publicly traded companies in which ineffective managers are less likely to be replaced because widely dispersed shareholders are not able to properly assess management's inability to respond to competitive pressures. Buyout equity provides a solution by taking the company private, which allows private equity owners to have more direct control over strategic decisions. Responses B and C are both incorrect as growth equity and venture capital are provided to private companies that do not face the same agency costs of equity.

VENTURE CAPITAL AND GROWTH EQUITY 3

☐ discuss characteristics of venture capital and growth equity investments

Buyout equity transactions among mature companies comprise roughly half of all private equity volume, with approximately one-third of total investment volume consisting of venture capital and a sixth involving growth equity. These two latter areas of private equity usually involve much smaller deals but entail greater risk as they occur in the early stages of a company's life cycle; however, they also offer investors higher potential returns in most economic scenarios.

Venture Capital

Venture capital investments are widely seen as a catalyst for new and emerging technologies and industries. These high-growth, high-risk investments in new companies are concentrated in a few industries, such as information technology or health care, and typically target startups seeking to either transform an existing market or establish a new one.

While new ventures were historically funded directly by wealthy individuals and families, among others, the most common approach today is for a VC general partner to solicit limited partner (LP) investors such as pensions, endowments, family offices, or high-net-worth individuals in a closed-end fund. These funds are usually composed of a portfolio of minority investments in startups with a drawdown, investment, and return harvesting. Exhibit 4 shows a typical distribution cycle.

Exhibit 4: Venture Capital Fund Life Cycle

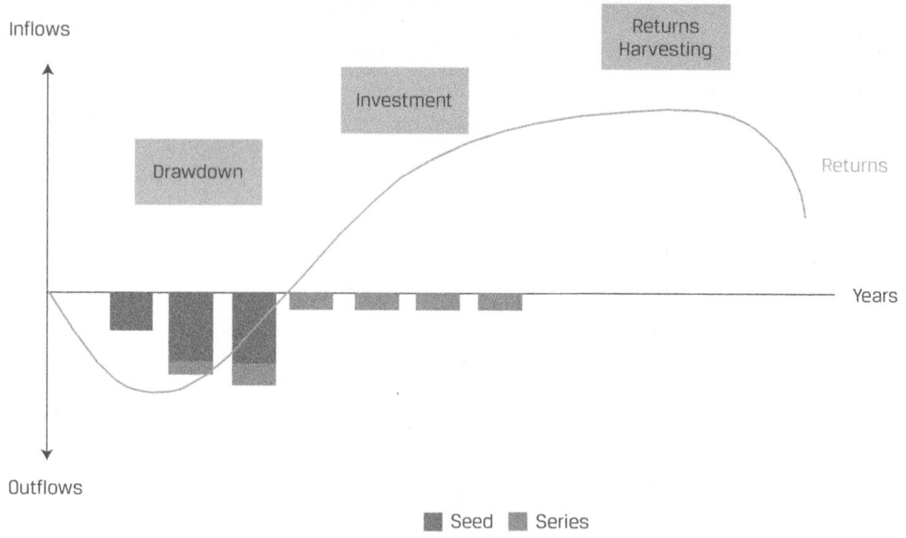

The typical drawdown or initial capital deployment phase of a VC fund usually starts with what is referred to as **seed capital**, which is used to launch new businesses. This committed capital is called over time. As new firms proceed to launch a new business idea, some fail, whereas others reach the next stage of development and require additional capital. This investment phase is often characterized by several follow-on equity injections or so-called **series financings** that are often staggered in phases over the next few years. Losses remain elevated over this period as firms often prove to be unable to commercialize what was originally deemed to be a sound business idea, as in the earlier case of Airware. Given the high failure rate among new companies, VC investors often refer to **100/10/1 rule of thumb**, which involves reviewing 100 startup pitches, conducting due diligence on just ten of the 100 reviewed and selecting only one of the ten as an investment. Despite the high degree of selectivity, VC investors still expect most investments to fail and very few to earn an outsized return, as shown below.

KNOWLEDGE CHECK

1. Estragon SA is a French VC fund whose investments have a 75% failure rate, with an average 15× capital growth rate among its remaining startup equity positions over a five-year period. If we assume no follow-on financing takes place over the period and ignore all fees and other costs, what is Estragon's expected IRR over this period?

Solution

Assuming an initial investment of EUR100 and a terminal value in five years of EUR375 (= 0.75 × EUR0 + 0.25 × EUR100 × 15), we may solve for an IRR of 30.26% by either discounting the terminal cash flow over five years,

$$\text{EUR100} = \frac{\text{EUR375}}{(1+\text{IRR})^5}; \text{IRR} = 30.26\%,$$

or, alternatively, using the Excel IRR function (= *IRR*(*Values, Guess*)) to solve for 30.26% = IRR({-100,0,0,0,0,375}).

The investment and payoff period of a VC fund is rarely as predictable as suggested in the prior numerical example. Since newly established firms face a very high failure rate with few to no assets or operating history, the initial focus of VC investors is often on founders and their credentials; their business, product ideas, and intellectual property; and the potential total addressable market, competitors, and barriers to entry. The stages of venture capital funding that startup firms may follow are shown in greater detail in Exhibit 5.

Exhibit 5: Venture Capital Funding Stages

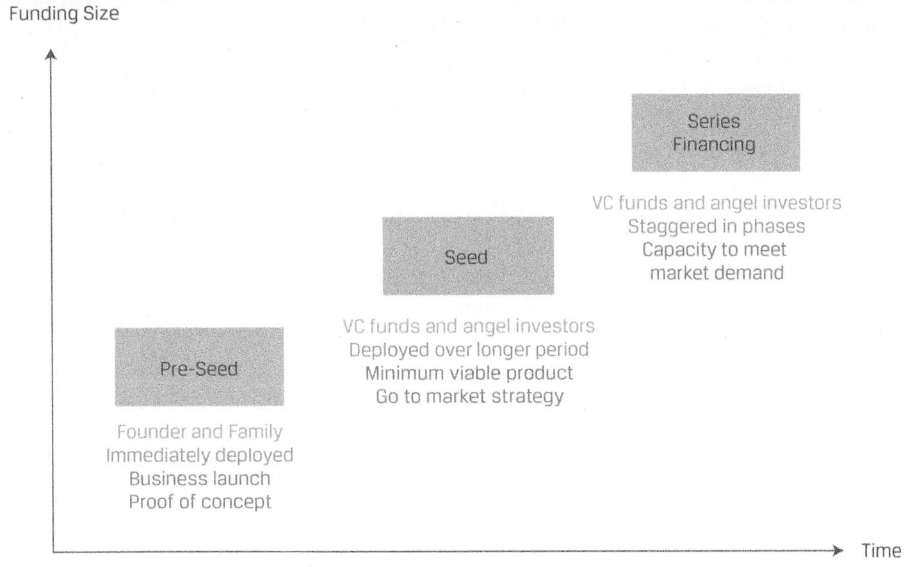

While individual cases can vary widely, the initial capital deployment phase of a new firm often occurs in two phases, namely, **pre-seed capital** funding and seed funding, as follows.

- *Pre-seed funding.* The initial source of equity capital is often simply the founder, family members, or friends. In addition to establishing a legal entity and other startup costs, pre-seed capital is typically used to determine the feasibility of a product and market need. This phase targets milestones such as establishing proof of concept and creating a product prototype over a brief period, usually less than a year.
- *Seed funding.* Once a startup firm has a proven idea and can demonstrate how a product prototype could meet that need, it may attract institutional investors as well as one or more high-net-worth individuals known as **angel investors**, who are also often entrepreneurs. This cash received from issuance of equity capital—typically in the form of common shares—is deployed over a longer period to achieve a product-market fit with key milestones, such as the creation of a minimum viable product to show to potential clients and a go-to-market strategy to generate initial revenue.

CASE STUDY

Kumartest LLP Seed Financing

Scientists at the Kumar Lab, a biomedical engineering research group with a focus on computer-based technology at a major Indian research university, developed a revolutionary process to conduct instantaneous testing of complex assays using mobile technology under laboratory conditions. Given the potential applicability of this new process in the fields of mining, environmental protection, and medicine, Dr. Sana Kumar establishes a new limited liability company (Kumartest LLP) to commercialize this technology.

As a first step, she raises USD1 million in pre-seed common equity capital from family members to replicate her team's lab results. Her goal is to detect trace amounts of chemical compounds on a timely and accurate basis using a handheld device and demonstrate the practical applications of this new technology.

Next, Kumar raises an additional USD2 million in seed capital to hire her first employees and approach environmental service firms and prospective investors with her prototype used to detect hazardous substances for environmental remediation projects. These funds will enable the company to gauge market receptivity for its product and also explore other applications in developing a go-to-market strategy.

Given the critical importance of non-financial milestones in the early stages of a company's development, venture capital general partners (GPs) typically apply more specific technical expertise and knowledge of industries and markets than financial analysis in evaluating prospective investments.

Once a new idea, technology, or product clears the initial hurdle of potentially addressing a customer need, young businesses shift to execution mode in seeking rapid growth by investing in resources necessary to establish markets for their new product.

In contrast to seed financing, investors in later stages of follow-on or series financing (often referred to alphabetically as Series A, B, or C financing) face lower risk than at the pure startup phase, given that the company generates some revenue, but also expect to pay a higher price per share than initial investors. These new investors often include, but may not be limited to, the original VC or angel investors from a prior funding phase, who often face ownership dilution in the event of follow-on financing. Uses of series funding differ markedly from startup phase financing as companies hire staff, purchase fixed assets, build inventory, and create capacity to meet initial market demand. Investor focus shifts from non-financial milestones to revenue, new customers, and other financial criteria to track company progress in reaching its market potential.

CASE STUDY

Kumartest LLP Series Financing

During its first year, Kumartest spends six months developing a product prototype and engages several pilot customers in environmental services. Initial user feedback on the functionality of Kumartest's handheld device is very positive, but Kumar believes the commercial potential in health care is far greater. She uses the remaining seed capital to test and pilot a second prototype to conduct on-demand diagnostic medical tests, which is initially well received but will require more client feedback and approval for use in major markets.

> Kumartest approaches VC investors with a health care focus, seeking funding to clear regulatory hurdles, establish production capacity, and hire a sales manager. After successful testing of its health care prototype, the company raises USD2 million in Series A financing from two investors, USD1 million each in common equity from the French VC firm Estragon SA and the privately held US medical device maker Sevastek Limited.
>
> Two years later, as product receptivity and sales continue to grow, Kumartest raises an additional USD2 million in Series B financing from its Series A investors.

While most series financing is provided as common equity as in the case study, in other cases, it is a hybrid involving the upside potential of equities and downside protection of debt-like fixed claims as shown below.

Growth Equity

As described earlier, growth equity is a distinct asset class within private equity that targets profitable earnings growth, most commonly via a minority equity investment. In contrast to venture capital focus on startups in few industries expected to expand very rapidly, growth equity is less industry focused and targets later-stage companies for expansion with established products and business models. While such firms may be profitable, they typically lack the cash flow necessary to fund major growth initiatives. This expansion may occur by increasing a company's scale of production, marketing, and distribution in an existing product or market, or to grow via business acquisition, new channels, or new markets, as in the case of last mile logistics.

Investors in growth equity often contribute capital in the form of **convertible preferred shares (CPS)** rather than ordinary shares due to several attractive features. As described earlier in the curriculum, convertible preferred shares are a form of preferred stock that may pay a dividend and be converted into common shares at a fixed **conversion ratio**, or number of common shares received for each preferred share, after a specific period. As a result, these shares have both debt- and equity-like features. Like debt, they represent claims senior to those of common shareholders and may receive a fixed dividend and/or a **liquidation preference payout**, or predefined cash distribution to preferred shareholders made in full before any payment to common shareholders. The conversion right to exchange preferred shares for ordinary shares in the future represents an equity-like return. Exhibit 6 shows the payoff profile of convertible preferred versus common shareholders as a function of exit value at the time of conversion.

Exhibit 6: Convertible Preferred and Common Share Payoff Versus Exit Value

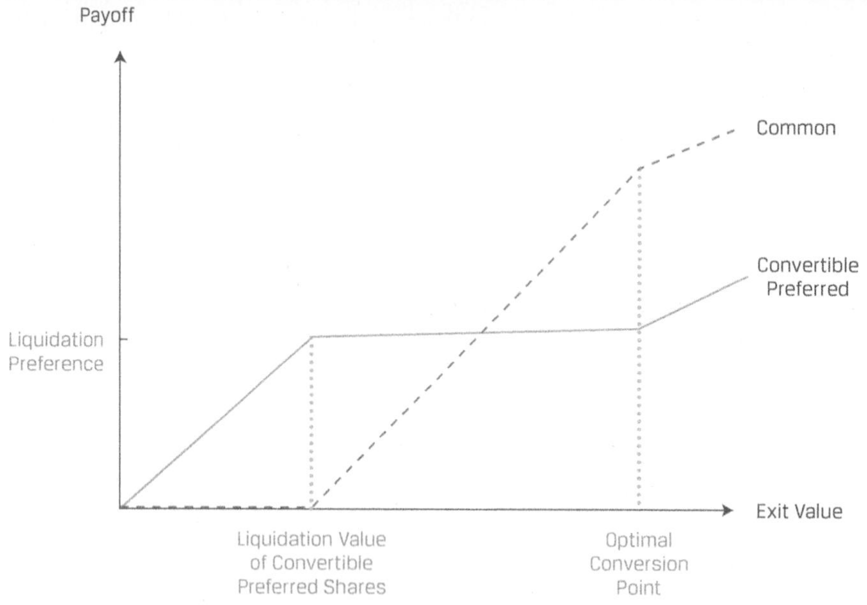

As shown in Exhibit 6, if the exit value remains below the liquidation value of convertible preferred shares, convertible shareholders receive a payoff equivalent to the exit value, whereas common shareholders receive nothing. As the exit value rises above the liquidation preference value, but remains below the conversion price, the payoff to convertible preferred investors is constant, whereas the value to common shareholders rises because common shareholders receive 100% of the incremental gains in exit value (i.e., the slope of the payoff line is equal to one). Once the exit value exceeds an implied equity price at which convertible preferred shares reach the conversion price, shown in Exhibit 6 as the **optimal conversion point**, preferred shareholders may be better off converting to common shares. The convertible preferred payoff rises with exit value beyond this point, while the slope of the common shareholder payoff line falls below one, given the conversion dilution. The relative slope of the two lines beyond the optimal conversion point reflects the fractional ownership of the original common shareholders and the shareholders converting their preferred shares. Fractional ownership is covered later in this reading.

The optimal conversion point may be determined as follows:

$$\text{Optimal Conversion Point} = \frac{\text{Total Liquidation Preference Value}}{\text{Conversion Ratio} \times \text{Number of Preferred Shares}}. \quad (1)$$

For example, given a USD100 million preferred share issuance at USD20 per share, 5 million preferred shares are outstanding (= USD100 million ÷ USD20). Given a liquidation preference value of 2.5× and a conversion ratio of 1.5×, we may solve for the optimal conversation point using Equation 1 as follows:

$$\text{USD33.33 per share} = \frac{2.5 \times 100 \text{ million}}{1.5 \times 5 \text{ million}}$$

$$= \frac{\text{Total Liquidation Preference Value}}{\text{Conversion Ratio} \times \text{Number of Preferred Shares}}.$$

Convertible preferred shares may include other investor rights such as **redemption rights**, **participation rights**, and **governance rights** in lieu of a conversion to common shares. Redemption rights grant an investor the ability to redeem preferred shares for cash, a form of downside protection that may be desirable when an early-stage company faces event risk such as regulatory or other approvals. Participation rights, on the other hand, offer preferred shareholders greater upside via similar distributions as common shareholders without a full conversion to common equity. Governance rights may be extended broadly among investors, or in the case of some private transactions, negotiated by convertible preferred investors who can convert their holdings into large (i.e., greater than 10%) common stock positions. Governance rights may include board seats, special voting rights, or simply the ability to observe board meetings. Finally, convertible preferred investors may be able to negotiate for the ability to force company liquidation within a predefined time frame.

Growth equity investments are not limited to private equity but may also take place in other private markets such as the real estate sector, as evidenced by the following case.

BLACKSTONE MILEWAY RECAPITALIZATION

One of the world's largest alternative asset managers, Blackstone, announced in 2019 the creation of Mileway, a private last mile logistics company composed of 1,000 European properties from its existing real estate portfolio. Given the rise of e-commerce as a fraction of total sales, the speed and efficiency of package delivery from local warehouses to their destination is of primary importance in scaling online businesses and ensuring customer satisfaction.

Three years later, as the company continued to expand in size and geographic scope across European countries, Mileway announced a capital raise, offering existing investors the chance to retain their investments, increase their share position, or sell for cash. The EUR21 billion recapitalization was also subject to a 75-day **go-shop process**, in which Blackstone solicited bids from potential third-party buyers after extending the offer to its current investors. However, most of the recapitalization was provided by existing investors, with Blackstone extending the remainder of the investment to other Blackstone funds. The growth equity from Mileway's recapitalization supported the company's expansion to over 1,700 properties including fulfillment centers, wholesalers, and air freight logistics providers.

Beyond an investment focus on profitable expansion, additional features that distinguish growth equity include investor dynamics and relative risk and return. While founders and venture capital investors have relatively concentrated stakes in startups with high failure rates and an unproven business model, the transition to growth once a business model is established allows early investors and founders to reduce their stake in a business and maintain control by attracting new private investors without selling the entire company or going public. Unlike venture capital, growth deals occur only once a firm's business model, market, and product fit are established, with equity proceeds used to scale the firm's production, sales, and distribution to achieve profitable growth. As a result, both the risk and return of growth equity is below that of venture capital.

CASE STUDY

Kumartest LLP Growth Equity Financing

Six years after it was founded and five years after its first series financing, Kumartest reaches USD70 million in annual sales and is close to earning a profit. That said, the company faces capacity limitations associated with manufacturing its testing devices and therefore has a limited ability to expand beyond a single region.

In seeking to capitalize on the company's growth potential while remaining private, Kumartest's senior management and existing investors agreed to raise USD30 million from a growth equity investor to be invested in manufacturing capacity as well as sales and distribution to achieve targeted earnings of just under USD50 million in five years.

Given the clearer financial targets involved versus the non-financial milestones associated with venture capital financing, growth equity financing is typically associated with a more detailed business plan mapping out a company's projected revenue and income and cash flow as well as balance sheet assets over the investment horizon. Growth equity investors typically target a specific return in money and percentage terms and then solve for incremental share capital necessary to achieve the young firm's profitability objective, as will be shown later in this reading.

QUESTION SET

1. The most common approach for a venture capital general partner to fund startup companies is:

   A. solicit limited partner investors to invest directly.

   B. solicit limited partner investors to invest in an open-end fund.

   C. solicit limited partner investors to invest in a closed-end fund.

   Solution

   Response C is correct. The general partner of the VC fund creates a closed-end fund and solicits capital commitments from institutional investors such as pension funds, endowment funds, family offices, and high-net-worth individuals as limited partners in the fund.

2. The French VC fund, Estragon SA, hopes to have four successful startups eventually emerge from its latest funding round. The typical failure rate of Estragon's investments is 75%, and Estragon adheres to the 100/10/1 rule of thumb. Which of the following is closest to the number of startup pitches Estragon must review?

   A. 400

   B. 1,600

   C. 2,000

   Solution

   Response B is correct. Estragon's failure rate is 75%, so 16 investments must be selected to have 4 successful ones. With 16 investments, the 100/10/1 rule of thumb implies that Estragon must review 1,600 startup pitches (= 16 × 100).

3. Which type of investor is most likely to provide pre-seed funding?

   A. Founder, family members, or friends

   B. Angel investors

   C. Venture capital funds

   Solution

   Response A is correct. Pre-seed funding is the earliest stage of capital deployment. As startups at this stage have not yet established a feasible business concept, the most likely investors are the founder and those closest relationally, such as family members or friends. Responses B and C are not correct as angel investors and VC funds provide seed funding after basic business feasibility milestones have been achieved following pre-seed funding.

4. Contrast the critical analytical roles played by the general partners of venture capital funds versus growth equity funds in analyzing potential investments.

Solution

Venture capital general partners are seeking investments with massive growth potential. Thus, general partners of VC funds typically apply more specific technical expertise and knowledge of industries when analyzing startup companies with less focus on financial analysis because of the high degree of uncertainty regarding the size of a market and the company's ability to capture market share. On the other hand, growth equity funds are focused on profitable growth potential of their investment opportunities, so general partners of these funds will create a detailed business plan with projected revenues, income, balance sheets, and cash flows over the investment horizon.

BUYOUT EQUITY 4

☐ discuss characteristics of buyout equity investments

In contrast to venture capital and growth equity, buyout equity investments involve the purchase of company or a company division with the intent to transform and improve existing operations and maximize return from the sale of the restructured firm upon exit.

Buyout equity targets are typically larger, profitable companies that might be publicly listed prior to a buyout equity transaction. Controlling private versus public ownership is an advantageous corporate governance structure in the case of rapid transformation, better aligning incentives to execute the targeted business plan within the prospective investment timeframe. Unlike early-stage equity investments, buyout transactions usually involve an initial high proportion of debt financing to fund the transformation over this period.

Buyout equity transactions may occur as a direct purchase, a co-investment, or through a private equity fund referred to as a **financial sponsor**, which takes a controlling stake in one or more companies distributed to investors in the form of limited partnerships. Company managers typically have some form of direct share-based compensation to closely align performance incentives to the business plan under a buyout scenario.

Firms that are likely targets for an equity buyout investment are distinguished by three key features:

- mature phase in the company life cycle,
- larger company size relative to industry peers and strong competitive market position, and
- management perceived as not maximizing company value.

Given the availability of historical financial statements, prospective investors in mature companies are able to engage in more thorough accounting due diligence, among other forms of assessment not available for startups or private firms with limited operating history. For example, prospective buyers are likely to conduct detailed comparisons between a targeted firm's revenue recognition and inventory management policies, depreciation methods, and the frequency and size of non-recurring items in operating profit versus industry peers. Unlike pre-revenue or pre-profit early-stage companies, buyout targets offer financial analysts the means to use more conventional valuation techniques, such as the method of comparables approach using market multiples when establishing a purchase price.

Larger firms with a stronger market position are more frequent targets for leveraged buyouts and financial sponsors. Company features associated with more predictable cash flows also include more regulated industries, those with higher barriers to entry, as well as firms with recurring, subscription-based revenues from a broad group of stable customers. In addition to consistent cash flows, firms with a significant asset base, which can be available as collateral for secured debt, or which can be undervalued versus replacement cost, are also attractive LBO targets.

LBOs typically involve either the purchase of a publicly held company by private investors known as a **take-private transaction**—the sale of a public company division to a buyout investor—or a divestiture or a private company sale. Buyers often target distinct features based upon a specific LBO scenario, such as the following.

Take-private (stock) transaction:

- A target company has an attractive public market value based on comparison to multiples of public company peers
- An acquirer has the ability to purchase outstanding public shares of the target company at a modest premium to the market price
- There is little to no company ownership among existing company managers
- There is potential for expense reductions and/or asset efficiencies that can produce meaningful improvements in profit margins and returns on capital

Corporate divestiture (stock or asset transaction):

- Target has few synergies with remainder of existing parent company
- High parent overhead costs or lack of manager focus and internal funding
- May be preferable to IPO, spinoff, or leveraged recapitalization

Private company sale:

- Opportunities for efficiency gains versus current owner-manager
- Ability to negotiate purchase price and obtain specific assets
- Address manager succession issues or insufficient access to funding

The change in ownership and capital structure of an LBO transaction typically takes place in two phases, as shown in Exhibit 7.

Exhibit 7: Mechanics of a Buyout Transaction

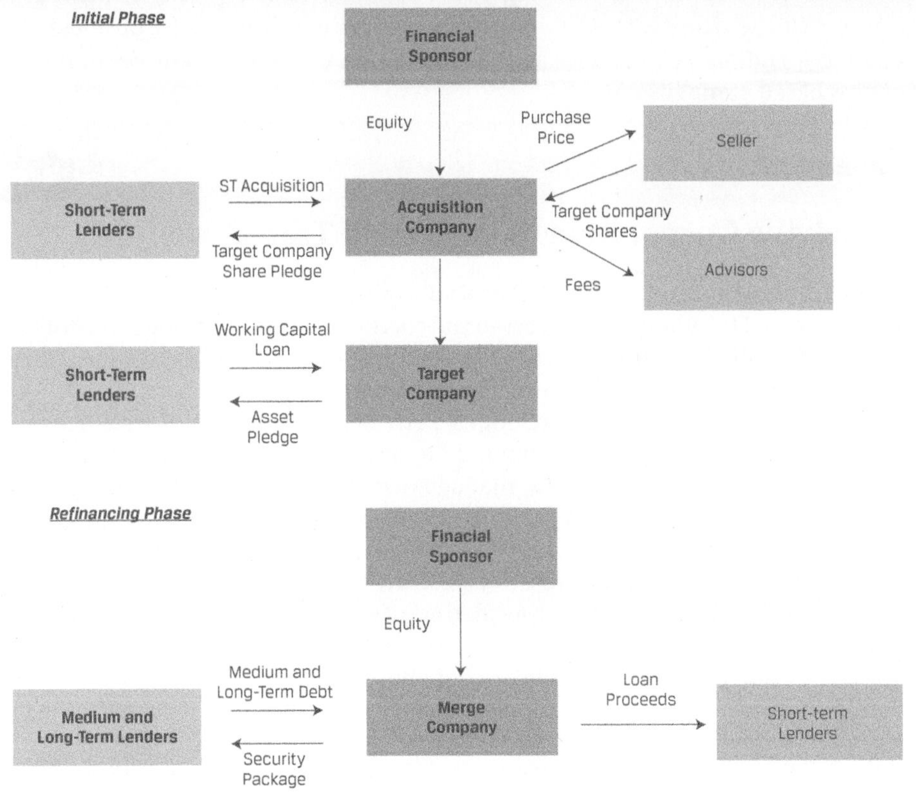

As shown in Exhibit 7, the financial sponsor or equity buyout fund first creates a new legal entity (AcquisitionCo) for the purpose of acquiring the target (TargetCo). AcquisitionCo receives equity from the sponsor and a short-term acquisition or bridge loan from lenders and uses the proceeds to pay the seller for TargetCo shares and fees to advisors. Change of control provisions, covenants, and other pre-existing TargetCo debt terms usually trigger debt repayment and therefore require full refinancing under the new ownership. The target will therefore often seek temporary debt financing to bridge the period over which the deal closes. This is followed by deal closure and refinancing, in which AcquisitionCo and TargetCo are combined in a merger, and the short-term bridge financing is replaced with medium- and long-term debt issued by the new legal entity.

It is important to distinguish the private buyout investment strategy illustrated above from those activities within an existing corporate issuer such as a **dividend recapitalization**, introduced earlier in the curriculum. Under a dividend recapitalization, also referred to as a leveraged recapitalization, a corporate issuer changes the mix of debt and equity outstanding by increasing leverage via debt-financed dividends or share repurchases. As an increase in debt and reduction in shares outstanding reduce the firm's **weighted average cost of capital (WACC)**, or the expected cost of debt and equity in the capital structure, with no change to the corporation's value, these transactions may be used to benefit existing shareholders.

In contrast, the investment focus of buyout equity is to purchase a controlling stake in a company where an acquirer sees an opportunity for significant return by *restructuring and improving operations* using debt financing over a specific period and then selling the company at a higher multiple upon exit. In contrast to the use of price-based multiples more common among equity-financed venture capital and growth equity investments, buyout equity multiples typically involve enterprise value-based valuation metrics, which consider the value of a firm to both debt and equity holders. Execution of the TargetCo business plan is typically entrusted with a proven management team with industry experience in integrating businesses and achieving operational efficiencies as well as aligning manager incentives in the form of equity-based compensation.

CASE STUDY

Maudville Corporation Take-Private Transaction

Maudville is a mature US public chemical company with current year EBITDA of close to USD1 billion. In contrast to the chemical industry average EV/EBITA of 6×, Maudville is trading closer to a 5× multiple due to a higher cost structure versus its competitors and fractious management.

Bardstown Partners, a private equity firm specializing in industrial buyout equity transactions, is considering a take-private purchase of Maudville and a restructuring plan under new management to make strategic changes to Maudville's operating model. Under this plan, Bardstown believes it could improve cash flows and profitability to bring Maudville's EV/EBITDA multiple in line with industry peers over a five-year investment period.

In its proposal, Bardstown is considering a Maudville purchase price of USD5 billion, with 20% of the purchase price contributed by Bardstown Partners via common equity, a 5% equity stake contributed by a limited partner buying convertible preferred shares, and the remaining 75% financed with debt.

Given the larger size, established market position and stable cash flows of LBO targets, buyout equity investors expect to face lower risk and return as compared to venture capital investments and growth equity. In contrast to the high failure rate of startups and execution risk of growth equity in achieving profitable expansion, buyout capital seeks to unlock the potential of an existing business by creating efficiencies, shedding non-core activities, and/or combining a company with others to build scale and synergies across similar lines of business. The evolution of a personal computer sales startup founded by Michael Dell to a multinational technology corporation illustrates the role of private buyout capital in the transformation of a mature business.

FROM DELL COMPUTER TO DELL TECHNOLOGIES

Michael Dell began building personal computers while a student at the University of Texas in 1984. He went on to found Dell Computer Corporation, which was part of the personal computer (PC) revolution during the 1980s and 1990s. However, by the early 2010s, PCs fell out of favor as the market moved toward smartphones and tablets. Dell Computer repeatedly missed its revenue projections during this time, and Dell reached the conclusion that taking the company private would help the company focus on a long-term strategy of customer-centric innovation.

Together with Silver Lake Partners, a private equity firm, Michael Dell took the company private in a USD25 billion transaction in early 2013. At the time of the LBO, Dell owned company shares worth USD3.6 billion. During the next three years, the company focused on using its cash flow to pay down debt of USD15 billion incurred in the buyout.

In 2016, Dell purchased the data management firm EMC in a USD67 billion transaction, giving the company a more diversified business profile across PCs, servers, and storage. Michael Dell contributed more cash and stock into the deal, reaching a total investment of about USD7.5 billion. Following the transaction, Dell was able to sell off selected divisions of the combined companies and begin paying down the USD46 billion in debt issued to fund the acquisition.

A key source of future value creation from the deal was EMC's 81% ownership of VMWare, a cloud computing company. Dell and Silver Lake listed a publicly traded tracking stock for VMWare, which proved to be a success as the shares soared in value. In 2018, the VMWare tracking stock was retired with a special dividend to its shareholders. Dell used his share of the special dividend, along with a portion of equity in the private company and USD5 billion in debt, to bring Dell back to the public market as Dell Technologies.

By early 2021, Dell was preparing to spin off VMWare as a publicly traded company and use some of the proceeds to continue to pay down the debt of Dell Technologies. The value of Michael Dell's shares in Dell Technologies had grown to USD39 billion. While Dell's core businesses remain slow in growth with limited profitability, the LBO of Dell Computers in 2013 allowed for a business trajectory that launched a major player in cloud computing, an area with far more growth potential.

A comparison of the features of venture capital, growth equity, and buyout equity investments are summarized in Exhibit 8.

Exhibit 8: Venture Capital, Growth, and Buyout Equity Characteristics

Feature	Venture Capital	Growth Equity	Buyout Equity
Life cycle stage	Startup	Growth	Mature
Industry	New, emerging, or disruptive to existing business models	Various	Various
Company size	Very small	Varies	Varies
Market position	None, small, or new market	Proven with significant growth potential	Established
Investment focus	Company launch, proof of concept, establish product, and market fit	Profitable expansion of established product	Purchase of undervalued asset, add value, and sell at higher multiple upon exit
Form of investment	Equity based	Equity and convertible instruments	Equity, convertible and debt instruments
Stake	Minority	Minority	Controlling
Relative risk and return	Highest	Higher	High
Investment size	USD1–10 million	Varies	Greater than USD10 million
Time horizon	5–10 years	3–7 years	3–7 years

In what follows, we revisit the valuation of private versus publicly owned companies introduced earlier in the curriculum with a distinct focus on each of these forms of private equity across the company life cycle.

QUESTION SET

1. Which of the following features is likely apparent in both growth equity and private buyout equity deals?

   A. High levels of debt used by the private equity firm to fund the deal

B. Potential for improved profitability of the firm being funded

C. Potential for significant revenue growth of the firm being funded

Solution

Response B is correct. Firms financed with growth equity funding are typically those with potential for significant improvements in both revenue and profit margin growth, and firms financed with buyout equity funding are typically firms with slower revenue growth but with potential for improved profitability growth. Response A is incorrect as high debt is a feature of buyout equity but not a feature of growth equity. Response C is incorrect as significant revenue growth is a feature of growth equity but not buyout equity.

2. Compare the financial leverage strategies and outcomes of a dividend recapitalization versus a take-private buyout equity transaction.

Solution

Both dividend recapitalization and buyout equity reflect strategies that increase the proportion of debt in a company's capital structure.

A dividend recapitalization strategy issues new debt to finance the reduction of a company's equity through a special dividend or share repurchases, and the outcome of the strategy is focused on optimizing the company's capital structure by reducing weighted average cost of capital.

A take-private equity buyout equity transaction is typically funded with high levels of debt, so the short-term outcome of the transaction may be similar to that of a dividend recapitalization. However, the buyout equity transaction aims to pay off significant amounts of debt over the private equity firm's investment time horizon. Thus, a company taken private in a buyout equity deal should eventually revert to a lower proportion of financial leverage in its capital structure in the long term.

3. Discuss the rationale for a two-stage process in the change of ownership and capital structure of a target company in a leveraged buyout (LBO) transaction.

Solution

The two-stage process is often necessary to repay existing debt in the first stage and then optimize the capital structure in the second stage. The target company's debt terms likely include change of control provisions, covenants, and other pre-existing debt terms, and these terms trigger debt repayment under the new ownership. In the first stage, both the target company and the financial sponsor (i.e., the private equity firm) will often need temporary debt financing to bridge the period over which the deal closes. In the second stage, the acquisition company created by the financial sponsor and the target company are combined in a merger, and the short-term bridge financing is replaced with medium- and long-term debt issued by the new legal entity.

PRIVATE EQUITY VALUATION

5

- [ ] estimate and interpret key inputs and calculate the value of a private equity investment for venture capital, growth equity, and buyout situations

In an earlier Level II Private Company Valuation reading, we considered the similarities and differences in the valuation of stable, mature private versus public companies. For example, common features under an income-based approach include the discounting of expected free cash flow to both debt and equity holders, or **free cash flow to the firm (FCFF)**, shown in Equation 2.

$$\text{FCFF} = \text{EBITDA}(1 - t) + \text{Depreciation } (t) - \text{Change in Long-Term Assets} - \text{Change in Capital} \quad (2)$$

where t is the firm's tax rate. Cash flows are projected over several periods, after which a terminal value or exit value, typically based on either constant growth or an expected market multiple, is assumed. The life cycle implications for company valuation in venture capital, growth equity, buyout, and special situations give rise to distinct approaches for these forms of private equity, as shown in Exhibit 9.

Exhibit 9: Private Equity Valuation Approaches Across the Life Cycle

Phase / Characteristic	Venture Capital	Growth Equity	Buyout Equity	Special Situations
Life cycle stage	Startup	Growth	Mature	Decline
Valuation approach	VC Method	Growth equity method	LBO model	Various
Primary valuation input	Revenue forecast	Income statement forecast	Three-statement financial model forecast	Three-statement model, asset values

Valuation approaches for special situations involving stressed, distressed, or event-driven investments will be covered in detail in a later reading.

Venture Capital and the VC Method

Venture capital investors face uncertain prospects given the lack of operating history and high failure rate of startup companies. The income, market, and asset-based valuation approaches common among mature firms are of little to no use for these early-stage companies. Instead, the so-called **VC method** is typically used to establish the current value of a young company in conjunction with new financing. Under the VC method, the initial or so-called **pre-money valuation**, or implied firm value prior to an incremental new equity investment, is determined using the expected terminal value of the firm (or **exit value of equity**) and the required ROI, as shown in Exhibit 10.

Exhibit 10: VC Method Inputs and Output

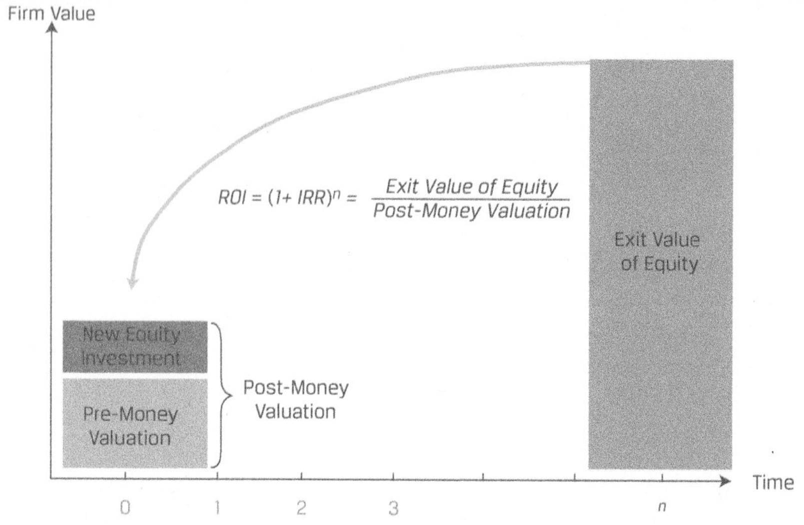

As shown in Exhibit 10, the **post-money valuation** is a combination of the pre-money valuation and new equity invested. Since startups are usually fully equity financed and make no distributions to shareholders over the investment time horizon, the post-money valuation is a function of the expected exit value of equity divided by the required return on investment, as shown in Equation 3.

$$\text{Post-Money Valuation} = \frac{\text{Exit Value of Equity}}{\text{ROI}} \tag{3}$$

VC-required rates of return on investment are communicated to the limited partners of the fund, thus the ROI presented in Equation 3 reflects the effective cost of capital to the VC general partner. In venture capital, typical ROIs range from 10× to 30× over a five- to eight-year period.

If we assume no intermediate investment returns and a single inflow upon exit, we may convert the ROI return over an investment time horizon to an equivalent internal rate of return for an n-year investment period in Equation 4.

$$\text{ROI} = (1 + \text{IRR})^n \tag{4}$$

While the path to revenue and profitability is highly uncertain for most startups, performance metrics such as the method of comparables, introduced earlier in the curriculum, are commonly used to gauge commercial success at the end of the investment horizon. For example, while a price to earnings ratio or multiple may be used if the firm is expected to generate significant profits by the time of exit value, price to sales or price to cash flow multiples are most appropriate for estimation of equity exit value of early-stage companies with no profits and no leverage, as shown in the following case.

CASE STUDY

Kumartest Series A Financing—Exit Value

Prior to its Series A financing, Kumartest successfully launched a new prototype for on-demand medical diagnostics. Given expected swift regulatory approval, Kumartest believes it can achieve USD75 million in annual sales in seven years following Series A financing. The price-to-sales ratio for medical devices is 3×.

1. Calculate the estimated exit value for Kumartest in seven years.

   Solution

   Given Kumartest's estimate of USD75 million in future annual revenue and an expected price-to-sales ratio of 3×, the company value upon exit in seven years may be estimated as USD225 million (= 75 million × 3).

2. Estimate a range of exit value possibilities for Kumartest in seven years if its annual sales may fall between USD50 million and USD100 million and the price-to-sales ratio for medical devices may fall between 2.5× and 3.5×.

   Solution

   At the low end of the range, with USD50 million in future annual revenue and a price-to-sales ratio of 2.5×, Kumartest's exit value is estimated at USD125 million (= 50 million × 2.5). At the high end of the range, with USD100 million in annual revenue and a price-to-sales ratio of 3.5×, Kumartest's exit value is estimated at USD350 million (= 100 million × 3.5). Thus, Kumartest's exit value may lie in a range of USD125 million to USD350 million.

Because of the high uncertainty associated with future revenue potential for startups and the variability of sales-based multiples over time, an important aspect of valuing companies with the VC method is to consider a range of potential scenarios in exit value estimation.

Recall that under the VC method, we are solving for the pre-money valuation, which is simply equal to the post-money valuation less new equity:

$$\text{Pre-Money Valuation} = \text{Post-money Valuation} - \text{New Equity}. \tag{5}$$

The fractional ownership stake of new investors is equal to the new equity contribution divided by the post-money valuation:

$$\text{Fractional Ownership} = \frac{\text{New Equity}}{\text{Post-Money Valuation}}. \tag{6}$$

Note that while these calculations are in money terms, we may express post-money valuation and ownership in terms of shares outstanding as follows.

$$\text{Post-Money Valuation} = \text{Total Shares Outstanding (Old and New)} \times \text{Share Price} \tag{7}$$

$$\text{Fractional Ownership} = \frac{\text{New Shares Issued}}{\text{Post-Money Shares Outstanding}} \tag{8}$$

We illustrate these concepts by revisiting Kumartest's Series A financing.

CASE STUDY

Kumartest Series A Financing, Fractional Ownership and Expected Return

Recall from earlier that Kumartest LLC began by raising USD3 million in seed financing from 1 million shares and subsequently raised USD2 million in Series A common equity, with USD1 million each from Estragon SA and Sevastek Limited.

Prior to Series A financing, Kumartest successfully launched a new prototype for on-demand medical diagnostics. Kumartest's management is projecting an exit value of USD225 million in seven years. Estragon SA and Sevastek Limited have a target ROI of 20× over the seven-year investment time horizon.

1. Calculate Kumartest LLC's post-money valuation based upon the information provided.

Solution

We may solve for Kumartest's post-money valuation using Equation 3:

$$\text{Post-Money Valuation} = \frac{\text{Exit Value of Equity}}{\text{ROI}}.$$

Given Kumartest's estimated exit value of USD225 million and the stated target ROI of 20×, we may solve for post-money valuation as USD11.25 million (= 225 million ÷ 20).

2. As a medical device company with strategic investments in startup companies within its sector, Sevastek's CEO has a stated objective to target VC investments with at least a 50% IRR. Evaluate whether the Kumartest Series A financing meets the CEO's objective.

Solution

Use Equation 4 to determine the equivalent internal rate of return, which reflects a 20× ROI over seven years:

$$\text{ROI} = 20\times = (1 + \text{IRR})^7;\ \text{IRR} = 53.4\% > 50\%.$$

The Kumartest Series A financing therefore meets the CEO's target ROI of 50%.

3. Calculate the value of Kumartest to its initial investors at the time of Series A financing in both money terms and price per share.

Solution

The value of Kumartest to its initial investors is the pre-money valuation, which, based on Equation 5, is simply equal to the post-money valuation less new equity:

$$\text{Pre-Money Valuation} = \text{Post-Money Valuation} - \text{New Equity}.$$

From Question 1, post-money valuation is USD11.25 million and new equity is USD2 million, so pre-money valuation is equal to USD9.25 million (= 11.25 million – 2 million). Given the original issuance of 1 million shares, the per share price is USD9.25.

4. Calculate Estragon's fractional ownership of Kumartest and the number of shares it receives.

Solution

Estragon's fractional ownership stake is equal to its USD1 million Series A equity contribution divided by the post-money valuation of USD11.25 million from Question 1 as per Equation 6, which amounts to 8.89%:

$$\text{Fractional Ownership} = \frac{\text{New Equity}}{\text{Post-Money Valuation}};$$

$$8.89\% = \frac{\text{USD1 million}}{\text{USD11.25 million}}.$$

We can solve for the number of total (old and new) shares outstanding by rearranging Equation 7:

$$\text{Total Shares Outstanding (Old and New)}$$
$$= \text{Post-Money Valuation} \div \text{Share Price};$$

1,216,216 = USD11.25 million ÷ USD9.25.

Recall that the initial investors hold 1 million shares and the incremental financing is split between Sevastek and Estragon. Estragon will therefore receive half of the new shares, or 108,108 shares (= (1,216,216 – 1,000,000) ÷ 2) in Series A.

In addition to the absence of debt and equity distributions, the VC method as shown above also assumes no equity dilution takes place over the remaining investment time horizon once the Series A financing is complete. The potential for equity dilution arises from three primary sources.

1. *Incentive-Based Equity Compensation.* In order to attract, retain, and incentivize employees, startup firms frequently offer employees equity options granting the right to purchase common shares at a fixed price in the future. As option exercises increase shares outstanding, VC firms typically calculate ownership and per-share price on a fully diluted basis.
2. *Follow-on Equity Financing.* New common equity issuance in a subsequent financing round as well as mergers and acquisitions where shares are used instead of cash also increase the number of shares outstanding and therefore reduce fractional ownership of earlier investors.
3. *Financing with Contingent Future Share Issuance.* Use of instruments such as convertible preferred shares may result in additional share issuance if converted. This dilution must be taken into consideration when determining fractional ownership for new investors.

Consider the following versions of the original Kumartest case, which include the first and second of these sources of dilution, with the third covered later under a growth equity scenario.

CASE STUDY

Kumartest Series A Financing with Option Pool and Price Per Share

Kumartest LLC began by issuing 1 million shares at USD3 each for USD3 million in seed financing. Kumartest subsequently raised USD2 million in Series A common equity, or USD1 million each from Estragon SA and Sevastek Limited.

Prior to the Series A financing, Kumartest granted its employees the option to purchase a total of 100,000 Kumartest shares at a strike price of USD6 starting in five years if they remain employed at the company. Exit value assumptions remain as in the earlier case study, with USD75 million in annual sales expected in seven years and a comparable price-to-sales ratio of 3×, with an investor target ROI of 20× over seven years. For the purposes of answering the following questions, ignore any potential effects of option valuation on Kumartest's company value as well as investor proportional ownership.

1. Recall that the intrinsic or exercise value of an option is the amount by which the option is in the money. Discuss the implications of the intrinsic value of Kumartest employee options after Series A financing.

Solution

From Question 3 above, Kumartest's share price at the time of Series A financing is USD9.25. Given the USD6 option strike price, the intrinsic value of the 100,000 options is USD325,000. As they cannot be exercised for several years, the intrinsic option value is an incentive for option holders to remain employed with the company.

2. Calculate the fractional ownership of Kumartest's management and the impact on firm value if the company reaches its expected annual sales target in Year 7 and all options are exercised.

Solution

When Kumartest's managers exercise 100,000 employee options, total shares outstanding increase by 100,000 and we may use Equation 8 to solve for Kumartest management's fractional ownership:

$$\text{Fractional Ownership} = 7.6\% = \frac{100,000}{1,000,000 + 216,216 + 100,000}.$$

Projected Kumartest exit value in Year 7 is USD225 million. When Kumartest's managers exercise 100,000 employee options at a strike price of USD6, the firm receives USD600,000 (= 100,000 × USD6), increasing firm value to USD225,600,000.

3. Calculate the fractional ownership of Sevastek Limited under the Series A financing on a fully diluted basis.

Solution

Recall from Question 4 above that Estragon was issued 108,108 shares in the Series A financing. Use Equation 8 to determine Estragon's fractional ownership on a fully diluted basis by adding the 100,000 employee options granted to the post-money shares outstanding:

$$\text{Fractional Ownership} = 8.21\% = \frac{108,108}{1,000,000 + 216,216 + 100,000}.$$

Estragon's fractional ownership falls from 8.89% to 8.21% on a diluted basis.

As early-stage companies engage in multiple equity rounds, it is important to track the *cumulative* fractional ownership of a private equity fund or investor as the ownership structure evolves. An investor's postfinancing fractional ownership (or FO_{post}) is equal to its prior cumulative stake (FO_{prior}) multiplied by the percentage of dilution in the current round, plus the percentage of the firm it acquires in the new equity round as shown in Equation 9.

$$FO_{\text{post}} = \left[FO_{\text{prior}} \times \frac{\text{Pre-Money Valuation}}{\text{Post-Money Valuation}}\right] + \frac{\text{New Investor Equity}}{\text{Post-Money Valuation}}$$
$$= \frac{\text{Pre-Money Valuation of Investor's Stake} + \text{Investor's Incremental Investment}}{\text{Post-Money Valuation}} \quad (9)$$

Consider the following extension of the Kumartest case to a new Series B financing.

CASE STUDY

Kumartest Series B Financing with No Option Pool

Kumartest decides to raise a total of USD2 million in Series B common equity funding, USD1 million each from Estragon and Sevastek, two years after its USD2 million Series A funding, in order to continue to build its capacity to serve the health care industry. In this second series financing, both Estragon and Sevastek have a 10× ROI target over five years, and the expected sales at the time of exit remains USD75 million with a price to sales multiple of 3×. We assume no employee options for the purpose of this example.

1. Calculate the share price at the time of Series B financing.

Solution

The exit value of Kumartest equity is USD225 million (= 75 million × 3) as shown earlier, while the new post-money valuation may be solved using Equation 3 (recall that the ROI target is 10×):

$$\text{Post-Money Valuation} = \text{USD22.5 million} = \frac{\text{USD225,000,000}}{10}.$$

Solve for pre-money valuation using Equation 7 and new financing of USD2 million:

$$\text{Pre-Money Valuation} = \text{USD20.5 million} = 22.5 \text{ million} - 2 \text{ million}.$$

Solve for the share price by dividing pre-money valuation by shares outstanding:

$$\text{USD16.86} = \frac{\text{USD20,500,000}}{\text{1,216,216 shares outstanding}}.$$

2. Calculate Estragon's fractional ownership following Series B financing.

Solution

Determine Estragon's post–Series B financing fractional ownership using Equation 9.

$$FO_{post} = FO_{prior} \times \frac{\text{Pre-Money Valuation}}{\text{Post-Money Valuation}} + \frac{\text{New Investor Equity}}{\text{Post-Money Valuation}}$$

$$FO_{post} = 8.89\% \times \frac{\text{USD20,500,000}}{\text{USD22,500,000}} + \frac{\text{USD1,000,000}}{\text{USD22,500,000}}$$

$$FO_{post} = 12.54\% = 8.10\% + 4.44\%$$

Current and prospective investors in early-stage companies often make use of a **capitalization table** to summarize changes in firm value and fractional ownership over the course of multiple equity rounds on a fully diluted basis. Exhibit 11 shows this evolution for the three Kumartest financing rounds. Readers should note that the calculations are conducted in a spreadsheet and numbers presented throughout reflect rounding.

Exhibit 11: Kumartest Capitalization Table

Panel A: Shares and Fractional Ownership (FO)

Investor	Seed Shares	Seed FO %	Post Series A	Post Series A FO %	Post Series B	Post Series B FO %
Estragon Series A			108,108	8.89%	108,108	8.10%
Estragon Series B					59,328	4.44%
Sevastek Series A			108,108	8.89%	108,108	8.10%
Sevastek Series B					59,328	4.44%
Subtotals			216,216	17.78%	334,871	25.09%
Founder	1,000,000	100%	1,000,000	82.22%	1,000,000	74.91%
Totals	1,000,000	100%	1,216,216	100.00%	1,334,874	100.00%

The fractional ownership shown in Panel A is often accompanied by changes in valuation over a series of financings. The higher share price at the time of Kumartest's Series B financing is referred to as the **price step-up**, either in multiple or percentage terms:

$$\text{Step-Up (multiple)} = \frac{\text{New Round Share Price}}{\text{Prior Round Share Price}}; \tag{10}$$

$$\text{Step-Up (percentage)} = \left(\frac{\text{New Round Share Price}}{\text{Prior Round Share Price}} - 1\right) \times 100. \tag{11}$$

The Kumartest Series B step-up is 1.822 $\left(= \frac{\text{USD16.86}}{\text{USD9.25}}\right)$, or 82.2% in percentage terms. Higher share prices in subsequent funding rounds indicate an early-stage company's progress in achieving targeted growth, as shown in Panel B.

Panel B: Valuation across Financing Series

	Seed Financing	Series A Financing	Series B Financing
Share price (USD)	3.00	9.25	16.86
Price step-up		3.08	1.82
Pre-money valuation (USD)	0	9,250,000	20,500,000
New equity (USD)	3,000,000	2,000,000	2,000,000
Post-money valuation (USD)	3,000,000	11,250,000	22,500,000

On the other hand, lagging company performance in reaching milestones or an adverse market environment may result in new financing at a share price below that of the prior financing round, which is referred to as a **down round**. To protect themselves against dilution at a lower share price at new issuance, private equity investors often seek to negotiate a so-called **ratchet provision**, which partially or fully reduces the conversion price of existing options or preferred shares to the new lower share issue price for a later financing.

Valuing Growth Equity

Recall that under the VC method, we derived the pre-money valuation using the exit value of equity and the ROI as inputs. In contrast to startups with a high failure rate, proof of concept risk, and undefined capital needs, growth equity involves scaling more developed and profitable, or near profitable, companies with known products and market opportunities over a defined investment time horizon. As a result, the **growth equity method** includes revenue and profit projections over the investment horizon necessary to achieve the desired financial results and quantifies the initial capital necessary to realize the plan.

Growth equity funds seek to invest as little capital as possible at the lowest pre-money valuation and sell at the highest valuation as soon as possible. Given the path to profitability as laid out in the business plan, the primary risk to these investors is the execution of the growth strategy within the forecast period.

CASE STUDY

Kumartest Growth Equity Using Common Shares

In its sixth year of operations, Kumartest is nearing its Series B revenue target of USD75 million but remains unprofitable, with the income statement below.

Kumartest Income Statement, Year 6

Position	Year 6 (USD)
Sales	70,000,000
COGS	60,000,000
Gross profit	10,000,000
SGA	10,000,000
Depreciation	2,000,000
EBITDA	2,000,000
Profit before tax	0
Net income	0

Kumartest identifies production and distribution capacity constraints as the key impediments to its further growth. To capitalize on Kumartest's high potential while remaining private, senior management and existing investors agree to approach Ventmax Partners, a growth equity fund, to finance expansion of its manufacturing capacity, sales, and distribution.

Ventmax typically seeks to invest in a minority common or convertible preferred equity stake for a five-year period with a minimum IRR of 35%. The Ventmax team conducts thorough due diligence on Kumartest, concluding that new equity of USD30 million is necessary to meet property, plant, and equipment; sales and distribution; and working capital needs to achieve targeted EBITDA in excess of USD65 million in five years.

In its detailed five-year business plan, Ventmax forecasts 30% annual sales growth; a 23% rise per year in both cost of goods sold (COGS) and sales, general, and administrative expenses (SGA). Depreciation expense is embedded within COGS and is added back to calculate EBIDTA, as shown below. We assume a 20% corporate tax rate. Readers should note that the following calculations are conducted in a spreadsheet, and rounding may occur throughout the case study.

Ventmax Partners Forecast of Kumartest Income Statement (Years 7 to 11)

Position	Year 7	Year 8	Year 9	Year 10	Year 11
Sales	91,000,000	118,300,000	153,790,000	199,927,000	259,905,100
COGS	73,800,000	90,774,000	111,652,020	137,331,985	168,918,341
Gross profit	17,200,000	27,526,000	42,137,980	62,595,015	90,986,759
SGA	12,300,000	15,129,000	18,608,670	22,888,664	28,153,057
EBITDA	7,900,000	16,397,000	27,529,310	43,706,351	66,833,702
Depreciation	3,000,000	4,000,000	4,000,000	4,000,000	4,000,000
Profit before tax	4,900,000	12,397,000	23,529,310	39,706,351	62,833,702
Net income	3,920,000	9,917,600	18,823,448	31,765,081	50,266,962

The Ventmax team has accepted the earlier 3× price to sales multiple to be used to establish the pre-money valuation and estimates an 18× price to EBITDA exit multiple after five years based on similar medical device firms.

Kumartest's pre-money valuation may be estimated as USD210 million given the current year (Year 6) revenue of USD70 million and a 3× price-to-sales ratio.

1. Calculate the price per share paid by Ventmax and its fractional ownership once the new financing is completed.

Solution

In order to establish the price per share, divide the pre-money valuation of USD210 million by the pre-financing number of shares outstanding (1,334,871) to solve for a share price of USD157.32 (= 210,000,000 ÷ 1,334,871). Recall that the post-money valuation is the sum of the pre-money valuation plus new financing:

USD240 million = USD210 million + USD30 million.

Since Ventmax Partners has no prior fractional ownership ($FO_{prior} = 0$), we may solve for its ownership stake using a simplified version of Equation 8.

$$FO_{post} = \frac{\text{New Investor Equity}}{\text{Post-Money Valuation}}$$

$$12.5\% = \frac{30,000,000}{240,000,000}$$

2. Discuss how the IRR calculation changes if we assume net income is distributed to shareholders on a pro rata basis and determine whether Ventmax is able to reach its minimum 35% target under the proposed five-year business plan under this assumption.

Solution

Unlike the initial investment and single exit cash flow to equity holders assumed under the VC method and in Equation 2, here we must take *all* cash flows to equity holders over the investment period into account when calculating the IRR.

First, we consider both the USD240 million from Year 6 and net income for Years 7 to 11. Next, we solve for the terminal value in five years by multiplying Year 11 EBITDA of USD66,833,702 by the 18× price to EBITDA multiple to arrive at an estimated exit value of equity of USD1,203,006,638 (= USD66,833,702 × 18).

Cash flows used to calculate IRR may be summarized as follows.

Position	Year 6	Year 7	Year 8	Year 9	Year 10	Year 11
Net cash flow	(240,000,000)	3,920,000	9,917,600	18,823,448	31,765,081	50,266,962
Terminal value						1,203,006,636
Total cash flow	(240,000,000)	3,920,000	9,917,600	18,823,448	31,765,081	1,253,273,599

We may solve for an IRR of 41.89% using a spreadsheet IRR function:

ROI = IRR({-240000000,3920000,9917600,18823448,31765081,1253273599})

= 41.89%.

Recall that ROI is the ratio of received cash flows to investments:

$$\text{ROI} = \frac{1}{240,000,000} \times [3,920,000 + 9,917,600 + \ldots + 1,253,273,599]X$$

$$= 5.49X.$$

Ventmax Partners is therefore able to reach its minimum 35% IRR target. The inputs and outputs under the growth equity method for Kumartest are summarized in Exhibit 12.

Exhibit 12: Kumartest Growth Equity Method Inputs and Output

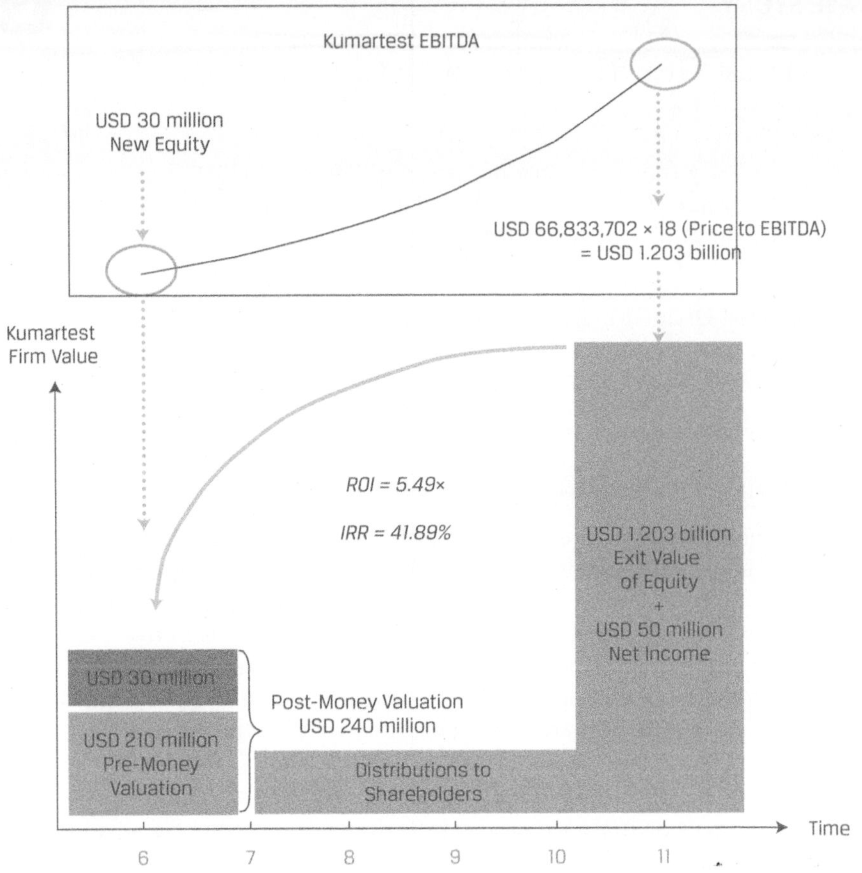

As the prior case study shows, the growth equity capital method has a few similarities with the VC method, with several key differences. For example, growth equity investments tend to be larger than those in venture capital, with a lower expected ROI over a shorter investment time horizon. A detailed financial plan focused on earnings growth replaces broad revenue expectations, and earnings-based multiples are preferred over sales-based measures used for early-stage pre-profit firms in establishing the exit value of equity. However, once the pre- and post-money valuations and exit value of equity are determined, the calculation of ROI and the corresponding internal rate of return are often the same.

However, complicating factors include the existence of employee options and other forms of potential dilution. For example, growth equity investors are more likely to provide capital in the form of convertible preferred shares, which result in additional share issuance upon conversion. We now turn our attention to this form of growth equity capital to finance Kumartest's expansion.

CASE STUDY

Kumartest Growth Equity with Convertible Preferred Shares

Here we modify the prior case of Ventmax Partners' USD30 million growth equity investment to capital contributed as convertible preferred shares rather than common equity. Brief terms of the convertible preferred shares are as follows:

Preferred Dividend: 5% per annum

Liquidation Preference Payout: 2× upon exit in five years

Conversion Ratio: 2× upon exit in five years

Convertible Preferred Share Price: USD400.00.

The 2× liquidation preference payout entitles preferred shareholders to receive a cash payment equal to double the preferred share price upon issuance (or USD800), while the 2× conversion ratio reflects that a preferred shareholder may convert each preferred share into two common shares in five years. Note that in this modified case, we have excluded employee options. Readers should also note that the calculations shown in the solutions to the questions below are conducted in a spreadsheet and numbers presented throughout reflect rounding.

1. Discuss the payoff profile of a Kumartest convertible preferred shareholder under different possible scenarios at the time of exit assuming no additional financing occurs.

Solution

The USD30 million financing involves the issuance of 75,000 (= USD30 million ÷ 400) convertible preferred shares. The payoff profile of a preferred shareholder involves three general outcomes as shown earlier in Exhibit 6 and described below.

Equity Value at Exit < Liquidation Preference. If the equity value upon exit is equal to or below the total liquidation preference payout due to preferred shareholders upon exit of USD60 million (= 2 × 30,000,000), then preferred shareholders will receive the entire firm value on a proportional per-share basis and common shareholders will receive zero. For example, if the firm value upon exit is USD52.5 million, then preferred shareholders will receive USD700 each upon liquidation (= 52,500,000 ÷ 75,000).

Liquidation Preference ≤ Equity Value at Exit ≤ Conversion Value. If the equity value upon exit is greater than the liquidation preference payout of USD60 million, but at or below the common share price of USD400, at which the 2× conversion right of preferred shares has a positive value, then preferred shareholders will receive the full liquidation preference payout of USD800 per share. Note that the common share price of USD 400 corresponds to an equity value upon exit of USD533,948,583 (or USD400 × 1,334,871 pre-money common shares outstanding) for the prior case.

Equity Value at Exit > Conversion Value. If the per unit equity value upon exit exceeds USD400, then the entire firm value upon exit is divided among pre-existing common shareholders and preferred shareholders (who have converted from one preferred to two common shares each). We may solve for the total number of shares outstanding post dilution as 1,484,871 (or 1,334,871 pre-money common shares + 2 × 75,000 preferred shares). For example, if the equity value upon exit is USD750 million, then the fully diluted share price is USD505.09 (= 750,000,000 ÷ 1,484,871) and the preferred shareholder payoff is USD1,010.18 (= 505.09 × 2).

2. Discuss the fractional ownership of Kumartest preferred shareholders.

Solution

Use of instruments such as convertible preferred shares was described earlier as financing with *contingent* future share issuance. As shown in Question 1, the fractional ownership of preferred shareholders therefore depends upon whether additional shares are issued upon conversion from preferred to common shares. We may solve for fully diluted share ownership issuance by solving for the number of new common shares upon conversion divided by post dilution shares outstanding. New common shares are 150,000 (or 75,000 original preferred shares × 2, the conversion ratio), and total shares outstanding post dilution is 1,484,871 (or 1,334,871 pre-money common shares + 150,000 new common shares). Solve for Ventmax's fractional ownership upon conversion as:

$$10.1\% = \frac{150,000}{1,484,871}.$$

3. Describe how Ventmax Partners might best seek to protect its interests as a preferred shareholder in the event of a future down round financing.

Solution

Antidilution or ratchet provisions may be negotiated by growth equity investors to reduce the conversion price of the new convertible preferred shares to the new, lower price at which down round shares are issued in a subsequent offering.

Use of the LBO Model to Establish Buyout Firm Value

Whether initiated as a take-private transaction, the purchase of a public company division, or the purchase of a private company, buyout targets have an established operating history and historical financial statements that support a distinct valuation approach. As buyout investors consider the relative attractiveness of one or more acquisition targets, they must establish a simplified means of evaluating not only the cash flow projections of the targeted company under the proposed business plan but also the capital structure composition and cost involved in generating a sufficient return for equity investors.

The so-called **LBO model** uses these parameters to establish the maximum price that can be paid to a seller while satisfying the targeted returns of financing providers. Exhibit 13 illustrates these inputs and outputs for the case with no interim distributions to shareholders.

Exhibit 13: LBO Method Inputs and Output

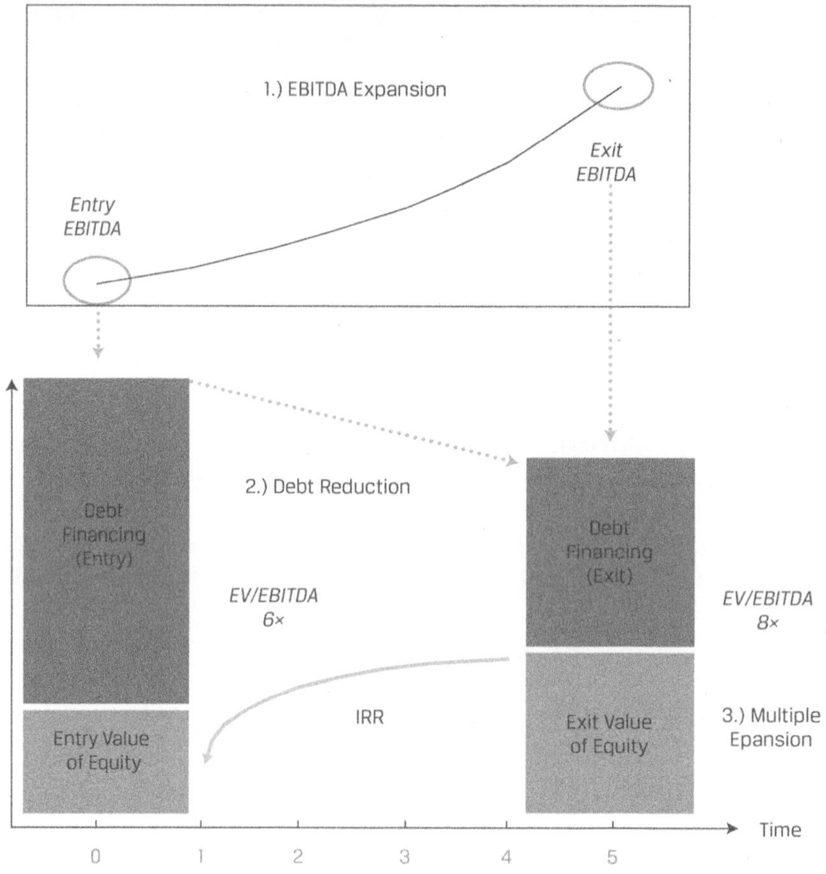

Unlike the simplified ROI approximation used under the VC method or the sole focus on profitable top-line growth financed by equity as in the growth equity method, the LBO model frequently uses an income- or relative value–based approach to establish a company's initial value, project the improved performance over the investment period, and consider expected changes in leverage until the time of exit. As Exhibit 13 showed, the value creation of an LBO transaction typically involves three elements, as follows.

> *EBITDA Expansion.* Like growth equity, increasing profitability over the investment period is an important element of value creation. In a buyout scenario, this is usually the result of increased efficiency or realizing synergies rather than simple expansion of scale or markets as in growth equity.
>
> *Debt Reduction.* While the initial high level of debt contributes to elevated expected equity returns because of the leverage effect, the high debt creates high risk for both debt and equity investors in the transaction. As the company generates improved cash flows consistent with the EBITDA expansion projections, this cash flow should be projected to reduce financial leverage over the investment period, reducing the risk to equity investors. Note that the use of debt in private market strategies will be covered in detail in a later reading.

Multiple Expansion. As the acquired company transforms from an undervalued target to a more profitable firm with declining leverage, its market multiple is expected to rise as future prospects improve. This form of value creation is typically validated using a method of comparables analysis of a peer group of comparable publicly traded companies.

We may use a simplified example to illustrate the effect of these three elements on the IRR of a proposed buyout transaction using the LBO method.

KNOWLEDGE CHECK

Saugerton Partners is considering the purchase of a controlling stake in Clevington Corporation to take the company private. Clevington is a publicly traded manufacturing firm currently trading at a 6× EV/EBITDA multiple.

Based upon thorough due diligence and a valuation analysis versus its publicly traded peers, a senior investment analyst at Saugerton draws the following conclusions about the Clevington buyout opportunity:

- A controlling stake in Clevington shares may be purchased at a share price close to the current market and financed with 75% debt and 25% equity;
- Under the proposed restructuring plan, Clevington can achieve 5% annual EBITDA growth and pay down a quarter of debt outstanding in five years, assuming no interim distributions to shareholders;
- Clevington may be sold in five years to a private or public buyer at an 8× EV/EBITDA multiple in line with industry peers.

1. Assuming current year Clevington EBITDA of USD100,000,000, calculate the purchase price and entry value of equity required for the buyout transaction.

Solution

Given Clevington's current EBITDA of USD100,000,000, an EV/EBITDA of 6× and no share price premium to the current market, the purchase price is USD600,000,000 (= 6 × 100,000,000) and the entry value of equity is USD150,000,000 (= 0.25 × 600,000,000), with the remaining USD450,000,000 as debt financing.

2. Calculate Clevington's enterprise value and equity value of exit in five years, under the assumption that outstanding debt will be valued at par.

Solution

We must first determine Clevington's expected EBITDA in five years' time. Given an assumed annual growth rate of 5%, we may calculate this to be USD127,628,156 (= 100,000,000 × $(1.05)^5$). Given the assumption of a future sale in five years at a price equal to 8× EV/EBITDA, we may estimate the future sale price to be USD1,021,025,250 (= 127,628,156 × 8).

This price is equal to *enterprise value*, or the value of the firm to *both* debt and equity holders. If we assume that Clevington has the ability to pay down debt by 25% in five years without significant penalty, the par value of Clevington's debt becomes USD337,500,000 (= 0.75 × 450,000,000). Solve for the exit value of equity of USD683,525,250 by subtracting remaining debt from enterprise value (= 1,021,025,250 − 337,500,000).

3. Discuss whether Saugerton can reach its targeted 30% IRR on the proposed Clevington transaction based upon the analyst's calculations, under the assumption that shareholders receive no distributions prior to exit. Assume that no interim cash flows are made to equity holders over the period.

Solution

Given the USD150,000,000 entry value of equity from Question 1 and the estimated exit value of equity of USD683,525,250 from Question 2, we may use Equation 2 to calculate the ROI:

$$\text{ROI} = 4.56\times = \frac{\text{USD683,525,250}}{\text{USD150 million}}.$$

Convert ROI to an equivalent IRR using Equation 4:

$$\text{ROI} = (1 + \text{IRR})^n;$$

$$4.56\times = (1+\text{IRR})^5;\ \text{IRR} = 35.44\%.$$

The Clevington opportunity therefore exceeds the expected 30% IRR hurdle.

Note that while the determination of LBO model inputs is far more complex due to the target company's mature stage in the life cycle, the use of financial statement analysis to determine the entry and exit value of equity as well as the complicating factor of changes in financial leverage, all three forms of private equity investments take a similar approach in determining the internal rate of return to investors.

We now return to the earlier Maudville Corporation case study to illustrate the valuation of buyout equity in greater detail. Earlier in the curriculum, three-statement model forecasts were used to value public equity and debt, and we take a similar approach below to create an income statement and balance sheet forecast for Maudville. Consistent with the focus on EBITDA expansion, debt reduction, and multiple expansion as outlined earlier, income statement and balance sheet forecasts are used to show the expected impact of Bardstown's restructuring plan as well as cash flow available from increases in expected profit due to margin expansion and use of cash to reduce Maudville's debt burden over the investment horizon. The financing structure includes multiple debt tranches and common and preferred shares; it also incorporates the potential dilution from stock options used to incentivize new management.

CASE STUDY

Maudville Corporation Valuation

Maudville Corporation is a mature US chemical company that generated nearly USD5 billion in revenues and USD1 billion in EBITDA in its most recent fiscal year. Bardstown Partners, a private equity firm specializing in buyout equity, is considering a go-private transaction at a purchase price of USD5 billion, of which Bardstown would contribute 20% as common equity, with 5% sourced from an LP as convertible preferred shares and 75% in three debt tranches. Bardstown targets a 35% IRR on buyout deals over five years, and the purchase is assumed to occur at the end of Maudville's current fiscal year.

Bardstown's managing partner has asked you, as an experienced analyst, to build a three-statement financial model for a five-year time horizon. Starting from Year 0 of Maudville's income statement, you are asked to assume a 5% annual sales growth rate. The managing partner believes that improved cost efficiencies can reduce COGS as a percentage of sales by one percentage point per year, from the current 55% to 50% of sales in Year 5. Additionally, the managing partner expects to achieve one percentage point annual SGA reductions as a percentage of sales (currently 25%) starting in Year 3 to 22% in Year 5.

Corporate taxes are assumed to be 25% of net income. The resulting five-year income statement forecast is shown below. Readers should note that the calculations shown in the case study are conducted in a spreadsheet and numbers presented throughout reflect rounding.

Income Statement (USD million)	Year 0	Year 1	Year 2	Year 3	Year 4	Year 5
Sales	4,988	5,237	5,499	5,774	6,062	6,365
COGS	–2,743	–2,828	–2,914	–3,002	–3,092	–3,183
SGA	–1,247	–1,309	–1,375	–1,386	–1,394	–1,400
EBITDA	**998**	**1,100**	**1,210**	**1,386**	**1,576**	**1,782**
Depreciation	–401	–421	–443	–465	–488	–512
Net interest	–17	–269	–262	–250	–231	–201
Profit before tax	**579**	**409**	505	671	857	1,069
Taxes	–145	–102	–126	–168	–214	–267
Net income	**434**	307	379	503	643	802
Dividends	–87	–25	–25	–25	–25	–25

The managing partner states that the cost efficiency assumptions are expected to improve Maudville's cash flow, which will be used to repay a portion of debt taken on at the time of the buyout transaction. Debt consists of three tranches, as follows.

Senior Debt. USD2.65 billion in seven-year senior secured debt at a 6.50% annual interest rate that may be prepaid at par starting in one year.

Junior Debt. USD600 million in seven-year junior subordinated debt at an 8.00% annual interest rate that amortizes in four equal installments, starting in Year 4.

Mezzanine Debt. USD500 million in ten-year mezzanine debt at a 12.2% annual interest rate that is fully repaid at maturity.

As the senior secured tranche has the greatest repayment flexibility, the managing partner asks you to prioritize pay down of this tranche until junior debt amortization begins in Year 4. Based on these instructions, you prepare the following balance sheet forecast for Maudville. Readers should note that the sales growth rate mentioned earlier is also assumed for growth in current and net fixed assets as well as for current liabilities.

Balance Sheet (USD million)	Year 0	Year 1	Year 2	Year 3	Year 4	Year 5
Panel A: Assets						
Cash	400	400	400	400	400	400
Current assets	599	628	660	693	727	764
Net fixed assets	3,242	3,404	3,574	3,753	3,941	4,138
Goodwill	1,258	1,258	1,258	1,258	1,258	1,258
Total assets	**5,499**	**5,691**	**5,892**	**6,104**	**6,326**	**6,560**
Panel B: Liabilities and Equity						
Current liabilities	499	524	550	577	606	637
Debt	3,750	3,635	3,457	3,163	2,738	2,165
Stock	1,250	1,250	1,250	1,250	1,250	1,250

Balance Sheet (USD million)	Year 0	Year 1	Year 2	Year 3	Year 4	Year 5
Retained earnings	0	282	636	1,114	1,732	2,509
Total liabilities and equity	**5,499**	**5,691**	**5,892**	**6,104**	**6,326**	**6,560**

The managing partner reminds you that the equity of USD1,250 million consists of not only the USD1 billion Bardstown common stock contribution (or 100 million shares at USD10 per share) but also the LP convertible preferred stock purchase of USD250 million (2,500,000 shares at USD100 per share). While Bardstown plans to forego dividends on common shares, convertible preferred share terms are as follows:

Preferred share dividend: 10% (USD10 per share);

Liquidation preference payout: 2.5× upon exit in five years;

Conversion ratio: 2× upon exit in five years.

Finally, as a management incentive, Bardstown introduces a plan to grant Maudville stock options to the new senior management team. These options grant managers the right to buy 5 million Maudville common shares at a strike price of USD10 per share at the end of the five-year investment horizon.

1. Calculate exit value of equity assuming 6× EV/EBITDA multiple and discuss whether equity value improvement meets Bardstown's required return goals. Assume outstanding debt may be repaid at its par value and ignore any potential dilution and exit payoff effects from convertible preferred or management options.

Solution

Based upon the income statement forecast, we see that Maudville's expected EBITDA in five years' time is equal to USD1,782 million. Given the assumption of a future sale in five years at a price equal to 6× EV/EBITDA, we may estimate the future sale price to be USD10,694,000,000 (= 1,728 million × 6).

Recall that this is the *enterprise value*, from which we must subtract the forecasted carrying value of debt to arrive at the expected firm value. Given the debt paydown forecast from USD3,750 million to USD2,165 million in Year 5, solve for the exit value of equity of USD8,529 million by subtracting remaining debt from enterprise value (= USD10,694 million – USD2,165 million).

The forecasted equity value improvement from the initial USD1,250 million (note that we include the convertible preferred shares in equity here as a simplifying assumption) to USD8,529 million easily meets Bardstown's required return goals of 35% IRR, assuming no interim dividend payments. Use Equation 3 to calculate the ROI:

$$\text{ROI} = 6.82\times = \frac{8,529}{1,250}.$$

Convert ROI to an equivalent IRR using Equation 4:

$$\text{ROI} = (1 + \text{IRR})^n;$$

$$6.82\times = (1+\text{IRR})^5;\ \text{IRR} = 46.8\%.$$

2. Discuss factors contributing to forecasted equity returns in the Maudville buyout transaction.

Solution

The 46.8% equity return forecasted from this model is an outcome of three primary factors assumed as part of the model. First, Maudville is expected to realize significant EBITDA margin expansion. Given the decline in assumed COGS and SGA expenses as percentages of sales, EBITDA margin increases from 20% (=100% – 55% – 25%) to 28% (=100% – 50% – 22%) in five years. Second, the improvement in EBITDA is further magnified in computing exit value by a higher assumed exit multiple of 6×, compared to Bardstown's 5× EV/EBITDA entry multiple (= 5,000 ÷ 998) calculated from the purchase price divided by Year 0 EBITDA. Finally, debt reduction from USD3,750 million to USD2,165 million over five years allows for a greater proportion of enterprise value to flow to equity holders.

3. Calculate the forecasted payoff to the convertible preferred shareholders at exit under the income statement and exit value assumptions presented earlier.

Solution

The forecasted payoff to convertible preferred shareholders upon exit is USD625 million, and the solution process is described below. Specifically, we use the critical points shown earlier in Exhibit 6 to analyze the payoff to the convertible preferred shares.

The maximum firm value at which the liquidation preference amount applies in this situation is equal to USD625 million (= USD250 million × 2.5× liquidation preference ratio), or the total capital from convertible preferred shareholders (i.e., USD250 million) multiplied by the liquidation preference payout. Note that the estimated firm value computed earlier is well above this threshold of USD625 million.

If the equity share price exceeds USD125 (= USD625 million ÷ (2 × 2.5 million shares)), then convertible preferred shareholders will choose to exercise their conversion option. The USD125 equity share price corresponds to the optimal conversion point from Exhibit 6. The corresponding firm value at the optimal conversion point is USD13,125 million (= 100 million × USD125 + USD625 million). Maudville's equity exit value under Bardstown's restructuring plan is estimated to be USD8,529 million, which lies between the USD625 million liquidation value of convertible preferred shares and the USD13,125 million optimal conversion point. Therefore, the forecasted payoff to convertible preferred shareholders upon exit is USD625 million.

4. Calculate Bardstown Partners' fractional ownership of Bardstown incorporating the dilution effects of both the convertible preferred stock and the management options.

Solution

Equity dilution of Bardstown's common shares may result from the possible conversion of convertible preferred shares and exercise of management options. Consider the following modified version of Equation 8, which shows Bardstown's fractional ownership under full dilution:

$$\text{Fractional Ownership} = \frac{\text{Common Shares}}{\text{Common} + \text{Newly Issued to Preferred} + \text{Option Exercise}}.$$

$$90.91\% = \frac{100,000,000}{100,000,000 + 5,000,000 + 5,000,000}.$$

The 2× conversion ratio for convertible preferred shares implies the potential issuance of 5 million shares (= 2.5 × 2) upon conversion, while management options may be exercised into 5 million shares of common stock.

While the Maudville case study shows the basic structure of a buyout equity analysis, investors usually assess potential deals under varying assumptions of potential revenue growth, cost improvements, paydown of debt, and margin expansion to identify the key risks affecting an investment's exit value. Scenario analyses often include sensitivity tables showing investment return given deviations from key base case assumptions. In addition, specific downside scenarios that may result in lower returns or the loss of capital may be worth considering in detail as shown below.

CASE STUDY

Maudville Corporation Valuation: A Downside Scenario

In an earlier case study, Bardstown Partners estimated a 47% IRR on a buyout equity investment in Maudville Corporation, a mature US chemical company. In addition to base case results and underlying assumptions, Bardstown's investment committee has requested a downside scenario analysis given concerns that a sharp economic downturn next year will significantly reduce demand for Maudville's products over the five-year investment period. In addition to lower revenue, senior management believes that significant profit margin pressures would lead to negative net income and EBITDA of approximately half of recent levels. While the investment committee believes that such a scenario has a low probability, they would like to understand its impact on Bardstown's estimated equity return. Given your familiarity with the Maudville base case forecast, the managing director asks you to create a forecast consistent with the recession scenario raised by the investment committee. After some changes to the model, you produce the following summary income statement and balance sheet five-year forecasts.

Income Statement (USD million)	Year 0	Year 1	Year 2	Year 3	Year 4	Year 5
Sales	4,988	4,589	4,359	4,272	4,315	4,444
COGS	(2,743)	(2,753)	(2,703)	(2,563)	(2,589)	(2,666)
SGA	(1,247)	(1,285)	(1,264)	-1153	-1165	(1,200)
EBITDA	998	551	392	555	561	578
Depreciation	(401)	(421)	(388)	(368)	(361)	(365)
Net interest	(17)	(269)	(260)	(260)	(260)	(248)
Profit before tax	579	(140)	(256)	(73)	(60)	(35)
Taxes	(145)	35	64	18	15	9
Net income	434	(105)	(192)	(55)	(45)	(26)
Dividends	(87)	(25)	(25)	(25)	(25)	(25)

Balance Sheet (USD million)	Year 0	Year 1	Year 2	Year 3	Year 4	Year 5
Panel A: Assets						
Cash	400	400	400	400	400	400
Current assets	599	551	523	513	518	533
Net fixed assets	3,242	2,983	2,833	2,777	2,804	2,889
Goodwill	1,258	1,258	1,258	1,258	1,258	1,258
Total assets	5,499	5,192	5,015	4,948	4,981	5,080
Panel B: Liabilities and Equity						
Current liabilities	499	459	436	427	431	444
Debt	3,750	3,613	3,613	3,613	3,463	3,313
Stock	1,250	1,250	1,313	1,335	1,584	1,872
Retained earnings	0	(130)	(347)	(427)	(497)	(549)
Total liabilities and equity	5,499	5,192	5,015	4,948	4,981	5,080

The managing director asks for a brief review of the key assumptions underlying the forecast. You assume 8% and 5% revenue declines during the first and second years of the forecast, consistent with a sharp economic contraction. Maudville's revenue ends the forecast horizon at a level approximately USD540 million below that of the base year. As revenues fall, you assume that Maudville's operations would generate close to current expense levels for COGS and SGA expenses. As a result, Maudville's EBITDA margin declines from 20% in the base year to a low of 9% in the second year of the forecast, before recovering to 13% in the final three years of the investment period. The profitability decline severely diminishes Maudville's ability to reduce its debt load.

Under these adverse economic conditions, you suggest that an EV/EBITDA exit multiple of 6× is unrealistic, assuming instead that no multiple expansion occurs over the five-year horizon and the EV/EBITDA exit multiple remains 5×. Based on a final year EBITDA forecast of USD578 million, the exit value of Maudville's enterprise value is USD2,889 million. As this amount is exceeded by Maudville's forecasted debt outstanding at the end of Year 5, it implies that the firm would be insolvent by the end of the forecast period and Bardstown's equity investment would therefore have a value of zero.

While this case ignores the possibility of asset sales, debt restructuring, or other measures taken in the case of financial distress, which are addressed in a later reading, it illustrates both the importance of macroeconomic conditions as well as their impact on key drivers of potential value creation in buyout equity strategies.

As both the case studies and real-world examples suggest, private equity strategies across venture capital, growth equity, and buyout situations often play a critical role outside of the public capital markets for startups launching a business, young firms pursuing rapid growth, or mature companies reaching their potential following a period of transformation.

Although the general valuation principles of these strategies across the investment life cycle have similarities, venture capital investments typically require more specific industry and technical knowledge given the initial importance of non-financial milestones associated with success. Growth equity often requires financial analysis to demonstrate the feasibility of EBITDA growth, which is usually financed with equity, while buyout equity transactions involve more detailed financial modeling and analysis given both the maturity of the companies involved and the combination of debt and equity more commonly used in these transactions. In what follows, we will consider the relative return and risk of all three forms of private equity as well as their strategic role in an investment portfolio.

QUESTION SET

1. Which of the following statements most correctly describes the estimation of exit value in the VC method of valuation?

   A. Exit value is estimated by using a single estimate of revenue potential and a single estimate of price-to-sales.

   B. Exit value is estimated in the context of a range of revenue potential and price-to-sales.

   C. Exit value is estimated by using a single estimate of forecasted earnings and a single estimate of price-to-earnings.

   Solution

   Response B is the most correct description of exit value estimation in the VC method. Because of high uncertainty of future revenue potential of a startup, a range of revenue estimates is desirable. Additionally, a range of price-to-sales also reflects the high degree of future uncertainty associated with the valuation environment of startups. Response A is less correct as this statement does not account for the high uncertainty of the startup environment. Response C is less correct as startups are less likely to have positive and stable earnings necessary to apply a price-to-earnings multiple.

2. Calculate the missing figures (indicated by "?") in the Series A Financing column to complete the capitalization table using the following information and the simple, incomplete capitalization table shown below.

   Scenario: A startup founder, Heinz Fernandez, invests USD450,000 into Nuca Group as its sole equity owner, and receives 90,000 shares in the startup. One year later, Fernandez attracts USD2,000,000 in new equity capital from an outside investor in Series A financing in exchange for a 10% ownership stake in Nuca Group.

Capitalization Table

Panel A: Shares and Fractional Ownership

Investor	Seed Shares	Seed FO %	Series A shares	Series A FO %
Outside investor			?	10%
Founder	90,000	100%	90,000	90%
Totals	90,000	100%	?	100%

Panel B: Valuation across Financing Series

	Seed Financing	Series A Financing
Share price (USD)	5.00	?
Pre-money valuation (USD)	0	?

Panel B: Valuation across Financing Series		
	Seed Financing	**Series A Financing**
New equity (USD)	450,000	2,000,000
Post-money valuation (USD)	450,000	?

Solution

The missing figures may be solved for, sequentially, as follows.

First, use the 10% equity stake and the USD2 million investment to calculate post-money valuation.

Post-money valuation: USD20,000,000 (= 2,000,000 ÷ 0.10)

Second, calculate pre-money valuation taking the post-money valuation minus the new equity investment amount of USD2 million.

Pre-money valuation: USD18,000,000 (= 20,000,000 − 2,000,000)

At any point in the process, we can use the 10% equity stake and the founder's shares of 90,000 to calculate the outside investor's number of shares and the total shares by solving for x below.

$10\% = x \div (90{,}000 + x)$

Outside investor number of shares = 10,000

Total shares =100,000 (= 90,000 + 10,000)

Finally, share price can be calculated by dividing pre-money valuation by the number of shares from the founder round.

Share price: USD200 (= 18,000,000 ÷ 90,000)

Panel A: Shares and Fractional Ownership				
Investor	**Seed Shares**	**Seed FO %**	**Series A shares**	**Series A FO %**
Outside investor			10,000	10%
Founder	90,000	100%	90,000	90%
Totals	90,000	100%	100,000	100%

Panel B: Valuation across Financing Series		
	Seed Financing	**Series A Financing**
Share Price (USD)	5.00	200.00
Pre-money valuation (USD)	0	18,000,000
New equity (USD)	450,000	2,000,000
Post-money valuation (USD)	450,000	20,000,000

3. Assuming that the liquidation preference multiple and conversion ratios are equal, convertible preferred shareholders are most likely to convert their shares if:

   A. aggregate common equity value at exit is greater than preferred stock price per share multiplied by the number of common shares outstanding post dilution.

   B. aggregate common equity value at exit is greater than common stock price per share multiplied by the number of common shares outstanding before dilution.

   C. aggregate common equity value at exit is greater than preferred stock price per share multiplied by the number of common shares outstanding before dilution.

   Solution

   C is the correct response. Using the equation below, total liquidation preference value equals the liquidation preference multiple times the number of preferred shares times the preferred stock price.

   $$\text{Optimal Conversion Point} = \frac{\text{Total Liquidation Preference Value}}{\text{Conversion Ratio} \times \text{Number of Preferred Shares}}$$

   If the liquidation preference multiple and conversion ratios are equal, then the above equation simplifies to be equal to the preferred stock price. The preferred stock price is fixed based on the issuance price while the equity value is based on a variable stock price. Equity value exceeds the term in response C if the common stock price exceeds the fixed preferred stock price, and at this point, convertible preferred stockholders will convert their preferred shares to common shares. Response A is incorrect because the equity value reflects the value of common shares before dilution. Response B is incorrect because equity value is always equal to this term.

4. Saugerton Partners, a private equity firm, considers a take-private transaction with the following assumptions:

   - 6× current EV/EBITDA multiple
   - Deal financed with 25% equity and 75% debt
   - 5% annual EBITDA growth
   - 25% of the debt is paid off during the investment horizon
   - 8× EV/EBITDA multiple at exit
   - 35.44% IRR > 30% required return

   Which one of the following factors important to LBO success seem least important in this example?

   A. Margin expansion

   B. Improved asset efficiencies

   C. Debt repayment

   Solution

   B is the most likely correct response. Both responses A and C are very clearly outlined in the assumptions. Assumed EV/EBITDA multiples increase from 6× to 8× between the deal closing and the exit date, so margin expansion is very clear. Twenty-five percent of debt is expected to be repaid over the investment horizon, so this aspect of equity value improvement is also clearly assumed. The EBITDA growth rate is relatively slow, so may reflect very modest margin expansion if sales growth rates are below 5%. Nevertheless, improvements in cost efficiencies are not clear as a driver to the high IRR of the example.

PRIVATE EQUITY RISK AND RETURN

6

☐ discuss the risk and return among private equity investments as well as versus other investments as part of a strategic asset allocation

Unlike some other private asset classes such as unlisted infrastructure projects, private equity investors have public equity market indexes at their disposal to gauge the relative risk and return of these investments. The role of private equity in a strategic asset allocation is to achieve high risk-adjusted returns that provide some degree of diversification benefits relative to public equity holdings due to the more specific investment focus of venture capital, growth equity, and buyout equity strategies. Investors also seek diversification within private equity strategies by allocating investments across different vintage years and various investment managers.

The diversification benefits of private equity versus public equity occur because private equity investments provide exposure to specialized areas of the economy. Early-stage VC targets are in new industries or have disruptive business models with an expected rapid growth trajectory often driven more by technological change rather than macroeconomic conditions. Similarly, growth equity investors seek above-trend profitable expansion by gaining market share or new markets, while buyout equity uses a controlling stake to drive a firm's relative performance improvement versus peers.

However, aggregate private equity returns are unlikely to diverge too far from those of public equity. Private equity returns can diverge from public markets under normal market conditions, particularly if the entry involves a take-private transaction and they exit an IPO. That said, in the case of a public market downturn, private equity markets face similar effects of adverse market conditions, which tends to increase correlation between public and private markets. For example, greater risk aversion among investors generally leads to a reduction in VC activity and value of startups, while higher interest rates dampen buyout activity given the higher cost of financial leverage.

High and less correlated expected returns of private equity investments across VC, growth, and buyout equity must be sufficient to offset the higher risks and higher costs of these investments, which include the following.

Liquidity Risk. Long investment periods of up to 10 years with limited sale opportunities versus public markets give rise to liquidity risk. While general partners and other investors increasingly offer secondaries for sale or purchase, the bid-offer spread on such transactions lacks the transparency of exchange-traded instruments and may widen substantially under adverse public market conditions.

Valuation Risk. Private market valuations for partnerships and co-investments are affected by the chosen methodology, inputs, and judgement of a general partner rather than an independent third party or as observed in public market prices. For example, private valuations often use income-based discounted cash flow (DCF) analysis based on risk free rates, public credit spreads, public market multiples, and recent public transactions. When interest rates rise or market multiples fall, private funds may avoid overreacting to adverse public market changes by limiting markdowns, thus reducing apparent correlation to public markets. Valuation risk arises not only due to this potential bias but also the delayed timing of private market valuations received by investors. Public market investors typically receive same-day valuations based upon net asset value (NAV) at the end of each trading day, whereas private equity investors commonly receive valuations with a quarterly time lag. This delays an investor's ability to weigh tactical rebalancing and other decisions versus public market allocations.

Agency Risk. While private equity ownership is a means of addressing the principal-agent issue between company managers and shareholders as described earlier, asymmetric information between a general partner and limited partners also gives rise to a potential misalignment of interests. Performance and other incentive-based fee structures for GPs and share-based compensation for private company managers are potential mitigants to this risk. However, private firms lack the corporate transparency of publicly traded firms, and investors are often unable to exercise voting rights similar to public company investments. Also, in earlier-stage deals under management control, owners may continue to enjoy private benefits of majority ownership versus minority investors. For example, private equity investors may have limited information on whether portfolio company investments meet similar environmental, social, and governance (ESG) criteria to their public company equity investments as described below.

PRIVATE EQUITY GOVERNANCE CONSIDERATIONS FOR PUBLIC INVESTORS

Public sector investors such as public pension funds are not only focused on maximizing risk-adjusted returns and generating a surplus for beneficiaries and stakeholders but are also keenly focused on environmental, social, and governance issues as they cast votes for publicly held shares and interact with investment managers. For example, public pension plans are significantly more likely to support ESG proposals as compared to general shareholders, according to a 2022 Morningstar report.

However, investing in private equity through a fund structure introduces an additional layer between these investors and the companies in which they invest. Specifically, private market investors have less influence and often lack the ability to vote on important ESG issues related to problems of investor concern such as climate change, pay equity, and board gender diversity, as well as a wide array of other ESG-related topics. Pension plans may lack the ability to sufficiently ensure that their private equity investments are consistent with mandates established by the plans. To mitigate this concern, in some cases large public pension plans implement policies in an effort to ensure that their specific goals are achieved through private equity investing.

As one example, CalPERS has a policy restricting investment in private equity funds holding portfolio companies connected to the outsourcing of US public sector jobs. As the largest public pension plan in the US, CalPERS likely has greater influence over private equity fund managers than many other plans to encourage compliance, but with investments in over 300 different private equity funds, the ongoing monitoring of such a policy may impose significant additional costs on both the plan and its managers.

Extraordinary Operating and Business Risks. The investment focus of venture capital, growth equity, and buyout situations may involve exceptional operating and business risks, which may result in a substantial loss of capital. Unrealized assumptions in the ex-ante financial analysis may have large impacts on realized returns.

Interest Rate and Leverage Risk. In the case of buyout equity where significant leverage is used, rising interest rates and credit spreads increase the cost of debt and potentially impair the ability to realize financing on attractive terms.

Macroeconomic and Public Market Risks. Private equity investments face unique risks related to the entry and exit value of equity. For example, in a strong market environment, competition for undervalued assets may be high and drive up the cost of investments, while in an adverse market scenario, depressed market multiples may reduce the potential return on investment for a planned exit.

Dilution Risk. As highlighted in earlier examples, the potential for dilution is also a consideration for investors, whether that includes later-stage series financing for early-stage companies or the dilution arising from share-based compensation to company managers in the case of buyout equity.

As described earlier in the curriculum, the costs and fees associated with private equity investments are substantially higher than those of public markets and must be factored into expected investor returns. In addition to higher management fees and performance-based compensation, these include the following.

Transaction Fees. Fees arising from extensive due diligence, bank financing costs, legal fees for arranging an acquisition, and the direct or indirect costs of arranging the sale of an investee company.

Fund Setup Costs. These mainly involve the legal costs of setting up an investment vehicle and marketing roadshows during fundraising, which are typically amortized over the life of the investment vehicle.

Administrative Costs. Custodian, accounting, and transfer-agent costs are generally charged as additional annual fixed fees, often as a fraction of the investment vehicle's NAV.

Investors seek to manage private equity risks via both thorough due diligence of fund managers for co-investment and limited partnership investments as well as diversification by geography, industry, vintage year, and investment strategy. Given the higher costs of these investments, investors often adjust expected return targets as shown in the following example.

CASE STUDY

Northern States Private Equity Investment Strategy

Northern States Pension Plan is a large US-based public pension plan with a long history of allocating to private equity as an asset class. The plan has an allocation target range of 10%–20% for private equity investment. Its current allocation to private equity investments is 19.3%. Northern States has established the following investment policy for its investments in private equity funds.

Private Equity Investments—Strategic Objectives:

- Achieve significant outperformance relative to a broad equity benchmark over a long (i.e., 10 year) time horizon
- Diversify among fund types and strategies
- Diversify across development stages, investment size, industry sectors, geographies, and vintage years
- Engage as a responsible investor to promote sound environmental practices
- Leverage manufacturing industry experience by strategically co-investing in this industry sector

Private Equity Performance Target:

The Plan has a performance target of exceeding a return on a broad equity benchmark plus 2.5% per annum net of fees.

Within the private equity asset class, Northern States has established the following policy ranges for the different categories:

- Venture capital: 30%–50%
- Growth equity: 20%–30%
- Buyout equity: 25%–45%

Recent declines in the valuation of venture capital investments have caused the value of Northern States' venture investment to decline, and its allocation to this category is currently at 32%. Both growth equity and buyout equity have shown stronger performance and the allocations are at 28% and 40%, respectively. The main economic drivers causing recent performance in private equity include (1) a concentration of venture capital money into startups focused on artificial intelligence applications at the expense of other types of industries that typically rely on venture funding and (2) a renewed emphasis on investments generating improved cash flow. The consensus among Northern States' senior management is a continuation of these two trends for at least the next year.

Brianna Jenkins, Head of Alternative Investments at Northern States, has asked you, as an analyst in her team, to prepare a memo related to a possible co-investment in Clevington Corporation alongside Saugerton Partners equity for the Investment Committee. Details of the potential Clevington LBO are shown below:

- Clevington Corporation is a manufacturing company.
- A controlling stake in Clevington shares may be purchased at a share price consistent with a 6× EV/EBITDA multiple and financed with 75% debt and 25% equity;
- Under the proposed restructuring plan, Clevington can achieve 5% annual EBITDA growth and pay down a quarter of debt outstanding in five years;
- Clevington may be sold in five years to a private or public buyer at an 8× EV/EBITDA multiple in line with industry peers.
- The expected IRR to equity investors of Clevington is 35.4%.
- The expected IRR of the public equity benchmark is 30.0% over the expected investment period.

1. Discuss two challenges faced by Northern States with respect to rebalancing its private equity portfolio in preparation for the next year.

   Solution

   One challenge relates to Northern States' overall allocation to private equity as it is currently at 19.3%, near the top of the allowable range of 10%–20%. While still within the allowable range, any further upward adjustments in private equity valuations may cause its allocation to go above the upper bound of its allocation range. Given that private equity investments are not liquid, Northern States may need to sell one or more of its investments using a secondary market transaction with wide bid-ask spreads.

   A second challenge relates to its allocation to venture capital, with 32% of its overall private equity investment being at the low end of its allowable range of 30%–50%. While being close to underweight may allow for a buying opportunity in venture capital, the need to potentially sell private equity investments in the other subclasses once again may require the use of a secondary market transaction.

   A related challenge in the venture capital space relates to lack of diversification by focusing new investments in artificial intelligence–related ventures at potentially inflated valuations versus allocating to underfunded VC opportunities in other venture-eligible industries. One other valuation-related challenge is whether Northern States should look to liquidate (or not reinvest distributions) in the cash flow generating areas of growth equity and buyout equity when those areas are forecast to perform well.

2. Evaluate a possible equity investment by Northern States into the Clevington Corporation take-private opportunity with respect to the pension fund's strategic objectives, performance target and allocation ranges.

   Solution

   The potential Clevington investment is consistent with the final bullet point of Northern States' strategic objectives. Specifically, Clevington operates in a line of business in which Northern States has expertise and they may be able to co-invest (thus avoiding the fees associated with investing through a private equity fund).

   The expected IRR of the Clevington equity investment is approximately 35%, and this appears consistent with the performance target of outperforming the broad equity benchmark by 2.5%.

   Finally, the Northern States' allocation to buyout equity is currently at 40% of its private equity portfolio. This allocation is at the higher end of its allowable range of 25%–45%. If the proposed investment size is sufficiently small in the scope of its overall private equity portfolio, the Clevington investment may be consistent with Northern States' allocation targets.

QUESTION SET

1. Which of the following statements about private equity investment compared to other private market investments, such as private infrastructure, is most correct?

   A. Private equity investment differs from other private market investments in that performance may often be benchmarked against a public market index.

   B. Private equity investments offer higher risk-adjusted returns with low correlations to other asset classes.

   C. Private equity investments are less prone to economic conditions affecting other private market investments.

   Solution

   A is the most correct response. As opposed to private market investments such as real estate or infrastructure, private equity returns can reasonably be compared against a public equity benchmark. Response B is not correct because this statement is likely true for multiple private market asset classes. Response C is not correct as private equity is affected by economic conditions, especially adverse conditions that broadly impact both public and private markets.

2. Secondaries offered by general partners or other private equity investors address which of the following risk factors?

   A. Valuation risk

   B. Macroeconomic risk

   C. Liquidity risk

   Solution

   C is the correct response. Investments in private equity have very long holding periods, sometimes as long as ten years. The market for secondaries provides opportunities for investors to liquidate their holdings although secondaries likely are offered at high bid-ask spreads. Response A is incorrect as valuation risks are associated with any aspect surrounding how a private equity investment is valued. Response B is incorrect because macroeconomic risk (also known as public market risk) relates to the economic environment affecting entry and exit multiples of private equity transactions.

3. Which of the following risk management objectives is least likely to be implementable for an investor allocating 100% of funds to venture capital?

   A. Diversification across geographic regions

   B. Diversification across industries

   C. Diversification across vintage years

   Solution

   B is the correct response. Venture capital investment is focused on a small set of emerging industries characterized by the potential for very high growth. As a result, industry diversification is not likely if investing only in venture capital. Responses A and C are not correct as startup opportunities are available for investment in many parts of the world and investment in venture capital can be diversified across time (i.e., investing in funds with different vintage years).

PRACTICE PROBLEMS

The following information relates to questions 1-4

Brianna Jenkins, Head of Alternative Investments at Northern States Pension Plan, has recently hired a new analyst, Cheng Zhu, to assist on its private equity allocations within its overall alternatives portfolio. Zhu has worked as a buy-side analyst in public equities for the last three years, and Jenkins hopes to find out what her new hire knows about private equity markets.

Jenkins begins by discussing the Northern States investment approach to identifying quality fund managers in the private equity market. Jenkins makes the following two statements.

Statement 1	"Northern States prefers fund managers that rely less on assumptions about multiple expansion in identifying good portfolio companies."
Statement 2	"Northern States prefers fund managers that apply more realistic assumptions about the potential for paying off the debt of a portfolio company over the investment horizon."

Zhu asks Jenkins about the ability of Northern States to liquidate portions of its private equity portfolio following periods of strong performance. Specifically, Zhu is curious as to what degree Northern States is able to liquidate a holding in an illiquid private equity fund.

Zhu discusses the increasing importance of voting rights in public equity markets and asks Jenkins how governance issues work when investing in private equity markets. In response to Zhu's question, Jenkins makes the following statements.

Statement 3	"Northern States participates as a co-investor in private equity investments in industries in which it believes it has strong experience."
Statement 4	"Northern States has included investment policy mandates associated with board diversity that restrict investment in private equity funds that own portfolio companies which are not compliant with Northern States' policy on board diversity."

1. Which of the following risks associated with private equity investing is most consistent with Statement 1 made by Jenkins?

   A. Liquidity risk

   B. Valuation risk

   C. Agency risk

2. Which of the following private equity strategies is most likely being discussed in Statement 2 made by Jenkins?

   A. Venture capital

   B. Growth equity

C. Buyout equity

3. Which of the following poses the least direct liquidity risk associated with owning a position in a private equity fund?

   A. A secondary market for private equity holdings created by a general partner

   B. The long holding period required by the private equity fund

   C. Adverse conditions in public markets

4. Discuss how Statements 3 and 4 address Northern States' response to agency risks associated with private equity investment.

The following information relates to questions 5-9

Suzette Moreau is a managing director of Estragon SA, a French private equity firm focused on venture capital investment. Moreau is working on strategies to improve the firm's overall rate of return (of approximately 30%) on its venture portfolio of 20 companies. The fund's current failure rate is 75% and its portfolio of successful investments earns 15× capital, on average, over a five-year investment horizon. Moreau believes that Estragon can improve its failure rate sufficiently without a material decline in its investment returns on its portfolio of successful investments.

Moreau meets with a new analyst beginning work on Estragon's venture capital portfolio. Moreau discusses some of the different financing mechanisms used in private equity and introduces convertible preferred shares. She shows the analyst Exhibit 1.

Exhibit 1

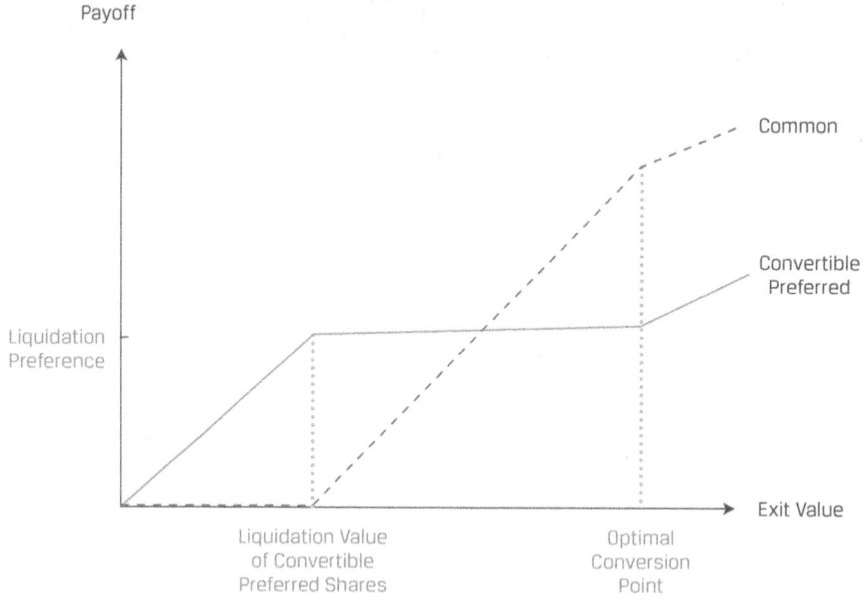

Moreau provides her new analyst with the following scenario to assess: Estragon is considering investing EUR2.5 million in Series A financing of a startup venture having seed capital already invested of EUR1 million. Estragon's estimated exit value of the startup's equity in five years is EUR150 million, and its target ROI is 8×.

Moreau continues her example as follows: Estragon makes its Series A financing investment of EUR2.5 million in a startup venture with a post-money valuation at the time of financing of EUR18.75 million. One year later, the startup seeks another EUR5 million in Series B financing and Estragon is willing to contribute an additional EUR2.5 million. The updated post-money valuation is EUR50 million.

As a final question, the new analyst asks Moreau about Estragon's participation in growth equity deals in the private equity market. Moreau responds that the firm will occasionally consider investing in growth equity, but only on a limited basis because the differences in analyzing venture capital and growth equity are sufficiently significant enough that Estragon believes that its expertise is better focused in the venture capital portion of the private equity market.

5. Demonstrate whether Estragon can reasonably improve its failure rate to increase its overall rate of return to 35%.

6. Discuss the economic reason for why the slope of the payoff to common shares declines at points greater than the conversion price on the x-axis of the chart.

7. Which of the following is closest to Estragon's expected fractional ownership of the startup if it makes this projected investment in the Series A financing?

   A. 13.3%

   B. 15.4%

   C. 71.4%

8. Which of the following is closest to Estragon's fractional ownership if it partici-

pates in the Series B financing?

A. 10.0%

B. 17.7%

C. 62.5%

9. Discuss two aspects of differences between venture capital and growth equity that may reflect Moreau's comments about preferring to focus on investing in venture capital rather than growth equity.

The following information relates to questions 10-13

Benrich Inc. is a US-based food services corporation with a long history in the industry, but recently has struggled to generate adequate growth or profitability. However, despite its relatively low net profit margins, Benrich generates a stable EBITDA of USD150 million, EBITDA margins of about 20%, and revenue growth of approximately 1% per year. Bardstown Partners, a private equity firm specializing in buyout equity transactions, believes that Benrich may be a good investment candidate for inclusion in its latest buyout fund.

The Bardstown Partners analyst assigned to this deal concludes that an assumption of additional revenue growth may be unlikely for Benrich. However, the analyst believes that an assumption of 6% EBITDA growth per year over the investment horizon is plausible.

Bardstown believes that Benrich can be purchased at an EV multiple of 5× EBITDA of USD150 million with 30% common equity contributed by Bardstown and 70% debt financing. The Bardstown analyst forecasts that Benrich can reduce its debt load following the transaction by USD40 million per year over a five-year investment horizon.

At the end of the investment horizon, Bardstown views the potential for exiting its investment by selling Benrich at a 6× EV/EBITDA multiple due to increased efficiencies. Bardstown has a 35% IRR target for a buyout equity deal of this risk level.

10. Discuss two characteristics that may make Benrich a suitable candidate as a target of a buyout equity fund.

11. Discuss and estimate assumptions necessary for 1% revenue growth and 6% EBITDA growth.

12. Calculate Benrich's estimated debt outstanding at the end of the five-year investment horizon and evaluate whether the debt reduction goal is likely realistic in the context of other aspects of the forecast.

13. Analyze the investment potential of the proposed transaction to take Benrich private under Bardstown's assumptions with no interim cash flows distributed to equity investors.

SOLUTIONS

1. B is correct. Both entry and exit multiples reflect valuation assumptions. Assumptions about multiple expansion reflect one path by which fund managers assume good returns from investment in a portfolio company. Multiples for private equity portfolio companies are likely to move less than benchmark public equity multiples. Less emphasis on margin expansion implies that Northern States prefers to avoid managers who may be overly influenced by increases in public market multiples in setting exit multiple assumptions. Responses A and C are incorrect as neither of these risks are related to assumptions about multiples.

2. C is correct. Buyout equity transactions typically involve significant debt as part of the initial purchase price of the portfolio company. In these types of deals, both the income statement and balance sheet are forecasted over the investment horizon. A key assumption made in the balance sheet forecast is the degree to which debt is repaid. Responses A and B are incorrect as neither venture capital nor growth equity include assumptions about balance sheet forecasts, so repayment of debt is unlikely to be a significant assumption in these types of private equity deals.

3. C is correct. Adverse conditions in markets do not, in isolation, create liquidity risk for private equity investors. Rather, an added element associated with private equity investments must be included to the statement to imply that adverse market conditions create liquidity risks. On the other hand, both Responses A and B reflect situations that are direct or indirect liquidity risks. Long required holding periods are the most direct form of liquidity risk of private equity. In response to investor demand for some liquidity, general partners may create a secondary market for fund investors to liquidate holdings, but they are likely to demand a wide bid-ask spread. This wide bid-ask spread properly reflects liquidity risk.

4. Statement 3 directly addresses agency risk. As a co-investor, Northern States has a direct ownership stake in a portfolio company rather than an indirect stake owned directly by a private equity fund. As a result, Northern States has the ability to interact directly with the portfolio company's management on areas of governance concern. Statement 4 addresses agency risk indirectly. By imposing a policy mandate on private equity funds, Northern States attempts to ensure that the funds will support board diversity proposals by only owning portfolio companies that comply with Northern States' policy. However, Northern States will face additional costs to ensure that its fund investments follow this policy.

5. Assuming an initial investment of EUR100, we would need to solve for the unknown failure rate to achieve an IRR of 35%. The unknown terminal value in five years may be expressed as follows: (= (EUR100 – EURX) × 15) and we use an IRR of 35% in the denominator, as shown below.

   $$\text{EUR}100 = \frac{X}{(1 + 0.35)^5}$$

   Solving for X in the equation above gives a result of 448.4 (= $100(1.35)^5$). Substituting 448.4 into the following and solving for x gives a result of 70.1:

   $$448.4 = (100 - x) \times 15.$$

   Thus, the failure rate would have to improve to 70% (from its previous level of 75%).

   Applying the 100/10/1 rule of thumb and the failure rates above to Estragon's situation with 20 portfolio companies implies that currently five of these (i.e., (=

1 – 0.75) × 20) are the drivers of Estragon's returns. If Estragon could improve its process to improve its portfolio to six successful companies (i.e., (= 1 – 0.70) × 20), then it could improve its IRR to 35%. NOTE: A simpler way to estimate this would be to note that the hoped-for IRR is 16.67% better than current (= (35 – 30) ÷ 30), so a 20% (= (6-5) ÷ 5) improvement in the number of successful firms in the portfolio would accomplish this if the additional successful firm can generate the 15× return.

6. The optimal conversion point is that at which the convertible preferred shareholders choose to convert their preferred shares to common shares. Above this point, the increase in firm value accrues to both the convertible holders who have converted preferred shares to common equity as well as existing common shareholders. The conversion of preferred shares into common shares causes the fractional ownership of the common shares to become diluted and the increase in value for common shareholders is reduced because of the dilution.

7. A is correct. The post-money valuation may be estimated as EUR18.75 million (= EUR150 million exit value ÷ 8× ROI). Estragon's fractional ownership is estimated at 13.3% (= 2.5 ÷ 18.75). Response B is incorrect as it uses the pre-money valuation of EUR 16.25 million (= 18.75 – 2.5) as the denominator in calculating fractional ownership. Response C is incorrect as it assumes EUR1 million as the pre-money valuation, so then assumes post-money valuation of EUR3.5 million.

8. B is correct. To calculate Estragon's fractional ownership, use the equation shown below:

$$FO_{\text{post}} = FO_{\text{prior}} \times \frac{\text{Pre-Money Valuation}}{\text{Post-Money Valuation}} + \frac{\text{New Investor Equity}}{\text{Post-Money Valuation}}.$$

The prior fractional ownership is equal to 13.33% (= 2.5 ÷ 18.75). Post-money valuation is given as EUR50 million and pre-money valuation is equal to EUR47.5 million (= 50 – 2.5). New investor equity is given as Estragon's planned investment of EUR2.5 million. Thus, the fractional ownership is equal to approximately 17.7% (= 13.33% × $\left(\frac{47.5}{50}\right) + \left(\frac{2.5}{50}\right)$).

9. In contrast to venture capital's focus on startups in the few industries expected to expand very rapidly, growth equity is less industry focused and targets later-stage companies for expansion with established products and business models. As such, Moreau may be concerned with the need to conduct due diligence across more industries and become more comfortable with researching companies later in their lifecycles. Additionally, the analysis required for modeling growth equity requires income statement modeling beyond the assessment of future revenue projections as is common in venture capital. Thus, investments in growth equity require more expertise in projecting feasible improvements in profit margins as well.

10. First, Benrich is a mature company in the late stages of its lifecycle in a slow-growth industry. Second, Benrich generates stable cash flows, and these are helpful in reducing debt typically taken on in buyout equity transactions.

11. To achieve 6% EBITDA growth with only 1% revenue growth, Benrich will need to achieve cost-cutting strategies related to the cost of goods sold and selling, general, and administrative expenses. The growth rates of both expense items must be below 1% to ensure improved EBITDA margins. To illustrate the margin assumptions necessary, assume Benrich's revenues grow from 1 to 1.01 (i.e., 1% growth). Benrich's EBITDA on revenue of 1 is 0.20, and 6% growth would reflect an increase in EBITDA from 0.20 to 0.212. Thus, the EBITDA margin required would be 20.99% (= 0.212 ÷ 1.01). Thus, the combined COGS and SGA expens-

es would need to decline from 80% of revenues (i.e., 100%–20%) to 79.01% in the first year. The combined COGS and SGA would be equal to 0.798 (= 1.01 – 0.212), and this represents a 25-basis point decline in costs from year to year. This pattern of declining costs would need to continue at slightly increased rates during each subsequent year over a multi-year time horizon to achieve the goal.

12. Given the EV/EBITDA multiple of 5× and EBITDA of USD150 million, the proposed transaction price to buy Benrich is USD750 million (= 5 × 150). With a 70% debt and 30% equity financing structure, the initial debt level of Benrich will be USD525 million (= 0.7 × 750). With USD40 million in debt repaid per year, the expected debt level at the end of five years is USD325 million (= 525 – 5(40)).

    The debt reduction target appears realistic. Given Benrich's EBITDA base year value of USD150 million and growth at 6% per year, the company likely can fund debt repayments of USD40 million per year as long as its capital investment needs are relatively small. If the asset base stays constant at USD750 million, Benrich's debt ratio declines from 70% at the outset of the transaction to 43.3% (= 325 ÷ 750) by the end of five years.

13. The goal is to assess whether the IRR of the proposed buyout deal of Benrich is greater than Bardstown's required return of 35%. Of the USD750 million purchase, Bardstown will commit USD225 million of equity contribution (= 750 × 30%). To compute the expected exit value of equity, we must first calculate the expected enterprise value upon exit based on the projected EBITDA in year 5 and the expected EV/EBITDA multiple of 6×. Projected EBITDA is approximately USD200.7 million (= $150 (1.06)^5$) and estimated enterprise value at exit is USD1,204.4 million (= 200.7 × 6). To obtain exit value of equity, we subtract the projected debt outstanding at the end of five years of USD325 million from the exit value of enterprise value. The exit value of equity is USD879.4 million (= 1204.4 – 325). Finally, we can obtain the IRR by dividing the exit value of equity by the initial equity contribution, taking this to the power of 0.2 (= 1 ÷ 5) to reflect the investment horizon, then subtract one. The resulting IRR is equal to 31.3% (= $(879.4 \div 225)^{0.2} - 1$). The expected IRR of the deal does not meet Bardstown's required return, so the Benrich deal does not show potential as a private equity investment.

LEARNING MODULE

4

Private Debt

LEARNING OUTCOMES	
Mastery	***The candidate should be able to:***
☐	discuss the use of debt financing in private market strategies over the investment life cycle
☐	discuss the use of leveraged loans, high-yield bonds, and convertible bonds in private market strategies
☐	contrast the use of mezzanine debt and unitranche debt in private market strategies;
☐	analyze private debt profiles and calculate and interpret financial ratios used to value private debt investments
☐	discuss the risk and return among private debt investments as well as versus other private market investments as part of a strategic asset allocation

INTRODUCTION

1

Fixed-income instruments such as loans and bonds are not only the most common source of capital for public issuers, but also play an important role in private markets.

The source of debt financing in private markets has evolved from being largely the domain of banks, bank syndicates, and public markets to non-bank sources of lending known as private debt, which have experienced rapid growth.

According to Preqin, an alternative investment data company, private debt capital raised has more than doubled over the past decade, led by a sharp increase in direct lending, and is expected to reach USD2.2 trillion in global assets under management by 2027.

Debt financing used in private market strategies differs from the non-callable, unsecured fixed-coupon bonds commonly used by mature public corporations and sovereign issuers. Lenders and borrowers in private corporate, real estate, or infrastructure debt transactions often incorporate characteristics such as equity-like features (to attract lenders when cash flows are less stable),, or prepayment features to give borrowers flexibility over situations such as company restructuring or managing a project development life cycle. This may involve prepayable variable-rate debt with lower effective duration than fixed-rate bonds of similar maturity, or fixed-rate bonds with explicit call or conversion features. Non-bank private debt funds offer distinct strategies such as venture debt and direct lending to small and medium-sized companies. They also offer funds devoted to event-driven or special situations, such as distressed debt, which are covered in a separate learning module.

In this learning module, we discuss how and why debt financing is used in private markets, from startups to growth companies and buyout situations, as well as real estate and infrastructure financing. We also investigate the similarities and differences in debt instruments offered by banks and non-bank sources, as well as mezzanine debt and unitranche debt. Next, we examine the role these debt instruments play in a private company's debt profile, applying fixed-income risk and return measures introduced earlier in the curriculum to estimate their value. Differences in debt features, underlying uses, and borrower profiles offer the potential for higher return and diversification with less correlation to traditional public fixed-income securities. Private debt also offers investors exposure to private market strategies with more predictable cash flows than equity. Investors must weigh these possible benefits against the unique risks of private debt when considering their role in an investor's portfolio.

LEARNING MODULE OVERVIEW

- Debt financing used in private markets includes venture debt for startups and mezzanine debt for growth and mature companies. Leveraged loans and high-yield bonds are commonly used for larger buyout equity situations, while direct lending is more prevalent for small and medium-sized firms.
- Leveraged loans involve senior secured, floating-rate debt prepayable by the issuer. This compares to high-yield bonds which are fixed-rate, subordinated debt instruments with a fixed-price call feature. Convertible bonds combine features of debt with equity by allowing investors to exchange debt for shares at a predetermined price.
- Subordinated mezzanine debt and unitranche debt are less liquid compared to most other private forms of debt. Both offer more flexible terms to lenders. Subordinated mezzanine debt often incorporates equity-like features. Unitranche debt facilities combine senior and subordinated debt.
- Private issuer debt profiles seek to ensure sufficient operating flexibility with adequate borrower protections, including covenants and other contingencies. In addition to fixed-income risk and return measures, private debt valuation involves a larger credit component than investment grade debt, increased complexity due to the use of security and subordination, and a high degree of illiquidity.
- Differences in private debt characteristics, such as contingency features, higher yield spreads due to credit, and liquidity and its use in private market strategies, contribute to the potential for higher return and diversification from traditional fixed-income exposures.

PRIVATE DEBT STRATEGIES

2

☐ discuss the use of debt financing in private market strategies over the investment life cycle

The investment life cycle for private markets, including private equity, real estate, and infrastructure, involves debt financing over a period of development or transformation. Private market debt use differs markedly from the use of commercial paper, unsecured revolving credit, and senior unsecured bonds among mature public companies with investment grade ratings.

Highly rated public companies with stable cash flows are considered far less likely to default, face few covenant or debt tenor restrictions, and enjoy a high degree of investor confidence that they will meet interest and principal payments from operating cash flow. Private equity strategies over the company life cycle, in contrast, involve either early-stage startup or growth firms with low or less predictable operating cash flow, or buyout companies where greater financial leverage increases the likelihood of default. To reduce the overall investment risk associated with debt financing, private equity borrowers must offer debt investors a higher return as well as protection in the form of restrictive covenants, security in the form of collateral, and/or equity-like returns to compensate lenders for greater risk.

Exhibit 1 shows common forms of debt used in conjunction with private equity strategies employed over the company life cycle.

Exhibit 1: Debt Financing in Private Equity Over the Company Life Cycle

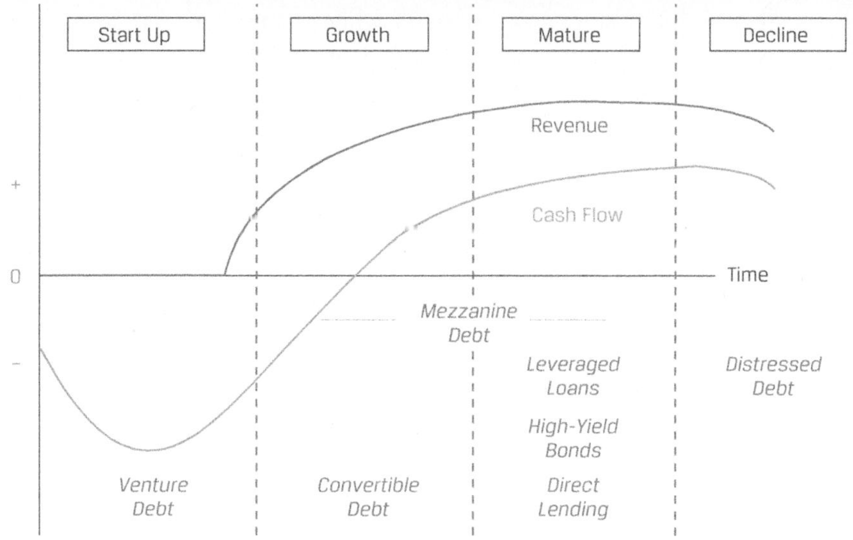

Venture Debt

Startup companies with little to no revenue, negative cash flow, and few assets available as collateral are unattractive candidates for traditional loan or bond financing, but in select cases, they can access **venture debt**.

When available, unsecured venture debt from non-bank lenders is typically offered to an early-stage, revenue-generating firm for up to three years at a relatively high interest rate given the lack of positive cash flow and high default potential. Venture borrowers usually have large cash balances, and their loan balances reflect low loan-to-value ratios, typically no greater than 10%. To minimize refinancing risk, venture debt is typically amortized over the loan period. Venture debt typically involves a loan plus a **warrant** granting a lender the right to purchase common equity shares issued by the company for a fraction (often 10–20%) of the loan amount at a predetermined price over a specific period.

Warrants have a similar payoff profile to equity call options but differ in two ways. First, they are usually outstanding for longer periods of up to several years. Second, warrants are issued directly by a company versus an exchange, and they result in dilution due to the issuance of new shares for settlement. This feature is used by borrowers to both reduce financing costs versus common shares and avoid the *immediate* dilution of equity while accepting *contingent* dilution if shares appreciate above the warrant exercise price.

As for lenders, despite the lack of revenue, cash flow, or tangible collateral, venture debt offers the potential for equity-like returns if shares appreciate, with potential additional equity series financing and in some cases a claim against intellectual property as additional default risk mitigants.

SILICON VALLEY BANK (SVB) AND THE VENTURE DEBT MARKET

Named after the Northern California region known as a global technology and innovation hub, Silicon Valley Bank was founded in the 1980s to serve the specific needs of technology startup companies.

SVB's business model deviated from that of more traditional cash flow–based and collateral-based bank lending, as it extended loans to early-stage companies and accepted founder shares as collateral while accumulating deposits from businesses financed through venture capital. As SVB pursued rapid growth over the next three decades, it began financing venture capital firms, expanding services, and connecting startups to legal and financial advisors.

At the end of 2022, SVB was estimated to hold nearly a quarter of the total US venture debt market estimated at approximately USD 30 billion, with over half of its loan portfolio comprised of loans to venture capital firms and private equity and used to invest in private firms.

The benefits of SVB's highly concentrated portfolio were sharply reversed amid the downturn in technology stocks and rising interest rates in 2022. In early 2023, social media posts based on rumors of substantial losses and risk management missteps resulted in a run on SVB's deposits. Both the sharp drop in deposits and the revelation of securities portfolio losses amid higher rates led SVB to be declared insolvent and was closed by regulators in March 2023.

Within a few weeks of SVB's failure, SVB filed for bankruptcy and First Citizens BancShares purchased SVB's loans, deposits, and branches. Notably, SVB's venture debt portfolio was included in this purchase, and the president of First Citizens confirmed that the company had hired the venture debt team from SVB in a statement of commitment to continuing the focus on venture lending.

The future of venture debt in the United States following SVB's failure remains uncertain. SVB's demise creates a new playing field in the venture debt market. While First Citizens BancShares' SVB acquisition may give it an early advantage in the event of a market rebound, this market faces a likely adjustment to new venture capital market conditions.

A special form of venture debt applicable to early-stage firms with subscription-based revenue is **recurring revenue financing** (also known as receivables financing or factoring). Under this structure, a private lender offers a loan to a software firm, for example, with an established software license subscriber base and an established track record of monthly cash flows. The loan, which consists of a discounted upfront monthly payment of expected subscription revenue, is extended in exchange for some or all of the monthly subscriber cash flows as they are received. Key determinants of cost and availability include the size, growth rate, and quality of the underlying subscriber revenue.

Mezzanine Debt

Also referred to as hybrid debt, or more broadly as junior debt, **mezzanine debt** represents long-term claims to interest and principal which are met only once all senior debt claims are satisfied but before any distributions to common equity or other shareholders.

In contrast to both high-yield and convertible bonds as well as leveraged loans, mezzanine debt is often of smaller size and arranged privately with non-standardized terms. The **contractual subordination** of mezzanine debt is usually established via an agreement among borrowers linking senior secured and subordinated mezzanine debt claims at the company level.

Mezzanine debt may include equity-like features such as call options, conversion rights, or warrants. This debt may be offered on a fixed or variable rate basis, with interest paid in cash—or **payment in kind (PIK)**, that is, via accrual which increases principal outstanding and is paid at maturity. As shown in Exhibit 1, mezzanine debt is used across the growth and mature phase of the company life cycle.

Convertible Debt

Convertible debt is a fixed-income instrument which combines the features of debt with equity via a contingent feature allowing debtholders to exchange their claim for common shares at a predetermined fixed price in the future.

Since this equity call option-like feature is embedded in the convertible bond's price, these long-term bonds pay little to no periodic interest and are used in private market strategies where lenders are willing to accept the credit risk of issuers with less certain cash flows in exchange for equity appreciation potential. For example, early-stage companies which lack the level and stability of cash flows needed to support traditional forms of debt may issue convertible bonds to increase financial flexibility and lower the cost of capital, while issuers pursuing an acquisition may also find the contingent dilution preferable to an equity-financed purchase while also lowering the cost versus standard debt.

Leveraged Loans

Leveraged loans are term loans with a tenor of four to seven years extended to sub-investment grade borrowers. These floating-rate loans are typically issued to borrowers with a higher degree of financial leverage on a senior secured basis. The periodic debt coupon is usually based upon some market reference rate (MRR) plus an issuer-specific credit spread, with principal which is either fully repaid upon maturity or amortized based on a predetermined schedule. Leveraged loans are typically callable at par (plus any accrued interest) at any time starting several months after issuance, offering issuers a high degree of financing flexibility.

The higher likelihood of financial distress among private buyout debt issuers usually leads leveraged loan investors to require a **first lien** or **second lien** on certain assets, an investor protection which increases the recovery rate in the event of default versus unsecured debt. A first or priority lien grants a lender the right to take possession of specific property from a borrower which fails to repay debt, while a second lien loan is secured by an asset with an existing lien and will only be repaid when the first lien creditor receives payment.

Additional constraints on issuers in the form of restrictive covenants are also common for leveraged loans. An issuer may face **maintenance covenants** requiring it to meet certain metrics for each financial reporting period, such as keeping debt outstanding *below* a certain total leverage ratio and operating cash flow *above* an interest coverage ratio. In competitive markets with strong demand for leveraged loans, these conditions may be loosened in what is known as a **covenant-lite** transaction. Note that the above maintenance covenants may instead be weakened when imposed as **incurrence covenants**, which are tested only when an issuer seeks to assume additional debt. For example, under a debt to EBITDA maintenance covenant, a borrower must remain below a given threshold in all reporting periods; however, under an incurrence covenant this test is only conducted if the borrower seeks to issue new debt.

Investors in leveraged loans face less duration risk due to changing benchmark interest rates than fixed-coupon bonds and will face higher or lower coupons as market reference rates rise or fall. It is important to note that many investors access the leveraged loan market by purchasing **collateralized loan obligations (CLOs)**, which were described earlier in the CFA Level I curriculum. CLOs raise capital to invest in a portfolio of leveraged loans and are separated into tranches with different priority claims on cash flow from the loan portfolio and exposure to losses based upon a waterfall.

High-Yield Bonds

High-yield bonds are fixed-income securities issued by sub-investment grade borrowers. These bonds represent more equity-like exposure as they are subordinated in the capital structure and therefore repaid after leveraged loans.

High-yield bonds have a fixed coupon and usually a longer tenor than leveraged loans of up to ten years, and include a call feature, available to issuers, allowing prepayment of the bond before maturity. In contrast to the prepayability of loans at par at almost any time, high-yield bonds typically offer investors a period of call protection, after which an issuer may call outstanding bonds at a fixed premium over par.

Although high-yield bonds are usually publicly traded debt instruments, they often play an important role in transactions involving private debt. For example, issuers in a buyout equity transaction assess borrower demand across markets and debt types when financing large, highly leveraged transactions as discussed below.

THYSSENKRUPP ELEVATOR'S 2020 LEVERAGED BUYOUT FINANCING

In February 2020, the publicly traded German conglomerate Thyssenkrupp agreed to sell its elevator unit to a private equity consortium, led by Advent International and Cinven, for EUR17.2 billion in Europe's largest leveraged buyout transaction since the Alliance Boots buyout in 2007. Thyssenkrupp Elevator was the world's fourth largest elevator manufacturer and the conglomerate's most profitable unit. Nevertheless, its profit margins lagged behind those of larger global competitors. The transaction closed in June 2020 and included EUR7.6 billion of debt financing.

Given the global nature of the division's cash flows, the private equity group was able to raise both secured and unsecured debt denominated in both USD and EUR, testing demand across private and public markets. The final deal raised

EUR3.265 billion from European investors and approximately EUR4.36 billion from US markets. The US leveraged loan market provided the largest proportion of debt, equivalent to approximately EUR2.56 billion, while the European leveraged loan market contributed the smallest portion, with EUR1.015 billion. The remaining EUR4.05 billion of debt was contributed from high-yield bond markets in Europe (EUR2.25 billion) and the US (EUR1.8 billion).

Yields ranged from 4.375% for European secured high-yield notes (based on B/B1/B+ ratings) to 5.73% on the US leveraged loans. The European leveraged loans priced at a yield of 4.68% and the US high-yield notes at a yield of 5.25%. However, a part of the structure included PIK notes in both EUR and USD priced to yield 11% and 12%, respectively.

Early in the capital raising process, leveraged loans were expected to comprise a greater proportion of the overall financing package. Ultimately, greater investor demand for fixed rates and high-yield bonds led to growth in these tranches at the expense of secured floating-rate and privately held debt. Overall, the deal underscored strength in the public high-yield market, greater relative demand from the USD leveraged loan market versus Europe, and somewhat weaker demand from private market debt investors.

By distributing the debt tranches across currencies and debt types, the private equity buyers of Thyssenkrupp Elevator were able to establish a flexible debt profile at the lowest cost of capital for the acquisition financing.

Direct Lending

A growing alternative to traditional bank intermediation, **direct lending** involves leveraged loans issued to small- and medium-sized companies with limited access to banks or public markets by private non-bank lenders. The debt instruments used in direct lending, such as leveraged loans and unitranche debt, are addressed in detail later in this learning module.

The rapid growth in private credit as an asset class following the Global Financial Crisis of 2008–9 stemmed from both tighter bank regulation and near-zero central bank policy rates. Stricter capital standards for banks and rising minimum public debt market issuance sizes reduced bank and public debt market access for smaller firms. Quantitative easing spurred investors to seek fixed-income returns from new sources. Private non-bank lenders filled this funding gap among small- and medium-sized firms, whose relatively illiquid debt offered higher coupons and enjoyed strong demand, with institutional investors explicitly adding this asset class to their strategic allocations for the first time.

Direct lending may involve a single senior secured loan on a floating-rate basis similar to a syndicated leveraged loan, or a hybrid loan combining senior and subordinated debt in one facility known as **unitranche debt**, addressed later in this learning module. In either case, direct loans are typically issued at a higher coupon than standardized loans to borrowers of similar seniority and credit quality. The higher spread also reflects a greater liquidity premium associated with these borrowers. Underwriters of these loans may include private credit funds or **business development companies** in the US, a form of closed-end investment vehicle which is often a publicly traded company specializing in private debt.

Direct loans are sponsored or non-sponsored. **Sponsored loans** are those for which a private equity firm with a controlling ownership stake in the potential borrower directly seeks to access debt for a company. In the case of traditional bank lending, financial institutions conduct periodic credit assessments, maintain transactional banking services, and impose constraints such as covenants on a borrower. Under a sponsored loan, lenders are typically able to source firm information and due diligence from the sponsoring private equity firm. In addition, the private equity sponsor usually closely monitors firm performance and supports the borrower, also soliciting additional debt and equity funding as needed. Lenders forego the use of a financial intermediary, dealing either with the private equity sponsor or directly with the borrower company's management. Given the existing due diligence, monitoring, and controlling relationship of the private equity sponsor, prospective lenders tend to have less bargaining power in negotiating terms and pricing for sponsored loans. Additionally, sponsored loans may generate a potential conflict of interest between a general partner (GP) and limited partners (LPs), arising from loan arrangement fees charged by GPs but not shared with LPs.

Non-sponsored loans, or those which lack a controlling financial sponsor, involve greater search, due diligence, and monitoring costs, given the lack of a controlling financial sponsor. In this case, lenders deal directly with a potential borrower's management team. Given the greater costs associated with identifying non-sponsored borrowers and analyzing and monitoring their creditworthiness, investors often expect higher returns in the form of wider credit spreads compared to private, sponsored borrowers of similar credit quality. Given the lack of financial sponsor support, non-sponsored borrowers may face less bargaining power than sponsored lenders as they may be less sophisticated or have fewer resources to focus on negotiating debt financing.

Project-Related Debt (Real Estate and Infrastructure)

Forms of debt used in other private markets, such as real estate or infrastructure development, often involve a project which has an initial period of negative net income over an initial development phase, as shown in Exhibit 2.

Exhibit 2: Use of Debt in Private Real Estate Development

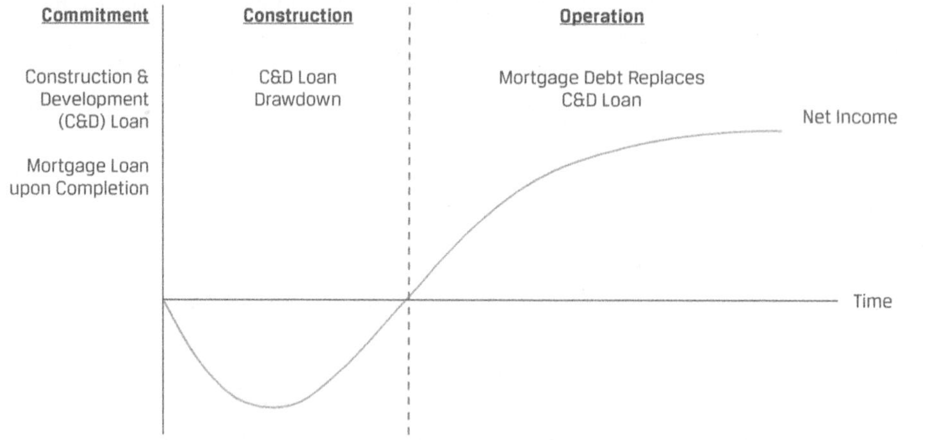

Debt and equity capital is committed prior to the initiation of a new real estate project and drawn from the time of site purchase through the construction period. Temporary debt in the form of a **construction and development (C&D) loan** shown in Exhibit 2 is disbursed in stages to finance building costs as specific project milestones are met, and the loan typically accrues interest over the construction period. The C&D loan is usually repaid upon project completion via a mortgage loan secured by the property and serviced by operating cash flows. While C&D loans are also typically secured by project assets, risks include the uncertain resale value of collateral during construction, as well as the potential for delays and cost overruns.

The use of debt in infrastructure is shown in Exhibit 3 using the example of a so-called **build-operate-transfer (BOT) project** which is sponsored by a public entity and transferred to its control after a finite operating period.

Exhibit 3: Debt in the Private Infrastructure Build-Operate-Transfer Cycle

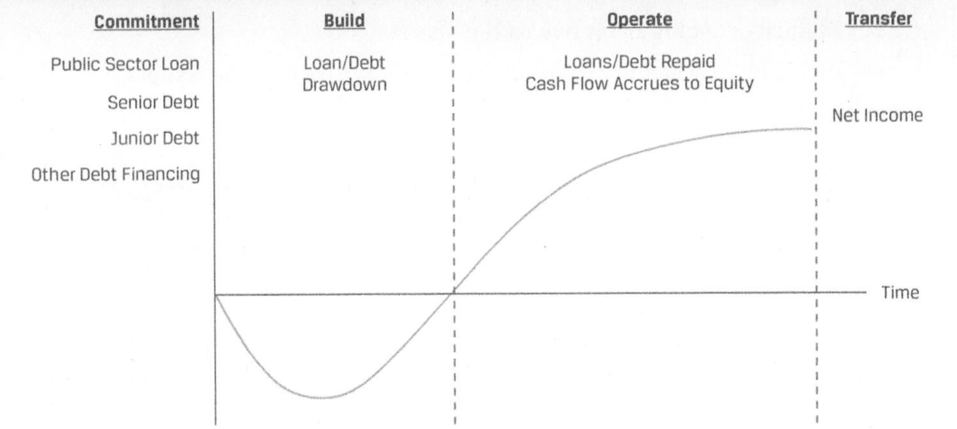

While similar to the real estate investment cycle at first glance, infrastructure debt use differs in several ways. As shown in Exhibit 3, in some instances debt financing may include public as well as private sources of debt. However, the key difference is that once in operation, real estate properties can support a high degree of financial leverage over time and may be held indefinitely or sold at the end of a targeted holding period. In the case of infrastructure projects with a finite operating period, such as a BOT project, the debt is paid down fully as operations begin, with cash flows accruing to equity holders until the asset is transferred to the public entity with a terminal value of zero. In both the case of private real estate and infrastructure, the use of loans over bonds is prevalent due to the greater flexibility of prepayment as described earlier.

Distressed Debt

Loans or bonds which face a high likelihood of non-payment or bankruptcy, known as **distressed debt**, will be covered in detail in a later learning module on Special Situations, while the use of debt financing in real estate and infrastructure will be shown in case studies in subsequent Private Real Estate and Infrastructure learning modules. The remainder of this learning module will primarily focus on debt used in private equity strategies across the company life cycle.

QUESTION SET

1. Which one of the following types of debt is least likely to be used as a source of funding a buyout transaction?

   A. Leveraged loan

   B. Convertible debt

   C. High-yield bond

   Solution

   B is the correct response. Convertible debt is unlikely to be used as a debt funding source in a buyout transaction but is more likely to be used in conjunction with a growth equity transaction. Responses A and C are both incorrect as these are both commonly used debt types in financing buyout transactions.

2. Which of the following is a typical feature of venture debt?

   A. Ability to convert the debt into common stock of the issuer

   B. Maturity ranging from five to ten years

   C. Inclusion of warrants to purchase common stock of the issuer

   Solution

   C is the correct response. Venture debt typically involves a loan plus a warrant granting the right to purchase additional common equity shares issued for a fraction (often 10–20%) of the loan amount at a predetermined price over a specific period. Warrants are issued directly by a company versus an exchange, and result in dilution due to the issuance of new shares for settlement. Response A is not correct as the statement refers to a conversion feature found in convertible debt, not venture debt. Response B is not correct as venture debt typically carries a shorter maturity of three years or less.

3. Discuss how the markets for leveraged loans and collateralized loan obligations are related to each other.

   Solution

   The market for leveraged loans is driven by the market for buyout equity transactions as these types of loans are a common source of funding buyout deals. Many investors in private debt markets access leveraged loans by investing in CLOs, which are created from pools of leveraged loans. Therefore, the markets for leveraged loans and CLOs are closely related as CLOs require pools of leveraged loans from which to create the CLO securities.

4. Consider two mature companies: one publicly traded and the other recently taken private in a buyout deal. Both companies have similar ratios of debt relative to assets. Discuss differences that are likely to be observed between these two companies with respect to their cash flows, credit ratings, debt covenants, and expected returns on debt securities.

   Solution

   Cash flows and credit ratings: The cash flow stability and predictability is likely superior for the publicly traded company compared to the newly private company. As a result, the publicly traded company may have a better credit rating and lower likelihood of default as compared to the newly private company.

   Debt covenants: The public company is more likely to face fewer covenant restrictions compared to the newly private company. As an example, the higher likelihood of financial distress among private buyout debt issuers usually leads leveraged loan investors to require a first or second lien on certain assets, an investor protection which increases the recovery rate in the event of default. Additional constraints on issuers in the form of restrictive covenants are also common for leveraged loans.

   Expected returns on debt securities: Investors in the debt of the newly private company likely face greater risk of default as well as more liquidity risk associated with their investment, and so they are likely to demand higher expected returns as compared to expected returns on the debt of the similar public company.

LEVERAGED LOANS, HIGH YIELD, AND CONVERTIBLE BONDS

3

- [ ] discuss the use of leveraged loans, high-yield bonds, and convertible bonds in private market strategies

The distinctive features of leveraged loans, high-yield bonds, and convertible bonds lead to specific benefits and risks of these fixed-income instruments to both private markets issuers as well as investors across the investment life cycle.

While these debt instruments are distinguished by either fixed or variable-rate coupons, as well as contingency features, all three incorporate spreads versus comparable risk-free government securities which compensate investors for the likelihood of issuer default, loss severity if a default occurs, and relative liquidity.

Credit spreads vary widely across issuers, seniority rank, and time periods, while liquidity tends to be higher for listed bonds than leveraged loans.

In contrast to investment grade loans and bonds, half or more of the total yield-to-maturity of high-yield bonds is often attributable to yield spread for private market issuers, which fall within the sub-investment grade category.

A comparison of the features of leveraged loans, high-yield bonds, and convertible bonds, as well as mezzanine debt introduced later in this learning module, is summarized in Exhibit 4.

Exhibit 4: Comparison of Private Market Debt Features

Feature	Leveraged Loans	High-Yield Bond	Convertible Debt	Venture Debt	Mezzanine Debt
Private equity phase	Buyout	Buyout	Early stage / acquisition	Early stage	Growth stage/ buyout
Tenor	4–7years	5–10 years	3–7 years	Up to 3 years	7–10 years
Debt coupon	Variable rate (MRR) plus credit spread	High fixed coupon	Zero or low fixed coupon	High fixed or floating coupon	High fixed or floating coupon
Seniority	Senior secured	Subordinated	Senior unsecured	Senior (usually)	Subordinated
Contingency	Callable by issuer at par shortly after issuance	Callable by issuer at a fixed price over par after a lockout period	Convertible to common shares at a fixed price	Warrants	Warrants and/or PIK coupon
Price appreciation potential	Often limited by issuer par call feature	Often capped by issuer fixed-price call feature	Often unlimited as issuer shares appreciate	Often unlimited if combined with warrants	Often unlimited if combined with warrants

Unitranche debt includes more than one of these debt types in a single facility.

Note that while high-yield bonds and convertible bonds are used in private market strategies, most private debt professionals and investors do not consider them as part of the private debt asset class.

Leveraged Loans

Earlier Fixed Income lessons distinguished floating-rate loan features from fixed-rate bonds. Debt coupons fluctuate over time as the MRR changes, while the issuer-specific credit spread is usually fixed for the entire loan term. As base rates adjust to market conditions, the price of a leveraged loan remains close to par if market credit spreads and issuer credit quality are unchanged. This interest rate feature, in addition to the right to prepay loans at par, provide issuers greater flexibility than other term financing alternatives. Leveraged loans are commonly used in private buyout situations as well as for acquisition financing in which the loan is secured by target company assets, as in the following case study.

CASE STUDY

Everfloat Limited Acquisition and Leveraged Loan

Everfloat Ltd. is a UK-based firm owned by a private equity sponsor which manufactures, sells, and distributes marine-based navigation and logistics equipment. As part of its restructuring plan, Everfloat has established a holding company (Everfloat Holdings) which fully owns an operating subsidiary (Everfloat Products). Everfloat Products has acquired Boatswain Industries—the computer-based navigation technology division of a separate public company–for a purchase price of GBP500 million. Everfloat Products intends to integrate Boatswain into its operations over three to five years and has access to the leveraged loan market based upon the following terms in Exhibit 5.

Exhibit 5: Everfloat Products Leveraged Loan Summary of Terms

Issuer:	Everfloat Holdings ("Everfloat")
Settlement date:	[T + 3 Business Days]
Maturity date:	[Five Years from Settlement Date]
Principal amount:	GBP500 million
Interest:	MRR plus 300 bps per annum (p.a.) MRR is reset and interest is paid semiannually
Interest payment:	Commencing six months from [settlement date] to be paid semiannually with final payment on [maturity date]
Seniority:	The notes are secured and unsubordinated obligations of Everfloat Products and rank *pari passu* with all other secured and unsubordinated indebtedness.

Maintenance covenant:	Issuer must maintain: (a) net interest bearing debt to EBITDA not greater than 5.50×, and (b) interest coverage ratio greater than 2.50× for each financial reporting period.
Business days:	London

The MRR on a leveraged loan often sets at the beginning of an interest period with payment at the end, which may be monthly, quarterly, or semiannually, as in the above case. For example, assuming an initial MRR in GBP terms of 4.40% and semiannual interest payable of MRR + 300 bps p.a., we may calculate Everfloat's initial interest coupon to be GBP18,500,000 (= GBP500 million × (4.40% + 3.00%)/2) if the interest period is exactly 0.5 years. Note that this payment will fluctuate with changes to MRR while the 300 bp spread is constant.

Consistent with the approach taken earlier in the curriculum, we consider the leveraged loan price (PV) without accrued interest on a given rate reset date. We further assume N evenly spaced periods to maturity, m equal periods per year, and a constant MRR for all cash flows. The 300 bp spread in the prior case is the **quoted margin (QM)** established at the time of loan issuance to compensate investors for issuer credit risk, while the **required margin** (or discount margin (DM)) is the market-determined yield spread over or under the MRR such that the leveraged loan is priced at par on a reset date.

Recall that the price of a fixed-rate, non-callable bond on a coupon date with the bond's future or par value of future value (FV), market discount rate r, and coupon payment PMT for N years is equal to:

$$PV = \frac{PMT}{(1+r)^1} + \frac{PMT}{(1+r)^2} + \ldots + \frac{PMT + FV}{(1+r)^N}. \tag{1}$$

The numerators in Equation 1 are constant, while the market discount rate r changes as the yield-to-maturity (comprising benchmark rates and credit spreads) changes. For a floating-rate loan in contrast, the *numerator* of the present value calculation changes each period as a function of the MRR and the *quoted* margin, while the market discount rate in the *denominator* depends on the MRR and the market-driven DM:

$$PV = \frac{\frac{(MRR + QM) \times FV}{m}}{\left(1 + \frac{MRR + DM}{m}\right)^1} + \frac{\frac{(MRR + QM) \times FV}{m}}{\left(1 + \frac{MRR + DM}{m}\right)^2} + \ldots + \frac{\frac{(MRR + QM) \times FV}{m} + FV}{\left(1 + \frac{MRR + DM}{m}\right)^N}. \tag{2}$$

We must divide by m periods per year in Equation 2, as MRR, QM, and DM are quoted as annual rates.

Note that an investor faces far less exposure to interest rate risk under a floating rate structure but remains exposed to credit spread risk.

Let us return to the earlier case of Everfloat to contrast the leveraged loan financing alternative with fixed, non-callable debt.

CASE STUDY

Everfloat Leveraged Loan vs. Bond Financing

Assume that Everfloat Holdings has a hypothetical choice between financing the Boatswain acquisition using the five-year leveraged loan shown earlier based upon MRR plus 300 bps p.a. and five-year, non-callable bonds at a fixed, semiannual coupon rate equal to 7.40%, comprising the five year gilt yield benchmark plus a 300 bp spread. Assuming a flat GBP yield curve (that is, both MRR and five year gilt yields at 4.40%) and similar changes to credit spreads across the two forms of debt with the same day count convention, consider the effect of the following scenarios on the leveraged loan and the fixed-rate bond.

1. Discuss the change in interest expense to Everfloat and value of the leveraged loan and non-callable bond debt outstanding if benchmark interest rates fall by 100 bps at the end of the first semiannual interest period and credit spreads remain unchanged.

Solution

Interest expense on the fixed-rate bond is a constant 7.40%, equal to GBP18,500,000 (= GBP500,000,000 × 0.074/2) at the initial 4.40% MRR regardless of interest rate changes. As for the leveraged loan, a 100 bps decrease in MRR to 3.40% reduces Everfloat's periodic interest expense to GBP16,000,000 (= GBP500 million × (3.40% + 3.00%)/2).

We can solve for the value of fixed-coupon debt outstanding in six months using Equation 1 for the fixed-rate bond with nine periods remaining and a new yield-to-maturity of 6.40% (= 7.40% – 1.00%):

$$PV = \frac{\text{GBP}18,500,000}{(1+0.064/2)^1} + \frac{\text{GBP}18,500,000}{(1+0.064/2)^2} + \ldots + \frac{\text{GBP}518,500,000}{(1+0.064/2)^9},$$

or, alternatively, the PV spreadsheet function (= –PV(*rate,nper,pmt,fv,type*), or (= –PV(0.064/2,9,18500000,500000000,0) to arrive at a price of GBP519,284,988, or a 3.86% price increase (= (519,284,988 – 500,000,000)/500,000,000) due to the 100 bps fall in the benchmark yield.

As for the leveraged loan, Equation 2 becomes:

$$PV = \frac{\frac{(0.064)\times 500,000,000}{2}}{\left(1+\frac{0.064}{2}\right)^1} + \frac{\frac{(0.064)\times 500,000,000}{2}}{\left(1+\frac{0.064}{2}\right)^2} + \ldots + \frac{\frac{(0.064)\times 500,000,000}{2} + 500,000,000}{\left(1+\frac{0.064}{2}\right)^9}.$$

We may solve for PV by first calculating the *PMT* of GBP16,000,000 (= (GBP500 million × (3.40% + 3.00%)/2) and then using a spreadsheet program or financial calculator to arrive at par, or GBP500,000,000, or no change in the price due to the benchmark yield change. Note the difference between the leveraged loan and the fixed-rate bond calculation is that while the denominators are identical, the leveraged loan numerator has also adjusted to the market rate, while the fixed-rate bond payment remains constant.

2. Discuss the relative change to Everfloat's interest expense and the value of debt outstanding at the end of the first semiannual interest period if Everfloat's required or discount margin were to rise 100 bps above the quoted margin, with benchmark rates unchanged.

Solution

Interest expense on the fixed-rate bond remains a constant 7.40% equal to GBP18,500,000 (= GBP500,000,000 × 0.074/2). While the *discount* margin has risen 100 bps, the *quoted* margin on which Everfloat's periodic leveraged loan debt coupon is still 300 bps and periodic interest expense remains at GBP18,500,000 (= GBP500 million × (4.40% + 3.00%)/2).

The 100 bps increase in discount margin in six months is reflected in a higher yield-to-maturity of 8.40% (= 7.40% + 1.00%) for the remaining 4.5 years.

Solve for the value of fixed-coupon debt outstanding in six months using Equation 1:

$$PV = \frac{GBP18,500,000}{(1+0.084/2)^1} + \frac{GBP18,500,000}{(1+0.084/2)^2} + \ldots + \frac{GBP518,500,000}{\left(1+\frac{0.084}{2}\right)^9},$$

or the PV spreadsheet function (= –PV(*rate,nper,pmt,fv,type*), or (= –PV(0.084/2,9,18500000,500000000,0) to arrive at a price of GBP481,579,922, or a 3.68% price *decrease* (= (481,579,922–500,000,000)/500,000,000) due to the 100 bps rise in the market credit spread.

In the case of the leveraged loan, the *quoted* margin used to calculate the periodic debt coupon in the numerator remains unchanged, while the *discount* margin in the denominator is higher due to the deterioration in the market's view of Everfloat credit risk. Equation 2 becomes:

$$PV = \frac{\frac{(0.074)\times 500,000,000}{2}}{\left(1+\frac{0.084}{2}\right)^1} + \frac{\frac{(0.074)\times 500,000,000}{2}}{\left(1+\frac{0.084}{2}\right)^2} + \ldots + \frac{\frac{(0.074)\times 500,000,000}{2} + 500,000,000}{\left(1+\frac{0.084}{2}\right)^9}.$$

We can solve for PV by first calculating *PMT* of GBP18,500,000 (= GBP500 million × (4.40% + 3.00%)/2) and then using a spreadsheet program or financial calculator to arrive at a PV of GBP481,579,922. Note the difference here is that the numerator of the leveraged loan and the fixed-rate bond calculations remain unchanged, while the denominators both rise to adjust to the market credit spread for Everfloat.

The case study above highlights key differences and similarities between interest rate exposure faced by issuers and investors for leveraged loans and non-callable fixed-rate bonds. For example, while changing short-term MRR rates result in adjusted debt coupons payable by leveraged loan issuers to investors, bond investors receive a constant coupon while facing capital gains (losses) in a lower (higher) benchmark rate environment.

The quoted versus discount margin on a leveraged loan on the other hand is an important determinant of its price on a reset date. As shown in the case study, a leveraged loan will be priced at par if the quoted margin and discount margin are equal, but at a discount if a higher margin required by investors under adverse credit conditions is not reflected in the loan coupon. In the earlier case, the GBP18,420,078 discount (= 500,000,000–481,579,922) equals the 100 bps annuity difference calculated for the remaining life of the Everfloat loan. The following exhibit summarizes the relationship between the quoted versus discount margin and a leveraged loan's price on any reset date.

Exhibit 6: Leveraged Loan Discount, Premium, and Par Pricing

Leveraged loan price	Description	Quoted Versus Discount Margin
Par	Loan trades at a price (PV) equal to its future value	QM = DM
Discount	Loan trades at a price below its future value	QM < DM
Premium	Loan trades at a price above its future value	QM > DM

As Exhibit 6 shows, leveraged loan price deviations from par *on a reset date* are due entirely to market spread changes. On a non-reset date, the *following* coupon payments are subject to both interest rate and market spread changes as the current period payment was fixed on the prior reset date.

As rising margins and growing cash flows translate into lower market credit spreads over a buyout restructuring phase, issuers have an incentive to refinance or prepay debt trading at a premium. The structural flexibility of leveraged loans also allows borrowers under a private buyout strategy to tailor debt terms to match business plan milestones. Examples include the renegotiation of covenants, extension of loan tenor, or setting a variable credit spread based upon financial leverage or coverage criteria targets to increase debt capacity or in exchange for fewer restrictive covenants.

Fixed-rate bond terms are more standardized and difficult to amend, with bond indenture changes often requiring the consent of a majority of bondholders to make changes. Early bond repayment also generally requires issuers to hold a **tender process** in which a voluntary offer is extended to all bondholders to repurchase outstanding bonds prior to maturity date at a specified premium to the market price within a specific timeframe. Highly rated bonds often include a so-called make-whole call protection allowing an issuer to pay bondholders a call price determined using a market discount rate close to that of a sovereign bond yield-to-maturity of comparable maturity. However, as the make whole call price usually far exceeds a bond's market price, they are rarely executed and have little to no impact on bond pricing.

High-Yield Bonds

As described earlier, high-yield bonds are fixed-rate debt instruments issued by sub-investment grade borrowers for a term of five to ten years on a subordinated basis, often at a holding rather than operating company level. These registered debt securities are subject to greater issuer disclosures and increased standardization, which also generally contributes to their greater liquidity versus leveraged loans.

Like other bonds, high-yield bonds are issued under an indenture specifying terms, conditions, and constraints imposed upon issuers by investors in the form of covenants. Given the aim of balancing investors' desire for basic bondholder protections and private issuer needs for flexibility to operate a business, high-yield bonds typically lack the maintenance covenants common in leveraged loans but retain restrictive covenants such as a **change of control provision** and include incurrence covenants such as those noted below.

A change of control clause typically requires the issuer to offer to repurchase outstanding bonds at a fixed price at or above par if a new owner acquires a predetermined percentage of voting shares. This provision gives lenders and bondholders the ability to put or sell back bonds to an issuer or renegotiate terms if they believe that ownership and management changes may adversely affect their ability to collect future interest and principal payments. Common high-yield incurrence covenants include those which limit certain borrower actions such as paying dividends, taking on additional debt, or selling assets under certain conditions.

An important distinguishing feature of high-yield bonds impacting their value is the fixed-price call feature. After a period of investor call protection of up to half of a bond's time to maturity, an issuer may call outstanding bonds at a fixed price over par starting at a premium equal to half of the coupon (which steps down over time). Since the issuer call feature is embedded in the price of the bond, an issuer pays a higher coupon than would be expected for a non-callable bond of the same maturity. We can compare leveraged loan and high-yield bond financing alternatives based upon the earlier Everfloat case.

CASE STUDY

Everfloat High-Yield Bond Financing for the Boatswain Acquisition

As Everfloat weighs financing alternatives for the Boatswain acquisition, it considers high-yield bonds issued at the holding company level (Everfloat Holdings) to increase its flexibility to sell non-strategic assets within Boatswain during the integration period and reduce reliance on secured leveraged loan financing. In addition, Everfloat believes it may achieve a lower credit spread on its secured leveraged loan financing backed by pledged assets given the smaller debt tranche size. To ensure the best execution of its new high-yield bond issuance, Everfloat's advisors recommend a GBP300 million minimum size transaction. Everfloat solicits investor interest based upon the terms in Exhibit 7.

Exhibit 7: Everfloat High-Yield Bond Issue Summary of Terms

Issuer:	Everfloat Holdings ("Everfloat")
Settlement date:	[T + 5 Business Days]
Maturity date:	[Seven years from settlement date]
Principal amount:	GBP300 million
Interest:	9.00% p.a. paid semiannually
Interest payment:	Commencing six months from [settlement date] to be paid semiannually with final payment on [maturity date]
Seniority:	The notes are unsecured subordinated obligations of Everfloat Holdings and rank *pari passu* with all other subordinated indebtedness.
Call provision:	Everfloat Holdings may redeem some or all of the notes on any business day before [maturity] starting three years after [settlement] based upon the call price schedule as a percentage of the principal amount plus accrued interest.
Call price schedule (% of par):	104.5% [3–4 years after settlement] 103% [4–5 years after settlement] 101.5% [5–6 years after settlement] 100% [6–7 years after settlement]

Incurrence test:	Test is met if issuer has (a) net interest bearing debt to EBITDA not greater than 5.00X and (b) an interest coverage ratio greater than 2.75× for each financial reporting period.
Change of control provision:	Bondholder has the right to sell bond to issuer at a price of 101 if (a) any person other than current holders or permitted holders become the beneficial owner of over 50% of issuer voting shares, or (b) all or substantially all of the assets of the restricted group are sold to any person other than to current or permitted holders.
Business days:	London

Similar to the prepayability of Everfloat's proposed leveraged loan, the high-yield bond grants the investor three years of call protection, after which the issuer may repurchase the bonds at a predetermined fixed premium.

Recall from earlier in the curriculum that the investor is long the bond and short the call option. Therefore, the call option value lowers the value of the high-yield bond relative to the value of a non-callable bond of similar tenor:

$$\text{Callable bond price} = \text{Value of straight bond} - \text{Value of issuer call option.} \quad (3)$$

The value of the non-callable bond may be obtained by discounting the bond's future cash flows at the appropriate rate (yield-to-maturity) or periodic discount rates as shown in Equation 1. For a high-yield bond, the call exercise is contingent upon future interest rates, and the issuer's decision to call depends upon its ability to refinance debt in the future at a lower cost.

In contrast to leveraged loans, the contingent call feature for a high-yield bond depends on the relationship between the bond's yield-to-maturity (comprising both benchmark rates and credit spreads) and its coupon rather than simply the difference between the quoted and discount margin. We illustrate the relationship between the callable high-yield bond and a hypothetical non-callable bond in the case of Everfloat.

CASE STUDY

Everfloat's High-Yield Bond Versus Non-Callable Fixed-Rate Debt

Consider Everfloat's proposed 9% seven year high-yield bond as of the first call date in three years. Under a simplified binomial interest rate tree approach adapted from earlier learning modules, we assume a flat yield curve, fixed interest rate volatility for the bond's yield for its remaining term, and annual interest rate changes based on a lognormal random walk to calculate the price of an identical, non-callable, fixed-rate bond.

That is, in one year, the remaining six-year bond's yield will either rise to a higher rate ($r_{1,H}$) or fall to a lower rate ($r_{1,L}$) with equal probability. Earlier in the curriculum, the relationship between these two rates was shown to be:

$$r_{1,H} = r_{1,L}e^{2\sigma}, \quad (4)$$

where σ is the standard deviation and e is Euler's number (i.e., the base of natural logarithms, which is a constant 2.7183). If we start with r_0 equal to the 9.00% bond coupon and σ = 10%, then we may solve for the higher and lower rate in one period, or $r_{1,H}$ and $r_{1,L}$, respectively, as follows:

$$r_{1,H} = r_0 e^{\left(\sigma - \frac{\sigma^2}{2}\right)}, \quad (5)$$

$$9.897\% = 9.00\% e^{(0.1 - 0.005)},$$

$$r_{1,L} = r_0 e^{\left(-\sigma - \frac{\sigma^2}{2}\right)}, \quad (6)$$

$$8.103\% = 9.00\% e^{(-0.1 - 0.005)}.$$

We may solve for the bond's price under each rate scenario ($PV_{1,H}$ and $PV_{1,L}$, respectively) assuming a par value of 100 by substituting the rate on a financial calculator or the PV spreadsheet function (= –PV(*rate,nper,pmt,fv,type*)):

$$PV_{1,H} = 96.014 = -PV(0.09897/2,12,4.5,100,0),$$

$$PV_{1,L} = 104.197 = -PV(0.08103/2,12,4.5,100,0).$$

We may show this relationship using the following one-period framework in Exhibit 8.

Exhibit 8: One-Year Binomial Tree Framework

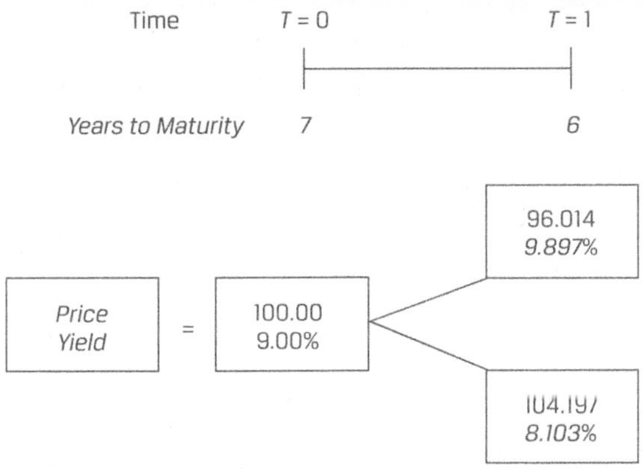

This analysis may be extended for another year by solving for $r_{2,HH}$, $r_{2,HL}$, $r_{2,LH}$, and $r_{2,LL}$ using a similar approach, noting that $r_{2,HL} = r_{2,LH}$ and the dispersion between the highest to lowest rates rises each period:

$$r_{2,HH} = r_{2,LL} e^{4\sigma}. \quad (7)$$

Exhibit 9 shows an example of possible bond yield and price scenarios in three years based upon a bond with four years remaining to maturity.

Exhibit 9: Three-Year Binomial Tree Framework

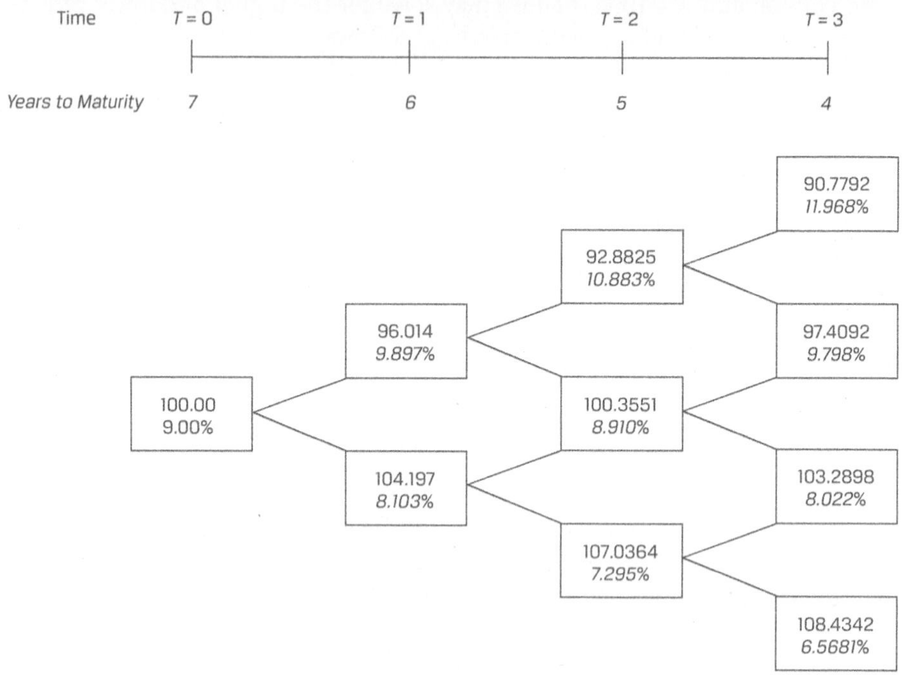

1. Discuss how the bond price and yield outcomes shown in Exhibit 9 would differ in the case of Everfloat's high-yield bond.

Solution

According to Everfloat's high-yield bond terms, the issuer has the right to repurchase the bond three years after settlement at a price of 104.5 per 100. Note that three consecutive rate declines in the binomial tree ($r_{3,LLL}$ = 6.5681%) results in a price which exceeds the call price by 3.9342 (= 108.4342–104.5). Since a high-yield bond investor foregoes the full price appreciation of the non-callable equivalent if the bond is called, we expect the high-yield bond to trade at a higher yield, lower price than a similar non-callable bond. Using the same non-callable bond price and yield scenarios from above, Exhibit 10 illustrates the scenario in which the bond would be called in three years.

Exhibit 10: Three-Year Binomial Tree Framework for Callable Bond

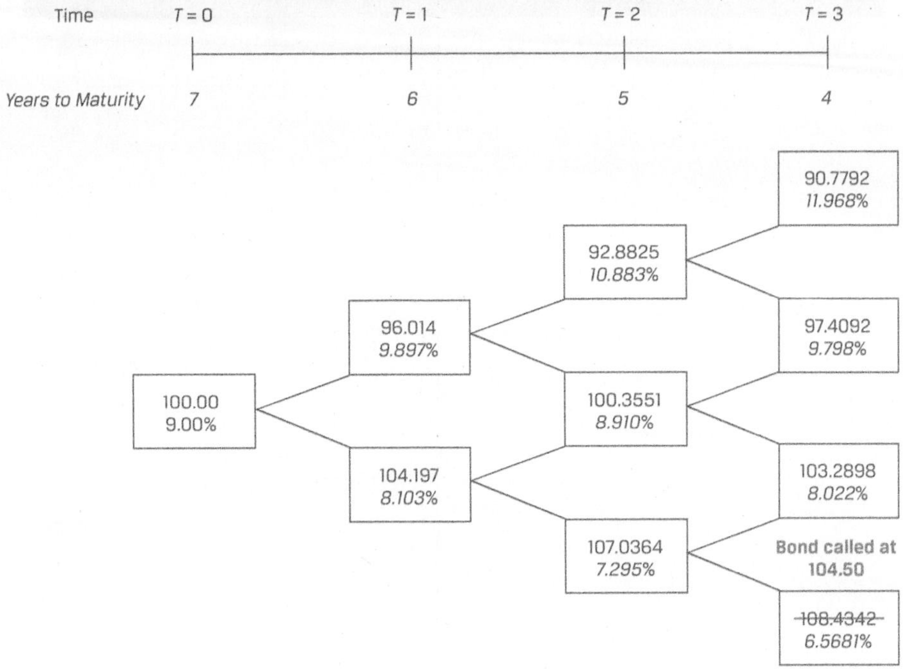

2. Evaluate the effect of higher interest rate volatility on the price and yield outcomes in Exhibit 9 for the case of Everfloat's high-yield bond.

Solution

As for any embedded or stand-alone option transaction, the value of the call option in Everfloat's high-yield bond increases in value as interest rate volatility rises. This is reflected in both a greater dispersion of bond yields and prices and an increased likelihood that the bond is called. We can show this effect by taking the same approach as in solution 1, using non-callable bond prices to illustrate the price and yield scenarios in which the bond would be called in three years under the assumption of 15% interest rate volatility. In this example with higher volatility, the bond would be called in the two lowest-yield outcomes as shown in Exhibit 11.

Exhibit 11: Three-Year Binomial Tree Framework for Callable Bond (15% Volatility)

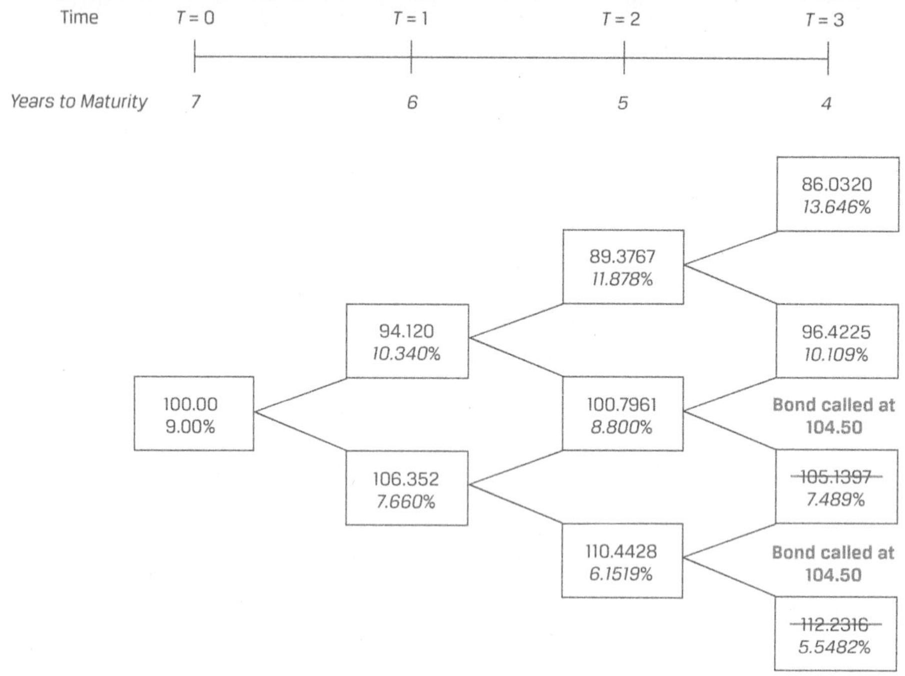

While the above case takes a simplified approach to comparing callable high-yield to non-callable bonds, practitioners typically evaluate risky bonds using either an issuer-specific yield curve with borrowing rates over different tenors, or a series of default risk-free zero rates plus a constant spread estimated using the market prices of comparable bonds for issuers of similar credit quality, known as the **zero-volatility spread (Z-spread)**, while also taking credit spread volatility into account. The **option-adjusted spread (OAS)** is a generalization of the Z-spread calculation that incorporates bond option pricing based on assumed interest rate volatility. The OAS measure is the constant yield spread over the zero curve, which makes the arbitrage-free value of a bond equal to its market price, allowing comparisons across callable, putable, and non-callable bonds.

Characteristics of the price–yield relationship for both leveraged loans and high-yield bonds are noteworthy for both private market issuers and investors. For fixed-rate bonds, it was established earlier in the CFA Level I curriculum under an analytical duration approach that the change in a bond's price for a given change in benchmark yield is the combination of a negative, linear first-order **duration** component and a usually positive, non-linear second-order **convexity** component, as shown in Exhibit 12.

Exhibit 12: Price–Yield Relationship for an Option-Free Bond

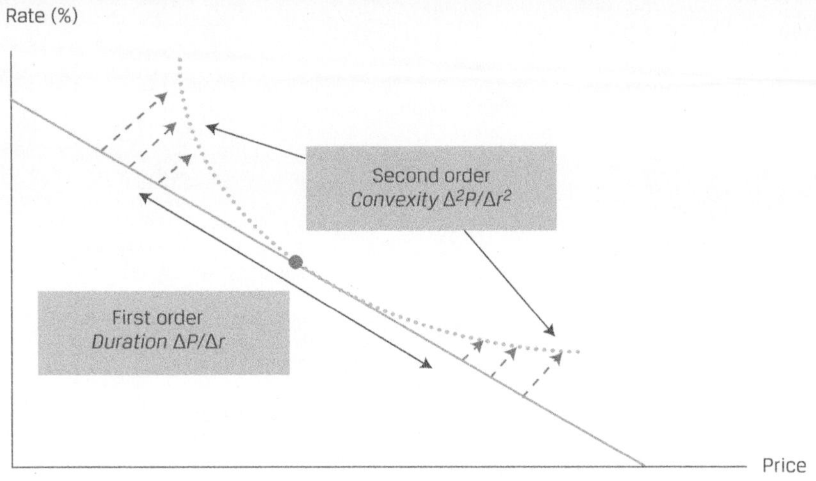

The price–yield relationship for default risk-free, non-callable government bonds and investment grade bonds with highly certain cash flows differs from that of leveraged loans and high-yield bonds. When future cash flows are less certain, the use of an effective duration measure is the relevant statistic to measure a bond price's interest rate sensitivity:

$$\text{Effective Duration (EffDur)} = \frac{(PV_-) - (PV_+)}{2 \times (\Delta\ \text{Curve})(PV_0)}. \tag{8}$$

This measure involves pricing the underlying bond or loan given an instantaneous parallel shift in the issuer-specific yield curve (ΔCurve), with a price increase (PV_+) or decrease (PV_-) from the initial price (PV_0).

For a high-yield bond, its non-callable equivalent will always have a higher price due to the call option value as shown in Equation 3. In the Everfloat case, it was shown that when interest rates are low relative to the bond coupon, the issuer is more likely to exercise the option to refinance its debt at lower prevailing rates. Exhibit 13 shows how this affects the price–yield relationship versus an option-free bond.

Exhibit 13: Price–Yield Relationship for a Callable High-Yield Bond

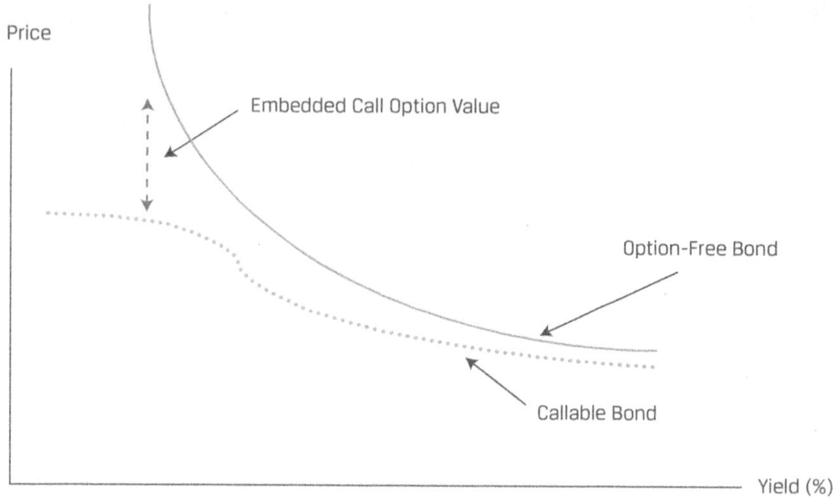

The price–yield sensitivity of floating-rate leveraged loans is a different story. Changing short-term MRRs result in adjusted debt coupons for floating-rate loans and notes, which is why leveraged loans demonstrate little to no price change for a given *benchmark* yield change. As noted earlier, leveraged loan price changes are largely driven by yield spread changes, with the **effective spread duration** (EffSpreadDur) being the appropriate measure:

$$\text{EffSpreadDur} = \frac{(PV_-) - (PV_+)}{2 \times (\Delta\text{Spread})(PV_0)} \tag{9}$$

Note the difference between Equation 7 and Equation 8 is that ΔSpread has replaced ΔCurve in the denominator for leveraged loans.

CASE STUDY

Effective Duration of Everfloat's Acquisition Financing Alternatives

Sue Park is a research analyst at a private debt fund considering an investment in Everfloat's acquisition debt financing. Although the leveraged loan and high-yield bond alternatives have features which differ from non-callable bonds, as a starting point she calculates the effective duration for both the non-callable, 7.40%, five-year bond and the 9.00% seven-year bonds priced at par for *ΔCurve* = 0.0005 using Equation 8:

$$\text{EffDur} = \frac{(PV_-) - (PV_+)}{2 \times (0.0005)(100)}.$$

7.40% Five Year:

PV_0 = 100 with a yield of 7.40%

PV_- = 100.206 with a yield of 7.35% (= −PV(0.0735/2,10,0.074/2×100,100,0))

PV_+ = 99.794 with a yield of 7.45% (= −PV(0.0745/2,10,0.074/2×100,100,0))

$$\text{EffDur} = 4.117 = \frac{(100.206) - (99.794)}{2 \times (0.0005)(100)}.$$

9.00% Seven Year:

$PV_0 = 100$ with a yield of 9.00%

$PV_- = 100.256$ with a yield of 8.95% (= −PV(0.0895/2,14,0.09/2×100,100,0))

$PV_+ = 99.745$ with a yield of 9.05% (= −PV(0.0905/2,14,0.09/2×100,100,0))

$$\text{EffDur} = 5.111 = \frac{(100.256) - (99.745)}{2 \times (0.0005)(100)}.$$

1. Discuss the relationship between the interest rate sensitivity of the non-callable, five-year bond and the proposed leveraged loan for the Boatswain acquisition.

   Solution

   This is a comparison between a non-callable, five-year, fixed-rate bond and a prepayable, five-year, floating-rate loan. Changing short-term MRR rates result in adjusted debt coupons for the floating-rate leveraged loans. The leveraged loan exhibits little to no price change for a given benchmark yield change, but the loan price changes when market credit spreads change as measured by effective spread duration. The non-callable bond price will change given changes in benchmark yields and spreads, so we would expect it to be more sensitive to overall interest rate changes than the leveraged loan.

2. Discuss the relationship between the effective duration of the non-callable, seven-year bond and that of the proposed Everfloat seven-year, high-yield bond.

   Solution

   Consider the interest rate sensitivity of a non-callable bond versus an otherwise identical callable bond. Interest rate changes will have a smaller effect on the callable bond price because at lower yields, price appreciation is limited by the possibility that the bond will be called by the issuer at the predetermined call price.

In general, as the prior case study shows, the effective duration of a non-callable fixed-rate bond always exceeds that of a high-yield bond of the same maturity due to the issuer call option, which increases in value as yields fall. In addition, the interest rate sensitivity of a leveraged loan's price is directly tied to yield spread changes only given the periodic MRR reset based upon market conditions. Note that this limited *price* sensitivity to yield changes does not shield issuers or investors from the risk of short-term yield or MRR fluctuations, which directly affect periodic coupons and therefore the interest expense of issuers and interest income of investors.

Under certain market conditions, the actual price movements of high-yield bonds may differ substantially from what analytical models based on benchmark rates and credit spreads would suggest. For example, issuer financial distress will have a much greater impact on a high-yield bond's price than benchmark rate movements. Also, under a "flight to quality" market stress scenario, investors shun risky assets, causing higher risk, lower rated bonds to fall in price as the price of default risk-free government bonds rises. This observed negative correlation between high-yield spreads and benchmark yields leads practitioners to apply statistical models and historical market data to estimate **empirical duration** as opposed to relying on analytical duration estimates.

The following case study from the COVID-19 pandemic illustrates the divergence between analytical and empirical duration for the high-yield bond market.

HIGH-YIELD BOND MARKET DURING THE COVID-19 PANDEMIC

Global flight restrictions in February of 2020 and the World Health Organization's declaration of a global pandemic in early March led to economic shutdowns in mid-March, a selloff in risk assets, and a sharp decline in both equity markets and US Treasury yields.

A strictly analytical duration approach would imply that a decline in benchmark yields leads to a lower all-in yield to maturity for a fixed-coupon corporate bond and therefore a higher price. Exhibit 14 shows the actual change in high-yield corporate credit spreads rated BB versus US Treasury yields.

Exhibit 14: US Treasury Yields Versus US Corporate BB Spreads, 2020

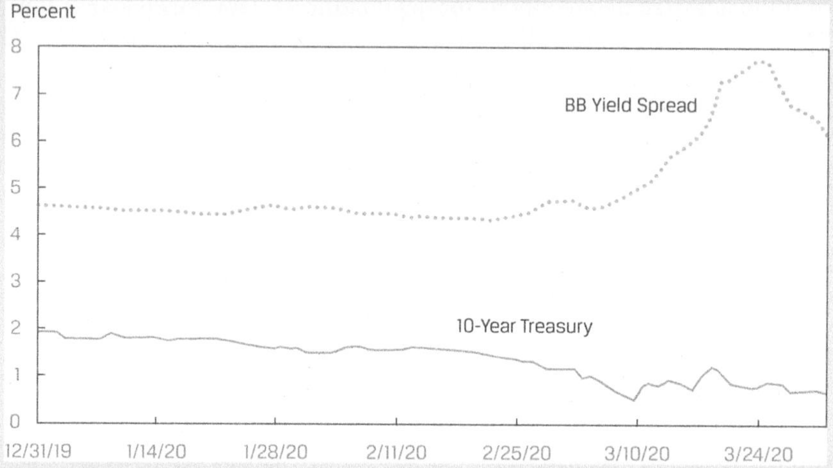

Source: Bloomberg

As investors rapidly shed risk in the wake of the COVID-19 pandemic in early 2020, macroeconomic factors driving government bond yields-to-maturity *lower* caused high-yield bond credit spreads to *rise* due to an expectation of a greater likelihood and higher severity of financial distress.

Convertible Bonds

Convertible bonds are long-term fixed-income instruments which allow investors to exchange debt into equity at a predetermined **conversion price** per share during a **conversion period** in the future. Exhibit 15 shows the payoff profile for a convertible bond introduced earlier in the curriculum as a function of the issuer's share price.

Exhibit 15: Convertible Bond Price Versus Share Price

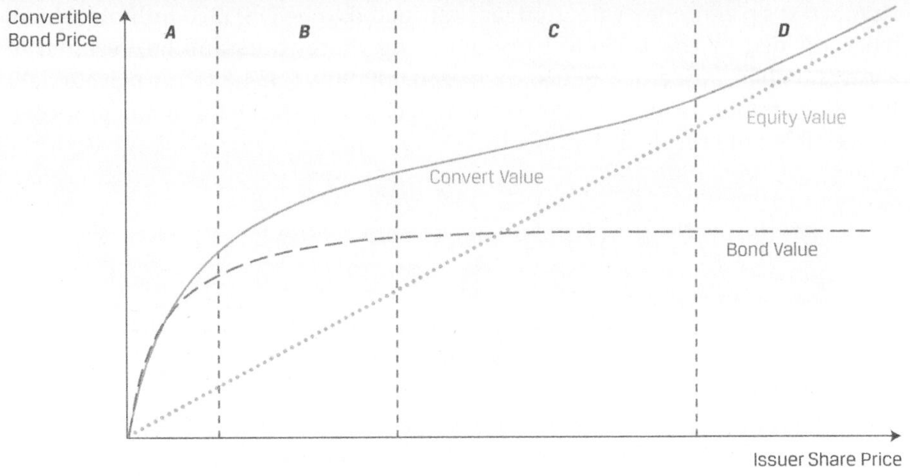

In contrast to Equation 3 for high-yield bonds, a convertible bond value is:

$$\text{Convertible bond value} = \text{Value of straight bond} + \text{Value of call option on issuer stock.} \quad (10)$$

Convertible bond prices exhibit fixed income characteristics when the conversion feature is unlikely to be exercised and have equity-like features as shares rise to near or above the price at which conversion occurs. From left to right in Exhibit 15, the first quadrant (*A*) reflects a distressed case as convertible and straight bond values are nearly equal and equity value is close to zero. Quadrant *B* shows the case in which the convertible bond's value is more closely aligned with expected interest and principal payments, while Quadrant *C* involves the hybrid case in which the share price is near the conversion price. As the issuer share price rises above the conversion price, the convertible bond price approaches the equity value as shown in Quadrant *D*.

Convertible bonds are more common in early-stage and growth strategies for private companies, where issuers may raise debt as a low-cost alternative to common shares. These bonds offer equity upside in the form of conversion rights to investors otherwise unwilling to lend to firms with less stable cash flows and few assets to secure debt. In contrast to both leveraged loans and high-yield bonds, convertible debt is typically senior unsecured with no financial covenants and a debt coupon well below that of non-callable debt. Given the lack of a publicly traded underlying share price, convertible debt issued by private companies is less liquid and typically in the form of privately placed convertible notes. Common convertible bond indenture terms include change of control protection as well as the right to trigger conversion at a discounted price to capture the effects of dilution in the case of new equity financing. Consider the startup company Kumartest LLC introduced in an earlier lesson module and its convertible note financing alternative to new equity issuance.

CASE STUDY

Kumartest LLC Convertible Note Offering

Six years after it was founded, the private medical device startup firm Kumartest LLC reached USD70 million in annual sales and is close to earning a profit. As the company lacks the manufacturing capacity to grow its business and expand to new markets, Kumartest is considering a USD30 million convertible debt offering as an alternative to common equity or convertible preferred shares. Given an estimated 3× price-to-sales ratio for comparable companies, Kumartest's pre-money valuation was estimated to be USD210 million, which, when divided by the 1,334,871 pre-financing shares outstanding, resulted in a current share price of USD157.32 (= 210,000,000/1,334,871). A private debt fund has provided Kumartest senior management with the following proposed convertible note terms in Exhibit 16.

Exhibit 16: Kumartest LLC Proposed Convertible Bond Terms

Issuer:	Kumartest LLC
Settlement Date:	[T + 3 business days]
Maturity Date:	Five years from settlement date unless the notes are redeemed earlier in a conversion.
Principal Amount:	USD30 million
Interest:	0% p.a.
Seniority:	The notes are a senior unsecured obligation of Kumartest and rank *pari passu* with any other unsecured debt.
Conversion Provision:	At its sole option, an investor has the right to convert a portion or the full sum of the principal amount, or any part outstanding at any time at the conversion price during the conversion period.
Current Price:	USD157.32 per common equity share
Conversion Price:	USD275.00 per common equity share
Conversion Period:	Any business day starting one year from the settlement date through the maturity date
Covenants:	Negative pledge of assets
Business Days:	London

Kumartest convertible debt investors are willing to forego a debt coupon in exchange for conversion rights. These investors have the right to exchange debt for Kumartest common stock at a price of USD275 per share, a 74.8% premium over the current Kumartest price of USD157.32 per share (= (275.00 – 157.32) / 157.32). The **conversion ratio** represents the number of common shares a bond may be converted into for a specific par value:

$$\text{Conversion ratio} = \text{Convertible bond par value} / \text{Conversion Price}. \quad (11)$$

For example, if the Kumartest note has a USD1,000 face value:

- The conversion ratio is equal to USD1,000 / USD275 or 3.64.
- An owner of one USD1,000 Kumartest bond may redeem the bond for 3.64 shares of common stock during the conversion period.

The **conversion value** is derived by comparing the convertible bond's price with its value if the bondholder were to exchange bonds for shares today:

$$\text{Conversion value} = \text{Conversion ratio} \times \text{Current share price}. \quad (12)$$

For example, if we assume that Kumartest is valued at a share price of USD350 in five years' time, a convertible noteholder could convert one USD1,000 bond to shares with a conversion value of USD1,274 (= 3.64 × USD350). While this value is used frequently when comparing a publicly traded issuer share price with the market price of a convertible bond, in the case of illiquid private convertible notes exchanged for non-traded private shares, conversion values are more difficult to estimate except at the time of an IPO of issuer shares, a private sale of the company, or a new equity financing.

CASE STUDY

Kumartest Growth Financing with Convertible Notes

As Kumartest's senior management weighs the convertible note proposal in order to finance its proposed growth strategy, it decides to consider both potential outcomes of the strategy as well as possible future equity dilution.

1. Discuss the payoff profile of Kumartest convertible bond under different possible scenarios at the time of maturity assuming no additional financing occurs.

   Solution

   The payoff profile of a preferred shareholder involves two possible outcomes:

   - Share price < Conversion price: If Kumartest's share price remains below the conversion price of USD275 per share, then Kumartest bondholders will receive the bond's face value equal to USD30 million at the time of maturity, assuming no default.
   - Share price > Conversion price: If Kumartest shares appreciate beyond the USD275 conversion price, then the debtholders will exchange the convertible note for shares and receive the conversion value as per Equation 12:

   $$\text{Conversion value} = \text{Conversion ratio} \times \text{Current share price}.$$

   For example, if Kumartest's share price is USD400, then a USD1,000 par value noteholder will receive shares valued at USD1,456 (= 3.64 × USD400).

2. Discuss the fractional ownership of Kumartest convertible noteholders if the notes are fully exchanged for newly issued shares.

   Solution

   Exchange of all convertible notes for newly issued Kumartest shares will lead to the issuance of 109,200 additional shares (= 30,000 × 3.64), or 30,000 USD1,000 bonds at a conversion ratio of 3.64. Given that Kumartest has 1,334,871 existing shares outstanding, post-conversion ownership by convertible noteholders is 7.56% calculated as follows:

   $$7.56\% = \frac{109,200}{(109,200 + 1,334,871)}.$$

   The convertible noteholders' fractional ownership dilutes the ownership stake of the existing equity holders such that their ownership has declined by 7.56%, from 100% to 92.44%.

Standard measures of interest rate sensitivity are not applicable to convertible bonds given their sensitivity to the issuer's stock price over time. In the next section, we will explore forms of debt financing, which are predominantly offered by non-bank lenders.

QUESTION SET

1. Which one of the following statements describes a typical contingency feature of a leveraged loan?

   A. Loan is callable at par.

   B. Loan is callable at a fixed price above par.

   C. Loan interest may be paid in kind.

   Solution

   A is the correct response. Leveraged loans typically have floating coupons with changing MRRs, which cause prices to remain close to par. A common contingency of leveraged loans allows for callability at a price of par, providing a borrower the flexibility to pay down debt. For example, if the issuer's credit quality improves, they may be able to access more favorable financing terms. Response B is incorrect as this contingency is typically associated with a high-yield bond. Response C is incorrect as this feature is associated with mezzanine debt.

2. An issuer has decided it makes the most sense to prepay an outstanding leveraged loan versus other outstanding debt obligations. Which of the following is the most likely reason?

   A. Decrease in the market reference rate

   B. Decrease in the quoted margin

   C. Decrease in the discount margin

   Solution

   C is the correct response. A decline in the discount margin occurs because the issuer's credit quality has improved. A leveraged loan's price increases with a decline in the market discount rate below the quoted margin (i.e., QM > DM), and the issuer is more likely to call the leveraged loan. Response A is incorrect as the coupon on the leveraged loan is floating at MRR plus QM. A decline in MRR causes the coupon to decrease, keeping the loan's price at par as the market discount rate declines. Response B is incorrect as the QM is fixed at the time the loan is made and is less likely to be changed unless the change in credit quality can be tied to achievement of a specified business milestone.

3. Suppose we observe two bonds that are identical other than two characteristics: bond value or coupon. Which one of the following statements best describes the likely relationship between a callable high-yield bond and an otherwise identical bond without a call feature?

   A. Callable bond has higher value or higher coupon.

   B. Callable bond has higher value or lower coupon.

   C. Callable bond has lower value or higher coupon.

   Solution

   C is the correct response. Suppose the two bonds have identical coupons. In this case, the value of a callable bond is equal to the value of an otherwise identical non-callable bond minus the value of the call feature to the bond's issuer. Given that the call feature is an option, its value is most likely greater than zero. Thus, the callable bond has a lower value than its identical non-callable bond. If we instead assume that the two bonds have equal value, then the issuer call feature is embedded in the price of the bond, an issuer pays a higher coupon than would be expected for a non-callable bond of the same maturity. Response A is incorrect as the call feature would have to add value to the non-callable bond for either higher value or higher coupon on the callable to be possible. Response B is incorrect as this statement is the exact opposite of the correct response. With the same coupon, the non-callable must have lower value because of the value of the issuer's call feature.

4. The price–yield sensitivities of leveraged loans and high-yield bonds are usually best measured by which of the following duration measures, respectively?

   A. Effective duration for leveraged loans and effective spread duration for high-yield bonds

   B. Effective spread duration for leveraged loans and effective duration for high-yield bonds

   C. Effective duration for both leveraged loans and high-yield bonds

Solution

Response B is correct. Leveraged loans are usually floating-rate notes, so their prices do not change with benchmark yields. Rather, their prices are only sensitive to changes in issuer-specific credit spreads. Therefore, an effective spread duration measure is more appropriate. The price–yield sensitivity of high-yield bonds, on the other hand, are reflective of changes in issuer-specific discount rates, so effective duration is a better measure.

5. Discuss features of convertible debt that make it an attractive financing choice for early-stage growth companies as compared to leveraged loans or high-yield bonds.

Solution

Issuers of early-stage growth companies may choose to raise debt as a low-cost alternative to common shares. Convertible bonds offer equity upside in the form of conversion rights to investors otherwise unwilling to lend to firms with less stable cash flows and few assets to secure debt. In contrast to both leveraged loans and high-yield bonds, convertible debt is typically senior unsecured with no financial covenants and a debt coupon well below that of non-callable debt.

MEZZANINE AND UNITRANCHE DEBT 4

☐ contrast the use of mezzanine debt and unitranche debt in private market strategies;

As described earlier, private market strategies often use mezzanine structures for subordinated borrowing while offering equity-like returns, or unitranche debt, which combines senior and subordinated debt components into a single facility. Leveraged loans, high-yield bonds, and convertible debt described earlier typically involve either traded public securities or loans underwritten by bank syndicates with standardized terms and disclosures.

In contrast, mezzanine and unitranche debt are highly flexible and tailored to specific issuer and investor needs. As they involve non-standard terms as well as private, confidential reporting, they are often unrated and highly illiquid. These debt forms are primarily the domain of non-bank lenders, with general partners frequently holding a large proportion of a single facility, which increases the ability to directly negotiate initial debt terms and make modifications over time as needed with a private borrower.

Mezzanine Debt

Mezzanine debt is generally subordinated and of a longer tenor than other forms of borrowed capital. Terms vary widely across transactions and regions, with North American structures often more bond-like in nature—that is, unsecured with fixed debt coupons—while European mezzanine debt tends to involve floating rates and often holds a second lien or subordinated claim to company assets, as in the case of leveraged loans. In each case, given its longer time to maturity with no amortization, deferred debt service in the form of paid in kind interest or the inclusion of warrants, mezzanine debt is commonly used to ease initial cash flow pressures in growth or buyout equity transactions as well as acquisitions.

The positioning of mezzanine debt claims after senior secured debt may occur in the forms of either contractual subordination or **structural subordination**.

Exhibit 17: Contractual Subordination

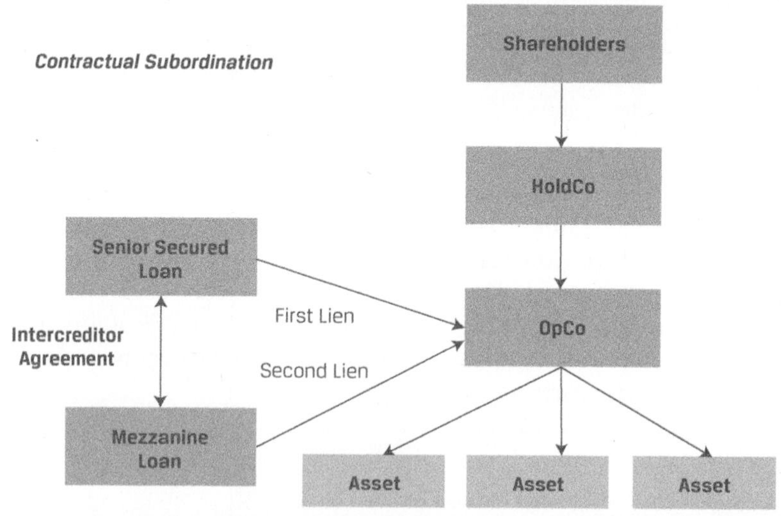

As shown in Exhibit 17, under contractual subordination, senior secured and mezzanine debtholders lend to the same OpCo and sign a contract known as an **intercreditor agreement**. The intercreditor agreement specifies priority of claims, details between lenders, and other key terms among debt tranches.

Exhibit 18: Structural Subordination

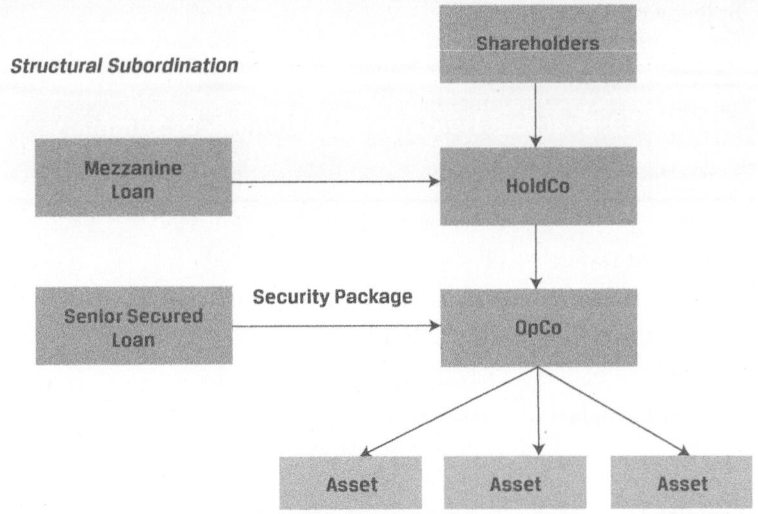

Structural subordination as shown in Exhibit 18 involves debt issued at the HoldCo level as in the case of high-yield bonds, or one step removed from direct access to the operating company cash flows and pledged assets.

Note that in the case of contractual subordination, OpCo lenders have a claim against the assets of OpCo, while under structural subordination, lenders to the HoldCo parent company only have an *equity* claim to OpCo assets as the owner of its common stock. If OpCo were to issue preferred stock to any party other than the parent, then the claims of those preferred stockholders rank ahead of the issuer's common stock claims. Mezzanine debtholders are excluded from the OpCo security agreement governing pledged assets but have a residual HoldCo debt which is satisfied once OpCo senior secured claims are met.

We now revisit the Everfloat case to evaluate a possible role for mezzanine debt in the Boatswain acquisition.

CASE STUDY

Everfloat Mezzanine Financing for the Boatswain Acquisition

Everfloat management has weighed two acquisition financing plans so far:

- Scenario 1: GBP500 million in five-year, senior secured leveraged loan financing at a yield of MRR + 300 bps (with initial MRR of 4.40%).
- Scenario 2: GBP300 million in 9.00%, seven-year, callable high-yield bonds, combined with GBP200 million in five-year, leveraged loans (with initial yield of MRR + 2.75%).

Given the smaller secured loan tranche, Everfloat believes it can realize a lower yield spread of 275 bps p.a. on its floating-rate loan under the second scenario. However, a third scenario emerges.

- Scenario 3: Initial discussions with Spleenwood Capital, a private debt fund, raise a third option, namely a longer term GBP100 million mezzanine debt tranche privately placed with the latest vintage Spleenwood Capital private credit fund and a GBP400 million senior secured leveraged loan (yielding MRR + 2.90%). Everfloat's management has received the following preliminary term sheet from Spleenwood in Exhibit 19.

Exhibit 19: Everfloat Holdings Mezzanine Debt Summary of Terms

Issuer:	Everfloat Holdings
Settlement Date:	[T + 5 business days]
Maturity Date:	[Ten years from settlement date]
Principal Amount:	GBP100 million
Interest:	10.00% p.a. paid semiannually
Interest Payment:	Commencing six months from [settlement date] to be paid semiannually with final payment on [maturity date]
Seniority:	The notes are unsecured subordinated obligations of Everfloat Holdings and rank *pari passu* with all other subordinated indebtedness.
Business Days:	London

1. Given its preference for staggered debt maturities and a balance between fixed versus floating-rate debt, Everfloat is leaning towards the second or third scenario. If Everfloat estimates that it will be able to realize a 290 bps p.a. spread for a GBP400 million loan tranche, calculate its expected annual interest rate savings under the third versus the second scenario (focus on the initial period before any principal is paid back and assume a flat yield curve).

Solution

Compare initial annual interest expense for the second and third scenarios:

- Scenario 2: GBP41,300,000 (= 500 million × (0.4 × 7.15% + 0.6 × 9.00%)).
- Scenario 3: GBP39,200,000 (= 500 million × (0.8 × 7.30% + 0.2 × 10.00%)).

Thus, Scenario 3 results in a GBP2,100,000 initial interest expense savings.

2. Discuss two possible mezzanine structure changes that Everfloat might propose (other than size and tenor) to reduce near-term interest burden and their expected effect on overall financing cost.

Solution

Two possible mezzanine debt features which Everfloat may use to reduce its near-term interest burden include a payment in kind feature or the inclusion of warrants.

A payment in kind feature involves investors foregoing several years of interest payments in exchange for an equivalent increase in debt principal. Given the greater risk associated with this deferred interest structure, Everfloat should expect to pay a higher overall debt coupon.

The use of warrants on the other hand may be used to reduce the fixed debt coupon. However, this lender right to purchase Everfloat's common shares at a predetermined price in the future introduces the possibility of future equity dilution as shares appreciate.

As the Everfloat case demonstrates, considerations beyond interest expense, such as staggered debt maturities, restrictions on asset sales, fixed versus floating interest rate exposure, seniority of debtholder's claim, loan covenants, and other contingencies, all play a role in establishing the most appropriate debt structure for private market strategies. As the most flexible form of subordinated debt, mezzanine structures may be tailored in several ways to meet issuer and investor needs.

Unitranche Debt

In contrast to more complex private company debt profiles combining leveraged loans, high-yield and/or convertible or mezzanine debt, unitranche debt offers a simpler alternative by combining senior and subordinated debt features into a single hybrid loan, as shown in Exhibit 20.

Exhibit 20: Unitranche Debt and Agreement Among Lenders

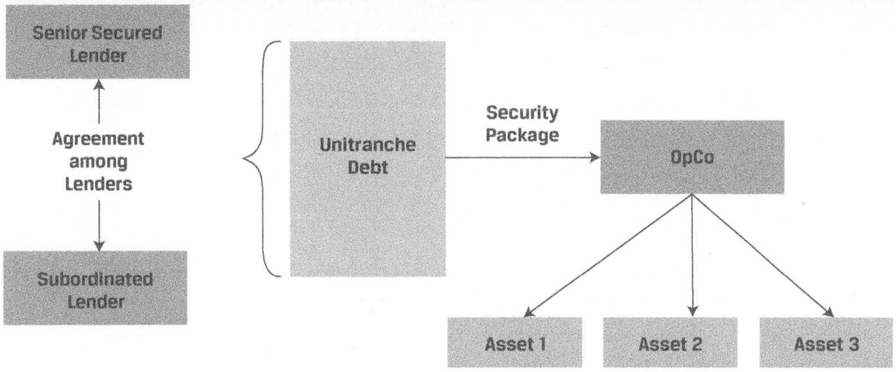

As is the case for other forms of private debt, unitranche debt is available in multiple forms, but often includes a combination of senior secured and subordinated or mezzanine debt. As shown in Exhibit 20, this single tranche loan may involve one blended interest rate reflecting the risk of combined tranches, with creditors separately agreeing to share differently in the risk and return of the consolidated loan exposure via an intercreditor **agreement among lenders**. As the name suggests, the borrower is not a party to this agreement.

The contractual arrangement between creditors may serve to reallocate the unitranche facility's interest and principal payments based upon a revised priority of claims among lenders with specific rights assigned to each, or exchange voting rights to make changes to the covenants or other loan terms. In other cases, the single unitranche debt facility contains two separate tranches or classes of debt: (1) a senior or so-called **first-out tranche**, which is at an interest rate below the blended rate with amortization prior to final maturity, and (2) a junior, subordinated, or **last-out tranche**, which is outstanding until maturity at a higher rate than the overall blended rate of a single tranche.

The most attractive feature of unitranche debt from a borrower perspective is the existence of one loan agreement, which can be executed more quickly and with lower fees than public securities or widely syndicated debt arrangements. The relationship among lenders can take several forms, ranging from *pari passu* treatment to redistribution of claims using an agreement among lenders. These lenders are often GPs who distribute debt to LPs within a closed-end private debt fund and can more directly engage with borrowers to renegotiate loan terms on a proactive basis as needed. That said, the non-standard terms of private debt facilities and complexity of agreements among lenders (to which the borrower is not a party) diverges from standard intercreditor agreements and traditional bond and loan structures, which have been widely tested in court. As a result, greater uncertainty exists as to how these private debt structures will perform in the event of financial distress, bankruptcy, and liquidation.

While initial demand for unitranche debt was from private equity firms financing buyouts for small and medium-sized firms with just one or very few lenders, use of this debt structure has become more widespread among larger private firms, as highlighted in the following example.

THE ACCESS GROUP'S UNITRANCHE DEBT TRANSACTION

The Access Group is a British company providing software application solutions to a variety of industries across the UK, Ireland, and the Asia-Pacific region.

In 2022, the Access Group borrowed GBP3.5 billion from a club of direct lenders to support its acquisition-focused growth strategy. The financing included a GBP2.3 billion unitranche facility in what is believed to be the largest unitranche debt deal in Europe to date, and a GBP1.2 billion acquisition facility.

The unitranche debt was priced at Libor plus 575 basis points with PIK. The direct lenders included twelve firms including well-known names such as Apollo Global Management, Blackstone, and GIC. In addition to more flexible terms, analysts cited lower pricing than for comparable public market transactions at the time.

As the company continued its acquisition strategy, plans for a GBP500 million add-on to the deal were under consideration the following year.

Let us consider a unitranche facility as an additional financing alternative in the Everfloat acquisition of Boatswain Industries.

CASE STUDY

Everfloat Products Unitranche Term Facility

As Everfloat management discusses the GBP100 million mezzanine debt proposal, Spleenwood Capital's managing partner raises the potential of combining the senior secured and mezzanine debt into a unitranche term facility. In addition to lower fees and more rapid execution than a traditional syndicated leveraged loan, the Everfloat team recognizes the potential benefit of renegotiating debt terms with a single GP in the future if it chooses to sell pledged assets or make other adjustments.

Spleenwood offers to fully underwrite the unitranche facility based on its observation of strong demand for mezzanine debt and has identified another private debt fund willing to split the senior tranche via a participation agreement. Spleenwood shares several terms with Everfloat in Exhibit 21.

Exhibit 21: Everfloat Products Unitranche Debt Summary of Terms

Issuer:	Everfloat Products
Settlement Date:	[T + 5 business days]
Term Facility:	A term loan unitranche facility consisting of a senior secured term loan facility ("first-out term facility") and a subordinated mezzanine tranche ("second-out term facility").
Maturity Date:	Ten years from settlement date
Amortization:	First-Out term facility: four years from settlement date
Principal Amount:	GBP500 million total, with first-out term facility of GBP400 million and second-out term facility of GBP100 million
Interest:	MRR + 350 bps p.a. until four years from settlement date 10.00% p.a. paid semiannually thereafter until maturity date
Interest Payment:	Commencing six months from [settlement date] to be paid semiannually with final payment on [maturity date]
Seniority:	The first-out term facility is a senior secured obligation of Everfloat Products and ranks *pari passu* with all other senior indebtedness. The second-out term facility is a subordinated obligation of Everfloat Products and ranks *pari passu* with other subordinated indebtedness.
Prepayment:	First-Out term facility prepayable at par starting one year after the settlement date
Business Days:	London

QUESTION SET

1. Identify and explain the seniority feature common between mezzanine and unitranche debt and discuss how this feature also differs between the two types of debt.

   Solution

   Mezzanine and unitranche both include debt contracts that are subordinated to other classes of debt issued by a company. However, unitranche debt is one debt facility that includes both subordinated and senior debt components into a single debt facility whereas mezzanine simply refers to a subordinated debt class.

2. In structural subordination, mezzanine debt is issued by the:

   A. operating company with a second lien on its assets.

   B. operating company with an intercreditor agreement.

C. holding company.

Solution

Response C is correct. Structural subordination involves debt issued at the holding company level, one step removed from direct access to the operating company cash flows and pledged assets. Responses A and B are both incorrect as these refer to contractual subordination.

3. Identify and discuss two features of mezzanine debt that may be attractive for early-stage growth company issuers.

Solution

Two possible mezzanine debt features which may be attractive for early-stage growth companies include a PIK feature and an attached warrants feature. A PIK feature capitalizes interest to increase the debt outstanding, thus avoiding cash interest expenditures. By attaching warrants to the debt, the issuer adds equity-like features to the debt, thus reducing the need for cash coupons. As early-stage growth companies seek to preserve cash for company growth purposes as opposed to servicing debt payments, both features may be attractive.

4. Discuss an attractive feature of unitranche debt from an issuer perspective.

Solution

The most attractive feature of unitranche debt from an issuer's perspective is the existence of one loan agreement, which can be executed more quickly and with lower fees than public securities or widely syndicated debt arrangements.

5 PRIVATE DEBT PROFILES AND VALUATION

☐ analyze private debt profiles and calculate and interpret financial ratios used to value private debt investments

Private market strategies such as private real estate, infrastructure, and buyout equity depend upon the use of borrowed capital in addition to equity to develop and operate an asset or restructure a company to increase valuation and improve cash flow. Important features beyond debt availability, cost, and tenor include restrictive covenants, contingencies benefiting issuers and investors, and the use of underlying project or company assets as a secondary repayment source.

An important distinguishing feature of private markets is the type of **debt profile**, or detailed breakdown of short-term and long-term liabilities by tenor, seniority, and other features, used in these strategies. Unlike mature investment grade corporate issuers with stable cash flows and broad access to unsecured debt across maturities and markets, private issuers with less stable cash flows are usually sub-investment grade or unrated and must accept constraints in the form of security, covenants, or contingencies imposed by lenders as issuers seek to maximize their value creation potential using leverage.

The composition of a debt profile is a critical consideration in ensuring sufficient operating flexibility with adequate borrower protections, as well as in valuing these instruments under different credit and economic scenarios.

Earlier in the curriculum, we distinguished between short-term forms of funding to meet working capital needs and longer-term funding using loans or bonds. **Revolving credit agreements** are the most common form of short-term bank borrowing facility and may be drawn and repaid as needed until maturity. Revolvers are sometimes available for under a year (usually 364 days) to minimize bank capital requirements, or for multiple years on either a secured or unsecured basis. In the case of leveraged buyout transactions, revolving credit is often made available on a secured basis by a bank based upon a pledge of fixed assets, or private lenders using specific claims to accounts receivable, inventory, or equipment as collateral. This latter form of secured revolving credit is often referred to as **asset-based lending**, as these lenders look primarily to the potential sale of underlying collateral rather than cash flow as the primary source of repayment.

We extend the earlier illustration of individual forms of debt by more closely examining how Bardstown Partners and Maudville Corporation arrive at a debt profile used to finance 75% of the take-private transaction.

CASE STUDY

Maudville Debt Profile

Maudville Corporation is a US chemical producer with nearly USD5 billion in revenue and USD1 billion in EBITDA. Bardstown Partners, a financial sponsor specializing in buyout equity, has offered to take Maudville private for USD5 billion with 20% in common equity, 5% in convertible preferred shares, and 75% in debt.

Working closely with Bardstown, Maudville's new management has established the following priorities in seeking to optimize establishing its debt profile:

- Maximize flexibility to prepay debt over the next three to four years.
- Strike a balance between fixed and floating-rate interest rate exposure.
- Maximize use of Maudville's significant fixed assets as collateral.
- Optimize pricing by tapping the more liquid syndicated bank market as well as private lender demand for junior and subordinated debt.
- Establish flexibility to renegotiate subordinated debt terms as needed by limiting the number of lenders and distribution of voting rights.

Given strong floating-rate leveraged loan market demand, Maudville maximizes the size of its senior secured first lien debt tranche while establishing a second lien junior tranche at a fixed rate, which is funded by Bardstown Partners' own private debt GP affiliate, Bardstown Credit Partners. Given the potential for conflicts between the two affiliates if Maudville were to face financial distress during the investment horizon, Bardstown has created clear written guidance governing information segregation across the two business units as well as policies as to how any resulting conflicts and Bardstown's handling of these will be communicated to LPs. As Bardstown is also building out its new mezzanine opportunity fund, it agrees to underwrite a non-amortizing mezzanine debt tranche at a higher fixed rate for a ten-year tenor, selling half of the debt facility to another private debt GP. In its debt sale agreement to a second private debt GP, Bardstown retains majority voting rights to amend mezzanine debt terms in exchange for a reduced interest rate.

Details of Maudville's debt structure are as follows:

Secured revolving credit facility. USD250 million, 364 day revolving credit facility priced at MRR + 150 bps p.a. on drawn amounts, which is secured by a first lien on Maudville's fixed assets and retained by Maudville's lead banks.

Senior secured leveraged loan tranche. USD2.65 billion in seven-year, senior secured debt at a debt coupon of MRR + 200 bps (current MRR of 4.50% and initial coupon of 6.50%). Loan may be prepaid at par starting in one year and is secured by a first lien on Maudville's fixed assets and ranked *pari passu* with other senior secured debt. Covenants include maintenance of a debt to EBITDA ratio of no more than 6×.

Junior second lien fixed-rate tranche. USD600 million in seven-year junior debt at an 8.00% annual fixed interest rate, which amortizes in four equal installments starting in Year 4. The junior tranche is secured by a second lien on Maudville's fixed assets, established via an intercreditor agreement between the leveraged loan and the junior tranche and ranks *pari passu* with other junior secured debt. Covenants include maintenance of a debt to EBITDA ratio of no more than 6×.

Mezzanine debt tranche. USD500 million in non-amortizing, ten-year mezzanine debt at a 12.2% annual fixed interest rate. The mezzanine debt tranche is an unsecured subordinated obligation of Maudville and ranks *pari passu* with all other subordinated indebtedness. Covenants include maintenance of a debt to EBITDA ratio of no more than 6.5×.

Recall from earlier in the curriculum that corporate creditworthiness is a function of qualitative factors, such as a company's business model, industry, size, and competitive position, and quantitative factors including profitability, debt coverage, and financial leverage.

Financial statement modeling and forecasting tools used throughout the CFA curriculum to evaluate future equity and debt performance also apply to private market debt profiles with a few specific areas of focus. For example, the same buyout equity model used to assess a company's ability to execute on its business plan of value creation via EBITDA expansion, debt reduction, and market multiple expansion may be applied to debt valuation, provided that it incorporates an expected debt paydown plan with the appropriate level of debt detail by tranche, including prepayment penalties and the priority of claims. Estimating expected loss under different scenarios is a key focus, as credit spreads comprise a higher proportion of sub-investment grade and unrated private issuer debt total yield and price, and potential restrictive covenant breaches or debt contingency triggers are additional considerations for these more highly structured types of debt. Finally, illiquidity is an important factor for private debt valuation as for other private market instruments.

The **credit valuation adjustment (CVA)** framework shown earlier in the curriculum and below in Exhibit 22 represents the present value of credit risk for a loan, bond, or derivative obligation.

Exhibit 22: Credit Valuation Adjustment

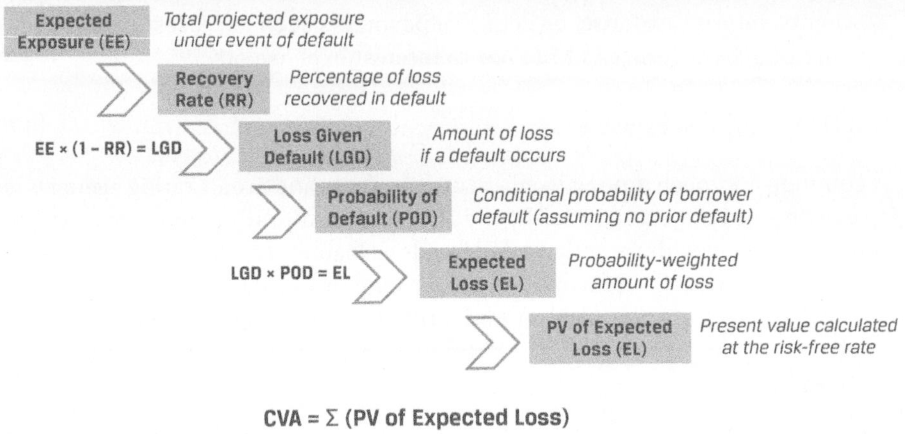

The CVA framework has two key credit risk components, namely (1) **probability of default (POD)**, or the likelihood that a borrower fails to make full and timely payments of principal and interest according to debt terms; and (2) **loss given default (LGD)**, or the amount a lender fails to recover if a default occurs. POD is usually shown in annual percentage terms, while LGD is expressed as a percentage of par value. Expected loss (EL) shown as the product of LGD and POD may also be considered as a simple one-period credit spread estimate, as shown in Equation 13:

$$\text{Credit spread} \approx \text{LGD} \times \text{POD}. \tag{13}$$

While the default probability for a given issuer applies across all debt tranches, recovery for a specific tranche under an event of default depends upon its relative position in the priority of claims among types of debt.

Key financial ratios used to evaluate corporate creditworthiness include profitability, debt coverage, and leverage are summarized below:

Profitability. Strong, stable earnings support cash flow generation as a primary source of repayment, with a focus on operating profits and recurring revenues. Macro factors, such as an unexpected cyclical downturn or declining market share, can adversely impact future profitability. The EBITDA margin is commonly used to gauge profitability:

$$\text{EBITDA margin} = \frac{\text{EBITDA}}{\text{Revenue}}. \tag{14}$$

That said, it is important to note that this non-GAAP measure of operating cash flow excludes capital expenditure and working capital changes.

Leverage. Buyout strategies often tailor an issuer's debt profile to support the highest possible degree of leverage, the timely reduction of which is among the key drivers of value creation. Leverage measures usually compare total debt to firm resources as gauged by assets, capital, profitability, or cash flow. Debt to EBITDA and **retained cash flow (RCF)**, or net cash from operating activities less dividends, to net debt, or debt less cash and marketable securities, are among the most common measures:

$$\text{Debt to EBITDA} = \frac{\text{Total debt}}{\text{EBITDA}}, \tag{15}$$

$$\text{RCF to net debt} = \frac{\text{Retained cash flow}}{\text{Debt} - \text{Cash and Marketable securities}}. \tag{16}$$

Coverage. This ratio assesses an issuer's ability to meet debt obligations from operations by comparing periodic income or cash flow to debt service payments, interest expense, or debt-like payments such as leases. A key measure of debt coverage is EBITDA to interest expense:

$$\text{EBITDA to interest expense} = \frac{\text{EBITDA}}{\text{Interest expense}}. \tag{17}$$

A common approach among fixed-income analysts and credit rating agencies is to group existing and projected ratios by industry and credit rating for comparison with peers or comparison with recently traded bonds or loans of similar tenor and seniority. This estimation process is a form of matrix pricing or evaluated pricing as shown in the Maudville case for a debt analyst evaluating the senior secured leveraged loan.

CASE STUDY

Evaluating Maudville's Senior Secured Leveraged Loan

A debt analyst evaluating Maudville's outstanding debt first conducts research on key financial ratios for the commodity-based chemical sector in North America where Maudville primarily operates grouped by credit rating category as well as her observations of traded credit spreads for similar senior secured leveraged loans in the same industry with the results shown in Exhibit 23.

Exhibit 23: Chemical Industry Financial Ratios by Rating and Spreads

Rating Moody's/S&P Global	EBITDA Margin	Debt to EBITDA	RCF / Net Debt	EBITDA / Int Exp	Senior Secured 7y Spread
Baa2 / BBB	18%–22%	2.25×–2.5×	23%–27%	10×–13×	150 bps
Baa3 / BBB–	15%–18%	2.5×–3×	20%–23%	8×–10×	165 bps
Ba1 / BB+	13%–15%	3×–3.25×	17%–20%	6×–8×	200 bps
Ba2 / BB	11%–13%	3.25×–3.75×	13%–17%	4×–6×	225 bps
Ba3 / BB–	9%–11%	3.75×–4×	10%–13%	2.5×–4×	250 bps
B1, B2, B3 / B	4%–9%	4×–6×	5%–10%	1.5×–2.5×	300 bps
Caa1, Caa2, Caa3 /CCC	1%–4%	6×–8×	1%–5%	0.5×–1.5×	375 bps

Based upon her estimated results from Maudville's first year of operations under new management, the analyst calculates the following financial ratios:

Financial Ratio	Maudville Corporation (End of Year 1)
EBITDA margin	21%
Debt to EBITDA	3.31
RCF / Net debt	22%
EBITDA / Int exp	4.1

Mapping her estimates of Maudville's key financial ratios at the end of Year 1 against those of ratings peers as well as observed traded spreads for similar debt, she concludes that both the issuance spread and ratings of Maudville's Ba1 / BB+-rated 200 bps senior secured issuance spread are consistent with the current leveraged loan market.

[redacted]

Rating Moody's/S&P Global	EBITDA Margin	Debt to EBITDA	RCF / Net Debt	EBITDA / Int Exp	Senior Secured 7y Spread
Baa2 / BBB	18%–22%	2.25×–2.5×	23%–27%	10×–13×	150 bps
Baa3 / BBB–	15%–18%	2.5×–3×	20%–23%	8×–10×	165 bps
Ba1 / BB+	13%–15%	3×–3.25×	17%–20%	6×–8×	200 bps
Ba2 / BB	11%–13%	3.25×–3.75×	13%–17%	4×–6×	225 bps
Ba3 / BB–	9%–11%	3.75×–4×	10%–13%	2.5×–4×	250 bps
B1, B2, B3 / B	4%–9%	4×–6×	5%–10%	1.5×–2.5×	300 bps
Caa1, Caa2, Caa3 /CCC	1%–4%	6×–8×	1%–5%	0.5×–1.5×	375 bps

Private debt valuation *changes* over time reflect a combination of top-down macroeconomic factors as well as bottom-up issuer-specific drivers.

From a macro perspective, the level and slope of credit spread curves change over the economic cycle. While the duration and magnitude of spread changes varies across cycles and industries, Exhibit 24 presents a stylized view of credit spread changes for investment grade (IG) and high-yield (HY) issuers, which represent most private debt issuers, over the economic cycle clockwise, starting in the upper left quadrant.

Exhibit 24: Credit Spread Curves over the Economic Cycle

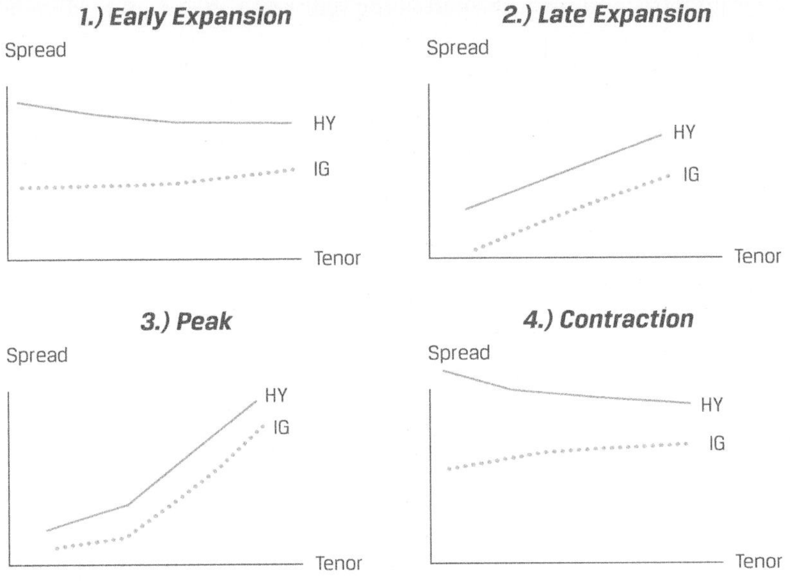

In an early expansion phase, as profitability rises while defaults remain elevated, high-yield spreads are relatively high and well above investment grade spreads, which often exhibit a flat to inverted spread curve.

Later in the expansion phase, default rates fall and profits continue to climb, causing credit spread curves to steepen. This steepening continues as the expansion reaches its peak amid higher leverage and rising inflation expectations.

As contraction begins, growth slows and the economy enters a recession while credit spreads rise and spread curves flatten, with the high-yield spread curve inverting in some cases due to lower profitability and higher defaults.

In addition to macroeconomic factors, we consider bottom-up factors, such as industry- and issuer-specific trends. For example, we would expect the chemical industry to reflect a relatively high degree of cyclicality given sector exposures to regional and global cycles as well as commodity prices, particularly for firms like Maudville as a commodity chemicals producer.

We revisit Maudville Corporation's buyout equity forecast from the Private Equity learning module with a closer look at factors affecting its debt to demonstrate the impact of a recession scenario on key financial ratios affecting the probability of default and therefore credit spreads as a driver of debt value.

CASE STUDY

Maudville Debt Valuation and Scenario Analysis

Recall that Bardstown Partners is pursuing a USD5 billion take-private transaction for Maudville, 75% of which is debt in the following term tranches:

- USD2.65 billion in seven-year, senior secured debt at MRR + 200 bps (current MRR of 4.50% and initial coupon of 6.50%) prepayable at par.
- USD600 million in seven-year, junior second lien debt at an 8.00% fixed rate which amortizes in four equal installments starting in Year 4.
- USD500 million in non-amortizing, ten-year, unsecured subordinated mezzanine debt at a 12.2% annual fixed interest rate.

Note that for modeling purposes, we assume the secured revolving credit facility is not outstanding at the end of the year and cost is captured in interest expense.

As prepayment of junior and mezzanine debt is likely to be more costly than the leveraged loan, we assume that any debt amortization occurring in the first three years involves paydown of the senior secured leveraged loan. Recall that Maudville's business plan to improve Maudville's operations over the next five years include the following assumptions:

- 5% annual sales growth
- Improved cost efficiencies, including:
    - Lowering cost of goods sold (COGS) as a percentage of sales by one percent per year from the current 55% to 50% of sales in Year 5, and
    - Selling, general, and administrative (SGA) expense reduction as a percentage of sales (currently 25%) starting in Year 3, to 22% in Year 5.

The analysis assumes no change in MRR over the period. Under the base case business plan forecast, Maudville's key financial ratios derived from income statement, cash flow, and balance sheet projections for the first three years are as follows:

Maudville Corporation Key Financial Ratios (Base Case)

Financial Ratio	Year 1	Year 2	Year 3
EBITDA margin	21%	22%	24%
Debt to EBITDA	3.31	2.86	2.28
RCF / Net debt	23%	26%	34%
EBITDA / Int exp	4.1	4.6	5.5

In addition to the base case forecast, the analyst decides to add a recession scenario to her assessment in order to evaluate Maudville's business plan in an economic downturn, with the following revised assumptions:

- 5% sales growth in Years 1 and 2, with a 5% *decline* in Year 3
- Cost efficiency gains impacted by the Year 3 recession:
    - COGS as a percentage of sales lowered by one percent per year in Years 1 and 2, with a rise to 58% in Year 3.
    - SGA rises from 25% in Years 1 and 2 to 30% in Year 3.

With other assumptions remaining the same, under the recession forecast, Maudville's key financial ratios for the first three years are as follows:

Maudville Corporation Key Financial Ratios (Recession Case)

Financial Ratio	Year 1	Year 2	Year 3
EBITDA margin	21%	22%	12%
Debt to EBITDA	3.31	2.86	5.37
RCF / Net debt	23%	26%	13%
EBITDA / Int exp	4.1	4.6	2.5

The analyst once again reviews her summary of key industry financial ratios grouped by rating along with current market credit spreads. She decides to apply these same assumptions in her base case analysis for these loans with four years to maturity, while factoring in a 100 bps rise in credit spreads at the end of Year 3 under the recession scenario.

Rating Moody's/S&P Global	EBITDA Margin	Debt to EBITDA	RCF / Net Debt	EBITDA / Int Exp	Senior Secured 4y Spread
Baa2 / BBB	18%–22%	2.25×–2.5×	23%–27%	10×–13×	150 bps
Baa3 / BBB–	15%–18%	2.5×–3×	20%–23%	8×–10×	165 bps
Ba1 / BB+	13%–15%	3×–3.25×	17%–20%	6×–8×	200 bps
Ba2 / BB	11%–13%	3.25×–3.75×	13%–17%	4×–6×	225 bps
Ba3 / BB–	9%–11%	3.75×–4×	10%–13%	2.5×–4×	250 bps
B1, B2, B3 / B	4%–9%	4×–6×	5%–10%	1.5×–2.5×	300 bps
Caa1, Caa2, Caa3 /CCC	1%–4%	6×–8×	1%–5%	0.5×–1.5×	375 bps

1. Discuss the implications of the Year 3 financial ratios for the expected value of Maudville's senior secured leveraged loan at that time under the base case scenario.

Solution

As Maudville executes on its business plan to increase EBITDA and pay down debt under its business plan in a stable macroeconomic environment, it is able to increase EBITDA margin and debt coverage (EBITDA to interest expense as well as RCF to net debt) while lowering leverage. In comparison to peer ratios, Maudville's improved credit measures suggest that it may move into a higher rating category with lower credit spreads, as shown below:

Rating Moody's/S&P Global	EBITDA Margin	Debt to EBITDA	RCF / Net Debt	EBITDA / Int Exp	Senior Secured 4y Spread
Baa2 / BBB	**18%–22%**	**2.25×–2.5×**	**23%–27%**	10×–13×	150 bp
Baa3 / BBB–	15%–18%	2.5×–3×	20%–23%	8×–10×	**165 bp**
Ba1 / BB+	13%–15%	3×–3.25×	17%–20%	6×–8×	200 bp
Ba2 / BB	11%–13%	3.25×–3.75×	13%–17%	**4×–6×**	225 bp
Ba3 / BB–	9%–11%	3.75×–4×	10%–13%	2.5×–4×	250 bp
B1, B2, B3 / B	4%–9%	4×–6×	5%–10%	1.5×–2.5×	300 bp
Caa1, Caa2, Caa3 /CCC	1%–4%	6×–8×	1%–5%	0.5×–1.5×	375 bp

We may therefore expect its senior secured leveraged loan to trade at a premium given the potential expected decline in its market credit spread or DM of 35 bps to 165 bps versus the quoted margin of 200 bps.

2. Discuss the implications of the Year 3 financial ratios for the expected value of Maudville's senior secured leveraged loan at that time under the recession scenario.

Solution

Given the cyclical nature of Maudville's business, the economic downturn adversely affects its business plan to increase EBITDA and pay down debt. The recession causes a decrease in Maudville's EBITDA margin and debt coverage while increasing leverage. In comparison to peer ratios, Maudville's weaker credit measures suggest that it may be downgraded, resulting in higher credit spreads compounded by an overall rise in high-yield spreads:

Rating Moody's/S&P Global	EBITDA Margin	Debt to EBITDA	RCF / Net Debt	EBITDA / Int Exp	Senior Secured 4y Spread
Baa2 / BBB	18%–22%	2.25×–2.5×	23%–27%	10×–13×	250 bps
Baa3 / BBB–	15%–18%	2.5×–3×	20%–23%	8×–10×	265 bps
Ba1 / BB+	13%–15%	3×–3.25×	17%–20%	6×–8×	300 bps
Ba2 / BB	**11%–13%**	3.25×–3.75×	**13%–17%**	4×–6×	325 bps
Ba3 / BB–	9%–11%	3.75×–4×	**10%–13%**	**2.5×–4×**	**350 bps**

Rating Moody's/S&P Global	EBITDA Margin	Debt to EBITDA	RCF / Net Debt	EBITDA / Int Exp	Senior Secured 4y Spread
B1, B2, B3 / B	4%–9%	4×–6×	5%–10%	1.5×–2.5×	400 bps
Caa1, Caa2, Caa3 /CCC	1%–4%	6×–8×	1%–5%	0.5×–1.5×	475 bps

We may therefore expect its leveraged loan to trade at a discount given an expected150 bps increase in the market credit spread to 350 bps versus the quoted margin of 200 bps.

QUESTION SET

1. Which of the following is the most correct description of an asset-based revolving credit agreement used as part of a borrower's debt profile in a leveraged buyout?

   A. Long-term bank or private lending facility with no collateral

   B. Short-term bank or private lending facility with operating cash flow pledged as collateral

   C. Short-term bank or private lending facility with inventories pledged as collateral

   Solution

   C is the correct response. In leveraged buyouts, revolving credit agreements provide a short-term borrowing facility in addition to the issuer's longer-term debts. These credit agreements include asset collateral such as receivables, inventories, or possibly fixed assets. Response A is incorrect. While the revolving facility can be longer-term, there will be assets pledged as collateral. Response B is incorrect because the revolving facility requires assets as collateral rather than operating cash flow.

2. Assuming no change in benchmark yields over time, which one of the following types of debt commonly used in a leveraged buyout is likely to be prepaid first if the company achieves cash flow goals over time?

   A. Mezzanine debt

   B. Leveraged loans

   C. High-yield bonds

   Solution

   B is the correct response. Leveraged loans are issued with a call provision at par and their floating coupon rates ensure that the price of the loans remains near par in the absence of an improvement in the issuer's credit spread. Response A is incorrect as mezzanine debt is not issued with a call provision. Response C is incorrect. While high-yield bonds likely include a call provision, the call price is set well above par value and usually not callable for a few years, suggesting that these bonds are unlikely to be the first choice for prepayment.

3. An analyst is assessing the current price of a private debt transaction. At inception, the debt was priced at a credit spread of 225 bps because the

profitability, leverage, and coverage ratios for the company imply a Ba2/BB credit rating based on the following table.

Rating Moody's/S&P Global	EBITDA Margin	Debt to EBITDA	RCF / Net Debt	EBITDA / Int Exp	Credit Spread
Baa2 / BBB	18%–22%	2.25×–2.5×	23%–27%	10×–13×	150 bps
Baa3 / BBB–	15%–18%	2.5×–3×	20%–23%	8×–10×	175 bps
Ba1 / BB+	13%–15%	3×–3.25×	17%–20%	6×–8×	200 bps
Ba2 / BB	11%–13%	3.25×–3.75×	13%–17%	4×–6×	225 bps
Ba3 / BB–	9%–11%	3.75×–4×	10%–13%	2.5×–4×	250 bps
B1, B2, B3 / B	4%–9%	4×–6×	5%–10%	1.5×–2.5×	300 bps
Caa1, Caa2, Caa3 / CCC	1%–4%	6×–8×	1%–5%	0.5×–1.5×	375 bps

In the current environment, the company's EBITDA margin is now 10%, its debt to EBITDA multiple is 4.0, its RCF to net debt is 12%, and its EBITDA to interest expense is 3.0. Based on the current ratios, estimate the company's current credit rating, and discuss the debt value implications associated with any change in the credit rating since the deal's origination.

Solution

Based on these updated ratios, the company's current credit rating has likely declined to Ba3/BB–. All four of the ratios fall into this classification, although the debt to EBITDA falls on the dividing point between Ba3/BB– and the category below. Based on the decline in credit quality, the private debt's discount margin should increase by 25 bps to 250 bps, and this should drive an appropriate valuation discount on the private debt.

6 PRIVATE DEBT RISK AND RETURN

☐ discuss the risk and return among private debt investments as well as versus other private market investments as part of a strategic asset allocation

Private debt investment funds have emerged as a significant source of debt capital as a result of tighter bank capital standards after the Global Financial Crisis of 2008–09. Private debt strategies primarily involve lending to sub-investment grade and unrated borrowers across the company life cycle, as well as private real estate and infrastructure projects. The rapid growth in private debt coincided with a period of very low sovereign yields following the Global Financial Crisis, coaxing many investors with a significant allocation to public fixed income to consider explicitly including private debt in their strategic asset allocations for the first time. For example, the higher return potential of private market debt compared to public market debt has made this asset class increasingly attractive for pension plans as discussed below, despite lower liquidity and lower transparency.

PENSION PLANS TRANSITION TO PRIVATE DEBT ALLOCATIONS

Traditional pension plan investment strategies have relied heavily on public market debt investments to provide low risk cash flows to match fund liabilities. However, after over a decade of low to negative sovereign debt yields as a result of quantitative easing following the Global Financial Crisis, many pension plans added private debt as a separate asset allocation category.

For example, as part of its periodic comprehensive review of its investment portfolio and actuarial liabilities, CalPERS, the largest US public pension fund, decided in 2021 to increase its target allocation to private debt from 0% to 5%, including the following categories:

- direct lending: 20% to 100% of the total allocation;
- specialty lending: 5% to 40%;
- liquidity financing: 0% to 25%;
- real estate financing: 5% to 40%; and
- private structured products: 0% to 25%.

Specialty financing involves non-bank lending to commercial and consumer borrowers, including areas such as credit card receivables, leasing, and installment loans. **Liquidity financing** includes private debt funds which seek to generate income by investing in a portfolio of short-term obligations to maintain a stable net asset value (NAV). According to Preqin, an alternative investment data company, private debt was identified as the fastest-growing allocation category among US public pension funds with an average allocation target of 5.7%, up from 3%.

As in the case of private equity, strategies employed by private debt funds require longer investment time horizons, given the need for capital commitments from investors which may not be immediately drawn. Private debt funds on the other hand must maintain a solid pipeline of acceptable loans to fulfill these capital commitments over time. Given the higher credit spreads, borrower contingencies, and illiquidity of private debt, investors in these funds expect to earn higher returns than those available from public debt investments. Private debt manager due diligence should include an evaluation of the manager's skill at constructing diversified portfolios that generate stable returns over business cycles. Investors must weigh the benefits of using a manager and incurring management fees versus seeking to create a portfolio of direct private loans or co-investments.

Key sources of risk and return unique to debt used in private market strategies include the following:

Credit risk. Investors in the debt of private issuers expect to be compensated for the likelihood of default and potential loss for all forms of debt used in private market strategies. The credit spread component typically comprises the bulk of investor returns given both the higher likelihood of borrower default as well as their relative position in the capital structure and expected loss under a default scenario. Even though private debt exhibits fixed income characteristics such as a fixed claim with finite maturity, periodic cash flows and a more senior position than equity investments, these investments have historically been categorized within the respective private market category (private equity, real estate, or infrastructure) rather than fixed income, as changes in credit risk and spreads are tied to the underlying investment life cycle and they are generally illiquid.

Interest rate risk. The inverse relationship between debt prices and yield is a key driver of risk and return for non-callable investment grade and sovereign debt, but as established earlier, this risk as measured by effective duration is lower for high-yield bonds and much lower for leveraged loans given the periodic reset of market reference rates than for publicly traded non-callable bonds.

Liquidity risk. Investors in non-traded private debt expect to receive a liquidity premium versus more widely held debt with otherwise similar characteristics. Unlike public debt funds, private debt funds generally originate new loans which are expected to be held to maturity. This approach together with a fund structure more closely aligned with that of private equity enables private debt funds to bear greater liquidity risk and target a higher risk-adjusted return as a result.

Inflation risk. Rising prices reduce the inflation-adjusted real returns associated with fixed-coupon debt instruments. However, because periodically resetting nominal market reference rates incorporate inflation expectations, the floating coupon structures present in leveraged loans and most direct lending facilities are especially attractive for institutions with inflation-adjusted liabilities.

Borrower and lender contingencies. Debt contingencies which benefit borrowers include loan prepayability and fixed-price call options on high-yield debt. While these features create investor uncertainty as to final debt maturities and reinvestment risk, investors expect to be compensated in the form of higher debt coupons versus non-callable debt. The hybrid nature of convertible bonds or mezzanine debt with embedded equity call options or warrants on the other hand represent contingencies which benefit lenders. The risk and return profile of these debt instruments are more equity-like and follow the investment life cycle, supporting their inclusion within the respective private market strategy allocation rather than fixed income.

Direct ending features. Public debt fund managers often supplement their own financial statement analysis with information from credit rating agencies and traded market prices for similar debt transactions. Direct lending in contrast requires private debt fund GPs to establish and maintain a high degree of expertise in finding new borrowers, conducting thorough due diligence, and structuring a properly documented loan facility which they monitor, manage, and periodically value through final maturity. In particular, non-sponsored loans involve higher search, due diligence, and monitoring costs and higher risks given the lack of a controlling financial sponsor. Despite their greater flexibility, newer structures, and documentation, such as agreements among lenders, they are untested in bankruptcy and therefore involve greater uncertainty as to their treatment in the event of financial distress.

As a new separate asset class which has rapidly emerged over a short period, institutional investors seeking to initiate or increase their private debt allocation face a number of challenges in the GP selection process. For example, the lack of sufficient data prevents them from performing a thorough long-term historical analysis of relative performance over time. Second, the period of rapid growth in private debt does not yet include a full credit cycle, which for sub-investment grade and unrated borrowers is a key factor affecting prospective returns for debt-based investments given the relatively high likelihood of loss under a financial distress scenario. Given these limitations on directly assessing fund manager quality based upon differences in performance, factors including the firm's track record in related private market equity strategies over the cycle, the prior experience of debt managers, as well as reviewing the GP's process of sourcing, conducting due diligence, structuring covenants and associated legal contracts, managing, and monitoring outstanding debt over time in detail are all of critical importance when evaluating managers. Many traditional banks whose involvement was historically limited to syndicated bank and public debt markets have also initiated private credit funds managed as limited partnerships, expanding the array of choices available to LPs.

Performing stringent due diligence of private debt fund managers and their performance net of fees is of particular importance given the relatively low allocation among many investors. Smaller investment sizes allow for fewer diversification opportunities across geography, industry, vintage year, and investment strategy, as is commonly observed for private equity investors.

The following case study addresses how a pension plan might consider these issues when establishing a private debt allocation target.

CASE STUDY

Northern States Private Debt Investment Strategy

Northern States Pension Plan is a large US-based public pension plan with a long history of investing in private markets. Nevertheless, private debt is a relatively new asset class and Northern States has not formally included these investments as part of its allocation targets in the past. Given the growing prominence of private debt, Northern States' Investment Committee decides to meet to discuss whether to include private debt in its private market allocation.

Northern States has excellent relationships with its broad array of general partners in other private market funds, and many of these organizations have developed high-quality private debt investment funds. The pension plan has been under considerable pressure to maintain or increase its overall portfolio return target while generating sufficient funds to meet the plan's liabilities, many of which are inflation-adjusted.

Current inflation is at 4.5% annually. Northern States' economic outlook is for inflation to either stabilize at current levels or potentially increase, and its expectation is that nominal interest rates will include changes in inflation.

Northern States currently has asset allocation and expected return targets as follows:

Asset Class	Target Allocation	Expected Return
Public equity	30%	9%
Private equity	25%	11%
Fixed income	20%	5%
Real estate and infrastructure	15%	9%
Other alternative investments	10%	9%
Total	100%	8.7%

Northern States currently owns investments in private debt, and these are included in its private equity allocation. The extent of its private debt portfolio amounts to 4% of the private equity holdings and is held in mezzanine debt and venture debt. These investments typically generate returns similar to the remainder of the private equity portfolio. Based on observations of the private debt market, the current consensus of the Investment Committee is that a diversified portfolio of private debt would have an expected return of 10%.

Brianna Jenkins, Head of Alternative Investments at Northern States, has been tasked with presenting arguments regarding the institution of a formal allocation target to private debt. Jenkins plans to discuss several key points as part of her argument. These include the following:

- The effect of banking industry shocks on the market for private debt.
- The current nominal interest rate environment and inflation expectations.

1. Discuss why the effect of banking industry shocks are a relevant point to discuss in Northern States' decision to allocate to private debt.

Solution

Banking industry shocks, such as the Global Financial Crisis of 2008–09 or the 2023 shock involving the failure of Silicon Valley Bank outlined earlier, reduce the supply of debt capital coming from traditional banks. The private debt market provides a potential funding solution for borrowers in this environment. Northern States can leverage its existing relationships with private market funds and supply funding no longer provided by banks by participating in this newer area of private markets.

2. Justify an argument for Northern States to invest in private debt fund focused on leveraged loans, given its outlook on the nominal interest rate environment.

Solution

Leveraged loans are typically floating-rate debt instruments with coupons that reset as the MRR changes. Because Northern States believes that nominal interest rates are at risk of moving higher, an allocation to a fund investing in leveraged loans may be a way of generating returns that will keep pace with higher benchmark yields and fund liabilities that adjust with inflation.

3. Discuss three possible rationales for why the expected return on private debt is significantly higher than that of the fixed income asset class.

Solution

Rationale 1: Private debt includes illiquid debt investments in lower credit quality companies, thus carrying higher spreads due to credit risk and illiquidity. The fixed income portfolio is more likely to invest in high-quality, liquid government and corporate securities with zero to low credit spreads.

Rationale 2: Private debt often includes features that are valued by the borrower (such as call provisions). To compensate the lender, borrowers must pay higher yields on the debt.

Rationale 3: Some private debt (such as venture funds) may include equity-like features which create a higher risk profile for the debt securities than provided by fixed income securities, as well as a higher expected rate of return.

QUESTION SET

1. A pension plan invested in a leveraged loan as well as a *pari passu* public market bond from the same issuer. After two years, the leveraged loan generated a higher return. Which one of the following statements is the most plausible explanation as to why this might have occurred?

   A. The leveraged loan's call at par contingency feature provided greater price appreciation.

   B. The leveraged loan's floating coupon rates improved inflation protection.

   C. The leveraged loan's price did not decrease as the issuer's credit spread increases.

   Solution

   B is the correct response. The floating coupons of a leveraged loan provide higher cash coupon returns to the lender when nominal rates increase with inflation. Response A is incorrect. The issuer has the right to call the loan at par value, but this does not provide greater price appreciation for the loan. Rather, the lender may demand higher yield on the loan by paying a lower price for the loan. Response C is incorrect. This statement is false as a leveraged loan's price declines with interest rate increases associated with credit spread increases (but not benchmark yield increases).

2. Which one of the following features is most consistent with private debt being riskier than public debt?

   A. More restrictive covenants on private debt

   B. Greater use of floating rates in private debt

   C. Credit rating differences between companies in private versus public debt markets

   Solution

   C is the correct response. Companies borrowing in private debt markets are likely lower-rated or unrated, thus implying higher risk in private debt markets. Response A is incorrect as more restrictive covenants are applied by the lender on the borrower to help offset the higher risk associated with lending to lower-rated companies. Response B is incorrect as floating rates only reflect changes in the underlying risks of debt markets in general. Greater use of floating rates does not reflect any difference in risk compared to public debt markets.

3. Discuss how both lower and higher interest rates may potentially be a risk factor for an investor in the private debt market.

   Solution

   The most obvious example of risks to private debt investing from higher or lower interest rates can be discussed using leveraged loans with floating coupons. An economic environment in which interest rates increase will cause leveraged loans to pay higher coupons if the interest rate increases occur because of benchmark yield increases. The higher cash flow burden associated with higher coupon payments may cause increased bankruptcies, thus lowering private debt returns. On the other hand, interest rate decreases may be associated with benchmark yield decreases associated with slowing growth. If the slowing growth becomes recessionary, corporate bankruptcies may increase in this circumstance as well. General partners must perform significant due diligence on their private debt target companies to ensure the ability to perform in a variety of economic scenarios.

PRACTICE PROBLEMS

The following information relates to questions 1-4

Brianna Jenkins, Head of Alternative Investments at Northern States Pension Plan, has asked an analyst, Cheng Zhu, to assist on the plan's proposed allocation of 5% of its overall portfolio to rivate debt. Jenkins first shows the following table summarizing Northern States' current allocations across asset classes:

Asset Class	Target Allocation	Expected Return
Public equity	30%	9%
Private equity	25%	11%
Fixed income	20%	5%
Real estate and infrastructure	15%	9%
Other alternative investments	10%	9%
Total	100%	8.7%

Jenkins informs Zhu that a diversified portfolio of private debt would have an expected return of 10%.

Zhu is curious as to why the expected return on private debt is much higher than that expected from the fixed income portfolio and asks Jenkins about the potential risks associated with private debt. Jenkins responds with the following two statements:

Statement 1 One of the major types of private debt exhibits greater price sensitivity to interest rate changes compared to straight debt instruments.

Statement 2 Higher interest rate scenarios may be associated with increased bankruptcy risk in the corporate sector.

Jenkins continues discussing possible risks in the private debt category and notes that historical private debt fund performance varies depending upon the strategy focus of different funds. However, historical performance differences are not particularly noticeable across fund managers investing in similar strategies within private debt.

Jenkins also notes that the due diligence process of private debt fund GPs is a very important aspect of Northern States' investment process. She identifies three major risks associated with investing in private debt funds: (1) the macroeconomic risks facing borrowers, (2) the illiquidity of private debt funds, and (3) the covenants underlying the debts in which private debt funds invest.

1. Demonstrate how an allocation to private debt may allow Northern States to increase its total expected return.

2. Which response below is correct about Statements 1 and 2 made by Jenkins?

   A. Statements 1 and 2 are both true.

B. Statement 1 is true, and Statement 2 is false.

C. Statement 1 is false, and Statement 2 is true.

3. Discuss why Jenkins believes that a lack of noticeable performance differences across private debt fund managers may reflect a risk of private debt investing.

4. Which one of the following return risks facing private debt investors is least likely to be potentially addressed through adequate due diligence of fund general partners?

   A. Credit cycle risks of private debt

   B. Private debt fund illiquidity risks

   C. Private debt fund covenant risks

The following information relates to questions 5-8

Bardstown Partners, a private equity firm specializing in buyout equity investing, is the financial sponsor of a USD2 billion transaction to take Peerland Company, a mature grocery chain, private. Bardstown's senior management debated whether to allow Peerland's management team to negotiate directly with potential direct lenders or not. Ultimately, they decide to financially sponsor Peerland's direct lending.

Leveraged loans play a primary role in the debt profile of the Peerland buyout. Bardstown has issued USD800 million of floating-rate leveraged loans with six-year maturity as part of the overall financing of the transaction. The leveraged loans pay coupons at MRR plus 250 bps, and MRR is currently 4.80%. The other debt in the financing is a USD500 million of fixed-rate 8.50% coupon, high-yield bonds with an eight-year maturity. Both tranches of debt include call features. Bardstown's projections suggest that Peerland will generate sufficient cash flow to begin prepaying its debt in the first year following the buyout to begin lowering its leverage ratio towards longer-term targets.

The high-yield debt issued as part of the Peerland buyout includes a change of control provision which requires Bardstown to offer to repurchase all outstanding high-yield bonds at a fixed price (above par) if a new owner acquires a predetermined percentage of voting shares.

Bardstown Partners has built detailed projections of Peerland's operations, which include significant improvements in its EBITDA margins, debt to EBITDA multiples, and interest coverage multiples over a five-year time horizon. Bardstown expects the credit spread on Peerland's debt to improve by 100 bps under their assumptions. On the other hand, Bardstown has no projections regarding benchmark yield changes over the time frame of their projections.

5. Which of the following most accurately describes the loan pricing of Peerland's direct loans, given Bardstown's decision to sponsor as compared to non-sponsored direct loans?

   A. Lower coupon rates

   B. No difference in coupon rates

C. Higher coupon rates

6. Which one of the following statements most correctly describes Bardstown's strategy to prepay Peerland's debt?
   A. Prepay the high-yield bonds first to avoid their higher coupon payments
   B. Prepay the leveraged loans first only if benchmark yields decline
   C. Prepay the leveraged loans first because the call provision has a very short lockup period.

7. Discuss why the buyers of the high-yield bonds may want a change of control provision included as a restrictive covenant.

8. Which of the following duration measures is most appropriate to assess the price–yield sensitivity of the Bardstown sponsored leveraged loans?
   A. Modified duration
   B. Effective duration
   C. Effective spread duration

The following information relates to questions 9-12

Spleenwood Capital, a fund management company specializing in private debt investing across a broad range of strategies, is evaluating an array of potential investments for several funds in which the company serves as general partner.

Many of Spleenwood's funds include direct lending arrangements structured as leveraged loan transactions. Leveraged loans are senior secured debt typically with floating-rate coupons and are made to borrowers with below investment grade credit ratings. In the current direct lending environment, Spleenwood is increasingly encountering companies able to access the leveraged loan market in covenant-lite transactions. Spleenwood's investment policy does not allow for it to engage in covenant-lite transactions.

Spleenwood has been actively pursuing fund opportunities focused on lending to younger growth-oriented companies. Spleenwood is attracted to these fund categories because the types of debt investments in these funds exhibit significantly different characteristics compared to most of the other private debt market. As part of its strategy to focus on growth-oriented companies, Spleenwood also seeks out companies that may consider issuing mezzanine debt. Spleenwood is attracted to the very high interest rates typically available from mezzanine issues.

Some of the growth companies that Spleenwood targets for mezzanine debt have indicated an interest in having the proposed mezzanine financing provided by Spleenwood included as part of a unitranche debt facility. Spleenwood considers the benefits and costs associated with being part of a unitranche structure.

9. Discuss the market conditions under which a covenant-lite transaction is likely to occur in private debt markets, and describe one example consistent with a covenant-lite transaction.

10. Which one of the following debt characteristics is most likely to be attractive to

Spleenwood in its strategy to lend to younger growth-oriented companies?

A. Coupon income

B. Warrants and conversion rights

C. Secured by asset collateral

11. Discuss how Spleenwood might structure 10-year mezzanine debt to avoid a high cash flow burden on the borrower during the first four years of the debt contract while ensuring that the debt has no equity-linked features.

12. Which one of the following is a likely concern for Spleenwood with respect to the unitranche structure?

A. Borrower pays one blended interest rate

B. Complexity of agreements among lenders

C. Borrower pays lower fees than for syndicated debt

SOLUTIONS

1. To increase portfolio return significantly, an allocation to private debt would be funded by reducing the allocation to fixed income. The expected return of private debt is 10% and this is 500 bps greater than the 5% fixed income expected return. Thus, a simple reallocation of 5% to private debt from fixed income is expected to yield an additional 25 bps of expected return (= 500 bps × 0.05). A reallocation utilizing other asset classes will reduce the potential for expected return and, in the case of private equity, a reallocation to private debt would reduce expected return. Note that this ignores any impact of different correlations between equities and fixed income and equities and private debt.

2. C is the correct response. Statement 1 is false because leveraged loans, a major category of private debt, are less price sensitive to interest rate changes than are straight debt. Statement 2 is true as higher interest rates may cause additional cash burdens on corporate borrowers with a potential that they may be faced with possible bankruptcy.

3. The inability to differentiate returns is likely associated with the lack of difficult economic circumstances facing private debt fund GPs over the historical reporting period in addition to their lack of liquidity. This creates an investment climate in which it may be difficult to assess fund manager quality based on differences in performance. Rather, investors must seek to manage their risks of private debt investing by performing stringent due diligence of fund managers on their entire investment process and portfolio construction process.

4. B is the correct response. While private debt has finite maturities in contrast to the underlying equity in the same issuer, private debt investors face significant illiquidity of private debt fund that cannot be addressed in their due diligence process. Response A is incorrect as investors should ensure that their due diligence process of GPs of private debt funds includes a thorough analysis of how the fund identifies borrowers who will be less susceptible to these sorts of macroeconomic risk factors. Response C is incorrect as private debt fund general partners able to negotiate adequate covenant protections are more likely to outperform their counterparts who include looser covenants on their transactions when economic stress events occur. As such, proper investor due diligence should review a GP's policies on drafting covenants as well as reviewing covenants of current portfolio investments.

5. A is the correct response. Prospective lenders tend to have less bargaining power in negotiating terms and pricing for sponsored loans. This implies that lenders must accept lower coupon rates, implying lower expected returns on direct loans. Because of the greater costs associated with identifying non-sponsored borrowers and analyzing and monitoring their creditworthiness, investors often expect higher returns in the form of wider credit spreads on these loans.

6. C is the correct response. Leveraged loans allow for the debt to be prepaid shortly after issuance at a price of par value. As a result of the low call price and the short lock-up period, leveraged loans can be prepaid almost immediately. Response A is incorrect as high-yield bonds have a longer lock-up period such that they cannot be prepaid in the first year after issuance. Response B is incorrect as declines in benchmark yields have little or no effect on the price of the floating-rate callable leveraged loans, so conditioning the prepayment on benchmark yields declining is not a necessary condition.

7. If Bardstown sells Peerland before the high-yield bonds mature in eight years, the bondholders will benefit from the change of control provision and will be able to collect a premium to par value. Without the provision, Bardstown could simply use the sale proceeds and buy back the debt at prevailing market prices.

8. C is the correct response. The price of floating-rate coupon leveraged loans is not sensitive to changes in benchmark yields but only to changes in credit spreads. Thus, effective spread duration is the most appropriate measure of price–yield sensitivity. Response A is incorrect as modified duration is not appropriate for bonds with embedded options and adjustable cash flows. Response B is incorrect as effective duration measures price–yield sensitivity for changes in the benchmark yield but not credit spread changes.

9. In competitive markets with strong demand for leveraged loans, the types of maintenance covenants typically required for leveraged loans may be weakened to make the loan terms more favorable to the borrower.

   One example of a covenant-lite transaction may be to include an incurrence covenant such as requiring the borrower having a debt to EBITDA below a certain level only if the borrower is seeking to issue new debt. This covenant is weaker than a maintenance covenant in which the debt to EBITDA multiple is assessed at each reporting period to ensure that the multiple is below the agreed-upon level.

10. B is the correct response. The typical debt instruments issued by younger growth-oriented companies are venture debt and convertible debt. Both of these debt types typically include equity-linked features such as warrants (venture debt) and conversion rights (convertible debt) which increase the risk and expected returns of the instruments. Response A is incorrect because one effect of the inclusion of equity-linked features is to lower the coupon rates on these types of debt to preserve cash flows. Response C is incorrect as the early-stage companies issuing venture debt likely do not own assets that would be good collateral and convertible bonds typically are not secured.

11. A PIK feature involves investors foregoing several years of interest payments in exchange for an equivalent increase in debt principal. Spleenwood could structure the mezzanine debt to defer the first four years of coupon payments by increasing the debt principal to account for the deferred interest. Because Spleenwood is taking greater risk with this structure, the stated interest rate is likely greater than if Spleenwood structured the mezzanine debt as a standard fixed-coupon bond.

12. B is the correct response. The unitranche structure creates one loan agreement which can be executed more quickly and with lower fees than public securities or widely syndicated debt arrangements. This benefit to the borrower creates a more complicated contracting problem for the different lenders that are parties to the structure. The non-standard terms of private debt facilities and complexity of agreements among lenders (to which the borrower is not a party) diverges from standard intercreditor agreements, and these agreements have not been widely tested in legal settings. As a result, greater uncertainty exists as to how these private debt structures will perform in the event of financial distress, bankruptcy, and liquidation. Response A is incorrect as the sharing of interest is addressed by the agreement among lenders. Response C is incorrect as this is a benefit to the borrower.

LEARNING MODULE

5

Private Special Situations

LEARNING OUTCOMES	
Mastery	*The candidate should be able to:*
☐	discuss the characteristics and risks of special investment situations
☐	discuss the features of distressed debt, financing alternatives for issuers in financial distress, and investment strategies in distressed situations
☐	discuss the features of complex investment situations involving financial dislocation or stress
☐	discuss the due diligence and valuation processes used to evaluate special investment situations
☐	discuss the risk and return among special situations and compared to other forms of private debt as part of a strategic asset allocation

INTRODUCTION

1

As described in earlier learning modules, private market strategies usually involve investments over a broad range of company life-cycle phases or project development stages with relatively long and illiquid holding periods. Private investment general partners (GPs) focus on adding value and generating returns over a multiyear investment life cycle in private equity, real estate, and infrastructure investments, among others.

Special situations investments, in contrast, are often of a shorter-term nature, focused on opportunities associated with events or market conditions that are expected to have a significant impact on the absolute or relative value of an issuer's private or public obligations. These events are most frequently associated with either financial dislocation or distress, although non-financial events such as fraud, litigation, or failed business combinations may be involved. This type of investment spans a wide range of corporate and sovereign issuers and investments, including private special situations funds, high-risk debt strategies within a private debt asset allocation, or as a separate category of opportunistic investments. Despite their investments in publicly traded securities in many cases, special situations funds are included here due to their predominantly private ownership structure. Given their episodic nature and limited scope, special situations represent a small but growing fraction of the overall private market universe. According to the alternative investment data provider Preqin, which includes such investments in its private debt category as either distressed debt or special situations and mezzanine debt, these strategies are expected to reach over USD1 trillion in global assets under management (AUM) by 2027, or just under half of all private debt investments under management.

This learning module builds on the foundation established in the Private Debt learning module in this pathway by first addressing the features of special situations investments. While the previous learning module highlighted the use of debt in private market strategies over a restructuring or project development life cycle, the focus here is on *events* that materially affect the value of an issuer's debt or equity securities. For example, financial distress, or a high likelihood that promised loan or bond payments will not be made in full on time, and its resolution via restructuring, bankruptcy, or liquidation are among the most common events associated with this investment subcategory. We will address the characteristics of distressed debt, which arise due to both adverse macroeconomic conditions and company- and industry-specific factors, as well as financing alternatives for distressed issuers. Investment approaches associated with special situations include short-term trading strategies related to credit events or business combinations, more active strategies seeking to control a firm as it emerges from bankruptcy, and more complex transactions involving capital structure or convertible arbitrage. As with other private markets, specialized GP knowledge and experience are critical to success in sourcing, evaluating, and executing special situations investments, which often include an understanding of the bankruptcy process. Valuation approaches are often supported by scenario analysis given the material impact of alternative outcomes. The combination of returns dominated by short-term price changes and the potential for less correlation and idiosyncratic sources of return are important drivers of the unique role of special situations in a strategic asset allocation.

LEARNING MODULE OVERVIEW

- Special situations involve opportunities associated with issuers in financial distress or events over a relatively short time horizon. Strategies include capitalizing on securities mispricing for distressed issuers, a corporate action such as a merger or acquisition, or a more complex investment situation, such as convertible arbitrage.
- Distressed debt involves issuers that are illiquid, insolvent, or at greater risk of not meeting debt obligations. Distressed financing alternatives include debt exchanges outside or within the bankruptcy process, as well as secured debtor-in-possession financing during the reorganization period.
- Structural models linking the price of equity and credit may be used to establish relative value across a firm's shares, bonds, and credit default swap (CDS) pricing. Capital structure and convertible arbitrage strategies seek to capitalize on pricing anomalies among these positions and within the capital structure in cases of financial dislocation.
- Investors in special situations often face a short time frame to conduct due diligence and have less information, which is subject to event-driven change. Given the challenges of incorporating the timing and magnitude of financial distress and other events into standard valuation approaches, scenario analysis is often applied to liquidation and going concern outcomes weighted by probability.

- As a subcategory of private debt for many investors, special situations investments seeking to capitalize on event-driven mispricing have the potential to provide diversification to debt portfolios where interest income and the return of principal are primary sources of return.

SPECIAL INVESTMENT SITUATIONS 2

☐ discuss the characteristics and risks of special investment situations

Earlier Private Markets Pathway learning modules characterized private investments in company debt or equity, real estate, or infrastructure as illiquid positions held for multiyear investment periods over a range of company life-cycle or project development phases. The area of private investment that targets return by investing in stressed, distressed, or event-driven opportunities, often over a shorter time frame, is referred to as **special situations**.

In contrast to the value creation process used in other private market strategies, these opportunities involve discrete events that have a significant impact on investment value. Investment professionals often refer to **financial dislocation** as a case in which market prices are misaligned on an absolute or relative basis due to economic crises, changes in liquidity, market constraints, or other industry- or company-specific factors. While many situations may fall into this category, we distinguish here between financial distress and other event-driven opportunities.

Financial Distress

The loan or bond obligations of issuers considered unlikely to meet promised future interest and principal payments in a timely manner are referred to as **distressed debt**. Events associated with financial distress include failure to pay a contractual debt obligation on time, violation of a financial covenant in a bond indenture or loan agreement, and/or a situation in which the market value of a firm's assets falls below that of its fixed obligations when valued as a going concern. When issuers are unable to meet their fixed debt obligations, debtholders may become residual claimants to a firm's remaining net assets, as shown in Exhibit 1.

Exhibit 1: Firm Value Distribution between Shareholders and Debtholders

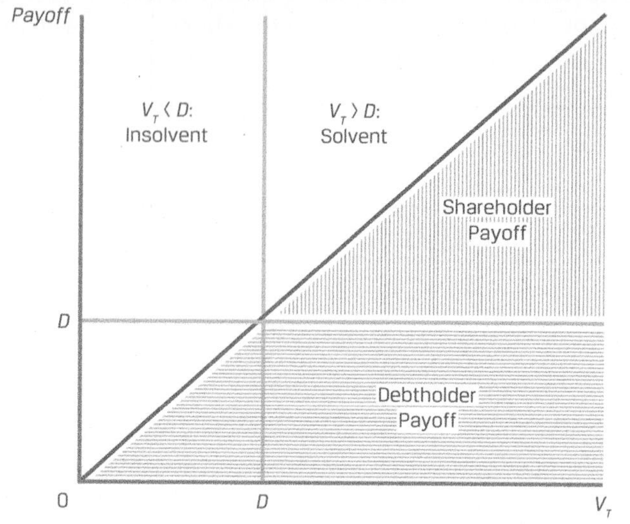

Exhibit 1 shows the example of a firm valued at time T (V_T), at which time the firm's zero-coupon debt (D) also matures. If the firm is solvent ($V_T > D$), debtholders are paid in full and shareholders capture the remaining firm value. In the case of **insolvency** ($V_T < D$), a situation in which total liabilities exceed the market value of assets, V_T is distributed to debtholders, who receive less than the promised interest and principal, while shareholders receive nothing. Earlier in the curriculum, it was shown that this relationship between shareholders and debtholders has option-like characteristics. That is, shareholders hold a long position in the firm's assets (V_T) and have purchased a put option on firm value with an exercise price of D from debtholders. The put option premium may be interpreted as the credit spread paid to debtholders.

A distressed investor might seek to capitalize on the expected outcome by either (1) purchasing the bonds of an issuer trading at a significant discount to par in anticipation of being paid in full or receiving a higher discounted price or (2) selling short the stock of an issuer that is expected to become insolvent. Beyond this short-term approach involving non-controlling trading positions, investors may seek a more active role in restructuring as a significant minority or controlling investor or use the process to acquire and eventually resell an entire company.

In practice, the assessment and allocation of firm value among investors is more complex than shown in Exhibit 1. For example, asset valuation may vary widely when considering a forced sale to a third party versus continued operations as a going concern. Firm liabilities typically involve many claims, with more complex debt profiles and staggered interest and principal payment schedules over time, as well as different levels of seniority, security, and other contingency features. The substantial time and cost associated with the **bankruptcy** process are important drivers of alternative approaches, described later in this learning module.

Causes of financial distress include economic downturns leading to poor operating and financial performance and company- or industry-specific factors adversely affecting a firm or industry. For example, Exhibit 2 shows global annual corporate default rates from S&P Global Ratings over several decades.

Exhibit 2: Annual Global Corporate Bond Default Rates (%)

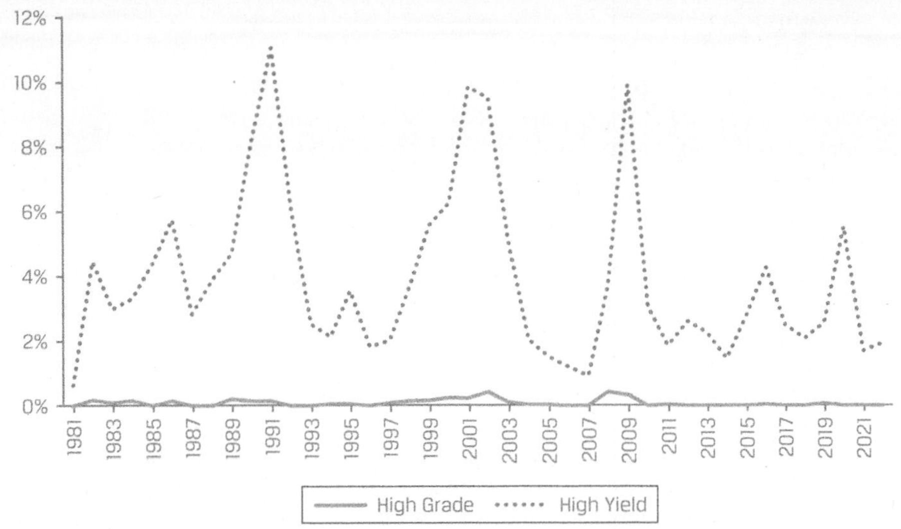

Source: S&P Global Ratings.

Exhibit 2 demonstrates that the likelihood of default rises significantly amid economic slowdowns, reaching highs during the 1990–91 and 2001 recessions, the Global Financial Crisis of 2008-2009, and, to a lesser degree, the COVID-19 pandemic. Defaults are also far more frequent among high-yield issuers, or those with sub-investment-grade ratings at the time of default. One measure of investor loss in a default scenario is the **credit loss rate**, the *realized* percentage of par value lost to default for bonds, equal to the bonds' default rate multiplied by the loss severity. According to Moody's Investors Service, the highest annual credit loss rate for US investment-grade corporate bonds since 1983 was close to 0.4%, with an average of 0.05%. For high-yield bonds, the average credit loss rate was around 2.5%, while in several years, usually around economic recessions, losses exceeded 5%.

Industry-specific factors often play a role in the financial distress of firms, even in periods of relative macroeconomic stability. Earlier in the curriculum, risk factors considered that affect overall industry performance beyond cyclicality included industry structure and concentration, competitive intensity, value chain dynamics, and long-term growth and demand. For example, commodity-based companies are often considered among the most cyclical due to the direct impact of underlying economic activity and consumer demand on prices. However, the impact of supply increases and technological change may also contribute to weaker industry performance, as highlighted in the following example.

EXAMPLE 1

Petroleum Industry Bankruptcies amid the Global Oil Price Collapse

Beginning in July 2014, global oil prices faced their most sustained decline of the 21st century. The US benchmark West Texas Intermediate (WTI) crude oil price fell from highs of well over USD100 per barrel through mid-2014 to just USD30 per barrel in early 2016, as shown below.

WTI Price per Barrel (USD), 2011–2018

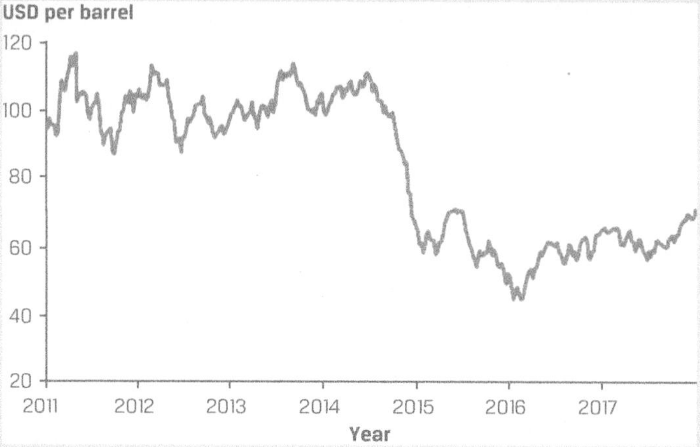

Source: Bloomberg.

Supply outpaced demand due in part to new discoveries in the Permian Basin in the United States, as well as drilling technology improvements using hydraulic fracturing (or fracking) that lowered breakeven prices for crude oil production. Given balance sheets that hold predominantly fixed assets financed heavily by debt, the sustained oil price decline drove oil and gas firm revenues and profits sharply lower, forcing several exploration and production companies to seek bankruptcy protection in 2015. By late 2016, over 200 petroleum industry companies had filed for bankruptcy.

Weak demand for oil production and refinery equipment also caused recovery rates to plunge. Prior to 2015, historical recovery rates in the oil and gas industry averaged 58%. For the industry bankruptcies in 2015, recovery rates averaged only 21% as the value of oil production assets declined due to these industry-specific circumstances.

In other instances, financial distress is isolated to a single company. Company-specific risk factors include a single firm's weak or deteriorating competitive position in an industry, product market risk, execution risk, and excessive operating leverage. A sharp deterioration in company performance in periods of economic growth and otherwise strong industry performance may result from specific adverse events, such as product recalls, litigation, isolated operating or supply chain disruptions, or management irregularities, including fraud.

EXAMPLE 2

Luckin Coffee's Accounting Fraud

Luckin Coffee Inc. was founded in Beijing in 2017 with a goal of surpassing global coffee retailer, Starbucks, by offering lower-priced coffee for takeout and delivery through its proprietary technology application. Within one year, the company experienced rapid growth and reached a valuation of USD1 billion, with venture capital (VC) funding from one of China's largest VC funds, as well as from Singapore's sovereign wealth fund, GIC. Luckin Coffee continued to raise new capital, including nearly USD700 million via a public offering on the US NASDAQ exchange in May 2019. By July 2019, the company was valued at USD4 billion, with 5,000 locations across China and plans to double the number of stores by the end of 2021.

The company's impressive growth reports prompted skepticism from some in the investment community. At the end of January 2020, a short seller released a research report based on customer traffic at Luckin Coffee locations compared to sales figures reported by the company. The research report suggested that Luckin had overstated 2019 revenues by as much as 88%. Luckin's auditor, EY, later found evidence of revenue overstatement in early 2020. China's market regulator initiated an investigation, concluding that Luckin had inflated revenues and misled investors.

Luckin shares were subsequently delisted from NASDAQ, and the US Securities and Exchange Commission imposed a USD180 million penalty on the company. In February 2021, Luckin Coffee filed for Chapter 15 reorganization in US bankruptcy court with plans to continue operations. When it emerged from bankruptcy, Luckin was able to find new investors and restart its revenue growth trajectory.

Special situations investors may take positions in the outstanding loans, bonds, or equity of distressed issuers to capitalize on expected price appreciation, as described above. More complex approaches may involve hybrid securities, such as convertible bonds, or combine short and long positions in instruments with different claims in the issuer's capital structure, as described later. Other strategies include the purchase of assets from forced sellers in liquidation at a discount to fair market value or the provision of special forms of secured financing to firms in distress.

Beyond the macroeconomic, industry, and company risks highlighted previously for corporations, distressed situations involve several additional risks unique to these investments, as described next.

Credit Risk

The **credit valuation adjustment (CVA)** framework introduced earlier in the curriculum is shown in Exhibit 3.

Exhibit 3: Credit Valuation Adjustment

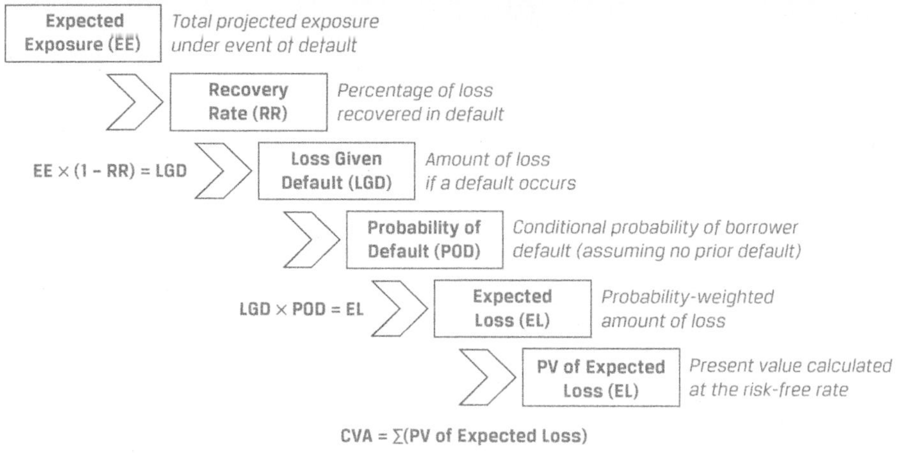

Recall that CVA measures the present value of expected loss (EL), or the product of the probability of default (POD) and loss given default (LGD).

$$EL = LGD \times POD. \quad (1)$$

Since distressed debt often involves issuers whose default may be imminent, as POD approaches 100%, expected loss rises to nearly equal the loss given default, with the underlying debt price (as a percentage of face value) approaching the expected recovery rate in a default scenario.

To properly diagnose sources of credit risk, analysts and investors typically distinguish between short-term issuer liquidity and longer-term solvency issues. Liquidity refers to the relative ability to convert a firm's resources into cash over an asset conversion cycle to cover its immediate obligations, while solvency assesses an issuer's cash flow generation potential over multiple periods to meet interest and principal payments.

Investor Liquidity Risk

Debt and equity instruments of issuers facing financial distress often face limited liquidity as price volatility rises. Many market participants are forced to sell if their investment policies preclude ownership of distressed debt or equity securities. Public equities failing to meet minimum exchange price requirements are often delisted as a firm approaches default.

Operational Risk

Firms facing financial distress may lose employees, customers, or suppliers unwilling to bear the greater risk of non-payment or liquidation while a firm restructures its debt or pursues bankruptcy.

Legal Risk

The costs and uncertainty associated with financial distress include creditor disputes and bankruptcy proceedings. As both the risks and costs associated with bankruptcy and other forms of litigation reduce the assets available to settle claims, distressed debt investors must weigh these costs against the potential benefits of pursuing such legal action.

Financial distress affects both corporate and sovereign issuers. A sovereign borrower's creditworthiness may deteriorate due to excessive fiscal deficits, inflexible monetary and exchange rate policies, or adverse economic conditions.

Sovereign borrowers in highly developed markets generally reflect the lowest credit risk among public sector borrowers. These issuers have the power to tax economic activity in highly diversified economies engaged in global trade with freely floating currencies widely held by external parties, including central banks, referred to as **reserve currencies**.

Sovereign issuers in *developing* markets, in contrast, are more susceptible to financial distress, for several reasons. These less wealthy economies often have limited economic diversification, fewer foreign trade partners, and less developed domestic financial markets. In addition, the restrictive, non-convertible, and often fixed exchange rate regimes in these economies limit policy effectiveness, magnify the impact of economic shocks, and increase the likelihood of financial distress. These countries with non-reserve currency regimes often rely on foreign direct investment and issuing debt denominated in major foreign currencies, which require sufficient currency reserves to service interest and principal and to pay for essential imports.

While distressed corporate issuers often enter legal bankruptcy proceedings to continue operations while restructuring debt, the principle of **sovereign immunity** limits the legal recourse of lenders to enforce debt claims against distressed sovereign borrowers. As a result, sovereign financial distress typically results in the restructuring of outstanding debt rather than asset sales or liquidation. On one hand, fiscal deficits and declining tax revenues are common sources of distress among sovereign bonds denominated in domestic currency. Foreign currency bonds, on the other hand, are more susceptible to weaker external conditions, which may involve domestic currency depreciation due to lack of competitiveness and/or falling foreign currency reserves. The unique example of El Salvador demonstrates the impact of a mismatch between a country's reserves and its outstanding debt.

EXAMPLE 3

El Salvador Averts External Debt Default

As a lower-middle-income developing country in Central America seeking to promote stable inflation and growth, El Salvador adopted the US dollar as its official currency over two decades ago following a period of pegging its currency to the US dollar. Despite a strong economic rebound following the COVID-19 shutdown, fiscal deficits remained high, and the country was heavily dependent on short-term external debt, with a debt-to-GDP ratio of over 80%.

In 2021, El Salvador's president, Nayib Bukele, made the country the first to adopt bitcoin (XBT) as legal tender, claiming it would ease the transfer of remittances from abroad and make digital transactions more accessible to an underbanked population. The country began actively purchasing the crypto-currency as part of its external reserves. However, the USD/XBT exchange rate suffered a decline from over USD60,000 per XBT to approximately USD20,000 by July 2022, which coincided with a plunge in the price of El Salvador's 5.875% US dollar–denominated sovereign bonds to just 30% of par, as shown in Exhibit 4.

Exhibit 4: USD/XBT vs. 5.875% 2025 El Salvador US Dollar Bond

Source: Bloomberg.

Sharp declines in XBT in the wake of pending near-term US dollar debt maturities cast doubt on El Salvador's ability to meet its external obligations, leading to ratings downgrades from S&P and Moody's to CCC+ and Caa3, respectively.

The price of El Salvador's external bonds rebounded in the latter half of 2022 as the government offered to buy back a portion of its outstanding debt using reserves and was also able to arrange a USD450 million loan from the Central American Bank for Economic Integration, a multilateral financial institution focused on regional economic development. With this partial debt repurchase, incremental new funding and a mild XBT rebound, El Salvador averted default on the January 2023 bond maturity as debtholders were repaid in full.

While sovereign immunity precludes such issuers from entering bankruptcy proceedings, investors in distressed sovereign debt face losses under a default scenario that often involves a debt restructuring plan in conjunction with a multilateral financial institution, such as the International Monetary Fund (IMF). While such plans are often accompanied by austerity measures, such as budget cuts and tax increases, debt investors incur losses in the form of interest and principal payment grace periods, extended payment terms, and other borrower concessions.

Reputational Risk

Investors in corporate or sovereign distressed debt face the potential of displacing workers, disrupting communities, and having an adverse environmental impact when forcing a firm to liquidate its assets or pursuing legal claims. Many public sector investors, such as pension funds and sovereign wealth funds, are wary of failing to meet their environmental, social, and governance (ESG) objectives when investing in such opportunities. For example, investors in sovereign debt obligations of **heavily indebted poor countries (HIPCs)**, a specific group of developing countries eligible for support from the IMF and the World Bank due to high rates of poverty and significant indebtedness, may be seen as taking advantage of such crises, as described in the following example.

HIPCS AND DISTRESSED DEBT FUNDS

The IMF and the World Bank launched the HIPC Initiative in 1996 to help HIPCs avoid unsustainable debt burdens.

Sovereign debt crises have posed a challenge to this goal when special situations funds use a strategy to purchase a portion of a country's distressed external sovereign debt in the secondary market at a deep discount. In some cases, a fund may elect not to participate in the restructuring process and use litigation to either attempt to recover the debt's face value or settle at a significant premium to the price originally paid. The offshore legal expenses and considerable time over which such litigation occurs impose a high burden on HIPCs. According to the African Development Bank Group, such fund efforts to target HIPC distressed debt are often successful, leading to annualized returns on investments ranging from 50% to 333%, among the highest for distressed debt investing.

Strategies to help HIPCs and other developing countries avoid financial distress and heavy indebtedness have been combined with environmental conservation initiatives. For example, in 2022, Belize and a subsidiary of The Nature Conservancy (TNC) agreed to a debt-for-nature swap under which the country was able to repurchase its external debt in exchange for fixed annual marine conservation expenditures during the 19-year loan term. Gabon entered a similar USD500 million debt-for-nature swap in the next year, repurchasing outstanding debt at a discount in exchange for an extended term loan at a lower interest rate contingent on promising to fund conservation efforts.

Corporate Actions and Other Event-Driven Opportunities

Special situations other than financial distress that drive investment opportunities include corporate actions such as business combinations, sales, and tender offers. In other cases, investors seek to capitalize on expected investment value due to litigation, regulatory sanctions, or significant issues adversely affecting an issuer's competitors, key suppliers, or customers.

Other than financial distress, mergers, acquisitions, and divestitures are the most common event-driven situations that drive significant valuation changes. Special situations associated with business combinations are often referred to as **merger arbitrage** opportunities, which involve investors seeking to capitalize on price discrepancies of one or more securities issued either by the target, the acquirer, or another party associated with a transaction. Unlike the risk-free arbitrage associated with the law of one price introduced earlier in the curriculum, this form of mispricing is related to informational inefficiencies associated with the likelihood, timing, and final terms at which a transaction occurs that may cause securities to trade at a different value. Merger arbitrage managers commonly use borrowed funds to generate leveraged returns. The use of borrowed funds depends on the expected payout and the degree of confidence in the merger successfully closing.

Merger arbitrage opportunities are typically triggered by the announcement of a potential transaction for which the target company (TargetCo) is often acquired using cash or stock, as shown in Exhibit 5.

Exhibit 5: Merger Purchase Method and Corresponding Arbitrage Positioning

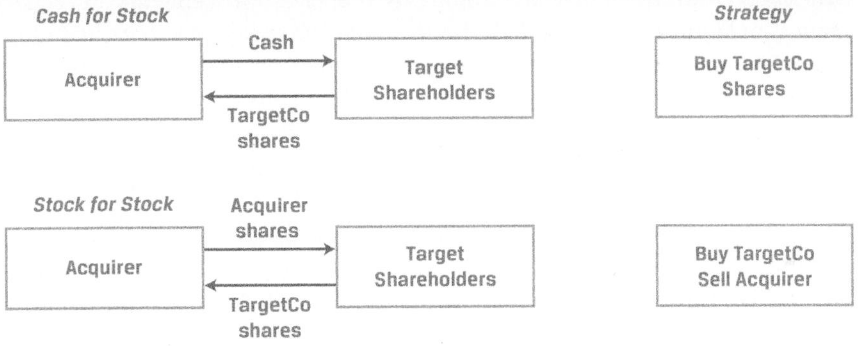

Whether a merger or acquisition is announced as an all-cash or all-stock deal, the market price of TargetCo typically remains below the announced price given the uncertainty associated with closing the transaction. The **arbitrage spread**, or the difference between the announced acquisition price and the post-announcement market price, represents the potential return opportunity of a merger arbitrage strategy if the deal closes based on original terms ignoring transaction costs. The simplest form of arbitrage is an all-cash transaction that involves the purchase of TargetCo shares in anticipation of deal closure, while an all-stock deal arbitrage strategy often combines a *purchase* of TargetCo shares and a *short sale* of the acquirer's shares, as shown in the following example.

KNOWLEDGE CHECK

Windslater Corporation seeks to acquire all the shares of Spruceneedle Company. Windslater's management team is considering two possible acquisition strategies: an all-cash purchase and an exchange of shares. Spruceneedle's share price prior to the acquisition announcement is CAD40 per share, and Windslater plans to offer a 25% premium. Windslater's current share price is CAD100 per share.

1. Calculate the arbitrage spread if Windslater announces an all-cash purchase of Spruceneedle's shares and the share price increases to CAD46 upon this announcement. Discuss one fundamental reason why the arbitrage spread is greater than zero.

Solution:

Given the 25% premium, Windslater is offering CAD50 per share for Spruceneedle [= 40 × (1+0.25)], so the arbitrage spread equals CAD4 per share (= 50 – 46). An investor engaging in merger arbitrage would buy Spruceneedle shares at CAD46 upon the acquisition announcement with a possible payoff of CAD50 when the acquisition is completed. The arbitrage spread is greater than zero because there is a significant probability that the acquisition will not be completed as of the acquisition announcement date.

2. Discuss the trade that a merger arbitrage investor would likely construct if Windslater announces a stock-for-stock transaction if Spruceneedle's share price increases to CAD46 upon announcement and Windslater's share price is unchanged.

Solution:

The merger arbitrage investor would buy shares of Spruceneedle and sell shares of Windslater. Given Windslater's CAD100 price per share and the CAD50 purchase price for Spruceneedle, Windslater would offer to pay 0.5 share for each Spruceneedle share. The merger arbitrage investor would construct a similar trade by selling 0.5 share of Windslater for CAD50 and buying one share of Spruceneedle for CAD46. This trade results in a CAD4 per share arbitrage spread if the acquisition closes as announced.

Acquirers with liquid shares that may attract short selling under such strategies frequently seek to minimize stock price declines following a merger announcement by offering to purchase a company with a combination of cash and stock. Regardless of whether a merger is announced using all cash, all stock, or a combination of the two, the main risk associated with merger arbitrage is the same—namely, that the announced transaction does not take place. While most mergers are ultimately consummated, many fail for various reasons, which include the following:

- Debt financing becomes unavailable or subject to far less attractive terms.
- Governments, antitrust and competition regulators, or foreign investment rules in a region or country prevent the merger's completion.
- Changes in economic or industry conditions make the merger less attractive.
- Merger due diligence uncovers cases of fraud or material misrepresentation.
- A third-party bidder makes a counteroffer, which may delay timing but still results in a higher purchase price.

CASE STUDY

Elon Musk's Twitter (X) Acquisition

In April 2022, billionaire investor Elon Musk announced plans to acquire the social media company Twitter in a USD44 billion transaction that valued the firm at USD54.20 per share. The price represented a 38% premium over Twitter's traded price on the day before the announcement. Initially, the proposed deal was considered hostile, but within two weeks, Musk had arranged financing and Twitter agreed to the terms in what became one of the most quickly arranged deals of its size. Twitter's share price ranged between USD45 and USD52 during the remainder of April as investors weighed the likelihood of deal completion. Exhibit 6 shows Twitter's share price from the beginning of April 2022 until the company was taken private.

Exhibit 6: Twitter Stock Price, April–October 2022

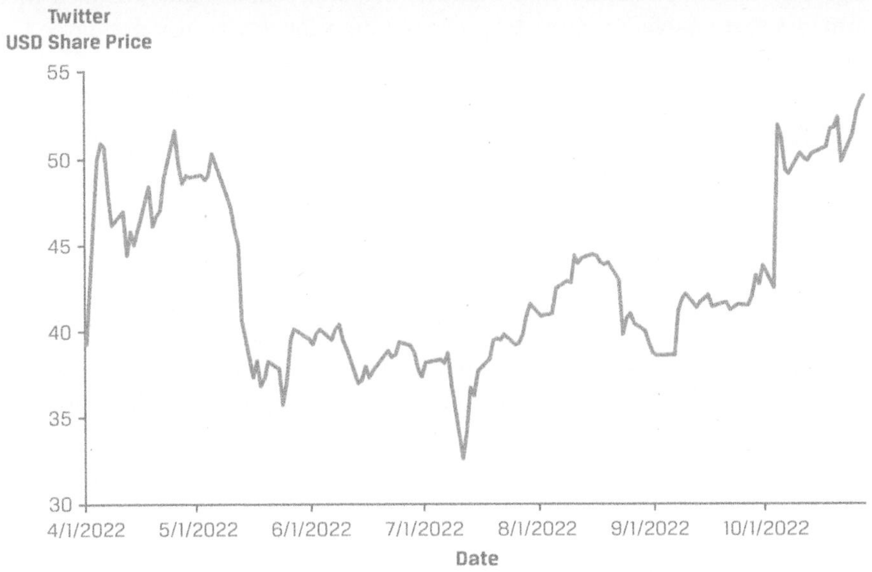

Source: Bloomberg.

Despite its initial rapid pace, investor doubts were raised in May about the merger closing when Musk posted a comment, using Twitter, that he was reconsidering his bid pending more information regarding the proportion of "fake accounts" being reported among Twitter's total users. Twitter's share price fell to below USD40 following Musk's comments, approximately where it had traded before the acquisition announcement.

In July 2022, Musk announced plans to end his bid for Twitter as the company provided misleading information regarding the number of fake accounts on the social media platform. The initial response to this news was a decline in Twitter's price to approximately USD33 per share, before rebounding back to around USD40 by later in July. In early October 2022, Musk reversed his decision to contest the original merger agreement, and the deal closed near the end of the month at the original purchase price.

Note that an acquirer assumes all the assets and liabilities of the target company once a merger is complete, including the target company's debt obligations. As a result, business combinations also give rise to several types of debt-related merger arbitrage opportunities.

For example, recall from earlier learning modules that a **change of control** clause typically requires the issuer to offer to repurchase outstanding bonds at a fixed price at or above par if a new owner acquires a certain percentage of voting shares. In a merger scenario, this allows lenders and bondholders to put or sell back bonds to an issuer at a gain or negotiate more favorable debt terms.

In the case of debt whose repayment may not be triggered by a change of control clause, an acquirer may initiate a **bond tender offer** to buy back outstanding debt at a premium to the current market price. This public solicitation of debt to be purchased at a predetermined price for a specified period may involve either an offer of cash or an exchange of outstanding bonds for newly issued securities of equivalent value.

More complex investments combining long or short debt, equity, and/or credit default swap positions to exploit significant mispricing in a single issuer's obligations are referred to as **capital structure arbitrage** strategies. Hybrid securities such as convertible bonds offer an additional opportunity to capitalize on the perceived mispricing of underlying risk components, including interest rate risk, credit, volatility, and equity risk, in what is known as **convertible arbitrage**. As in the case of merger arbitrage, these strategies also often use borrowed funds to increase returns using leverage. Recall from earlier learning modules that convertible bonds are fixed-income instruments that enable investors to exchange debt for equity at a pre-agreed price over a specific period.

QUESTION SET

1. Discuss one fundamental contrast between special situations investing compared to investing in other private market asset classes.

Solution:

The most fundamental contrast between special situations and other private markets relates to the time frame of the investment horizon. While most private market investing involves value creation over a long holding period, possibly 5–10 years or longer, the value creation from special situations investing is driven by the outcome of discrete events, typically occurring over much shorter time horizons.

2. Discuss the basic return-to-risk trade-off being considered by an investor in a cash-for-stock merger arbitrage opportunity in which an acquiror bids EUR70 for a target company and the target's stock price rises from EUR54 to EUR66 upon the acquisition announcement. Assume that the target stock falls to its original price if the merger does not close.

Solution:

The investor is considering whether a 6.06% (= 4 ÷ 66) return is a sufficient return for taking the risk that the acquisition will be successfully completed relative to the possibility of –18.18% (= –12 ÷ 66) return if the acquisition attempt fails and the target's stock price falls to its prior price.

3. Which one of the following best states the credit risk faced by an investor in the distressed debt of an issuer whose default is imminent?

   A. Probability of default (POD) by the issuer

   B. Loss given default (LGD) of the issuer

   C. Both POD and LGD

Solution:

B is the correct response. Because the distressed debt issuer's default is imminent, POD approaches 100%. Therefore, expected loss is equal to LGD, with the underlying debt price (as a percentage of face value) approaching the expected recovery rate in a default scenario. The investor is taking a view on how the realized recovery rate compares to the expected recovery rate priced into the security at the time of investment. A is not correct, because the POD is approximately 100% for the issuer of a distressed debt security whose default is imminent. C is not correct, because this response incorrectly includes POD.

DISTRESSED DEBT

3

☐ discuss the features of distressed debt, financing alternatives for issuers in financial distress, and investment strategies in distressed situations

As described earlier, distressed debt involves the fixed obligations of issuers that are insolvent, face the risk of insolvency, or have a higher likelihood of failing to meet interest or principal payments in a timely manner. While both sovereign and corporate borrowers experience financial distress, our focus here is on corporate distressed issuers.

Distressed Debt Features

No universally accepted definition of distressed debt exists, although practitioners often identify such issuers by the observed market price of outstanding debt or equity obligations. That is, issuers with a bond yield *spread* of over 1,000 bps above the risk-free rate for a similar maturity or a corresponding loan *price* below 90% of par are usually classified as distressed. Alternatively, an equity price near or below the minimum trading price required to meet listing rules (such as USD1 on the New York Stock Exchange) indicates a high likelihood of distress, often leading to balance sheet restructuring, bankruptcy, or liquidation of assets.

Companies facing financial distress vary widely by size, industry, jurisdiction, and financial circumstances. Specific events associated with distress include a **technical default**, or violation of the terms and conditions of a credit or loan agreement. These events include the breach of a financial covenant or an actual non-payment of interest and principal in a timely manner, which often includes a 30-day grace period.

A thorough understanding of the causes of financial distress are an important first step in assessing a likely path for resolution and strategies for distressed investors. Exhibit 7 outlines common drivers of financial distress, which often occur concurrently.

Exhibit 7: Common Causes of Corporate Financial Distress

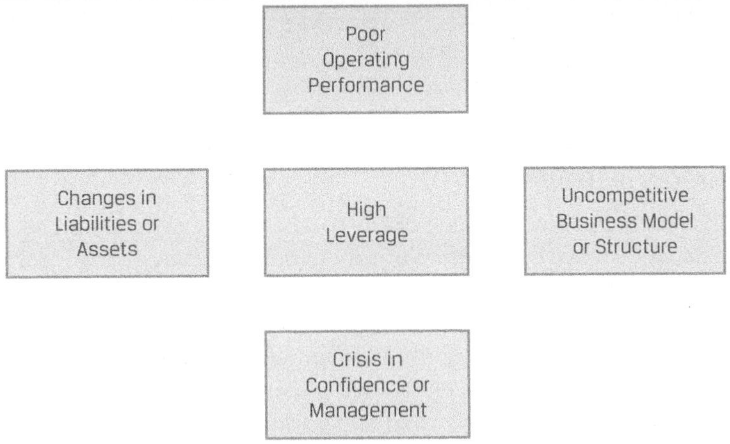

High Leverage

High leverage itself is often a necessary but not a sufficient condition to cause financial distress. However, the compound effects of high financial leverage and uneven operating performance over the economic cycle are a common source of financial stress among firms in cyclical industries. The expected duration and severity of these effects are important factors when considering debt restructuring alternatives and investment prospects. While minor debt adjustments may be sufficient to address liquidity constraints, solvency issues may warrant more significant capital structure changes.

For example, a retailer with strong market share and operating performance may become unable to meet current debt service obligations amid declining cash on hand, rising inventories from slower sales, and delays in accounts receivable collections. A lender might conclude that given the firm's otherwise strong performance, sales and margins will rebound quickly, opting to amend the terms of the company's short-term debt obligations to bridge the temporary shortfall in net cash flow generation. In other cases, a cyclical downturn may prompt an issuer to reduce leverage via asset sales, as in the following example.

EXAMPLE 4

Swedish Real Estate Firm SBB Sells Assets to Reduce Leverage

Samhällsbyggnadsbolaget i Norden (SBB), a Swedish property company known as the country's largest landlord, was long known as a favorite of individual investors because of its growth, financial stability, and strong history of dividends. In 2021, SBB announced plans to nearly triple the size of its property portfolio over the next five years, increasing its leverage substantially just as Sweden's housing market began showing a significant decline in value.

In early 2023, SBB was facing cash flow strains from interest payments and looming repayments of maturing debt. The firm lost its investment-grade ratings and was downgraded several times during the year, reaching a speculative CCC+ S&P rating. To address short-term cash flow pressures, SBB embarked on a strategy of selling properties at a discount to book value. By late summer of 2023, market prices of SBB's securities declined to levels suggesting that SBB was unlikely to remain solvent, with senior bonds maturing within a year trading at a 15% discount to par and subordinated hybrid notes trading at a 90% discount. However, SBB's prospects improved as it accelerated its strategy of asset disposals, including a USD720 million sale to a North American real estate investor, which provided a short-term boost to its bond prices.

Changes in Assets or Liabilities

Material adverse changes in the value of key balance sheet items are an additional catalyst for financial distress. Unforeseen non-debt liabilities triggering insolvency often result from litigation, product recalls, or other forms of product- or customer-related liability that exceed a company's liability insurance coverage.

Asset impairment, in contrast, involves an adverse change in the market value of an asset in which the value falls below that which is recorded on the firm's balance sheet. Examples include changes in current assets, such as uncollectible accounts receivable, and changes in the value of long-term tangible and intangible assets.

For example, the average market value of commercial aircraft plunged by a third in the wake of the COVID-19 pandemic amid widespread travel restrictions. While newer models still in production fell the least in price, airlines and aircraft lessors accelerated the retirement of older models approaching the end of their useful life.

Poor Operating Performance

While financial distress is often cyclical, in some cases underperformance reflects overall industry decline, poor management practices, or an uncompetitive business model. Insolvency due to high debt levels combined with poor operating performance may warrant more proactive measures to downsize or restructure a business.

Uncompetitive Business Model or Structure

In other cases, a company's new business model or strategy following a restructuring may be unable to support its balance sheet debt load. A new capital structure may depend on reaching financial milestones that prove to be unattainable. In the following example, this situation occurred in two phases.

EXAMPLE 5

Galeria Karstadt Kaufhof (GKK) Insolvency Proceedings

In 2023, Germany's largest department store chain entered insolvency proceedings, the German equivalent of US bankruptcy, for the second time in less than three years due to challenging market conditions and poor operating performance. Formed by a merger of Germany's two largest retailers (Karstadt and Kaufhof) in 2019, GKK's owners were slow to consolidate the combined firms' operations and realize the value of real estate holdings among its nearly 200 locations, facing resistance from its 34,000 unionized employees.

The firm first declared insolvency in July 2020 in the wake of the COVID-19 pandemic, emerging three months later with over EUR2 billion in debt writedowns, over 40 store closures, and several thousand employee layoffs. GKK was placed under new management with the goal of achieving growth in part by expanding its online sales from just over 4% of total revenue.

However, these measures did not prove sufficient to turn the company around, as it once again declared insolvency in March 2023. A second restructuring plan called for the closure of 50 additional stores, the downsizing of remaining locations in central business districts, and the release of an additional 4,000 employees from a level just half that at the time of the announced merger. Lenders were forced to accept a further EUR1 billion in debt losses.

Crisis in Confidence or Management

The discovery of fraud, aggressive accounting practices, or other financial irregularities often results in financial distress or bankruptcy. For example, the accounting fraud involving the falsification of Luckin Coffee sales data described earlier led to a delisting of the stock and a US bankruptcy filing in addition to investor lawsuits, from which the company successfully reemerged under new management.

Proper diagnosis of the causes and severity of declining creditworthiness is an important first step in determining appropriate steps to stabilize and improve performance. We return to the case study introduced in an earlier learning module to evaluate potential remedies to mitigate financial distress and identify associated investment strategies.

CASE STUDY

Maudville Corporation Take-Private Transaction

Maudville Corporation, a US chemical producer with USD5 billion in revenue and EBITDA of USD1 billion, was taken private for USD5 billion by the buyout equity firm Bardstown Partners; 20% of the purchase price was funded with private common equity, 5% in private convertible preferred shares, and 75% in private debt. These funds were used to buy and retire the USD5 billion of publicly held equity. Bardstown plans to restructure and sell the company, targeting a 35% internal rate of return (IRR) on its equity investment over five years.

Under new leadership, Maudville worked with Bardstown and both syndicated bank and private lenders to create the following debt profile.

Maudville Corporation Original Take-Private Debt Profile

Debt Tranche	Size	Pricing	Tenor	Terms and Conditions	Lender(s)
Secured Revolving Credit Facility	USD250 million	MRR + 150 bps p.a. on drawn amounts	364 days	Secured by first lien on Maudville's fixed assets	Syndicated bank group
Senior Secured Leveraged Loan	USD2.65 billion	MRR + 200 bps	Seven years; Prepayable at par starting in one year	Secured by first lien on Maudville's fixed assets; Ranks *pari passu* with other senior secured debt; 6× debt-to-EBITDA maintenance covenant	Syndicated bank group
Junior Second Lien Fixed-Rate Tranche	USD600 million	8.00% fixed	Seven years; Amortizing in four equal installments starting Year 4	Secured by second lien on Maudville's fixed assets; Ranks *pari passu* with other junior secured debt; 6× debt-to-EBITDA maintenance covenant	100% Bardstown Credit Partners
Mezzanine Debt Tranche	USD500 million	12.2% fixed	10 years	Unsecured subordinated obligation; Ranks *pari passu* with all other subordinated indebtedness; 6.5× debt-to-EBITDA maintenance covenant	50%: Bardstown Mezzanine Opportunity Fund; 50%: Another private debt GP. Bardstown retains majority voting rights to amend mezzanine debt terms

Maudville's five-year restructuring plan seeks to achieve 5% in annual sales growth while reducing cost of goods sold (COGS) as a percentage of sales by 1 percentage point per year from 55% in Year 0, with annual 1 point SGA reductions as a percentage of sales from 25% starting in Year 3. Since the leveraged loan is prepayable at par after a year, early debt amortization involves the senior secured leveraged loan.

1. Calculate Maudville's term debt maturity schedule, and evaluate possible events leading to financial distress over the five-year restructuring period.

Solution:

Maudville's term debt maturity schedule is as follows:

Year/Amortization (USD thousands)	Senior Secured	Junior Second Lien	Mezzanine	Total
0	0	0	0	0
1	0	0	0	0
2	0	0	0	0
3	0	0	0	0
4	0	150,000	0	150,000
5	0	150,000	0	150,000
6	0	150,000	0	150,000
7	2,650,000	150,000	0	2,800,000
8			0	0
9			0	0
10			500,000	500,000

While *voluntary* senior secured debt paydowns may occur earlier, note that no *mandatory* debt amortization is scheduled until Year 4.

Key potential events associated with financial distress over the five-year period include Maudville's failure to make timely interest payments, which may fluctuate in the case of the senior secured loan as the market reference rate (MRR) changes, and principal payments, which apply to the junior second-lien loan in Years 4 and 5. Also, Maudville must maintain at least a 6× debt-to-EBITDA ratio to avoid a technical default on its senior secured and junior second-lien loans and a 6.5× debt-to-EBITDA ratio to avoid a covenant breach on its mezzanine debt.

Distressed Debt Financing Strategies and the Bankruptcy Process

Credit risk, as defined earlier in the curriculum, refers to changes in the likelihood of default and loss severity under a default as reflected in market credit spreads. In contrast, actual technical or legal defaults must be addressed to avoid a contract violation triggering demand for full debt repayment. Issuers and investors have several alternatives and financing strategies to mitigate financial distress, as shown in Exhibit 8.

Exhibit 8: Financing Strategies for Firms in Financial Distress

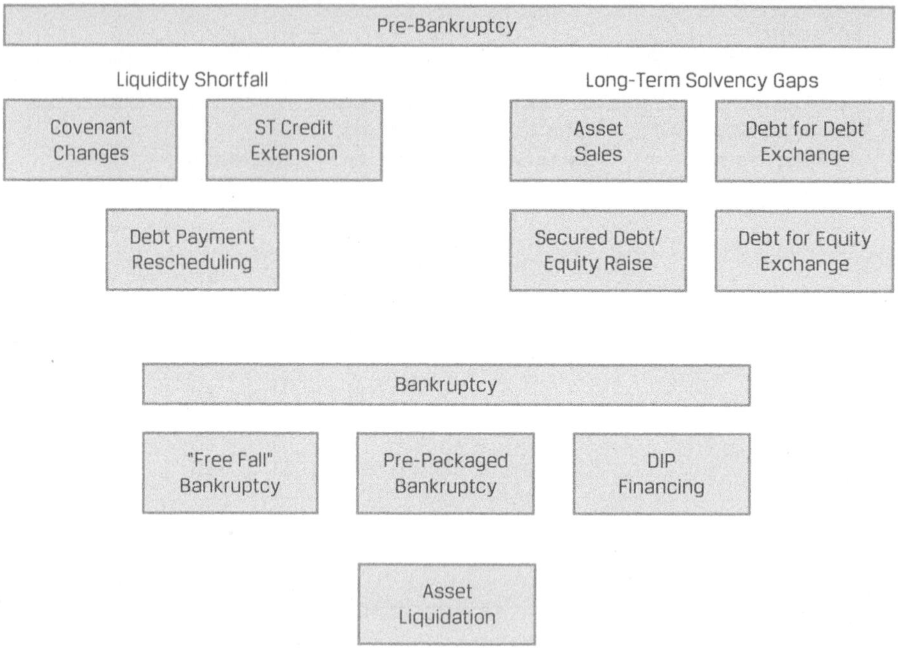

The use of alternatives outlined in Exhibit 8 varies widely based on different circumstances, including whether the issuer faces a short-term liquidity or long-term capital gap, as well as the possibility of a negotiated outcome with creditors without entering bankruptcy.

If the source of financial distress is limited to a temporary lack of short-term assets to meet obligations over an operating cycle, a solution is most often negotiated with liquidity providers. This may involve increasing the size of revolving credit agreements or working capital facilities, extending tenors, or waiving or changing covenants. For example, an issuer could agree to step up coupons or credit spreads if covenant levels are breached or seek less restrictive thresholds in exchange for higher pricing or other borrower restrictions or concessions.

Addressing long-term solvency gaps typically also requires a distressed issuer to negotiate additional sources of financing or reduce financial leverage. Common alternatives shown in the upper right of Exhibit 8 are as follows:

- *Sale or pledge of assets.* Given the general lack of cash among distressed firms, asset sales are a frequently used means of debt reduction. Whether considering the disposition of specific fixed assets or non-core businesses, pre-bankruptcy negotiation of sales provides sellers a greater opportunity to negotiate with strategic buyers and avoid forced sales at liquidation prices. Any assets used in ongoing operations previously excluded from secured debt collateral provisions may be included to improve the security position of lenders.
- *Secured debt or equity raise.* Raising additional debt or equity is another means of increasing capital, which for distressed firms is generally unavailable on an unsecured basis. Incremental borrowing may occur against assets that are not already fully encumbered under existing bond or loan agreements. Raising equity capital offers a debtor-friendly means of increasing

firm solvency, which in the interest of time is often sourced from existing shareholders, while a secondary equity offering to new investors takes more time and involves greater cost.

- *Debt purchase or exchange.* A distressed issuer with sufficient liquidity could enter open market purchases of discounted debt or make a formal tender offer to retire certain debt tranches. In practice, however, the limited liquidity available to such issuers usually leads to a debt exchange in which the issuer offers new securities for existing bonds with lower par values, longer maturities, and other measures to ease the firm's debt burden. This approach, known as a **distressed debt exchange**, is accepted by bondholders to avoid the cost and a potentially worse outcome in the case of a bankruptcy filing.

Let us revisit the case of Maudville to consider its possible alternatives in a financial distress scenario.

CASE STUDY

Maudville Faces Financial Distress

During the first two years under new management, Maudville successfully executes on its business plan to grow sales, increase EBITDA, and reduce debt amid a stable economic environment. However, in Year 3, the company experiences a sharp drop in performance, with sales falling 7% amid increasing labor and material costs, driving COGS to 60% of sales. Maudville's key financial ratios derived from its income statement, retained cash flow (RCF), or net cash from operating activities less dividends, and balance sheet for the first three years are as follows:

Maudville Corporation Key Financial Ratios

Financial Ratio	Year 1	Year 2	Year 3
EBITDA Margin	21%	22%	10%
Debt to EBITDA	3.28	2.82	6.46
RCF/Net Debt	22%	27%	11%
EBITDA/Int. Exp.	4.1	4.6	2.1

Maudville's Year 3 EBITDA is USD511 million, with USD3,302 million in remaining term debt outstanding following the paydown of USD448 million in senior secured debt. Maudville has pledged substantially all its fixed assets as collateral, except for USD75 million in railcars, trucks, and other vehicles.

1. Discuss the nature of Maudville's financial distress, as well as possible remedies to address the situation.

   Solution:

   Given its debt of USD3,302 million and EBITDA of USD511 million, Maudville's 6.46× debt-to-EBITDA ratio exceeds the 6× maintenance covenant on its senior secured and junior second-lien debt tranches, placing it in technical default.

   Technical default remedies include a one-time covenant breach waiver, requiring approval of the syndicated bank group and Bardstown Credit Partners for respective tranches; amendment of the covenant threshold to

> a less restrictive level in exchange for higher pricing; or agreement to other borrower restrictions or concessions. At current EBITDA levels, Maudville's debt load exceeds the covenant threshold by USD236 million. The company could consider reducing debt by using cash to purchase debt on the open market or selling assets. One possible borrower concession might involve an incremental pledge of rail cars, trucks, and other vehicles to increase the collateral asset base.

As shown in the case study, firms with an initial covenant breach often find small open-market purchases or incremental asset sales preferable to a full debt-for-debt exchange. These and other measures can reduce debt and help avoid the bankruptcy process.

A **debt-for-equity exchange** involves the extinguishment of debt rather than amendment of debt terms in exchange for a position in the issuer's shares. Key issues to address in the case of a debt-for-equity swap include the type of equity received by debtholders (common shares, preferred shares, or convertible bonds) and the rights and restrictions associated with the new securities. Unlike the debt-for-debt exchange, existing shareholders typically face dilution when new shares are exchanged for outstanding debt.

Earlier in the curriculum, it was shown that the tax benefit of greater leverage is offset by the costs of financial distress or bankruptcy. Once a firm faces distress, issuers and investors often prefer to address technical and legal defaults outside of the bankruptcy process to avoid the considerable cost and time involved. However, the ability to avert legal bankruptcy proceedings depends on several factors, including a firm's cash position, the timing and magnitude of the expected financial shortfall, the complexity of the issuer's assets and capital structure, and regulatory and other constraints.

Limited liquidity prevents firms from taking immediate steps to mitigate financial stress, such as open-market debt repurchases. When weighing other measures to reduce leverage, the time to liquidity is an important determinant of the feasibility of specific alternatives. For example, a debtor may temporarily delay trade payables or sell individual asset sales relatively quickly to raise cash, while the sale of an entire business division takes more time. The impact of a shortfall may also be magnified by a lack of time and business resources available to address the issue.

Complex business models and capital structures are more difficult to restructure with relatively short notice. For example, the inability to identify individual retail locations, fixed assets, or non-core business units for disposal can complicate the deleveraging process. Complex capital structures involving secured debt, covenant protections, layers of subordination, and intercreditor agreements restrict the flexibility of borrowers and lenders to negotiate a plan that is satisfactory to all parties. Significant regulatory or external constraints on businesses, such as labor contracts and significant pension commitments, are additional complexities that lead distressed firms to seek bankruptcy protection versus a pre-bankruptcy settlement of claims.

The bankruptcy process seeks to protect the legal rights of all parties involved, afford a distressed issuer protection from creditors when operating as a going concern is preferable, and allow for an orderly asset liquidation when it is not. The US bankruptcy process is shown in Exhibit 9.

Exhibit 9: US Bankruptcy Process

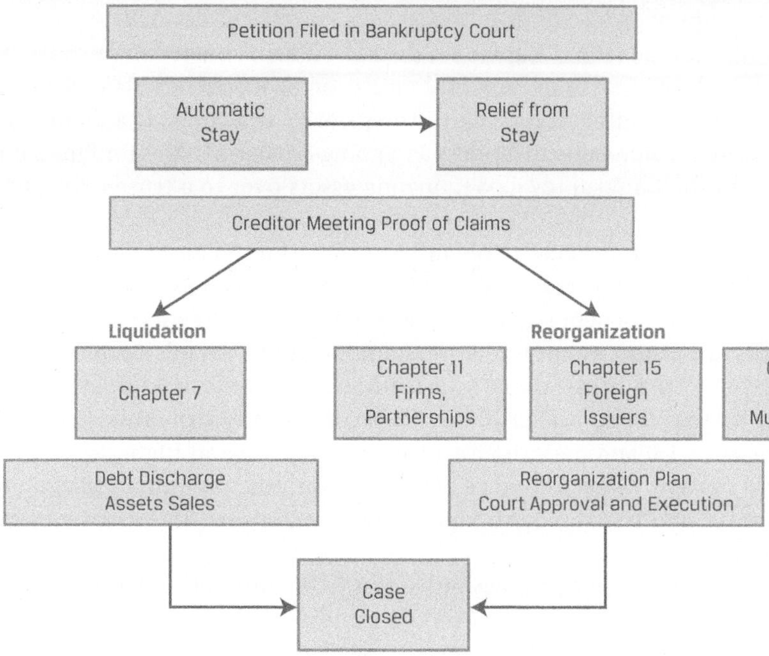

Once a debtor files for bankruptcy in a US court, it is granted an automatic stay, or protection, from lenders seeking to collect claims unless an exception (or relief) is granted. Legal protections extended to lenders in bankruptcy include strict limitations on **fraudulent conveyance**, or the transfer of assets to a third party to prevent creditors from reaching a borrower's assets. While local laws vary, US bankruptcy law allows the court to void such transactions for up to two years prior to bankruptcy filing and claw back funds to pay creditors.

FTX FRAUDULENT TRANSFERS

In November 2022, FTX, a Bahamas-based cryptocurrency exchange, filed for Chapter 11 bankruptcy protection under US law following a rapid decline in the value of its exchange token, FTT, causing a liquidity crisis. The company named a new CEO at the time of the bankruptcy filing to replace the company's founder.

Approximately eight months later, FTX Trading sued the founder of FTX as well as several other senior executives to recoup over USD1 billion in fraudulent transfers made by the company's senior executives during the two years prior to FTX's Chapter 11 filing. The complaint alleged that the defendants misappropriated funds to both offset losses of a trading affiliate and pay for luxury condominiums, political contributions, and speculative investments for personal gain.

Firms seeking to continue operations as a going concern propose a reorganization plan to be confirmed in court under a Chapter 11 bankruptcy filing. The company becomes a so-called **debtor in possession (DIP)**, remaining in control of the business under court supervision. A debtor may submit a proposal to the court to obtain **DIP financing**, a form of temporary debt financing senior to all other claims used to both cover ongoing bankruptcy costs and provide working capital and other financing to maintain operations while the firm is in bankruptcy.

A similar reorganization process exists for US governmental entities (Chapter 9), while a Chapter 15 filing, which involves foreign creditors, is generally conducted in parallel with bankruptcy proceedings in the issuer's country of domicile.

To successfully emerge from Chapter 11, distressed firms must demonstrate that all creditors will be better off than under a liquidation scenario net of costs if asset sale proceeds were distributed according to the priority of claims. If a debtor firm cannot demonstrate greater value to lenders as a going concern, it files for liquidation under Chapter 7 of the Bankruptcy Code, turning assets over to a trustee for sale to settle all claims.

Investors who have purchased or sold credit protection on an underlying issuer facing financial distress closely track those events that may trigger a settlement of such contracts. Failure to make a debt payment, debt restructuring, or a bankruptcy filing generally constitute a **credit event** under outstanding credit default swap contracts. As shown in Exhibit 10, a protection buyer transfers the credit risk of an issuer or reference entity to a protection seller in exchange for a periodic premium. Standard CDS coupon rates of 1% and 5% exist for investment-grade and high-yield issuers, respectively. The present value difference between a periodic premium based on the issuer's CDS spread and the standard coupon for the contract life is exchanged at contract initiation.

If the defaulting issuer is a reference entity in a CDS contract, a credit event will trigger a settlement payment equal to the LGD multiplied by the contract notional amount from the protection seller to the protection buyer.

Exhibit 10: Credit Default Swap Mechanics

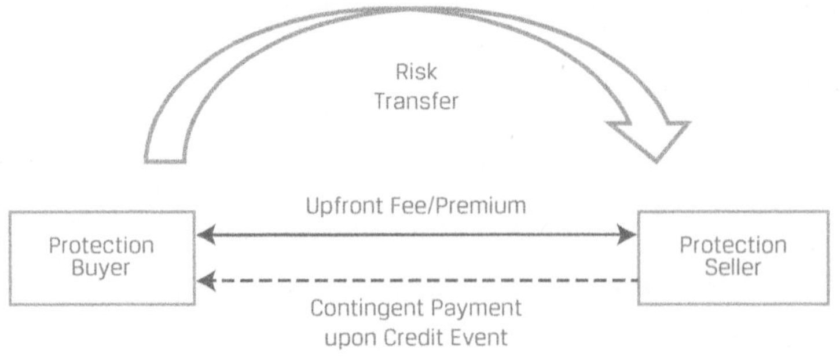

While US bankruptcy laws are generally considered more debtor friendly, many other jurisdictions have more stringent laws favoring creditors and are more likely to result in liquidation. In other cases, large companies considered to operate in the national economic interest may benefit from a form of direct or indirect government support such as loan guarantees or subsidies when facing financial distress to preserve domestic production and employment.

GLOBAL APPROACHES TO BANKRUPTCY

US corporate bankruptcy laws have a long history of allowing businesses to continue to operate following a bankruptcy filing, often with continuing management by the incumbent executive team. As a result, the United States has traditionally been viewed as the most debtor-friendly jurisdiction in the world. US law provides an extended period, typically 120 days, for management to file its plan of reorganization for review by the courts and creditors. Chapter 11 reorganizations commonly take well over one year in the best of circumstances and can last several years in complicated reorganization cases.

Insolvency laws and processes vary widely among the largest developed economies. For example, the UK bankruptcy process exhibits several contrasts to the US process. Overall, UK law is considered creditor friendly, with firm control in the reorganization process (known as administration) held by an administrator rather than company management. Nevertheless, historical empirical evidence on firm survival and creditor recovery rates are similar for the United States and the United Kingdom. Other countries' laws may focus more attention on protection of employment, such as in France, and research suggests that creditor recovery rates may be lower as a result. Germany and Japan have historically had strong banking sectors, resulting in more creditor-friendly processes. However, Japan's insolvency processes have evolved to focus more on restructuring firms to continue as going concerns, similar to the US approach.

The world's two most populous countries, China and India, continue to develop and improve their systems for resolving corporate insolvency cases. China's 2007 Enterprise Bankruptcy Law represented the nation's first comprehensive bankruptcy code, and for several years, bankruptcy filings remained relatively low, although these have increased over time. Similarly, India relied on a patchwork of different laws governing bankruptcy until 2016, when the country enacted its more comprehensive Insolvency and Bankruptcy Code.

Cross-border cooperation in reorganization processes is of growing importance as firms increasingly borrow and own assets in multiple jurisdictions. In 2005, the United States added Chapter 15 to its bankruptcy code to address insolvency cases involving more than one country.

An important consideration for financing strategies outside or within the bankruptcy process is the degree of control and expected timing associated with these alternatives. Successful out-of-court restructurings may be negotiated quickly but typically require agreement of all creditors to proceed.

As for settlements that occur *within* the bankruptcy process, an approach combining the expediency of pre-bankruptcy restructuring with favorable voting rules under a Chapter 11 reorganization—namely, the required consent of two-thirds of the volume and one-half of the investors for each claimant class—is referred to as a **prepackaged bankruptcy**.

A prepackaged bankruptcy involves a detailed business plan and exit strategy formulated by the debtor and agreed on with one or more major creditors in advance of bankruptcy filing. A prepackaged plan typically accelerates the process, reduces the likelihood of liquidation, and increases an issuer's ability to attract equity capital once it emerges from bankruptcy.

If the onset of financial distress is sudden or unexpected, an issuer is more likely to enter Chapter 11 bankruptcy in a **free fall bankruptcy**, or one with no plan or pre-agreement with creditors. While a debtor still controls company assets and typically has at least 120 days to file a plan, free fall bankruptcy is usually more expensive and time consuming, with a less certain outcome.

Distressed Issuer Investment Strategies

Many creditors and investors face pressure to dispose of distressed issuer obligations, including trade creditors, banks facing regulatory capital pressures for non-performing loans, and asset managers whose investment policy statement specifies credit quality minimums. In other cases, unconstrained investors see opportunity in distressed issuer debt and equity obligations. Three broad investment strategies are shown in Exhibit 11.

Exhibit 11: Common Distressed Investment Strategies

Strategy	Trading Non-Controlling	Active Non-Controlling	Active Controlling
Target Investment	Traded debt, equity, or credit default swaps	Senior secured or unsecured public or private debt	Controlling stake in secured or unsecured public or private debt
Goal	Buy and hold	Actively engage in bankruptcy process	Seek control
Approach	Seek price appreciation or capital structure arbitrage opportunity	Seek returns upon exit from bankruptcy	Retain equity stake to continue restructuring after bankruptcy exit
Typical Holding Period	Six months or more	1–2 years	Exit in 2–3 years

The first distinction among these strategies is whether an investor takes a short-term trading position based largely on public information or seeks to actively engage in the debt restructuring process over time to influence the outcome. The former approach is commonly taken by alternative investors, such as hedge funds, as outlined in earlier in the curriculum. Specifically, credit hedge funds are well positioned to capitalize on temporary security mispricing due to the credit quality and liquidity constraints faced by many institutional investors. For example, in the case of **fallen angels**, or formerly investment-grade-rated issuers whose bonds are downgraded to high yield due to credit deterioration, a trading strategy might involve buying just after the downgrade to high yield in the wake of forced selling by high-grade investors, with a subsequent sale as these same bonds appreciate as they are widely added to institutional high-yield bond portfolios.

When evaluating distressed investment strategies in general and distressed debt in particular, it is important to look beyond standard yield-to-maturity and credit spread measures given the high likelihood of default and recovery in a default scenario, as illustrated in the following example.

EXAMPLE 6

Fallco's Distressed Bonds

A distressed credit fund manager is evaluating a possible investment in the senior unsecured bonds of Fallco, a fallen angel with one-year 6.00% and three-year 6.50% fixed senior unsecured annual coupon bonds outstanding. Both bonds recently traded at a price equal to 75% of par value. The current risk-free rate for both maturities is 5.00%.

1. Calculate the respective yields-to-maturity on Fallco's outstanding bonds and discuss the limitations associated with this return measure.

   Solution:

   Using the spreadsheet RATE function [= RATE(*nper*,*pmt*,*pv*,*fv*,*type*)], where *nper* is the number of periods, *pmt* is the periodic coupon payment, *pv* is the present value, *fv* is future or face value, and *type* corresponds to payments made at the end (0) or beginning (1) of each period, we can solve for the Fallco bond yields-to-maturity as follows:

One-year 6% coupon: 41.33% = RATE(1,6,-75,100,0).

Three-year 6.5% coupon: 18.00% = RATE(3,6.5,-75,100,0).

Investors earn a rate of return on a bond equal to its yield-to-maturity only if

- the investor holds the bond to maturity and receives payment in full,
- no issuer default occurs, and
- the investor reinvests all coupon payments at the same yield-to-maturity.

Given the distressed nature of Fallco's debt, these assumptions underlying the yield-to-maturity calculation are less likely to be met, making this an unsuitable measure of return for such bonds.

2. The credit hedge fund manager notes a 40% historical recovery rate for senior unsecured bonds in Fallco's industry sector and estimates a one-third chance of a Fallco default in one year's time. Compare the recently traded price of Fallco's one-year bond to the estimated market price using these assumptions.

Solution:

To estimate the bond's market price, we first discount the 106 cash flow to the present at the 5% risk-free rate using a simple time-value-of-money calculation:

$$PV = \frac{FV_t}{(1+r)^t}.$$

$$100.9524 = \frac{106}{(1.05)^1}.$$

The price of 100.9524 represents the present value of bond cash flows at the risk-free rate, from which we must deduct the credit valuation adjustment. Recall that the CVA is the present value of expected loss, or the probability-weighted recovery in one period, as shown below in Exhibit 12.

Exhibit 12: Expected One-Year Return on Fallco Bond

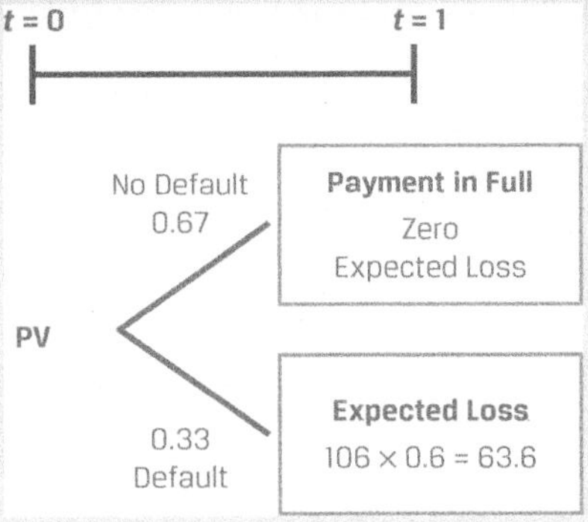

Solve for the expected loss using Equation 1:

$EL = POD \times LGD$

$= 20.99 = 0.33 \times (106 \times 0.6).$

Solve for the present value of expected loss and subtract from 100.9524:

$$PV(EL) = 19.99 = \frac{20.99}{1.05}.$$

Estimated market price = 80.96 (= 100.9524 – 19.99). The current trading price of 75% of par value presents an attractive buying opportunity given the estimated value of approximately 81% of par value.
Alternatively, one can probability weight each of the separate outcomes:

No-default: Value = 106.

Default: Value = $106 \times 0.4 = 42.4$.

Expected end value = $0.67 \times 106 + 0.33 \times 42.4 = 71.02 + 13.99 = 85.01$.

PV(Expected end value) = 85.01/1.05 = 80.96.

This simple example illustrates key parameters used to estimate the market value of a security, but the timing and likelihood of default is highly unpredictable in the case of financial distress. More complex capital structure arbitrage investment situations involving more than one security are addressed later.

Investors actively engaged in the restructuring process via either a controlling or non-controlling stake seek to create value by influencing the outcome of a distressed debt reorganization. These investment strategies are more closely aligned with private equity investments, except for the timing and method of investment.

In contrast to a more orderly take-private transaction in which a private equity sponsor contributes equity and raises debt for the remainder of the purchase price, an active distressed investor may acquire at least half of an issuer's outstanding loans and bonds, or a third in order to establish a blocking minority stake, with the goal of acquiring the firm in a debt-for-equity swap and likely contributing additional equity or partnering with another equity investor at a later stage.

Private equity GPs often view distressed situations as an attractive entry point to combine and consolidate companies within an industry following a cyclical downturn. For example, private equity played an active role in the oil and gas industry consolidation following the wave of bankruptcies described in an earlier example. By acquiring a controlling stake during the reorganization process, private investors can negotiate sweeping management changes, cost reductions, and other concessions that may contribute to a more rapid turnaround of a company than under stable market conditions. In some cases, a highly sought-after distressed firm may be purchased at terms favorable to the company's creditors, as in the following example.

HERTZ EMERGES FROM BANKRUPTCY

Hertz, a US rental car company, began Chapter 11 bankruptcy proceedings in May 2020 following the onset of the COVID-19 pandemic and the resulting decline in all travel-related businesses. In an interesting turn of events, used car prices soared in late 2020 because of global car shortages. Hertz took advantage of this opportunity to sell approximately a third of its fleet. As travel began to resume more quickly than anticipated in early 2021, the shortage of available vehicles caused car rental rates to soar.

In this environment, Hertz attracted interest from several private equity investor groups looking to bring the company out of bankruptcy. After a bidding war in spring of 2021, the winning investors paid approximately USD5.9 billion for Hertz. As part of their bid, both secured and unsecured claims in the company's Chapter 11 case received 100% payment and existing shareholders received small allotments of cash and equity stakes in the reorganized company.

Active controlling investors usually hold their positions for two to three years following the exit from bankruptcy.

Active investors who are *not* seeking to take a controlling stake in the company may also purchase distressed debt and participate in creditor committees, as well as provide post-bankruptcy financing. These investors typically hold smaller stakes, may partner with larger or smaller investors to influence restructuring outcomes, and are more likely to exit soon after the company emerges from bankruptcy.

QUESTION SET

1. Discuss the circumstance under which excessive leverage is likely to contribute to a company's financial distress and its potential severity.

   Solution:

   While excessive leverage can be a factor leading to financial distress for a company, a compounding factor such as poor operating performance is usually necessary to create distress. The severity of distress may depend on whether poor operating performance is of a short-term cyclical nature or is evident of longer-term performance issues. High leverage increases the amount of cash flow necessary to service a company's debt.

2. Which of the following is the most likely strategy for a company whose debt-to-EBITDA ratio rises above a level defined in maintenance covenants?

   A. Raise additional debt capital.

   B. Reschedule debt repayment.

   C. Sell operating assets to raise capital.

   Solution:

   B is the correct response. The violation of a maintenance covenant reflects a technical default, and the most likely response is a short-term liquidity strategy, such as rescheduling debt repayments. A and C are incorrect because both represent strategies that would be used if the default were characterized by a longer-term insolvency issue.

3. Contrast the seniority ranking of debtor in possession financing of a company filing Chapter 11 bankruptcy relative to that of its existing debt claims, and explain a rationale for the relative ranking of DIP financing.

   Solution:

   DIP financing is short-term debt senior to all other existing claims against the debtor. This temporary financing is used to both cover ongoing bankruptcy costs and provide working capital and other financing to maintain operations while the firm is in bankruptcy. Thus, lenders need senior status to be willing to provide this capital to the bankrupt company.

4. Evaluate the following investment opportunity available to a distressed debt investor: Failco has a one-year 8% coupon bond trading at 70% of par value. The investor estimates a 60% chance of default for Failco and a 55% expected recovery rate. The current risk-free rate is 4%.

   Solution:

   Expected loss if Failco defaults:

$EL = 0.60 \times (0.45 \times 108) = 29.16.$

Expected payoff in one year to buying Failco bond:

Expected payoff = $108 - 29.16 = 78.84.$

Fair market value for Failco bond:

Value = $78.84 \div 1.04 = 75.81.$

The bond trades at 70 and is worth 75.81, assuming the expected default probability and recovery rate given above, so the distressed debt investor should view this opportunity as potentially profitable.

4 OTHER SPECIAL SITUATIONS

☐ discuss the features of complex investment situations involving financial dislocation or stress

Financial distress arises as the value of an issuer's assets (V_T) declines compared to the face value of its debt (D). More complex investment situations associated with a company's capital structure require a closer examination of the building blocks of firm value.

Equity as an Option of Firm Assets: The Merton Model

As shown in Exhibit 1, a firm's value combines shareholder and debtholder claims. In theory, shareholder claims consist of assets (V_T) plus the right to deliver or "put" assets to debtholders upon default at an exercise price of D (p_0 at $t = 0$). Debtholders have a risk-free debt claim at maturity (D) plus the put option ($-p_0$) *sold* to shareholders. These components of firm value distributed between shareholders and debtholders are illustrated in Exhibit 13.

Exhibit 13: Shareholder and Debtholder Payoffs at Time *T*

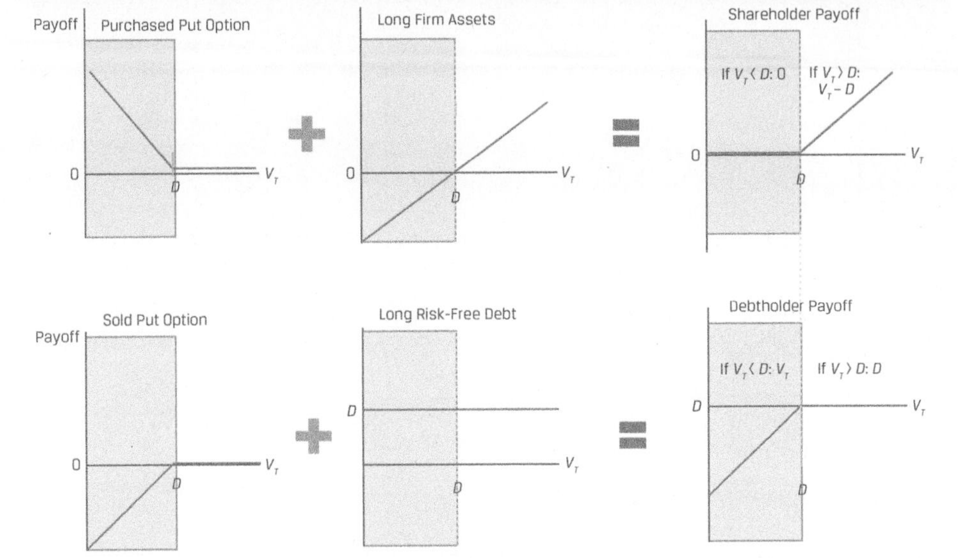

Earlier in the curriculum, it was shown that under put–call parity, at $t = 0$, the price of a long underlying asset plus a long put option must equal the price of a long call option plus the present value of a risk-free bond's face value (D) equal to the option exercise price. Substituting firm asset value as the asset and risk-free debt for the risk-free asset, we can show firm asset value under put–call parity (V_0) as

$$V_0 + p_0 = c_0 + \text{PV}(D).$$

$$V_0 = c_0 + \text{PV}(D) - p_0. \tag{2}$$

In Equation 2, the *shareholder* payoff is shown as a call option on firm value (c_0), while the debtholder payoff is equal to risk-free debt, PV(D), and the sold put ($-p_0$). This sold put option may be interpreted as the firm's *credit spread*, or the premium above the risk-free rate shareholders must pay debtholders to assume default risk.

This link between credit spreads to equity prices is the key feature of **structural credit risk models** introduced earlier in the curriculum. Structural models, or models using an option-based approach to evaluate a firm's market value of assets versus its fixed obligations, are commonly applied to evaluate default probabilities and complex investment situations. Exhibit 14 shows the features of a structural model, with the market value of equity, E_t, over time based on the market value of firm assets (V_t), a probability distribution based on asset value volatility (σ) and the face value of debt(D), also referred to as the default barrier.

Exhibit 14: Structural Model of Default

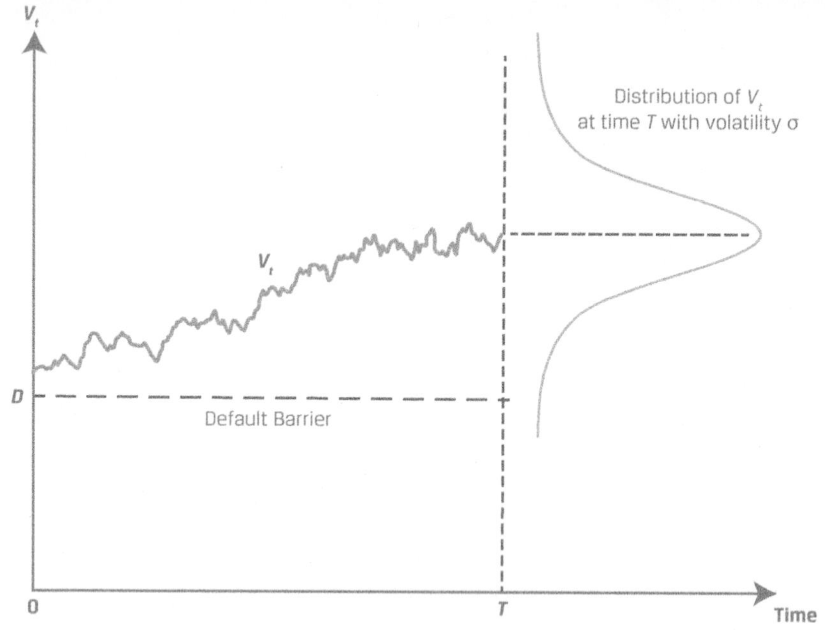

At time T, equity and debt values are as follows:

$$V_T = E_T + D_T, \quad (3)$$

where

$$E_T = \max[(V_T - D_T), 0] \quad (4)$$

$$D_T = V_T - \max[(V_T - D_T), 0] \quad (5)$$

Equation 3 shows firm asset value divided between equity and debt. Equityholders own a call option on residual assets (Equation 4), while debtholders own a covered call position on the firm's asset value (Equation 5).

Structural models are also often referred to as Merton models, because they are based on the same work and apply the same Black–Scholes–Merton (BSM) option pricing model introduced in an earlier learning module on derivatives. Since equity value E_t may be expressed as a call option on residual firm value $(V_t - D)$, we substitute this expression for the familiar $(S - X)$ denoting the stock price minus the exercise price used in the original BSM model. This theoretical application of the BSM model also uses the volatility of the value of the firm's assets rather than that of the firm's equity:

$$E_t = V_t N(d_1) - e^{-rT} DN(d_2), \quad (6)$$

where

$$d_1 = \frac{\ln(V_t/D) + [r + (1/2)\sigma^2](T - t)}{\sigma\sqrt{T - t}}$$

$$d_2 = d_1 - \sigma\sqrt{T - t}$$

$N(x)$ denotes the probability of obtaining a value of less than x based on a standard normal distribution. Debtholders expect to receive D at maturity, while the value of *risky* debt prior to maturity at time t (D_t) simply equals the difference between firm asset value (V_t) and equity value (E_t):

$$D_t = V_t - E_t. \quad (7)$$

Ignoring spread adjustments due to liquidity or other factors, the difference between the present value of risk-free debt ($e^{-rT}D$) and risky debt (D_t) represents the put option on firm value described earlier. The "price" of the put option is the present value of expected loss, or credit valuation adjustment.

Risky bond and CDS values are more easily compared when the put option price is shown as a spread over risk-free debt rather than based on the difference in present value of zero-coupon debt. The put option expressed as a periodic credit spread, or the difference between a risky yield R and the risk-free rate r, is shown in Equation 8 for a maturity of $T - t$.

$$R - r = \frac{1}{T-t}\left(\ln\left[\frac{D}{D_t}\right]\right) - r. \tag{8}$$

Since D_t is equal to face value of debt minus the value of the put option, we can see that the more valuable the put option, the higher the credit spread ($R - r$) becomes. Because of put–call parity, greater call option value implies greater put option value (i.e., higher equity value and lower debt value relative to asset value). These structural model relationships are illustrated in the following case study.

CASE STUDY

Cedere Corporation Equity and Debt Values Using a Structural Model

An analyst estimates that Cedere Corporation, a publicly traded company with 10 million shares outstanding, has assets with a market value of EUR3.25 billion and an estimated asset volatility of 20%. She observes that Cedere currently has a face value of EUR2.75 billion in debt outstanding and that the current risk-free euro interest rate is 5%.

1. Assuming a one-year time horizon, use the structural model to estimate the value of Cedere's equity, its risky debt, and its credit spread.

   Solution:

   Solve for Cedere's equity value using Equation 6:

   $$E_t = V_t N(d_1) - e^{-rT} D N(d_2).$$

   $$E_t = 3{,}250 \times N(d_1) - e^{-0.05} \times 2{,}750 \times N(d_2).$$

   $$d_1 = \frac{\ln(3{,}250/2{,}750) + (0.05 + (1/2)0.2^2)}{0.2} = 1.18527.$$

   $$d_2 = d_1 - 0.2 = 0.98527.$$

   Use the spreadsheet function NORM.S.DIST(*z*,*cumulative*) to solve for $N(d_1)$ and $N(d_2)$ given the respective values:

   $N(d_1) = 0.88204 =$ NORM.S.DIST(1.18527,*true*).

   $N(d_2) = 0.83775 =$ NORM.S.DIST(0.98527,*true*).

   Substituting these values into Equation 6, solve for E_t of EUR675 million, or a price per share of EUR67.50 (EUR675 million/10 million).

   Solve for Cedere's risky debt value using Equation 7:

   $D_t = 3{,}250 - 675 =$ EUR2.575 billion.

   Solve for Cedere's implied credit spread using Equation 8:

$$R - r = \frac{1}{T-t}\left[\ln\left(\frac{2,750}{2,575}\right)\right] - 0.05.$$

Solve for $R - r$ of 1.58% p.a.

2. Discuss how Cedere's equity, debt, and credit spread values change if the market value of the firm's assets were to fall to EUR2.5 billion.

Solution:

A decline in Cedere's market value of assets (V_t) from EUR3.25 billion to EUR2.5 billion would reduce the value of a call option on residual assets ($V_t - D$), reducing the value of equity and increasing the value of the put option and the credit spread. We can calculate the impact of this change as follows:

Solve for Cedere's equity value using Equation 6:

$$E_t = 2,500 \times N(d_1) - e^{-0.05} \times 2,750 \times N(d_2).$$

$$d_1 = \frac{\ln(2,500/2,750) + (0.05 + (1/2)0.2^2)}{0.2} = -0.12655.$$

$$d_2 = d_1 - 0.2 = -0.32655.$$

Use the spreadsheet function NORM.S.DIST(*z*,*cumulative*) to solve for $N(d_1)$ and $N(d_2)$ given the respective values:

$N(d_1) = 0.44965 =$ NORM.S.DIST(–0.12655,*true*).

$N(d_2) = 0.37200 =$ NORM.S.DIST(–0.32655,*true*).

Substituting these values into Equation 6, solve for E_t of EUR151 million, or a price per share of EUR15.10 (EUR151 million/10 million).

Solve for Cedere's risky debt value using Equation 7:

$$D_t = 2,500 - 151 = \text{EUR}2.349 \text{ billion}.$$

Solve for Cedere's implied credit spread using Equation 8:

$$R - r = \frac{1}{T-t}\left[\ln\left(\frac{2,750}{2,349}\right)\right] - 0.05.$$

Solve for $R - r$ of 10.76% p.a.

Note that the firm's share price fell but remained positive despite a decline in the market value of firm assets below the face value of debt ($V_t > D$). Consistent with an out-of-the-money call option on firm value, the positive equity price represents time value given the underlying volatility of asset prices.

Insights gained from structural models must be weighed against their limitations. In practice, the market value of a firm's assets and asset price volatility are not directly observable but instead are estimated using equity prices and equity volatility. Debt profiles with staggered maturities, different levels of seniority and security, and contingency features complicate the put option calculation, and it is difficult to calibrate models to sudden capital structure changes. Continuous trading and no-arbitrage pricing assumptions do not apply to firms in financial distress with less liquid debt and equity securities. In practice, the default probabilities and credit spreads resulting from the Merton model may require adjustments based on historical data or other factors to arrive at a default probability forecast. As a result, while useful in quantifying equity implied credit risk, structural models are usually complemented by other credit and equity valuation models and techniques.

Capital Structure Arbitrage and the Merton Model

As described earlier, capital structure arbitrage strategies involve taking more than one position, typically a long and a short position, to capitalize on security mispricing in different markets for the same issuer. Discrepancies may arise due to the presence of different participants in equity, bond, loan, and CDS markets, as well as varying speeds of price adjustment.

Structural models are used as a basis to compare implied credit spreads across equity, bond, and CDS markets and predict changes based on market movements. For example, we showed that an implied credit spread from the equity value (or $S_{Equity,Implied}$) is equal to $(R - r)$, where R is the yield-to-maturity on an issuer's debt and r is the applicable risk-free rate. We can derive implied credit spreads over a range of equity prices and compare them to observed bond market spreads ($S_{Bond,Observed}$) based on traded prices as shown in Exhibit 15.

Exhibit 15: Model Results vs. Observed Bond Credit Spreads

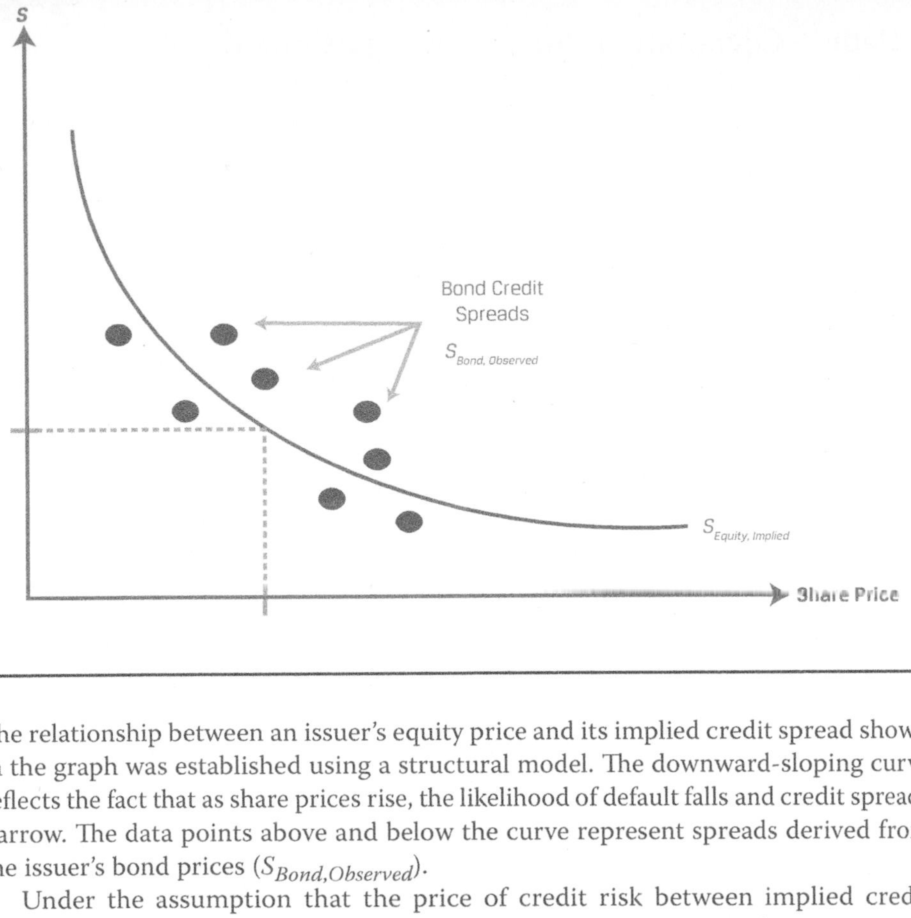

The relationship between an issuer's equity price and its implied credit spread shown in the graph was established using a structural model. The downward-sloping curve reflects the fact that as share prices rise, the likelihood of default falls and credit spreads narrow. The data points above and below the curve represent spreads derived from the issuer's bond prices ($S_{Bond,Observed}$).

Under the assumption that the price of credit risk between implied credit spreads from equity and bond spreads should generally be aligned ($S_{Equity,Implied} \approx S_{Bond,Observed}$), a simple capital arbitrage decision rule to take advantage of *relative* mispricing between implied equity and bond spreads is as follows:

$S_{Bond,Observed} > S_{Equity,Implied}$: Buy bonds, sell equity short

$S_{Equity,Implied} > S_{Bond,Observed}$: Buy equities, sell bonds short

If the observed bond spread $S_{Bond,Observed}$ exceeds the spread implied by the model, then the value of debt, D_t, and thus the bond price are *below* that predicted by the model. An investor who buys the bond and sells the stock short expects to gain as the mispricing ($S_{Bond,Observed} - S_{Equity,Implied}$) falls to zero.

A final consideration is the hedge ratio of this capital arbitrage strategy. Assuming the Merton model accurately represents the default probability, as in the case of other options, we can use the BSM model to derive the delta, or expected change in bond value for a given change in equity value, dD_t/dE_t, to determine this ratio as follows, using Equation 7:

$$\frac{dE_t}{dV_t} = N(d_1)\ ;\ D_t = V_t - E_t.$$

$$\frac{dD_t}{dE_t} = \frac{dV_t}{dE_t} - 1 = \frac{1}{N(d_1)} - 1. \qquad (9)$$

We consider a capital arbitrage strategy using the earlier case study.

CASE STUDY

Cedere Corporation Bond vs. Equity Capital Arbitrage Strategy

Recall that Cedere Corporation is a publicly traded company with 10 million shares outstanding. Cedere currently has one-year debt with a face value of EUR2.75 billion outstanding, and the current risk-free euro interest rate of 5% remains constant for the period under consideration.

1. Assuming a firm asset volatility of 20%, calculate the implied equity credit spread over a range from EUR10 to EUR100 per share using the structural model and interpret the results under the Merton model.

Solution:

Using the BSM model in Equation 6 and given that D equals EUR2.75 billion, r is 5%, $\sigma = 0.2$, and T is 1, we can solve for a given E_t, which when divided by 10 million gives us the respective price per Cedere share. For example, a EUR10 price per share implies E_t of EUR100 million. Solve for $\text{Spread}_{Equity,Implied}$:

$$\text{EUR100 million} = V_t N(d_1) - e^{-0.05} 2.75 \text{ billion } N(d_2),$$

where

$$d_1 = \frac{\ln(V_t/2.75 \text{ billion}) + [0.05 + (1/2)0.2^2](1)}{0.2}.$$

$$d_2 = d_1 - 0.2$$

Solve for V_t = EUR2.372 million by an iterative process, such as trial and error or the Goal Seek function in Excel.

lve for D_t using Equation 7:

$$D_t = 2{,}372 - 100 = \text{EUR2.272 billion}.$$

Solve for Cedere's implied credit spread using Equation 8:

$$R - r = \frac{1}{T-t}\left[\ln\left(\frac{2{,}750}{2{,}272}\right)\right] - 0.05.$$

Solve for $\text{Spread}_{Equity,Implied} = R - r$ of 14.09% p.a.

Using a spreadsheet to set up the calculation of Equation 6, Equation 7, and Equation 8, we can use a Data Table or Goal Seek function to solve for $\text{Spread}_{Equity,Implied}$ as a function of Cedere's equity price per share, as shown in the following table and Exhibit 16.

Cedere Equity Price (EUR)	$\text{Spread}_{Equity,Implied}$ (% p.a., σ = 20%)
10	14.09%
20	8.60%
30	5.75%
40	4.00%
50	2.83%
60	2.03%
70	1.46%
80	1.05%
90	0.76%
100	0.55%

Exhibit 16: Cedere Implied Credit Spread vs. Equity Prices

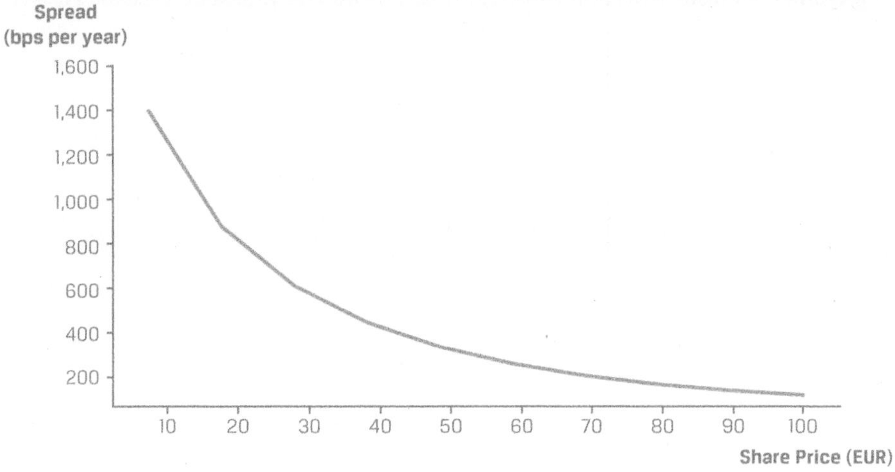

2. Assume an analyst observes that Cederes' shares are trading at EUR40 and its one-year zero-coupon debt is available for purchase at a price of EUR90 per EUR100 face value. Analyze the potential for capital structure arbitrage, and recommend a trading strategy incorporating an appropriate hedge ratio.

Solution:

Cedere's firm value is EUR2,875 million given equity value of EUR400 million (= EUR40 per share × 10 million shares) and debt value of EUR2,475 million (= 90% × EUR2,750).

Using Cedere's firm value of EUR2,875, we continue to assume that D equals EUR2,750 million, r is 5%, σ = 0.2, and T is 1. Next, we solve for d_1 and d_2:

$$d_1 = 0.5723 = \frac{\ln(2.875/2.75 \text{ billion}) + [0.05 + (1/2)0.2^2](1)}{0.2}.$$

$$d_2 = 0.3723 = 0.5723 - 0.2.$$

Then, we solve for $N(d_1)$ and $N(d_2)$ given the respective values:

$N(d_1) = 0.7164 = \text{NORM.S.DIST}(0.5723,\textit{true})$.

$N(d_2) = 0.6451 = \text{NORM.S.DIST}(0.3723,\textit{true})$.

Using this information in Equation 6 to solve for Cedere's equity value (i.e., the call option value):

$E_t = 2{,}875 \times 0.7164 - e^{-0.05} \times 2{,}750 \times 0.6451 = 372.$

Thus, Cedere's equity value according to the structural model is EUR372 million, which compared to the current traded price of EUR400 million suggests that Cedere's equity is overvalued. Subtracting Cedere's model equity value of EUR372 million from the asset value of EUR2,875 million implies a fair value of debt of EUR2,503 million, which implies the traded value of EUR2,475 is undervalued.

Therefore, there appears to be potential for a capital structure arbitrage by buying Cedere's bonds and selling short the company's stock.

To construct the trade, we use Equation 9 to find the hedge ratio (i.e., change in debt value per change in equity value), and we use the $N(d_1)$ term from the BSM model of 0.7164 to calculate a ratio of 0.3958 [= (1 ÷ 0.7164) – 1]. So, per EUR1 of bond value purchased, sell short EUR0.3958 in equity value.

The prior case study assumed a constant risk-free rate, but fixed-coupon bond prices change as both the level of interest rates and the market's view of an issuer's credit risk changes. Investors use interest rate hedging strategies, such as an **asset swap**, to isolate a bond's spread component.

Exhibit 17 shows a bond's periodic fixed coupon to a market reference rate MRR plus (or minus) a spread using an asset swap.

Exhibit 17: Asset Swap Mechanics

If we assume an investor purchases a risky bond at par, the asset swap transforms the risky fixed-rate coupon to an equivalent fixed credit spread over MRR for the life of the bond. As the swap offsets bond value changes due to interest rate risk, the combination of risky bond and pay-fixed swap exposure leaves the investor with price risk based on bond credit spread (S_{Bond}) changes. However, note that under a bond default scenario, the investor still faces a mark-to-market settlement of the pay-fixed asset swap.

Recall from earlier that a credit default swap is a derivative contract in which a protection *buyer* pays a periodic premium based on the CDS spread at inception to a protection *seller*. The seller makes a contingent payment equal to the difference between par and the recovery rate to the buyer under a credit event. Unlike interest rate swaps, credit default swaps are terminated and settled after a credit event, with no remaining interest rate swap exposure.

Under the no-arbitrage assumption that an investor can both borrow and lend at MRR as a reasonable approximation of the risk-free rate, *r*, Exhibit 18 illustrates the use of these strategies in taking a synthetic position in an issuer's bond or credit spread.

Exhibit 18: Bond vs. CDS Strategies in Managing Issuer Spread Risk

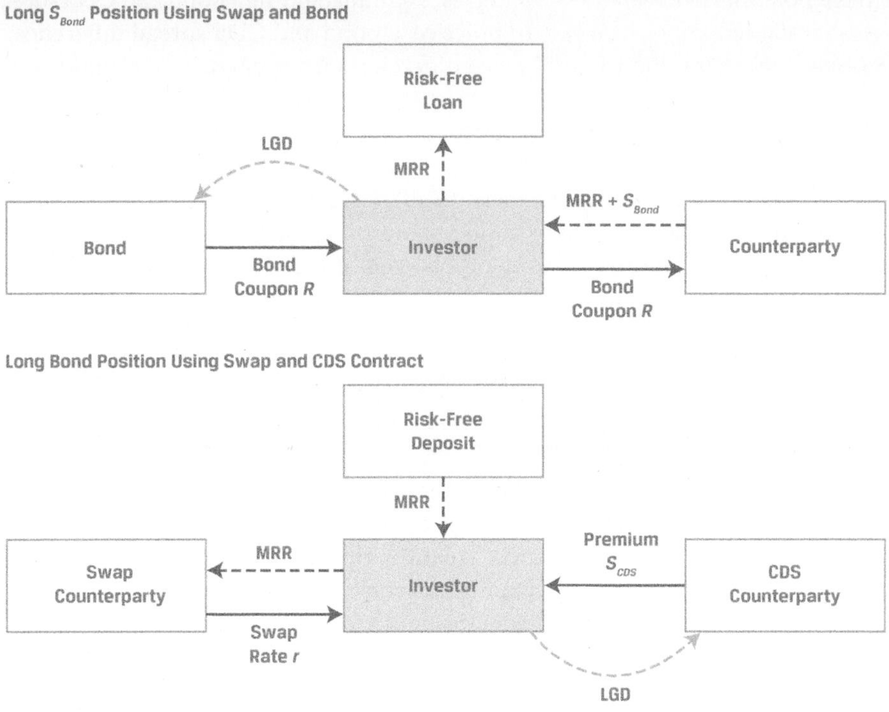

In the first instance, we demonstrate that an investor can create a long bond spread (S_{Bond}) position by borrowing at MRR for the life of the debt, buying the bond, and entering a pay-fixed interest rate swap. Alternatively, an investor may create a synthetic long bond position to earn the total rate of return, *R*, by depositing the bond purchase at a risk-free rate, selling CDS protection, and entering a receive-fixed swap. The cash flows of these two approaches are summarized in Exhibit 19.

Exhibit 19: Synthetic Bond Spread and Synthetic Bond Cash Flows

Cash Flows	Synthetic S_{Bond}	Synthetic Bond with CDS
At Inception	Borrow *D*	Lend *D*
	Purchase bond for *D*	Enter receive-fixed swap
	Enter pay-fixed swap	Sell CDS protection
	Net: 0	**Net: –*D***
Periodic Cash Flows	Bond: + *R*	Deposit: + MRR
	Swap: + MRR + S_{Bond} – *R*	Swap: + *r* – MRR
	Loan: – MRR	CDS: + S_{CDS}
	Net: + S_{Bond}	**Net: + $(r + S_{CDS}) \approx R$**

Cash Flows	Synthetic S_{Bond}	Synthetic Bond with CDS
At Maturity	Bond: Receive D	Loan: Receive D
	Loan: Pay D	
	Net: 0	**Net: D**

Arbitrage potential between these strategies is eliminated when bond and CDS spreads are closely aligned ($S_{Bond} \approx S_{CDS}$). In practice, a bond and CDS spread difference, or **CDS basis**, may arise due to bond price differences from par, accrued interest, and varying contract terms. For example, in the case of a *negative* CDS basis (where $S_{Bond} > S_{CDS}$), an investor might combine a synthetic long S_{Bond} position, shown above, with *buying* CDS protection on the same issuer to benefit as the basis declines over time.

As a protection *seller* realizes a mark-to-market *gain* when CDS spreads *narrow*, the position is equivalent to a long bond position. Capital structure arbitrage trades to take advantage of *relative* mispricing between implied equity and CDS spreads may be summarized as follows:

If:	Then:
$S_{CDS} > S_{Equity,Implied}$:	Sell CDS protection, sell equity short
$S_{Equity,Implied} > S_{CDS}$:	Buy equities, buy CDS protection

We have considered changes in implied asset values, as well as changes in equity values, to motivate capital structure arbitrage opportunities. However, these examples have assumed fixed volatility over time. Volatility changes in the structural model add a third dimension that may create capital structure arbitrage opportunities. We first consider how a volatility change affects the equity price versus implied credit spread relationship by revisiting our earlier case study.

CASE STUDY

Cedere Corporation Bond vs. Equity As Asset Volatility Changes

Cedere Corporation has 10 million shares and EUR2.75 billion in one-year debt outstanding. Rising uncertainty in Cedere's industry has caused the analyst to double the asset volatility assumption in her structural model to 40%.

1. Assuming a risk-free rate of 5%, calculate the implied equity credit spread for a share price of EUR10 per share using the revised structural model volatility assumption, and interpret the results.

   Solution:

   Using the BSM model in Equation 6 with D = EUR2.75 billion, r = 5%, σ = 0.4, and T = 1, solve for $\text{Spread}_{Equity,Implied}$ given E_t of EUR100 million (EUR10 per share):

   $$\text{EUR100 million} = V_t N(d_1) - e^{-0.05} 2.75 \text{ billion } N(d_2),$$

   where

   $$d_1 = \frac{\ln(V_t/2.75 \text{ billion}) + [0.05 + (1/2)0.4^2](1)}{0.4}$$

$d_2 = d_1 - 0.4$

Solve for V_t = EUR1.878 billion using an iterative approach as in the prior case study, and note a comparison to EUR2.372 billion when 20% volatility was assumed.

Solve for D_t using Equation 7:

D_t = 1,878 – 100 = EUR1.778 billion.

Solve for Cedere's implied credit spread using Equation 8:

$$R - r = \frac{1}{T-t}\left[\ln\left(\frac{2,750}{1,778}\right)\right] - 0.05.$$

Solve for $\text{Spread}_{Equity,Implied} = R - r = 38.64\%$ (versus 14.09% with 20% volatility).

The value of the call option held by shareholders on firm assets *rises* as volatility increases, causing the present value of firm assets at time t (V_t) to be lower for a given equity price and increasing the value of the put option sold by debtholders, both reducing the debt value (D_t) and increasing the credit spread ($R - r$) expressed as a percentage.

2. Revisit the arbitrage strategy used in Question 2 in the prior case study, and discuss an alternative interpretation of how a volatility change may impact the outcome.

Solution:

As Cedere's assumed asset volatility increases, the company's option values increase, holding asset value constant. Specifically, volatility increases imply higher fair values for Cedere's equity while the company's fair value of debt decreases, thus increasing the implied credit spread on Cedere's risky debt.

In a higher-volatility environment, Cedere's equity and debt values may move sufficiently that the company's stock becomes undervalued, and the debt overvalued. In fact, in the scenario of Question 2 in the prior case study, volatility above approximately 22.8% (which may be viewed as the implied asset volatility associated with Cedere's observed equity and debt prices) will create a situation in which the capital structure arbitrage would be to buy Cedere's shares and sell short the bonds.

An increase in volatility in the structural model leads to a shift in the equity price/implied bond spread relationship upward and to the right, as shown in Exhibit 20.

Exhibit 20: Volatility and the Credit Spread/Share Price Relationship

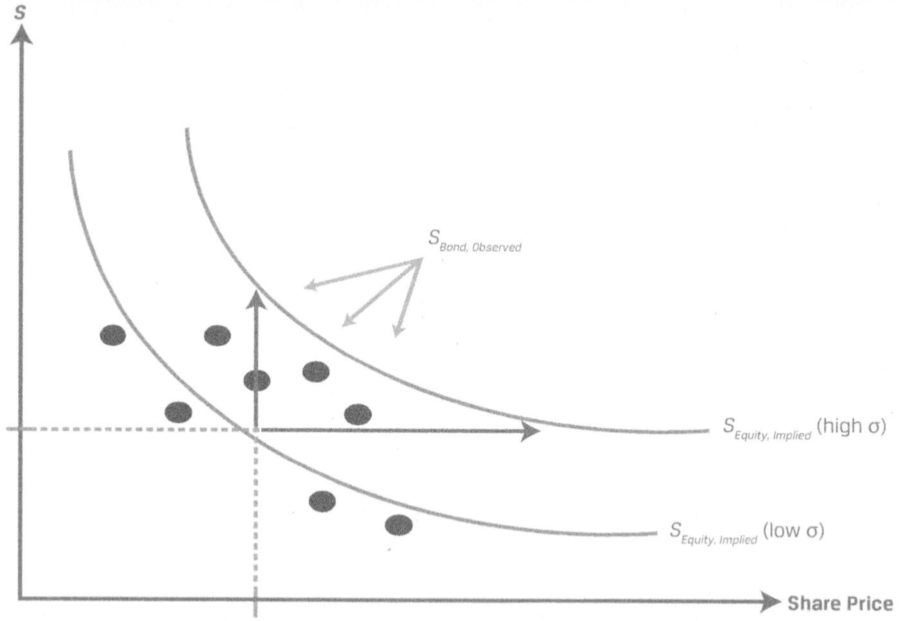

This shift in the equity price/credit spread relationship increases the expected credit spread ($S_{Equity,Implied}$) for a given share price, changing the relative mispricing of observed trades based on the original volatility assumption. For example, in Exhibit 15, a short bond/long equity position would have realized a gain given the shift from low to high volatility and a new equity/credit spread relationship.

Investors may also take an explicit capital structure arbitrage position based on a view that the *implied* equity volatility suggested by the credit spread/share relationship in the structural model deviates significantly from actual equity volatility, as observed, for example, in the traded equity options market.

Convertible Bond Arbitrage Strategies

As described earlier in the curriculum, convertible bonds combine a straight bond with an embedded call option on an issuer's shares sold to investors. Investors may exchange debt into equity at a predetermined **conversion price** per share, or the price at which the debt may be fully exchanged for shares, during a period in the future.

Convertible bonds are relatively illiquid securities typically issued by early-stage or high-risk companies, with the call option contingency feature attracting lenders who may not be willing to offer standard fixed-rate debt to the issuer. Convertible bonds are also often offered at a discount to investors to attract capital more quickly than through a typical equity or bond offering. Exhibit 21 extends the earlier exhibit showing a straight bond's building blocks in terms of interest rate risk and credit risk to the case of convertible bonds.

Exhibit 21: Convertible Bond Building Blocks

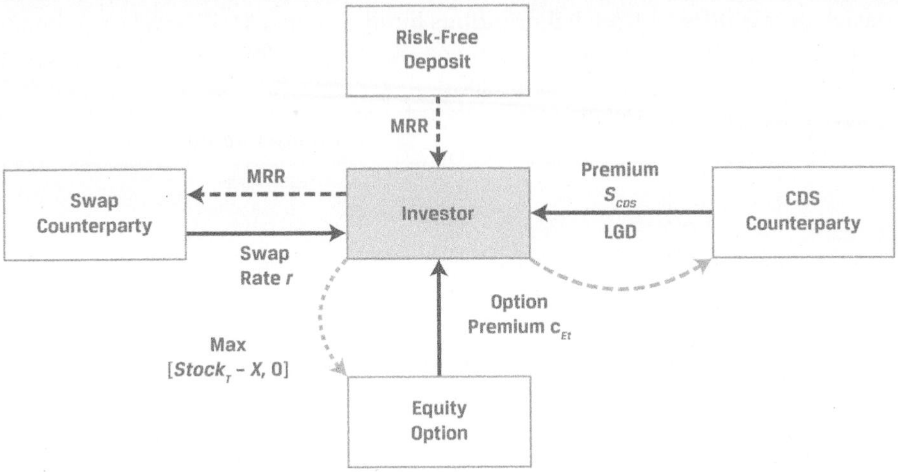

Extending the earlier synthetic long bond example, an investor may create a synthetic long convertible bond position by depositing the bond purchase price at a risk-free rate, selling CDS protection, entering a receive-fixed swap, and purchasing an equity call option that matches the bond's conversion terms.

The convertible bond issuer has sold equity volatility to the investor, typically in the form of a lower debt coupon versus standard non-convertible debt. This is demonstrated in Exhibit 21 by the investor's initial outlay of the straight bond purchase price *D* plus the equity call option(c_{Et}), which is greater than *D* in Exhibit 13 for the case of standard fixed debt.

Two key differences exist for capital structure arbitrage in the case of convertible debt versus straight debt. First, in contrast to the *indirect* impact of equity volatility on the relationship between credit spreads and share prices in the structural model, convertible bond investors hold a long equity volatility position in the form of an embedded call option. Increasing volatility results in gains to the convertible bondholder due to increases in value on the embedded call option. Second, the conversion feature associated with convertible bonds imposes arbitrage bounds on convertible bonds that do not exist in the case of straight bonds under the structural model. A wide range of capital arbitrage strategies may be used to isolate or offset equity, volatility, credit, and other exposures related to convertible bonds, three of which are listed below.

- *Credit risk.* An investor can purchase CDS protection to offset convertible bond issuer default risk.
- *Interest rate risk.* An investor can pay fixed on an interest rate swap to convert the fixed-rate exposure on the convertible bond to MRR.
- *Equity volatility risk.* An investor can use short equity positions or equity put options to hedge the equity market position of the convertible bond.

QUESTION SET

Laborantibus Partners manages a private fund specializing in distressed securities and is considering investments in public securities issued by Fracassar PLC, a British hotel chain encountering financial problems. Fracassar owns assets with a market value estimate of GBP6,500 million and has GBP7,500 million of zero-coupon debt outstanding that is scheduled to be repaid in six months (i.e., half of a year). Laborantibus estimates that Fracassar's annualized asset volatility is 50%. The current annualized risk-free rate is 5%. Based on this information, Laborantibus builds a structural model to estimate Fracassar's credit risk. As an analyst, you observe the following output from a spreadsheet estimate from this model.

Variable	Estimated Value
d_1	−0.1573
d_2	−0.5108
$N(d_1)$	0.4375
$N(d_2)$	0.3047
Call option value	GBP615 million

1. Calculate the estimated current value of Fracassar debt and the company's credit spread based on the results of the structural model.

Solution:

Fracassar's equity value is equal to the call option value of GBP615 million. So, Fracassar's debt value is GBP5,885 million (= 6,500 – 615), using Equation 7.

Next, we solve for Fracassar's implied credit spread using Equation 8:

$$R - r = \frac{1}{0.5}\left[\ln\left(\frac{7,500}{5,885}\right)\right] - 0.05.$$

$R - r$ equals 43.49%, which reflects Fracassar's implied credit spread.

2. Laborantibus observes the actual credit spread on Fracassar's bonds is 40.0% and their price is GBP5,885. Which of the following best describes a potentially profitable capital structure arbitrage strategy?

A. Buy Fracassar equity, and sell short Fracassar bonds.

B. Buy Fracassar bonds, and sell short Fracassar equity.

C. Buy Fracassar bonds, and buy Fracassar equity.

Solution:

A is the correct response. As shown in the solution to the prior question, a bond price of GBP5,885 implies a credit spread of 43.49%. When the observed credit spread is lower than the implied equity spread, the capital structure arbitrage strategy involves selling short bonds and buying equity. The investor expects spreads to widen to those implied by the structural model, causing the bonds to fall in value relative to equity. B is incorrect because it would be an appropriate strategy if the observed credit spread were greater than the implied credit spread. C is incorrect because this strategy implies that both securities are underpriced, which is not consistent with the structural model, because the two securities can only be mispriced in the opposite direction (i.e., one undervalued and the other overvalued).

3. Laborantibus revises its assumption about Fracassar's asset value given that it observes the market prices of Fracassar's equity and debt are GBP600 million and GBP6,000 million, respectively. The structural model is recal-

culated, and outputs of the model are shown below. Recommend a capital structure arbitrage strategy incorporating an appropriate hedge ratio.

Variable	Estimated Value
d_1	–0.1141
d_2	–0.4676
$N(d_1)$	0.4546
$N(d_2)$	0.3200
Call option value	GBP659 million

Solution:

Given that Fracassar's equity is valued at GBP659 million and can be purchased for GBP600 million, the equity is undervalued by GBP59 million. Thus, Fracassar's debt is overvalued by GBP59 million. The capital structure arbitrage strategy is to buy Fracassar equity and sell Fracassar debt.

To construct the trade incorporating the hedge ratio, we use Equation 9 to find the hedge ratio, and we use the $N(d_1)$ term from the BSM model of 0.4546 to calculate a ratio of 1.1998 [= (1 ÷ 0.4546) – 1]. So, per GBP1 of bond value sold short, buy GBP1.1998 of equity.

4. While Laborantibus believes that Fracassar's asset volatility will likely stay high, it has also built a scenario in which asset volatility declines considerably as uncertainty about the value of hotel asset fades. Which of the following capital structure arbitrage trades works best to capitalize on this scenario?

   A. Buy Fracassar equity, and sell short Fracassar debt.

   B. Sell short Fracassar equity, and sell short Fracassar debt.

   C. Sell Fracassar equity, and buy Fracassar debt.

   Solution:

   C is the correct response. A decline in asset volatility will reduce the call option value that is Fracassar's equity while the company's debt increases in value. A is incorrect because this strategy is appropriate in the event of increasing volatility. B is incorrect because this strategy is not an arbitrage; it is simply a bearish strategy on firm value

SPECIAL SITUATIONS DUE DILIGENCE AND VALUATION 5

☐ discuss the due diligence and valuation processes used to evaluate special investment situations

Special Situations Due Diligence

The types of market-, industry-, and issuer-specific information gathered and analyzed in the due diligence process for special situations investments is similar to that described in earlier Private Markets Pathway learning modules. Recall that more detailed analysis is common in private versus public markets given the role of analysis in establishing a business plan for value creation over a relatively long holding period rather than for short-term trading purposes.

Given the relatively short-term, cyclical, and/or event-driven nature of distressed situations, investors typically have far less time to conduct due diligence and evaluate prospective investments. As a result, screening opportunities to prioritize specific investments is a critical initial step in the process. Key criteria such as issuer ratings, company size based on market capitalization, observed market prices of distressed bonds, and leverage ratios, such as debt/EBITDA, can help narrow investor focus on fewer targets whose debt is currently priced lower than expected based on observed financial ratios.

Statistical credit analysis models to measure creditworthiness often use the structural credit models introduced earlier or **reduced form models**. Unlike structural models, such as the Merton Model, reduced form models are not based on capital structure assumptions. Reduced form models provide a probability of default over a specific time frame, typically using observable company-specific variables, such as financial ratios, and market-based measures. An early example of the reduced form approach is the **Z-score** established by Edward Altman, which includes the following factors:

Liquidity: Working capital/total assets

Profitability: Retained earnings/total assets

Asset efficiency: EBIT/total assets

Market to book: Market value of equity/book value of equity

Asset turnover: Sales/total assets

These factors are weighted by coefficients to form a composite, or Z-score, used to classify firms into those expected to remain solvent versus bankrupt firms.

The structural models introduced earlier are also applied to estimate an issuer's probability of default to be considered along with the expected loss given default when evaluating the price of a distressed issuer's securities. Structural credit models used by practitioners include Moody's Analytics' Expected Default Frequency (EDF) and Bloomberg's Default Risk (DRSK) models, both of which estimate an issuer's probability of default over a selected period. For example, the DRSK model estimate includes a market-based asset value measure derived from equity market capitalization, asset value volatility based on equity volatility, and a default threshold measured using the book value of liabilities. Exhibit 22 shows the Bloomberg DRSK screen for the Swedish real estate firm SBB, described earlier, which estimates a one-year POD of 14.41%.

Exhibit 22: Bloomberg DRSK Model for SBB

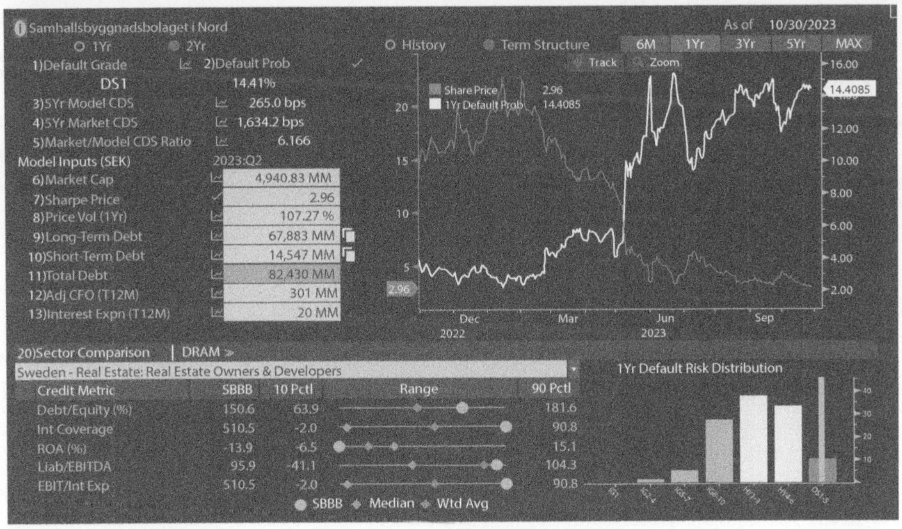

Source: Bloomberg.

Other important differences from the private markets due diligence process are the relative lack of information available to investors compared to a typical corporate acquisition and the more rapid change in a company's financial conditions due to market- or company-specific events.

For example, short-term, trading-based investors, such as credit hedge funds, are best positioned to capitalize on temporary mispricing due to forced sales among institutional investors. These short-term investors are typically limited to public information and have a greater focus on the relative liquidity of instruments under consideration given the higher price volatility associated with these investment opportunities.

Longer-term investors seeking to engage in the restructuring process via either a controlling or non-controlling stake use the due diligence process to gauge their influence over the outcome of a reorganization and ability to create value as the issuer emerges from bankruptcy. In some instances, an investor may establish a small initial investment position in a company because initial due diligence suggests an attractive buying opportunity. Over time, the investor may continue to build the position if ongoing due diligence suggests that a controlling stake is appropriate, while in other cases, the investor may trade the position or retain a minority position.

Valuable information for these prospective investors, such as customer lists, sales projections, or commercial contracts, is likely to be non-public, and company management may be unwilling or unable to share it with outsiders in times of distress. In other cases, access to restricted information may be limited to a bank or lending group and only available to existing creditors under a confidentiality agreement. Limitations on the use of confidential non-public information may restrict trading in public securities and other activities. In this situation or when no such lending group exists, prospective investors have limited bargaining power to obtain this information.

In addition to the financial due diligence common among private investments, including financial statement analysis, cash flow projections, and industry and competitive analysis, evaluation of distressed issuers should include a worst-case liquidation scenario in which the company is dissolved and its assets are sold individually rather than as a going concern. For companies already in bankruptcy, a detailed review of the initial and subsequent bankruptcy court filings and ongoing monthly operating reports provides vital information about the firm's current unsecured creditors, short-term cash flow projections, inventory liquidations, and material events.

Legal due diligence for distressed companies should extend beyond the evaluation of organizational, legal commitments and outstanding litigation to include a thorough understanding of firm structure, as well as loan agreements and indentures within different legal entities, to identify any consolidation, structural, or financial issues or restrictions that may impact a creditor claim as the firm seeks or enters bankruptcy. For example, in contrast to fraudulent transfers described earlier in which assets are moved out of the reach of all creditors, an issuer may have granted a preference to one creditor over another, which may be reversed in bankruptcy court in what is known as a **voidable preference**.

Special Situations Valuation Approaches

Special situations investors make use of valuation techniques similar to those for public and private companies when considering an issuer as a going concern. In addition to the option-based structural model described in this learning module, techniques introduced earlier in the curriculum include the following:

- Income-based approaches based on discounted projected cash flows and a terminal value using assumed constant growth or a terminal market multiple
- Relative approaches (or the method of comparables) based on price-based or enterprise value–based multiples of firms with similar features
- Asset-based approaches seeking to estimate the value of underlying assets less liabilities

The key issue in valuing special situations is how to incorporate the likelihood, timing, and financial impact of specific events that give rise to investment opportunities. As described earlier in the curriculum, firms may face future alternatives that may be considered **real options** under a distressed scenario that can alter firm value. Recall that real options grant a firm the right but not the obligation to decide or take an action in the future. A company will choose to pursue (or exercise) a real option only if it enhances shareholder value. These options might include the sale of individual assets or an entire division of a firm. A related approach involves a **sum-of-the-parts valuation**, which considers the value of a firm's individual business segments if they were to be sold separately.

In what follows, we focus on events related to financial distress, such as bankruptcy, restructuring, and liquidation.

Consider how the potential for financial distress affects the standard discounted cash flow (DCF) valuation approach, as shown in Exhibit 23.

Exhibit 23: The Effect of Financial Distress on DCF Valuation

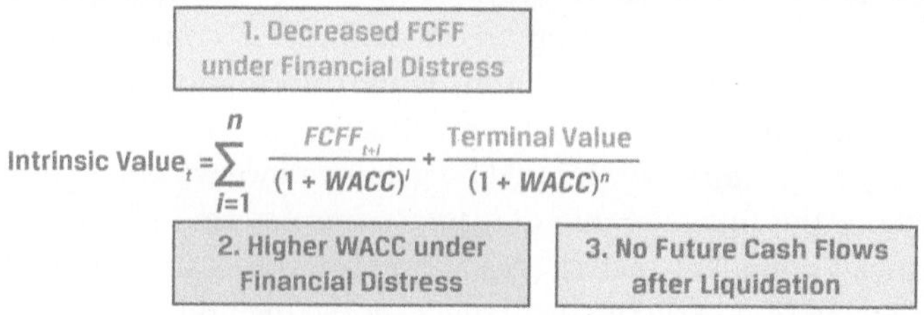

Exhibit 23 shows three key challenges associated with applying the standard DCF approach to the case of a distressed company:

- *"Numerator" issues.* Analysts must identify and adjust key balance sheet and income statement items due to expected financial distress affecting a company's normalized earnings. The timing and magnitude of event-driven changes to revenue and cash flow are difficult to estimate.
- *"Denominator" issues.* Rates of return used to discount future cash flows or earnings are a second challenge in a distress scenario. In addition to the relative illiquidity of debt and complex capital structures involved, recall that distressed debt yields are not reflective of an expected rate of return, since these bonds trade at a significant discount to par.
- *Terminal value issues.* Discounting future cash flows back to the present implies that a firm will remain a going concern, a questionable assumption in a case of financial distress. The assumption of a future terminal growth rate or market multiple based on non-distressed valuations results in further distortions when considering a firm that may be restructured or liquidated in the near term.

Relative value comparisons using market multiples also fail to adequately account for financial distress, because they are typically calculated using ratios from non-distressed industry peers. As in the case of exit multiples for private equity, a relative value approach can be applied if the firm is considered a going concern—that is, a scenario under which it has averted dissolution.

Asset-based valuation approaches hinge on whether the market value is estimated as part of an ongoing business—that is, incorporating the value of existing products, customers, suppliers, and relationships—or whether the assets are sold individually and separate from the business. As described earlier, if an issuer cannot restructure its activities and obligations to sufficiently meet creditor obligations as a going concern, the individual sale of its assets to settle claims is the best course of action. The liquidation value of a firm's assets therefore often represents a lower bound for valuation purposes.

Liquidation most often occurs when a firm is uncompetitive; its assets are inadequate, outdated, or in disrepair; or the company's management is ineffective. While specialized industry knowledge is critical in assessing asset values under these circumstances, little secondary market information exists for most fixed assets, and their sale price is highly dependent on whether a distressed or orderly sale process takes place.

Valuing a firm's outstanding securities under liquidation involves comparing the value of firm assets (V_t) to debt (D) based on the priority of claims. Exhibit 24 illustrates this scenario by contrasting the balance sheet with asset liquidation proceeds versus debt.

Exhibit 24: Liquidation Valuation Approach

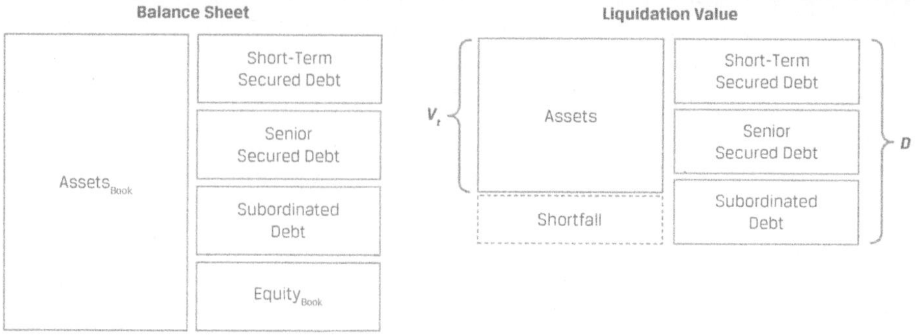

The balance sheet on the left shows the book value of assets, equity, and debt, while on the right we see a shortfall ($V_t - D$) between asset liquidation values and debt. As a result, while senior secured lenders in this example will likely be repaid in full from liquidation proceeds, subordinated lenders will face a settlement value below the face value of debt. Consider the following liquidation valuation based on the earlier Maudville case study.

CASE STUDY

Maudville Corporation Liquidation Valuation

Recall that Maudville Corporation is a US chemical producer with USD5 billion in revenue and EBITDA of USD1 billion that was taken private for USD5 billion using debt (75%), equity (20%), and convertible preferred (5%) financing. After two years of profitability growth, operational improvements, and senior secured debt paydown, Maudville's revenue and profitability decline sharply in Year 3, leading to debt investor concerns over the company's financial situation entering Year 4. Maudville's remaining debt outstanding at the end of Year 3 is as follows:

Maudville Corp. Year 3 Debt Profile

Debt Tranche	Size	Tenor	Amortization	Terms and Conditions	Lender(s)
Secured Revolver	USD250 million	364 days		Secured by first lien	Syndicated bank group
Senior Secured Leveraged Loan	USD2.2 billion	Seven years		Secured by first lien; Ranks *pari passu* with other senior secured debt	Syndicated bank group
Junior Second-Lien Debt	USD600 million	Seven years	Amortizing in four equal installments starting Year 4	Secured by second lien; Ranks *pari passu* with other junior secured debt	100% Bardstown Credit Partners
Mezzanine Debt	USD500 million	10 years		Unsecured subordinated obligation; Ranks *pari passu* with all other subordinated indebtedness	50%: Bardstown Mezzanine Fund; 50%: Another GP. Bardstown has majority voting rights.

An analyst constructing an end-of-Year-4 liquidation scenario observes Year 3 total assets of USD5,596 million and goodwill of USD1,258 million. She assumes that Maudville has fully drawn down its secured revolver and that goodwill should be excluded from the value of assets sold under her presumed distressed liquidation scenario.

1. Calculate the expected recovery of Maudville's outstanding debt by tranche under the liquidation scenario if the analyst assumes that assets are sold for 60% of their Year 3 book value.

   Solution:

   Year 3 assets of USD5,596 million minus goodwill of USD1,258 million results in assets for sale of USD4,338 million, 60% of which gives us liquidation proceeds of USD2,602.6 million (= 0.6 × USD4,338 million). Total debt outstanding with the fully drawn USD250 million revolver is equal to USD3,550 million (3,550 = 250 + 2,200 + 600 + 500), leading to an *average* debt recovery upon liquidation of 73.3% (= 2,602.6/3,550). Using the priority of claims, we first apply USD2,450 million to the first-lien revolver and senior secured debt claim, with the remaining USD152.4 million (= 2,602.6 – 2,450) in proceeds used to settle 25.4% (= 152.4/600) of the USD600 million in second-lien claims. Expected recovery by tranche may be shown as follows:

   First lien: USD250 million revolver 100% recovery

   USD2,200 million senior secured 100% recovery

   Second lien: USD600 million junior second lien 25.4% recovery

   Unsecured: USD500 million mezzanine 0% recovery

2. Discuss the impact of the distressed liquidation scenario described above on the company's convertible preferred shares.

   Solution:

   Because preferred shareholders are paid only once all debtholder claims are satisfied, convertible preferred shareholder claims will be zero under the distressed liquidation scenario.

An alternative to the liquidation case in the previous case study is a going concern scenario, or valuation of the firm under the assumption that it survives and continues to operate. The advantage of this approach is the avoidance of the valuation pitfalls described earlier, which can cloud the analysis by attempting to incorporate event-driven changes of unknown timing and magnitude. While the path to returning to profitability and competitiveness may be far from certain, the advantage to this approach is the ability to use valuation metrics such as market multiples for healthy industry peers.

CASE STUDY

Maudville Corporation Going Concern Valuation and Scenario Analysis

The analyst evaluating Maudville's value at the end of Year 4 assumes that after a challenging period, the company is able to reach a normalized EBITDA of USD750 million in two years' time (Year 6).

1. Assuming the 6× EV/EBITDA industry multiple for Maudville's industry and using a risk-free discount rate of 5%, calculate the implied value of Maudville as a going concern at the end of Year 4.

   Solution:

   Given the assumed normalized EBITDA of USD750 million, we can solve for an enterprise value at the end of Year 6 of USD4,500 million (= 750 million × 6).

   Using a simple time-value-of-money calculation, we can solve for a present value of USD4,081.6 million at the end of Year 4.

$$\text{PV} = \frac{\text{FV}_t}{(1+r)^t}.$$

$$\text{USD4,081.6 million} = \frac{4,500}{(1.05)^2}.$$

2. Assuming a one-third probability of a distressed liquidation at the end of Year 4, solve for Maudville's enterprise value at the end of Year 4.

   Solution:

   Given the liquidation value as of the end of Year 4 of USD2,602.6 million from the earlier case study and the present value of Maudville as a going concern of USD4,081.6 million, we may solve for the implied enterprise value using a weighted average based on the assumed 33.3% likelihood of liquidation:

$$\text{USD3,588.6 million} = (1/3) \times \text{USD2,602.6 million} + (2/3) \times \text{USD4,081.6 million}.$$

In practice, the default probability used in the simple scenario analysis shown in the case study may be derived from a structural or reduced form model, while the scenarios themselves may incorporate varying liquidation or restructuring assumptions. By isolating financial distress based on one or more specific scenarios and including a going concern recovery case in another, financial analysts can quickly tailor a valuation to changing market conditions.

QUESTION SET

1. Contrast the due diligence focus on distressed debt investments of credit hedge funds with investors looking to engage in the restructuring process.

   Solution:

   Credit hedge funds are short-term, trading-focused investors and will be focused on public information and the relative liquidity of credit instruments to assess their ability to take advantage of the price volatility. Investors engaged in the restructuring process are longer-term investors and use the due diligence process to assess how they may be able to influence the outcome of the reorganization process.

2. Explain the issues associated with estimating the cost of debt capital when valuing a distressed company using standard discounted cash flow analysis.

   Solution:

   The common approach to estimating the cost of debt capital used in the weighted average cost of capital (WACC) is to calculate a yield-to-maturity on the firm's debt. The yield-to-maturity reflects the promised rate of return on debt, rather than the expected rate of return, which incorporates expected loss E(L). As a result, the yield-to-maturity provides an inaccurate estimate of the cost of debt.

3. Discuss the potential for using each of the three standard approaches to company valuation for distressed companies.

   Solution:

   Income-based approaches are difficult to use for distressed companies because of challenges with numerator (i.e., cash flow), denominator (i.e., cost of capital), and terminal value estimates. Income-based approaches are best suited to valuing businesses that are a going concern. Thus, income-based approaches should be used only for distressed businesses with a high probability of continuing as a going concern.

   Relative valuations, or using comparables, may be complicated by the definition of a peer group. A non-distressed peer group may be suitable for estimating terminal value for a distressed company that has a high likelihood of continuing operations as a going concern. However, controlling for the near-term effects of distress may complicate the use of comparables.

   Standard asset-based valuation often determines the market value of a company under the assumption of continuing operations, while a distressed company likely to be liquidated should rather assume a liquidation value of the company's assets. As such, asset-based valuation is more appropriate where the company has a high probability of continuing operations, but liquidation value of assets should be used if there is a high probability of discontinuing operations.

SPECIAL SITUATIONS RISK AND RETURN 6

☐ discuss the risk and return among special situations and compared to other forms of private debt as part of a strategic asset allocation

Private market debt investment typically involves sub-investment-grade or unrated issuers and assets and often involves securities with restrictive covenants and contingencies such as callability or equity-like features. Macroeconomic, industry-specific, or company-specific events may create distressed circumstances for a subset of these investments, giving rise to idiosyncratic risks, but also the potential for higher return for investors who are able to fund these opportunities upon short notice if distress occurs.

To address these opportunities, private funds have increasingly initiated special situations funds to fund distressed firms while providing investors with acceptable risk-adjusted expected returns. Given their investment focus on distressed debt, special situations funds are generally classified as a subset of private debt. As mentioned earlier, the market for private special situations funds is expected to grow to roughly half of the private debt market by 2027.

Institutional investors, such as pension plans, face an allocation challenge in their private debt strategies because they must assess a manager's ability to profit from the potentially higher risk associated with special situations funds as compared to other forms of private debt structure. While the issuers targeted by special situations funds typically face either a cyclical downturn or a steady deterioration in performance in a declining phase of their life cycle, fund GPs seek to navigate distressed situations to achieve returns from the following risk factors.

Credit Risk

Fund GPs expect portfolio assets to result in lower expected losses than those implied by their discounted purchase prices. Lower expected losses must reflect lower default rates or higher recovery rates in the event of default than expected as part of the restructuring process. That is, special situations fund GPs rely on their ability to either identify mispriced assets or identify situations in which they can add value to purchased debt securities by improving recovery rates on distressed assets. The following example illustrates the GP's or fund manager's ability to pursue a strategy to improve recovery rates.

BUSINESS HOTELS AND DEFAULT RISK AFTER THE COVID-19 SHUTDOWN

Following economic shutdowns related to COVID-19, hotel occupancy rates struggled to return to pre-pandemic levels, causing continued distress risk for many hotel owners and their investors. Hotels focused on business and convention traffic were especially risk prone in this environment because of the rise of remote work, which reduced business traveler demand and business meetings that traditionally used hotel conference room space.

Occupancy rates were slow to recover. For example, while Marriott International's occupancy rates exceeded 70% before the COVID-19 pandemic, by 2022, its North American occupancy remained depressed and its international properties remained below 60% occupancy.

Business-focused hotels also faced property value declines as occupancy rates failed to recover, reducing the collateral value of hotel owners and creating debt financing challenges for these issuers, who typically refinance properties every three years. Furthermore, the underlying financing of these hotels consisted largely of floating-rate loans; thus, rising interest costs due to the end of quantitative easing in 2022 placed additional cash flow strains on hotel owners.

While 2023 began with several hotel bankruptcy filings, including the world's tallest Holiday Inn, located in New York City's financial district, other hotel owners bypassed the reorganization process, allowing distressed properties to be foreclosed on by their lenders. Opportunities for asset sales were limited because potential buyers, such as private equity and sovereign wealth funds, were largely waiting for signs of market stabilization before bidding for distressed assets. For example, Blackstone, a significant private equity participant in lodging transactions, did not commit to any hotel purchases in the second half of 2022.

Liquidity Risks

Because a proportion of investors may be forced to sell loans as the underlying assets become distressed, special situations fund GPs actively seek forced sale situations to take advantage of asset mispricing by bidding at prices below what they perceive as fair value.

Legal Risks

The complexity of issues arising from creditor disputes in a distressed environment highlights opportunities for fund GPs who have expertise and experience in navigating the bankruptcy process and negotiating to ensure acceptable recoveries in a distressed environment.

Fund GPs who can successfully manage these risks are more likely to generate significant price appreciation on their investments. Investors should note this difference between the primary source of returns in special situations as compared to private debt in which interest income and return of principal is assumed to be the primary return source. Thus, as a subcategory of private debt in most investor allocations, special situations investment is likely to provide diversification potential relative to private and public debt allocations. This is apparent when we consider the impact of inflation risk and interest rate risk on more traditional debt investments, neither of which is likely to significantly affect special situations returns.

Some private debt funds have a broader investment mandate that allows greater flexibility to pivot between distressed and non-distressed debt investments as industry and economic conditions warrant. This type of mixed focus by private debt funds may be advantageous to those investors with relatively small allocations to private debt and special situations relative to their overall asset allocation. In some cases, a closed-end fund may add an incremental fund to its existing structure to capitalize on a dislocation event, as described in the following example.

CONTINGENT DISLOCATION FUNDS

A contingent dislocation fund (CDF) is designed to invest capital upon the occurrence of a market disruption, or trigger, event. Such events might be defined as a financial or geopolitical crisis or a negative market signal. For private debt funds that typically lend to non-investment-grade companies within their main fund structures, events leading to financial distress offer attractive opportunities when additional capital is available in a timely manner.

Private debt funds often structure CDFs as a supplemental commitment to the primary debt fund, in which investor capital is only drawn if a dislocation event occurs. This provides a flexible mechanism in which the fund can access additional capital in the event of market stress. Typically, the CDF maintains an investment strategy similar to that of the primary debt fund.

The investor due diligence process for special situations fund managers shares common elements with that of a private debt fund manager but has several differences. Both seek to ensure superior credit analysis and structuring skills, as well as a manager's ability to adequately monitor, manage, and periodically value debt obligations. Special situations fund managers must demonstrate additional skills, such as managing legal and procedural aspects of the restructuring, bankruptcy, and liquidation processes important for issuers facing financial distress and dislocation. The following case study addresses a pension plan's evaluation process in considering a special situations fund investment as part of its overall asset allocation.

CASE STUDY

Northern States Evaluates a Special Situations Fund

Northern States Pension Plan is a large US-based public pension plan with extensive private market investment experience. Its investment committee has scheduled a presentation with Bywater Capital on its Special Situations Fund III, the firm's latest fund offering with a strategic focus on distressed debt and other event-driven strategies.

Bywater Special Situations Fund I was recently fully exited with a net IRR of 15.0% and TVPI (total value to paid-in) of 2.0, and Special Situations Fund II is currently on track for similar performance. Compared to other private distressed debt funds, Bywater's performance is in the top quartile. While Bywater has successfully invested in different sectors, its investments recently have been concentrated in hospitality-related industries, including aviation and hotel properties.

Northern States currently owns a diversified public and private market debt portfolio, with a 10% allocation to private debt. Private debt investments include funds invested in senior secured floating-rate, mezzanine, and venture debt, and the underlying securities are typically unrated or below investment grade. The current asset allocation is shown below:

Asset class	Target allocation
Public equity	30%
Private equity	25%
Public fixed income	15%
Private debt	10%
Real estate and infrastructure	15%
Other alternative investments	5%
Total	100%

Northern States' economic outlook has recently changed to incorporate increasing probabilities of financial distress in several global industry sectors. As a result, the investment committee is evaluating investment strategies that may benefit from such an economic environment.

Brianna Jenkins, head of alternative investments at Northern States, has been asked to lead the discussion regarding an investment in Bywater Special Situations Fund III. Jenkins plans a discussion focused on the relation of special situations investing to the larger mandate of private debt investing.

1. Discuss how Northern States' economic outlook may affect the allocation decision to include special situations investments in their private debt portfolio.

Solution:

Because Northern States forecasts increasing financial distress in several sectors, the pension plan may be expecting lower returns on a portion of its private debt portfolio as the credit quality of the underlying loan portfolio declines. Distressed opportunities may provide Northern States with opportunities to attempt to partially offset the effects of distress on its existing private debt portfolio. Thus, Northern States may be open to allocating capital to special situations funds such as Bywater to augment returns in its private debt portfolio over time.

QUESTION SET

1. Discuss how a special situations fund GP creates value for investors with respect to credit risk in distressed debt situations.

   Solution:

   Special situations fund GPs use specialized skills to identify situations in which they can either identify mispricing or add value to purchased debt securities. This involves capitalizing on purchases when existing investors are forced to sell and seeking ways to lower expected losses on their investments below expected losses implied by their purchase prices. Lower expected losses must reflect lower default rates or higher recovery rates in the event of default than expected as part of the restructuring process.

2. Discuss why a pension plan's due diligence process on a distressed debt fund manager should include a thorough review of the fund's ability to address legal risks of potential investments.

   Solution:

   Distressed debt funds generate returns by applying expertise in navigating legal environments associated with debt restructuring and insolvency laws. Thus, a fund's ability to assess legal risks as it considers potential investments will be critical to the ability to add value to the fund. The complexity of issues arising from creditor disputes in a distressed environment highlights opportunities for fund GPs who have expertise and experience in navigating the bankruptcy process and negotiating to ensure acceptable recoveries in a distressed environment.

3. Discuss why a special situations fund may focus on specific industries in its selection of portfolio assets.

   Solution:

   Special situations investors often focus on specific industries due to their more favorable characteristics for distressed investments, including cyclicality and the prevalent use of secured debt to finance fixed assets. For example, firms that face volatile cash flows during economic downturns can represent attractive investment opportunities if their securities are mispriced or certain investors are forced to sell debt or equity. A specialized industry focus is advantageous in understanding asset values in a liquidation scenario. Industries involving firms with complex debt profiles secured by assets, restrictions such as covenants, and other contingencies offer advantages to special situations funds with expertise in understanding the valuation, liquidity, and legal environments that are likely to occur in a specific industry.

PRACTICE PROBLEMS

The following information relates to questions 1-4

Brianna Jenkins, head of alternative investments at Northern States Pension Plan, is working on a presentation to the plan's investment committee to provide fundamental information to help the group consider investing in a distressed debt fund. As part of her work, she develops two visuals showing the contingent payoffs to both debt- and equityholders as functions of the asset value of a company and an equation demonstrating put–call parity.

Jenkins continues her presentation with a numeric example in which she shows a basic example of a structural model of credit risk. A company's asset value is CAD800 million, and it has zero-coupon debt with face value of CAD1,000 million maturing in two years. The volatility of the company's assets is 20% per year. The risk-free rate is 5% per year. Jenkins shows output from this model indicating that the value of a call option on this company's assets with an exercise price of CAD1,000 million is equal to CAD52 million and then states that the company's debt is trading at an observed credit spread of 10.4%.

Jenkins includes some examples of differing circumstances that may cause a company's debt to become distressed. Her examples include recessions, innovations that disrupt specific industries, and instances of company mismanagement and fraud. Jenkins follows this material with some discussion of additional operating risks faced by issuers in distress, such as loss of customers and employees.

Jenkins looks to close her presentation by providing some discussion of opportunities to invest in distressed debt funds. Northern States recently received a proposal from Bywater Partners to consider investing in its Bywater Special Situations Fund III. Bywater Partners has decided to focus exclusively on special situations investing. Alternatively, Northern States has an existing relationship with Spleenwood Capital, a firm with a broad private debt strategy. Spleenwood has begun including contingent dislocation funds (CDFs) as part of its private debt funds.

1. Which of the following best describes what Jenkins is seeking to illustrate with her visuals and the put–call parity equation?

   A. Equity value is zero any time that company asset value declines below face value of debt.

   B. Debt value is independent of equity value.

   C. Debt and equity values may be characterized as option values based on company asset value.

2. Analyze whether there is a profitable capital structure arbitrage trade available based on Jenkins's example.

3. Discuss the potential for a distressed issuer to suffer from excessive loss of employees depending on whether distress is more related to industry-specific conditions than company mismanagement.

4. Discuss one fundamental difference with respect to a distressed debt allocation

between committing capital to Bywater versus Spleenwood.

The following information relates to questions 5-8

Spleenwood Capital, a private market firm focused on debt-focused investment strategies, is exploring the possibility of starting an event-driven special situations fund. The firm desires to focus primarily on debt-oriented control strategies but is open to considering other types of event-driven strategies. Given Spleenwood's desire to specialize in taking controlling stakes, the firm's principals believe that other investment strategies focused on assessing business combinations, such as merger arbitrage, may fit well with the overall fund focus.

Spleenwood explores additional approaches to merger arbitrage strategies that may leverage their skills in buying corporate debt. Specifically, Spleenwood considers investing in the debt of target companies with associated change-of-control clauses.

Spleenwood's managing directors further discuss a strategy of investing in debt of companies in which perceptions of mismanagement have contributed to long-term solvency issues. Spleenwood believes that there are profitable opportunities to pursue active and controlling strategies in buying company debt in such an environment.

Spleenwood prefers to avoid situations in which portfolio companies need to enter Chapter 11 bankruptcy reorganization in the United States as part of its active, controlling strategy. Rather, it prefers to buy the debt of companies that can be restructured outside the court system. However, if Chapter 11 cannot be avoided, Spleenwood strives to negotiate for prepackaged bankruptcy filings.

5. Contrast the event risk associated with merger arbitrage strategies with the event risk typically associated with distressed debt investing.

6. Discuss how Spleenwood expects to profit from a strategy targeting companies with change of control clauses.

7. Discuss why Spleenwood may prefer to negotiate debt-for-equity exchanges as a financing strategy (compared to other possible strategies) for its portfolio holdings in which mismanagement perceptions exist, and explain a potential challenge to implementing the strategy.

8. Discuss one significant reason why Spleenwood prefers to avoid unplanned Chapter 11 bankruptcy filings for the companies in which it has invested in debt, and discuss briefly what must happen to avoid this outcome.

The following information relates to questions 9-12

Laborantibus Partners, a private market firm specializing in distressed debt, is considering investments in public securities issued by Fracassar PLC, a British hotel chain encountering financial difficulties. Fracassar's debt, maturing in six months, is currently trading at GBP6,000 million. While Laborantibus has valued Fracassar as a going concern using a relative valuation approach based on publicly traded European hotel chain comparables at an enterprise value of GBP9,000 million, it estimates a 30% probability that Fracassar defaults on its GBP7,500 million of debt in six months. Laborantibus assesses the liquidation value of Fracassar's assets at GBP3,000 million. Assume that the risk-free rate is 5% annually.

A few members of the Laborantibus investment committee express reservations about estimating Fracassar's enterprise value as a going concern using a relative valuation approach. They suggest that an income-based approach may be superior to use as a going concern valuation approach.

Laborantibus examines opportunities to trade across different seniorities of Fracassar's debt instruments. Fracassar's debt consists of GBP4,500 million of senior secured debt and GBP3,000 million of junior second-lien debt. The senior debt is trading at GBP4,200 million, and the junior debt is trading at GBP1,800 million.

Laborantibus observes that the credit default swap spreads on Fracassar's debt are higher than the associated bond spreads. Laborantibus considers the potential for a profitable trading opportunity.

9. Recommend whether Laborantibus should pursue an investment in Fracassar debt.

10. Evaluate the choice of estimating Fracassar's going concern value using relative valuation versus using an income-based approach.

11. Recommend a capital structure arbitrage trade involving Fracassar's senior and junior debt.

12. Explain how Laborantibus can create a synthetic Fracassar bond using a CDS.

SOLUTIONS

1. C is the correct response. Asset value may be written as $V_0 = c_0 + \text{PV}(D) - p_0$. The equation reflects put–call parity, and the shareholder payoff is shown as a call option on firm value (c_0), while the debtholder payoff is equal to risk-free debt, PV(D), and the sold put ($-p_0$). A is incorrect because equity value will often be greater than zero despite asset value falling below face value of debt because of the call option's time value. B is incorrect because the debt value and equity value are related as a result of put–call parity.

2. Given that the equity value of the company is equal to the call option value of CAD52 million, the company's debt value is equal to CAD748 million (= CAD800 million – CAD52 million). The company's implied credit spread is approximately 9.5% {= [(1/2) × ln(1,000/748)] – 0.05}. Because the observed credit spread is approximately 90 bps greater, a profitable capital structure arbitrage is to buy the company's debt and sell its equity.

3. An operating risk, such as loss of employees, may depend on whether the events leading to the distress are macroeconomic, industry specific, or company specific.

   Distress due to macroeconomic factors typically involves economic downturns leading to poor operating and financial performance.

   In the case of distress due to industry-specific causes (such as the distress that occurred during and following the COVID-19 pandemic in travel-related industries), employees may find limited job opportunities that align with their experience and training.

   In the case of distress due to a company-specific factor related to mismanagement of a company, employees are more likely to have the ability to find alternate job opportunities related to their experience and training.

4. By committing capital to Bywater, Northern States is making an explicit allocation to distressed debt. In contrast, a commitment to Spleenwood commits capital to a distressed debt allocation only if a dislocation event occurs.

5. A merger arbitrage strategy's returns are defined by whether an acquisition is completed. For distressed debt investing, the event is resolution of distress. Unlike the merger arbitrage investment, resolution of distress is not a simple "yes" or "no" solution. The resolution of distress may take many forms of outcome in terms of how a distressed company's assets are divided between claimants. As such, the event risk for distressed debt is more complicated compared to that of merger arbitrage.

6. A change-of control-clause included in a corporation's covenants requires the issuer to offer to repurchase outstanding bonds at a fixed price at or above par, conditional on a new owner acquiring a specified percentage of the issuer's voting shares. Thus, Spleenwood will identify issuers with change-of-control clauses on their bonds that are potential takeover targets. By buying the debt of the most likely takeover targets, Spleenwood expects to sell back purchased bonds at a profit once the change-of-control clause is triggered.

7. A perception of mismanagement may provide incentives for Spleenwood to convert debt holdings into equity stakes sufficiently large to force a change in management. Other approaches to financing a distressed firm cannot address the issue of poor management because none of the other strategies translate into

company ownership. The primary challenge for Spleenwood will be to buy a sufficiently large stake of company debt to ensure enough governance power after the debt-for-equity exchange to enact a management change.

8. An unplanned Chapter 11 bankruptcy filing is unlikely to be resolved quickly. A typical time frame for the company to successfully reorganize in this setting is likely to be two to three years or more, and this would reflect Spleenwood's investment horizon as an active, controlling investor. Avoidance of the unplanned Chapter 11 bankruptcy requires agreement among all creditors. For example, a prepackaged bankruptcy requires two-thirds of the volume and one-half of claimants to agree to terms, while out-of-court restructurings require all creditors to agree.

9. Based on the data given, Laborantibus would estimate that Fracassar's enterprise value is GBP7,200 million, as shown below.

   Enterprise value in six months = 0.3 × 3,000 + 0.7 × 9,000 = GBP7,200.

   If Laborantibus buys all of Fracassar's debt, the expected value is GBP6,150 million, as shown below.

   Debt value in six months = 0.3 × 3,000 + 0.7 × 7,500 = GBP6,150 million.

   Implied return for six months = (6,150 ÷ 6,000) – 1 = 2.5%.

   Laborantibus should not pursue an investment in Fracassar debt at its current price of GBP6,000 million. The expected return is approximately equivalent to the risk-free rate of 5% annually (i.e., 2.5% over half a year), which provides no compensation for the risks involved.

10. While both valuation approaches are more difficult to use for distressed companies, an approach using non-distressed comparables may be appropriate for assessing a going concern terminal value at the future date when the company either defaults or does not default. An income-based approach to valuation typically assumes several years of cash flows discounted at a risk-adjusted cost of capital. This approach likely creates several estimation challenges associated with both the cash flows (i.e., numerator issues) and the discount rate (i.e., denominator issues). Overall, the use of relative valuation is likely to be a less challenging approach to implement in valuing Fracassar as a going concern.

11. Using the default probability of 30% and the seniority structure of the two classes of debt, we estimate the value of the senior and junior debt in six months as follows:

    Senior debt value in six months = 0.3 × 3,000 + 0.7 × 4,500 = GBP4,050 million.

    Junior debt value in six months = 0.3 × 0 + 0.7 × 3,000 = GBP2,100 million.

    The future value of senior debt of GBP4,050 million is below its trading price of GBP4,200 million. Thus, the senior debt is clearly overpriced. The value of the junior debt implies a return of 16.67% over six months [= (2,100 ÷ 1,800) – 1]. Thus, a capital structure arbitrage would be to buy Fracassar junior debt and sell short its senior debt.

12. Laborantibus may create a synthetic long bond position in Fracassar by depositing the desired amount of the bond purchase at the market reference rate, selling CDS protection to collect the "high" CDS spread on Fracassar, and entering a receive-fixed interest rate swap to protect against interest rate risk from volatility in the MRR. The resulting return stream is the locked-in MRR plus the CDS spread received.

LEARNING MODULE

6

Private Real Estate Investments

LEARNING OUTCOMES

Mastery	The candidate should be able to:
☐	discuss important private real estate investment features
☐	discuss economic value drivers of private real estate investments and their role in a portfolio
☐	discuss the due diligence and valuation processes for private real estate
☐	discuss the distinctive investment characteristics of timberland and farmland
☐	discuss the risk and return among private real estate investments and as compared to other investments as part of a strategic asset allocation

INTRODUCTION

1

Real estate investments are heterogeneous building and property assets in illiquid and fragmented local markets. While earlier learning modules addressed income-producing properties and publicly traded real estate, such as real estate investment trusts (REITs), we now turn our attention to private real estate investments. While this asset class spans a wide range of investments, including diversified and core funds, we focus here on the features, economic drivers, valuation, and portfolio characteristics of value-add and opportunistic real estate investments. According to the alternative investment data provider Preqin, private real estate is the third-largest private markets asset class, of which roughly one-third involves value-add investments, one-third is opportunistic, and the remaining third involves privately held core or other assets. Private real estate is expected to exceed USD2 trillion in assets under management (AUM) by 2027 globally, over half of which is expected to be in North America, despite rapid growth in Asia and Europe. Private real estate equity and debt investments typically exhibit more equity-like return characteristics. They often involve major property renovation, repositioning, or new construction. In contrast, raw and less developed land used in agriculture and forestry represents distinct segments of the private real estate market.

In this learning module, we first distinguish key features of private real estate markets. These investments often occur over a property development life cycle, unlike the more stable, consistent cash flows associated with core real estate. Farmland and timberland, in contrast, involve fewer or no physical improvements and derive their economic value from current and future agricultural use or the timber growth cycle, as well as capital appreciation. These differences give rise to specific investment characteristics for private real estate debt and equity investors, unique due diligence and valuation challenges, and distinctive risk and return features that define the role of these investments in a strategic asset allocation.

LEARNING MODULE OVERVIEW

- Private real estate investments usually involve major property refurbishment, repositioning, or new development and exhibit more equity-like characteristics than income-producing property.
- Debt and equity instruments used in property development frequently differ from public real estate investments in terms of the timing, terms, and type of funding involved, which often vary over capital commitment, deployment, and distribution phases.
- Private real estate due diligence incorporates more complex private investment structure details and the capital and development life cycles, while valuation approaches often include scenario and sensitivity analysis in addition to income and sales comparison approaches.
- Timberland and farmland are unique forms of largely private real estate investment involving raw land whose value is derived from economic use associated with the timber growth cycle or agricultural use, as well as potential capital appreciation.
- Relative risk and return analysis of private real estate investments assesses the expected timing and volatility of expected income and price appreciation based on economic drivers and includes the complex compensation structures of these investments.

2 PRIVATE REAL ESTATE INVESTMENT FEATURES

☐ discuss important private real estate investment features

General Characteristics

Real estate investments span a broad spectrum, from portfolios of stable income-producing equity or debt property assets, such as publicly traded REITs or mortgage-backed securities, which are publicly traded, to private investments. These private investments may involve anything from repurposing, repositioning, or developing new properties to using raw or undeveloped land for agriculture or forestry. In this lesson, we will concentrate on private debt and equity investments, particularly those that fall in the upper right area of Exhibit 1.

Exhibit 1: Real Estate Investment Characteristics

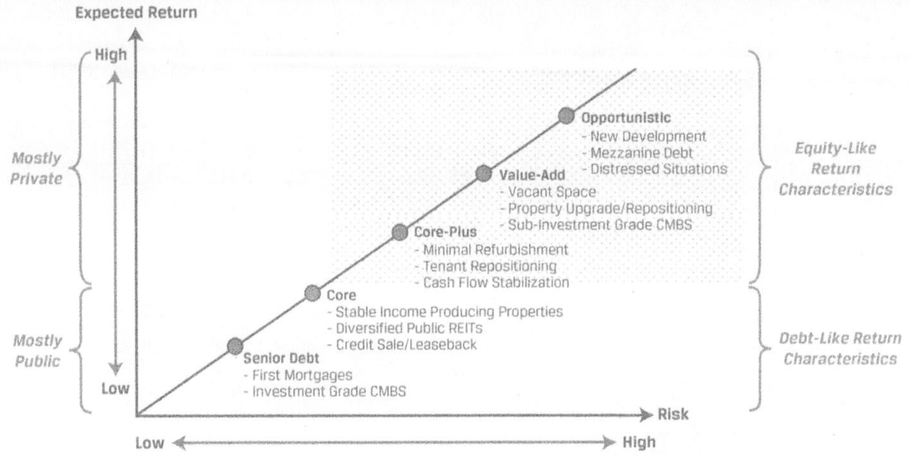

New property developments, particularly those requiring substantial improvement as part of opportunistic real estate strategies, entail higher risk. They also exhibit more equity-like return characteristics. Such investments are commonly undertaken through private real estate vehicles, such as limited partnerships. As in the case of other private markets, private real estate investments typically involve longer investment periods, reduced liquidity, and greater direct control due to the transformational nature of value-add and opportunistic investment. Private real estate funds are different from **open-end funds** in public markets, which allow investors to contribute or withdraw capital freely and have no predetermined end date. Private real estate funds can be either open-end funds with certain constraints, known as **interval funds**, or **closed-end funds**. Interval funds lack a predetermined maturity date but come with liquidity constraints, such as limits on the proportion of total assets that can be redeemed periodically. Closed-end funds, in contrast, have a finite lifespan, necessitating an upfront capital commitment, a lockup period, and the eventual sale of the property or properties to distribute returns to investors.

In the realm of closed-end funds, general partners (GPs) typically combine several properties into a real estate limited partnership or a limited liability company, which is then distributed to numerous limited partners (LPs). Alternatively, GPs might establish separately managed accounts that consist of bespoke investments tailored for specific investors. One distinguishing characteristic of newly developed properties is the distinct phases they undergo in the real estate development life cycle, as demonstrated in Exhibit 2.

Exhibit 2: Property Development Life Cycle

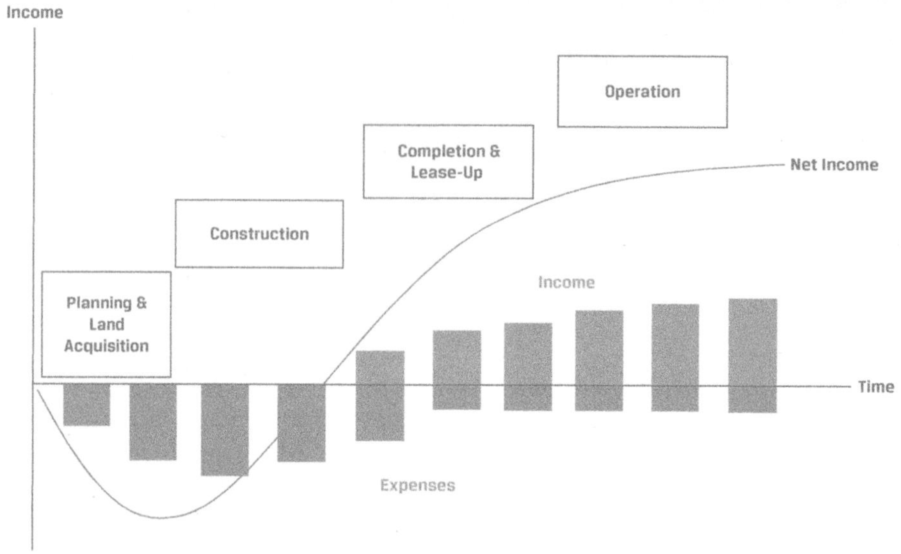

Although details of the development cycle vary for each property, there are five universal phases: planning, land acquisition, construction, completion and lease-up, and operation.

Planning

Developers constructing buildings on undeveloped or reclaimed land must first establish the physical and economic feasibility of a project. The initial step in the planning process is to assess a project's physical feasibility, or one that represents the site's best economic use, in compliance with local laws and regulations. For example, zoning requirements often restrict economic use and require provisions for **setback** or distance to property lines and **circulation**, such as security and emergency access to buildings or facilities. Consider the following case study, the first of several throughout this learning module that discuss the Pandan East project.

CASE STUDY

Pandan East Feasibility Study

A private real estate investor is assessing the physical feasibility of a vacant three-acre (130,680 ft^2) site for a 1,200-unit residential facility outside Kuala Lumpur, Malaysia, along the proposed Mass Rapid Transit Circle Line. Local zoning requirements dictate that 20% of the land must be set aside for setback and circulation, with the following apartment and parking plans:

- Apartments—Three 20-story towers with one 0.5-acre courtyard between the three towers,and each floor with an average of 20 units (1,200 ft^2 each) and 2,500 ft^2 of common space
- Parking—1,000 ft^2 per tower for surface parking, with additional space underground

1. Assess the Pandan East project site feasibility given zoning restrictions, the site plan, and building and parking requirements.

   Solution:

   Zoning restrictions include setback and circulation of 26,136 ft^2 (= 0.2 × 130,680) and an open courtyard of 21,780 ft^2 [= 130,680 × (0.5/3)], while parking requirements total 3,000 ft^2 (= 1,000 × 3) and the building footprint is 79,500 ft^2 {= 3 × [(20 × 1,200) + 2,500]}. Solve for 264 ft^2 in excess space:

Physical Feasibility	ft^2
Gross Land Area	130,680
Less: Setback and Circulation	(26,136)
Less: Open Area	(21,780)
Available to Develop	82,764
Parking Space Needs	(3,000)
Available to Build	79,764
Building Footprint	(79,500)
Excess Space	264

Economic feasibility involves weighing a property's future economic use by residential or commercial tenants versus construction and operating costs to determine whether the project will meet or exceed required rates of return for debt and equity investors upon completion. Recall from earlier real estate learning modules that **net operating income** (NOI) is a key property income measure that ignores financing costs and taxes, as shown in Equation 1:

NOI = Effective gross income – Operating expenses – Property maintenance allowance. (1)

We may estimate initial project return to both debtholders and equityholders on the basis of NOI versus project cost as follows:

Project return = NOI/Project cost. (2)

Consider Pandan East's expected NOI and project return upon completion based on cost and rental assumptions in the following case study.

CASE STUDY

Pandan East Expected NOI and Project Return

The Pandan East project plan includes 1,200 residential units averaging 1,200 ft^2 each. Project planners estimate a monthly rent per ft^2 net of expenses in Malaysian ringgit of MYR2.75, with no additional income. Occupancy is expected to be 95% upon completion in two years, with 30% of gross rent as expenses, including a small capital improvement allowance. Estimated costs are as follows:

Line Item	MYR
Land	25,000,000
On-site land improvements	10,000,000
Construction cost/unit	200,000

1. Calculate Pandan East's expected NOI upon completion.

   Solution:

   Calculate NOI using Equation 1. First, solve for effective gross income as equal to gross rent, or revenue from rental of the 1,200 units at full occupancy:

   $$\text{Gross rent} = \text{MYR}47{,}520{,}000 = 1{,}200\text{ft}^2 \times 1{,}200 \text{ units} \times 2.75 \text{ rent/ft}^2 \times 12.$$

   Next, subtract vacancies and operating expenses (5%, or 100% – 95%, and 30% of gross rent, respectively) from gross rent:

   $$\text{NOI} = \text{MYR}30{,}888{,}000 = (1 - 0.35) \times \text{MYR}47{,}520{,}000.$$

2. Calculate Pandan East's project cost and return based on NOI.

   Solution:

   Calculate project costs by adding construction costs of MYR240,000,000 (= 1,200 units × MYR200,000/unit) to other costs:

Line Item	MYR
Land	25,000,000
On-site land improvements	10,000,000
Construction cost	240,000,000
Project cost	275,000,000

   The return is equal to the NOI from Question 1 divided by project cost:

   $$\text{Rate of return} = 11.23\% = \frac{\text{MYR } 30{,}888{,}000}{\text{MYR } 275{,}000{,}000}.$$

Recall from prior learning modules that the required rate of return on a property is often referred to as the **capitalization rate**, or cap rate. The **direct capitalization approach** shown earlier in the curriculum divides a single year's net operating income by the cap rate to estimate a property's value:

$$\text{Property value} = \frac{\text{Expected NOI}}{\text{Capitalization rate}}. \quad (3)$$

Land Acquisition

A developer may acquire land using a combination of equity and debt secured by the property. In addition to ensuring a property is free of outstanding liens or tax obligations, the acquiror must also receive approval for project plans and obtain necessary building permits and zoning exemptions or amendments prior to initiating construction. A prospective buyer may enter into an option agreement to secure the right, but not the obligation, to purchase a property at a fixed price for the period over which these issues are addressed. Investors may also choose to buy and operate an existing property with the intention of renovating in the future, as shown in a later case study.

Construction

The land improvement and building phase involves far greater execution risk than property operation. Potential delays and disruptions include labor disputes, unanticipated slowdowns in the supply of materials or equipment, and adverse weather conditions. Also, changing market prices can drive cost overruns for building materials, as in the following example.

LUMBER PRICES DURING THE COVID-19 PANDEMIC

Lumber is an important commodity in US single-home residential construction, representing around 15%–20% of construction costs. Lumber price volatility increased during the COVID-19 pandemic. Exhibit 3 shows front-month lumber futures prices for a three-year period starting in March 2020.

Exhibit 3: Front-Month US Lumber Futures Prices, March 2020–March 2023

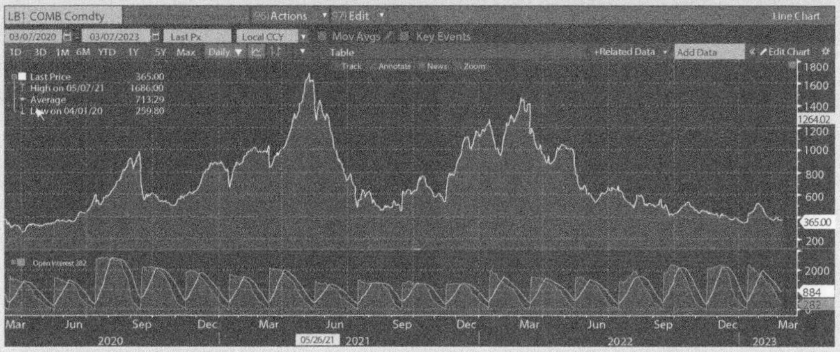

Source: Bloomberg.

As the pandemic began, lumber prices were close to USD400 per 1,000 board feet (1,000 board feet equals 2.36 m^3), surging until early May 2021, when the lumber futures price peaked at USD1,686, over four times the level from a year earlier. Note that the lumber futures contract specification has subsequently been amended to one-quarter of the original size, or roughly the amount of lumber used to build an average house in the United States.

While demand increased due to the impact of rising home prices on new construction starts and renovations, supply disruptions related to COVID-19 included labor shortages and decreased mill capacity due to health protocols. While lumber prices fell by late summer of 2021, another sharp price increase in the fall of 2021 coincided with a subsequent surge in COVID-19 cases, peaking in late winter before gradually declining, as Federal Reserve interest rate hikes dampened housing demand and lumber prices fell back to levels closer to historical averages.

In addition to changing market dynamics affecting project costs, construction delays pose risks for future income assumptions as market conditions change. Also, if a project encounters problems that require it to be sold during the construction phase, the sale price may be below total project costs incurred.

Completion and Lease-Up

Project risks continue to rise as a development nears completion given the need to offset rising costs with expected rental income. While some projects involve space built for a specific tenant, in the case of multiple commercial or residential tenants, developers often seek to pre-lease undeveloped or unfinished space using such incentives as reduced or free rent and free amenities for a given period in exchange for lease commitments.

Operation

Once the initial lease phase is complete, property risk declines, because longer-term tenant commitments are in place, and the property management phase begins. While public investment vehicles, such as REITs, often buy and hold such income-producing properties once normal occupancy is reached, private investors may play different roles over the life cycle, from developing a property on a speculative basis to be sold upon completion to selling a fully leased property on an opportunistic basis or owning and operating it indefinitely.

The features of private real estate debt and equity investments differ from those of public investments, usually consisting of income-producing properties, in several important ways. The first is timing, as debt and equity capital needs for new development rise from the time of site purchase through the construction period and completion phase. Second, the type of funding often varies over phases of the development cycle. For example, an **acquisition and development loan** (ADL) may be used to purchase and prepare land for a specific construction use, while a **construction and development loan** is outstanding during the building phase. ADLs and construction and development (C&D) loans disbursed over time typically accrue interest over the period of negative cash flow and are later replaced by a long-term mortgage loan. Equity also may be drawn down over time as a project meets certain milestones. Private real estate investments often follow capital commitment, deployment, and distribution phases over the development cycle, similar to many other alternative and private investments, as shown in Exhibit 4.

Exhibit 4: Sample Real Estate Development Financing Plan

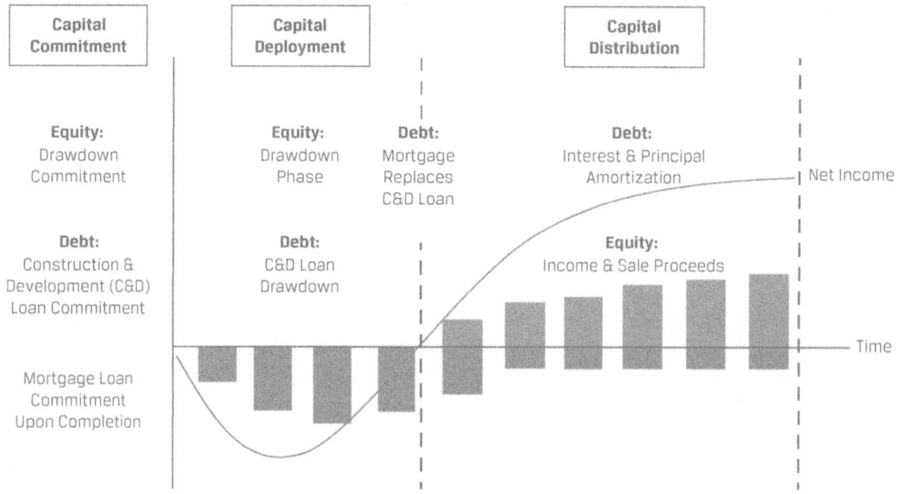

Earlier real estate learning modules addressed measures used by debt and equity investors to assess risk and return. For example, debt investors use leverage and coverage measures to evaluate creditworthiness, including the **loan-to-value ratio** (LTV) and **debt service coverage ratio** (DSC), respectively:

$$\text{LTV} = \frac{\text{Debt outstanding}}{\text{Current property value}}. \tag{4}$$

$$\text{DSC} = \frac{\text{Net operating income}}{\text{Debt service}}. \tag{5}$$

A lower LTV and a higher DSC indicate greater creditworthiness. For example, while levels vary, real estate lenders often target an LTV of 0.8 or lower, whereas a DSC of 2× or greater is generally considered strong, with a minimum target of 1.2× to 1.4×. Equity investors, in contrast, evaluate before-tax returns using actual or expected NOI less debt service using an **equity dividend rate**:

$$\text{Equity dividend rate} = \frac{\text{Before-tax cash flow}}{\text{Property purchase price} - \text{Debt outstanding}}, \quad (6)$$

where

$$\text{Before-tax cash flow} = \text{NOI} - \text{Debt service}. \quad (7)$$

We now examine the Pandan East project financing plan using these metrics.

CASE STUDY

Pandan East Financing Plan Details

Pandan East's MYR275,000,000 project financing plan is as follows:

Equity: 25% of cost, or MYR68,750,000 drawn in three steps. GP performance fees equal 20% of returns above a 15% hurdle rate upon completion.

1. Equity drawdown
   - Initial: MYR25,000,000 (land purchase and fees)
   - One Year: MYR25,000,000
   - Two Years: MYR18,750,000

Debt: 75% of cost, or MYR206,250,000 from private investors in two forms:

1. Construction and development loan
   - 10% annual interest
   - Monthly disbursements linked to construction milestones, such as zoning approval, foundation completion, and property inspections
   - Interest accrues monthly over a two-year construction period.
   - Loan is to be repaid from mortgage loan proceeds.
   - Secured by Pandan East land, property, and other project assets
   - End-of-month drawdowns as follows:
     - Month 1: MYR15,000,000
     - Months 2–6: MYR10,000,000
     - Months 7–20: MYR7,500,000
     - Months 21–23: MYR5,000,000
     - Month 24: MYR200,635
2. Mortgage loan
   - 20-year, MYR206,250,000 amortizing loan starting in two years
   - Drawn after final inspection and once construction claims and wages are paid and no property liens exist
   - 7% annual interest rate with fixed monthly payments of interest and principal repayment
   - Secured by Pandan East land and property

1. Calculate and show the ratio of equity to total capital monthly for the first year of the Pandan East project.

Solution:

Equity drawdown of MYR25,000,000 occurs both at inception and in one year's time, while C&D debt outstanding at month end is the sum of the loan drawdown to date and interest accrued on the initial period balance at the monthly equivalent of a 10% annual rate. Recall from earlier time-value-of-money lessons that this may be converted to a monthly rate, as follows:

$$R_{annual} = (1 + R_{monthly})^{12} - 1;$$

$$R_{monthly} = 0.7974\% = (1 + 0.10)^{1/12} - 1.$$

Therefore, at the end of Month 2, the outstanding C&D loan balance is equal to MYR25,119,612, calculated as follows:

- MYR15,000,000 drawn at the end of Month 1
- MYR119,612 interest on initial balance (= 0.79741% × 15,000,000)
- MYR10,000,000 drawn at the end of Month 2

MYR25,119,612 = 15,000,000 + 119,612 + 10,000,000.

Use a spreadsheet to calculate monthly debt and equity balances. The following table provides a summary for the first 12 months. Candidates should note that the numbers presented throughout this case study as well as later case studies may reflect rounding from the spreadsheet calculations.

Month	C&D Loan Drawdown	C&D Interest	C&D Loan Balance	Equity	Total	Equity/ (Debt + Equity)
1	15,000,000	0	15,000,000	25,000,000	40,000,000	0.63
2	10,000,000	119,612	25,119,612	25,000,000	50,119,612	0.50
3	10,000,000	200,307	35,319,919	25,000,000	60,319,919	0.41
4	10,000,000	281,646	45,601,565	25,000,000	70,601,565	0.35
5	10,000,000	363,633	55,965,199	25,000,000	80,965,199	0.31
6	10,000,000	446,274	66,411,473	25,000,000	91,411,473	0.27
7	7,500,000	529,574	74,441,047	25,000,000	99,441,047	0.25
8	7,500,000	593,603	82,534,651	25,000,000	107,534,651	0.23
9	7,500,000	658,143	90,692,794	25,000,000	115,692,794	0.22
10	7,500,000	723,197	98,915,991	25,000,000	123,915,991	0.20
11	7,500,000	788,770	107,204,761	25,000,000	132,204,761	0.19
12	7,500,000	854,866	115,559,627	50,000,000	165,559,627	0.30

2. Solve for the LTV at the end of 12 months if the project's value equals cost in terms of debt and equity, as well as the DSC for the first year upon completion using Pandan East's expected NOI from the previous case study.

Solution:

Use Equation 4 to solve for LTV at the end of 12 months as follows:

$$\text{LTV} = 0.70 = \frac{115,559,627}{165,559,627}.$$

Note that LTV equals 1 – Equity/(Debt + Equity) in the solution to Question 1.

To determine DSC upon completion, we must solve for the fixed monthly mortgage loan payment. Earlier fixed-income lessons showed that periodic payments (A) for a fully amortizing loan using an annual rate can be calculated as follows:

$$A = \frac{r \times \text{Principal}}{1-(1+r)^{-n}},$$

where

A = Periodic payment

r = Interest rate per period (0.005833 = 0.07/12)

Principal = Principal amount (MYR206,250,000)

n = Number of periods (240 = 20 × 12)

Solve for A of MYR1,599,054 per month as follows:

$$A = \text{MYR}1,599,054 = \frac{0.005833 \times \text{MYR}206,250,000}{1-(1+0.005833)^{-240}}.$$

We may also derive A using the Excel PMT function, PMT(*rate*,*nper*,*pv*,[*fv*],[*type*]), and solving for MYR1,599,054 using PMT(0.005833,240,206250000,0,0). The final entry of zero indicates that the mortgage loan settles at the end of the period.

Annual mortgage debt service is therefore MYR19,188,649 (= 1,599,054 × 12). Solve for DSC to be 1.61 using Equation 4 and NOI of MYR30,888,000 from Question 1 in the previous case study as follows:

$$\text{DSC} = \frac{\text{Net operating income}}{\text{Debt service}}.$$

$$\text{DSC} = 1.61 = \frac{\text{MYR}30,888,000}{\text{MYR}19,188,649}.$$

3. Calculate the equity dividend rate upon completion using Pandan East's expected NOI from the previous case study, as well as the GP performance fee.

Solution:

Using Pandan East's annual debt service of MYR19,188,649 from Question 2, solve for before-tax cash flow of MYR11,699,351 using Equation 6:

Before-tax cash flow = NOI – Debt service = 30,888,000 – 19,188,649.

Use Equation 6 to solve for the equity dividend rate:

$$\text{Equity dividend rate} = \frac{\text{Before-tax cash flow}}{\text{Property purchase price} - \text{Debt outstanding}}.$$

$$17.02\% = \frac{\text{MYR}11,699,351}{\text{MYR}275,000,000 - \text{MYR}206,250,000}.$$

GP performance fees are equal to 20% of the equity dividend rate in excess of the 15% hurdle rate. We first determine the before-tax cash flow threshold by multiplying the denominator of Equation 6 (MYR68,750,000 = 275,000,000 – 206,250,000) by the hurdle rate:

MYR10,312,500 = MYR68,750,000 × 0.15.

Next, we subtract this from the actual before-tax cash flow:

GP performance fee = MYR277,370 = 0.20 × (11,699,351 – 10,312,500).

The Pandan East financing plan illustrates the timing and sources of funding for real estate development projects, as well as their relative risk and return. Despite its shorter tenor and use of the same underlying project as security, C&D lenders expect to earn a higher interest rate than mortgage lenders due to the greater default risk over the construction and development phase. Potential delays and disruptions and changing market conditions involve far greater execution risk than managing an existing income-producing property. A forced sale prior to completion may result in a price well below total project costs incurred. These loans often involve non-standard terms and may be more speculative in nature if no upfront mortgage commitment is in place. While C&D loan repayment depends on timely project completion and the disbursement of more permanent mortgage financing, positive rental cash flows upon project completion are a more reliable primary source of debt repayment. Equity returns also rely on future project income and a property's future sale price, which, as we will see in the following lesson, depends on key value drivers and economic conditions.

QUESTION SET

Questions 1–3 are based on the following information.

Asiastruct, a private real estate fund based in Singapore, has identified a property outside Bangkok for a residential development similar to the previous Pandan East case studies. The following information provides a summary of expected financial information on the property, development costs, and financing, shown in Thai bhat (THB):

Property:

- 900 residential units averaging 1,400 ft^2 each
- THB0.65 monthly rent/ft^2 at 95% occupancy expected in two years
- Operating expenses (including improvements) = 33% of gross rent.

Cost:

- Expected construction costs per unit = THB50,000.
- Expected land cost = THB6,000,000.
- Cost of land improvements = THB3,000,000.

Financing:

- Equity: THB12,750,000 with THB5,000,000 drawn in both Months 1 and 12 and THB2,750,000 drawn in Month 24
- Debt: THB41,250,000
    - Two-year C&D loan at 10% annual interest accrued monthly
        - Drawdowns
            - Month 1: THB3,000,000
            - Months 2–6: THB2,000,000
            - Months 7–20: THB1,450,000
            - Months 21–23: THB1,000,000
            - Month 24: THB801,398
    - 20-year mortgage loan drawn to repay C&D loan:
        - 6.80% annual interest with fixed monthly payments
        - Fully amortizing loan starting in two years

1. Contrast the NOI and rate of return on the Bangkok opportunity to those from the Pandan East opportunity.

Solution:

To calculate NOI, first calculate annual gross rent of THB9,828,000 by multiplying the number of units (900) by average size per unit (1,400 ft^2) by expected monthly rent (0.65) by 12 months:

Annual gross rent: $9{,}828{,}000 = 900 \times 1{,}400 \times 0.65 \times 12$.

To solve for NOI, deduct vacancy costs equal to 5% of annual gross rent (or THB491,400) and deduct operating costs equal to 33% of annual gross rent (or THB3,243,240) to solve for NOI of THB6,093,360.

NOI: THB6,093,360 = $9{,}828{,}000 \times (1 - 0.05 - 0.33)$.

Use Equation 2 to solve for the project's rate of return:

Project return = NOI/Project cost.

Total project cost is equal to the sum of land costs, land improvements, and expected construction costs of THB45,000,000 derived by multiplying the THB50,000 per unit by 900 units:

THB54,000,000 = THB6,000,000 + THB3,000,000 + THB45,000,000.

Divide NOI of THB6,093,360 by total project cost of THB54,000,000 to solve for a project return equal to 11.28%.

Project return: 11.28% = (6,093,360/54,000,000)

The NOI and project returns for the Bangkok and Pandan East projects are as follows:

Measure/Project	Bangkok	Pandan East
NOI	THB6,093,360	MYR30,888,000
Project Return	11.28%	11.23%

While the NOIs reflect differences in currency values, the expected project rates of return expected on these two projects are nearly the same.

2. Use the following table derived from the C&D loan to solve for the Bangkok project's LTV ratio at the end of Month 12 of the project.

Monthly Interest: 0.79741%

Month	Project Costs	Interest	Loan Draws	Loan Balance	Equity	Total	Equity/Value	LTV
1	3,000,000	0	3,000,000	3,000,000	5,000,000	8,000,000	0.63	0.37
2	2,000,000	23,922	3,023,922	5,023,922	5,000,000	10,023,922	0.50	0.50
3	2,000,000	40,061	5,063,984	7,063,984	5,000,000	12,063,984	0.41	0.59
4	2,000,000	56,329	7,120,313	9,120,313	5,000,000	14,120,313	0.35	0.65
5	2,000,000	72,727	9,193,040	11,193,040	5,000,000	16,193,040	0.31	0.69
6	2,000,000	89,255	11,282,295	13,282,295	5,000,000	18,282,295	0.27	0.73
7	1,450,000	105,915	13,388,209	14,838,209	5,000,000	19,838,209	0.25	0.75
8	1,450,000	118,322	14,956,531	16,406,531	5,000,000	21,406,531	0.23	0.77
9	1,450,000	130,828	16,537,359	17,987,359	5,000,000	22,987,359	0.22	0.78

Month	Project Costs	Interest	Loan Draws	Loan Balance	Equity	Total	Equity/ Value	LTV
10	1,450,000	143,434	18,130,793	19,580,793	5,000,000	24,580,793	0.20	0.80
11	1,450,000	156,140	19,736,933	21,186,933	5,000,000	26,186,933	0.19	0.81

Solution:

To compute the project LTV ratio for the following month, use project assumptions or calculations to compile the data in the columns from left to right for Month 12 as follows:

- Project Cost (Month 12): THB1,450,000
- Construction Interest: THB168,948 (or 0.797414% × THB21,186,933, equal to the Month 11 loan balance)
- Loan Draws: THB 21,355,881 (Month 11 loan balance of THB21,186,933 + THB168,948 in Month 12 construction interest)
- Loan Balance: THB22,805,881 (total draws of THB21,355,881 + THB1,450,000, Month 12 project cost)
- Equity Drawdown: THB5,000,000 (Month 12 equity drawdown as assumed)
- Total Equity: THB10,000,000 (existing equity of THB5,000,000 + THB5,000,000 equity drawdown)
- Total Financing: THB32,805,881 (loan balance of THB22,805,881 + THB10,000,000 in total equity)
- LTV: 0.6952 (= THB22,805,881/THB32,805,811)

3. Contrast the equity dividend rate on the Bangkok project with that of the Pandan East project, both before GP performance fees and after fees. Assume GP performance fees are equal to 20% of returns above a 15% hurdle rate upon completion for both projects.

Solution:

Equation 6 and Equation 7 showed the equity dividend rate and before-tax cash flow:

$$\text{Equity dividend rate} = \frac{\text{Before-tax cash flow}}{\text{Property purchase price} - \text{Debt outstanding}}.$$

$$\text{Before-tax cash flow} = \text{NOI} - \text{Debt service}.$$

First, solve for before-tax cash flow by determining the Bangkok project's annual debt service. Calculate the monthly mortgage payment using

$$A = \frac{r \times \text{Principal}}{1 - (1 + r)^{-n}}$$

or the Excel PMT function. Given monthly interest of 0.56667% (= 6.80%/12), a term of 240 months, and mortgage principal of THB41,250,000, we can calculate the monthly mortgage payment of THB314,878:

$$A = \text{THB}314,878 = \frac{0.0056667 \times \text{THB}41,250,000}{1 - (1 + 0.056667)^{-240}},$$

or PMT(0.0056667,240,41250000,0,0).

Derive annual debt service of THB3,778,531 by multiplying this result by 12. Using NOI of 6,093,360 from Question 1, solve for before-tax cash flow:

Before-tax cash flow = THB2,314,829 = 6,093,360 – 3,778,531.

Next, we solve for the equity dividend using before-tax cash flow of THB2,314,829 as the numerator and the difference between total project cost of THB54,000,000 from Question 1 and mortgage principal of THB41,250,000 (equal to the equity investment) as the denominator:

$$\text{Equity dividend rate} = 18.16\% = \frac{\text{THB2,314,829}}{\text{THB54,000,000} - \text{THB41,250,000}}.$$

This is the Bangkok project's equity dividend rate before GP performance fees. To solve for the equity dividend rate after fees, we must first determine the before-tax cash flow threshold by multiplying the denominator of Equation 6 (THB12,750,000 = 54,000,000 – 41,250,000) by the hurdle rate: Cash flow hurdle = THB1,912,500 = 0.15 × THB12,750,000.

Next, solve for fees equal to 20% of before-tax cash flow in excess of the 15% hurdle rate and deduct this from the numerator:

GP fees: THB80,466 = 0.20 × (2,314,829 – 1,912,500).

Before-tax cash flow (after fees): THB2,234,363 = 2,314,829 – 80,466.

Recalculate the equity dividend using before-tax cash flow after fees:

$$\text{Equity dividend rate (after fees)} = 17.52\% = \frac{\text{THB2,234,363}}{\text{THB54,000,000} - \text{THB41,250,000}}.$$

We can summarize equity dividend rates for the two projects as follows:

	Equity Dividend Rate (before Fees)	**Equity Dividend Rate (after Fees)**
Bangkok	18.16%	17.52%
Pandan East	17.02%	16.61%

Because equity dividend rates for the Bangkok project are approximately 100 bps higher than those for the Pandan East project, we might conclude that the Bangkok project is a more attractive equity investment for Asiastruct than the Pandan East project based on this measure, assuming they are otherwise similar and involve comparable risks.

PRIVATE REAL ESTATE VALUE DRIVERS AND PORTFOLIO CHARACTERISTICS

3

☐ discuss economic value drivers of private real estate investments and their role in a portfolio

Private Real Estate Economic Value Drivers

Expected real estate income and price appreciation are determined by the current and expected future economic use of a property for residential or commercial purposes. Key economic value drivers include specific property features, such as location, age, and amenities, in addition to regional and local economic conditions.

Earlier real estate learning modules cited GDP, job growth, and wage growth as macroeconomic variables that tend to be positively correlated with rental rates and real estate prices. Local conditions enhancing the value of a property's economic use include an attractive business climate and infrastructure, favorable regulatory and tax policies, and the proximity of major suppliers, customers, and employers. Commercial real estate is an important production input for many industries, while rising employment, population growth, and consumer confidence increase demand for rental and owner-occupied housing.

Opportunistic private real estate investments involve a greater focus on expected price appreciation than income, which magnifies the importance of real estate cycle timing as an economic value driver. Earlier learning modules linked rising rental and occupancy rates as a signal to increase market supply. As private real estate investors weigh potential refurbishment and new development projects based on current market conditions, they must factor timing from project inception to completion and potential market changes into their investment decision. Exhibit 5 shows the relationship between project development phases and the real estate cycle.

Exhibit 5: Project Development and the Real Estate Cycle

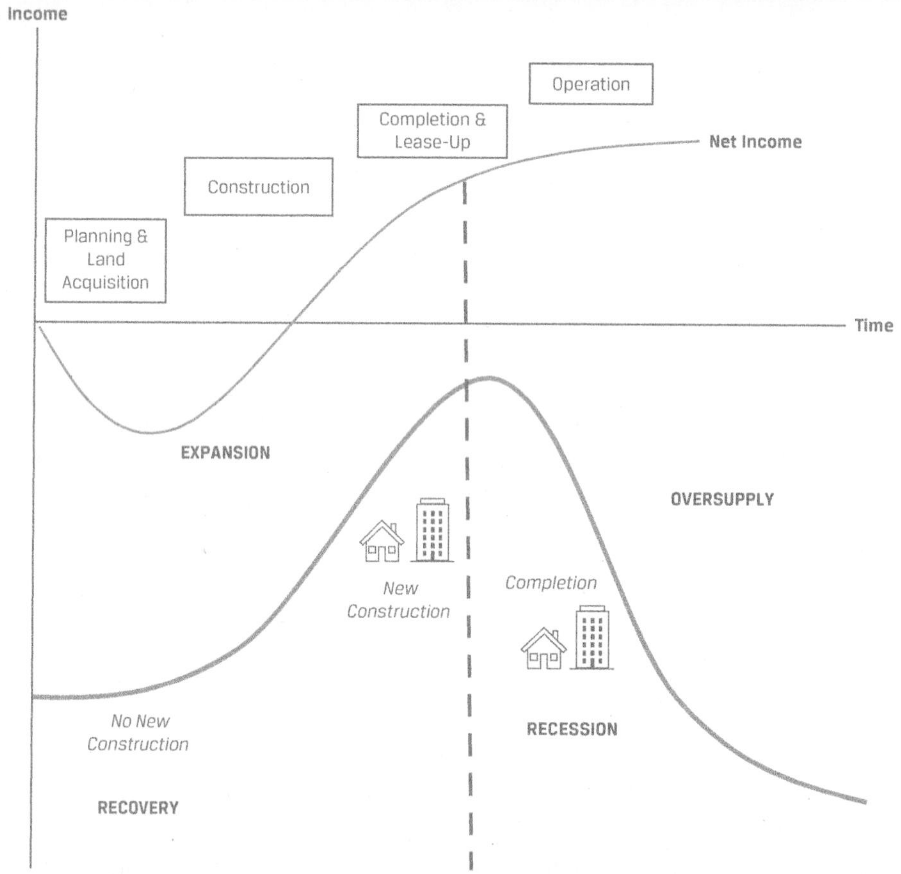

As Exhibit 5 shows, a multiyear project planned and built during real estate market recovery and expansion may reach completion at an inopportune time in the real estate market as rents decline and vacancies rise. The following case study shows how changing market conditions may affect project return.

CASE STUDY

Pandan East Return over the Real Estate Cycle

Assume the Pandan East project is completed during an oversupply phase in the real estate cycle. Due to the regional multifamily housing glut, the owners must reduce average rental rates to MYR2.50 per ft^2 to reach just 85% occupancy upon completion, while the owners are unable to reduce expenses as a fraction of gross rent despite lower-than-expected occupancy.

Recall that Pandan East includes 1,200 units averaging 1,200 ft^2 each, with expenses equal to 30% of gross rent. Assume the C&D loan has been repaid using the 20-year, 7% monthly MYR206,250,000 mortgage loan proceeds.

1. Calculate the revised before-tax cash flow and equity dividend rate for the Pandan East project under the new market conditions.

Solution:

Calculate NOI using Equation 1 by first solving for gross rent, or revenue from full occupancy rental of the 1,200 units at the average rent/ft^2:

$$\text{Gross rent} = \text{MYR}43{,}200{,}000 = (1{,}200\ \text{ft}^2 \times 1{,}200\ \text{units} \times 2.5\ \text{rent/ft}^2 \times 12).$$

Next, subtract vacancies and operating expenses (15%, or 100% – 85%, and 30% of gross rent, respectively) from gross rent:

$$\text{NOI} = \text{MYR}23{,}760{,}000 = (1 - 0.45) \times \text{MYR}43{,}200{,}000.$$

Recall from the previous case study that the annual mortgage debt service cost is MYR19,188,649. Solve for before-tax cash flow using Equation 7:

$$\text{NOI} - \text{Debt service} = \text{MYR}4{,}571{,}351 = 23{,}760{,}000 - 19{,}188{,}649.$$

Use Equation 6 to calculate the equity dividend rate:

$$\text{Equity dividend rate} = \frac{\text{Before-tax cash flow}}{\text{Property purchase price} - \text{Debt outstanding}}.$$

While the previous result is the numerator of Equation 6, the denominator (MYR68,750,000 = 275,000,000 – 206,250,000) remains unchanged:

$$\text{Equity dividend rate} = 6.65\% = \frac{\text{MYR } 4{,}571{,}351}{\text{MYR } 68{,}250{,}000}.$$

While the completed project in the previous case study generates sufficient cash flow to meet fixed debt service obligations, a key question is whether the lower NOI is a temporary cyclical phenomenon or reflects a more permanent level of the property's earnings potential over time (sometimes referred to as **stabilized NOI**). If we assume the latter case of lower operating income for the foreseeable future, consider how the new market conditions drive economic value changes for both debt and equity investors.

Using the direct capitalization method and assuming a capitalization rate equal to the original expected project rate of return of 11.23%, we estimate the project's new value to be MYR211,576,135, using Equation 3:

$$\text{Property value} = \frac{\text{Expected NOI}}{\text{Capitalization rate}}.$$

$$\text{MYR}211{,}576{,}136 = \frac{\text{MYR}23{,}760{,}000}{0.1123}.$$

We can break down the project's estimated value further by capitalizing the residual cash flows that accrue to equityholders only, which, in this case, includes before-tax cash flow after debt service of MYR4,571,351. If we consider the 15% hurdle rate mentioned earlier in the case study as a reasonable return on equity assumption for similar projects, we may solve for the market value of project equity by modifying the equity dividend calculation in Equation 6:

$$\text{Equity dividend rate} = 15\% = \frac{\text{MYR4,571,351}}{\text{Market value of equity}}.$$

Market value of equity = MYR30,475,676.

Because total project value is the sum of equity market value and the market value of debt, we can indirectly solve for the market value of debt as MYR181,100,459:

Total project value = Market value of equity + Market value of debt. (8)

MYR211,576,135 = MYR30,475,676 + MYR181,100,459.

Note that the 23% decline in total project value involves an estimated 56% decline in equity and a 12% decline in estimated mortgage loan market value.

Finally, we may show how changing market conditions affect mortgage debt coverage and leverage. Lower NOI reduces debt service coverage (that is, results in a lower DSC ratio) for lenders versus original project assumptions:

$$\text{DSC (Original)} = 1.61 = \frac{\text{MYR 30,888,000}}{\text{MYR 19,188,649}}.$$

$$\text{DSC (Revised)} = 1.24 = \frac{\text{MYR 23,760,000}}{\text{MYR 19,188,649}}.$$

A decline in market value gives rise to higher leverage, as shown by comparing expected LTV at completion using original project cost versus revised LTV under new market conditions:

$$\text{LTV (Original)} = 0.75 = \frac{\text{MYR 206,250,000}}{\text{MYR 275,000,000}}.$$

$$\text{LTV (Revised)} = 0.97 = \frac{\text{MYR 206,250,000}}{\text{MYR 211,576,135}}.$$

Details of differences in the base case and the oversupply case are as follows:

	Average Rent (MYR)	Occupancy Rate (%)	Equity Dividend	LTV	DSC
Original Case	2.75	95%	18.16%	0.75	1.61
Oversupply	2.50	85%	6.65%	0.97	1.24

Structural changes in demand are another important economic value driver for private real estate investments. Property owners can adapt their existing assets to the evolving needs of commercial and residential end users to maximize return on their investments. In doing so, they often invest in value-add strategies that involve upgrades or changes in the economic use of an existing income-producing property, as in the following case study.

CASE STUDY

Kingston Tower NOI and Sales Price

Kingston Tower is an aging 250,000 ft^2 office building on the outskirts of Toronto with few amenities and dwindling occupancy. Given the shift to hybrid work following the COVID-19 pandemic, a real estate GP is considering the purchase and renovation of the property to capitalize on market trends by creating a mixed-use, amenity-rich coworking and luxury apartment complex. The GP's analyst reviews the following NOI calculation in Canadian dollars (CAD) for the prior year given an average base rent of CAD40 per ft^2, 90% occupancy, and revenue and expense based on a percentage of gross rent:

Kingston Tower (Prior Year)	CAD	% Gross Rent
Revenue		
Gross Rent	10,000,000	100%
Operating Expense Recovery	1,000,000	10%
Other Income	400,000	4%
Less: Vacancy	(1,000,000)	10%
Concessions	(200,000)	2%
Effective Gross Income	10,200,000	
Less: Operating Expenses		
Taxes, Insurance, Maintenance	(5,000,000)	50%
Property Maintenance Allowance	(2,000,000)	20%
Net Operating Income	3,200,000	

1. Assuming a cap rate of 12%, use the direct capitalization method to estimate the property's value based on the prior-year NOI

   Solution:

   Use Equation 3 to solve for the property's value based on prior-year NOI:

$$\text{Property value} = \frac{\text{Expected NOI}}{\text{Capitalization rate}}.$$

$$\text{CAD}26,666,667 = \frac{\text{CAD}3,200,000}{0.12}.$$

2. The GP learns that current-year occupancy has fallen to 80% as tenants shifting to hybrid work policies fail to renew multiyear leases. Calculate expected current-year NOI and property value as in Question 1 for the current year using the same cap rate, revenue, and expense assumptions.

   Solution:

   The decline in occupancy to 80% doubles the effective gross income deduction for vacancy from 1,000,000 to 2,000,000 (= 20% × CAD10,000,000), while other revenue and expenses are unchanged since gross rent does not change.

Solve for current-year NOI of CAD2,200,000 by subtracting the CAD1,000,000 decrease in income from prior-year NOI (= 3,200,000 – 1,000,000).

$$\text{Property value} = \frac{\text{Expected NOI}}{\text{Capitalization rate}}.$$

$$\text{CAD}18,333,333 = \frac{\text{CAD}2,200,000}{0.12}.$$

3. Evaluate the appropriateness of using the direct capitalization method from a seller versus buyer perspective in this example.

Solution:

The direct capitalization method is appropriate if the NOI used in the numerator of Equation 3 reflects a normalized level of the property's earnings potential, which is expected to be constant over time. This may be a reasonable assumption from the seller's perspective if the seller believes the structural change in demand is permanent and there are no plans to change the property's economic use. While the GP buyer may use this method as an estimate of value to a seller based on current cash flows and economic use, the buyer may use other valuation approaches to determine the price it is willing to pay.

Investors in value-add real estate strategies aim to acquire an existing property and invest funds to implement changes that increase income and property value beyond expectations based on current economic use. A seller may be unable to identify such opportunities, may not be able or willing to capitalize on them due to a lack of expertise or financing, or have a limited risk appetite. The prospective buyer need not pay the seller a premium for the possible value it brings to a transaction. The highest bidder for a property expects the greatest return on those value drivers and is able and willing to assume the associated execution risk. The following case study shows the prospective purchase price a potential investor might be willing to pay based on a target hurdle rate.

CASE STUDY

Kingston Tower Refurbishment Project

The Kingston Tower renovation involves the conversion of upper floors totaling 50,000 ft^2 into luxury apartments and the remaining 200,000 ft^2 into high-end coworking spaces with full amenities based on the following timeline:

- Year 0: Purchase property
- Year 1: Operate office building at 80% occupancy while obtaining all permits and rezoning approvals. Assume first-year NOI (NOI_1) of CAD2,200,000 from the previous case study.
- Year 2: Renovate vacant floors while operating remainder of office building under existing leases. Renovation costs exceed second-year NOI (NOI_2) for a net cash flow of (CAD2,000,000).
- Year 3: Complete renovation and initiate new coworking and residential leases and operations. Renovation costs to exceed third-year NOI (NOI_3) for a net cash flow of (CAD2,000,000).
- Year 4: Coworking and residential space fully operational, with stabilized fourth-year NOI (NOI_4) of CAD6,412,500 based on

- Coworking base rent CAD55/ft^2, residential base rent CAD50/ft^2
- 95% occupancy
- Revenue and expense assumptions as follows:

Kingston Tower (Post-Renovation)	CAD	% Gross Rent
Revenue		
Gross Rent	13,500,000	100%
Operating Expense Recovery	1,350,000	10%
Other Income	607,500	4.5%
Less: Vacancy	(675,000)	5%
Concessions	(270,000)	2%
Effective Gross Income	14,512,500	
Less: Operating Expenses		
Taxes, Insurance, Maintenance	(6,750,000)	50%
Property Maintenance Allowance	(1,350,000)	10%
Net Operating Income	6,412,500	

1. Assuming a capitalization rate of 17%, solve for the expected property value at the end of three years based on the NOI once renovation is complete using the direct capitalization method.

   Solution:

   Use Equation 3 to solve for the property's expected value in three years based on NOI in Year 4:

$$\text{Property value} = \frac{\text{Expected NOI}_4}{\text{Capitalization rate}}.$$

$$\text{CAD37,720,588} = \frac{\text{CAD6,412,500}}{0.17}.$$

2. Given the expected project cash flows, what should the GP be willing to pay for the property today to achieve a hurdle rate of 17%?

   Solution:

   Given both the expected future cash flows and the 17% hurdle rate, we can use an internal rate of return (IRR) calculation to solve for the property value V_0 that would result in a 17% IRR:

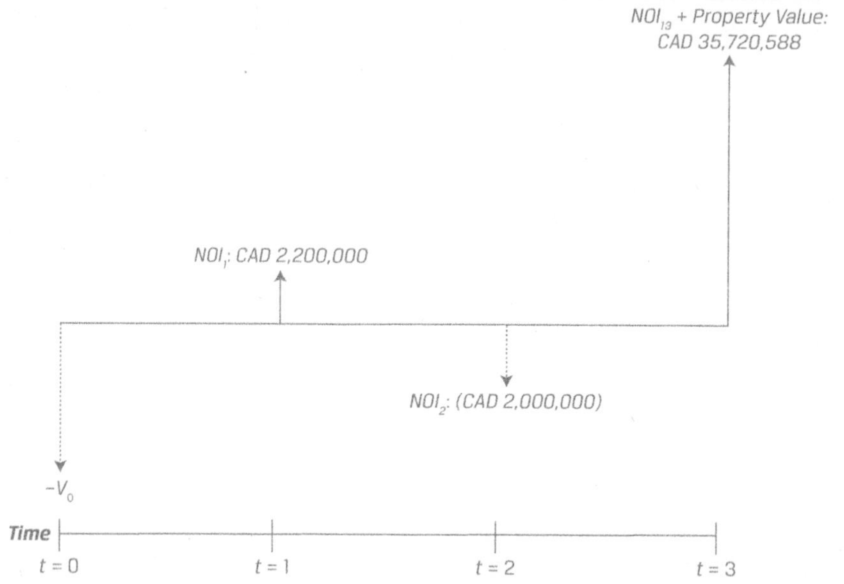

This may be solved using a financial calculator or the Microsoft Excel IRR function [=IRR(*values,guess*)]. We enter an estimated value for V_0 and solve for IRR, and then, using the Goal Seek function in Excel or trial and error on a calculator, we can iterate a new solution for V_0 for which the IRR of all cash flows is 17%. For example, assuming an initial price of CAD20,000,000, we enter IRR(-20000000,2200000,-2000000,35720588) and can solve for IRR of 22.28%. Using trial and error or the Goal Seek function to arrive at an IRR of 17% by changing V_0, we can solve for V_0 of approximately CAD22,725,000.

Private Real Estate Portfolio Characteristics

Private real estate investment projects typically involve construction or renovation following the acquisition of land or existing property to increase income and capital appreciation potential. Value-add investors usually focus on renovating and repositioning existing income-generating real estate assets, while opportunistic strategies entail new development or repurposed properties with longer periods of investment and negative cash flow. In both cases, these property changes over an investment life cycle entail greater risk but also higher expected return than the more stable, lower returns associated with operating and maintaining income-producing properties.

As in the case of other private markets where acquisition of assets or companies is followed by an investment or restructuring period to increase profitability, private real estate fund portfolios are typically characterized by multiyear cash calls or commitments, deployment of committed funds, and eventual realization of returns only once projects are completed and sold.

In addition to earmarking an existing investment allocation to fund future drawdowns, investors entering private real estate transactions must be willing to accept long investment time horizons over which the investment is illiquid and its net asset value (NAV) is relatively uncertain given the limited ability to sell a property during the construction or renovation phase.

While an underlying property or properties may be more difficult to buy or sell prior to completion, an increasing number of LP investors sell underlying fund interests to new investors in the secondary market. Similar to private equity secondaries, these transactions offer existing LP investors an ability to liquidate and diversify their holdings prior to a fund's termination date, while new investors may be attracted by shorter investment horizons, the ability to acquire a position at a price below the current NAV, and access to otherwise unavailable investments. General partners also often have an interest in leading secondary transactions to promote liquidity or rebalance an existing portfolio. In other cases, GPs offer interval funds with a limited number of fund redemptions or repurchases prior to termination. Many such open-end funds are offered for sale by LPs on the secondary market. While these GP provisions offer investors a degree of liquidity under normal market conditions, this source of liquidity may become unavailable during periods of market stress, as in the following case.

BLACKSTONE REIT (BREIT) REDEMPTION RESTRICTIONS

In 2017, Blackstone, the world's largest private real estate firm, launched the Blackstone Real Estate Income Trust (BREIT) in order to provide high-net-worth individuals access to private market real estate investments. BREIT grew to USD69 billion in assets under management over five years and contributed approximately 17% of Blackstone's earnings. As interest rates rose in 2022, publicly traded REIT prices fell, while BREIT continued to show significant positive returns. As a result, individual investors in BREIT increasingly sought to withdraw funds in late 2022, with the demand for withdrawals exceeding Blackstone's redemption limits. The contract underlying the BREIT fund allows for monthly investor redemptions of no more than 2% of fund value and quarterly redemptions of 5%. These limits were reached in November 2022, and as a result, less than half of investor repurchase requests could be satisfied by Blackstone for several months.

The BREIT situation highlights a number of issues related to private versus public real estate investments. The increased demand for BREIT redemptions led more investors to submit redemption requests for BREIT shares and other non-traded REITs. Investors who are able to move their money out of BREIT may find more attractive valuations in publicly traded REITs. Those investors whose redemption requests are not met often seek to offer their position on the secondary market. Alternative private trading platforms have sought to establish their own secondary markets for BREIT and similar non-traded REITs, reducing GP control over LP fund access previously controlled by selling agreements.

QUESTION SET

Questions 1–4 are based on the following information.

Alyssa Tan, a senior analyst at Asiastruct, considers how a debt or equity investment in the THB54 million Bangkok project would be affected if its completion coincides with an oversupply in the local real estate market. She develops the following table to compare data from the original project assumptions from the previous lesson with an oversupply scenario in which rents fall 10%, vacancies increase from 5% to 15%, and operating expenses rise from 33% to 35% of gross rent:

	Original Assumptions Year 3 (THB)	Oversupply Scenario Year 3 (THB)
Rent per ft^2 (monthly)	0.65	0.585
Gross Rent (total units)	9,828,000	8,845,200
Less: Average Vacancy	491,400	1,326,780

	Original Assumptions Year 3 (THB)	Oversupply Scenario Year 3 (THB)
Effective Gross Income	9,336,600	7,518,420
Operating Costs	3,243,240	3,095,820

We continue to assume that the project is financed with THB12,750,000 in equity and THB41,250,000 in debt financing with a 20-year 6.80% mortgage. Key calculations from the project base case are as follows:

Net Operating Income	6,093,360
Annual Debt Service	3,778,531
Before-Tax Cash Flow	2,314,829

Assume that the property's capitalization rate is 11.28% and the equity dividend rate is 18.16%.

1. By what percentage does before-tax cash flow decline from the original assumptions in the oversupply scenario?

   A. 22.0%

   B. 27.8%

   C. 72.2%

   Solution:

   Response C is correct. Subtract operating costs from effective gross income to solve for NOI of THB4,422,600 in the oversupply scenario versus THB6,093,360 in the original case. Deducting the debt service costs from the revised NOI results in before-tax cash flow of THB644,069. Comparing this number to the original before-tax cash flow of THB2,314,829, we find a 72.2% decline [= (2,314,829 – 644,069)/2,314,829].

2. Calculate and interpret the revised equity dividend rate of the Bangkok project.

   Solution:

   We can substitute the revised before-tax cash flow into Equation 6 to solve for the revised Bangkok project equity dividend rate:

   $$5.05\% = \frac{\text{THB644,069}}{\text{THB12,750,000}}.$$

   The equity dividend rate also declines by 72.2% from 18.16% to 5.05% as a result of the decline in before-tax cash flow.

3. Calculate and interpret the LTV ratio of the Bangkok project upon completion under the revised scenario. Continue to assume a capitalization rate of 11.28%.

   Solution:

   To determine the LTV ratio, we must first calculate the property value using expected Year 3 NOI as in Equation 3:

   $$\text{Property value} = \frac{\text{Expected NOI}_3}{\text{Capitalization rate}}.$$

$$\text{THB}39,200,000 = \frac{\text{THB}4,422,600}{11.28\%}.$$

Next, solve for LTV by dividing the THB41,250,000 loan amount by the revised property value:

$$\text{LTV} = 1.05 = \frac{41,250,000}{39,200,000}.$$

An LTV above 1 implies that the face value of the loan exceeds the property value. We would therefore expect the debt to be priced at a discount to its face value in this scenario.

4. Suppose that Alyssa Tan's oversupply scenario presented previously is a temporary rather than permanent market phenomenon in the local rental market. Discuss the bias created by the analysis conducted in Questions 1–3.

Solution:

The prior three questions used the oversupply assumptions to calculate a stabilized NOI and before-tax cash flow. If this situation is temporary, the analysis in Questions 1–3 generates an overly pessimistic view of the Bangkok property's long-term value. As future NOI and before-tax cash flow is expected to recover, a discounted cash flow analysis for the transition period to a higher stabilized NOI would reflect a more realistic and higher valuation for the property equity and debt.

4 PRIVATE REAL ESTATE DUE DILIGENCE AND VALUATION

☐ discuss the due diligence and valuation processes for private real estate

Earlier real estate learning modules stressed the importance of evaluating a property's physical attributes and costs of operation, as well as expected rental rates and future market dynamics affecting income and potential capital appreciation. More complex investment structures and the construction and financing life cycle of a refurbished or newly developed property add further dimensions to the due diligence process for private real estate. While real estate valuation approaches are like those for other private market assets, private markets may incorporate option- or scenario-based analysis in addition to more conventional income, cost, and sales comparison approaches.

Private Real Estate Due Diligence

Key elements of private real estate due diligence for a newly developed property are outlined in Exhibit 6.

Exhibit 6: Elements of Private Real Estate Due Diligence

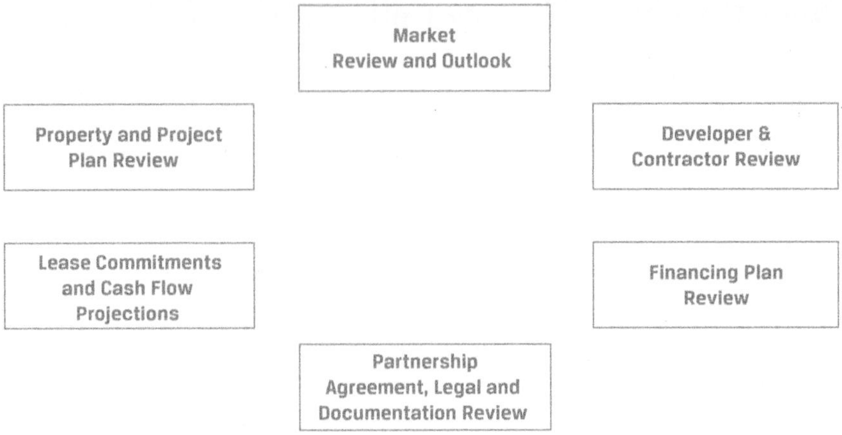

Market Review and Outlook

Regional and local business outlooks are an important gauge of future commercial and residential real estate demand. While due diligence for income-producing properties focuses primarily on current sale prices and lease rates and trends, opportunistic property investors also consider comparable prices of undeveloped land or properties targeted for refurbishment, as well as construction costs. Forward projections of real estate cycle dynamics as a project reaches completion are important for estimating future income, while in the case of value-add real estate renovation projects, improved local economic conditions may be necessary to generate higher rental and lease income following capital improvements. Community engagement, the anticipated arrival or departure of major employers, or similar development in the area, as well as changes to public infrastructure, are additional factors to consider.

Property and Project Plan Review

Investors typically review property surveys and physical, engineering, and environmental feasibility studies, as well as construction plans and details. In addition to the reputation and experience of the architecture and engineering (A&E) firm serving as technical consultant, coordination and integration of the design and construction process are key factors affecting the timely completion of a project within the original budget.

Developer, Contractor, and Supplier Review

Investors depend heavily on close cooperation between developers, general and specialty contractors, and suppliers during the construction phase. In some cases, an A&E firm or general contractor agrees to deliver a project on a **turnkey** or fully completed basis, which can streamline the process but also concentrates execution risk. In other cases, work occurs in stages, with progress payments made at key milestones. Important factors to consider include the experience of contractors on similar projects, past partnership with involved parties (as well as their financial strength), adherence to safety measures, alignment of incentives, and adequate liability insurance.

Lease Commitments and Cash Flow Projections

The level and variability of property income will vary widely depending on the business strategy, type of property, and lease commitments in place upon completion. For example, a project may be built to suit a single commercial tenant with a pre-signed rental contract, have one or two major retailers committed to leases in a multi-tenant shopping facility, or be constructed on a purely speculative basis with no predevelopment leases in place. Other base-case assumptions supporting income and expense forecasts should be critically evaluated, including possible construction or lease delays or other adverse events.

Financing Plan Review

Potential debt and equity investors may take a similar approach in assessing the level and variability of future cash flows but often view associated risks and considerations very differently based on their position in the project's capital structure and life cycle timing.

*ADLs and C&D Loans.*Investors in debt drawn during the land purchase, development, and construction phases of a project focus specifically on the nature of costs funded, expected financial leverage, and the commitment and timing of permanent debt financing. For example, these investors have greater risk when drawdowns are for fees or project management costs as opposed to land and building materials expenses, outlays that are more likely to be recouped in the sale of an unfinished project. The probability of default for such loans is greater for projects that rely more heavily on debt financing or that lack a firm mortgage commitment upon completion. Early-stage lenders pay particular attention to the financial condition of developers, loan covenants, and completion of project milestones over time.

Mortgage Loans. Permanent lenders evaluate the degree of upfront commitment, as well as the expected and actual debt coverage, leverage, and the profitability of the completed project. Firm loan commitments at rates or spreads fixed prior to project completion carry greater risk because they must rely on the value of the undeveloped land only, while standby commitments usually allow for adjusted market rates and other terms upon loan disbursal. Mortgage prepayment features give rise to reinvestment risk for lenders.

Equity. Prospective equity investors must balance the higher return of projects with greater leverage and financial flexibility with the risk-reducing benefits that financially sound debt providers able to meet debt drawdowns typically impose, such as leverage- and covenant-based constraints. Equity owners must understand the consequences of debt drawdowns not occurring or a loan not closing and be prepared to potentially inject additional equity to bridge the project or walk away and lose their existing equity investment.

Partnership Agreement, Legal, and Documentation Review

Private real estate investments often involve a partnership agreement that governs shareholder rights, such as voting or GP appointment rights; financial disclosures; and sale restrictions, such as lockup provisions. This review also extends to compensation arrangements seeking to align manager and investor incentives. Prospective LP investors must weigh the potential risks of earlier involvement, concentration in larger investments, and/or longer lockup periods against greater rewards offered by GPs for such positions. As in the case of public investments, a legal and tax review of ownership history ensures that a property is free of any liens or tax obligations to protect the new owner and secured lenders.

Private Real Estate Valuation Approaches

Private real estate valuation incorporates elements of the income, cost, and sales comparison approaches introduced in earlier learning modules that are used to value public real estate and other private market assets. Factors that distinguish the valuation of private real estate include property development life cycle dynamics, the future state of the real estate market, and the income and capital appreciation of a completed project. In addition, real options are associated with an investor's ability to alter a planned course of action in response to changing market conditions, as shown later.

Private real estate investors often apply more than one valuation approach to arrive at a price at which they may be willing to buy or sell a property over the development life cycle, with the preferred method varying based on an investor's position and property characteristics.

For example, an income-based approach is most appropriate when earnings are considered the primary source of value based on the property's current or future economic use. The single-year NOI in the numerator of the direct capitalization method described earlier and shown in Equation 3 implicitly assumes consistent earnings in the future. In the case of new development, direct capitalization was used earlier to gauge the Pandan East property's post-completion value based on future earnings under its new economic use. Given the lack of cash flows from the vacant three-acre plot used for the project, it is not current earnings but, rather, the potential for development from which the raw land derives its value. In this case, a market price comparison to other nearby comparable properties available for development is more suitable than an income valuation approach.

In the earlier Kingston Tower case study, an existing income-producing property is under consideration for major renovation under a value-add investment strategy. Recall that previously, the direct capitalization method was used to compare the difference in the value of the cash flow stream under the property's current use and the expected cash flows after renovation. Investors typically demand a higher return in the construction phase versus the cap rate for a stabilized NOI. In practice, both the seller and buyer are also likely to consider more than one valuation approach. For example, given uncertainty surrounding future office occupancy, the seller may look to a sales comparison or market approach by considering prices at which similar or comparable properties recently traded. In addition to considering other renovation targets, the buyer may also consider the cost of new development versus renovation. The cost approach involves evaluating the expense of buying the land and constructing a new property on the site that has the same economic use as the property being appraised (referred to as the subject property). The following case study illustrates these approaches.

CASE STUDY

Kingston Tower Seller and Buyer Valuation Approaches

The seller uses a sales comparison approach based on public records or other data sources to compare prices per square foot of three comparable properties, adjusting for differences from the subject property in terms of size, age, location, and market conditions at times of sale.

Measure/Property	Subject Property (Kingston Tower)	Compara-ble Prop-erty 1	Compara-ble Prop-erty 2	Compara-ble Prop-erty 3
Sale Date		6 months	9 months	18 months
Sale Price		28,895,000	21,295,000	13,575,000
Gross Annual Rent		13,500,000	9,250,000	8,795,000
Gross Square Feet	250,000	325,000	225,000	220,000
Rent/ft^2		24	26	27.27
Additional Distance from City Center	0 miles	3 miles closer	2 miles further	4 miles further
Age	25y	15y	20y	30y
Price/ft^2		88.91	94.64	61.70
Adjustments:				
Sale Date		0%	4%	8%
Square Footage		5%	−1%	−2%
Location		−5%	5%	8%
Age		−10%	−5%	5%
Net Difference		−10%	3%	19%
Adjusted Price		26,005,500	21,933,850	16,154,250
Adjusted Price/ft^2		80.02	97.48	73.43
Estimated Price/ft^2 for Subject Property		83.64		
Estimated Value (CAD)		20,910,759		

Using a cost approach, the buyer estimates the price of purchasing vacant land and developing a comparable property with the same rental space and economic use following the proposed renovation, while adjusting for the difference between a new building and an older, renovated building.

Estimate Components	Estimate (CAD)
Excavation and steel framing	1,000,000
Foundation	1,250,000
Façade (glass, brick, mortar)	2,400,000
Floor finishing	950,000
Roofing/ceiling/insulation	1,500,000
Interior walls and finishing	2,000,000
Electrical and lighting	1,750,000
Plumbing	1,175,000
HVAC (heating, ventilation, and A/C)	1,200,000
Interior furnishing	2,250,000
Parking and paving	500,000
SUBTOTAL	15,975,000
Architect/legal/tax/permits/accounting	1,250,000
Development period interest	1,250,000

Estimate Components	Estimate (CAD)
Contractor profit	2,700,000
SUBTOTAL	5,200,000
Comparable land cost	4,950,000
Cost estimate for new building	26,125,000
Adjustment for age of subject property (–15%)	22,206,250

Recall from the previous case study that the GP investor is targeting a 17% hurdle rate and expects the following cash flows during renovation and upon completion:

- Year 1: Assume NOI_1 of CAD2,200,000
- Year 2: Renovation costs exceed NOI_2, net cash flow of –CAD2,000,000.
- Year 3: Renovation costs exceed NOI_3, net cash flow of –CAD2,000,000.
- Year 4: Stabilized NOI_4 of CAD6,412,500 at 95% occupancy

1. Using estimated property price based on values derived under the sales comparison and cost approaches, determine whether the GP investor should pursue the Kingston Tower project given its stated hurdle rate.

Solution:

In Question 2 in the previous case study, we calculated a property price V_0 of CAD22,725,000 for which the IRR of all cash flows equaled the GP's hurdle rate of 17%. Given the lower estimated V_0 using the sales comparison and cost approaches—CAD20,910,759 and CAD22,206,250, respectively—the expected IRR is above 17% and the GP investor would pursue the project under either valuation scenario, as shown below:

Sales comparison approach:

IRR = 20.4% [=IRR(-20910759,2200000,-2000000,35720588)].

Cost approach:

IRR = 17.9% [=IRR(-22206250,2200000,-2000000,35720588)].

The valuation approaches shown thus far are relatively straightforward given their *static* nature; that is, they capture a property's value by discounting a single year's cash flow as a perpetuity or a ratio comparing sales based on a common unit of measure. When an analyst seeks to capture cyclical or multiperiod trends, a *dynamic* approach based on discounting a series of income projections and a terminal value to the present is more appropriate. The discounted cash flow (DCF) method is applied when an analyst has sufficient information to estimate property cash flows over several years. Earlier learning modules showed the property value using DCF as a combination of forecasted NOI and a terminal value on a future date.

$$\text{Property value} = \sum_{i=1}^{n} \frac{\text{NOI}_{t+i}}{(1+r)^i} + \frac{\text{Terminal value}}{(1+r)^n}. \qquad (9)$$

Terminal values can be derived by capitalizing the NOI of comparable properties or using the final year's projected NOI multiplied by 1 plus the constant growth rate, *g*, discounted by the cap rate:

$$\text{Terminal value} = \frac{\text{NOI}_n(1+g)}{r-g}. \tag{10}$$

We illustrate this for a secondaries LP investor evaluating the purchase of the beleaguered Pandan East development described earlier, where we assumed project completion amid a real estate market in an oversupply phase.

CASE STUDY

DCF Valuation of Pandan East Secondaries Purchase

Recall from earlier the situation in which Pandan East is completed during a real estate market glut, forcing the owner to rent new units at an average MYR2.50 per ft^2 and reach just 85% occupancy versus an expected MYR2.75 per ft^2 and 95%, respectively, under the original plan for the first year after completion.

Pandan East includes 1,200 units averaging 1,200 ft^2 each, with expenses equal to 30% of gross rent. The first full year's NOI may be shown as follows:

Pandan East (Year 0)	MYR	% Gross Rent
Revenue		
Gross Rent	43,200,000	100%
Other Income	0	0%
Less: Vacancy	(6,480,000)	15%
Effective Gross Income	36,720,000	
Less: Operating Expenses	(12,960,000)	30%
Net Operating Income	23,760,000	

While the GP contract and business plan foresee four more years of ownership before exit, an original LP investor is soliciting secondary market bids from new LP investors. An analyst conducting due diligence on the purchase of an equity stake in Pandan East projects the following rent and occupancy rates:

Period	Average Rent (MYR)	% Occupancy
Year 1	2.60	90%
Year 2	2.75	95%
Year 3	2.85	95%
Year 4	3.00	95%

The LP analyst assumes no added income and expenses equal to 30% of gross rent, as well as a required rate of return of 12% and a 2% constant growth rate starting at the end of four years.

1. Calculate the present value (PV) of NOI over the four-year holding period.

   Solution:

   First, project Year 1 to Year 4 cash flows based on LP analyst assumptions:

Pandan East NOI Projections

NOI Components	Year 1	Year 2	Year 3	Year 4
Average Rent	2.60	2.75	2.85	3.00
Occupancy	90%	95%	95%	95%
Gross Rent	44,928,000	47,520,000	49,248,000	51,840,000
Other Income	—	—	—	—
Less Vacancies	(4,492,800)	(2,376,000)	(2,462,400)	(2,592,000)
Effective Gross Income	40,435,200	45,144,000	46,785,600	49,248,000
Operating Expenses	(13,478,400)	(14,256,000)	(14,774,400)	(15,552,000)
NOI	26,956,800	30,888,000	32,011,200	33,696,000

Second, calculate the PV of NOI using the first expression in Equation 9,

$$\sum_{i=1}^{n} \frac{\text{NOI}_{t+i}}{(1+r)^i}, \text{ where } r = 12\%,$$

or in Excel using the NPV function [=NPV(*rate,value1,value2...*)] with a rate of 12% and values equal to each annual NOI to get MYR92,891,653:

$$\text{MYR}92,891,653 = \frac{26,956.800}{(1.12)^1} + \frac{30,888,000}{(1.12)^2} + \frac{32,011,200}{(1.12)^3} + \frac{33,696,000}{(1.12)^4}.$$

2. Calculate the terminal value based on Year 4 NOI and the expected price the new LP investor would be willing to pay for the property.

Solution:

Use Equation 10 to solve for terminal value using NOI_4 of MYR33,696,000, r of 12%, and g equal to 2% to derive a future terminal value of MYR343,699,200:

$$\text{Terminal value} = \frac{\text{NOI}_4(1+g)}{r-g}.$$

$$\text{MYR}343,699,200 = \frac{33,696,000(1.02)}{0.12-0.02}.$$

Substitute this result into Equation 9 to estimate the property's value to the LP investor by combining the PV of NOI with the terminal value PV:

$$\text{Property value} = \text{MYR}311,318,708 = \text{MYR}92,891,653 + \frac{\text{MYR}343,699,200}{(1.12)^4}.$$

A detailed cash flow forecast over multiple periods under a single likely economic scenario is most suitable for properties or companies with relatively stable income sources that do not change over the forecast period, as in the prior case study. When greater uncertainty exists over a development cycle coupled with potential real estate market changes during the construction phase, a valuation based on **scenario analysis** may be more appropriate. Scenario analysis combines a base case with alternative outcomes, allowing the incorporation of more favorable or adverse scenarios in the valuation process.

$$\text{Property value} = \sum_{i=1}^{n} \text{Probability}(i) \times \text{Property value}_i. \quad (11)$$

In Equation 11, the property's value under scenario i (Property value$_i$) is weighted by its respective probability, Probability(i), and $\sum_{i=1}^{n}$ Probability(i) = 1. For example, at project inception, a prospective investor might consider the three potential scenarios upon completion shown in Exhibit 7.

Exhibit 7: Private Real Estate Valuation Using Scenario Analysis

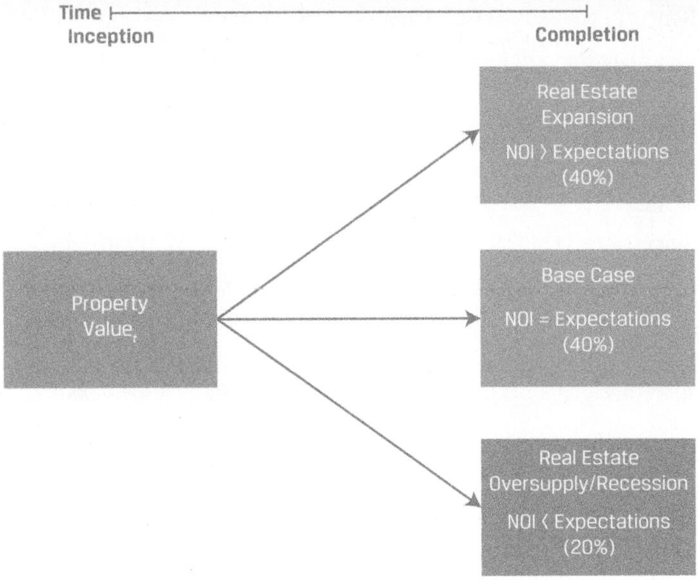

While the valuation method used in Equation 11 for all scenarios must be consistent, it may involve income-, cost-, or market-based approaches. We illustrate the use of scenario analysis by revisiting the Kingston Tower refurbishment project using direct capitalization.

CASE STUDY

Kingston Tower Scenario Analysis

An analyst weighing a Kingston Tower investment examines prospective returns under different market rent assumptions. Since she believes the high-end coworking rental market is more cyclical than residential real estate, she establishes three scenarios upon project completion under which coworking rent exhibits greater variability as follows:

Scenario/Probability	Coworking Rent (CAD/ft^2)	Residential Rent (CAD/ft^2)
Expansion (25%)	60	55
Base (40%)	55	50
Downside Case (35%)	45	50

The analyst assumes 95% occupancy in all three cases and similar income and expense assumptions as before. Recall the project includes 50,000 ft^2 of luxury apartment space and 200,000 ft^2 of coworking space developed over three years, with NOI_1 of CAD2,200,000 and net cash flow of –CAD2,000,000 in Years 2 and 3. The analyst calculates post-completion NOI in Year 4 under each of the three scenarios as follows:

Cash Flow Item/ Scenario	Upside Case (Expansion)	Base Case	Downside Case (Over-supply/ Recession)	% Gross Rent
Revenue				
Gross Rent	14,750,000	13,500,000	11,500,000	
Operating Expense Recovery	1,475,000	1,350,000	1,150,000	10%
Other Income	663,750	607,500	517,500	4.5%
Less: Vacancy	(737,500)	(675,000)	(575,000)	5%
Less: Concessions	(295,000)	(270,000)	(230,000)	2%
Effective Gross Income	15,856,250	14,512,500	12,362,500	
Less: Operating Expenses	(7,375,000)	(6,750,000)	(5,750,000)	50%
Less: Property Maintenance Allowance	(1,475,000)	(1,350,000)	(1,150,000)	10%
Net Operating Income	7,006,250	6,412,500	5,462,500	

1. Calculate the expected property value under the three possible scenarios at the end of Year 3 using a direct capitalization approach and a 17% required rate of return.

Solution:

We first calculate the property's value at the end of Year 3 under each scenario using Equation 3:

$$\text{Property value} = \frac{\text{Expected NOI}}{\text{Capitalization rate}}.$$

$$\text{Property value}_{Upside} = 41,213,235 = \frac{7,006,250}{0.17}.$$

$$\text{Property value}_{Base} = 37,720,588 = \frac{6,412,500}{0.17}.$$

$$\text{Property value}_{Downside} = 32,132,353 = \frac{5,462,500}{0.17}.$$

Next, solve for an expected property value of CAD36,637,868 using probability-weighted capitalized values as shown in Equation 11:

$$\text{CAD}36,637,868$$
$$= (0.25 \times 41,213,235) + (0.40 \times 37,720,588) + (0.35 \times 32,132,353).$$

Note that this expected value is less than the original base-case estimate of CAD37,720,588 from before due in part to the higher probability (35%) associated with the downside versus upside case.

2. If we assume a purchase price (V_0) of CAD22,000,000, determine the likelihood of the investor reaching or exceeding her 17% target IRR.

Solution:

We can determine the rate of return under each scenario using the same Excel IRR formula [=IRR(*values,guess*)] as before, with *value1* equal to V_0 of CAD22,000,000 and *value4* equal to the respective terminal value under each scenario:

Upside case (25%):

IRR = 22.10% [=*IRR*(-22000000,2200000,-2000000,39213235)]

Base case (40%):

IRR = 18.31% [=*IRR*(-22000000,2200000,-2000000,35720588)]

Downside case (35%):

IRR = 11.68% [=*IRR*(-22000000,2200000,-2000000,30132353)]

This implies that the investor has a 65% chance (= 25% + 40%) of reaching or exceeding a 17% IRR on the prospective investment under these assumptions.

A key advantage of scenario analysis is that it considers a range of future potential outcomes rather than a single point estimate. Establishing a range of outcomes allows analysts to incorporate changing market conditions or other factors more explicitly into a valuation approach. Given the heterogeneous and illiquid nature of real estate markets, pursuing a simpler approach by forecasting fewer scenarios and individual variables is usually preferable to the greater financial modeling detail used in valuing public market securities.

In addition, **sensitivity analysis** is often used to determine the impact of a change in one or more key variables affecting investment return. For instance, given the focus on both coworking and residential rent as two key drivers of expected property value in the previous case study, we may create a two-variable Excel data table to examine how different values of these variables affect the expected property value assuming a 17% cap rate, as shown in Exhibit 8.

Exhibit 8: Kingston Tower Sensitivity Analysis: Property Value

Coworking rent (CAD per ft^2)	Residential Rent (CAD per ft^2)		
	55	50	45
65	50,955,882	49,485,294	48,014,706
60	45,073,529	43,602,941	42,132,353
55	39,191,176	**37,720,588**	36,250,000
50	33,308,824	31,838,235	30,367,647
45	27,426,471	25,955,882	24,485,294
40	21,544,118	20,073,529	18,602,941

Base Case*:* CAD37,720,588

Note that the base case corresponds to the scenario under which coworking and residential rent are CAD 55 and CAD 50 per ft^2, respectively. An alternative use of sensitivity analysis in this example would be to consider how the expected IRR would vary if the property were purchased for CAD22,725,000 as originally assumed associated with different coworking and residential rent assumptions for the terminal value in Year 4 as shown in Exhibit 9.

Exhibit 9: Kingston Tower Sensitivity Analysis – Expected IRR

Coworking Rent (CAD per ft^2)	Residential rent (CAD per ft^2)		
	55	50	45
65	30.13%	28.80%	27.44%
60	24.64%	23.18%	21.70%
55	18.60%	**17.00%**	15.34%
50	11.88%	10.07%	8.19%
45	4.23%	2.13%	–0.06%
40	–4.76%	–7.29%	–9.97%

Base Case: IRR = 17%

As in Exhibit 8, the 17% IRR base case corresponds to the scenario with coworking and residential rent of CAD55 and CAD50 per ft^2, respectively.

Under the real estate valuation approaches described thus far, an investor chooses a single, pre-determined course of action. In practice, investors face multiple investment alternatives that can affect a property's value, known as **real options**. As described earlier in the curriculum, real options involve the right but not the obligation to take future action. A firm or investor should choose to pursue a real option only if it increases value.

In the case of real estate development, real options available to investors purchasing land or a property for possible upgrade often include the following:

- **Delay option**: Developers may increase a project's present value by postponing property construction until market conditions improve.
- **Sequencing option**: Dividing and executing a project in staggered phases rather than all at once may increase a project's risk-adjusted return by reducing exposure to market oversupply during the lease-up period.
- **Switching option**: The option to choose among alternative projects for a given plot of land or switch economic uses for an existing project, such as a mixed-use facility, may increase value.

Investors may use different methods to factor these alternatives into valuation:

1. Conduct a DCF analysis *without* options. If the project IRR meets an investor's hurdle rate without including options that would increase its NPV, then the NPV without options represents the *minimum* return.
2. Calculate NPV with real options. Under this approach, the firm calculates project NPV based on expected cash flows and then subtracts the incremental cost of real options and adds back its value, as shown in Equation 12:

$$\text{Project NPV} = \text{NPV (without options)} - \text{Option cost} + \text{Option value}. \qquad (12)$$

3. Use a decision tree or option pricing model. Either approach may be used to assess the value of a project involving future sequential decisions and alternative outcomes. These models often assign probability and expected timing to future outcomes used to calculate the project's NPV.

The decision as to whether to delay a project is illustrated in the Knowledge Check below.

KNOWLEDGE CHECK: PROJECT TIMING DECISION

An investor in vacant land is weighing the decision of whether to build today or delay construction for one year. Estimates of current and future costs and real estate market prices are as follows:

Build today: Construction costs today are USD95,000,000, and the completed building value is expected to be USD115,000,000 in present value terms.

Build in one year: The investor estimates a 70% probability of continued real estate market expansion and a 30% chance of a downturn, in which case the project will not be built, and the owner incurs USD250,000 in property taxes in either scenario. Under the expansion scenario, construction costs (including financing) are expected to rise 8%, while the completed building value will increase by 20%.

1. If the investor has a required rate of return of 17%, determine whether the investor should build the project today or delay for one year.

   Solution:

   The decision of whether to build today or delay involves a comparison of today's return to the present value of construction delay based on the following decision tree and modification of Equation 11:

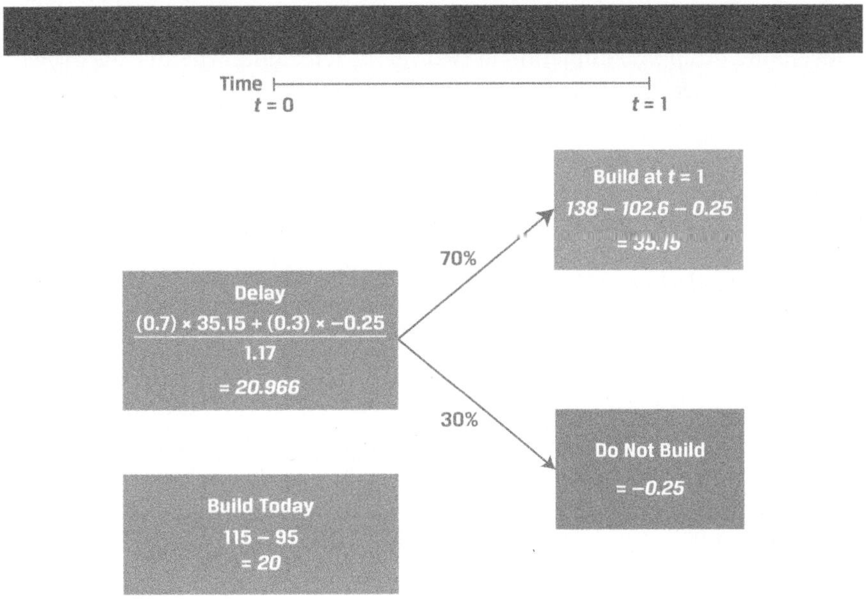

Build today:

USD20,000,000 = USD115,000,000 – USD95,000,000.

Build in one year:

PV(Delay) = USD20,965,812

$$= \frac{0.7 \times (138,000,000 - 102,600,000 - 250,000) + 0.3 \times (-250,000)}{1.17}.$$

The investor should therefore delay the project given the higher present value.

QUESTION SET

1. Alyssa Tan at Asiastruct has identified three property transactions in Thailand from the past two years comparable to the original 1.26 million ft^2 project (with 900 residential units averaging 1,400 ft^2 each) located in Bangkok from earlier in the learning module. Tan evaluated each property's key features, including their relative location, age, and size, which she combined in order to establish an expected net difference in price per ft^2. Selected data from these three properties and the new Bangkok project are summarized below.

Data/project	Bangkok	Comp 1	Comp 2	Comp 3
Gross square feet	1,260,000	1,000,000	1,400,000	1,100,000
Price per ft^2		THB 50.24	THB 61.58	THB 44.76
Location adjustment		−4%	+2%	9%
Age adjustment		−2%	+2%	0%
Size adjustment		−2%	+1%	−1%
Net difference		−8%	5%	8%

If the Bangkok project cost is THB54,000,000 today and the value derived from this sales comparison is used as a basis for the expected price of the development upon completion in two years, determine whether the project is likely to exceed Asiastruct's 10% hurdle rate.

Solution:

First, solve for the average adjusted price per ft^2 of the three properties:

Adjusted price per ft^2: Comp 1: THB46.22 = THB50.24 × (1 – 0.08).

Comp 2: THB64.66 = THB61.58 × (1 + 0.05).

Comp 3: THB48.34 = THB44.76 × (1 + 0.08).

Average adjusted price: THB53.07 = (46.22 + 64.66 + 48.34)/3.

Next, solve for the Bangkok property value upon completion in two years by multiplying the square footage by the average adjusted price:

THB66,872,652 = 1,260,000 ft^2 × THB53.07/ft^2.

Finally, calculate the return for an initial cash outflow equal to today's project cost and an inflow equal to the estimated property value in two years. We may use either the Excel PMT function or a discounted cash flow approach to solve for an IRR of 11.28%:

IRR = 11.28% [=IRR(-54000000,0,66872652)], or

$$FV = PV(1+r)^t;\ r = \left(\frac{FV}{PV}\right)^{\frac{1}{t}} - 1\ ;$$

$$11.28\% = \left(\frac{66,872,652}{54,000,000}\right)^{\frac{1}{2}} - 1.$$

The 11.28% estimated return exceeds the analyst's 10% hurdle rate.

2. Alyssa Tan is considering a scenario analysis to build on her earlier analysis of the Bangkok project. Her NOI forecast of THB 6,093,360 for the first full year of operation (Year 3) is the base case, and her oversupply scenario of a 10% fall in rents and vacancies and a 2% rise in operating costs, yielding an NOI of THB4,422,600, is the downside case. Tan adds a growth scenario in which a local shortage of rental housing results in 10% upside to rental rates, lower vacancies, and lower operating costs, resulting in Year 3 NOI of THB7,151,344. These three scenarios and their associated probabilities are summarized below:

Scenario	Probability	Year 3 NOI (THB)
Growth Scenario	25%	7,151,344
Base-Case Scenario	45%	6,093,360
Oversupply Scenario	30%	4,422,600

Assuming a direct capitalization approach with a 10% cap rate, determine whether the Bangkok project meets her 10% hurdle rate using scenario analysis and assuming the same initial investment of THB54,000,000.

Solution:

Use the same approach as in Equation 11 to solve for the expected NOI given the three scenarios and their associated probabilities:

$$\text{NOI} = \sum_{i=1}^{n} \text{Probability}(i) \times \text{NOI}_i.$$

$$\text{NOI} = \text{THB}5,856,628$$

$$= (0.45 \times 6,093,360) + (0.30 \times 4,422,600) + (0.25 \times 7,151,344).$$

Use Equation 3 to solve for the expected property value upon completion:

$$\text{Property value} = \frac{\text{Expected NOI}}{\text{Capitalization rate}}.$$

$$\text{THB}58,566,281 = \frac{5,856,628}{0.10}.$$

Note that this is the expected property value at the end of Year 2. Similar to Question 1, we may calculate the return using an initial cash outflow equal to today's project cost of THB54,000,000 and an inflow equal to THB58,566,281. Using the Excel PMT function or a discounted cash flow approach, we solve for an IRR of 4.14%:

IRR = 4.14% [=*IRR*(-54000000,0,58566281)], or

$$\text{FV} = \text{PV}(1+r)^t;\ r = \left(\frac{\text{FV}}{\text{PV}}\right)^{\frac{1}{t}} - 1\ ;$$

$$4.14\% = \left(\frac{58,566,281}{54,000,000}\right)^{\frac{1}{2}} - 1.$$

The 4.14% estimated return is below the analyst's 10% hurdle rate, and she should therefore not pursue the project based on scenario analysis.

3. As Asiastruct considers its alternatives, Alyssa Tan is exploring the Bangkok project today versus a one-year delay in construction. After considering all value estimates from earlier exercises, she decides on an appropriate future estimate of the property value upon completion. She notes the present value of the completed project at her 10% hurdle rate is THB59,090,909. The present value of construction costs if the project is initiated today is THB54,000,000. Tan has established two possible market scenarios if construction is delayed by one year:

   Growth scenario (60% probability): Construction costs rise by 12%, while the completed project value increases by 16%.

   Stable scenario (40% probability): Construction costs rise 3%, while the completed project value increases by 1%.

   Justify Tan's recommendation on whether Asiastruct should build the Bangkok project now, delay for a year, or not pursue the project at all.

   Solution:

   The justification for a recommendation to build now or delay is best conducted using an NPV analysis based on expected probabilities and using a discount rate equal to Asiastruct's hurdle rate.

   First, we evaluate whether to build the project now by comparing project costs to value upon completion in PV terms:

   PV of project construction cost: THB54,000,000

   PV of project upon completion: THB59,090,909

   Project NPV: THB5,090,909 = 59,090,909 – 54,000,000.

   Asiastruct would pursue the project today given its positive NPV of THB5,090,909, which we now compare to a one-year delay.

   Next, we evaluate the estimated return given a project delay by comparing construction costs to value upon completion under both scenarios weighted by probability as of the time the project starts in one year.

   Growth scenario (60% probability):

   Construction costs in one year: THB60,480,000 = 54,000,000 × 1.12.

   Project value in one year: THB68,545,455 = 59,090,909 × 1.16.

   Difference between project value and construction costs in one year: THB8,065,455 = 68,545,455 – 60,480,000.

   Stable scenario (40% probability):

   Construction costs in one year: THB55,620,000 = 54,000,000 × 1.03.

   Project value in one year: THB59,681,818 = 59,090,909 × 1.01.

   Difference between project value and construction costs in one year: THB4,061,818 = 59,681,818 – 55,620,000.

   Use probability weights to estimate the project's value in one year:

   Project value: THB6,464,000 = (8,065,454 × 0.6) + (4,061,818 × 0.4).

   Discount project value by the hurdle rate to compare to today's land price:

$$\text{THB}5,876,363 = \frac{\text{THB}6,464,000}{(1+0.10)^1}.$$

Since the delayed project's PV of THB5,876,363 exceeds that of pursuing the project today when discounted by Asiastruct's hurdle rate, Tan should recommend delaying construction by one year.

TIMBERLAND AND FARMLAND INVESTMENT CHARACTERISTICS

5

- [ ] discuss the distinctive investment characteristics of timberland and farmland

Timberland Investment Characteristics

Private timberland investment began as a shift in ownership from private forest product companies in the United States seeking greater tax and capital efficiency to tax-exempt pensions and other investors seeking portfolio diversification. While most private investable timberland is in the United States, these investments have expanded to regions including Central and Eastern Europe, Latin America, Australia, and New Zealand.

As in the case of other types of real estate, timberland derives its value from current and future economic use. Timberland use involves the biological growth and harvest of timber naturally grown or cultivated and managed on forest plantations for use in the paper, packaging, and construction industries. The suitability of land for timber production varies by climate, soil type, and the age, species, and density of existing tree cover. Thinned or harvested timber is logged by private firms, which pay a **stumpage fee** to timberland owners for the right to harvest. These logs are then transported and processed or milled and kiln dried for further use or sale at market prices that vary based on quality and potential end uses. **Pulpwood** consisting of lower-quality, small, and often thinned trees is the primary input for paper products, while higher-priced **sawtimber** is top-quality timber used for construction lumber and other building products, such as plywood and particleboard. Unharvested timber appreciates in value over time not only due to growth but also since a higher proportion of many older trees may be sold as sawtimber.

Given a harvest cycle that can span 25–100 years, timberland is usually evaluated based on a long-term investment horizon that combines income and capital appreciation. Exhibit 10 shows the cash flows associated with a simple timber growth and harvest cycle, as in the following case.

Exhibit 10: Timber Growth and Harvest Cycle Cash Flows

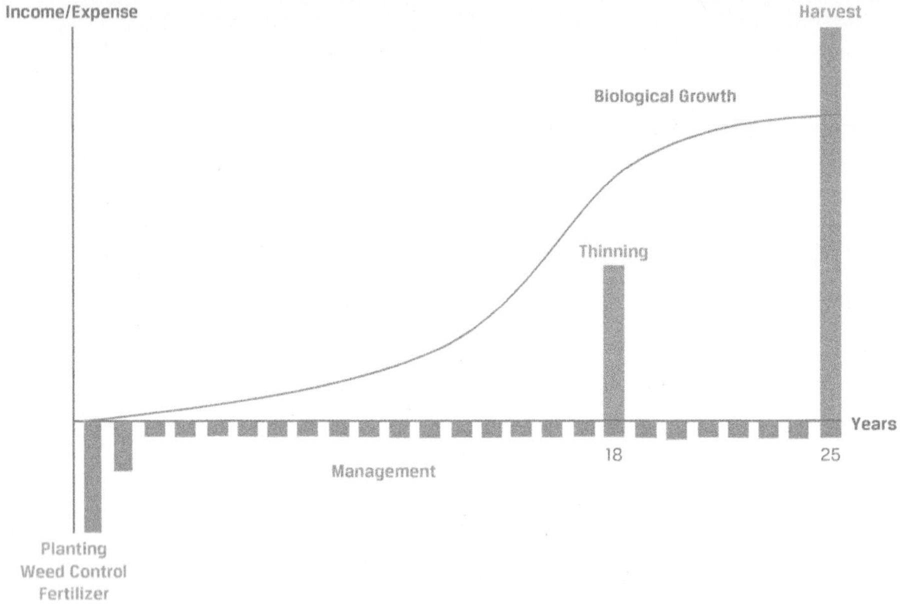

KNOWLEDGE CHECK: PINE PLAINS LLC TIMBER MANAGEMENT PLAN

Pine Plains LLC (PPLLC) is a private investment firm that owns a several thousand–acre pine plantation in the southern United States. PPLLC's 25-year timber rotation plan calls for the reforestation of recently harvested bare land, with thinning planned in 18 years and final harvest in 25 years. PPLLC forestry management establishes the following per-acre estimates of expected revenue and expenses:

Year	Description	USD per acre
Expenses:		
Annual (1–25)	Management fee	4.00
0	Site preparation and planting	500.00
1	Weed control and fertilizer	75.00
Revenues:		
18	Thinning revenue	725.00
25	Final harvest revenue	5,750.00

1. Assuming a 6.5% annual required rate of return, calculate the net present value of PPLLC's timber rotation plan.

   Solution:

   Recall from earlier time-value-of-money lessons that a single cash flow in n periods may be discounted to the present as follows:

$$PV(\text{Cash flow}) = \frac{\text{Cash flow}}{(1+r)^n},$$

where r is the required rate of return and n is the number of periods, and the present value of a series of fixed cash flows is calculated as

$$PV(\text{Series of fixed cash flows}) = \sum_{i=1}^{n} \frac{\text{Cash flow}}{(1+r)^i}.$$

Using r of 6.5%, we can calculate the PV of PPLLC's timber rotation as follows:

Year	Description	USD per acre	PV USD per acre
Annual (1–25)	Management fee	(4.00)	(48.79)
0	Site preparation and planting	(500.00)	(500.00)
1	Weed control and fertilizer	(75.00)	(70.42)
18	Thinning revenue	725.00	233.37
25	Final harvest revenue	5,750.00	1,191.04
	PV of timber rotation plan		USD805.20

Similar to NOI for a developed property, the present value in the prior example represents the return of a timber rotation through final harvest over 25 years. We can calculate the net future value (NFV) of the rotation per acre at the end of the 25-year period to be USD3,887.26:

$$NFV = USD3{,}887.26 = USD805.20 \times (1.065)^{25}.$$

If an acre of land remains in rotation indefinitely with constant costs and revenues, we would expect to earn NFV of USD3,887.26 at the end of each 25-year cycle in perpetuity. Since income is realized over a multiyear cycle rather than annually, we approach timberland valuation differently from other real estate assets by solving for the so-called **land expectation value** (LEV), or the value of an acre of bare land in perpetual timberland production, using the discounting formula for a perpetual periodic annuity, as follows:

$$LEV = \frac{NFV}{(1+r)^t - 1}, \tag{13}$$

where

NFV = Net future value of a single timber rotation

r = Required rate of return

t = Length of timber rotation in years

For example, we may solve for LEV in the case of Pine Plains LLC as follows:

$$LEV = USD1{,}015.56 = \frac{USD3{,}887.26}{(1.065)^{25} - 1}.$$

While LEV provides a valuation based solely on timber rotation cash flows under simple assumptions, in practice, additional factors, such as potential alternative land use or premiums paid by investors to capture carbon credits, may significantly affect timberland prices. As a result, the discounted cash flow approach is often complemented by sales comparisons when similar recent transactions exist.

The unique characteristics of timberland investments may be traced to their biological features. For example, cash flows derived from the harvest and sale of real assets used as inputs in basic industries offer inflation-hedging potential and tend to have low correlations with other asset classes. Forest management techniques may be employed to optimize age distribution of trees, the stocking of species, and the acceleration or deferral of harvests in response to market price changes at little or no cost. Environmental conservation efforts and other constraints on available global timberland supply combined with growing demand for pulp and wood products form the basis for continued demand. Timberland has favorable cyclical characteristics, because growing trees appreciate regardless of economic conditions and the real estate cycle and serve as a long-term inflation hedge as a real asset. Although thinning serves as a form of forest management, timberland owners face biophysical risks from drought, wildfires, pests, and disease. Beyond its attractive risk and return features, investor interest in timberland has also increased due to its environmental, social, and governance–related characteristics. A secondary source of timberland returns is the purchase of forests or carbon credits from forest owners as a form of **carbon offset**. Carbon offsets are investments that reduce or remove carbon dioxide and other greenhouse gases to compensate for emissions produced elsewhere to achieve reduction or net-zero emission goals.

TIMBERLAND INVESTMENTS AS A CARBON OFFSET

While timberland returns are primarily based on the harvest of trees over the growth cycle, the market for carbon offsets has increased financial incentives for timberland owners to leave their trees standing. As government mandates for carbon offsets through cap-and-trade systems continue to develop, many issuers and investors have initiated voluntary carbon offsets to achieve emission reduction targets. For example, carbon emitters such as oil and gas companies are eager to purchase voluntary offsets, while timberland owners may sell these credits in exchange for allowing continued growth in uncut timber.

New market entrants seeking to match buyers and sellers of carbon credits have developed sophisticated approaches to quantifying the carbon benefits of harvest deferral. For example, Natural Capital Exchange (NCX) in the United States combines satellite images with field measurements to establish the size and species of trees in each acre of forest using Microsoft's AI for Earth. Once a property assessment is completed, timberland owners may submit offers to NCX on the number and price of carbon credits they are willing to sell for one year and, once accepted by a bidder, receive compensation following verification of harvest deferral at the end of the year.

Timberland investors face a high degree of illiquidity and must therefore consider these investments as components of a long-term portfolio. The length of the timber growth and harvest cycle and the processing and delivery cycle used to convert raw timber into pulp, paper, and lumber dampen the effect of short-term market fluctuations for finished products. For example, rising market prices for pulpwood and sawtimber may not always be reflected in higher stumpage prices for landowners, as shown in the following example.

SUPPLY FACTORS AND LUMBER PRICES DURING THE COVID-19 PANDEMIC

An earlier example illustrated the sharp rise in US lumber prices during the COVID-19 pandemic. In addition to continued strong demand for lumber in the construction industry due to continued low interest rates and increases in home renovations and new residential building, supply chain issues unique to COVID-19, including a shortage of truck drivers, declining mill capacity caused by worker shortages, and increased safety protocols, were cited as causes for the spike in lumber prices.

Timberland owners, in contrast, receive stumpage prices upon harvest, which have remained largely stable over time and are far less volatile than the final product, which includes labor, transportation, and other processing costs, as shown in Exhibit 11. The exhibit shows stumpage spot and lumber futures prices from 2013 to 2023.

Exhibit 11: US Stumpage Spot Prices vs. Lumber Futures Prices, 2013–2023

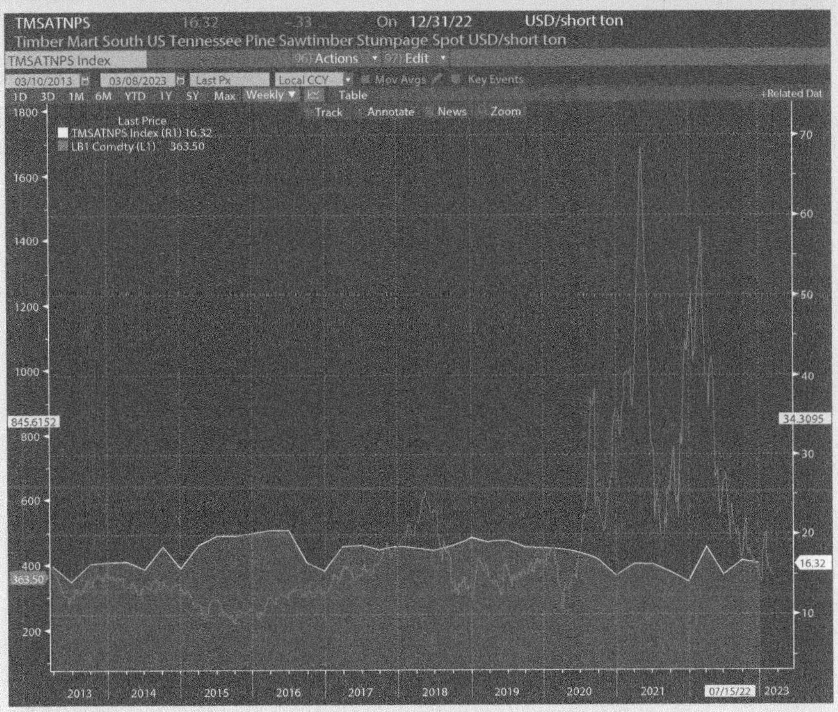

Source: Bloomberg.

The relatively stable Timber Mart South Tennessee Pine Sawtimber Stumpage spot price (TMSATNPS Index) is the US dollar price per ton as shown on the right axis, while the more volatile front-month lumber futures price ("LB1 Comdty") is shown on the left axis in US dollars per 110,000 board feet of random length lumber.

Farmland Investment Characteristics

In contrast to private timberland historically held by forest product companies, traditional farm ownership varies widely across regions, ranging from often smaller, family-owned and -operated farming enterprises in the United States to larger-scale, concentrated agricultural land ownership in such countries as Brazil or state-owned land in developing countries in Africa and Southeast Asia. In contrast to timberland, farmland investments may be of smaller size—perhaps tens or a few hundred acres or hectares. For example, 98% of US farmland is owned by families, excluding corporations, cooperatives, and external managers, and it remains a key source of global family wealth.

While institutional farmland investment has a history similar to that of timberland, with large US investors seeking portfolio diversification, the greater variety of agricultural products and operating models gives rise to a broader investment risk-versus-return spectrum, as shown in Exhibit 12.

Exhibit 12: Farmland Investment Risk/Return Spectrum

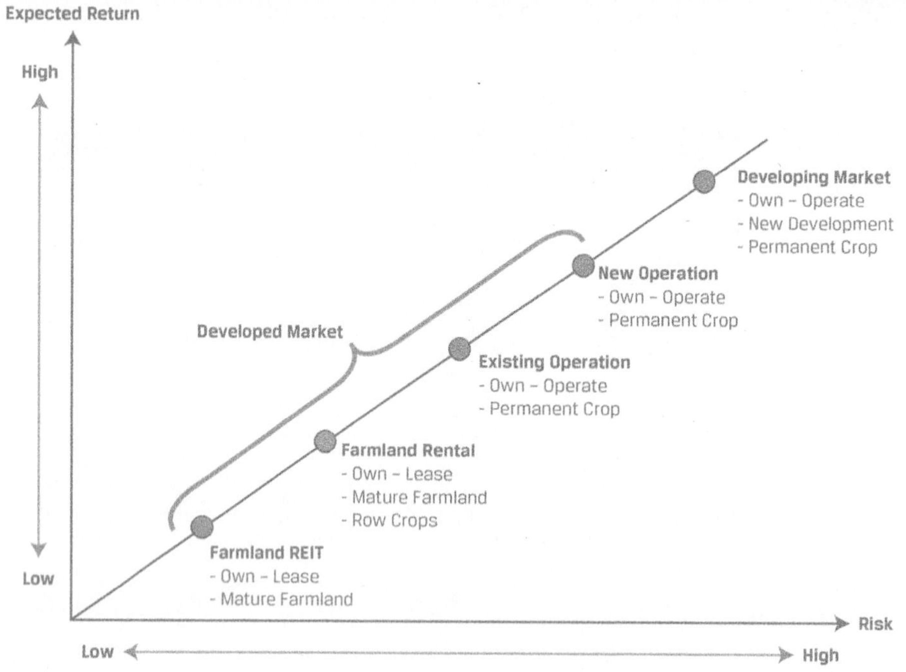

Similar to other forms of real estate, farmland derives its value from current and future economic use. The suitability of land for agricultural production varies widely based on temperature, soil type, rainfall, and available irrigation sources. A shorter growth cycle is measured in seasons for **row crops**, or those harvested annually and rotated, and in years for **permanent crops** planted for many seasons, such as orchards or vineyards, which typically generate a higher return per acre or hectare. Crops are used either directly as a raw material in food production or as an intermediate good when **feed crops**, such as grains, are cultivated for use in raising livestock.

A key distinction in farmland investment is the difference between **own–operate** approach and the **own–lease** approach to farmland ownership. The owner–operator model involves owning land, buildings, equipment, and other assets and operating an agricultural business. Under the own–lease model, far more common among financial investors, an owner or lessor receives fixed rental payments for undeveloped tillable acreage under a multiyear lease agreement from a farm operator lessee who assumes all other business risks. Owner-operated farms and agricultural businesses have cash flow features and risk–return characteristics similar to those of private companies addressed earlier in the curriculum, while own–lease farmland investments earn periodic rent, which offsets property tax, with no other significant income or expenses. As a result, financial returns on own–lease farmland are primarily in the form of capital appreciation instead of income.

The shift to private investable farmland began among tax-exempt pensions and other investors for several reasons, including

- portfolio diversification,
- long-term capital appreciation,
- an inflation hedge, and
- a relative lack of correlation with the economic cycle.

Steady and growing demand for food and other plant- and animal-based raw materials combined with government policies ensure stable demand for agricultural land use. Examples of government intervention in agriculture include production supports, subsidies, and other programs under the Common Agricultural Policy of the European Union, as well as US Renewable Fuel Standards mandating and subsidizing the production of biofuels from corn and other plants, which represents 10% of the country's gasoline supply. While farmland generally lacks the degree of carbon capture available from timberland, opportunities to reduce carbon emissions include environmental protection via expanded conservation areas; sustainable farming practices, such as reduced tillage; and soil and water protection.

Unlike other vacant land, farmland generates positive cash flow in the form of land leases less taxes with no capital improvements necessary, while also granting an owner a perpetual option to develop the property for an alternative economic use in the future. In addition to the inflation-hedging properties of tillable land whose economic use is based on the value of real assets, such as crops, the option to rezone and repurpose a property may be particularly valuable if land prices are volatile or the property is subject to increasing urban density or greater proximity to transportation infrastructure.

QUESTION SET

1. DugFir LLC is a private investor in timberland throughout the western United States. The firm intends to spend USD400 per acre today for site preparation and planting and an additional USD90 per acre on weed control and fertilizer in one year and expects thinning revenue of USD500 per acre in 15 years and harvest revenue of USD7,000 per acre in 25 years. Its annual management fee is USD3 per acre. Which of the following is closest to the correct land expectation value per acre (LEV) of this proposed timberland development assuming an 8% required return?

   A. USD664

   B. USD778

   C. USD815

   Solution:

   The correct response is B. The present value of the rotation plan is USD664.39 and may be calculated as the sum of its components, shown and summarized in the table that appears later in this solution.

   We can solve for the present value of the annual USD3.00 management fee as –32.02 in several ways—namely, as the PV of a series of cash flows:

   $$\text{PV(Series of fixed cash flows)} = \sum_{i=1}^{n} \frac{\text{Cash Flow}}{(1+r)^i} = \sum_{i=1}^{25} \frac{\text{USD3.00}}{(1+0.08)^{25}}.$$

   We can also use the same annuity calculation used for mortgage payments earlier by solving for the principal:

   $$A = \frac{r \times \text{Principal}}{1-(1+r)^{-n}};\ \text{USD3.00} = \frac{0.08 \times \text{Principal}}{1-(1+0.08)^{-25}}.$$

   Or we can use the Excel PV function [=PV(*rate,nper,pmt,[fv],[type]*)], or PV(0.08,25,3,0,0).

   All other fees and returns are single-period PV calculations:

   $$\text{Weed control and fertilizer costs: (USD83.33)} = \frac{\text{(USD90)}}{1.08}.$$

Thinning revenue: $\text{USD157.62} = \dfrac{\text{USD500}}{(1.08)^{15}}.$

Final harvest revenue: $\text{USD1,022.13} = \dfrac{\text{USD7,000}}{(1.08)^{25}}.$

Year	Description	Cost/return per acre	PV USD per acre
Annual (1–25)	Management fee	(3.00)	(32.02)
0	Site preparation and planting	(400.00)	(400.00)
1	Weed control and fertilizer	(90.00)	(83.33)
15	Thinning revenue	500.00	157.62
25	Final harvest revenue	7,000.00	1,022.13
	PV of timber rotation plan		USD664.39

Solve for the land expectation value by first calculating the net future value in the numerator of Equation 13 as follows:

$$\text{LEV} = \frac{\text{NFV}}{(1+r)^t - 1}.$$

The NFV of USD664.39 at the end of 25 years is equal to USD4,550.05 [= USD664.39 × $(1.08)^{25}$]. Dividing this amount by $(1.08)^{25} - 1$ yields an LEV result of USD777.99.

2. Which of the following valuation approaches is unlikely to apply to timberland?

   A. Sales comparison approach

   B. Cost approach

   C. Discounted cash flow approach

   Solution:

   The correct response is B. Unlike developed real estate, the asset (timber) cannot be bought and constructed; thus, the cost approach does not apply to timberland. Both the sales comparison and discounted cash flow approaches are typically used for valuing timberland, so responses A and C are incorrect.

3. Explain why short-term fluctuations in finished wood products, such as lumber, may not translate into similar fluctuations in stumpage fees.

   Solution:

   The length of the timber growth and harvest cycle and the processing and delivery cycle used to convert raw timber into pulp, paper, and lumber dampen the effect of short-term market fluctuations for finished products on stumpage fees. As an example, the sawtimber must be processed at a mill and then transported to a building site. If labor costs rise considerably, due to shortages of skilled labor for staffing mills and driving trucks, the price of lumber may increase significantly while stumpage fees for the sawtimber remain stable.

PRIVATE REAL ESTATE RISK AND RETURN

6

☐ discuss the risk and return among private real estate investments and as compared to other investments as part of a strategic asset allocation

Real estate investments were characterized in earlier learning modules as a source of diversification from public fixed-income and equity securities, a hedge against inflation as a real asset, and a source of cash flows and enhanced return due to their illiquid nature. While largely public and private core and core-plus investments consist of income-producing properties, value-add and opportunistic real estate returns primarily involve capital appreciation by increasing value through the upgrade of a property's economic use or creation of new capacity.

Institutional investors—such as pensions and sovereign wealth funds—and ultra-high-net-worth individuals or family offices are usually best suited to accommodate the larger investment sizes, lack of liquidity, and longer and less certain time horizons associated with private real estate. These investors align their allocation to such investments with their risk tolerance, return objectives, and market expectations, as demonstrated in the following case study.

CASE STUDY

XGT's Real Estate Investment Strategy

XGT, a large developed-market public pension plan, has the following investment policy for real assets, including real estate by segment:

Real Assets: Real Estate 15% (± 3%)

Inflation Sensitive 5% (± 3%)

Suballocation (Real Estate): Core 60% (± 5%)

Value-Add 20% (± 5%)

Opportunistic 20% (± 5%)

1. Benchmark and Restrictions

The portfolio benchmark is the NCREIF Open End Diversified Core Equity (ODCE) index net of fees. Portfolio allocations seek a long-term return in excess of the benchmark while remaining within target ranges.

2. Core Real Estate

Core investments include stable, well-diversified, income-producing properties in developed markets expected to produce a return net of fees of 7% per annum. Core portfolio leverage is limited to 40% of total asset value.

3. Value-Add Real Estate

Value-add investments include repositioned, renovated, or redeveloped properties with expected risk and return that exceed the expected risk and return of core real estate. These investments are expected to have limited income and greater capital appreciation, with expected return net of fees of 8% per annum. Value-add portfolio leverage is limited to 60% of total asset value.

4. Opportunistic Real Estate

Opportunistic real estate investments focus on development, extensive redevelopment, and land development and may include international or emerging markets. Opportunistic investments are expected to return 10% per annum net of fees, with portfolio diversification and leverage to be vetted individually in the due diligence process.

XGT's Investment Committee is considering changes to its allocation between value-add and opportunistic segments given expected distributions over the next six months. Following an extended period of low borrowing costs, rising rents, and new construction growth, XGT's investment consultant forecasts higher interest rates and an economic slowdown in the next 12–24 months.

1. Discuss XGT's decision between increasing value-add or opportunistic portfolio allocations in light of the consultant's economic forecast.

   Solution:

   Value-add and opportunistic investments entail the greater risk and return of upgrading or changing a property's economic use, which also involves higher leverage compared to core real estate. Under the consultant's forecast scenario, higher rates and a pending real estate market slowdown increase debt financing costs and required cap rates and reduce the income-producing potential of properties once completed. While value-add projects usually involve property redevelopment with existing current income and shorter development periods, opportunistic real estate investments typically involve initial negative income with greater leverage and the highest project risk as a project nears completion, magnifying the importance of real estate cycle timing as an economic value driver. This suggests that an increased allocation to value-add as opposed to opportunistic real estate is warranted under this scenario.

The prior case study illustrates the risk-versus-return trade-off across various real estate investments and over the property development life cycle.

General partners seek to construct an optimally diversified asset portfolio of value-add or opportunistic assets across different geographies, asset types, and expected cash flow timing designed to maximize the likelihood of achieving investor hurdle rates or preferred rates of return. Investors comparing the risk and return among private real estate investments to other private market opportunities typically focus on expected IRR, as shown earlier, or a simpler **multiple of invested capital** (MOIC), or money multiple, on total invested capital (or paid-in capital). This calculation ignores the timing of cash inflows and outflows, is typically calculated on a gross basis ignoring fees, and simply compares the total value of all realized investments and residual asset values (assets that may still be awaiting sale) relative to capital invested:

$$\text{MOIC} = (\text{Realized value of investment} + \text{Unrealized value of investment})/\text{Total invested capital}. \quad (14)$$

These return metrics are used to compare private real estate to other private investments, portfolio benchmarks, or target returns, as illustrated in the following case study.

CASE STUDY

XGT's Kingston Tower Investment

XGT's Investment Committee decides to increase its value-add private real estate allocation following the recommendation of its consultant, choosing an LP investment that includes the Kingston Tower project described earlier, an office tower conversion into apartments and coworking space. The GP investor expects the following cash flows during renovation and upon completion:

- Year 1: Assume NOI_1 of CAD2,200,000.
- Year 2: Renovation costs exceed NOI_2, net cash flow of –CAD2,000,000.
- Year 3: Renovation costs exceed NOI_3, net cash flow of –CAD2,000,000.
- Year 4: Stabilized base-case NOI_4 of CAD6,412,500 at 95% occupancy.

The GP plans to sell Kingston Tower at the end of three years at an expected property value of CAD37,720,588 assuming a 17% cap rate:

$$\text{Property value} = \frac{\text{Expected NOI}_4}{\text{Capitalization rate}}.$$

$$\text{CAD37,720,588} = \frac{\text{CAD6,412,500}}{0.17}.$$

GP fees include a 1% annual management fee plus a 20% performance fee determined at the end of the holding period based on property appreciation if the investment return after management fees exceeds a 10% hurdle rate. For purposes of this example, assume that Kingston Tower is purchased for CAD20,000,000 in Year 0 and the investment is financed by equity, with no further transaction costs.

1. Solve for XGT's base-case MOIC.

   Solution:

   Solve for MOIC using Equation 14:

   MOIC = (Realized value of investment + Unrealized value of investment)/Total invested capital.

   Given the expected sale of Kingston Tower at the end of Year 3, unrealized investment value is zero, with the MOIC equal to the sum of cash inflows divided by cash outflows, as follows:

   Cash inflows: NOI_1 + (Expected property value)4

   Cash outflows: (Purchase price)0 + NOI2 + NOI3

   $$\text{MOIC} = 1.663 = \frac{2,200,000 + 37,720,588}{20,000,000 + 2,000,000 + 2,000,000}.$$

2. Calculate XGT's base-case IRR both before and after fees.

   Solution:

   Using the Excel IRR function [=IRR(*values,guess*)] as shown earlier and the cash flows in the following table,

Year 0	Year 1	Year 2	Year 3
(20,000,000)	2,200,000	(2,000,000)	35,720,588

we can solve for IRR *before* fees, equal to 22.28%:

22.28% = IRR(-20000000,2200000,-2000000,35720588).

To solve for IRR *after* fees, we incorporate both the 1% annual management fee and the 20% performance fee to obtain net cash flows, as follows.

Year	Year 0	Year 1	Year 2	Year 3
Gross	(20,000,000)	2,200,000	(2,000,000)	35,720,588
1% Mgmt. Fee		(200,000)	(200,000)	(200,000)
20% Perf. Fee				(3,544,118)
Net Cash Flow	(20,000,000)	2,000,000	(2,200,000)	31,976,470

The 20% performance fee is CAD3,544,118, or 0.2 × (37,720,588 – 20,000,000).

We can solve for IRR *after* fees, equal to 17.14%:

17.14% = IRR(-20000000,2000000,-2200000,31976471).

3. Determine the breakeven Kingston Tower property value required at the end of Year 3 in order for XGT to meet the return requirements as stated in its value-add real estate investment policy.

Solution:

Recall from XGT's investment policy that value-add real estate is expected to earn a return of 8% per annum net of fees. We must therefore solve for an expected property value at the end of Year 3 that gives us an IRR *after* fees of 8%. Note that since the 8% IRR falls below the 10% hurdle rate required for the 20% performance fee to apply, the GP will earn only the 1% management fee. We therefore must solve for the gross cash flow in Year 3 given an 8% IRR after fees, as shown in the following table:

Year	Year 0	Year 1	Year 2	Year 3
Gross	(20,000,000)	2,200,000	(2,000,000)	? + (2,000,000)
1% Mgmt. Fee		(200,000)	(200,000)	(200,000)
Net Cash Flow	(20,000,000)	2,000,000	(2,200,000)	? + (2,200,000)

As shown previously, we can use the Excel IRR function, entering an estimated value for Year 3 net cash flow [= (Expected property value)$_3$ – 2,200,000) and solving for IRR, and then use the Goal Seek function to iterate a new solution for the Year 3 net cash flow for which the IRR of all net cash flows is 8%.

For example, assume that the property may be sold at the end of Year 4 for CAD28,200,000 with a Year 3 net cash flow of CAD26,000,000. Solve for IRR:

9.11% = IRR(-20000000,2000000,-2200000,-2600000).

Using Goal Seek to solve for an IRR of 8% by changing Year 3 net cash flow, we arrive at a Year 3 net cash flow of CAD25,248,590. Given that this includes the expected property value and NOI_3 of –CAD2,000,000 and CAD200,000 in management fees, we can solve for an expected property value of CAD27,448,590, or CAD25,248,000 + CAD2,200,000.

4. Interpret the breakeven property value from Question 3 in the context of the investment consultant's forecast, the earlier scenario analysis, and the sensitivity analysis in Exhibit 8.

Solution:

Based on project assumptions including Kingston Tower's expected purchase price, renovation costs, and cash flow, including the capitalization rate used to solve for the future sale price based on stabilized Year 4 NOI, XGT is expected to reach its target 8% return after fees if the property can be sold for at least CAD27,448,590 at the end of three years.

Given the investment consultant's forecast of a likely economic downturn, it makes sense to consider this expected property value in the context of the downside case established earlier by the LP analyst, under which it was assumed that coworking space rent would equal just CAD45 per ft^2 and residential rent would equal CAD50 per ft^2 in Year 4. However, the expected IRR from the earlier calculation is not directly comparable given the assumed higher purchase price and the absence of fees. Instead, we may consider the property value sensitivity analysis in Exhibit 8 based on different coworking and residential rental rates, which shows an expected property value at the end of Year 3 of CAD25,955,882 based on these downside-case assumptions. This suggests that XGT will fail to reach its minimum 8% return after fees under the downside case proposed by the analyst. We may confirm this by recalculating IRR after fees using the lower sale price of CAD25,955,882 at the end of three years and deducting –CAD2,000,000 Year 3 NOI and the CAD200,000 management fee for a Year 3 net cash flow of CAD23,755,882:

5.77% = IRR(-20000000,2000000,-2200000,23755882).

This example and those that precede it demonstrate the application of valuation tools along with scenario and sensitivity analysis used by financial analysts in practice to thoroughly evaluate the expected risk and return of these investments. When carefully and consistently applied in the context of investment policies and market analysis, private real estate investments can play an important role in meeting investor objectives and goals.

QUESTION SET

1. Which of the following real estate classifications is likely to have the highest return expectation?

   A. Value-add real estate

   B. Opportunistic real estate

   C. Core real estate

Solution:

The correct response is B. Opportunistic real estate, because of its focus on initial development of properties, carries the highest levels of risk in private real estate investing. Its returns are focused on the capital appreciation of the project during its development phase. Value-add real estate is riskier than core real estate; however, value-add projects are less likely to be in the development cycle for as long as opportunistic ones. Core real estate includes established income-producing properties and, as such, carries the lowest risk and return expectations among the major real estate categories.

The following information relates to Questions 2 and 3.

Alyssa Tan at Asiastruct approaches the Bangkok residential project analysis in earlier question sets from a different perspective, using the following simplified details:

Assume the property requires an investment of THB54,000,000 over the two years of property development and construction. Asiastruct contributes THB24,000,000 initially and an additional THB30,000,000 at the beginning of the second year. At the beginning of the third year, the property begins operations, with NOI of THB6,093,360 during the third year. Asiastruct is planning to sell the property upon its opening at the beginning of the third year, assuming a cap rate of 10%. Given that this project is an opportunistic investment, Asiastruct has return expectations of 10% net of fees.

2. Calculate the real estate investor's MOIC and IRR, and discuss the associated implications for Asiastruct as a result of these calculations.

Solution:

First, use the third-year NOI and the cap rate to compute an expected selling price of the property of THB60,933,600 at the end of the second year. The cash flows are as follows:

Year	0	1	2
Cash flows (THB)	(24,000,000.00)	(30,000,000.00)	60,933,600.00

MOIC = 60,933,600/54,000,000 = 1.13.

IRR can be calculated using the IRR function in Excel to arrive at IRR of 8.66%. Without comparable property MOICs to use for comparison purposes, it is impossible to assess the relative attractiveness of the MOIC of 1.13.

The IRR provides a better comparison because this measurement accounts for the timing of cash flows and can be compared more directly to return requirements. Given that the investor expects a 10% return on opportunistic real estate investments net of fees, it is clear that the 8.66% IRR (before fees) makes the Bangkok project economically unattractive.

3. Analyze how much improvement would be necessary in the Bangkok project's NOI to reach a 10% IRR (before fees).

Solution:

While this analysis may be solved by trial and error, the Goal Seek function in Excel allows for a quick solution methodology. The set cell is the one in which the IRR function is solved. Set the desired value to 10.00%, and allow the project NOI to change. If the Bangkok project NOI can be improved to THB6,203,806, then the 10% return can be met (ignoring fees). This is a 1.81% improvement in NOI, and the investor would need to assess the feasibility of such an increase.

PRACTICE PROBLEMS

The following information relates to questions 1-5

Northern States, a US multi-employer pension plan with USD80 billion in assets, has the following investment policy for real assets, including real estate by segment:

Real Assets: Real Estate 15% (± 3%)

Inflation Sensitive 5% (± 3%)

Suballocation (Real Estate): Core 60% (± 5%)

Value-Add 20% (± 5%)

Opportunistic 20% (± 5%)

Northern States' investment committee is discussing its planned real estate and real assets portfolio weights for the coming year.

The consensus view of committee members regarding the economy and the market for residential housing is summarized by the following two statements:

Statement 1	The US national economy is currently in or nearing a recession.
Statement 2	The lack of residential housing supply is a major concern for US adults.

The discussion shifted to Northern States' suballocations within real estate. Given the committee's expectations of a recession, they decided to maintain the current weight on core real estate while calling for a vote to re-allocate between value-add and opportunistic real estate.

The conversation turned to the due diligence process involved in opportunistic projects. The pension plan participates in all its private real estate investments as an LP. The investment committee's risk guidelines for participation as an LP include strict covenants regarding LTV and DSC for the GPs of all private real estate investments. The committee members discussed whether they should consider changes to the LTV and DSC guidelines in light of the economic climate.

Committee members also discussed the valuation environment in private real estate. Due to the residential housing supply situation, properties that were typically selling at high prices (based on price per square foot) using sales comparison valuation approaches tended to produce high valuations, while valuations of the same properties using direct capitalization approaches tended to produce lower value estimates.

The final discussion topic of the investment committee involves the pension plan's investments in timberland. Recently, lumber prices had become quite volatile, and some members of the committee suggested that they would prefer to reduce the plan's exposure to timberland investments as a result.

1. Which two phases of the real estate cycle are most likely reflected by Statements 1 and 2?

   A. Oversupply and recession

   B. Recession and recovery

C. Recession and expansion

2. Contrast the relative risks of private value-add versus opportunistic real estate suballocations faced by Northern States given its market view.

3. Which of the following would be the most appropriate changes to Northern States' LTV and DSC risk guidelines in the current economic climate?
   A. Increase LTV and decrease DSC benchmarks.
   B. Decrease LTV and increase DSC benchmarks.
   C. Increase LTV and increase DSC benchmarks.

4. Which of the following is the most likely argument for the discrepancy between the sales comparison and direct capitalization valuation approaches?
   A. Direct capitalization approach cap rates are currently too low.
   B. Rental revenues are strong in most housing markets around the country.
   C. The residential housing supply is temporarily too low.

5. Provide a counterargument to the statement made by committee members regarding the volatility of lumber prices and its effect on timber investments.

The following information relates to questions 6-9

BFW Invest Considers an Opportunistic Project

Sylvia Steinhaeuser, managing director of BFW Invest, a European fund with EUR12 billion in assets under management, is considering a new construction opportunity on a one-acre (43,560 ft^2) property in Lisbon, Portugal. The project is expected to cost EUR5,000,000 and generate NOI of EUR540,000 in its first full year of operation following a two-year construction period. BFW has recently hired Sven Walters as a new analyst, and Steinhaeuser has asked him to evaluate this as his initial project. Steinhaeuser introduces Walters to the process of opportunistic private real estate investment by describing several aspects of this type of investment and follows up with a series of questions.

Steinhaeuser begins the discussion of how new construction projects are financed. She learns that Walters is already familiar with publicly traded REIT projects but has had little exposure to new construction financing.

Portugal has become very popular with immigrants from other EU countries settling in the country as remote workers and retirees, and the conversation turns to the current state of the Lisbon rental market. Given the influx of new residents, developers are seeking opportunities to add rental housing in Lisbon.

Steinhaeuser turns her attention to valuation issues. The plan is to incur 50% of project cost immediately and the remaining 50% in one year. She informs Walters that the cap rate assumed upon completion will be 9.2%. BFW currently uses a 10% hurdle rate for new construction projects.

Steinhaeuser addresses possible risks that would adversely affect project return. For example, labor issues could easily delay the completion of construction, while inflation and the rising cost of construction materials could easily cause returns to fall below the project's base-case projections. Steinhaeuser mentions that, while unlikely, construction delays could potentially postpone the opening of the building by as much as one full year.

6. Describe two differences between the financing for a new construction project as compared with the acquisition of an existing income-producing property.
7. Identify the most likely current stage of the real estate cycle in Lisbon, and explain one possible risk associated with a new construction project in this market phase.
8. Based on the current assumptions regarding project cost, the construction schedule, future NOI, and the cap rate, calculate the IRR of the Lisbon project and evaluate the economic feasibility of this project.
9. Calculate the percentage by which NOI would need to increase if construction delays cause a one-year delay in the opening of the building (assuming all other assumptions remain the same with no cash flows in Year 2) for the building project to meet BFW Invest's hurdle rate.

The following information relates to questions 10-13

BFW Invest Considers a Value-Add Project

Because Sylvia Steinhaeuser at BFW Invest has been impressed with Sven Walter's work on the Lisbon project, she assigns him to another transaction in which the fund will buy an existing office building in Madrid slated for conversion to high-end residential apartments with retail space on the ground floor. The fund's hurdle rate on the project is 10%. Under its current use as office space, expected NOI during the next year is EUR1,400,000.

The purchase price is EUR15,000,000, and during the first year, Steinhaeuser estimates that NOI will be EUR1,000,000 as existing leases expire and office tenants relocate. Renovation will start in the second year, with net cash outflows of EUR4,000,000. New residential tenants are expected to occupy selected upper floors during the third year as renovation continues on lower floors, with net cash outflow of EUR1,000,000. By the end of Year 3, renovation is expected to be complete, with expected Year 4 NOI of EUR3,000,000 and expected property value after full renovation at the end of three years of EUR28,000,000.

After presenting the basic facts of the project, Steinhaeuser asks Walters about a contrast between this sort of renovation project and the new construction project that they recently discussed.

The analyst raises the issue of the possible effect of a recession on the renovation project returns. Steinhaeuser implies that such conditions may warrant an indefinite delay to the renovation. In such a case, the fund would plan to continue to operate the building in its current use as an office building.

Steinhaeuser realizes that she has not discussed the fund's fee structure with Walters. As a general partner, the fund charges annual management fees of 1.5% based on the size of initial investment and a performance fee of 20% based on returns in excess of the hurdle rate at the end of a three-year holding period. The performance fee is earned only if the investment performance exceeds a 10% hurdle rate, which occurs if Year 3 returns before fees are EUR23,153,000. The project will be financed only with equity and no additional transaction costs.

Steinhaeuser has noticed that the market for buildings in Madrid recently had been showing increased competition among buyers for the sort of property under consideration. As a result, she believes that a winning bid may need to exceed EUR15,000,000. She asks Walters to assess the maximum price that the fund could consider paying for the building.

10. Contrast the source of returns between a renovation project and a new construction project.

11. Evaluate whether the Madrid building purchase is economically feasible for the BFW Invest fund if it continues to operate as an office building.

12. Calculate the annual management fee and the performance fee for the Madrid property, and determine whether the after-fee performance of the investment meets BFW Invest's hurdle rate.

13. Determine the maximum price that BFW Invest could pay for the Madrid property while incorporating management fees.

SOLUTIONS

1. B is correct. Recession and recovery are both characterized by a lack of new construction that may likely result in an undersupply of residential housing. Response A is incorrect because the oversupply phase of the real estate cycle is less likely to coincide with a lack of housing. Response C is incorrect because these two phases of the real estate cycle do not coincide with one another; expansion usually moves into an oversupply phase prior to a recession.

2. Value-add real estate projects involve refurbishing or repurposing an existing income-producing property, while opportunistic real estate involves substantial development, such as new construction or redevelopment. Although both types of private real estate involve greater risk than stable income-producing properties included in core real estate, value-add properties typically generate income over some or all of the redevelopment phase, while opportunistic real estate usually generates no cash inflows until the project is complete and is likely to involve greater exposure to future lease rates upon completion. As a result, value-add real estate provides a less risky asset allocation during a recession.

3. B is correct. LTV refers to the loan to value ratio, with a higher LTV implying greater financial leverage and therefore higher risk. DSC refers to the debt service coverage ratio, with a lower ratio reflecting fewer resources available to service debt obligations and therefore greater risk. Given Northern States' expectation of a recession, the investment committee is most likely to amend its guidelines to reduce risk by lowering LTV and raising DSC requirements.

4. C is the best response. The lack of residential housing supply likely creates more competition between potential buyers, thus driving prices above what might be indicated by an income-based valuation model. Response B suggests that the NOI in direct capitalization models would be high, thus making the associated valuations high (not low). Response A also implies high valuations from a direct capitalization model.

5. As long-term investments that derive their value from the harvest of raw materials over the timber harvest cycle, timberland investment income is more closely related to the level of stumpage fees as opposed to lumber prices. Stumpage fees are much less volatile than lumber prices, because lumber is a finished product that also reflects costs associated with processing and transportation. For example, labor shortages throughout the supply chain can create lumber supply shocks while stumpage fees remain relatively constant.

   An additional revenue source from timberland investments comes from the purchase of carbon offsets in which carbon emitters pay timberland owners to delay harvests, which is similarly unaffected by lumber prices.

6. The first key difference relates to the timing of the financing. To purchase an income-producing building, the full proceeds of equity and debt financing must be available at the time of acquisition. A new construction project, in contrast, usually draws upon financing sources over time throughout the land acquisition and construction phases of the project based on the achievement of project milestones. Nevertheless, financing should be committed in advance.

   The second difference relates to the type of financing. The purchase of existing income-producing property usually involves a mortgage loan secured by the existing property. In the case of a new construction project, developers often initially draw upon an acquisition and development loan to finance the land acquisition and a construction and development loan to finance project construction costs. As the building nears completion, developers often replace these loans with a mortgage loan secured by the property.

7. Given the local market dynamics described by Steinhaeuser, it is most likely that the Lisbon market is in an expansion phase of the real estate cycle. A possible risk related to this stage of the real estate cycle is that Lisbon may move to an oversupply stage by the time the project is completed.

8. The expected project cash flows are as follows:

Year	0	1	2
Cash flows	(2,500,000)	(2,500,000)	5,869,565

The first two cash flows reflect construction costs, while the Year 2 cash flow is the expected value of the completed building using the direct capitalization method. We may calculate this using Equation 3 based on Year 3 NOI of EUR540,000 and the cap rate of 9.2%:

$$\text{Property value} = \frac{\text{Expected NOI}}{\text{Capitalization rate}}.$$

$$\text{EUR5,869,565} = \frac{\text{EUR540,000}}{9.2\%}.$$

Determine the economic feasibility of the project by comparing the IRR to BFW's 10% hurdle rate. Using the Excel IRR function [=IRR(-2500000,-250000000,5869565)], we may solve for the project IRR of 11.18%.

Because the IRR is greater than the hurdle rate, the Lisbon project appears to be economically feasible.

9. The construction delay shifts the final project cash flow from the end of Year 2 to the end of Year 3. We can solve for the Year 3 cash flow that generates a 10% hurdle rate using a trial-and-error process or the Excel Goal Seek function and confirm that the Excel IRR function [=IRR(-2500000,-2500000,0,6352717)] gives us a result of 10%. The original and revised cash flows are as follows:

Year	0	1	2	3
Original cash flows	(2,500,000)	(2,500,000)	5,869,565	—
Revised cash flows	(2,500,000)	(2,500,000)	—	6,352,717
IRR	10.00%			

Given a Year 3 cash flow of EUR6,352,717, we can show that Year 3 NOI (and expected building value) would need to be 8.23% higher than that in Year 2 for the project to achieve a 10% IRR:

8.23% = 6,352,717/5,869,565 – 1.

10. Value-add and opportunistic private real estate investments are less focused on the income component of returns (the primary component of public real estate investment returns) and are more focused on the potential for capital appreciation during the development phase of the project. A significant contrast between a renovation project compared to a new construction project is that renovation projects may allow for cash inflows after the building is purchased while a new construction project is purely focused on the potential for capital appreciation. This contrast may be important in that after a building is purchased for renovation, the buyer may find that deteriorating economic conditions make it prefer-

able to continue operating a building as is until the real estate market reaches a recovery phase.

11. Based on the expected NOI of EUR1,400,000 for the Madrid building during the next year and a purchase price of EUR15,000,000, the project return can be calculated using Equation 2:

    Project return = NOI/Project cost,

    which is just 9.33% (= 1,400,000/15,000,000). Since this return falls below BFW Invest's hurdle rate of 10%, the Madrid building purchase is not economically feasible for BFW Invest if it is expected to operate indefinitely under its current use in the current rental market. In order for the property purchase to reach the hurdle rate, BFW would have to either lower its offer price or consider the possibility of a delayed renovation if the market improves in the analysis.

12. The annual management fee is EUR225,000 per year (= 1.5% × 15,000,000).

    To calculate the performance fee, we must first solve for cash flow at the end of the three-year holding period, which combines the EUR28,000,000 expected sale price and the net cash outflow of EUR1,000,000 in Year 3.

    Year 3 cash flow: EUR27,000,000 = 28,000,000 – 1,000,000.

    The performance fee is therefore

    EUR769,400 = 20% × (27,000,000 – 23,153,000).

    The before-tax cash flow, fees, and after-tax cash flow are as follows:

Year	0	1	2	3
Cash flows before fees	(15,000,000)	1,000,000	(4,000,000)	27,000,000
Fees		(225,000)	(225,000)	(994,400)
Cash flows after fees	(15,000,000)	775,000	(4,225,000)	26,005,600

    Use the Excel IRR function to calculate the IRR after fees:

    13.96% = IRR(-15000000,775000,-4225000,26005600).

    The resulting IRR after fees is 13.96%, which exceeds BFW's hurdle rate.

13. Because an earlier question also involved the calculation of the Madrid project IRR after fees, we can use the same information to determine the purchase price (or Year 0 cash outflow) using the Excel IRR function for which the IRR equals BFW Invest's 10% hurdle rate:

    10% = IRR(*Year 0 cash flow*,775000,-4225000,26005600).

    We can solve for the purchase price (or Year 0 cash flow) as EUR16,750,000 using trial and error or the Excel Goal Seek function. The cash flows are as follows:

Year	0	1	2	3
Cash flows before fees	(15,000,000)	1,000,000	(4,000,000)	27,000,000
Fees		(225,000)	(225,000)	(994,400)
Cash flows after fees with IRR = 13.96%	(15,000,000)	775,000	(4,225,000)	26,005,600
Cash flows after fees with IRR = 10%	(16,750,000)	775,000	(4,225,000)	26,005,600

LEARNING MODULE

7

Infrastructure

LEARNING OUTCOMES

Mastery	*The candidate should be able to:*
☐	discuss important infrastructure investment features
☐	discuss infrastructure investment methods and investment vehicles and their uses
☐	discuss the infrastructure investment process over the project life cycle and the roles of infrastructure debt and equity financing
☐	discuss the due diligence and valuation processes for infrastructure investments
☐	discuss the risk and return among infrastructure investments and as compared to other investments as part of a strategic asset allocation

INTRODUCTION

1

Infrastructure investments involve capital-intensive, long-lived assets whose underlying economic use is associated with the provision of essential services, such as transportation or power generation.

While sovereign, regional, and local governments borrow and levy taxes to build and operate infrastructure assets using public funds, our focus in this learning module is the features, structures, process, due diligence, valuation, and portfolio characteristics of private unlisted infrastructure investments. As of October 2022, private unlisted infrastructure remained the fourth largest private asset class after private equity, private debt, and real estate, with over USD1.25 trillion in global assets under management (AUM). This private asset class is forecast by the alternative investment data company Preqin to reach USD1.9 trillion by 2027, approaching the size of private real estate AUM.

Infrastructure investments are characterized by unique, often project-based structures with distinct cash flows and risk and return characteristics resulting from contractual or regulatory arrangements associated with public use. Like other private assets, infrastructure assets are typically large and illiquid—in some cases, involving existing government assets that are privatized, and in other cases, involving new assets built, operated, and often transferred to public use at the end of a predefined operating period.

In this reading, we first distinguish important features of private infrastructure. Infrastructure assets share similar life-cycle characteristics with private real estate but have important differences. As in the case of private real estate, these investments involve an initial development phase with negative cash flows, followed by a longer operating period over which costs are recovered and returns are generated. That said, the inability to repurpose single-use, long-lived infrastructure assets often means that their value is solely derived from contractual or regulatory relationships that govern their specific economic use in providing essential services. These relationships usually dictate the capital structure and investment process for debt and equity investors. While infrastructure assets are usually far less liquid and adaptable to other economic uses than non-infrastructure investments, they often benefit from inelastic demand, direct or indirect subsidies, or competitive and regulatory constraints that reduce business and operating risks. The use of special purpose entities to allocate project risks among public and private entities gives rise to unique due diligence challenges and distinctive risk and return features. Long-term stable cash flows from infrastructure investments combine bond- and equity-like characteristics that drive market-based valuation approaches and define their role in a strategic asset allocation.

LEARNING MODULE OVERVIEW

- Infrastructure investments are single-use, long-lived assets that may be classified on the basis of the inherent business risk faced by investors. The business risk depends on the specific security's place in the capital structure and its claim on cash flows of the underlying project, as well as the project type, corporate governance features, and geoeconomic exposure.
- Single-asset infrastructure companies typically involve a special purpose company with debt and equity investments closely tied to specific commercial contracts, while investments in entities engaged in multiple projects are more closely aligned with a corporate structure.
- Unlike private equity or real estate investments, which typically seek an exit in several years following capital appreciation due to restructuring or development, infrastructure investments that use a build–operate–transfer structure transfer their assets at the end of an operating period and therefore have a terminal value of zero.
- Due diligence challenges unique to infrastructure investments include jurisdictional, legal, and regulatory considerations; technical aspects of the engineering, procurement, and construction phase; and the commercial terms of their operation as defined by contractual or regulatory relationships.
- Given the unique and illiquid nature of infrastructure assets, valuation approaches generally focus on discounting expected cash flows over the commercial term using risk-adjusted discount rates.
- Because infrastructure assets are characterized by a relatively high payout of cash flows following a construction phase and their returns are less correlated with public bond and equity returns, their inclusion in a strategic asset allocation most often seeks to benefit from both diversification and long-term liability matching.

INFRASTRUCTURE INVESTMENT FEATURES 2

☐ discuss important infrastructure investment features

Infrastructure assets share some features of private commercial real estate investments but have critical differences. Both involve large, heterogeneous, illiquid investments in real assets that often follow a distinct development life cycle. However, whereas value-add and opportunistic commercial or residential real estate investments ultimately generate market rents as a primary source of revenue, infrastructure investments have little or no economic value beyond the public goods or essential services they provide. The unique contractual relationships among public and private entities related to the use of infrastructure assets creates distinct risk–return profiles for private investors. These investments are often grouped by the underlying industry associated with the service provided, such as power generation or transportation, as well as the associated stage of development. For example, new infrastructure projects and assets are referred to as **greenfield investment**, while **brownfield investment** may involve the privatization or repurposing of existing public assets or an expansion of existing facilities providing the same service. As with real estate investments, infrastructure projects and investment funds are often grouped by core, value-add, and opportunistic criteria, as shown in Exhibit 1.

Exhibit 1: Infrastructure Investment Risk and Return Spectrum

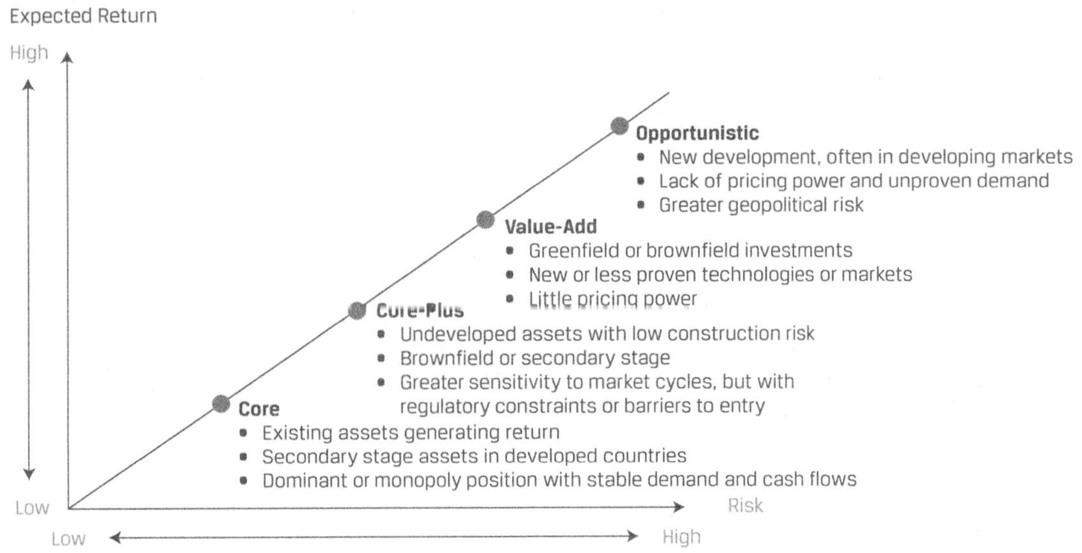

From an investment perspective, the source, type, and timing of compensation offered for the provision of these essential services or public goods is of primary importance. For example, in some cases, a local or regional government authority enters a **concession agreement** with a private firm that establishes terms and conditions to plan, build, operate, finance, and maintain an infrastructure asset, such as a toll road, bridge, or other facility. Under such an agreement, the public authority, often referred to as the **grantor**, provides the private developer or operator, also known as the **concessionaire**, the right to charge user fees over a predetermined operating period to both recover construction and maintenance costs and provide a return to investors once the facility is completed and meets specifications.

Infrastructure investment returns are primarily derived from an asset's income-generating potential, because most projects are single-use investments with little or no alternative economic value. Furthermore, they are often built on public land or land acquired under government authority for fair market compensation and are frequently transferred to the public entity at the end of an operating period with a terminal value of zero.

A key feature that distinguishes infrastructure from other investments is the underlying business model. In contrast to corporate issuers or real estate, long-term contractual arrangements clearly define services provided, as well as the economic terms. Infrastructure investors may act as private project developers and/or asset operators.

Private developers may agree to build a hospital, a bridge, or power generation facilities to certain technical specifications required to deliver services and receive progress payments during construction and upon completion. Asset operators generate revenue that usually involves one of three possible approaches:

> *Fixed or availability-based payment:* Public or private sector end users agree to payment of a fixed income stream over the period during which the asset is available for use. An operator must meet all construction, operating, and financing cash flows from this income stream. Under this arrangement common among **social infrastructure** investments, or those directed toward education, health care, and other government services, as well as the transport and energy sectors, the asset is often returned to the public sector entity and the terminal value is zero.
>
> *Commercial payment:* Under a commercial or so-called **merchant payment scheme**, the operator has the right to collect service or user fees over the operating period but remains exposed to the asset's business risk based on demand and other economic factors. Merchant payment schemes are frequently used for power generation and toll road assets.
>
> *Regulation-based payment:* In network-based industries where natural monopolies are common, such as power or water distribution, public authorities often seek to stabilize pricing or impose pricing restrictions. These measures may be designed to offer a specific return on investment, limit price adjustments to the rate of inflation or a predetermined rise in service charges, or encourage investment in a particular area or technology. While this approach has the effect of limiting potential returns, it also may be used to encourage investment by reducing business risk to investors.

Regulation-based payments are also used to promote investment in renewable energy. For example, the United Kingdom is one of several developed market countries that uses **contracts for difference (CfDs)** as a primary mechanism to promote investment in low-carbon electricity generation, such as wind and solar power. CfDs are used by the **Low Carbon Contracts Company (LCCC)** to stabilize a project's renewable energy income, as shown Exhibit 2.

Exhibit 2: Contracts for Difference in UK Renewable Energy

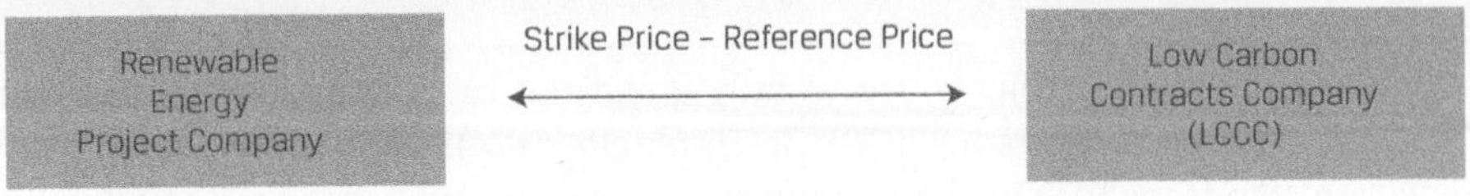

Strike Price > Reference Price: LCCC Pays Difference

Reference Price > Strike Price: Project Company Pays Difference

Qualified low-carbon energy project developers bid on a fixed, likely inflation-adjusted, indexed electricity rate for periodic future delivery over 15 years, with successful bidders entering a CfD with the UK government–owned LCCC. Under the CfD, a developer exchanges the difference between the **strike price**, or the fixed contractual rate agreed at a CfD auction for each period, and a **reference price**, or the average UK electricity market price for the period. For intermittent projects, such as wind power, market reference prices for a given day are set hourly based on the prior day's power auctions.

If the pre-agreed strike price exceeds the market reference price, the project company receives the difference from LCCC, while the project company must pay LCCC the difference when the market price exceeds the strike price, thus ensuring a stabilized electricity price for the contracted period and volume.

KNOWLEDGE CHECK: WYNDSIDE LIMITED CONTRACT FOR DIFFERENCE

Wyndside Limited is an onshore wind farm that was awarded a 15-year CfD at auction with a strike price of GBP230.18 per MWh for 25 MW (1MW = 1,000 kW) of power. The **intermittent market reference price (IMRP)** is the market reference price determined daily on the basis of the prior day's hourly electricity rates.

1. Explain how the CfD is used to determine Wyndside's income for the quarter (equal to 90 days) if the IMRP for the current quarter is GBP208 per MWh. Assume no CfD inflation adjustment, 24-hour daily operation, and constant 25 MW per hour output.

   Solution:

   If the pre-agreed strike price under the CfD exceeds the market reference price, then Wyndside receives the difference from LCCC. Wyndside's income is the sum of the electricity income based on IMRP plus the CfD settlement:

   Wyndside income (IMRP): 11,232,000 = GBP208 × 25 MW × 90 days × 24 hours.

   CfD settlement: 1,197,720 = (230.18 – 208) × 25 MW × 90 days × 24 hours.

   Wyndside income: GBP12,429,720 = 11,232,000 + 1,197,720.

   While this CfD settlement mechanism addresses a contractual volume for a given period, note that wind farms in practice are subject to output variability due to seasonal and weather conditions, among other factors, which prevent them from fully offsetting revenue-related risk.

Single, standalone projects are usually governed by a **special purpose entity (SPE)**, also referred to as a special purpose vehicle (SPV), established to undertake a project. This approach is similar to asset-backed securities, where a standalone SPV is created to purchase loans from an originator and issue securities backed by loan interest and principal payments. In the case of a project SPV, the entity's sole purpose is to facilitate the construction, operation, and financing of an infrastructure asset over its contractual life both by limiting the liability of private firms that build, operate, and maintain the asset in exchange for contractual or commercial operating cash flows and by limiting debt and equity investor claims to a project's net cash flows.

The long-lived, illiquid nature of infrastructure investments combined with the contractual and business risk characteristics we have outlined result in unique infrastructure cash flow, diversification, and exposure profile features:

Cash flow features: As long-lived, single-use assets, infrastructure investments typically offer investors a higher cash yield than other asset classes because there are limited opportunities for cash flow reinvestment into an existing project. As a result, equity investors can usually expect a higher proportion of revenues as dividends, while debtholders are often able to receive relatively high yields compared to similar investments with low credit risk.

Diversification features: Given the provision of essential or public services that often have few substitutes and inelastic demand, infrastructure asset returns typically exhibit lower correlation with other asset classes and tend to be less exposed to cyclicality or market downturns. For example, according to a study by PGIM, a global investment management firm, the total return correlation between private infrastructure equity assets and public equities from 2012 to 2021 was 0.57, which is higher than that of equities and fixed income but lower than correlations between types of private equity.

Exposure profile features: Given the distribution of relatively predictable cash flows over extended contractual periods, infrastructure assets offer the potential for cash flow or liability matching for long-term institutional investors, such as pension funds, as a source of income and portfolio duration.

Given the unique nature of infrastructure project risks, the EDHEC Infrastructure Institute initiated the **Infrastructure Company Classification Standard (TICCS)** in 2018, with the input of asset owners and asset managers, to categorize investments based on key characteristics affecting relative risk and return. These features include the form of business risk, the underlying industry, corporate governance, and geo-economic exposures, as shown in Exhibit 3.

Exhibit 3: The Infrastructure Company Classification Standard

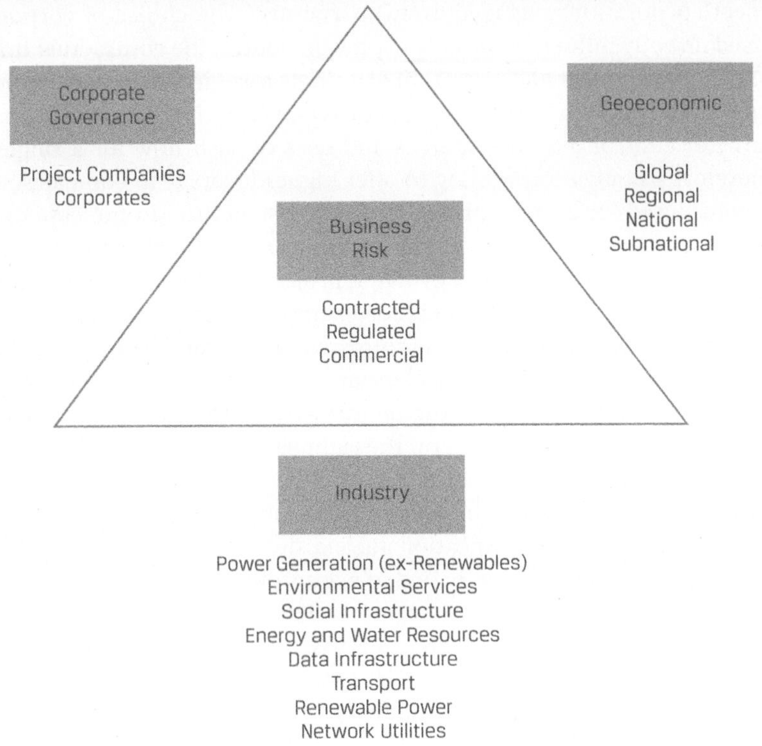

Business risk characteristics of infrastructure investments at the center of the exhibit were defined earlier by whether cash flows are fixed or availability based, merchant, or commercial, or regulation based. These cash flows constitute the income over the asset's period of operation used to cover upfront development and construction costs and ongoing maintenance upon completion and to compensate investors over an asset's life. Given their long useful life, regulatory risk in the form of political, legal, and governmental change is an additional feature of business risk for infrastructure assets. The anticipated level and volatility of cash flows affect not only the level of risk and return but also the degree to which leverage can be used to finance these long-lived assets.

The *industry* classifications shown at the bottom of Exhibit 3 used to group and evaluate private companies are important, but they often ignore key distinctions associated with the development and operation of infrastructure assets. Industry risk factors include cyclicality, concentration, and competitive intensity, as well as growth and demand. While an investment's technical and physical features may be similar to other investments in the same industry, relative risk and return are often dictated by the business model. For example, a power generation facility that delivers electricity to the power grid under a government-sponsored price stabilization scheme may face less business risk than an identical facility with a long-term power purchase agreement with a private manufacturing company, but it bears more regulatory risk. Also, while low-carbon energy solutions may benefit from income stabilization schemes as described earlier, traditional power-generation assets face the risk of tighter environmental restrictions over their useful life. Infrastructure assets in the same sector therefore often require groupings with greater specificity based on the types of services rendered, technologies employed, and customers, as well as the terms of service.

The type of *corporate governance* shown on the left side of Exhibit 3 refers to the use of single-asset project companies typically governed under SPEs, as opposed to multi-project corporations engaged in infrastructure. The choice of corporate governance used directly influences project capital structure; the contractual framework governing the development and operation of a single asset imposes tighter constraints on managers than under a corporate structure with multiple projects. Lenders can exercise greater control over the sources and uses of cash flow for a single project and are therefore usually more willing to offer higher leverage in comparison to debt financing considered for a multi-project corporate structure. In the case of publicly traded infrastructure companies involved in multiple projects, debt and equity investors in liquid securities are exposed to an evolving project portfolio over time as opposed to a single-use asset for a finite period. For example, in the case of Hochtief AG, a publicly traded construction and global infrastructure company based in Germany, the company has shifted its focus from German reunification projects in past years to such new areas as energy transition, digital infrastructure, and sustainable mobility.

Finally, *geoeconomic* classification on the right side of Exhibit 3 refers to the local, national, or global exposures associated with an infrastructure asset. For example, as with real estate assets where income depends on local economic conditions, investors often seek geographic diversification among similar infrastructure assets whose commercial revenue stream is closely tied to economic activity, such as traffic for toll roads and business and leisure travel for airports. In some cases, a project may directly hinge on the creditworthiness or counterparty risk of a local or national government, while in others—such as bridges, ports, or distribution networks—a project's viability may depend on the level of cross-border activity or global trade. These large, immobile assets depend directly and indirectly on national government policies to determine how public entities partner with private sector entities to develop and operate infrastructure. These so-called **public–private partnerships (PPPs)** take many forms but are usually defined as a long-term contractual relationship between the public and private sectors involving a concession agreement or other form of compensation in exchange for delivering an essential service or public good.

While private market solutions to address the provision of public goods are often seen as an attractive investable alternative to schemes funded entirely through fiscal budgets, PPPs often face unique and unforeseen risks when put into practice. For example, while the vast majority of transport infrastructure investment following German reunification was funded through taxation, the following private project example illustrates some of the challenges faced when estimating usage and revenue for any infrastructure project, whether publicly or privately financed.

WARNOW TUNNEL PROJECT

The Warnow tunnel, a 0.8 km road tunnel under the Warnow River in Rostock, was the first German toll road constructed following the passage of the Private Highway Construction Financing Act after reunification. Under the new law, a new form of PPP known as the F-Model was used; it transferred the right to collect tolls to private investors but involved a bidding process that took place prior to formal project approval.

Completed in 2003 at a cost of EUR220 million, the Warnow tunnel was nearly bankrupt within three years of completion. The investors and planners had overly optimistic traffic forecasts, particularly for trucks facing much higher tolls than passenger cars. Truck drivers chose instead to take a 10–15 km detour on public roads rather than incurring the EUR9.00 (or EUR17.50 in summer) toll per vehicle, and overall tunnel traffic remained at roughly half the level necessary for the project to be profitable. Following a two-year period of negotiation with the City of Rostock as grantor, the operating concession was extended from 20 years to 50 years and the toll structure was adjusted to make the project economically feasible for the operator.

This widely cited example is often used to describe the pitfalls of the so-called F-Model and to justify subsequent changes to German PPP transport structures.

The role of private infrastructure investments differs markedly in developed and developing countries for several reasons.

Developed markets are characterized by diversified domestic economies with a strong financial sector, extensive existing domestic transportation and energy networks, and fiscal budgets that provide essential services and public goods through taxation and borrowing. Private infrastructure is prevalent in industries in which public sector assets are privatized or a well-established regulatory framework governs activity, such as power and water utilities or transportation. In other cases, government intervention is used to promote either brownfield investment to revitalize disadvantaged areas or greenfield development to stimulate growth in such areas as renewable energy.

Developing countries, in contrast, face less economic diversification, few budgetary resources to provide public goods, evolving transportation and energy networks, and a less robust financial sector with a greater likelihood of domestic currency devaluation, which creates currency risk. In these cases, private infrastructure investment is more often greenfield than brownfield and tied to projects that seek to provide a catalyst for overall economic growth and development. Global and regional development banks and supranational financial institutions, such as the World Bank and its affiliate, the International Finance Corporation (IFC), frequently play a pivotal role in providing technical assistance to these countries for infrastructure investments, such as concession agreement terms, standard bidding documents, and legal and regulatory advice, as well as various forms of financing. Private investors in developing market infrastructure typically look to the engagement of these public and other private entities with experience and expertise with similar projects to mitigate country and political risk associated with long-term illiquid developing market investments.

In contrast to developed markets, infrastructure asset performance in developing economies often hinges on the market for a key global commodity or domestic industry that may be a driver of continued economic development, as well as a critical source of foreign currency reserves. While developing market investments are less frequently associated with brownfield investments, the following fictional case study provides a counterexample in which existing infrastructure may be repurposed to align resources to national government priorities using private investment.

CASE STUDY

Tay Bac Airport (Vietnam)

In response to growing cross-border travel and trade in the northwestern Vietnamese province of Tay Bac, the Vietnamese Ministry of Transport has proposed the repurposing of an abandoned military airport site for civilian use as a regional airport to primarily serve passengers on domestic routes and connecting flights to global destinations, promoting tourism, trade, and local economic growth.

The Ministry of Transport intends to work in conjunction with the IFC under a plan where private sector firms will design, build, finance, operate, and maintain the Tay Bac Airport (TBA) facilities over the next 20 years.

The proposed commercial arrangement between the Ministry of Transport and the airport operator foresees nominal concession payments related to airport operations, with the bulk of expected project revenue based on commercial payments tied to airport traffic, as well as the right to generate ancillary revenues from parking, duty-free shopping, and other sources on the property.

1. Describe TBA's infrastructure investment features using TICCS.

Solution:

Corporate governance: As a single standalone project, we would expect the Tay Bac Airport project to be built and operated using an SPE structure to accommodate long-term contractual relationships between public sector project sponsors and private sector parties involved in the design, construction, financing, operation, and maintenance of airport facilities.

Business risk: Tay Bac Airport's business risk and business model primarily involve a commercial payment scheme, because projected airport revenue is reliant on passenger and cargo traffic and other traffic-related revenue.

Geoeconomic risk: Because TBA is in the transport sector and associated with goals of promoting tourism, international trade, and economic growth via both domestic travel and connections to global routes, TBA's geoeconomic risk involves both global and national exposures.

Industry Risk: The project will have significant exposure to the tourism industry, as well as some exposure to ancillary industries related to the operation and upkeep of the facility.

Despite their obvious differences, the Wyndside and Tay Bac Airport projects share several common features, such as their lack of adaptability to alternative economic uses and a development period with negative cash flows followed by a period of contractual cash inflows available to pay development costs and generate investor returns. The investment methods and structures used to achieve the objectives of the public and private parties involved, as well as third-party investors, have similar features. Infrastructure investments span the development and operation cycles as shown in the following section.

QUESTION SET

1. Describe two possible rationales for establishing a special purpose entity for governing a private infrastructure project.

Solution:

In the case of a project SPE, the entity's sole purpose is to facilitate the construction, operation, and financing of an infrastructure asset over its contractual life. For private infrastructure projects, an SPE has the effect of both (1) limiting the liability of private firms that build, operate, and maintain the asset in exchange for contractual or commercial operating cash flows and (2) limiting off-balance-sheet debt and equity investor claims to a project's net cash flows.

2. Which of the following corporate governance structures in private infrastructure is likely to allow for greater debt financing assuming similar creditworthiness?

   A. Single-asset companies

   B. Multi-project companies

   C. Publicly traded infrastructure companies

   Solution:

   The correct response is A.The choice of corporate governance used directly influences project capital structure; the contractual framework governing the development and operation of a single asset imposes tighter constraints on managers than under a corporate structure with multiple projects. Lenders can exercise greater control over the sources and uses of cash flow for a single project and are therefore usually more willing to accept a higher degree of leverage than under a corporate structure (i.e., multi-project companies or publicly traded infrastructure companies).

3. Vento Anglio Limited (VAL) is a private 125 MW onshore wind farm project planned in western England. Because it expects to qualify as a low-carbon energy project developer, VAL intends to take advantage of the UK government's CfD scheme and deliver electricity to the local power grid. Describe VAL's infrastructure investment features using TICCS.

   Solution:

   Corporate governance: As a single, standalone project company, we would expect VAL to be governed by a special purpose entity) established solely to undertake the wind farm project as opposed to a corporate structure.

   Business risk: Given its intention to use a contract for difference (CfD) scheme to stabilize power revenue, we should classify VAL's business risk as involving regulation-based payments, since the CfD contract stabilizes electricity prices for the life of the contract for difference.

   Industry risk: VAL's underlying industry is the renewable power sector.

   Geoeconomic risk: Changes to the domestic UK government's programs to encourage investment in renewable energy are a form of geoeconomic risk.

INFRASTRUCTURE INVESTMENT STRUCTURES 3

☐ discuss infrastructure investment methods and investment vehicles and their uses

Infrastructure investments take several forms similar to those from other private markets, ranging from fund investments in a portfolio of infrastructure assets or projects, co-investment, or direct investment in a project or asset.

While smaller investors that are unable to accommodate sizable stakes in these often large-scale, highly illiquid, single-use assets typically invest as one of many limited partners, larger institutional investors frequently consider significant minority, majority, or 100% ownership, as in the following example.

PUBLIC SECTOR PENSION (PSP) INVESTMENTS IN INFRASTRUCTURE

PSP Investments was established in 1999 by the Canadian government to manage and invest the public sector pension plans of the federal Public Service, the Canadian Forces, the Royal Canadian Mounted Police, and the Reserve Forces. PSP's assets under management grew during its first 20 years of operation to over CAD200 billion.

Beyond public market equities and fixed income, PSP expanded to private market investments, including infrastructure, seeking to invest in large assets with stable long-term cash flows to match its liabilities for very long tenors with no exit requirements. PSP participates in both co-investment opportunities with significant minority ownership stakes and 100% direct investments, such as AviAlliance.

AviAlliance is a leading global airport investor and manager based in Germany, which PSP acquired from Hochtief AG, a publicly traded global infrastructure company, over a decade ago.

In contrast to other private market investments, infrastructure assets often require a high degree of technical, engineering, regulatory, and other expertise to ensure the physical and economic feasibility of a project over its life cycle. Smaller general partner (GP) funds and other investors who are unable to make large investments and lack the necessary depth of resources and sector- and asset-specific expertise often seek to co-invest in projects led by a major fund manager, sovereign wealth fund, or pension fund with greater experience. As infrastructure involves essential services or public goods created and supported in tightly regulated markets governed by regional or national authorities, public entities often play a key role in determining the investment method, types of financing, and parties involved. In other instances, especially in developing countries, regional development banks or supranational entities, such as IFC, offer technical assistance for engineering and financing proposals and bid processes.

Most developed market governments have created **export credit agencies (ECAs)** to promote the export of domestic goods and services via credit insurance, subsidized or guaranteed debt financing, which is often a key factor in reducing cost, extending the tenor, or increasing the availability of debt financing for capital goods used in developing market infrastructure.

In the case of a UK wind farm, the project requires assembly, installation, and operation of the wind turbines to generate and transmit electricity to the power grid at optimal levels and in compliance with the British Standards Institution and pricing regulated by the Office of Gas and Electricity Markets. The UK Department of International Trade has sponsored initiatives seeking to attract foreign investors to provide debt and equity financing for renewable energy.

As for Tay Bac Airport in Vietnam, introduced earlier, the facility must meet physical feasibility requirements of aircraft, passengers, and cargo. International passengers, airlines, and freight companies will also expect Tay Bac Airport to meet high global service requirements, such as the International Air Transport Association's standards of interoperability and technology. Transport linkages requiring local and regional authority agreements to provide road, rail, and other onward travel connections are important elements required to attract and accommodate traffic over the concession period.

These complex contractual relationships among developers, contractors, suppliers, private and public service providers, managers, and investors are usually governed through an SPE structure over a project's life cycle. Because no two projects are identical, the form of an infrastructure project SPE is often uniquely structured to follow its function in establishing and allocating sources and uses of cash, as well as risks, roles, and responsibilities among parties involved. Exhibit 4 provides a generalized structure of a special purpose entity.

Exhibit 4: Infrastructure Project Special Purpose Entity

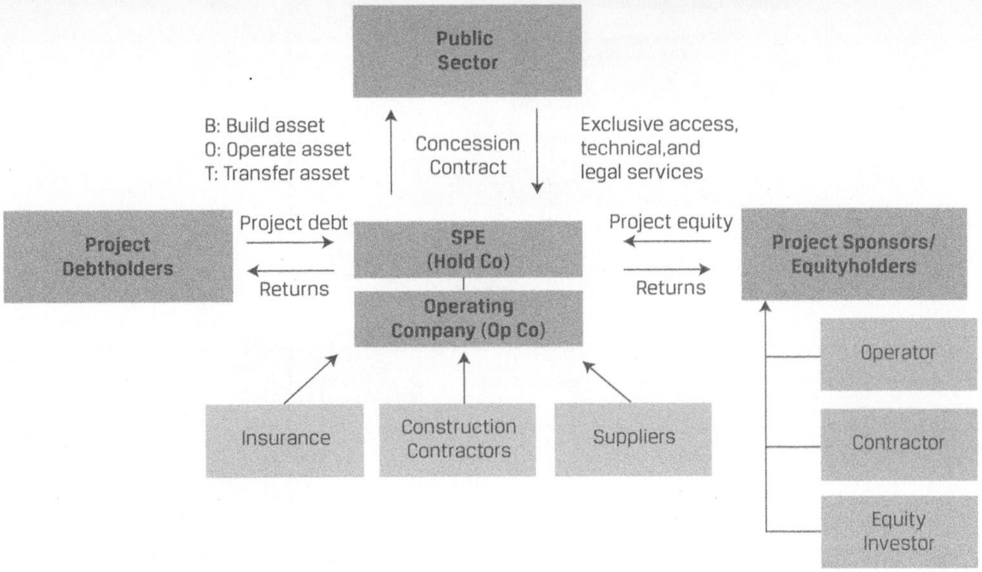

As Exhibit 4 shows, the project SPE is often a separate holding company (shown in the diagram as HoldCo) established for financing purposes that also has an operating company (or OpCo) that holds the assets, contracts with related parties, and generates cash flows. In some cases, both entities issue securities and investors must be aware of the seniority of their claim depending on the issuing entity and the project cash flows.

In addition to their legal segregation using SPEs, infrastructure investments are often governed by a set of standardized procedures for the selection of parties involved in the development, construction, operation, and financing of the project once its size, scope, and timing are determined. Key steps in the process are shown in Exhibit 5.

Exhibit 5: Infrastructure Project Bidding Process

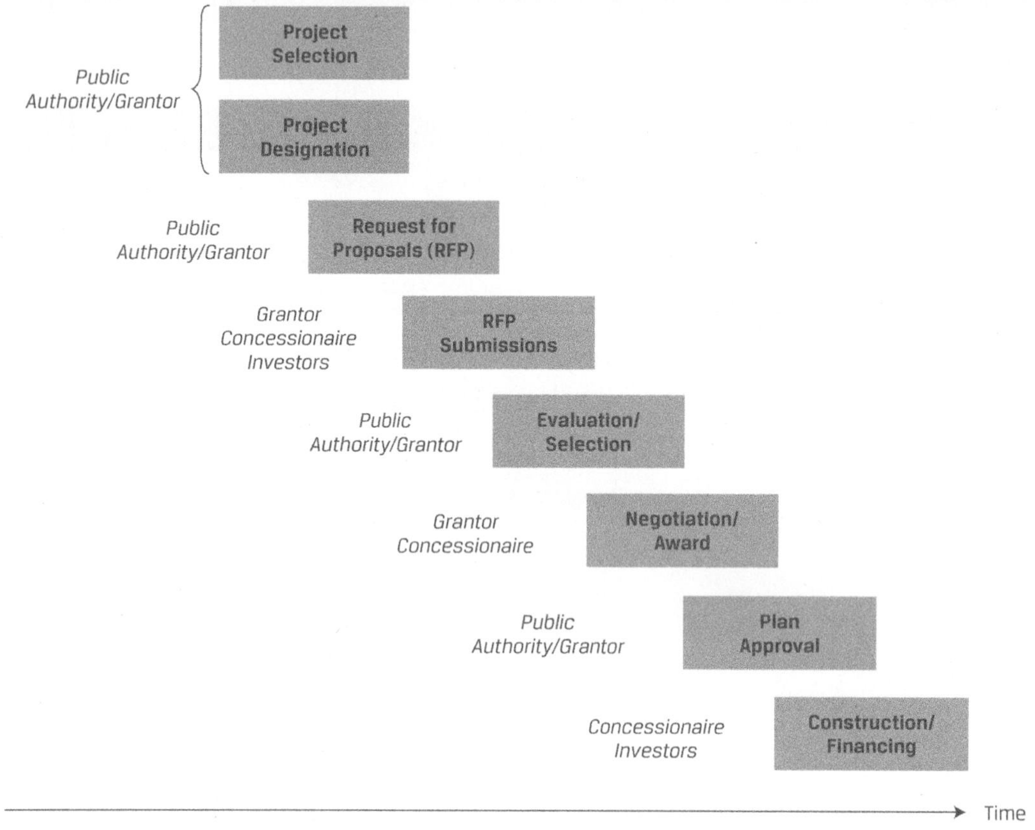

The **request for proposal (RFP)** outlines project details, requirements, and timing, as well as assessment criteria used to award contracts to successful bidders. In addition to laying out the size, scope, technical specifications, and the nature of essential services to be provided by an infrastructure asset to all interested parties submitting a sealed bid for the project, the RFP process also aims to promote a fair, competitive, and transparent process for all parties involved.

To better understand how these infrastructure methods and structures work in practice, we now return to the case of the Vietnamese airport introduced earlier. In the case of Tay Bac Airport, private investors engage with global institutions, public sector authorities, and private entities with extensive experience and expertise in developing and operating regional airports to mitigate associated geoeconomic risk, as shown in the following case study.

CASE STUDY

Tay Bac Airport Limited Investment Vehicle and Structure

The state-owned Airports Corporation of Vietnam (ACV), a subsidiary of Vietnam's Ministry of Transport and operator of Vietnam's existing international airports, has completed a successful RFP process for the design, construction, financing, and operation of the new Tay Bac Airport on 500 hectares of government land on an abandoned military site in northwestern Vietnam, and it was awarded the contract.

The project is co-sponsored by the IFC as a provider of both technical support and debt financing and AviAlliance, a private industrial airport investor, manager, and equity provider. Tay Bac Airport Limited (TBA Limited) was established as the project company and concessionaire, with ACV serving as grantor over the 20-year period, with ownership and control transferred to ACV at the end. TBA Limited's structure is summarized in Exhibit 6.

Exhibit 6: TBA Limited Structure

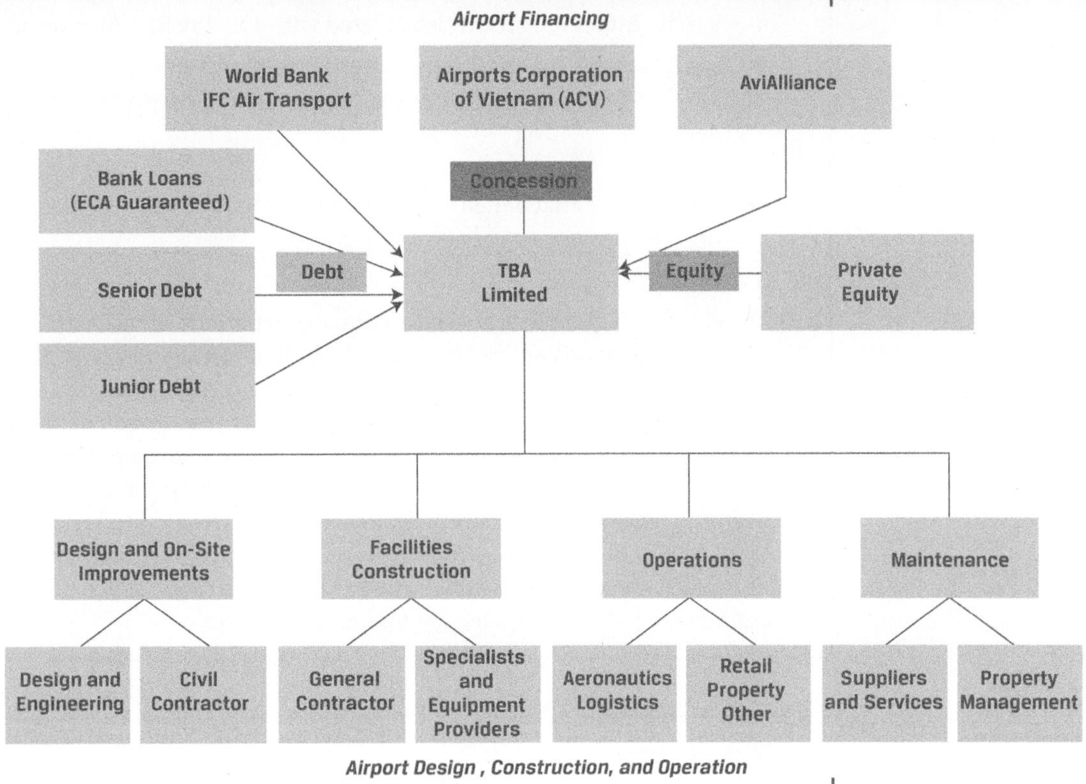

As shown in the diagram, TBA Limited has four sources of debt and two sources of equity financing and intends to directly contract with design and civil contractors in the initial development phase and general and specialist contractors over the facility construction period and for operations and maintenance once TBA is operational.

TBA is projected to cost USD900 million, as shown in the following table, with 65% of the project (or USD585 million) funded with debt and the rest with equity:

TBA Development Costs	USD
Facilities	515,000,000
Equipment & Systems	135,000,000
On-Site Land Improvements	100,000,000
Civil Engineering	90,000,000
Parking & Transportation	50,000,000
Upfront Costs & Reserves	10,000,000
Total	900,000,000

1. Explain the benefits to a TBA Limited debt or equity investor of investing directly with the special purpose company as opposed to the Airports Corporation of Vietnam over the concession period.

   Solution:

   The legal separation between TBA Limited (the SPE concessionaire) and the Airports Corporation of Vietnam (the grantor) provides important benefits to both debt and equity investors of the infrastructure project.

   First, investors are protected from cash flow risks arising from other assets (i.e., all other airports in Vietnam) associated with the grantor. The cash flows to investors are strictly associated with the Tay Bac Airport asset.

   Second, investors can focus any monitoring efforts solely on the operations of Tay Bac Airport as opposed to monitoring Airports Corporation of Vietnam.

2. Discuss the potential benefits of using ECA-guaranteed bank loans as debt for the TBA project.

   Solution:

   Developed market governments create export credit agencies to promote the export of goods and services via credit insurance and political risk insurance protecting against project expropriation and the inability to repatriate cross-border cash flows and subsidized or guaranteed debt financing. These features of ECAs assist in reducing cost, extending potential tenor, and increasing the availability of debt financing for capital goods used in developing market infrastructure. Thus, the use of the ECA-guaranteed bank loans likely comes at lower interest rates and with better loan terms than non-guaranteed debt. The guaranteed feature also should provide additional confidence to other possible lenders on the project.

QUESTION SET

A private equity GP initiates the 125 MW Vento Anglio project by entering into a GBP1.825 million land use contract for 12,000 acres of remote land to build and operate a wind farm following community engagement and receipt of local authority permits. The GP establishes Vento Anglio Limited (VAL) with the basic structure in Exhibit 7.

Exhibit 7: VAL Structure

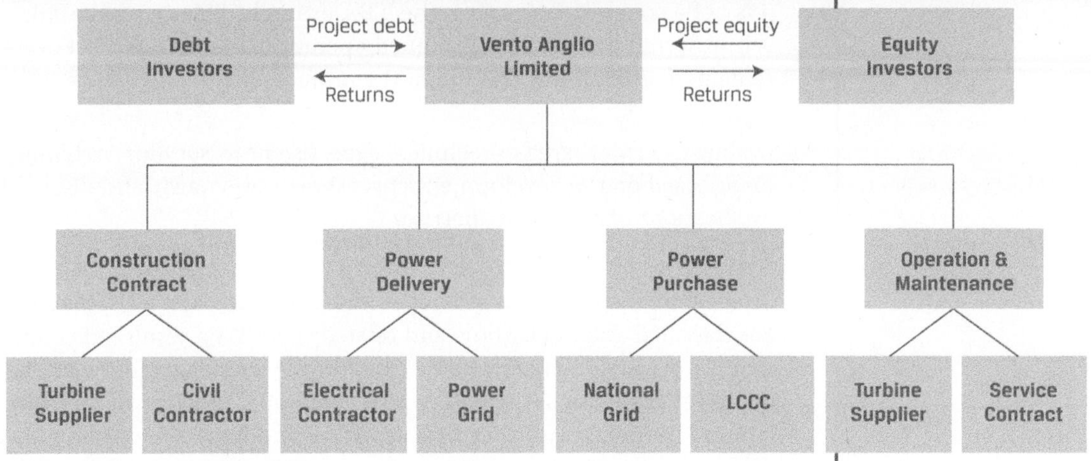

The VAL wind farm is projected to cost GBP160 million, as shown in the following table, using GBP50 million in equity and the remainder in debt financing:

VAL Development Costs	GBP
Land Use Cost	1,825,000
Wind Turbines & Related Costs	137,500,000
Site Setup Costs	1,600,000
Development Fees	2,300,000
Contingency	6,500,000
Interest Reserves	4,020,000
Operating Deficit Reserves	4,255,000
Miscellaneous Closing Costs	2,000,000
Total	160,000,000

The VAL wind farm has a 30-year expected life, after which the turbines are expected to be recycled to cover wind-down costs and the land will be returned to owner use.

1. Explain the benefits to wind turbine suppliers and LCCC of contracting directly with the special purpose entity VAL versus the private equity GP.

   Solution:

   Because of the specific and technical nature of an infrastructure asset like the Vento Anglio project, an SPE can be organized and staffed to provide the unique project knowledge required to interact with suppliers to the project (such as the wind turbine suppliers and LCCC). The private equity general partner, in contrast, is unlikely to be staffed with such asset-specific expertise.

2. Identify key differences between the structure of VAL compared to the structure from the TBA example presented earlier in the lesson.

   Solution:

   The VAL structure does not include a grantor as in the TBA scenario in which Airports Corporation of Vietnam (ACV) grants the concession to build, operate, and transfer Tay Bac Airport to ACV at the end of the contract. There is also no ECA supporting debt issuance.

While VAL will interact with government authorities through the process of providing electricity to the national power grid and obtaining local permits, it is not a concessionaire as in the TBA example. Finally, unlike TBA, which is transferred to ACV for continued operation, the VAL project does not remain in operation at the end of the project's life.

3. Evaluate a critical area of technical expertise necessary for VAL management based on the development costs shown previously and discuss the implications of a lack of expertise.

Solution:

Of the GBP160 million cost budget for the project, almost 86% of these costs are classified as wind turbine and related costs. As a result, it is imperative that the private equity GP ensure that the VAL management team has a high degree of expertise in the construction and operation of wind turbines. A lack of knowledge in this critical aspect of building a wind farm may cause delays, cost overruns, and other adverse events that may substantially reduce project returns.

4 INFRASTRUCTURE INVESTMENT PROCESS

☐ discuss the infrastructure investment process over the project life cycle and the roles of infrastructure debt and equity financing

Private market investments such as venture capital, growth or buyout equity, or value-add or opportunistic real estate projects are often characterized by value creation over a transformational life cycle. Several features of infrastructure assets affect their value creation process in the project life cycle, including their size, a higher degree of illiquidity, and lack of ability to repurpose, in contrast to other private market investments. As we have discussed, these large-scale fixed assets involve a development process with sizable sunk costs to deliver specific essential services or public goods under contractual relationships established with public entities. Unlike private equity investors who may alter restructuring or company exit plans based on market conditions or private real estate investors who may repurpose a property to meet changes in demand, infrastructure investments are usually more difficult to liquidate or convert to alternative uses.

Infrastructure asset inflexibility extends beyond the development phase to the period of operation and in many cases to the final asset transfer to public ownership, resulting in a zero terminal value to investors. The phases of such a **build–operate–transfer (BOT) project** are shown in Exhibit 8.

Exhibit 8: Infrastructure Project Build–Operate–Transfer Life Cycle

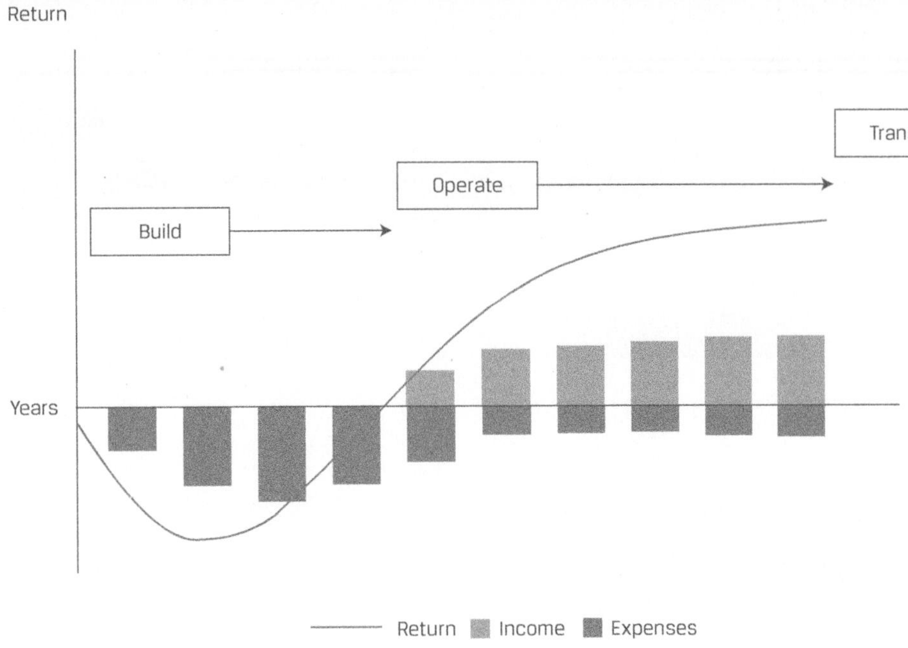

BOT projects are characterized by an initial construction or "build" phase, followed by a predefined operating period over which contractual or commercial cash flows are generated before the asset is transferred to a public authority. Given the high degree of sunk costs in these specialized fixed assets, the payout period of infrastructure assets typically spans several decades. In developed markets, BOT projects are most common in such sectors as transportation, energy and water resources, and other network utilities for which large-scale investment is required for projects with a high level of fixed assets and long operating periods. In developing countries, BOT structures are commonly used to attract foreign investors in partnership with multilateral funding agencies for selected projects necessary to support economic growth where public funds are inadequate.

The use of debt versus equity financing also differs over the infrastructure asset life cycle versus other private investments. Many private investments combine debt and equity financing over a development period characterized by negative cash flows, followed by an operating period where sustainable cash flows support a relatively high degree of leverage. While private equity and real estate investment returns come from cash flows over a holding period and a terminal value upon exit, infrastructure equity investors must receive their returns largely in the form of dividends given the minimal or zero terminal value of most infrastructure assets. As the infrastructure asset's equity cushion declines, the ability to support debt financing falls, with debt repayment occurring earlier in the project life cycle, as shown in Exhibit 9.

Exhibit 9: Infrastructure Project BOT Investment Life Cycle

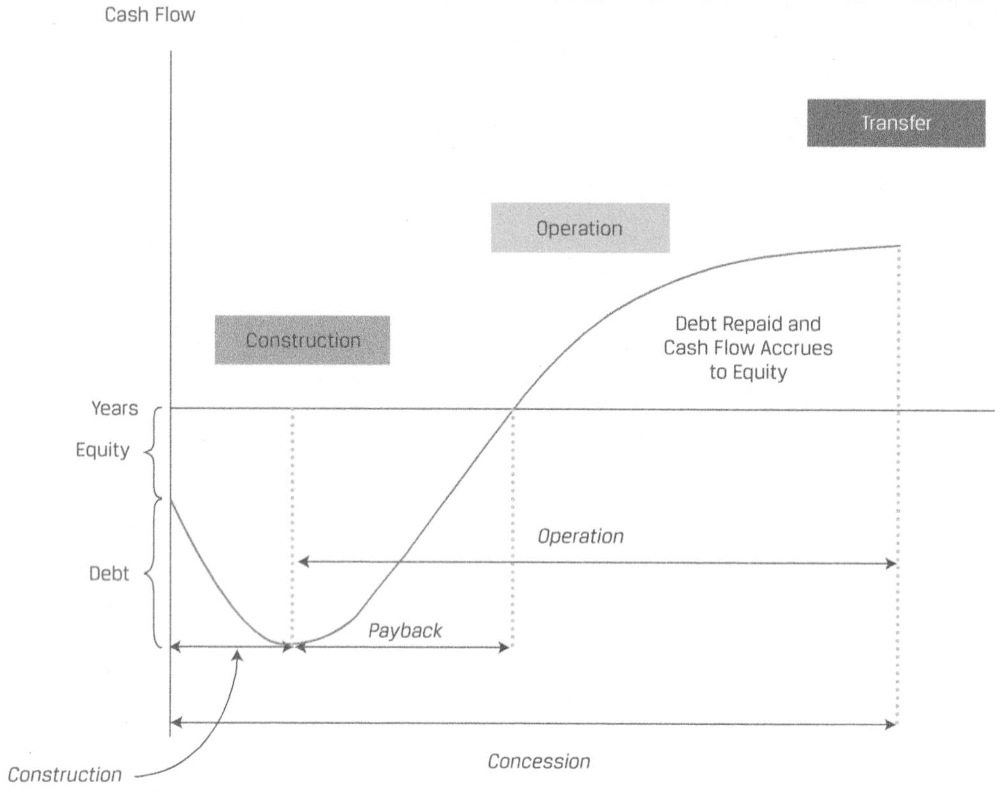

Once an infrastructure asset enters the operating phase, cash flows are used to pay debt service, operating and maintenance expenses, and other costs, after which funds are available to equityholders in the form of dividends. Given the limited growth options, limited opportunities for cash flow reinvestment, and contractual or regulated business model associated with infrastructure assets, most SPEs are characterized by a strict cash flow waterfall that dictates the prioritization and use of project cash flow to meet all obligations, as well as payments to debt- and equityholders, as shown in Exhibit 10.

Exhibit 10: Project SPV Sample Cash Flow Waterfall

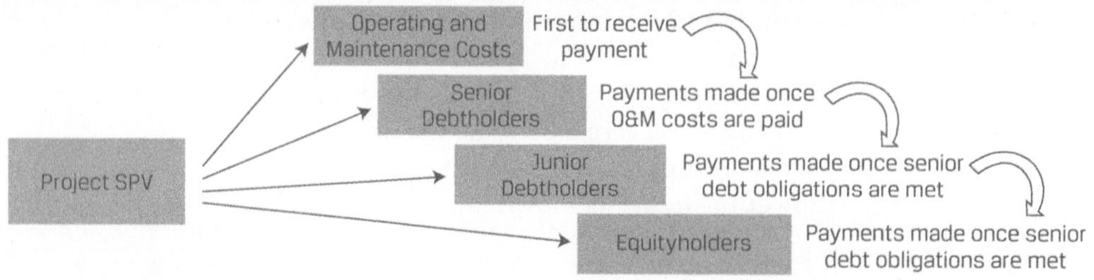

The SPV's debt may in some cases be enhanced by the establishment of reserve accounts for debt service and other obligations. For example, when project cash flows are less predictable, a **debt service reserve account (DSRA)** is often established, which accumulates sufficient cash in order to meet specific debt service requirements and from which funds are released when payments are due. Reserve accounts are often used for operating and maintenance costs and for decommissioning equipment at the end of its serviceable life. For example, the eventual closure and dismantling of a power generation facility and its equipment often involves a reserve account.

The roles of debt and equity financing in infrastructure projects can vary significantly depending on the business model, underlying industry, and public and private entities involved in a specific project. As with other private investments, such as real estate, debt investors often consider leverage and coverage measures to evaluate creditworthiness, such as **loan to value (LTV)** and the **debt service coverage ratio** (DSCR), respectively:

$$\text{LTV} = \frac{\text{Debt outstanding}}{\text{Current project value}}. \quad (1)$$

$$\text{DSCR} = \frac{\text{Net cash flow from operations}}{\text{Debt service}}. \quad (2)$$

Equity investors, in contrast, evaluate before-tax returns using actual or expected net cash flow from operations minus debt service to establish an **equity dividend rate**:

$$\text{Equity dividend rate} = \frac{\text{Before} - \text{tax net cash flow}}{\text{Equity invested}}, \quad (3)$$

where:

$$\text{Before-tax cash flow} = \text{Net cash flow from operations} - \text{Debt service}. \quad (4)$$

Note that this equity return calculation rate does not include fees. Recall from earlier in the curriculum that GP fees (R_{GP}) often involve a fixed percentage (r_m) of AUM as a management fee on end-of-period assets (P_1) and a GP performance fee (p) as a percentage of total period return ($P_1 - P_0$) in excess of a hurdle rate (r_h):

$$R_{GP\,(\text{Net with hurdle})} = (P_1 \times r_m) + \max\{0, [P_1(1 - r_m) - P_0 \times (1 + r_h)] \times p\}. \quad (5)$$

The infrastructure investment process and use of debt and equity are similar to other private markets during the development and construction phases with varying degrees of public sector involvement, while the predefined operating period places constraints on the use of leverage.

For example, in the earlier case of the UK wind farm, Wyndside, the public sector stabilized project cash flows under the contract for difference scheme used to offset electricity price volatility. However, more complex, larger-scale projects in developing economies designed to address national economic priorities (such as Tay Bac Airport) often rely on direct and indirect financial incentives, subsidies, and/or guarantees from multilateral institutions, developed market governments, and private partners to attract additional foreign debt and equity investors.

CASE STUDY

TBA Limited Financing Plan

The Tay Bac Airport project involves the reclamation of a former military base and construction of a 3,200 meter runway, as well as a new passenger terminal with the initial capacity to serve 5 million passengers per year with retail and other services, auto rental, and rail and road transportation links (to be established by the Transport Ministry), as well as fueling, maintenance, and cargo handling facilities. Expected project development costs over three years are as follows:

TBA Development Costs	USD
Facilities	515,000,000
Equipment & Systems	135,000,000
On-Site Land Improvements	100,000,000
Civil Engineering	90,000,000
Parking & Transportation	50,000,000
Upfront Costs & Reserves	10,000,000
Total	900,000,000

Upon completion, TBA will hold a 20-year concession under which it is due to receive periodic contractual payments for operating passenger and cargo aviation services while holding the right to operate retail, parking, and other airport-based services under a commercial or merchant payment scheme based on demand and other economic factors.

TBA Project Financing Plan

Equity: 35% of cost, or USD315,000,000, 25% of which is from AviAlliance, with the remaining 75% from other equity investors drawn in three stages. GP performance fees upon completion are 10% of returns above a 15% hurdle.

Equity drawdown:

- Initial: USD157,500,000 (AviAlliance equity is fully drawn)
- One year: USD78,750,000
- Two years: USD78,750,000

Debt: 65% of cost, or USD585,000,000, from public and private investors:

1. International Finance Corporation (IFC) senior loan (USD150,000,000)
   - 6% annual interest
   - Fully disbursed at the end of Year 2 linked to project milestones
   - Accrued interest is capitalized in Year 3 and paid in Year 4 on full balance outstanding.
   - Loan is repaid in 12 equal annual installments comprising principal and interest payments starting in Year 5
   - Secured by TBA project assets
2. Senior syndicated bank loan—Term Loan A (USD235,000,000)
   - 7.5% annual interest paid annually on balance outstanding
   - Fully disbursed at the end of Year 3 linked to construction milestones
   - Full balance outstanding for three years, with principal amortization in four equal annual tranches thereafter
   - Secured by TBA project assets
3. Bank loan (ECA guaranteed; USD100,000,000)
   - 6.5% annual interest paid annually on outstanding balance
   - Fully disbursed at the end of Year 3 linked to export and delivery of ECA-eligible equipment and systems
   - Interest is paid on full balance outstanding for 10 years, with full (bullet) loan repayment at maturity.

- Insured by developed market ECA against political and commercial risks and secured by equipment financed under loan agreement

4. Junior construction and development loan (USD100,000,000)
   - 9.5% annual interest accrued on outstanding balance
   - Immediate disbursal upon project initiation and equity drawdown
   - Capitalized interest and principal are paid in four equal installments starting at the end of Year 14.
   - Subordinated claim to TBA project assets, which is repaid only once senior creditor claims are paid

TBA Operations

In its first full year of operation, Tay Bac Airport expects to earn an average of USD40 in per-passenger total airport revenue from 5 million passengers and before-tax cash flow based on the following assumptions:

Tay Bac Airport Operations	USD
Total Revenue (5,000,000 passengers × USD40 each)	200,000,000
Operating Expenses (40% of Revenue)	80,000,000
EBITDA	120,000,000
Capital Expenditures (CapEx)	20,000,000
Net Cash Flow from Operations	**100,000,000**

1. Calculate the debt outstanding and the DSCR for the first full year of operation (Year 4) of the Tay Bac Airport project.

   Solution:

   The debt service coverage ratio is equal to net cash flow from operations divided by debt service, as shown in Equation 2:

$$\text{DSCR} = \frac{\text{Net cash flow from operations}}{\text{Debt service}}.$$

   Net cash flow from the first year of operations is given as USD100,000,000, and we must solve for Year 4 debt service as follows:

   1. IFC senior loan (USD150,000,000)

      As 6% interest is capitalized in Year 3 and paid in Year 4 on the full balance, we may calculate Year 4 debt outstanding and debt service as follows:

      Debt outstanding: USD159,000,000 = USD150,000,000 × (1 + 0.06).

      Debt service: USD9,540,000 = USD159,000,000 × 0.06.

   2. Senior syndicated bank loan—Term Loan A (USD235,000,000)

      7.5% annual interest is paid, and the full balance is outstanding:

      Debt service: USD17,625,000 = USD235,000,000 × 0.075.

   3. Bank loan (ECA guaranteed; USD 100,000,000)

      6.5% annual interest is paid, and the full balance is outstanding:

      Debt service: USD6,500,000 = USD100,000,000 × 0.065.

   4. Junior construction and development loan (USD100,000,000)

While 9.5% annual interest is accrued on the outstanding balance, interest is capitalized and not paid until installments begin at the end of Year 10:

Debt outstanding: USD143,766,095 = USD100,000,000 × $(1 + 0.095)^4$

Debt service: USD0

Debt outstanding is the sum of the four loans outstanding at the end of Year 4:

$$\text{USD}637{,}766{,}095 = 159{,}000{,}000 + 235{,}000{,}000 + 100{,}000{,}000 + 143{,}766{,}095.$$

No debt amortization occurs in Year 4, so debt service is the sum of the interest payments on the four loans at the end of Year 4:

Debt service: USD33,665,000 = 9,540,000 + 17,625,000 + 6,500,000 + 0.

Solve for DSCR to be 2.97 as follows:

$$\text{DSC} = 2.97 = \frac{\text{USD } 100{,}000{,}000}{\text{USD } 33{,}665{,}000}.$$

2. Solve for the LTV at the end of Year 4 if the TBA project has a value that has appreciated 10% above its original development cost.

Solution:

Use Equation 1 to solve for loan to value as follows:

$$\text{LTV} = \frac{\text{Debt outstanding}}{\text{Current project value}}.$$

Given Tay Bac Airport development costs of USD900,000,000, we can solve for an estimated project value of USD990,000,000 (= 1.1 × 900,000,000):

$$\text{LTV} = 0.644 = \frac{637{,}766{,}095}{990{,}000{,}000}.$$

Note that while capitalized interest decreases debt service, it increases LTV.

3. Calculate the equity dividend rate for the first full year of TBA's operation, as well as the GP performance fee (ignoring management fees).

Solution:

Using TBA's Year 4 debt service of USD33,665,000 from Question 1, solve for before-tax cash flow of USD66,335,000 using Equation 4:

$$\text{Before-tax cash flow} = \text{Net cash flow from operations} - \text{Debt service}$$

$$= 100{,}000{,}000 - 33{,}665{,}000.$$

Use Equation 3 to solve for the equity dividend rate by dividing before-tax cash flow by project equity.

$$\text{Equity dividend rate} = 21.1\% = \frac{\text{USD}66{,}335{,}000}{\text{USD}315{,}000{,}000}.$$

GP performance fees are equal to 10% of the equity dividend rate in excess of the 15% hurdle rate. We may use a simplified version of Equation 5 (where $r_m = 0$) to solve for the performance fee as follows:

$$R_{GP\text{ (Net with hurdle)}} = (P_1 \times r_m) + \max\{0, [P_1(1 - r_m) - P_0 \times (1 + r_h)] \times p\}.$$

$$R_{GP\ (\text{Net with hurdle},\ r_m=0)} = \max\{0, [P_1 - P_0 \times (1 + r_h)] \times p\}.$$

P_1 is equal to USD381,335,000, or the sum of the equity dividend and equity, with r_h of 0.15 and p of 0.10:

$$= \max\{0, [381,335,000 - 315,000,000 \times (1.15)] \times 0.1\},$$

which results in a GP performance fee of USD1,908,500.

QUESTION SET

The 125 MW Vento Anglio Limited (VAL) project involves the purchase and installation of 50 2.5 MW wind turbines at a cost of GBP1.1million per MW, with total development costs incurred either upfront or equally over three years, as follows:

VAL Development Costs	**GBP**
Wind Turbines & Related Costs	137,500,000
Contingency Reserve	6,500,000
Operating Deficit Reserves	4,255,000
Interest Reserves	4,020,000
Development Fees	2,300,000
Misc. Closing Costs	2,000,000
Land Use Cost	1,825,000
Site Setup Costs	1,600,000
Total	160,000,000

VAL turbines have a 30-year serviceable life, and VAL plans to contract with LCCC for fixed-price delivery under a 15-year CfD agreement when operations begin. Note that while wind power generation in practice often varies due to changing weather conditions over time and other factors, the wind farm capacity used for VAL modeling purposes is a probability-weighted measure of a minimal level for each wind turbine to produce over an average year with 90% probability, referred to in the renewable energy industry as a **P90 level**.

VAL Project Financing Plan

Equity: 31.25% of cost, or GBP50,000,000 drawn in three steps. Upon completion, GP performance fees are 15% of returns above a 12% hurdle rate.

Equity drawdown:

- Initial: GBP20,000,000
- One year: GBP15,000,000
- Two years: GBP15,000,000

Debt: 68.75% of cost, or GBP110,000,000 from private investors in two forms:

Construction and development (C&D) loan

- 8% annualized interest

- Monthly loan disbursements linked to construction milestones, such as site setup and timely commissioning of wind turbines as scheduled
- Interest accrues monthly over a three-year construction period.
- Secured by VAL land, equipment, and other project assets
- 36 end-of-month drawdowns (disbursements) equal to GBP2,725,108 each
- Loan is to be repaid from amortizing term loan proceeds.

Amortizing term loan

- 15-year, GBP110,000,000 amortizing loan starting in three years
- Drawn once 125 MW are fully operational and connected to grid
- 7% annual interest rate with 180 fixed monthly payments of interest and principal repayment
- Secured by VAL land, equipment, and other project assets

VAL Operations

VAL's expected revenue from its first full year of operation is shown in the following table.

Measure	Amount
Wind Farm Capacity (MW)	125
P90 Farm Capacity (kWh, 1,000 kW = 1 MW) (Wind Farm Capacity for 8,760 Hours)	1,095,000,000
Efficiency (%)	35%
Total Output (kWh)	383,250,000
Down Time (%)	5%
Actual Output (kWh)	364,087,500
Fixed Price for Delivery (GBP/kWh)	0.125
First Full Year of Revenue (GBP)	45,510,938
Operating Expenses (GBP)	(9,715,082)
Net Cash Flow from Operations (GBP)	**35,795,855**

VAL turbines are assumed to be 35% efficient in capturing wind power. With 5% expected down time and a starting contractual rate of GBP0.125 per kWh, first-year estimated revenue is GBP45,510,938 (= 125MW × 1,000 kWh/MW × 8,760 hours/year × 35% efficiency × 95% operating time × GBP0.125).

1. Calculate and show the ratio of equity to total capital monthly for the first year of the VAL project.

   Solution:

   Equity drawdown of GBP20,000,000 occurs at inception and does not occur again until the beginning of the second year, while C&D debt outstanding at month end is the sum of the loan drawdown to date and interest accrued on the initial period balance at the monthly equivalent of an 8% annual rate. Recall from earlier time-value-of-money lessons that this may be converted to a monthly rate as follows:

   $R_{annual} = (1 + R_{monthly})^{12} - 1;$

$R_{monthly} = 0.6434\% = (1 + 0.08)^{1/12} - 1.$

Therefore, at the end of Month 2, the outstanding C&D loan balance is equal to GBP5,467,750, calculated as follows:

- GBP2,725,108 drawn at the end of Month 1
- GBP17,533 interest on initial balance (= 0.6434% × 2,725,108)
- GBP2,725,108 drawn at the end of Month 2
- GBP5,467,750 = 2,725,108 + 17,533 + 2,725,108.

Use an Excel spreadsheet or Google Sheet to calculate monthly debt and equity balances. The following table provides a summary for the first 12 months.

Month	C&D Loan Drawdown	C&D Interest	C&D Loan Balance	Equity	Total	Equity/ (Debt + Equity)
1	2,725,108	0	2,725,108	20,000,000	22,725,108	0.88
2	2,725,108	17,533	5,467,750	20,000,000	25,467,750	0.79
3	2,725,108	35,180	8,228,038	20,000,000	28,228,038	0.71
4	2,725,108	52,939	11,006,086	20,000,000	31,006,086	0.65
5	2,725,108	70,813	13,802,007	20,000,000	33,802,007	0.59
6	2,725,108	88,803	16,615,918	20,000,000	36,615,918	0.55
7	2,725,108	106,907	19,447,934	20,000,000	39,447,934	0.51
8	2,725,108	125,129	22,298,170	20,000,000	42,298,170	0.47
9	2,725,108	143,467	25,166,746	20,000,000	45,166,746	0.44
10	2,725,108	161,924	28,053,778	20,000,000	48,053,778	0.42
11	2,725,108	180,499	30,959,385	20,000,000	50,959,385	0.39
12	2,725,108	199,194	33,883,687	20,000,000	53,883,687	0.37

2. Calculate the LTV at the end of 12 months if the project's value equals cost in terms of debt and equity.

Solution:

Use Equation 1 to solve for LTV at the end of 12 months as follows:

LTV= 0.63 = 33,883,687/53,883,687.

Note that LTV equals 1 – [Equity/(Debt + Equity)] in the solution to Question 1.

3. Calculate the DSCR *for the first year after completion* using VAL's expected first full year of revenue.

Solution:

To determine DSCR upon completion, we must solve for the fixed monthly mortgage loan payment. Earlier fixed-income learning modules showed that periodic payments (A) for a fully amortizing loan may be calculated as follows:

$$A = \frac{r \times \text{Principal}}{1 - (1 + r)^{-n}},$$

where

A = Periodic payment

r = Interest rate per period (0.07/12)

Principal = Principal amount (GBP110,000,000)

n = Number of periods (180 = 15 × 12)

Solve for A of GBP988,711 per month as follows:

$$A = \text{GBP988,711} = \frac{0.005833 \times \text{GBP110,000,000}}{1 - (1 + 0.07/12)^{-180}}.$$

We may also derive A using the Excel PMT function PMT(rate, nper, pv, [fv], [type]), giving us an answer of –GBP988,711 using PMT(0.07/12, 180, 110000000, 0, 0). The final entry of zero indicates that the amortizing term loan settles at the end of the period.

Annual debt service is therefore GBP11,864,533 (= 988,711 × 12).

Solving for DSCR gives 3.02 using Equation 2 and net cash flow from operations of GBP35,795,855 from above as follows:

DSCR = Net cash flow from operations/Debt service.

DSCR = 3.02 = GBP35,795,855/GBP11,864,533.

4. Calculate the equity dividend rate for the first full year of VAL's operation and the GP performance fee (ignoring management fees).

Solution:

Using VAL's annual debt service of GBP11,864,533 from Question 2, solve for before-tax cash flow of GBP23,931,322 using Equation 4:

Before-tax cash flow = Net cash flow from operations – Debt service.

GBP23,931,322 = 35,795,855 – 11,864,533.

Use Equation 3 to solve for the equity dividend rate:

$$\text{Equity dividend rate} = 47.9\% = \frac{\text{GBP23,931,322}}{\text{GBP160,000,000} - \text{GBP110,000,000}}.$$

GP performance fees are equal to 15% of the equity dividend rate in excess of the 12% hurdle rate. Solve as before using a simplified version of Equation 5:

$$R_{GP\ (\text{Net with hurdle},\ r_m=0)} = \max\{0, [P_1 - P_0 \times (1 + r_h)] \times p\}.$$

P_1 is equal to GBP73,931,322, or the sum of the equity dividend and equity, with r_h of 0.12 and p of 0.15:

$$= \max[0, (73,931,322 - 50,000,000 \times 1.12) \times 0.15],$$

which results in a GP performance fee of GBP2,689,968.

INFRASTRUCTURE INVESTMENT DUE DILIGENCE AND VALUATION

5

☐ discuss the due diligence and valuation processes for infrastructure investments

Infrastructure Investment Due Diligence

Infrastructure investments are distinguished by their greater complexity and longevity relative to other assets. Investors often develop or engage advisers with specific legal and sector-specific technical expertise to conduct due diligence.

In addition to specific jurisdictional, legal, and regulatory considerations, detailed technical issues associated with engineering, procurement, and construction contracts, as well as the details, scope, and commercial terms of the concession agreement, are among the unique elements of infrastructure due diligence, as highlighted in Exhibit 11.

Exhibit 11: Elements of Infrastructure Investment Due Diligence

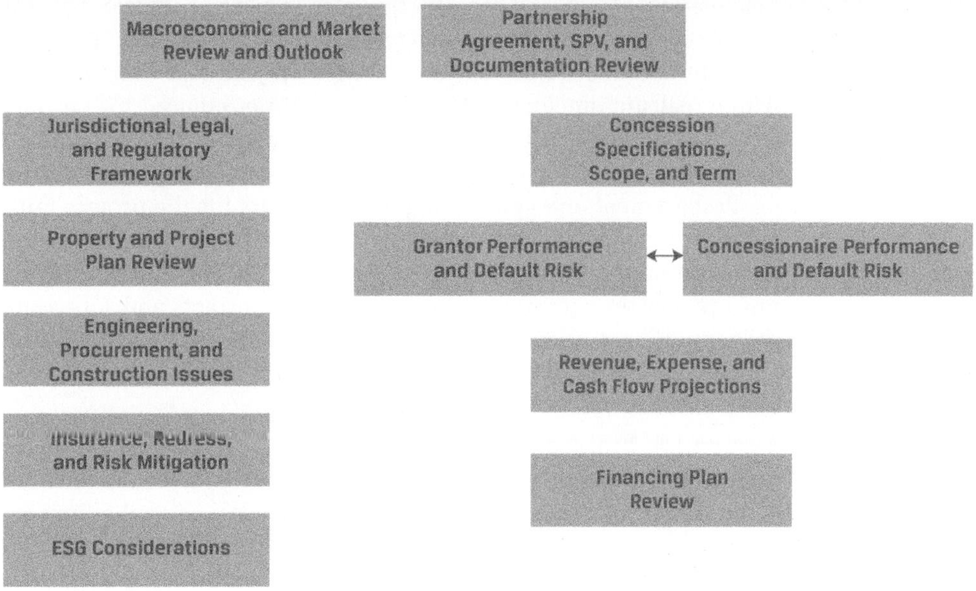

As in the case of other private markets, investors use a variety of sources to gather information about factors affecting the asset's future economic use, including forecasting demand and long-term growth. In private equity or real estate, asset appreciation over a several-year period of restructuring or development drives a greater focus on the market or real estate cycle. Infrastructure investors, in contrast, seek to ensure the protection of a project's long-term viability over multiple cycles with a greater focus on both jurisdictional and legal issues, as well as performance and default risk of the multiple parties involved. Three key areas of importance for infrastructure due diligence are highlighted next.

Jurisdictional, Legal and Regulatory Framework

The direct and indirect involvement of public authorities in infrastructure projects requires a broad knowledge of host country laws and a detailed understanding of regulations specifically pertaining to a project's grantor of property use, the right to construct and operate the asset under an associated concession, and key commercial terms. In particular, the legal status of the grantor and laws governing its authority, the means of dispute resolution, and possible sovereign immunity issues are considerations for investors to factor into their analysis.

Lenders must also thoroughly investigate financial recourse, such as the ability to assume control or take possession of project assets, cash reserve accounts, insurance proceeds, or other assets, as well as the right to take corrective action via negative covenants or other means when a project is in trouble.

When investing in developing markets, investors also consider the degree of technical and financial support from global or supranational financial institutions, governments, and globally active developers and operators, as well as the existence of currency controls or limitations on the repatriation of returns or capital investments.

Compliance with anti-corruption laws, ESG issues, and reputational risk issues also require evaluation.

Engineering, Procurement, and Construction Contract Issues

Investors must evaluate both a project's technical feasibility to meet service needs over the anticipated contract life and its adherence to legal and regulatory requirements. Engineering, design, and construction plans must be comprehensive and achievable by project developers and must meet all safety and regulatory requirements (both local and international standards). Reasonable project cost estimates must be combined with a realistic timeline that incorporates time required for permits and approvals, as well as potential delays, risks, and contingencies. Investors must also understand the likelihood and consequences of cost overruns and project delays.

Procurement and contracting arrangements for the project must follow specific guidelines and regulations, such as local labor laws; address the potential environmental and community impact; and comply with zoning and land use regulations. Investors must review procurement strategy, evaluate contracts and sub-contracts, and assess the reputation, track record, and financial stability of developers and contractors.

Concession Scope, Specifications, and Term

Beyond the broad distinction among fixed or availability-based, commercial, or regulation-based payment schemes outlined earlier, investors must thoroughly understand the specific size and timing of revenue flows, as well as any contingencies. For example, the concessionaire may be required to meet specific maintenance or operating standards to be fully compensated. The concessionaire may also be required to renew or upgrade assets or increase capacity as the concession term nears its end.

In other cases, total project receipts do not cover operating costs or additional investments, requiring the grantor to establish alternative forms of cost recovery, including subsidies, taxes, or other government sources. Consider the challenges faced by the new Berlin airport, which we will describe next.

BERLIN BRANDENBURG AIRPORT

Because Berlin's existing three airports lacked the capacity to meet expected future air traffic demand for the country's new capital, a new single airport, Berlin Brandenburg Airport, was proposed to expand capacity following German reunification in 1990.

After establishing a project company in 1991, federal, state, and local authorities reached a consensus on using one of the existing airports (Schönefeld) as the site for the new project over a five-year period.

Originally planned as a privately constructed and operated airport over a 50-year concession period, the initial consortium selected to build and operate the new airport was removed due to legal action by a losing bidder, and ultimately the privatization effort was abandoned in 2003.

Once the project shifted to the public sector, legal action by nearby residents adversely impacted by the airport expansion delayed the start of construction until 2006. Although the Berlin Brandenburg Airport was slated to open in 2011, five years after construction began, substantial cost overruns and poor construction planning, execution, and management led to nearly a decade of further delays, with the airport finally opening for commercial traffic in October 2020, nearly 30 years after official planning began. Over this period, the project planner became insolvent, the architectural firm was dismissed, and a host of technical and engineering problems arose over the construction period, from faulty wiring to an inadequate fire safety system.

Infrastructure Investment Valuation

Earlier learning modules have demonstrated the use of public market valuation approaches, such as discounted cash flow, relative value, or replacement cost methods, in private markets, which have varying degrees of applicability and typically require several adjustments among different asset classes.

In the case of private infrastructure assets, the preferred method is the discounted cash flow (DCF) approach with periodic equity distributions in the form of dividends (D_t) in the numerator and a series of discount rates in the denominator combining risk-free rates (r_t) with an asset-specific risk premium (γ_t) comprising relevant risk factors, as shown in Exhibit 12 and Equation 5.

Exhibit 12: Areas of Focus for Infrastructure Asset Valuation

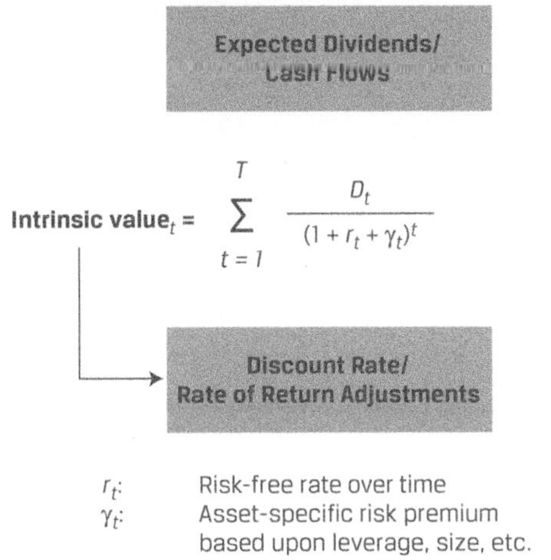

$$\text{Intrinsic value} = \sum_{t=1}^{T} \frac{D_t}{(1 + r_t + \gamma_t)^t}, \tag{6}$$

$$\gamma_t = \text{Risk factor}_{1,t} + \text{Risk factor}_{2,t} + \ldots; \gamma = \sum_{k=1}^{K} Risk\,factor_{k,t} \quad (7)$$

The predominant use of the DCF method is also often due to a lack of comparable infrastructure asset transactions severely limiting the application of relative value techniques, while the alternative of a replacement cost approach ignores a project's underlying business model, source of cash flows, and life cycle timing.

The Tay Bac Airport case study continues with expected cash flows for the project.

CASE STUDY

Tay Bac Airport Expected Cash Flows

Meg Zhu is a senior analyst at InfraEast, an infrastructure firm considering an investment in the Tay Bac Airport project. She notes the expected USD200,000,000 in initial operating year (Year 4) revenue from 5,000,000 passengers generating USD40 in gross revenue each. Based on her analysis of expected Vietnamese economic growth and existing airport cost structures, Zhu formulates the following assumptions to project future cash flows:

- For the first 10 years of operation (through Year 13), Tay Bac Airport passenger traffic grows 5% annually while revenue per passenger rises 1% per year. Starting in the 11th year of operation (Year 14) through the end of the concession period, the respective growth rates fall by 50%.
- Zhu estimates operating and other expenses equal to 50% of revenue and assumes a tax rate of 20%.

Zhu next uses the following debt details to determine annual debt service:

IFC Senior Debt

Year	Drawdown	Interest Accrued	Interest Paid	Principal Paid	Debt Service	Debt Outstanding
2	150,000,000					150,000,000
3		9,000,000				159,000,000
4		9,540,000	9,540,000		**9,540,000**	159,000,000
5		9,540,000	9,540,000	9,425,048	**18,965,048**	149,574,952
6		8,974,497	8,974,497	9,990,551	**18,965,048**	139,584,402
7		8,375,064	8,375,064	10,589,984	**18,965,048**	128,994,418
8		7,739,665	7,739,665	11,225,383	**18,965,048**	117,769,036
9		7,066,142	7,066,142	11,898,906	**18,965,048**	105,870,130
10		6,352,208	6,352,208	12,612,840	**18,965,048**	93,257,290
11		5,595,437	5,595,437	13,369,610	**18,965,048**	79,887,680
12		4,793,261	4,793,261	14,171,787	**18,965,048**	65,715,893
13		3,942,954	3,942,954	15,022,094	**18,965,048**	50,693,799
14		3,041,628	3,041,628	15,923,420	**18,965,048**	34,770,379
15		2,086,223	2,086,223	16,878,825	**18,965,048**	17,891,554
16		1,073,493	1,073,493	17,891,554	**18,965,048**	

Senior Term Loan A

Year	Drawdown	Interest Paid	Principal Paid	Debt Service	Debt Outstanding
3	235,000,000				235,000,000
4		17,625,000		**17,625,000**	235,000,000
5		17,625,000		**17,625,000**	235,000,000
6		17,625,000		**17,625,000**	235,000,000
7		17,625,000	58,750,000	**76,375,000**	176,250,000
8		13,218,750	58,750,000	**71,968,750**	117,500,000
9		8,812,500	58,750,000	**67,562,500**	58,750,000
10		4,406,250	58,750,000	**63,156,250**	

Bank Loan (ECA guaranteed)

Year	Drawdown	Interest Paid	Principal Paid	Debt Service	Debt Outstanding
3	100,000,000				100,000,000
4		6,500,000		6,500,000	100,000,000
5		6,500,000		6,500,000	100,000,000
6		6,500,000		6,500,000	100,000,000
7		6,500,000		6,500,000	100,000,000
8		6,500,000		6,500,000	100,000,000
9		6,500,000		6,500,000	100,000,000
10		6,500,000		6,500,000	100,000,000
11		6,500,000		6,500,000	100,000,000
12		6,500,000		6,500,000	100,000,000
13		6,500,000	100,000,000	106,500,000	

Junior Debt

Year	Drawdown	Interest Accrued	Interest Paid	Principal Paid	Debt Service	Debt Outstanding
0	100,000,000					100,000,000
1		9,500,000				109,500,000
2		10,402,500				119,902,500
3		11,390,738				131,293,238
4		12,472,858				143,766,095
5		13,657,779				157,423,874
6		14,955,268				172,379,142
7		16,376,019				188,755,161
8		17,931,740				206,686,901
9		19,635,256				226,322,156
10		21,500,605				247,822,761

Year	Drawdown	Interest Accrued	Interest Paid	Principal Paid	Debt Service	Debt Outstanding
11		23,543,162				271,365,924
12		25,779,763				297,145,686
13		28,228,840				325,374,527
14		30,910,580	30,910,580	70,626,722	**101,537,352**	254,747,755
15		24,201,037	24,201,037	77,335,315	**101,537,352**	177,411,440
16		16,854,087	16,854,087	84,683,265	**101,537,352**	92,728,175
17		8,809,177	8,809,177	92,728,175	**101,537,352**	0

1. Calculate the expected Tay Bac Airport revenue, net cash flow from operations, and after-tax dividend over the 20-year concession period.

Solution:

Using the assumptions provided, we can determine TBA's annual revenue. Initial operating (Year 4) revenue of USD200,000,000 grows at an annual rate of 6.05% [= (1.05 × 1.01) – 1] through Year 13 and 3.515% [= (1.025 × 1.005) – 1] thereafter. For example, Year 5 operating revenue is USD212,100,000, or 200,000,000 × 1.05 × 1.01.

Net cash flow from operations is half of revenue. Using the previous debt service analysis and Equation 4,

Before-tax cash flow = Net cash flow from operations – Debt service,

we can solve for before-tax cash flow, which when reduced by the 20% tax rate gives us the after-tax dividend. These figures are summarized for the full concession period as follows:

Year	Revenue	Net Cash Flow from Operations	Debt Service	Interest Payments	Before-Tax Cash Flow	Tax	After-Tax Dividend
4	200,000,000	100,000,000	33,665,000	33,665,000	66,335,000	13,267,000	53,068,000
5	212,100,000	106,050,000	43,090,048	33,665,000	62,959,952	14,477,000	48,482,952
6	224,932,050	112,466,025	43,090,048	33,099,497	69,375,977	15,873,306	53,502,672
7	238,540,439	119,270,220	101,840,048	32,500,064	17,430,172	17,354,031	76,141
8	252,972,136	126,486,068	97,433,798	27,458,415	29,052,270	19,805,531	9,246,740
9	268,276,950	134,138,475	93,027,548	22,378,642	41,110,927	22,351,967	18,758,961
10	284,507,705	142,253,853	88,621,298	17,258,458	53,632,555	24,999,079	28,633,476
11	301,720,421	150,860,211	25,465,048	12,095,437	125,395,163	27,752,955	97,642,208
12	319,974,507	159,987,253	25,465,048	11,293,261	134,522,206	29,738,799	104,783,407
13	339,332,965	169,666,482	125,465,048	10,442,954	44,201,435	31,844,706	12,356,729
14	349,555,370	174,777,685	120,502,399	33,952,208	54,275,286	28,165,095	26,110,190
15	360,085,726	180,042,863	120,502,399	26,287,259	59,540,463	30,751,121	28,789,343
16	370,933,308	185,466,654	120,502,399	17,927,580	64,964,255	33,507,815	31,456,440
17	382,107,674	191,053,837	101,537,352	8,809,177	89,516,485	36,448,932	53,067,553
18	393,618,668	196,809,334			196,809,334	39,361,867	157,447,467
19	405,476,430	202,738,215			202,738,215	40,547,643	162,190,572
20	417,691,408	208,845,704			208,845,704	41,769,141	167,076,563
21	430,274,361	215,137,181			215,137,181	43,027,436	172,109,744

Year	Revenue	Net Cash Flow from Operations	Debt Service	Interest Payments	Before-Tax Cash Flow	Tax	After-Tax Dividend
22	443,236,376	221,618,188			221,618,188	44,323,638	177,294,551
23	456,588,872	228,294,436			228,294,436	45,658,887	182,635,549

2. Contrast the risks of the Senior Term Loan A and the junior debt tranches in the context of TBA's debt profile and project phases.

Solution:

While Term Loan A interest and principal reflect a senior debt claim, the greater risks of the junior debt tranche are reflected in the fact that it is drawn earlier (Year 0 versus Year 3 in the case of Term Loan A), remains fully outstanding during TBA's construction and development phase, is repaid later (Years 13–17 for junior debt, Years 7–10 for Term Loan A), pays no interest until amortization, represents a subordinated claim to TBA project assets, and is repaid only once periodic debt service for the other three loans is paid.

Junior debt repayment occurs following the expected initial revenue growth phase of the project—that is, during a period after which the growth in the number of passengers and revenue per passenger has leveled off.

3. Discuss the project period or periods in which TBA is at greatest risk of being unable to meet its debt service.

Solution:

The debt service coverage ratio, shown in Equation 2, provides a measure of whether the project is able to meet its debt obligations from expected net cash flow from operations:

$$\text{DSCR} = \frac{\text{Net cash flow from operations}}{\text{Debt service}}.$$

As demonstrated in the following table, the project's DSCR is expected to reach a low of 1.17X in Year 7 as the amortization of Term Loan A begins. Note that the DSCR also remains relatively low (below 2X) during the years when Term Loan A principal is amortized (Years 7–10) and when the bank ECA loan and the junior loan are amortized (Years 13–17).

Year	Net Cash Flow from Operations	Debt Service	DSCR
4	100,000,000	33,665,000	2.97
5	106,050,000	43,090,048	2.46
6	112,466,025	43,090,048	2.61
7	119,270,220	101,840,048	1.17
8	126,486,068	97,433,798	1.30
9	134,138,475	93,027,548	1.44
10	142,253,853	88,621,298	1.61
11	150,860,211	25,465,048	5.92
12	159,987,253	25,465,048	6.28
13	169,666,482	125,465,048	1.35
14	174,777,685	120,502,399	1.45
15	180,042,863	120,502,399	1.49

Year	Net Cash Flow from Operations	Debt Service	DSCR
16	185,466,654	120,502,399	1.54
17	191,053,837	101,537,352	1.88
18	196,809,334		
19	202,738,215		
20	208,845,704		
21	215,137,181		
22	221,618,188		
23	228,294,436		

As illustrated in the case study, infrastructure projects often make use of multiple sources of public and private debt to optimize the cost and timing of debt service and outstanding debt over the project life cycle. These relationships are shown with net cash flow from operations in Exhibit 13.

Exhibit 13: Tay Bac Cash Flows and Debt

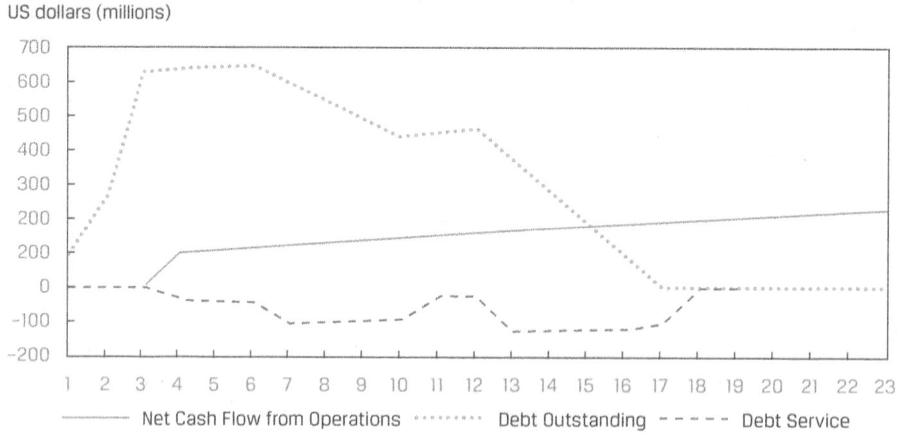

The IFC and ECA loans reduce debt costs compared to traditional private market sources. The senior term loan market has relatively standardized terms, while the junior loan offers private investors higher return in exchange for subordinated claims, capitalized interest, and full drawdown over the construction phase combined with a longer tenor.

The denominator used to discount infrastructure asset cash flows involves a combination of the term structure of risk-free rates and an asset-specific risk premium. Note that these risk premiums may vary over time based on changes over the project life cycle and market conditions. As in the case of private company valuation, the limited applicability of the capital asset pricing model using public company comparables results in the use of a buildup approach that combines a number of risk factors:

- *Size:* Larger infrastructure assets are less liquid, and therefore a higher liquidity premium is associated with owning such assets. This factor typically rises under adverse market conditions when investors seek greater liquidity.

- *Leverage:* While higher leverage generally commands a higher risk premium, falling leverage ratios over the life of an infrastructure project contribute to lower future discount rates. Note also that projects with a contractual, fixed cash flow business model are often able to support greater leverage than those with merchant payment schemes.
- *Profitability:* Profitability is inversely related to risk and is often believed to have a smaller impact on the discount rate than other factors. Higher profits lead to a lower and typically negative risk premium (that is, they receive less of a discount via a lower denominator in Equation 5), while lower profits have a higher risk premium.
- *Investment:* High capital expenditures as a proportion of project assets typically indicate an asset in the development phase of its life cycle, which is associated with the highest risk. This factor tends to be higher for greenfield investments than for brownfield investments.
- *Country risk:* As in the case of equities or other private assets, developing markets have higher project risk than do developed markets.
- *Currency risk:* If long-term project cash flows are in a foreign currency and remain unhedged, then a currency risk premium should be incorporated to address the risk of depreciation in the foreign currency cash flows and its impact on investor currency returns.

These aggregated risk factors are combined with each respective risk-free rate to derive a periodic discount rate used for valuation purposes as shown in the case of Tay Bac Airport.

CASE STUDY

Tay Bac Airport Discount Factors and Valuation

Meg Zhu at InfraEast continues her analysis of the Tay Bac Airport project at the end of Year 3 by estimating annual discount factors for the expected annual dividends to equityholders. As a first step, she observes the following US dollar risk-free zero rates that apply at the end of each period.

Year	US Dollar Risk-Free Zero Rates
4	3.0960%
5	3.2040%
6	3.2310%
7	3.2760%
8	3.3390%
9	3.4110%
10	3.4560%
11	3.5190%
12	3.6090%
13	3.7395%
14	3.8070%
15	3.9339%
16	4.0482%
17	4.1418%
18	4.2453%
19	4.3407%

Year	US Dollar Risk-Free Zero Rates
20	4.4568%
21	4.5216%
22	4.5459%
23	4.5657%

Next, Zhu analyzes the project in the context of key risk factors compared with transaction prices. Using a statistical analysis of past price observations and the key risk factors listed previously, she draws the following conclusions:

- *Size:* As a regional airport, Zhu considers Tay Bac Airport to be a mid-size project, which warrants a 1.50% risk premium above the risk-free rate over the project life.
- *Leverage:* Zhu assigns the highest (2.50%) project leverage risk premium for Years 4–6, which, given significant debt reduction due to amortization of Term Loan A and the maturing ECA bank loan, is reduced to 1.50% for Year 7 through Year 13. Zhu assigns a 0.50% leverage premium to Years 14 through 17 and 0.00% thereafter because debt will have been repaid.
- *Profitability and investment:* Tay Bac Airport's expected median profitability and relatively low investment levels (once construction is completed in the first three years) warrant a –1.00% and 0.50% risk premium adjustment, respectively.
- *Country and Currency Risk:* Based on Vietnam's status as a thriving middle-income economy and positive outlook, Zhu estimates the country risk for Vietnam to be a constant 4% throughout the concession period. Given that project cash flows are primarily in Vietnamese dong (VND) while financing is denominated in US dollars and the currency risk is unhedged, Zhu increases the risk premium by 1% based on potential future VND depreciation risk.

1. Calculate the respective annual discount rates for the Tay Bac Airport project concession period based on Meg Zhu's research.

Solution

We can solve for the respective annual discount rate by adding the risk-free zero rate, r_t, to the sum of the risk factors, γ_t, as shown in Equation 7:

$$\gamma_t = \text{Risk factor}_{1,t} + \text{Risk factor}_{2,t} + \ldots.$$

The respective discount factors ($r_t + \gamma_t$) are shown in the far right column in the following table:

Year	US Dollar Risk-Free Zero Rates	Size	Leverage	Profitability	Investment	Country and Currency Risk	Discount Factor ($r_t + \gamma_t$)
4	3.0960%	1.50%	2.50%	–1.00%	0.50%	5.00%	11.5960%
5	3.2040%	1.50%	2.50%	–1.00%	0.50%	5.00%	11.7040%
6	3.2310%	1.50%	2.50%	–1.00%	0.50%	5.00%	11.7310%
7	3.2760%	1.50%	1.50%	–1.00%	0.50%	5.00%	10.7760%
8	3.3390%	1.50%	1.50%	–1.00%	0.50%	5.00%	10.8390%
9	3.4110%	1.50%	1.50%	–1.00%	0.50%	5.00%	10.9110%
10	3.4560%	1.50%	1.50%	–1.00%	0.50%	5.00%	10.9560%

Year	US Dollar Risk-Free Zero Rates	Size	Leverage	Profitability	Investment	Country and Currency Risk	Discount Factor $(r_t + \gamma_t)$
11	3.5190%	1.50%	1.50%	−1.00%	0.50%	5.00%	11.0190%
12	3.6090%	1.50%	1.50%	−1.00%	0.50%	5.00%	11.1090%
13	3.7395%	1.50%	1.50%	−1.00%	0.50%	5.00%	11.2395%
14	3.8070%	1.50%	0.50%	−1.00%	0.50%	5.00%	10.3070%
15	3.9339%	1.50%	0.50%	−1.00%	0.50%	5.00%	10.4339%
16	4.0482%	1.50%	0.50%	−1.00%	0.50%	5.00%	10.5482%
17	4.1418%	1.50%	0.50%	−1.00%	0.50%	5.00%	10.6418%
18	4.2453%	1.50%	0.00%	−1.00%	0.50%	5.00%	10.2453%
19	4.3407%	1.50%	0.00%	−1.00%	0.50%	5.00%	10.3407%
20	4.4568%	1.50%	0.00%	−1.00%	0.50%	5.00%	10.4568%
21	4.5216%	1.50%	0.00%	−1.00%	0.50%	5.00%	10.5216%
22	4.5459%	1.50%	0.00%	−1.00%	0.50%	5.00%	10.5459%
23	4.5657%	1.50%	0.00%	−1.00%	0.50%	5.00%	10.5657%

2. Solve for the expected Tay Bac Airport project value at the end of Year 3.

Solution:

We can calculate the expected Tay Bac Airport project value at the end of Year 3 by first determining the present value (PV) of each annual dividend using the respective periodic discount rate and then adding the results. For example, because the Year 5 dividend is expected in two years, we solve for the PV of the Year 5 dividend as follows:

$$\text{USD}38,855,420 = \frac{\text{USD}48,482,952}{(1 + 0.11704)^2}.$$

The results for all expected concession period dividends are shown in the following table.

Year	Adjusted Rate	Discount Factor $(1 + r + y)^{-(t-3)}$	After-Tax Dividend	PV of After-Tax Dividend
4	11.596%	0.89609	53,068,000	47,553,676
5	11.704%	0.80142	48,482,952	38,855,420
6	11.731%	0.71693	53,502,672	38,357,864
7	10.776%	0.66408	76,141	50,563
8	10.839%	0.59777	9,246,740	5,527,460
9	10.911%	0.53722	18,758,961	10,077,691
10	10.956%	0.48300	28,633,476	13,829,884
11	11.019%	0.43333	97,642,208	42,311,566
12	11.109%	0.38749	104,783,407	40,602,181
13	11.240%	0.34467	12,356,729	4,259,055
14	10.307%	0.33991	26,110,190	8,875,161
15	10.434%	0.30393	28,789,343	8,749,895
16	10.548%	0.27154	31,456,440	8,541,572
17	10.642%	0.24273	53,067,553	12,881,303
18	10.245%	0.23153	157,447,467	36,453,096
19	10.341%	0.20712	162,190,572	33,593,391

Year	Adjusted Rate	Discount Factor $(1 + r + y)^{-(t-3)}$	After-Tax Dividend	PV of After-Tax Dividend
20	10.457%	0.18439	167,076,563	30,806,599
21	10.522%	0.16518	172,109,744	28,428,668
22	10.546%	0.14883	177,294,551	26,386,709
23	10.566%	0.13415	182,635,549	24,500,611

Next, we use Equation 6 to determine the expected project value:

$$\text{USD460,642,367} = \sum_{t=4}^{23} (\text{PV of after} - \text{tax dividend})_t.$$

3. Discuss the return to equityholders over the construction period.

Solution:

During the construction period (Years 1 – 3), equity investors contribute capital into the project while the asset is generating no positive cash flows. So, there is no cash yield earned during the construction period. The return to equityholders is estimated on the basis of the expected future cash flows occurring over the 20-year life of the project beginning in Year 4. As shown in the solution to the prior question, the value of the project at the end of Year 3 is USD460,642,367, and we can calculate a project internal rate of return (IRR) of 13.51% using the initial equity investment of USD315,000,000 and a three-year period. This can be calculated using the IRR function on a financial calculator or using the Excel RATE formula as follows:

Project return = RATE(nper, pmt, -pv, fv)

= 13.51% = RATE(3, 0, -315000000, 460642367).

While the previous example represents the analyst's base-case estimate of project value, uncertainty over an infrastructure project's life cycle often warrants the use of **scenario analysis** or **sensitivity analysis**, as in the case of other private market investments. Recall that scenario analysis involves the combination of a base case with more favorable or adverse alternative outcomes to determine expected value using the average of scenario values weighted by their respective probabilities, while sensitivity analysis measures the impact of changes in one or more key variables on investment value.

Scenario analysis is of particular importance when structural or regulatory changes can lead to an abrupt shift in an infrastructure project's economic return. For example, the value of long-lived power generation projects based on fossil fuels may be impaired by policy changes discouraging the use of fossil fuels in response to climate change or increased operating costs due to enhanced regulatory measures to protect the environment. However, a future reduction in subsidies or less favorable terms for stabilized pricing mechanisms, such as CfDs, may adversely impact the return on long-lived renewable energy projects. Note that infrastructure investments are often viewed as providing an inflation hedge because of the ability of these assets to generate additional revenues during inflationary periods.

Sensitivity analysis is frequently used as a valuation tool in the case of variable merchant-based cash flows, where changes to key business drivers are critical to understand potential investment value changes under different economic and market conditions. Sensitivity analysis is also important in renewable power infrastructure projects where short-term and long-term variations in wind speed, cloud cover, rainfall, and other factors can undermine project finances.

CASE STUDY

Tay Bac Airport Sensitivity Analysis

Meg Zhu at InfraEast takes an additional step in her analysis by stress testing the two key drivers of value in her earlier analysis—namely, the expected growth rates for both the number of passengers and revenue per passenger. She creates a two-variable Excel data table to examine how the starting values for these two growth rates affect the valuation and IRR of the project:

Passenger Growth Rate (%)	Revenue per Passenger Growth (%) Base-Case Value: USD460,642,367		
	0%	**1%**	**2%**
7%	520,983,041	594,196,594	674,084,447
6%	457,813,060	524,660,869	597,531,959
5%	399,597,144	460,642,367	527,121,640
4%	345,930,584	401,687,248	462,344,864
3%	296,441,420	347,378,578	402,734,563

Passenger Growth Rate (%)	Revenue per Passenger Growth (%) Base-Case IRR: 13.51%		
	0%	**1%**	**2%**
7%	18.26%	23.56%	28.86%
6%	13.27%	18.54%	23.79%
5%	8.25%	13.51%	18.72%
4%	3.17%	8.44%	13.65%
3%	−2.00%	3.32%	8.53%

1. Discuss how changes in the growth expectations in her sensitivity analysis might cause Zhu to revisit her assumptions affecting the *numerator* of the infrastructure valuation.

   Solution:

   In her expected dividend calculations that make up the numerator of the infrastructure valuation as shown in Equation 5, Zhu has made the simple assumption that operating expenses are directly proportional to revenues. In the case of lower-than-expected passenger volumes, Zhu may consider revisiting this assumption due to the fixed costs of operating the airport at lower-than-expected capacity. However, if passenger volumes are much higher than her base case, the facility may face capacity constraints that require additional capital expenditures, which would lower expected dividends versus original estimates.

2. Discuss how changes in the growth expectations in her sensitivity analysis might cause Zhu to revisit her assumptions affecting the *denominator* of the infrastructure valuation.

   Solution:

   As noted in the answer to Question 1, changes in expected passenger volume may have an impact on both profitability and investment levels over the Tay Bac Airport project life cycle. Large deviations from the base case assumptions may warrant an adjustment of the risk factors used to discount expected dividend cash flows. For example, lower-than-expected passenger growth might reduce the expected median profitability of the project and therefore imply a higher discount rate. However, higher-than-expected traffic may result in higher capital expenditure, increasing the investment risk factor and raising the discount rate.

3. Discuss how changes in inflation may affect the valuation of the Tay Bac Airport project.

Solution:

Inflation may be reflected by the growth in revenue per passenger shown at the top of the sensitivity tables. If an increase in inflation is accompanied by the ability of the Tay Bac Airport project to generate greater revenue growth per passenger, then subsequent improvements in cash flow from operations may assist in hedging Tay Bac Airport's value from the effects of inflation. While the sensitivity table shows value (and IRR) improvements as revenue growth per passenger increases, care must be taken to also assess inflationary effects on Tay Bac Airport's operating costs. Cost increases due to inflation may offset revenue increases. Furthermore, inflationary pressures may also negatively affect the demand for air travel, thus reducing the passenger growth rate. Overall, the effects of possible inflation on Tay Bac Airport's value are likely too complex to be reflected in the two-variable Excel table.

As the case study demonstrates, scenario and sensitivity analysis tools help investors and risk managers gauge the impact of changes in key value drivers but may also raise shortcomings of simplified model assumptions that warrant further refinement. In the following section, we will further address the drivers of relative risk and return among infrastructure investments and compare them to other private markets.

QUESTION SET

Meg Zhu at InfraEast continues her assessment of the sensitivity issues associated with the Tay Bac Airport project. Specifically, she wants to explore issues of cost overruns and delays in construction as they relate to valuation and debt service coverage, and she wants to review the discount rate assumptions.

Use relevant information from the Tay Bac Airport examples presented earlier to answer Questions 1–4.

1. Demonstrate the effect of a 10% cost overrun on the expected return to the equity investor of the Tay Bac Airport project, assuming that the cost overrun must be funded by an additional equity contribution in Year 3.

Solution:

A 10% cost overrun increases the amount of the overall project cost from USD900 million to USD990 million. We may use the Excel RATE function to calculate the revised project return. If the Year 3 project value remains at USD460,642,367, then the additional equity contribution of USD90,000,000 reduces the future value in Year 3 to USD370,642,367 (= 460,642,367 – 90,000,000) and we can calculate return as 5.57%.

Equity project return = RATE(nper, pmt, pv, fv)

= 5.57% = RATE(3, 0, -315000000, 437514322).

The IRR declines from 13.51% in the original scenario to 5.57% with the cost overrun.

2. Demonstrate the effect of a one-year delay on the expected return to the equity investor of the Tay Bac Airport project, assuming that all expected project cash flows remain in place (and assume for simplicity that debt can be renegotiated to delay debt cash flows for one year and that discount rates do not adjust for the delay).

   Solution:

   In this case, the value of the project (USD527,514,322) is delayed from the end of three years to the end of four years. Reverting the initial equity investment amount to USD315 million and changing the *nper* amount from three to four in the IRR formula result in

   Expected return = IRR(4, 0, -315000000, 460642367) = 9.97%.

   The IRR declines from 13.51% in the original scenario to 9.97% with the one-year delay.

3. Evaluate the one-year delay scenario if debt cash flows are not delayed by considering debt service coverage ratios of the Tay Bac Airport project.

   Solution:

   Given the growing cash inflows expected for the project throughout its life, the DSCRs are best considered at the times during the project when debt service reaches high points. In the earlier example in which debt service was examined, debt service reaches highs in Year 7 (USD101,840,048) and in Year 13 (USD125,465,048). So, a one-year delay in net cash flow from operations implies that the revised DSCR in Year 7 would be equal to the original Year 6 net cash flow from operations divided by 101,840,048. Similarly, for the DSCR in Year 13, the original Year 12 net cash flow from operations would be divided by 125,465,048.

   Revised Year 7 DSCR = 112,466,025/101,840,048 = 1.10.

   Revised Year 13 DSCR = 159,987,253/125,465,048 = 1.28.

   The one-year delay, while reducing the DSCRs for the Tay Bac Airport project, still allows for debt service to be fully covered from net cash flow from operations under the revised cash flow scenario.

4. Justify the pattern of declining discount factors used to determine the Tay Bac Airport project value.

   Solution:

   As shown earlier in the example, the discount rates decline over the life of the Tay Bac Airport project from 11.596% in the first year in which the asset generates positive cash flows to 10.5657% during the last year of the project. While several factors are used to determine the discount rate, including the size of the project, profitability, investment, and country and currency risk premiums, none of these factors vary over the project's life. Only the risk-free rate and the leverage factor show declines over the project's life. While the risk-free rate reflects an upward-sloping term structure, the increase is more than offset by the decline in the leverage factor premium. This reflects the decline in the project's debt outstanding that begins after Year 6 and continues throughout the life span of the project.

6 INFRASTRUCTURE RISK AND RETURN

- [ ] discuss the risk and return among infrastructure investments and as compared to other investments as part of a strategic asset allocation

Investment features contributing to the unique role of infrastructure among private market assets stem from the provision of services with relatively inelastic demand and less exposure to market cyclicality or economic shocks. While most infrastructure investments involve a high distribution of stable cash flows over long-term contractual periods, they may also benefit from significant barriers to entry, as highlighted in the following example.

MACQUARIE SUPER CORE INFRASTRUCTURE FUND

As the world's largest infrastructure general partner, Sydney-based Macquarie Asset Management closed the first series of its Super Core Infrastructure Fund in 2018 with EUR2.5 billion in initial investments. The fund's focus is on core regulated infrastructure assets in gas and electricity distribution in Western Europe. At the time of its launch, initial projections of the fund's target return were 7%–8% with a 5% cash yield. Given the focus on core assets, the risk profile is lower than diversified infrastructure funds (with target returns of 10%–12%).

In late 2022, Macquarie closed a follow-on offering of EUR2.3 billion. Since the fund's inception, it also raised additional capital of EUR7.8 billion in co-investment, increasing total capital raised from investors in the super core strategy to EUR12.6 billion. The fund has expanded its geographic footprint and now owns assets in countries including the United Kingdom, Germany, Finland, Spain, and Greece.

The Super Core Infrastructure Fund has been classified as an Article 8 fund under the Sustainable Finance Disclosure Regulation as part of the EU's Financing Sustainable Growth Action Plan. Article 8 funds are those that promote environmental or social features. This classification is attractive to European institutional investors and global investors seeking investments in private market assets with ESG characteristics.

The Super Core Infrastructure Fund's acquisition focus involves the ownership of assets that connect electricity and gas production facilities, thus improving the capacity to distribute power from existing generation facilities. For example, the Super Core Infrastructure Fund owns the operator of the national electricity distribution network in Greece. By improving the ability of the network to distribute the electricity produced by solar and wind on the Greek mainland to the Greek islands, Macquarie's Super Core Infrastructure Fund expands the electrical grid, lowers household energy costs, and improves network reliability.

While assets in core infrastructure equity, such as the fund in the previous example, offer the lowest risk and return among infrastructure equity assets, their stable cash flows and favorable duration characteristics are increasingly seen as a long-term liability-matching alternative to default-risk-free government bonds.

These infrastructure investments typically offer return levels well in excess of other long-duration investments, provided an investor is able to accept these assets' lack of liquidity.

For example, the infra300 equity index of unlisted infrastructure investments had a return over a 10-year period (from 2009 to 2019) of just over 12% per annum, with a 13.9% total return volatility and just a 24% correlation with the MSCI World Index.

This liability-matching feature is increasingly used by long-term institutional investors, such as pensions, sovereign wealth funds, ultra-high-net-worth individuals, and family offices. These investors align their allocation to such investments with their risk tolerance, return objectives, and market expectations as demonstrated in the following example.

CASE STUDY

Northern States Infrastructure Investment Strategy

Northern States Pension Plan is a large US-based public pension plan that added infrastructure investments as a suballocation in its overall asset allocation to private markets in the past five years. Northern States has established the following investment policy for infrastructure assets:

Infrastructure investment strategic objectives:

- Improve investment portfolio diversification.
- Earn yield above earnings assumptions and generate stable cash flows.
- Match future liabilities and expected long-term distributions.
- Preserve capital and hedge against inflation.
- Engage as a responsible investor to promote sound environmental practices.

Infrastructure investment performance target:

The plan has a performance target of exceeding a return of US CPI plus 5.00% per annum net of fees on its private unlisted investments and seeks to exceed the appropriate public market benchmark for publicly traded infrastructure assets.

Long-term target infrastructure allocation ranges:

- Core: 30%–70%
- Value-add: 20%–60%
- Opportunistic: 5%–25%
- Publicly traded: 0%–10%
- Co-investment and direct investment: 0%–10%

Long-term target infrastructure geographic allocation:

- United States: 25%–70%
- OECD, Ex-US: 20%–60%
- Non-OECD: 0%–25%

In addition to limited liability companies and limited partnerships, Northern States policy allows for co-investment or direct investment in infrastructure assets without an asset manager. Northern States currently has a 70% allocation to US-based core infrastructure via a single closed-end fund and 30% to a value-add closed-end infrastructure fund focused on assets in the EU, all of which are member countries of the OECD.

Brianna Jenkins, head of alternative investments at Northern States, has asked you as an analyst on her team to prepare a memo related to the Tay Bac Airport equity investment opportunity for the investment committee.

1. Evaluate a possible equity investment by Northern States into the Tay Bac Airport opportunity with respect to the pension fund's performance target and allocation ranges for infrastructure investments.

Solution:

First, Northern States has a performance target of exceeding a return of US CPI plus 5.00% per annum net of fees on its private unlisted investments. In an earlier section, the internal rate of return for the Tay Bac Airport project was calculated as 13.51%. As such, the Tay Bac Airport investment opportunity is likely to achieve the pension fund's performance target assuming inflation remains relatively unchanged.

Second, Northern States has a current 70% core infrastructure and 30% value-add infrastructure allocation. However, the pension fund is allowed to allocate between 5% and 25% to opportunistic infrastructure assets, and this is likely the classification to which the Tay Bac Airport project belongs.

Given that Northern States currently has no allocation to opportunistic infrastructure, an investment in the Tay Bac Airport project appears plausible in this component of the fund's target allocations.

Finally, Northern States has the potential to further diversify its portfolio internationally. Its current allocations are 70% to the United States (which is at the maximum of its target) and 30% to the EU (which is in the middle of its target). Northern States may allocate up to 25% to infrastructure assets in non-OECD countries.

Overall, an investment in the Tay Bac Airport project is feasible when considering Northern States' performance target and allocation ranges for infrastructure asset investment.

2. Evaluate a possible equity investment by Northern States into the Tay Bac Airport opportunity with respect to the pension fund's strategic objectives for infrastructure investments.

Solution:

Northern States has the following strategic objectives for its infrastructure investments:

- Improve investment portfolio diversification.
- Target return at or above earnings assumptions and generate stable cash flows.
- Match future liabilities and expected long-term distributions.
- Preserve capital and hedge against inflation.
- Engage as a responsible investor to promote sound environmental practices.

An investment in Tay Bac Airport would provide both asset-type and geographic diversification, as discussed in the prior solution, and its expected return of 13.51% appears likely to meet the performance target of 5% above US CPI.

However, the cash flow projections presented in an earlier section suggest that the Tay Bac Airport project may not generate stable cash flows, making long-term liability matching potentially difficult.

Future spikes in inflation may dampen leisure travel, thus reducing the project's cash flows. As such, this investment may be a less effective inflation hedge.

Finally, given Northern States' stated goal of promoting sound environmental practices, the analyst may need to weigh any potential environmental benefits of the airport project as a more efficient means of travel than, for example, road construction in promoting economic growth and tourism versus the expected increase in air travel often cited as a contributor to greenhouse gas emissions.

Despite their complexity and illiquidity, unlisted infrastructure investments can add diversified, stable cash flows to effectively match an investor's anticipated liability cash flows in the context of an investment strategy and policy. The examples in this learning module used to evaluate the structure, method, investment process over the life cycle, and estimated market value of these assets are similar to those used by practitioners to thoroughly evaluate the expected risk and return of these investments.

QUESTION SET

1. Using the case study and example from Infrastructure Risk and Return, evaluate whether Northern States Pension Fund would likely benefit from an investment in the Macquarie Super Core Infrastructure Fund relative to its current infrastructure allocation.

   Solution:

   Northern States would be unlikely to benefit from investing in the Super Core Infrastructure Fund.

   It has reached its current maximum allocation to core infrastructure asset investments, so any amount invested in the Super Core Infrastructure Fund would require a liquidation of its current US closed-end fund holding in core infrastructure. Although this change would improve the geographic diversification of its infrastructure portfolio, the return performance may be more related to the core feature.

2. Evaluate whether Northern States would favor an infrastructure asset investment with availability-based payments with respect to its strategic objectives.

   Solution:

   An infrastructure asset with availability-based payment provides a fixed income stream, so this would best allow for Northern States' goal of achieving a match between its liabilities and the cash flows from investment.

3. Which of the following strategic objectives listed in the Northern States example is least likely to be provided by an investment in Vento Anglio Limited, introduced in an earlier example for an investor heavily invested in core infrastructure?

   A. Improve portfolio diversification.

   B. Match future liabilities and expected long-term distributions.

C. Engage as a responsible investor by promoting sound environmental practices.

Solution:

A is the correct response. Because the VAL project produces electricity and is paid a fixed price through a contract for difference arrangement, its income stream is likely similar to core infrastructure in electricity generation.

B is incorrect because of the fixed price arrangement. C is incorrect because the wind farm project promotes sound environmental practices.

PRACTICE PROBLEMS

The following information relates to questions 1-5

Brianna Jenkins, head of alternative investments at Northern States Pension Plan, a large US-based public pension plan, is helping a new analyst become familiar with private infrastructure investment.

After covering basics of classifying infrastructure investments across the risk–return spectrum, Jenkins mentions that Northern States has a 70% allocation to US-based core infrastructure via a single closed-end fund and 30% to a value-add closed-end infrastructure fund focused on assets in the EU.

The analyst asks Jenkins about the revenue streams associated with private infrastructure assets, and Jenkins outlined the basics of the three types of payment streams that asset operators receive: availability based, commercial (also called merchant), and regulation based. Jenkins noted how these payment structures create differing levels of business risk for investors in these assets. Jenkins further discussed how private infrastructure assets fit within a broader diversified portfolio.

The analyst asked Jenkins about Northern States' history of private infrastructure investing, and Jenkins explained how Northern States had grown its expertise in infrastructure over the last five years and is now able to participate in the market as a direct investor in specific infrastructure industries. Additionally, Northern States continued to build related industry-specific expertise through its equity investments.

1. Which of the following allocation changes should Northern States consider in order to assume greater risk in its infrastructure suballocation?

   A. Add an allocation to core-plus assets while decreasing its value-add assets.

   B. Add an allocation to opportunistic assets while decreasing its core assets.

   C. Increase its allocation to core assets while decreasing its value-add assets.

2. Which of the following payment approaches is likely associated with the most business risk for a private infrastructure investment?

   A. Availability-based payment

   B. Commercial payment

   C. Regulation-based payment

3. Discuss the factors that are likely to make private infrastructure assets an effective portfolio diversifier.

4. Discuss how industry expertise factors into the methods by which Northern States may participate as an equity co-investor or direct investor in private infrastructure projects.

5. Contrast the cash flow assumptions of valuing a private infrastructure asset under the build–operate–transfer model relative to a private real estate investment.

The following information relates to questions 6-9

The 125 MW Vento Anglio Limited project involves the purchase and installation of 50 2.5 MW wind turbines at a cost of GBP1.1 million per MW, with total development costs incurred either upfront or equally over three years, as shown in the following table.

VAL Development Costs	GBP
Wind Turbines & Related Costs	137,500,000
Contingency Reserve	6,500,000
Operating Deficit Reserves	4,255,000
Interest Reserves	4,020,000
Development Fees	2,300,000
Misc. Closing Costs	2,000,000
Land Use Cost	1,825,000
Site Setup Costs	1,600,000
Total	160,000,000

VAL turbines have a 30-year serviceable life, and VAL has contracted with LCCC for fixed-price delivery under a 15-year CfD agreement at a rate of GBP0.075 per kWh when operations begin. While the vast majority of the total development costs consist of the outlay for the wind turbines, close to GBP15 million of the cost budget is set up as contingency and reserve funds.

VAL Project Financing Plan

Equity: GBP50,000,000

Debt: GBP110,000,000 from private investors in two forms:

C&D loan

- 8% annual interest
- Monthly disbursements linked to construction milestones, such as site setup and timely commissioning of wind turbines as scheduled
- Interest accrues monthly over a three-year construction period.
- The loan is to be repaid from amortizing term loan proceeds.
- Secured by VAL land, equipment, and other project assets
- 36 end-of-month drawdowns of GBP2,725,108 each

Amortizing term loan

- 15-year, GBP110,000,000 amortizing loan starting in three years
- Drawn once 125 MW are fully operational and connected to grid
- 7% annual interest rate with 180 fixed monthly payments of interest and principal repayment
- Secured by VAL land, equipment, and other project assets

VAL's expected revenue from its first full year of operation is shown in the following table.

VAL Operations	
Actual Output (kWh)	364,087,500
Fixed Price for Delivery (GBP/kWh)	GBP0.075
First Full Year of Revenue	GBP27,306,563
Operating Expenses (45% of revenue)	(GBP12,287,953)
CapEx	(GBP4,125,000)
Net Cash Flow from Operations	**GBP10,893,609**

With a contractual rate of GBP0.075 per kWh, first-year estimated revenue is GBP27,306,563 (= 364,087,500 × GBP0.075).

6. Discuss why an SPE such as VAL would establish reserve accounts.

7. Which of the following cash flow structures best characterizes VAL's business risk in the TICCS system?
   A. Availability-based payments
   B. Commercial payments
   C. Regulation-based payments

8. Discuss VAL's rationale for financing the wind farm with two different forms of debt.

9. Demonstrate that VAL's contract for difference with LCCC guarantees the same annual revenue regardless of the prevailing market price of electricity assuming no fluctuation in wind speeds.

The following information relates to questions 10-13

Meg Zhu is a senior analyst at InfraEast, an infrastructure firm considering an equity investment in the VAL wind farm project, and she has built a spreadsheet model based on facts shown in the previous Item Set.

Zhu is working on assessing the sensitivity of project value. The first issue with which she is concerned is the CfD rate. Rather than a rate of GBP0.0.075 per kWh, she has decided to lower the assumption of the CfD rate to GBP0.07 per kWh to reflect any potential decline in prices before the CfD terms are set. Zhu estimates the value of the project's equity given a CfD rate of 0.075 per kWh at GBP74,376,852, and her value estimate declines to GBP58,706,468 if she assumes a CfD rate of 0.07 per kWh. Zhu believes that 8% is an acceptable hurdle rate for a wind farm project in a developed market. Ultimately, she decides to base her valuation on a CfD rate of 0.075 per kWh.

Zhu is concerned about the effects on future electricity prices of continued expansion of solar and wind power capacity, so she decides to build in an assumption that after the CfD contract price for the first 15 years expires, VAL will have to contract for a lower market price for electricity for the latter half (Years 16–30) of the wind farm's life. She is uncertain as to whether and how the CfD scheme will change in the future. She believes that a GBP0.07 market electricity rate might be a real possibility at the end of 15 years. The following table shows selected data from the projections in Year 15 of the wind farm's operation (based on a rate of GBP0.075 per kWh). Revenue and operating expenses grow over time at a 1.5% annual rate.

Revenue (GBP)	Operating Expense + CapEx	Net Cash Flow from Operations	Debt Service
33,635,015	19,260,757	14,374,258	11,864,533

Zhu has also been carefully considering how to estimate discount rates for the valuation. She has decided to estimate zero-coupon GBP bond rates and then adjust each year's discount rate to reflect project size, leverage, profitability, and investment. She maintains a size premium of 1.0% and an investment premium of 0.5% for all 30 years of the project. During the first 15 years of the project, she includes a 3.0% leverage premium and a −1.0% premium (i.e., 1.0% discount) for profitability. During the final 15 years of the project, the leverage premium is set to 0.0%.

10. Recommend whether Zhu should view an investment in the VAL project's equity as acceptable given her two possible CfD scenarios and justify your recommendation.

11. Calculate the effect of the lower market electricity rate of GBP0.07 per kWh on VAL's expected revenue for the wind farm in Year 16. Assume a constant annual growth in demand factor of 1.5%.

12. Discuss whether the change in Zhu's assumptions about market electricity rates will affect the projected VAL equity dividend rate between Years 15 and 16 of the wind farm's operation. For simplicity, assume expenses grow in line with demand.

13. Discuss why Zhu decides to change the leverage premium in the discount rate for the final 15 years (Years 16–30) of the VAL project.

SOLUTIONS

1. B is the correct response. Opportunistic assets are the highest risk classification among the infrastructure categories. Changing its allocation to Opportunistic will increase its risk profile.

   Response A is incorrect because core-plus assets are typically lower risk than value-add assets. Response C is incorrect because core assets are lower risk than value-add assets.

2. B is the correct response. Commercial (or merchant) payments will vary based on demand for the infrastructure asset, such as in the case of collections on a toll road.

   Response A is incorrect because availability-based payments are fixed by the contract and thus create lower business risk. Response C is incorrect because regulation-based payments are fixed by government authorities to allow for a sufficient rate of return, such as in the case of power companies.

3. Private infrastructure assets are used to provide essential or public services with few substitutes and typically are characterized by inelastic demand. Infrastructure asset returns typically exhibit lower correlation with other asset classes and tend to be less exposed to cyclicality or market downturns.

4. Northern States participates as an equity investor as a limited partner in infrastructure assets in industries in which it has not yet built sufficient expertise to manage the investment process more directly. As it gains sufficient expertise in a specific industry, it is more likely to invest as a general partner or co-investor in infrastructure assets in that industry.

5. Both types of private asset categories require a cash flow forecast over a time horizon. The point of contrast is that a private real estate asset is expected to be sold at the end of the time horizon and cash is expected to be received. A private infrastructure asset is usually assumed to have zero value at the end of the cash flow forecasting time horizon because the asset is transferred from the concessionaire to the grantor at that point in time.

6. The SPE's debt may in some cases be enhanced by the establishment of reserve accounts for debt service and other obligations. For example, when project cash flows are less predictable, a debt service reserve account is often established that accumulates sufficient cash in order to meet specific debt service requirements and from which funds are released when payments are due. Reserve accounts are often used for operating and maintenance costs and decommissioning equipment at the end of the project's serviceable life, such as the eventual closure and dismantling of wind turbines in the case of VAL.

7. C is the correct response. Power companies are regulated by government entities, and the price that they are able to charge is based on these regulations. The CfD structure of VAL supplements the regulatory nature of the payment scheme by fixing a price per kWh for a specific volume, ignoring the impact of wind speed variability.

   Response A is incorrect because the payment can still fluctuate based on electricity demand. Response B is incorrect because commercial payments are more variable based on the demand for the infrastructure asset's usage.

8. The VAL wind farm is financed in two phases. The first phase provides the shorter-term financing required to build the asset, and this phase is expected

to last three years. Thus, the construction and development loan provides this financing, and repayment of the loan occurs from the second phase of financing: the amortizing 15-year term loan. Once construction is completed and the wind farm begins operation, the wind farm generates cash flows and VAL can make fixed repayments of principal and interest on this loan from the expected cash flows from electricity sales.

9. The CfD guarantees that VAL will generate revenue of GBP0.075 per kWh regardless of the price at which it sells electricity output. The intermittent market reference price is the market reference price, and for simplicity, we assume an annual IMRP; this is the price at which VAL will sell its electricity. If the IMRP is greater than GBP0.075 per kWh, then VAL will make a payment to LCCC for the difference. For example, suppose the IMRP is GBP0.09 per kWh on average for a full year. Then, VAL's revenue is GBP32,767,875 (= 364,087,500 × GBP0.09).

   However, VAL must make a payment to LCCC for the difference between the IMRP and the CfD rate. This payment is GBP5,461,313[= 364,087,500 × (GBP0.09 – GBP0.075)]. Subtracting the amount of this payment from VAL's revenue calculated previously provides VAL's guaranteed revenue of 27,306,563.

   If the IMRP is less than GBP0.075 per kWh, then VAL will receive a payment from LCCC for the difference. Suppose the IMRP is GBP0.06 per kWh on average for a full year. Then, VAL's revenue is GBP21,845,250 (= 364,087,500 × GBP0.06).

   However, VAL receives a payment from LCCC for the difference between the IMRP and the CfD rate. This payment is GBP5,461,313 [= 364,087,500 × (GBP0.075 – GBP0.06)]. Adding the amount of this payment to VAL's revenue calculated previously provides VAL's guaranteed revenue of 27,306,563.

10. The IRR of the VAL project's equity under the original assumption of GBP0.075 as the guaranteed rate for the full 30-year time horizon of the project is equal to 14.15% [= RATE(nper, pmt, -pv, fv) = RATE(3, 0, -50000000, 74376852)].

    The IRR of the VAL project under the updated assumption of GBP0.07 as the guaranteed rate for the full 30-year time horizon of the project is equal to 5.50% [= RATE(nper, pmt, -pv, fv) = RATE(3, 0, -50000000, 58706468)].

    The IRR of the VAL project exceeds the 8% hurdle rate at a CfD rate of 0.075 but fails to do so if the CfD rate is 0.07. As such, Zhu's assumption about future electricity rates is critical to her recommendation. If she fully believes that a CfD rate of 0.075 is attainable, then an investment in the VAL project is attractive.

11. Year 16 of the revised revenue forecast may be estimated by first calculating the percentage decline in revenue from Year 15 to Year 16 due to the price change. We first divide the new market rate of GBP0.07 per kWh by the prior rate of GBP0.075, then multiply the result by the constant annual growth factor of 1.015, and finally subtract from 1:

    $$5.27\% = \left(1 - \frac{\text{GBP0.07}}{\text{GBP0.075}} \times 1.015\right).$$

    We can calculate the revised Year 16 revenue by multiplying the expected Year 15 revenue by this result:

    Revised Year 16 revenue: GBP31,863,571 = (1 – 0.0527) × GBP33,635,015.

12. Recall from Equations 3 and 4 that the equity dividend rate is calculated as follows:

    $$\text{Equity dividend rate} = \frac{\text{Before} - \text{tax net cash flow}}{\text{Project cost} - \text{Debt outstanding}},$$

    where

Before-tax cash flow = Net cash flow from operations – Debt service.

The most notable aspect from these formulas is that debt service declines from its Year 15 amount of GBP11,864,533 to zero in Year 16. Thus, all else equal, the before-tax cash flow increases by over GBP11.8 million between Years 15 and 16 because VAL's debt service has been paid. As a result, we would expect a significant increase in the equity dividend rate in Year 16 compared to Year 15 despite the decline in revenue from a decline in the assumed electricity price.

We can also explicitly show this result by estimating the equity dividend rate in both years. First, solve for before-tax cash flow in Year 15 using the information from the table: GBP2,509,725 (= 14,374,258 – 11,864,533). This gives an equity dividend rate of 5.02% (= 2,509,725/50,000,000). Year 16 net cash flow from operations is estimated by subtracting estimated operating expenses and capital expenditures (which grow at a rate of 1.5% per year from the Year 15 amount of GBP19,260,757) from estimated Year 16 revenue:

Net cash flow from operations = Revenue – Operating expenses.

GBP12,313,903 = 31,863,571 – (19,260,757 × 1.015).

This result is equal to the before-tax cash flow in the numerator of Equation 3, while the denominator equals the equity contribution of GBP50 million. Solve for the equity dividend rate as 13.25%:

$$24.63\% = \frac{\text{GBP}12,313,903}{\text{GBP}50,000,000}.$$

13. The 15-year term loan is fully repaid following the first 15 years of the VAL wind farm project. During the first 15 years of the project, the discount rate warranted a premium to reflect the risk associated with the project's financial leverage. Once the debt is repaid, the discount rate can be reduced to reflect the lack of required debt service payments in the project's capital structure from Years 16 to 30.

Glossary

100/10/1 rule of thumb A VC investor's rule of thumb that demonstrates the high selectivity required, as one may review 100 startup pitches, conduct due diligence on 10 of those reviewed, and select just one for investment.

Acquisition and development loan A loan used to purchase and prepare land for a specific construction use.

Agency cost of equity A principal–agent problem which arises when company managers have more information about a company than public shareholders, limiting the ability to assess performance and take corrective action.

Agreement among lenders A contractual arrangement among lenders in a unitranche debt facility which may reallocate interest and principal payments, priority of claims, or voting rights on covenant or other credit agreement changes.

Angel investors High-net-worth investors who are also often entrepreneurs that provide seed financing to startup companies.

Arbitrage spread The difference between an announced acquisition price and the post-announcement market price, which represents the potential return to a merger arbitrage strategy prior to considering transaction costs.

Asset impairment An adverse change in the market value of an asset that falls below its balance sheet carrying value.

Asset swap Converts a bond's fixed coupon to MRR plus (or minus) a spread using an interest rate swap for the remaining life of the bond.

Asset-based lending Revolving credit facility extended on a secured basis using accounts receivable, inventory, or equipment as collateral.

Bankruptcy Legal proceedings, which vary by jurisdiction, allowing a firm whose liabilities exceed its assets to restructure existing debt obligations or liquidate assets in an orderly manner.

Bond tender offer An offer from a fixed-income issuer to repurchase outstanding loans or bonds.

Brownfield investment Infrastructure investments that involve existing rather than to-be-built facilities, which may involve the privatization or repurposing of existing public assets or an expansion of existing facilities.

Build-operate-transfer (BOT) project Infrastructure project whose construction and development is conducted by private entities sponsored by a public entity and transferred to public control after a finite operating period.

Business development companies A type of closed-end investment vehicle in the United States which are publicly traded and specialize in private debt.

Buyout equity Private equity investment in a mature company with the intent to transform, divest, or acquire businesses and sell the reorganized firm at a higher price to public or private investors.

Capital structure arbitrage An investment approach that combines long or short debt, equity, and/or credit default swap positions to exploit mispricing in a single issuer's obligations.

Capitalization rate The rate used to discount expected NOI, which combines the required rate of return on similar properties with an implied constant growth rate.

Capitalization table A detailed summary of changes in firm value, fractional ownership dilution, and prices paid by investors or stakeholders over the course of multiple equity rounds typically shown on a fully diluted basis.

Carbon offset Investments that reduce or remove carbon dioxide and other greenhouse gases to compensate for emissions produced elsewhere to achieve reduction or net-zero emission goals.

Carried interest A performance or incentive fee applied to private market fund investments based on returns above a hurdle rate.

Catch-up clause A clause in a limited partner agreement that specifies that a general partner will receive 100% of the distributions above a prespecified hurdle *until* the GP receives the carried interest percentage (such as 20%) of the returns generated and then every excess dollar will be split between the LPs and GP based on the carried interest percentage.

CDS basis Differences in bond and CDS spreads that arise because of bond price differences from par, accrued interest, and varying contract terms.

Change of control A debt clause that requires an issuer to repurchase outstanding bonds at a fixed price at or above par if a new owner acquires a predetermined percentage of voting shares.

Change of control clause Debt provision that requires an issuer to offer to repay outstanding debt if a new owner acquires a predetermined percentage of voting shares.

Change of control provision A restrictive covenant typically included in a high-yield bond indenture that requires the issuer to offer to repurchase outstanding bonds at a fixed price (above par) if a new owner acquires a predetermined percentage of voting shares.

Circulation Zoning requirement mandating provisions for security and emergency access to buildings or facilities.

Clawback provisions Limited partnership agreement provisions that involve returning GP performance fees to LPs in cases where transactions that are initially successful later face losses.

Closed-end funds Funds with a finite life requiring an initial capital commitment with a lockup period and eventual sale of the property or properties for distribution to investors.

Collateralized loan obligations (CLOs) Investment vehicle with exposure to a portfolio of leveraged loans separated into tranches with different cash flow claims and exposure to losses based on a waterfall.

Concession agreement A contractual arrangement under which an entity (also known as a grantor) establishes terms and conditions with a developer or operator (referred to as a concessionaire) to plan, build, operate, finance, and maintain an infrastructure asset for a specific period.

Concessionaire A developer or operator that is provided the right under a concession agreement to charge user fees over an operating period to recover construction, maintenance, and operational costs and compensate investors.

Construction and development (C&D) loan Debt financing for real estate development which is committed prior to project initiation and drawn through a construction phase, accruing interest over time, and typically repaid with a mortgage loan.

Construction and development loan A loan used to provide funds during the building phase of a real estate project.

Continuation funds New private investment funds established by GPs through the sale of existing assets in another limited partnership in GP-led secondary transactions.

Contracts for difference (CfDs) Contracts used as an income stabilization measure under which the difference between a pre-agreed, fixed contractual price (or strike price) for a service or good is exchanged for the current prevailing market price (or so-called reference price).

Contractual subordination Use of contract or intercreditor agreement between senior and subordinated lenders to establish seniority ranking of debt obligations.

Conversion period The period over which a convertible bond may be exchanged for equity at a predetermined price.

Conversion price Predetermined share price at which convertible debt may be fully exchanged for common shares during the conversion period.

Conversion ratio The number of common shares a convertible bond or noteholder may receive in exchange for a specific bond par value.

Conversion value The current contingency feature value derived by comparing a convertible bond's price with its value if a bondholder were to exchange bonds for shares.

Convertible arbitrage A special situations investment approach that involves capitalizing on the perceived mispricing of the underlying risk components of a convertible bond.

Convertible debt A fixed-income instrument which combines the features of debt with equity via a contingent feature, allowing debtholders to exchange their claim for common shares at a predetermined fixed price in the future.

Convertible preferred shares (CPS) A form of preferred stock that may pay a dividend and be converted into common shares at a fixed conversion ratio, or number of common shares received for each preferred share.

Convexity The second order, usually a positive change in the price of a bond for a given change in yield, which can be negative for a callable bond such as a high-yield bond.

Covenant-lite Debt transactions involving a relatively weak set of restrictive covenants imposed on an issuer due to competitive market pressures.

Credit event An occurrence that triggers the settlement of a CDS contract, including failure to make a debt payment, debt restructuring, or a bankruptcy filing.

Credit loss rate The realized percentage of par value lost to default for a group of bonds equal to the bonds' default rate multiplied by the loss severity.

Credit valuation adjustment (CVA) The present value of credit risk for a loan, bond, or derivative obligation.

Data room A repository used to store confidential company documents that may be accessed by potential bidders who sign a non-disclosure agreement.

Debt profile A detailed breakdown of short-term and long-term liabilities by tenor, seniority, and other features, used in a private debt market strategy.

Debt service coverage ratio A key indicator of credit performance equal to the ratio of net operating income to debt service.

Debt service reserve account (DSRA) A separate fund established to accumulate the cash flow necessary to meet debt service requirements from which cash is released when debt interest and principal payments are due.

Debt-for-equity exchange An exchange executed by distressed firms in which new shares are issued to debtholders in exchange for the extinguishment of existing debt claims.

Debtor in possession (DIP) A debtor that has filed for Chapter 11 US bankruptcy protection but remains in possession of company assets for the purpose of maintaining operations as a going concern.

Delay option Developers may increase a project's present value by postponing property construction until market conditions improve.

DIP financing Super senior debt financing obtained on a short-term basis to cover ongoing bankruptcy costs and provide funding to maintain operations as a company completes the bankruptcy process.

Direct capitalization approach A property valuation approach that divides a single year's net operating income by the cap rate to estimate a property's value.

Direct co-investment The direct purchase of an ownership stake or private debt investment with the use of one or more partners, one or more of whom may be a private fund manager.

Direct investment The purchase of an ownership stake or debt investment without the use of a partner or an investment intermediary.

Direct lending Providing capital directly from private debt investors.

Distressed debt Debt of mature companies in financial difficulty, in bankruptcy, or likely to default on debt.

Distressed debt exchange An exchange of existing bonds for new securities from the same issuer that involve lower par values, longer maturities, and/or fewer protective financial covenants than current outstanding bonds.

Distributed to paid-in (DPI) Also referred to as the cash-on-cash return, this ratio gauges an investor's realized rate of return via the ratio of cumulative distributions to limited partners to the capital invested.

Dividend recapitalization A change in the mix of debt and equity outstanding for an existing corporate issuer which increases leverage via debt-financed dividends or share repurchases to benefit existing shareholders.

Down round Venture capital financing of an early-stage company which takes place at a share price below that of the previous financing round.

Duration The first-order, linear change in a bond's price for a given yield change in yield, which is a negative or inverse relationship.

Effective spread duration Change in a loan or bond price for a given change in yield spread, with the spread typically defined as OAS.

Empirical duration Estimation of the price–yield relationship using historical bond market data in statistical models.

Equity dividend rate Equityholder return that considers the first-year return on equity on an income-producing property involving the before-tax cash flow divided by the property purchase price less the mortgage loan outstanding.

Exit value of equity The expected terminal value of an early-stage firm at the end of a holding period is determined by using the required return on investment or a market multiple if the firm is expected to be profitable.

Export credit agencies (ECAs) Quasi-government entities sponsored by developed market governments to promote the export of domestic goods and services via credit insurance, political risk insurance, or subsidized or guaranteed debt financing.

Fallen angels Formerly investment-grade-rated issuers whose bonds are downgraded to high yield due to credit deterioration.

Feed crops Crops such as grain used as either raw material in food production or as an intermediate good.

Financial buyer An owner seeking to earn investment returns from an existing company without identifying or capitalizing on synergies from a controlling interest.

Financial dislocation A situation in which market prices are misaligned on an absolute or relative basis due to financial market stress, changes in liquidity, market constraints, or other industry- or company-specific factors.

Financial sponsor A private equity buyout fund which purchases a controlling stake in a firm distributed to investors in the form of limited partnerships.

First lien Also known as a priority lien, this investor protection grants a lender the right to take possession of property from a borrower which fails to repay debt.

First-out tranche Senior debt tranche in a unitranche facility which is typically at an interest rate below the blended facility rate and repaid earlier than subordinated debt claims.

Fraudulent conveyance An unlawful transfer of assets by an issuer to a third party to prevent creditors from reaching a borrower's assets, which in some cases may be voided by a court under bankruptcy law.

Free cash flow to the firm (FCFF) Free cash flow to both debt and equity holders composed of after-tax EBITDA plus tax benefits of depreciation less changes in long-term assets and working capital.

Free fall bankruptcy A situation in which an issuer enters the bankruptcy process without a reorganization plan in place.

General partners (GPs) Private fund managers responsible for sourcing and deploying capital from limited partner investors over an investment life cycle and distributing returns to those investors over a finite investment holding period.

Go-shop process Provision in a sale or merger agreement in which the seller solicits bids from potential third-party buyers for a limited period after extending the offer to an initial buyer.

Governance rights Powers extended to preferred or minority shareholders which may include board seats, special voting rights, or the ability to observe board meetings, among others.

GP-led secondary A form of private market sale in which a general partner sells a private asset from an existing portfolio into a new fund.

Grantor Another word for "settlor," who is a person who creates a trust.

Greenfield investment New "to be built" infrastructure projects and assets created to provide a specific essential service or to supply a public good.

Growth equity Private equity investment in a young company with a business model and growing revenue used to reach its total addressable market and reduce concentrated ownership of founders and initial investors.

Growth equity method Valuation approach used for private companies engaging in profitable expansion which incorporates cash flow projections over an investment horizon required to achieve a desired exit valuation and initial capital necessary to reach a targeted investor ROI.

Hard hurdle rate The minimum rate of return in a performance-based fee arrangement in which the GP earns only fees on annual returns that exceed the hurdle rate.

Heavily indebted poor countries (HIPCs) A specific group of developing countries eligible for support from the International Monetary Fund (IMF) and the World Bank.

High-water mark A measure that reflects the fund's maximum value as of a performance fee payment date net of fees.

High-yield bonds Fixed-income securities issued on a fixed-rate basis by sub-investment grade companies, which are typically subordinate to leveraged loans and include call features.

Hurdle rate A predetermined minimum rate of return an investment fund must reach before a GP receives incentive-based compensation.

Incurrence covenants Restrictive debt covenants involving financial metrics which only must be met at the time the issuer seeks to take on additional debt.

Infrastructure Company Classification Standard (TICCS) A standard developed to categorize infrastructure investments based on key characteristics affecting relative risk and return with the input of asset owners and asset managers.

Insolvency A situation in which an issuer's total liabilities exceed the market value of its assets.

Intercreditor agreement Legal contract specifying details of the priority of claims and other key terms governing separate debt claims to the same assets and legal entity.

Intermittent market reference price (IMRP) The UK market reference price for intermittently produced power determined daily based on the prior day's hourly electricity rates.

Internal rate of return (IRR) The uniform discount rate for a series of cash flows over *n* periods that returns a net present value of zero.

Interval funds Open-end funds with certain constraints that have no predetermined maturity date but include liquidity restrictions, such as limits on the fraction of total assets available for redemption on a periodic basis.

J-curve effect Net income over a multiyear private investment holding period characterized by negative returns in an initial phase, followed by cash flow and income growth toward the end of the holding period.

Land expectation value Value of an acre of bare land in perpetual timberland production.

Last-out tranche Junior debt tranche in a unitranche facility which is at an interest rate above the blended facility rate and repaid after senior debt claims.

LBO model Valuation approach used for buyout equity which uses expected cash flows of a target acquisition, as well as expected capital structure composition and cost, to establish the maximum price that can be paid to a seller while satisfying targeted financing returns.

Leveraged buyout (LBO) A transaction in which a private acquiror uses equity and a high proportion of debt to acquire a public or private company in order to make changes to increase value over an investment period.

Leveraged buyouts Buyout equity transactions that utilize a high proportion of debt financing to make a company acquisition.

Leveraged loans Loans made to a borrower or issuer with relatively lower credit quality and/or higher leverage.

Limited partner co-investment Involves the purchase of an ownership stake or private debt investment in a single investment that is managed by a private fund manager or general partner.

Limited partners (LPs) Outside investors in a private market fund who own a fractional interest in a limited, closed-end partnership managed by a general partner based on the investment commitment and other terms set out in a limited partner agreement.

Limited partnership Closed-end form of ownership frequently used in private market funds in which private market fund investors, or limited partners, commit capital that is invested, managed, and distributed by a private market fund manager, or general partner, over an investment holding period.

Liquidation preference payout Predefined distribution of cash proceeds to preferred shareholders made in full before any distributions are made to common shareholders.

Liquidity financing Private debt funds which seek to generate income by investing in a portfolio of short-term obligations in order to maintain a stable net asset value.

Loan to value (LTV) A measure of leverage used by debt investors that equals the loan amount outstanding divided by the project value.

Loan-to-value ratio A primary measure of leverage involving the ratio of mortgage principal outstanding to the property's current value.

Lockup agreement A provision requiring a private equity investor to retain a material interest in the shares of a new public company for a predetermined period to protect the interests of institutional investors.

Loss given default (LGD) The amount a debtholder fails to recover if a default occurs, usually expressed as a percentage of par value.

Low Carbon Contracts Company (LCCC) UK government-owned counterparty for qualified low-carbon energy contracts for difference.

Maintenance covenants Restrictive debt covenants requiring an issuer to meet certain financial metrics for each financial reporting period.

Management buyout A private sale to a strategic buyer that includes a company's existing management. The management team commits their own equity capital along with other investors as an incentive to grow the firm's cash flows and value.

Merchant payment scheme Also referred to as a commercial payment scheme, under this structure frequently used for power generation and toll road assets, an operator has the right to collect service or user fees over an operating period but remains exposed to the asset's business risk based on demand and other economic factors.

Merger arbitrage Special situations investments related to business combinations in which investors seek to capitalize on price discrepancies of securities issued by the target company.

Mezzanine debt Refers to private credit subordinated to senior secured debt but senior to equity in the borrower's capital structure.

Mezzanine loan A debt claim that is serviced after all senior debt claims but before common shares and other forms of equity in the capital structure.

Multiple of invested capital A ratio in which the total value of all realized investments and residual asset values (assets that may still be awaiting sale) are divided by capital invested.

Multiple of invested capital (MOIC) Also referred to as the multiple of money or total value to paid-in, this private market performance measure incorporates both the cumulative distributions received and the net asset value of a fund as a proportion of invested capital.

Multiple of money (MOM) Also referred to as the multiple of invested capital or total value to paid-in, this private market return measure incorporates both the cumulative distributions received and the fund's net asset value as a proportion of invested capital.

Net operating income A commonly used measure of income-producing property returns prior to the inclusion of financing costs or income taxes.

Non-disclosure agreement A legal contract specifying that any confidential information received by a prospective company buyer is used only to evaluate a possible transaction.

Non-sponsored loans Direct loans to small- or medium-sized firms which lack a controlling financial sponsor and involve greater search, due diligence, and monitoring costs.

Open-end diversified core equity (ODCE) funds Private investment funds that hold portfolios of core income-producing properties.

Open-end funds Funds which allow investors to contribute or withdraw capital freely and have no predetermined end date.

Optimal conversion point The implied equity price at which convertible preferred shareholders are better off exercising their right to convert preferred shares into common shares.

Option-adjusted spread (OAS) A generalized constant yield spread over the zero curve that incorporates bond option pricing based on assumed interest rate volatility and may be used for callable, putable, and non-callable bonds.

Own–lease A farmland investing model more common among financial investors in which an owner or lessor receives fixed rental payments for undeveloped tillable acreage under a multiyear lease agreement from a farm operator lessee who assumes all other business risks.

Own–operate A farmland investing model which involves owning land, buildings, equipment, and other assets as well as operating an agricultural business.

P90 level Probability-weighted measure of the minimum amount of electricity an average wind turbine is 90% likely to produce over an average period given changing weather conditions.

Paid-in capital (PIC) Reflects the proportion of the limited partners' total committed capital that the general partner has so far deployed, following any capital calls, to total committed capital.

Participation rights Preferred share feature which offers upside gains to investors via similar distributions to those received by common shareholders instead of a conversion to common equity.

Payment in kind (PIK) Interest paid not in cash, but via accrual, increasing the debt principal outstanding, which is then paid at maturity.

Permanent crops Agricultural crops planted for many seasons, such as orchards or vineyards, which typically generate a higher return per acre or hectare.

Post-money valuation A combination of the pre-money valuation and new equity invested.

Pre-money valuation Estimated current value of a startup company prior to new financing derived using the VC method.

Pre-seed capital Initial equity capital for a new business, most often sourced from founders and angel investors, which is used to establish the feasibility of a product or market need.

Prepackaged bankruptcy A detailed business plan and exit strategy with a new capital structure proposal that is formulated and agreed on with major creditors prior to entering the bankruptcy process.

Price step-up Change in a company's price per share over a series of financings.

Private asset investment life cycle Refers to the multiyear investment holding period common among private investments that consists of capital commitment, deployment, distribution and exit phases.

Probability of default (POD) The likelihood that a borrower fails to make full and timely payments of principal and interest according to debt terms, usually expressed in annual percentage terms.

Public market equivalent A theoretical public market investment in which private fund cash outflows are invested in a public market index while cash inflows are sold from a public market index.

Public–private partnerships (PPPs) A long-term contractual relationship between the public and private sectors involving a concession agreement or other form of compensation in exchange for delivering an essential service or public good.

Pulpwood A timber product consisting of lower-quality, small, and often thinned trees that is the primary input for paper products.

Quoted margin (QM) Spread over the market reference rate for a floating-rate loan established at the time of issuance to compensate investors for issuer credit and liquidity risk.

Ratchet provision Antidilution provision negotiated by investors in early-stage companies that partially or fully reduces the conversion price of existing options or preferred shares to the price at which new shares are issued in a subsequent financing round.

Real options Refers to the right but not the obligation to take future action. The existence of such options may affect the value of a real estate investment.

Recurring revenue financing A form of venture debt in which a private loan is offered to a startup firm with an established subscriber base in the form of a discounted upfront monthly payment of expected subscription revenue in exchange for all monthly subscriber cash flows.

Redemption rights Grant an investor the right to redeem preferred shares for cash as a form of downside protection against adverse events.

Reduced form models Statistical credit models that solve for the probability of default over a specific time period, using observable company-specific and market-based variables.

Reference price The current prevailing market price for a service or good whose difference from a pre-agreed, fixed contractual price (or strike price) determines the settlement amount in a contract for difference.

Request for proposal (RFP) Standardized document used by public entities to choose parties involved in the development, construction, operation, and financing of infrastructure projects that outlines project details, requirements, and timing, as well as assessment criteria used to award contracts to successful bidders.

Required margin Also known as discount margin. The market-determined yield spread over or under the market reference rate such that a floating-rate loan is priced at par on a rate reset date following issuance.

Reserve currencies Freely floating currencies issued by central banks in major developed markets that are widely held by external parties, including central banks.

Residual value to paid-in (RVPI) A measure of an investor's unrealized return on investment equal to the fund's net asset value as a proportion of the total invested capital.

Retained cash flow (RCF) Net cash from operating activities less dividends, and often compared to net debt as a measure of financial leverage.

Return on investment (ROI) A simple performance measure equal to the ratio or multiplier of cash flows received versus those invested that ignores the time value of money and length of an investment holding period.

Revolving credit agreement The most reliable form of a short-term bank borrowing facility, which can be drawn and repaid based upon working capital needs and in effect for multiple years on either a secured or unsecured basis. Also known as revolvers.

Row crops Agricultural crops harvested annually and rotated.

Sawtimber Top-quality timber used for construction lumber, as well as other building products, such as plywood or particleboard.

Scenario analysis A variation of the valuation process combining a base case with alternative outcomes, allowing the incorporation of more favorable or adverse scenarios in the valuation process.

Second lien An investor protection which increases the recovery rate in the event of default versus unsecured debt. A second lien loan is secured by an asset with an existing lien and will only be repaid once the first lien creditor receives payment.

Secondaries Limited partnership stakes in existing mid-cycle private market funds that are purchased and sold among LPs, which in many cases involves the fund GP as an intermediary.

Seed capital Equity investment(s) used to launch a startup company once it has a proven business idea.

Sensitivity analysis A form of analysis used to determine the impact of a change in one or more key variables affecting investment returns or valuation.

Sequencing option Dividing and executing a project in staggered phases rather than all at once, which may increase a project's risk-adjusted return by reducing exposure to market oversupply during the lease-up period.

Series financing One or more stages of equity investment in young companies which occurs after the firm is established and before it is sold or goes public.

Setback Zoning requirement mandating provisions for distance to property lines.

Social infrastructure Infrastructure investments directed toward essential government services, such as education and health care.

Soft hurdle rate The minimum rate of return in a performance-based fee arrangement in which the entire return is subject to the fee once the hurdle is exceeded.

Sovereign immunity A principle that limits legal recourse of lenders from forcing a sovereign borrower to declare bankruptcy or liquidate its assets to settle debt claims.

Special purpose entity (SPE) Also referred to as a special purpose vehicle (SPV), this legal entity is created for a specific economic purpose. In the case of a project SPV, the entity's sole purpose is to facilitate the construction, operation, and financing of an infrastructure asset over its contractual life.

Special situations An area of private capital investment which targets return by investing in stressed, distressed, or event-driven opportunities.

Specialty financing Involves forms of non-bank lending to commercial and consumer borrowers such as credit card receivables, leasing, and installment loans.

Sponsored loans Debt funding in which a private equity firm with a large equity investment in a prospective borrower directly solicits debt investors for the company.

Stabilized NOI Normalized or expected long-term level of net operating income level used to value real estate properties.

Strategic buyer An investor seeking to capitalize on synergies by extending the value creation process initiated by a GP, combining a business with another portfolio company, or taking other actions to increase firm value.

Strike price A pre-agreed, fixed contractual price per period whose difference from the current prevailing market price (or so-called reference price) determines the settlement amount in a contract for difference.

Structural credit risk models Option-based models of a firm's market value of assets over time versus its fixed obligations used to link an issuer's likelihood of default to its equity price.

Structural subordination Refers to the positioning of debt, which is issued by a legal entity, typically a holding company, which is separate and therefore one step removed from an operating company, which holds assets pledged under a security agreement to senior secured debtholders.

Stumpage fee A fee paid to timberland owners by private firms for the right to harvest timber.

Subscription lines Short-term lines of credit extended to private market funds that are secured by LP investor fund commitments prior to drawdown.

Sum-of-the-parts valuation A valuation approach that considers the value of a firm's business segments if they are sold separately.

Switching option The option to choose among alternative projects for a given plot of land or switch economic uses for an existing project, such as a mixed-use facility, which may increase value.

Take-private transaction A purchase of a public company by private investors in which the target company's shares are no longer publicly traded.

Technical default A violation of the terms and conditions of a credit, loan, or bond agreement, such as the breach of a financial covenant.

Tender process Early bond repayment mechanism in which a voluntary offer is extended to bondholders by an issuer to repurchase outstanding bonds prior to maturity.

Total addressable market A measure of the industry-wide revenue potential for the company's product or service.

Total value to paid-in (TVPI) Also referred to as multiple of invested capital or multiple of money, this measure reflects the overall value to the limited partner by incorporating both the cumulative distributions received and the net asset value as a proportion of invested capital. TVPI is the sum of distributed to paid-in and residual value to paid-in.

Turnkey A type of construction project in which a general contractor agrees to deliver a project on a fully completed basis.

Unitranche debt A hybrid or blended loan structure combining different tranches of secured and unsecured debt into a single loan with a single, blended interest rate.

VC method Valuation method for startup companies in which the current value is determined using the expected terminal value of the firm (or exit value of equity) and the required return on investment.

Venture capital Private equity investment in a startup or early-stage company involving high risk and a high rate of failure.

Venture debt Private debt funding that provides venture capital backing to start-up or early-stage companies that may be generating little or negative cash flow.

Vintage year The initial year in which capital is deployed in a private market transaction used to benchmark relative performance across investments and over time.

Voidable preference A situation in which an issuer grants a preference to one creditor over another in violation of a loan agreement or bond indenture, which may be reversed in bankruptcy court.

Warrant Debt feature or security granting the right to purchase additional common equity shares issued by the company at a predetermined price for a given period.

Weighted-average cost of capital (WACC) A weighted average of the after-tax required rates of return on a company's equity, debt, preferred stock, and other long-term financing sources, where the weights are the fraction of each source of financing in the company's current market value or management's target capital structure.

Z-score A reduced-form statistical credit measure that uses company-specific and market-based ratios to create a composite score used to determine whether a firm is likely to default or remain solvent.

Zero-volatility spread (Z-spread) A constant spread which is estimated using the market prices of comparable bonds for issuers of similar credit quality of a bond over the benchmark rate.